The Cambridge Guide to
THEATRE

Edited by Martin Banham

Editorial Advisory Board

Professor James Brandon, *University of Hawaii at Manoa*
Professor Ruby Cohn, *University of California, Davis*
Dr. Peter Holland, *Trinity Hall, Cambridge*
Professor Christopher Innes, *York University, Ontario*
Professor Tice Miller, *University of Nebraska – Lincoln*
Professor Peter Thomson, *University of Exeter*
Professor Don B. Wilmeth, *Brown University*
Professor George Woodyard, *University of Kansas*

CAMBRIDGE
UNIVERSITY PRESS

Published by the Press Syndicate of the University of Cambridge
The Pitt Building, Trumpington Street, Cambridge CB2 1RP
40 West 20th Street, New York, NY 10011–4211, USA
10 Stamford Road, Oakleigh, Victoria 3166, Australia

© Copyright Cambridge University Press 1988, 1992

First published 1988 as *The Cambridge Guide to World Theatre*
Reprinted with corrections 1990

Revised paperback edition first published 1992

Printed in the United States of America

A catalogue record for this book is available from the British Library.

Library of Congress cataloging in publication data

The Cambridge guide to world theatre.
Bibliography: p.
Includes index.
1. Theater–Dictionaries. I. Banham, Martin.
PN2035.C27   1988   792'.0321   8825804

ISBN 0 521 26595 9 hardback
ISBN 0 521 42903 X paperback

The Cambridge Guide to
THEATRE

Editor's Introduction

This edition of *The Cambridge Guide to Theatre* reproduces the entire text of *The Cambridge Guide to World Theatre* first published in 1988, and allows us to bring various entries up to date and to reflect changes in the theatre world since the parent *Guide* was first planned. Some of these have been startling: in 1988 Václav Havel was to be noted as a dissident Czech playwright. By 1989 he was President of his country! In 1988 we wrote of South African theatre reflecting that country's unique social problems. Today we can record a theatre contributing to a people's understanding of a post-apartheid society. Old stars have been rediscovered, through the archaeological excavations in London of the Elizabethan playhouses, the Rose and the Globe. New stars, like Kenneth Branagh, have established themselves.

Our intentions in publishing the *Guide* were, and remain, to offer a comprehensive view of the history and present practice of theatre in all parts of the world, thus pointing to the dynamic interaction of performance traditions from all cultures in present day theatre. We also aim to celebrate the vitality and importance of popular theatre and popular entertainment, and the constructive relationship between 'high' and 'low' art in the theatre – the fusion that brings together the eccentric comedian Max Wall and Samuel Beckett's Vladimir, and which gives us equal interest in Shakespeare's famous clown Will Kempe and in his mastery of the jig!

As editor my aim is to offer both students of the theatre and the general theatregoer information, assessment and entertainment, and a base from which they may explore particular interests. The majority of the entries are concerned with theatrical practitioners, but we also offer entries on national traditions of theatre, from Russia to Ecuador, Canada to Nigeria. We are concerned, too, with a range of other important topics, such as Dramatic Theory, Criticism, Censorship, Copyright, Lighting, Sound, Design, Theatre buildings, as well as Puppets and Performing Animals, Fireworks, Waxworks, Acrobatics, Carnival and Cabaret. The *Guide* has been recognised as 'the single most useful volume of theatre in the language'. I'm pleased that we can now make it available in this updated form.

I have many acknowledgements to make. The distinguished members of the editorial advisory board have been no mere figure-heads. All have made major contributions to the *Guide* by their own entries and by their expert recommendation of subjects to cover and appropriate contributors. I express my deepest gratitude to them all. It has been a privilege to have worked with them. I am also grateful to the many other contributors to the *Guide* for their valuable input. A separate list identifies contributors against the initials found at the foot of each entry. I have felt it important to make this acknowledgement and not to subsume the work of so many individual scholars into collective anonymity. Equally I have tried to allow contributors to speak with their own voices within the constraints of our general style. At Cambridge University Press Sarah Stanton has commissioned and developed the *Guide* with her customary initiative, enthusiasm, energy and good humour, and her consistently perceptive advice has saved me from many errors. Ann Stonehouse and Ann Mason have supported, scrutinised and contributed in important and significant ways, and my gratitude goes to them too. Over the five years that this work has been in preparation a multitude of other people have given invaluable advice and support. In this context I especially wish to thank Judith Greenwood, my colleagues and students at the University of Leeds, themselves representative of theatre traditions from all continents, Mrs Stella Garside and Ms Nicola Duke. I must also acknowledge the debt that any editor of a work of reference owes to fellow editors of similar publications. Phyllis Hartnoll's editions of *The Oxford Companion to the Theatre* have long been standard works of reference and have always been to hand. The witty and wise *Everyman Companion to the Theatre* edited by Peter Thomson and Gamini Salgado has both informed and delighted. Philip Barnes' helpful *Companion to Post-War British Theatre* has also been drawn upon. Other bibliographical references are listed elsewhere. I am happy, too, to acknowledge on behalf of other contributors special assistance and advice. For the Australian entry thanks are due for material on Aboriginal dance to Margaret Clunies-Ross and Stephen Wild. For North America Don B. Wilmeth especially thanks his research assistant (UGC – please note!) Catherine Linberg, and John Frick, Kate Davy, Denis Salter, Richard Plant and Heather McCallum; also John Guare, Romulus Linney, Maurice Evans, Constance Cummings, Marian Seldes, Elizabeth Lecompte, Heather Patrick, Pat Brown, Trent Jenkins, Jan Geidt, Marion Simon and Rosalind Heinz. On behalf of other advisory editors and contributors I thank all who advised, answered queries, typed entries, checked details, brewed coffee and poured the drinks.

Finally, my warm thanks to my wife Kate and my family, who have long lived with the *Guide*, and a final dedication to the memory of my mother Mary Winifred (Molly) Banham who loved to act and go to the theatre, and to her great-grandchildren Tom Carlos Banham Lopez and Lucy Kate Lopez that they may have that enjoyment too.

Martin Banham
Leeds

Contributors

AA	Arnold Aronson	PHe	Paul Hernadi	PN	Penny Newman
JA	James Aikens	WH	Wil Hildebrand		
SMA	Stephen M. Archer			DP	Daniel Pires
		AI	Arni Ibsen	JP	Jørgen Pjettursson
AB	Alec Baron	CI	Christopher Innes	RP	Richard Pilbrow
ALB	Andrew Brown				
DB	David Bradby	AJ	Anthony Jackson	DR	Donald Roy
EB	Eugene Brogyány	KJ	Krishen Jit	FR	Francis Reid
FB	Frances Bzowski			FaR	Farley Richmond
GWB	George W. Brandt	CK	Christopher Kamlongera	GAR	Graham Runnalls
JMB	Jarka Burian	DK	Dragan Klaić	KR	Kenneth Richards
JRB	James R. Brandon	JK-D	James Kotsilibas-Davis	LR	Laura Richards
MB	Martin Banham	LK	Laurence Keates	LSR	Leslie du S. Read
WBB	W. B. Bland	MK	Margaret M. Knapp	MR	Maarten Reilingh
WOB	William O. Beeman	RK	Robert Kavanagh		
		REK	Richard E. Kramer	AS	Alisa Solomon
DC	David Collison			ACS	A. C. Scott
LDC	Larry D. Clark	BL	Bistra Lankova	CS	Christopher Scarles
OkC	Oh-kon Cho	CL	C. I. Lewis	ClS	Claude Schumacher
RC	Ruby Cohn	FHL	Felicia Hardison Londré	ES	Elsa Strietman
SC	Stephen Chifunyise	HL	Harry Lane	HS	Henri Schoenmakers
		PL	Peter Lewis	HaS	Hanna Scolnicov
LED	Leonard Doucette			IS	Ian Steadman
		BMcN	Brooks McNamara	JRS	J. R. Stephens
JE	John Elsom	DMcD	Douglas McDermott	LS	Laurence Senelick
ME	Michael Etherton	HDMcN	Howard McNaughton	LSh	Louis Sheaffer
		JMcC	John McCormick	MS	Maxine S. Seller
KF	Kathy Foley	MMac	Margaret Macpherson	RAS	Robert A. Schanke
				SS	Sarah Stanton
AEG	A. E. Green	BM	Bogdan Mischiu		
DG	Daniel Gerould	CPM	Colin Mackerras	GT	G. Thaniel
DGG	David G. Goodman	DM	Desmond Maxwell	JET	John E. Tailby
FG	Frances Gray	DMw	Dickson Mwansa	PT	Peter Thomson
IG	Ivor Guest	LM	Linda McKenny		
KG	Kimani Gecan	LRM	Lynette Muir	DV	Dev Virahsawmy
MG	Martin van Ginkel	MM	Monica Murray		
SG	Spencer Golub	NwaM	Ngugi Wa Mirii	CHW	Clive Wake
WG	William Green	PM	Peter Meredith	DBW	Don B. Wilmeth
		PMl	Penina Mlama	DJW	Daniel J. Watermeier
AH	Andrew Horn	PFM	Peter McDonald	GW	George Woodyard
EGH	Errol Hill	RM	Richard Moody	MW	Margaret Williams
FH	Foster Hirsch	TM	Tom Mikotowicz	SW	Simon Williams
GH	George Hauger	TLM	Tice L. Miller		
MCH	Mary C. Henderson	WJM	Walter J. Meserve	DSPY	Daniel S. P. Yang.
PH	Peter Holland				
		AJN	Andrea J. Nouryeh		
		IN	Irmeli Niemi		

Further Reading

Bibliographies

Bibliographies are to be found at the end of most national and general entries.

Encyclopedias and Guides: a select complementary bibliography

Enciclopedia dello Spettacolo, 9 vols., Rome, 1954–64; *Aggiornamento, 1955–1965*, Rome, 1966; M. Esslin (ed.) *Illustrated Encyclopaedia of World Theatre*, London, 1977; J. Gassner, E. Quinn (eds.), *The Reader's Encyclopedia of World Drama*, New York, 1969, London, 1975; P. Hartnoll (ed.), *The Oxford Companion to the Theatre*, 4th edition, Oxford, 1983; J. R. Taylor (ed.), *The Penguin Dictionary of the Theatre*, London, 1967; P. Thomson, G. Salgado (eds.) *The Everyman Companion to the Theatre*, London, 1985.

see also:

M. Anderson, J. Guicharnaud, K. Morrison, J. D. Zipes *et al* (eds.), *A Handbook of Contemporary Drama*, London, 1972; W. Matlaw, *Modern World Drama*, London, 1972; S. Melchinger, *The Concise Encyclopedia of Modern Drama*, New York, 1966.

A Note on less obvious entries

The list below, while not intended to be in any way exhaustive, is intended to point the reader to entries in various categories, and to indicate the range of topics that we aim to cover in the *Guide* beyond those one would normally expect.

Academic Theatre in the United States
American Theatre Societies & Associations
Collective Theatre Groups (US)
Ethnic Theatre in the United States
Gay Theatre
Resident non-profit theatre in the United States
Theatre Awards (United States)
Theatrical Training in the United States
Third World Popular Theatre
Unions, theatrical (US)
United States Theatre Clubs

Acrobatics
Animals as Performers
Animal Impersonation
Baiting
Cabaret
Carnival
Fireworks
Gag
Hippodrama
Jig
Juggler
Male Impersonation (and Female Impersonation)
Marionette
Medicine Shows
Pornographic Theatre
Shadow Puppets
Waxworks
Wild West Exhibitions

Censorship
Copyright
Criticism
Dramatic Theory
Sound
Stage Lighting
Theatre Buildings
Theatre Design

A

Abbey Theatre The Dublin theatre by whose name the Irish National Theatre Society Ltd is popularly known. The Society's predecessors were the Irish Literary Theatre (1899–1901), founded by **W. B. Yeats**, **Augusta Lady Gregory**, Edward Martyn, and George Moore; and the Irish National Dramatic Company of Frank and Willie Fay. The aim of the Society, formed by the Fay brothers, Yeats, Lady Gregory, and **J. M. Synge**, was to encourage new writers, in Synge's words, to 'work in English that is perfectly Irish in essence'. The Abbey Street theatre, converted from a former morgue, was the gift in 1904 of an English admirer of Yeats, Miss **Annie Horniman**.

The Fay brothers were amateurs, both capable actors with practical stage experience: Willie, the stage-manager, advocated simple sets and designs; Frank, an elocutionist, distinct, melodious speech and minimal 'business'. Yeats and the Fays had compatible approaches to theatre, but the demanding patronage of Miss Horniman exacerbated the ever-present administrative and political disputes.

In 1903, when Willie Fay withdrew **Padraic Colum**'s *The Saxon Shillin'*, according to him for artistic reasons, Maud Gonne took it as censorship of patriotic art and resigned. With Miss Horniman's subsidy the players became salaried employees and lost their voting rights. The disgruntled left, some of whom, with Padraic Colum and Edward Martyn, set up the rival Theatre of Ireland (1906–12), which though it never came to much seemed to pose a threat. By 1908 Miss Horniman had removed the Fays, whom she detested, and by 1911 her subsidy. With the death of Synge in 1909 Yeats was effectively in control.

The indisputable dramatic genius of these years is

The first production of *The Plough and the Stars* by Sean O'Casey, Abbey Theatre, 1926.

Synge, whose disreputable peasant characters provoked riotous nationalist demonstrations, expecially against *The Playboy of the Western World* (1907). It offended many of the Company as well; Yeats showed considerable courage in standing by it and outfacing the demonstrators. More to the Abbey audience's taste were Lady Gregory's many folk dramas, entirely lacking Synge's disturbing transfigurations of common life and speech. Synge's mantle passed to **Sean O'Casey** and his synthesis of a poetic vernacular and urban realism. His irreverent treatment of the patriotic myths of Easter 1916 in *The Plough and the Stars* (1926) caused more riots. 'You have disgraced yourselves again', Yeats told the audience. Sadly, O'Casey abandoned the Abbey when in 1928 it rejected his part-expressionistic *The Silver Tassie*.

Alongside the uncommon brilliance of Synge and O'Casey, the Abbey had consolidated a line of essentially realist drama on local themes, initiated by Padraic Colum (*Broken Soil*, 1903), **Lennox Robinson** (*The Clancy Name*, 1908), and **T. C. Murray** (*Birthright*, 1910). Robinson (play-director 1909–14, 1919–35) was receptive to this kind of play, although he also inaugurated the **Dublin Drama League** (1919–29), opening the Abbey stage to experimental European and American drama.

A series of American tours and in 1925 an annual Government subsidy mitigated the Abbey's chronic penury. The subsidy was due largely to Ernest Blythe (Board of Directors 1935–41, Managing Director 1941–72), a Government member and a Gaelic enthusiast. This relative security enabled the Directors to accommodate a little theatre, the Peacock. Their better-known players – Sarah Allgood, Barry Fitzgerald, **Cyril Cusack**, Siobhan McKenna – remained at risk to the rewards of London and Hollywood.

Under Blythe's autocratic rule, with Yeats now infrequently present, the Abbey languished but survived. In the 1930s and 40s the discipline of acting and direction slackened, vulgarizing perhaps its best writer of the period, **George Shiels**. A few substantial new playwrights – **Paul Vincent Carroll**, **M. J. Molloy** – emerged. **Hugh Hunt**'s tenure (play-director 1935–8) was too brief to establish reform. The captive audiences of the war years acquiesced.

The fire which destroyed the old Abbey in 1951 exiled the company for 15 years to the decrepit Queen's Theatre, a larger house requiring runs longer than the Abbey's practice, in all a debilitating location. Its new home, on the old site, is a 628-seat modern theatre with, like the 167-seat new Peacock, sophisticated stage and lighting facilities.

After an indecisive start, the new Abbey found its

confidence, enlivened by the considerable talents of the directors Tomas MacAnna, Alan Simpson, Joe Dowling, and a gifted company. It remains a writers' theatre – with some aberrant rejections – and was an important instrument in the dramatic revival which began in the 1960s. In recent years the Abbey has undertaken successful European and American tours; it has had the stimulus of distinguished guest directors: in 1968 Maria Knebel of the **Moscow Arts Theatre** directed *The Cherry Orchard*, Hugh Hunt the revival of *The Silver Tassie* in 1972; it has established **Shakespeare, Chekhov, Brecht**, in its programming. Among the contemporary Irish writers mainly associated with it are **Brian Friel, Tom Murphy, Tom Kilroy, Hugh Leonard, Tom MacIntyre** and, more recently, **Graham Reid**. In the 1980s the Abbey has renewed the best of its inheritance.   DM

Abbott, George (1887–) American director, playwright, and actor. In his 1963 autobiography, Abbott praises his Harvard drama teacher **George Pierce Baker** in a way that defines his own theatrical creed: 'Professor Baker gave you no nonsense about inner meanings and symbolism; he turned your whole thoughts and energies into the practical matter of how to make a show.' Taking Baker's lessons to heart, Abbott became the most practical showman in Broadway history. As performer, co-author, play doctor, and director, Abbott has entertained audiences more often and over a longer period of time than anyone else. He first acted on a Broadway stage in 1913; in the spring of 1985 he directed a workshop production of a new musical called *Tropicana*. As both director and co-author his specialities are racy contemporary melodrama (*Broadway*, 1926); split-second farce (*Three Men On a Horse*, 1935); and peppy musicals with vigorous choreography (*On Your Toes*, 1936; *Damn Yankees*, 1955). Gangsters, bookies, gold-diggers, politicians, baseball heroes, hoofers and hookers populate his work, providing colourful slices of Americana. Despite the occasional suggestion of sexual daring (as in *Coquette*, 1927, and *New Girl in Town*, 1957, his musical version of *Anna Christie*) and of political conflict (*The Pajama Game*, 1954; *Fiorello!*, 1959), the typical Abbott show is archly conservative. The famed 'Abbott touch' always kept his shows spinning at a brisk clip, but Abbott downplays his technique, claiming that all he does is make actors 'say their final syllables'.   FH

Abell, Kjeld (1901–61) Danish playwright. After studies in Paris and London, he began his career designing Balanchine's ballets at the **Kongelige Teater**. His first writing for the theatre, the ballet-scenario *The Widow in the Mirror* (1934), introduced a recurrent Abell theme, the anguish caused by alienation from life. Ballet undoubtedly influenced the non-verbal and non-realistic elements in the plays that followed, beginning with *The Melody that Got Lost* (1935) produced at the Riddersalen cabaret theatre, which Abell admired and wrote for. More substantial than cabarets, his early expressionistic plays, *The Melody* and *Eve Serves Her Childhood*, sharply depict the suffocating effect of bourgeois values. His plays during and immediately after the Second World War, such as *Anna Sophie Hedvig, Judith, The Queen on Tour, Silkeborg* and *Days on a Cloud*, identify activism as essential to freedom and escapism as self-annihilation. After the war, part of which Abell had spent hiding from the Gestapo, his plays generally became more complex, as he explored, in an increasingly mystical way, the spiritual linking of minds through time and space, as well as the desperation of those who resist such bonds, such as the deceased David in *Vetsera Does Not Bloom For Everyone*, Tordis in *The Blue Pekingese* and the organist Dan in Abell's last play *The Scream*.   HL

Abington, Frances (1737–1815) English actress. Born in a poor family, she worked as a flower-seller and for a milliner before she began acting, though she still managed to learn French and Italian. By 1755 she was working with **Theophilus Cibber** at the **Haymarket** Theatre and the following year joined **Drury Lane** on the recommendation of **Samuel Foote**. After a period acting in Ireland she returned to London to join **Garrick**'s company at Drury Lane. Garrick always admired her acting though irritated by her temperament – he called her 'the worst of bad women'. In 1776 she made the first announcement of her retirement but continued to act, playing Lady Teazle in **Sheridan**'s *The School for Scandal* (1777). Though very highly paid she retired on a whim in 1790, making an unsuccessful return in 1799 by which time she was overweight and 'her elegance somewhat unfashionable'. For much of her career she was a leader of fashion, popularizing hair-styles and hats named after her.   PH

Above Much used in the often-enigmatic stage directions of Elizabethan plays, the 'above' was a practical upper level, equally important in the public and private theatres of London. It is generally assumed that the gallery over the stage of the **Swan**, clearly visible in De Witt's drawing of that theatre, represents the kind of fixture normally used by actors entering 'above', although there are occasions on which a free-standing two-tier structure would have proved more satisfactory. There is precedent for such structures in medieval staging, which often calls for an upper level for the accommodation of God and angels. (See **Below**.)   PT

Absurd, Theatre of the see **Theatre of the absurd**

Academic theatre in the United States Study of theatrical production techniques, as opposed to dramatic literature, has flourished in American colleges and universities only in this century, although the beginnings of college dramatics predate the nation's founding. Although the earliest student-produced plays and shows are incompletely documented, the earliest indication of such dramatic interest is found in a Harvard University's President's diary in 1698. Students of William and Mary in Virginia staged a 'pastoral colloquy' in 1702, whereas much of New England, permeated by Puritan influence, considered theatre in any form to be vicious, ungodly, and unworthy of study. Perhaps this explains the students' frequent attraction to the theatre.

However, college faculties, such as Harvard's professors, saw in the drama a valuable tool for instruction; by 1781 the faculty wrote scripts to be 'exhibited' as 'academic exercises'. Commencement plays and dialogues were somewhat regularly included, and a few literary societies produced what might be termed extra-curricular plays.

The early 19th century saw 168 colleges founded, mostly church-sponsored. Orthodox religion re-established its dominance of American cultural life, but the people of the new nation grew steadily more tolerant toward the theatre. The Hasty Pudding Club of Harvard, founded in 1795, began theatrical production in 1844 with *Bombastes Furioso*. Faculties, it would seem, preferred tragedy; the students, if left to their own resources, gravitated toward farce, satire, and comedy. Still no classroom study of theatre can be found in this period.

After the Civil War, students began to form organizations for the express purpose of presenting plays. The Thalian Dramatic Association, founded at Brown University in 1866, was one of the earliest of these producing agencies. Such clubs frequently flourished, died out when the leadership graduated, and were in turn replaced by others. Benefit performances were common, the proceeds being turned over to some campus activity or other, but rarely for the continued production of plays. Still, production did increase in quantity, as did all the extra-curricular aspects of college life.

Harvard again led the way; the Hasty Pudding Club initiated musical burlesques, influencing many other campuses to do the same. As the production of foreign language scripts increased, Harvard produced, after six months' rehearsal, *Oedipus Rex* in May 1881, probably the first Greek tragedy done in the original in the United States. The continuing use of the drama by foreign language departments no doubt helped raise the respectability of the theatre in the public's eye.

The beginnings of formalized classroom instruction in theatrical techniques, leading to departments of theatre and drama, are somewhat vague. In 1886 William O. Partridge, a Columbia University Professor, pleaded for such departments, but most historians have dated the beginnings of formal theatre instruction from **George Pierce Baker**'s 1903 playwriting course at Radcliffe College. Certainly others had preceded him, most notably Thomas Dickinson's instructions in staging at Baylor in 1901–2. Later pioneers such as E. C. Mabie at Iowa and Alexander Drummond at Cornell began to influence their campuses and, after the First World War, the nation.

The first department of theatre in the United States was founded in 1914 at the Carnegie Institute of Technology in Pittsburgh, Pennsylvania. George Pierce Baker founded a more influential postgraduate Department of Drama at Yale in 1925. The American Educational Theatre Association was founded in 1936, attracting some eighty members; the same organization, later called the American Theatre Association, dealt with some 1,600 theatre departments in the United States.

Even colleges without theatre departments offer productions today. In 1977 the National Endowment for the Arts estimated that some 2,500 colleges and universities presented 30,000 presentations of 7,500 scripts for an estimated audience of nine million.

Theatre production and curriculum followed in secondary or high schools in America only a few years after its arrival on college campuses. First presented to raise money for some worthy cause, high school plays became recognized by some as an end in their own right as early as 1912. Few states offer separate certification for high school teachers of drama, but the growth of dramatic activity at the secondary school level has been impressive. By the beginning of this decade, the National Endowment for the Arts reported some 30,000 high school theatre programmes in the USA, offering about 150,000 performances annually to a total of 45 million audience members. 92.2% of American high schools are engaged in some sort of theatrical endeavour.

The American student, then, may encounter live theatre at any level of his or her education. Even in primary or grade school, children's theatre abounds, although figures are inexact. Course work in drama or theatre is more commonly encountered at the high school level, as are more fully mounted productions, often as extra-curricular activity. A student wishing to specialize in theatre vocationally may select from thousands of college programmes in the USA, usually pursuing a Bachelor of Arts or Bachelor of Fine Arts degree. Similarly, Master of Arts or Master of Fine Arts (the latter considered a terminal degree, comparable to the doctorate) are offered throughout the country, and several dozen Doctor of Philosophy degrees in Theatre are available. Such programmes are usually less concerned with production techniques than with the historical and theoretical aspects of theatre. SMA

Accesi Two acting companies of the Italian **commedia dell'arte**, both begun under the patronage of Vincenzo I Gonzaga, Duke of Mantua. The first may have been founded about 1595, the other around 1600 by Tristano Martinelli and Pier Maria Cecchini, who eventually took over its management. The troupe toured Italy and appeared several times in France with such players as Flaminio Scala and Drusiano Martinelli. They merged with **G. B. Andreini**'s troupe, the **Fedeli**, for a brief period, before dissolving about 1626, at which time **Silvio Fiorillo** was the company's outstanding player in his role as Captain Matamoros. LS

Achurch, Janet (1864–1916) English actress whose career is identified with **Ibsen** and **Shaw**. As a member of **Frank Benson**'s company in the 1880s, she established a reputation as a tragedian. On taking over the management of the Novelty Theatre in 1889 she played Nora in the first British production of *A Doll's House*, returning to play Mrs Linde as her final stage appearance in 1911. In 1900 she starred in the premieres of *Candida* and *Captain Brassbound's Conversion*, and her correspondence with Shaw was made the basis for a play in 1978. CI

Ackermann The most important family of German actors in the 18th century. After a career in the military, in 1740 **Konrad Ernst** (1712–71) joined the **Schönemann** troupe. He soon left to set up his own troupe, along with **Sophie Schröder** (1714–92), who was soon to be the mother of **Friedrich Ludwig Schröder**. After Sophie's husband died, Konrad married her. The Ackermann troupe toured widely in Central and Eastern Europe, acquiring a considerable name for itself, above all for introducing to the German stage the genre of the *bürgerliches Trauerspiel*. In particular, after **Ekhof** joined the troupe in 1764, it became widely known for the comparative realism of its acting. In 1767 the troupe, temporarily without the leadership of Ackermann, formed the company of the Hamburg National Theatre. When that project foundered, the troupe returned to the road. After Ackermann's death, Friedrich Schröder took over the leadership, eventually settling it permanently in the Hamburg Town Theatre. Ackermann's two daughters, Dorothea (1752–1821) and Charlotte (1757–74), promised, by their talent and beauty, to be among the greatest actresses of the German stage, but Dorothea disliked acting and left the profession for marriage in 1778. Charlotte, a great favourite with the Hamburg audiences, was driven too hard by her step-brother Friedrich; she died, possibly by her own hand, before she was 18.   SW

Acquart, André (1922–   ) French stage designer. Educated in Algiers at the Ecole Nationale des Beaux Arts, he came to Paris in 1951. Since then he has designed in Germany and France but is known primarily for his work in the 1960s for leading French directors. Such productions include *The Blacks* (1959), directed by **Roger Blin**, *The Resistible Rise of Arturo Ui* (1961), co-directed by **Jean Vilar** and Georges Wilson, and *Biedermann and the Firebugs* (1960), directed by **Jean-Marie Serreau**. His designs are abstract, utilizing skeletal structures such as tubes or movable flats and multiple playing levels. This style is best exemplified in his pivoting and folding flats designed for **Roger Planchon**'s *Troilus and Cressida* (1964), and in his use of steps and mobile paper screens for Roger Blin's version of **Genet**'s *The Screens* (1966).   AJN

Acrobatics One of the most ancient and prevalent forms of physical entertainment. Egyptian and Etruscan murals depict leapers and vaulters, who often performed at feasts, and the springboard itself was known to antiquity. The earliest work devoted to the subject is Arcangelo Tuccaro's *Trois dialogues de l'exercise de sauter et voltiger en l'air* (1599), which applied to the architectonics of the leap and the mastery of mind over body the same attention to physicality that was creating ritualistic etiquette at the court of Charles IX. In 1641 Tommaso Garzoni drew up a list of distinguished acrobats.

The Three Emersons, a clown acrobatic act active in European variety in the early 20th century.

The most basic move is the *salto* or leap into the air, in which neither hands nor feet must move. All sorts of combinations are possible, backwards, forwards, sideways (the Arab jump), the flip-flop (a backward somersault from a standing position), and from trampolines and flying trapezes. The *salto mortale* or death-defying leap is so called from its dangerousness. A double *salto mortale* was first performed by an Englishman named Tomkinson in 1840; a triple, two years later, at Van Amburgh's circus resulted in a fatal accident. The first successful triple from a high springboard was made by the American Billy Dutton in 1860 and later Alfredo Codona mastered it on the flying trapeze.

Other forms of acrobatics include the antipodean, in which one acrobat lies on his back and juggles the other performer with his feet; and its offshoot, the Icarian games, invented by the Englishman Cottrelly c. 1850, in which performers are tossed, balanced and caught by the feet of their partners, lying on specially constructed cushions. The most outstanding exponents were the Schäffers and the Kremos: Sylvester Schäffer (1860–1931) created a six-man column, balanced on the feet of the low man. Risley stunts, named after Professor Richard Risley (Carlisle), involve somersaults performed by two children, from foot to foot of the recumbent partner.

In popular amusements like the **commedia dell'-arte** and the harlequinade, acrobatics is at a premium, but is neglected by the dramatic stage, except in actor's training. **Tom Stoppard** in *Jumpers* (1972) used acrobatics as a metaphor for mental gymnastics, and the 12th-century fabliau of *The Tumbler of Our Lady* has been made into an opera (Massenet, 1902), a ballet (D. Howes, 1936) and several plays.   LS

See: Adrian, *En piste, les acrobates*, Bourg-la-Reine, 1973; G. Strehly, *L'acrobatie et les acrobates*, Paris, 1903.

Acting The impulse to make-believe and play is common to humanity. To act is both to do and to pretend to do. For both actor and spectator, the uncanny power of any performance springs from an ambiguous tension between what is actual and what is fictional. This ambiguity is present in all acting however much a particular society or individual may wish to resolve it. In the 20th century many Western theories of acting have stressed the integrity of the doing, while in the 18th century, for example, Europeans were more concerned with the authentic nature of the pretence, its style and social aptness.

Throughout history, the unease aroused by this ambiguity has been reflected in the status of the actor. Even in classical Greece, where acting had religious and political importance, there is evidence from the 4th century BC onwards that the *technitai* of Dionysus were viewed with ambivalence. Certainly in Rome acting was felt to be the work of slaves and aliens; while in modern Europe players long existed on the margins of law and religion (**Molière** could not be buried in consecrated ground). This ambivalence can be traced elsewhere. In Asia, outside the confines of local prestige, religious purpose, or court patronage, performers were, and often still are, equated with wanderers and beggars.

The social assimilation of the acting profession in the West, around the beginning of the 20th century, was paralleled by sustained and serious evaluation of its art. In England, for example, **Irving**'s knighthood in 1895, the first to be bestowed on an actor, was followed not only by further theatrical knighthoods (six before 1914) but also by the founding of the Academy of Dramatic Art (later RADA). Similar developments are evident throughout Europe, most notably in Russia where for **Stanislavsky** training combined with a radical analysis of the art. Stanislavsky's accounts of his psycho-physical method constitute the first systematic exam-ination of acting, in the West, written from the viewpoint of the actor. Earlier writings are either anecdotal or, as with **Diderot**, written from the perspective of the auditorium. In the East, such approaches to practice can be found in works like the *Natyasastra* (c. 200 BC) and Zeami's treatises on the **nō** (c. 1402–30).

The art of acting lies in showing and sharing an action, image, character, or story. It is rooted in the present tense encounter of actor with actor, and/or actor with audience. The material of the art is the body, voice, and being of the performer. Different styles demand different skills of this material. Bodily skills may range from the acrobatic and pantomimic, as in traditional Chinese theatre, through schematic languages of dance and gesture, as found in **Kutiyat-tam** or **Kathakali**, to the faithful reproduction of everyday motions, as in Western naturalism. Vocal skills likewise may range from song, through chant or declamation, to conversational speech. As for being, individual and group accomplishment may be openly celebrated or hidden. This is not simply a contrast between a presentational mode of acting with its emphasis on display and a representational mode with its stress on verisimilitude. It relates to human identity and human energies, to a range of percepts of which mask and trance are an ambiguous part. Acting works with living presence. This is of the utmost importance in performance and of the utmost contention in discus-sion. Contraries abound – inspiration versus technique, talent versus training, **Kean** or **Kemble**, Irving or **Coquelin**, **Duse** or **Bernhardt**? Theatre is a social art and attitudes to being and social relationships inform any idea or style of acting. LSR

Acting Company (USA) (originally, City Centre Acting Company) **John Houseman** and Margot Harley organized the first graduating class of the Drama Division of Juilliard School into a permanent repertory troupe, which began performing at the City Centre in New York in 1972. By 1984 it functioned as the touring arm of the **John F. Kennedy Centre for the Performing Arts** in Washington, DC. The company's fifteen members are selected nationally by auditions, and moulded into an ensemble by Houseman and his associates. Actors perform a variety of roles, classical and modern. The 1982–3 repertoire included: *The Country Wife, Twelfth Night, Tartuffe, Pericles*, and *Play and Other Plays* by **Samuel Beckett**. In 1984 it was reported that the Acting Company had performed 'a repertoire of 49 plays in 235 cities, in 44 states, before more than one million people'. Alumni of the company include **Kevin Kline**, **Patti LuPone**, William Hurt, and Christopher Reeve. TLM

Actors Studio, The Founded in 1947 by **Group**

Theatre alumni **Elia Kazan**, **Cheryl Crawford**, and **Robert Lewis**, the Actors Studio is a unique work-shop for professional actors. It is not a school; it charges no tuition; and once an actor is accepted (by a rigorous audition process) he or she becomes a member for life, for the Studio's basic assumption is that there is no terminal degree for an actor. Under **Lee Strasberg**, who joined the Studio in 1949 and who from 1951 until his death in February 1982 was its strong-willed artistic director, the Studio became renowned as the high temple of the Method. The popular notion of the Studio as a place where the mumble, the scratch, and the slouch are tokens of integrity derives from films directed by Elia Kazan (*A Streetcar Named Desire*, 1951; *On the Waterfront*, 1954; *East of Eden*, 1955) which feature moody, verbally inarticulate, spectacularly neurotic performances by such Studio members as **Marlon Brando** and James Dean.

Those who admire the Studio's naturalistic style praise it for psychological revelation. Opponents attack the Studio as a place where self-indulgence, manner-ism, and inaudibility are encouraged as actors examine their own emotions at the expense of the character or the play. Even Studio detractors, however, admit that the Method is a useful technique for the requirements of realistic film acting. The Studio's achievements con-tinue to be hotly debated but its influence is undeniable; its Method has come to be identified as the quintessen-tial American style. In 1963, after years of hesitation, the Studio formed its own short-lived theatre on Broadway; but its enduring legacy is the films directed by Kazan and in the vibrant film performances of its many illustrious members from Brando and Dean and Montgomery Clift to **Dustin Hoffman**, Robert de Niro, **Al Pacino**, Shelley Winters, **Geraldine Page** and Ellen Burstyn, who is the Studio's present artistic director. FH

Actors Theatre of Louisville One of the lead-ing American regional theatres, located in Louisville, Kentucky, most noted for encouraging and producing original scripts. Richard Block and Ewel Cornett founded the Actors Theatre in 1964. Although suc-cessful, Block was replaced at his request in 1969 by Jon Jory, who had previously worked at the **Cleveland Play House** and had co-founded New Haven's **Long Wharf Theatre**.

Jory's appointment and leadership proved beneficial. By 1970–1, season tickets accounted for 95% of the house's capacity. In 1972 the company moved to their present location, the Old Bank of Louisville Building. A $1.7 million conversion of the building resulted in the Pamela Brown Theatre (capacity 641) and the Victor Jory Theatre (capacity 160).

In 1977 the Actors Theatre achieved international acclaim by initiating the Festival of New American Plays. Scripts such as *Gin Game* and *Crimes of the Heart* premiered at the Actors Theatre, moved to Broadway, and won Pulitzer Prizes for Drama.

Jory and the Actors Theatre have received numerous awards and prizes as a result of their work. In 1978 they received the Margo Jones Award for achievement in regional theatres; the next year the **Shubert** Founda-tion's James N. Vaughn Award for encouraging new scripts. In 1980 they received a special Antoinette Perry (Tony) Award. SMA

Adamov, Arthur (1908–70) French playwright of Armenian origins who grew up speaking French as his first language, as was common in wealthy Russian families. Because of his father's passion for gambling, as well as Revolution and exile, the family passed from riches to rags, and settled in Paris in 1924. Adamov's twenties and thirties were marked by loneliness and neurosis, chronicled in *L'Aveu* (*The Confession*, 1946) and *L'Homme et L'Enfant* (*Man and Child*, 1968). After the Second World War he began writing plays, completing seven between 1947 and 1953. Influenced by **Strindberg**, to whom he devoted a monograph, these plays depict a world of terror and persecution stemming from Adamov's own dreams and neuroses, but with a remarkable feel for the telling stage image that can embody, in literal form, a whole state of mind. The masterpiece of this period is *Professor Taranne* (1953). In 1955, when the theatre of the absurd, with which he had been linked, was becoming well known, Adamov's *Ping-Pong* heralded a move towards a more politicized theatre. His *Paolo Paoli* (dir. **Planchon**, 1957) was praised as the first successful Brechtian play in France. Dogged by illness for ten years, Adamov did not achieve further success until *Off Limits* (dir. Garran and Grüber, 1969) and *Si L'Eté Revenait* (*If Summer Returned*) published 1970. His plays are complex and have not always been successful when performed, though his early work was championed by **Vilar**, **Blin**, **Serreau**, etc. His move towards political theatre was made in tandem with Planchon, whose productions have shown how powerful Adamov's work can be, given sufficiently imaginative direction, notably in *A. A. Théâtres d'Adamov*, a posthumous tribute performed at the **TNP** in 1975.   DB

Adams, Edwin (1834–77) American actor. He made his debut in Boston in 1853, and after almost a decade of acting in support of such stars as **Joseph Jefferson** and **E. A. Sothern**, he had his first important New York engagement in 1863 with **Kate Bateman**'s company. During the Civil War, he established himself as a travelling star especially distinguished for his playing of romantic or light comedy characters in such vehicles as *The Lady of Lyons* and *Narcisse*. In 1869, **Edwin Booth** selected him to play Mercutio opposite his Romeo for the opening of **Booth's Theatre**. He was subsequently featured at Booth's Theatre in several roles including the dual roles of Phidias and Raphael in *The Marble Heart* and most notably the title role in a dramatization of **Tennyson**'s *Enoch Arden*, perhaps his favourite characterization. In 1876 following a starring tour of Australia, he returned to the United States gravely ill, and made his last appearance at the California Theatre in San Francisco on 27 May 1876.   DJW

Adams (Kiskadden), Maude (1872–1953) American actress, daughter of Salt Lake City star Annie Adams. At five Maude was starring as Little Schnieder in *Fritz, Our German Cousin* in San Francisco. Her adult career began at 16 with a New York debut at the Star Theatre in *The Paymaster*. In 1890 she began an association with producer **Charles Frohman** which lasted until 1915. A box office favourite until 1932, despite an early retirement from 1918 until 1931, she emerged in 1897 as a star, capitalizing on her eternal youthfulness and whimsey, as Lady Babbie in *The Little Minister*, a character rewritten for her by **Barrie**. She also starred in United States productions of his *Quality Street* (1901), *Peter Pan* (1905), *What Every Woman Knows* (1908), *The Legend of Leonora* (1914), and *A Kiss for Cinderella* (1916). Other parts included **Rostand**'s *L'Aiglon*, the strutting hero in his *Chantecler*, and **Shakespeare**'s Viola, Juliet and Rosalind. In the 1920s she was lighting consultant for General Electric. In 1931 she toured with **Otis Skinner** in *The Merchant of Venice*. From 1937 to 1950 she taught theatre at Stephens College, Missouri.   DBW

Addison, Joseph (1672–1719) English playwright. He wrote only two plays in the middle of a busy career as essayist and politician. In his collaborations with Sir **Richard Steele** on the periodicals *The Tatler* and *The Spectator* he frequently wrote about drama and the practice of the theatres, often admiringly but frequently with a sharp mockery. His play *Cato* (1713) was the subject of an energetic controversy, partly over its alleged political allegory and partly over its success as a controlled neoclassical tragedy of dignity and grief. Cato, who will weep for Rome but not for the death of his son, is offered as an exemplar of political duty. Addison's comedy *The Drummer or the Haunted House* (1716) was not a success.   PH

Ade, George (1866–1944) American playwright and librettist. Born and educated in Indiana, Ade made a name for himself as a reporter in Chicago before turning his talents to the theatre. His most popular librettos, *The Sultan of Sulu* (1902) and *The Sho-Gun* (1904), were influenced by **Gilbert** and Sullivan, but he is best remembered for two dramatic comedies of small-town life, *The County Chairman* (1903) and *The College Widow* (1904). The latter introduced the subject of collegiate adventures and the game of college football to the American stage. Because he had an outstanding ear for current slang and a keen eye for characterizing the everyday residents of his native mid-America, his more than a dozen plays and librettos, although seldom revived, illuminate the social record of the turn of the 20th century.   LDC

Adejumo, Moses Olaiya (1936–) Nigerian actor-manager and founder-owner of the Alawada Theatre ('theatre of the one who entertains'). Moses Olaiya, whose stage name is Baba Sala, is the most popular comedian in Nigeria today and his registered company (both acting and trading) is the most commercially successful, despite performances being almost entirely in Yoruba. The Company has a licence to 'produce plays, run musical groups, run hotels, produce records and magazines' (Lakoju). Olaiya has recently made a feature film, *Orun Mooru* (1984). He and his Alawada Theatre perform extensively on television.

Moses Olaiya started his first theatre group in 1963. He developed what is now his unique comic format in 1965 when he won first prize (a tour of West Germany) in a Nigerian television drama competition. He was denied the prize (his Company were considered too coarse to represent Nigeria) but was compensated with a permanent slot on local television. Ironically, this made his name and ensured the future success of his travelling theatre. Since 1965 he has performed continuously all over Nigeria and coastal West Africa. He is a deeply religious Christian, with many wives and children. He works hard and disciplines his Company, many of whom are his family. His satirical comedies are improvised, 'built around an old pensioner called Baba Sala . . . poor, working with the Ministry of Works . . . Baba Sala is witty but does all the menial jobs at home' (Lakoju).

Jeyifo contends that despite the plays debunking all social pretensions, nonetheless 'the amoral, cynical, social vision of this gifted satirist and parodist' neutralizes his potential for social protest.   ME

Adelphi Theatre, London Of four theatres on the same site in the Strand, the first was built in 1806 and called the Sans Pareil. It was renamed the Adelphi in 1819 and attracted sudden attention in 1821 with the successful run – the first to exceed 100 performances – of **W. T. Moncrieff**'s *Tom and Jerry*. Under the management of Frederick Yates and Daniel Terry (1825–8), the Adelphi became known for its adaptations of Scott's novels and for nautical melodramas starring **T. P. Cooke**. During the long management (1844–74) of **Benjamin Webster**, the theatre was rebuilt to accommodate 1,500 (1858). It was well attended for most of this time, and the description 'Adelphi dramas' was familiarly attached to strong melodramas, well staged (the 'sinking stage' had been used at the Adelphi in 1834, for the first time in England) and powerfully acted by such as Cooke, Webster himself, his mistress **Madame Céleste** and O'Smith. **Buckstone** and **Boucicault** were among the featured dramatists. At the end of the century 'Adelphi dramas' still predominated, with **William Terriss** as swashbuckling hero. Terriss's murder at the stage door of the Adelphi in 1897 brought the great years of the theatre to an abrupt end. It was subsequently twice rebuilt, in 1901 and in 1930.   PT

Adler, Stella (1903–) American actress and teacher. Daughter of the Yiddish actor–producer Jacob Adler, Stella grew up surrounded by great plays and bravura acting. Always interested in the technique of acting, she studied with Richard Boleslavski at the **American Laboratory Theatre** in the twenties even after she had become an established performer. She joined the **Group Theatre** in 1931 because she believed in its founder, **Harold Clurman**, whom she married. A tall, statuesque blonde with imperial carriage and mid-Atlantic diction, Adler ironically had her greatest theatrical success playing downtrodden depression-era housewives in the Group's productions of **Clifford Odets**'s *Awake and Sing!* (1935) and *Paradise Lost* (1935). Her last appearance on a New York stage was in 1945 in *He Who Gets Slapped*, but since 1949, when she founded the Stella Adler Conservatory, she has served the theatre as a teacher. Reminiscing about her famous acting family and her husband, recalling her experiences studying with **Stanislavsky** in Paris in 1934, rising from her throne-like chair to demonstrate an action, continuing to flay the memory of her arch-rival **Lee Strasberg**, issuing threats and portents, and regaling students with advice about life as well as art, Adler is a witty, exhilarating teacher. Countering Strasberg's Method with its focus on self, she urges students to transcend their own experiences by developing their imaginations and by investigating the play's circumstances rather than their own.   FH

Adlers, the A family of actors of the Yiddish theatre. Jacob Adler and his small company from Riga were amongst the first to perform in London, from 1883 to 1887, before moving on to popular success in America. In addition to his wife Sara, six of their seven children, Celia, Luther, Stella, Charles, Jay, and Julia, became actors, the first three being exceptionally talented.   AB

Admiral's Men This company took its name from its patron, Lord Howard who was created Lord High Admiral in 1585, the year in which the Admiral's Men first appeared at Court. We do not know at which London theatre they performed in their early years. Probably they alternated between the **Theatre**, the **Curtain** and Newington Butts. But the emergence of the Admiral's Men as a distinct and distinguished company is properly associated with three men, **Philip Henslowe**, **Edward Alleyn** and **Christopher Marlowe**. It was Alleyn's acting in Marlowe's plays at Henslowe's **Rose** that established the company's reputation. It was only the formation of the **Lord Chamberlain's Men** in 1594 that nudged the Admiral's Men into second place in the Elizabethan theatrical hierarchy. Henslowe's financial involvement may not, in the long run, have been an advantage, although it provided a greater security than was common, and helped the company to evade the general prohibition of plays after the *Isle of Dogs* affair in 1597. The opportunistic Henslowe was quick to obtain for the Admiral's Men the services of several leading members of Pembroke's Men, jobless because of their involvement in the performance of *The Isle of Dogs*. His shrewdness was certainly an asset and his wealth a comfort in times of hardship. But Henslowe was not himself a member of the Admiral's Men. He was the owner of their theatre. When, in 1599, the Lord Chamberlain's Men opened the **Globe**, very close to the Rose, the Admiral's Men suffered in the competition for audiences. Unlike their rivals, they did not own their own theatre. Partly as a result, perhaps, they did not command the same loyalty from their actors. Alleyn's increasing involvement in his business partnership with Henslowe deprived them of a star. The move north of the river, to the **Fortune**, in 1600 brought a new audience and sufficient prosperity. As London's acknowledged second company, they were granted royal patronage and the title of Prince Henry's Men after the accession of James I. Regular writers included **Dekker**, **Munday**, **Chettle** and a host of lesser names, but the regular revival of Marlowe's plays and the sinking reputation of the Fortune during the second decade of the 17th century announced the company's creative impoverishment. As the Palsgrave's Men, they continued their occupation of the Fortune, rebuilt in 1623 after destruction by fire in 1621, without much success. By 1631, when some of the Fortune actors joined a newly formed Prince Charles's Men at **Salisbury Court**, the long tradition of the Admiral's Men had been broken.   PT

Adriani, Placido (d. c. 1740) An Italian Benedictine monk, residing in Naples, who specialized in the role of Pulcinella in monastery recitals and staged sacred performances, such as *S. Francesco di Paola* (1719). His importance lies in his manuscript collection, *Selva, overo Zibaldone di concetti comici* (1734), which was discovered by Benedetto Croce in the Public Library of Perugia in the 1890s. It is a rich repository of **commedia dell'-arte** scenarios, plots and *lazzi*.   LS

Aeschylus (525/4–456/5 BC) A native of Eleusis, Aeschylus is said to have produced tragedies as early as 499, and won his first victory at the Great Dionysia (see **Greece, ancient**) in 484. He fought against the Persians at the Battle of Marathon (490) and probably also at that of Salamis (480). He became the most popular tragedian of his day, winning a total of 13 victories at Athens and also visiting Sicily to produce plays for the tyrant Hieron I of Syracuse. It was on a later visit to Sicily that he died. As early as **Aristophanes**, who affectionately parodies his style in *Frogs*, he was regarded as the first of the great tragedians (*Frogs* 1004–5).

For at least part of his career he played the leading part in his own plays, as was normal until the time of **Sophocles**. He is said to have been responsible for reducing the role of the Chorus and for introducing the second actor – clearly a momentous innovation. Many, perhaps most, of his plays belonged to connected tetralogies, but it is uncertain whether these were a speciality of his or were standard in the early 5th century.

He is said to have written 90 plays; we know the titles of over 70; seven survive under his name. *Persians* (472), which depicts the despair of the Persian court on hearing of the Greek victory at Salamis, is the earliest drama we possess and the only surviving Greek tragedy on a historical subject. It did not belong to a connected tetralogy. *Seven against Thebes* (467) was the third play of a tetralogy about Oedipus and his family, the other plays being *Laius*, *Oedipus* and the satyr play *Sphinx*. *Suppliant Women* (once thought to be the earliest play but now dated between 466 and 459) almost certainly belonged to a connected tetralogy about the daughters of Danaus. *Agamemnon*, *Choephori* (*Libation-Bearers*) and *Eumenides* together form the *Oresteia* (458), the only connected trilogy that survives (the lost satyr play *Proteus* completed the tetralogy).

The seventh play, *Prometheus Bound*, was until recently accepted as authentic by most scholars, but detailed examination of its language, metre and stagecraft has made it very probable that it is post-Aeschylean, perhaps datable to the 440s. It was accompanied by the lost *Prometheus Unbound*, in which Prometheus was released from his torment by Heracles. The surviving play combines an extraordinary boldness of overall conception (the reason for its popularity among 19th-century romantics) with a distinct clumsiness of detailed execution. Like the *Oresteia*, it employs three actors.

Fragments also survive, not extensive but providing valuable evidence for Aeschylus' satyr plays, as well as for lost tragedies.

The authentic surviving plays, though so few in number, are so diverse that it is difficult to generalize about them. Each is fairly simple in plot, though those of the *Oresteia*, perhaps influenced by Sophocles, are more complex than the others. Each, except *Suppliant Women* and *Eumenides*, invests a single public event (such as the Persian defeat or the murder of Agamem-non by his wife Clytemnestra) with great moral and religious significance. Before it occurs, or is announced, the event is foreshadowed with foreboding or (in *Choephori*) with illusory hope, and we become more and more aware of the network of forces making it inevitable; afterwards its ethical implications are explored and its future consequences predicted. We can see in the *Oresteia*, and glimpse in the *Seven against Thebes*, how the significance of this central event could be further enriched through its relation to others in the same trilogy. Characterization tends to be subordinate to the deeds which the characters perform rather than being pursued for its own sake; but this does not prevent those characters from being fully intelligible in human terms.

The Chorus is constantly exploited throughout the authentic plays. Its songs, often longer and more elaborate than any in Sophocles or **Euripides**, carry much of the moral and emotional weight of the drama. It can also be seen as a counterpart, within the play, of the audience outside it, making the characters aware that their deeds are on public view and enabling them to project their speeches outward to the public. This may have been usual in Aeschylus' day; what can never have been usual, and was probably a bold experiment, was the use of the Chorus as a major party to the action, which we see in *Suppliant Women* and *Eumenides*.

An unusual richness of language, and boldness – often obscurity – of verbal imagery is apparent both in the choral songs and in much of the spoken dialogue. Powerful use is made of sustained image-patterns, especially in the *Oresteia*, where some images (such as the net, the hunt, the light in seen darkness) recur throughout the trilogy. Visual effects are also exploited, sometimes in symbolic ways, the classic examples being the so-called carpet in *Agamemnon* and the robe in *Choephori*. The impression given by some ancient (and modern) critics, however, that Aeschylus was addicted to grandiose spectacle for its own sake, is not to be trusted.

Divine and human causation work together (see e.g. *Persians* 472, *Agamemnon* 1505–8), so that events are intelligible in purely human terms (except in *Eumenides*, where the gods themselves take the stage) but the influence of divine forces can always be seen in them. The supremacy of Zeus is frequently stressed; but it is no longer fashionable to see Aeschylus as a champion of an 'advanced', almost monotheist religion. Zeus and the other gods ensure that crime is punished and are to that extent 'just', but they are less concerned to see innocence rewarded; indeed in some plays it seems that the punishment of crime must always involve further crime, creating an unbreakable cycle (*Seven* 742–65, *Agamemnon* 757–71). In *Eumenides*, however, Aeschylus expresses an emotional faith that the cycle can be broken, linking this to his faith in the future of Athens.

Aeschylus does not, any more than the other tragedians, fill his plays with contemporary political allusions. *Persians* cannot help making an appeal to Greek patriotic pride, but this is not allowed to detract from the sombre tragedy of Xerxes, ruined by his own folly. *Eumenides* is exceptional among Greek tragedies in not only having broadly political implications but appearing to be a reaction to a particular event – Ephialtes' democratic reform of the Council of the Areopagus in 462/1. Even here, however, Aeschylus does not take any clear stance for or against the reform. ALB

Afinogenov, Aleksandr Nikolaevich (1904–41) Soviet playwright.

One of **Gorky**'s would-be heirs apparent, Afinogenov searched for a new Soviet psychological drama in the post-revolutionary years of transition from primitive agit-prop to doctrinaire socialist realism. Raised by revolutionary parents, a Communist Party member from 1922, and a graduate of the Moscow School of Journalism (1924), the author of 26 plays seemed to be well-equipped for the task. His early plays – *Robert Tim* (1923), *The Other Side of the Slot* (adapted from Jack London, 1926), *At the Breaking Point* (1927), *Keep Your Eyes Peeled* (1927) and *Raspberry Jam* (1928) – were produced by the civic-minded Proletkult Theatre, where Afinogenov served as literary manager and director, and reflected the group's singleminded proletarian bias. Afinogenov tired of the schematic, predictable plots, the superficial character typing and telegraphic language which characterized the Proletkult dramatic style. He formally broke with the organization in 1928, joining the Russian Association of Proletarian Writers (RAPP), whose 'dialectical-materialist' approach to art he helped to define in his *The Creative Method of the Theatre: The Dialectics of the Creative Process* (1931). However, RAPP, which was dissolved by Stalin in 1932, proved to be equally unsympathetic to his artistic goals which had become clearer from 1929 with his drama *The Eccentric*. A character study of a romantic non-communist dreamer set against the backdrop of First Five-Year Plan ideological enthusiasm, the author had the temerity to cast communists as villains in counterpoint to his unallied hero. His best play, *Fear* (1931), further defined the nature and scope of the social psychological drama, separating it from the **Moscow Art Theatre**'s individualistic 'biological psychologism' and bringing some subtlety and humanity to a basically dialectic confrontation between a good communist and an unenlightened but salvageable elder scientist who is surrounded by the usual opportunistic and decadent types. Considered pivotal in the Soviet dramatic canon, it was successfully staged by **Stanislavsky** at MAT. His remaining plays include: *Distant Point* (1935), a Soviet philosophical drama; *Hail, Spain!* (1936), a heroically scaled popular romantic piece; and *Mashenka* (1940), a very popular amalgam of personal and patriotic dramas. Afinogenov was criticized throughout the 1930s for his insistence on psychological realism at the expense of ideological concerns, was charged with being a Trotskyite agent and lost his Party membership in 1937. His membership was restored in 1938, and he was made head of the Literary Department of the Soviet Information Bureau. SG

Africa (North) French-speaking see French-speaking North Africa

Africa: Portuguese-speaking (lusophone)

In the Portuguese colonies, European theatre was introduced very early on by missionaries. The plays were religious in character, their objective being the propagation of Catholicism. The religion of the Africans was not taken into consideration: the settlers imposed their own religion and culture on the natives.

The literary genre of drama, as seen from a Western point of view, is a more recent concept, which appeared much later than poetry and prose in the Portuguese-speaking African countries. This can be explained by the fact that the colonialists provided very little in the way of facilities needed to perform a play, and also because poetry could more freely express the violence felt by the colonized peoples.

When independence was declared in 1975 in Angola, Cape Verde, Guinea-Bissau, Mozambique and São Tomé e Príncipe, illiteracy was higher than 90%. This had affected literary production and the people's interest in drama. It was very difficult to publish anything and as the writers had little incentive to do so anyway, there came about a cultural stagnation.

Portuguese colonialism imposed a very severe censorship on newspapers and books, which meant that any expression of opinions contrary to those held by the ruling power would not be published.

The principles of negritude and Pan-Africanism formed the political and cultural background that led to the armed struggle for liberation in 1961 in Angola, 1963 in Guinea-Bissau and 1964 in Mozambique. This anti-colonial war led to their independence in 1975, after a coup in Portugal in 1974 that had overthrown the oldest dictatorship in Europe.

These principles influenced in part the dramatic production of these territories. Some plays directly challenged the ruling values. However, the vast majority of the plays performed before independence were vaudeville pieces that came from the metropolis, their objective being mainly to amuse the white spectators.

After independence, Marxist regimes were formed aiming to make good the damage done by colonialism and build a classless society. Consequently drama was often used as a means of politicizing people, as a political instrument supporting the principles of socialist realism.

Angola Western drama was introduced by Portuguese missionaries at the beginning of colonization. The subjects of the plays performed were based on Catholicism with no consideration for the natives' own religion. As Carlos Vaz reports, 'the roles of the Infant Jesus, of the Angels and of Joseph and Mary could only be performed by white people while the roles of Judas, Satan and even sometimes Herod were only performed by the blacks'.

On the other hand, vaudeville pieces were also acted out, mainly by theatre groups from the metropolis.

Important plays, as far as those that have actually been committed to writing are concerned, include Domingos Van-Dúnen's *Auto de Natal* (*Christmas Play*) (performed in Luanda in 1972 and written in *quimbundo*, a native language, as a reaction against the language imposed by the settlers and as a revalidation of the African culture); two plays of Orlando de Albuquerque, published in 1974, *Ovibanda* and *O filho de Zambi* (*Zambi's Son*), on religious themes that were genuinely Angolan and the children's play *Os pioneiros do futuro* (*The Pioneers of the Future*), written in 1974 by Júlio de Almeida and Elsa de Sousa.

On 11 November 1975, Angola became independent. A month later, the Union of Angolan Writers was formed. They promulagated:

> At this moment when our people have just taken over full responsibility for their future as a free and

At this moment when our people have just taken over full responsibility for their future as a free and sovereign nation, the Angolan writers take their stand at the forefront facing the enormous tasks of national liberation and reconstruction.

Our literary history bears witness to the generations of writers who were able in their own time to keep alive the process of our liberation by expressing the deep longings of our people, mainly those of its most exploited classes. Thus Angolan literature emerges not merely as an aesthetic need but also as a weapon for the affirmation of the Angolans.

The first step of direct armed struggle against colonialism has been made. The Angolan writers in many different ways answered the call to arms and some gave their lives on the field of honour for their fatherland.

Today, our people have entered into a new battle in this centuries-old war for our self-assertion as a free nation, in Africa and in the world. Once more, as is their duty and tradition, the Angolan writers are present at the heart of this popular resistance joining the battle of the cultural front.

This quotation sums up the themes that dominated literature in Angola during the first years of independence. This was confirmed by the President of the Republic, Agostinho Neto, himself an eminent poet, when he declared that 'literature in this independent country of Angola which is marching towards a superior form of social organization – socialism – must necessarily reflect this new situation'. However, two years later, Agostinho Neto qualified the principles of the cultural policy: 'I would say that we cannot be schematic or follow stereotypes as the theoreticians of socialist realism once did.' This position followed upon the realization that art had served politics, had no autonomy, and had often been reduced to political pamphleteering.

After the fall of the dictatorship in Portugal and during the period of transition that led to independence, there flourished in Angola a spontaneous theatre that reflected the social contradictions of a colonial society in open disintegration. In this period of transition the plays *As duas caras do patrão (The Two Faces of the Boss), A província de Angola (The Province of Angola), Manifestação no jardim da Celeste (Demonstration in Celeste's garden), Combate de box (Boxing Match)* and *Uma lição de Portugalidade (A Lesson of Portuguese-ness)* were performed by students and workers.

After independence, the fundamental objective of the Angolan theatre was to awaken the political consciousness of the people. In 1975, *Poder popular (Popular Power)* was performed by the Tchingange Group. In accordance with its didactic, political and doctrinal approach, it was presented in schools, factories and hospitals in Luanda and in rural areas. In 1976, the National School of Theatre was created. One of the groups of this school performed *Africa liberdade (Africa Freedom)*. In 1977, the group Xilenga-Teatro was formed, which resurrected from the vast and rich repertory of the oral tradition of the Tchokwe people four narratives. The activity of the group 'Ngongo' and the experiments that were made in the field of the puppet theatre are worth mentioning.

Bearing the same political lines are *A pele do diabo (The Devil's Skin)*, written by Manuel Santos Lima (1977), *A corda (The Rope)* by Pepetela (1978), *O círculo de giz de Bombó (Bombó's Chalk Circle)* by Henrique Guerra (1979), adapted from **Bertolt Brecht**'s play *The Caucasian Chalk Circle, No velho ninguém toca (The Old Man is Untouchable)* by Costa Andrade, and *A revolta da casa dos ídolos (The Revolt in the House of the Idols)* written by Pepetela and published in 1980. This last play shows a formal and thematic depth that contrasts with the naive spontaneity that was common in the vast majority of the plays previously mentioned.

Cape Verde The first known play is *Terra de sôdade (Land of Nostalgia)* written in the 40s by Jaime de Figueiredo. It is a nostalgic four-act ballet on the theme of emigration.

Before independence, nothing else is worthy of note except that, according to Carlos Vaz, there was a theatre group in the grammar school 'Adriano Moreira', in Praia.

After independence, which took place on 5 July 1975, theatre was a means of politicizing the people, as in the other Portuguese-speaking African countries. Basing himself, thematically speaking, on the history of Cape Verde – an uprising of slaves against the colonial domination – Oswaldo Osório wrote *Gervásio* heavily influenced by Bertolt Brecht.

Seeking to reveal the origins of the culture of Cape Verde, Kwame Konde founded the theatre group Korda Kaoberdi and combined acting with music and dance. In 1977 he performed *Os disanimados para os infernos (To Hell with the Pessimists)* written by Kaoberdiano Dambará. Later this group performed **Augusto Boal**'s play *A lua muito pequena e a caminhada perigosa (The Very Small Moon and the Dangerous Journey)*, which dealt with the political action and theory of Che Guevara.

In 1979, Donaldo Pereira de Macedo's play *Descarado (Shameless)* was published in the USA. Its importance lies in the fact of its being the first play from Cape Verde to be published in book form and also because it was written in Creole.

The present situation is not very encouraging. There are very few incentives to create and produce theatre and previous experiments are not being followed through. Some directors like Leão Lopes occasionally experiment in combining the traditional dramatic features – dance, masks, etc. – with audio-visual techniques, the thematic source being traditional tales, poetry and national literature.

Guinea-Bissau Besides the traditional theatre, the vaudeville pieces that flourished before independence and were based on the everyday life of the settlers must also be mentioned.

Some plays for children, based on traditional fables, were also performed.

Dances like *A dança do boi (The Dance of the Ox)* and the *Danças dos Bijagós (The Bijagós Dances)* have some underlying dramatic features.

After independence, no dramatic activity has been reported in this country.

Mozambique Before independence, censorship controlled all literary production, it was therefore difficult to write plays with clear political features. However, there were some plays that denounced the claustrophobic colonial status quo.

In 1959, Afonso Ribeiro wrote *Três setas apontadas*

son, who represents colonial values. Out of the conflict between these two philosophies of life emerges a movement towards a new society which will be more aware of human and universal values.

Lindo Lhongo's *Os noivos ou conferência dramática sobre o lobolo* (*The Engagement or the Dramatic Discourse of the Purchasing of a Bride*) follows the same basic principle of confrontation with colonial ideology. It was performed in 1971, and an excerpt was published in the literary magazine *Caliban*, banned soon afterwards by the political police. The emphasis of this text is on the renaissance and valorization of a genuinely African culture.

Not long before independence, other politically and culturally engaged plays were written: *As trinta mulheres de Muzelini* (*The Thirty Wives of Muzelini*) by Lindo Lhongo, *Filhos da noite* (*Children of the Night*) by António Francisco and *O feitiço e a religião* (*Sorcery and Religion*) by João Fumane.

Among the vaudeville pieces the following are worth a mention: *Crime Anica, Madalena, As aventuras de um herói* (*The Adventures of a Hero*), *Sua Alteza o Criador* (*His Highness the Creator*), *Os cavaleiros do arcabuz* (*The Knights of the Arquebus*), and *Era eu* (*It was I*) by Carlos da Silva; *Polana azul* (*Blue Polana*) and *Sete de março* (*The Seventh of March*) by Fernando Baldaque and Carlos Queirós de Fonseca, all written in the first 20 years of this century; *Ponta vermelha* (*Red Point*) by Fernando Baldaque and Arnaldo Silva (1931); *Ice-cream Today* by António Alonso Moreira, Fernando Baldaque and Arnaldo Silva (1932); *Renúncia* (*Resignation*) by Alexandre Cabral Campos (1932); *A palhota de Moçambique* (*The Thatched Hut of Mozambique*, 1937) and *Zona perigosa* (*Danger Zone*) written by Fernando Baldaque and Arnaldo Silva (1941); *Africa menina e moça* (*Africa Young and Lovely*) by Ruy Sant'Elmo, *Latitude sul* (*Southern Latitude*) by Luna de Oliveira, *Amor à vista* (*Love on the Way*) by José Mendonça and Fausto Ritto, *O mato* (*The Forest*) by Caetano Montez and *Infortúnio* (*Misfortune*) by Felisberto Ferreirinha, which were performed in the 40s.

According to the regime that emerged after independence in 1975, the principal task was then to 'heal colonial wounds' and build a fairer society. As in the other Portuguese-speaking countries, drama was a means of propagating the ideology of the party in power. The model followed was Soviet agit-prop. These pragmatic principles were displayed in the plays of Orlando Mendes *Um minuto de silêncio* (*One Minute of Silence*) and *Na machamba de Maria – sábado às três da tarde* (*On Maria's Small Farm – Saturday Afternoon at Three O'Clock*), published in 1975; in the radiophonic theatrical experiment elaborated by Alvaro Belo Marques, a Portuguese voluntary worker in 1978; in *A estrada* (*The Road*) by Leite Vasconcelos, in 1979; in *O destino inimigo do povo* (*Destiny: Enemy of the People*) performed by a collective of workers; in *A Comuna* (*The Commune*), created by the students of the University Eduardo Mondlane and the workers of the Mozambique Railway, in 1979; in *A Sagrada Família* (*The Holy Family*) written and performed by the 'Grupo Cénico das Forças Populares de Libertação de Moçambique'.

Other dramatic activities that deserve to be mentioned are the adaptation of Luís Bernardo Honwana's tale *Rosita até morrer* (*Rosita to my Dying Day*) by a group of Brazilian voluntary workers, Sant'Anna Afonso's

Eu não sou eu e outras peças (*I Am Not I and Other Plays*), *Memórias de um projecto* (*Memories of a Project*) by the Cuban voluntary worker Maité Vera. Currently in press is Pedro Paulo Pereira's *Tempo de mudança* (*Time for a Change*).

Theatre for children, with a basically didactic aim, was also pursued in the plays *Chiquinho malandrinho* (*Naughty Chiquinho*) by Mwaparra and *Coisas que só acontecem na flor de lótus* (*Things that only Happen in the Lotus Flower*) by Álvaro Belo Marques.

São Tomé e Príncipe As far as this country is concerned, the importance of *Tchiloli ou Tragédia do Marquês de Mântua e do Imperador Carloto Magno*, brought with them by the Portuguese settlers, must be stressed. It is a combination of European and African cultures, and to the Portuguese text African features were added: music, masks, dances and costumes.

O Auto de Floripes, performed in the island of Príncipe, was also brought over from Portugal.

In 1965 and 1969, two plays written by Fernando Reis were performed: *Os mangas de alpaca* (*The Red-Tapists*) and *D'Jambi*.   DP

See: J. M. Abrantes, 'A procura de um Reencontro com a Realidade', *Africa* 3, January/March, 1979; C. Andrade, *Literatura Angolana* (*Opiniões*), Lisbon, 1980; M. E. O. O. Assumpção, 'A Identidade Nacional na Dramaturgia Angolana. A Revolta da Casa dos Ídolos e a Pele do Diabo', *Les Littératures Africaines de Langue Portugaise. Actes du Colloque International*, Paris, 28, 29, 30 November, 1 December 1984, Paris, 1985; M. Ferreira, *Literaturas Africanas de Expressão Portuguesa*, vols. 1 and 2, Lisbon, 1977; R. G. Hamilton, *Literatura Africana Literatura Necessária*, vols. 1 and 2, Lisbon, 1981 and 1984; F. Reis, *Povô Flogá – O Povo Brinca*, São Tomé, 1969; B. Traoré, 'Le Théâtre Négro-Africain et ses Fonctions Sociologiques', *Présence Africaine* no. 14/15, June/September, 1957; C. Valbert, *Le Tchiloli de São Tomé. Un Exemple de Subversion Culturelle. Les Littératures Africaines de Langue Portugaise. Actes du Colloque International*, Paris, 28, 29, 30 November, 1 December 1984, Paris, 1985; C. Vaz, *Para um Conhecimento do Teatro Africano*, Lisbon, 1978.

Africa (South of the Sahara) see **French-speaking Africa South of the Sahara**

Afro-American theatre Afro-American theatre had a dual origin. First came the indigenous theatre consisting of folk tales, songs, music, dance and mimicry that blacks performed in cabins, at camp meetings, and in open parks like Congo Square in New Orleans. African in spirit, these expressions were transformed by the American environment. Then came the African theatre in imitation of white playhouses and scripted dramas that **William Henry Brown** established in 1821. Though Brown began with **Shakespeare** he also staged a sketch on slavery and his own play *The Drama of King Shotaway* (1823). His theatre produced two notable Shakespearian actors in James Hewlett and **Ira Aldridge**.

The African theatre had no successors in antebellum America except for two plays written by the ex-slave William Wells Brown and read by him on abolitionist platforms. One, *The Escape, or, A Leap for Freedom* (1858), survives. Black indigenous expressions, however, were by the 1840s adopted by white comedians and fashioned into blackface minstrelsy that caricatured black folk on Southern plantations. Ironically, the now-disdained minstrel show opened the professional stage to Afro-Americans. Billed as authentic Negroes, black minstrels inherited the burnt-cork stereotype characters created by whites and gave them validity. At the same time black performers were polishing acting skills in short farces which were added to their shows. Ernest Hogan, Billy Kersands and Sam Lucas were three leading minstrels while noteworthy black troupes included Charles B. Hicks's Georgia Minstrels (1865), Callender's Original Georgia Minstrels (1872) and Haverly's Coloured Minstrels (1878). Since black playgoers were segregated in an upper gallery section in most theatres, these shows played primarily to white audiences. Yet their success ensured perpetuation of the genre into the first decades of the 20th century.

Vying for popularity with the minstrels were ubiquitous 'Tom shows' based on the dramatization of **Uncle Tom's Cabin** (1852). Despite the novel's intent to eradicate slavery, stage versions seen throughout the land for 80 years reinforced the theatrical image of blacks as ignorant, submissive, happy-go-lucky creatures. Tom shows also began to employ blacks as slave characters and in plantation choruses but eventually the play was denounced by black leaders.

Black companies of higher calibre emerged after the Civil War. Anna and Emma Hyers, classically trained prodigies from Sacramento, California, toured the country in *opéra bouffe* and original musicals such as *Out of Bondage* (1877). The Astor Place Company of Coloured Tragedians under **J. A. Arneaux** came into being in 1884 with a Shakespearian repertoire and in 1889 Theodore Drury gave the first performance of his Opera Company. Professional concert artists and solo readers like **Henrietta Vinton Davis** appeared across the country.

In the popular theatre a shift in the minstrel pattern occurred with white-produced shows. Sam Jack's *Creole Show* (1891–7) introduced women in the line-up and as a dancing chorus. John W. Isham added a story-line to olio specialities in *The Octoroons* (1895) and operatic selections for the finale of *Oriental America* (1896). This last production prepared Broadway for the invasion of original black musicals such as *A Trip to Coontown* (1898) by the multi-talented **Bob Cole** and Billy Johnson and *In Dahomey* (1902) by **Bert Williams** and George Walker. Teamed with these star performers were the composer Will Marion Cook who wrote the operetta *Clorindy; or, The Origin of the Cake Walk* (1898), the playwright Jesse Shipp, and the versatile brothers J. Rosamond Johnson and James W. Johnson.

Also prominent at this time were long-lasting road companies in vaudeville, notably Sissieretta Jones's Black Patti Troubadours and Gus Hill's The Smart Set which was later acquired by the brothers Salem Tutt Whitney and J. Homer Tutt.

In straight drama William Edgar Easton wrote two historical plays on the Haitian revolution: *Dessalines* (1893) and *Christophe* (1911) which were produced by Henrietta Vinton Davis. Scott Joplin composed his opera *Treemonisha* (1911) but it remained unproduced for decades. In 1897 Bob Cole organized a stock company and training school at Worth's Museum in New York. Others followed, urged on by black critics Sylvester Russell of the *Freeman* (Indianapolis) and

Lester Walton of the New York *Age* who felt that resident companies in Afro-American theatres would encourage dramatic plays, provide regular employment to black actors and permit open seating. In 1906 Robert Motts of Chicago started the Pekin Stock Company whose success spawned other Pekins in Cincinnati, Ohio, and Savannah, Georgia. In New York the Negro Players were formed in 1912 and the **Lafayette Players** in 1915. Some of these companies staged original musicals and dramas while others contented themselves with popular Broadway revivals.

Blacks first appeared on Broadway in dramatic roles in *Three Plays for a Negro Theatre* (1917) by the white writer Ridgely Torrence. This auspicious start, cut short by America's imminent entry into the First World War, was confirmed by **Charles Gilpin**'s stunning performance for the **Provincetown Players** in *The Emperor Jones* (1920). However, the commercial success of *Shuffle Along* (1921) brought a resurgence of black musicals that stirred critics to rail against the pervasive image of black song-and-dance clowns on the professional stage. W. E. B. DuBois, editor of *The Crisis*, urged formation of a nationwide movement of little theatres presenting plays 'about us, by us, for us, and near us'. His magazine and *Opportunity* sponsored playwriting competitions and published prizewinning entries. In the years ahead black college drama professors like Randolph Edmonds, Owen Dodson and Thomas D. Pawley would begin writing and directing original plays with their students.

Three dramas by white playwrights demonstrated the reach of black histrionic talent. **Paul Green**'s *In Abraham's Bosom* (1926) shared Pulitzer Prize honours with an experienced cast including the gifted Rose McLendon, **Dubose** and **Dorothy Heyward**'s 1927 hit *Porgy* inspired the operatic version by **George Gershwin**, and **Marc Connelly**'s *The Green Pastures* (1930) with De Lawd magnificently played by Richard B. Harrison earned a Pulitzer Prize and a five-year run. The 1930s witnessed an upsurge of socially relevant plays like Hall Johnson's *Run Little Chillun* (1933), **Langston Hughes**'s *Mulatto* (1935) and *Stevedore* (1934) by white authors Paul Peters and George Sklar. The short-lived **Federal Theatre Project** through its Negro Units in 22 cities sponsored black playwrights and productions including Theodore Browne's *Natural Man* (1937) in Seattle, Theodore Ward's *Big White Frog* (1938) in Chicago, and **Orson Welles**'s production of the 'voodoo' *Macbeth* (1936) in Harlem.

In the 40s the American Negro Theatre made steady progress in training and production at its Harlem-based Library Theatre until its successful *Anna Lucasta* (1944) transferred to Broadway and caused the breakup of the company. Richard Wright's *Native Son* (1941), imaginatively staged by Orson Welles, revealed the driving, versatile talent of **Canada Lee** as Bigger Thomas and Theodore Ward's *Our Lan'* (1946), a moving historical drama about newly-freed slaves seeking a homestead, showed well Off-Broadway but lost its appeal when altered for a bigger house. **Paul Robeson**'s record-breaking *Othello* (1943) belongs to this decade.

After the Second World War the civil rights movement gained momentum. Plays such as Louis Peterson's *Take a Giant Step* (1953) on Broadway, William Branch's *In Splendid Error* (1954), **Alice Childress**'s

Trouble in Mind (1955) and **Loften Mitchell**'s *A Land Beyond the River* (1957) at the Greenwich Mews Theatre Off-Broadway dealt unambiguously with the racial problem and used racially mixed casts. Companies like **Joseph Papp**'s **New York Shakespeare Festival** began to cast black actors in traditionally white roles. The trend towards integration was reflected in **Lorraine Hansberry**'s award-winning drama, *A Raisin in the Sun* (1959) and **Ossie Davis**'s satiric comedy *Purlie Victorious* (1961). Nevertheless, the slow pace of social reform coupled with a controversial Vietnam War triggered unrest on college campuses and in black urban communities. Afro-American theatre revealed the frustration in a series of revolutionary dramas led by **Amiri Baraka**'s *Dutchman* (1964). As government and foundation funds were hurriedly released to ameliorate conditions in inner cities, black theatres mushroomed nationwide, generating a crop of new playwrights and productions and opening opportunities for directors, designers and technicians. The search for a black identity led to experimentation with new dramatic forms. In 1969 Lonnie Elder's *Ceremonies in Dark Old Men* just missed and **Charles Gordone**'s *No Place to Be Somebody* captured the Pulitzer Prize. Other significant playwrights of the period were **Ed Bullins**, Phillip Hayes Dean, **Adrienne Kennedy**, Ron Milner, Charlie Russell, Joseph Walker and Richard Wesley.

Among the few theatre groups to survive when funding was withdrawn were the **Negro Ensemble Company** of New York, the Free Southern Theatre in New Orleans, and the Inner City Cultural Centre in Los Angeles. Afro-American theatre had gained immeasurably from this period of upheaval but had made little headway in the Broadway commercial theatre which responded by staging a number of extravagant black musicals such as the revived *Hello Dolly* (1967), *The Wiz* (1975) and *Timbuktu!* (1978). Only *The Great White Hope* (1968) by white playwright Howard Sackler with a bravura performance by **James Earl Jones** as the prizefighter Jack Jefferson merits attention. Both Sackler and Jones received top awards for their work. Important black productions of recent years include **Ntozake Shange**'s *For Colored Girls . . .* and Vinnette Carroll's *Your Arms Too Short To Box With God*, both in 1976, Phillip Hayes Dean's monodrama *Paul Robeson* (1978), and **Charles Fuller**'s Pulitzer Prize-winning *A Soldier's Play* (1981).   EGH

Agate, James (Evershed) (1877–1947) British drama critic. Born in Manchester, he began his career as reviewer for *The Manchester Guardian*. It was as drama critic of *The Sunday Times* from 1923 until his death that Agate established himself as the most feared and most courted of theatrical judges. His exemplary determination to write well did not prevent an occasional waywardness in deciding what to say nor a preparedness to resist radical change in the London theatre. He became too conscious of his own personality, as is disarmingly confessed in the very title of his selection, in nine volumes, from his diary, *Ego* (1932–47). Among his volumes of selected criticism are *Brief Chronicles* (1943), *Red-Letter Nights* (1944) and *Immoment Toys* (1945).   PT

Agathon (c. 447 – c. 401 BC) A tragedian who produced plays at Athens for some years before departing c. 407, like **Euripides**, for the court of Archelaus of Macedon. **Aristotle** mentions a tragedy of his (*Antheus*) in which plot and characters were entirely invented (not drawn from myth), and another which contained enough material for an epic. He also says that Agathon was the first to write choral odes which were mere interludes irrelevant to the play's action. A few fragments survive.   ALB

Agit-prop Term used to describe theatre pieces devised to ferment political action (agitation) and propaganda.   MB

Aguilera Malta, Demetrio (1909–79) Ecuadorian dramatist, poet, novelist, short story writer, and diplomat. Born in Guayaquil, he was one-fifth of the famous literary 'Grupo de Guayaquil', a leftist literary group dedicated to social change but committed as well to literary excellence. His early reputation was based on *Don Goyo*, a vanguard novel published in 1933. In the early period his full-length plays, such as *España leal* (*Loyal Spain*, 1938), *Lázaro* (*Lazarus*, 1941), *Sangre azul* (*Blue Blood*, 1954) and *No bastan los átomos* (*Atoms Aren't Enough*, 1954), are realistic presentations with social denunciations and commitments. Aguilera Malta's best efforts clearly belong to his expressionistic period, with *El tigre* (*The Tiger*, 1955), a play of magical realism in the supernatural tropics, *Dientes blancos* (*White Teeth*, 1955) and *Honorarios* (*Fees*, 1957). Aguilera Malta served his country in various capacities in Ecuador, in the diplomatic corps in Santiago, in the Pan American Union in Washington, and for the last years of his life as Ecuador's Ambassador to Mexico. During this period he wrote *Infierno negro* (*Black Hell*, 1967) and *Muerte, S.A.* (*Death, Inc.*, 1970), both continuing the expressionistic tendencies but with mordant satire and the denunciation of discrimination.   GW

Agustín, José (1944–) Mexican playwright and novelist, who combines novelistic and dramatic techniques into interesting compositions. *Abolición de la propiedad* (*Abolition of Property*) was published in 1969 but first staged in 1979 because of the complexities of a text that relies on closed circuit TV, recordings and projections in dealing with an almost psychopathic perception of reality. *Círculo vicioso* (*Vicious Circle*, 1972) is an exposé of corruption in the Mexican penal system (using Lecumberri as an example). The play was censored by Mexican authorities for its gross language, but finally permitted.   GW

Aidoo, Ama Ata (1942–) Ghanaian playwright. Born in Ghana and graduated from the University of Legon in 1964. Her reputation as a playwright rests upon her two plays, *The Dilemma of a Ghost* and *Anowa*. *The Dilemma of a Ghost* was first produced at the University of Legon in 1964, and published in London a year later. It explores the problems of a marriage between a Ghanaian man who has achieved academic honours in the United States and a black American woman whom he brings home to Ghana. The play is concerned with their decision not to have children immediately, and the consequent relationship with the husband's proud Ghanaian family, who cannot reconcile the wife's slave ancestry with their prejudices. But there is eventually a reconciliation between the women and the husband is chided for his own insensitivity towards mother, aunts and wife. *Anowa* (1970), too, is concerned with slavery's legacy, and again is written from a woman's point of view. This time the perspective is not of reconciliation and of the good sense of traditional society, but of the social visionary, and the outcome is tragic. The play embodies a powerful poetic vision of social values in the context of slavery and the position of women.

Aidoo has written a collection of short stories, *No Sweetness Here* (1970); and a novel *The Killing of Sister Kiljoy*. She held the post of Secretary for Education in the Rawlings government.   ME

Aiken, George L. (1830–76) American playwright. Aiken is known for one play: **Uncle Tom's Cabin**, *or Life Among the Lowly*, a dramatization of Mrs Stowe's novel, presented at Troy, New York on 27 September 1852, with Aiken in the part of George Harris. In response to audience demand for more episodes from the novel, Aiken prepared a sequel, *The Death of Uncle Tom, or the Religion of the Lowly*, and in mid-November combined the two plays into one drama of six acts, now the standard version.

G. C. Howard, manager of the company and Aiken's cousin, rewarded the 22-year-old actor–playwright with a bonus of forty dollars and a gold watch for the 'week of extra work' required to devise a role (Eva) for his four-year-old daughter Cordelia.   RM

Aikenvald, Yuly Isaevich (1872–1928) Russian literary critic and theatre reviewer for *Russian Thought* and other journals, who became embroiled in the pre-revolutionary 'crisis in the theatre' debate over theatre's true nature and proper function. His article 'Rejecting the Theatre' (*Studio*, 1912) asserted that theatre had no value except as dramatic literature, no justifiable aesthetic as an independent art form and possessed an innate concreteness which defied all contemporary attempts – by the symbolists, **Meyerhold**, **Evreinov** and others – to poeticize, stylize, conventionalize or psychologize it. The author's intentions are better realized and his rights served by an intelligent reading of his play rather than by the meddling of interpretive artists such as actors and directors. Aikhenvald's broadside galvanized the loyal opposition – among them, directors **V. I. Nemirovich-Danchenko** and **Fyodor Komissarzhevsky**, critic D. N. Ovsyaniko-Kulikovsky and dramatist-actor A. I. Yuzhin-Sumbatov – who published a volume of their own, *Debating the Theatre* (1912), in which they defended their roles as artistic interpreters.   SG

Akalaitis, JoAnne (1937–) American actress/ director and founding and continuing member of the avant-garde group **Mabou Mines**. Her experimental works have been performed at major art centres and festivals throughout the USA and Europe, including the New York Public Theatre, The Kitchen (New York City), the Walker Art Centre (Minneapolis), the **Mark Taper** (Los Angeles), Théâtre St Denis (France), Teatro Goldoni (Italy), and the National Galerie (Berlin). In 1983–4 she directed a controversial production of **Beckett**'s *Endgame* with music by her former husband Philip Glass at the **American Repertory Theatre**.   DBW

Akimov, Nikolai Pavlovich (1901–68) Soviet designer, director, graphic artist, portraitist and teacher, whose distinctive graceful, whimsical and vibrantly colourful stage realizations, especially of **Evgeny Shvarts**'s political fables, defined the character of the Leningrad Theatre of Comedy, where he was the long-time artistic director (1935–49, 1955–68). Akimov studied under artists M. V. Dobuzhinsky, A. E. Yakovlev and V. I. Shukhaev (1915–19) and in 1922 began his design career at the Kharkov Children's Theatre. His Leningrad and Moscow design career, dating from 1923, includes work at the Free Comedy Theatre, the Leningrad Theatre of Satire, the Bolshoi Dramatic Theatre, the Leningrad Academic Theatre of Drama, the Moscow Theatre of the Revolution and the **Moscow Art Theatre**, on Soviet dramas by **Ivanov**, **Faiko**, **Olesha**, **Afinogenov** and Kron. He began directing in 1929 and in 1932 staged a controversial formalist production of *Hamlet* for Moscow's Vakhtangov Theatre, set at a decadent court with a not mad but drunk Ophelia and a Ghost invented by Hamlet. His sharp and witty style, a kind of satiric Hoffmannesque romanticism, was most clearly demonstrated in his Theatre of Comedy productions, particularly: Shvarts's *The Shadow* (1940, 1960), *The Dragon* (1944, 1962) and *An Ordinary Miracle* (1956) and in **Sukhovo-Kobylin**'s *The Case* (1964) and *Krechinsky's Wedding* (1966). From 1951 to 1955 he served as the Lensoviet Theatre's artistic director, where he staged **Saltykov-Shchedrin**'s *Shadows* (1953) and an earlier version of *The Case* (1955). He also designed for films, and his theatre posters are among the most famous in Soviet history. He was the author of many articles and two books – *About Theatre* (1962) and its revised and expanded successor *Not Only About Theatre* (1966) – in which he blended memoir material with discussion of theatre aesthetics and practice. In 1960 he was named a 'People's Artist of the USSR'.   SG

Akins, Zoë (1886–1958) Prolific American playwright, scenarist, and adapter of French and Hungarian plays, began her career with an experimental *vers libre* drama, *The Magical City* (1916). Her early sophisticated

Akimov's set in *commedia dell'arte* style, for Act I, *The Shadow*.

comedies and wistful tragedies about worldly and slightly jaded women were followed by a rash of typical popular comedies. Her first and best hit was *Déclassée* (1919). Others which had either critical or popular success were *Papa* (1919), *Greatness: A Comedy* (1921 – also called *The Texas Nightingale*), *Daddy's Gone A-Hunting* (1921), *The Greeks Had A Word for It* (1929 – later filmed as *The Golddiggers*). In 1935, in a controversial decision, Akins received the Pulitzer Prize for her adaptation of Edna Ferber's *The Old Maid*. Her successful screenplays include *Morning Glory* (1932) and *Camille* (1937).   FB

Aksyonov, Vasily Pavlovich (1932–) Soviet novelist and dramatist, who continues the intellectual tradition of literary parody, satiric fable and grotesque realism of **Gogol**, **Sukhovo-Kobylin**, **Saltykov-Shchedrin**, **Bulgakov**, **Erdman**, **Mayakovsky**, **Olesha** and **Shvarts**. The son of Evgeniya Ginzburg, whose *Journey into the Whirlwind* (1967) is a harrowing account of her imprisonment during the Stalinist purges, Aksyonov abandoned medicine for a literary career. As part of the 'Young Prose' movement centred around **Valentin Kataev**'s journal *Youth* (1955), he became a spokesman for the post-Second World War generation. His early novels – *Colleagues* (1960), *A Ticket to the Stars* (1961), *Oranges from Morocco* (1962), *It's Time, My Love, It's Time* (1963) – reflect the problems of youth and maturation in Soviet society and are characterized by a highly eclectic 1960s feel: racy dialogue; Western-style dress, music and colloquialisms; shifting and confused objective and subjective perspectives on reality. His later writing, of which his two major plays are a part, tends toward the experimental and fantastic and suggests a conscious throwback to the Russian avant-garde of the 1920s. *Always on Sale*, at once a realistic social satire and highly theatricalist pastiche of popular culture – masks, songs and dances, film and television – was a great success in **Oleg Efremov**'s 1965 production at Moscow's Sovremennik Theatre. *Your Murderer* (published in English, 1977), subtitled 'An Antialcoholic Comedy in Eight Scenes with a Prologue and an Epilogue', is a grotesque, fanciful parable of an artist who sells out, opts out and is destroyed by his own creation, an Ubu-esque monster-become-folk hero named 'Pork Sausage'. This play is an even greater mix of popular junk culture and literary allusions than his former. A third play, *The Heron* (unpublished), 'A Comedy with Intermissions and Rhymes', is a Chekhovian parody set at a health resort and containing familiar Aksyonovian erotic touches. It received a staged reading at the Theatre at St Clement's Church in New York City in spring 1985. Aksyonov emigrated to the United States in 1980 as a result of his involvement with the *Metropol* literary anthology, which had been banned the previous year in Moscow. He has become a ubiquitous literary presence in America, discoursing on Russian and Soviet writers past and present and on the problems of the transplanted artist.   SG

Aktie Tomaat (Action tomato or the tomato campaign) Late in 1969, tomatoes were thrown at actors during a performance by the Nederlandse Comedie at the municipal theatre of Amsterdam. Thus, students from the Toneelschool (Amsterdam School of Drama) launched a protest against the rigid theatrical opinions held by established theatre producers, who were accused of limiting their repertory to middle-of-the-road performances, lacking any form of social relevance. The protest was, moreover, aimed at the authoritarian status of the director, who subordinated everybody else, notably the actors, to his views.

This protest linked up with that of students and workers which had started in the late sixties in the United States and had crossed over to Europe, particularly Paris (May 1968). The call for democracy was general. Aktie Tomaat contributed to breaking through old structures: new companies emerged that were organized on democratic principles, and old ones disappeared. The director became a stimulator, assistant or member of a collective. Actors could start to explore their creative potential. Productions were made on the basis of themes that had come out of improvisation; dramatic texts had to be updated before they could be acted.

In general, much thought was given to the social function of drama and theatre: performances were geared to sections of the population that had not previously been in contact with drama, because form and content had not appealed to them. Aktie Tomaat created a climate in which new theatrical companies could come into existence: **Werkteater**; Sater (political educational theatre (1971–84), director Peter de Baan); Baal (musical theatre (1973–), director Leonard Frank); De Appel (modern stagings of classics such as the *Oresteia*, *King Lear* (1972–), director Erik Vos); Onafhankelijk Toneel (environmental theatre). MG HS

Alarcón y Mendoza, Juan Ruiz de (c. 1580–1639) Spanish dramatist, born in Mexico, who trained as a lawyer and settled in Madrid in 1615. In 1625 he abandoned playwriting and held a post in the Colonial Office till his death. He published two collections of plays, in 1628 and 1634, his total output being about 24.

Alarcón was an outsider, mocked for his physical deformities, and his plays stand out from those of his contemporaries for their clear moral purpose of castigating the vices of Spanish society and for the nonconformity of their protagonists. His best-known play is *La verdad sospechosa* (*Suspect Truth*) condemning the vice of lying, and is the source of **Corneille**'s *Le Menteur* and several English plays. While deceit forms the essence of most Spanish comedy of the period, a necessity resulting from social restrictions, for Alarcón it is a denial of honour and nobility. In this play and others he stresses that true nobility depends on personal worth rather than an inherited title.

Among other plays, *Las paredes oyen* (*Walls have Ears*) castigates slander, and *No hay mal que por bien no venga* (*It's an Ill Wind . . .*) portrays an outsider who refuses to conform to standards of behaviour which he sees as pointless. His plays are by no means all negative, however, and *Los pechos privilegiados* (*Privileged Hearts*) gives the ideal of what a king's favourite should be, while *Ganar amigos* (*Winning Friends*) promotes the virtue of returning good for evil.

In another society Alarcón's plays might have had the success which their quality merited, but they did not appeal to Spanish audiences of the period, having more influence outside Spain. CL

Alawada Theatre see Adejumo, Moses Olaiya

Albania Albania, about the size of Wales and with a population of just under three million, lies on the western coast of the Balkan Peninsula, between Greece and Yugoslavia. The history of the theatre in Albania goes back to ancient times: archaeologists have uncovered the remains of theatres dating back to the 4th century BC – that at Bylis in the south of the country having accommodation for an audience of more than 7,000 people.

For 500 years – from the 15th to the 20th centuries – Albania lay under the occupation of the Ottoman Empire, which discouraged the drama. The modern Albanian theatre came into existence only during the National Renaissance of the late 19th and early 20th centuries, when Albanians at home and abroad were engaged in a fierce struggle for national independence. This national struggle was naturally reflected in the arts, and the plays performed by the amateur dramatic groups which sprang up in the main towns at this time, as well as those written by playwrights of the Albanian communities abroad, were for the most part imbued with patriotic sentiments and played a significant role in the development of national consciousness.

The first known performance of a play in the Albanian language took place in the southern town of Gjirokastra in 1874, the play being *The Wedding in Lunxhëria* by the teacher Koto Hoxhi (1824–95).

In southern Italy the former priest Anton Santori (1809–94) wrote *Emira* (1887), a love story set among the Albanian community in the author's native Calabria. In Turkey Sami Frashëri (1850–1904), the youngest of the three distinguished Frashëri brothers, wrote the six-act play *The Vow* in Turkish, but it was translated into Albanian in 1902. The Orthodox bishop Fan Noli (1882–1965) – poet, historian, playwright, translator, composer and statesman (he was briefly Prime Minister in 1924 before settling in the United States) – made brilliant translations of a number of **Shakespeare**'s tragedies, as well as of **Ibsen**'s *An Enemy of the People*, and was the author of *Israelites and Philistines* (1902), ostensibly biblical in theme but in fact portraying problems of the contemporary Albanian national movement. In Egypt the lawyer-poet Andon Zako Çajupi (1866–1930) wrote several plays, including the one-act comedies *The 14-Year-Old Bridegroom* (1902) and *Post Mortem* (1910) and the classical verse tragedy *Man of the Earth* (1907), based on Albania's 15th-century leader of the resistance against the Turkish invaders, Skanderbeg. An émigré in Rumania and America, Mohal Grameno (1872–1931), was the author of the anti-clerical comedy *The Curse of the Albanian Language* (1905) and the historical drama *The Death of Pirro* (1906). In predominantly Catholic northern Albania, the Franciscan priest and poet Gjergj Fishta (1871–1940) translated plays by **Euripides** and **Molière** and was himself the author of the verse plays *The Civilized Albanian* and *Judas Maccabaeus*.

The proclamation of independence in November 1912 brought little development of the Albanian theatre, since it was quickly followed by foreign occupation during the First World War, by the dicta-torship of Zog, and by the further occupation of fascist Italy and Nazi Germany. During most of this period the arts were not encouraged – indeed, many amateur dramatic groups were victims of savage persecution – and the dream of establishing a professional national theatre did not come to fruition.

The contemporary situation National liberation from German occupation was achieved in November 1944 under the leadership of the Communist Party of Albania (now the Party of Labour) and the People's Republic of Albania (now the People's Socialist Republic of Albania) was established with a programme of building a socialist society on Marxist-Leninist principles. The new state adopted a policy of actively encouraging the arts and of making them available to a mass audience. Even during the War of National Liberation itself, partisan theatre groups presented plays aimed at stimulating national morale, and on 24 May 1944 the first professional theatre was established in the liberated town of Përmet; this company later moved to the capital to become the People's Theatre of Tirana.

Today almost every factory, cooperative farm, school and military detachment has its own amateur dramatic company, and frequent drama festivals and competitions are organized for these thousands of amateur groups. There are 8 professional theatres (apart from 15 variety theatres and 26 puppet theatres), the best-known of which are the People's Theatre in Tirana, the A. Z. Çajupi Theatre in Korça, the Migjeni Theatre in Shkodra, the Scampa Theatre in Elbasan, and the A. Moisiu Theatre in Durrës. The last-mentioned theatre is named after the famous Albanian actor **Aleksandër Moisiu** (1879–1935), who was compelled to carry on his profession outside Albania.

In 1946 the first art school with a drama department – the Jordan Misja School – was opened, and this was followed in 1959 by the inauguration of the Aleksandër Moisiu School of Drama, a department of the higher Institute of Art: this trains actors, directors and stage technicians.

Although each professional company has its own permanent theatre, it spends approximately 50% of each year playing to audiences in the countryside and in helping to raise the artistic standards of amateur drama groups. Those in the theatre who are considered the most outstanding artists may be awarded the decoration of 'Honoured Artist' or 'People's Artist'.

The Party of Labour, which is constitutionally the 'guiding force' within society, maintains that good art must be realist in form – and, in the case of contemporary art, must accord with the principles of socialist realism. Plays, whether Albanian or foreign, are selected for production on this basis. The most popular non-Albanian playwrights who figure in the repertoire of the contemporary theatre include **Brecht, Chekhov**, Euripides, **Gogol, Goldoni**, Ibsen, **Miller, Priestley, Schiller** and Shakespeare.

Prime attention has, however, been paid to the development of a national drama, and among the most successful plays in recent years have been *Our Land, Halil and Hajrija* and *The Great Flood*, all by Kolë Jakova, the founder/director of the People's Theatre in Tirana; *The Carnivals of Korça*, by Spiro Çomora; *The Fisherman's Family*, by Sulejman Pitarka; *Koste Bardhi's*

Mill, by Naum Prifti; *The Girl from the Mountains*, by Loni Papa; and *The Lady From the City*, by Ruzhdi Pulaha. A whole galaxy of gifted actors – such as Naim Frashëri, Pjetër Gjoka, Zef Jubani, Loro Kovaçi, Marie Logoreci, Violeta Manushi, Mihal Popi and Sander Prosi – and directors – such as Andrea Malo, Pirro Mani, Esat Oktrova and Pandi Stillu – has emerged, many of them having graduated from the ranks of amateurs. WBB

See: K. Bihiku, *A History of Albanian Literature*, Tirana, 1980; R. Brahimi, *Artet dhe zhvillimi i tyre në RPSSH* (The Arts and their Development in the PSRA), Tirana, 1981; T. Çaushi, *Për mendimin estetik të PPSH* (On the Aesthetic Thought of the PLA), Tirana, 1983; Directory of Statistics of the PSRA, *40 Years of Socialist Albania*, Tirana, 1984; Editorial Board of 'New Albania', *Albania: General Information*, Tirana, 1984; E. Hoxha, *Mbi letërsinë dhe artin* (On Literature and Art), Tirana, 1977; N. V. Jorgaqi, *Antologji e mendimit estetik shqiptar* (Anthology of Albanian Aesthetic Thought), Tirana, 1979; S. E. Mann, *Albanian Literature*, London, 1955; Dh. S. Shuteriqi (ed.), *Historia e letërsisë shqiptare* (History of Albanian Literature), Tirana, 1959.

Albee, Edward (1928–) American playwright. Albee made a spectacular debut with four one-act plays in an absurdist style (*The Zoo Story*, 1958; *The Death of Bessie Smith*, 1959; *The Sandbox*, 1959; and *The American Dream*, 1960) and capped his reputation with the Broadway productions of *Who's Afraid of Virginia Woolf?* (1962) and an audacious and belligerent metaphysical mystery, *Tiny Alice* (1964). He was greeted as the leader of a new theatrical movement and his name was linked with those of **Tennessee Williams**, **Arthur Miller**, and **William Inge** as a major American playwright. Refusing, however, to capitalize on the qualities that made *Virginia Woolf* so powerful – the lacerating wit and incendiary character conflict – Albee has pursued an increasingly rarefied style, one that is emotionally and sexually evasive and that often forsakes dramatic impact for mandarin elegance. Despite critical and commercial defeats, Albee has continued to write prolifically in three forms: adaptations (Carson McCullers's *Ballad of the Sad Café*, 1963, James Purdy's *Malcolm*, 1965, and Nabokov's *Lolita*, 1980); short chamber plays that are musical in their repetitions and juxtapositions of image and motif (*Box and Quotations from Mao-Tse Tung*, 1968, *Listening*, 1975, and *Counting the Ways*, 1976); and full-length plays in which ordered lives are invaded and transformed. His settings may appear realistic but Albee is at heart a fabulist; like the imaginary child in *Virginia Woolf*, surreal surprises hover over most of his work. In his wisest play, *A Delicate Balance* (awarded the Pulitzer Prize in 1966), Harry and Edna carry a mysterious psychic plague into their best friends' living room. The title character in *The Lady from Dubuque* (1979) is an angel of death. Talking sea creatures emerge from the water to confront sedate picnickers in *Seascape* (which won the Pulitzer Prize in 1975). His reputation is now at a low ebb but in the long run Albee will surely reclaim his place as an important stylist, a writer of wit and sensibility. FH

Albee, Edward F. see **Vaudeville, American**

Albery, James (1838–89) English playwright whose one outstanding success, *Two Roses* (1870), established **Henry Irving** as a star. Albery tried in vain to live up to the reputation *Two Roses* had gained for him as a true successor to **T. W. Robertson**, and undervalued his ingenious adaptations from the French. **Charles Wyndham**, who recognized the sophistication of Albery's dialogue, set him the task of making palatable for Criterion audiences the saucy marital farce *Les Dominos Roses*, and *The Pink Dominos* (1877), whilst raising a few hackles, was the effective outcome. *Where's the Cat?* (1880) was another vehicle for Wyndham and another disappointment for the critics who ruined Albery's talent by expecting too much of it. PT

Aldredge, Theoni (1932–) American costume designer; born in Athens, Greece. Aldredge studied and then worked at the **Goodman Theatre** in Chicago before coming to New York in 1958. From 1962 onwards she was a principal designer for the **New York Shakespeare Festival**. From the mid-1970s she has been part of the collaborative team – **Michael Bennett**, **Robin Wagner** and **Tharon Musser** – that produced *Chorus Line* and *Dreamgirls*, among others. Aldredge designed landmark productions such as *Who's Afraid of Virginia Woolf?* and *Hair*. She also designs for ballet, opera, television, and film, including *Network* and *The Great Gatsby*. Aldredge is an excellent collaborative artist and her designs are integrated with and supportive of the direction and overall visual statement of a production. AA

Aldridge, Ira (1807–67) Afro-American actor. Starting with the African Theatre in New York, Aldridge moved to England at the age of 17 and became a touring provincial actor in Britain and Ireland for over 25 years. In 1833 he replaced the mortally ill **Edmund Kean** as Othello at **Covent Garden** Theatre to a mixed press, and in 1852 began a series of highly successful appearances in Europe and Russia receiving several decorations from heads of state. His return to London's West End in 1865 was widely praised. Aldridge played over 40 roles, black and white, many of them Shakespearian. Equally brilliant in tragedy and comedy, he often performed Othello and Mungo (in **Bickerstaffe**'s comic operetta *The Padlock*) on the same bill. He introduced psychological realism in acting in the 1850s well before his European counterparts. He died on on engagement in Łodz, Poland, in 1867. EGH

Alegría, Alonso (1940–) Peruvian playwright, director and professor. Born in Santiago de Chile, he studied architecture from 1958–60, later organized theatre group Alba (1960–2). Between 1964–9 he received BA and MFA degrees in theatre from Yale, studied with John Gassner, and worked in the **New York Shakespeare Festival** with **Papp**. Director of the National Popular Theatre in Lima from 1971–5, later professor in the United States (Texas Tech, Florida International, and Kenyon College). Author of *Remigio, el huaquero* (*Remigio, the Huaco Collector*, 1965), his major play is *El cruce sobre el Niágara* (*Niagara Crossing*, 1969), a powerful rendition of existential values predicated on the 19th-century French tightrope walker **Blondin** and his assistant Carlo. Later plays include *El terno blanco* (*The White Suit*), rewritten as *El color de Chambalén, una novela fantaseosa para teatro* (*The Colour of Chambalén, a Vain Novel for Theatre*, 1981) and *Daniela Frank* (1982), the latter written in English.   GW

Alekseev, K. S. see **Stanislavsky, K. S.**

Aleotti, Giovanni Battista (1546–1636) Italian architect, engineer and stage designer who spent most of his working life in the service of the court of the Estensi at Ferrara, where he built the Teatro degli Intrepidi in 1605 (destroyed by fire in 1679). His finest surviving work is the Teatro Farnese in Parma. Constructed in 1618 in the Pilotta and one of the largest and finest of baroque theatres, its U-shaped auditorium has a seating capacity of 4,500. Its inauguration was delayed until 1628, when it opened with the tourney *Mercurio e Marte* with music by Monteverdi. To Aleotti is ascribed the introduction, possible as early as 1606, but certainly by 1618, of sliding flat wings; these rapidly came to replace the traditional Serlian (see **Serlio**) fixed angle wings and permitted frequent and rapid shifts of scene, particularly after **Torelli** developed on the system by devising machinery for synchronizing wing changes.   KR

Alexander, George (1858–1918) Anglo-Scottish actor and theatre manager. Born George Samson and intended by his parents for a respectable career in the city, Alexander turned actor in 1879 and was with **Irving** at the **Lyceum** from 1881–9, most notably as Valentine in *Faust* (1885). After a brief spell as manager of the Royal Avenue Theatre, he bought the lease on the **St James's** and retained it until his death. His declared policy was to encourage and support the writing of new plays by British authors. Alexander was the first English producer of **Oscar Wilde** – *Lady Windermere's Fan* (1892) – and the creator of Jack Worthing in *The Importance of Being Earnest* (1895). His greatest (and boldest) success was **Pinero**'s *The Second Mrs Tanqueray* (1893), which made a star of **Mrs Patrick Campbell** and confirmed Alexander's own quality as a strong-jawed 'straight' man in the part of Aubrey Tanqueray. Later Pinero premieres included *The Princess and the Butterfly* (1897), *His House in Order* (1906), *The Thunderbolt* (1908) and *Mid-Channel* (1909). **Henry James**'s *Guy Domville* (1895) did not long survive a disastrous first night, and it was the 1902 production of **Stephen Phillips**'s *Paolo and Francesca* which earned for Alexander an undeserved reputation as an upholder of literary standards. He was, in fact, a shrewd businessman and a punctilious and efficient theatre manager, who took risks only occasionally. He had a highly developed sense of 'fair play' – he was prosecuted in 1895 for defending a prostitute from police harassment – and was loyal to his company. He was knighted in 1911.   PT

Alexander (née Quigley), Jane (1939–) American actress who gained stardom as the white mistress of the black boxing champion in *The Great White Hope* (1968), a role she first created at the **Arena Stage** in Washington, DC. A New Englander dedicated to regional theatre, to which she returns frequently, she was critically acclaimed as Lavinia in *Mourning Becomes Electra* at the **American Shakespeare Festival** Theatre in 1971 and at the Eisen-

hower in Washington, DC, and the Huntington Hartford in Los Angeles in 1972. Other New York theatre appearances include *Six Rms Riv Vu* (1972), *First Monday in October* (1978), and **William Gibson**'s *Monday After the Miracle* (1982). She is married to the American stage director Edwin Sherin.   DBW

Alfieri, Vittorio (1749–1803) Italian dramatist and poet. Born into a noble family he was at first destined for an army career, but in 1766 abandoned military studies in Turin and spent the next few years travelling widely throughout Europe. It was after his return to Turin in 1772 that he began seriously to write in both French and Italian, his first tragedy *Cleopatra* appearing in 1775. Over the next decade or so he produced the bulk of his dramatic work, including 19 tragedies, a substantial amount of non-dramatic verse, and many highly personal social and political writings in which he challenged the authoritarian institutions of his day and the mass servility and passivity they bred. The tragic form in particular permitted him to tap a vein of melancholy deep-rooted in his temperament, and at their best his plays reveal a distinctively personal blend of the classical and romantic, his taste for the economy and austerity of classical models, and tight adherence to the Aristotelian rules, being balanced by powerful emotion and a highly individual insistence on the exercise of heroic will. Great poetic dramas, the prominence of the authorial voice limits their stageworthiness, and although 19th-century actors like **Salvini** performed some of the plays abroad, and several have survived on the modern Italian stage, none has entered the European repertoire. Of Alfieri's 21 tragedies perhaps the best are *Oreste* (1778), *Virginia* (1778), *Saul* (1782) and *Mirra* (1786); none of his six comedies now attracts interest.   LR

Algarotti, Franceso (1712–64) An Italian of wide culture, friend of many European artists and intimate of Frederick the Great who created him Count. His influential *Essay on Opera* (1755), originally published in Italy, appeared in English (1767), in German (1769) and in French (1773). It is still a striking account of the state of opera in the middle of the 18th century and makes reasoned proposals for its reform and development. One random illustration of its anticipation of the ideas of **Gluck**, **Calzabigi** and many others is its claim that it is almost impossible to convince the composer 'that he ought to be in a subordinate position, that music derives its greatest merit from being no more than an auxiliary, the handmaid to poetry'.   GH

Algeria see **French-speaking North Africa; Middle East**

Allen, Gracie see **George Burns**

Allen, Viola (1869–1948) American actress. She made her stage debut in *Esmeralda* in New York in 1882. In 1884 **John McCullough** engaged her to play his daughter in *Virginius*, then made her his leading lady. In subsequent seasons she played opposite W. E. Sheridan, **Tommaso Salvini**, and **Joseph Jefferson**. For four years she was leading lady in **Charles Frohman**'s Empire Stock Company. An intelligent and appealing actress, sometimes thought to be over-technical, she was, until her retirement in 1918, a popular touring star, highly regarded for such portrayals as Viola, the double roles of Hermione and Perdita, and Dolores (*In the Palace of the King*).   FHL

Alley Theatre, The   Established as an amateur organization in Houston, Texas, by Mr and Mrs Robert Altfeld and Nina Vance, who became artistic head, the theatre began production in November 1947 in a rented 87-seat dance studio, the name inspired by a narrow alleyway which led to the studio. The second home, an attic fan-manufacturing plant converted to a 231-seat arena theatre, opened on 8 February 1949 with a production of *The Children's Hour* utilizing professional actors. In 1954 the theatre became fully professional. The current building, which opened in November 1968, was named after Nina Vance following her death in 1980. Appointed in 1981, the current artistic director, Pat Brown, has attempted to fill the two theatres, including one seating 798 and another arena-style holding 296, in the complex (with a third under construction) with more adventurous and experimental fare than its previous conservative offerings. The Alley completed in June 1983 a landmark exchange with the Stephen Joseph Theatre in Scarborough, England; in July 1985 they presented **Ayckbourn**'s *Season's Greetings* at New York's Joyce Theatre.   DBW

Alleyn, Edward (1566–1626) English actor, known to have been with Worcester's Men in 1583 and with the **Admiral's Men** at the **Rose** by, at the latest, 1592. It was above all as the creator, for the latter company, of **Marlowe**'s towering heroes that Alleyn was celebrated. He shared with **Richard Burbage** the acknowledged leadership of his profession. But unlike Burbage, Alleyn did not remain an actor. A friendship with the Rose's manager, **Henslowe**, led to marriage to Henslowe's stepdaughter and a business partnership that eventually made Alleyn a rich man. He retired from the stage in 1597, presumably to join in some of Henslowe's enterprises. Together they ran the Bear Garden, possibly from as early as 1594, and built the **Fortune** as a new home for the Admiral's Men. When the Fortune opened in 1600, Alleyn returned to the stage. His highly rhetorical style may by then have seemed old-fashioned, but he was still with the Admiral's Men when the change of monarch saw the company renamed Prince Henry's Men. Alleyn's final retirement from acting probably came in 1604, when he and Henslowe received a joint-patent as Masters of the Royal Game of Bears, Bulls and Mastiff Dogs. By 1605, he was negotiating to buy the manor of Dulwich, where, in 1613, he began the building of the College of God's Gift. The papers he deposited in the library there, including Henslowe's *Diary*, are a unique record of the business side of the Elizabethan and Jacobean theatre. Assured of his social status, Alleyn took as his second wife the daughter of the Dean of St Paul's, the poet John Donne.   PT

Alpers, Boris Vladimirovich (1894–1974) Soviet theatre critic and scholar who, following the 1917 Revolution, adopted a Bolshevik bias in his writing. A former member of **Meyerhold**'s 'Dr Dapertutto' Studio on Borodinsky Street (1914–15),

Alpers, along with fellow 'Dapertutto' alumni V. V. Dmitriev, K. K. Tverskoi (pseudonym of Kuzmin-Karavaev), K. N. Derzhavin, A. L. Gripich and V. N. Solovyov (artistic director), established the Ligovsky Dramatic Theatre in Petrograd (1921–4), whose 'industrial programme' called for a more democratic actor–audience relationship. Renamed the Theatre of New Drama (1922–3), the company turned away from its original position and towards expressionism. Alpers and Gripich later helped to organize the Moscow Theatre of the Revolution, where Alpers headed the literary section (1924–7) and where many of the 'social themes' originally proposed at the Ligovsky were realized. He began his literary career in 1921, which included reviews, theoretical articles and books such as *The Theatre of the Revolution* (1928), *M. S. Shchepkin* (1933), *The Actor's Art in Russia* (1945) and *The Path of the Soviet Theatre* (1947). Most important was his *The Theatre of the Social Mask* (1931), written in the late 1920s, which presented the first conceptual, developmental assessment of Meyerhold's work to that point. Alpers believed that Meyerhold's art was always the art of 'type masks' which 'embrace the entire living variety of types from the past', and especially 'the ossification of a social type', drained of individual traits, schematized, generalized and resistant to 'character'. Although opposed in its own time by the trend toward concrete, individuated character psychology, the term is still quoted in contemporary Soviet criticism.   SG

Alta comedia see **Comedia**

Altweibermuehle 'The Mill for Old Women', a Tirolean **Fastnachtspiel**. The idea of a mill or forge which rejuvenates old women, traceable to the 16th century, in both dramatic and iconographic form, turns up in the work of the 18th-century showman Barzanti, and in Jugoslavian folk-paintings of the 18th and 19th centuries. In the Tirolean play, a series of local character-types drag their ageing wives to the miraculous mill, run by a clownish apprentice. The apparent sexism is turned on its head when the women, once more young and desirable, refuse to return to their husbands until a change of attitude and behaviour is negotiated.   AEG

Álvarez Quintero, Serafín (1871–1938) and **Joaquín** (1873–1944) Spanish playwrights collaborating on more than 200 plays and sketches over a period of 40 years. The brothers had an early success with *Esgrima y amor* (*Fencing and Love*, 1888) in Seville. After nine years in Madrid they gained success with *El ojito derecho* (*The Apple of his Eye*) followed by a stream of playlets, **zarzuelas** and sketches. Their works lean heavily on local Andalusian colour and custom, depicting a charming, optimistic world, but though shallow they are witty and easily acted, and have been popular with amateur companies outside Spain.   CL

Amalrik, Andrei Alekseevich (1938–80) Independent, outspoken Soviet dissident historian, memoirist and absurdist dramatist, in the tradition of **Gogol**, **Sukhovo-Kobylin** and the OBERIU of the 1920s. Amalrik was expelled from Moscow University in 1963 for attempting to convey his controversial diploma dissertation on foreign influence in 9th-century Kievan Russia to a Danish professor. He was exiled to a collective farm in Tomsk, Siberia (1965) for two and a half years on charges of 'parasitism' (vagrancy) and disseminating pornography (i.e., his plays and the avant-garde art of others). Following the commutation of his sentence and his release in 1966, he published *Involuntary Journey to Siberia*, which documented his experiences as a shepherd and cart driver. He was dismissed in 1968 from his job at the Novosty Press Agency for 'nonconformist dissident behaviour' and worked thereafter as everything from a translator of technical literature and private tutor to construction worker, cartographer and a timekeeper at sporting events. His long theoretical essay, 'Will the Soviet Union Survive Until 1984?' (1969), was a pessimistic rejoinder to those who foresaw a growing liberalization of Soviet society and predicted war between the USSR and China. His three-year labour camp sentence for spreading 'falsehoods derogatory to the Soviet state' (1970) was extended in 1973, and he emigrated in 1976. His *Notes of a Revolutionary* (1982), its title suggested by the memoirs of Prince Peter Kropotkin, is a personal biography and a cultural history of the USSR, 1966–76, focusing upon the individual's destruction by the governmental system. Amalrik's five short plays reflect his childhood interest in the puppet theatre, as well as the influence, in addition to those already mentioned, of the Russian transrationalist, futurist poet-dramatist, Velimir Khlebnikov, **Beckett** and especially, **Ionesco**. *My Aunt Is Living in Volokolamsk* (1963, 1964, 1966), *East-West: A Dialogue in Suzdal* (1963), *The Fourteen Lovers of Ugly Mary-Ann* (1964), *The Story of the Little White Bull* (1964), *Is Uncle Jack a Conformist?* (1964) and *Nose! Nose? No-se!* (adapted from Gogol's short story, 'The Nose', 1964), all one-acts, are characterized by the following traits: Freudian-based sex and violence; illogical character behaviour and plot structuring; role reversals and identity confusion; sudden appearances and disappearances of characters; language, ranging from aphoristic to freely associative to nonsensical; ritualistic patterning; parodied stage conventions. Amalrik was killed in an automobile accident while travelling to Madrid to testify at a conference examining Soviet compliance with the Helsinki Accords on Human Rights. At the time of his death, he was working on a biography of Rasputin. SG

Ambassador Theatre 215 West 49th St, New York City [Architect: Herbert J. Krapp]. Built in 1921, when prime sites in the theatre district were being rapidly used up, the **Shuberts'** architect, Herbert Krapp, was forced to design the new 1,100-seat theatre diagonally across the plot to make maximum use of the area. The Ambassador was intended to house operettas, the Shuberts' perennial theatrical product, but it was leased for non-musicals as well. In 1935, the playhouse was sold and thereafter it was used for live and film presentations as well as a radio and television studio. In 1956, it was reacquired by the Shuberts, who returned it to legitimate roles. MCH

American Conservatory Theatre (ACT) A non-commercial regional repertory company which combines performing with a training school. Founded in 1965 by William Ball, the ACT has made its home in San Francisco since 1967. Ball attracted critical notice in 1958 with an Off-Broadway staging of **Chekhov**'s *Ivanov*. Subsequent productions throughout the United States and Canada made him one of the most promising young directors in America, known for his 'flamboyant eccentricity'. In 1965 he established the ACT at the Pittsburgh Playhouse as an experimental and educational company with a more 'dashing style' than he saw elsewhere. Arrangements quickly soured and Ball took the ACT on the road for much of 1966, settling permanently in San Francisco for a January 1967 opening. Playing in two theatres, the downtown Geary and the Marine Memorial, the 50-member company offered 15 plays during the 1967–8 season including: *A Flea in Her Ear*, *The Three Sisters*, *The Devil's Disciple*, *Little Murders*, *A Delicate Balance*, and *Hamlet*. **Allen Fletcher** joined ACT in 1970 to head the Conservatory training programme. The company ran up deficits of $900,000 in 1973 which required reductions in the size of the company and its repertoire. TLM

American Laboratory Theatre Inspired by the first American appearance of the **Moscow Art Theatre** in January 1923, the American Laboratory Theatre (originally called the Theatre Arts Institute) was founded six months later by a group of wealthy American patrons as a school for training young actors in the **Stanislavsky** system. Providing a well-rounded three-year programme, the school was a significant first step in translating Stanislavsky's ideas about truth in acting into an American idiom. There were courses in mime, ballet, fencing, phonetics, and corrective gymnastics, but the school's focus was the classes taught by Richard Boleslavski and Maria Ouspenskaya, two impassioned émigrés from Stanislavsky's company.

From 1925 to 1930, with Boleslavski as its artistic director, the Lab sponsored a theatre, modelled on the Moscow Art but advertised as America's first native, creative theatre. Most of its productions, however, were of new and revived European plays rather than the original American drama its charter promised. The Lab (disbanded in 1933) and its theatre were an important link between the historic appearance of Stanislavsky's company and the establishment in 1931 of America's first true theatrical collective, the **Group Theatre**, co-founded by **Harold Clurman**, **Lee Strasberg** and **Cheryl Crawford** who had listened intently to Boleslavski's inspiring lectures. FH

American musical theatre The first musical performances on the American stage occurred during the Colonial period, when ballad operas were presented by touring companies of English actors. After the Revolution (1776–83) native composers and writers created the first American comic operas. Notable among these was *The Archers*, with book and lyrics by **William Dunlap** and music by Benjamin Carr.

By the 1840s several types of European entertainments were contributing to the growth of American musical theatre. Burlesque reached the United States in the 1830s, and by the 1850s there were numerous American burlesques on native subjects, such as **John Brougham**'s *Pocahontas; or, The Gentle Savage* (1855). Another imported form that proved popular with American audiences was the spectacle, which made use of lavish scenery and special effects as well as music and dance to tell its story.

Theatre activity in the United States was retarded by the Civil War (1861–5). After the war pantomime reached the height of its appeal in America with *Humpty Dumpty* (1868) starring **George L. Fox**, while burlesque received a boost from periodic visits by the English star **Lydia Thompson**, and from the success of *Evangeline* (1874), an extravaganza from the Longfellow poem.

Despite the popularity of these musical forms, the event most often singled out as the starting point of American musical theatre is the production of *The Black Crook* in 1866. This show, created when a melodrama on Faustian lines was augmented with dances by a French ballet company stranded in New York, is viewed as a primitive example of musical comedy because of its use of music and dance in the telling of its story.

French *opéra bouffe* had a vogue on the American stage in the 1870s and 1880s, where it competed with native entertainments such as the 'Mulligan Guard' series of musical plays created and performed by **Edward Harrigan** and **Tony Hart**.

The American premiere of **Gilbert** and Sullivan's *HMS Pinafore* in 1879 made comic opera the dominant musical form for the rest of the century. Most distinguished of the American composers of comic opera was **Reginald De Koven**, whose *Robin Hood* (1891) was frequently revived. Among the many fine comedians who performed in comic opera were **Jefferson De Angelis**, **De Wolf Hopper**, **Francis Wilson**, and **Eddie Foy**.

Backstage during *The Black Crook*, 1866. Ladies of the ballet preparing to 'fly'.

Most musical theatre librettos in this period were constructed in such a way as to allow for interpolations of unrelated songs and dances by members of the company. This taste for unrelated specialities encouraged the development of the revue, a form of musical theatre in which songs, dances, and comedy sketches were loosely connected by a plot or recurring theme. The first American revue was *The Passing Show* (1894).

In the last decade of the 19th century, comic opera and *opéra bouffe* declined, while burlesque was given a temporary reprieve in the shows of **Weber** and **Fields**. As the 1890s progressed, signs of change began to appear in the musical stage. In 1894, the Bostonians presented the comic opera *Prince Ananias*, which contained the first full score by **Victor Herbert**, destined to be one of the most important composers of operettas for the American stage. Also appearing in 1894 was *A Gaiety Girl*, an English musical that abandoned the exotic locales and stilted language of comic opera in favour of a contemporary setting and more topical humour. In 1898 two musicals written and performed by blacks made their appearance, *A Trip to Coontown* and *The Origin of the Cakewalk; or, Clorindy*. Despite the warm reception which these two shows received, few black artists were seen on the Broadway stage before the 1920s.

Comic opera, operetta, and musical comedy were the dominant forms on the American musical stage at the dawn of the new century. The most successful show of the decade was *Florodora* (1900), an English import. Victor Herbert continued to compose operettas such as *Babes in Toyland* (1903), *Mlle. Modiste* (1905), *The Red Mill* (1906), and *Naughty Marietta* (1910). The native comic tradition of Harrigan and Hart was continued by **George M. Cohan** in a series of musical comedies that emphasized contemporary characters and settings, wise-cracking humour, and a generous dose of patriotic sentiment.

With the arrival of Franz Lehar's *The Merry Widow* in New York in 1907, a vogue for Viennese operetta was launched which lasted until the advent of the First World War. In the same year, **Florenz Ziegfeld** produced the *Follies of 1907*, the first in a series of annual revues which gradually moved that form away from topical humour toward a greater emphasis on elaborate scenery, beautifully dressed chorus girls, and star comedians and singers.

Some significant innovations took place in the American musical stage in the period of the First World War. Several of the shows written during that era rejected European styles in favour of American musical idioms, most notably ragtime. Developed by black musicians, ragtime was first heard on the musical stage in the form of individual songs interpolated into shows. In 1914 **Irving Berlin** composed a ragtime score for the revue *Watch Your Step*. Although it has been argued that many of Berlin's songs were not true ragtime, the success of his work brought ragtime to the forefront of musical styles for the legitimate stage.

Meanwhile, composer **Jerome Kern** was revolutionizing musical comedy with his modest, charming 'Princess Theatre' shows. Designed to make the most of the intimate Princess Theatre in which they were performed, these musicals featured small casts, simple settings, and contemporary characters and situations. In the years immediately following the war such musicals as *Irene* (1919) and Kern's own *Sally* (1920), which starred **Marilyn Miller**, demonstrated that contemporary American characters and situations and fresh musical styles could be effectively employed in more elaborate musical comedies.

Despite the changes being wrought in American musical comedy, the demand for operetta did not abate. A new generation of European-trained composers, most notably Rudolf Friml and Sigmund Romberg, joined Victor Herbert in the creation of operetta for the American stage. Friml's scores during the 1920s included *Rose-Marie* (1924), *The Vagabond King* (1925), and *The Three Musketeers* (1928). Among Romberg's best works were *Maytime* (1918), *The Student Prince* (1924), *The Desert Song* (1926), and *The New Moon* (1928).

In the early post-war years a number of new revue series appeared, including the *Greenwich Village Follies*, *George White's Scandals*, the *Music Box Revues*, *The Grand Street Follies*, and *Earl Carroll's Vanities*. The early 1920s also marked the reappearance of the black musical on the American stage. Although there had been a few isolated efforts since the turn of the century, including *In Dahomey* (1903), *Abyssinia* (1906), and *The Shoo Fly Regiment* (1907), blacks had their greatest impact on the Broadway musical stage in the 1920s. Beginning with *Shuffle Along* (1921), a succession of black book musicals and revues popularized a form of jazz that replaced ragtime as the dominant musical comedy style, and also introduced many new dance steps to the musical stage.

During the 1920s a new generation of composers began to make their mark on the Broadway stage. Writing in the jazz-influenced style that had evolved in the years following the Princess Theatre shows, **George** and **Ira Gershwin** had a series of successes with *Lady, Be Good!* (1924), *Tip-Toes* (1925), *Oh, Kay* (1926), and *Funny Face* (1927). Their work during this period culminated in two political satires, *Strike Up the Band* (1930), and the Pulitzer Prize-winning *Of Thee I Sing* (1931). Among the shows created in the 1920s by the new songwriting team of **Richard Rodgers** and **Lorenz Hart** were *The Garrick Gaieties* (1925), *Dearest Enemy* (1925), *A Connecticut Yankee* (1927), and *Present Arms* (1928). Other composers writing musical comedies in the 1920s included Vincent Youmans and De Sylva, Brown and Henderson.

The pioneer of the style of contemporary musical comedy so popular in the 1920s, **Jerome Kern**, took musical theatre in another direction when he composed *Show Boat* (1927), an operetta that used American musical idioms to tell a serious dramatic story. With lyrics by **Oscar Hammerstein II**, *Show Boat* pointed the way to the serious musical plays of the 1940s and 1950s.

The 1927–8 season, with some 250 shows, was a high point in the history of the Broadway stage. Events outside of the theatre, including the advent of sound films and the stock market crash of 1929, would prevent it from ever again reaching that level of production. By the 1930–1 season there was a marked decline in the number of shows produced on Broadway, and those that did appear were usually presented on a more modest scale. Most revues now emphasized singing, dancing, and satiric comedy rather than expensive sets and costumes.

The musical theatre was invigorated at the end of the 1920s by the appearance of some new composers and lyricists. **Cole Porter** wrote insinuating melodies and clever lyrics for a number of frothy musical comedies, including *Fifty Million Frenchmen* (1929), *The New Yorkers* (1930), and *Anything Goes* (1934), while the songwriting team of Arthur Schwartz and Howard Dietz brought a new, more subdued and melodic sound to their scores for the revues *The Little Show* (1929), *Three's a Crowd* (1930), and *The Band Wagon* (1931).

Despite the appearance of these new contributors to the musical theatre, two of the more impressive musicals of the 1930s were created by composers, lyricists, and librettists who had begun their careers in the previous decade: *Porgy and Bess* (1935) by the Gershwins (with **DuBose Heyward**), and *On Your Toes* (1936) by Rodgers and Hart.

As the depression worsened, musicals began to reflect the country's growing unrest. In 1936 the **Group Theatre** produced *Johnny Johnson*, a musical with an anti-war message, and the **Mercury Theatre** offered Mark Blitzstein's controversial capitalist vs. labour parable, *The Cradle Will Rock*, in 1938. This interest in the issues of the day was short-lived, however, for with the advent of the Second World War the musical theatre once again turned its back on political and social commentary. Nevertheless, a few musicals of the early 1940s demonstrated that the seriousness of the 1930s had not been completely abandoned. Rodgers and Hart's *Pal Joey* (1940) had an amoral gigolo for its hero, while the Kurt Weill–Ira Gershwin musical, *Lady in the Dark* (1941), dealt with a mentally disturbed magazine editor whose problems were solved through psychoanalysis.

Musical theatre experienced another change in direction in 1943 as a result of the unprecedented popularity of *Oklahoma!*, the first musical by the new partnership of Richard Rodgers and Oscar Hammerstein II. *Oklahoma!*'s affirmation of the simple values of an earlier America gave it a broad and lasting appeal. Although it adhered in many ways to the traditions of operetta, its departures from standard musical theatre practice, such as allowing a murder to take place on stage and using a 'dream ballet' to amplify the dramatic action, made *Oklahoma!* the most influential and widely imitated musical of its day. Among the subsequent 'musical plays' created by Rodgers and Hammerstein were *Carousel* (1945), *South Pacific* (1949), *The King and I* (1951), *Flower Drum Song* (1958), and *The Sound of Music* (1959).

Despite the pervasive influence of Rodgers and Hammerstein, the traditional musical comedy continued to flourish in the 1940s and early 1950s. *Annie Get Your Gun*, with a score by Irving Berlin and a bravura performance by **Ethel Merman** as the backwoods sharpshooter Annie Oakley, opened to critical acclaim in 1946. **Frank Loesser** received enthusiastic notices for *Guys and Dolls* (1950), a musical about Broadway gamblers and their perennial girlfriends. *Wonderful Town* (1953), by the team of **Bernstein**, **Comden** and **Green**, dealt with life in New York's Greenwich Village in the 1930s. *Pajama Game*, a musical about management–labour strife in a pyjama factory, introduced the songwriting team of Richard Adler and Jerry Ross to Broadway in 1954. A year later *Damn Yankees*, also by Adler and Ross, combined the

Faust legend with baseball, and elevated dancer **Gwen Verdon** to stardom.

In 1956, **Lerner** and **Loewe** adapted **George Bernard Shaw**'s comedy *Pygmalion* into the musical *My Fair Lady*. Like *Show Boat* and *Oklahoma!* before it, *My Fair Lady* changed the course of musical theatre: it revived the vogue for operettas set in bygone eras; it created a trend toward hiring actors rather than singers for important musical theatre roles; and it led librettists to concentrate on adapting already successful plays, films, and novels rather than creating original librettos.

The two basic threads of musical theatre, operetta and musical comedy, continued to flourish from the mid-1950s through the mid-1960s. As usual, the operettas tended to be the more elaborate and ambitious works. Leonard Bernstein, **Arthur Laurents**, **Stephen Sondheim** and **Jerome Robbins** based *West Side Story* (1957) on the Romeo and Juliet legend. The songwriting team of **Jerry Bock** and **Sheldon Harnick** caught the flavour of European operetta with *She Loves Me* (1963), and in the following year created one of the most popular of all American musicals, *Fiddler on the Roof*. *Man of La Mancha*, based on **Cervantes**'s *Don Quixote*, received excellent reviews when it opened in 1965.

The creators of musical comedy tried to vary the traditional formulas by exploring new settings and subjects. *Gypsy* (1959) was based on the life of stripper **Gypsy Rose Lee**. *Fiorello* (1959) followed the career of New York mayor Fiorello LaGuardia. *How to Succeed in Business Without Really Trying* (1961) satirized corporate back-stabbing and in-fighting. *Hello, Dolly!*, while blazing no new trails in subject matter, made more extensive use of dance than was the custom in musical comedy. *Cabaret* (1966) was set in the decadent Berlin of the 1930s. *Hair* (1968) brought rock music and nudity to the Broadway musical stage.

By the end of the 1960s it had become clear that the musical theatre was failing to develop new artists and audiences. An increasing number of revivals of older shows, coupled with revues created out of the songs of veteran composers, held the stage. The only new composer–lyricist to contribute importantly to the musical theatre in the 1970s was Stephen Sondheim. His brilliant but often controversial shows of the 1970s and 1980s included *Company* (1970), *Follies* (1971), *A Little Night Music* (1973), *Pacific Overtures* (1976), *Sweeney Todd* (1979), *Merrily We Roll Along* (1981), and *Sunday in the Park With George* (1984).

The work of Sondheim in collaboration with producer–director **Harold Prince** popularized the 'concept musical', a show in which the director and designers, instead of attempting to translate a preexisting libretto and score into theatrical terms during rehearsals, collaborate with the composer, lyricist and librettist during the creation of the show, so that every element is conceived in terms of production. Because of the emergence of the concept musical, and because so few new composers, lyricists, and librettists of stature appeared during the period, the musical theatre of the 1970s and 1980s was dominated by the choreographer–director. Such shows as **Bob Fosse**'s *Pippin* (1972), *Chicago* (1975) and *Dancin'* (1978); **Michael Bennett**'s *A Chorus Line* (1975) and *Dreamgirls* (1981); and **Gower Champion**'s *42nd Street* (1980) benefited immeasurably from the imaginative and energetic staging that their director–choreographers created for them.

The period of the 1970s and 1980s was a time of reassessment of the musical theatre in the light of rising production costs and prohibitive ticket prices. Some artists and producers preferred to work in the more modest surroundings of Off or Off-Off Broadway, their more successful creations eventually finding their way to the Broadway theatre. Also contributing shows to Broadway were regional theatres, notably the Goodspeed Opera House in East Haddam, Connecticut.

Sometimes called the only uniquely American contribution to world theatre, the Broadway musical faces some severe economic and artistic tests in the years to come. MK

See: R. Baral, *Revue: The Great Broadway Period*, New York, 1970; G. Bordman, *American Musical Theatre: A Chronicle*, New York, 1978; S. Green, *Encyclopedia of the Musical Theatre*, New York, 1976; C. Smith and G. Litton, *Musical Comedy in America*, New York, 1981.

American Place Theatre   111 West 46th St, New York City [Architect: Richard D. Kaplan]. Founded as a producing organization dedicated to the presentation of new American plays by living authors, the American Place Theatre started at St Clement's Church on West 46th Street. Its founders were Wynn Handman and Reverend Sidney Lanier, the vicar of the church. In 1971, an underground complex of theatres, offices and workrooms at the rear of the Stevens building on 6th Avenue was presented to the group through changes in the building and zoning laws which permitted the builder of an office skyscraper to add extra storeys if he included a theatre within the structure. The company pays $5.00 per year for this space. Handman continues as artistic director assisted by Julia Miles, who runs the Women's Project founded in 1978. The company mounts full-scale productions as well as numerous works-in-progress during its ten-month season. MCH

American Repertory Theatre   The first company of this name, founded in 1946 by **Eva Le Gallienne** with **Margaret Webster** and **Cheryl Crawford**, was located in an obsolete theatre on Columbus Circle. Despite a notable company of actors and the objective to become New York's version of the **Old Vic** or the **Comédie-Française**, it was defunct by 1948. The second company of this name (ART) under **Robert Brustein** began an association in 1980 with Harvard University. Dedicated to neglected works from the past, new American plays, and innovative classical productions, the theatre has staged controversial productions (such as *Endgame* in 1984–5, disclaimed by **Beckett**), innovative direction and experimental work, such as the 1985 production of portions of **Robert Wilson**'s *the CIVIL WarS*, and inaugural productions, such as **Marsha Norman**'s *'night, Mother* (1982) and the 1985 Tony Award-winning musical *Big River*, later seen in New York. DBW

American Shakespeare Theatre   Founded in Stratford, Connecticut, in 1951 as the American Festival Theatre under the guidance of **Lawrence Lang-**

The American Repertory Theatre's production of Carlo Gozzi's *The King Stag*, directed by Andrei Serban, 1984/5 season.

ner, its name was changed in 1972. Designed by Edwin Howard, the octagonal shaped theatre reminiscent of the exterior of the original **Globe Theatre**, with a thrust stage and an auditorium seating about 1,500, opened on 12 July 1955 with *Julius Caesar* as part of an eight-week season. Under a series of artistic directors, approximately 74 productions have been staged, including non-Shakespearian works beginning with **Shaw**'s *Caesar and Cleopatra* in 1963. In 1959 special spring performances for students were added. Among the better known actors to have appeared here are **Morris Carnovsky**, **Jessica Tandy**, **Katharine Hepburn**, **Kate Reid**, **James Earl Jones**, **Christopher Plummer**, and **Alfred Drake**. In 1977 the Connecticut Centre for the Performing Arts was established to expand the season to include guest artists and touring companies. The most recent full summer season was 1979, followed by sporadic production and finally total inactivity since 1982. In January of that year the theatre filed for bankruptcy with a debt of almost $2 million, although a solution to its financial woes has been devised and future productions promised.   DBW

American Theatre Camp St, New Orleans. English-language theatre was successfully established in New Orleans with the American Theatre, which flourished from 1824 to 1840. A substantial brick structure, the house was built by **James H. Caldwell**, who served as its manager for eight years before leasing

it to others. Caldwell and his successors assembled competent companies, provided novelties along with the standard repertory and brought in whatever stars were available each season. After he had launched his larger and more opulent **St Charles**, Caldwell disposed of the 'pretty little playhouse' on Camp Street, which was rebuilt as the Camp St Exchange in 1840.   MCH

American theatre societies and associations
The *Encyclopedia of Associations* (Detroit: Gale Research Co., 1985) lists well over 130 theatrical societies and associations in the United States. Among the better known are the following:

1. American Society for Theatre Research (ASTR) Theatre Arts Programme –D1; University of Pennsylvania; Philadelphia PA 19102. Founded 1956, membership 620. ASTR is an organization for theatre scholars to promote knowledge of theatre history. It is affiliated with the International Federation for Theatre Research.

2. The American Theatre Association (ATA) 1010 Wisconsin Ave., NW, 6th Fl.; Washington DC 20007. Founded 1936 as the American Educational Theatre Association, disbanded summer 1986. Primarily but not exclusively an educators' organization, the ATA included the following divisions, some of which hope to re-form as separate organizations: American Community Theatre Association; Army Theatre Arts Association; National Association of Schools of Theatre;

National Children's Theatre Association; Secondary School Theatre Association; University and College Theatre Association; and the University Resident Theatre Association. The ATA founded the American College Theatre Festival, an annual competition with numerous awards granted at regional and national festivals.

3. American Theatre Critics Association (ATCA) 1326 Madison Ave.; New York NY 10128. Founded 1974, membership 251. ATCA seeks to foster communication between American theatre critics, encourages freedom of expression in the theatre and theatre criticism, and advances theatrical standards.

4. Catholic Actors Guild of America (CAG) 8768 Broadway, Suite 2400; New York NY 10036. Founded 1914, membership 500. CAG was founded for the spiritual and temporal welfare of theatre people.

5. International Theatre Institute of the United States (ITI/US) 1860 Broadway, Suite 1510; New York NY 10023. Founded 1948. The ITI/US was established by UNESCO to serve as an international theatre organization and clearing house for information and services. ITI/US maintains a library of international theatre covering 142 countries. Although the United States left UNESCO in 1984, ITI/US continues to function.

6. League of Historic American Theatres 1600 H St, NW; Washington DC 20006. Founded 1977, membership 175. The League is primarily concerned with the restoration of important historic theatres and maintains the Chesley Collection on American historic theatres.

7. League of New York Theatres and Producers 226 W 47th St; New York NY 10036. Founded 1930, membership 250. This organization negotiates labour contracts and government relations; it also conducts and sponsors theatrical research concerning the commercial theatre.

8. League of Off-Broadway Theatres and Producers (LOBTP) c/o **Circle in the Square**; 1633 Broadway; New York NY 10019. Founded 1957, membership 50. LOBTP seeks to advance the Off-Broadway theatre in New York.

9. League of Resident Theatres (LORT) c/o Center Stage; 700 N. Calvert St; Baltimore MD 21201. Founded 1965, membership 64. LORT seeks to advance the regional professional theatre in the USA.

10. National Theatre Conference (NTC) c/o Prof. William A. Allman; Art and Drama Center; Baldwin Wallace College; Berea OH 44017. Founded 1925, membership 120. NTC membership is limited to 120 leaders of the non-commercial academic and non-academic theatre; NTC seeks to collaborate on matters of policy and action with other major theatre organizations.

11. Negro Actors Guild of America (NAG) Founded 1936, membership 878. NAG seeks to provide for the specific care of Negro performers in particular situations arising from theatrical life.

12. New York Drama Critics Circle (NYDCC) c/o Allan Wallach; Newsday; 1500 Broadway; New York NY 10036. Founded 1935, membership 25. NYDCC seeks to uphold the standards of dramatic criticism in New York City.

13. Theatre Communications Group (TCG) 355 Lexington Ave.; New York NY 10017. Founded 1961, membership 220. TCG is a service organization for nonprofit professional theatres and performers, fostering interaction between members.

14. Theatre Historical Society (THS) c/o Dr Robert K. Headley, Jr; 6510 41st Ave., N; Hyattsville MD 20782. Founded 1969, membership 800. THS seeks to preserve and make available the history of the popular theatre in the USA.

15. Theatre Library Association (TLA) 111 Amsterdam Ave, Rm 513; New York NY 10023. Founded 1937, membership 500. TLA seeks to further the interests of gathering, preserving, and making available any records of theatre in all its forms. Its membership is composed of curators, librarians, and theatre scholars.

16. United States Institute for Theatre Technology (USITT) 330 W 42nd St, #1702; New York NY 10036. Founded 1960, membership 3,500. USITT seeks to serve those interested in the advancement of theatre techniques and technology.

Other theatrically oriented organizations in America include the American Theatre Society; Council of Resident Summer Theatres; Drama Desk; Episcopal Actor's Guild of America; Ford's Theatre Society; Institute for Advanced Studies in the Theatre; Institute of Outdoor Drama; National Costumers Association; National Playwrights Conference; National Theatre of the Deaf; New Dramatists; Outer Critics Circle; Society for the Preservation of Variety Arts; Theatre Development Fund; and the Yiddish Theatre Alliance. SMA

Ames, Winthrop (1871–1937) American producer and director. Ames, a wealthy Bostonian, was a leader in the art theatre movement. At Boston's Castle Square Theatre (1904–7), at New York's ill-fated **New Theatre** (1909–11), and finally at the two theatres he built: the **Little Theatre** (1912, West 44th Street), 'a little Pullman car of a place', he called it, and the **Booth** (West 45th).

Ames was the first American to make a serious study of the European art theatres. In 1907 he visited 64 theatres and saw 53 productions in Paris, London, Berlin, Vienna, and Munich and kept a detailed notebook including 154 sketches of scenic innovations. In 1912 Ames introduced the 'new stage-craft' to New York by bringing over **Reinhardt**'s production of *Sumrun*. He encouraged **Norman Bel Geddes**'s experiments in stage lighting at his two theatres.

Ames prepared minutely detailed prompt scripts – 'mother copies', he called them – for his productions and the results always reflected his lively imagination and his impeccable taste. Most notably: **Galsworthy**'s *The Pigeon* (1912), **Schnitzler**'s *The Affairs of Anatol* (1912), starring **John Barrymore**, **Shaw**'s *The Philanderer* (1913), *Snow White* (1913, his own adaptation), **Maeterlinck**'s *The Betrothel* (1918), and **Kaufman** and **Connelly**'s *Beggar on Horseback* (1924). RM

Amsterdamse Schouwburg In 1637, Jacob van Campen, a famous Dutch architect, built the first municipal theatre of Amsterdam, the famous Schouwburg, by order of the trustees of the orphanage and the old people's home. It was opened on 3 January 1638 with a performance of *Gijsbrecht van Aemstel*, written by **Joost van den Vondel** especially for this occasion. The event meant the beginning of a New Year's tradition that would continue for centuries. It was here in the Amsterdam theatre that in 1655 the first Dutch actress, Ariana Roozemond, appeared on stage.

In 1664, the trustees decided to have a new, 'modern' theatre built in the Venetian style. A system of baroque-style side-wings and backdrops was introduced, which enabled quick scene-changes. In 1772, the theatre was destroyed by fire. Two years later, in 1774, a new theatre was built at the 'Leidseplein', a wooden building, destined to go up in flames, which indeed happened in 1890. The present theatre, made of stone, was built in 1894 at the 'Leidseplein'.

The resident company in the Amsterdam Schouwburg chooses its repertory from the best of drama all over the world. The municipal theatre of Amsterdam faces stiff competition from the Muziektheater, the Stopera, built in 1986. In future, it is likely to take the central position.   MG   WH

Anderson, John Henry (1814–74) Scottish conjurer known as 'The Great Wizard of the North'. The son of an Aberdeen tenant farmer, he had a genius for publicity, broadcasting posters, staging parades and publishing newspapers to advertise his advent. After years of success in the provinces and London, he opened his 5,000-seat City Theatre in Glasgow in 1845, producing minstrel shows, operas and variety as a setting for his demonstrations of magic and second-sight. Anderson originated pulling rabbits from top hats and a live goose from 'The Magic Scrapbook' (Queen Victoria's favourite trick). Five months after the opening, the theatre was consumed by fire, and all his conjuring apparatus destroyed, so he resumed touring, taking in Europe (1846–7), the USA (1851, 1855–6, 1859–61) and Australia (1858). Two more stage fires helped reduce him to bankruptcy, prompting an unsuccessful appearance as Prospero in a burlesque, pro-Union *Tempest* (NY Winter Garden, 1861). His final performances were assisted by a bevy of daughters, some adopted.   LS

Anderson, John Murray (1886–1954) American producer, designer, and director. After beginning his theatrical career as a producer of pageants and civic masques, Anderson applied the new stagecraft of **Gordon Craig** and his followers to the American revue when he presented the *Greenwich Village Follies* (1919). The show's success, due largely to its simple, imaginative, and beautiful scenery and costumes, launched an annual series of revues that rivalled the *Ziegfeld Follies* in the taste and artistry of its *mise en scène*. The *Greenwich Village Follies* were also noted for their 'ballet ballads', poems and stories set to music and dance. Anderson was soon in demand as a designer, director and producer. Over the next 30 years he was primarily known as a facile director of musicals, night club floor shows, and circuses. Among his musical theatre productions were two editions of the revue *Murray Anderson's Almanac* (1929 and 1953). His autobiography was published in 1954.   MK

Anderson, Judith (née Frances Margaret Anderson-Anderson) (1898–) First Australian-born actress to be appointed DBE (1960). She has consistently excelled in powerful, tragic roles.

Failing in her planned singing career, she turned to acting, made her debut in Sydney in 1915, followed by a two-year tour with an American stock company. Her first New York appearance was in 1918; her first substantial success was as Elise in *Cobra* (1924), followed by the Unknown One in *As You Desire Me* (1931) and Lavinia in *Mourning Becomes Electra* (1932). In 1936 she was Gertrude to **John Gielgud**'s Hamlet in New York; in 1937 she made her London debut (**Old Vic**) as Lady Macbeth opposite **Laurence Olivier** (repeated with **Maurice Evans**, New York, 1941). She played the title role in Robinson Jeffer's adaptation of **Euripides**' *Medea* in 1947 (revived in 1974). At the Old Vic in 1960 she appeared as Irina Arkadina in *The Seagull*. In 1970, with minimal success, she toured as Hamlet. In 1984 she appeared regularly on the United States television daytime drama *Santa Barbara*.   DBW

Anderson, Lindsay (Gordon) (1923–) British director who began his career by making documentary films. He met **George Devine** through a mutual friend, Tony Richardson, at a time, 1956, when Devine was establishing the English Stage Company at the **Royal Court Theatre**. He became a forceful member of Devine's team, directing **Willis Hall**'s *The Long and the Short and the Tall* (1959) and **John Arden**'s *Serjeant Musgrave's Dance* (1959); but his qualities as a director were better revealed through his long association with the plays of **David Storey**, which began with *In Celebration* (1969) and continued through several lovingly detailed studies of contemporary life, *The Contractor* (1969), *Home* (1970), *The Changing Room* (1971), *The Farm* (1973) and *Life Class* (1974). In 1969, he became part of a three-man management running the Royal Court with Anthony Page and **William Gaskill**, but his talents did not lie towards administration. As a free-lance film and stage director, he has worked at the **National Theatre** and on Broadway and made a powerful screen impact with such films as *If* (1968).   JE

Anderson, Mary (1859–1940) American actress. At 16, in 1875, she made her debut as Juliet at Macaulay's Theatre in Louisville, and this quickly led to other engagements. Her major assets were her classical physical beauty and a rich, expressive voice. She made her New York debut in 1877. **W. S. Gilbert** wrote a short play, *Comedy and Tragedy*, for her. Americans proudly called her 'Our Mary'.

During her 14-year career on both sides of the Atlantic, she played 18 leading roles, including such favourites as Rosalind and Galatea in *Pygmalion and Galatea*. She was also the first actress to double the roles of Hermione and Perdita. In 1890 at the height of her career, she retired from the stage, settled in England, and married Antonio de Navarro. She returned to the stage during the First World War, however, appearing in various benefit performances. Her memoirs were published as *A Few Memories* (1896) and *A Few More Memories* (1930).   FHL   DJW

Anderson, Maxwell (1888–1959) American playwright and dramatic theorist. This prolific playwright's career spanned three decades, but the bulk of his critically acclaimed work came in the 30s. He won the Pulitzer Prize for *Both Your Houses* (1933), the

Drama Critics' Circle Award for *Winterset* (1935), the first such Award ever given, and another for *High Tor* (1937). He gained a reputation as an anti-war dramatist, and *What Price Glory?* (1924) (co-authored with Lawrence Stallings) pioneered by bringing onstage the realistic, salty language of men at war. Other Anderson plays with wartime settings or themes include *Valley Forge* (1934), *Key Largo* (1939), *Candle in the Wind* (1941), and *The Eve of St Mark* (1942). Anderson turned frequently to the lives of monarchs and other political leaders for the subject matter of his dramas. Important examples include *Elizabeth the Queen* (1930), *Mary of Scotland* (1933), *Knickerbocker Holiday* (1938) (a musical written in collaboration with Kurt Weill), *Joan of Lorraine* (1947), *Anne of the Thousand Days* (1948), and *Barefoot in Athens* (1951). Anderson also successfully adapted others' work for the stage. Examples are *Lost in the Stars* (1949) (also in collaboration with Kurt Weill) and *The Bad Seed* (1954). Anderson never tired of attempting to justify the use of blank verse in modern drama, and with *The Essence of Tragedy* (1939) became the first American playwright to publish a detailed theory of tragedy. An astute businessman, he was one of the founders of the Playwrights' Company (1938).   LDC

Anderson, Robert W[oodruff] (1917–)

American playwright. New York born and Harvard educated, Robert Anderson first drew attention as a playwright by winning the National Theatre Conference prize with *Come Marching Home* (1945). After an eight-year hiatus during which he taught playwriting and adapted 36 plays and several novels for the Theatre Guild of the Air, he burst upon Broadway with the long-running *Tea and Sympathy* (1953). This sensitive study of a young man's growth from innocence into experience is still considered his outstanding work. He was the only new playwright ever elected to membership (1953) in the Playwrights' Company, which produced three of his plays: *All Summer Long* (1953), *Tea and Sympathy*, and *Silent Night, Lonely Night* (1959). His play, *The Days Between* (1965), helped inaugurate the American Playwright's Theatre. He proved that an evening of one-act plays was still viable Broadway fare with *You Know I Can't Hear You When the Water's Running* (1967) and *Solitaire/Double Solitaire* (1970). He wrote screenplays based on several of his plays, including the autobiographical *I Never Sang for My Father* (1970) for which he was nominated for an Academy Award.   LDC

Andinet Theatre Club (Unity Theatre Club)

Ethiopian professional touring company, founded by Mattewos Bekele in 1953, consisting of traditional and modern dance and music groups and a drama company. It toured many of Ethiopia's provinces performing mostly Mattewos's own short verse-plays accompanied by music. It collapsed in the face of competition from the **Hagr Fikir** and City Hall Theatres. See also **Ethiopia** and **Kinet** for the Andinet Kinet, not connected.   RK

Andrade, Jorge (1922–84)

Brazilian playwright, born to one of São Paulo's most traditional rural aristocratic families. He was educated in the capital city and returned to work on the family estate, but discovered his vocation on enrolling in the Drama School of São Paulo where he finished in 1954. His plays divide into the 'rural' cycle and the 'urban' plays. In the 'rural' cycle: *O telescópio* (*The Telescope*, 1954), *A moratório* (*The Moratorium*, 1955), *Pedreira das almas* (*Stone Quarry of Souls*, 1956) and *Vereda da salvação* (*Path to Salvation*, 1964). Of the several urban plays, the best known is perhaps *Os ossos do Barão* (*The Baron's Bones*, 1963). Andrade specialized in showing the decadence of the Paulista society in its various phases with special emphasis on the coffee plantations that were a singular part of his heritage. The publication of *Marta, a arvore e o relógio* (*Martha, the Tree and the Clock*, 1970) climaxed his entire production, one of the most heterogeneous in Brazil. *Rasto atrás* (*Step Backwards*), his last major play, dealt explosively with an undercurrent that had permeated his other plays, that is, the autobiographical projection of a father–son relationship with a public confession of personal issues in a context of social class decadence.   GW

Andreev, Leonid Nikolaevich (1871–1919)

Prolific and controversial Russian prose writer, dramatist and journalist, who rivalled **Chekhov** and **Gorky** in popularity and importance during the pre-revolutionary period (c. 1905–17). Andreev is an extreme example of the soul-sickness, spiritual confusion and sense of isolation suffered by the Russian artistic intelligentsia of this era. In his work, one finds a growing pessimism bordering on nihilism and a concomitant hope for spiritual regeneration and a reprieve from mankind's dark fate. In his search for faith he assumed many roles: realist, pro- and anti-symbolist, pro- and anti-revolutionary, militarist and neo-romantic allegorist. Gorky's neo-realist Znanie (Knowledge) publishing house printed his early stories, but Andreev eventually rejected his sponsor's naive revolutionary politics. The symbolists, with the exception of **Blok** and **Bely**, disowned him. The futurists, with whom he shared a primitivist tendency, parted with him after 1915, when he proclaimed them philistines and bourgeois entertainers. His real kinsmen were **E. T. A. Hoffmann**, Poe, **Maeterlinck**, **Gogol** and Dostoevsky. His macabre short stories, like his metaphysical dramas, contemplate man's folly, vanity and brutality and life's horror and falsity and feature madness, death and all manner of sexual and spiritual perversion. On the basis of these stories and plays (he wrote some less interesting realistic and satirical dramas as well), Andreev has been lauded by some for his ambitious scope, his modernism and truthfulness and attacked by others for his pretence, abstract moralizing and humourless contrivance of theme, plot and character, which makes his people and situations inaccessible and unbelievable. Both assessments are partly correct. Despite the audacity of his conceptions, their realizations are too often melodramatic and in time redundant. His language tends also to be stilted and his tone self-important. Nevertheless, he is an artistic phenomenon. His most representative 'cosmic' dramas include: *The Life of Man* (1906), *Tsar Hunger* (1907), *Black Masks* (1908), *Anathema* (1909) and his international classic, *He Who Gets Slapped* (1915). *The Life of Man* utilizes puppet-like characters, stylized speech and action, *chiaroscuro* lighting effects (Andreev was a painter) and 'Someone in Grey', representing God-Fate-Death, to relate in schematic fashion the central episodes in the life cycle. **Meyerhold** and **Stanislavsky** gave it impressionistic mountings on grey- and black-draped stages in St Petersburg and Moscow, respectively (1907). *Black Masks*, a romantic *doppelgänger* tale, suggests the extreme subjectivism and externalization of psychic experience posited in **Evreinov**'s theory of 'monodrama', **Sologub**'s 'theatre of one will' and Andreev's own 'panpsychism'. *Anathema* depicts the struggle for man's soul between Satan's logic and God's irrational love. *He Who Gets Slapped* combines aspects of Russian folk puppet theatre, **commedia dell'arte**, Oriental theatrical conventionalism and romantic circus themes in a mythic-symbolic story of alienation, pain and humiliation. Andreev's sombreness was parodied in his time. His mysticism, eroticism, nihilism and eventual repudiation of the revolutionary cause have conspired to deflate his reputation in the Soviet Union today. SG

Andreini Family of Italian actors, originally from Tuscany. Its founder Francesco Dal Gallo (1548–1624) took the name Andreini when he entered a **commedia dell'arte** troupe. His best roles included a good Sicilian Dottore and a polyglot romancer, and as Capitano Spavento da Vall'Inferno he perfected the type of the braggart soldier. He headed the **Gelosi** company on its pioneering visit to Paris in 1603–4. His wife **Isabella** (born Canali, 1562–1604) played Innamorata with the Gelosi and was the most famous actress of her time. Much lauded for her grace, virtue and beauty, she lent her name to many *commedia* heroines. She was also celebrated as a writer of poetry and pastoral (*Mirtilla*, 1588). Their eldest son **Giovan Battista** or Giambattista (1576 or 1579–1654) played Innamorato under the name Lelio, and insisted on a form of stage naturalism and splendour. With **Tristano Martinelli** he founded the **Fedeli** troupe, which toured Italy (1613–14) and came to Paris, where he became a favourite of Louis XIII. He was a prolific playwright, his works comprising tragicomedies, comedies, mystery plays (*L'Adamo*, 1613, which was once thought to be Milton's inspiration for *Paradise Lost*) and pastorals (*La Florinda*, 1603). This last piece featured his wife **Virginia** (born Ramponi, 1583–1638), a frigid beauty who performed under the name Florinda. After her death, he married Virginia Rotari, known as Lidia. LS

Andrianoú, Kyvéli (?1887–1978) Greek actress. Together with the better known Katína Paxinoú and the more versatile **Maríka Kotopoúli**, Kyvéli or Kyría Kyvéli, as she was usually referred to ('Kyría' suggesting a respect similar to that evoked by 'Dame'), graced the modern Greek stage for decades. Her springboard was Constantíne Christomános's *Néa Skiní* (New Stage, or Theatre) (1901–5). She distinguished herself in innocent girl roles (*ingénue*) and played in a great number of bourgeois dramas, captivating audiences with her melodious voice and sentimental gestures. Eventually she acted in mature roles: Mary Stuart (against Kotopoúli's Elisabeth) in **Schiller**'s classical drama, Kontéssa Valéraina in Gregory Xenópoulos's best play *The Secret of Kontéssa Valéraina*, the mother in **Brecht**'s *Mother Courage*. Several Greek playwrights wrote dramas especially for her to act. Kyvéli's two

daughters, Alíki and Miránda, followed her example and became actresses. GT

Andronicus, Lucius Livius (d. ?204 BC) Early Latin dramatist, said to have been a freed slave from the Greek colony of Tarentum. His chronology was disputed by Roman scholars, but it is now generally accepted that he produced the first of all literary dramas in Latin in 240 BC. He wrote tragedies and comedies, all adapted from Greek originals, as well as non-dramatic works, and must have established the main conventions of Roman drama, though his work seemed crude to later generations. ALB

Anglin, Margaret (1876–1958) American actress. Daughter of the Speaker of the Canadian parliament, she trained at **Charles Frohman**'s Empire Theatre School, made her debut in 1893, and toured opposite **James O'Neill** and **Richard Mansfield**. She became leading lady of the Empire company opposite **Henry Miller** (1899–1905), and under their own management (1905–8), they produced *The Great Divide* by **William Vaughn Moody**. She then devoted herself to classical plays in productions designed by Livingston Platt in the manner of **Edward Gordon Craig**. Highlights were her summer productions of *Antigone*, *Electra* and *Medea* in the Hearst Amphitheatre at the University of California, Berkeley (1910, 1913 and 1915), and her tour in *The Taming of the Shrew*, *Twelfth Night*, *As You Like It*, and *Antony and Cleopatra* (1913/14). Except for a few revivals of her Greek productions, she appeared in modern plays from 1915 to 1943. In 1911 she married the actor, Howard Hull. A large, commanding woman, she lacked warmth and charm, but was unsurpassed at tears and dark interior emotions. DMCD

Animal impersonation May have been the earliest form of acting, as primitive tribesmen or their shamans disguised themselves as animal divinities to ensure successful hunts, evoke fertility daimons or propitiate malign influences. The painting of the deer dancer in the Trois Frères cave in Ariège probably shows such an impersonation, and the Indians of New Mexico preserved such a deer dance to the 20th century. Horns continued to appear on the Wild Men of Bavarian folk festivals and in the Abbots Bromley horn dance. The daimonic element can be traced in surviving folk customs, such as the whirling Padstowe horse and hobbyhorses of the mummers' plays, and particularly in the combats against dragons, usually portrayed by a collective. These range from the grotesque Balinese *barong* to the dragon marched in procession in Suffolk as late as 1903.

The folk plays of Attica were strong on animal impersonation, while the *maenads* in their ecstatic worship of Dionysus wore fox- and doeskins, and the satyr chorus from which tragedy is traditionally claimed to have sprung was clad in goatskins, horsetails and fox ears. Vase paintings of c. 500 BC show dancing men dressed as birds and horses. Vestiges of these practices recur in the fantasticated choruses of **Aristophanes**' comedies: birds, wasps and frogs. One of his legendary predecessors Magnes, a writer of beast-fable comedies, is said to have flapped wings and dyed himself green to amuse the Athenian audiences.

The Italo-American pantomimist Joseph Marzetti (d. 1864) as Jocko, the Brazilian ape.

The portrayal of animals as individual characters by human actors became immensely popular after the French Revolution, as a byblow of **Rousseau**'s ideas; the noble savage was held to exist even under the skin of an ape. Thus, the sensitive anthropoid in Gabriel and Rochefort's pantomimic scenario *Jocko; or The Ape of Brazil* (1825) was one of the most successful tear-jerkers of all time. A number of skilled performers, including the Frenchman **Mazurier**, the Englishman Gouffe, the Italo-American Marzetti, made careers of imitating the behaviour of simians in mimes, ballets, and plays, part melodrama, part farce, composed to feature them. Edward Klischnigg (1813–77), an English contortionist, lent his name to the *emploi* in the German-speaking theatre, and **Nestroy** wrote his *Ape and Bridegroom* (1836) for him.

English pantomime was another important setting for animal impersonation. Hogarth portrayed **John Rich** in a dogskin from *Perseus and Andromeda* (1730), and **Grimaldi** was almost killed at the age of three as he played a monkey swung round on a chain by his father. The 19-year-old **Henry Irving** practised villainy as a wolf in an Edinburgh panto. The leading artists in this field were **George Conquest**, George Ali and Charles Lauri. Conquest triumphed in such outlandish parts as an octopus, a crab and a giant porcupine whose costume consisted of 2,500 separate pieces; his son Fred is considered the greatest Goose of all time, and his son Arthur ended his career with the act 'Daphne the Chimpanzee'. Lauri was an expert at reproducing the

movement of a poodle, an ape, a bear, a wolf, an ostrich, a kangaroo, and especially a cat, in which role he introduced his famous walk round the dress circle balcony. The Brothers Griffiths kept music-hall audiences in stitches with their wrestling lion and the famous **Blondin** donkey, which seemed lifelike but contorted its legs in a cartoon fashion as soon as it was forced on to the tightrope.

Modern drama, fixated on realism, has been chary of this type of performance. In a playful mode, **Maeterlinck** made a dog and cat major characters in *The Blue Bird* (1908) and **Shaw** provided his Androcles with a waltzing lion (1913); but despite such fine actors as Lucien Guitry and **Maude Adams**, **Rostand**'s attempt in *Chantecler* (1910) to turn barnyard fowl and forest creatures into alexandrine-spouting humanoids could not be taken seriously by adult audiences. LS

Animals as performers From the dawn of time, man has used animal totems and established animal cults to achieve a dominance over nature. The training of animals not to perform an agricultural or military function but simply to entertain, most specifically by imitating human behaviour, blatantly advertises man as Lord of Creation. The earliest recorded example is the lion Antam-Nekht under Pharaoh Rameses II (1292–1225 BC); trained tigers who would allow a man to put his head safely in their mouths were known in early China and India (12–9th centuries BC). The Romans were more expert at slaughtering beasts than at schooling them, but the name of at least one of the *bestiari* or animal-trainers survives, the Gallic gladiator Paulus Superbus. Wandering performers both in the ancient and medieval worlds showed off simple tricks with bears and apes.

The most famous trained animal of **Shakespeare**'s day was the bay horse Morocco, shown by John Banks; as exhibited in the yard of the Belle Sauvage, London, it returned gloves to their owners, told the number of coins, and danced (warranting a mention in *Love's Labour's Lost*). Sir Walter Raleigh praised him, and **Ben Jonson**, referring to the rumour that beast and master had been executed for sorcery in Europe, described Banks as 'our Pythagoras,/Grave tutor to the learned horse; both which/Being, beyond the sea, burned for one witch'.

The heyday of the performing animal came in the 'Age of Enlightenment', when 'animaux savants' rivalled the noble savage as exemplars of natural perfectibility. The almanacs of Parisian fairs and boulevards (1773–87) report on the 'volatile troupe' of birds at the St Germain fair doing acrobatics and military exercises, rats that danced a saraband and Nicolet's ape Turco, a rope-dancer; during the Restoration the spaniel Munito was a celebrity. In England learned pigs were frequently on view solving mathematical puzzles. During the early romantic period of melodrama and pantomime, animals starred: Coco the stag, a headliner at the **Cirque Olympique**, was seriously compared to ballet dancers when he overleapt 16 horses in 1813. When Karsten of Vienna visited the Weimar Court Theatre in 1817 with *The Hound of Aubry*, featuring a poodle, **Goethe** gave up the management in disgust.

Covent Garden and **Drury Lane** admitted horses, lions and elephants to their pantomimic spectacles, with Chunee, the first pachyderm on the English stage,

An unidentified French clown with his troupe of trained dogs.

seen in the Garden's *Harlequin and Padmanaba* in 1811. Gasparo Spontini added an elephant to his opera *Olympia* (Berlin, 1821) and Mlle Djeck took the title-role as *The King of Siam's Elephant* (Cirque Olympique, 1829). Dog drama retained its favour on the Bowery and transpontine London stages well into the century. In the 1850s, when **Charles Kean** revived 'legitimate' drama at the **Princess's Theatre**, he followed the example of William Cooke, who had equestrianized Shakespeare at **Astley**'s, and put horses on stage. Contretemps were not infrequent: the horse starved to play Rosinante at the Cirque Olympique in 1843 died in rehearsal, and the operetta *Barkouf* by **Scribe** and Offenbach (1860) which featured a dog and music that imitated howling was damned by the critics as 'chiennerie'.

Meanwhile, the exhibition of wild animals at circuses was undergoing a change. Most trainers entered the cage and with more or less violence put the beasts through their paces. Isaac van Amburgh (1811–65) performed before Queen Victoria and was painted by Landseer, in his cage. Henri Martin was the first to break out of the cage into pantomime in *The Lions of Mysore* (Paris, 1831), and was followed by Thomas Batty at the Zirkus Renz (Berlin, 1861).

New training methods stressed animal psychology and work therapy, based on Pavlov's experiments and those of the Swiss psychologist J. Gaule. The result could be seen in the work of Carl and Wilhelm Hagenbeck who worked on the trust system and developed the round cage that filled the entire arena, allowing the animals more freedom (1888), Julius Seeth who let himself be eaten by lions nightly in *Quo Vadis?*, and the Russian clown **Vladimir Durov** whose rats and pigs made satirical political points. In the 20th century, although Clyde Beatty and Alfred Court continued to use the whip and chair as trademarks, the stress was now laid on glamour, culminating in the quasi-erotic displays of Günther Gebel-Williams.

Almost every kind of animal has been recruited into show business, from Fink's mules in American vaudeville to Floridian alligator-wrestling. Trained bees were shown by an Englishman at the St Germain fair in 1774, and the first recorded flea circus was opened by the Swiss Heinrich Degeller in Stuttgart in 1812. The variety stage housed boxing kangaroos (first shown by Prof. Landermann at the London Aquarium in 1892), Harald Winston's sea-lions dancing with chorus-girls in 1924, hyenas acting villains in 'The Shepherdess in the Desert' (1927), and Peter Alupka's (1905–18) cats singing 'O Tannenbaum'. The chimpanzee Consul, Lockhart's Elephants and Capt. Woodward's seals were public favourites for many years, but snake-charming was segregated into dime museums and side shows. Today live animals are still to be seen in grand opera and musical comedy: Billy Rose's *Jumbo* (1935) put down a spoor to be picked up by the dog Sandy in *Annie*. LS

See: A. Lehmann, *Tiere als Artisten*, Wittenberg, 1955; H. Thétard, *Les Dompteurs*, Paris, 1928.

Ankiya Nat *Ankiya Nat* is a form of religious theatre which originated and still exists in Assam, a beautiful but somewhat remote state in north-eastern India. *Ankiya Nat* was created by Sankaradeva (c. 1449–1568), an ardent devotee of Lord Vishnu who in his earthly manifestation as Krishna is worshipped by many Assamese Hindus. *Ankiya* means 'act' and *Nat* means 'drama'. Thus, *Ankiya Nat* means a one-act drama composed in a particular form.

Sankaradeva created *Ankiya Nat* and wrote many popular plays for the repertory as a means of maintaining and spreading the tenets of Vaisnavism among his people. He is also credited with establishing the practice that all leaders of religious orders should write at least one play about Krishna's life during their lifetime.

Performances of *Ankiya Nat* usually take place within the confines of the prayer halls (*nam-ghar*), roofed structures open at the side, located in the sacred confines of a monastery. The acting area is a long narrow corridor marked off by ropes running down the centre the length of the building. Usually, audiences sit on the ground or stand at the back facing each other while the players make their way up and down the narrow acting corridor. At times, scenes are played behind one side of the audience, literally enfolding them in the dramatic action.

At one end of the prayer hall is a shrine (*manikut*) where the sacred text (*Bhagavata Purana*) is kept, symbolizing the presence of Krishna's (Vishnu's) words, his teachings. Entrances are usually made at the end opposite the shrine and the players progress down the passageway in a slow ritual dance toward the text to begin most performances.

Usually, companies consist of about 15 amateur actors, either made up of monks who regard it as their sacred duty to portray the stories of their god or village artists who take particular pride in playing the roles of the gods and goddesses of the plays. Normally, men play all the parts of the monastery productions but women may participate in performances in communities where taboos against this activity are not rigidly enforced. The boys who take the role of Krishna and his brother Balarama are thought to be temporarily possessed by the spirit of god and are approached with great reverence, particularly by women among the spectators.

Shimmering white costumes are worn by the large orchestra of musicians which provide a hypnotic musical background during the overture and throughout a show. Leading characters wear colourful costumes and crowns to symbolize their particular station in life. Perhaps the most striking characters are the giant effigies made of bamboo and covered with papier-mâché painted to represent demons and animals. Some of the figures are at least 15 feet high and must be manipulated by several actors at once. Masks of birds, snakes, monkeys and bears are worn when a particular play demands the presence of such fanciful characters.

Typically, performances are organized to coincide with religious festivals, such as the birth of Krishna, the memorial day celebration of Sankaradeva or some local preceptor or on a full-moon night. The holiday season coincides with harvest and planting (mid-January to mid-April). A performance event usually begins around 9 pm and continues until sunrise.

Performances begin with an elaborate ritual of drumming, songs and dances commencing at the archway of lights (*agni-gad*) constructed on the acting area, opposite the sacred shrine. Special songs are sung in praise of Krishna and distribution of sacred food (*prasada*) to the musicians follows. At last, the stage manager (*sutradhara*) makes a spectacular entrance from behind a curtain at the archway accompanied by fireworks and dancing. A stately dance ensues during which he offers his humble respects to Krishna before the shrine. Then he recites a verse from the play to be enacted and concludes with a song. A red curtain is held up and Krishna makes his entrance by dancing majestically towards the shrine. Only then does the actual drama begin. Throughout the action which follows, the stage manager stands near the actors referring to the text of the play in order to make certain that they perform all the dialogue correctly. He inserts the necessary directions to the musicians and comments to the audience when need be to interpret the action of the play. In this respect, the stage manager reminds one of the medieval directors depicted in the famous painting of the martyrdom of Saint Apollonia.

Like other forms of traditional theatre, scenes of conflict between the forces of good and evil highlight an evening of *Ankiya Nat*. Brief songs and dances close the performance in the wee hours of the morning.

The strength of *Ankiya Nat* is in its close links to the religious beliefs of the Assamese people, particularly the devotees (*bhaktas*) of Krishna. It has sustained itself for centuries because it is prominent among the religiously minded Hindus of the state. It does not seem to have changed drastically over time, even though the state has undergone many dramatic changes in its economic and social organization in recent times. FaR

Annenkov, Yury Pavlovich (1889–1974) Russian designer, graphic artist, portraitist, art critic and memoirist, whose witty, sharp and eccentric style, suggestive of expressionism, cubo-futurism and constructivism, abetted noteworthy pre-revolutionary and early post-revolutionary theatrical experiments by **Nikolai Evreinov**, **Fyodor Komissarzhevsky** and others. He designed at two of the most popular 'theatres of small forms', **Nikita Baliev**'s Moscow 'Bat' (Chauve-Souris) and (from 1913) **Kugel**'s and Kholmskaya's St Petersburg Crooked Mirror Theatre, where Evreinov served as artistic director and resident playwright (1910–17). The Annenkov-Evreinov collaboration extended from Crooked Mirror parodies of classical and contemporary literature genres to a por-

trait, book covers and illustrations and expressionist designs for Evreinov's Soviet mass spectacle *The Storming of the Winter Palace* (1920) and *The Chief Thing* premiere at the Theatre of Free Comedy (1921). Annenkov also contributed large-scale designs to *The Field of Mars May Day Celebration* (1918) and *The Hymn to Liberated Labour* (1920), staged in front of the old St Petersburg stock exchange. He helped introduce futurist theatre ideas into Russia via his 1919 design-*mise en scène* for **L. Tolstoi**'s *The First Distiller* at the Petrograd Hermitage Theatre, his 1921 broadside 'Merry Sanitorium' and his 1921 manifesto 'The Theatre to the End', these two literary pronouncements owing much to **Marinetti**'s 'Variety Manifesto' (1913). Annenkov posited a 'Theatre of Pure Method', based upon gymnastic and circus performance and a kinetic stage space which would be anti-psychological and heroic. This approach inspired 'The Factory of the Eccentric Actor' (1922) of Kozintsev, Trauberg and Kryzhitsky and **Meyerhold**'s 1922 staging of *Tarelkin's Death*. In 1924 Annenkov emigrated to Germany and France, where he published articles, prose tales and an illuminating memoir of his Russian years, *Diary of My Acquaintances* (2 vols., 1965–6). SG

Annensky, Innokenty Fyodorovich (1856–1909) Russian symbolist-based poet, impressionist critic (he dubbed **Gorky** a symbolist), translator of all of **Euripides**' plays, neo-mythic dramatist, teacher, Hellenist and Slavist, he was one of Russian modernism's forebears and unallied elder statesmen. A man of exceptional classical erudition, he attempted in his four dramas to contemporize the Greek myths while maintaining their universality. Euripides was his model and master in the following ways: his questioning of religious belief (i.e., the classical myths) and search for a way to believe; his interest in human psychology and journalistic approach to the personalities, themes and events of the day; his hybridization of metre and style; his penchant for introducing music, dance, spectacle and melodramatic devices; his unabashed virtuosity. All four of Annensky's plays – *Melanippe, the Philosopher* (1901), *King Ixion* (1902), *Laodamia* (1906), *Thamira, the Cither Player* (1906) – deal in some sense with the conflict between art and life, beauty and suffering and display a well-developed auditory and visual sense. Only *Thamira* was staged, by **Tairov** in a cubist production at Moscow's Kamerny Theatre (1916). The story of Laodamia was retold by **Sologub** in *The Gift of the Wise Bees* (1907) and by **Briusov** in *Protesilaus Deceased* (1913). SG

Anouilh, Jean (1910–87) French playwright and script writer. Probably the most successful modern French playwright in financial terms, Anouilh worked in theatre (and films) since his first job, as secretary to **Jouvet**. **Giraudoux** and **Pirandello** were important influences on his work but his first plays were written in a naturalist vein e.g. *Le Voyageur sans Bagage* (*Traveller Without Luggage*) (directed by **Pitoëff** 1937) but he soon moved towards a more light-hearted style of bitter-sweet comedy, perfected in *Le Bal des Voleurs* (*The Thieves' Carnival*) (directed by **Barsacq**, 1938). This started a fruitful collaboration with Barsacq, which included his best-known play *Antigone* (1944). The play identifies role-play with fate: because she is called Antigone, the heroine must say 'no' to Creon; in this, the play is derivative of Pirandello and of revivals of Greek myth between the wars. Anouilh's *Antigone* lacks the political and religious elements of **Sophocles'** play and contains anachronistic references to contemporary life. As a result the 1944 production appealed both to Nazi sympathizers and to Resistance workers. After the war, Anouilh established a place as a writer of quality plays which could bridge the gap between the classics and the boulevard. His output in the 1950s and 1960s was voluminous but his themes, notably the contrast between youthful purity and adult compromise, varied little. His characters are mostly reduced to the dimensions of a single role or mask which lends a certain similarity to his plots whether they be set in the Middle Ages (*L'Alouette* (*The Lark*), 1953), the French Revolution (*Pauvre Bitos* (*Poor Bitos*), 1956) or modern times (*Cher Antoine* (*Dear Antoine*), 1969). The vapidity of his work has been partly concealed by his choice of familiar subjects (e.g. St Joan in *The Lark*, Thomas Becket and Henry II in *Becket* 1959) and by his unquestionably brilliant theatrical craftsmanship. Some of the credit for this must go to the directors with whom he worked: Barsacq during the 1940s, Roland Piétri in the 1950s and 1960s; but Anouilh showed his own acumen in directing revivals of **Molière** and of **Vitrac**'s *Victor*.   DB

Anski, Solomon (1863–1920) Russian-born writer immortalized by his play *The Dybbuk*, which resulted from research into small mystical ethnic sects, in this case the Chassidim. Written in 1914 in Yiddish, it was first produced with outstanding success by the **Vilna Troupe** two weeks after Anski's death, and subsequently toured throughout the world. Translated into Hebrew by the poet Bialik it became the outstanding success of **Habimah**.   AB

Anthony, Joseph (Deuster) (1912–) American actor and director. Born in Milwaukee, Anthony attended the University of Wisconsin and **Pasadena Playhouse** School (1931–5). He made his acting debut in a West Coast production of *Mary of Scotland*, after which he appeared in New York with the **Federal Theatre** in 1937, and later in numerous roles including Richters in *Skipper Next to God* (1948), Casanova in *Camino Real* and Prince Bounine in *Anastasia* (1954). In 1948 he made his New York directing debut with *Celebration*. Working in both films and the theatre, Anthony established himself as one of America's premiere directors. His stage credits include: *The Rainmaker* (1954); *The Lark* (1955); *The Most Happy Fella* (1956); *Winesburg Ohio* (1958); *The Best Man* (1960); *Mary, Mary* (1961); *Romulus* (1962); *110 in the Shade* (1963); *Slow Dance on the Killing Ground* (1964); and *Finishing Touches* (1973). In 1976 he was appointed Professor of Theatre Arts at SUNY-Purchase.   TLM

Anti-masque see **Masque**

Antoine, André (1858–1943) French actor and director who started life working for the Paris gas company. While a member of an amateur company, the Cercle Gaulois, he persuaded friends to perform some new plays and adopted the name Théâtre Libre (Free Theatre). In his first programme was an adapta-

tion of *Jacques Damour*, a story by **Zola**, with whom Antoine was friendly. Surprised by the success of this and a subsequent programme of new plays, Antoine turned professional. Between 1887 and 1894 his Free Theatre operated as a small experimental theatre club with a remarkable influence since it laid the foundations of stage naturalism, a form that was to dominate Western theatre for the next century. His lead was followed by **Otto Brahm** who opened his Free Theatre in Berlin in 1889 and J. T. Grein who founded the Independent Theatre in London in 1891.

Antoine was not a programmatic director, though his memory has become imprisoned in a myth of total stage illusionism. His prime aim was to free theatre from the constricting conventions of the time: instead of frivolous bedroom farce or spectacular melodrama, he wanted to be able to perform new plays dealing with contemporary issues. He taught his audience to enjoy evenings of short new plays known as *quarts d'heure* (quarter hours) though they lasted more than 15 minutes. He also introduced the work of major German, Scandinavian and Russian naturalists to the Paris stage, e.g. **Ibsen**'s *Ghosts* (1890), *The Wild Duck* (1891) and **Strindberg**'s *Miss Julie* (1893). In 1888 he saw performances by the **Meininger** and was deeply impressed by the ensemble playing, especially in crowd scenes. He aimed for similar effects, notably in **Hauptmann**'s *The Weavers* (1893).

In 1894 bankruptcy forced him to close down but in 1897 he was able to reopen as the Théâtre Antoine, and he received public recognition when in 1906 he was appointed director of the **Odéon**. In this period he revived many early successes but also developed and refined the techniques of naturalist theatre. He was the first director in France to do away with footlights, to lower house lights completely during performances and to treat the set like a real environment rather than a decorative background. He anticipated modern trends by always attempting to build the set in time for rehearsals so that the actors would be thoroughly familiar with it. Some rehearsal sets were even constructed with a fourth wall, later removed for performances. Above all, Antoine revolutionized acting in France, doing away with grand postures and declamatory speech and encouraging an intimate acting style and realistic use of space (e.g. being prepared to turn one's back on the audience).

Antoine was also the first French director of modern times to take **Shakespeare** seriously, beginning another trend that was to dominate 20th-century French theatre. During his time at the Odéon he produced the first unbowdlerized French *King Lear* (1904) as well as other plays little known at the time e.g. *Troilus and Cressida* (1912). For these he adapted his usual naturalistic settings to achieve a more fluid production style. After the First World War he worked in films for a while and continued to campaign for the ideals on which the Théâtre Libre had been founded.   DB

Anzengruber, Ludwig (1839–89) Australian playwright. After a disastrous career as an actor, Anzengruber turned to playwriting. He was happiest writing about the Austrian peasantry, whose dialect he was able to capture in a masterly way. Two of his greatest successes, *The Parson of Kirchfeld* (1870) and *The*

Cross-Markers (1872), reflect the conflict between orthodox Catholicism and liberalism in contemporary Austria, while *The Perjured Peasant* (1871) is a grim study of family life among the peasantry. Anzengruber's major achievement in the genre of the Viennese **Volksstück** was *The Fourth Commandment* (1877), a play that advocated the maintenance of traditional family values and loyalties. Anzengruber's plays were first produced in the commercial theatres of Vienna, not at the **Burgtheater**.   SW

Appia, Adolphe (1862–1928) Swiss theorist and designer who renovated theatrical and operatic scenography. 1880–1, musical studies in Geneva; 1882, first trip to Bayreuth and musical studies in Leipzig. 1882–90, extensive travels: Leipzig, Geneva, Paris, Bayreuth, Dresden, pursuing studies in music and drawing. Two suicide attempts (1888 and 90). In 1888, after a performance of **Wagner**'s *The Master Singers*, he resolved 'to reform the art of the theatre' (*la mise en scène*). Cosima Wagner invited him to design the costumes for Bayreuth (1888), but he declined the offer as too premature. It was not repeated. In 1891–2 he wrote his notes towards the production of *The Ring* and *La Mise en Scène du Drame Wagnérien* (published in Paris in 1895), and in 1892 he also wrote his most important work, *La Musique et la Mise en Scène* which was first published, with Appia's drawings, in German as *Die Musik und die Inszenierung* (Munich, 1899). In 1905 he saw the *Fête des Vignerons* in Vevey (which awakened his interest in popular festivals) and in 1906 he met Emile Jacques-Dalcroze, the creator of the system of eurhythmics. In 1909 he began sketches for his 'rhythmic spaces'. Appia and Dalcroze prepared plans for an ambitious school and festival in Hellerau (Germany), where singers, dancers, musicians, designers would work in creative harmony. The Institute operated from 1911 to 1914 and staged two festivals (1912 and 1913). In 1914 he exhibited 53 drawings in Zurich and met **Gordon Craig**: they respected each other's work and recognized a kindred spirit. **Copeau** became a personal friend in 1915 and the two men remained in close contact, although they never worked together. *L'Oeuvre d'Art Vivant* was published in 1921. Craig and Appia shared an exhibition in Amsterdam (1922). Eventually, on 20 December 1923, a full design by Appia for an opera by Wagner was completed, when the Scala of

Appia's design for Act II, The Elysian Fields, *Orphéus et Euridice*, 1926.

Milan under Toscanini performed *Tristan and Isolde*, to a mixed reception. In 1924, the young director **Wälterlin** asked him to design the whole of *The Ring* for his theatre in Basle. But after a few performances of *Rhinegold* and *The Valkyrie* the plan had to be abandoned, as Appia's work was deemed 'too revolutionary'. Although Appia's output as a theatre designer was pitifully small (his shyness and the establishment's philistinism combining to keep him away from the stage), his influence on designers and lighting designers cannot be overstressed. He abolished *trompe-l'oeil* scenery, called for non-naturalistic and symbolic, architectural sets, used light creatively and insisted on the alliance of music and action, of body and spirit.   CLS

Aquarium French theatre company which has successfully maintained the principle of *création collective* developed by many companies after 1968. Originally a student group, they turned professional in 1970 and moved to a permanent space in the Cartoucherie at Vincennes in 1972. Their work has been distinguished by a rigorous search for effective theatrical treatment of contemporary documentary material, e.g. *Marchands de Ville* (*Town Merchants*, 1972) about housing problems or *Un Conseil de Classe très Ordinaire* (*A Very Ordinary Staff Meeting*, 1981) about education.   DB

Arbuzov, Aleksei Nikolaevich (1908–) Soviet actor, director and one of the most prolific and popular dramatists at home and in the West. His plays employ the theatricalist devices of late 1950s 'new lyricism' to punch up a cagey mix of irony, sentimentalism, melodrama, fantasy, romanticism and self-consciously evoked Chekhovian character eccentricities and themes – time's passage, life's disappointments, youth's coming of age and the old becoming young again. An 'orphan of the Revolution', raised by an aunt – his father left home and his mother was hospitalized (1919) – Arbuzov's sense of love and fantasy as twin salvations from the fragility and cruelty of life, is reflected in his plays. He began by writing agit-prop skits for the Moscow Proletkult Theatre, having already performed in a mime troupe and in an amateur travelling company of his own. His first full-length plays – *Class* (1930), *Six Favourites* and *The*

Appia's design for The Magic Garden, *Parsifal*, 1922.

Distant Road (1935) – were followed by the extremely popular *Tanya* (1939; revised 1946; operatic version by G. G. Kreitner, 1954). A chronicle play centring on a negative, dependent woman, who through losing her husband transforms herself into a self- and socially aware heroine, *Tanya* is typical of Arbuzov's work and of much Soviet playwriting. Arbuzov's next plays, written for the Second World War front-line theatre, the Moscow Theatrical Studio, which he co-founded with **V. N. Plyuchek**, include: *Sunrise City* (co-written with the collective, 1940), *The Immortal One* (with A. K. Gladkov, 1942) and *The Little House in Cherkizovo* (revised as *The Little House on the Outskirts*, 1943). Following *A Meeting with Youth* (1947), a dramatization of **Turgenev**'s *On the Eve* (1948), and *European Chronicle* (1952), Arbuzov wrote the youth chronicle play, *The Years of Wandering* (1954), the strongly Chekhovian *The Twelfth Hour* (1959) and his most popular drama, *Irkutsk Story* (1959), which became the model for much of his later work. This simple, naive tale of young love, personal hardship and growth is given a socially resonant setting – a Siberian hydroelectric plant – and a flashback structure through which the story is told in part by a chorus, direct audience address and mime. In his international hit, *My Poor Marat* (English title – *The Promise*, 1965), Arbuzov compresses space (a claustrophobic Leningrad apartment) and expands time (1942–60), offers us dreams deferred and love redeemed with the individual assuming responsibility for his own life. His plays of the 1970s, published in the collection, *Choice*, called after the least memorable among the plays, focus upon more mature adults, either saved from loneliness by love or punished for withholding it when it was needed. These include: *Tales of the Old Arbat* (English title – *Once Upon a Time*), a 'comedy' featuring a puppeteer-Prospero battling his son for the love of a Hilda Wangel-type; *In This Pleasant Old House*, a 'vaudeville-melodrama' with songs and dances, in which an estranged wife is fittingly denied readmission to a warm, eccentric musical family she had earlier rejected; *My Eye-Catcher*, an 'optimistic comedy' of super-animated flat characters and improbable situations à la vaudeville; *An Old-Fashioned Comedy* (English title – *Do You Turn Somersaults?*), a gentle 'presentation' for two ageing and lonely people, set to romantic musical themes; *Evening Light*, a Chekhovian 'tale for the theatre', linking serious moral themes on personal and social levels. *Cruel Games* (1978), which takes its epigraph from **Albee**'s *Who's Afraid of Virginia Woolf?*, is a disturbing picture of disaffected youth passing through cruelty to kindness, which aroused considerable controversy when produced. His most recent plays, *Remembrances* (1981) and *The Victorious One*, return to the safe, familiar conflicts between extracurricular romance and family, professional and personal life. A long-time supporter of young talent, Arbuzov runs a theatre studio, which has graduated playwrights Lyudmila Petrushevskaya, Olga Kuchkina-Pavlova and Anna Rodionova. SG

Arce, Manuel José (1935–) Playwright and director, also one of Guatemala's best poets and the most read columnist of his generation. His best plays, *Delito, condena y ejecución de una gallina* (*Crime, Punishment and Execution of a Chicken*, 1968) and *Sebastián sale de compras* (*Sebastian Goes Shopping*, 1971), have been translated and performed in several countries. He has several one-act plays. Presently lives exiled in southern France. GW

Arch Street Theatre 609–615 Arch St, Philadelphia [Architect: William Strickland]. Believing that Philadelphians would support a newer, more elegant playhouse than the **Chestnut**, a group of citizens pledged the money to build the Arch Street Theatre and leased it to **William B. Wood**, late of the rival theatre. It opened in 1828, but Wood did not last long as manager and it passed to other hands. In 1861, it enjoyed its most prosperous and famous period when **Mrs John Drew** became manageress. For nearly a decade, she maintained a peerless company of actors in excellent productions. Early in the 1880s, Mrs Drew was forced to accede to the 'combination system', in which each play is individually cast and presented for as long a run as it has the public's interest. After she retired from the theatre's management in 1892, it was often closed. Before it was demolished in 1936, the theatre had been used by German and Yiddish companies. MCH

Archer, William (1856–1924) Scottish journalist and dramatic critic, whose alliance with **George Bernard Shaw** in the promotion of **Ibsen** was influential in the move to raise the literary standards of British drama at the end of the 19th century. The first of Archer's own translations from Ibsen was performed in London in 1880 under the title *Quicksands: or The Pillars of Society*. A collected edition in 11 volumes was published in 1906–8. Archer was a fierce defender of the best of contemporary drama against what he considered a dangerous and indiscriminate preference for the 'classics'. *The Old Drama and the New* (1923) is a vigorously argued and unashamedly partisan statement of his critical view that the plays of **T. W. Robertson** raised the English drama to a new level of excellence and that they, together with the work of Robertson's immediate successors, should command a dominant place on the stage. PT

Arden, John (1930–) British dramatist, whose first plays were seen at the **Royal Court Theatre** during **George Devine**'s pioneering seasons. *Serjeant Musgrave's Dance* (1959) about a band of deserting soldiers who try to recruit the inhabitants of a bleak Northern town into a dance of death is now widely regarded as a modern classic. Other Arden plays from this period such as *Live Like Pigs* (1957) and *The Happy Haven* (1960) reveal a blend of social concern and technical experimentation. For *Armstrong's Last Goodnight*, which came to the **National Theatre** in 1965, he invented a medieval Scottish dialect with regional variations to express a theme originally inspired by political events in the Congo. His Arthurian epic, *The Island of the Mighty* (1972), written with his wife Margaretta D'Arcy, was produced by the **Royal Shakespeare Company** only after violent disagreements; and since 1970, Arden's Marxist convictions have increasingly taken him away from the mainstream of British theatre. He writes with Margaretta D'Arcy for non-professional groups and lives in Ireland, whose troubled history has provided them with the content of several plays, such as *The Ballygombeen Bequest* (1972) and *The Non-Stop Connolly Show* (1975). The literary preoccupations of his early years, which lent him the reputation of being an English **Brecht** with a summary song for every moral, have changed towards a populist directness of speech, often harsh and polemical, but at best stirring and powerful. His views on the theatre have been collected into a book of essays, *To Present the Pretence* (1978).   JE

Arden of Feversham, The Tragedy of Mr An anonymous play, at one time attributed to **Shakespeare**, published in 1592 and probably first performed in the same year. It is of great interest as an early example of domestic tragedy and, insofar as it is based on an actual recent murder, as a forerunner of the popular criminal drama of the 18th and 19th centuries. **George Lillo** adapted and sentimentalized it for the audience of his day.   PT

Arena Stage   6th St and Maine Ave, NW, Washington, DC [Architect: Harry Weese]. In 1950, a group of six associated with George Washington University founded a theatrical company, Arena Stage, under the guidance of Professor Edward Mangum. They opened their first season in a movie house, presenting their plays 'in the round'. When most of the original group drifted away to other pursuits, Zelda Fichandler, one of the founding members, took over the reins of leadership and has remained its director ever since. In 1956, the company moved into an old brewery and gradually built an audience. In 1961, sharing the management with her husband Thomas, Mrs Fichandler moved into a new modern theatre with the help of grants from the Ford Foundation and others. In 1970, in Phase II of its development, a 500-seat modified thrust stage playhouse, the Kreeger, joined the 800-seat mainstage, and later, a cabaret theatre, the Old Vat Room was added. The Arena Stage Company supports a full company of actors, directors and designers and presents new American and European plays along with musicals and classical revivals.   MCH

Aretino, Pietro (1492–1556) Italian writer and dramatist noted for his vigorous satires against papal and secular figures and his scurrilous dialogues *I Ragionamenti* (1534–6). His early work was written in Rome under the patronage of Leo X, but the hostility it attracted later prompted him to move to the more liberal atmosphere of Venice. Although he wrote one tragedy, *L'Orazia* (1545), his wide-ranging interests, eye for social detail, and vigorous, colloquial language were better suited to comedy, in which genre he wrote some of the most lively and enduring of the period, among them *La Cortigiana* (*The Courtesan*, 1525) and *Il Marescalco* (*The Stablemaster*, 1527). For the production of his comedy *La Talanta* at Venice in 1541 **Vasari** prepared a theatre in the Casa di Cannaregio, one of the significant early developments in the evolution of indoor fitted stagings.   KR   LR

Argentina Buenos Aires, often referred to as the Paris of South America, was an insignificant city at the time of independence in 1816. Neither Argentina nor the River Plate, contrary to the connotations of the names, yielded up silver to the colonizers; neither did the explorers find gold as they did in many other Spanish colonies. Buenos Aires was founded in 1580 but the interior cities were more important in early years. In Córdoba theatre activity was documented as early as 1610 as the Jesuit missions worked with the local Indian population. Comedies, dramas and religious plays were performed by such authors as Luis de Tejeda, Valentín de Céspedes and Cristóbal de Aguilar, all from Córdoba.

In Buenos Aires the first permanent construction for musical theatrical events dates from 1757. The Teatro de la Ranchería (Settlement Theatre) was built in 1783 on the site of the present Manzana de las Luces (Block of Lights). Before it burned in 1792, one play now considered part of the early heritage was presented there: *Siripo* (1789) by Manuel José de Lavardén (1754–1801), an early tragedy of which only a fragment survives. The anonymous *sainete, El amor de la estanciera* (*Love of the Ranch Lady*), recognized as the precursor of gaucho drama for its popular verse form, rustic speech and setting on the pampa, is probably later (c. 1814). Existing records show that **loas** and other Spanish and French classics were also presented in several cities such as Santiago del Estero, Buenos Aires, Catamarca, Santa Fe, Corrientes, and Córdoba throughout the 18th century.

After independence the Sociedad del Buen Gusto del Teatro (Society of Good Taste in Theatre) (1817) aspired to create an autonomous theatre but internal dissensions over censorship issues caused it to cease operations after only two years. The theatre still reflected the 18th-century French neoclassical styles in such plays as the tragedy *Dido* (1821), a work inspired by the *Aeneid* and written by Juan Cruz Varela (1794–1839), whose *A río revuelto ganancia de pescadores* (*Turbulent River, Fisherman's Delight*), written during his student years, was a fresh comedy still of interest today. Luis Ambrosio Morante (1775–1837) was a major director and actor of this period, and several plays are attributed to him, in addition to various translations and adaptations. He captured the new spirit of independence in such plays as *25 de mayo* (*25th of May*, 1812) and *Tupac Amaru* (1817). A series of anonymous plays followed, written from a historical–political perspective and revivifying the revolutionary battles.

During the federal government (1829–53) of Juan Manuel de Rosas, theatre became a favourite entertainment with new buildings and good public support. Romantic theatre appeared in Buenos Aires following the satiric–costumbristic style established by Bretón in Spain. The circus was popular. Ten plays plus as many *sainetes* by local writers were performed. In addition to such authors as Bartolomé Mitre (1821–1906) and José Mármol (1817–71), the principal exponent was Juan Bautista Alberdi (1810–84) whose *El gigante Amapolas* (*The Giant Amapolas*, 1841) is a one-act farce satirizing Rosas and the myths of power. The play was comic and entertaining, it sowed the seeds of the grotesque theatre that was to follow, and it retained its popularity up to the present. A theatre in exile presented works critical of Rosas; after his fall Pedro Echagüe (1821–89) wrote his play *Rosas* (1860), a politically recriminatory caricature. Echagüe also marked the transition to a post-romantic period during the years of growth and expansion of Presidents Mitre and Sarmiento, but even so the theatre did not flourish. Instead, travelling shows and imported groups dominated. At least ten new theatres were built during the century, including the impressive Teatro Colón (1857–1944 in its first epoch), which regularly attracted world-class performers.

The year 1884 marked a turning point in the Argentine theatre. The distinguishing geographical feature of Argentina was the enormous pampa, originally an inland sea, a fertile agricultural area unbroken for miles that served as the heartland of the nation and produced myths and legends about the gaucho, the inimitable Argentine cowboy. The 19th-century literature included the play *Las bodas de Chivico y Pancha* (*The Wedding of Chivico and Pancha*, 1823), Mitre's poems (1840s) Sarmiento's historical–fictional account of civilization and barbarism in the life of Quiroga (1845) and especially the epic poem of José Hernández, *Martín Fierro* (1872–9). After the publication of Eduardo Gutiérrez's serialized novel, *Juan Moreira*, in 1884, the Carlo Brothers' Circus commissioned the author to prepare a pantomimic version which was performed with José J. Podestá in the title role. This popular figure representing the fates and fortunes of the gaucho, the free spirit of the pampas in conflict with civil authority, captured the Argentine spirit. The circus tradition became an integral feature of Argentine theatre, and in the centennial revival of the play in 1984, the circus tent was still a dominant scenographic reminder of this heritage. Martiniano Leguizamón's (1858–1933) *Calandria* in 1896 continued the tradition, as did many others who wrote *sainetes gauchescos* about rural conflicts. On the other hand, the *sainete urbano* revealed conflicts of the city in a stage of development.

20th century Before the turn of the century, impoverished European emigrants began to deluge Argentina in search of opportunities and prosperity. The fusion of the new arrivals with the national atmosphere provided the raw materials for the modernized *sainete*, the principal mouthpiece of this social class. For all their faults, the plays had the merit of depicting a typically Argentine reality. The theatre in Argentina cannot easily be separated from that of Uruguay, since the capital cities are only 100 miles apart and communication across the River Plate has been continuous. The realistic–naturalistic influence of the European theatre and the local *sainete criollo* tradition merged to produce the most renowned dramatist of South America: Florencio Sánchez (1875–1910). Born in Uruguay, the self-taught Sánchez was a faithful observer of daily life, of the customs and people of his time. During the so-called Golden Decade (1900–10) he wrote plays that reflected values in an age when the predominance of urban life and the immigrant population signalled rapid change in life styles. *La gringa* (*The Foreign Girl*, 1904) and *Barranca abajo* (*Down the Gully*, 1905) are his two masterpieces that depict characters struggling against insurmountable obstacles; Don Zoilo of the latter play is a memorable tragic figure whose despair leads him to suicide.

Other dramatists also captured the life of the times. Gregorio Laferrère (1867–1913) wrote popular theatre with spontaneous characters such as those in *Las de Barranco* (*Those of Barranco*, 1908) and Roberto J. Payró (1867–1928) also dealt with social injustices. The *sainete* maintained box-office success for many years through such authors as Alberto Vacarezza (1888–1959) who showed the picturesqueness of popular types in caricature. Throughout the first 30 years of the century, the Argentine theatre was dominated by these *sainetes criollos*. This term actually includes such diverse forms as drama, comedy, and political theatre. In a total production of possibly 5,000 plays, the following writers stood out: Nemesio Trejo (1862–1916), Carlos M. Pacheco (1881–1914), Enrique García Velloso (1880–1938) and José González Castillo (1885–1937). Other writers in a similar vein included Pedro E. Pico (1882–1945), Camilo Darthés (1889–1974), Carlos S. Damel (1890–1930), and Francisco Defilippis Novoa (1890–1930). Armando Discépolo (1887–1952) developed the creole grotesque, and served as the model for later generations.

Samuel Eichelbaum (1894–1967) was touted as a major force but his plays are at times exaggerated and unrealistic. His *La mala sed* (*The Bad Thirst*, 1920) dealt with hereditary sexual impulses, and *Dos brasas* (*Two Live Coals*) is an exercise in greed and moral misery. Conrado Nalé Roxlo (1898–1971), on the other hand, achieved a lyrical, poetical quality in plays such as *La cola de la sirena* (*The Mermaid's Tail*, 1941), a farcical examination of reality and egotism. Juan Oscar Ponferrada (b. 1907) played with folkloric material from the pagan *calchaquí* carnival in *El carnival del diablo* (*The Devil's Carnival*, 1943).

The rise of the independent theatre movement in 1930 gave new impulse to the Argentine theatre. The movement brought fresh life to techniques of stage performance. The first group formed was the Teatro del Pueblo (People's Theatre) by Leónidas Barletta, whose motivation was to develop a new public, to give new importance to the role of the director, and to impose vanguard techniques of production. In Argentina, this independent theatre also had a political commitment, inspired by Marxism, for addressing social concerns and vices. The Juan B. Justo group (1933) and La Máscara (The Mask) (1939) shared the problems, anxieties and successes of the Teatro del Pueblo, as did 50 other groups founded in Buenos Aires and the provinces as modern successors of the so-called *filodramáticos* (union groups, immigrant community groups, neighbourhood social clubs, etc.) that formed from 1890 to 1930. The usual foreign authors were presented – **Cocteau, Lenormand, Synge, Piran-**

Pacho O'Donnell's *Vincent y los cuervos* (*Vincent and the Crows*), Teatro del Bosque, Buenos Aires, 1984.

dello, O'Neill – as well as new national dramatists including **Roberto Arlt**, César Tiempo, Juan Oscar Ponferrada, Carlos Carlino, Tulio Carella, and others. Of these, Roberto Arlt (1900–42) was the author of the most consistent body of vanguard work. Better known by his contemporaries as a novelist, he mixed the possible with the impossible and the world of reality with the world of dreams. Of his eight plays, *Saverio el cruel* (*Saverio the Cruel*, 1936) has become a revisionist classic for its metatheatrical techniques and the experimentation with illusion and insanity.

The year 1949 was a turning point when **Carlos Gorostiza** (b. 1920) first staged *El puente* (*The Bridge*) in La Máscara, an independent theatre. The play metaphorically bridged two separate social classes with a common denominator – the pathos of death. From 1950 onward, the theatre in Argentina entered a new phase of growth and development. The costumbristic theatre continued to exist, but a greater consciousness of national social and political issues impinged on the creative arts. Gorostiza continued to be a major realistic writer with plays that reflected the changing milieu of Buenos Aires but that at the same time honoured traditional values. Gorostiza experimented with game theory form in *¿A qué jugamos?* (*What Shall We Play?*, 1968) and other plays, always faithful in language to the social stratum. **Agustín Cuzzani** (b. 1924) wrote what he called *farsátiras* that pointed out the deficiencies in the standards of middle class society, willing to sacrifice the most helpless fellow human beings. Another important author of the period was **Andrés Lizárraga** (1919–82), whose *Tres jueces para un largo silencio* (*Three Judges for a Long Silence*), *Santa Juana de América* (*St Joan of America*), and *Alto Perú* (*High Peru*) constituted a revisionist history of the 1810 Revolution under the common title *Trilogía sobre mayo* (*Trilogy about May*).

Osvaldo Dragún (b. 1929) captured international attention with his *Historias para ser contadas* (*Stories to be Told*, 1957), expressionistic, Brechtian-flavoured vignettes of dehumanization and exploitation that translated easily and were understandable around the world. Disillusioned with Peronism and more disillusioned with the political anarchy that followed, Dragún sought to translate the injustices of Argentine social and economic systems for the stage. *La peste viene de Melos* (*The Plague Comes from Melos*, 1956) and *Tupac Amarú* (1957) launched his career with the theatre group Fray Mocho, and marked his orientation as a committed realistic dramatist, a tendency he was to follow in many subsequent plays, some of which echoed the *Historias* model. Although his theatre has become more symbolic over the years, his insistence on portraying flaws in society has not waned.

In spite of, or ironically perhaps because of, the political turmoil in Argentina since the 1950s, the constant military intervention that interrupts civilian authority, the theatre has shown remarkable vitality. In addition to Gorostiza, Cuzzani and Dragún, other writers who dealt with the problems and issues of the Argentine middle class through a style of social realism that earned them the denomination of the 'new realist generation' were Julio Mauricio (b. 1919), Sergio de Cecco (b. 1931), **Carlos Somigliana** (b. 1932), **Roberto Cossa** (b. 1934), **Ricardo Halac** (b. 1935), **Ricardo Talesnik** (b. 1935), and **Germán Rozenma-**

cher (1936–71). In their early plays, many of them focused on the frustrations and rebellion of a disillusioned generation of youth, such as Halac's *Soledad para cuatro* (*Solitude for Four*, 1961) and Cossa's *Nuestro fin de semana* (*Our Weekend*, 1964). By constantly searching out the value systems within society, they captured the realities of their generation, becoming more cynical with time and veering toward the traditions of the Argentine grotesque, as in Cossa's *La nona* (*The Grandmother*, 1977) or Halac's *El destete* (*The Weaning*, 1978). In 1970 Cossa, Rozenmacher, Somigliana and Talesnik collaborated on a play, *El avión negro* (*The Black Airplane*), an episodic documentary in future time that foretells Perón's return from exile in a mythical black airplane. Mauricio's plays looked at the human condition to find a means of happiness in spite of the stresses of everyday existence. Rozenmacher, a talented and active journalist and writer, focused on the problems of the Jewish middle class with its hopes, fears, and generational and religious conflicts. Talesnik began in television and film; of his several works in theatre, he was brought international fame by *La fiaca* (*The Doldrums*, 1967), a poignant play about a man who tries to assert his independence one abulic Monday morning by not going to work.

Almost simultaneously with the generation mentioned earlier, another group of writers began to make its mark by adhering more to the vein of absurdist theatre and to theatre of cruelty. Principal among them were **Griselda Gambaro** (b. 1928), **Eduardo Pavlovsky** (b. 1933), Alberto Adellach (b. 1933), and **Ricardo Monti** (b. 1944). Gambaro's *Los siameses* (*The Siamese Twins*, 1967) and *El campo* (*The Camp*, 1968) are characteristic of the violence inherent in human nature and the dependency syndromes that penetrate love/hate relationships. Gambaro well deserves her reputation as one of the best women playwrights in all of Latin America. Pavlovsky, a psychiatrist trained in psychodrama, turned from his early experimentation with psychoanalytic situations toward the problems of the Argentine socio-political situation in *El señor Galíndez* (*Mr Galíndez*, 1973), a study of torture and physical/mental cruelty. His *Telarañas* (*Spiderwebs*, 1976) was banned during the height of the political repression. He used the brutality of Haiti and the Duvalier regime in similar fashion in *El señor Laforgue* (*Mr Laforgue*, 1982). Monti experimented with expressive and symbolic language in *Una noche con el señor Magnus e hijos* (*A Night with Mr Magnus and Sons*, 1970) as well as *Visita* (*Visit*, 1977) and *Marathón* (*Marathon*, 1980). All are restaged frequently and reveal his particular style of relating political and historical themes of Argentina. Oscar Viale (b. 1932), author of *El grito pelado* (*The Shriek*, 1967), *Chúmbale* (*Go get 'em!*, 1971) and *Convivencia* (*Living Together*, 1978), is an author of grotesque naturalism with black humour.

At a low point in Argentine political freedom, a group of authors and directors collaborated on a project known as **Teatro Abierto** (Open Theatre). Designed to revitalize the stagnant stage and to encourage new experimentation, the first cycle in 1981 resulted in 20 new one-act plays staged by different directors, three each night for a week on a repeating cycle. The theatre building, the Teatro Picadero, burned mysteriously at the end of the first week, but the project continued almost immediately in the Teatro Tabarís with determination and enthusiastic public support. Osvaldo Dragún was instrumental in organizing the movement which disclaims any relationship to **Joe Chaikin**'s 1963 experiment. The 1982 cycle was less successful aesthetically and unfortunately coincided with the Argentine–British dispute over the Falklands. Activities have been organized for subsequent years, but the election of Raúl Alfosín in 1983 returned democracy to Argentina and diminished pressures for maintaining the project.

The few authors and directors mentioned do scant credit to the multiplicity of themes, styles and techniques that characterize Argentine theatre in the 20th century. Economic and political problems have taken their toll, disrupting attendance and clouding the artistic atmosphere, but during the present regime new theatres are being constructed and new personnel are being formed. The national theatre (Cervantes), the municipal theatre complex (San Martín), The Manzana de las Luces and a host of independent theatres promote a wide variety of national, Latin American and world-wide plays. New playwrights and directors are emerging, such as **Beatriz Seibel** (b. 1934), Eugenio Griffero (b. 1936), Roma Mahieu (b. 1937), Enrique Pinti (b. 1940), Pacho O'Donnell (b. 1941), Susana Torres Molina (b. 1956), Aída Bortnik (b. 1938) and Jorge Goldenberg (b. 1941).

Theatre in the provinces has followed much the same history as that of Buenos Aires with *filodramáticos* groups and later independent theatres, although commercial or professional theatres are notably lacking. Important provincial dramatists include Miguel Iriarte in Córdoba, Oscar Quiroga in Tucumán and Hugo Laccoccia in Neuquén. With democracy a flurry of festivals and regional meetings has stimulated the theatre, especially in Córdoba.

A panoramic view of Argentine theatre could not be complete without mention, at least, of many other forms: ritual theatre in the Indian communities; creole circuses; radiotheatre companies; street theatre in the large cities; popular festivals and carnivals; and the innumerable religious festivals such as the Fiesta of Santa Ana in Tilcara. Argentores, the playwrights' theatre organization, as well as the Argentine Association of Actors, the Association of Critics and Researchers and other private and state institutions, continue to promote the dramatic arts and to sustain the long theatrical tradition which inheres in Argentina. GW

See: A. Blanco Amores de Pagella, *Iniciadores del teatro argentino*, Buenos Aires, 1972; *idem, Motivaciones del teatro argentino en el siglo XX*, Buenos Aires, 1983; R. Castagnino, *El teatro en Buenos Aires durante la época de Rosas*, Buenos Aires, 1944; J. Marial, *El teatro independiente*, Buenos Aires, 1955; N. Mazziotti, *El auge de las revistas teatrales argentinas*, Madrid, 1985; L. Ordaz, *Breve historia del teatro argentino*, Buenos Aires, 1985, *idem, Los artistas trashumantes*, Buenos Aires, 1985; J. L. Trenti Rocamora, *El teatro en la América colonial*, Buenos Aires, 1947; N. Tirri, *Realismo y teatro argentino*, Buenos Aires, 1973; P. Zayas de Lima, *Diccionario de autores teatrales argentinos (1940–80)*, Buenos Aires, 1981.

Aria A feature of opera, absent at the beginning of the 17th century, that achieved its peak in the first half of the 18th century and thereafter became increasingly modified. As distinct from recitative, an aria has a formal musical structure. It expresses feeling rather than presents information, reflecting rather than forwarding the action. The most prevalent type of aria during the 18th century was the *da capo* (literally 'from the beginning') aria in which there are three sections, the third being a repeat of the first. Musical rather than dramatic considerations prevailed in the *da capo* aria, although skilled composers were able to use such arias to dramatic effect. Arias were elaborately codified into a dozen or more types according to the feelings they expressed and the kind of music they involved. After the 18th century arias became more flexible and recitative more musically fluent and their abrupt distinction disappeared. GH

Ariosto, Ludovico (1474–1533) Italian poet and dramatist. One of the first major Italian dramatists to write in the vernacular, rather than Latin, his first play *La Cassaria* (*The Chest*, performed 1508), in addition to being important in its own right as perhaps the first *commedia erudita*, is significant in theatrical history for being presented with painted, perspective settings. His second, *I Suppositi* (1509, and mounted with settings by Raphael in 1519), was one of the first Italian prose comedies to be widely imitated and exerted considerable influence on the development of scripted comedy, not just in Italy but elsewhere, as in England through George Gascoigne's version, *The Supposes*. Both prose plays Ariosto later recast into verse. His *La Lena* and *Il Negromante* (*Lena* and *The Magician*, 1528 and 1529 respectively) were both done during Carnival at Ferrara. Ariosto's plays carried additional authority by virtue of the reputation he won by his non-dramatic, verse epic *Orlando Furioso*, one of the major poetic works of the Renaissance. This has several times been adapted for stage performance, notably by **Luca Ronconi** in 1968, the production later being transferred to film. LR

Aristophanes (active 427–after 388 BC) Aristophanes was regarded as the greatest poet of the Athenian 'Old Comedy' (see **Greece, ancient**), and is the only such poet whose work survives. He was probably born about 447, and spent most of his adult life during the Peloponnesian War (431–404), a bitter struggle between Athens and an alliance led by Sparta. His first play was performed in 427. Because of his youth he gave his first three plays (*Banqueters, Babylonians* and *Acharnians*) to another man to produce instead of doing so himself, and for some reason he did the same with some of his later plays. He seems to have been unsuccessfully prosecuted by the demagogue Cleon (see below) on a charge of slandering magistrates and citizens in his *Babylonians* (426), and again, perhaps after *Knights* (424), on a charge of falsely claiming to be an Athenian citizen. He wrote about 40 plays in all, some for the Great Dionysia and some for the Lenaea.

Eleven plays survive. In *Acharnians* (*Men of Acharnae*, a village near Athens; 425) an Athenian makes a private peace treaty with Sparta. *Knights* (424) is a savage attack on Cleon. *Clouds* (produced in 423, though the version we have was revised by its author c. 418) ridicules the philosopher Socrates. *Wasps* (422) satirizes the Athenians' alleged passion for jury-service. *Peace* (421) celebrates an imminent peace treaty with Sparta. In *Birds* (414) two Athenians found an ideal city among the birds. In *Lysistrata* (411) the women of Greece hold a 'sex strike' to force the men to end the war. *Thesmophoriazusae* (*Women Celebrating the Thesmophoria*, a women's festival; 411) travesties **Euripides**. In *Frogs* (405) the god Dionysus visits the underworld to fetch Euripides back. In *Ecclesiazusae* (*Women Holding an Assembly*; c. 392) the women take control at Athens. In *Plutus* (*Wealth*, 388) the god Wealth is cured of his blindness.

The plots of these plays are exuberant fantasies set in a world in which anything is possible – in which an ordinary citizen can make a private peace treaty and enjoy the blessings of peace while the city remains at war, or can fly to heaven on a giant dung-beetle to rescue the goddess Peace, or can join the birds to found the city of Cloudcuckooland. Typically the play centres on a 'comic hero', elderly (unless female) but lusty, and a 'Great Idea' for setting the world, or at least the 'hero's' own problems, to rights. The 'Great Idea' encounters opposition, and the Chorus is called in either to assist the 'hero' or to oppose him. At least once in each of the 5th-century plays the Chorus steps forward in a *parabasis* to address the audience directly; and the main issues of the play are usually debated in a formal *agōn* or battle of words between two characters. The 'hero' usually triumphs (but in *Clouds*, *Wasps*, and *Frogs*, where he has ideas that Aristophanes disapproves of, he is made to see the error of his ways); and the play often ends with a series of short, farcical scenes in which enemies or spongers are beaten off.

A bracing feature (or a deplorable one, according to taste) of all the plays except *Plutus* is their total lack of moral uplift. Honesty, decency and courage barely exist, and subjects for cheerful humour include torture, rape, blindness and starvation. The way to deal with enemies is sometimes to defeat them by argument (of a sort), but just as often to cudgel them from the stage. Even the 'hero' seldom rises above a certain shrewd peasant cunning (it takes some effort to apply the word 'hero' to the truly appalling Philocleon of *Wasps*, perhaps Aristophanes' funniest character). If we identify with him, it is because he contrives to enact with impunity our more disreputable fantasies. *Plutus*, however, which should perhaps be classed as Middle Comedy rather than Old, presents a rather sentimental idealization of honest poverty.

Aristophanes never allows considerations of relevance, dramatic illusion or consistency of character or motive to get in the way of a good joke; and his humour covers the widest possible range. There are passages (generally choral) of innocent and whimsical charm (notably in *Birds*); there is skilful parody of tragedy, implying close study of it (notably in *Acharnians*, *Thesmophoriazusae* and *Frogs*); but these things can exist side by side with sheer slapstick and the crudest of schoolboy jokes.

Though Aristophanes is capable of satirizing sentimental traditionalism (the personification of Right Argument in *Clouds* turns out to be the archetypal scoutmaster), he generally assumes that his audience is highly conservative in its attitudes. While he would certainly have called himself a democrat, and while he would not have dreamed of suggesting that any living politician was *not* a thief, foreigner and sexual pervert, the main targets of his political attacks are the so-called demagogues – politicians (including his arch-enemy Cleon) who depended on the support of the poorer classes in Athens. More attractive, perhaps, is his constant devotion to the cause of peace, a devotion that is surely sincere and not merely a function of the hedonism expected in comedy (it seems not to have been shared by his rival Eupolis).

Similarly among intellectuals, Aristophanes' favourite targets are the new-fangled sophists, whom he accuses of corrupting the morals of the young, and among whom (in defiance of all our other evidence) he includes Socrates. With these he associates Euripides, who also upset traditional assumptions, and who is the favourite object of Aristophanic parody.

While much of his abuse of living figures is obviously unfair, it is unclear how seriously it was taken. The Athenians appointed Cleon to the post of general shortly after awarding first prize to *Knights*; but Cleon himself seems to have reacted sharply to Aristophanes' attacks on him, and indeed these can hardly be dismissed as good clean fun. Plato's *Apology* holds Aristophanes partly responsible for popular prejudice against Socrates, but his *Symposium* portrays him with affection, and shows him at ease in Socrates' company. There is no doubt that his *main* purpose was to entertain his audience and win their applause, not to alter their views.   ALB

Aristotle

Aristotle (384–322 BC) Philosopher, pupil of Plato, and author of numerous works concerning logic, the natural world, and human activities. Though he often alludes to drama in the *Rhetoric* and elsewhere, his importance for World Theatre lies mainly in his *Poetics*, which probably dates from the 330s or 320s. From this we have only one book, on tragedy and epic poetry, a second book, on comedy, being lost. Moreover, what we have is (for whatever reason) preserved in such a compressed, disorganized and corrupt form that its meaning is often highly obscure.

Aristotle approaches poetry not as a literary critic but as an analytical philosopher. He regards it as a phenomenon among other phenomena, needing to be defined, accounted for and classified into its different varieties, each of which must itself be defined and analysed into its constituent parts (this, at least, is the plan, though it is very imperfectly realized in the work as we have it). Any phenomenon, however, is best exemplified by its highest forms, and Aristotle must therefore establish what is the highest form of poetry (in his opinion tragedy) and what is the best type of tragedy (exemplified for him by the *Oedipus Tyrannus* of **Sophocles**). It is in this way that literary evaluation enters in; though, when Aristotle is defending the existence of poetry or of tragedy (*Poetics* 4, 9, 26, etc.), we may often detect the ulterior motive of replying to the charges brought against them by Plato.

The factual information which Aristotle gives, especially on the origins of tragedy and comedy (see **Greece, ancient**), can seem contradictory and implausible, and it is doubtful how far it is based on evidence and how far on mere theorizing. His definitions, such as the famous definition of tragedy in chapter 6, tend to reflect his philosophical preoccupations rather than ordinary usage. The analysis of the structure of a tragedy in chapter 12 is unsatisfactory, and may not be his work at all. His literary judgements are often based on *a priori* reasoning rather than a direct response to literature – or at least, they *claim* to be so based, though at times it may be that a direct response to literature is being rationalized. His emphasis on the preeminence of plot over character (chapter 6 etc.) may reflect the priorities of the Greek dramatists, and his guidance on effective plot-construction (7–14) is of wide, though not universal, application. For anyone seeking to understand Greek drama, however, his unargued assumptions may be of greater interest than his conclusions.

Nevertheless, the influence of the *Poetics* – or of doctrines purporting to be derived from it – has been immense ever since it became known to Renaisssance Europe through a Latin translation by Giorgio Valla, published in 1498. One famous 'Aristotelian' doctrine is that of the Three Unities – of Time, Place and Action – which were considered canonical by, in particular, the 17th-century dramatists of France and England. The *Poetics* does insist on 'Unity of Action' (chapters 7–8 etc.), but the idea of 'Unity of Time' derives merely from a remark in chapter 5 that tragedy 'tries as far as possible to limit itself to a single revolution of the sun, or a little more', and 'Unity of Place' is not mentioned at all.

In more recent times certain terms which do occur in the *Poetics* have become clichés of literary criticism, notably *katharsis* ('purgation' or 'purification'?) from chapter 6 and *hamartia* ('sin', 'error' or both?) from chapter 13. What Aristotle himself meant by those terms is still hotly disputed. We may be fairly certain, however, that his *katharsis* had little in common with the Freudian ideas now associated with it, and that his *hamartia* was not the 'fatal flaw' of the 'tragic hero'. ALB

Arlecchino see **Commedia dell'arte**; **Harlequin**; **Zanni**

Arlequin see **Harlequin**

Arliss, George (George Augustus Andrews) (1868–1946) British-born character actor and playwright whose greatest successes occurred in the USA after 1901. Arliss, immediately recognizable due to his distinctive features (long, narrow face, pointed nose, habitual monocle, and charming voice), spent 40 years perfecting the playing of villains, great historical leaders, and wise old men with an apparent effortlessness that concealed his polished technique. **Louis Parker**, author of his best known vehicle, *Disraeli* (1911), said Arliss could 'express more with one finger than most actors can express with their entire bodies'. His most notable stage roles, in addition to Disraeli, were in *The Second Mrs Tanqueray* (1901) with **Mrs Pat Campbell**, *The Darling of the Gods* (1902) with **Blanche Bates**, *Hedda Gabler* (1904) and *Rosmersholm* (1907) with **Mrs Fiske**, *Paganini* (1915), *The Green Goddess* (1921), *Old English* (1924), and his last formal stage appearance as Shylock (1928). In 1923 he returned to London after a 22-year absence to appear in **Archer**'s *The Green Goddess*. His successful film career began in 1920 and during the decade of the 1930s he made over 20 films, portraying among other characters such historical figures as Voltaire, Rothschild (Meyer and Nathan), Cardinal Richelieu, and Wellington. He wrote or collaborated on six plays and wrote two important autobiographies: *Up the Years from Bloomsbury* (1927) and *My Ten Years in the Studio* (1940). DBW

Arlt, Roberto (1900–42) Argentine playwright. Also journalist and novelist, Arlt is the link between the celebrated Golden Decade (1900–10) of Argentine theatre and the contemporary movement. Arlt's experimental style and technique were apparent in his first novel, *El juguete rabioso* (1926), but were greatly refined in his later novels, which he peopled with anguished, non-conformist characters who anticipated later existentialist trends. His dramatic career spans the ten years from 1932 until his death. The essential characteristic of his dramaturgy is the transformation of a conventional reality by means of illusions, dreams, fantasies and the grotesque in order to create a new world. He denied the influence of **Pirandello**, although Pirandello's works were played in Buenos Aires during those years, and preferred to say that he had found his inspiration in the European master painters – Goya, Dürer, Brueghel. He wrote eight plays, most of which were premiered by Leónidas Barletta, the father of the Argentine independent theatre movement, in his Teatro del Pueblo. Major titles are *Saverio el cruel* (*Saverio the Cruel*), which shows strong influence of the *Quijote*, Arlt's favourite book, *La isla desierta* (*The Desert Island*, 1937), and *La fiesta del hierro* (*The Iron Fiesta*, 1940). GW

Armin, Robert (c. 1568–1615) Elizabethan actor, who may have attracted the attention of the great clown **Richard Tarlton** while serving an apprenticeship to a goldsmith. We do not know when Armin became an actor, though it was certainly some years before he succeeded **Will Kempe** as leading 'clown' in the **Lord Chamberlain's Men**. We know from Armin's own *Quips upon Questions* (1600) that he inherited some of Tarlton's (and Kempe's) skills as an extemporizer, but also that he considered himself a 'foolosopher'. The recognizable transition in **Shakespeare**'s plays from broad clown to wise fool must owe something to the contrasting playing styles of Kempe and Armin. The passage from Dogberry (Kempe's creation) to Feste (Armin's) is a change from rustic clown to motley jester. If, as is sometimes supposed, Armin was also the original Lavache, Pandarus and Fool to King Lear, he was obviously an actor whom Shakespeare trusted, as well as a talented singer. Armin's collection of comic tales, *Foole upon Foole, or Sixe Sortes of Sottes* (1600), was successful enough to earn a second edition in 1605 and republication in enlarged form as *A Nest of Ninnies* (1608). His play, *The Two Maids of Moreclacke* (1609), was performed by the Children of the King's Revels. PT

Arneaux, J. A. (1855–?) Afro-American actor. Born in Georgia of a white French father and a black mother, Arneaux received a good post-secondary education in northern cities and in Paris. A journalist by profession, he took to the stage, first as a song-and-dance artist at **Tony Pastor**'s Metropolitan Theatre on Broadway, then as a legitimate actor and manager of the Astor Place Company of Coloured Tragedians, the leading black dramatic troupe in America in the 1880s. Based in New York, the company performed there, in Philadelphia, and in Providence, Rhode Island, to great acclaim.

Arneaux's roles included Iago, Macbeth, and Pythias, but his favourite part in which he excelled was Richard III, being ranked with **Macready**, **Edwin Booth** and **Lawrence Barrett**. EGH

Aronson, Boris (1898–1980) Russian-American painter, sculptor and set designer. Aronson remains as perhaps the most respected American designer of the mid-20th century. He was born in Russia and studied with **Aleksandra Ekster**, a constructivist designer with the Kamerny Theatre. He left Russia for Berlin in 1922 and emigrated to the USA in 1923 where his first assignments were for the Unser Theatre and the **Yiddish Art Theatre**. By the 1930s he was designing major shows on Broadway and working with the **Group Theatre**. His early work reflected not only the influences of Ekster but of Marc Chagall and Nathan Altman who designed for the Moscow Jewish Theatre. Aronson greatly admired Chagall and the cubist-fantastic style characteristic of his paintings can be seen in much of Aronson's early work and even in later works such as the acclaimed 1959 set for *J. B.* Despite his enormous output and critical success for plays by **William Saroyan**, **Tennessee Williams**, **Clifford Odets**, and others, and hit musicals including *South Pacific*, he did not achieve widespread recognition until he teamed up with director **Harold Prince** on the 1964 musical, *Fiddler on the Roof*. This was followed by six more musicals including *Cabaret* and *A Little Night Music*. This collaboration seemed to bring out Aronson's creativity. His designs ranged from realistic detail for plays like *Awake and Sing* to technological fantasies such as *Company* that used steel and plexiglass and projections. His constructivist influences could be seen throughout his work. His sets always had a strong sense of line and form, and a generally subtle but evocative use of colour used symbolically to support the mood of the play. For the 1940 production of Ballet Theatre's *The Great American Goof*, Aronson employed, for the first time, a technique he called 'Projected Scenery' – a method of projecting coloured slides on neutral, abstract shapes in order to create and change the mood and space of a piece. This technique was displayed in the 1947 exhibition of his work at the Museum of Modern Art aptly titled 'Painting with Light'. AA

Arrabal, Fernando (1932–) Spanish/French playwright. Arrabal's work is dominated by the traumas of his Spanish childhood when his mother, a Catholic, betrayed his father, a Republican, to Franco's police. His early plays, published in 1958, are dream works in which naive characters behave according to basic Freudian drives. In the 1960s he achieved notoriety, especially with **Savary**'s production of *Le Labyrinthe* (1967). The same year Garcia produced Arrabal's *Automobile Graveyard* and Lavelli *The Architect and Emperor of Assyria*. Since then his voluminous work has appeared under the title 'Panic Theatre'. Designed to provoke psychological shockwaves in its audience, it often appears merely self-indulgent. DB

Arriví, Francisco (1915–) Puerto Rican dramatist, director, critic, essayist, major figure in Puerto Rican theatre. Studied pedagogy in Puerto Rico, radio

and theatre at Columbia University. Early plays *Club de solteros* (*Bachelors' Club*, 1940) and *El diablo se humaniza* (*Humanizing the Devil*, 1941) are fantastic and farcical. *María Soledad* (*María Solitude*, 1947) is a Jasperian search for absolute purity. The trilogy *Máscara puertorriqueña* (*Puerto Rican Mask,* 1956–9) deals with the complex racial and cultural heritage of the Puerto Ricans. Other major plays include *Cóctel de Don Nadie* (*Mr Nobody's Cocktail*, 1964) and the musical *Solteros 72* (*Bachelors 72*). Arriví founded the theatre group Tinglado Puertorriqueño in 1945 and was for years director of the theatre wing of the Puerto Rican Cultural Institute that sponsors the annual theatre festival. GW

Arrufat, Antón (1935–) Cuban playwright and poet, abandoned university studies to write. Initiated with two one-act absurdist plays *El caso se investiga* (*The Case is Being Investigated*) and *El último tren* (*The Last Train*) (both written in 1957 but without initial success). *El vivo al pollo* (*Chicken for the Living*, 1959) uses traditional **bufo** theatre to parody a natural fear of death in the case of a woman who embalms her husband. With *La zona cero* (*Zero Zone*, 1959) the illogical patterns and comedy routines he developed earlier reached a climax in a **Beckett**-style absurdism. After *La repetición* (*The Repetition*, 1963), a duplicative process that shows the influence of the Revolution, and *Todos los domingos* (*Every Sunday*, 1965), he wrote *Los siete contra Tebas* (*Seven against Thebes*) which won the UNEAC prize for 1968, but he was censured along with Herberto Padilla for a work considered antithetical to Revolutionary goals. He remains in Cuba and works as a journalist/writer. His later plays are unpublished and unstaged: *La tierra permanente* (*The Solid Earth*), *Retrato de Juan Criollo* (*Portrait of John Creole*) and *La divina Fanny* (*Divine Fanny*). His preoccupation with language and the search for language adequate to express new concepts are strong characteristics of his work. GW

Artaud, Antonin (1896–1949) French poet, actor, director and theoretician. Born in Marseille, Artaud came to Paris in 1920 where he acted in **Dullin**'s company and in productions by **Lugné-Poe** and **Pitoëff**. He sent some poems to Jacques Rivière, director of the *Nouvelle Revue Française*, who rejected them but published the correspondence that followed, in which Artaud attempted to explain the difficulties he experienced in expressing himself. This analysis of the gap between the poet's vision and the expressive means at his disposal stands as a paradigmatic statement for all 20th-century artists. Artaud was a member of Breton's surrealist group from 1924 until they expelled him two years later. He took acting roles in films, notably Abel Gance's *Napoléon* (Marat) and Dreyer's *Passion of Joan of Arc* (Brother Massieu). But his extraordinary influence on subsequent theatre is based largely on his two short-lived attempts at directing and on his volume of essays *The Theatre and its Double*. The first directing venture was in 1926 when he founded the Théâtre Alfred Jarry together with Robert Aron and **Roger Vitrac**. The manifestos for this theatre stressed the idea that theatre should no longer be mere entertainment but genuine action with real effects on the real world. A suggested model for theatre was a police raid on a red-light district, rounding up prostitutes on the streets and flushing them out of the brothels. The features of what he later called theatre of cruelty are all to be found here: violence, sexuality, social taboos, and the eruption of dramatic action outside the safe confines of the stage. The Théâtre Alfred Jarry never had its own premises and could only manage occasional productions, among which were **Strindberg**'s *Dream Play* and Vitrac's *Victor* (both 1928). In 1931 Artaud was dazzled by a performance of dances from Bali that he saw at the colonial exhibition. Under their influence, he published a series of articles later collected and published in 1938 as *The Theatre and its Double*. The double of theatre was life, the vital, metaphysical reality that shadows our everyday actions. Western society had lost contact with this life and so theatre had to be like the plague, a violent, overwhelming crisis, both socially and individually, from which people would emerge either dead or purged. In 1935 he founded his second theatre, the Théâtre de la Cruauté, which failed to outlive its first production, an adaptation of Shelley's *The Cenci*. Artaud's direction was precise, even balletic, but he was obliged to give the main part to an indifferent actress who put up the money for the production. The circumstances of the production were also to blame for its failure: primeval theatre did not harmonize with fashionable Parisian theatre-going. He travelled to Mexico and to Ireland but, with his health gradually deteriorating, he was committed by his family to an asylum at Rodez. He remained in institutions throughout the war and only emerged two years before his death. His last two years produced a torrent of work including an essay in which he identified with Van Gogh, and a radio programme of his own work which was banned at the last minute.

Artaud's writings do not form a coherent body of dramatic theory, but, rather, a visionary expression of the loss of the spiritual dimension in the life of Western civilization. His proposed remedy involves rediscovering the sense of danger and of total, physical commitment in both Art and Life. Artists, he says in the preface to *Theatre and its Double*, should be 'condemned men at the stake, signalling through the flames'. He dismisses clever, witty writing and the cult of the masterpiece, moving the emphasis from the writer to the director and stressing the essentially physical, three-dimensional quality of theatre. The director becomes a new kind of author, writing in space by means of sound, colour, lights, objects and, above all, actors, who take on the force of moving hieroglyphs. Though he himself failed, his work has been enormously influential, especially since the Second World War; many directors e.g. **Brook**, **Grotowski**, **Planchon**, **Blin** have acknowledged their debt to him. DB

Artef A New York proletarian Yiddish theatre collective of amateurs led by experienced professionals like Jacob Mestel, Nathaniel Buchwald and Benno Schneider. From the first 'studio' of 26 students in 1926, the collective grew to six 'studios' in 1936. Over 80 plays were produced, the most notable being P. Tchernov's *The Roar of the Machines* and Samuel Ornitz's *Haunch, Paunch and Jowl*, both exercises in agitational propaganda, although the non-political

plays proved the most successful. The collective folded in 1939. AB

Arthur, Julia (Ida Lewis) (1869–1950) Canadian-born, United States actress who played the leading feminine roles in about 200 plays, including the first Lady Windermere in America (1893). From her success in 1891 in F. R. Giles's *The Black Masque* at the **Union Square Theatre** until her first retirement in 1899, after her marriage to millionaire Benjamin P. Cheney, Arthur attained acclaim in numerous Shakespearian roles, as well as contemporary parts. During 1895–7 she appeared at the **Lyceum** under **Henry Irving**. She was most successful in roles featuring unbridled temperament, pathos, and tears. After a 15-year retirement she returned to the stage; her last appearance was on tour in 1924 in *Saint Joan*. DBW

Arts Council of Great Britain (ACGB) The agency through which funds from central government sources are distributed to the arts in Britain, the Arts Council was incorporated by Royal Charter on 9 August 1946. Like its wartime predecessor **CEMA**, the ACGB had links with the adult education movement and its aims were philanthropic – to improve artistic standards and to encourage the appreciation of the arts around the country. It was only allowed to subsidize non-profit-distributing companies, registered under the Charities Act. The Council itself consisted of up to 16 members, appointed by the government which was afterwards expected not to interfere with its decisions but stay 'at arm's length'. The day-to-day running of the ACGB's affairs was left in the hands of a Secretary-General and his staff, assisted by unpaid boards of expert advisers.

Initially the ACGB's funds, received directly from the Treasury, were very small, rising to little more than £3 million by 1964, of which a third was automatically allocated to the Royal Opera House, **Covent Garden**. But its influence during these early years was considerable. It helped ambitious new companies, such as the English Stage Company, encouraged local authorities to lay the foundations for a new regional repertory movement, supported the establishment of two national companies, opposed censorship which was abolished, and conducted an influential survey on *Housing the Arts* (1961). The ACGB was a significant factor behind the transformation of British theatre from its lacklustre 1950s image to the buoyancy of the 1960s.

With the arrival of Harold Wilson's Labour government and the publication of a White Paper on the Arts (1965), the role of the ACGB was itself transformed. It became the responsibility of the Department of Education and Science and its resources rose rapidly under both Labour and Conservative administrations, reaching £100 million by 1984. It became the main financial support for 12 Regional Arts Associations, instead of being a secondary one, and subsidized most forms of theatre, apart from amateur and narrowly commercial. It tried to streamline touring, with mixed results, and under its influence a new generation of theatre buildings came into existence, designed for 'an age of subsidy', with large foyers and uneconomically small seating capacities.

As the ACGB became more central to theatre in

Britain, the tensions within it, which had always been present, emerged as conflicts. The regions objected to the preferential treatment given to London, smaller theatres to the dominance of the national companies, commercial managements to the unfair competition with the subsidized sector. It became more difficult for the ACGB to stay at arm's length from governments and from being the champion of the arts, the ACGB seemed more like their whipping boy. Its modestly reformist document, *The Glory of the Garden* (1984), was treated with scorn.   JE

Arts Theatre, Belfast From 1982 the Belfast Civic Arts Theatre. Built in 1961 by government and private funding to house the Arts Theatre Studio by Hubert and Dorothy Wilmot. Founded in 1950, and occupying a series of converted buildings, the Studio presented mainly world drama – **Sartre, Tennessee Williams, Eliot** – employing local actors. The policy survived until the 1960s when the economics of the new theatre enforced the more popular fare of musicals, West End successes, and Sam Cree's local farces. The Arts Theatre Studio ceased its activities in 1977, the theatre becoming a venue for independent productions.   DM

Arts Theatre (London) Opening in 1927, the theatre gave private performances of unlicensed experimental plays for members. Successful from the first, with a series of productions transferring to the commercial theatre, including John Van Druten's first play *Young Woodly* in 1928, it continued this role until sold to the film producer Nathan Cohen in 1962. It hosted tours by foreign artists such as **Yvette Guilbert**, and the **Compagnie des Quinze** appeared there in 1931. Under the management of **Alec Clunes** from 1942 to 1950 it gained a national reputation, with premieres of work such as **Christopher Fry**'s *The Lady's Not For Burning* (1948). The intimacy of the small stage and 347-seat auditorium was particularly suited to the new wave of absurd drama in the 1950s, and **Beckett**'s *Waiting for Godot*, **Pinter**'s *The Caretaker*, and **Albee**'s *Zoo Story* were all given their first English performances there. The **Royal Shakespeare Company** leased it for a major season of new work and seldom-performed classics in 1962, and since then it has served as a West End transfer house for Fringe theatre productions, with Robert Patrick's *Kennedy's Children* from the King's Head (Islington) in 1975, and **Stoppard**'s *Dirty Linen* and *New Found Land* in 1976.   CI

Asch, Sholom (1880–1957) Polish-born American playwright and novelist who wrote in Yiddish. His plays mainly concern the conflict between orthodox and emancipated Jew, and he achieved early fame and notoriety with *The God of Vengeance* (1907). Other notable plays include *Downstream* (1904), *The Messiah Period* (1906), *Sabatai Zevi* (1908), *Wealthy Reb Shloime* (1913) and *Mottke the Thief* (1917). Several of his novels were dramatized and performed by **Maurice Schwartz**.   AB

Asche, Oscar (1872–1936) British actor, who worked with **Frank Benson** and **Beerbohm Tree**, from whom he took over the management of **His Majesty's Theatre**. He made his reputation in Shakespearian roles, though he also played opposite **Ellen**

Terry in **Gordon Craig**'s 1903 production of **Ibsen**'s *The Vikings*, and gained his greatest success in his own musical fantasy *Chu Chin Chow* (based on *Ali Baba and the Forty Thieves*), which ran from 1916 to 1921.   CI

Ashcroft, Peggy (Edith Margaret Emily) (1907–91) British actress, who first took the West End by storm as the innocent Naemi in *Jew Suss* (1929). Her special quality of radiant freshness caused some critics, including **James Agate**, to state that she was too simple and lightweight for major classical roles, but the 1932/3 **Old Vic** season revealed her range as an actress in such parts as Juliet, Rosalind, Lady Teazle and **Shaw**'s Cleopatra. Her subsequent career is remarkable for its versatility, command and, not least, her instinct for major challenges. Against all expectations, she was a brilliantly sluttish Cleopatra to **Michael Redgrave**'s Antony at the Shakespeare Memorial Theatre in 1953, an electric Beatrice to **John Gielgud**'s Benedict in 1950 and 1955, a savage Hedda Gabler in 1954, and Shen Teh in **Brecht**'s *The Good Person of Setzuan*. Her roles in contemporary plays ranged from Hester in **Terence Rattigan**'s *The Deep Blue Sea* (1952) to Beth in **Harold Pinter**'s *Landscape* (1969) and Winnie in **Samuel Beckett**'s *Happy Days* (1975). A committed socialist, Ashcroft has energetically furthered the interests of her profession by serving on the council of Equity, on the **Arts Council** and on the artistic committee of the English Stage Company. She became a director of the **Royal Shakespeare Company** in 1968 and among her many honours, she received a DBE in 1956. In 1962, a new theatre in her place of birth, Croydon, was named after her.   JE

Asia, South-East (Modern) (See also individual national entries.)

Introduction The idea of the 'modern' in South-East Asian theatre was, until two decades ago, hitched to notions of Western dramaturgy. The early playwrights were an educated elite, scions of a privileged colonial schooling, who congregated in metropolitan areas at the dawn of the 20th century. They were literary men steeped in the Western liberal tradition and in nationalist ideals. Impassioned by the prevailing revolutionary fervour, they wrote romantic spoken dramas redolent with symbol and allegory, presumably in the manner of their mentors, **Shakespeare, Goethe,** and **Schiller**. Their plays were written and performed for their peers: urban students, teachers, artists, journalists, and professional men. (Only the Philippine revolutionary dramas (1902–6) garnered responses beyond this small coterie.) The pioneer dramatists adhered to an amateur ideal, and stood proudly above and apart from the theatre professionals dispensing popular theatre in the burgeoning cosmopolitan towns and cities.

The playwrights of independent South-East Asia after the Second World War were, for the most part, as fervently elitist and amateur in their approach to theatre. But they rejected the histrionic themes and stances of their predecessors, and instead cultivated verisimilitude in drama. Their aesthetic models were **Ibsen** and **Chekhov**, and their principal goal was to publish rather than perform their plays. The gap that some of the realistic playwrights discovered between the high-flown rhetoric of their indigenous political leaders and the grim reality of the ruled, caused them to take refuge in dramas evoking disillusionment and alienation.

The initial break with Western realism and the hegemony of literature in theatre, was precipitated by experiences of severe political crises. Although traumatic, the series of political convulsions that began in the 1960s were liberating, in the sense that they led (in the words of the Nigerian playwright **Wole Soyinka**) to a groping towards 'self-apprehension'. Decolonization was and continues to be the primary impulse generating the experimental passion of what is called 'contemporary theatre' in South-East Asia. The avowed aim was to forge a theatre that was uniquely and identifiably home-grown. Few of the contemporary theatre practitioners are fully convinced that the objective has been achieved. The search for a crystalline and accessible form or forms persists, inducing contemporary theatre to be constantly regenerative and avant-garde.

The major modern theatre countries in South-East Asia are the Philippines, Indonesia, Malaysia and Singapore. Their present state of achievement is the outcome of a continuous modern theatre tradition, and the availability of adequate human creative resources, physical infrastructure, and other support systems. Contemporary theatre and its critical resolution, namely, the convening of a marriage between Western and Asian dramaturgies, have been mainly developed in Island South-East Asia.

On the other hand, the weight of tradition and the uncertainties created by protracted political wars (Cambodia, Vietnam), have hampered the growth of stable and continuous theatre cultures in mainland South-East Asia. Burma, for example, has yet to produce fertile ground for modern theatre. In Thailand, modern theatre has a fitful history. Never colonized, Thailand nevertheless nurtured an educated elite receptive to European influences. Spoken dramas were attempted by Thai royalty and aristocrats at the beginning of this century. The *natakam* (spoken drama) was promoted by Western-educated Thai intellectuals during the Westernization campaign of the first Phibulsonkram government (1938–44). An unexpected wave of street theatre was witnessed during the short-lived democratic period (1973–6). However in 1976, the noted theatre scholar, Brandon, concluded that: 'Modern drama is not a significant aspect of Thai theatrical life as yet.' The prospect for a fully-fledged modern theatre in Thailand has recently brightened, even though it continues to be university-centred, concentrated in the campuses of Chulalongkorn and Thammasat.

The Philippines The first scripted spoken dramas in South-East Asia were written by Filipinos. The so-called 'seditious plays' of 1902–6 emerged while the Philippines was engaged in brutal guerilla warfare with America, and caused its creators to be harassed, if not imprisoned. The Tagalog dramas were written by *ilustrados* (elite), such as Aurelio Tolentino, Juan Abad, and Juan Matapang Cruz, who regarded themselves as heirs to the committed literature tradition of Balagtas and Rizal. Couched in allegory, their inflammatory plays struck a responsive chord with the politicized Filipino populace. Juan Abad's 1902 play, *Tanikalang*

Ginto (*Golden Chain*), is considered typical of the genre. It tells of the persecution suffered by the damsel, Liwanang or 'Light' (the Philippines), at the hands of Maimbot or 'Greedy' (America), and the rescue attempt by her sweetheart, K'Ulayaw (Revolutionary Filipinos). Despite its short duration, the revolutionary drama period left a legacy of allegorical theatre and 'people's art' that is vivid with Philippine contemporary theatre practitioners.

Once the fury of the Filipino Revolution had been contained by the Americans, the spoken dramas sputtered into innocuity, and appeared in the 1920s as domestic tales of romance and moral persuasion. The *ilustrados* switched their allegiance to the new rule, and with the coming of 'the second American occupation', i.e. the American education system, they also turned from the vernacular to English. The result was doldrums in modern Filipino drama. American-sponsored educators thought of drama as efficacious only for speech and moral training. The ensuing self-conscious literary homilies could hardly compete with the increasingly popular *bodabil* (vaudeville) and movies of the 1930s.

Even after the Philippines achieved independence in 1946, the urban Filipino elite continued to write their plays in English. Psychological and social realism was essayed by playwrights such as Wilfrido Ma Guerrero, Alberto Florentino, Severino Montano, Estrella D. Alfon, and Nick Joaquin, who wrote mainly for magazines. Theatre was primarily based in schools, which staged Broadway musicals and Western classics. Theatre companies rose and fell with equal rapidity. By their Western-influenced standards, the indigenous product was found wanting. The introduction of playwriting competitions did not make a substantial dent in these attitudes, and plays languished while 'in search of a stage'. However, Joaquin's play, *A Portrait of the Artist as Filipino*, was staged soon after its publication in 1952. While flawed by overwriting, the tragicomic paean to a lost age of nobility and human compassion is often lyrical. The presence of the narrator–character, and (to the audience) unseen painting looming in spiritual potency during the course of the play, were clever and innovative images for its time.

Apart from Guerrero (leader of the University of the Philippines Dramatic Club for three decades) and Joaquin, the work of a few theatre directors, particularly that of Rolando Tinio, lent lustre to a theatre era (1946–66) that has been described as 'short-lived, merely transitional, and with an unfortunate alienating effect' (Fernandez, 1984). The maverick director, Tinio, anticipated a new age of theatre with his unconventional staging of conventional Western plays.

Two features in Philippine theatre since 1966 set it apart from the other contemporary theatres of South-East Asia. The first difference is that, at least the metropolitan Filipinos had to make a traumatic language change in theatre, from English to Tagalog. This was the initial Filipino route to a 'self-apprehension' that has been the wellspring of decolonization in contemporary South-East Asian theatre. Secondly, the intense and prolonged politicization of contemporary Philippine theatre is also uncommon. The process began with the student demonstrations in the late 1960s, and accelerated with the imposition of

Martial Law in 1972. Since then, there swelled a sense that: 'The present has too much urgency. It pressed on the playwright's consciousness too insistently. He had to respond' (Fernandez, 1984).

These unique sensibilities were foreshadowed even before Martial Law was declared. Beginning in 1966, Manila audiences were 'shocked' by the 'bold' Tinio translations and adaptations of **Miller**, **Williams**, and **Lorca**. In the next year, the Philippine Educational Theatre Association (PETA) inaugurated its 'national theatre' performance of indigenous and avant-garde foreign works in Tagalog. Theatre took to the streets and other open and crowded places in support of the students' demands for an end to 'American imperialism, feudal corruption, and bureaucratic capitalism'.

The exposure of injustice and the enactment on stage of kinship with the masses surfaced as persistent themes in contemporary Philippine theatre. By digging into themselves, Filipino playwrights and directors exhumed seemingly limitless theatre resources which they reshaped to suit their pressing needs. The resources excavated ranged from: ur-dramas, and epic plays of the pre-Hispanic period, Spanish-influenced religious and secular dramas, *sarsuwela* (musical play), and even its death-knell, *bodabil*. One of the earliest deconstructions of indigenous and indigenized performance texts was *Halimaw* (*Monster*, 1971) by Isagani Cruz, staged by PETA. While the traditional *sarsuwela* was being revived, Cruz fused it with a variety of epic, absurd, and Broadway musical devices, to convey his dire warning on tyrannical power. *Sinakulo* (Passion plays) were also refashioned for contemporary purposes by the revival-conscious Babaylan Theatre in the 1970s. The company's *sinakulo* series was climaxed in 1977 with the appearance of a radical Christ taking up arms against his imperialist persecutors. A Mass calling on the Filipino clergy to join 'the life-and-death struggles of the nation' was written by Bonifacio Ilagan. Called *Pagsambang Bayan* (*The Nation's Worship*), it was reconstructed street theatre, persuading the audience into communion through the rituals of collection, readings, and singing. The performance led to investigation of the playwright by the Martial Law authorities, and a second detention for the director, Behn Cervantes.

Conventional Western forms were not entirely rejected, instead they were selectively borrowed to serve indigenous ends. The constraints of Martial Law impelled naturalistic playwrights to camouflage their true intentions by 'sticking to the facts'. One of the best received plays of this genre was Orlando Nadres's *Paraisong Parisukat* (*Square Paradise*, 1974) about a female shoe-store employee.

The quest for effective and directly communicable forms of theatre produced, for example, the *dula-tula* (play-poem) by the University of Philippine Repertory Company, led by Cervantes. Asian in its suppleness, minimalism, and strategies of transformation, the didactic form requires only three performers: a narrator, principal actor, and a 'common man' playing multiple roles. Amelia Lapeña Bonifacio in her *Ang Paglalakbay ni Sisa* (*The Journeying of Sisa*, 1976) grafted Japanese **nō** drama techniques to *pasyon* (passion) style chanting poetically to express the anguish of Sisa, a character from Rizal's novel, *Noli Me Tangere*.

The spirit of the age was perhaps best encapsulated by PETA. A polyfunctional and private theatre organization, it is unique in South-East Asia. PETA is a performing company, and a training centre reaching out to the provinces and to some Asian countries. As a political action group, PETA is intent on creating political awareness among the masses. Guided by Cecile Guidote, PETA in 1967 built a challenging 'environmental' theatre encompassing the ruins of Manila's Fort Santiago. PETA's recent 'nuclear' rock operas sum up its means and ends. *Nukleyar* (1983) and *Nukleyar II* (1984), performed in song, dance, and mime, blended indigenous and empathetic Western dramaturgies, particularly the anti-bourgeois mischief of surrealism, the grotesque of the absurd, and the 'learning' devices of **Brecht**. The outcome was exhilarating theatre designed to transform the audience into active participants of the anti-nuclear cause.

Indonesia The 1926 verse drama written by Rustam Effendi, *Bebasari*, opened the curtain on modern Indonesian theatre. Rustam's allegorical tale recalls the famous episode about the kidnapping of Sita in the Hindu epic, *Ramayana*. Princess Bebasari (Indonesia) is abducted by Rawana (Dutch) but she is subsequently rescued by Bujangga (Indonesian Youth). Publication and performance of the play were obstructed by the Dutch colonial government. Rustam published the play himself, only to have it proscribed.

Young literary dramatists such as Rustam and Mohammed Yamin, and those who belonged to the influential 1930s literary group, Pujangga Baru ('New Literati'), were pioneer writers in the newly proclaimed (1928) national language of Indonesia. Collectively, they saw themselves as a beacon leading the nation towards the formation of a new culture. Their Western education had instilled in them progressive ideals, yet they were pulled towards '*dongeng ksyatria*', fables of legendary and historical warriors, gleaned from Indonesia's aristocratic classical literature. A leading figure of Pujangga Baru, Sanusi Pane, wove stories about imperious figures of the past in plays such as *Kertadjaja* (1932) and *Sandhyakala Ning Majapahit* (*Twilight of Majapahit*, 1933). But unlike Rustam's traditional hero, Sanusi's champions are flawed men, and vaguely tragic, surrendering either to fate or passion. Sanusi's ideal modern man, a synthesis of East and West, was raised in his only play with a contemporary setting (India), *Manusia Baru* (*New Man*, 1940). The most thoughtful play of the era was never performed.

Performance, however, was one of the main objectives of the theatre company, Maya, formed by Usmar Ismail in 1944 at the close of the Japanese occupation. A literary intellectual and playwright cut in the same mould as the Pujangga Baru writers, Usmar was also a director and theatre professional. But the short tradition of professional theatre disappeared when Usmar turned from theatre to film in the 1950s, and was not revived again until the contemporary period.

'Closet-dramas' regained their hold after Indonesia gained independence in 1949. The proliferation of one-act plays in the 1950s pointed to two realities: firstly the modest capacities of the playwrights; and secondly, the primary aim of writing plays: publication, mostly in literary magazines. Regarded as the father of Indonesian realistic drama, Utuy Tatang Sontani gained prominence because of his fecundity, deftness in creating verisimilitude, and his vision of the times. He wrote numerous one-act plays – one of the best-known, both in Indonesia and Malaysia, was *Awal dan Mira* (*Awal and Mira*, 1952) – and a few full-length dramas, that often alluded to that singular modern condition: alienation.

The inchoate in Indonesian realism was infused with a formal sensibility by the Indonesian National Academy of Theatre (Akademi Teater Nasional Indonesia, ATNI), instituted in 1955. The first modern theatre academy in South-East Asia, ATNI taught the Stanislavskian performance methods. Between 1955 and 1963, ATNI principally staged Western dramas, including **Molière**, **Gogol**, Chekhov, and **Sartre**. ATNI's choices reflected and reinforced theatre people's lack of confidence in indigenous modern plays. Nevertheless, ATNI raised the status of theatre in the national consciousness, and acted as a catalyst of increased theatre activity in major Indonesian towns and cities.

In the meantime, a doctrinaire 'social realism' in the arts was beginning to be preached in the late 1950s, following the ascendancy of the Indonesian Communist Party during Sukarno's 'Guided Democracy' government. The aggressive promotion of the Marxist-Leninist line in the arts compelled neutrals and anti-communists to protect themselves against the communist onslaughts. The consequences were an intense politicization and sectarianism of the arts, including theatre. The communists, and eventually Sukarno himself, were discredited by the attempted coup against the military generals on 30 September 1965. Soon after Suharto's New Order emerged in 1966, theatre too began to reveal a new visage.

In the growing mythology of contemporary Indonesian theatre, two persons are credited with its origins: W. S. Rendra and Arifin C. Noer. The watershed event was Rendra's staging of *Bip-Bop* in 1968. Nothing could have been more defiant of the literary realistic theatre than this improvised and starkly non-verbal theatre exercise. Its principal resources – an ensemble of performers and a leader – collectively assembled a succession of non-linear images made up of movement, sound (natural and human) and, occasionally, song. According to contemporary commentators, the overall impact of the piece was poetic, suggestive of a conflict between the mass and the individual. Generously featured in the national press and on TV, Rendra, also a considerable poet, soon rose in the national perception as a modern cultural hero. In subsequent years, his company, Bengkel Teater Jogjakarta, staged Rendra's original plays, and various 'confrontations' with Western classics. Rendra, for example, transplanted the ambience of the Javanese folk theatre clowns in **Beckett**'s *Waiting for Godot* (*Menanti Godot*, 1969). **Sophocles**' *Oedipus Rex* (1969) was mediated with a Balinese style of theatre, complete with Balinese masks and costumes.

Rendra's theatre became increasingly and explicitly political in the mid-1970s, as shown by the performances of *Kisah Perjuangan Suku Naga* (*The Struggle of the Naga Tribe*, 1974) and *Sekda* (*District Secretary*, 1977). Framed in the Javanese *wayang kulit* (shadow theatre) performance, the former warned that foreign exploitation, abetted by high-placed indigenous corruption, was jeopardizing the natural and harmonious order.

From May to October 1978, Rendra was detained by the Indonesian authorities, and subsequently prohibited from public performance for seven years. In 1986, he returned to the stage with *Panembahan Reso* (*Honourable Reso*), a seven-hour event just two short of the traditional all-night *wayang kulit* performance. Staged in Jakarta's Senayan Stadium, the performance emphasized that Rendra, a charismatic actor with a unique Indonesian epic manner, is the only Asian *avant-garde* theatre personality who can command a mass audience cutting across age and class barriers.

Folk (and popular theatre) have also been Arifin's resources in his explorations of a genuinely Indonesian theatre. His use of traditional sources is, however, informal, born of instinct and cunning, rather than of an *a priori* schema. He began his task with *Mega-Mega* (*Clouds*, 1964), and reached a momentary epiphany with *Kapai-Kapai* (*Moths*, 1970), the best-known South-East Asian play. The written text of *Kapai-Kapai* is as austere as a poem, but contemporary descriptions of the Jakarta premiere describe a multi-dimensional performance, profuse with non-linear events, crystallized by folk songs, children's games, irreverent popular theatre comedy, and stylized movement. By so doing, Arifin wrested freedom from the thrall of the literary text. The relentless images revolved around the worker, Abu, whose plight was raised to spiritual and metaphysical heights by the performance strategy. (All of Arifin's contemporary plays focus on the spiritual vitiation of the underdog.) Mercurial juxtapositions of events and images were the means that opened up entry points to a reflexivity: juxtapositions between illusion and reality, 'sense and nonsense', tragedy and comedy, horror and farce. In *Kapai-Kapai*, Arifin was the quintessential middleman, negotiating an autonomous status between Western and Asian theatre. The actor and playwright–director, Ikranagara, calls this stance, 'post-modern'.

Throughout the 1970s, Arifin and his theatre group, Teater Kecil, forged ahead with a widely emulated style of play and performance. In 1985, after six years spent almost exclusively in film, Arifin staged *Interogasi Atau Dalam Bayangan Tuhan* (*Interrogation Or In the Shadow of God*). His sense of play, provoking the contrasts in tone and sensibility, was still intact. But he showed a renewed faith in story and verbal theatre. He explained that words, after all, are the last refuge of human contact in a world gone excessively rational and materialistic.

Once Putu Wijaya formed his theatre group, Teater Mandiri, in 1974, it was possible to talk of a 'Yogyakarta School of Contemporary Theatre'. (At separate times in the 1960s, both Arifin and Putu worked in Rendra's Yogyakarta theatre company.) Prominent also as an innovative and prolific novelist, Putu brought a posture of severe detachment to Indonesian contemporary theatre. Conventional characters were entirely absent on Putu's stage: his people appeared as dislocated beings, dependent on the content of their dialogue to acquire 'character' (*Aduh* (*Ouch*, 1974); *Edan* (*Insane*, 1973)). His evocation of the 'tragedy of language' made a mockery of human communication (*Dag-Dig-Dug* (1972); *Anu* (*So and So*, 1974)). Most of his plays present assemblies of contentious people caught in a state of shock or 'terror' over the power that mysterious individuals and happenings have on their lives (*Anu*; *Tai* (*Shit*, 1983)). In contrast to his arid written texts, his performances were as sensual, irrepressibly playful, and grotesque, as the folk Balinese theatre he imbibed as a high-born Balinese child. His last performance, *Front* (1985), however, also hinted at Putu's return to a narrative theatre.

In contrast, Teguh Karya, theatre director, filmmaker, and the master of Indonesian formal realism, has expanded his vocabulary of non-realistic gestures in recent performances staged by his group, Teater Popular. *Randai* (Sumatran folk theatre) was the informing style of his revival of Lorca's *Pernikahan Darah* (*Blood Wedding*, 1987). The indigenous perception of Teguh as one of the prime movers of contemporary theatre is paradigmatic of its plural and remarkably tolerant aesthetics. An ATNI product, Teguh, since his repertory days in the Bali Room of Hotel Indonesia (1968–72), gained fame and following mainly for his formalistic and finely-wrought performances of Western dramas.

Direct contact with a 'concrete' audience was the root cause accounting for the ubiquitous and *kurang ajar* ('rough and rude') humour characterizing much of contemporary Indonesian theatre. A specific audience, mostly young, was created in the 1970s, particularly in Jakarta's Ismail Marzuki Park (Taman Ismail Marzuki, TIM), 'the most successfully conceived arts centre in Asia' (Brandon). Although financially supported by the Jakarta municipality, TIM is run by the artists themselves who, for the most part, have been immune from official interference. Since 1968, TIM has housed a stable, diverse, innovative, and frequently quality controlled repertory, including folk and popular theatre performances. The nursery of the mature theatre companies is TIM's annual Youth Theatre Festival. TIM is also the mecca of regional contemporary theatres, notably those led by Wisran Hadi (Padang, Sumatra), and Suyatna Anirun (Bandung, Java). Recently, a new audience, consisting of the middle and upper middle classes, has been packing Teater Koma's 'operas'. It may be because the *avant-garde* thrust of Koma's performances, created by N. Riantiarno, formerly of Teater Popular, albeit dwelling upon the miseries of the underclass, has been moderated by an overwhelming comic temper.

Malaysia Who wrote the first scripted Malay spoken drama and when, are questions yet to be resolved. But the consensus is that the schoolteacher and playwright–director, Shahrom Hussain, was among the pioneers of the early modern drama period (1940s to early 1960s). All but two of his plays are *purbawara*: plays based on the exploits and achievements of historical and mythical personages. Written mostly by students, teachers and journalists with a literary bent, *purbawara* re-enacted the glory and might of the Malay sultanate on stage. Off-stage, however, Malay power had been progressively dissipated by British colonial rule. By highlighting the contrast between ideal and reality, *purbawara* contributed to post-Second World War Malay nationalism, part of the aims of which were fulfilled by independence in 1957.

Immediately after independence, some *purbawara* playwrights reversed course, and critically scrutinized the orthodox feudal values glorified by their predecessors. The spirit of rational inquiry was manifested, for

example, in Shahrom's later works, particularly in his emblematic play, *SiBongkok Tanjung Puteri* (*The Hunchback of Tanjung Puteri*, 1961), which introduced the blatantly ugly, aggressive but probing anti-hero, SiBongkok. The poet, playwright and journalist Usman Awang elicited the modern rebel, garbed in the guise of the 15th-century warrior-'traitor', Hang Jebat, viewed in the play as the champion of truth and justice. Usman's Jebat, released in the intense and compact's verse drama *Matinya Seorang Pahlawan* (*Death of a Warrior*, 1964), was repeatedly resurrected as the archetypal rebel in the 1970s theatre.

In 1963, Mustapha Kamil Yassin, a teachers' training college lecturer, and later a university professor, pronounced that thematically and aesthetically, poetic dramas clung too much to the past. In the next decade, he launched a vigorous campaign promoting the 'dynamic', Western-influenced realistic drama, called *drama moden* (modern drama). His mostly comic plays, crowded with social types – the best of which is *Atap Genting Atap Rembia* (*Brick House, Nipa House*, 1963) – conclude reconciliations between the conflicting forces in post-independence Malaysian society: rural vs. urban values, old vs. young generation, Malay vs. Chinese. Mustapha and his colleagues, Usman Awang, Awang Had Salleh, Aziz Jahpin and A. Samad Said, drew the newly urbanized Malay literary elite towards acceptance of *drama moden*.

The ethnic riots of May 1969, which gripped the major cities of peninsular Malaysia, undermined the optimism of *drama moden*. In fact, the impact of the event has been so profound that it justifies the recognition of a post-1969 perspective on the arts, including theatre. Soon after the riots, some Malay playwright–directors set about reviewing the Malaysian past, in the hope that such an exercise would help them to understand the disturbing present. One of the earliest results of these steps towards 'self-apprehension' was Noordin Hassan's *Bukan Lalang DiTiup Angin* (*It is Not the Tall Grass that is Blown by the Wind*, 1970). Partially allegorical and replete with oblique references to May 1969, the non-linear piece was fuelled by Noordin's surrealistic imagination. It was calculated to uncover the ironies and ambiguities that lurk behind the mask of harmony, peaceful coexistence, and progress in multi-ethnic Malaysian society. Through an interaction between traditional and modern (or Western) performance modes and aesthetics, the piece strove to mediate between past and present in Malay experience. Most of the audience thought the performance was confusing, and in his deep need to communicate to the many, Noordin simplified his next two plays, *Tiang Seri Tegak Berlima* (*Five Braided Pillars*, 1973), and *Pintu* (*Door*, 1976). But he did not compromise on his multi-channelled approach to performance, nor on his mission to inculcate a Malaysian identity in the theatre. What was to be called *teater kontemporari* ('contemporary theatre') assumed the proportions of a movement by the mid-1970s, with the rise of playwright–directors Syed Alwi, Dinsman, Bidin Subari and Johan Jaafar. They were soon joined by Hatta Azad Khan, trained in performing arts from the University of Science Malaysia in Penang.

Syed's *Tok Perak* (1975), the first multi-media event in Malaysian theatre, juxtaposed folk theatre events, images from film and slides, and an intricately textured realistic theatre. The mixed means performance was an analogue of the protagonist's condition. A middle-aged street medicine seller, Tok Perak is trapped in the transition between tradition and modernity. When faced with the classic choice between the imperatives of society and self, he chooses the latter.

The troubled and ruminating self was also exalted in sensational theatrical images by the University of Malaya graduate, Dinsman, the only genuinely cult figure in contemporary Malay theatre. Dinsman created a series of startling *personae* – Jebat in *Jebat* (1973), Adam in *Bukan Bunuh Diri* (*Not Suicide*, 1974), and Ana in *Ana* (1976) – who echoed a young generation restive with traditional values, but uncertain about the modern persuasion. Dinsman's partially absurd performances beckoning at existentialism, found the measure of the post-book and television generation, and were frequently performed in the 1970s.

Nevertheless, the unhalting experimental zeal of contemporary theatre began to wear down the audience. Simultaneously, a resurgent Islam in Malaysia caught the contemporary theatre practitioners unawares and defenceless against attacks that they were harbouring the sins of polytheism and nihilism in their plays. In the 1980s, the Malay avant-garde attack has been (temporarily) blunted and, indeed, transferred to local English drama, as demonstrated by the performances of K. S. Maniam's *The Cord* (1984), and Kee Thuan Chye's politically controversial *1984 – Here and Now* (1985). Hitherto self-absorbed, Malay theatre, however, is witnessing a new tolerance towards foreign works in translation, staged principally by The Drama Centre led by Mustapha Nor. Noordin Hassan continues to experiment and is currently exploring an Islamic mode of theatre in performances such as *1400* (1981), and *Jangan Bunuh Rama-Rama* (*Don't Kill the Butterflies*, 1983).

Singapore Singapore has four official languages: Malay, Mandarin, Tamil, and English. The plural linguistic–cultural system of Singapore has led to the formation of four separate enclaves or 'streams' of theatre. Until recently, rapprochement between streams was rare. Each stream looked to outside sources for inspiration and models to help shape its aesthetics and repertory: Mandarin theatre to China, Tamil to India, and English theatre to the West.

Singapore Malay theatre, however, was an integral and, occasionally, leading part of Malaysian Malay theatre, i.e. until Singapore's separation from Malaysia in 1963. (Singapore joined The Federation of Malaysia immediately upon independence from the British in 1959.) For more than a decade after the Japanese occupation, Singapore was the virtual centre of Malay literary activities on both sides of the Causeway. The era spawned the durable theatre company, Sriwana, and the eclectic plays and performances, including *purbawara* and *drama moden*, of the idiosyncratic theatre professional, Kalam Hamidy. Separation caught the Singapore Malays as a cultural minority in a Chinese-dominated society. Sriwana assumed the role of bastion of the beleaguered theatre culture. Recent efforts to encourage an experimental sensibility, particularly by Nadi Putra, Sriwana's leader since 1965, have so far been thwarted by the group's conservatism. Significantly, Nadi's contemporary vision of Jebat, *Menara*

Gading (*Ivory Tower*, 1986), was staged by Teater Kemuning, a young theatre company drawn to Indonesian–Malaysian contemporary theatre.

Tamil theatre, also a distinct cultural minority, turned from its traditional historical–mythological plays to a reformist realistic theatre in the 1950s. Since then, it has not felt any urgency radically to change its aesthetic direction.

The firm foundations of a Mandarin-based realistic theatre were planted by the teachers and journalists leading the Singapore Amateur Players in the early 1950s. Their painstaking groundwork was rudely shaken by the local reverberations of the Cultural Revolution in China (1966–76). What ensued was a Singapore version of the Cultural Revolution's militant non-realistic theatre of heroic gestures and images exalting the common man. Kuo Pao Kun, a playwright–director trained in Australia's National Academy of Dramatic Arts, injected strong doses of professionalism and artistic responsibility to the revolutionary theatre. His epic-type plays, improvised and conceived collectively, demystified Mandarin playwriting in Singapore. Staged by the farmers, factory workers, and clerks enrolled in his theatre school (Practice Performing Arts School), his performances expounded on the social dislocations brought on by foreign investment in an increasingly corporate Singapore. In 1976, Kuo was detained during the government's massive anti-leftist drive. Upon his release in 1980, he immediately returned to the stage, disclosing a human and reflective dimension in his partially expressionist theatre. In 1985, he began the writing and directing of a successful series of Mandarin–English one-man theatre pieces, inspired by the Chinese oral story-telling tradition. Gently satirical and in convincing Singlish (Singapore English), *The Coffin is Too Big for the Hole* (1985), and *No Parking on Odd Days* (1986) rue the excessive homogenization and bureaucratization of contemporary Singapore society.

The early 1960s generation of Singapore playwrights in English was a politicized, nationalist-minded, university-trained literary elite, represented by Lim Chor Pee and Goh Poh Seng. The indifferent response to their pioneering plays was followed by a drought in local English drama, relieved only by the 1970s political plays of the poet Robert Yeo. At the end of the decade, an identity crisis was perceived by the theatre director and university lecturer, Max LeBlond, who lent his zest for the local *patois* (Singlish) to resourceful adaptations of foreign works in the early 1980s. Along with Kuo's mono-dramas, LeBlond's staging of Stella Kon's *Emily of Emerald Hill* (1985) elevated the status of the Singapore English play in the national estimation. Kon's Asian treatment of time and space in her bitter-sweet eulogy of the disappearing culture of the Chinese *peranakan* (Straits-born Chinese) was a rare experience for the ethnically dispossessed middle-class audience. Currently, an alternative theatre, directly influenced by the Philippine Educational Theatre Association (PETA), is proposed by Third Stage, which presents 'learning plays' on the ills of Singapore society to the young, 'high-rise' generation. The recent detention (May 1987) of Third Stage leaders by the Singapore government will surely lead to the paralysis of the company.

If current trends prevail, English promises to be the

dominant language of Singapore. Presently, the Singapore government has launched a rational support system for theatre, by way of providing physical infrastructure, grants and tax rebates, annual and biannual national and international festivals and playwriting competitions. In 1985, Singapore developed its first professional modern theatre in English, Theatre Works. Modern theatre in Singapore is brimming with potential. What direction it will take – Western, Asian, or a synthesis of the two – remains uncertain.

Conclusion Modern South-East Asian theatre began in the city and continues to be a predominantly urban phenomenon. The exceptions are to be found in the Philippines (PETA), and with a handful of young Indonesian contemporary theatre groups. (Singapore is an anomaly since its rural areas have practically disappeared.) Recently, however, the spreading tentacles of television have brought modern realistic theatre to the rural centres. Most South-East Asian governments ensure that *kitsch* television drama is sanitized of images and ideas contrary to its purposes. Alternative or opposing social and political attitudes in the performing arts often stem from contemporary theatres, thereby lending urgency and justification for their survival. The reluctance or failure of contemporary theatre to abandon its urban fortress renders it a minority art form. In fact, even in its natural domain, the city, it tends to have an enclave mentality, or as the writer Goenawan Mohamed has remarked about contemporary Indonesian theatre, it is a minority among diverse minorities.

The youthful character of modern South-East Asian theatre is also striking. This tendency is implicitly recognized by indigenous theatre histories, which tell of processions of succeeding generations of people and ideas. Continuity of theatre personalities is rare: theatre men and women who reach 30 and above are usually swallowed up by mounting career and family responsibilities. A few contemporary theatre people have demonstrated persistence of creative endeavour. They include: Rolando Tinio, Amelia Lapeña Bonifacio (Philippines), W. S. Rendra, Arifin C. Noer, Teguh Karya (Indonesia), Noordin Hassan (Malaysia), Kuo Pao Kun (Singapore). The current efforts made to professionalize modern theatre in part speak of the desire to break the age barrier. If they succeed, then excellence, often the handmaiden of creative continuity, will be widespread in the future modern theatre of South-East Asia. KJ

See: J. R. Brandon, *Brandon's Guide to Theatre in Asia*, Honolulu, 1976; D. G. Fernandez, 'Asian Theatre of Communion: A Look at Contemporary Philippine Theatre', *Continuity and Change in South-East Asia: Papers of Distinguished Scholars Series: University of Hawaii 1982*, South-East Asian Paper No. 23, South-East Asian Studies, Centre For Asian and Pacific Studies, University of Hawaii at Manoa, 1984; M. Goenawan, 'Sebuah Pembelaan Untuk Teater Indonesia Mutakhir' ('A Defence of Contemporary Indonesian Theatre'), *Seks, Sastera, Kita (Sex, Literature, Us)*, Jakarta, 1980; K. Jit, 'Towards an Islamic Theatre for Malaysia: Noordin Hassan and *Don't Kill the Butterflies*', *Asian Theatre Journal* Vol. 1, no. 2, Honolulu, 1984; N. G. Tiongson, 'What is Philippine Drama?', unpublished paper presented at the Asian Theatre Festival and Conference, Manila, 9–15 May, 1983; O. Yuthavong, 'The Emergence of Drama in Thailand' in L. Y. Yabes (ed. and intro.), *Asian Writers on Literature and Justice*, Manila, 1982.

Association of Producing Artists (APA)

Founded in 1960 by **Ellis Rabb** in an attempt to create a collective of theatre artists offering a wide range of material in a repertory structure, APA spent its first four seasons, in addition to touring, with residencies at Princeton, Milwaukee's Fred Miller Theatre, the Folksbiene Theatre in New York City, and at the University of Michigan. In 1964 it joined the Off-Broadway Phoenix Theatre, which had been organized in 1953 by T. Edward Hambleton and Norris Houghton (with Stuart Vaughan as artistic director, 1958–62) and had presented notable productions of standard plays and new works, including *Once Upon a Mattress* (1959) and **Kopit**'s *Oh, Dad, Poor Dad* (1962). For five years the APA at the Phoenix presented a wide range of plays, most notably *Man and Superman* (1964); *You Can't Take It With You* (1965); *Right You Are* (1966); *The Show-Off* (1967); *Pantagleize* (co-directed with **John Houseman**), *The Misanthrope*, and *Exit the King* (1968); *Cock-a-Doodle Dandy* and *Hamlet* (1969). Several seasons were spent at New York City's **Lyceum Theatre** prior to its dissolution in 1970. DBW

Astaire, Fred (1899–1987) and Adele (1898–1981)

American dancers, singers, and actors. As children the Astaires spent ten years in vaudeville, where they perfected their dancing and teamwork. In 1917 they made their New York musical theatre debut in *Over the Top*. Influenced by the ballroom dancing of Vernon and Irene Castle, the Astaires also studied with Broadway choreographer and director **Ned Wayburn**. Their dances were fluid, stylish, and often witty, in keeping with the frothy musicals in which they appeared. After featured roles in several shows, the Astaires were the stars of *Lady, Be Good!* (1924), for which **George** and **Ira Gershwin** wrote the score. The successful partnership with the Gershwins was repeated with *Funny Face* (1927). They starred with **Marilyn Miller** in *Smiles* (1930), and made their last appearance as a team in the Howard Dietz–Arthur Schwartz revue, *The Band Wagon* (1931). After Adele's retirement, Fred appeared alone in *The Gay Divorce* (1932) before leaving for Hollywood and a career in musical films. Critics generally considered Adele to be the stronger dancer and more vivid personality of the partnership. Equally popular in England, the Astaires brought several of their American successes to the London stage during the 1920s. MK

Astley, Philip (1742–1814)

English equestrian and manager, who first distinguished himself as a horse-breaking sergeant-major during the continental wars (1760). On leaving the cavalry, he opened a riding school outside London (1768), where he combined equestrianism with clowns and tumblers to constitute the first true circus. After a stint in Dublin, he erected his Royal Amphitheatre (1788). When a rival, Charles Hughes, built the Royal Circus and began staging plays without a licence, Astley followed suit. Both managers were closed by the authorities, and Astley sought new pastures in Paris where he prospered with his 'cirque'

Astley's Amphitheatre, 1808.

1782–9. The French Revolution forced him home, where he published his *System of Equestrian Education* (1801). His London amphitheatre burned to the ground in 1794, to be rebuilt the next year; it burned again in 1803 to rise phoenix-like as a splendid new house, seating 2,500 spectators, in 1804. He left this business to his son and then built the Olympic Pavilion from the timber of an old frigate at the cost of £800. It lost £10,000 its first season. His last enterprise was an Amphitheatre restricted to equestrianism in the Faubourg du Temple (Oct. 1814).

His son John Philip Conway (1767–1821), as a child equestrian, had been dubbed the English Rose by Marie Antoinette. Indolent and handsome, he excelled at devising fanciful equestrian pantomimes but, a prodigal businessman, he spent more than the Amphitheatre earned and died of high-living.   LS

Aston, Anthony (c. 1682 – c. 1753) English actor-manager. Born in a wealthy family, he abandoned law to become an actor. A strolling player with **Doggett** in the provinces and in Ireland in the late 1690s, he became a soldier and a lawyer in the West Indies and may also have acted in America. By 1709 he was acting again in Ireland, where his first play *Love in a Hurry* was performed. In 1710 he began performing the medleys for which he became famous. These were variety shows of short plays, scenes, songs and dances performed by Aston and members of his family and their success earned him the nickname Matt Medley. Though he attempted a full-scale production in London

in 1717 (closed down because of the monopoly of the patent companies) and briefly joined the **Lincoln's Inn Fields** company in 1722, he spent most of his career touring the country with the medleys, adding extra features such as animal impersonations from time to time. In 1735 he campaigned successfully against the proposed Playhouse Bill which would have strengthened the power of the patent companies against shows like his. He gave his last known performances in 1744. His play *The Fool's Opera* contains an autobiographical sketch. As a contemporary said, 'he is a monopoliser . . . he plays all characters, he fills none: he is the whole comedy in his single person'.   PH

Astor Place Opera House   Broadway, East 9th St and Astor Pl., New York City. In their pursuit of operatic pleasure, well-to-do New Yorkers built the Astor Place close to an exclusive enclave on Lafayette Street settled by the Astors and their friends, but opera did not remain long the house's principal fare and the 1,800-seat theatre was given over to other entertainments. In 1849, during an engagement by the English star **William Macready**, a riot was triggered from a long-smouldering feud between Macready and the American star **Edwin Forrest**, which was also fed by anti-English sentiment among the Irish denizens of the Bowery area. The militia was called in to quell the riot and the order was given to fire at the crowd. When the smoke had cleared, 31 people had died and 150 were wounded. In 1852, the theatre was renamed the New York to rid it of its tainted past, but in 1854, it was sold at auction to the Mercantile Library Association. It was known as Clinton Hall and stood until 1891, when it was torn down. MCH

Atelier Theatre (France) A 19th-century Melodrama theatre in Montmartre, it was a cinema from 1914 till 1922 when **Dullin** reopened it as L'Atelier. It became well known as one of the **Cartel** theatres, producing a wide repertoire, including the classics, the Elizabethans and modern playwrights, notably **Pirandello** and **Salacrou**. Alongside the producing company, Dullin ran a school in which many famous French actors and directors trained, e.g. **Artaud**, **Barrault**, **Barsacq**, **Blin**, **Vilar**. When Dullin moved to the Théâtre Sarah Bernhardt in 1940, Barsacq took over the theatre with his Compagnie des Quatre Saisons. He remained director of the theatre till his death, preserving a similar tradition to that of Dullin but with the addition of more light modern works. DB

Atkinson, (Justin) Brooks (1894–1984) American drama critic. Educated at Harvard University where he attended **George Pierce Baker**'s Workshop 47, Atkinson taught English for a year (1917–18) at Dartmouth College and worked as a reporter on the Springfield (Mass.) *Daily News*. A year later, he began a four-year stint as assistant drama critic to H. T. Parker on the *Boston Daily Evening Transcript*. In 1922 he became book review editor for the *New York Times*, followed in 1926 as the paper's drama critic succeeding **Stark Young**. When war broke out in 1941, he took an overseas assignment, and received a Pulitzer Prize (1947) for his reports on the Soviet Union. After the war (1946) he returned to reviewing the Broadway theatre. The most respected critic of his generation, Atkinson offered common sense opinions in a graceful style, and was known for both his fairness and candour. He thought that the theatre should reach out and relate to the world outside of the art. Therefore he did not mingle with theatre people or attend rehearsals believing that his reviews were for the 'Average guy who goes to the theatre'. At his retirement in 1960, the Mansfield Theatre was renamed in his honour. His many books include *Broadway Scrapbook* (1948), *Brief Chronicles* (1966), *Broadway* (1970), and *The Lively Years: 1920–1973*. TLM

Aubignac, François Hédelin, abbé d' (1604–76) French critic and dramatist. As a member of **Richelieu**'s household he came to share the Cardinal's passion for the drama and evolved an authoritarian view of its nature and current practice, to the extent of advancing a proposal for the radical reform of the theatre under state control. His principal work, *La Pratique du théâtre*, published in 1657 but begun much earlier, is a manual of dramatic writing and stage presentation in which he elaborates the neoclassical rules of composition into a systematic code of practice for the playwright. He insists on a strict division of the genres, the consequential decorum of character and incident to each, and above all the importance of *vraisemblance* (credibility) which inclines him to a severe interpretation of the unities of place, time and action, the presumed length of the latter being ideally compar-

able to the actual duration of the performance. For him, such rules are founded not on the authority of the ancients but on that of reason and will be conducive to the production of a satisfying artefact, capable of pleasing an audience in performance. Sadly they did not serve to enhance his own three tragedies, intended as models but indifferently received. The *Pratique* itself, however, had a profound influence on dramatists, extended by its translation into English as *The Whole Art of the Stage* in 1684. DR

Auden, W[instanley] H[ugh] (1907–73) British poet and dramatist, a founder member of the **Group Theatre** in London, which was responsible for the production of his first performed play, *The Dance of Death* (1934). A didactic celebration of the destruction of the bourgeoisie using music and ballet, and influenced by the agit-prop form of workers' theatre, its doggerel verse and Marxist themes point forward to his collaborations with **Christopher Isherwood**, *The Dog Beneath the Skin* (1935), *The Ascent of F6* (1936) and *On the Frontier* (1938). These political fables, mixing symbolic quests, epic techniques derived from **Brecht**, and satiric pastiche are among the most powerful English plays of the 1930s. Auden was awarded the Pulitzer Prize for his modern morality play *The Age of Anxiety* (1947), which explores loneliness as the human condition through characters derived from Jungian psychology. As well as translations of **Ernst Toller**, Brecht and **Cocteau**, Auden is known for his opera librettos – in particular *Paul Bunyan* (1941) for Benjamin Britten, *The Rake's Progress* (1951) for Igor Stravinski, and *Moralities* for Hans Werner Henze (1969). CI

Audiberti, Jacques (1899–1965) Prolific southern French writer of poetic rather than dramatic bent, his first play to be seen on the French stage, *Quoat-Quoat* (directed by Reybaz 1946) was written without thought of performance. However, his poetic exuberance led him to be linked with writers of the post-war avantgarde such as Schéhadé or **Vauthier**. Many of his plays were directed by Georges Vitaly and then enjoyed a second life in productions by **Marcel Maréchal** in Lyon in the 1960s. His multi-layered texts (including 26 plays) deal with the eternal conflict between forces of good and evil in settings often borrowed from history or myth. DB

Auditorium Theatre Congress St and Michigan Ave, Chicago [Architects: Sullivan and Adler]. Set within a multi-purpose building encompassing a hotel, offices and stores, the Auditorium was intended to be supported by the commercial enterprises in the complex. Designed by the experimental firm of Dankmar and Adler, it introduced no stunningly new concepts architecturally but was provided with near-perfect acoustics and sightlines, a flexible auditorium and stage, and striking interior decoration. It opened in 1899 and was in use as an opera house and theatre until 1942, when it was largely abandoned. When it was threatened with destruction, a civic campaign was launched to save it. It was restored and reopened in 1967. MCH

Augier, Emile (1820–89) French dramatist. Augier is the most important social dramatist and chronicler of society of the Second Empire and Third Republic. He exposes the bourgeoisie of the period in play after play for its hypocritical and false moral values. His plays helped move the French theatre in the direction of naturalism by offering serious examination of a number of topical issues – for example, *Madame Caverlet* (1876) dealt with the question of divorce. The 19th-century bourgeois's obsession with money and his confusion of moral and monetary values provided a favourite theme of Augier's, most strongly expressed in his last play, *The House of Fourchambault* (1878), in which a character states that 'marriage is the lowest of human institutions when it is no more than the union of two fortunes'. Augier's first play, *Hemlock* (1844), had a classical theme, but revealed a talent which he would soon turn to more contemporary issues. In *Le Mariage d'Olympe* (*The Marriage of Olympia*, 1855), which was booed by its first audiences, he attacked the romantic sentimentalizing of the courtesan. *Le Gendre de Monsieur Poirier* (*Monsieur Poirier's Son-in-law*), written with Jules Sandeau for the Gymnase in 1854 (it joined the repertoire of the **Comédie-Française** in 1864) explored the subject of the nouveau-riche bourgeois and the impoverished nobleman in a 19th-century version of **Molière**'s *Le Bourgeois Gentilhomme*. *A False Step* (*The Poor Lionesses*, 1858) showed the lengths to which the wives of the bourgeoisie were prepared to go to satisfy their taste for ostentation and luxury – and the risks which they might run. By the 1860s Augier was dealing with more and more contentious subjects, constantly attacking the frenetic pursuit of material wealth. In *Les Effrontés* (*The Shameless Ones*, 1861) he exposed the link between manipulation of the stock exchange and the press. This play created the character of Giboyer (brilliantly interpreted by the actor **Got**), and its success led to a sequel, *Le Fils de Giboyer* (*Giboyer's Son*). The play contained a strong dose of anti-clericalism. His virulent attack on the political manoeuvring of the Jesuits was continued in *Lions et Renards* (*Lions and Foxes*, 1869). *Maître Guérin* (1864), which had a long run, is a return to the comedy of manners, focusing on the character of a dubious lawyer who turns the law to his own advantage. The French critic, Gustave Lanson, felt that this was the most original and the most closely observed character to be put on the stage since Molière. Augier was elected to the French Academy in 1857. After *The House of Fourchambault* he virtually stopped writing because of a nervous complaint. JMCC

Auriol, Jean-Baptiste (1806–81) French acrobatic clown, son of a ballet-master; he studied under the rope-dancer Pierre Forioso and married the English performer Aurelia Belling, before taking his first job with **Ducrow**, performing his famous bottle-dance. After appearances throughout Europe he made his Parisian debut with Franconi (1847), where his leaps had a phenomenal success: he performed a *salto mortale* over 24 soldiers and a double *salto* over 12 horses. Auriol's non-use of makeup, his voice 'like a child's trumpet' and his jester's costume set the style for European clowns for two decades. He retired in 1862. LS

Australia

Aboriginal dance-drama In the 40,000 years the Aborigines are believed to have inhabited Australia, many forms of dance drama or 'corroboree' evolved. These dance traditions, which Aborigines believe are passed on from the spirits of ancestors, have religious significance and are associated with initiation, tribal, totemic and magic ceremonies. A fusion of music, dance and drama, they have varied from the large formal patterns of the south-eastern traditions to the looser formations and individual dancing of northern Australia. Sometimes only men dance; on other occasions both men and women dance, sometimes separately. Dance is usually accompanied by singing and clapsticks; in northern Australia a wooden trumpet (didjeridu) is also played. Dancers are painted with coloured ochres and decorated with feathers and plants, preparing themselves behind a screen of boughs and performing, often by firelight, in a specially prepared area. The dances often depict animal movements; among the distinctive steps are the 'leg quivering' movement and dancing on all fours. These dances combine religious rite and theatrical entertainment; those of the south-eastern areas, now largely inhabited by white settlers, have for the most part disappeared, but Aboriginal dance remains a living tradition in other parts of Australia.

Early colonial theatre, 1789–1850 European settlement of Australia began in 1788 with the founding of a British penal colony at Sydney, and for a generation afterwards theatre was largely a convict activity. The first theatrical performance took place in 1789 –

Tiwi dancer, Australia.

Farquhar's *The Recruiting Officer* staged in a decorated bark hut in honour of the King's birthday. In 1796 Robert Sidaway opened a theatre which convicts could attend for payment of meat, flour or spirits, but their rowdy behaviour spelt its closure two years later, and another theatre, for officers, in 1800 was also short-lived. But convict performances were permitted at Norfolk Island in 1793–4; in 1826 performances were held in the Debtors' Room at Sydney Gaol, and at Emu Plains a convict theatre group established in 1825 was patronized by free settlers until abruptly disbanded in 1830.

Professional theatre in New South Wales, however, emerged only after a struggle with officialdom and some community disapproval. In 1827 a stage-struck Sydney businessman named Barnett Levey advertised for share-holders in a theatre, and in 1829 began holding balls and entertainments in his mill and hotel complex known as the Colchester warehouse. After repeated applications and a change of governor he was finally granted a theatre licence, and professional theatre was born on Boxing Night 1832 with *Black Ey'd Susan* staged in the hotel saloon; his Theatre Royal opened on 5 October 1833 with *The Miller and his Men*. Many associated with Levey, including the actors Conrad Knowles, George Buckingham, and John Meredith, and the managers Joseph Simmons and Joseph Wyatt, helped consolidate the profession in Sydney and the other colonies in the next decade, while the lively actress Eliza Winstanley went on to perform with **Charles Kean** at the London **Princess's Theatre** in the 1850s. The Theatre Royal survived until 1838 when Sydney gained a second theatre, the Royal Victoria, seating almost 2,000 and with a solid professional company under Joseph Wyatt. The 1840s saw short-lived competition from Signor Dalle Case's Olympic Theatre (1842) and Joseph Simmons's Royal City Theatre (1843), but the Royal Victoria remained a major Sydney theatre until 1880.

Theatre was also established in the other Australian colonies in the 1830s and 1840s, with Sydney performers and others newly arrived from England, including the Samson Camerons, Theodosia Yates, Francis Nesbitt, Francis Belfield, Gustavus Arabin, and Anne Clarke, moving with surprising frequency between widely separated settlements. In Van Diemen's Land (Tasmania) John Phillip Deane held concerts in Hobart from 1826, and in 1833–4 the Samson Camerons at the Freemason's Tavern and Deane at the Argyle Rooms presented professional entertainments; by 1841 the provincial town of Launceston had regular performances. Though Tasmania was also a penal colony, unlike New South Wales its Colonial Secretary was one of the sponsors of a theatre, and in 1837 Hobart's Theatre Royal was opened. Though much altered, it still stands as Australia's only working theatre from early colonial days. Adelaide, a free settlement, gained a professional theatre in 1838, and two more under the Camerons and Buckingham, before the Queen's Theatre opened near the Shakespeare Tavern (later the New Queen's) in 1841. The English actor-manager **George Coppin** became Adelaide's most prominent theatrical figure in the late 1840s, managing the Royal Victoria (the old Queen's) with John Lazar, and opening a theatre in Port Adelaide in 1850. Melbourne was founded later in

1835, and not until 1841 did its makeshift Pavilion Theatre open next to the Eagle Tavern – another example of the common link between early theatres and public-houses. As the Royal Victoria it was managed by Knowles and Samson Cameron until 1845, when a New Queen's Theatre Royal opened under Francis Nesbitt. The nearby township of Geelong also had a thriving theatre from the 1840s. Perth had theatrical entertainments from 1839, and from 1842 Hodge's Hotel presented amateur performances; Brisbane was to wait till the 1850s for its earliest theatricals, and till 1865 for its first theatre.

The repertoire of such theatres was that of the British stage, from **Shakespeare** to melodrama, farce and burlesque – indeed Levey's original licence had specified 'such Plays and·Entertainments only as have been performed at one of His Majesty's Licensed Theatres in London'. But the indigenous drama dates from 1828 when David Burn wrote his melodrama *The Bushrangers* (staged at Edinburgh in 1829), based on a Tasmanian convict, Matthew Brady. Burn's other dramas were performed in Sydney and Melbourne during the 1840s, while the Melbourne Queen's Theatre staged several plays by local authors, including the actor Francis Belfield's melodramas. In Sydney, still cautious towards theatre because of its convict population, a system of licensing locally written plays on the pattern of the Lord Chamberlain's censorship in Britain developed in the 1840s, though it favoured plays with little or no local content. The convict Edward Geoghegan became Sydney's most prolific playwright, writing or adapting ten pieces for the Royal Victoria, including a charming musical trifle with a Sydney setting, *The Currency Lass* (1844). Most of his plays, however, like those of Conrad Knowles and Joseph Simmons, are romantic melodramas with exotic settings, as was the first locally written opera staged in Australia, Isaac Nathan's *Don John of Austria* (1847). Apart from Burn's drama, the most specific depiction of colonial society is the anonymous comedy *Jemmy Green in Australia* (c. 1845), attributed to the convict James Tucker, which transplants a naive cockney character from **Moncrieff**'s *Tom and Jerry* to confront bumbling constables and bushrangers in New South Wales.

Years of expansion The early 1850s saw theatre's expansion into a fully fledged entertainment industry with the discovery of gold in New South Wales and Victoria, and subsequently in Queensland. Melbourne, barely 15 years old, became almost overnight a cosmopolitan city, and with Bendigo, Ballarat and other goldmining centres provided a ready market for performers such as **Lola Montez**, who toured in 1855 with her notorious 'spider dance'. George Coppin quickly established himself as Australia's leading entrepreneur, with four theatres in Melbourne by the mid-1850s, and it was he who introduced the practice of importing noted artists to tour an established circuit of major cities and provincial towns, a policy which was to dominate the Australian theatre throughout the 19th century. Coppin's first overseas star was the Irish tragedian Gustavus Vaughan Brooke, his partner at the Melbourne Queen's Theatre in the 1850s, and over the next 20 years many theatrical celebrities toured Australia, most under Coppin's management. From the

British and European theatre came Charles Kean and Ellen Tree (1863), the Shakespearians Barry Sullivan (1862–6) and Walter Montgomery (1867–9) **Charles Mathews** the younger (1870–1) and Madame **Céleste** (1867), while from America came Joseph Jefferson for several years in the early 1860s, Adelaide and Joey Gougenheim (1856), **Edwin Booth** in the 1850s and again in 1872, and Avonia Jones (1859–61), among many others. Such theatrical celebrities, and others sometimes less well known, while undoubtedly raising theatrical standards, inevitably fostered the attitude that 'the best' came from abroad and consolidated the emerging Australian theatre in the mould of British and American tradition.

A number of Australian-based managements became well established in the 1860s–70s, preeminent among whom was William Saurin Lyster's Grand Opera Company, which established opera as the popular form it was to remain until after the First World War. But not surprisingly, in the light of so many imported plays and players, the local drama was even less evident than in the 1840s. Farces and comic afterpieces with local settings were sometimes staged, but pantomimes emerged as the form most readily adaptable to local colour and topicality. The prolific William Mower Akhurst, and later Marcus Clarke and Garnet Walch, wrote numerous pantomimes and extravaganzas which combined fairy tale and mythology with colonial characters to satirize the new pretensions to urbanity of Australian society, though in the most light-hearted and ephemeral way.

The golden years, 1870–1914 The period from 1870 to the First World War saw rapid growth in theatrical activity. Sydney, for example, which in the early 1870s had two or three regular venues, could boast six major theatres by the late 1880s, as well as several smaller venues for variety theatre. By the 1890s Australians had access to the full spectrum of 19th-century theatrical fare, from Shakespeare, grand opera and operetta to melodrama, farce and variety theatre. From the 1870s the Australian-born population outnumbered immigrants, producing homegrown stars such as the ravishing **Nellie Stewart**, but the theatre remained largely dominated by performers and managers who had come from abroad. Australia was still a provincial outpost of British theatre, and increasingly part of an international touring circuit. Some performers came for brief highly publicized tours – Julius Knight in 1891 and 1897, Henry Irving the younger in 1911, Emily Soldene and her showgirls in 1877, and Mrs Brown Potter and Kyrle Bellew in 1891, **Janet Achurch** in the controversial *A Doll's House* in 1889, soon after its London staging, the expatriate **Oscar Asche** with Lily Brayton in 1909, and most celebrated of all, **Sarah Bernhardt** in 1891. Others returned so often or stayed so long that they became identified with the Australian stage: the actor-manager George Rignold, the Majeroni family who had arrived with **Adelaide Ristori**, the Italian tragedienne, in 1875, the English actor George Titheradge and the American Grattan Riggs, among many others. The famous melodramatist **Dion Boucicault** arrived in 1885 with his son and daughter, and the younger Dion (Dot) remained to found in 1886, with Robert Brough, the Brough-Boucicault Company, based in Melbourne, which for a decade set the

standard for stylish productions of sophisticated new plays.

Many such performers were initially brought to Australia by Coppin's successor as Australia's foremost entrepreneur, the American **James Cassius Williamson**, who himself had first arrived as one of Coppin's imported stars in 1874. In 1882 Williamson formed a partnership with Arthur Garner and George Musgrove, known as the 'Triumvirate', which lasted until 1890 and led to the Williamson managerial 'Firm' which dominated Australian theatre for two generations. Williamson, a shrewd businessman with little interest in serious drama, and even less in that of his adopted country, consolidated the policy of importing proven successes with overseas stars, justifying it with the dictum that 'Australians don't want Australian' – a view that was almost unquestioningly accepted as fact until the mid-20th century. Williamson's middle-brow entertainment, leavened with spectacular seasons of 'high culture' such as the Melba Grand Opera tour in 1911, set the pattern for commercial theatre until the 1950s. Ironically his denigration of the local playwright came just as Australian authors were finding enthusiastic audiences in the melodrama theatres, though local drama was always heavily overshadowed by overseas successes. Walter Cooper, journalist, member of parliament and playwright, in the 1870s wrote comedies and sensation dramas depicting the 'new chum' immigrant's experience, sometimes with spectacle scenes of bushfires and floods, and George Darrell, an English-born actor-manager and author, consolidated the Anglo-Australian melodrama with pieces such as *The Forlorn Hope* (1879), showing a band of colonials coming to Britain's aid in a future European war, and *The Sunny South* (1883), in which an English aristocratic household 'strike it rich' on the goldfields and have various colonial adventures before returning triumphant to England. In the 1890s and early 20th century Alfred Dampier, Bland Holt and William Anderson staged local melodramas with bush settings and stock figures such as the bushranger, squatter, bushman, gold-digger and spirited colonial heroine in adapted melodramatic plots; Dampier's bushranging play *Robbery Under Arms* (1890) and the stage version of the chronicles of the hayseed Rudd family, *On Our Selection*, as dramatized by Bert Bailey and Edmund Duggan in 1912, remained popular favourites until well into the 1920s. There is no Australian genre equivalent to the 'society drama' of the British theatre, nor did there develop, despite the great popularity of musical theatre, a distinctively Australian strand of operetta or opera. Melodrama with a heavy weighting towards farce remained the predominant form of Australian popular drama until the advent of the 'talkies' virtually spelt its end.

The commercial theatre, 1920–60 The years after the First World War saw the transition from the last of the old actor-managements, providing a wide spectrum of entertainment, to a theatre run largely by entrepreneurs and presenting light entertainment with occasional seasons of culture from abroad. The J. C. Williamson management consolidated its dominance of Australian theatre by absorbing its major competitors, and in 1920 effected a merger with its most significant rival, J. & N. Tait. This virtually monopolistic 'Firm', in the tradition laid down by its founder, staged proven musicals, thrillers and light comedies, usually with imported stars. A number of talented Australians, including **Gladys Moncrieff**, **Robert Helpmann**, Madge Elliott and Dorothy Brunton, had their first opportunity in the lavish Williamson musicals of the 1920s, but in later years local performers were relegated to supporting roles, and many notable performers were lost to the British theatre. The procession of visiting stars continued – Pavlova toured in 1926, Dion Boucicault Junior and his wife Irene Vanbrugh made several visits in the 1920s, and in 1932 **Sybil Thorndike** and **Lewis Casson** toured in a memorable *St Joan*. Often the visiting stars were Australians who had made their names abroad: Melba made two farewell tours of her homeland in 1924–8, Oscar Asche returned in 1922–3, **Judith Anderson** returned from America for a season in 1927, and Cyril Ritchard and Madge Elliott toured in 1946, followed by Cicely Courtneidge two years later. In the 1930s two musicals presented by F. W. Thring, *Collit's Inn* (1933) and *The Cedar Tree* (1934), together with the Williamson production *Blue Mountain Melody* (1934), gave promise of an indigenous musical theatre which, apart from Williamson's much later success with *The Sentimental Bloke* (1957), was not fulfilled. By the 1950s the commercial theatre was even less grounded in Australian life than had been the popular theatre of the 19th century.

The vaudeville and variety theatre, however, developed its own indigenous quality. The variety and minstrel show had been popular since the 1870s, but large-scale vaudeville dates from 1892 when Harry Rickards (Benjamin Harry Leete), a London-born comic singer, opened the Sydney Tivoli theatre, first of a circuit which was to last 75 years. By 1915 Rickards's successor Hugh D. McIntosh was rivalled by the New Zealand management Fuller's (two brothers, Ben and John), who established their own city theatres while also working with the suburban theatre circuits and the travelling tent shows, such as Sorlie's and Barton's Follies, which carried entertainment to the widely dispersed rural populations. Where the Tivoli chain imported stars from the British and American music hall and variety theatre, including **Marie Lloyd**, Little Tich, **W. C. Fields** and the Australian-born Florrie Forde, Fuller's cultivated local artists. In 1916 their Australian pantomime *The Bunyip* at the Sydney Grand Opera House brought together two comedians whose legendary partnership as 'Stiffy and Mo' lasted until 1928. 'Mo', or **Roy Rene**, Australia's first national comedian, with a grotesquely insinuating manner, and his 'straight man' Nat Phillips, together with Jim Gerald, a clown and outrageous pantomime dame, and George Wallace, a 'hayseed' type who specialized in comic falls, turned the vaudeville theatre between the wars into the vehicle for a characteristically Australian style of broad humour and irreverence.

The depression was a major setback for the commercial theatre, with economic difficulties compounded by a crippling entertainment tax at both state and federal levels. Many larger theatres were forced to close, the Tivoli circuit was reduced to one theatre for a time, and Fuller's exchanged live theatre for film: but in the 1930s Rene led a Mike Connors–Queenie Paul company which merged briefly with the Tivoli management. A revival of local variety theatre during the Second World War created new stars such as Gloria Dawn, but in post-war years the Tivoli, under David N. Martin, reverted to imported artists, and many former vaudevillians ended their careers in radio.

The 'literary' drama, 1900–55 The serious drama was not entirely neglected, though it played to a small and fairly literate audience. The first repertory theatre was established in Adelaide in 1908 by Bryceson Treharne, followed in 1911 by **Gregan McMahon**'s Melbourne Repertory Theatre and later his Sydney semi-amateur groups; while Shakespeare was regularly performed from 1916 to the depression by **Allan Wilkie**'s touring company, and in the 1950s by the John Alden Company, at times with the backing of the Williamson management. But there was little if any place for the Australian playwright in the professional theatre. From 1904, when Leon Brodzky had attempted to organize an Australian Stage Society, there were moves to cultivate an indigenous drama of greater depth than the sensation melodramas. From 1909–12 William Moore held annual Australian Drama Nights in Melbourne, at which the earliest work of Australia's first realistic playwright, **Louis Esson**, was staged, and in 1922, influenced by the **Abbey Theatre**, Esson co-founded the Pioneer Players in Melbourne, to perform only Australian works. The group disbanded in 1926, and its attempt to create a folk theatre must be counted a failure, but it remained an inspiration to those committed to the indigenous drama.

From the early 1930s many small amateur and semi-amateur theatres were founded, many by talented women. Carrie Tennant opened her Community Playhouse in Sydney in 1930, and in 1932 the Independent Theatre, also in Sydney, was founded by Doris Fitton. May Hollingworth's Metropolitan Theatre in Sydney, the Little Theatre, Frank Thring Senior's Arrow Theatre, and Gertrude Johnson's National Theatre Movement, all in Melbourne, and the various branches of the left-wing New Theatre in several cities, kept alive the serious drama until the 1950s, and in some cases for much longer. These 'little theatres' were virtually the only outlet for the work of Australian playwrights, and fostered a large number of writers, including Oriel Gray and Mona Brand (both associated with the New Theatres), Henrietta Drake-Brockman, Sydney Tomholt, George Landen Dann, George Farwell, and Frank Hardy. Their plays, for the most part in the prevailing realistic style, drew on historical themes, or depicted the cultural clash between country and city folk, or whites and Aborigines, in the harsh 'outback'. Among the best plays are Betty Roland's *The Touch of Silk* (1928), the touching story of a French war bride whose marriage is destroyed by the tensions of drought and small-town bigotry, and Katharine Susannah Prichard's *Brumby Innes*, a study in black–white relations and unromantic sexuality written in 1927 but not performed until 1972. Many playwrights turned to radio, the major producer of Australian drama between the wars; of the radio playwrights the most important was Douglas Stewart, whose historical verse dramas, several of which were subsequently staged, extended the language of Australian drama beyond the realism of the vernacular. Most Australian plays were seen only by coterie audiences, but in 1948 the Independent Theatre's production of Sumner Locke-Elliott's *Rusty*

Bugles caused a minor furore when the New South Wales police investigated its alleged 'profanity'. The vigour and humour of its depiction of a group of soldiers stationed at an isolated ordnance depot in Northern Territory, cut off from both family life and the action of the war, won the play a wide audience throughout Australia.

The little theatres struggled against great difficulties, apart from their financial precariousness. The spectacular high-budget commercial productions inevitably made the amateur groups seem merely 'worthy' by comparison, while the lack of opportunity outside the overseas dominated commercial theatre led many actors and actresses who had gained their initial experience in the little theatres to pursue their careers abroad – Peter Finch, Coral Browne, Marie Ney, Frank Thring, Ray Barrett and later **Zoë Caldwell**, among many others – so that the smaller theatres were constantly depleted of their finest talent. Until well into the 1950s the highlights of Australian theatre were still the highly publicized tours of overseas stars and companies. The acclaimed **Old Vic** tour of 1948 with **Laurence Olivier** and **Vivien Leigh**, the 1949 and 1952–3 tours of the Stratford Memorial Theatre, the latter including the expatriate actors **Leo McKern** and **Keith Michell**, and the Old Vic tour of 1955 with **Katharine Hepburn** and Robert Helpmann, could only underline the deficiencies of a country unable to provide opportunities for its own talent.

The Australian Elizabethan Theatre Trust, 1954

From the 1940s increasing dissatisfaction was voiced about the theatre's stratification into entertainment industry and amateur substitute for a profession. In 1943 an Australian Council for Music and the Arts was established to take the arts to schools and country areas, and in 1947 the Australian government invited the British director **Tyrone Guthrie** to Australia to report on the feasibility of establishing a national theatre. Guthrie's report, suggesting that such a move was premature, was resented in some quarters, but helped to fuel nationalistic feeling. In 1954 Dr H. C. Coombs, Governor of the Commonwealth Bank, announced a theatre trust to be set up by public subscription and government *pro rata* payments. Named the Australian Elizabethan Theatre Trust to commemorate the Queen's recent Australian visit, it was formally inaugurated on 29 September 1954. Though initially the Trust came under some criticism for appointing an English director, **Hugh Hunt**, and presenting two English plays in conjunction with a commercial management, Garnet H. Carroll, as its opening season, the national aspirations for theatre and drama were acknowledged the following year with the return of Judith Anderson to play Medea, and the production in 1956 of Douglas Stewart's verse drama *Ned Kelly*, with Leo McKern in the title role of Australia's most famous bushranger.

Throughout the 1950s and 1960s the Trust set up theatrical structures through which, in time, an indigenous drama and theatre could mature. In 1956 the national Elizabethan Theatre Trust Opera Company was created, becoming The Australian Opera in 1969; and in 1962 The Australian Ballet under Peggy van Praagh was established after the demise of the Borovansky Ballet which had performed since the 1940s,

The first production of Ray Lawler's *Summer of the Seventeenth Doll*, Union Theatre Company, 1955.

often with the backing of the Williamson 'Firm'. When barely a year old the Trust was remarkably lucky to find what is still Australia's best-known and most-loved play – *Summer of the Seventeenth Doll*, by a then unknown author, **Ray Lawler**. *The Doll*, as it became known, co-winner in a competition run by the Playwrights Advisory Board (an organization for the encouragement of Australian drama set up by Leslie Rees in 1938), was an immediate success from its first production at the Union Theatre, Melbourne, in 1955, and after touring Australia under the Trust's auspices, went on to London and New York. The stimulus to Australian playwriting was immediate, and gave rise to a school of plays in *The Doll*'s mould of three-act realism, making vivid use of the vernacular and colourful working class characters. Of these the most lasting have been Richard Beynon's drama of immigrant Italians, *The Shifting Heart* (1957), Peter Kenna's underworld drama *The Slaughter of St Teresa's Day* (1959), and Alan Seymour's play of the conflict between generations over war remembrance, *The One Day of the Year* (1960). Most of them were staged by the Trust Players, a core company of eight actors under the director Robin Lovejoy, which was established in 1959 and performed widely throughout Australia until the rigours of touring brought about its disbanding in 1961.

The effects of subsidy

The 1960s saw radical changes in Australian theatre thanks to government subsidy of the performing arts, consolidated in 1968 with the formation of the Australian Council for the Arts (renamed the Australia Council in 1975). Fully professional subsidized companies were set up in each of the state capital cities, largely superseding the little theatres of the previous three decades. Two of these new 'state companies' grew directly out of links with universities; in 1968 the Union Theatre Repertory Company, initially at Melbourne University, became the Melbourne Theatre Company under John Sumner, while in Sydney the University of New South Wales Drama Foundation under Robert Quentin comprised Australia's first training school for theatre professionals, the National Institute of Dramatic Art (NIDA), founded in 1958, the first academic drama department, and the Old Tote Theatre Company. (The Old Tote was replaced as New South Wales's state company by the Sydney Theatre Company in 1980.) The creation of the South Australian Theatre Company (1965) in Adelaide, and Queensland Theatre Company (1969) in Brisbane, together with the National Theatre Company which had been formed from the Perth Repertory Club in 1956, and the Tasmanian Theatre Company (1973) in Hobart (the latter two now superseded by the Western Australian Theatre Company and the Tasmanian Theatre Trust), meant that within two decades of the Trust's foundation Australia had a professional theatre network providing regular employment for performers, directors and designers who in an earlier generation would have made their careers abroad.

The change came about not only at the expense of the little theatres – the 1960s saw the closure of many of the large commercial theatres. The vaudeville and variety tradition dating back to the 1890s virtually came to an end in 1966 with the closure of the Tivoli circuit, though its spirit had seen a revival in the 1950s and 1960s in the wickedly satrical Phillip Street Revues in Sydney. The J. C. Williamson management had become increasingly conservative in its musical entertainments, and the spiralling costs of its spectacular productions caused the almost century-old Firm to close in 1976, though the famous name continued to be used by a new management under Kenn Brodziak, Michael Edgley and several others.

The indigenous drama was slower to develop, The short-lived burst of realistic drama after *The Doll* had ended with several playwrights emigrating to Britain, but the early 1960s saw two significant developments – the rise to international stardom of **Barry Humphries**, whose archetypal housewife character Edna Everage had had a cult following since the mid-1950s, and the emergence of the celebrated novelist **Patrick White** as playwright. In contrast to the prevailing realism of the drama since the First World War, both writers, Humphries in particular, opened up a rich vein of satirical caricature, anticipating the cartoon style of a 'new wave' of playwrights later in the decade. (The rejection of White's first play, *The Ham Funeral*, as 'unpleasant' by the Adelaide Festival Committee, before its staging at Adelaide University and subsequent production by the Trust, epitomized the censorship battles of the 1960s, in which attempts to suppress such productions as the Sydney New Theatre's *America Hurrah!* in 1968 eventually led to the more liberal attitudes of the 1970s.) From 1966 seasons of new Australian plays were held in a small church, the Jane Street Theatre, initially under the University of New South Wales Drama Foundation with assistance from the Gulbenkian Foundation, and from 1969 under the management of NIDA. The Jane Street seasons, intended primarily as workshop experience for the authors,

staged the work of a number of new playwrights, including the novelist Thomas Keneally, **Dorothy Hewett**, and Rodney Milgate; but the response to an adventurous season of plays at the Old Tote in 1968 seemed to confirm the long-standing managerial scepticism towards the Australian playwright. By the late 1960s the performance of Australian plays by the professional theatre was still minimal. The new state companies based their repertoires firmly on the classics and recent British or American successes, and though not yet a decade old, were increasingly seen as the reactionary 'establishment' by a new generation of potential actors and writers.

The alternative theatres, 1967–75 A new era in Australian theatre began in 1967 in Carlton, a working-class and immigrant suburb of Melbourne with a large student population, when Betty Burstall opened an intimate coffee-theatre on the model of the alternative venues in New York, and named La Mama after one of them. La Mama quickly became a focus for new poets, musicians and actors, and a group of playwrights including **Jack Hibberd**, **John Romeril**, **David Williamson** and Barry Oakley. The La Mama Company of actors and writers also presented street theatre, often at the large anti-Vietnam-war demonstrations, and toured factories in agit-prop political pieces. In 1970 they moved to a large warehouse theatre, the Pram Factory, and renamed themselves the Australian Performing Group, reflecting their commitment to an indigenous drama and playing style; the Pram Factory quickly gained a reputation for robust and irreverent productions drawing on the old Australian vaudeville, variety, and pantomime traditions. For ten years the APG remained a theatrical cooperative and umbrella organization for factory tours, innovative versions of the classics, Soapbox Circus (antecedent of the internationally known Circus Oz), film-making and a writers' agency. Though essentially an actors' company and committed to collective creation, which produced such successes as *The Hills Family Show* (1975), a hilarious back-stage view of an old-time travelling theatre troupe, the APG also fostered a number of talented playwrights, some associated with the company since the La Mama days – Hibberd, Romeril, Oakley – and others, such as Barry Dickins and Tim Robertson, sharing the Pram Factory's radical political and theatrical commitment and often anarchic comic style.

Sydney's version of alternative theatre grew out of the blockbusting Jane Street success in 1970 of *The Legend of King O'Malley*, Michael Boddy's and Bob Ellis's revue-style portrait of a former political figure, which went on to an Australia-wide tour. Later the same year its director **John Bell**, with Ken Horler, founded the small Nimrod Street Theatre in the inner-city suburb of Darlinghurst. Unlike the APG, which even as a subsidized company remained 'anti-establishment' in philosophy and structure, Nimrod was a fully professional, if unconventional, theatre. Its early productions included irreverent musical treatments of Australian history, innovative productions of Shakespeare, and an outrageous transvestite pantomime, *Hamlet on Ice* (1972). It also attracted new Sydney playwrights such as Boddy and Ellis, Ron Blair, Jim McNeill, Dick Hall, and **Alex Buzo**, who, like their Melbourne counterparts, bypassed traditional

forms to create works of an almost journalistic immediacy, and in demolishing the pretensions and hypocrisies of Australian society quickly found a responsive
young audience. While the APG remained by choice an
alternative group until its self-dissolution in 1981,
Nimrod moved in 1974 to larger premises and established itself as a major mainstream company, often
more adventurous than the state companies with which
it stands comparison.

The acceptance of the new playwrights by the
professional theatre came about largely through the
work of David Williamson, whose *The Removalists* and
Don's Party, initially staged at La Mama and the Pram
Factory, had notable successes in Sydney – the former
in 1971 at Nimrod followed by a commercial production by Harry M. Miller, and the latter at Jane Street in
1972 prior to an Australian tour and production in
London. These, with *O'Malley* and the many long-
running productions of Jack Hibberd's participatory
wedding play, *Dimboola* (1969), removed any doubt
that audiences would respond enthusiastically to Australian plays. By the mid-1970s, after a century and a
half of theatrical activity, Australia had a theatre created
by its own actors, directors, and designers, and a drama
that, at least in part, reflected its own society.

Contemporary Australian theatre Today the theatre
has a range and diversity comparable to that of many
older cultures. Public acceptance of the performing arts
as an important part of Australian life is seen in the
building of large performance complexes in several
capitals, the most famous of which is the Sydney Opera
House. Built to a modified design by the Danish
architect Joern Utzon, it has some limitations as a
performance space, but since its opening in 1973 its
flamboyant white 'sails' on the edge of Sydney Harbour
have become a symbol of renewed interest in the
performing arts. Similar complexes, incorporating
large auditoria and intimate studio theatres, have been
opened in Adelaide, Melbourne and Brisbane. The
marked increase in theatrical activity is largely due to
the Australia Council, whose Performing Arts Board,
composed of theatre and music practitioners, distributes annual grants to the major companies (the Australian Opera and Australian Ballet are funded by
special grants) and to the many smaller companies,
fringe and community groups, and individual artists
through direct grants and Special Projects, Limited Life
and travel grants. State governments and some local
councils also offer assistance, and business sponsorship
is increasingly important. Until 1991 the Elizabethan
Theatre Trust remained an entrepreneurial body with
some Australia Council aid, while branches of the
federal Arts Council body promote touring and local
enterprises in various states. Two major international
arts festivals, the Adelaide Festival every two years and
the annual Perth Festival, provide first-class overseas
theatre as well as promoting Australian work.

The six state theatre companies are the mainstay of
traditional performance, though most state companies
present a wide spectrum of classical and modern work,
and have access to informal flexible venues for experimental productions. A number of smaller theatres in
each capital (Sydney's Q Theatre in the outer suburbs,
Ensemble theatre-in-the-round, and Off-Broadway
and Belvoir Street theatres; La Boite in Brisbane;

Playbox Theatre Company and Anthill in Melbourne;
Troupe and the Stage Company in Adelaide; the Hole
in the Wall in Perth) are important outlets for overseas
drama and new Australian writing. Australian material
is now integral at all levels of activity; directors of
European classics often commission Australian translations, while outstanding directors such as **Jim
Sharman**, **George Ogilvie**, Rex Cramphorn,
Richard Wherrett and Rodney Fisher have made their
reputations as much through Australian plays as the
classics and overseas works – Sharman has been
associated with the work of Patrick White, and Fisher
with that of David Williamson and **Dorothy Hewett**.
Since 1975 the annual National Playwrights Conference has provided workshops and readings of new
plays, many of which have subsequently received full
professional production, and certain theatre companies, such as the Griffin Theatre in Sydney, are
orientated towards staging Australian material.
Though David Williamson remains the most successful
playwright, the energetic, topical and celebratory
drama of the 1970s has to some extent been supplanted
by a more urbane, cosmopolitan and even cerebral style
in the work of **Louis Nowra** and **Stephen Sewell**;
other established playwrights include Steve J. Spears
(whose monodrama *The Elocution of Benjamin Franklin*
won the New York critics' Off-Broadway Award for
1980), Ron Elisha, Doreen Clark, Jennifer Compton,
David Allen, George Hutchinson, Alma de Groen,
Michael Gow, Hannie Rayson and the Nick Enright–
Terence Clark musical theatre team. The solo performers Reg Livermore, with his outrageous lampoons
of reactionary social attitudes, and Max Gillies, a brilliant mimic of political and public figures, are the successors in satirizing Australian society to Barry Humphries.

Three important areas of growth are youth,
women's and Aboriginal theatre. The Patch Theatre in
Adelaide, and numerous children's theatre and theatre-
in-education teams, including Arena in Melbourne,
and Jigsaw in Canberra, Toe Truck, Pipi Storm, Pact
and the Theatre of the Deaf in Sydney, the Magpie team
in Adelaide and Salamanca company in Hobart, and
puppet companies such as Handspan in Melbourne,
Spare Parts in Perth, and the Marionette Theatre of
Australia in Sydney have presented schools shows or
holiday entertainment. There are also participatory youth
theatres such as the Carclew Youth Performing Arts
Centre in Adelaide, and the Australian Theatre for
Young People and Shopfront in Sydney; the latter has
since 1977 conducted national Young Playwrights'
Conferences, and in 1985 initiated the first international
Young Playwrights' Conference in Sydney. Youth
theatre festivals are held in most cities, with the annual
'Come Out' festival in Adelaide as the major national
event. Women's theatre largely began in the early 1970s
when an offshoot of the Carlton alternative theatre, the
Women's Theatre Group, provided opportunities for
performers, directors and writers such as Val Kirwin,
Jan Cornall, Jenny Kemp, Kerry Dwyer and Fay
Mokotow, while in Sydney in 1981–2 a Women and
Theatre Project for established professionals was funded by the Australia Council. Among the many groups
featuring women's theatre have been the Canberra
group Fool's Gallery, directed by Carol Woodrow,
Home Cooking in Melbourne, and the Brisbane
Women's Theatre, while the singer–author Robyn

Archer has brought a wider public to theatre with a feminist orientation through shows such as *The Pack of Women* (1983), a cabaret-style evening of songs, poems and sketches first performed in London. In the early 1970s, following a revue titled *Basically Black* (1972) at Nimrod Theatre, a Black Theatre group was created under the direction of Betty Fisher in Redfern, a Sydney inner suburb with a large urban Aboriginal population. Its most notable production was Robert Merritt's *The Cake Man* (1975), a depiction of so-called 'benevolent' white influence on Aboriginal life which represented Australia at the World Theatre Festival in Denver, Colorado, in 1982. Perth poet Jack Davis has written several plays, one of which, *The Dreamers*, toured Australia in 1983 with great success; in Sydney a training school and company, the Aboriginal Islander Dance Theatre, and Eora, a new Redfern group, give promise of greater Aboriginal participation in the theatre.

The 1980s have seen a revival of 'fringe' and alternative theatre, though less directly political and writer-orientated than that of the 1960s. Political and popular groups such as the Popular Theatre Troupe in Queensland and Death-Defying Theatre in Sydney have performed in shopping centres, factories and schools, but the fringe theatre of the 1980s seems directed more to the exploration of theatrical styles, sometimes through evocative images, as in the All Out Ensemble's work, and sometimes in combination with mime and dance in companies such as Entr'acte and the One Extra Company in Sydney. (The Sydney Dance Company, under its director Graeme Murphy, has also been particularly innovative in combining modern dance with theatrical and dramatic qualities.) Numerous theatre restaurants and cabaret-style venues chiefly in Sydney and Melbourne have created a new brand of comedy from teams such as the Melbourne duo Los Trios Ringbarkus and the Sydney group Funny Stories, as well as many individual comedians, a number of whom, like Sue Ingleton, deal specifically with women's issues.

If the 1970s impetus was towards nationalism, the emphasis of the 1980s is on decentralization. Australia has 15 million people on a continent almost the size of the United States, but the concentration of population in the capital cities (Sydney and Melbourne together have over one-third of the population) has inevitably led to theatre's focus on the urban areas, and recently to a drift towards the largest city, Sydney, compounded in the view of some by the Australia Council's headquarters being in that city. Extensive touring in country areas has not always proved feasible, and regionally based theatres such as the New Moon Company in Northern Queensland and the Harvest Company in South Australia have been established to counter the isolation of country communities from the performing arts. The Australia Council's policy from 1986 is to limit grants to the major companies to an indexed 'ceiling', in order to promote a wider range of smaller groups more closely related to specific audiences. In some rural areas theatre-in-education teams and community theatres such as the Murray River Performing Group and Riverina Theatre Company have already developed a strong local identity, and regional growth of this kind is the present aim of funding. Community theatre groups, both urban and regional, are also encouraged, some fully professional companies focusing on local issues, and others participatory groups in which professional leaders work with local amateurs or disadvantaged groups such as the physically handicapped and unemployed. The Victorian College of the Arts, the second major training institution for theatre professionals (the third is the Western Australian Academy of the Performing Arts), and many of the training courses in the Colleges of Advanced Education, place a strong emphasis on community theatre arts in addition to traditional theatre skills. Regional and grass-roots growth, it is hoped, will bring the performing arts to those formerly isolated, either geographically or socially, from mainstream theatre, though the development has not been without its critics among those who see theatre in more traditional terms.

Television drama Australia gained television in 1956; besides a government-funded national network run by the ABC (Australian Broadcasting Corporation), there are a number of commercial networks – the larger cities each have three commercial channels – and since 1980 there has been a government-sponsored multi-cultural channel in several cities. Initially local drama was submerged by British and American imports, though Crawford Productions' police series *Homicide*, beginning in 1964, and the ABC's serial of country life, *Bellbird* (1967–77), had popular followings. From 1967 a quota for locally-produced drama was imposed on the commercial channels, initially 30 minutes per week, and currently 102 hours per year. This, with the founding in 1973 of a national Film and Television School in Sydney (there is a second training institution at the Swinburne Institute of Technology in Melbourne), has led to a marked increase in both the quantity and quality of local drama. Since the 1970s local serials and series, most created by the two major production companies, Crawfords and the Grundy Organization, have become a feature of commercial television. Among the longest-running have been *The Sullivans* (1976–83), showing a working-class family during war years, the hospital series *The Young Doctors* (1976–82), the domestic dramas *The Restless Years* (1977–82), and *Sons and Daughters* (1982–), *Prisoner* (1979–), set in a women's penitentiary, and *A Country Practice* (1981–), set in a country town. While similar to American soap operas, such serials are an important balance to the still dominant imported drama, and sometimes explore current social issues. The ABC has produced many high-quality shorter serials, including the goldmining story *Rush* (1973–4) in collaboration with France's Antenne 2 and Scottish Global Television; the bushranging drama *Ben Hall* (1974–5), a joint Australian–Canadian production; *I Can Jump Puddles* (1980–1), the story of a country youth between the wars, *Scales of Justice* (1983), an exposé of police corruption, and *Palace of Dreams* (1985), a story of Jewish immigrants in Sydney. It has also presented seasons of television plays and comedy series, though neither the self-contained play nor situation comedy has been as important in Australia as in some other countries.

The 1980s have seen a number of mini-series, thanks to the federal government's generous tax concessions since 1981 for investment in Australian films. Produced by companies such as Kennedy Miller for the commercial channels, some, like the Pegasus production *Against the Wind* (1979), have been set in the colonial past; others, including *Waterfront* (1985) and *Bodyline* (1984), have been set in the more recent past. Among the more controversial have been *The Dismissal* (1983), a semi-documentary depicting the 1975 Labour government's dismissal from office, *The Last Bastion* (1984), exposing the Allies' tenuous commitment to Australia in the Second World War, and *The Cowra Breakout* (1985), based on the escape attempt of Japanese prisoners-of-war in a country town. These mini-series have been culturally significant in bringing local drama to a wide audience, and sometimes in provoking heated reexamination of Australian history.

Much diverse theatrical activity has developed in the 30 years since the founding of the Elizabethan Theatre Trust. That the increasing respectability and acceptance of theatre in the 1980s has been gained at the expense of the nationalistic fervour and exuberance of the 1970s is perhaps inevitable after heady pioneering days, and perhaps also a reflection of grimmer economic times. In particular the more cosmopolitan drama of Nowra and Sewell, after the earlier 'folk' drama of the previous decade, has tended to polarize those who believe the theatre's function is to celebrate and explore Australian society, and those who see theatre in less localized terms. The vitality, irreverence and freshness of recent 'fringe' theatre, ranging from stylistic exploration to social comment, is evidence that the two aims need not be incompatible.

The future will almost certainly include other influences besides the still predominantly British and American traditions. Australia is closer to Asia than to anywhere except New Zealand, and immigration, business and travel contacts have greatly strengthened its ties with the Pacific region. Individual directors and groups such as Rex Cramphorn's Performance Syndicate in the 1970s have explored Asian styles, and playwrights including Buzo and Nowra have written on Asian themes. In Sydney the One Extra Company has had a Malaysian Chinese director, and in 1983–4 Chinese acrobats from Nanjing spent several months training the children of the Flying Fruit Fly Circus; Japanese artists have worked with Australian puppetry companies, and cultural exchanges between Australian and Asian companies are increasing. Australia itself has since the Second World War become the second most multi-cultural society in the world, after Israel. Established playwrights such as Louis Nowra and Janis Balodis have written of the immigrant experience, individual ethnic communities have created theatre groups performing in their own languages, and the Sydney company Sidetrack has cultivated a multi-cultural policy through employing performers from many national backgrounds. With an increasing number of performers and writers from non-British backgrounds, the mainstream theatre must increasingly reflect a wider range of cultural influences.

A feature of Australian theatre in the past decade has been the interaction of mainstream and fringe theatres, with many performers, writers and directors moving freely between them. This flexibility is the best guarantee that the Australian theatre will not relapse, as so often in the past, into merely reproducing the received traditions of overseas theatre, but will explore those qualities which make it a living expression of Australia's increasingly complex society.   MW

> *See*: M. Clunies Ross, 'North-Central Arnhem Land'; C. Ellis, 'Antatirinya Dance'; A. Grau, 'YOI: The Dance of the Tiwi'; M. Llinos Dail-Jones, 'Warlpiri Dance'; J. von Sturmer, 'Cape York Peninsula'; S. Wild, 'Australian Aboriginal Dance'; in *International Encyclopaedia of Dance*, New York, in preparation; J. Allen (ed.), *Entertainment Arts in Australia*, Sydney, 1968; P. Fitzpatrick, *After 'The Doll'*, Melbourne, 1979; P. Holloway (ed.), *Contemporary Australian Drama*, Sydney, 1987; E. Irvin, *A Dictionary of the Australian Theatre*, Sydney, 1985; E. Irvin, *Theatre Comes to Australia*, St Lucia, 1971; H. Love (ed.), *The Australian Stage: A Documentary History*, Sydney, 1984; H. Love, *The Golden Age of Australian Opera*, Sydney, 1981; L. Rees, *A History of Australian Drama*, Sydney, 1978; J. West, *Theatre in Australia*, Sydney, 1978; M. Williams, *Australia on the Popular Stage, 1829–1929*, Melbourne, 1983.

Austria

To 1914   The cultural traditions of Austria are quite distinct from those of her larger neighbour, Germany. This is clearly apparent in the history of their respective theatres. While professional theatre in Germany was, for much of the 18th century, an alien hybrid, the Austrian theatre was an indigenous phenomenon, growing spontaneously as a popular institution. Furthermore, unlike Germany, whose theatrical tradition has grown around several provincial cities, in Austria most significant developments in the theatre have taken place in the capital city, Vienna.

During the Middle Ages, Vienna had been a major centre for the production of religious drama, passion plays with massive casts being given in various locales of the city on Good Friday and Corpus Christi. The familiarity of the Viennese with theatre no doubt eased the way for the acceptance of secular, humanistic drama, based on Roman models, staged under the aegis of Konrad Celtis (1459–1508) at the University of Vienna early in the 16th century. But no continuous theatrical activity occurred at this time; indeed it was not until the mid-17th century that the three modes of theatre that would have a potent formative influence on the subsequent development of Austrian theatre had fully evolved. The first of these was the Jesuit drama (see **Jesuitendrama**) which was to give the Austrian theatre one of its most characteristic themes, the conflict between supernatural and human planes of experience; it flourished in the schools. The second was the **commedia dell'arte**, which engendered in audiences and actors alike a strong taste for improvisation, and could be seen in the work of several travelling Italian troupes and, occasionally, in the **Englische Komödianten**. Thirdly, there was Italian opera, first produced solely at the Habsburg court, but it gained in popularity and created among the Viennese a widespread taste for musical expression and lavish spectacle on stage.

These three forms of theatre were gradually united on the Viennese stage in the course of the 18th century, forming one of the most attractive theatrical cultures of Europe. The founding of the popular theatre has traditionally been dated as 1711 when **Josef Stranitzky**, an improvisational player who led his own wandering troupe, took over the Kärntnertortheater in Vienna from an Italian company. He instantly won the support of the populace for his racy plays on local life, which required considerable improvisation. Stranitzky was also famed for his creation of the generic figure of **Hanswurst**, a wily, coarse servant, initially of rustic origin, but after Stranitzky's translation to Vienna, he was made into an urban figure, who had much in common with his Italian counterpart **Harlequin**. The irreverent spirit of Hanswurst was the dominant influence on the early years of the Viennese popular theatre, but in the hands of Stranitzky's successor **Gottfried Prehauser** (1699–1769) and, later, the comic actor Josef Felix Kurz (1717–83) the tone was softened, even sentimentalized, greater attention being paid on the one hand to realistic characterization, on the other to the relationship between the human and magic world, a concern which links the Viennese popular drama with its Jesuit predecessors. During the middle of the 18th century, improvisation gradually disappeared from the stage. Though this change might initially seem to indicate a decline in energy, toward the end of the century the Viennese theatre produced one of the greatest works of any popular theatrical tradition, *The Magic Flute* (1791) by Mozart and **Schikaneder**.

The change in the popular theatre was caused in part by external pressure. **Josef von Sonnenfels**, one of the Viennese literati, was a follower of the German professor **Johann Gottsched**, and in his *Letters on the Viennese Stage* (1767), he advocated a decorous, unimprovised drama that could lead toward the education of the populace. These ideas were fundamental to the establishment by the Emperor Josef II of the Habsburg Court Theatre, the **Burgtheater**, as a national theatre. Despite early vicissitudes, this grew to be the pre-eminent theatre of the German-speaking world. During the 19th century, especially under the direction of **Josef Schreyvogel** and **Heinrich Laube**, the repertoire came to include all ages and styles of Western drama, while the elegant underplaying and ensemble of the Burgtheater's famous company became a byword in the German theatre. Although the Burgtheater has always regarded itself as an 'actor's theatre', it has also had some notable house playwrights, especially during the 19th century. By far the most important was **Franz Grillparzer**, whose adaptation of various foreign forms of drama, especially of the ancient Greek and Spanish baroque, was very characteristic of his country's international outlook. **Eduard von Bauernfeld**, whose skilfully written, light comedies of Viennese life were immensely popular in his time, was another of the mainstays of the Burgtheater repertoire during the 19th century.

The great resilience of Viennese theatre is demonstrated by the refusal of the popular theatre to be overshadowed by the successful and prestigious Burgtheater. In fact, despite Sonnenfels's wish to extinguish the popular theatre, the last decades of the 18th century and the first half of the 19th century represent the full flowering of this theatre. In addition to *The Magic Flute*, the 18th century saw other significant additions to the popular repertoire, most notably in the plays of Philipp Hafner, whose famous work *Megära the Terrible Witch* (1755) is possibly the first example of the Viennese **Volksstück** in which magic and human characters are mingled. The turn of the century saw countless additions to the repertoire, most significantly in the highly theatrical plays of the prolific Josef Gleich (1772–1841), Karl Meisl (1775–1853), and Adolphe Bäuerle (1786–1859). While the literary level of their works is not especially high, a colleague of these playwrights, **Ferdinand Raimund**, made out of the magic *Volksstück*, or *Zauberstück*, plays that are among the few masterpieces of the romantic theatre, especially *The Alpine King and the Misanthrope* (1828) and *The Spendthrift* (1834). Raimund committed suicide, possibly in apprehension of the rise of a new playwright, whose work seemed to threaten the fundamental assumptions and integrated vision of the *Zauberstück*, **Johann Nestroy**. Over the middle of the 19th century, in Nestroy's plays the satirical vein of the popular theatre, which had never entirely disappeared, reached complete fulfilment. In fact, Nestroy's dramatic work, both parodies and social comedies, possibly represents the most consummate achievement in stage comedy in the German language. After Nestroy's retirement in 1860, the energy seemed to leave the popular theatre. In its years of decline, the most characteristic genre of the popular theatre was the attractive though comparatively devitalized operetta.

During its heyday, the Viennese popular theatre, like the Burgtheater, maintained an unusually sophisticated level of acting. Several actors, like Stranitzky with Hanswurst, evolved generic comic figures; Kurz was responsible for introducing the figure of Bernadon, a young adventurer, Johann Laroche (1745–1806) introduced **Kasperl**, a figure with some affinities to **Punch**, and Anton Hasenhut (1766–1841) created the pathetic Thaddädl. These characters recurred in several of the hundreds of plays that composed the popular repertoire and the audiences' affection for them ensured well-packed auditoriums. The particular enjoyment of the Viennese audiences for the discipline of acting suggests that improvisation did not disappear entirely from the stage; in fact Nestroy, as versatile and celebrated an actor as he was a playwright, was occasionally in trouble for passages of action, for speeches and ripostes, that had not passed the censor's approval, as they had been made up on the spur of the moment.

The widespread popularity of theatre in Vienna meant a consistent expansion in the number of theatres. In its most flourishing years, three of the most famous 'suburban' theatres – i.e. those theatres not in the city centre like the Burgtheater – opened their doors; of these, two, the Theater in der Josefstadt and the Theater an der Wien, are still in use today. The third, the Theater in der Leopoldstadt, was replaced by the Carltheater in the middle of the 19th century. The abundance of theatres in Vienna has led several historians to characterize it as quintessentially a 'theatre city'. Although this epithet has been used to describe the supposedly Viennese trait of treating life as a play, as if in ironic denial of its more serious aspects, it also identifies the unique role of theatre in the city's social life. In the early 19th century, the suburban theatres and the Burgtheater dominated, but as the century progressed, several more theatres opened, such as the Stadttheater (1880) and the Deutsches Volkstheater (1889), which attempted a more serious repertoire than the declining popular theatre. In addition, the Court Opera, which opened a splendid new opera house on the Ringstrasse in 1869, was one of the centres of the city's closely aligned musical and theatre lives.

As the popular theatre declined during the latter half of the 19th century, the most successful works of Raimund and Nestroy passed into the Burgtheater repertoire. Meanwhile, a school of playwriting emerged which owed as much to European as it did to Viennese models. A deep concern with the injustices and deprivations of everyday life had been apparent in the rather grim, realistic plays of **Ludwig Anzengruber**, who wrote about the peasantry as well as about city life. However, both a more characteristically Viennese note and a European tone could be heard in the plays of **Arthur Schnitzler**, all of which are impressionistic or naturalistic dramatizations of Viennese life. In them the playwright's unceasing and stringent irony points toward, though never rigorously spells out, a moralistic judgement of the city's society, especially in matters of sexual morality. Early in life Schnitzler belonged to an informal group of writers known as Jung Wien (Young Vienna), who were set upon modernizing the city's literature. Among the most prominent writers in this group were **Hermann Bahr**, who achieved more as a contentious theatre critic and as an interpreter of contemporary literary theory than as a dramatist, and **Hugo von Hofmannsthal**. As a young man, Hofmannsthal wrote verse drama that showed clearly the influence of French symbolism. Later, having suffered a crisis of confidence in the ability of language to express his thoughts effectively, Hofmannsthal turned to writing librettos for the opera composer, Richard Strauss. Hofmannsthal did not, however, abandon the legitimate theatre, and his later plays are remarkable for their author's ability to combine a concern for the modern world with traditional dramatic material. In this respect his greatest and most Austrian play is *The Tower*. Not only does the play focus on the rise of totalitarianism, but thematically it expresses the tension between human and supernatural planes of experience. In this play, Hofmannsthal's rich, allusive technique reminds us of past ages of drama, of **Shakespeare**, the Spanish baroque (it is based on **Calderón**'s *Life is a Dream*), and the various indigenous forms of Austrian drama. This arouses in the audience a profound sense of what has been lost by the modern world. In doing so the play expresses in the most positive and humane way its country's characteristic, deep attachment to the past. sw

Since 1914   With the First World War and the destruction of the Austro-Hungarian Empire, Austrian theatre effectively lost its existence as an independent entity, becoming increasingly integrated with that of Germany. Sharing much of the same history of the dissolution of the monarchy and a weak republic, the Anschluss and fascism which drove almost all the leading writers into exile and shut down the stages completely in 1945, foreign occupation and, more recently, a high standard of material prosperity, Austrian dramatists have been preoccupied with the same kind of themes as their German counterparts, and adopted comparable styles of representation. In addition there has been a continual interchange of actors and directors, with **Max Pallenberg**, **Fritz Kortner**, or in the younger generation **Hans Hollman**, who estab-

lished themselves on the German stage, or **Berthold Viertel**, who eventually returned to lead the rebuilt Vienna Burgtheater after making his reputation at the **Deutsches Theater** in Berlin and working with the **Berliner Ensemble**.

Despite the dominance of Berlin as a centre for theatrical experimentation during the 1920s, however, this influence has by no means been one sided. It was an Austrian, **Max Reinhardt**, who became perhaps the most significant single figure in German theatre during the first part of the century with his eclectic range of productions. His stagings of **Wedekind** and **Strindberg** (1912–13) set the style for early expressionist works, and it was under his aegis at the Deutsches Theater that the plays of the Young Germany movement were performed, while productions like Karl Vollmoeller's *Miracle* (1917) brought the traditional Austrian religious themes and spectacular pageant production to Germany. But he also founded the modern Salzburg Festival together with Hofmannsthal in 1918, which under Reinhardt's direction became the leading festival theatre in Europe, characterized by his open-air productions of Hofmannsthal's *Everyman*.

Even in movements specifically identified with Germany such as expressionism, Austrian dramatists made significant contributions. **Oskar Kokoschka**'s work prefigured its violent sexual themes and psychological symbolism as early as 1910, **Arnolt Bronnen** and **Franz Werfel** were among its leading exponents, while the drama of Anton Wildgans (1881–1932), who also directed the Burgtheater during the 1920s, transposed expressionist elements into a distinctively Austrian form. Alongside this avant-garde work, traditional Austrian theatre continued to flourish with the revival of the miracle play by Max Mell (1882–1971), the historical tragedies of **Richard Beer-Hoffman** or **Ferdinand Bruckner**, both of whom turned to themes of radical persecution in response to the Jewish Holocaust, and the drama of ideas developed by **Fritz Hochwälder**.

Successful as they were, these traditional works seem dated from a modern perspective in contrast to the plays of **Ödön von Horváth**. Following **Karl Kraus** and Franz Csokor (1885–1969), he transformed the satiric popular theatre of Nestroy into highly political images of social hypocrisy and the corruption of cultural values. Rediscovered in the 1960s, his work inspired the modern *Volksstück* (Folk Play), one of the major forms of contemporary German drama, whose Austrian exponents are **Wolfgang Bauer**, Harald Sommer (b. 1935) and Peter Turrini (b. 1944). Another influence has been the Vienna Group, active between 1954 and 1964. Its playwrights Konrad Bayer (1932–64) and H. C. Artmann (b. 1921) adapted the traditional Kasperl figure for dialect dramas that prefigure the linguistic themes of **Peter Handke**, whose experimental 'speaking plays' have achieved an international reputation, while his later surrealistic drama – like the nihilistic symbolism of the other leading contemporary Austrian playwright, **Thomas Bernhard** – continues to be recognized as among the most significant work on the contemporary German-speaking stage.   CI

See: C. E. Williams, *The Broken Eagle: the Politics of Austrian Literature from Empire to Anschluss*, London, 1974.

Auto sacramental   A one-act religious allegory

performed on the Feast of Corpus Christi in Spain from the 16th to the 18th centuries. In Madrid four per year (till 1648, thereafter only two) were sponsored by the city authorities, **Calderón** being the sole author from 1648 till his death (1681). They were performed in the open air on a stage with scenery mounted on two carts (four after 1648) drawn up behind. Illustrating the central dogmas of the Catholic Church, they became more complex in form and staging under Calderón, with increasing use of special effects. Considered unsuitable by the Bourbon Enlightenment, they were suppressed in 1765.   CL

Averchenko, Arkady Timofeevich (1881–1925) Russian writer of humorous stories, *feuilletons* and dramatic miniatures satirizing contemporary mores, vulgarity, pretence and artistic trends. He contributed to and was eventual editor of St Petersburg's leading satirical weekly, *Satyricon* (1908–14), whose staff included writers N. A. Teffi, B. F. Geier and **M. A. Kuzmin** and artists **A. N. Benois** and M. V. Dobuzhinsky. He left in 1913 to edit *New Satyricon* until it was closed for publishing anti-Bolshevik satire. From 1912 to 1916 he contributed short comic sketches and vaudevilles to the Liteiny, Crooked Mirror and Troitsky Theatres in St Petersburg. These included parodies of **L. Tolstoi's** *The Power of Darkness* and of futurism (*Woe from Futurism*). He published four volumes of one-act plays and miniatures, a highly popular collection of stories, entitled *Jolly Oysters* (1910), the three-volume *Stories* (1910–11) and, in 1920 the anti-Bolshevik collection *Unclean Power*, which led to his emigration that same year, eventually ending in Prague (1922).   SG

Avignon festival Theatre festival established by **Jean Vilar** in 1947 in order to provide a context for theatre-going different from that of the Paris boulevard theatres. The festival was, and still is, held in July, when commercial and state theatres in France are closed. Vilar's work at Avignon successfully created an atmosphere of celebration and participation and laid the foundations for his production style at the **TNP** in the 1950s; his choice of Avignon helped give impetus to the **decentralization movement**. Avignon has played a significant role in the development of French theatre since 1947 (see **France**).   DB

Avilés Blonda, Máximo (1931–) Dominican Republic playwright, poet, with degrees in philosophy and law, founder and director of the University Theatre. *Las manos vacías* (*Empty Hands*, 1959) is a post-war study; *La otra estrella en el cielo* (*The Other Star in the Sky*, 1963) deals metaphorically with a 15th-century Italian struggle for power: *Yo, Bertolt Brecht* (*I, Bertolt Brecht*, 1966) is a vanguardist adaptation of epic scenes, and *Pirámide 179* (*Pyramid 179*, 1969) applies Brechtian techniques to national hatred over the Haitian boundary issue.   GW

Ayalneh, Mulat (*fl.* 1970s) Ethiopian playwright. After being director of the University of Addis Ababa Cultural Centre he assumed responsibility for culture in COPWE (Commission for the Party of the Working People of Ethiopia). One of the most consistent writers of pro-revolutionary material, including the Amharic plays *When the Fire is Burning* (1975), *Pumpkin and Gourd* (1979) and *The Peasant Woman's Beacon* (1977).   RK

Ayckbourn, Alan (1939–) British playwright and director, who began his career as a stage manager and actor with Sir **Donald Wolfit's** touring company, joined **Stephen Joseph's** theatre-in-the-round at Scarborough in 1959, became a drama producer with the BBC in Leeds and a founder of the **Victoria Theatre, Stoke-on-Trent**, before returning to Scarborough as Director of Productions in 1970. Ayckbourn has been the most successful writer of sharp comedies about middle-class manners and morals since the war and his only rival internationally would be the American dramatist, **Neil Simon**. Although his first play to reach the West End, *Mr Whatnot*, was written in 1963, Ayckbourn's major commercial successes began with *Relatively Speaking* (London, 1967) and *How the Other Half Loves* (1970). Throughout the 1970s, he was prolific – with a sequence of comedy hits which started with *Time and Time Again* (1971), *Absurd Person Singular* (1973), rose to the complicated heights of *The Norman Conquests* (1974), a trilogy of plays set in different areas of one house over one weekend, and was rewarded by productions at the **National Theatre** of *Bedroom Farce* (1977), *Sisterly Feelings* (1980), *Way Upstream* (1983) and his own production of *A Small Family Business* (1987). Ayckbourn's plays have received critical acclaim and popular approval, despite the predictable objection that they have concentrated on too narrow a class range in life. His success is partly due to a rare professionalism in writing plays, revealed through his brilliantly terse dialogue and intricate situations, but it also comes from his clear observation of how people behave. His humour is tinged with sadness and sometimes even bitterness. The sugary complacency of much boulevard drama has no place within Ayckbourn's plays which he tests in front of demanding Yorkshire audiences in the Stephen Joseph Theatre in Scarborough before releasing to the West End.   JE

Ayrer, Jacob (1543–1601) German playwright. Several of the plays of this popular and extremely prolific dramatist shared sources with the plays of **Shakespeare**. However, the quality of Ayrer's drama, written as it is in *Knittelverse* (irregular popular verse), is far from Shakespearian.   SW

Azenberg, Emanuel (1934–) American producer, called by the *New York Times* one of Broadway's 'most successful producers and one of its outspoken critics'. Although he works closely with the **Shubert Organization**, in the mid-80s he essentially left the Broadway establishment by walking out on the League of American Theatres and Producers. Although he has been producing in New York since 1961 (as of 1985, 35 Broadway plays in 19 years) his greatest successes have been since 1982 and his single major client has been **Neil Simon**, for whom he has produced 12 plays since 1972. Recent productions have included *Biloxi Blues*, a revival of *Joe Egg*, and **Sondheim's** *Sunday in the Park With George*.   DBW

B

Baba Sala see **Adejumo, Moses Olaiya**

Babel, Isaak Emmanuilovich (1894–1941) Odessa-born Russian Jewish short story writer and dramatist, noted for his textured and polished language, careful attention to character and environmental detail and vivid sense of historical time and place. His two famous short story collections, *The Odessa Tales* (1921–3) and *Red Cavalry* (1926), are based upon personal experience. The former is a rich tapestry of the Jewish underworld in Odessa. The latter evokes the brutality of the Russian Civil War. The stories are characterized by exoticism, eroticism, moral and political ambiguity, paradox and grotesque, all qualities which have impeded his full critical acceptance in the Soviet Union. His play *Sunset* (1928) borrows themes and characters from *The Odessa Tales* (which also appeared in his scenario for the film *Benya Krik*, 1926). It was successfully produced at the **Moscow Art Theatre** in 1928 and translated into Yiddish in 1929. His play *Mariya* (published 1935), set in Petrograd in 1920, dramatizes the disintegration of a family in the wake of the Bolshevik victory and evokes **Chekhov's** *The Cherry Orchard*. It was banned while in simultaneous rehearsal at the Vakhtangov Theatre and at the State Jewish Theatre, under the direction of **Solomon Mikhoels**. A third play, *The Chekist*, was seized and believed destroyed at Babel's arrest on undisclosed charges in 1939. The official Soviet account lists the date of his death in a prison camp as 17 March 1941. SG

Bacon, Frank (1864–1922) American actor and dramatist. A native of California, Bacon acted in melodramas such as *Ten Nights in a Bar-Room*, comedy and vaudeville sketches, mainly in the San Francisco area, until the earthquake in 1906 when he departed for New York. There he performed in such plays as *Alabama*, *Pudd'nhead Wilson* and Winchell Smith's *The Fortune Hunter*. His greatest success came in *Lightnin'* (1918), a play he wrote in collaboration with Smith and acted the role of Lightnin' Bill Jones, a charming rascal and ne'er-do-well who enjoys tall tales and strong drink. The plays ran for three years, breaking all existing records with 1,291 performances. WJM

Badel, Alan (Firman) (1923–82) British actor, who joined Sir **Barry Jackson's** companies in Birmingham and Stratford-upon-Avon after leaving the army in 1946. With his imposing presence and rich voice, he was quickly in demand for roles in classical theatre, joining Michael Benthall's company at the **Old Vic**, where his Romeo (1952) to **Claire Bloom's** Juliet

and his Hamlet (1956) are still remembered. His acting style, which often recalled the great actor-managers, fell out of fashion towards the late 1950s, with the arrival of new actors with regional or working-class images. In his later years, his stage roles were often those which demanded a certain flamboyance, such as John Tanner in **Shaw's** *Man and Superman* (1965) and the title role of **Kean** in **Sartre's** version of the play by the elder **Dumas**. But Badel was not merely an actor for the grand gesture, but one of subtlety and range as well; and his reputation sadly limited the parts he was called upon to play. In the 1960s, he turned increasingly towards films and television, where again his roles usually tilted towards the grandiose. But his *Othello* (1970) at the Oxford Playhouse was a powerful performance, if less haunting than his Stephen Dedalus in Marjorie Barkentin's *Ulysses in Nighttown* (1959), which he also produced in London. JE

Bagnold, Enid (Lady Roderick Jones) (1889–1981) British playwright and novelist, who became well known in the inter-war years through her novels, *Serena Blandish* (1925), which **S. N. Behrman** adapted for the stage (1929 New York), and *National Velvet* (1935), which was made into a film and dramatized by Bagnold herself for the theatre. She also adapted another of her novels, *Lottie Dundas* (1943), and her later stage plays, including *The Chalk Garden* (1955 New York, 1956 London) and *The Chinese Prime Minister* (1964 New York, 1965 London), retain a literary flavour, as if written by someone who was not closely in touch with the shifts of theatrical fashion. Of her plays, *The Chalk Garden* was the most successful, described by **Kenneth Tynan** as perhaps 'the finest artificial comedy to have flowed from an English (as opposed to Irish) pen since the death of **Congreve**'. *The Last Joke* (1960) and *Call Me Jacky* (1967) failed to find a public in either New York or London, although the latter was revived as *A Matter of Gravity* with **Katharine Hepburn** in 1976. JE

Bahr, Hermann (1863–1934) Austrian playwright and critic. After some years as a student in Germany, Bahr settled in Vienna, where he became a leading light of an informal group of writers known as Jung Wien (Young Vienna), whose intent was to introduce into Viennese literature themes and literary modes of the avant-garde writers in other European countries. Bahr, whose prime importance was as a dramatic critic, first introduced naturalism, which he quickly repudiated in an essay in 1891; he then acted as the harbinger of other literary movements for his Viennese readers. He was also a prolific playwright, but only his comedy *The*

Concert (1909) has proved to be durable. In 1918 he was briefly part of a directorial triumvirate at the **Burgtheater**.   SW

Baierl, Helmut (1926–) German dramatist and dramaturge. Born in Czechoslovakia, he began his career as a teacher of Russian in Köthen and lectured in 'Worker and Peasant' studies at Greifswald, before becoming the dramaturge for the **Deutsches Theater** in 1957. His first play, *The Finding* (1958), used techniques from the Brechtian 'Teaching Plays' to deal with peasant reeducation. In 1959 he transferred to the **Berliner Ensemble**, where his reworking of **Brecht**'s *Mother Courage* in the contemporary DDR context, *Frau Flinz* (1961), was staged with **Helene Weigel** in lead role. Entering politics in 1967, he was appointed Secretary of the Literary section of the Deutsche Akademie der Künste.   CI

Baiting An obsolete popular entertainment, notable for its cruelty. In the Roman games, specialized gladiators, the *venationes* and *bestiarii*, were set to kill exotic beasts in epic numbers, though we are told that an audience at Pompey's show pitied the massacred elephants in their frantic confusion. In the Middle Ages, the baiting of bulls was required by law as a hygienic measure prior to their slaughter by butchers, and survived in towns like Tutbury and Stamford as 'bull-running'.

Bear-baiting may have been introduced into England by Italians during the reign of King John; it began as an exclusively aristocratic pastime, a degenerate form of hunting, until the 15th century when nobles allowed their bear-wards to institute a commercial exhibition of bears at lesser manors. Erasmus wrote (c. 1500) of the 'many herds of bears kept in England for the purpose of baiting'. Under Henry VIII a certain John Cooper was licensed to put on public animal combats; prior to 1574, there were two baiting rings in London, but by **Shakespeare**'s day, they had merged into one, The Bear Garden, which was permitted to play on Sunday (when playhouses were closed) until 1603. This monopoly of Sunday amusement had led to a collapse of the building beneath an overflow crowd in 1583, and The Bear Garden was immediately rebuilt as a three-storey amphitheatre, managed by **Henslowe** of the **Rose**. In 1598, a German traveller, Hentzner, watched bulls and bears teased by dogs and a blind bear whipped there; its proximity to the playhouses may have enabled Shakespeare to use the genuine article when *The Winter's Tale* requires an 'Exit pursued by a bear'. Elizabeth I was a great enthusiast, and some bears enjoyed star status; in *The Merry Wives of Windsor*, Slender tells sweet Anne Page he has seen 'Sanderson' loose 20 times. The Queen's Treasury paid for the provisioning and replacement of the baiting animals, and the actor **Edward Alleyn** was made Royal Keeper of Bulls and Mastiffs in 1604, a source of considerable profit. Three bear-gardens existed in Restoration London. (Evelyn thought it 'a rude and dirty pastime') and one persisted in Birmingham until 1773. Parliament finally forbade the practice in 1835, but it was carried on in private for at least another 50 years.

Bears, boars and deer were baited by dogs in Dresden in the early 17th century, and tigers and buffaloes in the later part of the century. A special amphitheatre was built to house the combats in the 18th century. It was also carried on in Königsberg, Berlin, Moscow (till 1867), and Vienna, where a commercial baiting pit was opened in 1699. A new establishment was designed in 1735 by no less artists than **Antonio Galli da Bibiena** and Antonio Caradini. As late as 1828, John Orlando Parry saw dogs in Paris gored and tossed to a height of 12 metres by savage bulls, bears placed on a pole with a fire above and below them, wild asses and bulldogs tearing each other to pieces, and a bull chained to a stake fighting an elkhound. Such diversions were offered for three hours every Sunday afternoon to a crowded attendance. Rats killed by terriers provided a popular sport for Victorian gamblers, as Henry Mayhew attests in his reportage. More recently, deer-baiting has been observed at mid-western American county fairs.   LS

See: W. B. Boulton, *The Amusements of Old London*, London, 1901; O. Brownstein, 'The Popularity of Baiting in England before 1660', *Educational Theatre Journal*; Rolf von Ende, *Circenses. Spiele auf Leben und Tod*, Berlin, 1984.

Baker, Benjamin A. (1818–90) American playwright. 'Uncle Ben Baker' deserted his prompter's post at William **Mitchell's Olympic Theatre** and for his benefit on 15 February 1848 wrote *A Glance at New York in 1848* starring **F. S. Chanfrau** as Mose. Encouraged by the 'shouts of delight from the Bowery B'hoys in the pit', and a run of 74 performances, Baker created more adventures for Mose: *New York as It Is* (1848), *Mose in California* (1849), and *Mose in China* (1850).   RM

Baker, George Pierce (1866–1935) American educator. A year after graduating from Harvard University in 1887, Baker returned as an instructor in the English Department. In 1905, he began offering a course in playwriting entitled English 47. Three years later he founded the Harvard Dramatic Club and served as its sponsor. And in 1912 he established Workshop 47 as a laboratory theatre for plays written in English 47. The programme and Baker's growing reputation attracted to Harvard such promising talents as **Eugene O'Neill**, **Sidney Howard**, Thomas Wolfe, **Edward Sheldon**, and Philip Barry. He resigned and moved to Yale in 1925 as head of its first Department of Drama, retiring in 1933. Beginning in 1927 he worked to establish the National Theatre Conference, and served as its first president in 1932. He is remembered as a teacher and mentor to the generation of American playwrights who came to the front in the 1920s. His ideas about the craft of playwriting are set forth in *Dramatic Technique* (1919).   TLM

Baker, Josephine (Freda Josephine McDonald) (1906–75) American entertainer, who left her indigent family in St Louis at the age of 16 to play in all-black revues in Philadelphia and New York. Her outrageous comic antics had a *succès de scandale* in Paris in *La Revue Nègre* (Théâtre des Champs-Elysées, 1925). Some celebrated her as a combination of 'boxing kangaroo, sen-sen gum and racing cyclist' (*Candide*), while moralists condemned her as the decline of the West made flesh. 'La Baker's' rubber-limbed Charlestons and black-bottoms, and her cincture of phalliform bananas became a fixture of Parisian night life. Her repertory of American classics (*Always*), French nostalgia (*La Petite Tonkinoise*), and the signature tune *J'ai Deux Amours* was sung in a thin soprano. After the Second World War, when she had worked for the Resistance, she made many 'farewell tours' to raise money for the orphans she housed on her estate in Milandes. Needy and ailing, she died during the run of a revue at the Paris Bobino.   LS

Bakst, Léon (Lev Rozenberg) (1866–1924) Russian painter and designer; emigrated to Paris in 1909. He began his stage career designing at the Hermitage, the imperial private theatre. Bakst was a co-founder, with **Alexandre Benois**, of The World of Art Group and was one of the primary designers – many believe the most significant – of the first period of the Ballets Russes where he worked with Diaghilev until 1914. In Paris he also designed for Ida Rubinstein. Bakst's use of colour revolutionized all of Western design. Drawing on motifs, line, and palettes from ancient Greece, Egypt, central Asia and the Orient, he simplified the shape and line of costumes, designed costumes and sets that suggested free-flowing movement, and bathed decor in nearly overwhelming, deep, rich, sensual shades of blue, green, gold, orange and yellow. He believed that colour – and the fusion of colours – had significant emotional effects upon the spectators. This is most evident in *Scheherazade* (1910). Other significant designs include *Cléopâtre*, *L'Oiseau de Feu* (*The Firebird*, 1910), *Le Dieu Bleu* (1912), *Thamar* (1912), *L'Après-Midi d'un Faune* (1912), *Daphnis and Chloe* (1912), and *La Belle au Bois Dormant* (1921) with the Ballets Russes in London.   AA

Baldwin, James Arthur (1924–87) Afro-American novelist, essayist and playwright. The most widely read of contemporary black authors, Baldwin wrote two plays. In *The Amen Corner* (produced at Howard University in 1954 and on Broadway in 1965) a fanatical woman pastor tries unsuccessfully to turn her son against the father whose love she has rejected. Despite a convincing performance by Beah Richards, the play was coolly received by leading critics. In *Blues for Mr Charlie* (1964) Baldwin examined racial attitudes in the murder of an angry black youth by a white bigot. The writing is often shrill, characters' motivations are questionable, and the author's viewpoint remains ambivalent.   EGH

Bale, John (1495–1563) English playwright. His most notable play was *Kynge Johan* (1538) which combines elements of both the medieval theatre, with its abstract characters, and historical drama based on actual people. His contribution to the theatre ranged from morality plays to propagandist pieces of an anti-Catholic nature. He was the Bishop of Ossory in Ireland.   MB

Baliev, Nikita Fyodorovich (?1877–1936) Co-founder (with Nikolai Tarasov) of, director and jovial master of ceremonies at Moscow's 'The Bat' (1908–22), Russia's first real cabaret. The Bat grew out of the 'cabbage parties', the informal, in-house variety evenings held at the **Moscow Art Theatre** (MAT) in pre-revolutionary days during Lent when the theatres were officially closed. Baliev became part of the MAT

company (1906–11) after meeting **Stanislavsky** in Berlin during the theatre's European tour (1906). He appeared as 'Bread' in **Maeterlinck**'s *The Blue Bird* and as 'the Guest' in **Andreev**'s *The Life of Man*. The Bat began as a semi-independent, MAT-related enterprise, originally playing to an invited audience, but after 1910 and the first of two address changes, it opened its doors to the paying public. The Bat's main attraction was the rotund, moonfaced Baliev who, as Russia's first *conférencier*, was expert at improvising horseplay with the customers from the stage and cavorting in specially designed *entr'acte* numbers. The Bat did not imagine itself a serious artistic enterprise with an articulated aesthetic credo like the Crooked Mirror Theatre, for example. It catered to Moscow's *nouveaux riches*, not St Petersburg's intelligentsia. It offered lighthearted, slightly varied and occasionally uneven performances of sketches, mime, comedy and musical acts and especially, short dramatizations and modestly conceived parodies of Russian classics by **Pushkin**, **Lermontov** and above all, **Gogol**. In 1920 Baliev emigrated to Paris with part of the company. As the Chauve-Souris they offered 273 performances in Paris, 175 in London and nearly 1,000 in America (1920–4). After some success, its audience dried up, and the cabaret closed.   SG

Ballad Opera Although called a type of opera, Ballad Opera is more nearly a play interspersed with songs, the songs having new words set to already known tunes. The most famous example is *The Beggar's Opera*, which enjoyed phenomenal popularity in its own day and is now the only Ballad Opera to be regularly revived. Ballad Opera, strictly defined, disappeared after the middle of the 18th century. It was succeeded by what is often called English Opera in which many of the tunes were written by the person named as composer and others were extracted by him from various sources, including foreign operas, and interpolated in the work. Sometimes English Opera is for obvious reasons referred to as Pasticcio Opera, although the term is also used to indicate operas in which each act is by a different composer.   GH

Ballet

The development of court ballet Ballet as an art form of the Western theatre first took root in the Italian courts of the Renaissance, where dancing was harnessed to the needs of the reigning prince and a hybrid form of spectacle evolved whose objects were to entertain and also, and most importantly, to impress. The professional dancing master, whose task it was to create dances for important occasions, then emerged: men such as Domenico of Piacenza, Antonio Cornazano and William the Jew. When Charles VIII of France entered Italy in 1494 to claim the throne of Naples, these court entertainments were already well established and his courtiers were astonished by their magnificence. In the following century, largely through the influence of Catharine de' Medici, an Italian princess who married Henri II of France, this form of spectacle, in which singing and declamation were employed as well as the dance, was developed in the French court. The production in Paris of the *Balet Comique de la Reine* (1581) was an important landmark, not the first French court ballet

A scene from *Balet Comique de la Reine*, 1581.

but by far the most splendid to have been produced up to that time, and celebrated ever since as a result of the distribution of its libretto among the courts of Europe as an example of the superiority of French culture.

Under succeeding reigns ballet became an important feature of French court life, assuming a wide variety of forms and sometimes devised to make a political point. These ballets, to which the public was frequently admitted, were performed mainly by the courtiers, who from the reign of Louis XIII were joined by a leavening of professional dancers. The kings themselves did not consider it beneath their dignity to take part, Louis XIV being an exceptionally talented dancer in his youth and well into manhood. In the early part of his reign the French court ballet reached its apogee, being used almost as an instrument of state, to implant and drive home the notion of absolute monarchy, enshrined in the person of the king who, significantly, was to become known in history by one of his balletic roles, that of 'Le Roi Soleil'.

Ballet enters the theatre Louis XIV's interest in the arts, and the dance in particular, led him to establish the Paris Opéra under the composer **Lully**. The virtual disappearance at this time of ballet as a court entertainment coincided with a most austere outlook that was adopted as the King realized the passing of his youth, and as France became embroiled more and more in costly wars. In certain respects Lully's operas continued the traditions of the court ballet, particularly in the importance given to the dance, and this increased in the early years of the 18th century in the opera-ballets of Campra and Rameau. Being established in the theatre, the dance became professional, and its technical and interpretative potential was reflected in the appearance of the first great stars, notably the virtuosic Marie Camargo and the expressive Marie Sallé, and on the male side, Louis Dupré and Gaétan Vestris, who, each in his own way, developed the essentially French style of the *danse noble*.

The development of the ballet d'action The separation of ballet from opera that took place in the 18th century was a most crucial development. The idea of a dramatic performance, conveyed without words and entirely through pantomime and dancing, was not the invention of any one person, but arose, seemingly naturally, in the minds of several ballet-masters. Among its earliest practical manifestations were the productions of John Weaver in London, notably *The Loves of Mars and Venus* (1717). A generation or so later Franz Hilferding was staging mime versions of plays in Vienna, while in Paris Jean-François De Hesse, influenced by the **commedia dell'arte**, was producing ballet-pantomimes at the Théâtre Italien. These were the most important forerunners of the two choreographers who led the way to the establishment of ballet as a theatrical form in its own right on the opera-house stage: Gasparo Angiolini and Jean-Georges Noverre. Noverre was the more influential of these two, for he was to set forth his views in his *Letters on Dancing and Ballets*, first published in 1760 and recognized ever since as a seminal work on choreographic theory. After making his reputation in Stuttgart, he was engaged at the Paris Opéra, where his formula for what he called the *ballet d'action* was to be adopted after his departure by the Gardel brothers and Dauberval.

The Gardels were to dominate the Paris ballet until the eve of the romantic period. The elder brother Maximilien had a gift for making ballets out of *opéras comiques*, and this approach had a direct and wide appeal and did much to give ballet in its new form a firm foothold in the Paris Opéra repertory. Dying young, he was succeeded by his brother Pierre who was the unchallenged master of French ballet from 1787 until 1820. Pierre Gardel was very much a man of his time, his most successful ballets – *Télémaque* and *Psyché* (both 1790) – being distinctly neoclassical in flavour, but he also produced a comic ballet, *La Dansomanie* (1800) that remained in the repertory for a quarter of a century. Jean Dauberval, who had a warmer personality, was perhaps even more gifted, but he worked mainly in Bordeaux, preferring the freer conditions that reigned there. His fame has been perpetuated by his comic masterpiece, *La Fille Mal Gardée*, which has survived in various versions to the present day.

Ballet flourished all over Europe in the 18th century, and companies of dancers were attached to many of the great opera houses, notably the Scala, Milan, the Imperial theatres in Russia, and the Royal Theatre, Copenhagen. Ballet in Italy assumed a particular style of its own, relying heavily on mime, and at the end of the century produced a major choreographer in **Salvatore Viganò**, whose choreodramas attained a high level of homogeneity in their conception.

Ballet technique was also developing apace, and moving further and further away from that of social dance. By the end of the century it was beginning to

Marie Camargo.

crystallize into the form that Carlo Blasis was to record so clearly in his *Elementary Treatise upon the Theory and Practice of the Art of Dancing* (1820). A development that was to prove of supreme importance was the introduction of the heelless ballet shoe. This was to make possible the extraordinary extension of the ballerina's technique afforded by *pointe* work, that was to be exploited throughout the 19th century.

The male dancer retained his importance into the second half of the 18th century, Auguste Vestris and Charles Le Picq earning equal applause with that of their female companions. Among the ballerinas of note during these years were Anne Heinel, Madeleine Guimard, and Marie Gardel.

The romantic ballet The romantic movement, which infiltrated and transformed art in all its forms in the first half of the 19th century, found fertile soil in the ballet. The first sign of this extraordinary flowering that was to generate an unprecedented vogue for ballet came with the emergence of Marie Taglioni, a dancer whose style possessed an inner poetry perfectly in accord with the romantic image of the ballerina. She had the good fortune to be guided by a father who was to choreograph ballets that were tailor-made for her, the most celebrated being *La Sylphide* (Paris Opéra, 1832), which became the prototype of many other ballets produced in the romantic era and afterwards. Its theme – the love of a spirit and a mortal that is inherently impossible of realization – was essentially romantic, expressing, with extreme delicacy, the quest for the unattainable.

The mysterious forest scene of *La Sylphide* followed an act with a Scottish setting, an example of the *couleur locale* that was no less typical of romantic art. This was the other aspect of romantic ballet, an aspect personified by the Viennese ballerina, Fanny Elssler, who aroused audiences to frenzy with her rendering of the Spanish *Cachucha*. Both these ballerinas became international celebrities – a new possibility with the introduction of the steamship and the railway; their careers

took them, each in her turn, to Russia, and Elssler spent two years on a triumphant tour of North America.

Paris was still accepted as the main focus of ballet, but a stream of brilliantly trained ballerinas was beginning to emerge from Italy – in particular from the school at the Scala, Milan, which came under the direction of Carlo Blasis in 1837. The ballerina who succeeded Taglioni and Elssler in Paris, Carlotta Grisi, had received her early training there, and her style had been polished by Jules Perrot. She burst into fame when she created the title-role in *Giselle* (1841), a ballet that has survived with much of the original choreography intact and is accepted as the greatest masterpiece of the romantic ballet. It had been created to the formula set by *La Sylphide*, over which it had several advantages: a finer score, by Adolphe Adam, a scenario by the poet and critic **Théophile Gautier**, and the more important sections of the choreography arranged by Perrot.

Jules Perrot had been the star male dancer at the Opéra in the 1830s – 'the last man to have danced', in Gautier's phrase – and had turned his talents to choreography. He worked very little in Paris, London being the scene of his greatest compositions, which placed him in the forefront of his contemporaries. **Her Majesty's Theatre**, London, was run on a seasonal basis, and while not possessing the continuity afforded by a permanent ballet company and school, followed a policy of engaging a galaxy of stars of ballet and opera such as could not be seen elsewhere. Among Perrot's ballets were *Ondine* (1843) for Fanny Cerrito, *Esmeralda* (1844) for Grisi, and *Catarina* (1846) for Lucile Grahn, but even more extraordinary were his multistellar divertissements, the most famous of which was the *Pas*

Marie Taglioni in *La Sylphide*, Paris, 1832.

de Quatre (1845), in which Taglioni, Cerrito, Grisi and Grahn all appeared together.

Working on a smaller canvas in Copenhagen was a choreographer, half-French by birth and trained in the Paris school, who produced a large repertory of ballets, many of which have been preserved with much of their original choreography intact. This was August Bournonville, who directed the ballet at the Royal Theatre there from 1830 to 1877, with two short breaks. These ballets – notably his version of *La Sylphide* (1836), *Napoli* (1842) and *Conservatory* (1849) – may be seen as counterparts, though on a less lavish scale, of the lost masterpieces of Perrot.

The vogue for ballet began to diminish around 1850, but the impetus of romanticism remained strong and choreographers who had lived through the golden years continued to produce successful works. Arthur Saint-Léon, the husband of the ballerina Cerrito and in his prime a dancer of extraordinary virtuosity, was adept at producing entertaining ballets full of *couleur locale* in the form of national dances. During the 1860s he dominated the ballet scene in Russia and in Paris; his *Little Hump-backed Horse* (1864) was long a favourite in both St Petersburg and Moscow, while his last ballet, *Coppélia* (Paris Opéra, 1870), produced to a brilliant score by Léo Delibes, has lost none of its evergreen charm with the passing of the years. Marie Taglioni too turned her attention to choreography, producing a single ballet, *Le Papillon* (Paris Opéra, 1860), to music by Offenbach, for her ill-fated protégée Emma Livry, one of the many victims of fire in the age of gas-light.

Ballet in Tsarist Russia As the vogue for ballet declined in Western Europe, the focus of importance shifted to Russia, where the Tsars had established ballet companies on a lavish scale in St Petersburg and Moscow, the former remaining the more significant centre until the Revolution. In the 19th century much of the impetus was supplied by a succession of French-trained ballet-masters, headed by Charles Didelot, one of the greatest choreographers of the pre-romantic era, who reorganized the St Petersburg school, which then began to produce excellent Russian dancers. After Didelot came Perrot and Saint-Léon, and then the man whose name is indelibly associated with the great flowering of ballet in Russia at the end of the century, Marius Petipa.

Petipa had arrived in St Petersburg in 1847, and served his choreographic apprenticeship under Perrot and Saint-Léon. The former exerted the greater influence, and Petipa kept several of his ballets alive, notably *Giselle*, revising them to accord with contemporary taste and the developing technique of the dancers. The shift in taste was not accompanied by the vulgarization that was an unfortunate feature in the West, and in several of his early ballets Petipa was able to inject a truly poetic content. This was most noticeable in *The Bayadere* (1877), with its scene of 'The Shades', an act of pure dancing that is still considered a touchstone of classical dance in its purest form.

The growing public indifference to ballet that was even felt in St Petersburg was halted by the appearance in 1884 of the great Italian dramatic ballerina, Virginia Zucchi, who was followed by a succession of her fellow-countrywomen who introduced the virtuosity of the Milan school. Zucchi restored the vogue for ballet virtually single-handed, and this reawakening of interest was to lead, a few years later, to the masterpieces that Petipa created in his later years, and in particular to his celebrated association with Tchaikovsky. His first collaboration with Tchaikovsky was *The Sleeping Beauty* (1890). This was followed by *The Nutcracker* (1892), but owing to Petipa's ill health it was his assistant Lev Ivanov who was primarily responsible for the choreography, though working to his principal's plan. The third Tchaikovsky ballet, *Swan Lake* (1894–5) had been produced earlier in Moscow, but the version by Petipa and Ivanov totally superseded it. Another of Petipa's later ballets was *Raymonda* (1900), with music by Glazounov, created when the choreographer was over eighty.

Despite Petipa's enormous legacy, it was hardly surprising that a need for change was felt after his long domination. Russian ballet had become sufficiently secure to stand on its own feet. Its ballerinas were mastering the technical secrets of the Italians, and a young Russian choreographer, Michel Fokine, was already forming ideas that were to reform the art of ballet.

During the time that ballet was flourishing under Petipa in Russia, in Western Europe it had sunk to a sad level. In London it had even been ejected from the opera-house and forced to take root in the music-hall, and the only flash of brilliance came with the appearance of Adeline Genée at the Empire Theatre in the early years of the 20th century. Even in Paris ballet seemed to have lost its power to move and appeal. To some it may have seemed an art that had no place in the modern theatre, but a reawakening was imminent.

The Diaghilev Ballet The awakening was brought about by Serge Diaghilev, an extraordinary man, who first emerged as the dominant figure of a group of young intellectuals in St Petersburg, revealed a special talent for organizing exhibitions, and then, in 1909, brought a company of Russian dancers to Paris. If the course of history can ever be changed in a single day, it did so on the day of that company's first Paris performance. The Russian ballet was a revelation, and Paris, and soon all Europe, fell under the spell of Russian genius – the choreography of Michel Fokine, the décors of **Benois** and **Bakst**, the artistry of Tamara Karsavina, and above all the incredible technique of Vaslav Nijinsky, who amazingly attracted more interest than the ballerinas.

Over the next 20 years the Diaghilev Ballet awakened Europe to the potential of ballet as a serious and indeed major theatrical art, an art that based its claim on a collaboration between choreographer, musician and artist to an extent that had never been achieved before. Drawing its dancers from the Imperial Theatres and, after the Revolution, from dancers who had emigrated to the West, the company gained added strength from Diaghilev's unique flair in attracting artists, writers and musicians of the highest calibre to work for him. The company survived the vicissitudes of the First World War and the Russian Revolution, and though plagued by a chronic shortage of finance, was held together by the personality of its founder, who moulded it into a company that kept abreast of the latest artistic trends and never lost its glamour.

The seasons before the First World War were

dominated by two choreographers, Fokine and Nijinsky. Fokine, already established as the leading choreographer of the Imperial Russian ballet, produced a string of masterpieces: *Les Sylphides* (1909), *The Firebird, Scheherazade, Le Carnaval* (all 1910), *Petrushka* and *Le Spectre de la Rose* (both 1911). *The Firebird* and *Petrushka* also introduced a young composer who was to become a major figure in ballet for the next sixty years, Igor Stravinsky. Fokine became disillusioned when Diaghilev began to encourage Nijinsky's leanings towards choreography. Nijinsky produced three ballets before his career was cut short by mental illness; while there were differing views about his choreographic ability, two of them – *L'Après-Midi d'un Faune* (1912) and *Le Sacre du Printemps* (1913) – were the cause of celebrated scandals.

Neither Fokine nor Nijinsky was available when the Diaghilev Ballet resumed its European tours after the war. A new choreographer then emerged, Leonide Massine, who proved adept at producing amusing works such as *La Boutique Fantasque* (1919), but also created the impressive Spanish ballet, *Le Tricorne* (1919), to music by de Falla. In 1921 Diaghilev ventured all on a lavish revival of *The Sleeping Beauty* in London, designed by Bakst, but although it was an artistic success and awakened the growing ballet public to the glories of Petipa, it proved a financial failure. But, as always, Diaghilev survived. Massine was then succeeded as principal choreographer by Bronislava Nijinsky, whose *Les Noces* (1923) was a profound memory of the old Russia she had left for ever, and in sharp contrast to the more contemporary *Les Biches* (1924), a delicate evocation of the social pleasures of the Riviera set. In the company's last phase, George Balanchine produced some of his early works, including *Apollon Musagète* (1928) and *Le Fils Prodigue* (1929).

The list of the dancers of the Diaghilev Ballet included many of the greatest performers of the time – Karsavina, Spessivtseva, Danilova, Markova among the ballerinas, Nijinsky, Massine, Dolin, Lifar among the men – while the artists who designed the ballets included Benois, Bakst, **Picasso**, Larionov, **Goncharova**, **Derain**, Laurencin, Braque, Utrillo and Chirico.

Outside Diaghilev's orbit another Russian dancer was spreading the gospel of ballet, but appealing to a less sophisticated but much wider public. This was Anna Pavlova, who had been trained in the Imperial school and been a leading ballerina in St Petersburg before the Revolution. For more than twenty years she travelled the globe with her own company, entrancing millions with the poetry of her dancing.

Between them, Diaghilev and Pavlova laid the foundations on which the ballet in the West was to be rebuilt in the years to come. Unfortunately, neither was to see the result of their efforts, both of them died before their allotted span, Diaghilev in 1929 and Pavlova in 1931.

Post-Diaghilev companies Two streams of development followed Diaghilev's death: the foundation of international itinerant companies on the Diaghilev Ballet's model, and the emergence of national companies. The Diaghilev Ballet itself dissolved immediately it was deprived of its founder, and in 1932 a new company – the Ballets Russes de Monte-Carlo – was

formed under the direction of Colonel W. de Basil and René Blum around a strong nucleus of Russian dancers, with Massine and Balanchine as choreographers, and Serge Grigoriev, who had performed the same role for Diaghilev, as *régisseur*. This company rapidly established itself as the heir to the Diaghilev tradition, acquiring in the eyes of the public a glamour that added to its appeal. It launched a new generation of dancers, notably the 'baby ballerinas', Tamara Toumanova, Tatiana Riabouchinska and Irina Baronova, and its repertory was to be distinguished by two of Balanchine's earliest successes, *Cottillon* and *La Concurrence* (both 1932), and Massine's first symphonic ballets, which marked a novel development in choreography: *Les Présages* to Tchaikovsky's 5th Symphony and *Choreartium* to Brahms's 4th Symphony (both 1933).

In 1937 Massine left de Basil to become artistic director of a new company which confusingly bore the name Ballet Russe de Monte-Carlo. In 1938 London had a feast of ballet when both companies were appearing there simultaneously. The Ballet Russe de Monte-Carlo emigrated to the United States shortly after the outbreak of the Second World War and became progressively transformed into an American company, spending most of its time touring the States. Among the ballets which it created were **Agnes de Mille**'s *Rodeo* (1942), Balanchine's *Ballet Imperial* (1944), *Concerto Barocco* (1945) and *Night Shadow* (1945). The company continued in existence until 1962.

Meanwhile, de Basil's company, which became known as Original Ballet Russe from 1939, presented some of Fokine's last ballets, including *Le Coq d'Or* and *Paganini* (both 1939), featuring Riabouchinska, in the last years of peace. Following a successful tour of Australia, during which Lichine's *Graduation Ball* (1940) was created, it too made its way to America. Its later history was chequered. It spent four years in South America, and in 1947 returned to London, being the first visiting company to appear at **Covent Garden** after the war. The company was disbanded the following year.

The last of the great private companies was the Grand Ballet du Marquis de Cuevas, founded in 1947. Its artistic legacy was substantially less than that of its predecessors, but it remained an important feature of the European dance scene during the 15 years of its existence, bringing several American dancers, notably Rosella Hightower and Marjorie Tallchief, into international prominence. Its last achievement was to be the forum for Rudolf Nureyev's first appearance after his departure from the Kirov Ballet in 1961. The Marquis died in 1961, and the company ceased to exist the following year.

The growth of national companies The main thrust of activity since Diaghilev's death, however, has taken place in national or municipally supported companies. Ballet, like opera, has always tended to be a subsidized art, being recognized by governments for its prestige value as a cultural manifestation, and requiring expenditure on spectacular production, orchestra and supporting school that is generally too great to recover from a paying public.

In Paris the Opéra has long enjoyed financial subsidy of one sort or another, and the Paris Opéra Ballet had sufficient protection to survive the decadence into which it sank towards the end of the 19th century. When Diaghilev died it was already beginning to recover under the rule of an exceptional director, Jacques Rouché, who then seized the opportunity to engage Serge Lifar as ballet-master. It was a daring step but the risk proved justified, for Lifar was to dominate French ballet for nearly 30 years, until he resigned in 1958. During that period he not only inspired the company and gave the dancers a new pride in their art, but became a respected and influential figure in intellectual and artistic circles. He produced a great number of ballets, of which several are still occasionally performed: *Suite en Blanc* (1943), *Les Mirages* (1947), and *Phèdre* (1950).

Since Lifar's retirement the Paris Opéra Ballet has been eclectic in its choice of choreographers. Neither of the two leading French choreographers active today, Roland Petit and Maurice Béjart, have been willing to attach themselves permanently to the Opéra, although both have been engaged as guest choreographers. Petit first came into prominence as principal choreographer of the Ballets des Champs Elysées and the Ballets de Paris, independent companies that flourished shortly after the Second World War, and since 1972 he has directed the Ballet de Marseille. His most celebrated ballets have been *Le Jeune Homme et la Mort* (1946), produced in collaboration with the poet **Cocteau**, and *Carmen* (1949). Béjart has been director of the Brussels-based Ballet du XIXe Siècle since 1960, and has enjoyed great artistic freedom in developing his choreographic ideas. His leaning towards total theatre has gained him a wide circle of admirers, although his work arouses controversy in some quarters. His most widely known ballets are his version of *Le Sacre du Printemps* (1959) and *Nijinsky, Clown de Dieu* (1971)

Russia has benefited directly from her own great tradition of ballet, but has remained largely untouched by the developments that Diaghilev instituted in the West. In the early years of the Soviet era ballet was in serious danger of being jettisoned as a manifestation of the Tsarist regime, but happily the discovery was made that it could be moulded to accord with the social realism of the time while still following its hallowed traditions. Typical of this new approach was the ballet *The Red Poppy* (1927), based on colonial oppression, and Vainonen's *Flames of Paris* (1932), set in the French Revolution. The full-length ballet remained the accepted framework (in contrast to the position in the West, where shorter ballets had become the rule on the example of Diaghilev), but ballets were now constructed with a much stronger narrative that was conveyed in a newly developed realistic style of miming, the most notable example being Lavrovsky's *Romeo and Juliet* (1940), set to the now celebrated and frequently used score by Prokofiev. It was in the role of Juliet that the great Soviet ballerina, Galina Ulanova, gave her most moving interpretation.

Today the great schools of Leningrad and Moscow continue to flourish, and the companies they serve, including those in other cities, are a source of pride to an infinitely wider public than that which supported the ballet in Tsarist times. A more conservative spirit tends to reign than in the West. The Bolshoi Ballet in Moscow has since 1964 been directed by Yuri Grigorovich, choreographer of *Spartacus* (1968) and *Ivan the Terrible* (1975). Leningrad has taken second place to

Moscow in the Soviet era, but its Kirov Ballet still preserves the elegance of Maryinsky days and is renowned for its production of the classics.

In Britain, Diaghilev's death stimulated a surge of interest in its own dancers. Public interest was ready for such a development, and two companies, the Ballet Rambert and the Vic-Wells Ballet (later the **Sadler's Wells** Ballet) won an increasingly wide following in the 1930s under their respective founders, Marie Rambert and Ninette de Valois. During the Second World War, when there was no competition from abroad, they established themselves as firm favourites with the public. It fell to the Sadler's Wells Ballet to become the national company when it moved to the Royal Opera House, Covent Garden, in 1946 and was granted a royal charter and became the Royal Ballet in 1956. For some 30 years it enjoyed the possession of one of the greatest contemporary choreographers in Frederick Ashton, whose works long formed the mainstay of the repertory. Among these were *Symphonic Variations* (1946), *La Fille Mal Gardée* (1960), and *Enigma Variations* (1968). Many of Ashton's ballets were created for Margot Fonteyn, who was for long the company's prima ballerina, being considered in her prime one of the greatest living dancers. Her career was magically extended by a partnership with Rudolf Nureyev, who danced with the company for a number of years and inspired a notable improvement in the standard and status of the male dancers. The English choreographic tradition was carried on by John Cranko, whose major work was done in Stuttgart, and by Kenneth MacMillan, whose prolific output includes the full-length *Romeo and Juliet* and *Song of the Earth* (both 1965), and most talented of the latest generation, David Bintley.

As the Royal Ballet gained in stature, the Ballet Rambert inevitably fell into second place, but it played an important role in the growth of a native ballet tradition, providing a forum for the choreography of Antony Tudor, whose *Jardin aux Lilas* (1936) and *Dark Elegies* (1937) have stood the test of time. The Ballet

Margot Fonteyn and Rudolf Nureyev rehearsing *Marguerite and Armand*.

Rambert still survives, but has chosen to move outside the strict limits of classical ballet in the direction of modern dance. Another English company that has flourished since 1950 is the London Festival Ballet.

The USA was another beneficiary of the Diaghilev era, inheriting the most musically gifted choreographer of all time, George Balanchine. In 1933 Balanchine was invited to direct the School of American Ballet, from which grew the company known today as the New York City Ballet (founded in 1946 as Ballet Society), on which he created almost his entire choreographic output until his death in 1983. Balanchine enjoyed an intimate relationship with Stravinsky, with whom he had produced *Apollon Musagète* for the Diaghilev Ballet, and went on to create *Orpheus* (1948), *Agon* (1957) and other works for NYCB. His enormous output also included his perennial *Nutcracker* (1954) and the full-length *Don Quixote* (1965). Another choreographer, Jerome Robbins, produced ballets for the company, including *Dancers at a Gathering* (1969). Balanchine's predilection for tall, lean, loose-limbed, buoyant dancers had a decided influence on the general physique of his company, and virtually produced a new image of the ballerina.

The other leading American company, American Ballet Theatre, was formed in 1940 and has not been a reflection of one man's genius. Massine produced several ballets for it during the Second World War, but more important were a number of essentially American works, such as Robbins's *Fancy Free* (1944) and Agnes de Mille's *Fall River Legend* (1948). More recently ABT has engaged the Russian expatriate stars, Natalia Makarova and Mikhail Baryshnikov, the latter having been its director since 1980. Another company that is growing in importance is the Dance Theatre of Harlem, the first black ballet company, founded in 1971.

American ballet is also represented by a network of regional companies. Another important field of theatrical dance in the USA is modern dance, of which there are numerous forms, chief among them being that of Martha Graham. For a long time modern dance and classical ballet developed along quite separate lines, but recently there has been some cross-fertilization.

Copenhagen, although small in population, is internationally recognized as an important centre of ballet owing to the long unbroken tradition of its national company, the Royal Danish Ballet, and the preservation of the Bournonville heritage. Prominent among recent Danish choreographers have been Harald Lander and Flemming Flindt.

Germany, which earlier in the century was a cradle of modern dance, has made important contributions in the field of ballet in recent years. John Cranko raised the Stuttgart Ballet to international status, directing it from 1961 until his death in 1973 and producing many important works, including the full-length works, *Onegin* (1965) and *Taming of the Shrew* (1969). A decade later the spotlight turned to Hamburg, where John Neumeier has directed the ballet at the Hamburg State Opera since 1973, producing a series of major works, several of them based on **Shakespeare**, including *A Midsummer Night's Dream* (1977).

Among other ballet companies that flourish around the world, mention should be made of the National Ballet of Cuba, the Royal Canadian Ballet, and the Australian Ballet – evidence that ballet is truly an art that knows no frontiers.

Training and notation The well-being of the art of classical ballet is founded on the teaching of the technique that has evolved over the centuries and has developed an ever-increasing measure of virtuosity. Important schools have been established alongside permanently based companies in Paris, Milan, Russia, Copenhagen, New York and elsewhere, where many great teachers have moulded the successive generations of pupils who have carried on the traditions of their forebears. Among the most celebrated teachers, whose methods have been recorded and followed, have been Carlo Blasis, Enrico Cecchetti and Agrippina Vaganova.

In former times ballet teaching was purely a professional accomplishment, but in the present century many children and young adults have studied ballet without thought of a stage career. In England particularly, organizations have been set up to control and maintain teaching standards through examinations, the largest of these being the Royal Academy of Dancing, founded in 1920, which examines candidates around the world.

Another development, at present still in its infancy, is the use of notation. Many systems have been devised, but only two are used at all widely, Labanotation and Benesh Notation. A growing number of companies record their repertories, but the full benefits of notation, teaching it from childhood as an inseparable part of the dancer's education, have still to come.   IG

Balsam, Martin (1919–) An American film and stage actor, born in New York City, Balsam has specialized in major supporting roles, almost always sympathetic. He made his professional debut in *The Play's the Thing*, at the Red Barn, Locust Valley, New York, August 1941, and on Broadway as Mr Blow in *Ghost for Sale*, at Daly's Theatre, 1941. His awards include the Outer Circle Award and a *Variety* poll citation for performances in *You Know I Can't Hear You When the Water's Running*, 1967, and an Academy Award as best supporting actor in *A Thousand Clowns*, 1965.   SMA

Bances y López Candamo, Francisco Antonio de (1662–1704) The last notable Spanish dramatist of the Golden Age. Of Asturian origins but brought up in Seville, he became official playwright to Carlos II (1687–94), then resigned and became a treasury official, apart from a brief comeback, 1696–7. Many of his plays have strong political overtones, which probably brought about his resignation, especially *El esclavo en grillos de oro* (*The Slave in Golden Shackles*, 1692), whose plot resembles **Shakespeare**'s *Measure for Measure*, and *La piedra filosofal* (*The Philosopher's Stone*, 1693). *Por su rey y por su dama* (*For King and Lady*, 1685) remained popular until the 19th century, and his treatise *Teatro de los teatros de los pasados y presentes siglos* (*Theatre of the Theatres of Past and Present Ages*, 1689–93) is invaluable as the only work of dramatic theory in the age of **Calderón**.   CL

Bancroft, Anne (Anna Maria Luisa Italiano) (1931–) American stage and film actress, who made her Broadway debut as Gittel Mosca in *Two for the Seesaw* (1958). She secured her stardom with such roles as Annie Sullivan in *The Miracle Worker* (1959) and Mother Courage in *Mother Courage and Her Children* (1963). Other substantial Broadway roles were in *The Devils* (1965), *A Cry of Players* (1968), *Golda* (1977) and *Duet for One* (1981). Her awards include Tonys for Gittel Mosca and Annie Sullivan. She received the Oscar for best actress for *The Miracle Worker* (1962). She is married to film director Mel Brooks and has appeared in several of his films. At the time of her debut, she was described as 'the most engaging gamin to light up a stage'; later, critics spoke glowingly of 'her guts and her spirit, the elegance of her style, and the passion of her playing'. SMA

Bancroft, Squire (1841–1926) English actor-manager, who made his London debut in **T. W. Robertson**'s *Society* at the **Prince of Wales's** in 1865. Two years later, after creating the role of Captain Hawtree in Robertson's *Caste*, he married the theatre's lessee, **Marie Wilton**, thereby entering simultaneously into matrimony and theatre-management. The Bancrofts' tenure of the Prince of Wales's was a fashionable triumph, and Bancroft himself, tall, distinguished, habitually sporting a monocle, was a social success. His impeccable manners and snobbish elegance became hallmarks of the Bancroft companies at the Prince of Wales's until 1879 and subsequently at the **Haymarket** (1880–5). Despite their rigid sense of hierarchy, they had the good sense to play lesser roles in several productions, offering to theatregoers an ensemble alternative to the star-centred regime of **Irving** at the **Lyceum**. No less enamoured of pictorial staging than Irving himself, their feeling was for the exquisite, even the miniature. When he renovated the Haymarket in 1880, Bancroft took the picture-frame stage to its logical conclusion by providing a proscenium 'in the form of a large gold frame, with all four sides complete'. He retired, already rich, at the age of 44. The first of many books, all remarkably similar, *Mr and Mrs Bancroft, on and off the Stage*, was published in 1888. In 1897, Bancroft became the second actor to receive a knighthood. Irving had beaten him by two years. PT

Bandi Nata This is the name of an Indian dramatic form which lasts about three hours. It takes its name from Bandi, the nickname of the sister of Chandrasena, the husband of Radha in the mythological tales surrounding the life of Krishna. The form is acted by members of the untouchable community of central and western Orissa. The actors mix with the spectators and only join in the action when their turn comes. They are accompanied by the dhol drum. Dances, songs, actions and humour are freely mixed to keep the spectators entertained. The stories concern Bandi's self-sacrifice for her husband Krishna so that he may sport with Radha. FaR

Bankhead, Tallulah (1902–68) American stage, film, and television actress, noted for her vibrant energy, sultry voice, explosive speech, and impetuous behaviour. The daughter of one of the most famous political families of Alabama, she first appeared on Broadway in 1918 and achieved fame in 1923 with her appearance in London in *The Dancers*. She returned to the USA in 1923 for film work and reappeared on Broadway in 1933. After doing a revival of *Rain*, she was widely acclaimed for her work as Regina in *The Little Foxes* in 1939 and won the New York Drama Critics Circle Award for best actress as Sabina in *The Skin of Our Teeth*. In film, she won the best actress award from the New York Film Critics in 1944 for *Lifeboat*. She published her autobiography, *Tallulah*, in 1952. SMA

Banks, John (c. 1652–1706) English playwright. Trained for the law he turned to the theatre and wrote seven plays. After three heroic plays, of which the best is *The Destruction of Troy* (1678), Banks established an entirely new form of drama which was decisively influential. Using as his source British history, he centred his plays, dubbed she-tragedies, on the sufferings of the heroine, creating an overwhelming emphasis on pathos. *The Unhappy Favourite* (1681), on Queen Elizabeth and Essex, was markedly successful and Banks pursued the genre with plays on Anne Boleyn, Lady Jane Grey and Mary Queen of Scots. The latter two, *The Innocent Usurper* (1683) and *The Island Queens* (1684), dealing in threats of usurpation and the execution of monarchs, were far too politically sensitive and were banned from performance. PH

Bannister, John (1760–1836) English actor, son of the comedian Charles Bannister (1741–1804). 'Jack' Bannister was a student at the Royal Academy before making his acting debut at the **Haymarket** in 1778, and remained a close friend of his fellow-student Thomas Rowlandson until Rowlandson's death in 1827. After moderate successes in tragedy at **Drury Lane**, he began a new career as a comedian when he created the part of Don Ferolo Whiskerandos in **Sheridan**'s *The Critic* (1779). A popular light comedian with a genial temperament and a fair singing voice, he was particularly associated with the summer seasons at the Haymarket. The manager was **George Colman the Younger**, who wrote a part for Bannister in almost all his plays and who helped him to compile one of the first authentic one-man shows under the title of *Bannister's Budget*. The success of these performances enabled Bannister to retire in 1815. PT

Bannister, Nathaniel (Harrington) (1813–47) American actor who began his career in New York and Philadelphia before going to New Orleans in 1834 where he married the widow of **John Augustus Stone** and established his reputation as a playwright. After 1837 the Bannisters performed regularly in New York. The author of at least 40 plays ranging through ancient history (*Gaulantus the Gaul*, 1836), local incidents (*The Maine Question*, 1839), romantic comedy (*The Gentleman of Lyons*, 1838) and moral dilemmas (*The Destruction of Jerusalem*, 1837), Bannister wrote mainly spectacles to please the public. *Putnam, the Iron Son of '76* (1844), his best-known play, opened with 78 performances, enchanting audiences with horses on stage. An innovator who influenced the development of American drama and enriched theatre managers, Bannister died young and a pauper. WJM

Baraka, Amiri (1934–) Afro-American poet, essayist and playwright. Born Everett Leroi Jones, Baraka assumed a new name and mission in the 1960s when he became leader of the black arts revolutionary movement that viewed theatre as a weapon in the struggle for black liberation. He has produced some 20 plays, many of them one-act, that powerfully dramatize social and racial problems in expressive forms and with unnerving frankness. Hailed for his 'fierce and blazing talent', condemned for his blatant anti-white posture, Baraka was notwithstanding the most prominent American dramatist of the 1960s with such plays as the Obie Award-winning *Dutchman* (1964), *The Slave* (1964), *A Black Mass* (1966), and *Slave Ship* (1967). He founded the Black Arts Repertory Theatre/School in Harlem (1965-6) and Spirit House in Newark, New Jersey (1966-), where his plays are produced. Baraka's writings and speeches have had a profound influence on the younger generation of Afro-American playwrights.   EGH

Barba, Eugenio (1936-) Italian theatre director and theorist whose major work has been done with the **Odin Teatret**, exploring the possibilities of what he has called 'the Third Theatre', a socially aware, exploratory, actor-oriented drama, distinct from that of commercial boulevard theatre on the one hand, and director-dominated, dramatist-oriented art theatre on the other. After university study in Italy, and a period at the directors' school in Warsaw, he joined **Grotowski**'s Laboratory Theatre as an observer in 1961. The influence of the three years he spent there has remained fundamental in his later work, inspiring him to found the Odin Teatret, first in Oslo, then on a more firm and regular basis as a centre for theatre research at Holstebrö in Denmark. That research has been pursued in a variety of ways, including the mounting of international conferences at which like-minded groups can exchange information on aims and methods, working in communities traditionally deprived of drama other than that projected by the mass media, exploring the possibilities of 'bartering' entertainment, and founding, as a focal point for collective research, the International School of Theatre Anthropology in 1979. He edited and contributed to Grotowski's seminal *Towards a Poor Theatre* (English translation 1968), and has published many articles on actor research and theatre anthropology, some of which have been gathered in *The Floating Islands* (1984) and *Beyond the Floating Islands* (1986).   KR

Barbeau, Jean (1945-) Quebec playwright. He was one of the first to follow the lead of **Michel Tremblay** in the use of *joual*, the popular French of Quebec, in plays such as *Manon Lastcall* (1970) and *Joualez-Moi d'Amour* (*Speak to Me of Love*, with the forging of a new verb, *joualer*, to replace *parler*, 1970). These plays deal humorously with the cultural schizophrenia of Quebec, joined by shared social heritage with France but divided by an uncommon tongue. *Le Chemin de Lacroix* (*The Way of Lacroix*), 0-71 and *Ben-Ur*, all three published in 1971, deal in more serious fashion with the social victims of his province's malaise. Since the election of the Parti Québécois in 1976 Barbeau, like many another Quebec intellectual, has turned to more universal concerns in plays such as *Le Jardin de la Maison Blanche* (*The White House Garden*,

1979), which attacks the materialistic values of contemporary North American society.   LED

Barbette (Vander Clyde) (1904-73) American aerialist, born near Austin, Texas. He made his circus debut dressed as a girl as one of the Alfaretta Sisters, but soon developed his own single act, under the name Barbette. At the Paris Alhambra, 1923, his elegant trapeze artistry became a sensation when he snatched off his blond wig at the end to reveal that the slender aerial queen was male. He was taken up by **Jean Cocteau** who devoted an essay to him and used him dressed in a Chanel evening gown in his film *Blood of a Poet*. After a triumphant career in Europe, Barbette contracted a chill at Loew's State, New York (1938), which developed into a crippling bone disease, and he became a popular trainer.   LS

Barker, Harley Granville see **Granville Barker**

Barker, Howard (1946-) British dramatist, whose first plays were produced at the **Royal Court Theatre** and the Open Space in the early 1970s. His early plays looked at British society from the stance of the underworld as well as the underdog – of twin gangsters in *Alpha Alpha* (1972), of pimps in *Claw* (1975) and of the criminal in *Stripwell* (1975) who invades the house of the judge who condemned him. Barker is adept at choosing telling dramatic situations in which many different incidents can take place, but he reverses what might be regarded as the moral expectations. The prison governor in *The Hang of the Gaol* (1978) becomes an arsonist, while the entrepreneur who capitalizes on graveyard mementoes in *The Love of a Good Man* is the hero of a black comedy set in 1920, after the carnage of the First World War. In *No End of Blame* (1980), he debates the issue of the different censorships, East and West.   JE

Barker, James Nelson (1784-1858) Born into a politically and socially influential American family, Barker combined his love of country with his love of theatre. Among his plays are *America* (1805); *Tears and Smiles* (1807), a patriotic comedy; a defence of Jefferson's Embargo Act, *The Embargo* (1808); the first produced American play about Pocahontas, *The Indian Princess* (1808); and *Marmion; or, The Battle of Flodden Field* (1812) in which England's treatment of 16th-century Scotland was transferred to America. Barker's greatest contributions are his 11 essays on drama in the *Democratic Press* (18 December 1816-19 February 1817) and his remarkable tragedy of New England intolerance, *Superstition; or The Fanatic Father* (1824). Thereafter, Barker, an avid supporter of Andrew Jackson, absorbed himself in politics, contributing to literature with poetry rather than plays.   WJM

Barlach, Ernst (1870-1938) German sculptor and dramatist, whose work forms a bridge between the symbolist movement and expressionism. His mystical themes focus on the nature of salvation, exploring the opposition between material existence and spiritual development in complex visual imagery. Though written between 1903 and 1912, his first play *The Dead Day* only reached the stage in 1919. Transferring the typical expressionist conflict between parents and children into religious terms – father as God, earth mother – it was strongly autobiographical, as was his next drama, *The Poor Cousin*, performed the same year. Moving away from realistic dialogue, he experimented with a modern form of the Mystery Play and turned to a biblical subject for his most widely produced work, *The Flood* (1924). Awarded the Kleist prize in 1924, his reputation was confirmed by a poetic return to his earlier themes in *The Blue Bulb* (1926). But his writings were banned by the Nazis, his sculptures destroyed, and his final work *Der Graf von Ratzeburg* remained unproduced until 1956, when his plays were revived by Lietzau in Berlin.   CI

Barnay, Ludwig (1842–1924) German actor. Before he joined the **Meininger** company as an actor of heroic roles, Barnay had acquired a considerable reputation as a guest in theatres in Pest, Graz, Mainz, Vienna, Leipzig and Frankfurt am Main. After his years with the Meininger, he made tours of England and America. In 1883 he was a co-founder with **L'Arronge** of the **Deutsches Theater**, though he soon left the company to start his own Berliner Theater in 1887. His last years were spent directing the **Berlin Royal Theatre** and the Court Theatre in Hannover. Barnay is also noted as the founder of a fledgling German actors' union, the Genossenschaft Deutscher Bühnenangehörigen, in 1871.   SW

Barnes, Clive Alexander (1927–) English/American dance and drama critic. Born in London and educated at Oxford, Barnes established his credentials as a dance critic for *Dance and Dancers* (1950–) and for *The Times* (1961–5). In 1965 he came to the United States as dance critic for the *New York Times*, adding the drama post in 1967. A decade later he was replaced as drama critic, and within the year (1977) resigned from the *Times* to become dance/drama critic for the *New York Post*. Noted for his clever style, Barnes wrote of *Agnes of God*: 'Some plays are so concerned with being theatrical that they forget to be dramatic.' He has been accused of being pro-British and of supporting the avant-garde more than the Broadway theatre.   TLM

Barnes, Peter (1931–) British dramatist, whose plays combine trenchant satire with a delight in shock effects. Although his first play, *Sclerosis*, an attack on British colonialism, was seen in Edinburgh and London in 1965, Barnes achieved success with his second play, *The Ruling Class* (1968), which contained many distinguishing features of his style – a fierce parody of the English upper classes, rapid changes of mood and atmosphere from the farcical to the macabre, an unusual delight in rhetoric and several *coups de théâtre*, not least in the play's final moments, where a grotesque House of Lords with skeletal figures swings on stage. In subsequent plays, he has chosen major moral and historical themes as subjects for black comedy – the Spanish Succession in *The Bewitched* (1974), the Holocaust in *Laughter!* (1978) and the Black Death in *Red Noses* (1985). Barnes consciously looks back to the Jacobeans and to the German dramatist **Frank Wedekind**, for his technical style, despising naturalism; and he has adapted plays by **Ben Jonson** (whom he admires more than **Shakespeare**) and Wedekind's *Lulu* plays (1971).   JE

Barnum, P[hineas] T[aylor] (1810–91) American entrepreneur and showman, a hard-headed businessman of great personal integrity whose *modus operandi* used deceit and innovative methods of publicity to promote both popular and high culture. Starting as a shopkeeper and editor of a weekly newspaper in Danbury, Conn., he moved to New York in 1834 and the next year commenced as a showman by exhibiting an ancient black woman he claimed was 160 years old and George Washington's nurse. In 1841 he purchased Scudder's American Museum, where he mixed freakshows with 'moral' drama and brought out the midget Tom Thumb (Charles Stratton), whose European appearances in 1844 made Barnum and the notion of 'humbug' notorious. In 1849 the Museum became a stock company and the next year he organized the American tour of the Swedish soprano Jenny Lind, who received 1,000 dollars a night. Barnum retired in 1855, but soon resumed his business. He did not enter the circus trade until 1871, merging with James A. Bailey in 1881 to create 'The Greatest Show on Earth', a combination of circus, menagerie and side-show; the acquisition of the elephant Jumbo was his greatest feat there. Throughout his busy life, Barnum regularly issued versions of his life story and optimistic philosophy: these included his *Autobiography* (1854), *The Humbugs of the World* (1865) and *Struggles and Triumphs* (1869; the best edition is that edited by G. S. Bryan, 2 vols., 1927).   LS

Barnum's American Museum   Broadway and Ann St, New York City. In 1841, **P. T. Barnum**, America's greatest showman, bought Scudder's Museum and quickly turned it into a city landmark. As part of the price of admission to see real and fake curiosities and an assortment of human freaks and

P. T. Barnum kneeling before Mercy Lavinia Warren Bump (1841–1919), who became Mrs Tom Thumb.

oddities, Barnum provided concerts and light entertainment in a Lecture Room. In 1849, it was expanded into a full-scale theatre for dramatic performances. In 1850, the seating was increased to 3,000 for the presentation of *The Drunkard*, the temperance drama. Thereafter, Barnum presented a series of moral plays in a moral manner with a stock company of actors of unimpeachable morality. In 1865, the museum and theatre burned to the ground and Barnum moved to 559 Broadway, but never achieved the success of the first venture. It, too, was destroyed by fire after only a few years of operation. MCH

Baron (Michel Boyron) (1653–1729) French actor and protégé of **Molière**. The son of theatrical parents, he was orphaned in childhood and at the age of 13, while acting in a children's troupe, he so impressed Molière that the latter offered him individual coaching and took him into his own company, where he developed into a successful *jeune premier*. On Molière's death he moved to the **Hôtel de Bourgogne**, creating some of **Racine**'s young heroes, and thence to the **Comédie-Française** on its formation in 1680. In 1691, at the height of his powers, he inexplicably retired from the stage, not acting again, except for occasional private performances, until he made an equally unexpected comeback 29 years later, whereupon at the age of 67 he cheerfully resumed most of his former roles, including those of young lovers, and created a number of new ones. He continued to act until shortly before his death nine years later. At his peak his outstanding ability, allied to good looks, intelligence and an air of distinction, enabled him to take leading roles in tragedy and comedy alike and was apparently enough to ensure a sympathetic hearing for mediocre plays. Contemporary critics remarked upon his attention to detail and the relative simplicity of his playing – a quality he is supposed to have encouraged in the young **Adrienne Lecouvreur** – though he could also be self-important and disagreeable to his colleagues. He was the author of several comedies, the most interesting of which are *L'Homme à Bonnes Fortunes* (*The Philanderer*, 1686) and the one-act *Le Rendez-vous des Tuileries* (1685) in which several actors of the Comédie-Française appeared as themselves. DR

Barrault, Jean-Louis (1910–) French actor and director who has made a significant contribution to five decades of theatre. His first performances were at **L'Atelier** in the 1930s; one of these was hailed by **Artaud** as achieving his own ideal. In 1940 Barrault joined the **Comédie-Française** where he met Madeleine Renaud, an outstanding actress and later his wife and co-director. Here he began to direct as well as act: his production of **Claudel**'s *Le Soulier de Satin* (*The Satin Slipper*) in 1943 was a particular success. In 1946 he and Renaud left to found their own company. At the Marigny theatre as a private company and, after 1959, at the **Odéon** with state subsidy, their policy was to produce a mixture of new plays and classics. Barrault's greatest achievement is to have seen that Claudel's apparently wordy plays could succeed in the theatre given a sufficiently concrete and gestural production style: he produced six of his plays. He had learned much from the mime artist **Etienne Decroux** before the war (as he demonstrated in the role of **Deburau** in Carné's

film *Les Enfants du Paradis*) and his performances were outstanding for the detail and inventiveness of their physical action. He produced many new authors, including **Ionesco**, **Duras**, **Vauthier**, and made a number of his own adaptations for the stage. The most famous was *Rabelais* (1968) performed in a Montmartre wrestling hall. This production, celebrating freedom from authority, was his reply to Malraux, who had dismissed him from his post at the Odéon for allowing students to use it as a debating forum during the near-revolution. In 1972 he converted the former Orsay station into a performance space, erecting a circus tent inside the building and in 1981 he moved to the Théâtre du Rond Point, a former skating rink on the Champs Elysées. Originally identified with total theatre, Barrault has become, in old age, a star actor viewed with the same respect as **Laurence Olivier** in England. DB

Barrett, Lawrence (1838–91) American actor and manager. He made his debut as Murad in *The French Spy* in Detroit in 1853 and his first important New York appearances in 1857 as a member of **William E. Burton**'s Metropolitan Theatre Company. He subsequently was a member of Boston's Howard Athenaeum Company (1858–61). Barrett was often associated with **Edwin Booth** throughout his career. In 1863 he acted with Booth at the **Winter Garden Theatre** and in 1871–2 at **Booth's Theatre** he was the leading supporting actor appearing most notably as Adrian de Mauprat to Booth's celebrated Richelieu, but also alternating Othello and Iago with him. At Booth's Theatre, Barrett also starred as James Harebell in **W. G. Wills**'s *The Man O'Airlie* – one of his most acclaimed roles – as Leontes in a spectacular production of *The Winter's Tale*, and as Cassius with Booth's Brutus in a lavish revival of *Julius Caesar*. This last production was later toured by Barrett under the management of **Jarrett** and **Palmer**. Although a professional disagreement estranged them for the next seven years, Booth and Barrett were reconciled in 1880 and their relationship continued to be close for the rest of their lives. Barrett managed Booth's last starring tours from 1886 to 1891 and for the last three seasons, they made nationwide 'joint starring' tours. Barrett managed at one time (1866–70) the California Theatre in San Francisco with **John McCullough** and the Variety Theatre in New Orleans (1871–3). In 1884–5 he leased **Henry Irving**'s **Lyceum Theatre** during the latter's first American tour. Generally, however, Barrett spent most of his career as a touring star often with his own company. He was also keenly interested in encouraging American drama and dramatists, commissioning numerous original plays and adaptations during his career. He presented **W. D. Howells**'s first full length play *Counterfeit Presentment* (1877), William Young's *Pendragon* (1881) and *Ganelon* (1888), and successfully revived **George Henry Boker**'s *Francesca da Rimini* (1883).

Slender with a sensitive face, deep set expressive eyes, and an unusual vocal range. Barrett was regarded as a studious, sometimes compelling, but also overly technical actor. His most successful roles after Harebell were Lanciotto in *Francesca da Rimini*, Hernani, Cassius and late in his career Othello. DJW

Barrett, Wilson (1846–1904) English actor–manager, who too often wasted his good looks and fervour for greatness on inferior material, much of it written by himself. The supreme example is *The Sign of the Cross* (1895), a melodrama of frantic spirituality which requires a Roman patrician to face the lions for love of a Christian maiden. He opened the play in the USA, brought it to the Grand Theatre in Leeds, of which he was the first lessee (1878–95), and only then to London, where, outrageously, it was a huge success. Barrett was, at various times, manager of theatres in Leeds and Hull as well as in London (the Court, the **Princess's**, the **Globe**, the **Olympic**, the **Lyceum**). Among his Shakespearian roles, his Mercutio was better received than his Hamlet and his Benedick, but his real gift was in rampantly wholesome melodrama, preferably with religious overtones. He had major successes with George R. Sims's *The Lights o' London* (1881), the **Henry Arthur Jones**/Henry Herman collaboration *The Silver King* (1882) and with his own adaptations of *The Manxman* (1894) and *Quo Vadis?* (1900).   PT

Barrie, J[ames] M[atthew] (1860–1937) Scottish playwright whose journalistic career brought him to London in 1885. Barrie had already made a mark with a novel, *The Little Minister* (1891), when **J. L. Toole** staged his first successful play, *Walker, London* (1892). Ten years and several plays later, Barrie discovered, in *Quality Street* (1902) and *The Admirable Crichton* (1902), a profitable way of combining his own predilection for escapist romance with the contemporary dramatic interest in social problems. He was a craftsman who should not be too easily condemned as merely whimsical or classified as a permanent adolescent, unwilling or unable to join the adult world, like the leading character of his most famous play, *Peter Pan* (1904). If *Alice Sit-by-the-Fire* (1905) and *Mary Rose* (1920) are fatally flawed by mawkishness, *What Every Woman Knows* (1908) and *Dear Brutus* (1917) are strengthened by the quiet satire that is present in everything that Barrie wrote. Certain of his one-act plays, *The Twelve-Pound Look* (1910), *The Will* (1913) and *The Old Lady Shows Her Medals* (1917) among them, remain effective examples of that difficult form. Best of all, perhaps, is the teasing *Shall We Join the Ladies?* (1921), the first act of an uncompleted murder-mystery, which is a masterpiece of trail-laying. Barrie was knighted in 1913.   PT

Barrison Sisters, The Five (Bareisen) Swedish variety performers, who first appeared in 1893 at the Chicago World's Fair in a children's ballet. Despite their ages (one was married), they dressed in pink pinafores, ruffled petticoats and baby's caps. The contrast between this innocent exterior and the *double entendre* of their songs and dances, as they held black pussy-cats below their midriffs, created a sensation in Europe, especially at the **Folies-Bergère** and the Berlin Wintergarten, and founded a new genre of sisters act. Their best number was 'Linger Longer, Loo'. They retired in 1908, although the youngest, Gertrude, continued to dance in cabarets.   LS

Barry, Elizabeth (c. 1658–1713) English actress. According to tradition, after a poor start in the theatre, she was trained by the Earl of Rochester and became his mistress. Her first known role was in **Otway**'s *Alcibiades* (1675) for the Duke's Company and she quickly established herself as the outstanding actress of her day. Her great success as Monimia in Otway's *The Orphan* (1680) showed her ability to move the audience: **Downes**, the prompter, recorded 'she forced tears from the eyes of her auditory, especially those who have any sense of pity for the distressed'. By the late 1680s, she was effectively co-manager of the United Company with **Betterton** and joined his group of actors who seceded in 1695 to form a company at **Lincoln's Inn Fields Theatre**. She retired in 1710. Her acting was marked by an unusual control and intensity. She was praised for her identification with the role ('she is the person she represents') and for what **Cibber** described as her ability to 'pour out the sentiment with an enchanting harmony'. At her best in tragedy, she had many major parts written for her by Otway, **Congreve** and others. For nearly 30 years she proved her right to be regarded as the first great English actress.   PH

Barry, Spranger (?1717–77) Irish actor–manager. Born in Dublin, he began acting at Smock Alley Theatre in 1744, playing Othello at his debut. In 1746 he moved to **Drury Lane**, playing Othello and Macbeth in his first season. He quickly established a high reputation as an actor of sighing lovers, acting opposite **Garrick** in plays by **Otway** and **Rowe** with great success. In 1750 he joined **Covent Garden** and played Romeo in direct competition with Garrick's performances in Drury Lane for 12 successive nights, eventually giving way to Garrick, though praised for 'the amorous harmony of his features, his melting eyes and unequalled plaintiveness of voice'. In 1756 he played Lear with great majesty. The following year he took over a theatre in Dublin and built a new one, the Crow Street Theatre, but returned to London in 1767, nearly bankrupt. He remarried and often acted with his wife but he rowed incessantly with Garrick who accused him of avoiding performing whenever possible. In the 1770s, frequently ill, he moved again to Covent Garden and continued acting till his death.   PH

Barrymore see **Drew**

Barsacq, André (1909–) French theatre director of Russian origins who began as a designer for **Dullin**. With **Jean Dasté** and Maurice Jacquemont he founded the Compagnie des Quatre Saisons in 1937. In 1940 he took over from Dullin as director of the **Atelier** where he succeeded in continuing the work of the pre-war **Cartel** directors, like them largely unsubsidized and relying on exquisite revivals of classics, especially the Russians combined with popular modern playwrights such as **Anouilh**, Marcel Aymé, Félicien Marceau, René de Obaldia and occasionally a media-hyped author such as Françoise Sagan. He made a fine adaptation of Dostoevsky's *The Idiot* (1966).   DB

Bartoli, Francesco (1745–1806) Italian actor and writer who worked his way up in the trade, first directing amateur improvising groups, then in minor professional companies, and finally joining the major troupe led by Pietro Rossi. In 1769 he married one of the lead actresses of the time, Teodora Ricci, and with her two years later joined one of the most important companies of the age, that led by **Antonio Sacchi**. A competent, second string actor, at a time when most players were uneducated, in addition to his wide professional experience, he brought intelligence and a cultivated mind to his most important writing on the theatre, *Notizie Istoriche de'Comici Italiani che Fiorirono Intorno all'Anno MDL Fino a' Giorni Presenti* (*Historical Particulars of Italian Players who Flourished Around the Year MDL to the Present Day*, 2 vols., 1782). Although full of errors, it is an indispensable early source book for information on Italian performers and companies, particularly those of the **commedia dell'arte**. It was published in the year he left the profession and, abandoned by his wife, who in 1777 had left to pursue an independent career in Paris, he took up bookselling. He also wrote poetry and plays, and a study of Italian architects.   KR

Barton, John (Bernard Adie) (1928–) British director, who directed Marlowe Society productions in Cambridge while he was a Fellow of King's College during the 1950s. His particular strength lay in his detailed understanding of Elizabethan and Jacobean verse, and under his guidance the Society's **Shakespeare** productions were renowned for the vivid naturalness of the verse-speaking. In 1960, he joined the Shakespeare Memorial Company at Stratford (later, the **Royal Shakespeare Company**) under its new leadership from **Peter Hall**. Barton helped the company to present Shakespearian texts in ways that were immediately understood by modern audiences. Sometimes this involved a simplification or reduction of the original texts, as in *The Wars of the Roses* (1963), which condensed the *Henry VI* trilogy and *Richard III* into three evenings of power struggles. He devised recital performances for the RSC, such as *The Hollow Crown* (1961) and *The Art of Seduction* (1962) – and helped to bring the RSC's touring Theatre-go-round into existence. As a resident director with the company, he was responsible for many Shakespearian productions on the main stages and in the studio theatres. In 1980, he devised *The Greeks*, ten plays shown in a cycle which tell the story of the Trojan wars. In recent years, he has directed 19th- and 20th-century plays for the RSC by such writers as **Ibsen**, **Schnitzler**, **Granville Barker** and **John Whiting**.   JE

Bassermann, Albert (1862–1952) German actor. After acting in Mannheim and with the **Meiningen**, in 1899 Bassermann joined **Brahm**'s **Deutsches Theater** in Berlin. Here he was specially noted for his interpretations of **Ibsen**. Later he acted for several years with **Reinhardt**. Upon Hitler's rise to power, he emigrated to America. In 1944, he appeared on Broadway, then returned to Europe at the end of the war.   SW

Bateman family **Hezekiah Linthicum Bateman** (1812–75), American manager, first relied on his child-prodigy daughters, before managing London's **Lyceum Theatre** where he brought **Henry Irving** to prominence in *The Bells* (1871), and then in *Hamlet* (1874, for 200 performances).
His wife **Sidney** (1823–81) wrote *Self* (1856), assumed the Lyceum management at her husband's death, and later managed **Sadler's Wells** (1879).

Kate (1843–1917) and **Ellen** (1844–1936) began performing **Shakespeare** in New York (1849), when they were six and five, then in London (1851). Kate played Richmond, Portia, and Lady Macbeth; Ellen, Richard III, Shylock, and Macbeth. Kate later played in *Leah, the Forsaken* (1862, New York; 1863, London), then appeared with Irving. Ellen retired.
Virginia (1853–1940) and **Isabel** (1854–1934) made their London debuts in 1865, then joined Irving. Virginia married Edwin Compton and was the mother of Fay Compton and Compton McKenzie. Isabel co-managed Sadler's Wells before becoming Reverend Mother General of the Community of St Mary the Virgin at Wantage (1898).   RM

Bates, Alan (Arthur) (1934–) British actor, who played the passive Cliff to Kenneth Haigh's vitriolic Jimmy Porter in the **Royal Court** production of *Look Back in Anger* (1956). Bates here revealed his capacity for a taut stillness, an eloquent calm, which has stayed with him in more demanding roles, such as Mick in **Harold Pinter**'s *The Caretaker* (1960), the title role in **Simon Gray**'s *Butley* (1971), Simon in Gray's *Otherwise Engaged* (1975) and the Inquisitor in Pinter's *One for the Road* (1984). He quickly discovered how to use the prolonged pauses in Pinter's plays, the biting irony and the savage invective of Gray's characters, as of **Osborne**'s and **David Storey**'s. In 1985, he played the title role in **Peter Shaffer**'s *Yonadab* at the **National Theatre**.   JE

Bates, Blanche (1873–1941) American actress. Daughter of Frank Bates, manager of noted stock companies in Portland and San Francisco, she made her debut in the latter (1893) after an early marriage and a brief career as a school teacher. By 1895 she had become a leading lady there. A successful tour opposite **James O'Neill** (1899–1900) brought her to New York and the attention of **David Belasco**, who starred her as Cho-Cho-San in *Madame Butterfly* (1900), Cigarette in *Under Two Flags* (1901), Yo-San in *The Darling of the Gods* (1902) and Minnie in *The Girl of the Golden West* (1905). She retired in 1926. Full of power and humour, she portrayed a liberated woman who was always energetic, resourceful, and faithful.   DMCD

Baty, Gaston (1885–1952) French theatre director, the only member of the **Cartel** who was not also an actor. Baty brought the stage techniques of expressionism to the Paris theatre. Like **Craig**, he admired puppets and had an ambitious view of the director's art. Like **Artaud** he attacked the predominance of literary theatre in France between the wars. From 1930 to 1947 he ran the Théâtre Montparnasse, where he strove for complex staging methods with an emphasis on pictorial qualities.   DB

Bauer, Wolfgang (1941–) Austrian dramatist, whose work has helped to revive the **Volksstück** tradition in contemporary terms, extending the kind of realism established by **Horváth** in the 1930s. From *Pig Transport* in 1962, his dialect plays have presented increasingly violent images of a society stripped of cultural values by materialism in which sex, sadism, drugs and pop music are the only release for boredom. Designed as provocation, works like *Magic Afternoon*

(1968), *Sylvester or the Massacre at the Sacher Hotel* (1971), or *Magnetic Kisses* (1976), are deliberately unartistic in style with trivialized characters, crude plot development and fast pacing that transforms brutality into farce, apparently undercutting serious themes. CI

Bauernfeld, Eduard von (1802–90) Austrian playwright. Prolific writer of comedies of manners on Viennese life, most of which were produced at the **Burgtheater**. These plays are considered to capture the essence of Viennese society during the Biedermeier period. Best-known among Bauernfeld's plays, several of which were effective satires, are *Bourgeois and Romantic* (1833), *Of Age* (1846), *The Categorical Imperative* (1850), and *From Society* (1867). SW

Bax, Clifford (1886–1962) British playwright, poet and critic, heavily influenced by **W. B. Yeats**, whose major success was in historical tragedy. Besides his portrayal of Henry VIII in *The Rose Without a Thorn* (1932) or *The House of Borgia* (1935), however, he also adapted **Karel Čapek**'s *The Insect Play* (1922–3) together with Nigel Playfair, and experimented with **commedia dell'arte** and parody in *Midsummer Marriage* (1924). During the Second World War he turned to radio plays on mystical themes, and in 1945 published a work of theatrical theory that contained a strong plea for the establishment of a **National Theatre**. CI

Baxter, James K. (1926–72) New Zealand playwright. He was already established as a poet when his first radio play, *Jack Winter's Dream*, was produced in 1958, and other radio plays followed during a fellowship at the University of Otago (1966–7). His first stage plays were written for the director Richard Campion; *The Wide Open Cage* (1959) was the most successful of these. In Dunedin, the director Patric Carey encouraged him to write other plays on religious and social themes, notably *The Band Rotunda* (1967), *The Devil and Mr Mulcahy* (1967), and *The Day that Flanagan Died* (1969), and also plays derived from Greek myth, such as *The Sore-footed Man* (1967) and *The Temptations of Oedipus* (1970). HDMCN

Bay, Howard (1912–86) American stage and film designer. Bay's designs include *The Little Foxes, Show Boat, The Music Man, Finian's Rainbow*, and *Man of La Mancha*. He became associated with the sentimental musicals of the 1940s and 50s which were very painterly in style. But he virtually began his career with a super-realistic set, a tenement, for the **Federal Theatre Project**'s *One Third of a Nation*. Bay believes that a designer 'must not polish a single style' but rather, must be adaptable to any situation. Thus, he is known as a pragmatist and for his ingenious solutions to design problems. From 1965 to 1982 Bay taught at Brandeis University. He is the author of the well-respected book *Stage Design*. AA

Baylis, Lilian Mary (1874–1937) British theatre manager. Trained as a musician, she began her association with the Victoria theatre (popularly known as the **Old Vic**) when it was run as a temperance hall providing cheap family entertainment under her aunt, Emma Cons. Taking over in 1912, she mounted a complete cycle of **Shakespeare**'s first folio plays from *The Taming of the Shrew* in 1914 to *Troilus and Cressida* in 1923, an undertaking that no theatre had attempted before. Directed by **Ben Greet**, and with players of the stature of **Sybil Thorndike**, these established a reputation for the theatre that continued after her death up to 1963, when it became the temporary stage of the new **National Theatre** company. Appointed a Companion of Honour for her services to the arts in 1929, she reopened **Sadler's Wells Theatre** in 1931, founding the companies that eventually became the Royal Ballet and the English National Opera. CI

Bayreuth This Franconian city has two notable theatres. First there is the Margrave's Opera House, designed by members of the **Bibiena** family, opened in 1748, and regarded nowadays as a perfect example of rococo theatre architecture. Then there is the Festival Theatre, opened by **Richard Wagner** in 1876, built specifically for the performance of *The Ring of the Nibelungs* and, as it transpired later, for his other mature music dramas. The auditorium of the Festival Theatre is one of the first examples of the arrangement known in America as the 'European style'. It has a wedge-shaped auditorium, a sunken orchestra pit, and a proscenium arch, which is repeated on the side-walls of the auditorium. These features, combined with the unusually long acoustic reverberation of the wooden auditorium, have created a theatre space where Wagner's spectacular, large-scale works can be seen and heard under conditions of remarkable concentration, even intimacy. Wagner's music dramas are still performed at annual music festivals at Bayreuth, under the direction of the Wagner family. SW

Bear-baiting see **Baiting**

Beaton, Cecil (1904–80) British theatrical set and costume designer, photographer, and writer. Beaton's career as a designer began after he was permitted to photograph Edith Sitwell, who introduced him into theatrical circles. Beaton's neoromantic style is illustrated in his well-known designs for the stage which include costumes for the musical *My Fair Lady* (1956), and the play *Lady Windermere's Fan* (1946). He also created exuberant designs for film with *Gigi* (1958), *My Fair Lady* (1964), and *On a Clear Day You Can See Forever* (1970) (which he co-designed). Beaton's style, particularly suited to the ballet, is evident in his designs for Frederick Ashton's *Les Sirènes* (1946), *Swan Lake* (1952), and *Marguerite et Armand* (1963). TM

Beaulne, Guy (1921–) French Canadian actor, director and critic. His career began in amateur theatre in the Ottawa area. After appearing in several radio dramas in the 1940s, he studied theatre in Paris, 1948–50. On his return he immediately joined Radio-Canada's television department, directing the most successful serial in its history, *La Famille Plouffe* (*The Plouffes*, 1952–63). Longtime theatre critic for Ottawa's *Le Droit,* he continued to act professionally in major productions of works by **Molière**, **Shakespeare**, by Canadian authors such as **Marcel Dubé** and Felix Leclerc, and to direct major works by these and other playwrights. In 1958 he founded the influential Canadian Amateur Theatre Association, acting as its director until 1963. In 1970 he became director of Quebec City's Grand Théâtre, the first fully professional troupe established there. He served as director-general of the National Theatre School of Canada, 1981–4. LED

Beaumarchais, Pierre-Augustin Caron de (1732–99) French playwright whose work for the stage occupied only a fraction of his energetic life as government agent, financial speculator, litigant and commercial entrepreneur. Son of a Paris watchmaker, he used this skill to gain an entrée to court where he advanced himself with characteristic opportunism, giving music lessons to the king's daughters, acquiring a position and the title Beaumarchais by marriage to a rich widow and purchasing various royal charges. His dramatic career began with 'parades', short sketches modelled on those acted at the fair theatres and written for private performance, but with *Eugénie* (1767), a domestic drama, he produced his first serious work and published it with a supporting essay showing clearly the influence of **Diderot**'s advocacy of this new genre. The play was quite well received, but another in the same vein, *Les Deux Amis* (*The Two Friends*, 1770), proved a failure. With a display of tongue-in-cheek contrition he turned to comedy, contriving an exquisite confection of all the genre's traditional devices. This was the first of his Figaro plays, *The Barber of Seville*, which despite some initial difficulties with the censor was a huge success at the **Comédie-Française** in 1775, but the underlying note of seriousness in its sequel, *The Marriage of Figaro*, fell badly foul of censorship. It was considered dangerously critical of authority and permission to present it publicly was withheld for several years. The opening night at the Comédie-Française in 1784 was a keenly anticipated and historic occasion: ecstatic applause came from all parts of the house, not least from the aristocracy themselves, and a record run of performances ensued. Because of its proximity to the events of 1789 the play's political significance can too easily be overestimated, but as a comedy it is remarkable for having captured a sense of grievance and dissent in the air of its time. Beaumarchais's next work was an opera, *Tarare* (1787), with music by Salieri, and in 1792 he returned to heavy-handed domestic sentiment with the last Figaro play, *La Mère Coupable* (*The Guilty Mother*). Using the same central characters the trilogy as a whole thus charts in miniature a progression from 'artificial' comedy to 'realistic' domestic drama. Meanwhile he had founded the Société des Auteurs, introducing an author's royalty on all theatrical performances, established a printing press to publish the first complete edition of **Voltaire**'s works, and exported arms to the American colonies during the War of Independence. A protracted arms mission on behalf of the Revolution led to accusations of fraud, seizure of his property, temporary exile and disgrace for his entire family, but he still managed to avoid the guillotine and died peacefully in his bed. DR

Beaumont, Francis (1584–1616) English playwright and poet, a member of the rural gentry who left Oxford without a degree in 1598 and was a casual law-student at the Inner Temple after 1600. His first play, *The Woman Hater* (1605), is a comedy of humours written for the **Boys of St Paul's**. A second, the only other extant play of which he was sole author, was

performed by the **Children of the Chapel Royal**. This is the witty and splendidly good-humoured *The Knight of the Burning Pestle* (1607), in which the bourgeois taste for chivalric romance is kindly mocked. The rest of Beaumont's dramatic work was written in a famous collaboration with **John Fletcher**. They succeeded **Shakespeare** as leading playwrights for the King's Men in about 1609, providing the company with a sequence of popular successes including *Philaster* (c. 1609), *The Maid's Tragedy* (c. 1610) and *A King and No King* (1611). Perhaps because they shared a fashionably educated audience's fondness for mellifluous verse, spicy sexual encounters and neatly paralleled situations, Beaumont and Fletcher became leaders of refined theatrical taste. Their natural home was less the **Globe** than the King's Men's newly acquired indoor theatre in the **Blackfriars**. Beaumont's active involvement did not long survive his marriage in 1613, and of the many plays sometimes ascribed to the two friends, only a handful can be confidently attributed, in any significant part, to him. These include *Cupid's Revenge* (c. 1611), *The Coxcomb* (1612), *The Scornful Lady* (c. 1613) and *The Captain* (1613) in addition to the three finer works already mentioned. PT

Beaumont, Hugh (Binkie) (1908–73) British theatre impresario, who became the Managing Director of H. M. Tennent Ltd and its non-profit subsidiary, Tennent Productions Ltd. For a quarter of a century, from the mid-1930s to the early 1960s, Beaumont was one of the most powerful impresarios in British theatre, concerning himself mainly with dramas and comedies. His tastes were restrained: he liked fine writing in plays and helped such dramatists as **Christopher Fry** and **Terence Rattigan**. H. M. Tennent Ltd became associated in the 1950s with star-studded West End productions of small-cast, opulently dressed and staged plays, and, as such, became a target for such 'angry young men' as **Kenneth Tynan**. Beaumont became a governor of the Shakespeare Memorial Theatre in 1950 and was also a member of the **National Theatre** Board from 1962–8. A modest, retiring man, Beaumont was an astute business man and clearly understood the middle- and upper-middle-class tastes for which his productions were mainly intended. JE

Beck, Julian see **Living Theatre**

Beckett, Samuel (1906–) Irish and French playwright. Like **Adamov** and **Ionesco**, Beckett only became known as a playwright relatively late in life when, in 1953, *En Attendant Godot* was successfully produced by **Blin**. The play was both so brilliant and so different from anything audiences were accustomed to, that it became a great talking point in cultural circles. The British premiere of *Waiting for Godot* (directed by **Hall**, 1955) had a similarly explosive effect on English theatre. But when Beckett wrote *Godot* he had already completed the greater part of his prose *oeuvre*, including the trilogy (*Molloy*, *Malone Dies* and *The Unnamable*).

He had grown up in Dublin in a Protestant family, taken a job briefly teaching French at Trinity College. But he soon moved into self-imposed exile in London and then in Paris, where he has lived almost continuously since 1937. Some of his plays were written in French, some in English; in each case Beckett has done his own translations into the other language. In *Godot* and subsequent plays, especially *Endgame* (first performed as *Fin de Partie* directed by Blin in London, 1957), *Krapp's Last Tape* (1958) and *Happy Days* (1961), Beckett succeeded in creating rituals for celebrating nothing which are both philosophically uncompromising and theatrically inventive. He appears to have been influenced by the Dublin music-halls he visited in his youth and his characters' dialogue owes much to comic cross-talk acts. But Beckett's achievement is that through whittling away the traditional elements of plot, setting and character, he has created a dynamic image for the static experience of waiting, remembering, struggling with the characteristically modern sense of futility. His characters are often devoid of 'personality', possessing only the clown's self-conscious and anguished awareness that his sole function is to keep the game going. Their appeal on stage stems from Beckett's gift for creating literal images for degenerating life conditions and some of these have become proverbial: Hamm's parents living in dustbins (*Endgame*) or Winnie, buried in a mound, first up to her waist, then up to her neck (*Happy Days*). By such means, Beckett creates compressed images of the whole human situation. Since the late 1960s he has written only short dramatic fragments in which the clown figure has disappeared, to be replaced by ghostly shapes, only half seen, struggling to retain a feeble hold on their sense of themselves and of the space in which they move or speak. But Beckett has also become more involved in the production of his own works and records of his direction e.g. of *Waiting for Godot* in Berlin, 1975, have led to increased understanding of his dramaturgical originality. DB

Becque, Henry (1837–99) French dramatist. Becque's significance for the development of naturalism in the theatre is out of proportion to his actual dramatic output. His early play, *Michel Pauper* (1870), was already a committedly socialist piece. *La Navette* (*The Shuttle*), about a lady with three lovers, a foretaste of *The Parisienne*, disgusted audiences at the Gymnase in 1878. Two years later his Mussetish badinage *Les Honnêtes Femmes* (*Honest Women*) had a better reception. In 1882, five years after its writing, having been refused by a number of theatres, *Les Corbeaux* (*The Crows*) received its premiere at the **Comédie-Française**. This was a stormy event followed by long battles in the press, and signalled the arrival of naturalism in the national theatre. Becque had moved beyond the well-made play to the well-observed play, an accurate depiction of the less pleasant side of late 19th-century society. The 'crows' are birds of prey who descend on the women of a family after the death of the father. One of the daughters finally 'saves' the family by marrying the man whom she knows to have been the cause of their poverty. *The Parisienne* (1885) had even less plot, lacking exposition and denouement, and was the prototype of the 'slice of life' play. It presented a married woman with a complaisant husband, a jealous lover and another lover. In a short piece, *Veuve!* (*Widow!*), Becque explored the situation after the death of the husband. *The Parisienne* was first staged at the Renaissance with **Réjane**, and joined the repertoire of the Comédie-Française in 1890. Becque wrote

little in his later years apart from some one-act sketches and an unfinished work, *Les Polichinelles, ou le Monde d'Argent* (*Polichinelles, or The World of Money*) but in 1895 he published his *Memoirs of a Dramatist*. His two major plays heralded the bitter comedies, the *comédies rosses*, that would become a major feature of the Théâtre Libre repertoire, and his achievement is best measured by comparing him with such 'realist' dramatists as **Augier** and **Dumas**, still working within the framework of the well-made play.   JMCC

Beer-Hoffman, Richard (1886–1945) Austrian dramatist, director and novelist, one of the Young Vienna group with **Schnitzler** and **Hofmannsthal**. After writing poetic historical tragedy and pantomime, the first part of his major work appeared in 1919. This was an Old Testament cycle (*Jacob's Dream, Young David, The History of King David*) experimenting with symbolic tableaux and pageant elements. All his plays are variations on the theme of fate, and the later parts of the trilogy remain unperformed. Banned in 1933, their portrayal of faith as the acceptance of suffering, even persecution, has seemed unacceptable after the Holocaust.   CI

Beeston, Christopher (c. 1580–1639) English actor and theatre manager who may have been trained for the stage by **Augustine Phillips**, was briefly with the **Lord Chamberlain's Men** and then with Worcester's Men at the **Rose**. Beeston made his reputation at the **Red Bull** during that theatre's boisterous occupation by Queen Anne's Men, for whom, from 1612–19, he was an autocratic business manager. In 1616, Beeston acquired the lease of the **Cockpit** in Drury Lane, converting and renaming it the **Phoenix** in 1617. It was as manager and impresario at the Phoenix that Beeston exerted a major influence on the Jacobean and Caroline theatre. His dominance was acknowledged in the popular name of the last of the many companies he established there, Beeston's Boys (1637–40).   PT

Beeston, William (c. 1606–82) English theatre manager, the son of **Christopher Beeston**, from whom he inherited control of Beeston's Boys at the **Phoenix** in 1639. He was replaced by **Davenant** in 1640, after twice offending the authorities by his choice of plays. Certainly he maintained his theatrical ambitions during the Interregnum. His activities at the indoor theatre in **Salisbury Court** may have provoked its dismantling by soldiers in 1649. Beeston refurbished it for performance in 1660 and probably retained a managerial interest until the building's destruction in the Great Fire of 1666. In retirement, Beeston was a noted theatrical raconteur.   PT

Behan, Brendan (1923–64) Irish playwright. A child of the tenements, Behan credited his education to his prison terms, though he owed much to his family, well-read, and of strong Republican sympathies. At 14 he joined the IRA, and spent two years in an English Borstal, convicted in 1939 of carrying explosives. Released and deported, in 1942 he got 14 years for shooting at a policeman during an IRA ceremony.

Amnestied in 1947, Behan continued the writing begun in prison, mainly short stories in an inventive stylization of Dublin vernacular. His plays brought him celebrity. In 1954 the **Pike Theatre** presented *The Quare Fellow*, a grimly comic drama of the hours preceding a prison hanging. Much more than propaganda against judicial execution, it captures, with remarkable economy of form and neutrality of tone, the condition of the outcast and the emotions excited by barbaric revenge. **Joan Littlewood**'s 1956 Theatre Workshop production in London made Behan famous.

Success was unmanageable. Behan's irresolute discipline collapsed into international drinking bouts. *The Hostage* (1958), his next play, derived from his one-act Gaelic play *An Giall*, was acclaimed in London, Paris, New York. Much influenced by Joan Littlewood's improvisational theatre, it travesties with song and dance – and Behan's easy connivance – the tragic simplicity of its original. His last serious work, *Borstal Boy* (1958), is an imaginatively controlled account of his Borstal years, itself the testimony to a sophisticated creative power and great generosity of feeling.

A clamorous Dublin presence, belligerent or convivial, Behan illuminated the theatrical drabness of the 1950s. He subdued his vivid personality to an objective form, and his work, however brief, is continuous with a tradition, that of **O'Casey**'s urban drama.   DM

Behn, Aphra (1640–89) The first English woman to be a professional playwright. She lived in Surinam from 1663 to 1664, an experience on which her novella *Oroonoko* was based. In 1666 she was employed as a spy by the English government in Antwerp but, arriving back in London in 1667 penniless, she was imprisoned for debt and had to appeal for her government pay. She wrote at least 17 plays, mostly comedies but including one farce opera, *The Emperor of the Moon* (1687), which made use of massive stage spectacle and a French **commedia dell'arte** plot. Her comedies, well crafted and vigorous, return frequently to the miseries of mercenary, loveless marriages. She wrote political comedies of Tory propaganda, e.g. *The Roundheads* (1681), as well as satires on contemporary behaviour, e.g. *The Lucky Chance* (1686) and *Sir Patient Fancy* (1678). Her best play, *The Rover* (1677), was based on **Thomas Killigrew**'s *Thomaso* and sets the rake's freedom against the independence and wit of Hellena. She produced a sequel in 1681.   PH

Behrman, S[amuel] N[athaniel] (1893–1973) American playwright. Though Behrman came from a middle-class family, his plays are typically set in genteel upper-class drawing rooms. Dramatizing conflicts of conscience and values among wealthy, privileged characters, Behrman produced a steady series of urbane and curiously impersonal high comedies such as *The Second Man* (1927), *Biography* (1932), *End of Summer* (1936), *No Time for Comedy* (1939), and *But for Whom Charlie* (1964). Two recurrent character types haunt his salons: fashionable, tolerant matrons (often played, charmingly, by **Ina Claire**) and cynically detached self-made artists and sybarites. Not quite problem plays, or plays of ideas in the Shavian mould, Behrman's discussion dramas (notably weak in story and structure) chart the progress of his well-spoken characters toward a position of worldly compromise, a sophisticated *via media*. The **Theatre Guild** presented most of Behrman's work, and his smart comedies have

come to be identified as the Guild's prevailing house style.   FH

Béjart Name of a remarkable family of French actors whose careers were intimately linked with that of **Molière**. **Joseph**, the eldest brother (c. 1616–59), was a co-founder in 1643 of Molière's first theatrical venture, the Illustre-Théâtre, and subsequently shared his fortunes as a strolling player in the provinces but died prematurely in 1659 without participating in the years of success in Paris. Afflicted with a stammer on which he doubtless capitalized in comic roles, he was a useful and well-liked company member who also contrived to publish two books on heraldry. **Madeleine** (1618–72) was already an experienced actress when she helped to establish the Illustre-Théâtre and became Molière's touring companion as well as his mistress before returning with him to the capital in 1658. Her devoted support as performer (and for a time as business manager) was of incalculable importance to him for almost 30 years until she predeceased him by exactly a twelvemonth. She played tragic heroines (e.g. Jocaste in **Racine**'s first play *La Thébaïde* (*The Thebaid*)) and created several of Molière's outspoken soubrettes (e.g. Dorine in *Tartuffe*). Her sister **Geneviève** (1624–75), who adopted her mother's maiden name, Mlle Hervé, was another of the original members of the Illustre-Théâtre and thereafter a constant member of Molière's company, more noted for tragic roles though she played Bélise in *Les Femmes Savantes* (*The Learned Ladies*). **Louis** (1630–78), known as L'Eguisé on stage, joined the company later to play old men and supporting roles such as La Flèche in *L'Avare* (*The Miser*), where Molière made use of his limp and had Harpagon call him a 'lame devil'. When he retired in 1670 he was the first member of the company to be awarded a pension. **Armande-Grésinde-Claire-Elizabeth** (1641–1700), Madeleine's youngest sister or possibly her illegitimate daughter, was brought up as a member of Molière's itinerant company and became his wife in 1662. Gossip, articulated by the playwright's lampooned enemy **Montfleury**, suggested that Molière had thus married his own daughter by his mistress, though Louis XIV's willingness to stand as godfather to their firstborn two years later effectively stifled the aspersion. Although the marriage itself was not happy (and the widowed Armande later remarried), the parallel stage partnership was probably a vital element in her husband's success. Benefiting no doubt from his advice, she proved a fine actress and after her debut in 1663 she played most of Molière's young heroines (e.g. Célimène in *The Misanthrope*, Elmire in *Tartuffe*, Henriette in *The Learned Ladies* and Angélique in *Le Malade Imaginaire* (*The Imaginary Invalid*)), parts which he had fashioned for her. It was she too, with the help of **La Grange**, who rallied the company after his death.   DR

Bel Geddes, Norman (1893–1958) American set and industrial designer. Pioneered the use of lenses in stage lighting equipment. Bel Geddes is probably better known for his industrial designs ranging from cars to stoves; he is sometimes called 'the father of streamlining'. The number of his designs for the theatre was small in comparison to his contemporaries, but they were often visionary and influential. His most

Norman Bel Geddes's famous set for *Dead End* by Sidney Kingsley, Belasco Theatre, 1935.

ambitious design was for an unrealized project based on *The Divine Comedy*. The set was to include 70-foot towers and a performance area some 100 feet wide. His visionary designs are suggestive, emblematic, and possessed of towering grandeur, thus creating a theatrical sense of space. Most of his designs that were executed were detailed and naturalistic, such as *Dead End*, because of the demands of the theatre at the time. He is best known for transforming a theatre into a cavernous gothic cathedral for **Max Reinhardt**'s production of *The Miracle*. Bel Geddes also had projects for innovative theatre spaces that altered the traditional audience–performer relationship.   AA

Belasco, David (1853–1931) American director, playwright, manager. A San Francisco native, he made his acting debut there (1872), and toured the west as a supporting player, settling at San Francisco's Baldwin Theatre as stage manager and playwright (1878–82). There he collaborated with **James A. Herne** in writing and producing, and first worked with Gustave Frohman, who brought him to New York as stage manager and resident dramatist for the new Madison Square Theatre (1882). In 1884 he moved to **Daniel Frohman**'s Lyceum Theatre, performing the same tasks until 1890 when he became an independent producer. His long apprenticeship involved the staging of scores

of productions and the writing, alone or in collaboration, of more than three dozen plays. The first play of which he was sole author was *May Blossom* (1884), but his first successes were in collaboration with Henry C. DeMille, beginning with *The Wife* (1887). Until 1902 Belasco produced plays for booking by the **Theatrical Syndicate**. His most notable productions in this period were *Madam Butterfly* (1900), *Under Two Flags* (1901), *The Auctioneer* (1901) and *Dubarry* (1901). He broke with the Theatrical Syndicate in a dispute over fees, leased a theatre from Oscar Hammerstein, and entered into the richest phase of his career (1902–15). In this period he did 42 original productions and revivals in New York City and on tour. The most famous were *The Darling of the Gods* (1902), *The Girl of the Golden West* (1905), *The Rose of the Rancho* (1906), *The Easiest Way* (1909), and *The Governor's Lady* (1912). He also built a new theatre (1907) and kept both houses active for the rest of the period. Though he was responsible for another 35 productions between 1915 and his retirement in 1930, his influence had waned, and his work was treated condescendingly.

Though prodigiously active as a playwright, affixing his name to some 70 works, none still hold the stage. Even in playwriting his greatest contribution was in creating and managing stage effects. In collaborating with DeMille, Belasco would pace the stage, describing scenes and effects while DeMille took notes. DeMille would then write out the dialogue, which Belasco would polish during rehearsals. As a producer Belasco did nothing that had not been done before, but he did it more elaborately and carefully. Desiring to be realistic without being unpleasant, he combined a scenic realism, which demanded solid, three-dimensional pieces and actual objects whenever possible, with melodramatic action and sentimental idealization of character. Working with the designer Louis Hartmann and the technicians John H. and Anton Kliegl, he pioneered the use of electric lights to create mood. He selected talented but relatively unknown performers (**Blanche Bates**, **Mrs Leslie Carter**, **Frances Starr**, and **David Warfield**) whom he cast to type in vehicles created for them. Each piece was rehearsed for ten weeks (rather than the normal four), so that as nearly as possible the leading performers were playing carefully derived extensions of their own personalities on stage.   DMCD

Belasco Theatre New York City theatre at 111 West 44th Street. Designed by architect George Keister, it was opened on 16 October 1907, with a production of *A Grand Army Man*, starring **David Warfield** and directed by the new theatre's owner, producer **David Belasco**. (Until 1910 the theatre was called the Stuyvesant, to avoid confusion with another house bearing Belasco's name.) The theatre, which cost $750,000 to erect, was elaborately decorated. The stage and backstage areas were unusually well equipped, and the lighting system – a special interest of Belasco's – was considered to be particularly innovative. In 1909

Belasco added a penthouse, which contained offices and a lavish apartment for himself. Belasco continued to produce at the theatre until his death in 1931. Among his spectacularly conceived productions in the house were *The Return of Peter Grimm* (1911), with David Warfield; *The Governor's Lady* (1912), in which an accurate replica of a Child's Restaurant was built onstage; and a memorable 1922 presentation of *The Merchant of Venice*, with Warfield as Shylock. After Belasco's death the theatre was leased, at various times, to **Katharine Cornell**, **Elmer Rice**, the **Group Theatre**, and the National Broadcasting Company, which used it as a radio playhouse in the early 1950s. It became a legitimate house again in 1953. The Belasco, which seats approximately 1,000 spectators, is currently owned by the **Shubert Organization**.   BMCN

Belaval, Emilio S. (1903–72) Puerto Rican essayist, playwright, director and producer. Studied law at the University of Puerto Rico, later President of the Puerto Rican Atheneum and member of the Supreme Court. In 1939 he created Areyto, a popular but short-lived theatre group. Belaval was a major contributor to the development of modern Puerto Rican theatre because of his books and essays, his work in promoting theatre, and his plays: *La presa de los vencedores* (*The Victors' Prey*, 1939), *Hay que decir la verdad* (*The Truth Must be Told*, 1940), *La muerte* (*Death*, 1950), *La vida* (*Life*, 1958), and *Cielo caído* (*Fallen Sky*, 1960).   GW

Belgium The earliest history of Belgian theatre, particularly in Flanders, where Dutch was spoken,

The Darling of the Gods, written, produced and directed by David Belasco at the Belasco Theatre, 1902.

bears close resemblance to that of The Netherlands. In fact, the two countries, then called the Low Countries, were one until 1830. A major difference lies in the fact that in the South (present-day Belgium) two languages are spoken, namely Dutch and French (in the Walloon part).

The *Mons Passion-play*, written in French and dating from 1501, is an important point of reference for liturgical drama, just as the *First* and *Seventh Joy of Mary*, composed in Flemish and dating from around 1440, are early witnesses of miracle plays. Next to these, the miracle play *Mariken van Nieumeghen* and the miracle play *Elckerlijc* present two absolute highlights. (See **Medieval drama in Europe**.)

With the rise of the 'Rederijkers' ('Rhetoricians') in the 16th century, drama in the Low Countries became better organized, and came to the fore in Flanders. A leaning towards the didactic, and a preference for abstract characters, by means of allegorical presentation, dominated poetic and dramatic works of art. Particularly, the spectacular 'landjuwelen' ('country jewels'), in which the 'Kamers van Rhetorike' ('Chambers of Rhetoric') took part, and which covered several days, determined a large part of the cultural value of the activities held by these chambers.

Pyramus and Thisbe, written by Matthijs de Castelein (1488–1555), seems to give a first, if somewhat cautious, impulse to the Renaissance. However, a large number of these allegories exercised an ever-increasing impetus to the spread of Protestantism. As a result, the 'Rederijkers' fell into disgrace with the Roman Catholic authorities. Moreover, Spanish, Catholic rule claimed many victims, particularly among the 'Rederijkers', who remained loyal to their faith and country. Consequently, after the Fall of Antwerp in 1585, many artists fled to the North, to Amsterdam. As a result, this city became the new cultural centre of the Low Countries. Because of constant wars, the Renaissance in Belgium never flourished.

In the 17th and 18th century, there was hardly any theatrical activity; drama relapsed into medieval allegory and *vaudevilles*, modelled on French lines. Michiel de Swaen (1654–1707), however, proved an exception. His *The Blessed Cobblers or the Crowned Boot* (1688) showed force and originality.

In 1830, Belgium reached independence and French became the official language. In reaction to this development, the Flemish started to become more self-assured. Under the influence of the Vlaamse Beweging (Flemish Movement), a strong impulse was given to Flemish drama. The first official Flemish theatre, De Koninklyke Nationale Schouwburg (KNS) (The Royal National Theatre), was opened in 1853. In 1887, another theatre, De Koninklyke Vlaamse Schouwburg (KVS) (The Royal Flemish Theatre), followed in Brussels, a city mainly inhabited by French-speaking citizens.

Cyriel Buysse (1859–1932), a well-known novelist, was one of those who contributed to this gradual revival. In *The Paemel Family* (1903), the normal and economic decline of the Flemish labourers is portrayed in a sombre style, following the realistic–naturalistic tradition.

The best-known playwright from around 1900 is **Maurice Maeterlinck** (1862–1949). This Fleming, who wrote in French and reached international fame

through plays like *Les Aveugles* (1890), *La Princesse Maleine* (1889), and *Pelléas et Mélisande* (1892), represents the victory of symbolism over naturalism. Maeterlinck was fascinated by dimensions that make life elusive, such as mysterious forces and blindness. Only through contemplation, absolute silence, and inactivity could these be made visible. His plays are characteristic for their lack of action or conflict. This made him, in the eyes of some, a precursor of absurdism.

In *Le Cocu Magnifique* (1920), Fernand Crommelynck (1885–1970, in inimitable style, portrayed marital jealousy and the obsession with sin. **Meyerhold**'s famous staging of the play in 1922, acted in bio-mechanical style, is still a highlight in the history of modern theatre.

Another Fleming who wrote in French, **Michel de Ghelderode** (1898–1962), became known after the Second World War. In his comedies, he pictured a world in which madness and sanity, the tragic and the burlesque, meet and clash, and the power of death is everywhere: *Pantagleize* (1929), *Magie Rouge* (1931), *Hop Signor* (1935).

Herman Teirlinck (1879–1967) is important primarily as a theorist (he introduced **Appia** and **Craig**), and as a founder of the Antwerp school of drama, which now bears his name. As a playwright, he is an exponent of expressionism (*De Vertraagde film* (*The Slow-motion Film*, 1922)).

After the Second World War, the character of Belgian theatre was dominated by repertory companies such as the KNS and the KVS. The Vlaamse Volkstoneel (Flemish people's theatre) did not receive financial support, because, in the eyes of the suppliers of subsidy, it showed too much interest in social and political causes. Since 1922, this company became a household word, under the inspired leadership of Jan de Gruyter (1885–1929). He renewed the repertory and built up a solid company that lacked the star-system. However, after the war continuation proved difficult, and the most important author of this post-war generation is **Hugo Claus** (b. 1929).

Around 1968, in Belgium, too, a strong reaction took place against the established theatre and what were considered its rigid structures (see **Aktie Tomaat**, (politiek) **Vormingstoneel**). A group by the name of Kollektief **Internationale Nieuwe Scene** (New International Stage) was one of the companies to emerge from this source of dissatisfaction. They are a political theatre movement with a strong socialist tendency. Particularly, their performance of **Dario Fo**'s *Mistero Buffo* gave them an international reputation. The development in this period runs strikingly parallel to that in The Netherlands.

In the eighties, the development of Belgian theatre is mainly interesting due to a young generation of theatre artists who experiment with new forms of theatre, e.g. Jan Decorte.

In a very short time, Jan Fabre (b. 1958) has earned himself international fame with two performances, namely *Het is Theater Zoals te Verwachten en te Voorzien was* (*It is the Kind of Theatre one could Expect and Foresee*, 1982–3) and *De Macht der Theaterlijke Dwaasheden* (*The Power of Theatrical Follies*, 1984) performed also outside Belgium. Originally a plastic artist, he produces strongly ritualistic and visual theatre; during frequently lengthy plays (5–8 hours), Fabre puts the theatrical conventions under constant discussion, e.g. traditional differences between actor and character become unclear and traditional storylines or themes disappear. He prefers to work with people who have not been to drama school, whom he pushes almost to the limits of their physical endurance; the repetition of act and movement seems to express a post-modern sense of life.

In the field of dance, especially where minimal dance is concerned, Anne Therese de Keersmaeker plays an important part. In cooperation with Steve Reich, a quadtych came into being: *Phase, Four Movements on the Music of Steve Reich*. Her performances are characteristic in that music is linked to complicated dance constructions, which move in phases; the repeating movements which are used stand alone and abstract, and are stripped of all (traditional) dramatic impact. This is the field in which, as yet, a prominent part seems to be reserved for Belgian theatre in its widest sense. MG WH HS

> *See*: G. Cohen, *Le Théâtre Français en Belgique au Moyen Age*, Brussels, 1953; A. van Impe, *Over toneel: Vlaamse kroniek van het komediantendom*, Amsterdam/Tielt: Lannoo, 1978; M. van Kerkhoven, *De vernieuwing van het Zuid-Nederlands Toneel tussen 1950 en 1960*, Brussels, 1968; S. Lilar, *The Belgian Theatre since 1890*, New York, 1950; Th. de Ronde, *Het Toneelleven in Vlaanderen door de Eeuwen heen*, Leuven, 1930; C. Tindemans, 'Theater en Drama 1920–1970' in: *Een halve eeuw Kunst in België*, Brussels, 1973; C. Tindemans, *Mens, Gemeenschap en Maatschappij in de Toneelletterkunde van Zuid-Nederland 1815–1914* Kon. Ac. voor Nederl. Taal- en Letterkunde, 1973. *See also*: bibliography of **The Netherlands**.

Bell, John (1940–) Australian actor and director. After acting in student theatre and with the Old Tote Theatre Company in Sydney, a British Council scholarship took him to Britain in 1964, where he acted with the **Royal Shakespeare Company** from 1964–9, and acted and directed at Lincoln Repertory Theatre. A co-founder of Nimrod Theatre, Sydney, in 1970, he remained an artistic director there till 1985, directing several innovative Shakespearian productions. His major roles include Arturo Ui (1971, 1985), Hamlet (1973), Henry V (1964) and Cyrano de Bergerac (1980–1). He was awarded an OBE in 1978. MW

Bellamy, George Anne (?1731–88) Irish actress. Named George because she was born on St George's Day, she appeared as a child-actress at **Covent Garden** in 1741, playing Prue in **Congreve**'s *Love for Love* and she played with **Garrick** in private performances in Kingston. In 1744 she made her debut as an adult actress playing Monimia in **Otway**'s *The Orphan*. After a brief stay in Ireland she returned to London in 1748. Her life-style was already established: many lovers, extravagant spending, heavy gambling and furious rows with Garrick and others in the company. It did not help her acting: as a contemporary commented, 'were but her love to her profession, her application to its necessary studies and her patience . . . equal to her abilities, she would have few equals'. In 1750 she played Juliet to Garrick's Romeo. Performing as Euridice in *Oedipus* she was so 'overcome by the horror of the piece

that she was carried off in a state of insensibility'. She was severely ill in 1757 and by the 1760s, still only in her thirties, she looked old and wrinkled. She finally retired in 1770, returning to the stage for a single benefit performance in 1780. Her ghosted autobiography in six volumes was published in 1785. PH

Bellamy, Ralph (1904–) American actor born in Chicago. After touring with William Owen in 1921 he worked steadily in provincial theatre, directing his own stock company, the Ralph Bellamy Players. He made his debut in New York in 1929 as Ben Davis in *Town Boy*. Bellamy made his first appearance in film as *The Secret Six* in 1931. By 1943 he had made 84 pictures and for the rest of his career alternated between film and theatre with frequent work in television. In 1958 he won the New York Drama Critics Award, the Delia Austrian Award, and the Antoinette Perry (Tony) Award for his performance as Franklin Delano Roosevelt in *Sunrise at Campobello*. Between 1952 and 1964 he served four terms as President of Actors Equity. SMA

Bellerose (Pierre Le Messier) (?–1670) French actor–manager, one of the leading exponents of tragedy in the first half of the 17th century. Apprenticed to **Valleran le Conte** in 1609 he presumably remained attached to his master's itinerant company for several years but by 1620 he was leading his own company in Marseille. He joined the Comédiens du Roi under **Gros-Guillaume** at the **Hôtel de Bourgogne** in 1622 and succeeded the latter as director in 1635 before selling the position to **Floridor** in 1647 while remaining a member of the company for many years. He had a fine speaking voice which he used to good effect as company 'orator' in formal addresses to the audience and in a whole range of leading parts in tragedy and comedy, though some contemporaries, perhaps preferring the greater aggression of his arch-rival **Mondory** at the **Marais**, regarded Bellerose as insipid and somewhat affected. He was one of the actors appearing *in propria persona* in Gougenot's *La Comédie des Comédiens* (*The Actors' Comedy*, 1631/2). DR

Bellotti-Bon, Luigi (1820–83) Italian actor and company manager. Born into the profession he was acting from an early age and in his twenties acquired a wide range of experience with a number of companies, the enduring influence perhaps being that of **Gustavo Modena**'s young company in 1845 (together with **Tommaso Salvini**). In the 1850s he was a member of the Reale Sarda with **Ristori** and **Rossi**, and went with them to Paris, Dresden and Berlin, on what was one of the first 'international' tours undertaken by an Italian company since the decline of the **commedia dell'arte**. In 1859 he formed a company of his own, distinguished for the range and quality of the talents it included and the manager's own concern for high standards. He particularly encouraged new drama, and most of the leading and emerging playwrights of the day wrote for his company. The troup enjoyed great success, and in 1873 he expanded his single company into three. Unfortunately the bid was over-ambitious, stretching both his financial and artistic resources. He turned increasingly to French adaptations, but failed to hold his audience. Too late he attempted to cut back, reducing the companies first to two, then to one, but was unable to cover mounting debts. After delaying for several years the inevitable financial collapse, when a bank fore-closed on him, he shot himself. He was one of the most accomplished and innovative actor-managers of the century, and his tragedy sent a shock-wave through the Italian theatrical and cultural scene, prompting intense discussion of the problems confronting Italian drama and theatre.   KR

Below Sometimes used in Elizabethan stage-directions simply to indicate the location of a character on the main stage in contrast to a character '**above**', the 'below' was also the area underneath the trestle-stage from which access was possible through a trap. Very occasionally it was put to use by actors and dramatists, as, for example, by the Ghost in *Hamlet*. On medieval stages, the below could represent Hell, the abode of the Devil and his minions. Christ's harrowing of Hell could release the righteous pre-Christians from the below onto the platform.   PT

Bely, Andrei (pseudonym of Bugaev, Boris Nikolaevich) (1880–1934) Russian symbolist poet, novelist, critic, theorist and dramatist, whose 'crisis of consciousness' mirrored that of his society and produced works of stylistic brilliance. Vladimir Solovyov's moral philosophy (1905–10) engendered in him a belief in imminent apocalypse to be precipitated by the 1905 Revolution and resulting in a reconciliation with God. He embraced Rudolf Steiner's anthroposophic philosophy (1912–23), which gave scientific coherence to Christian doctrine and Eastern mysticism. He believed with the symbolists that the creative act makes life meaningful but wavered on the question of how conscious or intuitive creation should be. He found in poetry the desired synthesis between concrete space and abstract time and in poetry conceived as music a transcendent force. His dramas – *He Who Has Come* (1903) and *The Jaws of Night* (1907) – are from the period (1900–1906) in which he championed the mystery play as generator of religious experience. His 'mysteries' describe a portentous moment in time in which the earth is poised between apocalypse and the Second Coming, a situation recreated in his 1910 novel, *The Silver Dove*. Their imitative Maeterlinckian dialogue and settings are infused with Bely's intense, hallucinogenic orchestration of rhythms, sound, light and colour. Bely's prescient (pro-**Meyerhold**, anti-**Stanislavsky**) critical essay on *The Cherry Orchard* (1904) already pointed in a new direction, toward a more Ibsenite-Chekhovian symbolic realism in which the infinite is revealed in the instant, the eternal in the seemingly quotidian. His essay 'Theatre and Modern Drama' not only rejected the mystery play but announced that 'the theatre is no place for symbolist drama'. Bely's final experiences with theatre involved adapting his two city novels for the stage. The right to produce his Joycean symphonic *Petersburg* (1913) was awarded to **Michael Chekhov** over Meyerhold and **Tairov** and resulted in a much cut and altered stage version entitled *The Death of a Senator* (1925). Although Chekhov won rave reviews in the title role, the production at the **Moscow Art Theatre**'s Second Studio received mixed reviews. Impressed by Meyerhold's musically constructed theatricalist stagings of classics, Bely gave him his Moscow adaptation, but it never reached the stage.   SG

Bemba, Sylvain (1934–) Novelist and playwright. Born at Sibiti, Congo Popular Republic. Bemba was educated in the Congo and trained as an administrator, entering the Information Services on the completion of his studies. He also studied journalism in Strasbourg and has published extensively in that medium especially as a sports writer. During the 1970s, he published a number of plays, mainly for the radio, which have proved very popular. Drawing on a range of themes, from corruption in the old and new Africa to a historical play set in the colonial period and a dramatization of the intellectual's dilemma about involvement in a guerilla war, Bemba's plays reveal a lively sense of dialogue and situation which incorporates the use of traditional elements and popular speech. The plays are: *L'Enfer c'est Orféo* (*Hell is Orfeo*, 1970) (published under the pseudonym Martial Malinda), *L'Homme qui tua le Crocodile* (*The Man who Killed the Crocodile*, 1972), *L'Eau Dormante* (*Dormant Water*, 1975 – this play won the Listeners' Prize in the annual French radio playwriting competition for Africa in 1972), *Tarentelle Noire et Diable Blanc* (*Black Tarantula and White Devil*, 1976), *Un Foutu Monde pour un Blanchisseur trop Honnête* (*A Rotten World for an Over-Honest Laundryman*, 1979).   CW

Ben-Ami, Jacob (1890–1977) Russian-born American actor and director who achieved critical acclaim on both Yiddish and English-speaking stages. Born in Minsk, he worked with the Hirshbein Troupe in Odessa, the **Vilna Troupe**, and, for a short period, the Fineman Art Theatre in London. Ben-Ami emigrated to New York in 1912 and joined **Maurice Schwartz**'s Irving Place Theatre in 1918. Dissatisfied with the superficial quality of Yiddish theatre, Ben-Ami sought to modernize the repertoire. Differences with Schwartz in 1919 led him to found his own Jewish Art Theatre where he discarded the old starring system and offered works by **Sholom Aleichem**, **Tolstoi**, and **Hauptmann**. Discovered by **Arthur Hopkins**, in 1920 he was given his first English-speaking role as Peter Krumback in *Samson and Delilah*. His Broadway acting career extended to 1972 and included Michael Cape in **O'Neill**'s *Welded* (1924); Arthur Kober in *Evening Song* (1934); and Forman in *The Tenth Man* (1959). He was a member of **Eva Le Gallienne**'s Civic Repertory Theatre from 1929–31, portraying a memorable Trigorin in *The Seagull*. He acted and directed for the **Theatre Guild**, and toured his Yiddish productions to Africa and South America.   TLM   AB

Benavente y Martínez, Jacinto (1866–1954) Spanish playwright who abandoned law studies and became a circus impresario before turning to the theatre. His first full-length play, *El nido ajeno* (*Another's Nest*, 1894), was not well received, being considered too sharply critical of society. However, *Gente conocida* (*People of Importance*, 1896) established his career which was to last 50 years. He wrote 18 plays in the period 1901–4, *La noche del sábado* (*Saturday Night*, 1903) bringing an international reputation which was confirmed by *Los intereses creados* (*Bonds of Interest*, 1909). *Señora ama* (*M'lady*, 1908) shows patient feminine virtue triumphing over a husband's philandering. *La malquerida* (*Passion Flower*, 1913) on the other hand is a tragedy brought on by a man's passion for his stepdaughter. In 1909 Benavente helped found a short-lived Children's Theatre, which opened with his fairy-tale play *El príncipe que todo lo aprendió en libros* (*The Prince Who Learned Everything Out of Books*), an interesting work worthy of adult audiences.

Benavente supported Germany in the First World War and his later plays became more conservative. He became director of the Teatro Español in 1920, but his Nobel Prize in 1922 provoked almost as much protest as that of **Echegaray**. He declared for the Republic in 1936, but made his peace with the Franco regime and continued to pour out plays till his death.

Benavente's 175 plays include all types of drama, though many are mediocre and repetitive, especially after 1920. His eclectic style, and in particular his sharply satirical social comedies, broke with the melodrama of Echegaray and went some way to restoring the theatre, but stopped short in the interests of popular appeal. CL

Mario Benedetti's *Primavera con una esquina rota* (*Spring with a Broken Corner*), at La Comedia Theatre, Santiago de Chile, 1985.

Benchley, Robert (1889–1945) American humorist, actor, dramatic critic, and professional celebrity. Educated at Harvard University, Benchley wrote for the *New York Tribune* and *Vanity Fair*, before becoming dramatic editor of the old *Life* (1920–9), and of *The New Yorker* (1929–40). His short humorous sketches on minor problems of the middle class appeared in *Life*, *Liberty*, and other popular magazines. Many of these were recycled into vaudeville sketches, and later into short films in which Benchley appeared. In the 1930s, he appeared in numerous feature films. A charter member of the Algonquin Round Table and of the New York Drama Critics Circle, Benchley was noted for his sophisticated wit and urbanity. TLM

Bene, Carmelo (1937–) Italian actor, director and dramatist who began his career as an actor playing traditional roles in established theatre, but quickly went his own way to develop his combined talents of actor, writer and director. His stage presentations, often radical reorchestrations of classic drama, like his versions of **Shakespeare**, *Amleto* (1975), *Romeo e Giulietta* (1976) and *Riccardo III* (1977), or compositions like *Nostra Signora dei Turchi* (*Our Lady of the Turks*, 1973) and *S. A. D. E.* (1974) have been highly original, if often controversial attempts to evolve contemporary, post-Artaudian performance styles centred on the physical and vocal qualities of the actor, but exploiting all the technical facilities available to the modern stage, particularly light, sound and costuming. The range of his skills and the idiosyncratic nature of his work have won him considerable *succès d'estime* and a wide following, but have also drawn charges of empty flamboyance, exhibitionism and decadence. An intelligent, ambitious and always innovative writer, director and actor, his performance skills were remarkably demonstrated in his *tour de force* oratorio version of **Manzoni**'s *Adelchi* (1984), first presented on stage, then transferred to Italian television. KR

Benedetti, Mario (1920–) Uruguayan playwright, novelist, short story writer, and critic. After three plays, including *Ida y vuelta* (*Return Trip*, 1958), a bitter Pirandellian satire on problems of moral decay in the national identity, Benedetti left the theatre because productions fell short of his expectations. He subsequently wrote *Pedro y el capitán* (*Pedro and the Captain*, 1979), a virulent play about torture written during the worst period of Uruguayan political repression. ICTUS, a major professional theatre in Chile, adapted his novel, *Primavera con una esquina rota* (*Spring with a Broken Corner*, 1984), for the stage in order to portray the issues of exile and escape from political upheaval. GW

Benedix, Roderich (1811–73) German playwright and director. Managed theatres in Frankfurt, Cologne, and Leipzig. Prolific writer of light comedy in the manner of **Scribe**. Highly popular in their day, Benedix's plays have now disappeared totally from the repertoire. SW

Benelli, Sem (1877–1949) Italian dramatist and poet, his best work was done in the decade or so before the First World War: costume drama in the manner of **D'Annunzio** that exploited a fashionable taste for pseudo-Renaissance dash, colour and dastardly deeds. Most celebrated of such pieces in Italy and abroad was *La Cene delle Beffe* (*The Jest*, 1909), an exotic blank-verse tragedy of Renaissance court revenge. A prolific dramatist in his day, he was too much of his age to be of more than historical interest, although some have seen his *La Maschera di Bruto* (*The Mask of Brutus*, 1908) as anticipating later experimental drama, and his comedy *Tignola* (1908) retains a certain charm. LR

Bennett, Alan (1934–) British actor and dramatist, who was part of the highly successful *Beyond the Fringe* revue team (1960). As a character actor, Bennett specialized in woolly-minded English eccentrics, whose nursery language revealed political realities. The satiric qualities of Bennett's acting were more fully developed in his writing, which started with a revue-like play, *Forty Years On* (1968), recalling the changes in a minor public school. The school's pageant described the decline of Britain and while, in subsequent plays,

Bennett left behind the dependence on short satiric scenes, he retained his mournful obsession with the twilight of British imperialism. *Getting On* (1971) described the disillusionment of a Labour MP and in *The Old Country* (1977), **Alec Guinness** played a British traitor in exile in the Soviet Union. His small-town comedy, *Habeas Corpus* (1973), contained amusing jokes about British middle-class sexual inhibitions, while *Enjoy* (1980) offered the life-cycle of a working-class couple. JE

Bennett, (Enoch) Arnold (1867–1931) British novelist and dramatist, resident in France after 1903. After early romantic comedies (*Cupid and Common Sense*, 1908; *The Honeymoon*, 1911) he made his reputation with *The Great Adventure* (1911), based on his own novel *Buried Alive*. Dealing with an artist who fakes his own death to escape the pressure of fame, it was followed by his most successful play *Milestones* (in collaboration with Edward Knoblock, 1912), which covers the human and political machinations of an English industrial family over several generations. After the First World War, in which he served as director of propaganda for the Ministry of Information, he turned to more metaphysical themes in plays like *Sacred and Profane Love* (1919) or *Body and Soul* (1922), though these were less well received than his naturalistic comedies *London Life* (1924) or *Mr Prohack* (1927, with **Charles Laughton** in the title role), both of which again were written in collaboration with Knoblock. CI

Bennett, Michael (1943–87) American choreographer and director. He began his Broadway career as a dancer, creating his first choreography for *A Joyful Noise* (1966). Bennett served as both director and choreographer for *Promises, Promises* (1968) and *Coco* (1969). In the early 1970s he teamed with **Harold Prince** and **Stephen Sondheim** in the creation of two 'concept musicals', *Company* (1970) and *Follies* (1971), for which Bennett served as choreographer and co-director. He next directed and choreographed the more traditional *Seesaw* (1973), followed by the critically acclaimed *A Chorus Line* (1975). A concept musical about the lives of Broadway's chorus dancers, *A Chorus Line*'s brilliant dance sequences were the most vivid element of the production. Bennett went on to direct and choreograph *Ballroom* (1978) and *Dreamgirls* (1981). As a choreographer, Bennett most often employed a precise, rhythmic, but emotionally expressive style of jazz dance admirably suited to contemporary characters and situations. MK

Bennett, Richard (1873–1944) American actor, born in Deacon's Mills, Indiana. Bennett first appeared on the stage at the Standard Theatre, Chicago, in 1891, and made his debut on Broadway at **Niblo's Garden** in *The Limited Mail*. His first London appearance was as Jefferson Ryder in *The Lion and the Mouse* in 1906, and his film career began in 1913. Among his more successful roles were He in *He Who Gets Slapped*, Judge Gaunt in *Winterset*, Tony in *They Knew What They Wanted*, and Robert Mayo in *Beyond the Horizon*. Bennett excited considerable controversy by berating audiences and critics, even stopping shows to lecture the audience. Three of his daughters, Constance, Barbara, and Joan, had successful film careers. SMA

Benois, Alexandre (1870–1960) Russian painter, art historian, and designer; born in St Petersburg and emigrated to Paris in 1926. Except for a few productions at the **Moscow Art Theatre** and elsewhere, most of his design was for opera and ballet. Together with Serge Diaghilev he founded the journal *Mir Isskustva* (The World of Art) in 1898 which resurrected Russia's folk art and became a focal point for the The World of Art Group – the emerging modern artists of Russia. Benois served as artistic director for the early years of Diaghilev's Ballets Russes and together with **Léon Bakst** shaped the visual aesthetic of that group and thus exerted a profound influence on the development of European design and ballet. Benois's designs, which were often of 18th- and 19th-century scenes, exhibit deep, rich colours; an evocative, romantic – though non-sentimental – atmosphere; and an attention to detail and scale. He designed both sets and costumes since he considered them an inseparable scenographic unit. His crowning achievement with the Ballets Russes was *Petrushka* (1911). After the mid-1920s he designed throughout Europe, primarily with the Paris Opéra, the Ballets Russes de Monte Carlo, and especially at La Scala in Milan where his son Nicola (b. 1901) was resident designer. AA

Benson, F[rank] R[obert] (1858–1939) English actor–manager, whose lifelong interest in sport and in theatre was established while he was an Oxford undergraduate. In 1881, for example, he produced the *Agamemnon* in Greek and won the three-mile race against Cambridge. He made his professional debut in **Irving**'s **Lyceum** in 1882, joined a touring Shakespearian company whose manager absconded, bought the remaining assets and found himself, at the age of 25, manager of the F. R. Benson company. Engaged by Charles Flower to initiate an annual **Shakespeare Festival** at Stratford, Benson retained his association with the Festival from 1886–1919. When he was not at Stratford, he was touring the British Isles, providing for many provincial audiences their only experience of professional Shakespearian performances. Responses to Benson's acting were to remain mixed. **Beerbohm** found his Henry V beyond praise 'as a branch of university cricket', but less impressive 'as a form of acting'. For other critics, he was at his best in the History Plays. To his credit, he played an uncut *Hamlet* (1899) and all but two of Shakespeare's plays, and many actors did their apprenticeship in his busy company. Benson was knighted in the Royal Box at **Drury Lane** in 1916. PT

Bentley, Eric (Russell) (1916–) American drama critic, translator, editor, playwright, and director. Born in England, educated at Oxford and Yale (Ph.D., 1941), Bentley gained recognition in the late 1940s for his translations of **Brecht**'s plays. He worked in both the USA and European theatre, co-directing the German language premiere of *The Iceman Cometh* in Zurich (1950), and directing his translation of *The Good Person of Setzuan* in New York (1956). Drama critic of the *New Republic* from 1952 to 1956, Bentley also has held distinguished academic positions as Brander Matthews Professor of Dramatic Literature at Columbia University (1952–69) and Katharine Cornell Professor of Theatre at SUNY-Buffalo (1974–). He is a noted translator of Brecht, **Pirandello**, and **Schnitzler**; an author of ten original plays; and author or editor of numerous books including *The Playwright as Thinker* (1946), *The Life of the Drama* (1964), and *The Brecht Commentaries 1943–1980* (1981).   TLM

Beolco, Angelo see Ruzzante

Berain, Jean (1637–1711) French engraver, architect and designer whose style represents a transitional phase between baroque and rococo. He was appointed official designer to Louis XIV in 1674, his chief function being to devise the costumes and decorations for royal ceremonies such as marriages, baptisms and funerals and for all court entertainments. Given the king's taste these consisted predominantly of ballets, operas and the elaborate open-air *fêtes* arranged by **Lully** and his various associates in the gardens of Versailles and other royal palaces. He also collaborated with Lully at the Paris Opéra, where he succeeded **Vigarani** as designer-machinist in 1680. If Berain's approach to scenic spectacle was rather more restrained than that of his Italian predecessors, his costume designs were sumptuous and idiosyncratic, without the least regard for period accuracy or local colour but showing an inspired conjunction between fantasy and the line of contemporary dress which amounted to a truly personal style. It was inherited, along with his post, by his son Jean (1678–1726).   DR

Bérard, Christian-Jacques (1902–49) French theatrical and film designer, graphic artist, painter, and fashion designer. Bérard combined his painting with a theatrical career, much like **Eugene Berman** and **Pavel Tchelitchew**, two neoromantic artists with whom Bérard exhibited his works in Paris in 1926. His sketches of Paris fashions, which he submitted to such magazines as *Vogue* and *Harper's Bazaar*, were so recognized that he was said to have inspired fashion designer Christian Dior to create the 'New Look' in the mid-forties.

When he was 22, Bérard designed the ballet *Les Elves* (1924), for Michel Fokine. He subsequently worked for other famous choreographers and executed such works as George Balanchine's *Mozartiana* (1931), Roland Petit's *Les Forains* (1945), and Leonide Massine's *Symphonie Fantastique* (1936). Along with Petit and Boris Kochno, he founded and served as co-director of the Ballet des Champs-Elysées. His play designs included highly stylized productions such as **Jean Cocteau**'s *The Infernal Machine* (1934), the film *Beauty and the Beast*, and **Louis Jouvet**'s production of **Jean Giraudoux**'s *Madwoman of Chaillot* (1945). Bérard, a ubiquitous personality in the theatre world, was a short dishevelled man with an unruly beard whose appearance belied the stunning beauty of his stage designs.   TM

Berber, Anita see Nudity on stage

Berghof, Herbert (1909–) Actor, director, teacher. Born in Vienna, Austria, he studied with **Aleksandër Moisiu**, **Max Reinhardt**, **Lee Stras-**berg, and the **Actors Studio** (charter member). His professional debut was in *Don Carlos*, Vienna, 1927, and his New York debut was as Fool in *King Lear*, New School for Social Research Studio Theatre, 1941. He first appeared on Broadway in 1940, co-directing and performing in *Reunion in New York*. His first solo directing on Broadway was *From Vienna*, 1939. Berghof has taught acting at Columbia University, the New School for Social Research, the **Neighbourhood Playhouse**, and the American Theatre Wing. In 1946 he founded the Hagen-Berghof Studio, which he directs with his wife, **Uta Hagen**. In 1964 he founded the HB Playwrights Foundation.   SMA

Bergman, Hjalmar (1883–1931) Swedish novelist and playwright. He experimented with various dramatic styles before publishing his collection of one-act *Marionette Plays* (1917), of which the most intense is *Mr Sleeman is Coming*, a blend of the realistic and symbolic reminiscent of **Maeterlinck**. *An Experiment* (1919) is an uneasily playful social comedy echoing **Shaw**'s *Pygmalion*, but with *The Gambling House* (1916–23) and *The Legend* (c. 1920) he attempted ambitious symbolist fantasies on moral issues. Popular success in the theatre eluded Bergman until his final plays: *Swedenhielms* (1923), *The Rabble* (1928), *The Markurells of Wadköping* (1929) and *The Baron's Will* (1930), the last two being dramatizations of earlier novels. These are inventive comedies, unambitious, but with a spirited dialogue, well-prepared confrontations, sudden changes of mood and eccentric characters that make splendid acting vehicles. Their occasionally contrived quality is more than counterbalanced by their vitality.   HL

Bergman, Ingmar (1918–) Swedish director and playwright, best known for his films, but constantly active in the theatre. His early work was done at provincial city theatres: Helsingborg, including a stark anti-Nazi *Macbeth*; **Gothenburg** (1946–50), including *A Streetcar Named Desire* and an intensely physical *Caligula*; **Malmö** (1952–8), whose huge main stage he is one of the few directors to master, not only for large-scale works like *The Merry Widow*, but also for **Molière**, **Ibsen** and **Strindberg**. His stagings of *The Crown Bride*, *The Ghost Sonata* and *Erik XIV* there confirmed his special grasp of Strindberg. For three years (1963–6) Bergman headed **Dramaten**, introducing several positive innovations (open rehearsals, higher salaries and better programmes) and directing some extraordinary productions (including a stark *Who's Afraid of Virginia Woolf?* and his split-stage *Hedda Gabler*). However, his 1966 resignation began a period of little theatre activity, until he returned to Dramaten in the 1970s for major guest engagements, especially to direct Strindberg: an intimate *Dream Play* (1970), a remarkable grotesque *Ghost Sonata* (1973) and an adaptation of *To Damascus*, Parts I and II (1974). Suddenly, in 1976, erroneous charges of tax evasion resulted in Bergman's leaving Sweden for nine years and joining the Munich Residenztheater, where he staged another *Dream Play*, as well as works by Molière, Ibsen, **Chekhov** and **Gombrowicz**. The most ambitious was his 1981 triple production of *A Doll's House*, *Miss Julie* and his own *Scenes From a Marriage*, all opening on the same evening. He occasionally directed in Sweden (including a lavish

King Lear in 1984) and permanently rejoined Dramaten in 1985 to stage new productions of *Miss Julie* and *A Dream Play*.

While Bergman's range of playwrights is wide, three have been especially important to him: Strindberg, Ibsen and Molière. Rather than 'mere word fidelity', his approach often involves a radical reformulation of the text, to crystallize in modern terms his understanding of the playwright's fundamental vision. Consequently, in addition to daring theatricalism, his productions have depth and density. Seeing theatre as a form of conjuration, in which actor and text interact with spectator, he avoids literal realism, preferring to suggest, rather than reconstruct. Nevertheless, his stage productions have much in common with his films: they are strikingly picturesque and they mostly support acting that is courageously truthful. HL

Bergner, Elisabeth (1900–) Austrian actress, who made her reputation in the plays of **Wedekind** before being catapulted to international success by her portrayal of **Shaw's** *St Joan* in 1924. *Boy David* was written by **Barrie** specifically for her, and in 1963 she became the first actress ever to be awarded the Schiller prize. CI

Berkoff, Steve[n] (1937–) British playwright and performer. He established his reputation with three adaptations of work by Kafka, *The Penal Colony* (1968), *Metamorphosis* (1969) and *The Trial* (1970). Further adaptations included **Aeschylus'** *Agamemnon* (1973) and Edgar Allan Poe's *The Fall of the House of Usher* (1974). He formed the London Theatre Group in 1968 as a vehicle for his work both as writer and director/performer, and developed a style that combined verbal and non-verbal elements of theatre, parody and experiment. Original works include *East* (1975), *Greek* (1979) where he treats the Oedipus story, *Decadence* (1981) and a cockney *Beowulf*, *West* (1983). MB

Berlin, Irving (1888–1989) American composer and lyricist. With his family he emigrated to America from Russia at the age of two. He received little formal education, and held a variety of jobs before publishing his first song in 1907. Four years later his 'Alexander's Ragtime Band' became an international sensation, launching a vogue for popular songs written in a ragtime or pseudo-ragtime rhythm. Berlin wrote his first complete Broadway score for *Watch Your Step* (1914). After contributing songs to other musical comedies and revues, he created the score for an all-soldier show, *Yip, Yip Yaphank* (1918). In the following year, he wrote several songs for *The Ziegfeld Follies*. In the years 1921–24 Berlin and producer **Sam H. Harris** offered a series of *Music Box Revues* which introduced many of Berlin's standards, such as 'What'll I Do?' and 'All Alone'. His other shows of the 1920s were *The Cocoanuts* (1925) and *The Ziegfeld Follies* (1927).

In the 1930s Berlin responded to a trend toward treating social and political issues in musicals by creating the score to *Face the Music* (1932), a satire on police corruption. He also included in his score for the revue *As Thousands Cheer* (1933) the song 'Supper Time', a lament about the lynching of a southern black. After spending several years writing for Hollywood films, Berlin returned to Broadway with the score for *Louisiana Purchase* (1940), and an updated all-soldier show, *This is the Army* (1942). Four years later Berlin wrote the music for *Annie Get Your Gun*, proving that he, like **Rodgers** and **Hammerstein**, could write a score in which the song grew naturally out of the dramatic action. In 1950 he wrote the songs for *Call Me Madam*, and twelve years later Broadway heard his final score, written for *Mr President* (1962).

One of America's most successful composers of popular music, Berlin's most memorable contributions to the musical stage were individual songs rather than complete scores. Never interested in experimentation or innovation, Berlin's strength was his ability to adapt to changing musical styles and to reflect in his music the thoughts, feelings, and aspirations of average people. MK

Berlin Royal Theatre In 1786, **Döbbelin** took over the Komödienhaus on the Gendarmenmarkt in Berlin, where he received a royal patent to perform plays. In 1796, **August Iffland** was appointed director of this Court Theatre. Under him it achieved the status of a national theatre. Iffland's attention to production values, especially in the performance of plays with historical settings, did much to raise theatrical standards in Germany. After Iffland's death in 1812, the direction was taken over by Count Karl von Brühl (1772–1837), who cultivated the **Weimar style** of acting in the company, despite the presence in it of **Ludwig Devrient**. After Brühl's retirement and Devrient's death, the preeminence of the National Theatre began to decline, and, although actors such as **Karl Seydelmann** and **Adalbert Matkowsky** occasionally energized its work, its influence over the development of the German theatre fell off rapidly. SW

Berliner Ensemble German theatre company, founded under the direction of **Helene Weigel** in 1949 and dedicated to promoting the epic theatre of **Brecht**. In 1954 it gained a permanent base at the Theater am Schiffbauerdamm, and since then has proved to be the single most influential force in German theatre. Apart from productions of all his major plays, which form about half of the repertoire, Brecht used the stage to explore his concepts of acting and directing, and to encourage work by other playwrights along the same lines. Following his anti-illusionistic principles, designed to encourage a critical attitude in the audience, the company developed a uniquely clear and theatrical style of presentation – though discarding his concept of *Verfremdung* or 'Alienation'. Brecht's productions were recorded in *Modellbücher* for the guidance of other directors, and the company's extensive touring – Austria, Poland, France (1954, 1957, 1960, 1971), Britain (1956, 1965), Russia, Italy and most recently Canada – gave its methods international exposure which had a significant effect. From its opening the Ensemble attracted major actors, among them Therese Giehse, Leonard Steckel, Angelika Hurwicz, Ekkehard Schall and Ernst Busch; and a significant number of directors were trained there, including **Benno Besson**, **Peter Palitzsch**, and Manfred Wekwerth, the present manager of the company. His internationally acclaimed production of Brecht's adaptation of *Coriolanus* was followed by invitations to direct **Shakespeare** at the

London **National Theatre** (1971) and in North America, as practical examples demonstrating the value of Brechtian technique for staging the traditional repertoire. CI

Berman, Eugene (1899–1972) Set and costume designer and painter. Born in St Petersburg, Russia, lived in Paris 1918–39, then the USA. Berman first visited Italy in 1922 and his studies of Italian landscape and Renaissance and Baroque theatrical design influenced him greatly. His wispy, almost surreal sketches are filled with architectural elements such as arches and colonnades, and a strong sense of proportion, all reminiscent of Piranesi. In the 1920s he was classed with a group of artists known as neo-romantics. Most of his designs were for ballet and opera and he worked frequently with George Balanchine. Berman's design for Anthony Tudor's *Romeo and Juliet* with American Ballet Theatre is considered one of his best. AA

Bernal, Ligia (1930–) Guatemalan playwright and director, founder of the University Art Theatre (1950), she studied theatre in Paris. Her most important works are *Una piedra en el pozo* (*Stone in the Well*, 1959) and *Tus alas, Ariel* (*Your Wings, Ariel*, 1970). Presently director of AMARES, a student theatre institution. GW

Bernard, John (1756–1828) British actor-manager who had an extensive career in the United States. Born in Portsmouth, he played provincial theatres before his debut at **Covent Garden** in *The Beaux' Stratagem* in 1787. **Wignell** brought him to Philadelphia's **Chestnut Street Theatre**, where he remained until 1803, thence moving to Boston's **Federal Street Theatre**, which he co-managed from 1806 to 1810. He then toured the USA and Canada extensively, returning in 1819 to England, where he died in poverty. He describes his career as a leading low comedian in two books, *Retrospections of America 1797–1811* (1887) and *Retrospections of the Stage* (1832). SMA

Bernhard, Thomas (1931–89) Austrian dramatist and novelist who classifies his plays as 'musical theatre'. Analogous in some ways to absurd drama, he presents images of existence through grotesque figures, tramps, clowns and cripples, avoiding elements of plot and using clichés as the basis of dialogue. The mechanical nature of socially conditioned behaviour provides a farcical base to his drama, as in the senselessly repetitive family relationships of *Have We Reached Our Goal* (1981) where the only escape from the past is paralysing isolation. But his major theme is the alienation of the artist, which recurs in *The Ignoramus and the Madman* (1971), *Force of Habit* (1974) and *Minetti* (1976). Musical motifs represent the dead weight of culture or the irrational nature of art, and there is a strong element of self-parody in his work which uses symphonic structures. One of his latest plays, *Über allen Gipfeln ist Ruh* (1982: the title of a sentimental song popular in the Nazi era), gives this a clear autobiographical dimension with a dramatist as the central figure, whose major work is a tetralogy demonstrating the impotence of art. CI

Bernhardt, Sarah (1844–1923) French actress. Incontestably the greatest star of the 19th-century French theatre, the 'divine' Sarah's reputation depended partly upon her very great talent as an actress (notably the purity of her diction), partly upon her personal charisma and particular brand of femininity and partly upon her extravagant lifestyle and productions. Her tempestuous departure from the **Comédie-Française** in 1880, her well-publicized exhibitions of sculpture and painting, her liaisons and her 'scandalous' balloon ride in 1878 kept the journalists busy. Her numerous tours abroad especially to the States, but also to Russia and Australia, ensured that her reputation travelled well beyond the boundaries of France. Thanks to the highly-placed protectors of her mother, Sarah was able to go to the Conservatoire and to make her debut at the Comédie-Française in 1862 in the role of Iphigenia. This was unremarkable and she left under a cloud, having slapped a senior member of the troupe. In 1869 she appeared at the **Odéon** in the breeches part of Zanetto in François Coppée's *The Passer-by*, making both her own reputation and that of the young Coppée. By 1872 she was back at the Comédie-Française making a triumphant appearance as the Queen in the major revival of **Hugo**'s *Ruy Blas*, and by 1875 had risen to being a *sociétaire* of the company. She appeared in a number of roles including *Phèdre* (1877) which would become one of her greatest parts, *Andromaque* and *Hernani* (where she was much admired by Hugo and had a strong partner in Mounet Sully). She was at home in both the classical and the modern repertoire, notably in the plays of the younger **Dumas**,

Sarah Bernhardt as Hamlet.

especially as Mistress Clarkson in *The Outsider* (*L'Etrangère*) – and, later, Marguerite in *The Lady of the Camellias* would become one of her great parts. The Comédie-Française found her hard to contain on the occasion of their visit to London in 1878. After her departure from the troupe, she developed a pattern of long foreign tours. In 1882 she found one of her two major authors in **Victorien Sardou**, whose *Fédora* was written for her to perform at the Vaudeville. From now on she was virtually her own manager and it is noticeable how many of the plays chosen became vehicles for her talent, and opportunities for her artistic delight in sumptuous *mise-en-scène*. In 1883 she took over the Porte-Saint-Martin and showed her versatility by appearing in **Meilhac** and Halévy's light comedy, *Froufrou*, followed by Jean Richepin's much darker drama *Nana Sahib*. She was also involved in the Ambigu theatre through her son, Maurice. However, these ventures led her to bankruptcy. In 1884 she gave one of the finest performances of her career in *The Lady of the Camellias*, with her husband, Jacques Damala, as Armand. That autumn she was ill (her health was often a problem), but by December was appearing at the Porte-Saint-Martin in Sardou's *Théodora*, another sumptuous spectacle, for which her cloak alone was reputed to have cost 8,000 francs. In 1893 she took on the direction of the Renaissance, her intention being to have a theatre where she could prepare and launch productions which would then tour. It was here that she created Sardou's *Gismonda* (1894) – in which she was joined by **Coquelin**, who had left the Comédie-Française, *La Princesse Lointaine* (*The Distant Princess*) by **Rostand** (her other major author) and the first production of **Musset**'s *Lorenzaccio*, adapted for her by Armand d'Artois, in which she played Lorenzo. In 1899 she moved to the former **Théâtre des Nations** on the Place du Châtelet, which now became the Théâtre Sarah Bernhardt (a title it would retain until the Occupation). She opened with one of her great roles in Sardou's *Tosca*, revived Rostand's *La Samaritaine* (*The Woman of Samaria*), and appeared in Marcel Schwob's adaptation of *Hamlet*. The most significant production of this period was Rostand's *L'Aiglon* (another breeches part, as Napoleon's son). When Bernhardt went on tour that autumn she allowed the Comédie-Française, which had just suffered a serious fire, to use her theatre. During the First World War Sarah, who in 1870 had turned the Odéon into a field hospital, turned to fund-raising on a massive scale to help the war-wounded. She continued playing to the bitter end, even after the amputation of one of her legs, which often required her to be propped up on stage. After her death her son Maurice continued the management of the theatre for some years.   JMCC

Bernini, Gian Lorenzo (1598–1680) Italian architect, sculptor, stage designer, dramatist, actor and stage manager. Perhaps the greatest artist of the Italian baroque, throughout his life he was fascinated by, and involved in, theatrical activity; some would argue that his architecture and sculptures are essentially theatrical in tone and organization. No visual material has survived illustrative of his scenographic work, which was undertaken in his main work-place, Rome, in places like the Vatican Fonderia and the Teatro Barberini, as well as for private theatricals mounted at his own

house. Such baroque spectacles as *De'Due Teatri* (*The Two Theatres*, 1637) and *L'Inondazione del Tevere* (*The Tiber in Flood*, 1638) he stage-managed himself. His output also included plays, a particularly interesting example of which was discovered only in the 1960s and given the title *La Fontana di Trevi* (*Trevi Fountain*, 1966), a scripted treatment of subject matter in the **commedia dell'arte** tradition.   KR

Bernstein, Aline (1880–1955) American set and costume designer. Bernstein became involved in theatre as a founding member of the **Neighbourhood Playhouse** in 1915. Her successful designs there, such as *The Little Clay Cart*, led to work with the **Theatre Guild** and on Broadway and in 1926 actress **Eva Le Gallienne** asked her to design for a newly founded Civic Repertory Theatre. She first worked with producer Herman Shumlin on *Grand Hotel* and continued her association with him through the 1930s, most notably on the plays of **Lillian Hellman** including *The Little Foxes*. Bernstein's early designs utilized adaptable unit sets, while some of her later work employed mechanical devices for a cinematic change of scenes. Bernstein founded the Costume Museum which later was absorbed by the Metropolitan Museum of Art.   AA

Bernstein, Leonard (1918–90) American composer. Although his primary career was as a conductor of symphony orchestras, Bernstein wrote the scores for six musicals. In 1944 he composed the music for **Jerome Robbins**'s ballet 'Fancy Free', and when the ballet was expanded into the full-length musical *On the Town* (1944), Bernstein wrote the entire score. Critics complimented him for the fresh, lively sound of his music. Nine years passed before Broadway heard another Bernstein score. *Wonderful Town* gave him the opportunity to write a nostalgic score full of pastiches of the 'swing' music popular in the 1930s. In 1956 Bernstein wrote the music for *Candide*, a musical adaptation of the **Voltaire** novel. Although the show was not a commercial success, Bernstein's score, with its echoes of various classical composers and its dry, satiric sound, was recognized as one of the finest written for the Broadway stage. A 1974 revival of *Candide* proved to be more successful with audiences. Bernstein's most famous score, that for *West Side Story*, premiered in 1957. Critics praised the music for its ability to embody the tensions and passions of the show's teenage characters. Although his contributions to the Broadway stage were relatively few, Bernstein's musically sophisticated and inventive scores earned him a reputation as one of the foremost Broadway composers.   MK

Bertinazzi (or Bertinassi), Carlo Antonio, called Carlino or Carlin (1710–83) Italian actor, the last great Arlecchino in France. Already famous in Italy, he first appeared at the Théâtre Italien, Paris, as a replacement for the unpopular **Antonio Costantini**; unsure of his French, he chose **Luigi Riccoboni**'s *Arlecchino contrained to be mute* as his premier offering. His grace, elegance, precision of movement, and the wittiness of his mime and vocal inflexions won him approbation; the rapport between himself and his audience was so great that he was always chosen to make the addresses

to the public. He was admired by **David Garrick** and
by **Goldoni**, in whose *Arlecchino's Son Lost and Found*
and *Paternal Love* he played, but his best vehicles were
written by Jean-Pierre de Florian.   LS

Bertonov, Yehoshua (1879–1971) Hebrew actor.
Born in Vilna to poor parents, he joined **Habimah** in
1922 and was at the time the only member with
previous acting experience. Played Old Ekdal in
Ibsen's *The Wild Duck* (1954), and the title role in
Sholom Aleichem's *Tevye the Milkman* (1943). He was
noted for his readings, especially from the Bible.   HAS

Besson, Benno (1922–   ) Swiss director who, until
1982, was best known for his close collaboration with
Brecht and his work in East Germany. In 1942 he joined
Geneviève and **Jean-Marie Serreau** in Lyon, then
studied English and French at Zurich University,
where he met Brecht. In 1947–9, he toured the French
occupation zone in Germany with Serreau (*The Exception and the Rule*); in 1949 Brecht invited him to East
Berlin. His first *mise en scène* was **Molière**'s *Don Juan*, in
Besson's own adaptation (**Berliner Ensemble**, Rostock, 1952). He remained in East Berlin until 1977;
Berliner Ensemble, 1949–58; director of **Deutsches
Theater**, 1960–9; of **Volksbühne** 1969–77. During
these 25 years, Besson directed also in Rostock,
Vienna, Frankfurt, Stuttgart, Lausanne, Zurich,
Munich, Sofia, Avignon, amongst others. In 1982 he
was offered his first appointment in Switzerland as
artistic director of the Comédie de Genève. In 1985 he
received the Reinhart-Ring, highest Swiss award for
exceptional achievements in the theatre. Besson directed over 50 plays, bringing to his work a high degree of
visual inventiveness, insisting on the playful quality of
the art of theatre and on the need for true communication between actors and spectators. He has, like Brecht,
modernized the classics and staged the work of young
playwrights. His main productions are: Brecht, *The
Days of the Commune* (premiere, 1956), *The Good Person*
(1956, 1957, 1970, 1973), *Man is Man* (1958: two
different productions with the same cast), *Saint Joan of
the Stockyards* (1961, 1962, 1973, 1981), *The Caucasian
Chalk Circle* (1978); **Shakespeare**'s *The Two Gentlemen
of Verona* (1959, 1963), *As You Like It* (1975, Berlin and
Sofia; 1974, Paris), *Hamlet* (1977, Paris; 1983, Geneva
and Zurich; 1985, Helsinki). He premiered **Peter
Hacks**'s *Moritz Tassow* (1965), Gerhard Winterlich's
Horizons (1969), Flaubert's *Le Sexe Faible* (*The Weaker
Sex*, 1984) and Elie Bourquin's *Lapin Lapin* (*Rabbit
Rabbit*, 1986).   CLS

Betterton, Thomas (1635–1710) English actor,
manager, playwright. Without doubt the greatest actor
in England between **Burbage** and **Garrick**. He probably started acting with John Rhodes's company in
1659 and was immediately recognized as their leading
man and a major talent. By 1661 he had joined
Davenant's company as their star actor and also
became a shareholder in the company. Pepys frequently praised his excellence. Davenant trained him as
Hamlet: 'having seen Mr **Taylor** of the Blackfriars
company act it, who being instructed by the author Mr
Shakespeare, he taught Mr Betterton in every particle
of it'. In 1662 he married Mary Saunderson, one of the
first English actresses and a leading member of the

Thomas Betterton's Hamlet meeting his father's ghost in his
mother's chamber.

company. In the same year he visited Paris to learn
about French theatre machinery and stage design. He
starred in virtually every play his company put on:
playing, for instance, Bosola in **Webster**'s *The Duchess
of Malfi*, Sir Toby Belch, Macbeth and Henry VIII. On
Davenant's death he became co-manager of the company with particular responsibility for rehearsals and
for training young actors. He also began writing
comedies and adapting earlier ones for the Restoration
stage. He continued as manager when the two companies were amalgamated in 1682 into the United
Company. The following year he visited France again,
pursuing his interest in spectacular stage effects, and
brought over Louis Grabu, a composer who collaborated with him on a series of operas of great expense and
technical brilliance. After a series of arguments with
Christopher Rich, who was financial director of the
company, Betterton led the senior actors in revolt
against the management and by 1695, under licence
from the king, they established themselves in the
Lincoln's Inn Fields Theatre under Betterton's control. But, after an initial success, the company was a
failure, with Betterton failing to be sufficiently innovative and to preserve discipline. In 1704, when the
company moved into **Vanbrugh**'s **Haymarket
Theatre**, he retired as manager, continuing to act. Not

long after a famous benefit performance of **Congreve**'s *Love for Love* for him in 1709, he retired as an actor as well. Throughout his long career he played all the major parts available to him: over 120 roles can be specifically ascribed to him. He was known for his careful preparation of roles, always consulting the playwright, always ready to respond to criticism. His acting style in tragedy was majestic and restrained, with an impressive self-discipline, a long way from the excessive styles of his contemporaries. Some of his thoughts on acting may survive in a history of the stage, written largely by Gildon but published under Betterton's name (1710).   PH

Betti, Ugo (1892–1953) Italian dramatist, poet and critic, and after **Pirandello** regarded by many as the major Italian playwright of the 20th century. Although his legal training and practice are strongly felt in his major plays of the 1940s, he began as a poet, and for a period in the late 1920s essayed a number of experimental drama forms, including dance-drama. He achieved his first major success with what many consider his finest play, *Frana Allo Scalo Nord* (*Landslide*, 1936), cast in the form of a judicial inquiry following an accident, and concerned with the revelation and exploration of guilt, weakness and spiritual need. His standpoint is liberal and Christian, but he avoids moral and religious simplicities and dogmatic judgements, exploring, in his best work, the nature of social and individual responsibility. The austere tone of his work was for long little appreciated in Italy until he achieved international success with plays like *Corruzione al Palazzo di Giustizia* (*Corruption in the Palace of Justice*, 1944), *Delitto all'Isola delle Capre* (*Crime on Goat Island*, 1946) and *La Regina e Gli Insorti* (*The Queen and the Rebels*, 1949).   LR

Betty, William Henry West (1791–1874) Anglo-Irish actor, a child prodigy, who for two seasons (1804–6) threw the London theatre into an undignified flutter. Billed as the 'Young **Roscius**', he outshone **John Philip Kemble** at **Covent Garden**, threatening that theatre with bankruptcy when he was tempted over to **Drury Lane**. During those heady years, Betty played Hamlet, Romeo, Rolla in **Sheridan**'s *Pizarro* and Young Norval in **Home**'s *Douglas* to the utter delight of indulgent audiences, until the craze dwindled. Beautiful and, within limits, talented, Betty was first ignored and then hissed into oblivion, despite the endeavours of his grasping father. After an abortive spell at Cambridge University, he attempted a comeback in 1812, but the magic was gone. Disheartened by the struggle, he attempted suicide in 1821 and retired into a tolerably prosperous obscurity in 1824.   PT

Bhagat This is an obscure Indian dramatic form confined to Agra, the home of the Taj Mahal and an important historic city of north India. Headed by a leader (*khalifa*), a party performs for the benefit of the individuals in their area of the city. Competition between parties of players is known to take place for the benefit of enthusiastic partisans.   FaR

Bhagavata Mela (India) The term *Bhagavata* is a reference to the *Bhagavata Puranas* which are collections of epic stories about Lord Vishnu's incarnations. Those who perform these stories are known as *Bhagavatars* or

The entrance of an actor in a *Bhagavata Mela* production in Tamil Nadu, India. Note the painted scenery on wings and drop.

Bhagavatulus. Mela refers to a troupe of dancers or singers.

The origin of *Bhagavata Mela*, as found in the village of Melattur in the state of Tamil Nadu, is traced to the state of Andhra Pradesh where it appears to have been born from the **Kuchipudi** dance-drama around 1502.

After the fall of the Vijayanagar Empire in 1565, cultural activities in the northern region of south India came to a virtual standstill. About 500 Telugu-speaking Brahmin families who performed this version of Kuchipudi were left homeless. They travelled south to Tanjore, a Tamil-speaking region, and appealed to King Achyutappa Nayak (1561–1614) for support. The gracious ruler granted them cultivable land and six villages near the city of Tanjore. Today, the only village to retain *Bhagavata Mela* as an annual performance is that of Melattur. Other villages of the area are known to have given *Bhagavata Mela* performances on an annual basis and a few of them still present truncated versions during the annual festival season.

In Melattur, during the last few weeks of April or early May, two troupes of devotees present an annual performance before the Varadraja Perumala Temple and at the village tank in celebration of Narasimha Jayanti, a festival honouring Vishnu's terrifying man-lion incarnation which destroyed a demon king. Venkatarama Sastri (1759–1847) sparked new life in the form by creating appealing musical compositions to suit about a dozen of his dance-dramas. The object of Sastri's compositions was to spread the devotional movement of Hinduism (*bhakti*) which began in the Middle Ages and continues unabated up to the present day among the people of this region.

The traditional site for the so-called 'temple performance' is on a narrow raised proscenium stage erected in the street between rows of the houses of Brahmin families opposite the Varadraja Perumala Temple. A long protective roof of thatch is stretched from the top of the proscenium about 100 feet down the street. Before performances begin around 9.30 or 10.00 pm, the temple deity is carried in lavish procession through the streets of the town and installed on a special roofed structure opposite the stage, so that performances take place in the divine presence.

The performance begins with the entrance of the clown (*konangi*) who dances and jests with the spectators. Then musicians enter and sing songs of invocation principally praising Vishnu and songs appropriate to introduce the particular play to be enacted. Next, the chief teachers of the art are honoured with sandal paste and flowers. This is followed by the appearance of a small boy wearing the mask of Ganapati, the elephant-headed god of good fortune. It is said that the child is chosen because his parents have made a vow to present their son on the stage in this role. After brief dances and songs asking his blessings for the proceedings, the drama begins.

All the actors who participate in the production are men, the younger and more attractive of whom play the female roles. Elaborate entrances of each character are made behind a curtain held by two attendants. The dance entrances incorporate stylized gesture and intricate rhythmic patterns of movement characteristic of all the classical dance styles practised in India. The entrance songs (called *patra pravesha darus*) introduce each character.

The scenes that follow depict the episodes of the drama in dialogue, song and dance. Actors combine stylized and complicated patterns of gesture-language with naturalistic movement and gesture to convey the meaning of the texts. The climax of performance usually occurs in the early hours of the morning when a dramatic crisis is reached.

One particular drama is noteworthy for its dramatic impact and ritual significance – that of *The Story Prahlada (Prahlada Charitram)*.

This story demonstrates the faith of Prahlada, a youthful prince who worships Lord Vishnu. Forsaking his father's love for that of his god, Prahlada's faith is tested in various ways. With each successive test his wicked father becomes more and more furious. Eventually, Prahlada's father is tricked and loses his life when Lord Vishnu, in the form of a man-lion (*Hiranyakashipu*), rips open his guts and kills the tyrant king.

According to tradition, the actor who portrays the role of the man-lion fasts and prays before wearing a special mask depicting the god. The mask is said to possess special powers endowed by the deity. When the actor appears in the scene he goes into a trance becoming the violent man-lion. To protect the actors playing the other roles, this actor must be restrained by attendants. Eventually, after the ritual killing is completed, all the actors climb down from the stage and walk to the temple where they circumambulate the deity. Songs appropriate to the early hours of the morning are sung by the chief musician. Offerings of rice are then received at households along the street and the ritual ends with a visit to another temple on the outskirts of the village where the actor playing the man-lion takes off his mask. Immediately, he falls into another trance and lies motionless on the ground until revived by water sprinkled over him to restore him to consciousness and symbolically return him to his normal state. To conclude the ceremony, benedictory verses are chanted and the exhausted actors return to their homes.

Owing to family conflicts, two parties of performers now work in this tiny village. They share the performance space over a period of time considered sacred for the festival and each presents a dramatic work as part of the celebrations.

The music of *Bhagavata Mela* follows the Karnataka style of classical music and has garnered much praise from music critics throughout India. Musical instruments used in performance are those considered appropriate for the classical repertory – the *mridangam* drum, traverse bamboo flute, a violin played in the Indian manner and bell-brass cymbals. The voice of the singer is a particularly important instrument completing the musical ensemble.

The dance techniques are a mixture of those inherited from *Kuchipudi* and those adapted from the classical *Bharata Natyam* dance popular in Tamil Nadu.   FaR

Bhamakalapam (India) The word is composed of two parts: *Bhama* which is an abbreviation of the name of Lord Krishna's beautiful and jealous wife Satyabhama and *kalapam* which means dialogue or argument. *Bhamakalapam* like **Gollakalapam** is both a play and a theatre form. The play was created in the 17th century by Siddhendra Yogi for use as a devotional ritual by **Kuchipudi** performers. Several versions of the story have been created since that time but none as well known or as popular. *Bhamakalapam* is also known as Vithi Natakam by some scholars, although in form and content it is markedly different from **Veedhi Natakam**, the well-known street drama of this area of south India.

Bhamakalapam is enacted by various troupes (*melas*) which function throughout the state of Andhra Pradesh. Until recently, it was patronized by local landowners (*zamindars*) and other wealthy patrons. Owing to the general deterioration of folk arts and traditions in modern India, the form is in serious danger of disappearing altogether.

Unlike **Kathakali**, **Yakshagana** or **Therukoothu**, which emphasize the masculine dance movements (*tandava*), *Bhamakalapam* is a superb example of the wide range and potential beauty of graceful feminine dance movements (*lasya*).

The form is traditionally performed by male devotees as is its parent form *Kuchipudi*. Today, there is less scope for *Bhamakalapam* than *Kuchipudi* because it has gained little recognition among dance critics and scholars and the support of wealthy patrons has disappeared as tastes have changed.   FaR

Bhamakalapam performance in Andhra Pradesh, India. Male actor playing the heroine Satyabhama stands behind a half curtain which represents a balcony and is questioned by the stage manager. Musicians stand close to the rear of the scene.

Bhand Jashna (India) *Bhand* means clown and *Jashna* means festival. For several centuries this has been the popular form of rural theatre of Kashmir, a state at the northern tip of the Indian subcontinent. Like other forms of rural theatre popular among Muslims of north India, the form emphasizes farce and satire. Lively plays (*pather*) are improvised primarily in the Kashmiri language, but also with a free blend of words and phrases borrowed from other languages, such as Urdu, Hindi, Punjabi and Persian, to suit the particular political and social situation of a village. The actors mercilessly ridicule corrupt officials, money-lenders and the dowry system while making fun of everyone from the simplest peasant to the most powerful political leader. Many of the plays have semi-historical settings and concern popular folk heroes to avoid the accusation of slander but their contemporary relevance is made clear.

Performances may take place during the day, as well as in the evening. To the accompaniment of music, the actors make their entrances through the audience to the playing area, which may be any open space in the village. Unlike musical parties elsewhere in north India, the musicians stand and accompany the actors as they work the crowd seated around the playing area.

Performances begin with a ritual invocation (*pooza-path*) honouring Allah. This is followed by a farcical imitation of the solemnities performed by the clowns (*maskharas*). Costumes are a blend of contemporary local and semi-historical dress, indiscriminately mixed together. Colourful headdresses and cloth pieces are used to add flair.   FaR

Bharatlila Also known as *Dwara Nata*. This folk theatre form of Orissa, India, stresses episodes from the epic *Mahabharata*, particularly those concerning Arjuna and Subhadra, his wife. The character of Dwara acts as an interpreter of the events to the audience. The three actors are the main characters, exchanging remarks and adding considerable humour to the events which take three to four hours to enact.   FaR

Bhavai (India) Raucous, bawdy, obscene, satiric, poignant – all these terms describe *Bhavai*, a form of rural theatre once popular in western India. Local legend has it that *Bhavai*'s origin may be attributed to Asaita Thakar, an outcast Brahmin who lived during the mid-14th century in what is now Gujarat state.

The story goes that Asaita Thakar was born a Brahmin and served as the family priest of Patel Hema, headman of Unza, a small village in north Gujarat. One day Hema's daughter Ganga was abducted by a Muslim captain who had an eye for a pretty face. Asaita felt obliged to save the poor girl and so he sought audience with the captain on the pretext of entertaining him with his songs. After winning the captain's praise, Asaita begged that Ganga be released saying that she was his only daughter. The shrewd captain suspected that Asaita was lying but he agreed to release Ganga if Asaita dined with her in his presence. The wily captain knew that Brahmins were strictly forbidden to dine with lower caste Hindus, indeed it was considered an unpardonable act. To the captain's amazement Asaita readily agreed and did as he was bade, thus gaining Ganga's freedom. When Asaita returned to Unza with Ganga safely in tow he was promptly excommunicated

by his Brahmin brethren. In ancient India excommunication was considered a fate worse than death. It meant that Asaita could no longer practise his hereditary profession. A lesser man would surely have been ruined by this sudden reversal of fortune but Asaita accepted his fate and turned to singing and dancing for a living which has historically been considered an appropriate profession for many of India's outcasts. With the help of his sons and other outcast Brahmins he formed the first company of strolling players in Gujarat, the *bhaviyas* – those who arouse sentiment in the spectators through their performance. Later, the members of this community came to be known as the targalas, those of three castes. It is this community which still preserves the hereditary right to perform *Bhavai* in Gujarat.

In gratitude for the safe return of his daughter, Patel Hema bestowed a small plot of land and financial support on Asaita, thereby initiating a pattern of village patronage of *bhavaiyas* which persists even today.

Although no longer a popular art form, *Bhavai* may still be found today in North Gujarat and Saurashtra, in Malawa in the state of Madhya Pradesh and Marwad and elsewhere in Rajasthan state. Its wide geographic spread is due, no doubt, to the close ties among the peoples of this colourful region.

Bhavai is traditionally performed in connection with religious festivals in praise of mother goddesses, such as Ambaji and Bahucharaji, the latter of which is regarded as the patroness of the *Bhavai* actors. *Navaratri*, the nine-night festival in September–October honouring the goddess, is a particularly auspicious occasion for performance. Performances are normally arranged on Hindu holy days and in the sacred confines of a temple courtyard or a street in front of the temple. The performance space (*paudh*) is sanctified by the stage manager who draws a large circle of oil on the ground and lights a torch symbolizing the presence of the goddess. Songs in praise of the goddess are also sung prior to other ritual overtures and the actors and audience alike sometimes shout 'Long life to the Goddess!' during the show.

Despite the highly charged religious atmosphere of the place and occasion, the contents of most of the performances centre on the vices and virtues of members of various communities in village society. The Brahmin, the taylor, the potter, the scavenger, the money-lender – all are satirized in *Bhavai*. There are some performances which deal with Hindu mythology and others which provide vignettes of famous historical personages of the area but even these have an abundance of satire and an inevitable didactic message.

Humour is the dominant sentiment in *Bhavai*, although a variety of other emotions are evoked during the progress of many performances. The predominance of humour, however, makes *Bhavai* unique in the catalogue of traditional Indian theatre.

The language of performance is a generous mix of Gujarati, Hindi-Urdu and Marwadi, which further indicates the historical connection of many castes and communities throughout this wide geographic region. Songs in verse set to a wide variety of metres and prose dialogue characterize the structure of the stories.

Bhavai is linked to the past through performance rather than through written, printed or published texts, although stories were collected and published in Gujarat for the first time in the 19th century. The stories are

Audience of a *Bhavai* production in rural Gujarat before the entrance to a temple. Traditionally, the village barber holds a lighted torch during the performance.

known as *vesa* which literally means 'costume' and they bear the names of the chief characters around which they are composed. For example, *Ganapati-no-vesa* is the ritual introduction and dance of the elephant-headed god Ganapati; *Juthana-no-vesa* is the story about the trials of a Muslim crown-prince; *Zhanda Zulan-no-vesa* concerns the love affair between a Muslim policeman and a wife of a rich Hindu merchant; *Brahmana-no-vesa* depicts the mad antics of a priest, and so the catalogue goes on and on. There are said to have been 360 *vesa*, one for every day of the year, but far fewer actually survive in the repertory today.

The instruments most commonly used in the *Bhavai* are *bhungals*, *pakhawaja* or *tabla* drums, small cymbals (*jhanjha*) and the harmonium, a small keyboard instrument similar to an organ and the *sarangi*, a classical north Indian stringed instrument. The *bhungals* are unique to *Bhavai*. They are four-foot long copper pipes which provide a forceful cadence during the dance sequences and serve to announce the entrance of important characters. Normally, two *bhungals* are used, a male and a female instrument. On occasion, various other instruments are introduced for special effects.

Performances usually begin around 10 pm after the villagers have taken their evening meals. Music accompanies the action and initially serves to attract the spectators to the performance area. The Hindustani or north Indian style of music dominates but popular local tunes and rhythms are integrated throughout. When a sufficient number of spectators have been drawn to the playing area and the important guests have been seated, prayers to Ambaji commence. These are followed by a few songs describing the love affair of a famous couple from Marwad. The songs serve as a cue to the stage manager (*nayaka*) to enter the arena and begin the rituals.

Asaita Thakar must have considered this phase of the preliminaries important because he formalized the pattern of the preliminaries in a separate *vesa*. On cue from the musicians, an actor dressed to represent Ganapati, the elephant-headed god of beginnings and successes, enters holding a brass plate before his face. As he dances, the musicians sing his praises. Like all of the dances of *Bhavai*, the style is a watered down

version of *Kathak*, the classical dance of north India, combined with *garba*, a folk dance of the region. After Ganapati makes his exit, another actor enters impersonating the goddess Kali. The stage manager questions her as to her name and business but gets nothing other than monosyllables as a reply. Kali dances in a frenzy to loud songs of praise. At the end of the dance all the musicians implore her to remove all impediments that might hinder their performance which she symbolically does by forming a circle over their heads and cracking her knuckles on her temples.

To conclude the preliminaries, an actor dressed as a Brahmin priest comes from the dressing room through the crowds of spectators which circle the arena. He provides the first bit of humour in the show. When questioned by the stage manager as to his name and business he replies in a ridiculous manner using all kinds of obscenities to the delight of the spectators. His costume is a caricature of that of a Brahmin. Sometimes an actor portrays the role wearing small clay pots on his stomach and on his hips which are concealed under the folds of his costume. His appearance is grotesque and provokes roars of laughter. When he dances his movements are the very antithesis of grace. After his antics have been completed the Ganapati preliminaries are concluded by a song. Only then do the regular stories begin.

Although the rural interest in *Bhavai* has waned over the last several decades, urban theatre people have been attracted to it for a variety of reasons. First, in the wake of a national desire to preserve valuable and endangered folk traditions, urbanites have sought to support *Bhavai* performances and even to recruit some of the best actors as part-time teachers at the college level in a few prominent educational institutions. In this way, unique folk traditions are preserved and passed down to future generations in this rapidly industrializing society. Second, the form of *Bhavai*, its attention to comedy, satire and political details, accompanied by music with stylized movements and dance, have been imitated by urban theatre groups adapting the content to suit urban purposes. Troupes of actors have taken *Bhavai* and rendered their own versions of the form to the delight of many city dwellers. A few, more faithful imitators have attempted to replicate *Bhavai*'s rural flavour rather than adapting it wholesale by gutting its content. *Mena Gujari* and *Jasma Odan* produced by Deena Gandhi and Shanta Gandhi, respectively, two well-known theatre exponents, have been successfully produced in Ahmedabad, Bombay and Delhi in recent years. With all the expressed interest, no major movement has occurred which has led the way toward a genuine revival of *Bhavai*. And so, the original actors and the community continues to struggle to survive.   FaR

Biancolelli A family of Italian actors. **Isabella** Franchini (d. c. 1650), the daughter of the famous Pantalone Francesco Franchini and a famous Colombina in her own right, took as her third husband the Bolognese **Francesco** Biancolelli (d. c. 1640). Their son **Giuseppe Domenico** (c. 1636–88) played with Locatelli's company in Paris from 1659 and from 1680 acted at the newly founded **Hôtel de Bourgogne** in the **Comédie-Italienne**, under the stage-name Dominique. Short, svelte and supremely agile, he naturalized the Arlecchino type to the French stage with an admixture of dance, wise-cracks and acrobatic elements and a quantum of elegance. He was on bantering terms with Louis XIV, who permitted him to interject French dialogue in his harsh voice. He died of pneumonia, following a particularly strenuous exhibition. He had married (1663) Orsola Cortesi, called Eularia (c. 1632–1718), who took the veil at his death. Their children included three actors: Francesca Maria Apolline, called Isabella (1664–1747), a witty, brilliant *amorosa*, who made her debut in 1683; Caterina, called Colombina (1665–1716), who excelled her grandmother in that role and was painted by Watteau before her retirement in 1697; and Pier Francesco, called Dominique *fils* (1680–1734). He made his debut with an Italian troupe in Toulouse, toured the French provinces, and had an extraordinary success as Arlecchino in Venice and Genoa. On his return to Paris, he took over the management of the foundering Opéra Comique. When **Luigi Riccoboni** reopened the newly organized Comédie-Italienne in 1716 under the protection of the Duc d'Orléans, he joined it, soon becoming one of its favourite players. Contemporaries unanimously hailed him as the best Arlequin of his time; he wrote a number of scenarios for the improvised comedy. LS

Bibiena, Galli da An Italian family of theatre architects and scenic designers who took their name from the birth-place of Giovanni Maria (1625–65), known as *Il Vecchio*, a designer of modest talents who established the family connections with theatre and whose sons and grandsons acquired European celebrity. His eldest son, **Ferdinando** (1657–1743), is said to have begun his career with **Giacomo Torelli**, but quickly rose to prominence under the patronage of the Farnese at Parma, where he was chief court architect for many years. He went to Spain in 1708 to direct the festivities at Barcelona in celebration of the marriage of Charles III, and between 1712 and 1717 was in the service of the Emperor Charles VI in Vienna. His major contribution to scenic design, the scenes set at an acute angle (*scena per angolo*), revolutionized baroque staging: these were first used at Piacenza in mounting Lotti's *Didio Giuliano* (1687), and are described in his *L'Architettura Civile Preparata Nella Geometria* (1711). His brother **Francesco** (1659–1739) likewise worked widely throughout Italy and elsewhere on the Continent, at first often with Ferdinando, developing the latter's angled scenes, then on his own account. In 1702 he was responsible for the celebrations mounted to mark the arrival of Philip V in Naples; between 1708 and 1709 he built the splendid theatre at Nancy and, later in his career, the Teatro Filarmonico at Verona. Ferdinando's eldest son **Giuseppe** (1696–1757) long worked with his father at the Viennese court and was noted for the quality of his opera sets there, as well as those he did for major theatrical centres like Dresden, Prague and Venice: in 1740 he published a rich collection of his stage designs. He appears to have been the first to use transparent scenery lit from behind. His younger brother **Antonio** (1700–74) followed him as first court architect at Vienna, and in Italy designed a number of theatres including the Teatro Comunale in Bologna (from 1755) and the Teatro dei Quattro Cavalieri in Pavia, 1773. Giuseppe's son **Carlo** (1728–87) continued the family tradition, working with his father, for example, on the Opera-House of the Palgrave at Bayreuth, then at various courts, including those of Vienna and Dresden. KR

Bickerstaffe, Isaac (1733–?1808) Irish playwright. Born in Dublin, he was a page to the Earl of Chesterfield before coming to London in 1755. In 1760 his 'dramatic pastoral' or 'ballad farce' *Thomas and Sally*, with music by Arne, was performed. *Love in a Village* (1762) is probably the first English comic opera. Its success led Bickerstaffe to write many more, including *The Maid in the Mill* (1765). His collaborations with **Dibdin** were particularly successful, influencing the whole development of musical comedy as a dramatic form. Their play *Love in the City* failed at its first performance but succeeded when abbreviated as *The Romp*. He adapted **Wycherley**'s *The Plain Dealer* for **Garrick** in 1765 and his short farce *The Padlock* (1768) starred Dibdin as Mungo, the first black-face comic role seen in London. In 1772 he escaped to France to avoid prosecution after a homosexual affair and he lived abroad until his death. PH

Bidesia (India) The term means one who emigrates from his homeland. It refers to a relatively obscure form of theatre found in the villages of Bihar. Apparently, it was created in the early part of the century by Bhikhari Thakur, a barber who left the security of his home to form a company of itinerant actors. The plays depict the trials and tribulations of villagers, some of which concern the confrontation between the traditional values of rural life and the modern values of city dwellers. FaR

Bill-Belotserkovsky, Vladimir Naumovich (1884–1970) Soviet dramatist, whose propagandistic tales of heroic communism and decadent capitalism introduced many of the theatrical themes, devices and character types which were consolidated under socialist realism (1934–53). Bill-Belotserkovsky's work reflects his proletarian beginnings, his years at sea, his sojourn as an unskilled worker in the United States (1911–17, thus his American nickname 'Bill'), his active participation in the October Revolution and ensuing work on behalf of the Communist Party. As a member (in 1921) of the Proletkult (the Proletarian Culture Organization) and later the Glavrepertkom (the Central Committee for the Control of Repertory, 1929), he helped to develop and to police the new Soviet drama. Derived from the *agitka*, or agit-prop presentations of the Civil War period, his plays are naive, crudely energetic, episodically structured and transparently diagrammatic in character and thematic development, ranging in style from primitive psychological realism to heroic monumentalism. His first four plays – *Beefsteak, Rare* (1920), *Stages* (1921), *Echo* (1922) and *Steer to the Left!* (1926) – traverse the path to 'World Revolution' through Europe and America, underscoring, sometimes in allegorical terms, the inevitability of the climactic struggle. *Storm* (1924) is the author's classic Civil War play. Melodramatically conceived and martially scored at a brisk tempo, its tale of an heroic Party Chairman (the first 'positive hero' on the Soviet stage) battling to rid his quarter of class enemies and bring about a new order out of chaos gave birth to **Vishnevsky**'s genre-defining *An Optimistic Tragedy* (1933) and a host of

The first scene of Isaac Bickerstaffe's *The Maid of the Mill*, 1765.

socialist realist progeny. It was popular throughout Eastern Europe and was revised by the author for the 1952 **Yury Zavadsky** production at the Mossoviet Theatre. His second most influential work, *Life Is Calling* (1953), is an attempt to deal with the social problems of assimilation into and alienation from the new regime within the framework of a small-scale psychological realistic play. Its use of romantic sub-plots, pairings of ideological types and a climactic conversion speech, really a clarion call to the audience, became familiar elements in the theatrical language of the new Soviet drama. His other plays include *Calm* (1926), an attempt at NEP (New Economic Policy) satire, *Moon on the Left* (1927), a weak comedy about the positive hero and love and *The Voice of the Depths* (1928), a First Five-Year Plan reconstruction play, none of which were successful.   SG

Biltmore Theatre   261 West 47th St, New York City [Architect: Herbert J. Krapp]. Still believing that theatres represented a solid real-estate venture, the Chanin brothers, builders, erected the Biltmore with under 1,000 seats for serious plays and comedies. Unfortunately, the depression robbed them of their theatrical empire. After a year in which it was rented to the **Federal Theatre Project**, the playhouse was sold to Warner Brothers, who leased it to **George Abbott**. In the next 15 years, Abbott presented and often directed about a dozen or more of his own productions at the theatre. In 1951, the theatre was sold and became

a CBS-TV studio. In 1961, with another owner, seats were added to it and it was reclaimed for legitimate production. It is currently leased to the **Nederlander** Organization.   MCH

Birch-Pfeiffer, Charlotte (1800–68) German actress and playwright. Among the several plays she adapted from novels, *The Orphan of Lowood* (1856), based on *Jane Eyre*, was the most widely performed. Despite her considerable dramaturgical skill, Birch-Pfeiffer's plays disappeared soon after her death.   SW

Bird, Robert Montgomery (1806–54) American playwright. His major plays were prize-winners in **Edwin Forrest**'s playwriting contests and were per-formed by him: *The Gladiator* (1831), *Oralloosa* (1832), and *The Broker of Bogota* (1834). *Gladiator* and *Broker* were retained in Forrest's repertoire with extraordinary profits for him and only 2,000 dollars for Bird. *Pelopidas* (1830), another winner, was never produced. Discouraged by his bitter financial quarrels with For-rest, Bird turned to novels. *Hawks of Hawk Hollow* (1836), *Nick of the Woods* (1837) are the best known.

Bird received his medical degree in 1827, practised for a year, wrote two plays in 1827, *The Cowled Lover* and *Caridorf*, and taught at Pennsylvania Medical College (1841–3). At his death his notebook outlined plans for 11 tragedies, 12 comedies, 33 melodramas, and 25 novels.   RM

Birmingham Repertory Theatre This, the first purpose-built repertory theatre in Britain, was opened in February 1913. Seating 464, it was designed to be intimate, every seat in the steeply raked auditorium having an unrestricted view of the stage. Under **Barry Jackson**, the theatre's owner and artistic director, with John Drinkwater as its general manager, the resident company quickly gained a reputation for consistent, high quality and often adventurous productions of the 'uncommercial' drama, and notable successes included Eden Phillpotts's *The Farmer's Wife* (1916), Drinkwater's *Abraham Lincoln* (1918), modern-dress productions of **Shakespeare** (1923 onwards) and **Shaw**'s *Back to Methuselah* (1923). From 1925 Jackson added a series of London seasons to the work of a rapidly expanding company. Recurring financial difficulties, however, led in 1935 to a Board of Trustees taking over ownership of the theatre. In 1971 a new theatre was opened to replace the old. A 900-seat auditorium facing a wide stage, spacious foyers and backstage facilities and a small studio theatre for experimental work contrast markedly with the old building, though there has been some loss of intimacy too. Jackson's policy of an all-embracing repertoire of new, old and popular works continues but, now lacking a resident company and with serious cutbacks in the level of subsidy, the theatre's home-produced shows are fewer in number. Actors whose careers were launched at Birmingham include **Ralph Richardson**, **Laurence Olivier**, Cedric Hardwicke, **Paul Scofield** and **Albert Finney**. AJ

Bjørnson, Bjørn (1859–1942) Norwegian director and actor, son of **Bjørnstjerne Bjørnson**. After studies in Vienna, he first acted with the Saxe-**Meiningen** company. Joining Christiania Theatre in 1884, he introduced naturalistic acting and staging and in the next nine years, acted in or directed some 130 productions, including **Shakespeare**, **Molière** and **Ibsen** and several operas. His tremendous energies were then committed to the campaign for the new **Nationaltheatret**, which opened in 1899 with Bjørnson at its head. He again threw himself into almost every aspect of production and created a remarkable ensemble, until ill-health forced his resignation in 1907. Apart from a brief return to Nationaltheatret in the 1920s, he spent the rest of his life in Germany and Italy, returning frequently to Norway to act and direct. Although he was sometimes attacked for poor artistic taste, Bjørnson was a crucial figure in the modernization of Norwegian theatre. HL

Bjørnson, Bjørnstjerne (1832–1910) Norwegian playwright, novelist and journalist, winner of the 1903 Nobel Prize for Literature. He succeeded **Ibsen** as Stage Director of the Norwegian Theatre, Bergen (1857–9) and later successfully directed Christiania Theatre. He was also involved in journalism, editing several newspapers, and in politics he was a Nationalist and spokesman for the Left Party. His playwriting began in the 1850s with romantic history plays in the manner of **Oehlenschläger** and **Schiller**; the most enduring is *Sigurd the Bad* (1862). From the mid-1860s, his plays were more realistic, dealing with contemporary social problems: marital, as in *The Newlyweds* (1865), *Leonarda* (1879) and *A Gauntlet* (1883); business-related, as

in the successful *A Bankruptcy* (1874); and political, as in *The King* (1877) and *Paul Lang and Tora Parsberg* (1898). Frequently marred by Bjørnson's obvious plot manipulations, these plays are also limited by their good-natured sentimentality, which allows the solution of problems by characters' superficial changes of heart. Beginning with *Beyond Our Power, I* (1883), his plays occasionally explore more spiritual issues, but this is intermittent and limited. HL

Black, George (1891–1945) English impresario, noted for the rapid pacing of his shows. He originated the Royal Variety performances and injected the sumptuousness of revue into music-hall. As managing director of the General Theatre Corporation (1928) and Moss Empires Ltd (1933), he controlled 40 halls, including the Palladium, where, by conflating three teams of comedians, he created the **Crazy Gang** (*U-Kay for Sound*, 1936–7). His lavish revues at the **Hippodrome** include *The Fleet's Lit Up* (1938), *Black Velvet* (1939) and *Black Varieties* (1941). LS

Blackface minstrelsy see **Minstrel show**

Blackfriars Theatre, London Of the two theatres built in rooms formerly part of the Blackfriars monastery, the earlier dates from 1576, the same year in which **James Burbage** erected the **Theatre**. The private and public theatres of Elizabethan London were, thus, virtually twin-born. The prime mover in the Blackfriars enterprise was Richard Farrant, Deputy Master of the **Children of the Chapel Royal** and already an experienced instigator of their occasional plays at Court. Speculation on a basis of scant detail suggests that the room Farrant converted was the old refectory. The dimensions (46½ft × 26ft) are those of an intimate theatre, with a presumed capacity not much in excess of 100. The convenient fiction was that the choristers were there 'rehearsing' plays for performance before the Queen, but patrons were charged for admission and Farrant's boys were effective rivals to the **Boys of St Paul's**. After Farrant's death in 1580, the two **Boys' Companies** were briefly united under the creative leadership of **John Lyly**, but in 1584 the Blackfriars landlord, for reasons unknown, decided to recover possession of his property.

Speculation has again many gaps to fill in our knowledge of the second Blackfriars, but the outline of its story is discernible. When James Burbage was looking to replace the Theatre, whose lease was due to expire in 1597, he bought, from the same landlord who had evicted the Children of the Chapel Royal, several rooms in the Blackfriars, including the Parliament Chamber (66ft × 46ft). It was probably in this Chamber, rather than the lower paved hall beneath it, that Burbage set about his conversion work. That work was, however, halted late in 1596 when a petition from Blackfriars residents against the licensing of a public playhouse in their exclusive precinct was circulated. Burbage died in 1597, leaving the unusable Blackfriars to his equally practical son, the actor **Richard Burbage**, and it was he who, in 1600, leased it to Henry Evans, operating on behalf of the Children of the Chapel Royal. The residents evidently found it easier to stomach a 'private' playhouse, occupied by a Boys' Company, and Evans maintained his lease of the second Blackfriars for eight of its 21 years (1600–8). The Parliament Chamber was high enough to accommodate galleries, and its capacity was also increased by on-stage seating for privileged or showy spectators. The artificial lighting and scenic refinements of the indoor stage, together with a faddish interest in boy-performers, made the Blackfriars a formidable rival to the outdoor houses of the adult companies, but Evans, notoriously unscrupulous in his treatment of the choristers and possessed of a tabloid temperament, pushed his players too far into controversy. The repertoire included many of the finest plays of the period, but Evans came increasingly to miscalculate the amount of licence permissible to boys, and his management ended in disorder in 1608. It was then that Richard Burbage brought the King's Men into occupation of their prized indoor theatre, although their first performances there may have been delayed until 1610. The playhouse remained in the company's possession until the closure of the theatres in 1642. PT

Blake, Eubie see **Sissle, Noble**

Blake, William Rufus (1805–63) Canadian-born actor, playwright, and manager, noted for his portrayal of old men on the American stage. With the possible exception of **William Burton**, he was without equal in this line. Blake made his New York debut at the **Chatham Garden Theatre** in 1824 and subsequently appeared with great success in the United States and Britain. In the 1820s and 30s he managed successively the **Tremont Theatre**, Boston; the **Walnut Street** in Philadelphia; and with H. E. Willard the **Olympic Theatre**, New York. Later he was principal comedian in the New York stock companies of Burton, **Laura Keene**, and **Lester Wallack**. His final appearance was as Sir Peter Teazle at the Boston Theatre on 21 April. He died suddenly the next day. DBW

Blakely, Colin (George Edward) (1930–87) British actor, who turned to the theatre at the age of 28 in Belfast and was invited to join **George Devine**'s English Stage Company for a small part in **Sean O'Casey**'s *Cock-a-Doodle-Dandy*. He was invited to join the **National Theatre** company under **Laurence Olivier** in 1963, where he achieved immediate success as the rugged adventurer, Pizarro, in **Peter Shaffer**'s *The Royal Hunt of the Sun* (1964). The range of Blakely's work was impressive – equally successful as Titus Andronicus in a **Royal Shakespeare Company** production as in a play by **Harold Pinter** (*Old Times*, 1972) – and he starred in the West End, as with the national companies, in films, TV and in fringe theatres. Blakely's particular asset, however, was the feeling of authenticity which he brought to his various roles, a quality of being dramatically un-theatrical, so that, as with his performance in **Ayckbourn**'s *Just Between Ourselves* (1977), the audience was drawn into what seemed an intimate eavesdropping of human life. JE

Blakemore, Michael (Howell) (1928–) Australian born actor and director, who came to study at the Royal Academy of Dramatic Art in London. He started as an actor with several major regional repertory companies, including the **Birmingham Rep** and the Shakespeare Memorial Company at Stratford-upon-Avon. In 1966, he was appointed co-director of the **Glasgow Citizens' Theatre**, where his sensitive production of **Peter Nichols**'s *A Day in the Death of Joe Egg* (1967) attracted much attention. His *Arturo Ui* production in 1969 first drew the attention of many other directors to the potentiality of this **Brecht** play. His association with the work of Peter Nichols continued with successful productions of *Forget-me-not Lane* (1971), *The National Health* (1969) at the **National Theatre** and *Privates on Parade* with the **Royal Shakespeare Company**. **Laurence Olivier** invited him to become an Associate Artistic Director of the National Theatre in 1971; and there he directed several major NT successes in quick succession, including *Long Day's Journey into Night* (with Olivier as Tyrone), *The Front Page*, *The Cherry Orchard* and *Plunder*. He stayed on under **Peter Hall**'s regime at the National Theatre until the opening of the new theatre, but the relationship between them was never happy. After a brief spell as resident director at the **Lyric Theatre**, **Hammersmith**, in 1970, he returned to being a freelance director in Britain and Australia, directing **Michael Frayn**'s hit farce, *Noises Off* (1982), in Britain and the United States. His film, *A Personal History of the Australian Surf* (1981), is a splendid evocation of his boyhood, while his novel, *Next Season* (1969), provides a telling account of his life as an actor with the Shakespeare Memorial Company. As a director, Blakemore excels in coaxing actors to provide outstanding performances. JE

Blin, Roger (1907–84) French actor, director, designer. Drawn to stage acting as a way of overcoming a stammer, Blin acted with **Artaud**, **Dullin**, **Barrault** and the **October group** in the 1930s, also studying mime. After the war he began directing in avant-garde theatres producing two of **Adamov**'s plays as well as **Beckett**'s *En Attendant Godot* with which he made his name in 1953. He became the friend and trusted director of Beckett (*Fin de Partie* 1957; *La Dernière Bande* 1960; *Oh Les Beaux Jours* 1963) and also of **Genet** (*Les Nègres* (*The Blacks*) 1959; *Les Paravents* (*The Screens*) 1966). Genet's published letters to him about his production of *The Screens* testify to an unusually close collaboration between author and director. For Blin, the functions of director and designer were inseparable: to direct a play was to reveal reality in a new light, making every element in the production speak its own particular language. DB

Blinn, Holbrook (1872–1928) American actor. Born in San Francisco, Blinn first appeared onstage locally as a child in *Streets of New York* (1878). After a year at Stanford University (1891–2), he made his New York debut in *The New South* (1893), and his first London appearance in *The Cat and the Cherub* (1897). He began playing leading parts for **Arnold Daly**'s Company (1907–8) and afterwards for **Mrs Fiske** (1908–11), portraying Jim Platt in *Salvation Nell* (1908) and Karsten Bernick in *Pillars of Society* (1901). In 1911 **Harrison Grey Fiske** featured him as Michael Regan in **Edward Sheldon**'s *The Boss*. During the 1913–14 season he produced a series of 30 one-acts at the Princess Theatre, acting in several. Other starring roles included Lord Illingworth in *A Woman of No Importance* (1916) with **Margaret Anglin**; Georges Duval in *The Lady of the Camellias* in an all-star revival (1917); and

Pancho Lopez in *The Bad Man* (1920), a role which brought him recognition for his comic ability. Blinn was a versatile actor able to play a wide range of roles from the brutal Jim Platt to the aristocratic Georges Duval. TLM

Bloch, William (1845–1926) Danish director, who pioneered the introduction of naturalistic staging at the **Kongelige Teater** in the 1880s. In his richly textured **Ibsen** productions, he rapidly established himself as Denmark's most perceptive interpreter of the new drama. Criticism over his neglect of classical tragedy, for which he had little aptitude, and the rivalry of **Emil Poulsen** caused his resignation in 1893, until he returned in 1899 for a ten-year engagement during which he revolutionized the theatre's approach to **Holberg**. Anticipating many of **Stanislavsky**'s ideas, Bloch increased rehearsal time, planned and researched productions and, although he was working with actors trained in the romantic theatre, strove (not always successfully) for acting that depended on individuality, inner truth, and ensemble. He specialized in coordinating a mass of carefully planned details to create the 'atmosphere' of a play's specific time and place, as in his productions of *An Enemy of the People* (1883) and *The Wild Duck* (1885). HL

Blok, Aleksandr Aleksandrovich (1880–1921) Russian poet and dramatist considered 'the last romantic' and 'the greatest symbolist', who helped to define 20th-century self-conscious, conventional theatre. The latter half of his career is an ironic commentary on his earlier naive romance with symbolism and the mystical philosophy of Vladimir Solovyov. When the latter's 'Divine Sophia', 'God's ideal humanity', failed to materialize with the defeat of the 1905 Revolution, Blok underwent a spiritual crisis from which he never recovered. He rejected the 'decadent charlatanism' of symbolist mysticism, an impulse reinforced by the relationship that was forming between his wife (L. D. Mendeleeva) and symbolist colleague **Andrei Bely**. The *Lyrical Dramas* (1908) which resulted – *The Puppet Show*, *The King on the Square* and *The Unknown Woman* (all 1906) – along with his later plays offer a mixture of autobiographical existentialist drama, artistic and socio-political satire and elegy for what was lost, never was and might never be found. His tragifarce *The Puppet Show*, based on an earlier poem, casts Bely as Harlequin, Mendeleevna as Columbine – symbolist image recast as sensual betrayer – Blok as Pierrot and mystical God-seekers and apocalyptic seers from the symbolist ranks – Gippius, Merezhkovsky, **Briusov**, etc. – as the Mystics, whose philosophical drama here collides with **commedia dell'arte**. Infused with doubleness of vision, self-conscious role-playing, grotesque juxtapositions, direct audience address and 'laying bare the device', the play unites the Gogolian tradition with modern metatheatrical and absurdist perspectives, Blok's *liebestod* created an exceptional furore when staged by **Meyerhold** (Vera Komissarzhevskaya's Theatre, 1906) who appeared as Pierrot. *The King on the Square* was denied production by the censor, and *The Unknown Woman*, staged by Meyerhold in 1914, find the poet alienated from the untransformed society of post-1905 Russia and from his Eternal Feminine who has been transformed into a prostitute. The allegorical *The Song of Fate* (1908), dealing with similar themes, was rewritten by Blok in 1919 to make it more realistic, a change which **Stanislavsky** had thought necessary when he rejected it for production in 1908. Blok's verse drama *The Rose and the Cross* (1913) grew out of his libretto for a Glazunov opera and more generally, from his affinity for and knowledge of medieval culture. Drawing upon materials gathered for his translation of *The Miracle of Théophile*, produced at the Ancient Theatre in 1908, he again brings together joy (the rose) and suffering (the cross), concluding that the former is transient, while the latter if selfless yields true and lasting happiness. The play, planned for the **Moscow Art Theatre**, was not produced. In 1919 Blok served as chairman of the production board of Leningrad's Bolshoi Dramatic Theatre and was appointed to the repertory section of the Theatre Division of the People's Commissariat for Education. SG

Blondin, Charles (Jean-François-Emile Gravelet) (1824–97) French wire-walker. The son of nomadic performers, he studied with the **Ravel** family, taking his name from his tutor Jean Ravel Blondin and cultivating the bayonet spring-board. Fame came in 1859 when, on a USA tour with the Ravels, he crossed Niagara Falls on a tightrope; he later repeated this feat blindfolded or pushing a man in a wheelbarrow, or stopping halfway across to cook an omelette. He was much imitated, especially by 'Female Blondins'. His first London appearance at the Crystal Palace (1861) earned him £100 a performance, enabling him to buy an estate near Birmingham. He pursued his altitudinous profession till the age of 70. LS

Bloolips see **Female impersonation; Revue**

Bloom, Claire (1931–) British actress. She made her debut at the Oxford Repertory Theatre in 1946 and has developed a distinguished career that encompasses the stage, film and television. She has played an extensive repertoire of Shakespearian roles, including Cordelia to **John Gielgud**'s King Lear in the 1952–3 **Old Vic** season, and acted major roles in both classic and modern plays, such as Hedda in *Hedda Gabler* (1971), Blanche du Bois in *A Streetcar Named Desire* (1974), Mary Queen of Scots in *Vivat! Vivat Regina!* (1972). Her films have included Chaplin's *Limelight* (1952) and *Look Back in Anger* (1959), and for television more Shakespearian roles and *Brideshead Revisited*. Her acting has consistently been distinguished not only by her personal beauty, but by great sensitivity and intelligence. MB

Bloomgarden, Kermit (1904–76) American producer. Born in Brooklyn and educated at New York University, Bloomgarden made his producing debut in 1940 with Albert Bein's *Heavenly Express* which promptly closed. In 1945 he sponsored his first hit, *Deep Are the Roots*, a drama about racial conflict, followed in 1946 by **Lillian Hellman**'s *Another Part of the Forest*, beginning a long association with the playwright. Success continued with *Command Decision* (1947); *Death of a Salesman* (1949); *The Crucible* (1953); *A View from the Bridge* (1955); *The Diary of Anne Frank* (1955); *The Most Happy Fella* (1956); *Look Homeward*

Angel (1957); and *The Music Man* (1957). He presented Hellman's *Toys in the Attic* in 1960, but had few other productions of note until *Hot l Baltimore* in 1973, and the New York mounting of *Equus* in 1974. Bloomgarden believed that producers should interfere as little as possible with artists except to 'throw out sparks that will stimulate them to make better use of their own creativity'.   TLM

Blue Blouses The first of these Soviet Russian workers' groups was founded by Boris Yuzhanin in 1923 at the Moscow Institute for Journalism; the name derived from factory-workers' loose blue smocks. Essentially, it was a 'living newspaper', presenting a montage of current events skewed to a proletarian ideology in a music-hall format of songs and sketches. Because of its flexibility, a troupe could tour widely, performing agit-prop in factories, clubs and the open air. In their heyday, there were more than 5,000 of these groups, both professional and amateur collectives, with 100,000 members. **Sergei Tretyakov** promoted them, though he warned of the dangers of too much didacticism and stylization. After a tour of Germany in 1927 by a professional troupe, the Blue Blouses were forcibly merged with the more orthodox TRAM movement.   LS

Boaden, James (1762–1839) English dramatist and biographer. Educated for a career in commerce, Boaden became a journalist and editor. In 1794 his adaptation of Ann Radcliffe's *Romance of the Forest*, *Fountainville Forest*, was performed, one of the first transformations of a Gothic novel into Gothic drama. He led the attack on the **Shakespeare** forgeries of **William Henry Ireland** in 1796. The following year he adapted Mrs Radcliffe's *The Italian* as *The Italian Monk*. A great admirer of **Kemble** and **Mrs Siddons** he wrote important biographies of them in 1825 and 1827 as well as of **Mrs Jordan**, **Mrs Inchbald** and **Garrick**.   PH

Soviet Blue Blouse Troupe, Moscow, 1927.

Boal, Augusto (1931–) Brazilian playwright, director, theoretician. Boal premiered as an author with *Mulher magra, marido chato* (*Lean Wife, Mean Husband*) in 1957. His *Revolução na América do Sul* (*Revolution in South America*) in 1961 by Arena Theatre opened a new epoch of political protest theatre. Teatro Oficina in 1962 presented his third play, *José, do parto a sepultura* (*Joe, from the Womb to the Tomb*). During the 60s he worked closely with **Gianfrancesco Guarnieri** on various classical plays about **Lope de Vega**, **Gogol**, and in 1965 they launched their famous *Arena conta . . .* series (Zumbi, Tirandentes, Bolívar, etc.). An inveterate experimenter and Marxist ideologue, Boal encountered problems with the Brazilian political situation. After a period of imprisonment, he sought exile in Argentina and other countries, where he continued to develop new forms of radical theatre, such as the 'teatro jornal', a documentary-drama based on current events (newspaper events), and the 'teatro invisible', which consists of staged performances in public places before unsuspecting audiences. Boal has written theoretical works explaining his techniques of theatre: *Categorías de teatro popular* (*Categories of Popular Theatre*) (Buenos Aires, 1972), and *Técnicas latinoamericanas de teatro popular* (*Latin American Techniques of Popular Theatre*) (Buenos Aires, 1975). His *Teatro do Oprimido* (1975, translated as *Theatre of the Oppressed*, 1979) gained international recognition as a theoretical model of revolutionary theatre.   GW

Boar's Head Tavern, London Situated in Whitechapel, just outside Aldgate, the Boar's Head was the first of London's inns to undergo radical transformation for the purpose of accommodating plays (1598–9). Details of the conversion are known from a complicated legal wrangle involving the innkeeper Richard Samwell, a city haberdasher Oliver Woodliffe, the owner of the **Swan** Francis Langley and the actor **Robert Browne**. We know that a stage was erected on one of the long sides of a rectangular yard, that the galleries were extended to increase the capacity and that a tiring house was provided behind the stage. The ambitious plan was to combine three companies, Worcester's, Derby's and Oxford's, as serious rivals to the dominance of the **Lord Chamberlain's Men** at the **Globe** and the **Admiral's Men**, still at the **Rose** in 1599. The combined company, renamed Queen Anne's Men under James I, soon moved to the **Red Bull**, and the subsequent history of the Boar's Head is unimpressive. By 1621 it was no longer in use as a theatre. It may be that **Philip Henslowe**'s decision to bring the Admiral's Men north of the river to the **Fortune** in 1600, thereby challenging the geographical uniqueness of the Boar's Head, was too quick and too powerful a blow.   PT

Bobèche (Jean-Antoine-Aimé Mandelart) (1791–c. 1841) and **Galimafré (Auguste Guérin)** (d. c. 1870) These artisans' sons played together in *parades*, open-air performances given on trestle-stages before the showbooths of the Parisian boulevards. In his yellow shorts, red coat, stringy wig and tricorne hat with its butterfly cockade, Bobèche represented the naif whose half-closed eyes and caustic smile concealed shrewdness. His salty comments, unbridled puns and *non sequiturs* were taken up by society; and whenever he played with Galimafré, a tall scrawny figure with a fringe of hair and a Norman costume, the Boulevard du Temple was jammed with carriages. They separated in 1814; Galimafré became a stagehand at the **Odéon** for almost 30 years; Bobèche failed in theatre management in Rouen and Bordeaux and was reduced to playing the violin in low music-halls.   LS

Bocage (1797–1863) French actor. Bocage was a major figure in the establishment of the *drame romantique*, but for which he might never have made a serious career. He owed much to **Dumas** *père* who understood his talent and made use of it. His political views were strong and coloured his performance and, in the later 1840s, his management of the **Odéon** theatre. Bocage's career began with a travelling troupe. He was taken on at the Odéon in 1822 where the intensity of his acting was noticed. Attracted by the *drame* he moved to the Gaîté in 1829, playing Sir Jack in *Alice ou les Fossoyeurs d'Ecosse* (*Alice or the Scottish Grave-diggers*), then on to the Porte-Saint-Martin, where he played Shylock. Described as 'the boldest barnstormer of the capital' he reached the peak of his career in 1831–2 with Dumas's *Antony*, Didier in *Marion Delorme* and Buridan in *La Tour de Nesle*. Antony allowed him to display a sombre, melancholy and wildly passionate nature which established him as the romantic actor *par excellence*, but the **Comédie-Française**, where it was staged, was not the theatre for him and he returned to the Porte-Saint-Martin. He moved from theatre to theatre, appearing at the Ambigu in **Pyat** and Luchet's *Ango* in 1835 (performances were stopped by the censors), at the Porte-Saint-Martin in 1836 in *Don Juan de Marana*, at the Ambigu in 1839 in *Christophe le Suédois* and at the Gymnase in Souvestre's *L'Interdiction* (*Forbidden*) (a sort of modern-day *Hamlet*). In 1843 he made a huge success as Brute in **Ponsard**'s *Lucrèce*. During his brief and disastrous period as director of the Odéon, he staged George Sand's *François le Champi*, which decided her to write for the theatre. He was a great actor, a good director, but a mediocre theatre manager. In 1859 the last of his savings went into a brief management of the Saint Marcel theatre. In 1861 he was

Bocage in Dumas's popular melodrama *La Tour de Nesle*, Porte-Saint-Martin, 1832.

playing Buridan at Belleville. He was however to know one more great triumph with Paul Meurice and George Sand's play *Les Beaux Messieurs de Bois Doré* (Ambigu, 1862).   JMCC

Bock, Jerry (1925–) and **Sheldon Harnick** (1924–) American composer and lyricist. Bock and Harnick each began writing for the Broadway musical stage in the 1950s, but did not work as collaborators until *The Body Beautiful* (1958). In the following year their show *Fiorello* won the Pulitzer Prize for Drama. Among their other notable scores were *She Loves Me* (1963), *Fiddler on the Roof* (1964), *The Apple Tree* (1966), and *The Rothschilds* (1970). They ended their partnership after *The Rothschilds*. Writing in an era when most musicals had an exotic or period setting, Bock and Harnick were adept at varying their style to match the time and place of each show, while at the same time working within the traditional forms of Broadway show music.   MK

Boeuf sur le Toit, Le ('The Ox on the Roof') Parisian cabaret, founded by **Jean Cocteau** in 1921; the name derives from an orchestral suite by Darius Milhaud (1919), exploiting music-hall tunes. The club served as a retreat for avant-garde artists like Tristan Tzara who could hear Mozart or **Gershwin** played by virtuoso pianists. The Nazis closed it in 1943, but after the war it reopened featuring Resistance songs, and took on an existentialist aura in 1949, when Juliette Greco sang works by **Sartre** and Mauriac.   LS

Bogusławski, Wojciech (1757–1829) Polish actor, director, manager and playwright, who abandoned a military career for the stage. He is the father of the Polish National Theatre in Warsaw, which he directed from 1783 to 1814. There he staged the first opera sung in Polish, Salieri's *Axur*, playing the title role in 1793. In 1798 in Lwów he presented the first Polish *Hamlet*, adapting it from German and French versions. In 1811 he founded the first theatre school, where he taught and wrote a textbook on acting. Among over eighty original plays and adaptations, best known are his musical *Cracovians and Mountaineers* (1794), and the historical drama *Henry VI at the Hunt* (1792).   DG

Boileau-Despréaux, Nicolas (1636–1711) French poet and critic whose independent spirit, shrewd literary judgement and keen satirical style made him a powerful arbiter of contemporary taste and demolisher of individual reputations. In particular, his adroit exposition of neoclassical doctrine, *L'Art Poétique* (1674), conveniently and elegantly summarizes his own critical thinking on the various literary forms, giving prominence to tragedy and comedy. He was the friend and supporter of **Molière** and **Racine** and was elected to the Académie-Française in 1684.   DR

Boker, George Henry (1823–90) American playwright and poet. His principal play, *Francesca da Rimini* (1855), first performed by **E. L. Davenport** (Lanciotto), did not achieve major success until 1882 when **Lawrence Barrett** appeared as Lanciotto and **Otis Skinner** as Paolo. It was retained in Barrett's repertoire and was revived by Skinner (Lanciotto) in 1901. Boker wrote ten other plays. The best known: *The World a*

Mask (1851) and *The Bankrupt* (1855). Boker once confided to Bayard Taylor that he had no ambition to become 'a mere playwright', he wanted to be 'acknowledged as a poet'. He wrote several volumes of poetry: *The Lesson of Life* (1848), *Poems of the War* (1864) and *The Will of the People* (1864).

Boker served as Minister to Turkey (1871–5), as Minister Plenipotentiary to Russia (1875–8), and became President of Philadelphia's Union League (1878–84). RM

Bolger, Ray (1904–87) American dancer and singer. After making his debut with a musical stock company in Boston, Bolger spent a few years in vaudeville before appearing on Broadway in *The Merry World* (1926). His loose-limbed, comic dancing style was featured in several revues, including **George White**'s *Scandals of 1931*. In 1936 he created the part of Junior Dolan in **Rodgers** and **Hart**'s *On Your Toes* (1936), in which he performed George Balanchine's choreography for the 'Slaughter on Tenth Avenue' ballet. During the 1940s Bolger starred in such popular musicals as *By Jupiter* (1942) and *Three to Make Ready* (1946). In *Where's Charley* (1948), a musical version of *Charley's Aunt*, Bolger stopped the show with his rendition of 'Once in Love with Amy'. After a decade away from Broadway, Bolger returned to the musical stage in the 1960s for *All American* (1962) and *Come Summer* (1969), neither of which was a hit. MK

Bolivia Since the time of the Spanish conquest, and even before, there has been theatrical activity in this land-locked nation, although a sustained tradition is lacking. Possible causes include the imposing geography, relative isolation, a series of devastating wars that decimated Bolivia's spirit, and an unstable political climate that produced on average more than one head of state per year since independence. During the colonial period, plays focused on religious themes and important historical events before and during the conquest. Often trilingual – in Spanish, Quechua and Aymará – no individual plays of artistic merit can be cited. Upper Peru was part of the Viceroyalty of La Plata and for over 300 years supplied the Spanish with a steady supply of silver, tin and other riches. Bolívar and Sucre liberated this territory in 1825, relatively late in the independence movement in Latin America, and it was named Bolivia, but political independence did not sever Spanish cultural linkages. Traditional Spanish styles continued to dominate through the 19th century.

A major 19th-century play, *Plan de una representación* (*Plan of a Performance*, 1857) by Félix Reyes Ortiz, satirized military coups from university students' perspectives, an ominously prescient view of later Bolivian reality. Historical plays with bombastic verse and exaggerated situations were set vicariously in Argentina (about Juan Manuel de Rosas) and Mexico (about Iturbide). In the War of the Pacific (1879–83) with Peru and Chile, Bolivia lost valuable territory, including its access to the sea, but the theatre did not reflect major changes. An emphasis on verse monologue related to historical drama exalted such figures as Pedro Domingo Murillo, a La Paz revolutionary hero, and Simón Bolívar. Major playwrights of the period are José Palma y V. in the monologue, and Ricardo Jaimes

Freyre (1868–1933) and Franz Tamayo (1880–1956) in poetic drama.

20th century Modern Bolivian theatre began with Fabián Vaca Chávez's *Carmen Rosa* (1912), a play that portrayed human characters rather than glorified heroes. In a new flurry of interest during the 1920s, the young intellectuals tried to renovate poetry and the arts with vanguard European techniques, but their theatre still resonated with 19th-century romanticism. The Ateneo de la Juventud (Youth Atheneum) and the Sociedad Boliviana de Autores Teatrales (Bolivian Society of Theatrical Authors) in 1922 and 1923 respectively promoted the dramatic arts. The major contribution of these years was to raise the consciousness level regarding the Indian, as well as other national socio-political issues. Wenceslao Monroy, better known as 'Tío Ubico', taught actors and directors for three decades until 1954. The most prolific playwrights of the period are Mario Flores and Alberto Saavedro.

The War of the Chaco (1932–5) helped unify the country in the quest for a national identity. After the war, Antonio Díaz Villamil advanced the Bolivian theatre by incorporating the lively language of the lower classes, while Valentín Meriles and Joaquín Gantier experimented with the psychological play. A major transformation in government systems led to the National Revolution of 1952 that imposed agrarian reform, nationalized the mines, and introduced universal suffrage – traumatic events that failed nonetheless to stem the revolutions, political assassinations and disastrous economics that plague modern-day Bolivia. A new wave of theatrical activity was evident from 1967 forward that included the formation of new theatre groups such as the Experimental University Theatre, both of Santa Cruz and of Cochabamba. Since 1967 IBART (Bolivian Art Institute) has sponsored nine theatre festivals in Cochabamba.

Another generation of playwrights took a fresh look at age-old problems. Raúl Salmón in the 1950s and 1960s wrote social plays with a didactic purpose. One of them, *Tres generales* (*Three Generals*, 1969), places three presidents of the 19th century into contemporary Bolivia to emphasize the ubiquitous problems of Bolivian politics and governance. In *La lanza capitana* (1967) Raúl Botelho Gosálvez used a historical framework to advocate Indian rights. Sergio Suárez Figueroa, born in Uruguay, wrote two major plays, *El hombre del sombrero de paja* (*Man in the Straw Hat*, 1967) and *La peste negra* (*Black Plague*, 1967), the latter a medieval pestilence play with political overtones of modern-day Bolivian governments of terror. **Guillermo Francovich** pressed for educational reform by dramatizing Simón Rodríguez, the teacher of Simón Bolívar, in *Como los gansos* (*Like the Geese*, 1957). Other playwrights worthy of note are Guido H. Calabri Abaroa and Adolfo Costa du Rels (1895–1980), author of *Los estandartes del rey* (*The King's Standards*, 1956), the only Bolivian play to have won international recognition. In 1972 the play was selected over one by **Buero Vallejo** for the Gulbenkian Award, given by the Academy of the Latin World. Rose Marie (d. 1979) and Andrés Canedo actively promoted theatre in La Paz, but as yet no solid infrastructure for theatre exists in this 'American Tibet'. GW

See: E. M. Dial, 'The Military in Government in Bolivia: A View from the Theatre of Raúl Salmón', *Latin American Theatre Review*, IX, I, Fall 1975, 47–53; O. Muñoz Cadima, *Teatro boliviano contemporáneo*, La Paz, 1981; J. Ortega and A. Cáseres Romero, *Diccionario de la literatura boliviana*, La Paz, 1977; M. T. Soria, *Teatro boliviano en el siglo XX*, La Paz, 1980; C. M. Suárez Radillo, 'El teatro boliviano: De lo histórico a lo humano contemporáneo', *Cuadernos Hispanoamericanos*, vols. 263–4, May–June 1972, 1–16.

Bolt, Robert (Oxton) (1924–) British dramatist, whose first performed plays, *The Critic and the Heart* (1957), *Flowering Cherry* (1957) and *The Tiger and the Horse* (1960), kept closely to the requirements of serious, 'well-made' plays of the 1950s. **Ralph Richardson** and Celia Johnson were notably successful in *Flowering Cherry* which ran for 400 performances at the **Haymarket**. Bolt's training as a historian not only provided the material for later plays but also encouraged him to break away from the somewhat constricting formulae of his early work. In *A Man for All Seasons* (1960) about the life and death of Sir Thomas More, Bolt chose to link together short scenes by employing a narrator, the Common Man, in a style which was then dubbed Brechtian. Subsequent historical plays included *Vivat! Vivat Regina!* (1970) and *State of Revolution* (1977) and Bolt also wrote the screenplays for such films as *Lawrence of Arabia* (1962), *Dr Zhivago* (1965) and *Ryan's Daughter* (1970). Other sides to his talents were revealed in his children's play, *The Thwarting of Baron Bolligrew* (1965), and *Gentle Jack* (1963), a pantheistic parable. JE

Bolton, Guy (1883–1979) American librettist and playwright. He began writing plays in 1911, and soon after turned to writing librettos. In 1915 he joined composer **Jerome Kern** for the first of the Princess Theatre musicals, *Nobody Home*. The success of this modest and ingratiating musical comedy was repeated with *Very Good Eddie* (1915), *Have a Heart* (1917), *Oh, Boy!* (1917), and others. Bolton's Princess Theatre librettos were praised for their unusually coherent plots and well developed characters. His career as a librettist spanned forty years, encompassing such hits as *Sally* (1920), *Lady, Be Good* (1924), *Oh Kay* (1926), and *Anything Goes* (1934). With lyricist **P. G. Wodehouse**, Bolton was the co-author of an autobiography, *Bring on the Girls*, in 1953. MK

Bommalattam (India) Also known as *Gombeyata*. Mani Iyer's party of Kumbhakonam near Tanjore in Madras state, the Haluvagalu party and Padmanabhan Kamath in northern Mysore are the only groups in south India that still perform *Bommalattam*, a doll-puppet form, similar in some respects to the better-known Rajasthani dolls (**Kathputli**) of north India.

The form used by all the parties is very close in outline. It draws on themes from the *Puranas* and differs only in that each imposes the features of local forms of art over the outline. The Mysore troupes use *Yakshagana*, a form of rural theatre, as a base and the Tamil Party imitates *Bharata Natyam*, the classical dance. Both parties use puppets that are from one to three feet tall and manipulated by strings attached to the head and back of the figure and rods or strings attached to the arms and legs. The puppet's head and hands are constructed of light wood and the costume is stuffed with paper to give the figure a softer, round appearance.

The manipulators stand above the puppets and manipulate them in a rather small area about four feet high and eleven feet wide. The puppet area is created by black cloth stretched across benches or any improvised frame-work which forms a proscenium opening. Light from two petromax lamps or small oil lamps made of coconut shells illuminates the acting area from the front. Like the shadow manipulators, the doll-puppeteers wear bells on their ankles. The stories are told in song and dialogue with passages of dance added for colour. Usually, a cymbal player keeps time, the *mridangam* drum is played and the harmonium provides the base sound for the singers. In the Mysore form, a wind instrument (*ottu*) is used when songs are not sung.

The age and origin of the south Indian doll-puppets is as yet uncertain. The occasion for performance is usually a temple festival or some religious celebration. Puppets are also used to ward off evil, prevent epidemics and drought and to bring rain. FaR

Bond, Edward (1934–) British dramatist, whose second play, *Saved*, created a furore when it was first performed at the **Royal Court Theatre** in 1965. The most controversial scene involved the stoning to death of a baby in a pram, but Bond used this savage incident to illustrate the moral and cultural deprivation of contemporary life. The technical range and imaginative strength of Bond's plays are impressive. In *Early Morning* (1968), he offered a surrealistic farce on Victorian values and mock-heroism, set in a cannibalistic heaven, while in *Narrow Road to the Deep North* (1968) the Japanese *haiku* poet, Matsui Basho, is the central character in a myth about power-lords, good and bad, the worst ones being British imperialists. Despite his sombre views, Bond can sometimes be a funny writer, as in *The Sea* (1973), a lyric poet capable of portraying convincingly other poets, such as John Clare in *The Fool* (1976) and **Shakespeare** in *Bingo* (1974), and a persuasive naturalistic writer, as in his first play, *The Pope's Wedding* (1962), set in East Anglia. The intensity of his vision can verge on the apocalyptic, as in *Lear* (1972) and particularly his *War Plays* (1985) about life after the nuclear holocaust. Bond is the most celebrated and powerful dramatist to have emerged from a group of left-wing writers who were originally encouraged through the Royal Court in the 1960s and went on to write both for fringe theatre in the 1970s and for the national companies. In 1978, his version of the Greek myths, *The Woman*, was presented at the **National Theatre**. JE

Bonstelle, Jessie (?1872–1932) American director-actress, best known for directing the Detroit Civic Theatre. Born near Greece, New York, by the age of nine she could recite 150 selections, mostly Shakespearian. After attending a convent school, Bonstelle entered a road company of *Bertha, the Beautiful Sewing Machine Girl* and later worked for **Augustin Daly** and the **Shuberts**. In 1910 she founded a repertory company in Detroit which ran for 14 years. In 1925 she opened the Bonstelle Playhouse and later organized the Detroit Civic Theatre. The depression threatened the organization, for which she actively campaigned until the time of her death. Among the many stars she developed were **Katharine Cornell**, **Melvyn Douglas**, Frank Morgan, and William Powell. SMA

Book-holder In the Elizabethan theatre, the book-holder combined the functions of prompter and stage-hand. There is insufficient evidence to provide a detailed job-description. PT

Book-keeper In Elizabethan theatres, the company member responsible for the copies of the plays owned by the company was generally called the book-keeper. His first task, on receipt of the author's manuscript ('foul papers'), was to commission a fair copy and to supervise the preparation of the rolls on which individual parts, with short cues, were written out. He was then entrusted with the safe-keeping of the playhouse copy and the parts. Any inefficiency he displayed would have simplified the theft of a popular success by another company or by an opportunist publisher. The continuing reputation of a company might, on the other hand, have been sustained by his effectiveness. PT

Booth, Barton (?1679–1733) English actor and manager. At Westminster School with **Rowe**, he was praised for his performance in school productions of **Terence**. After performing in Dublin, he joined **Betterton**'s company in 1700, Rowe giving him a part in *The Ambitious Stepmother*. He played secondary roles until he joined **Aaron Hill**'s company at **Drury Lane** in 1710, taking over some of Betterton's old roles. Often arguing with Hill, he rioted against him with the other actors. He scored a great triumph as Cato in **Addison**'s play (1713) and became a partner in the management of the company. In the 1720s his laziness interfered with his success, though he could be inspired on occasions and was expected to take on a heavy acting load, leading to wrangling with **Cibber** and Wilks. He retired in 1728 due to ill-health. At his best in majestic roles in tragedy from the start (e.g. the Ghost in *Hamlet*), he thought it 'depreciated the dignity of tragedy to raise a smile in any part of it' (Cibber). PH

Booth, Edwin Thomas (1833–93) American actor and manager. He made his debut in 1849 at the **Boston Museum** as Tressel in support of his father's Richard III. Booth continued to act with his father accompanying him to California in 1852. When the elder Booth left California, Edwin remained, playing in San Francisco, Sacramento, and touring various small towns and mining camps. In 1854–5, he toured with **Laura Keene** to Melbourne and Sydney with a brief engagement in Honolulu on the return voyage. In 1856 he returned to the east, making starring engagements in Baltimore, Richmond, and Boston. He made his first major New York appearance at Burton's Theatre in May 1857. From this point until his retirement in 1891, his acting career was generally a series of unbroken successes. For ten years (1864–74), Booth was involved in the management of several theatres, most notably the **Winter Garden** (1864–7) and his own **Booth's Theatre** (1869–74). His management was particularly distinguished by his carefully mounted, visually splendid productions of *Hamlet*, *Julius Caesar*, *The Merchant of*

Edwin Booth as Hamlet, 1870.

Venice, *Othello*, and *Richelieu*. However, after Booth lost his theatre in 1873, the result of poor financial management, he abandoned management and spent the remainder of his career touring. Early in his career, in 1861–2, he had starred in London (where his only child Edwina was born) and in Manchester and Liverpool. In 1881–2, at the height of his powers, he played at London's **Princess's Theatre** and alternated Othello and Iago with **Henry Irving** at the **Lyceum Theatre**. He appeared in London again in 1883 and then toured the provincial circuit. In 1883 he also made a highly successful tour of several German cities. From 1886 to 1891, he completed several extensive national tours, in association with his close friend, **Lawrence Barrett**. Booth's last performance was as Hamlet at the Brooklyn Academy of Music in 1891.

Slender and darkly handsome with a clear, musical voice and luminous, expressive eyes, studious and thoughtful, Booth was the finest American tragedian of his time. Although justly celebrated for his richly nuanced Hamlet, he also excelled as Iago, Richelieu, and Bertuccio (*The Fool's Revenge*). Late in his career, his King Lear and Shylock came to be highly regarded. Throughout his career, he diligently tried to better not only his art, but also the theatrical profession. He eagerly shared the stage with fellow stars, including not only Irving and Barrett, but also **Bogumil Dawison**, **Tommaso Salvini**, **Helena** Modjeska (**Modrzejewska**), **Charlotte Cushman**, and **Fanny Janauschek**. In 1888, he established The Players as a social and cultural club for actors and others interested in theatre. DJW

Booth, John Wilkes (1839–65) American actor, brother of **Edwin**. He made his professional debut in 1855 at the Charles Street Theatre in Baltimore as Richmond in *Richard III*. He subsequently played supporting roles for several seasons, principally at the **Arch Street Theatre** in Philadelphia and the Richmond Theatre. By the early 1860s he was an established popular touring star, playing mainly in the midwestern and southern theatrical circuits. His first New York appearance was as Richard III in 1862 at the old **Wallack's Theatre**, while his last stage appearance was as Pescara in *The Apostate* at **Ford's Theatre** on 18 March 1865. Almost a month later (14 April 1865) in the same theatre, Booth assassinated Lincoln whilst the President was watching a performance of **Tom Taylor**'s *Our American Cousin*. His motive may have been a desire for notoriety or a misguided act of patriotism.

He was undoubtedly a talented, sometimes compelling, but also erratic and undisciplined actor, who was probably at his best playing romantic characters and melodramatic heroes and villains. DJW MB

Booth, Junius Brutus (1796–1852) Anglo-American actor who rose to stardom in London, but who spent the bulk of his career in America. Born in London, Booth tried various occupations before becoming an actor in 1813. After a continental tour in 1814–15, Booth performed at Brighton and Worthing before starring in 1817 at **Covent Garden**. **Kean**, concerned with a possible new rival, invited Booth to **Drury Lane** to play Iago to Kean's Othello. After one performance, Booth retreated to Covent Garden, where he starred for a few months, then toured the provinces, playing London only occasionally. In 1921 he deserted his wife and child and emigrated to America with Mary Ann Holmes.

Booth bought a farm in Maryland and toured the United States until his death, except for visits to England in 1825–6 and 1836–7. He sired ten children in Maryland, six of whom reached their majority. His London wife, Adelaide Dellanoy, learned of Booth's American family and in 1851 divorced Booth, who married Holmes a few weeks later.

As an actor, Booth was often compared to Kean, even accused of imitating him. Romantic, passionate, frequently seeming out of control, Booth gained such notoriety in the New World with his often aberrant behaviour as to be billed 'The Mad Tragedian'. Heavy drinking complicated his situation, but Walt Whitman said of him 'The words fire, energy, *abandon*, found in him unprecedented meanings. I never heard a speaker or actor who could give such a sting to hauteur or the taunt. . .'

About 1852 Booth began construction of Tudor Hall on his farm, a structure which still stands, based on an English design. He played San Francisco and Sacramento in 1852, appeared for the last time in New Orleans, and died on a Mississippi River steamboat near Louisville. He is buried in Greenmount Cemetery in Baltimore. SMA

Booth, Junius Brutus, Jr (1821–83) American actor and theatre manager. He made his debut in 1834 at the Pittsburgh Theatre as Tressel to his father's Richard III. After over a decade of playing stock at various theatres, including New York's **Bowery** and Boston's

Howard Athenaeum, he migrated to California in 1851 where he acted and managed several theatres in San Francisco until he returned east in 1864. At various times, he managed for his brother **Edwin**, the Boston Theatre, the **Walnut Street Theatre**, the **Winter Garden**, and for one season **Booth's Theatre**. He was a competent manager, but generally an undistinguished actor, although he was well regarded for his King John and Cassius. He was married three times – all actresses – first to Clementine DeBar, then to Harriet Mace (d. 1859) and finally to Agnes Land Perry (d. 1910) who was a successful leading actress for many years. Four of Junius's children pursued stage careers, Blanche DeBar, Marion, Junius Brutus III (d. 1887) and Sydney Barton (1873–1937). DJW

Booth, Shirley (née Thelma Booth Ford) (1907–) American actress whose career began in 1919 with the Poli Stock Company. Her first New York appearance was in *Hell's Bells* (1925). She is best known for her haunting portrayal of the anguished and slovenly Lola in **Inge**'s *Come Back, Little Sheba* (1950), for which she received a Tony Award and, for the film version, an Academy Award. In addition she has appeared in such productions as *Goodbye, My Fancy* (1948), *A Tree Grows in Brooklyn* (1951), *The Time of the Cuckoo* (1952), *By the Beautiful Sea* (1954), *The Desk Set* (1955), *Juno* (1959), and *Look to the Lilies* and *Hay Fever* (1970). In 1972 she toured as Mrs Gibson in *Mourning in a Funny Hat*. During the 1960s she played the comic strip character Hazel on television. DBW

Booth Theatre 222 West 45th St, New York City [Architect: Henry B. Herts]. Built by the **Shubert** brothers in partnership with producer **Winthrop Ames**, the Booth opened in 1913 with its sister house, the **Sam S. Shubert**, and completes the western wall of Shubert Alley, which originated as a fire passage behind the Hotel Astor. A small house, seating about 800, Winthrop Ames envisioned it for his productions of intimate dramas and comedies, which have been its staple ever since. When Ames retired in 1932, the theatre reverted to the Shuberts and has remained a Shubert house ever since. It has housed four Pulitzer Prize-winning productions: *You Can't Take It with You* (1936), *The Time of Your Life* (1939), *That Championship Season* (1972) and a musical *Sunday in the Park with George* (1984). MCH

Booth's Theatre Built for **Edwin Booth** at the corner of Sixth Avenue and Twenty-Third Street in New York. Opened on 3 February 1869 with a production of *Romeo and Juliet*. The theatre was designed by the architectural firm of Renwick and Sands. James Renwick Jr was a distinguished architect. Among his major buildings are St Patrick's Cathedral, the Smithsonian Institution, and The Main Hall at Vassar College. Booth's Theatre was built of granite in an ornate Second Empire style. The building measured 150 feet along Twenty-Third Street by 100 feet deep and rose to a height of 125 feet. Attached to the west end of the theatre was a five-storey wing, the ground floor of which was for commercial shops, with three floors above for artist studios and apartments and the top floor reserved for Booth's private flat. The lavishly decorated and appointed auditorium followed the standard 19th-century horseshoe-shaped configuration, although it had a fairly narrow apron and a sunken orchestra pit similar to that designed for the Bayreuth Fest Spielhaus some seven years later. There were a number of other mechanical innovations in the design of the theatre, including a forced-air heating and cooling system, a set of hydraulic ramps which raised vertically moving bridges or platforms for changing scenery, a sprinkling system for fire protection, and an electrical spark ignition device which for the first time in the USA permitted both the auditorium and stage lights to be extinguished during performances.

Some of the finest Shakespearian productions of the era were mounted at the theatre during Booth's four year tenure. After he lost control of it in 1873, the result of poor financial management, Booth's Theatre was leased and managed by various individuals including **Junius Brutus Booth**, **Henry C. Jarrett** and Henry David Palmer, **Augustin Daly**, George Rignold and **Dion Boucicault**. In 1883, the theatre was rebuilt as a department store which in turn was razed sometime in the 1960s.   DJW

Borchers, David (1744–96) German actor. Borchers was a celebrated intuitive actor who began in the **Ackermann** troupe, then played with **Schröder** in the Hamburg Town Theatre. He was noted for the elemental power of his stage presence and for his wild good humour. He never learnt his roles and often improvised. From 1782 to 1785, Borchers was the director of the Linz Town Theatre. He was notorious for his irregular private life. In particular, he once gambled with his wife as the stake and lost.   SW

Borchert, Wolfgang (1921–47) German dramatist and poet, whose reputation comes as much from the circumstances of his life as from his single play, *The Man Outside*. Drafted to the Russian front in 1941, he was imprisoned several times between 1942 and 1944 for public opposition to the Nazis, and invalided out of the army with frozen feet. As a conscientious objector, his semi-autobiographical passion play carried particular conviction in its denunciation of a corrupted society. First staged the day after Borchert's death, with 32 productions in 1948, it was performed over 130 times in the next 20 years.   CI

Borovsky, David (1934–) Soviet stage designer, best known for his work with director **Yury Lyubimov** at the Taganka Theatre in Moscow. Some of his more important productions include *Hamlet* (1972), *Comrade Believe*, **Gorky**'s *Mother* (1978), and *Valentin and Valentina* (1978). His design is characterized by the creation of highly textured, three-dimensional, interactive playing environments using real objects – related metaphorically to the play's themes – which can be transformed by the actors. A good example is the use of a wooden army truck in *The Dawns Are Quiet* (1972), which was transformed into trees, living quarters, and coffins. In *Hamlet*, a movable woollen curtain transformed the space into 12 different configurations.   AJN

Boston Ideal Opera Company (The Bostonians) American comic opera company. Founded by Miss E. H. Ober in 1879 in order to present an 'ideal' production of *HMS Pinafore*, the company,

made up primarily of church choir singers from the Boston area, was noted for its high standards in both the singing and the mounting of comic operas. Although based in Boston, the company toured extensively. Reorganized as the Bostonians in 1887, the company announced its intention of encouraging the development of American comic opera. They launched the career of composer **Reginald De Koven** with their production of *Robin Hood* (1891) and performed the same service for **Victor Herbert** with *Prince Ananias* (1894). After a defection by several members of the troupe in 1898, the company declined, ending its existence in the 1904–5 season.   MK

Boston Museum Tremont St between Court and School Sts, Boston [Architect: Hammatt Billings, 1846]. In 1841, Moses Kimball opened the Boston Museum and Gallery of Fine Arts at the corner of Tremont and Bromfield Streets to offer a collection of curiosities to the public at small admission charge. In combination with the museum was a 'concert saloon', which was transformed in 1843 into a regular theatre with a stock company. In 1844, after the phenomenal success of *The Drunkard*, which played 100 performances, it provided a steady diet of moral plays earning it the name of 'deacon's theatre'. In 1846, the entire enterprise was moved into its new building and under a succession of astute managers, particularly R. M. Field, it housed the finest dramatic corps in America during the 1860s and 1870s. In 1894, the company was disbanded when the era of the stock company drew to a close. Until the theatre was demolished in 1903, it was run by the **Theatrical Syndicate** which booked its touring shows into it.   MCH

Botswana, Lesotho and Swaziland Sharing the southern African subcontinent with the Republic of South Africa, Botswana, Lesotho and Swaziland have had much of their modern history determined by events taking place in that troubled stage. Established as discrete nations in the early 19th century, Lesotho (formerly Basotholand) and Swaziland developed quite differently. Moshoeshoe I of the Basotho welcomed immigrants of many ethnic backgrounds and encouraged his people to engage themselves in the emerging industrialization and urbanization of South Africa. This policy, however, had unfortunate results, as labour migrancy over the past 150 years has led to catastrophic soil erosion and the fracturing of the family unit. Religious divisions have created additional tensions within Lesotho, further worsened by the South African experience of many Basotho men. In Swaziland, a conservative ethnic exclusivity and the centralized power of the monarchy have been less encouraging to experimentation in the arts. Botswana (formerly Bechuanaland), with the most varied citizenry of the three, ranging from the Khoi-Khoi and San 'bushmen' of the Kalahari to the urbanites of the modern capital Gaborone, has also had the most pacific history and the greatest measure of political democracy. But the scattered nature of settlement over a large but sparsely populated territory has not, until recently, stimulated a great deal of theatrical activity beyond traditional forms. Botswana and Lesotho became independent in 1966; Swaziland, in 1968. The population of the three states totals some three million, including many who reside in South Africa.

Having shared a regional experience, playwrights of the three nations tend also to share thematic preoccupations: history (often exploring intra-communal dissonance, rather than conflicts with colonial authorities or settlers); strain between generations and between Western-Christian and customary ways, including the enduring dilemmas of bride-price, polygamy and traditional magic; the changing pattern of family relations; the life of the sojourner in South African cities; the corrosive effects of apartheid; and the social and psychological consequences of labour migrancy. Interestingly, while writers working in English have tended to be identified with their nations of citizenship, writers in African languages are often seen as members of a larger transnational ethnic community. Thus, South African Joseph M. Ntsime (b. 1930) is considered a Setswana-language playwright, while Sesotho-speaking B. L. Leshoai (b. 1920), who writes in English, is perceived as a South African.

Of the surviving traditional performance modes in the three countries, that with the most prominent dramatic component is the mimetic game-enactment of the hunter-gatherer Khoi-Khoi and San of Botswana's desert region. In sung and danced sketches, involving rudimentary forms of plot and characterization and the use of costuming and makeup, both animals and humans are represented. Like the cave-paintings for which these cultures are noted, such plays often deal with the processes and skills of hunting.

Written drama in Setswana, the language of the Batswana, dates only from the 1930s, with **Shakespeare** translations by South African Soloman T. Plaatje (1877–1932), and, later, the Motswana Michael O. Seboni (1912–72). The first original play published in Setswana was the work of the Botswana playwright Leetile Disang Raditladi (1910–71). *Motšasele II* (1937) deals with a critical moment in the history of Botswana's Bakwena people, and was eventually followed by the tragedy, *Dinšhontšho tsa Lorato* (*The Many Deaths of Love*, 1956) and *Sekgoma I* (1967), which recounts the events of a disruptive chieftaincy dispute amongst the 19th-century Amangwato.

A scene from *Kopana Ke Matla* (*Unity is Strength*), a play about the problems facing an agricultural co-operative, produced by the National University of Lesotho's Theatre in Community Development Project, 1984.

In the next generation, Ntsime's *Pelo e Ja Se Rati* (*A Loving Heart Knows No Bounds*, 1965) is a domestic comedy setting chiefly and paternal authority against decisions of the heart; *Kobo e Ntsho* (*The Black Robe*, 1968) is a darker and partly autobiographical study of the effects of a father's pressure on his son to become a clergyman; and *Pelo e Ntsho* (*A Black Heart*, 1972) is an attack on witchcraft.

But by far the most innovative theatrical initiative in Botswana in recent years has been the *Laedza Batanani* (*The Sun is Risen, Come Out and Work*) scheme, begun by Jeppe Kelepile in 1974, using theatre to encourage both discussion of and action on community problems (health, illiteracy, crime, economic issues) at village level.

Largest of the countries and the first to have a working printery, Lesotho has seen the greatest number of published plays, if disproportionately fewer stage productions. The first script published in Sesotho, Twentyman M. Mofokeng's *Sek'ona Sa Joala* (*A Calabash of Beer*, 1939), is concerned with the clash of cultures, traditional and modern. Later, numerous plays on moral and religious themes, many of them unproducible closet dramas, were circulated, often in cyclostyled form, by the Roman Catholic centre at Mazenod and the Evangelical Mission at Morija.

The emergence of Lesotho's first major playwright came in 1947, with the publication of B. M. Khaketla's *Moshoeshoe le Baruti* (*Moshoeshoe and the Missionaries*). Khaketla (b. 1913), a teacher turned politician and founder, in 1960, of the small Marematlon Freedom Party, is best known as a novelist, poet and polemicist. His stage pieces include the historical *Tholoana tsa Sethepu* (*The Fruits of Polygamy*, 1954), about a succession to kingship, and its sequel, *Bulane* (1958), in which the disinherited son finally becomes king. Khaketla's wife, Mrs N. M. Khaketla, is probably the most widely read Sesotho author today. Amongst her plays, which deal with both domestic and broader social problems, are *Mosali Eo U 'Neileng Eena* (*The Woman Thou Gavest Me*, 1956), in which a shell-shocked former seminarian returns from the First World War, survives difficulties in love and becomes a cleric; the two short pieces collected as *Ka U Lotha* (*I'm Posing You a Riddle*, 1976); the unpublished *Mahlopha a Senya* (*Creating and Destroying*, early 1980s), which mixes Sesotho and the local English of the streets; and the more recent *Ho Isa Lefung* (*Unto Death*).

Lesotho's best-known playwright, however, and one of Africa's major theatrical voices, is Zakes Mda (b. 1948). Son of a central figure in South Africa's banned Pan-Africanist Congress, Mda emigrated to Lesotho in 1963, and began writing for the stage while in secondary school. By the mid-1980s, his plays had been performed both within and outside Africa and translated into several languages. *We Shall Sing for the Fatherland* (1978), set in an unnamed African country, examines the disparity between the promises of nationalist politicians before independence and the reality of deprivation afterwards. In *Dark Voices Ring* (1978), Mda anatomizes the system of contracted prison labour in South Africa and the psychological cost to the family of a black farm overseer of complicity with apartheid. *The Hill* (1979), Mda's most finished piece is a powerful tragi-comedy on the social and ethical distortions created by labour migrancy. This theme is further developed in *The Road* (1982), a stark parable with resonances of **Brecht**, **Beckett** and **Genet**, in which a Lesotho migrant worker confronts an Afrikaaner farmer in a bizarre melange of misperception, hostility and desperate territoriality.

In the mid-1980s, Lesotho also saw the emergence of popular theatre with the Theatre for Community Development Project of the National University, combining the improvisional stage techniques of *Laedza Batanani* with radio, video-tape and narrative comic-book production directed to rural, urban and prison groups.

Swaziland's theatre remains the least developed in the region, with its best-known published play by a writer who is neither a Swazi nor primarily a playwright – anthropologist Hilda Kuper's statement on the position of women in Swazi society, *A Witch in My Heart* (1970). A great deal of work, however, has recently been done in participatory community theatre as part of public education campaigns. Swaziland also has a rich tradition of ritual and ceremonial performance, including the six-day sacred harvest and kingship rites of the *Ncwala* and the annual secular *Mhlanga* (Reed Dance) for young girls.   AH

> *See*: C. M. Doke, 'Games, Plays and Dances of the *Khomani* Bushmen', *Bantu Studies*, x (1936), 461–71; A. Gerard, *African Language Literatures*, London, 1981; A. Horn, intro., *The Plays of Zakes Mda*, Johannesburg, 1987; R. Kidd, M. Byram and P. Rohr-Rouendaal, *Laedza Batanani: Organizing Popular Theatre*, Gaborone, 1978; L. Nichols, *African Writers at the Microphone*, Washington, DC, 1984.

Bottomley, Gordon (1874–1948) British poet and dramatist, who wrote specifically for groups such as the Community Theatre and the Scottish National Theatre, though his early work also had some success on the London stage. Poetic dramas influenced by **Synge**'s realism, these dealt with subjects from Norse history (*The Riding to Lithend*, 1907 – first performed 1928), or **Shakespeare** (*King Lear's Wife*, 1915, *Gruach*, 1923). Discarding these as 'plays for the Theatre Outworn', he turned to experimental choral work based on Celtic legend, following **nō** drama in reducing scenery to a portable folding screen, which he called pieces 'for a Theatre Unborn'.   CI

Bouchardy, Joseph (1810–70) French dramatist and engraver. Beginning to write for the theatre in the mid 1830s, Bouchardy was often thought of as the direct descendant of **Pixérécourt**, and his name became almost a byword for the rather naive old-fashioned melodrama. His main output was a score of dramas, of which the most popular were *Gaspardo le Pêcheur* (*Gaspardo the Fisherman*, 1837), *Le Sonneur de Saint-Paul* (*The Bell-ringer of Saint Paul's*, 1838), and *Lazare le Pâtre* (*Lazarus the Shepherd*, 1840). Most of them were written for the Ambigu or the Gaîté, and their general tone is resolutely populist with their powerful villains who always meet their deserts. Bouchardy's plots are infinitely more complicated than those of Pixérécourt and generally revolve around the avenging of a crime committed either in a prologue, or 20 years before the beginning of the action proper. His avenging heroes are thus usually middle-aged men. Bouchardy's stagecraft helped ensure his popularity,

which lasted until the 1850s. His last play, *The Armourer of Santiago*, was performed at the Châtelet in 1868. Bouchardy's work as an engraver includes theatrical scenes for *Le Monde Dramatique*.   JMCC

Boucicault, Dion[ysius] (Lardner) (1820–90) Irish-born playwright, actor and theatre manager whose energy and facility combined with a flair for self-advertisement to make him a leading figure in both the English and the American theatre. The success of *London Assurance* (1841) at **Covent Garden** during the regime of **Madame Vestris** and **Charles James Mathews** brought Boucicault into youthful prominence. This artful five-act comedy, Regency rather than Victorian in tone and setting, held the stage throughout the 19th century and was effectively revived by the **Royal Shakespeare Company** in 1970. *Old Heads and Young Hearts* (1844) was a second and similar success. Like the cleverly contrasting two-act comedy *Used Up* (1844), it was staged at **Benjamin Webster**'s **Haymarket**. It was partly to provide Webster with plays 'from the French' that Boucicault went to Paris in 1845. Mostly on the strength of intelligent plagiarism, he continued to supply the London theatres for a further decade, most notably with *The Corsican Brothers* (1852) and *The Vampire* (1852) at **Charles Kean**'s **Princess's Theatre**. Not only as a playwright, but also as the actor of the sensational title-role in *The Vampire*, Boucicault was London's rising star in 1852, but the scandal of his liaison with the actress **Agnes Robertson** ended his contract with Kean. It was as Agnes Robertson's manager that the resourceful Boucicault began his career in the American theatre in 1853. As man and wife they toured the USA, managed theatres in New Orleans (1855), Washington (1858) and New York (1859) and made Boucicault's name familiar in the new world. With *The Poor of New York* (1857), he established the vogue of the sensation scene in melodrama, continuing it with *Jessie Brown* (1858), *The Octoroon* (1859) and *The Colleen Bawn* (1860). It was in the last of these that Boucicault and Agnes made a brilliant comeback in London in 1860, where they remained until 1872. Outstanding successes during this period included an adaptation of *Rip Van Winkle* (1865) for **Joseph Jefferson III**, a horse-racing melodrama *The Flying Scud* (1866) and a courtesan-play which scandalized the audiences it also delighted at **Drury Lane**, *Formosa* (1869). A second Irish melodrama, *Arrah-na-Pogue* (1864), was followed ten years later by a third, *The Shaughraun* (1874), which is among the best of the genre. Of Boucicault's remaining plays (he is credited with nearly 200), only *The Jilt* (1885) did anything to sustain his reputation. Always controversial, he had contributed to the establishment of a new copyright laws in the USA, to the development of fire-proofed scenery, to a profit-sharing system for playwrights which led in time to their receiving royalties and to the foundation of actor-training in the USA. His own style of acting was extravagant and idiosyncratic. Outstanding as the lovable Irish rogues he had written into his accomplished trio of melodramas, he also relished the oriental exoticism of the villainous Nana Sahib in *Jessie Brown* and the Indian chief Wahnotee in *The Octoroon*. Quite as roguish in his own life as his finest creation, Conn the Shaughraun, he made a bigamous marriage to an American actress 44 years his junior in 1885, defiantly claiming until his death that his common-law wedding to Agnes Robertson was not legally binding.   PT

Bouffe (1800–88) French actor. A performer of considerable sensitivity and simplicity, Bouffe was known particularly for his attention to nuance and accurately observed detail and for a tendency to underplay in the genre in which he excelled, the vaudeville. His first roles were at the Panorama Dramatique, playing La mère Simonne in *La Fille Mal Gardée* and the Chinese emperor in *La Petite Lampe Merveilleuse* (*The Wonderful Little Lamp*, 1822). With the closure of the Panorama he moved to the Cirque Olympique, and then to the Gaîté, where he showed a talent for cameo character parts. From 1827–31 he appeared in 52 plays at the Nouveautés, moving then to the Gymnase, where he was said to be the best comic actor in Paris. His great triumph there was in *Le Gamin de Paris* (*The Urchin of Paris*) which he played 315 times between 1836 and 1844 (Vanderbuck, one of the authors, was able to buy a chateau with his share of the royalties). In 1842 the Gymnase trapped him into a 15-year contract, which he managed to buy himself out of so as to move to the Variétés in 1843. His appointment there changed the deficit of that theatre into a handsome profit, and **Déjazet** was appointed to complement him. In 1848 his career was interrupted for five years by a nervous disease. He then began playing again in the provinces, appearing in Paris in 1854 at the Porte-Saint-Martin with *Michel Perrin*, and then in *La Fille de l'Avare* (*The Miser's Daughter*) which gave him one of his greatest roles. In 1855 the Cogniards invited him back to the Variétés, but without a fixed contract, because of his health. His last appearance was in a special matinée given for him in 1878, and in 1880 he published his memoirs.   JMCC

Boulevard In the late 19th century the term applied broadly to the commercial theatre in Paris purveying meretricious entertainment to the more affluent bourgeoisie. Between 1750 and 1830, the term had a more precise geographical reference, the Boulevard du Temple (sometimes called the Boulevard du Crime because of the violent melodramas shown there), and was associated with the popular theatres. Two fairground showmen, Nicolet (a harlequin) and Audinot (a puppet-showman), set up booths on the Boulevard which ultimately became the Théâtre de la Gaîté and the Ambigu-Comique, where the melodrama was born out of the 18th-century pantomime – a development greatly accelerated by the abolition of the monopoly of the **Comédie-Française** in 1791. The Gaîté, the theatre associated with **Pixérécourt** in particular, was rebuilt, and then demolished in 1862, when the Boulevard du Temple made way for the present Place de la République. The new Gaîté moved to the Square des Arts et Métiers, becoming more an operetta theatre than a melodrama one. The Ambigu, after a fire in 1827, moved to the adjacent Boulevard Saint-Martin and continued into the 20th century as a theatre for popular melodrama. Napoleon's decree of 1807 limited the number of theatres in Paris to eight (plus the Circus, where much equestrian melodrama developed). The four 'secondary', or Boulevard theatres were the Gaîté,

the Ambigu, the Variétés and the Vaudeville. The Variétés, going back to 1785, was occupying la Montansier's theatre in the **Palais-Royal**, but in 1807 moved into a new theatre, Boulevard Montmartre (the oldest extant theatre building in Paris). Its licence permitted 'short plays in the *grivois*, *poissard* or *villageois* genres, sometimes also containing songs set to popular tunes'. By the 1850s the Variétés had abandoned its popular repertoire (drag parts such as Madame Angot, played by Brunet) and under Hippolyte Cogniard introduced revues and operetta, including Offenbach's *La Belle Hélène*, with Hortense Schneider (1864). The Vaudeville opened in 1792, as a result of the liberty of the theatres. Its repertoire, like that of the Variétés, consisted largely of the *vaudeville*, short comic pieces with sung couplets, a genre which would find its highest expression in the plays of **Labiche**. In 1838 the Vaudeville was demolished but it re-opened in a theatre opposite the Stock Exchange, the unsuccessful Nouveautés (1827–32), where it remained until 1869, and where, in 1852, Eugénie Doche and Fechter appeared in the first production of *La Dame aux Camélias* (*The Lady of the Camellias*). The largest of the Boulevard theatres, the Porte-Saint-Martin, was originally built as a temporary opera house in 1781, opened as a melodrama theatre in 1802, closed for a time because of the 1807 decree, was burnt in the Commune of 1871, and rebuilt. In the early 1800s it was important for its *ballet-pantomimes*, forerunners of the romantic story-ballet. For the dramatists of the Romantic school (**Hugo**, **Dumas**, and even **Delavigne**), the Porte-Saint-Martin became a sort of alternative Théâtre-Français. After the first Empire the number of theatres gradually increased until 1864, when Napoleon III granted complete freedom to anyone wishing to build and run a theatre. As a result the latter part of the century saw a vast boom in theatre building, and the disappearance of the concept of theatres limited to a specific repertoire or genre.

In the 20th century these theatres changed their staple from melodrama to light comedy though some managers have attempted to include more literary plays in a repertoire mostly composed of commercial productions. The Boulevard's most flourishing period was the *belle époque* (1890–1914) before there was serious competition from the modern media. In this period the contemporary playwrights most favoured were **Georges Feydeau**, Tristan Bernard and Georges Courteline. These authors continued the tradition of the well-made sex comedy, designed to entertain a well-heeled after-dinner audience and providing a suitable vehicle for star actors such as **Sacha Guitry**, who himself wrote Boulevard comedies. Other writers whose plays partly fall into the Boulevard category also had higher ambitions, e.g. Edouard Bourdet, Henri Bernstein, Henri Bataille, Georges de Porto-Riche. Between the wars a sub-genre of psychological portrait theatre set in rural France was provided by Marcel Pagnol, Jean-Jacques Bernard and other comedy writers emerged, notably Marcel Achard. But the essential nature of boulevard theatre as an upper-middle-class club was maintained by the obligatory wearing of evening dress, the series of tips required from the *vestiaire* to the *ouvreuse*, and the fact that performances never started until at least half an hour after the advertised time of 9 pm. These were not favourable conditions for serious

Boulevard du Temple, Paris, mid-19th century.

drama, as reformers such as **Copeau**, **Antoine**, **Gémier** etc. never ceased to point out.

After the Second World War boulevard theatre again flourished, benefiting from the habit of theatre-going acquired by Parisians during the German occupation. New successful playwrights emerged, notably André Roussin and Félicien Marceau. Plays by more literary dramatists, especially **Salacrou**, **Sartre** and **Anouilh** were also performed on the boulevards in the 1950s and many private managers prided themselves on their commercial flair, fighting hard against every encroachment of subsidized theatre (e.g. the **TNP** of **Vilar**). But since the 1960s with escalating costs and the inexorable rise of the subsidized sector, the commercial theatres of the boulevards have gradually been reduced in number. Some have tried to broaden their appeal with imported successes from Britain and the USA, others have tried to develop a particular brand of whimsical, semi-cynical, semi-poetic humour through authors such as François Billetdoux, Romain Weingarten, René de Obaldia. Today the distinctive snob value of these theatres has largely disappeared and some are even able to claim government subsidy.   JMCC DB

Bowery Theatre   46–48 The Bowery, New York City [Architect: Ithiel Town; John Trimble]. When a

The Bowery Theatre, 1831.

sprinkling of wealthy and fashionable New York families began to settle near the Bowery, the link to the Boston Post Road, they decided to erect a playhouse more conveniently located for them than the **Park Theatre**. Pledging money and buying land on which Henry Astor's tavern had stood, they erected what came to be known as the Bowery Theatre, although it passed through a succession of names. Superior to the Park in appearance, both inside and out, it presented several seasons of drama, opera and ballet before its audience left it to return to the older house. In 1830, Thomas S. Hamblin secured its lease and for the next 20 years, dominated its policies. Hamblin's tenure included the highwater years for the playhouse, during which the greatest names of the American theatre (**J. B. Booth**, **Edwin Forrest**, the **Wallacks**, **Louisa Lane Drew**, **Frank Chanfrau**) appeared on its stage. Hamblin eventually bought the theatre, but bad times forced him to lose it. A succession of managers followed, who presented spectacle and melodrama to please the neighbourhood.

The district surrounding the theatre became the haven for the newly arriving immigrant groups, who poured into New York at the mid-century. The theatre began to reflect more and more the new populations of the area. Until 1879, the dramatic fare was in English; thereafter, it passed to German acting troupes, who renamed it the Thalia; then to Yiddish performers in 1891; next to Italian vaudevillians; and finally, at its fiery demise in 1929, it was playing Chinese vaudeville. The theatre had become the temple of entertainment for New York's Lower East Side. The theatre burned six times in its history, in 1828, 1830, 1836, 1838, 1845 and 1929. It was rebuilt five times and each reconstruction carried it further away from its original neoclassical facade into a strange mixture of architectural styles.   MCH

Boyd, John (1912–) Irish playwright. Honorary director **Lyric Theatre Belfast** (1972–) Boyd's major theme is the North's divided heritage, mainly in an urban setting and expressed in the local idiom paradoxically common to the antagonistic faiths. *The Assassin* (Gaiety, Dublin, 1969) explores the psychology of a clerical demagogue, *The Flats* (Lyric 1971, also produced New York and Germany) places domestic tragedy in the collective violence of the Belfast streets. These naturalistic plays, with *The Farm* (1972) and *The Street* (1977), are acutely discerning of the brutalities behind factional slogans and their travesty of political action. DM

Boyle, Roger, Earl of Orrery (1621–79) Irish playwright. He ended the Civil War as a favourite of Charles II and began writing plays after the King had suggested he try to write a tragedy in heroic couplets. The result, *The General*, was first performed privately in Ireland in 1662 and in London in 1664. He continued writing whenever recurrent bouts of gout interrupted his political career as one of the Lord Justices of Ireland. *Henry V* (1664), *Mustapha* (1665) and *The Black Prince* (1667) established his reputation for the creation of a new mode of heroic drama, placing the hero between love and honour. His work was much admired by **Dryden**, though his later comedies, written when heroic drama ceased to be fashionable, were unsuccessful. PH

Boyle, William (1853–1923) Irish playwright. **The Abbey**, to judge by the reviews, made uproarious comedies of Boyle's plays. Except for *The Eloquent Dempsey* (1906), a farce about dishonest politics, his plays are desolate enough. *The Building Fund* (1905) is a black study in avaricious competition for an inheritance, *The Mineral Workers* (1906) a kind of 'problem play' about the conflict between industrial development and rural values, their representatives equally unsavoury. Boyle broke with the Abbey in the row over **Synge**'s *Playboy*, but gave it his last two plays, *Family Failing* (1912) and *Nic* (1916). DM

Boys' Companies There are records of Court performances of plays by choristers as early as the 14th century, but the significant history of the two major companies, the **Boys of St Paul's** and the **Children of the Chapel Royal**, begins in the 16th century. The Paul's Boys were probably the first English company, adult or child, to have its own theatre (c. 1575) though they were quickly followed by the Chapel Children at the **Blackfriars** (1576). The early repertoire probably consisted of Morality Plays, but the engagement of **John Lyly** as the major writer for both companies (1582–90) brought a new sophistication to their work. Lyly's allegorical plays could be deciphered by alert audiences more readily than by the choristers themselves, and the dangerous precedent of employing boys to speak lines that would have been considered censurable if spoken by adults was established. But Lyly misjudged the mood of the established church when he used the Paul's Boys on its behalf in the Marprelate Controversy (1589–90), and the activities of the Boys' Companies were summarily curtailed. After a ten-year silence, during which Elizabethan drama had grown by leaps and bounds, the boys began a decade of astonishing and controversial activity. Only **Shakespeare** among the major dramatists of his day remained aloof. Others, like **Chapman** and **Marston**, wrote their best plays for the boy actors, demanding of them rhetorical skill in delivering lines whose import they cannot always have grasped. We must assume that audiences

took a mischievous delight in hearing pubescent boys mouth sexual innuendoes or satirical jibes. There was also the advantage of indoor performance and the sensible exploitation of the choristers' musical skills, which the adult companies could not match. Never far from controversy, the boys came under more vigilant scrutiny after the accession of James I. Diplomatic blunders mounted. Chapman, Marston and **Jonson** offended with *Eastward Ho* (1605), **John Day** with *The Isle of Gulls* (1606) and Chapman again with his *Biron* plays (1608). The Paul's Boys declined after 1606 and the Chapel Children were forced to abandon the Blackfriars to the King's Men in 1608. This was not the end of the Boys' Companies, but it marked the climacteric. As the Children of the King's Revels (1608–9) and of the Queen's Revels (1609–13), groups continued to perform at the less attractive **Whitefriars**, but without the special privileges of choristers they struggled to rival the adult troupes. The last of the major children's companies performed at the **Cockpit** from 1637–42, where they were familiarly known as Beeston's Boys after their manager, **Christopher Beeston**, but this, though a youthful company, was probably not composed of boys as young as the choristers of the early 17th-century ascendancy, when **Salathiel Pavy** had been three years a star on his death at the age of 13. PT

Boys of St Paul's Although the choristers of St Paul's may have acted in plays as early as the 14th century, the significant history of what is arguably England's first home-based drama company begins with the Mastership of Sebastian Westcott in 1553. Licensed to impress suitable children, Westcott seems to have been as interested in an aptitude for acting as an ability to sing. Recent scholarship has established the existence, but not the exact whereabouts or dimensions, of a playhouse within the precinct of St Paul's. The likeliest site is a corner of the Chapter House cloisters. We know that a portion, known as the shrouds, was roofed over to form a secure house in c. 1575, and this may in effect mean that an open-air playing space was converted into a private theatre. The ten choristers of St Paul's were sporadically employed as actors before Westcott's mastership. They 'recited' **Terence**'s *Phormio* for Cardinal Wolsey in 1528, and an earlier master, John Redford, probably wrote *Wit and Science* for them during his period of office (c. 1534–c. 1547). But Westcott, despite his defiant Catholicism, was favoured and protected by the Queen during his 30 years (1553–82) as Master. There are records of over 30 Court appearances by the Paul's Boys under his direction. We have, for example, the names though not the texts of seven plays they presented at Court for the Christmas celebrations of 1567–8. Westcott's successor, Thomas Gyles (1584–1600), was not discernibly interested in drama, and he entrusted their preparation to **John Lyly**. For a while (1582–5) the Paul's Boys combined with the **Children of the Chapel Royal** to present Lyly's courtly plays, which simultaneously increased the prestige and reduced the audience of the **Boys' Companies**. Even more disastrously, Lyly enlisted the boy-actors in the Marprelate Controversy, after which their right to perform was summarily removed. Only after a ten-year silence and under a new Master, Edward Pearce, did the Paul's Boys reemerge as an acting company. The major influence now was **John Marston**, who wrote his extraordinary *Antonio* plays (1599) for the choristers before plunging them into the adult **Poetomachia**, in which he was worsted by **Ben Jonson**. This time, though, the Paul's Boys benefited from the publicity of controversy. Major playwrights – **Dekker**, **Chapman**, **Middleton**, **Webster**, **Beaumont** – wrote for them, and they were popular enough to ruffle the adult companies. Around 1605, almost unaccountably, the tide began to turn against the Boys' Companies, and the St Paul's group was the first to crack. Reduced to sporadic performance from 1606–8, they ceased operation in later years. PT

Bracco, Roberto (1862–1943) Italian dramatist and critic whose prolific output spans a range of dramatic kinds: light, sophisticated comedies, naturalistic pieces, and explorations of social and domestic problems in the manner of **Ibsen**. It was for the last, with plays like *Tragedie dell'anima* (*Tragedies of the Soul*, 1899) and *Maternità* (*Maternity*, 1903), that he was particularly admired in his own day, although the play for which he is now best remembered, *Il Piccolo Santo* (*The Little Saint*, 1909), was more innovative than derivative in its Freudian-like treatment of the workings of the subconscious. In the 1920s his liberal views ran foul of Fascist opposition, which effectively put an end to his career in the theatre. LR

Bracegirdle, Anne (1671–1748) English actress who first appeared on the stage in 1688. From the beginning she chose parts as a pathetic heroine in tragedy and witty, sophisticated woman in comedy, particularly if the role called for her to be disguised in breeches. She also gained a considerable reputation as a singer. She worked for the United Company until 1695 when she joined **Betterton**'s group of seceding actors. **Congreve** wrote for her such roles as Angelica in *Love for Love* (1695) and Millamant in *The Way of the World* (1700). Her carefully made reputation for virtue and virginity was frequently challenged but never overthrown. She retired in 1707, probably recognizing that she could not compete with the talents of **Anne Oldfield**, and enjoyed a long and dignified retirement. PH

Brackenridge, Hugh H[enry] (1748–1815) American author and playwright. He wrote two plays to inspire his students at Maryland Academy: *The Battle of Bunker's-Hill* and *The Death of General Montgomery in Storming the City of Quebec* (1777). As teacher, legislator and chaplain in Washington's army, Brackenridge exhibited a sense of mission. Both plays, amateur attempts in blank verse, emphasized themes of patriotic virtue to encourage the colonists. Brackenridge's best-known novel is a satire entitled *Modern Chivalry*. WJM

Brady, Alice (1892–1939) American stage and film actress and singer. Making her New York debut as a chorus girl in *The Mikado* at 18, she appeared in major **Gilbert** and Sullivan roles for the next two years, then appeared as Meg in *Little Women* (1912). In 1914 she

entered silent pictures for Famous Players Company. By 1923 she had made 32 films, but continued working in the theatre. In 1928 she joined the **Theatre Guild**; her most memorable stage role was as Lavinia in **O'Neill**'s *Mourning Becomes Electra*. She returned to films as a singer-actress in 1933. SMA

Brady, William Aloysius (1863–1950) American manager and producer. Born in San Francisco, Brady made his first stage appearance in 1882, and his debut as a producer in 1888. He purchased the rights to *After Dark* from **Dion Boucicault** in 1899 and presented it at the **Bowery Theatre**. **Augustin Daly** sued him for plagiarizing the locomotive scene from *Under the Gaslight*. Brady eventually lost but attained publicity by hiring prize fighter James J. Corbett to appear in the cast and later featuring him in several vehicles. In 1896 he leased the Manhattan Theatre where he enjoyed several successes including *Way Down East* in 1898. A year later he married the actress Grace George and promoted her career. She opened his Playhouse in 1911 with *Sauce for the Goose*, and later appeared in *Divorçons* and *Major Barbara*. Brady managed the careers of numerous players including his wife's, and his daughter, **Alice**'s. His more than 260 productions included *Street Scene* (1929) which ran for 600 performances and won a Pulitzer. Also a sports promoter and film pioneer, Brady was recognized as a 'born gambler' with an 'uncanny instinct for drama'. TLM

Bragaglia, Anton Giulio (1890–1960) Italian theatre director and critic. Founder and director of the Teatro degli Indipendenti, an experimental avant-garde company working in Rome between 1923–30, and conceived radically to reform the conservative and conventional Italian stage of his day, he pioneered new staging techniques and introduced the work of innovative young playwrights, including **Brecht**. Early connected with the futurist movement, he looked to technology to revolutionize a moribund theatre by emphasizing the spectacularity of the art. A theorist as well as a practitioner, many of his early ideas found expression in his controversial *Del Teatro Teatrale, ossia del Teatro* (1927), a work which puts him among the major early 20th-century prophets of a new theatre to meet modern needs. His own experimentation as director, however, was handicapped, as were futurist experiments, by the technical backwardness of the Italian stage, as well as by his limited funds. During the Fascist period, he directed the Teatro delle Arti in Rome, seeking where possible to advance new work and encourage young directing talent: in both respects his positive longer term effects on the Italian stage were substantial, and he ranks as one of the few significant figures in the Italian theatre of the inter-war years. Like other members of the futurist movement he was interested in photography and the cinema making an early experimental film, *Perfido Incanto* (*Perfidious Enchantment*, 1916). His last years were devoted to theatre criticism and to studies of popular theatre. KR

Brahm, Otto (1856–1912) German director and critic. Brahm began his career as dramatic critic of somewhat conservative tastes on the Berlin newspapers

Vossische Zeitung and *Die Nation*. However, he became enthused by the European naturalist movement and, especially, by the plays of **Ibsen**. As a result, in 1889 he founded the **Freie Bühne** (Free Theatre), an organization devoted to the production of naturalistic drama on an irregular basis but in established theatres using well-known Berlin actors. In these years Brahm was substantially responsible for bringing the plays of **Gerhart Hauptmann** to public attention. In 1894 Brahm was appointed director of the **Deutsches Theater**. However, as a director, he was limited by his unremittingly naturalistic approach to production, so that he was unable to adapt to changing trends in theatre. In 1904, the more versatile **Max Reinhardt** took over the Deutsches Theater and Brahm's final years were spent as the director of the less prominent Lessingtheater. SW

Branagh, Kenneth (1961–) British actor, born in Belfast but living in England (Reading) from the age of nine. Trained at RADA, he graduated in 1981 and in 1982 won two awards as the most promising newcomer of the year for his role as Judd in Julian Mitchell's *Another Country*. With the **RSC** in 1984 he played Henry V and Laertes amongst other roles and in 1986 Romeo in his own production of *Romeo and Juliet* at the Lyric Theatre, Hammersmith. He established his television career at the same time, significantly in the BBC serial *Fortunes of War* in which he played Guy Pringle. In April 1987, together with David Parfitt, he formed the Renaissance Theatre Company and his work as an actor and director for this company (including playing Benedick, Touchstone and Hamlet in 1988, directing and playing in *King Lear*, and *A Midsummer Night's Dream* in 1990, co-directing *Uncle Vanya* in 1991) consolidated his reputation as a leading talent of his generation. In 1989 he played Jimmy Porter in **John Osborne**'s *Look Back in Anger* (directed by **Judi Dench**), a production created to support various social causes in his native Northern Ireland, and which transferred to London and was filmed for television. His 1988 film of *Henry V*, which he directed as well as playing the title role, brought numerous awards and Oscar nominations for Best Director and Best Actor, and other film work includes *Dead Again* (1990). His autobiography, *Beginning*, was published in 1989. He is married to the actress Emma Thompson. MB

Brandão, Raúl (1867–1930) Portuguese playwright. Before the vogue for literary existentialism caught on anywhere, Brandão wrote theatre which takes as its dominant theme the existential position of man, with the emotional accents on the pain, the deprivations and frustrations and the very brevity, pointless and tragic, of life. Two apprentice plays of the turn of the century were followed by *O Gebo e a Sombra* (*Hunchback and Shadow*, 1927), the only play performed professionally in his lifetime; two longish one-act plays; two dramatic monologues; and a tragicomedy, *Jesus Cristo em Lisboa* (1927). In spite of the exiguous repertoire, Brandão's burning compassion and his dramatic single-mindedness and power have ensured the growth of his reputation and influence in latter years. LK

Brandes, Georg (1842–1927) Danish critic and theorist, the major instigator in 1870s Scandinavia of the 'Modern Breakthrough' of rational, progressive thinking and naturalistic problem-orientated literature. As a theorist, Brandes was an assimilator, rather than an originator, his main contribution being the influential assertion in his published lectures *Main Currents in Nineteenth-Century Literature* that contemporary literature was alive insofar as it submitted problems to debate. The controversy caused by his own questioning of accepted social views led to his spending the years 1877–83 in exile in Germany, where he had frequent contact with **Ibsen**, who (like **Bjørnson** and **Strindberg**) was stirred to write his realistic plays by Brandes's campaign. Also significant for these dramatists was his analysis in the essay 'The Infinitely Small and the Infinitely Great in Literature' (1870) of the importance of characteristic details to **Shakespeare**'s realism. Through his prolific writings, Brandes was a major promoter of Ibsen, Kierkegaard, Strindberg, Bjørnson, J. P. Jacobsen and other Scandinavian writers, both at home and abroad. Equally importantly, he promoted within Scandinavia such diverse figures as John Stuart Mill, Taine, Dostoevsky and, above all, **Nietzsche**. HL

Brandes, Johann Christian (1735–99) German actor and playwright. An actor of little distinction, Brandes made his mark by his facile pen. His plays, thoroughly forgotten now, were successful in their day. However, he is best known now for his autobiography (1800) which is one of the chief sources for the theatre history of the late 18th century. Brandes was briefly, and unsuccessfully, manager of the Hamburg Town Theatre while **Schröder** was away in Vienna. SW

Brando, Marlon (1924–) American actor. Although his major reputation comes from his work as a film actor (*A Streetcar Named Desire*, *On the Waterfront*, *The Godfather*) it was as Kowalski in **Elia Kazan**'s stage production of **Tennessee Williams**'s *A Streetcar Named Desire* (1947) that Brando first made his mark as an actor of moody intensity. His style is often seen as the most famous product of the Method school of acting (see **Lee Strasberg**). MB

Branner, Hans Christian (1903–66) Danish novelist and dramatist, who began writing radio plays in the early 1930s, followed in the 1950s by three stage plays: *The Riding Master*, adapted from his 1949 novel (1950), *The Siblings*, known in English as *The Judge* (1952), and *Thermopylae* (1958). While his radio work is technically innovative, his stage plays are conventionally realistic, with occasional symbolic resonances. Their power stems from his passionate concern with such themes as the crisis of humanism in an alienated post-war world and the redemptive power of love, an idea that permeates his radio play *A Play of Love and Death* (1961). HL

Brassens, Georges (1921–81) French poet and singer. The son of a mason, he came to Paris in 1939, worked in a factory and after the war joined the anarchist movement. Although he already had an underground reputation for performing his unconventional compositions in clubs, he was 'discovered' in 1952 by Jacques Grello and his recordings soon became best-sellers. Accompanying himself on the guitar, Brassens would sing of friendship, atheism, self-sacrifice, losers and nostalgia in a gruff and ursine manner, that smacked a bit of the blues. The Académie-Française awarded him its poetry prize in 1967; he made his last public appearances at the Bobino in 1972 and 1976.   LS

Braun, Volker (1939–) German dramatist and poet. Trained in the **Berliner Ensemble**, where his celebratory parable of Communist utopia (*The Big Peace*, 1979) was staged, his most significant plays are critical analyses of contemporary political issues. As such they have been consistently censored in the DDR. His biting picture of factory conditions in *Tipper Paul Bauch* was banned in 1966, as was *Lenin's Death* in 1970, and in 1975 *Guevara*, technically the most interesting of his plays with its chronological reversal.   CI

Brazil In all of Latin America, Brazil is a unique phenomenon. This gigantic territory, occupying as it does nearly half the land mass of South America, was settled by Portuguese explorers after discovery in 1500. Even though it shares a border with every country in South America except Chile, the linguistic and cultural differences in formation have created a vast chasm that impedes close contact with Spanish-speaking neighbours. Brazil is remarkably heterogeneous: in addition to the Portuguese and the native Indians, Africans were brought to sustain slavery which endured until 1888. Waves of Italian, Spanish, and German immigrants, followed by the Japanese and various other nationalities, produced a melting pot of traditions and heritages in a country enormously rich in natural and human resources and with a strong international presence.

The theatre in this great land has developed separately from that of its neighbours but is similar in many respects because of dominant external influences over an extended period of time. The early immigrants included the Jesuit missionaries who incorporated indigenous elements, extracted from the flora, fauna and ethnology, into their productions that were designed to help catechize the native populations. One early example is the *Auto de pregação universal* (*Auto of Universal Prayer*, 1570), written by Padre José Anchieta, and considered a typical manifestation of the early religious plays. Autos, comedies and tragedies were all cultivated, written in combinations of Latin, Spanish and Portuguese with the native language, of which many existed in this vast territory.

The excitement of the conquest and settlement produced some dramatic activity, but the ensuing 17th and 18th centuries have been described by Brazilian critic Sábato Magaldi as the 'vacuum of two centuries'. This period marks the decline of the activities of the Jesuit theatre; in general the dramatic representations were linked to religious festivals or to other popular feasts and public occasions. Manuel Botelho de Oliveira (1636–1711) was one of the first Brazilians to publish his works, but they are Spanish in spirit, technique, themes and even in language. The other significant figure of the period was Antonio José de Silva ('The Jew') (1705–39). During his short lifetime, punctuated by persecutions from the Inquisition, he dedicated himself to satiric theatre as a reaction against the decadence of the Portuguese theatre which was dominated by a taste for Spanish comedy and Italian opera. His facility in caricaturing nobles and churchmen probably contributed greatly to his being beheaded and burned at the stake.

In 19th-century Brazil the political and social upheaval produced the same kind of theatrical anarchy that was evident in other countries. When King Dom João fled with his nobles to Brazil to escape Napoleon's invading armies, he ordered the construction of the Royal Theatre of St John in order to transplant to Rio the Italian opera he dearly loved. Through his protection and encouragement, governmental subsidies were granted to support dramatic enterprises. *Antonio José, ou o poeta e a Inquisição* (*Antonio José, or the Poet and the Inquisition*, 1838) by Gonçalves de Magalhães (1811–82) merited attention as the first work on a national theme written by a Brazilian. The author wrote his play as a classical tragedy to represent his violent reaction against the 'horrors of the modern school' of romanticism, the outmoded literary movement still dominant at that time in Latin America.

The first period of monarchy under King John was followed by that of Pedro I (1822–31) who failed to find favour with the Brazilian populace and abdicated his throne in disgrace. He left a young son Pedro II who after a period of regency (1831–41) ruled Brazil for nearly 50 years (1841–89) and despite all odds managed to keep the country intact. This unique political situation did not produce the kind of political and propagandistic drama often found in the other Latin American countries. Instead, the comedy of manners flourished under the inspiration of Martins Pena. His one-act comedy, *O Juiz de Paz de Roça* (*The Frontier Justice of the Peace*, 1833) revealed his unusual ability to capture the essence of the people. His plays, in fact, represented a compendium of the life and times of the first half of the century, and are still produced because of the humour and the agility of his dramatic constructions. Other writers of the period succumbed to the liberal excesses of romanticism. Their premature deaths reflected their ebullient spirits but cut short their production. Gonçalves Dias (1823–64) left one important work, *Leonor de Mendoça* (1847), a historical play based on jealousy and intrigue. In 1852 Alvares de Azevedo (1831–52) wrote *Macário*, a wickedly nightmarish dream. Castro Alves (1847–71) does not belong chronologically to the romanticists but his work reflected the aesthetics of the period. His masterpiece, *Gonzaga ou a Revolução de Minas* (*Gonzaga, or the Minas Revolution*, 1867), advocated his greatest aspiration, the abolition of slavery.

The second half of the 19th century has been divided into two stages: from 1855 to 1884, and 1884 to 1900. In 1855 Joaquim Heliodoro Gomes organized his new theatre, the Ginásio Dramático (Dramatic Gymnasium), which was modelled on the 'Gymnase' in Paris where the repertoire of French realism triumphed. The new works, thesis plays illustrating the important social questions of the time, were presented there and for a while were received enthusiastically by the public. The **comedia** more accurately reflected the true interest of the public, however, rather than the theatre of social thesis and psychological analysis, and the initial step towards realism fell short because of the intervention of the operetta and the musical *revue*.

Artur Azevedo (1855–1908), more than any other

writer, was responsible for the trend of the Brazilian drama during the latter half of the century. A prolific writer, his adaptations and translations were regularly performed in Rio de Janeiro. His most popular work, *A capital federal* (*The Federal Capital*, 1897), itself an adaptation of one of his earlier plays, turned on humorous contrasts between rural and urban life styles. The *revista* (revue) form he cultivated gained quick popular acceptance. A satire of customs, primarily political issues, the *revista* ranged from a unified plot to independent sketches without continuity. In either event, the *revista* attracted a greater public during those years than the more serious theatre, and Azevedo responded to his critics by pointing out the public choices. When Azevedo and Moreira Sampaio presented *O mandarim* (*The Mandarin*) in 1884, the *revista* was established as a literary–dramatic genre that has survived to the present day to a minor extent, although it was essentially discredited by the early 1940s. Although the quality was not exceptional, the operetta, the *revista* and parody were all popular forms at the end of the century.

20th century During the early years of the century, the greater degree of commercial success available to writers and impresarios of the *teatro ligeiro* (light theatre) inhibited the expansion of serious works. Reviews, burlesque, farces and operettas continued as the dominant forms, represented by Gomes Cardim, Coelho Neto, Cláudio de Sousa and João de Rio who continued these traditions after Azevedo's death in 1908. In the next two decades, several attempts were made to establish new theatre companies, most of which produced only fleeting impressions on national drama. The popular Cláudio de Sousa (1876–1954) continued the romantic, sentimental traditions of the past century in *Flores na sombra* (*Flowers in the Shadow*, 1916). The Semana de Arte Moderna (Week of Modern Art) (1922) brought to Brazil the post-war vanguard movement in literature and the arts, although the movement had little effect on drama. Alvaro Moreyra (1888–1964) and Oswald de Andrade (1890–1954), leading writers in 'modernism', failed to achieve public acceptance, although the latter's *O rei da vela* (*King of the Candle*), for example, revealed a technical virtuosity too early for its time.

The world-wide economic and social crises of the 1930s produced an incipient revolution in the theatre. **Joracy Camargo** (1898–1973) and Oduvaldo Vianna (1892–1972) wrote pompous, 19th-century-style thesis plays utilizing an anachronistic Camões language. The initiative to reform the theatre along the lines of the European vanguardists such as **Copeau**, **Reinhardt**, and **Stanislavsky** fell to several theatre groups knowledgeable about the new techniques, such as Colméia (1924), Alvaro Moreyra's Teatro de Brinquedo (Game Theatre, late 1920s), the Teatro Universitário (University Theatre, 1940s) and the Teatro do Estudante do Brasil (Brazilian Student Theatre, 1940s).

The new orientation took solid form in 1938 with the formation of Os Comediantes (The Comedians), an amateur group, later professional, that dared to disobey the traditional rules and customs by experimenting with new techniques of lighting, staging and acting. The arrival of the Polish refugee Zbigniew Ziembinski in 1941 provided substance to their efforts. Ziembinski was trained in German expressionism and brought with him experience in directing, acting and lighting as well as techniques for training new actors and a new theatre public. Their production of *Vestido de noiva* (*Bridal Gown*) in Rio in 1943 marked the beginning of the modern Brazilian theatre. This play by **Nelson Rodrigues** (1912–81) was ideally suited to the expressionistic techniques in lighting, rhythm and movement that enhanced the presentation of the psychic disassociations of a moribund woman in three levels of past and present time. Rodrigues' morbid attraction for shocking scenes and themes revealed an analogy with the theatre of the absurd. A prolific though not always popular dramatist, Rodrigues often lacked commercial success although he continued to write about the perversions, sexual and otherwise, he considered indicative of contemporary society. From that point forward, the Brazilian theatre began to reflect the aesthetic revolution that occurred in other genres during the modernist movement in 1922.

In the oft-repeated pattern of Latin American theatre, a number of amateur and experimental companies developed to accept the challenge of establishing a new theatre: Teatro de Amadores de Pernambuco (Amateur Theatre of Pernambuco) (1941), Teatro Experimental do Negro (Black Experimental Theatre) (1944), established in protest about the lack of blacks on the Brazilian stage, Grupo dos Quixotes (Quixote Group) (1951) and others. Without question the most significant group was the Teatro Brasileiro de Comédia (Brazilian Play Company), established in São Paulo in 1948, where it formed a permanent company of 15 to 20 actors with two Italian directors, Celi and Salce. By 1954 the TBC had acquired sufficient stability and a sound artistic and commercial base in order to open a parallel company in Rio de Janeiro, where it inspired rival groups along similar lines, such as the Teatro Maria Della Costa.

From the 1940s onward, the critics have commented on the dichotomies in the Brazilian theatre between the public that favours light, frivolous comedies and those who support serious artistic fare. Originally, the distinction was geographic, with the light farce and comedy associated with Rio de Janeiro and the serious comedy with São Paulo, although these lines are not severely drawn. In Rio the tradition of Martins Pena and Artur Azevedo was continued by Silveira Sampaio (1914–65) and Henrique Pongetti (b. 1898). Sampaio satirized the customs of marriage and middle class society in three comedies filled with irony and comic talent known as the *Trilogia do herói grotesco* (*Trilogy of the Grotesque Hero*, 1948–9). Two political satires followed: Pongetti also wrote farces disparaging politics and high society morals. Other playwrights of the Rio tradition included Raimundo Magalhães Júnior (b. 1907) and Pedro Bloch (b. 1914). Bloch was consistently popular with the public if not with the drama critics. His two-act monologue, *As mãos de Eurídice* (*Euridice's Hands*, 1951), achieved international acclaim, more for its interesting techniques than for the convincing psychology. He also wrote psycho-dramas with didactic tendencies.

The theatre in São Paulo began to develop a serious, realistic tradition. One of the major playwrights affiliated with the TBC was **Jorge Andrade** (1922–84), whose interest in the decadence of the rural Paulista society led to *A moratória* (*The Moratorium*, 1955), *Pedreira das almas* (*Stone-Quarry of Souls*, 1956), and a group of plays known as the 'coffee cycle'. Abílio Pereira de Almeida (1906–77) had already portrayed the decadence of the rural aristocracy in *Paiol velho* (*Old Barn*, 1951), but as the unofficial dramatist of the TBC, he lapsed briefly into sensationalism for commercial success before returning to criticism of venal public officials and the political, moral and economic corruption of the metropolis.

In the late 50s and early 60s various experimental theatre groups with the perspectives inspired by vanguard European and North American groups (such as the **Living Theatre**) launched new directions. Three groups were particularly important. In São Paulo the Teatro Arena (Arena Theatre) made initial efforts with both foreign plays (**Tennessee Williams** and others) and domestic productions. The focus was on politically committed theatre which would elaborate a unique and characteristically Brazilian dramatic 'language'. The founder and first director was José Renato; after the American-trained **Augusto Boal** joined the company in 1956, they staged a series of *Arena Conta . . .* (*Arena Tells . . .*) plays with an arena stage, actor/audience contact, nudity and daring language in an effort to Brazilianize **Brecht**. Their production of *Eles não usam black-tie* (*They Don't Use Tuxedos*) by **Gianfrancesco Guarnieri** (born in Italy in 1934) set new standards of realistic theatre by focusing on lower class problems of life in the *favela* (the Brazilian slum). The Teatro Oficina (Workshop Theatre) under the direction of José Celso promoted street theatre, staged **Gorky** and Brecht, and the first production in 1967 of *O rei da vela* (*King of the Candle*), the long-ignored 1929 play by Osvaldo de Andrade. The most important production since *Bridal Gown* in 1943, it again revolutionized Brazilian stagecraft. The Teatro Opinião (Opinion Theatre) in Rio functioned along similar lines, staging *Liberdade, liberdade* (*Freedom, Freedom*) by Flavio Rangel and Millor Fernandes in 1965.

The dominance of Rio and São Paulo as theatrical centres did not preclude the development or a religious and folkloric theatre in the Northeast, where unique combinations of cultural, social and religious elements produced moralizing and regionalistic farces. The principal playwrights were **Ariano Suassuna** (b. 1927) and **Alfredo Dias Gomes** (b. 1922). Suassuna's *Auto da Compadecida* (*The Rogue's Trial*, 1957) integrated the 17th-century-style **auto sacramental** with modern comedy, folklore and colloquial language. An instant success in Brazil, the play was soon known around the world in various translations. Dias Gomes achieved international recognition with *O pagador de promessas* (*Payment as Pledged*, 1960), a moving drama staged by the TBC in 1960 that reflected the insensitivity of the modern world towards an ingenuous peasant victimized by the hypocrisy and syncretism of his native region. The film version of this play won the Cannes Film Festival in 1962, and launched a long and productive career for Dias Gomes whose other plays included *O berço do heroi* (*The Hero's Cradle*, 1965) and *O Santo Inquérito* (*The Holy Inquisition*, 1966).

Deteriorating political conditions in Brazil in the 1960s led to major changes in the theatre. The military regime of General Castello Branco at first dealt lightly with the theatre, but after the world-wide protests of 1968 brought strikes and student demonstrations to Brazil, restrictions and censorship were imposed. **Plínio Marcos** (b. 1935) was the most sensational new playwright with *Dois perdidos numa noite suja* (*Two Lost Souls in a Dirty Night*, 1966), and *Navalha na carne* (*Knife in the Flesh*, 1967), plays that captured the marginal society of pimps, prostitutes and homosexuals with candour and scabrous language. In *O assalto* (*The Assault*, 1969), José Vicente painted the fragility of the human condition in a two-character play with homosexual motifs that turns violent and destructive. Homosexual themes coupled with revolutionary motifs are still in evidence in 1984 in such plays as *As três moças do sabonete* (*Three Girls on a Bar of Soap*) by Herbert Daniel.

During the radicalized period of the 1970s, the newspapers resorted to such absurd tactics as publishing recipes when articles were censored. In the theatre innovative groups such as Arena Theatre and Workshop Theatre disappeared. Plínio Marcos was unable to stage his plays. Augusto Boal after a period of torture and imprisonment went into exile, where he continued his vanguardist experiments with 'newspaper theatre' ('teatro jornal', a kind of documentary drama) or the 'invisible theatre' (street theatre in which the public is unaware of a rehearsed performance). Within Brazil, social commentary was permissible only if cleverly disguised, such as in the brilliant *Apareceu a Margarida* (*Miss Margarida's Way*, 1973) by Roberto de Athayde (b. 1949), a monologue by a frustrated and foul-mouthed school teacher lecturing to her students *Um grito parado no ar* (*A Scream in the Air*, 1974) was a symbolic, nationalistic piece by Guarnieri (in collaboration with Boal). Chico Buarque de Holanda brought his musical genius to notable productions such as *Gota d'agua* (*Drop of Water*, 1977), the tragic theme of Medea set in the Brazilian *favela*. His *Opera do malandro* (*The Rogue's Opera*, 1980), an adaptation of *The Threepenny Opera*, is critical of commercial relationships between Third World countries and the Unites States. The most important Brazilian theatre company in the 1970s was Rio's Asdrubal Trouxe Seu Trombone (Hasdrubal Brought his Trombone).

The new regime of General João Figueiredo in 1979 restored greater freedoms to the Brazilian people and to the stage, which led to a resurgence of activity. The spectacular productions of recent years include *Macunaíma*, a staged version of the recondite novel by Mário de Andrade, written in 1927 and staged in 1979 by the Grupo Pau Brasil, a group that subsequently adopted the name of its own production. Based on a cyclical and mythical journey by an ingenuous Indian from the innocence of the jungle to the sophisticated and wicked metropolis and back again, the play recreates with freshness and ingenuity the true genius of Brazilian theatre. Grupo Macunaíma has been Brazil's most successful company in the 1980s and has achieved international acclaim. Its subsequent productions are *O eterno retorno* (*The Eternal Return*), 1981, based on plays by Nelson Rodrigues, *Romeo and Juliet* (1984), and *Augusto Matraga* (1986), based on a short story by Guimarães Rosa. Cacá Rosset has directed such notable productions as a Brazilian version of Brecht's *Mahagonny* and, more recently, a clever, fascinating version of *Père Ubu* with all the humour, sensuality and freedom of expression that typify the Brazilian theatre.

Grupo Pau Brasil's *Macunaíma*, at The Fifth International Theatre Festival, Caracas, Venezuela, 1981.

Important women writers in Brazil include Maria Clara Machado, Rachel de Queiroz, Luiza Barreto Leite, and Leilah Assunpção. The Portuguese-born Ruth Escobar and the English-educated Barbara Heliodora have promoted theatre with productions and solid criticism.

In a country with a multiplicity of regional customs and traditions, the theatre is diversified and active. Although theatre companies in Brazil are notoriously unstable (the exceptions are Os Comediantes, TBC, Arena, Oficina and perhaps Grupo Macunaíma), and new companies are constantly being formed as only slightly older ones disappear, the level of theatre activity is high and the quality is good. Language differences continue to impede the transmission of recent Brazilian drama to the consciousness of the Western world, a serious loss.   GW

See: A. Boal, *Teatro do oprimido*, Rio de Janeiro, 1975; H. Borba Filho, *Fisonomia e espírito de mamulengo (O Teatro Popular do Nordeste)*, São Paulo, 1966; A. S. da Silva, *Oficina: do Teatro ao te-ato*, São Paulo, 1981; M. Garcia Mendes, *A personagem negra no teatro brasileiro*, São Paulo, 1982; D. George, *Teatro e Antropofágia*, São Paulo, 1985; A. Guzik (ed.), *Teatro brasileiro do comédia*, Rio de Janeiro, 1980; L. B. Leite, *A mulher no teatro brasileiro*, Rio de Janeiro, 1965; S. Magaldi, *Panorama do teatro brasileiro*, Rio de Janeiro, 1979; *idem, Um palco brasileiro: arena*, São Paulo, 1984; M. Silveira, *A contribuição Italiana ao teatro brasileiro*; São Paulo, 1976; *idem, A outra crítica*, São Paulo, 1976; *Teatro e realidade brasileira*, Caderno especial, *Revista civilização brasileira*, No. 2 (1968).

Bread and Puppet Theatre Founded in New York in 1961 by Peter Schumann, who had previously organized the New Dance Group in Germany, Bread and Puppet was never an orthodox group in manning, finance, or artistic policy. Not an ensemble, but a loose association of performers under Schumann's firm direction, and supplemented at need by amateurs, the company mistrusted the idea of purchasing entertainment deeply enough to offer its services free, whenever

possible, on the principle of its founder's maxim, 'theatre is like bread, more like a necessity' – an axiom literally enacted in the course of each performance by the giving of bread to the audience. Deeply involved in the contemporary reaction against what was perceived as the over-intellectualization of Western culture, as epitomized in its powerful tradition of literary theatre, Schumann and his associates worked with larger than life puppets to create a non-narrative theatre which addressed contemporary issues – notably the Vietnam War – through disturbing visual images rather than words. In performances such as 'The Cry of the People for Meat', and 'The Domestic Resurrection Circus' (the latter presented each summer since 1974) religious iconography and political message were combined in an attempt to offer a critique of contemporary society in terms of its own values. After a four-year residence at Goddard College, in 1974 Schumann moved to a farm near Glover, Vermont, and the company nominally disbanded. In practice it has continued to regroup for summer festivals at Glover, and for specific commissions such as the 1975 'Anti-Bicentennial' at the University of California, an angry and moving elegy to

Wooden puppets, by Bread and Puppet Theatre.

the last Indian survivor of white genocide in the state. More recently Schumann and his associates scripted plays such as **Büchner**'s *Woyzeck* (New York, 1981). AEG DBW

Brecht, Bertolt (Eugen Berthold Friedrich)

(1898–1956) German dramatist, director and poet, whose work dominated 20th-century German theatre and is perhaps the most influential force in Western theatre since the Second World War. Despite self-propagated myths, his 1918 military service was as a medical orderly in an Augsburg convalescent clinic and he played no part in the 1919 revolution. His first work to be staged, the iconoclastic *Drums in the Night* (1922), rejected political involvement while *Baal* (completed 1919) and *In the Cities' Jungle* (1923) are examples of nihilistic expressionism. These plays brought him notoriety with riots at their premieres and instant recognition with the Kleist prize in 1922. In his Munich staging of *Edward II* (adapted from **Marlowe**, 1924) and his anti-militaristic *Man is Man* (1925) he began to develop the anti-illusionistic staging methods and parable structures that later became the basis for his theory of epic theatre.

Moving to Berlin, he worked as a dramaturge under **Reinhardt** and collaborated with **Piscator**. His first popular success came with *The Threepenny Opera* in 1928, a modernization of *The Beggar's Opera* by **Gay** with music by Kurt Weill, who also provided the scores for *Happy End* (1929, produced under Brecht's name, though the text was by Elisabeth Hauptmann) and *The Rise and Fall of the City of Mahagonny* (1930). With musicians on stage, the use of placards to give spectators an objective perspective on the action, the separation of dialogue from song and a harshly cynical presentation of the material to prevent emotional empathy, these operas were designed as the antithesis to **Wagner**. They were the first consciously developed examples of the 'distancing' of *Verfremdungseffekt*, forming the basis of a new style of acting in which the performers demonstrate the actions of a character instead of identifying with their roles, and it was in essays written at this time that Brecht formulated his 'Non-Aristotelian' drama though the most complete definition comes in the 1949 *Small Organum for the Theatre*. Later Brecht was to modify these principles into a theory of 'dialectical' theatre, and came to regret that they had conditioned the interpretation of his drama, but they provided the basis for his mature work as well as his 'Teaching Plays' or *Lehrstücke*. Deriving in some ways from agit-prop theatre, these show Brecht's approach to his dramatic material at its clearest, abstracting political issues such as whether individuals should be sacrificed for the revolution (*He Who Says Yes*, 1929, *He Who Says No*, 1930, and *The Measures Taken*, 1930) or class exploitation (*The Exception and the Rule*, 1938), and presenting them in historically or geographically distant contexts where their essential nature could be displayed.

Forced to flee by Hitler's rise to power in 1933, Brecht attempted to recoup his finances with the team responsible for his operatic successes, Weill, Lotte Lenya and the scene designer, Caspar Neher, in a 'Ballet-Cantata' *The Seven Deadly Sins* (Paris 1933). In exile, first in Denmark, followed by Sweden and in 1940 Finland, Brecht began writing his major plays –

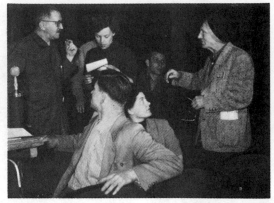

Bertolt Brecht (far left) rehearsing his play *The Life of Galileo*, Berlin, 1956.

the first version of *The Life of Galileo* (1938), *Mother Courage and her Children* (1939), *The Good Person of Setzuan* (1940), *Puntila and his Man Matti* (1940) and *The Resistible Rise of Arturo Ui* (1941). In 1941 he travelled via Russia to the USA, where he found employment in Hollywood. Though his film experience included *Kuhle Wampe* in 1932, the only script he wrote there was *Hangmen Also Die* for Fritz Lang, and until the defeat of the Nazis the drama he produced was minor – *The Story of Simone Machard* in collaboration with **Lion Feuchtwanger** (1943), *Schweik in the Second World War* (1944). Then in 1945 came what many consider his finest play, *The Caucasian Chalk Circle*, with its complex mixture of pathos and comedy, and in 1947 he directed *Galileo*, which he had revised for **Charles Laughton** to reflect the moral issues posed by Hiroshima.

Although some of his major plays had been produced at the Zürich Schauspielhaus during his exile, it was only after his return to Berlin in 1948 and with the establishment of the **Berliner Ensemble** under his wife and leading actress, **Helene Weigel**, that they achieved wide recognition. His international stature – as well as an Austrian passport and a West German publisher – preserved his artistic independence despite Marxist attacks on his 'formalism', but apart from *Turandot or the Whitewashers' Congress* (1954, staged by **Benno Besson** in Zürich, 1969) which remained unperformed in the DDR until after his death, his dramatic output during the last eight years of his life consisted of collaborations (*The Days of the Commune*) and classical adaptations (*The Tutor* by **Lenz**, **Shakespeare**'s *Coriolanus*, **Farquhar**'s *The Recruiting Officer*). However, his directorial work with these and his definitive productions of his own plays affirmed the viability of his earlier theatrical theory. The work of the Ensemble established his influential position in the contemporary theatre, and his continuing domination of the German stage can be indicated by figures for the 1963–4 season in which there were 1,393 performances in 74 productions of his plays. CI

Bredero, Gerbrand Adriaansz (1585–1618)

Dutch poet and dramatist, famous primarily for his comedies and farces. The impact of his plays lies in the apt portrayal of the middle classes, farmers, and citizens, seen in plays like *The Farce of the Cow* (1612), and *The Miller's Farce* (1613). In his *Moortje* (1616), based on **Terence**'s *Eunuchus*, and in *The Spanish Brabanter* (1617), too, his use of dialect, and the way in which he depicts ordinary Amsterdam life is striking. Today, his plays are still regularly performed. *The Spanish Brabanter* has been translated into English, and has been staged in England. Bredero wrote tragedies too. He was, however, less familiar with the genre, and, as a result, these plays have remained relatively unknown. MG WH

Breeches part This describes male roles played by actresses. **Peg Woffington**'s portrayal of Sir Harry Wildair in **Farquhar**'s *The Constant Couple* (1699) established a tradition that extends, in the English theatre, through to the Principal Boy in Pantomime. In the 19th century the breeches role often accommodated a roguish young man, of good if mischievous nature, as for instance in the part of Sam Willoughby in **Tom Taylor**'s *The Ticket of Leave Man*. MB

Brel, Jacques (1929–78) Belgian song-writer and performer, who renounced his middle class inheritance to sing in Paris. Originally, his songs were idealistic and tinged with Catholic pieties, but gradually grew more trenchant, misogynistic and obsessed with death. His performance technique used illustrative gesture to caricature his own lyrics, which he almost spat out at the adoring audience. Brel's fame spread to the English-speaking world with the musical *Jacques Brel is Alive and Well and Living in Paris* by Mort Shuman and Eric Blau (1968). He retired from the stage in 1972 and died of cancer six years later. LS

Brenton, Howard (1942–) British dramatist, whose first play, *Ladder of Fools*, was staged in 1965 in Cambridge where he was a student. After leaving university, he wrote for various fringe companies, winning **Arts Council** bursaries in 1969 and 1970, together with the John Whiting Award (1970) for his short play, *Christie in Love*. Brenton was influenced by a group of intellectuals in France, the 'situationists', who described Western liberal democracies as the societies 'of the Spectacle' in which politicians deceived the public with confidence tricks, aided by the mass media. Brenton saw his task as being to 'disrupt the Spectacle' and his full-length plays, such as *Magnificence* (1973), *The Churchill Play* (1974) and *Brassneck* (with **David Hare**, 1973), have all attempted to shock the British public out of their bourgeois complacency. In *The Romans in Britain* (1980) Brenton drew a parallel between the presence of British troops in Northern Ireland and the conquest of Britain by Julius Caesar, stressing the analogy with a graphic scene of homosexual rape. The ensuing controversy led to a private prosecution being brought under the Sexual Offences Act of 1956 – though it was eventually withdrawn. Brenton's vivid dialogue, his narrative flow of powerful incidents and his polemical attacks brought him quickly to the fore in the state-subsidized sector of British theatre, with productions at the **National Theatre**, the **Royal Court** and major regional reps. As a translator/adapter, he has provided the National Theatre with English versions of **Brecht**'s *Galileo* and **Büchner**'s *Danton's Death*. JE

Breuer, Lee (1937–) American actor and director. A founding director of the avant-garde theatre company **Mabou Mines**, Breuer began his career in the early 1960s with the San Francisco Actors' Workshop, moving to Europe in 1965 to study with the **Berliner Ensemble** and the Polish Theatre Lab. For Mabou Mines he serves as director, author, adapter, producer, and performer. His staging and adaptation of **Beckett**'s work has earned him three major awards (Obies); his trilogy *Animations* (1970–8) was published in 1979. Outside Mabou Mines his most notable effort has been *The Gospel at Colonus* (1983) which he conceived, adapted, and directed for the Brooklyn Academy of Music's 'Next Wave Festival' and which was performed later at Washington's **Arena Stage**. In the 1980s his focus has been on creating a new theatre that merges Asian and African arts with American performance techniques. DBW

Brice, Fanny (Fannie) (1891–1951) American comedienne and singer. Her gawky walk, repertoire of comic faces, and ability to sing both satiric and serious songs with equal success made Fanny Brice a star of revues for over a quarter of a century. After serving an apprenticeship in amateur shows and burlesque, Brice appeared in the *Ziegfeld Follies of 1910*. She remained with the *Follies* for six more editions through 1923, then switched to **Irving Berlin**'s *Music Box Revue* (1924). An attempt to star in a book musical, *Fioretta* (1929), was a failure. Brice appeared in four more revues: *Sweet and Low* (1930), *Billy Rose's Crazy Quilt* (1931), and two editions of the *Ziegfeld Follies* (1934 and 1936) produced by the **Shuberts** after **Ziegfeld**'s death. In most of her songs and sketches Brice affected a Yiddish accent that heightened her satirical treatment of such subjects as the ballet and silent film 'vamps'. MK

Bridges-Adams, William (1889–1965) British director, who toured the provinces as an actor and stage-managed for **William Poel** before taking over the Bristol repertory theatre, where he introduced a programme of **Shaw**, **Masefield** and **Stanley Houghton** between 1914 and 1915. From 1919 to 1934 he directed the Festival at Stratford-upon-Avon, where he founded the New Shakespearian Company and toured Canada and America with them after the old theatre burnt down in 1926. His last production was *Oedipus Rex* at **Covent Garden** in 1936. CI

Bridie, James (Osborne Henry Mavor) (1888–1951) Scottish playwright. Bridie was a doctor, and he certainly did much to keep Scottish theatre healthy, not only through his playwriting (which included *Tobias and the Angel* (1930), *Jonah and the Whale* (1932), *Mr Bolfry* (1943), *Daphne Laureola* (1949), *The Queen's Comedy* (1950)) but also through his association, as a founder, with the **Glasgow Citizens' Theatre** and with the establishment of drama training in the Royal Scottish Academy of Music and Drama. His playwriting, though often on serious themes, was distinguished by a very personal wit and charm, and he created roles relished by such performers as Alastair Sim and **Edith Evans**. MB

Brieux, Eugène (1858–1932) French dramatist. His

naturalistic dramas on social themes dealt frankly with matters ranging from syphilis to birth control. **George Bernard Shaw** wrote a famous introduction to the English translation of three of the plays, *Les Avariés* (*Damaged Goods*, 1902), *The Three Daughters of M. Dupont* (1897) and *Maternity* (1903) in which he compared Brieux to **Ibsen**. As a campaigner the comparison is valid.   MB

Brighouse, Harold (1882–1958) British playwright, who wrote prolifically and mainly about the people and affairs of his home county of Lancashire. The **Gaiety Theatre** in Manchester was the venue for much of his work, including his best-known play *Hobson's Choice* (1915). This play and *Zack* (1916) have established a firm place in the national repertory. His one-act plays are particularly well-crafted and form an important part of his work. See also **Stanley Houghton**.   MB

Bristol Old Vic Company Shortly after the war, the **Arts Council of Great Britain**, in association with the **Old Vic** in London, set up a permanent repertory company in Bristol, based at the recently re-opened Theatre Royal. Beginning in 1946, under the direction of **Hugh Hunt**, it soon became established as one of the country's leading theatre companies: a position it has continued to hold under its subsequent directors, with a record of many transfers of successful productions to London and world-wide tours. Notable productions have included *Salad Days*, *The Killing of Sister George*, *Conduct Unbecoming* and *A Severed Head*. Since 1972, when alterations to the Theatre Royal were completed, the company has also been able to present small-scale new and experimental work in a theatre studio, the New Vic. The Bristol Old Vic Theatre Trust, independent of the Arts Council since 1963 though still receiving substantial grant-aid, also runs the highly regarded Bristol Old Vic Theatre School.   AJ

Bristow, James (c. 1585–?) English actor whose experience provides unique information on the trade in boy-actors in the Elizabethan theatre. **Henslowe**'s *Diary* records the purchase of Bristow from William Augusten 'player' for £8. That purchase price is greater than Bristow's yearly wage as an employee of Henslowe's in 1600, when he received three shillings per week. Nothing is heard of him after 1603.   PT

British Drama League see **British Theatre Association**

British Theatre Association Founded by Geoffrey Whitworth in 1919 as the **British Drama League** to promote the development of theatre. Its early causes included the establishment of a **National Theatre**, the introduction of drama into the school curriculum and the winning of public support for the arts. Of special importance has been its Library and Information/Research Service. The BTA was dissolved for financial reasons in 1990. Its collection of play-scripts (presented by **Miss Horniman** and including the **William Archer** collection) are now held by the Theatre Museum.   AJ

Briusov, Valery Yakovlevich (1873–1924) Russian poet, novelist, critic, translator, scholar and chief theoretician of the symbolist movement, whose call for a conventional theatre of essence greatly influenced **Meyerhold** and other anti-realistic directors of the early 20th century. His symbolist activities included: the anthology *Russian Symbolists* (1894) which launched the movement; the editing of its journal *The Scales* (1904); numerous volumes of poetry and short fiction; theoretical and critical articles; the novel *The Fiery Angel* (1907–8); over 20 produced plays and sketches of many more. His comparison of **Stanislavsky**'s realistic approach to poetic drama at the **Moscow Art Theatre** (MAT) and the naive poeticism of the native folk theatre helped convince him that the latter's stylized conventionality better realized theatre's innately symbolic nature. In his seminal essay 'Unnecessary Truth' (*World of Art*, 1902) and later in 'The Theatre of the Future' (1907) and 'Realism and Convention on the Stage' (1908), he argued his preference for a conventional (*uslovny*) theatre which would give the actor the centrality he enjoyed in the ancient Greek and Elizabethan theatres. Stanislavsky attempted to adopt these ideas in his work on **Maeterlinck**'s, Hamsun's and **Andreev**'s dramas at MAT (1903–7), then sponsored Meyerhold's more dramatic experiments at the Theatre Studio on Povarskaya Street (1905), of which Briusov was literary head. Briusov attacked Meyerhold's mechanization of the actor in his production of Maeterlinck's *Pelléas and Mélisande*, which Briusov translated, at Vera Komissarzhevskaya's Theatre (1907). However, he supported **Gordon Craig**'s bid to stylize the acting in his *Hamlet* collaboration with Stanislavsky at MAT (1912). His own dramas have been labelled 'cosmic' and offer spectacular scenic and lighting effects, philosophical themes and heightened language, symbols and imagery rather than credibility. *Earth* (1904) is the only published one of four science fiction plays which Briusov wrote, the others being *Piroent* (*Pyroesis*), *The Dictator* (1921) and *The World of Seven Generations* (1923). The lone symbolist play set in the future, it is an urban apocalyptic tale with echoes of Plato and of **Goethe**'s *Faust*. *The Wayfarer* (1910) is a one-act 'psychodrama' resembling Evreinovian monodrama and featuring a Maeterlinckian 'silent stranger' (later used by Pinter) in a study of repressed female eroticism. *Protesilaus Deceased* (1911–12) is a version of the **Euripides**-dramatized myth, which was also the subject of dramas by **Annensky** and **Sologub**. Briusov's plays have had no meaningful production history in Russia. Briusov, who sided with the 'clarists' against the 'mystics' in the 1904–5 symbolist split, later broke with the movement (1908–10) and, in 1917, embraced the October Revolution.   SG

Broadhurst Theatre 235 West 44th St, New York City [Architect: Herbert J. Krapp]. Continuing their custom to name playhouses after prominent theatrical personages, the **Shuberts** opened another of their 1917-built theatres in honour of George Broadhurst, an English-born playwright, who enjoyed fleeting fame as the author of a string of successful modern melodramas. Broadhurst also often produced his own plays and managed the house in tandem with the

Shuberts. Seating about 1,200, its policy has alternated between musicals and dramas and among its more successful tenants have been *Beggar on Horseback* (1924), *The Green Hat* (with the young **Katharine Cornell**) (1925), *Broadway* (1926), *Men in White* (1933), *The Petrified Forest* (1935), *Victoria Regina* (with **Helen Hayes**) (1936) and the musicals *Fiorello!* (1959) and *Cabaret* (1967). It remains a Shubert theatre.   MCH

Broadway Broadway is to New York as the West End is to London – the district that is thought of as the traditional theatrical heart of the city. Centered on and around the street of that name in New York City since the 1890s have been the major theatres that have represented the professional and commercial theatrical core of the nation, extending, from the 1950s, into **off-Broadway** locations (to accommodate generally smaller and somewhat more innovative theatres) as economic pressures restricted work in the big old theatres. **Off-off Broadway** is distinguished from Broadway and Off-Broadway by a further diminution in scale and eclectic experimentation, by the different contractual relationship with actors based on non-profit-making companies.   MB

Broadway, Off-Off see **Off-Off Broadway**

Broadway Theatre *1* 326–8 Broadway, New York City [Architect: John M. Trimble]. The first important theatre in a succession of New York's playhouses to bear the name, the original Broadway was modelled on London's **Haymarket** and with 4,500 seats was the largest theatre built before 1847, when it opened its doors. Intended to replace the **Park Theatre** in public favour, and although many stars appeared on its stage, it never achieved the prominence of the earlier theatre and was torn down in 1859.
  2 Broadway and 41st St, New York [Architect: J. B. McElfatrick and Co.]. Built in 1888 when 41st Street was still 'uptown' for the rest of the city, it was dedicated to musical comedy, operetta and spectacle. Later, when the new theatre district began to coalesce around 42nd Street, the theatre was assimilated within its borders. Both **Edwin Booth** and Sir **Henry Irving** made final appearances in New York at the Broadway. Too large for the later dramatic and musical fare, it was used for motion pictures and vaudeville before being torn down in 1929.
  3 1681 Broadway, New York City [Architect: Eugene De Rosa]. Opened as B. S. Moss's Colony Theatre in 1924, the playhouse see-sawed between plays and movies for more than 25 years. Renamed the Broadway in 1930, it is a large 1,800-seat house, well suited for musicals. Among its outstanding tenants have been *This Is the Army* (1942), *Lady in the Dark* (1943), *Gypsy* (1959) and *Evita* (1979). Since 1943, it has been a **Shubert** theatre.   MCH

Brockmann, Johann (1745–1812) Austrian actor. Brockmann achieved prominence when, in 1776, he acted the title role in **Schröder**'s famous production of *Hamlet* in Hamburg. The grace and naturalness of his expression were highly admired. After successful guest appearances in Berlin, Brockmann was called to the **Burgtheater** where he remained for the rest of his life.

Here he helped form the characteristic style of the company.   SW

Brome, Richard (*c.* 1590–1652) English playwright, one of the many efficient professionals who continued to provide the Caroline theatre with plays until the closing of the theatres in 1642, Brome is known only by his writing. According to *Biographia Dramatica* (1764) 'his extraction was mean, he having originally been no better than a menial servant to the celebrated **Ben Jonson**', and a Jonsonian influence is certainly detectable in much of his work, though the geniality is Brome's own. Of his surviving plays, the best are *The Northern Lass* (1629), *The City Wit* (c. 1630), *The Antipodes* (1638) and *A Jovial Crew* (1641). That Brome's talent was recognized in his own time is clear from the earliest known playwright's contract, drawn up in his name on 20 July 1635. The document is nothing less than a Caroline playwright's job-description.   PT

Bronnen, Arnolt (1895–1959) Austrian dramatist and novelist, who made his reputation on the German stage with violently emotional examples of expressionism (*Parricide*, 1922, *The Birth of Youth*, 1925) before turning to comedy. His plays, although frequently taken as supporting the Nazi movement, were banned in 1943 and in 1955 he moved to East Berlin as a theatre critic.   CI

Brook, Peter (Stephen Paul) (1925–) British director. Born in London of Russian descent, Brook first attracted attention as an Oxford undergraduate staging ambitious plays under the difficult conditions of London's little theatre clubs during the war. **Barry Jackson** invited him to direct *King John* (1945) at the **Birmingham Rep**, whose success led to an engagement at the Shakespeare Memorial Theatre, Stratford-upon-Avon, then struggling to revive its summer festival seasons. His enchanting *Love's Labour's Lost* (1946), designed after Watteau, began his long association with what became in 1961 the **Royal Shakespeare Company** (RSC). The charm and visual style of Brook's early productions aroused the interest of West End and Broadway managements, for whom he directed plays by **Anouilh**, Roussin, and **Christopher Fry**; but the true power of his imagination was felt through the Stratford Shakespearian productions, notably of *Measure for Measure* (1950) and of *Titus Andronicus* (1955) which starred **Laurence Olivier** as Titus and featured Brook's own set designs and *musique concrète*. Later Brook productions for the RSC included *King Lear* (1962) with **Paul Scofield**, Peter Weiss's *The Marat/Sade* (1964), *US* (1966) a documentary attack on the United States's involvement in Vietnam and *A Midsummer Night's Dream* (1970), set in an adult adventure playground, with trapezes, stilts and spinning plates. During the 1960s, Brook was influenced by the seemingly contradictory theories of **Antonin Artaud** and **Bertolt Brecht**, shock tactics and analytical calm, and his reconciliation of these extremes became a feature of the RSC style. His collection of four brief essays, *The Empty Space* (1968), influenced many directors in Britain and overseas as an acute analysis of the basic problems facing contemporary theatre. By 1970, however, Brook was moving towards a style of performance which would have been equally out of place in a major subsidized company as on the West End stage. With the help of **Jean-Louis Barrault** and a Ford Foundation grant, he established an International Centre of Theatre Research in a deserted music-hall near the Gare du Nord in Paris where he assembled a team of actors, dancers, musicians, acrobats and mimes from many countries. He wanted to encourage a group approach which could transcend the boundaries of national cultures. His company took myths to remote villages in the Sahara, as in *The Conference of the Birds* (1976), and the experience of living on the verge of starvation back to Paris and London in *The Ik* (1975). Although the Centre has been acclaimed for its productions of *The Cherry Orchard* (1981) and *The Tragedy of Carmen* (1983), its most celebrated and daunting achievement has so far been to tell the entire story of the Indian religious epic, *The Mahabharata* (1985), in nine hours in a quarry outside Avignon. JE

Brooks Atkinson Theatre 256 West 47th St, New York City [Architect: Herbert J. Krapp]. When it opened in 1926, the third of the Chanin-built theatres was named after **Richard Mansfield**, one of the outstanding actors of a previous generation. After the playhouse reverted to the mortgage company early in the depression, it was leased to a succession of managements. In 1931, the **Group Theatre** launched its initial venture, *The House of Connally*, from its stage. In 1944, the theatre was sold to Michael Myerberg, who subsequently leased it to CBS-TV from 1950 to 1960. Thereafter, it was returned to legitimate use and renamed the **Brooks Atkinson** after the recently retired and revered *New York Times* drama critic. In 1964, **Tallulah Bankhead** made her final appearance in *The Milk Train Doesn't Stop Here Anymore* from its stage. Three years later, the theatre passed to the control of the **Nederlander** Organization. In 1975, the comedy *Same Time, Next Year* became its longest-running tenant for three years. MCH

Brougham, John (1810–80) Irish-American playwright and actor. Brougham's reputation rests principally on his outlandish Indian burlesques: *Po-ca-hon-tas, or the Gentle Savage* (1855), 'An Original Aboriginal Erratic Operatic Semi-Civilized and Demi-Savage Extravaganza', and *Metamora, or the Last of the Pollywogs* (1857). He poked fun at the stage version of the 'noble savage', particularly that of **Edwin Forrest** in *Metamora*. Brougham had a facile pen, too facile he once admitted. He wrote 126 wide-ranging pieces: adaptations, *Dombey and Son* (1848); gothic melodramas, *The Gun-maker of Moscow* (1857); tearful melodramas, *Night and Morning* (1855); sensational melodrama, *The Lottery of Life* (1868); social satire, *The Game of Love* (1856); and never with any 'gall in his ink', according to one critic. As principal actor in most of his pieces, he was praised for his joviality, versatility, his topical interpolations and his impromptu 'before-the-curtain' speeches.

Born in Dublin, he performed in amateur theatricals at Trinity College, appeared at London's **Olympic** (1830, with **Madame Vestris**), at **Covent Garden**, leased the **Lyceum** (1840), came to America (1842), appeared at the **Park**, toured the country, became stage-manager at **Burton**'s Chambers Street Theatre

(1848), had two flings at management (Brougham's Broadway Lyceum, 1850–2) and at the old **Bowery** (1856–7), and was employed as actor–playwright at **Wallack's** for seven seasons, 'the brightest part of my artist's life', he reported. He spent the war years in London, returned in 1865 to continue as actor–playwright at the **Winter Garden** and at **Daly**'s **Fifth Avenue Theatre**. RM

Brown, John Mason (1900–69) American drama critic. Educated at Harvard University, Brown began his journalist career on the *Louisville Courier-Journal* in 1917. In 1923–4 he reported on the European theatre for Boston and Louisville newspapers before becoming Associate Editor and dramatic critic for **Theatre Arts Monthly** (1924–8). In 1929 Brown moved to the *New York Evening Post* and established his column 'Two on the Aisle', which remained popular throughout the 1930s. In 1941 he accepted a similar position on the *New York World-Telegram* but the outbreak of the war prompted him to join the Navy in 1942. Two years later he became Associate Editor and dramatic critic of *Saturday Review* where his column 'Seeing Things' remained a standard for ten years. Brown wrote in an easy informal style which **John Simon** characterized as 'chatty urbanity'. His many books include *The Modern Theatre in Revolt* (1929), *Two on the Aisle* (1938), *Seeing Things* (1946), *Dramatis Personae* (1963), and *The Worlds of Robert E. Sherwood* (1965). TLM

Brown, William Henry (*fl.* 1820s) Afro-American theatre manager and playwright. An ex-West Indian seaman, Brown became the father of Afro-American theatre when he established the African Theatre in New York in 1821 with a repertoire that included condensed versions of plays such as *Richard III, Pizarro, Tom and Jerry, Obi, or Three-Fingered Jack*, and pantomimes. Brown also wrote and produced the first Afro-American play, *The Drama of King Shotaway* (1823), based on personal experience of the 1795 Black Caribs' insurrection on St Vincent. From his African Theatre emerged James Hewlett, the first black Shakespearian actor, and **Ira Aldridge**, renowned black actor in England and Europe in the 19th century. Brown may also have founded a theatre in Albany, New York, in 1823. EGH

Browne, E[lliot] Martin (1900–80) British director, instrumental in reviving poetic religious drama. Appointed Director of Religious Drama for the diocese of Chichester in 1930, he founded the Religious Drama Society and encouraged **T. S. Eliot** to write for the theatre, directing all his plays from *Murder in the Cathedral*, in which he also acted the Fourth Tempter (1935), to *The Elder Statesman* (1958). After directing the Pilgrim Players, who toured with works by Eliot and **Bridie**, he took over the **Mercury Theatre** in 1945, making it a centre for new poetic plays that included **Christopher Fry**'s first success, *A Phoenix Too Frequent* (1946). In 1948 he succeeded Geoffrey Whitworth as director of the **British Drama League**, and in 1951 produced the first revival of the York Cycle of Mystery Plays since 1572. CI

Browne, Robert (*fl.* 1593–1603) English actor, about whose career contradictory records survive. It may be that there were two actors of this name, one of whom was the active leader of a group of English players on the continent, particularly in Germany, from 1592–1620, and the other a leader of Derby's Men, prosperous enough to finance the innkeeper Richard Samwell's conversion of the **Boar's Head** in 1598–9) and then to buy Samwell's interest in the new theatre. This may be the 'Browne of the Boar's Head' referred to in 1603, in a letter to **Edward Alleyn** from his wife, as 'dead and died very poor'. PT

Bruant, Aristide (1851–1925) The first outstanding 'author-composer-performer' of the French cabaret. A former soldier and railway clerk, he sang in **cafés chantants** before opening his own cabaret Le Mirliton in 1885, where middle class audiences flocked to be insulted by him (one refrain ran 'All customers are swine!') and hear his 'Realistic Songs'. These ballads, couched in the authentic slang of the Parisian slums, hymn the desperate plight of the outcast and outlawed with sardonic impassivity. Bruant, a striking combination of *apache* and lion-tamer in his black sombrero, boots and red scarf, recorded by Toulouse-Lautrec, made a fortune and in 1900 retired to the bourgeois private life he had earlier attacked. LS

Bruce, Lenny (Alfred Schneider) (c. 1924–66) American stand-up comic, who became a martyr to his cult image. After serving in the Navy in the Second World War, he studied acting under the GI bill and began as a night-club comedian. Working out of small clubs in Greenwich Village, he first gained notoriety for his liberal use of four-letter words; gradually, he became noted for his savage attacks on establishment hypocrisy. As his act developed into intimate, improvisational harangues of the audience, he shocked the conventional and rejoiced the 'hip' with his free-wheeling satire of narcotics legislation, organized religion, sexual taboos and race relations. Frequently arrested for drug abuse and blasphemy (the Home Office refused to let him perform in England), he sank into paranoia and died of an overdose of narcotics. After his death, he became a totem, in **Kenneth Tynan**'s words, 'the man who went down on America's conscience', and a play, *Lenny*, was devoted to him. LS

Bruckner, Ferdinand (Theodor Tagger) (1891–1958) Austrian dramatist. After early experiments with expressionism his plays ranged from brutally realistic studies of suicide (*Malady of Youth*, 1926) or the persecution of Jewish students (*Races*, 1933) to historical dramas such as his best-known work *Elizabeth of England* (1930). In 1936 he emigrated to America, where he worked with **Piscator**, returning in 1951 to become dramaturge at the Schiller Theater in Berlin. Though technically innovative, his post-war attempts to revive verse tragedy in *Pyrrhus and Andromache* (1952) or *The Fight with the Angel* (1956) were unsuccessful. CI

Brun, Johannes (1832–90) Leading actor with the Bergen Norwegian Theatre (1850); he accompanied **Ibsen** on his 1852 study tour to Copenhagen. Brun joined Christiania Theatre in 1857 and stayed for 32 years, playing almost 400 roles, including several Ibsen premieres: Daniel Hejre in *The League of Youth*, the

Dovre King in *Peer Gynt* and Old Ekdal in *The Wild Duck*. His strength was in comedy, to which he brought simplicity, naturalness and a fundamental gravity. He was the leading Norwegian interpreter of **Holberg**'s Jeppe in his generation and, until illness restricted his range, a superb Falstaff. From the late 1870s he also directed, including the world premiere of *An Enemy of the People* (1883). HL

Bruno, Giordano (1548–1600) Italian philosopher and dramatist. A Dominican priest and one of the greatest philosophers of the Renaissance, he ran foul of the Inquisition, and after a peripatetic life was burnt at the stake in Rome. His only known play, the comedy *Il Candelaio* (*The Candlemaker*, Paris, 1582), is a subtle, complex and verbally difficult piece. It is one of the few great Italian Renaissance comedies, but is rarely performed, although for all its verbal density it stages well and was given an impressively theatrical production by **Luca Ronconi** in 1968. LR

Bruscambille (Jean Deslauriers or Du Laurier) French actor of the 17th century, who may have trained at fairgrounds and in Italy where he claimed to have learned 'la charlatannerie'. He was seen at Toulouse c. 1598 and joined the company of the **Hôtel de Bourgogne**, Paris, in 1606; he was playing there still in 1632, but no trace of him survives after 1634. His prime function was as a master of ceremonies, delivering vivacious satirical prologues. Several collections of jokes attributed to him were published between 1610 and 1619, including the famous sally that his was 'une vie sans souci, et quelquefois sans six sous'. LS

Brustein, Robert (1927–) American critic, actor, director, and founder of the **Yale** and **American Repertory Theatres**. He has served on the faculties of several universities and was the Dean of the Yale Drama School, 1965–79, years recalled in his book *Making Scenes*. The author of seven other important books on theatre and society (most notably *The Theatre of Revolt*, 1964, *Seasons of Discontent*, 1966, *The Third Theatre*, 1968, *Revolution as Theatre*, 1970, and *The Cultural Watch*, 1975), Brustein has been one of the most respected and controversial critics, primarily as drama critic for *The New Republic* since 1959 (on a regular basis until 1968). He was also sometime critic for the London Sunday *Observer*. He received the George Jean Nathan Award for dramatic criticism in 1962. In 1979 Brustein was unexpectedly released as Dean at Yale and moved to Harvard where ART was established. At Yale and Harvard, he has supervised over 150 professional productions. DBW

Bryden, Bill (William Campbell Rough) (1942–) British dramatist and director, who began his career as a documentary writer for Scottish television. He was drawn towards the theatre and was appointed Assistant Director at the Belgrade Theatre, Coventry (1965–7) and at the **Royal Court Theatre** (1967–9). From 1971 to 1974, Bryden was an Associate Director at the Royal Lyceum Theatre in Edinburgh and helped to raise the company towards the status of being Scotland's unofficial national theatre. Notable among many Lyceum productions were those of Bryden's own two plays, *Willie Rough* (1972), about the Greenock shop steward who led a shipyard strike during the First World War, and *Benny Lynch* (1974). Both plays were distinguished by the naturalistic detail, the clear handling of complex historical material and the socialist fervour which never became blindly polemical. **Peter Hall** invited him to join the **National Theatre** in 1975, where he became director of the Cottesloe Theatre in 1978. Bryden developed the flexibility of the space by exploring the possibilities of 'promenade' productions, as in *Lark Rise* (1978) and Tony Harrison's *Mysteries*, derived from the York Mystery Cycle, which were developed over four years from 1979 and presented in three parts. His play, *Old Movies* (1977), was also seen at the Cottesloe, as were his productions of 20th-century American plays, by **O'Neill**, **Odets** and **David Marmet**.   JE

Buatier de Kolta (Joseph Buatier) (1847–1903) French illusionist, who gave up studying for the priesthood to become assistant to the Hungarian presti-digitator De Kolta. Buatier's claim was that he never bought a trick but invented all the illusions in his act: scarves passing through bottles; a seated woman disappearing from her chair; the apparition of a giant black glove, and many others. His last great invention was 'The Growing Die', which expanded at the conjurer's command until it was the size of a trunk, at which point a woman stepped out of it.   LS

Büchner, Georg (1813–37) German dramatist. During his brief life, Büchner achieved notoriety as the leader of an abortive conspiracy to revolution in Hesse and distinction as a lecturer in comparative anatomy at the University of Zürich, a post to which he was appointed in 1836. His first play, *Danton's Death* (1835), reflects his disillusionment at revolutionary politics; Danton's humanity is the sole positive element in this nihilistic view of the French Revolution as being nothing but the power struggle of ambitious individuals and interests. *Leonce and Lena* (1836) is a lively satirical comedy, while *Woyzeck* (1837), a possibly incomplete drama, expresses Büchner's sympathy for the socially downtrodden. Because of his unorthodox dramaturgy, Büchner's plays were not performed for several decades after his death. *Leonce and Lena* was first produced in 1895, *Danton's Death* in 1903, and *Woyzeck* in 1913. It is possible that Büchner left another play in manuscript when he died, *Pietro Aretino*; this may have been destroyed by Büchner's fiancée, who objected to the obscenity in the play.   sw

Buckingham, George Villiers, 2nd Duke of (1628–87) English playwright. After service in the Civil War, exile with Charles II and imprisonment in the Tower, Buckingham became effectively chief minister of state from 1668 in spite of his notorious affair with the Countess of Shrewsbury whose husband he had killed in a duel. In 1668 his adaptation of **Fletcher**'s *The Chances* was very successful, with **Nell Gwyn** in a minor role. In 1669 he collaborated with Sir **Robert Howard** on *The Country Gentleman*, contributing a scene which mocked Sir William Coventry so accurately that Coventry succeeded in having the play banned. His best play, *The Rehearsal*, was first written in 1665, in collaboration with Clifford, Sprat and Butler, as a satire on **Davenant** and Sir Robert Howard but by the time the play was first performed in 1671 it

had become a satire on **Dryden** who was portrayed as Bayes, a pompous writer of heroic plays. A brilliant burlesque of the heroic drama then particularly popular, the play parodies plays and playwrights unmercifully. The form, a writer outlining his ideas to his friends during a rehearsal of one of his plays, was the model for burlesque drama thereafter and particularly influenced **Sheridan** in *The Critic*. Buckingham fell from power soon after his disastrous negotiations with France in 1674. He retired from politics after the accession of James II.   PH

Buckstone, John Baldwin (1802–79) English actor, playwright and theatre manager. After three seasons in the provinces, he made his London debut at the Surrey Theatre in 1823–4, establishing himself in the 'low comedian' line which he sustained for over 50 years. Of the 160 or so dramatic pieces Buckstone wrote between 1825 and 1850, most were short farces, operettas or burlettas – the staple accompaniment of melodrama at the minor theatres of London, but one of the earliest, *Luke the Labourer* (1826), helped set the fashion for domestic melodrama. *The Wreck Ashore* (1830) is a hyperactive adventure story, typically larded with low-life comic characters. Here, as in the lively comedy of *The Irish Lion* (1838) and *Single Life* (1839) and in the tear-jerking of *The Green Bushes* (1845), Buckstone upholds manly fortitude and decency, assuring his heroes and heroines the satisfaction of victory or of superior self-sacrifice in defeat. Most of his plays provided him with meaty comic roles during the years (1827–40) when he wintered at the **Adelphi** and played at the **Haymarket** during the summer months. It was with the Haymarket that he came finally to be identified, initially as part of **Benjamin Webster**'s company (1842–53) and from 1853–76 as manager. His announced policy was to make the Haymarket the home of comedy and prospective playwrights were expected to provide suitable parts for the resident company. **Tom Taylor**, **Westland Marston** and, after 1870, **W. S. Gilbert** were Buckstone's preferred playwrights.   PT

Buenaventura, Enrique (1928–) Colombian playwright, director and theoretician, born in Cali, studied architecture, painting and sculpture in Bogotá, all of which gave a plastic vision of dramatic art to his work. In 1955 he helped establish the TEC (Theatre School of Cali, renamed the Experimental Theatre of Cali in 1970), one of the most respected and enduring theatre groups in Latin America. His style and dedication to principles of Third World theatre (the so-called 'new theatre') have brought him international recognition. The early *A la diestra de Dios Padre* (*On the Right Hand of God the Father*, 1958) is modelled on folkloric versions of the Devil and St Peter, as told by Colombian novelist Tomás Carrasquilla. His later plays have stronger messages of social and political protest. The vitriolic one-act segments of *Los papeles del infierno* (*Documents from Hell*, 1968) and *Historia de una bala de plata* (*Story of a Silver Bullet*, 1980) are representative of this change in his theatre.   GW

Buero Vallejo, Antonio (1916–) Spanish playwright, one of the few important figures in the 1950s and 1960s. Born in Guadalajara, he studied art in

Madrid before the Civil War, afterwards serving six years in prison for his Republican sympathies. In 1949 his name was made with *Historia de una escalera* (*Story of a Staircase*) portraying the lives of the inhabitants of a poor tenement over 30 years. This was followed by *En la ardiente oscuridad* (*In the Burning Darkness*, 1950), a tragedy set in a home for the blind, and *La tejedora de sueños* (*The Weaver of Dreams*, 1952), a reinterpretation of Ulysses' return home. These plays established the themes of man's frustrated search for happiness and the obstacles of human frailty which prevent him achieving it. There followed a number of less successful plays, including *Hoy es fiesta* (*Today's a Holiday*, 1956) before the more socially oriented *Las cartas boca abajo* (*Cards Face Downwards*, 1957). A trio of historical plays followed; *Un soñador para el pueblo* (*A Dreamer for the People*, 1958) deals with Carlos III's idealist minister Esquilache, while *Las meninas* (*The Ladies-in-Waiting*, 1959) is described as a 'fantasy in the manner of Velázquez'.

Later plays include *Aventura en la gris* (*Adventure in the Grey*, 1963), *El tragaluz* (*The Skylight*, 1967), a symbolic tragedy, and *La doble historia del Dr Valmy* (*The Double Story of Dr Valmy*, 1964) whose portrayal of a torturer in the secret police meant that its first performance took place in England, at the Gateway Theatre, Chester in 1968. *Jueces en la noche* (*Judges in the Night*, 1979) deals with the right-wing manipulation of left-wing terror groups. His latest play, *Diálogo secreto* (*Secret Dialogue*, 1984), shows that the playwright has by no means exhausted his ideas, though since the relaxation of censorship he has tended to preach rather than suggest. Though hardly polemical and somewhat uneven, his plays are a courageous and sincere contribution to the sparse Spanish theatre of the Franco era. CL

Bufo The Caribbean, especially Cuban, equivalent of the **sainete**, a popular theatre form that incorporates the types, characters and language typical of lower social classes. *Bufo* also implies a criticism of some aspect of life and is normally presented with the intention of destroying false illusions. After a period of relative disuse, the form has been reincorporated into Cuba's new social theatre. GW

Bugaev, Boris N. see **Bely, Andrei**

Bugaku A formal Japanese court dance, dating from the 7th century, that originated in China. A rarefied art, *bugaku* is performed and taught primarily at the Music Department of the Imperial Household Agency and at large temples and shrines in Kyoto, Osaka, and Nara. Also several times a year public performances are given usually at the National Theatre in Tokyo. *Bugaku* is performed on a square, raised dance floor. Unroofed, its space is demarked visually by a red-lacquered railing on four sides and by a green silk cloth that covers its surface. The stage is often set outdoors, in a garden or over a pond, to enhance the beauty of performance. Performers, divided into 'left' and 'right' groups and performing different items of the repertory, enter between two enormous drums that stand at the rear of the stage. Masks are worn for some roles. Costumes are court dress of the 7th century: elegant silk robes, black hats, white *tabi* covering the feet. No scenery is used. Musicians playing flute

(*ryūteki*, *komabue*, and *hichiriki*), mouth organ (*shō*), gong (*shōko*), drums (*taiko*, *sannoko*, and *kakko*) accompany the dance while seated, often in small pavilions, offstage. There are no singers. The repertory of about 50 dances can be classified into pieces of Chinese or Korean origin; old or new; large, medium, or small cast; or, most commonly, into military or civil pieces, a classification well known in China.

Although performance today has lost almost all dramatic function, reminders of *bugaku*'s previous dramatic content can be seen in the grotesque mask worn by the young king Ranryō who wished to frighten his enemy in battle, in Batō where the dancer is supposedly mounted on a white horse, and in some now extinct pieces that were comic parodies of *gigaku* dances. Associated with the imperial court from its beginnings, the decorous, four-square movements and ethereal music of *bugaku* evoke, to a remarkable extent, the refined elegance of the Japanese court of 1,000 years ago (the dances from which *bugaku* grew have long since died out in China). *Bugaku* performance was structured into an opening (*jo*), a breaking apart (*ha*), and a fast conclusion (*kyū*). This fundamental aesthetic construct was later adopted in **nō** and other forms of Japanese theatre. JRB

Bulgakov, Mikhail Afanasievich (1891– 1940) Russian novelist, short story writer and dramatist who, perceiving post-revolutionary Russia as a spiritual vacuum for the artist-intellectual, attempted to maintain a continued relationship with a civilized past while defining an ethical response to the present. He was uniquely able to embroider mystical, allegorical and parallel historical threads into the fabric of his texts, successfully mixing all manner of literary allusions and styles. The medically trained son of a Kiev theologian, he soon embarked on careers in journalism and literature, the latter including such major narrative works as the story collection *Diaboliad*, the novelette *Heart of a Dog* and the epic and some say best Soviet Civil War novel *White Guard* (all 1925). His adaptation of this novel, *The Days of the Turbins* (1925) commissioned by the **Moscow Art Theatre** (MAT) which premiered it in 1926, realistically depicts the rush of events (1918–19) leading to the destruction and exile of a White officer's family in the author's native Kiev. Its sympathetic portrayal of the White enemy and its downplaying of the constructive role the Red Army played in these events resulted in Bulgakov's being labelled an 'internal émigré'. 'Former people' again are featured in his first major comedy, *Zoika's Apartment* (1926), a 'satiric melodrama' similar to those of the NEP period (e.g., by **Erdman** and **Faiko**), dealing with Khlestakovian deception, financial speculation and petty demonism in a time of severe economic shortages. It played 100 times at the Vakhtangov Theatre and elsewhere in Moscow before being totally banned with Bulgakov's other plays in 1929. *The Crimson Island* (1927), a comedy-allegory written for **Tairov**'s Kamerny Theatre where it ran briefly in 1928, parodies censorship and officially sanctioned drama. *Flight* (1927), his most ambitious play and the first to be banned before it premiered (at MAT), is a hallucinatory epilogue to *The Days of the Turbins*. Via a series of dreams and ever shifting time–space matrices the author creates the surreal experience of White émigrés in confused psychological and moral transit. The play received its Soviet premiere in 1957. Preceding his biography of **Molière** (1933), Bulgakov wrote *A Cabal of Hypocrites* (*Molière*, 1929), a cinematically structured, onstage-backstage retelling of the difficulties experienced by *Tartuffe*'s author in getting his play produced and in reconciling the tensions of his personal and professional lives. The obvious parallels with Bulgakov's own life and work together with **Stanislavsky**'s disapproval of the author's anti-heroic portrayal of this admired artist contributed to the play's difficulties, and it ran for only seven performances. Bulgakov satirized his uneasy tenure at MAT as playwright and as an assistant director (1930–6) in his *Theatrical Novel* (*Black Snow*, 1936). Of the remaining 30-odd plays written by Bulgakov that were not either burned by the author or confiscated by the government, some worth mentioning are: *Last Days* (1935), in which an unseen **Pushkin** is discussed as a victim of the tsarist police state; an apocalyptic science fiction play, *Adam and Eve* (1931); two fantasy-satires on time-travel, *Bliss* (1934) and *Ivan Vasilievich* (1935); his adaptations of *Dead Souls* (1932) and *Don Quixote* (1938); and *Batum* (1938), about the young Stalin. His brilliant novel *The Master and Margarita*, a veritable compendium of topical, literary (especially biblical) and personal themes and styles completed at his death, established him as a true heir to **Gogol**, **Sukhovo-Kobylin** and Dostoevsky. Long a Soviet underground classic, it was finally brought to the stage by **Yury Lyubimov** at Moscow's Taganka Theatre (1977). SG

Bulgaria Despite a scant history that extends back only to the mid-19th century, Bulgarian theatre thrives today on a par with the rest of European theatre.

The beginning of Bulgarian theatre is usually identified with two performances in 1856: (1) the 15 August performance of a Serbian comedy, *Mihal Mishkoed*, in Shumen where Sava Dobroplodni staged his farcical adaptation to a coffee-house audience; (2) the 12 December showing of a German melodrama *Longsuffering Genoveve*, in Lom, staged by Krastu Pishurka in his home before an audience of over 100.

The first Bulgarian theatrical troupe was founded by Dobri Voinikov in 1865 in Braila, Rumania. Its location outside the country reflects the long legacy of Bulgaria's political suppression under Turkish rule and the cultural hegemony of the Greek Church.

From its beginning the theatre in Bulgaria was devoted to two themes: national independence and cultural revival. The oral folklore tradition and the art of recitation, widely used in the schools, were fertile ground for the emerging dramatic form.

Two works stand out from the original plays written prior to the national liberation in 1878: *Ivanko, Assassin of Asen I* (1872), a historical play, by Basil Drumev (1840–1901), author of the first modern Bulgarian novel, and *Civilization Misunderstood* (1871), by D. Voinikov, a comedy satirizing the popular fashion for embracing all things French to the disdain of everything Bulgarian. Both plays retain a currency today that bears occasional performance.

From the arrival of national independence (1878) through the First World War the dominant influence in Bulgarian theatre was poet and novelist Ivan Vasov (1850–1921). Vasov's historical/patriotic plays *Khushove* (1894) and *Under the Yoke* (1910) were adapted from his novels. He also wrote several original plays, among them *Jobchasers* (1903), a colourful comedy ridiculing the widespread careerism of his day.

Two theatre companies, 'Foundation', established in 1888 in Sofia, and 'Tears and Laughter', established in 1892, led to the founding of the Bulgarian National Theatre, which moved into a new building in the heart of Sofia in 1907 and became the centre for theatrical life in the country. A nucleus of talented performers and directors, mostly educated in Europe and Russia, formed under the direction of poet and drama critic P. Slavejkov.

Dramatic literature as an independent form dates from the first two decades of the 20th century. Its founders were Anton Strashimirov (1872–1937), a novelist, Petko Todorov (1879–1916) and poet Peio Yavorov (1878–1914). Strashimirov is best remembered for a drama *Vampire* (1901) and *Mother-in-Law* (1907), a satiric comedy; Yavorov, artistic director of the National Theatre, foreshadowed his own suicide in *In the Foothills of Vitosha* (1911); Todorov invented a ballad-like genre combining mythic folk motifs with realistic characters in his *The Masons* (1902), *The Woodsprite* (1904) and *The Dragon's Wedding* (1911). Influences of the period include **Ibsen**, **Chekhov**, **Strindberg** and **Hauptmann**.

A series of catastrophes struck in the mid 1920s. The National Theatre building was destroyed by fire in 1923; the same year an abortive uprising against the regime led to the black-listing of many theatre professionals. Then, in 1925 an assassination attempt against the Bulgarian Tsar cost the lives of hundreds of intellectuals in the purge that followed.

Among those purged was Geo Milev (1895–1925), an avant-garde modernist poet who, as Director of the National Theatre, stressed highly experimental directorial methods and introduced Bulgarian audiences to the work of German playwright **Ernst Toller**.

A vital resurrection was signalled in 1929 by the opening of a new 1,150-seat modern theatre building. This theatre, standing on the site of the old, offered the most advanced technology of production; renovated in the 1970s it now bears the name of Ivan Vasov.

The dozen-odd years before the Second World War saw a new emphasis on directorial techniques (H. Tzankov, B. Danovski, N. Fol). In 1948 Bulgaria was declared a People's Republic and the theatre reaped the benefit of full state support together with the bane of supervised repertoire. The High Institute for Theatrical Arts (VITIS) offered a diverse curriculum for training actors, directors and dramaturges; specialized theatre companies were created and a film industry was founded.

The torpor of the post-war period gave way to a new vital phase for the theatre in the 1960s. The energy released generated a rebirth of the spirit that had infused the first quarter of the century. G. Ostrovski's 1961–2 productions of *When the Roses Dance*, a musical by V. Petrov, and *Improvisation* by V. Petrov and R. Ralin, both staged in the Theatre of Satire, started a series of innovative productions there. *Sumatoha*, written by Y. Radichkov, directed by M. Andonov, was not only a new kind of dramaturgy but an example of superb ensemble and character acting. In Andonov's revival of *Mihal Mishkoed* the actors were encouraged to improvise freely. The close collaboration of directors and

The US premiere of Yordan Radichkov's *An Attempt at Flying*, Yale Repertory Theatre, 1981.

playwrights shaped the modern drama. Such teams produced *We Are Not Angels* by N. Yordanov (directed by A. Shopov), *The Poet and the Mountain* by I. Teofilov (directed by L. Daniel), *The Prosecutor* by G. Gjagarov (directed by E. Halachev), *Romeo, Juliet and Petroleum* by I. Radoev (directed by A. Shopov), *The Old Man and the Arrow* by N. Russev (directed by M. Andonov).

In the 1970s and 80s Bulgarian drama showed its appeal before Western audiences. Director Andonov screened his feature film *The Goat's Horn*, scripted by playwright N. Haytov, at the 1972 Chicago Film Festival where it won the Golden Hugo; in 1981 M. Kisselov, a student of Andonov, staged a production of Radichkov's *An Attempt at Flying* at the Yale Repertory Theatre in New Haven, Conn., after staging it at the National Theatre in Sofia. *Official Status: Batman*, adapted from a short story by playwright G. P. Stamatov, directed by K. Kolarov, won the Golden Ear of Wheat at the 1980 Feature Film Festival in Valladolid, Spain.

Today Bulgaria has 56 repertory theatres spread around the country, against a pre-war maximum of 13. Bulgarian National Television has, from its beginning in 1958, featured a weekly TV drama series which has drawn from the best theatre professionals for its players, directors and playwrights. Bulgaria is a member of ITI. BL

See: B. Penev, *History of Bulgarian Literature*, Vol. I, II, III, 1933; *Bulgarian Encyclopaedia*, 1936; G. Konstantinov, *New Bulgarian Literature*, 1943; L. Tenev, 'Dramaturgy and Reality', *Literaturen Front*, 7 May 1981, p. 6; *Modern Bulgaria*, Sofia Press, 1981.

Bull-baiting see Baiting

Bullins, Ed (1935–) Afro-American playwright who began writing fiction but, seeing Baraka's plays on stage, felt drama was more effective in reaching black audiences. Since 1965 Bullins has written several dozen plays and is produced internationally. In 1967 he joined the New Lafayette Theatre as resident playwright, became its associate director, and edited its periodical *Black Theatre*. Among his best known plays are *Goin' a Buffalo* (1966), *In the Wine Time* (1968), *The Duplex*

(1970), *In New England Winter* (1971), and *The Fabulous Miss Marie* (1971). Bullins's experiments in form combine rhythmic, racy dialogue, black ritual, jazz and blues music as integral elements of his dramaturgy. His work has won several awards including the New York Drama Critics Circle award for *The Taking of Miss Janie* (1975). EGH

Buloff, Joseph (1899–) Gifted Yiddish theatre actor and director first with the **Vilna Troupe** where he distinguished himself in the title role of **Ossip Dimov**'s *Yoshke Musikant*, then in America where he acted with **Maurice Schwartz**'s **Yiddish Art Theatre** and directed for the **Folksbühne** etc., latterly forming the New York Art Theatre in 1934/5. He eventually moved to English-speaking roles on Broadway and was active in Israel during the 50s and 60s. AB

Bulwer, Edward (1803–73) English novelist, playwright and politician, who changed his name to Bulwer-Lytton on inheriting Knebworth House from his mother Elizabeth Lytton and was created Baron Lytton of Knebworth in 1866. Richly talented and damagingly vain, Bulwer found himself suddenly needy when his parents opposed his disastrous marriage, and he wrote to earn money. Already famous as the author of *Eugene Aram* (1832), a fashionable 'Newgate novel', and *The Last Days of Pompeii* (1834) when he wrote his first plays, Bulwer was also a far-sighted agitator for theatrical reform. As a member of parliament, he had led a Select Committee of Inquiry into the state of the theatre in 1832. The Committee's three aims were impeccable – to protect playwrights by establishing an effective copyright law, to investigate the propriety of the Patent Theatres' monopoly over legitimate drama and to challenge the Lord Chamberlain's role as dramatic censor. (The first was a limited success, the second bore fruit 11 years later and the third faded into obscurity.) Bulwer's perceptive analysis of contemporary theatre can be read in Book IV of his acute social survey, *England and the English* (1833). The best of his plays were solicited and performed by **Macready**. They are *The Duchess de la Vallière* (1837), a Gothic drama in verse, *The Lady of Lyons* (1838), a drama of mixed verse and prose which remained a favourite of audiences throughout the 19th century, *Richelieu* (1839), a polished verse drama which provided **Irving** as well as Macready with a major role, and the prose comedy, *Money* (1840), which offers a particularly sharp commentary on contemporary values. It was revived by the **Royal Shakespeare Company** in 1982. PT

Bunn, Alfred (1798–1860) English theatre manager whose scuffle with **Macready** (Macready punched him in the eye and Bunn bit Macready's finger) has earned him a partly merited notoriety. Bunn was appointed stage manager at **Drury Lane** by **Elliston**, whose view that there was nothing so special about the proud Patent Theatres he inherited. His simultaneous management of Drury Lane and **Covent Garden** (1833–5) gave him a unique opportunity to test his views, but his singular tactlessness aroused such vigorous opposition that he was never able to pursue a consistent policy, and by 1840 he was bankrupt. *The Stage: Both Before and Behind the Curtain* (1840) is an argumentative and by no means negligible self-justification in three volumes. Bunn, who was mockingly nicknamed 'Poet' Bunn in response to his published verse, loved comic opera more than he loved plays. He wrote several librettos, including one for Balfe's popular *The Bohemian Girl* (1843). PT

Bunraku The commercial doll-puppet theatre of Osaka, Japan. The name *bunraku* is relatively recent and derives from the 19th-century theatre manager, Uemura Bunrakuen (or Bunrakuken), who staged puppet plays at shrines and professional theatres in Osaka. His troupe was the only group of professionals to continue into the Meiji period (1868–1912), hence the association of the name with the genre. More formally, a chanted puppet performance is called *jōruri*, after the generic style of narrative music, or *ayatsuri* (puppetry) *jōruri* or, more rarely, *ningyō shibai* (puppet play).

Long before puppetry was joined to *jōruri* narrative chanting and *shamisen* music in the 1590s, narrative story-telling was widely practised in Japan. In *bunraku* chanting continues as the dominant performance element. The chanter has precedence in ranking (during the feudal era, only he was allowed to own property or live outside the entertainment district). Numerous styles of chanting were in competition in the early 17th century. In Edo (Tokyo), a bombastic chanting style, *kimpiri jōruri*, was joined to a violent style of puppet manipulation by Satsuma Jōun (1593–1672) and others. It is said the **kabuki** bravura acting style (*aragoto*) was in part inspired by puppeteer Izumi Dayū, a *kimpira* puppeteer who decapitated puppets with an iron bar in knockabout battle scenes. In Kyoto in 1614 the Emperor Go-Yōzei attended a puppet performance of the Buddhist miracle play, *The Chest-Splitting of Amida Buddha*. Episodes from the medieval epic, *The Tale of the Heike*, were fashioned into moving narratives that were accompanied by increasingly sophisticated *shamisen* melodies. Until 1629 there were female chanters of considerable popularity; they were banned from public stages in that year by the same prohibition that banned *kabuki* actresses.

Three professional puppet theatres were operating in Edo in 1652 (as well as four large and eight small *kabuki* theatres). Following the Great Edo Fire of 1657, most puppet troupes moved to Osaka. Since that time Osaka and neighbouring Awaji Island have been the undisputed centre of puppet theatre in Japan. In 1686 an obscure *jōruri* chanter Takemoto Gidayū (1651–1714) collaborated with the highly regarded Puppet Theatre in Osaka's entertainment district. Gidayū's beautiful melodies and powerful chanting style soon eclipsed all others and he became regarded as the greatest chanter of his time. His style became standard and today the common name for *bunraku* music is *gidayū* (or *takemoto* when played and sung in *kabuki*). Chikamatsu wrote both history (*jidai*) and domestic (*sewa*) plays. A history play was the major work on a programme. It was written in five acts, each act divided into two or three scenes, usually titled opening (*kuchi*), middle (*naka*), and conclusion (*kiri*). Chikamatsu's history play *The Battles of Coxinga* (1715) follows this form. The half-Japanese Coxinga invades China in order to dethrone a usurping emperor, which he does with the help of a tiger mount, miracles, and advice from Taoist Immor-

tals. In the concluding scene of act three (*san dan no kiri*) Coxinga's mother and sister sacrifice their lives to maintain his honour. The other four acts conclude in pitched battles. A domestic play, like Chikamatsu's *Love Suicides at Sonezaki* (1703) – in one act and three scenes – was a short afterpiece. Chikamatsu wrote narrative passages of great beauty and he created puppet characters of flesh and blood who wrestled with the same conflicts between feudal duty (*giri*) and human love and affection (*ninjō*) that his audience faced in life. Takeda Izumo I (d. 1747) and II (1691–1756), and other playwrights of the mid-18th century worked within these same dramatic forms, but they relied less on descriptive narrative and more on first-person dialogue. The realistic puppets created in the same years, up to around 1750, were capable of a wide range of visual expression. Puppeteers who first performed *The Treasury of Loyal Retainers* (1748) at the Takemoto Puppet Theatre in Osaka copied the movements of the *kabuki* actor Sawamura Chōjūrō III (1685–1756), who had had an enormous success the previous year in a *kabuki* play *The Forty-Seven Great Arrows* on the same topic of the vendetta of the 47 samurai.

In performance a different chanter (*tayū*) comes before the audience to speak and sing each succeeding scene (a programme lasted nine to twelve hours). Veteran chanters take act-concluding scenes (*kiri*), which are the most complex dramatically and musically, while younger chanters are given introductory, less important scenes. The poetic travel scenes (*michiyuki*) of domestic plays have always been reserved for high-ranking chanters. In certain scenes, such as the Ichiriki Brothel Scene in *The Treasury of Loyal Retainers*, multiple chanters take the voices of specific characters, as if they were actors. Chanters memorize the text which is written out in the form of a novel, rather than a play. Using a highly developed vocal repertory, the chanter distinguishes in the first place between spoken prose (*kotoba*) dialogue of puppet characters and poetic descriptions in which the voice moves back and forth between melodic song (*ji, jiai*, or *fushi*) and chant (*ji iro*). The latter occupies a middle ground between speech and song. In the second place, the chanter shows the full gamut of human emotions vocally: wailing in suffering, rhythmic laughing in joy, a tirade of anger, gentle tones of love. Chanting is a tour de force.

There are about 50 types of puppet heads matching a wide variety of character types; in a long play as many as five heads may be used for one character to show changes in emotion. Heads are carved of paulownia wood, hollowed to hold the mechanisms for moving eyes, eyebrows, and mouth, and painted in realistic detail. Fingers may be joined so the hand can open wide and close in a fist. Puppets of vigorous male characters have the most movable parts. A puppet is brought to life by the coordinated actions of three puppeteers, who surround, hold and move the puppet close to their bodies. The chief puppeteer (*omo zukai*) controls a puppet's head and body (with his left hand) and right arm (with his right hand). The second puppeteer (*hidari zukai*, left puppeteer) controls the left arm. The third puppeteer (*ashi zukai*, foot puppeteer) moves the feet. The puppet moves to the cadence of chanting and the rhythm of the *shamisen*. Puppeteers identify two types of movements: slightly stylized reproductions of human actions and emotions (*furi*, mime) and displays of technique that emphasize the beauty of line and form (*kata*, form). The former include actions such as sewing, smoking, walking or weeping and are as various as human life. The latter include standard displays of technical virtuosity, such as the one-hand pose of a female puppet looking over its shoulder (*ushiroburi*), intended to be gracefully beautiful. Both types of action are exaggerated beyond that of human life. Perhaps because inanimate figures of wood and cloth require extra energy to bring them alive, one's general impression of the puppets is that they seem remarkably life-like (while a living *kabuki* actor may seem unreal). JRB

Buontalenti, Bernardo (1536–1608) Italian architect and scenic designer. In 1547 he began service to the Medici court assisting designer and architect **Giorgio Vasari**. In addition to designing palaces, villas and fortresses, he organized firework displays and designed costumes and machinery for transformation scenes in festivals directed by Vasari (1565) and Lanci (1569). By 1574 he had succeeded Vasari as architect and supervisor of Florentine court entertainments. In honour of the marriage between Virginia de' Medici and Cesare d'Este (1585), he designed the Teatro degli Uffizi with a system of revolving *periaktoi* and elaborate stage machinery. His decors were used for Giovanni Bardi's *L'Amico Fido* and the accompanying six intermezzi written for the occasion. Another further achievement was direction of the month-long festivities honouring the marriage of Ferdinand I of Tuscany to Catherine de' Medici (1589). In addition to the animal hunts, masquerades, and *naumachia* on the Arno which he supervised for the occasion, he designed the production of Girolami Bargagli's *La Pellegrina* and its six intermezzi. Characteristic of his style, these elaborate and sumptuous productions were noted for the ingenious cloud machines, glories, traps, revolving *periaktoi* and moving side wings which facilitated the almost magical scene changes taking place in full view of the spectators. AJN

Burbage, James (*c.* 1530–97) English actor and tradesman, remembered and the builder of the first English theatre. Trained as a joiner, Burbage probably turned actor in middle life and is known to have been a leading member of **Leicester's Men** by 1572. Perceiving the spread of interest in plays, he borrowed money from his brother-in-law to finance the erection of the **Theatre** on the estate of the dissolved Holywell Priory. The Theatre opened in 1576 and for the rest of his life Burbage seems to have devoted himself to theatre management. Conscious that his lease would expire in 1597, he purchased and converted a large room in the old Blackfriars monastery in 1596, but his plans were frustrated by the opposition of Blackfriars residents. He died with the situation unresolved, leaving the Theatre and its problems to his elder son, Cuthbert, and the **Blackfriars** and its problems to his younger son, **Richard** (see **England**). PT

Burbage, Richard (*c.* 1569–1619) English actor, who, as the leading member of the **Lord Chamberlain's**/King's **Men** from 1594 until his death, created many of **Shakespeare**'s greatest roles. As the

son of **James Burbage**, he was involved in theatre management from an early age. His name is first encountered in a lawsuit of 1590, when, in defiance of a court order, he physically resisted the attempts of his father's business-partners to collect a share of the takings at the **Theatre**. The impression that Richard Burbage was strong and sturdily built is confirmed by a surviving portrait in the Dulwich library. Whether or not this is a self-portrait, Burbage is known to have been a talented painter as well as an actor. He was engaged for the important job of scene-painting at the Earl of Rutland's tilts in 1613 and 1616, and these are unlikely to be isolated occasions. In 1594, when **Strange's Men**, to which he belonged, either dissolved or moved out of London, Burbage remained in the capital as a founder-member of the new company, the Lord Chamberlain's Men, resident at the Theatre. Over the next two decades, he is known to have played Hamlet, Othello, Lear and Richard III, Ferdinand in **Webster**'s *The Duchess of Malfi*, Malevole in **Marston**'s *The Malcontent* and 'Jeronimo', probably in a lost play opportunistically exploiting the success of **Kyd**'s *The Spanish Tragedy*. Contemporaries, comparing him perhaps with **Edward Alleyn**, considered his acting true to life, though he was certainly faithful also to rhetorical conventions. With his brother Cuthbert, he owned half the shares in the **Globe** and, later, the **Blackfriars**, and he must be accounted, in the company's sharing system, *primus inter pares*. PT

Bürgerliches Trauerspiel ('Bourgeois Tragedy'). A genre that arose in the German theatre during the latter half of the 18th century, partially as a result of the introduction of English plays into the repertoire, partially due to the rise in economic power of the bourgeoisie. It is a tragedy set neither in princely or noble courts nor in a heroic period of history, but in the home of the bourgeoisie, who are regarded as serious subject matter for drama. The first significant examples of the genre are **Lessing**'s *Miss Sara Sampson* (1755), written under the influence of the English writers **George Lillo** and Samuel Richardson, and *Emilia Galotti* (1772). **Schiller** described his *Love and Intrigue* (1783) as a *bürgerliches Trauerspiel*. The genre is universally recognized as foreshadowing the work of **Henrik Ibsen**, **Gerhart Hauptmann**, and other late 19th-century naturalist dramatists. SW

Burgtheater Viennese theatre, founded in 1741 as the court theatre of the Habsburgs. In 1776, the Emperor Josef II declared it to be a national theatre; in so doing, Josef was influenced partially by the ideas of **Josef von Sonnenfels** on the educative potential of the theatre. Under the aegis of actors such as Stephanie the Elder (1773–98), J. H. F. Müller (1738–1815), **Brockmann**, and **Schröder**, the Burgtheater developed a style of acting noted for its moderation and evenness of expression among the whole ensemble. In the 19th century, under the directorship first of **Josef Schreyvogel**, then of **Heinrich Laube**, this style became widely admired and imitated throughout the German-speaking world. Among the greatest actors who perfected the Burgtheater style were Heinrich Anschütz (1785–1865), famous for his moving Lear, Bernhard Baumeister (1828–1917), a magnificently robust actor, Josef Lewinsky (1835–1907), a masterly player of villains, **Sophie Schröder**, Charlotte Wolter (1834–97), a great tragedienne, and Adolf von Sonnenthal (1834–1909), whose gracious bearing both on and off stage established him in the eyes of the public as the epitome of the Burgtheater. In 1888, the company moved from their intimate theatre in the Hofburg to a palatial construction on the Franzen-Ring. This threatened their traditional style of ensemble, but through the direction of Max Burckhard (1854–1912), then Intendant of the Burgtheater, and the acting first of **Mitterwurzer**, then of **Kainz**, this difficult period of transition passed without the company declining. The Burgtheater is still the preeminent theatre of the German-speaking world and continues to practise, in modified form, the ideals of acting developed during the 18th and 19th centuries. sw

Burian, Emil František (1904–59) Czech avant-garde theatre artist, began his career in the 1920s as composer, musician and actor. Concurrently he developed Voiceband, a synthesis of music and syncopated choral recitation. In 1933 Burian established his own theatre collective, D34 (the number changed annually to indicate the current season). There, his early work contained elements of **Piscator**-like agit-prop, but his most successful productions combined his musical talents more artistically with his heightened political concerns. Burian often created his own poetic scenarios, most strikingly in *War* (1935), a moving antimilitary work of village life. An auteur of the stage, he tended to regard every text as a libretto, for which he would be editor, composer, orchestrator, and conductor. Although he produced in very small spaces, he achieved sophisticated technical effects; e.g., Theatergraph, in 1935, a system that blended cinema projections with live action in poetic ways and thus anticipated the Czech **Laterna Magika** of the 1950s. JMB

Burk, John Daly (c. 1776–1808) American playwright. Burk is known for his patriotic spectacle, *Bunker-Hill, or The Death of General Warren* (Boston, February 1797; New York, September 1797) and for his detailed account of the primitive staging: 'Our twelve-minute battle . . . Charlestown on fire and Warren animating the Americans amidst the smoak [*sic*] and confusion produce an effect scarce credible'. For twenty years *Bunker-Hill* became the American theatre's standard offering for the Fourth of July and for Evacuation Day (25 November).

Burk was expelled from Dublin's Trinity College, came to Boston in 1796, and in 1808 was killed in a duel. He edited two newspapers, practised law, wrote six other plays – *Female Patriotism, or The Death of Joan of Arc* (1798) the best known – and a *History of Virginia* and a *History of the Late-War in Ireland* (1799). RM

Burlesque Burlesque, parody, and satire are often treated as synonyms for ridicule through distortion, but it is useful to suggest distinctions between them. None of the three words refers exclusively to drama; yet all have been applied to drama. Burlesque as derisive imitation enters the English language in the 17th century, *after* such signal achievements as the Pyramus and Thisbe scene in **Shakespeare**'s *Midsummer Night's Dream* and the mockery of romance in

Beaumont and **Fletcher**'s *Knight of the Burning Pestle*. In general, burlesque tends to be broader than parody, mocking a style, class, or genre. 17th-century France and 18th-century England showed a marked taste for burlesque, and plays of that genre were standard fare in the 19th-century theatres of most European countries. 20th-century burlesque survives in skits and reviews, but **Tom Stoppard**'s *Travesties* is a rare example of a full-length burlesque. RC

Burlesque show, American A raucous and bawdy style of variety performance, partly inspired by **Lydia Thompson** and her British blondes, partly by blackface minstrelsy and 'leg shows' like *The Black Crook*. The manager Michael B. Leavitt is credited with its invention by creating Mme Rentz's Female Minstrels (Rentz from a popular circus), later the Rentz–Santley troupe (after Mabel Santley, its star). One of its earliest personalities was May Howard who ran her own company in the 1880s. It rapidly developed a tripartite structure: in the first third, dance and song rendered by a female company was intermingled with low comedy from male comedians; part two was an olio of specialities in which the women did not appear; and part three comprised a grand finale. 'Clean' versions of these preponderantly female productions were widely sponsored by the Miner family. Sam T. Jack, who opened the first exclusively burlesque theatre in Chicago, pioneered 'dirty' burlesque or 'turkey show', which was especially popular in the Western 'honky-tonks'. The Empire and Mutual Circuits or Wheels revelled in such maculose entertainment, while the Columbia Circuit booked only clean shows, until 1925 when it too was forced by dwindling receipts to go dirty.

Leading entrepreneurs were the Minsky brothers: Abe who brought belly dancers (known as 'cootchers') and the illuminated runway from Paris; the publicists Billy and Morton; and Herbert who introduced opera. From the early 1900s to 1935, they moulded the image of American burlesque, at the Republic Theatre and the National Winter Garden, New York. By present-day standards, the offerings were tame, for the girls never disrobed completely. But the blatant *double entendres* in the dialogue between straight man and 'talking woman', and runway interplay between strippers and audience enraged moralists. The strip-tease which achieved extraordinary invention and daring entered burlesque in 1921 with 'Curls' Mason, and Carrie Finnell performed the first tassel dance, twirling the fringe from her nipples; the most memorable personalities among the strippers were Millie De Leon, the urbane **Gypsy Rose Lee** (a protégée of the gangster Waxy Gordon) and the indestructible Anne Corio. Among the comedians nurtured by the form were Sliding Billy Watson, Billy 'Beef Trust' Watson, Al Shean, **Willie Howard**, Phil Silvers, Abbott and Costello, and Jackie Gleason, while routines like 'Floogle Street' became classics.

Changing times brought about an end to classic burlesque. New York courts banned the runway in 1934 and all burlesque in 1942, and the Burlesque Artists Association had its charter revoked in 1957. Gogo dancing, the Las Vegas-style revue and television siphoned off the remaining talents, and revivals, like Corio's widely toured *This Was Burlesque*, tend to be

May Howard (Havill), Canadian-born burlesque performer, who became star of her own company and by 1897 was the first 'burlesque queen'. This portrait first appeared in the New York *Police Gazette*.

steeped in nostalgia. It has inspired **Arthur Hopkins**'s play *Burlesque* (1927), Ralph Allen's musical *Sugar Babies* (1979), and feminist dramas that stress the exploitation of the stripper as commodity. LS

> See: M. Minsky, *Minsky's Burlesque*, New York, 1986; B. Sobel, *Burleycue*, New York, 1931; I. Zeidman, *The American Burlesque Show*, New York, 1967.

Burma This South-East Asian country borders on India, Bangladesh, China, Laos and Thailand; the country is 600 miles by 800 miles in its major land area with a thin strip running another 500 miles down the Malay peninsula. The population numbers approximately 37 million and is composed of hill people and lowlanders. Though music and dance are important among the hill groups, drama is historically a development of the lowland areas where the Burmese predominate. The Burmese speak a Tibeto-Burman language and adopted cultural patterns from the ethnically related Pyu and Mon people who established themselves in the area prior to Burmese migration from Tibet. From the Pyu they learned Theraveda Buddhism which, mixed with animist elements, has been a belief system which has contributed to performance practice, in terms of aesthetics, performance occasions, and plot patterns. The recorded history of the Burmese begins with the founding of the kingdom of Pagan in the 11th century.

Though Indian, Chinese and Tibetan influences are evident in the music and repertoire, general South-East Asian features such as the assertion that human performance is modelled on the puppet theatre, the function of the clown, set character types of refined hero clashing with ogrely villains, and the dramatic structure that moves from court to the wilderness underlie the performance. Written records are rare, since theatrical practice is passed orally from teacher to student in training and performance. Four categories can be distinguished: (1) animistic performance, (2) Buddhist theatre, (3) court dance drama, and (4) popular performance.

Animistic performance Until the late 1700s, dance and music, especially in the context of animist performance, seem more significant for human performers than drama. Traditionally Burmese believe in spirits, called *nats*, which include spirits of heroes, ancestors, place spirits, criminals, etc. Throughout Burma 37 major *nats* are honoured, and female spirit-mediums (*nat kadaw*, 'spirit wives') enter trance to manifest them during spirit festivals or in private seances for divination. Set songs are used to summon specific spirits; female mediums dance till possessed, then speak in the voice of the possessing spirit. Male mediums, relatively rare before recent years, are transvestites. Shamanic patterns of sickness accompanying the call to the medium role are the norm.

The jerky movements of the ecstatic *nat* dances have probably contributed to the percussive nature of Burmese non-trance, theatrical dance. The persistence of this aesthetic in the area is attested by the poem of a T'ang dynasty official who saw dancing of Pyu performers at the court of the Chinese emperor in AD 802. The twirls and leaps, the crowns and gongs described would be appropriate to a contemporary performance. Trance performances may have established the aesthetic, and *nat pwe* (spirit shows) may have been the first format for drama activities, for legend claims that in the 1400s two outcast princes became the first secular performers, by emulating such seances of these female mediums.

Contemporary performances which relate to trance traditions include *nat pwe*, and *anyein pwe*. For the former, a group of mediums dress in theatrical garb: the chief medium in the costume of a prince, a junior medium in a princess's costume. These are, of course, the main types of theatrical performances too. *Anyein pwe*, which features a female singer-dancer in conjunction with a pair of clowns who perform while she rests, or engage her in repartee, may be a secularization of the female trance tradition. The structure and status of performance may also relate to *nat* dancing: the opening piece of all traditional drama is a *nat* dance, executed by a female performer. The low status traditionally accorded to actors may result from this association: *nat* mediums hold a devalued position in the Buddhist society.

Buddhist theatre Some Burmese scholars hold that the first dramas presented were of *jataka* stories, i.e. tales presenting prior lives of the Buddha. By being reconceived as stories of incarnations of the historical Buddha, plots and tales from older and indigenous sources were reincorporated into this tradition as well. Religious plays on *jataka* themes called *nibhatkhin* were presented by villagers on cart stages which stopped in various parts of the town to enact episodes using dialogue and action. Aside from *nat pwe*, these were probably the main dramatic presentations in the period prior to 1752. Stories were derived from *hawsa*, the story-telling tradition of Burma, in which a reciter told *jataka* tales, changing voices and gestures for the different characters. When enacted as *nibhatkhin*, scenes included a clown character (*lubyet*) who served the prince and added satirical comment. Like all South-East Asian clowns, the *lubyet* of today is free to break the story frame as he improvises freely on any topic. Though he may have come to the *nibhatkhin* from earlier genres, he became ensconced in the Buddhist theatre and associated with the *jataka* tradition. Because *jataka* were important themes, classical drama as a whole was called *zat pwe* (literally, '*jataka* show') and the name would be retained even after the repertoire widened to include historical episodes and legends. The *lyubet* character was to become a staple of the theatre.

Tradition relates that the puppet show (*yokthe pwe*) became the first non-devotional format for the presentation of *jataka*, and the repertoire and movements of the marionettes were later emulated by the human dancers. Puppet performance of *jataka* was common in the reign of King Bowpaya (1782–1819) when a court minister assigned to oversee theatrical activities gave the form considerable support. Some scholars think the form may only have been developed in this era, under the influence of Siamese puppeteers. But the use of marionettes rather than the shadow figures like the Thai *nang yai* puppet theatre and distinctive pre-play scenes peculiar to the Burmese puppet theatre may be evidence that supports the Burmese oral tradition which says the puppet form was already old.

Only a few *yokthe pwe* companies operate in contemporary Burma, but their practice is believed to reflect an old tradition. The puppets range from a little over two to three feet in height, and hidden manipulators operate them on a raised platform stage about 20 feet in length. The performance opens with the symbolic destruction/ recreation of the world; a *nat* votaress (*apyodaw*) then dances – reports of 60 strings on this most complex of puppets are available; then, animals battle; ogres battle; and an alchemist (*zawgyi*) appears. After these standard preliminaries, the play, which will be based on *jataka* or legendary themes, begins. Plots customarily begin in a court and move to the forest where ogres and spirits threaten the princely hero and the princess heroine. The action often ends with the hero's withdrawal to be a hermit, a sign of the Buddhist orientation of plot patterns, according to A. L. Becker. Further research is needed to establish how the opening sequence relates to the ritual openings of other South-East Asian theatres: the destruction/recreation scene may be related to the dance of the tree puppet in the Balinese *wayang parwa* (shadow theatre) performance, for it has a similar explanation, and the animal battles might be related to the battling monkeys in the Thai shadow puppet tradition (*nang yai*).

To summarize the traditional background of Burmese performance, it flourished in *nat* worship and festivals; patterns of music and dance and a pool of performers may have emerged in this context. The *jatakas* of Buddhism provided the plots for the puppet theatre and eventually actors emulated the puppets.

The refined female and male roles, the princess and the hero, performed by members of the Burmese National Theatre.

Court dance drama The human dance drama only seems to have emerged under Thai influence. The capture of the Siamese capital of Ayutthya in 1767 by King Hsinbyushin's troops and the subsequent carrying of the Siamese court dancers and musicians into exile is considered by some scholars the major impetus in the development of the indigenous Burmese theatre. A ready-made model of performance was available to Burmese artists who, over time, reworked the Siamese material into a distinct Burmese theatre, modifying the dance style, the instrumentation, and plot materials. It seems likely that the relatively high status of these captured performers as compared to *nat* dancers, and the sudden increase in court support of the arts helped raise the status of performance and performers as a whole.

The Thai female group dances probably became the basis for the *yein*, Burmese female court dance. The Thai mask dance *khon* with its Ramayana repertoire became the model for the Burmese court mask dance. The acceptance of this Vishnavite religious epic was facilitated by considering the hero Rama (Yama in Burma) as a previous incarnation of the Buddha. As in Thai court performance, professional dancers and courtiers soon mingled in the cast, ornate costumes and crown-like headdresses adorned the performers who mimed the actions as narrators and chorus sang the text to musical accompaniment. This court performance was called a *zat*.

Soon more than Ramayana texts were available: a minister, Myawaddi, created a version of the Panji story called *Inaung* which, like its Thai model, dwells on the amorous exploits of that Indonesian prince. Later court dramas written by U Kyin U (?–1853) and U Pon Nya (1807–66) are the most notable achievements of court literary activity. Their plots abound in political intrigue, murder, and betrayal. The Buddhist mistrust of worldly things, the murderous struggle for power that characterizes Burmese history, and the malaise in the wake of the first Anglo-Burman war in 1823 combined to create a dark world-view.

Three plays of U Kyin U, each of which takes its name from the hero, remain: *Mahaw*, *Dewagonban*, and *Papahein*. *Papahein*, which explores the intricacies of royal succession, is representative in its concerns. A junior queen has been promised by the king that her son will succeed to the throne. The unruly disposition of the designated heir, Papahein, causes his father to select his older brother over him. Papahein is first condemned to be a labourer and then exiled. Raising an army he marches on his brothers and kills his younger sibling. The righteous eldest brother mourns this death, and when the younger brother is resurrected by an alchemist, the two righteous princes retire from the world to become hermits.

U Pon Nya was a poet whose involvement in court intrigues ended with his execution in 1866. His plays, which again take their titles from the name or occupation of the hero, include *Pauduma*, *The Water Seller*, *Wizaya*, *Kanthala*, and *Waythandaya*. *The Water Seller* tells of a ruler who is impressed by the integrity of a poor water seller and makes him crown prince. The water seller is tempted to kill the king to gain the throne, but confesses these wicked thoughts to the monarch. The king, impressed, offers to abdicate, but the water seller opts to become the hermit himself and withdraws to the forest.

Popular performance As court support waned due to British control in the 1800s, the new dance drama took to the villages. To the present, the *zat pwe* (classical dance drama on *jataka* or historical themes) remains the major offering on a typical theatre programme. The characters of prince, princess, clown and ogre/villain became and remain the staple character types of the performance. But modern troupes have also found that their audiences hunger for *pya zat* modern stories that take contemporary events and common characters for their theme. So such plays have also entered the repertoire.

The foundations of modern theatre practice were laid by performers like Po Sein (1882–1952), who rejected the traditional, ground level dancing circle of earlier dance drama for a raised stage modelled on the puppet platform. He incorporated new Western-influenced techniques in lighting, scenery, and story; and his skill as a dancer and ability to keep one innovation ahead of his audience made him a theatrical legend. The troupe system currently in operation throughout Burma was created in his period. Troupes include 50–150 performers under the direction of the leading performer, who plays the refined male lead. The writer, who generates scripts, and the chief musician, who writes the musical accompaniment, are the other major figures.

Major troupes of the late 1970s and early 1980s included Golden Mandalay Troupe (Shwe-Man-tha-bin) led by Bo Win, noted for his romantic performances; Golden Mandalay (Shwe-Man) led by Kyaw Aung and Capital (Myo-daw) directed by Thein-Aung – both popular for their modern plays; while The Great Sein Troupe (Sein-Maha-tha-bin) carries on the tradition of excellence begun by Po Sein. Each town will

have a troupe, and large cities two or three. All troupes tour at least the surrounding countryside, and major groups tour nationally.

To understand current practice, one must consider the current training system and comprehend the requirements of a typical performance programme. Performers traditionally were trained in the troupes, but since independence Burma's Governmental Department of Performing Arts has founded two training schools at Rangoon and Mandalay, with programmes that last from six months to three years. These schools provide the seedbed for privately owned troupes, though a few performers may be selected as members of the two troupes supported by the Government or as teachers for these arts academies.

Performers need this sound training in music, dance, and traditional literature to carry out a performance. Preliminaries begin at 9 pm and the programme continues until dawn in the thatched enclosure built for the occasion – only in major cities are there permanent structures or actual enclosed theatres to utilize. Audience members bring rugs to lay on the mats inside, and space which may seat 700 will often be full for the seven nights that a troupe may stay in the area. Viewers may eat or nap during parts of the performance, attending to only those that particularly suit their interests. Different parts of the programme contain different admixtures of song, dance, comic patter, and dramatic episodes in modern and classical style.

The programme begins with the solo *nat* dance, followed by an *opaya* (opera) which is usually a *jataka* tale using classical music sung in a modern mode. This is followed by the *pya zat*, written by the troupe playwright, which generally takes contemporary life as its theme. Plots may, for example, deal with the dangers of modernization, and guitar-playing, liquor-drinking young people learn the error of their ways. Next comes the *thay-tha-yot-hpaw*, which literally means 'the performance to display the song'. This piece lasts about 30 minutes as actors mime the story of a song written by the chief musician as musicians sing. Finally comes the featured *zat*, the play in classical dance style. *Jataka*, historical, or mythical materials will be dealt with in this story, but the writer may take liberties to make the material significant to his audience. A plot, for example, may deal with the efforts of three Shan princes to win over the Mongols, a reference to the current need for unity against insurgents.

The major roles remain constant: heroes, princesses, clowns and ogres or villains. Long sequences of song and dance by the major characters, or comic improvisation by the clowns may disrupt the flow of dramatic events. These seeming interludes may have more to do with the original impulse and continued theatrical need of performers and audiences of Burma. Dance, song, and clowning have more seniority than drama.

The traditional orchestra, *hsaing waing*, consists of a drum chime of 21 tuned drums in a circular frame (*pat waing*), a gong chime of 21 gongs in a circular frame (*kyi waing*), 18 or 19 horizontal knobbed gongs on a five-row frame (*maung zaing*), an oboe with a conical body (*hne*), a set of six drums (*chauk-lon-bat*), a stick beaten slit drum (*byauk*), a clapper (*walet khok*), hand cymbals (*si*), and a large knobbed hanging gong (*maung*). Musicians play the traditional tunes appropriate to the type of scene enacted – a hero meditating in the forest would require one tune and audience scenes would need another song. Audiences are aware of nuances of the song choice. The music, the visual impact of the character type presented highlighted by the elaborate classical dance costume, and the stylization of the dance appropriate to that character combine to evoke the spirit that lies behind Burmese drama. KF

> *See:* M. H. Aung, *Burmese drama*, London, 1957 and *A History of Burma*, New York, 1967; A. L. Becker, 'Journey Through the Night: Some Reflections on Burmese Traditional Theatre', in *Traditional Drama and Music of Southeast Asia*, ed. M. Osman, Kuala Lumpur, 1974; J. Becker, 'Instrumental Ensembles', and '20th Century Practice', in 'Burma', *New Grove Dictionary of Music and Musicians*, New York, 1980; J. Brandon, *Theatre in Southeast Asia*, Cambridge, Mass., 1967; J. G. Scott (Schway Yoe), *The Burman, His Life and Notions*, 1895, repr. New York, 1963; K. Sein and J. Withey, *The Great Po Sein*, Bloomington, 1965; J. Withey, 'Burma' in *Readers' Encyclopedia of the Drama*, ed. J. Gassner and G. Quinn, New York, 1969, 96–103.

Burns, George (Nathan Birnbaum) (1896–) and **Gracie Allen (Grace Ethel Cecile Rosalie Allen)** (1895–1964) Burns and Allen was the paradigm of American male–female doubles acts, his wry underplaying setting in relief her staccato dizziness. Burns had been a trick roller-skater, dance teacher and song-and-dance man in vaudeville; Allen entered show business as a child in an Irish sisters act. They teamed up in 1923 and married in 1926, Burns playing the quizzical staight-man to her Dumb Dora. 'Lamb Chops', one version of their cross-talk act, was signed to a six-year contract in the Keith theatres (1926–32). They had their own radio show (1932–49) and moved successfully to television. After Allen's retirement in 1958, Burns, wielding his omnipresent cigar, continued to perform, a high point being his Carnegie Hall recital in 1976. LS

Burrakatha (India) *Burrakatha* is a popular form of theatrical entertainment, especially in the rural areas of the state of Andhra Pradesh. The form is thought to have been derived from bands of roving minstrels (*jangams*) who sang the praise of the god Shiva as they travelled the rural areas of this state in ancient times. As social and religious affiliations shifted and changed among the population, the minstrels responded by absorbing secular materials into their shows.

In these early days, *Burrakatha*'s predecessor was known as *Jangam Kathas*, literally, 'stories of the Jangams', in which a story-teller, accompanied by his wife, who assisted him in giving recitals of two or three days' duration, sang, danced and recited before the people of a village under the patronage of a village elder. At some undetermined point in its history, perhaps in the early 20th century, *Burrakatha* came into existence.

The term *burra* refers to the *tambura*, a stringed instrument worn across the right shoulder of the performer (*kathakudu*). The term *katha* means a story. The *kathakudu* plays the *tambura* with his right hand as he dances rhythmically forward and back on the stage reciting a story. The *kathakudu* also wears a hollow ring with metal balls inside over his right thumb and holds a similar metal ring in the palm of his hand. The rings are used to beat the basic tempo of the songs. At regular intervals during the narration, he addresses and responds to his co-performers, two drummers who play the earthen drums with two heads (*dakki*), which produce a distinctly metallic sound to accentuate the songs. The *dakki* is regarded as an indispensable ingredient of all *Burrakatha* performances.

The drummer to the right of the *kathakudu*, as he faces the audience, is known as the *rajkiya*. This drummer makes political and social comments on contemporary issues even if the story concerns historical or mythological events. To the left of the *kathakudu* is the *hasyam*, who cracks jokes and provides comic relief.

Performances begin in the evening with devotional songs in praise of various celestial beings. Then the *kathakudu* introduces the main story establishing the place, time and historical context of the action. During this section the *rajkiya* and *hasyam* simply repeat the refrain of the *kathakudu*'s narrative. When the introduction is concluded, the main plot begins in which all three individuals take an active role assuming various characters in the incidents, as well as providing narrative bridges between incidents. Dance, recitation, song and enactment of scenes provides variation to the strong narrative line of the story. Generally, the stories continue for two to three hours. Longer works may be serialized into several consecutive evenings of entertainment.

The *Burrakatha* stories fall into three categories of content – mythological, historical and socio-political. Although the form was originally improvised, today many of the most popular stories have been written down and committed to memory by the *Burrakatha* performers.

In the 1940s, the Indian People's Theatre Association (IPTA), which was closely associated with the Communist Party of India, made use of rural forms of theatre throughout many parts of India as a vehicle for conveying its political and social message. In the state of Andhra, the *Praja Natak Mandali* (IPTA) revised *Burrakatha* in order to reach vast numbers of voters. Soon, other political parties followed suit. Today, as a medium of traditional communication to attract audiences, *Burrakatha* parties are used by a wide range of political organizations and also by the state and central government.

Although the Communists maintain devoted *Burrakatha* performers who believe in their political persuasion, most artists are politically neutral but willing to work for anyone who wants them to convey social and political ideas through *Burrakatha*, provided the price is right.

Today, more than 200 troupes of artists are said to bring *Burrakatha* to rural and urban audiences of Andhra Pradesh. Many of them derive their living from performance and a few of the performers have become celebrities. A large number of other parties manage to combine performances with other means of livelihood. FAR

Burrows, Abe (Abram S.) (1910–85) American playwright, librettist, 'play doctor', and director. Born in New York City, Burrows moved to Holywood in 1939 and divided his time between these two entertainment centres for the rest of his life. Following a successful career in radio (he was the chief writer for 'Duffy's Tavern', for example), he first scored as a playwright in 1950 by co-authoring *Guys and Dolls* with Jo Swerling and **Frank Loesser**. This success (Drama Critics Circle Award) propelled him during the next decade into several assignments as lyricist or librettist for musicals including *Three Wishes for Jamie* (1952), *Can-Can* (1953), *Silk Stockings* (1955), *Say, Darling* (1958), *First Impressions* (1959), and *How to Succeed in Business Without Really Trying* (1961). The latter won the Pulitzer Prize. He also adapted *Cactus Flower* from a French comedy by Barillet and Gredy for a successful 1965 Broadway production. He made his debut as a director with *Can-Can* and soon became known for his ability to infuse stage comedies with the kind of wit and gentle humour that characterized his personality, and allowed him to work harmoniously with testy writers when called upon as an unbilled 'doctor' for shows in trouble.   LDC

Burton, Richard (Jenkins) (1925–84) Welsh actor. His early work for the stage in productions of Fry's *The Lady's Not for Burning* (1949) and *Hamlet* at the **Old Vic** in 1953 amongst others, established him as one of the most brilliant actors of his generation. He abandoned the stage for a life of film stardom which meant that his remarkable talent was never fully realized.   MB

Burton, William Evans (1804–60) British-born actor and manager who ran one of the best stock companies in the United States, earning at the same time the reputation, according to Laurence Hutton, as the 'funniest man who ever lived'. Burton's first professional appearance was in 1831 at London's Pavilion Theatre, followed the next year with an engagement opposite **Edmund Kean** at the **Haymarket** Theatre. In 1834 he made his American debut at the **Arch Street Theatre**, Philadelphia. In 1841 he entered management in New York at the National Theatre, short-lived due to the destruction by fire of the theatre seven weeks later. He also managed briefly the **Chestnut** and Arch Street theatres in Philadelphia, the Washington Theatre, and the Front Street Theatre in Baltimore. In 1848 he leased Palmo's Opera House, renamed Burton's Chamber Street Theatre, and in 1856, with increasing competition from **J. W. Wallack**, moved to The Metropolitan Theatre, Broadway, renamed Burton's New Theatre. He withdrew from management in 1858. Burton's Theatres operated successfully from 1848 to 1856 largely without visiting stars, boasting such company members as **Henry Placide**, **William Rufus Blake**, **George Holland**, Charles Fisher, **Lester Wallack**, and **John Brougham**, who also wrote numerous new pieces for Burton. Audiences, however, came primarily to see Burton perform such roles as Bob Acres, Tony Lumpkin, Bottom, Falstaff, and especially Timothy Toodles in his own *The Toodles*, Aminidab Sleek in Morris Barnett's *The Serious Family*, and Captain Cuttle in Brougham's stage version of **Dickens**'s *Dombey and Son*. His last New York appearance was at **Niblo's Garden** in 1959. Burton also wrote plays (non-extant). His biography, by William L. Keese, was published in 1885.   DBW

Bury, John (1925–) Senior British stage designer, who has three major affiliations in his career. For more than ten years immediately after the Second World War he worked with **Joan Littlewood**'s Theatre Workshop. From 1963 to 1973 he was chief designer at the Royal Shakespeare Theatre, and from 1973 to 1985 he was head of design at the **National Theatre**, in addition to free-lancing at other theatres in England and abroad. With no formal training in art or design, Bury developed a mode of selective, abstractly treated realism, eschewing the consciously decorative and theatrical in favour of stark, large-scale images, and relying on authentic materials rather than the artifices of the scene shop. *The Wars of the Roses* (1963) employed steel for most surfaces and shifted scenes by means of twin, mobile *periaktoi* towers. In later years a conscious sense of form and style became more apparent: *Tristan and Isolde* (1971), *Amadeus* (1979), *Yonadab* (1985). Throughout his career Bury has designed his own lighting in order to increase the expressiveness of his sets.   JMB

Bush Theatre A leading fringe theatre in London, with a remarkable record in the promotion of new plays and unknown dramatists. It was founded in 1970 by the actor Brian McDermott in the 'social functions' room of a public house. Originally self-financing, it quickly became the venue for many lively touring companies, including The People Show and Lindsay Kemp's company, whose hit show, *Flowers*, received its premiere at the Bush. In the mid-1970s the Bush Theatre received its first substantial **Arts Council** grants and, under the direction of (among others) the playwright Dusty Hughes and the director Simon Stokes, it evolved into a 'new plays' theatre, specializing in an imaginative use of its black-box auditorium and excelling in its acting standards. Among the many dramatists whose early plays were promoted through the Bush are **Stephen Poliakoff** (*Hitting Town, City Sugar*) and Tom Kempinski (*Duet for One*).   JE

Buzo, Alexander John (1944–) Australian playwright. His first success was *Norm and Ahmed* (1968), a dialogue between an old Australian and a Pakistani student. His subsequent plays tend to focus on misfit idealists in contemporary suburbia or historical settings; his style, sometimes misconstrued as realism, is a brittle comic-ironic surface with complex subtext and evocative images. His plays include *The Front Room Boys* (1969), *Macquarie*, written while he was resident playwright with Melbourne Theatre Company in 1972–3, *Coralie Lansdowne Says No* (1974), *Martello Towers* (1976), *Makassar Reef* (1978) and *The Marginal Farm* (1984).   MW

Byron, George Gordon, Lord (1788–1824) English poet and playwright, who scandalized and excited contemporary England to a degree rivalled only by Napoleon. Byron's interest in the theatre, and his admiration in particular for **Edmund Kean**, can be traced in his *Letters and Journals*. He was even appointed to the Committee of **Drury Lane** in 1815, shortly before the publicity surrounding his separation from his wife drove him out of the country. He wrote all his plays during his Italian exile. There is good reason to doubt his frequent claims that they were not intended for the stage, though his determination to write 'studiously Greek' tragedies was a conscious challenge to English theatrical tradition. Only *Marino Faliero* was performed in his lifetime, not only at Drury Lane (1821), but also in New York and Paris. **Macready**, who revived it in 1842, had long maintained *Werner*, a gloomy Gothic melodrama which Byron certainly wrote with performance in mind, in his repertoire. **Irving** selected *Werner* for a charity matinee at the **Lyceum** in 1887. It is Byron's worst play. His best is probably *Sardanapalus*. Macready was the first to stage it, in 1834, but the most famous revival was **Charles Kean**'s at the **Princess**'s in 1853, enriched by the pageantry of Thomas Grieve's 'historical' sets, based on Layard's *Nineveh and its Remains* (1849). *Manfred*, unmistakably a dramatic poem rather than a play, was wrestled into shape by **Alfred Bunn** for performance at **Covent Garden** in 1834, in a shameless attempt to capitalize on the vogue for witch-drama inspired by Weber's *Der Freischutz*. More surprisingly, **Samuel Phelps** chose to open his Drury Lane season of 1863 with his version of *Manfred*. *The Two Foscari*, tedious as a poem and clumsy as a play, was first staged by Macready in 1838. *Cain* was directed by **Stanislavsky** for the **Moscow Art Theatre** in 1920 and transformed by **Grotowski** in 1960. There is every chance that Byron's plays will be further revived.   PT

Byron, H[enry] J[ames] (1834–84) English playwright, actor, theatre manager and journalist, who abandoned legal training when his burlesque version of *Fra Diavolo* (1858) proved a popular success at the Strand Theatre. Over the next seven years, Byron had 40 pieces staged at the Strand and other London theatres, and he continued to write at much the same rate throughout his life. His prodigious punning and irreverent treatment of familiar stories made a distinctive contribution to the development of the British pantomime. (To his burlesque versions of *Cinderella* (1860) and *Aladdin* (1861), we owe the invention of Buttons and Widow Twankey.) In 1865, together with the star of many of his Strand burlesques **Marie Wilton**, Byron took on the management of the **Prince of Wales's Theatre** and it was at his instigation that the first of **T. W. Robertson**'s plays was staged there, but he resigned in 1867, when it became clear that Marie Wilton had no further interest in burlesque. He was, by then, manager of three Liverpool theatres, a venture that ended in bankruptcy in 1868. It was for Liverpool that he wrote *The Lancashire Lass* (1867), a melodrama full of the effects he delighted to burlesque. Other melodramas include *Blow for Blow* (1868) and, in collaboration with **Boucicault**, *Lost at Sea* (1869). They were less successful than the comedies, *Cyril's Success* (1868) and the phenomenally popular *Our Boys* (1875), which ran for over four years at the Vaudeville Theatre. Byron, who was an indifferent actor, made his London debut in his own *Not Such a Fool as He Looks* (1869), and he continued to make irregular appearances thereafter. More successful was his return to burlesque at the **Gaiety**. His delightful *The Gaiety Gulliver* (1879), for example, set the pattern for the famous quartette of **Nellie Farren**, **Edward Terry**, **Kate Vaughan** and **Edward Royce**.   PT

C

Cabaret (from the Spanish *caba retta* or merry bowl, then the French *cabaret* or tavern) A small-scale entertainment, occasionally improvised, for the presentation of songs, sketches, satires and speeches, usually commenting on social, political or artistic conditions. Strictly an urban form, it originated as an avant-garde amusement for a select audience but later became commercialized for a broader public.

In 1878 Emile Goudeau founded such a club for the Hydropathes (a polyglot pun on Goût d'Eau) at Le Sherry Cobbler in Paris, where poets read their own work. But it was the Chat Noir, a name taken from Poe's tale, that gave the generic term 'cabaret artistique' to programmes put on in cafés and pubs. It was founded on 18 November 1881 by the painter Rudolphe Salis, who called it a cabaret because the songs and sketches were set forth like courses on a menu. His Montmartre premises, seating 60, and designed in an antiquarian Louis XIII style, housed not only Friday night poetry readings but elaborate shadow plays, scripted, designed and musically accompanied by leading artists. When it moved to elegant new premises in 1885, the old building was taken over by **Aristide Bruant**'s Le Mirliton, one of the numerous Montmartre cabarets it inspired. The intimate milieu allowed performers like **Yvette Guilbert** to develop a subtle new manner of delivery and to treat 'naturalistic' subjects.

In Germany, the first true cabaret was the Bunte Bühne (Motley Stage), a self-styled *Überbrettl* (Supergaff) created by Baron Ernst von Wolzogen and Otto Julius Bierbaum in 1901 to offer a superior form of variety show. Its self-conscious artiness led Alfred Kerr to criticize it for philistinism. The same year saw the founding of Berlin's Schall und Rauch (Noise and Smoke) by young **Max Reinhardt** and actors of the **Deutsches Theater**; and of Munich's Elf Scharfrichter (Eleven Executioners), where **Frank Wedekind** sang his own macabre ditties to guitar accompaniment. The writers and artists connected with the satirical journal *Simplicissimus* performed at the homonymous cabaret of Kathi Kobus in Munich. These artistic cabarets mixed ballads, art songs, one-act plays, dance, puppet drama and instrumental music in a programme held together by a master of ceremonies. The primary aim was to amuse and to air new fashions in literature.

Similar goals were served in Barcelona at Els Quatre Gats (The Four Cats) and in Cracow at Zielony Balonik (The Green Balloon), evolved from painters' gatherings. In Russia, the associations were more theatrical. Letuchaya Mysh (The Bat) was developed by **Nikita Baliev** from the hilarious Cabbage Parties held by the **Moscow Art Theatre**, and rapidly turned into a miniature theatre presenting plays and tableaux based on classic Russian literature and folk art. As Le Chauve-Souris it became world famous after the Revolution. Krivoe Zerkalo (The Crooked Mirror), founded in St Petersburg in 1908, was, under the directorship of **Nikolai Evreinov**, a house excelling in parody and experimental forms such as monodrama. The most literary of these cabarets was Brodyachaya Sobaka (The Stray Dog, 1913–15), a haunt of futurists and acmeists. It was succeeded by the Prival Komediantov (Comedians' Rest, 1916–19), an intimate theatre whose presiding genius was **Vsevolod Meyerhold**.

The most extreme of these artistic playgrounds was the Cabaret Voltaire in Zürich (1916–17), where Hans Arp and Tristan Tzara enunciated dadaism, soon to branch out as an independent art movement. After the First World War, German cabarets grew more political, breeding-grounds for dissent, particularly in Berlin. Kurt Tucholsky coined the term *Kabarett* to describe the newly engaged cabaret, with an ensemble company and a programme founded on a given theme (in German, *Cabaret* suggests a less structured series of solo numbers). They included Trude Hesterberg's Wilde Bühne (Wild Stage, 1921), the Kabarett der Komiker (Comedians' Cabaret, 1924), the anti-fascist Katakombe (Catacombs, 1929) of **Werner Finck**, and Friedrich Hollaender's Tingel-Tangel (1930). Although these did not always pack the political punch they promised, by 1935 the Nazis had banned cabaret. Some performers like Finck were sent to concentration camps; others emigrated to carry on exile cabarets, such as the Pfeffer-Mühle (Pepper-Mill) of Klaus and Erika Mann and Therese Giehse (1933).

Post-war cabaret in Germany, both East and West, tried hard to renew its political activity. There was a tendency towards carefully structured programmes and precise staging at Munich's Schaubude (Showbooth), Düsseldorf's Das Kom(m)ödchen (The Commody) and Munich's Die Lach- und Schiessgesellschaft (Laugh and Shooting Society). But they, like West Berlin's Stachelschweine (Porcupine, founded 1949), found it hard to compete with television; and the East Berlin cabarets had to direct their satire exclusively at foreign targets. In times of political turmoil they proved to be less pungent than street theatre and agit-prop groups.

In the English-speaking world, cabaret had been equated with night clubs until the 1960s, when Chicago's Second City emphasized improvisation and devised sketches before the audience's eyes. It spawned a shoal of imitations, such as San Francisco's The Premise and Boston's The Proposition, manned by university graduates. Following the highly successful run of the revue *Beyond the Fringe*, the Establishment (1961), an after-hours club in London, tried to maintain the atmosphere of irreverence.

Recent developments include comedy clubs where untried performers air their material before uncritical audiences at little cost to the management. (This phenomenon had been foreshadowed in Berlin in 1926 by the Cabaret of the Nameless, where amateurs made fools of themselves.) The haphazard nature of the enterprise is a far cry from the programmatic intentions of the artistic cabaret. More in line with the avant-garde tradition has been the short-lived 'New Wave Vaudeville', a lunatic musical assemblage deriving from punk rock. LS

See: L. Appignanesi, *The Cabaret*, London, 1975; K. Budzinski, *Pfeffer ins Getriebe*, Munich, 1984; R. Hösch, *Kabarett von gestern und heute*, Berlin, 1967; H. Valbel, *Les chansonniers et les cabarets artistiques*, Paris, 1895.

Cabrujas, José Ignacio (1937–) Venezuelan playwright and director. One third of the Venezuelan 'Holy Trinity' (with **Chalbaud** and **Chocrón**), Cabrujas made his start with the theatre group of the Central University in 1956. Until he joined the **Nuevo Grupo** (New Group) in 1967, he participated as an actor, director and writer with various groups and was a founding member of the Teatro Arte de Caracas (Theatre Art of Caracas) in 1961. A committed writer with multiple talents, he has written for the New Group such plays as *Acto cultural* (*Cultural Act*, 1976) and *Profundo* (*Deep*, 1970), *El día que me quieras* (*The Day You Love Me*, 1979), the latter an enormously popular play that intermixes the Argentine tangos of Carlos Gardel with the Marxist movement of the 1930s. He has won many prizes for acting and directing, and since the early 60s has written and adapted for film as well. Other plays include *Los insurgentes* (*The Insurgents*, 1961), *El extraño viaje de Simón el malo* (*The Strange Voyage of Simon the Evil*, 1962) and *Fiésole* (1967). GW

Café chantant, Café concert The leading French variety entertainment of the 19th century. The first musical taverns that sprang up along the Parisian boulevards in the 1770s were called *musicos*, from the Dutch; their growth was fostered during the Revolution by a decree of the National Assembly which gave theatres total licence and they proliferated around the Palais-Royal and the Boulevard du Temple, becoming so popular that the singer Déduit of the Café Yon was dubbed the 'chansonnier national'. When theatrical freedom was suppressed under the First Empire, these cafés were supplanted by summer theatres along the Champs Elysées; they spread rapidly and by 1850 there were some 200 in Paris alone. However, by law, their actors had the status of fairground performers, were not allowed to perform in stage costume (until 1867), and had to pass the hat personally once or twice a night.

These open-air *cafés chantants*, which popularized the *vaudeville* traditions of the French stage, multiplied under the Second Empire, but when the Boulevard du Temple and its cheap theatres were torn down, they were replaced by *cafés concerts*, long rooms with a high stage, where popular performances combined with smoking and drinking were accessible to small budgets. The decline of the public dance-halls also contrib-

uted to their proliferation. The *caf' conc'*, as it was known, specialized in romantic ballads, erotic innuendo and *scies* or catchy, nonsensical choruses. Between 1870 and 1914 there were as many *caf' conc's* in Paris as there are now cinemas. The most important were the Eldorado and the Alcazar, which showcased the talents of **Thérésa**, **Judic**, **Paulus**, **Polin**, Dranem, **Mayol**, among others. The types of performers included the 'comic trooper', the 'dude' or *gommeux*, the 'naturalistic' singer of urban lowlife, and the sentimental balladeer.

A decree of 1864 allowed some of these houses to become *cafés-spectacles*, blending songs with farces and operettas, and by the turn of the century the largest had taken on the English name of 'music-halls'. The first was Joseph Oller's Olympia (1893) which, under Jacques-Charles's management, launched **Mistinguett** and introduced American jazz. The music-hall, which dominated the scene by the end of the First World War, banned smoking and drinking from the auditorium; it still offered a central role to song, but this became increasingly the *tour de chant*, a recital by a single performer, e.g., Georgius, Fréhel, later **Piaf**. In 1949 the historian Romi founded a nostalgic, amateur *caf' conc'* but it had scant success. LS

See: F. Caradec and A. Weill, *Le Café-concert* Paris, 1980; Romi, *Petite histoire des cafés parisiens*, Paris, 1950.

Caigniez, L. C. (1762–1842) French dramatist. Born into a legal family which suffered at the Revolution, Caigniez came to Paris in 1798 and had his first play, *La Forêt Enchantée* (*The Enchanted Forest*), a fairy extravaganza, performed at the Gaîté in 1799. The melodrama was the new popular genre, and the one in which he would excel. In 1802 his *Le Jugement de Salomon* (*The Judgement of Solomon*) ran for over 300 performances at the Ambigu. He followed it with *Le Triomphe de David* (*The Triumph of King David*, 1805) and then turned to the type of play favoured by **Pixérécourt**, *La Forêt d'Hermanstadt, ou la Fausse Epouse* (*The Forest of Hermanstadt or The False Wife*), set in a brigand-ridden Bulgaria and employing the souterrains and other devices of the early melodrama. *L'Illustre Aveugle* (*The Illustrious Blindman*, 1806), exploiting the dramatic possibilities of a physical defect and the device of switched identity, showed him at the height of his powers. His name is linked most closely with *La Pie Voleuse, ou La Servante de Palaiseau* (*The Thieving Magpie or The Servant of Palaiseau*, 1815), a re-writing of a play submitted by an unknown author to the Porte-Saint-Martin, which made the fortune of the theatre director, Saint-Romain, and later provided the plot of Rossini's opera. Caigniez remained popular until about 1830, but died in poverty. JMCC

Calderón de la Barca, Pedro (1600–81) Spanish playwright, ranking with **Lope de Vega** as the greatest of Spain's Golden Age. Born in Madrid into the lower ranks of the nobility, he attended a famous Jesuit school before studying Canon Law and Logic at the Universities of Alcalá and Salamanca (1614–20). His poor relations with his father led him to reject the priesthood planned for him and he led the life of a gentleman poet and playwright. His first successful play dates from 1623, and after a period of military service in Flanders he devoted himself to the theatre. By 1629 his reputation was made with the martyr-play *El príncipe constante* and two cloak-and-sword plays, *La dama duende* (*The Phantom Lady*) and *Casa con dos puertas* (*The House with Two Doors*). The period 1629–40 showed him at the height of his creative powers, writing comedies, tragedies of the classical and honour-play type, historical plays and *autos sacramentales*. These plays were written at first for the **Corrales**, but after the construction of the Coliseo theatre in the Retiro palace (1634) he wrote increasingly for the court, collaborating with the Italian Cosme Lotti on elaborately staged plays with music and later full-scale operas. He became a member of the Order of Santiago in 1636, and on the outbreak of the Catalonian Revolt in 1640 he served in the army for two years. His dramatic output decreased greatly in this decade, and with the closure of the theatres during most of 1644–50 and the death of two brothers and his mistress, he thought of abandoning the theatre and became a priest in 1651.

His talents were still in demand, however, and he wrote court comedies, mythological plays and especially *autos sacramentales* till his death.

Calderón's prolific output, more than 110 **comedias**, seventy *autos sacramentales* and other works, makes a balanced view of the man and his works difficult, and generally the serious and religious side of his plays and character have been emphasized, though half his plays are basically comic, and he was as popular with the groundlings as with the educated. To some degree his plays satisfied the moralist and the classicist through the greater decorum of the comedies and the didactic strain of some serious works. Nevertheless he owed more to **Seneca** than to **Aristotle** and rarely observed the classical unities.

He retained the three-act form of the *comedia* and Lope de Vega's rhyme-schemes, but combined them with a high-flown rhetorical style and cultured language. He was an adequate dramatic poet, making use of imagery using analogies with the four elements. His Jesuit training shows both in his rhetoric and the way his characters argue and attempt to prove their point with logical and pseudo-legal terminology.

Calderón left no *Ars poetica* and it is rare to find the author's own opinion clearly expressed in his works, though there is no reason to doubt his religious orthodoxy. The essence of his drama is a mental and spiritual struggle between conflicting demands, especially those of Love, Honour, and Religion. In the three controversial 'honour-tragedies' *El médico de su honra* (*Physician to his Own Honour*, 1635), *A secreto agravio secreta venganza* (*Secret Vengeance for Secret Insult*, 1636) and *El pintor du su deshonra* (*Painter of his Own Dishonour*, 1648?) honour is paramount. The fact that in each play a husband murders his wife because he suspects her of adultery (though in two of the plays she is patently innocent) and yet in each case the husband is vindicated by the king has given rise to heated discussion of the author's personal opinion on the subject. It may be however that Calderón was more interested in the tragic situation of the 'eternal triangle' than in judging the characters involved.

A less controversial play, unusual for its degree of realism, is *El Alcalde de Zalamea* (*The Mayor of Zalamea*, 1642?) developing the themes of Lope de Vega's peasant honour-plays, while other serious and religious plays deal with the conflict between a harsh father and a rebellious son. Amongst these is Calderón's most famous play, *La vida es sueño* (*Life is a Dream*, 1635) a profound play on the themes of horoscopes, predestination and free will.

In the cloak-and-sword comedies, love usually triumphs as the lovers attempt to meet secretly and overcome the confusion resulting from such secrecy, the interest deriving from their stratagems and quarrels and the wit of the *gracioso*. Some of these plays are 'dark' comedies in which sympathy is aroused for a lady accused of infidelity or forced to flee for her life.

Among the plays on religious subjects, *El Príncipe constante* (*The Constant Prince*) tells of the heroic martyrdom of a Portuguese prince who refused to surrender Ceuta to the Moors in exchange for his own life, while *El mágico prodigioso* (*The Wonder-Working Magician*, 1637) tells the Faust-like legend of St Cyprian. Calderón was undisputed master of the *auto sacramental*, his works in the genre showing an increasing elaborateness in structure and staging, so that the earlier *El gran teatro del mundo* (*The Great Theatre of the World*, 1645–50) or *La cena del rey Baltasar* (*Belshazzar's Feast*, 1632) are more appreciated by modern critics. In some later *autos* Calderón reworks classical myths in Christian terms.

Calderón's plays were much translated and adapted during his lifetime by French and English playwrights, but were largely forgotten outside Spain in the 18th century. Foreign interest was rekindled by **Schlegel**'s translations and the plays had a great influence on German romantics from **Goethe** to **Wagner**. In the 20th century an important Anglo-American school of criticism has done much to edit and evaluate the plays, but in spite of some good translations performances of Calderón's works are rare outside Spain.   CL

Caldwell, James H. (1793–1863) British-born actor-manager who pioneered the theatre in the Mississippi valley. He made his debut in Manchester, England, and came to the United States in 1816 to perform in Charleston, but soon began managing in Kentucky and assembled his own touring company. On New Year's Day, 1824, he opened the **Camp Street Theatre**, the first English-language house in New Orleans and the first USA theatre illuminated by gas. Caldwell built theatres for his companies in such cities as Mobile, Nashville, and Cincinnati, thus rising to dominate the Mississippi and Ohio river valleys. His success was such that in 1835 he opened the **St Charles Theatre** with a first-rate company and visiting stars of the highest magnitude. Intense competition with **Ludlow** and **Smith** fostered excellent theatre in the area, but in 1837 a financial panic ruined Caldwell, the St Charles Theatre burned down in 1842, and by 1843 he could no longer successfully compete and so retired from the stage. He held several official positions in New Orleans, fled to New York at the beginning of the Civil War, and died there in 1863.   SMA

Caldwell, Zoë (Ada) (1934–) Australian-born actress and director whose professional debut was with the Union Theatre Company, Stratford-upon-Avon, England, 1958–9; she made her London debut at the **Royal Court** in 1960. After seasons in Canada and Australia, her USA debut occurred in 1963 at the Tyrone **Guthrie Theatre** in Minneapolis followed by her New York debut in 1965 as the Prioress in **Whiting**'s *The Devils*. While remaining active in regional theatre, she is best remembered for the Tony Award-winning title roles in *The Prime of Miss Jean Brodie* (1968) and *Medea* (1982). Her directing credits include *An Almost Perfect Person* (1977) and *Richard II* (1979). A superb technician with great power on stage, she has avoided being type-cast, while leaning toward work in the classics. The wife of producer **Robert Whitehead**, she was awarded the OBE in 1970.   DBW

Callow, Simon (1949–) British actor who has worked in a variety of theatrical situations from the **National Theatre** (Mozart in **Shaffer**'s *Amadeus* – 1979) to the innovative Joint Stock theatre company. His book *Being an Actor* published in 1984 offers a lively and important debate on the relationship between the actor and the director in the contemporary British theatre.   MB

Calmo, Andrea (1509/10–71) Venetian actor and playwright, considered to be the leading literary influence on the **commedia dell'arte**. The son of a gondolier, he made his reputation playing fussy, amorous old men of the Pantalone type. His six comedies spice the intrigues of the **commedia erudita** with regional dialects, horseplay and comic invention. He is said to have retired in 1560 because pastoral and tragedy were dominating the stage.   LS

Căluş Rumanian Whitsuntide ritual dance of great semiotic complexity, performed by men who during the performance period abstain from sex and keep normal social contact to a minimum. It has a strong magical element, involving trance and the healing of people possessed by spirits. In one form, prevalent in Muntenia, the dances alternate with short comic plays, led by a paradoxical phallic clown, the 'mute' (he is not silent), on subjects such as money, sex, and fighting.   AEG

Calzabigi, Raniero de (1714–95) Italian man of letters, and something of an adventurer, who is principally remembered as **Gluck**'s collaborator. His early works were commended, with some reservation, by **Metastasio**. He went to Paris and, along with Casanova, established a lottery. Arriving in Vienna in about 1761, he there made the acquaintance of Gluck to whom he supplied three librettos, *Orpheus and Eurydice* (1762), *Alcestis* (1767), *Paris and Helen* (1769), of which the first two were the basis of Gluck's earliest successful essentially dramatic operas. Calzabigi aimed at the natural expression of genuine feeling and was skilled at keeping his main theme free from excrescences. His aesthetic and Gluck's were identical and there is much doubt as to how far Gluck's writings on opera are the composer's own work and how far they are unacknowledgedly Calzabigi's. A letter from Gluck to the *Mercure de France* in 1774, in which he comments on the success of his operas, is no doubt genuine. It contains the tribute, 'It is to Signor Calzabigi that the chief praise is due, and if my music has found approbation I think I must gratefully acknowledge that I am indebted to him, since it was he who gave me the opportunity to pour forth my art.'   GH

Camargo, Joracy (1898–1973) Brazilian playwright. A precursor of the reformation of the Brazilian theatre, his career began with the *revue*, later shifted to the serious play. A major contribution was *Deus lhe pague* (*May God pay you*) (1932), a play generally considered to mark the beginning of the social theatre in Brazil with its examination of bourgeois values under the microscope of Marx and leftist ideology during the heady years of the 1930s.   GW

Cambodia see **Kampuchea**

Cameroon Cameroon entered the colonial period as a German possession. Signs of this experience are to be found in some of the theatre: A. Kum'a N'dumbe III's play *Kafra – Biatanga* (1973) was first written in German, and R. Douala-Bell recalls one of the most infamous events in Cameroon's colonial history when he evokes in *Le Seigneur de la Terre* (*The Lord of the Land*, 1980) the hanging of Chief Rudolph Douala-Bell for resisting the Germans' annexation of tribal land. After the First World War, the German colony was placed under the wing of the League of Nations which divided it into two as a mandated territory, the bulk of the country being handed over to France and the smaller, northern region coming under British control. When the Cameroons were eventually granted independence in 1960, a referendum held in the English-speaking region chose federation with the French-speaking part of the country in preference to absorption into Nigeria. The English language and the culture associated with it have been seriously disadvantaged ever since, a factor that has been reflected in the relative absence of theatre in English. Creative writing in French in all the genres has, on the other hand, been amongst the most prolific and lively in French-speaking Africa, not least of all in the field of drama. The theatre itself has never been actively encouraged either by the colonial authorities or the government of independent Cameroon; apart from a good drama department at Yaoundé University, there is no national theatre or institute of the arts as in many of the other French-speaking countries of Africa. Theatre is essentially dependent on amateur troupes. In Yaoundé there is a very large auditorium in the Congress Centre built by the Chinese government and there are also facilities at the French Cultural Centre.

With four plays to his credit, and an outstanding awareness of theatrical technique, **G. Oyônô-Mbia** is not only an important dramatist in this his own country but in the whole of French-speaking Africa. His plays are constantly being performed. However, although he has the satirist's sharp eye for the comic potential of the practices and attitudes of modern African society, Oyônô-Mbia's approach belongs to the tradition of comedy going back to **Molière**, who clearly influences his work. Two successful plays in the same vein are *Le Fusil* (*The Gun*, 1970) by P. Ndedi-Penda and *Politicos* (1974), a political satire by J. Evina Mba. Bearing a closer resemblance to the grotesque of **Jarry**'s *Ubu* plays is R. Philombe's *Africapolis* (1978), a harsh piece of writing which was censored at the time of its first performance by actors afraid of upsetting the president of the day. The most significant Cameroonian playwright is, however, Werewere Liking, but she has left Cameroon to write and work in the Ivory Coast where there is more opportunity for her to put her ideas into practice. With a French colleague at the University of Abidjan, M.-T. Hourantier, she has developed and practised a theory of African theatre based on the centrality of ritual for all performance reminiscent of, and perhaps influenced by, the ideas of **A. Artaud**. Her two best-known plays are *La Puissance de Um* (*The Power of Um*, 1979) and *Une Nouvelle Terre* (*A New Earth*, 1980). These are not plays that can be appreciated on the basis of the written text alone; much more than the plays of Oyônô-Mbia, which can be more adequately assessed when read, Werewere Liking's plays can only be comprehended in performance.

The outstanding playwright in anglophone Cameroon is probably Victor Eleame Musinga. He is the author of over 20 plays and a brilliant actor. His theatre company, the Musinga Drama Group, MDG, is able to draw huge and appreciative audiences wherever it performs in the region. He has only an early play published, *The Tragedy of Mr No-Balance* (1975), a sprawling comedy full of insights about corruption among urban clerks. Many of his subsequent plays are about this stratum of society: men and women on the make in the lower ranks of commerce and the bureaucracy, the petty bourgeoisie, caught between marriage and sexual adventures, and tempted by ju-ju as the illusionary short-cut to promotion, money and sex. Examples are *Madame Magrano* (1968), *Incredible Madame Elonde* (1974) *Colofonco* (1970) and *The Director* (1978). This last is drawn from his own experience when bureaucracy prevented MDG from performing at FESTAC in Nigeria in 1977, after they had decisively beaten all the competition, including the francophone companies, with *The Trials of Ngowo* (1973), probably Musinga's most popular play. All his plays are linguistically rich, especially in the dramatic interweaving of pidgin and English, matching the delight of his audiences in linguistic extension. Untutored in theatre and with only his salary as a clerk in the Statistics Office, Musinga has managed to harness his dramatic talent to its social production: 'Musinga is simultaneously building a professional troupe and an audience to support it' (Arnold).   CW   ME

> See: M. Banham with C. Wake, *African Theatre Today*, London, 1976; R. Cornevin, *Le Théâtre en Afrique Noire et à Madagascar*, Paris, 1970; Stephen Arnold, 'A Comparative View of the Career and Aesthetic of Victor Musinga. . .', in L. A. Johnson et al. (eds.), *Towards Defining the African Aesthetic*, Washington, 1982.

Campagnol, Théâtre du

Campagnol, Théâtre du French Theatre company founded in 1975 by Jean-Claude Penchenat. Its most notable productions have been *David Copperfield* (1977) and *Le Bal* (*The Ball* or *Ballroom*, 1981). The latter relied entirely on gesture, mime, movement and dance, containing no speech at all. It was filmed by Ettore Scola in 1983. Like the **'Soleil'** (which Penchenat had helped to found) it often works through *création collective* and relies on meticulous observation of physical realities. In 1983 it became an official Centre Dramatique, based in south Paris.   DB

Campbell, Bartley (1843–88) American playwright. Born in a suburb of Pittsburgh and privately educated, he turned to journalism and then to playwriting. The first of his 35 plays was *Through Fire* (1871). From 1872 to 1876 he wrote and staged plays for R. M.

Hooley in Chicago. From 1876 until his mental breakdown in 1885 he was America's most popular melodramatist. His greatest success was the mining camp melodrama, *My Partner* (1879), which became a starring vehicle for Louis Aldrich as Joe and Charles Parsloe as Wing Lee. Though Parsloe went on to other parts, Aldrich, having purchased the rights to the play for a paltry $10 a performance, played it for the rest of his career. Campbell's other outstanding plays were *The Galley Slave* (1879) and *The White Slave* (1881).   DMCD

Campbell, Ken (1941–) British actor, director, clown and playwright. As the leader of the anarchic fringe touring group, Ken Campbell's Roadshow, which featured such unlikely acts as the World 'Ferret down Trousers' Competition, Campbell became a popular entertainer around the fringe circuit during the 1960s; but his talents drew him towards writing and directing, with a particular fascination for strange and wonderful tales, including science fiction. *The Great Caper* (1974) speculated about time warps, while in 1976, he adapted with Chris Langham the science fiction novel, *Illuminatus*, for the stage, which ran for seven hours. It was originally presented by the Science Fiction Theatre of Liverpool, but transferred to the **National Theatre** to open the Cottesloe auditorium in 1977. Its sequel, Neil Oram's *The Warp*, transferred to the ICA in London in 1979. In 1980, Campbell became the artistic director of the Everyman Theatre, Liverpool, for which he adapted and directed **Karel Čapek**'s novel, *The War with the Newts*, later seen at **Riverside Studios** in London.   JE

Campbell, Mrs Patrick (Beatrice Stella Tanner) (1865–1940) English actress, whose formidable personality sometimes hid or overshadowed her artistry. No more than a minor name before 1893, she became a star when she created the title role in **Pinero**'s *The Second Mrs Tanqueray* (1893) at the **St James's**. Playwrights clamoured to provide her with opportunities to repeat herself as the superficially urbane but secretly passionate *demi-mondaine* – Haddon Chambers with *John-a-Dreams* (1894), **Henry Arthur Jones** with *The Masqueraders* (1894) and Pinero again with *The Notorious Mrs Ebbsmith* (1895) among them – but she had higher artistic aspirations than such parts allowed. With **Johnston Forbes-Robertson**, who loved and encouraged her, she played Juliet (1896), Lady Teazle (1896) and Ophelia (1897). Her performances were considered dangerously modern against the classical purity of Forbes-Robertson. As Macbeth and Lady Macbeth (1897), they were attacked in England and applauded on a German tour. Mrs Patrick Campbell had made it a condition of her agreement to tour that she would stage the first English production of **Maeterlinck**'s *Pelléas and Mélisande* on her return to London in 1897. Forbes-Robertson, who thought the play morbid, gave Pelléas to **John Martin-Harvey**. It became Mrs Campbell's favourite part. She even played Mélisande in French to **Sarah Bernhardt**'s Pelléas (1904). It was a dangerous fondness for operatic roles that marred her career at its height and that spoiled her attempts at **Ibsen** (Rita in *Little Eyolf* (1896) and the title role in *Hedda Gabler* (1907)). **Shaw**, who recognized in her a supremacy in comedy, wrote *Caesar and*

Cleopatra for her and Forbes-Robertson, but she never performed it. Instead, nearing 50, she created Eliza Doolittle in *Pygmalion* (1914), the last and greatest scandal of her London career.   PT

Campion, Thomas (1567–1620) English poet and musician, best remembered as a writer of songs, though his versatility is exemplified also by his studies of poetic theory, the law and medicine. Campion's theatrical importance rests on his composition of words and music for three Jacobean masques, *Lord Hayes' Masque* (1607), the *Lords' Masque* and the *Squires' Masque* (both 1613).   PT

Campistron, Jean Galbert de (1656–1723) French dramatist whose work marks a decline in the power and rigour of 17th-century classical tragedy. His tragic situations, best exemplified by *Tiridate* (1691), are too often vitiated by a treatment which is tame and insipid, though occasionally affecting in an elegantly melancholy vein, and seem but a pale imitation of **Racine** and **Corneille**. He also wrote comedies and the text of two 'tragédies en musique' for **Lully**. He was sufficiently esteemed in his day to be admitted to the Académie-Française in 1701.   DR

Camus, Albert (1913–60) French novelist, essayist, playwright and director. Camus's plays, which were a significant part of the vigorous revival of French theatre following the Second World War, no longer seem as innovative as they did in the 1940s and 1950s. His reputation rested largely on *Le Malentendu* (*Cross Purpose*) and *Caligula* (1945), in which **Gérard Philipe** played the title role. But *Les Justes* (*The Just*, 1949) confirmed Camus's tendency to write extended debates rather than true dramatic actions. Camus had run an amateur theatre company in Algiers before the war and he directed his own adaptations of works by Faulkner and Dostoevsky in Paris in the 1950s; these were successful with audiences and critics alike. He appreciated the team work involved in theatre production and once said that the only places he felt really happy were the football field and the theatre.   DB

Canada: 1. English

The colonial theatre to 1879 The first record of theatrical activity in what is now Canada is probably found in Richard Hakluyt's *Principal Navigations* where Captain Edward Haies reports on his 1583 voyage with Sir Humphrey Gilbert's expedition to Newfoundland that 'we were provided of Musike in good variety: not omitting the least toyes, as Morris dancers, Hobby Horses, and Maylike conceits to delight the Savage people'.

Of course, these 'Savage people' had their own theatrical rites and ceremonies and had had them for many centuries, if not millennia before. By the time of the arrival of the first Europeans, some of these ceremonials had become very elaborate. The most interesting theatrically were those of the Nootka and Kwakiutl Indians of the west coast. Staged at night and indoors around a huge fire their ceremonial cycles recreated incidents from clan mythology. They were performed by members of dance societies wearing costume and intricately carved wooden masks. During the performances, masks opened to reveal other masks beneath, monsters flew through the air on strings, actors disappeared into tunnels and trap-doors and voices were transmitted through hollow kelp stems. These were stage effects unsurpassed in the Americas.

The European theatrical tradition had to await the arrival of permanent European settlers. New France was settled early in the 17th century but it was not until the mid-18th century that we find the first traces of theatrical production in English. In the constant state of war that reigned between England and France in the 18th century it is not surprising that the first English-speaking residents of Canada should be the military garrisons. A natural consequence is that the earliest English theatre was 'Garrison Theatre' staged by the officers and men for their own diversion and for that of the few settlers and traders in the vicinity. As the settlements grew larger the military men were often joined by local 'Gentlemen Amateurs'. Thus we find records of performances in Nova Scotia as early as 1743, though real theatrical activity had to wait for the founding of Halifax in 1749.

The first professional troupe to play in English Canada was the American Company of Comedians led by Mills and Gifford who spent an autumn season in Halifax in 1768. But this was only a brief visit. The main source of theatrical entertainment in the colonies continued to be provided by the garrison amateurs, such as the production of *The Suspicious Husband* by 'The gentlemen of the Army and Navy' in 1773. Another garrison production, *Acadius, or Love in a Calm*, performed in Halifax in 1774, was probably the first native English Canadian play.

The fall of New France in 1760 brought British military installations and theatricals to Quebec and Montreal, though the population remained overwhelmingly French-speaking. The real development of English Canada did not begin until the American revolution, especially after 1783 when thousands of United Empire Loyalists fled inhospitable surroundings and made new homes in British North America. The Atlantic colonies grew and prospered with this new wave of immigration and the first settlements were established in what is now Ontario.

While the earliest performances were given in inns and assembly rooms, soon various associations of garrison amateurs and local theatrical societies fitted up special buildings as playhouses. The first official theatre was constructed by military officers in Halifax in 1789. Besides housing their own performances, it was rented out to other amateurs and to occasional visiting professional companies. Thus there was constant, though not sustained activity. More than a hundred different pieces were presented in Halifax in the last 15 years of the 18th century.

As other centres grew, theatrical activity spread to them, beginning in Saint John, New Brunswick, with an amateur performance of *The Busy Body* in 1789. A company of English actors came from Albany, New York, and played seasons in Montreal and Quebec as early as 1786. Another company, led by a Mr Ormsby, 'from the Theatre Royal, Edinburgh', also came by way of Albany and constructed Montreal's first theatre in 1804. We find them again as the first professional company in Newfoundland, appearing in St John's in July 1806, presumably a stop-over on the way back to Britain.

Montreal and Quebec could be reached by sea, and consequently attracted many visitors. **Edmund Kean** played in Quebec and Montreal in 1826 and was made an honorary chief by admiring Huron Indians. **Charles** and **Fanny Kemble** appeared in 1833, and **Charles Macready** in 1844.

In Ontario the same pattern held true. In Kingston and Toronto, military and local amateurs performed in improvised settings until the population justified dedicating a building or part of a building to theatrical entertainments. This facility then attracted the strolling professional troupes. Throughout the first half of the 19th century this was the basis for theatre in all of British North America.

Garrison players were usually officers and, consequently, of a relatively elevated social class. The local amateurs were often men of the law, accustomed to public declamation. They represented a small coterie, in frequent contact with the home country, and imbued with the expected sense of decorum and respectability, only slightly marred by unprofessional attempts at female impersonation. It was with such amateurs that **Charles Dickens** acted during his visit to Montreal in 1842.

The professional companies were a very different story. They were usually small, led by a married couple, and often made up of other couples. Because extensive travel in early Canada could only easily be undertaken by water in the summer or by sleigh in the winter, we find these companies most often in the Atlantic provinces during the summer and in central Canada during the winter. When the size of the settlements warranted it, larger companies could come by water, and Halifax soon became a summer home for companies from Boston or New York. **E. A. Sothern** brought a company for long seasons in 1857 and 1858.

But transportation difficulties meant that the growing demand for more and larger scale entertainment could only be satisfied by resident repertory companies. Across the eastern part of the country substantial theatre buildings seating from 500 to 1,000 were constructed (Royal Lyceum, Toronto, 1849; Theatre Royal, Montreal, 1852) and these were owned or leased by managers who engaged good quality companies for an entire season. J. W. Lanergan in Saint John, the Bucklands in Montreal, and John Nickinson in Toronto established long and close relations with their respective communities. Variety was provided by a constant round of touring stars who joined these resident companies for a few nights or a few weeks. In Canada these visiting stars were more often English than American, but the supporting company usually came from New York.

The presence of a resident company in the community offered the possibility of local plays being produced. Unfortunately, Canadian writers did not seem to be attracted to the theatre, and the number of original pieces produced through this period is insignificant. While the theatre did not appeal to Canadian writers, the dramatic form did. But their works were either closet verse dramas such as Charles Heavysege's *Saul* (1857) and Charles Mair's *Tecumseh* (1886), or journalistic social and political satires, usually anonymous, such as *The Female Consistory of Brockville* (1856) or

The Theatre Royal and William's Creek Fire Brigade Hall, Barkerville, British Columbia, 1869.

Nicholas Flood Davin's *The Fair Grit; or the Advantages of Coalition* (1876) which were never intended for the stage.

The system of visiting stars impeded the development of any original drama and limited the repertoire to the standard London drama and **Shakespeare** – plays familiar to both the star and the company. Early in the century the bills were filled with short farces and burlettas which later gave way to **Sheridan** and **Goldsmith**; **Colman**'s *The Heir-at-Law*, **Kotzebue**'s *The Stranger*, **Home**'s *Douglas* and the plays of **Boucicault** were also great favourites. It is interesting, however, to note that the military men, with their frequent rotation, were often able to stage relatively recent London successes. **Edward Fitzball**'s *The Inchcape Bell*, first presented in London in May 1828, was staged by the garrison amateurs in Kingston in July 1830.

As the population grew, so did the number and size of the theatres. By the 1870s, playhouses seating close to 2,000 people appeared across the country (Grand Opera House, Toronto, 1874; Academy of Music, Montreal, 1875; Academy of Music, Halifax, 1877) and the larger cities had several theatres, each one appealing to a different audience segment: for example in Toronto in 1875 the Grand Opera House presented the standard drama, the Royal Opera House tended towards the melodramatic and sensational, while the Queen's theatre was what was known as a 'variety dive'. All these theatres had their own companies, generally engaged in New York and filled out with local residents, but they were very much a part of the community.

As the Canadian population spread westward across the prairies, so did the theatre. Garrison amateurs were active in the Red River settlements from 1866, and so were the employees of the Hudson's Bay Company. The first visiting professionals arrived in Winnipeg soon after a rail link was established with Minneapolis in 1878. E. A. McDowell's Shaughraun company from the Academy of Music in Montreal was a frequent visitor to most eastern Canadian cities and the first to make the long trek to Winnipeg. His company spent a month there in the summer of 1879 and two months in 1880. By 1883 Winnipeg audiences could support the 1,300 seat Princess Theatre.

On the west coast, the naval installations at Victoria saw the same kind of garrison theatre as had been performed in the east almost a century earlier, with the difference that performances were often given on board Her Majesty's war ships. But Victoria and the west coast also saw another remarkable kind of colonial theatre arise with the discovery of gold in the Fraser River in 1858. Thousands of treasure hunters flocked to the tent cities that sprang up along the rivers and creeks of British Columbia. Many of them wintered in Victoria or mainland towns such as New Westminster. Among various kinds of diversions provided to them the theatre played a surprisingly large role.

The first professional company to visit Victoria was George Chapman's Pioneer Dramatic Company in 1859, and Chapman built the city's first theatre, The Colonial, in 1860. Even the tiny mining settlements created playhouses for visiting and local entertainers. The pioneer theatre at Barkerville, for example, also served as headquarters for the local fire brigade. San Francisco was the main source for these visiting companies who often made Victoria the terminus of their route up the coast. Further developments quickly followed the established pattern in the rest of the country and by the end of the 1870s Canada could boast of a chain of large theatres and established repertory companies from coast to coast.

The touring era 1880–1945 The years from 1880 to the First World War were a golden age of popular theatre in Canada. At the end of the 1870s economic, artistic and technological forces combined to produce a sudden change in the way the theatre worked, not only in Canada but across North America. Almost overnight the system of resident companies and visiting stars was replaced by touring companies presenting a single play. This new system brought with it higher standards of production and a new and more varied repertoire. However, it was a North American, rather than a Canadian theatre, almost entirely focused on New York where companies were formed, productions mounted and tours booked. If there had been a chance of a Canadian drama emerging from the local repertory companies, it had now completely disappeared. The Canadian market was simply too small for the theatre industry to produce special products for it, for the theatre had become a major industry dedicated to the production of mass entertainment.

There had been touring companies before, of course, particularly opera companies. After mid-century, operetta, *opéra bouffe*, and other light musical concoctions were extremely popular in English Canada. The Holman English Opera Company, based in London and Toronto, regularly toured eastern Canada and the northern United States throughout the 1860s and 1870s

with works by Balfe, Lecocq, and Offenbach, as well as their own creations. It is no surprise, then, to find that the most successful original productions of the Canadian theatre in this period were musical entertainments. W. H. Fuller's attack on the Canadian government, *HMS Parliament* (1880), enjoyed a remarkable success in the hands of the McDowell company; another musical pastiche, *Bunthorne Abroad* (1883), assembled from **Gilbert** and Sullivan by Toronto caricaturist J. W. Bengough, survived several revivals before disappearing.

Local booking circuits had already begun to spring up in the 1870s to allow for more efficient planning of tours by the stars and their entourages. These circuits gradually became larger and more exclusive. Local entrepreneurs such as Ambrose Small in Toronto, the Whitney family in south-western Ontario, or C. P. Walker in Winnipeg with his Red River Theatre Circuit either associated themselves with the larger American chains or simply sold out to them. The resulting syndicate control of virtually all North American playhouses effectively dealt the death blow to any hopes for a distinctive Canadian theatre.

Canadians, however, participated fully in this North American theatre industry, and many became very prominent parts of it. There was room for small local companies within the continental scheme, and essentially Canadian troupes such as the Marks Brothers or Ida Van Cortland and the Tavernier Dramatic Company played on both Canadian and nearby American circuits. Harold Nelson's Canadian Dramatic Company played the classics regularly on the Walker circuit in the west, while 'The Dumbells', a vaudeville company that had grown out of a First World War army show, enjoyed international fame.

Many individual Canadian performers and producers such as **Margaret Anglin**, **Julia Arthur**, **Walter Huston**, **Marie Dressler**, **Henry Miller**, **Beatrice Lillie**, **David Belasco** and Mary Pickford began their careers in local stock companies. Among playwrights W. A. Tremayne of Montreal was the most successful Canadian, writing several farces and melodramas, including *The Secret Warrant* (1897), *The Dagger and the Cross* (1900) for Robert Mantell, and *The Black Feather* (1916). Canada's more serious writers such as Charles Mair and Wilfred Campbell still avoided the contemporary stage though they continued to write in dramatic forms.

But even as theatrical activity was at its peak satisfaction with the product was often lacking. The little theatre or art theatre movement was a widespread reaction to the state of commercial theatre at the turn of the century. In Canada, journalist Roy Mitchell made Toronto's Arts and Letters Club an important centre of theatrical experimentation from 1908, but the plays produced were those of **Maeterlinck**, **Yeats**, Tagore and **Synge**. The visits of the Irish Players from the **Abbey Theatre** provided an important model to those who were crying out for a Canadian theatre, and the art theatre movement in Canada soon became a decidedly nationalistic one.

When Mitchell was appointed the first director of **Hart House Theatre** in 1919, it became the focus of the little theatre movement in Canada. Mitchell soon left to teach and write, and his book, *Creative Theatre* (1929), is regarded as a seminal work. Under succeeding directors, more Canadian plays were produced at Hart House, though almost always one-act works. Merrill Denison, whose *Brothers in Arms* (1921) and *From their Own Place* (1922) were produced at Hart House and the Arts Club respectively, emerged as the first serious Canadian playwright to write about Canadian themes and Canadian places. In the 1930s **Herman Voaden**'s Play Workshop produced not only his experiments in symphonic expressionism but also the work of many local writers. The Playwrights Studio Group also produced dozens of original scripts at Hart House in the 1930s.

In Montreal, Martha Allan and Rupert Caplan were among the founders of the Community Players in 1921. W. A. Tremayne was their stage director. The Players disbanded after four years and Rupert Caplan joined the **Provincetown Players** before returning and becoming a major force in Canadian radio. Martha Allan went to the **Pasadena Playhouse** and returned to form the Montreal Repertory Theatre in 1929 which survived into the 1960s.

In the west, Carroll Aikens, whose poetic tragedy on Indian themes, *The God of Gods* (1919), had been produced at the **Birmingham Repertory Theatre**, constructed a marvellously equipped little playhouse on his Okanagan valley farm at Naramata, British Columbia, where he tried to create a professional troupe of Canadian Players in the early 1920s. He became director of Hart House Theatre at the end of the decade.

One of the reasons for all this indigenous theatrical activity was the gradual disappearance of the imported product. Just as Canadian writers were beginning to find some success on the stage, the stage was falling before the onslaught of vaudeville and the movies. The movies took over not only the theatre audience but also its buildings, and the great depression did the rest.

A consequence of the death of the road was the limited return of local stock companies presenting weekly rep. They were not really local, of course, for even they were bound to New York and the booking circuits, but in their long-term residencies in the larger cities they provided opportunities for local participation.

From the beginning of the century occasional companies had tried to avoid the cost of touring by spending long periods in one city or region, particularly in those parts of the country not well served by the major touring circuits. Among the more long-lived examples were the Permanent Players, who were a permanent institution in Winnipeg through the first two decades of the century. In Toronto the Vaughan Glaser Players played through the 1920s, for the first six years in the 3,000-seat Uptown Theatre. The John Holden Players, who grew out of a summer Actor's Colony near Toronto, played for several winter seasons in both Toronto and Winnipeg in the late 1930s. But by 1939 they were billing themselves as the only professional theatre in North America doing weekly stock on a year-round basis, and soon the Second World War put an end to such activity.

Outside the larger cities the professional theatre was virtually dead by the 1930s, but it was replaced to some degree by amateur theatre. The 1920s had seen the beginnings of a large number of little theatre groups across the country. Complementing the art theatres

they carried on the tradition begun in the military garrisons a century and a half before. In 1932 the Dominion Drama Festival was founded to provide a focus for this amateur activity with an annual competitive festival. Adjudicators such as Robert Speaight, **Harley Granville Barker**, and particularly **Michel Saint-Denis** contributed a great deal to the high standards of amateur theatre in Canada. The Barry Jackson Trophy, awarded from 1934 for the best Canadian play, stimulated the creation and production of works by Mazo de la Roche, **John Coulter**, **Robertson Davies** and **Gwen Pharis Ringwood**.

The thirties also saw the rise of the social theatre and agit-prop presentations by theatre groups associated with the leftist Progressive Arts Clubs in major cities across the country. The high point of this movement, *Eight Men Speak* (1933), a creation of Toronto's Workers' Theatre to protest the arrest and attempted prison murder of a Communist Party leader, was performed to great public controversy and subsequent attempts at suppression. These groups also brought Canadian audiences the works of radical American writers such as **Clifford Odets**, Sinclair Lewis, and Irwin Shaw.

Far more important for the future of the theatre in Canada was the establishment of the Canadian Broadcasting Corporation in 1936. Radio broadcasts of plays had begun as early as 1925, and in 1930 **Tyrone Guthrie** had come to Canada to produce 'The Romance of Canada', a series of historical plays written by Merrill Denison for the Canadian National Railways radio network. That network eventually became the CBC and, especially during the 1940s and 1950s under Andrew Allan, was a major producer of original drama. Playwrights and performers now were able to work professionally and consistently, though not on the stage. The talent pool that the CBC supported led directly to the post-war theatrical explosion that finally created an indigenous, professional theatre and an important body of Canadian dramatic work.

The new Canadian theatre The Canadian nation, formed in 1867, became almost totally independent in 1931. Its new nationhood was confirmed in the Second World War. Following the war there was an unmatched explosion of creative activity in all the performing arts. Recognizing the need for a comprehensive cultural policy the federal government in 1949 appointed a Royal Commission under Vincent Massey to study the role of the arts in Canadian life. The resulting Massey Report in 1951 was a major document in the evolution of Canadian culture. It recognized the importance of the arts and called for government subsidy to provide the necessary facilities for their growth. This recommendation led directly to the formation of the Canada Council in 1957, and later, various provincial Arts Councils, who provided 'arms-length' support to artists and arts organizations.

But long before the Canada Council and even before the Massey Report, Canadian theatre experienced a post-war rebirth from coast to coast. Sydney Risk's Everyman Theatre mounted a bus and truck tour of the west in 1946 and 1947 with a repertoire including Elsie Park Gowan's *The Last Caveman* (1946) before settling into its own studio theatre in Vancouver.

In Toronto, **Dora Mavor Moore**'s New Play

Society, founded in 1946, produced international classics as well as successful original works such as Morley Callaghan's *To Tell the Truth* (1949) and John Coulter's *Riel* (1950) in its first five years. When the NPS turned towards education and musical theatre, the Jupiter Theatre, founded in 1951 by Lorne Greene, John Drainie and other CBC artists, took over its original role, producing the works of **Brecht, Sartre, O'Neill** and **Pirandello,** but also Canadian plays such as Lister Sinclair's *Socrates* (1952) and *The Blood is Strong* (1953).

In Montreal, the Montreal Repertory Theatre renewed its activities after the war and was joined by the Canadian Art Theatre that presented ambitious productions at its Open Air Playhouse, including a 1950 *Cymbeline* directed by **Fyodor Komissarzhevsky** (Theodore Komisarjevsky). In the same year the first productions were mounted at the indoor Mountain Playhouse. Malcolm Morley went from Montreal to Ottawa in 1948 to join the Ottawa Stage Society and help turn it into the Canadian Repertory Theatre which produced full 34-play seasons of professional weekly rep in a school auditorium. And in Newfoundland a group of players from the Birmingham Repertory Company played long seasons from 1947 to 1957, first as the Alexandra Players then as the London Theatre Company. Most of those London players remained in Canada.

Summer theatre also flourished, from Quebec's Brae Manor Playhouse and Ontario's Red Barn and International Players to the Totem Theatre and Theatre Under the Stars in Vancouver. But undoubtedly the one event that catalysed and revolutionized theatre in Canada was the opening of the **Stratford Shakespearian Festival** in 1953. Almost overnight a major theatrical force was born that was to set standards of production for the whole continent. The intense post-war activity had produced a Canadian theatre community more than ready for the challenge of a world-class classical theatre. All but four of the first Stratford company were Canadians who had already been working in the nascent professional theatre and who were determined to continue. Among them were Robert Christie, Richard Easton, Amelia Hall, William Hutt, and Douglas Rain. Subsequent seasons included Frances Hyland, Lorne Greene, and **Christopher Plummer**.

A few months after the close of the first Stratford season, Donald and Murray Davis opened the Crest Theatre in Toronto to produce full winter seasons of two-week repertory. Over the next 12 years it provided a strong continuing presence that balanced many other short-lived theatrical enterprises. Among the 16 original works produced at the Crest were plays by Robertson Davies, Mavor Moore, Ted Allan, Jack Gray, and Bernard Slade. A few years later George Luscombe's **Toronto Workshop Productions** began offering a more radical alternative in both style and content.

The founding of the **Manitoba Theatre Centre** in 1958 marked the beginning of the regional theatre movement, and the next decade saw the establishment of a chain of relatively large, important theatre companies across the country. Vancouver's Playhouse and Halifax's Neptune presented their first seasons in 1962; Edmonton's Citadel Theatre opened in 1965, followed by the Glove in Regina the next year, The Saidye Bronfman Centre in Montreal in 1967, Theatre Calgary in 1968, and Theatre New Brunswick in 1969. In succeeding years professional theatres were established in almost every significant city in the country. Theatre critics such as **Nathan Cohen** and Herbert Whittaker made the whole country their 'beat'.

The year 1969 also saw the opening of the National Arts Centre in Ottawa and the next year the completion of the St Lawrence Centre in Toronto. The Stratford Festival was joined in 1962 by the Shaw Festival in Niagara-on-the-Lake, dedicated to the plays of **George Bernard Shaw** and his contemporaries. The Charlottetown Festival, established in Prince Edward Island in 1965, quickly found a role as the major producer of original musical theatre, presenting over 40 shows in its first 20 years, including the perennially popular *Anne of Green Gables* (1965).

Performers and theatre craftspeople were trained for these theatres at the **National Theatre School**, founded in 1960, other professional training programmes connected with the theatres themselves, especially in Vancouver, Winnipeg and Stratford, and a growing number of university theatre departments.

Funding came from a variety of sources. After 1957 the Canada Council and certain provincial bodies provided operating subsidies to established companies but these had to be supplemented by significant private fund-raising. The centennial of Canadian confederation in 1967 provided an impetus to the building boom, and many a theatre building or arts centre was designated a centennial project and thus eligible for special capital grants. While perhaps too much money was poured into concrete and not enough into art, the result was a living, reasonably healthy theatre network covering the country, providing professional production standards and popular entertainments. Show business had returned to Canada.

The centennial celebrations also provided an impetus to Canadian playwriting. The 1967 Dominion Drama Festival allowed only Canadian plays, and the regional theatres made determined efforts to find and produce Canadian scripts. The Vancouver Playhouse production of **George Ryga**'s *The Ecstasy of Rita Joe* was an important landmark in this new emerging Canadian drama. Also in 1967, the Stratford Festival staged **James Reaney**'s memory play, *Colours in the Dark*, at its Avon Theatre and the Manitoba Theatre Centre produced Ann Henry's *Lulu Street*.

But these large scale productions of new Canadian works were the exception, not the norm. The regional theatres were large, expensive and necessarily conservative institutions. Their subscription seasons were generally made up of a recent American or British success, a classic or two, and the occasional Canadian work. The most successful Canadian play of 1967, John Herbert's *Fortune and Men's Eyes*, had to look to New York for a full-scale production because its content was too disturbing.

The 1970s saw the arrival of the 'alternate theatre movement'. The energy and revolutionary idealism of the 1960s led to the growth of what were originally called 'underground' and later became 'alternate' theatres. Though unsanctioned by any dictionary, this phrase was widely used in Canada to suggest a movement diametrically opposed to the established regional theatres. On small and often improvised stages they explored new movements in the theatre of protest.

Their arrival was marked by a large Festival of Underground Theatre in Toronto in 1970 in which Canadian, American and European companies presented their work all over the city. While their initial impulse was not particularly nationalistic it quickly became so, especially after the Gaspe Manifesto issued by a meeting of Canadian playwrights in 1971. Toronto and, to a lesser extent, Vancouver were the centres of this movement. From the late 1960s to the early 1970s there was an explosion in theatre production and in the production of new Canadian plays in particular.

In the west, the Savage God experiments of John Juliani had begun in Vancouver as early as 1966, but with the establishment of the **New Play Centre** in 1970, a new generation of playwrights began seeing their works on stage and in print. The collective and improvisational found its outlet with Tamahnous Theatre, founded in 1971. West Coast Actors and the Arts Club Theatre occupied the middle ground between the established Playhouse Theatre and the experimenters.

In Toronto, Theatre Passe Muraille emerged from the parking garage of the radical Rochdale College and, under the direction of Paul Thompson, became a leader in a style of collective documentary drama which has become an important Canadian tradition. Ken Gass founded the Factory Theatre Lab in 1970 with a firm commitment to produce new plays, and in its first season introduced writers and plays as different as **George Walker**'s *Prince of Naples* (1971), Herschel Hardin's *Esker Mike and his Wife Agiluk* (1971), and David Freeman's *Creeps* (1971). Bill Glassco left the Factory Lab to found **Tarragon Theatre** which quickly became the most established of the alternates with successful productions of the works of David Freeman and **David French**, especially *Leaving Home* (1972), and English translations of Quebec playwright **Michel Tremblay**.

Much of the alternate theatrical activity was fuelled by special federal government employment programmes. Local Initiative Programs and Opportunities for Youth projects often turned into theatrical companies that flowered briefly before disappearing as quickly as they had arisen. One important survivor is the Toronto Free Theatre, founded in 1972 as literally a 'free' theatre with no admission charge. Toronto Free survived even though it is free now only in the artistic sense, its repertoire ranging from the new and shocking to **Middleton** and **Rowley**'s *The Changeling*.

Alternate theatres were not confined to the larger cities. Almost everywhere a regional theatre existed an alternate rose to challenge it, from Halifax's Pier One to Edmonton's Theatre Network and Calgary's Alberta Theatre Projects. In many cases the regionals themselves established second stages or workshops for the production of new and experimental works. Even such a small and remote city as Thunder Bay, Ontario, developed a mainstream company, Magnus Theatre, and an alternate, Kam Theatre Lab.

The result of all this activity was the production of over 200 new Canadian plays between 1970 and 1972. Many of them probably should not have been presented, but as a result, playwrights had a chance to learn. A whole new generation of writers found success, often continuing success, on the stage. Besides those mentioned already, Carol Bolt, Rick Salutin, **Sharon Pollock**, **Michael Cook**, **John Murrell** and **David Fennario** have established themselves as important and widely produced writers.

The trend towards collective creations, led by Theatre Passe Muraille's *Farm Show* (1972), found followers in the east and west; Newfoundland's Mummers' Theatre and Saskatoon's Twenty Fifth Street Theatre toured the country with productions such as *They Club Seals, Don't They?* (1978) and *Paper Wheat* (1977), both obviously deeply rooted in their environment.

Another trend evident in the early 1970s was the popularity of small-scale naturalistic looks at Canadian life. Although often most closely connected with the Tarragon Theatre, this style was a pervasive influence and not unrelated to the achievements of the Canadian documentary film-makers.

After such an orgy of playmaking it was inevitable that a certain retrenchment and consolidation would follow. The drying up of LIP and OFY funds after 1974 certainly helped, but there still remained a vigorous and active alternate theatre presenting a large proportion of new work. The survivors went through financial and artistic crises but they grew stronger each time. An 'edifice complex' took hold and the abandoned warehouses and factories that had housed these fledgling companies were bought, restored and equipped as playing spaces that would be the envy of similar companies in many other parts of the Western world.

As the alternates became more comfortable and more established, alternate alternates arose, catering to special groups or special philosophies of performance. A full spectrum of theatrical activity was now available to Canadians: a few remaining large touring houses for Broadway or West End successes, the established, traditional regional theatres, the more adventurous alternates, and the radical fringe. Theatre had once more become an industry in Canada. Awards such as the Doras in Toronto and the Jessies in Vancouver attract wide attention. The theatre companies themselves are coming closer together through tours, exchanges, co-productions and organizations such as the Professional Association of Canadian Theatres.

With the active encouragement of the Canada Council the regional theatres almost universally adopted subscription systems. Many of the alternates have followed suit. Subscription guarantees an audience but it also limits it. In the larger cities, the need for transfer houses where a successful production can have its run extended has become evident.

Despite the financial problems caused by recession, the situation of the Canadian theatre in the 1980s is a reasonably healthy one. But most of this theatre is still a non-profit, subsidized theatre, receiving anywhere from 10% to 50% of its budget from various governmental sources. There also exists and has always existed a commercial theatre. Even at the worst of times in the 1930s and 1940s there was always a market for comic and mildly satiric shows. Commercial revue and cabaret has continued to be strong, particularly in Toronto. Dinner Theatre is another thriving commercial aspect of contemporary Canadian theatre, providing jobs for actors if little else. Enough playing spaces and a large enough market now exist in Toronto and Vancouver that local producers have begun mounting high quality commercial productions, though rarely of new work. Nevertheless theatre in Canada, after four hundred years, is more than ever before presenting Canadian audiences with portrayals of their own problems, their own dreams. JA

See: J. Ball and R. Plant, *A Bibliography of Canadian Theatre History 1583–1975*, Toronto, 1976; M. Edwards, *A Stage in Our Past*, Toronto, 1968; R. Perkyns, ed., *Major Plays of the Canadian Theatre 1934–1984*, Toronto, 1984; R. Plant, ed., *The Penguin Book of Modern Canadian Drama*, Markham, Ontario, 1984; D. Rubin and A. Cranmer-Byng, *Canada's Playwrights: A Biographical Guide*, Toronto, 1980; E. R. Stuart, *The History of Prairie Theatre 1833–1982*, Toronto, 1984; R. Usmiani, *Second Stage: The Alternative Theatre Movement in Canada*, Vancouver, 1983; A. Wagner, ed., *Canada's Lost Plays* (4 vols.), Toronto, 1978–82; A. Wagner, ed., *Contemporary Canadian Theatre*, Toronto, 1985; R. Wallace and C. Zimmerman, *The Work: Conversations with English Canadian Playwrights*, Toronto, 1982; J. Wasserman, ed., *Modern Canadian Plays*, Vancouver, 1985; Periodicals: *Canadian Drama*; *Canadian Theatre Review*; *Theatre History in Canada*.

Canada: 2. French

Theatre in French Canada to the Second World War   The first record of theatrical activity in French and the first dramatic text come from Port Royal in Acadia (today's Annapolis Royal, Nova Scotia), where **Marc Lescarbot**'s aquatic pageant, *The Theatre of Neptune in New France*, was written and performed in November 1606. The text was composed to celebrate the return of the colony's leaders from a prolonged and dangerous mission: this function identifies it as a *réception*, a dramatic sub-genre long popular in France, performed mainly by students in Jesuit colleges to welcome visiting dignitaries. But Lescarbot's short verse-play has none of the stuffy formality associated with traditional *réceptions*: although relying heavily on neoclassical references, it is a good-natured frolic intended to amuse and entertain.

Only two other texts survive from the French regime, both belonging to this category: the *Réception for Governor D'Argenson*, written by the Jesuits and performed by their pupils in Quebec in 1658, to greet the arrival of the new Governor; and another *réception* with many elements of a *pastoral*, composed again by a Jesuit and performed by children for Bishop Saint-Vallier in 1727. A surprising characteristic of all three texts is their strong political component: their authors intercalate precise messages for the reader/spectator, advising strategies for colonization, recommending war against the Iroquois, pleading for administrative support of church projects. This characteristic would be an enduring one in French Canada.

Throughout its history, material conditions in New France were not conducive to the establishment of an enduring theatrical tradition. In Quebec fashionable plays (particularly those of **Corneille**) were staged for the social elite as early as the 1640s; such performances were surprisingly frequent at times, especially in the 1650s and early 1690s. But primary social factors: a sparse, transient population in a huge colony, the indifference and later the hostility of the powerful Catholic church, militated against sustained theatrical activity. These difficult conditions were exacerbated by

a direct confrontation between civil and religious authority in 1693–4. Word had spread that Governor Frontenac intended to stage, along with plays by Corneille and **Racine, Molière**'s *Tartuffe*. Bishop Saint-Vallier was scandalized, and used all the power of his office to block the plan. Their conflict ended with bishop bribing governor handsomely for not staging *Tartuffe*. Frontenac's cause was the loser, however: the bishop now forbade all public theatricals; and such was the authority of his office that there are only sporadic references to other performances after 1694: a light opera staged privately in 1706; the *réception* (already mentioned) of 1727; a Shrovetide comedy staged at Montreal in 1749 (first reference to theatre there); a farce written and performed by the garrison at Fort Niagara ten years later. Bishop Saint-Vallier's prohibition would create problems for theatre in French Canada for the next 200 years.

Soon after the formal cession of New France in 1763 the British garrison in Quebec was actively performing classical French plays (mainly by Molière), in French. Garrison theatre of this sort appeared in Montreal in the following decade, and would continue well into the 19th century, with frequent participation of local amateurs. After 1763 drama returned to the curriculum of schools and colleges as well, attested to by reports of such performances in newspapers and by surviving manuscripts of college plays from the 1780s. Independent amateur troupes appeared at this time also, the most important being Montreal's Society Theatre which, in the season 1789–90, staged eight separate plays, one of them written by a naturalized French immigrant, **Joseph Quesnel**, entitled *Colas et Colinette, ou Le Bailli Dupé* (*Colas and Colinette: or The Bailiff Confounded*), published in 1808.

At this point the Catholic church decided to intervene, first from the pulpit and then more effectively through the confessional. Its discreet strategy proved effective, and would continue to do so for the next half-century, with the result that theatre in French, unlike its English Canadian counterpart, would remain cyclical, endangered and amateur. In such conditions it is not surprising that the most successful dramatic form to evolve would be a literary-journalistic one: political theatre (or 'parateatre', since it would not be performed until the 1860s). Intensely partisan, it began appearing in French Canada's newspapers in the 1760s and would continue well into the 20th century. It represents the most original indigenous genre, and for good reason: surviving texts from the 1790s show that some at least were intended to be read aloud at public meetings, thus 'performed' in a sense, in a period when less than 5% of the francophone population could read. An apogee of this paradramatic form came in 1834, with the publication in rival newspapers of five amusing playlets, the *Status Quo Comedies*. Satirical, vituperative to the point of libel, they were an effective political weapon. Not being destined for performance, they could escape the church's ire, as could the religious-pedagogic theatre performed for a restricted public in educational institutions.

In the 1830s, as in the late 1780s, the public stage received much-needed catalysis from abroad. France's political turmoil of the early 1830s brought an influx of dissident intellectuals, the most notable being Firmin Prud'homme, Napoleon Aubin and Hyacinthe Leblanc de Marconnay. The latter helped found an Amateur Canadian Dramatic Society and composed two plays, *Le Soldat* (*The Soldier*, 1835), perhaps written in conjunction with Aubin, and *Valentine, ou La Nina Canadienne* (*Valentine: or The Canadian Nina*, 1836), both performed and published in Montreal. In 1837 came the first published play by a native French Canadian (apart from the closet political playlets mentioned above): *Griphon, ou La Vengeance d'un Valet* (*Griphon: or A Valet's Revenge*), written by **Pierre Petitclair**. It was never performed, but was followed by two others that were: his melodrama *La Donation* (*The Legal Donation*), first staged in 1842, making of it the first play by a native Canadian to be published and performed; and *Une Partie de Campagne* (*A Country Outing*, 1857), satirizing French Canadians who aped English speech and manners.

More solemn in intent, more formal in style is *Le Jeune Latour* (*Young Latour*) by Antoine Gerin-Lajoie, performed by him and his fellow students at the Collège de Nicolet in 1844. A verse tragedy dealing with the short-lived conquest of New France by the English in 1629–30, it is the first in a long line of patriotic historical works that would characterize the 19th century. It also signals a renaissance of drama in the institutions of secondary education in Quebec, from which would come the intellectual and social elite on which theatrical activity depended. Most of the college texts performed were, unlike *Young Latour*, either written by instructors who were usually priests (Father Hospice-Anselme Verreau's *Stanislas de Kostka*, 1855; *Archibald Cameron of Locheill*, by Fathers Joseph-Camille Caisse and Pierre-Arcade Laporte, 1865), or adapted by them from existing texts, the 'adaptation' consisting largely in the removal of all female roles, even for plays by Racine and Corneille. By mid-century the Catholic clergy, recognizing the propagandistic potential of theatre, took active measures to harness it to the church's ends: for combating heresy, in works such as the anonymous *Soirées du Village, ou Entretiens sur le Protestantisme* (*Village Evenings: or Conversations on Protestantism*, 1859–60); for alerting the faithful to the dangers of alcoholism, in *L'Hôte à Valiquet, ou Le Fricot Sinistre* (*Valiquet's Guest: or The Sinister Stew*) by Father Jean-Baptiste Proulx (1869); for attacking individual enemies, as in Father Alphonse Villeneuve's *Contre-Poison: Faussetés, Erreurs, Impostures, Blasphèmes de l'Apostat Chiniquy* (*Antidote: or Falsehoods, Errors, Deceits and Blasphemies of the Apostate [Charles] Chiniquy*, 1875); for eloquent pleas on behalf of colonization and social action, as in Father Proulx's *Les Pionniers du Lac Nomininque, ou Les Avantages de la Colonisation* (*The Pioneers of Lake Nomininque: or The Advantages of Colonization*, 1882) and Father Edouard Hamon's *Exil et Patrie* (*Exile and Fatherland*), performed in 1870.

Concomitant with the church's increasing use of dramatic forms was its growing tolerance of public theatre. **Louis-Honoré Fréchette**'s hyperpatriotic *Félix Poutré* (1862), dealing with the Rebellion of 1837–8, continued to be performed, even in educational institutions under church control, well into the 20th century, and college performances were opened to the general public, notably in the case of *Archibald Cameron of Locheill* (mentioned above), based on the most popular novel of the century, Philippe Aubert de

Gaspé's *Les Anciens Canadiens* (*Canadians of Old*): its premiere in 1865 at the Collège de l'Assomption was the cultural highlight of the decade. But native dramaturgy was slow to respond, its most significant evolution in this period being in the realm of political theatre: the unplayable, often wooden journalistic dialogues of the 1830s and 40s are enlivened with satirical songs in the following decade. In 1868 came Elzear Labelle's witty *La Conversion d'un Pêcheur de la Nouvelle-Ecosse* (*The Conversion of a Nova Scotian Fisherman*), no longer anonymous, no longer unilaterally partisan but directed at both sides in the Confederation debate. This play would continue to attract sell-out audiences to the end of the century. It points the way towards one of the few genres that would prosper in French Canada until the 1940s: the satirical revue, replete with music, dance and monologue, brimming with contemporary political allusions.

Another important factor influencing theatrical activity and eventually dramatic composition was the more and more frequent visits by touring companies from France. From 1858 professional troupes crossing to the USA began to add Montreal and occasionally Quebec to their itinerary as the continent's railway system developed sufficiently to allow this. Some of these troupes even remained in Canada, notably that of Alfred Maugard after 1871. The most celebrated of these tours were those of **Sarah Bernhardt**, beginning in 1880. She would return six times by 1916, arousing on each occasion great interest among French- and English-speaking audiences, and greater opposition from the church, scandalized by her choice of plays. This overall injection of lighter, more modern repertory fostered a sharp revival of amateur activity in both cities and led to the establishment of the first professional troupes in Montreal in the 1890s. Soon playwrights like Ernest Doin and J. George Walter McGown were 'adapting' successful Parisian fare to less worldly local tastes, thereby adding scores of ephemeral titles to Canadian repertory. Influenced also by imported tastes but much more original is the work of Félix-Gabriel Marchand, premier of Quebec, 1897–1900. His five plays, from *Fatenville* (1869) to *Le Lauréat* (*The Laureate*, 1899), brought welcome variety to a dramaturgy otherwise committed to solemn historical and patriotic themes. Similar in inspiration is the work of Régis Roy in popular comedies such as *Consultations Gratuites* (*Free Consultations*, 1896) and *Nous Divorçons* (*We're Divorcing*, 1897). But the most frequent source for dramatists remained the history of French Canada: the heroic age of exploration and conquest, as in Joseph-Louis Archambault's *Jacques Cartier, ou Canada Vengé* (*Jacques Cartier: or Canada Avenged*, 1879); the Conquest of 1759–60, in Laurent-Olivier David's *Le Drapeau de Carillon* (*The Flag from [the Battle of] Carillon*, 1901); the Patriote Rebellion of 1837–8, in Fréchette's *Félix Poutré* (1862) and his *Papineau* (1880); and contemporary national concerns such as the suppression of the French-speaking Métis under Louis Riel in 1885, which inspired in the following year two plays entitled *Riel*, one written in collaboration by two recent French immigrants, the other by Quebec-born Elzéar Paquin. This sometimes turgid nationalistic-historical vein would continue to be the mainstay of dramatic composition (but not, one must underline, performance), until the Second World War.

The result of this modest dramaturgic and theatrical activity was the establishment of the first permanent theatres in Montreal. The opening of the Monument National in 1894 and of the Théâtre des Nouveautés in 1898 marks an important progression, although it was mainly French actors who continued to play there, with only minor roles given to locals. In 1898 the first lay company officially sanctioned by the Catholic church was formed, appositely named Les Soirées de Famille (Family Evenings) dedicated to providing 'wholesome' theatre in more or less open opposition to the fare offered by touring troupes. The most important pioneer in the Canadianization of troupes and repertory at this time is Julien Daoust, founder in 1900 of the Théâtre National Français, actor, director, and composer of some two dozen works, most of them played but never published. The period 1898–1914 is frequently referred to as the 'Golden Age of Theatre in Montreal', an epithet that is only valid compared to the debased coinage that preceded it. And the glitter continued to be largely imported: of nearly 500 plays staged in French between 1890 and 1900, only 15 were composed by French Canadians; less than a third of the 85 plays composed by native playwrights between 1890 and 1914 were ever performed. In this respect the college stage remained exceptional, most of the works it offered continuing to be of local composition; but the public stage continued to prefer insubstantial comedies adapted for local tastes. By 1914 a noticeable change had occurred in the origin of source materials and models, however, and the Americanization of repertory becomes more and more apparent as vaudeville, burlesque and revues crowd out Parisian 'boulevard theatre'.

The First World War had a drastic effect, putting an end to international tours and sending most French professionals back to their homeland. After these barren years attempts to revive traditional repertory theatre were not successful: after 1918 the American genres mentioned above were the only ones capable of offering competition for cinema, a sad symptom being the regular conversion of theatres to movie-houses. This is when the dichotomy between dramaturgy and performance is most striking, as the favourite inspiration for local playwrights remained stubbornly patriotic and nationalistic. More than twice as many plays were published in French Canada in the 1920s as in any preceding decade, the majority of them belonging to this category. Yet most of the local texts performed were sketches and comic monologues. Drama remained primarily a literary form, with occasional exceptions such as Paul Gury's Le Mortel Baiser (Kiss of Death, 1923) and Léopold Houlé's Le Presbytère en Fleurs (The Presbytery in Flower, 1929), both staged with success before and after their publication. Best example of the tenuous link between performance and printed text is the case of Aurore l'Enfant Martyre (Aurora, Child Martyr), based upon a sensational crime that took place in 1920 in a Quebec village. First staged in 1921, this melodrama relying heavily on sadistic voyeurism was performed no less than 5,000 times by the late 1940s, yet remained unpublished until 1982.

Cinema had been a serious competitor with live theatre since its appearance in Montreal in 1902. When radio arrived in the 1920s its influence soon became pervasive, rapidly becoming the most important vehicle of cultural solidarity since for the first time the basic problem of demographic dispersion could be overcome. Initially radio's influence was pernicious to theatrical activity, but in the early 1930s broadcasts of plays and serials became immensely popular, providing fertile nurseries for indigenous authors and performers. Many passed with surprising ease from one medium to the other, notably Henry Deyglun and Henri Letondal. And since they could now live by their craft, they had spare energies to invest in keeping alive the unprofitable, 'serious' stage, as did actor-managers Fred Barry and Albert Duquesne in 1930, buying out a small movie-house and renaming it the Stella. During its five-year span this company provided the best theatrical fare Montreal had known for decades, staging some of the few home-grown plays of the period such as Yvette Mercier-Gouin's Cocktail in 1935. At the same time the Stella helped train future professionals on whom live theatre and radio would depend, through its subsidiary troupe, the Académie Canadienne d'Art Dramatique. This proved to be merely a holding action, however: the effects of the depression, along with increased competition from vaudeville, burlesque, film and radio, made the Stella's demise inevitable. Only the Americanized forms of popular theatre were secure, their principal practitioners (Olivier Guimond, **Rose Ouellette**, Juliette Petrie) becoming household names on whom any impresario could depend for a full house. On a non-competitive level, religious-pedagogical drama continued to thrive throughout the period in Quebec's educational institutions. In the 1930s it began to seek a broader public, primarily through the efforts of prolific writer-directors like Laurent Tremblay and **Gustave Lamarche**. With hundreds of participants, their creations took on the panoramic dimensions of medieval passion plays: Lamarche's La Défaite de l'Enfer (Hell Defeated, 1938), Notre-Dame-des-Neiges (Our Lady of the Snows, 1942) and Notre-Dame-de-la-Couronne (Our Lady of the Crown, 1947) are reported to have attracted up to 100,000 spectators for a single performance. With energetic, imaginative priests like Georges-Henri d'Auteuil at Montreal's Collège Sainte-Marie and **Emile Legault** at Collège Saint-Laurent, academic theatre came to the fore, rescuing the public stage from its own worst instincts. This is especially true in the case of Legault's Compagnons de Saint-Laurent: from their formation in 1937 to the time they disbanded in 1952 they would be a seminal group, providing most of the professional actors, directors and designers who would make possible a renaissance of stage arts after the Second World War. As that conflict approached, however, only what was peripheral to traditional theatre appeared to have any real chance of survival.

Theatre in Quebec since the Second World War Theatre historians have been almost unanimous in recognizing in the staging of **Gratien Gélinas**'s 'Tit-Coq (1948) the beginning of contemporary theatre in Quebec. In this play's theme of a foundling's frustrated search for identity, French Canadian audiences perceived something of their own quest, formulated in familiar language. Its 500 performances over the next few years attest to this, and its undeniable success immediately stimulated renewed interest in traditional theatre. Yet 'Tit-Coq was not the spontaneous phenomenon it has sometimes been made to appear: it is a mature outgrowth of processes observable over the preceding 60 years. Its premiere was at the Monument National, the opening of which in 1894 had marked a previous summit in Montreal's cultural history. Its cast included Fred Barry and Albert Duquesne, two of the founders of the Stella in 1930, as well as Juliette Béliveau, whose career had been launched at the turn of the century, during Montreal's so-called Golden Age. The author, who directed the play as well, had received a solid grounding in college theatre before going on to write and perform sketches in the 1930s. In the years 1938–46 he wrote annual revues called Fridolinades from their title-character Fridolin, a sort of Québécois Everyman played by the author himself; and from this character much of the essence of 'Tit-Coq's titular hero (also played by Gélinas) is distilled. One man had pulled together all these disparate threads, and his play came at an auspicious moment in Quebec's history.

The war years had brought changes, some of them beneficial to theatrical activity – the economic recovery it entailed, first of all, with money disposable for arts and entertainment after basic needs had been met; the partial eclipse of cinema, especially that hitherto imported from France. The European refugees with theatrical training like **Ludmilla Pitoëff**, who came to live for a time in Montreal; the visitors like **Jean–Paul Sartre**, who witnessed for the first time a performance of his own Huis Clos (No Exit) in that city in 1946. New troupes, especially L'Equipe, founded in 1943 by Pierre Dagenais, a disaffected member of Emile Legault's Compagnons, and Le Jeune Colombier, established by Jean Duceppe, whose contribution continues today in a theatre bearing his name. The most enduring of these companies is Montreal's Rideau Vert, established in the disused Stella in 1948 by Yvette Brind'Amour and Mercédès Palomino and still very much alive. Soon after the war young Québécois began returning to Paris to study stage arts under the great masters, as Emile Legault had done before them. Two such students in particular, **Jean Gascon** and **Jean-Louis Roux**, would play a central role on their return, founding the **Théâtre du Nouveau Monde** in 1951. This remains French Canada's most prestigious company: its influence has been pervasive, although it now represents an 'establishment' against which young troupes rebel. But the most significant event of the 1950s came from offstage: the establishment in 1957 of the Canada Council and of Montreal's Regional Arts Council, followed four years later by that of Quebec's Ministry of Cultural Affairs. By the very nature of their decision to fund one group at the expense of another, these three agencies, deliberately or not, have wielded much influence, not all of it positive, upon the repertory chosen. A stridently anti-establishment troupe or play has had less of a chance for subsidy, with the result that playwrights and theatre managers have sometimes had to compromise their principles. But positive effects have been many, including the establishment in 1960 of the **National Theatre School** of Canada (its first Executive Director was Jean Gascon, with **Michel Saint-Denis** as Artistic Director); and the differing criteria employed by the three granting agencies have frequently led to healthy rivalry.

In dramaturgy, the example of Gélinas was not immediately emulated. He himself did not compose another stage play until 1959, preferring to write for television and to concentrate on his career as director and actor. Other playwrights appeared in the 1940s and early 50s without achieving his sort of recognition: the singer-folklorist Félix Leclerc; the neoclassicist Paul Toupin; the novelist André Langevin; Robert Elie, Eloi de Grandmont, Yves Thériault: for all of them dramaturgy was an avocation, as it had been for those before 1948. More innovative were **Jacques Languirand** and **Jacques Ferron**, the former a bursary student who returned from Paris indelibly stamped by the theatre of the absurd in vogue there in the early 1950s. In works such as Les Insolites (The Unusual Ones, 1956) and Les Grands Départs (Great Departures, 1958), Languirand captured the attention of a public athirst for novelty, before the Quiet Revolution of the 1960s that would again turn its gaze inward. Ferron, on the other hand, had begun with satirical works such as Le Licou (The Halter, 1947) and L'Ogre (The Ogre, 1949), but in the following decade had anticipated Quebec's radical awakening with Les Grands Soleils (The Great Sunflowers, 1958), which centres upon the Patriote Rebellion and attacks the province's mythologized history. The most important and most productive dramatist of this period, however, is **Marcel Dubé**, author of more than 30 plays to date, many of them written for television and most of them visibly influenced by it, the most important being Zone (1955) and Un Simple Soldat (Private Soldier, 1958).

The Quiet Revolution brought with it an unprecedented flourishing, in quality as in quantity, of theatre arts. With the encouragement of state funding agencies new troupes thrived, their number in Montreal alone trebling between 1959 and 1968. Television provided a lucrative outlet for this exuberance, exercising in turn considerable influence on themes and structures of stage plays. Dubé continued to dominate both media in the 1960s, with plays such as Florence (1960), Octobre (1964), Bilan (The Accounting, 1968) and Au Retour des Oies Blanches (The White Geese, 1968), the latter often considered his finest play as well as a clear example of his steady progression away from the working-class characters and concerns of his early works. Many of the salient texts from this decade spring from the politico-social context: Gélinas's Hier les Enfants Dansaient (Yesterday the Children Were Dancing, 1966) portrays within one family the political scissions that existed on the national level; **Françoise Loranger**'s Le Chemin du Roy (The King's Highway, 1968) satirizes, in the guise of a penalty-filled hockey game between Ottawa and Quebec, the confrontation caused by President De Gaulle's visit during centennial year; **Robert Gurik**'s Hamlet, Prince du Québec (Hamlet, Prince of Quebec, 1968) is a parody of the same federal-provincial antagonism, close in form and inspiration to French Canadian political theatre of the 19th century. Yet the most revolutionary play of the decade has no direct reference to the political situation: **Michel Tremblay**'s Les Belles-Soeurs (Sisters-in-Law), composed in 1965, first performed in 1968. Its setting is a drab apartment in working-class Montreal, its characters all female, its theme that of cultural and economic dispossession. Most importantly, its language is unalloyed joual, the impoverished, eroded, heavily anglicized French of the urban proletariat, hitherto considered too ugly for public display except in vaudeville and burlesque. In Tremblay's stylized text, language itself becomes the metaphor of collective frustration and individual solitude. Its remarkable success led to an immediate proliferation of plays composed in Quebec's homely vernacular, the most notable being those of **Jean-Claude Germain**, **Jean Barbeau**, Michel Garneau and Victor-Lévy Beaulieu.

Les Belles-Soeurs had first been read and approved by the Centre d'Essai des Auteurs Dramatiques, a loose organization of young theatre professionals established in 1965 and whose activities would prove catalytic over the next decade. The CEAD and its spiritual successor, the Association Québécoise du Jeune Théâtre, assembled all the discordant voices of those opposed to the directions established theatre had been taking, an opposition that expressed itself most noticeably in an attack upon the traditional supremacy of the dramaturgic text and of the iniquitous 'star system' which militated against young actors. The movement it generated remains dynamic, and is called Jeune Théâtre (Young Theatre), best exemplified in the offerings of troupes such as Jean-Claude Germain's iconoclastic Grand Cirque Ordinaire, established in 1969, and his Théâtre du Même Nom (TMN), a parodic anagram of the Théâtre du Nouveau Monde (TNM), that most established of Canadian companies. Influenced by such groups as **Bread and Puppet**, **Living Theatre** and the Campesino theatre of California, some of these young experimental troupes adopted activist political ideology, as did the Marxist Théâtre Euh! (1970–8); others produce plays on demand for workers' unions, collectives and schools. Although the economic recession of the late 1970s brought the demise of many of them, there were still some 100 Young Theatre companies active in 1990, many of them clinging to a precarious existence. Their purgative influence has proven salutary for surviving groups and even for established theatre. The practitioners of 'young' theatre age ineluctably, however: if there is at present an 'establishment' in French Canadian dramaturgy, its most established author is the prolific Michel Tremblay, whose works have attracted national and international acclaim such as no Canadian before him had known.

Since the election of the independentist Parti Québécois government in 1976, the agressive political stance frequently visible hitherto in published texts has been mitigated. In recent years there has been less preoccupation with Quebec's problems and more interest in universal concerns. Most striking has been the rise of a group of immensely talented young authors whose themes are international in scope (René-Daniel Dubois, Normand Chaurette, Michel-Marc Bouchard), along with the sudden, full consecration of an older dramatist with truly universal vision, Roland Lepage (b. 1928). Some of the most successful plays have been apolitical comedies such as the bilingual *Broue/Brew* (1979), written in collaboration by seven authors and situated entirely in a Montreal tavern. Another interesting and largely apolitical phenomenon is the spectacularly successful Ligue Nationale d'Improvisation, its 'contests' vaguely reminiscent of the National Hockey League, with uniformed teams and referees, and an improvisational format that recalls both **commedia dell'arte** and American burlesque's comic 'bits'. A more universal revolution continues to produce far-reaching effects upon theatre in Canada: that of women. One of the earliest feminist voices was that of Françoise Loranger, in plays such as *Encore Cinq Minutes* (*Five Minutes More*, 1967), which portrays the identity crisis of a middle-aged, middle-class housewife. In the 1970s the first women's troupes appeared, producing collective works written by and for women, the most notable being Montreal's Théâtre des Cuisines (1973–81), the Théâtre Expérimental des Femmes (1979–) and Quebec City's Commune à Marie (1978–). The anonymous and collectivist preferences of these groups' productions underline their affinity with Jeune Théâtre, as does their iconoclasm. To date, their most remarkable production has been *La Nef des Sorcières* (*Ship of Witches*) in 1976, composed of eight monologues by different authors. More recently, individual feminist playwrights have come to the fore: Denise Boucher, whose *Les Fées ont Soif* (*The Fairies Are Thirsty*) led to a memorable confrontation between state funding agencies and the stage in 1978; Elizabeth Bourget; Marie Laberge; Jovette Marchessault, whose *La Saga des Poules Mouillées* (*The Saga of the Wet Hens*, 1981) attracted much scandalized attention nationwide.

The 1960s saw the serious gap between performed theatre and published texts diminish finally when the Montreal firm Leméac initiated an extensive collection of plays proven in performance. Partially as a result, the 1970s brought a heightened interest in theatre in colleges and universities across the nation. From a position subservient to that of poetry and the novel, drama has recently moved to a privileged rank in the curricula of post-secondary institutions, with the status of research and criticism enhanced accordingly. The first serious attempt at tracing the history of theatre had been made in 1958 by the critic Jean Béraud, in his *350 ans de théâtre au Canada français*. Although incomplete, it remained almost the only source of information on theatre before 1948 until the 1970s, when Baudouin Burger's *L'Activité théâtrale au Québec (1765–1825)* appeared, followed in 1976 by the irreplaceable fifth volume of Archives des lettres canadiennes, entitled *Le Théâtre canadien-français*. In 1978 came the first volume of *Dictionnaire des oeuvres littéraires du Québec*, the most ambitious and most useful literary-historical undertaking to date, now comprising five volumes and nearly 6,000 pages. Two specialized theatre journals, *Jeu*, founded in 1976, and *Pratiques théâtrales* the following year, have been followed by several recent monographs on the history of stage arts in French Canada.

Entering the 1990s, the stage remains troubled but vibrantly alive in Quebec. In the 1980s too many troupes were competing in a limited market (in 1984 there were more than 120 professional companies, and at least 450 amateur ones, the majority of them struggling for survival). At the same time, serious reductions were being made in funds available from municipal, provincial and federal agencies. In the present climate, it is difficult to forecast which of the competing options will find its place in the sun: 'established' theatre, Young Theatre, feminist, activist, collectivist–experimental or some other.

Theatre in French outside Quebec Although French-language theatre in North America began in Acadia in

1606 it did not return there for another 260 years; and it took an additional century before a viable theatrical tradition arose. The area's sparse population was too widely scattered for cultural centres to develop, and this dispersion was accentuated by the Deportation of the 1750s. But two years after the foundation of New Brunswick's Collège Saint-Joseph in 1864 a literary and dramatic society was formed, and when the Collège Saint-Louis was established in 1874, followed in the 1890s by the Collège du Sacré-Coeur and Nova Scotia's Collège Sainte-Anne, drama immediately became an integral part of their curricula.

At first the texts performed were imported, written mainly by clerics for college theatre in France and Quebec, with occasional use of adapted, expurgated classics, especially the works of Molière. By the 1870s theatre had extended to francophone parishes of the Maritime Provinces and New England, and the first Acadian texts, those of Pascal Poirier, were performed. Father Alexandre Braud's *Les Derniers Martyrs du Colisée* (*The Last Martyrs of the Coliseum*, 1898), and in particular his *Subercase* (1902), the latter commemorating the last French colonial governor of Acadia, attracted critical and popular acclaim in performances at the Collège Sainte-Anne. Amateur college and parish troupes would continue to provide the only sustained theatrical activity until the late 1950s, but this activity remained intensely popular, serving also as a vehicle of cultural renaissance.

In the late 1920s James Branch began composing the first of his five plays, two of which are remarkable for their provocative political stance: *Jusqu'à la Mort! . . . Pour nos Ecoles* (*To the Death! . . . For Our Schools!*, 1929) and *Vivent nos Ecoles Catholiques! ou La Résistance de Caraquet* (*Long Live Our Catholic Schools! or: Resistance at Caraquet*, 1932). Father Jean-Baptiste Jégo's works, such as *Le Drame du Peuple Acadien* (*The Drama of the Acadian People*, 1930), are also patriotic but less inflammatory in tone. These and similar plays continued to be performed by amateur groups in the 1940s, but it was not until 1960, when New Brunswick got its first Acadian premier, that a true cultural renewal brought with it gains for theatre. Chiefly responsible for this awakening is **Antonine Maillet**, Acadia's outstanding writer to date. Her first plays, *Entr'acte* (*Intermission*, 1957) and *Poireâcre* (1958), attracted local attention, but it was *La Sagouine* (*The Slattern*), first performed on radio in 1970–1, that fascinated national audiences in French and English, at the same time kindling interest in her people. She continues to compose plays now produced in Montreal but Acadian in theme, such as *Évangéline Deusse* (*Evangeline The Second*, 1976). Other contemporary playwrights of note are Laval Goupil, Jules Boudreau, Germaine Comeau, Herménégilde Chiasson and Claude Renaud.

In Ontario French-language theatre began in the Ottawa Valley in the 1860s, with the first theatre constructed in 1884. The fare offered was much the same as in Montreal, with no tradition of local dramatic composition. Theatrical activity in the Hull–Ottawa area remained vigorously amateur until after the Second World War, producing actor-directors like **Guy Beaulne** who had had to pursue professional careers elsewhere. Jacqueline Martin's *Trois Pièces en un Acte* (*Three One-Act Plays*) appeared in 1966, and the next decade witnessed a score of plays composed in

French, the most important being those of André Paiement and Jean-Marc Dalpé. The former is considered the major Franco-Ontarian dramatist to date. (His three volumes of plays were published posthumously in 1978).

In 1980 there were some two dozen French-language troupes active in the province, with Sudbury, Paiement's home, rapidly developing as a centre of cultural activity. Ottawa's importance was enhanced by the opening of the National Arts Centre, which stages plays in both languages, in 1969; and since 1968 Toronto's Théâtre du Petit Bonheur (renamed Le Théâtre Français de Toronto, 1987) has offered a succession of plays in French, mostly of Quebec origin.

In Western Canada theatre in French has also been surprisingly widespread, with virtually all the scattered francophone communities serving at one time or another as centres for local amateur activity. Theatre history begins in the educational institutions of Manitoba in the 1870s, many of the texts performed being composed by members of the local clergy such as Sister Malvina Collette, who taught at the Grey Nuns' boarding school in Saint-Boniface. After 1885 the Jesuit Collège de Saint-Boniface offered regular dramatic programmes that attracted spectators from all the tiny settlements along the Red River. Soon local amateur groups appeared in towns and villages, and continued to flourish until the Second World War. In Manitoba, the most famous of these is the Cercle Molière, founded in 1925 and still active today. Its success led to the establishment of Edmonton's Théâtre Molière in the following decade, and of Vancouver's active Troupe Molière, which flourished between 1946 and 1967. Belying their titles, these troupes' repertory has included everything from the French classics to musicals and light, modern theatre from Paris and Montreal.

Despite this healthy dramatic activity, only in Manitoba has a tradition of native dramaturgy developed. In the early 20th century an impressive number of plays were composed, in particular by Auguste-Henri de Trémaudan, author of five plays published between 1925 and 1930, and by André Castelein de la Lande, with some 50 titles to his credit, most of them performed but only four published, all in the mid-1930s. These and other playwrights from the period treat general, non-controversial themes. More recently, the tribulations of Manitoba's embattled francophone community have been the focus of plays such as Roger Auger's *Je M'en Vais à Régina* (*I'm Off to Regina*, 1976) and Rosemarie Bissonnette's *Une Bagarre Très Politique* (*A Very Political Quarrel*, 1981). Even works dealing with historical topics such as Claude Dorge's *Le Roitelet* (*Kinglet*, 1976) do so in contentious fashion. Theatre history in Manitoba is the subject of a monograph by Annette Saint-Pierre, *Le Rideau Se Lève au Manitoba* (1980). LED

See: Archives des lettres canadiennes, Vol v: *Le Théâtre canadien-français*, Montreal, 1976; J. Béraud, *350 ans de théâtre au Canada français*, Montreal, 1958; B. Burger, *L'Activité théâtrale au Québec, 1765–1825*, Montreal, 1974; *Dictionnaire des oeuvres littéraires du Québec*, Montreal, 5 vols, 1978–84; L. E. Doucette, *Theatre in French Canada: Laying the Foundations, 1606–1867*, Toronto, 1984; E.-F. Duval, *Anthologie thématique du théâtre québécois au XIXe siècle*, Montreal, 1978; J.-C. Godin, and L. Mailhot, *Théâtre québécois I*, Montreal, 1970; and *Théâtre québécois II*,

Montreal, 1980; J. Laflamme and R. Tourangeau, *L'Eglise et le théâtre au Québec*, Montreal, 1979; E.-G. Rinfret, ed., *Le Théâtre canadien d'expression française: Répertoire analytique des origines à nos jours*, Montreal, 4 vols, 1975–8.

Cañas, Alberto (1920–) Costa Rican playwright, director, Minister of Culture. Under Cañas's direction, the Costa Rican government launched a major new effort in the 1970s to promote theatre. In addition, Cañas is a major writer himself of at least ten plays, including such titles as *El luto robado* (*Stolen Mourning*, 1962); *En agosto hizo dos años* (*Two years Ago in August*, 1966), about an individual returned from the dead; *La segua* (1971), an untranslatable mythical creature in a play that used the Pirandellian techniques found in his earlier plays; and *Ni mi casa es ya mi casa* (*My House is No Longer My Home*, 1982), in which he dealt with the socio-economic crises produced by world inflationary and recessionary spirals.   GW

Cantor, Eddie (1892–1964) American singer and comedian. After spending his early years in vaudeville and English music-halls, Cantor made his legitimate theatre debut in a London revue. His first American appearance was in *Canary Cottage* (1917). **Florenz Ziegfeld** hired Cantor for his cabaret show, *The Midnight Frolic*, and then featured him in the *Ziegfeld Follies of 1917*. Cantor also appeared in the next two *Follies* (1918 and 1919). Like **Al Jolson**, he often appeared in blackface, a vestige of the American minstrel show. During his musical numbers he would skip across the stage and clap his hands while smirking his way through some slightly suggestive lyrics. Cantor also appeared in several *Follies* sketches as a timid but potentially hot-tempered young man. He switched to the **Shubert** management for a few years, after which Ziegfeld presented him in a book musical, *Kid Boots* (1923). Cantor appeared in two more Ziegfeld shows, the *Follies of 1927* (for which he collaborated on the libretto as well as being the star performer), and *Whoopee* (1928), a book musical. His final Broadway appearance was in *Banjo Eyes* (1941). In addition to his work in the theatre, Cantor appeared in numerous films and was a star of radio and television. His autobiography, *My Life is in Your Hands*, was published in 1928.   MK

Cao Yu (1910–) Chinese dramatist. (Pen name Wan Jiabao.) Born in Hubei he attended Nankai Middle School in Tianjin which had an excellent dramatic club. After graduating in Western literature from Qinghua University Beijing he taught at Tianjin Normal College for Women followed by a spell as professor at the new National Academy of Dramatic Art, Namjing. In 1934 he published his play *Thunderstorm* (*Leiyu*) which was nationally toured and received instant acclaim. He followed this with five other plays written within the next six years. Two of these, *Sunrise* (*Dichu*) and *Wilderness* (*Yuanye*), are usually linked with *Thunderstorm* as a trilogy constituting his major achievement. Their common theme is the decadence of Chinese pre-war society. During the war Cao Yu taught at Fudan University, which was evacuated from Shanghai to Chongqing. In March 1946, at the invitation of the State Department, he went to America with the novelist **Lao She** and stayed until November. He left Shanghai for Beijing in 1949 to serve on the presidium of the conference of writers, artists and theatre people called by the Chinese Communist Party for July. He held a number of cultural and administrative posts in the early 1950s but came under fire for his bourgeois thinking. He remained creatively inactive until 1956 when his new play *Bright Skies* (*Minglang de tian*) was staged at the Beijing People's Art Theatre of which he is today the director. The play was undistinguished both in content and production while being heavily propagandist. Cao Yu became a Party member in 1957 when there was a drive to recruit older intellectuals. In 1966 he was seized from his home at night and sent to a reform school in the country. He was rehabilitated like his fellow intellectuals after 1976 and today is recognized as a father figure of the modern theatre accorded support by the State. He has reverted to historical themes, the never failing resource of Chinese dramatists. His play *The Gall and the Sword* (*Dan jian pian*) published in July 1961 takes as its theme the wars between the two ancient kingdoms of Wu and Yue in the 5th century BC. The play has an ideological implication in its eulogizing of 'the people'. His early plays have been revived and in 1979 his full trilogy was revived to an enthusiastic reception. Recently he has been concerned with experimental use of conventions from traditional theatre for historical themes.   ACS

Capa y espada, Comedia de see **Comedia**.

Čapek, Karel (1890–1938) Czech dramatist. Educated at Charles University, he was a philosophic, ironic humanist deeply committed to the democratic ideals of his nation. After writing a variety of prose works including a major trilogy of novels, he achieved world recognition for several plays, especially *RUR* (1921), *The Insect Comedy* (written with his brother Josef in 1922), and *The Makropolus Affair* (1922), which became the libretto for Leoš Janáček's opera. These theatrically effective works displaying a fanciful, witty, yet compassionate vision of humanity coping with its own weaknesses amid the stresses of a high technology age were followed by the equally powerful *The White Disease* (1937), a disturbing parable of the seemingly inevitable devastation triggered by power-hungry dic-

Karel and Josef Čapek's *The Insect Comedy*, Prague National Theatre, 1965. The designer was Josef Svoboda.

tators, and *The Mother* (1938). More than any other Czech dramatist, he combined a talent for drama with acute insight into issues central to his time. JMB

Capon, William (1757–1827) British scene designer and architect. His first major employment was as scene designer for **John Philip Kemble** at **Drury Lane** (1794–1809). He impressed the critics with his design of a chapel of pointed architecture for Handel's *Oratorio* performed for the opening of the reconstructed theatre (1794) and his six gothic chamber wings designed for *Macbeth* that same year. During his tenure at Drury Lane his most impressive designs were for Kemble's melodramas: the gothic library and ancient baronial hall for *The Iron Chest* (1796), a chapel with side aisles and choir for *De Montfort* (1800), and a gothic castle for *Adelmorn, the Outlaw* (1801). When Kemble moved to **Covent Garden** in 1809 Capon joined him and designed many scenes for Shakespearian revivals including an Anglo-Norman hall for *Hamlet* (1812). The designs he contributed were intended not only to serve for a particular production, but also as part of the theatre's stock scenery. An antiquarian, he insisted upon accurate representations of the external construction materials and architectural features of existing historical buildings upon which he modelled his designs. His gothic and pregothic street scenes and building interiors, for which he was famous, remained part of the stock scenery used in productions at Covent Garden long after his death. AJN

Capuana, Luigi (1839–1915) Italian novelist, short-story writer and dramatist. A prolific writer, who began as a poet, and throughout his life produced a substantial body of journalistic writings, and literary and theatrical criticism, and in whose work the influences of many late 19th-century artistic movements can be felt, particularly that of symbolism; he is above all identified as a practitioner and theorist, with the development of Italian **verisimo**. Among his many plays, most enduring are his drama of peasant life, *Malia* (*The Spell*, 1895), and his study of the Sicilian petty bourgeoisie, *Lu Cavalieri Pidagna* (1909). LR

Caragiale, Ion Luca (1852–1912) Rumanian dramatist whose comedies are masterpieces of meticu-

Set design for an ancient street by William Capon, c. 1808.

lous craftsmanship. Associated with the conservative literary circle Junimea, he lashed out violently at the Rumanian society of his time. His sarcastic wit had its most celebrated expression in *A Lost Letter* (1884), the zenith of Rumanian playwriting, dealing with a corrupt provincial electoral campaign won unexpectedly by a hilariously doltish blackmailer, the basest and most empty-headed of all the candidates. His other comedy, *A Stormy Night* (1879), portrays the moral hypocrisy of the middle class, while the farce *Carnival Scenes* (1885), whose action takes place in a barber's shop, draws a ludicrous picture of the lower strata of urban society. Caragiale's scant dramatic output also includes the one-act farce *Mr Leonida Facing Reaction* (1880), in which a senile blockhead takes street-revellers for revolutionaries, and the less successful psychological drama *The Bane* (1890). A highly sophisticated use of colourful and often nonsensical language provides much of the appeal of his comedies, which, consequently, lose much in translation. Rumanian productions still invariably present these plays as period pieces, thereby reducing them to a critique of bourgeois society, and narrowing the universality of the playwright's vision. Caragiale also wrote many humorous short stories, a number of which were later performed as dramatic sketches. BM

Carballido, Emilio (1925–) Mexican playwright, director, professor, he has fomented theatre in Mexico since 1948. Born in Córdoba, Veracruz, his ties to the province remain strong although his professional career belongs to the capital. Founder of the theatre journal *Tramoya* (1975), he has taught, promoted and anthologized an entire generation of young playwrights in Mexico. Mexico's premier playwright, both in quantity and quality, his plays are marked by an inexhaustible creative spirit. Drawing on both the realistic and the fantastic, he has written more than 75 plays, several novels and cinema scripts. *Rosalba y los Llaveros* (*Rosalba and the Llavero Family*, 1950) is a psychological play that contrasts the moral codes of metropolis and province; *La hebra de oro* (*The Golden Thread*, 1955) integrates the fantastic into a provincial setting with existential intentions. *Yo también hablo de la rosa* (*I Too Speak of the Rose*, 1965) dramatizes the complexities of human experience and the process of creativity through a metaphorical rose. Later titles include *Las cartas de Mozart* (*Mozart's Letters*, 1974), *Fotografía en la playa* (*Photo on the Beach*, 1977), and *Mimí y Fifí en el Río Orinoco* (*Mimí and Fifí on the Orinoco River*, 1982). The distinctive notes in his theatre are the authentic language and an irrepressible humour. GW

Carey, Henry (1687–1743) English playwright. His early work was as a song-writer and librettist including songs for *The Beggar's Opera* (1727) and **Cibber**'s *The Provoked Husband* (1728). He wrote librettos for operas like *Amelia* (1731) and a farcical afterpiece *The Contrivances* (1715). In 1734 his brilliant parody of the bombast of contemporary tragedy, *Chrononhotonthologos*, was performed under the pseudonym Benjamin Bounce. In the wake of **Gay**'s *The Beggar's Opera*, Carey joined the attack on the excesses of Italian opera in England with his opera *The Dragonfly of Wantley* (1737), performed 67 times in its first season at **Covent**

Garden. Its sequel, *The Dragoness* (1738), was less successful. Carey committed suicide in 1743. PH

Cariou, Len (1939–   ) Canadian actor, director and singer. A classically trained actor whose career has been most closely associated with the **Stratford (Ontario) Shakespeare Festival** and the Tyrone **Guthrie Theatre** in Minneapolis, Cariou has received his greatest acclaim as a leading man in Broadway musicals. His first musical comedy appearance was in the role of Bill Sampson in *Applause* (1970). Critics praised Cariou's performance as Fredrik Egerman in *A Little Night Music* (1973), complimenting him for his acting ability and fine singing voice. Cariou returned to the musical stage in 1979 to portray the monomaniacal 'Demon Barber of Fleet Street' in *Sweeney Todd*. His bravura performance in one of the musical theatre's most demanding roles earned him the Tony Award as Best Actor in a Musical. In addition to performing, Cariou has directed several plays, and has served as Artistic Director of the Manitoba Theatre Centre. MK

Carle, Richard (1871–1941) American comedian, librettist and lyricist. Carle made his musical theatre debut in *Niobe* (1891), and quickly became a popular comedian and singer in such shows as *A Mad Bargain* (1893), *Excelsior, Jr.* (1895), and *Yankee Doodle Dandy* (1898). Unlike other comic opera performers, Carle's comic persona was that of a shrewd, worldly prankster rather than a butt or simpleton. Carle also wrote the scripts and lyrics for many of his shows. His last appearance was in *The New Yorkers* (1930). Although reviewers often criticized the *double entendres* in Carle's material, he toured constantly to appreciative audiences across America. MK

Carnival (see also **Trinidad Carnival**) Properly speaking the pre-Lent festival of the Christian and especially Roman Catholic world, its features occur in many seasonal festivities, varying according to both culture and climate, such as May Games, The Feast of St Bartholomew (25 August) (**Jonson**'s play gives a lively contemporary picture), the Jamaican Christmas masquerade of **Jonkonnu**, The Feast of Fools (28 December, Holy Innocents) or, outside Christianity, the Jewish **Purim play**. The word is known from the 11th century. Its Latin root signifies the 'removal' of flesh; Italian popular etymology gives us the literally equivalent but metaphorically more graphic 'farewell' to flesh – the meat about to be foresworn for the Lenten fast.

Julio Caro Baroja has shown that the wild indulgence of Carnival, though set immediately in opposition to the austerity of Lent, forms, in a larger context, the mediating term in a shift from the *alegría* of Christmas to the *tristeza* of Ash Wednesday to Easter Sunday, so that a secular celebration of carnality stands between the year's two key spiritual occasions, looking back to one and forward to the other. Nor is this a structuralist abstraction. Observers of the carnival in Trinidad, or the now heavily commercialized event in Rio de Janeiro, have noted their capacity to absorb, in planning and debriefing, more than their allotted span; and while, in principle, carnival is restricted to Shrove Tuesday, it has often tended to creep forward to *lundi gras*, *dimanche gras*, and sometimes further. In 1739,

Thomas Gray wrote from Italy that it 'lasts only from Christmas to Lent; one half of the remaining part of the year is passed in remembering the last, the other in expecting the future Carnival'.

In its activities, its visual imagery, and its verbal expressions, carnival is a bewildering set of variations on the theme of oppositions and their inversion or dissolution, which together create a **cockaigne**-like universe. **Living pictures** are processed through the street, illustrating versions of the world turned upside down: the judge sentenced by the accused, the horseman riding backwards, the husband spinning while his wife ploughs. Distinctions between rich and poor, high status and low, are dissolved in the promiscuous mingling of the crowd in the public square, or disguised behind zoomorphic and demonic masks and costumes. Men and women cross-dress, and the normal rules of sexual deference are relaxed or abandoned. Informal abuse and obscenity is the order of the day, together with its formal counterpart, the bawdy or satirical song. People throw things – fireworks, water, eggs, dirt – putting physical safety at risk and marring the very clothes that they have donned for the occasion. Animals are subjected to baiting, and so, sometimes, are minorities such as Jews. Competitive games may be organized, but even then they are virtually rule-free and extremely robust (like the Shrove Tuesday football at Ashbourne, Derbyshire, England), or tend to deny their own rules, by ensuring that the fattest and slowest man wins the foot-race. Informal associations of young men process, mount shows, or simply roam the streets – the **Schembartläufer** of Nuremberg, the Compagnie de la Mère Folle at Dijon, the Venetian Compagnie della Calza; even, though not in inception a carnivalic organization, the 17th-century London apprentices who used their Shrove Tuesday holiday to express trade rivalries in gang-fights and to make common cause against playhouses and brothels (not because they had anything against either, but because it caused a cheerful nuisance and offered the opportunity of stoning the constable and his men when they arrived to break it up). Such internally democratic and loosely constituted associations at once express the egalitarian ideal of carnival, and parody the guilds, societies and orders of the everyday, hierarchically organized world. Above all, people eat and drink as if there is no tomorrow – especially pork, hams, chitterlings, and innumerable variants of the phallomorphic sausage – turning on its head the usual cautious husbandry of the pre-industrial world, with the glorious excuse that if it is not eaten today, tomorrow we may not eat it.

The organization of all these activities, while obviously requiring planning and preparation, is on the day as loose and anarchic as is consistent with their occurring at all, and they go on simultaneously: a carnival is not primarily a spectator-sport, and has no need of the sequential patterning which audiences require. Its chronological frame of reference is external, not internal. Nevertheless, its activities cover a spectrum from wholly informal socializing and milling about, through the relatively formal processions of floats and perambulations of societies, to the wholly formal proto-dramatic or dramatic performance. Some of these derive directly from the parodic thesis of carnival – mock marriages, trials, burials (such as The Burial of the Sardine in Madrid depicted by Goya), jousts between Carnival and Lent (Brueghel's painting of 1559, though it should not be taken overall as a depiction of a Flemish carnival – it is a masterly synthesis of the festive calendar from winter to spring – shows in the foreground just such a combat between their gross and emaciated figures). Others extrapolate the ambiance of carnival into fully developed little farces, such as the **Fastnachtspiele** of southern Germany, or the *sottie* 'Le Jeu du Prince des Sots', which Pierre Gringore and his Enfants sans Souci gave in Paris in 1511. From plays such as these derive stock comic characters such as the German **Hanswurst**, and possibly the English Pickleherring.

This is carnival at its most organized, crystallized into a conscious aesthetic. At its least, always rowdy and rough, it could degenerate into serious public disorder or be used by conflicting interest groups as a violent expression of political and personal rivalry, as happened at Romans in 1580.

No single analytical strategy will explain a phenomenon as historically complex, semiotically diffuse, and intrinsically paradoxical as carnival. In a sense it is a ritual of revolt, and sometimes this has specific political connotations. But to equate its dialectic between official and popular culture with class struggle in a general sense is too simple, for patricians as well as plebeians are involved as organizers and participants, and share its symbolic vocabulary. Often it seems that a whole society is reacting against its own disciplinary framework, in order, as Victor Turner puts it, to break through the constraints of structure into the euphoria of *communitas*, to discard social norms in favour of human contact. Obviously some members of society have a greater interest than others in changing the norms more permanently, in establishing a free, equal and fraternal ideal of community as a basis for social life; whence the event's potential for political conflict. But for the most part, masters and servants alike seem willing to accept the collective hangover that follows the collective binge. Carnivals have led to riot and repression; they have never led directly to social revolution. Their indirect influence in posing questions of the relationship between the spiritual and the carnal, authority and equality, order and licence, and in offering an image of what the world might be like if it were turned upside down, remains a matter of speculation. AEG

> *See:* M. Bakhtin, *Rabelais and his World*, Cambridge, Mass., 1968; J. Caro Baroja, *El Carnaval*, Madrid, 1965; M. D. Bristol, *Carnival and Theater*, New York, 1985; P. Burke, *Popular Culture in Early Modern Europe*, London, 1978; C. Gaignebet, *Le Carnaval*, Paris, 1974; 'Le Combat de Carnaval et Carême', *Annales ESC*, 27, 1972; E. le Roy Ladurie, *Carnival in Romans*, London, 1980; V. Turner, *The Ritual Process*, London, 1969.

Carnovsky, Morris (1897–) American actor. Beginning his long career with the **Theatre Guild** in the twenties, Carnovsky departed in 1931 to join the **Group Theatre**. Among his many distinguished performances with the Group were those in **Clifford Odets**'s *Awake and Sing!* (1935), *Paradise Lost* (1935), *Golden Boy* (1937), *Rocket to the Moon* (1938), and *Night Music* (1940). With his mobile face, leonine profile and commanding voice, he played characters much older than himself. Like other Group members Carnovsky developed his own version of the Method; he disagreed

with **Lee Strasberg**'s emphasis on the actor's own emotions but believed that, used properly, the Method could help actors to create classic roles. Beginning in the mid-50s, in a series of acclaimed Shakespearian interpretations, Carnovsky achieved a fusion of the Method's psychological realism with the demands of poetic style. For the **New York Shakespeare Festival** and various universities he performed Lear, Falstaff, Prospero, and Shylock. Like all the Group alumni he is a lifelong student of the art of acting and has continued to be active as both a performer and a teacher. In 1983, with lovely simplicity, he portrayed Firs in *The Cherry Orchard* at New Haven's **Long Wharf Theatre**, and in 1984 he published a book of reflections, *The Actor's Eye*. FH

Carrillo, Hugo (1928–) Guatemalan playwright and director, studied in Paris and the USA, one of the founders of University Art Theatre (1950). Directed the National Theatre Company until 1968; since 1972 artistic director of the independent Theatre Club. A committed writer, his major works include *El corazón del espantapájaros* (*The Scarecrow's Heart*, 1962); *La herencia de la Tula* (*Tula's Inheritance*, 1964); *Mortaja, sueño, y autopsia para un teléfono* (*Shroud, Dream and Autopsy for a Telephone*), three one-act plays (1972); and *El señor Presidente* (*Mr President*, 1974) from the novel by Guatemala's Nobel Prize-winning novelist, Miguel Angel Asturias. Founded the Educational Theatre for school and college students for which he adapts classic Latin American novels to the stage. His plays are translated into many languages and presented widely. GW

Carroll, Paul Vincent (1900–68) Irish playwright, co-founder of **Glasgow Citizens' Theatre**. Emigrated when 21, taught in Glasgow until 1937, when his plays gave him financial independence. Carroll's early plays satirize the clerical authoritarianism of his youthful experience.

In 1932 the **Abbey** presented *Things That Are Caesar's*, in which a woman escapes from an odious marriage engineered with the approval of the local priest. *Shadow and Substance* (1937), acclaimed in Dublin and New York, is a study of Canon Skerritt, whose cold erudition disables his care of souls. In *The White Steed* (1939), Father Shaughnessy is a ruthless puritan vigilante, credibly sinister in the Europe of 1939.

Carroll's dialogue is robust and convincing, his satire precisely directed against subservience to power abused. Yet his first is his only play not to sentimentalize its conclusion: in *The White Steed* an implausibly benign Canon, previously implausibly inactive, defeats Shaughnessy's theocratic tyranny, displacing the antagonists who have really challenged it.

Apart from two lightly satiric comedies, *The Devil Came From Dublin* and *The Wayward Saint* (1955), Carroll's later work is heavily didactic. The acrid scenes from provincial life in his first three plays put him worthily in the line of **Colum** and **Murray**. DM

Cartel Name given to an association, formed in France in 1927, between **Dullin**, **Jouvet**, **Pitoëff** and **Baty**, originally to give mutual support in the face of hostile or frivolous drama critics; this grouping committed each director to publicizing the productions of the other three and to encouraging its audience to see theatre as an art rather than as mere entertainment. DB

Carter, Mrs Leslie (1862–1937) American actress. Mrs Carter and **David Belasco**, her tutor and director, discovered that striking beauty, emotional pyrotechnics, and a sensational divorce could make a star performer, in *The Heart of Maryland* (1895, for a three-year run) in which she swung on the clapper of a bell to keep it from ringing, then in such slightly lurid dramas as *Zaza* (1899), *DuBarry* (1901), and *Adrea* (1905). According to one critic, Mrs Carter would 'weep, vociferate, shriek, rant, become hoarse with passion, and finally flop and beat the floor'.

Although she continued to perform after breaking with Belasco (1906), on the road and sometimes under her own management, in *Camille*, *The Second Mrs Tanqueray*, and *The Circle*, she never matched her successes with Belasco. RM

Casarès, Maria (1922–) French actress of Spanish origins, she performed in *Cross Purpose* and *The Just* by **Camus**, in **Cocteau**'s film *Orphée* and was a permanent member of the **TNP** company 1954–9. Since then she has established a reputation as the outstanding French tragic actress, although her style is somewhat too violent for traditional tastes. Major performances include the Mother in *The Screens* (directed by **Blin** 1966, a role she repeated in **Chéreau**'s production of 1983), Medea in Lavelli's 1967 production and **Shakespeare**'s Cleopatra in 1975. DB

Casino Theatre Broadway and West 39th St, New York City [Architects: Francis Kimball and Thomas Wisedell]. Designed in a Moorish style complete with turret, the Casino was opened by Rudolph Aronson in 1882. During its long history, it presented musical shows of all varieties: comedies, operettas, comic operas and revues. In 1890, Aronson opened New York's first roof garden theatre atop the Casino, where light musical fare was served up with light after-theatre refreshments. The house is best remembered for *Florodora*, one of the most popular musical comedies of its day. The Casino was torn down in 1930. MCH

Casona, Alejandro (1903–65) Spanish poet and playwright, real name Alejandro Rodríguez Álvarez. Director of the Teatro del pueblo (People's Theatre), sponsored by the Republican government, 1931–6, in 1934 his comedy *La sirena varada* (*The Siren Castaway*) brought success and the Lope de Vega Prize. In 1937 he went into exile, and *Nuestra Natacha* (1936) on the need for educational reform, caused the Franco regime to ban his works. In exile he wrote *Prohibido suicidarse en primavera* (*No Suicide in Spring*, 1937), *La dama del alba* (*The Lady of the Dawn*, 1944) and *Los árboles mueren de pie* (*Trees Die Standing*, 1949). His plays, strongly poetic, contrast the escape into fantasy and the need to face up to unpleasant realities. CL

Cassidy, Claudia (1905–) American drama critic. Born in Illinois, Cassidy spent her girlhood in Chicago and attended the University of Illinois in Urbana. She began her career as a drama and music critic with the *Chicago Journal of Commerce* in 1925,

quickly gaining a reputation for being tough but fair. In 1941, she left the *Journal* to organize the music and drama departments of the new *Chicago Daily Sun* (now the *Sun-Times*). Within a year, she was hired by the *Tribune*. Until her retirement in 1965, Cassidy wrote a daily column, 'On the Aisle', plus contributing to the Sunday edition. She toured Europe during the summers, sending back to the *Tribune* her impressions of 'Europe on the Aisle'. Considered the most powerful Chicago critic, Cassidy was credited with stopping New York producers from sending weak companies on the road. Her major credo was that the 'only way to judge a play is to wait and see if the theatre brings it to life'. TLM

Casson, Lewis (1875–1969) British actor and director. From 1904 to 1907 he was a regular player at the **Royal Court Theatre** during the historic **Vedrenne–Barker** seasons, and Granville Barker's influence – on his directing and his commitment to the repertory movement – was life-long. In 1908 he joined **Miss Horniman**'s company in Manchester and was its director 1911–14. After the war he continued to mix acting (in plays ranging from **Shaw** to **Shakespeare** and **Euripides**) with directing, and with his wife **Sybil Thorndike** frequently toured abroad in both plays and recitals. During the Second World War he became a leading force in **CEMA** (Council for the Encouragement of Music and the Arts), directing and playing in *Macbeth* for the first tour of the Welsh coalfields in 1940. Knighted in 1945, he is remembered for his clear and subtly expressive stage speech, his catholicity of taste and his concern to extend the reach of the theatre. AJ

Castelvetro, Lodovico (1505–71) Italian dramatist and writer. Perhaps the most influential of the many Renaissance translators and interpreters of **Aristotle**, his liberal understanding of the unities, decorum and characterization in *La Poetica di Aristotele Vulgarizata et Sposta* (*Aristotle's Poetics Translated into the Vernacular and Explicated*, Vienna, 1950) generated intense critical debate on the degree of freedom that might reasonably be enjoyed by modern writers in adapting classical rules to contemporary needs and practice. KR

Castrato A mature male, castrated before his voice broke, singing in the soprano or contralto register. The original reasons for the occurrence of such singers have never been satisfactorily determined. They appeared in Italian opera from its beginning and achieved their greatest celebrity in the 18th century. It was claimed that their advantage over boys was that they were more amenable to discipline and, of course, their voices would not break after several years: also they were said to have more powerful voices than women. They were noted for their brilliant execution rather than for their dramatic accomplishment and they frequently ornamented their singing with the most elaborate embellishments, to the increasing anger of many serious composers. The castrati performed male roles, giving rise to such occasions as that on which a heroic character was sung by a castrato in a soprano voice and that of his wife by a woman contralto. The most famous of all operatic castrati was Carlo Broschi or Farinelli (1705–82). The comment, attributed to Lady Rich, 'One God – one Farinelli', was well enough known for Hogarth to include it in plate 2 of his *Rake's Progress*. The last of these celebrated singers was Giovanni Battista Velutti (1781–1861) who created the last operatic role written for his kind of voice in Meyerbeer's *Il Crociato in Egitto* (Venice, 1824). Castrati were sometimes referred to as sopranists (or contraltists), musici, or evirati.   GH

Castro y Bellvís, Guillén de (1569–1631) The most important Spanish dramatist of the Valencian school, writing first there and then from 1618 in Madrid. His novelesque plays set in Central Europe are probably his earliest, and he later borrowed plots from **Cervantes** (including *Don Quijote*) and from Spanish ballads, as well as writing comic plays of his own invention. He published two volumes of plays, in 1621 and 1625.

His most famous play is the two-part *Las mocedades del Cid* (*The Young El Cid*) based on ballad versions of the hero's life. The first part was adapted by **Corneille** as *Le Cid*, both versions being excellent examples of the differing national styles. His comedies include *El Narciso en su opinión* (*Narcissus in his own Eyes*) and the unbridled comedy of adultery *Los mal casados de Valencia* (*Unhappy Marriages in Valencia*).   CL

Catalan theatre Catalan, the language spoken in Catalonia, Valencia and the Balearic Islands by some eight million people, had a fine literature during the Middle Ages, but after the union of the crowns of Aragón and Castile to form modern Spain (1469) it fell into a period of decadence, surviving only as a spoken language, with dramatic production largely in Castilian until the 19th century apart from the bilingual **sainetes** of Josep Robrenyo.

The renaissance of the mid-19th century brought a return to playwriting, and Frederic Soler (Serafí Pitarra) wrote the first full-length play in Catalan in 1865. The only Catalan dramatist of stature in the late 19th century was **Guimerá**, whose plays were translated into Castilian and even had some success abroad. In the early 20th century Rusiñol i Prats wrote poetic drama and Ignaci Iglésies made contributions to working class drama. The only major talent of these years was Sugarra, writing a series of lyrical romantic plays divorced from reality.

During the Civil War Joan Oliver, writing under the pseudonym Pere Quart, began to make a reputation with a small number of plays showing his ability as moralist, satirist and entertainer. The resistance of Catalonia and Valencia had terrible consequences after the Civil War with the banning of Catalan in schools, restrictions on publications, etc.

Since the Civil War many of the most interesting contributions to the theatre have been made by novelists, for instance Manuel Pedrolo, Baltasar Porcel and Joan Brossa, mainly in the theatre of the absurd. In the 1960s, however, a reaction against the formal theatre led to the creation of such companies as Els Joglars (founded in 1962 by Albert Boadella and others), Els Comediants (founded 1970) and Dagoll-Dagom (1973). Group authorship and a total theatrical experience incorporating mime, dance, music and acrobats have gained these groups a tremendous reputation. The theatre cooperative of Teatro Lliure in Barcelona has also been most successful. With the autonomous status of the regions of Barcelona and Valencia since the return to democracy, it is to be expected that Catalan theatre will continue to flourish, if these groups can find the same stimulus under regional government support that they did under Francoist disapproval.   CL

Cavittu Natakam (India) In the mid-16th century, a form of theatre emerged in south India to satisfy the cravings of the Christian communities for an entertainment centred around Christian subject matter. This was the *Cavittu Natakam* of Kerala state, inspired by the zeal of Roman Catholic priests who proselytized the area under the watchful eye of the Portuguese military and political establishment which had recently consolidated its power along the eastern seacoast of the Indian subcontinent.

Quasi-historical and mythological characters of Christian history and epic romance filled the stage – figures like Charlemagne, St George and St Sebastian who are the equivalent of the great archetypal heroes of the Hindu myths and legends, such as Rama, Krishna and Arjuna. Among the plays, *The Play of Charlemagne* is the most famous and frequently performed. It is a rambling work requiring 15 nights to complete and includes a cast of nearly 80 characters. The play is based on **Ariosto**'s *Orlando Furioso* and deals with the heroic adventures of the 8th-century French emperor and his 12 valiant peers. Replete with battles and court scenes, it is the quintessential *Cavittu Natakam*. Other works created for the *Cavittu Natakam* stage present Old and New Testament figures, lives of the saints and contemporary plays with social and historical significance. The dominant sentiments of this form of theatre are, quite appropriately, heroism (*vira*) and love (*srngara*).

Cavittu means 'step' or 'stomping' and *natakam* refers to a play or drama. The performances themselves require a great deal of masculine dance movement in which the actors, who are all male, stamp their feet vigorously on the stage. In posture and walk, the actors exaggerate masculine movement patterns to an extreme. The battle scenes loosely incorporate the martial art techniques of the region (*kalarippayatt*) which have been corrupted to suit the demands of the plays, especially in the conflicts with swords and shields. The style of movement contrasts markedly with that of the Hindu forms of the theatre popular in the region, such as **Kathakali**, **Krishnattam** and **Kutiyattam**. Some hand gestures and facial expressions seem to have been borrowed from the more classically derived indigenous art forms but these are only faint traces of influence.

The master of the performance is the teacher (*asan*) who stage-manages the shows and trains the players in the martial arts, acrobatics, singing and dancing, not to mention the memorization of the plays, most of which are written in Tamil, not the language of the players, all of whom converse in their native tongue, Malayalam. The teacher sets up a schedule of work at his household, and after ritual initiation into the art, provides regular lessons in the specific roles that are to be learned. General training is not given. Those who play kings come from special families of Christians. Each of the actors is assigned to a character of an appropriate play according to his family connections.

The *Cavittu Natakam* stage is unique. Located in open

ground in a village or town near a church or cathedral, it may be 30 feet wide and 100 feet long. Flanking each end are tall wooden platforms that must be scaled from the stage by ladders. The kings hold court on the high platforms while the action scenes and battles take place centre stage. A door up-right serves for all entrances and that up-left serves as an exit. A small opening up-centre provides a clear view of the stage for the chorus and musicians who work backstage. A large bell-metal lamp fed by coconut oil and cloth wicks is located down-centre, although it is used more for ritual purposes than for illumination. The main illumination is provided by electric lights such as floods, scoops or fluorescent tubes.

Costumes are local versions of historical Western dress, sumptuous in appearance and very colourful. Makeup is realistic, except for the false beards and moustaches and wigs. Villainous characters often wear sunglasses and tennis shoes, which are thought to be appropriate for individuals with their evil nature. The clown character (*katiyakkaran*) keeps the spectators amused with various antics, especially when he parodies the songs and dances of the other characters. He even makes cutting remarks about the teacher, who stands on stage throughout a performance guiding the progress of the action. Through his interpretation of the action in Malayalam, the spectators are able to follow the meaning of the Tamil songs, as well as laugh uproariously at his satiric comments.

Chief among the musical instruments is the barrel-shaped drum played by two sticks (*centa*) and the large bell-brass cymbals (*elattalam*). The teacher controls the tempo of performance with small hand cymbals and sometimes resorts to a whistle to cue scene changes and entrances. A wide variety of other musical instruments are found in *Cavittu Natakam* – the harmonium, clarinet, *mridangam* drum, the *tamboora*, a stringed instrument made from a gourd, among several others. Even snare and trap drums make an appearance adding to the general chaos of sound that typifies the *Cavittu Natakam* performance.

Owing to the high cost of arranging a show and the changing tastes of the time, *Cavittu Natakam* is rarely seen today in Kerala. It is best known in Cochin and Quilon districts of central Kerala where the Latin Christians make their home. The season lasts from December through March coinciding with the major church festivals. A group of performers cannot count on more than a dozen shows a season; therefore, they all have other occupations and even the teachers have to resort to an outside income to survive. FaR

Cawthorn, Joseph (1868–1949) American comedian. As a child, Cawthorn performed in minstrel shows and in English music-halls. Returning to America, he appeared in comic operas as a 'Dutch comic', speaking fractured English with a German accent. After early successes in such musicals as *Excelsior, Jr.* (1895) and *Miss Philadelphia* (1897), Cawthorn played leading roles in *The Fortune Teller* (1898), *Mother Goose* (1903), *The Free Lance* (1906), *Little Nemo* (1908), *The Slim Princess* (1911), and many other shows. During the First World War he dropped his German accent. His last Broadway appearance was in *Sunny* (1925), which starred **Marilyn Miller**. MK

Céleste, Mme Céline (Céleste Keppler) 1810/11–82) French dancer, the majority of whose unusual career belongs to the English theatre. Most works of reference accept her own claim that she was born in 1814, but her marriage in Baltimore in 1828 and the birth of a child in 1829 make that improbable. She had visited the USA with a Parisian dance-troupe, and had already divested herself of husband and child when she made her English debut in 1830. A graceful dancer and mime, she solicited from English playwrights pieces that would either allow her to remain speechless throughout or would accommodate her unrepentant French accent. The first was **Planché**'s *The Child of the Wreck* (1837) at **Drury Lane**. Céleste was by now a wealthy woman, after several lucrative and wildly popular American tours, and her move to the **Haymarket** in 1838 was partly managerial and partly romantic. It signalled the start of a long relationship with **Benjamin Webster**, confirmed in 1844, when they became joint-lessees of the **Adelphi**, where Céleste became an acknowledged favourite. The part of the noble American Indian, Miami, in **Buckstone**'s *The Green Bushes* (1845) was to remain in her repertoire until her retirement. **Boucicault** and **Tom Taylor** also tailored parts for her at the Adelphi. After quarrelling with Webster, she became lessee of the **Lyceum** (1860–1), opening as Madame Defarge in Tom Taylor's version of *A Tale of Two Cities*. She returned to the Adelphi, after an extended foreign tour (1863–8), in 1870 to make her farewell appearance as Miami, a 'final' appearance which she repeated in 1872, 1873 and 1874. PT

Mme Céleste as Hamet, the Arab boy, in *The French Spy*.

CEMA (Council for the Encouragement of Music and the Arts) Formed in Britain in 1940 to provide entertainment for war-time factory and evacuation areas, CEMA was responsible for transferring the bombed out **Old Vic** Company to Burnley (1941) and sponsoring tours by the Pilgrim Players and **Ashley Dukes**'s Mercury Players. It took over the Bristol Theatre Royal in 1943 and through **James Bridie** founded the **Glasgow Citizens' Theatre**. In 1946 it was transformed into the **Arts Council of Great Britain**.   CI

Censorship The power of the theatre as a weapon in the armoury of propaganda has been recognized by all forms of authority from liberal democracies to totalitarian dictatorships. This belief in the persuasive impact of the public stage accounts for the longevity of dramatic censorship, sometimes in contrast to other forms. While literary censorship in Western Europe has been in most cases long abandoned (e.g. in Britain since 1695), censorship in the theatre survived in several major Western democracies into the 20th century. It has been equally useful to spiritual and temporal masters. Though often disguised under the cloaks of religion or morality, dramatic censorship is fundamentally a political act, which seeks to sedate (or suppress entirely if necessary) those elements in the drama which in the view of the authority that exercises it are harmful, heterodox, or otherwise disruptive of its interests. A tame theatre is an ally of the state machine; an unruly one potentially its bitterest enemy and critic.

All censorship (whether of the individual, group, government, or church) is by nature prescriptive and authoritarian. Sinister and ugly in its harsher aspects, irritating and ridiculous in its more capricious features, censorship today exerts a stronger grip on the theatre world-wide than perhaps ever before. Its agents are shadowy, Kafka-esque figures, whose decisions are rarely subject to question or appeal. Mainly (though by no means exclusively) the bulwark of dictatorships of the right and left, censorship of the stage now extends over much of Central and South America, large areas of Africa, the USSR and the Communist bloc, the Middle East, and parts of Asia. Even where formal censorship no longer exists (e.g. France, Britain) or has never properly existed (e.g. North America) recourse to the law is still normally open to individuals or groups whose paternalist instincts lead them to object to particular plays on grounds of profanity or offence to general morality. Censorship does not have to be institutionalized to have influence – but the substance of this comment will be principally concerned with pre-production censorship (the commonest and most effective form of dramatic censorship) which consciously and deliberately aims to define, control, and restrict the intellectual and artistic freedom of the playwright. In its more extreme forms it may involve an embargo on publication as well as performance.

Ancient Greece and Rome Perhaps the first true censors were the archons of ancient Athens who judged on purely artistic merits the entries of the great dramatic festivals, but evidence for the existence in classical antiquity of dramatic censorship in the modern sense is scarce and not wholly reliable. However, scattered references (e.g. Cicero, *De Republica*) suggest that the extent of personal satire in Attic comedy may

occasionally have led to attempts to bridle it, though certainly in no systematic way and not necessarily prompted by the state. On the other hand, free speech was a deeply-rooted Athenian concept and **Aristophanes** (e.g. in *The Birds, Lysistrata*) shows the limits, if any, were really very broad. Yet the somewhat more restrained nature of early Roman comedy may have been the result of the warning signalled by Naevius' imprisonment on orders of the powerful Metelli family, whom he allegedly insulted in his plays. Certainly Roman law on libel and slander (cf. the Twelve Tables) was very harsh, and it may have had an inhibitory effect on dramatists like **Plautus**. Some form of censorship is implied by Donatus' claim that in the *fabula togata* (native comedy) it was forbidden to show masters being outwitted by their slaves; but how widespread this prohibition was is not clear. Despite its popularity, the drama was sometimes the object of distrust, especially in the second century BC, when the Senate actively discouraged the spread of theatres. Towards the beginning of the end of the Roman Empire Tertullian (*De Spectaculis*) ventilates the growing animosity of the early Christian Church to the whole spectrum of dramatic activity.

Europe c. 1400–1900 The roots of modern European censorship lie deep within the medieval theatre, when conflicting forces, religious as well as political, local as well as national, were at work. In England the Catholic Church exercised considerable control over the content of the Mystery Cycles and it seems to have been responsible even before the Reformation for the removal of plays devoted to the life of the Virgin Mary from the York and Chester Cycles. But it was the local secular authorities at Chester who in 1531 sought to have removed from the Banns of the city's Cycle all references to the power of the Pope. In France as early as 1402 Charles VI tried to assert the authority of the court over the presentation of religious drama by granting the **Confrérie de la Passion** the right to stage *mystères* only on condition that his own officials kept a critical eye on the performances.

Such controls, limited in effect, were the beginning of more aggressive attempts to regulate the theatre in Western Europe as it became more secularized. Concern over profane elements adulterating religious drama was expressed in Spain at the Councils of Aranda (1473) and Henares (1480), while in France the cheekily satirical exploits of troupes like 'Les Basochiens' and 'Les Clercs' prompted edicts against them in 1442 and 1448. By the early 16th century some local authorities became increasingly impatient with itinerant troupes and their potential for disruption; at Lille in 1514 they prohibited 'farcer les princes', attacked the insolence of actors in 1522, and in 1544 suppressed 'des Jeux scandaleux'.

Religious drama, disinherited by the church and vexatious to the state, came under growing threat during the 16th century, especially in England and France. The French Parlement introduced a form of preventive censorship in 1538 which soon led to the withdrawal of the privilege of the Confrérie de la Passion in 1548 and a consequent ban on the performance of all mystery plays. In England, government regulation of the drama was a vital instrument of Tudor statecraft, serving the turn of the English Reformation under Henry VIII, the temporary reversion to Catholicism under Mary, and of Elizabeth's creation of a strong nation-state under the Protestant banner. The first attempt to fetter the drama on a national level dates back to the act 'for the advancement of true religion and for the abolishment of the contrary' (1543), one of the provisions of which banned all plays likely to challenge the newly-established religion. In 1548 the Feast of Corpus Christi (with all attendant dramatic activities) was suppressed; it was temporarily reinstated under Mary but by 1581 Elizabeth had managed to achieve a complete prohibition of the Mystery Cycles, followed by a ban (lasting for over 300 years) on any kind of scriptural or biblical drama.

The key to effective censorship was already centralized control. In many parts of Western Europe (e.g. Germany and Italy) the fragmented political situation made that impossible. France had some success via its Parlement in Paris, and Spain had its native-bred Inquisition (though the drama never figured prominently in the proscription lists); but the most skilful handling of stage censorship took place in Elizabethan England. In 1559 local authorities were empowered to prohibit plays 'wherein either matters of religion or of the governaunce of the estate of the common weale shall be handled, or treated', though Elizabeth always understood that proper control meant active supervision by the court itself. The powers of the **Master of the Revels**, nominally subject to the Lord Chamberlain, are first mentioned in the patent granted to the Earl of Leicester's troupe in 1574, which was allowed to perform only those plays 'sene & allowed' by the Master. The advent of the first permanent theatres in London in 1576–7 necessitated fuller definition of the powers of the Revels Office and in 1581 a royal patent gave the incumbent, Edmund Tilney, sweeping powers 'to order and reform, authorise and put down, as shall be thought meet unto himself, or his . . . deputy . . .' any piece considered prejudicial to the interests of the state. By the time **Shakespeare** came to London a centralized and remarkably effective system of censorship was operating. Further royal edicts of 1598, 1603 and 1622, and the 1606 act prohibiting profane oaths (3 Jac. I, c. 21), secured the Master of the Revels as principal arbiter of the drama until well into the 17th century, interrupted only by Cromwell's closure of the theatres from 1642 to 1660.

Court supervision had positive and negative effects on the theatre. While it gave acting companies welcome protection from interference by hostile local authorities, it also meant that plays were subjected to close official scrutiny before licensing. The text of *Sir Thomas More* (c. 1594) – of which it is likely Shakespeare was the part-author – bears the instruction: 'leave out ye insurrection and the cause'; and there is evidence of political censorship in a number of other plays of the period – e.g. *The Second Maiden's Tragedy* (1611), **Massinger**'s *Believe As You List* (1631) and *The King and his Subject* (1638) – though it is not certain in all cases that the censor (rather than the playhouse) was responsible. Some early printings of Shakespeare's plays seem to have suffered: the Quarto texts of *Richard II* (until Q4, 1608) lack the abdication scene and the Folio *Othello* omits the oaths present in the Quarto; but again the same caution applies, especially in the latter case. The substitution of Falstaff for Sir John Oldcastle

in *Henry IV Part 1* may indicate the censor's attempt to protect a prominent personality; but there are more definite examples of this practice later (e.g. **Shirley**'s *The Ball*, 1632), when censorship was under the firm control of Sir Henry Herbert (Master of the Revels, 1623–73). Some playwrights even went to prison for performing seditious matter – e.g. **Ben Jonson**, **Chapman**, and **Marston**, whose *Eastward Ho* (1605) aroused James I's wrath for its irreverent treatment of his Scottish courtiers.

The relative strength of the system of censorship in 17th-century England contrasts with its relative weakness elsewhere, even in France, where pre-production censorship had only limited returns. In 1609 the comic actors of the **Hôtel de Bourgogne** were prevented from staging 'aucunes comédies ou farces' without prior approval of the King's Procurator; but in 1641 Louis XIII abolished censorship altogether. Actors could still be punished for indecency, however, and, as **Molière** discovered in the 1660s, the playwright was still not wholly free. *Tartuffe* aroused such a storm of abuse from both Parlement and the Archbishop of Paris that Louis XIV, though privately sympathetic to Molière, was forced to ban the play. Only after much re-working was it allowed for public performance in the presence of the King in 1669.

During the 18th century, dramatic censorship became more firmly established in Western Europe, particularly in Britain and France, where measures were introduced which (with periodic remissions in the case of France) were to last well into the 20th century. On 31 March 1701 Louis XIV re-introduced formal censorship with an order that all new plays be officially scrutinized before performance. The principle was confirmed in another edict (November 1706), which effectively inaugurated the mechanism of pre-Revolution control of the stage, presided over by a successsion of censors – e.g. **Jolyot de Crébillon** and his son, Marin, and Suard (known for his moderate views) – who shaped 18th-century practice. Their victims included La Harpe, Lemierre, and (foremost of all) **Beaumarchais** (*The Barber of Seville* and *The Marriage of Figaro*, 1775, 1784).

Britain's system of censorship underwent dramatic and comprehensive revision in the early 18th century with the introduction of sweeping new powers in Sir Robert Walpole's 1737 stage Licensing Act (10 Geo. II, c. 19), hurriedly written into the statute books as a result of damaging lampoons on the government by **Henry Fielding** and others. Though drawing on the practice of the Revels Office, the new law centred on the Lord Chamberlain, who was empowered (in addition to certain licensing responsibilities for theatres) to forbid 'as often as he shall think fit' any dramatic piece acted 'for hire, gain, or reward' anywhere in Great Britain – an authority which, in the opinion of its arch-opponent Lord Chesterfield, was 'unknown to our laws, inconsistent with our constitution'. Modified only in details by the Theatre Regulation Act (6 & 7 Vict., c. 68) which replaced it in 1843, Walpole's act provided all the foundations for control of the theatre over the next 231 years. Although not normally applied retrospectively, the Lord Chamberlain's powers were occasionally used to prohibit performances of plays like **Otway**'s *Venice Preserv'd* and (during the madness of George III) *King Lear*.

In other parts of Europe also the theatre was coming under intense scrutiny. No formal system of censorship existed in Russia until the beginning of the 19th century but the tsars attempted to bring the drama into close alliance with the court, just as in England; the motives were the same, but the methods were different and more confining, since Russia relied on generous state patronage – in effect government sponsorship of the theatre – to ensure that what was performed was tailored to meet the political needs of the day. While there could be no centralized censorship in the politically confused climate of Germany and Austria, controls did operate at certain local levels. **Schiller**'s famous '**Sturm und Drang**' drama *The Robbers* (which **Hazlitt** described as the quintessence of all that was noble in the struggle for liberty) so frightened the director of the Mannheim production in 1782 that he deliberately camouflaged its revolutionary spirit by removing the action into the 16th century, thus forestalling action on the part of the authorities. Even so, the play was prohibited altogether in other parts of Germany–Austria (e.g. in Leipzig), while its premiere in Vienna was delayed until 1808, when it was given at the Theater an der Wien rather than at the more illustrious **Burgtheater** (where it was finally allowed in a cut version in 1850). Only in France was the play welcomed with unbridled enthusiasm as a salutary lesson for the times.

Censorship, inimical to the spirit of the French Revolution, was abolished by order of the Legislative Assembly 13–19 January 1791 but the free stage was short-lived. By 1794 censorship was reinstated and with it an attempt to 'republicanize' the theatre. Theatres were ordered to delete all references to 'duc', 'baron', 'marquis', 'comte', 'monsieur': no playwright was immune, not even Molière and **Racine**. During the summer of 1794 (at the height of the Terror) the unaccustomed aggressiveness of French censorship was clearly demonstrated; out of 151 scripts submitted over three months, 33 were suppressed and a further 25 severely cut. The fear of contamination by France's revolutionary spirit induced other countries to exercise sterner vigilance in political censorship than ever before. In England, under the watchful eyes of the Lord Chamberlain's deputies – John Larpent (1778–1824) and **George Colman the Younger** (1824–36) – revolutionary topics, regicide, allusions to oppression and patriotism were carefully excised from all play scripts. In some cases in which reform was impossible – e.g. Martin Archer Shee's *Alasco* (1824) and Mary Russell Mitford's *Charles the First* (1825) – plays were banned outright; and those concerned with subversive topics (e.g. Guy Fawkes, Chartism, or potentially insurrectionary subjects) stood little chance of being licensed unless with substantial cuts. A similar vigilance characterized the growing power of Habsburg censorship. The Vienna Order (1794) banned all dangerous political works and by the date of the notorious Karlsbad Decrees (1819) Metternich, supported by a spy system which had ramifications well beyond the dramatic and literary, sought to impose a rigid censorship through all the states of the Austrian Empire. With the assistance of his chief of police, Metternich banned **Franz Grillparzer**'s *King Ottokar, His Rise and Fall* (written 1819–23) as seditious; when in 1838 this was followed by a veto on *Thou Shalt Not Lie*, Grillparzer

refused to permit any further performances of any of his plays.

The theatre in tsarist Russia was already virtually a department of the state when formal censorship was established in 1804, followed by a progressive tightening of the regulations over the next 50 years. By 1828 censorship had been brought under the wing of the Third Department of His Majesty's Personal Office, which introduced new rules for censorship in Moscow, St Petersburg, and the larger provincial cities, and from 1842 embraced all provincial touring troupes. When Nicholas I set up a special secret committee for censorship (known officially as the Committee of April 2nd) in 1848, the tsar took over personal control of the system. Among the more notable victims of tsarist censorship (which permitted no representation of the tsar, no satire on the nobility, landowners, state, or local officials) were **Pushkin** (*Boris Godunov*, 1825; performed 1870 under the more flexible policies of Alexander II), **Turgenev** (*A Month in the Country*, 1850; performed 1872), **Sukhovo-Kobylin** (*The Case*, 1862, performed as *Obsolete Time*, 1882, and *The Death of Tarelkin*, 1869, performed 1900), **Tolstoi** (*The Power of Darkness*, 1886, performed 1895). **Gogol** rather surprisingly escaped a veto on *The Inspector General* (1836): the tsar seems to have been amused and counted on its frightening corrupt provincial officials.

On the European continent generally, political censorship was important as a weapon against the increasing use of the drama as a vehicle for expression of national libertarian sentiment. Metternich's spy system controlled from Vienna kept surveillance on the activities of a group of young radical writers known as the 'Junges Deutschland'; and **Johann Nestroy**'s opportunist *Freedom Comes to Krähwinkel*, crammed with ad-libbed political allusions, was predictably banned in October 1848, within a few months of its first performance. In France **Victor Hugo**'s *Le Roi S'Amuse* (1832) caused a riot at its premiere for supposed reference to Louis-Philippe; it was immediately prohibited and gave the excuse for the reimposition of state censorship after temporary abolition in the 1830 Revolution. The situation in Italy was, if anything, more chaotic than elsewhere. In some areas (e.g. Lombardy-Venetia) the Austrian censor was in control; in most other states and duchies there were more localized systems – a royal committee was set up in Naples in 1807 to supervise all aspects of theatrical production (including scenery and costumes), while at the Vatican, Pius VII appointed a censorship board of six *cavalieri* and a prelate. **Alfieri**'s tragedies were prohibited in the 1820s in Lombardy-Venetia and even in Piedmont, Victor Emmanuel, suspicious of their political allusiveness, ordered deletions of patriotic expressions from *Rosmunda* and *Oreste*. The fervent reception Verdi's *Nabucco* received at Milan in 1842 confirmed to authorities throughout Italy the necessity of anaesthetizing nationalist emotions and guaranteed Verdi close attention from Italian and other European censors thereafter. Among the numerous playwrights who suffered political censorship in the period before Unification were Monti (e.g. *Caius Gracchus*, Tuscany, 1847), Niccolini, D'Aste, and Pellico.

But the balance was slowly changing in Europe after c. 1850 towards a deeper and more persistent concern with moral issues, especially in the calmer political climates of France and Britain. After 1852 (and another brief respite from censorship in the wake of the 1848 Revolution), the French censors turned their attention to the supposed immoralities of the plays of, among others, **Alexandre Dumas** *fils*, **Victorien Sardou**, and **Emile Augier**. Since much of Britain's theatrical life in the 19th century was dependent on importation and adaptation of the latest Parisian novelties, and since its moral censorship was more restrictive than in France, the toll exacted by the Lord Chamberlain and his Examiner of Plays was relatively severe, reaching a peak in the 1870s and 80s. The process of disinfecting French plays for English consumption was common enough, but many comedies and dramas (especially when they seemed to attack the sanctity of family life) proved too *risqué* in language and situation to pass muster with the censor. Most notorious of all perhaps – indeed the benchmark of immorality – was the younger Dumas's *La Dame aux Camélias*, first banned in England in 1853 and several times thereafter in a variety of adaptations; but ironically Verdi's *La Traviata* was allowed in 1856 because, as a general rule, opera enjoyed more latitude than straight drama. The increasingly inhibitive nature of censorship was highlighted, however, by the arrival of the 'advanced drama', heralded by **Ibsen**, which accelerated the embryonic anti-censorship campaign led by **William Archer** and **Bernard Shaw**. This movement was fuelled in the period c. 1880–1910 with the suppression on moral grounds of several plays of European stature: Ibsen's *Ghosts*, Tolstoi's *The Power of Darkness*, **Maeterlinck**'s *Monna Vanna*, and some plays by **Eugène Brieux** (including *Damaged Goods*, also prohibited for a time in France). On the native front Shaw's *Mrs Warren's Profession*, **Harley Granville Barker**'s *Waste*, Edward Garnett's *The Breaking Point* were among the more prominent victims of a censorship which seemed utterly bemused by the idea of a drama seeking seriously to discuss moral and sexual issues on the stage. Conditions were hardly more favourable in Germany, where censorship took on renewed vigour after c. 1889: **Frank Wedekind**'s *Spring Awakening* (1891) and *Earth Spirit* (1895) were both banned from public performance until 1906 and 1902 respectively. One solution to the restrictions imposed on free artistic expression and which met with some success, especially in France, was the idea of a theatre dedicated to private (i.e. club) performances only, which would thus escape the attentions of the censor and, incidentally, be freed from the demands of commercial theatre. **André Antoine**'s Théâtre Libre, founded in Paris in 1887, was the model for similar enterprises in Germany (**Freie Bühne**, Berlin, 1889) and Britain (Independent Theatre Society, London, 1891). For the moment, however, only in France was the anti-censorship lobby victorious with the abolition of pre-production censorship for all practical purposes in 1906 (though formal abolition was delayed until after the Second World War). In Britain, after agitation by leading dramatists, a parliamentary committee met in 1909 (cf. earlier official inquiries into the theatre in 1832, 1866, and 1892) to consider the problem of stage censorship. Its conclusion that a voluntary system of censorship was a workable alternative found little support and the idea lapsed.

20th-century Europe The 20th century has seen a gradual contraction in the freedom accorded, in a world context, to the creative artist. Although dramatic censorship has to a large extent disappeared from nearly all Western democracies, it has inexorably advanced outside the European context to areas where its character, effectiveness, and severity is a function of the political complexion of the authorities that operate it.

British practice in the 20th century shows a gradual retreat by the censor from former embattled positions as public taste became more willing to accept what had been considered outrageous, indecent, or taboo. The rule on the ineligibility of scriptural drama on the stage was relaxed c. 1912 but even as late as 1958 **Beckett**'s *Endgame* was censored for its references to the non-existence of God (whereas the original 1957 French version had emerged unscathed). Political censorship was not wholly dormant either: Shaw's *Press Cuttings* and *The Shewing Up of Blanco Posnet* (there were also religious objections in this case) were both prohibited in 1909, but the latter was staged in Ireland at Dublin's **Abbey Theatre** after **Yeats** and **Lady Gregory** had managed to stave off threatened intervention from the Lord Lieutenant making use of his *ex post facto* powers of censorship. Where personalities were concerned the censor was always eager to intervene. The licence for **Gilbert** and Sullivan's *The Mikado* was temporarily suspended in 1907 for fear of giving offence to the Crown Prince of Japan, who was on a state visit; and in the 1930s all references to Hitler and Mussolini were scrupulously excised from play scripts. (The whole procedure was in fact rather a nonsense as the music-halls, immune from the Lord Chamberlain's jurisdiction, delighted in exploiting just the kind of material which the censors insisted on deleting.) However, the battle on personal allusion was more or less won by 1961 when a send-up of Harold Macmillan featured in the satirical revue *Beyond the Fringe*.

Moral concerns, the main ingredient of British censorship in this century, resulted in temporary prohibitions of varying lengths on a number of foreign plays (including **Strindberg**'s *Miss Julie*, **Pirandello**'s *Six Characters in Search of an Author*, **O'Neill**'s *Desire Under the Elms*, and Wedekind's *Spring Awakening* and *Earth Spirit*, which suffered the longest ban of all and was not licensed until 1964). Pressure from anti-censorship campaigners remained strong; private club performances remained a popular means of evading official interference. The flowering of institutions like the **Stage Society**, the **Gate Theatre**, the **Arts Theatre** Club, Cambridge Festival Theatre, **Joan Littlewood**'s Theatre Workshop, and the **Royal Court Theatre** all contributed in their special ways to the eventual abolition of censorship. After 1956 the Lord Chamberlain was very much on the defensive; dramatists such as **John Arden**, **Arnold Wesker**, and **John Osborne** – though they all had some difficulties with the censor (Osborne in particular) – steadily undermined the conservatism of the authorities and substantially widened the perspective of British theatre. Osborne's *A Patriot for Me* (1964) was considered too explicit, however, in its handling of the theme of homosexuality and was restricted to club performances at the Royal Court. Although much of the censor's work in the 1960s was confined to wrangles over the use of over-explicit language, the Lord Chamberlain's Office did occasionally bare its teeth (e.g. in 1965, three years before abolition of censorship, the production of **Edward Bond**'s *Saved* at the Royal Court was prosecuted for not fulfilling the proper conditions for a private performance). After the abolition of censorship under the 1968 Theatres Act, British theatre has exploited its new-found freedom in such productions as *Hair* (1968) and *Oh, Calcutta!* (1969) (both featured full-frontal nudity); but the deluge of immorality predicted by supporters of censorship never really arrived. The only notable private prosecution was in 1982, against Michael Bogdanov's **National Theatre** production of **Howard Brenton**'s *The Romans in Britain* (1980), which showed a simulated male rape. The case was unsuccessful and ended in confusion.

Outside Britain the pattern of European censorship has been mainly political. In Germany during the 1930s and 40s (and in Austria after the *Anschluss*) it was exceptionally severe. The Nazis took measures which not only prohibited the entire works of authors of whom they disapproved but sought directly to manipulate theatrical production and the choice of repertoire as part of their very sophisticated propaganda machine. Authors on the Nazi proscription lists included **Georg Kaiser** (Germany's leading expressionist playwright), **Arthur Schnitzler** (an Austrian Jew; his work was banned posthumously), Wedekind (on moral grounds) and **Bertolt Brecht** (who suffered police harassment until he fled the country in 1932 to temporary refuge in the USA). Proscriptions of a similar nature operated in Nazi-occupied countries and in Fascist Italy, where Alfieri's *Saul* was forbidden (because Saul was a Jew), as was **García Lorca**'s *Blood Wedding*, and a version of *Julius Caesar* (which was thought to reflect too critically on Mussolini). Official censorship ceased in West Germany at the end of the Second World War.

Equally repressive and longer-lasting was censorship in Franco's Spain, where pre-existent Catholic censorship was overlaid with an extreme right-wing political element. After Lorca was murdered by the Falangists at the end of the Civil War there was a mass exodus of intellectuals and artists, including **Fernando Arrabal** (who became a French citizen and henceforward wrote in French). Those who stayed included **Alfonso Sastre** and **Antonio Buero Vallejo**, both of whom endured terms of imprisonment under Franco. Buero Vallejo's *Adventure in the Grey* was banned in 1949 but allowed in a more critical version in 1963, when there was a slight relaxation in the rigours of censorship with the appointment of a new committee. In 1960 Sastre accused Vallejo of 'posibilismo' (i.e. of compromising his political stance in order to get his plays past the censor) at a time when Sastre had become so disillusioned with the stage that he had stopped writing for it. Buero Vallejo continued the struggle, however, and achieved some success in circumventing the censor, though *The Double Story of Dr Valmy* was suppressed in 1964, followed in 1970 by *The Sleep of Reason* (in which Goya's refusal to submit to tyranny by Ferdinand VII bore intentional parallels with contemporary resistance to Franco). As far back as 1961 Sastre and others had argued that censorship had had a profoundly damaging effect on the drama (cf. their manifesto entitled *Documento sobre el teatro español*). It was restrictive not only politically, but also morally, since the influence of the Catholic Church on the censor's office was still very

powerful. Most Spanish drama of any significance was produced abroad until the demise of Franco (1975), when censorship was relaxed.

East European censorship is naturally dominated by the model of the Soviet Union. Although there was a period of relative freedom for the theatre immediately after the Bolshevik Revolution, the USSR (taking much inspiration from the excesses of tsarist censorship) has since the 1920s engineered and perfected a system whereby the state is in absolute control of literature and the theatre. As a consequence much of the history of 20th-century Soviet drama is the history of its slow critical and intellectual emasculation in the name of 'socialist realism', a concept of uncertain definition but which nonetheless forces all writing into the mould determined by the state machine. All writers must belong to the institution now known as the Union of Soviet Writers, which is an organ of the Communist Party. 'Glavlit', the state censorship office, was established in 1922 and after c. 1930 it effectively became a branch of the security police. By 1934 'Glavlit' was empowered to read all plays at least ten days beforehand and to have its representatives allocated two seats (no further back than the fourth row) at every performance. 'Glavlit' and its sister 'Glavrepertkom' (which determined all theatre repertoires) were given responsibility for deciding what is art, since by definition anything not approved cannot be art.

Stalinist censorship was uncompromising and vindictive (e.g. in 1936–7 over half the plays earmarked for production at the main theatres were banned). Among the prominent dramatists to suffer in the late 20s and 30s were **Mikhail Bulgakov** (e.g. *Zoika's Apartment*, 1926, and his satire on 'Glavrepertkom' in *The Crimson Island*, 1928; on appeal to Stalin he was made resident playwright at the **Moscow Art Theatre** but further suppressions followed, including *Bliss*, 1934, *Ivan Vasilevich*, 1936 and *The Cabal of Hypocrites*, an attack on cultural dictatorship, 1936), **Vladimir Mayakovsky** (his imaginative satires on Soviet philistinism and bureaucracy *The Bedbug* and *The Bathhouse* were vetoed in 1929–30), and **Leonid Leonov** (e.g. *The Snowstorm*, suppressed during rehearsals in 1939). Some dramatists managed to emigrate (e.g. **Evgeny Zamyatin** in 1932) but the short story writer and playwright **Isaak Babel**, whose last play *The Chekist* disappeared after his arrest by the secret police, presumably shared a similar fate – death in a labour camp – to the director **Vsevolod Meyerhold**, a protégé of **Stanislavsky**'s, arrested during the same 1938–9 purge. The period came to be dominated by the hard-line orthodoxy of Andrei Zhdanov (Stalin's associate and ultimately Party spokesman on cultural affairs), who was responsible for the notorious 'Zhdanov Theses' (1946) and the drab, uniform mediocrity of approved Soviet drama until the early 1950s. Nearly all the suppressed plays and their authors were subsequently rehabilitated during one or other of the periodic post-Stalin cultural thaws (e.g. Babel in the late 1950s, but some of Bulgakov's work was not acceptable until 1965). In the 1960s several new dissident dramatists emerged – e.g. **Andrei Amalrik** and Aleksandr Solzhenitsyn, whose play *The Love Girl and the Innocent* (based on first-hand experience in a Stalinist labour camp) was banned after the dress rehearsal in 1962. Self-published, underground literature (*samizdat*), a long tradition in the Soviet Union, has served an important outlet for dissident expression (e.g. Amalrik's absurdist dramas and Muza Pavlova's satirical pieces *Boxes* and *Wings*, both eventually published in Frankfurt, 1970). Since the accession to power of Mikhail Gorbachev there have been signs of a more open policy (*glasnost*) towards the arts in general; and though no official announcement has been made, 'Glavlit' is said to have been abolished. Striking evidence of this liberalizing trend came in the summer of 1986 with the official approval of a populist, highly contentious play entitled *Sarcophagus* (by Vladimir Gubarev, a senior journalist with *Pravda*), based on personal observation of the aftermath of the Chernobyl nuclear disaster. It was widely performed in the USSR and extracts even appeared in official journals, among them *Sovietskaya Kultura*, the Communist Party newspaper.

All Soviet satellites operate systems of state censorship based on the parent model, though there are important differences of emphasis: generally speaking, East Germany and Bulgaria are among the more repressive, while Hungary (until 1956), Czechoslovakia (until 1968), and Poland (until the early 1980s) enjoyed degrees of relative independence. Following the Soviet invasion, the Czech theatre was put under harsh restraints: the plays of leading dramatists like Milan Kundera and Pavel Kohout were both banned, as was the entire work of **Václav Havel** (who had made a reputation in the mid-60s as an absurdist playwright). His later plays *Audience, Private View* (both 1975), and *Protest* (1978), all written in the knowledge that public performance was impossible and staged privately with friends, have since been professionally presented in the West. Havel spent over four years in prison following his arrest for subversion in 1979; Kohout now writes in exile in Vienna. In Poland, **Sławomir Mrożek**'s *Vatzlav* (written in the tense political climate of 1968) was denied its premiere until 1979, when the power of the popular movement known as Solidarity was strong. But after the imposition of military rule under General Jaruselski in late 1981, constraints were rapidly reimposed. A recent victim was Kazimierz Braun's *Dżuma* (based on **Camus**'s novel *The Plague* and drawing parallels with modern-day Poland) which was banned at the dress rehearsal in April 1983. It was then heavily censored and allowed two performances, only to be suppressed again shortly afterwards.

Outside Europe Dramatic censorship has never existed on a formalized basis in the USA, where free speech is guaranteed under the Constitution. However, that has not prevented occasional local action at community or state level, usually by the police, in closing down allegedly offensive productions which endanger public morals or are insulting to the state. In effect, theatre managers in the USA have been their own censors, as offences against public taste may well endanger their theatre licences. In general the southern states have shown more conservative attitudes than elsewhere. The absence of institutionalized censorship has allowed timely acts of courage (e.g. the world premiere of *Ghosts*, given in Chicago in 1882 as no theatre in Ibsen's native Norway would touch the play). But when Shaw's *Mrs Warren's Profession* was staged by **Arnold Daly** in New York in 1905 – it was

still banned in Britain – the actors were prosecuted; and in 1926 **Mae West**'s theatrical debut as a waterfront whore in *Sex* earned her an eight-day prison sentence for offence against public decency.

The widespread distribution of censorship is principally a modern phenomenon, but there are exceptions with earlier histories, such as Turkey and Japan, and some countries formerly under strong colonial rule, where forms of censorship were developed to suit local conditions at the time.

Censorship began in Australia soon after colonization. All theatrical performances by convict settlers were prohibited between 1800 and 1832; and in 1828, after the first permanent theatre was set up in Sydney, the Legislative Council was panicked into passing an act to regulate all places of public entertainment, which drew heavily on Walpole's 1737 Stage Licensing Act. By the 19th century the British authorities in India had begun to take an interest in native theatre, especially in Bengal, where the drama was used as an instrument for anti-British propaganda. Deenabandhu Mitra's *The Mirror of the Indigo* (1860) – on British exploitation of Bengali labour in the tea plantations – was eventually banned when taken on tour to Lucknow and Delhi. Censorship was generally very informal in the African dominions (mainly through the influence of the missionaries in the 19th century) but the authorities did have powers of intervention where necessary – e.g. some Yoruba-language operas by **Hubert Ogunde** (*Strike and Hunger*, 1945, and *Bread and Bullets*, 1949) were banned in certain areas of Nigeria for fear of public disturbances.

In the 19th century Turkish drama began to suffer censorship under the rule of Sultans Abdülaziz (1861–76) and Abdülhamit II (1876–1908): traditional shadow puppet theatre (**Karagöz**), often satirical in content, was as deeply affected as were the more westernized forms of theatre beginning to emerge (e.g. Namik Kemal's strongly nationalistic *The Fatherland: or Silistria*, 1873, which the Sultan, afraid of its inciting a revolution, banned with its author). Though in the early 20th century drama started to flourish once more – Antoine helped establish a National Theatre in Istanbul in 1914 – Turkey's record in political censorship was punctuated by periods of quite severe restriction. Only after the 1960 Revolution was political drama allowed relative freedom of expression.

In contrast, several Middle Eastern neighbours have enjoyed no such felicity. Among the more extreme is Iran. Having formerly enforced rigorous censorship under the Shah, it has since the early 1980s become even more repressive. Theatre directors are required to seek approval not only of text but of the manner of performance before rehearsals are even allowed to begin. Thereafter all productions are subject to unannounced visits by officials from the Ministry of Islamic Guidance, authorized in the name of Islam to make any changes they choose. A number of Iranian playwrights suffered under both regimes (e.g. Gholam Hoseyn Sa'edi, who died in exile in Paris in 1985).

Japanese censorship has a history dating back to the mid 17th century, when the Shōgunate, always distrustful of eruptions of popular feeling, imposed restrictions on **kabuki** theatre, the irreverent alternative to classical **nō** drama. From 1629 women were prohibited from acting on the stage; and they have reappeared only in the present century. For centuries Japanese theatre developed in virtual isolation from the rest of the world, yet the activities of its censors were strikingly similar to those of their European counterparts and were mainly of a political nature, occasionally disguised as moral concerns. After the Meiji Restoration in 1868, when Japan's contacts with the West assumed importance, the theatre was considered crucial to the country's dignity and prestige and was encouraged to project an image of wholesomeness and sobriety. It was at this time that *kabuki* theatre came under renewed attack for alleged superficiality and licentiousness. After the First World War Japan intensified its grip on the theatre: social criticism was severely restricted (e.g. Senzaburo Suzuki's *Burned Alive*, banned in 1921) and by the late 1930s political drama was outlawed completely. It began to re-emerge only in the 1950s.

China has laboured under strict censorship since the People's Republic was established in 1949 but even in the 1930s the theatre was made to serve the interests of the party in areas under Communist control. China's most intense (and chaotic) period of censorship began in the mid-60s with the Cultural Revolution, which was to some extent precipitated by attacks in 1964 on the play *Hai Jui Dismissed* (by Wu Han, deputy mayor of Peking) for its alleged veiled criticism of Chairman Mao. During the Revolution itself even Peking and Shanghai classical opera began to suffer and some of China's most distinguished playwrights (e.g. T'ien Han) fell from grace in a hysterical purge of modern drama. Although the injustices of the period have now been largely corrected, the Chinese theatre is still in a fluid state; and the drama is still a victim of the continuing debate between reactionary and liberalizing forces.

The restless and unstable political climate of Central and South America renders dramatic censorship an almost continually self-renewing feature of cultural life. It is as common to right-wing dictatorships (e.g. Chile) as to left-wing regimes (e.g. Cuba). Although the subcontinent has produced some dramatists of international repute, the predominance of military-inspired censorships has restricted (and in some periods stifled) growth – e.g. in Brazil between 1930 and 1960, when the Conservatório Dramático Brasileiro assumed absolute control over the theatre, and in the severe constraints imposed after the 1964 coup; also in Argentina, where particularly heavy-handed censorship characterized the Peronist regime and, more recently, the rule of the Generals. Anti-totalitarian dramatists have had little voice in modern Latin America; for some of them self-exile is the only alternative – e.g. the Chilean dramatist **Alejandro Sieveking** (who lived and worked in Costa Rica, 1974–84) and **Griselda Gambaro** of Argentina (who chose to live and write in Spain). Recent political changes have lightened the atmosphere somewhat, especially in Argentina, where Gambaro's plays have begun to be staged once more (e.g. *El campo*, which received its first performance for ten years in Buenos Aires in 1984).

Perhaps no system of modern censorship has kindled more adverse publicity and obloquy than South Africa's, where the laws abbreviating intellectual and artistic freedom have a comprehensiveness and rigour unmatched outside the Soviet bloc. They date back to the early years of Afrikaner rule but the Entertainments (Censorship) Act (1931) gave real force and substance to the earlier more haphazard arrangements. Since that time the system has been progressively modified and tightened, notably by the Publications and Entertainments Act (1963). The enforcement of apartheid has strangled much of the life from native drama. Several leading playwrights have been forced into exile (e.g. Alfred Hutchinson, Lewis Nkosi); others (e.g. **Athol Fugard**, a white writer hostile to the regime) have continued to produce under increasingly daunting conditions. Strict censorship also extends to the work of foreign dramatists (e.g. **Albee**'s *Who's Afraid of Virginia Woolf?*, banned in 1963). The censorship board considers plays from several view-points: whether they are likely to offend religious feelings, bring into ridicule or disrepute certain sections of society, and if they are generally contrary to the moral instincts or otherwise threaten the security of the white minority. There is an appeals procedure through the office of the Minister of the Interior.

Postscript Censorship is still endemic to most hard-line political and religious regimes world-wide; but profound political changes in the late 1980s resulted in liberalization of the theatre in South Africa and in the former Communist bloc. Officially abolished in the USSR in 1990, censorship ceased throughout Eastern Europe, including Czechoslovakia, where once dissident playwright **Václav Havel** became state president. JRS

Centlivre, Susannah (1669–1723) English playwright. Born in Lincolnshire she was a strolling player from c. 1685 and may have spent some time in Cambridge. In 1700 her first poems and letters were published and her first play produced. Her sharp attack on the contemporary addiction to gambling, *The Gamester* (1705), was her first significant success as a dramatist and its sequel, *The Basset-Table*, dealt with the same theme. She married in 1707. Of her 20 plays the most popular were *The Busy Body* (1709) and *The Wonder: A Woman Keeps a Secret* (1714) both of which lasted well into the 19th century. Her best work, *A Bold Stroke for a Wife* (1718), provides a virtuoso acting part for the hero in his multiple disguises. PH

Century Theatre see New Theatre

Cervantes, Miguel de (1547–1616) Spanish novelist and dramatist who found success in novels only after consistent failure in the theatre, to which his episodic style and lack of poetic talent were ill-suited. He wrote about 30 plays in the 1580s of which only two survive, each in four acts: *El trato de Argel* (*The Trade of Algiers*), drawing on his captivity there, and *El cerco de Numancia* (*The Siege of Numantia*), his best play in spite of its poor verse. Later he wrote eight more plays which it seems were not performed, but were eventually published with eight *entremeses* in 1615. These single-scene playlets, six of them in prose, are much superior to his full-length dramas. Cervantes initially supported the classical dramatic precepts, attacking **Lope de Vega** in Chapter 48 of *Don Quijote*, though by 1615 his opposition had turned to warm praise and unsuccessful imitation. CL

Césaire, Aimé (1913–) Martiniquan poet, politician, essayist and playwright. Césaire has enjoyed a successful career as a politician and author, being one of the founders (with Senghor) of the negritude movement in the 1930s. He is better known as a poet than as a playwright, but his plays are among the most important new French-language work of the 1960s. They administered a shock to the French theatre world very similar to that produced by **Soyinka**'s work in England. An early poetic play *Et les Chiens Se Taisaient* (*And the Dogs were Silent*) celebrates the themes of revolt to be found in his major plays, but remains essentially a poetic work. His three plays for the theatre were all written in the 1960s, partly under the influence of **Jean-Marie Serreau**, who directed them. In *La Tragédie du Roi Christophe* (*The Tragedy of King Christopher*, 1964) the historical figure of Christophe (King Henry of Haiti 1811–20) is used to present the conflicting views of black African liberation current in the 1950s and 1960s. They play has a vigorous, Brechtian epic structure, combined with a powerful and varied French poetic idiom, drawing on the language of Africa and the Caribbean as well as that of France. *Une Saison au Congo* (*A Season in the Congo*, 1967) centres on Patrice Lumumba's attempts to establish an independent Congolese Republic through the very different dramatic style of the African hero play. European critics misunderstood its intentions but it is as powerful, in its own way, as *Christophe*, and very much more critical of the effects of white decolonization. This theme is taken up in *Une Tempête* (1969), a brilliant re-working of **Shakespeare**'s *Tempest*, in which Prospero represents a white settler and Caliban a black slave, follower of Shango. The play ends differently from Shakespeare's with Prospero unable to leave the island, remaining locked in a power struggle with Caliban which he is doomed, in the end, to lose. Césaire turned to the theatre to reach a broader audience than the readers of his poetry and to deal directly with African politics. His plays were very widely discussed when produced but have not been as widely revived as they deserve. DB

Chaikin, Joseph (1935–) American director, actor, and producer. Born in Brooklyn and educated at Drake University (1950–3), Chaikin made his New York debut in *Dark of the Moon* (1958). He joined **The Living Theatre** the following year and appeared in *Many Loves* and *Tonight We Improvise* (1959); *The Connection* and *Jungle of Cities* (1961–2); and *Man Is Man* (1962). For the Writers' Stage (1964), he performed in **Ionesco**'s *The New Tenant* and *Victims of Duty*. Chaikin founded **The Open Theatre** in 1964 as an experimental company to build and perform new scripts. The success of *America Hurrah!* in 1966 (1967 in London) established his reputation. His workshop approach to composition also produced *Terminal* and *The Serpent* in 1970, the latter a series of episodes on the history of murder. Chaikin has directed for the **New York Shakespeare Festival**, **Manhattan Theatre Club**, Magic Theatre of San Francisco, and **Mark Taper Forum** of Los Angeles. An articulate spokesman for the 1960s avant-garde movement, Chaikin has won numerous awards including 5 Obies. TLM

Chaillot Theatre The first theatre on the Place du Trocadéro, opposite the Eiffel Tower in Paris, was a Second Empire monstrosity built for the exhibition of 1878. It was allotted to **Gémier** when he set up the first **Théâtre National Populaire** in 1920. Situated at the heart of the most fashionable residential district, it could never be the centre for a popular community theatre. Gémier could only arrange reduced price performances of productions by other companies. In 1935 it was demolished and the present complex of museums and theatres was built for the 1937 exhibition. The main theatre had a stage 23 metres wide and its auditorium held 2,800. It made a perfect debating chamber for the United Nations Organization which met there from 1947–51. Heading a revived TNP, **Vilar** managed to make a going concern of this theatre between 1951 and 1963 but audiences declined after Vilar's departure and in 1972 the theatre was closed for renovations. The interior was completely remodelled to designs commissioned by **Antoine Vitez** and Jack Lang, later Minister of Culture under Mitterrand. But the first director to be put in charge of the new auditorium, André-Louis Périnetti, claimed that it was too cumbersome to work with. It was left to Antoine Vitez, who took over in 1981, to regenerate something of Vilar and Gémier's vision with bold new productions of both new plays and world classics. DB

Chaita Ghoda Nata (India) This is a simple form of drama enacted by fishermen of Orissa state in northeastern India on full-moon nights in the spring. Three actors play all the roles and two musicians accompany them with drums and cymbals. One of the actors represents a horse-dancer. The *rauta* is the main singer-commentator who delivers discourses on mythological themes. The *rautami* plays his wife and acts as chorus and co-singer and dancer. Improvised dialogue and humorous episodes punctuate the evening event. FaR

Chalbaud, Román (1931–) Venezuelan playwright and director. One third of the Venezuelan 'Holy Trinity' (with **Cabrujas** and **Chocrón**), Chalbaud has written more than a dozen plays. A pioneer in film techniques, he has also been a leading figure in Venezuelan film since the mid-50s with a grotesque Buñuelesque reliance on abnormal and deformed characters. As a director of the **Nuevo Grupo** (New Group) since 1967, he has mounted both national and foreign plays, ranging from the classics to the absurd, in order to promote a national theatre movement. As a writer, he has been eclectic in both theme and style, but his plays often depict marginal characters within society and deal with poverty, social maladjustment, sexuality, and political and ontological problems. Often dealing with multiple issues at the same time, he characterizes the sociological concerns of Venezuelan society with a cinematic technique. *Caín adolescente* (*Adolescent Cain*, 1955) dealt with rural adaptation to an urban environment; later plays include *La quema de Judas* (*The Burning of Judas*, 1964), *Los ángeles terribles* (*The Terrible Angels*, 1967), *El pez que fuma* (*The Smoking Fish*, 1968) and *El viejo grupo* (*The Old Group*, 1984). GW

Champion, Gower (1921–80) American dancer, choreographer and director. Champion appeared as a

Production by El Nuevo Grupo of Román Chalbaud's *Los ángeles terribles*, Caracas, Venezuela, 1979.

dancer in *The Streets of Paris* (1939) and several other shows before turning to choreography with *Small Wonder* (1948). After dancing with his wife Marge in several Hollywood films, Champion returned to Broadway as the director and choreographer of *Bye, Bye, Birdie* (1960). The charm and energy of his staging led to further directing and choreography assignments for *Carnival* (1961), *Hello, Dolly!* (1964), *I Do! I Do!* (1966), *Irene* (1973), *Mack and Mabel* (1974), and others. Champion died just as his last show, *42nd Street*, was about to open in 1980. His initial directorial work evinced a fresh and inventive approach to staging a musical. *Carnival*, in particular, was praised for its imaginative, stylized production. Champion, along with **Bob Fosse** and **Michael Bennett**, made the choreographer-director the dominant figure in the musical theatre of the 1970s.   MK

Champmeslé (Marie Desmares) (1642–98) French actress, noted for her performances in the tragedies of **Racine**. First mentioned at Rouen in 1665, she came to Paris three years later and subsequently appeared at all the established theatres in turn, first the **Marais** from 1668, the **Hôtel de Bourgogne** from 1670 and after 1679 with **Molière**'s former company at the Hôtel Guénégaud, which became the first **Comédie-Française** in the following year. Although not beautiful she was renowned for her touching voice which could readily move an audience to tears and made her a potent attraction even in indifferent plays.

Having deeply impressed Racine as Hermione in *Andromaque* she became the playwright's mistress and created all his major heroines from Bérénice to Phèdre which he wrote expressly for her. Illness forced her to retire in 1698 and she died a few months later. Her husband Charles Chevillet, whose stage name she had taken after their marriage in 1666, was an actor with the same companies, also predominantly in tragic parts. He was a friend of La Fontaine and the author of a number of satirical comedies, notably *Crispin Chevalier* (*Crispin Knight*, 1673) and *Le Florentin* (*The Florentine*, 1685).   DR

Chancerel, Léon (1886–1965) French actor, director, playwright and researcher. After training with **Copeau** founded Les Comédiens Routiers in 1929, a semi-amateur touring company linked to the Scout movement. Like Copeau, he revived the style and spirit of the **commedia** for productions of **Molière** and of adaptations of medieval tales. He promoted the revival of medieval religious drama, established a children's theatre Le Théâtre de l'Oncle Sébastien and, in 1939, was put in charge of the Centre Dramatique de Kellermann, a research institute in which he continued to work after the war.   DB

Chanfrau, Francis (1824–84) American actor. A native of New York, Chanfrau was inspired by a performance of **Edwin Forrest** to become an actor and through his ability to imitate Forrest gained recognition and started on the tour of theatres and cities across America that eventually led him to the **Olympic Theatre** in New York in 1848. As Mose the fire b'hoy in *A Glance at New York*, written for him by **Benjamin A. Baker**, Chanfrau became the 'lion' of the town. Dressed in the red shirt, plug hat and turned-up trousers of the New York Fireman, Chanfrau was featured in several Mose plays, particularly *The Mysteries and Miseries of New York* by Henry W. Plunkett. Friends leased the **Chatham Theatre** for Chanfrau who renamed it the National and continued to perform the role of Mose for about three and a half years. After this popularity, Chanfrau performed 560 times as Kit Carson in a play by that title and played the lead character in Thomas de Walden's *Sam* 783 times. WJM

Chapelain, Jean (1595–1674) French scholar, critic and man of letters who played an influential part in the formulation of the neoclassical aesthetic in 17th-century France. As founder member of the Académie-Française in 1634 he guided its counsels for many years and was the principal, if not sole, author of the Academy's public censure of **Corneille**'s *Le Cid* for its irregularities. In this and other critical writings he staunchly upheld the formal conventions derived by Renaissance scholarship from the ancients, stressing the importance for drama of credibility (as distinct from truth to the facts), decorum, and the three unities, of time, place and action. In so doing he postulated two crucial factors, the existence of absolute rules for judging the quality of contemporary plays and the paternalistic role of the Académie-Française as the guardian of these standards, in effect the genesis of the 'academy-spirit': 'we must not say with the crowd that a work is good merely because it pleases, unless the learned and the expert are also pleased'. DR

Chapman, George (c. 1560–1634) English poet and playwright, as famous for his translations of Homer as for his idiosyncratic and often difficult plays. He was one of many writers associated with **Henslowe** and the **Admiral's Men** during the final decade of the 16th century. Surviving plays from this period are *The Blind Beggar of Alexandria* (1596) and *An Humorous Day's Mirth* (1597), which influenced **Jonson**'s more famous comedy of humours, *Every Man in His Humour* (1598). Francis Meres, in *Palladis Tamia* (1598), considered Chapman among the best poets for both tragedy and comedy, which strongly suggests that several of his plays have been lost. Those that survive date mostly from the first decade of the 17th century, when Chapman was writing for the sophisticated audiences of the **Boys' Companies**. They include *May Day* (c. 1601), *The Gentleman Usher* (c. 1602), *All Fools* (1604), *Monsieur D'Olive* (1604) and *The Widow's Tears* (c. 1605). These comedies yield less to the reader than does the work of many of Chapman's contemporaries. They are sometimes morally as well as linguistically complex. In his tragedies, Chapman writes repeatedly of deeply flawed Titanic heroes, distanced by their author's classical stoicism from the recent French history in which they figured. It is these overreachers who give their names to *Bussy D'Ambois* (1604), *The Conspiracy and Tragedy of Charles, Duke of Byron* (1608),

The Revenge of Bussy D'Ambois (c. 1610) and *Chabot, Admiral of France* (c. 1613). The second of these plays so offended the French Ambassador that Chapman was threatened with imprisonment, something he had already suffered for his part in the writing of *Eastward Ho* (1605). It is this lively collaboration with Jonson and **Marston** that has had the longest theatrical life of Chapman's plays. PT

Chapman family see **Showboats**

Chappuzeau, Samuel (1625–1701) French man of letters, author of a number of comedies and farces but pre-eminently of *Le Théâtre Français* (1674), the only contemporary account of its kind. Apart from presenting an apologia for the theatre in general and actors in particular, it contains a catalogue of dramatists and lives of many prominent performers, including a long section on **Molière**. Despite inaccuracies it is a valuable source of information on the 17th-century professional theatre. DR

Charivari The 'chalvaricum', as 14th- and 15th-century church bans refer to it, was originally a 'tumult' directed against a marriage the community disapproved of; remarried widows and unequal matches would be treated to a barrage of catcalls (the German 'Katzenmusik'). The term came to mean a procession of noisy maskers, dancers, drummers and singers who made the streets unsafe by night. Once the staid citizens realized the fun in singing and saying what one would under the anonymity of devil-masks, the charivari became organized as a mass 'happening' for its own sake. Among the *buffones* or masks were depraved monks with bare behinds and lion's manes, demons rattling pots and pans (as in the modern Fastnacht of Basel) and the wild man Hellequin or Herlequin whose name becomes transformed into **Harlequin**. In England this 'rough music' came to be performed by concerts of butchers on marrow-bones and cleavers at the weddings of members of their craft and, later, of the *beau monde*, as Hogarth shows in his illustrations to *Hudibras*. LS

See: R. Johannsmeier, *Spielmann, Schalk und Scharlatan*, Reinbek bei Hamburg, 1984.

Chatham Theatre (Chatham Garden Theatre) Park Row between Pearl and Duane Sts, New York City [Architect: George Conklin]. In 1823, Hippolite Barrière, proprietor of the Chatham Gardens, decided to dispense light entertainment along with summer refreshments on the property. He erected a tent theatre, perhaps America's first summer playhouse. The following year, he built a permanent structure and was for several seasons a formidable rival to the **Park Theatre**. After 1827, its vogue passed, it presented everything from **Shakespeare** to equestrian drama to French opera under a succession of managers, who failed to revive its fortunes. In 1832, it was converted to a Presbyterian chapel. MCH

Chayefsky, Paddy (1923–81) American playwright. A self-styled activist social critic, Chayefsky established himself as a writer during the heyday of live television drama, moved to the films with the highly honoured *Marty* (1955), succeeded briefly as a Broadway playwright, and finally abandoned the legitimate stage to concentrate again on writing for the motion pictures. His Broadway plays were *Middle of the Night* (1956), *The Tenth Man* (1959), *Gideon* (1961), and *The Passion of Josef D* (1964). His last play, *The Latent Heterosexual* (1968), was successfully produced in American regional professional theatres and at the **Bristol Old Vic** in England. The culmination of his film writing career came with *Network* (1976).   LDC

Chekhov, Anton Pavlovich (1860–1904) The most notable and celebrated 20th-century Russian dramatist in the West, his plays helped establish psychological realism, although possessing symbolist, impressionist and even proto-absurdist traits. By fragmenting the well-made play, scattering exposition throughout, compressing, internalizing and excising action, Chekhov created the so-called 'theatre of mood', of misdirection, noneventfulness and partially stated meaning. A physician by training, he was especially sensitive to the individual's predisposition toward wastefulness versus the conservationist potential of life. His short story writing career, begun at Moscow University Medical School (1879–84) and extending to his commissions for Suvorin's conservative newspaper *New Time* (1886–93) and beyond, taught him to select and delicately weave idiosyncratically revealing details, symbols, images and themes into a rhythmically constructed musical structure. His work reveals the influence of the great Russian realists – **Tolstoi**, Dostoevsky, **Turgenev**, the *bytovki* (those who wrote of everyday life) – as well as that of de Maupassant's and **Saltykov-Shchedrin**'s atmospheric character studies, **Maeterlinck**'s symbolist-rendered inner worlds, **Gogol**'s grotesquely stylized illogicality and **Pisarev**'s vaudevillian farces. Also, in such stories as 'The Steppe' (1888), 'A Dreary Story' (1889), 'The Duel' (1891), 'Ward No. 6' (1892), 'The Lady with the Dog' (1899) and 'In the Ravine' (1900), Chekhov learned to strike a balance between 'subjectively painful' and 'objectively comedic' perspectives on life, to link the catastrophic with the trivial, to create a sense of mystery, multiplicity, recurrence and nonoccurrence. Chekhov's earliest plays are farces, vaudevilles and 'comedy-jokes' based upon his stories: *On the Highroad* (1884), *The Harmfulness of Tobacco Smoking* (1886), *Swan Song* and *The Bear* (1888), *The Wedding* and *The Tragedian in Spite of Himself* (1889), *The Marriage Proposal* (1890) and *The Anniversary* (1891). In these succinct, dynamic and compassionate pieces, Chekhov began to erase the boundary between comedy and drama and to forge the tragifarcical approach built upon 'seeming irrelevancy' which so confounded the audiences and critics of his full-length plays, with the notable exception of **Nemirovich-Danchenko**, **Meyerhold** and **Bely**. Chekhov's ambivalence toward art as 'sacred mystery' or 'debased entertainment' and his uncertainty vis-à-vis his own career as a dramatist were reinforced by the failure of his early plays. *Platonov* (1878), *Ivanov* (1887) and *The Wood Demon* (1889) dealt with provincial Don Juans and Hamlets, 19th-century 'superfluous men' of the intelligentsia, sunk in the mire of false and disillusioned romance and realism. Chekhov's major plays – *The Seagull* (following a dismal 1896 production at the Aleksandrinsky Theatre), *Uncle Vanya* (a revised *Wood Demon*, 1899),

The Three Sisters (1901) and *The Cherry Orchard* (1904) – all staged by **Stanislavsky** at the **Moscow Art Theatre** (MAT) in what were for Chekhov unsatisfactorily sentimental and naturalistic productions, developed the full array of his characteristic dramaturgical devices: contrapuntal dialogue, structure and theme; offstage and inner action; spatial iconography; metatheatrical doubleness in settings, characters, time-and story-frames. Time moves relentlessly forward in his plays, while seeming simultaneously, via homecomings and departures, memories and fixations, to cycle endlessly back, and characters manage to waste what little time they have in the present. This describes both universal human folly and the situation of the pre-revolutionary Russian intelligentsia. The grandson of a serf, Chekhov well understood the necessity of change and the burden of legacy. A long-time sufferer of what would prove to be fatal tuberculosis, he lived more consciously than most with the reality of transience. **Gorky**, later to become the voice of Soviet Russia, was befriended and supported by Chekhov, who would have found the new world which he helped imagine utterly foreign to his spirit and intentions.   SG

Chekhov, Michael (Mikhail Aleksandrovich) (1891–1955) Russian stage and film actor, director, teacher and creator of an acting system which has become increasingly influential in the West. **Anton Chekhov**'s nephew, Michael (his professional name following emigration in 1928) was a self-styled mystical philosopher, who used the language of acting to reveal inner truth. A member of the **Moscow Art Theatre**'s First Studio from 1912 (later the Second Moscow Art Theatre, of which he became artistic director, 1924), his mentors were **Stanislavsky**, from whom he received personal training in the System, Leopold Sulerzhitsky, the Studio's head and the System's best teacher, and **Vakhtangov**, with whom he often quarrelled but who was perhaps his most influential director-teacher. A combined artistic-spiritual crisis led Chekhov to study Eastern philosophers and finally to embrace Rudolf Steiner's anthroposophy (1930), which pointed him in a more mystical symbolist direction. Chekhov's system of acting evolved into an alternative to Stanislavsky's, emphasizing more universal, imagistic and intuitively contacted and communicated spiritual resources of energy, rather than the historical, emotional and psychological details of the actor's life. Organized around the 'psychological gesture', an iconographic physicalization of inner thought and emotion which transforms rather than repeats itself in outer expression, the Chekhov approach is designed to be highly spontaneous, plastic and dialogic between inner and outer tempo-rhythms. Chekhov the actor was noted for his ability to transform himself into a simultaneously symbolic-realistic character mask and to animate his body, largely improvisatorily, into a varied code of precise gestures and movements. The major roles of his Russian career include: Caleb Plummer in **Dickens**'s *The Cricket on the Hearth* (1914), Malvolio in *Twelfth Night* (1917), the title role in Vakhtangov's production of **Strindberg**'s *Erik XIV* (1921), Khlestakov in *The Inspector General* (1921), Hamlet (1924) and Senatore Ableukov in *The Death of a Senator* (adapted from **Bely**'s *Petersburg*, 1925). His émigré career included acting for **Max Reinhardt**

(1928–30) and in Hollywood (Academy Award nomination for Hitchcock's *Spellbound*, 1945), directing the **Habimah** Theatre (1930) and several companies and studios of his own – the Chekhov-Bonner company (1931), the Moscow Art Players (1934) and the Chekhov Theatre Studio (1936–42) – through which he disseminated his ideas as actor–director–teacher. His books include *The Path of the Actor* (autobiography, 1928), *On the Actor's Technique* (in Russian, 1946), *To the Actor* (1953), *To the Director and Playwright* (1963). SG

Cheng Changgeng (c. 1812–80) Chinese *laosheng* actor. Born in Anhui he moved to Beijing in childhood and first studied acting under his maternal uncle, an actor. Cheng rose to become leader of the Sanqing Troupe – one of the four most prestigious acting companies in the capital. He was outstanding in the male roles portraying great statesmen and warriors. He created a style of acting which set precedents for the future. A man of great personal integrity and dignity he was well regarded at court. He was a seminal figure in a formative period of the Beijing theatre and the great master actor of his day. ACS

Cheng Yanqiu (1904–58) Chinese *dan* actor. Born in Beijing the son of an impoverished Manchu family. He studied both *jingxi* and *kunqu* techniques under leading teachers. Specializing in the women's roles he rose to professional recognition as one of the four great performers of his genre, the 'big four' as they were known in theatre circles. **Mei Lanfang** (1894–1961), Shang Xiaoyun (1900–76) and Xun Huisheng (1900–68) were the other three. Cheng developed a very individual style of vocalization and was noted for the grace and skill of his acting forms. In 1932 he was sent to Europe under the patronage of Li Shizeng, elder statesman and reformer, to study Western theatre and opera practices. In 1930 he was appointed head of the first coeducational Academy of Dramatic Art in Beijing. The school was the first of its kind marking an important step forward in theatre education methods. It had to close after the outbreak of the Sino-Japanese War (1937–45). A project for Cheng to lead a troupe to Paris at this time was cancelled. In its short existence the school was successful and set a trend for the future. In 1942 Cheng quit theatre for the duration. He made only a few appearances after the war. His last years were spent training a new generation of Beijing actors. He played in one film made expressly to record his technical expertise. ACS

Chéreau, Patrice (1944–) French director who made his name by winning the competition for young companies with **Lenz**'s *The Soldiers* in 1967. He joined **Planchon** as director of the **TNP** at Villeurbanne in 1972 and moved to the Théâtre des Amandiers at Nanterre in 1982. His productions are distinguished by great scenic brilliance together with an ability to create modern archetypes. His *Ring* cycle at Bayreuth 1976–80 recast the Norse legends in images of the industrial revolution and his revivals of **Marivaux**, **Ibsen** (*Peer Gynt*, 1981) and **Genet** (*Les Paravents*, 1983) have brought international recognition. DB

Chestnut Street Theatre Chestnut near 6th St,

Philadelphia [Architect: Inigo Richards?]. Prominent Philadelphians raised the capital to underwrite a theatre to replace the deteriorating **Southwark** and locate it in the centre of the city. It was leased to **Thomas Wignell** and Alexander Reinagle, who set about assembling an acting company. Completed in 1793, its opening was delayed for a year because of an outbreak of yellow fever. A handsome, well-appointed house, the exterior continued to be improved upon from plans furnished by Benjamin Latrobe. By 1805, it was considered the finest playhouse with the best acting company in America. In 1816, gaslighting was introduced for the first time in a theatre, but in 1820, the playhouse burned down. It was rebuilt in a version by William Strickland, which bore little resemblance to the original. The theatre's most prosperous years occurred under the management of **William Warren** and **William Wood**, which ended in 1828. Thereafter, it went steadily downhill as new theatres were built and better acting companies arose to challenge it. In 1855, the theatre was demolished. A new theatre bearing the same name was built six blocks away, but was unlike the original. It, too, was razed in 1917. MCH

Chettle, Henry (c. 1560–c. 1607) English playwright and pamphleteer, very few of whose plays survive. Forced into hack-work by financial need, Chettle had a hand in about 50 plays, including several for the **Admiral's Men**. The revenge tragedy, *Hoffman* (c. 1603), was probably his alone. With **Anthony Munday**, he wrote *The Downfall* and *The Death of Robert, Earl of Huntingdon* (1598), with **John Day** *The Blind Beggar of Bethnal Green* (1600) and with **Dekker** and William Haughton *Patient Grissel* (1600). Chettle is almost as well remembered as the printer of **Greene**'s *Groatsworth of Wit* (1592), and for dissociating himself from Greene's attack on **Shakespeare** in the preface to his own dream-fable, *Kind Heart's Dream* (1593). PT

Chevalier, Albert (Onésime Britannicus Gwathveoyd Louis) (1862–1923) English actor and music-hall singer, who made his professional debut under the **Bancrofts** at the **Prince of Wales's Theatre** in 1877. After a decade of work in the legitimate theatre, appearing with the **Kendals**, **John Hare** and Sir **George Alexander**, he reluctantly branched out in 1888 into recitals of comic songs and monologues, many written by his brother and manager Augustus (Charles Ingle). He first appeared on the 'halls at the London Pavilion, 5 February 1891, as a coster comedian and made an immediate hit; although or perhaps because he lacked the cockney authenticity of Gus Elen and Alec Hurley, he was a favourite with royalty and the upper classes, often performing in drawing-rooms, and widely appreciated outside London as well. A master of makeup and stage business, he introduced the now-traditional coster gestures in such songs as 'Knocked 'Em in the Old Kent Road' and the maudlin 'My Old Dutch', playing the latter as a full-scale *scena*. In 1906 he toured the USA and Canada with **Yvette Guilbert** who admired his technique but found his material old-fashioned. After his death, his wife Florrie (daughter of **George Leybourne**) wrote an account of her post-mortem conversations with him. LS

Chevalier, Maurice (1888–1972) French singer and

actor, who began his career at the age of 11. In music-hall, he imitated popular comedians before developing the character of a peasant aspiring to be a dandy. At the **Folies-Bergère** by 1908, he was later sponsored by **Mistinguett**, who became his mistress and his partner, leading to a phenomenal rise in revue, operetta and singing tours, with such numbers as 'Valentine' and 'Ma Pomme'. In the 1920s Chevalier's straw boater, dinner-jacket and casual soft-shoe stood for a sporty new generation. A stint in Hollywood (1928–35) earned him international fame and he cultivated a somewhat artificial French accent, much imitated. Because of his collaboration with the Vichy government during the Occupation, he temporarily fell out of favour, but he regained popularity with a series of one-man shows, begun in 1948. The chat gradually elbowed out the singing and he bade his final farewell to the stage at the Théâtre des Champs-Elysées in 1968. Chevalier's rapport with his audiences was a triumph of manner over matter: his trivial material, weak voice and bland personality were compensated for by abundant charm and a knowing use of *Sprechgesang*.   LS

Chiarelli, Luigi (1880–1947) Italian dramatist. In his early years he was primarily a journalist. His first tentative attempts to write short pieces for the theatre met with little success until in 1916 the company of **Virgilio Talli** produced his three-act *La Maschera e il Volto* (*The Mask and the Face*) in Rome. This ironic comedy, about the conflict between the individual and social conventions, helped to launch the theatre of the grotesque. Although he wrote many other plays in the twenties and thirties, these never enjoyed the same success, and indeed tended to expose the extent to which the thought underlying *La Maschera e il Volto* was essentially superficial.   LR

Chiari, Pietro (1712–85) Italian dramatist who worked mainly for the Venetian theatres and is remembered primarily for his literary and theatrical disputes with **Goldoni**. A prolific writer of competent but unambitious stock pieces, his work was enormously popular in its day, mingling as it did comic, tragic and satiric elements. Much of it turned on parody or ridicule of Goldoni's plays, notably *La Scuola delle Vedove* (*The School for Widows*, 1749), a parody of Goldoni's 'reform' play, *La Vedova Scaltra* (*The Cunning Widow*, 1748). A former Jesuit, and known as the *abate*, Chiari also wrote romances and *novelle*, and his writing output as a whole is a useful index to the tastes of the Venetian middle classes at the time of that city's theatrical heyday.   KR

Chicano theatre Chicano theatre belongs to the larger category of Spanish-speaking theatre in the United States. Its origins date from the arrival of the Spanish conquerors, including the priests interested in the spiritual conquest, in the 16th century. Dramatic performances were recorded in the South-west as early as 1598 when Juan de Oñate's band of explorers performed an early religious play near El Paso, Texas. Throughout the period of settlement and growth of the following centuries, the dominant Hispanic culture and language in the area gave attention to the theatre. During the 19th century, both San Francisco and Los Angeles were major centres of Hispanic theatre activity that sponsored visits by operatic companies even before the Gold Rush. As the railroad linked major cities throughout the South-west, especially Laredo, San Antonio and El Paso, the ethnic communities with a strong sense of their heritage and traditions maintained local cultural activities and hosted travelling road companies en route to and from Mexico City.

20th century By the 1920s Chicano theatre flourished from Los Angeles to Chicago. Productions of musical reviews and **zarzuelas** coincided with serious plays which addressed issues particular to the Chicano communities. The problems of adapting culturally and linguistically to a predominantly Anglo culture were standard themes. The level of activity subsequently subsided during the depression and Second World War years, although it did not disappear entirely.

The more recent Chicano theatre movement coincided with the activist movement in USA civil rights in the 1960s. In the summer of 1965, when **Luis Valdéz** joined César Chávez as he was organizing the farmworkers' strike in the fields of Delano, California, using politically-orientated improvisational theatre to underscore the migrant workers' cause, he became the acknowledged father of the new direction in Chicano theatre. His *actos*, as they came to be called, were short agit-prop pieces that dramatized the essence and spirit of the Chicano reality. The new Chicano theatre was, suddenly, a revolutionary theatre committed to social change. From this initial experience, Valdéz established the **Teatro Campesino** (Farm Workers' Theatre).

This group served as the model for a host of other Chicano theatre groups created throughout the West and South-west, and extending across the country into Illinois, Indiana and Wisconsin. Adrian Vargas created Teatro de la Gente (People's Theatre) in 1967. In 1971 **Jorge Huerta** developed the Teatro de la Esperanza (Theatre of Hope) in Santa Barbara, a group that has become the most stable after the Teatro Campesino. In 1972 Joe Rosenberg established the Teatro Bilingüe (Bilingual Theatre) in Kingsville, Texas. At the peak of the movement, as many as 100 groups were functioning throughout the USA. Rubén Sierra, Roberto D. Pomo, Romulus Zamora and Manuel Pickett are but a few of the other major directors. A national network was established in 1971 to maintain linkages among the groups. Called TENAZ (El Teatro Nacional de Aztlán/National Aztlán Theatre), it has sponsored the annual festivals that bring together groups from all over the USA as well as from Latin America to learn about their common heritage and to share their experiences. The road has not always been smooth; the differences in function and orientation were particularly evident at the Fifth Festival celebrated in 1974 in Mexico City, where Valdéz was severely criticized. Nevertheless, the festivals provided for a useful interchange and gave opportunity for fresh perspectives on techniques.

From its humble beginnings the Chicano theatre has climbed to impressive levels at some points in its history. Valdéz's *Zoot Suit* opened in Los Angeles in 1978 and was the first Chicano show to arrive on Broadway. After Valdéz, another generation of Chicano writers has picked up the cue, adding original notes derived from the rich traditions and folklore of the Chicano people. Other writers include Rubén Sierra, Carlos Morton and a promising Chicana playwright, Estela Portillo.

The Chicano theatre is normally written and performed in the peculiar linguistic mixture typical of the Chicano population. Words and phrases in the two languages are constantly interchanged depending upon the context. Most groups perform in the 'Spanglish' dialect most comfortable to their situation, although others, such as Rosenberg's Teatro Bilingüe, prefer to maintain the separation, alternating performances in either language. Economic difficulties have dimmed some opportunities for Chicano theatre, at the same time social advances have diminished some of the needs. The effort to educate the majority population in the United States while simultaneously serving the interests of the Chicano population itself continues, although not as many groups are functioning now as before. The translation and publication of play texts continues to be a high priority.   GW

> *See*: R. Garza, *Contemporary Chicano Theatre*, Notre Dame, 1976; J. A. Huerta, *Chicano Theatre: Themes and Forms*, New York, 1982; J. A. Huerta and N. Kanellos, *Nuevos Pasos: Chicano and Puerto Rican Drama*, Houston, 1979; N. Kanellos, *Hispanic Theatre in the United States*, Houston, 1984; C. Morton, *'Las muertes de Danny Rosales' and Other Plays*, Houston, 1984; E. Portillo, *'Sor Juana' and Other Plays*, New York, 1983; C. M. Tatum, *A Selected and Annotated Bibliography of Chicano Studies*, Lincoln, Nebraska, 1979; L. Valdéz (y el Teatro Campesino), *Actos*, Fresno, Calif., 1971.

Chichester Festival Theatre The first large thrust-stage theatre in Britain, seating nearly 1,400 people around its stage, it opened on 3 July 1962. It was also one of the first theatres to be built in a park, outside a small country city in the south of England. It was built largely by local subscriptions, raised by Leslie Evershed-Martin, who had been inspired by the example of the **Stratford (Ontario) Festival Theatre** in Canada. These two theatres share the ideals for theatre construction first argued by **Tyrone Guthrie** and derived from Elizabethan models, stressing close audience–actor contact, all-round visibility and the use of the whole auditorium as the stage set. Such ideas, radical in their day, were first put to the test at Chichester by **Laurence Olivier**, the first director, who was also appointed the director of the still embryonic **National Theatre** company at the **Old Vic**. The productions, including *Uncle Vanya* (1962), *The Royal Hunt of the Sun* (1964) and *Armstrong's Last Goodnight* (1965), transferred from Chichester to the Old Vic. In 1965, Olivier was succeeded by another famous actor–director, **John Clements**. The tradition of actor–managers at Chichester continued until Peter Dews's appointment in 1978. The theatre is unusual among now post-war civic theatres in that it receives comparatively little grant money but derives its income largely from the box-office and its large and enthusiastic supporters' club. Its programmes have not been noted for their avant-garde character, but for offering star actors in splendidly staged productions of major plays, many of which have moved to the West End.   JE

Chifunyise, S. J. (1948–) Zimbabwean playwright, educated in Zambia and the United States. A **Chikwakwa** product, he taught at the University of Zambia and was national Director of Culture. He is now Director of Arts and Crafts in the Ministry of Youth, Sport and Culture in Zimbabwe. His short plays and dance-dramas are extremely popular in both Zambia and Zimbabwe. Some of these have been published in his collection, *Medicine for Love* (1984).   RK

Chikwakwa Theatre An open-air theatre established at the University of Zambia in 1971 as a venue for practical drama work by students and in order to promote the democratic development of popular performing arts in Zambia as a whole. Plays produced there were original and indigenous in content and form and Chikwakwa pioneered the concept of taking theatre to the people with its tours into all parts of the country. Many of Zambia's playwrights and actors received their decisive training experience there. The spirit of Chikwakwa is perhaps best expressed by Michael Etherton, one of its founders, who wrote: 'Chikwakwa Theatre is more than an open-air theatre building in bush near Lusaka. It is a commitment to the development of theatre in Zambia from existing cultural roots as they are manifested in the performing arts and in ritual.' One of Chikwakwa's most influential productions was *Che Guevara* at the Third Summit of the Non-Aligned Movement in 1970. Chikwakwa also produced a theatre review.   RK

Children of Blackfriars, Children of the Queen's Revels, Children of Whitefriars see **Children of the Chapel Royal**

Children of the Chapel Royal Under the Mastership of William Cornish, the choristers of the Chapels Royal in Windsor and London supplied the young Henry VIII's demand for entertainment in a number of lost plays. **John Skelton**'s *Magnyfycence*, if not representative, at least underlines that most of them would have been in the Morality tradition, which also governed the elaborate disguisings in which Cornish and his King delighted. The mid-century Master, Richard Edwardes, putative author of the tragedy *Damon and Pithias* (1565), extended the dramatic range of the Chapel Children. He may have been the first to admit spectators to the 'rehearsals' of Court entertainments in the paved hall of the disused Blackfriars monastery, where the **Master of the Revels** previewed royal command performances. It was in the Blackfriars refectory that Richard Farrant, Deputy Master of the Chapel Children, established an indoor theatre in 1576. With a home of their own, Farrant's choristers became serious rivals to the **Boys of St Paul's**, with whom they teamed up under the creative leadership of **John Lyly** after Farrant's death in 1580 and that of Sebastian Westcott, Master of the Paul's Boys, in 1582. The Chapel Children shared the disgrace of the Paul's Boys after Lyly had drawn them into the Marprelate Controversy in 1589–90, and there is no evidence of further dramatic activity until 1600. It was then that Henry Evans leased the converted Parliament Chamber of the Blackfriars from **Richard Burbage** and led his choristers into eight years of intense and brilliant activity. The publicity provided by the **war of the theatres**, which lined **Jonson** and the Children of the Chapel against **Marston** and the Boys of St Paul's, turned Jonson's *Poetaster* (1600) into a *cause célèbre*. The talented boys, including at various times **Ezekiel Fenn**, **Nathan Field** and **Salathiel Pavy**, gave the first performances of major plays by Jonson, **Chapman**, **Middleton**, **Beaumont** and even Marston. Their repertoire was no less distinguished than that of the King's Men. It may be that playwrights as well as audiences took a perverse delight in the boys' utterance of bawdy or scurrilous material, but the authorities were increasingly unamused. *Eastward Ho* (1605) angered James I, as did **John Day**'s *The Isle of Gulls* (1606), and by 1608 the company was in crisis. Henry Evans surrendered his lease of the Blackfriars and fled to the continent, and Richard Burbage led the King's Men into the **Blackfriars Theatre**. A remnant of the Children of the Chapel Royal survived ingloriously at the **Whitefriars**, where they performed Jonson's *Epicoene* (1609) and other plays before being finally disbanded in 1615.   PT

Childress, Alice (1920–) Afro-American playwright. Born in Charleston, South Carolina, and raised in Harlem, Childress opened the New York stage to black women writers when her play *Gold Through The Trees* (1952) was professionally produced Off-Broadway. She had been for 12 years an actress with the American Negro Theatre and her most important play, *Trouble in Mind* (1955), voiced the protest of a veteran black actress against playing a stereotypical 'darkie' role in a Broadway-bound production. It won the Obie Award for best original Off-Broadway play. Other notable plays by Childress that feature strong black women of compassion and dignity are *Wedding Band* (1966) and *Wine in the Wilderness* (1969).   EGH

Chile Mexico and later Peru became the principal centres of commercial development and intellectual formation in the New World because the Spanish were able to build on well-developed indigenous cultures. In Chile, on the other hand, the native Americans had not achieved a high level of cultural development, and their fierce resistance made the conquest by the Spaniards extremely difficult. Much of the colonial literature in Chile dealt with aspects of heroic fighting on the part of the *araucanos*, and the names of the Indian leaders – Colocolo, Caupolicán and Lautaro, for example – survived as well as those of the Spanish *conquistadores* such as Pedro de Valdivia.

The earliest theatre representations recorded in Chile took place around 1612 when the King ordered the celebration of the Mystery of the Conception in the American colonies. Especially on Corpus Christi, **autos sacramentales** were commonly performed with elaborate processions, along with the 'mysteries' and **pasos**. Performances took place in the churches, convents and cemeteries until the corruption in the *autos sacramentales* invoked a ban by King Carlos III in 1765. The so-called 'divine' comedies were allowed to continue, but the strong position of the church impeded the development of secular drama. Women were not allowed to perform in the theatre, and strict regulations about seating arrangements were enforced. The essence of good drama present in epic poetry, nonetheless, was picked up in far-away Spain. Ercilla's *La araucana*

(1569–78–89), Pedro de Oña's *El arauco domado* (1596) and the chronicles of Don Cristóbal Suárez de Figueroa provided inspiration for at least three Spanish plays, one of which involved nine participating authors including **Mira de Amescua**, **Ruiz de Alarcón**, Vélez de Guevara and **Guillén de Castro**. Francisco González Bustos's play, *Los españoles en Chile* (*The Spanish in Chile*, 1655), which finally played in Chile after 1800, was a play of literary merit that showed the nobility of the *araucanos*. Toward the end of the 18th century Peruvian-born Juan de Egaña stimulated theatre in Santiago with translations of European plays, and it is significant that throughout the nearly 300 years of colonial rule no single play by a Chilean author captured critical attention as a major work.

In the period following independence in 1818, Camilo Henríquez (1769–1825) advocated governmental support of the theatre. One of his own plays, *La Camila, o la patriota de Sudamérica* (*Camila, or the South American Patriot*, 1817), is an early Chilean play but is poorly written and therefore did not gain much recognition. During much of this period Valparaíso, the port city, was a more important centre of theatre activity than Santiago, the capital, where the first permanent theatre building opened in 1820. In the new republic the major influences for promoting theatre came from Bernardo O'Higgins, the country's patriot and new leader, and Andrés Bello (1781–1865), a Venezuelan-born poet and philosopher who became rector of the university and reformed education throughout the country. During this period of transition between the aesthetics of neoclassicism and romanticism, Bello wrote plays, as did his son, Carlos Bello (1815–54). Other important foreign influences were Juan Casacuberta (1799–1849), an actor who arrived from Argentina with a repertory of romantic plays. Also from Argentina were Luis Ambrosio Morante, actor, director and sometime playwright, and Domingo Faustino Sarmiento (1811–88), a writer and essayist fleeing the dictatorial Rosas regime. The latter's critical editorials in *El Mercurio* of Valparaíso deploring the lack of culture produced a sharp reaction.

If the rest of the century did not produce transcendental works, it did see the emergence of nationalism and several plays and authors that attempted through the romantic mode to capture a Chilean ambiance. Rafael Minvielle (1800–87), with European background, achieved success with *Ernesto* in 1842. Alberto Blest Gana (1830–1920), better known as a novelist, attempted one play that in turn inspired the major playwright of the latter half of the century, Daniel Barros Grez (1834–1904). Barros Grez, in a sense the founder of the Chilean theatre and the first major **costumbrista**, wrote scores of plays and essays about the popular figures he wished to satirize with his moralizing, didactic tone. He is considered a successor of the Spanish **Moratín** and a precursor of **Pirandello**; one of his best plays is *Como en Santiago* (*As in Santiago*, 1874), a play revived and made popular in the 20th century for its engaging view of rural life that tries to emulate urban mores with its satirical and humorous view. Other writers of the century include Daniel Caldera y de Villar (1852–91), author of *El tribunal del honor* (*Honour of the Court*, 1877), a historico-nationalistic play, and Mateo Martínez Quevedo (1848–1923), author of *Don Lucas Gómez* (1885), an extremely popular play that highlighted rural/urban differences with great humour.

20th century The development of a Chilean middle class began to change the character of the theatre which at the beginning of the century belonged, for the most part, either to an outdated and romantic melodramatic style or to the reality of the incipient social class. The War of the Pacific (1879–84) not only ended the domination of the upper class, but it led as well to a period of great immigration and the foreign domination of Chilean economic interests, especially mining. A new sense of nationalism emerged, in spite of the strong foreign influences (French, German and British), and a rising consciousness of social problems. Antonio Acevedo Hernández (1886–1962) left home at age ten and learned the world through personal experiences. His plays focused on all aspects of the marginal classes in urban, rural, mining and other settings; while he criticized the social order he avoided the worst aspects of politically committed theatre. His major works are *Chañarcillo* (1936), *Los caminos de Dios* (*The Paths of God*), which premiered in Poland, and *El triángulo tiene cuatro lados* (*The Triangle Has Four Sides*).

The formation of the Compañía Dramática Nacional (National Drama Company) in 1913 fomented new interest in the theatre and barely preceded the opening of the Panama Canal (1914), which curiously had a negative impact on Chilean theatre. Foreign troupes that had traditionally visited Chile now could chose to by-pass the country, given the flexibility offered by the Canal. In 1915 the Sociedad de Autores Teatrales de Chile (Society of Chilean Playwrights) (SATCH) was formed, composed primarily of writers who followed the traditional lines of romantic melodramas as well as the satirical and costumbristic plays. Santiago's first theatre company, formed in 1917, was headed by actors Enrique Baguena and Arturo Burhle; it still adhered to the old styles of theatre (prompter's box, candles, painted sets, etc.). The other major writers of the period were Armando Moock (1894–1942) and Germán Luco Cruchaga (1894–1936). Moock broke with the naturalist/determinist school and anticipated the relevant themes of the 1950s in such plays as *Pueblecito* (*Little Town*), *Mocosita* (*Brat*, 1929) and *Rigoberto* (1935) which captured typical elements in the daily lives of urban dwellers concerned about education, family and especially the artistic existence. Luco Cruchaga is the author of the now classic play *La viuda de Apablaza* (*The Widow of Apablaza*, 1928) with its touching portrayal of loneliness, love and disappointment.

Throughout the 1920s and 30s the Chilean theatre continued along similar lines, unable to break with the strong traditions. A number of factors, including the world depression, Chile's relative isolation, and the rise of movies, contributed to the delay in creating an independent theatre in Chile, some 10 to 15 years after its development in Mexico or Argentina, for example. The visit by the famous Spanish company of Margarita Xirgú prepared the way for new concepts of staging with plays by **Shaw** and **Lenormand**.

With the creation of the Teatro Experimental de la Universidad de Chile (University of Chile Experimental Theatre) in 1941, renovation of the Chilean theatre began. Under the leadership of Pedro de la Barra, its first director (until 1958), the group (renamed ITUCH

in 1959, Instituto de Teatro de la Universidad de Chile) undertook to bring to the Chilean theatre the new conceptions of acting and staging that were implemented in Europe by **Piscator**, **Antoine**, **Copeau** and **Stanislavsky**. The famous French actor **Louis Jouvet** visited Chile with a French company in 1942 and provided additional impetus. The group's first major success was **Thornton Wilder**'s *Our Town* in 1945.

A similar thrust at the Catholic University led to the creation of the TEUC (Teatro Experimental de la Universidad Católica) in 1943, also with its own professional company and since 1956 its own theatre. Both ITUCH and TEUC brought together the most important theatre practitioners in the country and provided theatre training for a new generation of directors, actors, and technicians. In their formative years, both professional groups normally staged the best foreign plays. Plays by national authors were the exception as a new group of playwrights was being formed. In addition to Enrique Bunster, Fernando Cuadra and Pedro de la Barra, the most notable are María Asunción Requena's (1915–86) *Fuerte Bulnes* (*Fort Bulnes*), a drama of heroic proportions in the colonization of southern Chile (Magallanes), Fernando Debesa's *Mama Rosa* (1957), an engaging costumbristic middle class family story, and **Luis Alberto Heiremans**'s *Versos de ciego* (*The Blind Man's Verses*, 1961). Chile has produced exceptional women writers in addition to Requena, such as Isidora Aguirre (b. 1919) and Gabriela Roepke (b. 1920).

The solid quality of productions by ITUCH and TEUC brought about a new generation of Chilean playwrights who have dominated the Chilean scene since the mid-50s. The major theatrical mode has been realism that focuses on the socio-economic issues within Chilean society, drawing on representative psychological figures. **Egon Wolff** (b. 1926) and **Sergio Vodanović** (b. 1926) have exceptional plays. Wolff, trained as a chemical engineer, is the author of more than 20 plays, of which *Los invasores* (*The Invaders*, 1962) and *Flores de papel* (*Paper Flowers*, 1970) illustrate his technical control by combining pressing social concerns with artistic integrity. Vodanović was less experimental but achieved success with *Deja que los perros ladren* (*Let the Dogs Bark*, 1959) and *Nos tomamos la universidad* (*We Took the University*, 1970) in which he exposed corruption in the political sphere and hypocrisy in revolution. Another major realistic writer was Fernando Cuadra (b. 1926), author of *La niña en la palomera* (*The Girl in the Dovecot*, 1966), and **Juan Radrigán** (b. 1937), author of *Hechos consumados* (*Accomplished Deeds*, 1981).

The realistic overtone in the recent theatre has not precluded, however, a more abstract and symbolic theatre. **Jorge Díaz** (b. 1930), Chile's best-known playwright internationally, began in an absurdist vein with overtones of **Beckett** but even from the beginning demonstrated a concern about social issues which became more apparent in his later plays. His *El cepillo de dientes* (*The Toothbrush*, 1961) is a masterful two-character play of miscommunication within a circus atmosphere. Many of his later plays combine political and social topics with a constant experimentation for an adequate language of expression. His successor in this vein is Marco Antonio de la Parra (b. 1952), whose three plays to date have woven socio-political themes into an abstract technique. In a different vein, **Alejandro Sieveking** (b. 1934) has pursued vigorously and prolifically a popular theatre with social overtones that often depends on folkloric tendencies. A psychological, religious, and eclectic writer, he works in collaboration with his actress wife, Bélgica Castro.

The fall of the Allende regime in 1973 coincided with the death of Chile's Nobel poet laureate, Pablo Neruda, who himself had experimented with theatre in a curious work entitled *Fulgor y muerte de Joaquín Murieta* (*Splendour and Death of Joaquín Murieta*, 1966). The ensuing dictatorship of General Pinochet brought on a climate of repression difficult for the artistic community. Light comedies were admissible, but certain groups gradually became more insistent with socially-committed themes. After 1976 the plays became more daring, with such examples as *Pedro, Juan y Diego* (1976) by ICTUS and David Benavente; *¿Cuántos años tiene un día?* (*How Many Years in a Day?*, 1978) by ICTUS and Sergio Vodanović; *Los payasos de la esperanza* (*Clowns of Hope*, 1977) by Taller de Investigación Teatral; and *Tres Marías y una Rosa* (*Three Marys and a Rose*, 1979) by the same group in collaboration with David Benavente. De la Parra's *Lo crudo, lo cocido y lo podrido* (*The Raw, the Cooked and the Rotten*, 1978) created a sensation when it was banned at the Catholic University the day before its scheduled opening, ostensibly for its gross language. The collective work begun in 1967–8 with the so-called Teatro Taller (Theatre Workshop) was gradually transformed during these years into collaborative work that often incorporated a textual author into the process.

In 1984 a new political policy encouraged the return of the émigrés. The theatre has flourished, with many functioning groups and festivals. A pattern of self-censorship avoids massive confrontations, but generally the regime has not bothered the recent theatre which it treats as an intellectual safety valve. The current theatre is dynamic in dealing with psychological realism, socio-economic matters and problems of the émigré.

Among the most important functioning groups is ICTUS, directed by Delfina Guzmán and Nissim Sharim, a group established in 1956 and at present the strongest professional company in Santiago outside the universities. Teatro Imagen, Teatro del Angel and other smaller groups help maintain an active theatre fare. Two major novelists have entered the theatre in recent years: José Donoso (b. 1924) with his *Sueños de mala muerte* (*Second-Class Dreams*, 1983), developed in collaboration with ICTUS, and Antonio Skármeta (b. 1940) with *Ardiente paciencia* (*Burning Patience*, 1982), a poetic version of Pablo Neruda's final days that exalts his human qualities over his roles as diplomat and poet.

In the last 25 years Chile has benefited from an abundance of talented and productive directors such as Pedro Orthus, Agustín Siré, Pedro de la Barra, Fernando Colina, Eugenio Dittborn, Eugenio Guzmán, Fernando González, Raúl Osorio, Gustavo Meza and others. In addition to the young directors on the current scene, a new generation of writers is also emerging, including the original work of Ramón Griffero and Jaime Miranda.

Theatre of the marginal classes and an active programme of children's theatre complement the experiments of some of the more forward young playwrights

and directors. It is still true that most of the solid theatre activity is concentrated in Santiago. Theatre in the provinces is limited to small amateur groups, although cities such as Valdivia, which sponsored its first theatre festival in 1985, and Concepción, also in the south, have a tradition of active support.   GW

See: E. Castedo-Ellerman, *El teatro chileno de mediados del siglo XX*, Santiago, 1982; J. Durán Cerda, *Repertorio del teatro chileno*, Santiago de Chile, 1962; A. M. Escudero, *Apuntes sobre el teatro en Chile*, Santiago, 1967; T. Fernández, *El teatro chileno contemporáneo (1941–1973)*, Madrid, 1982; E. Pereira Salas, *Historia del teatro en Chile desde sus orígenes hasta la muerte de Juan Casacuberta*, Santiago, 1974; G. Rojo, *Muerte y res resurrección del teatro chileno (1973–1983)*, Madrid, 1985; O. Rodríguez and D. Piga, *Teatro chileno del siglo XX*, Santiago, 1964.

Chilly, Charles Marie de (1804–72) French actor and theatre manager, first appeared in the smaller theatres, making his debut at the **Odéon** in 1827. He then toured the provinces with a troupe run by Sabatier and **Bocage**, returning to the Odéon in 1829. He followed **Harel** to the Porte-Saint-Martin, where he attracted attention as the Jew in **Hugo**'s *Marie Tudor*. In 1837 he joined the Ambigu, taking on the parts of the late **Firmin**, and began to find his vocation in 'third roles', the villains of melodrama. His sharp features and clipped measured diction created a new type of villain, and his greatest role was that of Rodin in *The Wandering Jew*. In 1858 he became manager of the ailing Ambigu, and brought back audiences. From 1866–72 he was director of the Odéon, and was responsible for the triumphal revival of *Ruy Blas*.   JMCC

China

Introduction Theatre has been and remains an omnipresent force in the social life of the Chinese. They first described it by a single ambiguous term, *xi*, which originally was used to designate play, games and acrobatics. The name is still current but retains a connotation of plurality as an umbrella word covering a host of theatrical entertainments. When the Chinese speak of theatre specifically they use the names of the musical and dialectal forms which animate their numerous regional dramatic styles. These constitute the corpus of theatre in a national sense. A varying length of tradition lies behind them. Some, like the rice-planting song of northern China, persisted as simple forms of song and gestural expression with an uncomplicated musical accompaniment. Other styles practised within the orbit of the more sophisticated urban areas developed as the transmitters of polished theatrical form. Three seminal events mark the long time-span such progress involved. The rise of the Yuan theatre in the 13th century set precedents for structured stage practices which endured. The flowering of the **kunqu** in the 16th century ushered in a theatre of lyrical elegance and scholarly playwrights, while the domination of the Beijing theatre style in the 19th century proclaimed the triumph of an aesthetic for the man in the street.

Chinese traditional theatre is a presentational, secular style of performance essentially musical and choreographic in its basic structure. Synthesis of forms and variety of offering are operative factors. Dominant is the use of categorized, archetypal character roles each having its particular formalized speech and movement techniques together with makeup and costume styles.

The composition of a dramatic text and its interpretation by the actor is conditioned by an ordered arrangement of song, narrative and declamation. Their structural basis results from the dual relationship between musical sound and the spoken word arising from the homonymic nature of the Chinese language. Because of pitch variations, or tones, which differentiate the meanings of otherwise identically sounding words in Chinese, the sound pattern accruing from the formal organization of rhythm has acquired a particular literary significance. The number of syllables and tonal patterns contained by a line of text became a first element of verse and song composition for the traditional drama. Metrical pattern and rhyme schemes were given priority by the old Chinese dramatist in devising his text. Rhyme tables classifying words with the same tonal movement were the tools of his craft. The playwright did not set words to music, he sought appropriate words to match the auditory permutations of his lines and stanzas. Because of this, there has been handed down an extensive repertoire of tunes, that is to say metrical arrangements having their separate tonal patterns and rhyme schemes, which can be used over and over again in relation to specific emotional situations. Because of this also the stage musician can command stereotyped styles embodying fixed metrical patterns which complement the tonal–rhythmic format of a play text as stipulated by the dramatist. Dialect naturally affects compositional style so dependent on auditory effects. The melodic differences resulting from dialectal usage in regional dramatic forms were broadly classified as northern and southern styles by the Chinese in the past. A complex history of borrowing and cross fusion between the two divisions brought about the musical genres which identify major theatrical styles such as those of Suzhou or Beijing.

Antecedents of theatre Performance goes back to the earliest times in China. Shamanistic rituals from many centuries before the time of Christ probably involved a combination of song, dance, gesture and costume. The performing arts functioned also as entertainment. An example is shown in a wall painting in a tomb excavated in the early 1960s in Mixian, central Henan Province, dating from about AD 200. It shows a large-scale banquet, probably hosted by the main tomb occupant when alive. A series of small-scale performances is taking place between two long rows of guests. There are dancers, jugglers, plate-spinners and musicians.

The Tang dynasty (618–907) witnessed a climax in the political power and culture of medieval China. Although drama itself is not yet clearly mentioned, many quite developed forerunners certainly existed. An example is the 'adjutant plays' (*canjun xi*), which were light-hearted skits. They included dialogue, string and wind and perhaps percussion instruments as musical accompaniment, and role categories. Both actors and actresses took part, and sometimes there were three roles or even more. Puppet shows were not new to the Tang, but certainly flourished then and were popular in the market-places of the cities. The Emperor Minghuang (r. 713–56) loved to watch puppet shows in the inner palace. The 20th-century scholar Sun Kaidi has argued that drama in China imitates and derives from puppets. The arts of the story-tellers were also highly developed by that time. The late-Tang poet Li Shangyin records how story-tellers would expound the deeds and wars of the heroes of the Three Kingdoms period (220–65). These were later to be a major arm of the content of all popular Chinese theatre. It was already quite common for entertainers to mount high platforms or stages so that they could better be seen by their audiences.

Origins of drama The Song dynasty ruled all China from 960 to 1127 and the south only until 1279. Meanwhile the Jin dynasty, ruled by the Jurchen people, ancestors of the Manchus, seized the Northern Song capital Kaifeng in 1126, forcing the Song to relocate its centre of government in Hangzhou in the south.

The Song is notable for the rise of commerce. China's first fully developed theatre structures arose in an urbanized environment. Called *goulan* (lit. 'hook balustrades'), they were contained within amusement centres termed *wazi* ('tiles') or *washe* ('tile booths'). The largest amusement centre in early 12th-century Kaifeng held 50 theatres or even more, and the grandest theatre could accommodate several thousand people. They were covered, not open-air, structures and so not subject to the vagaries of the weather. All classes of people frequented them.

In the north, performances at such places were termed **zaju** ('various plays') or, under the Jin dynasty, *yuanben*, and these were variety shows which included dancing, acrobatics, the core play, comic patter and a musical conclusion. The terms *zaju* or *yuanben* refer also to the core playlet, which was short and funny and might concern a love affair or satirize officialdom. Apart from a musician, there were four or five characters in these playlets. Role categories included the clown (*fujing*) and jester (*fumo*). Masks were probably used for supernatural roles, and makeup was very common.

In the south, a new style arose from early in the 12th century: the 'southern drama' (*nanxi*). Its place of origin was Wenzhou in southern Zhejiang Province. Its music was based partly on folksongs and it may also have been influenced by Indian drama. The role categories of the 'southern drama' are the foundation on which most later Chinese theatre has built. There were seven types: the *sheng*, *dan*, *mo*, *wai*, *tie*, *jing* and *chou*. The *sheng* and *dan* were respectively the principal male and female characters, the *mo* and *wai* secondary male, and *tie* secondary female roles. The *jing* were strong male characters and the *chou*, according to our chief source commenting on early 'southern drama' Xu Wei (1521–93), had a 'face daubed with black powder and was very ugly'. The *jing* and *chou* were frequently interchangeable. In contrast to the *zaju*, all characters sang.

The 'southern drama' items were longer and with more complex story-lines than any earlier Chinese performances and in this sense they may be taken as the first stage of a fully developed Chinese theatre. The great majority appear to have been love comedies, although the two most famous, *Chaste Woman Zhao* (*Zhao Zhennü*) and *Wang Kui Renounces Guiying* (*Wang Kui fu Guiying*), both deal with unfaithful scholar-lovers who come to a bad end. Most items are anonymous, many having been written by 'writing societies'.

The first great age of Chinese theatre In 1234 the Mongols conquered the Jin and in 1279 the Southern Song. After the Mongol conquest of the south, the 'southern drama' lost popularity, although it did revive in the middle of the 14th century, not long before the fall of the Mongol Yuan dynasty (1368). The form of theatre which had replaced it was the Yuan *zaju*, considered by Chinese and foreign commentators to form the first great age of Chinese theatre. Within the reign-period of the Mongols the apex was probably the rule of Kublai Khan (1260–94), the man who reunited north and south China.

The texts of just over 160 *zaju* dramas survive from the Mongol Yuan dynasty. They are contained in two collections, the more important of them entitled *Selection of Yuan Songs* (*Yuanqu xuan*) collected and edited by Zang Maoxun and prefaced 1615. They deal with such topics as romance, courtesans, friendship between men, tyrannical rulers or rebels, recluses or supernatural beings. Many focus on politics or war, including the heroes of the Three Kingdoms period. Others centre around law cases, the main judge being the famous Bao Zheng (999–1062), an actual personality known for his harshness but canonized in the Yuan theatre for his benevolence and fairness. Although tragedy in the classical Greek sense is unknown, quite a few end sadly or with the death of the leading positive character.

The dramatists were mainly Han Chinese, but included also Uygurs, Mongols and others. They were minor officials, entertainers, traders and of other callings, but the main point to note is that they were not in general men of high social status. It has been suggested, by Chung-wen Shih among others, that Mongol rule blocked off opportunities for educated Han Chinese to enter the bureaucracy, through such measures as the suspension of the civil-service examinations (not reinstated until 1314), and that some wrote plays as an outlet for their literary talents.

The four most famous of the *zaju* dramatists were **Guan Hanqing**, Bai Pu (1226–after 1306), Ma Zhiyuan (1250–after 1321), and Zheng Guangzu (dates unknown). Bai Pu came from an official family which had been eminent under the Jin dynasty but been torn apart by the Mongol invasion. He was, not surprisingly, a Jin loyalist and refused an offer of service in the Mongol court. He wrote at least 16 dramas, of which three are still extant, the best known being *Rain on the Paulownia Tree* (*Wutong yu*). The love of Emperor Minghuang of Tang for his favourite concubine Lady Yang (Yang Guifei), which is the content of this drama, is among the most popular stories in Chinese literature; in Bai's version its ending is definitely sad.

In contrast to the texts of the Yuan dramas, there are no surviving musical scores. Possibly they were never used much, since the music could be transmitted from teacher to disciple. In any case Yuan drama music appears to have died out during the Ming dynasty (1368–1644). Musical accompaniment was mainly by string instruments, especially the four-string plucked lute (*pipa*). The famous wall painting of a scene from a Yuan *zaju*, dated 1324 and found in a temple in Shanxi province, shows no string players, but does include a player of a side-blown flute (*dizi*), and one of the clappers, as well as a drum, presumably in use.

The main role categories of the Yuan *zaju* were *mo* (male), *dan* (female), *jing* (villain), and *chou* (clown). There was one lead male and female character and a number of subsidiary ones. The categorization is similar but not identical to that of the *nanxi*. The costuming shown in the 1324 mural is colourful and fairly complex. Two of the characters there depicted have heavy black makeup on their eyebrows with white around the eyes. Several of the male characters are bearded, one with highly stylized whiskers. The stage shown there is tiled; there is a heavy backdrop, painted with two elaborate pictures, but no stage properties.

Performers of either sex acted either male or female roles. The heading of the 1324 mural informs us that a certain famous actress 'Elegance of Zhongdu performed here', while the main character depicted, in the centre of the front row and presumably the named female star, is male. Actresses may well have dominated the Yuan theatre. Certainly we know much more about them than the actors because Xia Tingzhi (1316–after 1368) wrote a work called *Green Bower Collection* (*Qinglou ji*) which is a set of biographies of actresses of the 13th and first half of the 14th centuries. Prostitutes as well as performers, they were wooed, sometimes even married, by high-ranking ministers, generals, literary figures and others. Although the Mongol rulers were initially favourably disposed to the acting profession, one of them later issued a ban on teaching or performing *zaju* and damned such entertainments as lewd. Probably few people took any notice of such an edict, but in general performers held a very low social status.

It remains a mystery why this theatrical tradition which had developed so recently should blossom so suddenly into the magnificent body of art which the Yuan *zaju* appears to have been. After all, Han Chinese scholars blocked from the bureaucracy might more easily have turned to another branch of art than to so new a form as drama. One recent interpretation is that of the American scholar James Crump. The Jurchen people of the Jin were very accomplished singers and dancers. Other component parts of theatre, acrobatics, pantomime, music, farce, were already flourishing and there was no shortage of good stories in Chinese literature and history. Yuan *zaju* represented the synthesis of several already existing fine traditions. The Mongols became acculturated and 'welcomed the dramas which were shaped by music probably already familiar to them and which incorporated the less sophisticated arts that had always delighted them'. It was from such processes, he concludes, that 'the golden age of Yuan drama began'.

The revival of southern drama; marvel dramas Under the last of the Mongol emperors Shundi (1333–68), the dormant 'southern drama' revived. The term used to refer to the form was one which had been in use to describe stories or novellas during the Tang dynasty: *chuanqi*. It means literally 'transmitting the marvellous' and can be translated in the present context as 'marvel dramas'.

The first of these marvel dramas was *The Story of the Lute* (*Pipa ji*) by Gao Ming (c. 1301–59). It is based on the same story as *Chaste Woman Zhao*, namely the abandonment by the writer and scholar Cai Yong (AD133–92) of his newly wed wife Zhao Wuniang. However, Gao Ming has altered the characterization to portray Cai in a positive light. In place of his bad end, Gao has him reunited with Zhao, redeemed and rewarded. Zhu Yuanzhang (r. 1368–99 the founder of the Ming dynasty, was an admirer of Gao and his play. Before his accession to power he had, early in 1359, conquered the area of eastern Zhejiang Province where Gao was living and offered the dramatist a job, but the latter declined it on the grounds of old age and ill health. Xu Wei records that, when Zhu had become the Hongwu Emperor, he regarded the drama highly enough to urge all noble families to possess a copy. He ordered his actors to perform *The Story of the Lute* every day. Regretting the lack of stringed accompaniment, he commanded members of his Academy of Music to rectify the weakness, so Liu Gao rearranged the orchestra adding the 15-string zither (*zheng*) and four-string lute.

In the late Yuan and early Ming, the 'four great marvel plays' appeared, following *The Story of the Lute*: *The Story of the Thorn Hairpin* (*Jingchai ji*), *The Moon Prayer Pavilion* (*Baiyue ting*), *The Story of the White Rabbit* (*Baitu ji*), and *The Story of Killing a Dog* (*Shagou ji*). The first two concern a scholar who leaves behind his faithful wife to sit for the examinations, does brilliantly in them and is reunited with his beloved. The marvel dramas tended strongly towards romantic themes, with scholars and beauties in central roles, and to lack the warlike content of the *zaju*.

One of the differences between the earlier southern dramas and the marvel dramas was that the former probably only sometimes but the latter always added a prologue before the action. Its functions were to explain the story and announce the title of the item to be performed. Sometimes, as in *The Story of the Lute*, it explains the moral of the drama. Another difference is that 'marvel dramas', at least in Ming editions, are divided into scenes, whereas the southern dramas were apparently performed without breaks. Yet there was a basic continuity of style, form and performance between the southern and marvel drama. Gao Ming and others built on, adjusted and strengthened what they found. They were basically transmitters rather than innovators.

The decline of the zaju The rise of the marvel dramas did not at first affect the *zaju* negatively in terms of quantity. On the contrary, the early Ming was a prolific period for the *zaju* and quality was also good. However, as the Ming progressed, the *zaju* declined in popularity quite sharply, and by the time the Ming fell in 1644, the *zaju* had died out as an actively performed branch of theatre, surviving only as a past genre of literature, still read but not much written.

Early Ming *zaju* authors include Zhu Quan (1378–1448), Zhu Youdun (1379–1439) and Yang Ne (dates unknown). Zhu Quan was the 17th son of the Hongwu Emperor Zhu Yuanzhang. He wrote twelve *zaju* dramas of which two survive. He also either wrote or had written a work entitled *Great Peace Table of Correct Sounds* (*Taihe zhengyin pu*), which not only lists the title of 689 *zaju* written from the Yuan to his own time, but also gives titles of 335 *zaju* melodies, each with poems

illustrating the appropriate tonal patterns, and arranges them into 12 modes. Zhu Youdun was one of the Hongwu Emperor's grandsons. He wrote over 30 *zaju*, all extant. Many deal with religious subjects, and women, either prostitutes or saints, are given great prominence in his work. Yang Ne was a Mongol who wrote 18 dramas, of which only two survive. One of them is *Journey to the West* (*Xiyou ji*) about Tripitaka's travels to India in search of sutras and the exploits of his three famous disciples, Monkey, Sandy and Pigsy. Yang Ne served for a time as adviser in the Ming palace. This fact and the prominence of the princely Zhu cousins suggests active early Ming court support for the *zaju*, and also that this form of theatre was changing from one with mass appeal to one popular more at the upper end of society than the lower.

A later *zaju* dramatist was Xu Wei, already mentioned as a source of information about early theatre in China. An eccentric man he was subject to distraught fits, which led him to attempt suicide many times and kill his second wife, for which crime he was imprisoned for seven years. His best known dramatic work is *Four Howls of the Ape* (*Sisheng yuan*), which in fact contains four *zaju*. Xu's plays were unconventional in two ways. Firstly, in several of them he departed from the rule that *zaju* should have four acts and a wedge. He was not the first to write a one-act *zaju*, but he also wrote two-acters and one in five, and his considerable influence on Ming drama signalled the collapse of the rigid *zaju* structure.

Secondly, Xu Wei combined northern and southern music in his *zaju*. Again, he was not the first to do this, and as early as the late Yuan the dramatist Shen He had used northern and southern tunes in the same work. What was different was that Xu's experiment led on quite soon to even more radical departure from *zaju* tradition when Wang Daokun (1525–93), in writing *zaju*, used southern music exclusively. The break was very important because it meant the abandonment of music which had imposed a quite clear northern stamp on the drama.

The southern theatre of the educated The Ming dynasty was the era when local drama rose to prominence. Along with the dialect used, it was the music which mainly identified the differences found from region to region.

One southern city with a particularly rich musical tradition was Haiyan, a major trading port in Zhejiang Province. Even before the Ming, the Music of Haiyan (*haiyan qiang*) flourished as a local form of southern drama. Xu Wei claims that in his own day it was 'in use' in four parts of Zhejiang Province and even Beijing, later in the 16th century. Dramas of the Haiyan Music were probably accompanied by percussion instruments only, but the singing was soft and melodious. Role categories followed the normal patterns of the southern drama. The audience came mainly from the educated classes, rich families and officials.

The Music of Haiyan had died out as an independent style by the end of the 17th century. However, Xu Wei lists it among those musical traditions absorbed into the *kunqu*, that drama form which by the end of the Ming was monopolizing the affections of those theatre-lovers among China's educated classes.

Credit for the creation of *kunqu* is often given to **Wei**

Liangfu, a 16th-century musician and actor. What Wei actually did was to adapt various already familiar musical styles, including not only *haiyan qiang* but also *zaju*, *yiyang qiang* and the local music of Kunshan, to a new form which was called the Music of Kunshan (*kunshan qiang*) and is now known simply as *kunqu*. It was Wei's achievement to impose on *kunqu* those main musical features which to this day make it instantly identifiable. These are the strong tendency towards slow-moving melismatic rhythmic melody, and the orchestration, dominated by the side-blown flute (*dizi*), but including also the four-string lute (*pipa*) and wind organ (*sheng*). The language of the librettos was classical and stilted with many unexplained literary allusions. Stage motions tended to be slow and action sparse. The overall effect was melodious, delicate, refined and even melancholy. The *kunqu* quickly came to be known as 'elegant drama'. Its language and style closed it off from the masses, whose theatre was known, by contrast, as 'flower drama'; the term covered more or less all styles other than *kunqu*.

Role categories in *kunqu* followed those of the marvel dramas closely. The *kunqu* companies took over stories from preceding styles, especially the marvel dramas and *zaju*. Many early pieces had 40 or 50 scenes, like the marvel dramas from which they had been adapted. Performance might require three days and nights. By the 17th century the practice of putting on a single scene separate from the others in the same item became the norm.

The most famous individual dramatists of the *kunqu* were Liang Chenyu, **Tang Xianzu**, **Hong Sheng** and **Kong Shangren**. These men and their works are treated separately.

Kunqu eventually spread throughout more or less the whole of China. This was because the working place of officials had no necessary connection with their place of birth. They had their own companies and invited guests to see their private actors perform. The style of drama was that proper to their class: *kunqu*.

Over its history the *kunqu* has spawned many famous professional companies. One worth special mention is the Jixiu of Suzhou. It was formed in 1784 to provide entertainment for the Manchu Qianlong Emperor (r. 1736–96) during his visit to the south in that year. Its members were drawn from among all the best actors of the cities of the Lower Yangzi Valley. It stayed together after the emperor's departure and survived until 1827.

Kunqu became the favourite drama style of the imperial court. The Hongwu Emperor of the Ming dynasty had founded a eunuch agency in 1390 to provide court entertainment, including theatre. Initially the favoured form was *zaju* but the court was happy to follow the fashion of the upper classes and patronize *kunqu* from the 16th century on. Early in his reign the Qianlong Emperor set up an organization to control court theatre. The official Zhang Zhao (1691–1745) wrote five lengthy and highly moralistic *kunqu* dramas for the imperial theatre, including *Golden Statutes for Encouraging Goodness* (*Quanshan jinke*) about Mulian's saving his mother from hell. The Manchu Prince Yinlu (1695–1767), an uncle of Qianlong's, adapted the stories of the Three Kingdoms to compile the *kunqu* piece *Annals of the Tripod* (*Dingzhi chunqiu*). During their heyday in the 18th century the court companies contained well over 1,000 actors, including both eunuchs and well-known artists especially imported from the south.

Popular theatre, yiyang qiang Originally a mass form of theatre, the *zaju*, or what was left of it, had been taken over by the educated elite by the 16th century. At about the same time, new forms of popular theatre began to emerge and prosper. They have developed by the 20th century into some 350 styles, the great majority popular in one or more particular locality, some major ones in whole provinces. Many belong to the *yiyang qiang* system.

Yiyang is the name of a place in eastern Jiangxi Province, near that point where the three provinces of Zhejiang, Fujian and Jiangxi meet. Southern drama and *zaju* were heard there about the 13th century and melodies from these combined with local folk music to form the Music of Yiyang (*yiyang qiang*). It is not known when a new style can be said to have arisen; however, reliable sources provide no evidence that it existed before the early 16th century. It quickly spread to other places, including the capital Beijing, and Jiangsu, Anhui, Hunan, Fujian, Guangxi and Guangdong Provinces. By the middle of the 17th century it was performed even in parts of the distant southwestern province of Sichuan.

Role categories and stories were similar to those of the southern and marvel dramas. Since *yiyang qiang* was popular drama, it was not normally written down. However, a few texts of dramas belonging to various local styles of the *yiyang qiang* system do survive from the 16th century. From them it is clear that the librettos were adapted from the marvel dramas, and performed in single short scenes.

Several features of the *yiyang qiang* styles are noteworthy. One is the practice of adding short sections in colloquial language to the original classical text. They came at the beginning, middle or end of a passage and took the form of explanations so that the audience could understand what was happening. Thus, a literary allusion to a classical poem in an original marvel drama text might be supplemented by a full recitation of the poem. An educated audience could be expected to recognize a literary allusion, but the ordinary masses who made up the audiences of the Music of Yiyang drama would not know it and would need to have it pointed out. These added passages, which were termed *gundiao* (literally 'rolling tunes'), could be either sung or, despite their name, spoken. One very important corollary of the *gundiao* was that librettos were much longer than for a corresponding *kunqu*. This made the use of excerpted scenes, rather than whole dramas, appropriate. Moreover, as the well-known 17th-century drama theorist **Li Yu** put it, 'characters are many but sounds are few'. What he meant was that, in strong contrast to the melismatic *kunqu*, the Music of Yiyang was syllabic. It was also rather fast-moving on the whole, so that in a comparable time the Music of Yiyang covered far more words than the *kunqu*.

A second feature of the Music of Yiyang drama styles, which applied to all popular theatre in China, was that they used local dialect. The ordinary people did not normally understand the 'official words' of the Music of Haiyan or of the bureaucrats.

A third feature, one apparently adopted from the earlier southern drama but not found in Ming or Qing drama systems other than the Music of Yiyang, was the 'helping' or offstage chorus (*bangqiang*). Li Yu writes that 'one person would start singing and then several would take up the tune'. The vague term 'several' means as few as one, usually two or three, but rarely more. The offstage chorus is still a strong feature in contemporary Music of Yiyang styles, such as Sichuan Opera (**chuanju**). The practice of accompanying solo singers in folksongs with a chorus is extremely ancient in China. It probably arose because instrumental accompaniment was impossible for people at work in the fields and 'labour songs' have always been a normal category of folksongs. *Yiyang qiang* styles, like the southern drama before them, lacked the accompaniment of string or wind instruments and had only percussion.

The initial net effect of these features was to irritate the refined members of the educated classes, who used terms like 'bawl' to describe the singing of the Music of Yiyang. Such contempt did not prevent the rapid and extensive spread of this mass drama and in any case, began to relax in the course of time. By the 18th century there were in Beijing six famous companies devoted to Capital Music drama (*jingqiang*), which belonged to the Music of Yiyang system, and the leading one was called Great Company of the Princely Mansions. So there were even members of the aristocracy willing to patronize this popular theatre.

Popular theatre, Clapper Opera   Another important system of popular theatre styles is the Clapper Opera (*bangzi qiang*). It appears to have originated in the border areas of Shanxi and Shaanxi just north of the great southern bend of the Yellow River. The time of origin is unclear, but the earliest written reference comes from late in the 16th century; a marvel drama of that time made use of a tune from Shaanxi known to belong to the Clapper Opera. The styles of this system were initially prevalent only in northern China. Still today they are found in almost all the provinces north of the Yangzi River. However, Liu Xianting (1648–95) mentions the Clapper Opera as 'new sounds' in a work on the southern provinces of Hunan and Hubei. By the late 18th century there was a thriving Clapper Opera tradition in Sichuan, and it was even popular in the lower Yangzi Valley in places like Suzhou and Yangzhou. It is known that merchants and bankers from Shaanxi and Shanxi traded all over the country and they might well have brought with them a demand for Clapper Opera, as well as private actors who could perform it.

As its name implies, the chief characteristic linking the styles of the Clapper Opera system is the use of the clapper, a datewood block struck with a stick, to beat out the rhythm. In contrast to the *kunqu*, the Clapper Opera emphasizes rhythmic change. In most styles there are eight different rhythms, the main one termed 'one beat, three eyes' (*yiban sanyan*) which corresponds to a quick, common time (4/4) in Western music. In the sung sections, the dominant poetic structure is seven- or ten-character couplets.

The other main characteristic, which separated the Clapper Opera from the Music of Yiyang or *kunqu*, is the dominance of string instruments in the accompaniment. The well-known scholar Li Tiaoyuan (1734–1803) writes that the four-string plucked moon-guitar (*yueqin*) 'responds to the clapper in rhythm which is either hurried or slow', but all Clapper styles also feature one kind of two-string bowed instrument or another.

The Clapper Opera attracted the attention of the scholar-official Yan Changming (1731–87) who, though originally from Jiangsu, lived and worked in Shaanxi late in his life. It is from him that we know of a flourishing Clapper Opera in Xi'an, Shaanxi's capital, in the 1780s, with 36 'famous' companies in operation, even more than in Beijing at the same time. The most distinguished of them was called Shuangsai.

It was in the early 1780s that Beijing was enjoying the performances of a group of *dan* Clapper actors from Sichuan. Wei Changsheng (1744–1802) and his followers went to Beijing in 1779, probably to take part in the Qianlong Emperor's 70th birthday celebrations, and stayed until 1785, when the court prohibited their performances as obscene. Although their sojourn in Beijing was thus only short, they exercised a tremendous influence on the theatre of the capital and many elements of their art were later absorbed into the Beijing Opera (**jingxi**). Among Wei Changsheng's innovations was the false foot worn beneath the actor's foot and tied to his leg with cotton bandage, enabling him to imitate the gait of a woman with bound feet. The Clapper actors were popular not only among the masses, but even the educated elite.

Popular theatre, the pihuang system   Following Wei's departure, a new group of actors came to Beijing in 1790 to take part in the celebrations for Qianlong's 80th birthday. This time the actors were members of companies from Anhui Province and the style performed belong to the *pihuang* system. Since this was the first time the *pihuang* had been given in the capital the event is usually regarded as the birth of the Beijing Opera, which is discussed separately under its Chinese designation *jingxi*.

Pihuang is actually a combination of two styles, *xipi* and *erhuang*, each of which remains identifiable and separately designated. Both styles can be varied greatly in their rhythm, melody and feeling. A. C. Scott wrote in 1957 that in general *erhuang* 'is used for more serious occasions' in Beijing Opera plays, while *xipi* 'is, on the whole, happy and spirited in feeling'. Each style includes 'counter' (*fan*) tunes which 'are used for sad and tragic occasions'.

Several theories have been advanced to explain the origin of *erhuang*. Although no final resolution is possible on the present state of knowledge, the most likely is that the term *erhuang* is a derivative of Yihuang, the name of a place in Jiangxi Province, and that the style originated there. It was adopted in Anhui Province and became far more popular there than in its original home. *Xipi* was a southern offshoot of the Clapper Opera which spread to Hubei and other provinces from its northern roots in Shaanxi and Shanxi. From the 18th century the two styles became inseparable and together they spread to all the southern provinces and Beijing. They formed at least 20 important styles, including not only Beijing Opera but also Anhui Opera (*huiju*), Hubei Opera (*hanju*), Guangdong Opera (**yueju**), and Jiangxi Opera (*ganju*). They also form part of such forms as Sichuan Opera (*chuanju*), and Yunnan Opera (*dianju*).

Although each of the *pihuang* styles has its own special points, such as the use of the local dialect and the influence of local folk music, they share many characteristics in common. These include several probably inherited from Clapper Opera: the use of seven- or ten-character couplets in the librettos, an emphasis on rhythmic change by comparison with *kunqu*, and, with the exception of a very few styles, the domination of the accompanying orchestra by a two-string bowed fiddle.

The actor mainly credited with the introduction of *pihuang* to Beijing was Gao Yueguan (c. 1770–c. 1830). He and his followers were *dan* performers and the early Beijing Opera flourished on a kind of slave trade by which parents in Jiangsu and Anhui sold sons to entrepreneurs who took them to Beijing to be trained for the stage. Within a short time after the first arrival of the companies from Anhui in 1790, four of them had established themselves as preeminent. Later known as the Four Great Anhui Companies, they were the Chuntai (Spring Stage), Sanqing (Three Celebrations), Sixi (Four Joys) and Hechun (Harmonious Spring). The one to last the longest was the Spring Stage which did not disband until 1900 when the Boxer uprising resulted in the burning down of the theatres of Beijing.

In the 1930s yet another wave of actors, this time from Hubei Province, entered Beijing. From this time we find a substantial change in the Beijing Opera art, from one in which the *dan* actors and 'civil' items were preeminent to an emphasis on *sheng*-dominated and 'military' plays. The most famous actors of 19th-century Beijing were all *sheng*: **Cheng Changgeng**, Yu Sansheng (d. c. 1875), and Zhang Erkui (d. 1860).

In 1860, the court for the first time brought Beijing Opera actors in from the city to perform. The initial experiment was short-lived but revived by the Empress Dowager Cixi in 1884 to celebrate her 50th birthday. She was an avid enthusiast of the Beijing Opera and ensured a continuing flow of fine actors from the city to the court.

The growth of the regional theatre in the Ming and Qing was paralleled by a similar expansion in local story-telling forms. The music, instruments and dialect varied from place to place, but on the whole the stories were constant and like those of the dramas. A particularly well-known story-telling form is the *pingtan*, popular in and near Suzhou, Jiangsu Province.

Ming and Qing society, stage and stage arts

Theatre in the Ming and Qing was very much a part of the people's life. Performers accompanied popular festivals and marked prayers to the gods for good harvests in the spring or thanksgiving in autumn. Rich families held performances to accompany sacrifices to their ancestors or banquets for their guests. Theatre was also tightly related to commerce. Temple or other fairs included performances which crowds watched between or even during business transactions. The government treated such occasions with suspicion. Authorities believed that large gatherings of people provided opportunities for political sedition and the planning of rebellion, or for sexual immorality; 'men and women mix unrestrainedly' is a phrase found constantly in the sources describing large crowds of people gathered to watch drama. Many edicts are recorded restricting or banning certain plays or practices associated with the theatre.

The site of performance in the Ming or Qing showed great variety. The *goulan* of earlier centuries tended to go out of fashion. Some temples and guild halls had permanent stages, but otherwise a temporary stage could be constructed as required. The market-place also provided a convenient venue, even without a stage. Performances given during the private banquets of the rich needed no stage, only an empty space near the banqueting tables, with a red carpet on the floor. A very high-ranking or rich family might have a stage especially constructed in its mansion. In Beijing a few of these were given over to the public as teahouse-theatres. The entry of Wei Changsheng and his Clapper Opera actors led to the repair of these buildings and the construction of others. The end of the 18th and all of the 19th century were the high point of the traditional teahouse-theatre in Beijing. All the best ones were concentrated in one part of town, just outside the main wall separating the masses' residential areas from that part of the city where the officials and imperial court abode.

The stage itself was very simple in Ming and Qing times. There was a curtain at the back but none at the front. Several records of Ming-dynasty plays describe elaborate scenery and stage properties, but these are about exceptional cases. The norm throughout the Ming and Qing dynasties was a nearly bare stage with no scenery and very simple or no properties.

The simplicity of the stage was balanced by the complexity and symbolism of the actors' art. Manners of walking, differing from character to character, hand gestures and the use of the fingers were all highly stylized and told the audience the nature and behaviour of the character. Costuming and makeup were extremely elaborate and expressive. Even apparently minor aspects of these assumed great theatrical significance, an example being the delicate way characters manipulate the very long and loose 'water' sleeves. All aspects of performance were integrated into a total theatre which to this day remains more or less unique.

It is not possible to trace the origins of all aspects of the performance of Chinese theatre. Certainly its totality predates the Ming dynasty, as do many of the particular features. Sleeve techniques in dancing were already an artistic skill before the time of Christ and figurines from the Tang provide evidence of the 'water' sleeve at that time. The 1324 mural shows that stylized beards and whiskers were already in use among actors before the Ming. Yet there was undoubtedly some change over the Ming and Qing periods, and it took the direction of refining performance techniques and the arts of the stage, making them more complicated and integrating them better into the totality of theatre.

The use of makeup is very ancient in the Chinese performing arts. In theatre it appears originally to have been simple. Only one of the characters in the 1324 wall painting has makeup over an area more extensive than that around the eyes. From early Ming times makeup became much more complicated and the practice of painting the whole face of *jing* characters with colour and design showing moral or other qualities became established. Pictures dating from the Ming and preserved by Mei Lanfang show that both in early *kunqu* and *yiyang qiang* dramas the face of the *jing* characters were fully painted. Red indicated loyalty and patriotism in generals, black honesty, and so on. The painted

Popular theatre performances. By an unknown painter of the Ming dynasty.

face has become a major feature of the Beijing Opera, where some of the colours hold essentially the same significance as in Ming times, but patterns are very much more complex.

For many centuries acrobatics have been a major form of entertainment in China. Tumbling, somersaults, and other gymnastics appear to have featured in the military items of the Yuan *zaju*, but they were not found in the southern drama with its emphasis on romantic stories and lack of warlike plays. In the Ming, *kunqu* included no acrobatics, but they became very well integrated into the performance of the *yiyang qiang* dramas and later other popular theatre forms, especially Beijing Opera. Military scenes climax in an acrobatics display, with rapid and numerous cartwheels, somersaults and finely timed throwing, kicking back and catching of spears and swords.

Ming *kunqu* emphasized the synthesis and synchronization of song and dance movements. The Clapper Opera system broke this unity, allowing actors not to dance while singing and *vice versa*. This process probably emerged late in the 18th or early in the 19th century. The change, added to the earlier absorption of acrobatics, made for much greater variety and liveliness in the stage movements of the popular theatre forms than in the *kunqu*.

Performers in the Ming and Qing The troupes which performed these dramas in the Ming and Qing were basically of two kinds: private and professional. The private troupes belonged to individual rich families and the members were drawn from among their servants or house-slaves. They could give private entertainment to the family or perform for invited guests. The great majority of such troupes specialized in the *kunqu* drama, but by the 18th century we find examples of

private companies which could perform popular regional styles, a very good example being the Chuntai (Spring Stage) Company in Yangzhou, Jiangsu Province, which belonged to the rich salt merchant Jiang Chun (1725–93).

Professional troupes tended mainly to be based in cities. Those named in the sources are concentrated in particular cities and times, especially Beijing in the 18th and 19th centuries, but they were very widespread throughout the country all the same. The normal pattern was for the professional companies to go wandering throughout the countryside in certain seasons of the year, especially before sowing and after the harvest had been reaped. They would stay at a particular place a few days, present a festival and then move on. They financed their activities by sending representatives from door to door collecting, the records claim sometimes extorting, money. Only the best companies were semi-permanent. The majority disbanded and reformed themselves from year to year, and the turnover of actors was substantial.

One type of professional company was that composed of female prostitutes. Performance was part of the skill of a good prostitute and several patrons have left behind records of their admiration for the beauty and skills of these women. Most excelled in *kunqu*; their bound feet made the gymnastic skills of military dramas impossible. The same artificial deformity prevented them from moving about away from their home base.

Acting companies of the Ming and Qing were thus either all-male, or all-female, the former being the great majority. The sources provide a few examples of individual males belonging to female companies and *vice versa*, but such cases were rare exceptions. Conse-

Peasant theatre in the Qing dynasty, 1875.

quently many actors excelled in the roles of women, actresses of men.

Training procedures were initially very rudimentary. Examples can be found from both the Ming and Qing of actors who in effect taught themselves the necessary skills by sheer determination. The normal procedure was for troupe managers to apprentice or buy small boys and have them taught the trade on a master–disciple basis. This purchase of small boys reached a high point late in the 18th and first half of the 19th century and supplied the Beijing Opera with a virtually limitless number of actors. The main companies in Beijing ran special training-schools (*keban*) which taught the slave-boys the necessary arts.

Performers held a very low status in society. One symbol of this was that they were forbidden to sit for the official examinations, which were the main gateway to the bureaucracy. Both the Ming and Qing issued edicts to this effect early in their rule (respectively 1369 and 1652), and in 1770 the prohibition was extended to their sons and grandsons. Actors were despised as vagabonds because they wandered about so much. Some members of the official classes were quite happy to take advantage of the sexual favours offered by performers, but these were still despised as immoral. Not only were actresses prostitutes, but homosexuality was extremely common among actors.

In the 19th century Qing law forbade government officials to visit female prostitutes, and as a result the boy actors became effective substitutes. It is true that there was a limited degree of social mobility among actors. Moreover, the age of the great stars from about 1780 on, especially in Beijing, may have raised the view society held about actors slightly. But in general the social status of the acting profession remained extremely low down to – and beyond – the fall of the Qing dynasty.

Traditional theatre in the 20th century The traditional stage during the first half of the 20th century was dominated by Beijing-style theatre. It retained an unequalled appeal on a national scale and had an enormous following among the ordinary public. This successful transition in an age of cultural iconoclasm was possible through a particularly talented body of actors. They bore the artistic integrity of the old theatrical tradition forward while adjusting to social change. A towering figure among them was the Beijing-born actor **Mei Lanfang**. His artistry and breadth of perception helped the old theatre attain a new pinnacle of public esteem. Not the least of Mei's achievements was his success in international cultural relations resulting from his tours to America and Russia in the 1930s. He stirred Western thinking to new aesthetic insights on theatre. **Brecht, Meyerhold** and Eisenstein admired and were deeply influenced by Mei's performances.

Two major reforms were accomplished in the professional world of Mei Lanfang and his peers during the 1920s and 1930s. An improved system of training and education for theatre apprentices was introduced and the actress began to achieve professional emancipation. Traditional theatre training had always begun at an early age. Prior to the 20th century, teaching was by direct transmission either from father to son or master teacher to indentured pupil. There were no academies or conservatories as such. A majority of apprentices were illiterate with little chance of being otherwise in a society where actors were regarded as outcasts. A first attempt at improved training conditions was the founding in 1903 of the Xiliancheng (later renamed the Fuliancheng) School in Beijing. Some of China's greatest Beijing actors graduated from this institution before it was closed down in 1937 by the Japanese war. Boys only were accepted for training and admitted at the age of seven. Auditioned entrants were taken on contract for a seven-year period. They lived in, and all training, board and lodging was free. In return the school demanded complete professional control. This meant performing in public by the graduating class to fill the school's coffers. The connoisseurs were keen patrons of these performances and sought to evaluate rising talents. It was a hard life demanding meticulous standards and intensive application. Many fell by the wayside. As an organized system it was an advance on older methods when boys could be victimized by unscrupulous individuals.

A revolutionary step came in 1930 when Li Yuying founded a coeducational conservatory for dramatic training in Beijing. The actor **Cheng Yanqiu** was appointed principal. Cheng was highly regarded both for his stage talents and personal integrity. He was second only to Mei Lanfang in public esteem. In 1932

The famous Beijing Opera actor Wang Yaoqing (1881–1954) in a military *dan* (*wudan*) role in *Qipan Mountain* (*Qipan shan*).

Cheng was sent to Europe on behalf of the school to study drama and opera for a year. The first of its kind to admit both sexes on an equal basis, the school provided a general education simultaneously with professional training. An ambitious syllabus was taught by special faculty. Professionals only were in charge of theatrical training. The first class graduated in 1937 but the outbreak of war shattered all plans for the school and it was closed down. A precedent was set for today's training methods, however, which follow a similar pattern. In 1934 a School for Experimental Drama was founded by Wang Bozheng at Jiinan in Shandong. It aimed to develop a new national form based on traditional methods but drawing scientifically on Western methods when required. A four-year course was set up with one year devoted to empirical experiment. War closed this institution also.

The professional rise of the actress in the 1920s and 1930s overcame long-standing prejudices. Women were excluded from the theatre either as performers or spectators during the 19th century. However in the early 1900s one or two all-women troupes were active in Beijing and Shanghai. They performed only at private gatherings and were not allowed into the theatres. By 1920 the prohibition against actresses began to change and women were performing at several Beijing theatres but never alongside actors. Mixed troupes were still taboo. During the 1920s several established actors began taking female pupils, a hitherto unknown practice. Wang Yaoqing (1881–1954), a teacher of Mei Lanfang, and Mei himself were among several who ignored old prejudices. This was an important step towards recognition for the actresses.

In 1928 two actresses Xue Yanqin and Xin Yanqiu appeared at the Great Theatre (*Da Xiyuan*) in Shanghai with male actors in a breakthrough performance. After 1930 Xue appeared regularly with mixed casts in Beijing. She came from Shandong but moved to Beijing when she was eight and studied under Jin Guorui and later Zhang Cailin, learning the women's roles, combat techniques and *kunqu*. She subsequently had a long acting career which began at the age of 15. She did much to enhance the theatrical prestige of the actress. In 1960 she assumed a teaching post with the Beijing School of Dramatic Art. Her contemporary Xin Yanqiu was from Beijing and began studying theatre when she was nine. She worked with Cheng Yanqiu whose professional name she took. At 17 she studied with Mei Lanfang and Wang Yaoqing before entering on her acting career.

Contemporary or near contemporary with these two pioneer actresses was a galaxy of accomplished women artists, including Yan Huiju and Meng Xiaodong (1907–77). Yan Huiju was the daughter of the leading Beijing actor Yan Jupeng (1890–1942). She began her studies at 12 and mastered both *jingxi* and *kunqu* techniques prior to embarking on a distinguished acting career. Before her death she was assistant director of the Shanghai Dramatic Training School. Meng Xiaodong, who died in obscurity in 1977 at the age of 70, was a brilliant actress who excelled in the male *laosheng* roles of the Beijing stage. The necessity for being self-sufficient in the past made women versatile in this way. Meng's father and grandfather, Meng Qi and Meng Hongqun, were both well-known Beijing actors and she herself was closely associated with Mei Lanfang in her early career. This new school of actresses which rose to prominence in the pre-war years brought new lustre to the artistry of the traditional theatre.

The rise of the modern theatre The 20th century began with a movement to create a new theatre inspired by Western example. Reform was in the air and the old theatre became a target for change. The Western impact on 19th-century China resulted in many young intellectuals being sent abroad to study. Thousands went to Japan where progressive modernization had followed the Meiji Restoration of 1868. Japan was geographically and culturally closer to the Chinese than the West. The synthesis of tradition with modernity they found there made cultural adjustment easier. Intellectuals who returned from Japan became a major influence on the early development of modern Chinese theatre.

In 1907 a Chinese group in Tokyo founded the Spring Willow Dramatic Society. Assisted by Fujisawa Asajirō, who ran an acting school in the city, they staged a version of *Camille* (*Chahua nü*) by **Alexandre Dumas** *fils* at the YMCA in February 1907. This play appealed to the emotional sentiments of the Chinese. The heroine's plight mirrored the rigidity of their own marital conventions and suitably echoed a dominant concern with social protest.

A five-act adaptation of **Uncle Tom's Cabin** followed in June. Entitled *The Black Slave's Cry to Heaven* (*Heinu yutian lu*) it was staged at the Hongo Theatre where *shimpa*, an early westernized Japanese genre, was featured. The play's action was expanded with extraneous interludes to please Chinese tastes. A curtain and scenery added novelty of effect. The production was well received and later given a second run. Harriet Beecher Stowe's theme offered a melodramatic vehicle for protest against racial discrimination from which the Chinese too had suffered.

Both plays were based on translations by Lin Shu, who first put **Shakespeare** into Chinese. Both used all-male casts. Hybrid productions, they nevertheless offered a stylistic if rudimentary substitute for the old song-declamation form. Precedents were set for a new genre eventually to be named *huaju*, spoken drama.

There had been short-lived efforts to devise Western-style drama in Shanghai before 1907. However in that year the city saw *The Black Slave's Cry to Heaven* staged by the Spring Sun Society under Wang Zhongsheng (d. 1911) who had studied in Japan. The wave of interest aroused led to a mushrooming of experimental drama groups.

In 1912, Lu Jingruo, also returned from Japan and a student of Tsubouchi Shoyo, father of the modern Japanese theatre, organized the New Drama Association. They performed at Chang's Garden, a popular Shanghai pleasure spot. In 1914 Lu revived the old Spring Willow Dramatic Society. They staged a series of productions including *Camille* in a Nanjing Road theatre until Lu's untimely death ended the venture.

Stage expertise remained provisional in these years. No significant playwright had emerged. Repertoires were devised from literary and journalistic texts freely rendered. Actors relied heavily on old conventions, including female impersonation. Familiarity with Western dramatic literature and stage techniques was slight.

The years 1915–19 marked a turning point. A Western-educated generation was agitating for cultural change. In 1916 the American-educated scholar, Hu Shi (1891–1962), spearheaded a movement to replace classical language – understood only by an educated elite – with a standardized vernacular intelligible to all. New journals proliferated supporting the New Culture Movement. Drama ignored by the old literati became recognized as a mouthpiece for social reform. *New Youth*, a monthly edited by Chen Duxiu (1879–1942), in 1918 devoted an issue to **Ibsen** whose work was discussed as an example to follow. Such promotion induced deeper study of Western dramatists and new translations multiplied. In May 1919 students protested in Beijing against the surrender of Chinese sovereignty proposed at the Paris Peace Conference; and when the Treaty of Versailles, signed on 28 June 1919, formalized the proposals to China's detriment, national outrage forced the Chinese government to refuse to sign. The new intelligentsia closed ranks in affirming an era of definitive cultural change called the May 4 Movement.

Succeeding events brought new impetus to theatre. The Shanghai Dramatic Association founded in 1921 by Gu Jiachen became a forceful sponsor of new drama. It was joined in 1923 By Ouyang Yuqian (1889–1962), actor-playwright-director. He had studied in Japan and performed with the original Spring Willow group in Tokyo and its Shanghai derivative. Trained in classical female impersonation techniques he turned professional on the traditional stage for a period. Quitting acting in 1918 he became head of the theatre training-school in the Nantong model community founded by the industrial benefactor Zhang Jian (1853–1926). The school sought to reform actor training and education. From this post Ouyang joined the Shanghai Dramatic Association to make his debut as a playwright.

He was followed by **Hong Shen** (1893–1955), stage director-playwright-teacher-film director. He studied in America from 1916 to 1922 and roused controversy on his return by refusing to countenance male playing of women's roles. Endorsed by conservative public opinion this convention remained a barrier to developing a naturalistic acting style. Hong Shen defied long standing prejudice by recruiting actresses from the more open-minded women of the universities and Shanghai film world. His productions of **Wilde**'s *Lady Windermere's Fan*, **Barrie**'s *Dear Brutus* and Ibsen's *Doll's House* were outstanding theatrical events of their day.

In 1928 Ouyang Yuqian and Hong Shen joined forces with Tian Han (1898–1968), playwright-teacher-film scenario writer. He also had studied in Japan where he associated with Guo Moruo and the literary group who in 1921 founded the Creation Society in Shanghai. Their journal *Creation Quarterly* began publication in May 1922, the first issue containing a play entitled *A Night at a Coffeehouse* (*Jiafei dian zhi yiye*) by Tian Han which was, in a sense, a theatrical causerie and drew immediate interest. Tian Han broke with the Creationists to teach and in 1928 organized the South China Society, a theatre training venture which had an impact during its short existence. A policy of studying acting under working conditions was pursued and the group toured its productions over a wide territory from their Shanghai base. Tian Han's own plays were in demand. Although none has survived the verdict of time they met a great need then. Serious study of acting was sustained and the little theatre movement so encouraged broke new ground for the future.

The South China Society was dissolved in 1930 by government order. The Japanese military threat compounded by the Nationalist–Communist political feud overshadowed intellectual life. People in literature and the arts responded to a new political awareness. In 1931 the League of Left Wing Dramatists, sister group of a literary predecessor, was formed. Tian Han and Hong Shen became active members. Plays were written and produced to portray current political–social problems and vigorously promoted in schools and factories. The Japanese attack on Shanghai in 1932 intensified theatrical protest. Government feelings were ruffled and a repression campaign was ordered forcing leftist theatre underground. Tian Han and other League members were arrested as a deterrent.

The Communists began organizing theatre for political action soon after the Party's establishment in 1921. In 1931 they set up the 'Chinese Soviet Republic' in Jiangxi with its capital at Ruijin. Troupes were trained at the Party school in Ruijin and then attached to army units for service in rural territory and the front line. Actors and actresses were recruited locally and provided with dramatic training, political education, their food, clothing and a subsistence pittance. This work culminated in the organization of a Workers and Peasants Dramatic Society.

Resources were primitive and emphasis given to histrionic ability. The 'living newspaper' presentation was a favoured technique while song, dance and mime were indispensable for audiences to whom these were their sole concept of theatre. An extensive dramatic network functioned on this basis. It contributed to establishing a permanent theatre-training school at the Communists' wartime base in Yan'an.

Advocacy of drama as a factor in social education was manifest on the Nationalist side in the work of Xiong Foxi (1900–65), playwright-teacher-producer. He had studied theatre in America. In 1932 the National Association for Advancement of Mass Education invited Xiong to initiate a theatre project in the rural district of Dingxian, Hebei Province. Living among the peasant community provided him with authentic material for writing and producing plays with the local people as actors. Within three years the troupe were staging self-supporting productions which attracted considerable notice. The Japanese invasion forced Xiong to lead his group to unoccupied west China. There, as the Farmers Resistance Dramatic Corps, they performed to mass audiences.

Political tensions notwithstanding, the 1930s witnessed the rise of a socially conscious theatre given credibility by the commitment of its practitioners. The flourishing university drama clubs and the Shanghai film studios which ran their own actress training-schools had eased the way for women on the modern stage. New dramatists were at work to capitalize on this advance.

Film, with its emotive capacity for evoking human values and national sentiment, gained new potential during the 1930s. Tian Han, Ouyang Yuqian and Hong Shen all turned to film as advisers, directors and scenario writers. A complementary and continuing relationship was established between the modern stage movement and the film studios. Xia Yan (b. 1900), Japan-returned dramatist and scenario writer, was representative of this trend. His two early stage plays

A county official as a *chou* character, showing the typical white patch on the face, headgear, whiskers and red garment.

Under a Shanghai Roof (*Shanghai wuyan xia*) and *Sai Jinhua* were considered major contributions to the modern repertoire. The first portrayed the alienation and suffering of tenement dwellers in a great city. The second concerned a celebrated Chinese courtesan, one of whose alliances was with Count Alfred von Waldersee the German commander of the allied forces which occupied Beijing to relieve the Boxer siege in 1900.

Cao Yu (b. 1910), playwright, a graduate in Western literature from a Beijing university, made theatre history with his first play, *Thunderstorm* (*Leiyu*). First staged in 1935 by the Fudan University Dramatic Club, Shanghai, it was directed by Hong Shen and Ouyang Yuqian. An immediate success it was then nationally toured by the China Travelling Dramatic Troupe. Cao Yu had studied Greek drama and admired **O'Neill** and **Chekhov**, influences discernible in his play. It was a dark commentary on the Chinese family system and the social degradation it caused. There were four acts with a prologue, epilogue and an involved plot covering a single day's events set against the menace of a gathering storm. A tangled history of seduction revealed through the interrelationships of a wealthy industrialist's household ended in tragedy when incest was exposed as a consequence of the misalliances. Credibility of characterization and realistic dialogue allied to an intuitive sense of theatre stamped this play as a breakthrough for an indigenous dialogue drama. Cao Yu's second play *Sunrise* (*Richu*) portrayed the corruptive power of materialism and won him a leading newspaper's literary prize. His four succeeding plays, *Wilderness* (*Yuanye*), *Metamorphosis* (*Shuibian*), *Peking Man* (*Beijing zen*) and *Family* (*Jia*), an adaptation, written within the half decade, established him as a dramatist with a social conscience.

The China Travelling Dramatic Troupe which toured *Thunderstorm* from Shanghai was founded in 1934 by Tang Huaiqiu. His goal was a modern repertory theatre on a financially viable basis. A cooperative unit, they achieved a homogeneous quality in their acting. *Thunderstorm* enabled them to turn the corner and all box-office records for modern theatre were broken. Hong Shen's version of *Lady Windermere's Fan* which they also staged at this time had equivalent financial success. The Troupe's aim seemed nearer realization when war in 1937 intervened. They moved their base to Hong Kong for a brief period but that too fell to the Japanese at the end of 1941.

An era had closed for modern theatre, henceforward subordinated to national propaganda needs. A call for resistance united theatre people as never before. Itinerant by vocation, they responded with travelling troupes to take propagandist theatre to the rural masses. Nationalists and Communists shared a common concept if with a divergent ideological intent.

In December 1937 theatre leaders, including Tian Han, met in Hankou to organize the National Dramatic Association to Resist the Enemy, an umbrella coverage for all wartime theatrical activities. In February 1938 Tian Han became director of the government's Cultural Work Committee and head of the Propaganda Section, divisional elements of the National Military Council. Government awareness of theatre as a spur to patriotic fervour was signified as also its critical potential. A zealous censorship was applied to all dramatic activity for the duration.

The rapid advance of the invading forces drove the Nationalist government to set up their capital at Chongqing, Sichuan Province. The universities and major educational organizations followed them together with those prominent in every field of the arts. Theatre became a vigorous assertion of public will. The emotional climate was typified by the manifesto of Xiong Foxi for his theatre students in west China. 'Cultivate modern drama with an artist's passion and a soldier's discipline to aid China's spiritual regeneration.'

Students of the coeducational Nanjing National Academy of Dramatic Art, newly founded in 1935 and evacuated to Chongqing, made their professional debut staging street plays and 'living newspaper' performances. A favoured technique entailed actors anonymously entering teahouses and drawing an audience by seemingly spontaneous dialogues on current affairs. Lack of permanent stages and technical equipment in wartime territory did not deter the hundreds of itinerant troupes. Academics and literary men frequently joined forces with the professionals. Urban intellectuals and the rural population shared a new direct relationship as the result of dramatic activities.

. Tian Han, official spokesman for theatre in wartime, encouraged these trends as a healthy portent for the future. He too toured the rural areas in charge of troupes performing the traditional Peking repertoire and adapting some of its plays for modern production purposes. This was questioned by some critics; nevertheless his version of *The White Snake (Baishe zhuan)*, an old favourite, became standard after the war. Ouyang Yuqian worked closely with Tian Han during those years and also led a touring troupe staging patriotic plays. Hong Shen combined running a theatrical troupe with teaching film and drama in the universities. It was a time of shared skills and commitments.

Xia Yan's plays successfully caught the public's mood. Typical was *City of Sorrows (Choucheng ji)* satirizing life in Japanese-occupied territory. *Put down Your Whip (Fangxia nide bianzi)* was based on an earlier one-act play of his. It denounced Japanese aggression and was outstanding among a mass of propaganda pieces being produced. Cao Yu, in contrast, wrote nothing after his adaptation in 1941 of Ba Jin's novel *Family* but taught in the universities for the duration. Xiong Foxi became disillusioned with government censorship policy after serving as head of the Sichuan Provincial College of Dramatic Arts. He left for Guilin in the south-west where he engaged in writing and editorial work until 1945.

Wartime Chongqing saw the germination of a national dance movement resulting from the work of Dai Ailian, a Trinidad-born Chinese danseuse. After studying ballet in England, patriotic motives led her to wartime China. While teaching in Chongqing she began studying local folk and minority nationality dances. With a team of pupil assistants she travelled to outlying areas researching and notating choreographic techniques, eventually forming her own company. Her pioneering work then prepared the way for organized dance education in China later.

The tangential ingredients of narrative, song and descriptive gesture in folk dance embodied primal elements of Chinese theatrical communication. They appealed directly to the uncomplicated emotive responses of peasant audiences. Both Nationalists and Communists sought profit from this factor in their wartime sensitivity to folk tradition. The Communists were the more uncompromising. The artistic criteria of folk genres were subordinated to theories of proletarian drama created to eliminate the aesthetic 'elitism' of the old theatre.

Following the Long March of 1934–5 the Communists set up their base in the loessic caves at Yan'an in Shaanxi Province. There in May 1942 Mao Zedong gave his 'Talks at the Yan'an Forum on Literature and Art'. In them he expounded his Marxist manifesto destined to become the bible of all Chinese cultural endeavour. He spoke at the Lu Xun Art Institute which provided dramatic training for the troupes sent out to different areas and developed adaptation of old folk performance methods to new content.

The *yangge*, rice-planting song, was an ancient form much utilized by the Communists. They applied the name collectively to the various forms they developed from it. Originally it referred to a simple series of rhythmic steps done to a chant with percussion accompaniment while planting the rice fields. When Communist troops entered the big cities in 1949 they were preceded by files of dancers performing this simple work form as a victory theme.

During the 19th century the style of *yangge* Dingxian prevalent in Hebei Province, gradually became elaborated as village performance: 20 to 30 dancers performed with a leader, male and female characters confronted each other with a question–response narrative followed by singing and dance movements were extended with representational gesture. Elemental themes on village life and ethics were introduced. A comic character frequently added the necessary touch of earthy humour. Drum, gong, flute and cymbals provided musical accompaniment.

Two scholars, Li Jinghuan and Zhang Shiwen, in 1932 did a government-sponsored field project on the Dingxian style, afterwards publishing an anthology of plays. It was this genre of performance the Communists found so adaptable and were quick to develop for their needs. *Yangge* troupes proliferated. More than 30 of them staged performances at a 1944 Yan'an spring festival. Their repertoire included a play called *The White-Haired Girl (Baimao nü)*.

Reputedly of ballad recitative origin based on some actual facts the play had undergone collective revisions prior to the 1944 presentation. In 1945 a new five-act version was prepared with a script and lyrics by He Jingzhi and Ding Yi. Music based on authentic folk sources was composed for it by Ma Ke and five colleagues. The theme of *The White-Haired Girl* was directed against abusive social practices long familiar to village tenant farmers.

The father of a peasant girl compelled to give his daughter in slavery to his tyrannical landlord killed himself in shame. Her village swain left the district to join up with the Communist forces. The girl was raped by her new master and became pregnant. To escape his murderous intent she fled to a mountain cave. In hiding from the outside world her child died and her hair turned white from her privations. She existed by taking the sacrificial rice from the altar of a small temple at night. Rumour spread of a white-haired spirit haunting the countryside. Communist troops occupied the area bringing back the girl's former suitor. After listening to the villagers' stories he set off to track down the 'spirit'. There was an emotional reunion and the couple returned to denounce the landlord who was publicly sentenced to execution.

This item became a theatrical symbol of the revolutionary cause and was constantly performed in the late 1940s and 1950s. The fusion of song, music, chorus work and ordinary speech allied to a contemporary setting marked *The White-Haired Girl* apart from either traditional Chinese or modern Western stage practices though both had clearly offered some inspiration. It appealed to an audience for whom theatre without song and music was inconceivable and dialogue drama in the Western vein meaningless in the context of their lifestyle. It was in effect an extension of ideas tried out in 1935 when the playwright Tian Han, collaborating with the composer Nie Er, used song and music with spoken drama in a play named *Storm Over the Yangzi River* (*Yangzi jiang de baofengyu*).

The White-Haired Girl was the first full-length representative of a new national genre named *geju*, song-opera. Flexible in subject matter and musical form it was contemporary but adaptable to regional traditions. It was one solution to a middle way between past and present, a long-standing problem of Chinese theatre.

Reestablishment of the Nationalist capital at Nanjing in May 1946 followed Japan's defeat in 1945. In 1946 full scale civil war broke out as the Communists began their drive for ultimate power. The hopes of a war-weary nation faded with the acceleration of a crippling inflation leading to economic chaos and social disintegration. The plight of the universities was desperate, the mood of the intellectuals one of despair.

In 1946 Xiong Foxi became head of the Shanghai Municipal Experimental School of Dramatic Art. Sharing the premises of a local museum and primary school it received negligible official aid and counted on receipts from its own productions to keep going. Xiong's faith in theatre was matched by that of his students and staff. Combining classroom study with working experience they sustained a continuing series of performances for the public. A venture of insight and promise, it symbolized the theatrical hopes of an era which perished in the tide of events.

Tian Han taught there after the war for a period, as did Hong Shen. Cao Yu joined the staff after his return from an invited visit to the United States in 1946. Xia Yen had given up playwriting for film work and Ouyang Yuqian worked for the Hongkong film studios after the war. Dai Ailian, the dancer, another guest of the United States during this period, returned to set up her own school in Shanghai. Conditions forced her to close it. When the Nationalist government left for Taiwan in 1949 this group of key personalities stayed on to work under the new regime. It was a decision which was shared by a large proportion of the people prominent in both traditional and modern theatre circles.

The People's Republic 1949 – Policy and theory On 1 October 1949 the Chinese Communist Party (CCP) established the People's Republic of China (PRC) under its Chairman Mao Zedong. In 1966 Mao launched his radical Cultural Revolution in an attempt to preserve revolutionary purity. With his death in

September 1976 and the fall of the radical 'gang of four' the following month, economic modernization soon assumed top priority in China's policy, and in 1981 both the Cultural Revolution and Mao's leadership from 1958 on were largely discredited.

Attitudes towards theatre reflect overall CCP policy, which means that there have been substantial changes from period to period. However, at no time has the CCP believed it should relax its concern with theatre activities altogether. As a result, the fact of censorship has been consistent, even though the extent has varied enormously.

Until 1981, the basic CCP policy and theory concepts of theatre (and other arts) were those Mao advanced in his 'Talks at the Yan'an Forum on Literature and Art'. Mao declared there that theatre reflected society but also influenced it as a means of propaganda, whether it intended to or not. He held all theatre as representing the interests of one class or another and advocated that it should oppose the bourgeoisie and favour the masses of workers, peasants and soldiers. Elsewhere, Mao pushed for the critical assimilation of traditional and foreign theatres.

In July 1950 the new government's Ministry of Culture set up a Drama Reform Committee to determine precisely how practice in the theatre should be brought into line with theory. Among traditional music-dramas it retained those which emphasized Chinese patriotism, peasant rebellion or heroism, equality between the sexes, or the political prominence of women. Newly arranged dramas on historical themes were expected to emphasize similar topics. On the other hand, many items considered 'feudal' and siding with the rich against the poor were banned. While the mannerisms, costumes and other aspects of the traditional actor's craft were retained, reform demanded the abolition of some 'unhealthy' usages. No people's hero should be shown in a position which humiliated him before a feudal person such as a monk. Kowtowing and the 'false foot' devised by Wei Changsheng were banned. The Great Leap Forward of 1958 gave strong emphasis to dramas of all forms on contemporary themes, but did not discourage traditional. Throughout the 1950s and early 1960s, although the theories of **Stanislavsky** were dominant among spoken drama circles, those of Bertolt Brecht also had a following, led by Huang Zuolin of the Shanghai People's Art Theatre.

At a meeting of heads of CCP Cultural Bureaux held in April 1963, Mao's wife Jiang Qing had a circular distributed calling for 'the suspension of the performance of ghost plays', by which she meant any traditional music-drama or newly arranged historical item. In mid-1964 a Festival of Beijing Opera on Contemporary Themes was held, signalling the near total disappearance of all such 'ghost plays' from the stage for 13 years. In February 1966 Jiang Qing held a forum on 'Literature and Art in the Armed Forces' which laid down the line on theatre demanded by the Cultural Revolution. It followed Mao's ideas closely in its emphasis on class and class struggle and the mass line, but placed an extreme interpretation on them. Thus 'critical assimilation' of tradition meant retention of little more than the name Beijing Opera. All content must praise the revolution and the CCP directly, almost all the traditional content, mannerisms and costumes were banned as espousing feudal ideas and class interests. The Forum also pushed the notion of a 'model' drama, one which encapsulated perfectly all the Cultural Revolution's theory of theatre. Over the following years a small number of these 'models' was devised, and professional drama companies were allowed to perform more or less nothing else. One of the main features of the 'models' was their characterization, which portrayed the heroes as faultless, and the villains as without redeeming features. Any positive character with weaknesses at the beginning had overcome them by the end of the play. Tragedy was excluded for, even if the hero or heroine is killed, the revolution must triumph. Love and humour shrank to near vanishing point, fantasy and magic were totally banned. Education, never entertainment, was pronounced the main aim of theatre.

Jiang Qing was the leader of the 'gang of four' and it was not long after its fall that the Cultural Revolution's theatre theory was discredited. In May 1977 several scenes of a newly arranged historical drama were restaged in Beijing. Early the following year the main power-holder of the new leadership, Deng Xiaoping, gave explicit approval for the revival of traditional music-dramas and these began to trickle back, very quickly becoming a veritable torrent which, as of 1985, had not subsided. Love-stories and patriotic dramas, as well as those about peasant rebels, again received encouragement and the theme of righted injustice set in the dynastic past became a useful propaganda weapon on behalf of the legal reform which has been so prominent a feature of Chinese society since 1979. Once again, humour became a dominant part of the Chinese regional drama, and entertainment was accepted as a main purpose of theatre.

The Changyin ge (Joyful Sounds Pagoda), a three-tiered stage in the Imperial Palaces of Beijing, home of the former imperial court.

The main linchpin in the CCP's theatre policy is the need for variety. The range of form and content has continued to broaden, on the whole with CCP approval. Up till 1985 attempts to hold back this trend towards liberalization, such as the Campaign against Spiritual Pollution in 1983, have proved short-lived. In 1982, Mao's 'Talks at the Yan'an Forum' were partly discredited. In theory, theatre should still serve the interests of the 'people' but the emphasis on its use as a propaganda weapon for socialism has tended increasingly to weaken. As a result, modern spoken dramas ignoring the role of the CCP in society, and those advocating no solution for its ills, have become common. Psychological drama has become popular among the urban intelligentsia, and the CCP tolerates it, though without enthusiasm. The theories of acting and theatre of Bertolt Brecht are increasing in influence especially among younger playwrights. Since 1979 various forms of foreign theatre have received CCP sponsorship, not only performed by foreign companies in the original language, but also by local troupes and translated into Chinese.

Form, performance   The main forms of drama in China since 1949 are traditional music-drama, newly arranged historical drama (*xinbian lishi ju*), spoken drama (**huaju**), song-drama (*geju*), dance-drama (*wuju*) and ballet.

Currently traditional music-drama is the most popular of the forms in the countryside, where some four-fifths of the people live. There are about 350 regional styles. The content is always from the distant past. As in the past, stage properties are simple, there is no scenery, but costumes and makeup are elaborate, mannerisms, posture and body movements stylized. An evening's entertainment will normally feature three or four short items. Reform and censorship have removed certain items and passages, but this is the form least affected by the modern age.

Newly arranged historical dramas are similar in many ways to traditional music-dramas. The music is strongly regionalized and follows the melodic patterns and texture of the particular regional style of which it is representative. Nevertheless, an individual composer writes music especially for each item. The costumes and makeup take their style from the traditional theatre, although with variations. On the other hand, there are complex scenery and stage properties and the tendency is for the drama to last a full evening. There is usually a definite structure in the plot, which rises to a climax and conclusion. Normally, the plot is set in the dynastic past, and, despite the term 'historical drama', is based either on a historical or mythological incident. There are cases of newly arranged regional music-dramas with modern and even contemporary themes. There is considerable room for a political message and the great majority carry a clear ideological viewpoint. Since 1978, the quantity of dramas written in this form is greater than for any other, with more and more themes and stories being dug up from the vastness of Chinese history and mythology.

Among Westernized forms, the most important is the spoken drama (*huaju*). Only of this form can it be said in the 1980s that most items are set in the present or even since 1949. It is the form which in the 1980s shows the greatest inventiveness and innovation, by comparison with China's past, and the most outside, mainly Western, influence. Social commentary remains strong, but among the avant-garde playwrights, propaganda of the type favoured by the CCP is becoming less and less direct, more and more subdued. Individualism and feminism are hallmarks of the plays of a contemporary female playwright such as Bai Fengxi. Experimentation with techniques new to China is gathering momentum, for example, variation in the colour and intensity of stage-lighting to show emotional or psychological atmospheres or qualities. Spoken dramas of the PRC normally use elaborate scenery and stage properties and in urban theatres curtains are drawn to mark the beginning, end or intermission. However, since 1982, a few plays have adopted extremely simple stage properties, and abandoned scenery and the curtain altogether. Body movements and postures are realistic, not stylized as in traditional music-drama. But whereas the plays with heavy propaganda content tended to show ideal characters through rather stilted, even stereotypical, movements and postures, natural style is becoming more popular in the 1980s to portray characters who themselves conform less to images laid down as good, mediocre or bad by the CCP.

The song-drama combines Chinese and Western techniques. The orchestra which accompanies the singing contains mainly Western instruments, but with an admixture of Chinese traditional. The melodies are Chinese in flavour but with Western influence in their structure, and the harmonic principles of the music are mainly Western. Complex scenery is used, and costumes and stage mannerisms, postures and gestures tend strongly to be realistic, although retaining the influence of traditional theatre. A single item usually occupies a full evening, but the practice of combining key scenes from several pieces into one session is not unknown. The first representative item *The White-Haired Girl* was adapted as a ballet during the Cultural Revolution and, its story somewhat changed to emphasize the class struggle, it became a 'model' drama. The form song-drama was totally suppressed during the Cultural Revolution decade, but *The White-Haired Girl* was repremiered in Beijing in that form in February 1977. While new items are still being written, they are not large in number, and the song-drama tends as a form to lack inventiveness and innovation.

Similar to song-drama in being a mixture of Western and Chinese styles is dance-drama. The instrumentation and flavour of the music are extremely close to each other. The essence of dance-drama is the combination of traditional Chinese folk dance and Western ballet. This form was quite popular in Chinese cities before 1966 but totally suppressed during the Cultural Revolution decade. Its return followed immediately upon the 'gang of four's' fall, and in Shanghai in January 1977 there were performances of *The Small Sword Society* (*Xiaodao hui*), a dance-drama praising the rebellious movement of the title, which took place in the middle of the 19th century.

The introduction of Western ballet is due principally to Soviet influence. Before 1966, ballet meant mainly items of classical European repertoire, especially *Swan Lake*. The 'model' dramas of Jiang Qing included two ballets: *The White-Haired Girl* and *The Red Detachment of Women* (*Hongse niangzi jun*). Since 1976, these items have disappeared as ballets and the classical works returned. At the same time, Chinese artists are making very tentative steps towards creating their own national ballet, including composing new works and training ballet-dancers. However, no high priority is given to this form, and it is most unlikely ever to gain great popularity in China outside a small urban intellectual elite.

Illustrative pieces Of all newly arranged historical dramas, none is more famous than *The White Snake* (*Baishe zhuan*). Originally a folk story about a white snake that turns into a beautiful woman, it underwent numerous adaptations, including to a *kunqu* by an anonymous playwright in the 18th century. Tian Han, one of the PRC's most famous dramatists, adapted it to a Beijing Opera, completing the work in 1953. A monk in the *kunqu* is a positive character who succeeds in curbing the power of the wicked snake, but Tian Han has changed the characterization to present him as evil, the snake-turned-woman as positive. Even though an element of magic is preserved, the item thus advocates a positive role for women.

The theme of patriotism supplements advocacy of equality for women in *Women Generals of the Yang Family* (*Yangmen nüjiang*), arranged into a Beijing Opera in 1960 by Lü Ruiming on the basis of the late-Ming novel and a Yangzhou music-drama (*yangju*) entitled *Centenarian Takes Command* (*Baisui guashuai*). Like all others on traditional themes, this item was banned during the Cultural Revolution. However it was revived on 1 January 1978. The item is set in the 11th century. A centenarian dowager surnamed Yang persuades the women of her family to resist an enemy aggressor from the north, and their forces win the final victory.

In the early 1980s several items appeared, both as spoken dramas and newly arranged historical music-dramas, on the subject of Li Shimin, one of China's greatest emperors (r. 626–49). He was the second ruler of the Tang dynasty (618–907) and held the imperial title of Taizong, and so is known also as Tang Taizong.

Scene from *Baisui guashuai* (*Centenarian Takes Command*), an item of *yangju*, the regional style of Yangzhou, Jiangsu Province. The 100-year-old woman Yu Taijun is third from the right. Note the two painted-faced characters on the right.

One of the music-dramas is the Beijing Opera *Tang Taizong*, arranged by Li Lun. It deals with Li Shimin's success in winning over a Turkish invader through mediation and popular support, not force, and in thus securing national unity. The incident which forms the core of the drama is historical, but the characterization and plot are adapted to advocate political lessons appropriate to the present.

More modern national heroes to be portrayed on the stage since the late 1970s are revolutionaries such as Zhou Enlai and Mao Zedong. In 1981, the 70th anniversary of the overthrow of the last dynasty by Sun Yatsen and his followers was the occasion for several spoken dramas about him. His wife Song Qingling, who died in 1981, figures prominently in them. The first of the plays was *Sun Yatsen's London Encounter with Danger* (*Sun Zhongshan Lundun mengnan ji*). Its focus was Sun's arrest by the Chinese legation in 1896 and later release through the efforts of his former teacher the British doctor Sir James Cantlie. This enables the playwright, Li Peijian, to emphasize not only the courage and unselfishness of Sun, but also the power and wisdom of the British people, represented by Cantlie and others, and Sun's good relations with his 'foreign friends'. The play is unusual in China, even now, in being set in a foreign country.

In 1979 a spate of spoken dramas was completed attacking official corruption, not in the past but in contemporary society. The one to gain most fame in the West was *If I Were Real* (*Rugu wo shi zhende*), by Sha Yexin and others, about a young man who gains great privileges by pretending to be the son of a high army officer. In China itself the play was banned and never shown publicly. *Power versus Law* (*Quan yu fa*), by Xing Yixun, was published late in 1979. The evil of corruption in the CCP looms large in the play but its thrust is to attack individuals, not the Party itself, and it was thus acceptable to the authorities. The central theme shows the law, supported by the good CCP leader and the people, victorious over corrupt officials. The play also denounces the acknowledged widespread seizure of privileges by officials for themselves and their families.

The necessity of law is a strong theme also in Liu Shugang's *Fifteen Cases of Divorce* (*Shiwu lihun an*), premiered in 1983, which probes the causes of divorce in contemporary China. The same two performers play the 15 couples suing for divorce. There is no curtain, and they change character on the stage by adding a layer to their costume. Racks on either side of the stage bear the clothes appropriate to the characters still to be represented in the play. There is no scenery but elaborate stage-properties which remain constant throughout the play. Mime, other acting techniques, and the context revealed by the dialogue, tell the audience what the properties represent.

No real solutions are offered to the problem of divorce, certainly not Party leadership. In *A Friend Comes in a Time of Stress* (*Fengyu guren lai*) by Bai Fengxi, premiered in December 1983, the CCP is ignored more or less totally. The play concerns a brilliant young mathematician who wins a scholarship to go to West Germany. The runner-up is her husband. Her mother-in-law places heavy pressure on her to withdraw in his favour. Her father arrives and successfully persuades her not to yield to sexist blandishments. Bai Fengxi believes that professional competition between married couples is frequent in Chinese cities. Her play appeals for a strong role for women in the professions in a society where Confucian sexist values remain very strong and have probably strengthened in the 1980s.

Among dance-dramas in the 1980s none is better known, either in China or outside, than *Tales of the Silk Road* (*Silu huayu*), first written in 1977 by members of the Gansu Song and Dance Ensemble, and performed frequently since 1979. The plot is set in the Tang dynasty and concerns a slave-dancer who is taken to Persia by a rich merchant of that country to escape an evil magistrate. The ending sees the magistrate punished and happy relations between Persia and China. What is distinctive about the piece is that the costumes and many of the dance movements derive from postures shown on the Tang-dynasty wall paintings of the Dunhuang caves in Gansu Province. The music, through a mixture of styles and melodies, attempts to capture the atmospheres of medieval China and Persia. Other dance-dramas of the 1980s include several based on the classical novel *A Dream of Red Mansions* (*Honglou meng*) and one adapted from Tang Xianzu's *The Peony Pavilion*.

Sites of performance, audiences Theatre performances can take place in a variety of sites in China, including workers' or rural clubs, a market-place or any open space. Street theatre is common only on special occasions such as festivals. In the cities and towns, cinemas are readily used as theatres for live performances. A major theatre encyclopaedia published in Beijing in 1983 stated that there were 891 theatres in China in 1949 and 2,227 in 1957. It claimed that 'after 1958 [we] continued to build quite a few new theatres' but gave no figures. In the main cities there are a few large theatres, of special note being one opened in Beijing in 1984 which has a 600-square-metre stage able to hold 1,000 performers.

Most theatres built since 1949 follow a somewhat stark Soviet architectural style, both internally and externally. In sharp contrast to the teahouse-theatres of the 19th century, the audience is expected to concentrate fully on the performance, and sits in rows facing one side of the stage. In the case of musical items, the text is projected beside the stage to facilitate comprehension. The seats are rarely padded. The large 1984 Beijing theatre has a stage with rising and revolving platforms, a stereo sound system, lamps, spotlights and curtains all controlled by computer. It is in this respect the first of its kind in China.

Some companies own their own theatre. Those not so fortunate negotiate with a local government Bureau of Culture, the jobs of which include that of coordinating the timetables of the various troupes and theatres. Tours are planned through an annual meeting organized by the central Ministry of Culture. In a few parts of China there are special theatres for balladeers or story-tellers. Here people, many of them old men, sip tea and listen to stories sung out by one or several performers, accompanying themselves on musical instruments. However, in most cases story-tellers perform singly in parks or squares, and the more formal companies are losing their audiences.

Advertisement of performances is partly through the local press. Theatres announce forthcoming items and

Teahouse-theatre of the late 19th or early 20th century.

performances through bills in the foyer. Most important of all, advertisements are stuck on special billboards, poles or any free space beside the streets or in the markets. This is especially necessary in small towns or villages which lack their own newspaper.

Tickets for professional performances are cheap and entry to amateur ones often free. During the early years of the Cultural Revolution all theatres were closed but when they reopened ticket-selling was on a rota system by which the local Bureau of Culture sold blocks of seats to organizations selected in turn; the relevant unit then drafted the number of members necessary to take up all the seats. This system began to be abandoned in 1977 in favour of individual free purchase but is by no means dead even in the mid-1980s.

Programmes are usually simple and very cheap, consisting of a single sheet of paper. For music-dramas the programme tells the plot and cast of each item to be shown, sometimes with brief commentary. In the case of spoken dramas the cast is given, occasionally with pictures of the performers. There is explanation of the play's significance but usually no account of the plot.

During the early 1970s performances were normally given to full houses, but that was because of the rota system of ticket-selling and small number of shows rather than because the people loved the model dramas. Full houses are still quite common, especially for good and well-performed pieces, but companies frequently complain of low attendances, and nearly empty theatres are distressingly common in provincial centres.

Those involved with the traditional and the newly arranged historical music-drama have become increasingly worried over the defection of young people from their audiences. Possibly the gap in performance of over a decade during the Cultural Revolution dealt a crippling blow to the youth's interest in such theatre. It was excluded from their education and cultural life for so long that by the time of its revival they simply did not understand it and saw no reason why they should

make the effort. Even in the early 1960s youth attendance of traditional shows was disappointing to performers. As a result there is rarely more than a sprinkling of those under 40 at urban traditional music-drama performances. The same problem affects the countryside, but is not nearly so advanced there.

Young theatre-goers prefer the spoken drama because they can understand it and it has more to say of relevance to their own lives. However, the forms of entertainment which are more and more attracting the largest audiences are not theatre at all, but cinema and television. The State Statistical Bureau's 1985 communiqué on the previous year's economy and society declared that there were 178,000 cinemas and film projection teams, and 466 television transmitting and relay stations, and that Central Television had aired 454 TV plays. Cinema and television are available not only in the cities but to large and rapidly increasing areas of the countryside. Ironically the screen does support all drama forms in the sense that both traditional and modern music-dramas and spoken dramas are shown both in the cinema and on television, but the fact is of little comfort to the average performer.

Audiences at traditional music-dramas tend to be noisy, possibly in part a reflection of their incomplete understanding of what is happening, but those of the spoken drama attend better and more quietly. Notices in many theatres forbid either spitting or smoking, but in provincial theatres infringements of the former prohibition, though less the latter, are common. Applause is reserved mainly for notes held an unusual length of time or an excellent acrobatics display. Even very good troupes are lucky to elicit more than a patter at the conclusion of the performance.

The performer The State Statistical Bureau announced in March 1985 that the number of full professional performing arts troupes in China in 1984 was 3,397. They are staffed with some 220,000 artists. The number of troupes in 1950 was 1,676 and in 1965 3,458, but fell to 2,514 by 1971 as a result of the policies of the Cultural Revolution. The year with the highest figure was 1980, with 3,533 troupes.

The nationalization of the professional troupes began in the mid-1950s and was completed during the Cultural Revolution. After the fall of the gang of four the process was reversed and in the early 1980s reform began to be introduced in the direction of free enterprise even in the state companies and, as of 1985, it appears to be gathering momentum rapidly. Under the new system, state subsidies to troupes are reduced, but correspondingly only a portion of the earnings is handed back to the state. Individual performers still receive a salary from the state but are given additional income commensurate with their contribution to a particular play. Box-office earnings thus assume a far greater importance in the work of the troupes and their members. This aims to 'break the iron rice bowl' and in theory improves quality because it intensifies competition among actors. In contrast to the earlier system, the possibility of dismissal becomes quite real for lazy or incompetent members. Above all, inequalities increase greatly because performers with big roles in successful plays can earn substantial sums from the box-office earnings, in addition to their salary, and thus become rich by Chinese standards quite quickly. Social securities for members of state professional troupes are quite good, and it is not proposed to weaken them under the reformed system.

Another major aspect of the reform lies in management. More decisions on such matters as to which pieces to perform and when, and who shall be in the cast, are handed over by the CCP branch to the director, who is a professional artist. The Party branches will certainly not withdraw, nor will their control be eliminated, but it will be reduced and shifted away from artistic to administrative matters.

Immediately after coming to power the CCP abolished the training system of the past and instituted the principle that potential performers should receive a general as well as theatrical education, in order to wipe out illiteracy among them. Much of the training of performers was suspended during the Cultural Revolution, including almost all that for traditional music-drama, but revived after 1976. Most professional companies run schools through which to recruit, train and educate new performers. There is also a network of formal academies for the training of personnel needed for theatre. These exist at central, provincial, municipal and other levels. For traditional music-drama, especially Beijing Opera, the main one at central level is the Chinese Music-Drama Institute (Zhongguo xiqu xueyuan). Initially set up as 'experimental' on 28 January 1950, it was confirmed as a school a few years later and raised to tertiary level as an institute in October 1978, with five departments: Beijing Opera performance, music-drama music, music-drama directing, arrangement of music-drama and music-drama stagecraft. Between 1956 and 1982 the institution produced some 1,300 graduates.

Entry into all training-schools at all levels is through examination and is extremely competitive. Only about 5 per cent of applicants gain admission. There is still a strong bias in favour of males, the rationale being that in the casts of most pieces men predominate.

CCP policy is to train women to sing female roles and men to sing male. In 1951 Premier Zhou Enlai told the famous *dan* Zhang Junqiu: 'up to you the male *dan*, and that's the end', meaning that, while the CCP would encourage those male *dan* brought up under the old regime, it would not train any more, so that eventually women would perform all *dan* roles. However, in December 1983 this writer learned, by meeting a male *dan* trainee at the Jiangsu Provincial Theatre School in Nanjing, that steps are being taken towards a very limited revival of the female impersonator's art.

The social status of performers has risen greatly under CCP rule. Among the reasons for this are the elimination of social discriminations which previously afflicted them, the more highly organized recruitment and training system, their much improved standard of living, and the government's high evaluation of 'art workers' as a profession. There are, however, still strong gradations in the status of performers. The stars may be among the most influential and respected members of the society, but there is still much serious poverty among ordinary performers and social disregard for them.

Since the earliest days of its existence the CCP always strongly encouraged amateur artists who, it considered, could assist its propaganda work among the masses to an extent even greater than the professionals. The slogan pushed was 'small in scale, rich in variety' (*xiaoxing duoyang*), meaning that long or complicated pieces requiring extensive training or elaborate and expensive costumes should be avoided. The spoken drama, simple songs and dances, or balladry items, were greatly preferred to traditional music-drama. The Cultural Revolution gave great priority to the 'mass amateur propaganda troupes' and for several years in the late 1960s they were more or less the only source of China's theatrical life.

Since the late 1970s these amateur troupes have declined markedly, although as of the end of 1983 they

The heroine Mu Guiying is the most important of the women generals of the Yang family and features in many music-dramas.

were by no means extinct. To fill their place semi-professional troupes have arisen everywhere in China, and especially in the countryside where fully professional theatre is much less accessible than in the cities. Peasants take their own initiative to form troupes, selection of members being rather careful so that only the most talented and skilled can obtain admission. They spend about half the year as peasants, and during the slack season they go around performing, mainly traditional regional music-dramas. The reward is financial, for although the performers do not receive salaries, they are paid from box-office returns according to their contribution to the particular drama. If they are good enough, they are also thrown tips from the audience. In 1983 there were about 3,000 of these semi-professional troupes in the single province of Anhui, and the number was still rising.

Conclusion Clearly the period since 1978 has brought enormous changes in the Chinese theatre in all respects and is likely to lead on to even greater transformation in the future. The major thrust is still socialist in that content tends to reflect the socialist society and many full professional troupes remain state-owned. On the other hand, the direction of change is unquestionably towards greater variety and liberalism in terms of form and content, and free enterprise in organization. A further expansion in innovation and variety would bode well for the future of the Chinese theatre. However, experience in other countries suggests that economic modernization affects traditional arts adversely. Despite the current revival of traditional regional music-drama, the same could easily happen in the next few decades in China. CPM ACS

See also: **Hong Kong; Taiwan.**

See: J. I. Crump, *Chinese Theatre in the Days of Kublai Khan*, Tucson, Arizona, 1980; W. Dolby (trans.), *Eight Chinese Plays from the Thirteenth Century to the Present*, New York, 1978; W. Dolby, *A History of Chinese Drama*, London, 1976; E. M. Gunn (ed.), *Twentieth-Century Chinese Drama: An Anthology*, Bloomington, 1983; E. Halson, *Peking Opera, A Short Guide*, Hong Kong, 1966; R. Howard, *Contemporary Chinese Theatre*, London, 1978; J. Huang Hung, *Ming Drama*, Taipei, 1966; D. R. Johnson, *Yuarn Music Dramas: Studies in Prosody and Structure and a Complete Catalogue of Northern Arias in the Dramatic Style*, Ann Arbor, 1980; B. S. McDougall (ed.), *Popular Chinese Literature and Performing Arts in the People's Republic of China 1949–1979*, Berkeley, California, 1984; C. Mackerras (ed.), *Chinese Theater from its Origins to the Present Day*, Honolulu, 1983; C. Mackerras, *The Chinese Theatre in Modern Times from 1840 to the Present Day*, London, 1975; *The Performing Arts in Contemporary China*, London, 1981; *The Rise of the Peking Opera 1770–1870, Social Aspects of the Theatre in Manchu China*, Oxford, 1972; W. J. and R. I. Meserve (eds.), *Modern Drama from Communist China*, New York, 1970; Ching-Hsi Perng, *Double Jeopardy: A Critique of Seven Yüan Courtroom Dramas*, Ann Arbor, 1978; A. C. Scott, *Actors are Madmen, Notebook of a Theatregoer in China*, Madison, 1982; *The Classical Theatre of China*, London, 1957; *Mei Lan-fang, Leader of the Pear Garden*, Hong Kong, 1959; A. C. Scott (trans. and ed.), *Traditional Chinese Plays*, 3 vols., Madison, Wisconsin, 1967, 1969, 1975; Shih Chung-wen, *The Golden Age of Chinese Drama: Yuan Tsa-chü*, Princeton, 1976; S. H. West, *Vaudeville and Narrative: Aspects of Chin Theater*, Wiesbaden, 1977; Wu Zuguang, Huang Zuolin and Mei Shaowu, *Peking Opera and Mei Lanfang, A Guide to China's Traditional Theatre and the Art of its Great Master*, Beijing, 1981; C. S. L. Zung, *Secrets of the Chinese Drama: A Complete Explanatory Guide to Actions and Symbols as Seen in the Performance of Chinese Dramas*, New York, 1937, 1964.

Chirgwin, G. H. (1854–1922) 'The White-eyed Kaffir'. English black-faced comedian, singer, multi-instrumentalist and eccentric dancer. London born, he got his early experience busking with his brothers both in the metropolis and at small seaside resorts, and subsequently as a nigger minstrel and cross-talk act at the minor halls. He seems to have made his London stage debut as early as 1861. He began to play solo at the Middlesex Music Hall, and became unfailingly successful after a booking at the Oxford in 1878. Tall and long-legged, he was a striking figure in black tights and leotard, floor length frock-coat and enormous stove-pipe hat, with a contrasting white lozenge over his right eye. In a stage career of over 40 years, the only variation in his appearance was that he sometimes appeared with the colours reversed. Though his act never changed, his instrumental versatility (and his ability to dance while playing the bagpipes) gave it variety, as did his habit of alternating baritone and falsetto delivery in both speech and song. He was also much given to topical rhymes and allusions, and liked to set up a relationship of impromptu banter with his audience. Best remembered for his performance of the old Christy Minstrel tear-jerker 'The Blind Boy' and the punning 'My Fiddle is my Sweetheart (and I'm her only Beau)'. AEG

Chocolat see **Foottit**

Chocrón, Isaac (1932–) Venezuelan playwright, director, critic and novelist. One third of the Venezuelan 'Holy Trinity' (with **Cabrujas** and **Chalbaud**), Chocrón has written more than a dozen plays plus several novels. Director of the **Nuevo Grupo** (New Group) since 1967, winner of the National Theatre Prize in 1979, in 1984 he was chosen by the Venezuelan

Grupo Rajatablas's production of Isaac Chocrón's *Simón*, at the Festival Latino, New York, 1985.

president to direct the newly formed National Theatre Company. Trained as an economist, he studied both in the USA and England. His first play, *Mónica y el florentino* (*Monica and the Florentine*, 1959), used an international guest house to manifest problems of isolation and difficulties of communication. Chocrón has experimented with a variety of styles: his popular *Asia y el lejano oriente* (*Asia and the Far East*, 1966), about the selling of a country, was restaged with music and dance added as the first offering of the National Theatre Company in 1985. *Okey* (1969) presented a *ménage à trois* addicted to consumerism and *La revolución* (*The Revolution*, 1971) dealt frankly with homosexuality. Later plays include *La máxima felicidad* (*Maximum Happiness*, 1974), *El acompañante* (*The Accompanist*, 1978), *Mesopotamia* (1979) and *Simón* (1983), the latter a view of young Bolívar and his mentor.   GW

Christie (Mallowan, née Miller), Agatha (1891–1976) British detective novelist and dramatist, whose dramatizations of her own novels have been successful both on stage and film, notably *Ten Little Niggers* (1943, produced in New York as *Ten Little Indians*, 1944) and *Murder on the Nile* (1946). *The Mousetrap*, which opened in 1952 at the Ambassadors Theatre and had already achieved the record for the longest continuous London run of any play before 1973, when it transferred to St Martin's Theatre, is still (1987) running. Although the most conventional of her plays, it was also seen in New York (1960), and has been running for the last 8 years in Toronto. Her work also established a record of another sort when *Spider's Web* was staged in 1954, while *Witness for the Prosecution* (1953) was still on, so that she had three plays running simultaneously in the West End.   CI

Chuanju (Sichuan Opera) The Chinese term for the form of music-drama found in Sichuan, China's most populous province, and one of the most important of the country's regional styles.

Initially there were five different styles, four belonging to the main systems of Chinese theatre and introduced from outside the province. The earliest is called *gaoqiang*. It is a variant of the Music of Yiyang drama and shares its main features such as the offstage chorus (see under **China**). It came to Sichuan probably in the 17th century. Slightly later was the Clapper Opera introduced from Shaanxi to the north, and known in Sichuan as *tanqiang* (strum music). It was this tradition which produced the great actor Wei Changsheng. Next was a variant of the *pihuang* system; called *huqin qiang* (the 'music of the *huqin*') in Sichuan, it clearly shares with other *pihuang* styles accompaniment by that two-stringed bowed instrument. The aristocratic **kunqu** was popular with the officials of Sichuan. A 19th-century governor-general of the province, Wu Tang (d. 1876), invited actors from Suzhou and set up his own private company, named Shuyi. The only style truly native to Sichuan was the *dengxi* ('lantern theatre'), a small-scale folk style based on the mask dances of village shamans.

Early in the 20th century a movement began to reform the Sichuan theatre. For the first time the five styles were performed on the same stage and regarded as a unity, though every item still retained its style of origin in its music. The first teahouse-theatres were

introduced into Sichuan's cities. Probably the greatest of the reformers was Kang Zhilin (1870–1931), a fine actor, teacher and leader of the Sanqing (Three Celebrations) Company. Set up in 1912, this was the most famous of the Sichuan Opera's troupes. Apart from the Cultural Revolution decade, the Sichuan Opera has flourished under the Communists, especially since 1978. As of 1983 the Sichuan Province *Chuanju* Research Institute held the texts of over 2,000 items. The great majority follow stories familiar from the literature and theatre of China as a whole rather than of the single province of Sichuan.

In its performance and stagecrafts, costuming and makeup, Sichuan Opera is essentially similar to other Chinese regional styles, including Beijing Opera. Some elements of Beijing Opera stage arts were in fact introduced from Sichuan through Wei Changsheng. It is important to note, however, that the Sichuan Opera does have its own distinctive stage arts tradition. For instance, Kang Zhilin devised a skill which enables an actor to kick up his foot, touching the middle of the lower forehead with it for a split second and leaving the image of a third eye there. This breathtaking art is still practised in Sichuan. Another example of Sichuan Opera's partial distinctiveness lies in the art of the painted face (*jing*), which is traditionally restricted to four colours, black, red, white and grey, as against the rather larger number of shades in Beijing Opera. The first three are used with significance similar to that in Beijing Opera, but whereas that style paints the faces of supernatural beings in green or gold the Sichuan Opera uses grey.   CPM

Churchill, Caryl (1938–   ) British dramatist, who started to write radio plays in the early 1960s about 'bourgeois middle-class life and the destruction of it'. Her husband was a barrister who came to work for a law centre, and a hatred of social injustice characterized Churchill's first major stage play, *Owners*, produced at the **Royal Court**'s Theatre Upstairs in 1972. While not at first a politically committed writer, she came to write for left-wing and feminist companies, such as Joint Stock and Monstrous Regiment, for whom she wrote *Light Shining in Buckinghamshire* (1976) and *Vinegar Tom* (1976) about 17th-century witchcraft. The historical background to current social-political problems, including sexual role-playing, fascinated her, and is most fully expressed in *Cloud Nine* (1979), developed through improvisation sessions with the Joint Stock company. Here British imperialism is revealed to cause sexual and racial stereotypes, and by swopping the roles, as well as shifting time, Churchill achieved a lively and highly intelligent comedy of manners. In *Top Girls* (1982), Churchill staged a dinner party for famous women of different ages, describing their various struggles and relating them with those of today. An imaginative and sceptical writer, Churchill does not tolerate political pedantry any more easily than conventional theatrical forms; and while her plays (such as *Objections to Sex and Violence*, 1974, and *Fen*, 1982) can seem untidy and even clumsy, they are sustained by the rigorous energy of her writing. *Serious Money* (1987) proved an effective comment on the people and practices of the 'City', coinciding as it did with an international financial crisis.   JE

Colley Cibber as Lord Foppington in Vanbrugh's *The Relapse*.

Cibber, Colley (1671–1757) English actor, manager, playwright. Son of Caius Gabriel Cibber, a sculptor, he joined the United Company as an actor in 1690. After the secession of the senior actors with **Betterton** in 1695, he stayed with Christopher Rich, recognizing the opportunity to take over major roles, and was successful as Fondlewife in **Congreve**'s *The Old Bachelor*. His first play, *Love's Last Shift* (1696), including a superb role for himself as a fop, Sir Novelty Fashion, contains a last-act repentance for the rake-hero and is often labelled the first sentimental comedy. He played Lord Foppington, Sir Novelty elevated to the peerage, in **Vanbrugh**'s rebuttal of the argument of *Love's Last Shift*, *The Relapse* (1698). In 1699 he produced his adaptation of **Shakespeare**'s *Richard III* and though his own performance as Richard was much ridiculed the adaptation was performed for the next 120 years: it, not Shakespeare's play, contains the famous line 'Off with his head. So much for Buckingham.' His best original comedy, *The Careless Husband*, with Lord Foppington again, was first performed in 1704. By this time Cibber was beginning to be involved in the management of the theatre and by 1708 he was taking a major share with **Doggett** and **Oldfield**. Triumphing over Rich, who lost the theatre, Cibber and his co-managers ran the Queen's Theatre for the owner, Swiney, and in 1710 the triumvirate, Wilks, Doggett and Cibber, took over the management of **Drury Lane**. Cibber was a broadly successful manager, with occasional blunders such as the rejection of **Gay**'s *The Beggar's Opera*; he was particularly good at teaching acting. His adaptation of **Molière**'s *Tartuffe* as *The Nonjuror* and his completion of Vanbrugh's *A Journey to London* as *The Provoked Husband* (1728) are his best plays of this period. Often mocked by satirists for his snobbishness and conceit, Cibber became an oddly

obsessive butt, after his appointment as Poet Laureate in 1730, both for **Fielding** and, especially Pope who made him King of the Dunces in *The New Dunciad* (1742). From 1733, when he retired as manager, he acted less frequently though he was still acting in 1745 in his adaptation of Shakespeare's *King John*. His brilliant autobiography, *An Apology for the Life of Colley Cibber*, was published in 1740.   PH

Cibber, Susanna Maria (1714–66) English actress who began her career as a singer at the **Haymarket** in 1732. Partly trained by **Colley Cibber**, she made her debut as an actress in **Hill**'s *Zara* with huge success. She had a small but carefully chosen repertoire of roles, including Desdemona, Cordelia and Monimia in **Otway**'s *The Orphan*, and was particularly famed for her use of her handkerchief in performances of tragedies. Her pathetic style led Aaron Hill to comment 'When Mrs Cibber weeps, who won't weep with her?' She was off the stage during the scandal of her husband's (**Theophilus Cibber**) suing her lover for damages for adultery but returned triumphantly in 1742 in Dublin and **Covent Garden**. She worked with **Garrick** and with **Rich** but recurrent illnesses frequently hindered her from acting, though she worked up to her death.   PH

Cibber, Theophilus (1703–58) English actor, manager and playwright, son of **Colley Cibber**. He joined the **Drury Lane** company in 1719 and was a precocious and appealing actor. From 1727 he assisted Wilks as

Theophilus Cibber as Pistol.

manager. He gained particular success as Pistol in *Henry IV Part 1* and *Henry V*, in spite of his over-acting. Distrusted by his father, who refused to appoint him his successor as manager, he led a rebellion of actors against the management and in 1734 was granted a licence for the **Haymarket Theatre**. His appalling treatment of his wife culminated in his attempt to sue his wife's lover for damages for adultery, though he condoned and encouraged the affair; he was awarded only £10 damages and was hissed off the stage. In spite of frequent attempts to take on other companies he never really succeeded. He drowned on his way to Ireland to act at Smock Alley Theatre.   PH

Ciceri, Pierre-Luc-Charles (1782–1862) French stage designer and painter. The most admired designer of the first half of the 19th century in Paris, Ciceri began studying drawing and painting with stage designer F. J. Belanger in 1802. In 1806 he became a staff painter to the Paris Opéra, specializing in landscapes. By 1818 he was promoted to chief painter and from 1822 to 1847 he was scenic director for the Paris Opéra. Imaginative landscapes and classical ruins painted on flats and backdrops using a central vanishing point were characteristic of his early designs. With the completion of the new opera house in 1822, dimming and brightening of gas footlights were incorporated into his designs. In 1826 for the **Comédie-Française**, he began designing detailed depictions of historical epochs. Some of his most important designs were executed in his scenic studio established in 1822: Liszt's *Don Sancho* (1825), *La Muette de Portici* (1828), *Guillaume Tell* (1829), *Robert Le Diable* (1831), and *Hernani* (1830). The romantic style developed at his studio dominated the scene designs of the next generation in France.   AJN

Cinquevalli, Paul (Paul Kestner) (1856–1918) Polish juggler. His debut took place in Odessa (1873) as an aerialist; but after a fall from a 75-foot height and eight months in hospital, he switched to juggling. He was first seen in London in 1885 and was soon a headliner on music-hall bills, as 'The Human Billiard Table'. He would often conclude his act by catching a cannon-ball on the nape of his neck. Absolute tops in his field, some of his tricks never copied, he retired in 1915, depressed by anti-German sentiment inaccurately directed at him.   LS

Circle in the Square (USA) New York's oldest company, founded in 1951 by **José Quintero**, Theodore Mann, Emilie Stevens and Jason Wingreen. Starting as the Loft Players in 1949 and specializing in theatre-in-the-round, the company is 'physically conceived and artistically committed to the art of acting', producing great works and 'plays that deserve re-examination'. On 24 April 1952, its now-famous revival of **Tennessee Williams**'s *Summer and Smoke* opened, launching Circle's success and Quintero's and **Geraldine Page**'s careers, and Off-Broadway's artistic heyday. In 1961, Circle opened its school, now offering a baccalaureate degree in association with New York University. In 1969–70, Circle produced six shows at Washington's **Ford's Theatre**, and in 1972, still maintaining its Greenwich Village house, occupied its Joseph E. Levine Theatre beneath the new Uris (now the **Gershwin**).

Under Artistic Director Mann, Circle produced many **O'Neill** works directed by Quintero, plays by **Terrence McNally**, **Israel Horovitz** and Murray Schisgal, and international classics, with such stars as **George C. Scott**, Cicely Tyson, **Jason Robards, Jr**, **James Earl Jones** and **Dustin Hoffman**. Its productions include Capote's *The Grass Harp* (1953), O'Neill's *The Iceman Cometh* with Robards (1956), **Thomas**'s *Under Milk Wood* (1961), **Fugard**'s *Boesman and Lena* (1970), *Medea* with Irene Papas (1973), a contemporary adaptation of **Molière**'s *Scapino* with Jim Dale (1974), Tennessee Williams's *The Glass Menagerie* (1975), **Ibsen**'s *The Lady from the Sea* with **Vanessa Redgrave** (1976), *Macbeth* directed by **Nicol Williamson** (1982), **Shaw**'s *Heartbreak House* with **Rex Harrison** (1983), and **Coward**'s *Design for Living* directed by Scott (1984). Many later ran on Broadway or were seen on public television.   REK

Circle Repertory Company (USA) An Off-Broadway theatre, founded in 1969 by **Marshall W. Mason**, Robert Thirkield, Tanya Berezin and **Lanford Wilson**, dedicated to rediscovering 'lyric realism as the native voice of American theatre'. The group, together since 1965 at Café **La Mama** and Caffé Cino, formed the American Theatre Project in a loft in 1968. Devoted to new American writers, Circle Rep operates a Playwrights' Workshop, Projects-in-Progress Series and Script Evaluation Service, in 1981 launching the Young Playwrights Festival (now at the **New York Shakespeare Festival**) for writers under 19. Circle Rep maintains an informal alliance of actors, playwrights and designers, and many established artists frequently return.

Under its Artistic Director Mason, Circle Rep produced many of Wilson's plays, moving several to Broadway (*The Hot l Baltimore*, 1972; *Talley's Folly*, 1979; *5th of July*, 1977; *Angels Fall*, 1983). Other productions include **Mark Medoff**'s *When You Comin' Back, Red Ryder?* (1973), **Tennessee Williams**'s *Battle of Angels* (1974), Edward Moore's *The Sea Horse* (1976), **Jules Feiffer**'s *Knock Knock* (1976), **Albert Innaurato**'s *Gemini* (1977), Marty Martin's *Gertrude Stein, Gertrude Stein, Gertrude Stein* (1979) and **Sam Shepard**'s *Buried Child* (1979) and *Fool for Love* (1983). Wilson won an Obie for *The Mound Builders* (1975), and *Talley's Folly* won a Pulitzer Prize (1980); the recording of *Gertrude Stein* won a Grammy for the spoken word (1980).   REK

Circus From the Latin for ring, but specifically from the Circus Maximus in Rome, it is defined by Marcello Truzzi as 'a travelling and organized display of animals and skilled performance within one or more circular stages known as "rings" before an audience encircling these activities'. The modern circus, which **Jean Genet** has called 'an instance of the ultimate truth', incorporates the individual acts into one serial, often simultaneous, presentation. It developed from the riding school in European cities of the late 18th century, often under the guidance of former cavalry officers. Fairs were declining, owing to newer forms of consumerism and tighter municipal licensing laws, and their entertainments could more easily be controlled within the rings of the equestrian shows. Unemployed rope dancers, acrobats and jugglers drifted to these arenas. Although

Jacob Bates had set up such a show, the 'Cirque équestre', in Paris in 1767, credit for the first true circus is usually bestowed on **Philip Astley** in London (1768), for he supplemented the horsemanship with clowns and trained animals and later added pantomimes. (The Royal Circus, founded in 1782 by **Charles Dibbin**, was the first theatre to use the term.) The circus of this period has been called 'one of the most abstract depictions of the ideals of the French Revolution' (Alexander Kluge), a picture which put man in an omnipotent position in regard to the world. The fairground, located in a natural setting, was less anthropocentric than the controlled space of the manège, which first resembled the theatres of its time with box, pit and gallery.

Once permanent buildings for the circus were created, its spontaneity diminished, but in recompense it provided an 'opera for the eyes' through its pantomime spectacles. The oval or race-track ring was characteristic, the round ring a later introduction by Americans. Astley's tradition of elegant riding was carried on in Paris by Antonio Franconi's 'exercices de grâce', in Vienna by de Bach, and in St Petersburg by Tourniaire. This so-called romantic period of the circus enjoyed considerable cross-fertilization with the ballet and pantomimic melodrama. But with an increasingly heterogeneous audience and larger buildings, elegant horsemanship gradually declined until the exclusively equestrian circus disappeared in 1897 with Berlin's Zirkus Renz. Meanwhile, new genres began to dominate, with an emphasis on sensation rather than grace; aerialism, wild-beast taming, and daredevil feats. Travelling circuses became a major concern only after the spread of railways, when it became easier to transport elaborate machinery, huge cages and a numerous troupe. With touring, which entailed an enormous staff of roustabouts and workers to set up and strike the tents, came the need for standardization, particularly so that the horses would not be upset by any deviation in environment. The standard European arena was invariably 13 metres in diameter, surrounded by a low barrier broken by two apertures on opposite sides, and strewn with sawdust or sand six to eight centimetres thick.

England Astley's Royal Amphitheatre (1798) burned in 1803 but was rebuilt the following year. Under the management of **Andrew Ducrow** (1830–41) and with a company of 150, it enjoyed a period of glory, especially hippodramas such as *The Battle of Waterloo* (1824), and survived as a building until 1893. These shows presented burlettas, pantomime, and *ballets d'action*, which used dramatic actors. Other managements include the Ginnetts, the Cookes, E. T. Smith, who starred **Adah Isaacs Menken**, and **George Sanger** who bought Astley's in 1871 to stage spectaculars. The circus empire of Charles Hengler, the son of a rope dancer, began in Liverpool when he converted the Argyll Street Theatre to an amphitheatre. At the turn of the century, competition from music-halls forced many circuses to convert to variety stages, although a reversal of this trend can be seen in the London Hippodrome, which was built to amalgamate the two genres. **C. B. Cochran** planned a circus building that could hold 6,000 spectators, but the war prevented its realization. Important modern managers

include Bertram Mills whose circus played at the London Olympia (1920–66) and on the road (1930–64); Billy Russell, Jimmy and Dick Chipperfield, Robert Brothers and Jerry Cottle. Circus at Christmas is as sure a tradition as the pantomime. Historically, the English influence in circus can be seen chiefly in the fields of equestrianism, gymnastics and clowning.

France The first true circus after Bates's was that of Astley's in the Rue des Vieilles-Tuileries (1772), later enlarged as the **Cirque Olympique** (1782), where a medley of equestrian acts (including a horse minuet), rope-dancing and pantomime was presented. Astley fled during the Revolution to be replaced by his erstwhile partner Antonio Franconi (1737–1836), a bird trainer turned horse trainer, who rented the circus in 1793 and produced elaborate pantomimes dominated by riding (such as 'The Death of Marlborough'). It was Franconi who first used the term 'cirque' in 1807 because of a Napoleonic ban on 'théâtre' to describe fairground entertainments. His sons Laurent (1776–1840) and Jean-Gérard-Henri (1778–1840), among the best equestrians of their time, opened the Cirque Olympique (1807–16), which featured stylish spectacles in Empire taste ('The Egyptian Pyramids', 'The Death of Bayard') and trained animals like Coco the stag and the elephant Baba. Their new building in the Boulevard du Temple was sold in 1835 to a banker, Louis Déjean, who called it the Cirque National and later opened the Cirque Napoléon (1852) and the Cirque de l'Impératrice, a summer circus in the Champs Elysées. These were veritable cultural centres that introduced the first English clowns and the aerialist **Léotard** to Paris; Déjean obtained a licence to stage plays there, provided the horses always took part. Victor Franconi carried on his family tradition with the Hippodrome (1846), a wooden oval some 108 metres long and 104 metres wide, which held an audience of 15,000; it excelled in military spectacles and Roman chariot races, arranged by Lucien Arnault. Victor Franconi also created the Cirque d'Hiver (1852) and the Cirque d'Eté. The Nouveau Cirque under Joseph Oller used tanbark (brown coconut matting) rather than sand, and featured naumachic (sea-battle) shows.

The Cirque Pinder, founded in 1854 in England by the brothers Pinder, was taken over by Spessardy in 1928 and carried on in partnership with the radio station ORTF until it was bought in 1972 by Jean Richard. Richard, a film actor, who founded his own circus in 1968, now runs a small empire, including the modern travelling Cirque Medrano, and is affiliated with the Grüss family of performers, who have expanded into management on their own. The Cirque Rancy et F. Lalanne, founded in 1856 by Théodore Rancy and F. Lalanne, was maintained until 1932, and revived 10 years later by Henry Rancy. The Cirque Bouglione, founded by Sampion Bouglione, played at the Cirque d'Hiver in winter and the Cirque de Montmartre in summer. The Cirque Amar, founded by the Algerian Ahmed Ben Amar as a menagerie, was active in the 1930s and was bought in 1973 by Bouglione.

Central and Eastern Europe Most German circuses followed the French pattern. The leading managements were and are Renz (1851–97), founded in Berlin by Ernst Jacob Renz (1815–92); Busch (1884–1960, after 1963 billed as the Roland Circus), founded by Paul

Busch; Sarrasani (1912–48, newly reopened 1956), founded by Hans Stosch (1874–1934); Krone (1905–49) (as a tent circus, then a winter building in Munich, a new building in 1962), founded by Carl Krone (1870–1943). The Circus Knie has become the unofficial Swiss national circus, and responsible for many innovations. The major Russian circus of Tsarist days was Salamonsky's, founded by the German Jew Albert Salamonsky (1839–1913); the building in Moscow which opened in 1880 is still in operation. Ciniselli's was its St Petersburg counterpart. In the Soviet bloc countries the circus has been nationalized and is heavily subsidized, organized, and promoted as a tool of popular enlightenment (Soviet State Circus, Zentral-Zirkus der DDR, etc.).

USA The first American circus performance may be that given by rope dancers in Philadelphia in 1724. A Mr Pool clowned in the first equestrian show in New York, Philadelphia and Boston in 1785. The first true circus was opened in Philadelphia on 9 April 1793 by John Bill Ricketts as a combination of riding academy and show; George Washington was among its patrons. Foreign troupes toured extensively, as did the pioneer companies of James West, Spalding & Rogers, and Van Amburgh, as travelling menageries began to be absorbed into circuses and 'mud shows' by 1824. New York's first circus building, which held 4,000 persons, opened in 1826. Native talent, such as the transvestite equestrian Ella Zoyara (Omar Kingsley) and the Shakespearian clown **Dan Rice** helped to naturalize the form, as did innovations like the circus parade and the **showboat**. The first railway circus to make a transcontinental tour was Dan Costello's in 1868; the last was the Cooper Brothers, which closed in 1936.

P. T. Barnum entered the circus business in 1871; two years later, W. C. Coup originated the two-ring arrangement in a Barnum show, and in 1881, James Bailey, who had combined with Barnum the previous year, instituted the three-ring circus, over his partner's protestations. The emphasis now fell on spectacle and intimacy was lost; this gigantism, as well as new methods of publicity and railway transport, were the major American innovations. When Barnum and Bailey's 'Greatest Show on Earth' went abroad in 1898, Europeans were most impressed by the quasi-military organization, the advance troops of press agents, and the whole notion of a gargantuan tenting show. As circuses began to run into competition from **Wild West exhibitions**, the five German-born Ringling brothers who managed the Forepaugh-Sells show cleaned up the act by banishing midway con-games in an attempt to bring respectability to the sawdust arena. Their sensational pantomimes, performed in Madison Square Garden in imitation of the **Kiralfys**, grew to hyperthyroid proportions; their *Cleopatra* required 1,500 performers and their 1919 show allowed 12,000 spectators to see seven manèges simultaneously in the confines of two-and-a-half acres. Such size naturally shifted the emphasis from clown patter, small-animal training and elegant equestrian pantomime, but made a strong impact on circus management throughout the world.

After a long period of competition, the Ringlings bought Barnum and Bailey's in 1907 and later, other rivals such as John Robinson, Hagenbeck-Wallace and Sells-Floto, to become the biggest concern in the world. These massive operations with their huge deployment of performers, labourers and animals continued until the depression. Ringling Brothers was reduced to only two tent circuses, with few baggage horses, parades or railway cars, and finally folded its tents in 1956, a year that also proved disastrous to Clyde Beatty and the King Brothers. Ringling now plays only indoors, with an infusion of show-business glitter, in an attempt to attract audiences weaned on television.

Historically, the appeal of the circus has derived in part from its variety, the romantic aura of its bohemianism, and the fact that it can be appreciated on many levels, from child-like wonder to the perception of a Laszlo Moholy-Nagy who envisaged acrobats as human machinery. It has had a powerful influence on the modern theatre, in reaction against the psychological drama of the late 19th century. The avant-garde was attracted to its physical skills and timing, clown routines, space-time continuum, the reduction of speech to merely one among many means of communication, and the arena itself. Although the circus is the setting for such plays as **Leonid Andreev**'s *He Who Gets Slapped*, Marcel Achard's *Voulez-vous jouer avec moâ*, Pavel Kohout's *August, August, August* and **Thomas Bernhard**'s *The Force of Habit*, a more important effect has been the use of the circus aesthetic in modern staging. **Oskar Schlemmer**'s *Triadic Ballet* (1912) was followed by his invention of the clown Mr Ey as an expression of physical mechanics (1933–7). As early as 1919, **Yury Annenkov** in Russia staged **Tolstoi**'s *First Distiller* as a circus-show, and **Gorky** provided a circus scenario in *The Hard-Worker Wordflow* (1920). The experiments of Eisenstein in his 'montage of attractions' and **Meyerhold** in biomechanics were grounded in circus gymnastics. **Jarry**, **Gordon Craig**, **Artaud**, the Futurists, and later **Peter Brook** with his ingenious *Midsummer Night's Dream* found inspiration in the circus ring.   LS

See: D. Amiard-Chevrel (ed.), *Du Cirque au Théâtre*, Lausanne, 1983; G. Bose and E. Brinkmann, *Circus: Geschichte und Aesthetik einer niederen Kunst*, Berlin, 1978; A. Hippisley-Coxe, *A Seat at the Circus*, London, 1951 (rev. ed., Hamden, Conn., 1980); M. J. Renevey, *Le Grand Livre du Cirque*, 2 vols., Paris, 1977; G. Speaight, *A History of the Circus*, London, 1980; H. Thétard, *La Merveilleuse Histoire du Cirque*, 2 vols., Paris, 1947 (rev. ed. 1 vol., Paris, 1978); R. Toole-Stott, *Circus and Allied Arts: A World Bibliography*, 4 vols., Derby, 1958–71.

Cirque Olympique/Théâtre du Châtelet

In 1782 **Philip Astley** established his equestrian amphitheatre in Paris. He left France at the Revolution, renting the establishment to Antonio Franconi and his two sons. Dramatic elements crept increasingly into the programmes. In 1798 and 1799 the Franconi troupe was engaged by the Théâtre de la Cité to provide equestrian scenes for pantomimes by J. A. G. Cuvelier. This led to the Franconis adding pantomime material to their own performances, especially after they opened a new circus at the Rue du Monthabor in 1807. They were not subject to the legislation restricting the number of theatres, as they counted as a circus. In fact they increasingly developed the old historical pantomime, now called a *mimodrame*, in

The Taking of Peking at the Théâtre Impérial du Cirque, 1862. The equestrian melodrama with combats was an important part of the repertoire of the Cirque.

which they celebrated all the major Napoleonic victories. In 1816 they moved to the more popular Temple suburb and, after a fire in 1826, to the Boulevard itself, the new theatre being built largely by popular subscription (with a handsome contribution from the royal family). The circus was a people's theatre, its dearest seats costing only 2 francs in 1835. It had a large and well-equipped stage which communicated with the arena. After the equestrian part of the programme, extra spectators came into the arena and an orchestra was pushed out from under the stage. In 1835 the name changed to the Théâtre National du Cirque. The repertoire had become increasingly the sumptuously mounted fairy extravaganza, with such popular successes as *Les Pilules du Diable* (*The Devil's Pills*) and *Rothomago*. In 1847 Adolphe Adam converted the circus into an Opéra National, but after the revolution of 1848, the repertoire reverted to the fairy extravaganza. In 1853 Napoleon III gave it the title of Théâtre Impérial du Cirque, and in 1862, with the demolition of the Boulevard du Temple, the whole establishment moved to a new theatre on the site of the old fortress of the Châtelet. This was the largest theatre of the time, with a stage 35 metres deep and excellently equipped for spectacular productions. Some lean years followed and the theatre closed in 1869, re-opening after the Commune of 1871, when a new management turned essentially to the dramas and melodramas of the Ambigu. In 1874 another attempt was made to create a popular opera theatre, but audiences were not interested. Finally the theatre found an appeal with the sensation drama, notably adaptations of Jules Verne, *Around the World in Eighty Days* and *Michel Strogoff*. JMCC

Citizen comedy The term is used to describe a group of Elizabethan and Jacobean plays whose setting is London and whose characters are predominantly the day-by-day tradesmen of the city. The satire of mercantile values and financial opportunism is, for the most part, good-humoured, but no quarter is given to social overreaching or the pursuit of commercial success by fraud. That is to say that citizen (or 'city') comedy is characteristically moral and determined to castigate whatever or whoever discredits the good name of London. Outstanding examples include **Dekker**'s *The Shoemaker's Holiday* (1599), *Eastward Ho* (1605), on which **Chapman**, **Jonson** and **Marston** collaborated and which outdoes the two joint-works of Dekker and **Webster**, *Westward Ho* (1604) and *Northward Ho* (1605), and **Middleton**'s *A Chaste Maid in Cheapside* (1611). The combination of a romantic plot and plain characters was sufficiently familiar by 1607 to provoke the lively mockery of **Beaumont**'s *The Knight of the Burning Pestle*, but citizen comedy was both durable and adaptable. It reflected the secure London base of many of the public stage's greatest dramatists. Jonson, too various and too original to be confined within a category, evoked the teeming life of the city in *Epicoene* (1609), *The Alchemist* (1610) and *Bartholomew Fair* (1614). The increasing tensions of London under the Stuarts, which contributed to the hardening tone and eventual decline of citizen comedy, are well represented by the distance between *Eastward Ho* and **Massinger**'s altogether darker version of the same plot in *The City Madam* (c. 1632). PT

Citizens' Theatre, Glasgow Founded in 1943 by **James Bridie**, who aimed at the establishment of a Scottish National Theatre, the Citizens' began operation at the small Athenaeum Theatre but in 1945 transferred to the Royal Princess's Theatre in the Gorbals where it has since remained. The policy continued to be the presentation of the best of British and European drama and the encouragement of new Scottish playwrights, until 1969 when Giles Havergal was appointed artistic director. Audience numbers had been dwindling and Havergal, together with (from 1970) his co-directors **Philip Prowse** and Robert David MacDonald, embarked on a radical new policy. Their aim was to find production styles that would make every performance, of whatever type of play, a fresh, eye-opening experience. Design (under Prowse) was accorded a high priority; naturalism was shunned; plays as far removed as *Hamlet*, *The Balcony* and MacDonald's *Chinchilla* (about Diaghilev) were invested with an assertively, sometimes outrageously theatrical style; within 10 years the Citizens' became one of the most distinctive of the country's theatre companies with an international reputation. AJ

Ciulei, Liviu (1923–) Rumanian director, scene designer, actor, and film-maker with a background in architecture. A seminal figure of the Rumanian stage, he worked at the Lucia Sturza Bulandra Theatre in Bucharest from 1948 until the late 1970s, when he took assignments as a guest director in Germany, Canada, Australia, and, finally, in the United States. Between 1981–5 he was the artistic director at the **Guthrie Theatre** in Minnesota. Ciulei's eclectic, idiosyncratic, and cerebral productions include *Leonce and Lena* (1970) and *Elisabeth I* (1974) at the Lucia Sturza Bulandra, and *The Tempest* (1981), *Peer Gynt* (1983), and *A Midsummer Night's Dream* (1985) at the Guthrie; and *Hamlet* (1986) at the Public Theatre in New York. BM

Claire, Ina (née Inez Fagan) (?1892–1985) American actress noted for her insouciant charm and high comedic sense and style, specializing from 1917, the year of her first appearance in a straight play, to 1954, her final appearance (in *The Confidential Clerk*), in what *Time Magazine* called 'highly varnished comedies of bad manners and good breeding in which the characters misbehave in venomous, perfectly timed epigrams'. Harold Clurman considered her 'the most brilliant comedienne of our stage' in vehicles such as **S. N. Behrman**'s *Biography* and *End of Summer*. She also had an active career in pre-First World War vaudeville, the *Ziegfeld Follies*, silent films, and later the talkies.   DBW

Clairon, Mlle (Claire-Josèphe-Hippolyte Léris de la Tude) (1723–1803) French actress,

considered the finest tragedienne of her age. After a brief engagement as a juvenile at the **Comédie-Italienne** and some years in provincial theatres she entered the **Comédie-Française** as an understudy and made a sensational debut as **Racine**'s Phèdre in 1743. This youthful success led to a whole series of major tragic roles for which her beautiful voice, graceful figure and range of feeling provided a natural endowment. Later she was persuaded by the critic Marmontel, whose mistress she had become, to moderate the solemn, declamatory style of the day in favour of a simpler, more conversationally direct form of diction and again at his instance and that of **Diderot** she tempered the worst excesses of fashion and ornament in her stage dress to make room for some sense of propriety and historical period, as did her contemporary **Lekain** for male costume. She was admired by **Garrick** and particularly by **Voltaire**, many of whose tragic heroines she created and in whose private theatre she gave performances during a visit to Ferney in 1765. In the following year she took a premature retirement, ostensibly on grounds of ill health but also perhaps because of friction with fellow members of the company, thereafter opening a school for young actors and appearing occasionally in private theatricals. Towards the end of her long life she published an interesting autobiographical work, *Mémoires d'Hippolyte Clairon et réflexions sur l'art dramatique* (1799) and died in virtual penury, her theatrical pension having lapsed under the Revolution.   DR

Clapp, Henry Austin (1841–1904) American

drama critic. Educated at Harvard, Clapp practised law in Boston, pursuing dramatic criticism as an avocation. He was music and drama critic of the *Boston Daily Advertiser* from 1868 until 1902, and of the *Boston Herald* from 1902 until 1904. An authority on **Shakespeare**, Clapp was viewed as an erudite, incorruptible, and fair critic. His *Reminiscences of a Dramatic Critic* (1902) provides an overview of late 19th-century Boston theatrical life.   TLM

Claque An organized band of applauders. Such bands

have been known since ancient Greek times, their members under the orders of someone in power or motivated by a common desire to further the interests of some writer, performer or cause. By the 18th century claques organized on a business footing had become established in European theatres, especially in France and Italy. The first three-quarters of the 19th century probably saw the claque at its peak.

Each claque had a leader, sometimes paid by the theatre but sometimes, as at the Paris Opéra, paying the theatre for acknowledging his office. He recruited

applauders by distributing free tickets, adding from time to time a free drink and, very rarely, a small amount of cash. The leader was paid by, or extorted payment from, the artists and authors who desired guaranteed public approbation. Some leaders had a list of charges for different lengths and intensities of applause. The kind of reaction required at any given moment was signalled by the leader to his claqueurs.

Leaders occupied a prominent position in theatrical circles and the most celebrated took their jobs very seriously, attending rehearsals and discussing both the appropriate moments for applause and the levels at which it should be given. Louis Castel's *Memoirs of a Claqueur* (1829) deals with 'the theory and practice of the art'. Even different ways of using the hands were a matter of concern, e.g. striking both open palms together, bringing the fingers of one hand against the palm of the other, snapping the fingers, etc.

Claques of unpaid enthusiasts continued to assemble from time to time, but it was the paid claque that persisted with regularity; however, even the paid claque began to disappear after the 19th century, leaving the playhouse before it left the opera house. Whether or not paid claques still operate on at least some occasions in some European theatres is unclear. Those on the outside have no direct evidence. Those on the inside are not forthcoming on the matter. By far the best, and most amusing, account of the modern claque is to be found in *Looking for a Bluebird* (1945) by Joseph Wechsberg.   GH

Clark, Bobby (1888–1960) and Paul McCull-

ough (1883–1936) American comedians. A comedy team that perfected its raucous, physical style in the circus and vaudeville, Clark and McCullough made the transition to musical theatre in a London revue, *Chuckles of 1922*. Their first Broadway show was *The Music Box Revue 1922–23*, and after other revue appearances they brought their acrobatic antics to a book musical, *Strike Up the Band* (1930). Following McCullough's suicide in 1936, Bobby Clark continued alone, appearing in revues such as *The Ziegfeld Follies of 1936*, musical comedies such as *Mexican Hayride* (1944), revivals of classical comedies such as *Love for Love* (1940), and revivals of operettas, such as *Sweethearts* (1947). His last engagement was in the touring company of *Damn Yankees* (1956). The crouching, scampering Clark, with his painted-on eyeglasses, ever-present cigar, and stubby cane, was perfectly matched with the tall, giggling McCullough, the straight man of the act.   MK

Clark, John Pepper (1936–) Nigerian play-

wright, poet, critic, academic. J. P. Clark (now Clark-Bekederemo) was born in Kiagbodo in Ijo country in the Niger Delta. In 1958, as an undergraduate at Ibadan University, he edited the poetry magazine *The Horn* which created both context and outlet for a new literary discourse in Nigeria by the young Nigerian 'euromodernists' (as they were later called). After a spell of journalism, Clark-Bekederemo held Research Fellowships at Princeton and Ibadan. Three early plays in English were widely acclaimed: *Song of a Goat*, a tragedy of two brothers, one of whom becomes impotent. His brother sleeps with his wife, resulting in both men committing suicide. *Masquerade*, which forms a diptych with it, is the tragedy of the child of that wife's coupling with the husband's younger brother. *The Raft*, the third play, is an existentialist play about four men adrift on the Niger on a lumber raft, and has been widely produced. (All published 1964.)

Clark-Bekederemo continued to publish poems in the 1960s. His reputation for fierce social criticism was confirmed by his account of his visit to America in *America, Their America* (1964). His years as an academic were marked by his creative and scholarly work on the monumental Ijo saga of *Ozidi*, a substantial piece of sustained research into the traditional antecedents for Nigerian theatre. This resulted in his own English-language play, *Ozidi* (1966), and a transcribed version of the full saga (1977).

In 1980, Clark-Bekederemo resigned his Chair of English at Lagos University; and in 1982 he founded with Ebun Odutola Clark the Pec Repertory Theatre in Lagos. It is a commercial venture committed to a professional presentation of outstanding African plays in English to a subscription audience, and through this initiative to the creation of a theatre industry in Nigeria. *The Bikoroa Plays* (a trilogy concerning one Ijo family in three ages) and a comedy, *The Wives Revolt* (1985), maintain and develop Clark's own creative writing. ME

Clarke, Austin (Augustine Joseph) (1896–1974)

Irish playwright, educated at University College Dublin. A major poet, realizing his full strengths in later life, Clarke was much under the shadow of **Yeats**, whose ideals for verse drama fascinated him. In 1940 Clarke founded the Dublin Verse-Speaking Society, giving readings on Radio Eireann and three drama seasons (1941–3) at the Peacock. His Lyric Theatre Company presented bi-annual evenings (1944–51) at the **Abbey**, putting on nine of Clarke's plays, reviving **Fitzmaurice**, and giving the first performances of Yeats's *The Death of Cuchulain* and *The Herne's Egg*.

Clarke's plays, set mostly in the 6th–12th centuries, turn, sometimes comically, on the nature of faith, on medieval and modern Catholicism, to the latter's disadvantage: *The Flame* (1930), *Black Fast* (1941), *The Moment Next to Nothing* (1953). They constitute another brave but unavailing attempt to bring verse to the 20th-century stage. DM

Clarke, John Sleeper (1833–99)

American actor and theatre manager. He made his professional stage debut in 1851 at Boston's Howard Athenaeum as Frank Hardy in *Paul Pry*. A friend of **Edwin Booth** since childhood, Clarke married Booth's sister Asia in 1859. Clarke was a popular, skilful comedian, highly regarded for his portrayal of eccentric characters like Major Wellington De Boots in Coyne's *A Widow Hunt*, Dr Pangloss and Zekiel Homespun in **Colman**'s *The Heir-at-Law*, and Bob Acres in *The Rivals*. In the 1860s Clarke was associated with Booth in the management of several theatres, including Philadelphia's **Walnut Street Theatre**, the Boston Theatre and the **Winter Garden**. In 1867, Clarke emigrated to England where he remained for the rest of his life, except for occasional starring tours to America. At various times he successfully managed several theatres including the **Haymarket**, the Charing Cross (Toole's) and for over a decade the Strand (1883–99). His sons Creston Clarke

(1865–1910) and Wilfred Booth Clarke (1867–1945) also had relatively successful careers in theatre. DJW

Claudel, Paul (1868–1955)

French poet, diplomat and playwright. A more unlikely figure for the major modern French playwright is hard to imagine. Claudel was authoritarian, pious, secretive, and wanted to be a priest not a writer. When he was turned down by the church he joined the diplomatic service, spending time in the Far East and experiencing an unhappy love affair that was to form the basis of *Partage de Midi* (*Break of Noon*, written 1905). His experience of Eastern Theatre and his interest in Ancient Greek Theatre (he made a fine translation of the *Oresteia*) helped him to develop a dramatic style of great theatrical resourcefulness and flexibility. At first influenced by symbolism, his plays were written, broadly, in three creative bursts. The first between about 1895 and 1905 include *Tête d'Or* (*Golden Head*, 1889), *La Ville* (*The Town*, 1890), *L'Echange* (*The Exchange*, 1893), *Partage de Midi* (1905) and *La Jeune Fille Violaine* (*The Young Girl Violaine*, 1892), later to become *L'Annonce Faite à Marie* (*The Tidings brought to Mary*). This was the first of his plays to be staged (directed by **Lugné-Poe** 1912); the second is a trilogy *L'Otage* (*The Hostage*, 1909), *Le Pain Dur* (*Hard Bread*, 1914) and *Le Père Humilié* (*The Humiliated Father*, 1916), and the third is *Le Soulier de Satin* (*The Satin Slipper*, 1924). They all rely for their power partly on Claudel's peculiar verse style. This is quite unlike anything before it in the French tradition, being based on the breath group, not on the number of feet in a line. Written for declamation, his verse nevertheless has a variety and subtlety that can fairly be compared with Shakespearian blank verse. Claudel admired the Spanish Golden Age and many of his plays deal with the discovery of the New World, but material confines can only restrict his ambitious characters who constantly yearn for other, wider worlds of the spirit. By picking subjects and characters of the Renaissance period, Claudel managed the improbable task of welding together elements of medieval mysticism, Renaissance optimism and modernist anguish. His most ambitious, and perhaps his theatrically most successful play *Le Soulier de Satin* includes a presenter figure whose linking commentary enables Claudel to achieve a striking alienation effect and also ties together the disparate elements of the play. These range from high tragedy to low farce, from soul-searching monologue to animated dialogue and include song, dance and mime. The play was thought unproducible because written at inordinate length and divided into four 'days'. But in 1942 the young **Barrault** persuaded Claudel to cut and rewrite his text for stage presentation and this production (**Comédie-Française** 1943) was a triumph. Claudel's work became one of the mainstays of Barrault's career as a director. Works written at the beginning of the century gradually took on a new life as their theatrical power was released in Barrault's productions. These included *Partage de Midi* (1948), *L'Echange* (1951), *Christophe Colomb* (1953), *Tête d'Or* (1968). The new generation of directors have made their own reinterpretations e.g. Jorge Lavelli *L'Echange* (1967), **Vitez** *Partage de Midi* (1975) and Gildas Bourdet *Le Pain Dur* (1984). Claudel is now widely recognized as the most important French dramatist of the last 100 years. DB

Claus, Hugo (1929–) Distinguished Flemish playwright, novelist, translator, and director of the postwar generation. His plays, written in Dutch, focus on themes such as loneliness, the purity of childhood in a corrupt world, love between brother and sister, and the Oedipus complex. The actions frequently bear a ritual nature. As a result, his plays rise above the Flemish surroundings in which they are set.

Particularly, his plays *Bruid in de Morgen* (*Bride in the Morning*, 1953), *Suiker* (*Sugar*, 1958), depicting the tough life of seasonal labourers in France, and *Vrijdag* (*Friday*, 1969) have established Claus's reputation as a playwright. He directed the film-version of *Vrijdag* himself. The story of the home-coming of a prisoner, who has been released from gaol and hears his wife confess that she has given birth to a child, after an affair with the neighbour, is presented in a sober way, almost as a factual account.

Claus has adapted several classical plays, e.g. **Seneca**'s *Thyestes* (1966), *Oedipus* (1971) and *Phaedra* (1980), **Jonson**'s *Volpone: De Vossenjacht* (*The Fox Hunting*, 1972), **De Rojas**'s *La Celestina: De Spaanse Hoer* (*The Spanish Whore*, 1970). Many of Clau's plays have been translated and are performed all over the world. MG HS

Claxton, Kate (1850–1924) American actress, sometimes called 'the **Sarah Bernhardt** of America'. Born in Somerville, New Jersey, she first appeared with **Lotta Crabtree** in 1870, then joined the stock companies of **Augustin Daly** and **A. M. Palmer**. Her most successful roles were in *The Two Orphans*, *Camille*, and *East Lynne*. After touring *The Two Orphans*, she retired in 1911. She was the heroine of a Brooklyn Theatre fire in 1876. SMA

Clements, John (Selby) (1910–) British actor, director and manager, began his acting career in 1930 and later founded the Intimate Theatre, Palmers Green, one of several small theatres around London which had a proud record in fostering talent during the 1930s. Handsome, with an aristocratic appearance and a rich expressive voice, Clements soon became successful in the West End, starring in **J. B. Priestley**'s *They Came to a City* (1943), and his second marriage, to the already well-known actress Kay Hammond (Dorothy Katherine Standing), began a theatrical partnership which lasted until Kay Hammond's death in 1980. In 1949, they appeared in a long-running production of **Farquhar**'s *The Beaux' Stratagem* at the Phoenix Theatre, which he also managed. He was in management briefly at **St James's Theatre**, the Saville Theatre (from 1955 to 1957) where the seasons excelled in classical comedy and, from 1965 to 1973, at **Chichester Festival Theatre**. Although his tastes were conservative, they were in tune with those of his Sussex audiences, who delighted in the elegant productions of Edwardian comedies (**Shaw**, **Pinero**, **Wilde**), the Shakespearian productions in which he starred (as Prospero in *The Tempest* and Antony in *Antony and Cleopatra*) and the sober modern dramas. He was knighted in 1968. JE

Cleveland Play House East 83–86 Sts between Euclid and Carnegie Aves, Cleveland [Architects: Philip Small, Charles Rowley and Francis Draz]. In 1915, Raymond O'Neil, a Cleveland journalist, founded a small amateur theatre group for the production of native plays. Out of it grew the Cleveland Play House, now the oldest producing regional theatre in America. In 1921, Frederic McConnell took over the amateur company and transformed it into a professional organization. Six years later, the company moved into its complex of two theatres, the 500-seat Drury and the 160-seat Brooks, plus offices and workrooms. When McConnell retired in 1958, he was succeeded by K. Elmo Lowe and more recently, by Richard Oberlin. In 1983, the 625-seat Bolton, designed by Philip Johnson, was added to the complex. The theatre maintains its policy of presenting classics, contemporary and new plays and musicals. MCH

Clive, Kitty (1711–85) English actress. Her debut in 1728 quickly led to success, particularly as a wry actress and singer in comedy, burlesque and ballad-opera. She was briefly married in 1732 to a lawyer. She performed at **Drury Lane** until 1769, apart from a brief spell at **Covent Garden** in the 1740s, enjoying a high reputation in spite of her long-running battles with **Garrick** over her choice of parts. Her performance as Portia in *The Merchant of Venice* was often attacked for its high comedy and its mimicry of contemporary lawyers but it was a popular success. Her long friendship with Horace Walpole led to her moving into a cottage near his home at Strawberry Hill in 1754; it became known as Cliveden (=Clive's Den). She retired there in 1769. PH

Close, Glenn (1947–) American actress who in only a decade established herself as one of the most respected actresses of her generation. Though best known for films such as *The Big Chill*, *The World According to Garp*, and *The Natural*, she is a versatile stage performer as well, noted for her 'charged stillness'. Her Broadway debut, Angelica in a revival of **Congreve**'s *Love for Love* (1974), was followed by a series of major roles in regional theatres, Off-Broadway appearances (including **Wendy Wasserstein**'s *Uncommon Women and Others* and an Obie Award-winning performance in Simone Benmussa's *The Singular Life of Albert Nobbs* at the **Manhattan Theatre Club**), and various Broadway appearances, including *The Crucifer of Blood* (1978), the musical *Barnum* (1980), and Annie in the American premiere of **Stoppard**'s *The Real Thing* (1984), for which she won the Tony. DBW

Closure of the theatres In England in 1642, a parliamentary ordinance signalling the imminent triumph of Puritan forces commanded the closure of all theatres. Although occasional surreptitious performances continued during the Interregnum and although Cromwell licensed certain private entertainments and approved school plays, the ordinance was surprisingly effective. It brought a great age of English drama to an end. PT

Clown The distinction between a clown and a comedian, said 'The Perfect Fool' **Ed Wynn**, is that the former does funny things, the latter does things funny. According to the social psychologist William McDougall, there are six primary components to clowning: the fall (slipping and sliding); the blow (slaps, custard pies); surprise (incongruity between what is expected and what happens); harmless and childish naughtiness; mimicry, usually with an element of parody; and stupidity which can turn out to be cleverness. This last trait may be the most basic, a false contrast: the clown's assumed clumsiness is revealed to be true virtuosity, his naïveté to be wisdom, his hilarity to be sorrow disguised. The mythic dimension of the clown may derive from this tension.

Some scholars have seen the clown's archetype in the arch-trickster of American Indian cults, who possessed fertility and healing powers. Others have identified it with a wonder-working but diabolic opponent to the divine Establishment, like Lucifer. There are no clowns in the Hindu epic the *Mahabharata*, but its stage version features Vidusaka, a bald dwarf with fangs and drooping limbs who speaks Prakrit, the language of women and low castes; he is teamed with Vita, a parasitic slyboots. This yoking of the dimwitted fallguy and the scheming conniver is constant in clowning: in China the contrast is between Wu Ch'ou and Wen Ch'ou, in Renaissance Italy between the two **zanni** Arlecchino and Brighella.

Clownish types appear in the ithyphallic satyr choruses of classical Greek drama, and in the phlyakes comedies of southern Italy in the 3rd century BC, and become discriminated in the Atellan farces into the pop-eyed boaster Bucco, the awkward Maccus and the hunchbacked Dossenus, and the Stupidus of the *ludi scenici*. In Roman comedy, the comic figure is usually the slave, for the clown is commonly in an underdog position, working within and hence against his social context.

This anti-social aspect was confirmed by medieval distrust of the itinerant entertainer. A Saxon law governing municipal outskirts declared that 'players and minstrels are not people like other men, for they have only the appearance of mankind and are almost akin to the dead'. The clown became the symbol of a lack, an absent quality, which enabled them to perform as 'constructive anarchists', and through their garish makeup and outlandish costume to assert that they are of another world. Typically, the clown of the miracle and mystery plays was a devil, and in the Moralities, the eloquently-named Vice, obtuse and buffeted, with his sword of lath. The first named German clown is Rubin, zany to the mountebank of the medieval Passion play; this function as stooge to a quack descends through the merry andrew and **Tabarin** to **Harpo Marx** and Lou Costello.

In the German **Fastnachtspiel** the low comic is usually a peasant. Indeed, the English word 'clown' first meant a country clotpoll, and this booby begins to be polished by the professionals of **Shakespeare**'s day, **Thomas Heywood**, **Richard Tarlton**, and **Will Kempe**. The Shakespearian comic is multiform: in *As You Like It* he runs the gamut from the thick ploughboy William to the professional jester Touchstone to the moody philosopher Jaques. (The jester or fool, native to courts, was distinctly not a clown in the modern sense; his comedy was more consciously verbal and ambiguous, and he has been seen by modern critics as the ancestor of the dandy and the art of high camp.) The Elizabethan clown was conveyed to Europe by the English Comedians (see **Englische Komödian-**

ten). Robert Reynolds introduced Pickelhering c. 1618; his bizarre costume, grotesque mask and movements were comic exaggerations of reality. Naturalized in Germany, he not only amused the audience and acted as a bridge between it and a play's action, but enlarged the scope of the pompous tragedies in which he appeared. Other clowns spawned by the English Comedians include John Posset (Jean Bouschet) invented by Sackville of the Brown troupe, who spoke a macaronic medley of broken German, witty English and Dutch; and Hans Stockfisch created by Spencer at Dresden (1617).

The Italian **commedia dell'arte** was immensely influential in disseminating its types, the *zanni*, the Dottore, Pantalone, the Spanish Captain, throughout Europe; but over time these types became submerged into complex dramatic characters with broader dimensions. **Molière**, for example, transforms Mascarille, Sganarelle and Scapin from masked clichés to recognizable human beings with individuated psychologies. Only Arlecchino as Arlequin and **Harlequin** managed to retain a being independent of the plot requirements; but even his diabolical vestiges began to be domesticated in the 18th century, in the *fêtes galantes* of **Marivaux** and Watteau and the more sophisticated figures of Figaro and Papageno. He was also gradually edged out by the melancholy **Pierrot**, created c. 1682 by G. B. Giaratoni as a foil to the turbulent Arlecchino. This pale-faced etiolation of Pedrolino evolved into the elegant white clown of the European circus.

As romantic and, later, realistic drama insisted on integrating the clown into a recognizable social entity (**Goethe**'s Mephistopheles may be seen as one surviving avatar of the Vice figure), he found a refuge in pantomime and then circus. **Joseph Grimaldi** established the type of the Joey, greedy, amoral, gloating over his triumphs and cringing at his defeats; henceforth the clown of the harlequinade would wear tufts and frills, brandish a red-hot poker, and butter slides for policemen. Successors to Grimaldi, like Tom Matthews and 'Whimsical Walker', embellished but did not substantially alter this outline, until music-hall comedians like **Dan Leno** assumed their function in the spectacular pantos of the 1880s and 1890s; then the clown was relegated to the vestigial harlequinade, and the comedian, in dame or villain role, reigned supreme.

The circus clown has also gone through several stages. In England he resembled the Grimaldi-type, trading cross-talk with the ringmaster. On the continent, under **Auriol**'s influence, he dressed as a jester and specialized in acrobatics; this culminated in the 1870s in the knockabout pantos of the **Hanlon-Lees** and the Byrne Brothers. The Shakespearian clown, exemplified in England by William Wallett and in America by **Dan Rice**, was possible only in a one-ring circus, exchanging puns and patter with the audience, and mangling hackneyed quotations from the Bard. Around 1869, according to tradition, Tom Belling (1834–1900) created the 'Dumme August' at the Zirkus Renz in Berlin, by making an impromptu appearance in a ringmaster's outfit and fright-wig; this radical innovation expanded the usual clown–ringmaster duet to a trio. (The invention was also claimed by Chadwick (d. 1889).) The term *august*, signifying a stupid grotesque clown, first occurs at the Cirque Franconi in 1877; it never caught on in English (the American Bozo is analogous).

Clown teams dominated the latter half of the 19th century: the exchange of slaps between **Foottit** and **Chocolat**, or the Price Brothers' 'Evening at Maxim's', with its demolition of a private room at a restaurant, injected social satire into the ring. Dan Rice had dabbled in political commentary; this factor became dominant in pre-Revolutionary Russia with the **Durov** brothers and has been carried on, in a carefully monitored form, under the Soviets (**Vitaly Lazarenko**, **Arkadi Raikin**). Harsh economic conditions, such as the American slump of the 1890s, spawned tramp clowns, like vaudeville's Nat Wills and the trick cyclist Joe Jackson; but they did not invade the circus until the Great Depression, when Otto Griebling with his rickety barrel organ and Emmett Kelly with his pathetic broom made their debut.

Although there was a recrudescence of genius in music-hall clowning with **Grock**, the **Fratellini** and **Charlie Rivel**, many of the clown's prerogatives were usurped by the silent film comics; circuses became overrun with Chaplin imitators. Contemporary clowns perform very much in the shadow of their illustrious forebears. Barring such exceptions as **Jango Edwards** who added a drug-culture anarchy to the tradition, and Coluche (Michel Colucci) who enlarged the clown's sphere of action by running for the French presidency in 1981, the clown today has become a hackneyed subject for Sunday painters, a huckster for hamburgers and cereal (not unlike the merry andrew who pitched for mountebanks), a filler between circus acts rather than a number in himself. In the USA, however, the so-called 'new vaudeville' has provided performance artists like Bill Irwin and Avner the Eccentric a chance to revive the clown as an eloquent mediator between age-old techniques and post-modern aesthetics.

The modern theatre has drawn deeply on the clown tradition, transmuting him into characters like **Brecht**'s Arturo Ui, Schweyk and Puntila, or absorbing his techniques, as **Dario Fo** has done. Germany, in particular, has been fascinated by the clown as a political symbol, and he is used by such playwrights as **Wedekind**, **Handke**, **Peter Weiss** and **Heiner Müller**; but the clown also informed the plays of **Mayakovsky**, **Beckett** and **Ionesco**, and the productions of the Brazilian **Augusto Boal**. LS

See: C. von Barloewen, *Clown*, Frankfurt, 1984; J. Fabbri and A. Sallée (eds.), *Clowns & Farceurs*, Paris, 1982; T. Rémy, *Les Clowns*, Paris, 1945; J. Schechter, *Durov's Pig: Clowns, Politics and Theatre*, New York, 1985; G. Speaight, *The Book of Clowns*, London, 1980; J. H. Towson, *Clowns*, New York, 1976.

Clun, Walter (d. 1664) English actor who began as a boy in women's parts and became a leading member of **Killigrew**'s company after the Restoration of Charles II. Much admired by **Pepys**, Clun played the lead in the opening production of the new playhouse in **Drury Lane** in 1663. The following year he was attacked and robbed in Kentish Town, where he bled to death in a ditch. PT

Clunes, Alec (Alexander S. de Moro) (1912–

70) British actor, director and theatre manager, who ran London's **Arts Theatre** for eight influential seasons from 1942 to 1950. Clunes was born into a theatre family and became a professional actor when he joined **Ben Greet**'s company in 1934. He was never a major star but he played a variety of roles at the **Old Vic** and at the Malvern Festival; and in the 1950s joined the Shakespeare Memorial Theatre at Stratford where he was Claudius to **Paul Scofield**'s Hamlet in 1955. His last acting appearance came in **Hochhuth**'s *Soldiers* in 1968. His main achievement, however, began during the war years when he ran an ambitious and intellectually demanding repertory at the tiny Arts Theatre in the heart of London's West End. In addition to pioneering the work of such writers as **Christopher Fry**, and creating the part of Thomas in *The Lady's Not For Burning* (1948), he unearthed forgotten English classics and searched for plays from abroad. JE

Clurman, Harold (1901–80) American director, critic, author, and teacher. Clurman left his mark on the American theatre as founder of the **Group Theatre** (1931–40). In 25 midnight sessions with New York actors and directors he 'talked the Group into existence', became its inspirational leader, and one of its principal directors. He nurtured the talents of **Clifford Odets** and directed five of his plays: *Awake and Sing* (1935), *Paradise Lost* (1935), *Golden Boy* (1937), *Rocket to the Moon* (1938), and *Night Music* (1940), also directed Irwin Shaw's *The Gentle People* (1939), and wrote *The Fervent Years* (1945), a history of the Group.

After the Group's demise Clurman continued directing: *The Member of the Wedding* (1950), *The Autumn Garden* (1951), *Bus Stop* (1955), *The Waltz of the Toreadors* (1957), *Incident at Vichy* (1965), and (in Tokyo), *Long Day's Journey into Night* (1965), and *The Iceman Cometh* (1968).

He was theatre critic for *The New Republic* (1949–52), *The Nation* (1953–80), and the London *Observer* (1955–63); assembled three volumes of essays: *Lies Like Truths* (1958), *The Naked Image* (1966), *The Divine Pastime* (1974); wrote *On Directing* (1968), *Ibsen* (1977), and *All People are Famous, instead of an autobiography* (1974); and was a professor at Hunter College (1964–80).

Born in New York, he was 'reborn in Paris in the 20s' (his words), and became a playreader for the **Theatre Guild** (1929–31). Among his awards, the Donaldson, the George Jean Nathan, four honorary doctorates, he was proudest of La Croix de Chevalier de la Légion d'Honneur. RM

Cobb, Lee J. (1911–76) American stage, film, and television actor, best remembered for creating the bewildered, dream-chasing Willy Loman in **Arthur Miller**'s *Death of a Salesman*. Born on New York City's Lower East Side, he decided at age 16 to become an actor, ran away from home at 17, and began playing small roles for the **Pasadena Playhouse**. In 1934 he joined the **Group Theatre**. After serving in the Second World War, he returned to Hollywood but went back to Broadway for *Salesman*. In 1969 he starred in a Broadway production of *King Lear*. SMA

Coburn, Charles Douville (1877–1961) American actor and manager, remembered for his films, who with his wife Ivah Wills founded in 1906 the Coburn

Shakespearean Players, touring major Shakespearian plays and other classics. Additional stage appearances included *The Better 'Ole* (1918), *The Yellow Jacket* (1921), *So This is London* (1922), *The Farmer's Wife* (1924), *Trelawny of the Wells* (1925 all-star revival), *Diplomacy* (1928), and *Three Wise Fools* (1936). The Coburns helped to found in 1934 the Mohawk Drama Festival at Union College, Schenectady, New York, performing there in the summers. He retired from the stage in 1937 on his wife's death, returning to play Falstaff in *The Merry Wives of Windsor* for the **Theatre Guild** in 1946, his final appearance on the Broadway stage. DBW

Cochran, Charles Blake (1872–1951) The leading English showman of his time whose enterprises ranged from roller-skating competitions to ballet. He began in the USA as an actor and then secretary to **Richard Mansfield**; his first production was **Ibsen**'s *John Gabriel Borkman* (New York, 1897). He returned to London in 1902. His taste was eclectic and not invariably tied to profit, capable of booking **Reinhardt**'s *The Miracle* into the London Olympia in 1911, and then housing Hagenbeck's circus there. From 1914 he was distinguished as a producer of smart revues: *Odds and Ends* (1914), *Pell Mell* (1916), *As You Were* (1918), *London, Paris and New York* (1920), etc. More highbrow efforts, including the first London showing of an **O'Neill** play (*Anna Christie*, 1925), led to bankruptcy, but he recouped his fortunes by collaborating with **Noël Coward** and producing *On with the Show* (1925), *This Year of Grace* (1928), *Bitter Sweet* (1929), *Private Lives* (1930), *Cavalcade* (1931), *Words and Music* (1932), *Conversation Piece* (1934). After the war, he seemed incapable of tapping into the new public taste. He published volumes of memoirs in 1925, 1932, 1941 and 1945, the best being the first, *The Secrets of a Showman*. In 1973 a musical comedy based on his career, *Cockie*, by Peter Saunders, opened at the Vaudeville Theatre, London. LS

Cockaigne Land of idleness and luxury known in Europe under various names (*cocagne, cuccagna, Schlarafenland,* lubberland, the *Land of Prester John*) since the 14th century. This popular utopia, in which houses are thatched with pancakes, people are paid for sleeping, and pigs run around with forks stuck in them looking for diners, is an important theme of European folk drama and carnival. AEG

Cockpit Theatre, London Built in Drury Lane in 1609 to house the popular 'game' of cockfighting, this small (c. 50ft square) tiered house was permanently converted for the performance of plays by **Christopher Beeston** in 1616. He renamed it the Phoenix, intending it as the indoor theatre of Queen Anne's Men during their popular tenure of the outdoor **Red Bull**. Beeston retained the management until his death in 1639, employing and dispensing with several companies, the last of which, nicknamed Beeston's Boys, was inherited by his son William. When the younger Beeston's choice of plays offended the Court, **Davenant** replaced him as manager. The Cockpit's irregular use for surreptitious performance during the Interregnum led to a raid by Commonwealth soldiers in 1649. More important to the future of English theatre (and

opera) was the licensed staging by Davenant of two musical spectacles, *The Cruelty of the Spaniards in Peru* (1658) and *Sir Francis Drake* (1659). After the Restoration, the Cockpit was quickly returned to regular use until the establishment of the Patent companies disenfranchized it. There is no record of performances there after 1665. PT

Cockpit-in-Court (London) Built in the Palace of Whitehall for the entertainment of Henry VIII and his Court, the royal cockpit was, from time to time, adapted to accommodate plays. Few records survive, though it can be reasonably surmised that the King's Men staged *The Merry Devil of Edmonton* there in 1618, shortly after **Christopher Beeston** had successfully converted the public **Cockpit** in Drury Lane. Beeston's attractive little theatre may have encouraged Charles I to undertake a similar permanent conversion in his own artistic Court. As Surveyor-General of the King's Works, **Inigo Jones** undertook the work, which was completed in 1629–30. His drawings of a ground-plan and an elevation, extant in Worcester College, Oxford, have recently been identified. They give us clearer information about this intimate theatre than we have about any other pre-Restoration theatre. An octagonal auditorium with tiers of seats and an upper gallery was set within a 58 ft-square frame. The semi-circular stage had five entrance-doors and was 36 ft wide at the front. Only from the royal box was there a central view across the stage to the large central arch of the *scaenae frons*. Even the placement of the candelabra (ten small and two large on stage) is known. What is not known is the repertoire nor the frequency of performances. Charles I would have wished to give pride of place to the King's Men in a theatre readily comparable to their own **Blackfriars**, but it is unlikely that they were the only users. Unused during the Interregnum, the Cockpit-in-Court was never again more than sporadically a playhouse. PT

Cocteau, Jean (1889–1963) French poet, novelist, essayist, cineast and playwright. Cocteau was at his best when indulging his highly developed sense of playfulness, well exemplified in the visual puns and gentle satire of *Parade* (1917), *Le Boeuf sur le Toit* (*The Ox on the Roof*, 1920) and *Les Mariés de la Tour Eiffel* (*The Eiffel Tower Wedding Party*, 1921). These were ballets or mime dramas written in collaboration with such luminaries as **Picasso**, Satie, Milhaud and were successful, especially with fashionable high society. Plays based on Ancient Greek models (*Antigone*) (directed by **Dullin** 1922), *Orphée* (*Orpheus*) (directed by **Pitoëff** 1926), *La Machine Infernale* (*The Infernal Machine*) (directed by **Jouvet** 1934) were very uneven, ostensibly seeking to develop a modern form of tragedy but in reality coming perilously close to parody. *Les Parents Terribles* (*Intimate Relations*, 1938) was a more vigorous, realistic tragedy of modern family life. It had the distinction of being banned under the Occupation as prejudicial to morality and public order. His later plays were weak, wordy and unoriginal: *Chevaliers de la Table Ronde* (*Knights of the Round Table*, 1937) an Arthurian fantasy; *Les Monstres Sacrés* (*The Sacred Monsters*, 1940) a technical melodrama, *La Machine à Ecrire* (*The Typewriter*, 1941) a thriller; *Renaud et Armide* (1943) a neoclassical fairy tale; *L'Aigle* *à Deux Têtes* (*The Eagle with Two Heads*, 1946) a neo-romantic love story and *Bacchus* (1951) a sub-Sartrean philosophical drama. His real genius was for the cinema, where his gift for organizing brilliant visual images was able to develop its full potential. His first full-length feature was *La Belle et la Bête* (*Beauty and the Beast*, 1945), followed by *Orphée* (1950) and *Le Testament d'Orphée* (1960).   DB

Codron, Michael (Victor) (1930–) British producer, whose adventurous promotion of new playwrights during the 1960s transformed the West End. His first London venture came in 1957, when he brought a college revue, *Share My Lettuce*, from Cambridge to London, re-casting it to include the then unknown actors, **Maggie Smith** and Kenneth Williams. In 1958, he staged the first plays of John Mortimer (*The Dock Brief* and *Shall We Tell Caroline?*) and **Harold Pinter**'s *The Birthday Party*, which ran for less than a week at the **Lyric Theatre, Hammersmith**. Codron retained his faith in Pinter and in 1960, produced *The Caretaker* at the **Arts Theatre** Club, which transferred to the West End and was recognized as one of the finest plays of its time. Other dramatists whose careers began with Codron productions include **Henry Livings**, Charles Dyer, **Alan Ayckbourn**, **James Saunders**, **Charles Wood**, **Frank Marcus**, **Joe Orton**, **David Halliwell** and **Simon Gray**, and he also enabled writers like **David Mercer** and **Christopher Hampton** to see their plays transferred from smaller subsidized theatres to the West End. Codron rarely produced musicals and for much of his career, he had no particular theatre with which he was associated. By the end of the 1960s, the West End contained a range of drama which could barely have been conceived when the decade began and Codron had led the way among the younger impresarios. He sat on advisory and governing boards in the subsidized sector, forming long-standing associations with **Hampstead Theatre**, the English Stage Company and other managements. In the 1980s, he became co-owner of the Vaudeville Theatre in London, where he produced **Michael Frayn**'s award-winning play, *Benefactors* (1984).   JE

Cody, William Frederick ('Buffalo Bill') see **Wild West exhibition**

Coe, Richard Livingston (1916–) American drama critic. Born in New York and educated at George Washington University, Coe served as assistant drama and film critic for the *Washington Post* from 1938–42. After military service in the Middle East, he returned to the *Post* in 1946 as its principal critic, a position he held until his semi-retirement in 1979. Coe has been regarded as one of the most perceptive, impartial, and supportive critics of the American stage. Joan Fontaine described him (1980) as 'the great rarity, a critic who loves actors and loves directors and loves playwrights and even, by God, loves producers'. He was named Critic of the Year in 1963 by the Directors' Guild of America.   TLM

Coghlan, Charles (1842–99) British-born actor who, after several successes in London, was brought to New York in 1876 by **Augustin Daly**. At the **Fifth Avenue Theatre** he became a favourite in leading roles

such as Alfred Evelyn in **Bulwer**'s *Money* and Orlando to **Fanny Davenport**'s Rosalind. Subsequent seasons found him at the **Union Square Theatre**, **Wallack's**, and in England again. In 1897 he created the part of Alex opposite **Mrs Fiske**'s Tess. He joined his sister, **Rose**, on several of her tours; together they were outstanding in **Sheridan**'s comedies. Coghlan died in Galveston, Texas, on tour in his own play, *The Royal Box*.   DBW

Coghlan, Rose (?1850/53–1932) British-born actress whose debut as a child was as one of the witches in a Scottish production of *Macbeth*. Her first New York appearance was in 1872 at **Wallack's**, where she would reign as leading lady during the 1880s. Her Lady Teazle and Rosalind were declared 'unsurpassed' on the American stage. During the 1890s and 1900s she appeared principally in London; and, after a 1907 United States tour in **Shaw**'s *Mrs Warren's Profession*, she divided her time between New York and London. At her retirement in 1921 she had completed a stage career of more than 52 years.   DBW

Cohan, George Michael (Keohane) (1878–1942) American performer, playwright, director, and producer who was born in Providence, Rhode Island, on 3 July while his parents were touring in vaudeville. He first appeared on stage as a child with his family's vaudeville team, the 'Four Cohans', and by 15 was writing material for their act. His New York debut came in 1901 with his first full-length play, *The Governor's Son*. In 1904 he formed a producing partnership with **Sam H. Harris**, which lasted until 1920. In 1911 he opened his own theatre, the **George M. Cohan Theatre**. Outstanding among the 50-odd plays and musicals credited to him are *Little Johnny Jones* (1904), featuring the song that most identifies Cohan ('Yankee Doodle Dandy'), *Forty-Five Minutes from Broadway* (1905), *The Talk of New York* (1907), *Get-Rich-Quick Wallingford* (1911), *Seven Keys to Baldpate* (1913), *The Tavern* (1921), and *The Song and Dance Man* (1923). His most famous song, 'Over There' (1917), won him a Congressional medal. His most notable performances in plays other than his own were as the father in **O'Neill**'s *Ah, Wilderness!* (1933) and as the President in **Kaufman** and **Hart**'s *I'd Rather Be Right* (1937). Although Cohan was always the archetype for the glories of turn of the century show business and the representation of a simplistic patriotism to his audience, he was also a complex and lonely man, rarely popular with critics and something of an outcast to his fellow performers when in 1919 he refused to support the establishment of an actors' union. His life story was filmed by Warner Brothers in 1942 (*Yankee Doodle Dandy*); a statue of Cohan was erected in 1959 in Duffy Square, New York; and a musical based on his career, *George M*, was produced on Broadway in 1968.   DBW

Cohen, Alexander H. (1920–) American producer. Born in New York, educated at NYU and Columbia University, Cohen made his Broadway producing debut in 1941 with *Ghost for Sale* and *Angel Street*. In 1950 his casting of *King Lear* with blacklisted actors established him as a producer of meritorious if not always commercially successful works. In 1959 he began a series called 'Nine O'Clock Theatre' and presented 11 successive hits including: *An Evening with Mike Nichols and Elaine May* (1960); *Beyond the Fringe* (1962); and a revival of **John Gielgud** in *The Ages of Man* (1963). A major importer of foreign productions, Cohen has presented in New York John Gielgud and **Ralph Richardson** in *The School for Scandal* (1963); the RSC's *The Homecoming* (1967); **David Storey**'s *Home*, starring Gielgud and Richardson (1970); *A Day in Hollywood/A Night in the Ukraine* (1980) directed by Tommy Tune; and **Peter Brook**'s *La Tragédie de Carmen* (1984). His numerous West End productions include **Arthur Miller**'s *The Price* (1969); and Peter Ustinov's *The Unknown Soldier and His Wife* (1973). He has served as Executive Producer of the Tony Awards telecast beginning in 1967. Married to the television producer, Hildy Parks, Cohen is a Trustee of the Actor's Fund of America.   TLM

Cohen, Nathan (1923–71) Canadian theatre critic.
The first important critical voice to cover Canadian theatre from coast to coast. On radio and television and as drama critic of the Toronto *Star* from 1959 to 1971, his often provocative and acerbic reviews chronicled the growth of the regional theatre movement across the country and the emergence of a new and substantial Canadian drama. They did so with rigorous and demanding standards that gained him many enemies but profoundly influenced not only audiences but those in the theatre and those who write about it. Nathan Cohen firmly established the idea in Canada that the theatre was something to be taken seriously and that to be taken seriously Canadian theatre must be measured against the highest international standards.   JA

Cokayne, Aston (1608–84) English dramatist. Born
in Derbyshire and educated at both Oxford and Cambridge he toured France and Italy in 1632. He wrote three plays, *The Obstinate Lady* (published 1657), a tragedy heavily influenced by **Fletcher**, *Trappolin Suppos'd a Prince*, a farce later successful when adapted by **Nahum Tate** as *A Duke and No Duke*, and *The Tragedy of Ovid*, an account of the poet's life in exile. It is not clear that any of the plays were ever performed. After the Restoration he wasted his wealth, had to sell off the family's estates, and died in poverty. His most important contribution to English drama may be the revelation in a poem that **Massinger** collaborated on many of the plays published under the authorship of **Beaumont** and **Fletcher**.   PH

Cole, Bob (1869–1912) and J. Rosamond Johnson (1873–1954) American lyricist and composer.
Pioneers in bringing black musicals to the New York stage, Cole and Johnson were prolific song writers, librettists, and performers. Cole, in conjunction with Billy Johnson, had written and starred in *A Trip to Coontown* (1898), the first musical entirely created and performed by blacks. Cole teamed with the classically trained composer J. Rosamond Johnson in 1900. In an era when it was a common practice for songs by several composers to be interpolated into a single musical, Cole and Johnson were in constant demand, providing songs for such shows as *The Belle of Bridgeport* (1900), *Mother Goose* (1903), and *Humpty Dumpty* (1904). Their biggest hit, 'Under the Bamboo Tree', was interpolated into *Sally in Our Alley* (1902). Cole and Johnson wrote and appeared in two musicals, *The Shoo Fly Regiment* (1907) and *Mr. Lode of Koal* (1909), but critics of the time were unwilling to accept black performers in musicals that had plots and sympathetic characters. After Cole's death, Johnson continued to write songs and sketches for musicals. Late in his career he appeared in the musicals *Porgy and Bess* (1935) and *Cabin in the Sky* (1940).   MK

Cole, Jack (1914–74) American choreographer and
dancer. Cole received his training in modern dance in the Humphrey-Weidman school and as a member of the Denishawn Company, after which he and his own company of dancers appeared in nightclubs. He danced in *Thumbs Up* (1934) and *Keep 'Em Laughing* (1942), and in 1943 was given his first choreographic assignment for *Something for the Boys*. Among the many other shows that he choreographed were *Alive and Kicking* (1950), in which he also appeared; *Kismet* (1953); *Jamaica* (1957); and *Man of La Mancha* (1965). Cole served as both director and choreographer for the short-lived *Donnybrook!* (1961). A student of the Chinese dancer **Mei Lanfang**, Cole frequently used Oriental movements and gestures in his choreography. He is most noted for creating 'jazz dancing', a form characterized by small groupings and angular movements. It became the dominant choreographic style of the 1950s and 1960s.   MK

Coliseum, The London music-hall and variety
theatre, seating 2,358 and the first English stage to be equipped with a revolve. Opened under Sir **Oswald Stoll** in 1904, performances included actresses of the stature of **Ellen Terry**, **Edith Evans**, **Sarah Bernhardt** or **Lillie Langtry**, and companies such as Diaghilev's Ballets Russes (in three seasons between 1918 and 1925). **Grock** (Adrien Wettach), the most accomplished clown of the period, presented his musical mimes there from 1911 to 1924. After 1931 it alternated between musical comedy, the most successful of which were *White Horse Inn* (1931) and *The Vagabond King* (1937), and spectacular ice-shows or Christmas pantomime. From 1945 to 1960 it housed a series of American musicals, including *Annie Get Your Gun* (1947), *Kiss me Kate!* (1951) and *Guys and Dolls* (1953). After some years as a cinema, it reopened in 1968 under the **Sadler's Wells** company as the permanent home of the English National Opera.   CI

Collective theatre groups (USA) During the
USA's burgeoning theatre movement throughout the 1960s, various performance ensembles formed to create an alternative to the prevalent commercial methods of producing. These groups produced a wide spectrum of work Off-Off Broadway, setting organizational precedents for groups that continue to be formed today. Collectives tended – sometimes explicitly, sometimes tacitly – to reject both the commercial aims of Broadway and Off-Broadway, as well as their hierarchical and increasingly bureaucratic organization. As actors especially became disenchanted by the exploitation of their talents in the service of commercial products in the mainstream theatre, they sought another working situation, one that would treat them as full artistic members of a creative endeavour. In many cases 'collective' is a misnomer since some groups have a

distinct director whose own style stamps the group's work and who makes the final artistic decisions. However, these ensembles involve actors and other company members in a collaborative process of developing plays, not bound by the short rehearsal periods of Broadway.

It is difficult to generalize about American collectives whose plays and processes vary tremendously; perhaps the American prototype was the **Living Theatre**, founded in 1948 by Julian Beck and Judith Malina. In many cases that followed, the plan to work collectively reflected overt political aims, as in the **Bread and Puppet Theatre**, started by the puppeteer Peter Schumann in the early 60s; the San Francisco Mime Troupe founded in 1959 by R. G. Davis, which produced open-air political **commedia**-like plays; **El Teatro Campesino**, a group of Chicano farm workers, founded by **Luis Valdéz** in response to the 1965 California grape strike; and, an outgrowth of the civil rights movement in the American South, the New Orleans-based Free Southern Theatre. During the same period groups placing more emphasis on formal experimentation like the **Performance Group**, Manhattan Project, **Mabou Mines**, and Wooster Group formed a major component of the New York avant-garde. Meanwhile the **Open Theatre** and the Talking Band concentrated more on the actor. Of course there is great overlap among these distinctions.

In the 70s the collective became the principal organizational approach for feminist theatres, among them, At the Foot of the Mountain in Minneapolis, and in New York, the Women's Experimental Theatre, Spiderwoman Theatre and Split Britches. AS

Collier, Jeremy (1650–1726) Educated at Caius College, Cambridge, he was ordained in 1677. In 1689 he refused to take the oath of allegiance to William and Mary and was briefly imprisoned. In 1697 he published the first volume of *Essays upon Several Moral Subjects* and in 1708 the first volume of *An Ecclesiastical History of Great Britain* – neither of which would earn him an entry in this *Guide*. In 1698 however he published *A Short View of the Immorality and Profaneness of the English Stage*, a lengthy, violent and combative attack on blasphemy, abuse of the clergy, abuse of sacraments like marriage and other offences he cited in contemporary drama, particularly the work of **Congreve**, **Dryden**, **D'Urfey** and **Vanbrugh**. The resulting pamphlet war was intense, rapid and acrimonious. By the end of 1698 Vanbrugh had written his defence, *A Vindication of The Relapse and The Provoked Wife*, Congreve his *Amendments of Mr Collier's False and Imperfect Citations* and been attacked in turn by Collier's supporters. Among Collier's subsequent contributions to the debate were *A Defence of the Short View* (1698), *A Second Defence* (1700), *A Dissuasive from the Playhouse* (1703) and *A Farther Vindication of the Short View* (1707). In addition to the battle in print, actors and playwrights found themselves prosecuted, from evidence collected by informers in the audience, for blasphemy, both in ad-libbed lines and in speeches previously licensed. Collier's attack also encouraged the establishment of Societies for the Reformation of Manners which monitored plays. Collier's diatribe was well-timed to catch the growing sense of middle-class morality and was undoubtedly a major contributory factor in the development towards unrealistic, sentimental forms.   PH

Collins, Lottie (Charlotte Louise Collins) (1865–1910) English music-hall performer, the daughter of a Jewish blackface minstrel. She began at the age of five as a skipping-rope dancer and joined her sisters Marie and Lizzie as a song-and-dance trio on the music-halls. In 1890 she leapt to fame with 'Ta-ra-ra-boom-de-ay', a laundered version of an American brothel song, which she introduced at the Tivoli Music-Hall, London. The infectious chorus and her high-kicking display of red petticoats for four years 'affected the country like an epidemic' (Holbrook Jackson) and has been interpreted as the revolutionary anthem of the Naughty 'Nineties. Collins toured America in 1892, and later became a sketch artist. Her eldest daughter Jose (1887–1958) was a popular musical comedy singer, best known for her Theresa in *The Maid of the Mountains*. LS

Collins, Sam (Samuel Vagg) (1824–65) 'Irish' comic vocalist and step-dancer, turned entrepreneur. Despite his stage persona, he was born in London and worked as a chimney-sweep before gaining fame at the tavern halls and concert rooms of the 1840s (such as Evan's Late Joys) with still celebrated songs such as 'Limerick Races', 'No Irish Need Apply' and 'The Rocky Road to Dublin'. Having increased his status and prosperity by bookings at **Charles Morton**'s Canterbury, he took over the Rose of Normandy in Edgware Road, turning it into the Marylebone Music Hall, and in 1861 initiated the venture which still bears his name (if only as a GLC blue plaque) by converting the Lansdown Arms, Islington Green, into a thousand-seater hall which opened in 1863 as Sam Collins's Music Hall.   AEG

Colman, George, the Elder (1732–94) English playwright and manager. Born in Florence where his father was an envoy, he was educated at Westminster School and Oxford, becoming a barrister in 1757. Considering theatre at this stage an amateur amusement, he began a long friendship with **Garrick** in 1760 when his first play, *Polly Honeycombe*, a satire on the sentimental novel, was produced. His first full-length play, *The Jealous Wife* (from **Fielding**'s *Tom Jones*), appeared in 1761. Disappointed in expectations of the will of his uncle, the Earl of Bath, in 1764, he was still able to give up law and turned to the theatre full-time. While Garrick was on tour he took part in the management of **Drury Lane**. His fine translation of **Terence** appeared in 1765 and the following year he collaborated with Garrick in writing *The Clandestine Marriage*, though arguing for years afterwards about the precise share each had in the play. The play, at times a serious consideration of social class and marriage, was a major success. In 1767 he invested both time and money in **Covent Garden**, becoming principal manager. In 1769 he beat Garrick in putting on a play about the **Shakespeare** Jubilee celebrations organized by Garrick in Stratford. Though he continued to write plays, none of them are more than hack work or adaptations, including a number of burlettas. In 1773 he was persuaded by **Goldsmith** to accept **Sheridan**'s *The School for Scandal* which Garrick had turned down.

He retired from Covent Garden in 1774 and negotiations for him to take over from Garrick at Drury Lane failed. In 1776 he bought the **Haymarket Theatre** from **Samuel Foote** and, in spite of heavy investment in scenery and costumes, made the theatre a financial and artistic success. From 1785 management began to pass to his son, particularly after a bad stroke in 1789, which led to his spending his last years in an asylum. PH

Colman, George, the Younger (1762–1836) English playwright and theatre manager, son of **George Colman the Elder**, from whom he inherited the Little Theatre in the Haymarket in 1794, having already assumed the responsibilities of management five years earlier. Gregarious, bibulous and personally improvident, Colman nevertheless defended and improved the status of the Little Theatre, with which he remained associated until 1817. His fourth play, *Inkle and Yarico* (1787), was a deserved success there. Described as an opera, it is a comedy with songs, humanely if uninsistently critical of the slave-trade. Colman's undoubted facility as a writer of comic verse (the collection of 'tales in verse', *My Nightgown and Slippers* (1797), has genuine merit) enlivens, with some strain of plausibility, the historical romances, *The Battle of Hexham* (1789) and *The Surrender of Calais* (1791), as well as colouring the otherwise sombre adaptation of Godwin's *Caleb Williams*, *The Iron Chest* (1796). Such impure writing from a man with a reputation as a superior dramatist forms a natural prelude to the wildness of the 19th-century theatre. Colman's more traditional five-act comedies, *The Heir at Law* (1797), *The Poor Gentleman* (1801) and particularly *John Bull* (1803), are not without incidental merits, but he was at his best as a popular entertainer. It is ironic that his appointment as Examiner of Plays in 1824, and his conduct in the office between then and his death, should have left him with the reputation of a spoiler of other people's entertainment. PT

Colombia Indigenous groups in the Americas often ceremonialized their myths and legends in dramatic form. Before the arrival of the Spanish, the Muiscas reached a modest level of development in the area known as New Granada in colonial times. In the colony itself, theatre records indicate presentations as early as 1580, and the first known play is *Laurea crítica* (*Critical Laurel*, 1629), a satirical sketch by Fernando Fernández de Valenzuela (1616–?). Only sporadic activity is recorded through the next two centuries, with an occasional religious play or **loa** for special occasions such as the canonization of St Thomas in 1660 and the crowning of Fernando VI in 1752. Nevertheless, the first theatre structure, the Coliseo Ramírez (Ramírez Coliseum), built in 1791 following Spanish models, attracted travelling companies presenting **zarzuelas**, dances and songs. In general the colonial period, however, was one of limited theatrical activity.

Independence in 1819 did not bring major changes. Luis Vargas Tejada (1802–29) and José Fernández Madrid (1789–1830) both wrote neoclassical historical tragedies with exalted Indian themes. Local authors imitated the Spanish costumbristic imports of **Moratín** and **Bretón de los Herreros**, followed later by the popular romantic movement. The prolific José María

Samper (1828–88) exercised both styles, perhaps never more successfully than in the musical version of *Un alcalde a la antigua* (*An Old-Fashioned Mayor*, 1856) that encapsulates the tension between tradition and progress in a rapidly changing society, a typical costumbrista theme of the period. The most important national theatre company at mid-century was that of Romualdo Díaz. José Caicedo Rojas (1816–97) and Santiago Pérez (1830–1900) were major writers of the late 19th century, a period that included Constancio Franco (1842–1917), José María Vergara y Vergara (1831–72), and Adolfo León Gómez (1858–1927).

20th century The creation of the Society of Authors of Bogotá in 1911 touched off a brief period of theatrical activity. The father of the modern Colombian theatre is considered to be Antonio Alvarez Lleras (1892–1956), the author of 15 plays. From his first effort in 1907 to his masterpiece, *El virrey Solís* (*The Viceroy Solís*) in 1948, he sought to internationalize Colombian themes with psychologically realistic plays that were didactic and often historical. Luis Enrique Osorio (1896–1966) promoted theatre with a quarterly journal, a national theatre company and his own plays that were openly critical of Colombian politics and manners. Other playwrights of this first half of the century included Angel María Céspedes (1892–1956), Jorge Zalamea (b. 1905) and Oswaldo Díaz Díaz (1910–67), and Gerardo Valencia Verjarano ('Chonta', b. 1911). The most important theatre group was Arturo Acevedo Vallanino's Benavente Company which toured the entire country.

The contemporary theatre movement in Colombia dates from the 1950s. The Experimental Theatre of the Institute of Fine Arts was created in 1950 in Medellín to promote acting and directing. In 1955 the Rojas Pinilla government invited the Japanese-born, **Stanislavsky**-trained and Mexico-based director, Seki Sano, to train actors and directors for the new television industry. Change came rapidly during his one-year stay (1955–6) before he was expelled in a governmental purge. The generation of writers and directors that emerged – **Enrique Buenaventura**, **Santiago García** and others – had new expectations about activist and committed theatre. Buenaventura aired **Brecht**'s *The Trial of Lucullus* on national radio, and El Buho (The Owl), one of the early experimental groups in Bogotá, staged a Brecht play in 1958. An incipient absurdist and escapist theatre disappeared under a rising tide of Brecht productions: Fausto Cabrera's version of *Man is Man*, Jorge Alí Triana's *The Guns of Mother Carrar* and Santiago García's *Galileo*.

During the 1960s the university theatre movement responded to the consolidated labour movement and the Cuban Revolution. In the National University, as well as the Universities del Valle, los Andes and Antioquia, theatre became the vehicle for a politicized student movement. In 1968 the first festival of university theatre was celebrated in the 3,500-seat ultra-modern theatre Los Fundadores (The Founders) in Manizales, with a blue-ribbon panel of judges (including Jack Lang of France and Pablo Neruda of Chile) and Guatemalan Miguel Angel Asturias as honorary president. Political disruptions closed this international festival after five years, but it was reinstated in 1984. The Festival of New Theatre sponsored annually after

1975 by Colcultura (Colombian Culture), was equally important in promoting national theatre with a strong socio-political commitment.

The history of the recent theatre in Colombia is closely related to several active groups. The TEC, established in 1955 under the direction of the Spaniard Cayetano Luca de Tena but soon taken over by playwright and director Enrique Buenaventura, was reorganized in 1969 as the Teatro Experimental de Cali (Experimental Theatre of Cali). Buenaventura was instrumental in restructuring theatre throughout Latin America by adapting Brechtian techniques and Marxist ideology from collective theatre to traditional dramatic theory. As university theatre became more ideological and less artistic, repressive measures brought to bear within the university led to the formation of the CCT (Colombian Theatre Corporation) in 1969, a new theatre union that embraced the 100 or more theatre groups in the country. Mostly non-professional and experimental in nature, the groups derived strength from each other in the absence of governmental or corporate support. Many groups have subsequently disappeared, but the spirit of solidarity and community was sustained by, among others, several core groups: The TEC of Buenaventura; Santiago García's La Candelaria (originally the Casa de Cultura but renamed for its sector of the city); Ricardo Camacho's Teatro Libre de Bogotá (Free Theatre of Bogotá); Miguel Torres's El Local (The Place); La Mama of Bogotá, established by Ellen Stewart in 1968 and directed by Edy Armando; and Jorge Alí Triana's TPB (Popular Theatre of Bogotá), also established in 1968, which merged in 1984 with **Carlos José Reyes**'s El Alacrán (The Scorpion).

The technique of collective theatre (*creación colectiva*) that appeared in Latin America around 1968 was particularly strong in Colombia and served to coalesce socio-political issues. The 'new theatre', as it was called, often dramatized historical issues. The TPB's *I Took Panamá* (1974) used an English title to document Teddy Roosevelt's imperialistic move to gain canal rights. La Candelaria's *Guadalupe, años sin cuenta* (*Guadalupe, Years without Number*, 1975) took advantage of a titular word play to focus on the years of 'The Violence' that marked the endemic struggle between liberals and conservatives that had devastated life and politics in Colombia since the 19th century. The TEC's *Nosotros los comunes* (*We the Peasants*, 1972) was also representative of the ongoing class struggle.

Street theatre is popular in Bogotá and other major cities in Colombia (Manizales, Cali, and Medellín, for example). Groups that are to some extent a product of the National Dramatic Arts School with inspiration from the USA's **Bread and Puppet** create lively and spontaneous performances. La Máscara (The Mask), El Globo (The Balloon), Nuevo Teatro de Pantomima (New Pantomime Theatre), Teatro Taller de Colombia (Workshop Theatre of Colombia), La Fanfarria and Pequeño Teatro (Little Theatre) (both of Medellín), Acto Latino (Latin Act), Súcubos, Tecal and others utilize puppets, masks and pantomime in combinations of Artaudian and grotesque forms that relate to popular native forms such as those Buenaventura used in *A la diestra de Dios Padre* (*On the Right Hand of God the Father*, 1958). Performances of *Gukup* by Teatro Taller de Colombia and *Blacamán* by Acto Latino (Latin Act), the latter based on a short story by Gabriel García Márquez, Colombia's Nobel-laureate novelist, are

Bread and Puppet Theatre (USA) performing *The Crucifixion and Resurrection of Archbishop Oscar Romero of El Salvador*, Manizales International Theatre Festival, Colombia, 1984.

La Candelaria in Santiago García's *Corre, corre carigüeta* (*Run, run carigüeta*), Bogotá, Colombia, 1985.

noteworthy. The coastal area has enjoyed its own theatrical forms, derived from the myths and traditions of the syncretic culture (black, white and Indian). Manuel Zapata Olivella's thoroughly-researched and documented *Rambao* (1975) is a good example.

Despite its problems, the Colombian theatre continues to be lively and dynamic. Younger authors include Fernando González Cajiao (b. 1938), also an important theatre historian, whose *Huellas de un rebelde* (*A Rebel's Tracks*, 1970) placed him in the mainstream. Jairo Aníbal Niño (b. 1941) is known for his *El Monte Calvo* (*Bald Mountain*). Esteban Navajas Cortés won the Cuban Casa de las Américas prize in 1978 for *La agonía del difunto* (*The Agony of the Deceased*). Fernando Peñuela's metafictional *La trasescena* (*Behind the Scenes*, 1984), written for La Candelaria, followed on the success of Santiago García's *Diálogo del rebusque* (*Hermetic Dialogue*, 1982), based on texts by the Spanish baroque poet Francisco de Quevedo.

An active theatre movement in the regional city of Medellín includes Gilberto Martínez, playwright, director and theatre journal editor; Rodrigo Saldarriaga, director of El Pequeño Teatro (The Little Theatre); and dramatists José Manuel Friedel, author of the vanguard *Las desdichas de la Bella Otero* (*The Misfortunes of the Beautiful Otero*, 1985) and Henry Díaz, whose *El cumpleaños de Alicia* (*Alice's Birthday*) won first prize in a Medellín University contest in 1985.

The theatre in Colombia includes a number of *café concierto* establishments; perhaps the most significant feature of the recent theatre is that it is not limited to political or engagé aspects.   GW

See: F. González Cajiao, *Historia del teatro en Colombia*, Bogotá, 1986; C. M. Suárez Radillo, 'Dos generaciones de la violencia en el teatro colombiano contemporaneo', *Anales de Literatura Hispanoamericana*, II–III, Madrid, 1973–4; M. Watson Espener and C. José Reyes, *Materiales para una historia del teatro en Colombia*, Bogotá, 1978.

Colum, Padraic (1881–1972) Irish playwright. A founder-member of the National Theatre Society, Colum was an influential figure in the movement. In 1906, he and other **Abbey** notables, disputing **Yeats**'s autocracy, formed the rival Theatre of Ireland (1906–12) under Edward Martyn. In 1914 he emigrated to

America, where he spent most of his life, celebrated for his poetry, children's stories, and travel books.

The Irish National Theatre Society's first season included Colum's first major play, *Broken Soil* (1903). There followed *The Land* (1905), *The Fiddler's House* (Theatre of Ireland 1907, a revision of *Broken Soil*), and *Thomas Muskerry* (1910). Colum's view of Ireland is represented in, respectively, Murtagh Cosgar, the man of the land surrounded by disenchanted youth; Con Hourican, the fiddler, the artist constrained by domesticity; Muskerry the official, workhouse Master, who dies in the workhouse infirmary stripped of his small authority. They are plays about individuals at moments of decision which reflect an era of social flux. The subdued lyricism of Colum's prose amplifies their essential realism, making them more than documentaries of historical circumstances.

Colum wrote few plays subsequently, none matching his early work. It had an influence out of proportion to its quantity, establishing a ground between **Synge**'s exuberant poetry and **T. C. Murray**'s plainer speech.   DM

Comden, Betty (1915–) and **Adolph Green** (1915–) American librettists, lyricists, and performers. After writing and appearing in a satirical nightclub act, Comden and Green made their Broadway debuts as librettists, lyricists, and featured performers in *On the Town* (1944). Their wry wit appeared to best advantage in the librettos and/or lyrics they created for shows with a satirical tinge, such as *Wonderful Town* (1953), *Bells are Ringing* (1956), and *Say Darling* (1958). When their fast-paced, wise-cracking style of musical comedy declined in popularity in the 1960s, Comden and Green's contributions to the Broadway stage became less frequent. As a taste for satirical books and lyrics returned in the late 1970s and 1980s, the partners were again successful with their work for *On the Twentieth Century* (1978) and *Singin' in the Rain* (1985). Comden and Green also wrote the screenplays for several popular musical films of the 1950s.   MK

Comedia In Spain from the 16th to the 18th century, the *comedia* was simply a full-scale play, whether comic or tragic in tone, as opposed to a one-act *entremés* or other short play. For the typical *comedia* of the Golden Age, see **Spain**.

Though often resisting categorization, the various types of *comedia* included the following:

Comedia de capa y espada (cloak-and-sword comedy). The cloak and sword were the distinctive feature of the *caballeros*, or lesser nobility. This type of play is the equivalent of middle class comedy in other countries, and a descendant of the New Comedy of **Menander**. The main elements of the plot, a mixture of comedy and thrills, were disguises, duels, misunderstandings and deceptions involved in the secret wooing of a noble lady.

Comedia de fábrica A court comedy involving the more refined wooing of princes, nobles and heads of state, often with long journeys and unusual events.

Comedia de figurón A type of comedy prevalent in the late 17th and early 18th centuries in which the main humour depends on a grotesque and ridiculous character (*figurón*), often personifying some vice.

Comedia de privanza   A play on the rise and fall of a royal favourite (*privado*), common in the first half of the 17th century.

Comedia de santo   A dramatization of scenes from the life of a saint.

Alta comedia   A late 19th-century form of bourgeois social drama, popularized by such playwrights as **Tamayo y Baus**. CL

Comédie-Française   Formed in 1680 by royal decree merging the troupes of **Molière** (d. 1673) and of the **Hôtel de Bourgogne**, the Comédie-Française is proud of its uninterrupted tradition as the oldest European theatre company. For most of its first 100 years it performed in a theatre constructed in 1688–9 on the site of a tennis court in the rue des Fossés St Germain des Prés, now rue de l'Ancienne Comédie. This was designed by François d'Orbay with a large parterre, a U-shaped amphitheatre at the back and 3 rows of boxes, giving a total audience capacity of around 1,500. Until the Revolution the company enjoyed a virtual monopoly on all new plays performed in the capital (only shared for some of the time with the **Comédie-Italienne**) and so the history of its repertoire was also the history of playwriting in France. The company has always retained a collective structure with shares held by full members of the company and decisions about repertoire etc. taken in common. At first the main influence was wielded by **La Grange**, one of Molière's main actors, together with **Armande Béjart**, Molière's widow. Other important players were Michel **Baron** and Noël-Jacques Hauteroche, both of whom followed Molière's example by writing comedies for performance by the company. As Madame de Maintenon's influence grew at court, life became more difficult for the company, who frequently had to close for periods of official mourning or religious observance. The accession of Louis XV brought easier times and the company was able to recruit powerful performers both in tragedy and in comedy, among whom were **Adrienne Lecouvreur**, **Mlle Clairon**, **Lekain**, and the **Poisson** family. They were received in society and their finances established on a sounder footing. For the repertoire, they continued to rely on the plays of **Racine**, **Corneille** and Molière but also enjoyed considerable success with the tragedies of **Voltaire** and the *comédies larmoyantes* of **La Chaussée**; their greatest success was *The Marriage of Figaro* whose opening night in 1784 had been delayed for several years by the censor. Between 1770 and 1782 the company performed in the **Salle des Machines** at the Tuileries palace, before moving into a new building designed for them by Peyre and Wailly, the present **Odéon**.

From the opening of the new theatre in 1782 to the burning of the Salle Richelieu in 1900, the Théâtre-Français had a chequered career. During the Revolution the title of the theatre was changed to Théâtre de la Nation (1789). In 1790 it went through a stormy period of internal dissension occasioned by Chénier's historico-political tragedy, *Charles IX*, which led to **Talma**, Dugazon, **Mme Vestris** and other revolutionary members of the troupe leaving to set up at the

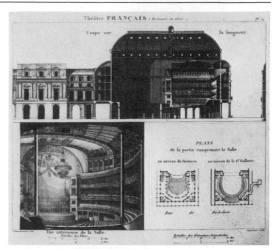

A plan of the Théâtre-Français in the nineteenth century. This is substantially Victor Louis's theatre. It is interesting to note how he placed a large theatre on a small site (vestibule under the auditorium, no large foyers or monumental staircase).

Théâtre de la République (Salle Richelieu, formerly the Variétés Amusantes). The situation of the Comédie was made more difficult by the law of the liberty of theatres of 1791, which abolished its monopoly, and, in 1793, by the arrest, and near execution, of the more conservative members as a result of performances of **Laya**'s moderate play *L'Ami des Lois* (*The Friend of the Law*) and François de Neufchâteau's *Paméla*. In 1798, the same François de Neufchâteau, now Minister for the Interior, arranged for the government to acquire both the old Comédie-Française (Odéon) and the Théâtre de la République, and to pay off the heavy debts incurred during the Revolution. A fire at the Odéon in 1799 brought the troupe together again. In 1800 the building of the Théâtre-Français became state property, and in 1802 a regular subsidy of 100,000 francs was established. An act of 1803 forbade the *sociétaires* to appear at any other theatre without special government permission. Napoleon had a great interest in the theatre, seeing the Théâtre-Français (where he attended some 270 performances) as essential to national prestige. The decree of Moscow of 1812 set forth the new organization of the theatre and removed some of the administrative authority of the actors by installing an imperial commissar whose job was to transmit to the actors the wishes of the *surintendant des spectacles*, even on such details as casting. After 1816 a not very happy attempt was made to revert to the organization of 1766. The theatre went through a difficult period – *Tartuffe* was banned and a series of rather dreary medieval tragedies was staged. Finally, in 1825, the new royal commissar, Baron Taylor, was appointed. Taylor had already been involved with the Panorama Dramatique, where he was co-author of the very successful adaptation of Maturin's *Bertram*. A widely travelled man and a keen archaeologist, he also produced a series of volumes illustrated by well-known artists called *Voyages pittoresques de l'ancienne France*. Taylor opened wide the doors of the Comédie to the romantic movement and also to a much more elaborate conception of *mise-en-scène* than had previously been contemplated at that theatre. In particular he was responsible for *Henri III et Sa Cour* (*Henry III and his Court*), *Le More de Venise* (*The Moor of Venice*) and *Hernani*. After the battle of *Hernani*, Taylor drifted off on long trips, leaving the company in a state of internal chaos which nearly led to its dissolution. In 1833 the Théâtre-Français abandoned its right to administer itself and a director was appointed, the first being Jouslin de la Salle, a former stage director, who saw himself as the saviour of the theatre and continued Taylor's policy, staging *Angelo* (**Hugo**), *Chatterton* (**Vigny**), *Les Enfants d'Edouard* and *Marino Faliero* (**Delavigne**), and introducing the repertoire of **Scribe**. He had to resign in 1837 over an illegal ticket racket. In 1838 **Rachel** was engaged and turned the classical repertoire into box-office. In 1840, Buloz (of the *Revue des Deux Mondes*) became director, introduced gas-lighting, discovered the plays of **Augier**, and tried to interest the theatre in ancient and foreign repertoires. 1843 saw the disaster of *Les Burgraves*. In 1847 an attempt was made to create an administrator who would be an almost all-powerful civil servant indepen-dent of the company itself. Buloz lost his post with the 1848 revolution and was replaced by a protégé of Rachel's, the actor Lockroy. A decree of 1849 estab-lished a commissar-administrator – in fact Arsène Houssaye, a man of letters – and in 1850 Louis Napoléon fixed the rights and duties of the administra-tor by decree. Houssaye met with hostility from the company, but when they offered to walk out, he simply told them he would employ Boulevard actors. The Théâtre-Français became very fashionable under the Second Empire, and Houssaye attached much importance to the presentation of new works. Under Empis (1856–9) there was a return to a more traditional repertoire. Edouard Thierry, appointed in 1859, intro-duced the repertoire of **Sardou** and Pailleron. In 1870 the theatre was set up as a field hospital, and the fall of the Empire brought considerable financial difficulties. After the Commune, Thierry was replaced by Emile Perrin, a former director of the Opéra, who brought back financial stability, introducing Tuesday subscrip-tion nights and Sunday matinees. It was also decided that actors should no longer be responsible for their own costumes in modern-dress plays. The troupe was now strong, but Perrin was criticized for attaching more importance to *mise-en-scène* than literary quality. Perrin was followed by Jules Clarétie, whose adminis-tration lasted for 28 years.

In 1900 a disastrous fire caused the death of an actor and the wholesale destruction of stage and scenery at the Salle Richelieu. A year later the company moved back into the renovated theatre, following the fashion of the times by performing mainly comedy of an undemanding kind. They continued to perform throughout the First World War, travelling to the front to entertain the troops. After the war, as **Copeau** and the **Cartel** directors tried to raise standards of produc-tion, the Comédie-Française lagged behind. An attempted improvement was the appointment of Bourdet as administrator in 1936 with four associate directors: **Baty**, Copeau, **Dullin** and **Jouvet**. During the German occupation the theatre's reputation rose again partly thanks to **Barrault**'s production of **Claudel**'s *Satin Slipper* (1943) but Barrault left with Madeleine Renaud in 1946 when they set up the independent Renaud–Barrault company. Since then the Comédie-Française, though strong in Boulevard comedy, has continued to be a conservative force in the French theatre, claiming to preserve the traditions of 17th-century performance. In fact its styles have changed, both in acting and production, but always considerably *after* rather than *with* the times. There are now 40 full *sociétaires*, who elect new members as vacancies occur from the 30 *pensionnaires* who are actors drawing a salary, not full shareholders. The current 350 technical and administrative staff account for the theatre's large subsidy, which is considerably higher than that of any other French theatre. Despite many reconstructions, the theatre retains **Victor Louis**'s basic lay-out with a horse-shoe shaped auditorium and four shallow superimposed balconies. Originally designed to hold 2,000 spectators it now contains seating for a maximum of 892. The stage, too, has had the latest technology installed without altering the fundamental design of the original building. The main training ground for actors, the Conservatoire, until recently employed almost exclusively Comédie-Française actors as its teachers which contributed to the company's conservative influence. After 1968 various reforms were introduced, notably in the Conserva-toire, and a policy of performing more contemporary plays was initiated. In 1983 **Jean-Pierre Vincent** was appointed director, the first to come to the post from a decentralized theatre (Strasbourg); however he left three years later without having been able to accom-plish the reforms he deemed necessary to make the Comédie-Française into a representative National Theatre. DB JMCC

Comédie-Italienne Italian **commedia** troupes were familiar visitors to France from the mid-16th century and increasingly into the 17th. Summoned to appear at court and entertaining the general public en route, companies led by **Ganassa**, Francesco and **Isabella Andreini**, **Tristano Martinelli**, **Tiberio Fiorilli** and others were so popular with Paris audi-ences that eventually Louis XIV resolved to establish the last-named under royal protection first at the **Petit-Bourbon** and then at the **Palais-Royal**. After a further spell in the rue Guénégaud they finally moved to the **Hôtel de Bourgogne**, made available by the formation of the **Comédie-Française** in 1680, where they took the name of the Comédie-Italienne. The company, which still featured the veteran Fiorilli alongside **Domenico Biancolelli**, his two daughters and the **Costantini** brothers, now went beyond occa-sional French interpolations in their performances to the adoption of whole scripted plays by such dramatists as **Regnard**, Dufresny and Palaprat and slowly their traditional reliance on improvisation diminished as they turned their attention to contemporary satire and comedy of manners. Their success suffered a setback in 1697 with Lenoble's *La Fausse Prude* (*The False Prude*), which was seen as an attack on Mme de Maintenon, the king's second wife, and the Italians were promptly banished. In 1716, after Louis's death, a new company under **Luigi Riccoboni** and numbering some of the finest *commedia* actors of the day returned to the Hôtel de Bourgogne, but the initial warmth of their reception soon cooled and they too were forced to abandon Italian for French. They were granted a royal pension in

1723 and despite competition from the fair theatres, the 'comédiens italiens ordinaires du roi' now enjoyed a period of great prosperity, thanks largely to their partnership with **Marivaux**, some 20 of whose plays they presented between 1720 and 1740, though their link with *commedia* became progressively more tenuous. Gradually the enormous popularity of *vaudevilles* and comic operas at the fair theatres induced the Italians to follow suit and led ultimately to their amalgamation with the Opéra-Comique under **Favart** in 1762. Most of the older actors had now retired and the traditional Comédie-Italienne had effectively ceased to exist by the time the joint company opened the new Salle Favart in 1783. DR

Comedy From classical Greek times, comedy has been viewed in contrast to tragedy, but by the late 20th century a considerable corpus of criticism has broken free of tragedy to comment independently on comedy and its several subgenres. Although **Aristotle** presents rival claims to the etymology of comedy, modern scholars agree that comedy means revel-song, and a correspondingly festive spirit has been associated with many forms of comic drama. Aristotle's definition of comedy as the painlessly ugly has proved less resonant than his definition of tragedy, and the centuries have brought scant agreement about the nature of dramatic comedy, its function, or its components. Critical consideration of comedy has often strayed into theories of laughter.

Played at the Dionysian Festival as well as the Lenaea in the 5th century BC, Greek comedy by the next century was classified as Old, Middle, or New. What the three forms shared were avatars of the laughable. Old Comedy, which is extant only in the plays of **Aristophanes**, was a rich blend of satire and fantasy, physical farce and subtle word play; it featured an ingenious trickster and closed on a lavish choral song and dance. Whatever Middle Comedy may be (scholars disagree), burlesque of heroes and divinities dilutes the comic brew. New Comedy depicted ordinary citizens beset by ordinary problems; the playwright's concern was with the individual. The plot of New Comedy was often structured on the most durable formula of all drama: young lovers separated by an obstacle are united by the grand finale. New Comedy thrived on asides, eavesdropping, quid pro quo, mistaken identity, and it evolved such comic types as the old grouch, the pedant, the braggart soldier – often the obstacle in the path of the young lovers. Although **Menander** may not have invented New Comedy, he was admired for his deft creations. Admiration took the form of imitation by Roman **Plautus** and **Terence**, and, through them, by a host of neoclassical European playwrights both in Latin and the vulgar tongues. The scheming slave of New Comedy was the ancestor of Italian Arlecchino, German **Hanswurst**, and the Spanish **gracioso**.

Before that harvest, however, dramatic comedy was eclipsed by comic theory, with Cicero offering a widely quoted definition of comedy as 'an imitation of life, a mirror of customs, and an image of truth'. In the Middle Ages comedy was associated with the vulgar tongue (as opposed to Latin) and with a happy ending; thus Dante called his great epic a comedy. On the late medieval stage – both amateur and professional – comedy displayed a spectrum of techniques from slapstick to puns, from topical satire to tropical fantasy. Moreover, in religious plays devils and Vice-figures were simultaneously funny and evil, implicitly contradicting an Aristotle they did not know – for the Medieval mind the comic was painfully ugly.

By the Renaissance neoclassical playwrights imposed decorum on comedy as on tragedy – the proverbial unities and five acts, as well as a realistic and prosaic tone. In contrast, neoclassical playwrights like **Shakespeare** rejected such constraints when they created what was later called romantic comedy. Both neoclassical and romantic comedies often ended in marriage, but different paths to wedlock might suggest different subgenres of comedy, even while comedy in the Romance languages gradually came to mean any play. Thus, Italian and Spanish drama introduced comedy of intrigue with elaborate plots. **Machiavelli**'s *Mandragola* may well be the pinnacle of this subgenre, but the anonymous *Ingannati* (*The Deceived*) became a fertile model. **Ben Jonson** in England created comedy of humours (named for the particular humour or body fluid which was believed to determine character), but in Jacobean times the broader panoply of 'city comedy' replaced obsessive monsters. In France **Molière** usually observed classical decorum but ranged from a farce like *The Flying Doctor* to character comedy like *The Misanthrope*. French comedy of morals crossed the English Channel as Comedy of Manners which ridiculed social foibles. Type characters from **commedia dell'arte** sprang across national boundaries into the written comedies of several languages.

Despite such gifted practitioners of comedy as Shakespeare, Molière, **Lope de Vega** and Jonson, critics and even practitioners tended to view comedy as a genre inferior to tragedy. In the 18th century, with the rise of the bourgeoisie, comedy tried to be serious in such subgenres as **La Chaussée**'s tearful comedy or **Steele**'s sentimental comedy (resurrected belatedly in today's sitcom). At approximately the same time, the stock type of the scheming servant towered above his master in **Beaumarchais**'s Figaro trilogy. Romantic dramatists preferred tragedy to comedy, but **Musset**'s bittersweet armchair comedies set the tone not only for **Büchner**'s *Leonce and Lena* but also for playwrights as different as **Chekhov**, **Lorca**, **Giraudoux**, **Barrie**. At the turn of the 20th century comedy gained stature – largely through **Bernard Shaw**, with his comedy of ideas. Although stage humour abounds in many times and places, the 20th-century commercial stage has been particularly hospitable to frivolous entertainment that goes by the name of comedy. In contrast, the zany humour of the dadaists and surrealists was only rarely seen in the theatre before the absurd exploded in the 1950s.

Is dramatic comedy still with us as a distinct genre? The reply will depend on how the viewer defines comedy: the new comedy formula holds in plays as different as **Harvey Fierstein**'s *Torch Song Trilogy* and **Neil Simon**'s *Barefoot in the Park*: wit scintillates in plays as bleak as **Samuel Beckett**'s *Endgame* and **Harold Pinter**'s *Betrayal*. Various comic subgenres linger residually as devices – burlesque, farce, parody, satire, even the grotesque – in such a play as **Stoppard**'s *Travesties*, of undesignated genre. Comedy has been the obstreperously preferred genre of political radicals from **Brecht** to **Fo**. What is hard to find today is the festive spirit implied by the etymology of comedy, which has been periodically revived in times less threatening and threatened than our own.　RC

Comedy of humours The distinctive style of English comedy of humours was popularized by the enormous success of **Jonson**'s *Every Man in His Humour* (1598) in its performance by the **Lord Chamberlain's Men**. Jonson peopled his play with characters, each of whom was dominated by a single attitude or 'humour'. It was a comic technique familiar from **Aristophanes**, and it was possibly the excellence of the acting that brought it into new prominence, denying what may have been a merited historical precedence to **Chapman**'s *An Humorous Day's Mirth* (1597). Jonson followed it up with the less successful *Every Man out of His Humour* (1599), written in the 'old comedy' style of Aristophanes and including satirical portraits of **Marston** and **Dekker**. The comedy of humours became a weapon in the **war of the theatres**, with Jonson countered by Dekker's *Satiromastix* and Marston's *What You Will* and himself striking back with *Poetaster*. Almost all contemporary and subsequent writers of comedy have been in various degrees reliant on the comic potential of 'humours'. **Shakespeare**, though exceptional, displays its influence in the creation of Jaques in *As You Like it* (1599) and *Twelfth Night* (c. 1600) as well as in the more slapdash *The Merry Wives of Windsor* (c. 1600). **John Day** looked back over a rich decade in the title and conduct of his *Humour out of Breath* (c. 1608), and the special tone of Restoration comedy is, in part, the result of a preservation of humours comedy alongside the sophisticated comedy of manners. Through the 18th and 19th century, professional dramatists, with an often-wearying predictability, deposited humours into farce, where the situation comedies of modern television have kept them.　PT

Commedia dell'arte 'Comedy of the profession', that is of the new acting companies which sprang up in northern Italy towards the middle of the 16th century, as distinct from the *commedia erudita* of gentlemanly dilettantes.

Its original setting was the simple booth-stage, easily portable or organized on the spot by a company on tour, and adaptable to any context from the public piazza to the courtly hall. On this uncluttered platform the actors improvised their plays (usually farcical comedies of sex, greed and status) from skeletal scenarios, ringing the changes on a set of masked caricatures and a repertory of traditional situations and gags.

Two centuries saw numerous changes of detail and nomenclature in its *dramatis personae*, sometimes in response to the success of particular performers (**Isabella Andreini** probably gave her own name to the first *inamorata* of the **Gelosi** company, and **Silvio Fiorillo** popularized Policenella), but its basic character-format remained the same: two contrasted male clowns or **zanni**, of low social status, the crafty and unscrupulous Brighella and the dim-witted and famished Arlecchino (**Harlequin**); two older male characters of high social status, bourgeois heads of household, the avaricious, lustful, and suspicious merchant Pantalone and the pedantic and ineffectual Dottore; and at least one pair of lovers, the *inamorato* (under a variety of names) and *inamorata* (often Isabella), the latter frequently the over-protected daughter or younger wife of one of the senior male characters. To this basic list were added the *capitano*, a braggart soldier; the witty serving-wench Colombina (who, as the genre developed, acquired a special stage relationship with Arlecchino); the obese and malicious Pulcinella; and numerous others, additional or alternative *zanni* such as Coviello, Pedrolino and Tartaglia, and further female characters, such as the widow, to complicate the sexual intrigue.

Most of the roles had their own half-mask and costume, so that they were instantly recognizable and the actor was freed from the need to establish his character, to concentrate on improvising the action. Arlecchino, whose rise in theatrical status (partly attributable to **Giuseppe Biancolelli**'s innovative fusion of the two *zanni* into a single, paradoxical character) is itself a miniature history of popular stereotypes, wore an unembellished black or dark brown mask, a patched and motley costume which subsequently became refined into the familiar overall pattern of lozenges, and carried a wooden slapstick. Brighella was identifiable by his green and white stripes and dagger, and sometimes played a guitar. Pantalone's attributes were a beard and long nose, loose gown, red stockings, Turkish slippers and brimless hat. The female characters were not invariably masked – or if so, not in character, but with the black velvet domino – but they were equally recognizable by clothes appropriate to their status, and could rely on a contemporary understanding of 'what colours signify love or hope or jealousy'. Such emblematic costuming, for both men and women, was reinforced in its visual impact by the actor's ability to relax into the characteristic posture and movement of a role which he or she was quite likely to inhabit throughout a professional lifetime.

An improvised masked comedy of traditional situation, social caricature, emblematic costume, and high visual impact, with no basis in a written script: it all points to a form in which action takes precedence over character, where physical skills are at least as important as verbal skills, and verbal skills are of a very particular kind. The impression is reinforced when we consider that Italian actors were able to play in France or Bavaria as successfully as on their Cisalpine stamping-ground. Further, in its early days, *commedia* made great play with local frames of reference and vernaculars, and its improvised texts must have been a pot-pourri of Italian dialects in an age when there was no spoken standard. Arlecchino hailed from Bergamo and Pulcinella from Benevento, near Naples, both Gothamite communities; Pantalone was a Venetian grandee, the Doctor a university man from Bologna, the captain a Spaniard. Not that the actors necessarily came from these places, but they presumably mimicked the dialects or broken Italian, and we cannot be sure that they were always wholly intelligible – for Arlecchino to speak virtual gibberish would be consistent with his role, and the parodied technical language of academicians and soldiers in itself approaches meaninglessness. Such classes of discourse are a common source of Renaissance humour. But on stage, if their appeal is not to wane through repetition, or be confined to an intellectual

French and Italian players in the *commedia dell'arte* style, c. 1670.

coterie, they must be allied with unflagging physical energy and narrative drive.

The basis for this was the scenario, a chronological plot-summary which was pinned up backstage. Though scenarios are sometimes referential – they were designed as an *aide-mémoire* for actors – they provide a schematic account of the intrigue (typically concerned with the ploys of tricksters in getting the girl, or the money, or both) and the interpolation of the stock comic device known as a **lazzo**. The *burla*, typically a practical joke, is a more developed form, though in practice the terms overlap. Either could be used as the action demanded or at the discretion of the players. The scenario was the framework which every improviser requires to support a performance, providing, in essence, given circumstances, lines of action, and needs. The performer brought to bear on this a physical training in acrobatics and comic business, and a verbal training in mimicry. We may also reasonably infer a formulaic technique of the kind widely used by oral improvisers from poets to preachers – certainly the extant *bravure* of the hyperbolical *capitano* suggest it – and perhaps certain memorized set-pieces such as the rhymed declarations of the lovers and the cross-talk acts of the *zanni*. Again, literary evidence exists for these, and combinations of memorization and improvisation are not unknown in other art forms.

The origin of the *commedia dell'arte* is unknown. Attempts have been made to trace it back to Roman comedy: certainly Pulcinella resembles the clown Maccus, Capitano Spavento da Vall'Inferno is *miles gloriosus* to the life, and **Plautus** would have recognized immediately the outwitting of masters by their servants. There is, however, no historical evidence to cover the millennium and a half that separate Plautus,

Terence and the Atellan farces from **Zan Ganassa** and his comrades, nor to bridge the gap between literary scripts and improvised action. There is no single, clear line of descent; in an age of syntheses, *commedia* is probably another. Plautus and Terence were known to the educated, and their conventions mediated into popular consciousness through the plays of **Calmo** and **Ruzzante**, who added elements of local vernacular language and anarchic comic business. Further material was readily available in printed *novelle* and chapbooks, not to mention oral literature. Professional entertainment was nothing new, and it is likely that the patter, story-telling, clowning, acrobatics, dancing and music of the minstrel and the mountebank contributed their techniques. As for improvisation, in 16th-century Italy, where most of the population had to rely on it for verbal expression of any kind, the opportunity to acquire its disciplines may be taken for granted, and even the elite culture's training in rhetoric probably played its part. Finally, models for dialogue might be acquired from the **flytings** associated with carnival, and the same source could have provided the concept of masked performance.

Most innovations are a form of *bricolage* under a given economic and cultural stimulus. The Mantua-based **Accesi**, the **Confidenti** who toured in Spain, the **Desiosi** whom Montaigne admired while visiting Pisa in 1581, and the **Fedeli** who played the **Hôtel de Bourgogne** in 1613 and 1614, were probably constructing a new artform from classical and traditional sources, just as they combined the old financial model of aristocratic patronage with the new supply-and-demand model of performing to popular audiences in the growing cities of the early modern world. Certainly there is nothing unambiguously old-fashioned about their way of doing business. They may sometimes be known as 'families', some actors were related, and some masks inherited; but the word should not be taken too literally. Performers such as **Francesco Gabrielli**, a musical Scapino, the great Arlecchino **Tristano Martinelli**, and the actor-manager and scenarist Flaminio Scala (whose collection of 1611 is the earliest printed source of scenarios), moved freely from company to company in pursuit of their own ends, as actors do today.

As modern Europe's first fully-fledged professional drama, the artistry of *commedia* rapidly created a demand outside its homeland. The first evidence of a company (its contracts), is from 1545: by 1568 Ganassa is working in Mantua and the Gelosi in Milan; and by 1577 **Drusiano Martinelli** was probably in London. Before 1600 the troupes had infiltrated every important European country, influencing actors and playwrights everywhere. France, particularly Paris, was their second home, and the later history of the form is as much French as Italian. The touring of earlier decades was consolidated, by the mid-17th century, in the long-term use of the **Petit-Bourbon** by **Tiberio Fiorilli**'s company. In 1680, the **Comédie-Italienne** was founded, occupying the Hôtel de Bourgogne as a permanent theatre, and including among its members **Domenico Biancolelli** and **Angelo Costantini**, as well as the ageing Fiorilli. Expelled in 1697 after a scandal, the company re-formed in 1716, 11 actors under **Luigi Riccoboni**. By 1720, when **Marivaux** wrote *Arlequin Poli par l'Amour* for them, they were, *ipso facto*, no longer a *commedia dell'arte* troupe in the old sense. This literalization of a performer's art was the inevitable conclusion of uprooting the *commedia* from its indigenous culture. Its potency of local and topical reference was inevitably lost, and replaced by the universalism of sentimental comedy; the performers began to work in a language that was not their own, and, unsurprisingly, relied increasingly on the memorization of macaronic texts; the permanent theatre building replaced the opportunistic venues of earlier days.

Nor was the process confined to France. In a world of growing literacy and literature, the *commedia* had its back to the wall. In its heartland, **Goldoni** wrote *The Servant of Two Masters* (1745) for **Sacchi**'s Venetian company, although he disliked masked acting and improvisation. **Gozzi** liked them, and his self-defeating response was to write another script, *The Love of Three Oranges* (1761). Fine plays both, but no longer *commedia dell'arte*.

The influences of *commedia* are many. Among the greats, **Jonson, Lope de Vega, Molière** and **Shakespeare** owe it a debt. The Anglo-German dramatic jig, the **Turlupinade** and the English Pantomime derive some of their characteristics from it. Even puppets, possibly including **Punch**, have been modelled on it. *Commedia dell'arte* may have been driven out by the literary theatre; in the 20th century's reaction against naturalism it has been rediscovered.

Meyerhold, and through him Eisenstein, were influenced by it, for reasons both technical and ideological. The notion of a non-naturalistic and non-individualistic mode of acting, demanding a range of performance skills, and based in recognizable social types rather than unique human personalities, had already attracted Meyerhold's attention before 1917; its salience after the Revolution was even greater, and the principles of *commedia* contributed to the formation of the bio-mechanical system. Others too have recognized the usefulness of *commedia* techniques in actor-training. **Jacques Copeau**'s school (founded 1921) was an early centre of mask-work as part of a programme for liberating the actor's physicality. Later, inside Italy, *commedia dell'arte* has been an important inspiration in the work of the Piccolo Teatro di Milano and of **Dario Fo**; outside, its techniques have been applied very successfully to modern situations and issues, on both sides of the Atlantic, by the San Francisco Mime Troupe (founded 1959) and the Belgian company **Internationale Nieuwe Scene**. AEG

See: G. Attinger, *L'Esprit de la Commedia dell'Arte dans le Théâtre Français*, Paris, 1950; P. L. Duchartre, *The Italian Comedy*, New York, 1966; K. M. Lea, *Italian Popular Comedy*, Oxford, 1934; C. Mic, *La Commedia dell'Arte*, Paris, 1927; A. Nicoll, *The World of Harlequin*, London, 1963; G. Oreglia, *The Commedia dell'Arte*, New York, 1968.

Community Arts Service Theatre New Zealand theatre organization active from 1947–62, touring productions extensively in the North Island. Organized from the Adult Education Centre of Auckland University, the company's professionalism was often in conflict with the amateur resources available on tour. Though only one New Zealand play was ever presented (Curnow's *Moon Section*), successive directors (Arnold Goodwin, Harold Baigent, and Ronald Barker) did introduce rural audiences to **Synge, Chekhov**, and **Beckett**, and stimulated amateur drama considerably. HDMCN

Community theatre (USA) Amateur dramatic groups in the United States have existed since the nation's beginnings but it was not until the 1910s that the community theatre (also called Little Theatre and Civic Theatre) movement became widely established. The reasons are many. Tent chautauquas (lecture meetings of an educational or religious nature) had built an audience for cultural events. **The Drama League** of America (1910–31) actively supported amateur theatre. **Percy MacKaye** and others organized dramatic pageants and wrote books which stressed community involvement. Mackaye called for a civic theatre as early as 1909 (*The Playhouse and the Play*), and in subsequent books – *The Civic Theatre* (1912) and *Community Drama* (1917) – explained how a community would benefit from the 'neighbourly ritual' of theatre. The poor quality of touring shows plus the increased competition from movies dried up professional theatre opportunities outside of major cities and promoted amateur ones. The **Little Theatre movement** in Europe spawned such pioneers in America as Maurice Browne's Little Theatre in Chicago (1912), and similar groups began to appear across the nation. According to one estimate (McCleery and Glick), there were about 40 community theatres operating in 1917 and 105 in 1938. The **Cleveland Play House** and the **Pasadena** Community **Playhouse** were the most prominent leaders in the 1930s and 1940s. According to the American Community Theatre Association (ACTA), nearly 100 theatres of at least 50 years duration were still producing in 1985 and included: The Footlight Club of Jamaica, Massachusetts (1877); the Players of Providence, Rhode Island (1909); Indianapolis Civic Theatre (1915); Le Petit Théâtre du Vieux Carré in New Orleans (1919); Theatre Memphis (1920); and the Omaha Community Playhouse (1925). Numerous attempts to organize community theatres into an association include a Little Theatre Conference at the Pasadena Playhouse in 1924; the National Theatre Conference in the 1930s; and the American Educational Theatre Association (AETA) beginning in 1936. In 1958 the National Association of Community Theatres joined members of AETA to form ACTA which continues in 1985 as a division of the American Theatre Association. The demise of ATA resulted in a new group, The American Association of Community Theatres, in 1985.   TLM

Community theatre (Britain) see Regional Theatre (Britain)

Compagnie des Quinze
French theatre company directed by **Michel Saint-Denis** and drawn from former pupils of **Copeau**. The company formed in 1929 when work with Copeau in Burgundy was no longer possible and gave performances at the **Vieux-Colombier Theatre** and the **Atelier** as well as on foreign tours between 1931 and 1934. Their aim was to create a style of theatre at once poetic and acrobatic; their success was partly due to close collaboration with **André Obey** who wrote several plays for them.   DB

Condell, Henry
(?–1627) English actor, a long-serving member of **Shakespeare**'s company, the **Lord Chamberlain's Men**. Condell is known to have acted the Cardinal in **Webster**'s *The Duchess of Malfi* and was in the cast-list of several other plays, all dating from before 1619, when he may have turned from acting to management. He shared with his colleague **Heminges** in the editing of the Shakespeare Folio of 1623 and in the churchwardenship of St Mary's, Aldermanbury. He accumulated sufficient wealth to buy a country house in Fulham.   PT

Confidenti
Company of Italian **commedia dell'arte** actors, 'confident of the public's indulgence', which travelled throughout Italy and to France and Spain between 1574 and 1620. In the early years it was headed by Vittoria Piisimi assisted by Giovanni Pellesini (Pedrolino) and for a brief time in 1584 merged with the **Uniti**. Its leading players were then Drusiano and **Tristano Martinelli** as Arlecchino. From 1612 until its breakup, the troupe was managed by Flaminio Scala (Flavio) who was also its scenarist.   LS

Confrérie de la Passion
(Confraternity of the Passion) Medieval guild of Parisian artisans and merchants, formed in the latter part of the 14th century for the performance of religious drama and recognized by letters patent of Charles VI in 1402. Their privileges, which included a monopoly on dramatic activity in the capital, were confirmed by successive French kings and by the Parlement in 1548. In the same year they built their own theatre, the **Hôtel de Bourgogne**, but were deprived of much of their repertoire by a Parlement decree banning the performance of 'sacred mysteries'. Turning to moralities, farces, romances and other secular pieces, they continued to perform until almost the end of the century, whereafter their occasional practice of leasing their theatre to itinerant companies rapidly became the norm and their own performances ceased. The Hôtel de Bourgogne was soon a hub of professional theatre, though as landlords the Confrères proved strict, imposing rigorous conditions and a stiff rental on their tenants and resolutely pursuing defaulters or those who sought to evade their monopoly by performing elsewhere without paying them the requisite fee. In this way they hindered the development of theatrical activity in Paris until the centralization of social and cultural life on the capital in the 1620s made change irresistible. With the establishment of the Comédiens du Roi in their theatre after 1629 and that of another company at the **Marais** in 1634 the Confrères' authority was slowly eroded and their monopoly was finally abolished in 1675.   DR

Congo Popular Republic
Before independence in 1960, a colony belonging to the French Equatorial Africa federation, the Congo Popular Republic is a small country with few resources, best known for the historical importance of its capital Brazzaville. Its practical achievements in the theatre are modest. In 1965, the two main theatre companies, the Association de Théâtre Congolais and the Théâtre Universitaire Congolais, joined forces to become the Théâtre National Congolais which has since presented the plays of its country's authors. The Congo Popular Republic has, in fact, been blessed with some of the best writers for the theatre in French-speaking Africa. At first, there was only Guy Menga, whose two plays *La Marmite de Koka-Mbala* (*Koka-Mbala's Pot*) and *L'Oracle* (*The Oracle*) in 1968 jointly won the first prize in the annual French radio-play competition for Africa and have since featured regularly in the repertoires of many African theatre companies. Both of these plays are social comedies based on the practices of a traditional African society subjected to the scrutiny of a critical modern generation. The following year a Congolese author, A. Letembet-Ambily, again won the first prize in the same radio competition, this time for a political allegory about colonialism entitled *L'Europe Inculpée* (*Europe Indicted*). More recently, Tchicaya U Tam'si, a major francophone African poet, has published three plays, *Le Zulu* and *Vwène le Fondateur* (*Vwene the Founder*, 1977) and *Le Destin Glorieux du Maréchal Nnikon Nniku* (*The Glorious Destiny of Marshal Nnikon Nniku*, 1979). U Tam'si has what can only be described as an aggressively creative approach to language which in general has so far been the least adventurous and least successful aspect of African theatre in French. This is evident, for example, in another Congolese play, on a similar theme to U Tam'si's *Nnikon Nniku* – M. N'Debeka's *Le Président* (*The President*, 1982), which has, however, had considerable success because of its direct popular appeal. It is **S. Bemba**, however, who has made the stronger cumulative impact, with five plays to date, all of which maintain a high degree of playability.   CW

See: M. Banham with C. Wake, *African Theatre Today*, London, 1976; R. Cornevin, *Le Théâtre en Afrique Noire et à Madagascar*, Paris, 1970.

Congreve, William
(1670–1729) English playwright. Born in Yorkshire, he was brought up in

Ireland and went to Trinity College, Dublin. In 1689 he wrote his first play *The Old Bachelor* before moving to London, ostensibly to study law. Through meeting **Thomas Southerne** he became known to **Dryden** and his circle. His novel *Incognita* was published in 1692. Southerne and Dryden helped Congreve revise *The Old Bachelor* which was a brilliant success when it was performed in 1693. Using the materials of earlier Restoration comedies, the play is a witty examination of courtship and marriage with the rake seen as an odd anachronism. Congreve's next play, *The Double-Dealer* (1694), published with a prefatory poem of high praise by Dryden, was less successful. Its claustrophobic atmosphere and contrast of good with evil rather than wit with folly was too different from the norm to be understood. When **Betterton**'s group split from the United Company, they opened their new theatre with Congreve's *Love for Love* (1695). Its blend of wit and generosity, with the rake in retreat for much of the play as his mistress seems about to marry his father, was immediately triumphant. Congreve's only tragedy, *The Mourning Bride*, much admired by **Dr Johnson**, was performed in 1697; its rhetoric is restrained and its action less exotically improbable than most Restoration tragedies. When **Jeremy Collier** launched the attack on the immorality of the stage Congreve was one of the dramatists singled out for especial attention: Congreve's reply, his *Amendments of Mr Collier's False and Imperfect Citations* (1698), does not show him at his wittiest for all its care in defending his practice. His last comedy, *The Way of the World* (1700), was not the success he had expected. It is the greatest of all Restoration comedies, exploring the battle for wealth and fortune as well as the search for security and constancy in courtship. Mirabell and Millament are both witty and serious in facing the difficulty in proving their love. His libretto *The Judgement of Paris* was set in 1701 but apart from collaborating with **Vanbrugh** and William Walsh on a **Molière** adaptation, *Squire Trelooby*, in 1704, Congreve did not write for the stage again. He briefly joined Vanbrugh in the management of the new Queen's Theatre in the Haymarket in 1704 but gave it up when he gained the sinecure of commissioner for wines. Failing eyesight did not prevent his attending meetings of the Kit-Kat Club and his *Works* were elegantly published in 1710. Financially secure when made Secretary for Jamaica in 1714, his long affair with the Duchess of Marlborough led to their daughter receiving his fortune in the form of a necklace after his death. In its brilliant wit and taut control his comic style marks the greatest achievement of its age.   PH

Connelly, Marc (Marcus Cook) (1890–1980)

American playwright, actor, producer, and director. Connelly first became known on the Broadway scene as a collaborator of **George S. Kaufman** on such plays as *Dulcy* (1921) and *Beggar on Horseback* (1924), the latter being the most successful of their work together. His greatest contribution as a playwright came with *The Green Pastures* (1930), a Pulitzer Prize adaptation of Roark Bradford's dialect stories. By holding the stage for 640 performances, this funny, touching, and naturally truthful work showed America that a play with an all-Negro cast could be good box office. Connelly's Broadway acting credits include the Stage Manager in a

1944 production of *Our Town* and Professor Osman in *Tall Story* (1959), a role he repeated for the motion picture. As a producer/director, his greatest success was *Having Wonderful Time* (1937).   LDC

Conquest English theatrical family, originally named Oliver. **Benjamin Oliver** (Conquest) (1804–72), a low comedian famous for his rendition of 'Billie Barlow', married the dancer Clarissa Ann Bennett (1803–67). He managed the Garrick Theatre in Whitechapel, from 1830 until 1946 when it burned down, and then took over the Grecian Theatre (1851–72), where he initiated a series of pantomimes featuring his son **George Augustus Oliver** Conquest (1837–1901). George was the most spectacular acrobatic performer of his day, excelling in grotesque characters, strenuous leaps and aerial combats; his best parts were *Spitz-Spitze the Spider Crab* (1875) and the Monkey in *Grim Goblin* (1876). He managed the Grecian, 1872–78, and then the Surrey Theatre, 1881–1901, specializing in pantomime and full-blooded melodrama, written in collaboration with Paul Merritt and Henry Pettitt. His biggest melodramatic successes were *Mankind* (1881) and *For Ever* (1882) in which he played the manmonkey Zacky Pastrana. His son **George Benjamin** (1858–1926) rose from acrobatics to roles as giants and carried on at the Surrey till 1904. His brothers were outstanding animal impersonators: **Fred** (1871–1941) excelled as the Goose in *Mother Goose*, while **Arthur** (1875–1945), after a successful career at **Drury Lane** and **Covent Garden**, appeared as Daphne the Chimpanzee on the music-halls in a double-act with his daughter Elizabeth.   LS

Conrad, Robert T[aylor] (1810–58) American playwright. A lawyer, judge, editor, politician and dilettante in the theatre, Conrad wrote at least three plays. Neither *Conrad of Naples* (1832), in which **James Wallack** acted the lead part, nor *The Heretic* (n.d.) has survived. Conrad revised *Jack Cade* (1835) for **Edwin Forrest** who produced it first in 1841 and kept it in his repertory for years. Variously called *Aylmere; or The Kentish Rebellion, Aylmere; or The Bond Man of Kent* or simply *Jack Cade*, it dramatizes the life of a villein named Cade who incites an insurrection to abolish the institution of villeinage. The theme of individual freedom was popular in Jacksonian America and added to Forrest's considerable prestige in the theatre. Conrad's later years were spent as a judge and an elected mayor of Philadelphia.   WJM

Contat, Louise (1760–1813) French actress, made her debut in 1776, and created the role of Suzanne in *The Marriage of Figaro* (1784). A particularly fine comic actress, she excelled in the plays of **Marivaux**, and was responsible for bringing *Les Fausses Confidences* into the **Comédie-Française** repertoire. A tendency to stoutness made her gravitate towards roles of mothers and duennas. An ardent royalist (one of her lovers was the Comte d'Artois), she belonged to the anti-**Talma** faction of the Comédie-Française, theatened to retire, and only reappeared (in *Les Victimes Cloitrées* (*The Victims of the Cloister*) 1793) after he had departed. She was one of the members of the troupe condemned to death in 1793, and she reappeared with the reunited troupe in 1798. Bonaparte disliked her for her royalist association and *ancien régime* style, but this also accounted for her popularity. JMCC

Cook, Barbara (1927–) American singer and actress. Possessing one of the finest soprano voices ever heard on the American musical stage, Cook made her Broadway debut in *Flahooley* (1954). She received critical acclaim for her performance as Cunegond in *Candide* (1956), and a Tony Award for her Marian Paroo in *The Music Man* (1957). Cook appeared in *The Gay Life* (1961), *She Loves Me* (1963), and *The Grass Harp* (1971). She also starred in major revivals of *Oklahoma!*, *Carousel*, *The King and I*, and *Show Boat*. In 1965 Cook replaced Sandy Dennis in the comedy *Any Wednesday*, and thereafter appeared in straight plays as well as musicals. She retired from the stage in the early 1970s and has since confined her appearances to concert halls and nightclubs. In addition to a singing voice of great range and expressiveness, Cook brought to her roles a winning personality and a deft touch for comedy. MK

Cook, Michael (1933–) English-born Canadian playwright. He spent twelve years in the British Army where he wrote, directed and acted in troop entertainments. After teacher training in drama at Nottingham University he emigrated to Canada and settled in Newfoundland where he was associated with Memorial University. He became deeply involved in local theatre and started writing radio plays. *Colour the Flesh the Colour of Dust* (1972), his first stage play, is a Brechtian examination of the political turmoil in Newfoundland in 1762 as it went from a British to a French to a British colony. *Head, Bones and Soundbone Dance* (1973) is a powerful folk play which captures both the colourful Newfoundland speech and the fatalistic attitudes engendered by the island's harsh life. *The Gayden Chronicles* (1979), commissioned by Festival Lennoxville, tells the story of a British Navy rebel who was hanged in St John's in 1812. Cook's plays are passionate and unsubtle attacks on the emotions that 'celebrate the elemental and instinctive', particularly as found in indigenous cultures. JA

Cooke, George Frederick (1756–1812) One of the first actors to achieve fame in England and America, Cooke was probably born in Berwick-on-Tweed rather than Westminster, as he claimed, or Dublin as his contemporaries supposed. He made his debut in 1773 in a Lincoln-based provincial company and remained a travelling actor for over 25 years. Cooke was most admired in roles that gave scope for satanic humour. The finest was Richard III, which he played regularly from 1774 until his death, but he was also notable as Shylock, Iago and, more controversially, as Macbeth, to all of which he brought a vivid relish for his own villainy. There were some critics who recognized in him a comic spirit, irreverently deployed in tragedy and better suited to such roles as Sir Pertinax MacSycophant and Sir Archy MacSarcasm, created for himself by the actor-playwright **Charles Macklin**. Precipitated later into London fame, Cooke was the star of **Covent Garden** from 1800–3, rival of **John Philip Kemble** at **Drury Lane**, but Kemble's move to Covent Garden in 1803 marked the beginning of a

serious decline in Cooke's health and fortunes. He drank prodigiously, coarsening a voice and style that were already rough in contrast to the stately Kemble. At least five times married and constantly in debt, Cooke broke his Covent Garden contract by sailing secretly for New York. Within two years, he had acted and drunk himself to death. His last recorded performance – as Sir Giles Overreach in **Massinger**'s *A New Way to Pay Old Debts* – took place in Providence in July 1812, two months before his death in New York. In 1820, **Edmund Kean** had his remains reinterred and erected a memorial over them. PT

Cooke, Thomas Potter (1786–1864) English actor, uniquely celebrated as a hero of nautical melodrama, an illusion aided by the fact that he had served in the Royal Navy during his teens. His most famous roles were Long Tom Coffin in **Fitzball**'s *The Pilot* (1825), William in **Jerrold**'s *Black-Eyed Susan* (1829) and Harry Hallyard in J. T. Haines's *My Poll and My Partner Joe* (1835). Cooke also provided the nautical interest in **Buckstone**'s domestic melodrama, *Luke the Labourer* (1826). His natural successor was **William Terriss**. PT

Cooper, Giles (1918–66) British playwright. Although best-known in his lifetime as a prolific adapter for television, notably the *Maigret* series for which he won a Writer of the Year award in 1961, he produced 70 original plays for radio, television and theatre. He had some critical success with the stage play *Everything in the Garden* (1962) and created one of the most spectacular television plays of its time, *The Other Man*, an alternative history of Anglo-Nazi relations, in 1964. His best work, however, was in radio, a medium whose extreme flexibility suited his acerbic mixture of the absurd and the naturalistic. Typically, the Cooper hero inhabits a world without meaning; he may be a small cog in an industrial machine of crushing pointlessness, or, often, a displaced soldier in a world with no room for his values. Cooper charted the decline of the British Empire in the post-war years with sardonic verve tinged with compassion; it symbolized for him the inability of the human race to make sense of itself. Despite their nihilism, his plays were charged with economical wit. Pushing out radio's technical frontiers, Cooper pioneered electronic sound effects to reinforce the cartoon-like nature of some of his stories; he moved adroitly between his characters' inner and outer lives, between dream and reality. Six of his radio plays were published by the BBC in 1966, a rare tribute to a single radio author. He also received distinctions for his radio work from Czechoslovakia and West Germany. FG

Cooper, Thomas Abthorpe (1776–1849) British-born American actor and manager who became the first star of the American stage and initiated the practice of travelling from one company to another performing only prominent roles. While in his teens Cooper performed in Edinburgh and at various provincial theatres; his London debut was as Hamlet in 1795. In 1796, unhappy with his English acceptance, he went to the **Chestnut Street Theatre** in Philadelphia. After the settlement of an alleged breach of articles with the Philadelphia management, he joined **Dunlap** at the **Park Street** in New York in 1801; from 1806 until 1815 he was in management at the Park. With **Stephen**

Price as his partner he played the eastern circuit, excelling in heroic characters in poetic drama, such as Pierre in *Venice Preserv'd*. His popularity continued into the 1820s but by 1830 it was waning and by 1835 'he had sadly become the seeker instead of the sought after'. DBW

Copeau, Jacques (1879–1949) French actor, director, critic, essayist and playwright. Generally considered to be the major influence on the development of French theatre since the First World War, Copeau was a tormented genius, never satisfied with what he achieved. He was a co-founder (with **Gide** and Schlumberger) of the *Nouvelle Revue Française*, which published art and theatre-criticism, until in 1913 he founded his own theatre company in the **Vieux-Colombier** on the then unfashionable Paris left bank. From here he planned to launch a renewal of theatre art, rejecting both naturalism and spectacular decorativism in favour of a concentration on the actor and a bare stage. His repertoire consisted mainly of **Shakespeare** and the French classics though he attempted to encourage new young playwrights. Associated with the theatre was a school in which an all-round training was given, not concentrating merely on theatre skills. Interrupted by the outbreak of war, Copeau was asked by Clémenceau to reconvene his company and perform in New York (Garrick Theatre 1917–19). They returned to Paris in 1920 and performed on a stage remodelled by **Jouvet** to achieve something close to an Elizabethan playing space. In 1924 a religious crisis led to Copeau's conversion and withdrawal, to the Burgundian village of Pernand-Vergelesses, accompanied by a few students. From 1925–9 he and the 'Copiaus' continued their quest, as much spiritual as theatrical, for artistic perfection. When Copeau again withdrew, some of his disciples formed the **Compagnie des Quinze**. His subsequent work consisted of isolated productions, especially of religious works in the open air, occasional productions, at the **Comédie-Française**, plus a brief spell as its director (1940–1), the writing of plays and of an influential essay *Le Théâtre Populaire* (1941) which articulated the theoretical foundation for the post-war **decentralization movement**. An extraordinary number of directors and actors (most notably **Dullin** and Jouvet) trained or worked with him at some stage, and underwent the influence of his charismatic personality. His search for a new performance style, truthful and direct, yet inventive and flexible, is still acknowledged as a source by contemporary groups such as the **Théâtre du Soleil**. DB

Coppin, George Selth (1819–1906) Australian actor–entrepreneur. A child performer and low comedian in England, Coppin arrived in Sydney with Maria Burroughs in 1843, and performed and managed theatres in several Australian colonies. By the mid-1850s he had four Melbourne theatres, including his famous 'Iron Pot', prefabricated in Manchester: based at the Melbourne Theatre Royal, he established a lucrative touring circuit for international performers. A member of the Victorian parliament and public figure for over 25 years, he retained his theatrical interests until the 1890s. MW

Copyright Copyright is one of those subjects which seem to become less comprehensible as you learn more about them. This is not because it is particularly 'difficult', but because of its inherent complexity (at least in its modern manifestations), and because of its tendency to mean different things at different times and in different countries and even in different minds. In terms of existing laws, for instance, copyright in the United Kingdom and in France shares many common characteristics but differs in important respects; and copyright in both countries differs significantly from copyright as a system of international protection. In historical terms, copyright (in different countries in different ways) is an evolving legal concept which has been and is being determined by the peculiarities of each particular nation's history, by the growing ease of international communications and by certain evolving practicalities (the invention of the gramophone, of television, of the photocopier; and so on). And in more general conceptual terms there is unresolvable debate as to whether copyright is properly seen primarily as a negative right (the right to stop), or as a monopoly, or as property, or as uniquely personal (dealing above all with the control of the creator over his creation). Copyright is fixed and final only in so far as it happens to be frozen, for the time being, within the laws of those countries which grant it recognition; and within certain international conventions. Beyond that, there is flux, the to-and-fro of debate as to the proper nature of copyright as an abstract entity which in turn affects debate as to the correct legislative balance to be struck between the interests of different parties.

To a large extent, the history of copyright begins when you want it to begin. Those who have been interested in dignifying the concept of author's rights with as long a genealogy as possible have gone back to classical Greek culture, to around the 6th century BC, when it is said that intellectual works began to be considered as coming from one hand rather than as the anonymous property of a whole society. Others have argued that 'true' copyright began in 1709, with the passing of the first national copyright act. However that may be, copyright has certainly been an important subject since the invention of movable type and has grown in importance, and continues to grow in importance, as the world finds more and better ways in which to multiply images, to record and to transmit and to receive. We are all copiers and receivers now – the large institutions with their rows of photocopiers and visual terminals; and the average individual, with an accessible photocopier at work or in the nearest library, a computer in his spare room, a video-cassette, a television and a radio in his living room, and a tape-recorder in his pocket. What is being devoured, insatiably, what is being copied, often illegally (knowingly or unknowingly, for private convenience or for great profit) – the plays, the novels, the films, the poems, the operas, the computer programmes – is the very lifeblood of our culture; and the main, almost the sole, legal safeguard of that lifeblood is the law of copyright.

Some general characteristics Fortunately, beneath the complexity and beyond the debate there are some fairly simple points which can be made about the nature of copyright which would fit in with the general tenor of the majority of national copyright laws.

Definition As a working definition, we can say that copyright is ownership of, and right of control over, all possible ways of reproducing a work; and that a work in this context is an object which is the product of an original creative act (by one or more people) and which is in a form which makes it subject to one or other means of copying. In particular (but by no means exclusively) copyright protection is given to literary works, dramatic works, musical works, artistic works (paintings, drawings, photographs, and so on), sound recordings, films, television and sound broadcasts, and various manifestations of the new technology.

Qualifications for protection There are two. First, that the work is capable of being 'in copyright' – that is to say that it was not in any event created or published at such a time in the past as to put it outside the period of protection offered by the law of the country in question. Second, that the work is 'original', which in the copyright world does not mean so much being novel in subject matter as being the product of some skill and labour in composition other than the skill and labour involved in mere copying. In the main, the emphasis here is on expression rather than content. The copyright in an article expressing a new philosophical theory, for example, is in its unique sequence of words rather than in the theory as such. You do not infringe copyright in paraphrasing this theory and publishing your paraphrase (although you may be guilty of plagiarism). Indeed, your paraphrase secures its own copyright protection as another sequence of words. A common, but oversimple, catchphrase in this context is 'copyright is in words and not ideas'. This is certainly true in the example that has just been given, and in the case of any single 'idea'. But if it were generally true, then to translate an English novel into French, or to turn it into a play, would not be an infringement of copyright. It is a matter of degree, and at one extreme a particularly distinctive sequence of events in a play, or whole collection of philosophical ideas, can be regarded as a substantial part of a work, and to express them, or a significant part of them, in other words, or with other characters, or in another medium, will be to infringe copyright.

Ownership The creator of a work is normally the copyright owner, and no special act (e.g. registration) is required in order to establish ownership. The main exceptions are where the creator has already assigned copyright to another party, via a contract entered into before the work was begun, or at least before it was finished, or where the act of creation was a legitimate part of the creator's role under a contract of employment (broadly speaking, what United States copyright legislation refers to as a 'work made for hire').

Duration of copyright In the main, copyright is finite: there comes a time when a work goes out of copyright and falls into the public domain. The term of copyright varies widely from country to country – from 20 years after first publication at one extreme to 80 years after the death of the author at the other. That copyright should be finite has not been the result of a logical and timeless sequence of thought, but it is probably true that all countries with a copyright legislation (no matter the term of protection they happen to offer) would now offer a similar justification, and that this would be along the lines that it is right for the author to control the use of his work during his lifetime and that his immediate dependants or successors should also have some measure of control of it, or at least some financial reward from it, but that it seems equally right that at some stage after his death the work should go out of copyright – for if copyright is still an issue at this stage, if the work is still in print, if the play is still being performed, then it must be assumed that the work has the makings of some kind of classic, is a candidate for permanent membership of a nation's culture, and should, in some sense, belong to everybody.

Transfer of rights 'Copyright' is really a bundle of rights, and the bundle grows as we invent more means of reproduction and dissemination. The copyright in an original play, for example, will contain the performing right, the right to publish in the original language, the right to translate and to perform and publish that translation, the right to quote, the right to turn into a film, and so on. The playwright is the original owner of all these rights by virtue of authorship; and in the normal run of events they are leased out on an exclusive basis, and possibly for a fixed period of time. An 'assignment of copyright', on the other hand, is the granting of the complete copyright to another: it is a transfer of ownership.

Dramatic copyright It is a surprising fact that the United Kingdom did not establish a performing right in a play (as distinct from a right as copy words on paper) until 1833. The moving force was **Bulwer-Lytton**, whose eloquence in Parliament led to a Committee of Inquiry into the laws affecting dramatic literature and the condition of the drama.

'The commonest invention in calico, a new pattern in the most trumpery article of dress, a new bit to our bridles, a new wheel to our carriages, may make the fortune of the inventor; but the intellectual invention of the finest drama in the world may not relieve by a groat the poverty of the inventor. The instant an author publishes a play, any manager may seize it, mangle it, act it, without the consent of the author, and without giving him one sixpence of remuneration.' Thus Bulwer-Lytton to the House of Commons. In addition to a dramatic copyright, Lytton urged the abolition of dramatic censorship (which 'invested the Lord Chamberlain with a power more absolute than that of the monarch himself') and the abolition of the patented theatres. In the event, he scored a remarkable two out of three (the Lord Chamberlain retaining his power, of course, for 135 years more), and the resultant Dramatic Copyright Act of 1833 is commonly known as Bulwer-Lytton's Act.

Other countries have their different histories; enlightenment came very early to some and very late to others. Roman law appears to have identified a performance right, for example, and playwrights sold this right to the organizers of games, whilst in pre-revolutionary France the monopoly of the **Comédie-Française** led to the poor author having neither rights nor payment . . .

Nowadays, the copyright laws of all countries contain specific protection for drama, and almost invariably a distinction is drawn between the right of publication and the right of performance. That much is straightforward. The differences and complexities arise when one starts to try to find out what each country means by 'performance', whether it takes some types of performance out of the realm of copyright, and what performance-protection it gives to works other than straightforward plays (to dance or mime, for example). We may take the case of the fairly recent United States Copyright Act as an example of the necessary distinctions and definitions. To 'perform' a work is 'to recite, render, play, dance or act it, either directly or by means of any device or process or, in the case of a motion picture or other audiovisual work, to show its images in any sequence or to make the sounds accompanying it audible'. The actual performing right is 'in the case of literary, musical, dramatic, and choreographic works, pantomimes, and motion pictures and other audiovisual works, to perform the copyrighted work publicly'. Some of the exceptions (that is, the cases where performance may take place without the copyright holder's permission) are 'performance . . . by instructors or pupils in the course of face-to-face teaching activities', performance as 'a regular part of the systematic instructional activities of a governmental body or a nonprofit educational institution', 'in the course of services at a place of worship', performances specifically for the blind or handicapped, and so on. Each country's laws, to a greater or lesser extent, will attempt to cover the same ground – what is performance? what is protected? under what circumstances is it not protected?; but, inevitably, there will be many variations on this complicated theme. In most countries, for example, copyright cannot be given to a work that is not fixed – in writing, symbols, or whatever. In Austria this is not so, and consequently the filming of an improvised pantomime would constitute an infringement of copyright. Again, and unlike nearly every other country, neither a Bulgarian nor a Mexican playwright needs to be approached for permission to perform once their plays have been published – although they must be paid (in Mexico, the tariff is fixed by the author's society). In Denmark, a performance is only a dramatic performance if the various characters ('if there be more than one') are distributed among several persons and the 'renditions of the characters are histrionic'; whilst in Finland and Hungary it is essential that at least two performers take part in the performance. The Italian copyright act states that dramatic works, although usually written, may be partly written and partly oral, or even wholly oral – improvised wholly or partly on stage, that is to say – and in all cases will be entitled to full copyright protection. In Spain, 'literary works in prose or verse, the recital of which has been announced on theatrical bills as forming an essential part of the performance' enjoy the same rights as an original one-act play. One could fill pages with these sorts of variation, and it will be seen that some of them are fairly substantial.

In all countries which recognize author's rights, the right to dramatize (a novel, short story, or whatever) is held by the author as part of his copyright. Some countries have it as a specific, named right; in others, it is presumed to be included in 'adaptation rights' – a general, catch-all phrase. Again, there are many variations from country to country, but the important point to stress is that the great majority assume that there is a point – however difficult to define – where a dramatization is so remote from the original novel (for example) as to take it outside the dramatization right

held by the novelist. In simple terms, we are talking here of a case where the dramatist is inspired by some dominant idea or theme in a novel, and ultimately produces a work which enshrines that idea but has its own set of characters and incidents. In any event, whether the work is a faithful dramatization of the novel or whether it is remote in everything but theme, the playwright will enjoy the dramatic copyright protection that is given to an 'original' play.

The need for flexibility *'An Act for the Encouragement of Learning, by vesting the Copies of printed Books in the Authors or Purchasers of such Copies, during the Times therein mentioned . . . WHEREAS Printers, Booksellers and other Persons have of late frequently taken the Liberty of printing, reprinting and publishing, or causing to be printed, reprinted or published, Books and other Writings, without the Consent of the Authors or Proprietors of such Books and Writings, to their very great Detriment, and too often to the Ruin of them and their Families . . .'* Thus the beginning of the United Kingdom Statute of Anne, 1709, the first national Copyright Act – a beginning which at once announces the two principal objects of copyright protection: 'the encouragement of learning' (we would now broaden this to 'creativity'), and the legitimate financial rewards of the creators and disseminators, the authors and the publishers, the composers and the record companies, the actors and the film studios. Clearly, these objects are not contradictory: in any society with a market economy, each flows from the other. Great differences can be achieved by different emphasis, however, as can be seen by contrasting French copyright law with that of the United Kingdom or United States. The latter laws stem essentially from a concern for the welfare of the entrepreneur rather than the creator. Their initial influence was the great powers given by the Crown, via the Star Chamber, to a designated group of printers, publishers and booksellers, the Stationers' Company: the 1709 Statute arose directly from the expiration in 1694 of the Act granting the Company a monopoly in the right to copy printed material. French copyright practice, on the other hand, stems from enactments dating from the French Revolution, and actually isolates the two objects of protection which we have talked about. There are the moral rights of the author (the right to prevent the author's work from being amended or distorted; the right to prevent others from claiming ownership) and there are the economic rights of the author; and the former are given more importance, in that they remain in the author's control after he has granted his economic rights (the *sine qua non* of publication). This distinction between moral and economic rights was taken up by the first major international copyright convention – the Berne Convention of 1866 – in one of its periodic revisions (Rome, 1928). Now, the British Government, in a White Paper which anticipates a new comprehensive Copyright Act to replace the Act of 1956, gives a firm indication that moral rights will be overtly recognized beyond the European mainland.

The Berne Convention was a necessary recognition that publishing had become international. National copyright laws were no longer enough: there had to be international agreements which respected the copyright of member nations. The problem with Berne was that it remained essentially European. In particular, it did not attract the USA, which moved very slowly in establishing copyright relations with Europe, but which established with its neighbours a pan-American copyright union, the Montevideo Convention. In the early 1950s, UNESCO set about devising a union that would be acceptable to the USA, and the outcome was the second great international copyright convention, the Universal Copyright Convention (UCC). It is via this convention that we have the familiar © symbol – the means by which member nations establish UCC protection.

In conclusion, all major countries (with the exception of the People's Republic of China) and most minor countries now possess a copyright law, and there are two international conventions which extend copyright protection to all member nations. The protective structure is in place. The problem is to hold it firm against the power and complexity and rapid development of the new technology, whilst at the same time allowing that technology its proper development and exploitation. It is a difficult balancing act, made all the more so because technical innovations proliferate almost daily, whilst the law remains constant for years, for decades. Laws change at snail's pace. New exploitations of the new technology are introduced, become commonplace, and are as like as not replaced by a second generation while copyright committees are still trying to come to terms with the last innovation but three. The copyright act in the United States became operative in 1978 after a gestation period of at least 40 years. The most recent major copyright act is the United Kingdom's Copyright, Designs and Patents Act, which was passed in 1988 after years of discussion and not a little procrastination. One could wish that it had come sooner, and that the legislatures, or more particularly the governments, of all countries would have the will to devise quicker and more flexible means of adapting and extending the protection which societies must give – incidentally and for good cultural and economic reasons to publishers and theatre companies and record manufacturers and the like – crucially and essentially and for the pleasure and enrichment of us all, to the writers and artists and composers of today and tomorrow.   CS

Coquelin, Constant (1841–1909) French actor. Coquelin's name is associated with Cyrano de Bergerac (1897), which he played over 400 times at the Porte-Saint-Martin. Essentially a comic actor he made his debut at the **Comédie-Française** in **Molière**'s Dépit Amoureux in 1860, but soon showed that his talents could be put to as good use in the modern as in the classical repertoire. One of his greatest successes was as Figaro. In 1886 he broke his career at the Comédie-Française to tour in Europe and America. He returned in 1889 for a brief period, which included the stormy reception of **Sardou**'s Thermidor, which had to be taken off after two nights in 1891 and replaced by a production of The Taming of the Shrew. The next year he joined **Sarah Bernhardt** at the Renaissance for Sardou's Gismonda. Their association was short, as the personalities of both were too strong to work together. The rest of his career was spent on the Boulevard. His last role was to have been **Rostand**'s Chantecler, but he died while studying it. His great parts included Tartuffe and Don César de Bazan in Ruy Blas (1879). An artist very

aware of his profession, Coquelin wrote an important manual of acting in 1880, in which he emphasizes the need for authenticity in performance and stresses that the actor must always be in control of his means and leave nothing to chance. For him the voice was fundamental. In his last years he founded a retirement home for old actors at Pont-aux-Dames, and died there himself. His brother Ernest (1848–1909), generally known as Coquelin 'cadet', or junior, was also an actor and tended to specialize in broader comic parts.   JMCC

Corneille, Pierre (1606–84) French dramatist and poet, one of the dominant figures in the evolution of 17th-century neoclassical drama. In the course of a long association with the Parisian theatres he produced over 30 plays and proved equally successful in tragedy and comedy. His first play Mélite, written while he was practising law in his native Rouen, was taken up by an itinerant company under Le Noir and **Montdory** and well received when they presented it in Paris in 1629. After an unfortunate foray into tragicomedy with Clitandre (1631) he returned to favour with a string of four comedies set in contemporary Paris, La Veuve (The Widow, 1631/2), La Galerie du Palais (The Palace Gallery, 1632), La Suivante (The Maidservant, 1633) and La Place Royale (1633), all performed by Montdory's company. Their success brought him to Paris, where his first tragedy Médée (1635), possibly inspired by **Mairet**'s regular tragedy Sophonisbe, was produced at the **Marais**, as was his most original, 'theatrical' comedy, L'Illusion Comique (The Theatrical Illusion, 1636). He had also become one of the group of five authors employed by **Richelieu** to write plays under his direction, but after a disagreement with the Cardinal over some point of plotting the engagement was terminated and he returned to Rouen, where he wrote his most celebrated play Le Cid, derived from his reading of Spanish literature. The triumph of this tragicomedy at the Marais early in 1637 signalled a resurgence in French drama, but it provoked the enmity of fellow writers, notably Mairet and **Scudéry**, and a polemical exchange of pamphlets for and against the play, the 'Querelle du Cid', ensued. In its wake Corneille wrote nothing for several years, but his series of 'Roman' plays, Horace (1640), Cinna (1641), Polyeucte (1642) and La Mort de Pompée (The Death of Pompey, 1643), followed by Rodogune, Théodore (both 1645) and Héraclius (1646), established him as the foremost tragedian of his day and led to his election to the Académie-Française in 1647. All were premiered at the Marais, where the leading roles were played by **Floridor**, who also appeared alongside **Jodelet** in Corneille's best comedy, Le Menteur (The Liar, 1643) and its sequel La Suite du Menteur (1644).

The remainder of his career was attended by rather mixed fortunes. An inferior 'heroic comedy', Don Sanche d'Aragon (1649), and a 'machine-play', Andromède (1650), designed to exploit **Torelli**'s new mechanical installations at the **Petit-Bourbon**, were followed by one of his finest tragedies, Nicomède (1651), but the failure of Pertharite in the following year induced him to abandon the stage and devote himself to verse and later to the preparation of a complete edition of his plays containing commentaries on each and a considered exposition of his dramatic theory, the three Discours sur l'art dramatique (1660). He resumed with further tragedies for the **Hôtel de Bourgogne** and the Marais, *Oedipe* (1659), *Sertorius* (1662), *Sophonisbe* (1663), *Othon* (1664), *Agésilas* (1666), while another machine-play *La Toison d'Or* (*The Golden Fleece*) was produced in honour of the king's marriage in 1660 and later re-staged at the Marais. Having finally settled in Paris in 1663 the veteran dramatist was now in a good position to witness the rise of a formidable young rival in **Racine**. He collaborated to good effect with **Molière** and **Quinault** on *Psyché*, a 'tragedie-ballet' presented at the Tuileries in 1671, but the two tragedies he entrusted to Molière's company at the **Palais-Royal**, *Attila* (1667) and *Tite et Bérénice* (1670), were both eclipsed by concurrent successes of Racine and Corneille's last two plays, *Pulchérie* (1672) and *Suréna* (1647), fared little better. Comparison with Racine is perhaps inevitable, if essentially unprofitable. As tragedians, the two evoke contrary responses in the spectator, Corneille's characters impressing us as emblems of nobility and heroic virtue and inspiring admiration above all else, Racine's as portraits of emotionally and psychologically divided individuals who arouse our appalled compassion. Not surprisingly, the latter's much smaller *oeuvre* is still largely familiar whereas Corneille holds his place in the modern repertoire with only a handful of tragedies and even fewer comedies. DR

Corneille (de l'Isle), Thomas (1625–1709) French dramatist, younger brother of the above, with whom he remained on close terms throughout his life. His first comedies were produced when he was in his early 20s and over the next 30 years he turned his hand with equal facility to a variety of genres, not least opera with librettos for **Lully**. Derivative but skilfully contrived, his plays followed the fashions of the day and proved consistently popular with audiences. In particular his tragedy *Timocrate* was a triumph at the **Marais** in 1656 and he scored further successes with two other tragedies, *Ariane* (1672) and *Le Comte d'Essex* (*The Earl of Essex*, 1678), a comedy for **Jodelet** entitled *Le Geôlier de Soi-même, ou Jodelet Prince* (*Jailer to Oneself, or Jodelet Prince*, 1655) and the machine-play *La Devineresse* (*The Fortune-Teller*, 1679). In 1681 he became co-editor of the *Mercure Galant* and in 1684 was elected to the Académie-Française in succession to his brother. DR

Cornell, Katharine (1893–1974) American actress. Called 'The First Lady of the Theatre' by **Alexander Woollcott**, Cornell, with **Helen Hayes** and **Lynn Fontanne**, was the reigning actress on the Broadway stage during the second quarter of the 20th century. An accomplished interpreter of romantic and character roles, she brought to her characterizations a resonant voice and a remarkably expressive face that captivated audiences; she could create the illusion that a memorable play was being witnessed when in fact the vehicle was weak. Her New York debut was with the **Washington Square Players** (1916); her London debut was as Jo in *Little Women* (1919). Prominence in the American theatre came with *A Bill of Divorcement* (1921). She is best remembered as Elizabeth Barrett in *The Barretts of Wimpole Street* (1931) and as **Shaw**'s *Candida* (1924). Other notable appearances included: *Romeo and Juliet* (1934), *The Doctor's Dilemma* (1941),

Antony and Cleopatra (1947), *The Dark is Light Enough* (1955), and *Dear Liar* (as Mrs Patrick Campbell) in 1959. In 1921 she maried **Guthrie McClintic**, who was responsible for most of her productions. On his death in 1961 she retired. DBW

Corrales de comedias (Sp. play-yards) The public theatres of Golden Age Spain were set in courtyards between houses. In Madrid in 1565 a charitable organization was allowed to sponsor plays in its own courtyards to raise funds for the maintenance of its hospital. Later, other courtyards were used and a second charity joined the scheme. The **commedia dell'arte** player **Ganassa** helped construct a covered stage in one of these in 1574. In 1579 the Corral de la Cruz was founded, and in 1582 the Corral del Príncipe, these two remaining as the two city theatres of Madrid until well into the 18th century. *Corrales* were also set up in other cities in the same way.

The *corral* was a courtyard with a stage at one end, projecting forward into the yard. Most of the theatre apart from the stage was exposed to the weather, though a cloth could be stretched across to provide shade. There were no seats in the pit (*patio*), but rows of benches (*gradas*) lined the sides, and above these boxes (*aposentos*) were formed from the rooms in the houses on each side which had windows giving onto the yard. The king had his own box, the others being rented by nobles. Entry, which was segregated by sex, was at the rear, as was the refreshment stall (*frutería* or *alojería*). Above this was a section for lower-class women (*cazuela*). Only in the expensive boxes were the sexes allowed to mix. A separate section for clergy (*tertulia*) was at the back at second-floor level.

The stage had no proscenium arch or curtain at the front, though a curtain behind separated dressing-rooms and an alcove for 'discoveries'. The gallery or balcony at first-floor level could also be used as the plot required.

All performances were in the afternoon, and had to be over before dusk. Fees were charged for admission and again to occupy a seat. The entertainment followed a set pattern. First would be music and songs, then the **loa** or prologue, perhaps ending with a dance. The **comedia** would then follow, with a brief *entremés* or *sainete* between the acts. Finally a lively *fin de fiesta* would end with a dance. Thus the entertainment was continuous but varied, perhaps more like a pantomime than a modern play performance.

The companies of actors for each *corral* were assembled in Lent ready to start at Easter. They were led by an actor–manager, who bought new plays outright from authors, or adapted old ones. Each company had 12 to 14 players. From 1587, as a result of the *commedia dell'arte* visits, women were allowed to appear on stage and boys forbidden to take women's roles.

The *corrales* declined from the middle of the 17th century as the more modern Coliseo theatre superseded them. CL

Corrie, Joe (1894–1968) Scottish dramatist. A miner, who wrote for the Scottish Community Drama Association and his own amateur group, the Bowhill Village Players, that toured the mining towns in Southern Scotland and (in 1929–30) Northern England. His first plays *The Shillin'-a-Week Man* and *The Poacher* were written for performance in the 1926 General Strike, but he rejected the more experimental techniques of agit-prop theatre, calling for 'old technique' to be applied to working-class Marxist themes. The majority of his plays were short political pieces depicting everyday scenes of mining and rural life in Scottish dialect, some of which gained an international reputation being translated into Russian, German and French, but he also completed two full length historical works – a drama on Robert Burns and *Master of Men* (1944).   CI

Cort Theatre 148 West 48th St, New York City [Architect: Edward B. Corey]. Built and named for John Cort, a West Coast producer, the new house was launched in 1912 with a hit production, Hartley Manners's *Peg o' My Heart*, which made a star of **Laurette Taylor**. With about 1,000 seats, it is best suited for comedies and realistic plays and has housed a series of long-running hits. Two Pulitzer Prize-winning plays premiered at the theatre: *The Shrike* (1951) and *The Diary of Anne Frank* (1955). From 1969 to 1972, it was turned into a television studio, but reverted to legitimate status thereafter. Since 1927, it has been a **Shubert** theatre.   MCH

Corvan, Ned (1830–65) English Tyneside comedian and song-writer. He joined **Billy Purvis**'s company in his late teens, played fiddle in his band, took bit-parts, and performed comic-songs, including his own compositions, between the scenes. Finding himself increasingly successful in this line, notably with the genially anti-militaristic 'He Wad be a Noodle', he left Billy's employ in 1850 to join the Olympic concert-hall, Newcastle, as a singer-composer. A great hit with his songs and patter on local issues such as 'The Toon Improvement Bill' ('But still thor's folks 'boot here that smells/The cash buik wiv its flaw') and the price of coal ('They ken hoo te swindle poor folks'), he went freelance, playing the growing number of north-east music-halls. After a short-lived and costly attempt to set himself up in business – as publican, impresario and leading artist at Corvan's Music Hall, South Shields – he went back to touring until his death from tuberculosis. A versatile performer, who incorporated impromptu cartooning into his act alongside self-accompanied song and character monologue, he stuck strictly to his north-eastern base. His work has a concrete precision of reference that is unusual on the British variety stage, as well as an anarchic imagination that looks forward to **Dan Leno**.   AEG

Cossa, Roberto (1934–) Argentine playwright and journalist, admirer of Florencio Sánchez, **Anton Chekhov**, and **Arthur Miller**. His first play, *Nuestro fin de semana* (*Our Weekend*, 1964), revealed him to be a major force in Argentine theatre, at the head of the so-called 'new realistic generation'. After several plays in the 1960s, he wrote, in collaboration with **Germán Rozenmacher**, **Carlos Somigliana** and **Ricardo Talesnik**, *El avión negro* (*The Black Airplane*, 1970), a collage of scenes dealing with the myth regarding Perón's possible return to Argentina. *La nona* (*The Grandmother*, 1977), the story of a voracious nonagenarian who metaphorically consumes and destroys, is perhaps the best-known play outside of Argentina. *Los compadritos* (*The Bullies*) describes a particular style of

urban strong man, and is based on the sinking of a German U-Boat off the coast of Uruguay at the beginning of the Second World War.   GW

Costa Rica Costa Rica is an anomaly within the Central American republics. With a high literacy rate, a record of stable democratic government, and no military force, Costa Rica has been a model imitated all too rarely. After the division of the United Provinces in 1838, this small country developed good working relationships between principal families and working class citizens. The coffee and sugar industries flourished, and the growth of the banana industry in the latter part of the 19th century was consolidated into United Fruit, led by railroad-tycoon Minor Keith. Petroleum shortages and inflationary trends in the 1970s and 1980s escalated the economic crises in Costa Rica, but the country remains decidedly stable in a geographic area characterized by political violence, socio-economic upheaval and class struggle.

The theatre before the 20th century has few national traits. Records exist regarding performances in the colonial capital of Cartago as early as 1722, but the few foreign troupes that presented plays did not provide sufficient impetus to create national theatre consciousness. Theatre houses were constructed by 1837 in San José, first in the Plaza Principal. Later constructions included the Teatro Mora, renamed the Teatro Municipal in 1861. The Costa Rican National Theatre, inaugurated in 1897 and renovated in 1974, bears testimony to cultural processes in this small democracy. Throughout the 19th century visiting theatre troupes, primarily from Spain, brought **Zorrilla** plays and other productions to enhance the scant activity being staged locally.

20th century In the 20th century the Costa Rican theatre began to assume national characteristics. The first national text is considered to be *Magdalena* by Ricardo Fernández Guardia (1867–1950), a costumbristic play of the Costa Rican coffee families in which the central theme is a marriage of convenience that exacerbates social class distinctions. A re-staging of this play by the National Theatre Company in 1983 affirmed the importance of value systems at the turn of the century. Emilio Pacheco Cooper also wrote plays about local customs, such as *Venganza de un poeta* (*A Poet's Vengeance*, 1902), a lyrical play about intellectual pur-

The National Theatre, San José, Costa Rica.

suits which won the author a laurel wreath. Raúl Salazar Alvárez's *San José en camisa* (*San José in Nightshirt*) and *El hombre que buscaba el verdadero amor* (*The Man who Sought True Love*) were major successes; the latter pointed up the problem of local women who marry foreigners with different expectations that such unions produce. The visit of Díaz de Mendoza and his company in 1912 stimulated local actors and writers such as Eduardo Calsamiglia (?–1918), who wrote a dozen plays, all in verse. José Fabio Garnier (1884–1956) studied in Italy and wrote plays in an Italian Renaissance style, notably *Boccacesca* (1910) inspired by the *Decameron*. During the period between the two World Wars, Costa Rica continued to be a regular stopping place for foreign theatre companies. Héctor Alfredo Castro Fernández (1889–1966), who used the pen name 'Marizancene', revealed a strong French influence and in fact often wrote his plays in French for later translation.

Major playwrights of recent years include the more traditional urban middle class theatre of **Alberto Cañas** (b. 1920) whose play, *Ni mi casa es ya mi casa* (*My House is No Longer My Home*, 1982), illustrated the devastating effects of inflation/recession in the modern world. Cañas is interested in folklore and popular myths. **Daniel Gallegos** (b. 1930), perhaps Costa Rica's most important playwright, wrote cosmopolitan theatre with more universal tendencies, as seen in *La colina* (*The Hill*, 1968), a penetrating play that raised important religious and metaphysical questions about the death of God. **Samuel Rovinski** (b. 1932), a more committed playwright in socio-political terms, wrote several plays that demand greater accountability of those in positions of authority. Historical theatre became an important form for a younger generation of writers that included Fernando Cerdas and Miguel Rojas, and Víctor Valdelomar dealt with drugs and violence in a metropolitan setting in *Como semilla e' coyol* (*Like Seed and Fruit*, 1982).

The congenial climate of Costa Rica causes foreigners to assimilate easily, and the country has extrapolated to good advantage the experience and talent of outsiders while developing a national theatre. Plays from London, New York, Paris, Mexico and Buenos Aires are commonly staged, and a series of annual theatre festivals and showcases has helped to disseminate theatre in San José. A popular theatre movement has gained momentum; the Grupo Tierra Negra which opened in 1973 with a *creación colectiva* called *La invasión* (*The Invasion*) celebrated its tenth anniversary with Fabián Dobles's *El barrilete* (*The Cylinder*), a Revolutionary play about a man who wanted to fly. A puppet theatre, the Moderno Teatro de Muñecos, was established by Juan Enrique Acuña in 1968. Since 1979, *Escena*, a major theatre journal, reports on theatrical activities and events in the country. For its size and population, Costa Rica has an active and vital theatre movement. GW

> See: Cajiao Salas and A. Herzfeld, *El teatro de hoy en Costa Rica; perspectiva crítica y antología*, San José, 1973; G. Fernández, *Los caminos del teatro en Costa Rica*, San José, 1977; L. Garrido, *La imagen teatral*, San José, 1972.

Costantini (in France, Constantini) Family of Italian actors. The earliest noticed Costantino (c. 1634–c. 1696) played first **zanni** under the name Gradellino and appeared in Paris from 1687. His son Angelo (c. 1654–1729) alternated Arlecchino with **Dominique Biancolelli**, but Dominique's death concentrated his powers on the role of Mezzetino, his red-and-white striped costume a contrast to the green and white livery of Brighella. He performed it in Paris (1683–97) and Dresden, where he was a successful rival in love to Duke August the Strong, who clapped him in prison for twenty years. Back in Paris, he was only sporadically successful. He wrote a life of **Tiberio Fiorilli**. His brother Giovan Battista (d. 1726) played second *amoroso* under the name Cintio, succeeding Marc Antonio Romagnesi in Paris in 1688. LS

Costumbrista/costumbristic theatre Spanish term which refers to the phenomenon of capturing the customs, style, characters and local colour of a particular area or region. Particularly strong in Spain in the early 19th century, it became characteristic of theatre in Spanish America in later periods. GW

Costume (European theatre) Theatre may have originated in the rituals of sympathetic magic. For this to involve the whole community a disguise is essential.

As drama broke away from this kind of magic it remained of the utmost importance for the actor to assume the outward appearance of the hero he was impersonating. Sometimes, due either to the sublime quality of the character – a god or a hero – or to the size of the theatre in which facial expression was lost, the actor assumed a mask thus making the disguise even more impenetrable. At other times, when the theatre had assumed an intimate or domestic character, and the plays set out to mirror the life of the times, the disguise was minimal and clothes in the same style as everyday wear were worn. Even then the actor, through clothing and makeup, attempted to appear a little wealthier, a little more exotic or a little more exciting than he would have done in the street.

Ancient Greece Athenian drama originated in the worship of Dionysus, fertility god of wine, with the

Figures from the Phlyax vase.

Figures from the Pronomos Vase.

establishment by Peisistratus of a competitive festival at the great city Dionysia in 534 BC. Thespis won the Sacred Tripod for an interpretation of one of the great myths, in which he played all the parts in dialogue with the dithyrambic chorus of *tragoi*, or goat-men, who are shown on vases as either nude or wearing scanty loin-cloths always with an uplifted tail. They are heavily bearded and have pointed ears. For these quick changes of character Thespis used masks which became an essential part of tragic costume.

While in ordinary life men wore short sleeveless tunics, in drama they are represented in long tunics with long tight sleeves heavily decorated with stylized bands of pattern, running both horizontally and vertically as in the Andromeda crater, giving a hieratical and venerable impression. Over the *chiton* (tunic) was worn a *himation* or oblong garment (approximately 15–18 ft x 5–6 ft), which could be draped in a variety of ways. This could show a marked development of emotional state by a change of colour (e.g. grey for mourning or purple for Agamemnon's victorious entrance). Patterns running along the long side were variations on stylized flowers, leaves and even animals, or on the traditional Greek key design. The gods and messengers of the gods are however often seen in short tunics with clearly recognizable symbols, such as the lion cape and head for Heracles who carries a bludgeon, the winged shoes and short *chlamys* (cape) for Hermes, and the *thyrsos* and garland, often with a saffron robe, for Dionysus. Apollo always carries a golden bow and arrow with which, for instance, he threatens the Furies in *The Eumenides*, Poseidon carries a trident and Zeus a winged shaft, signifying lightning. Travellers invaria-

bly wear a flat wide-brimmed hat or *petasos* and Asiatic people from all places east of the Aegean wear a peaked hood with some kind of neck and shoulder covering similar to the Phrygian 'Cap of Liberty' adopted in Europe at the time of the French Revolution.

Tragic masks, exaggerated by the high forehead called an *onkos*, were larger than life-size, and made in such a way as to act as a megaphone in the huge open-air theatres. Many represented the characters with great realism: particularly notable are the masks of the Furies which were sufficiently horrible allegedly to arouse panic in the theatre. The richly diverse masks listed by Pollux in the 2nd century AD can nearly all be recognized in vase paintings and descriptions dating from the classical period. This is especially true of tragedy from the time of **Euripides** when a more naturalistic approach was seen, and comedy in both its old and new forms.

Old Comedy derived directly from the songs of the *komasts*, or revellers, at the rural Dionysia and was not introduced into the city Dionysia until 486 BC. Its costume was lewd in every way. The chorus were originally animals as in **Aristophanes'** *Birds*, *Wasps* and *Frogs*, wearing animal masks and body disguise, but later, as the chorus changed to humans, they represented drunkards or obscene old men, who could make fun of any kind of authority. They wore ludicrously short tunics, tights, exaggeratedly padded stomach and buttocks with a large pendulous phallus covered in scarlet leather. Masks were similarly exaggerated, particularly when parodying tragic heroes.

Roman theatre Under the Roman Empire drama was subtly coarsened and vulgarized. As it no longer served a religious purpose tragic horrors were shown in a more melodramatic way. The tragic actor's costume was decorated in the Greek fashion but was built up with high boots called *cothurni*; masks became more exaggerated and formalized in design, with huge open mouths and an even higher *onkos*. These vertical

Roman New Comedy mask.

enlargements probably meant that the body was padded to preserve the scale, the whole person being in keeping with the high stages then in use which were copiously ornamented with outsize statuary.

New Comedy, on the other hand, became domestic and concerned with intrigue, and was therefore clothed in costumes more closely related to everyday dress with the toga being frequently seen in frescoes and mosaics; the actors retained hideously exaggerated masks but without the *onkos*.

Women were never allowed to act on any classical stage, but female dancers do seem to have amused some in nightclub-like establishments such as the tiny theatre in the precinct of the Egyptian Gods on the island of Delos.

The medieval world The fall of the Roman Empire and the chaotic conditions in Europe that followed led to the decline of the theatre. The Christian church newly emerging as the major power over all Europe could not accept or allow the pagan excesses of the Roman theatre so it is by a curious irony that the drama eventually resurfaced within the actual liturgy of the church. In England the earliest reference to what became known as the *Quem queritis* plays is contained in the Rule of St Ethelwold for the Benedictine Abbey of Winchester in AD 970 which tells us that the monk who was to represent the Angel at the empty tomb on Easter Day was dressed in an alb and the three monks who acted the Maries coming to anoint the body of Jesus were dressed in copes. Presumably they would also have had veils over their tonsured heads. Here we have the beginning of the great Mystery Cycles of the Middle Ages. All the parts were played by men, at first by clerics and later by laymen, members of the Guilds, so it was essential to differentiate the sex of the various participants by their clothes; women were distinguished by veils, cloaks and often by girdles. As the plays became more elaborate and the cycles grew, the pressure of space and personnel forced them to move outside the churches though they always (as at **Oberammergau** today) remained under clerical control and they were for the most part centred on the feast of Corpus Christi. Some of the costumes, depending on the wealth of the Guild and the rank of the characters presented, such as the Magi, were very richly ornamented as can be seen in paintings and stained glass windows of the period. M. D. Anderson, in *Drama and Imagery in English Medieval Churches*, draws particular attention to the Norwich roof bosses as a source of information. From these and copious written sources, it is clear that most of the characters were dressed in the usual clothes of the day, but identified by carrying or wearing appropriate, recognizable symbols such as St Peter's keys or Judas's money-bag; only slight indications were made of any geographical location in the Middle East and even slighter hints of any previous period; however, rarely, Moses, Caiaphas and other leading figures from the Bible have clothing covered with Jewish letters and symbols to give them what was considered an alien appearance. False hair, beards and wigs were an easy means of assuming a different identity and a wig served the practical purpose of disguising Abel's protective iron skull-cap worn to protect him from Cain's blow (Lucerne in 1583). Paint is frequently referred to; gold was used for the face of God and for Christ in Majesty;

in Coventry Gabriel had a crimson face with a white alb, while seraphs wear red clothing and have white faces. Damned souls have their faces blacked as have jailers and torturers. Red paint is, of course, used for blood, sometimes applied from below the stage through a trap in the course of the play, but at the Last Judgement Christ's wounds are sometimes shown in gold.

Angels, appearing in many of the plays, are shown very frequently in paintings, from Faras in Nubia, before 1200, to the late Renaissance, wearing wings of peacock feathers symbolizing their unique relationship with God, but the wings seem on occasion to have been capable of folding away so as to be unseen. In the account of the Annunciation Play in Florence in 1439, reprinted in *The Staging of Religious Drama* (Meredith and Tailby), Mary, in agitation, first mistakes the Angel for a young man who, after he has calmed her and delivered his message, returns to God in his Heaven, at the other end of the Church of the Annunziata, along a sort of ski-lift moving his hands about and beating his wings 'as if he were really flying'.

Nudity was another problem to be overcome since actual nakedness would have been quite unacceptable. A white leather 'cat-suit' symbolized nudity as can be seen quite clearly in the stained glass window of Adam and Eve in Thaxted, Essex, where, because the glass is incomplete, the difference between leather and clear glass is easily discernible. In Lucerne, Marcellus, having had his cloak seized, ran off 'in the naked garment'.

Devils provided the best opportunities for inventiveness. Sometimes they were clad all in feathers, as fallen

German medieval devil mask.

angels, sometimes the feathers had turned to snake-like scales suggesting serpents but the most remarkable features of their costumes were the masks of which many horrible and terrifying actual examples survive, as in the Ferdinandeum Museum in Innsbruck. Devils formed a link with the Morality Plays, with their eternal battles between good and evil, and with folk drama such as the plays of St George and the Dragon. Under the guise of Wild Men of the Woods they appeared in tournaments and many other quasi-dramatic forms of entertainment.

The Elizabethan age By a strange irony far less is known positively about the costuming of **Shakespeare**'s plays than about the previous period, though Stella Mary Newton has, in *Renaissance Theatre Costume*, made a very good case for far more awareness of the historic past in the 16th century than has hitherto been conjectured. It must, however, be pointed out that most of Shakespeare's plays, being set in the contemporary world, would have been dressed in the ordinary clothes of the day (see Janet Arnold's *Patterns of Fashion 1560–1620*). In spite of this there remain many problems for which no satisfactory answers can be given. What did Titania and her diminutive fairies wear and how was their scale conveyed? How were the Witches in *Macbeth* dressed – and the supernatural characters in *The Tempest*? Perhaps some hints can be gleaned from the masque designs of **Inigo Jones** and from the watercolours by John White in the British Museum showing American Indians about 1585–90. It does not seem too far-fetched to suggest that Jones's design for a lady, with wings (before 1606), might have had some analogy with Titania. Similarly the Furies in *Salmacida Spolia* (1640) may have been based on Macbeth's Witches.

We are on surer ground in examining the only contemporary illustration, that of *Titus Andronicus* (1595), that survives. Here can be seen the mixture of costume styles that were presumably accepted at the time. Tamara's dress hangs loose from the neck but her sleeves are the full, fashionable ones of the day; her long, fair hair and crown are reminiscent of the masquers at Sir Henry Upton's wedding feast (1597). Aaron and Tamara's kneeling, captive sons are shown in an approximation to Roman armour, though with Elizabethan sleeves made of fabric, while Titus wears the laurel wreath of a victorious Roman general with a Roman-type cuirass which looks more martial because it is sleeveless; over this he wears a knotted cloak which is interesting as it might have been an early attempt at suggesting a toga. One of his two sons, behind him, wears gothic armour of about 1480, which may have been a genuine piece that had somehow found its way into the theatre wardrobe – a not uncommon event, as at all times in its history the theatre has benefited from cast-off clothes which have been used with more or less authenticity. Thus may the whole cycle of Roman plays have been costumed, and perhaps Othello in Cyprus looked something like Aaron – blacker than black.

But what of the tragic heroes, such as Lear? C. Walter Hodges in *The Globe Restored* suggested that the short-sleeved, loose coat worn by Tragoedia in the frontispiece of **Ben Jonson**'s *Workes* may have been the typical dress of a tragic hero; in which case this may

have survived as an idea to resurface in **Garrick**'s day. There seems to have been only a vague or symbolic suggestion of any historically antique clothing and it is clear that many of the conventions of the medieval theatre survived, such as outsize turbans for Eastern characters, as in Hans Eworth's *Turk on Horseback*. It has long been believed that Shylock wore the red wig that had graced melodramatic villains such as Herod and Judas in the Mystery Plays, though in fact he probably wore the long, dark red gown and yellow cap of the Venetian Jewish merchant which would have made him instantly recognizable to his mercantile audience. These long gowns, generally black, and worn by all men of stature in Venice, would, incidentally, have made Portia's disguise – in a long, enveloping scarlet gown as a doctor of law in Act IV – more easily acceptable to the other characters.

We must imagine, therefore, companies of players, under the patronage of the greatest in the land, dressed in gorgeous clothes, very often given to them by their wealthy friends and supporters, using just enough by way of symbolic accoutrements to remove themselves from the everyday and to indicate, imaginatively, persons inhabiting a world outside the confines of the Wooden 'O'.

The 17th and 18th centuries Masques and Ballets de Cour form the major source of the extravagant and fantastical costumes of court entertainment in the 17th and early 18th centuries. Inigo Jones's work in introducing Italian Renaissance ideas of staging to England

Philippe Millot, a French actor at the court of Munich, c.1675.

is fundamental to the development of the English theatre when it was permitted to reopen after the closure during the Commonwealth, but his designs for costumes à *la romaine* in a curious blend of fantasy and contemporary taste, with strong classical overtones, were certainly outshone by the French designers for the court of Louis XIV, 'Le Roi Soleil'. Most notable of all these is **Jean Berain**, whose influence pervaded not only opera and ballet far into the 18th century, but also heroic tragedy and drama of the 'straight' stage. The channel for this influence in France seems to have been such ballet-mascarades as **Molière**'s *Le Bourgeois Gentilhomme* (1670) with its successive entrées or ballet-like interludes written in collaboration with the composer Lully. The lavish costume of this kind of production was possible in the court theatres of the continent because the performers were often members of the court circle who vied with one another to don the most magnificent and bejewelled clothes possible. This 'style Berain' continued to flourish throughout Europe until the French Revolution; such artists as **Burnacini** in Vienna, François Boucher in France, Desprez in Drottningholm and the many-branched **Bibiena** family were everywhere carrying on the tradition. Their work is immortalized for us in the paintings of Watteau and Fragonard.

While all this exuberance continued to flourish on the continent, England turned after the Puritan interregnum to a theatre in which the words and their meaning took precedence over spectacle. Court theatres did not appear at all, as in the rest of Europe, for though there were two theatres at the Whitehall Palace where the king, Charles II, could entertain his guests on occasions, he preferred to visit his players in his own Theatre Royal in **Drury Lane**, where their work had to be self-supporting and financially viable. Restoration comedy was dressed in the height of absurdity with perhaps 250 yards of ribbons adorning a man's garments, and wigs that came half-way down their chests, intending to ape fashionable clothes which the upper classes adopted as a reaction to the austerities of the previous period. The plays abound in quips about the placing of pockets, the width of cuffs, the set of a cravat, tight-lacing in pregnancy and so on to make the maximum possible satiric attack on the foibles of the day. Much of this clothing was given, or lent, to the actors by wealthy patrons.

For heroic or rewritten Shakespearian tragedy on the other hand, the actors adopted costumes à *la romaine* clearly derived from the continental court entertainments. Sometimes these achieved only ludicrous and incongruous results, as may be seen from **Addison**'s attack in *The Spectator* in 1711. He gibes at the tragic hero who claps a huge plume of feathers on his head which rises so very high that there is often a greater length from his chin to the top of his head than to the sole of his foot, and at a queen in a broad, sweeping train that follows her passions in a disordered motion, while a small boy (sometimes black) follows and 'spreads it to advantage'. Heroes seem also to have generally retained the tonnelet – a stiff, wideskirted tunic in outline like a ballet tutu – which is held up to ridicule in the engraving of **James Quin** in Thompson's version of *Coriolanus*. That this garment was not worn universally is indicated by another engraving in the British Theatre Museum, of Quin in the same part

Frontispiece to Shakespeare's *Henry VIII* in Rowe's edition (1709). Note that whereas the major characters are in historical costume, supporting actors wear contemporary dress.

with a skirt hanging loose like a genuine Roman tunic. Where any attempt is made at historical or geographical accuracy it is to be noted that this did not apply to any supporting characters, as is clearly illustrated in the frontispiece to *Henry VIII* in **Rowe**'s edition of Shakespeare's plays (1709) where the King and Wolsey are fairly correct (though Wolsey would not have worn a surplice at court!) but the courtiers behind are in the height of contemporary dress with long wigs and high-heeled shoes on feet turned out in balletic dancing positions.

The Georgian period Interest in the theatre moved away from the court during the Hanoverian period in England. Garrick, who epitomized the theatre in the 18th century, and whose death in 1779 was said by Dr Johnson to have 'eclipsed the gaiety of nations', played at Drury Lane surrounded by his friends, the nobility and the newly influential intelligentsia. In these circumstances the outrageous clothes of the previous era gave way to the best that the new social order could provide. Historical accuracy was still in the future but Garrick did bring his characters into the recognizable world in which he lived and played. For the first time statements were made about them through their costumes. Thus

An 18th-century German actor in Roman costume.

Macklin changed the whole understanding and perception of Shylock, who had, since 1660, been regarded as a figure of vituperative fun, to a heavy, silent cunning deceiver by dressing him in a long, black gown and long wide trousers as a contemporary Venetian Jew with black hair, while Garrick altered the balance of *Venice Preserv'd* by dressing the poverty-stricken Jaffier in a gorgeous waistcoat making him the hero of the play. Garrick had a huge wardrobe and an enormous collection of wigs so he was able to plan his appearance very carefully, even down to the dissipated ruckles in Sir John Brute's stockings in the famous portrait by Zoffany of him in his wife's new dress. There are two contrasting portraits of Garrick in the part of Macbeth, both with **Hannah Pritchard** as Lady Macbeth. The better known, by Zoffany, shows him in a sumptuous, green, court coat trimmed with six-inch wide bands of gold braid. His breeches are red, matching the very large red and gold cuffs, but his waistcoat is so lavishly ornamented in gold that it is almost impossible to guess at its basic colour. The other portrait, by Fuseli, shows him in the extremity of terror after the murder of Duncan, in a quite plain, unornamented coat and breeches which is very similar to the privately owned suit which was shown in the British Library Exhibition in 1979. This is said to have been sketched during a performance, so may represent more exactly what he actually wore during this scene. For Hamlet, according to Lichtenberg, he deliberately chose not to wear any kind of period costume, believing that the 'well-known diagonal crease from the shoulder to the opposite hip' of the back of a fashionable French coat was 'worth the play of facial expression twice over'. When, as Richard III, Garrick did make an attempt at authenticity, it is

noteworthy that while an Elizabethan ruff, short gown and much slashing (wrong, in fact, for 1485) are evidenced in Hogarth's painting, the doublet is cut with long skirts just like an 18th-century waistcoat. The one extant costume of the period, in the London Museum, which bears a slight resemblance to the portrait of Thomas Collins as Slender by De Wilde in the Maugham Collection at the **National Theatre** suggests that the 'slashings' were applied to the surface of the garment and not pulled through the surface as in the 16th century.

Women in the 18th century continue, at least until **Siddons**, to wear the most fashionable garments available, whatever the part or the period. There are innumerable portraits of women in parts as Greek heroines, through Cleopatra to Lady Macbeth and beyond wearing fashionable, towering wigs, tight-laced corsets and wide hoops. Their jewellery was frequently lent or given to them by wealthy patrons and worn regardless of the status of the characters they were portraying.

In vain did **Aaron Hill**, in *The Prompter*, plead for a more rational and consistent approach; it did not begin to show in the theatre until the dawn of neoclassicism nearly 40 years after his death in 1750.

The Kemble era With the long reign of the Kemble family at the two Theatres Royal a distinct change can be seen reflecting the growing interest in archaeology and the neoclassical devotion to historical truth. Not only did **John Philip Kemble** employ **Capon** to design his sets in true gothic style but, in 1794, he pointed the way towards a new conception of the role of costume by dressing Macbeth's Witches as spirits, truly evil, as may be seen in Fuseli's painting. His sister, Sarah Siddons, was influenced by Sir Joshua Reynolds to adopt the new neoclassical style of dress made fashionable by the French Revolution with its cry of 'back to Nature and the Greeks'. In abandoning hoops

Charles Macklin as Shylock.

Hogarth's painting of David Garrick as Richard III.

she is often extolled as a pioneer of historical dressing, but she was really only continuing the female foible of wearing fashionable clothes and having her hair as fashionably dressed as possible – only the fashion had changed! However she did wear white satin, the traditional garment of insanity on the stage, for the sleep-walking scene thus asserting that she believed Lady Macbeth had crossed the threshold into madness.

In Paris, in 1789, **Talma** outraged his fellow, bewigged, comédiens by appearing in a tiny part in **Voltaire**'s *Brutus* dressed for the first time for nearly 1,500 years in a toga based on an ancient statue. Kemble was not slow to copy. As Cato in Addison's play of that name, in 1791 he, also, wore a Roman tunic, thonged sandals and a toga-like drape, if the frontispiece of Bell's *British Theatre*, 1791, is to be believed.

The 19th century A dramatic change towards historical accuracy was made in 1823 with **J. R. Planché**'s designs for *King John* made for **Charles Kemble** at **Covent Garden**. For the first time serious research into the period costume was undertaken from original sources and put into practice in the theatre.

Victorian showmanship reached its highest point when **Charles Kean**'s antiquarian enthusiasm led him to mount magnificent Shakespearian productions full of authentic detail, sometimes at the expense of the text. One of his best-known productions is *The Winter's Tale*, partly because **Ellen Terry** made her first appearance in it as Mamillius. The engraving shows him in as nearly accurate a costume of a Greek actor as possible. However, he was less successful in imposing his ideas on his wife. Ellen Kean always insisted on wearing either a crinoline or voluminous petticoats under whatever shape had been designed for her.

In contrast to the exuberant exactitudes of Charles Kean, **Samuel Phelps** at **Sadler's Wells**, with far smaller resources, produced more imaginative effects. His use of a gauze curtain and green lighting lent an insubstantial quality to the figures in the wood in *A Midsummer Night's Dream* so that they appeared more like flitting shadows than human beings, which must have lent an added magic to the enchantment of the play. Gas lighting, with all the flexibility it brought to the theatre, had an almost incalculable effect on costuming, rendering the glitter of spangles, to be seen in

the costumes at Drottningholm, which was so necessary simply for visibility in the dim candle-lit theatres of the 18th century, a thing of the past.

The 19th century ended in a blaze of glory with sumptuous productions by the great actor–managers. **Irving** and, later, **Tree** brought the visual excitement of the theatre to a new high level. Irving was always scrupulously careful in recreating the past in terms that were artistically creative and not merely aridly accurate. Many of his costumes survive, most of them in the Museum of London; examination reveals the care with which he used 'trompe l'oeil' devices to achieve his effects, as, for example, his apparently long-peaked medieval hat cut short so as not to hide his face. His skill with lighting is legendary, and was nowhere better demonstrated than in the 'Brocken' scene in *Faust* which was cold, unreal and grey-green, the better to throw up the contrast with his own dramatically brilliant scarlet outfit. Also in *Faust* the great crowds who thronged the St Lorenz Platz were dressed in the most imaginatively varied clothes, from stiff, silk

Ellen Terry as Lady Macbeth, c.1888.

brocades to picturesque rags, but it was not as yet usual for all the costumes in a play to be designed together. Ellen Terry, for instance, went her own way, sometimes to superb effect as in the costume for Lady Macbeth, covered in beetle wings, and now in the Ellen Terry Museum at Smallhythe, which was designed by Mrs Comyns Carr and made by Mrs Nettleship and immortalized through Sargeant's painting. Occasionally, she was less successful as when, in the same production, Irving himself took over the cloak she had intended for the discovery scene realizing that it was too brilliant a ribbed silk and would distract the audience from the main action – and from himself.

However accurately designed any lady's costume at this period might be, the cut always ensured that the contemporary ideal of the corseted female figure was never completely obscured, even in the case of Ellen Terry who favoured the looser 'aesthetic' ideals.

Throughout the 19th century, excellence seems to have been judged against a standard of historical accuracy. This movement initiated by Planché and pursued by Charles Kean was carried to its logical extreme on the continent by the Duke of Saxe-**Meiningen** and in England by the pervasive influence of E. W. Godwin, **Edward Gordon Craig**'s father, who also made detailed researches into original sources, the results of which he then apparently put on the stage with no concessions to the exigences of theatre size, lighting or sightlines. For **Bancroft**'s *Merchant of Venice* (1875) when Ellen Terry played Portia he went back to Vecelli and 16th-century Italy; for **Wilson Barrett**'s *Hamlet* (1884) he went back to the reign of Cnut, while for Ellen Terry in *The Cup* (1881) and for *Claudian* he drew on the classical world. But, when designing on his own rather than copying, as in the *As You Like It* at Coombe House, his costumes look dull and amateurish.

Edward Gordon Craig's design for the mask of the Blind Man in Yeats's *On Baile's Strand*, 1911.

The 20th century A change was bound to come and, though it was slower in England than on the continent or America, it was nevertheless an Englishman, Edward Gordon Craig (son of Ellen Terry and E. W. Godwin) who was the leading pioneer of a change of mood. In the move away from the history/schoolroom idea one detects a growing attempt to interpret the inner meaning of the play. If overt symbolism was only occasionally fully successful it did influence the way the audience perceived a play. Striking early examples were to be found in Craig's designs for **Yeats**'s symbolist plays. In 1911, while working on *Hamlet* in Moscow where in the first court scene, Claudius wore an enormous gold cloak covering most of the stage, through slits in which appeared the sycophantic courtiers, Craig designed for Yeats's *On Baile's Strand* a mask head-dress for the Blind Man. It was an example of symbolism partly influenced by the Japanese **nō** theatre.

Meanwhile, back in England, Norman Wilkinson, working in close harmony with **Granville Barker**, achieved an imaginative unity of design in settings and costumes for *Twelfth Night* and *The Winter's Tale* (1912) and *A Midsummer Night's Dream* (1914) which clashed profoundly with the current ideas of realistic magnificence perpetrated at **His Majesty's Theatre** by Tree. The outbreak of the First World War put back any development along these lines for Shakespearian productions for many years.

In 1921 Claud Lovat Fraser went a stage further in symbolism in his designs for that 'Newgate Pastoral', as Swift called *The Beggar's Opera*, by adopting a method of simplifying 18th-century clothes, keeping faithfully to the outlines of the age but shorn of all ribbons, laces and yards of trimming that are generally superfluous and obscure the more important line. In this he was to point the way for many future artists and his untimely death was an irreparable loss to British theatre.

Another artist spanning the war years, Charles Ricketts, had his greatest success with designs for *St Joan* by **Shaw** in which **Sybil Thorndike** played the lead in 1924, while in 1933 three young women calling themselves 'Motley' exploited the glamour of medieval dress to the full for **John Gielgud** in *Richard of Bordeaux*. The last surviving member of the trio, Margaret Harris is, in 1987, head of the Design Course now at the Almeida Theatre, London.

In Europe, staging in the first half of the 20th century was dominated by the genius of **Max Reinhardt** for whom Ernst Stern designed a great deal in the stylized realism favoured by the great director, but for *The Miracle* in New York the costumes designed by **Norman Bel Geddes** evoked very clearly the mystical yet curiously pagan atmosphere of that extraordinary piece of pure theatre. It was Norman Bel Geddes with **Robert Edmond Jones** and **Lee Simonson** who first made a bid for international recognition of American staging and costume at the same time as **Eugene O'Neill** was making his mark as a dramatist. Plays such as his *The Emperor Jones* were a gift to the new expressionistic designers.

After the Second World War artists in Czechoslovakia provided (in some cases for older work, such as *Insect Play*) some of the most innovative costume designers in Europe, among whom Adolf Wenig and

The Witches and Macbeth (Ian McKellen), Royal Shakespeare Company, 1976.

Josef Jelinek must rank high; because of international tensions they are not sufficiently recognized in the West. **Josef Svoboda** who *has* an international reputation is more remarkable as a designer of scenery than costumes.

Many designers have worked in the revolutionary or political theatre of the 20th century but over all of them it has been the vision of directors – **Meyerhold**, **Piscator**, **Brecht**, **Peter Brook** – which has dominated attention, so that it is well-nigh impossible to distinguish the work of the designer from that of the director. This was particularly high-lighted in Brook's *'Dream'* (1970) where Sally Jacobs fully identified with Peter Brook in the creation of Chinese acrobat-like costumes of brilliant purple, yellow and green satin helping to give a breath-taking reappraisal of the play, in stark contrast to the richly delicious confections designed by Lila de Nobili for **Peter Hall**'s production of the same play some ten years earlier, and the sheer magic of inspiration by Deirdre Clancy for **Bill Bryden** at the National Theatre in 1982.

One feature of almost all reconstructions of period plays seen nowadays is a tendency to 'time-switch' – to look at a play through the spectrum of a time to which it did not initially belong, possibly in contrast to television which excels at detailed accuracy. Among earlier examples were the lovely *As You Like It* set in Watteau styles for **Edith Evans** in 1937 and the all-male version in modern dress with Ronald Pickup as Rosalind in 1967. It was accomplished with the most imaginative success in historical plays in 1963 by the **Royal**

Shakespeare Company with the marathon production of *The Wars of the Roses* in which, while the period line was still suggested, an overall use of homespun, leather and metal removed any sense of precise dating and gave the plays a universal application. This led to what could be called the company's 'black' phase with many productions dressed in shiny leather and heavy-looking armour. In the late 1970s a more abstract school showed itself with a *Macbeth* (**Ian McKellen** and **Judi Dench** in 1976) which was set in no particular time or place but in which the sense of evil was perceived as all-pervading through the threatening effect of jack-boots and polished trench-coats.

In the 1980s this move away from the discipline of historical accuracy and the consequent necessity to *wear* costumes correctly has resulted in a very free, but frequently sloppy, attitude to clothes with young actresses, for instance, being unwilling to wear corsets (necessary to achieve the correct shape) and unable to manage and control trains.

There may now be a slight swing, indicated in the new, 1985, *Othello* at Stratford, which returns to the earliest tradition of 'Eastern' characters wearing turbans; but, with so many brilliant artists at work in the theatre – Farah, Georgiadis, Maria Bjornson, **John Bury**, Alison Chitty, Bob Crowley and David Hockney, to name but a few of those with an international reputation there is an enormous richness of talent available which bodes well for the future history and development of theatre costume.   MM

See: S. Allen, *Samuel Phelps & Sadler's Wells Theatre*, Middletown, Connecticut, 1971; M. D. Anderson, *Drama and Imagery in English Medieval Churches*, London, 1963; G. A. Bellamy, *Apology for Her Life*, London, n.d.; M. Bieber, *The History of Greek and Roman Theatre*, London, 1951; M. Booth, *Victorian Spectacular Theatre*, London, Boston and Henley, 1981; J. Laver, *Drama, its Costume and Decor*, London, 1951; J. Laver, *Costume in the Theatre*, London, 1964; P. Meredith and J. Tailby, *The Staging of Religious Drama in Europe in the Later Middle Ages*, Michigan, 1983; S. M. Newton, *Renaissance Theatre Costume*, London, 1975; S. Orgel and R. Strong, *Inigo Jones. Theatre of the Stuart Court*, London, 1973; M. Summers, *The Restoration Theatre*, London, 1934; *Theatre Notebook, The Journal of The Society for Theatre Research*, Index to vols. 1–25, London, 1977; T. B. L. Webster, *Greek Theatre Production*, London, 1956.

Coulter, John (1888–1980) Irish-Canadian playwright, born in Belfast but taught for five years in Dublin where he was much influenced by the **Abbey Theatre**. His first stage play was published in 1917. He was editor of *The New Adelphi* in London when he met a Canadian writer, moved to Toronto, and married her. His play *The House in the Quiet Glen* (1937) won several awards at the 1937 Dominion Drama Festival. He wrote for radio, and later television, in Canada, the United States and Britain, as well as having several plays produced by Toronto companies. The Canadian Broadcasting Corporation commissioned librettos for two operas by Healey Willan: *Transit Through Fire* (1942) and *Deirdre* (1946), which was staged by the Canadian Opera Company in 1966. His best-known work is *Riel* (1950), an epic play about the leader of the 19th-century Métis rebellion in Western Canada. The same historic episode also yielded *The Crime of Louis*

Riel (1966) and *The Trial of Louis Riel* (1968). Though an immigrant, Coulter was an activist in support of a Canadian drama, and an early advocate of government support for the arts.   JA

Court theatres (England) The various entertainments at the Tudor and Stuart Courts were often elaborate enough to demand the temporary adaptation of indoor spaces. The Great Hall at Hampton Court, the Banqueting Houses as well as the Great Chamber at Whitehall and the Great Halls at Greenwich, Richmond and Windsor were all put to use, particularly during the Christmas festivities at which professional theatre companies were privileged to perform and well rewarded for doing so. Under Charles I, more permanent structures were adapted or built. **Inigo Jones** converted the **Cockpit-in-Court** (1629–30) into an intimate theatre along the lines already tested at the **Cockpit** in Drury Lane, and the Stuart delight in masques was gratified by the costly erection of the Masquing House (1637), close to Jones's magnificent Banqueting Hall (1619–22). Under Charles II and his successors, the custom of adaptation declined and the Court theatres dwindled into insignificance.   PT

Courtenay, Tom (Thomas Daniel) (1937–) British actor, who helped to change the image of English acting in the early 1960s. Not conventionally handsome, with a northern accent, Courtenay played Konstantin in an **Old Vic** production of **Chekhov**'s *The Seagull*, stressing not just the doomed romanticism but also the provincialism of Arkadina's son. Courtenay took over from **Albert Finney** in the title role of *Billy Liar* (1961) and established himself quickly as a brilliant deadpan comic, starring in two **Alan Ayckbourn** comedies, *Time and Time Again* (1972) and *The Norman Conquests* (1974) in which he played Norman, the 'gigolo trapped in a haystack'. In Manchester, where he was part of the 69 Company at the **Royal Exchange Theatre** for several seasons, the range of his acting was more visible and better appreciated than in London, for he played Hamlet, Peer Gynt and the title role in Ronald Harwood's *The Dresser*. Courtenay's style of acting adapts well to television and films, retaining its down-to-earth credibility. In 1964, he acted in the **National Theatre**'s production of **Max Frisch**'s *Andorra*, but his most memorable London role perhaps was as John Clare, the Northamptonshire poet-peasant, in **Edward Bond**'s *The Fool* (1975) at the **Royal Court Theatre**.   JE

Cousin, Gabriel (1908–) French playwright, poet and sportsman. Cousin's career has been entirely outside Paris in the theatres of the **decentralization movement**. His plays deal with major world problems of our time: hunger, racism, exploitation, the nuclear threat, but approached through the experience of communities of the working class, like himself, or the peasants. His first success, *Le Drame du Fukuryu Maru* (*The Drama of the Fukuryu Maru*) (directed by **Dasté** 1962), was a poetic evocation of the real experience of fishermen affected by a hydrogen bomb test in the Pacific in 1954. An original play about loneliness and exploitation used techniques reminiscent of the Absurd: *L'Aboyeuse et L'Automate* (*The Barker and the Automaton*) (directed by Lecoq 1961). *L'Opéra Noir*

(*Black Opera*) (directed by Garran 1967) is a musical about racial violence and *Le Voyage de Derrière la Montagne* (*The Journey Behind the Mountain*) (directed by Lepeuve 1966) is a powerful version of a Japanese tale about old age and poverty. His most accomplished play is *Le Cycle du Crabe* (*The Crab Cycle*) (directed by Cousin 1975) about the inhabitants of a shanty town in South America. His plays are filled with songs and movement; he believes that an essential element in *théâtre populaire* is festivity and celebration, however austere the subject. Since 1972 he has run a centre for encouraging creative activity, in Grenoble.   DB

Covent Garden, Theatre Royal (London) There have been three theatres on or near the Bow Street site, formerly part of a convent garden. The first was designed by James Shepherd for **John Rich**, then proprietor of the theatre in **Lincoln's Inn Fields** and holder of one of the two Royal Patents. With a greater capacity (nearly 3,000) than Lincoln's Inn Fields, it opened with a revival of **Congreve**'s *The Way of the World* in 1732. Rich's company was led by **James Quin**, though Rich himself continued to feature in the annual pantomime and his theatre's payroll had also to cater for followers of opera and ballet. Rivalry with **Drury Lane** intensified when **Spranger Barry** went to Covent Garden in 1750, though Barry rarely drew blood in his duels with **David Garrick**. For a few years after Rich's death in 1761, opera predominated at the theatre, but the stormy partnership of **George Colman the Elder** and Thomas Harris (1767–74) restored the balance. **Goldsmith**'s *The Good-natured Man* (1768) and *She Stoops to Conquer* (1773) belong to this period, as does **Charles Macklin**'s innovatory playing of Macbeth in Scottish costume (1773). Colman was eased out in 1774, but Harris remained active in the management of Covent Garden until 1809. His was the chief credit in the spotting of **Sheridan**'s promise in *The Rivals* (1775) and in the decision to ask Henry Holland to oversee the massive structural alterations and enlargement of 1792. **George Frederick Cooke** made his London debut at Covent Garden in 1800, and the first self-proclaimed melodrama, **Thomas Holcroft**'s *A Tale of Mystery*, was staged there in 1802. A major coup of Harris's was the theft of **John Kemble** from Sheridan's Drury Lane in 1803. Having bought a sixth share of the Patent, Kemble remained at Covent Garden until his retirement in 1817. It was he who engaged the prodigious Master **Betty** in 1804, suffering in silence the indignity of unfavourable comparison.

When the first theatre was destroyed by fire in 1808, a second, designed by Richard Smirke after the Temple of Minerva on the Acropolis, was speedily built and opened in 1809 with an ill-fated production of *Macbeth*. Smirke's Covent Garden (capacity 3,000) was slightly less capacious than Holland's remodelled auditorium and Kemble had agreed to a compensating increase in prices. The fierce Old Price Riots forced the management into eventual submission. **Sarah Siddons** gave her farewell performance at Covent Garden in 1812, four years before **Macready** made his unwilling debut there. Having already installed gas to illuminate the Entrance Hall and Grand Staircase in 1815, the management of Covent Garden was quick to follow the **Lyceum** and Drury Lane in the installation of gaslight

The interior of Covent Garden Theatre at the time of the 'Fitzgiggio' Riot, 1763.

for auditorium and stage (1817), an innovation which had an incalculable effect on the development of English acting. In 1821, John Kemble resigned his interest in Covent Garden to his brother Charles, who was to take responsibility for the staging of *King John* in historical costume (1823), according to the researches of **J. R. Planché**. It was an idea that caught the imagination of audiences in the era of the Waverley novels. It was a rare success for **Charles Kemble**, who was one among many to be impoverished by his involvement with Covent Garden. Even the popularity of his daughter Fanny, a reluctant actress from 1829–32, was insufficient to save him, and his appointment as Examiner of Plays in 1836 came as a welcome relief. Subsequent managers, Laporte (1832–3), **Alfred Bunn** (1833–5), Osbaldiston (1835–7), Macready (1837–9) and **Madame Vestris** and **Charles James Mathews** (1839–42), were no luckier. The Patent houses could no longer afford their supremacy. After the Vestris management, Covent Garden remained closed until 1847, when it entered on a new life as the Royal Italian Opera House, with its capacity increased to over 4,000. It was burnt to the ground in 1856.

The third theatre (capacity 2,141), designed by Edward Barry, opened in 1858 with a performance of Meyerbeer's *Les Huguenots* and has been associated with opera ever since. It has been known as the Royal Opera House since 1939.   PT

Coward, Noël (1899–1973) British playwright, actor. His most substantial work for the theatre was in the late 1920s to the early 1940s, with a series of rather precious but witty comedies (*Fallen Angels*, 1925, *Hay Fever*, 1925, *Private Lives*, 1930, *Design for Living*, 1933, *Blithe Spirit*, 1941, *Present Laughter*, 1942). The Second

World War brought from him some patriotic pieces that were successful in their time but seem somewhat excessive in retrospect (*This Happy Breed*, 1942, *Peace in Our Time*, 1947), reworking a flag-waving enthusiasm first seen in *Cavalcade* (1931). As a composer and song-writer he produced work that the messenger-boy whistled then and whistles still, and in the theatrical orbit he graced he was termed 'The Master'. He was knighted in 1970.   MB

Cowell, Joe Leathley (Joseph Hawkins Witchett) (1792–1863) English-born actor, manager and scene painter who, after an abortive career in the navy, became an itinerant actor, establishing a reputation as a low comedian. Emigrating to America in 1821, he became a well-known figure in the American theatre, both as an actor and a manager of both theatres and circuses. His memoirs appeared in 1844. In 1863 he returned to England. Through marriages he was related to the **Siddons** and the **Batemans**. His second son, **Sam**, became a music-hall star.   DBW

Cowell, Sam[uel] Houghton (1820–64) British actor/vocalist, born in the USA. Most music-hall stars came either from the working class or from a theatrical background. Cowell, one of the earliest recognized music-hall performers and an early star at the Canterbury, was the son of a **Drury Lane** actor, **Joe Cowell**, and began his career in the legitimate theatre, touring the USA with his father in the 1830s in Shakespearian productions, billed as 'The Young American Roscius'. Returning to England at the age of 20, initially he pursued his career as a straight actor, but rapidly converted himself to a comic vocalist (he had already done coon-songs as entr'actes in America) and burlesque performer. By 1850 he had abandoned the legitimate theatre entirely in favour of the song and supper rooms of the West End, though his early experience continued to serve him well in burlesques of **Shakespeare**. An ugly little man with a lugubrious expression, he specialized in cockney song-and-patter acts, notably 'The Ratcatcher's Daughter' and E. W. Blanchard's parody, 'Vilikins and his Dinah'. AEG DBW

Cowl, Jane (1884–1950) American actress. Born in Boston, Jane Cowl made her New York stage debut in 1903 in *Sweet Kitty Bellairs*. Her portrayal of the wronged woman, Mary Turner, in *Within the Law* (1912), established her as a star. Cowl appeared in plays that she wrote or co-wrote including *Lilac Time* (1917); *Daybreak* and *Information Please* (1918); and *Smilin' Through* (1920). In 1923 she offered a 'breath-taking' Juliet in a production which ran for 174 consecutive performances. Her successful rendering of Larita in **Noël Coward**'s *Easy Virtue* (1925) was followed by an 'appealing' Amytis in *The Road to Rome* (1927) and a 'brilliant' Lucy Chase Wayne in *First Lady* (1935). **Brooks Atkinson** praised her 'personal beauty, impeccability of manners, humorous vitality, and simple command of the art of acting'. The dark-haired, dark-eyed actress was regarded as a distinguished 'lady of the theatre' in London as well as New York. TLM

Cowley, Hannah (1743–1809) English playwright. Her first play, *The Runaway*, was produced by **Garrick** in 1776 after he had 'embellished' it. Prolonged battles with **Sheridan**, Garrick's successor at **Drury Lane**, and Harris at **Covent Garden** delayed production of her next play but her afterpiece *Who's the Dupe?* (1779) proved immensely successful in its vitality using traditional figures of comedy such as the pedant. Her best play, *The Belle's Stratagem* (1780), and *A Bold Stroke for a Husband* (1783) make extensive and unfashionable use of Restoration comedy as sources. In 1783 her husband moved to India (where he died in 1797) while she continued to pursue her writing career. PH

Crabtree, Charlotte (Lotta) (1847–1924) American actress. Born in New York, she and her mother followed her father to the gold mining town of Grass Valley, California, in 1853. She soon learned to dance and sing and became a featured performer in mining camp variety troupes. She conquered San Francisco in 1859 and headed east. She achieved widespread popularity when she made the transition to legitimate drama in the dual leading roles of *Little Nel and the Marchioness* (1867), dramatized for her from **Dickens**'s *The Old Curiosity Shop* by **John Brougham**. Though she later had other vehicles, they were only excuses for this tiny, red-haired, black-eyed elf to exhibit her skills at mimicry, banjo-picking, and clog dancing. She never married and retired with comfortable wealth in 1891. DMCD

Craig, Edith (1869–1947) British actress and director, sister of **Gordon Craig** and daughter of **Ellen Terry**, who began her career performing with **Henry Irving** at the **Lyceum** in 1890. She constructed the costumes designed by her brother for his productions in 1900–1 and stage-managed her mother's 1907

American tour. She designed and directed for the Pioneer Players (between 1911 and 1921) and in London. CI

Craig, (Edward Henry) Gordon (1872–1966) British theorist, director and stage designer. Trained under **Henry Irving**, about whom he later wrote a definitive study (1930), he established a reputation as one of the leading young actors before leaving the **Lyceum** in 1897. Influenced by Hubert von Herkomer and the symbolists, he directed and designed a series of highly praised but financially unsuccessful productions, ranging from opera (*Dido and Aeneas*, 1900; *The Masque of Love*, 1901; *Acis and Galatea*, 1902) to **Laurence Housman**'s nativity play *Bethlehem* (1902) and **Ibsen**'s *The Vikings* (1903), before leaving for Germany where he designed productions for **Otto Brahm** and **Eleonora Duse** and influenced **Max Reinhardt**, as well as beginning his association with Isadora Duncan.

In 1905 he published his first and most famous essay *The Art of the Theatre*, calling for the development of a non-naturalistic aesthetic through which the theatre could become an art form equivalent to music or poetry, and establishing the dominant position of the modern director. This was followed by one of the first proposals for an English **National Theatre** and an attack on conventional acting, apparently demanding the elimination of the human performer, which was published in the first volume of *The Mask*. From 1908 until 1929 this quarterly journal, published and largely written by Craig himself using over 30 pseudonyms, ranged over the whole history of the stage, arguing for an abstract and ritualistic theatre that would have an equivalent spiritual significance to the tragedy of classical Greece or the Japanese **nō** drama, and against the literary elements of drama as well as realism. Comparable in some ways to his contemporary **Adolphe Appia**, the basis of his new drama was to be light and rhythmic movement. In attempting to realize this, he pursued the notion of a flexible stage by means of which an endless variation of architectural shapes could be created during a performance (*Scene*, 1923). He founded a school of theatre in Florence in 1913 (closed by the First World War in 1915), and invented movable screens to substitute for scenery. These were used by **W. B. Yeats** at the **Abbey Theatre**, Dublin, in 1911, and by Craig himself in the famous 1912 *Hamlet*, which he directed for **Stanislavsky**'s **Moscow Art Theatre**.

Although, apart from this production, he only directed one other play – Ibsen's *The Pretenders* for the **Poulsens** at the Royal Theatre in Copenhagen (1926) – and only a single set of designs for live performance – **George Tyler**'s 1928 production of *Macbeth* in New York – the originality of Craig's writings and the visionary nature of his designs have had a lasting impact on 20th-century theatre. CI

Crane, William Henry (1845–1928) American actor. After a long apprenticeship with a small touring opera company, Crane achieved his first major success in *Evangeline* at **Niblo's Garden** in 1873. From 1877 to 1889, Crane and **Stuart Robson** joined together to produce a series of very popular American domestic comedies such as *Our Boarding House, Our Bachelors,* and *The Henrietta*. Crane was also noted for his Dromio, his Falstaff, and his Sir Toby Belch. In 1890, he began a successful career as a producer–actor in his own vehicle productions when he appeared as Senator Hannibal Rivers in *The Senator*, with which he was to be associated for the rest of his career. In 1896 he toured in **Joseph Jefferson**'s 'All Star' production of *The Rivals* as Anthony Absolute. Crane, a thoughtful artist who contributed a number of essays on acting and the theatre to popular journals of the day, published his autobiography *Footprints and Echoes* in 1927. MR DJW

Cratinus (active c. 450–c. 423 BC) The most prominent poet of Old Comedy (see **Greece, ancient**) in the generation before **Aristophanes**. He was noted for his invective, uninhibited even by Aristophanes' standards. Numerous brief fragments survive. ALB

Craven, Frank (?1875–1945) American actor, playwright, and director, best known for creating the Stage Manager in **Thornton Wilder**'s *Our Town* in 1938. Born in Boston of theatrical parents, Craven was a child actor. At 16 he played in repertory in Philadelphia and won his first New York success in 1910 as James Gilley in *Bought and Paid For*. He later wrote several successful scripts for the stage, such as *Too Many Cooks* and *This Way Out*. He played leading roles in several films, adapted some of his scripts to film, and wrote dialogue for Laurel and Hardy. He last appeared on Broadway in 1944. **Brooks Atkinson** called him 'the best pipe and pants-pocket actor in the business'. SMA

Crawford, Cheryl (1902–86) American producer. As executive assistant to **Theresa Helburn** at the **Theatre Guild** in the late twenties, as co-founder with **Harold Clurman** and **Lee Strasberg** of the **Group Theatre** in 1931, as creator of the **American Repertory Theatre** (1946) with **Eva Le Gallienne** and **Margaret Webster**, and as co-founder with **Elia Kazan** and **Robert Lewis** of the **Actors Studio** in 1947, Crawford was at the centre of the most vital and idealistic enterprises in the American theatre. A wry, poker-faced Midwesterner, she was a remarkably self-effacing impresario. Surrounded by high-strung, visionary colleagues, she always remained level-headed. She kept the peace between Clurman and Strasberg, whom she called Old Testament prophets; she raised money, trimmed budgets, found rehearsal space, arranged theatre rentals, and could always be counted on for a frank opinion of the artistic merit and commercial appeal of both plays and players. For all her commitment to serious theatre she thought of plays as potential hits or flops, and she withdrew from the organizations she helped to foster in order to pursue a career as an independent stage producer with a particular interest in musicals. Her biggest commercial success was *Brigadoon* (1947); other notable Crawford productions include the 1942 revival of *Porgy and Bess*; *One Touch of Venus* (1943); *Paint Your Wagon* (1950); *Mother Courage* (1963); and four plays by **Tennessee Williams**, *The Rose Tattoo* (1951), *Camino Real* (1953), *Sweet Bird of Youth* (1959), and *Period of Adjustment* (1960). FH

Crazy Gang, The A troupe of British comedians,

who brought comedy techniques from variety and circus to create a unique brand of knockabout satirical farce. (Bud) Flanagan (Chaim Reuben Weinthrop) and (Chesney William) Allen, Jimmie Nervo (James Holloway) and Teddy Knox (Albert Edward Cromwell-Knox), Charlie Naughton and Jimmy Gold (James McConigal), with 'Monsewer' Eddie Gray, were brought together by **George Black** for 'crazy weeks' at the London Palladium in 1932. These improvisations developed into a popular series of revues from *Life Begins at Oxford Circus* (1935) to *These Foolish Things* (1938); and their success was repeated at the Victoria Palace from 1947 (*Together Again*) to 1960 (*Young in Heart*). CI

Crébillon, Prosper Jolyot de (1674–1762) French dramatist whose work offers an early hint of 18th-century sensibility and taste for the macabre. As if to galvanize audience response or to eclipse the memory of **Racine**, he cultivated the most passionate and sensational of subject matter. His most wildly successful tragedies, *Atrée et Thyeste* (1707), *Électre* (1708) and *Rhadamiste et Zénobie* (1711), are rhetorical tissues of pathos, horror and complicated plotting, which in retrospect offer at best a melodramatic *frisson*. He became a member of the Académie-Française in 1731. DR

Criticism: 1. European

There is little theatre criticism in a modern sense before the 16th century in Europe, due to the lack of an established theatre or of pamphlets. What criticism there was confined itself to academic discussions of the merits of classical dramatists; and the classical bias accordingly entered into the first major critical discussions which emerged during the 17th century. In Britain, Sir **Philip Sidney** (1554–86) entered into a debate with a minor playwright, **Stephen Gosson**, who had become convinced of the sinfulness of all fiction; and the result, Sidney's *Apologie for Poetrie* (or *Defence of Poesie*), published in 1595 but written before 1583, became a model defence for the theatre (and all art) against the charge of lying. Nevertheless, the immorality or otherwise of the theatre has preoccupied much critical discussion until today, and has been well documented in Jonas Barish's *The Anti-theatrical Prejudice* (1981).

In France, theories of classical drama were discussed in Jacques Grevin's *Bref discours pour l'intelligence de ce théâtre* (1561) and Jacques de la Taille's *L'art de la tragédie* (1573); while in 1630, **Jean Chapelain** (1595–1674), a founder member of the French Academy and a friend of **Cardinal Richelieu**, wrote a *Letter on the Twenty-four Hour Rule* to his fellow Academician, Abbot Godeau, which starts to apply classical rules to contemporary texts, emphasizing among other matters *bienséance* (decorum). This letter suggests that of the famous Three Unities (of Time, Place and Action), only that of Time had yet been formulated. Chapelain also took the dramatist **Pierre Corneille** (1606–84) to task over his triumphantly successful tragedy, *Le Cid* (1637), and the following 'Querelle du Cid' prepared the way for the formation of neoclassical opinion. This was still textual criticism and confined to a limited social circle; but by the 1650s, public pamphlets on stage performances began to appear. A collection of these loose sheets, started in 1650 by Jean Loret, were published in 1656 as *Muse Historique*; while Charles Robinet's *Lettres*, begun in 1654, contained some theatre criticism. The most important of these gazetteers was **Donneau de Visé**, who from 1672 onwards started seriously to discuss criteria suitable for the public performance of plays in his *Le Mercure Galant*; and he, together with Charles de Saint-Denis Saint-Evremond (1613–1703), were the real pioneers of neoclassical criticism in Europe, rather than the better-known **Nicolas Boileau-Despréaux** (1636–1711).

Boileau's *L'art poétique* (1674) was originally conceived in four cantos as a witty commentary on his fellow poets; and Mme de Sévigné has described the amusement caused by its early readings in 1672. In comparing his contemporaries, often unfairly, with classical writers, Boileau described the three unities, which specified that plays should concentrate on single situations which might (in real life) have occurred in one place in a time span not exceeding one day. These rules, which suited Boileau's friend, **Jean Racine**, better than anybody else, became incorporated (together with decorum in speech, manner and moral behaviour) into the general tenets of neoclassicism, which spread from the court of the Sun King, Louis XIV of France (1638–1714), to other European monarchies, affecting the Enlightenment associated with the reign of Frederick II (the Great) of Prussia (1712–86) and the Age of Reason in Britain. Boileau himself became known throughout Europe as 'the lawgiver of Parnassus'.

Among British writers strongly influenced by Boileau was **Joseph Addison** (1672–1719), whose essays on theatre topics for *The Tatler* and *The Spectator*, a periodical which he edited with Sir **Richard Steele**, mark the rapid transformation from Restoration pamphleteering with its polemical tone into the urbane journalism of the Augustan age. Addison's tragedy, *Cato* (1713), is modelled on Boileau's precepts. Addison was not, however, a theorist and, as the successor to the poet, dramatist and critic, **John Dryden** (1631–1700), could not be regarded as a pioneer of criticism. The success of *The Spectator* led to many imitations, and aesthetic discussions, together with gossip, became a familiar feature of 18th-century literary life. Alexander Pope's *Essay on Criticism* (1711) and *The Dunciad* (1728) have in their satirical sketches and their conventional neoclassical wisdoms much in common with *L'art poétique* which Pope greatly admired. While Dr **Samuel Johnson**'s *The Lives of the Poets* (1781) represents the pinnacle of Augustan criticism – sane, terse and moral without being sententious – the capacity to take part in critical discussion at a high level was shared by most men of letters of his time, despite the fact that in Britain the Theatres Act of 1737 had severely restricted the development of the theatre.

Among the German-speaking countries, Boileau's influence spread through the Enlightenment critic, **Johann Christoph Gottsched** (1700–66), who became a professor at Leipzig University. He not only introduced neoclassical criticism into German dramaturgy through his *Versuch einer kritischer Dichtkunst* (1729) and compiled a bibliography of German drama from the 16th century onwards, but also translated (with his wife) plays from French and English sources, including Addison's *Cato*. He found the existing German repertoire lacking in seriousness, and he particularly disliked the touring bands of players with their slapstick comedies, in which the commentator clown, **Hanswurst**, so frequently figured. In France, Britain and the German-speaking countries, neoclassicism was soon to come under attack for being rule-bound, snobbish and inhibiting to the creative spirit; but at best, the critics were not dogmatic but sought to combat barbarism with the standards of the two highest civilizations of which they were aware, those of the Greek city-states and of Rome in the time of Augustus. They also pursued a reconciliation between Reason and Nature, for Reason was deemed mechanical and lifeless by itself, just as Nature was wild and anarchic without Reason. The critic sought a judicious balance, the harmony of opposites, which was also held to be the secret of behavioural and moral decorum.

The challenge to neoclassicism The first major challenge to neoclassical opinion came from **Gotthold Ephraim Lessing** (1729–81), who attacked Gottsched's reforms in *Briefe, die neuste Litteratur betreffend* (1759). He became the dramaturge to the National Theatre at Hamburg (1767–8), publishing a series of papers as *Hamburgische Dramaturgie*. The aesthetic principles described in *Laokoon* (1766), of which only the first part was finished, were developed through his own plays, which range in style from the early prose comedy, *Minna von Barnhelm* (1767), to his final tragedy, *Nathan the Wise*, not produced until two years after his death. Lessing, with the von **Schlegel** brothers, **August Wilhelm** (1767–1845) and Karl Wilhelm Friedrich (1772–1829), first proposed the theories which became known as romanticism. Gottsched was criticized for importing artificial French rules into Germany, and Lessing cited the example of **Shakespeare** as a dramatist who followed no sterile formula but achieved a directness of utterance unparalleled since the ancient Greeks. This enthusiasm for Shakespeare was shared by all the romantic critics and August Wilhelm von Schlegel's translations of Shakespeare's plays still hold pride of place on the German stage.

Naturalness and sincerity became key words in the critical vocabulary; and although Lessing anticipated and lawless aspirations of the **Sturm und Drang** movement, he was too steeped in classical humanism to endorse them. Johann Georg Hamann (1730–88) and his one-time pupil, Johann Gottfried Herder (1744–1803), finally broke with classical doctrine and declared that only the unfettered creative imagination could contemplate God and His works. In *Kritische Wälder* (1769), Herder argued that plays have to be seen in relationship to the prevailing circumstances of their times, not judged by any absolute standards, although the *Kraft* (energy, power) of the poet could transcend social conditioning. Herder championed not just Shakespeare but folk poetry and those early German plays which Gottsched had despised; and he influenced the great romantic writer, **Johann Wolfgang von Goethe** (1749–1832), who brought him to Weimar in 1776.

Herder was also an early admirer of **Jean-Jacques Rousseau** (1712–78), who in a tormented life came to reject the debilitating effects, as he saw them, of urban civilization, calling for a return to simpler, more primitive human values. Through Rousseau's *Du contrat social* (1762), romanticism acquired a political stance (for populism, democracy and folk loyalties) which it never subsequently lost. Romanticism reversed the neoclassical doctrines, perhaps too neatly. It was anti-academic, anti-monarchical, individualistic, passionate rather than polite, stressing the aspirations of the human soul. The artist became a prophet and a seer, the 'unacknowledged legislator of mankind', while the critic was his apostle and interpreter.

In Britain, until the restrictions of the Theatres Act were partially lifted in 1843, the theatre was damned in the eyes of many romantic critics by its aristocratic leanings and state censorship. Shakespeare, however, was exempt from these strictures and Samuel Taylor Coleridge, among others, wrote eloquently about him. **William Hazlitt** (1778–1830), the finest theatrical essayist to have emerged in Britain, described Elizabethan drama and Shakespeare's characters in powerful articles, as well as providing vivid portraits of actors like **Kemble** and **Kean**, for which he is best remembered. Hazlitt's collection of essays, *A View of the English Stage* (1818), remains a model for British critics; and he excelled in describing the social contexts of drama, which he dubbed (translating from German) the 'spirit of the age'. *Tales from Shakespeare* by **Charles Lamb** and his sister Mary introduced generations of schoolchildren to the basic plots. Among academics in Britain, Shakespearian interpretations owe a considerable debt to German romantic scholarship. Even A. C. Bradley's *Shakespearian Tragedy* (1905), a standard university textbook for 50 years, referred back to the pioneering work of Lessing and the Schlegels, and in particular adopted Lessing-like interpretations of the Tragic Hero and the importance of empathy and *catharsis*.

In France, what became bardolatry among lesser critics was slower to arrive and existed side by side with conventional neoclassical opinion, which received a new lease of life through the boulevard drama of **Eugène Scribe** (1791–1861) and the formulae of the 'well-made play'. Nevertheless, Mme de Staël's *De l'Allemagne* (1813) and Stendhal's *Racine et Shakespeare* (1823, 1825) paved the way for the flowering of French romanticism in the works of Vicomte François-René de Chateaubriand (1768–1848) and particularly of **Victor Hugo** (1802–85), whose *Préface de Cromwell* (1827) went out of its way to reject two of the three unities, retaining only that of action in a modified form. He praised Shakespeare's alternative technique which organized a play through contrasts, tone-colour and the juxtaposition of themes. Hugo's passion for Shakespeare is fully expressed in *William Shakespeare* (1864). By the 1840s, however, a reaction against romanticism had begun to be expressed through the writings of Charles Augustin Sainte-Beuve (1804–69), who came strongly to deplore the vaunting of egoism as inspiration. His *Chateaubriand et son groupe littéraire sous l'Empire* (1860) scathingly denigrated the romantic movement in France and proposed a new role for theatre critics, who should aim towards the sophisticated broadmindedness of Montaigne, the 16th-century essayist whom he particularly admired.

One consequence of the romantic movement was that aesthetics became detached from ethics or from any classical concept of civilization. Criticism necessa-

rily became more subjective, the reflection of the likes and dislikes of the individual critic; and in the early 19th century, magazines and periodicals which appealed to the new middle classes developed, whose pages contained the work of critical essayists whose personalities defined their aesthetic standards and whose charm became a major selling point. **Jules Janin** (1804–74) was one such, the critic of *Journal des Débats*, who could make and break theatrical reputations following no guide other than his own instinct. His main rival, Gustave Planche of *La Revue des Deux Mondes*, specialized in iconoclasm. Das Junge Deutschland (with Lüdwig Börne, 1786–1837, the dramatist **Karl Gutzkow**, 1811–78, and briefly Heinrich Heine, 1797–1856) was a literary and political movement in the 1830s, which sought to direct the idealism of the romantics towards specific political ends, anticipating social realism. Its main principles were expressed in Ludolf Wienbarg's *Aesthetische Feldzüge* (1834). Apart from such political movements, which were reflected to different degrees in other countries, the main feature of European criticism at this time lay in the growth of those elegant, personal descriptive essays which became known as *feuilletons*, a word still used to describe the review sections of newspapers in some parts of Europe; and the master of the *feuilleton*, who preached 'art for art's sake', was **Théophile Gautier** (1811–72), who wrote for *Le Monde Dramatique* and *La Presse*.

Despite the popularity of the *feuilletonistes*, criticism aspired towards a greater precision of thought, something of that discipline which had been lost with the decline of neoclassicism. One of Sainte-Beuve's disciples, Hippolyte Taine (1823–93), turned to science as the method for the objective description of a work of art, which could 'tackle the human soul' as well as the surrounding social history. Such faith in science was criticized by even his supporters, such as Paul Bourget (1852–1935) and Ferdinand Brunetière (1849–1906), who came to theorize about tragedy from a neo-Darwinian point of view, in his lectures at the Ecole Normale in 1889. Nevertheless, Brunetière eventually proclaimed the bankruptcy of science as an approach to art. Other French critics, such as Jules Lemaître (1853–1914) of the *Journal des Débats* and 'Anatole France' (1844–1924), the pseudonym of Anatole-François Thibault who wrote extensively for many papers but particularly for *Le Temps* from 1887–92, scrupulously avoided scientism, adopting an impressionistic style of considerable brilliance in which the first consideration was of an epicurean delight, and the second vaguely left-wing sentiments.

In the 43 years which separated the birth of the Third Republic in France in 1871 and the First World War, the growth of theatre criticism defies short, comprehensive analysis. In Paris, major poets and dramatists wrote regular columns, such as Alphonse Daudet (1840–97), Catulle Mendès (1841–1909), Jean-Jacques Weiss (1827–91) and even **Emile Zola** (1840–1902), whose contributions to *Le Bien Public*, together with his propagandist *Le Roman experimental* (1880), argued a fundamental, if extreme, case for naturalism. By 1911, there were no less than 150 theatre columns in Paris; and in 1907, a daily newspaper, *Comoedia*, was exclusively devoted to the theatre. Paul Léautard (1872–1956), Léon Blum in *L'Echo de Paris* and *La Grande*

Revue, Henri Bordeaux in *Revue Hebdomadaire* and *La Revue des Deux Mondes*, Paul Souday in *Le Temps* and Anatole France all had reading publics which spread beyond the borders of France.

In Germany, the proliferation of newspapers was one factor in the development of a split between ordinary theatre reviewing and academic criticism. Whereas the academics increasingly sought to apply scientific criteria, or at least sustainably objective ones, to the study of drama, the daily critics had neither the time nor the inclination to do so, although they tended to be more academic than the British critics. Before 1870, much German criticism was political in character, with Wolfgang Menzel (1798–1873) insisting that the critic should confront the nation with major moral questions and such writers as Theodor Vischer (1807–87), Robert Prutz (1816–72) and **Hermann Hettner** seeking to combine historical and social analysis with politics and aesthetics. The establishment of the Kaiserreich in 1870 and the new commercialism of the press changed the context in which critical discussions took place. As the theatre itself, under censorship, lost its political bite, so such journalists as Karl Frenzel of the *Nationalzeitung*, Berlin, concentrated on drama as entertainment, ignoring its other dimensions. As in France, there were brilliant *feuilletonistes*, such as Theodor Fontane (1819–98) and **Paul Lindau** (1839–1919), whose stylistic excellence compensated for their unwillingness to take part in wider speculation. Their approach was challenged, however, by those critics who came to embrace naturalism, led by Julius Hart (1859–1930), and whose arguments, as expressed by **Otto Brahm** (1856–1912), Paul Schlenther (1854–1916) and Alfred Kerr (1867–1948), laid the foundations for contemporary German criticism. Through Brahm and Kerr, criticism recovered its wider interests, notably in the avant-garde, without losing its journalistic panache – although their approaches could still be attacked as too subjective. A Marxist critic, such as Franz Mehring (1846–1919), would turn any aesthetic discussion into a political seminar, while Herbert Ihering (1888–1977), an early supporter of **Bertolt Brecht**, stressed the importance of a factual examination of the performance. Between 1933 and 1945, all criticism under the Nazis in Germany had to be dedicated to the goals of nationalism.

British theatre criticism, like British theatre itself, was slower to develop than in France or Germany; and less space was devoted to it within its press. Matthew Arnold (1822–88) attacked what he dubbed the philistinism of Victorian smugness and its moral values and the coarse popularity of proletarian theatre. His essay, 'The French Play in London', for the August issue of *Nineteenth Century* (1879), based on a visit of the Comédie-Française to London, called for the establishment of a British **National Theatre** – and was continually cited by those who wanted to establish continental-style repertory theatres in Britain. Clement Scott (1841–1904), the theatre critic for the *Daily Telegraph* for 30 years and a minor dramatist, became notorious for his attacks on **Ibsen** and the naturalistic writers, mainly on the grounds of preserving a moral decorum of language and subject matter within the theatre. Scott also edited *The Theatre*, which he founded in 1877, but withdrew in 1890 after a dispute with **William Archer** (1856–1924), the dramatist and critic

of the *World*, who was Ibsen's champion and translator in Britain. Archer with **Harley Granville Barker** (1877–1946) provided a blueprint for a British National Theatre (1907), which offered the model for fund-raisers and other enthusiasts for 50 years. The most brilliant and successful theatre critic, however, and the best since Hazlitt, was **Bernard Shaw**, whose columns for the *Saturday Review* from 1895 to 1898 combined wit, seriousness of intent and a voluminous, if superficial, general knowledge. His successor was almost equally remarkable, Max Beerbohm (1872–1956), the half-brother of **Herbert Beerbohm Tree** the actor-manager who wrote for the *Saturday Review* from 1895 to 1910, and was also an essayist and playwright.

Themes of 20th-century criticism From this welter of turn-of-the-century criticism, certain themes emerged which often transcended national boundaries and sometimes derived from ideas promulgated through romanticism. The great debating issue was that of the new naturalistic drama, pioneered by Zola and **Antoine**'s Théâtre Libre in Paris but which came to be associated with Ibsen and the Scandinavians. Systematically attacked by conventional moralists and often censored in Britain, the new naturalists were stoutly defended by most left-of-centre critics, including Shaw, who used the evident seriousness of Ibsen, **Brieux** and Zola as a means to attack the superficiality of state censorship. Censorship itself was an issue which divided critics around Europe. But naturalism was only one manifestation of the avant-garde which preoccupied critics. In some countries, such as Ireland still under British rule, nationalism and the rediscovery of national languages dominated critical discussion; and straight patriotism was incorporated into the aesthetic theories of Russia, Italy, Norway and the several nations which comprised the Austro-Hungarian empire (1867–1918). In line with romantic theory, the folk origins of their national theatres were discussed, usually praised at the expense of those from other countries and, for example, the Polishness of being Polish was debated, with the different imperialisms of France, Britain and Prussia coming under attack.

There was also a European growth of interest in Shakespeare, with the first translations appearing in Hungary (1864), Spain (in the 1870s), Belgium (1884), Denmark, Sweden, Norway and Russia. Shakespeare Associations developed in many countries, while in Britain, the interest in Shakespearian scholarship and production led to the foundation in 1894 of the Elizabethan Stage Society, under the actor-director, **William Poel**, whose experiments with open stages and minimal settings profoundly influenced Shakespearian performances in the 20th century. British Shakespearian scholarship moved away from its German intellectual roots towards practical staging – exemplified in Granville Barker's *Prefaces to Shakespeare* (1927–47), in which his experience as a director and actor is of paramount importance – and towards sensitive research and the brilliantly imaginative work of G. Wilson Knight and Caroline Spurgeon, whose analysis of Shakespeare's poetic images provided the **Royal Shakespeare Company** in the 1960s with a supply of set designs. The Polish-born critic **Jan Kott** (b. 1914) bravely attempted to strip 19th-century moralizing away from the canon in his *Shakespeare, our*

Contemporary (1964), in which the absurdity of Shakespeare's world and its power struggles was stressed and related to modern preoccupations.

But theatre criticism was also indebted to romanticism in other, less direct ways, for the romantics had uncovered problems and ideas which continued to haunt all intellectuals until the 1950s, whether they considered themselves to be part of the romantic movement or not. One such major theme was that of individualism and the search for the self. While many turn-of-the-century critics derided the spectacle of the doomed tragic hero, as hammed by actor–managers in countless melodramas, nevertheless they continued to be confronted by the consequences of individualism, such as the conflicting demands of the state, the private conscience and religious belief. **Nietzsche**'s assertion that God was dead was capable of many interpretations, one consequence being that without God there could be no inherent order within the universe. Edmund Husserl (1859–1938), the mathematician-philosopher, in common with some British empiricists, argued that the true study of philosophy lay in the accurate description of consciousness, which he christened 'phenomenology'. One of his pupils was the existentialist, Martin Heidegger (1889–1976), although Husserl's impact on criticism was more evident through the dominance in post-war Paris of **Jean-Paul Sartre** (1905–80). Sartre's particular contribution lay in his attempt to reconcile the apparently irreconcilable faiths in existential individualism, an individualism which discovers its own 'essence' through the act of being, and Marxist collectivism.

While such philosophical speculation coloured European criticism particularly in the 1950s, there were other less abstract ways in which individualism affected aesthetic theory. One was the growth of expressionism, which began in Germany in 1910, a movement of social revolt and a reaction against naturalism in which the playwright or director is considered to speak directly to the audience, albeit in a variety of ways, including agit-prop imagery. The Swedish critic, **Pär Lagerkvist** (1891–1974), who received the Nobel Prize for Literature in 1951, cogently argued the case for the expressionism in **August Strindberg** (against the naturalism of Henrik Ibsen) in *Modern Teater* (1918); but the greater international impact came from the work of the German expressionists, **Toller** and **Wedekind** among them, who influenced a generation of writers and directors, of whom the most systematic in developing his ideas was the dramatist–critic, Bertolt Brecht (1898–1956). Brecht's theoretical writings were considerable and appeared in essays and dialogues throughout his life; but the ideas on 'epic' theatre, 'alienation' (*Verfremdungseffekte*) and the 'gest' were summarized in *Kleines Organon für das Theater* (1949). Brecht borrowed some techniques from expressionism to provide the basis for what was essentially an instructional theatre, devoted to furthering Marxism, although his own theatrical sense and poetic instincts prevented his plays from being narrowly propagandist. With customary thoroughness, however, he argued the case for his epic theatre from the roots of dramatic theory, attacking the Aristotelian concept of theatre, as he understood it.

Brecht's views were not initially well received in the Soviet Union, whose official views, after the outpouring of modernism in the early 1920s, remained wedded to social realism, in which naturalistic stagings were wedded to socialist analysis. The first Commisar for Education in Soviet Russia was **Anatoly Vasilievich Lunacharsky** (1875–1933), a dramatist and comparatively liberal in his views, who furthered the cause of theatre under the intellectually restricted circumstances of Stalinism. The main purges of intellectuals, however, took place after his death and continued throughout the Eastern bloc until long after the death of Stalin. A particular target for Soviet attacks was, however, not Brecht, not even bourgeois theatre, for operetta houses still comprise a third of the theatres in the Soviet Union, but another and more fundamental offshoot of expressionism, the theatre of the absurd.

Absurdist theatre has many roots, well described in Martin Esslin's *The Theatre of the Absurd* (1962), but what all its different manifestations had in common was a hatred of conventional bourgeois theatre, scientific logic and middle-class ethical restrictions. While **Alfred Jarry**'s *Ubu Roi*, conceived as a marionette play in 1888 but performed as a stage play in 1896, is generally regarded as the seminal work, leading to the mock-scientific theories of Jarry's Pataphysics and to French surrealism, the leading theorist was **Stanisław Ignacy Witkiewicz** (1885–1919), 'Witkacy', a Polish dramatist and artist, whose impact on post-war absurdist writers and directors, including **Samuel Beckett**, **Eugène Ionesco** and the director, **Tadeusz Kantor**, was considerable. His use of visual imagery, for Witkacy had studied as an architect and painter, remains (despite the plays of **Picasso**) the most effective dramatic extension of surrealism; and as a philosopher, he was able to connect his ideas with those of existentialism. The French theorist, poet and playwright, **Antonin Artaud** (1896–1948), was more violent in his rejection of bourgeois codes, both in the theatre and outside it, declaring in his collection of essays, *Le Théâtre et son double* (1938), that the theatre would 'never find itself again . . . except by furnishing the spectator with the truthful precipitates of dreams', in which crime, erotic obsessions and savagery loomed large. Artaud in turn influenced **Jerzy Grotowski** (b. 1933) whose book, *Towards a Poor Theatre* (1968), and his example as a director working solely through those means supplied by the expressiveness of actors, made a great impact on the fringe theatres of the 1960s.

This often bewildering variety of theories and philosophies became absorbed into critical journalism, sometimes as little more than useful terms employed without questioning their background or meanings. In the inter-war years in Britain, it was possible for critics such as **James Agate** (1877–1947), who wrote for the *Sunday Times* from 1923 until his death, or W. A. Darlington (1890–1979) who was with the *Daily Telegraph* for 48 years, to be resolutely anti-intellectual, relying on their flair for judging the theatrical moment and their good-humoured relationship with their readers. 'Touchstone' criticism was in fashion: for Agate, **Irving** was the touchstone by which he judged great acting. Agate's successor at the *Sunday Times*, Harold Hobson (1904–   ), was another touchstone critic, although in his case Edwige Feuillère represented a kind of acting excellence. **Kenneth Tynan** (1927–80), the last flowering of the *feuilletoniste* tradition in Britain, employed touchstone criticism in his early essays, published in *He That Plays The King* (1950), which much impressed Agate.

1960s to the present day   In the 1960s, however, journalists were confronted with many genres of theatre and needed to develop a wider range of vocabulary in order to cope with them. An understanding of what was intended by the term 'alienation' was necessary to discuss Brecht's plays; and in such ways, a new technical language was developed which critics like **Irving Wardle** of *The Times* and Michael Billington of *The Guardian* could use skilfully, without losing their readership. British criticism, however, remained pragmatic and descriptive, not given to dogma; and Benedict Nightingale, who made his reputation through the *New Statesman*, was more adept at images than arguments. French, German and Italian critics, however, were more guided by intellectual beliefs, and would stake their claims to be Marxists, existentialists or structuralists in advance, approaching the act of criticism from the appropriate angle. British critics tended to be good at observing but weak at thinking, whereas continental ones were strong in argument but slack at observation.

Few post-war European theatre critics, however, could retain week after week the kind of high reputation enjoyed by their turn-of-the-century ancestors, partly because in the modern press less space is usually given to theatre criticism and partly perhaps because the theatre itself is considered less important. What may also be a contributory factor to the decline of theatre criticism lies in the fact that one powerful, intellectually cogent and embracing form of criticism has had no impact on journalism whatsoever, nor can it have. It derived from the universities and the systematic study of language. Ferdinand de Saussure (1857–1913) was a Swiss linguistic philosopher, who was a professor in Geneva from 1891 until his death, and his lectures were published posthumously. *Cours de linguistique générale* (1915, Paris; 1959, New York) described language as a system of signs, in which every item both defines and is defined by its surrounding signs. The study of signs, which do not have to be verbal signs, became known as 'structuralism' or 'semiology'. The work of the French anthropologist, Claude Lévi-Strauss, applied the principles of Saussurean linguistics to the problems of communication in many cultures, from primitive societies to modern ones, and his *Les Structures élémentaires de la parenté* (1949, Paris) remains a classic study of social structures and their origins. Roland Barthes (1915–80) approached literature from a similar point of view. His first book, *Le Degré zéro de l'écriture* (1953), describes the cultural conditioning which is inherent in all writing and in his various essays, including *Sur Racine* (1963) and *Essais critiques* (1964), he attempted to analyse certain works following the semiological methods. In *Critique et vérité* (1966), he gave a phrase-by-phrase analysis of a Balzac story, described the act of reading and the relationship of the reader's experiences while following the language of the text. Semiology, which is so concerned with the total experience, would not find the description of an audience in a theatre, or the surroundings of that theatre, as being any the less worthy of its attention than the play or performance itself. It attempts to incorporate all the disciplines – philosophy, anthropology, sociology, psychology and linguistics – into one overall study of how man communicates with man; and while Barthes himself championed Brecht and the 'nouveau roman', his methods could equally well be applied to all kinds of social transactions, as in 'transactional analysis'.

Barthes's impact on French criticism was immediate and profound, while Sartre's influence, which had dominated the intellectual debates in post-war Paris until the 1960s, declined after his arrival. But for everyday journalism, semiology is far too cumbersome and exacting a science to be of much practical help, although sometimes it offered a useful corrective to the prejudices and slipshod opinions of theatre critics. Indeed, after the arrival of the semiologists, no journalist critic could claim to be in the vanguard of opinion, although some semioticians, such as Carlos Tindemans at Antwerp University, succeeded both in journalism and as a Professor of Semiotics.

With the growth of semiology, academic or 'scientific' criticism finally was forced to break from its journalistic counterpart, for the methods of one were inherently unsuitable to the other. This split runs the risk of weakening journalism by separating it from serious intellectual debate and of rarefying academic criticism by narrowing the number of subjects which it can tackle at any one time. Semiology, like psychoanalysis, is a process which takes a long time before it arrives at any conclusions or results.   JE

Criticism: 2. USA

The critic experienced a difficult time establishing himself as an important force in the American theatre. Since the theatre itself was considered a dangerous public institution in the late 18th century, his role was seen more as censor than critic to guard against violations of social and moral laws. The earliest extant review of a play appeared anonymously in the *Maryland Gazette* (1760) at a time when papers usually 'noticed' a performance with little or no critical evaluation. The subject prompted **William Dunlap** in his *History of the American Theatre* (1832) to devote a chapter to critics, explaining that in 1796 a group of six 'gentlemen' organized themselves into a 'band of scalpers and tomahawkers' to write anonymous reviews about New York productions. A few years later, Washington Irving wrote the charming and lightly satirical 'Letters of Jonathan Oldstyle, Gent.' (1802–3), to comment upon the New York stage. Irving also penned reviews for *The Salmagundi* (1807) and *Select Reviews*, later the *Analectic Magazine* (1815). He is regarded as the first American dramatic critic of importance.

Few daily newspapers published reviews on a regular basis until the 1850s, and even fewer allowed by-lines by their critics until the end of the century. Theatre notices and criticism became associated more with short-lived dramatic magazines such as *Theatrical Censor* (1806); *Rambler's Magazine and New York Theatrical Register* (1809); *Mirror of Taste and Dramatic Censor* (1810); the *Broadway Journal and Stranger's Guide* (1847); and sporting weeklies such as *Spirit of the Times* (1831) and *New York Clipper* (1853). The first important theatrical weekly was the *New York Dramatic Mirror* founded in 1879. Play reviewing, like the theatre itself, was held in low esteem. It was not uncommon for editors to send untrained reporters to 'write up' the opening night of a play, nor was it uncommon for critics to review only productions which advertised in their papers. In 1836, Edgar Allan Poe called professional reviewers 'illiterate mountebanks'. Walt Whitman, writing in 1847, blamed the vulgarity and coarseness of the theatre upon the paid puff system.

The expansion of the newspaper business in the 1850s prompted separate 'amusement' departments and separate dramatic columns of news and reviews. Moralists and puffers tended to dominate the profession although Henry Clapp, Jr, returned from France in 1855 or 1856 to set up a coterie of critics at Pfaff's Restaurant to rail against tradition and convention. He advocated that the theatre be judged on aesthetic rather than moral grounds, and wrote bright and witty essays for the *Saturday Press* and other weeklies. The Civil War destroyed the movement, however, and what emerged afterwards was a highly moralistic and conservative school headed by **William Winter**, **John Ranken Towse**, and **Henry Austin Clapp**. Winter made his reputation on Horace Greeley's *New York Tribune* from 1865–1909; Towse headed the dramatic department of the elitist *New York Evening Post* from 1874–1902. Clapp wrote for the *Boston Daily Advertiser* from 1868–1902. These 'genteel' critics shared the values of the cultured elite and endured until these values changed.

The popular press demanded bright and clever reviews, not moralistic essays, however, and the innovations introduced by Henry Clapp, Jr, were carried on in the aggressive and colourful writing of Nym Crinkle (**Andrew C. Wheeler**) in the New York *Sun, World*, and 'lesser' dramatic and sporting journals. **Alan Dale** (Alfred J. Cohen) popularized his 'School of the Flippant Remark' from coast to coast for Hearst publications in the late 1890s and early 1900s. Other critics sought reform. Stephen Ryder Fiske of *Wilkes' Spirit of the Times* (1879–1902) ridiculed shoddy business practices and productions. He viewed the theatre as a worthwhile place of amusement which should be conducted in a professional manner. Epes W. Sargent served vaudeville in a similar way, writing for a number of trade papers including *Variety* in 1905. **Harrison Grey Fiske** of the *New York Dramatic Mirror* (1880–1911) worked to improve business practices and sought a charity (the Actor's Fund) to help the profession. He fought to protect the legal rights of playwrights, and to bring an end to the blackmailing efforts of the *New York Dramatic News*. Still other critics worked to improve the American drama. **William Dean Howells** in the 1880s sought a realistic native drama from his editor's desk at *Atlantic Monthly*, and encouraged **James A. Herne** and **Bronson Howard**. Edward Dithmar of the *New York Times* (1884–1902) encouraged American dramatists and broke with tradition by refusing to judge a play on moral grounds. Academicians such as Clayton Hamilton, Walter Prichard Eaton, and **Brander Matthews** wrote books about the history, practice, and theory of the drama thus educating the public. An important voice for change, **James G. Huneker**, promoted the new European drama of Ibsen and Shaw, and insisted that art be judged on aesthetic rather than moral grounds. Huneker influenced a generation of writers including **George Jean Nathan**.

As dramatic critic of *Smart Set* (1909–23) Nathan attacked the shop-worn dramatic devices of **Belasco**, the pomposity of the cultured elite, and the ignorance of the masses. He used ridicule, sarcasm, and satire to rid the theatre of stultifying tradition and convention. Like Huneker, he championed Ibsen, Shaw, Strindberg, **Maeterlinck**, and **Hauptmann**, and unlike Huneker he found value in the new American drama. He discovered **Eugene O'Neill** and published his early work in *Smart Set*. While he never wielded the power of his New York peers on the daily press, he commanded the respect of the young intellectuals in the 1910s and 1920s. His unwillingness to find value in the political theatre of the 1930s eroded his influence as a vital force in the theatre.

The exuberant **Alexander Woollcott** established the power of the *New York Times* in the 1910s with his enthusiastic prose and his battle with the **Shuberts**. **Percy Hammond** moved from the *Chicago Tribune* (1908–21) to the *New York Tribune* (1921–36) and brought his urbane and satirical style to bear upon that theatre's pretensions. He could dismiss a Shakespearian actor with the flick of his pen by noting: 'he wore his tights competently'. **Burns Mantle** provided good journalistic prose and sound opinions for the *New York Evening Mail* (1911–22) and *Daily News* (1922–43). **Brooks Atkinson** served for 34 years as chief critic of the *New York Times* (1926–60), enhancing the paper's reputation and his own for fairness and accuracy. Unlike Nathan he encouraged the more revolutionary theatre of the 1930s as did other critics including John Anderson (*Post* and *Journal*), Gilbert Gabriel (*Sun* and *American*), **John Mason Brown** (*Post* and *Saturday Review*), and **Richard Watts, Jr** (*Herald-Tribune* and *Post*). In 1950 **Walter Kerr** began reviewing for *Commonweal*, and a year later for the *Herald-Tribune*. A former drama professor, Kerr brought to his position a historical perspective lacked by most of his colleagues. Upon the retirement of Atkinson in 1960, Kerr was acknowledged as the foremost New York critic, a position he held until his retirement from the *New York Times* in 1983.

Outside New York, the reputation of critics has usually remained local or regional reflecting the institutions they review. Exceptions include: Henry Taylor Parker of the *Boston Transcript* (1905–35); **Claudia Cassidy** of the *Chicago Tribune* (1942–65); **Elliot Norton** of the *Boston Post* (1934–56) and other papers; and **Richard Coe** of the *Washington Post* (1946–79). These critics have gained wide-spread recognition because their writings have had an impact upon the national theatre.

As the number of New York newspapers declined after 1920 (15 in 1920; 7 in 1950; 3 in 1970), magazine critics gained in importance. **Stark Young** appealed to educated tastes in the *New Republic* (1921–47) as did Joseph Wood Krutch in the *Nation* (1924–52), and Kenneth Macgowan, Rosamond Gilder, and Edith J. R. Isaacs in **Theatre Arts Monthly** (1916–64). Discriminating readers also have turned to **Harold Clurman** in the *Nation*; **Eric Bentley**, Stanley Kauffmann, and **Robert Brustein** in *New Republic*; Henry Hewes in *Saturday Review*; **Robert Benchley**, Wolcott Gibbs, Brendan Gill, and Edith Oliver in *The New Yorker*; and **John Simon** in *New York Magazine*. The general public has depended more on Louis Kronenberger and T. E. Kalem in *Time* magazine and Jack Kroll in *Newsweek* while members of the theatrical profession have relied on *Billboard* and *Variety*. *Village*

Voice critics John Lahr and Michael Feingold have kept its readers abreast of the avant-garde. Television critics have been part of the Broadway scene for over a decade but there is no agreement over their role and influence. In the 1980s, the *New York Times* remains the most important and powerful newspaper to review the American theatre, and their daily critic the most powerful individual. In 1981 Frank Rich began his tenure in the position.   TLM

Cronyn, Hume (1911–) American actor, director, and writer, born in London, Ontario, Canada. Cronyn studied acting at the New York School of the Theatre and the American Academy of Dramatic Art, and made his professional debut with Cochran's Stock Company in Washington, DC, in 1931. He also worked for the Barter Theatre during their second season. His Broadway debut was as the Janitor in *Hipper's Holiday* (1934).

Cronyn soon became a much sought after character in Hollywood, where he married **Jessica Tandy** in 1942. While in Los Angeles, Cronyn directed Tandy as Miss Collins in **Tennessee Williams**'s *Portrait of a Madonna* (1946). This exposure led to Tandy's being cast as Blanche Dubois in 1947 on Broadway.

Cronyn and Tandy appeared together for the first time in 1951 in *The Fourposter*, in which they were 'compared to the **Lunts**, in that the team had enough grace, skill, and wit to hold a stage and an audience by themselves'. They have since co-starred in *The Physicists* (1964), **Albee**'s *A Delicate Balance* (1966), *The Gin Game* (1977), *Noel Coward in Two Keys* (1974), and *Foxfire* (1982), of which Cronyn was co-author. Between these projects, Cronyn and Tandy played several seasons at the **Guthrie Theatre** and at the **Stratford Festival** in Ontario. In 1964 Cronyn played Polonius to **Richard Burton**'s Hamlet, winning a Tony.   SMA

Crosman, Henrietta (1861–1944) American stage and film actress. Born in Wheeling, West Virginia, she began acting at 16 with **John Ellsler**. She scored her first success as Celia in *As You Like It* under **Daly**. After successes in *Gloriana* and *Mistress Nell*, she became the outstanding Rosalind of her time, and also scored a hit in *Sweet Kitty Bellairs*. From 1932 to 1936 she appeared in films, retiring in 1939.   SMA

Crothers, Rachel (c. 1878–1958) American actress, playwright and director whose commercially successful plays chronicled the tension in early 20th-century women between their new economic and sexual freedom and their old traditional values. Her first success, *The Three of Us* (1906), was followed by some 30 Broadway plays, most of which she directed and staged herself. Although she wrote some sentimental plays in the teens, her best works were her serio-comic, women-centred plays: *Myself Bettina* (1908), *A Man's World* (1910), *Ourselves* (1913), *Young Wisdom* (1914), *He and She* (1920 – first produced 1911), *Expressing Willie* (1924), *Let Us Be Gay* (1929), *As Husbands Go* (1931), *When Ladies Meet* (1932), and *Susan and God* (1937).

Crothers's other accomplishments include the founding of the Stage Women's War Relief Fund (1917), United Theatre Relief Committee (1932) and American Theatre Wing for War Relief (1940 – best known for the Stage Door Canteen). In 1939 she received the Chi Omega National Achievement Award.   FB

Crouse, Russel (1893–1966) American playwright, librettist, and producer. Crouse began his stage writing career as librettist for *The Gang's All Here* (1931), but it was only after he teamed with **Howard Lindsay** on *Anything Goes* (1934) that he achieved continued success. Crouse and Lindsay became prolific collaborators. Their first straight play was *Life With Father*, a nostalgic bit of Americana that captured the hearts of the Broadway audience for a contemporary long-run record which held until the 1970s. Working with Lindsay throughout the remainder of his career, Crouse helped write more than 15 plays and librettos, a highly successful example of the latter being *The Sound of Music* (1959). They also teamed to produce many plays in New York including several of their own and the profitable *Arsenic and Old Lace* (1941).   LDC

Crowne, John (c. 1640–1712) English playwright. Emigrated to America in 1657, when his father was granted estates in Nova Scotia by Cromwell, and educated at Harvard, he returned to England in 1660 when the family lost the estates at the Restoration. He began writing in the 1660s and his first play was performed in 1671. In 1675 he wrote the last court masque *Calisto*. His heroic play *The Destruction of Jerusalem* was successful in 1677. His finest tragedy, *The Ambitious Statesman* (1679), is a serious study of political power. A favourite of the King, Crowne was given the subject for his popular comedy, *Sir Courtly Nice* (1685), by Charles himself. His political comedy, *City Politiques* (1682), mocked leading lawyers and politicians. *The Married Beau* (1694), Crowne's last comedy, is a cynical satire on the torture of marriage. He died, poor and obscure, in 1712.   PH

Cruelty, Theatre of see **Artaud, Antonin**

Cuadra, Pablo Antonio (1912–) Nicaraguan poet, historian, journalist and playwright. Also lawyer, professor of history and literature, and founder of important cultural periodicals in Managua, such as *Vanguardia* (*Vanguard*) and *Trinchera* (*Trench*). His dramatic work includes *El árbol seco* (*The Dry Tree*), *Satanás entra en escena* (*Satan Enters on Stage*, 1938), *Pastorela* (1939) and his masterpiece, *Por los caminos van los campesinos* (*Along the Roads Go the Peasants*, 1937). The latter is set during the intervention of the USA in Nicaragua during the 1920s and protests the injustices committed against the poor in the name of politics. During the Sandinista government, Cuadra served as editor of the opposition newspaper, *La Prensa*.   GW

Cuba Early manifestations of theatrical activity in Cuba parallel those of the other Caribbean islands. The *areytos* of the indigenous peoples were complex theatre–dance forms that incorporated music with full dress costume to recount the historical, religious and cultural repertoire of the society. When the Spanish colonizers banned the *areytos* in 1512 on grounds of primitive hereticism, they extinguished an important part of the indigenous culture and took another step in obliterating the native population itself. Later, when black slaves were imported to work the developing sugar plantations, other traditions of culture and art forms came to exert an influence.

Cuba's strategic location generated a long struggle for military and economic control. The British occupied Havana in 1762–3; French refugees from Haiti arrived in the late 18th century. For centuries, sugar has been the single most important product, and its fluctuating price determined the local prosperity. Theatrical activity existed only sporadically during the first two centuries (1500–1700). The first Cuban play is considered to be *El príncipe jardinero y fingido Cloridano* (*The Presumed Gardener Prince Cloridano*) by Santiago Pita. Published in Spain around 1730, this play treats chivalry in a mythical Grecian setting far removed from Cuba's reality. Beginning late in the century, a round of theatre construction facilitated local productions: the Coliseo (Coliseum) (1775), later restored as the Teatro El Principal (The Principal Theatre) (1803), the Diorama (1829), the Tacón (1838), and others. The acknowledged father of the Cuban national theatre is Francisco Covarrubias (1775–1850). Impresario, actor and author of more than 20 plays, he was famous for his representation of the 'negrito' (the white actor in black face), probably before the famous roles created by **Thomas Rice** and Daniel Decatur Emmett in the USA. Covarrubias integrated popular Cuban figures into forms of the Spanish *sainete* without political implications or character development, but no play has survived.

During the 19th century Cuba continued to chafe under colonial domination, since the Spanish American struggle for independence (1810–25) excluded the island. In other countries the new freedom ushered in the unrestrained liberties of romanticism and Cuba also was touched as early as 1836 with the production of *Don Pedro de Castilla* by Francisco Javier Foxá (1816–65). This Dominican exile's play drew a storm of protest and censorship. José María Heredia (1803–39), Cuban poet and patriot who spent years of exile in the USA and Mexico, wrote romantic poetry, but his plays, translations and adaptations retained neoclassical styles and techniques. José Jacinto Milanés (1814–63) later took the figure of *El conde Alarcos* (*Count Alarcos*, 1838) as a dramatic symbol of tyranny and oppression; in his later plays he turned toward picturesque popular figures presented in natural language, such as *El mirón cubano* (*Cuban Busybody*, 1840), which consists of several scenes of a costumbristic nature in which Milanés censures habits and customs of the age. The outstanding figure of the period was **Gertrudis Gómez de Avellaneda** (1814–73), an extraordinary poet, novelist and playwright. With 20 plays, she was a major woman playwright of the Americas who dominated both tragic and comic form, and knew how to create solid characters while avoiding the excesses of romanticism.

At mid-century the theatre was replete with writers whose humour and comic intrigue reflected the foibles of a developing society, and the problems created by politics, social status, and racial mixtures. José Agustín Millán wrote his *Una aventura, o El camino más corto* (*An Adventure, or the Shortest Route*) in 1842, a play considered to be the beginning of the national comedy, a form characterized by its humble, popular language and comic intrigue. Joaquín Lorenzo Luaces (1826–67)

was Cuba's best playwright of the 19th century. His plays, *El becerro de oro* (*The Golden Calf*), *La escuela de los parientes* (*School for Relatives*), *Dos amigas* (*Two Friends*) and *El fantasmón de Aravaca* (*The Ghost of Aravaca*), are of good quality with Cuban characteristics. His plays captured the same comic style and anticipated the **bufo** theatre that took Havana by storm in 1868. The USA minstrel shows that visited Havana shortly before (1860–5) left an influence on this musical-dance theatre that specialized in parody, caricature and satire. The linguistic salad of the *bufo* drew on a French, English and black cuisine, and though their popular format excited the Cuban public, the colonial regime was not pleased. The havoc of the Ten Years' War (1868–78) suspended the Bufos Habaneros (Havana *bufos*), but they returned for a second cycle from 1879 to 1900.

Late in the century, the great Cuban poet and patriot, José Martí (1853–95), who also wrote patriotic and moralistic plays, spearheaded an invasion by the government in exile. Martí was killed in battle. Spain was ready to concede defeat, but the episode of the battleship *Maine* provoked American intervention, and in 1898 Spain relinquished Cuba as well as Puerto Rico and the Philippines to United States control.

20th century The United States ruled Cuba militarily for four years and withdrew as planned, leaving Cuba to self-rule under the Platt Amendment, although the USA reserved the right to intervene 'as necessary'. A series of inept and corrupt presidents led to the dictatorship of Fulgencio Batista from 1934 to 1959, when he himself was ousted by Fidel Castro and the Bearded Ones, an event that ushered in a period of Marxist domination. The century also ushered in the Alhambra Theatre which served as the centre of popular theatre in Havana. The music and dance revues programmed by Regino López as principal actor and Federico Villoch as impresario championed the popular Cuban character types in lavish and colourful productions that entertained Cubans for 35 years.

Efforts to organize a serious theatre movement came in 1910 with the formation of the Sociedad de Fomento del Teatro (Society for the Promotion of Theatre), later redesignated the Sociedad del Teatro Cubano (Society of Cuban Theatre), but in spite of the efforts of such distinguished participants as José Antonio Ramos (1885–1946) and Max Henríquez Ureña (b. 1885), the effort failed. Ramos did write serious plays, and his *Tembladera* (*Trembler*, 1917) was a precursor of the theatre of protest against exploitative bourgeois policies.

Another impetus came in 1928 when Luis A. Baralt (1892–1969) launched the Teatro La Cueva (The Cave Theatre) that represented an early effort to bring vanguard European techniques to the Cuban theatre. The Academia de Artes Dramáticas (Academy of Dramatic Arts) was established in 1941, the Patronata del Teatro (Patrons of Theatre) in 1942, and the Teatro Experimental (Experimental Theatre) of the University of Havana in 1949, all fundamental to the development of an internationalized theatre capable of stimulating national playwrights and directors. Nevertheless, authors such as Carlos Felipe (1911–75), **Virgilio Piñera** (1912–79) and Rolando Ferrer (1925–76), the most established playwrights during the 1950s, wrote without benefit of an atmosphere conducive to serious theatre. The decadence of Havana during the later Batista years yielded to prostitution and commercialized, semi-pornographic shows catering primarily for the tourist trade. In the years immediately preceding the Castro Revolution, few theatre companies existed and few serious plays were presented.

The revolutionary years The Revolution brought a new perspective on theatre and the arts. Under the new regime, government support was available and theatre became, in fact, an arm of the Revolutionary process. Salaries were provided for writers, directors, actors and technical crew. Buildings, some of them old movie houses, were converted or adapted for use as theatre space, but the theatre also took to the streets and parks. The Escuela de Instructores de Arte (School of Art Instructors) was established in 1961 and the Escuela Nacional de Arte (National School of Art) in 1962. By the mid-70s a wide network of sites offered instruction in theatre, music, plastic arts, ballet and dance to nearly 5,000 students. An active publication programme accompanied the literacy campaign; plays were published in great numbers and the theatre journal *Conjunto* (1964) began publishing criticism, plays and information about theatre from countries throughout the Americas.

Abelardo Estorino (b. 1925) joined the Teatro Estudio (Studio Theatre) group in 1960 and became a professional writer in 1961. His *El robo del cochino* (*The Theft of the Pig*, 1961) signalled his ability to create true-to-life characters in the tense political situation that anticipated the Revolution. His subsequent plays such as *La casa vieja* (*The Old House*, 1964), *Los mangos de Caín* (*Cain's Mangoes*, 1967), *La dolorosa historia del amor secreto de don José Jacinto Milanés* (*The Tragic Story of the Secret Love of don José Jacinto Milanés*, 1974), *Ni un sí ni un no* (*Neither a Yes nor a No*, 1981), and *Morir del cuento* (*To Die from the Story*, 1983), lived up to the original promise, as he became the only writer who continued over an extended period. **Antón Arrufat** (b. 1935) performed an absurdist play, *El caso se investiga* (*The Case is Being Investigated*) as early as 1957, which was followed by several plays during the early Revolutionary years. When his *Los siete contra Tebas* (*Seven Against Thebes*) won the UNEAC prize in 1968, the play was censured for its alleged counter-Revolutionary spirit, along with Herberto Padilla's poetry. Arrufat continued writing for the theatre but his later plays have not been staged.

José Triana (b. 1931) became Cuba's best-known writer internationally for his *La noche de los asesinos* (*Night of the Assassins*, 1965), an intriguing metatheatrical play of three adolescents playing various roles as they prepare for the ritual murder of their parents. Triana resumed writing for the theatre after 1980. Other writers of the early years of the Revolution included José Brene (b. 1927) whose *Santa Camila de la Habana vieja* (*St Camille of Old Havana*, 1962) dramatized the ideological reorientation of a parasite in the society and the precocious Nicolás Dorr (b. 1947) whose first work at age 14 was a remarkably mature picture of human relationships captured in a farcical and even absurdist style. In this vein are Dorr's *Las pericas* (*The Parrots*, 1961), *El palacio de los cartones* (*The Cardboard Palace*, 1961) and *La esquina de los concejales* (*The Councillors' Corner*, 1962), although later works are more realistic, such as *La Chacota* (*The Racket*, 1974) and *Confesión en el barrio chino* (*Confession in the Chinese Quarter*). As director of Teatro Popular Latinoamericano (Popular Latin American Theatre) Dorr launched an ambitious programme for Cuban theatre and continued writing ideologically-orientated plays about the new society. In 1967 the Cuban theatre was shaken by the appearance of *María Antonia*, a tragedy by Eugenio Hernández Espinosa (b. 1936) rooted in the mythical Afro-Cuban universe that reflects the marginal society preceding the 1959 Revolution. Hernández is the Cuban playwright who reflects with greatest authenticity the world of the blacks in such recent works as *Oba y Shangó* (*The King and Shango*) and *Odebí el cazador* (*Odebí the Hunter*).

By 1968 the theatre in Cuba entered a second phase. The Teatro Escambray (Escambray Theatre), established that year by Sergio Corrieri in the province of Las Villas, was representative of the search for the methods and contacts that would lead to the so-called 'new theatre'. The term refers to the anti-bourgeois theatre that grew out of close interaction between theatre groups and the public they served. The Escambray group, for example, developed a model of interviewing regional people about their concerns, attitudes and values in order to develop meaningful dramatic experiences for them. The plays relied on local language and colour, almost always with music. Other groups with a similar orientation soon followed: La Yaya (1973–6), Cabildo Teatral de Santiago (1973), Teatrova de Santiago (1974), Cubana de Acero (Cuban Steel) (1977), Teatro Juvenil Pinos Nuevos (Pinos Nuevos Children's Theatre) (1974) and others. Cuban Steel operated directly out of the steel factory, and performances took place between shifts. Juglares y su Peña Literaria performed in Lenin Park in Havana. The very first revolutionary group, the Studio Theatre, was consolidated in 1959 after the Revolution and dedicated to Marxist-Leninist principles.

Even though the Cuban theatre has operated in a collective style, individual authors have played a prominent role. In addition to those cited, others of note are Flora Lauten, Herminia Sánchez, Albio Paz, Francisco Garzón Céspedes, Roberto Orihuela, Lázaro Rodríguez, Rafael González, Freddy Artiles, and Abra-

Cabildo Teatral de Santiago in Raúl Pomares's *De cómo Santiago Apóstol puso los pies en le tierra* (*About how the Apostle James put his Feet on Earth*), Santiago, Cuba, 1975.

The Cubana de Acero in Albio Paz's *Huelga* (*Strike*), Havana, Cuba, 1981.

ham Rodríguez. The immediacy of the Revolutionary process called special attention to aspects of societal change, education, male/female roles and relationships, work ethics, and individual commitment to revolutionary goals in a rapidly changing economy and society. The theatre did not merely reflect the process, but because of its popular nature actually became instrumental in helping to shape attitudes and opinions. Especially since the 1970s Cuban playwriting signals a frequent recognition of current themes by means of a critical investigation of reality. The Cuban government has continued to invest in theatre and art programmes and since 1980 has sponsored an international theatre festival on an alternate year basis. A new journal *Tablas* (Boards) (1982), edited by Rosa Ileana Boudet, complemented the long-standing publication of the Casa de las Américas. Ideological theatre still dominated in Cuba and the search for new forms continued in the mid-80s.   GW

> *See*: N. González Freire, *Teatro cubano (1927–61)*, La Havana, 1961; R. Leal, *Breve historia del teatro cubano*, La Havana, 1980; M. Montes Huidobro, *Persona, vida y máscara en el teatro cubano*, Miami, 1973.

Cueva, Juan de la (?1550–1610) Spanish dramatist, writing before the **comedia** reached its established form under **Lope de Vega**. His 14 extant tragedies and comedies, written in four acts, were performed in the public theatres of Seville around 1579–81. His best constructed plays are three on classical themes, but he was probably the first to adapt successfully plots from Spanish history and ballads for the stage, including the *Tragedia de los siete infantes de Lara* (*Tragedy of the Seven Princes of Lara*). His collected plays were published in 1588, and he wrote a poem on dramatic theory, the *Ejemplar poético*, in 1609.   CL

Cumberland, Richard (1732–1811) English playwright. Born in Trinity College, Cambridge, where his grandfather was Master, and educated there, he entered politics as secretary to Lord Halifax in 1751. After a successful career with Halifax, he began writing plays in 1761 and became a prolific dramatist. He is best remembered as the original of Sir Fretful Plagiary, **Sheridan**'s caricature of him in *The Critic*, but he was rapidly and deservedly successful, particularly after **Garrick**'s production of *The West Indian* (1771), a highly moral account of an essentially good rake making his way through London society, a domestic comedy with a strong dose of sentimentalism. Among his outpouring of dully conventional plays, Cumberland's best work is intriguingly original, particularly *The Mysterious Husband* (1783), a prose tragedy set in contemporary London among the fashionable aristocracy, and *The Jew* (1794), a reasoned argument against contemporary anti-semitism, a play which restored Cumberland's reputation after some years of only moderate success. Secretary to the Board of Trade from 1775 to 1780, he retired to Tunbridge Wells on its abolition continuing to write plays until his death.   PH

Cummings, Constance (née Halveerstadt) (1910–   ) American-born actress who, because of her marriage to English playwright Benn W. Levy, has spent most of her career in England. Her first London success, *Sour Grapes*, was followed the same year (1934) by her first important New York appearance (*Accent on Youth*). During her long career she has appeared in modern and classical plays, including *Madame Bovary* (1937); *Goodbye, Mr Chips* (1938); *Romeo and Juliet* and *Saint Joan* (1939), both at the **Old Vic**; *The Petrified Forest* (1942); **MacLeish**'s *J. B.* (1961); *Who's Afraid of Virginia Woolf?* (replacing **Uta Hagen** as Martha in London, 1964); **Noël Coward**'s *Fallen Angels* (1967); and *Hamlet* (Gertrude in Tony Richardson's 1969 production). In 1971 she joined the **National Theatre** of Great Britain, playing Volumnia in *Coriolanus*, Leda in *Amphitryon 38*, Mary Tyrone in *Long Day's Journey Into Night*, Mme Ranevsky in *The Cherry Orchard*, and Agave in *The Bacchae*. She won a Tony Award in **Arthur Kopit**'s *Wings*, first seen in New York (1978) and the following year in London. Since then, she has appeared in *Hay Fever* and *The Golden Age* in London, *The Chalk Garden* in New York, and *Mrs Warren's Profession* in Vienna.   DBW

Curtain Theatre, London Erected not far from the **Theatre**, possibly by the Henry Lanman who was its proprietor from 1582–92, the Curtain was London's second purpose-built playhouse. Almost certainly polygonal and constructed after the model of the Theatre, it had a surprisingly long and almost entirely undistinguished life. For a brief period, between the dismantling of the Theatre and the opening of the **Globe**, it was probably the home of the **Lord Chamberlain's Men**. If, as is often claimed, it was the theatre which first staged **Shakespeare**'s *Henry V*, the apologetic Chorus may be drawing attention to the shortcomings of a theatre that was already old-fashioned in 1599. Even so, it was the home of Queen Anne's Men for a short period after 1603 and remained open and in occasional use by many other companies until the Restoration.   PT

Cusack, Cyril (1910–) Irish stage and film actor, director and playwright, who performed with the **Abbey Theatre** in Dublin from 1932 to 1945, and again from 1968, when he started the revival of **Boucicault**'s plays in the Abbey production of *The Shaughraun* at the World Theatre Season in London. He directed the Gaelic Players in 1935–6, and in his own play *Tareis an Aifreann* (*After the Mass*) at the Dublin **Gate Theatre** in 1942. After taking over the Gaiety Theatre, Dublin, in 1945, he formed his own company, with which he presented **Synge**'s *Playboy of the Western World* at the first International Drama Festival in Paris in 1954, and in 1960 he won the International Critics' Award for his performance in **Beckett**'s monologue, *Krapp's Last Tape*.   CI

Cushman, Charlotte Saunders (1816–76) American actress. As the first native-born actress of the top rank, Cushman was considered the most powerful actress on the 19th-century stage. Appearing somewhat masculine, with a tall, strong body, unusual voice, and a powerful personality, her stage characterizations emerged in heroic outline. Trained as an opera singer, she misused her voice and was forced to alter her career. Her acting debut was as Lady Macbeth in New Orleans (1836), repeated the same year in New York. Her first sensational success was as Nancy Sykes in *Oliver Twist* (1839). After appearing opposite **W. C. Macready** on his American tour in 1843–4, she went to London, appearing first in 1845 at the **Princess's Theatre**. By her return to the USA in 1849 she was

Charlotte Cushman and her sister Susan as Romeo and Juliet.

considered by many the greatest living English-speaking actress. During her long career she played over 200 roles but excelled as Meg Merrilies in *Guy Mannering*, Romeo opposite the Juliet of her sister Susan, Lady Macbeth, and Queen Katharine in *Henry VIII*. From 1852 to 1869 she gave a series of farewell appearances, returning permanently to the stage in 1869 to forget the pain she suffered from cancer. Her definitive biography, *Bright Particular Star* by Joseph Leech, was published in 1970.   DBW

Cuzzani, Agustín (1924–) Argentine playwright, novelist and lawyer. Famous for his *farsátiras* in the 1950s, he wrote several major plays: *Una libra de carne* (*A Pound of Flesh*, 1954), based on the Shylock story, *El centroforward murió al amanecer* (*The Centre Forward Died at Dawn*, 1955), and *Sempronio* (1958). The latter presents a man who has become radioactive from his Japanese stamp collection but is redeemed by the power of his family's love over the vindictive state bureaucracy. His plays depend on farcical situations to advocate positions of individual liberty for mankind within oppressive situations.   GW

Czechoslovakia

The beginnings to the 18th century The evolution of theatre in Czechoslovakia falls into several periods, most of which have been demarcated by religious, political, or military events. Evidence of a flourishing medieval religious drama gradually incorporating secular and comic elements, as well as vernacular Czech by the 14th century, is found in many sources; e.g., two 'Mastičkář' texts from c. 1350 that present a quack healer and his scolding wife with not only the three Marys but also Abraham and Isaac. The social comment and theatricality in such surviving fragments suggest a lively theatre culture, but its potential growth was aborted by the Hussite wars in the 15th century.

Theatre revived with Renaissance humanism in the 16th century. **Terence** and **Plautus** were performed in schools and occasionally in public by students, almost always in Latin, but biblical dramas based on the lives of saints were performed in Czech. Pavel Kyrmezer, a Slovak, but the first known playwright in Czech, composed several, with comic characterization and realistic detail, from the 1560s to the 1580s.

Several other forms of theatre emerged in the second half of the 16th century. Jesuit school drama developed rapidly after 1566 in Bohemia and was an important force in Czech theatre for two hundred years. Eventually incorporating Czech history and other secular themes, the Jesuits also expanded the use of scenery, costumes, and other production elements, as well as the use of Czech in performance. Theatricality also marked Italianate spectacles that reached a peak in Prague with the first movable scenery north of the Alps (*Phasma Dionysia*, 1617). Additional foreign influence came with touring Italian, German, and English companies toward the end of the 16th century. Concurrently, the indigenous folk tradition in theatre revived in the form of Shrovetide processions, skits, and plays in Czech that mixed moralizing and social satire with peasant farce. *The Feast at Sedlec* (printed 1588) is the best known. More formal and purely secular drama includes Jan Campanus Vodňanský's *Břetislav* (1603) and the first known Czech interlude, *The Apprehended Infidelity* (anon., 1608).

The vital theatre implicit in these examples ended with the Czechs' defeat at the Battle of White Mountain (1620). Not only Czech theatre but Czech culture and national identity were virtually erased for a century and a half as the Czechs languished under Habsburg authority.

Although no professional theatre in Czech was to exist until the National Revival in the late 18th century, other forms of theatre bridged the gap. Foreign theatre companies introduced Neapolitan opera, **commedia dell'arte**, and marionettes. Equally important, they brought technical advances in staging; e.g., for the coronation of Charles VI in Prague in 1723, **Giuseppe Bibiena** designed the total outdoor, nocturnal theatre and scenery for *Costanza e Fortezza*. Drama and theatre of native origin took two forms. Jan Ámos Komenský wrote Latin plays in the 1640s based on classical or biblical themes, to be performed by schoolboys as part of their education. Later in the 17th century Václav Kocmánek wrote a Christmas play and numerous interludes in Czech; Karel Kolčava composed several plays in Latin but based on Czech history. Of greater significance for Czech theatre, the folk theatre reappeared after 1650 in the form of amateur, village productions in Czech of primarily religious material but also comprising pre-Christian elements as well as theatrical techniques indirectly derived from Jesuit and foreign productions. This fascinating blend of naive and sophisticated theatre was profoundly important in sustaining the faith, culture, and language of the Czechs.

The national revival to 1900 Playing a leading role in the revival movement, which began in the 1780s, theatre became intimately linked with Czech national and cultural aspirations. One symptom of the increasing interest in theatre was the building of the Nostitz Theatre in Prague in 1783; later known as the Estates Theatre and surviving to this day as the Tyl Theatre, it embodied the latest technical equipment of its day and was the site of the original production of *Don Giovanni*, directed and conducted in 1786 by Mozart himself. The first performance in Czech at this theatre occurred in 1785.

Of greater consequence for Czech culture and theatre was the establishment by a group of Czech actors of the Bouda (Hut) Theatre in 1786 in order to be able to perform in Czech on a more regular basis, usually four times a week. That season included the performance of the first play in nearly two hundred years with Czech subject matter written and performed in Czech: *Břetislav and Jitka*, by Václav Thám, the first of many indefatigable Czech actor-writer-translators dedicated to the cause of reviving theatre in their native tongue.

The Hut Theatre lasted two years, but sporadic Czech performances continued into the 19th century in similar temporary, bilingual theatres as well as in the Nostitz Theatre. Jan Nepomuk Štepánek, playwright, translator, and theatre producer-administrator, was instrumental in increasing the number and regularity of Czech performances on the professional stage in Prague. Václav Kliment Klicpera was the first Czech playwright of undisputed talent. Whether in the genre of history, comedy, or parody-farce, Klicpera had a sure theatrical sense and special gift for characterization and sharp social observation, as is evident in *Hadrian of Rimsy* (1821) and *Everyone Does His Bit for the Homeland* (1829). Widespread marionette theatre activity by touring professional groups also sustained the public use of Czech, most notably in the years 1820–50. Matěj Kopecký was a leading practitioner.

Surpassing the achievements of all others at this time in the cause of theatre and emergent nationalism was Josef Kajetán Tyl; as actor, playwright, dramaturge, director, editor, publisher, and even representative to the Habsburg Assembly, he devoted himself entirely to his countrymen and his art. He was the first to formulate the concept of a Czech National Theatre, in the 1840s, when he was also a leading figure in Prague theatres and writer of some dozen major plays; e.g., *The Bagpiper of Strakonice* (1846), *The Miners of Kutna Mountain* (1848), and *Hardheaded Woman* (1849), works that blend patriotic romanticism with wry comedy and socially realistic detail.

In 1850 a committee for the establishment of a National Theatre became the focal point for the entire national revival movement. From then until the 1880s, when the dream was realized, most of the funds came from voluntary contributions by the Czech people. In the meantime, the Provisional Theatre was built in 1862, and thus became the first exclusively Czech professional theatre with a regular schedule. The National Theatre itself had two inaugurals: two months after the first one in 1881 the theatre burned down, but two years later it reopened with the premiere of Bedřich Smetana's opera *Libuše*. From then until now its motto, emblazoned above the proscenium arch, has been 'A Nation's Gift to Itself'.

Smetana was the most significant artistic force in the National Theatre movement, and his operas were the strongest productions during the years leading up to the opening of the theatre and even later. Nevertheless, playwrights and other theatre artists were also developing talents and experience necessary for so demanding a project. **Shakespeare** and **Schiller**, idealized models for the Czech theatre of the 19th century, were especially influential in the career of Josef J. Kolár, a major actor, producer, playwright, and translator of Shakespeare. French, Russian, and German theatre also became influential; Emanuel Bozděch was known as the Czech **Scribe**. A cluster of other playwrights reflected the shift to critical social realism sweeping Europe in the second half of the century. Among the realist playwrights and their chief works were L. Stroupežnický, *Our Hotheads*, 1887; F. V. Jeřábek, *The Servant of His Master*, 1869; the Mrštík brothers, Alois and Vilem, *Maryša*, 1894; and G. Preissová, *The Housewife Slave*, 1889. A counter-movement towards deliberately poetic, imaginative drama was evident in the work of Jaroslav Vrchlický, whose prolific output included lyrical treatments of Czech history, *A Night at Karlštein* (1884), and classical myth, the *Hippodamia* trilogy (1890–1). Similar neo-romantic impulses were evident in the poetic dramas of Julius Zeyer, *An Old Story* (1882) and *Radúz and Mahulena* (1898), while Jaroslav Hilbert strove to combine an **Ibsen**-like ethical realism with symbolist overtones: *Guilt* (1896), *About God* (1898).

Theatre practice was also maturing and becoming more sophisticated. With the National Theatre serving as prime inspiration and showcase, and with opportunities to observe visiting luminaries like the **Meiningen** players, Czech performers were able to build a promising foundation for a genuinely world-class Czech theatre in the 20th century. F. A. Šubert, playwright and director of the National Theatre until the turn of the century, led Czech theatre toward the mainstream of European theatre; 20th-century directors plunged it into that current and guided it to a leading position.

The 20th century Although other Czech theatres existed by 1900, the Prague National and Municipal theatres (the latter built in 1907) dominated Czech theatre during the first two decades of the 20th century. Each of the two major Prague theatres was led by a director with a distinctive creative personality.

In his concern with the total integration and harmony of all components of production, Jaroslav Kvapil was the first modern Czech director. At the National Theatre from 1900–18, he raised the level of performance to European standards. A gifted lyric poet, he brought his sensitivity to language, form, and nuance to the stage, where he was particularly drawn to Ibsen and **Chekhov**. His most notable productions, however, were of Shakespeare, especially his cycle of Shakespeare's plays in 1916. He mounted a similar cycle of Czech historical dramas in 1918 to support the hope for an independent state, which in fact materialized in October 1918 with the overthrow of the Habsburg regime. Kvapil worked with a number of great actors, above all the legendary Eduard Vojan, whose Hamlet (1905) is regarded as the highwater mark of Czech acting, Hana Kvapilová, his peer in Shakespearian and modern psychological roles, and Marie Hübnerová, whose forte was earthier genre types.

Kvapil's successor at the National Theatre was **Karel Hugo Hilar**, who had established a reputation for bold staging at the Municipal Theatre. More flamboyant and forceful than Kvapil, Hilar repeatedly attracted international attention to the National Theatre in the 1920s and early 1930s. Hilar had a notable collaborator in his chief designer, Vlastislav Hofman, whose stage settings based on both painting and architectural techniques matched the expressiveness of Hilar's vision.

Several Czech playwrights in the early 1900s reflected the growing maturity of Czech dramaturgy. Although primarily a novelist, Alois Jirásek brought skill and imagination to the writing of historical drama, particularly his plays known as the *Hussite Trilogy* (1903–14), and a lighter, fanciful touch to a play of Czech folk life, *The Lantern* (1905). Less social in its orientation was the work of the poet Fráňa Šrámek, who dealt sensitively with themes of youthful eroticism and other subjective states: *Summer* (1915), *Moon Above the River* (1922). Irony and disenchantment characterized the plays of Viktor Dyk: *The Coming to Wisdom of Don Quixote* (1913) and *Revolutionary Trilogy* (1917), on the French Revolution.

Overlapping the work of Hilar and Kvapil in the 1920s and 1930s was the work of another group of important theatre artists primarily associated with smaller, avant-garde Prague stages. At the crossroads of Europe, these artists were sensitized not only to theatre in Germany, France, and Soviet Russia but also to the political forces that threatened their new state.

Jindřich Honzl was a major theoretician and critic of theatre as well as an active director whose work encompassed Communist proletarian mass spectacles and small-scale experimental staging of surrealistic and other unorthodox texts; e.g., **Jarry**'s *Ubu Roi* and **Cocteau**'s *Orphée* in the 1920s. For a brief period in 1926, Jiří Frejka joined with Honzl in the leadership of the most active of the avant-garde groups, The Liberated Theatre. Frejka was a more lyrical, intuitive director; inspired by the *commedia dell'arte*, he was less intellectual and politically committed than Honzl. He leaned towards a more fanciful theatre and worked more intimately with actors. In the 1930s Frejka moved to the National Theatre, where he began to work on a larger scale and eventually directed productions that clearly took a stand against the growing threat of fascism in Europe; e.g., **Aristophanes**' *The Birds* (1933) and *Julius Caesar* (1936). Collaborating with Frejka on *Caesar* and many other major productions at the National Theatre was František Tröster, a stage designer with an architectonic approach to the handling of stage space. Other highly creative stage designers of the 1920s and 1930s included Bedřich Feuerstein, Antonín Heythum and František Muzika.

A distinctive new form of theatre was created by **Jiří Voskovec** and **Jan Werich**. In 1927 their semi-improvised entertainment, *Vestpocket Review*, became an overnight sensation in Prague. Authors, librettists, and chief actors of their reviews, they eventually took over the Liberated Theatre and renamed it the Liberated Theatre of V+W, where they continued to mount provocative socio-political combinations of music, dance, and Aristophanic farce. Particularly in the 1930s their productions became a rallying point against the fascist threat to the brief independence of Czechoslovakia. Among their successes were *Executioner and Fool* (1934), *Heavy Barbora* (1937), and *A Fist in the Eye* (1938).

Probably the most important avant-garde theatre artist of the inter-war period was **Emil František Burian**. In the 1930s he combined his talents for music and theatre with his political activism and established D34, a theatre that gained international recognition for its stage artistry and social relevance.

Other directors of the 1920s and 1930s included Jan Bor and Karel Dostal, who did important work at the Municipal and National theatres, respectively; Viktor

V. Hofman's set for *Hamlet*, Prague National Theatre, 1926.

Šulc, noted for his expressionistic productions in Bratislava and his interest in **Brecht**; and Oldřich Stibor, an eclectic, politically engaged director most of whose work was done in Olomouc.

The single best-known theatre figure in Czechoslovakia in the inter-war years was **Karel Čapek**, whose highly imaginative, provocative plays (e.g., *RUR*) achieved world-wide production in the 1920s and 30s. František Langer, who explored questions of ethical choice and social implications in more conventional ways, also achieved international recognition; e.g., *Camel Through the Needle's Eye* (1923), *The Periphery* (1925), *Grandhotel Nevada* (1927).

From the Munich capitulation in October 1938 to the liberation in May 1945, a censored theatre subsisted at the discretion of the German forces of occupation. Several of the leading theatre artists survived this period to extend their creativity for varying lengths of time, but none surpassed his pre-war achievements. One reason may be found in still another radical socio-political dislocation, in 1948: the fall of the post-war Republic, the ascension to power of the Communist Party, and the establishment of the Czechoslovakian Socialist Republic. Private enterprise in theatre was abolished and all theatre activity brought under state control. In the arts, a dogmatically imposed policy of Socialist Realism stifled for some ten years virtually all creativity not in accord with ideological guidelines. Then Czech theatre gradually began still another revival, which in several respects surpassed even the accomplishments of the inter-war era before being reined back again by the events of 1968.

As in the inter-war period, the most recent blooming of Czech theatre was principally evident in the work of directors and designers, who mounted a stream of highly imaginative, powerfully executed productions in both large institutional theatres and small studio environments.

Two directors stand out for their large-scale work. Otomar Krejča, who began as an actor under Burian and Frejka, eventually became chief director and head of drama at the National Theatre in the late 1950s. In 1965, he became head of his own producing organization at the Gate Theatre. In both places his most frequent collaborator was the designer **Josef Svoboda**; they formed a creative team that was reminiscent of Hilar and Hofman. While maintaining fidelity to a text, Krejča would subject it to exhaustive analysis, define his concepts and interpretations meticulously to his cast, and encourage his designers to bold stage embodiments of their shared vision. Some of Krejča's memorable productions included Chekhov's *Seagull* (1960) and *Three Sisters* (1966), *Romeo and Juliet* (1963), Topol's *Their Day* (1959) and *End of Carnival* (1964), and his own conflation *Oedipus-Antigone* (1971). After directing abroad exclusively between 1976–89 because of political pressures, Krejča returned to Prague and revived his Gate Theatre in 1990.

Alfred Radok also gained experience with Burian, as an assistant. His subsequent major work at the National Theatre and the Municipal Theatre of Prague in the 1950s and 1960s was distinguished by subjective, highly metaphoric production concepts, which often altered original texts and lent themselves to untraditional stage settings designed to interpret Radok's special vision. An outgrowth of Radok's creativity in the late 1950s was a unique fusion of live action and projected film called **Laterna Magika**, which he evolved with the aid of Josef Svoboda. Other collaborations with Svoboda included **Osborne**'s *The Entertainer* (1957) and **Gorky**'s *The Last Ones* (1966). Radok's single most outstanding production, however, was his adaptation of **Rolland**'s *The Game of Love and Death* (1964), designed by Czechoslovakia's other leading scenographer, **Ladislav Vychodil**. Radok worked abroad after 1968.

Josef Svoboda, who has designed over 500 productions of drama, opera, and ballet in Czechoslovakia and abroad since the 1940s, continues to experiment with innovative techniques in lighting, projections, and kinetically expressive forms.

Other lively theatre in the 1960s occurred on smaller stages that provided an outlet for creative energies dormant during the previous decade. One of the earliest examples was the Balustrade Theatre; established in the late 1950s, it reached its peak of creative production under the leadership of Jan Grossman in the last half of the 1960s with productions of **Kafka**'s *Trial*, Jarry's *Ubu Roi*, **Beckett**'s *Godot*, and the plays of **Václav Havel**. Sharing the theatre was the internationally known mime troupe of **Ladislav Fialka**. The Drama Club, founded in 1965, is relatively more an actor's theatre compared to the text-oriented Balustrade Theatre. The Semafor Theatre, under Jiří Suchý, has since the late 1950s specialized in satiric revues with heavy emphasis on music, echoing the prototypal V+W revues of the 1930s. Krejča's Gate Theatre (1965–72) was the other outstanding small theatre operation in Prague.

As Čapek's plays brought world attention to Czech theatre in the pre-war years, so too did the plays of Václav Havel in the 1960s. Echoing the implications of Čapek's works, Havel's themes centre on the plight of civilized values in a dehumanized world. Josef Topol is essentially a poet whose work is highly suggestive, intuitive, at times cryptic in its explorations of complex sensibilities. His chief works (all directed by Krejča) include *Their Day* (1959), *End of Carnival* (1964), *Cat on the Rails* (1965), and *Hour of Love* (1968). His work was banned between 1969 and 1990, after which time newer works such as *Goodbye, Socrates* and *Voices of the Birds* were staged. František Hrubín, like Topol a poet and Krejča collaborator, presented more traditionally drawn characters and incidents with Chekhovian overtones; for example, *Sunday in August* (1958) and *Starry Night* (1961). Other interesting authors include František Pavlíček, *The Heavenly Ascension of Šaška Christ*, 1967; Pavel Kohout, *August, August, August*, 1967; Milan Kundera, *Owners of the Keys*, 1962; Ivan Klíma, *The Castle*, 1964; and Ladislav Smoček, *Cosmic Spring*, 1970.

Slovak theatre Retarded in its development by its people's centuries-long vassalhood to Hungary and Austria, Slovak professional theatre began in 1918 with the formation of the Czechoslovak Republic. Prior to that time, theatre activity was limited to amateur performances, which dated back to 1830 and echoed the nationalistic aspirations of the Czech theatre. Early playwrights included Ján Chalupka and Ján Palárik, authors of satiric comedies; the major poet P. O. Hviezdoslav; the prolific, extremely popular Ferko Urbánek, and the naturalistic social critic J. G. Tajovský.

directors. Two men were especially significant in building the foundations of a truly Slovak professional theatre: Andrej Bagar and Ján Borodáč, both of whom were central to National Theatre activity from the 1920s to the 1960s as actors, directors, and administrators. Ján Jamnický was a strong, more overtly theatrical director in the early 1940s.

The most notable playwright of the inter-war years was Ivan Stodola, whose sharp sense of social satire went together with a firm grasp of theatre values; his work ranged from contemporary satire, *The Career of Jožka Púčik* (1931), to Slovak history, *King Svatopluk* (1931). Julius Barč-Ivan, a religiously oriented playwright, attempted to blend expressionism with neo-realism: *3000 People* (1934), *Mother* (1943).

The dominant figure in Slovak playwriting after the Second World War was Peter Karvaš, whose plays were especially effective in dealing with the problems of wartime morality in Slovakia (*Midnight Mass*, 1959; *Antigone and the Others*, 1962) and the follies of the 1950s (*The Big Whig*, 1964). Ivan Bukovčan was another socially concerned playwright of the 1960s (*Until the Cock Ceases to Sing*, 1969).

Two directors stood out in the post-war era. Jozef Budský developed into Slovakia's most expressive director, employing great imagination and theatrical metaphor in his bold stagings. Beginning his directing career in the 1940s, he endured the limitations of the socialist realism era and was the first to reintroduce conscious art into production. Karol Zachar had a special talent for fantasy and lyricism.

Slovakia's preeminent scenographer Ladislav Vychodil has been chief designer and technical chief of the Slovak National Theatre in Bratislava since the end of the Second World War. Less prolific than Svoboda, Vychodil also differs in being more emotive and lyrical in his designs and in not using complex technical methods as extensively. Vychodil also established the stage design training programme in the School of Fine Arts in Bratislava.

The present   The radical military and political events of August 1968 did not dramatically truncate theatre activity in Czechoslovakia; challenging, creative work occasionally surfaced for the next season or two. But the main flow was turned off, and although some of the principal writers and artists continued to work, theatre in Czechoslovakia (except for some interesting work by new studio theatres such as the Ypsilon in Prague and the Theatre on a String in Brno, once again marked time during a creatively unfruitful period that lasted until the liberation of 1989, after which a major reform in the leadership and operation of theatres began.   JMB

See: J. M. Burian, *The Scenography of Josef Svoboda*, Middletown, Ct, Wesleyan University Press, 1971; F. Černý, F., gen. ed., *Dějiny Českého Divadla* (The History of Czech Theatre), 4 vols., Prague Academia, 1968–83 (the most recent and most definitive study, but available only in Czech); M. Goetz-Stankiewicz, *The Silenced Theatre*, Toronto, University of Toronto Press, 1979; J. Honzl, ed., *The Czechoslovak Theatre*, Prague, Orbis, 1948; M. Rutte, and F. Bartoš, *The Modern Czech Scene*, Trans. Arthur R. Weir, Prague, Vladimir Zikes, 1938; P. Trensky, *Czech Drama Since World War II*, White Plains, NY, M. E. Sharpe, 1978; O. Vočadlo, 'The Theatre and Drama of Czechoslovakia', *The Theater in a Changing Europe*, ed. Thomas H. Dickinson, NY, Henry Holt and Company, 1937, 330–62.

D

D'Alton, Louis (1900–51) Irish playwright, associated with the **Abbey** from 1937 as playwright, actor, director. His plays, in a Shavian manner, were an enhancement in the Abbey repertoire of new plays of the 1940s and 50s: *The Money Doesn't Matter* (1941), *They Got What They Wanted* (1947), and *This Other Eden* (1953), a witty treatment of romantic English ideas about Ireland and of Irish about England.   DM

D'Annunzio, Gabriele (1863–1938) Italian poet, dramatist and novelist. A prolific writer, whose literary and theatrical activities, and adventurous life, made a powerful, if not always positive, influence on his contemporaries. A poet and novelist of *fin de siècle* decadence, his flamboyant writing and life style rapidly made him a prominent figure in the 1880s, particularly after the publication of *Canto Novo* and *Terra Vergine*, volumes of verse marked as much by stylistic experimentation as exotic language and subject matter. His theatrical activity began comparatively late in 1896, after the start of his seven-year relationship with the actress, **Eleonora Duse**, with whom he projected a revitalization of theatre that turned its face boldly against the constraints of bourgeois naturalism. The ideals of this new theatre he passionately described in his novel, *Il Fuoco* (*The Flame of Life*, 1900), and he wrote the one-act *Sogno di un Mattino di Primavera* (*Dream of a Spring Morning*) and *Sogno di un Tramonto d'Autunno* (*Dream of an Autumn Sunset*) for Duse in 1898. Audiences remained indifferent, and he won no substantially greater success with the full-length pieces which immediately followed, *La Città Morta* (*The Dead City*), first produced in Paris by **Sarah Bernhardt** in 1898, and *La Gioconda* and *La Gloria* (*The Glory*), both mounted by Duse and **Ermete Zacconi** in 1899. D'Annunzio's search for a poetic drama led him to abandon prose, and with his next play, *Francesca da Rimini* (1901) he attempted a verse tragedy in the historical vein. It proved enormously successful and was widely imitated. Even more popular was his next piece, *La Figlia di Iorio* (*Iorio's Daughter*, 1904), a modern peasant drama set in his native Abruzzo and considered today to be by far his best stage work. Later plays, enjoying variable success, included *La Nave* (*The Ship*, 1908) and *Le Martyr de Saint Sebastien* (*The Martyrdom of St Sebastian*) produced with music by Debussy in Paris in 1911, where D'Annunzio had gone into self-imposed exile to escape critical hostility and debts.

During the First World War D'Annunzio became increasingly a man of action, involved in Italian political and military affairs. He remained as flamboyant a figure as ever, never more so than during the Fiume adventure: with a group of volunteers he occupied the disputed city and held it for a year, defying the European powers and embarrassing the Italian government. In the 1920s he retired to his exotically decorated and furnished villa, Il Vittoriale, on Lake Garda. Of his last work perhaps the most effective was the libretto he wrote for Mascagni, *Parisina*. Increasingly from 1913 he wrote more for the cinema than the theatre, collaborating on the scenario for *Cabiria* (1913) and writing others independently. Many films have been made from his novels, stories and plays. These last, like *La Città Morta* and *La Gloria*, turned away from the concerns of contemporary naturalistic drama, to treat of the struggles of Nietzschean exceptional individuals in a language verbally rich but too often flamboyant, precious and replete with neologisms and antique terms and turns of phrase. The best of his plays are not wholly lacking in dramatic power, but they are often marred by contrived conflict and vapid grandiloquence. Invariably active in the preparation of his own plays for performance, his emphasis on detail and accuracy in the reconstruction of historical settings was obsessive to the point of pedantry, and his attempts to wed stage upholstery to the quasi-mystical and symbolic suggest that his rejection of naturalism was partial rather than complete, as too perhaps does his dependence on familiar love triangle conflicts in *La Città Morta*, *La Gloria*, *La Gioconda*, *Francesca da Rimini* and *La Figlia di Iorio*. Some of his work is occasionally revived in the Italian theatre today.   LR

D'Urfey, Thomas (1653–1723) English playwright. Born in Devon and probably trained for the law, he settled in London, becoming a close friend of the King, Charles II, and of all his successors, in itself an achievement. Constantly mocked for his stutter and his ugliness, he became best known for his songs, collected as *Pills to Purge Melancholy* (six vols., 1719). Making his living as a professional writer, he wrote 33 plays, including five poor sensationalist tragedies and four equally weak operas. But his comedies, beginning with *Madam Fickle* in 1676, have an energy far beyond their frequently imitative plots. D'Urfey often adapted earlier plays by **Fletcher** and others, including a version of **Shakespeare**'s *Cymbeline* as *The Injured Princess* (1682), but his best work is sharp contemporary satire, particularly on the connection between financial intrigue and marriage in *Love for Money* (1691) and *The Richmond Heiress* (1693), both plays combining a nascent sentimentalism with a harsh cynicism. His most ambitious work was a three-part adaptation of **Cervantes** as *The Comical History of Don Quixote* (1694–5), partly faithful recreation of his source and partly delightfully coarse invention like Sancho Panza's daughter, Mary the Buxom. The plays' bawdiness made them a particular target for the attacks of **Jeremy Collier**. PH

Da Silva Silverblatt, Howard (1909–86) American actor, director, and producer. Born in Cleveland, Ohio, Da Silva studied at the Carnegie Institute of Technology and made his debut in **Eva Le Gallienne's** Civic Repertory Company, New York, 1929, remaining for five years. His 1936 film debut was in *Once in a Blue Moon*. The same year he directed on radio the Great Classics Series for the **Federal Theatre Project**. He was twice nominated for Academy Awards. Among his outstanding stage roles were Benjamin Franklin in *1776* and Ben Marino in *Fiorello!* Da Silva won an Emmy in 1978 for *Verna–USO Girl*. SMA

Dadié, Bernard Binlin (1916–) Born in Assinie, Ivory Coast, Dadié began his education in the Ivory Coast before going on to the Ecole Normale William Ponty in Senegal to train as an administrator. It was here, and at this time (in the early 1930s), that theatrical activity in the French colonies was in the process of being initiated. Dadié contributed one of the first plays, *Assémien Déhylé, Roi du Sanwi* (*Assémien Déhylé, King of the Sanwi*), which, after performance at the Ecole Normale, was taken to Paris and produced at the Théâtre des Champs Elysées in 1937. After completing his studies, Dadié worked from 1936–47 at the Institut Français d'Afrique Noire (IFAN). He returned to the Ivory Coast where he held a series of increasingly senior posts in the fields of Information and Cultural Affairs which, with his growing reputation as one of francophone Africa's most respected writers, gave him the opportunity to exert a positive influence on the country's cultural development. Although he wrote a second play while a student in the 1930s, entitled *Les Villes* (*The Cities*) (it has never been published), Dadié abandoned drama for a number of years to concentrate on poetry and fiction. He returned to writing plays in the 1950s in order to offer practical encouragement to the theatre in the Ivory Coast. During the 1960s and 1970s he published a number of plays which made him not only the most prolific African playwright in French but also the best known and most widely performed. In 1969 his most celebrated play, *Monsieur Thôgô-gnini* ('thôgô-gnini' means 'the opportunist' in Malinke), was acclaimed at the Pan-African Festival in Algiers, and *Béatrice du Congo* (*Beatrice of the Congo*) was directed by **Jean-Marie Serreau** at the **Avignon festival** in 1971. Dadié's plays depict historical, social and political themes, arising mostly from the contact between white and black, but their success lies in his ability to express protest and satire in accordance with the language of the theatre. Dadié has a sound appreciation of the European and African theatrical traditions along with a striking imaginative inventiveness. None of his plays has yet been published in English translation. The titles, with dates of publication, are *Assémien Déhylé, King of the Sanwi* (1936 and 1979), *Min Adja-O* (*That's My Inheritance*), *Serment d'Amour* (*Love Vow*) and *A Difficult Situation* (1965), *Beatrice of the Congo* (1970), *Mr Thôgô-gnini* (1970), *Les Voix dans le Vent* (*Voices in the Wind* 1970), *Iles de Tempête* (*Islands of the Storm* 1973),

Papassidi maître escroc (*Papassidi, Master Crook* 1975; first version 1969), *Mhoi-ceul* (*Me Alone*, 1979). CW

Dagerman, Stig (1923–54) Swedish novelist and playwright. Dagerman was considered the most promising Swedish dramatist since **Lagerkvist**, a promise only partly fulfilled at the time of his suicide in 1954. His theory of 'de-dramatized drama', emphasizing words and ideas, rather than theatrical effects, led to plays that tend to be static, slow-moving and verbose, although he excels at building tension. Dagerman needs unusually vigorous direction, as in the case of his best (and first) play *The Condemned* (1947), brilliantly staged by **Alf Sjöberg** at **Dramaten** as a kind of Kafkaesque fantasy. HL

Dale, Alan (Alfred J. Cohen) (1861–1928) American drama critic. Born in England, Dale came to New York in the early 1880s to write for the *Dramatic Times*. In 1887 Joseph Pulitzer employed him as dramatic critic for the *World*. Dale switched to Hearst's *Morning Journal* in 1897 and *Cosmopolitan* Magazine in 1904. Except for the period 1914–17, he remained a Hearst regular until his death. Dale popularized an aggressive and 'smart' style of reviewing. *Who's Who in the Theatre* (1914) concluded that his opinions 'probably carry more weight than any others in New York'. TLM

Dallas Theatre Center 3636 Turtle Creek Blvd, Dallas, Texas [Architect: Frank Lloyd Wright]. Founded in 1959 by Baylor University professor Paul Baker and a group of Dallas citizens, the Dallas Theatre Centre sprang into being housed in the only theatre designed by Frank Lloyd Wright that he ever lived to see built. A gift of Dallas businessmen and named after a Texas actress who was killed in a plane crash, the Kalita Humphreys Theatre consists of a geometric poured concrete structure set into a hilly, wooded area a few miles from the centre of the city. Its original stage was set at one end of the auditorium and was equipped with a revolve and two side stages. Professor Baker's plan to assemble a permanent acting company to present classics, contemporary plays and introduce new works in conjunction with a graduate programme at Baylor, later at Trinity University, where he transferred his activities, was largely fulfilled but has been discontinued. The original 516-seat theatre was augmented by a tiny 56-seat theatre, Down Centre Stage, which presented experimental works within a proscenium stage. Under the leadership of Adrian Hall (1983), 'DTC' has become an Equity company utilizing new and renovated spaces. MCH

Dalrymple, Jean (1910–) American producer, director, and publicist. She began her career as an actress in vaudeville, then became personal representative with John Gòlden, and in 1940 formed her own publicity organization. Her initial venture as producer was in 1945 when she presented *Hope for the Best* by William McCleery. Associated with the New York City Centre Light Opera Company and the City Centre Drama Company from its inception in 1943, in 1953 she became its general director, a position she held for the next 15 years. This experience was recorded in her book *From the Last Row* (1975). From 1968–70 she was executive director of the American National

Theatre and Academy, and, in 1958, she was coordinator of the performing arts for the United States at the Brussels World's Fair.   DBW

Daly, (John) Augustin (1838–99) American dramatist, managing director, and critic who dominated the theatrical scene in the United States during the last half of the 19th century. His plays and especially his productions set a new standard for American theatre and exerted a strong influence in England, beginning with a first European tour in 1884 and culminating with the opening of Daly's own theatre in London in 1893. He began his theatre career as a critic, writing between 1859 and 1867 for five newspapers. During this period he also wrote or adapted his first plays, most notably *Leah the Forsaken* (1862) and the melodrama *Under the Gaslight* (1867). From the inception of his writing career he was assisted at every turn by his brother Joseph, though this collaboration was kept secret. Ultimately, the Dalys had over 90 of their plays or adaptations performed. Of this large number few are significant literary accomplishments though many show Daly to have been an exceptional contriver of effects and theatrical moments and during the 1870s and 80s a writer of melodramas and sentimental comedies superior to most of his contemporaries. Among his more successful productions were *A Flash of Lightning* (1868), *Frou-Frou* (1870), *Horizon* (1871), *Divorce* (1871), *Article 47* (1872), *Needles and Pins* (1880), *Dollars and Sense* (1883), *Love on Crutches* (1884), and *The Lottery of Love* (1888). He also produced adaptations of English classics and **Shakespeare**, one of the most successful of which, *The Taming of the Shrew*, was presented at Stratford-upon-Avon in 1888, supposedly the first performance of the play given there. Many of his more notable productions featured **Ada Rehan**, **John Drew**, **Mrs G. H. Gilbert**, and James Lewis, known as the 'Big Four'. Daly was usually adept at discerning and developing talent. Over 75 prominent actors owed their success to Daly's training. Daly also managed and built several important theatres, beginning with the rental in 1869 of the **Fifth Avenue Theatre**, and took over briefly the Grand Opera House. In 1879, with these theatres behind him, he took over the old Wood's Museum, which he opened as **Daly's**, remaining there until his death. Constantly striving for an ensemble effect in his productions, Daly was one of the first directors in the modern sense and the first American *régisseur*.   DBW

A poster advertising the sensation scene from Augustin Daly's *Under the Gaslight*, 1867.

Daly, (Peter Christopher) Arnold (1875–1927) American producer and actor. Daly should be remembered as **Shaw**'s first truly effective champion in the USA. Even as he was establishing himself as a player of supporting roles in England and America, he pursued his interest in Shaw by directing and acting in a trial matinee of *Candida* which opened for a regular run in New York in 1903 and then went on tour with *The Man of Destiny*. After visiting Shaw, Daly returned for the 1904–5 season to produce *How She Lied to her Husband* (written for Daly), *You Never Can Tell*, *John Bull's Other Island*, and *Mrs Warren's Profession*. The first performance of the latter play in New York was cause for Daly's arrest on morals charges, although he was acquitted. In 1906, Daly added *Arms and the Man* to his repertory and, under the management of the **Shuberts** conducted a successful national tour. Somewhat dismayed by the vitriolic response of conservative critics, Daly abandoned Shaw for a time to pursue more conventional roles.   MR

Daly's Theatre 1221 Broadway, New York City. Built to be a museum in 1867, John Banvard became manager and opened it mornings as a museum and used its three-tier, 2,000-seat auditorium for theatrical performances in the afternoons and evenings. A year later, it was taken over by George Wood, who renamed it Wood's Museum and Metropolitan Theatre, in which he presented plays, comic operas, burlesques and variety for the next few years. In 1876, Banvard reclaimed the lease and renamed it the Broadway Theatre. Its most significant period occurred when **Augustin Daly**, responding to the uptown drift of the theatres, took it over in 1879, renovated it extensively and transformed it into Daly's Theatre. Here, he and his stock company made their last stand against the new system of booking single plays into a theatre to try for a long run. Even Daly resorted to leasing the theatre to outside producers and summer rentals to keep it afloat, but when he died in 1899, the house passed to a succession of managers, including **Daniel Frohman** and the **Shubert brothers**. It met an inglorious end as a burlesque house when the new theatre district was amalgamating around Times Square. In 1920, it was razed and was replaced by a commercial structure.   MCH

Dame role see **Pantomime, English; Female impersonation**

Dancourt (Florent Carton) (1661–1725) French actor and playwright who, after several years with provincial companies, joined the **Comédie-Française** in 1685. Between then and his retirement in 1718 he pursued a dual career and wrote over 80 plays, including many in one act. Most are comedies of manners in prose, closely based on the contemporary scene and depicting an unscrupulous and pleasure-seeking society, as in *Le Chevalier à la mode* (*The Fashionable Knight*, 1687) and *Les Bourgeoises à la mode* (1692), which was imitated by **Vanbrugh** in *The Confederacy* (1705). Amongst the characteristic types surveyed – social-climbing bourgeois, financiers, magistrates, aristocratic gamesters and adventurers – there are few sympathetic figures and the perspective offered looks forward to **Lesage**, if in a less sardonic and more light-hearted mood.   DR

Dandanata In the state of Orissa, in north-eastern India, this form is thought to be the oldest example of drama. It begins with dances, music and dramatic episodes in the evening. Various mythological characters are introduced through song and dance in an open arena. Loosely connected episodes link the characters that appear during the evening. Moral lessons and religious messages are reinforced by the characters, some of whom are Jogi, Shiva, Krishna and the Gopis. FaR

Dane, Clemence (Winifred Ashton) (1888–1965) British dramatist and novelist, once hailed (by the critic **St John Ervine**) as 'the most distinguished woman dramatist'. Trained as a portraitist, she began her theatrical career as an actress (under the stage name of Diana Cortis) before turning to melodramatic 'problem plays' focusing on sexual issues from a female perspective. *A Bill of Divorcement* (1921) was followed by *The Way Things Happen* (1924), and a morality play on adultery, *Granite* (1926). She also used biblical subjects (*Naboth's Vineyard*, 1925; *Herod and Mariamne*, 1938) or historical settings (a dramatization of the lives of the Brontë sisters, *Wild Decembers*, 1932; *The Golden Age of Queen Elizabeth*, 1941) to illustrate her themes. She also wrote a seven-play religious cycle for radio, *The Saviours*, part of which was adapted for the stage (1942, with **John Mills** and **Sybil Thorndike**). Her last work, *Eighty in the Shade* (1959), was specially written for Sybil Thorndike and **Lewis Casson**, who had played the leading roles in the premiere of *Granite*. CI

Daniel, Samuel (1562–1619) English poet and occasional playwright, who enjoyed the patronage of many noble benefactors and was thus spared the rough and tumble of the public theatres. Daniel wrote two Senecan tragedies, *Cleopatra* (1594) and *Philotas* (1604), supervising the production of the second by the **Children of the Chapel Royal**. James I was among those troubled by supposedly covert references in the play to the fate of the Earl of Essex, and Daniel fell into further disfavour when the Children of the Chapel Royal, over which he exercised formal control, presented *Eastward Ho* (1605), the joint work of **Jonson**, **Marston** and **Chapman**, offensive to the King for its anti-Scottish jibes. But Daniel knew the virtues of timely sycophancy. The composition of a number of court entertainments, including the pastoral *The Queen's Arcadia* in the dangerous year of 1605, reestablished him at Court. We do not know why, nor precisely when, he retired from public life to a farm in Somerset. PT

Dashavatara (India) The term refers to the ten incarnations (*avataras*) of Lord Vishnu, one of a trinity of deities, two of whom are widely worshipped in India. The term also refers to a form of theatre popular in rural areas of the Konkan and Goa, on the western coast of the Indian subcontinent.

Although the history of the *Dashavatara* is not certain, it is thought to have been introduced to the area by a Brahmin 400 years ago. Some claim that it was derived from **Kuchipudi**; others maintain that it owes its origin to **Yakshagana**. The actors who preserve *Dashavatara* worship a small image of a diety at Walaval

which is said to have been brought from Kerala from where the form is also thought to have been derived.

Most of the actors come from the lower strata of society, although there are a few Brahmins who also perform. The troupes are itinerant, moving from village to village half the year, carrying their simple baskets and trunks in whatever way they may and sleeping out in the open most of the time. All of the actors are male and their earnings are generally rather poor.

Performances usually begin around 11 pm with songs in praise of Ganapati, the elephant-headed god, sung by the stage manager (*sutradhara*). A Brahmin enters and comic dialogue ensues. Dances are performed by two men dressed as women. An elementary dance is then performed by an actor who impersonates Saraswati, goddess of learning. After the dance, two women enter symbolizing rivers. With them is Madhavi, a comic Brahmin. Next, the frightening figure of Shankhasura bursts on the playing area dressed from head to foot in black and sporting a red cloth representing a long tongue. Shankhasura is thought to be capable of exposing the scandals and private lives of the villagers. He carries on a lively improvisational conversation with the stage manager. Then an actor playing the god Brahma, the creator, enters and a story about the theft of the sacred *Vedas* is related in which Shankhasura and the stage manager participate. The events of the elaborate overture described above continue for approximately two hours.

Finally, the drama (*akhyana*) begins. It usually carries the action forward until sunrise. The drama includes well-known episodes from the epic literature and introduces mythological and historical characters with whom village audiences are familiar. The decision about what episodes should be performed is negotiated between the village patron and the stage manager, sometimes less than an hour before the show.

A small boy dressed in the costume of a woman moves among the spectators during the performance soliciting contributions from the villagers. The job is said to help cure the boy of stage fright and his costume gives him access to the women, who usually huddle together apart from the village men.

The musical accompaniment for the dances and songs is simple. A harmonium and *mridangam* drum generally assist the actors with their songs and set a lively tempo for the simple dances. Tunes of popular film music have been liberally incorporated to accompany the lyrics of the songs and the dances are hardly more than simple rhythmic movements.

The stage, too, is simple – an open space in a temple hall or an open area in the village where a temporary raised platform is surrounded on three sides and roofed by thatch and leaves. A rough wooden bench obtained from the local town council hall or school serves as the only piece of furniture. Special properties, such as swords, spears and clubs, are introduced by the actors when the need arises. A few wooden masks are also part of their collection. An elaborately carved ten-headed wooden mask depicts Ravana, the demon-king of Lanka, and one representing Ganapati's elephant head is also part of a company's belongings. Costumes and ornaments are rather elaborate, considering the simple means the actors have of transporting them. Various cloth pieces, saris, jewellery and headdresses are worn to symbolize the nobility, gods and goddesses; use of red and white makeup helps to distinguish the characters from their simple village patrons.

Very little has been written about this form and only recently have scholars begun to reveal the full extent and characteristics of its impact on village life in this area of India.   FaR

Daskathia (India) This is a two-person dramatic form unique to Orissa in north-eastern India, in which several hundred groups of performers work, primarily in the Ganjam district of the state. The main singer, called *Gayaka*, is accompanied by the *Palia* who chants the name of Rama, the epic hero and incarnation of Lord Vishnu, in rhythmic refrains. A mythological story of about three hours' duration is related in which artists play many roles and accompany themselves with cymbals and wooden clappers or castanets. Social commentary and humorous anecdotes help to enliven the action. The artists wear regal attire. Ankle bells add additional percussive effects to their rhythmic stories.   FaR

Dasté, Jean (1904–) French actor, director. One of **Copeau**'s original band of disciples (he married Copeau's daughter, Marie-Hélène), Dasté was a pioneer in the **decentralization movement**. After working with the Compagnie des Quatre Saisons (he was a co-founder with **Barsacq** and Jacquemont in 1936) and a touring offshoot of this group under the Occupation, Dasté established a touring company of his own in Grenoble after the Liberation. Local opposition led to his departure for St Etienne in 1947, where he remained until 1971. His repertoire followed Copeau's lead but included new dramatists (**Cousin, Gatti**) and **Brecht** (his *Caucasian Chalk Circle*, 1956, was that play's French premiere). His policy involved vigorous prospection of a working-class audience. St Etienne's Maison de la Culture, built in consultation with Dasté, was denied him because of a disagreement with the local board of management. He played many character roles in French films, notably Truffaut's *L'Enfant Sauvage* (*The Wild Child*, 1970), in which he played the role of Professor Pinel.   DB

Daubeny, Peter (Lauderdale) (1921–75) British impresario, best known as the artistic director of the World Theatre Seasons in London from 1964 to 1973. He began his career as an actor, studying with **Michel Saint-Denis**'s London Theatre Studio and joining the **Liverpool Playhouse** under William Armstrong. During the war, he served as a lieutenant in the Coldstream Guards and lost a left arm during the Salerno invasion in 1943. This injury caused him to abandon his acting career and concentrate on management. He staged his first production, of William Lipscombe's *The Gay Pavilion*, at the Piccadilly Theatre in 1945, but his first major successes as an impresario came in the early 1950s, when he brought over to London a dazzling array of dance companies from Spain, India, France, Yugoslavia and Soviet Russia. He concentrated at first on those forms of theatre where language was no barrier, but following the triumphant success of Compagnie Edwige Feuillere in *La Dame aux Camélias* (1955), he looked to major drama companies as well. The **Berliner Ensemble** was brought over to

the Palace Theatre in 1956, providing British audiences with their first opportunity to see **Brecht**'s company, which was then little known. Other major visiting companies included the **Comédie-Française**, the **Moscow Art Theatre**, the Malmo City Theatre Company in **Ingmar Bergman**'s production of *Urfast*, Zizi Jeanmaire and her company and **Vittorio Gassman**'s Teatro Popolare Italiano. He introduced London audiences to the new wave of American theatre with Jack Gelber's *The Connection* (1961). As a result, he managed to build up an audience prepared to look at forms of theatre as various as the Classical Theatre of China and Dublin's **Abbey Theatre** in a **Sean O'Casey** play. This public provided the financial basis, for Daubeny received no government grants, for the World Theatre Seasons which ran usually at the Aldwych Theatre for two to three months in the spring. These became an established feature of London's theatrical year, a major reason for the new-found cosmopolitanism in British drama. Daubeny travelled tirelessly and the success of the World Theatre Seasons was due to the width and perceptions of his tastes, his energy and his outstanding diplomatic skills. He was knighted in 1973 but after his death in 1975, there was nobody who could adequately succeed him in running the World Theatre Seasons. He was the author of *Stage by Stage* (1952) and *My World of Theatre* (1971).   JE

Davenant, William (1606–68) English playwright, manager. He claimed to be the illegitimate son of **Shakespeare**. He joined the household of Fulke Greville and was soon a member of the circle of writers including **Shirley** and Suckling. His first play, *The Cruel Brother*, was performed in 1627 and in the 1630s he produced a steady stream of plays including comedies *The Platonic Lovers* (1635) and *News from Plymouth* (1635) and court **masques** (especially *Britannia Triumphans* (1638) and the last Caroline masque *Salmacida Spolia* (1640)). After a bout of syphilis his nose collapsed. In 1638 he succeeded **Jonson** as Laureate. In 1639 he secured a patent from the King to open a theatre and the following year on **Beeston**'s imprisonment he ran the **Cockpit Theatre** in Drury Lane. After active service during the Civil War and imprisonment when captured attempting to sail to Maryland he joined the King's circle in Paris. In 1656 he avoided the government's prohibition on plays by performing operas at Rutland House, including his own heroic play *The Siege of Rhodes* which marked a major advance in the development of English opera and was produced with changeable scenery by **John Webb**. He followed these performances with one at the Cockpit in Drury Lane in 1658. In 1660 he leased Lisle's Tennis Court in Lincoln's Inn Fields and converted it into a theatre. With **Killigrew** he persuaded the King to grant them a patent giving them a monopoly on theatre performances in London. Davenant's troupe, the Duke's Company, after eliminating the rival companies apart from Killigrew's, began acting at **Lincoln's Inn Fields** in 1661, the first professional company in England to act in a theatre equipped with changeable scenery. In his agreement with the company Davenant controlled the rent and production costs and maintained the actresses in return for two-thirds of the company profits. Shorn of rights to almost all pre-Restoration drama Davenant began adapting plays: *Hamlet* in 1661, *The Law against*

Lovers from *Measure for Measure* and *Much Ado About Nothing* in 1662, and operatic versions of *Macbeth* (1663) and *The Tempest* (with **Dryden**, 1667). He also carefully encouraged new work by **Etherege**, **Boyle** and others. Carefully identifying the tastes of his middleclass audience, he gave them spectacular dramas and good farces, establishing the success of his company which continued under his widow's management. PH

Davenport, Edward Loomis (1815–77) American actor. Davenport was known for his versatility, grace, good taste, musical voice, and gentlemanly manners. **Mrs Mowatt** said that he simply looked like a leading man. He began his career in Providence (1835), became **Anna Cora Mowatt**'s leading man (1846), went with her to London, remained there for seven years, often playing in support of **Macready**, and returned to be acclaimed for his 'intelligent and impressive' conception of Lanciotto in **Boker**'s *Francesca da Rimini* (1855). From then until his final season (1875–6, playing Brutus to **Lawrence Barrett**'s Cassius), he became known for his extraordinary versatility. He was equally effective as Bill Sykes, Hamlet, Sir Lucius O'Trigger or Othello.

He was the father of the actress **Fanny Davenport**, and three of his descendants have been active in recent years: Anne and **William Seymour** as actors, and the late May Davenport Seymour as theatre curator at the Museum of the City of New York. RM

Davenport, Fanny (1850–98) English-born American actress. Daughter of actor **E. L. Davenport**, 'Miss Fanny' was a popular child actress before her adult debut in 1862 at New York's **Niblo's Garden Theatre**. In 1869 she joined **Augustin Daly**'s **Fifth Avenue Theatre** company and demonstrated remarkable versatility in light comedies, Shakespeare, and finally serious dramatic works like Daly's *Pique* (1876) in which she created Mabel Renfew, one of her most popular roles, along with Nancy Sykes in *Oliver Twist*. A beautiful, 'spirited' actress, she formed her own company and gave the American English-language premieres of four **Bernhardt** vehicles by **Sardou**: *Fedora* (1883), *La Tosca* (1888), *Cleopatra* (1890), and *Gismonda* (1894). FHL

Davies, Hubert Henry (1876–1917) British dramatist. A journalist who wrote a series of social comedies between 1899 and 1914. These included a depiction of female domination, *The Mollusc* (1907), and *Outcast*, his last and most successful play, about sexual double standards. CI

Davies, Robertson (1913–) Canadian novelist, essayist, teacher, theatre historian and general 'man of letters' who has had a lifelong attachment to the theatre. Born in Thamesville, Ontario, he was educated in Canada and at Oxford, where his B.Litt. thesis was published as *Shakespeare's Boy Actors* (1939). He remained in England at the **Old Vic** and the Old Vic School before returning in 1940 to Canada and a career in journalism. Besides plays, his published writings consist of essays, novels, and chronicles (with **Tyrone Guthrie**) of the early years of the **Stratford Festival**, of which he was a founding Governor. His first play, *Overlaid* (1947), was published with several others in

the collection *Eros at Breakfast and Other Plays* (1949). These were one-acters primarily destined for amateur production. His first three-act play, *Fortune My Foe* (1948), an ironic look at the treatment of the artist in Canada, won the Best Canadian Play award at the 1949 Dominion Drama Festival. Among his later plays, the Welsh comedy *A Jig For The Gypsy* (1954), and *Hunting Stuart* (1955) were produced by Toronto's Crest Theatre. *Love and Libel* (1960), an adaptation of his early novel, *Leaven of Malice*, was produced unsuccessfully by the **Theatre Guild** of New York, but later a more successful version was produced by the **Shaw** Festival under the original title.

Davies made important contributions to the Report of the Massey Commission, stressing the need for a strong professional theatre. In 1966 as Master of Massey College he helped establish the University of Toronto's Graduate Centre for the Study of Drama. In the 1970s he achieved international fame as a novelist, but continued to write for and about the theatre. Just as his novels often have deep roots in the theatrical tradition, his later plays such as *Question Time* (1975) develop many of the Jungian ideas that permeate his novels. JA

Davis, Henrietta Vinton (1860–1941) Afro-American actress. For 35 years a preeminent actress and solo elocutionist, Baltimore-born Davis was 'a singularly beautiful woman . . . with illustriously expressive eyes [and a] rich, flexible and effective voice'. She was universally hailed by audiences across America for her powerful and moving interpretations of a range of dramatic heroines including Juliet, Portia, Ophelia, Rosalind, Lady Anne, Desdemona, Lady Macbeth, Cleopatra, and others. Excluded by racial prejudice from the established professional stage, Davis gave concert readings and performed dramatic scenes with other black actors. She produced and played leading roles in three plays by Afro-American dramatists: *Dessalines* (1893) and *Christophe* (1912), both by William Edgar Easton, and *Our Old Kentucky Home* (1898), written for her by the journalist John E. Bruce. From 1919 to 1931 Davis held a major office in the Marcus Garvey movement, working for racial equality and the establishment of a black nation state in Africa. EGH

Davis, Ossie (1917–) Afro-American actor and playwright who began acting with the Harlem-based Rose McClendon Players and made his Broadway debut in the title role of *Jeb* (1946). Davis joined the national tour of *Anna Lucasta* (1947) and played in various New York productions including *Stevedore* (1949), *The Green Pastures* (1951) and *No Time for Sergeants* (1955), before succeeding Sidney Poitier in *A Raisin in the Sun* (1959). In 1961 Davis assumed the lead role opposite his wife **Ruby Dee** in his hilarious comedy *Purlie Victorious* that pungently ridiculed racial stereotyping. The film version, *Gone Are the Days* (1963), was unimpressive but success was renewed with the musical *Purlie* (1970). Davis also wrote *Curtain Call, Mr Aldridge, Sir* (1963) and has appeared in numerous films and television shows, some of which he scripted and directed. Louis D. Mitchell has called him 'one of the most gifted men in the modern American theatre'. EGH

Davis, Owen (1874–1956) The most successful American writing melodrama at the turn of the 20th century. From *Through the Breakers* (1899) to *The Family Cupboard* (1913) he wrote scores of plays such as *Convict 999* and *Nellie, the Beautiful Cloak Model*. Then he stopped and in an essay entitled 'Why I Quit Writing Melodrama', *American Magazine* 78, September 1914, pp. 28–31 explained his art. Later, he elaborated in a book, *I'd Like to Do It Again*, 1931. Having abandoned his Harvard-trained writing style, he changed again and wrote realistic plays. *Detour* (1921) suggested the extent of his reformation, and *Icebound* (1923), concerned with the lost illusions of a New England family, won a Pulitzer Prize. Among later plays, only his adaptation of Edith Wharton's *Ethan Frome* (1936), with his son Donald Davis, had much success. He could not keep pace with the new rank of American dramatists after the First World War. WJM

Dawison, Bogumil (1818–72) Celebrated Polish virtuoso actor, whose career was spent mainly in the German theatre. He was a member of the Vienna **Burgtheater** from 1849 to 1852 and of the **Dresden Court Theatre** from 1852 to 1864. Dawison was noted for his aggressive, often unpolished interpretations of Shakespearean and other classic roles. As he was a bitter rival of **Emil Devrient**, his acting was widely regarded as the antithesis of the **Weimar style**. Dawison was one of the first German actors to tour America. SW

Day, John (1574–1640) English playwright and poet whose recorded theatrical activity is confined to the period 1598–1608. He was, for a time, one of **Henslowe**'s circle of writers, part-author with **Chettle** of one of the **Admiral's Men**'s major successes, *The Blind Beggar of Bethnal Green* (1600). Two satirical comedies for **Boys' Companies**, *Law Tricks* (1604) and *The Isle of Gulls* (1606), were followed by another collaboration, with **William Rowley** and George Wilkins, on the ramblingly peculiar romance, *The Travels of the Three English Brothers* (1607), based on the adventures of the extraordinary Shirley family and including an interesting scene in which the Shakespearian clown **Will Kempe** displays his extempore skills. Day's known dramatic work is completed by an attractive comedy, *Humour out of Breath* (c. 1608), and the poetic pastoral dialogues that make up *The Parliament of Bees* (published 1641). Day's is a minor talent, but a pleasing one. PT

De Angelis, Jefferson (1859–1933) American comedian and singer. One of the most beloved stars of comic opera, De Angelis performed in vaudeville as a child, and later on tried his hand at dramatic acting. In 1887 he joined the McCaull Opera Company, appearing as a featured performer in comic operas such as *The Lady or the Tiger?* (1888). For several years he was a regular member of the Casino Theatre company, along with **Lillian Russell** and **Francis Wilson**. His first solo starring part was in *The Caliph* (1896). De Angelis brought to his comic opera roles both an ability to create consistent and individualized characters and the physical skills of an acrobat. His greatest successes were in *The Jolly Musketeer* (1898), *The Emerald Isle* (1902), *Fantana* (1905), and *The Girl and the Governor* (1907).

From 1910 until his death, he performed in revivals of comic operas and in straight plays such as *The Royal Family* (1927). His autobiography was published in 1931. MK

DeBar, Ben (1812–77) American actor and manager. Born in England, he came to America as an equestrian performer in 1837, but soon specialized in low comedy. He was also stage manager for **Noah Ludlow** and **Sol Smith** at **St Charles Theatre**, New Orleans. When they retired (1843) he assumed management of their New Orleans and St Louis theatres. At the outbreak of the Civil War he moved to St Louis. He retained ownership of the St Charles until 1876. In St Louis he moved from the St Louis Theatre to DeBar's Grand Opera House in 1873. He remained active as a performer, touring the Mississippi River valley as a star every season, and was the most influential manager in the region. DMCD

De Filippo A family of Italian actors, directors and playwrights. **Eduardo** (1900–85), like his sister **Titina** (1898–1963) and brother **Peppino** (1903–80), was born into the profession and at an early age acted in the **Scarpetta** troupe. In 1932 the three formed their own company which lasted until 1945 when Peppino left to work independently, and Eduardo and Titina set up Il Teatro di Eduardo.

A brilliant comic actor, with an economic, realistic style of playing, Eduardo had an engaging stage presence and a wide range of technical skills honed to perfection by his apprenticeship in the Neapolitan theatre. From the late 1920s until his death he was a prolific dramatist, acting in and directing much of his own work; indeed many of his plays have been most effective on the stage when he has performed them with his own troupe. The best of them rank as the most vital in the modern Italian theatre, and attest to the enduring invention of the Neapolitan dialect stage. He wrote some 40 plays, several of the finest of which, like *Filumena Maturano* (*Filumena*, 1946), *Sabato, Domenica, e Lunedì* (*Saturday, Sunday, Monday*, 1959) and, at least in its film version, *Napoli Milionaria!* (*Affluent Naples!* 1945), have enjoyed not only great popularity in Italy, but considerable success abroad. They draw on a wide range of popular forms, and on the Italian and dialect 'prose' theatre traditions. Detailed stage directions show the hand of the professional practitioner, and for all that there are strong literary dramatic influences, notably that of **Pirandello**, the plays are very much of the theatre. But they are firmly placed too in the language, life and attitudes of the Neapolitan pettybourgeois and working class, and character and situation are handled in basically naturalistic ways. Eduardo's view of the world is essentially tragicomic: in many of his plays the action turns on the attempts of a good-natured, even naive individual to change a society that is rapacious and materialistic. A darker, more melancholy tone tends to emerge in his later work. At the centre of nearly all of it however is the family, and familial ties and obligations remain the one certainty in an otherwise unstable world. At times this can prove treacherous subject matter, and some of the plays are marred by sentimentality and a simplistic moral didacticism. One play, *L'Arte della Commedia* (*The Art of Comedy*, 1964), stands rather apart, its subject being the condition of the modern Italian theatre. Eduardo demonstrated his concern for the stage too in practical ways, notably in his renovation of the Teatro San Ferdinando in Naples, which he undertook at his own expense. He both acted in and directed a number of films.

Eduardo's brother, Peppino, after forming his own company came increasingly to specialize in Italian light comedy and farce, and excelled in much foreign comic drama, from **Molière** to **Pinter**. He too wrote plays and was a well-known film actor, often appearing with the comedian **Totò**. His son Luigi has continued in the family's actor–management tradition. Titina de Filippo worked mainly with Eduardo interpreting many of the female lead roles in his plays, notably Filumena Maturano.   LR

De Koven, Reginald (1859–1920) American composer. After an extensive musical education in Europe, De Koven, in partnership with librettist **Harry B. Smith**, set out to prove that Americans could write a comic opera in the European style. Their first show, *The Begum* (1887), while not an unqualified success in New York, drew large audiences in Chicago, De Koven's home town. In 1891 De Koven composed the score of *Robin Hood*, the most popular American comic opera of the era. Carefully mounted by the **Bostonians**, *Robin Hood* was an immediate hit and the song 'O Promise Me—' became an enduring American standard. Although he continued to compose comic operas until 1913, De Koven never had another success of the stature of *Robin Hood*. While his music was largely imitative of European modes, De Koven is remembered for his courage in challenging the supremacy of European comic opera composers on the American stage.   MK

De Liagre, Alfred Jr (1904–   ) American producer and director. Educated at Yale University, De Liagre began his professional career in 1930 as stage manager at the Woodstock Playhouse. In 1933 he began producing professionally and has worked in both New York and London. De Liagre has produced or co-produced more than 30 plays, a number of which he also directed. His more noteworthy credits include: *The Voice of the Turtle* (1943); *The Madwoman of Chaillot* (1948); *Second Threshold* (1950); *The Golden Apple* (1954); *The Girls in 509* (1958); *J. B.* (1959), which won a Pulitzer Prize; *Photo Finish* (1963); *Bubbling Brown Sugar* (1976); *Deathtrap* (1978); and *On Your Toes* (1983).   TLM

De Loutherbourg, Philip James (1740–1812) Scene designer. Born in Strasbourg, he studied painting in Paris, becoming particularly interested in the use of colour. In 1771 he moved to London to work with **Garrick** and proposed improvements in the lighting and scene systems at **Drury Lane**, particularly in the quantity of theatre lighting available. In 1773 he began designing extravagant theatre spectacles, like a naval review for Arne's *Alfred*. His new techniques concentrated on transformation scenes and on light effects (e.g. sunlight, castles in moonlight) as well as on developing a landscape and perspective style of exotic romantic views of England for, e.g., **Sheridan**'s *The Wonders of Derbyshire* (1779). In 1781 he left the theatre to set up the Eidophusikon, a display of scenes as

Scenic pieces by De Loutherbourg for the creation of a boat/cliff scene.

panoramic pictures, scenery for its own sake, using rear-lit transparencies and experimenting with coloured plates. His later years were obsessed with faith-healing. His brilliant developments of stage lighting and of naturalistic romantic landscapes enabled the actor to step back into the scenic spaces and prepared the ground for the development of pictorial modes of theatre.   PH

De Mille, Agnes (1905–   ) American choreographer and director. Trained in the techniques of classical ballet, de Mille appeared as a dancer in the *Greenwich Village Follies* (1928). After choreographing two shows in London, she returned to New York to create the dances for *Hooray for What* (1937), and *Swingin' the Dream* (1939). In 1943 **Rodgers** and **Hammerstein** hired her to choreograph *Oklahoma!*, and her use of modern ballet techniques revolutionized musical comedy dance. In particular, the success of *Oklahoma!*'s dream ballet made such sequences a common feature of 1940s musicals. De Mille went on to choreograph *One Touch of Venus* (1943), *Bloomer Girl* (1944), *Carousel* (1945), and *Brigadoon* (1947). Her choreography for *Brigadoon* was acclaimed for its dramatic intensity and its use of traditional Scottish dances. De Mille served as both choreographer and director for *Allegro* (1947) and *Out of This World* (1950). In the 1950s she created the dances for such shows as *Paint Your Wagon* (1951), *The Girl in Pink Tights* (1954), and *Goldilocks* (1958). Less active in the 1960s, de Mille choreographed *Kwamina* (1961), *110 in the Shade* (1963), and *Come Summer* (1969). Best remembered for her pioneering work in musicals of the 1940s, de Mille is credited with demonstrating dance's potential for furthering a musical's dramatic action.   MK

De Wahl, Anders (1869–1956) Swedish actor, popular until the late 1920s, when his preeminence was challenged by the more natural style of **Lars Hanson**. A personality actor, whose lyricism and physical grace precisely reflected the ideals of fin-de-siècle romanticism, he excelled in emotionally troubled roles, including **Strindberg**'s Erik XIV (1899) and King Magnus (1901), or in plays on religious themes, such as *Everyman* (1916) or **Eliot**'s *Murder in the Cathedral* (1939). Firmly rooted in 19th-century tradition, he was outspokenly opposed to modernism in theatre, although the early popularity of **Pirandello** in Sweden probably resulted from De Wahl's performances in *Six Characters in Search of an Author* (1925), *Henry IV* (1926) and *The Pleasure of Honesty* (1930). HL

Dean, Basil Herbert (1888–1978) British actor, director and producer. He joined **Miss Horniman**'s company in Manchester in 1907 as an actor where he stayed, until in 1910 he was invited to help start a new repertory theatre in Liverpool. Appointed director of productions in 1911, Dean soon established the theatre as a major force in the repertory movement before leaving in 1913. From 1919 to 1926 he was in partnership with Alec Rea and, as the 'ReandeaN' management, they were responsible for a series of major productions on the London stage, including *The Skin Game*, *R.U.R.* and *Hassan*. Dean continued both to produce and to direct, staging, among others, the premieres of several plays by **Priestley**. In 1939, he started and became director of **ENSA** (Entertainments National Service Association); and in 1948 organized the first British Repertory Theatre Festival in London. He directed a number of films, including *Lorna Doone* and the films of **Gracie Fields**. The two volumes of his autobiography are *Seven Ages* (1888–1927) and *The Mind's Eye* (1927–72); and his *Theatre at War* is the official history of ENSA. AJ

Dean, Julia (1830–68) American actress. Her mother, Julia Drake, was the daughter of pioneer Kentucky manager, **Samuel Drake**, and her father, Edwin Dean, was a pioneer manager in Buffalo. Making her debut at the age of 11, she was the leading American tragic actress by 1846. Marriage to Samuel Hayne in 1855 was disastrous, so she went west in 1856 and established herself as a star in California and Utah for the rest of her life. She specialized in suffering heroines, such as **Shakespeare**'s Juliet and **Bulwer-Lytton**'s Pauline, in which her height, her blonde good looks, and her deep voice were assets. DMCD

Dearly, Max (Lucien-Max Rolland) (1874–1943) French actor and variety artist, trained in an English circus at Marseilles. At his Paris debut at the Concert Parisien, his ingratiating manners, lantern-jawed face and 'British' elegance made him a favourite. In his heyday, 1905–10, he launched the 'valse chaloupée' with **Mistinguett** and mimed an entire horse-race in his 'Jockey américain'. As his vocal powers diminished, he abandoned operetta and revue for the plays of De Flers and Caillavet, and the screen, where he was seen as Homais in Jean Renoir's *Madame Bovary* (1934). LS

Deburau, Jean-Gaspard (Jan Kaspar Dvorak) (1796–1846) French mime, born in Bohemia; in 1812

Max Dearly and Mistinguett in an apache dance.

he came to Paris with his family, long active as acrobats and fairground performers. From 1816 he appeared at the **Théâtre des Funambules**, rapidly becoming a favourite of the working-class audiences in such pantomimes as *Harlequin Doctor*, *The Raging Bull* (1827), *The Golden Sleep* (1828), *The Whale* (1832), *Pierrot in Africa* and *The Old Clo' Man* (1842). He developed the secondary character **Pierrot** into a versatile protagonist, hapless, ingenious, often macabre and aggressive; puffed by the literati, including Nodier, **Gautier**, Baudelaire and Heine, his pale-faced, elongated hero took on mythic proportions. Personally taciturn and touchy (he once killed a youth who molested his wife), on stage Deburau extended the physical vocabulary of mime into broadly lyrical directions; most modern mimes, **Marceau** especially, acknowledge their debt to him. Deburau was the subject of a play by **Sacha Guitry** (1918) and Marcel Carné's film *Les Enfants du Paradis* (1945) incarnated 'Baptiste', the Deburau figure, in **Jean-Louis Barrault**. His son, Jean-Charles (1829–73), succeeded him at the Funambules and sublimated Pierrot into an elegant moonstruck romantic. LS

Decentralization movement Theatre in France has always been more centred on the metropolis than theatre in other European countries but it was the conversion of provincial theatres into cinemas in the early years of the 20th century that led to a situation where almost no producing company existed outside Paris. **Gémier** formed a Théâtre National Ambulant (National Touring Theatre) in 1911 to try to fill this provincial vacuum. He was followed by **Copeau**, **Chancerel**, and others between the two World Wars, who began to feel that a move away from Paris was a necessary prerequisite for theatrical renewal. In 1937 **Dullin** was commissioned by the Popular Front Government to produce a plan for decentralizing the theatre. His plan was for provincial centres of dramatic excellence, each with the responsibility for touring their region. The project was interrupted by the war years, but formed the basis of the policy vigorously pursued by Jeanne Laurent, who worked for the Ministry of Culture 1939–54. Under her guidance the first provincial Centres Dramatiques were established in Alsace at Colmar (later moving to Strasbourg and becoming a Théâtre National in 1968) at St Etienne, at Rennes, at Toulouse and at Aix-en-Provence. **Vilar**, who had founded the successful **Avignon theatre festival** in 1947, was installed as director of the **Théâtre National Populaire** at the **Chaillot Theatre**. No more official centres were established until De Gaulle came to power in 1959 and appointed Malraux his minister of culture. Malraux dreamed of creating a modern equivalent of the medieval cathedrals: Maisons de la Culture devoted to interdisciplinary practice of the arts. In reality, many of the first Maisons were constructed around an existing theatre company (e.g. Gabriel Monnet's at Bourges, Jo Tréhard's at Caen) although subsequent differences of opinion sometimes led to these directors being deprived of the building. The dual funding of the Maisons, half by the Ministry, half by the Municipality, often led to the Maison becoming a political football. The near-revolution of 1968 brought these differences into the open and the seventies were a period of stagnation from which the 15 Maisons were rescued by the socialist government's injections of cash and enthusiasm after 1981. Malraux also promoted the network of Centres Dramatiques, entirely funded by the Ministry, and introduced the status of Troupes permanentes de la décentralisation for young provincial companies serving a particular area. Among important companies to emerge in the sixties, following the Théâtre de la Cité at Villeurbanne, were companies based in Angers, Beaune, Besançon, Caen, Carcassonne, Grenoble, Lille, Limoges, Lyon, Marseille, Nice, Reims and Tourcoing. A number of new theatre companies were also established in the 'red belt' of workers' suburbs around Paris, notably the Théâtre des Amandiers directed by Pierre Debauche at Nanterre; the Théâtre de la Commune directed by Gabriel Garran at Aubervilliers; the Théâtre Gérard Philipe directed by José Valverde at Saint-Denis and the Théâtre de Sartrouville where **Patrice Chéreau** was beginning to make his name. The title of Théâtre de l'Est Parisien was conferred on the company of Guy Rétoré working in the East End of Paris. In the 1970s, **Planchon**'s company became the TNP while remaining in Villeurbanne and a new generation of directors and actors began to make their names in the decentralized theatres, notably **Jean-Pierre Vincent** at Strasbourg; Michel Dubois at Caen; Georges Lavaudant at Grenoble; **Marcel Maréchal** at Lyon, then at Marseille; Gildas Bourdet at Tourcoing; and, in the Parisian red belt, Bernard Sobel at Gennevilliers and **Antoine Vitez** at Ivry. In the mid-eighties there were 29 Centres Dramatiques in the provinces or Paris suburbs which had benefited from the Mitterrand government's determination to breathe new life into the decentralization movement.

Basing itself on the ideas articulated in Copeau's *Le Théâtre Populaire* (1941) and on Vilar's vision of theatre as a public service, the decentralization movement has had an important influence on the development of directing, acting and playwriting in France and has encouraged a greater level of social and political awareness among theatre artists. The theatre school attached to the Strasbourg centre by **Michel Saint-Denis** has trained a whole generation of actors and directors who have gone out to work in the decentralized theatres. New playwrights have been slower to emerge: while the new theatre of the absurd was the glory of the Parisian stage, the decentralized theatres were digesting the lessons of **Brecht**. But in the 1960s new work by French playwrights began to be performed. Some of these have acquired national reputations, e.g. **Adamov**, **Cousin**, **Gatti**, others have had a more local following, identified with a particular community e.g. Pierre Halet at Bourges. In the 1970s the decentralized theatres were in the avant-garde of new playwriting, promoting the work of the **Théâtre du Quotidien**.   DB

Decroux, Etienne–Marcel (1898–1991) French actor, who, according to **Gordon Craig**, rediscovered mime'. A student of **Charles Dullin** (1926–34), he developed a systematic grammar of physical expression he called 'mime corporel' or 'pantomime de style', a method of corporal extension geared to make abstract statements. He had a strong influence on **Jean-Louis Barrault**, playing **Deburau** *père* to the latter's Baptiste Deburau in the film *Les Enfants du Paradis* (1945). In 1941, he opened a school, performing for tiny audiences of two or three persons, and through his students Eliane Guyon, Cathérine Toth and **Marcel Marceau** his ideas were diffused throughout modern mime. He toured the Western world and Israel (1949–58) and ran a studio theatre in Paris. His son Maximilien was also a mime.   LS

Dee, Ruby (1923–) Afro-American actress. Born Ruby Ann Wallace in Cleveland, Ohio, Dee first acted with the American Negro Theatre and took over the title role for the tour of *Anna Lucasta* (1944). She appeared in various New York productions, attracting attention as Ruth Younger in *A Raisin in the Sun* (1959) after which her reputation advanced. She was acclaimed as Lutiebelle, the innocent pawn in *Purlie Victorious* (1961) and as the long-suffering Lena in *Boesman and Lena* (1970) for which she won the Obie and Drama Desk awards. Her performance in **Alice Childress**'s *Wedding Band* (1973) also earned a Drama Desk award. In **Shakespeare**, Dee has played Katharina in *The Taming of the Shrew* (1965), Cordelia to **Morris Carnovsky**'s King Lear (1965), and Gertrude in *Hamlet* (1975). Dee possesses an irresistibly enchanting stage personality and is infectiously funny in comedy.   EGH

Déjazet, (Pauline) Virginie (1798–1875) French actress. After a debut at the Variétés in 1817, she appeared in Lyon and Bordeaux, and, in 1821 was taken on at the Gymnase, where her roles included a number of **breeches parts**. In 1828 she joined the Nouveautés, playing the youthful Napoleon in *Bonaparte à Brienne ou Le Petit Caporal* (*Bonaparte at Brienne, or the Little*

Corporal, 1830). In 1831, now a 'star' she was at the Montansier (**Palais-Royal**), playing a series of *grisette* roles with a strong element of sexual suggestiveness. By 1844, she was earning 20,000 francs a year, with a fee of 20 francs for every act performed, four months' holiday and three benefit performances. In 1843, Béranger's *Lisette* provided her with a monologue she would use for the next 30 years. From 1844 to 1850 she was at the Variétés then on to the Vaudeville, still playing breeches parts, but she had herself freed from her contract because of the long run of *La Dame aux Camélias*, and became freelance. In 1857 she took over the Folies Nouvelles, which was managed by her son. She intended to produce the young **Sardou**'s *Candide*, but this was banned by the censorship, so she fell back on her old repertoire. In 1866 she had to give up her theatre and resume touring, playing the 15-year-old Richelieu at the age of 70. Her frenetic touring was largely forced on her by her exploitative son and daughter. In 1874 a huge benefit performance was given for her to create a pension, and her funeral, the following year, attracted some 30,000 people.   JMCC

Dekker, Thomas (c. 1570–1632) English playwright and pamphleteer whose vivid accounts of London life support the view that he was a Londoner by birth and upbringing. There are frequent references to Dekker's plays (and to his debts) in **Henslowe**'s *Diary* for 1598–1602. He was prodigiously busy – Henslowe lists 16 plays in which he had a hand in 1598 – but even such industry could not keep pace with his expenditure. Dekker was briefly in prison for debt in 1599 and again from 1613–19. Of the 50 or so plays on which he is known to have worked, some 20 have survived. The earliest, *Old Fortunatus* (1599), is a rambling moral comedy. The second, *The Shoemaker's Holiday* (1599), is his masterpiece. Its exuberant plotting and vivid portraits of London tradesmen established the distinctive form of citizen comedy. The other plays of which Dekker was sole author are, by comparison, disappointing. *Satiromastix* (1601) is a broken-backed rejoinder to **Jonson**'s abuse of Dekker (in *Poetaster* as well as in the earlier caricature of Orange in *Every Man out of His Humour*), notable only for its contribution to the **war of the theatres**. It was probably with an eye to the profitability of controversy that the King's Men chose to stage it. Careless construction (the outcome of too much haste?) also mars *The Whore of Babylon* (1606), *If It Be Not Good the Devil Is in It* (c. 1610) and *Match Me in London* (c. 1611). Needing to accept all commissions, Dekker was involved in numerous collaborations: with **Chettle** and William Haughton on *Patient Grissel* (1600), with **Webster** on *Westward Ho* (1604) and *Northward Ho* (1605), with **Middleton** on *The Honest Whore* (1604) and *The Roaring Girl* (c. 1610), with **Massinger** on *The Virgin Martyr* (1620) and with **William Rowley** and **Ford** on *The Witch of Edmonton* (1621). His lively satirical pamphlet, *The Gull's Hornbook* (1609), contains some telling observations of audience behaviour in the London theatres.   PT

Delaney, Shelagh (1939–   ) British dramatist. Her first and most successful play, *A Taste of Honey*, about a girl abandoned by her lover, who rears her child with the help of a maternally minded gay, was written when she was only 17 and staged in 1958 by **Joan Little-wood** at the Theatre Workshop, Stratford. The freshness of the writing and Littlewood's dynamic production took *A Taste of Honey* to the West End and afterwards to Broadway where it won the New York Drama Critics Award. Delaney's second play, *The Lion in Love* (1960), was less successful, and she turned away from the theatre to writing screenplays, *The White Bus* (1966) and *Charley Bubbles* (1968), and for television, *Did Your Nanny Come from Bergen* (1970).   JE

Delavigne, (Jean François) Casimir (1793–1843) French dramatist. Delavigne, who aligned himself with the liberal, anti-clerical bourgeoisie of the Restauration, began his career with a volume of patriotic poems, *Les Messéniennes*. His play *Sicilian Vespers* was refused at the **Comédie-Française** in 1818 and ran for some 300 performances when staged at the **Odéon** in 1819. Delavigne followed timidly in the wake of the romantics in his choice of medieval themes, but remained a second-rate (if much more frequently performed) dramatist, giving the audience what they wanted and avoiding shocking. His uninspired style continued the poetic diction of the 18th century with its inversions and periphrases. In *Le Paria* (1821) he introduced an important element of local colour with the Indian setting and used Brahmin fanaticism as a way of attacking Catholic fanaticism, a theme he would pick up again with *Une Famille au Temps de Luther* (*A Family in the Time of Luther*, 1836). The liberalism of Delavigne's sentiments lost him his job, but gained him the good opinion of the Duke of Orleans, who offered him a post of librarian. At the 1830 revolution, Delavigne's popular patriotic song, *La Parisienne*, was sung in all the theatres. *Marino Faliero* (1829) converted **Byron**'s model heroine into an adulterous wife (played by **Marie Dorval**). It was meant to be a tragedy, but drew heavily on the effects of melodrama, and even had to be described as such for its first performances at the Porte-Saint-Martin, with music by Rossini. *Louis XI*, seen sometimes as his greatest play, moved towards the romantic mixture of genres. In England, in **Boucicault**'s adaptation, it offered a splendid role to **Charles Kean** and later **Henry Irving**. One critic saw the play as a modern tragedy and a response to the excesses of the romantics. With *Les Enfants d'Edouard*, the romantic mixture of genres was taken further in a play that reduced *Richard III* to three acts, concentrated on the element of pathos and played down anything that might shock. His other main plays are *Don Juan d'Autriche*, *La Fille du Cid* (*The Daughter of the Cid*), and an opera, *Charles VI*, with music by Halévy. Delavigne was elected to the French Academy in 1825. His brother Germain was also quite well known as a dramatist.   JMCC

Della Porta, Giambattista (1535–1615) Italian dramatist, scientist and philosopher. A prolific writer on a wide range of subjects, his output included three tragedies, a tragicomedy and 29 comedies (of which 14 have survived). The best-known of his plays are *Olimpia* (1589) and *Il Moro* (*The Moor*, 1607) which, like most of his dramatic work, show the influence both of the classical tradition, and of the later *novelle* and romances, uniting the example of the ancients in structure and characterization with elements more reflective of Renaissance life and assumptions. Particularly interesting is his *L'Astrologo* (*The Astrologer*,

1606), and *La Trappolaria* (*The Comedy of Trappoia*, 1596), of which both scripted and scenario versions exist indicating some of the ways in which the Italian *commedia erudita* and **commedia dell'arte** interconnected. LR

Delpini, Carlo Antonio (1740–1828) Italian

dancer, clown and scenarist. He was first seen at **Covent Garden** in 1776 as **Pierrot** in *Harlequin's Frolicks* and for the rest of the century was involved in performing and creating pantomime there and at the **Haymarket**. Willson Disher credits him with having invented the Regency pantomime by stressing character and scenic transformation, as in the dumb show of *Robinson Crusoe* (**Drury Lane**, 1781). He also worked at Hughes's Royal Circus where, in the panto *What You Please*, he contrived a spectacular exhibition of 'The Four Quarters of the World' (1788). LS

Dench, Judi (Judith Olivia) (1934–) British

actress, who first attracted critical acclaim as Ophelia to **John Neville**'s Hamlet at the **Old Vic** in 1957. She was invited to join the **Royal Shakespeare Company** in the exciting first season, 1961, after its transformation from the Shakespeare Memorial Company, and became an established leading actress in **Peter Hall**'s team, playing Anya in *The Cherry Orchard*, Isabella in *Measure for Measure* and Dorcas in **John Whiting**'s *A Penny for a Song*. Her association with the RSC has continued for more than 20 years, during which time she has played a wide variety of great classical roles, from the Duchess in *The Duchess of Malfi*, Beatrice in *Much Ado* and Lady Macbeth, as well as Mother Courage in **Brecht**'s play. She has also appeared in the West End as Sally Bowles in *Cabaret* (1968), her first musical. Among the actresses of her generation, Judi Dench is technically the best equipped, with a naturally soft and expressive voice, an appearance versatile enough to match an imposing beauty for one play and dowdiness the next, and a keen intelligence which provides fresh insights into the most familiar texts. JE

Denmark Danish theatre probably began in medieval

churches, with liturgical tropes inserted into Easter and Epiphany masses. Physical evidence, such as sepulchres for the ritual burial of crosses or wooden effigies of Christ, indicates such activity in the 15th century, but nothing disproves the common assumption of an earlier tradition. Outdoor miracle plays, celebrating the lives of saints, began in the 15th century, as did visits by German travelling players, performing popular farces. (See **Medieval drama in Europe**.) While the Reformation (1536) ended liturgical drama, it encouraged school drama as an improver of behaviour and in schools and universities **Terence** and **Plautus** were acted, as well as modern derivations, such as the biblical *Susanna* (1576) and the satirical *Niding the Niggard* (1606). Meanwhile, 16th- and 17th-century monarchs mounted lavish festivals with Italianate scenery, allegorical processions and *ballets de cour*. Both Christian IV (reigned 1596–1648) and Frederik III (1648–70) were especially supportive; the marriage of Christian's eldest son in 1634 occasioned 13 days of festivities, including a huge production of *The Tragedy of Virtues and Vices* in Copenhagen's Castle Square.

Influence from abroad continued in 1662, when a

visiting Dutch actor, Andreas Joachimsen Wolf, obtained a patent to build Copenhagen's first shortlived public theatre, called the Schouwburg after its Amsterdam model. The end of the century witnessed the opening of Denmark's first opera house (1689) and at court a succession of French troupes, among whom was René Magnon de Montaigu, son of a close associate of **Molière**. In 1722, his company occupied a new theatre in the street called Lille Grønnegade and after a few months of French performances he obtained permission for Danish-language performances, beginning with Molière's *The Miser* and *The Political Tinker*, the first of the 27 comedies written for the Grønnegade company by **Ludvig Holberg**. This company survived (with interruptions) until 1728, when the great Copenhagen fire (followed in 1730 by the accession of the pietistic Christian VI) put a complete stop to theatrical activity. However, his successor Frederik V (1746–66) vigorously supported its revival, with an opera company at court, French and German troupes in the city and the Danish company, with Holberg as adviser, performing from 1748 in the new Danish Playhouse, later called the **Kongelige Teater** (The Royal Theatre), on Kongens Nytorv.

Its repertoire consisted primarily of comedies, including Molière and Holberg, acted by gifted comedians, such as **Gert Londemann**, N. H. Clementin and Caroline Thielo. Attempts in the 1770s to introduce tragedy in the French style produced Denmark's most brilliant literary parody, Johann Wessel's *Love Without Stockings* (1772). Nevertheless, the end of the century was a transitional period, witnessing the success of tragedies, sentimental dramas and the serious *singspiele* of Johannes Ewald, matched by the heroic acting of the popular Michael Rosing. In 1790, the Kongelige Teater first presented **Kotzebue**, beginning a flood of 1,000 performances of 73 plays over the next three decades. **Shakespeare** was first acted in Denmark in 1792, in Odense, and reached the Kongelige Teater in 1813, with *Hamlet*. The early 19th century was also dominated by the plays of **Oehlenschläger** and the impressive, declamatory acting of J. C. Ryge, N. P. Nielsen and his wife Anna Nielsen, inaugurating a period of virtuosity that reached its peak in the 1840s, under the aegis of the poet and critic **Johan Ludvig Heiberg** and his celebrated actress-wife **Johanne Luise Heiberg**. The Heibergs promoted European culture, as exemplified by **Goethe**'s concept of classical, idealized beauty and the polished urbanity of early French boulevard comedy. Kotzebue and Oehlenschläger faded in popularity, replaced by **Scribe**, Heiberg's own vaudevilles and comedies, some Shakespeare and **Schiller**, and the sentimental dramas of Henrik Hertz. A new, lighter acting style was in vogue, exemplified by the work of Fru Heiberg, her partner **Michael Wiehe** and actors such as C. N. Rosenkilde and J. L. Phister. However, by the 1850s the Heibergs were challenged by actors like Frederik Høedt, who demanded a more realistic style and repertoire.

The Kongelige Teater's first competitor was the privately owned Casino (1848), providing mostly popular entertainment, but also helping some major dramatists begin their careers. H. C. Andersen was unofficially house dramatist in the 1850s, **Ibsen**'s first Copenhagen production was at the Casino and the world premiere of **Strindberg**'s *The Father* took place

Goethe's *Faust*, at Gladsaxe Theatre, Denmark, 1978.

there in 1887. Meanwhile, Folketeatret, another rival, had opened in 1857, specializing in folk comedies and operettas, but from the 1880s presenting important plays rejected by the Kongelige, such as **Bjørnson**'s *Leonarda* and Ibsen's *Ghosts* (in a Swedish touring production); an even more serious rival was Dagmarteatret (1883). Crucial for these private theatres was the relaxation in 1889 of the Kongelige's monopoly on every play it had ever performed. In 1874, the Kongelige had moved to its present building, where the struggle to introduce naturalistic staging methods would be fought, particularly in **William Bloch**'s carefully orchestrated Ibsen productions in the 1880s, with actors who at least partly mastered the new style: **Betty Hennings**, Anna Bloch, **Emil Poulsen** and Karl Mantzius.

The 20th century began with the opening of new provincial theatres in Århus and Odense and of the New Theatre in Copenhagen, followed in 1917 by the Betty Nansen Theatre, which pioneered the production of new plays until **Nansen**'s death in 1943. In the 1920s the Dagmar enjoyed particular success under the direction of Thorkild Roose, with Bodil Ipsen and **Poul Reumert** as its stars. Although the predominant style was still realistic, a vogue for **Reinhardt**-style spectacle encouraged **Johannes Poulsen** to successfully mount a two-evening extravaganza built around Oehlenschläger's *Aladdin*, followed by similar approaches to Shakespeare and, in 1928, by Ibsen's *The Pretenders*, with designs by **Edward Gordon Craig**. However, it was in the 1930s that the theatricalized theatre gained ground, with directors like Per Knut-

zon, Holger Gabrielson and Svend Methling, theatres such as the experimental Riddersalen and a new generation of actors such as Bodil Kjer, **Mogens Wieth**, John Price and Ebbe Rode. After the war, the New Theatre, under Peer Gregaard, seriously challenged the preeminence of the Kongelige with outstanding productions of both classics and new foreign plays. Although the Kongelige's bicentenary celebrations in 1948 were largely retrospective in nature, it presented some innovations in the 1950s, such as **Brecht**'s *Mother Courage* and **Beckett**'s *Endgame*. However, it was at Århus Theatre that the absurdists found their most fertile ground.

The 1960s were marked by rapid expansion and diversification. In 1962 Fiolteatret opened, presenting **Pinter**, **Albee** and Beckett, as well as Danish modernists such as Klaus Rifbjerg. However, rather than plays, the 60s saw a proliferation of satirical (and increasingly political) revues, such as Erik Knudsen's celebrated *Freedom – The Best Gold* (1961). The Kongelige quickly joined this trend with *Teenagerlove* (1962), a barbed satire on the pop generation by Ernst Bruun Olsen, who remains Denmark's most eminent living playwright. Danish theatre's growing political consciousness was felt most heavily in the many 'group' theatres that were established: Svalegangen in Århus, Comediehuset and Boldhusteatret in Copenhagen, the Jomfru Ane Theatre in Aalborg. Fiolteatret increasingly sought to communicate a clear political stance and to provoke debate, as did the Debate Theatre, which like Banden in Odense, sought to take theatre out to schools and workplaces. Political theatre reached an extreme in the 1970s with the 'action theatre' of Solvognen, which mounted elaborate 'Happenings' to make political or social points; *Santa Claus Army* (1974) demonstrated the impracticality of Christmas charity under capitalism by having Santas distribute 'gifts' from department-store shelves.

In contemporary Denmark, the Kongelige Teater still dominates, if only because of its vast resources. However, it is challenged, at least in terms of repertoire, by the Folketeater and the three Provincial Theatres in Århus, Aalborg and Odense. Since 1975 most of the private Copenhagen theatres have combined in the Greater Copenhagen Provincial Theatre, with government subsidies and using the national ticket agency Arte to sell advance subscriptions. The resulting security has freed some of them, such as the Gladsaxe, Betty Nansen and Aveny theatres, to be very courageous in their programming, as are some of the smaller experimental stages that have emerged from the group theatre movement, such as the Boldhus and Båd theatres. Outside Copenhagen, group theatres have begun to collaborate with amateurs in 'local plays', such as Baggård Theatre's 1981 documentary about Svendborg, *Life in the Poorhouse*. **Odin Teatret** in Holstebro remains Denmark's most unique and internationally regarded theatre. Led by **Eugenio Barba**, since its arrival from Oslo in 1966, it has achieved remarkable results in its research into the fundamental nature of performance.

Playwriting seems in a healthier state now than ever since Abell's death in 1961. Bruun Olsen continues his ingenious political parables, often directed by the author; Rifbjerg's commitment to theatre seems to be growing; Ulla Ryum writes and directs increasingly for women; and many poets and prose writers are turning successfully to the theatre: Vita Andersen, Kirsten Thorup, Sten Kaalø and Svend Åge Madsen. Outstanding directors seem scarce. At 75, Sam Besekow continues, apparently unjaded; his talented successors include Kaspar Rostrup, Hans Rosenquist and Peter Langdal. Denmark continues to have actors of great virtuosity, including Bodil Kjer, Lise Ringheim, Kirsten Olesen, Ulla Henningsen, Søren Spanning, Erik Mørk and Henning Moritzen.   HL

See: H. Fenger and F. J. Marker, *The Heibergs*, New York, 1971; A. Henriques, *The Royal Theatre Past and Present*, Copenhagen, 1967; F. J. Marker, *Hans Christian Andersen and the Romantic Theatre*, Toronto, 1971; and Kjeld Abell, Boston, 1976; F. J. and Lise-Lone Marker, *Edward Gordon Craig and 'The Pretenders': A Production Revisited*, Carbondale, 1981, and *The Scandinavian Theatre*, Oxford, 1975; P. M. Mitchell, *A History of Danish Literature*, Copenhagen, 1957; *Modern Nordic Plays: Denmark*, intro. Per Olsen, New York, 1974.

Dennery (later D'Ennery), Adolphe (1811–99) French dramatist, Dennery was author or co-author of some of the best-known melodramas of the 19th century. *Emile, ou le Fils d'un Pair de France* (*Emile, or the Son of a Peer of France*, 1831), written with Charles Desnoyer, was the first of some 200 plays. He had an excellent sense of theatre and of dramatic situations, and many of the plays had a strong populist appeal which ensured them hundreds of performances on the Boulevard. His first major success, *Gaspard Hauser* (1838), based on recent real life events, showed the inhumanity of social convention in respect of illegitimacy. *La Grâce de Dieu* (*The Grace of God*, 1841), perhaps the greatest sentimental tear-jerker of the century, depended heavily on the opposition of the social classes. *Marie-Jeanne, ou la Femme du Peuple* (*Marie Jeanne, or the Woman of the People*, 1843) provided **Marie Dorval** with her most pathetic role and looked at the social problems of a drunken husband who will not work. *Les Deux Orphelines* (*The Two Orphans*, 1874) written in collaboration with Eugène Cormon, with its persecuted heroines, is his best-known play. Its popularity continued into the 20th century, ultimately becoming the D. W. Griffith film, *Orphans of the Storm*. In the latter part of his career Dennery moved heavily into the spectacular sensation drama with his adaptations of Jules Verne's novels – *Around the World in Eighty Days* (1874), *Captain Grant's Children* (1878), *Michel Strogoff* (1880), with its thrilling theme, impossible hero and astounding pyrotechnic effects. Other popular Dennery plays were *Les Bohémiens de Paris* (*The Bohemians of Paris*, 1843), *Don César de Bazan* (1844), *La Prière des Naufragés* (*The Prayer of the Castaways*, 1853), *Uncle Tom's Cabin* (1853), *Cartouche* (1858), *Le Lac de Glenaston* (*The Lake of Glenaston*, 1861) – an adaptation of *The Colleen Bawn – The Taking of Peking*, with much equestrian excitement (1861), and *Les Mystères du Vieux Paris* (*The Mysteries of Old Paris*, 1865). In addition Dennery was the author of some of the most celebrated *Féeries* or extravaganzas, of the century: *Les Sept Châteaux du Diable* (*The Seven Castles of the Devil*, 1844), *La Poule aux Oeufs d'Or* (*The Hen with the Golden Eggs*, 1848), *Rothomago* (1862) and *Aladin, or the Magic Lamp* (1863); and he wrote librettos for Adam's opera *Si J'étais Roi* (*If I were King*, 1852) and Massenet's *Le Cid* (1885). He also provided the first stage version of Balzac's *Mercadet, le Faiseur* (*Mercadet, or the Financier*), reducing it from five acts to three for the Gymnase in 1851.   JMCC

Dennis, John (1657–1734) English critic and playwright. After studying in Cambridge he settled in London in 1680. His early criticism, e.g. *The Impartial Critic* (1693), established his reputation as an intelligent and tolerant neoclassicist. He began writing plays in 1696 with a comedy *A Plot and No Plot* and wrote a spectacular opera *Rinaldo and Armida* (1698). He defended the state in the **Collier** controversy in his pamphlet *The Usefulness of the Stage* (1698). He put his principles to the test in the classical tragedy *Iphigenia* (1699) and in the restrained version of *Appius and Virginia* (1709). Of his other plays, he wrote two poor **Shakespeare** adaptations, *The Comical Gallant* (1702, from *The Merry Wives of Windsor*) and *The Invader of his Country* (1719, from *Coriolanus*), and a heroic drama set among Canadian Indians, *Liberty Asserted* (1704). His later critical writings, e.g. *Remarks upon 'The Conscious Lovers'* (1723) and *The Causes of the Decay of Dramatic Poetry* (1725), are remarkable for their nostalgic admiration for the drama of the Restoration against the anaemic contemporary specimens.   PH

Dennis, Nigel (Forbes) (1912–) British dramatist, novelist and critic, whose first three satirical plays were produced at the **Royal Court Theatre** under **George Devine**'s directorship. Unlike most other Royal Court writers, Dennis criticized society from a right-wing stance, deploring the debasement of standards under facile democracies and denouncing left-wing totalitarianism. In *Cards of Identity* (1956) which he adapted from his novel, the target is the manipulation of mass opinion, while in *The Making of Moo* (1957) he derides the idolatry of religions, Christianity included. *August for the People* (1961) concerns an aristocratic landowner who attacks the common man and finds himself besieged by common men who agree with him. A brilliant journalist, Dennis devoted less time in recent years to plays and novels, but the clarity of his writing style, with his acid wit, emerged from his reviews and columns for the *Sunday Telegraph*. JE

Denver Center Theatre The $13 million Helen G. Bonfils Theatre Complex opened on New Year's Eve, 1979, as part of the Denver Center for the Performing Arts. The Bonfils complex consists of three separate theatres: the 550-seat thrust; the 450-seat environmental; and a 150-seat theatre laboratory/rehearsal hall for new American works. Edward Payson Call served as the first artistic director from 1979–83 followed by Donovan Marley from 1983– . Maintaining a professional resident company, the Denver Theatre in its inaugural season (December–April) performed five plays: *The Caucasian Chalk Circle, Moby Dick–Rehearsed, The Learned Ladies, A Midsummer Night's Dream*, and *Passing Game* by Steve Tesich. **Allen Fletcher** was hired in 1984 to head the conservatory training programme. The company maintains both a classical and modern repertory with its production of *Quilters* appearing briefly on Broadway in 1984. TLM

Derain, André (1880–1954) French theatrical designer and artist. Derain's entry into the theatre came about in 1919 when Serge Diaghilev recruited him and other Paris-based painters to design for the Ballets Russes. He successfully designed *La Boutique Fantastique* (1919) for Leonide Massine, and *Jack-in-the-Box* (1926), for George Balanchine. Derain's theatrical design career lasted well into the 1950s and was distinguished by a 'painterly' style which simplified reality into a highly decorative stage picture. This style is evident in such productions as *Mam'zelle Angot* (1947), and *Les Femmes de Bonne Humeur* (1949). As an artist, his 'Fauvist' style was said to have influenced early modern painting, and he was also known as an accomplished illustrator and sculptor. TM

Derwent, Clarence (1884–1959) English actor and director. Born in London, Derwent fled his home to become a provincial bit player. By 1910 he appeared in London; in 1915 he came to the United States to appear with Grace George in *Major Barbara*. He went on to appear in some 500 plays, several movies, and occasionally directed. In 1945 he founded the Clarence Derwent Awards in London and New York for the best performers in supporting roles. Among his many professional offices were two terms as president of Actors' Equity and the presidency in 1952 of the American National Theatre and Academy. He also chaired the National Centre of the International Theatre Institute and had been president of the Dramatic Workshop. His autobiography, *The Derwent Story*, appeared in 1954. SMA

Deschamps, Yvon (1935–) French Canadian actor and comic monologuist. His stage career began in 1958, with a minor role in **Racine**'s *Andromaque*, and for the next ten years he continued to appear in traditional stage plays and in television dramas. In 1968 he wrote and performed a monologue for *L'Osstidcho* (*Damn Good Show*), a heterogeneous revue written by several authors in collaboration that proved enormously successful. Since then he has specialized in monologue performance, live and for television, writing all his own material and becoming by far the best-known comic artist and author in Quebec today. Deschamps's satirical monologues attack all subjects, sacred and profane, in a style and a popular language inimitably his own. His recordings have sold hundreds of thousands of copies. LED

Desiosi, Compagnia dei ('those desirous', i.e., of pleasing the public) A **commedia dell'arte** troupe first noted in 1581, when Montaigne saw them in Pisa and admired their comic Fargnoccola. The company also included the celebrated Arlecchino, **Tristano Martinelli**, and Flaminio Scala served in it both as comedian and manager; but its star from 1585 was Diana Ponti who acted under the name Lavinia. When she joined the **Accesi** in 1600, the Desiosi dispersed. LS

Deslys, Gaby (Gabrielle Caïre) (1881–1920) French revue artiste of scant talent but blonde good looks and elegant manner, who made her debut at the Parisiana in 1898. From the start, her alleged romance with the ex-King of Portugal and her regularly imperilled pearls were the stuff of press-agents' fables. Her importance lies in introducing Europe to American jazz styles in the revue *Laissez-les tomber* (1910): dancing with her American partner Harry Pilcer to such exotic instruments as xylophones, saxophones and banjos, she literally opened a New World to Paris. She was also the first to make a grand entrance descending a staircase in ostrich plumes and pearls, setting the style for **Mistinguett**, who was her stand-in when her health failed. LS

Dessoir, Ludwig (1810–74) German actor. A virtuoso noted for the contrast in his acting between restraint and carefully judged outbursts of passion. From 1849, Dessoir was a member of the **Berlin Royal Theatre**. In 1853, he appeared with **Emil Devrient** at the **St James's Theatre**, London. SW

Destouches (Philippe Néricault) (1680–1754) French dramatist whose early career was divided between writing for the stage and diplomatic service for the Regent, Philip of Orleans, whose protection probably ensured his admission to the Académie-Française in 1723. Thereafter he devoted himself exclusively to playwriting, producing about 30 plays in all, in which he gradually threw off a Molièresque manner and discovered a more individual and more obviously moralizing voice. The most characteristic, and certainly the most successful, were *Le Philosophe Marié* (*The Married Philosopher*, 1727) and *Le Glorieux* (*The Conceited Count*, 1732). DR

Deutsches Theater A theatre company in Berlin,

founded by **Adolph L'Arronge** in 1883 to provide the city with a repertory company that had standards of ensemble similar to those of the **Meininger**. Due to the contribution of actors such as **Josef Kainz** and others, L'Arronge succeeded in his efforts. In 1894, the direction was taken over by **Otto Brahm**, who developed a naturalistic approach to the performance of the classics and established the plays of the naturalists firmly in the repertoire. In 1904, **Max Reinhardt**, who had been a member of Brahm's ensemble, assumed the direction. In the following year he established a theatre school and built a chamber theatre. The Deutsches Theater remained the centre of Reinhardt's Berlin operations until his withdrawal from Nazi Germany in 1933. It is still one of the most prominent theatre companies in East Berlin. SW

Devant, David (Wighton) (1868–1941) 'The greatest magician of all times' as *The Times* called him, was presenting his first original illusion, 'Vice-Versa', a man-into-woman transformation, on the London music-halls, when he was discovered by **J. N. Maskelyne**, who took him on as assistant and, in 1905, partner. Devant discarded the hitherto indispensable magic wand and other suspect apparatus, appeared in the first Royal Command Variety Performance of 1912, and withdrew from co-managing St George's Hall in 1915 to offer a series of matinees at the Ambassador Theatre. His illusions, always eschewing the gruesome, included 'The Giant's Breakfast', in which a girl dressed as a chicken materialized from a huge egg; 'The Magic Mirror' wherein the figures of Devant, a volunteer from the audience, and Satan changed position around a mirrored frame; and 'Bif', in which a rattling motorcycle and its rider were pulled into the air and made to vanish. He retired in 1919 after the onset of a nervous palsy that reduced his sleight of hand to nil. LS

Devine, George (Alexander Cassidy) (1910–65) British actor and director, who established the English Stage Company at the **Royal Court** as a 'writers' theatre'. Devine was drawn towards the theatre at Oxford University where, as President of OUDS, he invited **John Gielgud** to direct *Romeo and Juliet* in 1932, in which he played Mercutio. This led to an early professional engagement with the **Old Vic**, before joining Gielgud's company at the New Theatre in 1934 to act the Player King in what was recognized to be the most celebrated *Hamlet* of the time. He met **Michel Saint-Denis**, the innovative French director, who had founded the London Theatre Studio. The partnership between them, at the Studio from 1936 to 1939, and at the Old Vic School with Glen Byam Shaw after the war, was fruitful both in the testing of new theatrical ideas and in the training of the next generation of actors. The Old Vic Centre, with its school and **Young Vic** theatre company, was intended to become the experimental heart of the proposed new **National Theatre**, but was axed in 1951. Devine returned to being a free-lance actor and director, playing Tesman in a memorable *Hedda Gabler* with **Peggy Ashcroft** in 1954 and directing at **Sadler's Wells** and Stratford-upon-Avon with the Shakespeare Memorial Company. But he became convinced that the conditions within British theatre had to change before good new

work could be achieved and in 1954, he joined forces with the playwright Ronald Duncan and the business man Neville Blond who, together with the director Tony Richardson, founded the English Stage Company for the purpose of staging contemporary plays. In April 1956, the English Stage Company began its first season at the Royal Court Theatre in Sloane Square, an event which had an immediate impact upon the course of British theatre. The success of the first season was the premiere of **John Osborne**'s *Look Back In Anger*, an unknown play by a then unknown writer, which lent the tone of crusading radicalism, often bitter and angry but never lazy or complacent, to the Royal Court's programmes. The subsequent years provided new plays by **Samuel Beckett**, **N. F. Simpson**, **Arnold Wesker**, **John Arden** and **Ann Jellicoe**; and Devine provided as artistic director a stabilizing influence in what were often stormy times, supporting his young protégés while helping them with sound common sense. He bore the main burden (with Tony Richardson) of directing the early seasons, staging plays by **Brecht**, **Arthur Miller** and **Jean-Paul Sartre**, and also acting with the company, notably in **Ionesco**'s *The Chairs* (1957) and in John Obsorne's *A Patriot for Me* (1965), his final role. The George Devine Award was instituted in his memory in 1966 to encourage young professional workers in the theatre, and has been awarded primarily to playwrights. JE

Devrient The most famous family of German actors in the 19th century. **Ludwig** (1784–1832) is almost universally regarded as the quintessentially romantic actor, due mainly to his celebrated interpretations of roles such as Franz Moor in **Schiller**'s *The Robbers*, Shylock, and Lear. His ability to bring the unconscious of the characters he played to the fore fascinated and often disturbed his audiences. He was also celebrated for his comic roles, among which was a matchless Falstaff. His early career was spent in the Dessau Court Theatre and the Breslau Town Theatre. In 1815 he joined the **Berlin Royal Theatre**, but soon his powers began to wane due to chronic alcoholism. Nevertheless, he continued to act both in Berlin and on numerous tours, acquiring for himself a legendary reputation until his early death. His three nephews were the most distinguished perpetuators of the family name. **Carl** (1797–1872) was a solid, heroic actor.

Ludwig Devrient as Shylock.

Eduard (1801–77) was a distinguished director of the Karlsruhe Court Theatre, where he raised standards of ensemble and production; he was also author of the great *History of German Acting* (1848–74). **Emil** (1803–72) was an idolized virtuoso, his acting being considered as the finest expression of the **Weimar style** in the mid-years of the century. Later family members continued the tradition into the 20th century. SW

Dewhurst, Colleen (1926–91) Canadian-born American actress whose robustness qualified her ideally for certain **Eugene O'Neill** heroines, most notably Josie in *A Moon for the Misbegotten*, for which she received a Tony in a 1973 revival directed by **José Quintero**. 'I love the O'Neill women,' she said. 'They move from the groin rather than the brain. To play O'Neill . . . you can't sit and play little moments of sadness or sweetness.' Ironically, her professional New York career began as one of the Neighbours in *Desire Under the Elms* in 1952 (in 1963 she played Abbie Putnam at **Circle in the Square**). Other O'Neill productions of note included *More Stately Mansions* (1967) and a 1972 revival of *Mourning Becomes Electra*. She also appeared in three **Edward Albee** plays including a 1976 revival of *Who's Afraid of Virginia Woolf?* In 1960 she received her first Tony Award for Mary Follet in *All the Way Home*. Dewhurst was also praised for her work in the classics, especially **Shakespeare**, most notably for **Joseph Papp**'s **New York Shakespeare Festival** in the 1950s. In recent years she appeared at Papp's Public Theatre in several roles including *O'Neill and Carlotta* (1979). DBW

Dexter, John (1925–) British director, who joined the English Stage Company at the **Royal Court** in 1957 primarily as an actor but quickly became their most innovative director. He established his reputation with productions of new plays by **Arnold Wesker**, including the *Roots* trilogy (1958, 1959, 1960), *Chips with Everything* (1962) and, in 1959, *The Kitchen*, where Dexter brilliantly choreographed the preparation of restaurant meals. His skill at mime and movement drew him towards a West End musical, *Half a Sixpence* (1963), and he was one of two Royal Court directors to be invited to join **Laurence Olivier** in the formation of the **National Theatre** company. From 1963 to 1966, Dexter was an Associate Director at the National Theatre, responsible for such revivals as *St Joan*, *Hobson's Choice* and *Othello* (with Olivier in the title role). But his most striking NT achievement was his production of **Peter Shaffer**'s *The Royal Hunt of the Sun* (1964), which had been rejected as unplayable by most London managements. Dexter directed the NT company into such feats as miming the ascent of the Andes, the invention of an Inca language, musical as well as spoken, and the convincing desecration of an empire. This triumph led to other Dexter/Shaffer collaborations, particularly on *Equus* (1973). After leaving the National Theatre as its Associate Director, Dexter directed on Broadway and in the West End, returning sometimes to the National Theatre on a free-lance basis, for **Trevor Griffiths**'s play *The Party* (1973), *Phaedra Britannica* (1975) adapted by Tony Harrison from **Racine**'s play and **Brecht**'s *Galileo* (1980). From 1974 to 1981, Dexter was Director of Productions at the Metropolitan Opera House in New York. JE

Dhanu Jatra (India) This is an open-air passion play depicting events in Krishna's life staged at Baragarh in Sambalpur district, Orissa. Villages, towns and countryside are incorporated into the dramatic action and symbolically become places in the mythological story. Processions, enactment of scenes using elephants and large-scale replicas of palaces and characters require the spectators to participate in the action. FaR

Dias Gomes, Alfredo (1922–) Brazilian playwright from Bahia, he began writing in the 40s, and by the 50s had published several novels and written ten plays. Problems with Brazilian censorship turned him towards radio and television, but did not dampen his interest in the theatre. In 1960 he catapulted into national prominence with his play *O pagador de promessas* (*Payment as Pledged*), the story of a simple peasant whose efforts to repay a religious promise bring down upon him the entire religious and civic authority of his town. In 1962 the film version of the play won him the coveted Gold Palm at the Cannes Film Festival. A series of successful plays followed. *A invasão* (*The Invasion*, 1962) depicted problems of the urban poor, *A revolução dos beatos* (*The Revolution of the Devout*, 1962) dealt with political and religious fanaticism and intrigue; *O berço do herói* (*The Hero's Cradle*, 1965) emphasized the humour, satire and expressionistic vein of early plays; and *O santo inquérito* (*The Holy Inquisition*, 1966) dealt with a historical figure burned at the stake in the 18th century who served as a metaphor of the political repression in Brazil at that time. Dias Gomes continued with *Dr Getulio, sua vida e sua glória* (*Dr Getulio, his Life and his Glory*) written in collaboration with Ferreira Gullar; *O rei de ramos* (*The King of Boughs*, 1979), a musical collective; and *Campeões do Mundo* (*World Champions*, 1980); all have a political current strongly based in contemporary Brazilian military repression, censorship, political intrigue and hypocrisy. *Amor em campo minado* (*Love in a Mine Field*, 1984), first published as *Vamos soltar os demonios*, chronicles the last hours of an intellectual accused of subversive activities and consists primarily of a verbal battle between the protagonist and his wife over levels of commitment. Erotic elements turn obscene as political issues are interrelated with sexuality. GW

Díaz, Gregor (1933–) Peruvian playwright, actor and director. Born in Cajamarca, Peru, he received his theatre training first in Lima in the National Institute of Dramatic Art, later in Chile in the University Experimental Theatre. Affiliated with the Theatre Club, he has won national prizes for many of his plays. His major works are *La huelga* (*Strike*, 1966), *Los del 4* (*The Ones in 4*, 1969), *Sitio al sitio* (*Siege of the Site*, 1978), and *El mudo de la ventana* (*The Mute at the Window*, 1984). Committed to redressing political and socio-economic injustices, his theatre presents the evils of oppression with artistic sensitivity. GW

Díaz, Jorge (1930–) Chilean playwright. Born in Argentina of Spanish parents, he became a naturalized Chilean citizen. After studying architecture at the University of Chile, he began his theatre career as a set designer with the group ICTUS in Santiago in 1959. In

1965 he moved to Spain, and currently holds dual Chilean–Spanish citizenship. His early plays fell into the following categories: those written with ICTUS, which showed the strong influence of European absurdism, such as *El cepillo de dientes* (*The Toothbrush*, 1961); and those from the first years in Spain, which still carried a strong Latin American influence, such as *Topografía de un desnudo* (*Topography of a Nude*, 1966). After 1970 Díaz wrote plays of strong political protest such as *Americaliente* (1971), a bombastic collage about US intervention in Latin America, and commentaries about contemporary life in Spain, such as *Mata a tu prójimo como a ti mismo* (*Kill Thy Neighbour as Thyself*, 1975). A prolific writer of more than 40 major plays, he also wrote children's theatre (more than 20 works) and television scripts. Díaz is an inveterate experimenter with language who loves to challenge societal conventions regarding basic aspects of human existence. His major themes are love, sex, violence and death.   GW

Dibdin, Charles (1745–1814) English actor, dramatist and composer. After early success as a chorister in Winchester and as a singer and song-writer in London (by his death he had written 1,400 songs), he began to collaborate with **Isaac Bickerstaffe** on comic operas, for example for **Garrick**'s **Shakespeare** Jubilee in 1769, an event which was part of his endless feuding with Garrick. In 1768 he starred as Mungo, a black-faced servant in his own play *The Padlock* with such success that he gave his son Charles the name Mungo. In 1776 he left **Drury Lane**, sacked for his neglect of rehearsals or because of Garrick's dislike of his mistress, and settled in France for two years in debt. Apart from numerous works for **Covent Garden** he also flirted with popular entertainments, creating a riot at a puppet play in 1780 when the audience had expected live actors, and becoming a partner in 1782 in an equestrian theatre, the Royal Circus, later the Surrey Theatre, another financial failure that landed him in a debtors' prison. From 1789 he began to perform one-man shows of songs, playlets and monologues. From 1796 he wrote plays and entertainments for the Sans Souci Theatre, which he managed. He was granted a civil list pension in 1803 for his songs celebrating the British sailor.   PH

Dickens, Charles (John Huffam) (1812–70) English novelist whose dependence on the theatre can be sensed even where it cannot be documented. His famous gift for eccentric characterization owed much to his youthful observation of actors and he repaid the debt by providing actors with unrivalled opportunities in the countless adaptations of his novels. Outstanding examples include **Irving**'s Jingle, **Joseph Jefferson III**'s Caleb Plummer (also in the repertoire of **J. L. Toole**), **Beerbohm Tree**'s Fagin and **John Martin-Harvey**'s Sydney Carton. Among the playwrights to have dramatized Dickens are **W. T. Moncrieff**, **Tom Taylor**, **T. W. Robertson**, **Boucicault**, **James Albery**, **W. S. Gilbert** and, most recently, **David Edgar** (*Nicholas Nickleby*, 1980). The famous public readings, with which Dickens boosted his income in his declining years, served only to confirm that it was partly as an armchair actor that he created characters and dramatic episodes. No novelist of stature has so fed

off the world of melodrama. Dickens's own plays – he had two burlettas and a farce performed in his lifetime – are lightweight, but he was immensely serious about his amateur theatricals in the small private theatre in his London home, Tavistock House, where he relished the opportunity to act on a real stage instead of only in his imagination.   PT

Diderot, Denis (1713–84) French philosopher, novelist, playwright and critic whose dramatic theory represents an attempt to liberate the 18th-century stage from the artificial constraints of neoclassical dramaturgy and to provide it with a moral rationale. Between the mutually exclusive poles of classical tragedy and traditional comedy of intrigue there is, he argued, a vast neglected territory ripe for dramatic exploration: the 'conditions' of men, their professions and trades, their conjugal and family lives, their social virtues, are susceptible to treatment either in the form of 'serious' comedy or domestic tragedy. Both are related aspects of what he calls the 'genre sérieux', in which tears and laughter should mingle as they do in the real world. With its recognizable situations and characters such drama will correspond to the audience's own experience of life, will touch them to the heart and thereby make them better people. His thinking exerted a widespread influence on European drama and proved, in fact, more compelling than the plays which he wrote to illustrate it, *Le Fils Naturel* (*The Natural Son*, published 1757 and performed 1771) and *Le Père de Famille* (*The Father of the Family*, 1758 and 1761) which are implausibly elevated in style and moralizingly over-sentimental in tone. Most memorable of all his theoretical work, perhaps, is his dialogue on the nature of acting, *Paradoxe sur le Comédien* (published posthumously in 1830), which assesses the relative importance to the performer of genuine feeling and conscious control by the intellect.   DR

Digges, Dudley (1879–1947) Actor and director, born in Dublin and a member of the original Abbey Players. He made his New York debut in 1904 with **Minnie Maddern Fiske**. In 1919 he appeared in *Bonds of Interest* for the **Theatre Guild** and appeared more than 3,500 times for them, including the role of James Caesar in *John Ferguson*. He also staged four plays for the Guild. Reviewing Digges's final appearance as Harry Hope in **O'Neill**'s *The Iceman Cometh*, **Brooks Atkinson** remarked that Digges's 'command of the actor's art of expressing character and theme is brilliantly alive; it overflows with comic and philosophical expression'. Digges also appeared in over 50 films and served as vice-president of Actors' Equity Association.   SMA

Dimov, Ossip (1878–1959) Russian-language writer of over 30 Jewish plays, at first for the **Moscow Art Theatre**, later in America. Devoted to improving the literary quality of Yiddish theatre both as a writer and producer, his best known plays are *The Eternal Wanderer*, *Hear O Israel*, *Yoshke Musikant* and *Bronx Express*.   AB

Dingelstedt, Franz von (1814–81) German director. After several years as a journalist with ideas akin to those of the liberal writers of the Junges Deutschland

(Young Germany) movement, Dingelstedt underwent a conversion to royalist beliefs. For some years, he was a librarian at the royal court in Stuttgart, then in 1851 he was appointed director of the Munich Court Theatre. Here he staged productions of unusual splendour, which were so expensive that in 1857 he was dismissed for running the theatre deeply into debt. He was immediately appointed director of the Weimar Court Theatre, where his most significant achievement was the production in 1864 of all of **Shakespeare**'s history plays. This created such a name for him that, in 1867, he was appointed director of the Vienna Opera and, in 1870, of the **Burgtheater**. Here he repeated his success with Shakespeare's histories and staged numerous other classical plays in a notably spectacular manner. Dingelstedt is regarded by many historians as a forerunner of both the Duke of Saxe-**Meiningen** and **Max Reinhardt**. SW

Directing Directing is part of that complex of seeing and doing which makes theatre. At all levels the need to intervene to shape the theatrical event can be felt but, because of the processual nature of play, the best of directing comes from within the activity. However, throughout the history of theatre, a need can be discerned for unification, direction, and encouragement from without – for leadership.

The authority to intervene on behalf of others has been, in the past, mainly the prerogative of playwright or actor (sometimes the same person as with Zeami and **Molière**). Social and economic power, though often influential, has rarely been directly responsible for the crafting of play. For example, in 472 BC at Athens, the politics and wealth of the young Pericles as *choregos* must have affected the ideology and spectacle of *The Persians*, but the teaching of the songs and dances, the vision and government of the overall event, was in the hands of **Aeschylus** who was both playwright and leading actor. By Hellenistic times there is evidence to suggest that training was a separate professional business, but by then directorial authority had been abrogated by the 'star' performer. Likewise in Rome, the *dominus gregis*, as chief actor of the troupe, was responsible for production. In the Middle Ages the *maître de jeu* or book-keeper worked both on the preparation and the smooth-running of the show, although often it is unclear how separate such figures were from poet or player. Many must have been similar to the 'property players' of early 16th-century England, actors engaged from the metropolis to supervise and furnish material for provincial productions; but some were, without doubt, separate managers and machinists like the two *conducteurs des secrets* of the *Mons Passion-play*. With the growth of scenic illusion in the West, such stage-management increased, but it is not until late in the 19th century that the figure of the director can be discerned.

The modern concept of the director grew from the work of the Duke of Saxe-**Meiningen** and his stage-manager Chronegk. It was nurtured by pioneers like **Antoine**, **Stanislavsky**, and **Reinhardt**. The latter gave up acting completely in 1903 to devote all his time to directing. The new authority, fundamental to the thoughts of **Appia** and **Craig** on the coherence of theatre as Art, is exemplified in the careers of **Meyerhold**, **Vakhtangov**, and **Tairov**, **Copeau** and **Piscator**. The work of such masters heads a rich and varied

tradition, of which more recent exponents include **Brook**, **Grotowski** and **Peter Stein** (all of whom began as directors). This tradition shares with film a parallel development and a common notion of the director as *auteur*. While this notion may be valid in film where a final intervention is made in the cutting room, in theatre the live performance mocks its grandeur. In many ways the hegemony of the director, the director seen as an authority separate and separable from either actor or dramatist, is problematic. Reliance on this authority can too often sap the creativity, intelligence, and initiative of the player; while for the playwright, production more and more usurps the power once held by the play. Interpretation is all! The idea of the director is the most dominant feature of Western theatre in the 20th century. LSR

Discovery space It is clear from numerous stage-directions that Elizabethan theatres, both public and private, had the capacity to conceal and reveal actors and scenes. The assumption that the platform had a large alcove or 'inner stage' at the back was undermined by the publication in 1888 of De Witt's drawing of the **Swan**, which shows a blank wall between two large stage-doors in the tiring-house façade. It would have been possible to create a small discovery space by hanging a curtain between the inward-opening doors of the Swan, an easy solution which would have had the advantage of increasing visibility for observers above or beside the thrust stage. For some scenes, as is suggested by the 1633 title-page drawing in **Kyd**'s *The Spanish Tragedy*, a separate free-standing structure would have been more appropriate. What is certain is that, once the concealed scene or character had been revealed, the action was brought out onto the platform proper. Having served the story, the discovery space was not allowed to contain or constrain it. PT

Dmitrevsky (Dmitrevskoi), Ivan Afanasievich (1734–1821)

The first Russian actor of real artistic distinction and social prominence, Dmitrevsky began his career with **Fyodor Volkov**'s acting troupe in Yaroslavl (1750) and continued with the Moscow company co-founded by Volkov and playwright **A. P. Sumarokov** in 1756. Known as 'the Russian **Garrick**', whose acting he studied along with **Lekain**'s and **Clairon**'s while abroad (1765–8), Dmitrevsky is credited with having introduced into Russia the loud, artificial declamatory acting style which **Mikhail Shchepkin**'s simple, natural approach replaced in the 1830s. Dmitrevsky's intelligent but unemotional approach to acting contributed to the success of his second career as teacher-director-administrator, beginning in 1780 with one of Russia's first private acting companies, the Free Knipper Theatre in Moscow, and extending through various enterprises over the next 38 years. Among Dmitrevsky's most distinguished pupils were such leaders of the next generation of actors as **P. A. Plavilshchikov**, **A. S. Yakovlev**, **E. S. Semyonova** and **I. I. Sosnitsky**. Dmitrevsky wrote more than 40 dramas, comedies and operas and regularly advised his more influential contemporary playwrights Sumarokov, **Ya. B. Knyazhnin** and especially **D. I. Fonvizin**, in whose comedy *The Minor* he had scored a notable acting success as Starodum. His co-translations of Tacitus, play analyses, contributions to joint scholarly projects and individual research efforts, including an unpublished history of the Russian theatre (1792), earned Dmitrevsky election to the Russian Academy on 3 May 1802. SG

Döbbelin, Carl Theophil (1727–93) German actor. After some years in **Schönemann**'s troupe, where he practised the **Leipzig style**, in 1756 Döbbelin founded his own troupe. This gave the first performance of **Lessing**'s *Götz von Berlichingen* in 1774. From 1775 on, this troupe formed a permanent company in Berlin; in 1786, this was established, still under Döbbelin's leadership, as the Berlin National and Court Theatre, later to become the important **Berlin Royal Theatre**. SW

Dockstader, Lew (George Alfred Clapp) (1856–1925) American comedian, who preserved the minstrel show's vitality while injecting it with political satire. He had begun in blackface as a teenager and formed his own company with Charles Dockstader in 1876, retaining the name after his partner retired in 1883. His new partnership with George Primrose created the most popular turn-of-the-century minstrel troupe in the USA (1898–1913). Dockstader performed in two-foot-long shoes and a coat with a 30-inch tail; his best song was 'Everybody Works but Father'. Before he became a solo monologuist on the Keith Circuit, he had given a start to **Al Jolson**. LS

Dodsley, Robert (1703–64) English playwright and publisher. He ran away from his apprenticeship to a stocking weaver and became a footman in London where encouraged by Alexander Pope he became a writer and book-seller. His first play, *The Toyshop* (1735), was a light farce. He had his greatest success with *The King and the Miller of Mansfield* (1737), a folk-tale comedy, and with *Cleone* (1758), an emotionally violent tragedy with **George Anne Bellamy** in the title role. But Dodsley's most important contribution to drama was as editor and publisher of *A Select Collection of Old Plays* (12 vols., 1744), a major attempt to rescue the work of many renaissance dramatists from obscurity – the work was re-edited by **Hazlitt** in 1874. He also turned **Day** and **Chettle**'s *The Blind Beggar of Bethnal Green* into a ballad opera in 1741. PH

Dog drama see **Animals as performers**

Doggett, Thomas (c. 1670–1721) English actor, manager, playwright. He performed in Ireland in the 1680s but joined the **Drury Lane** company by 1691, scoring a great success as Solon in **D'Urfey**'s *The Marriage-Hater Matched* (1692) and being nicknamed Solon thereafter. He was praised by **Dryden** for his intelligence as an actor and by **Aston** as 'the best face-player and gesticulator'. He was careful in his costuming and in his observation of life. Though he joined the secessionists in 1695, he could not settle with them and oscillated between the companies and touring outside London. In 1709 he joined Wilks and **Cibber** in running the Queen's Theatre and later Drury Lane. He left the triumvirate in 1714 in an argument over **Barton Booth**'s joining them. In 1716 he established a race for Thames watermen from London Bridge to Chelsea for a cap and silver badge: it is still rowed annually. PH

Domínguez, Franklin (1931–) Dominican Republic playwright, director, actor. A graduate of the National School of Dramatic Art in 1949, he was instrumental in creating the experimental theatre movement in the Dominican Republic. With degrees in philosophy (1953) and law (1955) he occupied important positions in national theatre and culture. He has served as director of the Fine Arts Theatre and has his own theatre group, Franklin Domínguez Presents. An eclectic writer, his works have been translated and staged in French, German, English, Portuguese, Flemish, and Chinese. Among his more than 30 plays are the following: *El último instante* (*The Last Moment*, 1957), the anguished monologue of a suicidal prostitute, *Se busca un hombre honesto* (*The Search for an Honest Man*, 1963), and *Lisístrata odia la política* (*Lysistrata Hates Politics*, 1965), a socially committed play based on **Aristophanes**. His plays have won prizes in many countries. GW

Dominican Republic On this Caribbean island, one of Columbus's first settlements, the native *taínos* practised both the *areyto*, a historical music–dance drama that transmitted the cultural heritage orally, and the *cohaba*, a priestly ceremonial dance induced by hallucinogenic drugs. The early extinction of the indigenous population through the imposition of a Spanish hierarchical system and the importation of European diseases reduced the demand for catechetical theatre. In the colonial years, theatre tended to reflect religious concerns in the form of **loas**, *entremeses* and **comedias**, although a secular theatre, realistic and comic, sometimes in open opposition to Catholic dogma, was performed and naturally censured by the church.

Cristóbal de Llerena is the first playwright of record born in the New World. Author of several works, only his *entremés* performed in 1588 survives. The work reflected social conflicts and corruption within the Dominican society during a period of external and internal pirating. Sir Francis Drake had sacked the city shortly before this date, and Llerena's brief, two-scene play resulted in his immediate but temporary deportation. In 1616–18 **Tirso de Molina**, the famous Spanish playwright of the Golden Age, lived on the island, but there is no record that his plays were performed there or that his idealistic conception of the world left any lasting impact on Dominican theatre.

New governors, slave rebellions and political instability produced by invasions and the wars among Spain, France and England characterized life on the island during the 17th and 18th centuries. Theatrical events took place in the churches, plazas, and viceregal houses and palaces, but no plays are preserved. The 19th-century foreign occupation by the Haitians (1822–44) and the Spanish (1861–5) perpetuated the turbulence, but such theatre groups as The Trinitarians, The Philanthropics and The Dramatic Society attempted to maintain a semblance of activity, generally with foreign plays by such authors as **Alfieri** and Francisco Martínez de la Rosa.

Don Felix María del Monte is considered to be the first national playwright, with a work that criticizes the first president of the nation for the assassination of the patriot, *Antonio Duvergé, o Las víctimas del 11 de abril*

(*Antonio Duvergé, or The Victims of 11 April*, 1856). Indigenous and heroic tendencies, embedded into a romantic framework, were typical of the other major authors of the period, such as Javier Foxá (1816–65) and Javier Angulo Guridi (1816–84), the latter the author of *Iguaniona* (1867). Groups such as La Juventud (Youth) (1868) and Amigos del País (Friends of the Nation) (1871) contributed to the theatre movement.

20th century After 1911 the cultural societies began to produce comedy sketches, and the North American occupation of the island (1916–24) inspired some political plays. Rafael Damirón's (1882–1946) *Alma criolla* (*Creole Soul*, 1916) continued the romantic tradition with elements of the **zarzuela**, however. For the most part the early years of the century saw little new development.

In the 1940s the arrival of Spanish immigrants, refugees of the Civil War, gave new impulse to the theatre and promoted local authors such as **Manuel Rueda** and **Héctor Incháustegui Cabral**. The contemporary theatre movement dates from 1946, the year that Generalissimo Trujillo's wife urged the creation of the Fine Arts Theatre. The theatre occupies a handsome building; the government provides regular, though minimal, salaries. The experimental theatre movement in Santo Domingo dates from 1952; **Máximo Avilés Blonda** (b. 1931) and **Franklin Domínguez** (b. 1931) were instrumental in using the latest production techniques to stage translations of foreign plays, along with their own works. Both are major authors with a commitment to serious theatre; Domínguez, the island's best known playwright internationally, has for years directed the Fine Arts Theatre. Other writers of importance include Marcio Veloz Maggiolo, Carlos Esteban Deive (b. 1935), Iván García Guerra (b. 1938), Carlos Acevedo, Rafael Añez Bergés, Juan Carlos Mieses (b. 1947) and Efraím Castillo. The latter has two published plays: *Viaje de regreso* (*Return Trip*) and *La cosecha* (*The Crop*).

The experimental movement spawned such groups as the Jockey Club Group, the Popular Experimental Theatre (1976), Intec Projection (1978) and Chispa (Spark). Domínguez created his own independent group, and the Gratey Theatre, directed by Danilo Ginebra and others, has been responsible for a wide range of publications and activities, including the first national popular theatre festival in 1983. Rafael Villalona, Delta Sota and María Castillo have done important work with the Nuevo Teatro (New Theatre). In 1985 Reynaldo Disla won the coveted Casa de las Américas prize in Cuba for the best new play, *Bolo Francisco*.

Theatre activity continues to be sporadic, centred mostly in the capital city of Santo Domingo which embraces the non-professional, independent and university theatre activity, such as the Autonomous University of Santo Domingo, Pedro Henríquez Ureña National University and the Technical Institute of Santo Domingo. Isolated movement in the provinces includes the work of Rubén Echavarría and Lincoln López in the theatre programme of the Catholic University Madre y Maestra. The Dominican theatre still suffers from a lack of infrastructure, and the many extant groups encourage false expectations about the availability of staged performance. GW

See: D. Ginebra (ed.), *Teatro dominicano*, vol. I, Santo Domingo, 1984; P. Henríquez Ureña, *Obras completas: El teatro de la América española*, vol. VII, Santo Domingo, 1978; J. Lockward, *Teatro dominicano: Pasado y presente*, Santo Domingo, 1959.

Donleavy, J[ames] P[atrick] (1926–) Irish dramatist and novelist, who adapted four of his novels for the stage, *The Ginger Man* (1959), *A Singular Man* (1967), *The Saddest Summer of Samuel S* and *The Beastly Beatitudes of Balthazar B* (1981). As these titles suggest, Donleavy enjoys a literary rumbustiousness which is not always suitable for the theatre, although *Balthazar* provided **Simon Callow** with a lively, scandalous role for the West End. Donleavy's most successful excursion into playwriting came with *Fairy Tales of New York* (1961), describing the sad homecoming of an American whose English wife has died on the voyage. These four short plays illustrate different aspects of New York, telling, fantastic and often witty. *Fairy Tales* won Donleavy the Evening Standard Most Promising Playwright Award for 1961. JE

Donneau de Visé, Jean (1638–1710) French man of letters, critic and journalist who fomented the hostile reaction to **Molière**'s *L'Ecole des Femmes* (*The School for Wives*) in 1663 with a critical article, followed by a one-act play *Zélinde* and possibly the highly injurious *La Vengeance des Marquis* (*The Marquises' Revenge*) which commented on the playwright's private life. Nevertheless several of de Visé's later plays were performed by Molière's company, and he collaborated to good effect on others with **Thomas Corneille**, notably on the very successful machine-play *La Devineresse* (*The Fortune-Teller*, 1679). In 1672 he founded *Le Mercure Galant* which became the quasi-official gazette of French social and literary life. DR

Döring, Theodor (1803–78) German actor. A natural and versatile imitator, Döring was known for the realism and completeness of his characterizations. He had a refreshing vital energy, though at times he became so absorbed in a role, it was difficult to hear him. Before joining the **Berlin Royal Theatre** in 1845, he acted in companies in Mannheim, Hamburg, Stuttgart, and Hannover. SW

Dorset Garden Theatre London theatre, begun in 1669 by Wren on a frontage facing the river with a site measuring 140 feet by 57 feet. It had seven boxes on each of the lower and middle galleries with an undivided upper gallery above. It opened in November 1671 for use by the Duke's Company with a production of **Dryden**'s *Sir Martin Mar-All*. It was soon apparent that the theatre's acoustics were poor and it was increasingly used only for spectacular productions of operatic extravagances. It was finally demolished in 1709. PH

Dorst, Tankred (1925–) German dramatist. Early works such as *Grand Tirade at the Town Wall* (1961) united techniques derived from **Brecht** and absurd themes in a highly original way with the aim of theatricalizing reality, dealing with the characters who impose their imaginary worlds on a mechanized or automaton-like society. Although he has denied the validity of ideas in drama and rejects ideology, *Toller*

(1968) aroused strong political passions. His first major play, this deals with the playwright **Ernst Toller**'s role in the short-lived Munich Soviet and uses agit-prop elements derived from the period to undercut expressionist quotation from the real-life protagonist's dramas. But a revue structure transforms the documentary into grotesque farce, and this questioning of the relationship between art and reality is continued in *Ice Age* (1973) through the figure of **Knut Hamsun**. One of the most interesting contemporary dramatists, who has recently turned to film directing, Dorst's range can be illustrated by the contrast between *Merlin or the Wasteland* (1981), an eight-hour perspective on the gap between utopian myth and the realities of progress, and the children's fairy tale *Ameley, the Beaver and the King on the Roof* (1982). His most ambitious work is the still incomplete multi-media cycle subtitled 'German History', comprising the retrospective epilogue *On the Chimborazo* (1970), a novel, *Dorothea Merz*, a film, *Klara's Mother* (1978 – also directed by Dorst) and *The Villa* (1984). Basically naturalistic, this cycle traces the fortunes of a representative group from the early years of the Weimar Republic to the present. CI

Dorval, Marie (1798–1849) French actress who best represented the romantic movement in the French theatre. Her passionate temperament and instinctive playing, defying the 'rules' of good acting, opposed her to the great classical actress, **Mlle Mars**, with whom she shared the stage in **Hugo**'s *Angelo* (1835). Dorval was the offspring of travelling players and made her first appearances at the age of eight in such popular melodramas as *Les Deux Petits Savoyards* (*The Two Little Savoyards*). At 15 she married a poor ballet-master, Allan Dorval, and having been noticed in Strasbourg by the actor **Potier**, was taken on at the Porte-Saint-Martin in 1818. Her greatest triumph there came in 1827 with **Victor Ducange**'s *The Hut on the Red Mountain; or, Thirty Years of a Gamester's Life*, in which she played opposite **Frédérick Lemaître**. This gave her the sort of strong dramatic role that suited her talent. **Casimir Delavigne**'s *Marino Faliero* (1829) established her as the first actress of the Boulevard. She moved briefly to the Ambigu, then back to the Porte-Saint-Martin to play Adèle d'Hervey with **Bocage** in **Dumas**'s *Antony* (1831). Her role was that of a passionate woman forced by society into a loveless marriage and trapped into an adulterous affair. In Hugo's *Marion de Lorme* she incarnated the golden-hearted courtesan. Her style of play, with a tremor in her voice, could send a wave of emotion through audiences. From 1833 to 1835 she had a liaison with **Vigny**, who wrote *Quitte Pour la Peur* (*Getting Off With a Fright*) and *Chatterton* (1835) for her. She made her debut at the **Comédie-Française** in 1834, taking on some of Mlle Mars's parts, but she was not really a Comédie-Française actress, and left again in 1835. In *Chatterton*, as the silent and pathetic Kitty Bell, she introduced an unforgettable final stage effect fainting at the top of a flight of stairs and allowing her inanimate body to slide the entire length of the bannisters. After the Comédie-Française she had a brief period at the **Odéon** and then moved to the Gymnase in 1837. It was mutually agreed that her talents were not suited to Gymnase comedy and the contract was cancelled in 1840. She returned for a time to the Comédie-

Française, appearing at the request of George Sand, who admired her, in the latter's *Cosima*, then moved back to the Odéon to appear in the title role of **Ponsard**'s *Lucrèce* (1842). In 1845 she was back on the Boulevard in her final huge triumph, the melodrama *Marie-Jeanne*. By this stage her health was undermined and, after some further appearances at the Odéon and a revival of *Marie-Jeanne* in 1848, she died in poverty. JMCC

Dotrice, Roy (1923–) British actor, who made his reputation after joining the **Royal Shakespeare Company** in 1958, where he demonstrated his versatility with memorable performances in the contrasting roles of Gaunt, Hotspur and Justice Shallow, all presented on a single day in the first half of **Peter Hall**'s history cycle, *The Wars of the Roses* (1963). He made an international reputation with his solo adaptation of John Aubrey's *Brief Lives* (1967), which has been followed by other one-man shows. CI

Douglas, James (1929–) Irish playwright. Douglas made an impressive debut with *North City Traffic Straight Ahead* (Gaiety 1961), apart from ironic echoes of **Synge**, a sparely written drama of wasted urban lives. Since then he has written many television works, including a long-running series, and a play, *The Bomb* (1962), in whose brief span a faded Ascendancy lady's life embodies great social changes. Douglas's later plays – *The Ice Goddess* (1964), *The Savages* (1968) – more realistically scripted than *North City Traffic*, have never quite recaptured its force. DM

Douglas (Hesselberg), Melvyn (1901–81) American actor, director, and producer. Douglas toured the Middle West in repertory and stock, then spent two years with **Jessie Bonstelle**'s company, headed his own company for a time, and made his debut on Broadway in 1928. His first hit, *Tonight or Never* (1930), co-starred Helen Gahagan, whom he married. From 1931 to 1942 he starred in 45 movies, then returned to the theatre in 1952 with *Time Out for Ginger* and in 1955 replaced **Paul Muni** as Drummond in *Inherit the Wind*, winning critical acclaim. Douglas had begun as a debonair and dapper leading man in romantic comedies, but matured into a forceful character actor of considerable stature. He won the Antoinette Perry (Tony) Award in 1960 for *The Best Man*. SMA

Douglass, David (?–1786) British-born actor-manager, who became the central figure in the history of the American theatre from his marriage in 1758 to the widow of **Lewis Hallam, Sr** in Jamaica, until the American Revolution. Douglass returned to New York in 1758 as head of Hallam's Company of Comedians from London (renamed in 1763 The American Company of Comedians). For 17 years Douglass's company played up and down the East Coast, erecting temporary theatres in most towns. In 1766 he built the first permanent theatre in the United States, the **Southwark** in Philadelphia, followed in 1767 by the **John Street** Theatre in New York. In April 1767 Douglass announced the first professional production of a play by a native American, a comic opera called *The Disappointment*, which was replaced at the last minute by Thomas Godfrey's *The Prince of Parthia*, the first native tragedy to be presented professionally. Before the outbreak of hostilities, Douglass and his company returned to the West Indies in 1775, where he became a justice, an officer in the militia, and a member of the Council. Douglass, America's first Falstaff and King John, though a poor actor, was a superb manager. DBW

Dowling, Eddie (Joseph Nelson Goucher) (1889–1976) Pulitzer Prize-winning American producer, playwright, songwriter, director, actor, who began his career doing a song and dance act in his native state of Rhode Island. His Broadway debut was in **Victor Herbert**'s *The Velvet Lady* in 1919; he appeared in the *Ziegfeld Follies* of 1919, 1920 and 1921. In 1945, after rejecting a sure-fire commercial project, he co-produced, co-directed (with **Margo Jones**) **Williams**'s *The Glass Menagerie*, in which he also played Tom. The production made theatrical history and brought Williams out of obscurity. Dowling produced *Richard II* in 1937 with **Maurice Evans** and during his long career worked with such playwrights as **William Saroyan**, **Paul Vincent Carroll**, **Sean O'Casey**, and Philip Barry. DBW

Downes, John (*fl.* 1661–1719) English prompter. He began as an actor but failed because of severe stage-fright in a performance of **Davenant**'s *The Siege of Rhodes* in 1661. He became prompter for the Duke's Company and worked for the United Company and **Betterton**'s Company until 1706, being responsible for writing out actors' parts, attending all rehearsals and all performances. In 1708 he published *Roscius Anglicanus*, a brief history of the stage from the Restoration. PH

Downstage Theatre, Wellington New Zealand theatre established in 1964 as a restaurant theatre specializing in local plays. The enterprise was initially precarious, but served as a stimulus for the foundation of other professional community theatres in many New Zealand cities. In 1974 Downstage moved into the new Hannah Playhouse, seating about 200, and its policy of promoting New Zealand scripts continues in the 1990s. HDMCN

Drag shows see **Female impersonation**

Dragún, Osvaldo (1929–) Argentine playwright and director. Born in San Salvador, Entre Ríos, he is committed to denouncing social injustices and has consistently censured the materialism and hypocrisy of our times. His *Historias para ser contadas* (*Stories to be Told*, 1957) were written with a **commedia dell'arte** flavour to be performed by his theatre group, Teatro Popular Fray Mocho. Internationally known, these vignettes with long titles condemn the sacrifices of human dignity on the altar of economic survival. Other titles, *La peste viene de Melos* (*The Plague comes from Melos*, 1956) and *Tupac Amarú* (1957) show perverted economic and moral values in classical settings. Later titles include *Y nos dijeron que éramos imortales* (*And They Told Us We Were Immortal*, 1963), *El milagro en el mercado viejo* (*Miracle in the Old Market*, 1964), *El amasijo* (*The Hodgepodge*, 1968), and sequels to the *Historias* (*Stories*). Dragún played a major role in the creation of

the **Teatro Abierto** (Open Theatre), an experiment organized in 1981 to produce viable theatre during the most repressive years of the military government. Recent works include *Al violador* (*To the Rapist*, 1981), *Hoy comen al flaco* (*Today They Eat the Thin Man*, 1981), *Mi obelisco y yo* (*My Obelisk and Me*, 1981), *Al perdedor* (*To the Loser*, 1982), *Al vendedor* (*To the Seller*, 1982) and *Arriba corazón!* (*Upward Heart!*, 1987). GW

Drake, Alfred (1914–) American singer and actor. One of the most versatile leading men of the American musical stage, Drake began his musical career in **Gilbert** and Sullivan revivals, and made his Broadway debut in the chorus of *White Horse Inn* (1936). After featured roles in such shows as *Babes in Arms* (1937) and *The Straw Hat Revue* (1939), Drake created the role of Curley in **Rodgers** and **Hammerstein**'s *Oklahoma!* (1943). Five years later, he played Fred Graham in *Kiss Me, Kate*. Praised by critics for his romantic, swaggering portrayal of a Shakespearian actor, Drake's comic abilities received a large share of the acclaim. Among his subsequent musical theatre appearances, only his performance as Hajj in *Kismet* (1953) was notable. Drake's career as an actor included performances as Othello and Benedick at the **American Shakespeare Festival Theatre**, and Claudius opposite **Richard Burton** in *Hamlet* (1964). MK

Drake, Samuel (1769–1854) American actor-manager. Born in England, where he became a provincial manager, Drake brought his family of performers to America in 1810. After a few years in Boston, the Drakes joined **John Bernard**'s company in Albany in 1813, and in 1815, at the invitation of Luke Usher, Drake took his three sons, two daughters, and five assistants as a company to Frankfort, Kentucky. From there he spread his influence to Louisville, Lexington, and Cincinnati, forming a circuit which he controlled for many years. While not the first company in the American West of the time, Drake's group improved the level of theatre in the area and firmly established the frontier theatre. Drake was the grandfather of **Julia Dean**, an outstanding American actress. SMA

Drama League, The (USA). The Drama League was founded in 1909 by an Evanston (Illinois) ladies' literary society, the 'Riley Circle'. Their first national gathering was held at a church in Evanston (1910), and at their constitutional convention (1910) at the Chicago Art Institute, attended by some 200 delegates representing 63 local centres, Mrs A. Starr Bast was elected president and proclaimed their goals: 'to stimulate interest in the best drama'; 'to awaken the public to the importance of the theatre as a social force'. The organization expanded rapidly: in 1911 they had 12,000 members in 25 states, in the early 20s, 23,000 members, 100,000 affiliated members, and 114 centres throughout the country. They published *The Drama* (1911), a quarterly 'to cultivate a deeper understanding and appreciation for American drama and theatre' with W. P. Eaton, **G. P. Baker**, **Brander Matthews**, **Stark Young**, *et al.* as editors, issued 250 bulletins (1910–16) endorsing current productions, sponsored tours of the Hull-House Players, the Irish Players, **Mrs Fiske**, **George Arliss**, *et al.*, published 20 volumes of 'good' plays, conducted summer instructional institutes, and held annual conventions in Chicago, New York, St Louis, Pittsburgh, and Detroit. After the national organization was disbanded (1931), local centres continued to function, and the New York Drama League was still active in 1985. RM

Dramaten The Royal Dramatic Theatre in Stockholm was founded in 1788 by Gustav III for the performance of original Swedish plays. It performed in various temporary playhouses (a converted tennis court, the royal arsenal) before acquiring the New Theatre in 1863. However, until 1842 it enjoyed a 50-year monopoly of spoken drama in the capital. It depended on royal and parliamentary subsidies until 1888, when it was denationalized and run by an association of actors, against strong competition from Albert Ranft's Svenska and Vasa Theatres. Dramaten moved to its present building and regained its subsidies in 1907 and has since become one of the world's most celebrated companies, especially under the leadership of **Per Lindberg**, **Olof Molander**, **Alf Sjöberg** and **Ingmar Bergman**. **Strindberg** has naturally been important in the modern repertory, but so have **Ibsen**, **Brecht** and **O'Neill**, several of whose premieres were entrusted to Dramaten. The theatre opened its Little Stage in 1945, followed in the 1970s by the converted Paint Room and the tiny 'Fyran', high under the theatre's roof. HL

Dramatic theory Most theorists of drama agree that one of their tasks is to define dramatic theory itself. In many instances, the agreement stops there because individual theorists often hold divergent views of both theory and drama. This is not to say that dramatic theory ought to be, or even could be, done without. Anyone arguing against dramatic theory would have to make some general statements about theory, drama, and their proper relationship (if any). He or she would thus add arguments to the growing body of dramatic theory which, for the purpose of these comments, may be defined as follows: systematically generalizing discourse about the nature and function of plays, about their genres, modes, and styles, and about their production by performers and reception by readers or spectators including theorists and other critics.

Such a broad definition is needed if we are to account for both guises in which drama can appear to its audience. Some theorists view the text, others the performance, as a play's ultimate reality. In both camps, however, there tends to be sufficient willingness to heed both the literary and the theatrical dimension of drama. Even the most devout believers in drama as literature hardly ever deny that the potential for being performed sets plays apart from other kinds of literary works. Conversely, even the most fervent proponents of the view that the 'playscript' is a mere recipe for a more or less delicious production stop short of suggesting that the assignment of readings in a drama course is like the serving up of loose leaves from a cookbook at the dinner table. On the evidence of 2,500 years of dramatic theory and practice in the West it is reasonable to conclude that plays need not be considered as *either* performable texts *or* scriptable performances. They can be, and usually are, both.

Whether designed for the page or the stage, many plays themselves contain theoretical observations about drama and performance. Since the Roman times of **Plautus** and **Terence**, prologues and epilogues have proved to be the most convenient dramatic sites for such self-reflective theorizing. But **Shakespeare** was by no means the only playwright to put elements of dramatic theory into the mouth of a major character, as when Hamlet tells the Players that the theatre's purpose has always been 'to hold, as 'twere, the mirror up to nature'. Hamlet's memorable phrase merely echoes the opinion, often expressed since Plato and **Aristotle**, that art in general and drama in particular 'imitates' or 'reflects' reality. Yet playwrights have also been known to initiate debates about important theoretical issues, and not only in prefaces, postscripts, or other writings designed to vindicate their own dramatic practice. For example, the contest in Hades between **Aeschylus** and **Euripides** at the thematic climax of *The Frogs* by **Aristophanes** foreshadows one of the fundamental dilemmas of later theory: is the playwright's first commitment to morality or reality, is he mainly to improve or to inform his audience?

As subsequent theorists pondered drama's impact on its audience, they often described or prescribed several distinct but combinable goals for the endeavours of playwrights and performers. On the whole, they tended either to share **Horace**'s view that plays like other poetic constructs may 'benefit' or 'delight' us or else to agree with Cicero's Renaissance disciple, Bishop Minturno, that plays like other rhetorical constructs should 'instruct, delight, and move' us. **Castelvetro** was a rare exception, and not only among 16th-century theorists, in that he rejected the didactic function of drama altogether, insisting that 'poetry was invented solely to delight and to recreate'. Disparate rankings of the two or three widely endorsed objectives of drama did, however, occur. In the preface to his edition of Shakespeare's plays, for example, **Samuel Johnson** subordinated delight to instruction as a means to an end ('the end of poetry is to instruct by pleasing') without explicit mention of the all-too-human need for motivation. The latter had, however, been stressed two centuries before in **Philip Sidney**'s *Defense of Poesy*. According to Sidney, the potential achievement of poetry (including drama) is 'of higher degree' than that of philosophy because imaginative works are more adept at the crucial task of 'moving' their audience, yet for any moral teaching to occur and be effective, it is necessary for us 'to be moved with desire to know' and 'to be moved to do that which we know'. Recent proponents of a politically activist theatre (e.g. **Augusto Boal**, **Dario Fo**, **Ariane Mnouchkine**) hold comparable views even if, following **Brecht**, they pay more attention than Sidney to the especially strong motivating power of the theatre to trigger the desired audience response during or after a live performance. The theory and practice of **Antonin Artaud** and some of his American followers (e.g. Julian Beck and Judith Malina of the **Living Theatre**, **Joseph Chaikin** and Viola Spolin of the **Open Theatre**, Richard Schechner of the **Performance Group**) in turn demand of the stage an almost hypnotic ability to 'move' performers and spectators alike – not toward specific intellectual, moral, or political commitments but, through participatory search for personal liberation, ultimately beyond them.

Plato's rejection of the theatre in *The Republic* and

elsewhere was tangential to his summary censure of poets and other artists for imitating transient objects (rather than contemplating eternal ideas) and for exciting the passions (rather than promoting truth, patriotic courage, and the love of justice). By contrast, Aristotle's *Poetics* defended the arts against such charges with frequent and specific reference to tragic drama. He argued that tragedy's skilful representation of events, linked together into a unified action by probability or necessity rather than mere chance, makes it 'more philosophical than history'; and he appears to have held the paradoxically profound view that the tragic poet's artistic arousal of pity and fear serves to purge us – perhaps by clarifying their causes – of the potentially harmful intensity of such emotions. Later theorists have made countless attempts to elucidate Aristotle's key concepts including the two just mentioned: representation (*mimesis*) and purging (*catharsis*). But untutored theatre-goers, too, are in the Greek philosopher's debt for a good deal of their pertinent vocabulary. In most languages spoken today in Europe and the Americas, even informal conversations about plays and productions heavily rely on words whose ancient Greek prototypes prominently figure in the *Poetics*: theatre and drama, tragedy and comedy, poet and critic, scene and rhythm, to name a few. Aristotle did not coin any of those terms, but his usage contributed greatly to establishing their future currency.

The extant text of the *Poetics* is terse, fragmentary, and enigmatic in several respects. Yet no single work has had a comparable commanding influence on almost all subsequent theorizing about plays the vast majority of which was, of course, unknown to its author. Needless to say, the critical tradition has been appropriating Aristotle according to its historically changing needs and circumstances. Following Robortello, some neoclassical theorists of the 16th and 17th centuries were to derive, for instance, iron-clad rules of the 'unity of time' from Aristotle's empirical observation that 'tragedy attempts, as far as possible, to remain within one circuit of the sun or, at least, not to depart from this by much'. Some pre-romantic and romantic critics of the 18th and early 19th centuries (e.g. La Motte, **A. W. Schlegel**, Coleridge) were in turn so dissatisfied with their predecesors' 'mechanical' application of supposedly Aristotelian rules that they even replaced Aristotle's explicit demand for the unity of dramatic action by what they felt was a more flexible and more natural organizing principle: the unity (or totality) of 'interest'. The major spokesmen for the various 'isms' of the late 19th and early 20th centuries (the naturalist **Zola**, the symbolist **Maeterlinck**, the futurist **Marinetti**, the surrealist Apollinaire, the expressionist Pinthus, and the dadaist Tzara, for example) neither used nor abused the *Poetics* as a frequent point of reference in their respective manifestos. Yet few theorists today doubt that Aristotle's overview of the principles of Greek drama has considerable relevance to the analysis and evaluation of most later plays as well. His preference for heroes that are neither completely virtuous nor completely evil is one good example. His insistence on the desirability of connecting the tragic figure's conduct and his or her fate through some grave 'error', 'transgression', or 'flaw' (*hamartia*) is another. Still more impressive is the degree to which some of the most basic conceptual tools of all later theorizing about

drama have been anticipated by Aristotle's magisterially simple delineation of the 'six parts' of tragedy: plot (*mythos*), character (*ethos*), thought (*dianoia*), diction (*lexis*), music (*melos*), and spectacle (*opsis*).

Five of the six Greek terms on the list are clearly recognizable ancestors of modern English and foreign words (myth, ethics, lexicon, melody, and optics, for example). All six Aristotelian concepts, however, relate to what still appear to be the most essential components of a performed play. The first three concepts encompass three aspects of the fictive world represented by a dramatic text or performance: what is done ('plot'), by and to whom ('character'), and why ('thought' as the characters' reasonings or as the playwright's and director's thematic message). The last three in turn apply to three aspects of theatrical world-making whose chief vehicles are, indeed, either verbal ('diction') or nonverbal and either acoustic (sometimes even 'musical') or visual (sometimes even 'spectacular').

Of the six categories, the first two have received privileged attention from both Aristotle – he called plot 'the soul of tragedy' – and the majority of later theorists. As a rule, 'plot' has prompted structural explorations in quasi-Aristotelian terms such as exposition, complication, denouement; deserved or undeserved suffering; rising or falling action; conflict, suspense, change of fortune; crisis, climax, reversal, and catastrophe. 'Character' has in turn been approached most frequently from the vantage point of the theorist's own system of psychology and morality. Theories of 'thought' (or theme) usually address the spiritual or ideological implications of drama and the socio-political relationship between a play's world and the worldview of its author or audience. Primary concern with 'diction' prompts theorists to stress the literary aspects of drama, while close study of 'music' and 'spectacle' (in the extended sense of the words as the acoustic and visual features of an actual or imagined production) points them toward every play's theatrical dimension. The last two 'parts' were relatively neglected by Aristotle but take centre stage among theorists of the opera, ballet, the pantomime, the cinema, and various forms of unscripted theatre (including 'happenings' and other types of partially improvised performance in both literate and oral cultures).

Theories of staging – whether articulated or merely implied – likewise vary in orientation. They may be principally geared toward a unified plot of human interaction (**Stanislavsky**'s atmospheric ensemble style); toward a few highlighted characters (the almost exclusive attention paid to 'leading men' and 'leading ladies' in some periods and many histories of acting); toward the direct communication of thought to the audience (Brechtian *Verfremdung* or estrangement); toward the unimpeded enactment of diction (**Jacques Copeau**'s almost 'bare boards' on which highly literate actors declaim the precious lines of dramatic masterpieces); toward the lavish forthpouring of nonverbal or partly verbal sound (the practice, if not the theory, of most operatic performances); or else toward the markedly non-literary creation of an imaginative visual design (**Gordon Craig**'s artistic sets and light effects and his proposed reduction of each performer to a masked *Über-Marionette*). In pure theory it seems possible and desirable to achieve a 'total work of art' through the mutual enhancement of all relevant components (**Richard Wagner**'s operatic *Gesamtkunswerk*) or through their mutual subordination (**Jerzy Grotowski**'s 'poor theatre'). In actual practice, however, the attention of most spectators (and of most theorists) is likely to remain riveted to just one of the six 'parts' as the dominant factor in a particular performance (or in a certain type of drama or production). The acknowledgement of such dominance need not lead to theoretical claims for absolute supremacy, of course. In most plays and performances, each 'part' significantly contributes to drama's representation of a world and its communication of a worldview.

Theorists seeing drama chiefly as communication aspire to varying degrees of precision as they explore just who does the communicating. Many assume that author and director – the ultimate senders of the dramatic 'message' – are absent from each part of the play while present in its total design by way of implication. For most purposes, the view expressed by Stephen Dedalus in Joyce's *Portrait of the Artist as a Young Man* is accurate enough: the playwright, 'like the God of the creation, remains within or behind or beyond or above his handiwork, invisible, refined out of existence, paring his fingernails'. On closer inspection, however, the image of an absent deity appears to do better justice to the director's role in individual performances than to the actual or implied author's concrete ubiquity in the text of his or her play. In their search for the concealed author, various modern theorists have been concentrating on a number of different components and aspects of drama in and through which that elusive spirit may have assumed material existence after all: stage directions and poetic diction (Roman Ingarden), Greek chorus and Elizabethan soliloquy (Una Ellis-Fermor), prologues, epilogues, narrator figures, and other devices of an 'epic' theatre (Peter Szondi). Somewhat more impressionistically, **T. S. Eliot** in *The Three Voices of Poetry* even wondered whether Macbeth's speech beginning 'To-morrow and to-morrow and to-morrow' especially moves us because 'Shakespeare and Macbeth are uttering the words in unison'.

A similar interplay of presence and absence has long been discerned in the representation of characters: each human participant in the action evoked by a performed play is, at the same time, magically present in and tantalizingly absent from the performer of the role. To give a particular example, the man we see on the stage is *neither* Hamlet *nor* **Laurence Olivier** but Olivier *as* Hamlet, which means that both character and performer simultaneously are and are not what they seem to be. To be sure, actors and actresses are merely implied when a play is being read rather than performed. Yet readers of a dramatic text imaginatively substitute their minds and bodies for the 'missing' performers whose assigned roles they enact on the mental stage of their reading experience. Theories of acting thus have considerable bearing on our understanding of the reception of printed drama as well. When, for disparate reasons of their own, Horace and Stanislavsky recommend – while **Diderot** and Brecht reject – the performer's emotional identification with his or her role, they thereby propose or presuppose very different methods of properly playing the implied reader's role. As a result, they also offer quite different views of drama as the textual basis of various kinds, degrees, or mixtures of empathy and distance.

Distinguishing among different kinds of plays tends to be an important part of theorizing about them. Often enough, the contrast outlined by Aristotle between tragedy and comedy has served as the principal model for drawing generic distinctions. Since the extant portions of the *Poetics* say far too little about comedy, some aspects of the contrast had to be reconstructed or constructed by other theorists in the light of Greek and later examples of comic drama. In any event, tragedy and comedy have remained the conceptual poles between which many sparks of genre criticism have been generated even beyond the confines of dramatic literature. For example, elementary observations about plot structure – happy *versus* unhappy ending – sufficed for Dante and Chaucer to subsume narrative texts under their respective concepts of comedy and tragedy. The majority of more recent, and usually more complex, attempts at defining the 'essence' or 'spirit' of tragedy and comedy likewise point beyond drama and the theatre in their theoretical implications. Even in middle-brow conversations, it is not uncommon to characterize the mood of poems and novels – or paintings and symphonies – as either 'tragic' or 'comic' (sometimes called 'comedic' to avoid the connotation of being unintentionally laughable).

The experience of tragic and comic drama has prompted numerous profound thinkers to evolve elaborate explanations as to why we find the contemplation both of grave suffering and risible levity both pleasurable and edifying. To name just a few, Plato, Augustine, Descartes, Hobbes, Hume, Kant, Schopenhauer, **Nietzsche**, Bergson, and Freud all have addressed at least one side of the puzzling fact that humans are rather proud of being able to indulge themselves in certain kinds of tears and laughter. It is, however, in Hegel's posthumously published lectures on aesthetics that tragedy and comedy have received their most ambitiously systematic treatment. In brief, Hegel sees drama as the artform best suited to make visible the dialectical truth that the universal World Spirit or Ethical Substance exists dispersed in a multiplicity of particular beings and conflicting values. Tragedy (especially the kind of Greek tragedy exemplified in **Sophocles**' *Antigone*) shows the ultimate victory of the undivided Substance over the human representatives of particular and thus one-sided moralities. When both Creon, who embodies the principle of the state, and Antigone, who stands for the principle of family, are crushed we pity each doomed hero and fear the ethical principle he or she has violated by embracing an equally divine yet momentarily opposed principle. Comedy in turn asserts the subjective right of what *is* by declining to relate it too closely to what *should* be, that is, to the objective goals of the Ethical Substance. In particular the comedies of Aristophanes and Shakespeare show the victory of the 'serene subjectivity' of individuals who are able to laugh at themselves as their more substantive aspirations (should they have any at all) remain unfulfilled.

Hegel's views of tragedy and comedy have been received with much admiration, as well as irritation, by later critics who have not stopped offering their own new perspectives on that old, and somewhat odd, couple. Susanne K. Langer's *Feeling and Form* may well contain the best-known 20th-century attempt by a philosopher to interrelate tragedy and comedy. Langer considers the two 'great dramatic forms' not only in the more conventional terms of a 'tragic theme' (guilt leading to expiation) and a 'comic theme' (vanity leading to exposure). Rather, she argues that tragic and comic works bear the marks of one of two fundamental 'rhythms' of life; they contrast the human awareness of individuation and death to the survival of species. While comedy exhibits the vital rhythm of nature's self-preservation, tragedy imprints on the dramatized events the rhythm of self-consummation – the 'death-ward advance' of multicellular life through the irreversible phases of growth, maturity, and decline.

Throughout the centuries, quite a few playwrights have reacted to the constraining tragic–comic dichotomy by turning into theorists of various alternatives. In the prologue to his *Amphitruo*, Plautus made the god Mercury (disguised as a slave) call the play a 'tragicomedy' because such traditionally tragic figures as gods and kings and such comic figures as slaves would appear in it. With different arguments (and under different historical circumstances) **Guarini**, **Fletcher**, and **Hugo** also spoke out in favour of their respective versions of a 'mixed' genre. **Dryden**, Diderot, **Beaumarchais**, and **Goethe** were in turn among the many playwrights who wished to fill what may be called the dramatic gap between tragedy and comedy by contributing to the theory and practice of such 'middle' categories as the heroic play, *le genre sérieux*, *le drame*, or *das Schauspiel*. More recently, **Dürrenmatt**, **Ionesco**, and **Pinter** were among the numerous modern authors claiming that there isn't, or need not be, any essential difference between tragedy and comedy. By contrast, **Arthur Miller** insisted on his *Death of a Salesman* being a tragedy even though the play had not met some critics' expectations as to the social status and intellectual stature of its central character. In 'Tragedy and the Common Man' Miller argued that for tragic feeling to be aroused in us it is sufficient that a character be 'ready to lay down his life to secure his sense of personal dignity'. Recalling that Miller gave the first name 'Willy' and the last name 'Loman' to his tragic anti-hero, one might sum up his position as follows: *man*, however *low*, can rise to tragic height if he has the *will* to do so. Among earlier defenders of bourgeois or even working-class tragedy, **Friedrich Hebbel** may have anticipated Miller's argument most closely when he suggested that all tragedy, whether 'high' or 'low', exemplifies some universal human conflict through a significant clash of individual wills.

Major modern attempts to account for and then transcend the tragic–comic polarity include Northrop Frye's *Anatomy of Criticism* and **Eric Bentley**'s *The Life of the Drama*. According to Frye's view of tragedy, similar acts of 'narrowing a comparatively free life into a process of causation' are performed by Macbeth when he accepts the logic of usurpation, by Hamlet when he accepts the logic of revenge, and by Lear when he accepts the logic of abdication. The typical plot structure of comedy reverses the process and leads the hero out of bondage into a 'stable and harmonious order' which at the end of most comic works, turns out to have been only temporarily 'disrupted by folly, obsession, forgetfulness, "pride and prejudice"'. Frye's theory goes well beyond drama in its range of cross-

disciplinary reference and textual illustrations; he uses the terms tragedy and comedy (as well as romance and satire) to designate narrative categories 'broader than, or logically prior to, literary genres'. Modelled on mythic narratives rather than their 'displaced' literary or dramatic versions, the four 'pregeneric' story patterns represent archetypal movements within a highly desirable world (romance), within a painfully defective world (satire), downward from innocence through hamartia to catastrophe (tragedy), or upward from the threatening complications of the fallen world of experience to 'a general assumption of post-dated innocence in which everyone lives happily ever after' (comedy).

Bentley favours a more theatrical fivesome of generic types: melodrama, farce, tragedy, comedy, and tragicomedy. While melodrama derives its basic formula – innocence surrounded by malevolence – from 'more or less paranoid phantasies', farce reveals the fierce pleasure of aggression with which 'innocence' retaliates. Tragedy thwarts our impulse to identify with innocence and exacts identification with the hero's guilt, thereby promoting self-knowledge instead of melodrama's wishful gratification of the ego. Comedy also promotes self-knowledge when, unlike farce, it makes us face the misery of the human condition before it allows us 'to look the other way'. As for tragicomedy, Bentley distinguishes two kinds. The first is, really, 'tragedy with a comic sequel' (e.g. Shakespeare's *Measure for Measure* and Goethe's *Faust*); it celebrates forgiveness instead of tragic justice, which is a higher form of melodramatic revenge. In the second and more harrowing strain of this complex genre, dark and bitter comedy either refuses 'to look the other way' (e.g. **Ibsen**'s *The Wild Duck*) or else permeates the entire play with the grotesquely zestful despair of 'gallows humour' (e.g. **Beckett**'s *Waiting for Godot*).

Most 20th-century critics addressing the question of dramatic kinds subscribe to Frye's view that 'the purpose of criticism by genres is not so much to classify as to clarify traditions and affinities, thereby bringing out a large number of literary relationships that would not be noticed as long as there were no context established for them'. For better or worse, however, the majority of playwrights, directors, and theorists today show relatively little explicit interest in problems of genre. Perhaps because nature abhores a vacuum, two other concerns have begun to hold sway in the dramatic theory of the last decades. The first prompts structuralist-semiological scrutinies of how everything in the theatre – the text, the performer, the decor, the music, and so forth – functions as a constructed sign of something else. The second leads to hermeneutic-phenomenological studies of how all those things, while functioning as decodable signs, manage to retain their phenomenal thingness or existentially interpretable humanity.

Readers wishing to explore both approaches and to become acquainted with the views of some influential and current proponents of each should consult the books by Keir Elam, Bert O. States, and Bruce Wilshire listed below. Some vital issues raised in those recent books are not restricted to 'dramatic theory' as defined at the beginning of this article. But this is precisely what we should expect. Theatrical enactment shares its reliance on semiotic codes and hermeneutic horizons not only with ceremonies, rituals, sporting events, and the like. Our ordinary acts of self-presentation in the socially assigned roles of daily life must likewise be decoded and interpreted. Recognizing their mutual affinities, philosophy, psychology, sociology, anthropology, and other human sciences have in recent years been interacting with dramatic theory very forcefully indeed. As a result, each alert participant in the ongoing cross-disciplinary dialogue has become increasingly aware of the many ways in which every stage is a world and in which, as Shakespeare's Jaques has put it, 'all the world's a stage' (*As You Like It*). PHE

See: Aristotle's Poetics, trans. L. Golden, commentary by O. B. Hardison, Jr, Englewood Cliffs, NJ, 1968; E. Bentley, The Life of the Drama, New York, 1967; Brecht on Theatre, ed., J. Willett, New York, 1964; M. Carlson, Theories of the Theatre: A Historical and Critical Survey, from the Greeks to the Present, Ithaca, NY, 1984; K. Elam, The Semiotics of Theatre and Drama, London, 1980; N. Frye, Anatomy of Criticism, Princeton, NJ, 1957; G. W. F. Hegel, Philosophy of Fine Art, transl. F. P. B. Osmaston, London, 1920; P. Hernadi, Beyond Genre: New Directions in Literary Classification, Ithaca, NY, 1972; S. K. Langer, Feeling and Form, New York, 1953; B. O. States, Great Reckonings in Little Rooms: On the Phenomenology of Theatre, Berkeley, California, 1985; B. Wilshire, Role Playing and Identity: The Limits of Theatre as Metaphor, Bloomington, Indiana, 1982.

Draper, Ruth (1884–1956) American actress and monologuist who created and performed a repertoire of 54 different characters in some 35 sketches. The range of personalities which she assumed was broad, as was the scope of her travels and reputation. In addition to accolades for her finely wrought characterizations of women of all ages, types, and cultures were plaudits for her ability to evoke throngs of other 'unseen' characters. Prior to her professional debut in 1920, at the Aeolian Hall, London, she had been perfecting her craft before family, friends, and charity audiences. In the three and a half decades that followed, she performed almost non-stop, on every continent, and often at the command of royalty. Her letters, edited by Neilla Warren, were published in 1979. DBW

Dresden Court Theatre The first record of performances in Dresden dates from 1585, when the **Englische Komödianten** visited the court. In the late 17th century, **Johannes Velten** was employed with some regularity at the Dresden court. Operatic and dramatic performances continued regularly throughout the 18th century, but the high point in the Court Theatre's history was the long intendancy of August von Lüttichau (1785–1863), which lasted from 1824 to 1862. During these years Dresden became known as the theatre where the **Weimar style** was most assiduously cultivated. From 1831 until his death in 1872, **Emil Devrient** was an idolized member of the company, though his preeminence was challenged between 1853 and 1864, when **Bogumil Dawison** was also in the company. In 1841, the Dresden Court Theatre was housed in a splendid new theatre designed by Gottfried Semper. This was in use until its destruction in the Second World War. The restored theatre was reopened in 1985. SW

Dressler, Marie (Leila Koerber) (1869–1934) Canadian comedienne, daughter of an itinerant musician. At

An advertising card for Marie Dressler in *Tillie's Nightmare*, on tour 1910.

14 she joined the Nevada Stock Company playing ingenues, but her mastiff-like features and stocky build soon relegated her to farcical roles. She entered New York vaudeville with coon songs and impersonations, and had a real success as the music-hall singer Flo Honeydew in the comic opera *The Lady Slavey* (1896). **Joe Weber** invited her to join his company in *Higgledy-Piggledy* (1904). Her most memorable role was the day-dreaming boarding-house drudge Tillie Blobbs, in *Tillie's Nightmare* (Herald Square Theatre, 1910), singing 'Heaven Will Protect the Working Girl'. This led to a film contract with Mack Sennett for *Tillie's Punctured Romance* (1914), in which she was wooed by Charlie Chaplin; but she never flourished in silent pictures. She was prominent in the Liberty Loan drives of 1917–18 and the Actors' Strike of 1919, but reached such a low ebb in her career by 1927 that she contemplated opening an hotel in Paris. Fortuitously she returned to Hollywood and won a new public with *Anna Christie* (1930), *Dinner at Eight* and *Tugboat Annie* (both 1933). LS

Drew-Barrymore family The name 'Barrymore', with Lionel, Ethel and John its foremost exponents, stands as a synonym for acting. Franklin Delano Roosevelt was called 'a newsreel Barrymore'. Mahatma Gandhi was 'the Barrymore of the talking newspapers'. *Time* Magazine coined 'Barrymorishly' to describe how Ethel held the stage. Thirty years after she, the last of the triumvirate, died in 1959, the Barrymores remain the undisputed royal family of a kingdom called Broadway.

Their theatrical pedigree is genuine, traceable to 1752 and, according to family tradition, to strolling players in **Shakespeare**'s time. Their maternal grandmother, **Mrs John Drew** (1820–97), was born Louisa Lane in London to Thomas Frederick Lane, an actor of some provincial fame, and Eliza Trenter, a sweet singer of ballads. After her father's early death, the child toured provincial theatres, playing such roles as Prince Agib in *Timour, the Tartar*, before sailing for America with her mother. After playing such roles as the Duke of York to **Junius Brutus Booth**'s Richard III and Albert to **Edwin Forrest**'s William Tell (ten years later, she would graduate to Lady Macbeth opposite Forrest's Thane), she made her debut as a child star in 1828, playing Little Pickle in *The Spoiled Child* and five characters in *Twelve Precisely*.

In 1850, after a distinguished adolescent and adult career, she married her third husband, **John Drew** (1827–62), whose father managed Niblo's Theatre in New York. Famous for such popular Irish characters as Dr O'Toole (*The Irish Tenor*) and Tim O'Brian (*The Irish Immigrant*) and Shakespeare's Andrew Aguecheek and Dromio, Drew briefly managed Philadelphia's National and **Arch Street** theatres. Mrs Drew undertook the management of the Arch in 1861, one year before her husband's untimely death. During 30 subsequent years at the helm, she essentially contributed to the achievement and acceptance of theatre in America, while continuing to act, by popular demand, in such roles as Mrs Malaprop and Mistress Quickly.

Two of her children by Drew began illustrious careers at the Arch. **John Drew** (1853–1927) trained under his mother's stern supervision before joining **Augustin Daly**'s **Fifth Avenue Theatre** company in New York (1875). Among his most popular old and new comedy parts were Orlando, Petruchio and Charles Surface. By the mid–1800s, he and his fellow Fifth Avenue players, **Ada Rehan**, James Lewis and **Mrs G. H. Gilbert**, were called 'the Big Four'. In 1892, Drew agreed to star for manager **Charles Frohman** at the unheard of salary of $500 per week. Following his sensational debut in *The Masked Ball*, his naturalistic acting, elegant bearing and sartorial correctness won him the uncontested title 'First Gentleman of the American Stage' and kept him a reigning star for 35 years.

Georgiana Drew (1856–93), after a strict Arch Street apprenticeship, followed her older brother to the Fifth Avenue in 1876. She made an immediate hit with her breezy manner and unique way of tossing lines like nosegays to an audience, a technique which established her as a popular comedienne in such subsequent hits as *The Senator* (1889) with **William H. Crane** and *Settled Out of Court* (1892) with Frohman's Comedians. Her Fifth Avenue debut, in Daly's popular *Pique*, cast her opposite a young newcomer from England, **Maurice Barrymore** (1847–1905), whom she married in 1876.

The son of a British district commissioner in India, Barrymore left Oxford, became Amateur Middle-Weight Boxing Champion of England, changed his name from Herbert Blyth to spare his proper family

and tried acting. After his 1872 debut at the Theatre Royal, Windsor, he toured the provincial theatres for three years before sailing for America. His early years there were distinguished by successive inclusion in the companies of America's foremost managers: Augustin Daly, **Lester Wallack**, and **A. M. Palmer**. His striking beauty, sharp wit, and carefree manner made him a popular matinee idol and a sought-after leading man. His most successful characterizations included Orlando (particularly opposite **Helena Modrzejewska**), and the title roles in *A Man of the World* and *Captain Swift* (1888), which reviewers considered his 'Monte Cristo' – a role in which he, like **James O'Neill** as the count, might have toured profitably for years. But Barrymore's volatile temperament and profligate ways precluded such security. Although three of the eight plays he wrote – *Reckless Temple*, *Roaring Dick & Co.* and *Nadjezda* – also were potentially durable vehicles, the author never exploited them. He died of paresis at the age of 58, deranged and unfulfilled, leaving a legacy of three children by Georgie Drew.

Ethel (1879–1959) became the first of the three siblings to achieve stardom. At the age of 21, after six years of apprenticeship with her grandmother, her uncle John Drew, and **Sir Henry Irving** in England, her name went above the title during the Broadway run of *Captain Jinks of the Horse Marines* in 1901. Under the astute management of Charles Frohman, she became a darling of fin-de-siècle society on two continents; the term 'glamour girl' was coined for her; sons of American millionaires and English peers courted her. Declining Winston Churchill's proposal of marriage, she explained, 'I didn't think I could live up to his world. My world was the theatre.' Her world remained the theatre as 'Ethel Barrymore vehicles' such as *Alice-Sit-By-the-Fire*, *Cousin Kate*, *Lady Frederick* and *Déclassé* alternated with the stronger stuff of *A Doll's House*, *The Second Mrs Tanqueray*, *The Constant Wife*, Lady Teazle, Camille, Portia and Juliet. By birth she

Ethel Barrymore in *Captain Jinks of the Horse Marines*, her debut as a star, 1901.

Lionel Barrymore in *The Copperhead*, by Augustus Thomas.

was queen of the royal family; by achievement, with regal bearing and fluid style, she became the First Lady of the American Theatre – a fact underscored in 1928 when the **Shuberts** opened the **Ethel Barrymore Theatre** with Ethel interpreting three ages of woman in *The Kingdom of God*. After the climax of her stage career in *The Corn Is Green* (1940), she opted for lucrative, less taxing movie work until her death in Hollywood two months before her 80th birthday.

Her older brother **Lionel** (1878–1954) began acting at 15 under the tutelage of his grandmother and his uncle **Sidney Drew** (1868–1919); Sidney was Mrs Drew's illegitimate son – probably by Robert Craig, an actor in her Arch Street company. Sidney became a noted stage and vaudeville comedian, usually opposite his first wife Gladys Rankin, daughter of actor-manager McKee Rankin and his actress wife Kitty Blanchard. Lionel, in support of his uncle John Drew in *The Mummy and the Humming Bird* (1903), excelled in the small role of an Italian organ grinder without speaking a word of English. His inspired gift for characterization flourished in several subsequent productions – notably as boxer Kid Garvey in *The Other Girl* (1904), written for him by his father's friend **Augustus Thomas**. But in 1906, Lionel retreated to France with his first wife, Doris Rankin (Gladys's sister), to indulge his first love – painting. Three years later they returned to America and what Lionel called 'the family curse': acting. Interspersed with his pioneer acting in the 'flickers' from 1912, his foremost stage vehicles – *The Copperhead* (1917), *The Claw* (1921) and *Laugh, Clown, Laugh* (1923) – were eclipsed by two co-starring ventures with his brother: *Peter Ibbetson* (1917) and *The Jest* (1919). 'To the future of such actors', predicted the New York *Times*, 'it is impossible

to set any limits'. But after the failure of his *Macbeth* in 1921 and a series of mediocre plays, Lionel turned irrevocably to Hollywood. The elder Barrymore became acting's unchallenged Grand Old Man after nearly 200 film roles – the last 40 played in excruciating rheumatic pain, but with no less power, on crutches or in a wheelchair until his death at the age of 76.

His younger brother **John** (1882–1942) was even more resistant to acting. After a brief stint as a newspaper illustrator, he half-heartedly pursued, with the help of family and friends, a career as a stage comedian, while whole-heartedly pursuing debutantes and chorus girls. (Among his conquests in the former category: Katherine Harris, who became his first wife in 1913; in the latter, Evelin Nesbit and Irene Fenwick, who later became Lionel's second wife.) Then, after a run of light comedy roles like *The Fortune Hunter* (1909), John stunned critics and theatregoers with his expert delineations of tragic roles in *Justice* (1916) and *Redemption* (1918). He followed them with two of the theatre's towering achievements: the **Arthur Hopkins/ Robert Edmond Jones** productions of *Richard III* (1920) and *Hamlet* (1922), illuminated by his poetic beauty, vocal grandeur and subtle strength. 'The new prince was entering his kingdom', observed Hopkins. But at the height of his powers, touted as America's greatest actor, the crown prince of the royal family abdicated. He left the stage for films, returning only once after alcohol and self-indulgence had diminished his talents, playing a parody of himself in a travesty of a play (*My Dear Children*, 1939) three years before his death at 60.

Artistry and industry, combined with the colour and glamour of their private lives, earned the Barrymores a unique niche in the annals of American theatre. Subsequent Drew-Barrymore generations have pursued theatrical careers with considerably less distinction. Ethel's three children from her marriage to socialite Russell Colt made attempts: two sons, half-heartedly; a daughter, **Ethel Barrymore Colt** (1912–77), with some success, particularly as an opera singer and acting teacher. John's daughter **Diana** (1921–60), by his second wife socialite/poetess Michael Strange, had a brief, promising acting career curtailed by excesses similar to those of her father. John's only son, known as John Barrymore Jr or **John Drew Barrymore** (b. 1932), by his third wife, actress Dolores Costello, also sacrificed a promising screen and stage career to alcohol, drugs and self-indulgence. But his daughter, named appropriately **Drew Barrymore** (b. 1975), gained stardom, as her great-great-grandmother Mrs Drew had, at the age of seven in the film *E.T.* (1982). JK-D

Drexler, Rosalyn (1926–) American absurdist playwright whose Off-Off Broadway, avant-garde plays satirize sex, violence and domestic life. Drexler's first play, *Home Movies* (1964), blended Drexler's 'camp' humour with music by Al Carmines, a partnership which proved successful again with *The Line of Least Existence* (1968). Drexler continued her anarchic humour in such plays as *Hot Buttered Roll* (1966) and *The Writer's Opera* (1979), but she also wrote naturalistically (*The Investigation*, 1966); a feminist history of Hatshepsut (*She Who Was He*, 1974); and a poignant study of two lesbian wrestlers (*Delicate Feelings*, 1984).

She has won three Obies, most recently for *Transients Welcome* (1985). FB

Drinkwater, John (1882–1937) British dramatist, director, poet and biographer; best known for his part in the revival of poetic drama, although he made a more lasting contribution to the theatre as a founder member of Sir **Barry Jackson**'s Pilgrim Players and as the first general manager of the **Birmingham Repertory Theatre**. There he directed over 60 productions as well as acting under the stage name of John Darnley. He experimented with masques before writing his first full-length play, *Rebellion* (1914), an allegorical attack on Victorian morality. This was followed by *The Storm* (1915), inspired by **Synge**'s *Riders to the Sea*, but after his bitter lament against war, *X=O: A Night of the Trojan War* (1917), he abandoned verse. His most successful work was in historical drama, in particular *Abraham Lincoln* (1918), though he also wrote a popular comedy, *Bird in Hand* (1927), the first play in which **Peggy Ashcroft** and **Laurence Olivier** played major roles. CI

Drottningholm Court Theatre As one of the summer palaces of the Swedish kings, Drottningholm had temporary theatres from at least the 1740s and from 1753 a permanent playhouse for Italian opera and French drama. After fire destroyed this in 1762, Carl Fredrik Adelcrantz designed the present building, which opened in 1766. It has an extremely deep stage, with elaborate machinery in the Italian manner by Donato Stopani: wing-chariots, a glory, movable traps and cloud and wave machines. The auditorium, adjustable in size, is itself a painted setting, designed to mirror

the illusory world on stage. The theatre's most brilliant era was the reign of Gustav III (1771–92), when the royal opera and acting companies spent the summers there. After Gustav's assassination, it gradually fell into disuse (which paradoxically ensured its survival), until rediscovered in 1921, miraculously preserved and with a store of about 30 complete 18th-century settings by such artists as **Carlo Bibiena** and Louis Jean Desprez. It reopened in 1922, inaugurating a tradition of summer seasons that have recently, under Arnold Östman's leadership, become important musical events. HL

Drury Lane, Theatre Royal (London) For nearly two centuries, any of the four buildings erected along the network of narrow streets including Drury Lane, Bridges Street and Catharine Street could reasonably have claimed to be London's leading theatre. The first, generally known as the Theatre Royal, Bridges Street, opened in 1663 with a performance of **John Fletcher**'s *The Humorous Lieutenant*. It was a small theatre (capacity c. 700), built at the behest of **Thomas Killigrew** to house the King's Men, one of the two companies licensed by Royal Patent to perform the legitimate drama in the city of Westminster. A strong company included Charles Hart, Michael Mohun and, for a while after 1665, **Nell Gwyn**. It was destroyed by fire early in 1672.

A second theatre (capacity 2,000), probably designed by Sir Christopher Wren, opened in 1674. Its foundations are still visible under the present stage. The building was rectangular, 114 feet in length. Nine rows of backless pit benches were ringed by boxes on three sides and the stage (c. 66 feet from the probably curved front of the apron to the rear wall) in front. There were

Drottningholm Court Theatre, opened in 1766.

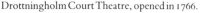

two galleries, the upper probably open as a 'footman's gallery'. The prominence of the stage doors, two on either side, emphasizes the fact that the action would have been confined to the apron, where it could be illuminated by chandeliers more concentrated than those in the auditorium. The middle section of the stage accommodated the grooves and shutters of the new scenecraft and the rear section was available for 'vistas'. Despite the compact elegance of its design, **Dryden** was not alone in considering this important theatre 'plain built – a bare convenience only'. Restoration audiences preferred the Duke's Men at the rival **Dorset Garden Theatre**, and Drury Lane experienced three decades of struggle, exacerbated by the unpopularity among actors of the new patentee, Christopher Rich. Its fortunes were restored in 1711, when three actors, Robert Wilks, **Thomas Doggett** (replaced by **Barton Booth** in 1713) and **Colley Cibber**, assumed the active management and **Anne Oldfield** was in her prime. But the costs of satisfying public demand for opera, ballet, pantomime and scenic spectacle as well as constant novelty in drama were cripplingly high for the Patent theatres, and Drury Lane experienced a series of crises from 1733–47, only temporarily alleviated by such outstanding events as **Charles Macklin**'s startlingly original playing of Shylock (1741) and the debut of **David Garrick** in **Otway**'s *The Orphan* (1742). It was Garrick himself, in association with **James Lacy**, who inaugurated the greatest years in the whole history of Drury Lane. His long management (1747–76) was a model of combined caution and daring. Although he failed in his attempts to abolish the custom of half-price admission – always an invitation to drink first and make trouble at the theatre afterwards – he succeeded in much else, not least in removing audience members from the stage. But it was in the practices of the stage that Garrick's regime most notably advanced the cause of the British theatre. He took rehearsals seriously, challenged assumptions about individual actors' 'possession' of their roles, treated the texts of the classical repertoire with a new respect and, particularly in association with **Philip De Loutherbourg**, raised the status of scenic design and explored the field of stage lighting. He surrounded himself with a strong company, including at various times **Spranger Barry**, Charles Macklin, **Kitty Clive**, **Peg Woffington**, **Susanna Cibber**, **Hannah Pritchard** and such comedians as Harry Woodward, Ned Shuter and Richard Yates. He was also responsible for the alterations to the interior of the theatre, undertaken by Robert Adam in 1775.

Garrick's unlikely successor was the playwright **Sheridan**, a man temperamentally unsuited to the chores of management. He began well with the production of his own *The School for Scandal* (1777), the most successful opening in the theatre's history. The following year, he engaged John Henderson in an attempt to replace Garrick as well as writing *The Camp*, and in 1779 he produced his last major work, *The Critic*. It was after the damage caused to Drury Lane during the Gordon Riots of 1780 that a detachment of Guards was posted nightly at the theatre, a custom not discontinued until 1896, though insufficient to prevent the attempt on George III's life in 1800. Sheridan's financial problems were eased by the success of **Sarah Siddons** in 1782 and of her brother **John Kemble** in

1783. It was to Kemble that Sheridan entrusted the effective management in 1788, but the theatre had so deteriorated that Sheridan decided to demolish it in 1791.

The third Drury Lane, designed by Henry Holland and opened in 1794, was a massive building with a capacity of 3,611. Better suited to spectacle than to drama, it marked a low point in theatrical taste. To judge from his last play, *Pizarro* (1799), Sheridan was aware of its limitations. No less aware of Sheridan's limitations, Kemble defected to **Covent Garden** in 1803, taking Sarah Siddons with him. Increasingly occupied with parliamentary affairs, Sheridan presided over a declining theatre, whose destruction by fire in 1809, notwithstanding the iron safety-curtain proudly exhibited at its opening, threatened him with utter ruin. Whilst a committee of management, ably chaired by the brewer Samuel Whitbread, set about raising funds for rebuilding, the Drury Lane company performed at the **Lyceum** from 1809–12.

The fourth theatre (original capacity 3,060), designed by Benjamin Wyatt, opened in 1812 with a prologue by **Lord Byron** and with a performance of *Hamlet* with **Robert Elliston** in the title role. The manager was Samuel Arnold, hampered by a committee of well-connected amateurs. It was the sensational debut of **Edmund Kean** in 1814 that delayed inevitable financial disaster, the joint fate of both Patent houses in the last decades of their monopoly. For nearly five seasons, Kean reigned supreme, but high living and scandal increasingly damaged him after 1819, the year in which the equally boisterous Elliston became manager of Drury Lane. By 1826, Kean was past his best and Elliston bankrupt. The improvident manager, **Charles Lamb**'s 'Great Lessee', had arranged for the addition of the portico in 1820 (John Nash's colonnade would be moved to Drury Lane from Regent Street in 1831) and Samuel Beazley's extensive remodelling of the interior in 1822. Equipped with gas-lighting since 1817, the Drury Lane which ruined successive managers until the abolition of the Patent monopoly in 1843 was a superb but costly toy. Even **Macready**'s admired attempt to restore it to its place at the head of English drama (1841–3) resulted in a loss to him of about £20,000. It was as a house of spectacle that Drury Lane survived the vicissitudes of the mid-century, a trend fully endorsed by the famous managements of Sir Augustus Harris (1879–96) and Arthur Collins (1896–1923). Their prosperity was based on sensation drama and the annual pantomime, though both men were hospitable to incursions of high art – provided they were profitable. Under Alfred Butt (1924–31), Drury Lane became the home of the English musical as it did of the American musical in the years following the Second World War, with Ivor Novello dominating the years between. A 1980 guide to London theatres described as the policy of London's greatest theatre: 'To present top musicals with wide appeal and likely to enjoy long runs'. PT

Dryden, John (1631–1700) English playwright. Educated at Westminster and Trinity College, Cambridge, he settled in London in 1657 and worked as a professional writer. Though he wrote, adapted and collaborated on at least 30 plays, they do not represent his greatest achievements as poet nor the best drama of the period. But they are marked by a consistently incisive intelligence and a seriousness that is invigorating. His first play, a comedy *The Wild Gallant*, was a failure at its first performances in 1663 – he revised it in 1668. He collaborated with Sir **Robert Howard** on *The Indian Queen* (1664), an attempt to create the new genre of heroic tragedy, depending on the hero's choice between love and honour in an exotic setting. His sequel, *The Indian Emperor* (1665), is a better and fully formed example of the genre, teetering on the edge of bombastic self-parody. In 1667 he experimented with mixing heroic tragedy and contemporary comedy in *Secret Love*, a form he returned to frequently. *Sir Martin Mar-All*, a bright comedy, possibly written with William Cavendish, Duke of Newcastle, marked a shift of allegiance from **Killigrew**'s **Drury Lane** to **Davenant**'s **Lincoln's Inn Fields** and he followed it with an adaptation of **Shakespeare**'s *The Tempest*, written with Davenant, playing up the spectacular and creating erotic frissons with new characters to balance Shakespeare's so that Miranda and Caliban each acquire sisters. In 1668 he was appointed Poet Laureate and published his major critical study, *An Essay of Dramatic Poesy*, constructed as a debate on the merits of French and English plays and establishing new principles of neoclassical judgement as applied to English drama. *Tyrannic Love*, on the martyrdom of St Catherine, was performed in 1669 but his largest-scale heroic drama, *The Conquest of Granada*, appeared in two parts in 1670 and 1671. Of his later tragedies, *Aureng-Zebe* (1675) is noticeably more restrained and points towards *All for Love*, a version of Shakespeare's *Antony and Cleopatra*, fully embodying neoclassical unities and morality to tearful effect. He adapted Milton's *Paradise Lost* into an unperformed and unperformable opera *The State of Innocence* (1677), and produced a blood-filled *Oedipus* with **Nathaniel Lee** (1679). Of his comedies, *Marriage A-La-Mode* (1672) is as witty and perceptive as *The Kind Keeper* (1678) is coarse. In 1685 he became Roman Catholic and while this earned him prestige under James II he lost the laureateship in 1689 on the accession of William and Mary. His best two plays date from this late period of his work: *Amphitryon* (1690) is a virtuoso retelling of the myth with an energy and lightness of wit that is continually surprising: *Don Sebastian* (1689), for all its comic subplot, is a dark and depressing tragedy of a king defeating rebellion but abdicating on discovering himself guilty of incest. Dryden also wrote operas at this time, notably *King Arthur* (1691) with music by Purcell. Dryden contributed numerous prologues and epilogues to others' plays and frequently engaged in literary pamphleteering on theatrical matters, particularly over **Settle**'s *The Empress of Morocco* and Rymer's attack on Shakespeare. In the range of his work over 30 years he dominated English drama of the Restoration.   PH

Držić, Marin (1508–67) Croatian playwright from Dubrovnik, educated in Siena, holder of minor offices in his Adriatic city-state, traveller to Italy and Austria. He ploted the overthrow of the patrician rule in Dubrovnik and solicited Florentine help for this purpose. He died in Venice as an exile. But between 1548–59, Držić was the main animator of amateur theatricals in Dubrovnik and creator of a small repertoire of pastorals and comedies. Some are lost, others are preserved only in incomplete form. Most famous and probably the best of these is *Uncle Maroje*, rediscovered and restaged for the first time by Marko Fotez in Zagreb just before the Second World War. *Uncle Maroje* became a regular feature in the Yugoslav repertoire and the national play most frequently produced abroad – in Scandinavia, Eastern Europe, Belgium, Holland, Turkey and America. In *Uncle Maroje*, *Tirena*, *The Farce of Stanac* and *The Miser*, Držić fuses the motifs and style of Italian Renaissance drama with local traditions, circumstances and temperament, but instances of melancholy and bitterness occasionally break through the spirit of merriment.   DK

Du Maurier, Gerald Hubert Edward (1873–1934) British actor–manager, who began his career under **Forbes-Robertson** and made his reputation with **Beerbohm Tree**. He specialized in popular drama of the clubland heroes variety (Raffles, Arsène Lupin, Bulldog Drummond), though his most important roles were in the premieres of **Barrie**'s *The Admirable Crichton* (1902), *Peter Pan* (1904) and *Dear Brutus* (1917). In 1910 he took over the management of Wyndham's Theatre, and was knighted in 1922.   CI

Du Ryer, Pierre (c. 1600–58) French dramatist, one of a group of young writers who emerged in the late 1620s in response to the establishment of permanent theatre companies in Paris. His workmanlike output, which evolved from romance-like tragicomedy, pastoral and one interesting comedy of manners, *Les Vendanges de Suresnes* (*The Grape Harvest at Suresnes*, 1633) to a more regular, heroic tragedy, as in *Alcionée* (1637) and *Scévole* (1644), which compares well with **Corneille**'s Roman plays, is a convenient barometer of trends in dramatic taste at the time. He was elected to the Académie-Française in 1646.   DR

Dubé, Marcel (1930–) French Canadian playwright, poet, novelist. The most prolific and most popular dramatist of the 1950s and 60s, he began writing for Radio-Canada in 1950 and for national television two years later. His first stage play, *Le Bal Triste* (*The Sad Ball*), was produced by a troupe he helped found, La Jeune Scène, in 1950, but he first attracted critical acclaim with *Zone*, winning first prize at the Dominion Drama Festival in 1953. This play, highly successful in its televised adaptation the same year, is typical of the first 'hungry' period of Dubé's work, portraying economically and culturally dispossessed urban youth in their defiance of social norms – in this case as smugglers on the USA/Quebec border. A second important play from this period is the even more popular *Un Simple Soldat* (*Private Soldier*, 1957), first produced on television, then revised for stage performance in 1958. His mastery of cinematic technique is evident in all his published work: no other Quebec dramatist passes as easily from one medium to the other. His themes and plots are realistic, yet his prose is infused with a poetic quality that heightens its symbolic strength, particularly in plays such as *Le Temps des Lilas* (*Lilac Time*, 1958), a depiction of love and disillusion in a decaying urban rooming-house.

Following his personal financial success, Dubé's attention turned to middle-class characters and concerns. In the 1960s his vision remained tragic, in works such as *Bilan* (*The Accounting*, 1960), *Florence* (1960), *Les Beaux Dimanches* (*Fine Sundays*, 1965) and, especially, in *Au Retour des Oies Blanches* (*The White Geese*, 1966), generally considered his finest play. In the 1970s, despite frequent illness, he has turned his hand to comedy, in *L'Eté S'appelle Julie* (*The Summer Named Julie*, 1975) and *Dites-le Avec Des Fleurs* (*Say It With Flowers*, 1976), the latter written in collaboration with **Jean Barbeau**. Author of more than 30 plays to date, plus a score of radio and television scripts, Dubé dominates his age as no previous Quebec dramatist has done. LED

Dublin Drama League Founded in 1919 by **Lennox Robinson**, with **Yeats**'s support. Managed by subscribing members, the League was allowed to use the **Abbey** stage on Sundays and Mondays, when the Abbey did not play. As a complement to the Abbey's almost wholly Irish repertoire the League presented **Pirandello**, **Toller**, **Strindberg**, **Chekhov**, **Andreev**. Abbey actors participated with amateurs, including **Denis Johnston**. The League was an enthusiastic venture, successfully bringing world drama to a Dublin audience, **Sean O'Casey** among them. The League dissolved itself in 1929, recognizing the legitimate succession of the Edwards–MacLiammóir **Gate Theatre**. DM

Dublin International Theatre Festival Emerged in 1957 from the general entertainment of An Tostal, its purpose to have plays by Irish and foreign dramatists staged annually by local and imported companies. Because of clerical objection to **O'Casey**'s *Drums of Father Ned* and a dramatization of Joyce's *Ulysses*, its second year was cancelled. Despite hand-to-mouth funding – there was no 1984 Festival – it has admirably realized its intentions and seen many notable Irish premieres. In recent years particularly its range has greatly extended beyond conventional theatre to Brazilian, Indian, Japanese, and German dance and mime. DM

Ducange, Victor (1783–1833) French novelist and dramatist. Ducange is historically important for his hostility to the restored monarchy and his activity as a political journalist. Ducange began to write for the stage in 1812 and his first real success was *Calas* (1819), a melodrama on the theme of religious fanaticism. Ducange's hallmark was his emphasis on strong emotional effect provoked by horror and pathos, well exemplified by the persecuted heroine of *Theresa ou L'Orpheline de Genève* (*Theresa or the Orphan of Geneva*). His most lasting success was *Thirty Years of a Gamester's Life* (1827), a piece on the evils of gambling. His anti-clericalism resurfaced in *Le Jésuite* (*The Jesuit*, 1820), and his final play *Il y a Seize Ans* (*Sixteen Years Ago*, 1831) was another famous tear-jerker. His own novels provided sources to some of the plays, and he also drew on Sir Walter Scott. JMCC

Duchesnois, Catherine Joséphine Rafuin (1777–1835) French actress. Born in Valenciennes, she first appeared in an amateur production there in 1797. After a debut in Versailles in 1802, she joined the **Comédie-Française** where she made up for lack of physical advantages by warmth, verve, instinct, and a strong and flexible voice. **Talma** found her an ideal partner, and audiences loved her, even calling her back on stage (which was not the custom at the time). There was a celebrated rivalry between Mlle Duchesnois and **Mlle George**, which was fed by the press. Both became *sociétaires* the same day, but Duchesnois really came into her own in 1808 when George ran off to Russia. From 1804 to 1829 she created 36 roles, including Andromaque in *Hector* (1809), Marie Stuart (1820) and Clytemnestra (1822). JMCC

Ducis, Jean-François (1733–1816) French dramatist and man of letters. Ducis is best known for his adaptations of **Shakespeare**'s plays according to the rules of the 'unities' and French neoclassical taste. His *Hamlet* (1769) was very successful and, despite the indignation of **Voltaire**, who felt that Shakespeare was a desecration of the French stage, remained popular into the 19th century. Ophelia is the daughter of Claudius; Hamlet shames his mother by presenting her with the urn containing his father's ashes; and at the end of the play he decides that the best thing he can do is to live and reign. Ducis also adapted *King Lear* (1792), *Macbeth* (1783), *Othello*, with two possible denouements (1792), as well as a *Romeo and Juliet* and *King John*. Ducis's own most popular play was *Abufar ou la Famille Arabe* (1795), which provided **Talma** with one of his greatest roles. In 1778 Ducis succeeded Voltaire at the Académie-Française. JMCC

Ducrow, Andrew (1793–1848) This uneducated son of a Belgian strongman was, in his way, a genius: an exquisite mime, and outstanding acrobat, a superb equestrian and an absolutely peerless contriver of spectacular shows. He won his fame in London at **Astley**'s in 1814 as Eloi the dumb boy in *The Forest of Bondy*, in Paris at Franconi's circus, where he was noted for his quick changes on horseback as in *The Peasant's Frolic or The Flying Wardrobe*, and his Poses Plastiques Equestriennes in which he impersonated Greek statuary on horseback. He managed Astley's with great success from 1830 to 1841, introducing brief dramas played entirely on horseback and such spectacles as his leading attraction, *The Battle of Waterloo* (1824), based on field research. Despite his theatrical acumen, he was scorned as a surly illiterate by many, who quoted his rehearsal directive, 'Cut the dialect and come to the 'osses.' His brother John (1796–1834) played at Astley's as Mr Merryman the clown from 1826, serving tea for his ponies Darby and Joan; and his second wife Louisa Woolford (1814–1900) was a distinguished equestrienne. LS

Dudley, William (1947–) British stage designer whose work ranges from grand opera to small, intimate environmental creations suggestive of street theatre, and who has in recent years been affiliated with London's **National Theatre**. After early training in landscape painting, he gained stage experience in London fringe theatre before working for five years at the **Royal Court Theatre**. Eventually tiring of the Court's stripped down, unostentatious style, Dudley moved on to work that was more reflective of 19th-century romanticism expressed with contemporary techniques. Representative productions include small-scale promenade stagings of *The Passion* (1977) and

William Dudley's design for Keith Dewhurst's *Lark Rise*,
National Theatre, London, 1978.

Lark Rise (1978) to the grander dimensions of the operas
Billy Budd (1976), *Tales of Hoffman* (1980), and **Wagner**'s *Ring* cycle at Bayreuth (1983).   JMB

Duff, Mary Ann (Dyke) (1794–1857) American
actress born in London, known as 'the American
Siddons'. She seems to have made her debut in Dublin,
but came to America with her husband, John Duff, in
1810 and made her first appearance as Juliet on New
Year's Eve that year. Until 1817 she went relatively
unnoticed, then suddenly changed her style, showing
the 'true fire of genius', and emerged as a star. She
won fame in Philadelphia and Boston rather than New York
as a tragic actress, noted by critics for her 'uniformity of
excellence'. The death of her husband in 1831 left her
with seven children; she then married the actor Charles
Young, but the marriage was soon annulled. She
married again in 1835 and retired in 1838, but returned
to the stage sporadically, appearing as late as 1850 in
Toronto. Many of the leading actors of the time
considered her the greatest actress in America.   SMA

Dukes, Ashley (1885–1959) British theatre manager, dramatic critic and dramatist, who founded the
Mercury Theatre in 1933 as a permanent base for the
ballet company run by his wife, Marie Rambert. In his
critical writing he consistently championed new
dramatists, becoming editor of **Theatre Arts
Monthly** in 1926. He adapted plays by **Anatole
France** (1914), **Georg Kaiser** and **Ernst Toller**
(1920–3 – thus introducing German expressionism to
the British stage), **Leon Feuchtwanger**, **Ferdinand
Bruckner** and **Carl Sternheim**, as well as **Niccolo
Machiavelli**'s *Mandragola* (1939). His most successful
original play was *The Man with a Load of Mischief*
(1924). In 1935 he organized a Poets' Theatre Season at
the Mercury in cooperation with the **Group Theatre**,
at which **T. S. Eliot**'s *Murder in the Cathedral* was given
its successful London premiere. Plays by **W. H.
Auden** and **Christopher Isherwood** followed, and
the theatre continued its reputation for poetic drama in
1945–6 with work by Norman Nicholson, Ronald
Duncan and **Christopher Fry**, produced by **Martin
Browne**. In 1941 Dukes joined **CEMA**, and later
became a member of the building committee for the
National Theatre.   CI

Dullin, Charles (1885–1949) French actor and director. After performing in melodrama and at the Théâtre
Antoine, Dullin was part of **Copeau**'s first company at
the **Vieux-Colombier**. He went to America with
Copeau but on his return he left to join **Gémier**, being
interested in *théâtre populaire*. He took on responsibility
for Gémier's theatre school and when, in 1922, he
assumed direction of **L'Atelier**, he retained the school,
in which many notable actors and directors including
Artaud, **Barrault**, **Blin** and **Vilar** received training.
At L'Atelier he emphasized acrobatic training, employing techniques from Music-Hall, **commedia dell'-
arte**, Japanese theatre. His repertoire followed
Copeau's, attempting to combine vigorous versions of
the classics with modern plays. He directed plays by
Salacrou and **Romains** and was one of the first to
perform **Pirandello** in France. He helped found the
Cartel in 1927. His most famous performances, often
revived, were in the central roles of **Molière**'s *The
Miser* (1922), **Jonson**'s *Volpone* (adapted by Romains,
1928) and **Shakespeare**'s *Richard III* (adapted by
Obey, 1933). In 1937 he compiled a report which
became the basis for the post-war **decentralization
movement**. In 1941 he moved to the large Théâtre
Sarah Bernhardt (renamed Théâtre de la Cité under the
German Occupation), hoping to reach a broader, more
popular audience than was possible in the tiny Atelier.
He produced a demanding repertoire there, including
Sartre's first play *The Flies* (1943), but did not achieve
the popular success he had hoped for.   DB

Dumas, Alexandre (1802–70) French dramatist and
novelist, known as *père* to distinguish him from his son.
Son of a Napoleonic general who had fallen from
favour with the emperor, he was first attracted to the
theatre by a provincial production of **Ducis**'s adaptation of *Hamlet*. By the early 1820s he had written some
vaudevilles, and a meeting with **Talma** finally decided
him on his career. His first major historical drama,
Christine, ou, Paris, Fontainebleau, Rome, was accepted
by the Théâtre-Français in 1828, but was not performed
until 1830, in a revised version, at the **Odéon**. *Henri III
et Sa Cour* (*Henry III and his Court*, 1829) was the first
great romantic drama to be staged at the Théâtre-
Français. The play, which contains many elements of
the melodrama, opened the way at the first French
theatre to a staging which attempted in costumes and
scenery to recreate a given historical period, and thus to
an overall concept of *mise-en-scène*. The 1830 revolu-

tion led to a wave of new plays about Napoleon (no longer a forbidden subject). Dumas's contribution was *Napoléon Bonaparte; ou, Trente Ans de l'Histoire de France* (*Napoleon Bonaparte; or, Thirty Years of French History*), a six-act drama in 23 scenes, with **Frédérick Lemaître** in the title role. His first real triumph was a modern-dress play *Antony* with **Bocage** and **Marie Dorval**, at the Porte-Saint-Martin in 1831. This powerful play with its theme of the outsider is an exciting melodrama, but the villain is society with its prejudices against illegitimacy. It is the first great 'problem play' of the 19th century. In 1834 it was banned at the Théâtre-Français. In 1831 the Odéon staged another major historical drama by Dumas, *Charles VII chez Ses Grands Vassaux* (*Charles VII with his Great Vassals*). In 1832, Dumas rewrote Gaillardet's play submitted to **Harel** at the Porte-Saint-Martin, *La Tour de Nesle*, a cloak-and-dagger piece in which crime from the past catches up on its perpetrators in the most horrible manner possible. This piece, which afforded Bocage, as the avenger/villain/hero Buridan, one of the most flamboyant roles of the 19th century, remained immensely popular and continued to be revived well into the 20th century. Further dramas included *Angèle* (1833), *Catherine Howard* (1834) and *Kean; or, Disorder and Genius* (1836), another actor's vehicle, about the English actor **Edmund Kean**, in which the most striking scene is a defiant insult hurled from the 'stage' at the Prince of Wales.

Dumas had long wanted a theatre of his own for the 'new' drama and in 1837 he and **Victor Hugo** rented the Ventadour and renamed it Théâtre de la Renaissance, opening it with Hugo's *Ruy Blas*. The popularity of the *drame romantique* was on the wane and this venture lasted less than three years. In 1839 Dumas's talents as a writer of historical comedy were shown in the successful *Mademoiselle de Belle-Isle* at the Théâtre-Français. The 1830s saw the rise of the serial story in newspapers. In 1838, Dumas adapted Fenimore Cooper's *The Pirate* as *Le Capitaine Paul* for *Le Siècle*, increasing the number of subscribers by 5,000 in three weeks, and in 1844 his two most famous novels appeared in serial form: *The Three Musketeers* and *The Count of Monte Cristo*. In 1846 there was *The Chevalier de Maison Rouge* and *The Lady of Monsoreau*, in 1848 *The Viscount de Bragelonne*, in 1849 *The Queen's Necklace* and in 1850 *The Black Tulip*. His second venture into theatre management came with the creation of the Théâtre Historique (1847) on the Boulevard du Temple, built according to his specifications, which opened with his *Reine Margot*, and presented a series of adaptations of his own novels, often written in collaboration with Auguste Maquet. The theatre closed in 1851, becoming an opera house until its demolition in 1863. Dumas's later years were largely devoted to the 20 volumes of his *Mémoires* (1852–54), to eight volumes of *Souvenirs de 1830–1842* (1855) and his *Souvenirs dramatiques* (1868), interesting, if inaccurate, sources of theatre history. He also launched his own newspaper, *Le Mousquetaire* (1853–7 and 1865–6) and *Le Monte Cristo* (1857–62). Dumas's own life was as colourful and extravagant as his fiction, and in total contrast to that of his rather puritanical illegitimate son, author of *The Lady of the Camellias*. JMCC

Dumas, Alexandre (1824–95) French novelist and dramatist, known as Dumas *fils*. The younger Dumas's main area of interest was the wealthy society of the Second Empire and Third Republic, which he examined with the eye of a severe moralist whilst dealing with themes considered 'risqué' at the time. In 1844 he met Alphonsine Duplessis, a high class courtesan, who became his mistress and was the model for his novel *La Dame aux Camélias* (1848), which he adapted for the stage, was accepted at the Vaudeville in 1850, but rejected three times by the censors before a change of Minister of the Interior made performance possible in 1852. The play subsequently became the basis for the libretto of Verdi's *La Traviata* (1853). His comedy *Le Demi-Monde* (Théâtre du Gymnase 1855) virtually created a new term for the French language – the woman with a past who will appear so frequently in the drama of the late 19th century. In 1865 the Théâtre-Français opened its doors to Dumas (and his collaborator Emile de Girardin) for his drama *Le Supplice d'Une Femme* (*A Woman's Torture*). His other most important play for this theatre was *L'Etrangère* (1876) which explored the theme of marital infidelity. The same year, under the pseudonym Pierre Newsky, his rewriting of a play by an amateur author, *Les Danicheff*, became one of the greatest and least expected successes of the 19th century at the **Odéon** (the cast included **Sarah Bernhardt**'s dog). JMCC

Dumb show Dumb shows as a feature of serious drama flourished in Tudor England. In the actionless tragedies that followed in the wake of *Gorboduc* (1562), they were a spectacular element. Early dumb shows were characteristically allegorical, employing symbolic figures rather than actual characters from the play, but the professional playwrights of Elizabethan England perceived the theatrical advantages to be gained by exploiting dumb shows to focus the attention of the audience on significant deeds outside the strict sequence of the play's narrative. There are famous examples in **Kyd**'s *The Spanish Tragedy* (c. 1589), **Peele**'s *The Old Wives Tale* (published 1595) and the anonymous *A Warning for Fair Women* (1599). **Munday**, like many other writers of plays on legendary heroes, found the dumb show particularly useful in the control of an awkwardly spreading plot. **Shakespeare** was less addicted than many of his contemporaries, though the dumb show that introduces the play-within-the-play in *Hamlet* is the most familiar of all. It is deployed in a consciously archaic way, since the vogue for introductory dumb shows had long passed. Still more unusual is its description of the whole play rather than of a single episode. **Webster** and **Middleton** continued to exploit dumb shows to sensational effect after they had been incorporated in the more spectacular masque, but they ceased to be a feature of tragedy during the reign of James I. PT

Dunlap, William (1766–1839) American playwright and manager. Dunlap has often been called 'the father of American drama'. He wrote or translated and adapted more than 50 plays. Half of them were originals; the other half adaptations from the French and German, principally from **Kotzebue**. He managed the **Park Theatre** (1798–1805), an undertaking that ended disastrously. He was apparently too good-natured to be hard-headed about financial matters. Still he persisted, managing the Park again (1806–11) for the actor **Thomas A. Cooper**. Even if poor at business, he was the first manager to write and present his own plays, the first to champion native subject matter and native dramatists, and the first to record his experiences and those of others in his *History of the American Theatre* (1832).

Most notable among his original plays: *Darby's Return* (1789), *The Father* (1799), *André* (1798) which he later transformed into a patriotic spectacle for holiday performance as *The Glory of Columbia* (1803) with backdrops and transparencies by Charles Ciceri, *Leicester* (1806), and *A Trip to Niagara, or Travellers in America* (1828) with a diorama of 18 scenes along the Hudson as a steamboat moves up the river from New York to Catskill landing. His most popular adaptations: *The Stranger* (1798), *False Shame* (1799), and *Pizarro in Peru* (1800), all from Kotzebue; and from the French: *The Wife of Two Husbands* (1804, **Pixérécourt**), and *Thirty Years, or the Life of a Gamester* (1828, Goubaux and **Ducange**).

Born in Perth Amboy, New Jersey, Dunlap began his artistic life as a painter, studied with Benjamin West in England (1784–7), became fascinated with the theatre when he saw *The School for Scandal* and *The Critic* with their original casts, and on his return to New York where he saw **Royall Tyler**'s *The Contrast*. Besides his work in the theatre, he painted a host of miniatures, portraits (one of George Washington), and monumental religious canvases such as *Christ Rejected* (12 by 18 feet). He was director of the American Academy of Fine Arts (1817), a founder of the National Academy of Design (1826), and a professor of historical painting at the National Academy (1830–9). He wrote biographies of the actor **George Frederick Cooke** (1813) and the novelist Charles Brockden Brown (1815), a *History of the Arts of Design* (1834), *Thirty Years Ago, or Memoirs of a Water Drinker* (1836), and a *History of New York for Schools* (1837). RM

Dunnock, Mildred (1900–91) American actress and director who first appeared in New York in 1932, after which she played several seasons of stock. After a number of Broadway appearances, she achieved stardom with such roles as Linda Loman in *Death of a Salesman* (1949) and Big Mama in *Cat on a Hot Tin Roof* (1955). She played a number of seasons with the **American Shakespeare Festival** in both classic and modern roles and in 1965 directed *Graduation* on Broadway. She usually appeared in major supporting roles, relying on a slight stature and tremendous voice to project an ineffectual gentility.

She made her film debut in *The Corn Is Green* (1945), and later appeared in such successful films as *Death of a Salesman* (1951), *Viva Zapata!* (1952), *The Jazz Singer* (1953), *Baby Doll* (1956), and *Sweet Bird of Youth* (1962). She also appeared on many television series and specials. SMA

Dunsany, Edward John Moreton Drax Plunkett (Lord) (1878–1957) Anglo-Irish dramatist, novelist and critic, whose ironic fantasies in exotic settings were connected with the Irish literary revival. After *The Glittering Gates* (1909) and *King Argimenes* (1911) at the **Abbey Theatre** in Dublin, his later work was mainly produced at the **Haymarket** and **Every-**

man **Theatres** in London and in the USA, the most successful being *If* (1921) in which time is reversed and telescoped. CI

Durang, Christopher (1949–) American playwright and actor, born in Montclair, New Jersey, and educated at Harvard and Yale, Durang had his first play produced in 1971, emerging as a substantial American dramatist in the late 1970s and early 1980s. His best-known scripts include *When Dinah Shore Ruled the Earth* (with **Wendy Wasserstein**, in 1975), *A History of the American Film* (1976), the highly controversial *Sister Mary Ignatius Explains It All for You* and *The Actor's Nightmare* (1982), *Beyond Therapy* (1982), *Baby with the Bath Water* (1984), and *The Marriage of Bette and Boo* (1985). For *Sister Mary Ignatius* Durang won the Obie Award in 1980. SMA

Duras, Marguerite (1914–) French novelist, script writer and playwright. Duras's contribution is to have blurred the distinctions between the genres: her disembodied voices speak hauntingly through novels and films as much as through the theatre. Her plays, sometimes adapted from her stories like her first, *Le Square* (*The Square*, 1956), present a stream of discourse, through which characters seek to make contact with one another but seldom succeed. Her plays have been successful on radio, where their lack of dramatic action is less of a disadvantage. Madeleine Renaud has performed in many of her plays, including *Des Journées Entières dans les Arbres* (1956) (*Days in the Trees* starred **Peggy Ashcroft** at the Aldwych in 1968) and *Eden-cinéma* (1977). DB

Durov Family of Russian clowns and animal trainers. The brothers **Vladimir Leonidovich** (1863–1934) and **Anatoly Leonidovich** (1864–1916), scions of the gentry, left school and played in showbooths and menageries in several capacities before discovering their proper role as satiric clowns. Vladimir was renowned as a trainer, using new principles based on Pavlov's experiments; with his pigs, rats and dogs in such sketches as 'The Pied Piper of Hamelin' and 'The Russo-Japanese War' he attacked bureaucratic corruption and administrative malpractice. Both brothers frequently got into trouble with the police and authorities, but it was Anatoly, the more sardonic and poetic satirist, who was gaoled in Berlin for *lèse-majesté* to Wilhelm II. Wearing almost no makeup, Anatoly always began his act with a monologue in verse; he toured Europe from 1890, and anunciated a theory of comedy.

After the Revolution, Vladimir, who had founded his own menagerie in 1912, retired to experiment in animal behaviour. Of his progeny, four children and two grandchildren went into the circus, as did two children and two grandchildren of Anatoly. These successors, the most important being **Yury Vladimirovich** (1910–71), **Anatoly Anatol'evich** (1894–1928), and **Vladimir Grigor'evich** (1909–72), concentrated on animal tricks rather than satire under the Soviets. LS

Dürrenmatt, Friedrich (1921–90) Swiss playwright, novelist and essayist, arguably the best known 'German' dramatist of the 20th century beside **Brecht**.

Born in Konolfingen, son of a Calvinist pastor. Studied classics, German literature and philosophy at the Universities of Berne and Zurich (1941–5), leaving without taking his exams. Interested in drawing and, especially, caricatures. His first play *It is Written* was presented at the Zurich Schauspielhaus in 1947, and caused a scandal because of the satirical nature of the work. Scandal and controversy attend many of Dürrenmatt's best plays as he cynically asks uncomfortable questions about the complacency of post-Second World War Switzerland. Success came with *Romulus the Great* (1949), 'an unhistorical historical comedy', compound of **Jarry**'s *Ubu Roi* and **Pirandello**'s *Henry IV*, containing already the quintessential mixture of sour comedy and unfulfilled tragedy which is Dürrenmatt's hallmark. *The Marriage of Mr Mississippi* (1952) plays freely with theatrical conventions and turns a string of murders into so many comic events. In *The Visit* (1955) which triumphed the world over and *The Physicists* (1962) Dürrenmatt casts a desperate look over mankind and concludes that hope is not reasonable. The bleakness of the parables is redeemed, as often in his plays, by a dazzling theatrical inventiveness. *The Visit* concerns millionaire Claire Zachanassian's return to her small home town where, in her youth, she was seduced and abandoned by Ill. She seeks revenge and, to get it, she bribes the entire population: every man, woman and child will be rich for the rest of their lives if they agree to put Ill to death. After a feeble moral struggle and a travesty of a trial, the people of Güllen condemn and execute the erstwhile lover. In so doing they condemn themselves and Dürrenmatt condemns society as a whole. In *The Physicists* a Pirandellian device cleverly blurs the edges separating reality from fiction, sanity from reason: the confusion between the sane world and the asylum presented on stage and between the responsible scientists and the mad atomic physicists is never 'happily' resolved. *Frank V* (1959), 'opera for a private bank', is an indictment of the modern totalitarian state and mocks the derisory situation of the individual. For the Basle Stadttheater, Dürrenmatt adapted **Shakespeare**'s *King John* (1968–9), directed by Werner Düggelin, and **Strindberg**'s *The Dance of Death* which became *Play Strindberg* (1969), an even sparer and harsher drama than the original, now Dürrenmatt's most performed play. *Woyzeck* followed in 1972. *The Partaker* (1973), a bleak descent into a putrid, post-Dachau netherworld where injustice rules supreme, had little success. Recently Dürrenmatt has been concentrating on prose writing. He is also the author of a number of important essays on playwriting and theatre theory. His scenically pyrotechnic style is caustic, iconoclastic and relies on the exploitation of the grotesque. Like **Ionesco**, he is convinced that the profound tragedy of our time can only be expressed through farce.   cls

Duse, Eleonora (1858–1924) Italian actress. Born into the profession, as a child she acquired considerable stage experience touring throughout Italy with her parents, who were poor players of modest rank. Her apprenticeship was long and hard, and more than once she came close to abandoning the profession. In 1879 she joined the company of **Giovanni Emanuel**: her parts opposite him included Desdemona and Ophelia. Later she achieved notable success in **Zola**'s *Thérèse*

Raquin (1879), which gave her status in the profession, but did not deliver her of the need, standard in the Italian theatre of the day, to tour constantly from one city to another. Such touring was particularly demanding on Duse, for her health was poor and she suffered frequent illness. Again she was tempted to leave the stage, but persevered when she saw performances by **Sarah Bernhardt**, during one of that actress's Italian visits. In Turin, in 1884 she achieved a major triumph, in **Verga**'s *Cavalleria Rusticana* (*Rustic Chivalry*). Following this she toured for the first time abroad, to South America, and in 1887 formed with the lead actor, Flavio Andò, the Compagnia Città di Roma, playing in 19th-century stock-pieces, particularly adaptations from French dramatists like **Sardou** and **Dumas** *fils*, as well as in **Goldoni** and **Giacosa**.

Duse had a long and intimate relationship with the composer and librettist **Arrigo Boito**, who questioned the worth of her stock repertoire and encouraged her to undertake artistically more ambitious work. He translated **Shakespeare**'s *Antony and Cleopatra* for her; first performed at the Teatro Manzoni in Milan in 1888, and brought to London in 1893, though not to the satisfaction of English critics. Her first significant triumph abroad was in 1891, when she opened in St Petersburg with *La Signora dalle Camelie* (*The Lady of the Camellias*); it was the start of a long international career that took her to most parts of Europe and to the United States and won her wide acclaim.

If it was in the 1890s that Duse established her international career, it was in the late 90s too that she entered into one of the most influential and painful relationships of her life: that with the Italian poet and dramatist, **Gabriele D'Annunzio**. For several years from 1896 she devoted much of her time, art and money to seeking to realize D'Annunzio's dream of a new, revolutionary, poetic drama that would achieve in modern times a theatre comparable to that of classical Greece. Notwithstanding her disappointment that D'Annunzio gave his first play, *La Città Morta* (*The Dead City*), to Bernhardt for performance in Paris, in 1898, in the same year she acted in his short pieces, *Sogno di un Mattino di Primavera* (*Dream of a Spring Morning*) and *Sogno di un Tramonto d'Autunno* (*Dream of an Autumn Sunset*), and went on to produce his *La Gioconda* (1899), *La Gloria* (1899) and *Francesca da Rimini* (1901), playing these abroad as well as in Italy. Her later repertoire expanded to include other serious modern drama, notably the work of **Ibsen**, including *A Doll's House*, *Hedda Gabler*, *Rosmersholm* (for which **Edward Gordon Craig** did the scenery), and *The Lady from the Sea*, the part of Elida being one of her last major roles. After the break up of her relationship with D'Annunzio, she continued to tour both in Italy and abroad into the 1920s.

In Italy at least however Duse was considered by many to be more than just a 'star' performer: her very individual talent, her high seriousness of purpose, and her working associations with many of the leading cultural figures of the age in Italy and abroad seemed to bring an intellectual prestige to the Italian theatre which it had long lacked. Certainly her acting style was felt by many to embody something new. Commenting on Duse in an interview **Adelaide Ristori** perceptively, if rather waspishly, characterized the stage *persona* of her younger colleague as that of the archetypal *fin de siècle* woman: 'Duse has created for herself her own mannerisms, she has created a kind of convention peculiar to herself: according to this she is the modern woman with all her maladies of hysteria, anaemia and neurosis, and with all their consequences.' A keen admirer, **Bernard Shaw**, defined her 'modernist' style more generously, seeing it as the application of the grand tradition of theatrical romantic realism, the disciplined, restrained force of a Ristori or a **Salvini**, to interpretations appropriate to the new age: Duse was, claimed Shaw, 'the first actress whom we have seen applying the method of the great school to characteristically modern parts, or to characteristically modern conceptions of old parts'. KR LR

Duym, Jacob (1547–?1612–20) In the career of Jacob Duym the history of the Low Countries in the second half of the 16th century is reflected. Duym, of a noble Brabant family, was invalided out of the army of William of Orange after having been in Spanish captivity and moved to Leyden in 1588, where he became poetic leader (*keizer*) of the Flemish Chamber of Rhetoric in exile, The Orange Lily (founded 1590). In that capacity he wrote 12 plays, using classical and national historical material. Duym created a new type of play which combined the allegorical character and the didactic moralizations of the *spel van sinnen* with the narrative epic character of secular and religious 16th-century drama. The plays are no longer merely dramatized disputes, the characters more than allegorical abstractions or collectives. The traditional *sinnekens* develop into characters of flesh and blood, who keep to some extent their usual role of scandal-mongers and entertainers, but are portrayed as servants of the main characters and take on the role of reporters for and informers of the audience. New too is Duym's frequent use of comic intermezzi, similar to the comic interludes in Elizabethan drama and employing lower-class characters. The *rondeau*, often used in *sinneken* scenes, is here employed for the comic interlude.

Each of Duym's plays is accompanied by elaborate stage directions. Costumes, decor and special effects are carefully described and often fairly complex. Duym uses three different types of staging according to the kind of play performed. Allegorical abstract plays, less abstract plays or siege plays are respectively performed on a stage with neutral entrances and mansions, a stage with more and specific entrances and mansions or a larger stage with specific and realistically rendered locations. ES

Dybwad, Johanne (1876–1950) The greatest Norwegian actress of her generation, Dybwad trained at the **Nationale Scene**, Bergen, before moving to Christiania Theatre and **Nationaltheatret**, where she acted for some 50 years, often opposite **Egil Eide** and August Oddvar. Her best work was under the direction of **Bjørn Bjørnson**, who encouraged her simplicity and naturalness. Later in her career, she was often accused of overexploiting her virtuosity to create sensational effects. Among her 20 **Ibsen** roles were a complex, serious Nora, Hedvig, a very natural Hilde Wangel, Mrs Alving and Aase. Other celebrated roles included the name parts in **Gunnar Heiberg**'s *Aunt Ulrikke* and **Bjørnstjerne Bjørnson**'s *Paul Lang and Tora Parsberg*. From 1906, she also frequently directed, sometimes with herself in the lead. Intense and demanding, she took great liberties with the text to reinforce her sometimes eccentric interpretations. HL

E

Echegaray, José (1832–1916) Spanish playwright who combined a prolific output with high office in Government finance. His first produced play was *El libro talonario* (*The Chequebook*, 1874) and this was followed by more than 60 further plays, mostly great popular successes with bourgeois theatre audiences. They combine melodramatic and sentimental plots with exaggerated solutions. In *El hombre negro* (*The Man in Black*, 1898) for instance, an elderly guardian causes his beautiful ward to contract leprosy and persuades her to enter a convent to prevent her from marrying a young sculptor, who wins her after blinding himself to prove the purity of his love. Echegaray's historical verse melodramas such as *El hijo de don Juan* (*The Son of Don Juan*, 1892) have lasted better than his plays in the *alta comedia* style, such as *El gran Galeot* (*The Great Galeoto*, 1881) in which malicious gossip forces two lovers together despite themselves. His Nobel Prize in 1904 aroused great protest from the new literary generation, and his domination of the Spanish stage for 30 years delayed the revitalization of the theatre evident in other countries.   CL

Ecuador The territory of the Incas extended into what is present-day Ecuador, but because the centre of power was located in Peru, that rich cultural heritage is affiliated more with Ecuador's neighbour to the south. Rich in natural resources but poor in development, Ecuador sits astride the Equator, for which it is named, with four major divisions in its geographical configuration, ranging from the tropical coastlands to the remote and exotic jungle regions. Progressively diminished in size over the years by avaricious neighbours, Ecuador has been overshadowed by a combination of foreign exploitation, overt admiration of France, and internal politics that have systematically, since the time of independence, wreaked havoc with the socio-economic structure of the country. Of all the South American countries, Ecuador may be among the poorest in early cultural development, although both Quito, the capital, and Guayaquil, the coastal city, are important metropolitan centres. Ricardo Descalzi, an indefatigable researcher and playwright as well, has documented the history of the Ecuadorian theatre in six volumes, even though an independent theatre activity from the early period is notably lean.

As with other colonial sites, however, visiting troupes brought theatre to the area. They performed primarily in the grand rooms of manorial houses or in churches and plazas. There is evidence of some original local production, but many texts have been lost. The earliest pieces preserved were an *entremés* and some **loas** by the priest Diego Molina, performed around 1732.

After independence in the early 19th century the internationally-known poet José Joaquín de Olmedo (1780–1847) wrote plays that were performed in Lima where he was studying, but all have been lost with the exception of one small *loa*. Throughout the 19th century a broad array of dramatists was active, including Juan Montalvo (1832–89) who wrote five plays in *The Book of the Passions*. Much of the work of the period, however, now appears to have had little transcendental value.

20th century The first decades of the 20th century continued the hyperbolic romantic tendencies of the previous century. In 1925 the National Dramatic Company was created in Quito and produced plays of **Jacinto Benavente** and Florencio Sánchez, Spaniard and Uruguayan, respectively. After a 1926 contest for dramatic companies, however, in which the National won first place, it soon ceased to exist. Jorge Icaza (b. 1906), who later achieved international fame for his Indian novel *Huasipungo* (1934), wrote six plays between 1928 and 1932 that combined psychoanalytical techniques and social class consciousness.

The so-called Generation of 1930 and the Guayaquil Group had a major impact on arts and letters in Ecuador. The five creative individuals who comprise the Group were dedicated to leftist, social reforms. The important theatrical figure to emerge from the Group was **Demetrio Aguilera Malta** (1909–79), also novelist and diplomat, whose earliest play is from 1938, *España leal* (*Loyal Spain*). His plays revealed both his dedication to social justice and to artistic integrity, as he experimented with techniques of expressionism and magical realism, seen especially in *El tigre* (*The Tiger*, 1955) and *Dientes blancos* (*White Teeth*, 1955). Another novelist, Pedro Jorge Vera (b. 1914), followed with *El Dios de la selva* (*God of the Jungle*) in 1941 and *Luto eterno* (*Eternal Mourning*, 1954), an adaptation of a homonymous novel in which he satirized the family rituals that accompany death.

The creation of the Teatro Experimental Universitario (University Experimental Theatre) in 1955 brought some coherence to the Quito theatre movement when Sixto Salguero with his ties to the Generation of 1930 provided new impetus to the popular theatre movement. Francisco Tobar García had organized the Teatro Independiente in 1954 and the group functioned until 1970. In Guayaquil the Teatro Experimental Universitario Agora was founded in 1958 by Francisco Villar, later directed by Ramón Arias. In this formative period many other groups were also created and gave rise to what Gerardo Luzuriaga has described as the Generation of 1960, when the Ecuadorian theatre for the first time achieved a sense of national identity.

In 1962 the Casa de la Cultura (House of Culture) requested through UNESCO a technical director who could infuse fresh life into the Ecuadorian theatre. In October 1963 the Italian director Fabio Pacchioni arrived under the auspices of the Ministry of Education to organize theatre seminars and to begin the process of building a new artistic expression. When the first seminar was concluded in 1964, the Teatro Ensayo (Rehearsal Theatre) was formed to train actors and other theatre personnel. The Teatro Ensayo staged several plays in each of the succeeding seasons, drawing on classical works by **Lope de Rueda** and **Cervantes**, while at the same time mounting both old and new works by Ecuadorian writers such as Aguilera Malta and **José Martínez Queirolo** (b. 1931). The latter's *Requiem por la lluvia* (*Requiem for the Rain*, 1960) is a socially-committed monologue with international appeal. The group went on tour within the country in an effort to raise the consciousness of theatre on a wider national scale. Antonio Ordóñez was a member of the original group and became the functional director in 1968.

Other groups that have influenced the direction of Ecuadorian theatre include the Teatro Experimental Ecuatoriano, established in 1971 and directed by Eduardo Almeida. A popular theatre group with a strong socio-political commitment, it has participated in many national and international festivals, including those of Rennes, Oporto, Amsterdam and Stockholm. Carlos Villalba has worked tirelessly with the Colegio Luciano Andrada Marín (CLAM) to form groups of actors who have at times splintered off to form other groups. Mojiganga was formed by a Belgian, Carlos Theus, in 1977. Other groups include the Ollantay (directed by Carlos Villarreal), El Juglar (directed by Ernesto Suárez) and the Taller de Teatro Popular (Popular Theatre Workshop) directed by the talented Ilonka Vargas, an actress and professor at the Central University. For the most part, these groups share in a commitment to develop a serious popular theatre that can respond to the needs and aesthetic sensibilities of the Ecuadorian public.

The functioning groups have not only promoted national theatre, but, as a part of the consciousness-raising process, have presented a range of Latin American works by such authors as **Agustín Cuzzani**, **Osvaldo Dragún** and **Andrés Lizárraga** of Argentina, **Jorge Díaz** of Chile, and Millor Fernandes and João Cabral de Melo Neto of Brazil. **Enrique Buenaventura** of Colombia and **Augusto Boal** of Brazil have worked with groups to develop techniques of collective or group theatre, common throughout Latin America in the 1970s. As the Ecuadorian groups have become more disciplined, and more exposed to regular participation in international theatre festivals in Manizales, Caracas and Europe, for example, the impetus for the growth and development of a national theatre has been even greater. After José Martínez Queirolo, whose later works include *Los unos vs. los otros* (*Some Against Others*, 1968), a story of rich vs. poor set in a boxing context, younger authors worthy of mention are: Jorge Dávila Vásquez with *Con gusto a muerte* (*With a Taste of Death*, 1977), Hugo Salazar Tamariz's *En tiempos de la colonia* (*In Colonial Times*, 1979) and Eliécer Cárdenas's *Polvo y ceniza* (*Dust and Ashes*, 1980). The Ecuadorian theatre is still struggling in its

process of self-identification and self-realization, but the efforts of talented individuals in the two major cities of Quito and the port city of Guayaquil, not to mention smaller cities in the interior, spur new levels of excitement and activity. The repressive political climate has taken its toll over the years, and military dictatorship alternating with unenlightened despots have not fostered the development of much activity. Nevertheless, the movement is growing and becoming more firmly established.   GW

See: R. Descalzi, *Historia crítica del teatro ecuatoriano*, Quito, 1968; G. Luzuriaga, *Del realismo al expresionismo: El teatro de Aguilera Malta*, Madrid, 1971; *idem*, 'La generación del 60 y el teatro', *Caravelle*, No. 30 (1980).

Edgar, David (1948–) British dramatist, one of several left-wing writers who were 'politicized' at university by the events of 1968, including the riots in Chicago and Paris. After a spell as a journalist on the Bradford *Telegraph and Argus*, Edgar turned to writing agit-prop plays for The General Will, a touring political theatre company, whose targets included the Conservative government of Edward Heath, the rent act and a strike on the Upper Clyde. These illustrated Edgar's gift for quick research, lively writing and the telling image, the skills of a cartoonist. In two years, from 1971 to 1973, he wrote ten plays and collaborated on two others, *England's Ireland* (1972) and *A Fart for Europe* with **Howard Brenton** (1973). Edgar's best work from this period came when he found a vivid popular form which matched the ideas and political views which he was so eager to express, as in the pantomime *Tedderella* (1971 and in London, 1973), or the melodrama *Dick Deterred* (1974) about the Watergate scandal. In 1973–4, Edgar started to move away from agit-prop towards a more complex theatrical language, social realism, taking as one of his subjects the growth of fascism within Britain. *Destiny* (1976) concerned the rise of a fictitious political party, Nation Forward, based on the real National Front. The **Royal Shakespeare Company** produced it at Stratford (1976) and then on their main London stage at the Aldwych Theatre in 1978. *Destiny* demonstrated Edgar's audacious ability to write an epic play with a large theme and spreading over a substantial span of time, which was later proved again by *Maydays* (1983) in which Edgar charted the growing disillusion of British socialists since the war. Edgar also adapted *Nicholas Nickleby* for the Royal Shakespeare Company, which became a major success for the RSC both in Britain and the United States. Most recently (1987), his *Entertaining Strangers*, first devised for the town of Dorchester as a community play, has been staged in promenade form by the **National Theatre**.   JE

Edinburgh Festival The Edinburgh International Festival of Music and Drama (1947 to the present day) presents a programme of first class international music and drama, as well as art exhibitions, opera and dance, in August and September each year. It is primarily an international occasion, but it has also provided a focus for Scottish theatrical achievement. Here, its most notable success was **Tyrone Guthrie**'s production of Sir David Lindsay's medieval morality play, *An Satyre of the Thrie Estaites* (first performed at the Assembly Halls on the Mound in 1948). From the very beginning, the official festival attracted a large number of smaller events. Their presence was ultimately recognized by the formation of the Edinburgh Fringe Festival Society. The Fringe offers a wide range of theatrical activities in halls and on the streets throughout the city. It has long been seen as a spawning ground for new talent and, on occasion, outshines its official counterpart.   LM

Edwardes, George (1852–1915) Irish-born theatre manager whose first important job was that of manager of the newly opened Savoy in 1881. Under direction from Richard D'Oyly Carte, he there supervised the staging of three **Gilbert** and Sullivan operas. In 1885, Edwardes entered partnership with **John Hollingshead** at the **Gaiety**, becoming sole manager the following year. His flair was immediately apparent in his employment of **Fred Leslie** as his leading comedian. Almost from the start, Edwardes was known as the 'Guv'nor'. He trained and made famous the chorus of Gaiety Girls and was the supreme impresario of the new style of musical comedy, which he introduced not only at the Gaiety, but also at the other London theatres he came to manage, Daly's, the **Adelphi**, the **Prince of Wales's** and the Apollo. Among the many stars who first made their name under Edwardes's management were Gertie Millar, Ellaline Terriss, **Seymour Hicks**, Marie Tempest, Constance Collier and Gladys Cooper, and among the many musicals he promoted were *The Merry Widow* (1907), *Our Miss Gibbs* (1909) and *The Quaker Girl* (1910).   PT

Edwards, Jango (Stanley Ted Edwards) (1950–) American clown. After phases as a student and a hippy, he studied clowning in London in 1971, when he founded his first theatre group; this eventually developed into the 'Friends Roadshow', which toured Europe regularly. Obscene, anarchic and using rock-concert techniques, Edwards revolutionized the European concept of clown shows and in 1975 organized a mass international gathering of clowns, musicians and fringe theatres at his Amsterdam headquarters, a 'Feast of Fools' which became an annual event.   LS

Efremov, Oleg Nikolaevich (1927–) Soviet stage and film actor, director in the **Stanislavsky** tradition of inner-directed emotional experiencing (*perezhivaniye*). Upon graduating from the studio school of the **Moscow Art Theatre** (1949), he joined the Moscow's Central Children's Theatre as an actor, making his directing debut in 1955. In 1957 he founded and directed the 'Studio of Young Actors', composed of actors from various theatres as well as students from the MAT studio school. In 1958 this became the Sovremennik (Contemporary) Theatre, so named because it sought to become the voice of the post-Thaw generation of the later 1950s. In intimate, psychologically based realistic plays through which the actors engaged in lyrical self-expression, they paid homage to the Stanislavskian collective ideal while opposing the moribund 'realism' which then characterized MAT productions. The company, performing at first in the ballroom of the Moskva (Moscow) hotel, opened with **Viktor Rozov**'s family war drama *Alive Forever*, which became the theatre's signature piece. Rozov and **Aleksandr Volodin**, whose *Two Flowers* (1959), *The Elder Sister* (1962) and *The Appointment* (1963) they also

produced, became house playwrights. Other notable Sovremennik productions included: **Evgeny Shvarts**'s *The Naked King* (1962) and *The Dragon*, which was removed from the repertoire after only four performances; Rozov's *On the Wedding Day* (1964), *The Reunion* (1967) and *From Night to Noon* (1969); **Vasily Aksyonov**'s social satire *Always on Sale* (1965); contemporary Western plays such as **William Gibson**'s *Two for the Seasaw* (1963), **John Osborne**'s *Look Back in Anger* (1966) and **Edward Albee**'s adaptation of Carson McCullers's *Ballad of the Sad Café* (1967); an adaptation of Ivan Goncharov's classic novel *An Ordinary Story* (1967); and a trilogy on Russia's revolutionary history, consisting of **Leonid Zorin**'s *The Decembrists*, A. Svobodin's *The Populists* and Mikhail Shatrov's *The Bolsheviks* (1967), commemorating the 50th anniversary of the October Revolution. The brilliant young company, once thought to be the best in Moscow if not Russia – Efremov, Igor Kvasha, Evgeny Evstigneev, Oleg Tabakov, L. Tolmachova, Mikhail Kazakov, etc. – divided in 1971, some following Efremov to MAT, where he became artistic director (succeeding Boris Livanov), some staying on under actors Oleg Tabakov and Galina Volchyok and some joining other companies. Appropriately, Efremov's final productions at the Sovremennik included MAT perennials, *The Lower Depths* (1969) and a purposely crowded staging of *The Seagull* (1970), in which a stuffed seagull, thrown at the stage curtain by the actor playing Treplev, hung ingloriously in mockery of MAT's emblem and the spiritual and artistic ideals that theatre no longer served. In the hope of reviving MAT but with some trepidation arising from the institution's prescribed social role and under some official pressure, Efremov accepted his new position and produced such plays as: Volodin's *Dulcinea of El Toboso* (1973), about Don Quixote's legacy; **Buero Vallejo**'s *The Sleep of Reason*, about Goya's last days; **Mikhail Roshchin**'s *Old New Year* (produced 1973) and *Echelon* (1975); and G. Bokrev's *Steel-Workers* (1974), an industrial ethics play whose claim to fame was its realistic-looking open-hearth furnaces, shower room with running water and functional elevator. In 1973 MAT moved into its new 1,370-seat theatre on Tverskoi Boulevard which increased audience expectations of Efremov's directorship, although his play selections and stagings were fast disappointing the *cognoscenti*. In recent years, many of the theatre's successful productions have been guest-directed.   SG

Efros, Anatoly Vasilievich (1925–) Soviet Moscow-based director of distinctive productions in which the kinetic enactment of actor temperament through character speaks to contemporary Soviet man's problem with expressing his personality and maintaining his humanity. Trained by N. V. Petrov and M. O. Knebel at the Moscow State Institute of Theatrical Art (GITIS), Efros began his directing career in Ryazan and has been the artistic director of several Moscow theatres: the Central Children's Theatre (1954–63); the Lenin Komsomol Theatre (1963–7), where he lost his position due to 'ideological deficiencies' (i.e., placing individualistic innovation above collective ideology) in his productions; and as the exiled **Yury Lyubimov**'s replacement at the Taganka Theatre (1985). From 1967 to 1985 he served in a reduced official capacity as staff director at the Theatre on Malaya Bronnaya, where he mounted some of his most celebrated productions. With an ensemble of like-minded performers assembled over the course of the past 25 years, Efros has forged a uniquely athletic style of play in which characters seem always to be running or otherwise violently physicalizing, and 'machines for acting', most successfully designed by David Borovsky and Valery Levintal, make strongly tactile, mobile, sculpted, non-decorative statements, somewhat reminiscent of 1920s constructivism. The stage itself is conceived as a boxing ring where the actors-characters' anxieties escalate via absurd repetition into weird rituals of alternating and simultaneous acceptance and denial. Efros has sensitively staged contemporary Soviet plays dealing with confused and disaffected youth and spiritual crisis, including: his most frequent collaborator **Viktor Rozov**'s *On the Wedding Day* (1964) and *Brother Alyosha* (adapted from Dostoevsky's *The Brothers Karamazov*, 1972); **Edvard Radzinsky**'s *104 Pages about Love* (1964) and *Making a Movie* (1965); and **Aleksei Arbuzov**'s *My Poor Marat* (1965). His staging of **Bulgakov**'s *A Cabal of Hypocrites* (*Molière*, 1967), a Soviet classic on talent-as-crown-of-thorns theme, was repeated for television with embattled Taganka director Lyubimov in the title role and recreated at the invitation of Minneapolis's **Guthrie Theatre** in 1979. His highly controversial production of **Chekhov**'s *The Three Sisters* (1967) emphasized enervation and repressed sexuality, dealt ironically with dreams of the future (i.e., the Communist utopia) and transformed characters into convulsively moving puppets. His *Romeo and Juliet* (1970), which pitted violently expressive youth against their indolent, banal and spiritually corrupt parents beneath the scenically rendered wings of death, was called a distortion of **Shakespeare**'s intentions. Efros interpreted **Molière**'s *Don Juan* (1973) as the last rites of a self-destructive, anti-heroic man, victimized by his own myths. His best production, **Gogol**'s *Marriage* (1974; restaged at the Guthrie Theatre, 1978), is a hyperbolic and alternately frenzied and dream-like evocation of fear and loneliness engaged in a violent tug of war and features overpopulated tracking stages and revolving scenic panels reminiscent of **Meyerhold**'s 1926 production of *The Inspector General*. Efros's rendering of Chekhov's *The Cherry Orchard*, as guest director at the Taganka (1975), is a study of heightened neurasthenia mounted in a white island-graveyard (perhaps the **Moscow Art Theatre** tradition's burial ground) in an empty white sea. His version of Molière's *Tartuffe* (1981), at the revitalized Moscow Art Theatre (filial), views Orgon's household as a madhouse and features such **Marx Brothers**-inspired antics as Elvire hiding from Tartuffe in the theatre's prompter's box and Orgon disappearing from underneath the table (which splits in half) where he has been seen to be hiding. Since taking over as head of Taganka, Efros has fallen somewhat out of favour with the *cognoscenti*. He has written two books: *Rehearsals are My Passion* (1975) and *Profession: Director* (1979). SG

Egypt see **Middle East**

Eichelbaum, Samuel (1894–1967) Argentine dramatist who dominated the Buenos Aires stage for nearly 50 years with more than 30 productions. *Un guapo del novecientos* (*A 1900s Dandy*, 1940) marks the beginning of a second period in his writing when he departs from the earlier introspective, often abstract, plays in order to concentrate on more localized themes. Major titles include *Divorcio nupcial* (*Nuptial Divorce*, 1941), *Rostro perdido* (*Lost Face*, 1952), *Dos brasas* (*Two Live Coals*, 1952) and *Subsuelo* (*Underground*, 1966). GW

Eide, Egil (1868–1946) Norwegian actor; a leading member of **Nationaltheatret** in the first decades of the century. He progressed rapidly from lyrical roles to his speciality, heroic figures such as **Ibsen**'s Julian (in *Emperor and Galilean*), Ørnulf (in *The Vikings at Helgeland*) and Olav (in *Lady Inger from Østråt*). While he had little aptitude for intellectual roles, Eide was unmatched for the emotional power of his performances, as in his 1899 Brand and 1907 Oedipus. Even when his technique seemed heavy-handed, as in *When We Dead Awaken* (1934) and *King Lear* (1937), his emotional commitment carried great conviction. HL

Ek, Anders (1916–79) Swedish actor, known internationally for his work in the films of **Ingmar Bergman** (especially as Frost in *Sawdust and Tinsel/The Naked Night*) but primarily active in the theatre, from 1941 to 1979. Much of this was also in collaboration with Bergman, for whom he gave an extraordinary virtuoso performance as **Camus**'s Caligula in 1946. With less than perfect diction, he possessed great emotional and intellectual intensity, and his very wide range encompassed roles by **Aeschylus**, **Shakespeare**, **Molière**, **Chekhov**, **Strindberg**, **Brecht** and **Fugard**. HL

Ekerot, Bengt (1920–71) Swedish actor and director, who began in Malmö and Gothenburg, where he directed influential productions of **Brecht** and **Lorca**, before he joined **Dramaten** in 1953. As an actor he is known internationally for his work in **Ingmar Bergman**'s films, especially as Death in *The Seventh Seal*. In 1956, he directed the world premiere of **O'Neill**'s *Long Day's Journey Into Night* at Dramaten, a brilliant orchestration of the elements of realistic theatre. Mainly interested in the modern repertoire, Ekerot also staged **Sophocles**, **Euripides**, **Shakespeare** and **Molière**; his commitment to new Swedish drama was crucial to the early career of playwright **Lars Forssell**, from *The Coronation*, which flopped in 1956, to the much more successful *Sunday Promenade* (1963) and *The Madcap* (1964). HL

Ekhof, Konrad (1720–78) German actor. Ekhof acted mainly with the travelling troupes of **Johann Schönemann** (from 1740 to 1764), **Konrad Ackermann** (from 1764 to 1771), and Abel Seyler (from 1771 to 1774). He was the leading actor of the short-lived Hamburg National Theatre project, where his performances led **Lessing** toward many of the insights into acting recorded in the *Hamburg Dramaturgy*. From 1774 to his death, Ekhof was director of the first troupe of actors to become permanently resident in a German court theatre, at Gotha. Deeply concerned about raising the social status of the acting profession and exploring the fundamental principles of performance, while he was in the Schönemann troupe, Ekhof attempted without much success to found an 'academy' among the actors to study these matters. In Gotha he was able to train young actors systematically. On stage Ekhof always gave performances that were realistic in contrast to the stiff, rhetorical '**Leipzig style**' then in vogue. He was often profoundly moving. He had a major influence over the development of German acting at a crucial point in its development.   SW

Ekman, Gösta (1890–1938) Swedish actor, whose erratic career alternated between periods of relatively superficial personality acting, which exploited his charm and charisma, and periods in which he achieved great depth and complexity, especially in collaboration with **Per Lindberg**, under whose direction he gave many of his most creative performances: Kurano in **Masefield**'s *The Faithful* (1931), Hamlet, Peer Gynt and the title role in **Lagerkvist**'s *The Hangman* (all 1934), Shylock, Hjalmar Ekdal and Fedja in **Tolstoi**'s *The Living Corpse* (all 1935).   HL

Ekster, Aleksandra Aleksandrovna (1884–1949) Soviet painter and theatrical designer, who helped to introduce cubist and futurist ideas into Russia and lyrically to adapt the constructivist concrete aesthetic in her work with **Tairov**. Ekster's outlook was highly cosmopolitan, a result of training and studio work in Paris (following the Kiev Art School), where she met **Picasso**, Braque, Apollinaire and **Marinetti**. Her sense of solid forms bursting out of three-dimensional space led her to Tairov's Kamerny Theatre, where she designed sets and costumes for **Annensky**'s *Thamira, the Cither Player* (1916), **Wilde**'s *Salome* (1917) and **Shakespeare**'s *Romeo and Juliet* (1921). Her cubist-influenced designs contributed to Tairov's concept of a 'synthetic theatre' in which all visual elements were extensions of the actor's will. This was expressed via a carefully orchestrated three-dimensional score of saturated and symbolic colours, rhythmic shapes, levels and spatial planes. This attempt to avoid both decorative illusionism and two-dimensional stylization coincided with Ekster's interest in exploring the 'dynamic use of immobile form' and the architectural potential of the stage. She designed constructivist costumes from 'industrial materials' (in collaboration with Vera Mukhina) for the film of **Aleksei Tolstoi**'s science fiction novel, *Aelita* (1923), as well as the costumes for **Michael Chekhov**'s 1924 MAT Second Studio production of **Calderón de la Barca**'s *The Phantom Lady*. She emigrated to France in 1924 and pursued an international career as a theatre, ballet and fashion designer and book illustrator. Her legacy to Russian design includes the 'Kiev school' of artists she trained – Pavel Chelishchev, Aleksandr Tyshler, Nisson Shifrin and Anatoly Petritsky – who had distinguished careers of their own.   SG

El Salvador If theatre existed in Salvadoran territory during the three centuries of colonial rule (16th through 18th centuries), no records documenting it have survived. The first play of record is titled *La tragedia de Morazán* (*The Tragedy of Morazán*). Written by Francisco Díaz (1812–45) and staged posthumously, it dramatizes the life of the Honduran Francisco Morazán, the general who served briefly as president of the United Provinces of Central America. During the 19th century the principal force in the Salvadoran theatre was Francisco Gavidia (1863–1955). A contemporary and friend of the Nicaraguan modernist poet Rubén Darío, he established the National Theatre with the help of Francisco Antonio Galindo, and over a 60-year period wrote a dozen plays about conflicts from the national past using romantic and symbolist styles. One of his best efforts was *Júpiter esclavo o Blanca Celis* (*Jupiter Enslaved or Blanca Celis*, 1895), on the issue of education as a means of personal freedom. Another playwright of the period was José Emilio Aragón (1887–1938).

20th century Visiting Spanish and Mexican troupes began to bring modern European influences to El Salvador during the 1920s. In 1927, the Guatemalan-born José Llerena (1895–1943), long-term resident of El Salvador, established the Escuela de Prácticas Escénicas (School of Dramatic Practice) along with the actor Gerardo Neva. He also wrote plays protesting the encroaching North American influence, but the realism of his satire was tempered by weak constructions and excessive moralizing. In 1952 the government established a Department of Theatre within the programme of Fine Arts. The impetus brought new playwrights to the fore. Walter Béneke (b. 1928) served as his country's ambassador to Germany and Japan, and wrote two prize-winning plays. *El paraíso de los imprudentes* (*Paradise of the Imprudent*, 1956) with its disconcerting look at the 'lost' post-war generation in Paris was the first play published in the series Colección Teatro (Theatre Collection) of El Salvador. The English title of *Funeral Home* (1958) reflects its setting in the United States where an anguished young widow faces an existential choice between happiness or adherence to a meaningless standard of values. A contemporary of Béneke's was Roberto Arturo Menéndez (b. 1931) who shared with him first prize in the national culture contest of 1958 for *La ira del cordero* (*The Ire of the Lamb*), a modernized version of the Cain and Abel story rooted in the jealousy and envy produced by parental favouritism. His later plays, *Prometeo II* (*Prometheus II*, 1965) and *Nuevamente Edipo* (*Oedipus Once Again*, 1968) showed his affinity for classical motifs in modern guise. Alvaro Menén Desleal (Alvaro Menéndez Leal) (b. 1943) author of the surrealistic *Luz negra* (*Black Light*, 1966) represented El Salvador in the Olympic Theatre Festival in Mexico in 1968. In the play the two 'severed' heads that compare death with life showed clear ties to **Beckett**'s theatre but with more humour. Roberto Armijo (b. 1937) won first prize in the Central American Theatre contest of 1969 for his *Jugando a la gallina ciega* (*Playing Blind Chicken*), a chilling story about entrapment in the modern world. A group formed in 1982, Teatro del Alba (Theatre of Dawn), presented an ambitious work by a new author, José Roberto Cea (b. 1939), in 1983. His *Escenas cumbres* (*High Points*) dramatized the anguish, solitude and rebellion of man in contemporary society searching for his authenticity.

Theatre in El Salvador has not yet achieved much international recognition, although the serious efforts of a few dedicated authors and directors are promising.   GW

Elder, Lonnie, III (1932–   ) Afro-American playwright who turned to theatre after working variously as a waiter, docker, gambler, political hack, and numbers-runner. Elder met **Douglas Turner Ward** in the cast of *A Raisin in the Sun* (1959), acted in Ward's *Day of Absence* (1965), was a fellowship playwright at the Yale University School of Drama, then joined the **Negro Ensemble Company** as director of its Playwrights' Unit. He already had five plays produced when his *Ceremonies in Dark Old Men* (1969), about a Harlem family's struggle to survive with dignity, was presented by the Negro Ensemble Company with Ward in the leading role. The play, 'poised between comedy and tragedy', received rave notices and won an Outer Critics Circle award and a Drama Desk award. Elder moved to California where he has become a successful scriptwriter for film and television. His screenplay *Sounder* (1972) received an Oscar nomination. EGH

Eldridge (McKechnie), Florence (1901–) American actress. Eldridge made her debut on Broadway in 1918 in the chorus of *Rock-a-Bye Baby*. After several appearances on Broadway, she toured with her husband, **Fredric March**, in the **Theatre Guild**'s productions of such scripts as *Arms and the Man*, *The Silver Cord*, and *The Guardsman* in 1927–8. She made her film debut in 1929 in *Studio Murder Mystery* with her husband. She frequently appeared with March, as in *The Skin of Our Teeth* (1942) and again in **Ruth Gordon**'s *Years Ago* (1946). One of her greatest successes, again with March, was as Mary Tyrone in *Long Day's Journey into Night* (1956), for which she won the *Variety* New York Drama Critics Poll. SMA

Eliot, T[homas] S[tearns] (1888–1965) American born British poet and dramatist born in St Louis, Missouri, educated at Harvard, the Sorbonne and Oxford, who settled in London after 1915, and whose plays mark the high point in the modern revival of English poetic drama. A founder-member of the **Group Theatre**, his first short stage pieces portraying the spiritual wasteland of 20th-century social values and political movements, the fragmentary 'Aristophanic melodrama' *Sweeney Agonistes* (1928) and the choral burlesque *The Rock*, were produced by Rupert Doone and **Martin Browne** in 1934. They reflected Eliot's suggestion that poetry might be restored to the theatre by adapting popular forms or music-hall techniques, as did his first major play, *Murder in the Cathedral*, with its incorporation of jazz rhythms and direct address as well as liturgical structures. Commissioned for the 1935 Canterbury Festival and performed in the Chapter House of the Cathedral, it is the clearest expression of the integral connection between verse and religious experience that characterizes Eliot's work. Despite its medieval subject and static form, it transferred successfully to the commercial theatre and has been more frequently revived than any of Eliot's other plays. However, he came to see it as a dead end in his attempt to create a contemporary poetic language for the stage, and from *The Family Reunion* (1939) he increasingly disguised the verse, spiritual themes and archetypal paradigms of his drama. Based on the *Oresteia*, this play retained visionary choral passages and the supernatural machinery of the Eumenides in the context of a modern country house detective drama.

But in *The Cocktail Party* (1949), *The Confidential Clerk* (1953) and *The Elder Statesman* (1958), all of which were first performed at the **Edinburgh Festival**, the rhythms of the dialogue become progressively closer to prose. The incongruity of overtly ritual elements in a realistic setting is avoided. There are no direct references to alert the audience to the mythical basis of the plots – drawn respectively from the *Alcestis* and *Ion* of **Euripides** and **Sophocles**' *Oedipus at Colonus* – and designed to work on a subconscious level. Instead the surface situation is that of a conventional comedy of manners or modern problem play, and they suffer by comparison with more normal examples of these genres since the underlying religious significance tends to flatten the characters and remove dramatic tension. Even so, with Eliot's prestige as a Nobel Prizewinner for his poetry (1948) and the intrinsic interest of his continuing theatrical experimentation, these plays ran successfully in London and New York as well as attracting considerable critical attention.

At the beginning of his career Eliot also edited a literary quarterly, the *Criterion*, becoming a director of the Faber publishing house in 1925, and the difficulties of his first marriage have recently formed the subject of a successful play, *Tom and Viv*, by Michael Hastings. A revival of *The Cocktail Party* (London 1986) and the production of the musical *Cats*, based on Eliot's 1939 poems *Old Possum's Book of Practical Cats*, suggest a renewed interest in Eliot in the 1980s. CI DBW MB

Elizabethan theatre companies The richer households of 14th- and 15th-century England customarily included minstrels and other entertainers among their numerous servants. The playing of Interludes at feasts in great halls encouraged the development of small troupes (four men and a boy) like Henry VII's Lusores Regis. Protected by the livery of a noble patron, these players avoided the stringent penalties inflicted on rogues and vagabonds in Tudor England. There was prestige to be gained for the Lord of an impressive acting troupe. **Leicester's Men** (1559–88) proclaimed the munificence of their patron as well as their own special skills. Other companies – Sussex's, Oxford's, **Strange's**, Worcester's – operated along similar lines. They performed before visiting dignitaries in the great halls of their patrons' homes, toured the provinces in his livery and aspired to the honour of playing at the Queen's Court. Performance in London was more likely to catch the eye of the Lord Chamberlain, and so it was to London that the companies gravitated, playing in inn-yards like the Saracen's Head, the Red Lion and the **Boar's Head**. It was a former member of Leicester's Men, **James Burbage**, who first tested the potential profitability of a purpose-built playhouse. His erection of the **Theatre** in 1576 began a change in the priorities of the household companies. The command of London audiences proffered a new financial independence to any company that could seize it. As more theatres were built, leading companies became associated with particular homes – the **Lord Chamberlain's Men** with the Theatre, the **Admiral's Men** with the **Rose**, Pembroke's Men (disastrously) with the **Swan**, Worcester's and Oxford's Men with the Boar's Head. The theatre owner would claim his share of the takings but the companies were artistically independent. The custom was for senior members to become sharers (in the risks as well as the profits). Buying and dealing in such shares was hazardous, since London's theatres were threatened by competition, by hostile authorities and by the recurrent plague epidemics, but prudence and good fortune brought riches to some sharers. A loyal and successful company like the Lord Chamberlain's Men probably included six actor-sharers, four hired men and two boys apprenticed to a sharer. But the Chamberlain's Men stole a march on all their rivals when they moved to the **Globe** in 1599. For the first, and probably the only, time the actors owned their own theatre.

Although briefly (1583–94) the nominal patron of her own company, **Queen Elizabeth's Men**, Elizabeth I endorsed the household groups of the Tudor aristocracy. James I was anxious to centralize and assert the cultural ascendancy of the Court. He adopted the Chamberlain's Men as his own King's Men and the Admiral's Men became Prince Henry's Men. London's third company, playing at the Boar's Head, became Queen Anne's Men and moved to the **Red Bull**, where they gratified a boisterous audience with violence and spectacle. Other companies formed and disbanded and other theatres, both public and private, opened and closed in London. The challenge of the **Boys' Companies** faded after 1608, and the adult companies, once the principle of higher admission charges for small indoor theatres had been established, vied for the privilege of performing under cover. The King's Men maintained their outdoor supremacy at the Globe and added indoor success at the **Blackfriars** after 1609. **Christopher Beeston** caused dissension when he tried to provide Queen Anne's Men with an indoor home at the **Cockpit**, and became instead an autocratic theatre manager, who hired the Cockpit to any high-bidding company before establishing there his own troupe, nicknamed Beeston's Boys. The last theatres to be built before the Civil War, the **Salisbury Court** and the **Cockpit-in-Court**, were both small indoor houses, which suited a Caroline taste for decorous display. The Salisbury Court was successively the home of Prince Charles's Men (1631–35) and Queen Henrietta's Men (1636–42). The Cockpit-in-Court was used primarily but not exclusively by the King's Men during their regular royal command performances. With the closure of the theatres, the great theatre companies were perforce disbanded. The great majority of the actors, conscious of the hand that buttered their bread, took and fought on the Royalist side. A few remained in London to seek out opportunities for surreptitious performance at the abandoned theatres.   PT

Elliot, Michael (1931–84) British director. In 1959 he formed the 59 Theatre Company at the **Lyric Theatre, Hammersmith**, for which he directed his highly acclaimed production of **Ibsen**'s *Brand*. He directed at Stratford in 1961–2, was appointed artistic director of the **Old Vic** for its final season in 1962–3 and directed for the **National Theatre** in 1965. In 1968, together with several members of the original 59 Company, he founded the 69 Theatre Company in Manchester which in 1976 metamorphosed into the **Royal Exchange Theatre** Company. He aimed from the start to make the new theatre of front-rank quality, independent of current London trends. His own pro-

ductions of (for example) *Uncle Vanya*, *The Lady from the Sea* and *The Dresser* all helped to guarantee the success of the enterprise. He won a deserved reputation as England's foremost interpreter of Ibsen and **Strindberg** and also directed many successful productions for television.   AJ

Elliott, Gertrude (Dermot) (1874–1950) American actress. After making her New York debut in 1894, Elliott acted with Marie Wainwright (1895) and **Nat Goodwin** (1897–9), playing Emily in *In Mizzoura*, Lucy in *The Rivals*, and Angelica Knowlton in *Nathan Hale*. She made her London debut in 1899 as Midge in *The Cowboy and the Lady*, and remained in England to play Ophelia to **Forbes-Robertson**'s Hamlet. After the two were married in 1900, she returned to America several times, playing Maisie in *The Light that Failed* (1903), a character in the mould of Hedda Gabler, and creating the role of Cleopatra in **Shaw**'s *Caesar and Cleopatra* (1906). Critics praised her girlish spirit, playful humour, eloquent speech, and husky beauty. After her husband retired, she managed the **St James's Theatre** in London (1918).   TLM

Elliott, Maxine (Jessie Dermot) (1871–1940) American actress and stage beauty. After making her New York stage debut at **Palmer**'s Theatre in 1890, Maxine Elliott rose rapidly in the theatre spending a season each with **Rose Coghlan**'s and **Augustin Daly**'s companies (1894, 1895) before her London debut as Sylvia in *Two Gentlemen of Verona* (1895). After an Australia tour with **Nat Goodwin** (1896), she became his leading lady (1897) and his wife (1898). They co-starred in numerous successes including her first big hit as Alice Adams in *Nathan Hale* (1899). They separated in 1902, after which she established herself as a star with Georgiana Carley in *Her Own Way* (1903) written for her by **Clyde Fitch**. Two years later, her Georgiana attracted the attentions of Edward VII in London. She built the Maxine Elliott Theatre in New York (1908) with help from the **Shuberts**, and appeared there in numerous comedies including *Myself, Settina* and *The Chaperon*. In 1911 she retired to England, making only occasional stage appearances afterwards. She was praised as a 'rare comedienne of the drawing room' during her 1918–19 American tour of *Lord and Lady Algy*. While she appeared stiff and mechanical to some critics, all praised her dark and lustrous beauty, and her statuesque stage presence. She retired to the Riviera after 1920 to live out her life as a 'lady of society'.   TLM

Elliston, Robert William (1774–1831) English actor and theatre manager, who disappointed his respectable uncles by running off to make a stage debut at Bath. Known for his versatility, since he was at home in tragedy as well as comedy, Elliston is remembered as 'the Great Lessee', lauded for his good spirits by **Charles Lamb** and a redoubtable opponent of the Patent Theatres' monopoly over the legitimate drama during his years in management of such minor theatres as the Royal Circus (1809–14), which he converted and renamed the Surrey, and the **Olympic** (1813–19), where he was the first manager to install gas in a theatre auditorium (1815). Having failed to beat the powerful Patent houses, he did the next best thing by assuming management of **Drury Lane** (1819–26). The company was led by **Edmund Kean**, whom Elliston had been the first London manager to recognize, and was in full-scale rivalry with **Covent Garden**. Elliston relished the competition and set about securing the best actors by raising salaries. For the first few years the policy paid off, but the end was bankruptcy. The failure owed as much to Elliston's private life – he had followed his watchmaker-father into alcoholism and was required to maintain at least three bastards as well as a wife and nine children of his own. His policy, which he bequeathed to the notorious **Alfred Bunn**, was to run Drury Lane as he had run the Surrey (and would run it again from 1827 until his death), as a home for spectacle and pantomime as well as the classical drama. The secret of his acting was the bond he established with his audience (as Charles Surface or Falstaff, in particular), and he managed his theatres the same way. Almost alone among Regency managers, Elliston had the common touch.   PT

Ellsler, John (1822–1903) American manager. Originally an actor, he assumed management of his own company at Cleveland's Academy of Music in 1855. He opened his lavish Euclid Avenue Opera House in 1875, but the Academy of Music remained his centre of operation until 1885. His company toured extensively to surrounding towns in the summers, and between 1871 and 1887 he managed at least one theatre a year in Pittsburgh. His theatre was noted as a nursery of talent. **Clara Morris**, **James O'Neill**, James Lewis, and **Mrs G. H. Gilbert** apprenticed there. His daughter, Effie, became a leading lady of the next generation, creating the title role in **Steele MacKaye**'s *Hazel Kirke*.   DMCD

Eltinge, Julian (William Dalton) (1883–1941) American female impersonator, first seen professionally in *Mr Wix of Wixham*, a musical comedy (1904). His biggest hit was *The Fascinating Widow* (1911 and subsequent tours), to whose success a grateful producer built the Eltinge Theatre on 42nd St, New York. With his own company, the Julian Eltinge Players, he worked in vaudeville 1918–27, and starred in silent films. A large man with a passable singing voice, Eltinge was a favourite primarily with female audiences, not least for the *chic* of his wardrobe. His last variety appearance, at the White Horse, Los Angeles, 1940, was a dismal fiasco, owing to a police ban on public transvestism.   LS

Emanuel, Giovanni (1848–1902) Italian actor–manager. He early became a lead player opposite the principal actresses of his day, formed his own company and, in the way of Italian players of the age, toured widely abroad, as far as Latin America and Russia. He was noted for his strongly naturalistic style in interpreting the classics, including **Shakespeare**, being particularly strong as Othello and Lear. The care with which he prepared productions, and the scrupulous attention he gave to detail in the roles he played are well evidenced in his extant prompt books.   KR

Emery, Gilbert (Emery Remsley Pottle) (1875–1945) American dramatist who made a moderate career writing social dramas. After serving in the First World War and working as an actor, Emery wrote *The Hero* (1921) which dramatized the effect a war hero had upon the wife of his brother who stayed home. An exciting melodrama, *The Hero* has outlasted its moderate sucess. *Tarnish* (1923), concerned with a naive young woman's confrontation with a lover's past, *Episode* (1925), dealing with a husband's acceptance and forgiveness of his wife's infidelities in order to maintain his conventional social life, and *Love-in-a-mist* (1926), written with Amelie Rives, reflect American society of a certain period.   WJM

Emery, John (1777–1822) English comic actor, the son, father and grandfather of notable actors. Emery completed his apprenticeship under **Tate Wilkinson** in the York circuit, and was, from 1798 until his death, a leading low comedian at **Covent Garden**. He is the first actor known to have been encored for his playing of a scene, that of Fixture's jealousy in **Thomas Morton**'s *A Roland for an Oliver* (1819). Emery had spent much of his childhood in Yorkshire, and his preeminence in rustic roles established the Yorkshire dialect as an acceptable alternative to 'Mummerset' for comic country bumpkins. His Tyke in Morton's *The School of Reform* (1805) was famous in his time, and the play died with him. His melancholy end is tersely recorded in James Winston's *Diary*: 'Emery is given over. Emery became latterly incapable of fulfilling his duty. He drank excessively, was in a public house great part of his time'.   PT

Emmett, Dan see **Minstrel show**

Empire Theatre 1430 Broadway, New York City [Architect: J. B. McElfatrick and Co.]. In 1893, when **Charles Frohman** built the gem-like Empire some 25 blocks north of the theatre district at Union Square, the spark was ignited to create a new theatre district uptown. The theatre remained the headquarters of Frohman's activities until he died on the *Lusitania* in 1915. During his lifetime, Frohman was Broadway's principal starmaker, a member of the **Theatrical Syndicate** and the Napoleon of the American theatre. The roster of the stars who appeared at the Empire is etched into a plaque which is affixed to the wall of the characterless office building which replaced the theatre after it was torn down in 1953. The theatre was managed by Alf Hayman for the Frohman estate on a run-of-the-play basis and was later leased to producer **Gilbert Miller** until 1931. With just over 1,000 seats, it was a compact, well-designed playhouse and a favourite among actors and audiences. It enjoyed a latter day reputation as a house of hits, which was crowned by the arrival of *Life with Father* in 1939, which did not leave its stage for six years. The theatre changed ownership several times before its demise. At the time it closed, it was presenting *The Time of the Cuckoo* with **Shirley Booth**.   MCH

Encina, Juan del (?1468–?1530) Spanish poet, musician and playwright, sometimes called the Father of Spanish Drama. Born and educated in Salamanca, he served the Duke of Alba in several capacities, then lived in Rome 1498–1509, returning several times in later life. Encina published eight dramatic *églogas* (eclogues) with his poetry and songs in 1496, and later six more, exercising considerable influence on later dramatists.

The early *églogas* are little pastoral playlets performed on high feastdays by Encina himself and other courtiers, with comic shepherds, topical allusions, songs and dances. The later works are longer, more complex, and influenced by secular Italian Renaissance forms. CL

Engel, Johann Jakob (1741–1802) German playwright and aesthetician. A minor figure at best, Engel's most important contribution to theatre was his book *Ideas on Mimesis* (1786), which catalogued in detail gestures and poses of characteristic emotions. From 1787 to 1794, he was director of the **Berlin Royal Theatre**. SW

England see also **Medieval drama in Europe**

The Tudor period The English theatre owes more than can be accurately determined to the fondness for display of the Tudor family. Henry VII had his own company of players. Grandiloquently called the Lusores Regis, the group probably comprised four men and a boy, all adept at quick costume changes and the doubling or trebling of parts. But it was not only, not even primarily, through the patronage of plays that the Tudors announced their theatricality. The elaborate Disguisings that greeted the arrival of distinguished guests, the royal progresses and tournaments often placed the monarch at the centre of the spectacle. Although such events were 'amateur', they were planned and managed with professional thoroughness and observed, or participated in, by the men who would later plan and manage the Elizabethan companies of professional players. The taste for display and spectacular expenditure (or the appearance of spectacular expenditure) should be recognized by any student of English drama under the Tudors and Stuarts.

The irregular but persistent increase of professional actors is a feature of the 16th century. Their attachment to noble families protected them from the worst effects of religious and political turbulence, which threatened and finally silenced the amateur performers of Mystery plays. The suppression of the Feast of Corpus Christi in 1548 was a sign of the new times. In the midlands and the north, remote from the centres of power, the Mystery Cycles continued for three decades, but by 1581 they had been effectively destroyed. The English theatre's secular history was decisively launched, and the fraternity of professional actors was ready for it.

Their readiness was owed in part to the slender growth of secular drama during the first half of the 16th century. The influence of Roman comedy persisted, despite the sudden disfavour with which everything Italian was viewed after the Reformation, but the audience for such plays was restricted. *Ralph Roister Doister* (written 1534–52, printed c. 1566), the first English comedy to capture successfully the comic vitality of **Plautus** and **Terence**, was probably intended by its schoolmaster-author, **Nicholas Udall**, for performance by the boys of Eton or Westminster. The more homespun *Gammer Gurton's Needle* (written 1552–63, printed 1575, the year in which its putative author, William Stevenson, died) was probably first performed by schoolboys, too. Like comedy, English tragedy was nurtured by a privileged audience. **Thomas Norton** and **Thomas Sackville**, men of substance whose involvement lent lustre to the craft of the playwright, wrote *Gorboduc* (1562), under the conscious influence of the Roman **Seneca**, for performance at the Inner Temple before the Queen. It was the scholarly study of classical form, supremely exemplified in the drama by Seneca and Terence, that established the formal, five-act discipline of tragedy and comedy in England. Since they were much studied at the grammar schools, it is reasonable to assume that Seneca and Terence were included in **Shakespeare**'s 'little Latin'.

If the outstanding plays of the mid-century were written for private performance, there were competent writers to cater for the immediate needs of professional players. In 1574, while the death-knell of religious drama tolled, regular weekday performances of plays were legitimized in London. One man who took particular notice was **James Burbage**, a master-carpenter eager to raise himself, and a member (or former member) of the most prominent of early Elizabethan household companies, Lord **Leicester's Men**. Burbage calculated that there was sufficient interest in and around London to justify the erection of a building specially designed for the performance of plays. He was guided less by continental precedent than by simple commercial considerations. Whilst professional players could expect *ex gratia* payments for entertaining the nobility, the collecting of money from casual audiences, particularly at open-air performances, was unreliable. We can reasonably assume that Burbage's main interest was the box-office, not the stage. Like many Elizabethans – explorers, alchemists, quack-doctors – he was a speculator, bold enough to risk all in a project. What he had not got, he borrowed, and his new playhouse, known simply as the **Theatre**, was completed in 1576.

There is no more significant date in the history of English drama. Had Burbage's project failed, it is difficult to see how the great plays of the next 50 years could have been written. The circumstances of his success merit attention. There is, firstly, the question of location. The city of London was governed by men much less sympathetic to games and plays than was the Tudor nobility. Prudence dictated that the Theatre be built outside the city walls, beyond the immediate jurisdiction of the city fathers. Burbage took a lease on a site north of Bishopsgate, in Shoreditch, on land vacated by the dissolution of Holywell Priory. Since no records survive, the nature of the building must be inferred, partly from our knowledge of Burbage's likely models and partly from information on subsequent theatre-building. Plays had been performed in public places for long enough to provide the first theatre-architect with certain guidelines. A raised stage, for instance, was of proven value. Simply mounted on barrels or trestles, it could be quickly removed to clear space for such popular entertainments as animal-baiting. Although he built the Theatre to house plays, Burbage was too good a businessman to neglect the advantages of adaptability. The new drama had still to capture public attention. Meanwhile, the medieval confusion of 'games' and 'plays' held good. Tiered seating, like that in contemporary cockpits, suited spectators of both. The Theatre was on a grander scale than the cockpits and more serviceable than the yards of coaching inns, whose open plan and first-floor walkways were familiar to Tudor actors, but it incorporated features of both. Arguing from later evidence, scholars propose that the first English playhouse had three galleries circling an open yard, about half of which was occupied by a removable scaffold-stage. The tiring house (dressing rooms) lay behind the stage, and entrances were made through either of two doors in the tiring house facade. This would have brought the actors into close proximity with the standing audience, who had paid one penny for admission to the yard, and also with the spectators seated in the lowest gallery, who had probably paid a further penny for the privilege of resting their legs.

This proximity was something with which audience and actors were familiar. There is disagreement among students of Elizabethan acting about the comparative formality or realism of performing styles. Either way, the actors had to confront a boisterous audience in an atmosphere closer to that of a public meeting than a decorously hushed modern theatre. On a wide stage (the later **Globe** and **Fortune** had platforms at least 43ft wide x 23ft deep), timid acting had no place. The Elizabethan player needed to dominate both platform and audience. The Theatre, like later Elizabethan playhouses, was no setting for inward acting. Passion had to be shown, not contained, and stories had to be told with emphasis and clarity. It was all too easy for a dissatisfied audience to make its feelings plain. The best Elizabethan actors were supreme showmen, many of them skilled swordsmen, athletes or musicians. Some learned their trade as apprentices, and the likelihood is that bodily prowess was as prominent in the training programme as rhetoric. No Elizabethan company could afford to neglect the drawing power of spectacle, and, since scene design and mechanical aids were in their infancy, that spectacle had to be provided by the actors themselves. Their chief support, in an age extravagantly interested in clothes, was costume. The actor had no scenery to shelter in, no atmospheric lighting and no proscenium arch to protect him from the rude encounter with his audience. Sharing a confined space under the open sky with paying customers, he needed a good costume and a good voice. The great playwrights of the age could afford to write as they did because actors spoke well and audiences were used to listening. It is hard for us, in a period so dependent on visual stimulus, to recapture the priorities of an aural culture, when vital information was still conveyed by proclamation and the town-crier not yet a colourful archaism, when street ballads attracted crowds and, even in sophisticated court circles, it was the custom for poets to read their work aloud.

It is easy, with hindsight, to see that London was ready for a theatre in 1576, but Burbage's boldness should not be underrated. The repertoire of plays, now that religious drama was frowned on, was pitiably small. The rapid creation of a national repertoire is the most astonishing achievement of the period, but the innovatory work of **Christopher Marlowe** was still a decade away – *Tamburlane* dates from c. 1587 – and we have no record of the plays presented at the Theatre in its early years. Burbage probably leased it, at a fixed rent, to his old company, Leicester's Men, and, on demand, to other groups. Like-minded promoters soon followed his lead. The **Curtain** was built nearby in 1577, and an obscure theatre in the south-bank

village of Newington was active by, at the latest, 1580. In addition, several inns remained in irregular use – the Bell and Cross Keys in Gracious (now Gracechurch) Street, the **Boar's Head** in Whitechapel, the Saracen's Head in Islington, the Bull in Bishopsgate, the Red Lion in Stepney and the Bel Savage in Ludgate Hill among them. By 1587, the enterprising **Philip Henslowe** was running the newly built **Rose** on the south bank of the Thames, where, like all Elizabethan public theatres, it was outside the jurisdiction of the city fathers. By 1595, Francis Langley, probably the most grasping of all Elizabethan theatrical entrepreneurs, had opened the **Swan** in nearby Paris Garden. It is from the chance preservation of a drawing of the Swan's interior by a visiting Dutchman, Johannes De Witt, that we derive our only concrete evidence of the physical outlines of the stage during the early years of the public theatres.

The year 1576 is notable for another theatrical enterprise, one which introduces an important Elizabethan distinction. 'Public' theatres of the kind pioneered by Burbage were, initially at least, polygonal buildings enclosing covered galleries and a yard open to the sky. The partial covering of the stage, observable in De Witt's drawing, was a later refinement, copied at the first and second Globe (1599 and 1614), the square Fortune (1600), the adapted inn known as the **Red Bull** (1605) and Henslowe's last great enterprise, the **Hope** (1614). But there was to be competition, after 1576, from a rival tradition of indoor 'private' theatres. In that extraordinary year, Richard Farrant, Master of the **Children of the Chapel Royal**, supervised the conversion of rooms in the dissolved **Blackfriars** monastery for use as an indoor playhouse. His actors were choirboys, whose regular involvement in the performance of plays at Court had been affirmed by such earlier 16th-century Masters as William Cornish and Richard Edwardes. Not to be outdone, the **Boys of St Paul's**, under the active Mastership (1557–82) of Sebastian Westcott, had formed an effective rival company. The fondness for boy actors, sometimes in preference to adults, is mysteriously related to aristocratic cult-interest in pubescence, and Farrant's Blackfriars plans were opportunistic. Although within the city walls, the Blackfriars precinct was constitutionally outside the jurisdiction of the civic authorities, and it had the extra advantage of being within easy reach of the Inns of Court, whose wealthy and pleasure-seeking residents became a staple audience of the private, as well as of the public, theatres.

The first innovative Elizabethan playwright, **John Lyly**, whose earliest plays were staged at the Blackfriars in 1584, can be claimed by the **Boys' Companies**. Lyly was prominent among the group of **University Wits** (others include **Peele**, **Nashe**, **Greene**, Lodge and Marlowe) whose alert response to theatrical expansion soon plumped out the meagre repertoire of plays. Proud of their sophistication, they poured scorn on the rising generation of professional playwrights, who eagerly peddled their work to boys and adults alike. Lyly went so far as to involve himself at managerial level, burning his own fingers as well as those of the Boys' Companies by involving them on the anti-Puritan side in the Marprelate Controversy of 1588–9. Under the Tudors, as under the Stuarts, it was a perilous thing for actors to involve themselves in politics. The Boys' Companies lay low for a decade, and when, under a new Master, Nathaniel Giles, the Children of the Chapel Royal returned to the Black-friars, it was to new premises. The second Blackfriars theatre had been leased and converted by James Burbage in 1596, for adult use, but the precinct's residents petitioned against the unruly intrusion and the enterprise foundered. That Giles should have been allowed to present plays there after 1600 is evidence of the social status attached to Boys' Companies. For a while, as the famous references in *Hamlet* show, the children were a threat even to the best of the adult players, but more political indiscretions, together with a shift in taste, led to their disintegration. By 1608, the heyday of boy-acting was over and the adult companies could take their pick from the choristers willing to play female roles in a single-sex profession.

Over one thousand professional players are known by name in the period 1590–1642, and there were probably at least as many again. Of the several companies under noble patronage (Pembroke's Men, Oxford's Men, Worcester's Men etc.), two had established a clear supremacy by the end of the 16th century. Of these, the **Admiral's Men** had been so called since 1585 and the **Chamberlain's Men** since 1594. The former became associated with Henslowe's theatres (the Rose and the Fortune) and the latter with Burbage's (the Theatre and the Globe). It was during the 1590s that the English theatre came of age, but the status of the playwright remained anomalous. 'Haply some plays may be worth the keeping: but hardly one in forty', wrote the book-loving Sir Thomas Bodley in 1612, and his point can be supported by reference to careless publication or, more often, by the lack of publication. Even so, we can estimate that well over 2,000 new plays were written between 1590 and 1642, each one a commodity for which a company would pay £6. Playwrights were employed by actors, and since speed of composition was vital, with several theatres competing for a limited audience and new pieces guaranteed a larger following at their first performance than ever again, the task of turning an agreed plot into a complete script was customarily shared by two or more writers. Unlike the University Wits, the new generation of playwrights came often from within the profession. Shakespeare and **Jonson**, the two greatest, were both actors, and Shakespeare would never have achieved such prosperity if he had confined himself to writing. His name was sufficiently familiar by 1592 to inspire Greene's jealous abuse, but it was his purchase of a share in the newly formed Chamberlain's Men in 1594 that gave him a secure hold on an insecure profession. Until his retirement in c. 1608, he remained an active member of London's leading company, adding outstandingly successful plays to a repertoire that also included work by Jonson, **Marston**, **Dekker**, **Webster**, **Middleton**, **Tourneur**, **Fletcher** and **Beaumont**. It was a repertoire that the Admiral's Men could not match, except with the often-revived plays of Marlowe. Evidently averse to collaborative composition, Shakespeare was adept at snapping up and improving popular styles. When Senecan tragedy (*Titus Andronicus*) was modified by the success of **Kyd**'s *The Spanish Tragedy*, he could lift revenge tragedy to new heights in *Hamlet*. When the rough chronicle plays were challenged by Marlowe's *Edward II*, he produced *Richard II* and the finest of history plays, *Henry IV* in two parts and *Henry V*. *Julius Caesar* was a response to a revived interest in Roman history. The late comedies, from *Pericles* to *The Tempest*, were written in full awareness of the popular romances of Beaumont and Fletcher. Even the uniquely Jonsonian comedy of humours is alluded to in *Twelfth Night*, and citizen comedy, of which Dekker's *The Shoemaker's Holiday* is the outstanding example, is embraced by *The Merry Wives of Windsor*. Shakespeare's greatest comedies and tragedies belong to no school, and the countless attempts through history to imitate them only serve to demonstrate their inimitability. But it should be stressed that they were written for performance by his known fellow-actors. **Richard Burbage** and others enhanced the greatness of Shakespeare's plays, establishing their claims on contemporary audiences as surely as **Edward Alleyn**'s playing established Marlowe's pre-eminence a few years earlier. By any reckoning, the Chamberlain's Men were, during Shakespeare's years as a member, one of the finest companies of players the English theatre has known.

The Stuart Period Within two months of his accession, James I had taken the Chamberlain's Men into his personal patronage, renaming them the King's Men. The Admiral's Men were assigned to his heir, Prince Henry. Unlike the Tudors, the Stuarts were anxious to centralize and specify cultural supremacy. Royal interest would prove a mixed blessing for the London theatre, but initially it was a lovely light in a dark world. The year 1603 would otherwise have been a financial disaster. Closed in March as a token of respect to the dying Queen, the theatres had scarcely opened after the period of national mourning when London was struck by plague. While 30,000 citizens died between May 1603 and April 1604, the theatres remained closed, as they always were when plague deaths reached 40 in any week. James, who had prudently delayed his arrival in the capital, summoned the King's Men to Wilton House, rewarding them for their December performances with a generous £30. But his displeasure could be equally decisive, as the authors of the anti-Scottish tags in *Eastward Ho* discovered in 1604. Two of them, **Chapman** and Jonson, were briefly imprisoned, and the third, Marston, took refuge abroad.

Some critics have perceived a darkening tone in Jacobean drama, a pervading cynicism about the preponderance of time-servers in corrupt courts and an unhappy recognition, shared with John Donne, that 'new philosophy' has 'put all in doubt'. The view is attractive but over-simple. The first Stuart decade encompasses the bitter work of Webster and Tourneur, the great tragedies of Shakespeare, Jonson's most biting comedies and the emergence of the distinctively caustic Middleton, but also the happy vogue for tragicomic romance, spearheaded by the gentleman-playwrights, Beaumont and Fletcher, who, together or singly, wrote with an easy grace that demonstrates the astonishingly rapid maturity of a national drama that was scarcely 30 years old.

The same decade saw important developments in staging techniques. In 1608, James Burbage's dream was posthumously realized when the King's Men took possession of the indoor theatre in the Blackfriars. Given the climate, indoor performance was certain, sooner or later, to become the norm in England, and it is appropriate that the King's Men should have led a move towards it. But the Globe, their home since 1599, was not abandoned. On the contrary, it was rebuilt after its gutting by fire in 1613, and the King's Men continued to conduct outdoor and indoor performances in tandem. This was nothing new. Actors were accustomed to presenting plays in a variety of spaces. The palace of Whitehall had several – the Great Hall (c. 40ft wide), the splendid Banquet House (50ft wide x 110ft long) and the compact **Cockpit-in-Court** were all familiar to the King's Men, whose adaptability to the Royal Command was certainly enhanced by their possession of the Blackfriars. But the greatest transformation was not strictly in the field of drama.

James I and his Danish wife, though interested in drama, took particular delight in the elaborate courtliness of the masque. Through the genius of one man, that royal preference came to exercise a decisive influence on the future of the English theatre. **Inigo Jones** brought first-hand experience of Italian theatres to his appointment in the household of Prince Henry (1604). For *The Masque of Blackness* (1605) he provided the first English example of perspective scenery behind an artificial proscenium arch. In tune with the Stuart preparedness to spend lavishly on Court entertainment, scenery came increasingly to dominate text in the masques that preceded the Civil War. Ben Jonson, who as court-poet wrote at least eight of them, was predictably resentful, and his quarrels with Jones culminated in his angry withdrawal in 1634. But Jones's experiments with changeable scenery, involving the use of decorated shutters run in grooves parallel to the line of the proscenium arch, had already created the conditions that would govern the pictorial stage for well over two centuries.

Some spin-off effect on the drama was inevitable. It is observable in the visual and musical techniques of *The Tempest* as well as in the more riotous spectacle associated with the performances of Queen Anne's Men at the Red Bull (1605–17). Even so, the new generation of playwrights, of whom **Massinger**, **Ford** and **Shirley** are the best known, were recognizably the inheritors of a sturdier Elizabethan tradition, embodied in Jonson's combative person. Typical of a group of minor dramatists, mocked in their time as 'Sons of Ben', is **Richard Brome**, whose contract as resident (or 'attached') playwright to Queen Henrietta's Men at the **Salisbury Court Theatre** (1635) provides valuable insights into the writer's world. The contract stipulates that Brome shall write three plays per year and publish none of them, that he will provide epilogues, prologues, inductions, songs and new or rewritten scenes for old plays, and that he will receive 15 shillings per week so long as he does no writing for other companies. We can reasonably assume that other attached playwrights, like Shakespeare, worked under similar conditions. It was only gradually that they achieved independence from actors or acting companies, and not until the end of the 17th century did their names figure on playbills. Jonson's publication of his own plays in the splendour of a Folio edition (1616) was unprecedented assertiveness, and the King's Men's decision to celebrate their late colleague, Shakespeare, in the same rich format (1623) must, in context, be seen as a vividly generous acknowledgement.

Concentration on theatrical activity in London gives a misleadingly narrow view, which recent scholarship is adjusting. It is, however, probably true that the centralizing disposition of the first two Stuart kings postponed the full development of provincial theatre, forcing would-be actors into the capital. The traveller Fynes Moryson recorded in 1626 that 'The City of London alone hath four or five companies of players with their peculiar theatres capable of many thousands, wherein they all play every day in the week but Sunday, with most strange concourse of people . . . as there be, in my opinion, more plays in London than in all parts of the world I have seen, so do these players or comedians excel all others in the world'. English actors were admired on the continent, particularly in Germany and the Low Countries. A visitor to the 1592 Frankfurt Autumn Fair wrote to his wife: 'Here are some English actors whose plays I have seen. They have such splendid good music, and are perfect in their dancing and jumping, whose equal I have never seen. There are ten or twelve of them, all richly and magnificently clothed.' It was probably **Robert Browne**'s company that he saw – specialists in jigs, the popular and often bawdy afterpieces in which **Richard Tarleton** and, after him, **William Kempe** featured in England. The Swiss visitor, Thomas Platter, was more struck by the jig that followed the Globe performance of *Julius Caesar* (1599) than by the play itself, although he thought that 'very well acted'. The theatre of Elizabethan and Jacobean London was popular, not purist, and a farcical jig had as rightful a place on the programme as a tragedy or one of the sour, satirical comedies written by, or in imitation of, Jonson that displaced Shakespearian lyricism during the troubled early years of the 17th century. It was the Court entertainment that displayed an alternative, elitist approach to theatrical art, adumbrating the distinction between a boisterous public form and a sophisticated private one that has bedevilled English drama ever since. The division is implicit in the architecture of the last two Caroline theatres. Invited to remodel the Cockpit-in-Court in about 1630, Inigo Jones incorporated Palladian features after the refined Italian model, and the Salisbury Court theatre, though public, was a neoclassically severe brick structure, which might well have intimidated a popular audience.

Puritan opposition to the theatre gathered force under the Stuarts. William Prynne's *Histriomastix* (1632) is the best known of many attempts to expose in print the moral dangers of the lascivious stage. The city fathers, resentful of royal privilege, were in general alliance with the Puritans, though paradoxically prepared to employ playwrights and actors in the elaborate annual pageants at the inauguration of the Lord Mayor. Dekker, Jonson, **Thomas Heywood**, Middleton and Webster all wrote Lord Mayor's Shows, and these civic spectacles can be seen, in part, as the city's emulation of the masques at Court. But if the evidence is contradictory, the outcome of Puritan hostility is clear. Soon after the outbreak of Civil War, the London theatres, public and private, were closed (1642–3).

This rupture of historical process is significant above all for its effect on audiences. Under Charles I, there had been a discernible drift among writers and entrepreneurs away from public theatres towards the more exclusive, though not formally or officially exclusive, private theatres. The enforced closure of the open-air houses broke the habit of popular playgoing in England. That remains true despite the fact that the closure was intermittently defied. Surreptitious performances of the kind that certainly occurred at the Red Bull, **Cockpit** and Salisbury Court are likely to increase an audience's sense of its own exclusiveness. With few exceptions, actors took the Royalist side in the Civil War, and the King's defeat cost some their lives and all their livelihoods. The Puritans, Cromwell included, permitted the performance of plays in schools and, on occasions, in private houses, before discriminating audiences. It was the mixed crowds of the public theatres that they feared, their objection to plays being quite as much political as moral. By 1656, attitudes had sufficiently softened to allow **William Davenant**, knighted by Charles I in 1643 for services to the Royalist cause, to resume an adventurous theatrical career. *The Siege of Rhodes* (1656) at Rutland House was followed, at the 'public' Cockpit, by *The Cruelty of the Spaniards in Peru* (1658) and *Sir Francis Drake* (1659). It is sometimes argued that *The Siege of Rhodes* was the first English opera, but its greater importance lay in its theatrical innovations. Assisted by Inigo Jones's pupil, **John Webb**, Davenant imported the changeable scenery of the masques into the public theatre. Wings, grooves and painted backcloths, augmented by machinery on demand, would become the stock-in-trade of the English stage before the 17th century ended.

The Restoration period The theatre during the period 1660–1700 was so markedly different from its pre-Cromwellian self that it has been habitually distinguished as 'Restoration Theatre' and its drama as 'Restoration Drama'. There was, of course, some continuity, provided not least by the two men who led the reform of the stage under Charles II, Davenant and **Thomas Killigrew**. Davenant had written masques for Charles I and managed the Cockpit in the years immediately preceding the Civil War. Killigrew had written modish tragicomedies and acted at the Red Bull during the same period. Advised of the dangers of an unlimited theatre, Charles II rewarded the loyalty of these middle-aged men by granting them a monopoly over the performance of plays in the city of Westminster. He could not have predicted the effect that the Letters Patent, issued to Davenant and Killigrew in 1662, would have on the English theatre from then until the Theatres Act of 1843. His intention, quite simply, was to control the excited professionals who had greeted his Restoration by reoccupying abandoned theatres and staging plays from the old repertoire. Such unrestricted growth threatened the precarious balance of the monarchy, and the Letters Patent were a decisive reaction. Killigrew led his King's Men to a newly constructed theatre in **Drury Lane** and Davenant the Duke's Men to a converted tennis-court in **Lincoln's Inn Fields**, where he had installed the public theatre's first proscenium arch.

The greatest single difference between the Restoration stage and all that had preceded it lay in the debut of the professional actress. The first outstanding names are those of **Elizabeth Barry**, creator of **Thomas Otway**'s tragic heroines, and **Anne Bracegirdle**, creator of **William Congreve**'s liveliest ladies. From the outset, actresses occupied an ambiguous place in society. In the Green Room, the highest in the land would talk and flirt with them. It was probably the rakish Earl of Rochester's child that Elizabeth Barry bore. Anne Bracegirdle was the mistress of the gentlemanly Congreve. **Nell Gwyn**'s liaison with Charles II was the most notorious of several rags-to-riches progresses, nor was she the only actress to nestle in the royal bed. It was not until late in the 19th century that actresses were given patriarchal leave to pursue their new profession in acknowledged contradistinction from the oldest profession. Their presence on the Restoration stage made overt the latent sexuality of performance, and it elicited from the fashionable audience a seedy voyeurism that is an unattractive feature of the new theatre. The displacing of male actors from female roles was not completed overnight – **Edward Kynaston**, for example, was considered by Samuel Pepys 'the loveliest lady that ever I saw' in a revival of Fletcher's *The Loyal Subject* – but it was rapid, and it brought with it a measurable shift in the tone of English drama.

The best known of the 'old' playwrights in the post-Interregnum theatre were Beaumont and Fletcher. A large Folio edition of their work had been published in 1647 – it was, in fact, an anthology of plays, few of them jointly written by the named authors, and some by neither – and it provided a treasury of Jacobean plays to energize the Restoration theatre. Its influence is apparent in the escapades of **Aphra Behn**'s intrigue comedies, in Samuel Tuke's *The Adventures of Five Hours* (1663) and in the forgotten work of **Thomas D'Urfey**, in which Spanish plots are grafted onto English manners. More solidly 'English' were **Thomas Shadwell**'s attempts to revitalize the Jonsonian comedy of humours, though Shadwell was also one of the many Restoration writers to plunder **Molière** without remembering to steal the clarity of his moral vision. Released from Puritan restraints, the fashion-conscious intellectuals of Restoration England tested the scope of human liberty. The great poets and thinkers of the mid-century, men like Milton and Hobbes, had dared to enquire into the sources of human behaviour and to question the legitimate power of governments, and the Restoration quest for knowledge is exemplified at its best by the cool intelligence of John Locke. But, as in all permissive societies, the honest quest can be easily diverted, and it is such a diversion that is recorded in the Restoration's most original contribution, the comedy of manners.

Adultery, either plotted or achieved, and acquisitive sexuality are common themes of what has come to be known as Restoration Comedy. Even where the tone is satirical, the cumulative tendency of these plays is to condone quick-witted conquests and easy virtue. The losers are usually less intelligent than the winners, and the dialogue sparkles most in contests of wit. Many of the female characters, like the actresses who played them, are willing sinners, plagued only by the fear of being found out, and the lords, knights and gentlemen stake their reputations on their effectiveness as seducers. The milieu is courtly and the *dramatis personae* predominantly aristocratic, though clever servants are often on hand to aid or thwart their betters' schemes. True to the spirit of comedy, the plays usually end with the imminent marriage of at least one couple, but the institution of marriage has taken such a battering by then that this represents the shape rather than the substance of a happy ending. There is something feverish about the anxiety of the characters to maintain their place in a society which threatens to corrupt all whom it has not already corrupted. To be forced out of town, away from fashionable assemblies, is a dread prospect. (To a dog that bit him, the Earl of Rochester said, 'I wish you were married and living in the country.') The status of Restoration Comedy is still a matter of debate, but the artfulness, wit and ingenuity of its best writers, **Etherege**, **Wycherley**, **Vanbrugh** and Congreve, is undeniable.

The style and subject matter of these comedies was controversial. The actor-playwright **Colley Cibber**, a gifted sycophant, provided an antidote in *Love's Last Shift* (1696), whose rakish hero ultimately resolves to reform and to honour his marriage vows. Cibber lost face in the short term, when Vanbrugh's hurriedly written but brilliant *The Relapse* showed Cibber's repentant hero's speedy fall from grace, but he won in the long term. In retrospect, *Love's Last Shift* can be seen as a harbinger of the imminent triumph of sentimental comedy over the Restoration comedy of manners. A crucial blow was struck by **Jeremy Collier**, whose *Short View of the Immorality and Profaneness of the English Stage* (1698) focused hostility on Vanbrugh and Congreve. Congreve was stung into action, and a pamphlet war ensued, with points scored on either side, but Congreve withdrew from the theatre after writing *The Way of the World* (1700), and it was left to the more genial **George Farquhar** to preserve the spirit of Restoration Comedy. When Farquhar died in poverty in 1707, a dramatic style died with him.

The change in taste was dictated by a changed audience. The early Restoration theatres were small and fashionable, but when the first Drury Lane was destroyed by fire (1672), it was replaced by a grander building, probably designed by Sir Christopher Wren, with a capacity increased from 700 to 2,000. The Duke's Men, led by the actor **Thomas Betterton**, had already moved from Lincoln's Inn Fields to a more capacious theatre in **Dorset Garden** (1671). The city's prosperous bourgeoisie could now exert its claims on the theatre. Less easy to particularize is the influence of Betterton, widely acknowledged as the age's greatest actor and accepted by colleagues as their leader. Respected and respectable in the loose world of the theatre, Betterton's image is solidly middle-class. When the Duke's and King's Men united at Drury Lane in 1682, it was Betterton who smoothed the rough passage, and it was he who, in protest against the malpractice of Drury Lane's Patent-holder Christopher Rich, led a breakaway group of actors to Lincoln's Inn Fields in 1695. Cibber's finest service to the English theatre is his generous record of Betterton's acting in his *Apology for the Life of Mr Colley Cibber, Comedian* (1740). The long dominance of the school of Betterton, formal, rhetorically measured in its delineation of the passions, given to heightened verse-speaking not far from chanting, was about to face the decisive challenge of **David Garrick** when Cibber's book was published. But, in his own time, Betterton was admired as Hamlet and Falstaff and for his mastery of the awkward language of heroic tragedy.

The tragic drama of Restoration England is not, for the most part, impressive. Over-affected by the niceties of neoclassical theory, the courtly poets of the period tried to import into English heroic couplets the crisp language and high sentiments of **Corneille** and **Racine**. The outcome, even from a writer as fine as **John Dryden**, was bombastic in a way that would have horrified Racine. Written at the height of the fashion for heroic tragedy, the two parts of Dryden's *The Conquest of Granada* (1670–1) exemplify the best and worst of the style. A notable theatrical consequence was the brilliant satire of the **Duke of Buckingham**'s *The Rehearsal* (1671), which pilloried Dryden and accelerated the decline of heroic tragedy, though Dryden had still to write one of his best, *Aureng-Zebe* (1675). More admired today is his *All for Love*, a blank verse reworking of Shakespeare's *Antony and Cleopatra* according to the more 'correct' taste of the Restoration. Otway, whose early ventures into heroic tragedy were moderately successful, turned to blank verse for *The Orphan* (1680) and *Venice Preserv'd* (1682), in which he revealed a rhetorical gift that recalls the riches of Elizabethan dramatic poetry. Otway, melancholy victim of an unrequited passion for Elizabeth Barry, died young. **Nathaniel Lee**, of whose ranting and death-strewn tragedies *The Rival Queens* (1677) proved most durable, was not much older when he died, confined in Bedlam as a lunatic. Having held their place in the theatrical repertoire into the 19th century, Lee's plays dropped into obscurity when the melodramatic taste for spectacle and triumphant virtue challenged his commitment to vaulting verse and death-throes. Unlike Otway's, they have not been successfully revived in the 20th century.

No survey of Restoration theatre can ignore the impact of dramatic theory. Dryden's *Essay of Dramatick Poesie* (1668) and Thomas Rymer's *Short View of Tragedy* (1693) provide a convenient frame. Both men, Rymer myopically, were partisans of French neoclassicism and of the rationalizing tendency of the 'new' philosophy. It was a movement on which Bishop Hurd would look back from the next century with a mixture of pride and ruefulness: 'What we have gotten by this revolution is a great deal of good sense. What we have lost is a world of fine fabling.' What were such 'ruly' critics to make of the unruly Shakespeare? Dryden's preparedness to admire him was characteristically generous, but characteristic also was his pragmatic decision to carry reproof of Shakespeare's barbarities to the point of improvement. It was during the Restoration period that the long tradition of rewriting Shakespeare began. Dryden contributed not only *All for Love* but also a corrected *Troilus and Cressida* (1679) with an influential critical Preface. A version of *The Tempest*, on which he collaborated with Davenant, was further modified by Shadwell as an opera, *The Enchanted Island* (1674), in which scope was offered to the new excitement of changeable scenery. **Nahum Tate**'s *King Lear* (1681), which displaced Shakespeare's for 150 years, cut the Fool, preserved Lear and Gloucester and married Cordelia to Edgar. Cibber's *Richard III* (1700), which held the stage for even longer, imported passages from several other plays by Shakespeare, clearing all obstructions to Richard's absolute domination of the piece. Such alterations are of immense importance in the history of English acting. The testing of an actor's greatness by reference to Shakespearian roles, already emergent in 1700 and soon to become mandatory, was carried out under the controlled conditions supplied by rewritten texts.

The 18th century In 1700, the Patent theatres were in familiar disarray. At Drury Lane, Christopher Rich's unpopular regime continued, whilst the best actors remained with Betterton at Lincoln's Inn Fields. It was already difficult to trace with precision the legal status of the Patents since the custom of purchasing shares in them was established. The issue would haunt the London stage until 1843, when the power of the Patents was abolished by Act of Parliament. The opening of non-Patent theatres, irregular throughout the 18th century, would become a regular occurrence in the early decades of the 19th century. Despite the efforts of the Patent-holders, it was soon clear that the monopoly over the acted drama did not carry with it a monopoly over those forms of dramatic entertainment that could not be strictly categorized as 'drama', and as the popular taste turned more and more towards these 'illegitimate' forms, the holding of the Royal Patent for the presentation of legitimate drama teetered towards the condition of empty splendour. But that condition was still many years away when, in 1705, Betterton led his company into a lavish new theatre, designed by the architect-playwright Vanbrugh for erection in the Haymarket. Within a few years, this unwieldy Queen's Theatre had become the home of opera, and the Patents had reverted to Drury Lane and Lincoln's Inn Fields. Drury Lane entered a controversial but comparatively prosperous period (1710–33) under a triumvirate of actor-managers, Cibber, Robert Wilks and **Thomas Doggett** (later replaced by **Barton Booth**). Ousted from Drury Lane, Christopher Rich took his share in the Patent to Lincoln's Inn Fields in 1714. He died before the renovations he initiated were complete and was succeeded by his son, whose regime proved more innovative than his father's could ever have been. **John Rich** had taken part in Drury Lane dumb shows, imported from **commedia dell'arte** by the dancing-master, John Weaver. Under the stage name of John Lun, he became a famous **Harlequin**, figuring in the annual pantomimes which he inaugurated at Lincoln's Inn Fields in 1717. They were soon to be emulated at Drury Lane and elsewhere. Rich made sufficient money from his pantomimes and from the popular success of **John Gay**'s *The Beggar's Opera* (1728) to undertake the construction of a new theatre, close to Drury Lane. The running rivalry of the Theatres Royal in **Covent Garden** and Drury Lane is a *leitmotif* in the subsequent history of the Patent houses.

The legitimate drama over which the patentees squabbled is now largely confined to the bookshelves of collectors of the voluminous anthologies of British plays – Cumberland's, Bell's, Inchbald's, Lacy's, Dick's and eventually French's. The moralizing comedies of Sir Francis Steele, from *The Funeral* (1701) to *The Conscious Lovers* (1722), are competently crafted but over-earnest. There is more life and less substance in the work of his contemporary, **Susannah Cent-livre**. Like most of the finest writers for the next 250 years, Steele was an uncertain dramatist. It is as an essayist and as the founder of the first English theatrical periodical, *The Theatre* (1719), that his reputation is most secure. The mid-century intellectual vogue for

sentimentality found Steele's successors in comedy well-equipped to exploit it. **Goldsmith**'s *The Good-Natured Man* (1768) has a sentimental hero, but Goldsmith subjects his behaviour to a scrutiny beyond the range of opportunistic playwrights like **Hugh Kelly**, whose *False Delicacy* (1768) eclipsed Goldsmith's play in London, and **Richard Cumberland**, whose hero in *The West Indian* (1771) is an 18th-century man of feeling bereft of any pupose beyond benevolence. This play was one of the great successes during Garrick's management of Drury Lane, bestowing on Cumberland a leadership of taste that stung **Sheridan** into caricaturing him as Sir Fretful Plagiary in *The Critic* (1779). Sheridan's own career as a playwright began auspiciously with *The Rivals* (1775), reached its peak with *The School for Scandal* (1777) and the glorious theatrical burlesque *The Critic*, dwindling after his election to Parliament in 1780 to culminate sadly in *Pizarro* (1799). Literary historians have tended to present Sheridan as an isolated phenomenon, supported in his struggle against sentimental comedy only by the excellence of Goldsmith's *She Stoops to Conquer* (1773). The truth is less bleak. The comedy of manners had other exponents, **Arthur Murphy**, **George Colman the Elder**, **John O'Keeffe** and the actor-playwrights Garrick and **Charles Macklin** among them.

It was in tragedy that the 18th century was worst served. Essays at poetic tragedy were frequent, but few attracted audiences. **Nicholas Rowe**, better remembered for his regularizing edition of Shakespeare (1709), provided strong roles for women, particularly in *The Fair Penitent* (1703) and *Jane Shore* (1714). They were still in **Sarah Siddons**'s repertoire as the century neared its end. As much for topical as for dramatic reasons, **Joseph Addison**'s neoclassical tragedy *Cato* (1713) had a celebrated run at Drury Lane, but Addison's essays are a securer monument. The best-known, though not necessarily the best, of later poetic tragedies include **Samuel Johnson**'s *Irene* (1749), **John Home**'s *Douglas* (1756) and Murphy's *The Grecian Daughter* (1772), but none is great. The perennial problem for writers of tragedy has been the example of Shakespeare and his contemporaries. Throughout the 18th and 19th centuries, the writers' search for a voice of their own in poetic tragedy had drifted too soon into an attempt to sound like Shakespeare. The exceptional case is that of domestic tragedy, pioneered by **George Lillo**. That Lillo was conscious of Elizabethan precedent is evident from his adaptation of *Arden of Feversham* but his plays belong firmly to their own age. The best, *The London Merchant* (1731), is a Hogarthian warning to idle apprentices. Its bourgeois author, speaking confidently to a bourgeois audience, commends industry, thrift and satisfaction with a middle station in life. Lillo's plays belong to an age that, in poetry, produced Pomfret's *The Choice* (1700) and Henry Baker's prayer: 'Grant me, ye gods, before I die / An happy mediocrity', and whose representative novel is Richardson's *Pamela* (1740). He had few followers in England – **Edward Moore**'s dreary play *The Gamester* (1753) is usually cited – though sentimental comedy shares his priorities, differing only in outcome. It was on the continent, particularly in the German states, that his influence was felt. Lillo had, after all, dared to challenge the Aristotelian conviction that tragedy requires noble protagonists. Dull himself, he nevertheless initiated a movement that would provide the 19th century with **Ibsen**'s plays.

It was outside the established modes of comedy and tragedy that the 18th century produced its liveliest drama. Ballad opera, boosted by *The Beggar's Opera*, retained its theatrical hold throughout the century. Gay had intended to mock the fashionable cult of Italian opera by providing popular songs with comically inappropriate orchestral and harmonic frills. Instead, he fashioned a genre which, on the one hand, profoundly strengthened the world of 'illegitimate' drama and, on the other, offered to homegrown English opera a new, non-Italianate direction. That the political gibes of *The Beggar's Opera* had struck home was proved by the banning of its sequel, *Polly*, and ballad opera remained a convenient container for social and political satire even as the censors grew more vigilant. The best, and most irritating, exponent was **Henry Fielding**, in militant occupation of a small unlicensed theatre in the **Haymarket**, where he staged a series of his own ballad operas and burlesques, as well as work by his friends and political allies. The main target was Robert Walpole, financial wizard of the Whig administration, but even the royal family felt Fielding's lash, hilariously plied in *The Welsh Opera* (1731). Without the advantages of the Patent houses, the Haymarket was also free of their constraints. Not since Middleton's *A Game at Chess* (1624) had contemporary political leaders been so openly attacked in the theatre as they were in Fielding's *Pasquin* (1736) and *The Historical Register for the Year 1736* (1737). Walpole took offence (or fright) and engineered a counter-attack, choosing as his weapon a scurrilous play called *The Golden Rump*. The provenance of this piece, or even whether it ever existed outside the fertile brains of Walpole and his fellow-schemers, is not known. It had, purportedly, been submitted to Henry Giffard, manager of another unlicensed theatre in **Goodman's Fields**, who thought it his patriotic duty to show it to Walpole. It is to be hoped that Giffard was well rewarded, for it was by means of judicious 'quotation' from *The Golden Rump* that Walpole persuaded Parliament of the need to curb the freedom of the turbulent theatre. One result was Lord Chesterfield's exemplary speech on the dangers of censorship, but a more repressive one was the Theatre Licensing Act of 1737. The Act aimed to consolidate the monopoly of the Patent theatres and to define for ever the terms of the Lord Chamberlain's control over the contents of performed plays. It was immediately effective on both fronts. Fielding's Haymarket operations were brought to an end and even Giffard had to close his theatre. In the longer term, though, it was only the processes of censorship that were adhered to. Once the heat was off, Giffard reopened his theatre – it was there that Garrick made his sensational debut in 1741. Deprived of an outlet for his plays, Fielding contributed his genius to the developing English novel, and it was the maverick **Samuel Foote** who reopened the Haymarket in 1747, charging patrons for tea and offering theatrical entertainment 'free'. The laws governing dramatic censorship were not so easily subverted. The Chamberlain's office retained legal authority over English drama until 1968, varying its rigidity according to the views of successive Chamberlains and Examiners of Plays. (The Examiner of Plays was appointed by the Crown to do or supervise the actual reading under the Lord Chamberlain's *imprimatur*. None distinguished himself.) However liberal the individual Examiner, the effect on English drama was unfortunate. To be confident of uncensored performance, playwrights had to avoid religious or political controversy. That is to say that they had to disengage themselves from the vital questions of their age. It is no surprise that the greatest writers of the next 200 years chose the freedom of the novel and of poetry.

Perversely perhaps, the theatre did not shrivel under the Lord Chamberlain's scrutiny. There was always the refuge of innuendo or the risky exhilaration of altering the written text in performance. Working playwrights tailored their plays to suit the public. It was common practice for the author of a comedy to abbreviate it as an afterpiece when it had served its turn in full-length form. Afterpieces, knowingly contrived by professionals like Garrick, Foote, Murphy and Colman, were often deployed to sustain the run of a faltering tragedy. It was an opportunistic, pragmatic theatre, in which the actor shone more brightly than the dramatist. The early years of the 18th century saw the rise of **Anne Oldfield**, supreme in Drury Lane comedy opposite Robert Wilks and Barton Booth. **James Quin**, Betterton's successor in Shakespearian roles, made his London debut in 1714. The year 1741 was a watershed. At Drury Lane in February, the fiery Macklin defied the pundits by playing Shylock as a serious, even dignified, figure. For Alexander Pope, 'This was the Jew that Shakespeare drew'. In October, a charismatric Midlander drew fashionable audiences to see his (and Cibber's) Richard III at Giffard's theatre in Goodman's Fields. David Garrick was launched in London.

Garrick's impact on the English theatre was greater than any single person's before or since. There was nothing that he did not touch. Versatile enough to play tragedy and comedy, he also wrote prolifically, adapted Shakespeare, inaugurated the glorification of Stratford-upon-Avon as birthplace of the bard (though the English climate turned his 1769 Jubilee into a fiasco), and established by his own conversational brilliance the actor's right of entry to intellectual society. But it was above all as manager of Drury Lane (1747–76) that Garrick raised the theatre. His supervision of stage business, though by no means that of a modern director, was unprecedentedly disciplined, and his clearing of the audience from the stage together with his ill-fated attempt to abolish the custom of half-price admission after the third act of the main piece – a custom which virtually invited roisterers to come drunk to the theatre – show the professionalism of his approach. Even on vacation, Garrick was at work. After a continental holiday, he invited the Alsatian painter **De Loutherbourg** to Drury Lane. As scenic director, de Loutherbourg began the transformation from the old system of flats and wings to the new one of exquisitely painted back-drops and the breaking of the stage-surface by load-bearing levels. His lighting innovations enhanced the illusion of reality in, for example, storms, fires and moonlit scenes. Garrick, although unashamedly conscious of himself as a star, built up a strong company at Drury Lane. Among many actresses who shared his glory were **Peg Woffington**, a trendsetter in **breeches parts**, the pert **Kitty Clive**, **Hannah Pritchard**, **Susanna Cibber**, **George Anne Bellamy** and **Frances Abington**. More chary of male competition, Garrick released **Spranger Barry** to Covent Garden in 1750. This fine-voiced and handsome Irishman was openly ambitious to usurp Garrick's crown, and their rivalry briefly brought competition between the Patent houses to a head.

A more serious problem was the alacrity with which financial backers greeted the increasing size of audiences by increasing the size of the theatres: Henry Holland's designs for the reconstruction of Drury Lane (1791) and Covent Garden (1792) raised both to a capacity in excess of 3,000, thus capping a steady growth over several decades. A parallel broadening of acting styles was unavoidable, and many discriminating actors and spectators came to prefer the reduced scale of the Haymarket. This theatre had undergone a significant change in status since its reopening by Samuel Foote. Foote's legendary improvidence had already lost him two fortunes when, in 1776, he also lost a leg. In remorse, or perhaps to buy Foote's silence, the Duke of York, who had been party to the prank that resulted in the amputation, procured for Foote a 'limited licence' to stage the legitimate drama during the summer months, when the Patent theatres were closed. By the end of the century, the 'little theatre in the Haymarket' was able to mount a formidable challenge to its overgrown rivals. It was then being managed, in succession to his father, by the clever but indolent **younger Colman**. After wintering in the vastnesses of Drury Lane, many actors found the summer intimacy of the Haymarket a blessed relief, and dramatists were easily persuaded that their plays had a better chance to be heard there. The new generation, whose writing would span the centuries – **Thomas Morton**, **Elizabeth Inchbald**, Frederick Reynolds, the younger Colman himself – accustomed themselves to writing scenic spectacles for the Patent theatres and plays for the Haymarket, and the new generation of actors, particularly those in the comic line – Joseph Munden, **Dorothy Jordan**, **John Liston**, **Charles Mathews** – had to make a virtue of inconsistency, or risk penury. The all-purpose actors, like Colman's favourite, **John Bannister**, were natural products of this confused period in English theatre history. The established genres of tragedy and comedy split into numerous sub-divisions, not least because unlicensed theatres sought to evade the law by mingling music and songs with the spoken text. Anything with music was 'illegitimate' and could, therefore, be performed anywhere. The range was wide, covering **Isaac Bickerstaffe**'s *Love in a Village* (1762), which, given original music by Thomas Arne, links ballad opera and English operetta, Colman's *Inkle and Yarico* (1787), which is closer to modern musical comedy, and countless 'straight' plays interrupted without rhyme or reason by sudden solos or glees. The curious word 'burletta' was often applied to such pieces. Asked to define 'burletta' during his undistinguished tenure of the office of Examiner of Plays, the younger Colman could suggest only that it was a play with at least five songs in each act.

It was a difficult task to maintain the Patent theatres amid such confusion. At Covent Garden (1774–1820), Thomas Harris displayed for 50 years a greater interest in business than in art, whilst Sheridan, who had succeeded Garrick at Drury Lane, showed small concern with either, deputing effective control to **John**

Philip Kemble in 1788. Kemble and his sister, **Sarah Siddons**, were dominant figures in the London theatre, to which they brought an Augustan dignity. Kemble excelled as Shakespeare's Roman heroes, in each of whom he found and embodied a ruling passion. Mrs Siddons, the most Racinian of English actresses, chilled audiences as Lady Macbeth and made them sob as Constance in *King John*. Their combined social prestige was still a rarity in an unstable profession. As a manager, Kemble found his belief in high art troubled by the demands of accountancy. Exasperated by Sheridan's interference, he moved to Covent Garden in 1805, and his last active years were scarred by the Old Price Riots (1809), the ridiculous craze for the 'young Roscius' **William Betty** (1804–5) and the sudden rivalry, after 1814, of **Edmund Kean**.

The Kembles' careers began, as was by now almost invariably the case, in the provinces. It was during the 18th century that the English provincial theatre became established. The practice was for a stock company to occupy a theatre in one town or city and use it as a base from which to tour a circuit of theatres. Thus, the Lincoln circuit embraced Grantham, Boston, Peterborough, Wisbech, Huntingdon, Spalding and Newark. From Nottingham, the stock company visited Worcester, Wolverhampton, Derby, Retford and Stamford. The Norwich circuit included Ipswich, Colchester, Bury St Edmunds and Yarmouth. Particularly famous, both in their own right and as launching-pads for London fame, were the companies based in Bath and in York. **Tate Wilkinson**, who managed the York circuit (Hull, Leeds, Doncaster, Wakefield, Pontefract) for about 30 years, is one of the 18th-century theatre's most colourful figures. It became customary for London stars to appear in favourite roles in provincial theatres, where they were supported by the local stock company. On one such occasion, the majestic Mrs Siddons needlessly commiserated with the diminutive Edmund Kean: 'You have done well, sir – very well. It is a pity there is too little of you to go far.'

The 19th century With English acting reaching new heights and English drama in a trough, there was a vacuum to be filled. The leading name as the 19th century began was that of the German playwright, **Kotzebue**. His *Menschenhass und Reue*, decently disguised to satisfy English modesty, had appeared in Benjamin Thompson's adaptation as *The Stranger* (1798), and in the same year Mrs Inchbald had turned *Das Kind der Liebe* into *Lovers' Vows*. Even watered-down Kotzebue was shocking enough to flutter domestic peace, as the younger generation discover in Jane Austen's *Mansfield Park* (1814), when their rehearsal of *Lovers' Vows* is interrupted by Sir Thomas Bertram's return. For the splendidly bad-tempered critic Thomas Dutton, this foreign domination of the English stage was deplorable, and in 1800 he filled successive numbers of his journal, *The Dramatic Censor*, with a celebration of the English renaissance as exemplified by Thomas Morton's new play, *Speed the Plough*. It is worth asking why Dutton should have so overrated a play which is now noted only for its invention of **Mrs Grundy**. *Speed the Plough* has five acts – the length is significant because a five-act structure implied an attempt to write within one of the major genres, tragedy or comedy – and at least three plots, forced together rather than linked. Its main plot is a gallimaufry of castles, lost heirs, secret guilt, locked chambers and remorse. Its obvious reference is to the contemporary novels of such as Ann Radcliffe and Matthew 'Monk' Lewis, the latter of whom had recently succeeded with a Gothic play, *The Castle Spectre* (1797). The secondary plot centres on the domestic life of a salt-of-the-earth farmer, whose good-hearted wife, a little too anxious to keep up appearances, is plagued by fears about what Mrs Grundy (who never appears) will say if she fails. The sentimental view that simplicity is synonymous with goodness had already a long history in the theatre, and would have a long future. A third plot, involving the mismatched and uxorious Sir Abel Handy, is a grotesque comedy of manners. There are no songs, but the play is otherwise characteristic of the mixed drama familiar to contemporary audiences. It is not great literature, but it fairly represents the best that can be expected – though better work might sometimes have been achieved – from a national drama whose hands were tied by a predominantly philistine censorship. Its virtues are those of good story-telling, its limitation a reliance on the existing stock of theatrical characters and situations.

Morton called *Speed the Plough* a 'comedy', but it belongs to the world of melodrama, into which Kotzebue had already guided the English theatre. The first self-styled melodrama on the London stage was **Thomas Holcroft**'s *A Tale of Mystery* (1802), adapted from a French play by **Pixérécourt**. Melodrama in its many guises is a distinctively 19th-century genre. It gratified the greed for spectacle, which was met also by the hippodramas at **Astley**'s Amphitheatre, the dioramas and panoramas, *tableaux vivants*, waxworks, magic lanterns, freaks and machines that added to the proliferating shows of London. But melodrama also responded to the emotional needs of an increasingly humdrum industrialized society. Playing on the nerves rather than the feelings, it replaces tragic catastrophe with peril. Its threatened heroines, resisting 'a fate worse than death', wrapped eroticism in an acceptable disguise. Its thrills and spills aroused the excitability of the superficially placid 19th-century middle classes, that same erethism that fed on Newgate novels and the supremely 'theatrical' work of **Charles Dickens**. Melodrama is a broad category, and there is little similarity between the rough justice of Isaac Pocock's *The Miller and his Men* (1813) or **Douglas Jerrold**'s *Black-Eyed Susan* (1829) and the crafted composition of **Dion Boucicault**'s *The Shaughraun* (1874) or **Henry Arthur Jones** and Henry Herman's *The Silver King* (1882), but the audience for such plays remained broadly the same. Every journeyman-dramatist of the century needed to know how to turn a melodrama. There was ready employment for facile journeymen at London's now-numerous theatres. **Sadler's Wells** had been active since 1765 and Astley's Amphitheatre since 1784. After 1806, the **Olympic**, the **Adelphi** and the rebuilt Surrey led the illegitimate charge, to be joined in 1809 by the more stately **Lyceum**, in 1818 by the Coburg (better known by its later nickname, the **Old Vic**) and in 1832 by the Strand. For these and other rivals to the Patent theatres, melodrama was the staple fare.

The quest for great tragedies continued alongside the spread of melodrama, and the claims of Joanna Baillie, Thomas Beddoes, Henry Milman, Richard Sheil, Henry Taylor, Thomas Talfourd and **W. G. Wills** were, at various times, vaunted. Most of the century's poets, from Wordsworth to Hardy, tried their hand at drama, with no one working harder on their behalf than the actor-manager, **William Macready**. But even Macready could make nothing of Browning's plays, and the only one of **Byron**'s that he found marketable was the Gothic melodrama, *Werner*. Of Byron's 'studiously Greek' tragedies, *Marino Faliero* flopped at Drury Lane in 1823 and the 1853 revival of *Sardanapalus* at the **Princess's** owed its cult-success to the lavish pedantry of **Charles Kean**'s archaeological research. Even **Tennyson**, despite his hold on the popular imagination, faltered in the theatre. His *Becket*, doctored and superbly performed by **Henry Irving**, was one of the glories of the century's last decade, but Irving died performing it and the play died with him. The only 19th-century tragedies to share literary and theatrical acclaim in their own time were those of **James Sheridan Knowles**, which now read poorly and have not been revived.

The condition of comedy was only a little healthier. One of the best, Colman the Younger's *John Bull* (1803), is typically dependent on the creation of eccentric 'characters', culled from past plays and loosely regrouped round an extravagant plot. The basic theme of comedy, as of melodrama, was money, a fact which **Edward Bulwer** frankly acknowledged in the title of his proficient *Money* (1840). Knowles's comedies, much better than his tragedies, were neglected even in his own time. Like Boucicault's *London Assurance* (1841) and *Old Heads and Young Hearts* (1844), and like **Tom Taylor**'s *The Overland Route* (1860), they derive from the comedy of manners, maintaining a tradition that would culminate in the 19th century's single dramatic masterpiece, **Oscar Wilde**'s *The Importance of Being Earnest* (1895). A significant, even revolutionary, step was taken when, at the previously unfashionable **Prince of Wales's**, under the bold management of **Marie Wilton**, a succession of plays by **T. W. (Tom) Robertson** was staged. *Society* (1865), *Ours* (1866), *Caste* (1867), *Play* (1868) and *School* (1869) are exceptional only in manner. For the first time, English comedy was allowed to settle snugly into prose. Knowing his limitations, Robertson let his characters talk like real people and diverted the sensation-scenes of melodrama into domestic routines: the pouring of tea, the carrying of milk-cans, the preparation of a roly-poly pudding. The recent innovation of the box-set permitted the use of doors – with real handles, and encouraged the fundamentally middle-class Robertson to depict the fundamentally middle-class. In his charming homage to the mid-Victorian theatre, *Trelawny of the Wells* (1898), **Pinero** portrays, through Tom Wrench, Robertson's delight in the mundane detail of stage business. Pinero was a beneficiary of the Robertsonian reformation, an inheritance which he used to guide comedy into the new territory of the social-problem play. *The Second Mrs Tanqueray* (1893), described as a 'drama' and certainly not a comedy, is the most famous example of the *fin-de-siècle* genre. Pinero wrote several more, as did Henry Arthur Jones among others.

More dependent on melodrama than on tragedy, the

19th-century stage was also more dependent on farce than on comedy. The long theatrical bills would conventionally end with a one-act farce, work for facile writers from Theodore Hook to **W. S. Gilbert**, and full-length farces 'from the French' were a frequent feature during the latter half of the century. The delight in childlike 'fun', which is so enigmatic an aspect of Victorian escapism, was expressed also in travesty, burlesque, extravaganza and pantomime, expertly composed by **J. R. Planché**, **H. J. Byron**, F. C. Burnand and others. The growth of the music-hall and the continuing development of comic opera, operetta and ballet are further evidence of the urban hunger for entertainment. The Patent theatres, forced to retain vast companies to cater for the variety of public taste, lost their distinctiveness and eventually, in 1843, their privilege. By 1900, Drury Lane was known as the home of pantomime and Covent Garden as the head-quarters of opera.

The Patent theatres had narrowly survived the first four decades of the 19th century through the drawing power of actors and the opportunism of managers. For six seasons (1814–19), Drury Lane had the best of Edmund Kean, but after that, he and his equally profligate manager, **Robert Elliston** (**Charles Lamb**'s 'Great Lessee'), slid together towards disaster. Macready, Kean's immediate successor, did his best to repair the damage done to the reputation of actors, with a dogged and thoroughly Victorian determination to improve the theatres he grudgingly adorned. Although Macready was a conscientious manager, he had too little respect for his fellow-actors to be a great one. The story of the 19th-century theatre is elsewhere strung together by a succession of impressive actor-managers. Daniel Terry and Frederick Yates established melodrama at the Adelphi (1825–9). **Madame Vestris** brilliantly staged Planché's extravaganzas at the Olympic (1831–9), where stylish costume and scenic invention were part of the routine. Vestris engaged **Charles James Mathews** in 1835, and it was at the Olympic that his relaxed comic style first challenged the gagging and caricatured oddness of his predecessors in comedy. The installation of gas-lighting in London's theatres (the Lyceum and Drury Lane led the way in 1817) allowed actors to perform within rather than in front of the scenery, inviting the evolution towards a greater naturalism, which Mathews accelerated. Charles Kean, the roguish Edmund's ultra-respectable son, made the Princess's a museum of pictorial staging (1850–9). Lavish productions and souvenir programmes that were illustrated records of research helped disguise the limitations of Kean's own acting. **Benjamin Webster** at the Haymarket (1837–53) and his successor, **J. B. Buckstone** (1853–79), built up a comic ensemble that lasted long enough to become old-fashioned. Marie Wilton and **Squire Bancroft** at the Prince of Wales's (1865–80) not only staged Robertson's comedies, but also changed the style of theatregoing. Their replacing of the old pit benches with individual stalls was an influential innovation that, by quietening the audience closest to the actors, aided the development of unforced acting. The standards of Shakespearian production were raised by **Samuel Phelps** during his astonishing years at Sadler's Wells (1844–62). Taking immediate advantage of the abolition of the Patent monopoly, Phelps staged all but four of Shakespeare's plays in an avowedly low-brow theatre. Henry Irving's long tenure of the Lyceum (1878–1902) exceeded even such outstanding precedents. The theatre was his temple, and he laboured to perfect each part of it, from dim-lit foyer to dressing-rooms. His decision to lower the auditorium lights during performance produced another major shift in theatregoing. Although Irving acted in several of Shakespeare's plays and brought their pictorial staging to its height, the Lyceum, particularly during the great years of his partnership with **Ellen Terry**, was dedicated to the actor's art. Irving's Hamlet was fine, but so was his Mathias in **Leopold Lewis**'s melodrama of secret guilt, *The Bells* (1871). It was not the quality of a play but the quality of a role that determined his repertoire. For nearly 30 years, in all but name, the Lyceum was a national theatre, and Irving's knighthood (1895) acknowledged as much. The century ended with two notable actor-managers still in office, **George Alexander** at the St James's (1891–1917) and **Beerbohm Tree** at **Her Majesty's** (1897–1915).

Actor-managers worked closely with designers, inheriting from such as **William Capon** a concern for settings that were both grand and appropriate. William Beverley's was a major contribution to the success of Madame Vestris's Olympic seasons. The painter **Clarkson Stanfield** worked for Macready and others. The **Grieve** family brought flair and industry to the Patent Theatres. Hawes Craven realized Irving's visions as William Telbin had realized Charles Kean's. Scenery and machinery were vital parts of the Victorian spectacular theatre, in which elaborate scene-changes prolonged intervals and drew attention to the importance of refreshment facilities and hospitable foyers.

It was not easy to accommodate the rapid scenes and multiple locations of Shakespeare's plays in such a theatre, and the rearrangement of scenes was a normal practice. But a growing reverence for the bard was variously expressed through the 19th century. **Charles Kemble** staged *King John* at Covent Garden (1823) in costumes researched and designed by the ubiquitous J. R. Planché, inaugurating a new concern for historical accuracy. Macready restored the Fool to *King Lear* (1838), albeit played by a woman. (Edmund Kean had played Shakespeare's ending in 1826.) Samuel Phelps was more faithful to the received text than any of his predecessors and most of his immediate successors. Irving, for example, surrendered to public pressure by cutting the final act of *The Merchant of Venice*, a play which, in the 19th century, rarely survived the departure of Shylock. The publication in 1888 of the newly discovered De Witt drawing of the Swan invited antiquarian interest in simpler Shakespearian staging, but **William Poel**'s was the only significant response. His 1895 *Twelfth Night* for the Elizabethan Stage Society was the first of several bare-stage productions by this singular prophet, whose influence on **Harley Granville Barker** had a greater impact on Shakespearian production than anything he did himself. Meanwhile it was individual actors rather than great playwrights who continued to draw the public to the theatres.

It is an anomaly of which historians have to take account that, during a period whose drama has generally been derided, the theatre was more popular than ever before or since. Great acting and ingenious stage-design are the real theme of the age, and our understanding of this is enhanced by the unique brilliance of 19th-century theatre criticism. The record of Shakespearian performances, from **George Frederick Cooke**'s Richard III in 1800 to **Forbes-Robertson**'s Hamlet in 1897, was kept by the descriptive genius of **William Hazlitt, Leigh Hunt, George Henry Lewes, Westland Marston** and **George Bernard Shaw**. Given generous space in the journals for which they wrote, these men thought it the business of criticism to say what was seen and heard before encapsulating their own opinions. Even Shaw, for whom opinion was daily bread, is scrupulous to describe as well as to discriminate.

The 20th century Locked in its own past, the English theatre traditionally stole from abroad only those goods which could be confidently marketed at home. Against the strident advocacy of **William Archer** and Shaw, actor-managers carried into the 20th century a 'native' dislike of continental naturalism in general and of the 'wretched, deplorable, loathsome' (Clement Scott in the *Daily Telegraph*) Ibsen in particular. The dominance of the 'long runs', supported by elaborate staging and the new suppleness of electric light, downgraded experiment, and it was left to small semi-professional groups, like J. T. Grein's Independent Theatre (founded in 1891) and the **Stage Society** (1899–1939), to pioneer the 'theatre of ideas'. It was the Stage Society's 1902 production of Shaw's prostitution-play, *Mrs Warren's Profession*, that established the right of 'private' clubs to perform works banned by the Lord Chamberlain. Earlier examples, like the Shelley Society's 1886 production of *The Cenci*, had been more discreet, but even such discretion has its admixture of valour. Much of the initiative in the 'modern' English theatre belongs to individuals operating in isolation from the mainstream. **Janet Achurch**'s tours of Ibsen and Shaw took her all over England and as far afield as Cairo. **Edith Craig**, the elder of Ellen Terry's two children, took a lead in the women's theatre movement as director of the Pioneer Players (1911–21). The younger, **Edward Gordon Craig**, was one of the rare English theatrical visionaries. Always a maverick, he had done little work in the English theatre, which he found stodgy, when he began his long residence in Italy, but his journal, *The Mask* (1908–29), was a source of inspiration to many people. Craig's aesthetic interest in the actor as one element in the kinetic sculpture of theatre led him to the concept of the *Über-Marionette*, a creature wholly subservient to the totality of the work of art, and he found his unlikely model in the disciplined regime of Irving's Lyceum productions. Irving's example, very differently perceived, also inspired the Shakespearian tours of **F. R. Benson**, whose annual visits to Stratford (1886–1916) established the provincial eminence of Shakespeare's birthplace. More immediately significant than any of these was the sequence of seasons at the **Royal Court** (1904–7) under the joint management of **J. E. Vedrenne** and Granville Barker. Committed to repertory rather than to long runs, Vedrenne and Barker not only introduced to London several continental dramatists (**Hauptmann, Maeterlinck, Schnitzler**), but also affirmed the centrality of Ibsen, provided a platform for English naturalism in the plays of **Galsworthy, St John Hankin** and Barker himself and established Shaw as the chief playwright of the new English theatre.

Shaw's plays, though touched by many 'schools', belong to none. Passionate to argue, he would contradict himself in the absence of intelligent contradiction from others. His childlike exuberance and his conviction that ideas important outside the theatre have a proper place inside it go some way towards explaining the tone of English drama, part-boyish and part-knowing, during the first half of the 20th century. The best, like the most successful, plays of this period are not really Shavian, but they occupy the adult playground that he helped to build. It was a playground for the fantasies of **J. M. Barrie** and the time-plays of **J. B. Priestley**, for **Somerset Maugham, Frederick Lonsdale, Ben Travers, R. C. Sherriff**, John Van Druten and **Noël Coward**. Maugham pleased Edwardian audiences – he had four plays running in London in 1908 – with social comedies, brittly brilliant like Lonsdale's *On Approval* (1927) and Coward's *Private Lives* (1930), but in *For Services Rendered* (1932) he provided a harsh view of the effects of war that neatly balances Sherriff's depiction of war's conduct in *Journey's End* (1928). Travers carried into the thirties the frivolity of the twenties with the sequence of farces (1925–33) he wrote for the talented Aldwych company. Controversial subjects, although they had to be charily handled to avoid censorship, were not avoided. Youthful sexuality, for instance, was displayed with some frankness in Coward's early plays, *The Young Idea* (1923) and *The Vortex* (1924), and in Van Druten's *Young Woodley* (1925), which the Chamberlain's office inanely banned. (It was given its first English performance 'privately' in 1928.) These plays have in common a comfortable acceptance of the conventions of stage reality. Shaw, by contrast, was constantly exploring the same conventions in order to draw attention to realities outside the theatre. When **Barry Jackson** founded the Malvern Festival in 1929, he gave Shaw a regular provincial base from which to launch on London *The Apple Cart* (1929) and its successors. Jackson had already taken the extraordinary *Back to Methuselah* (1922) from Birmingham to London.

The development of provincial theatre is a striking feature of the 20th century. The old stock companies had been thrown into disorder by the rail-based mobility of the 19th-century touring companies. A pre- or post-London tour extended the life of a play by many weeks, which suited managements whilst jostling provincial centres into theatrical parasitism. It was against this background that the Repertory Movement began (see **Regional theatre, Britain**). Its champions aimed to hold several plays in repertoire instead of retaining one play for as long as its audience held. In the event, this continental repertory system proved too much for English theatres, hit by inflation after the First World War, and it was quickly adapted to accommodate a sequence of short runs. Such a system had already been tested in London, by Florence Farr at the Avenue (1894) as well as Vedrenne and Barker at the Royal Court. The provincial initiative was taken by the tea-heiress, **Annie Horniman**, who had supported Florence Farr at the Avenue and financed the conversion of Dublin's **Abbey Theatre** (1904). Horniman bought the old **Gaiety Theatre** in Manchester and presided over its repertory company from 1908–17. The company, which included **Sybil Thorndike** and **Lewis Casson**, staged several plays by Manchester-based writers, including **Stanley Houghton, Harold Brighouse** and Allan Monkhouse. Other cities followed suit – Liverpool (1911), Birmingham under Barry Jackson (1913), Sheffield (1923), Oxford under J. B. Fagan (1923) and Cambridge (1926), where the idiosyncratic **Terence Gray** made the Festival Theatre an influential, though sadly short-lived, centre for experimental staging. A post-war lull in new theatre-building ended with the opening of the Belgrade Theatre in Coventry (1958). A modest revival of theatre-in-the-round, strenuously advocated by **Stephen Joseph**, was represented by the **Victoria Theatre, Stoke-on-Trent** (1962 and in new premises from 1986), the Stephen Joseph Theatre in Scarborough (1970) and the remarkable **Royal Exchange Theatre** in Manchester (1976), a glass module suspended from four pillars in the vast hall of the city's former cotton exchange. All these theatres are notable for the production of new plays in a period when few repertory theatres dare to risk the unknown. Other theatres of architectural interest include the Mermaid in London (1959), which has an end-stage unprotected by a proscenium, the cylindrical Nottingham Playhouse (1963), and the thrust-stage **Chichester Festival Theatre** (1962) and Sheffield Crucible (1971).

The heyday of the repertory and civic theatres of England, which followed hard on the foundation of the **Arts Council** in 1946 and began to falter under challenge from the radical Fringe after 1968, is over. Most companies, feeling the pinch of monetarist strategies in the eighties, have taken refuge in 'safe' plays, preferably with small casts. The Arts Council, under-funded itself, has passed along the under-funding to the regions, with the ironic result that its policy of regional growth, portentously outlined in *The Glory of the Garden* (1984), is likely to be a prelude to regional attenuation. It is not easy to see how the Arts Council can preserve, let alone strengthen, the best of live theatre in England. Without subsidy, few theatres outside London's West End can survive. High rents, spiralling production costs and the wage increases negotiated by Actors' Equity (founded in 1929) have seen to that. For a while, subsidy kept pace with inflation, but the signs are that this tendency will be reversed. Selected regional theatres may be allowed to die (*pour encourager les autres?*) and the two major companies, the **National** and the **Royal Shakespeare**, whose development is a feature of the post-war theatre, preserved just below the level of significant growth.

When the Gothic Memorial Theatre that had housed Benson's Stratford performances was destroyed by fire (1926), it was replaced by the building which, with significant modifications, still stands. Under successive artistic directors – **W. Bridges-Adams** (1920–34), **Ben Iden Payne** (1935–43), Sir Barry Jackson (1945–8), **Anthony Quayle** (1948–56) and Glen Byam Shaw (1956–61) – the prestige of Stratford grew. Quayle was particularly successful in attracting major actors, like **Peggy Ashcroft**, **John Gielgud** and **Michael Redgrave**, away from London. But the real leap came with the appointment of the ambitious, young **Peter Hall** in 1961. Hall negotiated a change of name to the Royal Shakespeare Theatre and rented a London base at the Aldwych. Now, whilst Shakespeare remained the staple diet at Stratford, the Royal Shakespeare Company could display its skills, in plays old and new, in London. Notable revivals have included Boucicault's *London Assurance* (1970), O'Keeffe's *Wild Oats* (1976) and several plays by **Gorky**. **Trevor Nunn**, who succeeded Hall in 1969, continued to blend revivals and premieres, signalling his interest in experiment by adding studio theatres in London – the Place (1971–4) and the Warehouse (1977–82) – and Stratford – the Other Place (opened 1974). With its occupation of the spacious Barbican Centre in London (1982), the Company stated its claims for parity with the National Theatre. The conversion of the old museum at Stratford into the open-stage Swan Theatre (1986), designed to stage post-Shakespearian classics, gives the RSC an important new venue.

The long-delayed establishment of a National Theatre Company finally came about in 1962, with a production of *Hamlet* at the Old Vic. The appointment of **Laurence Olivier** as artistic director was a tribute to the man himself and to the acting profession as a whole. In collaboration with his literary manager, **Kenneth Tynan**, Olivier determined on an eclectic repertoire, with English and foreign classics balancing new work by **Tom Stoppard**, **Peter Shaffer** and **Trevor Griffiths**. In 1973, with work on the south-bank site well advanced, Olivier was replaced by Peter Hall, under whose supervision the three separate theatres – the Lyttelton, the Olivier and the small Cottesloe – were opened in 1976–7. The situation of the huge complex designed by Denys Lasdun to house the National Theatre is splendid, but size brings its own burdens. In unpredicted ways, the pains of the old Patent Theatres have come back. Nunn and Hall, like earlier managers of Drury Lane and Covent Garden, have to reconcile artistic aims with the constant drain of an ever-lengthening permanent pay-roll.

The single most distinctive invention of the 20th century theatre is the non-acting director. Not that the actor-manager disappeared overnight. Beerbohm Tree, **Charles Wyndham**, **John Martin-Harvey**, **Oscar Asche** and others imported to the new century the customs of the old, which perished splendidly with **Donald Wolfit** and Anew McMaster. We cannot name the first English 'director'. Actor-managers from Betterton onwards attended to the stage-picture. T. W. Robertson's concern for detailed business influenced actors as well as playwrights. Irving took to heart the example of the visiting **Meiningen company** (1881), and his subsequent mastery of crowd-scenes was an admired feature of Lyceum productions. But *quis custodiet ipsos custodies?* Modern purism would question the ability of an actor to direct himself. For Poel, and above all for Craig, the unifying vision had to be that of the artist-director. Granville Barker was the finest early master, above all in his Shakespeare productions at the Savoy (1912–14). Together with his designers, Charles Ricketts and Norman Wilkinson, Barker cut away the clutter of 'pictorial' Shakespeare to release the poetry of Shakespearian comedy. The escape from scenic realism was carried further by Claude Lovat Fraser during Nigel Playfair's 1920 season at the **Lyric, Hammersmith**. Fraser died, young and full of promise, in 1921, but Playfair, who had played Bottom in Barker's Savoy production of *A Midsummer Night's Dream*, continued at the Lyric until 1931, sharing with Norman MacDermott at the Hampstead Everyman (1920–6) an infectious optimism. More influential than either of these notable ventures was the long regime (1912–37) of the extraordinary **Lilian Baylis** at the Old Vic. From 1915–23, the Old Vic staged all the plays in the Shakespeare Folio, many of them starring Sybil Thorndike, but it was during the thirties that it became England's leading theatre. The Old Vic was, above all, an actors' house. Ashcroft, Wolfit, Olivier, Redgrave, Gielgud, **Charles Laughton**, **Ralph Richardson**, **Edith Evans**, **Flora Robson** and **Emlyn Williams** all played there. It was a directors' theatre, too. **Tyrone Guthrie**'s bold *Measure for Measure* (1933) and uncut *Hamlet* (1937), which, with Olivier in the title role, toured to Elsinore, were important productions. **Michel Saint-Denis** was brought from France to revive *The Witch of Edmonton* (1936), and remained to provide a vital focus for the reappraisal of theatrical values in England. Among the teachers at the London Theatre Studio, which he founded in 1936, was **George Devine**, who would later rejoin him at the influential Old Vic School. Other émigrés to bring flair and seriousness to the English theatre were **Michael Chekhov** and Theodore Komisarjevsky (**Fyodor Komissarzhevsky**), whose Stratford productions (1933–9) were controversial enough to turn heads that way. Komisarjevsky liked to design his own productions, and his interest in the material as well as the appearance of his scenery anticipated by many years the original work of designers like Sean Kenny, **John Bury** and **Ralph Koltai**. Since the Second World War, the primacy of the director has been increasingly taken for granted. The one undoubted genius, **Peter Brook**, began young, with Barry Jackson's companies at Birmingham and Stratford (1945–6), where he established the rapport with **Paul Scofield** that culminated in a wonderful *King Lear* (1964). Two of his productions for the Royal Shakespeare Company, **Peter Weiss**'s *Marat/Sade* (1964) and *A Midsummer Night's Dream* (1970), are already part of international theatre history, and Brook's explorations continue from the Parisian base to which he moved in 1970. The difficulty for lesser directors is the constant demand that they should inspire. Those without genius have too often to cultivate the appearance of having it.

For a while, after the Second World War, English drama retained its air of genteel irrelevance. **Agatha Christie**'s *The Mousetrap* began its unprecedented run at the Ambassador's in 1952, when **Brian Rix**'s seasons of farce at the Whitehall were in their third year. Christie and Rix provided material to bring bus tours to London theatres after the vogue for Ivor Novello's moonlit romanticism had passed. The initiative in musical comedy was briefly wrested from America by Sandy Wilson's *The Boy Friend* (1953) and Julian Slade's *Salad Days* (1954), as it would be again by Lionel Bart's *Oliver!* (1960). But it was the craftsmanlike realism of **Terence Rattigan** that best represented English drama during a period of nervous stasis. No one doubted that a change had to come. Poetic drama, briefly prosperous at the beginning of the century in the largely forgotten work of **Stephen Phillips**, **Gordon Bottomley** and **John Masefield**, was made suddenly newsworthy by **T. S. Eliot**'s later plays and the verbal fireworks of **Christopher Fry**'s *The Lady's Not for Burning* (1948),

but a growing impatience with plays written on the retreat from social confrontation, brilliantly spearheaded by Kenneth Tynan in the *Observer* (1954–58), swept the poetic revival aside. Three names previously unfamiliar to English theatregoers were being increasingly heard – **Beckett**, **Ionesco** and **Brecht**. *Waiting for Godot* opened at the **Arts Theatre** in 1955 to mingled bewilderment and fascination, and in 1956, *The Bald Prima Donna* introduced the comic despair of Ionesco's absurdism to London at much the same time as the **Berliner Ensemble** was bringing Brecht to the Royal Court. The triviality of English theatre was suddenly highlighted.

It has become almost axiomatic to date the revival of English drama from the performance of **John Osborne**'s *Look Back in Anger* at the Royal Court in 1956, and although this overrates the play, it allots proper credit to the vision of George Devine and the English Stage Company. Within a few years, the Royal Court had staged early work by **John Arden**, **Arnold Wesker**, **Ann Jellicoe** and **Edward Bond**, and its writers' workshops generated an intense commitment to new plays and a preparedness to give offence when necessary. That the theatre might contribute to political debate, even under the eye of the Lord Chamberlain, had been proved by the socialist **Unity Theatre** in the thirties and by the Manchester Theatre Union, run by **Joan Littlewood** and Ewan McColl (1935–9). Regrouped after the war as the Theatre Workshop, this company moved from Manchester to the Theatre Royal, Stratford East in 1953. The high-spirited brashness of Joan Littlewood's productions caught the interest of West End managers and, largely to her disgust, her working-class community theatre was swept into the mainstream. Joan Littlewood's methods were her own, but she shared Brecht's ripe delight in provoking the complacent into thought and having fun while doing it. A more solemn commitment to Brechtian dramaturgy guided **Robert Bolt**'s *A Man for All Seasons* (1960), in which the versatile Paul Scofield excelled, and Brecht has also exerted a strong influence on Arden and Bond, as well as on the generation of political dramatists who came into prominence after the abolition of the Lord Chamberlain's powers of censorship (1968). More mannered playwrights – **Harold Pinter**, **James Saunders**, **N. F. Simpson**, Tom Stoppard – tend towards the philosophical buffoonery of Beckett or Ionesco, reflecting the incongruities of human behaviour rather than the political structure which may, but may not, affect it, whilst Wesker, the most Shavian of recent playwrights, continues, in the face of critical disapproval, to try almost anything.

During the radical sixties, the theatrical establishment spread to the repertory theatres where it was shored up by the 'closed shop' strategies of Actors' Equity. Articulate minorities looking for a hearing, rented outlying buildings on the 'fringe' of the annual **Edinburgh Festival**. By 1968, Fringe theatre-groups had completed their apprenticeship and were ready to launch an adult challenge against politicians in and outside the theatre. At their best, they brought a new vitality and originality to a still-timid profession. Portable Theatre staged plays by the young **Howard Brenton** and **David Hare**. **John McGrath** founded and wrote for 7:84 Theatre Company, which also revived Trevor Griffiths's *Occupations* and premiered

David Edgar's *Wreckers* (1976). The Pip Simmons group interwove theatrical imagery and familiar stories. Monstrous Regiment was one of the many groups alert to the values of feminism. Belt and Braces, Red Ladder and North West Spanner strove to raise the political consciousness of the exploited work-force. Many groups worked collectively on a presentational style, Shared Experience specializing in story-telling techniques, Hull Truck developing plays through improvisation (as does **Mike Leigh**), Moving Being combining dance and drama in an associational theatre of their own devising. Welfare State International continue to plan large-scale environmental events, calling themselves 'Civic Magicians and Engineers of the Imagination'. They were pioneers of the community theatre movement, which spread to all the English regions during the seventies. Many once-flourishing groups have ceased to exist. The Arts Council, having surprised them with subsidy, found it necessary to kill some in order to conserve its thinning funds. The eighties have seen a weakening of alternative theatre. Three tendencies are discernible – an interest in a music-theatre that is responsive to popular culture, the development of a distinctive Performance Art classically exemplified by the work of Impact Theatre and a preparedness among larger, play-centred groups to operate almost as touring repertory theatre rather than as permanent ensembles.

The theatre of the late 20th century is not in easy command of audiences. Competition from the cinema has dwindled, to be replaced by the stay-at-home temptations of television. Few theatres have succeeded in holding down the price of tickets. Rising petrol costs and the decline of public transport are further discouragements. It is, however, to the credit of British television that it has continued to provide opportunities for original playwrights. John Hopkins, **David Mercer**, Trevor Griffiths and **Dennis Potter** are among those who have generally preferred the wide and more popular audience of television to the diminishing and predominantly middle-class audience of the theatre. The modern actor has to learn to cope with television. Admired abroad and underrated in its own country, the English theatre treads uncertainly towards the 21st century. PT

See: E. L. Avery et al., *The London Stage, 1660–1800*, 11 vols., London, 1960–8; P. Barnes, *A Companion to Post-War British Theatre*, London and Sydney, 1986; G. E. Bentley, *The Jacobean and Caroline Stage*, 7 vols., Oxford, 1941–8; E. K. Chambers, *The Medieval Stage*, 2 vols., Oxford, 1903; *idem*, The Elizabethan Stage, 4 vols., Oxford, 1923; C. Leech and T. W. Craik (eds.), *The Revels History of Drama in English*, 8 vols., London, 1975–83; A. Nicoll, *History of English Drama, 1600–1900*, 6 vols., Cambridge, 1952–9; *idem*, *English Drama 1900–1930*, Cambridge, 1973; G. Rowell, *The Victorian Theatre 1792–1914*, 2nd edn, Cambridge, 1978; E. B. Watson, *Sheridan to Robertson*, Cambridge, Mass., 1926; G. Wickham, *Early English Stages 1300–1660: A History of the Development of Dramatic Spectacle and Stage Convention in England*, 3 vols., London, 1959–81.

Englische Komödianten Troupes of actors from the London theatres who toured Germany from the 1580s on, initially only when the London theatres were closed because of plague. By the start of the 17th century, however, their presence was more permanent and they enjoyed some aristocratic patronage. They performed plays of the Elizabethan and Jacobean dramatists in English, but soon German came to be substituted and the troupes took on German actors. By the end of the 17th century, all identification of the troupes with England had vanished, though the persistence of the **Haupt- und Staatsaktionen** in the repertoire until the mid-18th century represents a continuation of English influence in the German theatre. SW

Ennius, Quintus (239–169 BC) One of the most important of early Latin authors, active in various genres. His comedies seem to have been insignificant, but his tragedies, mostly adapted from **Euripides**, were admired and influential. They are represented by 20 titles and over 400 surviving lines. ALB

ENSA (Entertainments National Service Association) An organization formed in 1938 so that performing artists could contribute to the war effort by sustaining the morale of troops and support staff, wherever they were stationed, in the British Isles or abroad. The Services counterpart of **CEMA**, working through the NAAFI (Navy, Army and Air Force Institute), its first performance took place immediately following the outbreak of hostilities in 1939. Under the directorship of **Basil Dean** and from its headquarters in the **Drury Lane** Theatre, it provided a touring programme that ranged from symphony orchestras, ballet companies and Shakespearian acting troupes to variety shows, comedians, popular singers and mobile cinemas. CI

Entremés see **Género chico**

Enzensberger, Hans Magnus (1929–) German dramatist and poet, who has attacked conventional theatre for substituting rhetoric for political action. He has attempted to counter this with an extreme form of documentary drama in which dialogue is taken unaltered from legal transcripts or the news media and the stage itself becomes the set. His most characteristic subject has been Latin American revolution in such plays as *The Havana Enquiry* (1970), dealing with the Cuban show trial that followed the Bay of Pigs invasion, or *The Short Summer of Anarchy – Buenventura Durrah's Life and Death* (1972), but with the material presented as a media event his thematic focus is on the manipulative effects of journalism. More recently his range has extended to cover historical subjects like *The Sinking of the Titanic* (1978). CI

Epic theatre The very juxtaposition of these two words would have horrified **Aristotle**, and it was against Aristotle that **Erwin Piscator** and **Bertolt Brecht** rebelled in their respective uses of the term. The Greek critic declared tragedy a higher form of art than epic partly because of its economy and concentration. Reacting against expressionism's focus on emotion, Piscator and then Brecht separately wished theatre to embrace the larger social context of the epic. Towards this end, Piscator made varied and innovative use of film.

As early as 1924, in his adaptation of *Edward II*, Brecht introduced such epic elements as scene-by-scene summaries of the action and common soldiers in whiteface. In 1928 Brecht and others collaborated with Piscator in dramatizing the Hasek novel *Adventures of the Good Soldier Schweik*; another collaborator, Gasbarra, refers to the novel's 'epic breadth', 'epic movement' and 'epic development' which Piscator translated to the stage with the help of film, treadmills and moving cartoons by George Grosz. But Brecht in a 1927 newspaper article had already announced epic theatre as the contemporary theatrical style: 'The essential point of the epic theatre is perhaps that it appeals less to the feelings than to the spectator's reason.' By 1930, in connection with a production of his opera *Mahagonny* Brecht published an essay on epic theatre, in which he tabulated the contrasts between dramatic and epic theatre. In Brecht's 1931 production of his (revised) *Man is Man* he first introduced the devices that were thereafter associated with epic theatre – half-curtain, half-masks, summary projections, few props, visible stage machinery, songs that punctuate the action, and 'cool' or estranged acting. Brecht demanded that the spectator use reason to reflect upon the performance. Although the term rarely refers to theatre other than Brecht's, or adaptations of novels, the concept and devices of epic theatre have influenced playwrights as different as **John Arden**, **Thornton Wilder**, **Robert Bolt**, **Peter Weiss**, **Arthur Adamov**, **Roger Planchon** and **Michel Vinaver**. It can be argued that every post-war director of stature is aware of the staging techniques of epic theatre.   RC

Epicharmus (6th–5th centuries BC) Sicilian comic dramatist, active at Syracuse in the reign of Hieron I (478–467 BC) and probably earlier. Surviving fragments of his plays, written in Doric Greek, show that they included burlesque treatments of myths as well as scenes from contemporary life; but many features are obscure (see **Greece, ancient**).   ALB

Equestrian drama see **Hippodrama**

Erdman, Nikolai Robertovich (1902–70) Soviet dramatist who, in the tradition of **Gogol** and **Sukhovo-Kobylin**, brought grotesque satire, intellectual irony and knowledgeable theatricalism to bear on the socio-political theme of the little man alienated from his technocratic society. Erdman began his theatrical career as a writer of revue sketches and speciality numbers for cabaret and music-hall performers. The topical revue 'Moscow from a Point of View' (1924), co-written with Vladimir Mass, Viktor Tipot and David Gutman, helped found the Moscow Theatre of Satire. Erdman's adaptation of Lensky's 1839 vaudeville *Lev Gurych Sinichkin* ran for nearly 10 years at the Vaktangov Theatre in the 1930s. Erdman wrote two major plays – *The Mandate* (1924), **Meyerhold**'s most successful production at the Meyerhold Theatre and an influence on the work of **Mayakovsky**; and *The Suicide* (1928), planned by the **Moscow Art Theatre** and brought to dress rehearsal by the Meyerhold Theatre (1929) before it was closed. *The Laughter Conference*, a work in progress, is rumoured to exist. His two major works cast ineffectual, anachronistic pre-revolutionary types – romantics, narcissists, prostitutes, intellectuals, artists, financial speculators and petty bourgeois – i.e., individualists and malcontents – adrift in the so-called

worker's utopia in search of what was promised them. They find that although society has progressed, man has been left behind without material means, his faith which has been usurped by science, or even the right to protest. Erdman spent 1933–40 in Siberian exile and devoted the remainder of his career to stage adaptations of Russian classics and to writing scripts for children's, animated and other films, for which he received two Stalin Prizes. *The Mandate* was again produced in Russia in 1956 during the 'Thaw' period. *The Suicide*, which premiered in Sweden in 1969, played elsewhere in Europe, Canada and America throughout the seventies and into the eighties and was finally produced in Russia at the Moscow Theatre of Satire in 1982.   SG

Ermolova, Mariya Nikolaevna (1853–1928) Daughter of a prompter at Moscow's Maly Theatre, she became its leading tragedienne and with **Glikeriya Fedotova**, one of the two most prominent Russian actresses of her day. **Stanislavsky** called her 'the heroic symphony of the Russian stage' and the equal of **Salvini** and **Duse**. She belonged to the realistic acting tradition in the Russian theatre which includes **Shchepkin**, whom she revered, Savina, Dedotova, Stanislavsky and **Komissarzhevskaya**. She brought feminine strength, a mixture of inspiration and self-control, romantic idealism and a love of freedom to some 300 roles, excelling in those which emphasized heroic suffering: **Lessing**'s Emilia Galotti (her earliest success, 1870); Judith in **Gutzkow**'s *Uriel Acosta* (1879); **Schiller**'s Joan of Arc (*The Maid of Orleans*, her greatest success, 1884) and Maria Stuart (1886); **Racine**'s Phaedra (1890); and **Shakespeare**'s Ophelia (1878, 1891), Lady Anne (1878), Hermione (1887), Lady Macbeth (1896) and Volumnia (1902), among others. In 1876 her incandescent, politicized portrayal of Laurentia in **Lope de Vega**'s tale of popular rebellion, *Fuenteovejuna*, made her famous, endeared her to progressive youth and resulted in the play's banning from the Russian stage for many years to come. She interpreted her favourite native writers, many of whom were radical – **Pushkin**, Nekrasov, Belinsky, Chernyshevsky, Dobrolyubov and **Pisarev** – as well as **Gogol** and **Ostrovsky** on the stage, the concert platform and in progressive literary circles. The Maly Theatre administration sought to dismiss her in later years, but her career revived following the 1917 Revolution via a series of anti-bourgeois roles. She was the first actress to be given the honorary title of 'People's Artist of the Soviet Republics' (1920) as well as 'Hero of Labour' (1924). In 1930 one of the Maly Theatre's studios was named after her. In 1937 it became the Ermolova Theatre.   SG

Ervine, St John (John Greer) (1883–1971) Irish playwright. Emigrating to London in 1900, Ervine met **Shaw**, flirted briefly with Fabianism, and remained ineradicably Unionist. Gifted, cantankerous, Ervine when appointed **Abbey** manager (1915–16) considered Ireland 'nearly a lunatic nation' and its theatre unexceptionally – his strictures had some justice – part of British theatre. Having sacked the entire company he resigned.

Ervine was a prolific and quarrelsome drama critic, emerging in the 1920s as a consequential figure in English theatre, author of many successful drawing-room comedies, faded now, such as *The First Mrs*

Frazer (1929). His imagination finds a grip in the Northern Irish plays he gave the Abbey: *Mixed Marriage* (1911); *The Magnanimous Lover* (1912); *John Ferguson* (1915); *Boyd's Shop* (1936); *William John Mawhinney* (1940); *Friends and Relations* (1941).

A craftsman of the 'well-made play', Ervine in his Irish plays relieves its contrivances, and his own melodramatic tendency, by authentic characterization. Though lacking psychological depth, his people fairly exhibit not only the intolerance and acquisitiveness of Northern Protestantism, but a conviviality, and, in some of his women especially, a charity beyond dogma. *Mixed Marriage* anticipates **O'Casey**'s urban realism, in a vigorous, less flamboyant vernacular, a Northern equivalent of **T. C. Murray**'s.   DM

Esperpento see Valle-Inclán

Esslair, Ferdinand (1772–1840) German actor. As an actor of the romantic school, Esslair was second in popularity only to **Ludwig Devrient**. His grand stature, his good looks, and his expressive, powerful voice, made him an ideal interpreter of heroic roles. Reminiscent of **Fleck**, he was actually more reliable and methodical. Before settling at the Munich Court Theatre in 1820, Esslair acted in several companies throughout Germany.   SW

Esson, Thomas Louis Buvelot (1879–1943) Australia's first realistic playwright. His early plays include *The Woman Tamer* (1910), *Dead Timber* (1911), and a Shavian political satire, *The Time is Not Yet Ripe* (1912). Between 1922 and 1926 his own company, the Pioneer Players, co-founded with Vance Palmer and Steward Macky, staged his *The Battler, Mother and Son, The Drovers* (written in London in 1919) and *The Bride of Gospel Place*, all sensitive studies of outback or underworld life, written under the strong influence of **Yeats**, **Synge** and the **Abbey Theatre**. Disillusioned artistically and politically, Esson eventually abandoned playwriting.   MW

Estorino, Abelardo (1925–) Cuban playwright, director. Born in Matanzas, studied at the University of Havana, and practised dental surgery for three years. In 1960 he joined the Studio Theatre, Cuba's first revolutionary theatre group, and in 1961 was contracted by the government as a professional writer. He often directs and occasionally acts and designs sets. Estorino interprets contemporary situations and immediate problems of Cuban reality into transcendent theatrical pieces. The constants in his work are the focus on family units and marital issues, the need for openness, fairness and equality in human relationships. Essentially a realistic writer, he has remained loyal to the Revolutionary ideals while experimenting with meta-theatrical techniques in later plays. His best known works are *El robo del cochino* (*The Theft of the Pig*, 1961), *La casa vieja* (*The Old House*, 1964), *Los mangos de Caín* (*Cain's Mangoes*, 1967), *La dolorosa historia del amor secreto de don José Jacinto Milanés* (*The Tragic Story of the Secret Love of don José Jacinto Milanés*, 1974), *Ni un sí ni un no* (*Neither a Yes nor a No*, 1981), and *Morir del cuento* (*To Die from the Story*, 1983).   GW

Ethel Barrymore Theatre 243 West 47th St, New York City [Architect: Herbert J. Krapp]. **Ethel Barrymore**, the actress, was lured into the management of the **Shuberts** with the promise of Ethel Barrymore, the theatre. Opening late in 1928, it was one of the last playhouses to be built in the theatre district before the depression. An intimate, well-designed house, it seats just under 1,100 and is well suited to the realistic play and comedy. Although a number of failures have appeared at the Barrymore, it has also housed a fair share of history-making productions, among which have been *The Women* (1936), *Pal Joey* (1940), *A Streetcar Named Desire* (1947), *Look Homeward, Angel* (1957) and *A Raisin in the Sun* (1959). It has remained a Shubert house.   MCH

Etherege, George (1636–92) English dramatist. Apprenticed to a lawyer, he went on to study at the Inns of Court in London. He may have been in France before appearing in London in 1663, already a friend of aristocrats. He quickly became an important member of the group of courtier-wits centred on Rochester and Sedley. His first play, *The Comical Revenge, or Love in a Tub* (1663), is a brilliant mixture of four separate plots, ranging from a serious action of high honour to a broad farce about a syphilitic servant. In 1668 *She Would If She Could* demonstrated Etherege's brilliance in a witty and thoughtful investigation of the problems of love and courtship; it was highly influential on the development of Restoration comedy. Immediately after its success Etherege was sent to Constantinople as a diplomat, returning in 1671. His last play, *The Man of Mode* (1676), is a complex exploration of the conflict between sexual appetite and genuine love in the rake-hero Dorimant, combined with a depiction of one of the great stage-fops, Sir Fopling Flutter. In 1685 he became ambassador to Ratisbon and stayed abroad after the 1688 revolution.   PH

Ethiopia Like its history, little is known of the existence and scope of Ethiopia's theatre outside its borders. At the present time Addis Ababa has four full-time professional state theatre houses each with 'traditional' and 'modern' music and dance companies and an acting company. Similar state theatre houses are being developed in all the provincial capitals. The university has a fully-fledged Theatre Arts Department and numerous mass organizations throughout the country have performing groups. A provisional list of original staged productions this century comes to over 225.

Ethiopia is divided topographically into a highland plateau in the north, extremely hot and dry lowland areas to the east and fertile, well-watered areas to the west and south. The Christian Amharic and Tigrinya-speaking peoples who inhabit the highlands originally came from Saudi Arabia, subsequently absorbing the local population and establishing the early civilization of Axum and later developing a Christian feudal society, which under Menelik II in the late 19th century expanded to take in the peoples of the west, south and east of the country. Under Menelik II and especially Haile Selassie I the feudal ruling class began to modernize and introduce capitalist relations into restricted sections of the economy. From 1935 to 1941 Ethiopia was occupied by the Italian Fascists but with the restoration capitalism made increased inroads into the economy, bringing new social forces into play, culminating in the 1974 revolution and the establishment of the Provisional Military Administrative Council. In 1984 the Ethiopian Working People's Party was established in order to prepare for the birth of the People's Democratic Republic of Ethiopia.

It is claimed that theatre existed in the highlands 'during Axumite times'. With the coming of Christianity 'pagan' theatre was officially suppressed but the theatre tradition was kept alive within the church in the form of passion plays and other ritual dramatic forms. In addition, the feudal courts and their military functions gave rise to dramatic forms, notably the performances of the professional musician–singers, the *azmareewoch*.

Throughout the country the rural society had its own cultural activities containing more or less developed dramatic elements, in ritual ceremonies, story-telling, songs and dances. The whole question of dramatic activity in the early societies of Ethiopia requires research.

As in other parts of Africa the growth of 'modern' theatre was stimulated by the introduction of schools of the Western type and the education of Ethiopians in Europe. The first Ethiopian playwright in this tradition was Tekle Hawariat (*The Comedy of Animals*, 1903, a satire based on La Fontaine), followed by Yoftahe Negussie, who wrote numerous plays including *Afajeshegn* (1933), an allegory of the Italian invasion and Ethiopia's ultimate liberation.

At the restoration the **Hagr Fikir** (Patriotism) Theatre was established in Addis Ababa and many plays were performed there, some scripted, others improvised and accompanied by the *begena* or *masenko*, traditional stringed instruments. Yoftahe's students, Mattewos Bekele and Beshah Tesfamariam, and others, notably Iyoel Yohannes and Mekonnen Endalkachew (later to become Prime Minister) and the women writers, Sendu Gebru and Romanewerk Kassahun, wrote for the theatre. Mattewos Bekele was particularly prolific, as was Iyoel Yohannes, who, it is reputed, wrote 60 plays, mostly 'situation comedies' dealing with 'present-day strains on Ethiopian society caused by conflicts of value between the old and new'. Another dominant theme in this period was the Italian invasion and Ethiopian patriotism. In the 1950s new playwrights emerged, Tesfaye Tesemma and Melaku Ashagre, for instance, with plays that began to point fingers at abuses in the feudal system.

A second theatre, the City Hall Theatre, was founded in 1946. Meanwhile Mattewos Bekele had established the **Andinet** (Unity) **Theatre Club** whose aim was to take theatre into the countryside, touring Wello, Tigrai, Gonder and Eritrea. In 1955 the Haile Selassie I (now the Ethiopian National) Theatre was opened. The first directors were foreigners but in 1960 **Tsegaye Gebre-Medhin** returned to Ethiopia after studying theatre in Britain and France and was appointed director. With Tsegaye returned another important playwright, actor and director, **Tesfaye Gesesse**. Other influential playwrights were Kebede Mikael and **Mengistu Lemma**. Also, outside the capital, Asmara in Eritrea province was a centre for theatrical and musical performances.

Theatre in the feudo-bourgeois period faced great difficulties, beginning with Menelik II's banning of the first play, *The Comedy of Animals*. Censorship was Byzantine in its obsessive suspicion of every allusion. Tsegaye Gebre-Medhin, director of the Haile Selassie I Theatre, was frequently imprisoned and ultimately sacked. In these circumstances it was understandable that the 'established' theatre in the capital, with very few exceptions, restricted itself to religious, patriotic or uncontroversial subject matter. In addition audiences were exclusively drawn from the educated and well-off elite. However in the schools a much more outspoken and dynamic theatre of criticism and comment reached much wider audiences in many regions of the country.

The revolution of 1974 and its socialist direction ensured substantial state patronage of the arts. Cinemas were nationalized and four state theatres established, the Ethiopian National Theatre, the Hagr Fikir, the City Hall and the Ras. The mass audience in Addis Ababa and throughout the country became exposed to theatre as it was used by the revolutionary mass organization as an instrument of class struggle in the upheaval which was sweeping the entire country. The Amhara chauvinism of the imperial regime was replaced by this proclamation of the National Democratic Revolution: 'the history, language and religion of each nationality will have equal recognition in accordance with the spirit of socialism' and the languages, songs and dances of Ethiopia's many nationalities were now officially encouraged and performed.

In Addis Ababa the year of the revolution saw the staging of one of Tsegaye's greatest plays, *Ha-Hu Be Siddist Wer* (*ABC in Six Months*). After 1976 numerous plays appeared on themes of class struggle, the activities of counter-revolutionaries or ultra-left tendencies, the civil war in the countryside, the Somali invasion and relevant periods or personalities in Ethiopian history, with Tsegaye Gebre-Medhin, **Ayalneh Mulat**, **Getachew Abdi**, Tesfaye Gesesse and Tesfaye Abebe being the foremost playwrights of the period.

In the 1980s non-political plays were seen again, including translations of **Shakespeare**, **Molière**, **Chekhov**, **Goldoni** and the Cameroonian playwright, **Oyônô-Mbia**. The earlier playwrights continued to write and they were joined by others, including graduates from the Theatre Arts Department at the University established in 1978. The University's Cultural Centre was active in staging plays and musical shows and the Theatre Arts Department produced a spate of original and translated works. The 'established' urban theatre is becoming more and more characterized by petit-bourgeois ideology and aesthetic while retaining its traditional emphasis on dialogue and language at the expense of music, dance and all elements of the popular culture.

In contrast to the 'established' urban theatre, the revolutionary mass organizations took theatre into their hands and launched a massive cultural drive, affecting the lives of millions, as part of the class war that was raging throughout the country to extend and defend the gains of the revolution. **Kinet** groups were formed in all the revolutionary workers', peasants', women's and youth associations. Even the previously despised traditional performers, the *azmareewoch*, were formed into the Andinet (Unity) Kinet. These groups stimulated drama among the masses who had previously been totally excluded from the arts. Plays such as *Land to the Tillers* and *The Refugees Journey* by the

Lalibela Kinet of Wello province laid the basis for a whole new tradition of revolutionary drama, full of song, dance and mime and grounded in the people's own cultural forms.

Unfortunately the state has been forced to rely heavily on its petit-bourgeois theatre 'experts' with the result that the dynamism of the popular revolutionary theatre of the kinets has been allowed to decline.

A radical move away from the expensive and under-productive minority theatres of the urban petit-bourgeoisie to reactivating the peasants' and workers' kinets could revitalize that extremely inspiring chapter in the history of Ethiopian theatre and ensure the revolutionary directions of Ethiopian theatre in the future – a move favoured by the ruling Ethiopian Working People's Party. RK

> See: Ministry of Education, Ethiopia, *Ethiopia Today – The Arts*, Addis Ababa, n.d; Haile Selassie I Theatre, *The Storehouse of Ethiopian Music, Drama and Dance*, Addis Ababa, n.d.

Ethnic theatre in the United States Ethnic theatre in the United States is theatre by and for minority communities, whose cultural heritages distinguish them from the Anglo-American mainstream. A pluralistic nation with an indigenous population and immigrants from every corner of the earth, the United States has been host to a rich variety of ethnic theatres. Ethnic theatres have helped to meet the intellectual and emotional needs of people separated from the mainstream by language, culture, poverty, and discrimination. They have reinforced indigenous or 'old world' languages and traditions, helped immigrants adjust to the United States, provided an arena for talented ethnic actors, directors, and playwrights, and introduced new personalities and techniques to the Anglo-American stage.

Ethnic theatres sprang from a variety of historical conditions. Native American drama is rooted in communal celebrations and ancient rituals reflecting the religious outlook and shared values of the indigenous nations that created it. Unlike Western drama, it is charged with cosmic significance that sets it apart from events in the ordinary world, and the 'audience' are participants rather than passive spectators. Because the native population contains many distinct nations, Native American theatre is diverse, ranging from the polished one-person dramas of story-tellers and the improvisations of the shamans to the Navajo chantways, 100-hour long celebrations involving the entire community in which no costume, word, gesture, movement or song is left to chance.

White Americans were introduced to black performance as early as 1664 when captive Africans were forced to dance and sing for the crew of the English slaveship *Hannibal*. Autonomous black theatre began in 1821 in lower Manhattan where the African Theatre, founded by William Henry Brown, performed Shakespearian drama for audiences of whites and blacks. In the 19th century whites in 'black face' gave minstrel shows, a racist parody of black entertainment, but independent black theatre persisted and by the early 20th century musicals written and performed by blacks were appearing on Broadway and in Harlem.

French theatre entered the country in 1803 when the United States purchased Louisiana from France, and Mexican American theatre entered with the conquest of the south-west from Mexico in 1848. Immigrants from Europe and Asia established theatres soon after their arrival. German theatres appeared in the rural mid-west in the early 1840s and in New York and New Orleans even earlier. Chinese theatre opened in San Francisco in 1852, and Japanese troupes entertained in Seattle several decades later. Polish, Yiddish, Italian and other southern and eastern European theatres were active in urban centres by the turn of the century.

Native American theatre encountered enormous difficulties. Conquest by whites destroyed entire nations including, of course, their drama. The confinement of native peoples to reservations and the increasing dominance of Western culture often had a negative influence on the drama of nations that survived. The potlatch drama of the north-west coast, for example, in which the wealthy distributed gifts, degenerated from a mechanism for cementing the interrelationships of family and village into ostentatious displays of hierarchy and privilege. Nevertheless, many dramas such as the Plains Sun Dances, the Cheyenne Sacred Arrow Ceremony, the Iroquois False Face Drama, and the Navajo chantways survived into the 20th century and continued their time-honoured functions of uniting their communities and reinforcing traditional beliefs.

Immigrant theatres faced significant if less critical problems, including lack of money, quarrels among the actors, directors, and playwrights, and opposition from inside and outside the community: Scandinavian theatre was opposed by the conservative Lutheran clergy who associated it with drinking; civil authorities closed Chinese theatres for performing on Sunday (when working class audiences were free to attend); German theatre was devastated by boycotts during the First World War.

Nevertheless, as the number of immigrants rose to a million a year in the decade before the First World War, immigrant theatres flourished. Actors trained in the homelands pursued their careers in the United States, joined by enthusiastic amateurs who spent long days in the workplace and then rehearsed far into the night. Audiences with sparse resources saved their pennies for tickets. Large communities supported commercial theatres and virtually every group enjoyed amateur theatre sponsored by lodges, athletic groups, schools, and cultural, nationalist, and socialist societies. Road companies brought theatre to isolated farm and mining communities.

Moved by the same desire for economic opportunity and personal freedom that brought immigrants from foreign countries to the United States, native born blacks migrated from the rural South to the industrial and commercial cities of the North in the opening decades of the 20th century. A burst of black theatrical creativity was part of the cultural and intellectual flowering of the 1920s known as the Harlem Renaissance. While black theatre flourished in many cities, its centre was Harlem, where race conscious plays by, for, and about black America were produced in the 20s and 30s by companies such as the Krigwa Players (founded by W. E. B. Dubois), the Harlem Experimental Theatre, the New Negro Theatre, and the Harlem Suitcase Theatre (founded by **Langston Hughes**).

An integral part of the life of the immigrant 'ghettos' of the early 20th century, ethnic theatres supported the educational, charitable, and political causes important to their communities. Theatre benefits financed Italian parochial schools in St Louis, social services for Danes and Japanese in Seattle, and orphanages and hospitals in the Ukraine. Their actors unionized, Yiddish theatres supported the 'Uprising of the 20,000', the historic general strike of the largely Jewish shirtwaist makers in New York City in 1909. Thaddeus Dolega-Eminowicz, star and founder of Polish theatres in many American cities, produced and acted in an original play, *With Whom to Side?* in Detroit in 1917 to raise funds for the Polish Legion's participation in the First World War.

Immigrant theatres provided a place where the young and old, the educated and the uneducated, the newcomer and the oldtimer, the poor and the upwardly mobile could gather and share a common experience. To the inhabitants of cramped, dreary, tenements, theatres were attractive places to court, gossip, quarrel, eat, joke, and nurture friendships. To actors, directors, and playwrights, the theatre was a self-sufficient social world in which marriages took place and children were reared, sometimes appearing on stage as soon as they could walk and talk. This world was especially important to intellectuals, whose lack of English cut them off from the professions they had pursued in the homeland. It was also important to women, who found in it an alternative to traditional domestic roles and a chance to win money and recognition and adopt unconventional lifestyles with relative impunity.

Ethnic theatre made the history and folklore of the homelands accessible to immigrants, many of whom had been deprived of education in the homelands, and introduced American born children to the heritage of their parents. Based on the complex novel *Romance of the Three Kingdoms*, Chinese opera transmitted traditional Cantonese values of loyalty, self-reliance, and personal integrity. Yiddish plays depicted episodes from centuries of Jewish history. German theatre dramatized the exploits of Frederick the Great. Polish theatres presented so many plays on historical and national themes that a Polish journalist called them 'schools of patriotism'.

Immigrant theatres introduced dialect-speaking audiences to the 'standard' pronunciation and vocabulary of their native languages and, through use of English expressions and performance of American plays, to the language and culture of the United States. Many also introduced the classics of world theatre. **Shakespeare** was performed in Yiddish, German, Swedish, and Italian. Yiddish theatres performed the works of **Molière**, **Schiller**, **Goethe**, **Tolstoi**, **Gorky**, **Sudermann**, **Hauptmann**, **Ibsen**, **Strindberg**, **Molnar**, and **Shaw**, as well as those of Jewish playwrights such as **Jacob Gordin**, Leon Kobrin, and **Sholom Asch**.

Theatre groups of politically progressive Germans, Jews, Swedes, Finns, Hungarians, Latvians, Lithuanians, and others used the works of Shaw, Ibsen, and Strindberg as well as original plays to explore temperance, pacifism, and the problems of workers, women, and the aged. Latvian socialist theatres in New York, Chicago, Cleveland, Detroit, San Francisco, and Boston produced dozens of agit-prop-type plays, including original political dramas such as Sīmanis Berģis's *They Will Overcome*, and Dāvids Bundža's *Celebrating May*. Theatres were prominent features in Finnish 'Labour Temples' (socialist community centres) across the nation, where plays, both original and imported from Finland, were used for the political education of children and adults. The first Polish play in Chicago was *The Emancipation of Women* (1873), by feminist actress, writer, and community activist Theofilia Samolinska. Translated or adapted versions of Ibsen's controversial drama *A Doll's House* explored the 'woman question' in many immigrant theatres.

Despite the importance of educational and ideological plays, most immigrants attended the theatre for entertainment, glamour, diversion, and emotional release. Folk dramas depicting the regional music, dance, and customs of the homeland were popular in German, Swedish, Danish, Hungarian, and Ukrainian theatres, appealing to nostalgia and the desire to escape urban life. A musical folk play, *The People of Varmland* (text by Fredrik August Dahlgren), was the most popular Swedish play, performed at least 62 times in Chicago alone between 1884 and 1921; 90% of all Danish productions were folk plays or operettas.

'Formula' plays in which wily peasants outwitted landlords, true love triumphed, and villains were punished and heroes rewarded were popular among audiences for whom the problems of life were not so easily resolved. Also popular were vaudeville, comedy, and satire. Comic characters such as Olle i Skratthult (Olle from Laughtersville) created by Hjalmar Peterson and Farfariello, created by Eduardo Migliaccio, satirized the immigrant community itself, especially 'green ones' (new immigrants), using wit and irony to help audiences understand, laugh at, and thus transcend their own often painful adjustment to the United States.

Plays filled with violence, revenge, suicide, and murder were well received, both classical tragedies and original melodramas. These plays moved audiences because they dealt with familiar problems, though in exaggerated form; Jacob Gordin's *The Jewish King Lear*, for example, about a pious father abused by heartless daughters, brought tears to the eyes of immigrants less than satisfied with the behaviour of American-born children. Tragedy, like comedy, provided emotional release, allowing immigrants to

The Olle i Skratthult Troupe in *Lars Anders och Jan Anders och deras Barn*, early 1920s.

express their grief at the absence of loved ones and the frustrations of American life.

European and Asian immigrant theatres active in the early 20th century declined after 1930, undermined by the immigration restriction laws of 1924, the Americanization and geographic dispersion of audiences, and the rise of movies, radio, and television. Federal assistance through the Works Project Administration helped some immigrant and black theatre to survive during the Great Depression of the 1930s; and a few companies with an interest in artistic experimentation, such as the Folksbühne (Yiddish) theatre in New York City and the Swedish Folk Theatre in Chicago, continued into the mid-century. Meanwhile many actors, directors and writers from ethnic theatres passed into mainstream American entertainment, bringing elements of their traditions with them.

Ethnic theatre revived after the Second World War, stimulated by large scale migration of Puerto Ricans to the mainland, and, with liberalization of the immigration laws, new immigration from Eastern Europe, Mexico, Latin America, and Asia. The black civil rights movement touched off increased political activism and ethnic awareness not only among blacks but also among Hispanics, Native Americans, and Asian Americans, stimulating new 'Third World' theatre activity across the nation. Many older southern and eastern European theatres were rejuvenated in the 1960s and 1970s not only by newcomers, but also by the nostalgia of ageing immigrants, the desire of acculturated children and grandchildren to explore their roots, and the 'new ethnicity', a heightened appreciation of cultural pluralism as an antidote for the anomie and homogenization of modern society.

In the mid-1960s black theatre rose to new prominence in communities throughout the nation. In the late 1960s Miriam Colón's Puerto Rican Travelling Theatre began bringing bilingual productions to the Spanish-speaking neighbourhoods of New York City and by the early 1970s provided a laboratory theatre and an actors' training programme as well. In the late 1970s four Asian-American companies were performing in New York City. On the West Coast the East-West Players were presenting original Asian-American plays and training actors of Chinese, Japanese, Filipino, Korean, and Pacific Island backgrounds. Original plays about contemporary ethnic life as well as productions of Armenian, Latvian, Lithuanian, Polish, and Yiddish classics (in the original languages or, frequently, in English) were mounted by ethnic churches and community centres, universities, and professional companies.

Overshadowed by the mass media (now often available in ethnic languages), theatre in the post-Second World War decades was not as central to ethnic community life as it had been half a century earlier. Nevertheless it continued to educate as well as to entertain. In the 1970s Hanay Geiogamah's Native American Theatre Ensemble used 'western' style drama to transmit Native American traditions, values, and aesthetics. Byelorussians, Hungarians, Latvians, Ukrainians, Slovaks, and others used theatre in schools, summer camps, and youth groups to teach ethnic language and history to a new generation.

Post-war ethnic theatres informed their communities about social and political issues and were more active than their predecessors in reaching out to inform the mainstream community as well. Dramas from the Baltic nations dealt with political oppression and resistance to tyranny in Eastern Europe and, by implication, everywhere. The Theatre for Asian American Performing Artists in New York City gave a series of skits about anti-Asian discrimination for the United States Commission on Civil Rights and produced a satirical review based on those skits at Lincoln Center during the 1976 Bicentennial. **Luis Valdéz**'s **El Teatro Campesino** (the Farm Workers' Theatre) developed original 'actos' to unionize migrant workers in California and elaborated them into full-length plays that won national and international acclaim.

Ethnic theatre allowed Asian-American, black, Native American, Mexican American and other minority actors to move beyond the stereotypical roles usually assigned them in mainstream entertainment. It gave a new generation of playwrights an opportunity to use the language of the ethnic ghetto and to express sensibilities rooted in the unique historic experience of their own communities. 'America is illiterate . . . deadset against the Chinese American sensibility', wrote the militant Frank Chin, a seventh-generation Chinese American whose award-winning play *The Chickencoop Chinaman* was produced in New York in 1972; 'nothing but racist polemics have been written about us . . . I don't like that . . . All my writing is Chinaman backtalk.'

Ethnic theatre offered ethnic and mainstream audiences insights into minority experiences which, despite an increase of ethnic material in mainstream theatre, remained unavailable elsewhere. **René Marqués**'s celebrated play *The Oxcart*, whch describes a family's disintegration as it moves from rural Puerto Rico to San Juan to New York City, helped Puerto Rican migrants evaluate their gains and losses. The problems of the black family, the impact of the Vietnam War on the Asian-American soldier, the destruction of ethnic neighbourhoods through 'urban renewal', Turkish genocide against Armenians in 1915, the impact of the Holocaust on Jewish survivors, the realities of growing up, or getting old, or being a woman in ethnic America, discrimination, assimilation, and the survival of ethnic identities – these and similar themes were explored in post-Second World War ethnic theatre.

The future Some of the older theatres, the Italian and German, for example, did not revive in the post-Second World War decades, and by the mid-1980s the future of those that had revived seemed problematic. Funding provided to some theatres in the 1960s and 1970s by public and private foundations such as the Rockefeller Foundation, the National Endowment for the Arts, and state cultural agencies was discontinued due to budget cutbacks and changing priorities. The political and social climate supportive of pluralism in the 1960s and 1970s eroded. The Simpson–Rudino Act, passed in 1986 to stop illegal immigration, seemed likely to slow the growth of Spanish-speaking communities and, consequently, of their theatres.

Nevertheless, reasons for optimism remained. Regardless of immigration policy, identifiable ethnic communities would remain part of the American social landscape for the foreseeable future. Community theatre, including ethnic theatre, increased in popularity in the 1980s as the cost of mainstream Broadway-type productions soared. Moreover, in the 1980s ethnic theatre gained increased recognition in university theatre programmes, national theatre associations, and academic journals as well as among ethnic and mainstream audiences. Collections of ethnic plays and scholarly works about ethnic theatre were published. Actors, playwrights, and directors experimented with new forms and materials and explored new outlets for their work through the media. These developments provided grounds for hope that ethnic theatre would survive, not as a curiosity or exercise in nostalgia, but as a living force in American culture.   MS

See: Bridge: *An Asian American Perspective*, summer 1977; R. J. Garza, ed., *Contemporary Chicano Drama*, Notre Dame, 1976; H. Geiogamah, *New Native American Drama: Three plays*, Norman, Oklahoma, 1980; N. Gonzales, *Bibliografía de Teatro Puertorriqueno, Siglos XIX y XX*, San Juan, 1979; J. V. Hatch and T. Shine, eds., *Black Theatre USA: Forty-Five Plays By Black Americans 1847–1974*, New York, 1974; L. C. Walsh Jenkins, 'The Performances of Native Americans as American Theatre', PhD Dissertation, University of Minnesota, 1975; E. Kahn, *The Merry Partners: The Age and Stage of Harrigan and Hart*, New York, 1955; F. A. H. Leuchs, *The Early German Theater in New York 1840–1870*, New York, 1928; D. Lifson, *The Yiddish Theatre in America*, New York, 1965; R. L. Marquez, 'The Puerto Rican Travelling Theater Company: The First Ten Years', PhD Dissertation, Michigan State University, 1977; W. Mattila, ed., *The Theater Finns*, Portland, 1972; H. C. Koren Naeseth, *The Swedish Theater of Chicago 1868–1950*, Rock Island, Illinois, 1951; L. Rosenfeld, *Bright Star of Exile: Jacob Adler and the Yiddish Theatre*, New York, 1977; M. Schwartz Seller, *Ethnic Theatre in the United States*, Westport, Connecticut, 1983; A. Straumanis, ed., *Baltic Drama: A Handbook and Bibliography*, Prospect Heights, Illinois, 1981; L. Valdez, *Actos*, San Juan Bautista, California, 1971.

Eugene O'Neill Theatre 230 West 49th St, New York City [Architect: Herbert J. Krapp]. In 1925, the **Shuberts** opened another theatre and named it the Forrest in honour of America's first star **Edwin Forrest**. They sold it in 1945 to City Playhouses, a real estate holding company, which refurbished it and renamed it the Coronet. It was sold again to Lester Osterman, a Broadway producer, who changed its name again to honour America's greatest playwright **Eugene O'Neill**. Six years later, it was acquired by **Neil Simon** and David Cogan and served as a showcase for eight of Simon's plays and one of his musicals. As sole owner in 1982, Simon sold it to the Jujamcyn Organization. Its early history was inauspicious and contained a long string of flops, but its later history, particularly the Simon era, has included its share of successes.   MCH

Euripides (?485/4–407/6 BC) Euripides the tragedian came from Phyla in Attica, and was certainly of respectable birth; no attention need be paid to the allegation of comic poets that his mother was a greengrocer. Most of the anecdotes concerning his life are equally unreliable; it is doubtful, for instance, whether he became embittered at his lack of success at Athens, and whether he was prosecuted for impiety by the demagogue Cleon. Unlike his rival **Sophocles** he

seems to have taken little part in public life. In 408 or 407 he left Athens for the court of Archelaus, King of Macedon, and it was there that he died.

He produced his first plays in 455 but did not win a victory in the competition (see **Greece, ancient**) until 441. He is said to have produced 92 plays (we know the titles of about 80), but won first prize only four times in his life (and once after his death with plays that he had left unperformed). He did not usually write connected tetralogies, but there was a loose connection between the plays he produced in 415 (*Alexander*, *Palamedes*, the surviving *Trojan Women* and *Sisyphus*).

Nineteen plays survive under his name. One of these, the melodramatic *Rhesus*, is generally reckoned to be spurious, the only extant example of 4th-century tragedy. Another, *Cyclops*, is not a tragedy but a satyr play (the only one that survives in full), probably one of his later works. Several of the remaining plays are securely dated, and progressive changes in Euripides' metrical practice enable scholars to fix the relative chronology of the rest within quite narrow limits, giving the following list. *Alcestis*, 438 (a tragedy performed in the position normally occupied by a satyr play). *Medea*, 431. *Heraclidae* (*Children of Heracles*), 430–428. *Hippolytus*, 428 (a revision of an earlier version). *Andromache*, c. 425. *Hecabe*, c. 424. *Suppliant Women*, c. 423 (concerning the burial of the 'Seven against Thebes'). *Electra*, c. 422–416. *Heracles*, close to 415. *Trojan Women*, 415. *Iphigenia in Tauris* (*Among the Taurians*), c. 414. *Ion*, c. 413. *Helen*, c. 412. *Phoenician Women*, c. 409. *Orestes*, 408. *Bacchae* and *Iphigenia at Aulis*, both posthumously produced (the latter probably left unfinished and completed by a later hand). In addition we are well informed about many of the lost plays through numerous fragments and plot-summaries.

The tragedies tend to contain certain stereotyped structural units, each developed for its own sake. A formal 'prologue speech' at the beginning, delivered by a god or a mortal character and placed outside the action, serves to set the scene and sometimes to foreshadow what will happen. A rhetorical *agōn* or debate occurs in every play, and is more self-consciously marked out than it would be in Sophocles; the same is true of the formal messenger-speech. At the end a god generally appears, not so much to tidy up loose ends in the drama as to remove the misapprehensions of the characters and to predict future mythical events. The Chorus tends not to be closely involved in the action, and in the later plays, especially, its songs are often evocations of a world remote from the characters' sufferings (though this need not be seen as mere light relief, as those sufferings may seem all the more poignant by contrast).

Euripides was not always greatly interested in organic plot-construction (as **Aristotle** complains). While the plot of *Medea* shows 'Sophoclean' concentration and that of *Iphigenia in Tauris* is a neatly worked-out adventure story, *Trojan Women* hardly has a plot at all (being held together rather by unity of theme and mood), and some of the late plays, such as *Phoenician Women*, are highly episodic (though this is not true of *Bacchae*, which in many ways shows a reversion to earlier techniques).

Despite the uniformity of structure and style, the plays present a wide, even bewildering variety of tone.

From the grim exploration of the mentality of child-murder in *Medea*, or the bleak evocation of the sufferings of a captured city in *Trojan Women*, the plays range all the way to such light-hearted romances as *Iphigenia in Tauris* and *Helen*, with their daring rescues and happy endings. Between these extremes come various types of melodrama, such as *Hecabe* and *Orestes*, where the characters' emotions and misfortunes are serious enough, but where the reader senses a certain detachment and lack of moral commitment in Euripides' portrayal of them. Some of these plays must simply be accounted failures (it takes a determined apologist to do anything for *Andromache*). There are also 'problem plays' of which the tone is variously assessed; should *Alcestis* and *Ion*, for instance, be read as cheerfully romantic or as bitterly ironic?

The plays leave a general impression, however, of men and women adrift in a world over which they have no control, at the mercy of passion, illusion and chance. Religion does not help, for, whatever the characters might wish (*Hippolytus* 120, *Bacchae* 1,348), the action of the plays reveals the gods as behaving no better than mortals. Nor is the world redeemed by the possibility of noble self-sacrifice, like that of Alcestis or Iphigenia at Aulis, owing to the lack of worthy causes in which this can be displayed.

In characterization Euripides is particularly fond of paradox and moral ambivalence, creating conflicts of sympathy in the audience. In some cases this involves abrupt shifts in behaviour, with little continuity of character (e.g. Alcmene in *Heraclidae*, Hecabe in *Hecabe*); in others it involves real psychological complexity (e.g. Medea, Phaedra in *Hippolytus*, Pentheus in *Bacchae*, all these being studies in the power of passion over reason).

The rhetoric of Euripidean speeches tends to broad generalization and theorizing, and characters can express highly unconventional views (e.g. questioning the subordinate position of women at *Medea* 230–51 or the nature of Zeus at *Trojan Women* 884–8) which show the influence of the sceptical 5th-century thinkers called sophists. Such passages cannot be assumed to represent Euripides' personal opinions (no one wishing to promote feminist ideas would be likely to place them in the mouth of Medea), and it is hard to extract simple morals, whether modern or conventional, from the plays seen as wholes. The mere expression of sophistic ideas in tragedy, however, could evidently be regarded as subversive. **Aristophanes**, who picked Euripides as one of his favourite targets (presenting him in person in *Acharnians*, *Themophoriazusae* and *Frogs*), portrays him as a pretentious, atheistic intellectual, who degrades tragedy by depicting trivial and vulgar subjects. After his death, however, he became by far the most popular and influential of the tragedians.   ALB

Evans, Edith (1888–1976) British actress, awarded the DBE in 1946. After working with **William Poel** and **Ellen Terry**, she established a leading reputation in Restoration and Shakespearian comedy with Millamant (1924) and Lady Wishfort (1948) in *The Way of the World*, and Rosalind in *As You Like It* (1926 at the **Old Vic**, a role she returned to in 1959 with the **Royal Shakespeare Company**). Her most famous performance, using her superb voice to best advantage, was as Lady Bracknell in **Wilde**'s *The Importance of Being Earnest* (first played in 1939, filmed in 1951); but she also gave definitive interpretations of **Shaw** and **Chekhov** and toured widely with **ENSA** between 1942 and 1944. Her last stage appearance was in *Edith Evans . . . and Friends* in 1974.   CI

Evans, Maurice (Herbert) (1901–) English-born actor-director-producer who became an American citizen in 1941, following a 15-year acting career in England, most notably as Raleigh in *Journey's End* (1929) and with the **Old Vic–Sadler's Wells** company in 1934 (including a full-length *Hamlet*). In the United States he appeared with **Katharine Cornell** as Romeo (1935) and in 1936 as the Dauphin opposite her Saint Joan. A series of notable Shakespearian performances, most directed by **Margaret Webster**, followed, including Richard II (1937), gaining him the reputation as the foremost Shakespearian purveyor on the American stage. During World War II he entertained the troups with his so-called *GI Hamlet*. After the war (between 1947–59) Evans played major roles in four Shavian comedies, most notably John Tanner in *Man and Superman*. In 1952 he acted the uncharacteristic role of Tony Wendice in *Dial M for Murder*, in 1960 Rev. Brock in the musical *Tenderloin*, and in 1962 *The Aspern Papers*. In the 1950s he presented **Shakespeare** on television and produced several Broadway shows. In the 1970s and 80s he appeared mostly in films and television, although at the age of 80 he played Norman in *On Golden Pond* in Florida.   DBW

Eveling, Stanley (Harry S.) (1925–) British dramatist, who is a lecturer in Philosophy at Edinburgh University. Eveling's plays first began to appear in the programmes of the adventurous Traverse Theatre in Edinburgh during the late 1960s, occasionally transferring to fringe theatres like the Open Space in London. *The Lunatic, The Secret Sportsman and The Woman Next Door* (1968) and *Dear Janet Rosenberg, Dear Mr Kooning . . .* (1969) were two short plays ideally suited to the intimate, student surroundings of alternative theatre clubs. The dialogue is stimulating, the situations and images intellectually provocative, the opportunities for actors tantalizing. While not necessarily a dramatist of the absurd, for Eveling writes in many styles, he was concerned with that meaninglessness which leads to a comic despair. In the early 1970s, several plays concerned suicide in some form, such as *Caravaggio, Buddy* (1972), *Shivvers* (1974) and *The Dead of Night* (1975); while his farce, *Union Jack (and Bonzo)* (1973), which successfully transferred to London, turned a Boy Scout camp into a graveyard behind bushes.   JE

Everyman Theatre (London) Founded by Norman Macdermott in 1920 as a non-commercial experimental playhouse, it became a showcase for **Shaw**'s plays and mounted **Noël Coward**'s first successful work, *The Vortex* (1924). Macdermott was also responsible for introducing many foreign dramatists to the English stage, including the first London performances of **O'Neill**'s early work, **Chiarelli**'s *The Mask and the Face* (1924) and **Pirandello**'s *Henry IV* (1925), as well as important productions of **Ibsen**'s naturalistic dramas. This role was continued when **Raymond Massey** took over the management in 1926 and under Malcolm Morley, who directed the first English production of

Ostrovsky's *The Storm* in 1929. After that the building was used by various small companies such as the **Group Theatre** (1932 and 1934), and even when converted into a cinema in 1947 it retained the line set by Macdermott, specializing in non-commercial and foreign films.   CI

Evreinov, Nikolai Nikolaevich (1879–1953) Evreinov was a prolific and versatile anti-realist pre-revolutionary Russian man of the theatre. The central premiss of his work as director-dramatist-theorist-historian was 'theatricality', which consisted of: the need to revitalize theatre (and not solely to stylize it as he believed had **Meyerhold**) by rediscovering its origin as pre-aesthetic, imaginative play; the theatricalization of life (as opposed to the reexperiencing of life onstage as **Stanislavsky** proposed) in order to cure man's and society's ills, which largely derive from a fear of death. Evreinov evolved this concept from the following influences: Schopenhauer's 'the world as presentation'; **Nietszche**'s 'superman'; Bergson's 'creative evolution' or self-perfection; the symbolists' extreme subjectivism, which posited the artist-individual as the hero of his own life; the quasi-religious doctrine of transcendence via transformation; **commedia dell'arte**'s spontaneity and creation of the theatrical mask as real-life persona. Evreinov developed these themes in his interlocking theoretical treatises *An Introduction to Monodrama* (1909), *The Theatre as Such* (1912), *The Theatre for Oneself* (3 vols., 1915–17) and *Pro Scena Sua* (1915). 'Monodrama' seeks to reestablish the audience as co-creator of the theatrical event as a first step in erasing the border between theatre and life. The expressionistic transformation of characters and scenic effects to externalize the protagonist's consciousness in order to make him more accessible had little immediate impact but foreshadowed cinematic and absurdist theatrical techniques. *The Presentation of Love* (1910) and *In the Stage-Wings of the Soul* (1911) are his earliest and best monodramas, respectively. His most significant *commedia*-based plays are *A Merry Death* (1908) and *The Chief Thing* (1921). The former, a 'tragi-farce' after **Blok**'s *The Puppet Show*, and the latter, a 'dramatic paradox' and compendium of Evreinovian aesthetics and devices (and his one international success) based on **Gorky**'s *The Lower Depths*, feature the author's alter-ego Harlequin as death-defier and life-transformer. In all Evreinov wrote over 30 plays. Like his playwriting, Evreinov's early directing as Meyerhold's successor at Vera Komissarzhevskaya's Theatre (1908–9) was an embryonic combination of symbolist and mono-dramatic tendencies. His interest in 'cultural retrospectivism', in contemporary vogue, led to his co-founding the Ancient Theatre (1907–8, 1911–12) with theatre administrator-censor-editor Baron Nikolai Drizen. The theatre's basic philosophy, 'artistic reconstruction' as opposed to antiquarianism, was manifested in its Medieval and Spanish Golden Age cycles of productions. Evreinov's penchant for pedantry was balanced by a highly parodistic nature, which he displayed at the Merry Theatre for Grown-up Children, co-founded with **Fyodor Komissarzhevsky** (1908–9), and especially at the Crooked Mirror Theatre, co-founded by editor-critic **A. R. Kugel** and his wife, Maly Theatre comedienne Z. V. Kholmskaya, where Evreinov

served as artistic director, 1910–17. Here he directed, wrote, adapted, translated and composed scores for some 100 plays – satirical monodramas, harlequinades, pantomimes and theatrical and literary parodies – which helped transform a late-night cabaret into one of Russia's leading 'theatre of small forms'. Of these compositions, *The Inspector General* (1912), parodying various directors' conceptual approaches to **Gogol**'s play, and *The Fourth Wall* (1915), which reveals the ludicrousness of applying Stanislavskian aesthetics and devices to the staging of opera, are of particular note. The summary achievement of Evreinov's Russian theatrical career was his scripting and staging of the Soviet mass spectacle *The Storming of the Winter Palace* (1920) with a cast of 10,000 on Uritsky Square in Petrograd, which realized his dream of merging theatre and life via heroic man. In 1925 he emigrated to Paris, where he continued his multifaceted theatrical career but with less impact and originality.   SG

Expressionism In 1901, fittingly ushering in the new century, the French painter Julien-Auguste Hervé wanted to distinguish his painting from impressionism and coined the word expressionism, a word that soon found its way into several European languages. Not until the *Supplement to the OED*, however, do we find a formal definition in English: 'a style of painting in which the artist seeks to express emotional experience rather than impressions of the physical world; hence, a similar style or movement in literature, drama, music, etc.'. Despite the confusion of 'drama' with 'theatre', that definition points to one widespread use of expressionism as non-realism; sometimes, expressionism is loosely used as a synonym of surrealism. The other, more rigorous, use of expressionism in the context of theatre describes Central European, especially German, productions between 1907 (date of **Kokoschka**'s *Murderer, the Hope of Women*) and the mid-1920s, with productions of plays by **Sorge**, **Hasenclever**, **Kaiser**, **Goering**, **Toller**, Koffka, Unruh, **Bronnen**, **Barlach**, **Kornfeld**, directed by **Reinhardt**, **Jessner**, **Falckenberg**, Barnowsky, **Martin**, Fehling, Hartung.

Although a few expressionist dramas pre-date the First World War most of them bear the scars of that war. Aesthetically, the plays are marked by antimimetic predecessors, like Munch and Van Gogh in painting; **Wedekind**, and especially **Strindberg** in drama. Expressionists aimed at no less than the spiritual regeneration of mankind. Young men rebelling against the proprieties of the Hohenzollern Empire, they wrote of conflicts between generations, sexes, and classes. They boldly treated taboo subjects, such as incest and patricide. In their plays, which verbalize emotions rather than dramatize conflicts, an autobiographical protagonist is involved not in a plot but in an apocalyptic quest – often for his essential identity. The protagonist sometimes meets avatars of himself (expressionist protagonists are unregenerately male), and other characters are schematically designed as nameless types. Short, often static scenes are not causally linked, and the dialogue, varying from short phrases (telegraphese) to long rhapsodies, lacks interpersonal communication.

Originating in the visual arts, expressionism in the theatre was also highly visual. A strong directional hand would light for atmosphere, stage crowd scenes, block for jagged lines, colour garishly, and distort the architecture. Staircases, revolves, treadmills, traps, and bridges extended the domain of the stage. And on that stage a new generation of actors rejected verisimilitude on the one hand, and declamation on the other, in order to express passion for its own sake; a strident voice and cadaverous face became hallmarks of the expressionist actor.

It was mainly through the theatre that expressionism travelled from Germany, so that its most triumphant playwright was the American **Eugene O'Neill**. The critic John Willett believes that O'Neill was the one great expressionist dramatist in any country; but expressionism is the creditor of all frankly theatrical exploitation of the modern stage.   RC

Eyre, Richard (1943–   ) British director. While at the Royal Lyceum Theatre, Edinburgh (1967–72), and later as a freelance director, Eyre gained widespread notice for his staging of contemporary drama. In 1973 he was appointed director of Nottingham Playhouse where he remained for five years. His policy was to commission many new plays and, with premieres of such works as *Brassneck* (**Brenton** and **Hare**) and *Comedians* (**Griffiths**), the Playhouse quickly acquired a reputation as one of the major centres in the country for adventurous and often radical new drama. In 1978 he became producer of BBC TV's 'Play for Today', and in 1982 Associate Director at the **National Theatre**. Here, he demonstrated a mastery of the stage musical with productions of *The Beggar's Opera* and the long-running *Guys and Dolls*, other recent successful productions including *The Inspector General* and, for **The Royal Court**, *Hamlet*. His several full-length feature films include *The Ploughman's Lunch* and *Loose Connections*. In 1986 he was appointed to succeed Sir **Peter Hall** as artistic director of the National Theatre.   AJ

Eytinge, Rose (1835–1911) American actress, author, teacher. Her professional debut was in 1852 as Melanie in **Boucicault**'s *The Old Guard* in Syracuse, New York. Considered temperamental and often unmanageable, she acted in England and the USA, specializing in high comedy and tragedy. She worked under **Lester Wallack**, **Augustin Daly**, and **A. M. Palmer**. Although she excelled in roles such as Cleopatra (1877), she was best known for her Nancy in *Oliver Twist* (1867) opposite **E. L. Davenport**'s Bill Sykes and the younger **James Wallack**'s Fagin. She dramatized several novels, wrote a play, a novel, and recorded her colourful life in *The Memories of Rose Eytinge* (1905).   DBW

F

Fabbri, Diego (1911–) Italian dramatist notable particularly for his plays of Catholic emphasis written mainly in the 1950s, like *Inquisizione (Inquisition*, 1950), *Processo di Famiglia (Family Trial*, 1953) and *Processo a Gesù (The Trial of Jesus*, 1955). The very titles of these indicate something of their concern with the serious, probing analysis of spiritual and religious issues, somewhat in the manner of the 'problem' play, but under strong Pirandellian influence. Their tone and subject matter however have limited their appeal outside Italy. Although the relationship between drama and religion, and the ways in which the theatre can be used to explore religious issues have been major preoccupations, as indicated too by his collection of essays, *Ambiguità Cristiana (Christian Ambiguity*, 1954), not all his work has been in so serious a vein: more in the mainstream of boulevard theatre are his light comedies of manners and matrimony, *Il Seduttore (The Seducer*, 1951) and *La Bugiarda (The Liar*, 1954). He has also been an impressive stage adapter of novels, particularly those of Dostoevsky, and has worked on scripts for film and television. The Italian dramatist with whom he is most frequently compared, and who shared many of his concerns, is **Ugo Betti.** LR

Fagan, James Bernard (1873–1933) British director and playwright, born in Northern Ireland. Beginning as an actor with **Frank Benson**'s company and with **Beerbohm Tree**, he took over the management of the **Royal Court Theatre** in 1918, where he mounted the British premiere of **Shaw**'s *Heartbreak House* (1921) and a pioneering series of **Shakespeare** productions. As well as a *Shakespeare vs Shaw* revue (1905) he also wrote over 15 plays, some specifically for Sir **George Alexander** and **Mrs Patrick Campbell**, and his adaptation of *Treasure Island* became a regular Christmas show from 1922 until 1931. But his main contribution was in founding the Oxford Playhouse, where between 1923 and 1929 he directed a repertoire that included **Ibsen**, **Strindberg**, **Synge** and Shaw, and a 1925 production of *The Cherry Orchard* that was responsible for **Chekhov**'s acceptance on the English stage. Here he developed a 'presentational' non-naturalistic style, and trained such young actors as **John Gielgud**, **Tyrone Guthrie**, **Raymond Massey** and **Flora Robson**. After directing the Irish Players he abandoned the theatre for the American film industry. CI

Faiko, Aleksei Mikhailovich (1893–1978) Soviet author of quasi-expressionist plays that were meant to counter the poster-sloganism and schematization of agit-prop scenarios of the 1920s with clear, complex, emotionally saturated plots and characters. Following a brief career as teacher, actor and director and some minor dramatic efforts – *Dilemma* (1921); *The Career of Pierpont Black* (1922), *Evgraf, Seeker of Adventures* (1926) – he wrote three plays which are remembered more for the artistic and social contexts in which they were produced than for the skill with which they were created. *Lake Lyul*, a detective melodrama staged by **Meyerhold** at the Theatre of the Revolution (1923), interwove 'pictures of capitalist bacchanalia', representing decadent individualism, with the then pervasive sense of 'NEP intoxication', the Soviet audience's consciousness that the momentary liberal respite engendered by the New Economic Policy must be seized and lived to the fullest. Viktor Shestakov's three-tiered, caged, laddered and platformed set, featuring fully operative vertically and horizontally running elevators (a first on the Soviet stage), combined with slide projections and rapidly shifting action to create the effect of cinematic montage and anxious urbanism which, along with 'social mask' characterization (see **Alpers, Boris**), fulfilled the director's if not the author's intentions. Meyerhold again strove for a 'theatre of social masks' in his 1924 staging of Faiko's *Bubus the Teacher*, which transformed that work from a naive vaudeville-operetta into a pretentious social melodrama with a brilliantly visual and aural *mise en scène*. I. Shlepyanov's set, a semi-circle of bamboo hangings topped by intermittently flashing neon advertisements and a piano in a gilded half-shell on which a pianist performed live 46 'decadent' musical interpretations (Chopin, Liszt and jazz), combined with Meyerhold's experimental 'pre-acting' (pantomime preludes to and commentary upon dialogue) to produce an overall impression of alienation in the audience, akin to that experienced by the contemporary Soviet intelligentsia. *The Man with a Briefcase* (1928), a melodramatic treatment of the rise and fall of a ruthless careerist doomed by a pre-revolutionary tsarist military upbringing, is considered by the Soviets to be his best play and was popular during the Purges of the late 1930s. Faiko wrote six additional plays, two operetta librettos and several screenplays, including *Aelita* (with F.Ostep, from **A. N. Tolstoi**'s novel, 1924). SG

Falckenberg, Otto (1873–1947) German director and dramatist, whose work bridged symbolism and expressionism. After visionary plays like *Deliverance* (1899) and satirical cabaret, he became the artistic director of the Munich Kammerspiele from 1917 to 1947, establishing its reputation as one of the leading theatres for contemporary drama with productions of

Brecht's *Drums in the Night* (1922) or **Barlach**'s *The Dead Day* (1924). CI

Fantoccini see **Marionette**

Farce Farce as a technique is common to many forms of theatre, but it has been since the Middle Ages a popular genre which was neglected or scorned in criticism. Although the word 'farce' is of medieval origin, the performance of raucous comedy is as old and as widespread as theatre. European farce has its provenance in elements of Greek and Roman theatre, for instance the satyr plays of Greece and the comedies of **Plautus**, with their inventive manipulation of incident and character; the cook was evidently a staple of classical farce. The English word 'farce' derives from a culinary word in French, and ultimately from Latin 'farsa' which means 'stuffing'. The genre may therefore have its origin in the medieval theatre custom of 'stuffing' the programme with several plays of various kinds, or of stuffing the liturgy with comic scenes. French scholars have affixed the label of farce to some 200 short plays, mainly dating from the second half of the fifteenth century, but a minority of these carried genre tags in their own time. Consisting of a scene from daily life, these medieval farces in octosyllabic couplets (300 to 500 lines, on the average) were simple in setting, sparse in properties, but inventive in acting – even though they lack scenic directions. Scholars debate whether the purpose was entertainment or edification (portrait of a fallen world), but the short plays are amazingly durable in evoking laughter. The two main subjects of medieval farce were the cuckolded husband and the deceiver deceived. The earliest extant farce – *The Boy and the Blind Man* – is a brutal but funny example of the latter. Over 50 medieval farces focus on conjugal conflict, of which *The Washbasin* is a fine example, typically reflecting medieval misogyny. *Master Pathelin*, the anonymous 15th-century masterpiece, is so nuanced in its character depiction, and so brilliant in its linguistic strategies that it has led to the critical paradox that the best French farce is not a farce. French farce influenced 15th-century German and English playwrights like **John Heywood**. After the Middle Ages, farce was perpetuated in a performing rather than a literary tradition, to which both **Shakespeare** and **Molière** in their different countries are indebted. In a celebrated essay (of 1901) the scholar Gustave Lanson traced Molière's greatness not only to Italian *commedia lazzi* of Scapino, Scaramouche, and Brighella, but more importantly to the great French farceurs **Gros-Guillaume**, **Tabarin**, **Gaultier-Garguille**, and **Turlupin**. Lanson inaugurated critical appreciation of farce – after a half-century of its popularity in the theatre – in the form called *vaudeville*, whose circumstantial plots hinged on preserving the fragile sexual proprieties. Characters were rudimentary, but sets and props were elaborate in the frenzied chase that might circle back to its point of origin. In France, **Labiche** must have worn out a series of collaborators to produce some 175 farces, some of which were preposterous but many were grounded in the daily life of the rising bourgeoisie in its pursuit of brides, pleasure, and money. By the turn of the 20th century, **Feydeau**'s farces grew increasingly sour and cynical in his variations on bedmanship. To succeed in Britain, farces had to emerge from bedrooms and terminate in weddings, but **Jones** and **Pinero** were able to accomplish this feat. By the 1920s the surrealists sang the praises of farce, e.g. **Artaud**'s delight in the **Marx Brothers**. Across the Channel the Aldwych farces (mainly by **Ben Travers**) thrived on deception and manipulation. In the 1950s and 1960s farce was triumphant at the Whitehall Theatre, London, under the actor-manager **Brian Rix**. Silent films gave an international impetus to farce, through the brilliance of Buster Keaton, Laurel and Hardy, Harold Lloyd, and especially Charlie Chaplin. Farce is still the favourite genre on the Boulevards – Achard and Roussin – Shaftesbury Avenue – **Ayckbourn**, **Frayn** – and Broadway – **Simon**. Since the end of the Second World War, however, playwrights have deftly assimilated the devices of farce to expose a serious view, e.g. **Beckett**'s music-hall tramps in *Waiting for Godot*, **Ionesco**'s proliferation of chairs in *The Chairs*, **Genet**'s clownshow in *The Blacks*, **Pinter**'s games in *The Collection*, **Stoppard**'s acrobats in *Jumpers* or travesties in *Travesties*, **Griffiths**'s comic turns in *Comedians*, or **Mamet**'s burlesque in *A Life in the Theatre*. Farce has acquired its ablest critic in **Eric Bentley** in several essays, as well as *The Life of the Drama* (1964). RC

Farquhar, George (1677–1707) Irish playwright. Born in Londonderry and educated at Trinity College, Dublin, he tried a career as an actor at Smock Alley Theatre in Dublin, abandoning the stage when he wounded a fellow actor during a performance of **Dryden**'s *The Indian Emperor* in 1697 by forgetting to use a blunted sword. Moving to London that year, his first play, a conventional comedy, *Love and a Bottle*, was produced in 1698. The following year, *The Constant Couple* was a phenomenal success, the greatest of the Restoration, mainly through the performance as Sir Harry Wildair of Robert Wilks with whom Farquhar had acted in Dublin. Farquhar followed its success with a weaker sequel, *Sir Harry Wildair* (1701), an adaptation of **Fletcher**'s *The Wild Goose Chase* as *The Inconstant* (1702), a savage comedy in *The Twin Rivals* (1702) and a farce from a French source, *The Stage Coach* (1704). But none of these repeated his earlier success and a disastrous marriage to a penniless widow under the illusion that she was wealthy led to severe financial crisis – though the marriage surprisingly became an affectionate relationship. As a way out of his money troubles he became a lieutenant in the Earl of Orrery's regiment in 1704 where, though he did not make money, his experiences in recruiting soldiers in Shropshire became the source of his next play, *The Recruiting Officer* (1706). In spite of its success, Farquhar, poor and ill, rapidly wrote his last comedy, *The Beaux' Stratagem*, in 1707, dying soon after the first performance. A lasting success, *The Beaux' Stratagem* set in a country community of inn-keepers and highwaymen, explores the problems of a loveless marriage, recommending a solution of divorce by mutual consent derived from the apparently unlikely source of Milton's divorce pamphlets. PH

Farrah, Abdelkader (1926–) A native Algerian, most of whose work as a British freelance stage designer has been with the **Royal Shakespeare Company**. Self-trained as a painter, he became a protégé and

Farrah's design for *As You Like It*, Royal Shakespeare Company, 1980.

collaborator of **Michel Saint-Denis** in France and later in England. Farrah's scenography is marked by an architectonic and theatrically expressive shaping of stage space (especially evident in *The Balcony*, 1972, *Henry V*, 1975, and *Coriolanus*, 1977), and a painter's talent for bold design and colour in costumes and props (*Doctor Faustus*, 1968, *As You Like It*, 1980, and *Poppy*, 1982). Notable instances of Farrah's interest in stylized masks occurred in *The Tempest* (1963) and *Richard III* (1970), as well as the 1968 *Doctor Faustus*.   JMB

Farren, Elizabeth (1762–1829) English actress. She worked on the Midlands theatre circuit with her mother and sisters in the 1770s and then joined Younger's company at Liverpool. By 1777 she was in London where she had little success in **breeches parts**, lacking the figure for them. From 1780 she acted at **Drury Lane**, becoming very successful in the fine lady roles previously played by **Mrs Abington**, praised for her charm, beauty and art. Very successful and highly paid, she began an affair with the Earl of Derby in 1785 and started to move in high society. On the death of his first wife in 1797 she retired from the stage and married him.   PH

Farren, Nellie (Ellen) (1848–1904) English actress, born into a famous theatrical family, who made her London debut in 1864. Known above all as a queen of burlesque, she was a star of the **Gaiety** from 1868 until her retirement in 1891 and a member of the famous Gaiety Quartette, with **Edward Terry**, **Kate Vaughan** and **Edward Royce**. 'She was', wrote **H. J. Byron** in a poetic tribute, 'a peal of laughter, ringing its way through life.'   PT

Fassbinder, Rainer Werner (1945–82) German dramatist, cinema and theatre director. Although his reputation rests on a series of brilliant films (*The Marriage of Maria Braun*, 1978, *Veronika Voss*, 1982, *Querelle*, which was released posthumously, or the documentary *Berlin Alexanderplatz*, 1979), Fassbinder was one of the originators of the contemporary **Volksstück** (Folk Play) and produced film versions of plays by its leading exponents, **Kroetz** and **Sperr**. As a founding director of the Action-Theater and the 'antiteater' in Munich (1967–8) he rediscovered the work of **Marieluise Fleisser**, which provided the catalyst for the movement, as well as staging **Büchner**, **Weiss**, **Handke** and (in his own adaptation) **Jarry**. These represent a cross-section of the major influences on his

Elizabeth Farren as Hermione in *A Winter's Tale*, c. 1780.

fashionable theatregoers, and she was an admired Juliet, Desdemona and Cordelia. After her marriage to the writer (and friend of the royal family), Theodore Martin, in 1851, she made only occasional appearances on the stage. Her husband was knighted in 1880, and it was as Lady Martin that she published her book *On Some of Shakespeare's Female Characters* (1892), an arch example of the 19th-century tendency to speculate on the unwritten biographies of *dramatis personae*.   PT

Favart, Charles-Simon (1710–92) French playwright and librettist who wrote principally for the **Comédie-Italienne** and the Paris fair theatres of St Germain and St Laurent. In a long career stretching from the 1720s to the 1770s he produced some 150 pieces, mostly in the form of comic operas, 'balletpantomimes' or similar *divertissements* and frequently parodying other dramatic or operatic works. Many were devised in collaboration with such writers as Panard and the abbé de Voisenon and some, apparently, with his wife, a vivacious actress and singer who under the name of Mlle Chantilly (1727–72) appeared in most of his plays at the Comédie-Italienne and is reputed to have anticipated **Mlle Clairon** in incorporating touches of realism into her stage costume. Amongst the greatest of Favart's successes were *La Chercheuse d'Esprit* (*The Adventuress*, 1741), *Les Amours de Bastien et Bastienne* (*The Loves of Bastien and Bastienne*, 1753), a parody of **Rousseau**'s *Le Devin du Village* (*The Village Soothsayer*), *La Fée Urgèle* (*The Fairy Urgèle*, 1753) and *Annette et Lubin* (1762). In 1757 he replaced Monnet as director of the Opéra-Comique, a position he retained when it amalgamated with the Comédie-Italienne five years later. His lengthy correspondence in the 1760s with the intendant of court theatres in Vienna is a mine of information about Parisian theatrical life at the time.   DR

Faversham, William (1868–1940) American actor. Born in London, he appeared briefly on the stage there before migrating to America in 1887. He was in the companies of both **Daniel** and **Charles Frohman** and played opposite **Mrs Fiske** and **Maude Adams** before he became a leading man. His physical attractiveness and buoyant personality earned him the label of a 'matinee girl's idol'. Among his successful Shakespearian roles were Mark Antony in *Julius Caesar* and the title roles in *Romeo and Juliet* and *Othello*. He won his popularity, however, playing vigorous and masculine heroes in such plays as *Lord and Lady Algy*, *The Squaw May*, and *The Prince and the Pauper*. His last role came in 1933 when he played Jeeter Lester in the long-running *Tobacco Road*.   RAS

own dramatic writing, which ranges from surrealism to brutally realistic images of social exploitation in his best plays, *Bremen Coffee*, 1971; *Blood on the Cat's Neck*, 1972. In 1974 he became artistic director of the prestigious Theater am Turm in Frankfurt, but devoted himself entirely to the cinema after the anti-semitism furore during rehearsals for his last play *The Garbage, the Town and Death* (1975: unperformed).   CI

Fastnachtspiel The carnival or Shrovetide play of German-speaking Europe, known from the 15th century, popular in origin and content, though incorporating some learned elements. They are usually farcical comedies, as the term *Schwänke* ('jests'), sometimes applied to them, indicates. Generally supposed to have been performed by students and artisans, the guild of Mastersingers was also connected with them – Hans Folz, a member of the Nuremberg guild, is one of the few known 15th-century authors, and the 16th-century shoe-maker and Mastersinger Hans Sachs wrote a large number.   AEG

Faucit, Helen Saville (1817–98) English actress, remembered primarily for her performance as **Macready**'s leading lady. She made her debut at **Covent Garden** in 1836, as Julia in **Sheridan Knowles**'s *The Hunchback* and was the creator, with Macready, of leading roles in the best-known plays of **Edward Bulwer**, *The Duchess de la Vallière* (1837), *The Lady of Lyons* (1838), *Richelieu* (1839) and *Money* (1840). Her refined portrayal of romantic passion attracted

Fechter, Charles Albert (1824–79) Actor, born in London to a German father and English mother, educated in France and speaking French as his first language. He made his debut in Paris in 1840 and became a leading melodramatic actor, particularly at the Porte-Saint-Martin. Restless and erratic, Fechter moved to London in 1860 and opened at the **Princess's** in a version of **Hugo**'s *Ruy Blas*. Despite (or because of) his French accent, the performance was a sensational success. He followed it with an equally melodramatic version of *Don Caesar de Bazan* (1861) and then floored the English public with a Hamlet that had all the ease

Charles Albert Fechter as Hamlet.

and elegance of Ruy Blas. **G. H. Lewes** spoke for Fechter's female adorers in calling him 'lymphatic, delicate, handsome', and the ecstatic reception owed much to the innovatory blonde curls and the contrasting black suit, carefully tailored. The innovations of his 'logical' Othello (1861) were more controversial, and Fechter returned to French melodrama for *The Duke's Motto* (1863). But his iconoclasm was something more than mere display. As manager of the **Lyceum** (1863–7), he initiated a mechanical revolution, substituting for wings and grooves the solid walls of an enclosing set and installing a system of lifts which allowed the sinking and lifting of complete scenes. His Lyceum repertoire mixed gentlemanly melodrama with *Hamlet* and *Othello*, but his vogue passed. In 1870, he sailed to the USA, where he remained, with the exception of a short season in London in 1872, for the rest of his life. He toured for some time, then opened the Globe Theatre in Boston as Fechter's Theatre, again with many innovations. His managerial ventures in America, however, failed, owing to his personal vanity and what his fan and friend **Charles Dickens** called 'a perfect genius for quarrelling'. Excessive drinking and a bigamous marriage forced him into retirement. He died in Quakertown, where he had tried to set up a farm. PT SMA

Fedeli, I ('the faithful') A troupe of **commedia dell'arte** actors founded (c. 1603) and led by **Giovan Battista Andreini** (Lelio), under the protection of the Duke of Mantua. Once allied to and often competing with the **Accesi**, it specialized in sumptuous court spectacles and featured Florinda (**Virginia Andreini**) as its languishing prima donna in her husband's plays. It turned down Marie de Medici's invitation to give performances at the French court in 1611, but three years later played publicly in Paris at the **Hôtel de Bourgogne**, when the company included **Tristano Martinelli** (Arlecchino), Barbieri (Beltrame) and **Gabrielli** (Scapino). Other French appearances occurred in 1623 and sometime between 1643 and 1647. The last notice of it mentions a performance of Andreini's *Magdalene Lustful and Repentant* (1652) in which a new young actress Eularia Coris enjoyed great personal success. LS

Federal Street Theatre Federal St at Franklin Pl., Boston [Architect: Charles Bulfinch]. When the 1750 law prohibiting playacting was overturned, prominent Bostonians pledged money by shares to erect the city's first theatre. In 1794, a handsome brick building by one of America's first architects opened under the management of Charles Stuart Powell. In 1798, the theatre burned and was rebuilt by Bulfinch the following year. After a succession of managers, the theatre known as 'Old Boston' was supplanted by newer theatres and was not used consistently. It closed in 1852 and was replaced by stores. MCH

Federal Theatre Project Established under the Works Progress Administration (WPA) in 1935 by an act of the United States Congress, this was the first example in the USA of officially sponsored and financed theatre, and, as such, the subject of much political controversy. Under the national direction of the indefatigable and intrepid Hallie Flanagan, head of the experimental theatre at Vassar, the FTP's objectives were to give meaningful employment to theatrical professionals out of work during the depression and to provide 'free, adult, uncensored theatre' to audiences throughout the country. Indeed, 10,000 people were employed at its peak, with theatres in 40 states. During its almost four years of existence, the FTP launched or established the careers of such notable theatre artists as **Orson Welles**, **John Houseman**, Joseph Cotton, Arlene Francis, Will Geer, John Huston, **Arthur Miller**, Virgil Thomson, **Howard Bay**, **Paul Green**, Mary Chase, Marc Blitzstein, **Canada Lee**, and **Elmer Rice**. Audiences were provided at inexpensive prices with a large variety of fare, ranging from classics to new plays, children's theatre, foreign language productions, puppet shows, religious plays, a Negro theatre, musical theatre, a circus, and a controversial innovation called the **Living Newspaper**, designed to deal with issues of the day utilizing documentary sources. In January 1936, with the urging of Helen Tamiris, a separate Federal Dance Project was established, although congressional cutbacks forced a merging with the FTP in October 1937. The FTP played to millions of people throughout the country; it is estimated that over 12 million attended performances in New York alone. Of the hundreds of productions presented by the FTP, those by the black theatre were among the most innovative and included the voodoo *Macbeth* (1936), *Haiti* (1938), and *The Swing Mikado* (1939). In 1936 Sinclair Lewis's *It Can't Happen Here*, written for the FTP, was produced simultaneously in 22 cities. The United States premiere of *Murder in the Cathedral*, which had been rejected by the **Theatre Guild**, was successful in 1936 at popular prices. Paul Green's outdoor historical pageant *The Lost Colony*'s 1937 premiere was in a WPA-built outdoor theatre in North Carolina, where it has been seen every summer since. The FTP was endlessly willing to take chances in its selection of plays and was, in **Harold Clurman**'s words, 'The most truly experimental effort ever undertaken in the American theatre.' Censorship was a problem frequently faced by various units of the FTP; its outspoken criticism, interpreted especially by conservative Congressmen as left-wing, ultimately led to a heated debate and the disbanding of the project on 30 June 1939. The epic and convoluted history of the FTP was first recounted by Flanagan in *Arena* (1940). Since then, a number of excellent sources have appeared, including Jane Mathews, *The Federal Theatre* (1967), Tony Buttitta and Barry Witham's *Uncle Sam Presents* (1982), and, drawing on the Federal Theatre Project Research Centre at George Mason University established in 1974, *Free, Adult, Uncensored* (1978) by John O'Connor and Lorraine Brown.   DBW

A reproduction in figurines for the stereopticon viewer of Act II, scene 4 of the *féerie*, *La Biche aux Bois* (*The White Fawn*).

Fedotova, Glikeriya Nikolaevna (1846–1925) The leading Russian actress of her day, protégée of **Shchepkin**, the father of Russian realistic acting, and with her husband, actor-director A. F. Fedotov, **Stanislavsky**'s teacher at the Moscow Society of Art and Literature. Her range was broader than that of the tragedienne **Ermolova**, the other great Maly Theatre actress, extending to comedy and drama, both domestic and historical. She excelled in a series of 29 character roles from the **Ostrovsky** canon, requiring emotional depth and truth-to-life. She was also memorable as many of **Shakespeare**'s strong women – Beatrice (1865), Isabella (1868), Katherina (1871), Portia (1877), Lady Macbeth and Mistress Page (1890), Volumnia (1902) – and as Queen Elizabeth opposite Ermolova's Maria Stuart in **Schiller**'s play.   SG

Féerie A type of French spectacular show, whose action derives from magical, fantastic or supernatural elements; heavy on production values and stage machinery. Its forebears are the *pièces à machines* produced at the **Théâtre du Marais** in the mid-17th century, with classical mythology supplying the plots. The Abbé Boyer's *Ulysse dans l'Ile de Circe* (1648) was a grandiose example, while **Molière** and **Corneille**'s *Psyché* (1670) represents a pocket version. In the late 18th century, the fantastic infiltrated fairground pantomimes, as in *Arlequin dans un Oeuf* at the Théâtre des Jeunes-Artistes, to produce in the 19th century the synthetic *féerie*. The first true success was *Le Pied du Mouton* (Gaîté, 1806), a much revived extravaganza in which a magic sheep's trotter unleashes a host of miracles. It was superseded by *Les Pilules du diable* (**Cirque Olympique**, 1839) and a succession of invariably successful shows, such as *La Biche au Bois* (known in the English-speaking world as *The White Fawn*), *La Chatte Blanche*, *Peau d'Âne*, etc., based on fairy tales and romances. Since the transformations, tricks and apotheoses required a large stage, the Châtelet and then the Porte-Saint-Martin under Marc Fournier became its favourite haunts. Romantic authors appreciated the dream-like qualities of the *féerie* (even Flaubert turned his hand to writing one, which

went unproduced); it exercised an important influence on the development of burlesque, musical comedy and early cinema.   LS

See: P. Ginisty, *La Féerie*, Paris, 1908).

Feiffer, Jules (1929–) American playwright and cartoonist. Born in New York, Feiffer studied at the Arts Students' League and Pratt Institute. Since 1956 his cartoons have appeared in *Village Voice* and have been widely syndicated. His first play, *The Explainers*, a musical review of his cartoons, was presented at the Second City, Chicago, in 1961. *Little Murders*, his first full-length script, won honours in London (1967), and an Obie in New York. Other major works include: *God Bless* (1968); *Feiffer's People* (1968); *The White Murder Case* (1970), which also won an Obie; *Knock Knock* (1976); *Hold Me!* (1977); and *Grownups* (1981). His screenplays include: *Carnal Knowledge* (1971), *Little Murders* (1972), and *Popeye* (1980). A satirist with a keen wit, Feiffer depicts the anguish which underlies middle-class American life.   TLM

Female impersonation Among certain American Indian, African and South Sea Island tribes, the androgynous shaman or *bardache* serves an important function as intermediary with the supernatural which some scholars consider is, in civilized societies, sublimated in the actor. The origins of theatre in religious cults meant that women were barred from performance, a prohibition sustained by social sanctions against their public exhibition in general. Therefore, in Europe, before the 17th century, and in Asia, before the 20th, female impersonation was the standard way to portray women on stage, and was considered far more normal than females playing females. The Greek and Roman theatre accepted the convention, and scandal arose only when an emperor lost caste by becoming a performer. Suetonius tells us that Nero enacted the incestuous sister in the mime-drama *Macaris and Canace*, giving birth on stage to a baby that was then flung to the hounds; according to Ælius Lampridius, Heliogabalus played Venus in *The Judgement of Paris* with his naked body depilated.

In the Oriental theatre, the female impersonator constitutes a distinct line of business. The *Tan* of Chinese opera, instituted for moral reasons in the reign of Chi'en Lung (1735–96), must be an exceptionally graceful dancer. It was the *emploi* of the great **Mei Lanfang**, voted the most popular actor in China on 1924, for whom Ts'i Zhou-chan wrote a special repertory. The *onnagata* role of Japanese **kabuki** drama came about when women and boys were banished from stage, lest they promote wantonness; mature men with shaven foreheads had to take over the female roles. Many specialists in *onnagata* parts possess an extensive range and are capable of dozens of distinct characters; in the past they were expected to behave offstage in as womanly a fashion as they did on.

Men dressing as women was a tradition of saturnalia, Feasts of Fools and medieval New Year's celebrations, still to be seen in rag weeks and end-of-term revels. Cross-dressing is a usual accompaniment to carnival time, when norms are turned upside-down; men giving birth was enacted at some Hindu festivals, and even Arlecchino in the late **commedia dell'arte** was shown in childbed and then breastfeeding his infant. Just as the Catholic Church attacked unruly carnivals, Protestant clerics and Puritans censured the 'sodomitical' custom of the boy-player on the Elizabethan and Jacobean stage. **Boys' companies** dominated the English theatre until 1580, and **Nathan Field** as Ophelia, Alexander Cooke as Lady Macbeth, and Robert Goffe as Juliet and Cleopatra shaped the image of these characters in the minds of **Shakespeare**'s contemporaries. **Edward Kynaston** was the last of the line, playing well into the Restoration when **Pepys** saw him in skirts.

Women were members of *commedia dell'arte* troupes from the 16th century but the comic characters occasionally donned petticoats to the delight of audiences, and this travesty aspect (already present in **Aristophanes**) grew more important as actresses gained popularity. If beauty and sex appeal were to be projected from stage by a real, nubile woman, the post-menopausal woman could as easily be played by a comic actor; parts like Mme Pernelle in **Molière**'s *Tartuffe* and the nanny Yeremeevna in **Fonvizin**'s *The Minor* were conceived as male roles, and **Nestroy**'s mid-19th-century farces contain several of these 'dame' parts. The comic dame had become a fixture of the **English pantomime** by the Regency period, and would be a showcase for such comedians as **Dan Leno**, **George Robey** and George Graves; some performers like George Lacy and Rex Jamieson ('Mrs Shufflewick') played nothing but dames. The tradition was maintained on the American popular stage by Neil Burgess as Widow Bedotte and Gilbert Sarony (d. 1910) as the Giddy Gusher; in France, Offenbach's operetta *Mesdames de la Halle* (1858) created three roles of market-women to be sung by men.

Nor was it unusual in the circus for boy athletes to be disguised as girls to make their stunts seem more phenomenal: the American equestrian Ella Zoyara (Omar Kingsley) and the trapezist Lulu (El Niño Farini) were celebrated examples in the 19th century, the aerialist **Barbette** in the 20th. Such transvestite performers were said to be 'in drag', a term from thieves' cant that compared the train of a gown to the drag or brake on a coach, and entered theatrical parlance from homosexual slang around 1870. 'Dragging up' provides the central plot device in **Brandon Thomas**'s *Charley's Aunt*, **William Douglas Home**'s sex-change play *Aunt Edwina* (1959) and **Simon Gray**'s *Wise Child* (1968).

A new development arose in 19th-century variety with the glamorous impersonator, who might be a comedian but dressed and made-up to resemble a woman of taste, beauty and chic. In America they were stars. The baritone **Julian Eltinge** usually selected vehicles that allowed him to vary sexes, accomplished by quick-change (one act required 11 separate changes); this 'ambi-sextrous comedian', as **Percy Hammond** called him, wore costumes that rivalled those of the fashion-plate Valeska Surratt, whom he parodied in *The Fascinating Widow* (1911). Bert Savoy (Everett Mackenzie, 1888–1923), of Savoy and Brennan, introduced an outrageous caricature, garish and brassy, gossiping about her absent girlfriend Margie and launching such catch-phrases as 'You mussssst come over' and 'You don't know the half of it, dearie'; his arch camping influenced **Mae West**. Francis Renault (Anthony Oriema, d. 1956), billed as 'The Slave of Fashion' and 'Camofleur', sang in a clear soprano, and Karyl Norman (George Podezzi, 1897–1947), 'The Creole Fashion-Plate', starred in musical comedy.

During the Second World War, all-male drag revues were popular in the British armed services, and persisted as post-war shows like *Soldiers in Skirts* and *Forces Showboats*. By the mid-1950s this activity had transferred to after-hours clubs, while East-End pubs with

El Niño Farini, the English trapeze and highwire artist, in his transvestite costume as Mlle Lulu.

their drag amateur nights were frequently subject to raids. In the USA, annual extravaganzas like the Jewel Box Revue arose. Drag ensembles sprang up in West Berlin (Chez Nous, 1958; Chez Romy Haag, 1972) and in Paris (Alcazar, 1972; L'Ange Bleu, 1975; Chez Madame Arthur and Le Carrousel), often featuring transvestites such as the Bardot-clone Coccinelle who had taken hormone treatments to improve the likeness.

The mid-1960s to 1970s saw a resurgence of female impersonation as a virtual article of theatrical faith. **Danny La Rue**'s (Carroll) club in Hanover Square (1964–70) was a resort of fashion, and drag mimes, lip-synching to tapes, were ubiquitous. This style reached an apotheosis in Paris's La Grande Eugène, seen in London in 1976. The drag ball in **Osborne**'s *A Patriot for Me* (**Royal Court**, 1965) hastened the demise of dramatic censorship in England, thus enabling such impressive impersonations as Tim Curry's Dr Frank'n-'furter in *The Rocky Horror Show* (1972). Androgyny had infiltrated the rock-music scene with Alice Cooper and David Bowie and reached a logical terminus in the asexual Boy George. More anarchic uses of 'gender-fuck' came from the American group The Cycle Sluts, hairy bruisers in net-stockings, and the 'radical drag queens', Bloolips (founded 1970), while the Lindsay Kemp company and the **Glasgow Citizens' Theatre** adapted female impersonation to the interpretation of classical texts. Comedy persisted in the cod ballet of the all-male Ballets Trockadero de Monte Carlo (founded 1974) and the Trockadero Gloxinia Ballet, impersonators like Charles Pierce and Craig Russell, and dames, such as **Barry Humphries** as Edna Everage and the piano-entertainers Hinge & Brackett (George Logan and Patrick Fyffe). LS

See: R. Baker, *Drag: A History of Female Impersonation*, London, 1968; K. Kirk and E. Heath, *Men in Frocks*, London, 1984; C. Shaw and A. Oates, *A Pictorial History of the Art of Female Impersonation*, London, 1966.

Feminist theatre (USA) An outgrowth of the 1960s New Left, avant-garde theatre and the Women's Liberation Movement, which sprang from women's dissatisfaction with their roles in American life and American theatre. More than 100 feminist theatre groups have followed the first, New Feminist Theatre, founded in 1969 by Anselma Dell'Olio.

The difficulty of defining the phenomenon of feminist theatre stems from its still emergent nature, the variety of its grass-roots and the range of its ideology. All feminist theatre is radical since it seeks to upset the status quo by scrutinizing women's position in a sexist society. However, feminist theatre groups vary between those more traditional ones designed to fight discrimination by providing a wide range of experiences for women in theatre, and the revolutionary groups that seek a total upheaval of theatrical techniques and subjects. These latter groups reject hierarchical structures, often creating their works by collective improvisation and experimental methods and drawing their political themes from their personal experiences, similar to the consciousness-raising of the Women's Liberation Movement. Many such groups exclude men and prefer female-only audiences, which join in post-performance discussions of the issues presented. Their plays generally reject standard characterizations and, instead, create women who serve as metaphorical figures to present highly didactic messages.

Feminist theatre groups since their beginning have considered a variety of women's subjects. These range from the trivial – leg shaving, bras, ironing – to the essential – abortion, rape, domestic violence, motherhood and entrapment in the nuclear family. Many early feminist groups reflected women's anger at the start of liberation and their perception of man as the enemy. Sometimes through the use of gender role reversal, their plays exposed the oppression of women in patriarchal society (*But What Have You Done for Me Lately?* by Myrna Lamb). Other feminist plays reject the destructiveness of male history and insist on a woman-oriented, visionary world of nurturing, continuity and life. These plays sometimes rework classical myths from a woman's point of view; create women's rituals; consider positive relationships between women as mothers and daughters, sisters, and friends; rediscover women's history, or insist upon total lesbian separatism.

Many feminist theatre groups were short-lived, suffering from problems of disorganization, lack of money and media oversight. Yet the successful ones, such as Rhode Island Feminist Theatre, At the Foot of the Mountain, Women's Experimental Theatre, Theatre of Light and Shadow, The Interart Theatre, Omaha Magic Theatre, Lavender Cellar Theatre, Spiderwoman Theatre Workshop, have shown themselves to be resilient and persuasive. Many have moved from a straight agit-prop style to more sophisticated, in-depth treatments of issues, including broader, humanistic ones such as pacifism. Generally, feminist theatre has created a new excitement in American theatre and has remained true to feminist goals as expressed in a statement from At the Foot of the Mountain: 'As witnesses to the destructiveness of a society which is alienated from itself, we are a theater of protest. As participants in the prophecy of a new world which is emerging through the rebirth of women's consciousness, we are a theater of celebration.' FB

See: J. Brown, *Feminist Drama: Definition & Critical Analysis*, Metuchen, N. J. and London, 1979; D. L. Leavitt, *Feminist Theatre Groups*, Jefferson, North Carolina, 1980; E. J. Natalle, *Feminist Theatre: A Study in Persuasion*, Metuchen, N. J. & London, 1985.

Fenn, Ezekiel (1620–?) English actor who, in 1635, played two demanding female roles for Queen Henrietta's Men at the **Cockpit**, that of Sophonisba in Nabbes's *Hannibal and Scipio* and that of Winifred in a revival of *The Witch of Edmonton*, by **Dekker**, **Ford** and **William Rowley**. He remained at the Cockpit as one of **Beeston**'s Boys, and is the subject of an interesting poem by Henry Glapthorne (1639), 'For Ezekiel Fenn at his first Acting a Man's Part'. Glapthorne makes clear the magnitude of the transition from female to male roles. Since nothing further is known of Fenn, we cannot be sure that he accomplished it successfully. PT

Fennario, David (1947–) Canadian playwright, born in a working-class section of Montreal, he drifted through the 1960s youth subculture before finally returning to school where he was encouraged to write. He became a writer-in-residence at Montreal's Centaur Theatre in 1974, learning about the theatre and writing his first play, *On the Job* (1975), based on his own experiences as a low-paid worker. His fourth play, *Balconville* (1979), a bilingual work, treats life among the working poor of a Montreal slum. It has played across Canada and at the **Old Vic**, and won an award as the outstanding Canadian play of 1979. Fennario's plays have a strong, sometimes annoying, autobiographical base, and fall into the naturalistic, 'kitchen-sink' school. Although acclaimed as a leftist political writer, he regards the political contents of his work as an inevitable result of the milieux and characters he likes to write about. JA

Fennell, James (1766–1816) A London-born actor who had a substantial career in America. Fennell first studied law, but made his debut in Edinburgh in 1787 as Othello, which became his most successful role, and soon appeared at **Covent Garden** with minimal success. **Wignell** brought Fennell to Philadelphia in 1792, where he soon became a star. Well over six feet tall with an expressive, handsome face, Fennell brought considerable dignity to such roles as Othello, Lear, and Jaffier in *Venice Preserv'd*; he was also much admired as Hamlet, Glenalvon in *Douglas*, and Iago. Fennell, however, invested his theatrical income in various unsuccessful money-making schemes, including various salt-manufacturing schemes, was arrested for debt, and spent a time in prison. He retired from the stage in 1810 and in 1814 published his memoirs. In 1815 he attempted Lear, but his memory was gone and the exhibition was one of 'pitiable imbecility'. SMA

Fernández de Moratín, Leandro (1760–1828) Spanish playwright of the 18th century, son of **Nicolás**. His five original comedies established the neoclassical French model in Spain for 50 years. Apprenticed to a goldsmith 1780–5, he wrote *El viejo y la niña* (*The Old Man and the Young Girl*) in 1786. Between employment in the diplomatic service and travel abroad he secured the patronage of Godoy and had great success with *La comedia nueva o el café* (*The New Play, or, The Café*, 1792), satirizing establishment dramatists. This was followed by *El barón* (*The Baron*, 1803) and *La mojigata* (*The Religious Hypocrite*, 1804). His best play, *El sí de las niñas* (*The Maidens' Consent*) (written 1801, produced 1806), supports free choice in marriage. In spite of its immense success it brought the attack of the Inquisition and Moratín abandoned the theatre. CL

Fernández de Moratín, Nicolás (1737–80) Spanish playwright and poet, father of **Leandro**. A critic of Golden Age theatre and supporter of French neoclassicism, his comedy *La petimetra* (*The Fashionable Lady*, 1762) differs little from the forms of the previous century except for its observation of the unities, and the rational triumph of love over honour. Much superior are his tragedies, *Lucrecia* (1763) on the rape of Lucretia, and *Hormesinda* (1770) set in Medieval Spain. They are moral in the stoic manner with a clear condemnation of tyranny. *Guzmán el bueno* (1777) is a patriotic and more traditionally Spanish tragedy. CL

Ferrari, Paolo (1822–89) Italian dramatist whose long career and substantial output provide an index to many of the tastes, characteristics and deficiencies of the mid-19th-century Italian stage. The range of his work was wide, and included dialect pieces, comedies of manners, historical dramas and plays concerned with contemporary social and moral issues. The influence of French example, particularly the bourgeois *drame* of **Augier** and **Dumas** *père*, is pronounced in much of his later writing, little of which has continued to hold the stage, although in their time plays like *Goldoni e le Sue Sedici Commedie Nuove* (*Goldoni and His Sixteen New Comedies*, 1853), *La Satira e Parini* (*Parini and Satire*, 1856), *Il Duello* (*The Duel*, 1868), *Cause ed Effetti* (*Cause and Effect*, 1871) and *Il Suicidio* (*The Suicide*, 1875) enjoyed considerable success and esteem, and at its best his drama, notwithstanding a tendency to prolixity and artificiality, is marked by wit and lively characterization. LR

Ferreira, António (1528–69) Portuguese playwright. He is known mainly for his *Tragédia de D. Inês de Castro* (*The Tragedy of Lady Inês de Castro*), usually known simply as *A Castro* (*The Castro*) to underline its great affinity with the plays and heroines of classical Greek tragedy, performed in Ferreira's lifetime at Coimbra, but published only in 1587.

The Castro, based on a real-life episode of Portuguese history, portrays the illicit love of the heir to the throne, D. Pedro (Prince Peter), for the Lady Inês, a liaison which, as in **Racine**'s *Bérénice*, is perceived as being completely at odds with reasons of state. The two lovers have their own dilemmas, but they are not so cruel as that faced by the King, whose choice is between kingly prudence and compassion. The King, spurred on by counsellors, first condemns Inês to death, then rescinds his sentence and finally (Pilate-like) washes his hands of the responsibility while the counsellors, like chief priests, take the guilt upon themselves. Inês is dispatched, and the Prince in the last short act threatens vengeance and that serious social disjunction that high tragedy characteristically entails. The fine management of tensions, the poetic atmosphere of foreboding, the Chorus's highly dramatic evocation of pity and terror make this one of the most theatrically effective and enduring of neoclassical tragedies – it played to packed houses in 1982 at the Lisbon Comuna theatre.

Ferreira also wrote two comedies. *O Cioso* (*The Jealous Man*) and *O Bristo* (protagonist's surname), both pleasant, actable plays. LK

Ferrer, José (Vicente) (1912–) American actor, director, and producer, born in Santurce, Puerto Rico. His professional debut was in a showboat melodrama on Long Island Sound in 1934. He made his debut on Broadway in 1935, but his first substantial role came in *Brother Rat* (1936), and he achieved stardom in *Charley's Aunt* (1940). Ferrer employed his rich and powerful voice in two subsequent revivals, as Iago to **Paul Robeson**'s Othello (1943) and in the title role of *Cyrano de Bergerac* (1946). In the latter role, critics praised his 'throbbing, vigorous performance'. Ferrer directed the New York Theatre Company at the City Centre for a time, appearing in several classical revivals.

Two other acting successes were *The Silver Whistle* (1948) and *The Shrike* (1948). Among his directing assignments have been *Stalag 17* (1951), *My Three Angels* (1953), and *The Andersonville Trial* (1959). Ferrer appears often in films and won an Oscar for his filmed

Cyrano. He has also appeared in opera. He is the ninth president of the Players Club. SMA

Ferron, Jacques (1921–85) French Canadian playwright, novelist and essayist. A physician by profession, he early began to write satirical plays such as *Le Licou* (*The Halter*, 1947) and *L'Ogre* (*The Ogre*, 1949), pointing towards the nationalist political commitment of his later works. Chief among these are *Les Grands Soleils* (*The Great Sunflowers*, 1958), which reexamines the Patriote Rebellion of 1837–8 in Lower Canada and the myths that had distorted it; and the even more political *La Tête du Roi* (*The King's Head*, 1963), dealing on intersecting historical planes with the 19th-century Métis Revolt and contemporary revolutionary violence in Quebec, crystallized in the decapitation of the statue of Edward VII, Symbol of Empire. A major novelist and essayist, Ferron played an active role in the formation and victory of the separatist Parti Québécois in 1976. He was also the founder of the parodic Rhinoceros Party, an iconoclastic grouping which perished with him. LED

Feuchtwanger, Lion (1884–1958) German dramatist and novelist. After early historical dramas such as *Jew Süss* (1917 – rewritten as a novel in 1925) he turned to contemporary political themes with a 'dramatic novel' *1918* which caused an uproar when staged in 1924. He collaborated with **Brecht** on several plays, including *Edward II* (1924) and the adaptation of his novel, *The Story of Simone Machard* (1957). CI

Feydeau, Georges (1862–1921) French dramatist. Often thought of as the father of 'French farce', Feydeau took over the 19th-century *vaudeville*, as perfected by **Labiche** and others. His subject and audience was the wealthy bourgeoisie of the Third Republic, whose sexual and matrimonial activities he examines with great accuracy. Feydeau understood the mechanics of farce supremely well, moving his plot with enormous speed, invariably bringing the wrong people together at the wrong moment, and usually leaving a character caught, literally, with his trousers down. The world of Feydeau presents man helplessly out of control of his destiny, caught in situations for which he ultimately is responsible, in settings with multiple doors, any of which may open at any moment to reveal disaster, and surrounded by objects which seem to take on a perverse life of their own. Feydeau's dramatic output was relatively limited. His first full-length play to be staged was *Tailleur pour Dames* (*A Gown for his Mistress*) at the Renaissance in 1886. The formula of matrimonial infidelity prepared in act I, of all the characters coming together at the same place of assignation in act II, and of sorting out the situation to everybody's 'satisfaction' in act III was firmly established. Feydeau's subsequent plays were unsuccessful until 1892, when *Monsieur Chasse* (*Monsieur is Hunting*) was accepted by the **Palais-Royal**, and *Champignol Malgré lui* (*A Close Shave*) was staged at the Nouveautés, which would become the main theatre associated with his work. *Cat Among the Pigeons* (*Un Fil à la Patte*, 1894) shows the attempt of a young man to dispose of his *cocotte* mistress (a forerunner of the later 'Môme Crevette' of *The Lady from Maxim's* or of Amelia of *Look After Amelia* (1908)), in order to marry a

Act II of Feydeau's *A Flea in her Ear*, showing the complex hotel set with split-stage and bedroom with revolving bed. The set is an integral part of the mechanism of the farce.

young lady of large fortune. This was written on his own, unlike *Hotel Paradiso* (*L'Hôtel du Libre Echange*, 1894), on which he collaborated with Maurice Desvallieres, who had also collaborated on some of his earlier plays. *Hotel Paradiso*, like *A Flea in her Ear* (1907), his other most popular play, brings all the characters to an extremely dubious hotel in the second act, much of the comedy being derived from the respectability of the characters and the hypocrisy of their attitudes. With *Sauce for the Goose* (*Le Dindon*, 1896) Feydeau was moving towards a more serious portraiture of the mores of the bourgeoisie of the Belle Epoque. Increasingly his focus is on marriage itself as an institution. *The Lady from Maxim's* (1899), one of the most popular plays running during the 1900 Exhibition (so popular that he wrote a 'sequel', *The Duchess of the Folies-Bergère*), exposes social snobberies by setting up a situation in which a group of respectable provincial ladies emulate the speech of a Parisian *cocotte*. In his later years Feydeau's view of marriage (perhaps as a result of the failure of his own) became darker, with wives seen as invariably nagging and trivial. He wrote several shorter plays, including *Feu la Mère de Madame* (*Madame's Late Mother*, 1908) and *On Purge Bébé* (*We're Giving Baby a Laxative*, 1910), in which the emphasis is no longer on complexity of plot, but on conjugal relationships. In these and *Mais n'te promène donc pas Toute Nue!* (*Don't Walk Round With Nothing On!*, 1911) and *Hortense dit 'Je m'en Fous'* (*Hortense Says, I Don't Give a Damn!*, 1916), Feydeau was far closer to the naturalist theatre than to the fashionable boulevard. JMCC

Fialka, Ladislav (1931–91) Czech mime. Trained as a ballet dancer, he was one of the founders of the Prague Balustrade Theatre (1958), where he directed and starred in pantomimes wearing the traditional white-face of **Pierrot**. Working with a regular ensemble, he based his mimodramas mainly on traditional material: *Les Amants de la Lune* (1959) from **Deburau**; *The Castaways* (1959) in the style of silent films; *The Fools* (1965), which traced the type from the Bible to Kafka. He also worked in *Hamlet* (1959) and *Ubu* (1964), and toured Europe and America. LS

Field, Nathan (1587–c. 1620) English actor and playwright whose father was a Puritan clergyman of vehemently anti-theatrical views. Field was probably impressed into the **Children of the Chapel Royal** in 1600 and quickly made a reputation as an outstanding boy actor. By 1613, he was the leader of the adult Lady Elizabeth's Men from which he transferred to the King's Men in about 1615. Praised by **Ben Jonson**, the flamboyant Field was well suited to the role of **Chapman**'s Bussy d'Ambois, in which he excelled. That he was himself something of an overreacher is implied by his relationship with the Countess of Argyll, who bore his child in 1619. Field's two surviving comedies, *A Woman Is a Weather-Cock* (c. 1609) and *Amends for Ladies* (c. 1610), are competent exercises in the style of Jonson and he is known to have collaborated with **Massinger**, in *The Fatal Dowry* (c. 1618) and other plays, as well as with **Fletcher**.   PT

Fielding, Henry (1707–54) English playwright. His first play was produced before he went to study in Leyden but his reputation as the finest satirical dramatist of his age effectively began with the production of *The Author's Farce* in 1730, a ballad-opera which in its experimentation with dramatic form and the brilliance of its satire established the model for his later work. His mockery of contemporary tragedy, *Tom Thumb* (1730), was later revised under the grandiose title *The Tragedy of Tragedies* (1731). After trying full-length farce, Fielding turned to political satire on both parties and the royal family in *The Welsh Opera* (performed 1731), revised as *The Grub Street Opera*, again using the ballad-opera form as a vehicle for satire. His only attempt at a serious play on sexual intrigue and marriage, *The Modern Husband* (1732), analyses marriage as prostitution and adultery by consent. Of the 15 plays before 1734, only *The Welsh Opera* was openly political satire but, with Walpole's Excise Bill threatening, Fielding moved openly into the Opposition, and into political drama again, attacking Walpole in *Don Quixote in England* (1734). For the next three years he made his attacks on the government clearer and clearer in plays like *Pasquin* (1736) and *The Historical Register for the Year 1736* (1737). He used the Little Haymarket Theatre, which he managed, as a platform for his and others' attacks on the government. Walpole was provoked to limit the freedom of the theatres and using a particularly vicious attack, *The Golden Rump*, a play scheduled for production at **Goodman's Fields Theatre**, as a convenient pretext for action, his government rushed through the Licensing Act which created censorship over plays through the Lord Chamberlain's office which lasted until 1968. Fielding, censored and with his theatre closed because unlicensed, turned to the law and to writing novels, with a few infrequent plays.   PH

Fields, Gracie (Stansfield) (1898–1979) 'Our Gracie' was born over a fish-and-chip shop in Rochdale, Lancs, England, and worked part-time as a mill-girl and shopclerk, while she sang in working-men's clubs. Her professional debut at a local cinema, as a member of a juvenile troupe, came in 1908. In 1915 she joined the revue *Yes, I Think So*, at the Hulme Theatre, Manchester; three months later she made her London debut as Sally Perkins in *Mr Tower of London*, which enjoyed a phenomenal run (1918–25) at the Alhambra, Leicester Sq. She was a headliner in variety by 1928, played the New York Palace in 1930 and in 1931 first sang her signature tune 'Sally'. Audiences adored her for her clogs-and-shawl manner and her ability to move smoothly from the vocal clowning of 'The Biggest Aspidistra in the World' to the mawkishness of 'Ave Marie'. She received a CBE in 1937.

When Britain went to war, her second husband, an Italo-American, was deported as an enemy alien, and she attracted much opprobrium by moving to Hollywood. Even though she raised £1,500,000 in the USA for the war effort in 1941, adverse comment also attached to her leaving her **ENSA** tours to honour American contracts. She played ten Royal Variety performances, before retiring to Capri in 1959; by the time she was made Dame of the British Empire in 1979, all was forgiven and she was appreciated for her wartime efforts, with their theme-song 'Wish Me Luck As You Wave Me Goodbye'. Eric Morecambe opined that she and George Formby were the only show-business persons 'really loved by the public'.   LS

Fields, Lew see **Weber, Joseph**

Fields, W. C. (William Claude Duckenfield) (1880–1946) American comedian, who ran away from home at the age of 14 and taught himself to juggle. As an eccentric tramp juggler he was the first American headliner at the **Folies-Bergère** (1902) and a great hit at the London **Hippodrome** (1904) for his trick pool game and frustrating golf lesson. Taking his cue from **Harry Tate**'s music-hall persona, the bibulous, bottle-nosed Fields developed the character of a grandiloquent but seedy curmudgeon, muttering indignant asides. He starred in *The Ziegfeld Follies* (1915–18, 1920, 1921, 1925) and in 1923 in *Poppy* created the type of the moth-eaten but brazen showman he would later repeat on film. His earliest film appearance had been in a short of 1915, and after 1925 he settled in Los Angeles, filming a series of comic masterpieces.   LS

Fierstein, Harvey (1954–) American playwright, actor, producer and gay activist. Educated at Pratt Institute, Fierstein made his debut as an actor at **La Mama** in Andy Warhol's *Park* (1971). He garnered sudden fame in 1981 with the success of his *Torch Song Trilogy*, a play presenting various views of male homosexuality. With the commercial success of the musical *La Cage Aux Folles* (1983), of which he wrote the book, Fierstein has become the most successful Broadway playwright concerned with gay themes.   TLM

Fifth Avenue Theatre West 24th St between Broadway and Sixth Ave, New York City. Amos Eno, the owner of the Fifth Avenue Hotel, erected a small structure adjoining it for surreptitious and illegal stock exchange activities, which he was forced to abandon. In 1865, he decided to convert it into a theatre and for several years, it functioned as a minstrel hall. The railroad magnate James Fiske took it over, gutted the interior and transformed it into a handsome little theatre, which eventually fell into the hands of **Augustin Daly** for his introduction into theatrical management. From 1869 to 1873, Daly assembled an attractive company, staged comedies and dramas in perfectly tuned productions and made the theatre the most fashionable and popular playhouse in New York. When it went up in flames in 1873, Daly transferred his company to the New Fifth Avenue Theatre at 728 Broadway. In 1879, **Steele MacKaye** rebuilt the old house, renaming it the **Madison Square**. MCH

Finck, Werner (1902–78) German cabaret performer, co-founder of Berlin's Die Katakombe, where he was a cheeky and courageous compère and actor from 1929 to 1935. His puns and word-games constituted a veritable critique of his times, for which he was interned in a concentration camp in 1935. But he survived to make numerous post-war appearances as a solo cabaretist, particularly at Die Mausefalle, Stuttgart (1948–51). LS

Finland There exist no records of the very beginnings of theatrical activity in Finland. The main emphasis in the rich heritage of folklore is epic in nature, and no investigations have been made into the possible dramaturgy of the narrative event. The shaman was a locally sanctioned performer in primitive Finnish society. The bear-hunting and wedding-ceremonies certainly included role-playing. From the late 18th century onwards, one finds descriptions of games and ring-dances with an elementary plot structure.

Although the church in the Middle Ages first allowed and even organized religious performances and processions, a ban was imposed on all theatrical activities in the 17th century. The Finnish theatre thus lacks entirely the courtly traditions that have characterized the development of the theatre in other European countries.

At the end of the 18th century, when Finland was still part of Sweden, the first in Swedish theatre companies started to extend their tours to include Finnish cities. At the same time amateur acting became popular in upper middle class families. The plays were all in Swedish and later also in German, when German touring companies entered the country via St Petersburg.

Interest in plays and spectacles was also considerable among the lower classes, but the popular performances in market-places and public gardens were not generally considered to have any artistic value.

After Finland had become a Grand Duchy of Russia in 1809, the interest shown in drama as an art form was one manifestation of the rising ambition to create a national literature, both in Finnish and in Swedish. A vigorous, and successful, effort was made to develop Finnish, which had not earlier been used at all by upper class people, in such a way that it could compete with Swedish as a cultural language. Russian was never used as an artistically creative language in Finland.

For all these reasons literary and verbal elements have always been strong in the Finnish theatre, and realism its main performing style. The first important themes were found simultaneously in Finno-Ugric mythology and in regional history. Aleksis Kivi wrote the first tragedy in Finnish (*Kullervo*, 1864), the protagonist being one of the heroes of the 'Kalevala' and the Swedish poet J. J. Wecksell dramatized a complicated sequence of 16th-century Finnish–Swedish relations in *Daniel Hjort*. Both acknowledged their debt to **Shakespeare**. The first comedies, notably Kivi's *Cobblers on the Heath*, were influenced by the moderate rationalism of **Holberg**.

In the 1860s, theatre enthusiasts accepted the idea of founding a bi-lingual theatre, but their plans turned literally to ashes, when the new theatre house in Helsinki burnt down. Soon after that, the time seemed ripe for strengthening the position of the Finnish language in the performance of drama. The first professional theatre was founded by Dr Kaarlo Bergbom, a playwright and scholar, in 1872.

The Finnish Theatre, which in 1902 became the National Theatre, had an extensive and ambitious programme for building a theatrical culture based both in 'straight' drama and opera. Its primary objective was the promotion of drama in Finnish. Almost equally important was the task of making the great classical works available to Finnish audiences. This led, among other things, to the translation of the entire Shakespeare canon by the poet Cajander.

The next outstanding Finnish dramatist after Aleksis Kivi was Minna Canth (1844–97), who wrote most of her plays in collaboration with Bergbom. Canth protested against the injustices of woman's position in society and created a series of remarkable studies in social conscience, for example *The Worker's Wife* and *The Parson's Family*. The rebellious gipsy girl in *The Worker's Wife* was played by Ida Aalberg, who became the first great actress of the Finnish Theatre. She came of a humble family, her father being an employee on the railways, but soon she was playing all the great tragic parts. Later she toured with her own company and became internationally known, in Scandinavia, Russia and Germany. Greatly loved and greatly envied, Ida Aalberg was in the tradition of **Eleonora Duse** and **Sarah Bernhardt**.

The Finnish Theatre toured the country extensively until it finally settled down in its present house in Helsinki in 1902. Meanwhile, professional or semi-professional theatres were founded in its wake. The newly-urbanized workers were especially interested in theatre. They wanted to produce plays for their own amusement as well as for the social enlightenment of their fellows. Out of this interest there sprang up a number of Workers' Theatres, simultaneously with the 'bourgeois' houses. By the year 1920, after the deadlock of the Civil War, almost every city had two theatre companies, with professional status and a measure of support both from the central government and the local authorities. The economic burden involved in all this became soon very heavy, and because of the generally right-wing policies that prevailed, the theatres were progressively amalgamated. Only the biggest industrial city, Tampere, has succeeded in maintaining an independent Workers' Theatre, now having almost the status of a National Theatre.

Living drama in the Swedish language was for long dependent on visits by touring companies from Sweden. There was uncertainty as to whether the Swedish spoken in Finland was sufficiently refined for the stage. The first 'national' Swedish theatre was founded in Turku in 1894, but it was not until 1915 that it became fully established in its own house in Helsinki.

When Finland became an independent state in 1917 and the Civil War was over, the theatre was needed both to consolidate the strong new cultural base and also to open the windows to current cultural ideas elsewhere in Europe. The principal influences came largely from Germany and France and were mixed with the **Stanislavsky**-influenced 'national' realism.

The Workers' Theatres were particularly eager to embrace expressionism. This brought about a remarkable change in the style of acting. Expressionism gained a foothold through the success of various German plays, but it was soon to receive also Finnish and Swedish voices in plays by Lauri Haarla, Arvi Kivimaa and Hagar Olsson. Stage decor was relieved of the burden of stock realism and soon became an important element in dramaturgy itself, attracting both artists and architects (e.g. Wäinö Aaltonen, Alvar Aalto).

There existed simultaneously a quite different tradition, based on old Finnish folk characters. Scepticism and irony were characteristic of the comedies of Maria Jotuni and Maiju Lassila. These two dramatists created vivid social types, Jotuni, a woman herself, mostly women, and Lassila mostly men, and their plays were often built on a triangle of love, money and death. Lassila, a socialist journalist and novelist, was killed during the Civil War, but his comedies have shown enduring qualities. Jotuni continued writing right up to the 1940s, towards the end of that time composing sombre and powerful tragic plays.

The most important directors in the period between the two great wars were Eino Kalima and Eino Salmelainen. Kalima was familiar with the style of acting of the **Moscow Arts Theatre**, and it was he who introduced Stanislavsky principles to Finland. He was also influenced by the ideas of **Copeau** and in the 1960s he presented a series of **Chekhov** productions which have become legendary in Finnish theatre history. The special atmosphere of these performances was the result of a thorough study of Russian life and the nostalgia of the upper classes combined with an implied criticism of the futility of their way of life.

Another director, Eino Salmelainen was active in the People's Theatre of Helsinki and as director of the Tampere Workers' Theatre. He was largely responsible for bringing to the stage the life of Finnish peasants and workers in plays depicting their social conflicts especially through the works of Hella Wuolijoki (1886–1954). Wuolijoki's series of 'Niskavuori' plays, a family story centred on the heritage of agrarian culture, has become an apotheosis of the strength of Finnish womanhood.

The Second World War put a brake on the development in the theatre which sent its troupes to tour the fronts with lightweight comedies. Soon after the war the Finnish theatre saw a remarkable renaissance. Directors like Arvi Kivimaa, who had succeeded Kalima as the director of the National Theatre, Wilho Ilmari and Sakari Puurunen all displayed an interest in moral and psychological problems. It was difficult to produce such plays because the theatres were usually too large and the audience too remote from the actors. The demand for a more intimate type of drama led to the building of studio and workshop stages. The first to be constructed was the small stage of the National Theatre, which, by presenting a repertory of plays by authors like **Sartre**, **Beckett**, **Osborne** and **Pinter**, paved the way to similar developments elsewhere, and also served as an inspiration for young Finnish directors and playwrights. The new interest in man's inner life became visible e.g. in the plays of Eeva-Liisa Manner

(b. 1921), Paavo Haavikko (b. 1931) and Veijo Meri (b. 1928).

Arvi Kivimaa was active in building up international relationships, which led to membership of the ITI in 1959, foreign tours by Finnish companies and also visits to Finland by famous troupes from abroad. The native avant-garde was represented by the Intimiteatteri, which saw a period of splendid acting and fearless and original direction during its first decades 1950–70. In the Finnish Theatre School, directed by Wilho Ilmari, training was in the 1950s largely based on an adaptation of the methods of Stanislavsky. The School has produced generations of talented actors and actresses, well acquainted with the demands of psychological character study. Eeva-Kaarina Volanen (b. 1926) is a fine actress who, during the course of a long career, has moved on from her earlier portraits of soulful youth (**Anouilh**) to interpretations of the experienced and care-worn women in modern American and Scandinavian drama. Lasse Pöysti (b. 1927), who began his career as a greatly admired child actor, went on to become a skilful interpreter of the psychological problems of 20th-century man. Later still he worked for a period as director of the Tampere Workers' Theatre and finally as director of the Royal Dramatic Theatre, Stockholm.

The situation today In the sixties a new emphasis on the theatre's social utility and its importance as a political tool became as evident in Finland as elsewhere. The new viewpoint was encouraged by a number of different factors. Democratization of culture was seen

Vaasan Kaupungin Teatteri's production of Brecht's *The Good Person of Setzuan*.

as one of the tasks of society and public funds were allocated for the support of art and artistic institutions. It was recognized that although the audience the theatre attracted was eager, it was predominantly middle class, and whole sectors of society had become almost totally alienated from the theatre. At the same time, young people, influenced by the ideas of **Bertolt Brecht**, began to apprehend the theatre's potential for influencing the thinking of audiences.

The style and use of music also underwent a change; where homely folk melodies had been associated with comedy, and music had been used to point up the nuances of psychological relations, it now became possible to use music directly in cabarets and in plays in agit-prop style. The theatre first became a place for political debate in 1966, in Arvo Salo's Lapau Opera, which, despite the name, was not really profoundly Brechtian in character. Here was a clearly pacifist proclamation, inspired by memories of Finland's history in the thirties and American peace songs. This production, directed by Kalle Holmberg, with the Helsinki Students Theatre and music by Kaj Chydenius, represented a final breakthrough for the winds of change in theatrical thinking. Now, over 20 years later, almost everyone who was associated with that production has an established position in the Finnish theatre, either as director, actor or stage designer – which does not mean, however, that all of them still propound the same ideas.

The radical theatre of the young people was not easily accepted by the institutions, which had a more conservative bent. The result was the formation of new, independent theatre groups which emerged in the sixties and seventies. The most vigorous of them still survive, such as KOM, which started as a subgroup of Helsinki's Swedish Theatre, but soon became independent of it and gave performances in Finnish; Raatikko, now an internationally-known dance theatre, and the Swedish-language Skolteatern, which performs mainly to children. The Ryhmäteatteri, which was founded by the students of the Theatre Academy and has had a chequered existence, is now, under the direction of Arto aof Hällström and Raila Leppäkoski, the most radical of the avant-garde groups, presenting experimental plays by its own group of dramatists.

Meanwhile many of the institutional theatres have felt a need to modify and reorganize their work. The Turku City Theatre reached remarkable heights of achievement during the years 1973–7, when both Ralf Långbacka and Kalle Holmberg worked there as directors. Långbacka is a Brecht specialist and has directed many of the plays with a firm grasp of their message. He has also used Brechtian insights to create a new, critical way of producing Chekhov. Holmberg has directed a series of analytical plays on the social and moral conflicts in Finland. His 'rag' adaptation of the classic novel *The Seven Brothers* by Aleksis Kivi was immensely popular on the Turku stage and was taken on international tours.

Since the early 80s, Långbacka and Holmberg have worked together at the Helsinki City Theatre, which, with its up to four stages and high artistic standards, has become the flagship of the Finnish theatre. Since 1965 it has been housed in a palatial new building, which, together with the new theatres of Rovaniemi and Jyväskylä (both designed by Alvar Aalto), Lahti and Tampere, is eloquent testimony to the strong position of the theatre in Finland's cultural life.

During its short history, the Finnish theatre has had a number of important female directors. The tradition established by Mia Backman and Glory Leppänen has been continued by Vivica Bandler (long time director of Stockholm City Theatre), Rita Arvelo, Kaisa Korhonen, Ritva Siikala, Kristin Olsoni and Eija-Elina Bergholm. Their work has included new interpretations of the Finnish classics, notably the plays of Jotuni and Wuolijoki, and they have also brought a new vitality to the stage through study of current development in both European and Oriental theatre.

The greatest jolt to Finnish theatre traditions, and to the Finns' ideas of themselves, has recently been given by Jouko Turkka. He has been working at the Helsinki City Theatre and more recently as head of the Theatre Academy. He is a man of exceptional talent, who uses the stage as a musician uses his instrument, exploiting to the full its possibilities for expression. To the physical and emotional education of young actors and directors Turkka has brought a dark and passionate ethical outlook. In his productions, for example *Runar and Kyllikki* by Jussi Kylätasku and the plays of Hannu Salama, he has elicited the bleak and cruel side of the Finnish character.

It is the avowed aim of Finnish cultural policy to combat the all-pervasive influence of television and video. Theatre policy in Finland is largely directed by the wish to ensure that there will still be audiences in the theatre in the 21st century. The government subsidizes the touring activities of some 12 professional theatres which have their traditional base in one of the smaller theatres, but now also take their productions to the remote villages. The regional theatre of Lapland (Rovaniemi) makes three or four annual tours, to places as much as 500 miles away; in the south, the Swedish regional theatre of Åboland (Turku) has an equally demanding touring area in the archipelago off the south-west coast. These theatres have been extremely important for the children in those regions. Some good work is also done by the drama section of Finnish television. Radio drama, which has a long and honourable tradition of attracting talented actors and promising new playwrights, also has a nation-wide audience. Numerous educational organizations exist to foster an interest in the theatre and to guide amateur groups which arrange annual festivals at which their best work is presented.

A special feature of the Finnish theatre is the open-air stages on which popular plays are produced in the summer time notwithstanding the vicissitudes of the Finnish summer weather. In Savonlinna there is a special summer festival for opera at which both Finnish and classical operatic works are mounted.

Music has always had a prominent place in the Finnish theatrical tradition. Several works by Sibelius were originally composed for the stage (*The Tempest Suite* is perhaps the best known). Finnish opera has recently been enriched by the prestigious works of Joonas Kokkonen (*The Last Temptations*), Ilkka Kuusisto (*The Moomin Opera, War for the Light*), and Aulis Sallinen (*The Horseman, The Red Line, The King Goes Forth to France*). The dance theatre is a rapidly expanding sector of theatre life, and there are interesting new groups which strive to find an appropriate modern mode of expression, involving mythological materials, modern jazz drama as well as the visual arts. IN

See: Finnish Theatre Today, Helsinki, 1974; Maija Savutie, Finnish Theatre, Helsinki, 1980.

Finlay, Frank (1926–) British actor, who first attracted national attention as a versatile member of the English Stage Company at the **Royal Court** in the late 1950s. He was a memorable Harry Khan in **Arnold Wesker**'s *Chicken Soup with Barley* (1958), Attercliffe in **John Arden**'s *Sergeant Musgrave's Dance* (1959) and Hill in Wesker's *Chips with Everything* (1962). **Laurence Olivier** invited him to join the **National Theatre** Company, where he played such major roles as Willie Mossop in *Hobson's Choice*, Iago in *Othello* and Joxer Daly in *Juno and the Paycock*. Finlay acquired a certain identity as an actor, playing mainly middle-aged characters, often quiet and passive, but with a controlled power which rose to emotional climaxes. As Bernard Link in **David Mercer**'s *After Haggerty* (1970) and the paterfamilias in **De Filippo**'s *Saturday, Sunday, Monday* (1973), Finlay retained the audience's attention with what seemed to be minimal effort until he reached the explosion of despair and anger towards the end of the play. This gift for pacing a performance proved especially useful to the director in such discursive plays as **John Osborne**'s *Watch It Come Down* (1976) and **Howard Brenton**'s *Weapons of Happiness* (1976) at the National Theatre. After taking over from **Colin Blakely** in De Filippo's *Filumena* and from **Paul Scofield** as Salieri in *Amadeus* (1981), Finlay turned towards a West End musical, *Mutiny!*, in which he played Captain Bligh (1985). JE

Finney, Albert (1936–) British actor, who led the post-war generation of actors towards a less upper-class, less cerebral and more physical style of playing. He had an early opportunity to take major roles with the **Birmingham Repertory Theatre** where he was one of **Barry Jackson**'s protégés from 1956 to 1958; and then moved to the Shakespeare Memorial Theatre at Stratford-upon-Avon to play Edgar to **Charles Laughton**'s King Lear and to take over as Coriolanus from **Laurence Olivier**. He became nationally known in 1960 when he created the title role in *Billy Liar*, the North Country comedy by **Keith Waterhouse** and **Willis Hall**, and in 1961, played Luther in **John Osborne**'s historical epic at the **Royal Court Theatre**. He starred in major British films such as *Saturday Night and Sunday Morning* (1960) and *Tom Jones* (1963); and his rugged physique, stocky determined manner and rich voice attracted the hero-worship of teenagers. He joined the **National Theatre** Company in 1965 to play a variety of parts, ranging from the rebellious border baron, Armstrong, in **John Arden**'s *Armstrong's Last Goodnight* (1965) to the limp-wristed antiques collector in **Peter Shaffer**'s *Black Comedy* (1966). He started to direct both plays and films, notably *Charlie Bubbles* (1967), and was considered to be one of several possible successors to Olivier as director of the National Theatre. He co-presented **Peter Nichols**'s *A Day in the Death of Joe Egg* (1967) in London and New York, and became an Associate Director at the Royal Court Theatre from 1972 to 1975. When **Peter Hall** took over from Olivier at the National Theatre, he invited Finney to star in the first

NT seasons in their new home on the South Bank, as Hamlet, Tamburlaine and Macbeth. Finney's many-sided talents have never, however, been matched by a single creative challenge which could absorb his full energy and concentration. JE

Fiorilli, Tiberio (called Scaramuccia or Scaramouche) (c. 1600–94) Italian comedian, putative son of **Silvio Fiorillo**, popularized the character Scaramouche, an amalgam of the **zanni** and the Capitano, in a sober black costume, with no mask and a guitar in lieu of a sword. Despite his squint, deafness and withered arm, his French and Italian contemporaries were charmed by his naturalness and comic power; one mute scene of fear in *Colombine lawyer pro and con* (1685) kept a Parisian audience dying of laughter for 15 minutes. In 1658 he alternated performances at the **Petit-Bourbon** with **Molière**, who suggested a repeat of this experiment at the **Palais-Royal** in 1661. Fiorilli enjoyed success in London in 1673 and 1675. A picaresque but untrustworthy biography, *La Vie de Scaramouche*, was written by **Angelo Costantini** in 1695. LS

Fiorillo or **Fiorilli** Family of Italian actors. **Silvio Fiorillo** (d. 1633), began in the **commedia dell'arte** playing Captain Matamoros, then c. 1609 appeared in Naples as the first Policenella, brandishing a cuckold's horn; his success led to this episodic servant becoming a lead comedian. He also published some scenarios. His son **Giovan Battista** (*fl.* 1614–51) played second **zanni** under the name Trappolino; his wife Beatrice Vitelli (*fl.* 1638–54) played first amorosa. LS

Fireworks As a dramatic auxiliary, fireworks were used in 14th-century religious plays, particularly for hell mouth, and became a standard requisite of the medieval and baroque theatres. Vanuzzi Biringuccio and Bishop Abram of Suzdal testify to wooden figures and metal cylinders shooting off fireworks in plays produced in Siena and Florence on the Feast of St John and the Assumption, in the 16th century. In England, the 'wild men' of the Lord Mayor's show were associated with pyrotechnics; in George Whetstone's *Historie of Promos and Cassandra* (1578), green men enter with their clubs spouting fire. By the 18th century, fireworks displays, now with coloured lights, had been transferred to pleasure gardens, and only the **Comedié-Italienne** in Paris still employed them indoors. That they had become old-fashioned claptrap is clear in *Nicholas Nickleby* when Crummles proposes that a fireworks display, 'awful from the front', could be bought for 18 pence. A brief resurgence in their use came in the late 19th century in the spectaculars of the **Kiralfy** brothers and their competitors. LS

See: A. St H. Brock, Fireworks, London, 1949.

Firmin (1784–1859) French actor. Firmin first appeared with the Théâtre des Jeunes Elèves c. 1800. His talents suited him to comedy rather than tragedy and he joined **Picard**'s troupe at the Louvois in 1806, having an immediate success in *Le Jeune Homme à l'Epreuve* (*The True Young Man*) and *L'Amour et La Raison* (*Love and Reason*). He moved to the **Odéon**, where Napoleon noticed him in *Les Querelles des Deux Frères* (*The Quarrels of the Two Brothers*) in 1810 and had him transferred to the **Comédie-Française**. He was a lively, intelligent and sensitive actor, playing **Marivaux**'s lovers remarkably well. He ventured into the *drame* in 1829 as Saint Mégrin in *Henri III et Sa Cour*, and was the original Hernani the following year. In 1831 he left the Comédie to play in the provinces and abroad, but returned in 1833. From 1813 to 1843 he created at least 100 parts at the Comédie, including Torquato in *Tasse* (1826), Frédéric in **Scribe**'s *Bertrand et Raton* (1833) and Richelieu in *Mlle de Belle-Isle* (1839). In 1845 he retired as his memory was failing and died in rather mysterious circumstances at his country property in 1859. JMCC

Fiske, Harrison Grey (1861–1942) American dramatic editor, critic, producer, manager, and playwright. Born of wealthy parents, Fiske served an early apprenticeship on the *Jersey City Argus, New York Star*, and *New York Dramatic Mirror*. He left New York University after his sophomore year (1880) to edit the *Dramatic Mirror* when his father bought him one-third interest in it. He made the paper an important theatrical journal by attacking corruption in the profession and working to raise the tone of the American stage. He led a crusade in 1880 to establish the Actors Fund. In 1890, he married the actress Marie Augusta Davey (**Minnie Maddern Fiske**) and managed her career as well as that of a number of leading actors. For her he wrote or adapted numerous plays including *Hester Crewe* (1893), and *Marie Deloche* (1895). He leased the Manhattan Theatre in 1901 for Mrs Fiske, and formed the Manhattan Company to support her. His producing successes included *Kismet* in 1911 starring **Otis Skinner**. Financial problems forced him to sell the *Dramatic Mirror* in 1911, and he declared bankruptcy in 1914 although he was discharged the following year. The death of Mrs Fiske in 1932 effectively ended his career. Fiske fought commercialism in the theatre, and did much to establish **Ibsen** on the American stage. TLM

Fiske, Minnie Maddern (née Marie Augusta Davey) (1864–1932) American actress and director. From a theatrical family, she began her career at age three, remaining in steady demand as a child actress. Her adult New York debut was in Charles Callahan's *Fogg's Ferry* (1882). After a brief first marriage, she wed her second husband, **Harrison Grey Fiske**, editor of the *New York Dramatic Mirror*, in 1890, retiring for four years after her marriage. During this interlude she wrote several one-act plays and became interested in the realistic movement, focusing her energies after 1893, despite opposition, on plays of this ilk and working toward what she called 'natural, true acting' in her productions, especially with her Manhattan Theatre Company (1904–8). At the turn of the century she fought, almost alone, the **Theatrical Syndicate**, and became a noted humanitarian, fighting against cruelty and abuse to animals. Some of her notable stage appearances were in *Hester Crewe* (1893), *A Doll's House* (1894), *Tess of the d'Urbervilles* dramatized by Lorimer Stoddard (1897), *Vanity Fair* adapted by **Langdon Mitchell** (1899), *Becky Sharp* (1899), *Hedda Gabler* (1903), *Leah Kleschna* (1906), *The New York Idea* (1906), *Rosmersholm* (1907), *Salvation Nell* (1908), *The Pillars of Society* (1910), and *Ghosts* (1927). She is considered today one of the most distinguished actresses ever to have performed on the American stage and its chief promoter of **Ibsen**. A contemporary critic noted that 'She had a peculiar gift of emotion, uniting tears and smiles in the same breath, which was more pathetic than undiluted grief and more diverting than undiluted laughter.' DBW

Fitch, Clyde (1865–1909) American playwright. Fitch was extraordinarily successful and prolific: 60 plays from *Beau Brummell* (1890), starring **Richard Mansfield**, to *The City* (1909). In 1901 four plays were running simultaneously in New York: *Lover's Lane, Captain Jinks of the Horse Marines*, with **Ethel Barrymore**, *The Climbers*, and *Barbara Frietchie*. Best known among the others: *The Moth and the Flame* (1898), *Nathan Hale* (1898), *The Cowboy and the Lady* (1899), *The Girl with the Green Eyes* (1902), *Her Great Match* (1905), and *The Truth* (1907). Fitch was a master of sprightly dialogue and documentary-like scenes from contemporary life, and as director he meticulously controlled every detail of the staging. One critic said that his plays gave a better idea of American life than newspapers and historical records.

He was born in Elmira, New York, graduated from Amherst (1886) where he was a leader in the dramatic club, frequently playing female roles, and died at Châlons-sur-Marne in France. RM

Fitzball, Edward (1793–1873) English playwright, the author of at least 150 plays as well as four novels, six volumes of bouncy verse and an informative autobiography, *Thirty-Five Years of a Dramatic Author's Life* (1859). Most famous for his spectacular melodramas, some of which advanced the patriotic taste for nautical heroism, Fitzball wrote nothing better than *Jonathan Bradford* (1833), based on a recent murder and provided with special music by Jolly, musical director of the Surrey Theatre. Particularly striking was the scenic innovation of showing four separate rooms in an inn simultaneously. Fitzball's quest for gallery-gripping effects can be read in his titles, *The Burning Bridge* (1824), *The Earthquake* (1828), *The Negro of Wapping* (1838), *The Wreck and the Reef* (1847). It was the bursts of red and blue fire rather than the skeletal text that brought *The Flying Dutchman* (1827) its phenomenal popularity. But managers thought highly enough of his feeling for what would 'go' on the contemporary stage to make him reader of plays for **Covent Garden** (1835–8) and **Drury Lane** (1838–51). His output, in both quantity and quality, is typical of the journeyman dramatist's work in the busy London theatres. Adaptations of popular novels, Fenimore Cooper, **Bulwer**, **Victor Hugo**, thefts from the French stage, comic operas, burlesques, whatever was wanted he provided at the rate of six a year. From the fact that he added the prefix Fitz- to the plain Ball he was born, some *amour propre* is discernible, but his autobiography disarmingly records an occasion on which the manager and actors neglected to invite him to a first-night celebration of one of his own plays. It was not a writer's theatre during Fitzball's heyday. PT

Fitzgerald, Geraldine (1914–) Irish-born American actress and director. Born in Dublin and educated at the Dublin Art School, Fitzgerald made her stage debut at the **Gate Theatre** in Dublin (1932) and her first appearance in New York as Ellie Dunn in

Heartbreak House (1938). While working in both films and the theatre, she has played onstage an impressive array of classical and modern characters: Jennifer Dubedat, *The Doctor's Dilemma* (1955); Goneril, *King Lear* (1956); Gertrude, *Hamlet* (1958); Queen, *The Cave Dwellers* (1961); Mary Tyrone, *Long Day's Journey Into Night* (1971); Jenny, *The Threepenny Opera* (1972); Juno, *Juno and the Paycock* (1973); Essie Miller, *Ah, Wilderness!* (1975); Amanda Wingfield, *The Glass Menagerie* (1975); Felicity, *The Shadow Box* (1977); Nora Melody, *A Touch of the Poet* (1978); and a one-woman show, *Songs of the Streets: O'Neill and Carlotta* (1979). One of America's most distinguished character actresses, Fitzgerald has been widely acclaimed for her 1973 portrayal of Juno. Mel Gussow (*New York Times*) wrote: 'Geraldine Fitzgerald is exactly the actress to play her, managing to be resilient without sacrificing her vulnerability. Informed of her son's death, she marshals her resources, calms her hysterical daughter and then with a spasm of anguish reveals her own personal loss.' Fitzgerald has made over 30 films including *Wuthering Heights* (1939); *The Pawnbroker* (1965); *Arthur* (1981); and *Pope of Greenwich Village* (1984).   TLM

Fitzmaurice, George (1877–1963) Irish playwright. A civil servant, increasingly a recluse, Fitzmaurice, having served in the First World War, rarely left Dublin. His plays are not flawless. There is some clumsy exposition, and the over-reachingly elaborate set speech. Nevertheless, he is now regarded as being surpassed in early **Abbey** only by **Synge**, with whose metamorphosis of peasant speech his work has much in common.

Fitzmaurice's first play, *The Country Dressmaker* (1907), a fairly realistic satire of peasant chicanery, was a success. His next two plays, both one-acters, *The Pie-Dish* (1908) and *The Magic Glasses*, establish his fantastic 'folk-world' of reality and legend. The latter concerns witchcraft, quack and sinister, diabolic possession, and the killing of the fey Jaymony by his enchanting, murderous magic glasses.

In *The Dandy Dolls*, discourteously rejected by **Yeats** in 1913, Roger Carmody and his dolls are the prize in an occult feud (or alliance) between the Gray Men and the Hag. With splendid confidence, the play assumes its wondrous duality of human and supernatural, domestic and magical. Its 'rhythmic, gibing speech' (**Austin Clarke**'s phrase) materializes its fabulous world, realized again in the extravagant comedy of *The Enchanted Land* (published 1957), where matchmaking goes astray in the Land-Under-Wave.

Unencouraged by Yeats's regime, Fitzmaurice withdrew into silence, a loss to the poetic impulse Yeats desired to foster. His later, solitary work includes *One Evening Gleam* (1949). Uncharacteristically in a realistic, urban setting, it is a sombre, moving tale.

Fitzgerald's was an imagination of the most unusual temper, uniting the macabre and the exuberant, as an English reviewer of *The Pie-Dish* said, reaching, 'through the surface of common life into the great forces beneath'. Austin Clarke's Lyric Theatre Co. restored it to the stage in the mid and late 1940s and more recently, in belated tribute, the Abbey has put on productions.   DM

Flanders, Michael (1922–75) British variety performer, who contributed lyrics for such London revues as *Air on a Shoestring* and translated Stravinsky's *A Soldier's Tale* for the **Edinburgh Festival** (1954), but is best remembered for *The Drop of a Hat* (1956) and other entertainments created and performed with Donald Swann.   CI

Fleck, Ferdinand (1757–1801) German actor. After a few years in Hamburg, from 1786 to his death Fleck acted with the **Berlin Royal Theatre**. He was adulated for his powerful, spontaneous interpretations of roles in both the classics and contemporary romantic drama. **Ludwig Tieck**'s ideas on acting were profoundly influenced by his experience of Fleck's acting. Fleck's performance as Wallenstein provided a standard for most 19th-century actors.   SW

Flecker, James Elroy (1884–1915) British poet and dramatist. The sensuous lyricism of his two plays, *Don Juan* (1911, not publicly performed until 1950) and *Hassan* (1914), owes more to the decadent movement at the end of the 19th century than to the modern revival of poetic drama. However, the colourful exoticism of the second play that lends itself to spectacle, together with incidental music by Delius and ballets by Fokine, gave it considerable popularity when it was first produced (in Germany, then in London by **Basil Dean**) in 1923, and it has since been revived in 1931 with **Peggy Ashcroft** and, less successfully, as part of the Festival of Britain in 1951.   CI

Fleisser, Marieluise (1901–74) German dramatist and novelist, whose most influential works were *Purgatory*, completed with the help of **Brecht** and **Feuchtwanger** (1926), and *Pioneers in Ingolstadt* (1929). This play, exposing the exploitation of the proletariat and the manipulation of language in realistic terms, became one of the major models for **Kroetz** and **Fassbinder** when it was revived in a revised version by Fassbinder in 1971.   CI

Fletcher, Allen (1922–85) American director and teacher. Born in San Francisco, Fletcher studied at Stanford and Yale Universities, the **Bristol Old Vic** Theatre School, and LAMDA, on a Fulbright. He made his directing debut in 1948 at the Oregon Shakespeare Festival and returned there each year through 1956. Other directing credits include the Antioch Shakespeare Festival (1957); the Old Globe in San Diego (1955–66); and the APA (1960–1). From 1962–5 he served as principal director and head of the professional training programme for the American Shakespeare Festival, Stratford, Conn. In 1966 he took a similar post with the **Seattle Repertory Theatre** where he modernized the company and ended the rotating repertory. Ousted in 1970, he founded the Actor's Company, and became Director of the Conservatory for ACT (where he had guest-directed since 1965). He left ACT in 1984 for a similar post with the **Denver Centre Theatre**. A premiere classical director, Fletcher is remembered for his 1963 *King Lear* with **Morris Carnovsky**.   TLM

Fletcher, John (1579–1625) English playwright, son of a Bishop, who wrote elegantly and prolifically for

London's theatres for at least 20 years. Probably after writing for **Boys' Companies**, he became associated with the King's Men and may have collaborated with **Shakespeare** on *Henry VIII, The Two Noble Kinsmen* and the lost *Cardenio* (all c. 1613). By then, Fletcher's famous collaboration with **Beaumont** had provided the King's Men with such outstanding successes as *Philaster* (c. 1609), *The Maid's Tragedy* (c. 1610) and *A King and No King* (1611). Themselves 'gentlemen', Beaumont and Fletcher easily gratified the gentlemanly taste for undemanding poetry, sexual intrigue and patterned composition. Their success tempted contemporary publicists and later publishers to ascribe to the partnership far more work than properly belongs to it. Thus, a 1647 edition includes 34 plays and a masque, and a 1679 revision adds a further 18. Fletcher's hand is present in most of these, but Beaumont's in only about ten. It was **Massinger** who became Fletcher's most frequent collaborator in plays for the King's Men. Among the best of their joint work are *Sir John van Olden Barnavelt* (1619), *The Custom of the Country* (c. 1619), *The Beggars' Bush* (1622) and *The Spanish Curate* (c. 1622). A happy combination of industry and facility allowed Fletcher to write, singly or in collaboration, at least four plays per year, and his single-minded commitment to drama makes him a rarity among contemporary poets. His was the major influence on the post-Restoration development of intrigue comedy. An immensely flexible writer, he eased into the Jacobean theatre a taste for romantic tragicomedy which perfectly suited the sophisticated audiences of the private theatres. Among the best of the plays for which he may have been singly responsible are *The Chances* (c. 1617), *The Humorous Lieutenant* (c. 1619), *The Wild-Goose Chase* (c. 1621) and *Rule a Wife and Have a Wife* (1624).   PT

Fletcher, Laurence (d. 1608) Scottish actor, a leader of the English players in Edinburgh at the end of the 16th century, and a favourite of the Scottish King. On inheriting the English throne, James I seems to have brought Fletcher south and enrolled him as one of the King's Men. We do not know what **Shakespeare** and his colleagues thought of this arrangement, but there is no record of Fletcher's performing with the company.   PT

Florence, William 'Billy' Jermyn (or James) (Bernard Conlin) (1831–91) American actor. He made his professional stage debut in 1849 at the Marshall Theatre in Richmond, Virginia, as Peter in *The Stranger*. In 1853 he married Malvina Pray, the sister of Maria Pray Mestayer Williams, wife of actor **Barney Williams**. For almost 40 years, the Florences were a successful starring team in both England and America, often in Irish-American roles such as *The Irish Boy and the Yankee Girl*. Florence was a skilful comedian noted for his striking, convincingly human characterizations. After his Irish roles, his outstanding performances were as Bob Brierly in **Tom Taylor**'s *The Ticket-of-Leave Man*, Barwell Slote in Benjamin Woolf's *The Mighty Dollar*, Sir Lucius O'Trigger in *The Rivals*, and Zekiel Homespun in **Colman**'s *The Heir-at-Law*. Florence also presented the first American production of **T. W. Robertson**'s *Caste* in 1867, only four months after its London premiere.   DJW

Floridor (Josias de Soulas, sieur de Primefosse) (c. 1608–71) French actor-manager, scion of the minor aristocracy who opted for the life of a strolling player. First mentioned in 1635 as leader of a company of French actors in London where they played before the Court and at the **Cockpit** in Drury Lane, he made his debut at the **Marais** in 1638. Having prospered there, notably in the plays of **Corneille**, he purchased **Bellerose**'s position as director of the rival Parisian company, as well as his wardrobe, and moved to the **Hôtel de Bourgogne** in 1647, which may well have persuaded Corneille, with whom he was on friendly terms, to entrust his later plays to that theatre. His career continued to flourish until the very year of his death and he was much admired by Louis XIV, who granted him some remunerative commercial concessions. Of noble bearing, with a sonorous voice and an unforced delivery he was most successful in roles calling for dignity and authority and some critics found him too cold, though he created the role of Nero in **Racine**'s *Britannicus* (1669). Significantly he was the one leading actor of the Hôtel de Bourgogne whom **Molière** forbore to ridicule in his *Impromptu de Versailles* (1663). In fact, he seems to have been universally esteemed in his profession and to have led a blameless private life.   DR

Flyting A stylized exchange of insults, or formalized debate, often in verse or formulaic prose. At its simplest it appears as 'kidding' among friends. It is more obviously rule-bound among young American and West Indian blacks ('playing the dozens' or 'sounding'), and calls for considerable poetic skill among Eskimos, whose impromptu obscene verses are a favourite form of entertainment, and in Italy where contests in the satirical stanzas known as *contrasto a braccio* are sometimes organized enough to have a panel of judges. The pattern of the *contrasto*, in which each contstant takes on one role in an oppositional theme (wine versus water, atheist versus priest etc.), is common in carnival plays, and influenced the dramatic work of **John Heywood** and Hans Sachs.   AEG

Fo, Dario (1926–) Italian actor, director and dramatist. A versatile mime, improviser and satirist, he began his career as a writer and performer in comic sketches and political cabaret. In 1957 he and his wife, Franca Rame, herself from a family of popular entertainers, formed a company that worked a comic repertoire that included materials drawn from 19th-century farce and the techniques and strategies of popular street, fair and club theatre. Although this repertoire incorporated political satire, it was crafted principally for bourgeois audiences: it was mocking, irreverent and anarchic, but essentially amiable, and included pieces like *Aveva due Pistole daglia Occhi Bianchi e Neri* (*Had Two Pistols with White and Black Eyes*, 1960), and *Settimo: Ruba un Po'Mena* (*Seventh: Steal a Bit Less*, 1964).

In the mid and later 60s, Fo established a national reputation as a writer and performer of satirical pieces, the barbs of which became increasingly sharp in their cuts at capitalism, imperialism and the scandals and abuses of Italian government. The political disturbances of 1968, however, brought an important shift in the direction of Fo's work: abandoning mainstream theatre, he and his wife formed a new company, Nuova Scena (New Stage), and under the auspices of the Communist Party toured factories, clubs and halls in search of working-class audiences. His search for a genuinely political theatre issued in some quasi-Brechtian didactic pieces like *L'Operaio Conosce 300 parole, il Padrone 1,000; per Questo Lui e il Padrone (The Worker Knows 300 words, the Boss 1,000; That's Why He's the Boss)*. At the same time too he mounted the spectacular *Grande Pantomima (The Great Pantomime*, 1968), a satirical presentation of Italian politics since the fall of Fascism, and the highly original *Mistero Buffo* (1969), a unique one-man spectacle performed with great success in Italy and abroad.

But tensions between him and the Party led Fo to break with the orthodox left, and in 1970 he and Franca Rame formed the theatre collective La Comune and turned their skills to the service of the New Left. The work of this group was more aggressively revolutionary, dramatizing topical political issues and seeking to expose the corruption, oppression and incompetence of bourgeois capitalist governments. Products of this new direction of Fo's work came in the later 70s and 80s to attract attention throughout Europe, notably plays like *Morte Accidentale di un Anarchico (Accidental Death of an Anarchist*, 1970), *Non Si Paga! Non Si Paga! (Can't Pay, Won't Pay*, 1974) and *Female Parts* (1981) written jointly with Franca Rame.

Fo is perhaps foremost a brilliant actor and exploiter of theatrical means for politico-satiric purposes: most notably in *Mistero Buffo*, in which his consummate skill at drawing on a wide range of popular materials and traditions of improvised performance was put to the service of an ideological engagement that transcended merely national political concerns. In the view of some critics his deep political commitment at times co-exists uneasily with theatrical needs, creating a gap between ideological content and dramatic form: criticism levelled at, for example, the ending of *Clacson, Trombette e Pernacchi (Trumpets and Raspberries*, 1981). But no one in the contemporary theatre has more effectively wedded comedy and savage political comment than Fo in pieces like *Mistero Buffo* and *Morte Accidentale*. LR

Folies-Bergère A Parisian music-hall that opened in 1869, offering pantomime and operetta. Léon Sari, who managed it until 1885, indulged the prostitutes who haunted its promenade so that it became a fashionable resort of young men-about-town. Under various managements, 1885–1918, it alternated singers like **Maurice Chevalier** and **Yvette Guilbert** with speciality acts like **Little Tich** and Loïe Fuller. Paul Derval, who took it over in 1918, endowed it with the style that made it world-famous: lavish *revues à grand spectacle* with cohorts of naked women, exotic tableaux, monumental staircases, and acres of sequins and ostrich plumes. The titles, always of 13 letters, had to include the word 'folie'. This 'hypertrophy of sumptuousness', as Roland Barthes called it, became the tourist trap *par excellence*, a must-see for French provincials and foreigners alike. Since 1974, it has been managed by Hélène Martini. LS

Folk drama (European and European based) 'Folklore' was not identified as an autonomous area of cultural activity until 1846, under the stimulus of romanticism, nationalism, and rapid social change. The ensuing burst of collecting soon found its theoretical underpinning in cultural evolution, a bastard offspring of Darwin, which held that all societies pass through Savagery and Barbarism on their way to Civilization. In the process, much is discarded in favour of more adaptive ways of living and thinking; but some relics of earlier patterns live on into the modern world, particularly among the more conservative members of society, notably the peasantry (rightly or wrongly so called). The interest of these 'survivals in culture', to the 19th-century intellectual, lay in the light they shed on the prehistory of a people; that they might have a meaning in the present, for the 'peasants' who cherished them, rarely occurred to anybody. Meaning was consigned to the past, usually so remote that no documentary source could be used to test the scholar's analysis. Thus it came about, especially in the English-speaking world, that folk drama, rather than being treated as artistic genre, with its own development and conventions, was regarded as a corrupt and misunderstood ritual corpus. Where it could be shown that other phenomena – such as the chapbook press – had influenced it, these influences were rejected as late accretions. This idea of folk drama is still with us, not least among theatre historians, for all that professional folklorists have abandoned it, along with the general theory of culture from which it derived.

Not that folk drama contains no ancient elements; but, for the most part, we neither know nor are ever likely to know. Sometimes we do know, or may reasonably infer. The occasional association of ritual healing with folk drama (notably in the Rumanian **Căluş**) may be of considerable antiquity. For certain, the zoomorphic trend in folk drama takes us back a long way.

There is graphic evidence of animal impersonation from prehistory; written sources show it in the classical period; and by the early Christian epoch we find churchmen embarking on a litany of complaints against animal guisers which they will waste their breath on for the next millennium and more. There even exists a clay mask of a calf, clearly designed to be worn, and thought to date from about AD 400. It was found in Liechtenstein, and would not be out of place in an Alpine carnival in the 20th century. As the graphic and documentary sources of medieval art, scholarship and administration pile up, so does the evidence for zoomorphic masquerades. Of course, we never know exactly what the maskers were doing, though we sometimes know it was seasonal (New Year being a favourite time, just as it was in pre-Christian Rome, and still is for the youngsters in Derbyshire and Nottinghamshire who take their **Old Tup** play around the pubs). But seasonality does not, in itself, imply religious observance whether Christian or pagan (which is what the ritual survival thesis is about); ritual can be secular as well as sacred, and that St Augustine denounced a masquerade as ungodly in the 5th century no more makes it so than when Erasmus did the same in the 16th. What we have is a satisfying combination of archaeological, iconographic, and written sources which support a continuous history of a particular kind of dramatic manifestation from the earliest times to the present day.

It does not therefore follow that all folk drama is

ancient, and we merely lack the evidence to show it. Lying above this ancient cultural stratum are others demonstrably more recent. An important group of plays in Europe, and in Catholic Central America, celebrates major Christian feasts by the enactment of Bible stories; self-evidently, nothing pre-Christian about these. Though their age is unknown, they are analogous to and in some cases possibly derived from the liturgical drama of the late Middle Ages and Renaissance. They are not, however, cyclic, but concentrate rather on a specific event such as the arrival of the Magi (recorded in Germany from the 16th century and in Norway from the 17th); or the adoration of the Shepherds, known in Italy, Germany and Spain from the 16th century, in Czechoslovakia, Hungary and Poland from the 17th, and France from the 18th, as well as passing from Spain to Mexico, where *Los Pastores* is still performed. The overwhelming popularity of the Nativity and Epiphany as subjects is no doubt attributable to the growing importance of Christmas, as against Easter, in the modern world. Old Testament plays are less common, though folk redactions of Hans Sachs's *Tragedy of the Creation, the Fall and Expulsion of Adam from Paradise* have survived into the 20th century in Germany and Austria.

Cognate with these scripturally based plays in the secular domain are the numerous performances which are related to popular, or more rarely, elite literature. The English **Hero-Combat play** (often called the Mummers' Play) owes something textually to Richard Johnson's *The Seven Champions of Christendom*, which went through at least 26 editions between 1596 and 1770; the Swiss *Tellspiel* (Play of William Tell) derives from ballad and literary sources of the 15th and 16th centuries; the Wandering Jew Ahasuerus wanders off the pages of the *bibliothèque bleue* into a Liège Passion Play for puppets; and the so-called *Pastorales* of the Basque country draw on a variety of hagiographical and romance sources for their content. Boccaccio's tale of Patient Griselda, probably mediated through chapbooks, gives rise to Austrian folk plays. The northern Greek *Panaratos* (a sensational tale of forbidden love, judicial murder, and revenge, framed by a prologue and epilogue from Charos, the personification of death) is a heavily cut and reworked version of the five-act tragedy *Erophila*, written in c. 1600 by the Italianate Cretan Georgios Kostatzes. Even **Congreve**'s *Love for Love* lends a few lines to the admittedly unusual text of the Ampleforth Sword Dance: the contribution is important neither quantitatively nor dramatically, but it is a useful indication of folk drama's tolerant exploitation of the most unlikely looking material.

Each tradition, or group of related traditions, needs to be carefully scrutinized for its autochthonous elements, its debt to official traditions of religious expression (including the parody of them), and its borrowings from the great tradition of literacy, at high social and aesthetic levels as well as low, without granting theoretical precedence, *a priori*, to any one of these.

If the 'folk' element in folk drama is problematic, the 'drama' element is no less so. Everyone would agree, in principle, that it cannot be conceptualized according to an Aristotelian thesis of plot-construction, or to the literary theatre's preoccupation with character and motive. Even in the elite theatre, the presence or absence of a text is not easy to use as a criterion of 'drama', and in folk theatre we are faced with the question of what a text is. Some folk actors (for that they unquestionably are, and if drama is what actors do, the problem is solved) may not use language at all, or speech may be optional: processional characters in carnival, the New Year Dziady (vagabonds) of Poland, the Slovenian Kurenti with their animal-skin coats, long-nosed masks, and feathered head-dresses. But they may vocalize: grunts, snorts, roars, gibberish. Is this a 'text', and, if not, what is it? In any case, their behaviour, though apparently idiosyncratic to the point of anarchy, is neither unplanned nor incoherent. It has its own set of performance conventions, founded on the principle of reversing everyday behaviour. Other maskers, though they do not offer a 'play' in the sense that the literary theatre uses that term, engage in an improvised dialogue with their audience. This may be a guessing-game, in which the 'audience' (now effectively performers) have to identify the actors (**Tolstoi** incorporated it in *War and Peace*, since when it has been reported in Ecuador, Trinidad, Ireland and maritime Canada – in Newfoundland the mummers frustrate their efforts by speaking ingressively); or an interrogation of the audience by their disguised visitors (Norwegian Julegeita – Christmas goats – and in Labrador the Eskimo **naluyuks** – literally, 'heathens' – question children about their behaviour). Again, these dialogues, though improvised, follow entirely predictable lines, and occur within a recognized pattern of symbolic behaviour. We can, if we wish, deny these activities the status of 'drama', for pragmatic or ideological reasons; but then we are confronted by the Strawboys of County Fermanagh, who would follow their performance of a Hero-Combat play with the guessing-game – not to mention singing and dancing at their hosts' request, and eating and drinking at their expense.

Unless we are to risk overlooking vital conceptual links in a performance tradition (the Strawboys, masked, enter as 'strangers' and, in role, perform their play; through the guessing-game they become 'not-strangers'; only then can they be invited to sit and eat) it is essential that we be prepared to take events as a whole, rather than force them into the procrustean bed of an alien classification. Because folk traditions are so protean, not only among themselves (variation in space) but within themselves (variation in time), it makes sense to think in terms of a continuum of performance behaviour, rather than of clear demarcations.

Structurally, folk drama lies between two poles. One is the silent or non-verbal performance by masked actors, often constantly on the move, acting the goat (interesting phrase), frightening the children, grabbing girls, making mischief. The other is the virtually Aristotelian narrative of the sub-literary *Panaratos*, or the *Tellspiel*, which covers the fundamental elements of the legend – Gessler's imposition of the apple-shot, Tell's success and disclosure of the second arrow's destination, his arrest as a subversive and subsequent escape, his assassination of the tyrannical landgrave. Between them lie a multitude of forms, with more or less emphasis on text or narrative development. The Italian *I Mesi* (Play of the Months) is a cavalcade of the 12 months personified, each with a laudatory verse, and an emblematic property (a posy of flowers for May, figs for September, a pot of soup for December), introduced by New Year and the **commedia dell'arte** figure of Pulcinella. The whole text is addressed directly to the audience. This highly formal succession of speeches of equal length is also used in **flytings**, such as the Swiss *Sommer-und-Winterspiel* (Play of Summer and Winter); here, however, two allegorical characters are set in dialogue against one another, each praising himself and denouncing the other, until Winter concedes. Greater narrative development is seen in the Hero-Combat play, but the Aristotelian expectations of its first phase (quarrel – conflict – killing – cure) are frustrated by its second phase, a pageant of apparently unconnected characters using only direct address. Traditional farces, such as the Tirolean carnival-play **Altweibermuehle** (*The Mill for Old Women*) or the Russian **Pakhomushka**, by definition develop character-relationships within a plot, though often as much through the playing of variants on the same theme, as through a steady and integrated forward movement.

At any point in this continuum the dramatic action may be interrupted by or culminate in music and dance. The Basque *Pastorales* are interspersed with dances, selected from an independent repertory, regardless of whether the play is of St Eustace or Roland. The Papa Stour (Shetland) Sword Dance uses its text, a presentational pageant of characters, simply as a prologue to the dance. The important tradition of the **Moresca**, a spectacular and bellicose Mediterranean-based dance-drama, also uses its text as a prologue, but one in which, through dialogue and character-interaction, the conflict is established which will culminate in a choreographic battle.

Various as its sources and dramatic structures may be, the other formal properties of folk theatre are remarkably consistent. It is an open space form: fit-up stages are occasionally used, as is simple stage-furniture. But the normal performance environment is a street, square, public house or domestic interior, unaltered but for the presence of costumed actors. The relationship between performer and audience follows from this. Dramatic performance is in itself abnormal; but for its abnormality to be acceptable within an environment created, in the first instance, for other reasons, the performers incorporate in their performance certain fundamental elements which belong to that environment. When we go into somebody's house, we do not ignore the occupants; in the street or the public house, if we merely talk amongst ourselves, politeness dictates that others present ignore us. Folk actors have the same way of dealing with both constraints, namely direct address: even those performances which rely exclusively on dialogue, as many flytings do, are so formal in their construction and language as to invite a declamatory style which expressly includes the audience. Intimacy between characters is foreign to folk drama; interestingly, in the 20th century, when some traditions have been influenced in their content by film and television, the fourth wall seems to have had no effect. This must indicate, within folk drama, a powerful artistic principle in favour of constructing a relationship of mutual acknowledgement between actor and audience. Characterization also militates in favour of this. It is without exception stereotypical: culture

heroes and villains (including scriptural and hagiographical ones), allegorical figures, foolish old men and ugly old women, quack doctors, soldiers, schoolmasters, vagabonds. Costume and hand props either immediately represent these stereotypes, or are totally abstract. Finally, language and movement rarely pretend to realism. Rhymed verse, or a mixture of verse and prose, are typical, often ideographic (a fight may take the form of a metrical clashing of swords, a character decapitated may simply bow his or her head), and may become heightened into dance. Much of this also applies to performances by puppets, such as **Punch** or the Turkish **Karagöz**, which points to a high degree of stylization. Even the convention and implications of direct address, though they cannot literally apply to puppet-theatre, can be approximated by a skilful puppeteer.

If the style of folk drama is strikingly consistent, its content is not, and the analysis of it requires, strictly speaking, close attention to particular traditions. No more than a few introductory generalizations can be advanced here.

The first, and possibly the most fundamental, is that folk drama is frequently seasonal in its performance, that is, it is one item in a festive calendar. Since there is intrinsically no reason why folk plays should not be performed on demand, their calendric context must be significant. This may be marked in any of three ways: by reference to the official calendar whether liturgical (Christmas) or secular (New Year), or by reference to the pastoral or agricultural year (Anatolian shepherds perform their plays during the pregnancy of their ewes). Seasonality is sometimes a play's whole content; more frequently it is referred to in a prologue or epilogue.

The idea of continuity through change is central, obviously so in the religious plays which, through the re-enactment of, say, the Nativity, make concrete the community's commitment to a particular version of human history and its meaning. Small wonder that the shepherds have been so popular. The opportunities they offer for a certain level of realism in dialect speech and local costume, together with their representation of the poor and lowly, underscore the relationship – unmediated by a priest – between God and ordinary people.

In plays on secular themes may be seen a similar use of the past to validate the present, or particular values in relation to the present which are not necessarily those of the ruling class. The Russian plays which deal with the 17th-century peasant leader Sten'ka Razin embody an idea of justice which takes on a metaphysical dimension in the superhuman qualities attributed to him. Likewise the many plays about outlaws – **Robin Hood**, the Catalan Joán de Serrallonga, the Mexican Agustín Lorenzo – all of them likely to be regarded as historical figures by actors and audience, invariably show the hero as just, magnanimous and brave, thereby implying a critique of a law that makes such men criminals; and, through the setting of the action in the past, the persistence of an alternative set of values through thick and thin. As for the widespread dramatic traditions based on death and resurrection (the Hero-Combat, the Thracian *Kalogheroi*, some versions of *Căluş*), their metaphorical correspondence to the clash and synthesis of past and future is self-evident.

The definition of a community in time is complemented by the representation of desirable and undesirable social types, and of insiders and outsiders. At its simplest, the behaviour of culture heroes and saints expresses positive social values, and that of villains and fools negative values. But not all norms are so obviously stated, and a lot of plays seem preoccupied with defining the normal by reference to its opposite. In the *Moresca* both terms of the proposition are present in the defeat of blacks by whites. The Anatolian *Play of the Old Man* complicates the issue by making equally undesirable two suitors for a young woman's hand, the dangerous Arab, from an alien race and culture, and the foolish old man who demonstrates his unsuitability to claim the bride by his inability to fight for her. It is worth remembering that this violent comedy of sexual mis-match is set in the vital seasonal context of the reproduction of the flocks. The British Hero-Combat deals with two problematic social types, the untrustworthy stranger (soldiers, the itinerant mountebank, the light-fingered tramp) and the neighbour who is not fully integrated (the village idiot, the sexually ambiguous old woman).

The zoomorphic figure, where it occurs, is a central metaphor. It invariably has both human and animal attributes, an ambiguity which gives it special potency in a play of taxonomy. In the Anatolian plays the speaking characters are accompanied by non-speaking animal maskers. They represent both domestic animals such as the camel, and wild animals such as the hare and fox, echoing at an ecological level of imagery the outsider–insider dialectic which the text represents at a social and racial level. The hobby-horse who closes the Antrobus (Cheshire) Hero-Combat play is at once living and dead, domestic and wild, animal and human. Folk plays celebrate their community through a ludic representation of its definitions, including the parody of the dominant culture's institutions. Usually this remains at a fictional level, but there are examples in which play and real life merge. The Labrador *naluyuks* reward good children, and harass social undesirables. The Basque *Tobera Mustrak* is a highly developed **charivari** – based on the common carnivalic genre of the mock trial – in which a play is constructed specifically to hold up to public ridicule particular persons and their offences against society.

This extreme example illustrates the close relationship between folk drama and its community. It is there in the seasonal context, in the value-laden texts, in the informal socializing that invariably accompanies them, in their strong sense of reciprocity among friends and neighbours. Fermanagh mummers use the proceeds of their collection to throw a party for everybody; a Polish Herod speaks of 'the good times we share together'. An Antrobus soulcaker puts it succinctly: 'We're all one.' Theirs is an art in which text and context merge. AEG

See: V. Alford, *The Hobby Horse and other Animal Masks*, London, 1978; G. Cocciara, *The History of Folklore in Europe*, Philadelphia 1981; H. Glassie, *All Silver and No Brass*, Bloomington, 1975; A. E. Green, 'Popular Drama and the Mummer's Play', in Bradby *et al.* (eds.), *Performance and Politics in Popular Drama*, Cambridge, 1980; H. Halpert and G. M. Storey, *Christmas Mumming in Newfoundland*, Toronto, 1969; *Journal of American Folklore*, 94, 1981; G. Kligman, *Călus*, Chicago, 1981; L. Schmidt, *Das Deutsche Volksschauspiel*, Berlin, 1962; *Le Théâtre Populaire Européen*, Paris, 1965; *The Drama Review*, 18, 1974 (Indigenous Theatre Issue); P. Toschi, *Invito al Folklore Italiano: le Regioni e le Feste*, Rome, 1963; Arnold Van Gennep, *Manuel de Folklore Français Contemporain*, Paris, 1939–58; E. Warner, *The Russian Folk Theatre*, The Hague, 1977.

Folksbühne, The An amalgam of several New York amateur companies, formed in 1915, using professional directors of the stature of **Joseph Buloff**, Benno Schneider, **David Herman**, Jacob Rotbaum, Nahum Zemach and **Jacob Ben-Ami**. Dedicated to the highest ideals of play selection, acting and production, Folksbühne presented at least one painstakingly prepared play each winter season, achieving the reputation of a genuine folk theatre and serving as an inspiration to the professional Yiddish theatre. AB

Fonda (Jaynes), Henry (1905–82) American actor. Born in Nebraska, Fonda made his first stage appearance in 1925 at the Omaha Community Playhouse, and his Broadway debut in 1929. He established himself as a leading actor in *The Farmer Takes a Wife* (1934) before turning almost exclusively to making films. After service in the Second World War, he played the title role in *Mister Roberts* (1948), which won him a Tony. Working in both Hollywood and New York, Fonda won critical acclaim on Broadway in 1954 with his portrayal of Barney Greenwald in *The Caine Mutiny Court Martial*. He starred with **Ann Bancroft** in *Two for the Seesaw* (1958), and with Barbara Bel Geddes in *Silent Night, Lonely Night* (1959). Other important stage appearances include the comedy hit, *Generation*, in 1965, and the one-man show, *Clarence Darrow*, in 1974. Fonda's screen image as the quiet, unassuming man of integrity and strength dominated his appearances on stage. TLM

Fontanne, Lynn see **Lunt, Alfred**

Fonvizin, Denis Ivanovich (1745–92) The creator of Russian national comedy, linking **Sumarokov**'s neoclassicism and the satirical, social realism of **Gogol**, **Ostrovsky**, **Saltykov-Shchedrin** and **Chekhov**. Fonvizin's social libertarianism and fierce moralism, influenced by the French Enlightenment philosophers Montesquieu, **Voltaire**, **Rousseau** and **Diderot**, foreshadowed the social philosophy of art espoused by the critic Belinsky and the playwright-ideologue **Gorky**. An outspoken and periodically censored critic of Catherine the Great's regime, his favourite targets were the egoism and Gallomania of the provincial gentry, the institution of serfdom and especially the harmfulness and abuses of foreign education (the 'tutors' in his plays are French coachmen and manicurists) – a snobbish attitude and dehumanizing behaviour directed at one's own culture and its people. Fonvizin's satirical sensibility was sharpened by his reading of the Dane Holberg's fables, 183 of which he adapted and translated while a student at Moscow University (c. 1760–2). He had joined the gymnasium of the university as a student in 1755, moving later into the main university. In the early 1760s he served as a translator of Latin, French and German in the Ministry of Foreign Affairs, where he was involved with the circle of writers and translators headed by the writer and cabinet minister I. P. Elagin, whose secretary he became. Fonvizin's verse comedy *Korion* (1764), an adaptation for the Russian company of Gresset's *comédie larmoyante Sidney* (1745), set the pattern for his later work, blending to an unprecedented degree Russian character and linguistic traits, scenic and quotidian details with such themes and conventions of European sentimental comedy as characters derived from vices, romantic entanglements and parental interference. In his major neoclassical comedies, *The Brigadier* (written 1769, produced 1780) and *The Minor* (1782), he individuated such familiar character types as the servant and foolish old woman and created such staples of the Russian actor's repertoire as Starodum ('Old Sense'), Mitrofan, Mrs Prostakova ('Simple'), the brigadier (whose rank has been laughable ever since) and his wife. He continued the practice of comedic portraiture (*na litso*, or drawn from life) while developing character and exposition via dialogue and action, a technique which would be perfected by **Griboedov**. His remaining plays include *Alzire, or the Americans* (1762, adapted from Voltaire's verse tragedy), *A Friend of Honest People, or Starodum* (1788) and *The Choice of a Tutor* (1790). In 1782, Fonvizin followed his protector, the liberal ministry head Nikita Panin, into what was essentially for him a forced retirement from public life and devoted himself to satirical essays, correspondence, an autobiography and an abortive journal project.   SG

Foote, Samuel (1721–77) English actor, playwright and manager. After an extravagant youth ended with his being imprisoned for debt, he studied briefly with **Macklin** in 1743 and began acting with some success at the **Haymarket** and at Smock Alley in Dublin. In 1747 he published two interesting pamphlets on acting and dramatic theory, *A Treatise on the Passions* and *The Roman and English Comedy Considered*, and began writing plays. He evaded the conditions of the Licensing Act with *The Diversions of the Morning*, a satirical revue, by inviting the audience to tea and staging the performance as a noon matinée. His next dodge, *The Auction of Pictures*, was similarly briefly legal and successful. While in Paris between 1749 and 1751, the basis for his play *The Englishman in Paris* (1753), he was incensed by **Garrick**'s permitting Woodward to mimic him in a performance of *Friendship in Fashion*, though most of Foote's own plays include similar pieces of personal caricature. His revue, renamed *Taste* (1752), was not a success and Foote tried fortune-telling, puppet-plays and acting as well as theatre management in Dublin. In 1760, with his satire on Methodists, *The Minor*, he was at last a success in London and became the summer manager at the Haymarket. Thrown by a horse in 1766 he lost a leg but continued to act. In 1767 he brought and remodelled the Haymarket. His satire on doctors, *The Devil Upon Two Sticks* (1768), exploited his own amputation. *The Nabob* (1722) attacked the East India Company. Apart from continued experiments with puppet-shows, Foote's career as manager of the Haymarket was a success. His drama, with its recurrent concern with personal satire, led to his being nicknamed the English **Aristophanes**.   PH

Foottit, George (Tudor Hall) (1864–1921) and **Chocolat (Raphaël Padilla)** (1868–1917) French clown act. Foottit, an Englishman trained in pantomime and travelling shows, had already made a name for himself in Paris as a combination of the **Grimaldi** clown and the pattering French Jocrisse when, in 1886, he teamed up with the black Cuban Chocolat at the Cirque Médrano. For 15 years, they delighted audiences with routines displaying Chocolat as 'he who gets slapped' and Foottit as his arrogant oppressor. They played the Nouveau Cirque, the Hippodrome and in the revue *En Selle pour la Revue* (1888). After they retired, their sons carried on the tradition.   LS

Forbes, James (1871–1938) American playwright. Beginning with domestic farce in *The Chorus Lady* (1906), which developed from a vaudeville sketch, and plays emphasizing small-town living – *The Travelling Salesman* (1908) and *The Commutors* (1910) – Forbes made his greatest contribution with *The Famous Mrs Fair* (1919), which explores the problems of a woman whose war career overshadows her return to civilian life until she understands what her place in life must be. Later plays dealt with social situations, such as small-town people trying to gain social status in New York – *The Endless Chain* (1922) – and the problems of youth in *Young Blood* (1925).   WJM

Forbes-Robertson, Johnston (1853–1937) English actor who rejected the preferred but uncertain career of an artist when **Samuel Phelps** offered him six guineas a week to act with him. Forbes-Robertson became Phelps's pupil (his portrait of Phelps as Wolsey hangs in the Garrick Club) and credited the old actor with the training of the voice that, with Henry Ainley's and **John Gielgud**'s, has been the most praised in the English theatre. After working for **Buckstone** at the **Haymarket**, Henry Neville at the **Olympic** and the **Bancrofts** at the **Prince of Wales's**, he was invited by **Irving** to join the **Lyceum** company. Irving may have seen in the ascetically gaunt features of Forbes-Robertson an image of his own youth, but his new recruit was a classical actor, not, like Irving, an idiosyncratic romantic. Irving had made a virtue of his physical awkwardness. Forbes-Robertson was graceful in movement and elegant in repose. In the event, it was during Irving's absence that he found his best opportunities, as Romeo to **Mrs Patrick Campbell**'s Juliet (1895) and above all as Hamlet (1897). Forbes-Robertson was unquestionably the Hamlet of his generation, and the surviving silent film shows why. Grave and decorous, he displayed a feeling intelligence throughout the play. The part remained in his repertoire for the remaining 16 years of his theatrical career and he made his farewell appearance in it at **Drury Lane** in 1913. He was less suited to the emotional violence of other Shakespearian roles – Shylock, Leontes, Othello – though his admirers found no fault with him in them. It was the impish **Shaw** who perceived the classical Caesar in him and cajoled him into opening *Caesar and Cleopatra* during an American tour (1906) with his American wife, **Gertrude Elliott** (1874–1950), as Cleopatra. Forbes-Robertson's last famous creation was the Stranger in **Jerome K. Jerome**'s *The Passing of the Third Floor Back* (1908). He was knighted in 1913, the year of his retirement from the stage. In his autobiography, *A Player under Three Reigns* (1925), he confesses that he never really enjoyed acting.   PT

Ford, John (c. 1586–1640) English playwright of whose life very little is known. The order and precise dating of his work is the subject of scholarly debate, but it is generally believed that he wrote the sub-plot of *The Witch of Edmonton* (1621) and that he again collaborated with **Dekker** on *The Welsh Ambassador* (1623) and *The Sun's Darling* (1624). This may mean that, by about 1620, he had abandoned a legal career and attached himself to an acting company. If so, the known products of his pen are surprisingly few. His subsequent fame rests on three plays. *Perkin Warbeck* (published 1634) may have revived in its original audiences memories of the old-fashioned chronicle play, but the characterization of the feckless hero is Ford's particular achievement. A startling interest in morbid psychology and emotional excess distinguishes his two major tragedies, *The Broken Heart* (c. 1629) and *'Tis Pity She's a Whore* (c. 1631). The second is the Caroline theatre's masterpiece. Its emotional centre is incestuous love, which Ford dares to treat with compassion and with a rhetorical delight in ethical paradox. His other surviving plays include three comedies, of which *The Lover's Melancholy* (1628) is the most interesting, and a tragedy, *Love's Sacrifice* (c. 1632), most notable for its creation of the villainous D'Avalos, almost the last in a dramatic line of machiavellians. PT

Ford, John T. (1829–94) American manager. A book store owner in Richmond, Virginia, he became the agent for a variety troupe, and in 1855–6 leased theatres in Richmond, Baltimore, and Washington, DC. The Richmond theatre closed at the beginning of the Civil War. In Washington he built **Ford's Theatre** in 1861. As a result of Lincoln's assassination, it was closed by the army and purchased for offices by the government. He continued to manage one or two theatres in Baltimore, and from 1873 to 1886 he also managed the Grand Opera House in Washington, DC. In the 1880s he became the major producer of combination companies for the entire south. DMCD

Ford's Theatre Washington, DC. The site of the assassination of President Abraham Lincoln by **John Wilkes Booth**, 14 April 1865. The building had opened in 1834 as the First Baptist Church; in 1861 **John T. Ford** converted it into Ford's Atheneum, which burned down in December, 1862. He reopened it on 27 August 1863 and successfully engaged many of America's leading performers, including John Wilkes Booth. After the assassination the government converted the building to a storage facility, which collapsed in 1893 during **Edwin Booth**'s funeral in New York. In 1968 the government-restored theatre reopened for public performances. Ford's Theatre also houses a Lincoln Museum. SMA

Foreman, Richard (1937–) American director who began the Ontological-Hysteric Theatre in New York in 1968 where he has presided as a sort of theatrical *auteur* presenting only his own avant-garde works. Until roughly 1975, Foreman was concerned with 'putting [an object] on stage and finding different ways of looking at it'. In plays like *Total Recall* (1970), Foreman used untrained performers directed not to show emotion; dialogue was disjointed, often recorded, and spoken without inflection. Furniture and props, which were suspended from the ceiling, were accorded as much focus and expressiveness as actors. Foreman ran the show like a conductor. Perched above the stage, he periodically sounded a loud buzzer that separated phrases of the attenuated action. More recently Foreman has created pieces based directly on the ideas and sketches he collects in notebooks, often featuring a recurring character called Rhoda and played by Kate Manheim. Plays like *Pandering to the Masses* (1975), *Le Livre de Splendeurs* (Paris, 1976), *Penguin Touquet* (1981) and *Egyptology* (1983) have a relentlessly rapid pace. Using stop-and-go action, an accelerated parade of images, and his recorded comments on the performance, Foreman seeks to disrupt the audience's logical and teleological thought processes and 'force people to another level of consciousness'. Representative scripts and essays are collected in his *Plays and Manifestoes*, edited by Kate Davy (1976). AS

Fornes, Maria Irene (1930–) American playwright and director who so well exemplifies the concerns and style of Off-Broadway theatre that she has won six Obies since 1965, including one for sustained achievement (1982). Although her plays and musicals deal with serious individual, national and global problems – *Tango Palace* (1964); *Promenade* (1965); *The Successful Life of Three* (1965); *Dr Kheal* (1968); *The Danube* (1984); *The Conduct of Life* (1985) – they are most acclaimed for their zany, whimsical humour and the use of innovative, cinematic techniques. Fornes's greatest critical success, *Fefu and Her Friends* (1977), is a feminist perspective on female friendship and women's roles in patriarchal society. FB

Forrest, Edwin (1806–72) American actor. Forrest, the first native-born star, dominated the American stage for the middle years of the century as Othello, Lear, Richard III, Coriolanus, Hamlet, Macbeth, Shylock, Richelieu, and in his repertoire of American plays: **Stone**'s *Metamora*, **Bird**'s *The Gladiator* and *The Broker of Bogota*, and **Conrad**'s *Jack Cade*, all of which had been winners in his playwriting contests (1829–47). Lear and Metamora were regarded as his best. Forrest's power derived from his commanding physique, his penetrating voice, his magnetic presence, and his strenuous realism in characters whose driving passions paralleled his own. Although only five feet ten inches in height on stage his muscular frame seemed to tower like a giant. He was steady and predictable, in top form at every performance.

Born in Philadelphia, Forrest was stage-struck as a youngster, at 15 studied the playing of **Thomas A. Cooper**, **Edmund Kean**, and **J. B. Booth**. Six years later, after appearing in Lexington, Louisville, Cincinnati, and New Orleans, he performed with Kean and Cooper, and the next year alternated with Booth as Iago and Othello. He was quickly recognized as a star in the East, in the South, along the inland waterways, and later in the far West. He appeared in London in 1836 and again in 1845 when he challenged his British rival (**Macready**), a rivalry that precipitated the disastrous Astor Place Theatre riot (1849) in which 31 people were killed.

A super-patriot, Forrest was a colourful figure off-stage and on. The lurid details of his divorce trial

Edwin Forrest as *King Lear*.

(1850) – Forrest vs. Catherine Sinclair (she became a theatre manager in San Francisco) – filled the newspapers. He made a fortune, built Fonthill Castle on the Hudson, had a spacious home in New York and another in Philadelphia which was to become the Edwin Forrest Home for 'decayed' actors. He closed his career with Shakespearian readings in Philadelphia, New York, and Boston in 1872.   RM

Forssell, Lars (1929–) Swedish playwright and poet, a member of the Swedish Academy since 1971. His plays vary in style and structure, but frequently reflect his interest in socially-committed cabaret and popular song. Many explore the modern dilemma of disengagement, often suggested through historical parable, as in *The Coronation* (1956), *The Madcap* (1964) and *Pirates* (1982). While his early plays, such as *Mary Lou* (1962) and *The Sunday Walk* (1963), emphasize the anti-hero's cowardice, plays such as *At the Sign of the Hare and the Hawk* (1978) and *The Power and the Honesty* (1984) concern characters who overcome both their own insecurities and manipulation by society.   HL

Forte, Dieter (1935–) German dramatist, resident in Switzerland, whose success was established by *Martin Luther and Thomas Münzer or the Bookkeepers of the Reformation* in 1971. Uniting documentary with polemic farce, this deals with the relationship between finance and revolution to challenge accepted views of history, a line continued in *Jean-Henri Dunant or the Introduction of Civilization* (1978). His irreverently iconoclastic work has systematically covered the major factors conditioning established views of Western society, dealing most recently with Hitler and the

psychology of mass murder in *The Labyrinth of Dreams or the Separation of the Head from the Body* (1982).   CI

Fortune Theatre, London Built in 1600, just outside Cripplegate in the Liberty of Finsbury, the Fortune was intended by **Henslowe** and **Alleyn** to replace the **Rose** as the home of the **Admiral's Men** and rival to the **Globe**. The surviving building contract makes it abundantly clear that Henslowe had the Globe very much in mind and wished to copy many of its dimensions. In view of the fact that the Fortune was a square building, not a polygonal one, this emulation of the Globe posed (and poses) certain architectural problems. We know that the frame was to be 80 ft square and the inner frame 55 ft square. There were three tiers for spectators, and the covered stage was to be 43 ft wide and 22–3 ft deep, 'in all other proportions contrived and fashioned like unto the Stage of the said Play house called the Globe'. The venture was comparatively successful, and the Fortune was sufficiently prosperous to justify its rebuilding after destruction by fire in 1621. The second Fortune was probably polygonal. An important innovation was the use of brick in its building. It seems to have been an unlucky house whose reputation had declined some years before the closure of the theatres in 1642. Partially dismantled in 1649, it was demolished in 1661.

London's third Fortune was opened near Covent Garden in 1924. Successive managements have struggled to make it profitable largely because its capacity (424) is small for a commercial theatre.   PT

46th Street Theatre 226 West 46th St, New York City [Architect: Herbert J. Krapp]. Originally known as Chanin's 46th Street Theatre, it was one of six playhouses built in five years by the Chanin brothers and opened in 1924. For several years, it was a theatre in search of a hit and when it received one, it was more often than not moved to another house. In 1939, **Ethel Merman** appeared on its stage as a full-fledged star in *DuBarry Was a Lady* and returned the following year in *Panama Hattie*. Thereafter, the theatre housed a string of successful musicals beginning with *Finian's Rainbow* (1947) and continuing more recently with '*Nine*' (1982). When the Chanins lost their theatre to creditors in the early depression, the lease was acquired by the **Shuberts**, who ran it until 1945, when it became part of City Playhouses. It is now part of the **Nederlander** chain.   MCH

Fosse, Bob (1927–87) American choreographer and director. After beginning in vaudeville and burlesque as a teenager, Fosse appeared as a dancer in touring companies of *Call Me Mister* and *Make Mine Manhattan*. He made his Broadway debut in *Dance Me a Song* (1950). Fosse's first choreography, created for *The Pajama Game* (1954), was influenced by **Jack Cole**'s style of jazz dancing. His success with *The Pajama Game* was followed by choreography for *Damn Yankees* (1955) and *New Girl in Town* (1957). With *Redhead* (1959) Fosse began to direct as well as choreograph. In the 1960s he staged a number of successful musicals, including *Sweet Charity* (1966). During the 1970s he created three unusual shows, closer in spirit to the concept musicals of **Sondheim** and **Prince**: *Pippin* (1972), *Chicago* (1975), and *Dancin'* (1978). Fosse's frequent use of small groups, jerky, rhythmic steps, and sinuous, slow-motion movement, often coupled with derby hats and white gloves, became his choreographic trademark.   MK

Fourteenth Street Theatre 105–109 West 14th St, New York City [Architect: Alexander Saeltzer]. Although it began as the Théâtre Français for the presentation of French-language drama and opera in New York, the house was known as the Fourteenth St Theatre for most of its existence. After it opened in 1866, it embarked on an exceedingly rocky course as it changed owners, managers and policy many times. It became, however, the only 19th-century playhouse which enjoyed a renaissance late in its history. After being virtually abandoned in 1911, the actress **Eva Le Gallienne** rediscovered the 1,000-seat house in 1926 and installed the Civic Repertory Company in it, presenting well-cast, well-chosen plays in repertory at affordable prices for five years. When she left the theatre, it was only sporadically used and was pulled down in 1948.   MCH

Fox, George Washington Lafayette (1825–77) American comedian who came into his own as a comic actor during his tenure at New York's National Theatre (1850–8), where his uproarious caricatures made him a favourite. He became influential in management by introducing his family's production of *Uncle Tom's Cabin*, with Fox in the role of Phineas Fletcher. He temporarily managed the Old **Bowery**, the New Bowery and **Wallack**'s **Fifth Avenue**, losing as lessee what he earned as a comic star. Between 1862–7 he staged pantomimes at the Old Bowery, with himself as Clown and his brother Charles Kemble Fox as Pantaloon. More an expressive mime artist than an acrobat, Fox tempered the stage trickery of the **Ravels** with his own antic drollery to create a purely American brand of pantomime. This culminated in the immensely successful *Humpty Dumpty* (Olympic Theatre, 1868), which ran for more than 1,200 performances. Fox also made a hit in burlesques of *Faust*, *Macbeth*, *Richelieu*, and **Edwin Booth**'s *Hamlet*. After recurring fits of insanity, he was forcibly removed from a performance in 1875 for committal to an asylum. Fox was reputed to be the funniest performer of his time; he contrived to raise American pantomime to a level of popularity it has never regained.   LS

Foy, Eddie (1856–1928) American comedian and singer. Beginning as a child performer in vaudeville, Foy brought his acrobatic style of comedy and his amusing delivery of comic songs to musicals produced at the Chicago Opera House in 1889 and 1890. His performance in *Bluebeard, Jr* (1890) received praise in both Chicago and New York. After appearing as a featured performer in several other comic operas, Foy was hired as the principal comedian for *The Strollers* (1901). He starred in a number of musicals in the first decade of the 20th century, including *The Wild Rose* (1902), *Mr Bluebeard* (1903), *Piff! Paff!! Pouf!!!* (1904), *The Earl and the Girl* (1905), *The Orchid* (1907), *Mr Hamlet of Broadway* (1908), and *Up and Down Broadway* (1910). Always a popular favourite in vaudeville, Foy spent most of his time on the variety stage after 1910, when he began to include his children, billed as 'The

Seven Little Foys', in his act. He published his autobiography, *Clowning Through Life*, in 1928.   MK

Fragson, Harry (Leon Vince Philip Pott, orig. Fragmann) (1866–1913) Anglo-French music-hall performer, the son of a Belgian brewer. His career in England meeting with scant success, he tried his luck in Paris in 1891 and became an instant hit. His English accent, *chic* wardrobe, eloquent gesture and self-accompaniment on the piano (a novelty at the time) won him great popularity. Returning to London in 1905, he assumed a French accent and mannerisms. In the pantomime *Cinderella* (**Drury Lane**, 1906), the character Dandini was dubbed Dandigny in his honour. In France, his repertory had been comic and sentimental; in England it was dominated by such patter songs as 'The Other Department, If You Please'. The singer of the *Entente Cordiale*, as he was billed, was shot by his deranged father, who coveted one of his female admirers.   LS

France The edict of the Paris Parlement which in 1548 banned the performance of 'sacred mysteries' amounted to more than just the end of religious drama in France. It terminated a period in which theatre performance had given expression to the common beliefs held by all classes in the feudal order. The Roman Catholic church, until then the biggest patron of the drama, became its most implacable enemy: for more than a century French actors were not even allowed a church burial unless they made a death-bed renunciation of their profession. Farces and morality plays continued to be performed, but they too were much restricted, especially in the capital, where the **Confrérie de la Passion** was given a monopoly on all dramatic activity. Any company not performing in their new theatre, the **Hôtel de Bourgogne**, or with a licence obtained from them, was liable to a heavy fine. One consequence of this was to silence the theatre as a voice of popular political protest: Pierre Gringore (d. 1538) was the last performer of the century to be able to comment freely on affairs of State, though Brioché's puppet theatre on the Pont-Neuf indulged in mild satire of Henri IV. Theatrical activity that survived in France through the 30-year period of civil war and religious persecution was precisely shaped to meet the needs of particular sectional interests. The Swiss protestant Théodore de Bèze used biblical material, as the Mysteries had done, for his *Abraham Sacrifiing* (1550) and had a certain following among protestants, e.g. the *Tragédies Saintes* (Holy Tragedies) of Louis de Masures (1563). Later Roman Catholic humanist writers were to turn to biblical subjects, but treated in a more classical manner, e.g. **La Taille**'s *Saul Enraged* (1572) and **Garnier**'s *The Jewish Women* (1583). The rapidly expanding Jesuit Colleges also put on annual performances of religious plays, though the texts were, at first, in Latin. In academic and court circles a more important influence was the group of humanist poets known as the Pléiade. For the humanists the only suitable models of good dramaturgical practice were the authors of classical Greece and Rome, although their plays show them to have been at least as much influenced by the Italian *commedia erudita*. The first French tragedy of this kind was **Etienne Jodelle**'s *Cleopatra Captive*, performed before the king in 1552 with the 20-year-old author in the role of Cleopatra, but the first to be written in Alexandrines (the 12-syllable line advocated by the Pléiade) was *The Death of Caesar* by Jacques Grévin in 1560. The main inspiration for these tragedies was **Seneca**; they were short on dramatic action and long on monologue. Moreover their slavish imitation of the ancient world meant that reference to 16th-century France was almost entirely absent. The one author who managed to inject some contemporary urgency into his tragedies was Robert Garnier, whose *Antigone* (1580) was thus the first in a long line of French plays of that title using the downfall of the house of Oedipus as an oblique reference to contemporary events. Garnier's *The Jewish Women* also makes a powerful comment on cruelty at times of religious strife.

Many of the humanist authors also published theoretical statements of their dramaturgical aims: La Taille's treatise on the art of tragedy (1562) echoes **Aristotle** and **Horace**; the same author's prologue to *The Rivals* (1574) heaps scorn on the native farce tradition, advocating a return to the methods of classical **New Comedy**. Jodelle's *Eugene* (1552) was the first such comedy, but although written in five acts and respecting the unity of time, the play's subject, cuckoldry, and its octosyllabic verse form were indistinguishable from those of French farce. **Pierre de Larivey**'s comedies (the first six published in 1579) were close copies of the Italian *commedia*, but transposed into a vigorous French idiom; Odet de Turnèbe's *The Happy Ones* (1584) managed a more original plot and characters while respecting the new humanist rules. The French humanists derived from their study of the Classics and of the Italians the idea of theatre as an autonomous, stylized world, not as a simple transposition or symbolic representation of real life. The key factor was the change in the playing space. The medieval simultaneous staging, with actors visible throughout, had made no radical distinction between the world and the stage. By copying the Roman stage, and by building sets representing a public square or cross-roads set in perspective, the Italians had introduced a new kind of space: one which did not represent a particular location but which functioned as an empty space to be transformed by the presence of an actor. In France, however, although authors were trying to apply new methods, the precarious state of the professional theatre made real progress difficult until the 1630s. In staging, especially, it was a long time before the medieval system of simultaneous staging gave way before Italian influence, as is shown by the manuscript of **Mahelot**. Henri IV attempted to improve the state of the theatre, even authorizing the performance of mystery plays, but the Parlement confirmed its earlier veto. There is evidence of the existence of several itinerant companies working in the provinces at this time. In 1595 performances by such companies were permitted at the Paris fairs of St Germain in the Spring and St Laurent in the Autumn and in 1598 the Confrérie allowed Pierre Venier's company to move from the St Germain fair into a hall at the Hôtel d'Argent on payment of a tax for each performance given. A year later **Valleran le Conte** brought his company from the provinces to Paris, signing a three-month lease at the Hôtel de Bourgogne. Valleran's company dramatist was **Alexandre Hardy**, an immensely prolific playwright and

the first to make this a professional career. He was more interested in lively dramatic action than in theoretical rules. In addition to the *commedia erudita*, he had been influenced by the **commedia dell'arte** (the first of these Italian companies visited France in the 1570s, after which they were frequent visitors) and by the Italian vogue for pastorals. Hardy wrote many pastorals which, with their idealized worlds and analysis of emotional states, have been seen as the major source for French classical comedy. Hardy also borrowed from Spanish models and began another influential vogue for tragicomedies, often drawn from Spanish romance, filled with sensational action and quite unconcerned to observe the unities.

For the first quarter of the 17th century, the theatrical profession continued precarious, theatres being associated with low life and crude performance. The favoured court entertainment was the ballet: Henri IV and Marie de Medici commissioned large numbers of allegorical ballets and passed their love of dancing on to Louis XIII and Louis XIV. But in the 1630s and 1640s **Richelieu** showed what could be achieved by determined patronage. Under a famous farce player, **Gros-Guillaume**, a company had established itself as the 'Comédiens du Roi' at the Hôtel de Bourgogne. Richelieu put an end to their monopoly in 1634 by encouraging **Montdory** to bring his itinerant company to Paris and settle at the **Marais** theatre. This building was a former tennis court, previously hired out for occasional performances, which Montdory now rebuilt. Richelieu encouraged a spirit of rivalry between this new company and the Comédiens du Roi. He gave practical assistance to both by commissioning a group of five authors including **Mairet**, **Rotrou** and **Pierre Corneille** to write tragedies, and he promoted a decree which, in 1641, recognized the legal status of the acting profession. Other important factors in making the theatre more socially acceptable were the salons, devoted to raising standards in literature, and the Académie-Française, which received its royal charter in 1635.

Encouraged by improved conditions, a group of new playwrights emerged; the definitions of tragedy formulated by La Taille's generation were taken up and refined, for example in Mairet's *Sylvanire*, whose preface formulated the three unities and advocated 'the study of a sudden psychological crisis'. Mairet's *Sophonisbe* (1634) and **Tristan l'Hermite**'s *Marianne* (1636), tragedies of high-flown verse and sentiment, were considered successful exemplars by contemporaries, which explains why the prodigious success of Pierre Corneille's tragicomedy of love and revenge, *Le Cid* (1637), sparked off the flurry of pamphlets and discussion known as the 'Querelle du Cid'. Corneille was mortified by the doubt cast on his work's classical credentials and followed it with four tragedies drawn from Roman history in the early 1640s. These were perfectly regular, exalted duty and concern for honour, but also justice and clemency and were written in sonorous Alexandrines of great rhetorical power, well exploited by **Floridor** and other members of the Marais company who performed them. Corneille had at first attracted attention with his comedies at the Marais in the 1630s. Characterized by elegant style and elevated tone, but also by a new realism, both in setting and in depiction of character, they were quickly perceived as models of classical comedy, owing little to farce and much to **Terence** and the *commedia*. **Scudéry**'s *The Actors' Comedy* (1635) and Corneille's *The Theatrical Illusion* (1636) demonstrate theatre's growing self-awareness concerning its own artistic and aesthetic means. These comedies at the Marais eclipsed the performances at the Hôtel de Bourgogne by the celebrated trio of farce players Gros-Guillaume, **Gaultier-Garguille** and **Turlupin**, which were a mixture of lewd jokes, expressive mime and verbal comedy, the latter being the main inheritance from the old French farce tradition. While Gros-Guillaume retained the traditional floured face, Turlupin exhibited the influence of the Italian comedians with a costume similar to that of Brighella. Two other traditional stand-up comics, also known to act in plays, were **Tabarin** and **Bruscambille**, both of whose comic monologues were sufficiently popular to be published during their life-times. The last of the old-style comic actors was **Jodelet**, for whom **Scarron** wrote a vehicle-play, *Jodelet, or the Master-servant*, in 1645, and for whom **Molière** later wrote a leading role in *Les Précieuses Ridicules* (1659).

After the death of Gros-Guillaume in 1634 **Bellerose** took over management of the Hôtel de Bourgogne but he and his resident dramatist Rotrou were no match for the Marais with Corneille as dramatist and actors such as Montdory and Floridor. The Marais theatre was extensively rebuilt after a fire in 1644. In 1647 the Hôtel de Bourgogne followed suit, also inducing both Floridor and Corneille to move there, after which the Marais lost its pre-eminence, turning more to machine plays. The first building to be constructed specifically for theatre performance this century was the Palais Cardinal, built by Lemercier for Richelieu and inaugurated in 1641. After the Cardinal's death in 1642, it reverted to the crown, becoming known as the **Palais-Royal**. Paris thus had three modern theatres by the 1640s and to these was added the auditorium in the **Petit-Bourbon** palace, equipped by **Torelli**, whom Cardinal Mazarin summoned from Italy in 1645 to instal the latest machinery for spectacular scene changes, flying effects, etc. This was at first used for Italian opera, but later also for machine plays. It was demolished in 1660 to be replaced by an even grander **Salle des Machines** at the Tuileries palace, equipped by Torelli's great rival **Vigarani**. During this period provincial companies continued to prosper: after the financial collapse of the Illustre-Théâtre founded by the **Béjarts** with the young Molière in 1645, they had earned their living touring the provinces for 13 years before returning to Paris in 1658. The centralizing tendencies of Louis XIV were to redress the balance in favour of the Paris region in the second half of the century, though Versailles did not acquire a permanent theatre building until just before the Revolution (1770). Under Louis XIV the lavish court festivities were given on large improvised stages. These provided the extensive acting areas required for the ballets in which Louis himself liked to dance. Many of Molière's plays and 'comédies-ballets' were first performed as part of such festivities. In the town theatres the stages were more confined: long and narrow with the acting area further reduced by the young nobles who would pay a high price for a seat on the stage. The practice of selling seats on the stage seems to have started at the Marais during the immensely popular run of *Le Cid* (1637). At first limited to about 30, the seating on the sides of the stage later expanded to more than 200. This crowd of spectators on the stage was a constant annoyance to actors, designers and playwrights. Not until 1759 was the practice abolished, after a campaign led by **Lekain**.

In the 1650s and 1660s the range of Parisian theatrical entertainment developed rapidly. As well as burlesque comedy, whose major exponent was Scarron, and comedies of intrigue based on Italian or Spanish models by such writers as Rotrou, **Quinault** and **Thomas Corneille**, the Italian company of **Tiberio Fiorilli** took up permanent residence, sharing a theatre with Molière. There was also a vogue for romanesque tragedy, with plots borrowed from contemporary novels, notably the influential and interminable pastoral *L'Astrée* by Honoré d'Urfé, but also the writings of Madeleine de Scudéry and La Calprenède. But the genre with most prestige (and the one in which Molière wanted to excel) was tragedy. This period saw Corneille's late tragedies of political power in the ancient world and his eclipse by his younger rival **Racine** who, in the ten-year period 1667–77 wrote the seven plays now considered to be the crowning glory of French classical tragedy. In these, he largely avoided the romanesque, borrowing most of his plots from classical antiquity and effortlessly observing the rules. Even when depicting the most extreme characters or situations, he strove to maintain *vraisemblance* – the quality of verisimilitude, without which, he held, it was impossible to touch the spectators' emotions. His own tragic formula was expressed in the preface to *Bérénice* (1670) as 'a simple action sustained by the violence of the passions, the beauty of the sentiments and the elegance of the language'. Unlike Molière, whose prose plays are as effective as those written in verse, much of Racine's power in the theatre stems from his supreme mastery of the Alexandrine verse form. Racine's first two plays were staged by Molière, but he transferred to the Hôtel de Bourgogne because of its pre-eminence in tragedy. He took with him, as his mistress, Molière's best tragic actress, Mlle du Parc, but again transferred his affections to **Marie Champmeslé**, another Marais actress, for whom he wrote his major female roles from Bérénice to Phèdre. After *Phèdre* (1667) he withdrew from the theatre, was reconciled with the church, and only wrote two further tragedies, both on biblical subjects at Mme de Maintenon's request for performance by the girls at the Saint-Cyr school.

The works which have survived best from this period are the comedies of Molière, first written and produced in 14 years of intense activity from 1659 till his death in 1673. Their rich use of situation and dialogue, often exploiting traditional farce schemas to develop sophisticated comedy of character and ideas, has led to constant revivals in subsequent centuries. Part of their success at the time was doubtless due to the excellence of Molière's company, which included **La Grange**, whose register of daily takings is one of the main sources of information about the company. Molière received a stream of royal commissions for court entertainments; because of his powerful protector he was also able to tackle dangerous subjects such as religious hypocrisy in *Tartuffe*. But Molière had to contend with intense professional jealousy, both from rival companies and from the composer **Lully**, who also enjoyed the unstinting support of Louis XIV. Although Lully collaborated with Molière on many 'comédies-ballets', his ambition was to create a French opera in which pride of place would go to the music, reducing the role of the dramatist. He achieved this on Molière's death when he took possession of his theatre, the Palais-Royal. Vigarani converted the stage, which remained the home of Paris opera until 1763. Some of Molière's company went to the Hôtel de Bourgogne, the rest were merged with the Marais company which moved, with the Italians, into a theatre in the rue Guénégaud. In 1680, on the death of La Thorillière, manager of the Hotel de Bourgogne, the king merged the two companies so as to create La seule troupe des comédiens du roi. The new troupe contained 15 actors and 12 actresses who were none too pleased, at first, to be merged. But Louis rewarded them with a regular subsidy and monopoly of French-language performances in the capital; they quickly became known as the **Comédie-Française** to distinguish them from the **Comédie-Italienne**, which moved to the Hôtel de Bourgogne. The Italians continued to be popular and began introducing more French material but as Louis came under the influence of the devout Mme de Maintenon the Italians' brand of comedy became less acceptable. They were finally banished in 1697, to return in 1716 with the accession of Louis XV. The Comédie-Française also suffered from prevailing attitudes when in 1687 the king ordered them to leave the rue Guénégaud because a new College was to be opened nearby and there were fears for the students' morals. They were allowed to buy an old tennis court in what is now the rue de l'Ancienne Comédie, St Germain des Prés, where they had a new theatre built. Their repertoire during the remaining years of the century consisted largely of plays by Molière, Corneille and Racine, to which were added Molièresque comedies written by members of the company, including the leading actor, **Michel Baron**, whose most successful comedy was *The Philanderer* (1686) and Charles Champmeslé and Noël-Jacques Hauteroche, both of whom exploited the figure of the comic valet Crispin, originally developed by the actor **Raymond Poisson**. Molière's example was to dominate comic playwriting for a long time to come; without entirely escaping from his shadow, a group of playwrights including Dufresny, **Regnard**, **Dancourt** and **Lesage** established a brilliant if cynical comedy of manners giving an uncomfortably realistic portrait of contemporary French society. Among the most effective are Lesage's *Crispin Rival of his Master* (1707) and *Turcaret* (1709), the latter exposing a society motivated entirely by greed through its central character, a tax-farmer.

If Molière's example dominated the comic dramatists, writers of tragedy were completely overshadowed by Racine and Corneille. Their influence was reinforced by the work of critics, notably **Boileau** and **d'Aubignac**, whose *Practice of Theatre* (1657) developed the neoclassical rules into a systematic code of practice for the playwright. Corneille himself published three *Discourses on Dramatic Art* in 1660 and the result of so much critical and theoretical analysis was that all subsequent writers of tragedy found themselves obliged to follow a formula. Nevertheless new tragedies written in this way were a successful part of the Comédie-Française's repertoire throughout the 18th

century, the most prolific author being **Voltaire**, whose worthy but dull plays combined respect for the rules with crusades against bigotry. Voltaire helped to promote greater respect for the acting profession, protesting at the church's refusal to bury **Adrienne Lecouvreur** and assisting Clairon and Lekain in their campaign to clear the audience off the stage (this was partly to make room for the crowd scenes which he introduced under the influence of **Shakespeare**). **Crébillon**, while also respecting the rules, introduced more sensational subject matter, pointing the way towards melodrama. But despite undistinguished tragic writing, the century marked a high point in the influence of French theatre throughout Europe. In aristocratic cultural circles the aesthetic purity and elevated tone of French tragedy in particular was widely admired. Comedy was marked by more innovation, partly because of the outstanding qualities of two playwrights, **Marivaux** and **Beaumarchais**, but mostly because of the growing importance of fairground theatres and other forms of entertainment. Soon after the Comédie-Italienne returned under Riccoboni they were permitted to perform plays in French and it was for them that Marivaux wrote the great part of his comedies. These at first exploited stock types such as **Harlequin** in *Harlequin Refined by Love* (1720) but rapidly developed an original vein of psychological dialogue concentrating exclusively on the process of self-discovery occasioned by young love. Although not overwhelmingly successful in his own time, Marivaux has always remained in the repertoire and has enjoyed a great vogue among recent directors including **Planchon** and **Chéreau**. More successful in Marivaux's day were the *comédies larmoyantes* or sentimental comedies of **Destouches** and **La Chaussée**. This new genre constituted the main French contribution to the development of comedy in the 18th century although the plays have not weathered well. Their demonstrations of uncomplaining virtue rewarded after long trials soon palled, although they were the mainstay of the Comédie-Française repertoire in their time. Their generally improving tone paved the way for **Diderot**'s demand, in his treatise published with his play *The Natural Son* (1757), for a new genre mid-way between comedy and tragedy named *le drame* – serious domestic drama investigating the real conditions in which people live. **Rousseau**'s celebrated condemnation of theatre for its frivolous and corrupting influence only led playwrights to make more emphatic claims for their moral seriousness; one of the few to match these claims with a good play was **Sedaine**, whose *A Philosopher Without Knowing It* was first performed at the Comédie-Française in 1765.

The bulk of Sedaine's output was written for the more theatrically vital Comédie-Italienne and the fairground theatres, home of the more vigorous forms of popular entertainment. In the course of the century, companies playing at the fairs became progressively cleverer at evading the monopoly, using mime, dance, songs and placards to get round the ban on spoken dialogue. The *comédie-vaudeville* style they evolved became so popular that it led the Italians to copy them, developing their own form of comic opera. In 1762 the Italians amalgamated with the Opéra-Comique, which had been playing at the fairs for many years and had experienced particular success under **Favart** since 1757.

In 1783 the combined troupe moved from the Hôtel de Bourgogne into a new theatre on the Boulevard des Italiens, so named in their honour. During this period the theatre booths of the Boulevard du Temple were also becoming more successful. The first person to establish a regular theatre here (despite opposition from the Comédie-Française) was **Nicolet** with a troupe of acrobats and performing monkeys. He built a new theatre, named the Gaîté, and was followed to the Boulevard du Temple by Audinot, who, in 1769, moved his marionettes to the Ambigu-Comique, and by Fleury de l'Ecluze, who opened the Variétés-Amusantes in 1779 (see **Boulevard**). By the early 1770s, both Nicolet and Audinot were flouting the monopoly laws by broadening their repertoires but both were successful with all classes of theatre-goers and were even invited to perform before Louis XV at Versailles. After the Revolution, restrictions on these theatres were lifted: article 1 of a law passed in January 1791 stated that 'any citizen will be able to open a public theatre and to have performed there plays in all genres'. Equally important was the lifting of a heavy tax these theatres had been obliged to pay to the Opéra since 1784. French opera, like French tragedy, was widely admired in the 18th century as first Rameau then **Gluck** transformed it into a dramatic form in its own right. A similar development occurred in dance under the influence of Noverre. Together with the brilliant displays of the designer **Servandoni**, these developments help to explain the number of new theatres erected throughout France in the second half of the century. These included Gabriel's opera house at Versailles (1770), Ledoux's theatre at Besançon (1784) and **Victor Louis**'s theatre at Bordeaux (1780). The last major comic dramatist of the century was Beaumarchais. Influenced, like Sedaine, by Diderot, he wrote several serious domestic dramas but is remembered for his comedies *The Barber of Seville* and *The Marriage of Figaro*. Their combination of traditional comic devices with an underlying note of serious social and psychological comments makes them models of comic drama and suitable for setting to music, as Rossini and Mozart have shown. An astute business man, Beaumarchais tried to institute a system of royalty payments to playwrights, something that became legally established early in the following century. *The Marriage of Figaro* was considered dangerously anti-authoritarian and permission for performance at the Comédie-Française was withheld for 9 years. This only served to magnify the play's success when it was performed in 1784. More than any other play of its time, *The Marriage of Figaro* heralded a period when theatre was once again to become a focus for challenging political ideas.

As well as liberating the theatres, the French Revolution set up open-air festivities organized by the painter David, at which the crowd were not merely spectators, but participants as in the medieval mysteries. Rapidly a new theatre audience emerged, made up of citizens eager for powerful emotions and strong dramatic situations. These needs were met by melodrama. Early French melodrama brought together the movement and energy of popular entertainment with the social concern of the late 18th-century domestic drama and the love of the picturesque characteristic of romanticism. The companies who performed the early melodramas were those who, before the Revolution, had relied on acrobatic turns or comic dance acts. When they doubled as actors, their performances were characterized by large, precise gestures tending to flow into grand spectacular tableaux. This was obviously appropriate for the popular comic vaudevilles but also helped to shape the more tragic melodramas. The outstanding writer of melodramas was **Pixérécourt**, who claimed he wrote for 'those who cannot read' and often directed his own plays, attaching great importance to the visual aspects of production. Pixérécourt's protagonists are caught up in a cosmic battle between the forces of good and evil, often building up to a spectacular climax such as the eruption of Vesuvius on stage at the end of *Death's Head or the Ruins of Pompeii* (1827). Another dramatic genre which found favour with new audiences was equestrian drama performed in a circus ring with a stage behind. The first such permanent circus was erected by **Astley** in 1780. After the Revolution he abandoned it to the Franconi brothers, whose success led them to build the **Cirque Olympique** in 1807. Here they put on mass spectacles celebrating the Napoleonic Empire, incorporating both equestrian acts and dramatic tableaux. In 1815 the Restoration put a stop to Napoleonic myth-making, but after 1830 such shows became even more popular and others followed, celebrating colonial conquest e.g. *L'Empire* (1845) which concluded with an apotheosis of Napoleon. In the second half of the century circuses reverted to acrobatic, clowning and animal acts (at one time there were 5 permanent circuses in Paris) while large Hippodromes were constructed for the performance of mass spectacle.

During the late 18th and early 19th centuries fruitful links grew up between the pictorial and dramatic arts, boosted by Diderot's concept of domestic drama as a succession of truthful pictures and by the popularity of the spectacular. In 1800, for example, a staging of Salieri's *Les Horaces* brought to life David's painting *The Oath of the Horatii*, a scene which had already been enacted at the Festival of the Supreme Being in 1794. This was also the period of the Panorama and the Diorama, in which audiences viewed tableaux displaying the skill of such scene-painters as Daguerre, inventor of photography. Further evidence of the renewed importance of visual aspects in theatre performance can be seen in the success of **Deburau** whose mime plays at the **Funambules** theatre were continuously successful in the 1820s and 1830s. The Revolution also sparked an enormous increase in the number of French theatres: in 1791 alone more than 20 new theatres were opened in Paris. But Napoleon soon limited this new-found freedom, reintroducing censorship in 1804 and limiting the number of Paris theatres to eight (plus the circus) in 1807. Napoleon took a keen interest in the theatre and was a friend of **Talma**, the actor who had led the pro-Revolutionary faction of the Comédie-Française. By appearing in Voltaire's *Brutus* (1789) dressed in Roman garb, Talma had started a fashion for authentic costume which spread rapidly; delight in historical detail marks another point of contact between the visual and performing arts at this time.

Despite the vitality of theatre life after the Revolution, it was not until the 1830s that a major challenge to the literary tradition of classical tragedy appeared in the

Daguerre's setting for Act II of Ducange's *Elodie*, showing how he carried over the basic principles of the panorama and diorama into his stage-design, by dividing the stage into two main areas and varying lighting intensity to give a sense of considerable depth. Ambigu-Comique, 1822.

form of the romantic verse dramas of **Hugo** and **Dumas** *père*. The riots in the theatre at the first performance of *Hernani* in 1830 were occasioned not merely by Hugo's open scorn for the classical rules. They were also a response to the introduction into the Comédie-Française of elements associated with popular drama: Pixérécourt's use of local colour had clearly influenced Dumas and Hugo. Other more respectable influences like **Schiller** and Shakespeare were still deemed barbarous by French aesthetic criteria and also had demonstrable connections with melodrama – Schiller's *The Robbers* was the model for one of the earliest melodramas, Lamartellière's *Robert the Robber King* (1793). The first complete edition of Shakespeare's works in French had appeared in 1776–82 and he was to be a pervasive influence on dramatic writing, reinforced by visits of English theatre companies to Paris. A third important element in the controversy surrounding *Hernani* was Hugo's standing as a political writer: his earlier historical drama *Marion de Lorme* had been banned by the censor and many of his plays, especially *Ruy Blas* (1838), contain a meditation on the nature of political power clearly applicable to the contemporary French situation. The theoretical basis for romantic drama had been set out three years earlier by Hugo in the preface to his play *Cromwell* (1827). It involved mixing the genres which had been so carefully separated by the French classical theatre, combining elements of the sublime and the grotesque in the same play. It also advocated a Shakespearian flexibility in the use of time and space and looked to European rather than to Roman history for its subjects. For ten years, both at the Comédie-Française and at the Porte-Saint-Martin theatre, the plays of Hugo and Dumas drew enthusiastic audiences. Together with **Vigny**, whose *Chatterton* (1835) gave **Marie Dorval** one of her greatest roles, they were responsible for establishing a new dramatic genre. But it was surprisingly short-lived – Hugo's *Les Burgraves*, a failure at the Comédie-Française in 1843, was the last of its kind, although **Edmond Rostand**'s verse plays, written some 50 years later, rely on many of the same qualities. Allied to the romantic dramatists through his historical epic

Lorenzaccio (written 1834), **Musset** did not at first imagine that this play could be staged and he aimed many of his distinctive short comedies at the reader rather than at the spectator. He was, however, a skilful dramatist, successfully achieving a fluid, Shakespearian style and his works have enjoyed frequent revival; **Sarah Bernhardt** played the title role of *Lorenzaccio* in 1896 and this play was important in the early success of **Vilar** at **Avignon** and the **Théâtre National Populaire** with **Gérard Philipe** in the title role in 1952.

The most prolific comic dramatist of the early 19th century was **Scribe**, who strengthened the somewhat unstructured *vaudeville* form, turning it into the comedy situation, subsequently dubbed 'well-made play' by the critic **Sarcey**. Scribe was a master of complicated intrigue and *coups de théâtre* and his methods were copied by the equally successful **Sardou**. **Labiche** took this form and used it for a biting satire of the mid-19th-century bourgeoisie in plays whose visual qualities provoke comparison with Daumier. Labiche's combination of accurate social analysis and sense of the grotesque has led to recent revivals presenting him as a forerunner both of the absurd and of political theatre. Other successful comic dramatists were the partnership of **Meilhac** and **Halévy** who wrote witty librettos for Offenbach's operettas and **Feydeau**, who developed the form known as French Farce – a comic satire of the sexual mores of the bourgeoisie. Melodrama continued popular throughout the century, with **Bouchardy** and **Dennery** taking over from Pixérécourt. For a prolific author, this genre could provide rich earnings, but the people who profited most were the new breed of star actors or *monstres sacrés*, the most famous of whom was **Frédérick Lemaître**. Frédérick, as he was known, achieved fame in 1824 by parodying a feeble melodrama and, in the process, creating the figure of Robert Macaire, who took on a life of his own. Like other successful actors and actresses of the period – see e.g. **Bocage**, **Coquelin**, **Déjazet**, Dorval, **Mélingue**, **Potier**, **Réjane** – his services were disputed by the different theatres. He performed in all types of play, from high romantic drama to popular melodrama, sometimes running into trouble with the censor for introducing political satire into his performances. Frédérick never performed at the Comédie-Française, which for many performers constituted the summit of their art. **Rachel**, for example, had her greatest successes playing Racine and Corneille there and Sarah Bernhardt rose to become a *sociétaire* before her reputation became so great that she was able to branch out on her own, becoming both star, director and theatre manager.

In 1864 Napoleon III removed the last restrictions on the exploitation of theatres and the result was an enormous boom in theatre building especially along the new *grands boulevards* being constructed under Baron Haussmann. The most elaborate new theatre to be erected was the Paris Opéra designed by Charles Garnier with the encouragement of Napoleon III. Opera played an important role in the theatrical life of 19th-century France, an importance reflected in the four Parisian theatres – Opéra; Opéra-Comique; Théâtre Lyrique; Bouffes Parisiens – which gave regular performances in the second half of the century. Most successful were the light operas of composers Meyerbeer and Jacques Halévy, for both of whom

Scribe wrote librettos. Georges Bizet had less success, initially, in his attempts to promote a taste for realism e.g. with his music for Alphonse Daudet's *L'Arlésienne* (1872) and his opera *Carmen* (1875). The realist movement in the other arts found a faint dramatic echo in the plays of **Augier** and **Dumas** *fils*, but it was left to naturalism to bring about a real change in acting, production and playwriting. The force of naturalism as a cultural movement stemmed from its assertion that it was based on scientific principles. **Zola**, its main spokesman, borrowed ideas from contemporary medical and social theory as well as from Darwin. In addition to his novels and other writings, he mounted a campaign for the theatre to be treated seriously as a kind of laboratory of social relations. But, like Diderot in the previous century, though a powerful novelist and thinker, Zola was not a good dramatist. The French contribution to naturalism was largely the work of the pioneering director **Antoine**, who aimed to present new plays dealing with contemporary issues. He encouraged writers to attempt short one-act plays representing social conditions and promoted a generation of minor dramatists including Ancey, **Becque**, **Brieux**, Bernstein, Courteline, **Romains** and Mirbeau. Lacking major new French plays, he introduced the work of the German, Scandinavian and Russian naturalists to the French stage and also produced several of Shakespeare's plays for the first time. Antoine was a sensitive director of actors, encouraging an intimate, truthful performance style, and was also the first director to treat the stage setting as a realistic environment rather than a decorative or spectacular background. As a reaction against naturalism Paul Fort set up the Théâtre d'Art in 1890 to promote poetic and symbolist work, an aim that was continued by **Lugné-Poe** at the Théâtre de l'Oeuvre from 1893. Lugné-Poe staged the work of several important new dramatists, including **Claudel**, Crommelynck and **Maeterlinck**. He also put on the first performance of **Jarry**'s *Ubu Roi* (1896), a play which was to be an inspiration to the 20th-century theatrical avant-garde.

Although the innovations of both naturalism and symbolism were to prove influential, little seemed changed during the period of the *belle époque* (1890–1914). The majority of French theatres were devoted to light comic entertainment that could do nothing to shock the sensibilities of their newly prosperous bourgeois patrons. **Jacques Copeau** explicitly condemned this state of affairs as corrupt and set up his **Vieux-Colombier** theatre in 1913 to restore the dignity of an art form that had once been the central expression of society's religious and social beliefs. Like Antoine, he failed to call forth any major new dramatists and his repertoire was based on the classics, especially Shakespeare and Molière. Under his guidance, **Jouvet** rebuilt the stage of the theatre to resemble the Elizabethan playing space; on this bare stage, almost devoid of scenery, he encouraged his actors to develop a performance style that was physically inventive (based on researches into the *commedia dell'arte*) but also truthful and direct. He also set up an influential theatre school, where many outstanding actors and directors of the century were trained. Two of Copeau's original group, **Dullin** and Jouvet, set up their own companies soon after the end of the First World War; in 1927 they joined together with **Pitoëff**, a Russian

émigré, and **Baty** to form the **Cartel**. This group of actors and directors was responsible for introducing new standards of production and for creating an identifiable form of art-theatre in the inter-war years. Internationalist in their outlook, their productions included work from Russia, Germany, Britain and America. They also brought a major new influence to bear on French playwriting with their productions of plays by **Pirandello**, whose shadow hovers over the work of most successful dramatists of the 1930s and 1940s, notably **Salacrou** and **Anouilh**. A long-lasting partnership between Jouvet and **Giraudoux** helped the latter to develop into the outstanding dramatist of the inter-war period. Urbane and witty, many of his plays return to the classical sources of 17th- and 18th-century settings, achieving their effects from unexpected juxtaposition. Despite their considerable achievements, the Cartel did not affect the majority of French theatre output between the wars; this continued to consist of Boulevard plays by such writers as Bataille, Bernstein, Bourdet and **Guitry**. The success of the Boulevard play continued well into the 1950s and 1960s, sustaining a large number of commercial theatres in Paris, including some of considerable artistic merit like the **Atelier** which, under **Barsacq**, produced an impressive number of new plays including the work of Anouilh, Marcel Aymé, Félicien Marceau, René de Obaldia. Other successful authors of the Boulevard, such as André Roussin and Marcel Achard, were able to build up a personal following, but with the growing importance of the French cinema and television industry, star actors have been tempted away from the stage. This, combined with the growth of subsidized theatre, has contributed to the demise of French Boulevard theatres. Those which survive do so mostly on sex comedies imported from the English-speaking theatre.

By the end of the 1930s the reforms of Copeau and the Cartel had helped to create conditions in which theatre was seen once more as a significant element in French cultural life; there was a revival of interest in Catholic theatre and the Popular Front government promoted mass performances of socialist inspiration. Authors began once again to turn to the stage as a forum for serious political and philosophical ideas. Begun by Giraudoux in the 1930s, this continued in the 1940s and 1950s when **Sartre**, **Camus** and Anouilh helped to promote the theatre to the forefront of French intellectual life. Sartre adopted old-fashioned dramaturgical models, revivifying the 19th-century melodramatic structures by an emphasis on existentialist choice. His first director was Dullin, who was permitted to put on *The Flies* in 1943 despite its clear call to resistance. In the following decade Sartre wrote a number of commercially successful plays dramatizing the problems of personal identity in the light of both moral and political choices. Similar concerns found expression in the plays of Camus and Anouilh, whose *Antigone* (1944) was interpreted by some as justifying collaboration, by others as encouraging resistance.

The four years of German occupation (1940–4) were an important period for the subsequent development of both commercial and subsidized theatre in France. The commercial theatre experienced a boom whose momentum carried it beyond the years of post-war austerity. In addition the foundations were laid for the post-war **decentralization movement** by men such as Vilar, **Dasté**, **Cousin** who shared a vision of theatre as a cultural force for freedom extended to all Frenchmen, not just the cognoscenti of the capital. They looked back to the pioneering work of **Gémier**, who had founded the Théâtre National Populaire in 1920 and to the work of **Léon Chancerel** and the **Compagnie des Quinze** in the 1930s. The immediate post-war years saw a flowering of new theatre work both in Paris and the provinces based on an affirmation of traditional French cultural values. In Paris, **Jean-Louis Barrault**, with Madeleine Renaud, set up a company whose high reputation was built partly on brilliant productions of the classical French repertoire, partly on more recent playwrights, especially Claudel. With **Marcel Marceau** and Jacques Lecoq, he also helped to revive the tradition of mime. The Grenier-Hussenot company breathed new life into the traditional French farce with inventive, acrobatic productions, half-way between theatre and cabaret. In the provinces five new centres of dramatic creation were established supported by local and central government funding; strongly influenced by the example and writings of Copeau, these at first concentrated on the classical repertoire.

It was not until the 1950s that a major new dramaturgical form appeared, giving expression to the modern sense of anguish and despair by means of stage images both stark and concrete. The theatre of the absurd (or new theatre by analogy with the *nouveau roman*) was the work of playwrights who were all outside the mainstream of French tradition: **Beckett**, **Ionesco**, **Adamov**, **Genet**, and of actors and directors with roots in the surrealist avant-garde: Nicolas Bataille, **Blin**, **Serreau**. The surrealist movement between the wars had taken little active interest in theatre but it had revived the work of Jarry and influenced **Artaud** and **Vitrac** who founded their Théâtre Alfred Jarry in 1926. Here they performed Vitrac's *Victor* (1928), a surreal satire of boulevard theatre and the bourgeois world it mirrors. Artaud went on to found the short-lived Theatre of Cruelty (1935) and to publish *The Theatre and its Double* (1938), in which he drew an analogy between theatre and plague, suggesting that theatre's effect should be that of a great collective nightmare from which few would emerge unscathed but which would leave society purged; theatre should be able to break through the encrusted shell of cultural tradition and fine discourse to discover a new language, essentially physical, concrete, spatial. Although Artaud did not specifically influence the dramatists of the absurd, he helped to form the practitioners who, like Blin, were able to recognize the originality of these plays whose complex theatrical images combined tragedy and farce of the most extreme kind, thus decisively burying the great French tradition of separating the genres. At first misunderstood by the critics, plays such as Ionesco's *The Bald Prima Donna* staged by Bataille in 1950 or Beckett's *Waiting for Godot* staged by Blin in 1953 achieved rapid fame and have been constantly revived. Their influence also spread quickly in the English-speaking theatre world thanks to fine translations of Beckett's work by himself and of Ionesco's by Donald Watson. In the course of the 1950s and 1960s both authors continued to write plays but while Beckett's became shorter and starker, Ionesco's grew progressively longer and more verbose. Genet wrote only three full length plays, *The Balcony*, *The Blacks* and *The Screens*; all were associated with scandal and protest, the first directed by **Brook** and the other two by Blin. Adamov's work acquired a more political slant without abandoning the techniques of the new theatre. **Fernando Arrabal**, Robert Pinget and **Marguerite Duras** (better known for her *nouveaux romans*) also wrote plays which have been seen as part of the new theatre.

The triumph of the new theatre playwrights was almost exclusively confined to Paris. With a few exceptions, such as **Planchon** who produced Adamov and Ionesco at Lyon in the early 1950s, those working in the decentralized theatres at first shunned the absurd. Their aim was rather to rediscover theatre with a universal, popular appeal and to face up to issues of urgent political importance. The man who best represented this aim was Vilar, who had founded the Avignon theatre festival in 1947 and who, in 1951, became director of the Théâtre National Populaire at the **Chaillot Theatre**. His choice of plays, drawn from the international classic repertoire, was made in order to comment on the current political situation and he was among the first to produce **Brecht**'s work in France. Both Brecht's plays and his company, the **Berliner Ensemble**, exerted a powerful influence over the decentralized theatres of the 1950s and 1960s. This was evident in a new playing style, more down-to-earth and less declamatory than traditional French acting, and in the renewed urgency with which theatre companies tried to identify and serve the cultural needs of the working class. A new school of political dramatists emerged, including Adamov, **Césaire**, Cousin, **Gatti**, Planchon and **Yacine**. Although these playwrights were left-wing in their sympathies, the theatres at which they were performed were funded by a Gaullist government. Under de Gaulle's minister for culture, André Malraux, large sums of money were made available to subsidize theatre, especially outside Paris. By the end of the 1960s there were more than 30 permanent subsidized theatre companies working in provincial centres. Most were dedicated to an ideal of *théâtre populaire* inherited from Copeau, but becoming increasingly politicized. The near-revolution of 1968 persuaded many of these that they had lost touch with the people whom they were trying to serve. The result was a ferment of experimentation into new performance spaces, from the circus to the street and new forms of actor–audience relationship. Cafés provided an ideal location for occasional small-scale performance; this fashion caught on and café-theatres of a more permanent kind were established. Many theatre companies now abandoned the traditional repertoire in favour of *création collective* – collaboratively devised shows, the outstanding example being the **Théâtre du Soleil**'s *1789*, performed to packed audiences in a disused Vincennes warehouse from 1971 to 1973. This play, about the first year of the French Revolution, was acted on five separate stages placed around the audience and marked the start of a decade of experiment into different actor–audience relationships: each new show by the Théâtre du Soleil involved a new arrangement of the spaces for performers and spectators. Similar experiments, emphasizing personal rather than political liberation, produced the Grand Magic Circus of **Savary** and the panic theatre movement of Arrabal, whose work was produced by the South American directors Victor García and Jorge Lavelli.

Theatre was not favoured by governments from 1968 to 1981. Many provincial directors were dismissed for their part in the events of 1968 and even the apolitical Barrault was removed from the **Odéon**. Spending on theatre was stagnant, although it continued to sustain a large body of work. In the French system the subsidy is paid straight to the director who thus has complete control of artistic policy. Influenced by the work of Italian designers, particularly those who had worked for **Strehler**, many directors have developed styles of great visual complexity. At its best, as in Chéreau's production of *La Dispute* by Marivaux, or in Planchon's productions of Racine and Molière, this produces work that is both compelling and profound, although it can also lead to productions that are scenically brilliant but intellectually vapid. The plays produced are frequently drawn from the classic repertoire. Today the major names in French theatre are no longer those of the new dramatists, nor of the star actors, but those of directors: Barrault, Planchon, Mnouchkine, **Vitez**, Chéreau, **Vincent**, Lassalle, Lavaudant. The one major institutional change of the 1970s was the transfer of the title Théâtre National Populaire to the company of Planchon and Chéreau at Villeurbanne. Some of the decentralized theatres continued to produce new work. Those at Caen and Strasbourg, for example, were among the first to promote the school of playwrights influenced by recent German-language drama, known as **Théâtre du Quotidien** and including Michel Deutsch and **Michel Vinaver**. Under Jack Lang, minister for culture in the Mitterrand government, 1981–6, large sums of money were once again injected into the arts. The decentralized theatre received incentives to encourage the performance of work by new playwrights. The massive growth of decentralized theatre since the Second World War has transformed the pattern of theatrical activity in France so that the most exciting new work is no longer available to Parisians only but to audiences throughout the country. DB

See: D. Bradby, *Modern French Drama, 1940–1980*, Cambridge, 1984; M. Carlson, *The French Stage in the nineteenth century*, Methuen, New Jersey, 1972; L. Champagne, *French Theatre Experiment since 1968*, Michigan, 1984; W. Deierkauf-Holsboer, *Histoire de la mise en scène dans le théâtre français de 1600 à 1673*, Paris, 1960; J. Guicharnaud, *Modern French Theatre from Giraudoux to Genet* (rev. ed.), New Haven, 1975; W. D. Howarth, *Sublime and Grotesque*, London, 1975; D. Knowles, *French Drama of the inter-war years 1918–1939*, London, 1967; H. C. Lancaster, *A History of French Dramatic Literature in the seventeenth century*, 9 vols., Baltimore, 1924–42; T. E. Lawrenson, *The French Stage in the seventeenth century*, Manchester, 1957; M. Lioure, *Le Drame*, Paris, 1973; M. Meisel, *Realizations*, Princeton, 1983; J. Morel, *La Tragédie*, Paris, 1964; L. Moussinac, *Le Théâtre des Origines à nos jours*, Paris, 1966; P. Peyronnet, *La Mise en scène au XVIIIe siècle*, Paris, 1974; M. Root-Bernstein, *Boulevard Theatre and Revolution in eighteenth century Paris*, Michigan, 1984; J. Scherer, *La Dramaturgie Classique en France*, Paris, 1959; A. Simon, *Dictionnaire du Théâtre Français Contemporain*, Paris, 1970; P. Voltz, *La Comédie*, Paris, 1964.

Franconi family see **Circus**

Francovich, Guillermo (1901–   ) Bolivian playwright, lawyer, university president and diplomat. In addition to numerous philosophical essays, he has written more than a dozen plays, including *Como los gansos* (*Like the Geese*, 1957), *Un puñal en la noche* (*A Dagger in the Night*, 1953), and *El monje de Potosí* (*The Monk from Potosí*, 1954). GW

Frankel, Gene (1923–   ) American director. Born in New York and educated at New York University, Frankel made his New York directing debut in 1949 with *They Shall Not Die*, followed closely in 1950 with *Nat Turner*. He received Obies for his direction of *Volpone* (1957) and *Machinal* (1960). Other important New York productions include: *The Enemy of the People* (1959); *The Blacks* (1961); *Brecht on Brecht* (1962); *The Firebugs* (1963); *A Cry of Players* (1968); *To Be Young, Gifted and Black* (1969); and *Indians* (1969). Frankel has directed *The Blacks* at the Akademie der Kunst, Berlin, and at the Teatro la Fenice, Venice (1964). His production of *Oh, Dad, Poor Dad* was seen at the Atelje 212 in Belgrade (1965). Other notable productions include *Pueblo* at the **Arena Stage** (1971), and a revival of *The Diary of Anne Frank* at the Hartman Theatre (1979). Founder of the Berkshire Theatre, Frankel is also artistic director of the Gene Frankel Theatre Workshop in New York. TLM

Fratellini Italian circus family, best-known for the '3 Fratellini', a clown act composed of brothers, sons of the acrobat Gustavo Fratellini (1842–1905). Paul (Paolo 1877–1940) was the subtle comedian, dressed as a parody of bourgeois respectability. François (Francesco 1879–1951) was the elegant white clown in his spangled costume, strumming the guitar and mandolin. Albert (Alberto, 1886–1961) played the patsy with his huge nose, fright wigs, and musical instruments that were prone to squirt water or burst into flames. The trio first formed in 1905 and settled in Paris at the Cirque Médrano and then the Cirque d'Hiver, periodically touring Europe and America. They were so successful that in 1922 they were invited to join the **Comédie-Française** as affiliates. Their descendants carry on the tradition. LS

Frayn, Michael (1933–   ) British dramatist, who began by writing amusing columns for *The Guardian* and *The Observer*, before turning his attention to the stage. While at Cambridge University, he contributed sketches to such revues as *Share My Lettuce* (1956) which transferred to London, and wrote *Zounds!* with John Edwards and the composer Keith Statham. But journalism and writing witty novels took precedence over his early theatrical enthusiasms, until in 1970 he wrote four short plays which were presented together as *The Two of Us*. His next play, *The Sandboy* (1971), was less successful, although both comedies demonstrated Frayn's instinct for funny dialogue. His true strengths, however, were not revealed until, in the mid-1970s, he wrote three comedies, *Alphabetical Order* (1975) about mayhem in a newspaper cuttings library, *Donkeys' Years* (1976) about university loves and *Clouds* (1976), two of which had long West End runs. *Clouds* was perhaps the most original, based on Frayn's experiences as a journalist on a visit to Cuba. In *Liberty Hall* (1979), Frayn is concerned with socialist-versus-capitalist perceptions, here satirizing a writers' collective established by the state at Balmoral Castle. He translated and adapted **Chekhov**'s *The Cherry Orchard* and **Tolstoi**'s *The Fruits of Enlightenment* for the **National Theatre**, but his greatest commercial success came with *Noises Off* in 1982, a backstage comedy about an appalling touring company, which opened at the **Lyric Theatre, Hammersmith**, and transferred to the West End and Broadway.   JE

Fréchette, Louis-Honoré (1839–1908) French Canadian poet, essayist and playwright, author of the most popular 19th-century Canadian play, *Félix Poutré* (1862), performed hundreds of times by amateur troupes well into the 20th century. The work draws heavily upon published memoirs of its titular hero, a participant in the 1837–8 Patriote Rebellion who feigns madness to escape the gallows, exacting delicious vengeance onstage against stereotyped representatives of British rule. When research by historians proved Poutré to have been a double agent and liar, Fréchette shunned association with the work.

Two of his other three surviving plays have been shown to be suspect in origin: *Le Retour de l'Exilé* (*The Exile's Return*, 1880), whose plot comes from a popular French novel, and *Véronica* (1903), written for a fee by the French author, Maurice de Pradel. Even his only original drama, dealing with the leader of the Patriotes, *Papineau* (1880), relies too heavily on the latter's published speeches. Only *Félix Poutré* has attracted critical and popular acclaim.   LED

Fredro, Aleksander (1793–1876) Polish dramatist who between 1815 and 1835 wrote over 20 comedies in octosyllabic rhymed couplets that have become a central part of the national repertory. Often set in pre-partition Poland, they depict the life of the landed gentry and feature lively plots and colourful, eccentric characters. Major works are *Ladies and Hussars* (1825), *Maiden Vows* (1833), *Vengeance* (1834).   DG

Freedman, Gerald (1927–) American director and producer. Born in Ohio and educated at Northwestern University, Freedman began his professional career in 1956 as an assistant for *Bells Are Ringing*, and made his New York directing debut in 1959 with the first revival of *On the Town*. In 1960 he began a long association with the **New York Shakespeare Festival** with an Obie-winning *Macbeth*, and served as artistic director from 1967–71. Other notable productions for the Festival include *Hair*, which opened the Public Theatre in 1967; and *Hamlet* in 1972, starring **Stacy Keach, James Earl Jones**, and **Colleen Dewhurst**. He was co-artistic director of the **Acting Company** from 1974–7 with acclaimed productions of *School for Scandal* (1972), and *The Robber Bridegroom* (1975) which was transferred to Broadway. In 1978–9 he was artistic director for the American Shakespeare Festival in Stratford, Conn.; and in 1985 Freedman was appointed artistic director of the Great Lakes Theatre Festival.   TLM

Fregoli, Leopoldo (1867–1936) Italian quick-change artist, who began by singing both male and female parts as an amateur actor. In 1896 he created the Fin-de-Siècle Company to present his one-man shows; it travelled round the world with a staff of 23, 370 trunks and 800 costumes until his retirement in 1925. In the course of a three-hour performance, Fregoli would perform a one-act play, taking all the roles; then present imitations of 60 well-known music-hall performers, singing, dancing, performing magic tricks, ventriloquy and hypnotism; and end by screening 10 films he had directed and starred in, the 'Fregoligraph'. Using stand-ins and dummies to effect illusions of his presence, he became synonymous with proteanism, and **Nikolai Evreinov** used his name to baptize the mercurial hero of his play *The Chief Thing* (1921).   LS

Freie Bühne (Free Stage) A society in Berlin that was stimulated in part by the foundation of the Théâtre Libre in Paris. Its purpose was to stage new plays that could not be seen, for a variety of reasons, in the repertoires of the commercial and state-subsidized theatres. Under the direction of **Otto Brahm**, the Freie Bühne staged, with professional actors, **Ibsen**'s *Ghosts* in September 1889 and the first performance of **Hauptmann**'s *Before Dawn* in October 1889. Later productions included more plays by Hauptmann and works by, among others, **Tolstoi**, **Strindberg**, and **Zola**. The Freie Bühne was dissolved in 1894 when Otto Brahm was appointed director of the **Deutsches Theater**. Here he continued to pursue his mission of producing naturalist drama, though on a more permanent basis.   SW

French, David (1939–) Probably Canada's most produced playwright. Born in Newfoundland he was raised in Toronto and began his career as an actor and writer for television. *Leaving Home* (1972), his very successful first stage play, and *Of the Fields Lately* (1973), both produced under the guidance of Bill Glassco at Toronto's **Tarragon Theatre**, explore archetypal family conflicts in the specific context of the Mercers, an 'immigrant' Newfoundland family in Toronto. French returned to the Mercers for a third work, *Salt-Water Moon* (1984). The same autobiographical impulse, but in a very different genre, lies at the base of his most widely produced and highly praised play, *Jitters* (1979), a backstage comedy which offers an affectionate view of theatrical life as it is coloured by the specific problems and insecurities of producing theatre in Canada.   JA

French-speaking Africa south of the Sahara
With the exception of Senegal, which was colonized rather earlier, the French acquired their African colonies, along with the other European states involved, mainly in the late 19th century. By the end of the First World War French authority extended in a continuous band from Cape Verde to the Congo River. From there the influence of the French language continued across the vast territory of what eventually became the Belgian Congo and then independent Zaire well into the southern hemisphere. Off the east coast of Southern Africa lay the French colony of Madagascar, with its pre-European cultural roots both in Africa and in Polynesia. When independence came in and around 1960, the continental federations of West and Equatorial Africa broke down into a series of separate states but the influence of the French language and its culture remained. The colonizer's simplistic notion that black Africa had no culture of its own before the arrival of the

European has long been replaced by a knowledge and recognition of the African culture that existed before colonial times and has to some extent managed to survive into the 1980s. This survival is fragmentary and uneven, but much of the old culture continues to be deeply rooted in the consciousness of most Africans and to influence the shaping of the new, modern culture that is emerging out of contact with the West. Traditional African culture, with its religious awareness of man's relations with his environment and the universe, has a profound sense of the theatrical which is expressed in a variety of ways, from religious and social ritual to simple entertainment.

The modern African theatre, sometimes self-consciously but often perfectly naturally, incorporates many features of the traditional drama in its forms of expression. The most common element is the role of the traditional 'griot' – the 'troubadour', musician, praise-singer and story-teller, who is the repository of the past and its wisdom as well as the commentator on whom the whole community can focus its preoccupations and anxieties. Reminiscent of the Greek chorus, the griot plays a crucial functional role in many modern African plays, those of **Cheik Ndao**, for instance, or especially, in Sory Konaké's play *Le Grand Destin de Soundjata* (*The Great Destiny of Soundjata*, 1971), in which Djeli ('griot') Madi presents the events of the play and its characters through his own narrative, in the traditional manner. Dance, and with it mime, are widespread and essential features of African life and theatre. Whether or not they are written into the play by the author, directors make great use of this medium in their productions. Because traditional dances are never arbitrary but belong to specific rituals and activities, thereby carrying with them a symbolic meaning which an audience can recognize, dances are rarely mere decoration in a modern African play but add to its texture in performance. The Bambara people of Mali have an ancient theatrical tradition called the *koteba*, which combines a style of dance which takes on the 'shape' of the spiralling shell of the snail (somehow symbolic of the mysterious movement of life itself), with mime, gesture and straightforward social comedy. The Institut National des Arts in Mali has adopted this traditional theatre as the basis of its own practice, and so too has Souleymane Koly with his Koteba Ensemble in the Ivory Coast. Many authors and directors feel that reference to traditional African theatrical principles will be essential in the creation of a true popular theatre in Africa. Language is, of course, an important feature here. There is much village drama in the vernacular languages, but writers, directors and companies that aim at wide audiences, or at tours that can take in all the many language groups that exist in most African states, realize the importance of the international language of song, dance and mime and the use of French as the only possible 'lingua franca'. But the command of French itself is still very uneven, so if a play is very dependent on dialogue, it is not likely to travel well, and as a result there is a certain type of drama that is suited only to the cities with their educated middle classes and university communities. Here and there, writers are beginning to experiment with the use of the local brand of French, generally far more widely spoken than the standard form of the language – as for example, **S. Bemba** in his play *Un*

Foutu Monde pour un Blanchisseur trop Honnête (*A Rotten World for an Over-Honest Laundryman*) – or directors will build it into their own production of a play.

It is significant that an account of pre-European theatre in Africa leads naturally into a discussion of its influence on post-independence theatre. European-style theatre began in French-speaking Africa in the early 1930s at two educational establishments almost simultaneously: the Ecole Primaire Supérieure at Bingerville in the Ivory Coast, and the Ecole Normale William Ponty, then on the island of Gorée off Dakar in Senegal. The link between the two was Charles Béart, who taught at both institutions in the 1930s, although theatrical activities had begun at the Ponty school before he arrived. He is, however, the person who gave the greatest encouragement and direction to the theatre in French-speaking Africa in these early days. The Ivory Coast owes the Ponty and Bingerville schools a particular debt of gratitude since three of the people who contributed most to the development of theatre in the Ivory Coast – François Amon d'Aby, Coffi Gadeau and **Bernard Dadié** – were students at both schools consecutively at this crucial time. The pupils of the Ponty school wrote, directed and acted in their own plays, mostly based on historical events or legends of their countries of origin, and in 1937 paid a very successful visit to Paris, where they performed at the Théâtre des Champs Elysées. The Ponty school went into decline as a centre for theatre after the Second World War and, although the French colonial authorities began to encourage the establishment of drama schools in some of the African territories and thanks to Amon d'Aby the theatre retained a certain vigour in the Ivory Coast, there was very little activity, let alone development, until the 1960s.

The establishment at this time of annual prizes for plays in a competition organized by the French broadcasting service provided a very significant fillip to playwriting at least, and to performance to some extent as well, since many of the prize-winning plays were broadcast as radio plays before, in some cases, reaching the stage proper. The second important development in this period was the establishment after independence, in several states, of institutes of the arts whose drama sections provided training in a wide variety of theatre skills, and national theatres which, alongside European plays, performed the increasing number of African plays being written. The success of these ventures depended on the willingness or ability of governments to provide adequate resources. The three countries that appear to have achieved most in this respect are Senegal, Mali and the Ivory Coast. In Senegal, the Ivory Coast, Cameroon and the Congo Popular Republic, the presence of a university institution in the capital has been a great encouragement to theatre, while in these countries and others, such as Zaire, the determination of amateurs has played a vital role in maintaining theatrical activity. Tours made by French actors, directors and academics such as J. Scherer, R. Hermantier and G. Toussaint have, from time to time, had a very positive influence on the theatre in French-speaking Africa. **Jean-Marie Serreau** made what has probably been one of the most valuable contributions to black theatre by his productions of plays by black writers and his work with black companies in Europe.

Although several plays were written, and even published (mostly in the official colonial journal *Traits d'Union*) before independence, it was only after 1960 that the number of plays available written by African authors quite suddenly began to increase. Many of these were of the highest quality and have found their way into the repertoires of companies all over French-speaking Africa. They include plays by Cheik Ndao, **G. Oyônô-Mbia**, S. Bemba, B. Dadié, Guy Menga and Jean Pliya. There are three main sets of themes (although the emphasis varies from country to country): history, conflict between traditional and modern social practices, and social and political corruption since independence. The historical plays (of which Cheik Ndao is one of the leading exponents) are largely a reaction against colonialism through the depiction of heroic figures from African legend and history; although the Ponty plays were mostly historical, they differed from the new wave of historical plays in their avoidance of criticism of colonialism. The conflict between traditional and modern social practices is, as one might expect, a rich source of comedy and satire, although tragedy or serious drama is not unusual. The plays of the best-known writer in this field, G. Oyônô-Mbia, are performed all over French-speaking Africa, and indeed in English-speaking Africa as well since he provides his own English versions of his work. This genre is likely to be the most endurable, since it transcends historical periods and expresses the African's experience of Europe at its most profound and, in spite of the comedy, at its most traumatic level. Dissatisfaction with the social, administrative and political corruption of post-independence governments has encouraged a flourishing industry in satirical plays and tragedies on this theme. Although there are some good illustrations of this genre, it is not one that produces many really successful plays from the theatrical point of view; but they will continue to be written and, if they can get past the censor, to be performed and published for so long as Africa is unable to resolve its problems of government. CW

See: M. Banham with C. Wake, *African Theatre Today*, London, 1976; D. S. Blair, *African Literature in French*, London, 1976; R. Cornevin, *Le Théâtre en Afrique Noire et à Madagascar*, Paris, 1970; U. Edebiri, 'The Development of Theatre in French-speaking West Africa', *Theatre Research International*, vol. 9, no. 3, Autumn 1984, pp. 168–80; M. Schipper, 'Traditional Themes and Techniques in African Theatre and "Francophonie"', *Theatre Research International*, vol. 9, no. 3, Autumn 1984, pp. 215–31; B. Traoré, *Le Théâtre Négro-africain et ses fonctions sociales*, Paris, 1958; G. Warner, 'The Use of Historical Sources in Francophone African Theatre', *Theatre Research International*, vol. 9, no. 3, Autumn 1984, pp. 180–94; H. A. Waters, *Black Theater in French. A Guide*, Sherbrooke, 1978; 'Black French Theatre Up-date', *World Literature Today*, vol. 57, no. 1, Winter 1983, pp. 43–8; 'Black French Theatre in the Eighties', *Theatre Research International*, vol. 9, no. 3, Autumn 1984, pp. 195–215.

French-speaking North Africa

French-speaking North Africa Algeria, Morocco and Tunisia are all Muslim countries and, in spite of the complex vicissitudes of Mediterranean history, have been so since the Arab conquest of North Africa in the 7th and 8th centuries. The dominant European influence – most profoundly effective in Algeria – is that of France which, starting with the annexation of Algeria in 1830, eventually brought Tunisia (1883) and most of Morocco (1912) under its control as well as protectorates. The resistance to the French occupation was as unrelenting as it had been to the conquest and led to independence for Morocco and Tunisia in 1956 and, after a violent eight-year-long war of independence, for Algeria in 1962.

It has not been easy for theatre to flourish in these three countries. The Muslim tradition gave it little encouragement. French censorship was always ready to suppress criticism of the colonial authority. Theatre tended to come therefore largely from outside the region. In the 19th century shadow theatre from Turkey was popular. Theatre companies from Egypt visited from time to time and after the First World War gave a significant impetus to the development of modern Moroccan literature, albeit mainly in genres other than drama. Visiting French theatre companies, although often of a high quality, provided entertainment chiefly for French expatriates (or citizens, in the case of Algeria) and the French-speaking Arab elite; their offerings were almost by definition drawn from the Parisian boulevard theatres. Since independence, there has been more indigenous activity, especially in Algeria. National Theatres have been established in Algeria and Tunisia, not without difficulty. All three countries were well represented in the drama section of the 1969 Pan-African Festival, which was held in Algiers. The Moroccan entry won the third prize with a play by Ahmed Taïeb El Alj entitled *Les Moutons Répètent* (*The Sheep Rehearse*), which dealt with the theme of oppression through the medium of a fable. The Algerian entry, *Rouge l'Aube* (*Red the Dawn*), by Assia Djebar and Walid Garn, was directed by Mustapha Kateb, who has had an important influence on the development of post-independence theatre in North Africa. In addition to the difficulties created in pre-independence North Africa by religious and political restrictions, the development of the theatre has also been hampered, even into the present, by the firm hold of classical Arabic on literary production and the barrier to communication with the ordinary people that this causes. This is particularly harmful to the spread of theatre. Algeria did, however, have the major advantage of the work of Rachid Ksentini who, between the wars, wrote and directed plays in spoken Arabic with considerable success. Directors and writers committed to the nationalist movement before independence realized the importance of Ksentini's work for the development of a people's theatre after independence. His ideas were adopted by Bachtarzi Mahiedine and Mustapha Kateb in particular; as directors of the Conservatoire Municipal d'Alger and the Théâtre National Algérien respectively they were both in a very good position to exercise real influence. Mahiedine has also written plays which have been performed before enthusiastic audiences of workers, traders and women. They include *El Keddaïnes* (*The Traitors*), *Beni-oui-oui* (*The Yes-man*) and *Faqo* (*They Have Awoken*), as well as adaptations of **Molière**, which are always popular: *El Mech-hak* (*The Miser*), *Sliman Ellouk* (*The Hypochondriac*).

The French-speaking Algerian playwright and novelist **Kateb Yacine** (b. 1929) is well known in France where he has in the past more than once fallen foul of the authorities and French public opinion for his realistic and frank attacks on French colonialism in North Africa. His first play, *Le Cadavre Encerclé* (*The Encircled Corpse*, 1958), was directed by **Jean-Marie Serreau** and performed in Brussels after it nearly provoked a riot in Paris. Jean-Marie Serreau directed another of his plays, *Les Ancêtres Redoublent de Férocité* (*The Ancestors Redouble their Ferocity*), published under the title *La Femme Sauvage* (*The Savage Woman*); it was produced at the **Théâtre National Populaire** in Lyon, where once again there was a strong reaction from the French. Along with a third play, *La Poudre d'Intelligence* (*The Powder of Intelligence*), these plays have been published together in a volume entitled *Le Cercle des Représailles* (*The Circle of Reprisals*). *L'Homme aux Sandales de Caoutchouc* (*The Man in Rubber Sandals*) appeared in 1971, and also in the early 1970s an Algerian company presented his bilingual comedy about immigrant life in France, *Mohamed, Prends ta Valise* (*Mohamed, Take your Suitcase*), to immigrant audiences in Paris. Yacine's often violent language and style is as much that of the poet as the dramatist, and his theatre, like his novels, offers a vision of human behaviour which is far more nuanced than the simple portraits of political theatre. CW

Freytag, Gustav (1816–95) German playwright, novelist, and theorist. A writer of liberal sympathies, in his day Freytag was very widely read. His play *The Journalists* (1854), a genial comedy about the interrelationship of journalism and politics, was immensely popular and is still occasionally revived today. In his influential essay *The Technique of Drama* (1865), Freytag constructed a famous model by which each play was described as being structured like a pyramid; in essence, this was a refinement of the theory of the well-made play. SW

Friedman, Bruce Jay (1930–) American playwright. Born in the Bronx, educated at the University of Missouri, and primarily known as a writer of novels filled with his own particular brand of black humour, Friedman has ventured his talents into the theatre only twice. His first effort, *Scuba Duba* (1967), won the Obie Award for the outstanding Off-Broadway production of the season. Some critics have called this zany, jaundiced look at Jewish intellectual liberalism one of the best comedies of the decade. Friedman's other play, *Steambath* (1970), was an absurd comedy set in a steam room, later identified as Limbo, featuring God, personified by a Puerto Rican steambath attendant. Friedman was also one of the several contributors of sketches for *Oh, Calcutta!* (1969). LDC

Friel, Brian (1929–) Irish playwright. Teaching in Derry (1950–60), Friel began writing short stories, mainly for the *New Yorker*, and radio plays for the BBC. The earliest play he regards with any favour is *The Enemy Within* (**Abbey** 1962), based on the exiles of St Columba. *Philadelphia, Here I Come!* brought his first wide recognition. It played at the 1964 **Dublin Theatre Festival**, continuing to a long Broadway run.

The territory of Friel's short stories stretches from Co. Tyrone to west Donegal. For all their humour and devastating satire of Irish cant, their tone is elegiac, commemorating the solace of illusions that do not wholly deceive, a moment that may enshrine a whole relationship. Friel's plays inhabit the same region.

Since 1964 Friel has written the most impressive body of work in contemporary Irish drama. Its variety, taking on new strengths since the late seventies, is to be seen in *Philadelphia, Lovers* (1967), *Crystal and Fox* (1968), *The Freedom of the City* (1973), *Aristocrats* (1979), *Faith Healer* (1979), *Translations* (1980), *The Communication Cord* (1982). While they constitute a pattern, it is re-cast by each succeeding play.

The figments of memory have always absorbed Friel. In *Philadelphia*, Gar's 'Public' and 'Private' voices interrogate the past – his father, dead mother, lost sweetheart – which has brought him to the eve of exile. Fox, in *Crystal*, destroys his pitiable travelling show for a past which, if it ever existed, is irrecoverable. In *Aristocrats*, Casimir's fables of the Catholic Big House of his childhood collapse into the ruin of its decline confirmed.

'But that's another story', says Frank Harvey, faith healer, early in the play. Its boldly demanding form consists of four monologues, modulating with total assurance from comedy to grief and loss, an equivocal reconstruction of Frank's career, a parable of the artist's capricious powers. A wider loss informs *Translations*, that of the old Gaelic culture, its dissolution reinforced by the naming into English of the Irish place-names in the 1833 ordnance survey; and mirrored in the love between an Irish girl and an English soldier. All the Irish characters speak Irish and are assumed to be doing so on stage, where in fact they speak English, a richly effective illusion. That tragic scene is then farcically parodied in *The Communication Cord*, in the coarsened inheritance of a 'restored' peasant cottage. These are in a sense political plays, but like *The Freedom of the City*, set in the present-day violence, they compose a metaphor of individuals caught in a fragmenting society.

While working in the essentially realist proscenium stage, Friel's plays question its conventions: by Gar's double presence on stage in *Philadelphia*, the play-within-the-play in *Crystal*, by the linguistic fiction of *Translations*; and by their command of a dramatic language which perfectly represents the various 'realities' professed by the characters.

In 1980, Friel founded the Field Day Theatre Company in Derry. It has presented his own plays, assembling a company for each of its annual seasons, and more recently translations of **Molière** and **Sophocles** by the Northern Irish poets Derek Mahon and Tom Paulin. Its aim is to encourage the regional idiom within which Friel's drama has found its generalizing power. Most recently (1987) Friel has written an adaptation of **Turgenev**'s *Fathers and Sons*. DM

Fringe theatre A movement which began in the 1960s in Britain and corresponds to the Off-Off Broadway theatres in New York and to the 'free theatre' groups in Europe. Although London has a long tradition of adventurous little theatres, fringe theatre developed from the many small companies which gathered around the main festival offerings at the **Edinburgh Festival**. The term came into use in the late 1950s and the revue, *Beyond the Fringe*, was first seen in 1960 in Edinburgh before transferring to London and New York. In 1963, Jim Haynes, an American bookseller, started the **Traverse Theatre** Club in Edinburgh which became the unlikely centre for many small groups from America and Europe, including such companies as the **La Mama** troupe, **Grotowski**'s 13 Rows from Opole and, later, **Szajna**'s Studio Theatre from Warsaw. The Traverse Theatre received state support and a new theatre in 1969, but Haynes was less successful in establishing his Arts Laboratory in London. Another American, **Charles Marowitz**, who with **Peter Brook** ran the Theatre of Cruelty season at LAMDA's little theatre in 1964, opened his Open Space Theatre in Tottenham Court Road in 1968; and by then, the fringe theatre movement had become a major force in British theatre, developing not just in Edinburgh and London but in studios around the country, sometimes attached to repertory theatres but often just in back rooms of pubs or even converted garages.

Much fringe theatre has its origins in political protest movements, notably against the war in Vietnam. In the 1960s, the 'hippy' and 'flower power' movements, led by Julian Beck's **Living Theatre**, were primarily American in origin, although they had many imitators in Britain. After 1968, and the May events in Paris, many young British writers, including **David Hare**, **Howard Brenton** and **David Edgar**, turned to fringe theatre companies to present left-wing agit-prop plays. Not all fringe theatre, however, was political. In small theatre clubs, such as the Ambiance and the Almost Free, various kinds of experimentalism could be attempted which might otherwise have fallen foul of the censor, theatrical censorship only being abolished in 1968. Improvisatory drama, environmental theatre, plays with strong sexual impact or sometimes violent spectacles were staged in clubs to avoid the restrictions of the law. Companies like The People Show, which started in 1966, developed a powerful imagistic language of their own.

At first fringe theatres were unsubsidised, although by the early 1970s many had started to receive small subsidies. The financial crisis in 1973–4 caused many companies to close, while the better established fringe theatres survived. Of these, the **Bush Theatre** and the King's Head, Islington, became 'new plays' theatres, encouraging unknown writers. The touring fringe companies which survived included the left-wing 7:84 and Red Ladder Companies, while Shared Experience, under its director Mike Alfreds, turned the limitations of non-theatrical halls to their advantage, establishing a remarkable rapport with their audiences. The daring adventurousness of fringe theatres, the secret of their attraction in the 1960s, became less wild in the late 1970s, although the standards of production undoubtedly rose. It ceased to be polite to describe them as 'fringe', for most companies preferred the word 'alternative'. They regarded themselves as being different from mainstream theatre but not on its edges. JE

Frisch, Max (1911–91) Swiss playwright, novelist and essayist. Born in Zurich, son of an architect. Studied, briefly, German at Zurich University in 1931, but abandoned course to travel extensively across Europe. Returned to read architecture (1936–41). After graduation, he opened his architect's office where he worked until 1954. His major project was a large municipal swimming pool (Zurich, 1948). He started writing seriously (novels, diaries) in his early 20s, but his first play dates from 1945: *Santa Cruz* (staged in 1946). His second play, *Now They Are Singing Again*

(1945), was the first to be seen: it deals with the problem of individual guilt in war, the dichotomy of spirit and power. *The Great Wall of China* (1946) is a 'farce of the incommensurable', a structurally complex 'parody of consciousness' in which the contemporary (Swiss) intellectual comes face to face with totalitarianism in the wake of Hiroshima and Nagasaki. *When the War Was Over* (1949) and *Count Oderland* (1951) are two transitional plays. *Don Juan or The Love of Geometry* (1953) is an ironic comment on the mythical character treated as an anti-hero and a playful study of the relationship between fiction and reality. His Don Juan, yet another intellectual, refuses at first to wear the mask, thus unmasking the hypocrisy of bourgeois society, until the mask is forced upon him and willingly accepted by him: Don Juan renouncing his individuality sinks into the comfort of conformity. Frisch's two most important and successful plays are harsh and uncompromising indictments of Swiss mentality and Swiss blindness to the world outside. *The Fire Raisers* (*Biedermann und die Brandstifter*, 1958), a Brechtian parable or, according to Frisch, 'a morality without a moral', brought him international recognition. Biedermann, a complacent owner-occupier, worried about his property because of a recent series of crimes of arson in the neighbourhood, not only invites two 'tramps' to settle in his attic, but also stocks them with petrol and finally gives them the matches to set his house alight. Beyond the deliberately grotesque situation itself, the most powerful theatrical ingredient is language: the disaster stems from 'the continual discrepancy between phraseology and reality'. *Andorra* (1961) proved to be Frisch's most contentious play, critically and politically, as it concerns the growth and explosion of anti-Semitism in a small peaceful and peace-loving country. *Philipp Hotz's Fury* (1958), *Biography* (1968) and *Triptych* (1979) continue, in their various styles, the charting of the clash between the individual and society and the questioning of the position of man in the world. Frisch received many literary prizes and academic awards in Switzerland, Germany, Israel and the USA. cls

Frohman, Charles (1860–1915) American producer, theatrical manager. After a decade in theatrical business in various capacities, Frohman achieved his first major success as a producer in 1889 with **Bronson Howard**'s *Shenandoah*. In 1893 Frohman formed the **Empire Theatre** Stock Company with **John Drew** as his leading actor. Frohman now began to develop and exploit the 'star and combination' system. Members of his company would be made 'stars' as quickly as possible and sent, with a supporting cast, on national tours after opening in a Frohman theatre in New York. Frohman successfully employed similar methods in London, principally at the Duke of York Theatre after 1898. Stars who benefited from Frohman's patronage included **Maude Adams**, **William Gillette**, **Arnold Daly**, **Annie Russell**, **Ethel Barrymore**, **Margaret Anglin**, **Julia Marlowe**, John Drew, **William H. Crane**, **Otis Skinner**, and many others. In 1896 he joined in association with Al Hayman, Abe Erlanger, and Mark Klaw and Fred Zimmerman to organize a monopoly known as the **Theatrical Syndicate**. With the security and efficiency afforded by such control, Frohman produced many contemporary playwrights and helped many aspiring actors to achieve stardom giving him significant influence in matters of taste and method in the commercial theatre. After 1896 he regularly produced over a dozen shows a year including **Wilde**'s *The Importance of Being Earnest* (1895), Gillette's *Secret Service* (1896 in New York, 1897 in London, 1900 in Paris), **Barrie**'s *The Little Minister* (1896 in New York, with Maude Adams), **Clyde Fitch**'s *Barbara Frietchie* (1899, with Julia Marlowe), and Barrie's *Peter Pan* (1899 in New York with Maude Adams, 1904 in London). Frohman died with the sinking of the *Lusitania* in 1915. MR DJW

Frohman, Daniel (1851–1940) American theatre manager. With his brothers, **Charles** and Gustave, Frohman first came to prominence as business manager in 1880 with **Steele MacKaye**'s organization at the **Madison Square Theatre** where he developed the system of 'auxiliary road companies' which toured the country while the original production was playing in New York. Frohman should be noted for his tenure as the producer–manager of the old **Lyceum Theatre** at 4th Avenue and its stock company from 1887 to 1902, and in the new Lyceum on 45th Street from 1902 until his retirement in 1909. Enlisting the talents of a fine acting company from which **E. H. Sothern**'s career was launched and that over the years included **Henry Miller**, **William Faversham**, Effie Shannon, **Richard Mansfield**, **Maude Adams**, and **James H. Hackett**, Frohman presented a fashionable repertory from contemporary authors including **Clyde Fitch**, **J. M. Barrie**, **Pinero**, **Henry Arthur Jones**, **Wilde**, and **Sardou**. Notable productions which featured Sothern included *Lord Chumley* (1888), *The Charity Ball* (1889), and *The Prisoner of Zenda* (1895). The elaborate new Lyceum opened with Barrie's *The Admirable Crichton*. In 1899, Frohman began a four-year term as manager and lessee of **Daly's Theatre** where he imported many musical comedies from London. Frohman served as president of the Actor's Fund from 1903 until his death in 1940. Through his association with the Famous Players–Lasky Film Company after 1912, he brought many theatre stars to the infant film industry. MR

Frontier theatre (USA) Just as the frontier has been described as the single most distinguished feature of American history, it also left a distinguishing mark on American theatre history. Theatre in America began in the early settlements on the eastern seaboard, the frontier of the New World; and after Philadelphia, New York, and Boston became theatrical centres, troupes of actors advanced into the western regions quick on the heels of the pioneers.

The first theatre opened in Williamsburg (Virginia) in 1718, the second, the Dock Street in Charleston (South Carolina), in 1736, and when the **Lewis Hallam** company arrived from London in 1752 they performed in a new Williamsburg theatre. The Hallams and other troupes took to the road, found makeshift halls in such settlements as Annapolis, Norfolk, Newport and Providence, and set the pattern for the western trek that was soon to follow.

Thespian societies were a part of the cultural life of Lexington (1799), Cincinnati (1801), and St Louis (1815), even before professional troupes arrived. These troupes began their journey from Albany or Philadelphia to Pittsburgh and thence by flat boat down the Ohio River to Cincinnati and Louisville, and, as the frontier expanded, down the Mississippi to St Louis, Memphis, Nashville, Montgomery, Mobile, and New Orleans.

The James Douglass troupe arrived in Lexington, Louisville, and Frankfort in 1810 and the **Samuel Drake** company in 1815. Typical of the accommodation they found was Luke Usher's Lexington theatre, a large room (30 by 60 feet) on the second floor of his brewery. Two actors in Drake's company, **Noah Ludlow** and **Sol Smith**, became the leading managers on the frontier, first as competitors and then as partners and both wrote detailed first-hand accounts of their adventures: *Dramatic Life as I Found It* (1880, Ludlow) and *The Theatrical Journey* (1854) and *Theatrical Management in the South and West* (1868, Smith).

Cramped and improvised quarters were common: a stage ten feet wide and eight feet deep, a Memphis theatre where only the women could be seated, another that had formerly been a livery stable. Even proper theatres like the Columbia Street in Cincinnati (1821) boasting a 'spacious gallery', 'commodious lobbies', and 'two tiers of boxes', squeezed the stage and 800 spectators into a small area (40 by 100 feet). **James H. Caldwell** was the first to provide adequate facilities with his three New Orleans theatres: the **American** or Camp Street (1824), the **St Charles** (1835), and a second St Charles (1843). The Camp seated 1,100 on stuffed seats, had a proscenium opening of 38 feet, and was lighted with gas (Caldwell owned the gas works). The St Charles (said to be equalled in size and grandeur only by the opera houses in Naples, Milan, and St Petersburg) seated 4,000 in a pit and had four tiers of boxes. It had a 55-foot proscenium opening and a central chandelier with 23,000 cutglass drops lighted by 250 gas jets. When the theatre burned down (1842, a common occurrence), Caldwell built a second St Charles (1843), less ornate and seating 1,500, and turned the management over to Ludlow and Smith.

Frontier theatres were not all land-based. Showboating on the Ohio and Mississippi began early and continued into the 20th century. First with Ludlow's 'Noah's Ark' (1817), then with William Chapman's 'Floating Palace' (1831). **Showboats** lured audiences with their calliopes and their picturesque names: 'French's New Sensation', 'Snow Queen', 'Wonderland', 'Goldenrod', 'Cotton Blossom', and 'Majestic'.

Theatres appeared almost immediately after a community was settled. In Chicago: John B. Rice's first theatre (1847), his second (1851), and **McVicker's** (1857). The California miners who had struck gold in 1848 were well supplied: the Eagle in Sacramento (1849), Maguire's Opera House in Virginia City (1850), his first Jenny Lind in San Francisco (1850), his second in 1851 (both were destroyed by fire), his third (1851), and his Metropolitan (1853). In the early fifties there were a dozen theatre and music halls in San Francisco. The Mormons, always theatre enthusiasts, built an elegant Salt Lake Theatre (1861, said to have cost 100,000 dollars) shortly after they settled in Utah.

The provincial companies who opened the frontier were quickly followed by the star players from New York and Philadelphia: **J. B. Booth**, **Edwin Forrest**, **William Macready**, **Edwin Booth**, **Anna Cora**

Mowatt, **Joseph Jefferson**, **Laura Keene**, Tyrone Power, **Lotte Crabtree**, **Adah Isaacs Menken**, **James Murdoch**, **George Hill**, **Dan Marble**, **John McCullough**, *et al.* Both the early and later players ranged over a wide repertoire: **Shakespeare**, the standard British plays, the American plays of **Dunlap**, **Payne**, Mowatt, and **Bird**, and most frequently, the latest sentimental and spectacular melodramas. RM

Fry, Christopher (1907–) British playwright. His charming and witty verse plays of the 1940s and 1950s – *A Phoenix Too Frequent* (1946), *The Lady's Not for Burning* (1948), *Venus Observed* (1950) and *The Dark is Light Enough* (1954) – were gentle successes that touched upon real concerns via unreal situations. Fry's view of mankind is marked by a tolerant Christianity that has sometimes made his plays unfashionable, especially as the poetic form is of rather specialized appeal. His translation of **Anouilh**'s *L'Invitation au Château* (*Ring Round the Moon*, 1950) and *L'Alouette* (*The Lark*, 1955) and plays by **Giraudoux**, **Ibsen** and **Rostand** offered his skill with words more substantial plots. MB

Fuchs, Georg (1868–1949) German director. Influenced by **Jocza Savits**'s experiments with the Shakespeare-stage in the Munich Court Theatre, in 1908 Fuchs founded the Munich Artists' Theatre. This had a relief stage, on which no attempt was made to create a realistic illusion. Fuchs's ambitions for the theatre are to be found in his most frequently read book, *Revolution in the Theatre*. SW

Fugard, Athol (1932–) South African playwright. Born in Middelburg, Cape Province, of an Afrikaans mother and an English father, he studied philosophy and anthropology at the University of Cape Town. After periods of diverse employment – including two years as a merchant seaman and a short period as a stage manager for South Africa's National Theatre Organization – he settled into a career as a playwright in the late 1950s. His plays are written in English but incorporate many regional dialects and slang derived from the vernaculars. His first plays and a novel (*Tsotsi*) were written from 1958 to 1960 while Fugard associated with black writers and intellectuals in the freehold suburb of Sophiatown in Johannesburg. In the mid-1960s he wrote what are often referred to as 'the family plays' – including *The Blood Knot* (1961), *Hello and Goodbye* (1965) and *Boesman and Lena* (1969) – about the effects of South Africa's laws and social attitudes on working-class people of different races. In the early 1970s he worked through improvisation with actors to create what are referred to as 'the workshop plays', like *Sizwe Bansi is Dead* (1972) and *Statements After an Arrest under the Immorality Act* (1972). In the second half of the decade he began writing alone again, and this period produced plays like *Master Harold. . . and the Boys* (1982) and *The Road to Mecca* (1984). His plays are permeated by the South African political context, but Fugard maintains that he is simply a 'regional' writer, and that his concern is with individual loneliness and pain in specific situations: politics, he suggests, is merely the background. But by the 1990s Fugard had chosen to grapple more directly than ever before with the realities of South African politics, and his play *My Children! My Africa!* (1990) dramatized the political implications of a rapidly changing apartheid society. With the opening up of the society in the 1990s, it is unlikely that political matters will be entirely absent from Fugard's theatre. Castigated by some for being a white liberal out of touch with the realities of black suffering and resistance, Fugard nevertheless successfully dramatizes the effects of the political system of South Africa upon its diverse peoples. IS

Fulda, Ludwig (1862–1939) German playwright. As a young man, Fulda was closely associated with the naturalist movement. His later plays were in verse. SW

Fuller, Charles (1939–) Afro-American playwright. When *A Soldier's Play* (1981) dealing with the murder of an unpopular black army sergeant received the Pulitzer Prize, Fuller was only the second black playwright to be so honoured. Philadelphia-born Fuller had several plays produced Off-Broadway, notably by the **Negro Ensemble Company** that nurtured his talent with productions of *In the Deepest Part of Sleep* (1974), *The Brownsville Raid* (1976), the Obie Award-winning *Zooman and the Sign* (1980), as well as *A Soldier's Play*. Although this play received fine ensemble acting and a strongly favourable press, black opinion had been reserved, holding that the play's resolution was cleverly contrived to appease white sensitivities. EGH

Fuller, Isaac (1606–72) English scene-painter. A successful painter of portraits in the 1650s and 1660s, Fuller contracted with the King's Company in 1669 to paint 'a new scene of Elysium' for their production of **Dryden**'s *Tyrannic Love*, agreeing to complete it in two weeks. It took much longer and the company sued him for £500 for the delay. He claimed he worked nonstop on it for three weeks and was awarded £325, 10s. as payment for the work. The case demonstrates the colossal expenditure on sets for the Restoration stage. PH

Funambules, Théâtre des (Paris) As the name indicates, this theatre was licensed only for rope-dancing and acrobatics when it opened in the Boulevard du Temple in 1813. Two years later it was allowed to stage harlequinades, provided that no word was spoken. It was still more a showbooth than a playhouse when it was taken over by Nicolas Michel Bertrand, who put on topical farces and pantomimes centred around **Harlequin** as played by Bambochinet. The young, unknown **Frédérick Lemaître** appeared there, as did **Mme Saqui** the rope-dancer. **Jean-Gaspard Deburau** joined around 1820 and soon his pale-faced **Pierrot** was attracting huge crowds. After the 1830 Revolution, Bertrand was enabled to add *vaudevilles* to his bill and rapidly became a millionaire.

The 500-seat theatre boasted a well-trapped stage that could accomplish instantaneous scene changes; since there were no intervals (the proletarian public got too restless), an average of 15 changes took place in two hours. Bertrand's nephew Billion expanded the house to 773 seats but raised prices as well. When the popular Deburau died in 1846, he was succeeded by his son Charles and by Paul Legrand. The theatre was demolished in 1860 to make way for Baron Hauss-mann's 'improvements', but by that time it had become legendary as a temple of fantasy for the Parisian populace.   LS

Furttenbach, Josef (1591–1667) German architect and scene designer. Having studied architecture and theatre design in Italy, he absorbed the ideas utilized by **Giulio Parigi** and took them back to Germany. In 1631 he became municipal architect at Ulm and ten years later he designed and completed the city's Theater am Benderhof, which was used primarily for school performances. His designs are noted for their reliance upon a central vanishing point, *periaktoi*, a rear pit for the housing of special effects, and pictorial bow-shaped framing devices. He published several works on Italian architecture: *Civil Architecture* (1628) which only touched on theatre architecture and design; *Recreational Architecture* (1640) which illustrates *periaktoi*, cloud borders, flying machines, and the chariot-and-pole mechanism for shifting scenery; and *The Noble Mirror of Art* (1663). The importance of these works is that they preserve and illustrate in great detail both the function and construction of scene changing devices and stage machinery used in the Italian baroque theatre.   AJN

Futurism An artistic movement primarily of the second and third decades of the 20th century. Founded by **F. T. Marinetti** in 1909, the ideas and strategies of the futurists were rapidly diffused through manifestos, journals, exhibitions, and the so-called 'futurist even-ings'. The movement falls roughly into two phases, the first and most vigorous dating from Marinetti's 'The Founding and Manifesto of Futurism', published in the Paris *Le Figaro*, 20 February 1909, through to the early 1920s; the second during the period of Fascism when it was little more than a nominal avant-garde. Asserting an aesthetic of the 'new', and calling for an art attuned to the century of science and technology, futurism exalted what it claimed to be the essential characteristics of 'modernism': speed, movement, dynamism and spontaneity. It rejoiced in the machine – particularly in the motor car, aeroplane, speed boat and motor–cycle – and demanded a machine-age art. To achieve this it ruthlessly jettisoned the past, stridently denouncing most received artistic traditions, along with the confor-mism and academicism of museums, art galleries, concert halls and the regular 'prose' and 'musical' theatre.

Theatricality was of its essence, and the movement quickly developed a futurist theatre: the highly conten-tious 'futurist evenings' included readings, displays of painting and sculptures, and presentations of futurist performance 'works'. The presentations were deliber-ately calculated to provoke the verbal and physical wrath of audiences. Although they rejected most traditional forms of theatre, futurist practitioners recognized that their techniques had much in common with popular café and variety entertainment, as Mar-inetti acknowledged in his important manifesto *Teatro di Varietà* (*The Variety Theatre*, 1913).

A distinct advance came with the synthesis proposed in *Il Teatro Sintetico Futurista* (*The Synthetic Theatre*, 1915). Syntheses were highly compressed dramatic pieces, intended to be demonstrations of that dynamic, autonomous, alogical, anti-psychological, abstract theatre and the futurists advocated as an ideal. The movement produced about 500 such syntheses, the best of which are more than mere musical gags and pat cabaret sketches, and anticipate certain themes and motives developed later by surrealist and absurdist theatre, and by dramatists like **Pirandello** and **Beck-ett**. It inspired too some notable scenic design work, major figures in this field including the sculptor Giacomo Balla, the designer Fortunato Depero and the painter, and one of the leading theorists of the move-ment, **Enrico Prampolini**. Futurist staging sought a dynamic use of chromatic effects in which the role of the human was either absent altogether or relegated to a robotic-like function. An impressive example of futur-ist scenic design is that of Balla for Stravinsky's *Feu d'Artifice* (1917), but most futurist scenic projects were never realized on the stage.

Marinetti early proposed the use of revolves to achieve that synthesis of activities and effects that should characterize futurist presentations. But as Prampolini later admitted, the movement lacked mechanical means, just as it lacked performers of skill, and an air of the amateurish invariably enveloped the theatre work it actually succeeded in mount-ing.   KR LR

Fuzelier, Louis (1672–1752) French playwright and librettist, a prolific author of comedies, comic operas, *vaudevilles*, 'ballet-pantomimes' and other *divertisse-ments*, many of them parodies of existing works and totalling almost 200 in all. Apart from certain more formal works performed at the **Comédie-Française** or the Opéra, the vast majority were written for the **Comédie-Italienne** or for the Paris fair theatres where they were subject to an injunction outlawing spoken dialogue, imposed by the Parlement at the instance of jealous actors of the legitimate stage. Accordingly the text was either set to music and sung or delivered in successives monologues or again, in the so-called 'pièces à écriteaux', written on hand-held scrolls and on placards suspended from the flies, to which the actors mimed and the orchestra supplied a musical accom-paniment of familiar airs enabling the audience to join in. Fuzelier frequently collaborated with other play-wrights (notably Panard, d'Orneval and **Lesage**) or composers (Gilliers, J. B. Quinault, Rameau and Campra) and wrote on theatrical topics in the weekly *Mercure de France*, which he co-edited for several years in the 1720s and 1740s.   DR

G

Gabrielli Family of Italian actors. **Giovanni** (d. between 1603 and 1611), under the name Sivello, excelled at solo pantomimes in which he presented a whole troupe of characters. His son **Francesco** (?1588–?1636), who amplified the **zanni** Scapino, toured Italy and France from 1612, mostly with the **Accesi** and **Confidenti**, though he was with the **Fedeli** under **G. B. Andreini** in Paris 1624–5. Accomplished at a dozen instruments, he was noted for virtuoso musical numbers. His daughter **Giulia** was seen in Paris under the name Diana in 1645. Girolamo Gabrielli, a famous Pantalone, and Ippolita Gabrielli, who was managing a troupe in 1663, may or may not be his children. LS

Gag Originally, words interpolated by an actor into his part. The term derived from *gag* as something forced into the mouth and was current theatrical slang in the 1840s. **Dickens** uses it in *Bleak House* (1852). It came to mean a comic improvisation, and then, in silent film, a surprising or unmotivated wrinkle in the plot, often an elaborately structured piece of physical comedy. Now it is used to designate any joke or creative inspiration ('What's the gag?'). LS

Gaiety Theatre (London) Opened in 1868 on the site of the Strand Music-Hall by **John Hollingshead**. It established a reputation for burlesque, comic opera with the first collaboration of **Gilbert** and Sullivan, *Thespis* (1871), and then musical comedy after *In Town* (1892: generally considered the first of this genre), which survived the move to a new building in 1903 and continued until the theatre closed in 1939. Its initial popularity was partly due to a famous 'quartette' of comedians – **Nellie Farren, E. W. Royce, Edward Terry** and **Kate Vaughan** – then during the 1890s to the 'Gaiety Girls'. These were initially introduced in a parody form as part of *Ruy Blas; or, the Blasé Roué* (1889), a burlesque which featured C. Danby, **Fred Leslie**, Ben Nathan and Fred Story as ballerinas made up to resemble the actor-managers **Henry Irving, John Toole, Wilson Barrett** and **Edward Terry**. But the name came to refer to the musical chorus line of the 1890s, who were selected as much for their legs and looks as their singing and dancing ability. Among the later stars who made their name at the Gaiety, the best known were Gertie Millar and Leslie Henson. After standing empty for almost 20 years, the theatre was demolished in 1957. CI

Gaiety Theatre (Manchester, England) Built in 1884, the theatre achieved fame with the establishment there in 1908 of **Miss Horniman**'s repertory company – marking the beginning of the British repertory movement. Miss Horniman rebuilt and refurbished the theatre interior and reduced its seating from 2,500 to a more comfortable 1,250. The first full season set the pattern for the next six years, offering plays by (among others) **Euripides, Shaw** and **Galsworthy** and some one-act plays by Lancashire writers Allan Monkhouse, **Stanley Houghton** and **Harold Brighouse** – the core of what was later to be known as the 'Manchester school'. The Gaiety under the artistic direction of **Ben Iden Payne** and then **Lewis Casson** soon built a reputation for its ensemble playing and its fostering of new writing, boosted further by a series of London seasons and tours to Canada and the USA. Success however brought its own penalties: the company over-extended itself and standards became inconsistent. During wartime the theatre's quality of output and its audiences declined, until in 1917 the company was disbanded. The theatre became a minor touring house until Miss Horniman sold it in 1920. Thereafter it served as a cinema until finally demolished in 1952. AJ

Galich, Manuel (1913–84) Guatemalan playwright, born to a theatrical family, he studied law at the University of Guatemala, directed an experimental theatre group (1938–42), participated as a young revolutionary against Ubico. Subsequently Minister of Education under Arévalo, Minister of Foreign Affairs under Arbenz, and Guatemala's ambassador to Argentina. His early plays were both historical and costumbristic, but his principal thrust was anti-imperialistic, political theatre. Major titles are *El tren amarillo* (*The Yellow Train*, 1954), *El pescado indigesto* (*The Undigested Fish*, 1960) and *Míster John Tenor y yo* (*Mr John Tenor and I*, 1975). Attracted by the Castro Revolution, he played a major role in the development of Revolutionary theatre in Cuba and served from 1964 to 1984 as the general editor of the theatre journal *Conjunto*. GW

Galimafre see **Bobeche**

Gallegos, Daniel (1930–) Costa Rican playwright, director, professor and actor. Educated at home and abroad (USA and Europe), Gallegos was a major influence in the development of the Costa Rican theatre as director of the Teatro Universitario and professor at the University of Costa Rica. His major plays are *Ese algo de Dávalos* (*Davalos' Certain Something*, 1964), *La colina* (*The Hill*, 1968), a metaphysical play about the death of God, and *En el séptimo círculo* (*In the Seventh Circle*, 1982), about violence in the current world situation. GW

Galsworthy, John (1867–1933) British novelist and

dramatist; awarded the Nobel Prize for literature in 1932 and best known for his novel-sequence *The Forsyte Saga* that received international acclaim in a television dramatization. His first plays, *The Silver Box* (1906), *Strife* (1909) and *Justice* (1910), were all produced by **Granville Barker**. Dealing with the inequalities of justice in a class system, the causes of industrial unrest, and the psychological effects of the prison system, their objective depiction of topical moral issues and social conscience made Galsworthy's plays a popular staple of the provincial repertory movement as well as West End successes. These themes were extended in *The Fugitive* (1913), dealing with the social victimization of women, or *The Mob* (1914), denouncing war hysteria, and repeated in a series of plays during the 1920s: *The Skin Game, Loyalties, Escape, Exiled*. His call for social reform was most effective in *Justice*, which had a significant impact on the campaign for prison reform, and *Strife* was successfully revived at the **National Theatre** in 1978. But in general, like most 'problem drama', his plays have dated badly because the issues are defined too specifically in terms of a particular social context and the 'well-made' plots, several of which end with the protagonist's suicide, are overtly conventional.   CI

Gambaro, Griselda (1928–) Argentine playwright, novelist and short-story writer, perhaps the foremost woman playwright in Latin America. Her hard-hitting psychological plays strike at the violence and oppression which have not only characterized Argentine politics and daily life in recent years but are inherent in the human condition. *Los siameses* (*The Siamese Twins*, 1967) contrasts aggression and passivity in two mutually-dependent individuals and *El camp* (*The Camp*, 1968) bears the stigma of a concentration camp whose leader is named Franco. Both earlier and later plays decry the trivialization and show the absurdity of contemporary life-styles. During virulent periods of repression, she sought refuge in Spain; some of her plays have still not been performed in Argentina. Recent titles include *Decir sí* (*To Say Yes*, 1981) and *La malasangre* (*Bad Blood*, 1982).   GW

Gambon, Michael (1940–) Irish-born British actor. Gambon has become one of the most respected actors on the British stage, especially through his work at the **National Theatre** which he first joined in 1963 (at the **Old Vic**) and to which he returned in 1978, and for the **Royal Shakespeare Company**. He played King Lear for the RSC in 1982–3 and – as a comparable pinnacle in television – had the title role in **Dennis Potter**'s play *The Singing Detective* (BBC 1986). His is a quiet and unassuming talent, and a major one.   MB

Ganassa (or Zan Ganassa) (Alberto Naseli or Naselli) (?1540–?1584). One of the first Italian **commedia dell'arte** actors to perform beyond the borders of Italy. A specialist in **zanni** roles, he first crops up in 1568 as head of a troupe in Mantua. After giving private performances in France (1571, 1572), the latter occasion at the invitation of Charles IX, he spent nearly a decade in Spain (1574–84). There his success was so extraordinary that the municipal authorities of Seville revoked his company's licence because workers were slacking off to attend the shows. He is often mentioned by **Lope**

de Vega, who may have based his comic 'gracioso' on *commedia* figures. Fifty years after Ganassa's departure, he was still cited in Spanish folk-sayings.   LS

García Guerra, Ivan (1938–) Dominican Republic playwright, director short-story writer, professor. Active in all phases of Dominican theatre, his first play was *Más allá de la búsqueda* (*Beyond the Search*, 1963), a Promethean existentialist exercise. Other major plays include *Don Quijote de todo el mundo* (*Don Quixote of the World*, 1964), a modernized revolutionary version of the idealistic dreamer, and *Fábula de los cinco caminantes* (*Fable of the Five Travellers*, 1965), a symbolic work representing major forces of contemporary society.   GW

García Lorca, Federico (1898–1936) Spanish poet and dramatist, perhaps the best known of this century outside Spain. Born in the province of Granada, he frequented artistic and literary circles in Madrid during his studies there. He travelled widely in Spain, and also visited France, Britain and the United States in 1929–30. His first play, *El maleficio de la mariposa* (*The Butterfly's Evil Spell*, 1920), a short symbolic piece, was a failure, but his historic verse-drama *Mariana Pineda* (1923), recounting the life and death of the revolutionary Liberal heroine, was a great success, although such plays were no longer fashionable. Lorca continued to experiment with various styles, writing *La zapatera prodigiosa* (*The Prodigious Shoemaker's Wife*, 1926) as a puppet-like farce set in rural Andalusia, and *El amor de don Perlimpín con Belisa en su jardín* (*The Love of Don Perlimpín With Belisa in His Garden*, 1928), a combination of the lyrical, fantastic, and farcical. During his stay in the United States he wrote a surrealistic play, *Así que pasen cinco años* (*As Five Years Pass*, 1929–30), whose events take place in the mind of a man with only a few minutes to live, and the brief *El público* (*The Audience*, 1930).

During 1932–3 he was involved with the university theatre group La Barraca, touring rural Spain, and he went on to evolve a mature style with his three great peasant tragedies of passion and frustration, *Bodas de sangre* (*Blood Wedding*, 1933), *Yerma* (1934) and *La casa de Bernarda Alba* (*The House of Bernarda Alba*, 1936). The first of these fuses the poetry of the *Romancero gitano* (*Gypsy Ballad-book*) collection with the plot of an unwilling bride who elopes with her lover on her wedding night, leading to a tragic climax in which the husband and lover kill each other. *Yerma* deals with the tragedy of a woman whose longing for a child becomes so unbearable that she murders her indifferent husband. In *La casa de Bernarda Alba*, a mother orders her daughters to mourn their father's death for eight years before marrying, her obsession with decorum producing a tragedy of jealousy and frustration. A further play exploring the oppression and frustration of Spanish women is *Doña Rosita la soltera, o el lenguaje de las flores* (*Doña Rosita the Spinster, or the Language of the Flowers*, performed 1935) whose protagonist waits 20 years for her fiancé to return from South America, fading like the rose her uncle cultivates, and unable to reveal that she knows he will not return.

Lorca's murder by Falangists at the outbreak of the Civil War aged only 38 was a severe loss for Spanish literature. But Lorca's reputation abroad has been established by *Bodas de sangre* and *La casa de Bernarda Alba*. CL

García, Santiago (1928–) Colombian playwright and director. Studied in Czechoslovakia, France and the United States. Founder of various theatre groups: El Buho (The Owl), Teatro Estudio (Studio Theatre, of the National University), and the Casa de la Cultura, (1966–72) later renamed La Candelaria (1972). Also the prime force behind the Colombian Theatre Corporation that organized the 100 or more theatre groups in Colombia into a new union. The first Colombian director to stage **Brecht** and **Peter Weiss**, he promoted socio-political theatre with Marxist themes and structures. A major director, critic and theoretician, with close ties to other experimental theatre groups throughout Latin America. Major productions include *La ciudad dorada* (*The Golden City*, 1974), *Guadalupe, años sin cuenta* (*Guadalupe, Years without End*, 1975) both dealing with war and violence in Colombia. *Morte y vida severina* (*Life and Death Severina*) and *Los diez días que estremecieron el mundo* (*Ten Days that Shook the World*) are adaptations of the Brazilian play by João Cabral de Melo Neto and the John Reed documentary on Russia, respectively. *Diálogo del rebusque* (*Hermetic Dialogue*, 1983) adapts the Spanish baroque poet Francisco de Quevedo. GW

Garnier, Robert (c. 1545–90) French dramatist and poet, who divided his time between writing and the legal profession. His seven tragedies, though largely based on Greek mythology or Roman history, betray his own moral and religious concerns and may owe some of their power to his dismay at the doctrinal strife and civil wars then ravaging his native country. Despite their Senecan manner, relying heavily on monologue and exaggerated pathos, they contain impressive choruses and other passages of lyrical and imaginative eloquence, particularly in the later works such as *Antigone* (1580) and *Les Juives* (*The Jewish Women*, 1583) which deals with Nebuchadnezzar's cruelty to Zedekiah and his family after the siege of Jerusalem. In *Bradamante* (1582), a tragicomedy derived from **Ariosto**'s *Orlando Furioso*, he anticipated the genre that was to dominate the early part of the next century and it continued to be acted for many years. At its best Garnier's writing looks forward to **Corneille** and **Rotrou** and two of his Roman plays were even translated into English in his own time. DR

Garrett, João Baptista de Almeida (1799–1854) Portuguese playwright and theatrical motivator. After writing a neoclassical piece, *Catão* (*Cato*), in 1821 and putting on a play about the putting on of one of **Vicente**'s masques, *Um Auto de Gil Vicente*, which pointed the way to a renewal of Portuguese theatre, Garrett tried his hand with a couple of moderately successful historical plays. He was chosen in 1836 to implement, as Inspector-General of Theatres (a post he held from 1836 to 1841), a plan to renew the national stage, set up acting schools, build a National Theatre (eventually the **Teatro Nacional D. Maria II**) etc. He set to work with great energy, built the theatre, provided its first repertoire – the aforementioned plays and five additional comedies, as well as the century's finest drama.

This, *Frei Luís de Sousa*, first performed in 1850, is classical tragedy with careful attention to detail of setting, correctness of costume – spelled out in long stage directions – and to historical events and atmosphere that would have been more typical of contemporary romantic theatre. Based on the true story of a nobleman, presumed killed in battle, who returns to the Portugal of the Spanish captivity under the Philips, to the consternation of his daughter, his re-married wife and her noble-minded husband, the play is strongly patriotic and instinct with a psychological truth which increases the impact of its *dénouement*. With 239 performances in the first hundred years of the Teatro Nacional D. Maria II, it was the most often revived of all plays. LK

Garrick, David (1717–79) English actor, manager and playwright. Born in Hereford, he was educated at Lichfield, enrolling in **Dr Johnson**'s school at one stage. In 1737 he and Johnson moved to London where he opened a wholesale wine business with his brother. His first play, *Lethe*, a satire, was performed at **Drury Lane** in 1740. He began acting as an amateur but his family disapproved and he acted under a pseudonym in Ipswich. In 1741 at **Goodman's Fields Theatre** his performance as Richard III won him immediate success and he followed it with Bayes in **Buckingham**'s *The Rehearsal* and King Lear (coached by **Macklin**). The triumph continued when he transferred to Drury Lane in 1742 and in Dublin where he played Hamlet opposite **Mrs Woffington** with whom he lived in London. He also began to perform one of his greatest roles as Abel Drugger in **Jonson**'s *The Alchemist*, a realistic study of a low comedy role. Drury Lane was in deep financial trouble and Garrick joined the actors rebelling against the management. His willingness to capitulate infuriated Macklin. In 1744 Garrick prepared the way for his performance of Macbeth by publishing a pamphlet, *An Essay on Acting*, a satire on his own intentions. If he was always far from acting a true Shakespearian version of the text, Garrick was a careful restorer of many parts of **Shakespeare**'s plays that had traditionally been cut or adapted. Even his notorious version of *Hamlet* in 1772 which cut Ophelia's madness and the gravediggers in giving the play a remarkably rapid ending, put back numerous lines elsewhere. The *Macbeth* was advertised 'revived as Shakespeare wrote it'. During a season at **Covent Garden**, Garrick produced the best of his 20 plays, the afterpiece farce *Miss in her Teens*. In April 1747 Garrick and **Lacy** signed an agreement of partnership in Drury Lane Theatre and its patent, inaugurating Garrick's 29 years as the Theatre's manager. Opening with a prologue by Dr Johnson assuring the audience that 'The drama's laws the drama's patrons give,/For we that live to please must please to live', Garrick, with a strong company, established Drury Lane as a standard of excellence in production and acting. In 1748 he added Benedick in *Much Ado About Nothing* and Romeo to his repertory, giving *Romeo and Juliet* its first production in London for 80 years and allowing the lovers a brief reunion in the tomb. Never at his best as young lovers he still won the battle of the Romeos in 1750 when **Spranger Barry** played the same role at Covent Garden. His production of Malet's *Alfred* (1751) inaugurated the spectacular Drury Lane pantomimes. In 1754 Garrick bought an estate at Hampton with gardens laid out by Capability Brown and a new riverside temple dedicated to Shakespeare. His status was already far beyond any previous English actor's, a friend of the highest in London society, acclaimed as an intelligent critic as much as a performer. In 1755 Garrick coped with riots at the theatre over the employment of a French dance troupe as war broke out. Most of his own Shakespeare adaptations date from this period with versions of *The Taming of the Shrew*, *The Winter's Tale*, *The Tempest*, *King Lear* and *Antony and Cleopatra* (its first performance since the Restoration).

Always ready to reform theatrical abuses Garrick abolished the right of half-price admission after the third act but the consequent riots forced him to give way. Frustrated he left the stage for two years, travelling to France with his wife and lionized by French writers, players and society. His effect on the **Diderot** circle transformed the attitude to acting in France. For his part Garrick learnt about scenic innovations, for instance wing lights which he introduced at Drury Lane on his return. He collaborated with **George Colman the Elder** on *The Clandestine Marriage* in 1766 but refused to play Lord Ogleby and argued with Colman about their shares in the work.

In 1769 he was invited by the town council at Stratford to organize the Shakespeare Jubilee. Garrick, flattered and seizing the chance to display his idolatry of Shakespeare, arranged a massive series of processions, orations and entertainments at his own expense, nearly all of which were ruined by torrential rain. Undaunted he mounted the pageants at Drury Lane as *The Jubilee* and recouped his losses. Suffering increasingly from gout and migraines, he began to withdraw from management, eventually selling the patent and his shares to **Sheridan** and retiring from acting with a

series of farewell performances ending with **Mrs Centlivre**'s *The Wonder* in 1776. On his death he was accorded a grand funeral at Westminster Abbey. Among other bequests he left his remarkable collection of English plays to the British Museum. An assiduous collector of drama, he was generous in making his library available to scholars like Dr Johnson and Steevens to help their study of Shakespeare and his contemporaries; the bequest extended his generosity.

As manager, Garrick's career often seemed marked by disputes with other actors and playwrights but, if some showed him intransigent, he was firm in his policy of refusing bad plays even from friends and refusing actors parts which they could not successfully perform. If he was willing to satisfy public demands for spectacle he also inaugurated new forms of scenery and design, for example in his encouragement of **De Loutherbourg**. His cautious balance of commercial acquiescence and artistic responsibility carefully shaped public taste to his own standards and the result was a rare combination of profit and artistic integrity. As a sustained success his management of Drury Lane is unparalleled.

As writer, his original work was usually no more than pragmatic and he aspired no higher. But his adaptations of earlier drama kept a broad range of major plays in the repertory in forms that the audience would accept. The adaptations show the consistent intelligence of the actor, crafting scenes to maximum effect, giving the cast (and himself) the best opportunities. They also show the producer recognizing in a new way on the English stage how to create a consistent interpretation of a play through cutting, rewriting and the use of scenery and costume, a prototype for a much later concept of the director.

As actor, Garrick was incomparable, his range in

David Garrick 'delivering his Ode at Drury Lane Theatre, on dedicating a Building and erecting a Statue, to Shakespeare', 1769.

classic and new plays unequalled, his virtuosity and daring brilliant and his effect on the audience profound. His terror as Hamlet meeting his father's ghost terrified the audience; his easy charm as Archer in **Farquhar**'s *The Beaux' Stratagem* was infectious; his portrayal of Drugger as gentle simpleton was endearing.

Garrick's dominance of the English stage for over 30 years was absolute. His influence was as much social as theatrical; as Dr Johnson said, 'his profession made him rich and he made his profession respectable'. PH

Garrick Theatre 63–67 West 35 St, New York City [Architect: Francis H. Kimball]. In 1890, **Edward Harrigan** built his own theatre just above Herald Square and named it after himself. After five years, he relinquished the house to **Richard Mansfield**, who changed its name to the Garrick by having his signmaker revise the letters at a minimum cost and effort. In 1896, the Garrick changed hands again and was leased to **Charles Frohman** until his death in 1915. When it looked as if the house would be torn down, it was rescued by the millionaire-philanthropist Otto Kahn, who installed **Jacques Copeau**'s Théâtre du Vieux Colombier in it in 1917. Two years later, he placed it at the disposal of the infant **Theatre Guild**, in whose hands it remained until it built its own theatre in 1925. Within a few years, it descended into cheap burlesque and gradual abandonment as a theatre. In 1932, after extensive fire damage, it was razed for safety purposes. MCH

Garro, Elena (1922–) Mexican playwright and novelist, an imaginative writer who finds abstract means of expressing external realities. *Un hogar sólido* (*A Solid Home*, 1956) is the title play of a collection dealing with characters and situations beyond the grave. *La señora en su balcón* (*The Lady on the Balcony*, 1963) is the dramatic encounter of an older woman with haunting illusions of her past. Garro stands as one of the best women writers of Mexico. GW

Gascon, Jean (1921–) French Canadian actor and director. He acted with **Emile Legault**'s Compagnons de Saint-Laurent in the 1940s before studying professional theatre in Paris, 1948–51. One of the founders of the **Théâtre du Nouveau Monde** on his return, he was its artistic director until 1966. This is the period when the TNM attracted international acclaim for its interpretation of French classics, particularly the works of **Molière**, many of them directed by Gascon and staged with the assistance of **Robert Prévost** and **Jean-Louis Roux**. Named first director-general (1960–3) of the **National Theatre School** of Canada, he has also been active in English Canadian theatre and television, acting and directing at the **Stratford (Ontario) Festival**, of which he was artistic director, 1969–74. LED

Gaskill, William (1930–) British director, who joined the **Royal Court Theatre** in 1957. Gaskill, whose experience had previously been as an actor and stage manager in rep, was confronted by **N. F. Simpson**'s absurdist farce, *A Resounding Tinkle*, together with *The Hole* as his first assignment, whose unlikely success led to an engagement as Assistant to the Artistic Director, **George Devine**. He directed plays by

Simpson, Donald Howarth, **John Osborne** and **Arnold Wesker** at the Royal Court, *Richard III* (1961) and *Cymbeline* (1962) for the **Royal Shakespeare Company** and, in London, **Brecht**'s *The Caucasian Chalk Circle* and *Baal* (1963). **Laurence Olivier** invited him to join the newly formed **National Theatre** company in 1963 as associate director and he provided a memorable production of their first season, **Farquhar**'s *The Recruiting Officer*. His particular skill lay in encouraging the group acting of the new company through such methods as improvisation and discussion. After directing such National Theatre successes as Brecht's *Mother Courage* and **John Arden**'s *Armstrong's Last Goodnight*, he returned to the Royal Court, succeeding George Devine as Artistic Director. From 1965 to 1972, he led the company through some adventurous seasons, distinguished by the production of **Edward Bond**'s first plays, *Saved* (1965), *Early Morning* (1968), *Lear* (1971) and *The Sea* (1973), which he also directed. After leaving the Royal Court, he helped to found a theatre co-operative, the Joint Stock Company, which brought actors and writers together in the production of radical plays for what became the leading alternative theatre company in Britain. New plays by **David Hare**, **Howard Brenton** and Stephen Lowe were premiered by Joint Stock. He returned to the National Theatre as a guest director for **Granville Barker**'s *The Madras House* (1977). JE

Gassman, Vittorio (1922–) Italian actor and director. After studying at the National Academy of Dramatic Art in Rome, he made his debut in 1943 and rapidly emerged on the post-war scene as a major stage actor. His handsome presence and strong, expressive voice made him particularly suited to classic parts like the titles roles in **Alfieri**'s *Oreste*, 1950 (directed by **Visconti**), and **Shakespeare**'s *Hamlet*, 1952 (which he jointly directed with **Squarzina**) and *Othello*, 1956. He later formed and directed the Teatro Popolare Italiano, for which he played a range of lead roles. Not only classic, but modern Italian and European drama has been prominent in his repertory, including the **Dumas–Sartre** *Kean*, and plays by Zardi, Pasolini and others. His film career flourished after the international success of *I Soliti Ignoti* (*Unidentified People*, 1958, directed by Monicelli) in which he revealed a hitherto unsuspected talent for comic character roles. Among his most notable recent achievements have been *Richard the Third* and *King Lear*. KR

Gate Theatre (Dublin) Created in 1928 by Micheál MacLiammóir and Hilton Edwards to diversify Irish theatre. MacLiammóir (1899–1978) – actor, designer, director, playwright – born in Cork, studied at the Slade. Edwards, an Englishman and **Old Vic** actor, had settled in Ireland.

In 1930 the Gate moved from the Peacock to its own theatre, becoming noted for its brilliant production and catholic variety: world classics, experimental plays (decreasingly), West End successes, farces. In 1936 its major patron, Lord Longford, formed Longford Productions, sharing the theatre until the 1960s on a half-yearly basis. Among the Gate's Irish playwrights, it encouraged **Denis Johnston**, presented MacLiammóir's own romances, and in 1964 **Brian Friel**'s first international success.

The Gate continues, but without the idiosyncratic constitution of its founders' long, productive collaboration. DM

Gate Theatre (London) First a loft near Covent Garden then (after 1927) occupying part of the former Charing Cross Music-Hall, the Gate was opened in 1925 by Peter Godfrey, a variety performer who had been a member of **Ben Greet**'s Shakespearian troupe, as an experimental theatre for presenting the work of the expressionists. Over the next nine years, attracting performers of the calibre of **Flora Robson** and Eric Portman or Hermione Gingold, he staged approximately 350 plays ranging from **Strindberg**, **Wedekind**, **Toller** and **Kaiser** (*From Morn to Midnight*, 1928, being the most successful) to **O'Neill**'s banned work, *Desire Under the Elms*, and parody performances of plays like **Uncle Tom's Cabin** or *Little Lord Fauntleroy*. When **Norman Marshall** took over in 1934 the theatre lost its experimental significance, though it continued to produce new work – Sewell Stokes's *Oscar Wilde* (with **Robert Morley**, 1936), **John Steinbeck**'s *Of Mice and Men* (1938), **Cocteau**'s *Les Parents Terribles* (with **Cyril Cusack**, 1940) – until destroyed by bombing in 1941. CI

Gatti, Armand (1924–) French playwright, poet, journalist, script writer, film maker. Having experienced a German concentration camp, Gatti struggled, in much of his early work, to come to terms with the survivor complex. He has tried to write plays that could intervene as incisively in world events as political journalism does. His autobiographical *Vie Imaginaire de L'Eboueur Auguste Geai* (*Imaginary Life of Auguste Geai*) (directed by Rosner 1962) was his first big success, after which his plays were hotly disputed by the decentralized theatres. These plays explode the normal conventions of time and space, creating a revolutionary dramaturgy for revolutionary subjects. Since the 1970s, he has moved away from straight plays towards involvement of whole communities and the use of many different media at once, especially video. A series of hard-hitting documentary films was broadcast by French television and in 1983 he was put at the head of an audio-visual Atelier de Création Populaire at Toulouse. DB

Gaultier-Garguille (Hugues Guéru) (1572/3–1633) French actor, one of the most famous farceplayers of his generation. A member of **Valleran**'s troupe at the **Hôtel de Bourgogne** in 1606, he returned there in 1612 to join the company led by another of Valleran's ex-associates, **Gros-Guillaume**, thus cementing an acting partnership which was to endure until his death in 1633. In farce he was always masked and wore a tight-fitting black doublet with bright red sleeves, narrow black breeches and stockings. A round skull-cap, a cane and a belt holding a pouch and a wooden dagger completed the costume, which clearly owed something to the Pantalone of **commedia** and in which he played the old men of farce. In serious plays he adopted the name of Fléchelles but appeared under his farcical alias in Gougenot's *La Comédie des Comédiens* (*The Actors' Comedy*, 1631/2). Just as popular as his comic acting were the engagingly crude and licentious songs that he contributed to the

performance, a collection of which was published and went through several editions. DR

Gautier, Théophile (1811–72) French poet, novelist, critic. Gautier's main importance to the theatre is as a critic of drama and ballet. His first important review appeared in *Le Monde Dramatique* in 1835. From 1837–55 he had a regular column in *La Presse* and from 1855–71 in *Le Moniteur Universel*. He published a major collection of his theatre criticism in his *Histoire Dramatique en France Depuis Vingt-Cinq Ans* (1858). He originally trained to be a painter. In 1830 he became actively involved with the romantic 'cohort', supporting **Hugo**'s *Hernani* and sporting his celebrated red waistcoat. He soon distanced himself from the excesses of the romantic movement, and his criticism is marked by its common sense and honesty. He contributed to a number of minor dramatic works and librettos, but is best known for providing the scenarios for two major romantic ballets, *Giselle* (1841) and *La Péri* (1843). As a poet he is known for association with the Parnassian movement and for his volume *Emaux et Camées* (1852). JMCC

Gay, John (1685–1732) English dramatist. A school-friend of **Aaron Hill**, Gay was apprenticed to a silk mercer in London before finding employment with the Duchess of Monmouth and becoming a writer. His topical farce *The Mohocks* (1712) was unacted and his Chaucer adaptation *The Wife of Bath* (1713) was performed but proved a failure. A member of the Scriblerus Club with Swift and Pope from 1714 he aligned himself with the Tory party and sought court patronage fruitlessly. In 1715 his burlesque of contemporary tragedy *The What D'Ye Call It* (1715), written with help from Pope, was successful as was the satire on other writers he wrote with Pope and Arbuthnot, *Three Hours after Marriage* (1717). After writing the libretto for Handel's *Acis and Galatea* (1719) and a pastoral tragedy *Dione* (1720), Gay produced the first volume of *The Fables* (1727). In 1728 **John Rich**, manager of **Lincoln's Inn Fields** Theatre, produced Gay's balladopera *The Beggar's Opera* with music by Pepusch, a success that made 'Gay rich and Rich gay'. Gay invented a new form with the work, using ballads to create a music theatre and setting his love story in the criminal world through which he could attack sentimental drama and contemporary politics with immense verve. The work was later adapted by **Brecht** as *The Threepenny Opera*. Walpole, stung by the portrayal of him in *The Beggar's Opera*, banned performances of Gay's sequel *Polly* (1729) which moved Macheath to the West Indies; it was not performed until 1777 in a version by **George Colman the Elder**. None of Gay's later satiric plays match the brilliance of *The Beggar's Opera*. PH

Gay theatre The generic term for a modern theatrical movement dating from the 1960s dedicated to the writing, performance, and publication of plays dealing with the problems and lifestyles of the homosexual community. Ambiguity can arise over the label because although it usually applies only to gay male theatre, sometimes it includes lesbian drama and theatre. The main bastions for gay theatre have been the United States of America and Great Britain.

Hogarth's painting of Act III, scene 2 of Gay's *The Beggar's Opera*. Note the audience on stage, right and left.

Several modern English-language plays do exist which through their focus on homosexuality may be considered forerunners of the gay drama movement. In the United States, the earliest of these are two little-known plays by **Mae West**: *The Drag* (1927) and *The Pleasure Man* (1928). The first significant American exposure to gay drama, however, came in 1933 with the importation to Broadway of the London hit *The Green Bay Tree* (see below), the first major play about homosexuality. More overt treatment of the subject than Shairp makes is found in **Lillian Hellman**'s *The Children's Hour* (1934), in **Robert Anderson**'s *Tea and Sympathy* (1953), and, peripherally, in **Arthur Miller**'s *A View from the Bridge* (1955). Yet these dramatists, writing from a heterosexual point of view, study lesbianism and homosexuality as aberrations from societal norms.

In the 1960s, the treatment of homosexuality on the American stage began to change. There are two key reasons for this. First, theatrically, the emergence in New York of the Off-Broadway and Off-Off-Broadway movements of the 1950s and 1960s encouraged the production of plays which were non-commercial or controversial and which could be performed before small groups at modest cost. And second, sociologically, the sexual revolution of the 1960s and 1970s, with the freer attitude towards sexual morality and life styles it engendered in the United States, affected the homosexual world as well as the heterosexual. This, in turn, laid the groundwork for the appearance of plays which seriously portrayed the lives and problems of the gay community regardless of whether the form of the plays was comedy, realistic social drama, agit-prop or even a musical.

Gradually in the sixties a body of gay plays appeared and began receiving performances, particularly in the years 1960–7 at the Caffé Cino in New York's Greenwich Village. Doric Wilson became the first outstanding gay playwright to be nurtured at the Cino, his first four plays receiving their premieres there in 1961. Subsequently such gay playwrights as Robert Patrick, William Hoffman, Claris Nelson and David Starkweather had Cino performances of their plays. In 1968, *The Boys in the Band* by Mart Crowley stirred tremendous interest among New York theatregoers during an Off-Broadway run for its frank portrayal of homosexuals – the strongest treatment yet seen on the American stage – and for its bold use of gay language.

Building on the groundwork of the sixties, gay theatre made further advances in the decade of the 1970s with the establishment of gay producing companies in New York dedicated to the presentation of plays by gay playwrights primarily for gay audiences. The first of these was the TOSOS Theatre Company, which was founded by Doric Wilson and which lasted from 1973 until 1977. Next came The Glines, a gay arts centre founded by John Glines in 1976. Although devoted to all the arts, it was particularly noted for its productions of gay plays. It remained active in various guises until 1982. John Glines, retaining the organizational name, was still functioning in 1985 as the primary producer of gay theatre in New York, both on and off Broadway. With the demise of The Glines, the Meridian Gay Theatre, founded by Terry Miller and Terry Helbing, became the major gay theatre company in New York as of 1982.

Outside New York the gay theatre movement was also growing during the seventies, particularly in San Francisco, with its large gay population. There the major companies were the San Francisco Gay Men's Theatre Collective and Theatre Rhinoceros. Other representative companies across America include The Janus in Phoenix, the Carpenter's Children in San Diego, Diversity in Houston, the Lionheart in Chicago, the Out-and-About Theatre Company in Minneapolis, and the Triangle in Boston.

The growth of the gay theatre movement manifested itself in other ways. In 1978, the Gay Theatre Alliance was founded in New York dedicated to the promotion and development of gay and lesbian theatre. In 1980 in New York, the First Gay American Arts Festival was held, with gay theatre prominently featured. Publication of anthologies of gay plays began in the mid-seventies, giving further recognition to gay theatre as a movement.

As its own entity, gay theatre was well established by the late 1970s. And the output of plays both in America and England had picked up considerably, regardless of quality. But it was not until the end of the decade that a new note could be heard in the treatment of subject matter. That note was sounded by **Harvey Fierstein** in his three one-act plays *The International Stud* (1978), *Fugue in a Nursery* (1979) and *Widows and Children First!* (1979) which collectively became *Torch Song Trilogy* (1981) and by Martin Sherman in *Bent* (1979). Both playwrights, gays themselves, extended the range of treatment of subject matter in these works by reaching beyond a parochial gay community to deal with matters of universal concern though rooted in problems of the gay world. In *Torch Song Trilogy* Fierstein succeeded so well in what he was saying that this comedy of contemporary life moved from Off-Off-Broadway to Off-Broadway to Broadway. There it became the first gay play to have a long Broadway run, from 1982–4, and it won a Tony Award in 1983 in the best play category. *Bent* had actually preceded it to Broadway. Coming from a successful London run in December 1979, it became the first play on the commercial/establishment New York stage to focus on the persecution of homosexuals and to place that persecution in a historical perspective. For the play deals with the plight of gays under the Nazi regime.

A more deadly enemy than the Nazis came upon the gay community in 1981 when AIDS was diagnosed as a new fatal disease and when it was learned that homosexuals were its prime target. Gay drama responded to this horrible awareness with several works on the subject which began appearing Off-Off and Off-Broadway in 1984 and 1985. Two are of particular note: *As Is* (1985) by William M. Hoffman and *The Normal Heart* (1985) by Larry Kramer. Both are plays of anger, works that shout at the audiences about the consequences of AIDS, but with different dramatic tech-

niques. *As Is* is a bitter comedy, and *The Normal Heart* an agit-prop drama. When *As Is* transferred to Broadway (where it had a seven-month run in 1985), it became the first play dealing with AIDS to be presented on the commercial stage.

Musicals also became part of the gay theatre movement. The most notable in this genre is *The Faggot* (1973) by Al Carmines, which had an Off-Off-Broadway run. On Broadway, the strictly mainstream *La Cage aux Folles* began its fourth year in 1986, attended by scores of heterosexuals who willingly accept its gay characters and story line with little knowledge of the existence of a gay theatre movement.

In Great Britain, gay theatre developed along lines parallel to its American counterpart. Initially occasional mainstream dramas appeared. First among these was that landmark of modern British plays on homosexuality, Mordaunt Shairp's *The Green Bay Tree* (1933), which was received as enthusiastically by London audiences as it was later that year in New York. In the play, the homosexual relationship between Mr Dulcimer and Julian is never explicitly stated, nor is the word *homosexual* used – undoubtedly to have assured the work's production. Twenty-five years later homosexual characters could be honestly and sympathetically portrayed on the British stage as they were in 1958 in **Shelagh Delaney**'s *A Taste of Honey* and in **Brendan Behan**'s *The Hostage*. Following these, outstanding examples include **John Osborne**'s *Inadmissible Evidence* (1964) and *A Patriot for Me* (1966), a play concerned with homosexuality in the pre-First World War Austrian army, and **Joe Orton**'s *Entertaining Mr Sloan* (1964), **Frank Marcus**'s *The Killing of Sister George* (1967) – a lesbian-centred play – and Charles Dyer's *Staircase* (1968).

An aid to the freer treatment of homosexuality on the British stage was the repeal in 1967 of the law concerning criminal penalties for committing homosexual acts by consenting adults. Shortly after that came the development of an independent gay theatre movement as part of the growth of Fringe theatre. Gay companies began appearing in the 1970s, the most important being the Gay Sweatshop. Formed in 1975 under the leadership of Drew Griffiths and Gerald Chapman, Gay Sweatshop tours throughout Britain presenting plays dealing with all aspects of the gay lifestyle. Although it has undergone some organizational changes over the years, it remains the prime gay theatre company in Britain.

Apart from the embrace of the Fringe theatre by gay companies, plays with homosexual characters and themes continue to appear on the mainstream British stage as illustrated by Tom McClenaghan's *Submariners* (1980) and Michael Wilcox's *Accounts* (1981), and Hugh Whitemore's *Breaking the Code* (1986). WG

See: 'Caffé Cino – And its Legacy.' Exhibition catalogue, Library and Museum of the Performing Arts at Lincoln Center, New York, 1985; W. Green, '*Torch Song Trilogy*: A Gay Comedy with a Dying Fall' in *Maske und Kothurn* 30 (1984), 217–24; R. Hall, *Three Plays for a Gay Theater: & Three Essays*, San Francisco, 1983; T. Helbing (ed.), *Directory of Gay Plays*, New York, 1980; W. M. Hoffman (ed.), *Gay Plays: The First Collection*, New York, 1979; T. Miller, 'Gay Theatre: Is it Still Dangerous?' *Stages* 1 (June 1984), 7; Michael Wilcox (ed.), *Gay Plays*, London and New York, 1984.

Gélinas, Gratien (1909–) French Canadian playwright, actor and director. He began to write and perform radio scripts in the 1930s, creating in 1937 the comic character Fridolin, a satiric but sympathetic observer of contemporary Canadian foibles. The creation proved durable: from 1938 to 1946 he wrote annual stage reviews entitled *Fridolinons!* (published collectively as *Fridolinades* in 1980–1), interpreting the major role himself. Their immense popularity led to his first stage play, *'Tit-Coq* (1948), from which critics generally date the birth of modern Quebec theatre.

Much of Fridolin's character carries over into that of the titular hero, played by the author who also directed the play. A foundling defeated in his quest for social identity by military service in the Second World War and by an intransigent Catholic Church on his return, 'Tit-Coq (*Lil' Rooster*) incarnated, for many *Québécois*, their own frustrated aspirations at the end of that conflict. The play had more than 500 performances, in French and English. *Bousille et les Justes* (*Bousille and the Just*, 1959), painting the bankruptcy of middle-class morality, was also an outstanding success, as was *Hier les Enfants Dansaient* (*Yesterday the Children Were Dancing*, 1966), which depicts a Quebec family riven by the same political forces that then threatened to sunder Canada. Founder of the Comédie Canadienne in 1958, chairman of the Canadian Film Development Corporation in 1969, Gélinas continues to make a major contribution to the performing arts. LED

Gellert, Christian Fürchtegott (1715–69) German playwright. Gellert is best known for his *Fables*, but his effective sentimental comedies are among the more significant achievements of the early German theatre. Of these, *The Affectionate Sisters* (1747) and *The Sick Woman* (1747) are probably the best. SW

Gelosi, I ('the jealous', i.e., of praise) A troupe of Italian actors, headed by **Francesco** and **Isabella Andreini**, which collaborated with **Tasso** on *Aminta* in 1573 and undertook numerous tours from 1576. It was the first professional Italian company to visit Paris, at the invitation of Henri III; seen there in 1576–7, 1588, 1600 and 1602, it demonstrated the superiority of professional playing and had a great influence on the development of the French stage. Its repertory included both **commedia dell'arte** and *commedia erudita*. The troupe had long been troubled by internal dissension – the Arlecchino (**Tristano Martinelli**) was thought to have planned the murder of the Fritellino (Piermaria Cecchini) – and after Isabella died in 1604, her husband disbanded it. LS

Gémier, (Tonnerre) Firmin (1869–1933) French actor and director. At first a noted actor, Gémier was the first King Ubu in 1896. But the literary avant-garde interested him less than his vision of a mass theatre for the masses. In 1911 he bought a circus tent and built a mobile touring theatre with an audience capacity of 1,650. In 1919, at the Paris Winter Circus he directed large-cast spectaculars and in 1920 he was put in charge of the first **Théâtre National Populaire**, but was never given the means to run a permanent producing company. From 1921–30 he was director of the **Odéon**, where he distinguished himself by his productions of **Shakespeare**. He founded a Société Universelle du Théâtre, a forerunner of today's International Theatre Institute. DB

Gems, Pam (Iris Pamela) (1925–) British dramatist who turned to writing plays comparatively late in life after bringing up four children. She was involved in a Women's Theatre Season at the Almost Free in 1975 which included her full-length play, *The Amiable Courtship of Ms Venus and Wild Bill*. Two other lunchtime plays had been staged at the same theatre, *My Warren* (1973) and *After Birthday* (1973). Her first great success, however, came with the production in 1977 of *Dusa, Fish, Stas and Vi*, a study of four girls rooming together in a London flat, which transferred to the West End from **Hampstead Theatre Club**. The accuracy, good humour and specific awareness of feminist (as well as feminine) issues brought her recognition as a leading woman playwright, although her appeal was never confined to female audiences. The **Royal Shakespeare Company** produced *Queen Christina* at the Other Place in Stratford in 1977; but it was her musical biography of *Piaf*, which provided a splendid part for Jane Lapotaire, which moved in the RSC's production to the West End and New York (1980/81). Further productions with the RSC included *Camille* (1984) and *The Danton Affair* (1986). JE

Género chico Spanish generic term for the short one-act play, having its origin in the medieval church, but by the 16th century entirely secular. The essence of these works, including the *paso*, the *entremés*, and the *sainete*, is that they provided comic relief and variety between the acts of a full-scale **comedia**.

Paso is a term used by **Lope de Rueda** for his comic interludes depicting low-life characters and urban settings. It does not differ essentially from the *entremés*, which was usually performed after the first act of the *comedia*, the term first being found in 1565. Of many contributors to the genre, **Cervantes** published eight, though the greatest exponent was **Quiñones de Benavente**.

The *sainete* was originally similar, the term first being used in 1639. Music was an important element, as to a lesser degree in the other two forms. In the 18th century it was revived by Ramón de la Cruz (see **Spain**) who used it to parody the neoclassical tragic style. By the 19th century the genre was dominated by *costumbrismo*, the optimistic and conformist depiction of colourful low-life, the heyday of the genre being 1890–1910, with authors such as Carlos Arniches.

Both the *sainete* and the **zarzuela** served to inspire the popular theatre forms that began to develop in the River Plate (Argentina and Uruguay) area at the end of the 19th century. The *sainete criollo* depended on popular themes of the lower and middle class through an authentic language and presentation of customs, typical figures, and oftentimes political satire. The *sainete gauchesco* was attuned to the specific issues of the regional cowboy of the pampa, while the *sainete urbano* focused on popular types and themes within the rapidly changing urban environment. CL GW

Genet, Jean (1910–86) French poet, novelist, playwright. An orphan, Genet grew up to a life of crime and made his reputation with novels of homosexual eroticism written in prison. He wrote five plays: *Les Bonnes*

(*The Maids*), produced by **Jouvet** in 1947; *Haute Surveillance* (*Deathwatch*) (directed by Genet and Marchat 1949); *Le Balcon* (*The Balcony*, 1956) (directed by **Brook** 1960); *Les Nègres* (*The Blacks*) (directed by **Blin** 1959) and *Les Paravents* (*The Screens*) written in 1961 but considered too subversive to be produced until 1966 when Blin was invited to direct it at the **Odéon** by **Barrault**. His plays embody a brilliant interplay of different levels of illusion which suggest both the interdependence and the potential treachery of all social roles, stressing the links between power and theatricality. But although considered subversive by right-wing forces in France, which made it difficult for many of them to be staged, his plays do not advocate revolutionary political solutions. The Algerians of *The Screens*, the Negroes of *The Blacks*, the revolutionaries of *The Balcony* are all caught in a similar self-destructive circle and the transformations which occur in these plays are mystic rather than material. Genet's work has been very influential, partly because it comes close to realizing some of **Artaud**'s ideals: it does not rely on traditional plot or psychology, it is based in ritualized movements, dances, parades, interchanges of identity and a carefully worked contrast between the sumptuousness of poetic dialogue and the sordidness of dramatic situation. Genet was contemptuous of theatre as mere entertainment; he professed admiration for children's games and the Catholic Mass. Among the many significant productions of his plays was *The Maids* produced by the **Living Theatre** in 1965, *The Balcony* by Victor Garcia at São Paulo in 1969, *The Screens*, revived by **Chéreau** in 1983 and *The Blacks* by **Stein** the same year.   DB

Gentleman, Francis (1728–84) Irish actor, playwright and critic. After a brief career in the army and an acting debut in Smock Alley Theatre, he left for London on receiving a legacy and tried to ingratiate himself with **Garrick**. A notorious self-publicist, he acted in the provinces in the 1750s, returning to London as a journalist in the 1760s. Most of his plays of this period were adaptations, e.g. of **Jonson**'s *Sejanus* (1750) and *The Alchemist* (as *The Tobacconist*, 1760) and **Southerne**'s *Oroonoko* (as *The Royal Slave*, 1760). His dramatic criticism for the journal *The Dramatic Censor*, which he edited, was collected in 1771. Often pretentious and affected and with a concern for piety, his criticism provides remarkable descriptions of contemporary actors. In 1771 his satire on the theatre attacked Garrick for plagiarism. In 1772 he prepared an edition of **Shakespeare** for Bell's British Theatre incorporating much material about stage business from the prompt books in use at the Patent theatres.   PH

George, Mademoiselle (1787–1867) French actress. Marguerite-Joséphine Weymer (known as George), daughter of travelling players, appeared on the stage at Amiens at the age of five, was noticed by Mlle Raucourt who brought her to Paris to train her for the **Comédie-Française**, where she made her debut in 1802 in the unusual role of Clytemnestra. She had a celebrated liaison with Napoleon, for whom she retained a deep affection. Like **Talma**, she was the incarnation of the great classical roles to which her statuesque figure and sculptural beauty suited her. In 1808 she abandoned the Comédie-Française to go to

Mlle George in *La Tour de Nesle*, Porte-Saint-Martin, 1832.

Russia, where she was immensely popular. Back in Paris in 1813 she had to suffer the jealousy of her rival, **Mlle Duchesnois**. In the late 1820s a new career opened up with the romantic drama: **Dumas**'s *Christine* (1829) and **Vigny**'s *La Maréchale d'Ancre* (1830). Under the director **Harel** at the Porte-Saint-Martin, her greatest roles were Marguerite de Bourgogne in *La Tour de Nesle* (1832) and Lucrèce Borgia and Marie Tudor (1833) in **Hugo**'s plays. After 1842 her voice deteriorated, her majestic manner was out of fashion, and her weight problem had become chronic. She fell back on her old roles and in 1849 gave her farewell performance (a further one was given in 1853 at the Comédie-Française, when she played Rodogune).   JMCC

George M. Cohan's Theatre 1482 Broadway, New York City [Architect: George Keister]. Even by Broadway's standards, the active life of George M. Cohan's Theatre was brief. Built in 1911 for the musical comedy star then at his peak, it was part of the Fitzgerald building, which also housed Gray's Drugstore, for years a gathering place for unemployed actors. Joe Leblang, who ran a shoeshine stand at the rear of the drugstore, also established a business in buying and selling producers' leftover tickets at cut rates. He did so well that in 1914, he bought the drugstore and eventually, the building and theatre. During the depression the theatre was leased for movies and in 1938, the entire building was razed.   MCH

Germain, Jean-Claude (1939–) French Canadian playwright, critic and director. Born Claude-Jean Magnier, he became involved with stage arts while still a student, founding the Théâtre Antonin Artaud at the Université de Montréal in 1958. As drama critic for *Le Petit Journal* he remained active in avant-garde and experimental theatre, founding in 1969 the Théâtre du Même Nom (TMN), a parodic anagram of the **Théâtre du Nouveau Monde** (TNM), the most established of French Canada's troupes. Thereafter he devoted himself mainly to composing iconoclastic scripts for TMN. Relying heavily on *joual*, Quebec's popular idiom, and laden with ingenious puns, his works are virtually untranslatable. Most remarkable are *Diquidi, Diquidi, Ha! Ha! Ha!* (1969); *Le Roi des Mises à Bas Prix* (*King of Discount Sales*, 1971); and *Un Pays dont la Devise est Je M'Oublie* (*A Country Whose Slogan is 'I Forget'*, 1976), the latter a satiric reworking of history and of Quebec's provincial motto, *Je Me Souviens* (*I Remember*).   LED

Germany

(to 1914) Even though there was a vigorous religious and popular theatrical tradition in German-speaking countries during the Middle Ages, in contrast to England, France, and Spain, the professional theatre in Germany was late in its development. (See also **Medieval drama in Europe**.) Some historians have attributed this delay to the Thirty Years War and to the disastrous effect the war had on the German economy. However, it can also be argued, perhaps with more justification, that the absence of a regular professional theatre was primarily because there were no large cities that could nurture a permanent theatre in the way that London, Madrid, and Paris did.

In several respects, in its early years the modern professional theatre was a phenomenon alien to Germany. Its origins can be traced first to the **Englische Komödianten**, who, from the late 16th through to the mid-17th century, could be seen periodically on tours through the small towns and courts of Germany. Their repertoire consisted mainly of contemporary English plays, though from the very beginning of their tours comic scenes in Low German were inserted. Soon whole plays came to be given in German, especially as the companies were composed more and more of German actors. Italy also had a formative influence on German theatre, for the **commedia dell'arte** troupes were frequent visitors. As these two national traditions of theatre were unified in the troupes of wandering German players toward the end of the 17th century, a unique dramatic hybrid emerged to form the basis of their repertoire, the **Haupt- und Staatsaktionen**, plays that combined the episodic structure of the English chronicle play with the improvisational flexibility of the *commedia dell'arte*. Popular comic prototypical figures as, for example, 'Pickelhering' were evolved in this drama. Performances were normally given under rather primitive conditions, generally in spaces in the open air where it was possible to erect a stage structure. This may have borne some resemblance to the stage structure of the Elizabethan theatre.

Given the very lowly nature of the theatrical profession, it is not surprising that there were few German dramatists willing or capable of producing works of quality for the stage. **Jacob Ayrer**, a late 16th-century playwright whose work has not endured, was the only significant contributor. In the 17th century, when Germany seemed ready to produce drama of some quality, primarily in the work of the classically influenced dramatist **Andreas Gryphius** and the comparatively skilled baroque playwright **Caspar von Lohenstein**, there were no adequate professional companies to perform their plays. Gryphius's plays were occasionally staged by schoolboys. Indeed, it is in the performance of the Jesuit drama (see **Jesuitendrama**) in the schools of Bavaria that the most continuous tradition of theatre exists for much of the 17th century.

If England and Italy were the major formative influences on whatever popular theatrical tradition there was in 17th-century Germany, France exercised the dominant influence on the development of theatre as a high art. Early in the 17th century, **Martin Opitz**, a somewhat dry theoretician and translator, advocated that the German theatre model itself on the French and that dramatists respect the unities and classical decorum. His writings had little immediate effect but, by the end of the century, the actor–manager **Johannes Velten**, who received some patronage from the Duke of Saxony, began to introduce adaptations of French tragedy and comedy. He also attempted, without much success, to control the frequently unpredictable and unruly improvisational actors in his company. By this time, the adoption of French dramatic form and actorial mannerisms carried with it potential social prestige, as the richer courts of German-speaking Europe were hiring companies of French actors in an attempt to impose a civilized culture on a society that was widely regarded by the courtly aristocrats as backward in matters pertaining to art and social customs.

However, it was not until well into the 18th century that the court theatre began to influence the public theatre and then in a way that not all practitioners welcomed. This came about primarily through the efforts of **Johann Gottsched**, who, with the aid of **Caroline Neuber**, the most prominent actress of the time and the leader of Velten's old troupe, attempted to 'regularize' the public stage by introducing French classical tragedy in German adaptations, by abolishing improvisation (**Harlequin** was 'banished' from the stage in a formal ceremony in Leipzig in 1737), and by adopting a stiff, rhetorical manner of acting, known as the **Leipzig style**.

The endeavours of Neuber and Gottsched were thwarted by internal dissension and by an eventual lack of interest on the part of the public, who preferred the old *Haupt- und Staatsaktionen* and appreciated the freedom of the improvisational actors. Furthermore, actors in the public theatre failed at this time to attract the patronage of the aristocratic courts, who continued to prefer French actors and to enjoy the spectacle of Italian opera. In fact, despite the prestige earned by the troupe of **Konrad Ackermann**, it was not until well into the second half of the century that German actors began to enjoy regular aristocratic patronage. Through the middle of the 18th century, the number of touring troupes increased, but no permanent home was offered any troupe until 1776, when the Duke of Saxe-Gotha invited the actor **Konrad Ekhof** to settle in his capital with his band of travelling players and to form the first regular Court Theatre staffed by German actors.

Although the Gotha Court Theatre lasted only three years, as it was disbanded on Ekhof's death, its foundation was a highly significant event as it was the first step in the 50-year creation of a network of permanent, standing theatres that was eventually unequalled in Europe and gave the German theatre unique social prominence and prestige. In the late 1770s other important, standing theatres devoted to the production of German drama and foreign drama in German translation were founded. The most notable of these were the Hamburg Town Theatre, formed in 1776 on a commercial basis by **Friedrich Schröder** out of the Ackermann troupe, which had already attempted to form a National Theatre in Hamburg in the 1760s, and the **Mannheim Court** and National Theatre founded by the King of Bavaria in 1778 under the directorship of Baron Dalberg (1750–1806). In its early days this latter theatre had one of the greatest actors of the time, **August Iffland**, as the leading member of its company. During the next two decades, national, court, and municipal theatres came to be founded in most of the major German provinces and cities, so that by the early 19th century Germany possessed well over 65 permanent theatres, each of which was staffed with a company of actors. This network formed the basis for the present day system of regional theatres in Germany.

As a result of these momentous changes, acting became a socially acceptable and, for those who were successful in it, a financially reliable profession. Partially as a consequence of the burgeoning prestige of theatre, the period from the late 1760s through to the late 1820s saw an increase in the volume and quality of playwriting, which ensured that Germany had a native popular and classic repertoire upon which to build. During the 1760s and 1770s **Lessing**'s *bürgerliche Trauerspielen*, written under the influence of the comparatively realistic English drama, allowed the theatre to become a forum for the dramatization of issues close to the interests of the rising bourgeoisie. Lessing's plays, along with the *bürgerliche Trauerspielen* of other dramatists, encouraged a subdued style of realistic acting that was an alternative to the rather strident rhetoric of the Leipzig style. The 1770s saw the sudden eruption of the young **Sturm und Drang** playwrights, whose works, though infrequently performed, both introduced themes of social protest into the drama and demonstrated the potent influence **Shakespeare** was to have on the imagination of the German playwright. Among the most significant works of this movement were **Goethe**'s widely admired *Götz von Berlichingen*, first produced in Berlin and Hamburg in 1774, **Lenz**'s *The Tutor*, produced in Hamburg in 1778, and **Schiller**'s *The Robbers*, which received its immensely successful premiere in Mannheim in 1782. But the most significant achievement in playwriting occurred at the end of the century, at the Weimar Court Theatre, which was directed by Goethe between 1791 and 1817. Here the great tragedies of Schiller's maturity and several of Goethe's generically various plays were first performed. Although neither Goethe nor Schiller rejected the influence of Shakespeare (though Goethe became increasingly sceptical about the viability of Shakespeare's plays on stage), their plays from this period also show other foreign influences, primarily ancient Greek and French neoclassical drama. However, Schiller's tragedy of idealism and Goethe's humanistic theatre had its own brand of uniqueness. Indeed, the first national drama of Germany was created in Weimar over the turn of the century. The plays of one of Germany's greatest dramatists, **Heinrich von Kleist**, also date from this period, though due to the unpalatability of Kleist's outlook they went almost entirely unperformed in his lifetime and were only 'discovered' some decades after his death by **Ludwig Tieck**. During this same period, an extensive popular repertoire was also being created, primarily in the plays of the actor Iffland, who specialized in writing *Rührstücke*, sentimental domestic melodramas, and of **Kotzebue**, whose melodramas were performed not only in

Germany but widely in England and the United States. The works of these two dramatists were to hold the stage for much of the 19th century.

The 50 years that span the end of the 18th and the beginning of the 19th centuries represent a major flowering of theatre, not only in the area of playwriting, but also in the field of performance. Standards of acting and production underwent radical improvement. Iffland was perhaps the most technically consummate and certainly the most popular actor of the time, touring Germany ceaselessly, giving model performances of roles from his own plays and from some classics. **Ferdinand Fleck** and **Ludwig Devrient**, though radically different from Iffland as they seemed to act from seemingly intuitive bases, served to focus public interest on the actor as a performing artist: in particular, they managed to bring to the surface the unconscious motivation of the characters they played. All three of these actors tended to encourage solo virtuosity at the expense of ensemble work. In contrast, Goethe at Weimar trained his actors both to respect the ensemble and to conduct themselves with great dignity on stage. The '**Weimar style**' of acting that he evolved, which demanded that when the actor was performing tragedy he observe a formal aloofness from his audience, was to have a major influence on German actors for the next 100 years. Indeed, in the course of the 19th century, German acting developed in the tension between the formality of the Weimar school and the realism of the so-called Hamburg school, first practised by Friedrich Schröder in the late 18th century. Standards of physical production also improved significantly. When Iffland was appointed director of the **Berlin Royal Theatre**, in 1796, he received a substantial subsidy from the Prussian court. He used this money to stage productions of Shakespeare, Schiller, and other dramatists who used historical settings, under conditions of lavish splendour, achieving a level of spectacle previously unequalled in the German theatre. Although not all theatres could afford such luxury, Iffland's productions set the standard for the 19th century. In the German theatre as elsewhere in Europe, there was an increasing focus on spectacle, often at the expense of the impact that could be created by the individual actor and of the dramatic text itself.

As German cities grew in the course of the 19th century, so too did the theatres that serviced them. Although in contrast to the theatre of Austria, France and England, German theatre remained provincially oriented, Berlin, as the capital of Prussia and after 1870 of a united Germany, saw the greatest growth and the most vigorous theatre. Early in the century, the Royal Theatre, under the direction first of Iffland and then of Goethe's disciple Count Carl von Brühl (1772–1837), had a monopoly on the performance of drama, similar in some ways to the royal patents possessed by **Drury Lane** and **Covent Garden** in London. However, this was soon abolished. The Königstädttheater was established by royal patent in 1824, with the specific purpose of providing competition for the Royal Theatre and soon several other theatrical establishments sprang up in the city. Such expansion was common to other major German cities, in particular Hamburg and Munich. The growth of the German theatre did not, however, go unhampered. Until 1870, when Germany was united under Bismarck's rule, theatres could only be opened with governmental and police permission, which was not always forthcoming; after 1870, while freedom in building theatres was allowed, fairly stringent censorship of the plays that were staged in them remained the rule.

After the achievements of Weimar classicism, the development of German playwriting during the 19th century might be regarded as disappointing. The romantic movement made little contribution to the lasting dramatic repertoire. There was no lack of effective light comedies, melodramas, and sentimental family pieces, written by such excellent dramatic craftsmen as **Roderich Benedix** and **Charlotte Birch-Pfeiffer**. The plays of the Junges Deutschland (Young Germany) movement of the 1830s and 40s included themes of social protest but, because of the stringent censorship and the attachment of its major playwrights, **Heinrich Laube** and **Karl Gutzkow**, to the form of the well-made play, the work of Junges Deutschland lacked the urgency and exciting theatricality of the earlier *Sturm und Drang*. The most original playwrights of the age, and the only ones whose works have endured, were not widely performed. **Georg Büchner**, whose plays are generically similar to those of *Sturm und Drang*, never had one of his plays performed in his lifetime or for several decades after, while **Christian Dietrich Grabbe**, an eccentric but brilliant dramatist, also went unrecognized. Only **Friedrich Hebbel**, whose historical plays have complex characters drawn with remarkable psychological accuracy and whose *Maria Magdalena* is normally regarded as a forerunner of realism, achieved some degree of success and esteem in German theatres. **Gustav Freytag**'s comedy *The Journalists* and **Otto Ludwig**'s grim melodrama *The Hereditary Forester* are among the better plays of the mid-century.

Trends in performance in Germany during the 19th century demonstrate the same tension as in other countries. On the one hand, the rise of the virtuoso encouraged an approach to production that served mainly to highlight the principal star, on the other an increasingly sophisticated technology seemed to militate against the predominance of the single actor in the interests of spectacle. Not many theatres could afford to stage magnificent spectacles and most of the medium-sized and smaller theatres had relatively mediocre actors in their companies. Therefore they often had to rely on travelling stars to attract audiences. Thus, as the theatre expanded in the course of the century, increasing opportunities for skilled solo actors to make considerable fortunes opened up. Iffland and Ludwig Devrient were the important solo actors in the early decades of the century, but the great age for the travelling virtuosi was in the middle years of the century. Although actors such as **Karl Seydelmann**, **Emil Devrient**, the greatest solo perpetuator of the Weimar style, **Bogumil Dawison**, **Theodor Döring**, and Friedrich Haase were all members of major theatre companies, they would spend well over half the year touring both the provincial theatres and the major court and national theatres. As the century progressed and the American theatre developed, several of them crossed the Atlantic to make their name and sometimes a considerable sum of money by guest performances in the United States, often, like Dawison, acting in German to the English of his colleagues on stage.

Even though the solo actor was frequently the centre of audience attention, evidence suggests that most theatre managers and directors would, whenever they had the resources, devote their energies to spectacle. In this regard, the most characteristic mid-century director was **Franz von Dingelstedt**, who ran the Munich Court Theatre into debt because of his prodigiously extravagant productions. He then went on to Weimar and the Vienna **Burgtheater**. In both theatres he was especially noted for his magnificent production of the two Shakespeare history tetralogies. The main attraction of these productions for contemporaries was the sense that the whole physical apparatus of the stage operated like a machine, while the actors were little more than well-functioning cogs within it. Spectacle was also one of the ultimate goals of grand opera and, even though he claimed to be a theatrical revolutionary, **Richard Wagner**'s idea of the *Gesamtkunstwerk* existed in theory only when it came to staging. While the *Ring* Cycle was of quite remarkable novelty in matters relating to the music drama and to the characterization, when it was presented in 1876 in Bayreuth, the staging bore all the traditional trappings of the 19th-century spectacle theatre. Georg II, Duke of Saxe-Meiningen, has often been acclaimed as the first stage director in the modern theatre. While this may be true in respect of the relationship adopted in his theatre between the actor and the director, the actor being allowed less freedom than was normally given him, one might well argue that aesthetically the Duke's work was no more advanced than that of his predecessors, a fact pointed out by several contemporary theatre critics. Even **Max Reinhardt** can, for all the technological innovations he achieved on stage, be regarded as the heir to the traditional 19th-century stage director, in that his final ambition was to achieve on stage the impression of a physically dazzling performance that struck his audiences as a seamless whole.

Although theatre managers and *régisseurs* generally catered to the public appetite for spectacle, there were some who attempted to keep alive the ideal of ensemble, either as had been practised by Goethe at Weimar or by Schröder in Hamburg. Brühl, Iffland's successor at the Berlin Royal Theatre, perpetuated the Weimar style, though his productions were considerably more elaborate than Goethe's ever could have been at Weimar. August von Lüttichau (1785–1863), intendant at the **Dresden Court Theatre**, was also another notable perpetuator of Weimar acting; in fact, his theatre was nationally celebrated as a result. However, the spirit of Goethe's work was possibly better preserved in the work of **Ernst Klingemann** at the Brunswick Court Theatre and, above all, of **Karl Immermann** at the Düsseldorf Town Theatre. Immermann, in trying to focus attention on the actor, simplified the stage setting and encouraged an intimate ensemble among his actors that was more natural than that achieved by Goethe in Weimar. Toward the end of his life, Immermann also tried to revive the technique of open staging associated with theatres in England and Italy during the Renaissance. Immermann's private production of *Twelfth Night* in 1840, while it was seen by only a handful of people, was important as in it he rejected illusionistic scenery and multiple scene changes in order to achieve a simple, continuous production in which the ensemble was preeminent. Consequently the dramatic text was unfolded with remarkable simplicity. Immermann was influenced by the ideas of Ludwig Tieck, who had been interested in the plays of the Elizabethan theatre since the late 18th century and, after a trip to England in 1817, also in the physical arrangement of that theatre. During his long career as playwright, critic, and dramaturge, at the Dresden Court Theatre and, late in life, at the Berlin Royal Theatre, Tieck laboured without too much success to introduce simplified staging and natural ensemble. He did this in reaction both to the star system and to the emphasis on spectacle. His efforts reached their peak in 1843 when he staged, at the Berlin Royal Theatre, an epoch-making production of *A Midsummer Night's Dream* with a staging that owed much to the Elizabethan theatre, even though it was far from being historically accurate. Although the challenge that arose from this, of greater simplicity in production and a denial of the prevalent illusionism of the stage, was not taken up again until close to the end of the century by **Joczsa Savits** in Munich, the idea of a non-spectacular theatre remained an ideal for some directors, most prominent among whom was Heinrich Laube. Laube's achievement as a stage director in Vienna and Leipzig was, arguably, of greater significance than his playwriting, for he developed to a higher degree of perfection than his predecessors or contemporaries the art of conversational ensemble on stage among settings that were severe in contrast to those normally seen in the conventional theatre. **Eduard Devrient**, the nephew of Ludwig, also created a highly admired ensemble theatre in Karlsruhe. No doubt it was the work of such theatre men that led **George Henry Lewes** to comment, after a visit to Germany, that the quality of ensemble even in the smallest theatres was far in advance of that of theatres in England.

If many historians have seen in the work of the Duke of Saxe-Meiningen the start of modern theatre, it is possibly because he asserted the preeminence of the director in the rehearsal process. Audiences, in perceiving the rigorous discipline of the company, became aware of this. The example of his well-drilled ensemble inspired **Adolph L'Arronge** and a few like-minded actors to found the **Deutsches Theater** in Berlin in 1883, in order to provide the capital city with a regular ensemble theatre of the quality of the **Meininger**. This project succeeded due mainly to the quality of the company, which included actors such as **Josef Kainz** and **Agnes Sorma**. Some years later, in 1889, the drama critic **Otto Brahm**, an enthusiastic advocate of the plays of **Ibsen** and the naturalists and stimulated by the example of the Théâtre Libre in Paris, founded the **Freie Bühne**, an informal company of professional actors who performed the works of the naturalist dramatists in the ensemble style that suited them. Their performances took place in regular theatres at times that these theatres were not being used for conventional, commercial productions. Brahm's productions appealed not to the broad audiences of the commercial theatre but to specific interest groups, especially the intelligentsia and the fledgling Social Democratic party. Political rivalries quickly led to a split in the Freie Bühne movement, so that the more left-wing of Brahm's associates started the Freie Volksbühne, to be followed by yet a further splinter group, the Neue Freie Volksbühne, organizations that formed the basis of the present-day **Volksbühne** movement, which, closely associated with trade unions, provides subsidized seats at performances in regional theatres for union members. Brahm was unsympathetic to the political aspirations of his colleagues so, in 1894, he gladly accepted the appointment of director of the Deutsches Theater, where he produced both modern and classical plays in the naturalistic style.

While Brahm was initially inspired by Ibsen, his innovations would not have been possible without the work of the German naturalist dramatists, of whom **Gerhart Hauptmann** was undoubtedly the most important. Not only did Hauptmann successfully introduce onto the German stage both the subject matter and style advocated by **Zola** in his essays 'Naturalism in the Theatre', he also conducted a social polemic that was as capable of exciting and infuriating his contemporaries as were the plays of Ibsen. No other contemporary German playwright was as prolific as Hauptmann, not did any master such a variety of styles, for Hauptmann wrote successfully in the symbolist and neoromantic vein as well. But all contemporary playwrights were influenced by him to the extent that subsequent German drama exhibited greater attention to individual psychology and, in most cases, a heightened awareness of the inequalities that vitiated German society. By far the most controversial playwright of this turn of the century period was **Frank Wedekind**, whose play *Spring Awakening*, which is about the effects of society's ignorance of the nature of puberty on adolescents, was written in 1892, but could not be performed, and then only in a severely modified version, until 1906. Wedekind, who found Hauptmann's relentless realism pedestrian, constructed his plot in disjointed episodes, in a manner reminiscent of *Sturm und Drang* and, as it transpired, anticipatory of the later expressionist movement in theatre. Wedekind never lost his position as an outsider in German theatre and society, as he unceasingly dramatized the sensational though socially tabooed topic of sex. This caused him to become the most celebrated writer of the German theatrical avant-garde in the early 20th century. In the final year of his life, he sang in the company of the young **Bertolt Brecht** at a cabaret in Munich.

The years before the First World War were dominated by the work of the director Max Reinhardt. Reinhardt began his career as an actor in Brahm's ensemble at the Deutsches Theater. In 1903, ambition drove him to direct independently; in 1904, he took over the direction of the Deutsches Theater from Brahm and for the following decade made it into the most celebrated theatre in Germany. Here, utilizing the work of designers influenced by the seminal theory and renditions of **Adolphe Appia** and **Edward Gordon Craig**, Reinhardt staged productions that were noted for their extraordinary polish and for an illusionistic spectacle that was perfect to the last detail. While Reinhardt claimed to enjoy working in chamber theatre conditions, he made his name staging vast spectacles, first in Berlin, then Vienna, then in London and other European capitals. By the outbreak of the war, his name was the byword for all that was respected internationally in German theatre – superlative ensemble, seamless spectacle, and a company repertoire that embraced a breadth of classics and modern work in a way unequalled elsewhere in Europe.   sw

See: R. Hayman, *The German Theatre: A Symposium*, London, 1975; G. H. Huettich, *Theatre in the Planned Society: contemporary drama in the German Democratic Republic in its historical, political and cultural context*, Chapel Hill, 1978; C. Innes, *Modern German Drama: A Study in Form*, Cambridge, 1979; R. Pascal, *From Naturalism to Expressionism: German Literature & Society, 1880–1918*, London, 1973; M. Patterson, *The Revolution in German Theatre 1900–1933*, London, 1981; L. R. Shaw, *The Playwright & Historical Change: dramatic strategies in Brecht, Hauptmann, Kaiser, Wedekind*, Wisconsin, 1970.

Since 1914 Reinhardt, whose pioneering productions had established the pre-expressionistic work of Wedekind and **Sternheim** on the stage, was also responsible for promoting the dramatists of the Young Germany group between 1918 and 1921. Named after the 19th-century revolutionary movement, the work of **Reinhard Sorge**, **Walter Hasenclever**, **Reinhard Goering** and Fritz von Unruh defined the themes of German expressionism – the revolt against authority, the rejection of a materialistic society, pacifism and the liberation of the instincts. This anti-illusionistic form, derived from **Büchner** and the post-Inferno plays of **Strindberg**, dominated the German stage for almost a decade after the war, reaching its peak in the messianic pathos of **Georg Kaiser** and **Ernst Toller**. The dynamic symbolism of **Leopold Jessner**'s staging, or the rhetorical exaggeration of **Fritz Kortner**'s acting, was developed to reflect the new dramatic values incorporated in episodic plots, highly elliptical language and metaphysical abstraction.

Arguably, the real contribution of expressionism was in introducing non-naturalistic stage techniques, design and lighting. The more extreme work of its playwrights has little lasting value, and its significance is not in the work of individuals but as a broad general movement. It provided the starting point for directors such as **Karlheinz Martin** and **Erwin Piscator**, or dramatists like Bertolt Brecht, who later reacted against its subjective emotionalism and apolitical idealism. But indeed, with the failure of the Spartacist uprising in Berlin and the crushing of the short-lived Soviet republics set up in 1919, the 'ecstatic' proclamation of the 'New Man' that characterized expressionist drama of the immediate post-war period rapidly became transformed into grotesque and satiric pessimism.

Piscator, who established the criteria for the Neue Sachlichkeit (New Objectivity) movement, developed two contrasting and highly influential modes of theatre. The first, agit-prop or 'Agitation and Propaganda', took radically simplified and utilitarian performances out of the conventional stage. Designed for presentation at working-class gatherings or political party conventions, agit-prop could incorporate direct commentary on immediate topical events and borrowed revue elements from cabaret. It provided a model for the 'Teaching Plays' of Brecht or Carl Credé, though the form could also be expanded to fill the Grosses Schauspielhaus or 'Theatre of the Five Thousand', originally the arena of the Schumann Circus where Reinhardt had staged his spectacular mass

productions of *Oedipus Rex* or the *Oresteia*. At the other end of the theatrical spectrum Piscator mounted a series of productions between 1927 and 1929 that used all the mechanical resources of the modern stage and incorporated film, photo-montage, amplified sound recordings, projected texts, even the mutograph to create a technological and factual form of 'Total theatre' capable of handling political issues on a global scale. His company included many of the outstanding actors of the period, Ernst Deutsch, Alexander Granach, or **Max Pallenberg**, as well as Ernst Busch and Brecht's wife **Helene Weigel**, who later became key members of the **Berliner Ensemble**; but the full effect of Piscator's work was delayed until the Documentary Drama of the 1960s.

The other major figure in the period was Brecht, who developed his own version of Neue Sachlichkeit in his theory of 'epic theatre'. These objective, openly presentational and non-Aristotelian principles, using placards and minimal scenery, were worked out between his 1922 production of *Edward II* and his short, didatic 'teaching plays' of the 1930s. Although this new theatrical form was partially illustrated in *The Threepenny Opera*, which was an immediate success when it was performed in 1928, it required a style of acting very different from both the realistic method of **Stanislavsky** and the emotive symbolism of the expressionists. This could only be explored and his drama fully realized on stage when Brecht attained his

The figures on stilts in Brecht's production of *Man is Man*, 1931.

own company – and in 1933 political events put an end to the revolutionary experiments that made Weimar theatre a vital creative force. Under the Nazis the work of almost all the leading playwrights was banned. Brecht himself, together with Kaiser and Sternheim, was driven into exile, as were **Carl Zuckmayer** and **Lion Feuchtwanger**, who had used historical subjects to illustrate contemporary issues, and religious expressionists like **Ernst Barlach** or **Hans Henny Jahnn**, along with Toller, Hasenclever and Reinhard Goering, all three of whom committed suicide.

Friedrich Wolf continued to write political plays on topical issues in Russia, while Brecht completed all his major dramas in Scandinavia or America. But the German stage was closed to them, and apart from spectacular pageants glorifying fascist ideals (the *Thingspiel*) the only significant dramatic work under the Third Reich was **Gustaf Gründgens**'s productions of the classics. The theatres, closed completely by the Nazis from 1944 to 1945, were mainly destroyed by the end of the war, and with the exception of a single play by **Wolfgang Borchert** new work was slow to emerge. It was a tabula rasa.

In the immediate post-war years work by exiles like Zuckmayer or the Austrian, **Fritz Hochwälder**, were presented in Zürich, the only German-speaking theatre centre that had remained free of Nazi censorship; and it was from Switzerland that the first new dramatic initiatives appeared with the plays of **Friedrich Dürrenmatt** and **Max Frisch**. Brecht was the first major exile to return, and in 1949 his East Berlin production of *Mother Courage* was designed as an antidote to the empty rhetoric and self-indulgent emotionalism of theatre under the Nazis. It marked the opening of the Berliner Ensemble, which reestablished modern German drama on the international stage with its European tours in 1954–6. But partly because of the Cold War suspicion of Communism with which Brecht was identified, its influence was delayed in West Germany until directors like **Peter Palitzsch** or **Benno Besson**, who had trained under him, left the DDR at the beginning of the 1960s. However, almost all of the leading East German dramatists began their careers at the Berliner Ensemble, including **Helmut Baierl**, **Volker Braun**, **Harmut Lange** and **Erwin Strittmatter**, as well as the two playwrights whose work has established itself on the West German stage, **Peter Hacks** and **Heiner Müller**. All began with dialectical dramas before branching out into historical documentaries (Braun and Lange), poetic comedy (Hacks) or collages of violent fantasy (Müller). It is not accidental that the only contemporary director of note in the DDR is **Manfred Wekwerth**, who became artistic manager of the Berliner Ensemble in 1977, although during the 1960s Walter Felsenstein gave the Komische Oper in East Berlin a brilliant reputation for theatrically inventive and satirical interpretations of Mozart and Offenbach.

For post-war West German dramatists the catalyst was Gruppe 47 (Group 47), which for the next 20 years provided a forum for new work and spawned over a dozen literary journals, including the influential *Akzente*, *Kursbuch*, and *Text + Kritik*. It is partly due to its annual meetings that such a homogeneous progression of styles has appeared on the modern German stage. The absurd drama of **Wolfgang Hildesheimer**

or the early plays of **Günter Grass**, the early interior monologues of **Martin Walser** and Ilse Aichinger's poetic radio pieces, all of which were read at the Group's annual meetings between 1954 and 1957, appeared in response to the attention paid to Kafka in the early 1950s. Discussion of the political function of literature following the impact of the Berlin wall, the Eichmann trial and the Frankfurt War Crimes Tribunal between 1961 and 1964 was a major factor in the development of **Peter Weiss** from the *Marat/Sade* to *The Investigation*. It was also responsible for Grass's switch from surrealism to politically oriented drama in *The Plebians Rehearse the Uprising*, and conditioned the work of **Hans Magnus Enzensberger**. It provided the context for the Documentary Drama that Piscator developed at the newly opened Freie Volksbühne from 1962 to his death in 1966 through the plays of **Heinar Kipphardt** and **Rolf Hochhuth**. The final stylistic innovation from within Group 47 was the anti-theatre of the Austrian, **Peter Handke**, which concentrated on exposing the structures of political exploitation through language.

This also formed the basis of the new **Volksstück** (Folk Play) of **Franz Xaver Kroetz**, **Martin Sperr** and Jochen Ziem. The brutal and sometimes sensationalist realism of this school was influenced by the revival of work from the 1920s by **Ödön von Horváth** under Palitzsch, and by **Marieluise Fleisser** under **Rainer Werner Fassbinder**. But recently it has moved away from anti-idealistic pictures of peasant life to the analysis of the industrial consumer society. The Folk Play represents one of the major directions taken by contemporary German drama. Others are the development of Documentary Drama into a highly theatrical comic-strip form by **Dieter Forte** and **Tankred Dorst**, whose work has become identified with the most iconoclastic of the contemporary directors **Peter Zadek**; and the type of collective theatre evolved by **Peter Stein**, whose meticulous productions of the classics have gained an international reputation.   CI

See: H. Braun (trans. W. Mass), *The Theatre in Germany*, Munich, 1956; R. Hayman (ed.), *The German Theatre: A Symposium*, London & New York, 1970; C. Innes, *Modern German Drama*, Cambridge, 1979; M. Patterson, *German Theatre Today*, London, 1976; idem, *The Revolution in German Theatre 1900–33*, London, 1981; R. Samuel and R. H. Thomas, *Expressionism in German Life, Literature and the Theatre*, Cambridge, 1939.

Gershwin, George (1898–1937) and **Ira** (1896–1983) American composer and lyricist. George's first connections with the musical stage were as a song-plugger and rehearsal pianist. In 1918 he teamed up with his brother Ira, who had written prose and verse for various periodicals, to write their first song, 'The Real American Folk Song'. A year later, George collaborated with lyricist Irving Caesar on one of the most popular songs of the day, 'Swanee'. For their first ventures in musical theatre, the brothers worked with other collaborators, George contributing songs to *La, La Lucille* (1919), *Morris Gest's Midnight Whirl* (1919), and the 1920–4 editions of *George White's Scandals*, while Ira wrote lyrics for *Two Little Girls in Blue* (1921). George's early show music was steeped in the idioms of jazz, a form which he had learned from listening to black musicians. In 1924 the brothers collaborated on *Lady, Be Good!*, a musical starring **Fred** and **Adele Astaire**. Encouraged by the show's success, the Gershwins turned out a number of other popular 1920s musicals including *Oh, Kay!* (1926), *Funny Face* (1927), and *Rosalie* (1928). Their songs of the 1920s were characterized by George's infectious, driving music and Ira's clever, slangy lyrics.

In the early 1930s, the Gershwins created three satirical musicals, *Strike Up the Band* (1930), *Of Thee I Sing* (1931), and *Let 'Em Eat Cake* (1933). Acclaimed for its trenchant political satire and its good-humoured score, *Of Thee I Sing* was the first musical to be awarded the Pulitzer Prize for Drama. The brothers did not totally abandon more light-hearted forms of musical comedy, however. *Girl Crazy* (1930) had a frivolous book, but contained some of the Gershwins' best songs, such as 'I Got Rhythm' and 'Embraceable You'.

In 1935 the **Theatre Guild** produced the Gershwins' 'American folk opera' *Porgy and Bess*. Receiving mixed reviews from both drama and music critics, the original production of *Porgy and Bess* was not a success. Nevertheless, its magnificent score has proven to be the Gershwins' most enduring work, and the show has entered the repertoires of a number of opera companies.

After George's untimely death in 1937, Ira collaborated with other composers. *Lady in the Dark* (1941), which had a score by Kurt Weill, was innovative in confining its musical numbers to a few elaborate dream sequences. *The Firebrand of Florence* (1945), which Weill also composed, and *Park Avenue* (1946), with a score by Arthur Schwartz, were failures. In addition to composing for the musical stage, the Gershwins wrote a number of motion picture scores, and George also composed for the concert hall.

As a composer, George Gershwin helped to popularize jazz on the musical stage in the 1920s. His more serious compositions for the concert hall prepared him to write *Porgy and Bess*, one of the most ambitious scores ever created for the American musical theatre. Ira's abilities as a lyricist also grew from the facile rhyming of his 1920s songs to the deeper, more eloquent style of his later work. Together, the Gershwins were major forces in raising the level of musical theatre composition. MK

Gershwin Theatre 1633 Broadway, New York City [Architects: Theatre Planning Associates, Ralph Alswang]. The Uris Theatre was the first large Broadway playhouse to be built under the relaxed zoning constraints in the building code which permitted theatres to be incorporated within commercial structures. Erected by the Uris Corporation, the 1,900-seat theatre is under longterm lease to the **Nederlander** Organization and Eugene Ostreicher and opened in 1972 with a spectacular but unsuccessful rock musical. Since then, its policy has fluctuated between musical productions and a series of concert appearances of well-known popular performers, dance presentations and opera productions. In 1979, it received its first critical success with *Sweeney Todd*, the **Stephen Sondheim** musical. In 1983, it was renamed the Gershwin Theatre in honour of **George** and **Ira Gershwin**. The theatre also encompasses the Theatre Hall of Fame within its spacious public areas. MCH

Gerstein, Bertha (*fl.* c. 1900–20) Leading musical comedy and straight actress of the American Yiddish theatre, notably with **Boris Thomashevski**'s National Theatre and later with **Maurice Schwartz**'s company. Married to the actor **Jacob Ben-Ami**, she frequently played leads opposite him. AB

Gert, Valeska (Samosch) (1892–1978) German cabaret dancer, an exponent of grotesque pantomime. After study with **Aleksandër Moisiu**, she made her Berlin debut in 1916 and appeared at the Schall und Rauch from 1920. Her pugdog features and whirling movements were seen to advantage in macabre numbers like 'The Girl from the Mummy's Cellar'. Kurt Tucholsky called her harlot's dance, 'La Canaille', 'the boldest thing I ever saw on a stage'. She collaborated with **Brecht** on a 'Red Revue' and emigrated to New York (1928) where she founded the Beggar Bar. Back in West Berlin, she ran two more clubs, the Hexenküche (Witch's Kitchen, 1950) and the Ziegenstall (Goat Pen, 1978), adding parodic recitations to her dance repertory. LS

Getachew Abdi (*fl.* 1970s) Ethiopian playwright and director, at present director of the Ethiopian National Theatre. Trained in the Soviet Union. Author of a number of pro-revolutionary plays in Amharic including *The Mirror* (1979). RK

Ghana Ghana, in West Africa, achieved independence under Kwame Nkrumah in 1957, the first of Britain's African colonies to do so. Nkrumah's Convention People's Party was effectively organized at the grass roots and in the first years of independence proposed radical reform at the base of the society. Nkrumah himself was a committed pan-Africanist, eager to promote the liberation of the whole continent. His speeches and actions inspired millions in Africa. However, Ghana seems to frame new discourses which are fulfilled elsewhere. Nkrumah was overthrown by the military in 1966 and died in exile in 1972. Political and economic factors have a direct effect on modern Ghanaian drama, for Ghana is one African country in which its playwrights have, from time to time, played an active role in central government, rather than finding themselves consistently in opposition to it. From 1957, one of the key Ghanaians involved in the development of Ghanaian theatre, **Efua T. Sutherland**, was associated with Nkrumah. She tried to translate some of the early ideals of the State into a socially-based programme for the development of drama and performance out of traditional forms and professionalism. She founded the Ghana Drama Studio in Accra in 1957; and was involved, with J. K. Nketia, in the establishment of the School of Music and Drama under the aegis of the Institute of African Studies at the University of Ghana in Legon. Later, playwrights **Ama Ata Aidoo** and Asiedu Yirenkyi who had worked at the Ghana Drama Studio and with the University's Studio Players held Ministerial appointments in the military administration of Jerry Rawlings.

The continually deteriorating economy has meant that State funding for the performing arts has always been diminishing. Just as new ideas have been promoted which make virtue out of stringent economies the funding has been further reduced. The result is that dramatic talent has been nurtured and then forced into exile, sometimes for economic reasons only but always with a great deal of creative frustration. This has happened to Aidoo herself, as well as to another leading playwright and director, Joe de Graft. They have had to work as expatriates in other African countries, and their creative output has dwindled, away from the vigorous drama discourse within Ghana in which they were participating.

The influence of Ghanaian dramatists extends beyond their own artistic products, and to many African countries. However, the Ghanaian playwright in another African country is still classed as an expatriate and therefore caught in a contradiction: he or she is of the African culture politically, and yet politically separated from it. This can be particularly difficult for Ghanaian playwrights whose creative work has explored the political fusion of the traditional and the modern.

The traditional roots of drama in the oral culture are seen in Ghana as being highly significant for the forms, themes and tone of the new drama. Sophia Lokko, after J. K. Nketia, lists the Ghanaian sources of theatre as Dance-Drama, Ceremonies and Story-telling. There are different traditions among ethnic groups but research suggests that their dramatic elements all tend to emphasize the community as the basis for domestic well-being. The community can bring to light what the family may be tempted to hide to its cost. This can be seen in *Aboakyer*, the Deer-Hunt Festival in Winneba (researched by A. A. Mensah) which is a Lord-of-Misrule festival. The captured or killed deer is ceremonially sequestered while the entire community participates in an immense procession which contains bands, dancers, skits, satire, transvestism. Another feature of the oral tradition is the participation of the audience, especially in the story-telling performances. The traditions of *Anansesem* (Spider stories), described by Lokko, and others, have been extended into a modern form of performance by Efua Sutherland. She describes the conventions of *Anansegoro* in the Foreword to her play *The Marriage of Anansewa*. Others, like Yirenkyi, have also been involved in developing *Anansegoro*. Sutherland's development of this and other interesting forms of story-telling theatre and musical performance has led her also to develop the architecture of performance space, like the Atwia *Kodzidan* (the 'Story House' in the village of Atwia).

Charles Angmor divides modern dramatic expression in Ghana into operatic drama and literary drama. Under the former he lists the folk opera, cantatas (of various Christian congregations) and the Concert Parties. Folk opera may have developed out of the staging of **Gilbert** and Sullivan operettas in the schools, although the Ghanaian intelligentsia also developed a taste for European Grand Opera. Saka Acquaye, in particular, wanted to indigenize the operatic form and compose operas in Ghanaian languages. In a similar way, perhaps, the cantatas reflected a theatrical indigenizing of Christianity in the particular circumstances of fund-raising. However, it is in the Concert Parties that we find the most exciting development of theatre and dramatic form.

The Concert Parties of coastal Ghana and the neighbouring Republic of Togo are the only professional theatre, with the members of the many companies earning their livelihoods from their travelling shows. The Concert Parties are also called 'Trios', their performers 'Comedians' and their improvised performances 'Comic Plays'. The content of the plays is contemporary, depicting the actuality of the lives of their rapt audiences. Concert Parties are reputed to have started in 1918 with a headmaster who performed solo, Master Yalley; but the most famous company was that of 'Bob' Johnson in the 1930s. They were first known as the 'Two Bobs and their Carolina Girl' and then as the 'Axim Trio'. Sutherland states that they did not compose *Anansegoro*, but that Johnson 'took ordinary life stories and then composed plays by the method of *Kasa-ndwon*. . . (Speech and song. . .)'. The Trios flourished in the 1960s and 70s. Each company travels extensively with a large repertory of plays, which although improvised are actually maintained in a fairly stable performance 'text'. They have been researched by K. N. Bame in Ghana; and in Togo by Alain Ricard who has published a performance on sound-tape of *Mister Tameklor* by the Happy Star Concert Band of Lomé. The great popularity of the Concert Parties has inspired writers like Patience Addo and Derlene Clems whose plays, *Company Pot* and *Scholarship Woman* respectively, were broadcast by the BBC (1972).

The literary form which developed in the 1960s reflected in both content and form some Western models, but also strongly showed a movement away from these, especially as theatre practice attempted to link the depiction of Ghanaian attitudes to the sensibilities of the audiences. This literary drama 'does not operate as a rule on conflict and its resolution, but generally on consensus and consummation' (Angmor). It continues to advance the discourse of traditional performance. These literary plays were prefigured by Kobina Sekyi's *The Blinkards* (1915; published 1974) which attacked European cultural influences; and, in the 1940s, by the literary and philosophical plays of J. B. Danquah and F. K. Fiawoo. But the real flowering only came after independence. Although the corpus of published texts is small (about 30 plays, by fewer than 15 playwrights) the drama discourse has developed with depth and consistency, despite the divergent experiences and personalities of the playwrights. The plays deal with themes and ideas which are often far-reaching in their moral and political implications. *Foriwa*, by Efua Sutherland (1962), explores the transition from the old to the new, and the social mechanism for the transformation of the community at the grass roots. *The Mightier Sword* by Martin Owusu (1973) explores history for the sake of the present, as does de Graft's *Through a Film Darkly* (1966) offering a painful analysis of black racism. *Anowa*, by Ama Ata Aidoo (1970), considered by many critics to be one of the finest modern African plays, historicizes the present by exploring the implications of slavery for people's psyche. De Graft's *Muntu* (1975) mythologizes the present. The ordinary yet important domestic problems resulting from social transformations are expressed in Aidoo's *Dilemma of a Ghost* (1964), in *Sons and Daughters* by de Graft (1964), in *Laughter and Hubbub in the House* by Kwesi Kay (1972) and in Yirenkyi's *Blood and Tears* (1973). On the other hand, the extraordinary domestic crises that result from secret and dubious short-cuts to material prosperity are variously explored in *Kivuli* by Yirenkyi (1972), *Amari* by Jacob Hevi (1975), Owusu's *The Sudden Return* (1973), *Edufa* by Sutherland (1967), and in a humorous vein in Sutherland's *Anansegoro, The Marriage of Anansewa* (1975). These plays are concerned with relationships and responsibilities within the household, which is almost always contextualized by a particularized community perspective. This is usually created 'off-stage' by the drama on-stage. Though often not seen, the community is forever pressing in on the compound walls; and because of its absence it can also symbolize the nation-state, the well-being of which cannot be guaranteed until the family adjustments are properly made. In addition, the status of the women in the plays is often effectively problematized, by both male and female playwrights. The insights which this yields are perhaps Ghana's most important contribution to the development of African theatre. ME

See: C. Angmor, 'Drama in Ghana' in Ogunba and Irele (eds.), *Theatre in Africa*, Ibadan, 1978; K. N. Bame, *Come to Laugh: a Study of African Traditional Theatre in Ghana*, Legon, n.d.; M. Etherton, *The Development of African Drama*, London, 1982; S. Lokko, 'Theatre Space: a History Overview of the Theatre Movement in Ghana' in *Modern Drama*, XXIII, 1980; A. Yirenkyi, 'Bill Marshall and the Ghanaian Theatre of the Early Seventies' in *Journal of the Performing Arts*, Accra, I, I, 1980.
See also: N. Akam and A. Ricard, *Mister Tameklor, suivi de Français-le-Parisien, par le Happy Star Concert Band de Lomé (Togo)*, Paris, 1981.

Ghelderode, Michel de (originally Martens, Ad(h)émar-Adolphe-Louis) (1898–1962) The most powerful and significant Belgian dramatist of the inter-war years, as well as many stories and essays he wrote some 60 plays. His originals are in French but a number of his plays were first performed in Flemish or Dutch translations. They are the work of a national dramatist – not that they are nationalistic, but they are essentially the product of a Belgian, heir to a mixed Flemish and French culture, with a powerful sense of his country's long and violent history. Ghelderode's plays (several not performed until years after they were written, several still unperformed) can be divided very inexactly into three groups: those set in the past, as *Escorial* (Théâtre Communal, Brussels, 1929), *Chronicles of Hell* (Théâtre de l'Atelier, Paris, 1949), *The School for Fools* (Théâtre de l'Oeuvre, Paris, 1953); those with biblical origins – although these are far from being 'religious dramas' – e.g. *Barabbas* (Vlaamsche Volkstooneel, Ostend, 1929), *Miss Jairus* (Théâtre de l'Atelier, Paris, 1949), *The Women at the Tomb* (Théâtre Universitaire, Paris, 1953); and those with their roots in burlesque and the music-hall, e.g. *The Death of Doctor Faust* (Théâtre Art et Action, Paris, 1928), *Christopher Columbus* (Théâtre Art et Action, Paris, 1929), *Pantagleize* (Vlaamsche Volkstooneel, Saint-Trond, 1930). All vividly display a theatre of sights and sounds as well as of words, a theatre of the senses, **Artaud**'s theatre, and very much a theatre of cruelty wrought from the irresistible demands of the flesh, the agony of the spirit and the massacre of the innocent, frequently provoking laughter, but a very uneasy laughter. It has been well noted that much of the avant-garde theatre of the post-war years had already appeared in Ghelderode's plays, which had nevertheless to wait many years

before they escaped from print and from the obscurity of small cult theatres. His work has found appreciative audiences in both Eastern and Western Europe and in the USA, but he is still largely unknown in England. It is noteworthy that one of his most successful fictions was his account of his life and works. The true facts have been painstakingly established by Roland Beyen in *Michel de Ghelderode ou la hantise du masque* (Brussels, 1971). Ghelderode, of whom **Jean Cocteau** said, 'His genius in the theatre is unsurpassed', has not yet received the honour that is his due. He was robbed even by death of his nomination for a Nobel Prize. GH

Gherardi Family of Italian actors. **Giovanni** (c. 1645–83), a **commedia dell'arte** player, who won his sobriquet Flautino from his virtuosity on the flute and guitar, came to Paris in 1674 or 1675. His son **Evaristo** (1663–1700) entered the **Comédie-Italienne** there as Arlequin in **Regnard**'s *Le Divorce* in 1689 and soon rose to manage it, often running foul of the police for his outspokenness. He wrote numerous scenarios for the **Hôtel de Bourgogne** and when the Italian actors were turned out of Paris in 1697, he published 56 of them as *Le Théâtre Italien*, the fullest edition being that of 1700. They comprise one of the most important sources for the history of the *commedia dell'arte* in France. LS

Ghudiki Nabaranga Nata (India) Also known as *Dhukuki Nabaranga Nata*. The *Ghudiki* is the name of a local drum played during the performance in Orissa state. Eight to ten actors sing, dance and act in the midst of spectators. The *Ghudiki* player acts as the director, jesting with the other players, commenting on the dramatic action and dancing simple steps to add variety to the show. Various improvisational skits characterize the three-to-four-hour event. FAR

Giacometti, Paolo (1816–82) Italian dramatist, prolific in a range of play types but most important for his social dramas of which his finest, *La Morte Civile (Civil Death*, 1861), is one of the more considerable Italian plays of the 19th century and was a main piece in the repertoire of many leading actors, including **Salvini**, who after first producing it at the Teatro dei Fiorentini at Naples, played it successfully in both Britain and the United States. LR

Giacosa, Giuseppe (1847–1906) Italian dramatist. Began as a poet and published 'a theatrical legend', *Una Partita a Scacchi (A Game of Chess)*, in the journal *Nuova Antologia* in 1872. In the course of the seventies he wrote a number of historical plays, with mainly medieval and Renaissance settings, like *Il Trionfo dell'Amore (The Triumph of Love*, 1875), and comedies in a light Goldonian manner, like *Il Marito Amante della Moglie (The Husband and His Wife's Lover*, 1877). But his best work was written under the influence of naturalism in the 1890s: middle-class psychological dramas, the best known of which are *Tristi Amori (Sad Loves*, 1887) and *Come le Foglie (Like the Leaves*, 1900), both of which were later made into films and still hold the Italian stage today. His best work is tightly constructed and is characterized by a mood of subtle melancholy. He was a distinguished librettist, collaborating with Luigi Illica on several pieces set by **Puccini**, including

La Bohème (1896), *Tosca* (1899) and *Madame Butterfly* (1904). LR

Gibson, William (1914–   ) American playwright. Gibson first made it to Broadway with *Two for the Seesaw* (1958), and he scored again in 1959 with a stage adaptation of his television play, *The Miracle Worker*. This uncompromising account of Annie Sullivan's struggle to teach the deaf and blind Helen Keller the power of words is now firmly established as a modern American standard. No other Gibson play has come close to the success of his first two. He is also the author of *The Seesaw Log: A Chronicle of the Stage Production*, an agonizing account of the compromises necessitated by the collaborative nature of American commercial theatre. LDC

Gide, André (1869–1951) French novelist, essayist and playwright. As a playwright, Gide was one of a group of writers concerned to reintroduce classical myth on the modern stage, as shown by his *Oedipus* (1931). He was a friend of **Copeau** and interested in the **Vieux-Colombier**, but his talents were essentially those of an introspective *moraliste* and novelist, not a dramatist. DB

Gielgud, John (1904–   ) British actor and director, knighted in 1953. In his first roles under **Granville Barker** in 1921 and with **James Fagan**'s Oxford Repertory Company between 1924 and 1925, when he had his first London success as Trofimov in *The Cherry Orchard*, he developed the elegant style and expressive clarity of voice that won him immediate acclamation as the leading interpreter of Shakespearian tragedy on his appearance with the **Old Vic** in 1929. His most famous role was Hamlet, which he returned to in his own production in 1933 and performed more than 500 times during his career. Another key role was John Worthing in **Wilde**'s *The Importance of Being Earnest*, which he first played in 1930, while Gordon Daviot's *Richard of Bordeaux* (1932, under his own direction) established him as a popular star in the West End commercial theatre. His brilliant performances of *The Seagull* (1936), *The Three Sisters* (1937), *The Cherry Orchard* (1961) or *Ivanov* (1965), all of which he also directed, made a major contribution to **Chekhov**'s acceptance on the English-speaking stage. During the 1950s he promoted the work of such modern playwrights as **Terence Rattigan**, **Graham Greene** and **Enid Bagnold**, both as an actor and director, in addition to extending his Shakespearian repertoire with the **Royal Shakespeare Company** (Lear, Angelo, Leontes: 1950–1) or at the Old Vic, and presenting his internationally acclaimed Shakespeare recital *Ages of Man* (1958). Since 1974 he has appeared frequently at the **National Theatre**, his most striking performances being in *The Tempest* (Prospero, 1974) and in **Pinter**'s *No Man's Land* (1975), and his four books of theatrical reminiscences offer a wealth of material on the development of the English theatre in the modern period. CI

Gilbert, John (Gibbs) (1810–89) American actor famous for comic roles in classic English comedy. Gilbert was born in Boston and made his debut there at the **Tremont Theatre** as Jaffier in *Venice Preserv'd* in 1828. He played the frontier theatres until 1834 and made his New York debut in 1839. Although he started as a leading tragedian, his greater successes came in comedy, especially as old men. For a time he managed the **Chestnut Street Theatre**. For 26 years he was with **Wallack**'s company. A very traditional actor, he resisted almost any theatrical change. He died on the road. SMA

Gilbert, Mrs George H. (née Anne Hartley) (1821–1904) British born actress and dancer, who married a dancer-manager in 1846 and moved to America in 1849. Gilbert spent most of her career playing 'dear old ladies, foolish virgins and peppery viragos'. For 30 years, from 1869 to 1899, she acted in **Augustin Daly**'s company, inevitably playing opposite the comic James Lewis and with **Ada Rehan** and **John Drew** (the 'Big Four'). Gilbert, a polished technician, was admired for her cooperative spirit and was venerated by the public. After Daly's death she appeared under **Charles Frohman**'s management until her death. DBW

Gilbert, Sir William Schwenck (1836–1911) English playwright, famous above all for his collaboration with Sir Arthur Sullivan in the series of Savoy Operas that made them both (and Richard D'Oyly Carte, their sponsor) rich. Gilbert was already well known as a writer some years before *Thespis* (1871) brought the two men together for the first time. He trained as a lawyer and was called to the Bar in 1863. Two years earlier he had begun contributing comic verse to the magazine *Fun*, under the pseudonym 'Bab'. The 1869 collection of *Bab Ballads* (other collections followed in 1873 and 1877) was illustrated by the author. It earns him an honoured place among Victorian 'nonsense' poets, but Gilbert's nonsense has often a satirical edge. Gilbert wrote his first play in 1863 and was consistently active in the theatre from 1866–97, during which time he wrote well over 60 plays, burlesques, operas and extravaganzas.

Although he wrote plays in many different styles, Gilbert's pessimistic assumption that manners and politeness are a mask for fundamental human selfishness is rarely absent from his work. This, certainly, is the basis of most of the successful 'fairy' plays, from *The Palace of Truth* (1870) through *Pygmalion and Galatea* (1871) to *The Wicked World* (1873), all written in blank verse that welcomes bathos. The vein of mockery that enlivens Gilbert's best work was happily exploited in the collaborations with Sullivan, *The Sorcerer* (1877), *HMS Pinafore* (1878), *The Pirates of Penzance* (1879), *Patience* (1881), *Iolanthe* (1882), *Princess Ida* (1884), *The Mikado* (1885), *Ruddigore* (1887), *The Yeomen of the Guard* (1888), *The Gondoliers* (1889), *Utopia Limited* (1893) and *The Grand Duke* (1896). The fame of the Savoy Operas has eclipsed that of even his best plays, notably *Sweethearts* (1874), *Engaged* (1877), which certainly influenced **Shaw** and **Wilde**, and *Rosencranz and Guildenstern* (1891), a witty swan-song of Victorian burlesque. When Gilbert was knighted in 1907, he was proud to claim that he was the first to be so honoured 'for dramatic authorship alone'. PT

Gilford, Jack (1907–90) American actor-comedian. Gilford began his career as a comedian, appearing in night clubs, revues, and vaudeville. His most successful appearances on Broadway include the roles of Bontche Schweig in *The World of Sholom Aleichem* (1953), Mr Dussell in *The Diary of Anne Frank* (1955), King Sextimus in *Once Upon a Mattress* (1959), Hysterium in *A Funny Thing Happened on the Way to the Forum* (1962), and Herr Schultz in *Cabaret* (1966). He appeared in the films of *Funny Thing* and *Catch 22*. He also starred in televised versions of *Sholom Aleichem* and *Anne Frank*. SMA

Gill, Peter (1939–) British director and dramatist, who joined the **Royal Court** company as an actor in 1959 but became best known there as the director of three hitherto underrated plays by **D. H. Lawrence**, presented as a group in 1968. In 1969, the Royal Court also produced two of his first plays, *The Sleepers' Den* and *Over Gardens Out*, which revealed that Gill could evoke with economy of means but with lyrical skill the circumstances of his Cardiff boyhood. In 1977, Gill was appointed the Director of **Riverside Studios** which he transformed into a major arts centre. On its rudimentary stages he directed classical productions of **Chekhov**'s *The Cherry Orchard* (1978), **Middleton** and **Rowley**'s *The Changeling* (1978) and *Measure for Measure* (1979), as well as encouraging new dramatists and new forms of theatre. In 1980, he joined the **National Theatre** under **Peter Hall**, where as well as directing such productions as **Turgenev**'s *A Month in the Country* (1981) and **Büchner**'s *Danton's Death* (1983), he pioneered new writing at the Cottesloe Theatre, running a season of premieres there in 1985. His best play, *Small Change* (1976), received its premiere at the Royal Court under his own directing. JE

Gillette, William (Hooker) (1853–1937) American actor and playwright. Born into a prominent Hartford, Connecticut, family, Gillette left home in 1873 to seek a career on the stage. As an actor he is remembered for his performance in his own *Sherlock Holmes* (1899), which he played over 1,300 times, although his Civil War spy melodrama, *Secret Service*

William Gillette playing the title role in his *Sherlock Holmes*, first staged in 1899. Also in the photograph is George Wessells as his thwarted adversary, Professor Moriarty.

(1895), with its fast-moving action, suspense, and the tension between the demands of love and duty, was his most significant achievement as a playwright. Gillette was the author of numerous adaptations and dramatizations and several original plays in which he frequently appeared himself, in the USA and England. In addition to Holmes, he played Blane in *Held by the Enemy* (1886), Billings in *Too Much Johnson* (1894), and Thorne/Dumont in *Secret Service*. His other notable appearances were in **Barrie**'s *The Admirable Crichton* (1903) and *Dear Brutus* (1918). Other Gillette plays include *The Private Secretary* (1884), *All the Comforts of Home* (1890), *Clarice* (1905), and *Electricity* (1910). In 1913 Gillette delivered his influential lecture, subsequently published, *The Illusion of the First Time in Acting*, which explains his cool, understated approach to acting, a contrast to the florid and romantic style that dominated the theatre up to his time. *Sherlock Holmes* was successfully revived in 1974 by the **Royal Shakespeare Company**, first in London at the Aldwych and in New York in the same year; *Secret Service* was revived in 1976 by the Phoenix Theatre Company in New York. DBW

Gilpin, Charles Sidney (1878–1930) Afro-American actor. Introduced at school to amateur theatricals, Gilpin left school aged 14 to become a vagabond vaudevillian, his meagre earnings supplemented by sporadic jobs as printer, porter, barber and elevator boy. In 1907 he joined the all-black **Pekin** Stock Company of Chicago and later acted at the Lincoln and Lafayette Theatres in Harlem. His impressive Broadway performance as the slave Custis in **Drinkwater**'s *Abraham Lincoln* (1919) led to the title role in *The Emperor Jones* (1920) in which he scored a resounding triumph. A victim of sudden fame and racial prejudice, Gilpin took to drink which cut short his career. The black critic Theophilus Lewis lamented: 'He rose from obscurity to the peaks, lived his hour of triumph, and returned again to the shadows.' EGH

Gilroy, Frank D[aniel] (1925–) American playwright. Gilroy first gained attention with his solid drama, *Who'll Save the Plowboy?* (1962), which won the Obie Award. His next effort was *The Subject Was Roses* (1964), a story of the rivalry of a mother and father for the affection of their son who has just returned from the war. Although thinly funded and with a relatively unknown cast for the time, this play became one of the most honoured serious dramas of the past thirty years (Pulitzer Prize, Outer Circle Award, Drama Critics' Award, and Tony). Gilroy continues to write plays, but success has eluded his recent efforts. LDC

Giraldi, Giovan Battista, called **Cinzio** (1504–73) Italian dramatist, short story writer and literary theorist. A prolific and influential writer, his nine plays in the tragic or tragicomic modes, exploiting Senecan motives of violence and the supernatural, were much admired in Italy and abroad, particularly *L'Orbecche* (1541), and his short stories provided plot lines or suggestions to many dramatists, among them **Shakespeare**, who drew on his *Ecatommiti* (1565) for *Othello* and *Measure for Measure*. His theoretical writings on the unities of time, place and action, and the morality proper to dramatic subject matter and treatment, were no less influential, particularly in France. KR

Giraudoux, Jean (1882–1944) French diplomat and writer. Giraudoux's success as a dramatist was largely due to his partnership with **Jouvet**, who directed and acted in almost all his plays from the first, *Siegfried* (1928), to the last, *La Folle de Chaillot* (*The Madwoman of Chaillot*, 1945). At the time this pairing seemed the realization of **Copeau**'s dream of bringing poetry back to the modern stage and each new production was eagerly awaited by Jouvet's audience. In fact much of Giraudoux's work is ill suited to the stage, verbose and lacking action, though it has great wit and charm. Largely unsuccessful in his attempt at tragedy, Giraudoux seems at his best in light-hearted entertainments such as *Intermezzo* (1933) or *L'Apollon de Bellac* (*The Apollo of Bellac*, 1942) which combine brilliant humour with subtlety and occasional depth. Only perhaps in *La Guerre de Troie N'Aura Pas Lieu* (*Tiger at the Gates*, 1935) did he succeed in tailoring his style to a subject of contemporary importance. Hitler's power was increasing and this story of civilized Trojans and Greeks dragged unwillingly into war struck a prophetic chord. Giraudoux's frequent use of classical mythology encouraged a vogue for myth on the French stage in the 1930s and 1940s. DB

Glaspell, Susan (1876–1948) Perhaps best known as one of the founders of the **Provincetown Players** (along with her husband, George Cram Cook), Glaspell was also a playwright, second only to **Eugene O'Neill** in the founding of a modern American drama which combined contemporary American ideas with European expressionistic techniques. Glaspell's early one-act plays satirized contemporary attitudes and interests, such as pop psychology (*Suppressed Desires*, 1915) and ultra-idealism (*Tickless Time*, 1918) (both written in collaboration with Cook). But her *Trifles* (1916), one of the most frequently anthologized one-act plays, skilfully portrayed hidden, psychological motivation by using realistic settings and dialogue to reveal women's inner conflicts. This play was also her first to use the device of keeping the central female character off-stage. She repeated this technique in *Bernice* (1919) and in her most controversial play, *The Verge* (1921), in which she experimented with symbolism and expressionistic settings to reveal the state of mind of a 'new' woman striving for both abstract idealism and individual fulfilment.

Throughout her career Glaspell never feared to tackle the new and the immediate. In *The Inheritors* (1921) she contrasted post-First World War narrow Americanism with earlier ideals of individual freedom and tolerance, again creating a female character who sacrifices ease and comfort to remain true to her idealism. In 1931, Glaspell won the Pulitzer Prize for *Alison's House*, loosely based on the life of Emily Dickinson.

Glaspell's contribution to American drama includes her role in the founding of the **Little Theatre movement**, as well as her creation of modern female characters portrayed through new and experimental dramatic techniques. FB

Globe Theatre, London When the lease ran out on **James Burbage**'s **Theatre** in 1598, members of the **Lord Chamberlain's Men** had the building dismantled and most of its timbers carried across the Thames to a south-bank site close to **Henslowe**'s **Rose**

where they were thriftily deployed in the construction of a new theatre. The Globe was a polygonal structure with a three-tiered gallery surrounding an open yard. Attempts to 'reconstruct' it are based on De Witt's drawing of the **Swan**, which it probably resembled, and on references to it in the **Fortune** contract. Restricted excavations, begun on the site in 1989, are too inconclusive to settle disputes about its dimensions and capacity (3,350 according to John Orrell's 1983 argument), but it was certainly larger than the Rose, its chief south-bank competitor. Of more general interest is the system of sharing costs and profits devised by the company at the Globe. **Shakespeare** was among the six responsible 'housekeepers', and it was at the Globe from 1599–1608 that most of his finest plays were first publicly performed. The Globe continued in use after its resident company took possession of the indoor **Blackfriars Theatre** in 1608–9. That it was a profitable asset is emphasized by the speed with which it was rebuilt after destruction by fire in 1613. The second Globe remained active until the closure of the theatres in 1642. It was demolished in 1644.

Two later London theatres have shared the famous name. The first opened in 1868 with a production of **H. J. Byron**'s *Cyril's Success* but was demolished in 1902 as part of the scheme for widening the Strand. The second, originally called the **Seymour Hicks** after its first star, was opened in 1906 and still stands on Shaftesbury Avenue. PT

Gluck, Christoph Willibald (1714–87) German composer of many operas, the finest of which exhibit great dramatic power. In his later works Gluck dealt forceful blows at the decorative entertainment which opera had become in the 18th century. He was steeped in the aesthetic of the second half of the 18th century but created works that strongly foreshadow romanticism. In an age in which opera had become a mere succession of elaborate musical ornaments, he was preoccupied with opera as drama and sought to assign the libretto to its rightful position. He claimed that when composing he forgot that he was a musician. In fact he acted as an outstanding musician. His claim must be understood to mean that he did not aim to write music that proceeded in complete freedom but music that bore a reciprocally supportive relationship with the libretto. His most successful operas were on classical themes, as had been the earliest of all operas and as were most serious operas in the 18th century. They are *Orpheus and Eurydice* (Vienna 1762, revised Paris 1774), *Alcestis* (Vienna 1767, revised Paris 1776), *Paris and Helen* (Vienna 1769), *Iphigenia in Aulis* (Paris 1774), *Armida* (Paris 1777), *Iphigenia in Tauris* (Paris 1779). The librettos of the first three are by **Calzabigi** whose influence on Gluck was profound, probably decisive.

In the prefaces to the scores of *Alcestis* and *Paris and Helen* and in letters to the *Mercure de France* Gluck stated his aims in operatic composition. Insisting on the necessity of a meaningful libretto and, in true 18th-century fashion, on the imitation of Nature, he declared that the overture should not be a free-standing musical item but a suitable introduction to the subsequent drama, that dramatically unnecessary vocal ornamentation and instrumental interpolation should have no place, and that the sharpness of distinction between recitative and aria should be reduced, a matter that was to be pursued by opera composers until it eventuated in **Wagner**'s 'continuous melody'. Gluck's grasp of the nature of theatre music as against concert or salon music is well illustrated by his comment that if someone up in the dome of the Invalides closely examining the paintings were to ask, 'What is intended here – a nose, an arm?' the proper reply from the painter at ground level would be, 'Come down here and judge for yourself.'   GH

Goering, Reinhard (1887–1936) German dramatist. An exponent of expressionism, best known for *A Sea Battle* (1918), which was the first play to deal directly with the war on the German stage and introduced the anonymous characterization and telegraphic dialogue that mark the plays of **Kaiser** and **Hasenclever**.   CI

Goethe, Johann Wolfgang von (1749–1832) German playwright, director, novelist, and essayist. Goethe's achievement in the theatre was as varied and as significant as his accomplishment in other fields of the arts, humanities, and sciences. From his childhood in Frankfurt, where he eagerly attended both French tragedy and Punch and Judy shows, he demonstrated an active interest in all things theatrical. He was a prolific playwright, but he is difficult to categorize as his work both typified and developed most genres current in his time. Hence while his early play *Götz von Berlichingen* (1773) reflects contemporary enthusiasm for the works of **Shakespeare** and provided the young **Sturm und Drang** writers with a model for their own dramas, after his removal to Weimar, Goethe's drama gradually came to express a more classical outlook. *Egmont* (completed in 1788) is still Shakespearian in structure, but Goethe's view of his hero, whose 'daimonic' personality and trust in the goodness of those around him leads to his death, shows a distrust of the values that had enthused him in his *Sturm und Drang* period. Perhaps Goethe's most effective works for the theatre are the classical verse plays *Iphigenie on Tauris* (1787) and *Torquato Tasso* (1790), the former reflecting Goethe's belief in the superiority of moral strength and humanitarian impulse above barbarism, the latter, which may well indicate Goethe's dissatisfaction with his position in the Weimar court, showing a profound scepticism as well as appreciation of the romantic spirit of the artist. Goethe's masterpiece, *Faust Part 1* (1808) and *Part 2* (1832), while cast in dramatic form and exhibiting command of a vast range of dramatic styles, was not written with performance in mind. *Part 1* has, however, often been produced successfully; it focuses mainly on the private experience of Faust and on his erotic misadventures with Gretchen. *Part 2*, a far more formidable theatrical undertaking, has a wider scope, leading to meditations on such lofty and weighty subjects as the future of the human race.

From 1791 to 1817, Goethe executed, along with several other official duties in Weimar, the post of director of the Court Theatre, a position he shared for some years with **Schiller**. Apart from developing an admirably balanced approach to repertoire that was to be imitated by other court and municipal theatres, Goethe evolved the so-called 'Weimar School' of acting, embodied in his 'Rules for Actors', that was to

have a fundamental influence on the performance of tragedy in the German theatre until the end of the 19th century. Goethe's attempt to make the actor into a model of deportment and elegant speech might be regarded as a denial of the distrustful attitude he often expressed toward the acting profession, an attitude to which he gave vivid realization in the great *Bildungsroman Wilhelm Meister's Apprenticeship* (1795–6). Despite Goethe's obvious suspicion of the artistic integrity of the actor, the novel is still one of the liveliest accounts of theatre life yet written.

Goethe's attitude toward Shakespeare underwent much modification during his lifetime. Initially, under the influence of J. G. Herder, he was in the forefront of the German Shakespeare revival. Latterly, most notably in his essay 'Shakespeare und kein Ende' (1815 – 'No End to Shakespeare'), he argued that Shakespeare's plays were best read and not performed. His notorious adaptation of *Romeo and Juliet* shows a lack of sympathy with Shakespeare's dramatic strategy and a distinct preference for French dramaturgy.   SW

Gogol, Nikolai Vasilievich (1809–52) 19th-century Russia's greatest comic writer and dramatist, whose special brand of grotesque realism and stated belief in the moral and social obligation of art influenced two centuries of artists, including **Tolstoi**, Dostoevsky, **Sukhovo-Kobylin**, **Turgenev**, **Chekhov**, **Bely** and Nabokov. His early exposure to the puppet plays and folk tales of his native Ukraine with their mystery, superstition and coarse humour and his psychological pleasures and embarrassments – spiritual health versus physical uncleanliness, food and sexuality, anonymity and exposure, the perfidy of Woman and the hegemony of the Devil – mingled to produce his tormented art. His St Petersburg career (1828–36) as lowly civil servant, bumbling history professor and developing writer, broadened and deepened his fears for humanity and the Russian people in particular. This period produced three volumes of short stories and miscellany – *Evenings on a Farm Near Dikanka* (1831–2), *Arabesques* and *Mirgorod* (1835), the last two containing his so-called 'Petersburg Tales'. He also composed three short comedies which feature his inimitable linguistic verve and fluidity, farceur's sense of pace and

'If they want a celebration . . .', a scene from Gogol's *The Inspector General*. The picture demonstrates one of Meyerhold's famous concentrated 'piling together' scenic effects on a small, movable platform.

plot and his relentless dissection of opportunism, eccentricity, self-delusion and social and moral hypocrisy. These include *The Marriage* (1835), *The Gamblers* (1836) and *Decoration of Vladimir of the Third Class* (1832), the last concerning an upwardly mobile bureaucrat which Gogol left unfinished for fear of censorship. *The Inspector General* (1836) is his dramatic masterpiece. In it he creates a satirical–allegorical phantasmagoria of tsarist Russia in the form of a woebegone provincial town whose greed, fear, pride, incomprehension and need for confession are awakened by the arrival of a nonentity mistaken for the titular government official. Variously regarded in Russia as the best early specimen of social realism and as a precursor of late 19th-/early 20th-century symbolism and formalist experiments, the play is pure Gogolian hyperbole. It amused the tsar but confused and alienated many of the critics, upsetting the author who fled to Rome, where he remained for 13 years. His paranoia, political conservatism and messianism intensified in his final years, as is reflected in his *Selected Passages from Correspondence with Friends* (1847) and in the picaresque epic *Dead Souls* (1842–52). The latter, a projected trilogy in the tradition of Dante's *The Divine Comedy* calling for the spiritual regeneration of Russia, was incomplete and partially burned prior to his death. The 20th century has seen several celebrated productions of his work: **Meyerhold**'s and **Tovstonogov**'s *The Inspector General* (1926 and 1972, respectively), **Efros**'s *The Marriage* (1974) and **Lyubimov**'s *The Inspector's Recounting* (1978).   SG

Golden Age (Spain) A period in Spanish Literature and the Arts corresponding roughly to Spain's greatness as a European power, and dated as broadly as 1492–1700 by some, though in the theatre 1580–1680 is more realistic.   CL

Goldfaden, Abraham (1840–1909) Affectionately known as the father of Yiddish theatre, Goldfaden presented the first public performance of a Jewish play, in Mark's Biergarten in Jassy, Rumania, during the first week of October 1876. This event unleashed an immediate mushrooming of Yiddish theatre companies and set the pattern of a combination of laughter, tears and music in each play. Though musically uneducated, some of his many songs have become Jewish folk music. Playwright, poet, composer, producer and elegantly dressed impresario, his early rather naive plays were consciously directed at the masses of poor, simple and oppressed people around him. He wrote over 40 plays, or more correctly operettas, the most notable of the earlier ones being *The Two Kuni Lemels*, *Shmendrik* and *The Witch*, all of which appeared in 1877. His popularity established, Goldfaden became more ambitious in his writing and his two greatest works approached operatic form. These were *Shulamith* (1882), based on the Talmudic legend of the love story of Shulamith and Absalom, and *Bar Kochba* (1883) a historical drama of the warrior who led the last tragic revolt of the Jews against the Romans. Later, in America, he found his work being frequently performed to large audiences, but without payment of royalties. He died in poverty, although it is reported that 30,000 people followed his funeral cortège. His last play *Ben Ami*, produced five days before he died, proved a popular success.   AB

Goldin, Horace (Hyman Goldstein) (1873–1939) Polish-born magician who emigrated to the USA at the age of 16. He started with a comic magic act, but owing to his heavy accent and stammer, converted it to a rapid-fire silent routine, '45 tricks in 17 minutes', baffling audiences with a quick succession of illusions. He appeared in a musical comedy *The Merry Magician* (Theatre Royal, Brighton, 1911) and was the first conjurer to play the Palace, New York (1913). His most famous illusion was an improvement on P. T. Selbit's 1879 trick, 'Sawing a Lady in Half': Goldin eliminated the box and used a buzz-saw.   LS

Goldoni, Carlo (1707–98) Italian dramatist and librettist, his career is primarily associated with the theatres of his birth-place, Venice. Although he qualified at the Venetian bar, and intermittently practised law, he early had literary and theatrical ambitions: his tragedy for music, *Amalasunta*, he destroyed when it was rejected by the Milan opera; but he had better fortune with a tragicomedy, *Belisario*, produced in Venice by the company of Giuseppe Imer in 1734. Goldoni became the company's house dramatist at the San Samuele Theatre, writing mainly comic interludes and scenarios for improvising actors who worked in the tradition of the **commedia dell'arte**. His literary aspirations led him to write tragedies, tragicomedies and librettos for *opera seria*, and in 1737 he became for a time literary director of the most distinguished Venetian opera-house, the San Giovanni Grisostomo. Financial problems caused him to flee Venice in 1743 and for several years he practised law in Pisa, only occasionally writing dramatic pieces on demand. One such was *Arlecchino, Servitore di Due Padroni (Arlecchino, The Servant of Two Masters)*, re-worked in 1745 from an old scenario at the request of the improvising actor **Antonio Sacchi**: consisting part of scripted dialogue and part left for improvisation, in 1753 Goldoni fully scripted the play into the form in which it now survives.

It was another improvising actor, the Pantalone Cesare d'Arbes, who brought Goldoni back to the theatre in 1748 by introducing him to the actor–manager **Girolamo Medebach**. Goldoni joined Medebach's company (disparagingly called a troupe of 'rope-dancers') as house dramatist at the little Sant' Angelo Theatre in Venice. There, between 1748 and 1752, he effectively began his reform of Italian comedy by gradually banishing the crudities and excesses of the old improvised comedy, subordinating on the one hand the traditional improvisation of masked types, and on the other the overly ornate language of baroque drama, to the needs of a scripted comedy more firmly located in a recognizable social milieu. He sometimes eliminated masks and improvisation altogether in order to focus, in a quasi-naturalistic way, on local morals and manners. The plays of this period include *La Vedova Scaltra (The Cunning Widow)*, *La Famiglia dell'Antiquario (The Antiquarian's Family)*, *I Due Gemelli Veneziani (The Venetian Twins)*, *La Putta Onorata (The Respectable Girl)* and *La Locandiera (The Mistress of the Inn)*. In the celebrated season of 1750–1, in a successful attempt to revive flagging attendance at his theatre, he produced 16 comedies: among them *Pamela Nubile*, a version of Richardson's novel, and *Il Teatro Comico (The Comic Theatre)*, a dramatized discussion between performers and company manager, in which Goldoni outlined the nature and principles of his reform. In these years after 1748 too he contributed significantly to the comparatively new musical form, *opera buffa*, most notably in collaboration with the composer Baldassare Galuppi, who set more than 20 of Goldoni's librettos.

After quarrelling with Medebach over royalties and publication rights, in 1753 Goldoni moved to the larger San Luca Theatre run by the Vendramin family, achieving notable success there with a run of plays in the novel, if ephemeral, vein of exotic, Oriental tragicomedy; beginning with *La Sposa Persiana* (*The Persian Bride*, 1753) these capitalized on the size and facilities of the San Luca, and an audience taste for the strange mysteries of the East fostered by romances and travel writings. His comic drama became increasingly refined, subtle and ambitious in the ways in which it reflected mid-18th century Venetian social mores, particularly those of the middle, and even lower, classes, both in comedies scripted in Venetian dialect, and in plays which, while they rejected the external manifestations of the received tradition of improvised comedy like masks and impromptu performance, yet absorbed its comic strategies, type figures and intricate balletic organization. Among the most important comedies Goldoni wrote between 1753 and 1762 are *Il Campiello*, *La Casa Nova* (*The New House*), *Gli Innamorati* (*The Lovers*), *I Rusteghi* (*The Boors*), *La Villeggiatura* and *Le Baruffe Chiozzotte* (*The Chioggian Squabbles*). Goldoni's librettos for *opera buffa* show a similar accommodation of inherited *commedia dell'arte* elements to a comic action rooted in a recognizable middle-class society and engaged with more local and immediate concerns. Goldoni helped give a new direction to such librettos by deftly translating mere stock types into engaging characters, investing *arie* with ironic undertones, and building out ensembles and grand finales. His librettos became sought after and included two pieces which were among the century's most successful musical comedies throughout Europe: *Il Filosofo di Campagna* (*The Country Philosopher*, 1752) set by Galuppi, and *La Buona Figliuola* (*The Good Girl*), in the Piccinni setting of 1760. Goldoni's contribution was substantial then to the establishment of *opera buffa* by the 1770s and 1780s as a form of musical theatre as acceptable as *opera seria*. His reform of 'prose' comedy similarly transformed the status of the genre in the Venetian theatres, elevating the 'prose' theatre to a level equal to that of the musical stage, and helping to create an audience taste for the simpler and the more verisimilar that was strongly felt in stage scenography and performance.

From the beginning Goldoni's success, and even more his attempts to reform comedy, provoked envy and hostility. In the late 1740s and 1750s his chief rival was the dramatist **Pietro Chiari**. The bitter hostility between the two (expressed in savage dramatic parodies, verse lampoons and offensive manifestos) led, in 1749, to the introduction of censorship to the Venetian theatre. In the late 1750s another, and more dangerous, enemy appeared in the figure of the aristocratic writer and dramatist, **Carlo Gozzi**, defender of social, literary and linguistic tradition and champion of that masked and improvised comedy supposedly undermined by the Goldonian reform. Gozzi's *fiabe*, fantasy spectacles which exploited the talents of the improvis-

ing comedians, won considerable immediate success, and at the end of the 1761–2 season Goldoni left Venice to join the **Comédie-Italienne** in Paris. It is unlikely, however, that Gozzi's success alone led to his departure: Goldoni was now in his mid-fifties, he had exhausted much of his inspiration and he had a wife to support; the Venetian theatre offered a professional dramatist little long-term financial security, and Venetian patronage gave even less in the way of place or preferment. The Parisian theatre and French royalty had a reputation for generosity to foreign, particularly Italian, artists; he knew many Italian players in Paris, those close to Louis XV had invited him, his work was known there, and Italian *opera buffa* was becoming fashionable. But whatever hopes he may have entertained, they were only partially realized. He remained in France to the end of his life, but his work never really adjusted to the cultural change: significantly, the best play he wrote there, *Il Ventaglio* (*The Fan*, 1766), was done for a Venetian company, although plays he wrote in French, once he had mastered the language, have distinct quality, and *Le Bourru Bienfaisant* (*The Beneficent Bear*) was highly successful at the Comédie, when done there in 1771. He accepted a post as Italian tutor to Louis XV's eldest daughter, and in 1769 was given a small court pension and joined the entourage at Versailles. There, and in Paris, in the 1780s he wrote his entertaining but not wholly reliable *Mémoires* (1787). He died destitute after the Revolution when his pension was abolished, a decision later reversed to the benefit of his widow.   KR

Goldsmith, Oliver (1728–74) Irish playwright.

After studying at Trinity College, Dublin, he trained as a doctor at Edinburgh. He toured Europe in 1755 and settled in London, attempting to work as a physician. He began earning a living as a writer in 1757. His first play, *The Good Natured Man*, first performed in 1768, was a serious attack on sentimentalism; the play's hero, Honeywood, suffers from an excess of good nature, though money always resolves the play's problems. *She Stoops to Conquer* (1773) mocks the snobbery of London through the manipulations of the country, embodied in Tony Lumpkin. The play's geniality mocks Marlow's inability to woo a woman unless he thinks she is a servant, celebrating the virtues of 'laughing comedy', that Goldsmith advocated in an important essay over the prevalent sentimental forms.   PH

Gollakalapam (India) *Golla* means a 'female cowherd' (*gopi*) and *kalapam* is a 'dialogue' or an 'argument'. *Gollakalapam* is both the name of a play and also a theatre form. It was created in Andhra Pradesh, in the late 19th century by Bhagavatulu Ramayya who evolved the form out of the **Kuchipudi** dance-drama tradition which used to be executed by female dancers of courtesan families. *Gollakalapam* is also known as *Vithi Bhagavata*, religious street stories. Unlike *Kuchipudi*, which is now the exclusive province of Brahmin men and boys, *Gollakalapam* is performed by both women and men and has developed its own teachers and exponents knowledgeable in Sanskrit and the *Natyasastra*.

A typical performance proceeds as follows: A Brahmin acting as stage manager (*sutradhara*) performs the preliminaries and announces the beginning of the performance. Then the main dancer comes to the playing area and dances behind a curtain held by two attendants; she is the *golla*. Her dance is performed to the entrance songs of the singers, including the Brahmin. Eventually the curtain is pulled aside and the dancer performs stylized dance patterns (*jatis*) which are essentially the same as *darus* used in other dance-drama forms of the area. The dancers require intricate and precise footwork. The songs are interpreted visually through elaborate gestures. Following this, the *Vidushaka*, or clown, played by the same Brahmin who takes the role of stage manager, comes forward and converses with the dancer. They talk of the futility of religious rites, superiority of the soul over the mind, the ideal family, and so forth. The object of their conversation is to satirize the foibles of society and its conventions. A secondary female usually accompanies the chief dancer and performs less elaborate dances throughout the show.

The songs used in the performance are set to classical Karnatic melodies (*ragas*) and the *mridangam* drum produces a lively rhythmic accompaniment. Verbal recitations of the rhythmic patterns repeated in the dance (*jatis*) make for very exciting moments and enrich the variety of an evening's performance.

Originally, *Gollakalapam* was an all-night show which continued for three consecutive evenings. But today the form has almost disappeared, owing to the absence of sympathetic patrons. At its inception, it was a popular part of temple festivals and rich families even invited parties to their homes to celebrate marriages or other happy family occasions. Unlike *Kuchipudi*, its parent form, it is somewhat less complicated to perform and there are fewer restrictions regarding the time, place and process of performance.   FaR

Gombeyatta (India) This is the shadow puppet theatre of Karnataka, a state in the south-western part of the subcontinent. The puppets are made of goat skin. The largest puppets (30 to 40 inches tall) require a complete skin and additional skins are needed to complete the head, torso and limbs. When constructing puppets of Ganapati, the elephant-headed god, and the epic hero-gods Krishna and Rama, the puppeteer performs ritual sacrifices and takes care in preparing and cutting the hides.

At least 50 puppets are used in a performance and a puppeteer may have more than a hundred figures in his puppet set. Puppet size generally indicates social rank and puppets fall into the following categories: divinities, demons, humans, monkey generals, clowns, animals of various kinds and natural objects, such as plants and trees. Groups of characters are also to be found clustered together to form one puppet for the purposes of conveying some stories. As in other forms of shadow theatre, several puppets may be needed to represent the various moods of a single character.

Generally, a company of shadow players consist of the puppeteer, several male members of his family, his wife who plays the harmonium, sings and speaks the female roles and a *tabla* drummer who speaks some of the roles of the male characters. Three or four manipulators are needed to produce a shadow puppet show and the number of instrumentalists may vary, depending on the wealth of the company.

It is thought that about 300 families of shadow puppeteers make their living in Karnataka. The Karnataka Chitrakala Parishath of Bangalore has pioneered collection and preservation of puppets and supports the artist in maintaining their art.

The construction of the stage, its size, shape and location, follows the pattern of the **Tollu Bommalu**.

The shadow theatre of Karnataka is closely connected to religious holidays and the companies which are affiliated to particular temples must perform on demand, since the temple authorities financially support them during the year. The main season for religious festivals of the area is from February to April and again in September and October. Plays are adapted from stories in the *Ramayana* and the *Mahabharata* epics.   FaR

Gombrowicz, Witold (1902–69) Polish playwright, novelist and memoirist who from 1939 lived in Argentina and France. His plays are grotesque theatricalist fables that oppose conflicting images of reality in a struggle between socially imposed, restrictive forms and creative immaturity. Since the mid-1970s, *Ivona, Princess of Burgundia* (1938), *The Marriage* (1947) and *Operetta* (1966) have been central to the national repertory.   DG

Gómez de Avellaneda, Gertrudis (1814–73) An extraordinary poet, novelist and playwright whose work reflected little of Cuban reality. Twice-widowed, beset with major personal problems and mostly unappreciated in her native Cuba, she spent most of her life in Spain where she aspired to courtly grandeur. Her theatre belongs primarily to Spain although she is considered one of the major women playwrights of the Americas. With 20 plays, she is a major figure who dominated both tragic and comic form. Her principal tragic works are *Munio Alfonso* (1844) and *Baltasar* (1858), the latter relating the Spanish crown to its biblical antecedents. On the lighter side, *La hija de las flores (Daughter of the Flowers*, 1852) and *El millonario y la maleta (The Millionaire and his Suitcase*, 1870) are entertaining comedies with good humour. For the most part, Tula, as she was called, managed to avoid the excesses of romanticism and create developed characters with good psychological basis.   GW

Goncharova, Natalya Sergeevna (1881–1962) Goncharova was a talented and prolific Russian painter-designer of the pre-revolutionary period who, with her companion, the artist Mikhail Larionov, helped establish neo-primitivism (1910–14) as a trend in Russian art. Neo-primitivism returned to native-painted, handicraft art – the woodcut, primitive icon, toys, etc. – and Russian folkloric motifs to counter realist-naturalist illusionism, traditional perspective and proportion, the World of Art's *style moderne* with its decorative eclecticism and the symbolists' refined mysticism, all of which reflected the influence of the West. Goncharova embraced old Eastern forms – the Russian *skomorokhi* (mummers) and *balagany* (puppet shows) – with their frank and vital theatricality and spirit of buffoonery at a time when this idea was becoming attractive to Russia's most innovative directors – **Meyerhold**, **Evreinov** and **Tairov**. Her movement toward rayonism (light rays as analogue for spatial linear dynamic) and futurism ('the visual representation of time'), c. 1912–16, led to the incorporation into her work of a forced perspective of subjective contemporaneity – what the Russian cubo-futurists called 'shift' and the Russian formalists dubbed 'making it strange'. She designed sets and costumes for Diaghilev's production of the opera-ballet *The Golden Cockerel* (Paris, 1914) and the ballet *The Firebird* (London, 1926), Tairov's Kamerny Theatre production of **Goldoni**'s *The Fan* (Moscow, 1915) and for **Baliev**'s *Chauve-Souris* (New York, 1931). Her work also included book and fashion design. She and Larionov emigrated to Paris in 1917.   SG

González Dávila, Jesús (1942–   ) Mexican playwright, born in the capital, he has succeeded with several prize-winning plays. *La fábrica de juguetes* (*The Toy Factory*, 1970), *Muchacha del alma* (*A Girl with Soul*, 1983) are representative of his efforts to penetrate the contemporary Mexican psyche with realistic, often brutal, plays.   GW

Goodman Theatre Located in Chicago, the Goodman is America's second oldest regional theatre, founded in 1925. Originally funded as a memorial by the parents of playwright Kenneth Sawyer Goodman, the 683-seat theatre was to house both a resident professional company and a School of Drama, but the depression forced the company to disband, while the School continued.

In 1969–70 a professional company returned to the Goodman to varying critical and popular reception. In 1978 leadership was assumed by Gregory Mosher, who emphasized new works and classic revivals. Mosher frequently commissions scripts from leading American playwrights and in 1985 became co-director of Lincoln Center in New York City.

In 1977 the Goodman Theatre ceased its affiliation with the Chicago Art Institute to become a self-sustaining operation, and in 1978 the School of Drama affiliated with De Paul University.   SMA

Goodman's Fields Theatre (London) Built in 1729 by Odell in Ayliffe Street, Goodman's Fields, the opposite end of London from the usual location for theatres. It was licensed but after protests the King withdrew approval in 1730. Henry Giffard took over as manager and built a new theatre which opened in 1732, with a spectacular ceiling depicting the King surrounded by **Shakespeare**, **Dryden**, **Congreve** and **Betterton**. It was used until 1736 when it was offered for sale and again in 1740 to 1742 when it was the scene of **David Garrick**'s spectacular London debut.   PH

Goodwin, Nat(haniel) C(arl) (1857–1919) American actor and manager. Born and educated in Boston, Goodwin began his career as a mimic for drawing-room theatricals. In 1874 he made his professional stage debut at the Howard Athenaeum in Boston, and in 1875 his first New York appearance at **Tony Pastor**'s Opera House. He enjoyed a major success in 1876 at the New York **Lyceum** in *Off The Stage* by giving imitations of popular actors. While Goodwin excelled as a mimic and eccentric comedian, he also was effective in serious parts such as Jim Rayburn in *In Mizzoura* (1893), and the title role in *Nathan Hale*

(1899). Married 5 times, he gained notoriety for his off-stage antics. With his third wife **Maxine Elliott** he starred in numerous plays including *Nathan Hale*, *When We Were Twenty-One* (1900), and *The Merchant of Venice* (1901). He attempted Bottom in 1903 but was not successful in Shakespearian roles. In his autobiography, *Nat Goodwin's Book* (1914), he took revenge upon his many enemies.   TLM

Gopalila (India) This is a rare form of glove puppet theatre once seen with greater frequency in the villages of Orissa. *Gopa* refers to the cowherd boys and *lila* means 'play'. The puppets are made of wood and paper and their bodies are padded with cloth, the lower half of which is covered with a long skirt.

Puppeteers usually travel in pairs from village to village carrying their basket of puppets and a small box-like stage, just large enough to mask the performer who sits in a cramped position and manipulates the puppets above his head. The second member of the party sits nearby, playing the *pakhavaj* drum, singing and narrating incidents from the life of Lord Krishna.

Religious occasions, especially those related to Krishna, provided the puppeteers an opportunity to entertain the villagers and to earn a living. Today, the form has all but disappeared.   FaR

Gordin, Jacob (1853–1909) Russian-born radical Yiddish playwright, much influenced by **Ibsen** and **Hauptmann**. Appalled by the low standard of Yiddish popular theatre on his arrival in America in 1890, he began writing for the theatre, his plays being immediately hailed by the intellectuals and the socialists. *Siberia* (1891), *The Jewish King Lear* (1892) *Mirele Efros* (1898) and *God, Man and Devil* (1890) are the best known of some 90 plays, including translations into Yiddish of the great European classics.   AB

Gordon, Ruth (née Jones) (1896–1985) American actress and playwright. Her New York debut in *Peter Pan* (1915) was followed by a succession of relatively insignificant roles, until a revival in 1936 of **Wycherley**'s *The Country Wife*, in which she was the first American cast in an **Old Vic** (London) production, changed the direction of her career. Her Pinchwife led to roles that exploited her individualistic technique, whirlwind vivacity, and split-second timing. In 1937 (New York) she played Nora in *A Doll's House*, adapted for her by **Thornton Wilder**; in 1942 she was Natasha in *The Three Sisters*. Her most memorable stage creation was Dolly Levi in *The Matchmaker* (1954 London; 1955, New York), a role written for her by Wilder. Her last stage role was Zina in *Dreyfus in Rehearsal* (1974). Gordon was also a successful screen actress, playwright (*Over 21*, *Years Ago*) and especially screenwriter in collaboration with her second husband Garson Kanin. She was the author of three lively autobiographies.   DBW

Gordone, Charles (1925–   ) Afro-American playwright. With his only successful stage play *No Place To Be Somebody* (1969), Gordone became the first black playwright to win a Pulitzer Prize. A drama major at Los Angeles State College, he came to New York and acted bit parts while working as a bar-room waiter. This experience inspired him to write the play. At a time of militancy in black theatre, Gordone dramatized in a number of highly theatrical scenes the murder of an incorrigible black pimp by his closest friend. The **Negro Ensemble Company** rejected the play which was eventually staged at **Joseph Papp**'s Public Theatre in New York.   EGH

Gorelik, Mordecai (1899–1990) American stage and film designer; born in Russia. Gorelik studied with **Robert Edmond Jones**, **Norman Bel Geddes**, and Serge Soudeikine and began his career with the **Provincetown Players** in 1920. His 1925 design for *Processional* was a rare example of successful expressionism on the American stage. During the 1930s he was the primary designer for the **Group Theatre** including *Men and White* and *Golden Boy*. He was an organizer of a short-lived leftist group, the Theatre Collective. Gorelik also designed *All My Sons* and *A Hatful of Rain*, among others on Broadway. He was a strong advocate of **Brecht**'s epic theatre which he emphasizes in his book, *New Theatres for Old*. Much of his design can be classified as suggestive realism.   AA

Gorky, Maksim (pseudonym of Aleksei Maksimovich Peshkov) (1868–1936) Soviet novelist, memoirist, short story writer, dramatist and critic, the 'stormy petrel' of the Revolution and the official hero of Soviet art. Born seven years after serfdom's abolition but within its memory into an extremely ignorant, cruel and impoverished milieu, Gorky learned about life on the road and soon became a self-educated rebel artist. His early romanticized peasant tales, leading to his first St Petersburg success, the short story 'Chelkash' (1895), transformed the author into a tramp-poet folk hero for the urban artistic intelligentsia, who sought to emulate his primitivism in their work. Always self-critical, even embarrassed by the clumsiness of his art and ambivalent toward the illiterate peasant life from which literature provided him an escape, Gorky devoted his career to reconciling the classes into an enlightened society built upon education and communication. His humanist philosophy – basically to speak of what man can become by being made to believe in his goodness or potential for good – extended into the realistic literature which formed the basis of his developing art and his growing role of mediator between art and society. His publishing house Znanie (Knowledge) (1900), although it specialized in neo-realism, encouraged such writers as **Andreev**, Blok and Bunin, whose aesthetics did not always agree with Gorky's own. Gorky was in turn befriended and championed (and also sharply criticized) by **Chekhov**, whose plays he sought unsuccessfully to emulate. Gorky's involvement in the 1905 and 1917 Revolutions, which led to arrest and an inevitable movement toward Bolshevism, focused and delimited the remainder of his career. He wrote 12 plays between 1901 and 1913, having already established himself as a short story writer (*Sketches and Stories*, 2 vols. 1898), novelist (*Foma Gordeev*, 1899), revolutionary poet (*Song of the Stormy Petrel*, 1901) and social force. His dramas are all socio-politically slanted, lacking in psychological and stylistic subtlety, at times philosophically murky and morally ambivalent, mixing naive idealism with neo-puritanism, faith and cynicism. They offer stereotypically 'good', i.e., strong-willed, productive peasants and workers juxtaposed with 'bad' i.e., ineffectual, self-serving, unenlightened, morally dishonest and effete intellectuals, clerics and petty bourgeois. Plots are dialectically constructed so as to economize and maximize these conflicts and the theme of alienation between the classes. Language is often rhetorical, building towards and often interrupted by ideological tirades that are meant to educate the audience. While Gorky garners raw power from his group portraits and folkloric elements, he is less effective with individuals, unless they inspire his rage or enthusiasm. His first play, *The Petty Bourgeoisie* (1902), beginning Gorky's long association with the **Moscow Art Theatre** (MAT) which today bears his name, presents the traditional Russian generational conflict theme, here emblematic of revolutionary societal change, resulting in the birth of the proletarian hero. *The Lower Depths* (1902) was celebrated in its time for the novelty of its tramp characters in an exotically downtrodden flophouse as well as for the ensemble opportunities it afforded the MAT company, but it suffers from all of Gorky's ideological and dramaturgical faults. *Summer Folk* (1904), *Barbarians* (1905) and *Enemies* (1906) deal in various ways with philistinism and alienation among the classes, with culpability invariably falling upon the intelligentsia and the merchants. These and other plays such as *Children of the Sun* (1905) and *Queer People* (1910) introduce romantic subplots and an overall spiritual malaise suggestive of **Turgenev** and Chekhov, while Gorky's *Vassa Zheleznova* (1910), *The Zykovs* and *Counterfeit Money* (both 1913), the critically respected *Yegor Bulychov and Others* (1932) and its sequel *Dostigayev and Others* (1933) more directly suggest **Ostrovsky**'s dramatic portraits of merchant characters. Gorky's most fully realized human drama may well have been his own life, recorded in his autobiographical trilogy – *My Childhood* (1914), *In the World* (1916) and *My Universities* (1924). The dramatic final chapter saw the humanitarian idealist returning from self-imposed exile (1921–8) to become first president of the newly formed Union of Soviet Writers and the somewhat unwitting artistic point man for the government's policy of 'socialist realism' in literature. His death in 1936 has been variously ascribed to tuberculosis and, more dubiously, to Stalin-instigated assassination.   SG

Gorostiza, Carlos (1920–) Argentine playwright, actor and director. Gorostiza made theatre history when his play, *El puente* (*The Bridge*, 1949), spanned the gap between the independent theatre and the commercial theatre in Buenos Aires, and opened a new epoch in realism on the Argentine stage. Other major works include *El pan de la locura* (*Bread of Madness*, 1958) and *Los prójimos* (*The Neighbours*, 1966), the latter based on the famous Kitty Genovese incident in New York in which unconcerned witnesses to an assault failed to intervene. *¿A qué jugamos?* (*What Shall We Play?*, 1968) uses a metatheatrical structure to investigate contemporary problems, especially those of the younger generation. Gorostiza has written novels, worked in television, and in the Alfonsín government was named Secretary of Culture with broad responsibility for governmental support of the arts. Recent theatre titles are *Los hermanos queridos* (*Beloved Brothers*, 1978), *El acompañante* (*The Accompanist*, 1981), *Hay que* *apagar el fuego* (*We Have to Put Out the Fire*, 1982), and *Papi* (1984). GW

Gorostiza, Celestino (1904–67) Mexican playwright, director. A major figure in the independent movement of the 1930s, Gorostiza interpreted expressionist tendencies in vogue in the European theatre in such plays as *Ser o no ser* (*To Be or Not to Be*, 1934). In a later wave, he dealt with the taboos of racism in Mexican society in *El color de nuestra piel* (*The Colour of Our Skin*, 1952) and took a new look at the story of Cortés and Malinche in *La Malinche*, later retitled *La leña está verde* (*The Firewood is Green*, 1958). GW

Gosson, Stephen (1554–1624) English antitheatrical pamphleteer, who renounced his youthful interest in drama – he is known to have written some pastoral plays – under Puritan persuasion. His *The School of Abuse* (1579), attacking poets and actors, was dedicated, without permission, to Sir **Philip Sidney**, whose *The Apology for Poetry* (written c. 1580) was written partly to confute Gosson. The controversy was still at its height when Gosson wrote *Plays Confuted in Five Actions*. PT

Got, Edmond (1822–1901) French actor. Got's entire career of over 50 years was at the **Comédie-Française**, where he made his debut in 1844, having received a first prize at the Conservatoire. In 1848 he played the Abbé in **Musset**'s *Il Ne Faut Jurer de Rien* (*Nothing is Certain*). This part (which he retained for 50 years) gave full rein to his specific vein of whimsical comedy. He created some 200 parts, being equally at home in both the modern and the classical repertoire. An unforgettable Tibia in *Les Caprices de Marianne* (1851), his greatest successes were in *Le Duc Jacob* (1859), **Augier**'s *Les Effrontés* (*The Shameless Ones*, 1861), **Ponsard**'s *L'Honneur et L'Argent*, *Le Fils de Giboyer* (1862) and the splendid 1868 revival of Balzac's *Mercadet*. In 1870, he steered the Comédie through a difficult period by organizing a tour to London. In 1873 he became *doyen*, and in 1877 was appointed to teach at the Conservatoire. He played Bernard in *Les Fourchambault* in 1878, created an interesting Harpagon in 1879, was made chevalier of the Légion d'Honneur in 1881, played Triboulet in *Le Roi S'Amuse* (*The King's Fool*) (which had been banned since its first performance 50 years earlier) in 1882, and gave his last performance in 1895. JMCC

Gothenburg City Theatre and **People's Theatre** (Sweden) Gothenburg has a long theatrical tradition, with permanent playhouses throughout the 19th century and in 1916 the opening of one of Europe's most well-equipped theatres, the Lorensberg, used by the City Theatre company, founded in 1917, until it moved to its present building in 1934. Artistic achievement has varied, depending on leadership: **Per Lindberg**'s modernistic productions (1918–23) made the Lorensberg the theatrical focus of Scandinavia; Torsten Hammaren (1926–50) emphasized new writing, especially anti-fascist plays; Mats Johansson (1962–82) developed its social and political profile, through productions by Lennart Hjulström, Ralf Långbacka and Peter Oskarson and the remarkable work of its two splinter-companies, the suburban Angereds Ensemble

and the Backa young people's theatre. However, conflict in the early 1980s over artistic and political aims caused long-lasting problems. The People's Theatre (founded 1954) collaborates technically and financially with the City Theatre, but preserves its own vigorous artistic profile. Its links with the Labour movement are reflected in its repertoire (80% new Swedish plays, many by working-class writers or about local Labour concerns and history) and its ancillary services: inexpensive editions of new scripts, outreach theatre and educational programmes. HL

Gottsched, Johann Christoph (1700–66) German playwright, critic, and essayist. One of Germany's first significant men of letters, Gottsched wished to elevate German culture by modelling its literature and drama on the French. In his theatrical endeavours, he was aided by **Caroline Neuber**, whose troupe attempted to put into practice his tenets of acting, which were essentially abstracted from the acting of French companies in the German courts and developed from Gottsched's own conception of classical, rhetorical gesture. It became known as the **Leipzig style**. His play *The Dying Cato* (1732), despite its woodenness, had some success when performed by the Neuber troupe. Gottsched was a man of little humour and had a limited idea of what could be achieved in the theatre. Hence, after his rupture with the Neubers in 1741, even though he had some communication with **Schönemann**, his effective connections with the theatre were severed. SW

Goulue, La (Louise Weber) (1860–1919) French cancan dancer at the **Moulin Rouge**, Paris, 1889–95. A former washerwoman, she was notorious in her day for her hot temper, vast appetite, lesbian attachments and huge salary. Her high kicks performed with her partner Valentin le Désossé (Jacques Renaudin) and red topknot remain familiar through the art of Toulouse-Lautrec. She later descended to belly-dancing, ran a showbooth as a lion-tamer and died alcoholic, obese and all but forgotten. LS

Gozzi, Carlo (1720–1806) Italian writer and dramatist who wrote plays primarily for the theatres of his birth-place, Venice. Although brought up in modest circumstances and largely self-taught, he was a younger son of an aristocratic family and patrician attitudes strongly conditioned his views of society and the theatre. With his brother, the journalist Gasparo, he was a founder member of one of the most conservative Venetian academies, the Accademia dei Granelleschi, concerned to preserve the purity of traditional language, thought and artistic activity against the threatening incursions of the enlightenment. In the late 1750s, hostile to the bourgeois realistic and reformist tendencies of contemporary dramatists like **Carlo Goldoni** and **Pietro Chiari**, he engaged first in vigorous literary polemics, then in the deliberate creation of an opposition drama. In this he sought initially to restore to the stage the masks and improvisation of the traditional **commedia dell'arte**, supposedly undermined by the Goldonian reform of comedy, and later, drawing inspiration from Spanish drama, to reassert the courtly values of the aristocratic past. In neither was he successful for long, for all that much of his work was a product of his 25-year association with one of the finest Venetian acting companies of the 18th century, the troupe of **Antonio Sacchi**. For them he wrote the most enduring of his work, the *fiabe*, which included *L'Amore delle Tre Melarance* (*The Love of Three Oranges*, 1761), *Il Corvo* (*The Raven*), *Il Re Cervo* (*The King Stag*, 1762), *Turandot* (1762) and *La Donna Serpente* (*The Snake Woman*, 1762) and *L'Angellino Belverde* (*The Green Bird*, 1765). These fantastic and scenically spectacular romances often wedded the comic strategies and masked figures of the improvised drama to the fairy tale materials of exotic Oriental stories. Goldoni had capitalized in the mid-1750s on the Venetian taste for tales of the mysterious East, and Gozzi's highly theatrical concoctions proved equally successful in the 1750s – so much so, it is said, that they helped to drive his rival from Venice. Underpinning Gozzi's work was his hostility to the local realism, scenographic simplicity and idiomatic language of Goldoni's new comedy, which in his eyes breached artistic decorum by mingling characters of high and low place, extolling the virtues and values of the Venetian bourgeoisie, and banishing imagination and invention from the stage. Significantly, his *fiabe*, although they have long provided plot lines for opera and ballet, only began to attract the attention again of the non-musical stage with the rediscovery of a primarily non-verbal, theatrical theatre in the stagings of **Meyerhold** and **Vakhtangov** in the early years of this century, and in the avant-garde visual theatre of the 1970s and 80s. Gozzi's witty and waspish memoirs, *Memorie Inutili*, are a mine of information on the 18th-century Venetian theatre and provide an invaluable if one-sided account of his dispute with Goldoni and his association with the actors and actresses of Sacchi's company. KR

Grabbe, Christian Dietrich (1801–36) German playwright. Grabbe had ambitions first to be an actor, then a professional playwright, but was forced to earn his living as an army lawyer in his native town of Detmold. Despite this, he was a prolific writer. However, as his plays were written in a manner that anticipated both the epic theatre of the 20th century and absurdism, it is not surprising they were not produced. His most significant works are large-scale dramas on great men of history, most notable among which are two plays from a projected cycle on the Hohenstaufen family, *The Emperor Friedrich Barbarossa* (1829) and *The Emperor Henry VI* (1830), *Napoleon, or The Hundred Days* (1831) and *Hannibal* (1835). The only one of Grabbe's plays to be produced in his lifetime was *Don Juan and Faust* (1829), a study of the difference between the idealistic and realistic personalities. Grabbe is probably best known today for his grotesque comedy, *Joke, Satire, Irony, and Deeper Significance* (1827), though several of his plays have been revived with quite considerable success in the modern German theatre. SW

Gracioso A comic servant, one of the chief sources of humour in the Spanish **comedia** (see **Spain**). CL

Graetz, Paul (1890–1937) German cabaret artist, who made a name for himself in **Schnitzler** roles before appearing at the Schall und Rauch and Kabarett der Komiker in Berlin. With his deep raw voice and slow movements, he excelled at Berlin loudmouths and chatterboxes, his performances spiked with mother-wit. He collaborated with **Arnolt Bronnen** on the play *Katalaunische Schlacht* and worked for **Piscator**, before emigrating to the United States in 1935, where he died. LS

Gramsci, Antonio (1891–1937) Italian politician, political theorist and critic. As well as being an active politician and co-founder of the Italian Communist Party in 1921, he was a seminal commentator on a broad range of social and cultural matters, including the theatre. Between 1915 and 1920 he was theatre critic for *Avanti!*, and his penetrating articles, treating of drama and the stage from a firm and sophisticated ideological position hostile to the bourgeois and boulevard values of the day, have since exercised considerable influence on thinking about the functions of theatre both in Italy and abroad. LR

Grand Duke's Opera House, NY see **Penny theatres**

Grand Opera This term was commonly used in England during the late 19th and early 20th centuries to describe any serious opera that contained no spoken dialogue. Properly it indicates opera of the kind presented at the Paris Opéra from about 1830 to 1865. This had no spoken dialogue, was on historical themes, and included extensive choral writing, ballets and elaborate stage spectacle. The most assiduous composer of Grand Opera for Paris was Giacomo Meyerbeer, whose librettist was **Eugène Scribe**. GH

Grand-Guignol Founded in 1895 as a 'Théâtre salon' by Oscar Métenier, the Théâtre de Grand-Guignol moved to its premises in the rue Chaptal, Paris, four years later, under the leadership of Max Maurey. At first merely a naturalistic theatre alternating one-acts of brutality and farce, it eventually specialized in horror, drawing on the works of E. A. Poe in particular. Its chief playwright was André de Lorde, nicknamed 'The Prince of Terror', who preferred psychological suspense to gore, though he was not averse to the eye-gougings and acid-baths that were popular features of the genre. This skilled sensationalism pleased the Parisian public, but attempts to acclimate it to England and America were not successful. By the Second World War, it was drawing heavily on detective fiction and finally closed its doors in 1962. LS

Granville Barker, Harley (1877–1946) British actor, playwright, director and critic, who exerted a major influence on British drama and theatre both during and after his lifetime. As an actor he toured with various stock companies but became increasingly discontented with the low standards of commercial touring. Contact with **William Poel**, **William Archer** and **Bernard Shaw**, however, at the turn of the century, together with membership of the **Stage Society**, opened up new possibilities. He began acting in a new range of challenging roles (notably Marchbanks in *Candida*), and in 1900 directed his own first major play, written the year before, *The Marrying of*

Ann Leete. In 1904, with **J. E. Vedrenne** as his business manager, Barker took a lease on the **Royal Court Theatre**, Sloane Square, and initiated three historic seasons of the new 'uncommercial' drama, presenting 11 plays by Shaw together with new plays by continental and British authors and new translations of three plays by **Euripides**. The enterprise proved the viability of such a programme on the public stage and gave a major boost to the repertory movement.

During this period Barker wrote his second main play *The Voysey Inheritance* (1903–5; produced at the Court, 1905), and the publication during the next few years of *Waste* (1906–7) and *The Madras House* (1909) established him as an important dramatist of the new, realistic English drama. By 1907 he had practically abandoned acting, although his restrained, subtle and natural method of performance had made him an ideal player for the contemporary drama. His attention now focused upon directing and upon the promotion of the repertory movement in England. In 1910 he directed the experimental repertory season at the Duke of York's Theatre, London, which proved an artistic success but financial failure – underlining for Barker the case for subsidy of repertory. In 1912 the pinnacle of his directing career was reached with productions at the Savoy Theatre of *The Winter's Tale* and *Twelfth Night*, followed in 1914 by *A Midsummer Night's Dream*. He abandoned the elaborate, conventional methods of staging **Shakespeare**, including the domination of 'star' actors, and produced instead ensemble performances of the highest quality. An apron stage was used, scenery and costumes were simple, colourful and impressionistic and emphasis was given to the continuity of action, the full text being spoken with swiftness and intelligence. The freshness of interpretation and the vitality of the performances surprised and excited audiences and critics alike and stimulated a new approach to Shakespeare in the theatre.

From 1918, Barker devoted himself almost totally to writing, lecturing and scholarship. In 1919 he joined the newly formed **British Drama League** and was its chairman for 13 years. He wrote several more plays and published many works on the role of theatre in society (e.g. *The Exemplary Theatre*, 1922; *A National Theatre*, 1930) and the nature and function of dramatic art (e.g. *On Dramatic Method*, 1931; *The Use of Drama*, 1944). But his most important and pioneering work of scholarship was his *Prefaces to Shakespeare* (in six volumes, 1927–46), in which he bridged the gap between the academic and theatrical approaches to the plays. AJ

Grass, Günter (1927–) German dramatist and novelist, who uses deliberately naive perspectives to bring out the monstrosity of the Nazi period and its distorting effect on contemporary German society. A leading member of the influential Group 47, early dramas like *Flood* (1956) or *The Wicked Cooks* (1961) present political violence and moral coercion in images derived from absurd theatre. His novel *The Tin Drum* (1959) has become a modern classic, with its picture of fascism through the eyes of an insane dwarf; and *The Plebians Rehearse the Uprising* (1966), which dramatizes the problematic relationship between political art and actuality through the figure of **Brecht**, won an interna-

tional reputation. Since 1983 Grass has been the president of the Berlin Akademie der Künste. CI

Grasso, Giovanni (1873–1930) Italian actor-manager. Born into a Sicilian family of marionette specialists he turned to acting and after a long apprenticeship formed his own company with an emphasis on the performance of Sicilian plays, and the work of contemporary Italian dramatists in dialect versions. He was one of the last Italian stage actors to tour extensively abroad where the realism of his productions of dialect plays was particularly admired. He won notable success too, at home and abroad, as Othello, his version of the Moor out-doing **Salvini**'s for emotionalism and sensationalism, qualities little approved by English critics when he brought the play to London in 1911. KR

Grau Delgado, Jacinto (1877–1958) Spanish playwright whose works reflect his desire to raise Spanish theatre from the comfortable shallowness of **Echegaray** and **Benavente**. As a result his many fine plays were rarely successful in Spain, though he had some success abroad, *El señor de Pigmalión* (*Mr Pygmalion*, 1921) for instance being produced in Paris and Prague before Spain. His early plays, reworking historical or biblical themes (*El hijo pródigo* (*The Prodigal Son*, 1917) etc.), are classically simple. After 1918 they follow European trends, especially German expressionism and the concept of superman, as in *El señor de Pigmalión* and *El caballero Varona* (*The Knight of Varona*, 1925). In exile in South America after the Civil War, he experimented with farce and other forms. His complete works, 25 plays, were published in Buenos Aires, 1954–9. CL

Gray, John (1946–) Canadian playwright, composer, director, and one of the founders of Vancouver's Tamahnous Theatre. He began writing while musical director of Toronto's Theatre Passe Muraille. His works, *18 Wheels* (1977), *Billy Bishop Goes to War* (1981), and *Rock and Roll* (1982), are uniquely shaped musical plays, both literate and entertaining. *Billy Bishop*, the story of a legendary Canadian First World War flying ace, has been immensely successful across Canada, in Britain and the USA, and was seen on Canadian and British television. JA

Gray, Simon (James Holliday) (1936–) British dramatist, whose first stage play in the West End, *Wise Child* (1967), featured **Alec Guinness** as a transvestite. Gray's comedies often depict lonely, alienated men, rejected by society either because of their sexual inclinations or from shyness. His first major success came with *Butley* (1971) in which **Alan Bates** played a university lecturer torn between his disintegrating marriage and love for a male student. Bates also took the central role in Gray's *Otherwise Engaged* (1975), as a publisher surrounded by people whom he dislikes or distrusts, and seeking solace in music. In *Close of Play* (1978), a distinguished academic stays silent during his last hours, while his family bicker around him, while in *Quartermain's Terms* (1981), an ineffectual but good-hearted bachelor teacher in a Cambridge language school is left defenceless against the loss of friendships and the dislocation of school routine. In *The Rear Column* (1978), Gray presented a picture of institutionalized violence with an episode from British colonial history. *The Common Pursuit* (1984) provides a group portrait of Oxbridge arts graduates, with their failures and successes in later life. Gray's instinctive sympathy with the private individual usually suggests that the outside world is a frightening, even barbaric place. His diary of one production, *An Unnatural Pursuit* (1985), describes the suffering endured by the lonely playwright.   JE

Gray, Spalding (1941–) American actor and playwright. A product of the avant-garde theatre movement of the 1960s, Gray spent five years as a traditional actor before joining Richard Schechner and the **Performance Group** in 1970. With the disbanding of that group in 1980, Gray, along with his collaborator and director **Elizabeth LeCompte**, Jim Clayburgh, Willem Dafoe, Libby Howes, and Ron Vawter, became known as the Wooster Group. Gray's reputation, however, has transcended the Group, primarily because of *Three Places in Rhode Island* (*Sakonnet Point*, 1975; *Rumstick Road*, 1977; *Nayatt School*, 1978), a trilogy devised by Gray, who says he is extremely 'narcissistic and reflective', and LeCompte from his biography, and since 1979 a series of monologues drawn from Gray's past (*Sex and Death to the Age of 14*, *Booze, Cars and College Girls*, *A Personal History of the American Theatre*, *India and After*, *Interviewing the Audience*, and *Swimming to Cambodia*). Theodore Shank calls Gray's pieces 'the most literally autobiographical work that has been presented in the theatre'.   DBW

Gray, Terence (1895–) British director and stage designer, heavily influenced by **Gordon Craig**. In 1926 he founded the Cambridge Festival Theatre, where he worked with **Norman Marshall** and the lighting expert Harold Ridge, mounting productions of classical Greek drama, German expressionism, **Elmer Rice**, early **O'Neill**, **Pirandello** and **W. B. Yeats**. His non-naturalistic style, which disregarded dramatic texts (*Twelfth Night* on roller-skates – an idea recently appropriated in one of **Andrew Lloyd Webber**'s musical spectaculars – or a 'flamenco' treatment of *Romeo and Juliet*), was accompanied by 'isometric scenic design', using pale grey or luminous screens and columns as neutral architectural shapes for the play of light, together with arrangements of steps and multi-level rostra reminiscent of **Leopold Jessner**. **Tyrone Guthrie** took over the theatre for a season in 1929–30; and after Gray's final production, the first English performance of **Aeschylus**' *The Suppliants* in 1933, it finally closed in 1939.   CI

Greece, ancient

1 Dramatic festivals most of the Greek plays which survive were performed at Athens in the 5th century BC. All dramatic performances at this period took place at festivals of the god Dionysus. The main festival was the Great or City Dionysia, held in March or early April and centred on the temple and theatre of Dionysus (see **Greek theatres**) beneath the Acropolis. The principal features were probably established in the late 6th century by the tyrant Pisistratus.

Every year three tragedians competed for a prize, each producing four plays on one day; and five comic poets (in wartime perhaps only three) competed for another prize, each producing one play. The four plays by a tragedian usually comprised three tragedies followed by a satyr play (but there were exceptions; see **Euripides**). The four plays might be connected in theme to form a tetralogy in the proper sense (see **Aeschylus**), or might be wholly separate. The set of three tragedies from a tetralogy is called a trilogy.

The Great Dionysia also incorporated religious ceremonies and performances of dithyrambs (a form of non-dramatic choral song). The plays, however, were not religious rituals; they had no ritual function and their content had no necessary connection with Dionysus. At the beginning of the festival the competing dramatists paraded with their actors and choruses at a *proagōn*, a preliminary ceremony at which they probably announced the themes of their plays.

The plays were mass entertainment, performed before an audience of several thousand (perhaps as many as 15,000) drawn from all social classes. In the 4th century at least, and perhaps earlier, the democratic state paid a small allowance to enable poor citizens to attend. Whether women attended is uncertain.

The festival was presided over by the principal *archōn* or magistrate. It was he who selected the competing dramatists and assigned to each a *choregus* – a wealthy citizen who volunteered, or was coopted, to pay for the Chorus and for most other features of the production. Actors, however, were professionals paid by the state.

The prize-giving was taken very seriously, ten judges being nominated by an elaborate process from the ten 'tribes' into which the citizen body was divided. From 449 there was a prize for the best tragic protagonist (leading actor) as well as one for the best tragedian. Official records (*didaskaliai*) were kept of the plays performed each year and the prizes awarded. These records dated from c. 501 for tragedy (though we hear of a victory by **Thespis** as early as c. 534), from c. 486 for comedy.

The dramatists normally produced their own plays (though **Aristophanes** did not always do so). Indeed the Greeks generally spoke not of a 'writer' but of a 'teacher' of tragedy or comedy, since his essential task was not simply to compose a text but to instruct the Chorus and actors in the performance through which his play was to be realized. Revivals of plays already performed did not become usual at the Great Dionysia until the 4th century, though Aeschylus is said to have received the unique distinction of a decree allowing his plays to be revived after his death.

All actors and Chorus-members were male, and wore masks. The music to accompany songs was provided by the only unmasked figure, the player of the *aulos*, which was a double pipe with reeds. The Chorus normally sang in unison (though its leader could take part in spoken dialogue with actors), and danced in formation as it sang. Occasionally a second, subsidiary Chorus was used, and occasionally (but much less than in most modern productions) a song was divided between semichoruses or individual Chorus-members.

Another festival of Dionysus, the Lenaea, was held around the beginning of February. From c. 442 it too was the occasion for dramatic competitions in the Theatre of Dionysus, with two tragic poets producing two plays each and five comic poets producing one play each. It was more important for comedy than for tragedy.

In the villages of Attica (the territory of Athens) plays were performed at the Rural Dionysia, usually held in December. In the 4th century and later we hear of touring companies who would go the rounds of theatres in Attica and beyond.

2 Tragedy: origins, development, form The origin of tragedy has been the subject of endless discussion. The tendency among recent scholars has been to abandon the elaborate theoretical constructions which had earlier been built around enigmatic remarks in **Aristotle**, and to concentrate instead on the links between tragedy and various known types of non-dramatic poetry.

Tragedy contains two principal types of verse: spoken dialogue in iambic and trochaic metres, usually delivered by actors, and songs in lyric metres, usually delivered by the Chorus. There were non-dramatic precedents for both types. Iambic and trochaic poetry was composed for delivery by the poets themselves, for such purposes as attacking their enemies and giving moral and political advice to their fellow-citizens. Choral songs, sometimes long and elaborate and incorporating mythical narratives, were performed on various religious and ceremonial occasions. Tragedy as we know it was born when these two traditions were combined together, verse spoken by the poet (who was at first the sole actor) being interspersed with songs sung by the Chorus. This innovation probably occurred at Athens in the second half of the 6th century, and the man responsible was probably Thespis.

Our sources do provide faint hints that before Thespis' time something called 'tragedy' may have existed outside Athens, in the northern Peloponnese. 'Tragedy' is attributed to the poet Arion, who was active at Corinth c. 600, and we hear of 'tragic choruses' in 6th-century Sicyon. But this Peloponnesian 'tragedy', if it existed at all, was presumably a purely choral and non-dramatic form.

One feature which Thespis could not have borrowed from existing poetic traditions was the use of masks, enabling actor and Chorus to take on roles from the mythical past. Indeed, ancient sources claim that masks were his own invention. In other cultures, however, they are commonly employed in religious rituals, and there is some evidence for this in early Greece also. But any such ritual should be seen as at most another influence on the development of tragedy, not as its sole origin. There is no evidence that masks were ever used in the dithyramb, the form which Aristotle names (wrongly?) as the source of tragedy (*Poetics* 4).

The word 'tragedy' itself (*tragōidia*) remains most mysterious. It should mean something like 'goat-singing', but the Greeks themselves seem to have had no idea how tragedy was ever connected with goats. The sacrifice of a goat on the occasion of a tragic performance is a more likely explanation than any connection between tragedy and goat-like satyrs.

As long as the poet himself was the only actor, the dramatic possibilities must have been restricted. The important step of introducing a second actor is said to have been taken by Aeschylus, who also, according to Aristotle, 'reduced the choral element and gave dialogue the leading role', and who is often regarded as the true father of tragedy. The introduction of the third actor was ascribed to **Sophocles** by most authorities but to Aeschylus by some, and evidently occurred

around 460, in the period when both poets were competing. The three actors – protagonist, deuteragonist and tritagonist – shared the parts in any play between them. A fourth actor may have been employed on occasion, but it seems never to have come into general use. In addition there were mute extras, generally functioning as attendants but sometimes portraying named characters; and Euripides sometimes has short singing parts for boys. The Chorus is usually thought to have numbered 12 in the extant plays of Aeschylus, 15 in those of Sophocles and Euripides, but neither figure is quite certain.

The great majority of tragedies dramatized events from the Greek myths. These traditional tales were believed to be historically true in essence, but were also felt to provide paradigms of human fortunes, against which men could measure their own experience. The mythical material was usually taken from existing poetry, whether epic, lyric or tragic, but non-poetic traditions may have been used on occasion. The use of this familiar material meant that the outline of the story was always known to the audience in advance, and this knowledge could be exploited for purposes of dramatic irony. Nevertheless, the tragedian had great freedom in shaping his plot, and very different plays could be based on the same myth, as can be seen by comparing the *Choephori* of Aeschylus and the *Electras* of Sophocles and Euripides.

A few plays portrayed events in recent history (Aeschylus' *Persians* is the only surviving example, but see also **Phrynichus**). These, however, were events that had already attained 'mythic' status, and the plays were set in exotic locations; no living Greek is mentioned by name in any tragedy.

The style of tragedy can be supple, lively and, up to a point, colloquial, but always retains a certain dignity; it avoids the jokes and indecencies associated with comedy and is enriched by poetic words and expressions unknown in ordinary usage. In theme and plot not all tragedies have the concentrated seriousness of Sophocles' *Oedipus Tyrannus* or Euripides' *Medea*; for those of Euripides also include sensational melodramas and plays of romance and intrigue, even of gentle humour. And there are happy endings, not only in these romantic tragedies but in such serious ones as Aeschylus' *Eumenides* or Sophocles' *Philoctetes*. The fact that a Greek tragedy *can* end unhappily, however, and can contemplate death and acute suffering without escapism or false consolation, is a remarkable feature of the genre, distinguishing it from most independent dramatic traditions in other cultures, and doubtless owing much to the example of Homer's *Iliad*.

The scene of most tragedies is set in the open air in front of a palace or other building (exceptions include Aeschylus' *Persians*, apparently set *inside* a council-chamber, and Sophocles' *Oedipus at Colonus*, set in a rustic grove). Occasionally (as in Aeschylus' *Eumenides* and Sophocles' *Ajax*) there is a change of scene, marked by the departure and reentry of the Chorus. In Aeschylus there can also be a certain vagueness about the imagined location, allowing it to 'refocus' while the Chorus remains visible.

Events on the tragic stage never include acts of violence, and seldom include deaths. Violence and death, however, were central to most of the myths portrayed, and the tragedians dealt with this by means

Hellenistic terracotta figure, 'Parasite'.

of messengers, who come to report what has happened inside the palace or elsewhere. Every play of Sophocles and Euripides contains at least one formal messenger speech, and the dramatists make the most of the opportunities which these provide for vivid and exciting narrative. Aeschylus uses messengers in rather different and more varied ways.

In structure a tragedy consists of several acts or 'episodes', normally separated by the major choral songs, which are preceded by exits of actors (though it is not uncommon for an actor to remain on stage) and followed by entrances. Most of the spoken dialogue takes the form either of extended speeches (often highly rhetorical) or of line-by-line exchanges (stichomythia), though more irregular patterns also occur. Besides spoken dialogue, an act may contain a sung (or partly sung) exchange between actor and Chorus (*amoibaion* or *kommos*) or a solo song by an actor (monody). *Amoibaia* become rarer and monodies more common in the course of the 5th century.

The rhetorical style of tragic speeches becomes most marked in the set-piece debate (known to scholars as an *agōn* or contest) between two characters. There is at least one such debate in almost every play of Sophocles or Euripides.

A choral song can have various functions. It can influence the audience's feelings by means of moralizing comments on what the Chorus has witnessed (though such comments are usually made from the viewpoint of the man in the street, not from one of exceptional wisdom). It can broaden the scope of the play by exploring the connections between present and past events (especially in Aeschylus). It can work ironically, evoking a mood of hope and joy before disaster strikes, or one of despair before salvation comes (especially in Sophocles). It can wistfully describe a remote and idyllic world which contrasts painfully with present realities (especially in Euripides). In Aeschylus the Chorus is always closely involved in what is happening on stage, and many of the actors' speeches are addressed to it (though it seldom intervenes decisively in the plot, outside the special cases of *Suppliant Women* and *Eumenides*). In Euripides (especially his later work) its role becomes less integral; its presence is ignored for long stretches (and can even be an embarrassment), and some of its songs are little more than interludes.

In the 4th century the tendencies seen in late Euripides (and **Agathon**) – melodramatic plot, episodic structure, a decline in the role of the Chorus – were apparently carried further. The period was evidently one of decline; Aristotle treats contemporary tragedians with respect, but already regards the plays of Sophocles and Euripides (which were regularly revived) as classics.

In the Hellenistic period (from 323 BC) tragic performances, though widespread in the Greek world, were probably no longer attended by a wide public. While comedy remained popular and continued to develop, tragedy became fossilized. The stylized costume and narrow stage must have made performances very static and statuesque. A five-act structure seems to have been usual, and the Chorus, when employed at all, was wholly detached from the action. We hear of a 'Pleiad' of seven admired tragedians in 3rd-century Alexandria, but the only Hellenistic tragedy of which we can form any impression is an oddity, the *Exagoge* (a play about Moses and the Exodus) of the Hellenized Jew Ezechiel.

3 Comedy: origins, development, form The word *kōmōidia* means singing connected with, or suitable for, a *kōmos* or drunken revel. The comedy of 5th-century Athens – 'Old Comedy' – combines the same principal types of verse as tragedy, namely iambic or trochaic dialogue and choral song. The combination of these elements can hardly be independent of the example of early tragedy. The earliest known comic dramatists were Chionides and Magnes, who seem to have competed in the earliest recorded contest, at the Great Dionysia c. 486. Before this, according to Aristotle, there was informal comedy performed by 'volunteers' and derived from 'phallic songs'. The poet Susarion, who was claimed by some as the inventor of comedy, probably did not write comedies at all.

Matters are complicated, however, by the undoubted existence of a type of comedy in the Greek colony of Syracuse in Sicily. The chief exponent of this 'Doric Comedy' was **Epicharmus**, whom Aristotle places 'much earlier' than Chionides and Magnes, but who seems in fact to have been their contemporary. It is not clear whether his plays had a chorus and whether they influenced, or were influenced by, the comedy of Athens. Equally imponderable is the evidence of archaic vases showing dancers disguised as animals of one kind or another, which seem to provide a precedent for the animal choruses found in many comedies.

At Athens, though Aristotle assigns a formative role to one Crates (mid-5th century), the most admired poets of Old Comedy were **Cratinus**, Eupolis and Aristophanes; and only the work of Aristophanes survives. All his extant plays have fantasy plots set at the time of their production, but burlesque treatments of mythical themes were also common.

Comedy evidently saw itself from the first as the

antitype of tragedy, which it constantly parodies; and we may suspect that neither the sustained dignity of tragedy nor the sustained buffoonery of comedy would have been possible if each form of drama had not been able to react against the other. Comic poets are much less concerned than tragedians with coherence and consistency of plot, and several of Aristophanes' plays degenerate by the end into a series of slapstick routines. An actor is always allowed to come out of character for the sake of a joke or a topical reference, and the 'dramatic illusion' may be deliberately broken for the sake of insulting the audience or playing with theatrical convention. There is no attempt at unity of place, a few lines of dialogue being sufficient to transform the imagined setting completely.

Actors are used less economically than in tragedy, some plays requiring at least four. The language of comedy (when it is not parodying tragedy or other literature, or foreign dialects) is an entirely colloquial Attic Greek.

A startling feature is the scurrilous and often quite unfair abuse which the comic poets heaped on contemporary individuals, from defenceless private citizens to powerful politicians (even gods are treated with scant respect). Attempts seem to have been made to restrict by law the freedom which comedy traditionally enjoyed in this regard, but no such attempt had any lasting effect. And there was certainly no restriction on the explicitness of the sexual and excremental jokes.

A play is usually called after the character assumed by its Chorus (24 in number), which may be human (e.g. *Men of Acharnae*), animal (e.g. *Frogs*) or even inanimate (e.g. *Clouds*). In the middle of most of Aristophanes' plays there is a long section (sometimes two sections) called the *parabasis*, in which the plot simply stops and the Chorus addresses the audience directly. In part of each *parabasis* it comes out of character altogether to act as the mouthpiece of the poet. The earliest examples have a strict and complex form, but this is progressively simplified in the course of Aristophanes' career,

Hellenistic terracotta figure, 'Mason'.

until finally the *parabasis* disappears completely. Formal complexity can be found elsewhere in the earlier plays, notably in the conventional *agōn* or battle of words, the structure of which is marked out by a pattern of interspersed stanzas from the Chorus.

The last two extant plays of Aristophanes, *Ecclesiazusae* and *Plutus*, dating from the early 4th century, exhibit the transition to Middle Comedy, which prevailed at Athens until about the 320s. We have only fragments, however, from such prolific 4th-century poets as Antiphanes, Anaxandrides and Eubulus. The importance of the Chorus declines rapidly; in *Plutus* only one of its songs is written out, others being marked by a mere stage direction. Obscenity and satirical abuse also decline to some extent, and the pervasive cynicism of Aristophanes' earlier work is replaced by homely moralizing. Fantasy plots and burlesque treatments of myths remain popular, but familiar figures from daily life, such as cooks, parasites and courtesans, start to appear in stereotyped roles.

New Comedy, which prevailed from the late 4th century to the second, is a gentle, whimsical comedy of manners, very different indeed from the anarchic fantasy of Aristophanes, and showing the influence of the romantic tragedies of Euripides. The great name here is **Menander**; other popular poets included Alexis (whose very long career spanned the transition from Middle to New), Philemon and Diphilus.

The only sign of the Chorus is now a stage direction between acts (which always number five) and a conventional warning that revellers are approaching, which signals its first entry. The scene is always set in front of two bourgeois houses in contemporary Greece, and the romantic plot, while it may be highly improbable, contains no actual impossibilities. Love, an almost unheard-of phenomenon in Old Comedy, is normally the mainspring of the action, and this proceeds through intrigues and misunderstandings to a happy ending, in which the sympathetic characters receive their reward. The situation is made clear to the audience by a formal prologue-speech (not always situated at the very beginning), and most of the humour (and pathos) derives from the mistakes which the characters make and the human plausibility of their reactions. Somewhat broader humour is provided by slaves, cooks and the like, but indecency and topical allusions are very rare. While not all the sententious moralizing is to be taken at face value, an atmosphere of conventional decency and tolerance prevails.

The plays of New Comedy remained very popular throughout antiquity, but were lost in the Middle Ages. Our knowledge of them derives from imitations by **Plautus** and **Terence** (through which they influenced the comic traditions of the Renaissance and later periods) and from more or less fragmentary texts (almost exclusively of Menander) excavated in Egypt in recent times.

4 *Satyr play* Satyrs are mythical subhuman creatures of the Greek countryside, drunken and lustful and often portrayed in the retinue of Dionysus or in pursuit of nymphs. On 5th-century vases they are depicted as men with bald heads, pointed ears, snub noses and horses' tails.

Nothing can be made of Aristotle's claim (*Poetics* 4) that tragedy developed from some 'satyric' form (a claim which seems to contradict much else that he himself says). More plausible is the tradition that the satyr plays were introduced at Athens by Aeschylus' contemporary Pratinas, who perhaps knew them in some form at his native town of Phlius in the Peloponnese.

The 5th-century satyr play was always composed by a tragedian, and normally formed a humorous tailpiece to a set of three tragedies. It consisted of a burlesque treatment of a mythical theme, which often concerned a popular figure such as Heracles, Dionysus or Odysseus, and always had a happy ending. Into this myth the satyrs (together with their father Silenus, who was regularly a character) had to be more or less artificially introduced. In metre and construction the plays were similar to tragedies, but less strict. The plot and 'dramatic illusion' were more carefully sustained than in Old Comedy, and the humour was less broad; indecencies did occur, but contemporary allusions did not.

The only example to survive complete is Euripides' *Cyclops*, but we also have about half of Sophocles' *Ichneutae* (*Trackers*) and some interesting scraps by Aeschylus, who was regarded as the greatest exponent of the form.

In the 4th century satyr plays became separated from tragedies, and were used for political satire.

5 Mime and Phlyax Play The Greek colonies of Sicily and southern Italy evidently had a long and rich tradition of sub-literary humorous drama, of which we can catch only glimpses. The Doric Comedy of Epicharmus (see section 3) will be an early offshoot of this tradition.

A mime (*mimos*) was a short monologue or (later) dialogue on a low-life theme, normally in prose and delivered by a single unmasked performer, himself called a mime. We possess brief fragments of the work of the most admired mimographer, the 5th-century Sophron of Syracuse, and some portions of anonymous mimes from later periods, when the form became widespread in the Greek world.

In the 3rd century a literary form of mime was composed in verse and in archaic dialect by Herodas (or Herondas). It is uncertain whether this was intended for performance. The eight surviving examples mostly portray women, engaged in such unladylike activities as flogging slaves or shopping for dildoes. Some of the poems of his more refined contemporary Theocritus

A scene from a Phlyax Vase showing Chiron and slaves.

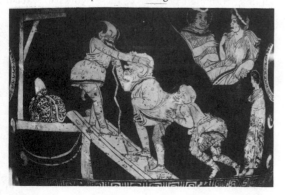

are also, in effect, mimes, or strongly influenced by the mime form.

The Phlyax Play of southern Italy is barely known from literary sources, but is taken to be the inspiration for a series of vivid and lively vase-paintings from the 4th century. The plays illustrated present either mythical burlesque or themes from contemporary life, and were evidently influenced by Athenian comedy. In their turn popular dramas of this type influenced the comedy of early Rome.

6 Actors and acting It is uncertain whether *hypokritēs*, the Greek for 'actor', originally meant 'answerer' (of the Chorus?) or 'interpreter, expounder'. Aeschylus may have taken the leading role in all his own plays (we are told the names of certain actors he employed, but not necessarily as protagonist). Sophocles, however, is said to have given up acting because of a weak voice, and the institution of a prize for actors shows that tragic poets did not act after the middle of the 5th century.

Tragic acting must have required considerable stamina and flexibility, since the same actors were used for all four plays which a tragedian presented on one day, and the roles assigned to a single actor might differ widely. The indications are that, as far as possible, the most important parts were given to the protagonist and the least important to the tritagonist, with little or no type-casting. It is uncertain whether a single part was ever divided between two or more actors (this would be necessary in Sophocles' *Oedipus at Colonus* unless a fourth actor was employed).

Strength and clarity of voice were naturally considered important. Tragic texts sometimes call for quite vigorous movements (running, collapsing in agony, grasping another's knees in supplication), but we cannot know how realistically these were performed; there was doubtless some stylization, in keeping with the size of the theatre. Various anecdotes indicate that a certain naturalism was prized, but such things are relative, and we cannot assume that Greek acting would have appeared at all naturalistic to a modern audience. Old Comedy is full of such lively activities as dancing for joy, beating opponents, and chasing them off the stage. It is not likely that tragedy contained any significant actions not signalled by the words of the texts, but there are some passages of comedy that are hard for us to understand without the accompanying gestures.

7 Music and dance These were integral parts of a Greek dramatic performance, but are impossible for us to reconstruct (we have a scrap of musical notation for Euripides' *Orestes*, but even this may not be Euripides' own). The metre shows that songs were often rhythmically complex but usually had a simple overall structure of paired stanzas (AABBCC...), the rhythms of the first stanza in each pair (the strophe) being recapitulated in the second (antistrophe). Where a song does not serve to separate two acts (often in comedy, more rarely in tragedy), the stanzas may be separated by dialogue passages. A freer form of song, without recapitulation, is also found, and becomes common in late Euripides.

Besides true song and spoken dialogue, there was an intermediate type of verse (often referred to as 'recitative'), accompanied, like the songs, on the *aulos*. This is often assigned to the Chorus-leader, but sometimes to actors and sometimes perhaps to the whole Chorus.

Late sources tell us that a rectangular formation was employed for the entrance and the dances of the dramatic Chorus, but it is hard to believe that it was always as regimented as this. Sometimes the Chorus's movements can be imagined from its words (beating of the breast and head at Aeschylus *Choephori* 423–8, kicking out at Aristophanes *Peace* 331–4), but many songs do not obviously call for imitative gestures.

8 Masks, costumes and properties The Greek mask covered the whole head, with holes for the eyes and mouth. It was probably made of linen on a wooden frame. Vase-paintings of the 5th century show that tragic masks of this period were realistic and undistorted. There must have been a range of types to show differences of age and sex, together with some special masks for such figures as the blinded Oedipus or the Phrygian in Euripides' *Orestes*. The mask of Old and Middle Comedy seems typically to have been ugly, with goggling eyes, wide nose and gaping mouth, but here again there must have been a wide variety according to needs of the play; and there is evidence that portrait masks were used by actors playing real people.

Some 5th-century paintings of tragic actors show them wearing ordinary tunics and cloaks; but it seems that the *syrma*, a long, richly embroidered robe with sleeves, which had been worn by the *aulos*-player from the first, was progressively adopted by the actors also, becoming the standard tragic costume by the end of the century. Aristophanes repeatedly taunts Euripides with presenting his heroes in rags, and there are plays by other tragedians in which ragged costumes seem to be called for (e.g. Aeschylus' *Persians*, Sophocles' *Philoctetes*), but we cannot tell how realistically ragged these were. The standard footwear was a calf-length boot, not normally worn by men in daily life.

Actors of Old and Middle Comedy wore the tunics and cloaks of everyday life, often with padding of the stomach and buttocks. It is disputed whether all comic actors wore a leather phallus (except when playing women or effeminates); it is likely that they did, but that this could be concealed beneath clothing on occasion. It is unclear whether the Chorus (when human) wore phalluses also.

In satyr plays the human characters wore tragic costume, while the satyrs wore drawers, usually of fur, equipped with phallus and horse's tail, and Silenus had a full-length costume covered with tufts of wool.

From the latter part of the 4th century the appearance of tragic actors became more stylized. The mouth of the mask opened wider; the forehead was unnaturally raised, to make the actor appear taller; and, for the same reason, the sole of the boot was thickened, until the actor was walking on stilts which raised him several inches from the ground. Since most surviving representations of tragic masks and costumes date from a late period, it must be emphasized that they are very different from those worn in the first performances of the surviving plays.

At the same period comic masks and costumes became more lifelike, in keeping with the greater realism and decorum of New Comedy. The phallus ceased to be worn. The late writer Pollux describes an extensive repertory of comic masks for the various

stock characters, and scholars have attempted to relate these both to the masks shown on terracottas and other monuments and to the characters in the plays themselves.

For stage properties (as distinct from sets and stage machinery, discussed under Greek theatres) we are dependent on the evidence of the plays. It is hardly likely (though possible in theory) that properties not mentioned in the text were used simply to create a realistic ambience. Those few which the tragic texts mention, however, are always dramatically significant and often memorably used (e.g. the carpet and the robe in Aeschylus' *Agamemnon* and *Choephori*, the urn and the bow in Sophocles' *Electra* and *Philoctetes*, the letter and the head of Pentheus in Euripides' *Iphigenia in Tauris* and *Bacchae*). The properties used by Aristophanes are more numerous, and include the scientific instruments of *Clouds* 200–17 and the arms-dealer's wares at *Peace* 1210–64.   ALB

See, in general: P. E. Easterling and B. M. W. Knox (eds.), *The Cambridge History of Classical Literature I*, Cambridge, 1985; *Greece & Rome New Surveys in the Classics* 13 (*Aristophanes*, 1979), 14 (*Euripides*, 1981), 16 (*Sophocles*, 1984), 18 (*Aeschylus*, 1986); A. Pickard-Cambridge, *Dithyramb Tragedy and Comedy*, 2nd edn rev. T. B. L. Webster, Oxford, 1962; E. Simon, *The Ancient Theatre*, trans. C. E. Vafopoulou-Richardson, London, 1982. *Festivals*: A. Pickard-Cambridge, *The Dramatic Festivals of Athens*, 2nd edn rev. J. Gould and D. M. Lewis, Oxford, 1968. *Tragedy*: A. Brown, *A New Companion to Greek Tragedy*, London, 1983; C. J. Herington, *Poetry into Drama*, Chapel Hill, 1985; A. Lesky, *Greek Tragic Poetry*, trans. M. Dillon, New Haven, 1983; O. Taplin, *Greek Tragedy in Action*, London, 1978. *Comedy*: K. J. Dover, *Aristophanic Comedy*, London, 1972; R. L. Hunter, *The New Comedy of Greece and Rome*, Cambridge, 1985; F. H. Sandbach, *The Comic Theatre of Greece and Rome*, London, 1977. *Satyr play*: D. F. Sutton, *The Greek Satyr Play*, Meisenheim am Glan, 1980.

Greece, modern

Crete, still under Venetian rule, experienced its literary and artistic renaissance in the 16th to 17th centuries, and this is where modern Greek theatre began. Little is known about how plays were produced, but there exist a number of remarkable pieces of theatre in verse from that period: three tragedies, the best of which is *Erophíli* (from the name of the heroine) by George Hortádjis, three comedies, a pastoral comedy and a religious drama. Although derivative, these works in Cretan dialect are often superior to their Western, mostly Italian models.

The Ionian islands (an area which never fell under the Turks) seem to have known, in the 18th century, a flowering of theatre with open air performances of 'Omilíes' (literally, 'speeches'), skits, in the vernacular Greek, often improvised, or of parts of the Cretan plays. The comedy *Hássis* (*The Loser*, 1795) by D. Gousélis, in 15-syllable lines, excells over all other works of the period, which also produced classicizing dramas in purist Greek by Phanariot writers (educated Greeks associated with the 'Phanari', the Greek district of Constantinople).

The two traditions, the popular and the 'loyía' (learned one), continue through the 19th century, with the former eventually gaining the upper hand. *The Basil Plant* (1830) by the Zanteot A. Mátesis is a social drama in prose and dialect. *Vavilonía* (*The Din of Babel*, 1836) by D. Vyzántios, in purist Greek but with heavily idiomatic dialogue (since the theme of the comedy is the very multiplicity of Greek dialects which supposedly makes communication among speakers impossible) has something of the spirit of *Karaghiózis*, the shadow theatre which, with its set characters and farcical predilections, becomes popular towards the end of the century. The influence of **Shakespeare** is evident on the scholar D. Vernardákis's archaicizing tragedies, such as *Merópi* (1866), and *Fáusta* (1893) which was performed simultaneously at two different theatres in Athens. Closer to reality is a type of popular theatre, in prose with inset songs, the so-called *Komidílion* (1888–c. 1900), that treats down-to-earth themes with everyday characters. This is often coupled with the *Pimenikón Idílion* (pastoral idyll), a more romantic type of play, also popular at the time. An outgrowth of both is the Greek *Epitheórisis* (Revue), skits with songs satirizing the social and political mores of the day.

Bourgeois theatre, which is represented by few plays in the 19th century (like *The Grocer's Daughter* by A. Vláhos, and *The Late Evening Visit* by Il. Kapetanákis), makes great advances in the first half of the 20th thanks to a number of talented writers who creatively adapt to modern Greek realities the techniques and spirit which they find in **Strindberg**, **Ibsen**, **Chekhov**, **Maeterlinck**, **Hauptmann**, and other European playwrights. **Wagner** influences *The Ring of the Mother* (1898) by J. Kambísis – a play which was turned into an opera by M. Kalomiris – and **Nietzsche** and **D'Annunzio** inspire the early plays of **N. Kazantzakis**. *The Three Kisses* (1908) by C. Hristomános, subtitled 'A tragic sonata', is rather sentimental, but its author played a key role in the promotion of the performing aspects of modern Greek theatre and by launching actors who eventually dominated the Greek stage. The great actress Kyvéli started at Hristomános's *Nea Skiní* (New Theatre) (1901–5), while **Maríka Kotopoúli** and other fine actors first appeared at the Greek Royal Theatre (1901–8), whose founding also helped to encourage young writers and the translation of classical dramas, as well as contemporary European comedies and tragedies, into modern Greek.

It was a new era for Greek theatre. Special schools trained professional actors and more attention was given to the direction and staging of plays. It was in this climate that the leading poet of the day Palamás wrote his poetic drama *Thrice Noble* (1903) and Grégory Xenópoulos *The Secret of Kontéssa Valéraina* (1904). Xenópoulos together with Spíros Melás, Pantelís Horn and some other writers enriched Greek theatre, in the decades following, with many new plays which proved rewarding both artistically and commercially.

The dominant trends were realism and naturalism. Xenópoulos wrote about 40 plays, tragedies and comedies, establishing himself as a great technician of the theatre (a kind of **Noël Coward** of the Greek stage): *The Soul Father* (1895), *Fotiní Sándri* (1908), *Stélla Violándi* (1909), *The Temptation* (1910), *The Flower of the Levant* (1914) and many other plays. Melás's works were heavier but equally well-crafted. The early pieces: *The Son of the Spectre*, *The Red Shirt* and *The Ruined Home* have a poetic flavour and echo Ibsenic and

Nietzschian ideas. More realistic are *The White and the Black* (1916) and *One Night, One Life* (1924). With themes from Greek history are *Papafléssas* (1937), *The King and the Dog* (on Alexander the Great and Diogenes) (1953) and *Rígas Velestinlís* (1962). Melás also wrote a successful comedy, *Dad Gets an Education* (1935), and for several years in the twenties and thirties he was also active as a theatre director. Horn's most memorable play is *To Findanáki* (*The Young Plant* – an allusion to a pretty young woman – 1921), a drama of social conflict set in a poor neighbourhood of Athens.

The writer and critic Fótos Politis, who had a serious, idealistic view of theatre, became the first director of the Greek National Theatre (1932). This event plus the establishment by Károlos Koun of the 'Popular Stage' and later (1942) of the 'Art Theatre', by Sokrátis Karandinós of his 'New Dramatic Stage' (1933), and the operation of good private companies helped advance the cause of the Greek theatre considerably. It held its own during the periods of the war and the Greek civil war to blossom again in the fifties and sixties. There is also a new development. What used to be sporadic and amateurish, that is the revival of ancient Greek dramas (as, for instance, in the Delphic festivals of 1927 and 1930 sponsored by the poet Ángelos Sikelianós and his wife Eva Palmer), is now practised on a regular basis and with elaborate productions in the ancient theatres of Epidaurus, Herodes

Katírina Paxinoú in Aeschylus' *Oresteia*, National Theatre, Greece, 1965.

Atticus (by the Acropolis), and in other extant theatres in Greece. Directors like Aléxis Minotís (d. 1990), Dimítris Rondíris, Aléxis Solomós and Károlos Koun, and performers like Katirína Paxinoú, Anna Sinodinoú, Thános Kotsópoulos, Mános Katrákis, and many others have distinguished themselves in this field.

At the same time, many of the successful plays in the theatres of London, Paris, and New York have been translated and presented in Greece, while writers of the generation of the thirties, like Ángelos Terzákis and **Pantelís Prevelákis**, and many younger writers have continued established traditions and also adapted fresh influences from abroad. The most popular types of theatre still are the *Epitheórisis* (Revue) and the so-called *Farsokomodía*, a light comedy. But dramas of ideas as well as poetic plays are also presented frequently by various companies, often with the financial assistance of the state. Composers, like Míkis Theodorákis and Mános Hadjidákis, have contributed musical scores for the production of particular plays, and painters like Yánnis Tsaroúhis have specialized in stage and costume designing.

Opera and operetta have not fared as well as other types of theatre in Greece, and the cinema and television have reduced the appeal of live theatre in general and of the Greek shadow theatre, *Karaghiózis*, in particular. This is the era of the popular music concerts and of the big spectacular productions of drama and ballet by foreign companies visiting Greece, mostly in the summer. But modern Greek theatre has come a long way from its start in 16th- and 17th-century Crete. GT

See: N. J. Laskaris, *Le Théâtre Néo-Grec*, Athens, 1930; F. M. Pontani, *Teatro Neoellenico*, Milan, 1962; Y. Sidéris, *et al.*, *The Modern Greek Theatre. A Concise History*, trans. from the Greek by L. Vassardaki, Athens, 1957; M. Valsa, *Le Théâtre Grec Moderne, de 1453 à 1900*, Berlin, 1960.

Greek theatres (See also **Theatre buildings**) According to tradition the first tragedian, **Thespis**, performed his plays on wagons with which he travelled, and seats were set up for performances in the *agora* (market-place) of Athens. By the end of the 6th century BC, however, a permanent *theatron*, 'watching-place', was set up in the precinct of Dionysus on the south slope of the Athenian Acropolis.

Since at first any construction above ground-level was of wood, and since the theatre was later rebuilt many times, the surviving remains of this earliest Theatre of Dionysus are extremely scanty. (The remains to be seen on the site today are largely of the Roman period.) It has therefore to be reconstructed on the analogy of other Greek theatres and on the evidence of the plays performed there. The only features which *necessarily* existed in the early 5th century are wooden seats for spectators on the hillside and a level, earth-floored *orchēstra*, 'dancing-area', in the centre. The *orchēstra* is usually believed to have been circular, like a threshing floor and like the *orchēstra* at Epidaurus (see below), with a diameter of perhaps 20 metres; but some have argued that it was rectangular, like that at Thoricus.

Most of the surviving plays also make use of a building, the *skēnē* or scene-building, behind the *orchēstra*. This was used as a changing-room for actors and as a sounding board, but also served to represent the palace or house in front of which most plays are set. There seems to be no reference to it in the three earliest surviving plays, **Aeschylus'** *Persians*, *Seven against Thebes* and *Suppliants*, but it certainly existed by 458, the date of his *Oresteia*, in which it is very prominently used. It may at first have been a temporary building reerected each year (*skēnē* means merely 'tent' or 'hut'). The number of doors in its facade is disputed; most tragedies require only one, but some of **Aristophanes'** plays could more easily be performed with more, and it is likely that there were in fact three. Actors and choruses could also enter by paths, called *parodoi* or *eisodoi*, to right and left of the *skēnē*. The roof of the building could be used as an acting area; it was probably there that gods entered when they appeared to mortal characters.

There has been much dispute as to the existence of a stage in front of the *skēnē*, raising the actors above the floor of the *orchēstra* where the Chorus performed. Though the evidence is sparse, it is probable that this stage existed, but it will not have been so high as to prevent easy interaction between actors and Chorus. Other features of the *orchēstra* were a central altar and several images of gods, which could be noticed in the plays when required.

A sentence in **Aristotle** connects painting of the *skēnē* with **Sophocles**, and another tradition attributes it to the painter Agatharchus working for Aeschylus. If these traditions are of any value, they must refer to permanent painting, perhaps with *trompe-l'oeil* architectural effects, and not to sets for individual plays, which seem not to have existed even at later periods.

A variety of stage machinery is mentioned by late authors, but the only devices for which there is 5th-century evidence are the *ekkyklēma* and the *mēchanē*. The former was a low platform on wheels, which could be pushed into view to reveal, in the form of a tableau, the consequence of events (normally killings) within the palace. It is a quite artificial device, but it seems to be an accepted convention as early as the *Oresteia*, and is used in many tragedies and in comic parodies of tragedy. The *mēchanē* was a kind of crane which could transport an actor through the air to give an effect of flying. It seems to be little used in surviving tragedy, though there are probable instances in the anonymous *Prometheus Bound* and *Rhesus*, as well as in Aristophanes; 5th-century tragedians probably did not use it for epiphanies of gods, though the 'god from the machine' (*deus ex machina*) became proverbial at an early date.

In the mid-5th century, at the instigation of the statesman Pericles, the Odeum, a square, roofed building for musical recitals, was built beside the theatre. Rather later (perhaps not until the 4th century) a long stone portico was built along the south side of the theatre, and the wooden *skēnē*, now at least 30 metres in length, backed directly onto this. Italian vase-paintings of the 4th century show dramatic scenes played in and around porches or booths, consisting of a roof on narrow columns; such structures may or may not have existed in Athens. Around 330 the theatre was largely rebuilt in stone by the statesman Lycurgus; thrones were provided for priests and officials in the front row of the audience, and the ends of stone *skēnē* were now equipped with forward-projecting wings, *paraskēnia*.

The lower rows of seats surrounded the *orchēstra* in approximately a semicircle and further rows extended up the slope of the Acropolis behind. The capacity of the theatre has been calculated at a theoretical maximum of some 17,000, but this figure may not have been reached in practice.

Meanwhile drama spread rapidly outside Athens. The oldest theatre to survive in approximately its original form is a small one at Thoricus in Attica, with an *orchēstra* in the form of an irregular rectangle. This is dated to the mid-5th century (the earliest remains have been dated to the late 6th, but it is questionable whether the site could have been used for drama at that period).

Particularly well preserved, and famous for its beauty and its acoustics, is the theatre at Epidaurus in the Peloponnese, built about 300 BC by the architect Polyclitus. This is similar in size to the Theatre of Dionysus at Athens, ut a hollow in the hillside allowed a more symmetrical design than was ever possible there. A circular *orchēstra*, marked by a stone rim, is surrounded by seats for just over half its circumference. The *skēnē* was probably of two storeys, with a long, narrow stage projecting at the level of the upper storey, so that the actors on the stage were better seen by the upper rows of the audience but were cut off from the Chorus in the *orchēstra*.

This type of design became standard in the Hellenistic period (3rd and 2nd centuries), when every town in the Greek world came to have its theatre. The front wall of the stage, the *proskēnion*, as well as the facade of the upper storey behind the actors, was often richly decorated with painted panels. ALB

See: M. Bieber, *The History of the Greek and Roman Theater*, 2nd edn, Princeton, 1961; A. W. Pickard-Cambridge, *The Theatre of Dionysus in Athens*, Oxford, 1946; E. Simon, *The Ancient Theatre*, trans. C. E. Vafopoulou-Richardson, London, 1982.

Green, Adolph see Comden, Betty

Green, Paul (1894–1981) American playwright. A student of Frederick Koch at the University of North Carolina, Green understood that he must write about the life he knew in his native South. In *The Last of the Lowries* (1920) he recreated the rhythmic language of the Negro and Southern folk characteristics. His best play, *In Abraham's Bosom* (1926), portrays the tragedy of a Negro idealist, defeated by his own limitations and the people he chooses to help. In both *The Field God* (1927), showing the spiritual disintegration of a man condemned by the religiosity he rejected, and *Shroud My Body Down* (1934), he dramatized the fascination and violence of religious mania. A man of strong opinions, Green became involved in the protest drama of the 1930s. *Hymn to the Rising Sun* (1936) is a condemnation of the chain-gang system. In *Johnny Johnson* (1936), America's most imaginative anti-war play, Green satirized warmongers through a hero who is confined by society for having 'peace monomania'. With *The Lost Colony* (1937), a symphonic drama about Sir Walter Ralegh's colony, Green's career changed. He continued throughout his life to celebrate American history through such pageants as *The Common Glory* (1947), the efforts of Jefferson during the Revolution; *The Founders* (1957), the story of the Jamestown colony; *Cross and Sword* (1965). WJM

Greene, Graham (1904–91) British novelist and playwright, whose characteristic theme is the emptiness of modern life and the rediscovery of religious belief. After dramatizing his own novel *The Heart of the Matter* in collaboration with **Basil Dean** (1950), he wrote a series of plays on adultery and the loss of faith (*The Living Room*, 1953; *The Complaisant Lover*, 1959), the effect of a miracle on an atheistic family (*The Potting Shed*, 1957) and the spiritual pride of an untalented artist (*Carving a Statue*, 1964). Though conventional in form, these offered satisfying roles for a number of leading performers – **Dorothy Tutin**, **Ralph Richardson** and **John Gielgud** – and *The Return of A. J. Raffles* was produced by the **Royal Shakespeare Company** in 1975. His plays *Yes and No* and *For Whom the Bell Chimes* were staged in 1980, and he also wrote several film scripts, notably *The Third Man* (1948). CI

Greene, Robert (c. 1558–92) English pamphleteer and playwright, one of the most voluble of the **University Wits**. His romance, *Pandosto* (1588), provided **Shakespeare** with the plot of *The Winter's Tale*, but Greene is better known for his attack on Shakespeare as 'an upstart crow, beautified with our feathers'. The attack appeared in *Greene's Groatsworth of Wit, Bought with a Million of Repentance* (1592), a death-bed pamphlet confessing and bemoaning his dissipated life. Of the five extant plays ascribed to him, the best is the comedy *Friar Bacon and Friar Bungay* (c. 1589), a light-hearted treatment of the experiments with magic conducted by two 13th-century Oxford Franciscans. *James IV* (c. 1591) combines Scottish history and fairy romance. *A Looking-Glass for London and England* (c. 1590), written with Thomas Lodge, is a satirical dramatic treatment of material handled with more confidence in Greene's pamphlets. PT

Greenland Theatre is deeply rooted in the Inuit culture. Drama has always been an important vehicle of entertainment, celebration and communication. During folk festivities songs were used partly as community singing, partly performed solo, and created by the singers themselves. The songs were accompanied by movement, dancing, highly developed gestures and mime. In various rituals and other activities performance skills were called upon. The shaman – Angakoq – maintained his confidence by spiritual songs, expressed in the special language which urges and conjures the helping spirits of the shaman. Grave disagreements and disputes were settled by a unique kind of duel – drum-dancing and singing created by the disputants themselves for their defence, expressing their opinion of the conflict and at the same time trying to ridicule their opponents. The contestant who most convinced the audience won the case. The wonders of life were praised by singing: a child's birth, special events in the child's life would be marked by a song composed by the child's 'special protector' – perhaps the grandmother. Likewise the death of a loved one would be mourned in elegies of sorrow. In these various ways drama was used in the culture of the Inuit people.

Christian missionaries found these habits of spontaneity heathen and not suited for their congregation and fought them to such a degree that the last representatives of these cultures had to perform their arts secretly.

During the 1930s a new kind of drama was introduced into Greenland. Some younger poets began writing plays in accordance with the European tradition, plays which became extremely popular with audiences, performed by amateur actors. Authors such as Pavia Petersen, Hans Lynge and Karl Heilmann are especially remembered for their works. During the following 20 to 30 years theatrical performances were strongly reestablished with successful plays such as Jorgen Pjetturssons's *Itersamit qaqivoq* (*Out from the Deep*). Today professional theatre is established in Greenland. The first professional actors were trained in Denmark with the **Tukak** (or **Tuukkaq**) **Theatre**, which worked on ancient Inuit legends and myths and developed a strongly non-verbal approach. Many of the actors from that theatre have returned to Greenland. In the main town, Nuuk, they have formed the company 'Silamuit' which enjoys great success. JP

Greet, Ben (Philip Barling) (1857–1936) British actor–manager, who founded his own touring company in 1886 after playing in the provinces with Sarah Thorne and in London at the **Lyceum** under **Lawrence Barrett**. Best known for his open-air performances of **Shakespeare**, particularly of *Midsummer Night's Dream*, he followed **William Poel** – with whom he had co-produced the 1902 revival of *Everyman* – in returning to the simplified staging techniques of the Elizabethan theatre. He toured widely in America and mounted a season at the New York Garden Theatre in 1910, before returning to become one of the leading directors at the **Old Vic**, where he directed 24 Shakespeare plays between 1915 and 1918. Knighted in 1929, in 1930 he re-opened the Oxford Repertory Company (which had closed after the departure of **J. B. Fagan**). CI

Gregory, André (1934–) American director and producer, identified closely with the 1960s avantgarde. After beginning his career in 1959 as an Off-Broadway producer, Gregory turned to directing at The Writer's Stage in 1962. He founded The Manhattan Project, an environmental theatre group which adapted performance spaces to suit each script. In 1970 he acquired sudden fame and international attention with the success of the company's *Alice in Wonderland*. *Endgame* in 1973 also attracted considerable interest, after which **Joseph Papp** presented the company at the Public Theatre in (The) *Seagull* (1975) and *Jinx Bridge* (1976) Always controversial, The Manhattan Project consisted of six actors performing in a highly eccentric style. Words were articulated in a strange and often comic manner, and gestures were exaggerated as the actors played the sub-text more often than the text. While **Clive Barnes** found Gregory 'One of the most interesting and innovative directors in the world', **Walter Kerr** dismissed the company as self-indulgent, slovenly in speech, and childish in antics. Gregory also starred in the film *My Dinner with Andre* (1982), with Wallace Shawn. TLM

Gregory, Johann Gottfried (1631–75) A Lutheran minister, born in Germany and practising in Moscow from 1662, who, at the behest of Tsar Aleksei Mikhailovich, founded and directed the first official court theatre in Russia (4 June 1672). A special wooden theatre was erected, an acting company of 64, mostly the sons of German merchants, was trained, and a selection of plays on biblical themes (Esther, Judith) and adapted from English sources (**Marlowe**) was drawn from the German dramatic repertory. Scenic, costume and musical effects were elaborate for their day, including perspective painting by the Dutch designer Engels. Attempts to educate the sons of Russian merchants as actors proved less successful as did the theatre's general operation following Gregory's death, under former assistant George Huebner and later Latin teacher Stefan Chizhinsky. The tsar's death in 1676 ended this theatre's brief career. SG

Gregory, Lady Augusta Isabella (1852–1932) Despite her Ascendancy background a staunch nationalist, Lady Gregory was a prime mover in founding and sustaining the Irish Literary, later the **Abbey, Theatre**. She translated voluminously from Gaelic folk tales and legends, rendered into the Kiltartan region English dialect, the idiom of most of her many plays – folk comedies and tragedies, histories, translations. Very popular in their time, particularly the comedies, and highly praised by **Yeats**, Lady Gregory's plays suggested, notably to **Synge**, the theatrical potential of Hibernicized English. DM

Grenfell, Joyce (Joyce Irene Phipps) (1910–79) British actress, who first made her name in intimate revue. She had entertained her friends privately with gently satiric sketches and monologues, which revealed her gifts for sharp observation and telling mimicry. Her first professional stage appearance in *The Little Revue* (1939) was successful; and throughout the war, she broadcast and toured, becoming one of Britain's best-loved comediennes. She appeared in **Noël Coward's** revue, *Sigh No More* (1945), in *Tuppence Coloured* (1947), *Penny Plain* (1951) and in her one-woman show, *Joyce Grenfell Requests the Pleasure*, which went to New York in 1955. Her one-woman sketches were similar to those of the American actress, **Ruth Draper**, and if Draper possessed a greater dramatic range, then Grenfell undoubtedly enjoyed the sharper comic instinct and unlike Draper, was successful within a team. She was a memorable Gossage, the gawky games mistress, in the film version of John Dighton's *The Happiest Days of Your Life*. She could sing in a wistful, appealing soprano songs of her own devising, and was the author of three books, *Nanny Says* (with Sir Hugh Casson) (1972), an autobiography *Joyce Grenfell Requests the Pleasure* (1976) and *George, Don't Do That* (1977). JE

Griboedov, Aleksandr Sergeevich (1794–1829) Dramatist, diplomat and founding father of Russian stage realism. Interested in the theatre from his youth, Griboedov wrote and collaborated on a series of largely undistinguished adaptations of and variants on French comedies while advancing from doctoral studies at Moscow University to a career in the Foreign Service. His early plays include: *The Young Marrieds* (1815), an adaptation of Creuzé de Lesser's *Le Secret du Ménage*; *All in the Family*, or *The Married Fiancée* (1818), his best play of the group; *Feigned Infidelity* (1818), a translation of Nicolas Berthe's *Les Fausses Infidélités*; *The Student* (written 1817, produced 1904); and *Who's the Brother, Who's the Sister, or Deception for Deception*, the libretto of a vaudeville opera, co-written with Prince Peter Viazemsky (1823), among others. Dispatched to Teheran as Russian minister in 1829, Griboedov was literally torn apart by a mob incensed by the harsh terms of a treaty which he had negotiated to end recent Russo-Persian hostilities. Griboedov's reputation as a dramatist is based upon the verse comedy *Woe to Wit* (1824), the first truly classic Russian play. An indictment of tsarist society etched in irony and melancholia, it is at once a romantic comedy of manners, psychological *comédie de caractère* à la **Molière**, 'spiritual drama' of disaffected, revolutionary youth, progressive and grotesque socio-political satire and *drame à clef*. Chatsky, the Byronic-Hamlet-Alceste-type protagonist, is a positive variant of the generally parodistic neo-*philosophe* character type and the ambivalent thematic core of the play. His relationship with Sofia, daughter of the ridiculous, conservative government official Famusov (a starring vehicle for **Shchepkin** and **Stanislavsky**) forms one-half of the play's 'double intrigue'. The second is Chatsky's disenchantment with and eventual fierce rejection of contemporary Russia's conservatism and Gallomania. Despite the play's pointedness of theme and characterization, Griboedov largely eschewed the didacticism and moralizing of contemporaries like **Prince Shakhovskoi** with whom and under whose influence he wrote some of his early works. Technically, he improved upon the French models of *haute comédie* as well as the Russian models of **Fonvizin**, employing dialogue and action to advance character and Russian phraseology to texture witty verse form. The play's evocation of antigovernment secret societies, especially the Decembrists with whom Griboedov was associated, earned its banning and underground celebrity prior to 1831. In the years following the 1917 Revolution Lenin and **Lunacharsky** characterized the enemies of the proletariat with images drawn from this play and declared

this to be one of the earliest 'people's creations'. **Meyerhold** staged a memorable production at his theatre in 1928. The most famous recent staging was by **Gregory Tovstonogov** at Leningrad's Gorky Theatre (1962) with Sergei Yursky as Chatsky.   SG

Grieg, Nordahl (1902–43) Norwegian poet and playwright, instrumental in the introduction of modernism in Norwegian theatre. Educated partly in Oxford, he was a journalist in China before turning to playwriting with *A Young Man's Love* (1927). His mature (and controversial) plays *Our Power and Our Glory* (1935), *But Tomorrow!* (1936) and *The Defeat* (1937) reveal his admiration for Soviet theatre techniques (studied during a two-year visit in 1932–4), his anti-fascism and his belief that theatre must activate the spectator. During the German occupation, Grieg was close to the Free Norwegian Government in London and died as an observer on a bombing raid over Berlin.   HL

Grieve, John Henderson (1770–1845) The first of a notable English family of scene-painters, long associated with **Covent Garden**. Grieve was one of the major contributors to the vogue for picturesque **Shakespeare** productions, encouraged under the management of **John Kemble**. Grieve was joined at Covent Garden by his sons Thomas (1799–1882) and William (1800–44). They were superior artisans, adept at adding to their moody landscapes slight antiquarian touches to gratify scholarly members of the audience. Like **Clarkson Stanfield**, they were quick to exploit the theatrical potential of the moving diorama, making them a feature of the annual Covent Garden pantomime after the sensational success of their 1820 'seacrossing from Wales to Ireland'. Only William Grieve and Thomas's son, Thomas Walford Grieve (1841–82), showed any evidence of an individual talent to rival

The Dining Room scene, from Griboedov's *Woe to Wit*, 1928.

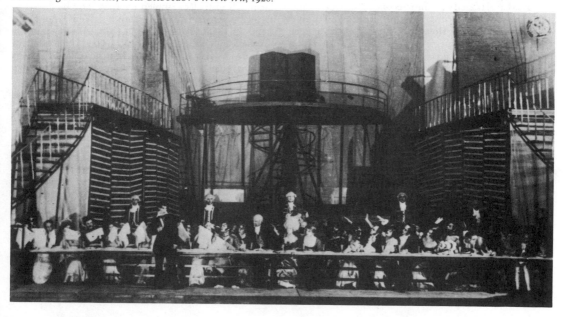

showed any evidence of an individual talent to rival Stanfield's. Particularly admired for his command of moonlight, William was called for by the audience after the first performance of Meyerbeer's *Robert le Diable* at Covent Garden in 1832. In the last years of his life, he deserted the family to work at **Drury Lane**. Over 700 designs by members of the Grieve family have survived, but so few are identified that it is difficult to distinguish the work of the individual members.   PT

Griffiths, Trevor (1935–) British dramatist, whose debate plays for stage and television reveal his training in Marxist dialectic and his sensitivity to working-class life. His first major play, *Occupations* (1970), was tried out at the Manchester fringe club, the Stables, before the **Royal Shakespeare Company** brought it to London. It concerned the 1920 Fiat motor strike in Italy and the contrasting ideologies of the Marxist theorist, **Antonio Gramsci**, and the Soviet agent, Kabak. *Sam, Sam* (1972) describes the careers of two brothers, one who stays happily loyal to his roots and the other who becomes a member of the new bourgeoisie. The most ambitious Griffiths study of the class basis to social behaviour came with *Comedians* (1975), which concerned an ageing music-hall comic, Eddie Waters, teaching his trade to some aspiring comedians in a night school. In 1973, the **National Theatre** produced *The Party*, an analysis as to why the 1968 events of May found so little response in Britain, which featured **Laurence Olivier** as Tagg, a Glaswegian Trotskyite. Griffiths has since turned to television as the better medium for the wider transmission of ideas, writing the *Bill Brand* series (1976) about a disillusioned Labour MP.   JE

Grillparzer, Franz (1791–1872) Austrian dramatist. The eclecticism of Grillparzer's work is typical of the variety of his country's dramatic tradition. Grillparzer's first success was a grim *Schicksaltragödie*, *The Ancestress* (1817), but it is a measure of his talent that he did not repeat himself. His next play, *Sappho* (1819), was a classical tragedy on the irreconcilability of art and life, a work that earned him the position of house dramatist at the **Burgtheater**. Until 1838, Grillparzer wrote plays of a diverse nature. *The Golden Fleece* (1821), a mighty trilogy about Medea and Jason, contains a study of male–female relationships that, it might be argued, foreshadows the work of **Ibsen**. The last play of the trilogy, *Medea*, equals in power the Euripidean original. *Waves of the Sea and Love* (1829) has a classical setting as it is a dramatization of the story of Hero and Leander. Grillparzer was also noted for his historical tragedy *King Ottokar's Rise and Fall* (1823), while his play *A True Servant to His Master* (1826) owes much to the work of **Lope de Vega**. Calderonian drama in an unlikely combination with the Viennese **Volksstück** inspired the most popular of Grillparzer's work with his contemporaries, *A Dream of Life* (1832). As a result of the failure of his comedy *Woe To Him Who Lies!* (1838), Grillparzer withdrew from writing for the public stage. His later plays, *Family Strife Among The Habsburgs*, *The Jewess of Toledo*, and *Libussa*, were only performed after his death. Although Grillparzer's plays incorporate wide-ranging themes on political and social matters and, in *Libussa*, on the whole development of human civilization, their strength derives from their author's acute knowledge of human relations, especially in the sphere of sexuality. This was partially the result of Grillparzer's tormented private life: he could never find the fulfilment in love he was constantly searching for. His personal unhappiness was aggravated by the necessity for him to spend most of his life working in the Austrian civil service. Nevertheless, on his death he was publicly recognized as the preeminent dramatist of his country and is still regarded as such today.   SW

Grimaldi, Joseph (1778–1837) 'King of Clowns', grandson of the Italian dancer John Baptist 'Iron Legs' Grimaldi, known as Nicolini (*fl.* 1740–2), and illegitimate London-born son of Giuseppe (?1710–88), a dancer and Pantaloon, noted for his agility and bad manners. He made his debut at **Sadler's Wells** or **Drury Lane** at the age of four, and played sprites and fairies throughout childhood. Awkward in drama, he gravitated to pantomime and first won acclaim as Clown in Dibdin's *Peter Wilkins or Harlequin in the Flying World* (Sadler's Wells, 1800), when he wore a costume more extravagant and particoloured than usual and changed the standard ruddy complexion for a white face with two red half-moons on the cheeks. His great success came in *Harlequin Mother Goose or The Golden Egg* (**Covent Garden**, 1806; much revived). Grimaldi's clown was a greedy, amoral schoolboy, out to satisfy his appetites; his exuberant optimism was that of the survivor, and the fun derived from the overthrow of everyday inhibitions. His entering cry of 'Here we are again!', his songs 'Hot Codlins' and 'Tippitiwitchet' shared with the audience, his tricks of construction, assembling living creatures from assorted props, and, especially, his thieving, gluttony and violence, stealing sausages and attacking watchmen and police with a redhot poker, became hallmarks of the panto clown or Joey. Lord High Chancellor Eldon himself exclaimed, 'Never, never did I see a leg of mutton stolen with such superhumanly sublime impudence as by that man.' Over-exertion rendered Grimaldi virtually crippled by 1823, and he gave two farewell performances, at Sadler's Wells and Drury Lane, in 1828. His son Joseph (1802–32) in whom he invested much hope of succession died of alcoholism, and the clown's last days were, as he described them, 'grim-all-day'. His *Memoirs* were edited, somewhat half-heartedly, by **Charles Dickens** in 1838; his grave in Pentonville is annually commemorated by a conventicle of clowns.   LS

Grimaldi as Clown in *Harlequin and the Golden Fish*, feeding and playing leapfrog with a giant frog.

Grock (Charles Adrien Wettach) (1880–1959) Swiss clown. He began as his father's partner in cabaret, and after 14 years as an acrobat took the name Grock when part of a musical-clown tour of Europe and S. America in 1903. Originally he played the dumb August to such white clowns as Antonet (Umberto Guillaume), but seldom got on with his partners, so he developed a solo act which gradually stretched to a half-hour. A virtuoso on 13 instruments, Grock in his routine demonstrated his inability to play properly on anything; concertinas, miniature fiddles, grand pianos turned into instruments of mental anguish in his hands. Combining the elegance of the white clown with the crude childishness of the August, he made his sketches parables of the malice of inanimate objects and human fecklessness. Personally pedantic and financially astute, on stage he tinged the hilarity with melancholy. His trademarks were an oversized coat, an egg-bald pate, a simian countenance, and frequent cries of (in France) 'Sans blague!', (in Germany) 'Nit möööglich!' and (in England) simply 'Oooh!' He founded his own circus in 1951, retiring three years later. His acts have been preserved on film (1931, 1948, 1949).   LS

Gropius, Walter (1883–1969) German artist and architect. In the 1920s, Gropius founded the Staatliches Bauhaus in Weimar, Germany, a school of Fine Arts and Arts and Crafts which focused on architecture, painting, sculpture, industrial design, and theatre. Working with **Oskar Schlemmer** who was in charge of the theatre workshop, Gropius hoped to fuse art with everyday life. In 1926, Gropius conceived a new type of theatre building which he called the Total-theatre. This facility was intended through its design to change the actor–audience relationship and was going to be used by director **Erwin Piscator**. Gropius believed that there were only three types of theatrical stages: the thrust, the arena, and the proscenium. In his new theatre design all three existed. Elliptically shaped, the 2,000-seat arena featured a proscenium stage that was fronted by a circular thrust performing area which could be rotated to the centre of the auditorium to create a theatre-in-the-round. In addition, the Total-theatre was designed to have a domed ceiling on which projections could be shown. This ceiling was supported by 12 pillars between which were additional projection screens. There was also a transluscent cyclo-rama for projections at the rear of the proscenium stage. When the Nazis came to power, the controversial Bauhaus was disbanded and thus the Total theatre was never built. Nevertheless, its influence can be seen in many subsequent theatres.   TM

Gros-Guillaume (Robert Guérin) (?–1634) French actor-manager, particularly celebrated under this guise in farce but who played in the remainder of the repertoire as La Fleur. First heard of at the **Hôtel de Bourgogne** in 1598, he joined **Valleran**'s company there in 1610 and formed his own two years later. After some time in the provinces he returned as director of the Comédiens du Roi who from 1622 took out successive leases of the Hôtel de Bourgogne before settling there permanently in 1629. A short, fat man, he accentuated his shape for comic effect by strapping two belts tightly round the midriff to give himself the appearance of a walking barrel; on his head he wore a flat cap askew and a sheepskin chin-strap while his face, in the French theatrical tradition, was covered with flour, which by moving his agile features he would sprinkle over any actor who accosted him. Thus attired he was a perfect foil to the other popular farce-players with whom he regularly acted in the 1620s and 30s, **Gaultier-Garguille** and **Turlupin**, and like them he appeared under his stage-name as a character in Gouge-not's comedy about a company of actors, *La Comédie des Comédiens* (*The Actors' Comedy*, 1631/2).   DR

Grosbard, Ulu (1929–) Belgium-born, American director. Grosbard emigrated to the United States in 1948, and attended the University of Chicago, Yale School of Drama, and **Actors Studio**. He began his directing career in 1957, making his New York debut in 1962 with *The Days and Nights of Beebee Fenstermaker* at the Sheridan Square Playhouse. His notable productions since include: *The Subject Was Roses* (1964); *A View from the Bridge* (1965); *The Investigation* (1966); *The Price* (1968); *American Buffalo* (1977); *The Wake of Jamie Foster* (1982); and *Weekends Like Other People* (1982). Since 1961 he has worked also in films and television.   TLM

Grossmith, George (junior) (1874–1935) British actor and co-author of revues for the Empire and **Gaiety Theatre**. The son of George Grossmith, who was a regular performer in the Savoy Operas, he introduced the stock figure of the 'dude' to musical comedy, in which he starred between 1893 and 1912.   CI

Grotowski, Jerzy (1933–) Polish director, teacher and theoretician of the theatre, who from 1982 has lived in the United States. After studying at the State Drama School in Cracow and in Moscow, and directing in Cracow, he established the Theatre of 13 Rows in Opole, where from 1959 to 1964 he staged poetic works played against the texts as arguments with past cultural monuments and designed to transform traditional actor–audience relationships: **Byron**'s *Cain*, **Goethe**'s *Faust*, **Mayakovsky**'s *Mystery-Bouffe* and Kalidasa's *Shakuntula* in 1960; **Mickiewicz**'s *Fore-fathers' Eve* in 1961; **Słowacki**'s *Kordian* and **Wyspiański**'s *Acropolis* (co-created with **Jozef Szajna**) in two versions in 1962; **Marlowe**'s *Faustus* in 1963; a third variant of *Acropolis* in 1964. In 1965 he moved the group to Wrocław, adopting the name Laboratory Theatre. From 1965 to 1973 he created a fourth and fifth variant of *Acropolis*, three versions of **Calderón**'s *The Constant Prince* (in Słowacki's translation), and three variants of *Apocalypsis cum figuris*, his final production. Since the early 1970s, he has engaged in paratheatrical activities, seminars, and teaching in Poland, Western Europe and America. Grotowski's productions and theories, concept of a 'poor theatre', and work on the training of actors have had a major impact on world theatre. *Towards a Poor Theatre* (1968) is a collection of his theoretical writings.   DG

Group Theatre, The Founded in 1931 by **Harold Clurman**, **Lee Strasberg** and **Cheryl Crawford**, the Group was a pioneering attempt to create a theatre collective, a company of players trained in a unified style and dedicated to presenting new American plays

Grotowski's production of *Faust*, Poznan, Poland, 1960.

of social significance. With **Stanislavsky**'s **Moscow Art Theatre** as their model, Group members began a systematic study of an art that had few guidelines and virtually no written record. Prodded by their exacting teacher, Lee Strasberg, and fired by Clurman's messianic fervour, the actors experimented with improvisation, emotional and sensory memories, private moments and exercises in relaxation and concentration. The inner technique they worked on, which became the basis of the American Method and which Strasberg continued to develop during his 35 years at the **Actors Studio**, resulted in acting that was more natural and earthy, more private, more intense, and more psychologically charged than previous styles. Debates over method erupted in the summer of 1934 when Group member **Stella Adler** returned from her studies with Stanislavsky in Paris to announce that the Master had abandoned his earlier emphasis on inner work in favour of a new external technique, the method of physical actions. Adler and Strasberg squared off in a craft war whose wounds have never healed, Strasberg and his followers continuing to focus on the actor's own emotional resources while Adler and her colleagues have concentrated on the play as opposed to the player.

Among the superb realistic actors the Group helped to develop were John Garfield and Franchot Tone (both of whom defected to movies), Margaret Barker, Ruth Nelson, **Morris Carnovsky**, Phoebe Brand, Art Smith, and Sanford Meisner. Decades after the Group disbanded in 1941, Strasberg, Adler, Meisner, and Carnovsky continued to be influential teachers, offering their own individual variations of the Method.

Although less successful than its actor-training programme, the Group's literary achievement was also substantial. The Group was not a political theatre and in fact was strongly criticized by more militant com-

panies, but over a ten-year period it produced 22 new American plays on subjects of contemporary relevance. If only a few of these – **John Howard Lawson**'s *Success Story* (1932) and **Clifford Odets**'s *Awake and Sing!* (1935) and *Paradise Lost* (1935) – have enduring literary value, all of the Group's plays rose above the level of propaganda and in Odets the company yielded an American original.   FH

Group Theatre (Belfast) Three amateur companies amalgamated (1939–40) to form the Ulster Group Theatre, unified in 1940 under a board of directors including Harold Goldblatt and James Tomelty. Although it presented **Sheridan**, **Ibsen**, **Chekhov**, **Odets**, it concentrated on Northern playwrights: **Ervine**, **Shiels**, Tomelty (*The End House* 1944, *All Souls' Night* 1949). The theatre attained high standards and initiated some distinguished actors: Patrick Magee, J. G. Devlin, Stephen Boyd, **Colin Blakely**, James Ellis. The major cause of the Group's demise was internal dispute over **Sam Thompson**'s controversial *Over the Bridge* (1960). Its final flourish was **Stewart Parker**'s *The Randy Dandy* (1960).   DM

Group Theatre (London) Founded by Rupert Doone, a choreographer who had danced with Diaghilev's Ballets Russes, together with Ormerod Greenwood and **Tyrone Guthrie**, as an ensemble company dedicated both to the performance of poetic drama and to socialist ideals comparable with the Workers' Theatre Movement. Its first successful production was the first revival in over 400 years of the recently discovered interlude *Fulgens and Lucrece* by **Henry Medwall**. It provided a stage for *Sweeney Agonistes* (1935) by **T. S. Eliot**, who also wrote a choral piece *The Rock* in collaboration with its members; and the verse plays of **W. H. Auden** and **Christopher Isher-wood** – *The Dog Beneath the Skin* (1936), *The Ascent of F6* (1937, re-staged at the Arts Theatre, Cambridge, in 1938 and at the **Old Vic** in 1939) and *On the Frontier* (1938) – were written specifically for the Group. Louis MacNeice also provided texts, as did Stephen Spender (*The Trial of a Judge*, 1938), while Benjamin Britten contributed musical scores for many of the productions. It also functioned briefly between 1950 and 1954, presenting the first English production of a **Sartre** play, *The Flies* (1951).   CI

Grumberg, Jean-Claude (1939–) French actor, director and playwright. Outstanding example of a playwright who successfully combined the styles of absurdist theatre and the social concern of the decentralized theatre in the 1970s. His use of theatre within the theatre (*Dreyfus* directed by Rosner 1973) and of autobiographical material (*L'Atelier* (*The Workshop*) directed by Bénichou, Rosner and Grumberg 1979) shows a craftsmanship similar to that displayed by the young **Anouilh**.   DB

Gründgens, Gustaf (1899–1963) German actor and director, whose work epitomized the classical tradition in opposition to the realism of **Stanislavsky**. After working with **Reinhardt** in 1928, he established his reputation as the leading German actor with his performance of Mephisto in **Goethe**'s *Faust* in 1932, a role he had played as early as 1922 and which he repeated in his famous 1957 production. Appointed director of the Berlin Staatsteater under the Nazis from 1934 to 1944, he was attacked as a fascist collaborator in the novel *Mephisto* by Klaus Mann (in whose 1925 play *Anja and Esther* he performed). But his war-time productions of **Schiller** or **Lessing** had drawn contemporary parallels as an oblique form of political protest – an approach continued as artistic director at Düsseldorf in 1947 and Hamburg from 1955, that has had a significant influence – and at **Brecht**'s request he directed the premiere of *St Joan of the Stockyards* in 1959.   CI

Grundy, Mrs The invention of the playwright **Thomas Morton**, Mrs Grundy is a character who never appears in his popular success *Speed the Plough* (1800), but whose approval is constantly sought and disapproval dreaded by Farmer Ashfield's worthy wife. The original Mrs Grundy is more like the Joneses, with whom the middle classes are constantly trying to 'keep up', than the ogre of prudish repression she has subsequently become.   PT

Grundy, Sydney (1848–1914) English playwright, born and educated in Manchester, where he was working as a barrister when his first play, *A Little Change* (1872), was staged at the **Haymarket**. Grundy's normal practice was to adapt, and if necessary clean up, French plays. The bowdlerized and reshaped versions of **Alexandre Dumas** *père* – *A Marriage of Convenience* (1897), *The Silver Key* (1897), *The Musketeers* (1898), *The Black Tulip* (1899) – are typical, as is his best-known work, *A Pair of Spectacles* (1890), an adaptation from *Les Petits Oiseaux* by **Labiche** and Delacour, which provided **John Hare** with a popular success as Benjamin Goldfinch. An outspoken oppo-nent of the 'demoralizing' **Ibsen**, Grundy nevertheless provided **Lillie Langtry** with a *succès de scandale* in *The Degenerates* (1899), and enjoyed playing with fire in *A Fool's Paradise* (1889), a response to the Maybrick trial, and *Slaves of the Ring* (1894), in which he brushed with the adulterous passion of Tristan and Isolde. In the year of his death, he published an outrageously reactionary booklet, *The Play of the Future: by a Playwright of the Past*.   PT

Gryphius, Andreas (1616–64) German play-wright. Although Gryphius's plays were not per-formed during his lifetime, they are now generally considered to be among the most significant achieve-ments in German drama during the baroque period. His tragedies, classical in style and structure, deal with the sufferings of high-born nobility and royalty, though *Cardenio and Celinde* (1647) is closer to middle-class drama. *Murdered Majesty, or Charles Stuart* (1649) dramatizes, not very effectively, the execution of the English king. Of Gryphius's comedies, *Horribilicribri-fax* (1663) and *The Beloved Rose With a Thorn* (1661) are the most refreshing and lively.   SW

Guan, Hanqing Chinese dramatist. His dates are controversial and known biographical facts minimal. He was probably born about 1230 and died towards the close of the 13th or very early in the 14th century. He was from Dadu, site of the present day Beijing. It is thought that he had experience as an actor which would have contributed to his dramatic prescience. He is regarded as the foremost of the Yuan *zaju* playwrights. The 700th anniversary of his work was celebrated with a fanfare of tributes in China in 1958. Emphasis was laid on his affinity with the everyday life of his times. Of his plays, 18 are extant out of a presumed output of 63. Eight have been translated into English, including *Injustice to Dou E* (*Dou E yuan*), perhaps his best known piece written towards the end of his life. It was constantly performed on the Beijing stage before 1949. The theme concerns the tragic fate of a young woman wrongly executed as the victim of false witness and a corrupt Prefect. Her innocence is established by cosmic intervention called down with her dying cry that Heaven and Earth have failed to ensure justice in the world. The emotional vigour of the characterization and expressive lyrical style of the original text exempli-fies the formative contribution Guan made to the early stage in China.   ACS

Guare, John (1938–) American playwright whose work is characterized by frank theatricality, lyrical quality, autobiographical base, and satiric vivacity. Some critics have found his plays too cerebral or abstract, lacking focus, but few have failed to praise his use of language. Recognized first for his one-act play *Muzeeka* (1968), he received wide acclaim for his first full-length play, *The House of Blue Leaves* (1970). Since then his major plays have included the adaptation and lyrics for *Two Gentlemen of Verona* (1971), *Rich and Famous* (1974), *The Landscape of the Body* (1977), and *Bosoms and Neglect* (1979). A notable screenplay, *Atlan-tic City*, written for Louis Malle's 1981 film was followed by *Lydie Breeze* and *Gardenia* (1982), two parts of a projected tetralogy set in 19th-century New England. *Women and Water*, chronologically first in this series, was seen in various drafts during 1984–5 in Los Angeles, Chicago, and Washington, DC.   DBW

Guarini, Giovan Battista (1538–1612) Italian poet, critic and dramatist. He obtained a European-wide reputation with his most important work, *Il Pastor Fido* (*The Faithful Shepherd*), written in the early 1580s in imitation of **Tasso**'s pastoral play *Aminta*, but seeking to ring changes on that work by exploring the new vein of tragicomedy. Guarini's play caught the taste of European courts, and his Preface, in which he set out a defensive theory of the genre against his critics, became widely influential: in England **John Fletcher**'s *The Faithful Shepherdess* was a version of the new tragicomic pastoral kind, and Fletcher's Preface, in which he defined tragicomedy as a form that 'wants deaths, but brings some near it', was indebted to Guarini's theory.   LR

Guarnieri, Gianfrancesco (1934–) Brazilian playwright, born in Milan, Italy, but arrived in Brazil as an infant. From a family of musicians, he became a major influence in the development of Brazilian realistic theatre during the 1950s. Affiliated with the Arena Theatre in São Paulo as actor and director, he participated in the development of the *Arena Tells . . .* series (Zumbi, Bolívar, Tiradentes, etc.), which depended on concepts of open stage, simple sets, realistic dialogue and close interaction between actor and public. His *Eles não usam black-tie* (*They Don't Use Tuxedos*, 1958) became a Brazilian classic for its portrayal of the social problems of the slum areas. His other plays include *Gimba, presidente dos valentes* (*Gimba, President of the Brave*, 1959), *Um grito parado no ar* (*A Scream Silenced in Air*, 1973), *Botequim* (*Tavern*, 1973), and *Ponto de partida* (*Point of Departure*, 1976). Guarnieri has emphasized Brechtian techniques in portraying the reality of Brazilian political and socio-economic situations with protest against military censorship and economic repression.   GW

Guatemala Home of the only authentic pre-Colombian theatre piece, the **Rabinal Achí**, Guatemala is a land rich in Indian tradition and folklore, a land where only about 50% of the present-day population are native speakers of Spanish. As a major capital during the colonial period, Guatemala enjoyed religious presentations on special occasions. One form, the *Loas del diablo* (*Loas of the Devil*), with fireworks and devils is unique to the region. In 1793 the first theatre constructed in the present capital (Antigua was largely destroyed by the 1772 earthquake) was named Camato after its impresario and designed for comedies. Through the 19th century a moderate level of theatrical activity was recorded. Although no plays of true dramatic value are known, several playwrights were active, especially Tiburcio Estrada (alias Tata Bucho) a talented actor, director, set designer, and even ticket seller. The Carrera Theatre, originally built in 1859, became the National Theatre in 1871 and was renamed the Colon Theatre in 1892, on the 400th anniversary of discovery. Various travelling companies brought operas, operettas and **zarzuelas** to Guatemala.

20th century The visiting troupes of the early part of the century (María Guerrero and her husband Fernando Díaz de Mendoza from Spain; Virginia Fábregas of Mexico, and others) helped inspire the formation of local groups: the National Artistic group (1912, later renamed Renaissance in 1918), and Salomé Gill (1930). During these years the theatre provided light comedy or classical plays. Social and political criticism was inadmissible, especially during the Ubico dictatorship (1931–44). Rafael Arévalo Martínez (1884–1970) and Adolfo Drago Bracco (1894–1965) formed Tepeus in 1930 and wrote vanguardist Italian-style mechanistic plays, but the dominant pattern was costumbristic with social criticism, and generally isolated from the main currents of North American and European theatre.

After the Ubico regime the Guatemalan theatre gained new strength in the October Revolution of 1944, responding to international theatre styles while often conserving elements of its rich folklore. New groups were created (Guatemalan Art Theatre and University Art Theatre, to name only two) and the Guatemalan theatre festivals sponsored by the Popular University annually since 1962 have promoted new authors. Two of Guatemala's major playwrights, **Carlos Solórzano** and **Manuel Galich**, made their reputation in exile. A new generation of directors, actors and designers, some formed by Chilean director and actor Domingo Tessier who established the National Theatre School in the University's Department of Fine Arts in 1957, have struggled against repression and political and economic upheavals to keep the theatre alive. Principal playwrights are **Hugo Carrillo**, **Manuel José Arce** and **Ligia Bernal**, who in 1959 opened the first Young Playwrights Season with their plays *Green Sex Street*, *Stone in the Well*, and *Orestes and the Apostle*, respectively, and defined the new profile of contemporary Guatemalan theatre.

Several permanent groups now work year round in Guatemala City. Some later present their productions in the interior. Some, such as the Teatro Club, Teatro Centro, and Grupo Diez, are independent; others such as Los Comediantes and the Popular University Theatre work with funds provided by the government through different educational and cultural departments. Since 1975 the Theatre Department in Fine Arts has organized annual theatre events in different regional cities where the best groups perform; of those the best are later invited to perform in a theatre in Guatemala City.   GW

See: M. A. Carrera, *Ideas políticas en el teatro de Manuel Galich*, Guatemala, 1982.

Guignol A marionette of the Lyons puppet-theatre, presumably invented by the puppeteer Laurent Mourguet (1745–1844). Distinguished by a sharply satirical tongue and an earthy use of the vernacular, Guignol, costumed as a Lyons silk-weaver, was forbidden to improvise by the police of the Second Empire, became a parodist of opera, and eventually supplanted Polichinelle. The term *guignol* is now generic for any French Punch-and-Judy show.   LS

Guilbert, Yvette (Emma Laure Esther Guilbert) (1865–1944) French song-stylist and *diseuse*, whose mordant attitude and clipped pronunciation revolutionized cabaret singing. She first appeared at the Théâtre des Variétés, Paris, 1889, and after various music-hall engagements, became a star in 1892 at the-

Divan Japonais and the **Moulin-Rouge**, singing verses by **Aristide Bruant** and Léon Xanrof. Her gaunt figure, long nose and neck, mop of red hair and invariable black gloves contrasted with the voluptuousness of her competition and were celebrated by Toulouse-Lautrec. According to Moeller van den Broeck, she had three styles: the lyrical, gruesome and coquettish. After 1901 she developed a fresh repertory of old French and English songs, religious and secular; made frequent appearances in revue and theatre (Mrs Peachum in the French *Threepenny Opera*, 1937); and in 1920 founded a school in New York. Her *How to Sing a Song* (1918) was the first textbook on the subject. LS

Guimerà, Àngel (1845–1924) Catalan poet and dramatist, one of the chief figures in the literary renaissance of Catalan and the only one till recent times to have had considerable success in translation. His 39 plays, following European trends, generally portray the Catalan peasantry in romantic, occasionally melodramatic plots. His first plays were historical verse love-dramas, of which perhaps the finest is *L'ànima morta* (*The Dead Soul*, 1892). He then turned to contemporary realism in such plays as *Terra baixa* (*The Lowlanders*, 1896) contrasting the morals of the lowlanders and highlanders of Catalonia, and considered his finest play. Later he wrote psychological dramas with less success, before returning to historical sources. CL

Guinness, Alec (1914–) British actor. His first stage appearance was in 1934, and in 1936 he joined the **Old Vic** theatre, playing various classic roles including Aguecheek in *Twelfth Night*. In 1938 he played Hamlet in the Old Vic's innovative modern dress production, a performance which firmly established his reputation. After war service in the Royal Navy he returned to the theatre, rejoining the Old Vic company and playing a wide variety of modern and classic roles ranging from Lear's Fool to Klestakov in **Gogol**'s *The Inspector General*. He also began to direct, with a production of *Twelfth Night* in 1948 and *Hamlet* in 1951, in which he also played the lead. A constantly busy actor Guinness displayed his range and ingenuity in parts ranging from Macbeth in **Gaskill**'s experimental production for the **Royal Court Theatre** (1966) to Dr Wickersteed in *Habeus Corpus* by **Alan Bennett** (1973). Guinness's film and television career developed alongside his work for the stage. His quizzical features became familiar in films such as *Kind Hearts and Coronets* (1949), *The Lavender Hill Mob* (1951) – the famous post-war Pinewood Studios comedies – and with *The Bridge on the River Kwai* (1957) his international stardom was established. For television his roles as a spy-catcher in John Le Carré's *Tinker, Tailor, Soldier, Spy* (1979) and *Smiley's People* (1982) were tailored for his enigmatic presence. He was knighted in 1959. MB

Guitry, Sacha (1885–1957) French actor, playwright. Son of Lucien-Germain (1860–1925), sometime manager of the Renaissance, and himself an actor and playwright. Sacha was a prolific playwright predominantly of rather flimsy plays, many of them on vaguely historical themes. MB

Gundersen, Laura (1832–98) One of the first Norwegian actresses to be engaged at the Danish-speaking Christiania Theatre, where she spent almost her entire career. With her grand, declamatory style, she excelled in tragedy and romantic drama, creating leading roles in many of **Ibsen**'s early plays: Blanka in *The Burial Mound*, Hjørdis in *The Vikings at Helgeland* and especially Lady Inger. **Bjørnson** roles included his Mary Stuart and Borghild in *Sigurd Jorsalfer*. Later in her career, she adapted sufficiently to the new realistic style to succeed as Ibsen's Mrs Borkman and Ellida (in *The Lady from the Sea*). HL

Gunn, Moses (1929–) Afro-American actor. Gunn's first professional engagement was with the remarkably talented Off-Broadway company presenting **Genet**'s *The Blacks* (1962). Thereafter, he performed five Shakespearian roles at the 1964 Antioch, Ohio, festival and three additional roles with the **New York Shakespeare Festival**, winning an Obie Award for his portrayal of Aaron the Moor in *Titus Andronicus* (1967). Gunn became a founder member of the **Negro Ensemble Company** and appeared in several productions, gaining a second Obie for his performance in *The First Breeze of Summer* (1975). His 'sensual-melodic' Othello for the **American Shakespeare Theatre** in 1970 elicited ecstatic reviews from major New York critics. EGH

Gunter, Archibald Clavering (1847–1907) Playwright and novelist. Born in England and educated as a mining engineer in San Francisco, where he wrote his first play, *Found the True Vein* (1872), he moved to New York in 1879. During the next decade he wrote a number of moderately successful plays showing the Western influence upon his European heritage. *Courage* (1883) starred Effie Ellsler; *Prince Karl* (1886) gave **Richard Mansfield** his first starring role as a prince who became a guide. Following the success of his novel, *Mr Barnes of New York* (1887), the adventures of a rich, imprudent American, which he dramatized in 1888, Gunter wrote mainly fiction. WJM

Gunter, John (1938–) British stage designer, who worked for years on the continent and in English regional theatre before establishing himself as a successful realistic designer at London's **Royal Court Theatre** in the late 1960s. Since then his work has been seen at both the Royal Shakespeare Theatre and, especially in recent years, at the **National Theatre**, in addition to productions in the West End and abroad. From 1974 to 1982 Gunter served as head of the theatre design programme at London's Central School, his own *alma mater*. Based on painstakingly selective detail, his work has lately exhibited more conscious theatricality and metaphoric imagery. Outstanding recent productions have included *All's Well that Ends Well* (1981), *Guys and Dolls* (1982), *The Rivals* (1983), and *The Government Inspector* (1985). JMB

Gurik, Robert (1932–) French Canadian playwright and novelist. Born in France, he came to Canada in 1950 and was soon active in amateur theatricals. His first play, *Le Chant du Poète* (*Poet's Song*, 1963), attracted only local attention, but *Le Pendu* (*The Hanged Man*, 1967) won the Dominion Drama Festival prize for best play, along with general critical acclaim. With

Hamlet, Prince du Québec (*Hamlet, Prince of Quebec*, 1968), a savage parody of the political rivalry between Quebec and Ottawa, Gurik moved towards current social issues, a commitment continued in subsequent works, such as *Le Procès de Jean-Baptiste M.* (*The Trial of Jean-Baptiste M.*, 1972) and *La Baie des Jacques* (*Jacques's Bay*, 1976), the latter consciously emulating **Bertolt Brecht**'s *Mahagonny* (1927) and depicting the dehumanizing effects of modern industrial development upon the individual. LED

Gurney, A. R. (1930–) American playwright. The American theatre's John Cheever, Gurney writes feelingly about what he fears is an endangered species, well-to-do or at least well-bred Anglo-Saxon Protestants. His wry comedies unfold in a nostalgic haze. Typically, his plays are set in a time and place of poignant transition: at the end of summer, of adolescence, of an era. While his characters reluctantly confront the need for making changes, they also lament the passing of an enclosed and carefully regulated way of life. In his best play, *The Dining Room* (1981), place is more important than any of the rotating cast of characters who pass through it; his dining room is a cultural artifact threatened with extinction, a metaphor for genteel traditions. In *The Middle Ages* (1983), the library of an exclusive club serves a similar thematic purpose. Other deft Gurney works include *Children* (1976), suggested by a Cheever short story, in which a matron chooses duty over pleasure, and *What I Did Last Summer* (1982), about a teenager torn between propriety and bohemianism. FH

Guthrie, Tyrone (1900–71) Anglo-Irish director. From the 1930s onward Guthrie was an innovative and popular international director, working extensively in Britain, the United States and Canada. His Shakespearian work included **Laurence Olivier**'s *Hamlet* and *Henry V* (1937) and a modern dress version of the former play in 1938 with **Alec Guinness**. He was to repeat this experiment at the theatre named after him, the **Guthrie Theatre** at Minneapolis, USA, in 1963. His other productions included a notable *Peer Gynt* (1944) in which **Ralph Richardson** starred, **Lindsay**'s *The Three Estates* (**Edinburgh Festival**, 1948) and, with **Donald Wolfit**, *Tamburlaine the Great* (**Old Vic**, 1951). He was director of the **Stratford** (Ontario) **Festival** theatre in Canada from 1953 to 1957, and it was here that he developed (together with **Tanya Moiseiwitsch**) his thrust stage theatre form that was later permanently enshrined both there and in Minneapolis, and which was widely copied in new theatre building in Britain (Sheffield Crucible Theatre, Leeds Playhouse). Guthrie was impressive in both stature and manner and (in Ronald Bryden's words) 'made his mark not only with adventurous productions, but also by gaining public acceptance for alternatives to the proscenium arch'. The architecture of his theatres indicated his devotion to the Elizabethan relation between actors and audience. He was knighted in 1961. MB

Guthrie Theatre 725 Vineland Place, Minneapolis, Minnesota [Architect: Ralph Rapson]. Conceiving the idea of founding a theatre away from New York, Oliver Rea and Peter Zeisler searched the country for a hospitable city which would support such an enterprise. Enlisting the aid of the director **Tyrone Guthrie**, they eventually chose Minneapolis as their site and brought forth the Tyrone Guthrie Theatre after much effort in 1963. Part of the Walker Art Centre, the 1,400-seat Guthrie features a thrust stage, favoured by the late director, and in the early seasons, it presented mainly well-cast productions of classics and significant modern plays. After Guthrie's departure, his place was taken by his assistant Douglas Campbell until 1967 and a few years later by Michael Langham (1971–5). In 1981, after years of declining audiences, the direction of the theatre fell to Liviu Cilieu, the Rumanian-born director, who has materially changed its policy. The stage has been enlarged, the exterior of the theatre altered and the production of new American and European plays in addition to the classics in a different mode have contributed to a new spirit within the enterprise. In 1986 Cilieu was succeeded by Garland Wright. MCH

Gutzkow, Karl (1811–78) German playwright, novelist, and journalist. As a young man, Gutzkow was associated with the group of liberal writers Junges Deutschland (Young Germany) and was briefly imprisoned for his views in 1836. After his imprisonment, he turned from journalism to writing plays, many of which have a historical setting, but refer to contemporary politics. Among his most widely performed works were *Richard Savage* (1839), the comedies *Pigtail and Sword* (1844) and *A Model for Tartuffe* (1845), and the powerful verse tragedy *Uriel Acosta* (1846), which has racial and religious intolerance as its theme. Gutzkow was briefly dramaturge at the **Dresden Court Theatre** (from 1846 to 1848), but after the 1848 revolution he seemed to lose interest in the drama and turned to novel writing. SW

Gwyn, Eleanor (Nell) (?1642–87) English actress. After an early career as a herring-seller and, famously, an orange-seller in the theatre, she was taken up by

Nell Gwyn and her son, the Duke of St Albans, as Venus and Cupid, by Sir Peter Lely. It is said to have been painted for the personal delectation of Charles II.

Charles Hart and taught dancing by **Lacy**, probably beginning to act in 1664. Her success as Florimel in **Dryden**'s *Secret Love* led Pepys to praise her 'both as a mad girl, then most and best of all when she comes in like a young gallant and hath the motions and carriage of a spark the most that ever I saw any man have'. She left the stage briefly in 1667 during her affair with Charles Sackville, Lord Buckhurst. She often attemp-ted but was rarely successful in tragedy. In 1669 she played in Dryden's *Tyrannic Love*, speaking the epilogue with its mock epitaph on herself: 'Here Nelly lies who, though she lived a slattern,/Yet died a princess, acting in St Cathar'n.' Shortly after then she became mistress to the King, though she continued to act even after the birth of her first child, finally leaving the stage in the 1670s.   PH

H

Habimah (Hebrew for 'The Stage') The national theatre of Israel, in Tel-Aviv. Originally founded by **Nahum Zemach** as the Habimah Studio in 1918, in Moscow, it was the first Hebrew-speaking professional theatre. (See **Hebrew Theatre**.) It soon won international acclaim with the production of **S. Anski's** *The Dybbuk* in 1922.

Zemach recruited many gifted actors, among them Menahem Gnessin, **Hanna Rovina**, **Yehoshua Bertonov** and **Aaron Meskin**. They formed a collective singularly devoted to their art, which the great Russian directors **Stanislavsky** and **Vakhtangov** found exciting enough to bestow their energies upon. **Maksim Gorky** wrote that 'they have the element of ecstasy; theatre for them is a rite, a worship'.

The problem of repertoire haunted the Habimah from the very beginning, because of the scarcity of original Hebrew plays. The debate over Habimah's future was formulated by the poet H. N. Bialik and the philosopher Martin Buber. While Bialik maintained that the Habimah should turn its back on the Diaspora and forge a new culture for the nation in the making, looking to the Bible as a source, Buber contended that culture cannot be artificially created but can only grow through interaction with the foreign arts, and therefore advocated the translation of the best of world drama.

Habimah travelled extensively and became essentially a homeless wandering troupe until they finally settled in Palestine in 1931, where they found at last their natural audience. In 1958 Habimah became Israel's national theatre. Habimah's visit to the USSR in 1990, one of the consequences of *perestroika*, closed a circle in its history. HAS

Hackett, James Henry (1800–71) American actor, master dialectitian, manager, and the first American to appear in London as a star. Although he played classical tragedy, audiences preferred him in frontier and Yankee roles. He first succeeded in New York as Sylvester Daggerwood in *New Hay at the Old Market*. In 1827 he appeared at **Covent Garden**, but failed to win public esteem. Returning to the USA he repeated his triumphant Dromio of Ephesus. Greater success followed his frontier and Yankee roles, especially Nimrod Wildfire in *The Lion of the West* and Rip Van Winkle. He secured his reputation as the finest Falstaff of his time, first playing the role in 1828. Hackett periodically essayed management and was manager of the Astor Place Opera House at the time of the **Forest–Macready** riot.

His son James Keteltas Hackett (1869–1926) was a member of **Frohman**'s **Lyceum** company, starring in such vehicles as *The Prisoner of Zenda*. In 1906 he opened Wallack's Theatre in New York. In 1914 he and

James Henry Hackett as Falstaff.

Joseph Urban collaborated on a scenically historic production of *Othello*. SMA

Hacks, Peter (1928–) German dramatist and poet, who with more than 25 plays and over 10 adaptations is the leading contemporary playwright in the DDR. Invited to Berlin by **Brecht** in 1955, his early work, *The Chapbook of Duke Ernest* (1953, premiere 1967) or *The Battle of Lobositz* (1956), derives from epic theatre with its satiric picaresque structure and anti-mythologizing themes. Following the 'Bitterfeld line' or 'writing worker's movement' proclaimed in 1959, he turned to the realistic depiction of topical issues such as production norms and falling industrial quality in *Anxieties and Power* (1960) and *Moritz Tassow* (1964), before developing his distinctive style. Attempting to formulate a 'post-revolutionary dramaturgy', he rejected both naturalism and epic theatre in favour of highly poetic comedies updating traditional forms. His adaptations of **Aristophanes**, **Shakespeare**, **Goethe** and **Synge** indicate his models, but ostensibly classical, historical or mythological subjects (*Amphitryon*, 1967, and *Prexaspes*, 1976; *Margarete in Aix*, 1966, and *Seneca's Death*, 1978; *Adam and Eve*, 1973) are used to present contemporary themes. Sometimes considered escapist by West German dramatists, his work has great elegance and comic power. However, its densely textured verse is almost impossible to translate, which has contributed to his neglect by the international theatre.   CI

Hagen, Uta (1919–) American actress and teacher. Hagen made her debut in 1938 in the Lunts' production of *The Seagull* and has acted only sporadically since then, though almost always in circumstances as notable: in **Maxwell Anderson**'s *Key Largo* (1939); with **Paul Robeson** and **José Ferrer** in *Othello* (1945); opposite Anthony Quinn in *A Streetcar Named Desire* (1950); as the lead in **Odets**'s *Country Girl* (1950); and, most memorably, as tortured, caustic, vulnerable Martha in **Edward Albee**'s *Who's Afraid of Virginia Woolf?* (1962). Known as an actor's actor, Hagen performs in a clean, masterly style; she has an earthy, assertive presence and a deep voice that suggests enormous power in reserve. Although her understatement is ideally suited to film, she has chosen to appear on screen only twice (in *The Other* and *The Boys from Brazil*). Since 1947 she has taught at the HB Studio in New York, which is run by her husband **Herbert Berghof**. Famous for the brevity and incisiveness of her comments, she speaks in technical code words – an actor's shorthand – that her students learn to interpret. Like most American teachers she derives her method from **Stanislavsky**; unlike **Lee Strasberg**, another Stanislavsky disciple, she is strongly opposed to the use of emotional memory, which she considers both self-indulgent and self-destructive. Her book, *Respect for Acting* (1973), has become a standard reference for both students and professionals.   FH

Hagr Fikir (Patriotism) Ethiopian theatre house. The National Patriotic Association was founded before the Italian invasion to prepare the people for resistance. At the restoration it was subverted by the emperor and revived as a propaganda instrument and housed in an abandoned Italian recreation centre. Programmes were largely musical though many short plays were performed. Today, full-length plays and music and dance shows are performed there to popular audiences at least every Sunday afternoon.   RK

Halac, Ricardo (1935–) Argentine playwright. A member of the realistic generation of the 1960s. Halac studied in West Germany under the auspices of a Goethe Institute fellowship. His first play, *Soledad para cuatro* (*Solitude for Four*, 1961), dealt with the anxieties and frustrations of a younger generation in confronting an incomprehensible and valueless society, themes echoed in *Estela de madrugada* (*Morning Wake*, 1965) and *Fin de diciembre* (*End of December, 1965*). Halac moved away from the realistic tradition and towards the grotesque with *El destete* (*The Weaning*, 1978), recovering some of the Brechtian tendencies he observed in his youth. A more recent play is *Lejana tierra prometida (Distant Promised Land*, 1981).   GW

Halbe, Max (1865–1944) German playwright and novelist. A prolific writer, Halbe was associated with the naturalist movement. His sole enduring success was the tragedy *Youth* (1893), one of the major works of German naturalism.   SW

Halévy, Ludovic see **Meilhac, Henri**

Hall, Peter (Reginald Frederick) (1930–) British director and theatre manager, who was largely responsible for the creation of two British national theatres, the **Royal Shakespeare Company** and the **National Theatre**. At Cambridge University, Hall was an energetic amateur director, who in 1953 received a professional production at the Theatre Royal, Windsor. He inherited the mantle of **Alec Clunes** at the Arts Theatre Club in 1954, where, like Clunes, he directed many British premieres of new plays from overseas, including **Samuel Beckett**'s *Waiting for Godot* (1956). He went as guest director to the Shakespeare Memorial Theatre in Stratford-upon-Avon where, after a successful *Love's Labour's Lost* (1956) and *Cymbeline* (1957), he was invited to become the new artistic director, taking up this post in 1960.

His plans for the Shakespeare Memorial Theatre were radical, ambitious and pursued with a dramatic speed. He wanted to transform what was then a prestigious regional festival theatre into a national company modelled on continental lines. The company would be semi-permanent, a substantial nucleus of actors offered two- or three-year contracts, and in order to offer them a metropolitan shop-window, Hall negotiated to take over the Aldwych Theatre in London. This enabled him to present a programme of new plays, as well as the **Shakespeare**-based repertoire at Stratford-upon-Avon. He calculated that such a company would require subsidy on a level previously unknown in Britain; and accordingly, with the approval of the Governors, he drew upon the accumulated reserves of the Shakespeare Memorial Theatre Company to launch the company's residency at the Aldwych Theatre. The company's name was changed to the Royal Shakespeare Company in 1961.

This managerial gamble was supported by an artistic vision, which transformed the verse-speaking at Stratford, encouraged contemporary interpretations of Shakespeare's plays along the lines of **Jan Kott** and backed proposals from innovative directors, such as **Peter Brook**. Although the RSC never received the state support which Hall thought the company required, it became the second largest recipient of subsidy to non-operatic theatre and throughout the 1960s, the RSC was the major 'directors' theatre' in Britain, although the National Theatre could be regarded as the 'actors' theatre'. Hall himself was responsible for several key RSC productions, including *The Wars of the Roses* (1963), adapted from the *Henry VI* trilogy and *Richard III*, and *Hamlet* (1965) with David Warner. He also directed **Harold Pinter**'s plays, *The Homecoming* (1965), *Landscape* and *Silence* (1969) and *Old Times* (1971).

In 1968, he resigned as Managing Director of the RSC, becoming a free-lance director in both the commercial and the subsidized sector, and extending his range of interests to opera. In 1970, he was appointed Director of Productions at the Royal Opera House, Covent Garden, but he left after a year claiming that too much money was being spent on an élitist art form. He was immediately (if privately) offered the post of **Olivier**'s successor at the National Theatre, although it was several months before this news became known even to Olivier. Hall took over from Olivier at the National Theatre under acrimonious circumstances and his task there was not helped by the delays to the opening of the new building on the South Bank. The climate of opinion too had changed by the mid-1970s. Demands for more state money, which had seemed swashbuckling when the RSC was founded, began to look selfish when almost every regional theatre was struggling to stay open.

As the National Theatre's Director, Hall was responsible for the programmes in three contrasting theatres, the Olivier, the Lyttelton with its proscenium arch stage and the Cottesloe, the smaller studio theatre. One of his early policy decisions was to place individual directors, or teams of directors, in charge of the separate theatres, instead of retaining one large company structure. He himself directed such NT successes as **Marlowe**'s *Tamburlane* (1976) which opened the Olivier Theatre, **Ayckbourn**'s *Bedroom Farce* (1977) and **Peter Shaffer**'s *Amadeus* (1979), which he also directed on Broadway. In 1983, he became artistic director of the Glyndebourne Festival, held jointly with his post at the National Theatre. In 1977, he was knighted for his services to the theatre.   JE

Hall, Willis (1929–   ) British dramatist, who also writes in partnership with Keith Waterhouse. Hall and Waterhouse both came from Leeds in Yorkshire and their plays often are set in Northern towns. These include *Billy Liar* (1960), which was based on a Waterhouse novel, *Celebration* (1961) about two different kinds of family parties and *All Things Bright and Beautiful* (1963). They collaborated on a comedy of adulteries, *Say Who You Are* (1965), and on an adaptation of **Eduardo de Filippo**'s *Saturday, Sunday, Monday* (1973) for the **National Theatre**. Hall himself started by writing plays for radio, but his first stage hit came with his military drama set in Malaysia, *The Long and the Short and the Tall* (1958). He also adapted François Billetdoux's *Chin Chin* (1960) which received a long London run. He has written prolifically for television, devising and contributing to several drama series, including *Budgie* (1971–2), *Three's Company* (1973) and *Billy Liar* (1973–4). With Waterhouse, he adapted de Filippo's *Filumena* for a West End run in 1977.   JE

Hallams, The A family of English actors and the first substantially documented company of professional players to appear on the North American continent. Hallams had apparently been in the English theatre from 1707, one being killed by **Macklin** in a Green Room brawl at **Drury Lane** in 1735. By 1750 **William Hallam** (d. 1758), had suffered serious financial reverses while managing **Goodman's Fields**, but creditors allowed him to try to raise his shortages. He therefore sent an advance agent, Robert Upton, across the Atlantic with considerable money to investigate theatrical conditions and potentials. Hallam never heard again from Upton, who joined the Murray-Kean company, took charge of the company, headed an engagement in New York in 1751, and then returned to England. The Murray-Kean company soon afterwards disappeared.

In the meantime, William Hallam sent his brother, **Lewis Sr** (1714–55), Lewis's wife, their three children, and an undistinguished company of ten to America. After a six-week voyage aboard the *Charming Sally*, the Hallam Company opened in Williamsburg, Virginia, on 15 September 1752 with *The Merchant of Venice* and *The Alchemist*. They remained in Williamsburg for about 11 months, presenting a repertory consisting of **Shakespeare**, **Rowe**, **Lillo**, **Moore**, **Farquhar**, **Addison**, **Cibber**, **Vanbrugh**, **Steele**, and **Gay**. They next played New York, opening 17 September 1753 with *The Conscious Lovers*. Although they faced considerable hostility from local Quakers, the company opened a Philadelphia engagement on 15 April 1754 with *The Fair Penitent* and *Miss in Her Teens*, but played only two months. After a three-month engagement in Charleston, the Hallams arrived in Jamaica about January 1755, where they joined forces with a company managed by **David Douglass**. After the elder Hallam's death, Douglass married **Mrs Hallam** (?–1773) in 1758, also securing **Lewis Jr** (1740–1808) as a leading man.

Mrs Hallam starred in the American Company, as Douglass called his group, being the first actress in New York to play such roles as Juliet, Cordelia, and Jane Shore. Lewis Jr remained on the stage for some fifty years, playing almost every significant role in the repertoire of the time. He appeared in Godfrey's *The Prince of Parthia* (1767), the first script by an American to be given a professional production. After Douglass's death in 1786, the younger Hallam assumed leadership of the American Company with various partners. He retired from management in 1797, but continued to act until his death. His second wife, Miss Tuke, joined the company, but her quarrelsome and intemperate habits caused considerable friction.

Adam Hallam, the younger brother of Lewis Jr, left Jamaica with the company, but his name soon disappears from the bills. Helen and Nancy Hallam eventually joined the company, as well.   SMA

Halliwell, David (William) (1936–   ) British dramatist and actor, whose first (and most successful) play was a comic study of a student Hitler, *Little Malcolm and his Struggle Against the Eunuchs* (1965), which was produced in New York as *Hail Scrawdyke!* (1966). In 1966, he started the adventurous fringe company, Quipu, which produced (as well as his own plays) new works by other young writers, including **Stephen Poliakoff**. Halliwell turned towards what he called 'multiviewpoint' drama in which, as in *K. D. Dufford . . .* (1969), different versions of the same incident, the rape and murder of a child, were played side by side. The technical problems of multiviewpoint drama preoccupied Halliwell as a director and writer for many years and although he wrote such plays as *Muck from Three Angles* (1970), *A Last Belch for the Great Auk* (1971) and *A Process of Elimination* (1975), he never reached the wider audiences of *Little Malcolm*.   JE

Halm, Friedrich (1806–71) Pseudonym of Freiherr von Münch-Bellinghausen, Austrian playwright. Halm wrote several romantic verse tragedies, which were produced at the **Burgtheater**. Of these, *The*

Gladiator of Ravenna (1854) was the sole, undisputed success of his career. Between 1867 and 1870 he was unhappily intendant of the Burgtheater. sw

Hamburg style A realistic approach to acting, initially associated with **Friedrich Ludwig Schröder** and generally posited as the opposite to the **Weimar style**. Although few German actors in the 19th century can have completely realized the 'unvarnished realism' normally suggested by the term, it was a valuable conception as it provided a point of reference for the discussion of various actors' styles. sw

Hammerstein, Oscar II (1895–1960) American lyricist and librettist. Born into a theatrical family, Oscar Hammerstein II began his career as a lyricist while a student at Columbia University. In the early 1920s he wrote lyrics for four shows with music by Herbert Stothart and two shows composed by Vincent Youmans. His first big success came with the lyrics for *Rose-Marie* (1924), an operetta with music by Rudolf Friml. Among other shows of the 1920s for which Hammerstein provided lyrics were *Sunny* (1925) and *The Desert Song* (1926). In 1927 Hammerstein wrote both the lyrics and the libretto for the era's most ambitious musical, *Show Boat*, which had a score by **Jerome Kern**. After writing several other musicals with Kern, Hammerstein teamed up with the composer **Richard Rodgers** in 1943 to create one of the most influential of all American musicals, *Oklahoma!* The collaboration continued through the 1940s and 1950s, resulting in *Carousel* (1945), *South Pacific* (1949), *The King and I* (1951), *Flower Drum Song* (1958), and *The Sound of Music* (1959).

While Hammerstein's lyrics have sometimes been criticized for their sentimentality, he is generally credited with making major innovations in the form and subject matter of the American musical through his contributions to *Show Boat* and his later musicals with Richard Rodgers. MK

Hammond, (Hunter) Percy (1873–1936) American dramatic critic. Born in Cadiz, Ohio, and educated at Franklin College (1892–6) Hammond began as a reporter and later drama critic for the *Chicago Evening Post* (1898–1908); after which he served as dramatic critic of the *Chicago Tribune* (1908–21). In 1921 he began a 15-year career as critic of the *New York Tribune* establishing his reputation as a master of irony and urbane humour. He wrote of the producer Al Woods: 'The anguish which Mr Woods experiences when he does a thing like *Gertie's Garter* . . . is assuaged by the knowledge that with its stupendous profits he may speculate in the precarious investments of the worthier drama' (1921). TLM

Hampden (Dougherty), Walter (1879–1955) American actor. Though American born, Hampden began his career learning the classical repertory and the grand manner acting style in the British company of **F. R. Benson** from 1901 to 1904. After playing leading and supporting roles in London and the provinces, he came to the USA in 1907 in support of **Alla Nazimova** in her repertory of **Ibsen** and other modern plays. Always more successful in poetic and romantic roles,

his desire to act in *Hamlet* and similar plays was not realized until he was able to assume the financial risks for their presentation in 1918. In the 1920s and 1930s he brought **Shakespeare**'s plays to appreciative audiences in many American cities. In 1923, he added **Rostand**'s *Cyrano de Bergerac* to his repertory and played the dauntless hero more than 1,000 times in 15 years. From 1925 to 1930 he leased his own theatre, adding the title character from **Bulwer-Lytton**'s *Richelieu* to his repertory in 1929. An active performer for most of his life, Hampden played Cardinal Wolsey in the **American Repertory Theatre** production of *Henry VIII* in 1946 and Danforth in **Arthur Miller**'s *Crucible* in 1953. MR

Hampstead Theatre Club (London) The theatre opened at Moreland Hall in 1959 but moved in 1962 to a prefabricated shed by Swiss Cottage underground station. It provides a historical link between the little theatres of pre-war London and the fringe theatre clubs of the 1960s. Its premises offered a plain end stage in a small auditorium, seating about 150, although its most recent theatre, which opened in 1970, is marginally more spacious with a more sharply raked seating. Within this simple setting, successive directors, who have included James Roose-Evans, **Michael Rudman** and Michael Attenborough, have been able to pursue an adventurous policy of new plays, often tried out before West End runs, and visiting small companies. The Hampstead locale provides the club with loyal supporters and its list of achievements, which include West End transfers of plays by **Michael Frayn**, **Pam Gems**, **Brian Friel** and **James Saunders**, has resulted in the club's high reputation. JE

Hampton, Christopher (James) (1946–) British dramatist, whose first play, *When Did You Last See My Mother?* (1966), was produced in London and New York while he was still an undergraduate at Oxford. From 1968 to 1970, he was resident dramatist at the **Royal Court Theatre** where his finely balanced study of the relationship between Rimbaud and Verlaine, *Total Eclipse* (1968), was staged, together with his comedy of linguistic misunderstanding, *The Philanthropist* (1970). Hampton was not a typical Royal Court playwright in that he disliked and resisted left-wing polemics. His plays were cool, poised, witty and cosmopolitan in outlook. An excellent linguist and, as a modern languages scholar, aware of the problems of translation, he sought to provide modern, actable versions of European classics, abused in many familiar English texts. He adapted *Uncle Vanya* (1970), *Hedda Gabler* (1970) and *A Doll's House* (1971) and later, for the **National Theatre**, **Molière**'s *Don Juan* (1972), **Ibsen**'s *The Wild Duck* (1979) and two plays by an Austrian dramatist, **Odön von Horváth**, then little known in Britain, *Tales from the Vienna Woods* (1977) and *Don Juan Comes Back from the War* (1978). Horváth's memory also inspired Hampton to write *Tales from Hollywood* (1983), set in the émigré community in California during the war, in which Horváth, Thomas and Heinrich Mann, and **Bertolt Brecht** appear as characters. Hampton can be a technically inventive writer, as his play, *Savages* (1973), revealed, in which a British diplomat is captured by guerillas in South America who, despite their populist ideology, despise and maltreat the native population. His most distinctive voice, however, comes through the cleverly crafted, amusing but thoughtful, conventionally structured comedies, of which *Treats* (1976) is a good, and underrated, example.   JE

Handke, Peter (1942–) Austrian dramatist and novelist, who won immediate recognition with his first 'Speaking Plays' *Offending the Audience* and *Self-Accusation*, performed at the Experimenta festival in 1966. As consciousness-raising exercises, these questioned all the conventional elements of theatre and focused on the manipulative effect of language, influenced by Handke's law studies and by **Horváth**. *Kaspar* (1968) extends this theme in exploring the social conditioning of the individual by linguistic education. Overtly theatrical, the archetypal protagonist (Kaspar Hauser, a historical figure drawn upon by expressionist poets and by the film maker Werner Herzog) is a clown, the traditional 'Kasperl' puppet, and the imposition of conformity results in schizophrenia. The use of theatre-figures as characters was continued in *The Ride Across Lake Constance* (1970), a surreal image of the stereotypes created by stage and screen peopled by famous actors, including **Elizabeth Bergner** and Erich von Stroheim. The psychological analysis of politics in Handke's anti-illusionistic drama is perhaps clearest in *They Are Dying Out* (1973), with its double action where the surrealist second half reveals the breakdown of the personality that underlies the preceding naturalistic presentation of capitalism. Handke's most ambitious work to date is the *Slow Homecoming* tetralogy (1982), an openly symbolic perspective on modern consciousness that epitomizes his approach. A 'dramatic poem' set in semi-abstract locations – an urban building site, the wall outside a village cemetery – the plotless action, in which even the characters' memories are interchangeable, focuses on the recognition of self and its renunciation.   CI

Hands, Terry (Terence David) (1941–) British director, who helped to found the lively Everyman Theatre in Liverpool in 1964. Two years later, he joined the **Royal Shakespeare Company**, initially to direct its travelling off-shoot, Theatre-go-round, which took Shakespearian productions and anthologies to schools. His first production at the Shakespeare Memorial Theatre at Stratford came in 1968 with *The Merry Wives of Windsor* which transferred to the Aldwych in London and returned to Stratford for the following season, proof of its popularity. In the following seasons, he directed *Pericles* and *Women Beware Women* (1969), *Richard III* (1970) and *The Merchant of Venice* (1971) at Stratford, and *Bartholomew Fair* (1969) and *The Man of Mode* (1971) at the Aldwych. Hands was then an established RSC director, but his Stratford Centenary productions of *Henry IV* and *Henry V* (1975) and his *Henry VI* cycle in 1977 indicated his love of major challenges. In 1978, he was appointed joint artistic director with **Trevor Nunn** of the RSC. Hands, unlike other RSC directors, was not noted for his interpretations of Shakespearian texts, but he had a fine command of spectacle, particularly when he worked with the designer Farrah, a panache in staging crowd scenes and developed a close working relationship with the actor **Alan Howard**, who played Henry VI, Henry

V, Coriolanus, Richard II and Richard III. From 1975 to 1977, he was consultant director at the **Comédie-Française** where he staged a triumphant *Richard III* in 1972. His flamboyant directing, however, sometimes led to excess, as in his staging of **Peter Nichols**'s satirical pantomime, *Poppy* (1983), intended as a tatty Victorian show parading jingoism, but which in Hands's version became a glamorous West End musical. In 1986 Hands took over the artistic leadership of the RSC.   JE

Hankin, Edward Charles St John (1869–1909) British dramatist and critic, who wrote social satire and, influenced by **Brieux** and **Shaw**, *The Return of the Prodigal* (1905 – revived by **John Gielgud** in 1948).   CI

Hanlon-Lees Six English brothers, aerialists and knockabout comedians, who introduced a new style of stage farce. The sons of Tom Hanlon, manager of the Theatre Royal, Manchester, **Thomas** (1836–68), **George** (1840–1926), **William** (1842–1923), **Alfred** (1844–86), **Edward** (1846–1931), and **Frederick** (adopted; 1848–86) took the name Lees in honour of their trainer, the carpet acrobat John Lees (d. 1856). After touring Europe as children, they created a sensation at **Niblo's Garden**, New York (1860) with their daring trapeze stunts, including Zampillaerostation, and visited both Americas and Europe 1862–6. Thereafter the troupe split up, and using lads they had trained, George, William and Alfred founded the Hanlon-Zanfretta company, while Frederick and Edward teamed with the French juggling clown Henri Agoust, and performed in a series of slapstick pantomimes, seen in Paris in 1867. Reconsolidated in 1868, they made a smash in St Petersburg and Berlin, and at the **Folies-Bergère** in 1878, where their original mixture of spring-heeled acrobatics, sadistic sight-gags and poker-faced slapstick were hailed by Edmond de Goncourt and **Emile Zola** as a new era in theatrical fantasy. This phase culminated in *Le Voyage en Suisse* (1879), a farce comedy enlivened with mechanical stunts which played 400 nights in Paris before moving to the Gaiety, London, 1880, and the Park Theatre, New York, 1881. William and Edward settled in Massachusetts and working from their superbly-equipped studio developed and promoted the comic extravaganzas *Fantasma* (1884) and *Superba* (1890), which briefly revived the American taste for spectacular pantomime. George Jr, teamed in vaudeville with Ferry Corwey in a clown act, the Hanlons, was a gagman much in demand (**Ed Wynn**'s *Hurray for What*, 1937).   LS

Hansberry, Lorraine (1930–65) Afro-American playwright. Born into a comfortable middle-class home but surrounded by poverty in Chicago's Southside, Hansberry early confronted the plight of black families living in ghetto conditions that formed the background for her landmark drama, *A Raisin in the Sun* (1959). This first play on Broadway by a black woman had a black director, Lloyd Richards, and predominant black financing It ran for 530 performances and won the New York Drama Critics Circle Award. Hansberry's next play, *The Sign in Sidney Brustein's Window* (1964), about uncommitted white intellectuals in Greenwich Village, was not successful.

After her early death from cancer her former husband completed and produced two plays from her unfinished manuscripts, *To Be Young, Gifted and Black* (1969) and *Les Blancs* (1970).   EGH

Hanson, Lars (1886–1965) Swedish stage and film actor, a leading exponent of the complex psychological realism which made **Dramaten** famous from the 1930s to the 1960s. His technical virtuosity was prodigious, enabling him to play Lear at 35 and Romeo at 49, but his acting was chiefly distinguished by its inner subtlety, especially in his many **Strindberg** roles, from his early Gustav III (1916) to a series of Dramaten performances, including Master Olof (1933), The Officer in *A Dream Play* (1935), The Unknown in *To Damascus* (1937 and 1944), Hummel in *The Ghost Sonata* (1942) and The Captain in *The Father* (1953). He excelled in **Shakespeare**, above all as Richard III (1918 and 1947). His work in **O'Neill**'s plays included James Tyrone in the 1956 world premiere of *Long Day's Journey Into Night*.   HL

Hanswurst (German, 'Jack Sausage'). The most indigenous of German clown figures. The name first appears in literature as 'Hans Worst' in a Dutch translation of Sebastian Brant's *Ship of Fools* (1519), and was used abusively by Martin Luther in disputations of 1530 and 1541. The earliest use of the name for a stage clown was in a **Fastnachtspiel** of 1553 and in scholastic German in 1573. He became a permanent type under the influence of the **Englische Komödianten**'s Pickelhering and the Italian Arlecchino during the 17th and 18th centuries.

Hanswurst received a distinctive format from **Josef Stranitzky** in Vienna, who turned him into a phlegmatic Salzburg peasant of coarse instincts, low cunning and mother-wit, clad in yellow trousers trimmed in blue, a bright red jacket with wide sleeves, a blue bib with an arsenic-green leather heart monogrammed HW, a white ruff, a green pointed hat; he wore a short black beard, his hair in a topknot and wielded the wooden sword or *pistolese*. In competition with the touring Italian **commedia**, the scurrilous, improvising (one stage direction reads, 'Here Hanswurst can perform his lazzi and fopperies') Hanswurst was interpolated into the pompous doings of the **Haupt- und Staatsaktionen**, to the delight of audiences and the outrage of academics, scandalized by his sexual and scatological ad libs. With the aid of **Caroline Neuber**, **Gottsched** in Leipzig tried to expel him from the stage with their *Play of Hanswurst's Banishment* (1737) and **Josef von Sonnenfels** in Vienna followed suit, but to no avail. He soon returned under other names, such as Hänschen, Kasperl or Claus Clump, usually in servant roles.

Stranitzky's chosen successor was the 26-year-old **Gottfried Prehauser** who made Hanswurst more Viennese: 'gallant, charming, agreeable'. Other outstanding Hanswursts were Phillip Hafner (1735–64) and Johann Josef Felix von Kurz (1715–84), who, under the name Bernardon, sang improvised verses in rapid patter. Gradually, Hanswurst was effaced by the figure of **Kasperle**, introduced by Johann Laroche in 1769, and his qualities were diffused among various Viennese comic figures, Larifari, Staberl, Thaddädl, until he wholly lost his improvisational clownishness in the comedies of **Raimund** and **Nestroy** and dwindled into a dramatically integrated character, usually a comic small tradesman.   LS

Hardy, Alexandre (c. 1575–c. 1632) French playwright, almost certainly the first to pursue a full-time career within the professional theatre. He probably began writing in the 1590s and by 1611 was attached as stock author to the itinerant company of **Valleran le Conte**, a position he still held with the Comédiens du Roi under **Bellerose** in 1625. Two years later he undertook to supply plays regularly to another troupe in return for one share as a company member. In all he reputedly wrote or adapted over 600 plays, though only 34 survive, predominantly tragedies and tragicomedies, which were published between 1623 and 1628. A further ten were still in the repertoire of the **Hôtel de Bourgogne** in the 1630s and their staging is described in the *Mémoire* of **Mahelot**. Drawing his subject matter eclectically from mythology and history and disdaining the neoclassical unities, he showed a true dramatist's instinct for propelling the action forward, promoting conflict or confrontation between protagonists and exploiting the possibilities of spectacle and violent incident, but as a writer of verse he was facile and was doubtless ill-served by contractual pressures and the easy popular success he achieved. In retrospect his real importance is to have animated the largely static, Senecan dramaturgy of the French Renaissance and thus prepared the way for the generation of young playwrights emerging in the 1620s and 1630s in response to the establishment of permanent theatre companies in Paris, who disparaged but profited from his example.   DR

Hare, David (1947–) British dramatist and director, a co-founder with Tony Bicat of the influential fringe company, Portable Theatre (1968–72). After three apprentice plays, of which the best was *Inside Out* adapted (with Bicat) from Kafka's diaries, Hare began his assault on male-dominated, capitalistic society with *Slag* (1970) about three teachers in a girls' school who abstain from sex as a protest. *The Great Exhibition* (1972) concerns a middle-class Labour MP who tries to opt out of parliamentary life but finds that the world's corruption pursues him; while *Knuckle* (1974), a neat Raymond Chandler pastiche set in the Home Counties of Britain, describes how the hard-bitten Curly tries to discover who killed his sister, concluding that capitalism itself is the real villain. With **Howard Brenton**, he wrote *Brassneck* (1973) about corruption in local government and, as a good team man, he contributed to several group plays, *Lay By* (1971), about the origins of pornography in capitalism, and *England's Ireland* (1972) about British imperialism across the water. Hare was a leader of the younger generation of dramatists politicized by the events of 1968 and was quickly absorbed into subsidized theatre establishment. From 1970–1, he was resident dramatist at the **Royal Court**, while in 1973 he became the resident dramatist at the Nottingham Playhouse. He was a founder member of Joint Stock for whom he adapted William Hinton's book about the Chinese Revolution, *Fanshen* (1975). After the success of *Teeth 'n' Smiles* (1975), in which **Helen Mirren** played a drunken lead singer performing at a Cambridge May Ball to an audience she despises, Hare started to write for the **National Theatre** which produced *Plenty* (1978), *A Map of the World* (1983) and *Pravda* (1985), with Howard Brenton, about the subservience of journalists towards the power-mad tycoons dominating Fleet Street. Hare was appointed an associate director of the National Theatre in 1984 and has directed several productions there, including Howard Brenton's *Weapons of Happiness*.   JE

Hare, John (1844–1921) English actor and theatre manager, who was part of the famous **Bancroft** company at the **Prince of Wales's** (1865–75), where he created parts in all the **T. W. Robertson** comedies (Sam Gerridge in *Caste* being the most famous). He was what would now be known as a 'character actor', with a meticulous eye for stage detail that made him *avant la lettre* an admired director. He was successively manager of the **Royal Court** (1875–9), the **St James's** with the **Kendals** (1879–88) and the **Garrick** (1889–95), where he created his best-known role as Benjamin Goldfinch in **Grundy**'s *A Pair of Spectacles* (1890). He was one of the first to recognize **Pinero**'s talents as a playwright, and was rewarded, late in his career, by the chance to create the title-part in *The Gay Lord Quex* (1899). Hare was knighted in 1907 and retired in 1911.   PT

Harel, Jean Charles (1790–1846) French theatre manager. Harel began his career as secretary to Cambacerès and was nominated sub-prefect at Soissons in 1814. With the return of the Bourbons, he left France, meeting **Mlle George**, with whom he would have a life-long liaison. In 1820 he returned to France and founded a paper, *Le Miroir* (*The Mirror*), in which he attacked the restored monarchy. During the 1820s he managed various provincial theatres, and in 1829 was appointed to the **Odéon**. He remained there until 1832. Harel was an extravagant manager who enjoyed scenic effect: **Dumas**'s *Napoleon Bonaparte, or thirty years of French History* (1831), starring **Lemaître** as the Emperor, cost 80,000 francs and, after a few performances, had to be shortened from 23 scenes to 14. Harel was heading for bankruptcy when he became manager of the Porte-Saint-Martin in 1831 and promptly moved part of his troupe to that theatre. One of his most successful productions there was Dumas's *Richard Darlington*, which he then transferred back to the Odéon, which he kept going for nearly a year with boulevard melodramas. His great period was the 1830s at the Porte-Saint-Martin, which he tried to make into an alternative **Comédie-Française**. Unfortunately, although their plays were staged by Harel, the great romantic dramatists felt the lure of the Comédie-Française, and some of his actors were also drawn there. Harel had to give up the Porte-Saint-Martin in 1840 and leave Paris to escape his creditors. In his last years he became insane and died in poverty. As a dramatist, he contributed to Théaulon and Alboize's popular play, *The War of the Servants* (1837). He also wrote a curious *Theatrical dictionary, or, 1,258 truths about various managers, actors and actresses*. He was an excellent conversationalist and publicist. Good at extracting money from people, he was less precise about paying his actors or creditors. He had a reputation for uncleanliness and kept a pig in his apartment.   JMCC

Harlequin The English name of a comic character who has persisted throughout the modern theatre. The names Herlekin and Hellequin occur in French folk literature as early as 1100 to denominate diabolic ragamuffins, and Adam de la Halle uses them in 1262 for spirits of the air. The Italian Arlecchino may, however, derive from *al lecchino*, the glutton. The character first appears as a doltish rustic from Lower Bergama, teamed as a **zanni** with the shrewder Brighella; an early portrait, in **Tristano Martinelli**'s *Les Compositions de Rhétorique de M. Don Arlequin* (1601), shows him in a loose white blouse and trousers, covered with patches, a flat cap and a black moustachioed half-mask; his dagger of lath was clearly descended from the ancient comic phalloi. By nature greedy, cowardly, slow-witted but inventive under compulsion, he retained the earthiness of his origins. **Zan Ganassa** is one of the first actors reputed to have played the role, which soon became a leading feature of any **commedia dell'arte** company, usually entrusted to one of the more skilful players.

Arlecchino's further metamorphoses took place in France, where he was first played by Tristano Martinelli, **G. Andreini** and **Angelo Costantini**. It was **Dominique Biancolelli** who naturalized him as Arlequin and fused the two *zanni* by making his Arlecchino witty, neat and fluent in a croaking voice, which became as traditional as the squawk of **Punch**. His Arlequin was endowed with a motto by the poet Santeuil: *Castigat ridendo mores*. Biancolelli's successors carried on the polishing process: **Evaristo Gherardi** bestowed the power of macaronic speech, a *patois* of French and Italian, and Vicentini-Thomassin added the element of pathos, the ability to evoke tears as well as laughter.

With the dissolution of the **Comédie-Italienne** in 1697, Arlequin moved to the fairground theatre, where he appeared in plays by **Marivaux**, Boissy, Delisle, **Lesage** and others; by this time, he was the leading character in these pieces, but with the return of the Italian players, was relegated to subservient status in the high comedies of Marivaux and Lesage. This prettified Arlequin is preserved in the porcelain figurines of Kändler. In Italy, **Goldoni** penned vehicles for the popular Arlecchini **Sacchi** and **Bertinazzi**, but tried to confine them to the written text; his opponent **Gozzi**, in his attempts to revive the improvised comedy, made Arlecchino merely one of a team of comics, no more important than Tartaglia or Truffaldino. In post-Revolutionary Paris, Arlequin settled into the popular boulevard theatres: at the Variétés-Amusantes he was played by Lazzari, at the Vaudeville by Laporte who enacted him in 500 plays. The last important French Arlequin was Bergamasque at the **Théâtre des Funambules**, but the character was already effaced by the **Pierrot** of **Jean-Gaspard Deburau**.

Harlequin in England first appears in **John Day**'s *The Travailes of the Three English Brothers* (1607) and Ravenscroft's *Scaramouch* (1644). **Aphra Behn** adapted a French scenario into *The Emperor of the Moon* (1686) for the comedian Tom Jevon, who played the famous **lazzi** of suicide in it; but Harlequin did not catch on in England until the introduction of the pantomime by John Weaver and **John Rich**. Rich, under the name Lun, presented an acrobatic Harlequin stripped of his complex French background, an antic mute most remarkable for his pantomimic tricks; this version was carried on by Henry Woodward, James Byrne who devised the close-fitting costume bespangled with glittering lozenges, John Bologna Jr, and Tom Ellar. By the time of the latter two, Harlequin had been elbowed aside by the popular Clown of **Joe Grimaldi**, and his chief functions were dancing with Columbine and effecting transformations with a touch of his magic bat. Despite his powers of invisibility, he performed chiefly as straightman to Clown and Pantaloon.

In modern times, Harlequin has become emblematic of a bygone theatre, despite attempts to revive him at the **Vieux-Colombier** and the Piccolo Teatro di Milano with Marcello Moretti in the part. Jacques Fabbri had a limited success in Santelli's *La Famille Arlequin* (1955). Fokine's use of Harlequin in his ballets *Arlequinade* (1900) and *Carnaval* (1910) is typical of the svelte, dandified character conjured up by many artists. The San Francisco Mime Troupe is one of the few groups to adapt Harlequin to the needs of contemporary satire, while **Dario Fo** has managed to absorb the *commedia* in a comic persona all his own.   LS

> See: G. Attinger, 'L'évolution d'un type en France: Arlequin', *Rivista di studi teatrali* (1954); F. Nicolini, *Vita di Arlecchino*, Milan, 1958; T. Niklaus, *Harlequin Phoenix*, London, 1956.

Harlequinade see **Pantomime, English**

Harnick, Sheldon see **Bock, Jerry**

Harrigan, Edward (1844–1911) American playwright and actor, and **Tony Hart** (1855–91), American actor. Harrigan and Hart became the most popular comedy team on the American stage (1871–85). They sang, danced, and played the principal roles (usually Harrigan as the amiable, fun-loving Irish adventurer Dan Mulligan and Hart, in blackface, as the Negro wench Rebecca Allup) in Harrigan's high-spirited 'melees': *The Mulligan Guard Picnic* (1878), *MG Ball* (1979), *MG Chowder* (1879), *MG Christmas* (1879), *MG Nominee* (1880), *MG Surprise* (1880), *MG Silver Wedding* (1881), *Old Lavender* (1877), *The Major* (1881), *Squatter Sovereignty* (1882), *Cordelia's Aspirations* (1883), *Dan's Tribulations* (1884), and *Investigation* (1884). Harrigan's farces were not all 'knockdown and slambang'. His documentary explorations of New York's Lower Eastside and his striking portraits of the Germans, Italians, Negroes, and particularly the Irish in his 40 plays promoted **W. D. Howells** to write: 'Here is the spring of a true American comedy, the joyous art of the dramatist who loves the life he observes.' Another critic called his plays the 'Pickwick Papers of a Bowery **Dickens**'.

Harrigan was born on the Lower Eastside, appeared first as an Irish comic singer in San Francisco (1867), in 1871 met Tony Hart (Anthony J. Cannon), a falsetto-voiced singer from Worcester, Massachusetts, wrote 'The Little Fraud' (1871) which alerted Boston to their extraordinary talents, turning out 60 more sketches, most notable of which was 'The Mulligan Guard' (with music by David Braham, his future father-in-law and thereafter his musical collaborator), a satire on New York's pseudo-military companies. Their antics drew boisterous crowds to the Théâtre Comique (514

Publicity poster for Harrigan and Hart.

Broadway) and then to Harrigan's Théâtre Comique (728 Broadway).

When the second Comique burned down (1884), the partners separated. Hart stumbled in and out of three plays, was committed to an asylum and died at the age of 35. Harrigan continued writing and acting: *The Leather Patch* (1886), *McNooney's Visit* (1887), *et al.*, and opened a new Harrigan Theatre on Herald Square with *Reilly and the Four Hundred* (1890).

Three of his children, 'Eddie', William, and Nedda (Mrs Joshua Logan), became actors.   RM

Harris, Jed (1900–79) American producer. At the height of the twenties Harris presented four plays celebrated for their crisp modern style: *Broadway* (1926), a raucous backstage melodrama overrun with wise-cracking gangsters and gum-chewing chorines; *Coquette* (1927), a tearjerker about the risks of Flaming Youth; *The Royal Family* (1927), a satire about a flamboyant theatrical dynasty modelled on the **Barrymores**; and *The Front Page* (1928), a whirlwind comedy-melodrama set in a newspaper office. Growing quickly bored with his success, Harris was content to rest on his laurels; he worked only sporadically thereafter, most notably on *Uncle Vanya* (1930), a response to critics who complained that he wasted his talents on light entertainment; *The Green Bay Tree* (1933), with **Laurence Olivier** as a kept homosexual; *Our Town* (1938); and *The Heiress* (1947), based on Henry James's *Washington Square*. After retiring to San Francisco, he broke silence with two books: *Watchman, What of the Night?* (1963), a crusty and self-justifying account of the backstage warfare on *The Heiress*, and *A Dance on the High Wire* (1979), a curiously muted memoir.

There are two enduring legends about Harris: one,

obviously untrue, that he had a golden touch that turned every play he handled into a hit; and the second, which has much greater validity, that he was a monster. Harris directed only a few of his plays (including *Uncle Vanya* and *Our Town*) but all of his productions had superb taste and showmanship, achieved at great cost to his collaborators. **George Abbott** called him 'the Little Napoleon of Broadway', and stories of Harris's wild mood swings, his withering sarcasm and cruelty, are part of theatrical folklore.   FH

Harris, Julie (1925–) American film, stage, and television actress, whose Broadway debut was as Atlanta in *It's a Gift* (1945). She rose to stardom with such roles as Frankie Adams in *The Member of the Wedding* (1950), Sally Bowles in *I Am a Camera* (1951), and Joan in *The Lark* (1955), performances she later filmed. In 1976 she successfully performed a one-woman show, *The Belle of Amherst*, subsequently touring the show and playing a season at the Phoenix, London. Critics have been won over by her air of vulnerability and fragility, coupled with remarkable stage techniques. Her Emily Dickinson in *Belle* was called 'astonishing in its sagacity and passion . . . shining'. She received an Antoinette Perry (Tony) Award for *Forty Carats* (1969) and for *The Last of Mrs Lincoln*. She frequently revives *Belle*, and in 1980 played the lead in *On Golden Pond* on the West Coast. Harris has also won many awards during her illustrious career in film and television. She is the author of a highly acclaimed and partially autobiographical text for beginning performers, *Julie Harris Talks to Young Actors*, 1972.   SMA

Harris, Rosemary (1930–) British actress who has appeared in over 140 roles in more than 30 years on the English and American stage, including affiliations with some of the great theatre companies (in England the **Bristol Old Vic**, **Old Vic**, the **National Theatre**, **Chichester Festival**; in the USA the **Association of Producing Artists**, Lincoln Center, Brooklyn Academy of Music, **American Shakespeare Theatre**, and **Williamstown Theatre Festival**). A versatile actress, who once described herself as 'a chameleon on a tartan', she has appeared prominently in **Guthrie**'s 1956 production of *Troilus and Cressida*, *Man and Superman*, *Much Ado About Nothing*, *The School for Scandal*, *The Seagull*, *Twelfth Night*, and *The Broken Heart* (first Chichester season, 1952), *Hamlet* (Ophelia in National Theatre's inaugural season), *The Lion in Winter* (1966 Tony award), *Old Times*, *Major Barbara*, *A Streetcar Named Desire*, *The Royal Family*, *All My Sons* (1981 London revival), *Pack of Lies* and the Broadway revival of *Hay Fever* in the 1985–6 season.   DBW

Harris, Sam H[enry] (1872–1941) American producer. Harris began his theatrical career in 1899 as a stagehand. The following year he became a partner in the firm of Sullivan, Harris, and Woods (1900–4), which produced eight melodramas and burlesques including a hit, *The Fatal Wedding*. He began a 16-year partnership with **George M. Cohan** in 1904, producing more than 50 plays including Cohan's own *Little Johnny Jones*, *Forty-five Minutes from Broadway*, and *Seven Keys to Baldpate*. After the partnership was dissolved in 1920, Harris independently produced *Rain*

(1922), *The Jazz Singer* (1925), *Animal Crackers* (1928), *Dinner at Eight* (1932), *The Man Who Came to Dinner* (1939), and *Lady in the Dark* (1941). His productions of *Icebound* (1923), *Of Thee I Sing* (1932) and *You Can't Take It with You* (1937) won Pulitzer Prizes; and *Of Mice and Men* won the 1938 New York Critics Circle Award. He preferred comedies and musical comedies to serious drama and was noted for paying attention to the smallest details of a production.   TLM

Harrison, Rex (Carey) (1908–90) British actor who will always be associated with the role of Henry Higgins in the musical version of **Shaw**'s *Pygmalion*, *My Fair Lady* (by **Lerner** and **Loewe**). In many ways this was a part made for him – the urbane English gentleman, stern yet sentimental, raffish yet decent. He started his professional career at Liverpool Playhouse in 1924, and arrived in London in 1930. His roles were not only in the comedies of **Coward**, **Rattigan** and Van Druten, but also in less obvious parts for an actor of his type-casting: he was the Uninvited Guest in **Eliot**'s *The Cocktail Party* (1950), Henry IV in **Pirandello**'s play (1973 and 1974) and played in **Shaw**, **Fry**, and **Chekhov**. He made acting look easy, and rather the profession of the officer class.   MB

Hart, Heinrich (1855–1906) and **Julius** (1859–1930) German critics and playwrights. The brothers Hart did much to prepare the critical ground for naturalist theatre in Berlin in the late 1880s. Their most important essays are collected in *Critical Conflicts* (1894).   SW

Hart, Lorenz (1895–1943) American lyricist and librettist. His first theatrical assignment was as a play translator for the **Shuberts**. In collaboration with **Richard Rodgers**, who was to be his partner for the rest of his career, Hart contributed four songs to the Broadway musical comedy *Poor Little Ritz Girl* (1920). The first complete scores by Rodgers and Hart were for *The Garrick Gaieties* (1925) and *Dearest Enemy* (1925). In the next eighteen years they created an almost uninterrupted string of successful shows, including *The Girl Friend* (1926), *A Connecticut Yankee* (1927), *America's Sweetheart* (1931), *On Your Toes* (1936), *Babes in Arms* (1937), *The Boys from Syracuse* (1938), *I Married an Angel* (1938), *Pal Joey* (1940), *By Jupiter* (1941), and a 1943 revival of *A Connecticut Yankee*. Hart's clever, sometimes sardonic lyrics, often employing complicated internal rhyme schemes, are considered among the finest ever written for the musical stage.   MK

Hart, Moss (1904–61) American playwright, librettist, and director. Although he had written several unsuccessful plays on his own, it was Hart's teaming up with **George S. Kaufman** during the decade of the thirties that established his career. These two wits delighted American audiences with such hits as *Once in a Lifetime* (1930), *You Can't Take It With You* (1936; Pulitzer Prize), and *The Man Who Came To Dinner* (1939). On his own in the forties, Hart wrote, among other offerings, the book for the landmark musical about psychoanalysis, *Lady in the Dark* (1941), and the funny theatre in-joke about a play in rehearsal, *Light up the Sky* (1948). Hart devoted much of the latter decade of his career to directing, winning the Tony Award for his work on *My Fair Lady* (1956).   LDC

Hart, Tony see **Harrigan, Edward**

Hart House Theatre A small Canadian professional theatre created within a student building given to the University of Toronto by the Massey family. During the 1920s and 1930s, under directors such as Roy Mitchell (1919–21) and Edgar Stone (1929–34), it was a major centre of new Canadian drama, introducing important new playwrights such as Merrill Denison. After the Second World War it became a student theatre and, under the direction of Robert Gill (1946–66), a vital training ground for a whole generation of professional actors, directors and designers. Since 1971 it has been closely linked with the University's Graduate Centre for the Study of Drama.   JA

Harte, Bret (Francis Brett Harte) (1836–1902) American writer. Raised in Brooklyn, he moved to California in 1853 and became famous for stories and poems in *The Overland Monthly* (1868–71). His popularity declined as rapidly as it rose, and after 1878 he lived abroad. His best work combines sentiment and low humour in the manner of **Charles Dickens**. He wrote *Two Men of Sandy Bar* (1875) for **Stuart Robson**, and collaborated with Mark Twain on *Ah Sin* (1877), a vehicle for Charles Parsloe. Though both failed, they established a genre that **Bartley Campbell** perfected in *My Partner*.   DMCD

Hartleben, Otto (1864–1905) German playwright, poet, and short story writer. His plays, of which by far the most successful was *Rosenmontag* (*The Monday Before Lent*, 1900), focus primarily upon the incompatibility of sexual attraction and social class.   SW

Harwood, John Edmund (1771–1809) British-born American comic actor who was brought to the **Chestnut Street Theatre** by **Wignell** in 1793, remaining in Philadelphia until engaged by **Dunlap** for the **Park** in New York in 1803, where he acted until his death. Among his better roles was Falstaff, which he played first in 1806 opposite the Hotspur of **Cooper**. Dunlap, who called him a man of wit and refinement and highly endowed as an actor, but indolent and careless of study, compared him to the British actor **John Bannister**. He married a grand-daughter of Benjamin Franklin and fathered Admiral Andrew Allen Harwood.   DBW

Hasenclever, Walter (1890–1940) German dramatist, novelist and poet, whose first play, *The Son* (1916), was one of the key works of expressionism. Semi-autobiographical in conception, it established conflict between the generations as a typical subject and contains the most directly political rendering of the parricide theme. His adaptation of *Antigone* as an anti-war piece was produced by **Reinhardt** in the mammoth 'Theatre of Five Thousand' (1920), but already a play like *The Decision* (awarded the Kleist prize in 1919) had put forward the thesis that action on a political level was irrelevant to real social change. In 1924 he abandoned expressionism for social comedy, *A Man of Distinction* (1926), *Marriages Are Made In Heaven*

(1928), which gained an international reputation with their tragic perception of existence underlying the irreverently witty surface. Forced into exile by the rise of Hitler, he turned to the biblical story of Esther for his last work, *Scandal in Assyria* (performed under the pseudonym of Axel Kjellström in London in 1939). **Olivier** planned a production of this dramatic denunciation of National Socialism in the USA, but the project was abandoned for fear of political demonstrations. Imprisoned by the Vichy French on the invasion of France, Hasenclever committed suicide.   CI

Hauptmann, Gerhart (1862–1946) German playwright and novelist. From the production of his first play *Before Dawn* (1889) at the **Freie Bühne**, Hauptmann was celebrated as the leader of naturalism in the German theatre. The play shows the unmistakable influence of the theories of **Zola** and the dramaturgy of **Ibsen**, a legacy from which Hauptmann found it difficult to escape. *Lonely Lives* (1891) was clearly inspired by *Rosmersholm*, though with *The Weavers* (1892), a play of epic structure dramatizing the plight of Silesian workers during the riots of 1844, Hauptmann found a more individual tone. Although he continued to write naturalistic plays into the 20th century – *The Beaver Coat* (1893), *Carter Henschel* (1899) and *Rose Bernd* (1903) are notable examples – he also experimented with other genres and modes. *The Sunken Bell* (1896) was a widely performed, neoromantic allegory that gave actors such as **Kainz** an ideal opportunity to display their vocal skills. Hauptmann, who was awarded the Nobel Prize in 1912, continued to expand his range, producing historical dramas, fantasy plays, and tragedies written in both the Greek and Shakespearian forms. Up until his death after the Second World War, Hauptmann remained one of the most respected German men of letters. However, his work never fulfilled the promise of the 1890s, when he was recognized, both in Germany and abroad, as a dramatist of primary significance.   SW

Haupt- und Staatsaktionen Plays performed by travelling troupes of actors in Germany during the 17th and early 18th centuries. They were derived from the Shakespearian drama that had been performed by the **Englische Komödianten**, from the German literary drama, and from the improvised drama of the **commedia dell'arte** troupes that toured Germany then. By all accounts, this was a debased form of theatre that encouraged bombastic acting, sensational and gory manifestations on the stage, and frequent gross obscenity. As the German theatre became 'regularized' under the influence of Gottsched and the quality of drama improved due to the efforts of such writers as **J. E. Schlegel** and **Lessing**, both the style and the genre of representation began to decline. Although *Haupt- und Staatsaktionen* continued to be performed sporadically into the 1760s by the troupes of **Koch** and **Döbbelin**, by the end of that decade they had disappeared entirely from the repertoire.   SW

Havel, Václav (1936–) Czech playwright, and President of Czechoslovakia since 1990. A native of Prague, he studied at the Prague Theatre Academy and eventually became dramaturge and resident playwright at the Balustrade Theatre, for which he wrote all his plays until 1968. In his best-known plays,

Havel focused on deformations in patterns of thinking (ideological and bureaucratic power stratagems run amok or become sclerotic). Havel's stage world is essentially abstract, schematic, and cerebral, characterized more by wit and farce than by humour, as is seen in *Garden Party* (1963), *Memorandum* (1965), and *The Increased Difficulty of Concentration* (1968), which form a triptych of variations on a theme. A frequently confined dissident, he continued to live and write in his homeland, although his only outlet for productions since 1969 was abroad; e.g., *A Private View* (New York, 1983), *Largo Desolato* (Vienna, 1985), *Temptation* (**RSC**, The Other Place, Stratford-upon-Avon, 1987). JMB

Hayes, Helen (1900–) American actress. With **Katharine Cornell** and **Lynn Fontanne**, Hayes has often been called 'the First Lady of the American Theater'. Diminutive and homespun, she is distinctly less glamorous than the other Great Ladies; and the qualities of modesty and common sense that she projects help account for her enduring appeal. A stage star for over 50 years (she retired in 1971), she has continued to act occasionally in films and on television and now hosts a radio programme addressed to senior citizens.

As a youngster she appeared with **John Drew** and **William Gillette** and worked for such fabled producers as **Charles Frohman** and **George Tyler**. Opposite **Alfred Lunt** in **Booth Tarkington**'s *Clarence* (1919), she played a saucy flapper, as she did again in the **Theatre Guild**'s *Caesar and Cleopatra* (1925) and *Coquette* (1927). In the thirties, she had her greatest critical success as the gallant monarchs in *Mary of Scotland* (1933) and *Victoria Regina* (1935). In the forties and fifties she starred in showy vehicles like *Harriet* (1943), an episodic biography of Harriet Beecher Stowe; *Happy Birthday* (1946), in which she was a librarian turned siren; and *Mrs McThing* (1952), in which she was a society matron transformed into a scrubwoman. In her most memorable later work, the Phoenix Theatre revival of *The Show-Off* in 1967, she played **George Kelly**'s no-nonsense mother-in-law with bracing tartness.

Often criticized for her choice of material and for being cloyingly demure, Hayes is more resourceful, more modern and witty, than her current reputation allows. She has a remarkably clear, low-pitched, resonant voice, and she has none of the hamminess that flawed the star acting of the tradition she grew up in. FH

Haymarket, Theatre Royal This London theatre, which was the chief rival of the Patent houses for almost a century, opened inauspiciously in late 1720, scarcely justifying the speculative ambitions of its carpenter-builder, John Potter. It gathered notoriety in the 1730s, when **Henry Fielding** leased it to stage a series of anti-Walpole satires. Walpole was sufficiently stung to engineer the passage of the Licensing Act in 1737, and the Haymarket was the most prominent of the illegitimate victims of this repressive legislation. After a fallow period, it was leased by **Samuel Foote** in 1747. After ingeniously circumventing the law for several years, Foote was awarded a limited licence for the Haymarket in 1766, probably in compensation for

The Theatre Royal, Haymarket, 1821.

the accident that cost him his leg. By the terms of the licence, the Haymarket was permitted to stage the legitimate drama during the summer months, when the patent theatres were closed. Under the successive managements of **George Colman the Elder** (1776–94) and his son (1794–1817), the Haymarket provided a summer home for almost all the greatest actors and most popular plays of the period. The present theatre, with John Nash's famous portico, was built in 1820, though its interior has been refashioned many times since then. Among its best-known managers have been **Benjamin Webster** (1837–53), **Buckstone** (1853–79), the **Bancrofts** (1880–5), **Beerbohm Tree** (1887–96) and Cyril Maude (1896–1905). PT

Hayward, Leland (1902–71) American producer responsible for two dozen plays and musicals on Broadway between 1941 and his death, two-thirds of which were unqualified successes both critically and financially. Two of his productions (*State of the Union*, 1945; *South Pacific*, 1949) won Pulitzer Prizes. Prior to becoming a producer in 1944 with *A Bell for Adano*, Hayward had established a successful talent agency in Hollywood and New York. Other significant plays produced included *Mister Roberts* (1948), *Anne of the*

Thousand Days (1948), *Call Me Madam* (1950), *Gypsy* (1959), *The Sound of Music* (1959), and *The Trial of the Catonsville Nine* (1971). Hayward was also a film and television producer, a pilot and airline executive, and a photographer. In 1936 he married the actress Margaret Sullavan, divorcing in 1948. **Oliver Smith** said that Hayward represented everything which was best in the theatre, being 'tenacious and at the same time elegant'. DBW

Hazlitt, William (1778–1830) English essayist and critic whose unpredictable temperament, alternating from extremes of morbidity to extremes of enthusiasm, disqualified him from a potential role as the Boswell of the English romantics. Stirred almost equally in childhood by the promise of the French Revolution, the acting of **Mrs Siddons** and a reading of **Schiller**'s *Die Räuber*, Hazlitt retained a fondness for the theatre, despite his clear perception of its faults and his literary refinement. 'We occasionally see something on the stage that reminds us a little of **Shakespeare**', he wrote in his *Champion* review of **Eliza O'Neill**'s Juliet (1814), and yet, from so sceptical a stance, he could praise the grandeur of Mrs Siddons, the intensity of **John Philip Kemble**, the gusto of **Edmund Kean** and the extravagance of **Liston**. Hazlitt was most active as a dramatic critic – for the *Examiner*, the *Champion*, the *Morning Chronicle* and *The Times* – from 1813–18. It was in 1818 that he published a selection of his reviews under the title, *A View of the English Stage*. But his theatrical writing is by no means confined to that volume. He filled out and largely wrote the unfinished *Memoirs of the Late Thomas Holcroft* (1816), his famous *Characters of Shakespeare's Plays* (1817) is dotted with theatrical references, the metaphor of public life as a stage binds together the disparate essays of his most original work, *The Spirit of the Age* (1825), and he pursued with fascination the dangerous disparity between the actor, lofty in performance, and the actor, diminished in private, most notably in two essays, 'On Actors and Acting' (*The Round Table*, 1817) and 'Whether Actors Ought to Sit in the Boxes?' (*Table Talk*, 1824). PT

Heavens From the symbolic association of the 'heavens' above the stage and the 'hell' beneath it, the Elizabethans derived the custom of calling the canopy over the stage of the public theatres, supported as in De Witt's drawing of the **Swan** by two pillars, the 'Heavens'. It is probable that they decorated it with sun, moon and stars. PT

Hebbel, Friedrich (1813–63) German playwright. After a childhood of abject poverty and an early manhood of dependency on various patrons, Hebbel settled in Vienna and, in 1846, married the **Burgtheater** actress, Christine Enghaus (1817–1910). The marriage gave him much-desired stability, both financial and emotional. Though most of Hebbel's plays have mythical or historical settings, his characters are recognizably figures of his time, struggling, not always with success, to come to terms with disturbing impulses that frequently border on the psychotic. The early prose drama *Judith* (1841) is an unorthodox treatment of the biblical myth, while *Maria Magdalena* (1844), a play with a contemporary setting, has been

seen by many as anticipating **Ibsen**. *Herodes and Mariamne* (1849) treats the themes of trust and jealousy in marriage, *Agnes Bernauer* (1852), a powerful historical drama, has as its theme the guilt inherent in perfect beauty, while *Gyges and his Ring* (1856), a striking play about sexual tensions, also involves much discussion of political and moral issues. Hebbel's final work was a trilogy, *The Nibelungs* (1862). Though **Laube** at the Burgtheater was unwilling to stage Hebbel's work, he had little difficulty in finding theatres elsewhere in German-speaking Europe to accept his plays. SW

Hebrew theatre Hebrew theatre is a relatively young theatre. Its history is intimately related to the national rebirth of the Jewish people and of the Hebrew language in the modern era. Although Hebrew, the language of the Bible, was continuously used by the Jews in the Diaspora for prayer, religious study and literature, it practically died out as a spoken language. Until the revival of Hebrew as an everyday language, since the turn of the century, Hebrew drama was handicapped by the lack of natural sounding dialogue. This was not the case with drama written in Yiddish, the spoken language of the Jews of Eastern Europe (see **Yiddish theatre**).

The growth of Hebrew theatre is also a concomitant of the gradual secularization of Jewish culture, for the Jewish religion was traditionally inimical to the theatre. The sages of the Talmud disapproved of it for a number of reasons, primarily because of the sacrifices offered in the theatre to the idols. In their eyes it was also a scurrilous and bawdy place where the actors trespassed the Deuteronomy injunction against men wearing female dress. During the Hellenistic and Roman periods many theatres were built in Palestine, but they were regarded as gentile institutions, symbols of Hellenistic culture. Only in periods in which the Jewish community opened up towards its surroundings could it find interest in this essentially alien form of art.

The modern Hebrew theatre, closely tied as it is to the revival of the Hebrew language, has no theatrical tradition of its own. It consciously dissociated itself from the immediate heritage of the Yiddish theatre, which represented the culture of the Diaspora. Instead, the founders of the modern Hebrew theatre looked towards the European theatre for inspiration. But this relationship with foreign theatrical traditions on which it depends is often problematic. Where it finds the aesthetic form pleasing, it may yet find the ideology or religious values unpalatable and even offensive. This painful dialectic is especially poignant when the contemporary Israeli theatre grapples with antisemitic drama, such as **Shakespeare**'s *Merchant of Venice*.

Western dramatic art has often rejuvenated itself by reinterpreting classical drama. But Judaism saw Hellenism as a threatening alien and pagan culture to be opposed and rejected. Hence the Jews could not share in neoclassical movements. Instead, they could resort to a parallel stratagem and use the Bible as their artistic and moral paradigm and source of tales and themes. But for all its literary merit, the Bible could not teach dramatic structure and theatrical technique. For these, the Hebrew playwright had to turn to the works of other nations and languages.

The Purimspiel (Yiddish for 'Purim play'). Most

scholars see the folk origins of Jewish theatre in the Purim festival, the commemoration of the delivery of the Jews as recorded in the Book of Esther. It was traditionally celebrated with drink and revelry, dressing up and fooling, song and dance. The earliest recorded Jewish plays, dating from the 16th and 17th centuries, were meant for performance during the festival. Beside plays that retold the story of Esther, there were others on various biblical heroes, such as Joseph or Samson. These were written in Hebrew, Italian, Spanish, Portuguese, Provençal and Yiddish. Although not many of these plays have survived, we know about them from occasional catalogues of private libraries.

The beginnings in Italy, Holland and Eastern Europe
It was his wish to show that it was possible to write drama in Hebrew that brought **Yehuda Leone de' Sommi** (Leone Di Somi) to write the first original play in Hebrew, *A Comedy of Betrothal* (c. 1550). In this comedy he successfully combined elements from both the *commedia erudita* and the **commedia dell'arte** with a traditional Jewish story from the Midrash. Proud of his Judaism, de' Sommi attempted to prove in his *Four Dialogues on Scenic Representation* that it was the children of Israel rather than the Greeks who invented the tragic form, ingeniously arguing that the Book of Job is a tragedy in five acts. De' Sommi's singular enterprise does not seem to have influenced other Italian Jews and his work was forgotten until it was rediscovered by modern scholarship.

But at the beginning of the 17th century, due to the persecution of the Spanish Inquisition, a large number of marranos left Spain and settled in Amsterdam. Here they revived their faith as well as the Hebrew language, in which they wrote not only religious treatises but also literary works and translations. Some of them, influenced perhaps by the Spanish **comedia**, attempted to write plays in Hebrew.

The famous kabbalist Mosè Zaccuto, born in Amsterdam of Spanish descent and later rabbi in Venice and Mantua, also wrote some Hebrew poetry and two dramatic works: *The Foundation of the Universe* (c. 1650), ostensibly based on the Genesis story of Abraham and on the Midrash, but whose real theme is the martyrdom of the Spanish Jews; and *The Inferno Set Out* (date unknown), a poetic masterpiece but only questionably a play, exposing the tribulations of a recently deceased criminal who finds himself in the nether world faced with damnation.

His younger contemporary, Josseph Felix Penso de la Vega, emigrated with his family from Spain to Amsterdam, where he returned to the Jewish faith. He wrote in both Spanish and Hebrew and is reputed to have been the first to publish a book on the workings of the Stock Exchange, *Confusión de confusiones* (1688), a witty series of four conversations between a clever philosopher, a wary merchant and a knowledgeable stock-holder. As a 17-year-old student at a religious school, Penso de la Vega produced a play called *Prisoners of Hope* (1667), an allegory about a king who must choose between good and evil, somewhat like a morality play. Another renowned kabbalist who was also an occasional playwright was Moshe Hayim Luzzatto, from Padua. In his three plays he wrote about love's joys and pains: *The Tale of Samson* (1720), an

adolescent biblical play intended perhaps as a Purim play, and two wedding-plays, *The Tower of Strength* (c. 1727), a pastoral play based on **Guarini**'s *Il Pastor Fido* (1596), and the highly allegorical *Praised be the Just* (1743).

Playwrights like Zaccuto and Luzzatto wrote against a background of a developing culture of plays performed at festivals and weddings. But at the end of the 18th century the Hebrew language lost favour with the Italian Jewish community as a literary medium, and the theatrical impulse died out.

The 19th century was a period of Jewish cultural renaissance in Eastern Europe. The *Haskalah* (Hebrew for 'Enlightenment') was a basically humanist and liberal movement, which aimed at introducing the Jews to the modern culture and science of other nations while at the same time effecting a revival of their own national culture. These new ideas, emanating from Germany, many of them put forth by the philosopher Moses Mendelssohn, swept through Eastern Europe in the second half of the 19th century. While the Yiddish theatre blossomed during this period, the Hebrew drama, heavily influenced by Luzzatto, remained didactic and moralistic, and devoid of theatricality.

The growth of the modern Hebrew theatre in Russia
The growth of the modern Hebrew theatre from the turn of the century onwards is closely associated with Zionism and its insistence on the return to Hebrew as an everyday spoken language. Unlike earlier cultural revivals, which produced occasional dramatic spurts, the Zionist movement was a national movement which succeeded in achieving its political goals with the founding of the State of Israel in 1948.

The first professional Hebrew theatre, **Habimah** ('The Stage'), was established in Moscow in 1918 by **Nahum Zemach**. The founding of a Hebrew theatre was a truly visionary undertaking at a time when even in Palestine the language was spoken only by a few, and certainly in Russia, where only small groups of intellectuals understood it. While the Yiddish theatre enjoyed large popular audiences, there was no broad Hebrew-speaking audience. But Hebrew had become inextricable from the Zionist dream and more and more literature was being written in it. Despite the ambivalent attitude of the Soviet authorities towards the use of Hebrew, Zemach obtained both recognition and financial support, and the Habimah became one of the three studios affiliated to the **Moscow Art Theatre**, under the direction of **Konstantin Stanislavsky**, and later grew into the Hebrew State Theatre Habimah.

Stanislavsky shaped the troupe's realistic acting technique, but it was **Evgeny Vakhtangov**'s production of **Anski**'s *The Dybbuk* (1922) that brought Habimah international recognition. Other notable early productions were *The Eternal Jew* by **David Pinski**, a play based on an ancient Talmudic legend, and *The Golem* by H. Leivik. In 1931 Habimah settled in Palestine.

Theatre in Palestine and Israel
The successive waves of Zionist immigration brought with them also the impetus to found a Hebrew theatre in Palestine. The first local group was The Lovers of the Hebrew Stage, who performed from 1904 to 1914. Various groups were formed in the early twenties: the Hebrew Theatre, the Dramatic Theatre, and the TAI (acronym for the Theatre of Eretz Israel).

The Ohel ('Tent') was founded by Moshe Halevi, a Habimah veteran, in 1925. It was organized as a cooperative, much like a cultural kibbutz, and aimed at presenting plays on socialist themes. But it soon abandoned the idea of proletarian art in favour of national art, with a repertoire similar to that of Habimah. It remained the official theatre of the Histadrut (The General Labour Federation) until 1958, and closed down in 1969. The Ohel's most memorable production was Jaroslav Hašek's *The Good Soldier Schweik* (1935), starring the outstanding comedian **Meir Margalit**.

While Habimah remained revered for its great past, a certain conservatism that had set in, a refusal to admit young actors into the collective and to face changes in Israeli society and in the spoken language, brought about the creation of the Cameri ('Chamber') theatre, in 1944, by a group of young actors with a West European orientation, headed by Yosef Millo. Two of his recruits, **Hanna Maron** and Yosef Yadin, were destined to become leading Israeli actors.

The Cameri's most important contribution to the theatrical scene was the performance of the first play by a *sabra*, a native Israeli, about a *sabra*. *He Walked the Fields*, by Moshe Shamir, was a topical play about the personal conflicts of the young heroes of the Israeli struggle for independence. The premiere took place in 1948, just two weeks after the proclamation of the State of Israel and in the midst of the war. The acting was devoid of the pathos that had come to be associated with the Habimah. Millo staged the play in a non-illusionistic Brechtian manner, with sets changed by the actors in front of the audience. Habimah followed suit with another play about the War of Independence, Yigal Mossinson's *The Wastes of the Negev* (1949), a thinly veiled stage reportage of a recent war episode.

Besides the three 'legitimate' public theatres there were also smaller ventures, such as the satirical theatres the Kumkum ('Kettle', 1927–8) and the Matateh ('Broom', 1928–54), which lampooned the British mandatory authorities.

The latest trends in avant-garde and experimental theatre were introduced in 1949 by Michael Almaz and his Zirah ('Arena') theatre. In 1955, only three years after the Paris world premiere, the Zirah staged **Beckett**'s *Waiting for Godot*, and in 1957 it produced **Ionesco**'s *The Bald Prima Donna* and *The Lesson*. But the theatre closed down after seven years, Almaz himself settling in England.

In 1961 the Hammam theatre opened in a disused Turkish bath in Jaffa. The Onot ('Seasons') theatre was established in 1962, Bamat Hasahkanim ('The Actor's Stage') and Tzavta ('Together') in 1966.

All theatrical activity continued to be centred in Tel-Aviv until the opening of the Haifa Municipal Theatre in 1961, with Yosef Millo as artistic director. In its first years it hardly performed any original plays, but mounted a number of memorable productions, among them **Brecht**'s *Caucasian Chalk Circle* (1962) with Zaharira Harifai as a marvellous Grusha, and *Richard III* (1966) with Millo himself in the title role.

Jerusalem, although the fast-expanding capital of Israel, has remained a theatrical backwater. In 1967 the Municipality decided to convert an old Khan into a theatre and to develop a local troupe. The Jerusalem Sherover Theatre is a striking modern edifice which has no troupe of its own but serves as the main auditorium for guest performances.

Theatrical life in Israel also takes less conventional forms. For many years army troupes provided initial training for young actors and developed a distinctive style of acting and special brand of humour. The kibbutzim maintain their own semi-professional theatre, Bimat Hakibbutz ('Kibbutz Stage'). But perhaps its most striking feature is the government-sponsored tours of the established theatres bringing performances to the remotest settlements.

Drama in the early years of the state The War of Independence and the establishment of the State of Israel (1948) made an enormous impact on the development of the theatre. A vogue of reportage-like drama followed the war plays of Moshe Shamir and Yigal Mossinson. Ben-Zion Tomer wrote in *The Children of the Shadow* about the encounter between refugees from Europe and the *sabras*. The failings of the new state were satirized by **Ephraim Kishon** and, in a lighter vein, by Aaron Megged (*Hedva and I*, 1954, *I Like Mike*, 1956).

From her broad European cultural perspective the poetess Leah Goldberg dramatized the struggle between the old European culture and the new one being forged in Israel in *The Lady of the Manor* (1955). Nathan Alterman wrote a number of poetic plays, among them *The Inn of Ghosts* (1963), about the place of the artist in the world, and *Kinneret, Kinneret* (1962), on the early pioneers. Plays in the manner of the theatre of the absurd were written in the fifties and sixties by Nissim Alloni (*Most Cruel Is the King*, *The American Princess*, *Eddie King*, *The Bride and the Butterfly-Hunter*, and several others) and by Amos Keenan (*That's the Man!*).

The contemporary scene While many successes from abroad continue to be imported for cultural as well as commercial reasons, the by now firm roots of the Israeli theatre have fostered the growth of new talent. The Haifa Municipal Theatre has been the most adventurous in soliciting new works with remarkable returns, such as Ya'acov Shabtai's *Spotted Tiger* (1974) about the idealism of the early builders of Tel-Aviv and A. B. Yehoshua's *A Night in May* (1968) about the effects of the pre-Six Day War tension on a Jerusalem family. Especially fruitful has been the association between the Theatre and Yehoshua Sobol (*Soul of a Jew*, 1982, *Ghetto*, 1984). Sobol has excelled in his imaginative use of historical and documentary material, and his plays have been well received abroad. Another outstanding Israeli playwright is **Hanoch Levin**.

The international vogue of adapting stories for the stage has not passed over Israel, where a number of plays based on stories by the two Nobel Prize-winners S. I. Agnon and Isaac Bashevis-Singer have coloured the local stage with nostalgia for the extinct Jewish culture of the Diaspora. The religious revival movement has also been reflected in a number of pieces, notably in Yossi Yizraeli's production of *The Seven Beggars* (1979), based on the Hassidic tales of Rabbi Nahman of Breslau.

The Israel Festival in Jerusalem has familiarized the Israeli public with the latest experimental work from abroad, while the young Acre Festival serves as a greenhouse for local alternative theatre.   HAS

See: G. Abramson, *Modern Hebrew Drama*, London, 1979; M. Kohansky, *The Hebrew Theatre: Its First Fifty Years*, Jerusalem, 1969; E. Levy, *The Habima – Israel's National Theatre 1917–1977*, New York, 1979; J. Schirman, *Studies in the History of Hebrew Poetry and Drama*, Jerusalem, 1979 (in Hebrew).

Hedgerow Theatre Founded in 1923 in Moylan-Rose Valley, Pennsylvania, by Jasper Deeter, this theatre was for many years the only true professional repertory theatre in the USA, operating year round with no stars and frequent changes of bill. By 1985, although the repertory scheme was dropped in 1956, the theatre had amassed a repertory of over 200 plays. Functioning as a cooperative, the theatre operated in a small converted mill with fewer than 170 seats. Standard plays, with those of **Shaw** most popular, have dominated. The future of the theatre is uncertain since the destruction by fire of its playhouse, late 1985.   DBW

Heeley, Desmond (1931–) British stage and costume designer. Heeley began his career at the **Birmingham Repertory Theatre** Company and then at the Shakespeare Memorial (now **Royal Shakespeare**) **Theatre** where he became designer in 1955. His first shows were *Toad of Toad Hall*, notable for its masks and headdresses and depiction of animals' hands and feet, and *Titus Andronicus* under the direction of **Peter Brook**. He subsequently became an internationally known designer working at the **Old Vic**, the Shakespearian Theatre of Stratford, Ontario, the **Tyrone Guthrie Theatre** in Minneapolis, and **Covent Garden**. He was hired to design *Norma* at the New York Metropolitan Opera (1970) after Rudolph Bing saw his sets and costumes for the Broadway production of *Rosencrantz and Guildenstern Are Dead* (1968). He has subsequently designed many operas there. Heeley's lush, textured, layered, and subtle but provocative use of colour in costumes has influenced a whole generation of designers. His style has been described as impressionistic symbolism combined with the texture of collage and junk art. Heeley's designs are most successful in the theatrical, larger-than-life world of **Shakespeare** and opera.   AA

Heiberg, Gunnar (1857–1929) Norwegian director, critic and playwright. As a critic, he argued for a more modern repertoire and acting style at Christiania Theatre and from 1884 attempted to realize them at the **Nationale Scene**, Bergen, where he directed the world premieres of *The Wild Duck* and *Rosmersholm*. In 1888 he began a new career as a dramatist and essayist, only occasionally returning to play directing. His 14 plays are influenced by **Ibsen**'s in their handling of ideas, but are experimental in their tendencies towards theatricalism, satire and formalized characterization. *Aunt Ulrikke* (1894) and *The Tragedy of Love* (1904) have been the most enduring.   HL

Heiberg, Johan Ludvig (1791–1860) Danish poet, playwright, critic and manager, married to the actress **Johanne Luise Heiberg**. His extraordinary influence on Denmark's cultural life depended primarily on his promotion of the thought and literature of France and Germany, through which he hoped to bring his country aesthetically and intellectually into Europe. He praised 18th-century French classicism and **Goethe**'s Weimar classicism for their emphasis on form in literature; he popularized Hegelian philosophy and admired **Calderón de la Barca** (the subject of his doctoral thesis) and the Jena romantics for their embodiment of speculative philosophy in drama; as an initial means of bringing sophistication to Danish theatre he promoted and wrote *vaudevilles*, mostly for his wife to perform; more enduring have been his comedies *Elves' Hill* (1828) and *A Soul After Death* (1841). His management of the **Kongelige Teater** (1849–56) was bitterly controversial, as he found himself opposed over repertoire by younger, more progressive minds.   HL

Heiberg, Johanne Luise (Pätges) (1812–90) Celebrated Danish actress who spent her entire career at the **Kongelige Teater**, where she began as a ballet apprentice. Her career was linked to that of her husband, **Johan Ludvig Heiberg**, who wrote a large number of *vaudevilles* specifically to suit her personality, while she shared his conviction that theatre should embody idealized beauty, rather than reality. Her ironic, graceful style suited the *vaudevilles* and Scribean comedies that dominated the Kongelige's repertoire in the 1830s, increasingly supplemented by the sentimental plays of Henrik Hertz in which she frequently co-starred with **Michael Wiehe**. Despite frequent criticism of her artificiality, she echoed the ideas of her main opponent Frederik Høedt in her demand that stage characters be complex and consistent. After her husband's death in 1860, she began her 'second career', playing Lady Macbeth and **Schiller**'s Mary Stuart with depth and humanity and directing several early plays by **Bjørnson** and **Ibsen**.   HL

Heijermans, Herman (1864–1924) Dutch playwright and theatre director, who reached international fame through his socio-realistic plays. As pseudonym he used the name Samuel Falkland. As a convinced socialist, he wrote plays to protest against bad social conditions, under which particularly the lower classes suffered. Although he was a Jew himself, he had a strong dislike of orthodox Judaism (*Ghetto*, 1898), in the way he generally opposed social and religious conventions and prejudices that forced man into a strait-jacket.

In the 1900s, Heijermans was a man of controversial opinions. Nevertheless, his plays were very popular with the audience, due to their social involvement. Today, his plays are still regularly performed. Popular plays are: *Schakels* (*Links*, 1903), *Uitkomst* (*Relief*, 1907), *De opgaande zon* (*The Rising Sun*, 1908), *De wijze kater* (*The Wise Cat*, 1917).

Ahasverus (1893) was staged in Paris by **Antoine**. *Op Hoop van Zegen* (*The Good Hope*, 1900) and *In de Jonge Jan* (1903) were performed in England, the United States, and Russia. *Op Hoop van Zegen*, his best-known play, deals with the oppression of poor fishermen by powerful ship-owners. The character of Kniertje, the old mother, has become a household word. His work has been compared with **Ibsen**, **Hauptmann** and **Chekhov**.   MG HS

Heiremans, Luis Alberto (1928–64) Chilean playwright, born to an illustrious and wealthy Santiago family with French ancestry. A talented and industrious student, he had early training in literature and languages (French and English), and discovered theatre at an early age. He received a medical degree, but preferred to devote his time and talents to literature and the arts. In addition to some 15 plays, Heiremans also published novels and short stories as well as translating and adapting French and English language plays for the Chilean stage. At the Teatro de Ensayo of the Catholic University he served as professor and promoted Chilean theatre. The Heiremans Foundation, created after his premature death by cancer, continues to provide benefits for theatre students and the arts. Interested in the vanguard theatrical techniques, Heiremans dealt with existentialist themes of anguish, frustration, solitude and alienation in his early plays. His *Esta señorita Trini* (*This Miss Trini*, 1958) was the first Chilean musical comedy, a play that enjoyed tremendous commercial success. Heiremans's most mature plays are his final trilogy, *Versos de ciego* (*The Blind Man's Verses*, 1961), *El abanderado* (*The Standard Bearer*, 1962) and *El tony chico* (*The Little Clown*, 1964), representing a combination of religious mythic, poetic and folkloric elements that point toward a higher Christian ideal.   GW

Helburn, Theresa (1887–1959) American director and producer. Born in New York, Helburn received her BA from Bryn Mawr in 1908, attended **George Pierce Baker**'s English 47 at Radcliffe, and studied in Paris for a year at the Sorbonne. After a brief career as an actress, she pursued a writing career, becoming dramatic critic of *The Nation* (1918). Two years later she took over the administration of the struggling **Theatre Guild** with the title of Executive Director. In 1933 she left for a year in Hollywood but returned as administrative director with **Lawrence Langner**. She was responsible for bringing **Alfred Lunt** and **Lynn Fontanne** together for *The Guardsman* in 1924, which established them as the leading dual acting team in America. With Langner she brought *Oklahoma!* to the stage in 1943, and in the same year *Othello* with **Paul Robeson**. A woman of outstanding executive ability she was described by Langner as possessing nerves 'like whipcord' and will power 'like steel'.   TLM

Helen Hayes Theatre *1* 210 West 46th St, New York City [Architects: Herts and Tallant]. Originally conceived as a New York counterpart of the Parisian original, the playhouse was opened in 1911 as the Follies Bergère, a restaurant-theatre, by producers Henry B. Harris and Jesse Lasky. Five months later, recognizing its failure, they rebuilt the interior and renamed it the Fulton without the restaurant for the production of legitimate fare. With fewer than 1,000 seats, it became the ideal house for intimate plays. During the depression decade, it changed owners and policy several times, but in 1941, it came back as a legitimate house. In 1955, it was renamed the Helen Hayes in honour of one of Broadway's first ladies of the stage. In 1982, despite strong protest from the theatrical community, the theatre was torn down to make way for a hotel. Its most famous tenant was the posthumous

production of **Eugene O'Neill**'s autobiographical play, *Long Day's Journey into Night* (1956).

2 238 West 44th St, New York City [Architects: H. C. Ingalls and F. B. Hoffman, Jr]. In 1912, producer **Winthrop Ames** built a 299-seat house named the Little for the production of unusual plays. Five years later, when it became a strain on his finances, he leased it to a succession of producers. To make it a viable Broadway house, a balcony was added and its seating was almost doubled. In 1931, it was sold to the *New York Times* and was thereafter used mainly as a concert-lecture hall and a television studio, but was returned to legitimate production in 1974. In 1983, under different ownership, the theatre was renamed the Helen Hayes during the run of *Torch Song Trilogy*.   MCH

Hellman, Lillian (1906–84) American playwright. Hellman was one of America's leading playwrights, and since 1963 when she ceased writing for the theatre, revivals of her plays are performed regularly throughout the country. Now she is also known for her books of memoirs: *An Unfinished Woman* (1969), *Pentimento* (1973), and *Scoundrel Time* (1976).

The Children's Hour (1934), based on an episode from William Roughead's *Bad Companions*, shocked and fascinated Broadway with the evil machinations of a child who destroys her teachers by whispering about their 'unnatural' relationship. Hellman was labelled a 'second **Ibsen**', 'the American **Strindberg**', and the play ran for 691 performances. Vigorous and unyielding confrontations became her dramaturgical trademark here and in: *The Little Foxes* (1939), *Watch on the Rhine* (1941), *The Searching Wind* (1944), *Another Part of the Forest* (1946), *The Autumn Garden* (1951), *The Lark* (1955, adapted from **Anouilh**'s *L'Alouette*), *Candide* (1956, from **Voltaire** with music by **Leonard Bernstein**), and *Toys in the Attic* (1960). Her plays were always given high-quality productions, first by Herman Shumlin and then by **Kermit Bloomgarden**. Only three plays failed at the box-office: *Days to Come* (1936), *Montserrat* (1949, adapted from Emmanuel Roblés's play), and *My Mother, My Father and Me* (1963, adapted from Burt Blechman's novel, *How Much?*).

Born in New Orleans, she became an editorial assistant to Horace Liveright in New York; a theatre press agent, a play-reader, and (in 1931) a script-reader in Hollywood where she met detective-story writer Dashiell Hammett who was to become her constant companion until his death in 1961. She wrote scripts for such films as *Dark Angel* (1935), *These Three* (1936, based on *The Children's Hour*), *Dead End* (1937), and *The North Star* (1943). In 1952 she was called before the House Un-American Activities Committee and her name was automatically added to Hollywood's blacklist.   RM

Helpmann, Robert Murray (1908–86) Australian dancer, actor, director and choreographer. As a youth he toured Australia with Pavlova in 1926, and became principal dancer in **J. C. Williamson** musicals. Joining the Vic Wells/Sadler's Wells Ballet in 1933, he remained principal dancer until 1950, also working as dancer, choreographer and director at **Covent Garden** from 1946. Since appearing as Oberon at the **Old Vic** in 1937 he has played many Shakespearian roles at the

Old Vic and Stratford-upon-Avon, and directed and acted in many modern plays. He was co-artistic director from 1965–76 of the Australian Ballet, which staged his ballets *The Display* (1964), *Yugen* (1965) and *Sun Music* (1968); he also directed the 1970 Adelaide Festival of Arts. He was awarded a CBE in 1964 and created a Knight of the British Empire in 1968.   MW

Heminges, John (d. 1630) English actor and company manager whose claim to have been the original Falstaff is based on nothing more than the memory of a rumour. He was a sharer in the **Lord Chamberlain's/King's Men** from the company's foundation in 1594 until his death. He was an unexceptional actor, but his immortality is assured by his initiative in the publication of the **Shakespeare** Folio of 1623. The task may have fallen to him in his role as business manager of the King's Men. After 1611, Heminges acted rarely, if at all. An ambiguous contemporary reference afflicts him with a stutter. There is no doubt that he was a reliable and widely respected administrator. He accumulated wealth and property, despite costly problems with at least two of his 14 children, and was for many years churchwarden of St Mary's, Aldermanbury. There was nothing of the 'rogue and vagabond' about Heminges.   PT

Henley, Beth (1952–) American playwright in the Southern Gothic tradition, whose comedies create empathy for bizarre characters who survive their disastrous experiences in outlandish ways. Her first professionally produced play, *Crimes of the Heart*, won the Pulitzer Prize in 1981. A family drama gone awry, the play portrays with absurdist wit and compassion the rallying of three eccentric Mississippi sisters because one of them has shot her husband. Henley's subsequent plays include: *The Wake of Jamey Foster* (1982), *Am I Blue?* (1982), and *The Miss Firecracker Contest* (1984) – another black comedy about a Mississippi woman's effort to redeem her calamitous life by winning a beauty contest.   FB

Hennings, Betty (1850–1939) Danish actress, noted for her performances of **Ibsen** at the **Kongelige Teater**. She specialized in ingenue roles, playing Agnes in *The School for Wives*, and Selma in *The League of Youth* before creating Nora in the world premiere of *A Doll's House* in 1879. Her revelation of Nora's growing inner tension was a turning point in Hennings's career, leading to her casting as other, even more complex Ibsen characters: Hedda Gabler, Hilde Wangel, Hedvig Ekdal and Mrs Alving. Although her strength was in naturalistic modern drama, by the turn of the century her style had begun to seem too mannered for modern taste.   HL

Henry, John (1738–94) Early American actor, born in Ireland and working in London and the West Indies before joining **Douglass**'s American Company. Henry made his first American appearance in Philadelphia on 6 October 1767. The matinee idol of his time, Henry was the first actor in America whose lamentable morals were seized on by opponents of the theatre. A chronic sufferer from gout, Henry was also the first American actor to keep a carriage. He first married a Miss Storer;

after her death lived with her sister, Ann, and finally married a third Storer sister, Maria.

After the Revolutionary War, Henry co-managed the American Company with **Lewis Hallam Jr** and in 1792 imported **John Hodgkinson**, who shortly forced Henry into retirement. A tall, handsome Irishman, Henry was most successful in comedy, especially Irish characters. **Dunlap** considered him 'one of the best performers in the colonies', but his arrogant manner made him many enemies.   SMA

Henslowe, Philip (c. 1550–1616) English businessman whose many enterprises included theatre management. Henslowe was apprenticed to a dyer, whose widow he married and whose daughter married the actor **Edward Alleyn** in 1592. By then, Henslowe already held the lease of the **Rose Theatre**, and may also have been in control of the theatre in Newington Butts. He and his son-in-law formed the most consistently successful partnership in the field of Elizabethan entertainment. When the Rose began to suffer under competition from the newly built **Globe**, they built the **Fortune** on the other side of the Thames (1600). In 1604, they purchased the Mastership of the Royal Game of Bears, Bulls and Mastiff Dogs, and ten years later they sought to combine their interests in drama and animal-baiting by erecting the adaptable **Hope Theatre** on Bankside. Henslowe became involved in drama because he believed in its profitability. He was an energetic and not over-scrupulous businessman. Apart from maintaining some share in his brother's mines in Ashdown Forest, he was also engaged in the manufacture of starch, in real estate, in pawnbroking and in money-lending. It was partly by usury that he controlled his contracted actors and playwrights. Evidence of his dealings has survived in the uniquely valuable *Diary*, the gatherings of papers deposited by Alleyn in the Dulwich Library.   PT

Hepburn, Katharine (1909–) American stage and film actress, educated at Bryn Mawr, whose professional debut was in *The Czarina* in Baltimore, Maryland, 1928; her New York debut was in *Night Hostess*, 1928. In 1950 she played Rosalind in *As You Like It*, then toured. In 1971 she toured in the musical comedy *Coco* after a successful Broadway run. Later stage appearances include *A Matter of Gravity* (1976) and *West Side Waltz* (1981). Her first film role was as Sydney Fairfield in *A Bill of Divorcement* (1932); she has won four Oscars as Best Actress.

Hepburn has invariably enchanted audiences by appearing in sophisticated comedy, in which her finesse and timing serve her well. In response to *A Matter of Gravity*, critics termed her 'radiant . . . enchanting', calling her a 'bright, classy, likeably smug, sassy lady'. Among her biographies is Charles Higham's *Kate: The Life of Katharine Hepburn* (1976).   SMA

Her/His Majesty's Theatre (London) There have been four theatres on the Haymarket site and their names have varied with the sex of the reigning monarch. The first, designed by Sir **John Vanbrugh** and named the Queen's Theatre, was intended as a home for the dissenting **Drury Lane** players under the leadership of **Thomas Betterton**. It opened in 1705, with Vanbrugh and **Congreve** in joint management, and soon proved more hospitable to opera than to drama. Handel wrote 29 of his 35 operas for performance there, and in its Georgian heyday, the King's Theatre was a Mecca for the fashionable adherents of the Italian opera. It was destroyed by fire in 1789.

The second King's Theatre (capacity 2,500), designed by Michael Novosielski, opened in 1791 and was recognized as a rival to La Scala in Milan (built 1788). After two seasons of drama (as host to the homeless Drury Lane company), it reverted to opera in 1793, remaining the undisputed centre of (predominantly Italian) opera until 1847, when **Covent Garden** proclaimed itself the Royal Italian Opera House. Renamed Her Majesty's Theatre on the accession of Queen Victoria in 1837, the second theatre was destroyed by fire in 1867.

The third theatre, known throughout as Her Majesty's, had an undistinguished history. Designed by Charles Lee to house an audience of nearly 2,000, it was completed in 1869, remained unused until 1874, when it was sold by auction, occupied from 1875–7 by the American evangelists Moodey and Sankey, first used for opera in 1877 and demolished in 1891.

The present theatre (capacity 1,263), designed by C. J. Phipps for **Herbert Beerbohm Tree**, opened in 1897 and remained under Tree's adventurous control until his death in 1917. It was there, in 1904, that he opened the drama school that would evolve into the Royal Academy of Dramatic Art, and there that he presented his spectacular **Shakespeare** productions. The more typical future of Her Majesty's (His Majesty's between the death of Queen Victoria and the accession of Queen Elizabeth II) was foreshadowed by the phenomenal success of **Oscar Asche**'s *Chu Chin Chow* (1916). Later spectacular successes have included **Flecker**'s *Hassan* (1923), **Coward**'s *Bitter Sweet* (1929) and such American musicals as *Brigadoon* (1949), *Paint Your Wagon* (1953), *West Side Story* (1958) and *Fiddler on the Roof* (1967). PT

Herbert, Jocelyn (1917–) British stage designer in the austere, poetic tradition of **Copeau** and **Saint-Denis**, by whom she became influenced while an art student in France and, later, as a theatre student in Saint-Denis's London Theatre Studio. Not until her 40th year did Herbert begin a theatre career, as stage designer at the **Royal Court Theatre** in London during its most creative years, under the leadership of **George Devine**, a former associate of Saint-Denis. Her work also came to reflect the spare functionality of Brechtian theatre. In later years her scenography in England and abroad became more complex but has never lost its essential purity and fine sense of spatial proportion. Distinctive productions include *Sergeant Musgrave's Dance* (1959), *Saint Joan of the Stockyards* (1964), *The Abduction from the Seraglio* (1979), *Galileo* (1980), and *The Oresteia* (1981), the last two at the **National Theatre**. JMB

Herbert, Victor (1859–1924) American composer. Born in Ireland and educated in Germany, Herbert came to America at the age of 27 to perform as a cellist with the Metropolitan Opera Orchestra. He became interested in composing for the theatre, and in 1894 his first score, *Prince Ananias*, was heard. The following year, his show *The Wizard of the Nile* had a long run in New York and on tour. After composing the music for several shows for comedian Frank Daniels, Herbert created the score for *The Serenade* (1897), which benefited from an excellent production by the **Bostonians**. In the last years of the 19th century Herbert served as musical director of the Pittsburgh Symphony Orchestra. Some of his most enduringly popular songs were written for *Babes in Toyland* (1903) and *Mlle. Modiste* (1905), the latter created as a vehicle for opera star Fritzi Scheff. Herbert's biggest commercial success came with *The Red Mill* (1906), which was also a big hit when it was revived on Broadway in 1945. Among Herbert's other popular musicals were *Naughty Marietta* (1910), *Sweethearts* (1913), and *Eileen* (1917). He also contributed songs to the 1921 and 1923 *Ziegfeld Follies*. Herbert was one of the founding members of the American Society of Composers, Authors and Publishers.

Trained in the conventions and traditions of European operetta, Herbert was adept at composing music that appealed to American audiences. Equally at home writing for comic operas, operettas, and musical comedies, he raised the level of American theatre music through the richness and variety of his scores. MK

Herman, David (1876–1937) One of the first and most influential of Jewish Art Theatre directors, starting with **Hirshbein**'s Troupe in Odessa in 1908, followed by the Arts Corner in Warsaw in 1910 and then the celebrated **Vilna Troupe** from 1917, where his most memorable of many productions was a stylistic production of *The Dybbuk*. After periods in Warsaw and Vienna he emigrated to America in 1934, exerting a profound influence on the Yiddish theatrical scene with his inspired direction of the **Folksbühne**. AB

Hernández, Luisa Josefina (1928–) Mexican playwright and novelist, she occupied the theatre chair at the National University vacated by her professor and mentor, **Rudolfo Usigli**, when he accepted a diplomatic position. A prolific contemporary writer, she achieved early success with both *Los frutos caídos* (*The Fallen Fruit*, 1957) and *Los huéspedes reales* (*The Royal Guests*, 1957), the latter a brilliant study of incest. Always concerned with problems of history, she adapted several major works to the stage, such as *Clemencia* (the Altamirano novel) (1963), and *Popol-Vuh* (1967), based on the Mayan myths and legends, and *Quetzalcoatl* (1968). Hernández has integrated Brechtian techniques into many works and has been an early and steady advocate of women's rights and social justice. GW

Herne, James A. (1839–1901) American actor, manager and playwright. Responding to the forces of science and democracy that challenged contemporary society, Herne developed realistic themes and characters in his plays and created a realistic creed for drama. Beginning his acting career in 1854, Herne became a stage manager in San Fransisco, where he wrote melodramas with **David Belasco** – *Within an Inch of His Life* (1879), *Hearts of Oak* (1879). Among his own plays, *The Minute Men of 1774–75* (1879) suggested the New England local colour that was developed in *Drifting Apart* (1888), a temperance play, and *Shore*

Acres (1892) in which Uncle Nat Berry, with his language and action, personified the Downeaster and made Herne a millionaire. With the help of **William Dean Howells** who rented the hall, Herne's best known play, *Margaret Fleming* (1890–1), was performed in Boston. This insightful play about a philandering husband whose illegitimate child is accepted by his morally strong and emotionally sensitive wife showed Herne's interest in realism and social determinism, but it was not successful. *The Reverend Griffith Davenport* (1899), based on a novel by Helen Gardner, dramatized the struggle of a slave holder who opposed slavery during the Civil War.

Relating drama to contemporary literature, Herne wrote 'Art for Truth's Sake in the Drama' (*Arena* XVII, February 1897, pp. 361–70) to emphasize the 'humanity' and 'large truth' in the drama which has a 'higher purpose' than to amuse. Praised by Howells for his 'epoch marking' drama, *Margaret Fleming*, Herne's work, frequently compared to **Ibsen**'s, began the period of modern drama in America   WJM

Hero-Combat play, the

The most widespread of the several British and Irish mumming plays. A comic drama of armed conflict, death and resurrection, performed seasonally, it is frequently described as medieval, or even pre-Christian, though there is actually no hard evidence of it until 1737. Its text appears to be based on one of the many editions of Richard Johnson's *Seven Champions of Christendom*, and on 17th-century broadside lampoons against mountebanks. It is probably a 17th- or 18th-century synthesis of popular literature with elements of indigenous traditions of mumming. Extensively revived in the present century under the aegis of the folk song and dance movements, traditional gangs still perform at Antrobus, Bampton, Chipping Campden, Marshfield, Ripon and Uttoxeter.   AEG

Heron, Matilda

(1830–77) American actress. Heron made a life's work of *Camille*. Fascinated by Mme Doché's playing of Marguerite Gautier in Paris (1854), she made her own adaptation of the play, opened it in New Orleans (1855) and then at **Wallack's** (1857). New Yorkers were captivated by Heron's 'elemental power', her 'animal vivacity', her uninhibited exploitation of a woman's sexual life, her life-like naturalness (even turning her back to the audience), and when Camille coughed her way to the grave, tears flowed throughout the house. After an initial run of 100 performances, she toured the play for the next 20 years.

Born in Ireland, she played Juliet to **Charlotte Cushman**'s Romeo (1852), made her New York debut as Lady Macbeth (1852), and appeared at **Drury Lane** (1854) before she discovered Camille.   RM

Herrmann family see Magic

Hettner, Hermann

(1821–82) German professor of literature. Hettner's most significant contribution to the theatre was his brief book *The Modern Drama* (1852), which, in validating the advances made by the bourgeois tragedy, prepared the way for the drama of **Ibsen** and the naturalists.   SW

Hewett, Dorothy

(1923–) Australian playwright. Initially a poet and novelist; her first play was the working class drama *This Old Man Comes Rolling Home* (1967). Her plays, mainly epic expressionistic works featuring music and poetry, depict complex women characters trapped in ageing, domesticity, and the stereotyped images of women, or evoke an idyllic pastoral world. They include *The Chapel Perilous* (1971), *Bon-Bons and Roses for Dolly* (1972), *The Tatty Hollow Story* (1974), *Pandora's Cross* (1978), *The Man from Muckinupin* (1979) and *The Fields of Heaven* (1982). She was made a Member of the Order of Australia in 1986.   MW

Heyward, Dorothy

(1890–1961) and **Du Bose** (1885–1940) American husband and wife playwriting team, in which he primarily supplied stories from his novels and she supplied dramatic craftsmanship. Although Du Bose wrote one other play and Dorothy had five others produced, their reputation rests on their folk dramas of Negro life – *Porgy* (1927) and *Mamba's Daughters* (1939) – both praised for their realistic depiction of the lives of Southern blacks. *Porgy*, the love story of a crippled black man and an erring woman, became an American legend, particularly after its conversion into a folk opera, *Porgy and Bess* (1935) by Du Bose and the **Gershwins**. The Heywards are credited with providing dramatic opportunities for black actors (**Ethel Waters** was the first black woman to star in a Broadway drama in *Mamba's Daughters*).   FB

Heywood, John

(1497–1580) English playwright. As a writer of interludes he is of importance in charting the development of the English theatre between the medieval period and the full fruition of the Elizabethan age. His plays *The Play of the Weather* (1533) and *The playe called the foure P.P.* etc. (*The Four P's*, c. 1543) are seen as his best. They, like the rest of his work, are jolly and simple. He was the son-in-law of **John Rastell**, and therefore the nephew-in-law of Sir Thomas More, which probably helped.   MB

Heywood, Thomas

(1573–1641) English playwright, actor, poet and pamphleteer, who was, at various times, actor and attached dramatist with the **Admiral's Men** and Worcester's Men and Queen Anne's Men. Heywood wrote industriously for money. Much of his work has been lost, and much that remains is ephemeral. Interest in his numerous mayoral pageants, for example, is likely to be confined to scholars. An early work, *The Four Prentices of London* (? 1592), is a far-fetched chivalric romance. It was presumably a revival of this uncommonly popular work which inspired the jolly parody of **Beaumont**'s *The Knight of the Burning Pestle* (1607). Heywood wrote plays of many kinds. His masterpiece is certainly the domestic tragedy, *A Woman Killed with Kindness* (1603), which rises to emotional heights without seeming to strive for them. Heywood's zest for the detail and range of Elizabethan life enriches the two-part chronicle of Elizabeth I's early years on the throne, *If You Know Not Me, You Know Nobody* (1605), and the eventful adventure-play, *The Fair Maid of the West* (Part I, c. 1610; Part II, c. 1630). The dramatizations of Greek mythology in *The Golden Age*, *The Silver Age*, *The Brazen Age* and *The Iron Age* (1611–13) are, by contrast, oddly perfunctory. Heywood wrote them for Queen Anne's Men at the rough-and-tumble **Red Bull Theatre**, and they are tuned to an audience that liked its poetry interrupted by spectacular action. By his own count, Heywood wrote, singly or in part, 220 plays, of which some 30 have survived. That he remained alert to topical issues is shown by a late play, written with **Richard Brome**, *The Late Lancashire Witches* (1634). He was well qualified by temperament and experience to write a defence of his profession, which he did in *An Apology for Actors* (1612). *The Fair Maid of the West* was the play chosen by the **RSC** to perform before Queen Elizabeth II when she officially opened the new Swan Theatre in Stratford-upon-Avon in 1986.   PT

Hibberd, Jack (John Charles) (1940–   ) Australian playwright. Studied medicine at Melbourne University where his first play, *White With Wire Wheels*, was staged in 1967: he later wrote for the Melbourne alternative theatres La Mama and the Pram Factory. His plays are characterized by caricature, black humour and flamboyant language: they include *Dimboola* (1969), *The Les Darcy Show* (1974) and *A Toast to Melba* (1976), both celebrations of famous Australians, the monodramas *A Stretch of the Imagination* (1972) and *Odyssey of a Prostitute* (1984), and a satirical opera, *Sin* (1978).   MW

Hicks, Edward Seymour (1871–1941) British actor–manager and dramatist, who toured America with the Kendals before producing *Under the Clock* in 1893, the first revue staged in London. A versatile performer starring in everything from music-hall to **Barrie**'s *Quality Street* (1904), he was a prolific author of light comedy such as *Sleeping Partners* (1917) or Christmas plays, one of which (*Bluebell in Fairyland*, 1901) was given regular performances until 1937, and collaborated with the novelist Ian Hay on satiric farce (*Good Luck*, 1923). In 1905 he built the Aldwych Theatre, then the Globe in 1907, both of which he opened with performances in his own plays. Awarded the Legion of Honour in 1931 for his promotion of French drama on the English stage, he took over Daly's Theatre in 1934 and was knighted in 1935.   CI

Hilar, Karel Hugo (1885–1935) Czech director. After early work as poet, critic, and literary editor, he began his directing career in 1910 at Prague's Municipal Theatre, where he soon established himself as a director of great force attracted to the expressionistic mode. By his dynamic personality and artistic vision, he eventually surpassed the achievements of Kvapil as head of drama at the National Theatre (1921–35). After the mid-1920s his work became less extravagant and more reflective. Among his principal achievements were *Hamlet* (1926), *Oedipus* (1932), and *Mourning Becomes Electra* (1934).   JMB

Hildesheimer, Wolfgang (1916–   ) German dramatist, novelist and painter. After a comedy based on *Turandot*, *The Dragon Throne* (produced by **Gründgens** in 1955), he became the leading German exponent of absurd theatre with plays such as *Behind Schedule* (1961) and *Nightpiece* (1963), before turning to historical subjects like *Mary Stuart* (1970).   CI

Hill, Aaron (1685–1750) English playwright, manager and critic. A schoolfriend of **Barton Booth** and **John Gay**, he toured Europe and the Middle East from 1700 to 1702. In 1709, as a complete novice, he was appointed manager of **Drury Lane** and wrote his first plays, *Elfrid* and *The Walking Statue* (a good farce). He closed the theatre in 1710, after disputes with the actors, and moved to manage the **Haymarket Theatre**. His libretto for *Rinaldo* (1711), Handel's first London opera, and the spectacular machinery in the production ensured Handel's success. After only one season he was forced to give up management. Of his next plays, *Fatal Vision* (1716) is significant for its use of **Bibiena**'s angular perspective for the first time in England and *Fatal Extravagance* (1721) for its attempt at domestic bourgeois tragedy, though neither are good plays. Occasionally involved in theatre management in the 1720s, Hill continued to make interesting, if failed, experiments in playwriting and production. *Athelwold* (1731), a revision of *Elfrid*, was an early attempt at historical authenticity in design, with Hill producing drawings of 'old Saxon dress'; *Zara* (1735) is a translation of **Voltaire**'s *Zaïre*, the first of Hill's four translations from Voltaire. Apart from his numerous inventions and speculations, Hill also founded one of the most important periodicals to be concerned with theatre, *The Prompter* (1734–6), and wrote a poem *The Art of Acting* (1746) encouraging the actor to develop the imagination to experience the emotions of the part and then reproduce the emotions in the physical appearance.   PH

Hill, Arthur (1922–   ) Canadian actor who has had a substantial career in America. His stage debut was in London as Finch in *Home of the Brave*. He played Cornelius Hackl in *The Matchmaker* at the **Haymarket** in 1954, later making his Broadway debut in the same role. In 1962 he starred as George in *Who's Afraid of Virginia Woolf?*, repeating the role in London in 1964. His George was referred to by one critic as 'a superbly modulated performance built on restraint'. He later appeared as Simon Harford in *More Stately Mansions* (1967). For *Who's Afraid of Virginia Woolf?* Hill received the Antoinette Perry (Tony) Award in 1963.   SMA

Hill, George Handel 'Yankee' (1809–49) American actor. In the 1830s and 40s Hill was the leading exponent of the 'Yankee' roles in **William Dunlap**'s *Trip to Niagara*, **Samuel Woodworth**'s *The Forest Rose*, and **J. S. Jones**'s *The Green Mountain Boy*. Audiences delighted in his plausible cunning, his great industry, and his pliant honesty. One critic said he was 'the funniest actor, and cleverest fellow in the Yankee signification of the word – in Christendom'. He appeared in London in 1836 and 1838. He first undertook Yankee impersonations with solo recitations of 'Jonathan's Visit to Buffalo', and 'The Yankee in Trouble; or, Zephaniah in the Pantry'.   RM

Hill, Jenny (1851–96) English serio-comedienne ('The Vital Spark') and the first female artist to achieve recognition as a music-hall star. She and her contemporary Bessie Bellwood broke with the gentility of the lady duettist to create racy and original solo character acts which paved the way for **Marie Lloyd**, **Vesta Tilley**, and **Nellie Wallace**. Though details of her early life and career are sparse, it is clear that she had a hard time. The daughter of a cab-minder at a rank in Marylebone High Street, she began work at an artificial flower factory until transferred, under articles which bound her for five years, to the Bradford Tavern, one of the early 'sing songs', where, not yet in her teens, she 'had to be up with the lark to clean the bars' and 'by noon . . . dressed and in the singing-room to provide harmony for the early-afternoon drinkers'. The long hours of virtual slavery while still a child may have contributed to the decline in her health and early death, but evidently did not break her indomitable spirit; and it is likely that the experience of the tough performance conditions of the tavern halls contributed to her vibrant stage-personality and gave depth to her later comic and melodramatic realizations of suffering and oppression.

Following a disastrous early marriage to an acrobat, who abandoned her on the birth of their daughter, she talked her way into an engagement at the London Pavilion (c. 1869) and from then on her brief career was made. She played all the big London halls, performed in New York, was a popular principal boy in pantomime, did burlesque, and even tried her hand at the legitimate theatre. Though not a success in the latter, even her failure moved the theatre manager **John Hollingshead** to describe her as 'one of the greatest female geniuses who ever appeared on the music hall platform'; specifically, he paid tribute to her 'sense of character – low life, of course – and her dramatic power of conjuring up solid pictures of men and women who never appear bodily on the stage'. The last remark probably refers to her emotive performance of narrative songs incorporating dialogue, but may also allude to the classic solo technique of inviting the audience to imagine the presence of other characters on stage.

Tiny in stature, with a generous smile, she had a powerful and flexible singing voice, danced well, and excelled in character songs both male and female, concentrating on representations of the poor and downtrodden: factory girls, slaveys, coster boys, and street vendors. Among many fine performances perhaps the most popular was as the eponymous hero of 'The Little Stowaway', a melodramatic song–sketch in which she played a small boy placed on board ship for Halifax, Nova Scotia, by his father who was unable to keep him. It is telling that no classic music-hall song is associated with her name; her fame came not from her material but from the power and generosity of her performance. AEG

Hillberg, Emil (1852–1929) Swedish actor, important for the breakthrough of **Strindberg**'s plays in the 1880s. Recognized as a leading practitioner of the realistic style, his impressive voice and effortless authority enabled him to excel in larger-than-life roles: Strindberg's Gustav Vasa, Bishop Brask and Gert Bookprinter and **Ibsen**'s Bishop Nicholas. As Brand (1883) he was reportedly sublime, but at the expense of the role's humanity. Other major roles were Shylock, Iago and Knox in **Bjørnson**'s *Mary Stuart in Scotland*. HL

Hingle, Pat (1924–) American actor. His professional debut was as Lachie in *Johnny Belinda* in 1950; he made his debut on Broadway as Koble in *End As a Man* in 1953. Among his Broadway hits were the brawling

and brusquely considerate Rubin Flood in *Dark at the Top of the Stairs* (1957) and the Job-like, anguished title role of *J. B.* (1958). Later starring roles included the failed brother in *The Price* (1968) and the bewildered Coach in *That Championship Season* (1975). Hingle has appeared in many feature films, as well as numerous television series and programmes. SMA

Hippodrama In A. H. Saxon's words, 'a play in which trained horses are considered as actors, with business, often leading actions of their own to perform'. Horses had occasionally been brought on stage before the 19th century – **Pepys** had seen some at the King's Playhouse in 1668 in a revival of **Shirley**'s *Hyde Park* and a live Pegasus was flown in **Corneille**'s *Andromède* in 1683. But the hippodrama first caught on at the turn of the 18th century, possibly due to cavalrymen, riding-masters and stable grooms made redundant after the Continental Wars and to the gradual closing of fairs. The innovation found a home in London at **Astley**'s Amphitheatre, 1803, the Royal Circus and the Olympic Pavilion, and in Paris at the **Cirque Olympique**. In Vienna, Christoph de Bach (1768–1834) presented equestrian pantomimes, such as *The Triumph of Diana* or *Marlborough's Heroic Death*, which constituted a synthesis of theatre and circus, and introduced a broader public to mythology and history.

Astley's *The Blood Red Knight* (1810) made £18,000, prompting **Covent Garden** to follow suit with **Colman**'s *Blue Beard* and 'Monk' Lewis's *Timour the Tartar* (1811), and **Drury Lane**, reluctantly, with *The Cataract of the Ganges*. The outstanding performer was **Andrew Ducrow**, but women took the title role in the frequently revived *Mazeppa or The Wild Horse of Tartary*, in which the young Prince, stripped to his fleshings, is strapped to a horse set loose on a treadmill and attacked by stuffed vultures and similar impedimenta. **Adah Isaacs Menken** made her notorious name in the part.

The hippodrama, fallen into disuse by the mid-century, enjoyed a revival of sorts at the Châtelet, Paris, with military spectaculars like *Marengo* (1863) and the immensely popular *Michel Strogoff* (1880). The invention of a graduated treadmill that could simulate races inspired one final burst of horse-play in America with *The Country Fair* by Charles Bernard (Union Square Theatre, New York, 1889) and Lew Wallace's *Ben Hur* (Broadway Theatre, New York, 1899). Thereafter, equine stardom passed to the movies where Trigger and Rex the Wonder Horse had fan clubs of their own. LS

See: A. H. Saxon, *Enter Foot and Horse. A History of the Hippodrama in England and France*, New Haven and London, 1968.

Hippodrome (London) Built as a circus in 1900, with a large water-tank for aquatic spectacles, it was reconstructed as a music-hall in 1909, where Tchaikovsky's *Swan Lake* was first danced in England by the Russian Ballet (1910). Its reputation was for revue and musical comedies, among them *Mr Cinders* (1929) and Ivor Novello's *Perchance to Dream* (1938), and from 1949 to 1951 it became the London equivalent of the **Folies-Bergère**. In 1958 it was reconstructed again, becoming a dinner-cabaret The Talk of the Town until it closed in 1982. CI

Hippodrome Theatre Sixth Ave between 43rd and 44th Sts, New York City [Architect: J. H. Morgan]. The Hippodrome was conceived and built by Frederic W. Thompson and Elmer S. Dundy, who had created Coney Island's Luna Amusement Park. Advertised as the world's largest theatre, its auditorium seated 5,000 and its stage was equipped with every device known to create magnificent spectacles. The costs of production and the maintenance of the house overwhelmed even the canniest of producers like the **Shuberts** and Charles Dillingham. In 1923, it was taken over by the Keith–Albee vaudeville chain, then leased for popular-priced opera, then as a sports arena. In 1935, Billy Rose presented his production of *Jumbo* at the theatre, the last notable event in its history. In 1939, it was torn down, but the site was not developed until 1952, when it was covered by a garage and office building. MCH

Hirsch, John (1930–) Hungarian-born director who went to Winnipeg, Canada, in 1947 as a war refugee. Active in local theatre, he was co-founder of the **Manitoba Theatre Centre**. As Artistic Director of the MTC from 1958–66 he established a continent-wide reputation for himself and the theatre with productions of *Mother Courage* (1964) with **Zoë Caldwell**, *Who's Afraid of Virginia Woolf?* (1964) with **Kate Reid**, and *Andorra* (1965) with William Hutt.

In 1965 he was invited to direct *The Cherry Orchard* at the **Stratford Festival**, which was followed by many other productions, particularly **James Reaney**'s *Colours in the Dark* (1967), a remarkable *Midsummer Night's Dream* (1968), and a highly successful swashbuckling version of *The Three Musketeers* (1968). During 1968–9 he was Associate Artistic Director (with **Jean Gascon**) of the Festival.

At the same time he was showing himself one of the few directors capable of mastering the stage of the Beaumont Theatre in New York's Lincoln Center. Notable productions were **Lorca**'s *Yerma* (1966), **Brecht**'s *Galileo* (1967) and **Sophocles**' *Antigone* (1971). He worked on and off Broadway and, further afield, his production of *The Seagull* (1970) opened the new home of Israel's **Habimah** National Theatre. His stage adaptation of the Yiddish parable *The Dybbuk* (1974) was immensely successful in Winnipeg, Toronto and Los Angeles.

From 1974–8 Hirsch served as Head of Television Drama for the Canadian Broadcasting Corporation before returning to the theatre. In 1981 he was named Artistic Director of the Stratford Festival.

Described by an American writer as 'one of the few major international artists this continent has produced', Hirsch is a controversial and tempestuous director, ruthless in his demands for the highest standards possible. But that intensity masks the irrepressible popular entertainer who has written delightful children's plays and staged many musical comedies and even night-club acts. JA

Hirsch, Judd (1935–) American actor who in over 20 years has established a major reputation as a versatile actor in film, television, and on stage, beginning with his Broadway debut in 1966, the Telephone Repairman in *Barefoot in the Park*. Unlike many of his successful contemporaries in film or television, Hirsch returns frequently to the New York stage, as the following partial list of credits illustrates: *The Hot l Baltimore* (1973) as Bill, the night manager; **Feiffer**'s *Knock, Knock* (1976); **Neil Simon**'s *Chapter Two* (1977); **Lanford Wilson**'s *Tally's Folly* (1979) as Matt Friedman, an immigrant Jewish accountant; **Circle Repertory Company**'s *The Seagull* (1983) as Trigorin; and Herb Gardner's *I'm Not Rappaport* (1985) at the **American Place Theatre**, which was later transferred to Broadway. According to one interviewer, Hirsch has a rugged 'street face, a face of interchangeable ethnicities and professions'. His career to date supports such a description. DBW

Hirschfeld, Kurt (1902–64) German director, whose major influence was in Switzerland where he staged the premiere of **Brecht**'s *Puntila* and helped to shape the drama of both **Dürrenmatt** and **Frisch**. CI

Hirshbein, Peretz (1880–1948) Yiddish playwright of great sensitivity. Raised on a farm in Lithuania, his first plays, written in Hebrew, deal with the extreme poverty he saw around him, but his later and important plays, written in Yiddish, are idyllic bucolic plays about simple country people. *The Haunted Inn* (1912), *A Forsaken Nook* (1913), *The Blacksmith's Daughter* (1914) and *Green Fields* (1916) were amongst the greatest successes, both artistically and financially, of the two leading American companies **Maurice Schwartz**'s **Yiddish Art Theatre** and **Jacob Ben-Ami**'s Jewish Art Theatre. His work exerted a strong innovative influence in elevating the standards of Yiddish theatre generally. AB

Hispanic theatre in the United States Before the impetus of **Chicano theatre** popularized in the mid-1960s by **Luis Valdéz** and the **Teatro Campesino**, the Spanish-speaking theatre had an extended history in the United States. The first recorded performance took place in a Spanish mission near Miami, Florida, in 1567, in which the Spanish settlers and soldiers utilized the feast day of St John the Baptist to present a religious play designed to catechize the local Indian population. In 1598 Juan de Oñate's colonizers en route to establish the regional capital at Santa Fe, New Mexico, performed religious plays near what is today El Paso, Texas. This Spanish-speaking theatre antedates by about 100 years the first performance of English-speaking theatre in the British-American colonies, estimated to be around 1700. The strong religious orientation of the Spanish conquest often manifested itself in theatrical performances such as the Magi play (*pastorelas*) still performed in Mexico and in communities throughout the South-west, in contrast with the guarded attitude of the Anglo-Saxon colonizers who generally avoided the theatre because they considered it to be a sinful enterprise.

From this early beginning to present times the Hispanic theatre in the United States is grouped as follows: the Chicano theatre, primarily in the West and South-west; the Cuban-American theatre, mostly in New York and Florida; and the New York theatre, which is strongly Puerto Rican. Caveats apply in all three cases since neither the ethnicity nor the geography is unilateral.

Chicano theatre The theatre of the Mexican-American population stretching across the United States has been known since 1965 as 'Chicano theatre'. This material can be found under a separate heading.

Cuban-American theatre As the turmoil in Cuban politics, especially in the latter part of the 19th century, brought to the USA a wave of immigrants seeking better political and economic conditions, the same travelling companies from Havana and Madrid that visited New York often stopped first in Tampa or Key West. By the 1920s the musical comedy, strong in the tradition of the Spanish **zarzuela** or the Cuban **bufo**, was the normal fare, although some productions included the 19th-century Spanish classics of psychological realism. The depression was particularly hard on Hispanic theatre in the USA, and the only company supported by the WPA **Federal Theatre Project** was the Tampa Company, a group that had been strong since the turn of the century. The Cuban Revolution of 1959 generated another migration as thousands of Cubans sought refuge in south Florida and other parts of the United States. By the late 1960s a new Spanish-speaking theatre, written by authors with a Cuban perspective, attempted to deal with a variety of issues. The principal concerns, at least in the early plays, were the sense of anguish and nostalgia over separation from the homeland. Language and communication problems were key to the psychological trauma of adjusting to an alien culture as were the generational differences between parents with a Cuban identification and the new 'American' generation too young to remember. Major authors, writing in exile, included Matías Montes Huidobro (b. 1931), José Sánchez-Boudy (b. 1928), Julio Matas (b. 1931) and Celedonio González (b. 1923). Most continued to write in Spanish, although some attempted English, especially in those cases where the subject matter had broad appeal. In New York, Omar Torres (b. 1945), Iván Acosta (?) and Dolores Prida (b. 1943) are younger writers dealing with current topical issues. Theatre groups such as La Comedia (The Comedy), Las Máscaras (The Masks) and Teatro Avante were at the centre of the Cuban-American theatre movement in Miami. Acculturation of the Cuban 'exile' diffused to a large extent the early impact of the Cuban-American theatre as an artistic movement.

New York theatre New York is clearly the neurological centre of theatre in the USA, and at times has played a major role in fomenting Hispanic theatre. During the early part of the 20th century, travelling companies from Spain and Cuba brought Spanish melodrama, zarzuelas, bufos and musical variety shows to entertain the predominantly peninsular and Cuban population. From the 1920s to the Second World War, the New York Hispanic stage was more important than San Antonio and Tampa, and second only to Los Angeles. Long Island developed one of the first centres of Hispanic movie production, feeding in large part on the resident Hispanic theatre artists. The large immigrations of Spanish-speakers from Spain (because of the Civil War) and also from Puerto Rico increased the level of theatrical demand and in the late 60s generated the descriptive term 'Nuyorican' or 'New Rican' theatre.

The sporadic activity of the 1950s and 60s later coalesced into different phenomena. Several established companies offered both classical and experimental plays in Spanish and English. Gilberto Zaldívar and René Buch's work with the Spanish Repertory Theatre Company ranged from the *Celestina* to recent Puerto Rican, Mexican and Argentine plays. Miriam Colón's Puerto Rican Company, originally an outdoor travelling company, later operated from a central location while sub-groups organized theatre in the barrios and offered seminars on acting and direction. The Teatro 4, so-named for its original location on 4th Street on the Lower East Side, was geared towards popular, radical theatre; its Argentine director Oscar Ciccone collaborated with **Joseph Papp** in sponsoring the Festival of Latin American Popular Theatre, held five times in New York between 1976 and 1985. Other groups, such as INTAR on West 42nd Street and Nuestro Teatro, responded on the interests of their own publics.

In addition to the best plays Spain and Latin America had to offer, the groups presented original works by local playwrights, such as Eduardo Gallardo's *Simpson Street* or Dolores Prida's *Beautiful señoritas*. Miguel Piñero's *Short Eyes* was developed in a workshop of The Family, directed by Marvin Felix Camillo, and later produced Off-Broadway by Joseph Papp. Given the heterogeneous public, these plays tended to be written in English with sufficient Spanish to capture the flavour and mood. Themes included problems of discrimination, economics, drugs, sex, crime in the streets and other issues that constituted the reality of this large sub-culture in New York. The objectives were as varied as the groups themselves, ranging from the most plastic, artistic experiences to an aggressive theatre dedicated to social change.   GW

See: N. Kanellos (ed.), *Hispanic Theatre in the United States*, Houston, 1984; *idem*, *Mexican American Theatre: Then and Now*, Houston, 1983.

History plays Because critics sensed a distinction between the plays **Shakespeare** wrote on subjects drawn from English history and, for example, those he wrote on subjects drawn from Roman history, they came gradually to accept the invented term, 'history play'. Despite its specious appropriateness, the description is not particularly useful except as a convenient way of dividing Shakespeare's plays into sub-groups, as has also been tried with 'problem plays', 'Roman plays', 'last plays' etc. The difference between the style of the Roman plays and that of the history plays owes more to the distinctive styles of Shakespeare's sources, Thomas North's translation of Plutarch for the Roman stories and Holinshed's *Chronicles* for the English, than to decisive authorial strategy. Nor could it be reputably maintained that the *Henry VI* trilogy has much in common with the great tetralogy comprising *Richard II*, the two parts of *Henry IV* and *Henry V*, whilst the untidy *King John* and the brilliantly melodramatic *Richard III* demand independent assessment. The Elizabethans would not have understood the modern distinction between history and legend, seeing both in terms of story. There is, however, some justice in the view that Shakespeare's history plays have, as a counterpoint to the story of English kings, the story of the country over which they ruled, and that they are further strengthened by the conviction, shared by playwright and original audience, that the story is still in progress. Even so refined, a term that may exclude **Tennyson**'s *Queen Mary* (1875), *Harold* (1876) and *Becket* (1884) but not plays as various as **John Bale**'s *Kynge Johan* (1538), **Marlowe**'s *Edward II* (c. 1592) and **John Arden**'s *Left-Handed Liberty* (1965) is of limited use. PT

Hjortsberg, Lars (1772–1843) Popular Swedish comic actor, who trained with Monvel's French troupe, brought to Sweden by Gustav III, and from 1788 to 1834 became a leading member of **Dramaten**. Admired for his powers of mimicry, improvisation and attention to detail, he specialized in playing eccentrics, such as the pendantic chatterbox Captain Puff, the daydreaming tailor in *The Imagined Prince* and Orgon in **Molière**'s *Tartuffe*. Short and somewhat plump, Hjortsberg was unsuited to tragedy, but succeeded in serious and sentimental drama, such as the name part in **Richard Cumberland**'s *The Jew*. HL

Hochhuth, Rolf (1931–) German dramatist, resident in Switzerland. More than any other single work, his first play *The Representative* (1963 – staged in New York as *The Deputy*, 1964) focused international attention on post-war German drama with 73 productions in 27 countries. Accusing Pope Pius XII of complicity in the extermination of the Jews, its factual subject and historical characters were explosively controversial, and led to its classification as documentary theatre. However, despite its mammoth length, due to the substantiating evidence incorporated both in stage directions and dialogue, its form is that of verse tragedy in the tradition of **Schiller**. The protagonist, an amalgam of two Catholic priests who died in the concentration camps, and the antagonist, modelled on Mengele, are presented as sacrificial Christ-figure and the devil. In light of this mythologizing treatment, the true focus of the play is the assertion of individual responsibility, even in the depersonalization of mass murder; a theme made more explicit in *Soldiers* (1967). This had an explicit political aim – to persuade public opinion in the signatories to the Geneva convention to outlaw air attacks on civilian targets – and it presents the fire-bombing of Dresden as a war crime equal to the Jewish Holocaust. Here the traditional nature of Hoch-huth's approach was explicit in his use of a Morality Play prologue to frame the quasi-documentary action. Again the figures are both historical and presented as symbols, with Bishop Bell as the moral conscience and Churchill's scientific adviser Cherwell as 'the Great Cremator', but the indictment of Churchill for the murder of Sikorski is less relevant to the main argument than the accusation levelled at the Pope in his first work. In England the play's production at the **National Theatre** was initially banned (as well as in Communist countries, where performance is still forbidden), and the controversy contributed to the abolition of stage censorship in 1968. Lacking the guiding inspiration of **Piscator**, who died in 1966, Hochhuth's subsequent attempts to deal with topical issues such as the anti-CIA play *Guerrillas* (1970) or *Lysistrata and NATO* are marred by utopian fantasy. His later work is more conventionally imaginary, though it continues to attack areas of social concern – the pharmaceutical industry and the legal system: *Female Doctors*, 1982; *Lawyers*, 1980 – and occasionally deals with real figures,

as in *Death of a Hunter* (1982), a monodrama on Ernest Hemingway's final hours. More highly regarded internationally than in Germany, his latest play *Judith* was performed at the **Citizens' Theatre** in Glasgow. CI

Hochwälder, Fritz (1911–) Austrian dramatist with Israeli citizenship, resident in Switzerland since 1938, and the first playwright to deal with the Nazi extermination of the Jews in *Esther* (1940), presenting it through the Old Testament parallel of their persecution under Haman in Persia. Hochwälder's characteristic plays are conventional dramas of ideas focusing on general moral themes in historical examples. As in *The Public Prosecutor* (1947), where Fouquier-Tinville is forced to recognize that his ideals of justice have made him 'the enemy of the people' in the French Revolution, analogies to contemporary political situations are left unstated – although *The Command* (1968) reuses this plot in a post-war Austrian context. His most successful play *The Strong Are Lonely* (*Das heilige Experiment*, 1947) uses the destruction of the autonomous Jesuit state in 18th-century Paraguay as a highly theatrical focus for discussing paradoxes about the relationship between spiritual and religious utopias or the right of pacifism to self-defence. But in form it is the modern equivalent of the 19th-century well-made play, and the moral questions are left unresolved. The traditional sources of his drama have led him to propose a revival of the **Volksstück** (Folk Play) on the model of **Raimund** and **Nestroy**, and to experiment with the Mystery Play form in *Thursday* (1959). His most recent play *The Princess of Chimay* was performed in 1981. CI

Hodgkinson (Meadowcroft), John (1767–1805) British-born actor and manager who after some provincial experience accepted an offer in 1792 from **John Henry** to join the American Company and spent the rest of his career in the USA. Although his personal reputation has been much maligned, his private life after his arrival in America seems to have been without blemish. He never became a star, but was a tall, handsome man with an exceptional voice and memory who excelled in high and low comedy, playing during his 24-year career at least 379 roles. From 1794 until 1798 he was joint manager of the **John Street Theatre**. Later he acted in all the principal cities of the Atlantic seaboard until his death from yellow fever. DBW

Hoffman, Dustin (1937–) American film and stage actor. Hoffman worked with the Theatre Company of Boston before his 1965 New York debut as Immanuel in *Harry, Noon, and Night*. The next year he played Zoditch in *The Journey to the Fifth House*. Also in 1966 he appeared in *Eh?*, winning several awards, as he did in 1968 in the title role of *Jimmy Shine*. After an extraordinarily successful stint in films, he starred in a Broadway revival of *Death of a Salesman* (1984) and was acclaimed as a performer of genius and demonic intensity. SMA

Hoffmann, Ernst Theodor Amadeus (1776–1822) German poet, novelist, composer, and stage director. Known primarily as a writer of romantic short stories and novels, Hoffmann nevertheless had important theatre experience. From 1808 to 1813, he directed the theatre at Bamberg where, in cooperation with Franz von Holbein (1779–1855), he attempted to create a theatre in which all elements, the actor, the design, and the lighting contributed toward a vision of life beyond the appearance of everyday reality. While at Bamberg, Hoffmann was among the first German directors to introduce the works of **Calderón** to the stage. After his return to Berlin in 1814, where he joined the Prussian Civil Service, Hoffmann became a close drinking companion of **Ludwig Devrient**. His poetic dialogue, *Strange Sorrows of a Theatre Director* (1818), apart from being an invaluable source for the acting of Devrient, also contains some of the liveliest accounts of the theatre of the time. Hoffmann was also a talented opera composer, his most famous work in this regard being the fairy-opera, *Undine* (1814).   SW

Hofmannsthal, Hugo von (1874–1929) Austrian poet, playwright, and essayist. In the 1890s, as the youngest member of the Jung Wien (Young Vienna) circle, Hofmannsthal's writings typified fin-de-siècle neoromanticism and decadence. Among several plays he wrote at this time, *Death and the Fool* (1893) is notable for its elaborate verse and poetic atmosphere. As he matured, Hofmannsthal developed a profound awareness of the importance of traditional European culture and, throughout his career, worked to preserve its values in a period of radical, often violent change. Hence he looked to the theatre of the past to provide him with both the structure and substance of his work. *Elektra* (1906) and his two Oedipus plays (1906 and 1907), while reflecting modern interest in psyche, clearly derive from classical sources. In plays Hofmannsthal wrote for the Salzburg Festival, *Everyman* (1911) and *The Salzburg Great Theatre of the World* (1922), he borrowed from medieval and Spanish baroque theatre. In *The Tower* (1925), his great festival play, the central situation is taken from **Calderón**'s *Life is A Dream*, though thematically it relates to the destruction caused in Europe by the First World War. Hofmannsthal also adapted **Otway**'s *Venice Preserv'd* (1905) and in his late comedy *The Difficult Man* (1921) he showed the influence of **Congreve**. He is possibly best remembered today for his librettos for operas by Richard Strauss. In addition to *Elektra*, these included *Der Rosenkavalier* (1911), *Ariadne auf Naxos* (1912), *The Woman Without a Shadow* (1919), *The Egyptian Helen* (1928), and *Arabella* (1931).   SW

Holberg, Ludvig (1684–1754) Norwegian-born playwright, satirist, historian and philosopher, who spent most of his life in Copenhagen, where he held several university positions. Although his major impact on Danish letters has been in the theatre, his playwriting occupied only short periods of his life. When Copenhagen acquired its first professional Danish-speaking theatre (in the street called Lille Grønnegade) in 1722, Holberg provided 27 comedies before it closed in 1728, and then six further plays for its successor, the new Danish Playhouse that opened on Kongens Nytorv in 1748. Often referred to as 'the **Molière** of the North', Holberg certainly owes much to the French playwright, but also directly to **Plautus**, **Ben Jonson** and **commedia dell'arte**. Holberg's most enduring comedies are those, such as *Jeppe of the Hill*, *Erasmus Montanus*, *The Political Tinker* and *The Fussy Man*, which focus on the irrationality of human

behaviour. In Denmark the many plays that are built around *commedia*-like intrigues have been almost as popular, while those that satirize contemporary literary and social excesses have had a limited theatrical life. The traditional scholarly view of Holberg's comedies is that they embody, at least by implication, an affirmative view of human rationality typical of the Enlightenment. This has recently been challenged by arguments that Holberg is a complex ironist, presenting a chaotic, amoral world, in which reason is threatened by irrational and antisocial forces.   HL

Holbrook, Hal (Harold Rowe Holbrook) (1925–) American actor and writer. He made his debut with a Cleveland stock company in 1942 and spent four seasons in stock. With his first wife he toured for six seasons, presenting famous scenes from the classics, from which developed his immensely successful one-man show, *Mark Twain Tonight!* He first appeared as Twain in New York in 1955 and has revived the show periodically to immense critical and popular acclaim.

Holbrook spent the 1964 season with the Lincoln Center Repertory, alternating Quentin with **Jason Robards, Jr**, and playing Marco Polo in *Marco Millions*.   SMA

Holcroft, Thomas (1745–1809) English playwright, the self-taught son of a shoemaker. Holcroft's life was a catalogue of disasters, sufficient to destroy a lesser man. After working successively as a pedlar, stable-boy, shoemaker and schoolteacher, he entered the theatrical profession in 1770 and was, for ten years, a strolling player. During this period of poverty, his first wife left him and his second died in childbirth, his first work, a comic opera called *The Crisis* (1778), was produced at **Drury Lane** and he published a novel based on his own theatrical experience, *Alwyn* (1780). The success of his comedy *Duplicity* (1781), at **Covent Garden** encouraged Holcroft to commit himself to writing. Having taught himself French, as well as German and Italian, he went to Paris in search of plots and was lucky enough to witness an early performance of **Beaumarchais**'s *The Marriage of Figaro*. Within two months, Holcroft's version, *The Follies of a Day* (1784), was staged at Covent Garden. It was followed by further adaptations, *Seduction* (1787) from Laclos's notorious novel *Les Liaisons Dangereuses*, *The German Hotel* (1790) from the German of **Johann Christian Brandes** and *The School for Arrogance* (1791) from *Le Glorieux* by **Philippe Destouches**. The source of Holcroft's best known play, *The Road to Ruin* (1792), is not known. A moral comedy, with excellent character roles, it held the stage for a century and was revived in London in 1937. Still dogged by tragedy, Holcroft witnessed the suicide of his only son in 1789 and the death of his third wife in 1790, and was himself partially paralysed by a stroke in 1792. As a friend of William Godwin and defender of Thomas Paine (*The Rights of Man* was published in 1791–2), Holcroft was one of the 12 indicted for High Treason in 1794, and although all were acquitted, Holcroft found his access to the theatre restricted for the rest of his life. Forced to avoid contentious topics, he mixed insipid comedies with the Gothic melodramas now in vogue in Paris. His first in this kind was *Deaf and Dumb* (1801), but the first to be advertised as a melodrama, thereby importing the word into the English theatre, was *A Tale of Mystery* (1802), hurriedly adapted from **Pixérécourt**'s *Coelina*. It is a shoddy monument to an extraordinarily vigorous man. Holcroft's *Memoirs* (1816), posthumously and grudgingly completed by **William Hazlitt**, offer better evidence of his worth. PT

Holland, George (1791–1870) British-born actor called a 'comedian of peculiar and irrepressible drollery'. After seven years on the London stage, he came to the United States in 1827, making his debut at the **Bowery Theatre** in *A Day After the Fair*. For 16 years he toured, gaining immense popularity, especially in the south, where he also entered for a time into management with **Noah Ludlow** and also **Sol Smith**. In New Orleans, where he remained from 1835 until 1843, he worked with **James H. Caldwell**. For the next six years he played in comedies and burlesques at **Mitchell's Olympic**. Beginning in 1855, and for a total of 14 years, he was low comedian with **Wallack**'s company, leaving in 1869 to join **Daly**. Of Holland's six children, four became actors, most notably Edmund Milton and Joseph Jefferson. DBW

Holland Festival In June 1947 in Amsterdam the first Holland Festival was held, as a result of plans made under German occupation during the Second World War to organize an annual manifestation of the arts. The Holland Festival is a member of the European Association of Music Festivals. However, in the course of time it has grown into a festival at which other artistic forms are presented as well, such as dance, plastic arts, and drama and theatre. The aim is to investigate new artistic values. Hence, the Holland Festival features experimental and controversial performances, and has done so particularly in recent years. Companies that specialize in drama, theatrical arts in general, music and dance, as well as individual artists both from The Netherlands and abroad are invited on the philosophy that The Netherlands, being a small country, should direct its attention to international developments. The Holland Festival, which is regarded as a cultural highlight, is held in June, a period in which the previous season has just ended, and the new one has not yet begun.

Significant performances have been **Botho Strauss**'s *Gross und Klein* by Schaubühne am Hallischen Ufer, Berlin (1980); MacDonald's *Chinchilla* by **Glasgow Citizens' Theatre** (1981); **Shakespeare**-trilogy, by La Compagnia del Collettivo/Teatro Due, Parma (1982); *Rosas danst Rosas* by Anne Terese de Keersmaeker (1983); *De Macht der Theaterlijke Dwaasheden* (*The Power of Theatrical Follies*) by Jan Fabre (1984); *Fairground '84* by **Mickery-theater** (1984); *King Lear* by **Dramaten**, Stockholm (1985) and *Sihanouk* by **Théâtre du Soleil**, Paris (1986).

The Holland Festival is subsidized by both the government and local authorities; further financial support is supplied by sponsorship.

The larger part of the Holland Festival takes place in Amsterdam. Now that television and radio show a growing interest in the festival, nationwide distribution takes place, both broadcast live and recorded in advance. MG HS

Hollingshead, John (1827–1904) English theatre manager and journalist who was, for a while, a leading contributor to **Dickens**'s *Household Words* and dramatic critic of the *Daily News*. Fascinated by the theatre, Hollingshead was also a radical thinker, committed to improving the life of London's workers. As stage manager of the Alhambra, he sought to broaden its audience and to entertain it. If girls were the answer, girls he would employ. He was instrumental in introducing the cancan to England, and it was in the same spirit of daring that he opened his own theatre, the **Gaiety**, in 1868. Almost accidentally, the Gaiety became the home of a new style of burlesque, revolving round the talents of a famous Quartette, **Nellie Farren**, **Edward Terry**, **Kate Vaughan**, and **Edward Royce**. But it was also the first theatre in London to stage a play by the shocking **Ibsen – William Archer**'s translation of *Quicksands: or The Pillars of Society* (1880). Illness and financial troubles forced Hollingshead to sell out to **George Edwardes** in 1886, but his love for his old theatre is vividly recorded in the books he wrote in his retirement, *Gaiety Chronicles* (1898) and *Good Old Gaiety* (1903). PT

Hollmann, Hans (1933–) Austrian director, whose productions have tended towards sensationalism. He has made a reputation for adapting the classics to reflect contemporary political issues, particularly **Shakespeare**, and his influential productions of **Horváth** between 1967 and 1971 helped to inspire the contemporary **Volksstück** (Folk Play). CI

Holm, Celeste (1919–) American film, stage, and television actress, who professional debut was in *The Night of January 16* in a Deer Lake, Pennsylvania, summer theatre in 1936. Her first New York appearance was as Lady Mary in *Gloriana* in 1938. She created Ado Annie in *Oklahoma!* in 1943. Her first film was *Three Little Girls in Blue*, 1946. Her awards include an Oscar for *Gentlemen's Agreement*, 1947, and the Sarah Siddons Award for her performance in the national touring company of *Mame*, 1969. In 1979 she was knighted by King Olav of Norway. SMA

Holtei, Karl von (1798–1880) German actor and dramatist. Holtei's comedies were extremely popular, especially his comedies *The Viennese in Berlin* (1824) and *The Berliners in Vienna* (1825). Holtei had less success as an actor, but he held several important administrative positions in various German theatres. His autobiography, *Forty Years* (1843–50), provides an especially lively account of the theatre of his time. SW

Holz, Arno (1863–1929) German poet and playwright. Holz is best known for his collaboration with Johannes Schlaf (1862–1941) on the naturalist play *The Selicke Family* (1892). Initially identified with naturalism, his later plays were poetic. SW

Home, John (1722–1808) Scottish playwright. Born near Edinburgh, Home was educated at Edinburgh University and was ordained a minister in the Church of Scotland in 1745. In 1746 he took up a living and began a friendship with David Hume, the philosopher. His first play, *Agis*, was rejected by **Garrick** in 1749 as was his second, *Douglas*. But his friends mounted the latter at the Canongate Theatre in Edinburgh in 1756. It was an extraordinary and lasting success, making Home the first major Scots playwright: as someone in the audience said, 'Whaur's yer Wullie Shakespeare noo?' *Douglas* is perhaps the first romantic tragedy, a non-didactic exploration of the love of mother for long-lost son. The church was outraged at a minister writing plays and had it denounced from pulpits. There was a prolonged pamphlet war for and against the play. Brought to **Covent Garden** by **Rich** it was equally successful. As a result Home gave up the ministry and became secretary to the Prime Minister, Lord Bute. *Agis* was mounted at **Drury Lane** by Garrick in 1758 but neither it nor Home's four subsequent plays were successful. They all aim at a romantic pathos intensified usually by remote British settings. In 1778 Home fell from a horse with consequent brain damage. He moved to Edinburgh till his death. PH

Home, William Douglas (1912–) British dramatist, whose upper-middle-class comedies and dramas have made him a natural successor to **Frederick Lonsdale** in the post-war West End theatre. He began his career as an actor, which helps to explain why his plays contain not only amusing dialogue but star parts. He is an actor's playwright, whose first political comedy successes, *The Chiltern Hundreds* (1947) and *The Manor of Northstead* (1954), were vehicles for the eccentric talents of A. E. Matthews. **Sybil Thorndike** starred in *The Reluctant Peer* (1964), Alastair Sim in *The Jockey Club Stakes* (1970), **Ralph Richardson** and **Peggy Ashcroft** in *Lloyd George Knew My Father* (1972), Celia Johnson in *The Dame of Sark* (1974) and **Rex Harrison** in the New York version of *The Kingfisher*, a part played by Ralph Richardson in London. His skill came in calculating exactly what the stars of his generation could achieve, but it was supported by a sound playwriting technique whose main weakness lay in a facile sentimentality. *Now Barabbas . . .* (1947), however, showed his ability with a serious theme about prison life, while *The Secretary Bird* (1968) remains a thoughtful *ménage-à-trois* comedy. JE

Honduras During the early years only the most sporadic evidence indicates some *pastorelas* written and performed by Fray José Trinidad Reyes (1797–1855) who arrived from Nicaragua and founded the University of Honduras. During the stormy years between independence from Spain and the creation of the five separate Central American republics, the young Fransisco Morazán governed from 1829 to 1838 over the united provinces in the classic struggle between conservatives and liberals, between church and state. Morazán was the subject of a successful 1852 play by the Salvadoran Francisco Díaz, as well as two patriotic plays by the Honduran Jorge Fidel Durón (b. 1902), one-time rector of the National University. J. M. Tobías Rosas also wrote children's theatre during these years. The Casa de la Cultura (Cultural Institute) was inaugurated in 1916 with another play on the Morazán period, *Los conspiradores* (*The Conspirators*), but no theatrical tradition was yet established.

After 1950 the theatre activity belonged primarily to some active experimental groups that tried to establish a new consciousness of theatre in Honduras. Many, such as Teatro Ensayo (Rehearsal Theatre), Talía and Arlequín, soon ceased functioning; others had a longer life. The Grupo Dramático Tegucigalpa (Tegucigalpa Drama Group) was established in 1956. The émigré Andrés Morris created TESP (Teatro de la Escuela Superior del Profesorado/Faculty High School Theatre) which merged with the newly-formed Teatro Nacional de Honduras (National Honduran Theatre) in 1965. Francisco Salvador, who studied acting in Mexico, became director, created an active programme for the National Theatre, by offering classes in acting, diction and history and by mounting four plays each year. Various groups brought for the first time to Honduran state productions of **Shakespeare**, **García Lorca**, **Sartre**, **Camus** and other theatre classics.

Honduras has not yet produced internationally known playwrights. Medardo Mejía's *Cinchonero* and Francisco Salvador's *El sueño de Matías Carpio* (*The Dream of Matías Carpio*) have limited merit. Andrés Morris (born in Spain in 1928, arrived in Honduras in 1961) is the author of a so-called 'tetralogy of underdevelopment': *La ascensión del busito* (*The Raising of the Little Bus*), *El Guarizama* (1966), *Oficio de hombres* (*Men's Job*, 1967) and *La miel del abejorro* (*Bumblebee Honey*, 1968) all point out too clearly the violence, corruption, and single industry operations characteristic of an underdeveloped nation. Morris recently left Honduras but he was recognized as an outstanding playwright for *Oficio de hombres* (*Men's Job*) and *La tormenta* (*The Storm*); the latter won the National Prize for Literature in 1955.

Recent activity includes a theatre movement with popular appeal. The Comunidad Hondureña de Teatristas (Honduran Theatrical Community) sponsored its first national congress in 1982 for the purpose of creating solidarity among the various groups with specific revolutionary objectives. The Teatro Taller Tegucigalpa (Tegucigalpa Workshop Theatre) and Teatro La Fragua (Forge Theatre), founded in Progreso in 1979, work closely with their public to develop folkloric and popular theatre. At the national theatre congress in July of 1982, a dialogue among five active Honduran theatre participants (Saúl Toro, Rafael Murillo Selva, Emmanuel Jaen, Hermes Zelaya and Francisco Salvador) attested to the deplorable lack of organization and cohesion. The national theatre festival in November in 1982, the first in 14 years, stimulated new levels of activity, and was followed in November 1983 by the third such festival. Awards were given in 1983 by the Camino Real Theatre Foundation to, among others, dramatist Francisco Salvador and critic Conrado Enríquez for their efforts to promote theatre. Nevertheless, the theatre in Honduras continues to operate on a precarious level at best with little or no institutional or governmental support. GW

See: A. Caballero and F. Salvador, *Teatro en Honduras*, 2 vols., Tegucigalpa, 1977; M. Fernández, *El Teatro en Honduras*, Nicaragua, 1976.

Hong Kong Hong Kong is a British colony on the south coast of China. It has a population of 5.6 million people, 98 per cent of whom are Chinese. Most of them come from the neighbouring Guangdong province in China and speak the Cantonese dialect. After the Communist takeover of mainland China in 1949, many refugees came to Hong Kong. These mainlanders plus the British, Americans, Europeans, Australians, Indians, Japanese, and Portuguese have made Hong Kong a true melting pot of Eastern and Western cultures. Drama and theatre in Hong Kong also reflect this mixture of two cultures.

The traditional theatre of Hong Kong is basically the Cantonese Opera – a regional drama of South China with a basic form of stage presentation quite similar to the more renowned and refined Peking Opera. The great difference is the use of the Cantonese dialect, which means disparities in the style of singing and rhythmic emphasis. Just as the Cantonese is a regional dialect, so is the theatre there related to but different from its parent form. The Cantonese Opera, as a pure dramatic form in the Guangdong region, is inferior to the Peking Opera in artistic quality and technical sophistication. The Hong Kong version of the Cantonese Opera is considerably worse, especially as it reflects the influences of novelties introduced in performances before the 1960s which permeated the art and removed it considerably from its original, characteristically Chinese atmosphere. Music for the Hong Kong version of the Cantonese Opera is often called 'yellow music', meaning that it is mock classical and bears the same relationship to the art that the 'yellow press' has to respectable journalism. It does pay a measure of homage to the classics, but it injects a note of sentimentality and softness into each aria, and often the tunes are even danceable in a Westernized ballroom way. Western instruments have become part of the traditional theatre orchestra. Costumes are vulgarized, with sparkling sequins to keep the show glittering. Realistic settings, alien to the classical Chinese theatre, are often used, showing everything from castle walls to gardens, temples, and palaces. Stylized gestures and movement patterns are still employed though often sloppily rendered. Such debasement of the traditional art has given the Cantonese theatre of Hong Kong a bad reputation.

Living side-by-side with the Cantonese Opera is the Western-style modern Chinese drama, called **Huaju** or 'spoken drama'. Since Hong Kong, in addition to its Chinese orientation, is a British colony in which English is an accepted and quite popular language, the Western-style drama in Hong Kong has been developing in two directions: one is English-language productions mounted by Caucasian actors for the foreign expatriates, and the other is Chinese-language productions staged by local theatre groups and by visiting mainland companies for the vast majority of the Hong Kong populace. The first known Western-style drama performance was staged in 1844 by some British soldiers and their families stationed in Hong Kong. In 1911, two local amateur theatre groups were formed, staging Chinese plays such as *Zhuang Zi Testing His Wife* and *Flesh for the Debt of Gold* (possibly an adaptation of *The Merchant of Venice*). It is important to note that these productions of 'spoken dramas' were mounted only four years after 1907 – the year marking the beginning of the Chinese modern drama movement, when *La Dame aux Camélias* and **Uncle Tom's Cabin** were staged by some Chinese students in Tokyo belonging to an amateur theatre organization called the Spring Willow Society. Later on, members of the Spring Willow Society went back to Shanghai and

staged more of such modern Chinese 'spoken dramas'. These plays were called 'enlightened dramas' or 'civilized drama' because they followed the more 'civilized' traditions of Western-style drama and dealt with more 'enlightened' social themes. The earliest 'enlightened drama' performed in Hong Kong was believed to be *Leung Tin-lai* which was premiered in 1928.

During the Sino-Japanese War between 1937 and 1945, patriotic Hong Kong youths did a lot to popularize the spoken drama. Over 200 amateur groups were formed at one time or another to stage over 300 productions for patriotic causes. A great number of these plays were original one-acts with anti-Japanese themes. Performances were done in school gyms or classrooms, and sometimes at street corners or sports fields following a sporting event. The most popular play of that period was *Lay Down Your Whip*, an agit-prop piece about the suffering of Chinese people during the Japanese invasions of the mainland. In 1942 Hong Kong was occupied by the Japanese. Before the arrival of Japanese soldiers, many theatre workers in Hong Kong burnt their mimeographed scripts to avoid later persecution. Most of the original plays written in this period were therefore lost. After the war the Hong Kong modern drama scene became alive again, with many productions of standard works such as *Thunderstorm*, *Family*, and *Sunrise*, by the noted Chinese playwright **Cao Yu** (b. 1919), which had become extremely popular on the mainland. Three professional theatre companies from the mainland also took residence in Hong Kong after the war to stage large-scale productions. *Sorrows of the Noble Family*, *The Story of Ah-Q*, *The Wedding March*, *Girls Apartment*, *Hell on Earth* (adapted from **Gorky**'s *The Lower Depths*), and *The Imperial Inspector* (adapted from **Gogol**'s *The Inspector General*) were the most often staged plays of that period.

In the 1950s and 1960s, local dramatists wrote some works of considerable maturity and sophistication. Three deserve mention. Hu Chun-bin wrote *Li Po the Poet* and *Dream of the Red Chamber* (adapted from the famous Chinese novel of the same title) and was perhaps the most respected theatre worker in Hong Kong. S. I. Hsiung was noted for his adaptation of classical Chinese plays into spoken dramas, such as *Lady Precious Stream* and *The West Chamber*. The English version of the former had been a London and Broadway hit in the 1930s, which had made S. I. Hsiung a celebrity in the English-speaking world. Yao Hsin-nung, trained at Yale Drama School, was the youngest among the three. Besides being a playwright and stage director, he was also a film producer and a script-writer in both Shanghai and Hong Kong in the 1940s and 1950s. His play *The Poorman's Alley* was a social drama in the realistic vein which became a hit on the mainland and in Hong Kong during the post-war era.

The contemporary situation The most important development of the contemporary Hong Kong theatre scene is perhaps the establishment of its first permanent, professional repertory theatre company for the spoken drama – the Hong Kong Repertory Theatre. Founded in 1977 by the Urban Council, its aim is to promote and raise the standard of Cantonese-language drama in Hong Kong through professional production, management, and training. The Repertory Theatre employs full-time actors and staff members and does high quality works. It produces six to seven major productions and two to four minor productions a year, totaling around 160 performances. It has an extensive touring programme to local schools and community centres. Every summer it sponsors a Drama Festival, inviting 60 to 70 local theatre groups to compete. Over half of these entries present original plays. The Repertory Theatre aims to offer a balanced programme of Chinese and Western plays. In recent years the staging of original plays by local playwrights on Hong Kong themes has also been successfully attempted. All productions are done in the Cantonese dialect, the only exception being the 1984 production of **Oscar Wilde**'s *The Importance of Being Earnest* which was done in both the Cantonese and the Mandarin dialect (the national dialect of China today) playing in nightly rotation. Western plays in translation comprise 50 per cent of the Repertory Theatre's offerings, including period classics, modern classics, current West End and Broadway hits, and occasional musicals. Most of the Repertory Theatre's performances are given in the City Hall Theatre. Plans are being drawn to make use of the two new theatres in the Hong Kong Cultural Centre after its projected opening in the autumn of 1989. Although it enjoys an extremely healthy attendance average of 98 per cent, receipts from the box office comprise only 20 per cent of its total income, making the Hong Kong Repertory Theatre one of the best subsidized (by the Urban Council) theatres in the world. The Repertory Theatre was first under the artistic leadership of Chung King-fai, a Yale trained native director, actor and teacher who contributed much to the contemporary Hong Kong theatre scene. In 1983 Daniel S. P. Yang, Production Director of the Colorado Shakespeare Festival, became its first full-time Artistic Director. After Yang's return to Colorado in 1985, Joanna Chan, a Maryknoll Sister who had worked for years in New York Chinatown community theatres, succeeded him.

Other leading theatre companies in contemporary Hong Kong include the Chung Ying Theatre Company and the Seals Theatre Company. Chung Ying is a bilingual professional theatre group formed in 1979 with funding first from the British Council then from the Hong Kong government. Its original intention was to do English-language Theatre-in-Education, so at the beginning the Company was entirely British. Now Chung Ying employs six actors and a few technical and administrative staff of local Chinese. The actors perform mostly in Cantonese and occasionally join the guest British actors for the English-language productions. Most of the Chung Ying performances are done in area schools and community centres. The Seals Theatre Company is a semi-professional theatre group established in 1979. Its Artistic Director is a Lecturer in English at Hong Kong University. Actors are engaged on a show-to-show basis from professionals and amateurs in the community. With one rare exception, all Seals Company productions are performed in Cantonese. Foreign plays in translation are balanced by Chinese plays classical or original.

There are close to 100 registered community, college, and school theatre groups currently in Hong Kong, among which the Amity Theatre Company, the Living Theatre Ensemble, and the Zuni Icosahedron

Hong Kong Repertory Theatre in *The Story of Ah-Q*, adapted from the famous Chinese novel by Chen Baichen and Daniel S. P. Yang, 1983.

are the most active. The Amity Theatre Company (Chi-Kwan) was formed in 1970 and is the most respected amateur theatre group in Hong Kong. The Living Theatre Ensemble is known for its high-quality productions featuring radio and television personalities. The Zuni Icosahedron is an avant-garde experimental group whose daring and controversial productions have enjoyed a small following in Hong Kong and attracted considerable attention in other Asian countries due to its touring activities.

In the traditional theatre, there seems to be a happy sign of increase of interest in Cantonese Opera among young people in Hong Kong today. Although there are few professional troupes in residence, the interest is being kept alive by amateur activities. In recent years the Urban Council has been promoting Cantonese Opera by providing funds and venues for amateur productions. New troupes are being formed to accommodate budding young talent. In January 1980 a Cantonese training school was formed by the Pak Wo Association, an umbrella organization for the traditional theatre in Hong Kong. The graduates of this School later formed their own company called the Yat Yuet Sing (Sun Moon Star) Operatic Troupe. Led by the renowned actress Li Heung-kam, they have already made their stage debut. These talented young actors are likely to become the next generation of professional actors for Cantonese Opera in Hong Kong. Today, the most celebrated Cantonese Opera company in this territory is the Chung Sun Sing Cantonese Opera Troupe, which was formed in 1965 by Lam Kar-sing – currently the most respected Cantonese Opera star in Hong Kong. This company is noted for its strictly professional standards and the precision of its performances.

Hong Kong did not have a School of Drama for vocational training of actors, directors, designers, technicians, and playwrights until 1985 when the Hong Kong Academy for Performing Arts was officially opened. The Academy has four Schools: Music, Dance, Drama, and Technical Services. The 1,200-seat Lyric Theatre in the Academy complex is currently the best performance venue in Hong Kong. The Academy aims to pursue the highest international standards and to heighten community awareness in the performing arts. Since Hong Kong is at the crossroad between East and West, the Academy designs its curricula to take advantage of the performing traditions of both the Asian and Western countries. In the School of Drama, for instance, a good portion of the curriculum is on the study of the traditional theatre of China, with courses in T'ai Chi, Peking Opera acting and acrobatic training, traditional Chinese dance and music.

Another impressive addition to the contemporary Hong Kong theatre scene is the construction of the Hong Kong Cultural Centre. Its Auditoria Building will house a 2,250-seat Concert Hall, a 1,860-seat Grand Theatre and a Studio Theatre with variable stage formats and seating configurations for from 300 to 500 audience members. Also, in the last decade the Urban Council has constructed several district theatres to accommodate cultural events in these areas. The 3,000-seat Ko Shan Theatre, which opened in 1983, and the 1,450-seat Tsuen Wan Town Hall, which opened in 1980, are but two examples. There are a dozen more district theatres under construction, all built by the Urban Council and each having a 450-seat auditorium. It is estimated that by the year 2000 there will be at least a five-fold increase of theatre-seating capacity in Hong Kong, promising a considerable growth of theatre activities in this territory.   DSPY

> *See:* F. Bowers, *Theatre in the East*, New York, 1956; J. R. Brandon, *Brandon's Guide to Theatre in Asia*, Honolulu, 1976; A. Leigh, 'A Report on Drama in Hong Kong' (unpublished document of Hong Kong Government), Hong Kong, 1983; Li Wan-wa, 'Man-tan Xianggang huaju fa-zhan' (Random talks on the development of spoken drama in Hong Kong), *Hong Kong Literature Monthly*, vol. 3 (March 1985), 86–91; A. C. Scott, *Literature and the Arts in Twentieth Century China*, New York, 1963; Selected Documents of Council on Performing Arts, Hong Kong Government, 1984 and 1985; S. P. Yang, 'The Hong Kong Repertory Theatre: Its History, Structure, Budget, Artistic Policies, Performance Activities, and Outlooks for the Future' (unpublished paper for the 2nd Asian Theatre Conference/Festival, Manila), 1983.

Hong Sheng (1645–1704) Chinese dramatist. Born in Hangzhou he was appointed to the Imperial Academy in Beijing where he made a reputation as a poet and playwright. His masterpiece *The Palace of Eternal Youth* (*Changsheng dian*) first drafted in his home town in 1679 was completed in 1688. It came to the notice of the Kangxi Emperor (r. 1662–1723) and thereafter was performed frequently before court society. The plot concerns the love affair of the Tang Emperor Minghuang (r. 713–56) and his favourite concubine Yang Guifei. The theme has been a constant inspiration to poets and dramatists in China. Hong's play is still regarded by the Chinese as one of their great lyric dramas. In 1689 a group of actors staged a special performance of the play in Hong's honour. It happened to coincide with a period of mourning for an imperial family member and was therefore a serious breach of public etiquette according to the protocol of those days. Punishment was meted out to all concerned and Hong was dismissed from the Academy. He spent his remaining days in poverty. Hong was regarded as one of the two major dramatists of his time, the other being **Kong Shangren.**   ACS

Hooft, Pieter Cornelisz (1581–1647) Together with **Vondel, P. C. Hooft** was amongst the most distinguished men of letters of the Golden Age in The Netherlands. The themes of his tragedies go back to the classics, notably **Seneca**, yet even more so to Dutch history. *Geraert van Velsen* (1613) and *Baeto* (1616), although composed in conformity with Renaissance stylistic conventions, bear witness to a strong sense of individuality. His play *Warenar* (1617), a comedy after **Plautus**' *The Pot of Gold*, was very popular on the stage in Amsterdam during the 17th and 18th centuries.

He was the central figure of the so-called 'Muiderkring', a group of talented artists, who had regular meetings at Hooft's official residence, the Muiderslot.   MG WH

Hope Theatre, London   **Philip Henslowe**, who was the chief instigator in the building of the Hope, intended that his new theatre should house animal-baiting as well as plays. The surviving contract stipulates that the stage should be removable and that its roof (or **'Heavens'**) should be cantilevered rather than supported by the familiar pillars. Since 1604, Henslowe had shared with **Edward Alleyn** the Mastership of the Royal Game of Bears, Bulls and Mastiff Dogs, and there is some evidence that animal-baiting soon took precedence over acting at the Hope. The best-known play to be performed there was **Jonson**'s *Bartholomew Fair* (1614). After the death of Alleyn in 1626, the Hope probably ceased to be used for plays. It was probably demolished in 1656.   PT

Hopkins, Arthur (Melancthon) (1878–1950) American producer and director. Hopkins began his career as a newspaper reporter, then worked as a vaudeville press agent, and finally booked attractions himself. His first Broadway production was *Poor Little Rich Girl* (1913) which ran for 160 performances. Other early successes include *On Trial* (1914), *Good Gracious Annabelle* (1916), *A Successful Calamity* (1917), *Redemption* (1918) with **John Barrymore**, and *The Jest* (1919) with John and **Lionel Barrymore**. He featured **Alla Nazimova** in revivals of **Ibsen**'s *Wild Duck*, *Hedda Gabler*, and *A Doll's House*. In the 1920s, Hopkins directed **O'Neill**'s *Anna Christie* (1921) and *The Hairy Ape* (1922); Stallings and **Anderson**'s *What Price Glory?* (1924); and Philip Barry's *Paris Bound* (1927) and *Holiday* (1928). His output decreased after 1930 but he staged a successful *The Petrified Forest* in 1935 with Leslie Howard and Humphrey Bogart, and *The Magnificent Yankee* in 1946. His notable productions of **Shakespeare** include John Barrymore in *Richard III* (1920) and in *Hamlet* (1922), and Lionel Barrymore in *Macbeth* (1921). Hopkins discovered Pauline Lord and **Katharine Hepburn**, and contributed to the success of **Robert Edmond Jones**. He studied theatrical production in Europe and returned home to develop the revolving stage in America. He placed artistic above commercial merit. While many of his directing methods were modern, his reliance upon pictorial effect made his later productions seem old-fashioned.   TLM

Hopper, De Wolf (1858–1935) American comedian and singer. His abnormally long legs, loose-jointed movements, and strong singing voice made Hopper one of the most beloved performers in comic opera. His debut was in *Our Daughters* (1879), after which he appeared in a number of shows under the aegis of the McCaull Opera Company. Hopper left the McCaull company in 1890 and under a new management was given his first starring role in *Castles in the Air* (1890). His two greatest successes, *Wang* (1891) and *Panjandrum* (1893), followed. After forming the De Wolf Hopper Opera Company, he appeared in *Dr Syntax* (1894), *El Capitan* (1896), and *The Mystical Miss* (1899). Hopper then joined the **Weber** and **Fields** company for two shows, then starred in *Mr Pickwick* (1903), *Happyland* (1905), *The Pied Piper* (1908), and *A Matinee Idol* (1910). In 1911 Hopper made the first of a number of successful forays into the **Gilbert** and Sullivan repertoire with a revival of *HMS Pinafore*. As the vogue for comic opera waned, Hopper's work was confined to revues, such as *The Passing Show of 1917*, and, on occasion, operettas. His last New York appearance was in *White Lilacs* (1928). Beginning his career at a time when comic opera was at its height, Hopper found ample opportunity to exercise his comic gifts and his forceful singing voice. He was especially noted for his ability to handle long comic speeches and involved patter songs, and for his amusing use of props. Hopper published his autobiography in 1927.   MK

Hopper, Edna Wallace (1874–1959) American actress and singer who began her stage career at the **Boston Museum** in 1891. As Edna Wallace, she appeared in a number of straight plays produced by **Charles Frohman** before making her comic opera debut as a replacement for Della Fox in *Panjandrum*. Soon after, she married **De Wolf Hopper**, and as Edna Wallace Hopper starred in *Dr Syntax* (1894), *El Capitan* (1896), *Yankee Doodle Dandy* (1898), and *Chris and the Wonderful Lamp* (1900). She played Lady Holyrood in the American production of *Florodora* (1900). Subsequently, she made the transition from comic opera to musical comedy in such shows as *About Town* (1906), *Fifty Miles from Boston* (1908), and *Jumping Jupiter* (1911). Hopper's popularity in comic opera was generally attributed to her sparkling and vivacious personality rather than to her singing voice, which was too small and delicate. Audiences especially enjoyed her appearances in trousers roles.   MK

Hopwood, Avery (1882–1928) American playwright. A remarkably successful playwright with eighteen 'hits' in fifteen years, four of them running simultaneously in New York theatres in 1920, Hopwood understood the slight and ephemeral nature of his artistry. Some of his best works were written in collaboration with the others – *The Bat* (1920) with Mary Roberts Rinehart and *Getting Gertie's Garter* (1921) with Wilson Collison. Other plays demonstrate the clever, *risqué* character of his work – *The Gold Diggers* (1919), *The Demi-Virgin* (1921), and *The Grand Illusion* (1920) from the French. Hopwood drowned in a swimming accident on the French Riviera.   WJM

Horace (65–8 BC) Quintus Horatius Flaccus, Augustan poet. Though he wrote no drama himself, his verse epistle *Ars Poetica* (*The Art of Poetry*) includes advice on the writing of tragedies, comedies and satyr plays in the Greek manner (see **Greece, ancient**). There is no evidence that this advice had any effect in his own day, but it influenced neoclassical drama from the Renaissance onward.   ALB

Hordern, Michael (Murray) (1911–) British actor, who made his professional debut in 1937. Despite being a popular actor in comparatively minor roles for 20 years, he first became a major London star with his portrait of the incompetent barrister in John Mortimer's *The Dock Brief*. This performance provided a general identity for the characters which Hordern came to play, of absent-minded, good-hearted, English eccentrics. He played Riley in **Tom Stoppard**'s *Enter a Free Man* (1968) and George Moore, the traditional moral philosopher trying hard to defend his position in a world of materialists, in Stoppard's *Jumpers* (1972). He was the hippy vicar in **David Mercer**'s *Flint* (1970) and Pinfold in an adaptation of Evelyn Waugh's book, *The Ordeal of Gilbert Pinfold* (1977), which transferred from Manchester to London's Round House. He has also appeared with major repertory companies such as the **Royal Shakespeare Company** and Nottingham Playhouse in a variety of classic roles, notably Malvolio at the **Old Vic** in 1954, as King Lear in **Jonathan Miller**'s production of **Shakespeare**'s tragedy (1969), seen later on British television, and as Prospero in *The Tempest* in the 1978 Stratford version. He was knighted in 1983.   JE

Hornblow, Arthur (1865–1942) English-born American editor and author. Born in Manchester, Hornblow studied in Paris and worked as a correspondent for English and American newspapers before coming to the United States in 1889. He pursued a career as a journalist, working first for the *Kansas City Globe* and then the *New York Dramatic Mirror*. He was foreign editor for the *New York Herald* from 1894–9, and copy-editor for the *New York Times* in 1899. From 1910–26 he served as editor of *Theatre Magazine*, frequently reviewing opening nights. Afterwards, for two years, he held the post as Dean of the **John Murray Anderson**–Robert Milton School of Theatre and Dance in New York. Hornblow's greatest financial success came from novelizing popular plays including *The Lion and the Mouse*, *The Easiest Way*, and *Bought and Paid For*. His two-volume *A History of the Theatre in America* (1919) remains a standard reference work.   TLM

Horniman, Annie E. F. (1860–1937) British theatre manager and patron. Born of a prosperous tea merchant's family, she inherited a large legacy in 1893 which she began, discreetly, to invest in theatrical enterprises that excited her. The first was a season at the Avenue Theatre, London, in 1894, which included **W. B. Yeats**'s *Land of Heart's Desire*. She became Yeats's private secretary for five years and in 1904 financed the opening of the **Abbey Theatre**, Dublin, for the Irish National Theatre Society. She continued to subsidize the theatre until disagreement with the organizers led her to transfer her capital to Manchester where in 1907 she founded a new repertory company (the first in England), opening its first season at the Midland Hotel Theatre. She purchased the nearby **Gaiety Theatre** and made it, from 1908, her company's permanent home. Under her watchful eye the theatre became a major force in the repertory movement until the outbreak of the war when the fortunes of the theatre fell and never recovered: she sold the building in 1920. In 1921 she donated her extensive library of plays to the **British Drama League**.   AJ

Horovitz, Israel Arthur (1939–) American playwright. Educated at Harvard University, Horovitz spent two years at the London Royal Academy of Dramatic Art (1961–3), and a year as resident playwright with the **Royal Shakespeare Company** (1965). He attracted critical attention in 1968 with the New York production of two one-acts: *It's Called the Sugar Plum* and *The Indian Wants the Bronx*, plays about urban violence in America. Also in 1968, his one-act *Morning*, appeared on Broadway together with short pieces by **Terrence McNally** and Leonard Melfi. Other Horovitz plays include: *The Good Parts* (1982); *The Wakefield Plays* (1974–9), which includes *The Alfred Trilogy* and *The Quannatowitt Quartet*. Horovitz deals in a realistic way with the angst of American life.   TLM

Horváth, Odön von (1901–38) Austrian dramatist and novelist. Moving from naturalistic depictions of contemporary issues in *Revolt on Côte 3018* (1927) or *Sladek the Black Reichswehr Man*, subtitled 'History of the Inflation Era', which dealt with the assassination of Weimar socialists and caused a riot at its premiere in 1929, Horváth became the first exponent of the modern **Volksstück** (Folk Play). Influenced by **Nestroy**, his highly ironic comedies use sentimental kitsch to contrast idealized concepts of the common people with the brutal reality of a disintegrating society. Cliché, whether verbal or in cultural images like the Oktoberfest or Strauss waltzes, exposes the corruption of cultural values. The socially conditioned language of the dialogue provides a powerful commentary on the crippling emotional effect of exploitation, and the interweaving of short scenes gives a panoramic overview of the problem without losing specificity. *Italian Night* was awarded the Kleist prize in 1931, and *Tales from the Vienna Woods*, which has become a modern classic and has been translated by **Hampton** for the London **National Theatre**, was performed the same year. But when *Kasimir and Karoline* was staged in 1932 Horváth felt compelled to issue guidelines to control how his plays should be produced, and in 1933 the production of *Faith, Love, Hope* was banned. *The Divorce of Figaro* and *Day of Judgement* were performed in Czechoslovakia, but his work vanished almost completely from the German stage for almost 40 years. With the difficulty of dialect translation his plays have had little international exposure, although his 1937 novel *Youth Without God* has been published in 15 languages. Productions in 1949, 1952 and 1967 caused violent controversy, and his work was only really rediscovered in the 1970–1 season, when Horváth's plays appeared in 23 German theatres as well as five in Austria and Switzerland. The most significant productions in this revival were those by **Palitzsch** and **Hollmann**, which influenced such dramatists as **Kroetz** and **Sperr**. Horváth was killed by a freak accident in Paris a few hours before leaving to take refuge in Switzerland.   CI

Hôtel de Bourgogne Theatre in the rue Mauconseil, Paris, built by the **Confrérie de la Passion** in 1548 on the site of a former residence of the Dukes of Burgundy. Used for their own performances until the end of the century, it then became the principal focus in the capital for the rapidly developing professional stage and was leased to a variety of itinerant French and foreign companies, amongst them that of **Valleran le Conte** and many from Italy. After 1629 it became the permanent home of the Comédiens du Roi, who occupied it continuously, under the successive leadership of **Bellerose**, **Floridor** and **Hauteroche**, until their incorporation into the **Comédie-Française** in 1680 and who performed there much of the most important dramatic writing of the 17th century, including many of **Corneille**'s later plays and most of **Racine**'s work. As originally constructed, it was a long, rather narrow building, more than 108 ft long by a little under 45 ft wide, with a raked stage measuring some 35 ft from the back wall and occupying the entire width of the building (minus wing space) and a smaller upper stage which, as the *Mémoire* of **Mahelot** makes clear, was also used during the action, notably for mechanical effects. A large pit for standing spectators dominated the auditorium, which also contained boxes along the side walls, tiered benches facing the stage and galleries, giving a probable capacity well in excess of 1,000. In 1647 the stage was extended forward by ten feet, raised slightly and fitted with a front curtain, and modifications were made to the auditorium modelled on seating arrangements at the **Marais**. In 1680 the vacated building was taken over by the **Comédie-Italienne** who remained associated with it until 1783.   DR

Hou Baolin (1917–) China's most popular exponent of *xiangsheng*, a branch of the story-telling genre involving comic dialogue, wisecracks and mimicry which customarily reduces Chinese audiences to hilarious laughter. Hou was born in Beijing and became the adopted son of an indigent family whom he had to help make ends meet. He was apprenticed to a street singer and eventually joined a troupe skilled in reciting complete plays from the Beijing repertoire to the street crowds. He then studied comic monologues and dialogues. After hard years spent working the street pitches and market places he was accepted as a legitimate apprentice by the *xiangsheng* guild. He left Beijing in 1940 with an invitation to perform at a well known Tianjin theatre where by dint of hard application he eventually rose to be top of the bill. After the war he returned to Beijing where for many years he was partnered by Guo Qiru as his stage foil, making an irrepressible pair. Denounced during the Cultural Revolution he left the stage, like many others. Guo died during this period but Hou has become a national celebrity today. He is a skilled master of a craft whose seemingly improvisatory nature is deceptive. It demands a fine knowledge of verbal manipulation and an assured familiarity with all the technical intricacies of both orthodox and dialectal usage as well as a keen sense of characterization. Huo remains unsurpassed in the art of taking the audience by surprise, the essence of comic genius on the stage.   ACS

Houdar de la Motte, Antoine (1672–1731) French dramatist, poet and critic. In his theoretical writings on drama he adopted an openly modernist stance, proclaiming the virtues of prose, even in tragedy, rejecting slavish conformity to rules and conventions derived from the ancients, and identifying the pleasure given to an audience as the ultimate dramaturgic criterion. His own dramatic work, comprising six comedies, four tragedies, of which the most interesting and successful was *Inès de Castro* (1723), and numerous librettos, was far more conservative in character and he was elected to the Académie-Française in 1710. DR

Houdini, Harry (Erik Weisz) (1874–1926) American magician and escape artist, born in Budapest the son of a rabbi; his stage-name was a homage to **Robert-Houdin**. Starting in dime museums and circuses as the self-styled 'King of Cards' he gained prominence in 1895 with his escapes from handcuffs and straitjackets. A genius at self-promotion, he was soon challenging police forces throughout the world to keep him pent up, and once escaped from a chained packing crate at the bottom of a river; these escapes were often engineered by concealed keys, one passed in a kiss from his wife. Other tricks involved making an elephant vanish and swallowing 70 needles and 20 yards of thread and bringing them up threaded. Houdini was also the first to fly an airplane in Australia (1910), enjoyed a career as a silent-film star, and, after his mother's death in 1913, exposed fraudulent mediums. **G. B. Shaw** called him one of the three most famous persons in the world (the other two being Jesus Christ and Sherlock Holmes). *Houdini* a 'circus-opera' by Adrian Mitchell and Peter Schat was performed in Amsterdam in 1977. LS

Houghton, Stanley (1881–1913) British playwright, one of the Manchester playwrights associated with the **Gaiety Theatre**. *Hindle Wakes* (1912) is typical of the genre, a good Lancashire tale told with wit and care. *The Younger Generation* (1910) shows the radical social concern that is also evident in the clearly argued woman's point of view in *Hindle Wakes*. See also **Harold Brighouse**. MB

Houseman, John (Jacques Haussman) (1902–) American director, producer, and actor. Born in Bucharest, educated in England, Houseman began producing in New York in 1934. He was affiliated for a time with the **Federal Theatre Project**. Some of his finest work was with **Orson Welles** and the **Mercury Theatre**, which he co-founded in 1937, notably his production of *Julius Caesar* in modern dress. He has served as artistic director for such producing agencies as the **American Shakespeare Festival** (1956–9), the Professional Theatre Group of the University of California at Los Angeles (1959–64), and the Drama Division of the Juilliard School of the Performing Arts (1968–76). In 1972 Houseman founded the **Acting Company**, originally known as the City Centre Acting Company. Since then he has directed several productions for them.

Houseman won great popular acclaim by playing an acerbic law professor in the television series 'Paper Chase'. He has published three detailed and valuable accounts of his life in the theatre: *Run-Through* (1972), *Front and Center* (1981), and *Final Dress* (1983). SMA

Housman, Laurence (1865–1959) British dramatist and novelist, most of whose work was banned from the public theatre because it presented the Holy Family or the Royal Family on the stage. His early play *Bethlehem* formed the basis of a brilliant production by **Gordon Craig** in 1902, and *Prunella*, written in collaboration with **Granville Barker**, was one of the successes in his 1910 repertory season at the Duke of York's Theatre. Three series of one-act dramas with the general title of *The Little Plays of St Francis* (1922, 1931, 1935) have retained their popularity on the amateur stage, but his best-known work was *Victoria Regina. A Dramatic Biography*. A loosely connected sequence of ten vignettes from before Queen Victoria's accession to her Diamond Jubilee, this was first presented privately by **Norman Marshall** at the London Gate Theatre and in a much acclaimed New York production with **Helen Hayes** in 1935. CI

Howard, Alan (Mackenzie) (1937–) British actor, who became a star leading man in the **Royal Shakespeare Company** which normally prefers to emphasize its ensemble playing. He came from a theatrical family and his uncle was the film actor, Leslie Howard. He joined Bryan Bailey's company at the Belgrade Theatre, Coventry, going to the **Royal Court** with the transfer of **Arnold Wesker**'s *Roots* (1959). He stayed at the Royal Court for the Wesker trilogy (1960) and for *The Changeling* (1961), but his aristocratic good looks, diction and stage presence were not ideally suited to the Royal Court's programme of angry, working-class plays. After playing Simon in *A Heritage and its History* (1965), adapted by Julian Mitchell from the Ivy Compton-Burnett novel, he joined the RSC, where his first major role was as Lussurioso, the voluptuary, in **Tourneur**'s *The Revenger's Tragedy* (1966), an early **Trevor Nunn** production. In 1968, he played Benedick in *Much Ado About Nothing*, then in 1970 Hamlet, before touring Europe as Theseus/Oberon in **Peter Brook**'s revolutionary *A Midsummer Night's Dream*, where his natural athleticism was turned into circus skills on the trapeze (1970). In 1975, he played Prince Hal and Henry V in the Stratford Centenary productions of *Henry IV* and *Henry V*, which led to a remarkable association with the director **Terry Hands**, who wanted to direct him into what almost amounted to the full span of kingly roles in **Shakespeare**'s History plays, including Richard II, Richard III and in 1977, Henry VI in Shakespeare's early trilogy, which Howard invested with a saintly innocence and dignity. In contemporary plays with the RSC, he took the leading role of the liberal German professor who cooperates with the Nazis in **C. P. Taylor**'s *Good* (1981) and appeared in revivals of plays by **Gorky** and **Ostrovsky**. JE

Howard, Bronson (Crocker) (1842–1908) The first professional American playwright; the first to emphasize systematically the businessman in drama and to frame his principles of dramaturgy – 'The Laws of Dramatic Composition'. Among his businessman plays are *Young Mrs Winthrop* (1882), about a neglected wife; *The Henrietta* (1887), a satire of life on the stock exchange; and *Aristocracy* (1892), which ridiculed new and old American wealth. Howard's awareness of social classes in *Saratoga* (1870), which was adapted to

English circumstance as *Brighton* (1874), and *One of Our Girls* (1885) pointed toward future American plays. *The Banker's Daughter* (1878), given notoriety by Howard's lecture, 'Autobiography of a Play' (1886), and his Civil War melodrama *Shenandoah* (1888) epitomized Howard's success. Although aided by his association with the Theatrical Syndicate, Howard raised the status of the American playwright with his plays and as a founder of the American Dramatists' Club in 1891.   WJM

Howard, Robert (1626–98) English playwright. Knighted for bravery at the battle of Newbury in 1644, he was imprisoned during the Interregnum at Windsor Castle. At the Restoration he began a successful political career, becoming Auditor of the Exchequer in 1677, and a Privy Councillor in 1688. In the 1660s he wrote six plays and indulged in a prolonged argument with his brother-in-law, **John Dryden**, about the relative merits of rhyming couplets and blank verse for tragedy and the desirability of writing tragicomedies, an early controversy in British dramatic theory. Of his plays *The Committee* (1662), a bitter play on the work of the Sequestration Committee during the Civil War, introduced the comic Irish servant Teague to the English stage. He collaborated with Dryden on *The Indian Queen* (1664), one of the most important plays in the creation of the genre of heroic play in England, an exotically set struggle between love and honour. *The Country Gentleman* was banned in 1669 because of a scene by **Buckingham** satirizing Sir William Coventry. Howard's brothers Edward and James were also both successful dramatists.   PH

Howard, Sidney (1891–1939) American playwright. In the twenties Howard was a crucial figure in lifting American drama from provincial entertainment to an authentic native literature. In a group of provocative plays – *They Knew What They Wanted* (which won the Pulitzer Prize in 1924), *Lucky Sam McCarver* (1925), *The Silver Cord* (1926), *Ned McCobb's Daughter* (1927), and *Half Gods* (1929) – he looked at such subjects as sex, mother love, psychiatry, and prohibition with a fresh point of view. Like **Eugene O'Neill**, Howard helped to popularize Freudian ideas about family and sexual relationships, but unlike O'Neill's, his focus was intimate and his tone essentially comic. His best play, *They Knew What They Wanted*, advocates moral and sexual compromise, and in *Ned McCobb's Daughter* he created one of the era's most appealing New Women, a heroine with more sense than any of the men in her life. Because Howard thought of himself as a skilled craftsman rather than as an artist with a distinctive voice, he was a jack of all trades who wrote in a number of genres: spectacle, romance, the war story, and both urban and rural comedy. He frequently collaborated, and he translated and adapted the work of other writers (*The Late Christopher Bean*, 1932, and *Dodsworth*, 1934, were both acclaimed). He was also an active screenwriter, winning Academy Awards for *Arrowsmith* (1931) and *Gone With the Wind* (1939). His remarkably productive career – 27 plays and 13 screenplays – ended suddenly in 1939 when he had a fatal tractor accident on his Massachusetts farm.   FH

Howard, Willie (1886–1949) and **Eugene** (1880–

1965) American comedians. Like many comedians of their day, the Howard brothers developed their comic personae in vaudeville. Their first joint appearance on the legitimate musical stage was in *The Passing Show of 1912*. Eugene served as the straight man for the act, while the sad-faced Willie got most of the laughs. Their talents were best displayed in revues; in addition to appearing in six of the *Passing Shows*, they starred in six editions of *George White's Scandals*. Willie's abilities as a mimic made him especially valuable in revues that emphasized travesties of the latest performers and shows. In addition to their comic talents, both brothers had fine singing voices, which they often displayed in parodies of grand opera. After Eugene's retirement in 1940, Willie continued as a solo performer, but never again had the success that the brothers had achieved as a team.   MK

Howard family American performers. **George Cunnabel Howard** (1820–87), a Canadian-born actor, was engaged at the **Boston Museum** where he met and married (1844) the actress **Caroline Emily Fox** (1829–1908). With a stock company that included Caroline's mother and three brothers, they toured New England in abbreviated versions of *The Drunkard* and *The Factory Girl* intermingled with an olio of songs and dances. As a respectable family unit they acclimatized theatre in towns that had hitherto condemned all playacting as devilish. The Howards achieved their most durable success with an adaptation of **Uncle Tom's Cabin** (1852) carpentered by their cousin **George Aiken** featuring Howard as St Clare, Caroline as Topsy and their daughter Cordelia as Eva. When it played in an expanded text at the National Theatre (New York, 1853), it captured the imagination of the times. Cordelia became the star of the family, also creating Katy the Hot Corn Girl and Little Gerty in *The Lamplighter*.   LS

Howells, William Dean (1837–1920) American novelist, critic and author of 36 plays. A proponent of commonplace realism who supported the work of **Edward Harrigan**, **James Herne** and **Henrik Ibsen**, Howells contributed to the rise of realism in drama and the development of social comedy. *A Counterfeit Presentment* (1877) and *Yorick's Love* (1878) were acted successfully by **Lawrence Barrett**. Howells's best work appears in 12 one-act farces featuring social events in the lives of two couples (the Robertses and the Campbells) – *The Garroters* (1885) in which Roberts mistakenly garrots a friend, *Five O'Clock Tea* (1887) as Campbell becomes engaged, *The Unexpected Guest* (1893). With charming dialogue but slight action, Howells also pictures such man–woman struggles as broken engagements – *An Indian Giver* (1897), *Parting Friends* (1910). A gentle satirist of Boston manners, who became bitter in later plays – *The Impossible* (1910) and *The Night Before Christmas* (1910) – Howells's work appealed more to amateur than professional performers.   WJM

Hoyt, Charles (Hale) (1860–1900) American dramatist. A major writer of farce and satire that usually degenerated into hilarous confusion, Hoyt wrote some 20 plays, drawing his material from his own interests and experiences – small-town life (*A Rag*

Hoyt's *A Trip to Chinatown* Company.

Baby, 1884), his father's early occupation of hotel management (*A Bunch of Keys*, 1882), superstitions (*The Brass Monkey*, 1888), corrupt politics (*A Texas Steer*, 1890), prohibition (*A Temperence Town*, 1893), the hypocrisy of home guard companies (*A Milk White Flag*, 1893), baseball (*A Runaway Colt*, 1895). *A Trip to Chinatown* (1891) had the longest run of any play produced in America to that date, 650 performances. Theatre was strictly a business with Hoyt, who made £100,000 in a good year and had a reputation for generosity. His life, however, was very stressful. Committed to the Retreat for the Insane in Hartford, Connecticut, in his native New England in 1900, he died that year. WJM

Hrotsvitha of Gandersheim (c. 935–73) German noblewoman living voluntarily within an order, but not a 'nun', authoress of six plays, *Abraham, Calimachus, Dulcitius, Gallicanus, Pafnutius* and *Sapientia*, concerned with martyrdom for the Christian faith and the triumph of virginity over the temptations of the flesh. She wished to provide a Christian counterbalance to the plays of **Terence**, but despite successful modern productions both in the original Latin and in translation it remains uncertain whether she had any idea of theatrical performance. JET

Huaju The Chinese generic description for dialogue plays in the Western style. Literally 'spoken' or 'speech drama'. *Huaju* had its tentative debut in the first decade of this century. Early inhibiting factors were public prejudice against women on the stage and an inability to dispense with old acting conventions. Since its appeal was primarily to Western-educated intellectuals it at first offered no vital challenge to the mass appeal of the old theatre beyond the great cities. They remain the established centres of operation for this genre even today. The period 1915–19 was one of intellectual revolt against the old Chinese social–cultural order. Sweeping language reforms were introduced. Western literature was being read and translated, including the dramatists. **Ibsen** made a powerful impression and taught the intellectuals to use theatre as an art of social protest. It was the thirties, however, which marked the first significant advance in making *huaju* credible theatre. The actress was coming into her own, due in part to the rise of a film industry in Shanghai, while a number of talented writers and directors with Western experience were then at work. An epoch-making event in *huaju* history was the staging of **Cao Yu**'s play *Thunderstorm (Leiyu)* in 1935. Treating Chinese social problems with a new sense of Western realism, the play was toured nationally by a cohesive travelling repertory company, a pioneer of its kind, together with a highly successful adaptation of **Wilde**'s *Lady Windermere's Fan* by Hong Shen who also directed it. This combination of events encouraged new hopes for the future of *huaju*, had not war intervened.

The war years were dominated by the subservience of theatre to patriotic propaganda in the Nationalist camp and Party needs on the Communist side. While there was intense dramatic activity in both cases it was a case of marking time rather than any significant advance on the bright hopes of the thirties. In the event *huaju* remained the poor relative of theatre after the war, the prerogative of school and university drama clubs until the foundation of the People's Republic in 1949 and a concerted attempt to reorganize *huaju* training. On 2 April 1950 the Central Drama Institute was set up in Beijing with Ouyang Yuqian as President. It was the first school of its kind, equipped to train actors, directors and set designers for *huaju* theatre. Sino-Soviet relations were then at their zenith and Russian advisers and teachers presided over the modern theatre scene. The Chinese were given exposure in depth of **Stanislavsky**'s theories according to current Russian interpretation. The after effects of this immersion are revealed in the work of many Chinese actors and directors today. However, during the Cultural Revolution (1966–76) Jiang Qing denounced Stanislavsky as bourgeois, along with virtually all spoken dramas performed in China since 1949. Companies were disbanded, their members dispersed and training institutions closed.

Following Jiang's downfall in 1976 there has been an enthusiastic renaissance of *huaju* in the struggle to make up for the lost years. Stanislavsky has been rehabilitated and training facilities reorganized.

An eclectic choice of productions has marked the years of rehabilitation. Directors have ranged over a galaxy of both classical and modern plays from the Western repertoire. A major event was the staging of **Arthur Miller**'s *Death of a Salesman* by the Beijing People's Art Theatre in 1983. It was directed by Ying Ruocheng, one of China's most talented and forward-looking actor-directors, and Miller himself. Ying's translation was used. The play was given a passionate reception by the audience. Western observers present were impressed by the profound understanding of the theme evinced by Chinese theatre-goers. ACS

Huerta, Jorge (1942–) Chicano director and critic. Born in east Los Angeles, he worked as a child actor in television. In 1971 he founded the Teatro de la Esperanza (Theatre of Hope) in Santa Barbara, California, and served as its artistic director until 1975. Founding member in 1971 of TENAZ (El Teatro Nacional de Aztlán), the national **Chicano theatre** network. Editor of various anthologies and newsletters (*TENAZ Talks Teatro*); author of books *Chicano Theatre, Themes and Forms*. Co-artistic director of The Old Globe's Teatro Meta and professor at the University of California, San Diego. GW

Hughes, Barnard (1915–   )American actor. Born in Bedford Hills, New York, and educated at Manhattan College, Hughes made his New York debut in 1934 as the haberdasher in *The Taming of the Shrew*. After minor roles and military service, he developed his range and diversity in major supporting roles: *The Teahouse of the August Moon* (1956); *Enrico IV* (1958); *Advise and Consent* (1960); *A Doll's House* (1963); *Nobody Loves an Albatross* (1963); **John Gielgud**'s *Hamlet* (1964); *Hogan's Goat* (1965); *How Now, Dow Jones* (1967); and *Sheep on the Runway* (1970). Since 1970, Hughes has become one of America's most distinguished character actors, acclaimed for his Dogberry in *Much Ado* (1972); Alexander Serebryakov in *Uncle Vanya* (1973); Falstaff in *The Merry Wives of Windsor* (1974); the title role in *Da* (1978); Father William Doherty in *Angels Fall* (1983); and Philip Stone in *End of the World* (1984). Mel Gussow (*New York Times*) regarded his award winning Da as the high point of his career: 'he takes a most ordinary man . . . and makes him lovable to his sardonic son and to the audience'. T. E. Kalem (*Time* Magazine) viewed his Da as 'an expansive field marshall of lifelong defeat who acts with the authority of an uncaged lion'. TLM

Hughes, James Mercer Langston (1902–67) Afro-American poet, story writer and playwright. Hughes was brought up by his grandmother whose first husband died in John Brown's raid at Harper's Ferry. From her he acquired racial consciousness and a love of literature. He published his first play, *The Gold Piece*, in 1921 and gained his first Broadway success with *Mulatto* (1935), a melodrama on race relations in a Southern town. Hughes achieved substantial New York runs with his folk musical *Simply Heavenly* (1957) and with *Tambourines to Glory* (1963). He received several premieres at the inter-racial Karamu Theatre in Cleveland where Hughes attended public school. Among these plays are *Little Ham* (1936), *Troubled Island* (1936), *Joy To My Soul* (1937), and *Front Porch* (1938). In addition, Hughes wrote librettos for four produced operas and the book and lyrics for Kurt Weill's musical version of *Street Scene* (1947). Hughes founded three short-lived theatres: the Harlem Suitcase Theatre where his polemical *Don't You Want To Be Free?* (1938) ran on weekends for 135 performances, the New Negro Theatre in Los Angeles (1939), and the Skyloft Players in Chicago (1949). Hughes's plays are most appealing when his righteous anger is tempered by gentle satire, humour and lyricism. EGH

Hugo, Victor (1802–85) Poet, dramatist, novelist. Hugo was the literary colossus of the French 19th century. Son of a Napoleonic officer, he developed an early interest in theatre and particularly in the historical melodrama. His *Inez de Castro* was scheduled for production at the Panorama Dramatique in 1822, but forbidden by the censors. In the 1830s a number of Hugo's plays would have problems with censorship, as he used historical themes to comment on the government and society of France at the time, expressed uncomfortable populist ideas, and harked back to Napoleon as an idealized ruler. His first play to be performed was *Amy Robsart* (under the name of his brother-in-law, Paul Foucher) at the **Odéon** in 1828, with costumes by Delacroix. One of a number of adaptations of Scott's *Kenilworth*, it was not a great success and was Hugo's last attempt to adapt a novel for the stage. As Napoleon could not be represented on the stage in the 1820s, Hugo's great analysis of the legitimacy of power received its first expression in his unperformed play *Cromwell* (1827), originally intended for **Talma** (d. 1826), which developed his idea of a historical drama creating an understanding of its period and not simply concentrating on great historical protagonists. *Cromwell* was eclipsed by its preface, often seen as the manifesto of romantic drama. Many of the ideas of the preface were not new, but common practice in the popular melodrama theatres of the boulevards. However, Hugo was trying to find a new dramatic idiom to replace the played-out neoclassical tragedy which was still favoured at the Théâtre-Français. Hugo's master was clearly **Shakespeare** (though his plays are not particularly Shakespearian). He advocated a verse rather than a prose drama, but his practice was to free the Alexandrine rhythmically, to do away with 18th-century poetic diction and to introduce banal and unpoetic vocabulary. The most famous aesthetic thesis of the preface, significant in that the Théâtre-Français believed in keeping the genres separate, was the idea of the mixture of genres, the idea that the same play could contain elements of the 'sublime' and the 'grotesque'. Hugo also attacked the constrictions of the unities of time, place and action (the boulevard melodrama simply ignored them). Hugo's plays, with their slower speed and political purpose, though full of melodramatic scenes, situations and devices, differ from melodrama in their emphasis. Hugo's first play to be accepted by the Théâtre-Français was *Marion de Lorme*, but its courtesan heroine and its attack on the power of the church caused it to be banned. Finally, in 1831, after the 1830 revolution, it was performed at the Porte-Saint-Martin, slightly upstaged by **Dumas**'s *Antony* which has some resemblances to it. Meanwhile, *Hernani*, written at about the same time, was given an elaborate production at the Théâtre-Français in 1830, once the censors of Charles X had been satisfied by the excision of a number of lines expressing populist sentiment or harking back to the 'great' Emperor, Charlemagne. The battle of *Hernani* was one of the famous theatre riots of history, representing the irruption into the temple of conservatism and classicism of the 'angry young men' of the romantic school. Ultimately the 'battle' was more symbolic than real. *Le Roi S'Amuse*, source of the libretto of Verdi's *Rigoletto*, received a single performance at the Théâtre-Français in 1832, and was then banned because of the unfavourable light in which it showed King François I. Hugo took court proceedings, which he lost, and the play was not revived until 1882. Hugo's next three dramas were in prose. *Lucrèce Borgia*, a triumph at the Porte-Saint-Martin for **Mlle George** and **Frédérick Lemaître** in 1833, resembled *La Tour de Nesle* with a sinful mother accidentally murdering her son. His *Marie Tudor* at the same theatre the same year was a flop. In 1835 he returned to the Théâtre-Français with *Angelo, Tyran de Padoue* which offered two very strong female roles played by **Mars** and **Dorval**. *Ruy Blas* opened Dumas and Hugo's Théâtre de la Renaissance in 1838. Despite a melodramatic framework, with clearly defined good and bad characters, the play continued a serious meditation on the nature of political power. A moderate success at the time, when revived with **Sarah Bernhardt** in 1872 it ran for 300 performances. Hugo's last major romantic drama, *Les Burgraves* (Théâtre-Français. 1843), was of epic proportions, but audiences failed to take its 100-year-old lovers seriously, and this type of play was now clearly out of fashion. In 1845 Hugo was elected a peer of France and in 1852 he had to go into exile for his opposition to Napoleon III. His later years were devoted to more novels (*Les Misérables*, 1862, *Les Travailleurs de la Mer*, 1866 and *Quatre-vingt-treize*, 1874) and to some of his major poetic works, including *La Légende des Siècles*. He also wrote a study of Shakespeare in 1864. During the years of exile he turned to armchair theatre, the plays of the *Théâtre en Liberté* – a freedom from censorship as much as from stage conventions. The most important of these was a modern play, *Mille Francs de Récompense* (*1000 Francs Reward*), a melodrama in the style of *Le Chiffonnier de Paris*, which proved very playable when first performed in 1961. Hugo received a state funeral when he died in 1885. JMCC

Hume, Samuel J. (1885–1962) American set designer and founder of the Detroit Arts and Crafts Theatre. Hume was one of the pioneers of the New Stagecraft and the **Little Theatre movement**. He studied with **Edward Gordon Craig** in Florence and subsequently applied Craig's idea of movable screens into 'adaptable settings' – unit sets utilizing flats, platforms, draperies, arches, and pylons that could be rearranged, changed, or altered by lighting to fit individual scenes. It was thus a move away from naturalism towards simplification and suggestion as well as being economical. AA

Humphries, (John) Barry (1934–) Australian actor and author. He created his archetypal Australian housewife Edna Everage while working as an actor in the 1950s; his other characters include the ageing suburbanite Sandy Stone and the gross member of parliament Sir Les Patterson (Australia's 'Minister of Culture'). His satirical one-man shows, characterized by banter with the audience and a gladioli-waving finale, include *A Nice Night's Entertainment* (1962), *Excuse I* (1965), *At Least You Can Say You've Seen It* (1974), *Isn't It Pathetic At His Age* (1977), *An Evening's Intercourse with Barry Humphries* (1981) and *Tears Before Bedtime* (1985). He created the comic strip and film character Barry McKenzie. MW

Huneker, James G. (1857–1921) American critic who brought serious public attention to continental dramatists in the 1890s and early 1900s. Huneker made his debut as a music critic in 1875 for the *Philadelphia Evening Bulletin*. In 1886, after studying piano in Paris, he moved to New York and a position as music critic for the *Musical Courier*. He began writing dramatic criticism during his tenure with the *New York Recorder* (1891–5). In 1895 he became music and drama critic for the *Morning Advertiser*, and between 1902–4 he held the drama post for the *New York Sun*. He also wrote for *Metropolitan Magazine*, *Puck*, *Smart Set*, and *New York Times*. His 22 books include *Iconoclasts: A Book of*

Barry Humphries as the 'megastar' Dame Edna Everage.

Dramatists (1905) and his autobiography *Steeplejack* (1920). Huneker opposed the Genteel Tradition and championed the plays of **Ibsen**, **Strindberg**, **Shaw**, **Maeterlinck**, and **Schnitzler**. He brought a lively and impressionistic style to American criticism, and influenced a generation of writers including **George Jean Nathan** and H. L. Mencken. TLM

Hungary As a medieval Christian kingdom, Hungary participated in the European tradition of mystery plays and biblical passions. The Renaissance in the 16th century yielded two noteworthy plays: *Electra* by Péter Bornemisza, a reworking of **Sophocles**, and *A Fine Hungarian Comedy* by Bálint Balassi. Reformation-inspired college dramas became the main theatrical venue of 17th-century Hungary, a strife-torn country fighting both Turks and Austrians, with no urban centres in which a theatrical culture could develop. The colleges kept theatre alive until the emergence of professional Hungarian theatre companies in the late 18th century. Though at first in Latin, Jesuit college drama created the pantheon of heroes that enabled the nation to identify with its past. Protestant college plays were mostly in Hungarian, as were Jesuit dramas by the mid-18th century. From that time on college performances attracted a wide audience including peasants.

During the 18th century the ideas of the French Enlightenment flourished in Vienna, and influenced members of Empress Maria Theresa's Hungarian Guards, one of whom, György Bessenyei, initiated a national programme of cultural resurgence. This was followed by the language reform, a movement led by Ferenc Kazinczy, which reinvigorated native Hungarian culture, eliminating Latin as Hungary's official language, and countering German influence. As part of his programme Bessenyei wrote plays such as *The Tragedy of Agis* (1772), which marks the traditional beginning of modern Hungarian literature, and the comedy, *The Philosopher* (1777), which delighted audiences when performed more than a decade after its publication. Mihály Csokonai, leading poet of his time, also contributed to early developments with plays like *The Dreamy Tempefői* (1793), a critique of class distinctions which abounds in social satire. Both Bessenyei and Csokonai used drama as a means of social criticism.

The German-speaking middle class of Pest and Buda of the 18th century had two theatres: Pest (1774) and Buda (1784). Political, social, and economic conditions impeded the emergence of a Hungarian urban middle class. Nevertheless from 1780 to 1830 Pest became the Hungarian cultural centre of the country with its University, National Museum, Academy of Sciences, and several publishing firms. Periodicals also flourished. Increasing numbers of impoverished noblemen moved to Pest as professionals, and the German-speaking middle class was gradually assimilated. Establishing Hungarian theatrical hegemony over Austrian colonial theatre became a national cause, especially after the building in 1812 of a large, German-language theatre in Pest.

In 1790, under the management of László Kelemen, a Hungarian acting troupe began performing in various locations in Pest, the repertoire consisting largely of translated German plays. The company received some local official support, which was withdrawn during the period of terror following the uncovering of the Martinovics conspiracy of 1794, an anti-monarchist plot. The company ceased functioning in 1796; a second attempt lasted from 1807 to 1815.

On the initiative of the leading Transylvanian Enlightenment intellectual, György Aranka, a Hungarian theatre company began performing in 1792 in Kolozsvár. This company survived through support from the aristocracy and the largely Hungarian-speaking Transylvanian urban middle class. Also, as an autonomous province of the Empire, Transylvania was less affected by the aftermath of the Martinovics conspiracy. In 1821 the company acquired in Kolozsvár the first permanent home of any Hungarian theatre.

Hungarian theatrical activity in Pest from 1815 to 1833 consisted of ten guest appearances by travelling troupes from other parts of Hungary. By the late 1820s about 15 such companies were touring the country, and several noteworthy troupes, based in Kassa, Miskolc, and Székesfehérvár, emerged. The premiere in Pest of Károly Kisfaludy's *The Tartars in Hungary* (1819) by the Székesfehérvár troupe marked the beginning of a new era in Hungarian theatre. Kisfaludy's historical dramas satisfied the intense interest, characteristic of Hungarian romanticism, in the early history of the nation. Kisfaludy also popularized comedy (e.g. *The Suitors*, 1817) whose characters were recognizable Hungarian types. The plots, though standard, presented the clash of the social and cultural backgrounds of the characters, and made for social commentary.

The Academy of Sciences, founded in 1825, endeavoured to popularize the newly codified literary language by promoting the construction in Pest of a permanent home for Hungarian theatre, commissioning the translation of plays of international excellence, and holding competitions for original Hungarian plays. Mihály Vörösmarty, the leading romantic poet, turned to writing plays in the 1830s. His one masterpiece is *Csongor and Tünde*, written in 1831, but not performed until 1879. This verse play describes Csongor's search for Fairyland, where he hopes to be reunited with his love, Tünde. Csongor is symbolic of the idealist who meets disillusionment and attains wisdom. At this time the greatest Hungarian play of the century, **József Katona**'s *Bánk Bán*, was not accorded its deserved recognition. Written in 1815, this tragedy of an honourable palatine undone by conflicting loyalties was premiered in Kassa in 1833, but its merits were not recognized until 1845 at the National Theatre.

In 1833 the newly revived Hungarian Theatre Company of Pest took control of the former German theatre in Buda, and in 1837 moved into its new home in Pest, built with donations by citizens. At the Academy, Vörösmarty became head of the Drama Supervisory Committee, and steered the repertoire toward **Shakespeare**, **Schiller**, and original Hungarian works. In 1840 the Theatre of Pest became the National Theatre under the management of József Bajza, renowned critic; he was succeeded in 1843 by Endre Bartay, a proponent of French romanticism. In 1847 the German theatre building in Pest burned down, an event signalling the rapid decline of German-language theatre in the capital, while in provincial cities assimilation led to the transfer of theatres to Hungarian companies. Between 1854 and 1867 six new theatres were built in provincial cities.

Hungary's Age of Reform (1825–48) was characterized by liberal political ideas and economic growth. By the 1840s there was widespread demand for the emancipation of the peasantry, and the National Theatre became a platform for these strivings. Hungarian political comedy was created by Ignác Nagy, whose *The County Election* (1843) satirizes social stereotypes and ridicules local political corruption. Comedies commenting on contemporary society became the vogue as interest in historical subjects waned. Károly Obernyik received an Academy award for his *Aristocrat and Serf* (1843), an open attack against class privilege. Zsigmond Czakó, influenced by French romanticism, depicted in *The Will* (1845) a hero who loses his social standing and sanity when it turns out he is not, as he thought, of noble descent. In 1843 Ede Szigligeti emerged as the creator of a new type of play whose influence was apparent for half a century. *The Deserter* was the first *népszínmű* (roughly: folk play). This genre portrays peasant life with the aim of arousing sympathy for the peasantry; major ingredients are dialects, folk costumes, folk song and dance. Before the 1849 defeat of the War of Independence, the *népszínmű* was serious. Later the trappings and comic effects began to dominate as the genre lost its reforming mission. Eventually the *népszínmű*, among whose practitioners was József Szigeti, degenerated into pseudo-operetta. During the National Theatre's first four decades one-third of its repertoire consisted of plays by Ede Szigligeti. *Liliomfi* (1849) remains his most highly regarded comedy. He was the National's manager from 1873 to his death in 1878. Directorship was then assumed by Ede Paulay, who premiered Vörösmarty's *Csongor and Tünde* in 1879 and **Imre Madách**'s *The Tragedy of Man* in 1883.

The reign of terror following the defeat of the War of

Independence (1848–9) crushed Hungarian intellectual life, and the gradual literary resurgence of the 1850s was much influenced by disillusionment over the present and future of the nation. This pessimism influenced Imre Madách's dramatic poem, *The Tragedy of Man* (1860), which nevertheless transcends national concerns, and gives expression to man's inherent metaphysical insecurity. The work has proved to be one of the most enduring successes of the Hungarian theatre.

Political tensions eased following the Compromise of 1867, which established the Austro-Hungarian Dual Monarchy. In the final decades of the century the middle class grew rapidly as Budapest became a major European city, and the demand for theatre grew. Between 1896 and 1907 five theatres were built in the capital, all in private hands except for the National. Regional theatre was also experiencing an upsurge; by 1911, 38 theatres were operating throughout the country. But little of value was performed. The most popular domestic playwright of the period, Gergely Csiky, a keen observer of Hungarian society, has been called the **Sardou** of the Hungarian stage.

At the beginning of the 20th century, drama was the weakest branch of Hungarian literature. In 1904 a group of intellectuals founded the Thalia Company, which championed the works of **Ibsen**, **Strindberg**, **Hauptmann**, **Shaw**, etc. Its director, Sándor Hevesi, brought naturalism to the Hungarian stage. Though disbanded in 1909 the influence of the Thalia helped usher in a new breed of Hungarian playwrights, some of whom acquired international reputations. Their work, often called commercial drama, is based on a mastery of stagecraft and often a cosmopolitanism to which urban audiences in Europe and America could respond. These qualities are evident in the work of **Ferenc Molnár**, whose dramatic situations betray the influence of Freud, his sparkling dialogue that of **Wilde**, and whose treatment of reality versus illusion is reminiscent of **Pirandello**. But Molnár's technical brilliance is not matched by depth of philosophical insight. The best known of his nearly 30 plays are *The Devil* (1907), *Liliom* (1909), *The Guardsman* (1910), and *The Play's the Thing* (1926). Another popular playwright of the period was Ferenc Herczeg. Whereas Molnár dealt mainly with the bourgeoisie, Herczeg in his historical dramas was an apologist for feudalism and the court of Vienna; in other plays he glorified the nationalist, conservative gentry. He is best known for *The Blue Fox* (1917). Menyhért Lengyel achieved international acclaim with *Typhoon* (1909), a play about the clash of Eastern and Western world outlooks. Lengyel's attraction to oriental themes is demonstrated by his 1917 scenario for Béla Bartók's ballet, *The Miraculous Mandarin*. It was thanks to Bartók that Béla Balázs (later known as a film theorist) attained world fame with his symbolist play, *Bluebeard's Castle* (1910), which Bartók set to music. Lajos Bíró was also a popular, prolific, commercial playwright, best known for *Yellow Lily* (1909). After the collapse of the short-lived Hungarian Republic of Councils in 1919 he settled in London and became a successful screenwriter. Dezső Szomory's historical dramas, many about Habsburg monarchs, are known for their use of lofty, ceremonious language. Jenő Heltai recorded his characters' foibles, social games, and moral compromises with indulgence and cynicism. He is best known for

The Tündérlaki Girls (1914) and *The Silent Knight* (1936). Zsigmond Móricz, primarily a prose chronicler of peasant and small-town life, in his play *Judge Sári* (1910) gave one of the most true-to-life portrayals of peasant life ever to reach the Hungarian stage. Zoltán Thury and Sándor Bródy tried to bring genuine psychological conflict and social criticism to the stage, but could not compete with commercial drama. Thury was concerned in plays like *Soldiers* (1889) with revealing the passions behind false facades of social stability. Bródy's targets were middle-class families who corrupted and exploited their peasant maids. His best-known plays are *The Nanny* (1902) and *The Schoolmistress* (1908).

The First World War and its aftermath, the 133-day Republic of Councils followed by the White terror, and the loss of two-thirds of the country's territory along with over three million ethnic Hungarians to the successor states, help explain why the legitimate theatre became the bourgeoisie's outlet for escapist entertainment and nostalgia. It was left to the cabaret, the most vital Hungarian theatrical forum of the inter-war years, to provide room for experimentation, political satire, and at times resistance. The cabaret was a phenomenon of Budapest, but had roots in folk traditions. Endre Nagy ran a cabaret from 1907 to 1929 in which some of the country's best performers, composers, and writers including Móricz, Heltai, and Molnár experimented. Between 1916 and 1936, 18 cabarets opened in Budapest. The cabaret pieces of Frigyes Karinthy, e.g. *The Magic Chair* (1917), foreshadowed absurdist drama. Cabaret continued to flourish under the new social order imposed after the Second World War.

Following the Second World War, playwrights who had left the country or were silenced by the White terror, the rise of fascism, or intolerance toward experimentation, returned or reemerged. The most significant were Tibor Déry, Gyula Háy, Lajos Kassák, Áron Tamási, and Béla Balázs. Their work was officially discredited, however, because the theatre was proclaimed a school for educating the masses in the new social order. In 1949 all of Hungary's theatres were nationalized. In the next five seasons 66 new Soviet plays, 13 Russian classics, and only six Western plays were mounted, in addition to examples of domestic socialist realism conforming to the Party's aims. The pattern was broken by Tibor Déry's *The Sycophant* (1954), which ridiculed the over-eager Party functionary, and by Imre Sarkadi's *September* (1955), which in its realism broke with the Party's formula for the peasant-play.

Following the 1956 uprising the Party required plays justifying the crushing of the insurrection. Imre Dobozy, Lajos Mesterházy, and József Darvas wrote plays performed in 1958–9 in which the hero is presented with a moral dilemma brought on by the uprising, and makes the 'correct' choice. The fact that drama had returned from schematic statements to the depiction of individuals in the throes of moral conflict signalled an innovation. By the early 1960s plays appeared that questioned Hungary's socialist system. Endre Fejes's *Scrap Yard* (1963) is a chronicle of a working-class family leading a meaningless life amidst the system's promises. Imre Sarkadi, concerned with the post-1956 intellectual's problem of being an unwilling member of the ruling class, painted a bleak picture of the intellectual in *Simeon Stylites* (1967). István Csurka's *Strip Poker* (1967) lays bare, during an all-night card game, the lost souls of four intellectuals. Csurka has achieved great success in recent years with plays like *Lamentations for a Custodian* (1980), which throw together disparate members of modern Hungarian society. In **István Örkény**'s popular *Catsplay* (1966) a lyrical evocation of the pre-First World War period frames a presentation of the dilemma of a nation split in two: those who emigrated to the West, and those who stayed. Örkény's other plays are in the absurdist vein, as are plays by Miklós Mészöly, István Eörsi, Gábor Görgey, and **Géza Páskándi**. Hungarian absurdist drama tends to be concerned with the individual's relation to power. A more traditional school of drama has also been thriving. Its main representatives are Gyula Illyés, László Németh, **András Sütő** and János Székely. Their plays, mostly historical dramas, reflect a concern with the nation's history and destiny. Illyés's play about the Albigensian Crusade, *Cathars* (1969), 'is about a nation that has perished, written for peoples and communities still alive'. Theatre is vital to the cultural existence of the Hungarian populations of those territories of historical Hungary which now form parts of neighbouring states. But while playwrights in Hungary are increasingly open in treating national problems, minority playwrights write under severe constraints. Rumania's alarming assimilationist policy toward its Hungarians may not be openly treated. Thus when the Transylvanian András Sütő, perhaps the most revered living Hungarian playwright, creates vast historical dramas about rebellion against forces that threaten the individual's identity, he is expressing the deepest concern of the Hungarians of Rumania. At the same time, the need to resort to indirect means of expression, such as historical analogies, contributes to the universal significance of his plays. Similarly, the 'absurdoid' plays of Géza Páskándi, another Transylvanian, are grotesque reflections of the state's intrusion into the individual's daily life; at the same time the plays express the *angst* of universal modern man.

In Budapest 20 theatres are active, not counting opera, operetta, or university theatre, and 12 cities in the provinces of Hungary have theatre companies. The theatre in Kaposvár has attracted national attention for its excellence and innovativeness. The over two million Hungarians of Rumania are served by seven Hungarian theatre companies, mostly sections of Rumanian companies, and their future is uncertain under the state's assimilationist policies. In Slovakia the approximately one million Hungarians have two Hungarian theatres, (Komárom, Kassa), as do the 600,000 Hungarians of Yugoslavia (Szabadka, Újvidék).

The fact that Tibor Déry's 1926 Dadaist masterpiece, *The Giant Baby*, had to wait until 1969 to reach the stage is indicative of the missed or crushed opportunities that characterize Hungarian theatre history. Openness to innovation since the mid-1960s, however, bodes well for the future of Hungarian theatre.   EB

See: L. Czigány, *The Oxford History of Hungarian Literature*, Oxford, 1984; I. Goldstein, 'A History of Hungarian Drama between 1945 and 1970', Ph.D. dissertation, City University of New York, 1974; F. Hont (ed.), *Magyar színháztörténet*, Budapest, 1962; T. Klaniczay (ed.), *A History of Hungarian Literature*, Budapest, 1983; A. Szerb, *Magyar irodalomtörténet*, Budapest, 6th edn, 1978.

Hunger artist A sideshow performer who fasts publicly for extended periods. Starvation had been used as a tragic theme in H. W. Gerstenberg's *Ugolino* (1768) and public fasting exploited by female charlatans passing themselves off as saints. Showmen took to it after 1880 when Dr Henry Tanner (d. 1893) of New York fasted 40 days to win a bet. Most hunger artists did drink during their ordeals, among them the leading performer of the turn of the century, Giacomo Succi of Milan. The phenomenon caught on in Germany during the Inflation period, when the populace was starving anyway; Succi's record was broken in 1926 by Ventego (47 days). As late as 1950 fasting could still be seen at European fairs, though it has now become a property of political protest in prisons. **Tadeusz Róẑewicz**'s play *The Hunger Artist Departs* (1976), based on Franz Kafka, converts the starveling into a metaphor for the visionary artist in an uncomprehending world.   LS

Hunt, Hugh Sidney (1911–) British director, dramatist and critic. After directing a wide variety of plays in Repertory Theatre, he became a director at the **Abbey Theatre**, Dublin, from 1935 to 1938, where his first play written in collaboration with Frank O'Connor *The Invincibles* (1937) was performed. In 1946 he was appointed the first director of the **Bristol Old Vic Company**, moving to the London **Old Vic** in 1949, where he directed a series of **Shakespeare** and **Shaw** productions. From 1955 to 1960 he played a significant role in the development of the Australian theatre as director of the Elizabethan Theatre Trust in Sydney, where he founded the Trust Players, the Young Elizabethan Players and the Elizabethan Opera Company. Returning to England in 1960, he directed a tour of **Peter Shaffer**'s *Five Finger Exercise* for the **Arts Council**, and was instrumental in creating the Contact Company in Manchester, now the **Royal Exchange Theatre Company**. He was Professor of Drama at Manchester University, 1961–73, and between 1969 and 1971 also was Artistic Director of the Abbey Theatre.   CI   MB

Hunt, (James Henry) Leigh (1784–1859) English dramatic critic, essayist and poet. Hunt's father emigrated from the newly independent USA, where his vehement loyalty to the English crown had made him too many enemies. His sons, John and Leigh, inherited his defiance. Leigh Hunt's first dramatic criticism was written for the *News*, of which John was editor. The volume of *Critical Essays on the Performers of the London Theatres* (1808) is a selection of these early reviews, the product of independent observation, seriousness and verbal facility. The absence of evident bias and the willingness to admire the art and chastise the artfulness of actors combined to enhance the status of dramatic criticism in England. When his brother founded the *Examiner*, Hunt became its editor (1808), continuing his systematic visits to London theatres. The paper was prosecuted three times. On the first two occasions (they had exposed abuses in the British army) the Hunts were acquitted, but in 1813 they were imprisoned for two years following what was adjudged a libel on the Prince Regent. As a result, Hunt missed the London debut of **Edmund Kean**. Released in early 1815, he saw Kean as Richard III and wrote one of his finest pieces of measured criticism to express his disappointment. Almost equally fine is his speedy recantation after watching Kean as Othello – 'the masterpiece of the living stage' was his conclusion. Hunt was the father of a large and often hapless family, and he undertook far too much work in order to support it. He was probably mortified that so many of his friends – they included, at various times, Keats, Shelley, **Byron**, **Lamb**, Carlyle, Browning, **Tennyson** and **Dickens** – were better writers than he. Of the ten or so plays he wrote, or started, two were staged in his lifetime, the verse tragedy *A Legend of Florence* (1840) at **Covent Garden**, and a verse comedy, *Lovers' Amazements* (1858), at the **Lyceum**. To the end, Hunt aspired to be more than he actually was, a superior journalist. His *Dramatic Criticism, 1808–31* can be read in an excellent collection by L. H. and C. W. Houtchens (1949).   PT

Hunter, Kim (Janet Cole) (1922–) American stage, film, and television actress. Her stage debut was in *Penny Wise* (1929); her Broadway debut was as Stella in *A Streetcar Named Desire* (1947). She recreated Stella on film in 1951, winning an Oscar for Best Actress. Hunter has acted for the **Shakespeare Festival Theatre** and various stock companies in such roles as Catherine Reardon in *And Miss Reardon Drinks a Little*.   SMA

Hunter, N[orman] C[harles] (1908–71) British dramatist, whose two dramas of middle-class households in decline, *Waters of the Moon* (1951) and *A Day by the Sea* (1953), gave him the reputation of being an English **Chekhov**. He began by writing amusing comedies of which *All Rights Reserved* (1935) and *A Party for Christmas* (1938) reached the West End, but the plotting and dialogue seemed slick, without being particularly original or effective. After the war, however, his style became more leisurely, intricate and concerned with shifts in mood. The casting of *A Day by the Sea*, with **John Gielgud**, **Ralph Richardson**, **Sybil Thorndike** and **Irene Worth**, illustrates the esteem in which this autumnal play was held, and its command of atmosphere rewards the outstanding, actor. Its dialogue now seems pedestrian, not like Chekhov but closer to minor **Rattigan**, but interest is retained through the interweaving of emotional themes. *A Touch of the Sun* (1958) and *The Tulip Tree* (1962) were less successful; and the fashion for N. C. Hunter's plays was one casualty of the new **Royal Court**-led wave of angry young writers.   JE

Hurwitz, Moishe (1844–1910) and **Jacob Lateiner** (1853–1935) The two main writers of **Shund** theatre, characterizing the lowest quality of popular American Yiddish theatre during the 1890s. Deliberately writing down to the tastes of the most uneducated and unsophisticated of the 'green' immigrants, 'Professor' Hurwitz (as he called himself) wrote about 90 plays and Joseph Lateiner turned out over 150.   AB

Hussein, Ebrahim (1943–) Tanzanian playwright. Published plays include *Kinjeketile* (1970) originally in Swahili and translated into English, *Wakati Ukata* (*Time is a Wall*, 1970), *Alikaona* (*The One Who Got What She Deserved*, 1970), *Mashetani* (*Devils*, 1971), *Arusi* (*Wedding*, 1980), *Jogoo Kijijini* (*The Cock in the Village*, 1976), *Ngao ya Jadi* (*The Traditional Shield*, 1976). Hussein's themes are closely related to the struggle for a just society in Tanzania, from the depiction of the Maji Maji uprising against the Germans in *Kinjeketile* to his portrayal of the unfulfilled dream for a better society in *Arusi*. Not only are his themes relevant to the Tanzanian situation but in many cases so are his forms, particularly his use of the traditional story-telling structure. Professor Hussein is Associate Professor in Theatre Arts at the University of Dar es Salaam.   PMl

Huston, Walter (1884–1950) American stage and film director, noted for his artistic integrity, lack of affectation, and economic style. Born in Toronto, Canada, he began acting in 1902, returned to school, then re-entered the theatre in 1909. For almost 18 years he toured the United States and Canada. His New York debut was in 1924 in the title role of *Mr Pitt*, and in the same year he achieved stardom as Ephraim Cabot in *Desire Under the Elms*. **Stark Young** called Huston's Ephraim 'trenchant, gaunt, fervid, harsh', lauding his 'ability to convey the harsh, inarticulate life' of the role. Later **Brooks Atkinson** called Huston 'the most honest of actors – plain, simple, lucid, magnetic'. He was also acclaimed for his title role in Sinclair Lewis's *Dodsworth* and for his work in *Knickerbocker Holiday*, in which he introduced 'September Song'. In 1948 he won an Academy Award for best supporting actor in *The Treasure of the Sierra Madre*, a film directed by his son, John. His other films included *Dodsworth* and *Duel in the Sun*.   SMA

Hyman, Earle (1926–) Afro-American actor. Renowned in classical and contemporary roles, Hyman began with the American Negro Theatre and at 17 appeared in *Anna Lucasta* (1944) on Broadway and in London's West End. His earliest Shakespearian role was Hamlet (1951) at Howard University, followed by the first of six Othellos played over a 25-year period in Antioch (Ohio), New York, Connecticut, Norway and Sweden. Hyman performed ten other roles with the **American Shakespeare Theatre** (1955–60), received rave notices for his Broadway performance in *Mr Johnson* (1956), and the State Award in Oslo, Norway, for his portrayal of the title role in *The Emperor Jones* (1965).   EGH

Ibsen, Henrik (1828–1906) Norwegian playwright and poet. His playwriting benefited greatly from his early practical experience in the theatre. Having written only *Catiline* and *The Warrior's Barrow* (the latter staged at Christiania Theatre), he was appointed resident dramatist and then stage director at the new Norwegian Theatre in Bergen, Norway's first theatre to use Norwegian actors and attempt Norwegian (rather than Danish) speech; his next plays were written to meet his contract for a new play every year. In 1852, the theatre sent Ibsen on an important study tour to Dresden and Copenhagen, where he learned much from the methods and principles enforced by **Johan Ludvig Heiberg** at the **Kongelige Teater** and from its acting ensemble, led by **Johanne Luise Heiberg** and **Michael Wiehe**. He also discovered Herman Hettner's book *The Modern Drama*, which stressed psychological conflict as the basis of drama; from Heiberg he probably learned a new respect for the dramaturgical mechanics of **Scribe**. The Bergen years were valuable but difficult and in 1857, Ibsen took the opportunity to move to Christiania (now Oslo) to manage the recently opened Norwegian Theatre, where conditions were even worse. When it closed in 1862, he was briefly engaged at Christiania Theatre to direct his own *The Pretenders*, his final direct involvement in practical theatre ever. Moreover, in 1864 he moved to Rome, the beginning of a 27-year voluntary exile.

Apart from the contemporary *St John's Night* (1852) and *Love's Comedy* (1862), his early plays (including *The Pretenders*) owe much to **Oehlenschläger** and to the national romantic movement's fascination with Norway's past. His major transformation as a playwright occurred abroad, first in the magnificent dramas *Brand* (1865) and *Peer Gynt* (1867) dealing with the dilemmas created by both the claims of the absolute and the temptations of compromise. The immediate impulse was Ibsen's dismay at Norway's failure to assist Denmark in its struggle with Bismarck over Schleswig-Holstein. However, the plays' themes reach back to *Catiline* and resonate, with increasing complexity, in the later plays. Ibsen's characters are typically caught in a tension between the possible and the impossible, driven to strive for the latter and tormented by guilt when they give in to the former. Despite his disclaimers, Ibsen's mature plays are imbued with the ideas of Kierkegaard, particularly his differentiation between the aesthetic, ethical and religious ways of life and his use of Abraham as a representative 'Knight of Faith'. The motif of vocation, seized but imperfectly understood by Brand and evaded (but perhaps partly understood) by Peer Gynt, is also drawn from Kierkegaard and was to hold together the sprawling two-part *Emperor and Galilean* completed in 1873. Ibsen uses Julian the Apostate (AD 331–63) to explore the ironies of a confused search for a vocation, while history progresses regardless.

Despite Ibsen's protests that he was a poet, rather than a social reformer, his next plays were widely understood to be primarily blows struck in favour of social and political reform. For example, *A Doll's House* (1879) seemed to be a feminist tract (shocking to many), rather than a study of self-realization and vocation. *Ghosts* (1881) was taken to be about venereal disease, rather than the more insidious social diseases it exposes. *An Enemy of the People* (1882) provoked more discussion of its supposed political targets than of its theme of the vocation to truth. However, with *The Wild Duck* (1884), the critics were bewildered. Ibsen had entered a new phase, in which his normally ambivalent perception of life became mysterious, raising more questions (both of fact and of principle) than he answered. In the character Gregers Werle, the motif of vocation was perceived in a satirical and sinister light, an effect to be echoed in *Rosmersholm* (1886) and *Hedda Gabler* (1890), in which the female protagonists pursue missions that lead to disaster. Ibsen's plays were now concerned more with individual destinies than with general moral or social principles and his focus narrowed (and intensified) even more in *The Lady from the Sea* (1888) and the plays that followed: *The Master Builder* (1892), with its complex interweaving of guilt, ambition and fantasy; *Little Eyolf* (1894), in which Alfred and Rita seem possessed by a confused blend of guilt and frustrated personal ambition; *John Gabriel Borkman* (1896) which exposes the frustrating failure of a family to live through others. Finally, in 1899, came the play that Ibsen once called the 'Dramatic Epilogue' to the sequence of plays beginning with *A Doll's House* and later seen as the conclusion to his *entire* dramatic output: *When We Dead Awaken* (1899). It does indeed seem to reach back through his 50 years of playwriting, drawing together many of the images and themes employed in earlier plays. However, he does not achieve a resolution of his characters' spiritual conflicts, but rather a final statement of their dilemma, caught between the temptations of the possible and the terrible demands of the ideal.   HL

Iceland Under Norwegian and Danish rule respectively for seven centuries, Iceland regained independence, becoming a republic in 1944. Christianity was adopted in 1000, although heathen worship was tolerated. Roman Catholic until 1550, Iceland is now Lutheran Protestant. Iceland has 255,000 inhabitants half of which live in the Reykjavík area.

Unlike with the rich tradition of story-telling, evidence for early performance is scant. A definitive history of theatre goes back to the early 18th century, when students at The Cathedral School at Skálholt began performing the 'Herranótt', an annual ritual resembling The Boy Bishop tradition in England. This gave birth to Icelandic drama, as by 1790 the festivities included the performance of a play, the first significant dramatist being Sigurdur Pétursson, whose satirical comedies resemble **Holberg**'s plays. Danish authorities eventually found these activities offensive and banned them from 1799 until 1820. Plays were annually performed at the school after it moved to Reykjavík in 1846, and soon there were fairly regular amateur performances of plays and vaudevilles both in Danish and Icelandic in Reykjavík and various villages around the country.

During the latter half of the 19th century, theatre became the most popular form of entertainment, a status it still retains. The chief exponent of theatre at the time was painter Sigurdur Gudmundsson. While studying in Copenhagen, Gudmundsson developed a keen interest in theatre, realizing its potential against foreign oppression, which led him to express the need for a national stage from which the people could be enlightened and made aware of their national identity. Gudmundsson became the first stage designer and may also be the first stage director, as he frequently used to place the actors to create tableaux.

Gudmundsson prompted poets to create a national drama from Icelandic folklore, suggesting the craft could be learned by translating great works of world theatre. Under his influence two students wrote plays from folklore. Matthías Jochumsson wrote *The Outlaws* (1862), and Indridi Einarsson wrote *New Year's Eve* (1871) inspired by **Heiberg**'s *Elverhöj* and **Shakespeare**'s *Midsummer Night's Dream*. *The Outlaws*, a popular comedy, remains the most frequently produced Icelandic play, but its initial success owed greatly to Gudmundsson's pioneering stage design depicting Icelandic landscape. Jochumsson and Einarsson made several translations of Shakespeare, which were not superseded until Helgi Hálfdanarson's translations of the complete plays began appearing after 1950, as well as writing historical plays in his fashion. These include Jochumsson's *Jón Arason* (1899) and Einarsson's *Sword and Crosier* (1899). Einarsson, a lesser writer than Jochumsson, was the first to concentrate on playwriting and his folklore-plays include *The Cave Dwellers* (1897) and the Faustian *The Dance at Hruni* (1921). Einarsson's major contribution, however, is his dedication to Gudmundsson's national theatre ideal. Through his tireless efforts money was secured to begin construction of a National Theatre around 1930.

By the 1890s there were three main amateur companies in Reykjavík, two of which joined forces in 1897 to establish the Reykjavík Theatre Company (RTC) aiming to secure the growth of Icelandic drama and raise the standard of productions. The company, officially supported, found a permanent home with an intimate stage and Einarsson became the first stage director. In 1903 the RTC produced their first Icelandic play, Einarsson's realistic *The Ship is Sinking*, while the 1904–5 season featured **Ibsen**'s *Ghosts* and *A Doll's House*, with **Molière**, **Schiller** and **Shaw** crowning subsequent seasons. From 1908 to 1920 there were productions of 11 new plays, all but one directed by actor Jens B. Waage. In this period **Jóhann Sigurjónsson**, **Gudmundur Kamban** and Einar H. Kvaran, three outstanding playwrights, were established, the first two gaining international reputations. The RTC, strong and ambitious although amateur, was joined by the first professional actors arriving from training abroad, mostly from Copenhagen, during the 1920s and early 1930s. These were Haraldur Björnsson, Anna Borg Reumert, Lárus Pálsson, Indridi Waage and Thorsteinn Ö. Stephensen. Björnsson, Pálsson and Waage became leading directors, while Stephensen also headed radio drama for almost thirty years. Anna Borg Reumert soon returned to Copenhagen to become a leading actress there. In 1926 Waage directed *Twelfth Night*, the first Shakespeare production in Iceland.

The existence of the RTC was threatened in 1950 when the National Theatre opened, as nearly all the actors were recruited for the new theatre. A few idealists, including leading actors Stephensen and Brynjólfur Jóhannesson, decided to persevere, with Danish-born Gunnar R. Hansen as director. The RTC became fully professional in 1963 under artistic director Sveinn Einarsson and has since proved a vital alternative to the National Theatre. Vigdís Finnbogadóttir, now president of the republic, took over as artistic director in 1972. The present director is Sigurdur Hróarsson. The RTC moved into the new City Theatre in 1989.

The National Theatre opened with three productions on consecutive nights. Einarsson's *New Year's Eve* was followed by Jóhann Sigurjónsson's *Eyvind of the Mountains* (1911) and Lárus Pálsson's adaptation of Halldór Laxness's epic *The Bell of Iceland* (1943–6). Playing new works and classics, both Icelandic and foreign, it was not until the 1970s that new Icelandic drama became the backbone of the repertoire. Although the RTC had fine achievements to their credit, fully professional theatre only begins with the National Theatre. The NT-Drama School (1950–70) offered the opportunity of professional training within the country and the NT-Ballet School eventually made it possible to establish the Icelandic Dance Company in 1973, making ballet part of the repertoire, while opera has been included since 1951, the theatre being the only opera house until the Icelandic Opera was formed in 1982. The National Theatre has an auditorium with 661 seats and, since 1964, a small experimental stage. The ensemble consists of 40 versatile actors. Björnsson, Pálsson and Waage were leading directors in the 1950s, but since 1960 main directors have been Baldvin Halldórsson, Benedikt Árnason, Brynja Benediktsdóttir, Sveinn Einarsson, Stefán Baldursson, Bríet Hédinsdóttir, Thórhildur Thorleifsdóttir and Thórhallur Sigurdsson. Artistic directors have been Gudlaugur Rósinkranz, Sveinn Einarsson, Gísli Alfredsson and Stefán Baldursson.

The 1960s saw a renaissance of playwriting and ever since Jökull Jakobsson's successful *Hard-a-Port* (1962), Icelandic plays have been predominant. This period has produced a variety of playwrights, including Jakobsson with his impressionistic studies, absurd-satirist Oddur Björnsson, popular comedy writer Jónas Árnason, the versatile Kjartan Ragnarsson, the lyrical Nína Björk Árnadóttir, Birgir Sigurdsson with his psychological dramas, and **Gudmundur Steinsson** with his allegories and tragicomedies. Laxness also wrote a few absurd-satires in the 1960s and dramatizations of his novels have proved popular.

'The theatre of the absurd' was influential in the 1960s, traces of which are detectable in nearly all the playwrights, but Icelandic 'absurdism' is satirical rather than metaphysical, closer to early **Albee** and **Ionesco** than to **Beckett**, while Jakobsson's plays echo **Pinter**. Now most writers have found different departures from the absurd, some towards realism, others towards social satire and expressionism.

Fringe theatre has made an impression since the 1960s, beginning with the Gríma-Theatre, which, active throughout the 1960s, proved the need for an adventurous alternative theatre through productions of new avant-garde drama, whereas short-lived 'Leiksmidjan' (Theatre Workshop) made its mark, under director Eyvindur Erlendsson, by a return to folklore motifs. Fringe theatre has gained a stronger foothold in the 1970s and 1980s, especially after the Icelandic Drama School was founded in 1973, training many promising young actors who have been unable to find work with existing theatres. In 1973 the amateur theatre in Akureyri became the only professional theatre outside Reykjavík and in 1975 The People's Theatre was established which, initially a touring company, now performs in Reykjavík. Other fringe theatres include The EGG-Theatre and the semi-professional University Theatre. AI

See: A. Boucher, *Modern Nordic Plays*, Oslo, 1973; S. Einarsson, *A History of Icelandic Literature*, Baltimore, 1957; E. Haugen, *Fire and Ice: Three Icelandic Plays*, London, 1967; S. A. Magnússon, *Iceland Crucible*, Reykjavík, 1985.

Ichikawa Danjūrō Twelve generations of actors in the Ichikawa family of Japanese **kabuki** actors have attained the illustrious name Danjūrō. Because of the importance of this acting family and its long history, Danjūrō is sometimes called the 'emperor' of *kabuki*. A brief description of the genealogy of this one acting name tells us much about *kabuki*'s hereditary acting system in general. Danjūrō, as family head (*soke*), is responsible for preserving the Ichikawa family's famous *aragoto* acting style and passing it to the next generation. The Danjūrō name was rather often given to child actors in the past, but more typically the expectant heir was awarded successively higher-ranking names during his early career (making identification of actors in historical sources a puzzle to unravel): the present Danjūrō XII was given the name Ichikawa Natsuō for his stage debut when he was three, Ichikawa Shinnosuke when he was 12, and Ichikawa Ebizō X when he showed his mature acting stature by playing the lead in *Sukeroku: Flower of Edo* at 23. He took the Danjūrō name at a three-month-long ceremony in the summer of 1985. Several Danjūrōs were adopted to continue the family acting line when there was no son.

Danjūrō I (1660–1704). Son of a country samurai, he was 13 when he played the boy-hero Sakata Kintoki in the play *The Four Guardian Gods* at the Nakamura Theatre in Edo (Tokyo) in bravura style marking the beginning of *aragoto* acting. He wrote heroic roles for himself in a dozen plays under the pen name Mimasuya Hyōgo – an infatuated priest turned thundergod in *Thundergod* (1684), the superhero Kamakura Gongorō in *Wait a Moment* (1697), the fierce protective god Fudō

in *Immovable* (1697), the powerful priest Benkei in *The Subscription List* (1702). He was murdered on stage by a jealous actor when he was 44.

Danjūrō II (1688–1758). The eldest son of Danjūrō I he became Danjūrō II when he was 17. Over his long lifetime, he originated more than half the plays in the Eighteen Favourite Plays (*jūhachiban*) collection – *Sukeroku: Flower of Edo* (1713), *Medicine Seller* (1718), *Arrow Maker* (1725), and *Whisker Tweezers* (1742) among them. He introduced grace and gentleness into *aragoto* acting, especially in the dashing title role of Sukeroku, borrowing from the Kyoto-Osaka soft style of acting (*wagoto*). Having no son, he passed the Danjūrō name to a pupil and acted for the last 23 years of his life as Ichikawa Ebizō II.

Danjūrō III (1721–42). An adored child actor at 6, he became Danjūrō III when he was 14. He had a beautiful voice and an elegant acting style. He died at the age of 21, after becoming ill while performing in Osaka with his adoptive father.

Danjūrō IV (1711–78). After Danjūrō III died, no successor was named for 12 years. The elderly Ebizō II (Danjūrō II) adopted 43-year-old Matsumoto Koshirō II, a specialist in villain roles, as his heir. A progressive intelligent actor, Danjūrō IV added a dark tinge to *aragoto* acting in his role of the malicious warrior Kagekiyo, a role he played 16 times in his life.

Danjūrō V (1741–1807). The son of Danjūrō IV, when he was 29 he changed his name from Matsumoto Koshirō III to Ichikawa Danjūrō V. He was the first actor to announce his new name in a formal name-taking ceremony (*shūmei hirō*). His boast that his name was known 'in all the corners of the world' (*sumi kara sumi made*) is now repeated by every Danjūrō. He addressed the audience, 'I will now cross one eye over the other' thus beginning the custom of demonstrating the Ichikawa family pose (*mie*) and eye-crossing glare (*nirami*), trademarks of each Danjūrō name succession. When he was 49 and at the height of his powers he gave the Danjūrō name to his son and retired as Ichikawa Hakuen, to a life of leisure and writing.

Danjūrō VI (1778–99). The son of Danjūrō V. Four magnificent prints by the woodblock artist Sharaku show a sensuously attractive teenage Danjūrō VI. He took his famous name when he was 13 and at 20 he was actor-manager (*zagashira*) of the Nakamura Theatre, a remarkable honour. Audiences loved his 'modern' acting as Heiemon in *The Forty-Seven Loyal Retainers* (1748) in which he expanded the range of the Ichikawa family acting style (*ie no gei*). His brilliant career ended the following year when he died on stage at the age of 21.

Danjūrō VII (1791–1859). He was probably the child of Danjūrō V's daughter Sumi and the actor Maruya Shichibei. Precocious, he was three when he first acted in *kabuki*, became Ebizō at five, starred as Gongorō in *Wait a Moment* at the Kawarazaki Theatre at seven, and at the ripe age of nine became Danjūrō VII, only months after Danjūrō VI's sudden death. The greatest actors of the time – Matsumoto Koshirō V, Iwai Hanshirō V, Onoe Kikugorō III – spoke at his name-taking ceremony. He was highly original. He created gangster (*kizewamono*) roles, like the scoundrel Yoemon in Tsuruya Namboku's *Kasane* (1823). He was a master at playing several roles in a play, accomplished by quick costume changes: he played four leading roles in Tsuruya Namboku's *The Scarlet Princess of Edo* (1817). He premiered new dance-dramas based on **nō**, such as *The Subscription List* (1840). Proud and ostentatious in his manner of living, the government banished him from Edo for seven years (1842–9). In all, he spent 15 years playing in the provinces.

Danjūrō VIII (1823–54). The eldest son of Danjūrō VII, he took his father's name when he was 9 years old. He was idolized in such romantic roles as Sukeroku, but his father's banishment and the consequent burden he carried as head of the Ichikawa family led him into deep depression. He committed suicide when he was 31.

Danjūrō IX (1838–1903). The fifth son of Danjūrō VII had no reason to believe he would inherit his father's name. For 30 years he was an adopted actor in the Kawarazaki acting family, where he attained that family's highest name, Gonnosuke VII. Twenty years after the death of Danjūrō VIII and when he was 36 years old, he returned to carry on the Ichikawa family line as Danjūrō IX. He supported the Society for Theatre Reform that strove to modernize *kabuki* in the late 1880s. Danjūrō played Benkei in *The Subscription List* in the presence of the Emperor Meiji, the first time *kabuki* had been honoured by the imperial presence. He was a star of the Kabuki-za, a new theatre in the Ginza, which attracted a fashionable audience and helped make *kabuki* 'respectable' in society. Danjūrō IX possessed energy, courage, and artistic vision; unquestionably he was the greatest *kabuki* actor of the modern era.

Danjūrō X (1882–1956). Danjūrō IX had no son and no adoptive heir when he died. His eldest daughter was a talented performer but being a woman she could not act in *kabuki*, so responsibility for continuing the Ichikawa Danjūrō family line fell on her husband, a banker. Untrained in theatre, nonetheless he courageously revived long-forgotten plays in the Ichikawa repertory – *Immovable*, *Seven Masks*, *Pushing and Pulling*, and others – thus perpetuating the family acting style through a difficult period of Japanese history. He was awarded the name Danjūrō X posthumously.

Danjūrō XI (1909–65). Danjūrō X, too, had no son. For 60 years there was no Danjūrō on the *kabuki* stage. Danjūrō XI was the eldest son of Matsumoto Koshirō VII, a former pupil of Danjūrō IX, so it was considered appropriate that Koshirō's son should be adopted by the Ichikawa family. By nature he was reserved and modest, but on stage he excelled in dashing, romantic roles like Sukeroku or the Shining Prince Genji. He died, after a short illness, after holding the Danjūrō name for three years.

Danjūrō XII (b. 1946). Twenty years after Danjūrō XI died, his eldest son became Danjūrō XII in a name-taking ceremony (*shūmei hirō*) that continued for three months in summer 1985. A modern person, he has combined a college education with a career as a classical *kabuki* actor. He had already attracted a youthful following as a teenager performing with Onoe Tatsunosuke and Onoe Kikunosuke (the present Kikugorō VII). When he took the name Ebizō, at the age of 23, he was a veteran of 100 major roles. He is a genuine star, admired for restrained acting in modern plays as well as bravura performances of *aragoto* classics in the family line.   JRB

Iffland, August Wilhelm (1759–1814) German actor, régisseur, and playwright. After being trained by

Ekhof at Gotha, in 1779 Iffland joined the new **Mannheim Court Theatre**. He left in 1796 to become the director of the **Berlin Royal Theatre**, where he remained until his death. Iffland was honoured throughout Germany for the extraordinary versatility of his acting. Although not a performer of exceptional power, he was noted for the completeness of his characterization, his subtlety, and his finely judged transitions. **Goethe** was among his greatest admirers, though **Schiller**, who had approved of his Franz Moor at the first performance of *The Robbers* in 1782, later found him to be cold and artificial. Iffland was also a prolific playwright, specializing in *Rührstücke*, sentimental, melodramatic pieces, generally with a domestic setting. Of these, *The Huntsmen* (1785) may be seen occasionally in Germany today. As director of the Berlin Royal Theatre, Iffland presented the plays of **Shakespeare**, Schiller, and contemporary historical dramatists in extremely spectacular productions, which foreshadowed the work of later directors such as **Dingelstedt** and the Duke of Saxe-**Meiningen**. Iffland was decorated by the Prussian king. All in all, the eminence he achieved did much to elevate the professional status of the theatre in the eyes of the public.   SW

Imbuga, Francis (*fl.* 1970s) Kenyan playwright, author of a number of plays, including *Betrayal in the City* which was Kenya's entry to the Second World Black and African Festival of Arts and Culture in Lagos, 1976. The play is a satire on 'the problems of independence and freedom in post-colonial African states'.   RK

Immermann, Karl (1796–1840) German director, playwright, and novelist. Immermann's most important contribution to the German theatre occurred during his directorship of the Düsseldorf Town Theatre between 1835 and 1837. Here, despite modest resources, he developed a company that achieved national renown for the standards of its ensemble playing. At this time most German theatres were subject to the preeminence of the virtuoso actor. In February 1840, Immermann staged *Twelfth Night* on a specially constructed stage that incorporated features of the Elizabethan and Italian Renaissance stages, a highly unusual enterprise in those days. As a playwright, his work tended to be too reliant upon **Shakespeare** and only his tragedy *Andreas Hofer* (1834) has any individual distinction. Immermann is remembered today primarily for his novel *Münchhausen*.   SW

Imperial Theatre 249 West 45th St, New York City [Architect: Herbert J. Krapp]. Built by the **Shubert brothers** to house their special brand of musical theatre, the playhouse opened in 1923 and since then, has booked fewer than 60 productions, giving it a reputation as a 'lucky house'. Among its most interesting non-musical tenants have been Leslie Howard's *Hamlet* (1936), Jean Arthur's *Peter Pan* (1950) and **John Osborne**'s *A Patriot for Me* (1969). Leading the list of its extraordinary musical successes have been *Oh, Kay!* (1926), *On Your Toes* (1936), *Annie Get Your Gun* (1946), *Fiddler on the Roof* (1964) and *Dreamgirls* (1981). The 1,500-seat theatre remains a Shubert house.   MCH

Incháustegui Cabral, Héctor (1912–79) Poet, critic, fiction writer and playwright. Born in Baní, Dominican Republic, he practised journalism in his youth. He belonged to the so-called group of independent poets who produced important social poetry during the 30s to the 50s. His *Miedo en un puñado de polvo* (*Fear in a Handful of Dust*, 1968) is a collection of three plays based on Greek classics that express universal constants of the human spirit, but his theatre is more theatre of ideas than of action.   GW

Inchbald, Elizabeth (1753–1821) English playwright and novelist, whose determination to become an actress, despite a speech impediment, led her to run away from home in 1772. Little is known of her marriage to Joseph Inchbald (d. 1779), a minor actor. That she loved the much greater actor, **John Philip Kemble**, is well known, not least from the reasonable inference that he served as the model for Dorriforth in her novel, *A Simple Story* (1791). Inchbald's acting career continued until 1789, after which time she devoted herself to writing. Her first play, *A Mogul Tale* (1784), cleverly exploited the current craze for hot-air balloons. It was followed by a number of comedies, of which the most successful included *I'll Tell You What* (1785), *Everyone Has His Fault* (1793), *Wives as They Were, and Maids as They Are* (1797) and *To Marry, or Not to Marry* (1805). *The Child of Nature* (1788) is a more ambitious piece, derived from **Rousseau** by way of Madame de Genlis. A more famous adaptation is that of **Kotzebue**'s *Das Kind der Liebe* as *Lovers' Vows* (1798), the play whose rehearsal in the Bertram household causes such consternation in Jane Austen's *Mansfield Park* (1814). Inchbald defied male prejudice by editing three collections of plays, *The British Theatre* (25 vols, 1808), *Farces* (7 vols, 1809) and *The Modern Theatre* (10 vols, 1809).   PT

India India is among the world's most populous nations, with nearly 800 million people inhabiting a vast and contrasting land bordered on the north and east by the Himalayan mountain range, on the west by the Great Thar Desert with the southern half of the nation a peninsula surrounded by the Arabian Sea on one side and the Bay of Bengal on the other. Because of its strategic location, Indian civilization has been shaped over time by a multitude of social, political and religious forces which, in turn, have had a direct bearing on the shape of its theatre.

The Indus Valley Civilization dating from 2300 BC was the first great culture to inhabit areas of the north, along the Indus River basin. The advanced city states that were formed there came to an abrupt and unexplainable halt by 1750 BC. Eventually, India was populated by Indo-Aryans who migrated from Persia.

Over the centuries, the Aryans developed a body of rituals and religious customs which came to be known as Hinduism. The Sanskrit language was the medium of communication among the priests and kings who dominated the social life of the times. Myths developed which reinforced their ideas and the resulting society prospered and grew to take its place among the world's great ancient civilizations. Sanskrit drama and theatre came into being and flourished during this relatively peaceful period between the 1st and the 10th centuries AD, reinforcing the beliefs of the civilization.

India also served as the cradle of other great religions – Buddhism, Jainism, Sikhism and, though it did not originate there, India became the adopted home of Zoroastrianism. Even the Christian faith took root and flourished in India.

Among the social and political influences that have had a major bearing on the development of Indian theatre was the introduction of Islam to the Indian subcontinent. After an initial period of conquest around the 10th and 11th centuries, the Middle Eastern people who introduced Islam integrated with the Indo-Aryans and produced powerful empires centred in Delhi, such as that of the Emperor Akbar. Owing to their religious convictions, the followers of Islam discouraged, or forbade entirely, the performance of theatre. Under the threat of mass conversion to Islam, the decline of Buddhism as a popular religion, and the loss of social and political power, a new movement of Hinduism was born known as Vaisnavism. As a result of renewed faith in the values and ideas which were essentially indigenous to India, Vaisnavism nurtured the growth of theatre in village settings throughout the subcontinent. Theatre grew to service the needs of millions of people in a multitude of regional languages (by some counts today, there are 16 major regional languages in India). The period of development and growth of rural theatre forms began about the 15th century and continued through to the 19th century.

The British came to India in the 17th century, although they did not dominate the country until 150 years later. They established a presence at strategic locations on the subcontinent. Through their effort, modern urban society was born. The colonial period extended from the mid-19th to the mid-20th centuries which witnessed the centralization of power, industrialization, development of mass systems of transportation and communication, as well as staggering growth in the population. During the colonial period, modern theatre developed. It continues to develop in all the major regional languages as a reflection of the ideas and concerns of urban Indian audiences.

In order to understand Indian theatre, it is necessary to investigate each stage of its growth separately, beginning with the Sanskrit theatre, continuing through the rural theatre forms and concluding with modern theatre.

It is difficult to affix an exact date, or even to determine the precise century, of the origin of Sanskrit theatre. Fragments of the earliest known plays have been traced to the 1st century AD. And yet the sophistication of the form of the fragments suggests that a living theatre tradition must have existed in India at a somewhat earlier date. The earliest traces of civilization in India date from between 2300 and 1750 BC and yet the enormous wealth of archaeological evidence provides no hint of the existence of a living theatre tradition. Dance and music seem to have been enjoyed by the people of those times, perhaps as part of religious celebrations, but theatre is not in evidence. A search of the *Vedas*, sacred hymns, among the world's earliest literary outpourings, dating from approximately 1500 to 1000 BC, yields no trace of theatre, even though a few of the hymns are composed in a short, elementary dialogue. Some of the ritual practices of the Vedic age have the potential of developing into drama but do not seem to have sparked a theatre tradition.

The period between 1000 BC and 100 BC saw the rise of the great Hindu epic literature, particularly the *Mahabharata*, the longest and arguably the most comprehensive document of ancient Indian life, the *Ramayana*, a somewhat shorter but no less important epic work, which, like the *Mahabharata*, still provides rural and urban dramatists with source material, and the *Puranas*, a major collection of stories dealing with the life and exploits of Krishna, incarnation of the god Vishnu, all of whose incarnations have provided inspiration for dramatic compositions. Reference to a class of performers who may have been actors is to be found in major epic stories but no clear cut reference to theatre and drama exists.

Some scholars conjecture, without any proof, that the Sanskrit theatre owes some, or all, of its inspiration to contact between ancient Indian poets and ancient Greek actors. Alexander the Great is known to have been fond of actors and may have taken troupes of them with him on his campaigns to north-eastern India in 327 BC.

The earliest reference to events which may have been the seeds of Sanskrit drama is in 140 BC by Patanjali in his *Mahabhasya*. The work itself is a text of grammar. In order to make a point, Patanjali indicates that action may be determined in several ways; through: 1. Pantomime, 2. Recitation, 3. Song, and 4. Dance. Although drama (*natya*) is not specifically mentioned, reference is made to individuals who recite and sing (*natas*). Coupled with the existence of dramatic rituals, ample epic stories which were later interpreted in dramatic form and the existence of traditions of song, dance and recitation, firmly established in Indian tradition, it is feasible that Sanskrit drama came into being about this point in time. What is lacking is a specific reference to that fact.

Unfortunately, unlike Greek and Roman theatre which left physical evidence of its presence in the ruins of theatre structures, Sanskrit theatre has left no tangible evidence of its early history. Only in the plays and dramaturgical texts which survive in palm leaf manuscript and descriptions from other sources may one glean the outlines of the Sanskrit theatre.

The most important single source for establishing the character of the Sanskrit tradition in ancient India is the *Natyasastra* of Bharata, a work which has been variously dated between 200 BC and AD 200. As we have seen *natya* means 'drama' or 'theatre'. *Sastra* is a generic term referring to any authoritative text. The author of the *Natyasastra* bears the name of the first tribe of India and his name has come to mean 'actor' as an occupational group.

The mythological origin of theatre is related in the *Natyasastra*. Theatre is said to have been the inspiration of Brahma, the god of creation, and Bharata figures prominently in its origin. In chapter one, Bharata describes a charming story of how theatre came into being:

When the world was given over to sensual pleasure, Indra, king of the gods (one of India's earliest major deities), approached Brahma and asked that he create a form of diversion that could be seen as well as heard and that would be accessible to the four occupational (colour) groups (*varnas*) – priests, warriors, tradesmen and peasants. Out of his state of meditation, Brahma created drama (*natya*), which he referred to as a fifth *Veda*, or sacred text.

Brahma requested that Indra compose plays and have the gods enact them. Not considering it appropriate for gods to act, Indra asked that the priests (*brahmanas*) be recruited to take on this task. Bharata and his sons were summoned by Brahma and persuaded to serve as the first actors, which they willingly agreed to do. And Brahma, knowing what he had in mind when he created theatre, taught them the art himself.

To fulfil additional personnel needs, Brahma created heavenly nymphs to act and dance and musicians were recruited to play and sing to accompany the show. The occasion of the first performance was established to depict and coincide with the defeat of the demons by the gods, celebrating Indra's victorious leadership.

All seemed well until malevolent spirits disturbed the dramatic action. Eventually, Brahma summoned Visvakarma, his architect, to devise a space which would be sanctified and prevent spirits from bringing harm to the actors and the action to a complete halt. The architect did as he was bid and produced a facility all the parts of which were consecrated with rituals, from the very groundbreaking to the inauguration ceremony.

The show resumed in the newly sanctified theatre structure but the evil spirits continued to plague the actors. At last, Brahma summoned the demons and in a mood of reconciliation explained the purpose of drama and the objective for which it was intended. In short, he indicates that no class of individuals is excluded from seeing it, including the demons, and that it is meant to educate and entertain, and thus no subject may be excluded from consideration, even the defeat of the demons in battle. As a final step to silence the objections of the malevolent spirits, Brahma proclaims that those who correctly observe the ritual sacrifices connected with performance will be protected from evil and will enjoy a success in their undertakings.

Bharata's simple story reveals many important facts about Sanskrit theatre: 1. It is composed of sacred material. 2. A specialist should witness it. 3. At least as far as Sanskrit drama is concerned, it should be performed by members of the priestly caste, the top rank in the hierarchy of the caste system. 4. It requires special knowledge and skill to execute it. 5. Training is a hereditary process coming from father to son and descending directly from God. 6. Special skills are necessary to execute theatre, such as dance, music, recitation and ritual knowledge. 7. It should be performed on consecrated ground. 8. Its purpose is to entertain as well as to educate.

It is difficult to measure the influence of the *Natyasastra* in its historical context and virtually impossible to compare the multitude of dictum in it with actual stage practices. Perhaps a measure of its importance to scholarly concerns today is that it sheds light, sometimes the only light available, on many subjects of importance to a comprehensive understanding of the theatre in ancient India. Perhaps we cannot hope for more.

The work is broad in scope, broader than **Aristotle**'s *Poetics*, the other major document of theatre practice surviving from the ancient world. The *Natyasastra* covers acting, theatre architecture, costuming, makeup, properties, dance, music, play construction, as well as the organization of theatre companies, audiences, dramatic competitions, the community of actors and ritual practices, to name only a few of the more important subjects of the book. Coupled with the extant texts of plays, it is possible to develop a picture, incomplete though it may be, of the classical Indian theatre.

At the heart of the theatre companies was the stage manager (*sutradhara*) who may have also been a leading actor. It was his job to direct the players; perhaps he also served as their teacher. Like Bharata in the mythological story of the origin of theatre, he literally held the strings of the performance within his grasp (i.e. *sutradhara*, literally means 'holder of the threads or strings', e.g. a puppeteer, an architect or a manipulator). He also seems to have been assisted in his duties, perhaps by an apprentice who may have been one of his sons.

The actors studied under the guidance of a drama teacher (*natyacharya*), probably the stage manager, who was usually an older and respected individual, perhaps like Bharata, the father of the actors. Under his guidance, it was their job to keep physically and vocally fit for performance by undergoing rigorous periods of training. Also through observation, they gained much insight from their elders in performance practices.

Men and women both seem to have been permitted to act together or in separate troupes of their own sex. They either played characters their own age or they played those of a contrasting age range. Younger actors might play the roles of older people and older actors might portray the young. Actresses were regarded as better suited to enact certain sentiments, not considered appropriate for men to perform. Given the plays, it may be assumed that the actors and actresses needed to be highly skilled in speech and singing, as well as adept at bodily movement, both realistic and abstract. The ability to dance may also have been required.

The Sanskrit plays that survive confirm the use of stock character types. Thus actors may have specialized in a particular role category, such as a hero (*nayaka*), a heroine (*nayika*), a clown (*vidushaka*), and so forth.

The Indian system of acting is laid out in considerable detail in the *Natyasastra*. Many chapters are devoted to its discussion, more than any other subject covered by the book. Two styles of acting appear to have been common – the realistic (*lokadharmi*) and the conventional (*natyadharmi*), the latter of which receives almost exclusive attention in the text.

Acting (*abhinaya*; literally, 'to carry towards') is defined as having four elements – bodily movement (*angika*), voice (*vacika*), spectacle (*aharya*), and sentiment or emotion (*sattvika*). Of these, bodily movement receives lavish attention in the *Natyasastra*. Five chapters are devoted to its discussion. Although the text reveals an enormous amount of detail about the subject, it is not always clear whether they are addressed to dancers or actors.

Whatever their application, the material is thorough. The body is divided into major and minor parts which are discussed in relation to the way they convey emotions to the spectators. A wide variety of hand gestures are described, indicating that a sophisticated language of communication had to be studied and perfected in order to act in the conventional style. Specific glances, movements of the eyebrows, cheeks, lips, chin and neck are all discussed according to their ability to communicate meaning.

Broad categories of movement involving the whole body are described, such as poses (*caris*) and gaits (*gatis*) thought suitable in various situations depending on the age, sex, rank and temperament of a character.

Although five chapters of the *Natyasastra* are devoted to voice, little of the information is applicable to acting on the stage. Instead, the information concerns questions of grammar, language and metres. Forms of address appropriate for characters of various ranks are discussed and regional dialects, thought appropriate to various characters according to their rank and station in life, are mentioned.

The ancient Indians do not seem content to limit acting to the study of voice, body and sentiment, as is frequently the case in the Western world; instead, they clearly consider the costumes, ornaments and makeup of the actor a vital part of character. Even stage properties are seen as an extension of acting and receive treatment in several chapters of the *Natyasastra*. A curtain (*yavanika*), held by two attendants, was used to mark entrances of characters and became a theatrical device for exposing the character to the public.

Elaborate decorations (*alamkara*) of the body are described in detail – garlands, ornaments and costumes. From the top of the head to the tip of the toe, hardly any part of the human body was not decorated according to the caste, station in life and occupation of the character. Real ornaments were considered inappropriate for stage use since their weight might tire the actor. Instead, ornaments were crafted of light wood and painted to resemble the actual object. It is not clear if the costumes were reproductions of historically accurate apparel, if they were the actual dress of the times or whether they were fanciful in shape, size and colour. There is no visual evidence depicting actors on stage to give us a clue of the stage practices of the day.

The well-rounded actor of Sanskrit plays was expected to go beyond external representation of character through correct execution of movement, speech and ornamentation. Although the *Natyasastra* is not crystal clear about this special attribute of performance skill, it states that there is something invisible (*sattva*) about performance, an intangible quality, that transcends externals and reaches the hearts and minds of the spectators. This process has to do with conveying sentiments and emotions (*sattvika*) of the play through the content of the work. It is this intangible something which completes the Sanskrit actor's circle of obligations.

Although acting is obviously a very important part of theatre, the social status of the actors does not seem to have been particularly high in ancient India. Bharata may have been a Brahmin priest, but Sanskrit actors were classed with bandits and prostitutes, according to most ancient authorities. In the final chapter of the *Natyasastra*, Bharata and his sons are cursed by respected sages who took offence at the caricatures of themselves by the actors. On the verge of suicide, the outcast actors were patronized by kings in order to preserve the art from extinction; thus began the historic practice of royal patronage which seems to have survived through ancient times.

It appears that dancers and musicians may have been commissioned to participate in performance, but there is room to argue that they, too, may have been regular members of ancient companies of players. Among the musicians were male and female vocalists, flautists, who performed on bamboo instruments, players of stringed instruments, like the *vina*, a classical south Indian instrument, drummers and cymbal players. Ankle bells worn on the feet of dancers helped to accentuate the rhythmic patterns of the music and further contributed to the sophistication of the sound.

When reading a Sanskrit play it is not possible to determine how dance and music might have been integrated into the fabric of performance. Indeed, at first glance, the plays appear to be dialogue dramas. The stage directions do not indicate places where music is to be inserted nor do they reveal when a dance should occur or whether a particular poetic passage is to be danced or sung. The *Natyasastra* does mention that songs (*dhruvas*) were to be composed in the Prakrit language and inserted for specific purposes. Apparently these songs were composed for introducing characters, to mark a character's exit, to establish the middle or end of an act, to reinforce a dramatic mood, to establish the change of dramatic moods and to fill the gap when a temporary halt occurred in the action, for instance, when a costume had to be adjusted and the actor was forced to leave the stage.

None of the *dhruvas* have survived the passage of time and it appears that the music in which they were composed may have differed considerably from that which we now know as Indian classical music, owing to the influence of Middle Eastern music after the Muslim invasions beginning in the 10th century AD.

Sanskrit theatre was performed to celebrate important religious occasions, in connection with temple festivals. The *Natyasastra* calls the performance of plays a visual sacrifice (*yajna*) to the gods and thus clearly identifies it as a sacred event. And yet we also know that performances were organized to celebrate coronations, marriages, the birth of children and the return of a traveller and to celebrate the defeat of an enemy.

The audience for theatrical events was known as 'those who see' (*preksaka*), clearly implying that seeing a performance was as important as hearing it. Owing to the sophistication demanded of the actors, it is not surprising that the *Natyasastra* identifies spectators in terms of certain ideal characteristics. Those of good character, high birth, quiet and learned, partial, advanced in age, alert, honest, virtuous, knowledgeable in drama, acting, music, dance and the arts and crafts which figure in their execution, were considered to have the attributes of an ideal spectator. Perhaps few if any individuals measured up to that ideal. Perhaps that is why God is the ultimate witness to the dramatic event, for he alone possessed all the attributes demanded.

Dramatic competitions are known during the classical period in which critics judged the merits of the acting and awarded prizes to those who excelled. Ultimately, those whose occupation was depicted were thought the best judge of the actors. Kings were thought fit to judge actors who portrayed kings, courtesans might judge those who played courtesans and so forth.

In contrast to the practices in the Greek theatre, prizes were not awarded to the playwrights (*natyakara*). Although the *Natyasastra* categorizes playwrights among the members of theatre companies, historical evidence suggests that they were more likely to have

been members of the courts of kings, if not kings themselves.

Literally hundreds of plays were written from the 1st century to the 10th century AD, the high point of the Sanskrit dramatic outpouring. Relatively few plays from this period have survived. The earliest are those of Asvaghosa whose fragmentary works of the 1st century AD came to the attention of scholars in the early part of our own century. His plays concern Buddhist teachings and follow the rules pertaining to dramatic composition laid down in the *Natyasastra*.

The author for whom we have the greatest abundance of works is Bhasa whose 13 surviving plays cover a wide range of subject matter and at least one of which, *The Vision of Vasavadatta* (*Svapnavasavatta*), is among the best and most important works of Sanskrit dramatic literature.

Although the actual period of his life is still in dispute and virtually nothing is known about his personal life, most probably he worked between the 4th and 5th centuries AD in the ancient city of Ujjain in north central India. He composed plays based on dramatic incidents from the *Ramayana*, the *Mahabharata* and the *Puranas*, as well as semi-historical tales. He also originated stories of his own. Bhasa's works follow many of the dramatic rules of the *Natyasastra*, although he violates some of them, at times with outstanding results. Bhasa seems to have been a man of the theatre, as well as a capable poet. His works are as fresh today as they must have been when he first composed them and his characterizations range from competent to exceptional.

Among the major dramatic works of classical India, the most monumental and perhaps one of the most popular is *The Little Clay Cart* (*Mrcchakatika*) attributed to Sudraka. No other works have been traced to Sudraka and yet it is hard to believe that a writer could have produced only one brilliant work and remained silent the rest of his life. The preface to the play describes the author in considerable detail, indicating that he was a king, a mathematician, knowledgeable in love and skilled in the training of elephants. According to the verse, he was a hundred years old when he committed suicide. Obviously, it is impossible that a writer could discuss his own death in the preface to one of his plays, thus raising numerous questions about the authenticity of the preface and the author of the work.

The Little Clay Cart is similar to Bhasa's unfinished work *Charudattam*. But there is no way of knowing whether Sudraka and Bhasa were one and the same individual, or whether Sudraka borrowed Bhasa's play and added his own poetic style to it, as well as embroidered the political plot into the fabric of the story. Whatever the circumstances, Sudraka may have lived about the 5th century AD and certainly produced a masterpiece.

The plot of *The Little Clay Cart* is original. It involves Charudatta, a hapless Brahmin merchant who is generous to a fault, brave and virtuous and who is in love with Vasantasena, a rich, beautiful and faithful courtesan. Their deep affection for each other is nearly spoiled by Samstanaka, a jealous ne'er-do-well brother-in-law of a corrupt king who is the very antithesis of Charudatta. He attempts to murder Vasantasena and blame the crime on Charudatta only to find his plot is spoiled by fate. Despite its serious moments, the play basically centres on love and humour and historically has been one of the few popularly staged pieces of the classical Indian repertory.

Arguably, India's greatest playwright is Kalidasa whose life and dates remain a mystery. He could have been court poet of King Chandragupta II of Ujjain in the mid-5th century AD. He is known to have written the plays *Malavikagnimitra* and *Vikramorvasiya*, the dramatic poem *Meghaduta*, and the epic poems *Kamarasambhava* and *Raghuvamsa*. However, his undisputed literary masterpiece is *Abhijnanasakuntala* (*Sakuntala and the Ring of Recognition*), which, like *The Little Clay Cart*, has been produced frequently in modern times.

Kalidasa's craftsmanship is regarded as the best example of the adherence of a Sanskrit poet to the classical rules without sacrificing his own artistic integrity. The play is a delicate exploration of human love. The source of the story may be found in the *Mahabharata*.

Kalidasa took liberties with the epic sources to suit his own particular needs. The plot surrounds King Dusyanta, his infatuation, love, marriage, separation and reunion with Sakuntala, daughter of a heavenly nymph and a sage. When the play opens, Sakuntala is a young girl on the verge of womanhood. Her unspoiled beauty attracts Dusyanta, who is sporting in a forest nearby Sakuntala's hermitage home. The first three acts explore the delicate relationship between the dashing king and the modest young maiden. After agreeing to a marriage by mutual consent, Sakuntala prepares to follow her husband to the city to take up residence in his palace as his chief queen. Her departure from the sacred grove provides ample food for some of the most beautiful lyrics in all of Sanskrit literature. They also parallel the anguish that parents experience when their children leave home for good.

Due to a seemingly minor offence to a saintly guest, on her arrival at court Sakuntala is punished when the king forgets her. Suffering from anguish, she is whisked away by a heavenly nymph and, up to the final act, the story revolves around the torments of the king whose memory is restored only too late to learn that Sakuntala has disappeared. Ultimately, fate intervenes and the king finds Sakuntala in the hermitage of the mother and father of the gods. She has given birth to a handsome son, his only child, who bears the marks of royalty. Dusyanta identifies the child, finds Sakuntala and experiences a tearful but happy reunion.

Among the major playwrights of a later period of Sanskrit drama, Bhavabhuti stands out above the others. He appears to have lived around AD 700 and was a member of the court of a north Indian king. His *The Latter History of Rama* is among the best plays of Sanskrit drama. The work adapts incidents from the epic *Ramayana* and develops unique and creative twists to the plot. Like other later writers, Bhavabhuti succumbs to the temptation to embellish his writing with lengthy poetic expressions.

Although there are other distinguished playwrights worth mentioning, none of them achieved the reputation of Bhasa, Sudraka, Kalidasa and Bhavabhuti. For all practical purposes, Sanskrit plays which deserve critical attention were not written after the 10th century AD.

The *Natyasastra* laid down rules for the composition of plays and for rituals connected with their presenta-tion. Published editions of the plays normally include a short benedictory verse (*nandi*) and a prologue (*prastavana*) along with the text of the work, if the original text contains a benediction and a prologue; however, the *Natyasastra* lists 18 separate preliminaries (*purvaranga*) among the steps that may have taken place prior to the first lines of a text, including the benediction and prologue. These preliminaries provide a gradual bridging between the world of the audience and that of the play. It begins with musical performances followed by dances and ritual observances. Eventually, events like those of the prologue occur in which the audience is addressed directly by the characters and their conversation leads to the introduction of the first character of the play. This special method of introduction to a play accomplishes the goal of warming the performers and the audience to the events at hand, sanctifying the performance area, blessing the proceedings, introducing the story in a novel way and focusing attention on the dramatic action.

Sanskrit playwrights had ten types of drama in which they could choose to compose their work. The best-known and most frequently used was the *nataka* which was a well-known story concerning a hero who might be a king or a royal sage. The theme of the *nataka* might exploit the sentiments of love and heroism. This type of drama was restricted to between five and seven acts. *Sakuntala*, *The Vision of Vasavadatta* and *The Latter History of Rama* are three of the better known examples of this dramatic type.

Although the *prakarana* was regarded as another major type, only two examples of this form survive. *The Little Clay Cart* is the better of the examples. According to the *Natyasastra*, it was to have an invented story; a Brahmin, merchant or minister was to serve as the hero; a courtesan was to serve as the heroine; and, love was to be the dominant sentiment. It was restricted to between five and ten acts.

The other types of plays listed in the *Natyasastra*, examples of which are best seen in the works of Bhasa, are *anka*, *vyayoga*, *bhana*, *samvakara*, *vithi*, *prahasana*, *dima* and *ihamrga*.

The smallest possible unit of a play was an act (*anka*) in which the hero's basic dramatic situation might be portrayed. Acts were to be made up of a series of incidents surrounding the main characters; the concerns of minor figures were not permitted to dominate an act. Curses, marriages, battles, loss of a kingdom or death were strictly prohibited from being depicted on the stage. Events such as these might be reported, but they could not be shown.

The plot (*vastu*) was considered the body of the play. Each stage in its development was carefully identified and thought to follow a prescribed pattern. Normally, the seed (*bija*) of the plot concerned the desire of the hero to achieve a specific end. The plot moved the dramatic action toward that goal with a reversal of fortune as an inevitable stumbling block to its achievement. Finally, the goal which was reached was to relate to one of the three ends of Hindu life – duty (*dharma*), pleasure (*kama*) or wealth (*artha*).

Rather than serving as a reflection of life in ancient India, Sanskrit drama served as a model of ideal human behaviour. The idealization of the characters, their values and actions, all point to this lofty ultimate aim. Sanskrit drama is not a drama of protest or of reaction but a theatre of elevated ideals. Guided by the *Natyasas-tra*'s rules, the writers cooperated and lived within their society rather than breaking down barriers or exhibiting individualistic points of view.

Among the unique contributions of Sanskrit drama to world literature is its aesthetic theory. The theory of sentiment (*rasa*) relates to the audience perception of the theatre event, as well as the contribution of the theatre artists to the process. According to the *Natyasastra*, which first articulated the theory of *rasa*, human experiences are divided into eight basic sentiments – erotic (*srngara*), comic (*hasya*), pathos (*karuna*), rage (*raudra*), heroism (*vira*), terror (*bhayanaka*), odiousness (*bibhatsa*) and the marvellous (*adbhuta*). These sentiments are aroused in the audience by corresponding emotions or feelings (*bhava*) represented by the actors. These emotions are achieved with the aid of 32 transitory feelings (*vyabhicaribhava*) and eight states of emotion or feeling (*sattvika*).

Every play has a dominant emotion (*stayibhava*) which produces a corresponding sentiment (*rasa*) in the audience. And yet the play of the other *bhava* and resulting *rasa* are permissible in a work, as long as balance is maintained and one sentiment dominates the others.

The theory of *rasa* is much like the experience of savouring a good meal, excellently cooked and served, with contrasting complementary tastes abounding. The playwright provides the basic menu which the performers translate into an appropriate presentation. Given the refinement of the system, it is little wonder that spectators were expected to be cultivated and well educated in the arts, as well as in other aspects of life.

The place of performance of these refined works of art is still something of an enigma. No sketches remain, no drawings, floor plans, paintings or models, no ruins to contemplate. The *Natyasastra* is our only guide for a description of the physical facilities of the Sanskrit theatre building. And it speaks of the structures that are described as though they were ideal models rather than actual edifices.

Because the medium-sized rectangular building (*vikrstamadhya*) is spoken of in great detail, it may have been the favoured model. Bharata regards it as the most suitable space to see and hear a performance. The structure is comparatively small, perhaps holding between two, and certainly no more than, five hundred people. Although ideal for achieving intimacy between spectators and players, it seems to have been an exclusive space in contrast with the theatre structures of Ancient Greece and Rome, or those of the great public theatres of Elizabethan England.

The *Natyasastra* sets out specific steps in the selection and preparation of a site for a theatre structure. Rituals accompanied its construction and sanctification, following the plan described for the first theatre structure created by Visvakarma, the heavenly architect. A roof with high windows protected it from the elements and the walls and pillars were decorated with paintings.

Half of the 48 x 96 ft structure was assigned to the spectators. It may be that they sat on risers. Different castes were assigned different seating locations according to their rank.

The stage and dressing room made up the other half of the building. The stage space was 48 x 24 ft and further subdivided in half. A space 48 x 12 ft rose above the floor of the building, perhaps a foot. The 48 x 12 ft space near the dressing room was elevated still further. Two doors separated the dressing room from the acting area. The space between the doors was reserved for the musicians and one of the doors may have been used for entrances and the other assigned for exits. Curtains could have covered the doors.

Little is known about the dressing room and about the acting area. It appears from the plays that the acting area was regarded as a neutral space endowed with symbolic meaning depending on the dramatic action. By walking around (*parikramana*) the actors symbolically changed the locale of the action. The stage was also thought to be divided into separate zones (*kaksya*), although just how this was achieved is not clear from the text. There is no evidence that furniture was used to identify place. Perhaps a stool was the only item of furniture needed to symbolize various objects, such as thrones, benches, etc.

The *Natyasastra* also describes square and triangular theatre structures and indicates that there were small, medium and large varieties of all these shapes.

The 10th century marks the end of the Sanskrit theatre as an active force in Indian art. Internal and external forces were at work several centuries prior to that time which brought about its demise. The successive invasions of Mohmmed of Gazzni weakened the kingdoms of north India, threatening their way of life. Eventually, the temples and kingdoms of the north could not withstand the external pressure. Also the exclusivity of Sanskrit theatre must have weakened its ability to survive. The language of the courts and temples was Sanskrit, but various regional languages and literary traditions were on the verge of emerging in the rural areas. Then too, the rules laid down by the *Natyasastra* exerted a strangle hold on the creative imagination of some later writers. Few were able to make use of them without stifling their creativity. The flexibility that existed in the earlier period disappeared later, and the possibility of new ideas was suppressed.

The period between the 10th and the 15th centuries was one of political and social unrest, particularly in north India. Old social orders were crumbling and new ones took their place. The Muslim invasions of the 10th century eventually led to consolidation of power and the great Mogul empires of the 15th century. In those areas where Islam became the state religion, theatre no longer thrived because the religion did not condone it. Only at the southern tip of the subcontinent did a form of Sanskrit theatre manage to survive – the **Kutiyattam** of Kerala.

Thus with the 10th century, a relatively dark period began in Indian theatre history. Little is known about the theatre of this period. For example, it is not known if the actors, once securely patronized at the court of Hindu kings, took to the road, abandoned Sanskrit and performed plays in vernacular languages of the rural areas, catering to the less sophisticated tastes of village spectators. To have done so would have been inconsistent and uncharacteristic but entirely possible, given the will to survive.

As with the dark ages in medieval Europe, there is evidence of the existence of jugglers, acrobats, storytellers and singers who are mentioned in various texts of the period. Certainly, entertainment did not totally disappear. However, the fortunes of theatre once again eluded us.

Theatre emerged again in India with a dazzling array of village theatre forms, each with its own unique manner of presentation and, more importantly, in the vernacular language of a particular region to service the needs of the people of that region. Unlike Sanskrit theatre, which exhibited a national character because of the widespread use of Sanskrit at the court and in the temple, the rural theatre forms that surfaced after the 15th century did not travel beyond the boundaries of the communities in which they were created. Village troupes which sprang into being were either made up of amateurs or composed of professionals. Many were itinerant groups that worked a particular area, sometimes only one community or religious group. From the 15th to the 19th century, forms of theatre sprang into being in virtually every pocket of the subcontinent. Some of the earlier forms have disappeared today, but a large number of them still survive and continue to serve as a testament to the richness and variety of the creative minds of the people who invented them and invested them with a unique life.

A major catalyst for the reemergence of theatre was Vaisnavism, a religious movement which centres on devotion (*bhakti*) of man for god, in the person of Krishna, the incarnation of Vishnu. Unlike orthodox Hindus, followers of Vaisnavism believe that man may approach god directly, rather than with the aid of rituals. The simple act of repeating god's names is regarded as an act of faith. Thus, theatre became an excellent vehicle for communicating the faith by depicting the acts of god. Those who witnessed it, as well as those who performed it, were engaging in a religious act. Many theatre forms arose at different times and in different places to address the needs of Vaisnavism. Among them are the **Ankiya Nat** of Assam, **Bandi Nata** of Orissa, **Bhagavata Mela** of Tamil Nadu, **Bhamakalapam** of Andhra Pradesh, **Dashavatara** of the Konkan and Goa, **Dhanu Jatra** of Orissa, **Gollakalapam** of Andhra Pradesh, **Krishnattam** of Kerala, **Kuchipudi** of Andhra Pradesh, **Nondi Natakam** of Tamil Nadu, **Prahlada Natakam** of Orissa and **Ramlila** and **Raslila** of various north Indian states.

Most rural theatre forms in India begin with preliminaries and conclude with rituals. Some of these forms arose as an expression of religious zeal and have since made the transition to more secular concerns. Others were originally secular in inspiration. These forms are: **Bharatlila** of Orissa, **Bhavai** of Gujarat, **Bidesia** of Bihar, **Burrakatha** of Andhra Pradesh, **Chaita Ghoda Nata**, **Dandanata**, **Daskathia** and **Ghudiki Nabaranga Nata** of Orissa, **Jatra** of Bengal, Bihar, Orissa and Tripura, **Kariyala** of Himachal Pradesh, **Kathakali** of Kerala, **Khyal** of Uttar Pradesh and Rajasthan, **Kuravanji** of Andhra Pradesh and Tamil Nadu, **Maach** of Madhya Pradesh, **Naqul** of Punjab, **Nautanki** of Uttar Pradesh, Punjab, Rajasthan, Hariyana and Bihar, **Pala** of Orissa, **Rasdhari** of Uttar Pradesh and Rajasthan, **Svanga** of Harayana, Uttar Pradesh and Punjab, **Tamasha** of Maharashtra, **Therukoothu** of Tamil Nadu, **Veedhi Natakam** of Andhra Pradesh and **Yakshagana** of Karnataka, Andhra Pradesh and Tamil Nadu.

Most of India's rural theatre forms were created by Hindus for Hindus and their content is derived from Hindu mythology. However, **Bhagat** of Agra, and the **Bhand Jashna** of Kashmir were created for Muslim consumption and **Cavittu Natakam** of Kerala focuses on Christian concerns.

All of the forms of theatre mentioned above have their own unique form. In execution, organization, costume, makeup, staging and acting style, they differ one from the other; yet, there are some broad similarities that may be noted here. The south Indian forms lay stress on dance; indeed, some of them qualify as dance-dramas, such as the *Kathakali* and *Krishnattam* of Kerala. The north Indian forms emphasize song, among them the *Khyal* of Rajasthan, the *Maach* of Madhya Pradesh, the *Nautanki* of Uttar Pradesh and the *Svanga* of the Punjab. Those that lay stress on dialogue are the *Jatra* of Bengal, the *Tamasha* of Maharashtra and the *Bhavai* of Gujarat. The last two mentioned forms are among the few which emphasize comedy and satire.

An amazing array of puppet theatre forms are also part of the heritage of Indian village life. Shadow, glove, doll, and string puppets have a place in various regions of the country. The shadow forms are **Gombeyatta** of Karnataka, **Pavaikuthu** of Kerala, **Ravana Chhaya** of Orissa and **Tollu Bommalu** of Andhra Pradesh. The glove forms are **Gopalila** of Orissa and **Kundhei Nata** of Orissa, **Pavai Kathakali** of Kerala and **Pavai Koothu** of Tamil Nadu. The doll forms are **Bommalattam** of Tamil Nadu and Mysore State and, **Putul Nautch** of Bengal. The string forms are **Kathputli** of Rajasthan and **Sakhi Kundhei** of Orissa.

The proliferation of forms of performing arts does not end here. Dramatic content may be found in the various solo forms of Indian classical dances, such as the *Bharata Natyam*, *Kathak*, *Odissi* and *Mohiniyattam*, and in folk forms, such as the *Gambhira* of Bengal, the *Seraikella Chhau* of Bihar, *Mayurbhanj Chhau* of Orissa and *Purulia Chhau* of Bengal. Also, dramatic content is richly woven into the ritual ceremonies of some areas, particularly those of Kerala with its Mudiyettu and Teyyam. Story-telling, too, is part of the dramatic heritage of India. The acting in Cakyar Koothu of Kerala, the dance, acting and singing of solo performers of the Ottan Tullal, also of Kerala, and the songs and simple dances of the Khavads of Rajasthan, provide hints of the enormously rich variety of India's rural areas.

Modern theatre The seeds of the modern Indian theatre were sown in the late 18th century with the consolidation of British power in three distinct areas of the subcontinent – Bengal, Maharashtra and Tamil Nadu. More particularly, the British developed fortifications and centralized authority in villages which were later developed into the thriving metropolises of Calcutta, Bombay and Madras. There they introduced their own brand of theatre, based on London models. In those days, the playhouses tripled as performance spaces, meeting houses and storage rooms. Initially, theatre was meant to provide entertainment for the soldiers and citizens who were serving out their days in an alien land and climate.

Before long it became evident that elaborate machinery was needed to govern a country much of which was already under British control. India, at that time, was a nation of a multitude of princely states most of whom were weak and governed by ineffectual leadership in Delhi. To achieve their ends, the British introduced the English system of higher education as a means of developing a class of Indians educated in British ideas, tastes, morals and values. The theatre became an extension of that aim – a tool for conveying the British way of life.

Not content simply to watch the performance of British works, in the mid 19th century, the rich young Bengalis of Calcutta established their own private theatres in their homes which had space large enough for temporary acting areas and auditoria. There they produced plays for the consumption of their friends and family. Eventually they began to write plays following British models which wove in Indian music and songs. The work of Rabindranath Tagore, the Nobel Prize-winning poet, was the product of this initial effort. Among his dramatic achievements were *Red Oleanders* (*Raktakurabi*) and *The King of the Dark Chamber* (*Raja*).

Experiments of this kind could not last, and eventually public theatres came into being during the last quarter of the 19th century, managed by Indian artists and designed to appeal to Indian urban taste. Thus, the modern Indian theatre was born.

The pattern of the development of modern theatre differs from region to region but it ultimately led to the same thing – construction of proscenium arch stages, lighting with equipment suited to the needs of the space, audience control through sale of tickets, a

Manohar, actor-producer of Madras's National Theatre productions performing the role of the gluttonous epic character Kumbakarna.

sophisticated system of theatre management, an acting style suited to the demands of an enclosed building, separation of the audience from the actors by a raised stage and a front curtain, scenery designed to establish the place and time of the dramatic action, costumes, ornaments and makeup geared to the particular lighting effects, organization of the text into units which provided intermissions, and content which addressed issues pertinent to audience concerns. And, perhaps, more importantly, the works were composed in the local regional languages. In Calcutta, Bengali was the language of the new and thriving theatre, in Madras it was Tamil and in Bombay, which was more cosmopolitan than the other cities, plays were composed in Marathi, Gujurati, Hindusthani, Urdu and sometimes in a blend of all these languages, plus English.

Dissatisfaction with British rule led some early patriots to produce works critical of the unfair and harsh treatment of Indian labourers. An itinerant band of Calcutta actors produced *Nildaparna* in Lucknow in 1875 which criticized white planters for their cruel treatment of the Indian peasants. The attempt led British audiences to send the actors packing. Sensitive to the potential of theatre to foment resentment and protest, the government passed the Dramatic Performances Act of 1879 which began a practice of censorship that persisted until recently. Nevertheless, many Indians resorted to masking their protests under the guise of history and mythology. This practice continued, more or less unabated, until independence was achieved in 1947.

The period of the late 19th and early 20th centuries saw the proliferation of theatre buildings, touring companies and an entrepreneurial spirit. Theatre was a popular art in the urban areas and in the small towns influenced by city commerce and trade. Not all companies were successful, however. Poor management, over-extension of resources and weak productions spelled the end of many groups that were initially enthusiastic. Those that survived encountered a far more fundamental threat to their existence, the introduction of the cinema. Sweeping changes in taste were afoot in the early 20th century. The enormous popularity of cinema with the middle classes and its easy access led to the closing of live theatres virtually everywhere in the country. Artists abandoned the stage in large numbers seeking more lucrative careers in films. India quickly developed into one of the world's largest producers and consumers of films. Great studios thrived in Bombay, primarily creating films in Hindi, the language which constituted the largest potential market. Those in Tamil followed a close second. Today, there are film studios in almost every major city and in every major language in the country and, while theatre retains some of its vigour, particularly in Calcutta and Bombay, it is not as popular as it once was in the early part of the century.

Today, there are relatively few commercial theatre companies. Calcutta has the largest number. Most of them are confined to north Calcutta in the heart of the Bengali-speaking section of the city. The Star Theatre is among the oldest and best known, working out of a building constructed in 1888 renowned for the famous theatre personalities that once performed there. Commercial companies also work in the Circarina, Rangmahal, Biswaroopa, Minerva, Rangana and Bijon. In

Tripti Mitra and Sombhu Mitra, well-known actors of the Calcutta stage, in Rabindranath Tagore's *Visarjan*, produced by Bohurupee.

Kerala, the Kerala People's Arts Company (KPAC) and Kalidasa Kalakendra, both Communist organizations, operate itinerant groups. The National Theatre of Madras still clings to 19th-century staging techniques producing slick shows throughout the city, the state and even abroad. Trivandrum's Kalanilaya Vistavision Dramascope Company follows along the path of the National with melodramatic 19th-century fare still popular with a segment of Kerala's population. Given India's vast size, commercial theatre is amazingly small and diffuse.

The heart of the live theatre in India today is the amateur companies. Among the better known are Calcutta's Bohurupee, Little Theatre Group, and Nandikar and Bombay's Goa Hindu Association's Theatre wing, Abhishek, Indian National Theatre, Theatre Unit and Theatre Group. Many of the players who work with these organizations are actually professionals who eke out a living performing a wide variety of jobs in films, television, advertising, as well as working on the stage. The groups retain their amateur status in order to benefit from tax concessions and, frankly, because they cannot make enough money at the box office to support the players on a continual basis.

Calcutta is said to have some three thousand registered amateur groups; Bombay may have as many as five hundred; Madras boasts of at least fifty and Delhi several dozen. No doubt every large city in India has amateur theatrical activity.

Characteristically, each amateur organization has a director, or core of directors at its head who serve as the artistic director, organize productions and provide momentum for its activities. Without a director these groups would collapse for lack of continuity and leadership. Distinguished directors with national reputations in the amateur theatre are Sombhu Mitra, Utpal Dutt and Rudraprasad Sen Gupta of Calcutta; Kamalkar Sarang, Mansukh Joshi, Satyadev Dubey, Alyque Padamsee, Pearl Padamsee, Vijaya Mehta of Bombay; and Ebrahim Alkazi, Habib Tanvir, Bansi Kaul and M. K. Raina of New Delhi; Manohar and Cho of Madras; and Kavalam Narayan Pannikar of Kerala.

Productions are normally produced by the amateur groups on a show by show basis. Subscription seasons are virtually unknown. If a show is successful, it is repeated as many times as audiences will come to see it in sufficient numbers to warrant a showing. Often shows are kept in a group's repertory for years on end.

The bane of amateur theatre is the fact that virtually all the groups must rent the theatre facilities which are owned by cooperatives, government and private individuals. Only one theatre group, Theatre Centre of Calcutta, owns its own building and that too is a tiny space seating less than a hundred people. This means that groups in all the cities vie with each other for bookings. In Bombay in recent years, the situation has led the amateur theatre producers to consolidate their efforts and to agree to a booking schedule that gives the busiest and most popular groups access to prime booking dates in the better houses.

Among the most popular amateur theatre houses are the Academy of Fine Arts of Calcutta; Shivaji Mandir, Ravindra Natya Mandir, Gadkari Nangayatan, Baidas, Bhirla, Tejpal, Prithvi, Patkar and the Tata Theatre of the National Centre for the Performing Arts of Bombay; Kamani Auditorium, Gandhi Memorial Theatre, Sri Ram Centre and Sapru House of New Delhi.

Production expenses are also relatively high for amateur theatre. Few of the groups have access to space to build scenery and props. Costume storage is virtually unheard of. What lighting equipment there is must

Goa Hindu Association in *Raigadala Jevha Jug Yete*, Bombay, 1962.

Goa Hindu Association in *Sandhya Chhaya*, Bombay, 1978.

lighting. Single set shows in Bombay and Calcutta cost between two and three thousand dollars. Multi-set shows range between three and five thousand dollars and historical plays or musicals demand an investment of between five and ten thousand dollars. In cities with a lower cost of living, such as Madras, Bangalore, Ahmedabad and Hyderabad, production costs are somewhat lower.

One of the largest expenses is that of advertising. Newspaper advertisements are virtually prohibitive. Each one may run into hundreds of rupees for a small space on a single day. Negotiations for concessions are virtually always going on between editors and heads of amateur groups. Word of mouth is considered the best, and certainly the cheapest, means of advertising a production.

If a show fails at the box office, it may mean the demise of an amateur theatre organization. In recent years, clever organizers have realized that once a production has met with some degree of success in a large and prominent urban theatre, then it must be marketed to organizations in smaller towns and cities. So-called 'call' bookings have become a lucrative source of income for many groups and make the difference between financial success and failure. Yet, they are hard on the organizers and performers, many of whom hold down jobs or have other commitments that must be taken into consideration when bookings are made outside the city. By its very nature, amateur theatre in India is itinerant. But the 'call' bookings impose an added hardship on all concerned. The only incentive for the players is that they may earn an additional income from 'call' bookings.

The plays that provide grist for the commercial and amateur theatre mill vary greatly from group to group, depending on the demands imposed by the organization. In the 19th century, plays were a blend of music, song and dialogue. During the 20th century music and song were dropped in favour of dialogue. Theatre came to mean dialogue. Today, the trend is towards the incorporation of music and song into performance either as a primary or a secondary ingredient. Dialogue plays are still popular but plays which click with city audiences are often those that introduce music into them. The playwrights who create this work are as varied as the works themselves. Hack writers whose names do not appear on any marquee or in any

programme are often engaged to develop an idea for the commercial theatres of Calcutta and Madras, much as hack writers do for films and television in the Western world. Socially committed playwrights like Thopil Basi are often commissioned by Communist groups in Kerala. They frequently serve as playwright–director negotiating script changes directly with the actors. Utpal Dutt is also known for his contributions to the socially committed theatre of Calcutta. Dutt usually works as a playwright, director and actor. Badal Sircar, Girish Karnad, Vijay Tendulkar, G. Sankara Pillai and K. Narayan Pannikar, join Utpal Dutt among a small band of playwrights who have achieved national prominence and whose works have been produced beyond the confines of their own language and area of the country. The work of these individuals concerns social and political issues which is primarily serious in tone.

Examples of playwrights who deliver safer more predictable works designed to appeal to the taste of the vast majority of urban audiences in their respective languages are N. N. Pillai of Kerala, Jaywant Dalve of Bombay and Cho of Madras. These writers focus on material which centres on family life, society and the plight of the individual in a modern mechanized country. Comedy and melodrama are freely mixed in their work leaving audiences satisfied at the conclusion of the show rather than disturbed or moved to take radical action.

Experimental work with limited public appeal has been presented in various areas of the country. Badal Sarkar launched experimentation in Calcutta with his Satabdi group by producing work in so-called 'found' spaces rather than in rented theatre halls, with the benefit of expensive lighting equipment, scenery and elaborate costuming. The work is presented every Friday evening on a regular basis with little or no advanced advertising. A mere pittance is charged for admission. The Living Theatre of Khardah, a theatre group in a suburb outside Calcutta, attempts the same thing – a theatre of ideas, accessible to the public but free of commercial constraints. Experimental work has also been attempted in Bombay by Avishkar in a rented school hall and at the moderately expensive Prithvi Theatre in north Bombay. Work that is expected to

Andanun Adakodanum by G. Sankara Pillai, Kerala playwright, with the Calicut University Repertory Company.

The National School of Drama Repertory Company of New Delhi in *Jasma Odan*.

attract limited audiences is also found in New Delhi and Madras. And in Kerala the work of Kavalam Narayan Pannikar has achieved critical acclaim for its integration of folk and classical theatre traditions.

Educational theatre is limited in India. For several decades the National School of Drama of New Delhi has been a leader in the training of young actors, directors and designers in modern theatre techniques. Under the guidance of Ebrahim Alkazi, it gained a national and international reputation during the 1960s and 1970s. Theatre is taught at the university level at the M. S. University of Baroda in Gujurat state, Rabindra Bharati University in Calcutta, Calicut University in Trichur, Kerala and Chandigar University in the Punjab.

Short training programmes, workshops and retreats are among the various methods used by educational theatre teachers and leaders of the amateur theatre organizations for promoting theatre among the young. Regional and state competitions are also conducted to encourage interest in theatre.

The state and national governments help in a limited way to support the study of traditional and modern Indian theatre through grants to teachers, students and organizations and the awarding of annual prizes to distinguished individuals for their accomplishments. The government has helped to focus national attention on theatre. FaR

See: M. Ashton and B. Christie, *Yakshagana*, New Delhi, 1977; Suresh Awasthi, *Drama: The Gift of Gods: Culture,*

Performance and Communication in India, Tokyo, 1983; R. Van M. Baumer and J. R. Brandon (eds.), *Sanskrit Drama in Performance*, Honolulu, 1981; Bharata, *Natyasastra*, ed. Manomohan Ghosh, Calcutta, 1961; Rustom Bharucha, *Rehearsals of Revolution*, Honolulu, 1983; G. K. Bhat, *The Vidusaka*, Ahmedabad, 1959; C. M. Byrski, *Concept of Ancient Indian Theatre*, New Delhi, 1974; *Classical and Folk Dances of India*, Bombay, 1963; Sudha R. Desai, *Bhavai*, Ahmedabad, 1972; Utpal Dutt, *Towards a Revolutionary Theatre*, Calcutta, 1982; Balwant Gargi, *Folk Theatre of India*, Seattle, 1966 and *Theatre in India*, New York, 1962; J. S. Hawley, *At Play with Krishna*, Princeton, 1981; M. Hein, *The Miracle Plays of Mathura*, New Haven, 1972; C. R. Jones and B. T. Jones, *Kathakali: An Introduction to the Dance-Drama of Kerala*, San Francisco, 1970; K. Shivarama Karanth, *Yakshagana*, Mysore, 1974; A. B. Keith, *The Sanskrit Drama in its Origin, Development, Theory and Practice*, London, 1964; M. Khokar, *Traditions of Indian Classical Dance*, Delhi, 1979; J. C. Mathur, *Drama in Rural India*, Bombay, 1964; B. S. Miller (ed.), *Theater of Memory, the Plays of Kalidasa*, New York, 1984; S. K. Mukherjee, *The Story of the Calcutta Theatres, 1753–1980*, Calcutta, 1982; M. Neog, *Sankaradeva and His Times*, Gauhati, 1965; G. Panchal, *Bhavai and its Typical Aharya*, Ahmedabad, 1983 and *Kuttampalam and Kutiyattam*, New Delhi, 1984; K. Kunjunni Raja, *Kutiyattam: An Introduction*, New Delhi, 1964; A. Rangacharya, *The Indian Theatre*, New Delhi, 1971; R. Schechner, *Performance Circumstances from the Avant Garde to Ramlila*, Calcutta, 1983; I. Shekhar, *Sanskrit Drama: Its Origin and Decline*, Leiden, 1960; K. Vatsayan, *Classical Indian Dance in Literature and the Arts*,

New Delhi, 1968; *Indian Classical Dance*, New Delhi, 1974 and *Traditional Indian Theatre: Multiple Streams*, New Delhi, 1980; H. W. Wells, *The Classical Drama of India*, New York, 1963 and *Six Sanskrit Plays*, Bombay, 1964; P. B. Zarrilli, *The Kathakali Complex: Actor, Performance, Structure*, New Delhi, 1984.

Indonesia This performance-rich South-East Asian nation has a population of about 170 million located on over 3,000 islands which extend from Sumatra to Irian Jaya (West New Guinea). Although most of the some 300 ethnic groups which speak over 250 languages have distinctive performance traditions, research in Western languages is just beginning to clarify the nature of these. However, the highly developed theatres of Java, Bali, and Sunda (West Java), where drama, dance, and music are wed, have been much studied by Western scholars in the last century. Information on the arts has largely been passed on by oral tradition, but archaeological and performance evidence, in conjunction with this tradition, allows reconstruction of the probable evolution. Descriptions here are however based on current practice, and, despite the indigenous tendency to preserve the archaic at the same time as new forms are developed, changes have inevitably occurred.

To understand the major theatres of Indonesia, it is important to comprehend four concepts: *wayang*, type, *gamelan*, and structured improvisation. The generic name for most theatre performance is *wayang*, possibly derived from *bayang* (shadow), since the oldest mode is said to be a shadow puppet theatre, Javanese *wayang kulit purwa*. The term *wayang* has come to be applied to many other genres modelled on this *wayang kulit purwa* form, for like it they use a *dalang* (puppet-master, story-teller) and a *gamelan* (gong chime orchestra). Genres are generally differentiated from each other by medium (puppet, mask, unmasked dancer, etc.) and the epic presented. The stories based on the Indian *Mahabharata* and *Ramayana* are considered the oldest, and are, hence, called *purwa* ('original'). Other major story cycles include *Panji* (which tells of the amorous adventures of Panji, prince of an east Javanese kingdom, as he searches for his lost love) and *Amir Hamzah* (which tells of an Arab king and uncle of Mohammed). The performance practice of *purwa* tales has been adopted for them as well.

In the descriptive name of any genre, *wayang* identifies it as part of this *dalang*/*gamelan*/story complex. The other terms imply the medium of performance and the exact epic. Hence, *wayang kulit* (leather) *purwa* uses leather puppets to tell the Indian-derived stories, while *wayang topeng* (mask) *purwa* uses masked dancers and *wayang orang* (human) *purwa* uses unmasked dancers to relate the same Hindu tales. In contrast, *wayang klitik*, *wayang golek cepak*, and *wayang gedog* all tell stories based on *Panji*, *Amir Hamzah* or other Javanese chronicle tales (*babad*), but the first uses flat wooden puppets (*klitik*); the second, three-dimensional wooden figures (*golek*); and the last, leather figures.

Second comes the concept of type. Actors strive to present the essence of a character type rather than a realistic portrait. A very refined character, a proud-refined one, a strong male warrior, an ogre king, and a clown generally appear in what is considered the oldest form of dance/acting, *topeng* (mask dance, literally, 'press' – the wood masks were held in place by biting a piece of leather tacked to the mask's mouth). Later genres developed from this mask form and, despite refinements, these five basic character types still form the substructure of theatre in the area. The range from *alus* (refined) to *kasar, gagah* (rough, strong) characters underlies everything. Stylized gestures for mimetic action – walking, adjusting costume, gesturing – and more pure dance movements are set for each type. Since all classical dance portrays one of these basic character types, all dance is dramatic. The hero, be he Rama from the *Ramayana*, Panji, Amir Hamzah, or Arjuna (from the *Mahabharata*), will be identical in terms of movement, vocal usage, and demeanour. Only the costume and the dialogue will betray the individual identity.

Thirdly, music is a necessary component of all traditional performance. A tune, a tempo, a particular percussive pattern will alert a blind audience member that a character like Rama is onstage and is doing a specific gesture. In former times particular scales were probably linked with certain story materials: the five tone *selendro* scale is widely found with the Hindu-derived tales, and the seven-tone *pelog* scale is more consistently used for Panji, Amir, Hamzah, and the Javanese tales. In current central Javanese practice, however, larger ensembles that can play either tuning have developed, blurring the earlier division. Most theatre forms are accompanied by some variant of *gamelan*, a gong chime orchestra in which instruments are a set tuned to each other rather than any absolute pitch. Hanging and horizontal gongs on racks generally sound on specific beats of the cyclical musical patterns. Smaller metallophones and xylophones play more melodic patterns in interconnected parts. Drums provide the rhythmic lead – signalling starts, stops, and changes of tune – and may make sound effects or accent the moves of the dance. Singers, flute, or a bowed lute (*rebab*) may provide an elaborate melody within the more structural frame the other instruments supply. The *dalang* cues the musicians with a wood mallet and/or metal plates. Specific tunes are associated with set scenes, character types, or dramatic action (i.e., battle). The *dalang* sings mood songs which have similar dramatic specificity. The *gamelan*'s singer, if present, will try to choose lyrics that reinforce the atmosphere of the scene. Voices of character types may be pegged to specific notes of the scale and defined by set vocal patterns.

Finally, one must consider the role of structured improvisation: traditional performances have no written text, nor are the songs to be played during a show preplanned by the troupe. The genre's set dramatic structure in conjunction with the scenario and rules of type allow performers to generate the text and song sequence in performance. A traditional epic episode or even a newly devised story can be presented by a good troupe at a moment's notice, and rehearsals are rare as a result. Indeed, the whole performance event has an air of structured chaos about it. Performances traditionally take place outdoors or in the pavilion of an aristocrat's house, and food stalls and other entertainments sprout just outside the performing area. Children wake up for clowning and battles, others wait for love scenes or philosophical discussions to turn their attention to the stage. Audience members come and go, eat, gamble, sleep, or visit with neighbours throughout the night.

The drama is only a part of a larger event in which audience and performers improvise within their set constraints.

These organizing principles provide a basis for considering theatre history. Four major categories of performance exist: (1) proto-theatrical practices (2) traditional court/folk performance (3) popular urban drama of the last 100 years, and (4) modern spoken drama. By considering each of these strata as representing stages of development, a sense of the history of theatre may be deduced, though admittedly the interplay of strata is more complex than this evolutionary model implies.

Proto-theatrical practices Throughout the archipelago features that characterize performance in most Malay cultures can be seen, notably (1) epic recitation (2) poetic dialogue games, and (3) use of performance for spirit communication. Singing of verse epics is found in many Indonesian cultures, and this custom seems to have continued with new content and metres as new cultural influences are accepted. For example, among the Sundanese of West Java, a *pantun* story-teller composes, in performance, his tale based on indigenous legends. Singing octosyllabic, metred lines, he accompanies himself on a zither (*kecapi*) in the nightlong performance. Similar entertainments may have been a base from which puppet theatre developed after the adoption of Hindu culture about the first century AD.

Javanese written epics of the 9th–12th centuries were probably presented in oral performance by the reciters mentioned in early court records. These *kakawin*, stories based on Indian epic in Sanskrit-derived metres and language, are still sung in Bali. Tales include the *Ramayana*, which chronicles Sita's rescue by her god-incarnate husband, Rama, when she is kidnapped by the demonic Rawana. Other *kakawin* are based on the *Mahabharata*, telling of the exploits of five heroes, the Pandawa brothers, who fight their hundred Kurawa cousins in the *bharata yudha*, a great war that leaves the heroes heartbroken in their hour of victory. Middle Javanese language *kidung* were stories written in indigenous verse forms, dealing with the story of *Panji* and other indigenous tales. Although these texts, by virtue of being written, are more set than traditional theatre genres of today, they correspond to the story materials of current theatre. Such texts, presumably growing from and intended for oral performance, may have had interplay with theatrical enactment from an early period. Indeed, a few mood songs of the shadow theatre repertoire correspond to passages from such texts.

Poetry games using indigenous verse forms are a root of some folk theatre forms. The Sundanese *sisinderan*, four-line riddle poetry, is an example. These verses could be improvised courting games in which a male singer would vie with a female, or sung in other contexts. A number of Sundanese folk theatre forms, such as *godang*, *dog-dog*, *calung* (each of which uses a different kind of musical instrument to accompany such singing), expand on such games, by adding humorous, improvised skits about village life.

Also significant is the use of performance for communicating with spirits. Trance performance is common throughout the islands, since such dances allow spirits to enter the world in a controlled mode. The Balinese *sanghyang dedari* is a trance performance done in times of epidemic or difficulty in which two small girls are put into trance by the chant of a male chorus and allowed to speak for the spirits. In West Java *Sintren/lais*, the trance dance of a child medium, is probably a related form. In central Java, entranced dancers may rock a doll figure, a *nini towong*, to make rain. In other islands of Indonesia, too, masks and puppets are used in rites for the dead, and the preference for puppet and mask in this culture may relate to such forms.

In other performances entranced dancers may be entered by the spirit of a tiger (*pamacan*) or monkey (*pamonyet*) while doing martial arts (*pencak silat*) dance in Sunda. Horse trance dances are found in Bali (*sanghang jaran*), Java (*kuda kepang*, *jatilan*) and Sunda (*kuda lumping*): dancers are entered by horse spirits and can eat glass or walk on hot coals. Another animal figure that is sometimes associated with trance performance is a lion-like being, a *barong*, perhaps derived from a Buddhist protective figure and related to the Chinese lion. In Bali the image has become linked to a magico-religious dance drama in which the protective *barong* pits its power against the malevolent witch, Rangda ('widow'). She prompts entranced dancers to turn their weapons against themselves; however, trance prevents wounds.

In most of these trance performances a *dukun* (ritual specialist in dealing with spirits and curing) or a priest will be the significant figure who, by mantras and incense, calls the appropriate spirit into the performer. Often an assistant makes sure the trancers remain within the acceptable bounds and adds comic quips to the possession rite at the same time. These roles have

Balinese *baris*, the dance of a strong warrior, has been elaborated into a dance drama, *baris melamphan*.

some features in common with *dalang* who control performances, but do not act themselves and the important clown characters who are part of every genre.

Content too is significant for placating the spirit world – the use of *wayang* to play out the exorcistic story, *The Origin of Kala*, is a case in point. In Java, Sunda, and Bali certain individuals are believed to be threatened by this demon Kala. Unless a *dalang* plays the story of how the first *wayang* exorcism (*ruwatan*) calmed the wrath of this demon, the potential victim lives in danger of misfortune. Another story, *Menkukuhan*, was used to prevent diseases threatening rice crops in Java and Sunda, while *Watu Gunung* was used in East Java to make rain. The Balinese *Calonarang* tells how a king of East Java foiled the machinations of the powerful witch-widow of the title role. It may be presented in Bali as a shadow play or in conjunction with *rangda-barong* dance drama.

Performances are traditionally part of rites of passage ceremonies for the group or individual, and this tradition seems to have persisted through times of spirit worship, of Hinduism, and of Islam. In areas like Cirebon, once a year a performance of wooden rod puppets presenting local chronicles (*wayang golek cepak*) is played at the graves of the village ancestors. Indeed some scholars believe pre-Hindu performances told of ancestral exploits to gain their aid in promoting fertility. In Bali much performance takes place in the context of temple festivals when Hindu and local spirits are thought to be visiting earth. Throughout Muslim Java and Sunda performances are most often held for a wedding, circumcision, ceremony for an unborn or newly born child, or a ritual cleansing of the village from bad spirits. Many performances last all night, since that is when spirits are nigh. Performances require some kind of offering for spirits, and open with mantras and music meant for spirit propitiation. Most performances today are primarily intended for the amusement of the audience who attend for free, while the family celebrating the rite of passage pays the troupe. But such evidence hints that the archaic relationships of dancer and spirit medium, *dalang* and shaman have given the performer an aura of power.

Traditional court and folk performance   The elaboration of early performance practices into strong theatrical traditions seems largely to have come after Hindu-Buddhist religion was adopted by the ruling elite. In the kingdom of Sriwijaya (7th–13th centuries), centred in Sumatra but having influence in Java and the Malay peninsula, the ruler used ceremony as a mode of dramatizing his magico-religious power, perhaps under the influence of Javanese models. In Java various dynasties perpetuated syncretic animistic-Hindu-Buddhist practices. By the 9th century Javanese inscriptions indicate that female dancers, clowns, mask performers, and shadow players were resident in courts and temples. Indian influence may have been stronger in this early period, for dancers in temple reliefs assume strong stances more like current Indian performance than anything seen today, though the usage of *mudras*, the sign-mime language of India, is not very apparent. Local aesthetics must soon have remoulded any strong outside stimuli: by the 13th century temple reliefs show scenes in which the costume, spacial usage, and charac-

ter typology bear striking resemblance to current Balinese performance.

From the 9th–15th centuries distinctive Javanese versions of the *Ramayana* and *Mahabharata* were developed; events of the epics were believed to have occurred at specific sites in Java, and the heroes were considered ancestors of the Javanese. Masked dance, female dance, and shadow theatre became integral parts of ritual to enhance the aura of the king in magico-religious, as well as aesthetic dimensions. The importance of performance to such systems has led anthropologist Geertz to characterize such cultures as 'theatre states': court performance and ceremony became the way rulers acted out their power and, thereby, were empowered. The concept that *gamelan*, dances, puppets, masks, and performers focused spiritual power and hence were necessary regalia for kings seems to have crystallized in this era. Kings in Kampuchea, Thailand, and Malaysia eventually adopted similar strategies for articulating their glory, influenced, in part, by Sriwijayan and Javanese models.

Scholars currently debate the impact of Indian and Chinese culture in developing the arts. For example, female dance, shadow puppetry, and mask theatre are all found in India. Though these are the oldest performance modes in Indonesia, each of these arts manifests itself in quite a different way. It seems likely that the archipelago largely reinforced indigenous performance tendencies, upgrading them with Indian stories and the aura of a higher culture. However, theatre only developed strongly in areas where Hindu culture was firmly implanted, implying that the impact was, indeed, strong. Trade with China was a significant feature in developing the economic base of the major kingdoms in Indonesia, and it is possible that puppetry techniques and typology of character were influenced by Chinese practice. Martial arts dance and wooden rod puppet techniques, for example, are often associated with Chinese communities.

Muslim in-roads began in the 13th century, and gradually all Java accepted Islam. The aristocrats of the last Hindu-Buddhist court, Majapahit, retreated to the neighbouring island of Bali around 1520. Balinese performance has developed greatly since these culture bringers slipped across those two miles of ocean, yet it seems likely that the aesthetic of Bali today may give a glimpse of that time. The Balinese hold that their theatre is the legacy of Majapahit, and that forms like *gambuh* dance drama have passed unchanged from generation to generation since the 16th century. Let us pause temporarily with Javanese history to consider current practice and oral traditions of Bali.

The *gambuh* is said to have been developed in Majapahit Java and was perpetuated in the Balinese courts to 1906. Despite lack of court support since that year when the Dutch seized the island, some groups have continued to present *gambuh* at village temple festivals. The plays, presented in the inner temple courtyard, last all day or all night and tell stories drawn from Javanese legends, notably the *Panji* cycle. The heroic characters speak Kawi (old Javanese), which the audience cannot understand, while the clowns use colloquial Balinese, and the narrator mixes Kawi and Balinese. This linguistic difference between epic characters and clowns is a significant part of all but the most recent Balinese performance. The orchestra is composed of four long flutes (*gambuh suling*), *rebab*, drums, cymbals, bells, gongs, and a *gumanek* (struck idiophone used in some of the oldest Javanese dances).

The structure of each story is predictable: the maid dances, followed by ladies-in-waiting, and the princess. Finally they speak, then, in the next scene, two portly ministers and four retainers dance, preceding the refined hero, Panji, and his clown servant. In the third scene the antagonist, a strong but greedy king, and his ministers appear. The conflict ensues. Other Balinese dramatic forms, including *legong*, *topeng*, *wayang wong*, *arja*, *baris melamphan*, are said to derive from this *ur*-genre, which is preserved at Batuan Gianyar, and a few other places.

The other form considered as a direct legacy of Majapahit is *wayang parwa*, the hide shadow puppet theatre of Bali telling *Mahabharata* tales. The figures, the music ensemble, and performance technique are less refined than current Javanese style, perhaps indicating an older practice. Using a screen about 6ft x 4ft a single *dalang* manipulates hide figures ranging from about 1–2ft in height, doing all the dialogue, narration, and mood songs, and cueing his musicians by rapping on the wooden puppet chest with his foot. The Kawi distances the heroic characters, but the ever present clowns provide colloquial equivalents for their noble visions.

The *dalang* opens the play with incantations as the 'tree of life' (*kayon*) puppet dances the creation of the world. Swinging the oil lamp he lets the shadows of the puppets quiver: he represents God breathing life into man and woman. Then he raps for the second 'tree' dance and the ensemble of four *gender*, metallophones with tube resonators, strikes up again. The dance represents the new imbalance in the universe, now that human desire has been born. Then the story of the evening can begin. Performances last from about 9pm–1am and usually take place in the context of a temple festival, cremation, or similar ceremony.

The *wayang parwa* is currently practised by 300 *dalang*, most male, and born in *dalang* families. Since 1974 however, a few women have been trained, primarily under I Nyoman Sumandhi, from the Denpasar High School of Traditional Music (SMKI/KOKAR). Performers of sufficient spiritual power can make holy water used for curing and exorcisms, play ritual stories like those of Kala and Calonarang, and comprehend the mantras of the *dalang*'s handbook, *The Book of the Wayang*. Almost all shadow puppet performances are of *Mahabharata* stories, but related genres do tell *Ramayana* and *Panji* tales.

Though not a direct legacy of Majapahit, the *legong* dancer, with darting eyes, high elbow placement, and dynamic changes of position, offers a more energized vision of the female than Muslim Java cultivates. The most abstract of dramas is hidden in the choreography done by three pre-pubescent girls to *gamelan pelegongan*. The form as currently practised developed only around 1800 when a prince, I Dewa Agung Made Karna, dreamt he saw heavenly maidens dancing in a style similar to the sacred trance, *sanghang dedari*, and ordered that girls be trained accordingly. As other rulers elaborated on this first attempt the *legong* was established. Perhaps the most frequently performed story today is an episode from the *Panji* cycle in which a rival, who has kidnapped Panji's betrothed, encounters a bird

of ill omen. In times past, *legong* dancers often became wives of the ruler when they reached puberty.

Topeng is the mask dance of Bali: the stories are taken from Javanese and local legends. The major characters wear full masks, while the clowns, who translate, wear half-masks. Some masks are said to be magically charged, and the oldest masks in the island are said to have been brought back from East Java in the Majapahit era by a Jelantik aristocrat. His descendants eventually used these masks and added new ones that tied at the back rather than being held by the teeth as in Java. The oldest form of Balinese *topeng* is a one-person form, *topeng pajegan*, performed in the inner courtyard of the temple. After dancing each of four introductory masks, the story is played by the solo dancer alternating noble and clown masks. Finally, he puts on the mask of an old man, Sidha Karya ('Accomplishing the Task'), and enacts a dance ritual to bring the desired blessing. Few ritually potent *topeng* dancers remain today: I Made Jimat is a noted performer, but I Nyoman Kakul's death in the early 1980s was a major loss.

In the last hundred years two new *topeng* forms have become popular for entertainment rather than ritual value. *Topeng panca* ('five' person *topeng*) uses a larger group, to present the traditional repertoire with more interaction and clown scenes. The Sidha Karya maskritual is not presented in this version nor in the eclectic *topeng prebon* ('combination' *topeng*), created around 1940. This form presents the *topeng* repertoire and clowns in conjunction with females from *arja* (dance opera), and the prime minister from *gambuh*.

Gambuh, *wayang parwa*, and, to a lesser extent, *legong* and *topeng* may clarify Majapahit aesthetics. Other Balinese genres are more recent, yet draw on these older forms. *Wayang wong* uses masked humans to tell tales derived from the *Ramayana* and was created in the late 1700s when the king of Klungklung asked performers to use ancient masks in his collection. *Wayang (orang) parwa* uses unmasked dancers (clowns only are masked) and tells *Mahabharata* stories. Sukawati was a centre for this genre, but the currently active group is in

Sintren, a trance dance of the Cirebon area of West Java. The entranced dancer is said to be possessed by a goddess who is called into her body by the *dukun*, here holding an incense burner in his hand.

Bonkasa, Badung. Both these forms use a *dalang* and follow shadow theatre performance practices.

More modern genres include *arja, kecak, baris melamphan,* and *sendratari. Arja* is the dance opera developed in the late 1900s and, currently, the most popular genre. Though first an all-male form, by the 1920s, women had taken over the major roles, since their voices seemed appropriate for the *tembang* singing style used. Noted singers rose to star status, especially after radio broadcasts began in 1958. Currently the troupe from the Radio Republic Indonesia station performs throughout the island, and cassette versions of the stories from Hindu, Javanese, Balinese and even Chinese sources are sold in shops.

Kecak is a modern creation devised for tourist audiences. Chant used to put *sanhyang* dancers into trance was combined with a *Ramayana* pantomime in the 1930s. The 150-strong male chorus, making interlocking 'cak' calls and playing a chorus of monkeys, creates a stirring background to the kidnapping of Sita. The performances in the dim light of the oil lamp made an impact on the tourist audiences; soon many villages were in the *kecak* business. Today a generation of Balinese have grown up doing the form, and younger choreographers have even created *kecak* for Balinese viewers.

Baris melamphan (warrior dance drama) is a male equivalent of the *legong. Ramayana* and *Mahabharata* stories are danced out by male performers using strong male style and Kawi. The dancers are not distinguished from each other by costume or characterization, but by action and the talk of the translator-clowns.

Sendratari (dance drama) is a form of pantomimic dance drama developed in the High School of Traditional Music (KOKAR, now SMKI) in 1962. This genre developed simultaneously in Java and Sunda in the government art schools, for it smashed the language barrier that kept members of other ethnic groups from understanding regional theatre. In Bali, the use of the popular *gamelan* style of the last 25 years, *kebyar,* 'lighting' style – so named for its brilliant tone and quick transitions – heightened its appeal. The expert performance of the young dance students who often come from the best families of traditional dance, the proscenium stage, theatre lighting, and costumes adapted from traditional dance apparel, all make the form popular. *Sendratari* as choreographed by I Wayan Beratha, I Wayan Dibia, and I Made Bandem show much continuity with the past, but the imposition of a set choreography, the lack of the Kawi and *dalang* show movement from the older pattern.

With the energized Balinese drama as a perspective, the transitions in 15th–17th century Java become clear. A generation of Muslim teacher–rulers rose in cities along the north coast. Rather than abandoning the arts, these leaders promoted them. Johns has suggested that Sufi mystical orders introduced the Islam, hence the affinity of performance. Further research is required to test the hypothesis: for example, a close comparison of *wayang kulit purwa* with the dervish-related Kargoz shadow puppet theatre of the Arab world, supposedly created in 1366 by a sufi mystic, Mehmend Kushteri, might establish firmer links.

Although documentation from earlier periods proves that shadow, mask, and dance performance developed in the Hindu-Buddhist period, traditional Javanese artists invariably trace the origin of their theatre practice to the *Wali Sangga,* the 'Nine Saints' who converted the island to Islam. Wali Sunan Kalijaga is credited with devising *wayang kulit purwa,* performing in mosques and requiring the Muslim confession of faith as the price of viewing.

Though not necessarily historical facts, these statements reveal inner truth – the local tradition was redefined, and new features characterized Muslim-Javanese as opposed to Hindu-Balinese arts. A greater stylization of puppet and mask was introduced, supposedly to circumvent the Islamic prohibition on representing the human form. A more inward-turning focus and flowing dance style were adopted, especially for refined character types. The Kawi language was abandoned for Javanese, though traces of the older tongue haunt mood songs and narration. The *Mahabharata* cycle, on which 95% of current stories are based, was revised to suit a Muslim ethos: Indian religious figures were devalued and the polygyny of the five Pandawa and their wife, Drupadi, edited out. New content was introduced, including the Amir Hamzah stories, supposedly from Persia, and tales chronicling deeds of the nine *wali* themselves. Pan-Islamic forms like *dikir* (sufi chanting with movement) and *dabus* (Muslim trance dance in which performers stab and cut themselves with impunity) also began in this era.

Many changes were made in the *wayang* tradition, leading toward the well-known *wayang kulit purwa* of today. On an expansive screen *dalang* presents the monodrama, manipulating about 50 figures involved in the complex plot lasting from 8.30pm till morning. He cues his *gamelan* players who play the appropriate tunes on the martial sounding *selendro* or more melancholy *pelog* scale instruments in the *patet,* key or mode, appropriate to that part of the story. The pitch of the three *patet* used in the successive sections of each performance is progressively higher, underlining the rising tension of the plot. The glamorous female singer was not part of the early period, but an innovation of the last hundred years.

The Hindu epic material is normally presented, but most performances are not events of the Indian versions, but 'branch' episodes that show the epic character in moments not defined by those 'trunk' stories. Typically, Arjuna or some other refined knight, with the counsel of his clown-servants, struggles with ogres to restore balance to the order they threaten. The *dalang* develops his performance according to a set dramatic

The front of the screen in a *wayang kulit purwa* performance.

A Cirebonese woman *dalang* lighting her oil lamp in a *wayang kulit purwa* performance.

structure from the story outline acquired in one of four ways (1) his teacher told it to him in a few paragraphs (2) he saw it performed (3) he read it in a *dalang* manual, or (4) he devised it himself. The plot will usually contain the following standard scenes.

As in Bali, the opening mantra-like narration and a 'tree' puppet dance begin the show. The action opens in a palace with a court audience scene; a problem is discussed, and an army is sent to deal with it. The next major audience scene often takes place in some rival palace. The various armies despatched in two or three such palace scenes will meet in the first of the evening's three major battles.

The *patet* changes, now the scene is a mountain where clown-servants of a refined prince wait as he undertakes a meditation causing cosmic imbalance. In this *gara-gara* (world in disorder) scene, which comes about midnight, clowns comment freely on current politics and events, in contrast to the other characters who live in epic time and cannot refer to the present. Semar, the chief clown, farts and frets – but the audience knows that this fat old hermaphrodite's insights veil deep truth, since Semar is a high god sojourning in the world. After a hermitage scene, the hero goes down from the mountain where he encounters four ogres in the 'flower battle' (*perang kembang*) – the manipulation highlight of the show. The first blood of the evening is Cakil, a boastful ogre who serves a giant king. He dies every *wayang* proving the hero is spiritually prepared for future challenges.

With the hour advancing toward 2am, the less structured scenes of the third *patet*, required by the plot of the particular story (*lakon*), come. The performance climaxes in the 'great' battle as the hero defeats all opponents. The 'tree' puppet is planted in the banana-log puppet-stand as the dawn approaches, ending the final audience scene. Certain scenes may be omitted and others, not noted here, added, but most performances are improvised within this frame.

The meanings of these plays are multiple: for example, the three parts of the night correspond to youth, adolescence, and adulthood: the child's precarious first steps become firm in the testing of youth, the 'flower battle'. There we overcome 'ogres' of greed and sensuality if we are to succeed in life. Another mode of looking at plays is to understand that the classes of characters correspond to different categories of Javanese society: the heroes are the Javanese elite; the clowns are the common people; the ogres, the demonic and non-Javanese powers/peoples. The myths of the Pandawas – fighting their own cousins – remind Javanese of their colonial experience. The Dutch used royal family rivalries, splitting the royal house in 1755 into Surakarta and Yogyakarta rulers and subdividing each of these two again later. The inter-family quarrels helped make the rulers weak, and have given these stories deep resonance. Other scholars have seen old tribal patterns or spirit communication, royal propaganda, and philosophical tolerance as important features of the form.

Less popular forms of Javanese *wayang* tend today to follow the structural–musical model of the *wayang kulit purwa*. The now infrequently played *wayang beber*, which tells various cycles using picture scrolls, may actually be older than the *wayang kulit purwa*. The oral tradition holds that this was the genre used to tell the exorcistic Kala tale until the early 1600s. Since *Dalang* still fear changing this magically powerful story, earlier practices of it might have been maintained longer. Another genre that follows the *wayang kulit purwa* style is *wayang gedog* which uses *pelog gamelan* and leather puppets to tell *Panji* and other Javanese tales. It was supposedly created in 1553 by the wali, Sunan Giri. *Wayang golek cepak*, which uses wooden doll-like rod puppets to tell Javanese chronicles and Amir Hamzah tales, was credited to Sunan Kudu's innovation in 1584. This form continues to thrive along the north coast, where currently Aliwijaya of Cirebon claims to be the 27th generation of his family to present the art. In East Java *wayang klitik* uses flat wooden puppets to tell Javanese tales. One feature that distinguishes some of these genres from *wayang purwa* is that there is no concept of 'branch' stories, and therefore *dalang*, in general, need to be better versed in all the particulars of the epic than the young *purwa dalang*, who may invent many of his tales. Another distinction is that puppet headdresses and costumes vary from *purwa* style, and are reminiscent of Javanese court dress of the 17th century.

Some newer shadow forms are found only in the palaces or government offices, since they validate and glorify those rulers: *wayang madya* uses leather puppets to tell tales of historical central Javanese kings. *Wayang suluh* was created in 1947 and tells of figures like Sukarno who forged the new Republic of Indonesia. There are many other *wayang* forms, but none rival the *wayang kulit purwa*, which remains a favoured entertainment for weddings and circumcisions. Cassettes of performances by super-stars like Narto Sabdho (1925–85) can be found in every record shop. At institutions like Habiranda, a puppetry school founded by the Bureau of Performing Arts of the Yogyakarta palace in 1950, one can find many students studying formally what *dalang* of past generations learned by apprenticing themselves for a number of years.

Also attributed to Sunan Kalijaga is the mask dance of the north coast (*topeng babakan*), in which a single dancer dances a series of four or five masks in an eight-hour performance. Though most current *dalang* specialize only in dance, in times past performers, who may be male or female, performed shadow plays as well. *Topeng* performances would be given during the day and *wayang kulit purwa* would be presented in the evening. The white-faced refined Panji, conceptually an innocent infant, yet spiritually perfected, opens the presentation. Then comes Pamindo ('two'), often a blue mask – a refined but proud and flighty adolescent; the third figure is a strong, mature male, Tummenggung ('minister'), whose mask has a reddish cast; and the final figure is Klana a red-faced figure with bulging eyes and fangs – furiously grasping for life, even in the moment of death. A fifth mask, Rumiang, may sometimes be added. A second dancer plays the clown, and his half-masks let him engage in verbal as well as physical humour. The abstract story is less significant than the types which represent the different aspects of the personality that lie behind and within each person. The symbolism of the masks is complex; they are correlated with the four directions, the elements and emotions, and may be derived from pre-Hindu ritual. The masks and their movements are probably the source of the typology of all dance drama. Today Sujana Ardja of Salangit, Cirebon, is a major performer of this genre.

The second major mask theatre of Java is said to have evolved from this solo tradition. *Wayang topeng* uses multiple masked dancers to tell shadow puppet stories. A *dalang* is required: he may deliver all the dialogue or just do narration, mood songs and cueing. This form persists in rural areas, while the courts and commercial theatre have largely abandoned it for unmasked dance drama.

The final legacy of this early Muslim period is the female dance of Java. Even more abstract than *legong*, it remains a potent symbol of past court glory. In *bedaya* nine refined female dancers execute in slow, stylized movements intricate floor patterns. Somewhere within the piece a highly stylized struggle may be enacted, representing both an actual combat in some story and the extinction of worldly desire in the soul of the true aescetic. The interplay of eroticism and enlightenment that colours some practices of Tantrism may have affected the genre, and the choreography seems to create a mandala-like floor pattern that works on a magico-religious level to simulate enlightenment in the ideal spectator – the ruler. The dancers would often become the wives and ladies-in-waiting of the ruler, and he might take them along to battle to unleash the spiritual forces they represented against his enemy.

The oldest *bedaya* choreography still performed dates from the 16th century, but the genre is believed to be related to Hindu-Buddhist forms. The *Bedaya Ketawang* is the inheritance of the Surakarta court of central Java. It is said that Sultan Agung of Mataram (1616–45) was meditating on the shores of the southern ocean when the goddess of the seas tried to seduce him with this dance. Thereafter, it has been ritually performed once a year on the anniversary of the coronation day of his kingly descendants, perpetuating the spiritual compact between goddess and ruler. The goddess herself is believed sometimes to appear among the dancers.

Other *bedaya* exist, though the *Bedaya Semang*, the similar ritual performance of the Yogyakarta court, lapsed around 1920. The *Bedaya Madiun* presents the suppression of a rebellion by the Mataram monarch, and the *Bedaya Arjuna Wiwaha* re-enacts the ritual union of the *Mahabharata* hero, Arjuna, with a heavenly nymph. In recent years *bedaya* has become a popular choreographic genre for new dances. A related form, *srimpi*, is a genre for four (or in *Srimpi Renggawati*, five) female dancers, dating from the 17th century. Performers were traditionally daughters of the rulers and, again, present a stylized battle. *Srimpi Renggawati* shows the battle between two princesses in love with the Amir Hamzah.

Solo female court dances do not have the same aura of the sacred as these group dances. It seems likely that they rise from the *ronggeng* (female singer/dancer) tradition which has given birth to forms like *tayuban*, a dance party in which a female dancer opens the performance by dancing classical character types but which ends up with the lady (or, in some instances, a female impersonator) doing partner dances with the various men. *Ronggeng* forms, found in many areas of Indonesia, always have an aura of prostitution attached, but the role has a significance that Western society does not accord the courtesan. Some scholars attribute these forms to archaic links between female dancers and fertility rituals, which are still found in some villages and require the presence of such a performer.

Beksan lawung (lance dances) are 17th-century male court dances depicting military prowess. Both Surakarta and Yogyakarta have full *beksan lawung*, but perhaps because of the military expertise of its founder, Hamengku Buwana I, the Yogyakarta sultanate is more noted for these dances which recreate the pageantry and battles of the court. The Surakarta court, with its legacy of *bedaya*, is felt to excel in female style dance.

Unmasked dance drama *wayang orang* or *wayang wong*, too, is a speciality of Yogyakarta since it was supposedly created there after the split of the royal line. The first court dance drama, *Gondowerdoyo* (*Sent of the Heart*), was presented under the direction of Hamengku Buwana I himself. Then, as today, the performance used *wayang kulit purwa* and *wayang topeng* as models. Therefore a *dalang* is needed and the dramatic structure is well defined. Dancers took the puppet roles, and the flat plane of the blocking and the flowing quality of movement probably derived from the shadow aesthetic. Female impersonators were used, a theatrical norm in Yogyakarta style until the 1920s. Dance was at the time considered a necessary study for royalty, since it refined the spirit. Hence, princes were often fine dancers and apt to play major roles in dance dramas. Performers were cast according to body type and personality, and would play the same role type for life. Though the conceptualization of available type was expanded from four to 12, the increased role types can be considered a refinement, rather than a rejection of the old system.

The resources of the court prompted precision and dedication inconceivable in the village performance that later used it as a model. In this century performances would run three to four days with hundreds of dancers rehearsing up to a year in advance. Twelve such epics were staged in the 1920s–30s, with the repertoire primarily drawn from *Mahabharata* material. The distinctive headdress of the mask dancer, the *gambuh* constructed of matted hair, was abandoned in favour of headpieces like those of *wayang kulit purwa* figures. Exquisite batiks with set designs designated for specific characters wrapped the bejewelled dancers. The dance scarves which are tossed and held as part of the dance technique were also prescribed for each role. The 'green room' area where dancers waited to make their entrance to the *pendapa* of the palace was called by the same name as the puppet chest of the *wayang*. Yet the splendour at court hid the fact that the *dalang* role of the ruler was already in decline.

In the first quarter of this century two major alterations occurred. Firstly, Krida Beksa Wikrama, an organization for the promotion of classical dance, was founded in Yogyakarta by Prince Surjodiningrat and Prince Tedjokusumo in 1918 and began to train dancers in court arts for performances outside the palace. Secondly, palace performers began producing *wayan orang* for a ticket-buying public in Sriwidari, a park in Surakarta opened in 1899. First travelling *wayang orang* companies played there, but by 1920 palace dancers took over the venue. The box office went into the palace treasury, and performers got a set salary. The democratization and commercialization of palace arts had started and has accelerated since 1949, when with independence the court resources diminished. Sriwidari itself came under city administration at that time.

Current *wayang orang* uses a proscenium stage with wing and drop scenery. Women often play refined male roles, a practice introduced in the 1930s in Surakarta. As audiences waned, troupes shortened the five-hour performance to three and began doing a new repertoire, Javanese legends, in addition to *purwa* tales, to attract houses. Actors find these new materials difficult and must undertake unaccustomed rehearsals: *purwa* materials are easily improvised from the scenario, since actors generally play the same set character from performance to performance. Though the 1980s have seen a continued decline in audiences, troupes like Sriwidari and Ngesti Pandawa in Semarang may still include 60 performers.

Today other Yogyakarta court dramas have largely disappeared. *Langendriya* is a dance drama with sung dialogue presented by a female troupe and telling the story of Damar Wualan, a 14th-century Majapahit ruler. The form was created in 1876 by Raden Tummenggung Purwadiningrat and Prince Mankubumi. Another vanishing form is *langen mandro wanara*, created by Danureja VII in the same era to present the *Ramayana* story.

As in Bali, the textless *sendratari* has grown popular. Major tourist performances can be seen in the dry season at Prambanan and Pandaan temple complexes, where *Ramayana* and East Javanese tales, respectively, are presented. Today noted choreographers, including Wisnu Wardhana, Bagong Kussudiardjo, Sudharso Pringgobroto, Sardono, and Sudarsono, have created innovative *sendratari* for Javanese audiences, sometimes using techniques from Sundanese, Balinese, or even Western experimental dance. Story materials, music, and costume may also diverge from traditional sources. Still, the strong continuity with the classical tradition is apparent in most performances, which can often be seen at the government supported academies of dance in Yogyakarta and Surakarta.

Since the 18th century the Sundanese, a distinct ethnic group living on the western half of Java, have developed a rich artistic tradition. The developments have, as in Bali, occurred in response to Javanese models, but taken a very different form. The genres are related to Java's but the aesthetic, movement style, music, and language are Sunda's own. The performance strikes the viewer as being the middle ground between the almost frenetic dynamism of Bali and the mesmerizing, flowing aesthetic of Java. The drummer accents the dancers' steps with drum patterns appropriate for the movement, rather like the drum–dance syllables of Indian performance. This makes the movement and sound system seem more transparent than Java's. This in conjunction with the lively musical style, the constant calls, and quips that musicians are free to add to the performance make Sunda's arts seem earthy and spontaneous. This changed aesthetic probably results from the fact that palaces have had little part in forming the Sundanese arts – these are village arts.

Although story-telling, harvest rituals, and poetry traditions involving skits were part of the indigenous culture, elaborate theatre was not. But in the early 19th century Javanese officials assigned to govern parts of this area began importing *dalang* from the Cirebon area. About the same time itinerant troupes from the north coast availed themselves of the road the Dutch colonial administration had opened into Sundanese highlands. *Topeng* dancers and *ronggeng* singers might be found as part of market day entertainments. As these artists settled in Sunda and intermarried with Sundanese, a new hybrid of *wayang ronggeng* and *topeng* performances developed.

Wayang golek purwa is the rod puppet theatre of Sunda in which the *dalang* performs amazingly realistic dances and gestures with his doll-like figures as he presents *Mahabharata* and *Ramayana* based tales in a nightlong performance. This genre serves the same ritual and entertainment functions as shadow puppetry in Bali and Java. The puppet screen, of course, has vanished and figures are merely placed in the banana-log stage. The 11 performers are seated on a 15ft x 15ft wooden stage which is constructed for the occasion and faces the porch of the host's house.

The *slendro*-tuned *gamelan* ensemble is much smaller than that of central Java, and requires only about nine musicians. The music and the dancing are exuberant, and distinct from Java's repertoire and technique. Plot interpretations reflect a peasant's perspective on the court ethos, and clowns receive more prominence. The structure of the performance is looser than in Java – the 'flower battle' with its set ogres are gone. It is possible that the simpler pattern reflects a form from which the more complex Javanese shadow theatre evolved within the court context.

Tradition reports that the genre was created in the 19th century by command of the regent of Sumedang. Until that time only leather puppets had been used to tell the *purwa* story, but the local preference for the comparative realism of the three-dimensional figures used to tell Javanese and Muslim stories prompted the regent to commission a set of wooden puppets with the distinctive *purwa* headdress. At present some performers do Sundanese chronicle tales and Amir Hamzah stories as well as Indian-based stories using the *purwa* style figures. These tales are the speciality of

Bogor area *dalang* who find Islamic fundamentalist audiences favour such material.

Today the Sunarya family of the Bandung area is probably the most popular *dalang* family, with five major performers in two generations of the family currently active. The eldest *dalang* in such a family that decends from *dalang* of yore can make holy water, used to cure and bring luck, or perform the spiritually dangerous exorcisms. However, since major *dalang* are culture idols and command high fees, many boys who do not come from families of *dalang* now aspire to the role, creating a current pool of about 2,000 trained in the art via the apprentice system. The female singer (*pesinden*), who was incorporated into the form around 1900, is given more prominence than her Javanese counterpart, and the audience requests songs during interludes in the story. The first *pesinden* was, reportedly, a *ronggeng* dancer–singer who married a *dalang*. The popularity of these dynamic women rivals that of the *dalang* themselves.

Many Sundanese folk theatres are linked to the *ronggeng* tradition. Throughout Sunda there are forms like *topeng banet* and *ronggeng gunung*. These genres often open with solo character dances by a female, lead into short sketches on village life, and culminate with performers dancing *ketuk tilu* partner dances with male audience members. Songs by the performers may come between sketches. The featured roles are the female actress/singer/dancers and the clowns.

Until the past generation the only masked dance of the Sundanese was the red-faced ogrely Klana character, which might be danced prior to a *wayang golek* performance, and was thought to bring good luck. Currently however the whole repertoire of the *topeng babakan* is spreading in Sunda, as a result of this form being included in the curriculum of the government dance schools in Bandung.

Wayang orang developed in Sunda, as in Java, by substituting people for puppets, and corresponds in most particulars to the *wayang golek purwa*. Costuming is similar to Javanese dance drama, but the dance of the performers has the grounded, three-dimensional feel of the wooden rod puppet that the dancer tries to emulate. *Sendratari* has emerged in the last 25 years, with Enoch Atmadibarata, Abay Subarja, and Endo Suwanda as important choreographers. Though *purwa* stories are sometimes presented, the Sundanese legends and history prevail. Tales of Pajajaran, the Sundanese kingdom that retreated to the spirit plane rather than accept the domination of the Javanese, may be presented with haunting Sundanese songs derived from the old *pantun* (story-telling) tradition. Where Javanese and Balinese may look for new materials from other areas, the Sundanese tend to look back.

Popular urban drama In the last hundred years popular drama forms which emphasize dialogue over dance, performed in permanent theatres for a ticket-buying audience have arisen in the cities. Many of these forms developed in response to companies of *bangsawan* players touring from Malaysia in the early part of this century. These troupes presented a model of a commercial theatre where entertainment was the prime aim and new plot materials standard practice.

In current forms actors still play set character types and generate the script from a scenario posted back-stage. But *dalang* are not needed, and the archaisms of language, rituals for spirits, and formulaic phrases that characterize *wayang* are gone. Plots may even be set in modern, rather than epic times. Given the plot and language emphasis, movement tends to be pedestrian, and the whole performance much more realistic than the forms discussed previously. The prominence given clown characters and tendency of many more recent plots to turn on problems of lovers and their parents make the forms reminiscent of **commedia dell'arte**. Usually performances will be given in structures that boast a proscenium stage, painted scenery, and a darkened auditorium. Though some forms, like *ketoprak*, show considerable continuity with *wayang*'s epic world, others, like *ludruk*, look more at the present.

Ketoprak is a form created in the early 20th century based on musical rhythms elaborated from pounding rice. The music became a craze in court and villages around Surakarta, and dialogue-oriented, improvised dramas based on Javanese chronicle tales became associated with it in the 1920s. By 1927 *gamelan* replaced the original musical instruments. Current troupes like Ketoprak Mataram and Sapta Mandala in Yogyakarta perform nightly, and the backstage visitor will see actors checking the posted scenario before their entrance. The plot structure and character types correspond in many ways to the *wayang orang* minus its dance and archaic language.

Sandiwara, Sunda's response to *bangsawan*, has two major forms. The first is comparable to *ketoprak* and combines indigenous *gamelan*, Sundanese history tales, and *wayang*-like dramatic structure. The second variant is now more common and focuses on domestic melodramas climaxing in martial arts scenes. A village girl may be kidnapped by a bandit, but rescued by her sweetheart, or the attempts of parents to marry a daughter for money will be foiled by her true love with her clownish servant's good offices.

Ludruk is the urban popular theatre of Surabaya in East Java developed from folk entertainments into a more drama-oriented genre under the influence of *bangsawan*. Performances begin with a dance, a clown sequence, and singing and dancing of the female impersonator. Then comes the story, usually a domestic melodrama with comic interludes, though some traditional stories are still presented. Though the female impersonator dances in a style rudely recalling the traditional female court dancer, the core of the show is the realistic spoken drama that probes problems of the modern urban audience.

Other examples of such 20th-century improvised forms are found in Sumatra (*randai*), around Jakarta (*lenong*), in Cirebon (*tarling*), and in Kalimantan (*mamanda*). Many troupes, however, have folded in recent years under the competition of rock bands, film and television.

Modern spoken drama (see also **Asia, South-East (Modern)**) Modern drama is the youngest dramatic genre, a 20th-century creation of university-educated authors writing under the influence of Western dramatic models. The dynamic author–director W. S. Rendra's politically committed theatre of the 1960s–70s galvanized audiences of the educated elite and gained government censorship because of its critique of political corruption. His theatre workshop was the breeding-ground for other major writers like Ikranagara, Arifin C. Nur, and Putu Wijaya. Plays are performed in major cities in permanent theatres, like that of Taman Ismail Marzuki (TIM), the Jakarta Arts complex. Spoken drama is presented in Indonesian, rather than the regional languages that characterize other dramatic forms. A trend started by Rendra in 1975 has been to incorporate music, dance, and traditional theatre practices increasingly into performance, but as with the urban popular theatre, the word and its message remains the focus of this theatre. It demands that the audience look at the real world around them and take action against pressing social problems confronting their modernizing nation. The traditional theatre comments on this world through the voice of the multi-faceted clown; but music, dance, types, and formulaic patterns communicate its message. It asks the audience to look at epic and archetypical worlds beyond and within them assuming the performance crafted by their forebears will make them see a reality that the real world obscures.   KF

See: Abdurachman, *Cerbon*, Jakarta, 1982; I. M. Bandem and F. deBoer, *Kaja and Kelod*, Kuala Lumpur, 1981; J. Brandon, *On Thrones of Gold*, Cambridge, Mass., 1970; and *Theatre in Southeast Asia*, Cambridge, Mass., 1967; J. Emigh, 'Playing with the Past: Visitation and Illusion in the Masked Theatre of Bali', *The Drama Review* 23, 2 (1979), 1–36; K. Foley, 'Of Dalang and Dukun – Spirits and Men: Curing Performance in the *Wayang* of West Java', *Asian Theatre Journal* 1, 1 (1984), 52–75; and 'The Sundanese Wayang Golek: The Rod Puppet Theatre of West Java', Ph.D. Univ. of Hawaii, 1979; C. Geertz, *Negara*, Princeton, 1980; C. Holt, *Art in Indonesia*, Ithaca, 1967; A. H. Johns, 'Islam in Southeast Asia: Reflections and a New Direction', *Indonesia* 19, (1975), 33–55; C. Kulhman (ed.), 'Indonesia', *Selected Great Theatre Companies of the World*, Westport, Ct, 1986; R. Long, *Javanese Shadow Theatre: Movement and Characterization in Ngayoyakarta Wayang Kulit*, Ann Arbor, 1982; Mangkunegoro VII of Sukarta *On the Wayang Kulit (Purwa) and its Symbolic and Mystical Elements*, Ithaca, 1957; J. Peacock, *Rites of Modernization: Symbolic and Social Aspects of Indonesian Proletarian Drama*, Chicago, 1968; B. de Zoete and W. Spies, *Dance and Drama in Bali*, Kuala Lumpur, 1973 (1938); T. Pigeaud, *Javaanse Volksvertoningen*, Batavia, 1938; W. S. Rendra, *Struggle of the Naga People*, trans. M. Lane, New York, 1979; Soedarsono, *Wayang Wong*, Yogyakarta, 1984.

Inge, William Motter (1913–73) American playwright. On the strength of his first play, *Come Back Little Sheba* (1950), the critics touted Inge as having the promise to join **Arthur Miller** and **Tennessee Williams** in a triumvirate of outstanding American dramatists. Although he never fulfilled that promise, he made considerable impact on American theatre with *Picnic* (1953), *Bus Stop* (1955), and *The Dark at the Top of the Stairs* (1957). *Picnic* won the Pulitzer Prize, the Drama Critics' Circle Award, and the Outer Critics' Circle Award. Born in Independence, Kansas, and educated at the University of Kansas, he taught at Stephens College in Columbia, Missouri, and at Washington University in St Louis, and he toured for a season under canvas with a **Toby** show. He was thus a product of mid-America, and his works reflected this background. He seemed to cherish his lonely characters; even as he laid

bare their weaknesses, he surrounded them with love and understanding. He also recorded their speech with an accurate, appreciative ear. His later works, such as *A Loss of Roses* (1959), *Natural Affection* (1963), and *Where's Daddy?* (1966), drew neither critical acclaim nor much of an audience. He suffered from depression and alcoholism, and his death was by suicide.   LDC

Innaurato, Albert (1948–   ) American playwright educated at Temple University and the Yale School of Drama. Drawing on his south Philadelphia background, Innaurato's most successful play, *Gemini*, produced in 1976, deals with an Italian and Catholic family (with the hero, Francis Geminiani, home from Harvard) in this ethnic neighbourhood. Other plays include *The Transfiguration of Benno Blimpie* (1973) and *Earth Worms* and *Ulysses in Traction* (New York productions, 1977). In 1980 a collection of his plays appeared appropriately titled *Bizarre Behavior*.   DBW

Inner stage see **Discovery space**

Inns used as playhouses The yards of coaching inns were often used by touring players in 16th-century England. A simple trestle-stage was set up along one side of a square or rectangular yard, and spectators accommodated in the first-floor walkways as well as in the yard itself. Innkeepers benefited from the extra custom, but the players probably had to rely on 'bottling' (taking a collection) for their remuneration. London inns known to have served as temporary playhouses include the Saracen's Head in Islington (first mentioned in 1557), the Red Lion in Stepney (first mentioned in 1567), the Bull in Bishopsgate and the Bell in Gracechurch Street, which were both used by **Queen Elizabeth's Men**, and the Bel Savage in Ludgate (first mentioned in 1579). The Cross Keys in Gracechurch Street may have undergone some conversion for use by **Strange's Men**. It was no longer satisfactory for the increasingly professional companies to settle for bottling once **James Burbage** had demonstrated a safer way at the **Theatre**. The public theatres of Elizabethan London had many features in common with inn-yards, as the enterprising speculators who converted the **Boar's Head** near Aldgate (1597–9) and the **Red Bull** in Clerkenwell (1605) clearly knew. If Burbage used his experience of inns in planning the Theatre, they used their knowledge of theatres in planning the radical transformation of inns.   PT

Inter-Action A charitable trust founded in London by the American director, Ed Berman, in 1968, designed to be an umbrella organization for a variety of community activities, particularly concerned with theatre and play projects. Berman began with a little lunchtime theatre, the Ambiance in Queensway, West London, which put on new plays by mainly British and American authors, including **Tom Stoppard** and **Ed Bullins**. When the lease ran out, the Ambiance moved to another short-term property and became the Almost Free in Piccadilly. At the main Inter-Action base in Kentish Town, North London, a bewildering range of little companies grew up around Berman, a Fun Art Bus, the Community Media Van, City Farm I (which created a farm in a city area), BARC (the British American Repertory Company), Professor Dogg's Troupe, Infilms (a professional film production company), Imprint (a small publishing house) and the International Institute for Social Enterprise. JE

Interlude The first recorded use of the term, at the beginning of the 14th century, is a theatrical one: the title of the fragmentary English play of *The Clerk and The Girl* (*Interludium de Clerico et Puella*). It seems not to have been used elsewhere in Europe. During the 14th and 15th centuries it is applied to a variety of entertainments, some solo (e.g. the 1494 account of King Alfred disguised as a minstrel performing 'enterludes and songes' to the Danes). It is often associated with singing but there are references which clearly indicate that it was also used of plays proper. The first-known named 'interlude' is **Medwall**'s *Fulgens and Lucres* (late 15th century) and thereafter during the 16th century it is used for any type of play: comedy, tragedy, biblical play, morality. It goes out of use in the later 17th century and was revived, as a critical term, by J. P. Collier to refer specifically to **John Heywood**'s plays. Now refers to the miscellaneous, short, often comic, English plays of the first half of the 16th century. PM

International Centre of Theatre Research see **Brook, Peter**

Internationale Nieuwe Scene (New International Stage) Antwerp-based bilingual political theatre company founded in 1973. Its main theoretical influence is **Brecht**; its main practical influence comes through personal and professional contact with **Dario Fo** and Arturo Corso. The company's first production was a re-working of Fo's *Mistero Buffo*, with the writer-actor's disquisitions on popular culture replaced by Flemish workers' songs. For preference the INS performs in a circus-tent, whose connotations of popular entertainment and informal pleasure suit it better than a purpose-built theatre. The techniques of **commedia dell'arte** are central to the company's work, in that they enable the actor to fulfil Brecht's criterion of showing rather than identifying with the character. However, their plays are in no sense archaeological exercises. The style (in itself impressively precise and imaginative) is one element in a thoroughly considered socialist aesthetic, seen at its most mature in *De Herkuls* (*Hercules*, 1980). AEG

Ionesco, Eugène (1909–   ) French playwright. The child of separated parents, Rumanian father and French mother, Ionesco's youth was divided between France and Rumania, but Paris has been his home since before the Second World War. His first play, *La Cantatrice Chauve* (*The Bald Prima Donna*), was inspired by an English phrase-book, but when performed (directed by Nicolas Bataille, 1950) astonished its author by its comic force: he imagined he had written 'the tragedy of language'. A stream of one-act plays followed, e.g. *La Leçon* (*The Lesson*) (directed by Cuvelier, 1951), *Les Chaises* (*The Chairs*) (directed by Dhomme, 1952) which merit the author's epithet 'tragic farce'. In them language becomes reified and both physical and metaphysical elements fuse to generate strong concrete images of anguished mental states. Story-line, charac-

The Chairs, by Ionesco, Studio des Champs Elysées, 1956.

ter and discussion are abandoned: events of a hallucinatory, surrealist quality take their place. With *Tueur sans Gages* (*The Killer*, 1959), Ionesco wrote his first three-act play and his subsequent work e.g. *Rhinoceros* (directed by **Barrault**, 1960) or *Le Roi Se Meurt* (*Exit the King*) (directed by Mauclair, 1962) became more conventional in form, returning to some of the dramatic traditions that his earlier work had castigated. Into a number of plays written during this period, Ionesco introduced a character named Bérenger: naive, imaginative, alternately ecstatic or depressed for reasons he cannot identify, Bérenger is a transparently autobiographical figure and one with whom audiences could identify more easily than with the earlier, puppet-like figures. In the 1960s Ionesco's plays were performed all over the world, including the **Comédie-Française**, *La Soif et la Faim* (*Hunger and Thirst*, 1966). He was elected to the Académie-Française in 1970. Since then he has been less prolific, writing memoirs and a novel. In 1981 a new play *Voyages chez les Morts* (*Journeys to the Homes of the Dead*) recaptured the hallucinatory quality of the early work using autobiographical material. It formed the basis of **Planchon**'s massive biographical production *Ionesco* starring Jean Carmet as the author in 1982. DB

Iran and **Iraq** see **Middle East**

Ireland Literature in Irish – epic, saga, and lyric – goes back some 1,500 years to the Early Christian period. There is no equivalent in Gaelic culture to the European development of drama from the church to the secular stage. By the beginning of the 17th century the Gaelic social system, its aristocracy, and the Bardic culture that depended on it had succumbed to the increasingly efficient repression by the Tudor colonizers. In its place, 'the English born in Ireland', descendants of the original invaders, supplied the ruling class: the Anglo-Irish, the Protestant Ascendancy, in a largely Catholic country.

The development of Irish theatre reflects the country's divisions. The drama cultivated by the Ascendancy was detached from the population outside its enclaves. Theatres were built in Dublin, the first in 1637 and the most celebrated, the Smock Alley, in 1662; and eventually in the provincial towns. It was a colonial theatre: touring English companies gave English plays.

In time, Irish players emerged: **Thomas Doggett** (1660–1721), **Peg Woffington** (1714–60), **Charles Macklin** (1697–1797). Inevitably, their profession took them to England. London was the theatrical arena too for Irish dramatists – or, to make a necessary distinction, for playwrights of Irish birth: **Farquhar**, **Congreve**, **Goldsmith**, **Sheridan**, **Wilde**, **Shaw**. Though one may catch inflections from their native country in their work, it belongs essentially to the English dramatic tradition – albeit within that tradition constituting almost a tradition of its own.

Effectively, Irish drama began in 1897 with the conception of the Irish Literary Theatre by the poet **W. B. Yeats** and two landowners in the west of Ireland, Augusta **Lady Gregory** and Edward Martyn. Shortly afterwards, George Moore the novelist, a landlord also, joined the trio.

Though the enterprise allied itself with, in Douglas Hyde's phrase, 'the necessity for de-Anglicizing Ireland', it proposed a drama written in English. The long cohabitation of the two languages had produced a Hibernicized English. Authentically a national speech, it supplied a medium through which 'to build up', in the words of the theatre's prospectus, 'a Celtic and Irish school of dramatic literature'. Lacking any native precedent and contemptuous of English commercial theatre, the founders had their several approaches to this end.

Lady Gregory's translations of Irish heroic legend and peasant tales attracted Yeats to their dramatic potential: images of Irish life to displace the caricatured 'stage Irishman' of the popular theatre. Yeats was confident of restoring verse, and a poetic, non-realistic theatre to their bygone primacy: 'the theatre of **Shakespeare** or rather perhaps of **Sophocles**'. Moore advised the example of **Ibsen**. So, ardently, did Martyn. Yeats did not demur, although privately he thought Ibsen a modish realist whose fashion would pass. More to his taste was the symbolist drama of Villiers de l'Isle Adam's *Axël* (1894). These divergent aesthetic claims were of less moment to the Theatre's prospective audience than the exigencies of nationalist politics. Among them, sentiment required of an Irish theatre, as a corrective to English disparagement, faithful, indeed flattering, portrayals of Irish piety.

The Irish Literary Theatre's three Dublin seasons (1899–1901) were a balance of its theories. Heroic verse drama was represented by Yeats's *The Countess Cathleen* (1899) and (in fretful collaboration with Moore) *Diarmuid and Grania* (1901); Ibsenite socio-psychological drama by Martyn's *The Heather Field* (1899) and *Maeve* (1900) – reverential travesties of Ibsen – and Moore's negligible *The Bending of the Bough* (1900), which was originally Martyn's *The Tale of a Town*, until Martyn refused his name to Moore's imperious 'collaboration'. Douglas Hyde contributed an entertaining one-act peasant comedy, *The Twisting of the Rope* (1901). The experiment arrived at a rudimentary map of possible courses; circumstances directed its elaboration.

Disgruntled by Yeats's indifference to presenting Continental drama, Martyn withdrew; Moore wearied of the venture and returned to England. Yeats took up with the brothers Frank and Willie Fay, enthusiastic amateurs. Where the Irish Literary Theatre had imported English companies, the Fays had assembled and trained a body of amateur players. They shared with Yeats the conviction that speech should be the governing presence on stage. In 1902 their Irish National Dramatic Company put on Yeats's *Cathleen ni Houlihan*, and the next year joined forces with Yeats and Lady Gregory to form the Irish National Theatre Society. This, when it acquired a permanent house in Abbey Street in 1904, became the Irish National Theatre Society Ltd, commonly known as the **Abbey**. In 1903 it had presented Yeats's *The Hour Glass* and *The King's Threshold*, James Cousins's *The Racing Lug*, Lady Gregory's first play, *Twenty-Five*. Most significant of a future pattern were **Padraic Colum**'s *Broken Soil* and **J. M. Synge**'s *In the Shadow of the Glen* (1903).

Through Yeats's work in these years verse drama was still holding its own. Colum and Synge, however, signal a shift, soon confirmed, to a drama whose medium was prose, whose settings were peasant and, increasingly, small-town life. They were in their different ways realist. Synge insisted on authenticity of sets and properties, and used the conventional proscenium stage. His prose, however, was a dramatic rhetoric which stylized and elevated peasant speech. Yeats recognized its enriching, poetic power. It occupied cottages and shebeens with a fabulous life, like that of Christy in *The Playboy of the Western World* (1907), a parable of the artist/outcast and his dangerous, liberating inroads on community decorum.

Colum's prose is less elaborately figured. Yeats saw it as the issue of a common speech discoloured by migration from the land, formal education, and the newspapers; and denied the possibility of its access to any comprehensive range of expression. It is true that Colum's plays are more circumstantially placed than Synge's on a map and in a period, but Colum's prose has a subdued poetry, to which Yeats was deaf.

Irish drama accepted the shape prescribed by the theatre available to it: the 19th-century proscenium stage. Colum's successors established the dominance of the realist manner, of which Yeats said in 1919, 'its success has been to me a discouragement and a defeat'. **William Boyle** (*The Building Fund*, 1905) and **T. C. Murray** (*Birthright*, 1910) had inaugurated a line of playwrights who took their subjects from contemporary social issues and employed a prose close to the common speech of their characters' real-life counterparts.

With a couple of interesting exceptions – the strange fantasy plays of **George Fitzmaurice** (*The Pie-Dish*, 1908) and the verse plays of **Austin Clarke** (*The Son of Learning*, 1927) – the general run of Irish drama from the 1920s to the 50s was of that kind. It sustained the adventures of dramatists whose use of the realist convention questioned its apparent solidity. This subversion of the accepted form is particularly notable in the early plays of **Sean O'Casey** (*The Shadow of a Gunman*, 1923) and **Denis Johnston** (*The Old Lady Says 'No!'*, 1929).

In the work of both these dramatists, as in Synge, it is language which challenges the simply coded signals of a realist theatre whose aim is to put on stage readily identifiable representations of external reality. In the best Irish drama words assert their own primacy; instead of running imitatively alongside life, so to speak, words create a rival world which may displace the world of facts, or alter it.

Though not unique to Irish drama, the claim to a 'sovereignty of words' – Yeats's phrase – is pervasive in it. It is an assertion not only by the dramatists of an aesthetic principle, but by their characters as a fact of life. In Denis Johnston's *The Old Lady* the Republican youth, responding to the old man's 'you can't change the world by words', answers 'we can make this country whatever we want it to be by saying so'. That the language used is English is itself a political consequence: displacing the mother tongue, it finds a sanction in its Gaelicized nature. In Irish drama, the subjects on which it bears are often political too. O'Casey's subjects are overtly so, as is much of Yeats, Johnston, and most recently **Brian Friel**. Even **Samuel Beckett**'s desolate, unlocalized landscapes open fleetingly on an inheritance of ruined, Irish hinterlands. A language which is in a sense politicized turns to political matter.

The work of **George Shiels** (*Paul Twyning*, 1922) and **Paul Vincent Carroll** (*Shadow and Substance*, 1937), which centres on the social usages of post-independence Ireland, is also in a broad sense political. The society they regard is in many ways a creation of Victorian notions of respectability, ubiquitous in the Northern Protestant middle class, and in the South when a Catholic bourgeoisie was consolidating itself. It was an ethos perfectly congenial to churches in whose teaching the major immoralities were sexual. Again the realist stage accommodated widely disparate treatments, from Carroll a rather indecisive crusading against the pieties, in Shiels the strangely modernist effect of noncommittal report on a world where base actions are the norm.

The contemporary scene The Abbey Theatre, throughout its career frequently and at times justly attacked for inert conservatism, has been the continuing home of Irish drama and the major nursery of its playwrights. Other enterprises have been less concerned to foster new writing. The **Ulster Literary Theatre** (1904–34) was located in Belfast, and remained amateur, never acquiring a house of its own. It developed in kitchen comedy and kitchen tragedy a regional variant on the Abbey style, built a reputation for imaginative staging, and in **Rutherford Mayne** found an interesting writer.

A major Dublin presence was the **Gate Theatre**. Founded in 1928 by Micheál MacLiammóir and Hilton Edwards, it was committed to a repertoire and a stagecraft more diversified than the Abbey's. Less ambitiously, Austin Clarke inaugurated his Lyric Theatre Company in Dublin in 1944 for occasional presentations of verse drama.

The beginning and end of the Second World War saw two companies founded in Belfast, respectively the **Group** and the **Arts Theatre**. Like the Ulster Literary Theatre, the Group had a regional emphasis; the Arts drew on a range of international drama. Mary O'Malley's **Lyric Theatre**, founded in Belfast in 1951, shared some of the aims of the Arts and gave a special place to verse drama, Yeats's specifically.

None of these ventures did much to stir the emergence of new dramatists. The 1940s and 50s, apart from the work of **M. J. Molloy**, were particularly drab. In 1954, however, Alan Simpson's tiny **Pike Theatre** put on **Brendan Behan**'s *The Quare Fellow* and in 1955 shared the London premiere of Beckett's *Waiting for Godot*. So far as Irish drama in general was concerned these events, although they had no immediate results, were perhaps harbingers of revival.

Simple equations between artistic and political developments are more likely than not misleading. However, it is tempting to surmise some common genesis in the revival of drama in the mid-1960s and the attack at the end of the decade on the mould and prerogatives of the Northern state. Certainly, much of the work of the newer dramatists seeks out, in domestic settings and individual lives, the assurances and instabilities of social and political inheritances no longer sure of themselves. **Sam Thompson** (*Over the Bridge*, 1960), **John Boyd** (*The Assassin*, 1969), have taken directly political approaches. **Thomas Murphy** (*A Whistle in the Dark*, 1961), **Eugene McCabe** (*King of the Castle*, 1964), Brian Friel (*Philadelphia, Here I Come!*, 1964), **Thomas Kilroy** (*The Death and Resurrection of Mr Roche*, 1968) anatomize lives in which spiritual stresses obliquely reflect political futilities. The underlying question of what is 'home' attracts both scepticism and celebration, often together. The Field Day Theatre Company, founded by Brian Friel and others in 1980, has as its aim to foster the dramatic expression of such concerns.

Irish drama is a long experiment, sometimes descending to stretches of mechanical self-duplication, with the boundaries of realist theatre. At its heights it engages realist theatre in poetic transformations, beyond the traffic with mere documentary paraphrase. It is remarkable that its history is essentially the flowering of an indigenous experience and imagination. It develops manners of presentation which are not discursive or sequential, which move away from literal portrayal: towards, in short, modernist attitudes and methods.

The experimental drama of Europe was known in Ireland at the turn of the century. In Ireland it was suggestive, not prescriptive. Synge rejected it. It interested Yeats, but he drew upon it, as he did upon the Japanese **nō** plays, quite arbitrarily to confirm his own propositions. Denis Johnston, the Irish dramatist perhaps most consciously receptive to the drama abroad, gave to his borrowings from German expressionism a peculiarly Irish character. These are cavalier alliances within a self-sufficiency which continues to the present, informed by the sense of language as both reflecting and supplanting reality.   DM

See: U. Ellis-Fermor, *The Irish Dramatic Movement*, London, 1939, rev. edn 1954; D. E. S. Maxwell, *A Critical History of Modern Irish Drama 1891–1980*, Cambridge, 1984; K. Worth, *The Irish Drama of Europe from Yeats to Beckett*, Atlantic Highlands, 1978.

Ireland, William Henry (1775–1835) English forger. In 1794, desperate to please his father, Samuel Ireland, an obsessive idolizer of **Shakespeare**, he began to forge legal documents with Shakespeare's signature. The papers early convinced a number of experts and other writers including **Boaden** and Boswell, who knelt before them. Encouraged, Ireland went on to produce manuscripts of *King Lear*, part of *Hamlet* and a new play, *Vortigern*, which was accepted for production at **Drury Lane** by **Sheridan**. Samuel Ireland published the documents as *Miscellaneous Papers* in 1795 but credulity had begun to wane, with Boaden now leading the attack. Two days before the first performance of *Vortigern* Edmond Malone, the most noted Shakespeare scholar of his day, published *An Inquiry into the Authenticity of Certain Miscellaneous Papers* which convincingly proved the forgery. *Vortigern* was performed on 2 April 1796, a day later than **Kemble** had wickedly intended, and was a disaster with Kemble delivering Ireland's line 'And when this solemn mockery is o'er' with calculated irony. Ireland's *Henry II*, another supposed Shakespeare play, was never performed. He admitted the fraud in his pamphlet *An Authentic Account* but his father believed in the authenticity of the papers until his death. Ireland continued to write voluminously, but only one further play, *Mutius Scaevola* (1801), his best though unperformed. His full *Confessions* were published in 1805.   PH

Irons, Jeremy (1948–   ) British actor. After training at **Bristol Old Vic** Theatre School he gained experience in repertory. His reputation was initially established through films (*The French Lieutenant's Woman*) and television (*Brideshead Revisited*). In 1986 he joined the RSC at Stratford-upon-Avon playing the title role in **Shakespeare**'s *Richard II* and **Aphra Behn**'s *The Rover* (at the first season of the Swan Theatre), staking positive claim to be regarded as a stage actor in the same way he is regarded in other media.   MB

Irving, Henry (1838–1905) English actor, born John Henry Brodribb. Risking (and receiving) the disapproval of his sternly Methodist Cornish relations, he escaped from a London counting-house onto the professional stage in 1856. For most of the next ten years he was a busy provincial actor, notably in Edinburgh and Manchester, distinguished from his colleagues only by the intensity of his ambition. In 1866, he played in **Hannah Cowley**'s *The Belle's Stratagem* and **Boucicault**'s *Hunted Down* at the **St James's** with sufficient success to encourage him to stay in London. He acted with **Ellen Terry** for the first time in an 1867 revival of **Garrick**'s *Katharine and Petruchio*, but it was his playing of Digby Grant in **James Albery**'s *Two Roses* (1870) that gave the first sure indication of his idiosyncratic genius. The American manager of the **Lyceum**, **H. L. Bateman**, engaged Irving at a critical point in his theatre's fortunes. As Jingle in Albery's *Pickwick* (1871), he was asked to do little more than repeat Digby Grant, and the public response was luke-warm. It was when Bateman yielded to Irving's suggestion that they stage **Leopold Lewis**'s version of *Le Juif Polonais* that the fortunes of the Lyceum changed decisively. *The Bells*, as Lewis agreed to call it, gave Irving his first great part, that of the guilt-ridden burgomaster Mathias. It held a central place in Irving's repertoire for the rest of his life. Secret guilt was again the basis of his next major success, as Eugene Aram in **W. G. Wills**'s indifferent play of that name (1873). In a revival of **Edward Bulwer**'s *Richelieu* (1873) it was his embodiment of will-power that mesmerized audiences. His tender, sensitive Hamlet

(1874) was an unexpected contrast and the public had to be weaned before accepting it as the generation's classic portrayal. It was in the sinister and the aloof that they most readily recognized Irving – as Philip of Spain in **Tennyson**'s *Queen Mary* (1876), as Richard III (1877), as the villainous Dubosc rather than his virtuous double Lesurques in **Charles Reade**'s version of *The Lyons Mail* (1877), as a coweringly senile Louis XI in Boucicault's play and as Vanderdecken in the Wills/Fitzgerald dilution of **Wagner**'s *The Flying Dutchman* (1878).

At the end of 1878, Irving bought Bateman's widow out of management of the Lyceum. For over 20 years he consecrated it as a temple to the actor's art, himself the high priest. His first decision was to open with a revival of *Hamlet*, his second, vastly more significant for the future, was to invite Ellen Terry to play Ophelia. She, all grace, charm and flowing lines, was aptly complementary to his angular eccentricity. All their Shakespearian triumphs were shared – Shylock and Portia (1879), Iago and Desdemona (1881), Benedick and Beatrice (1882), Malvolio and Viola (1884), Wolsey and Katherine of Aragon (1892), Lear and Cordelia (1892), Iachimo and Imogen (1896). So were their failures – Romeo and Juliet (1882), perhaps Macbeth and Lady Macbeth (1888), certainly Coriolanus and Volumnia (1901). Irving's **Shakespeare** productions were pictorially splendid and always embellished with commissioned music. Sir Arthur Sullivan composed incidental music for *Macbeth*, Edward German for *Henry VIII*, and the Lyceum musical directors (Hamilton Clarke,

Henry Irving as Mathias in Leopold Lewis's *The Bells*: 'Take the rope from my neck . . .'.

1878–81 and Meredith Ball, 1881–99) provided overtures as well as musical effects. Impressed by the staging techniques of the **Meininger** players at **Drury Lane** in 1881, Irving became a master of crowd scenes. In addition to his resident designers, Hawes Craven and Joseph Harker, he employed such luminaries as Alma-Tadema, Edwin Abbey and Burne-Jones. There was a regular orchestra of 30 at the Lyceum (35 for the lavish production of Wills's *Faust* (1885) together with a Chorus of 43 in the Brocken scene) and the payroll for *Robespierre* (1899) amounted to a staggering 639, comprising 355 performers and musicians, 236 technical staff and 48 administrators and their assistants. Despite his reputation as an interpreter of Shakespeare and the intellectual leader of his profession, Irving was primarily a showman, quite as likely to stage a tired melodrama like Watts Phillips's *The Dead Heart* (1889) as a classic revival, provided only that it contained a part in which he could startle audiences. It was for this reason that he selected Mephistopheles in Wills's shoddy *Faust*, the dual role of Fabien and Louis dei Franchi in Boucicault's *The Corsican Brothers* (1880) and the title role in Tennyson's *Becket* (1893). **George Bernard Shaw**'s repeated complaints that Irving did nothing to advance the English drama are just, not least because no other man was better placed to do so. It was acting that interested Irving, not writing. To that extent, he earned the knighthood bestowed on him in 1895, the first actor to be so honoured.

Irving's two sons (his marriage to Florence O'Callaghan, though maintained in name, formally ended in 1871) were both active in the theatre. The elder, Henry, known as H. B. Irving (1870–1919), made his debut in 1891, eventually forming his own company in 1906 and touring in many of his father's famous parts. His wife, Dorothea Baird (1875–1933), who had shot to fame as the creator of George Du Maurier's Trilby in 1895, was a member of the company until her retirement in 1913. Irving's younger son, Laurence (1871–1914), had aspirations as a playwright as well as an actor. There was some parental indulgence in the staging at the Lyceum of his unwieldy epic, *Peter the Great* (1898) and his adaptation of **Sardou**'s *Robespierre* (1899), but much was left unrealized when he was drowned in a shipwreck on the way to Canada. H. B. Irving's son, Laurence Irving (1897–1983), was a regular designer for stage and films (he designed the first London production of **T. S. Eliot**'s *Murder in the Cathedral* (1935)) and the author of an excellent biography of his grandfather (1951) and an account of the family's subsequent history, *The Successors* (1967).   PT

Irving, Jules (1924–79) American producer and director. Born in New York, Irving was educated at New York and Stanford Universities. While teaching at San Francisco State College (1949–62), he, together with a colleague Herbert Blau, founded the San Francisco Actors Workshop (1952–64), which became known for its experimental productions. In 1965 they became co-directors of the Repertory Theatre of Lincoln Center, and after Blau resigned in 1967, Irving continued as director until 1972. From 1972–9 he worked in Hollywood as producer–director of television movies. During his controversial tenure at Lincoln Center, Irving became known for his carefully crafted productions of the classics and for innovative

presentations of plays by **Brecht**, **Beckett**, and **Pinter**. In 1971 he staged the United States premiere of Pinter's *Landscape* and *Silence*. His daughter, Amy Irving, acts for films, television, and the theatre.   TLM

Irwin, Bill (1950–) American actor, entertainer and playwright. Irwin represents a new kind of American performing artist, and the best known, who has focused on the creation, often in collaboration, of theatre works which draw upon American popular entertainment traditions, from the circus to vaudeville, and experimental theatre techniques. Others in this disparate group would include Doug Skinner and Michael O'Connor, Irwin's frequent collaborators, the Karamazov Brothers (acrobats and jugglers), Avner the Eccentric (a clown), Michael Moshen (juggler), Paul Zaloom (puppeteer and modern-day medicine show talker), and the performers of such groups as the Pickle Family Circus and the Big Apple Circus. Irwin might be termed a 'post-modern clown'. Like others in the group, he attempts to make innovative use of his clown skills to create exciting visual metaphors for the broader actions and emotions of a play. He moved from conventional theatre training at UCLA to experimental theatre training with Herbert Blau, to the Ringling Brothers Clown College, the Pickle Family circus, and the avant-garde Oberlin Dance Collective before evolving what Ron Jenkins, a former circus clown, calls Irwin's 'metaphysical slapstick' and categorizes as 'New vaudeville'. Irwin's best work to date has been *The Regard of Flight*, a 1982 performance at the **American Place Theatre** that effectively and comedically satirized the so-called 'new, relevant theatre'. In 1984 he became the first American performing artist to receive the prestigious MacArthur Foundation Fellowship.   DBW

Isherwood, Christopher (1904–) British novelist and dramatist, who collaborated with **W. H. Auden** between 1935 and 1938 on the series of expressionistic verse plays that established the reputation of the London **Group Theatre** – *The Dog Beneath the Skin*, *The Ascent of F6* and *On the Frontier*. His novel *Goodbye to Berlin* (1939) won the New York Drama Critics Circle Award in the dramatization by John Van Druten, *I am a Camera*, and formed the basis for the film *Cabaret* (1966). Moving to Hollywood in 1940, he became an American citizen in 1946.   CI

Isola Brothers, Emile (1860–1945) and Vincent (1862–1947) French impresarios who began as conjurers in their native Algeria and made a Parisian debut at the **Folies-Bergère** in 1892 in a thought-transference act. That same year they founded the Théâtre Isola and were hailed for such illusions as 'The Muscovite Trunk'. Succumbing to competition, they gave up magic to become the managers of, in succession, Parisiana, the Olympia, the Folies-Bergère, the Gaieté-Lyrique, the Opéra Comique (for 12 years), the Mogador and the Théâtre Sarah-Bernhardt, which they ran with taste and acumen. Failing to create a music-hall monopoly after the British model and losing their money in the depression, they returned to magic. Vincent, with his aristocratic profile and monocle, presented grand illusions, while Emile specialized in shows of dexterity with cards and scarves.   LS

Israel see **Hebrew theatre**

Italy One of the difficulties in writing about Italian theatre is that until the middle of the 19th century Italy existed as a geographical, but not as a social or political entity. Administrative divisions were reinforced by cultural and linguistic divisions: regional associations were strong, local customs, habits and assumptions informed most modes of artistic expression, and in the absence of an established national language dialects, like Neapolitan and Venetian, enjoyed the status of quasi-independent languages with their own distinctive popular literatures. Conditions then for theatre differed quite considerably from region to region in terms of the pace of development, shaping influences, and even the organizational structures and kinds of innovation. No city in Italy enjoyed a status comparable to London or Paris as the administrative and cultural centre, and although Rome was made the national capital in 1870, the extent to which it is the *cultural* capital would even today be much disputed.

This political and cultural fragmentation in large measure accounts for one of the enduring features of much theatre in Italy since the formation of the professional acting companies, the **commedia dell'- arte**, in the mid 16th century: itinerancy. For all that many of the major troupes of the 17th and early 18th centuries turned regional differences and enforced travelling somewhat to their advantage, cultural divisions and the nomadic life endured by most theatre professionals were for long, and increasingly in the 19th and early 20th centuries, seen as artistically and economically debilitating, frustrating the development of a national drama and an effective organizational structure. Foreign political presences in the peninsula too helped to make the drama unduly dependent upon, or the more readily influenced by, foreign literary and dramatic norms; French cultural hegemony in particular being strong from the mid 17th century to at least the mid 19th. Yet if the Italian theatre produced no significant body of dramatic literature, save for brief efflorescences at the early *cinquecento* courts, in *settecento* Venice, and in the early 20th century, it was for long technically the most original in Europe. Renaissance Italy may not unreasonably be called the seeding-ground of the modern European theatre, breeding the genres of tragicomedy and pastoral, *opera seria* and *opera buffa*, and effecting a radical revolution in staging conventions, scenic design and theatre building. In the improvised drama too it produced an altogether unique actor-based theatre. Italian predominance in most of these fields remained supreme for more than two centuries and was widely influential throughout Europe, all the more so perhaps as the rapid economic decline of the peninsula during the 17th century helped to drive much of its most original talent abroad. Modest as has been Italy's contribution to European dramatic literature, in the arts and crafts of stage show perhaps no theatre in Europe since the Renaissance has been so consistently innovative for so long.

The Renaissance (a)The humanist theatre Post-*quattrocento* drama and theatre were in large measure shaped by the Renaissance rediscovery of ancient Greek and Roman achievement. Medieval literary example and stage materials were not wholly ignored, but the work of humanist scholars and enthusiasts in the 15th century, aided by the invention of the printing press and the growth of aristocratic patronage, proved decisive. A new and keen interest in classical models and ancient authority was generated as work unknown to the Middle Ages increasingly came to light: the first edition of **Terence**'s plays was printed in 1470, the first collected edition of **Plautus** in 1472. Printing permitted the wide dissemination of texts, and this in turn encouraged stage production and translation.

Production inevitably generated curiosity about classical theatre structures and staging practices, a curiosity all the more excited by the publication of Vitruvius' study of ancient theatres, *De Architectura* (particularly in the Barbaro translation of 1567), while the ready availability of printed editions of **Horace**'s *Ars Poetica* and **Aristotle**'s *Poetics* raised questions about dramatic structure and composition. Rediscovery of the ancients was not just locally seminal, but of European-wide significance, and came gradually to permeate all fields of drama and theatre, although in some countries, notably England, the Reformation prevented the new classicism from gaining a secure hold. In Italy it tended to license academicism.

(b)The vernacular drama Nowhere was the dead hand of classical imitation more icily felt than on drama of tragic emphasis. Numerous tragedies were written in the vernacular during the period, and some were performed, but none has survived for other than historical reasons. The first regular Italian tragedy was **Trissino**'s *Sofonisba* (1515), tightly organized on Greek lines in its observance of the unities and use of chorus, song and spectacle, but artificially rhetorical and inert. So too is **Giraldi Cinzio**'s *Orbecche*, first performed in 1541. It established the motives of Senecan tragedy as fit for the *cinquecento* stage, initiating a vogue for revenge plots widely influential beyond Italy. One of the best of the 15th-century Italian tragedies, **Aretino**'s *Orazia* (1546), points up the limitations of tragedy in this period: even though it jettisons some of the classical trappings, like the chorus, and is effectively plotted to achieve an unusual happy ending, it is stilted, remote and unfelt.

With comedy the case was somewhat different. Its structures, dramatic strategies, and some of its materials were likewise drawn from classical precedent, particularly Plautus and Terence. But classical precedent gave comic dramatists more freedom in their choice and use of language and subject matter, and although nearly all the comedies of the period are of historical interest only, like, for example, two of the first Italian vernacular comedies, **Ariosto**'s *La Cassaria* (*The Chest*, 1508) and *I Suppositi* (*The Supposes*, 1509), several, like **Bibiena**'s *La Calandria* (*The Follies of Calendro*, 1521) and **Machiavelli**'s *La Mandragola* (*The Mandragola*, c. 1518), had their roots in contemporary Italian life. The pool of stock classical characters was enriched by figures more particular to the age, like the devious priest, the hypocritical pedant, and the sham doctor. Machiavelli's play well illustrates this fruitful mingling of classical and more indigenous materials: its plot turns on a folk motive, and the stock Latin types, like the young people, the *senex* and the *servus*, are augmented by more distinctively Renaissance figures like an accommodating friar. In its language, mocking wit, local reference and amoral tone *La Mandragola* is very much a comedy of its age as too are the best comedies of Aretino, like *La Cortigiana* (*The Courtesan*, 1525) and *Il Marescalco* (*The Stablemaster*, 1527), plays both picaresque and vibrant of local street life. Occasionally revived too on the modern Italian stage is the anonymous *La Venexiana*, a cutting and earthy low-life comedy written about 1550 mainly in the Venetian dialect. In the second half of the 16th century the quality of scripted comedy markedly declined: only one play is occasionally revived today: *Il Candelaio* (*The Candle Maker*, 1582), a tough bitter comedy not performed in Italy in its own day, and the sole play by the greatest Italian philosopher of the age, **Giordano Bruno**.

The drama mentioned above was for the most part literary, was played in socially exclusive cultural centres and was often acted by amateurs. Since the 18th century many scholars have for convenience classified this drama as the *commedia erudita*, to distinguish it from the *commedia dell'arte*, acted by professional players in a wide range of performance places, from the streets and squares of towns, to halls and the formal theatres of royalty and nobility. The *commedia dell'arte* is discussed fully elsewhere, but here must be mentioned a drama that does not fall easily into either of these categories, *erudita* or *dell'arte*: the work of dramatists who wrote dialect comedies distinctive for their use of peasant characters or familiar local types. The 'popular' nature of their materials has encouraged some to see in their plays anticipations of the *commedia dell'arte*. Among these dramatists **Andrea Calmo** (c. 1510–71) acted as well as wrote, employed a wide range of dialect-speaking characters and developed a Venetian stage *vecchio* somewhat akin to the later Pantalone of the improvised comedy. But by far the most impressive writer of rustic comedy was Angelo Beolco, again an actor as well as a dramatist, who was known by the name of one of his stage characters, the boisterous peasant **Ruzzante**. Beolco's plays have a vitality wanting in much *cinquecento* literary comedy, and express, though without any self-conscious didacticism, a sympathy and concern for the habits, pleasures and hardships of poor country people.

Virtually at the opposite pole to this rustic comedy, in content, organization, characterization and verbal tone, was the pastoral drama that enjoyed a remarkable vogue in Italy, and indeed throughout Europe, for at least a century and a half after its first tentative appearance with the *Orfeo* of Angelo Poliziano (1454–94) in 1480. Although many pastoral plays were written and produced in Italy in the 16th and 17th centuries, only two now merit serious consideration: **Torquato Tasso**'s rich and complex masterpiece, the *Aminta*, first performed in 1573, and **Giovan Battista Guarini**'s *Il Pastor Fido* (*The Faithful Shepherd*, 1590), a tragicomic pastoral highly influential throughout Europe for its subject matter, its emotional and verbal extravagance, and the critical justification Guarini gave for his use of the tragicomic form. Aside from the influence Tasso and Guarini exercised on the development of pastoral drama proper, their refinements of the form contributed significantly to the later development of other dramatic kinds, including melodrama, tragicomedy, the French *ballet de cour* and, however indirectly, the English court masque.

(c) 16th- and early 17th-century festivals, staging and theatres Italian Renaissance festivals had their roots deep in medieval religious drama, pageant and display, but came increasingly in the second half of the 15th century to be organized under the aegis of the courts, concerned symbolically to affirm their status and authority in public and private entertainments. Such festivals, whether devised to celebrate carnival, or visits by foreign dignitaries, or the baptisms or nuptials of members of the nobility, provided the occasion for the staging of plays, both scripted and improvised. Prodigious sums were spent on these entertainments which might spread over days or weeks, and were expressly designed to serve social and political purposes: whether public or private they demonstrated the wealth, generosity and influence of a patron, or of a ruler; they were used to assert political authority, underscore independence, affirm allegiances, or orchestrate possible new alliances.

The late 16th-century master of Florentine spectacle was **Bernardo Buontalenti**: the six *intermezzi* designs he did in 1589 for a play, *La Pellegrina*, indicate something of the high quality of his work. His successor at the Medici court was **Giulio Parigi**, responsible for such major shows as that of 1608, which included striking *intermezzi* designs for Buonarroti's *Il Giudizio di Paride* (*The Judgement of Paris*) and for the elegant equestrian ballet, *La Guerra d'Amore* (*The War of Love*, 1615). Parigi's designs, not least through the wide dissemination of festival books, which included engravings of the shows and descriptive accounts pointing the symbolic content of the elaborate decorations, exercised wide influence beyond Florence, notably on the work of **Inigo Jones** in England. Many were engraved by the Frenchman Jacques Callot who worked at the Medici court until 1621, and designed too for plays like Bonarelli's *Il Solimano* (1619).

Surviving illustrative material is most rich for the *feste* in Florence, but sumptuous shows were mounted too in many other major Italian cities during the period, most frequently and strikingly perhaps in Venice and Rome. It is records of these aristocratic festivals and processions which for the most part have survived; but the richness and abundance of these, and the fact that they often appealed to and addressed all social levels, should not conceal the continuing importance too of more expressly popular festivals, like weddings and May Day revels, a distinctive and socially significant feature not just of the major cities, but of towns and villages.

The theatre of the festivals came in due course to contribute to a fundamental shift in staging conventions, from the multiple fixed or perambulatory stagings of the medieval drama, to the presentation of a play in a purpose-built theatre with end-stage and picture-framed perspective changeable settings. Recourse to perspective for stage settings had its roots in the work of *quattrocento* painters, and was furthered by the theoretical inquiries of the humanist academies. The first description we have of a perspective setting is of Pellegrino da Udine's set for Ariosto's *La Cassaria* done at Ferrara in 1508. Other plays known to have been performed with painted settings in the early *cinquecento* include Bibiena's *La Calandria* (1513 in Urbino, and 1514 in Rome), Ariosto's *I Suppositi* (1519 in Rome) and Machiavelli's *La Mandragola* and *Clizia* (1521 and 1526 respectively in Florence). Early designers included

Raphael, Andrea del Sarto, **Bastiano da Sangallo**, **Baldassare Peruzzi**, and **Sebastiano Serlio** the second book of whose *Dell'Architettura* (Paris, 1545) treated of theatres, stage effects and settings – notably the comic, the tragic and the pastoral (strictly, the satyric).

Perspective settings gave an illusion of depth and enhanced the three-dimensionality of the stage picture. Serlio's settings were achieved by spacing pairs of fixed angled wings at regular intervals on a raked stage, their painted fronts and the diminishing size of the wings at the rear of the scenic area, together with a painted back cloth, simulating distance. Later in the 16th century, such wings were set in continuous perspective. Perspective effects were achieved too by use of *periaktoi*: prisms with painted surfaces which could be rotated from face to face. Perspective settings were the response to a need generated by the new drama to establish unity of place for the stage action. That response, by focusing spectator attention on the action within and before a stage picture, made particular demands of the spectator, and turned the play in performance into a special event, while the special nature of the event came to require in its turn particular conditions of presentation.

Early stages were temporary wooden structures set up in courtyards or halls. Performance places in the courts, like those of say Florence, Mantua and Parma, were often decorated with tapestries and hangings, and were enhanced by diverse lighting effects. Elsewhere, however, as in the semi-private play performances given by Ruzzante, Calmo and others in the early decades of the 16th century around Padua and Venice, the venues were undoubtedly more modest in ambience and decoration. Permanent theatre buildings, the first known of which was that devised by Ariosto in 1531 at the Ferrarese court, were mainly a development of the second half of the century. Theatres were built at Mantua and Sienna, and in 1585–6 Buontalenti erected a permanent theatre in the Uffizi at Florence. By then the most famous of the Italian Renaissance theatres had been completed: the Teatro Olimpico at Vicenza, begun by **Palladio** in 1579 and finished according to his design by his pupil **Vincenzo Scamozzi**; with its permanent *scaenae frons* it stands rather apart from the main thrust of later Italian development which was to favour the end-stage, housing changeable perspective scenery boxed behind a picture-frame proscenium. That direction was partly foreshadowed in 1588 when Scamozzi undertook the building of a small court theatre at Sabbioneta for the Duke of Mantua, moving the fixed architectural perspective behind a single arch that took in the entire stage opening.

The 17th century (a) *Melodrama* The last decade of the 16th century saw the beginnings of theatrical baroque and its most characteristic dramatic form, *melodramma* or drama with music. The origins of *melodramma*, first called *opera* by the composer Pietro Francesco Cavalli (1602–76), are much disputed, but the form *sui generis* evolved gradually and in complex ways from a variety of theatrical kinds: from the musical spectacle that was an element of the *sacre rappresentazioni*, from the *intermezzi* of music, dance and scenic display which punctuated the acts of plays given at courts, and which gradually became semi-independent entertainments;

from the pastoral drama, in which music, dance, decoration and verbal lyricism were distinctive features; and from attempts by scholars and musicians to revive the musical dimension of classical staging.

Important beginnings were in Florence, but opera developed apace at Mantua where Monteverdi, *maestro di cappella* to the Gonzagas, composed *Orfeo* in 1607 and *Arianna* in 1608. The success of opera rapidly spread to other Italian courts; nor was its appeal confined to the social and cultural elites: the first public performances of opera were given in 1637 at the Teatro di San Cassiano in Venice; Monteverdi's *L'Incoronazione di Poppea* inaugurated the opera house in Naples in 1651; houses were soon opened in other major cities throughout the peninsula. The rapid advance of opera offered stiff competition to the improvised drama and, indeed, with the exception of brief periods when the regular theatre temporarily flourished, was to constitute perhaps the most signal Italian contribution to European theatrical life until well into the 20th century.

(b)*Scenic design and theatre buildings* The baroque theatre was preeminently one of expensive show and scenic marvels. In the early 17th century angle wing sets were displaced by sliding flat wings and back shutters, again spaced and painted for perspective effect, but now slotted through the stage floor and fixed to wheeled carriages which ran on rails under the stage. These movable 'flats' gave opportunity for increasingly sophisticated scenic changes. Increasingly elaborate ways of varying the settings were complemented by the rapid development of stage machinery, notably cloud machines and flying devices which could raise, lower or transport across the stage whole groups of performers or choirs of celestial beings. Ever more refined too were the mechanical contrivances for moving dragons, birds, chariots and ships, and for simulating storms at sea, cities on fire, and disturbances in the heavens.

The early development of sliding flat wings is usually ascribed to **Giovanni Battista Aleotti**. They were further developed by practitioners like Alfonso Parigi at Florence and, notably, **Giacomo Torelli** who in Venice and elsewhere developed an integrated wheel and roller system that allowed a single stage machinist to effect the synchronized movement of whole sets of wings and shutters. In 1645 Torelli translated his skills to the French court; he was but one of many Italian architects, designers and machinists who dominated baroque theatre throughout Europe, nowhere more so perhaps than in Vienna where particularly outstanding work was done by the **Burnacini**. Italian staging techniques, already disseminated by these native artists abroad, were further spread by technical treatises and handbooks, the most celebrated of the latter being **Nicola Sabbattini**'s *Practica di fabricar scene e machine ne'teatri* (1638).

Aleotti is said to have first employed flat wings in 1618 at the magnificent theatre he built in Parma, the Teatro Farnese. This playhouse combined elements of the old and the new: its architectural *scaenae frons* formed an elaborate, decorated proscenium frame for the deep, square single stage opening within which eight or more sets of wings and shutters could be housed. It prefigures what was to become the basic shape of later baroque and 18th-century playhouses. As in the previous century, the construction of theatres, temporary or permanent, continued to be in the charge of distinguished engineers, designers and architects, among them the greatest artist of the age, **Bernini**, and by 1650 many Italian courts could boast permanent theatres. But theatres were not built exclusively for courts and the elite. The public presentation of opera at the San Cassiano in Venice generated the development there of many public theatres. Both in Venice and elsewhere the design of public theatres posed architects with special problems, not least in the need to increase seating and to provide social segregation. Traditional performance places too were refashioned into fully-fledged permanent theatres, as was an erstwhile inn, the Teatro Falcone in Genoa (1653).

(c) The drama If Italian *melodramma*, scenography and stage mechanics could scarcely be rivalled elsewhere in Europe during the 17th century, as much cannot be said for Italian scripted drama. The only dramatist of any real note was **Giovan Battista Andreini**, and he is perhaps significant more as a resourceful *homme du théâtre* than as a playwright proper. A capable actor and leader of the **Fedeli** troupe, in addition to his religious verse pieces, the *Adamo* (1613) and *Maddalena* (1617), he wrote tragedies and comedies which exploited ingenious stagecraft, striking *coups de théâtre* and fresh re-workings of stock materials. Although his comedy-tragedy-pastoral novelty *La Centaura* (1622) and the dramaturgically interesting if facilely bawdy comic play-within-a-play, *Le Due Commedie in Commedia* (*Two Plays Within a Play*, 1623) have been revived in the modern theatre, like his other plays, which included *Lo Schiavetto* (*The Little Slave*, 1612) and *L'Amor nello Specchio* (*Love in the Mirror*, 1622), they survive essentially as historical curiosities. Much the same must be said of the work of Michelangelo Buonarroti (1568–1646), whose plays reflect his concern less with the theatrically viable than with the variety of Italian dialects – nowhere more so than in the monstrously lengthy *La Fiera* (*The Fair*) performed in 1618, a comedy in five parts, each part of five acts, that treats of the multitude of types and social groups who swarm in the play's fair-ground setting.

The extent to which Buonarroti's academician interests conditioned his dramatic writing is a fair measure of the extent to which virtually all 17th-century Italian scripted drama was governed by extra-theatrical considerations, to the detriment of authentic dramatic life. Vitality in drama lay elsewhere, at least during the early decades of the century, with the work of the improvising players. Increasingly in the course of the century however, the major companies travelled abroad, as if in search of markets no longer so readily available at home. The increasing popularity of opera may have contributed to that decline. Whatever the causes, by mid century no further records are found in Italy of the great troupes of the early decades – the **Uniti**, the **Accesi**, the **Confidenti** and the Fedeli.

The 18th century *(a) Early 18th-century developments* Well before the end of the 17th century the Italian theatre had become debilitatingly a prisoner of French influences: Paris drew off much of its best acting and scenographic talent, and French literary example and theatrical precepts strongly conditioned scripted drama. In the early years of the century, the actor-manager **Luigi Riccoboni** made earnest but largely abortive attempts to reform the theatrical climate by touring a quality repertoire including the best serious Italian play of the early and mid 18th century, **Maffei**'s *Merope* (1713). But although the Riccoboni troupe achieved a certain *succès d'estime*, it made little perceptible impact on the generally moribund Italian regular stage.

The lyric stage however remained very much alive, and produced a new theatrical form: *opera buffa*, or comic opera. Although the roots of *buffa* are hard to trace, a convenient *terminus a quo* is the decision in 1709 of the ailing Teatro dei Fiorentini in Naples to mount a season of comic musical entertainments in dialect. Gradually other cities took up the idea, if without the same emphasis on dialect and broad popular appeal, and with greater refinement of means in performance and presentation. Comic opera came quickly to appeal at all social levels. *Opera seria* meanwhile had been reformed by Zeno and others at the end of the 17th century according to French-inspired neoclassical notions of artistic decorum. The greatest serious librettist of the 18th century, **Metastasio** (Pietro Trapassi), took advantage of this reform to secure an international reputation as a poet and dramatist. Classical in spirit and subject matter, the best of his work is fluent, mellifluous and skilfully crafted for theatrical effect.

In another regard opera was particularly important. The 18th century in Italy saw the emergence of the fully-fledged professional dramatist who worked for the most part independent of patronage. The market for opera *librettos* was considerable and paid better than did writing for the regular theatre. It is no accident that **Carlo Goldoni**, the first major Italian professional dramatist, wrote for *opera seria* and *buffa* throughout his working life. Opera had become an important part of the entertainment business, most obviously in a tourist city like Venice.

(b) The Venetian theatre By the early 18th century Venice had about 14 active theatres, of which some 7 were in regular commercial competition. Musical drama of course predominated, at theatres like the San Giovanni Grisostomo and the San Benedetto, but in the middle decades of the century several dramatists revitalized the Venetian regular theatre. One was **Pietro Chiari**, a tough and combative polemicist with a sharp eye for the immediately effective. Another was the aristocrat Count **Carlo Gozzi**, who sought to revivify the ailing professional improvised comedy, the *commedia dell'arte*, in his *fiabe* – or fable plays – part-scripted, part-improvised. These enjoyed great success in the 1760s and some survive on European stages today, like *Il Re Cervo* (*The King Stag*) and *La Donna Serpente* (*The Snake Woman*). A third was their slightly older and decidely greater contemporary Carlo Goldoni.

Goldoni is important for his decisive reform of comedy: a reformation that entailed disciplining the crude and self-indulgent licence of the *commedia dell'arte* improvising players and reasserting the role of the dramatist in the Italian theatre. In the course of his career Goldoni essayed many kinds of comic play: 'low' comedy, comedy of middle- and upper-class life, comedy with a bias towards intrigue or towards character delineation, and tragicomedy that exploited the romantic, remote and mysterious settings of the Orient or the Americas. In many of his finest plays he gradually evolved a drama of character and manners with a certain emphasis on naturalistic depiction of persons and place, particularly in the Venetian dialect plays, like *Il Campiello* (1756), *Le Baruffe Chiozzotte* (*The Chioggian Squabbles*, 1760) and *I Rusteghi* (*The Boors*, 1760). But although his best drama is rooted in a recognizably Venetian social *milieu*, the determining influence remained the theatrical dimension. He was always a dramatist, never a mere documentarist. Much of his liveliest comedy, including *Arlecchino, Servitore di Due Padroni* (*The Servant of Two Masters*), *Due Gemelli Veneziani* (*The Venetian Twins*) and *Il Ventaglio* (*The Fan*), is distinguished by a highly developed sense of theatrical craftsmanship, learnt in his apprentice years in the theatre providing scenarios for masked improvisers.

The century saw a proliferation of acting troupes, most of them probably of mediocre quality, although their history has never been adequately investigated. Among them were companies led by Giuseppe Imer, Giuseppe Lapy, Pietro Rossi, Carlo and Maddalena Battaglia and, preeminently, by two actor–managers who were long based in Venice, **Girolamo Medebach** and **Antonio Sacchi**. The former is primarily remembered today as the manager who brought Goldoni back to the theatre in 1747, but his career as a whole merits more attention than it has received. Active as a manager for more than 30 years, and employing at various times most of the lead players of the period, Medebach was an astute impresario with a professional buoyancy that enabled him to survive in what was an increasingly competitive market. Sacchi, whose stage-name was Truffaldino, was probably the leading Italian player of the century. Long associated with Carlo Gozzi, most of whose plays were first staged by his company, Sacchi was noted for his histrionic agility, invention and improvising skill and his death, while sailing from Genoa to Marseilles in 1786, is often taken as marking the final demise of the *commedia dell'arte* and the end of the great age of the Venetian theatre.

(c) Theatres and scenic design The 18th century saw too the final efflorescence of Italian achievement in theatre architecture, mechanics and scenic design. In all areas opera set the pace. By the end of the century few major Italian cities were without a theatre. The traditional conjunction of architecture and design was maintained in the work of many members of the great artistic families, like the Galli da Bibiena, the Mauri and the Galliari. The design and construction of theatres was very much the preserve of such professionals, but on one occasion at least the guiding spirit was an amateur: a lawyer, Benedetto Alfieri, carried through, on the initial plans of **Filippo Juvarra**, the design and construction of the Teatro Regio in Turin (1738–40), an eclectic but harmonious conflation of baroque ideas that set a standard for many theatres elsewhere in Europe.

Theatre architecture throughout the century was preoccupied with the accommodation of classical inspiration to social needs, and to achieving a balance between the decorative and the functional in auditoria size, shape and organization. Experiment produced a variety of theatres, from Luigi Vanvitelli's elegant Neapolitan court venue at Caserta (completed 1768) to Cosimo Morelli's modest little theatre at Imola (1779). By the late 18th century civic pride was invested in theatre buildings, and great emphasis was placed on internal comfort, notably in the great opera–houses of La Scala in Milan (1778), La Fenice in Venice (1792), and the San Carlo in Naples (1810).

By the early 18th century recognition had been accorded to scenic design as a distinctive art form: some of the great designers published examples of their work, and others produced descriptive manuals of theatre architecture and design. Revolutionary in staging was the introduction in the 1690s of the *scena per angolo*, which broke with the traditional single perspective treatment of setting. These angled scenes helped to free the stage for more imaginative uses of space and were soon exploited by designers like Juvarra and the Bibienas, forming the base for a great deal of later scenic innovation. Although opera design remained sumptuous, elements of delicacy and refinement began to displace the ostentatious extravagances of the mythologically peopled stages of the 17th century. New influences too came to be felt: more naturalistic rustic landscapes, and the novel, exotic tones of *chinoiserie*. Restraint was probably more characteristic of design in the later 18th-century regular theatre, if the illustrations to the Zatta edition of Goldoni's plays can be taken to reflect at least something of stage practice. But with the exception of special and court occasions financial exigencies had always obliged the regular professional stage to be modest of decorative and mechanical means.

(d) Alfieri If Goldoni was the greatest Italian dramatist of the 18th century, the most highly esteemed serious dramatist in Italy by the beginning of the next was **Vittorio Alfieri**: his independent political and patriotic stance caught the mood of the times, and helped to fuel that search for a national as opposed to a local or regional identity that lay at the heart of the Risorgimento. He sought to fashion a language and a structure for serious drama, and to bring to it intellectual and literary dignity. But despite its pre-romantic notes his work looks back rather than forward: taking initial inspiration from French tragedy, absorbing elements from **Seneca**, and paring structure by the elimination of sub-plot and chorus, he sought more to refine the received literary tradition than to make any radical theatrical innovations. Certainly Alfieri did what he could to encourage a reform of acting, emphasizing the need for discipline and restraint, but he met with little support either within the profession or from audiences apparently content with flamboyance and excess. Significantly, although his first tragedy, *Cleopatra* (1775), was staged by the Medebach Company, all his other plays were performed privately before socially exclusive audiences. Even the best, like *Saul* and *Mirra*, for all their grandeur of theme and economy of statement, tend to the formal and static and survive more as literary works than as stage pieces. They heralded no Italian dramatic renaissance.

The 19th and early 20th centuries (a) The drama Like so much else in the arts, the early 19th-century Italian theatre was dominated by the struggle for national independence and unification, all the more fuelled by the sentiments of the romantic movement which in Italy was a revolt not only against French-oriented classicism, but against foreign domination, political fragmentation, economic retardation and intellectual obscurantism. More perhaps than elsewhere, romanticism too had strong nationalist and popular emphases. Yet it cannot be said that cultural ferment generated any strikingly original or vital new drama, and for much of the century the theatre was dominated by translations, adaptations or imitations of French melodrama or the well-made play.

Perhaps the most distinctive of the comic dramatists was Giovanni Giraud, whose best plays have perceptible roots in the Italian social world in their criticism of clerical influence and bourgeois hypocrisy. In serious drama Alfierian influences were strong, and the Italian discovery of **Shakespeare** was increasingly felt as the century progressed, particularly in the treatment of historical and biblical subject matter. Prominent among those dramatists whose work bore Alfierian classical tones were Vincenzo Monti (1754–1827), notably in *Galeotto Manfredi* (1788) and *Caio Gracco* (1802), and the lyric poet Ugo Foscolo (1788–1827), who ran foul of censorship and police intervention with his *Aiace*, performed at La Scala in 1811. Greater and more consistent stage success was enjoyed by the plays of the writer and critic Giovanni Battista Niccolini (1782–1861) and Silvio Pellico, whose *Francesca da Rimini* (1815) remained a stock-piece in the repertoires of touring companies throughout the century. But perhaps the only dramatist of the first half of the century to rise above literary mediocrity in drama was the poet and novelist **Alessandro Manzoni** who wrote two plays, *Il Conte di Carmagnola* (*The Count of Carmagnola*, 1816–19) and *Adelchi* (1820–2), neither of which however can be said to have succeeded in performance in its own time or since, notwithstanding evident Shakespearian influences.

The achievement of political independence and unification in 1870 led to intermittent attempts by central government to stimulate the growth of a national drama in the Italian language by the offer of official competitions and monetary prizes, but no dramatic revival followed. Dialect theatre occasionally threw up interesting and distinctive work, including in Piedmontese *Le Miserie d'Monssu Travet* (*The Troubles of M. Travet*, 1863) of Vittorio Bersezio (1828–1900), in Venetian the strongly Goldonian-influenced light dramas of Giacinto Gallina (1852–97) and, most notably, the plays devised in or re-worked from French farces into Neapolitan by the actor-dramatist **Eduardo Scarpetta**. For a time hopes for drama in the national language were pinned on Achille Torelli (1841–1922), whose *I Mariti* (*The Husbands*, 1867) won considerable success, but the promise was little realized. Among other distinctive Italian plays of the middle decades may be mentioned **Paolo Giacometti**'s *Elisabetta Regina d'Inghilterra* (*Elizabeth, Queen of England*, 1853) and *La Morte Civile* (*Civil Death*, 1861), both stock vehicles in the repertoires of leading players throughout the century, and the neatly crafted work of the versatile **Paolo Ferrari** in comedy, historical drama and plays of Goldonian-inspired social observation. In virtually all this work however the influence of French boulevard drama was strongly felt in plotting, characterization and theatrical emphases.

From France too came at least the initial inspiration for Italian theatrical *verismo*, triggered by the first Italian production of **Zola**'s *Thérèse Raquin* in 1879. *Verismo* however was distinctively Italian in its use of regional materials and subject matter and its particular focus on the social psychology of bourgeois life.

Foremost of the verist dramatists was the Sicilian **Giovanni Verga**, in whose *Cavalleria Rusticana* (*Rustic Chivalry*) **Eleonora Duse** secured a triumphant reception in 1884. Among other dramatists who worked in this line perhaps the most interesting was the Milanese, Carlo Bertolazzi, who in plays like *El Nost Milan* (*Our Milan*, 1893) and *La Gibigianna* (1898) treated of communal and lower-class life. Other serious and competent work was done by dramatists like **Marco Praga** and Gerolamo Rovetta (1851–1910), but perhaps the finest dramatist of the movement was **Giuseppe Giacosa**, whose *Tristi Amori* (*Sad Loves*, 1887) and *Come le Foglie* (*Like the Leaves*, 1900) remain the most durable plays of the 19th-century theatre. Limited as was the achievement of the *veristi*, they at least brought to the late 19th-century Italian theatre an attempt to treat serious themes, depict a recognizable social life, and eschew contrived and formulaic staginess. Not even the best of their plays, however, can compare with what was the greatest strength of the 19th-century Italian theatre: the musical drama from Donizetti and Bellini, through Verdi, to Mascagni and Puccini.

(b) The condition of the stage If dramatic talent was in short supply, working conditions in the Italian theatre did little to encourage it. Throughout the century most acting companies remained, as they had been in the past, itinerant, touring the major cities, renting theatres for short seasons, and transporting props and scenery with them as they moved from place to place. The theatre never lacked either champions or enthusiastic new recruits even if mainly *figli d'arte* (children of the profession), but its public was casual in attendance, conservative in attitude and all too prone to support modish foreign imports. A few companies enjoyed subsidy in permanent theatre buildings as did the Compagnia Reale Italiana, first in Milan, from 1806 to 1815, then in Naples until 1827, and the Turin-based Reale Sarda, perhaps the most celebrated company of the century, which from 1821 produced nearly 600 plays by Italian dramatists, until the Piedmontese state withdrew its subsidy on the ground that theatre was essentially entertainment and not an educative art. Ironically, the greatest Italian actor of the early decades of the century, **Gustavo Modena**, a tireless supporter of reform in acting, staging and dramatic content, urged just such an educative purpose in his utopian *Teatro Educatore* (1836).

This was the great age of 'star' performers, as much on the regular as on the operatic stage, and few acquired such wide international celebrity as did the major Italian players of the middle and later decades of the century: **Adelaide Ristori, Ernesto Rossi, Tommaso Salvini** and Eleonora Duse. They were followed in the first decade or so of the next century by **Giovanni Grasso**. By the time of the latter, however, taste for the novel realism and powerful emotionalism characteristic of much Italian playing was beginning to wane, as too was the domination exercised over international stages by the great 'star' performers. None of these 'stars' travelled as far and as frequently as did the Italians, north to Moscow and London, south to Egypt, and even more widely abroad to North and South America. Some, like Rossi and Salvini, came to spend as much if not more time playing abroad than in touring through Italy itself. Not least among their motives for travelling so much was the continuing instability and insecurity of acting company life in the peninsula itself, although by the final decades of the century the voices of players and managers were noticeably more concerted in their call for reform, and they were aided by the emergence of a new figure, the professional theatre critic.

(c) Theatres and scenic design Nowhere is the decline of Italian theatrical influence beyond the peninsula more evident than in the very limited contribution it made to 19th-century developments in theatre architecture, mechanics and scenic design, areas in which hitherto the work of Italians had been prominent and seminal. Throughout the century many new opera-houses were built and other major musical theatres were renovated, but for the most part Italian activity on these was either traditional or imitative of French and German models. The only really substantial new opera-house built in the century was the Teatro Massimo at Palermo, which the Basile completed over a 20 year period in 1897. Little was done to increase the number or quality of theatres catering primarily for acting companies. Radically new ideas for theatres, lyric or regular, were for the most part confined to visionary writings like Benevello's *Azioni Coreographiche* (1841) with its interesting anticipations of some of **Wagner**'s ideas for Bayreuth.

What was distinctive too in Italian scenic design, like the work of Antonio Basoli (1774–1843), Gaspare Galliari and Carlo Ferrario (1833–1907), was done for the musical stage. In the regular theatre production values were for the most part shoddy, their utilitarian nature dictated by limited funds and the requirements of constant touring: scenes consisted mainly of practicable and easily transportable flats and backdrops often showing, as the dramatist Marco Praga complained in 1912, all the signs of excessive wear and tear, while the advanced technology found in many theatres elsewhere in Europe was unavailable in Italy. Reviewing an exhibition at La Scala in 1894 mounted as part of *Le Esposizioni Riunite di Milano*, the theatre critic of *Corriere della Sera*, Giovanni Pozza, delivered a broadside against the all-pervasive architectural and staging inadequacies of the Italian theatre.

(d) Turn of the century developments Although the Italian theatre's traditional strengths had lain in acting and stage decoration rather than in scripted drama, it was the work of playwrights in the final years of the 19th century and the first decades of the 20th that offered promise of something new. Audaciously constructive were the dreams of the foremost Italian writer of the period, **Gabriele D'Annunzio**. Primarily a poet and novelist, D'Annunzio's interest in the theatre was sparked by his meeting in 1896 with the actress Eleonora Duse; for some years she was his artistic partner in an ambitious project to provide Italy with a great tragic drama. D'Annunzio took as his models the Greek classical theatre, the experiments of the Renaissance Florentine *camerata* with musical drama, the theory and practice of Wagner and the ideas of **Nietzsche**. With Duse he sketched plans for this new theatre and its future home – an open-air amphitheatre on the shore of Lake Albano where classical tragedy and his own plays would be produced. But although he wrote a number of highly individual plays, like *La Città Morta* (*The Dead City*, 1898) and *La Nave* (*The Ship*, 1908), his ideal of a total theatre that would fuse words, move-

ment, spectacle, music and dance was never adequately realized. The artistic and economic demands of D'Annunzio's programme were characteristically inflated, and were too remote from what could actually be achieved in the Italian theatre of his day. His ambitions however helped open up the Italian theatre to new staging ideas.

So too did the ostentatiously destructive experiments undertaken by the theatre practitioners of futurism. Where D'Annunzio had sought to fashion a new theatre by drawing creatively on the ideas and practices of the past, the futurists very deliberately rejected the past and called for an art appropriate to the new age of technology. In theatre that art would reject not just bourgeois naturalism, but traditional genres, subject matter, structures and verbal means, in favour of syntheses, or highly concentrated dramatic sketches. Much less aggressive and iconoclastic than the work of the futurists, but nonetheless charting distinctly new and promising territory, were the plays written by the dramatists of the **teatro del grottesco** whose cultivation of bizarre or absurd elements within the apparently traditional love-triangle situations of boulevard drama challenged the validity of naturalism. All these activities can be seen as attempts to revitalize a theatre widely acknowledged to be hide-bound and unimaginative. Unfortunately what new ideas and artistic movements could not contribute was what the Italian theatre needed, economic support. Unfortunately too, when that economic support did in some measure materialize there were political strings attached.

The later 20th century: Fascism to the present (a) *Theatre under Fascism* With the exception of **Pirandello**'s work, drama in Italy between the two World Wars was undistinguished: the new directions taken by D'Annunzian, futurist and grotesque theatre led nowhere. Bourgeois naturalism and undemanding boulevard diversion prevailed. If any stage activity can be said to have been vital it was that of the popular cabaret entertainers like **Petrolini** and **Totò**. Dialect theatre too remained strong, particularly in the Neapolitan plays of **Viviani** and the young **Eduardo de Filippo**. What changed quite significantly after the Mussolini government took power in 1922 was the manner in which some theatre was organized: the *laissez-faire* structure and economy of the actor–manager system was partially modified by state intervention. Pirandello's acting company, the Teatro d'Arte, was established with a small grant from the state, and some encouragement was given to **Bragaglia**'s experimental Teatro degli Indipendenti. From 1929 through to the early 1940s direct state encouragement of theatre was most evident in the activity of the so-called *carri di Tespi* (literally Thespian carts, i.e. mobile theatres) which toured theatrical entertainment through the provinces. Although the support of this theatre shows that drama was now recognized as fulfilling an educative role in society, few of these itinerant shows were notable for their intellectual or artistic qualities, and although some may be seen as politically propagandist, particularly after censorship became centralized in the early 1930s, most were merely conformist, escapist and innocuous. A decidedly significant development of these years however was the founding in 1935 of the Accademia d'Arte Drammatica in Rome, a commitment to the idea of organized training for the stage that not only acknowledged the national importance of the profession, but implicitly challenged the more casual and arbitrary preparation provided by the *figli d'arte* system. Some of the ground-work was thus done in the 1930s for that reorganization of the structures and the economy of the Italian stage that for a century or more so many of its champions and practitioners had been demanding.

(b) The post-war stage and the stabili In the years immediately following the Second World War important new initiatives began significantly to modify the traditional system of private management far beyond anything that had occurred in the 1930s. The attractions of the *teatro stabile*, the permanently established company, had long been advocated by theatre reformers, and several *stabili* had been set up for short periods, as in 1898 were the Stabile Romana and the Teatro d'Arte in Turin, but subsidy had never been generous or regular. From 1947 onwards a more substantial attempt was made to pursue the idea. The first company funded was the Piccolo Teatro in Milan, under the joint direction of Paolo Grassi and **Giorgio Strehler**: the emphasis they placed on exploring the European classic repertory in studied but imaginative productions gradually won for the Piccolo an international as well as a national reputation, and the Milan *stabile* remains today one of the great theatres of Italy. Other early established *stabili* have similarly survived with distinction, like the Teatro d'Arte of Genoa (1951) and the Teatro Stabile of Turin (1955). Although most major Italian cities pioneered *stabili* in the late 1940s and 1950s not all survived, for reasons artistic, economic and political.

While the development of *stabili* was of major importance, much significant work continued to be done by the independent actor-managed companies, one of the finest in the immediate post-war years being the Compagnia Morelli–Stoppa for which **Visconti** directed important new and classic drama. In the provinces too the centuries-old tradition of touring was maintained by stock companies often of very variable quality. Such advances as theatre made in the decade or so immediately after the war were achieved in the face of severe competition first from cinema then, in the later 1950s, from television.

(c) Actors, directors and dramatists The Italian regular theatre has traditionally been dominated by performers, and although the post-war stage has seen the emergence of the director the influence of lead actors and actresses has remained strong. This has been to the advantage of theatre when the ability and charisma of the 'star' performer have been allied to intelligent and imaginative reinterpretation of classic roles, or been put to the service of new drama or radical reorchestrations of the received repertoire: such is the case with the contributions of actors as very different as **Vittorio Gassman** and **Carmelo Bene**. On the other hand the persistence of the 'star' system has elsewhere, and not only in boulevard theatre, hampered the development of ensemble acting, as too some would argue has the increasing domination of the stage by 'star' directors. Aside from the work of between-the-wars pioneers like Bragaglia and **Talli**, the director in the Italian theatre is very much a product of the post-1945 stage: figures like Visconti, Strehler and **Squarzina** are not only the most distinguished, but in effect the first Italian directors,

and many of the most significant events in the modern Italian theatre are associated with them: Visconti's work on Goldonian comedy, Squarzina's treatments of Shakespeare, Strehler's productions of **Brecht**.

Much in modern Italian theatre has been shaped by foreign influences: the drama of **Miller, Williams** and **Sartre** in the late 1940s and early 50s, the impact of Brecht in the late 50s, a decade or so of radical experimentalism prompted from the mid-1960s onwards by the work of the **Living Theatre** and the inspiration offered by **Grotowski**. Much emphasis in Italian avant-garde theatre has been put on the non-literary: Bene's stage re-workings of classics, **Ronconi**'s explorations of performance space, the experiments with light and sound characteristic of much Italian alternative theatre staging. Significantly, the contemporary Italian dramatist best known internationally, **Dario Fo**, is considered by many to be less a playwright than a performer or an *homme du théâtre*, and although the modern stage has seen interesting work by dramatists like **Betti** and **Fabbri**, and one-off pieces by artists best known for their work in other fields, like Moravia and Pasolini, Italian drama has in the main been undistinguished, the strength of Italian theatre continuing to lie in the work of its actors, directors and designers. KR LR

See: M. Apollonio, *Storia del Teatro Italiano*, 2 vol. edn, Florence, 1981; M. Carlson, *The Italian Stage, from Goldoni to D'Annunzio*, North Carolina, 1981; A. D'Ancona, *Origini del Teatro Italiano*, 2 vols., Turin, 1891; *Enciclopedia dello Spettacolo*, 9 vols., Rome, 1954–62; *Enciclopedia dello Spettacolo: Cinema, Teatro, Balletto, TV*, Milan, 1976; V. Mariani, *Storia della Scenografia Italiana*, 1930; L. Rasi, *I Comici Italiani*, 3 vols., Florence, 1897–1905; G. Ricci, *Il Teatro d'Italia*, Milan, 1971; V. Vivani, *Storia del Teatro Napoletano*, Naples, 1969.

ITI (International Theatre Institute) A UNESCO-based organization dedicated to furthering the cause of theatre world-wide. It was founded in 1948 and is based in various national centres. Like many such organizations it is a good idea in principle but has difficulties being as effective as it should be in practice. The present (1987) honorary head of the ITI is the Nobel laureate **Wole Soyinka**. MB

Ivanov, Vsevolod Vyacheslavovich (1895–1963) Soviet prose writer and author of 15 plays, mostly relating to the Russian Civil War, in which he fought on the Red side, and to his native Siberia and Asiatic Russia. He led an itinerant early life as circus fakir, day labourer, etc., much like **Gorky**, who encouraged him in his early naturalistic short story writing (1915) and introduced him to Petrograd's Serapion Brotherhood (1920). Reflecting Gorky's and **Zamyatin**'s influence, his personal experience and his knowledge of Russian folklore, his early work included: the novelistic Civil War trilogy *The Partisans* (1921), *Coloured Winds* (1922) and *Armoured Train 14–69* (1922), the last of which he adapted for the stage in 1927 and became his most important play. Commissioned by the **Moscow Art Theatre** for the 10th anniversary of the Revolution, directed by **Stanislavsky** (along with Sudakov and Litovsev) and starring **Kachalov**, it was the first Soviet play to be successfully produced by MAT. In it a group of partisans, led by a peasant only

A scene from Ivanov's *The Armoured Train*, 1927.

recently converted to the Bolshevik cause, seize a train of White refugees in Siberia during the Civil War. It contains heroism and noble sacrifice, idealized Bolsheviks and nefarious Japanese interventionists, ideological themes – the people must win the battles of the Revolution – virile action and earthy humour, inflammatory iconography – a martyred comrade's body borne upon the train in inspirational evocation of Lenin. Ivanov's other plays include: on Civil War themes – *Blockade* (1929), *The Compromise of Naib-Khan* (1931), *The Doves See the Departing Cruisers* (1937) and *Uncle Kostya* (1944); on Russian historical themes – *Twelve Youths from a Snuffbox* (1936), on Tsar Paul I's assassination in 1801; *Inspiration* (1940), set in the 17th century in the time of the false Dmitry; and *Lomonosov* (1953), on the 18th-century Russian scientist–man of letters. Ivanov's plays and narrative fiction after 1930 bear the unmistakable imprint of socialist realism.   SG

Ivanov, Vyacheslav Ivanovich (1866–1949) Russian poet, dramatist, theorist and Hellenic scholar, Ivanov was the leader of the St Petersburg symbolists. His major area of inquiry was the Dionysian cult, which he linked to later Christian mysteries in an effort to establish a philosophical foundation for a modern liturgical theatre. He here differed from **Nietzsche** – one of his ideological mentors, along with **Goethe**, **Wagner** and Vladimir Solovyov – who had stressed their differences. In Ivanov's theatre of myth-creation and communal action the actor-priest and audience-

congregants would co-create the sacred rite of performance. He criticized those Russian symbolist mystery plays that were conceived according to purely aesthetic principles. He contributed two plays of his own – *Tantalus* (1905) and *Prometheus* (1919) – which imitated **Aeschylus** in structure, mythological subject matter and obscure, archaic language. The most scholarly and profound of the symbolists, his ideas greatly influenced **Meyerhold**'s thinking about conventional (*uslovny*) theatre. Meyerhold mounted a reconstruction of **Calderón de la Barca**'s *The Adoration of the Cross* at the Tower literary salon-theatre in the apartments of Ivanov and his poetess-wife, Lidiya D. Zinovyeva-Annibal (1910), where gathered the leading lights of St Petersburg artistic society. **Blok** dramatized his poem 'The Puppet Show' to launch another Ivanov-conceived symbolist theatrical (and journalistic) venture, 'The Torches', but this never materialized. Apart from contributing to the major symbolist journals of the day – *The Scales* and *The Golden Fleece* – and publishing several volumes of poetry, he collected his major aesthetic essays in the volumes *Along the Stars* (1909) and *Furrows and Landmarks* (1916). He emigrated to Italy in 1924.   SG

Ivory Coast The Ivory Coast is the largest and wealthiest of the French-speaking states of West Africa and it has had a solid modern theatrical tradition since the 1930s. François Amon d'Aby, Coffi Gadeau and **Bernard Dadié**, who have contributed most to the establishment of the theatre in the Ivory Coast, were all educated at the Ecole Primaire Supérieure at Bingerville (Ivory Coast) and the Ecole Normale William Ponty in Senegal at the time when these centres were laying the foundations of the modern theatre in French-speaking Africa. While Dadié remained behind in Senegal for some years, Amon d'Aby and Coffi Gadeau returned to the Ivory Coast where in 1938 they founded the Théâtre Indigène de la Côte d'Ivoire which continued its activities throughout the war period. Political and other difficulties after the end of the war led to the group's ceasing to function in 1946. It had, however, been eight very active years during which Amon d'Aby and Gadeau wrote a number of plays (to add to the Ponty repertoire which had initially formed the basis of their repertoire). In order to make their plays accessible to their mainly illiterate audiences, they wrote them in a language which combined literal translation from the vernacular and standard French. The themes were those that were to remain characteristic of the French-language theatre of Africa – the heroes of the African past, traditional social practices and the impact of Western culture; at this stage, the war and the fact that the Ivory Coast was still a colony did not allow for the possibility of overtly political themes. Between 1946 and 1953, there was something of a vacuum in Ivorian theatrical activities, until Amon d'Aby and Coffi Gadeau, joined now by Bernard Dadié who had since returned, founded the Cercle Culturel et Folklorique, which went on to have a considerable success at the Théâtre des Nations in Paris in 1956 and 1960 – the 1956 visit was followed by an equally successful tour of the French provinces. The 1950s and especially the 1960s saw the establishment of a number of troupes, such as the Troupe Houphouet-Boigny, the Troupe Théâtrale Kourouma Moussa and the Troupe Guézabo. In 1959, just before the country obtained its independence, the French Minister of Education authorized the establishment in Abidjan of an Ecole Nationale d'Art Dramatique; some of its best students eventually went on to France to pursue further training and not all returned to the Ivory Coast. In 1967, the Ivorian government created an Institut National des Arts which was helped in its initial stages by a visit from the French director Georges Toussaint: he gathered together a troupe of former drama students who performed Bernard Dadié's new play, M. Thôgô-gnini, with considerable success both in the Ivory Coast and on tour in other parts of French-speaking Africa. At about this time, the recently founded university in Abidjan began to play what was to become an increasingly significant role in the development of theatre in the Ivory Coast by attracting very committed staff, not only from the Ivory Coast itself but also from France and other parts of Africa, such as Barthélemy Kotchy, Marie-José Hourantier (France) and Werewere Liking (Cameroon).

Following an important Colloquium on African theatre held at the University of Abidjan in April 1970, there was much debate within the Ivory Coast about the way traditional African theatre could be used in the context of 'total theatre'. This led to the development of the concept of a ritual theatre by M. J. Hourantier and Werewere Liking who, with Jacques Scherer, set out their ideas in a book entitled From Ritual to the Stage, as well as writing and directing their own plays.

Approaching the subject from another side, Porquet Niangoran advocated a theatre based on the tradition of the griot story-teller incorporating song, dance and mime. The plays were called 'griot dramas' and the style itself was designated as La Griotique, a term which is not readily translatable. One of Porquet's plays, Soba ou Grande Afrique (Soba or Great Africa), has been published (1978) but the printed text cannot convey the real character of the work. Souleymane Koly, creator of the Koteba Ensemble, bases his approach on the Bambara koteba theatre of Mali, with its emphasis on a particular kind of dance, as well as mime and social comedy, while Bernard Zadi Zaourou, who teaches at the University of Abidjan, prefers to emphasize the traditional use of symbolism. Two of the latter's best-known plays are Les Sofas (The Sofas) (the 'sofas' were the warriors of the emperor Samory, who is the subject of the play) and L'Oeil (The Eye), a modern political satire, a part of which was censored for political reasons when it was staged in 1974 by another influential Ivorian director, Sidiky Bakaba. Bakaba bases his approach on the techniques of the traditional story-teller, emphasizing particularly strongly the involvement of the audience in the 'narrative' through their verbal participation as a group in what is happening on the stage.

The vitality of theatre in the Ivory Coast has all along depended on the energy of the directors who have founded troupes or associations whose primary purpose has been to bring about performance. Play texts have largely followed this underlying urge. This is why in discussing theatre in the Ivory Coast one thinks of plays largely in relation to performance; this has for instance been the real motivation behind the writing of plays by Bernard Dadié, the best-known Ivorian playwright (although not the most prolific – that honour belongs to Amon d'Aby). The playwright Charles Nokan starts from an essentially left-wing political standpoint and his mainly historical plays are aimed at expressing revolt at the condition of the black man. Even his two best-known plays, Abraha Pokou (the name of the legendary founder of the Baule tribe) (1970) and Les Malheurs de Tchakô (The Misfortunes of Tchakô, 1968), have not been much performed. R. Atta Koffi's historical play, Le Trône d'Or (The Golden Throne), won a prize in the 1967–8 French radio-play competition for Africa.   CW

See: M. Banham with C. Wake, African Theatre Today, London, 1976; R. Cornevin, Le Théâtre en Afrique Noire et à Madagascar, Paris 1970; B. Kotchy, 'New Trends in the Theatre of the Ivory Coast (1972–83)', Theatre Research International, vol. 9, no. 3, 1984, pp. 232–53.

Izenour, George (1912–) American theatre designer and engineering consultant. Inventor of the electronic console for theatre lighting control, the synchronous winch system, and the steel acoustical shell. He has been a design and engineering consultant for over 100 theatres around the world since the 1950s and as such is a dominant force in theatre design and technology. Because economics dictates that a single theatre must be employed for many uses (spoken drama, opera, concerts, etc.), he is an advocate of the multiple-use and multiple-form theatre in which the size and shape and auditorium can be altered for different needs and acoustical requirements.   AA

J

Jackson, Barry Vincent (1879–1961) British theatre director, manager and patron. Born in Birmingham of a prosperous merchant grocer's family, he founded the amateur Pilgrim Players in 1907 and the professional **Birmingham Repertory Theatre** in 1913 for which he financed the building of a purpose-designed theatre. As owner and artistic director, and with extraordinary dedication, he established the theatre as the country's leading repertory venture committed to both new and classic plays. He occasionally designed and directed productions himself. Disappointed by lack of consistent public support, however, he threatened closure twice and in 1935 handed ownership of the theatre to a public trust. He was founder and director of the Malvern Theatre Festival from 1929 to 1937 and director of the Stratford Memorial Theatre, 1945–8. He also wrote, co-wrote and adapted a number of plays for adults and children, and was knighted in 1925. AJ

Jackson, Glenda (1936–) British actress, who took part in a seminal Theatre of Cruelty season, organized by **Peter Brook** and **Charles Marowitz** with the **RSC** at LAMDA (the London Academy of Music and Dramatic Art) in 1964. This prepared the way for her performance as Charlotte Corday in Peter Brook's production of **Peter Weiss**'s *The Marat/Sade* (1965), celebrated on both sides of the Atlantic for its intensity and eroticism. In 1967, she was a notable Masha in **Chekhov**'s *The Three Sisters* at the **Royal Court Theatre**, became known to wider audiences through her film appearances, such as in *Women in Love* (1970), and in 1975 she played Hedda Gabler in the RSC's production of **Ibsen**'s play, which toured Britain, the USA and Australia. Not conventionally pretty, Jackson nonetheless could radiate an emotional directness and intellectual honesty which transformed her *gamine* attractiveness into outright beauty. Her independence of mind, however, prevented her from working consistently within the structure of a permanent company, such as the RSC. She returned to Stratford in 1978 to play Cleopatra in Peter Brook's production of *Antony and Cleopatra* with less than her usual success: but she has complained about the lack of good roles for actresses over 40. Of her several starring West End performances in recent years, in *Stevie* (1977), *Rose* (1980), *Summit Conference* (1982) and **Botho Strauss**'s *Great and Small* (1983), she achieved her most notable triumph in **Eugene O'Neill**'s *Strange Interlude* (1984). JE

Jacobi, Derek (George) (1938–) British actor. His debut was at **Birmingham Repertory Theatre** in 1960, and in 1963 he joined the **National Theatre** at the **Old Vic**, playing Laertes in *Hamlet*, Cassio in *Othello* and Lodovico in *The White Devils* among various other major roles. He joined the Prospect Theatre Company in 1972, working with them for six years. He played Hamlet in 1978, memorably, and Peer Gynt and Prospero for the **RSC** in the 1982–3 season. He made a major popular impact as Claudius in the television drama serial, *I, Claudius*. MB

Jahnn, Hans Henny (1894–1959) German dramatist and novelist, whose early work *Pastor Ephraim Magnus* (1917 – first produced 1923 then, adapted by **Brecht** and **Bronnen**, in 1925) is the most extreme example of the violent, anti-idealistic line in expressionism. Later plays, in which the tragic artist is a frequent figure, reestablished his reputation with productions of *Thomas Chatterton* by **Gründgens** (1956) and *The Dusty Rainbow* by **Piscator** (1961). CI

Janauschek, Francesca (Fanny) (1830–1904) Czech actress. She made her debut at 16 at the Royal Theatre of Prague and two years later was engaged as leading actress at the State Theatre, Frankfurt, where she remained for ten years. Subsequent triumphs on the continent established her as an eminent tragedienne. For her 1867 New York debut, she performed Medea in German while the rest of the cast acted in English, as did **Edwin Booth** opposite her German Lady Macbeth in 1868. After a year devoted to learning English, she launched her English-speaking career in 1870. With her statuesque figure, emotional power, and vibrant but controlled voice, she excelled in heroic roles like Brunhilde, Deborah, Mary Stuart, and later Meg Merrilies. But the public preferred her dual role as the coquettish French maid Hortense and the haughty Lady Dedlock in *Chesney Wold* adapted from **Dickens**'s *Bleak House*. She was one of the last great actresses in the 'grand style', but after 1898 she was reduced to playing in cheap melodramas. FHL

Janin, Jules (1804–74) French critic. Known as the 'prince of critics', Janin commanded enormous influence and respect. He began his career as a journalist in 1825 with *Le Figaro* (a small satirical paper) and then moved to the *Journal des Débats* as political correspondent. He temporarily took over from Duviquet for the theatre column, and became so popular that he remained in this position for 41 years. He was particularly important for his championship of **Rachel** and actively supported **Ponsard** (largely because he disapproved of **Hugo**). His disapproval of the **Comédie-Française** was expressed indirectly in a curious volume devoted to the pantomime artist **Deburau** (1832), an invaluable source of information on the Funambules. His theatre criticism appeared in two collections, *Histoire de la littérature dramatique* (1853–8) and *La Critique dramatique* (1877). He also published volumes on **Mlle Mars** (1843), on **Mlle George** (1862) and on **Alexandre Dumas** (1871).   JMCC

Japan

1. Ancient and traditional Theatre permeates Japanese culture. Today, in spite of a surfeit of television and film, live theatre continues to be supported in major cities – Tokyo, Osaka, and Kyoto – and in villages (through folk festivals). There are arguably more theatre buildings in Tokyo than any other city in the world, with new theatres being built constantly. Perhaps because of strong social strictures against emotional display in daily life, sophisticated theatrical expression of emotion is valued and theatre-going is a normal facet of life for millions of modern Japanese.

Japanese share with most Asians the attitude that theatre is an open-ended enterprise, with room for dialogue, song, music, dance, and expressive elocution. The mode of expression may be first-person enactment, in third-person narrative voice, with a chorus as substitute for the actor, or a combination of modes. Masks and puppets are important expressive media. With few exceptions, traditional theatrical performance is exceptionally dynamic and based almost equally on textual and performance elements. The traditional word for theatre in Japanese is *geinō*, 'artistic skill', indicating linguistically that theatre arose primarily from the body and the voice of the performer. The Japanese conception of theatre as a complete performing art thus stands in marked contrast to Western critical analysis in which historically, precedence has been given to drama (**Aristotle**'s plot, character, thought) while performance (Aristotle's spectacle, song, diction) has been felt to be unworthy of philosophic concern. With the exception of European opera and American musical comedy, the main line of Western performance development has been toward specialized arts: concert music, ballet, spoken drama. The naturalism of **Zola** and **Stanislavsky**, which took life, not art, as both subject matter and medium, was a movement consistent with the Western emphasis on dramatic content and its corollary disdain for performance as an expressive art. Western visionaries such as **Artaud**, **Meyerhold**, Eisenstein, and **Brecht** responded to the wholeness of Asian, and Japanese theatre, a wholeness that embraced all possible expressive means. Even today Japanese scholarship rarely treats play scripts as literature (*bungaku*) – not even **nō** texts. Text and performance together make up a single art which is understood to be quite distinct from written literature.

Significant theatre genres include Shintō-based celebratory dances and sketches (*kagura*), Buddhist dances and sketches (*gigaku*), semi-dramatic dances of the imperial court (**bugaku**), serious masked dance-dramas of the samurai class (*nō*) and their companion comic plays (**kyōgen**), flamboyant commercial urban theatre (**kabuki**), commercial puppet theatre (**bunraku**), and modern spoken drama inspired by Western models in this century (*shinpa* and *shingeki*). Each genre reflects the historical period in which it was first created

and the interests and the tastes of the social class which patronized it. A unique feature of this 2,000-year historical process in Japan, is that it was not 'cannibalistic', as has been the Western experience: succeeding genres did not devour existing genres, but rather came to occupy different but coexisting niches in society. The performing traditions of the genres of theatre mentioned above (with the exception of *gigaku*) continue unbroken down to the present day. To see performances of traditional theatre in Japan is akin to entering a theatrical time capsule that transports the spectator into a milieu from the past that is living and complete.

Early religious performance: kagura Written history began in Japan in the 6th century, long after the beginnings of theatre, so we can only speculate about the origins of Japanese theatre. Excavations of Yayoi period settlements (350 BC to AD 250) have uncovered clay miniatures of flutes, stringed instruments (*koto*), drums, and masks. Clay *haniwa* figures of the same era represent men and women singing, dancing, and playing musical instruments. The great variety of folk dances and skits (*kagura*) with which thousands of villages today celebrate Shintō festivals of the new year, rice planting, and harvest, leave no doubt that the performing arts trace their ancestry back to ancient times. The earliest written records of theatre are in the *Records of Ancient Matters* (712) and *Chronicles of Japan* (720). They describe the origin of performance in Japan in a proto-shamanic myth. The Sun Goddess, Amaterasu, angered, has withdrawn from the community of deities into a rock cave, thus plunging the islands of Japan into darkness. Another goddess, Ame-no-Uzume, tries to lure her from the cave by showing her breasts, lowering her skirt, and dancing with a joyful beat of her feet. The assembled gods and goddesses laugh and cry out with delight. Hearing their laughter, Amaterasu leaves the cave to see what is causing the merriment and thus light is restored to the world. This is the 'first *kagura* performance'. But it is not only a mythological description of how theatre in Japan began, it also shows the basic reason for theatre coming into existence: as a joyful entertainment offering welcome to a deity with the aim of assuring the continuing life and prosperity of the community. All *kagura* performances and Shintō festivals (*matsuri*) have the same function of mediating between man and animistic deities (*kami*).

Kagura came to be written with the Chinese characters meaning god-entertainment, but its original meaning was a deity's residence. *Kagura* performances were, and are, done where the deity resides. The centrality of *kagura* to Shintō worship is clear from the fixed three-part structure of Japanese festivals: summoning the deity, entertaining the deity, and bidding the deity farewell. Simply stated, *kagura* are any type of performance that entertains a deity during the mid-section of a Shintō festival ritual. *Kagura* exist in many forms. In the lion dance (*shishi kagura*), the deity is present in the large lion mask and it brings protection to those who invite it onto their premises. In folk *kagura* (*sato kagura*) a villager wears the mask of a deity and enters the village compound. Possession, role playing, and the enactment of a story, the fundamentals of drama and theatre, exist in prototypical form in village *kagura*.

Female shamanic dance (*miko kagura*) by shrine priestesses uses music and dance to induce trance and to evoke a deity who speaks prophetically through the mouth of the priestess-dancer. *Mikagura*, court *kagura*, are performed by court musicians and dancers (courtiers in the past) as part of major Shintō rites sponsored by the imperial court to assure the prosperity of the land and the continuity of imperial rule.

A number of significant characteristics of Japanese theatre are first found in *kagura*. The journey of the deity along a sacred path, from the spiritual to the mundane world where the performance occurred, was marked out as a passageway of the gods. Open passageways to the stage – the bridgeway in *nō* and the flower path in *kabuki* – have their origins in this deeply ingrained conception of god–man relationships. In subsequent theatre forms, scenes of travel, journeys, and impressive entrances became normal, indeed essential, parts of dramatic structure. *Kagura*'s square, raised wooden stage is Japan's earliest theatre structure. It sometimes was temporary and set in the garden of a shrine and sometimes it was permanently placed within the main worship hall. In the form that influenced the development of *nō* and early *kabuki* theatres, it was covered with a roof to become a free-standing dance pavilion (*kagura den*), usually located at the entrance to the inner shrine compound. Humour continues to be celebratory and joyous in *kyōgen* and in *kabuki*, as befits an entertainment of gods, rather than social (satire) or psychological (farce), the forms humour usually takes in Western theatre. There is no clown or buffoon role in Japanese theatre, as there is in Indian, South-East Asian, Chinese, and Western theatre. The buffoon is a social outcast and the butt of humour, often cruel, that is based on ineptitude and failure, characteristics that do not fit the communal, egalitarian, felicitous nature of *kagura*. The easy acceptance of theatrical performance as part of both community and religious ritual carries forward into Japanese attitudes toward theatre today. We do not know whether the masking found in some *kagura* derives from prehistoric practices or is a later adoption under the influence of Chinese and Korean theatre.

Early popular theatre: dengaku, sangaku, sarugaku Other early, popular entertainments are variously described as field entertainment (*dengaku*), miscellaneous entertainment (*sangaku*), and monkey music (*sarugaku*) in the diaries and records of local dignitaries and imperial court officials in the 10th–12th centuries. It is difficult to know what kind of performances the terms refer to because sacred and secular, village and country arts are mentioned first under one term and then under another. In part they referred to acrobats, tight-rope walkers, jugglers, and magicians, secular artists who worked the streets of Nara and Kyoto. Some of these arts were indigenous, but *sangaku*, a term borrowed from China, suggests others were introduced by Chinese (and Korean) artists. Until the 15th century, *dengaku* dramas were as popular as *nō* plays. Sacred *dengaku* rice-planting songs and dances have celebrated spring festivals as far back as records go; they are still performed as imperial rituals today. Professional *sarugaku* troupes gave variety shows in this early period. They set up in shrine or temple compounds at festival times or performed by invitation at the homes of court

nobles. Only later did *sarugaku* actors develop the serious dramas that came to be called *nō*.

Chinese and Korean influence: gigaku, bugaku Between the 7th and 10th centuries, Chinese and Korean culture, including theatre, was widely admired and imitated in Japan. Chinese ideographs were adopted for writing and Chinese poetic forms and styles were learned at court. In 612, a Korean performer Mimaji (Mimashi in Japanese) brought the Buddhist dance-play *gigaku* from China, where he had studied, to the Japanese court (*gigaku* masks, musical instruments, and costumes may have been brought from China as early as 550). The Japanese regent, Prince Shōtoku (r. 593–621), ordered him to establish a school of music and dance at the imperial court and assigned boys to be his pupils. Other Korean musicians and dancers followed Mimaji to Japan. *Gigaku*, elegant entertainment, propagated Buddhism, a religion new to Japan which Shōtoku avidly proselytized during his reign. A 13th-century account of *gigaku* performance describes a typical performance: first, ritual Buddhist music (*netori*) played on a flute, drums, gong, and cymbals, then a procession (*gyōdō*) of chanting monks masked as Buddha figures, followed by a second procession of ten or more actors wearing masks of a Chinese woman, a king, Baromon (an Indian Brahman), Karora (Garuda, the King of Birds in Indian myth), lion tamers, and others. Finally, the masked figures mounted a temporary outdoor stage where they enacted comic skits cautioning against Buddhist sins. By the 12th century, *gigaku* had lost imperial support and performances gradually ceased – an unusual case in Japan of a significant theatre form dying out. Some 250 *gigaku* masks are preserved in temple collections; the oldest dates from the 7th century, the time when *gigaku* was first introduced, and may be of Chinese make. They are beautifully carved and painted and are rare works of art.

A rival form of dance entertainment, *bugaku*, was also introduced to the court from China via Korea in the 7th century. In 701 an Imperial Music Bureau was established at the court for instruction in *bugaku* and its music (*kangen*). (The composite dance–music art is called *gagaku*, musical entertainment.) From the beginning, *bugaku* was an eclectic art. The Bureau had divisions for Chinese music and dance (*tōgaku*) and for Korean (*komagaku*) and apportioned its 255 performers to various specialities within the two divisions. In 736, performers were assigned to learn and perform new dances introduced from southern India and from Vietnam. The Emperor Ninmyō (r. 833–49) was so devoted to *bugaku* he journeyed to the T'ang court of China to study the original music and dance. He also composed many new dances. From the 13th to the 16th centuries *bugaku* entered a period of serious decline. The imperial court lost political power to the rising samurai class and, impoverished, it could not support hundreds of performers as it had in the past. Financial support and dance education were taken over by large Buddhist temples and Shintō shrines. Many pieces in the repertory were lost and the early dramatic vitality of the genre was largely forgotten. The oldest dance pieces, such as Bunomai, a martial dance, suggest the present style of performing is considerably less dynamic than in the past. The dance Genjōraku presents an intensely dramatic situation: a hero of Indian myth fights a poisonous snake, is victorious, and returns triumphant to his castle. A number of the *bugaku* dances were borrowed and then absorbed into provincial performance genres, such as Buddhist longevity dances (*ennen*), because of their dramatic qualities. Today, however, *bugaku* is danced to instrumental music only and there is virtually no role playing or dramatic interaction. Unison or mirror-image dancing in geometric patterns by two or four dancers is typical. Thus the earlier story-telling elements, song lyrics (and possibly dialogue) have not survived. *Bukagu*'s serene, stately qualities derive from the art's exclusive patronage by the imperial court and large shrines and temples closely associated with the throne, an association that has been maintained to the present time.

Theatre of the samurai: nō, kyōgen In Japan's medieval period (1185–1600), samurai generals wrested power from the imperial court and assuming for themselves the title of Shōgun, or General, they ruled from lavish courts first in Kamakura and then in Kyoto. The chief theatre forms patronized by the samurai class were *sarugaku*, also called at that time *sarugaku nō*, and then later simply *nō* (skill), and its companion form comic *kyōgen*. In the middle of the 14th century, dozens of professional *sarugaku nō* troupes were attached to important shrines and temples. Four large troupes were based in Nara, the ancient capital city, where they performed for festival occasions and in public (*kanjin nō*). The head of one of these troupes, Kan'ami Kiyotsugu (1333–84), is credited with transforming *sarugaku* into *nō*. A skilled actor and troupe head, he conceived of combining a popular narrative song of the time (*kuse*) with rhythmic dance (*mai*) and used the resulting narrative sung-dance (*kuse mai*) as the climactic scene of a performance. He structured his plays as virtual monodramas (in contrast to multi-role plays of competing *dengaku nō* troupes), in which the crucial event in the life of the chief character (the *shite*, or Doer, role), often the grieving spirit of a dead person, was remembered and reenacted in a *kuse mai* scene. Kan'ami's son, Zeami Motokiyo (1363–1443), was an actor of singular genius whose superb acting focused even more attention on the Doer role. Kan'ami stressed convincing physical and vocal characterization through observation of real people, hence he is considered the father of acting, as opposed to dancing and singing, in Japanese theatre.

Kan'ami's troupe, competing with other *sarugaku nō* and with *dengaku nō* troupes, had the good fortune to act before the Shōgun Ashikaga Yoshimitsu in 1374. The 14-year-old Shōgun was attracted by the playing of Zeami, who was 11 at the time, and he invited Zeami to be his companion in the palace. During the ensuing 50 years, Zeami performed at court and received shogunal patronage. Zen Buddhism was the official religion of the Ashikaga court, and under Zeami's guidance Zen artistic principles of restraint, austerity, and economy of expression were incorporated into *nō* performance and plays. The unadorned stage, the deliberate pace of performance, masks for major characters, and the significant gesture reflect Zen ideals. Zeami's advice to the actor to 'move seven if the heart feels ten' is a succinct expression of Zen precepts. Suggestive beauty (*yūgen*) was the quality sought by Zeami in performance. Zeami became troupe leader

when his father died and in his later years wrote some 20 'secret' treatises on *nō* aesthetics and acting intended for his successors. Among the 40–60 plays attributed to him that rank high in the current repertory of 240 plays are *The Damask Drum*, *Kiyotsune*, *The Well Curb*, *Takasago Shrine*, and *Lady Yuya*. He was succeeded by his eldest son Kanze Motomasa (?1394–1432), author of the play *The Sumida River*, and, following his early death, by his scholarly son-in-law Komparu Zenchiku (1405–?), author of sophisticated Buddhist interpretations of *nō* aesthetics and richly poetic plays such as *Yang Kuei-fei*, *The Plantain Tree*, and *Teika*. The last of the great *nō* performer-playwrights was Kanze Nobumitsu (1435–1516). He composed highly dramatic plays (*Benkei in the Boat*, *The Ataka Barrier*, *The Maple Viewing*) that used large casts and pitted Doer (*shite*) and Sideman (*waki*) in direct conflict (originally he was a *waki* actor).

During civil wars that lasted through most of the 16th century Kyoto was burned and shogunal patronage, in the form of sponsored professional performances, drastically declined. Troupes fled to the provinces where they found support from provincial samurai lords. To support themselves actors gave instruction in singing and dance to samurai, priests, and wealthy commoners, and amateur performances were popular. Texts for chanting (*utaibon*) were first published and sold to the public in 1512. Soon hundreds of *nō* plays were available in print, as well as descriptions of staging, costumes, masks, and music. During this period, knowledge of *nō* spread among all classes and into remote areas. Many surviving provincial *nō* styles trace their origins to this time. *Nō* troupes returned to the centre of political power once again at the end of the 16th century when the country was unified under powerful generals. Toyotomi Hideyoshi (1537–98) studied *nō* and played himself in *nō* plays that he had written about his battlefield victories. Tokugawa Ieyasu (1543–1616) patronized the Kanze troupe even before he became Shōgun in 1603. His successors, ruling from the new capital of Edo (Tokyo), designated *nō* the 'ceremonial art' (*shikigaku*) to be performed on formal occasions through the long Tokugawa era (1600–1868). The third Tokugawa Shōgun, Iemitsu (1604–51), codified every aspect of *nō* and forbade deviation. *Nō* actors were given samurai rank and only the sons of actors were allowed to become performers. The troupe head (*iemoto*) was given absolute authority, and was held responsible for every member of the troupe. The freshness of performance (*hana*) that Zeami had prized was smothered by tradition and regulation. Popular audiences were forbidden to see or study *nō* (although they did nonetheless). Actors devoted themselves to ever greater refinement and subtlety in their acting until, by the close of the 19th century, a play took two and three times as long to perform as during Zeami's time.

Nō evolved eclectically, its plays based on borrowed stories and its poetic forms mirroring earlier literature. Zeami advised playwrights to dramatize well-known figures and events from history and legend for these would be familiar and easily grasped, hence the many plays taken from Chinese legend and Japanese history, especially the civil war between the Heike and Genji clans in the 12th century. *Nō*'s sonorous singing style derives from Buddhist chant (*shōmyō*) and early popular songs (*imayō*) and its dance from professional female entertainers (*shirabyōshi*). The refined masks that mark *nō* as a uniquely suggestive art have antecedents in *gigaku* and *bugaku* masks of the court tradition and in village *kagura* masks as well. Especially beautiful are the masks for women's roles. Often said to be 'neutral' in fact they express, usually in subtle fashion, a wide range of human emotions – happiness, pride, innocence, melancholy, elegance, grief. Except for lavish costumes of the Doer role, dress is restrained in keeping with Zen precepts. Few properties are used and these tend to be symbolic – a fan as a drinking cup, a cloth-wrapped frame for a boat, for example.

Kyōgen, inspired or mad speech, is a performance genre that is both related to and separate from *nō*. *Kyōgen* actors perform in *nō* plays and they enact independent celebratory, often comic, plays that alternate in performance with *nō* plays. (The term *nōgaku* encompasses the art of *nō* and *kyōgen* together.) *Kyōgen* plays and acting style are at least as old as *nō*. Some accounts trace *kyōgen*'s origins to comic dances – such as Ame-no-Uzume's – from the prehistoric Age of the Gods. The ritual play *Okina*, performed as an auspicious prayer for longevity at the beginning of a *nō-kyōgen* programme, is in both the *nō* and the *kyōgen* repertories and there is some evidence that the latter version is the older. The humorous titles of 11th-century *sarugaku* plays (*A Nun Seeks Baby Diapers*, *Pranks by a City Boy*) show that *kyōgen* plays were a vital part of the *sarugaku* repertory. During Zeami's time specialist performers of *nō*, of *kyōgen*, of drums, and of flute were combined into a comprehensive *sarugaku nō* troupe. When *kyōgen* actors of the Ōkura, Sagi, and Izumi families received direct patronage of the Tokugawa rulers, toward the end of the 16th century, they became semi-independent of *nō* troupes. As with *nō*, all performers are men and acting is generally a hereditary profession passed down from father to son.

Within a *nō* play, the role of a commoner, servant, or labourer is played by a *kyōgen* actor. Rarely is more than one *kyōgen* actor called for in a *nō* play, but in dramatic plays, such as *Benkei in the Boat*, the role is major and essential to the play's plot. The *kyōgen* role is also important in the interlude (*ai* or *ai kyōgen*) between parts one and two of the typical two-part *nō* play. When the Doer retires from the stage to change costume, the *kyōgen* actor recapitulates the story, in a monologue or in dialogue with the Sideman. Published *nō* texts do not contain the interludes, for these sections are the sole prerogative of *kyōgen* performers. Finally, *kyōgen* actors perform all roles in the independent comic plays that make up the separate *kyōgen* repertory. Most plays have two to four characters, a major role (*shite*), a second role (*ado*), and subsidiary roles (*koado*, small *ado*). In all roles, the *kyōgen* style of acting, in contrast to *nō* acting, calls for a clear and lively voice and movements that are active and precise. Actors improvised *kyōgen* in performance until at least the 17th century. Scenarios of 165 texts were written in manuscript form in 1578 and a collection of 203 texts of plays as they were performed were transcribed by Ōkura Toraakira, head of the Ōkura acting family, between 1638 and 1642. These were secret texts, shown outside the acting family only under exceptional circumstances. Some 200 *kyōgen* plays were published for the general public in 1660.

A *nō-kyōgen* programme is made up of thematically unrelated plays chosen from the *nō* repertory of 240 plays and the *kyōgen* repertory of 260 plays. Each programme is given a single performance. Plays are chosen to match the season, the occasion, and the aesthetic principle of ever-increasing emotional tension and tempo (*jo-ha-kyū*) that regulate performance. The *nō* repertory is divided into five groups based on the nature of the Doer role and the order in which the plays appear on a programme. A typical programme contains, in order, a play with a Shintō deity (*kami*), a male warrior (*asura*), a court lady (*katsura*), a mad woman (*kyōran*), and a demon (*kichiku*) in the major role. The *kyōgen* plays that follow each *nō* play have as main roles a deity (*kami*), a wealthy land owner (*daimyō*), a small landholder (*shōmyō*), a bridegroom or son-in-law (*muko*), a Buddhist priest or mountain ascetic (*shukke* or *yamabushi*), or a demon (*oni*). A day-long programme in Zeami's time consisted of eight to ten *nō* plays and five or six *kyōgen* plays. Even a complete but shorter programme of five *nō* and four *kyōgen* is too long for modern audiences; shorter programmes, of as few as two or three *nō* and one or two *kyōgen*, fit the busy schedules of urban audiences. All-*kyōgen* programmes have gained acceptance in recent decades as the social status of *kyōgen* actors has grown.

Popular theatre of the Edo (Tokugawa) period: kabuki, bunraku Professional, commercial *kabuki* and *bunraku* puppet theatre are products of a restless, assertive, mercantile society that flourished in the great cities of Kyoto, Osaka, and Edo (Tokyo) under the xenophobic rule of successive Shōgun of the Tokugawa family (1603–1868). Troupes of the two genres competed for the same audiences. They performed in theatres side by side and over the decades they borrowed each others' successful plays. Alike in certain ways, nonetheless they evolved out of different antecedents and they follow mutually distinct artistic aims even today.

Kabuki grew out of popular, urban dances and sketches of contemporary life. In the 16th century vagabond troupes congregated in Kyoto, then the capital, where they performed secularized forms of religious dances (*ennen*) and folk dances (*yayako odori* and *kaka odori*). Around 1600 one of these dancers, a woman named Okuni and advertised as a priestess of the Grand Shrine in Izumo, made a great success in a new dance called *kabuki*. She performed on a temporary stage set up first in the grounds of Kitano Shrine and later along the dry bed of the Kamo River (hence the disparaging term for *kabuki* actors, 'beggars of the riverbed'). *Kabuki* was unorthodox. It was the rock entertainment of the 17th century. Okuni performed the first Japanese plays of contemporary urban life: numerous painted screens and scrolls show her outrageously garbed as a handsome young warrior, exotic Christian rosary draped on her bosom, conducting an assignation with a prostitute. The Portuguese were newly arrived and licensed quarters for prostitution had only recently been established in Kyoto. Okuni's chief imitators were professional prostitutes who performed *kabuki* dances and songs on public stages as a come-on for their evening profession. Paintings of the early 17th century show prostitutes seated sensuously on tiger skins playing the *shamisen*, a lute recently introduced from China via Okinawa, as bevies of girls circle the stage.

The shogunate banned women from public stages in 1629 as part of its general policy of restricting each person to a single occupation; prostitutes could not be actresses as well. Early *kabuki* was also performed by troupes of young boys, doubling as catamites, but boy performers (*tobiko*, travelling boys) were banned in 1652 as well. It was only after these events that *kabuki* began to develop as a serious art. *Kabuki*'s major characteristics became established by the early 18th century: all-day multi-act plays, adult male casts (and therefore the evolution of the art of the *onnagata* or actor of female roles), a yearly season of five or six productions, and unique musical, dance, and acting styles appropriate to various styles of play. Standard scene types are identifiable in the 1680s and 1690s: the brothel assignation (*keiseigai*), the swaggering parade of a hero (*tanzen roppō*), the flight of lovers (*michiyuki*), the choreographed fight between a hero and a group of opponents (*tachimawari*). Government officials restricted the number and location of *kabuki* theatres and forced actors to live apart from others. Plays about samurai clans were forbidden, leading playwrights to disguise contemporary events as history. In spite of government suppression of *kabuki*, samurai lords and their ladies, rich merchants, priests, workers, and servants all attended the theatre and the despised art flourished as a major attraction of Japanese urban life.

Unique plays and acting styles developed in *kabuki*'s two centres, Kyoto-Osaka and Edo. Sakata Tōjūrō (1644–1709) performed in Kyoto for relatively cultivated audiences. In 1678 he portrayed Izaemon, the pampered scion of a wealthy merchant in the play *Love Letter from the Licensed Quarter*. Audiences were captivated by the play's domestic scenes (*sewamono*) and Tōjūrō's gentle acting style (*wagoto*) that was both comic and sensuous. Tōjūrō repeated the role 16 times in his career. The playwright Chikamatsu Monzaemon (1653–1724) wrote two dozen *kabuki* plays for Tōjūrō, most of them in *wagoto* style. When Tōjūrō became old and his popularity faded, Chikamatsu left *kabuki* to become the puppet theatre's premiere playwright.

The Edo actor **Ichikawa Danjūrō** I (1660–1704) wrote bravura history plays (*jidaimono*) in which he played the superman hero. His flamboyant acting style (*aragoto*) suited the audience of samurai and adventurers in the raw new city. The bold red and black makeup (*kumadori*) and exaggerated costumes that mark *aragoto* acting date from Danjūrō's first stage appearance as a boy. Danjūrō's powerful poses (*mie*) and gestures are said to have been suggested by Buddhist guardian statues (the present Danjūrō XII worships at the same temple Danjūrō I did, dedicated to the Guardian Deity Fudō Myōō). Titles of plays he and his son Danjūrō II (1689–1758) starred in are amply descriptive – *Immovable, The Thundergod, Wait a Moment!, Indestructible, Pulling the Elephant, Repel!, Arrow Maker*. Danjūrō II blended the bravura and gentle styles when he created the role of the dandy hero in *Sukeroku: Flower of Edo* (1713), written by Tsuuchi Jihei II (1679–1760). The wonderfully dramatic confrontations, erotic byplay, impromptu comedy verging on farce, and brilliant settings of the licensed quarter justly make this *kabuki*'s most popular play. Later generations added to these,

making the Eighteen Favourite Plays (*jūhachiban*) of the Ichikawa family.

Professional puppet troupes proliferated in the large cities during this same period, but puppet theatre did not grow from the same sources as *kabuki*. In the late 16th century, puppet manipulation and narrative storytelling – both ancient but separate performing arts in Japan – were joined with the new music of the *shamisen*. This new puppet theatre was called *jōruri*, after its musical style, or more commonly *bunraku* (from the name of the puppet chanter Bunrakuen). Puppetry skills may have been learned in part from travelling troupes of Korean artists in medieval times. Narrative skills have long been admired in Japan and numerous religious and secular story-telling forms existed. Today comic and epic story-tellers (*rakugo* and *kōdan*) regularly perform in variety halls. Early commercial puppet performance (*sekkyōbushi* and *kojōruri*) was built around the narrative, sung, chanted, and spoken by a narrator (*tayū*). Buddhist morality stories, epic romances, and chronicles of feudal wars were narrated by a solo chanter, who also spoke incidental dialogue that might be in the text, while small dolls, each held overhead by a puppeteer, crudely illustrated the story. Puppeteers, chanter and *shamisen* musician were concealed from the audience.

The first important commercial puppet theatre was the Takemoto Theatre in Osaka, founded by the playwright Chikamatsu Monzaemon and the chanter Takemoto Gidayū (1651–1714) whose name (*gidayū*) identifies the musical style used in *bunraku*. Chikamatsu wrote beautiful love suicide plays (*shinjūmono*), such as the *Love Suicides at Amijima* (1720), in which thwarted lovers are only able to find escape from social obligations in death. The simple techniques of early puppet theatre presented no serious competition to *kabuki*. However, in the 1730s and 1740s *bunraku* adopted a number of characteristics of a first-person theatre that brought it closer to *kabuki*. An extremely complex, life-like doll was invented that had movable eyes, eyebrows, mouth, hands, and fingers. Three puppeteers moved the puppet in full audience view. The amount of narrative was reduced and dialogue was increased. Multiple chanters were assigned specific roles in some scenes, so that each major character had its own voice. Puppets moved realistically within homes and castles and forests that were more elaborate than *kabuki* scenery. Revolves and traps were developed at this time for *bunraku* and later taken into *kabuki*.

Exceptionally popular new plays were written to capitalize on the expressive power of the new puppets. A team of playwrights led by Takeda Izumo I (?–1747) and II (1691–1756) jointly composed the Three Great Masterpieces of *bunraku*, *The House of Sugawara* (1746), *Yoshitsune and the Thousand Cherry Trees* (1747), and *The Treasury of Loyal Retainers* (1748), for the Takemoto Puppet Theatre. These are history (*jidai*) plays, with some domestic (*sewa*) elements, whose convoluted plots are based on conflicts between duty (*giri*) of samurai and their love for family (*ninjō*). In *The Treasury of Loyal Retainers* the stalwart hero Yuranosuke abandons his wife and debauches himself, all in loyalty to his slain lord. The plays contain spectacular theatrical effects (a flying fox, a statue coming to life) but they are most compelling in florid scenes of overpowering emotionalism. Usually written in five acts, the emotional climax occurs at the end of act three (*san dan no kiri*), typically a ritual disembowelment, the verification of a severed head, or the forced killing of a beloved relative. In *The Battle of Ichinotani* (1751), composed by Namiki Sōsuke and others for the Toyotake Puppet Theatre in Osaka, the Genji general Kumagai Naozane slays his teenage son in order to save the life of the emperor's son, Atsumori. Unable to bear the horror of his act, Kumagai abandons his rank and becomes a mendicant Buddhist monk.

The plays were enacted with remarkable verisimilitude – real water and mud were used in staging the domestic play *The Summer Festival* (1745). (That human *kabuki* should be stylized and puppet *bunraku* realistic is explained by the *yin-yang* concept of balance through opposites.) These productions were tremendously popular: *The Battle of Ichinotani* ran 12 months. Within a month or two of their openings *kabuki* troupes put on pirated versions, thereby introducing puppet movement techniques, the heavy emotionalism of *gidayū* music, the bloody moral choices between duty and love, and third-person narration into *kabuki* for the first time. The plays were well crafted and it was interesting to watch actors play puppets. Eventually puppet plays provided a third of the *kabuki* repertory. The mid-19th century was *bunraku*'s golden age. Thereafter, creativity declined and audiences increasingly patronized rival *kabuki*. At the beginning of the 20th century there was one *bunraku* theatre, in Osaka.

A new dramatic dance form (*buyō geki*) was developed in *kabuki* by the playwrights Horikoshi Nisōji (1721–81?) and Sakurada Jisuke I (1734–1806) that emphasized male and female roles. Prior to this time, character dances had been the prerogative of *onnagata* actors. In Namiki Gōhei III's dance-drama *The Subscription List* (1840) for example, all the roles were male. Danjūrō VII (1791–1859) created the lead role of Benkei in this play, a role which is the most difficult in the entire dance repertory. *The Subscription List* is based on the *nō* play *The Ataka Barrier*, and it was the first of a score of dance-dramas, serious and comic, to follow closely the stories of *nō* and *kyōgen* plays and to use staging and acting techniques of these forms. One of the most prolific writers of dance-plays for *kabuki* was Kawatake Mokuami (1816–93), also known for writing grotesquely humorous gangster plays (*kizewamono*) for the actors Onoe Kikigorō V (1844–1903) and Ichikawa Kodanji (1812–66). Tsuruya Namboku IV (1755–1829) was perhaps the most typical playwright *kabuki* produced. Among the 120 plays of all types that he wrote through his long career, his masterpiece is *The Scarlet Princess of Edo* (1817), first staged at the Kawarazaki Theatre in Tokyo and revived in recent decades with great success. Namboku brilliantly wove together historical and outcast worlds, humour and gore, soaring passages of dialogue and wonderfully visual moments. His imperial princess becomes a prostitute, his gangster becomes an official, and a samurai lord is impudently slain. Without moralizing he showed the corruption and decline of the late feudal era.

The Western room: traditional theatre in the modern world
Western warships forced Japan to open its society to foreign trade and European cultural influences in the mid-19th century. The last Tokugawa Shōgun was defeated in a brief civil war by citizen soldiers loyal to the new Emperor Meiji. Cultural, political, and economic changes during the Meiji period (1868–1912) profoundly altered the social and economic basis of all existing theatre forms. Traditional genres – *bugaku*, *nō*, *kyōgen*, *kabuki*, and *bunraku* – are still adjusting to the requirements of gaining and holding an audience in the modern world in competition with film, television, and other entertainments.

Nō and *kyōgen* actors suffered greatly when the Meiji emperor proclaimed the abolition of feudalism in 1868. Overnight actors became unemployed ex-samurai. Great actors were reduced to selling precious masks and costumes to keep alive (hence the fine collections of *nō* masks and costumes in some Western museums). Minor actors supported themselves as charcoal sellers and weavers of bamboo hats. But enterprising performers quickly turned to the public for support. A low-ranking actor of minor roles (*tsure*), Umewaka Minoru (1828–1909) charged admission to performances in his home beginning in 1869 and soon established the right to perform major (*shite*) roles on the basis of his public accomplishments. He persuaded the reigning *nō* actor Hōshō Kurō to return from retirement on his farm and to join him in public performances. In Kyoto, monthly public performances were started by actors of the Kongō school in 1877. New *nō* theatres were built in Tokyo's Aoyama Palace in 1878 and in Shiba Park in 1881, both encouraged by the statesman Iwakura Tomomi who, returning from a study trip to Europe, realized that *nō* could be Japan's equivalent to Western opera. Former President Ulysses Grant, visiting Japan, praised *nō* and urged that it be preserved. Gradually *nō* came to occupy an elite position in the new society. Paradoxically, official government support, including imperial command performances, lasted for only a few decades while public support (of an art form so refined that few can comprehend it) has continued down to the present.

Today, the thousand or so professional actors that belong to the five *nō* and two *kyōgen* schools support themselves primarily by teaching hundreds of thousands of devoted amateurs and only a portion of their income derives from performance (theatres seat 400–500 and performances are relatively few). Each of the *nō* schools owns its own theatres and the head actors of each school exercise strong control. The repertory and style of performance is, on the surface at least, unaffected by the modern world. With rare exceptions, new plays are not performed (the actor Kanze Hideo was expelled for acting in modern plays).

The livelihood of *kabuki* and *bunraku* performers was not directly threatened by Meiji period reforms; actors and puppet performers had always depended on popular audiences and these did not change overnight. Government regulations controlling the theatre were only slowly removed: in 1872 officials informed *kabuki* playwrights and actors of the emperor's 'command' that entertainment not suitable for family groups or foreign spectators was banned. But theatres were freer than they ever had been and *kabuki* in particular was profoundly changed as it adapted to the modern world. Throughout its 300-year history, *kabuki* had been 'contemporary theatre'. Like film and television today, everything new in society had been eagerly placed on the stage. Responding to the new life and ideas around them, staff playwrights like Mokuami wrote plays featuring locomotives, balloon ascensions, and Japanese tourists in exotic India and Europe. He created contemporary roles for the actor Onoe Kikugorō V in cropped-hair plays (*zangirimono*), so-called because of the Western haircuts of the heroes. Ichikawa Danjūrō IX played in living history plays (*katsureki geki*) that aimed at historical truth. Most critics found the plays and acting style dull. Danjūrō agreed, at least for a time, with the calls of the Society for Theatre Reform, formed in 1886, to modernize and sanitize *kabuki* in line with Western theatre practice. Together with leading literary scholars, he advocated abolishing traditional music, the wooden clapper sound effects (*hyōshigi*), and even the *hanamichi*. It was argued that actresses should replace the 'unreal' *onnagata* actor. None of these reforms came to pass.

New *kabuki* dramas (*shin kabuki*) were written by literary men from outside the theatre, a significant development which marked the end of the self-contained *kabuki* troupe. Plays such as Tsubouchi Shōyō's *A Paulownia Leaf* (1904), Okamoto Kidō's *Love Suicides at Toribeyama* (1915), and more recently *kabuki* scripts by novelist-playwright Mishima Yukio are notable primarily because they achieved de facto the aims of the discredited reform movement. *Kabuki* dramaturgy (seven-five dialogue, poetic name-saying speeches, act and scene structure) is abandoned in them and their authors did not know how to incorporate *kabuki* performance techniques (*mie* poses, *shamisen* music, stylized battles, dance, elocution). New *kabuki* plays continue to be staged at the Kabuki-za in Tokyo almost monthly but rarely do audiences like them, rarely are they revived, and rarely do they in any way deserve the name *kabuki*.

A handful of superb performers of *bunraku* sparked renewed interest in the puppet theatre during the Meiji era. The chanter Takemoto Harudayū (1808–77) was greatly admired for his powerful and expressive voice. He moved between two newly opened theatres in Osaka, the Bunraku Theatre (opened 1872) and its competitor the Hikoroku Theatre. One of the few *shamisen* players to achieve personal fame in the world of puppet theatre, Toyozawa Danpei (1827–98) revolutionized the art of *bunraku* music. He composed complex scores that closely supported the emotional nuances of scenes rather than merely serving as accompaniment to the chanter. It was said a listener could understand the emotions of a character just by hearing Danpei play the *shamisen* even if no words were chanted. He was a demanding perfectionist who inspired his collaborating chanters and puppeteers to outdo themselves. He wrote the popular play *Miracle at Tsubosaka Temple* (1897) with his wife. The chanter Takemoto Settsu-Daijō (1836–1917) performed for members of the imperial family and in 1902 was honoured with an imperial title. A decade before this, Settsu-Daijō began the rage for chanting puppet texts without puppets. Amateurs studied chanting under the instruction of professional *shamisen* teachers; in 1889 perhaps a thousand amateurs were chanting in theatres and halls in Osaka. Mass performances by 400–500 chanters were not uncommon. Women chanters (*onna jōruri*) gained enormous success performing in commercial variety theatres (*yose*) in the early decades of the 20th century. Settsu-Daijō also attempted to restore

'historical truth' to classical plays (in the same way the actor Danjūrō IX had commissioned 'living history plays' for *kabuki*). He placed the old plays in their proper historical period and called characters by their real names. Lovers of *bunraku*, however, did not want their plays tampered with and by 1891 Settsu-Daijō had abandoned his reforms. *Bunraku*'s Meiji-period revival did not last when its charismatic performers passed from the scene. In 1909 the only remaining puppet theatre, the Bunraku Theatre of Osaka, was purchased by the Shōchiku Theatrical Corporation. Government subsidy of *bunraku* began in 1963 and continues to the present. Performers divided into two rival groups shortly after the war, but in 1963 they rejoined to form a single troupe under the auspices of the Bunraku Association. This troupe performs in its new home, the National Bunraku Theatre in Tokyo. The troupe draws a stable, moderate-sized audience.

Early in the Meiji period the owners of the majority of large *kabuki* theatre owners moved their theatres into elite locations in up-town Tokyo. In 1872 actor-manager Morita Kanya XII (1846–97) moved the Morita Theatre, which had opened in old Edo in 1660, into the heart of Tokyo and three years later rebuilt it as the New Tomi Theatre, equipped with Western seats and gas lights for night performances, for the first time in *kabuki*. Many foreign dignitaries, including former President Grant, went to this 'modern' theatre. The Kabuki-za, now the premiere *kabuki* theatre in the country, opened next to the fashionable Ginza district in 1889 and the Imperial Theatre, inspired by the design of Western opera houses, was built in 1911 almost adjacent to the imperial palace. *Kabuki* managers were successful in drawing the new upper middle class, but they also abandoned their traditional audience of merchants, artisans, and workers. Audiences for both *kabuki* and *bunraku* declined drastically during the Second World War. Performers were drafted into the army or sent out on war-related entertainment tours.

Theatres were burned or gutted by bombing. In the early post-war years, 'feudal' *kabuki* and *bunraku* plays were banned by American occupation censors and for a brief time the survival of both forms was in doubt. The appeal of *kabuki* to a large segment of the Japanese public remains strong, however, and audiences returned to the Kabuki-za, the Shinbashi Dance Theatre, and the National Theatre (opened 1966) in Tokyo where *kabuki* is most often performed. The Minami Theatre in Kyoto and the Naka Theatre in Osaka retain the flavour of old *kabuki* more than Tokyo's theatres, for they remain in the entertainment districts that have been their home for three centuries.

Family acting traditions were carried into the mid-20th century by a group of charismatic and talented post-Second World War actors: Ichikawa Danjūrō XI (1909–65), Living National Treasure Onoe Shōroku II (1913–89), Matsumoto Koshirō VII (1910–75), Nakamura Kanzaburō XVII (1909–88), former President of the Kabuki Actors' Association Ichikawa Sadanji (1898–1964), Morita Kanya (1907–75), and two great *onnagata*, Living National Treasure Nakamura Utaemon VI (b. 1917), and Onoe Baiko VI (b. 1915). Today's young actors Bandō Tamasaburō (b. 1950), Kataoka Takao (b. 1944), Onoe Kikugorō VII (b. 1942), Ichikawa Danjūrō XII (b. 1946), and Onoe Tatsunosuke (b. 1946) are idolized by fans. They have done much to attract a younger audience in the 1970s and 1980s. Today *kabuki* is a classical, orthodox theatre in which little change occurs.

The imaginative staging by actor-director Ichikawa Ennosuke, who insists upon reinterpreting each classic to make it interesting to a modern audience, is unusual. Today's audience is heavily middle class and a first class ticket costs US $40–60. Once a despised theatre, it calls itself Grand Kabuki on foreign tours. Actors work exceptionally long hours: matinee and evening bills, usually different, begin at 11 in the morning and end at 10 at night. The programme changes monthly, performances are daily for 25 days, and four or five days at the end of the month are spent in intensive rehearsals on the next month's plays. Theatre owners and producers run *kabuki* today and the 500 or so professional actors rotate among theatres each month as needed. There no longer is a functioning troupe system.

Government support for traditional theatre in the modern period has been negligible. *Bugaku* is the chief exception: the main troupe continues as part of the Imperial Household Agency. *Bunraku*, as noted, began receiving government subsidies 50 years ago. A distinguished artist who is named an Intangible Cultural Asset or Living National Treasure receives a small government annuity. Perhaps most significantly, in the past two decades the government has built a National Theatre for *kabuki* and a National Noh Theatre in Tokyo and in Osaka a National Bunraku Theatre. They are modern and beautifully equipped. Theatre staffs, but not the actors or musicians, are on government salary.

For 20 years traditional performances have been televised regularly throughout Japan (*kabuki* most often), thereby reaching audiences outside the large cities that normally would never have the chance to attend the theatre. *Kabuki*, *bunraku*, *nō*, and *kyōgen* troupes are regularly sent out on international tours, so that traditional theatre is no longer isolated.

Transition to modern theatre: shinpa Each significant social class in Japan developed its own theatre: *bugaku* was the theatre of the imperial court, *nō* and *kyōgen* of the samurai, and *kabuki* and *bunraku* of the townsmen. *Shinpa*, new school, is the theatre of the half-Westernized half-traditional urban middle class that rose to prominence during the Meiji era.

It was a transitional theatre whose rationale for existence was the rejection of the 'old' represented by *kabuki*. In fact, however, *shinpa* has less in common with later Western-derived 'new theatre' (*shingeki*) than it has with traditional theatre. The first *shinpa* plays were staged by the failed politician Kawakami Otojirō (1864–1911) who used patriotic events, such as the Russo-Japanese war, as subjects for melodrama. His troupe's performances in the United States and Europe in 1899–1901 were the first glimpses of Japanese theatre in the West. In spite of the troupe's insignificant standing in Japan, the controlled but emotional performances of Sada Yakko, Kawakami's wife and a trained geisha, received astounded acclaim from Western critics and theatre artists. She was compared to **Sarah Bernhardt** for the 'realism' of her death scenes. Because of Sada, the 1629 law banning women from the public stage was repealed.

Between 1900 and 1915 new style *shinpa* troupes performed in Tokyo and Osaka. Following his return from Europe, Kawakami successfully adapted Western plays such as *Othello*, *Hamlet*, and *The Count of Monte Cristo* to Japanese settings. He introduced **Maeterlinck** and **Sardou** and he produced Japan's first children's drama in 1903 at the Hongō Theatre. Kawakami appeared in major theatres, including the venerable Nakamura Theatre, one of the great *kabuki* houses, and at the new Kabuki-za. Rival *shinpa* troupes staged topical plays that had great popular appeal. Titles of plays produced in 1904, the year that the Russo-Japanese war began, suggest their intense nationalist flavour: *The Fall of Port Arthur*, *The Imperial Army That Vanquishes Russia*, *The Great Russo-Japanese War*, *Battle Report*, and *Submarine*. *Shinpa* producers successfully shortened performance hours, brought actresses back to the stage, and abolished the theatre teahouses that used to control ticket sales. Cinema had been introduced to Japan in 1896 and *shinpa* managers, seeing the huge country audiences that flocked into cinema theatres, tried putting live performances in front of film backgrounds in 1910. But most important, new Japanese playwrights were given an opportunity to see their plays produced. *Shinpa* actors presented Tsubouchi Shōyō's *The Cuckoo* in 1904. Tsubouchi (1859–1935) was a seminal figure in early modern Japanese theatre – translator of **Shakespeare**'s canon, playwright, acting teacher, director, and founder of the influential Literary Arts Society. Satō Kōroku (1874–1949) wrote five plays in the space of two years (1907–8) for *shinpa* actors and Mayama Seika (1878–1948) dramatized contemporary novels for *shinpa* performance. But by the 1920s *shingeki* had laid claim to Western drama and *shinpa* was reduced to producing domestic tragicomedies, usually about domestic travail in the middle class, marked by sentimental nostalgia for an era now past. The superlative actress Mizutani Yaeko (1905–79) assured the popularity of the one remaining *shinpa* troupe through the post-war years but her recent death casts doubt on *shinpa*'s future. Often today, *kabuki* and *shinpa* actors give joint performances, indicating the affinity of the two genres. JRB

2. Modern Japanese theatre The history of modern Japanese theatre, known as *shingeki* (literally 'new theatre'), has been characterized by a break with traditional theatre forms in the early 20th century and attempts since the Second World War to recapture some of the resources lost in that rupture. In essence, the plethora of gods and demons who had populated classical *kabuki* and *nō* were exiled from the modern stage in the early period, only to return in force since the war. Four periods may be discerned in this process: 1887–1928, the establishment of a modern theatre; 1928–45, the politicization of modern theatre; 1945–60, modernism becomes orthodoxy; and 1960–85, the rejection of modernism.

Exile of the Gods, 1887–1945: the classical legacy In 1887, the government of Meiji Japan formed a blue-ribbon Committee for the Reform of the Theatre (Engeki Kairyō Kai) to clean up *kabuki* and make it acceptable to a Western audience. The Japanese oligarchy was self-conscious about *kabuki* because it was a highly erotic and frequently violent form of popular theatre that had provided a relatively harmless release for plebeian libido in the repressive Tokugawa period (1600–1868).

The government's goal was to recast *kabuki* in the mould of 19th-century European realism. A number of attempts were made to achieve this end, including the *katsureki* or 'living history' plays performed by Ichikawa Danjūrō IX (1838–1903) in the 1890s and the experiments of Ichikawa Sadanji II (1880–1940) and Osanai Kaoru (1881–1928) in the first decades of the 20th century; but these experiments failed because the 'irrationality' that they sought to extirpate from *kabuki* was its very essence. *Kabuki* was simply not compatible with realism.

Nō and *kabuki*, Japan's premier traditional theatre forms, evolved in a pre-modern milieu where little distinction existed between art and religion. While very different from each other, *nō* and *kabuki* are nevertheless both religio-aesthetic forms. *Nō* is a sacred theatre where, typically, a god will appear and catharsis will be achieved through epiphany, contact with the divine. By contrast, *kabuki* is a profane theatre, where catharsis is achieved through exposure to evil. What the Committee for the Reform of the Theatre and other would-be reformers tried to do was deny the religious function of *nō* and *kabuki* and re-establish them as purely aesthetic forms.

Bungei Kyōkai and Jiyū Gekijō Exiled from the classical stage, the gods found little refuge in the emerging modern theatre. Troupes dedicated to producing Western plays and their Japanese equivalents appeared in the first decade of the 20th century. The Literary Arts Society (Bungei Kyōkai) was founded in 1906 by Tsubouchi Shōyō (1859–1935); the Free Theatre (Jiyū Gekijō), named after **Antoine**'s Théâtre Libre, was founded in 1909 by Osanai Kaoru and Ichikawa Sadanji.

While the two troupes differed in their approach to modern theatre, there was little room in either of them for the displaced spirits of the Japanese pantheon. Tsubouchi, one of the Meiji period's outstanding men of letters, was professor of English literature at Waseda University and a translator of Shakespeare. As its name implied, his troupe took an academic and literary approach to the theatre and concentrated on performing Tsubouchi's translations of Shakespeare, including *The Merchant of Venice* (1906), *Hamlet* (1907, 1911), and *Julius Caesar* (1913). In contrast, the Free Theatre concentrated on the works of contemporary European writers, staging **Ibsen**'s *John Gabriel Borkman* in 1909 and **Gorky**'s *Lower Depths* the following year.

The two troupes agreed that a new style of acting would be necessary successfully to perform Western drama (including the training of actresses, who had been banned from the Japanese stage more than 250 years earlier), but they differed on how this goal was to be achieved. The Literary Arts Society hoped to develop a new breed of actor by exposing amateurs to great works of dramatic literature; the Free Theatre sought to reeducate professional actors like its co-founder Ichikawa Sadanji to perform European works.

Neither approach was successful. *Kabuki* actors never successfully adapted to the realistic style of acting required by the modern European works staged by the Free Theatre; and the actors Tsubouchi helped to train were unwilling to remain dedicated to his stoic literary philosophy. The Free Theatre continued to perform sporadically until 1919. The Literary Arts Society collapsed in 1913, when the troupe's leading actress, Matsui Sumako (1886–1919), left the troupe with Tsubouchi's erstwhile disciple, Shimamura Hōgetsu (1871–1918), to found their own Art Theatre (Geijutsu-za), a more commercially oriented company that capitalized on Matsui's popularity as modern Japan's first actress.

En-no-Gyōja The real issue involved in the rise and fall of these first two *shingeki* troupes was more profound, however. It involved the conflict inherent in introducing the foreign ideas implicit in Western drama, ranging from Christianity to women's rights, while banishing from the stage the Japanese gods and the conceptions they embodied.

This conflict was trenchantly expressed in Tsubouchi's 1913 play *En-no-Gyōja* (*En the Ascetic*). The play ostensibly concerns a 7th-century religious figure, but the relationship between En and his disciple Hirotari, who falls prey to feminine charms and perverts his master's teachings, seems clearly modelled on Tsubouchi's relationship with Shimamura and Matsui. In the final scene of the play, the ascetic vows never to compromise and transforms himself into an image of Kongō Zaō, a Nietzschean image of transcendent power that can serve as a model for future generations.

Tsubouchi's play was very much in the spirit of its times. The Emperor Meiji had died the previous year, and his death had stimulated some of the most significant literary activity of the early 20th century, including novels like Mori Ogai's *Abe Ichizoku* (*The Abe Clan*, 1913; tr. 1977) and Natsume Sōseki's *Kokoro* (1914; tr. 1957), which deal with the theme of *junshi*, the feudal practice of self-immolation upon the death of one's lord. Tsubouchi's play should be read in this context, and En's metamorphosis into a Buddhist divinity should be construed as an attempt to reassert through a kind of symbolic self-destruction the playwright's dedication to the ideals of the Meiji era, his unswerving loyalty to the Japanese spirit even in his pursuit of Western knowledge and technique. Tsubouchi attempted to manifest a Japanese god on the modern stage, but it was already inert and inorganic.

The Tsukiji Little Theatre Although written in 1913, *En the Ascetic* was not performed until 1926. The circumstances of the production tell a great deal about the history of the theatre in this period.

The 1910s and early 1920s were an era of much literary but little theatrical activity. Many plays were written but few performed with distinction. Among those writing plays during these years were Kikuchi Kan (1888–1948), Kume Masao (1891–1952), Yamamoto Yūzō (1887–1974), and Tanizaki Junichirō (1886–1965), all of whom are as well or better known for their work as novelists.

It was at the end of this period of literary activity that the Tsukiji Little Theatre (Tsukiji Shōgekijō) was founded. Ordinances had prevented the construction of new theatres in Tokyo, but after the Great Kanto Earthquake destroyed much of the city on 1 September 1923, the municipal administration eased restrictions in the interest of rebuilding the capital. Osanai organized and Hijikata Yoshi (1898–1959) financed the project. A wealthy young nobleman and theatre devotee who had just left for an intended ten-year tour of Europe,

Hijikata hastened home when he heard that a theatre could be built and placed the funds earmarked for his stay abroad at Osanai's disposal.

The Tsukiji Little Theatre opened on 13 June 1924. It had a seating capacity of just under 500 and was constructed along the most modern lines. The most renowned feature of its stage was a *Kuppelhorizont* that made sophisticated lighting design possible.

Construction of the Tsukiji Little Theatre was greeted with enthusiasm by Japanese playwrights. They had been publishing their work, first in *Shinshichō* (New Trends in Thought), a journal founded in 1907 by Osanai himself, and later in *Engeki Shinchō* (New Trends in Drama), and had every reason to believe that the Tsukiji would stage it. They were thunderstruck, therefore, when Osanai announced at Keio University on 20 May 1924 that for a period of two years the Tsukiji would produce only works by Western playwrights.

Osanai's action precipitated a deep split in the *shingeki* movement. After his frustrating experience with the Free Theatre, his travels in Europe, and his contact with Stanislavsky's **Moscow Art Theatre**, however, Osanai was determined to create a viable production system for modern plays in Japan, and he was convinced that this required a clean break with traditional methods and sensibilities. Even the remnants of Japaneseness found in the ostensibly 'modern' works of Japanese playwrights could subvert this project, he feared. Only by actually producing European plays in the European manner for an extended period could the goal of a modern theatre for Japan be achieved.

The first play by a Japanese playwright to be staged at the Tsukiji Little Theatre was Tsubouchi's *En the Ascetic* (21 March–11 April 1926). The choice of this play by a sexagenarian only exacerbated the sense of alienation felt by the younger Japanese playwrights whose works Osanai had passed over, but Osanai had chosen it for a purpose: he wanted to test the production system the Tsukiji troupe had been developing against the most adamantine example of traditional Japanese sensibilities in modern dramatic form in order to prove that Japanese plays could now be produced by the Tsukiji without fear of recidivism. A modern theatre had been established in Japan.

Politicization of modern theatre, 1928–45: factionalism By the time of Osanai's untimely death on 25 December 1928, the Tsukiji Little Theatre had established a modern system of theatre production in Japan. It had produced a diverse repertory of representative European works by playwrights including Ibsen, **Chekhov**, **Turgenev**, **Strindberg**, **Čapek**, **Pirandello**, and **Georg Kaiser**; and it had trained an entire generation of theatre practitioners. With Osanai's passing, however, the tensions inherent in a troupe so diversely conceived immediately came to a head, and the company collapsed in less than three months.

The Tsukiji Little Theatre split into factions that continued to define the *shingeki* movement into the post-war period. Hijikata Yoshi led the New Tsukiji Troupe (Shin Tsukiji Gekidan), the 'political' faction, which incorporated the activist members of the original company, including such actors as Maruyama Sadao (who died in the atomic bombing of Hiroshima),

Yamamoto Yasue (later to become Kinoshita Junji's favourite actress and to create the role of Tsū in his *Twilight Crane*), Susukida Kenji (a founder of the Mingei company after the war) and others. Aoyama Sugisaku (1889–1956) represented the Tsukiji Little Theatre Company (Gekidan Tsukiji Shōgekijō), the 'artistic' faction, which included such notable actors as Higashiyama Chieko (later of Haiyūza), Tomoda Kyōsuke and Tamura Akiko (husband and wife, who later joined Bungakuza), and Sugimura Haruko (also of Bungakuza and one of the post-war period's finest actresses). Takizawa Osamu, one of Japan's most accomplished actors, originally belonged to the Tsukiji Little Theatre Company, but later shifted his allegiance to the politically engaged group.

Playwrights also helped to define the *shingeki* movement in the thirties. Nagata Hideo (1885–1949), Murayama Tomoyoshi (1901–77) (who was also a talented stage designer and director), and Kubo Sakae (1900–57) were left-wing writers associated with the political mainstream of the movement; Kubota Mantarō (1889–1963), Iwata Toyoo (1893–1969), and Kishida Kunio (1890–1954) were representative writers for the artistic group. Kubota, Iwata, and Kishida jointly founded The Literary Theatre (Bungakuza) in 1937; and it was the only pre-war *shingeki* troupe allowed to perform continuously through the war.

Kubo and Kishida Kubo and Kishida are often proposed as the greatest pre-war playwrights. Kubo was closely identified with Osanai and the Tsukiji Little Theatre. He had worked closely with Osanai as a translator of German drama, rendering some 30 plays into Japanese, ranging from **Goethe**'s *Faust* to works by Kaiser, **Wedekind**, and **Hauptmann**. Kubo delivered the eulogy at Osanai's funeral, wrote Osanai's biography, and dedicated *Land of Volcanic Ash* (*Kazanbaichi*, 1937–8; tr. 1986), his magnum opus, to his mentor.

Kishida, by contrast, had been one of those young playwrights alienated by Osanai when he announced that the Tsukiji would produce only foreign works. He had spent several years in France in the early 1920s and had been influenced by the work of **Jacques Copeau** and the **Vieux-Colombier**. In 1932, he founded *Gekisaku* (Playwriting) magazine as a literary showplace for younger playwrights deemed insufficiently committed by the left-wing troupes. Among the playwrights associated with Kishida's journal were

Kubo Sakae's *Land of Volcanic Ash*, 1938.

Tanaka Chikao (b. 1905), Uchimura Naoya (b. 1909), and Morimoto Kaoru (1912–46). The journal was so influential that the whole literary faction of playwrights in the 1930s is often referred to as the *Gekisaku-ha* or 'Playwriting faction'.

The plays of Kubo and Kishida could hardly be more different. *Land of Volcanic Ash* is a gargantuan work in seven acts with dozens of characters. It describes in minute detail the complex sociological relationships in an impoverished area of the underdeveloped northern island of Hokkaido. Kubo's intention in *Land of Volcanic Ash* was to combine science with art, and the play succeeded so well that it served as an inspiration to an entire generation of Japanese intellectuals.

By contrast, Kishida's *Mr Sawa and His Two Daughters* (*Sawa-shi no Futari Musume*, 1935; tr. 1986), often regarded as his finest work, is less than one-fifth the length of Kubo's play and has only three major characters. It is an intense, claustrophobic work, that describes the deteriorating relationship between Sawa, a retired diplomat, and his two very different daughters. The play was not produced until 1951, when it was directed by Tanaka Chikao, and its influence and appeal have been primarily literary.

Kubo and Kishida can both lay claim to being Japan's best pre-war playwright. Kubo is certainly the best representative of the style of theatre developed by the Tsukiji, which was realistic, scientific, and increasingly left-wing. Kishida was the writer most intensely devoted to the possibilities of drama as literature. Kubo's work expressed an intense faith in man's ability to shape his own future; Kishida's work has rightly been described as nihilistic.

Despite their differences, however, Kubo and Kishida were united in their devotion to the idea of realism in the theatre – Kubo to sociological realism, Kishida to a psychological variety. Taken together, their work represents the pinnacle of pre-war drama, which had, by the late 1930s, not only created a production system independent of traditional theatre, but also playwrights able to write completely rational, realistic works that accurately portrayed both the inner and outer intricacies of contemporary Japanese life. The gods are completely absent in the work of Kubo and Kishida, and even the conflicts over abandoning them, so evident in the drama of men like Tsubouchi, have no place in their work.

In the highly charged political atmosphere of the time, however, realism did not mean neutralism; every artistic act was political. In August 1940, the government ordered the New Tsukiji and Shinkyō troupes, the two remaining left-wing companies, to disband and imprisoned their leaders, including Kubo. Kishida, on the other hand, became head of the cultural section of the Imperial Rule Assistance Association in 1940, the year it supplanted all political parties, and after the war he was purged by the Occupation as a collaborator in the war effort.

Modernism becomes orthodoxy, 1945–60: the post-war situation For a brief period after the war, it seemed that *shingeki* would become the centre, not only of Japanese theatre, but of Japanese culture as a whole. Of all the arts, its ardent devotion to realism had kept it relatively immune to the ultranationalist contagion. It was this same commitment to realism, however, that hobbled modern theatre's attempts to answer the profound questions raised by the war and defeat.

The post-war scene was dominated by three *shingeki* troupes that reflected the alliances that had existed in the Tsukiji Little Theatre. Mingei (The People's Art Theatre) represented the left wing; Haiyūza (The Actors' Theatre), led by the brilliant actor, director, and translator of Brecht, Senda Koreya, most closely approximated the catholic, academic approach of Osanai; and Bungakuza continued to represent the literary faction.

With the easing of political tensions and the recovery of the post-war economy, the differences between these troupes became more apparent than real, however; and the post-war period was marked by a growing consensus on what modern theatre should be. Modernism, in short, became an orthodoxy. Among the tenets of this orthodoxy were a commitment to proscenium arch realism, a belief in the primacy of the text and the actor's subservience to it, a commitment to a tragic and humanistic dramaturgy, and a conviction that the principal function of theatre is didactic.

When the war ended, Japanese theatre, both modern and traditional, faced a severe crisis. Most theatres had been destroyed, and troupes lacked the wherewithal to mount productions. After an initial period of confusion, *kabuki* was taken under the protective wing of Tōhō and Shōchiku, two large commercial promoters; and *shingeki* developed a national system of audience organizations known as Rōen (Workers' Theatre Councils) modelled after the German **Volksbühne**.

Kinoshita Junji The most important playwright to emerge in the immediate post-war period was Kinoshita Junji (b. 1914). Kinoshita's work epitomizes the bifurcation between the commitment to realistic dramaturgy and the need to come to terms with the mythic aspects of the Japanese imagination that has characterized *shingeki* in the post-war period.

Kinoshita was a disciple of Kubo Sakae and thus the legitimate heir to the tradition of *shingeki* realism established at the Tsukiji Little Theatre. His first work, *Fūrō* (*Turbulent Times*, 1939–47), which deals with the ideologies competing for the allegiance of young Japanese minds in the 1870s, was clearly shaped by the dramatic method developed by Kubo in *Land of Volcanic Ash*. Kinoshita has continued to write plays in this vein, characterized by meticulous research and documentary precision.

Immediately after the war, Kinoshita also began to write 'folktale dramas', plays based on traditional Japanese sources. The best known of these is *Twilight Crane* (*Yūzuru*, 1949; tr. 1956), which related the ancient legend of a crane who transforms itself into a woman to reward the man who saved its life. The most significant feature of the folktale plays is Kinoshita's effort to recapture the means to realize the Japanese gods on the modern stage.

A recent example of this bifurcation in Kinoshita's work is *Between God and Man* (*Kami to Hito to no Aida*, 1970; tr. 1979), which consists of two separate plays, both dealing with the issue of Japanese war crimes. The first play uses verbatim transcripts from the Tokyo War Crimes Tribunal in a manner not dissimilar to **Peter Weiss**'s *The Investigation*. The second play takes a very different tack, exploring the question of crime and punishment, sin and expiation, from a religious perspective that syncretizes Christian and Shintō beliefs, and features a female shaman's mystical intercourse with the dead. Kinoshita has been searching for a means to reconcile his realistic, documentary dramaturgy with his attempts to return gods to the modern Japanese stage, but his difficulties in this undertaking have been more revealing than his successes.

Hiroshima and Nagasaki The bifurcation in Kinoshita's work is characteristic of *shingeki* drama in the post-war period. After the defeat, many playwrights felt that they could not explain what had happened to Japan in the war without acknowledging the activity of the gods, those subliminal forces that had been at play; but their efforts were compromised by their commitment to realism and the other tenets of *shingeki* orthodoxy.

Nowhere is this problem more apparent than in plays dealing with the atomic bombing of Hiroshima and Nagasaki. The first play to treat the subject was *The Island* (*Shima*, 1955; tr. 1986) by Hotta Kiyomi (b. 1922). The play is an excellent example of orthodox *shingeki* realism, but it also presents a strong Buddhist message of salvation through resignation for victims of the bomb. Similarly, Tanaka Chikao's *The Head of Mary* (*Maria no Kubi*, 1959; tr. 1986) is an essentially realistic work that interprets the bombing of Nagasaki from a Catholic perspective, as a theophany, a manifestation of God's will in history. Both Hotta and Tanaka attempt to address the urgent issues of life and death, meaning and absurdity, raised by the war. In order to do so, they find it necessary to refer to a transcendent dimension, but like Kinoshita they are only partially successful because of the contradiction between their fundamentally secular realism and their religious imagination. Thus, it is hard to take seriously the concluding scene in Tanaka's play, for example, when the severed head of a statue of the Madonna turns and speaks to a small band of prayerful believers.

Literary playwrights Kinoshita and Hotta belong to the main, political stream of the *shingeki* movement. Playwrights like Tanaka, affiliated with the literary stream of Kishida Kunio and Bungakuza, have also been active. These writers have included Fukuda Tsuneari (b. 1912), known for his 15-volume translation of the works of Shakespeare; and Mishima Yukio (1925–70), whose *Five Modern Nō Plays* (*Kindai Nōgaku Shū*, 1956; tr. 1957) offers modern adaptations of the *nō* classics as eerily effective one-act plays.

Return of the Gods: 1960–85: emergence of the post-shingeki movement When the United States–Japan Mutual Security Treaty came up for renewal in 1960, the limitations of orthodox *shingeki* became painfully apparent to the emerging younger generation. Massive nationwide demonstrations had been organized to oppose renewal of the treaty, which permits the stationing of American military forces on Japanese soil and places Japan under the United States 'nuclear umbrella', and *shingeki* groups had taken an active part in them. When the demonstrations failed to prevent the renewal of the treaty, however, younger members of the movement began to feel that *shingeki* orthodoxy could no more effectively explain what had happened to them than it had been able to explain the war, and this led to a thoroughgoing reassessment of theatrical priorities and

goals that precipitated a countermovement in modern Japanese theatre called the post-*shingeki* movement.

The Youth Art Theatre (Seigei) company provided the transition from orthodox *shingeki* to the post-*shingeki* movement. It had been organized by youthful members of the Mingei troupe in November 1959. The Youth Art Theatre's leading playwright was Fukuda Yoshiyuki (b. 1931), whose early works, including *A Long Row of Tombstones* (*Nagai Bohyō no Retsu*, 1957), were written under the strong influence of Kubo Sakae and Kinoshita Junji. The experience of the 1960 demonstrations, street theatre in a real sense, changed the perspective of Fukuda and other members of the troupe, however, and Seigei began to develop an independent style that rejected proscenium arch realism and the other major tenets of *shingeki* orthodoxy.

Seigei became a spawning ground for many of the writers and actors in the post-*shingeki* movement. Among the playwrights who were in some way connected with the troupe were Betsuyaku Minoru (b. 1937), Kara Jūrō (b. 1940), and Satoh Makoto (b. 1943).

In 1965, Seigei restaged Betsuyaku's 1962 play *The Elephant* (*Zō*, 1962; tr. 1986), which eloquently articulated the new generation's frustration with the passivity of the orthodox movement and their desire to create a newly empowering rationale for action. The play deals with survivors of Hiroshima, but it was understood as a protest against a world in which God or the gods, the ultimate source of legitimacy for any kind of action, were absent.

The dramaturgy of metamorphosis There was a widespread feeling after 1960 that if the past was to be successfully explained and a rationale for future action formulated, the dramatic conventions of a half-century would have to be discarded and some means found to make the gods once again appear on stage. In play after play, the writers of the post-*shingeki* movement engineered epiphanies, moments when gods once again came to populate the Japanese stage. This was their means of escaping the debilitating sense of enforced passivity and stasis they had been experiencing.

The mechanism was apotheosis: ordinary men and women were metamorphosed into gods before the audience's eyes. In 1964, Seigei produced Fukuda Yoshiyuki's *Find Hakamadare!* (*Hakamadare wa Doko Da*, 1964; tr. forthcoming), one of the first plays to clearly employ the dramaturgy of metamorphosis as an empowering theory of action. Based on a 12th-century legend, the play describes how a band of oppressed peasants take their fate into their own hands and become Hakamadare, their long-awaited saviour, when Hakamadare himself turns out to be a rapacious villain.

Kaison the Priest of Hitachi (*Hitachibō Kaison*, 1965; tr. 1973) by Akimoto Matsuyo (b. 1911), a playwright influenced by *shingeki* renegade Miyoshi Jūrō (1902–58), describes the metamorphosis of a young man in the early 1960s into the immortal Kaison, a warrior from the 12th century who is still reputed to wander through north-east Japan doing penance for sins committed centuries ago. Through his metamorphosis the young man escapes from history into mythic time and is saved from the excruciating burden of guilt he carries from his experience as a child during the war. Kara Jūrō's *The Beggar of Love* (*Ai no Kojiki*, 1970; tr. 1970) describes the

Satoh Makoto's *Nezumi Kozō* (*The Rat*).

metamorphosis of oppressed urbanites into their redeemer, an avenging peg-legged sailor named Silver. And Satoh Makoto's *Nezumi Kozō: The Rat* (*Nezumi Kozō Jirokichi*, 1970; tr. 1986) describes the transformation of a rag-tag band of lumpen proletarians into their awaited messiah, a Robin Hood-like figure from the early 19th century named Nezumi Kozō.

A special feature of the post-*shingeki* dramaturgy of metamorphosis is that 'salvation' in each of these plays is virtually indistinguishable from damnation. Apotheosis into Kaison or Silver or Nezumi Kozō means abandoning historical time and responsibility and being sucked back into the maelstrom of eternal redundancy. This restatement of the existential situation of the Japanese, torn between the cruel reality of history and the ambivalent promise of salvation through assimilation to mythic time, has challenged the tragic-humanistic formula of orthodox *shingeki* and has been the major contribution of post-*shingeki* dramaturgy.

This contribution has been accompanied by innovations in stagecraft that break decisively with orthodox *shingeki* practice. Gone is the hegemony of the proscenium stage: two of the post-*shingeki* movement's major troupes, Kara Jūrō's Situation Theatre (Jōkyō Gekijō) and Satoh Makoto's Black Tent Theatre 68/71 (Kuro Tento 68/71), perform in tents. Suzuki Tadashi's SCOT (Suzuki Troupe of Toga), formerly the Waseda Little Theatre (Waseda Shōgekijō), abandoned Tokyo in the late 1970s for Toga village, a mountain retreat eight hours from the city, where the company lives and works together in a manner similar to **Jerzy Grotowski**'s Laboratory Theatre in Wroclaw, Poland, or **Eugenio Barba**'s Odin Teatret in Holstebro, Denmark. SCOT also organizes an international theatre festival each year in Toga. The primacy of the text has been replaced by a renewed emphasis on the creative role of the actor, and Suzuki in particular has made a lasting contribution to actor training by creating a system of exercises that adapts techniques from *nō* and *kabuki*.

These three companies continue to perform today. An additional troupe from a slightly different lineage that contributed to the revolt against *shingeki* orthodoxy was Terayama Shūji's Tenjō Sajiki, which collapsed after Terayama's death in 1983. Terayama, who was born in 1935 in Aomori prefecture in north-eastern Japan, was deeply influenced by the French avant-garde, particularly Antonin Artaud and Lautréamont; and his first dramatic work, *Blood Sleeps Standing Up*

(*Chi wa Tatta Mama Nemutte Iru*, 1960), was produced by the Four Seasons (Shiki) company headed by Asari Keita, which gained fame in the 1950s for its productions of playwrights like **Giraudoux** and **Anouilh**. (Shiki is today a multimillion dollar enterprise specializing in the production of musicals like *Jesus Christ Superstar* and *Cats*.) The multitalented Terayama, who was also a renowned poet, essayist, and director, was a true scion of the European avant-garde. His principal aim was to shock the bourgeoisie, and he succeeded in this with happenings, street theatre, multimedia events, and themes ranging from incest to transvestitism.

Recent developments In recent years, the post-*shingeki* movement has achieved legitimacy and recognition. Orthodox *shingeki* troupes have accepted their work, and a still younger generation has emerged for whom the innovations of the post-*shingeki* movement have become conventions. Important younger playwright-directors include Tsuka Kōhei (b. 1948), Takeuchi Jūichirō (b. 1947), Yamazaki Tetsu (b. 1947), and Noda Hideki (b. 1955).   DGG

(a) Ancient and traditional
Bugaku: M. Togi, *Gagaku: Court Music and Dance*, Tokyo, Weatherhill/Tankosha, 1971; C. Wolz, *Bugaku: Japanese Court Dance*, Providence, R.I.: Asian Music Publications, 1971. *Nō*: D. Keene, *Nō: The Classical Theatre of Japan*, Palo Alto, Calif.: Kodansha, 1966; K. Komparu, *The Noh Theatre: Principles and Perspectives*, Tokyo, Weatherhill, 1983; *Japanese Noh Drama*, Rutland, Vermont: Charles E. Tuttle, 1955. *Kyōgen*: Richard N. McKinnon, *Selected Plays of Kyogen*, Tokyo, Uniprint, 1968; Shio Sakanishi, *Japanese Folk Plays: The Ink-Smeared Lady and Other Kyogen*, Rutland, Vermont: Charles E. Tuttle, 1960. *Kabuki*: J. R. Brandon, ed., *Chūshingura: Studies in Kabuki and the Puppet Theatre*, Honolulu, University of Hawaii Press, 1982 and trans., *Kabuki: Five Classic Plays*, Cambridge, Mass.: Harvard University Press, 1975; Earle Ernst, *The Kabuki Theatre*, Honolulu, University of Hawaii Press, 1974; Masakatsu Gunji, *Kabuki*, Palo Alto, Calif.: Kodansha, 1970. *Bunraku*: B. Adachi, *The Voices and Hands of Bunraku*, Tokyo, Kodansha, 1978; D. Keene, *Major Plays of Chikamatsu*, New York, Columbia University Press, 1961.   JRB
(b) Modern Japanese theatre
D. G. Goodman, ed. and tr., *After Apocalypse: Four Japanese Plays of Hiroshima and Nagasaki*, New York, Columbia University Press, 1986; and D. G. Goodman, ed. and tr., *The Return of the Gods: Japanese Drama in the 1960s*, forthcoming; A. Horie-Webber, 'Modernisation of the Japanese Theatre: The Shingeki Movement', in W. G. Beasley, ed., *Modern Japan: Aspects of History, Literature, and Society*, Berkeley, University of California Press, 1977; Kubo Sakae, *Land of Volcanic Ash*, tr. D. G. Goodman, Ithaca, NY: Cornell East Asian Papers, 1986; B. Powell, 'Japan's First Modern Theatre – The Tsukiji Shōgekijō and Its Company, 1924–1926', *Monumenta Nipponica* (1975), 30(1):69–85;'Shingeki Under the Occupation' in *The Occupation of Japan*, MacArthur Memorial, forthcoming; J. T. Rimer, *Toward a Modern Japanese Theatre*, Princeton, Princeton University Press, 1974.

Japanese stage designers The stage designer emerged as an identifiable member of the production staff in Japanese theatre only in the mid-1920s. The first and most influential Japanese stage designer was Itō Kisaku (1899–1967). Brother of dancer Itō Michio and director

Senda Koreya, Itō made his debut at the Tsukiji Little Theatre in 1925 with a modernistic set for *Julius Caesar*. He was strongly influenced by the work of **Edward Gordon Craig** and **Adolphe Appia** but turned to more realistic designs in the 1930s. His realistic set for *Yoakemae (Before the Dawn*, 1934), an adaptation of a novel by Shimazaki Tōson, was perhaps his greatest pre-war achievement. After the war, Itō returned to designing more abstract sets. His suggestive design for Kinoshita Junji's *Twilight Crane (Yūzuru*, 1949) is justly famous.

Itō influenced Kanamori Kaoru (1933–80), Takada Ichirō (b. 1929), and Asakura Setsu (b. 1922), three of the most prominent post-war stage designers. Kanamori, who died prematurely of cancer at the age of 47, designed many productions of modern French drama for the Shiki troupe. He is remembered for introducing new materials like steel and glass into his abstract sets for productions of works by **Giraudoux** and **Anouilh**. Kanamori's sets for commercial productions like *Jesus Christ Superstar* and *The Elephant Man* also attracted widespread attention.

Takada and Asakura are among the most active designers working today. Takada is professor of design at Musashino University of Art in Tokyo, and Asakura is a professor at the Kuwasawa Institute of Design. Takada's work has been primarily in orthodox shingeki productions. His two-storey set for Tanaka Chikao's *The Head of Mary (Maria no Kubi*, 1959) is representative of his style.

Asakura, by contrast, has been working with directors like Ninagawa Yukio, who emerged from the post-*shingeki* movement and who has stressed spectacle in his work. Asakura's mammoth two-storey set complete with miniature lake for the 1981 production of Kara Jūrō's *Shitaya Mannen-chō Monogatari*, directed by Ninagawa, is typical of her recent work.

Hirano Kōga (b. 1938) is best known as a book designer, but his stage designs for the Black Tent Theatre 68/71 have innovatively exploited the potential of the tent theatre while avoiding aesthetic compromise. Hirano's design for the 1980 production of *Saiyūki (Journey to the West*) was representative.

Finally, architect Isozaki Arata's work with director Suzuki Tadashi should be noted. Using concrete and aluminium, Isozaki (b. 1931) helped convert a traditional farm house in the remote village of Toga in Toyama prefecture into a theatre for the Suzuki Troupe of Toga (SCOT). Inspired by the clean, ritual space of the **nō** stage, the Toga theatre successfully blends contemporary and traditional Japanese architecture and creates a unique theatre space.   DGG

Jardiel Poncela, Enrique (1901–52) Spanish novelist and journalist who later turned to the theatre with great success, writing more than 40 comic plays whose combination of word-play and absurd situations were intended to parody the trivial normality of the Spanish theatre. Among his successes were *Eloisa está debajo de un almendro (Eloisa is Under an Almond Tree*, 1940), *Los ladrones somos gente honrada (We Thieves Are Decent Folk*, 1942) and *Los habitantes de la casa deshabitada (The Inhabitants of the Uninhabited House*, 1944). His complete works were published in 1958.   CL

Jarrett, Henry C. (1828–1903) American theatre manager. His career began in 1851 when he purchased

the Baltimore Museum. At various times, Jarrett managed several major theatres in the USA, including Washington's **National Theatre**, the Brooklyn Academy of Music, and **Niblo's Garden**. When **Edwin Booth** lost his Theatre in 1874, Jarrett joined with Henry David Palmer (d. 1879) to manage **Booth's Theatre** until 1877. **Jarrett** and Palmer also produced the popular musical fantasy *The Black Crook* at Niblo's Garden in 1866 and in 1875–6, they mounted a spectacular production of *Julius Caesar* at Booth's Theatre with **Lawrence Barrett** as Cassius and **E. L. Davenport** as Brutus.   DJW

Jarry, Alfred (1873–1907) French author and dramatist, the creator of King Ubu, a grotesque, puppet-like figure who embodies every mean, destructive ignoble quality. Ubu started life as a schoolboy send-up of Jarry's physics teacher at his school in Rennes; but he rapidly became a character in his own right, first in puppet performances given by Jarry and his friends, then, in 1896 in a performance by **Firmin Gémier**, directed by **Lugné-Poe** with costumes, masks and scenery by Jarry, Bonnard, Vuillard and Toulouse-Lautrec. The play's two performances caused a legendary stir in literary circles. Jarry wrote three other Ubu plays, as well as an *Almanach du Père Ubu* and associated writings, but none of them matched the brutal simplicity of *Ubu Roi*. This Shakespearian parody, in which a lazy 'little man' is goaded by his wife into terrible acts of violence, had a prophetic quality. Ubu is quite without scruples because he thinks only of his own satisfaction. But he is also devoid of imagination: *merdre* (shite), the scandalously famous first word of the play, sums up Ubu's philosophy. Jarry's stagecraft was simple and inventive, challenging the sacred cows of both naturalists and symbolists. Jarry drank himself to death at the age of 34 but his work was championed by the surrealists and finally achieved 'classic' status in the 1950s, when the theatre of the absurd adopted similar techniques and characters.   DB

Jatra (India) This is easily the most popular form of theatre in the rural areas of Bengal and among the Bengali-speaking people of eastern Bihar, Orissa, Assam and Tripura. It also holds sway over the villages of Bangladesh (formerly East Bengal before the partition of India in 1947). Versions of the form have been created in Oriyan and will be discussed later.

Jatra means procession. It may have come into existence in the 16th century as a part of the Vaishnava devotional movement introduced by Chaitanya, which swept the population into its fold through songs, dances and plays designed to propagate the faith. The earliest extant plays (*palas*) in Bengali date from the late 18th century, with the advent of the British presence in the state. Prior to that the plays were preserved as a part of the oral tradition of the region.

Up to the early 19th century, *Jatra* was primarily focused on religious themes and was instructive and moralistic in tone. The companies of actors were owned and managed by the chief singer or actor. Then, in the early to mid-19th century, amateurs, mostly the sons of the bourgeois of Calcutta, developed their own *Jatra* groups and chose secular themes for their subject matter rather than the traditional religious fare. This led the older companies to adapt the secular stories and resulted in a serious decline in the moral character of the stories and the companies, as well. With the advent of the modern theatre movement in the mid-19th century, the *Jatra* borrowed the scenic displays of the proscenium arch stage and imitated the Western style of acting and writing that was beginning to be popular among the middle- and upper-class citizens of Calcutta. *Jatra* fell out of favour with the urban audiences because of its music, tone and style which were viewed as old fashioned and corrupt and it did not return to favour in urban areas until well after independence in 1947 when the Communist Party employed it to win sympathetic support for its cause. Throughout the period from the late 19th to the mid-20th century, *Jatra* remained a rural art form.

Jatra companies are generally professional itinerant concerns that have an organizational structure and mechanism for booking their shows throughout the Bengali-speaking regions of India. Around 20 major troupes operate from their central heaquarters in Calcutta. There, an agent books shows over the telephone confirming engagements in the tea estates of Assam, in the steel towns and coal mining centres of the northeast or anywhere along the way that a group can afford to pay for the services of a *Jatra* company. Troupes are dispatched to a locale for a flat fee, including food, shelter and miscellaneous items. Bookings are arranged to make the maximum use of the tour route, playing shows at different locations along the way between major stops. Actors are hired by the company manager by the season, written contracts protect the interests of both parties and wages are paid according to a scale. The more important characters and the star performers receive the highest wages, which are handsome by comparison with Indian standards. Comedians and vocalists are paid somewhat less but are considerably better than the fledgeling apprentices who provide little more than manual labour.

The owner–managers of the companies are not normally artists themselves but entrepreneurs who take a large share of the profits and consider their investment a profitable business. In the early history of Jatra, actor–managers ran the companies and exercised greater artistic control over the final product. Today's owner–managers have little motive other than to please the public no matter what the artistic consequences.

Generally, the actors come from the lower strata of society. Many of them run away from their village homes to join companies at an early age because they fall in love with the romance of fame, fortune and travel. Boys aged 11 and 12 who join *Jatra* companies are put through rigorous training by the older actors to teach them to sing, dance and act in the *Jatra* style. Frailer youths eventually train to play the female characters and those with powerful voices and strong bodies act the heroes and villains. Actors with a natural sense of humour become the comedians.

The *Jatra* begins in earnest in September, at the end of the monsoon, and extends to late May or early June when the heavy rains return. A lucrative time for *Jatra* in the Bengali villages coincides with the major religious festivals, such as *Durga Puja* in late September and early October, *Kali Puja* three weeks later, *Ratha Jatra* and *Manasa Puja*, both later in the year. The marriage of a daughter, the birth of a son, the winning of a lawsuit – these, too, serve as an occasion of rejoicing and reason for sponsoring a *Jatra* performance by a family or wealthy village merchant or headman.

Jatra is highly melodramatic in character, with a liberal dose of songs and dramatic scenes. The actors are essentially adept at vocal projection and often play to many thousands of patrons out of doors without the aid of microphones. Among the more interesting of the old Jatra characters is the Conscience (*bibek*) who is an allegorical figure that moves in and out of the action, commenting on its meaning and foretelling the consequences of evil deeds. The character of Fate (*niyati*), like that of the Conscience, comments on the action and warns characters of potential dangers. Traditionally, this character is depicted by a female.

The acting area (*asar*) is usually on the ground level, covered with cloth mats (*durries*) or carpets and bounded by short bamboo poles linked together by string. In many places a low, square wooden platform is used. The platform is connected to the dressing room by a rampway marked by bamboo posts or made of wood built in the shape of a ramp. The ramp serves as an extension of the acting area and is used for dramatic effects, similar to that of the *hanamichi* of the **kabuki** theatres of Japan.

The audience enfolds the whole acting area creating a sense of intimacy in the playing, even when thousands of spectators gather on the ground or sit on chairs, stand on the verandas of nearby houses or hang from the boughs of trees to watch. Women usually sit separately from the men.

The dressing room (*shaj ghor*) is a small area bounded on four sides by canvas walls and sometimes covered with a temporary roof. Major actors sit on top of their costume trunks in a prescribed order of importance and put on their makeup, chew *pan* (a special leaf and alum preparation popular in India) or smoke cigarettes in anticipation of their entrances.

The scenes follow one after another, punctuated by songs which separate them into acts. The acting area is regarded as a neutral space to which meaning is assigned depending on the play's action. Scenery is not necessary and, indeed, intrudes on the event. Although experiments with scenery were undertaken in the 19th century in imitation of Western theatre practices, ultimately they failed. Today, *Jatra* continues the practice of using a neutral acting area for its performances, even when it is performed in proscenium theatres in urban areas.

Jatra music is provided by a *pakhwaj* drum, a harmonium, a violin, a clarinet or flute and bell-metal cymbals. The musicians normally sit at one side of the acting area so that they have a full view of the stage, the ramp and the dressing room. Normally, a prompter sits with them, following the action in the script.

The show begins with a musical concert which continues for an hour or two before the dramatic action starts. The concert is divided into two parts. In part one, evening melodies (*ragas*) are played. Part two emphasizes faster pace rhythms and virtuoso drumming. The concert helps to attract spectators to the playing area, as much as it does to entertain those who have already gathered there. Mood music is inserted throughout a performance to accentuate a bit of dramatic business, to heighten the melodramatic sentiments of a scene or to underscore a character's emotional state.

The performance space is lit by a variety of means, ranging from simple oil torches in remote villages, to petromax pressure lamps, electric bulbs and even fluorescent lights in areas where there is access to better equipment. No attempt is made to vary the intensity of the illumination or to control the colour.

A chair is the only furniture found on stage. Like the stage itself, it is regarded as a neutral object until it is endowed with meaning. It may serve as a throne, a bed, the steps of a temple, the shrine itself, whatever is demanded by the action.

In the early 1960s, *Jatra* underwent something of a revival among the middle classes of Calcutta. Before that time, it had been regarded as 'folksy' and not worth the attention of serious theatre patrons. In 1961, a *Jatra* festival was held in the palace courtyard of the Shabhabazar Rajas in north Calcutta. It was a great success and has been repeated yearly with renewed acclaim.

Periodicals and newspapers devote space to *Jatra*. *Jatra* scripts may be found in paperback editions in little stalls and shops along the streets of Calcutta. And in 1968 Phanibhusan Bidyabinod became the first *Jatra* artist honoured by the Sangeet Natak Akademi in New Delhi for his services to the art.

The Communist Party made use of *Jatra*, as it did with other popular forms of rural theatre elsewhere in India, to propagate its political messages. In the 1930s and 1940s, plays were written in the *Jatra* style and artists were recruited to the Communist cause. Since that time, artists have taken a neutral political position so they please the widest possible audience base. In their headquarters, it is not uncommon to find pictures of Communist Party leaders at home and abroad alongside those of popular Western politicians and Indian and Western religious leaders and prophets. In recent years, the form has served as the model for various contemporary stage directors, actors and playwrights who have experimented with the application of contemporary social issues through the adaptation of the form.

The *Jatra* of Bengal was introduced to the state of Orissa in the 19th century and quickly became popular in the rural areas. It is similar to the Bengali version in most respects. However, the parties of actors prefer to use the words Opera and *Natya* to describe their work rather than the term *Jatra*.

The acting area is a low temporary wooden platform surrounded by spectators. An entrance and exit passageway, literally the 'flower way' (*puspa patha*), connects the dressing room (*vesha ghara*) with the stage. The flower path is also used for acting various scenes. Entrances and exits are sometimes forged through the spectators at different sides of the acting area to achieve special dramatic effects. A simple chair generally serves as a neutral property used to suggest a throne, a cot, a tree, a hiding place or even a weapon. Other hand props are carried on and off the stage by the actors. Like the *Jatra* of Bengal the whole platform stage is a neutral acting area, bare of scenery, endowed with meaning through the songs and dialogues of the characters.

Plays were written in the style of the Bengali *Jatra* but instead of Bengali, the Oriyan language was used as a medium of expression. The plays range from farces to mythological and semi-historical tales. During the independence movement from the early 20th century up to 1947, *Jatra* companies in Orissa launched veiled attacks on their British rulers. Like the Bengali *Jatra*, the Oriyan works emphasized virtuous upright characters pitted against villains and blackguards. Comic scenes add variety and spice to an all-night performance sustaining the interest of the audience.   FaR

Jeffersons, The A famous Anglo-American acting family, traced back to **Thomas Jefferson** (1732–1807), an actor with **Garrick** and for a time manager of various provincial English theatres. One of his children, **Joseph Jefferson I** (1774–1832), went to America in 1795 and remained there. He became a favourite at the **John Street** and **Park Theatres** in New York, although somewhat overshadowed by **Hodgkinson**. In 1803 he moved to the **Chestnut Street Theatre** in Philadelphia, remaining there until 1830. Most of his children worked in the theatre, including **Joseph Jefferson II** (1804–42), who succeeded far more as a scene painter than an actor. His marriage to the actress Cornelia Thomas in 1826 made him the step-father of actor Charles Burke (1822–54).

The greatest of the Jeffersons, however, was **Joseph Jefferson III** (1829–1905), who first appeared on the stage at the age of four, in support of **T. D. Rice**. He toured with his family, winning some fame by the mid-century and visiting Europe in 1856. He then joined **Laura Keene**'s company, winning approval with such roles as Dr Pangloss in the younger **Colman**'s *The Heir-at-Law*. He spent some time at the **Winter Garden Theatre** in New York, toured Australia for four years, and in London in 1865 first performed the role for which he was most noted, Rip Van Winkle, dramatized for him by **Dion Boucicault**. In this role, Jefferson's dignity and sympathetic personality soon won him popular and critical acclaim. Of him, the critic **William Winter** said: 'The magical charm of his acting was the deep human sympathy and the liveliness and individuality by which it was irradiated – an exquisite blending of humour, pathos, grace and beauty. . . '

Jefferson also succeeded as Bob Acres in *The Rivals*, Caleb Plummer in *Dot*, and Salem Scudder in *The Octoroon; or, Life in Louisiana*. In 1893 he succeeded **Edwin Booth** as President of the Players Club. His autobiography, published in 1890, indicates much of Jefferson's warmth and humanity.

Of his children, four went on the stage, the most successful being **Charles Burke Jefferson** (1851–1908), who served for a time as his father's manager.   SMA

Jellicoe, Anne (1927–) British dramatist and director, whose first full-length play, *The Sport of My Mad Mother* (1956), came joint third in a playwriting competition organized by the *Observer* newspaper and was subsequently staged at the **Royal Court Theatre**. Its speech rhythms, defiantly non-literary, were based on listening to young teenagers at play and the 'mad mother' of the title was Kali, the Hindu goddess. Jellicoe, who trained at the Central School of Speech and Drama, was a pioneer of community theatre in Britain and sought to release in her casts impulses towards drama which might be otherwise confined by formal texts. Her first successful plays, however, were conventionally written, notably *The Knack* (1961), contrasting two young men, one who has the knack of attracting women, the other who has not. *Shelley* (1965) was a clear, almost documentary account of the poet's life. In contrast, *The Rising Generation* (1967), originally written for but not performed by the Girl Guides' Association, was conceived in a spirit of orgiastic feminism. She was a founder-director of the Cockpit Theatre Club in 1950 and the literary manager of the Royal Court from 1973 to 1975. She founded the Colway Theatre Trust in Dorset in 1979 to stage community plays in village areas and West Country towns, but resigned as its Director in 1985 as a protest against grant cuts.   JE

Jerome, Jerome K[lapka] (1859–1927) English playwright, novelist and journalist, remembered for the comic idyll *Three Men in a Boat* (1889). He was the author of several comedies and farces, two of the best, *The Prude's Progress* (1895) and *The MacHaggis* (1897) written in collaboration with Eden Phillpotts, in which pleasingly credible characters are asked to cope with pleasantly incredible situations. Of his social dramas, none has survived, though *The Passing of the Third Floor Back* (1908) gave **Johnston Forbes-Robertson** a famous part as the Christlike stranger whose presence in a Bloomsbury boarding-house transforms the lives of his fellow-lodgers. Jerome's early experience as an actor is amusingly embroidered in *On the Stage – and Off* (1885) and the stock characters of 19th-century melodrama are wittily anatomized in *Stage-Land* (1890).   PT

Jerrold, Douglas William (1803–57) English playwright and journalist, who was the leading contributor to *Punch* from its foundation in 1841 until his death. Jerrold was the son of an actor and the author of some 70 plays, many of them betraying his humane concern for the poor and oppressed in an uncaring society. He took more care over his comic and satiric sketches for *Punch*, of which the serial *Mrs Caudle's Curtain Lectures* is an outstanding example, than over his plays, but several are worthy of revival. A representative collection, published in 1854, contains one embarrassingly sentimental piece, *The Painter of Ghent* (1836), five charming comedies, *Nell Gwynne; or, The Prologue* (1833), *The Housekeeper* (1833), *The Wedding Gown* (1834), *The Schoolfellows* (1835) and *Doves in a Cage* (1835), a domestic drama which approaches its grim subject with unfamiliar glimpses of realism, *The Rent Day* (1832), and the incomparably ebullient nautical melodrama, *Black-Eyed Susan* (1829). The addition of another domestic drama, *The Factory Girl* (1832), would provide a fair basis for assessment of Jerrold's dramatic output.   PT

Jessner, Leopold (1878–1945) German director. One of the early exponents of naturalism, who later made his name by replacing representational scenery with multiple acting levels arranged in ascending steps on a bare stage (*Jessnertreppe*). These facilitated symbolic rhythms that reinforced the dramatic action. He transformed **Schiller**'s *Wilhelm Tell* and **Shakespeare**'s *Richard III* into key examples of expressionism in 1919 and 1920, using a selection of single colours and lighting to represent different moods, and developing a rhetorical acting style, in which exaggerated gesture and facial masking were designed to project inner vision.   CI

Jesuitendrama Drama performed at Jesuit colleges throughout Europe, but associated generally with colleges in Bavaria and Austria. It was performed from approximately the mid-16th century through to the mid-18th century. The purpose of these dramas was to educate the student-performers in the art of speaking and rhetoric and to instil in both audiences and actors a belief in the values of the Catholic Church, as propagated by the Society of Jesus after the Counter-Reformation. Initially the plays were in Latin, but in the course of the 17th century, performance in the German vernacular became increasingly common. Jesuit drama demonstrated an increasing tendency toward spectacular and musical embellishment; in this regard, it has been considered as a forerunner to the tradition of spectacular opera, which became established in several Austrian and southern German cities in the latter part of the 17th century. The most notable writers of Jesuit drama were Nikolaus Avancini (1611–86), an Austrian Jesuit of noble birth, and Jakob Bidermann (1578–1639), whose *Cenodoxus* (1609), written initially in Latin, might stand revival today. (See also **University** (Jesuit) **drama**.)   SW

Jewish Art Theatre, The A company closely modelled on **Stanislavsky**'s **Moscow Art Theatre**, set up by **Jacob Ben-Ami** in 1919 at the New York Garden Theatre, with **Emanuel Reicher**, associate of **Reinhardt** and a founder of the German **Freie Bühne**, as Play Director. Rave reviews greeted **Peretz Hirshbein**'s *The Haunted Inn* and *Green Fields*, with Ben-Ami scoring a personal triumph in both. In spite of further successes including **David Pinski**'s *The Dumb Messiah*, **Ossip Dimov**'s *Bronx Express* and **Tolstoi**'s *The Power of Darkness*, internal dissension brought the venture, which had reached probably the high point of Yiddish theatre, to a close after two seasons and 14 productions.   AB

Jewish theatre see **Yiddish theatre**; **Hebrew theatre**

Jig The Elizabethan jig, which was a popular item in the public theatres of London, developed from the song-and-dance acts of an older folk tradition and gained its name from the type of dance best known to its audiences. It was an inclusive term, used to describe a broadside ballad (danced as well as sung), a short satirical scene with music and rhyme and, most frequently, a broad and often bawdy farce in which doggerel and dance played a prominent part, and in which a clown was the central figure. The first great exponent of the theatrical jig was **Richard Tarlton**, and it was his example that provided the model for later clowns, of whom **William Kempe** is the most notable. As an afterpiece, the jig was, for a while, the necessary conclusion to an afternoon performance. Kempe's unexplained resignation from the **Lord Chamberlain's Men** in c. 1599 has led to speculation that **Shakespeare** and his colleagues downgraded the jig, but Richard Knolles noted the continuing demand for a jig at the end of a tragedy in 1606, and the disorderly crowds that attended the **Fortune** for the jig only led, in 1612, to an Order 'for the suppressing of jigs at the end of plays'. The subsequent history of the theatrical jig is obscure, but it retained its popularity in fairgrounds and among strolling players until well into the 18th century.   PT

Jingxi Drama of the Chinese capital i.e. Beijing. Also known as *jingju*. Before 1949 it was designated *guoxi*, national drama. Loosely named Beijing Opera in English it is more specifically known as *pihuang* drama in Chinese theatre circles. This is a telescoping of *xipi* and *erhuang*, two musical styles with a complex history and controversial origin, quite likely in Hubei and Jiangxi respectively. Both styles have been freely adapted in other regional areas and they constitute the musical basis of the *jingxi*. In 1790 Anhui troupes visiting Beijing for the Qianlong Emperor's birthday celebrations staged innovatory performances incorporating the *pihuang* modes. They made a great impact and a new style was born. By the early 19th century *jingxi* dominated the Beijing stage and eventually usurped the national popularity of **kunqu**. Brought to maturity in the venue of the stage connoisseurs, enthusiastically patronized by the Court, it was essentially an urban entertainment. Flourishing along an axis defined by the traditional bastion of Beijing and the westernized sophistication of Shanghai it achieved more than regional popularity and its actors a national following. Until 1949 it remained the adored entertainment of a vast segment of the ordinary Chinese public dominating all other traditional styles. Accepted as the national form of dramatic expression it achieved international recognition when a Beijing troupe led by **Mei Lanfang** toured America in 1930.

The great success of the *jingxi* was due in part to a style which was neither too complicated nor precious by prevailing dramatic standards. Literary and musical content were easily memorized and touched the collective unconscious. The plays were derived from the historical epics and romantic novels of China's past familiar to everybody. The musical content is limited and repetitive in form serving a strictly theatrical function. Before 1949 the orchestra was seated downstage left, the playing being aurally and visually integrated with the placing and timing of the actors. The two principal styles are the prototypes for a prescribed number of metrical arrangements defined in terms of the accented and unaccented beat within the measure. The theatre musician requires no printed notation reacting instinctively to a particular rhythmic combination designated by its beat structure. The leader of the orchestra uses a pair of wooden clappers manipulated rather like castanets and a hardwood drum with a skin head to beat out the measures. Singing is accompanied by a bowed two-stringed instrument, *huqin*, which has a florid, rippling line. The bowing is characterized by *vibrato* and *glissando* effects. Brass gongs and cymbals are used to mark entries, exits and emotional climaxes in the song and action of a play. They are particularly evident in the combat scenes, acrobatics and dance passages which are integral to all *jingxi* performance. Singing is used to indicate human emotions and psychological reactions as they are melodramatically accentuated by musical rhythms conveying mood. Each role category is vocally identified by specific qualities of pitch, volume and enunciation. Rhyme patterns are created from a system of 13-character groupings which provide a compositional key for the dramatist. The rhyme sounds themselves contain elements from the dialects of Anhui, Sichuan and Hubei in the interests of euphony and intensity of dramatic speech. Stanzas of four lines rhyming alternately are standard practice whether in monologue or dialogue. The opening two lines are often recited in monotone with the third rising to a long drawn out utterance of the final syllable and the fourth taken smoothly or else given briskly indicating further action to follow. Rhyme and melismatic effects serve a vital euphonic function in vocalization.

After the establishment of the People's Republic in 1949 *jingxi* was reformed along the lines directed by the Chinese Communist Party. During the Cultural Revolution (1966–76), all items were forbidden performance, except a few 'models'. It has revived today and is once more being staged in its integrity. Though unrealistic to assume it can regain the old following, an honourable place in China's traditional arts seems assured.   ACS

Jodelet (Julien Bedeau) (c. 1590–1660) Celebrated French comedian who adopted the floured face traditionally asociated with farce. First heard of with a provincial touring company in 1603, he had graduated to the **Marais** by 1634 before being transferred with other members of **Montdory**'s company to the **Hôtel de Bourgogne** at the king's behest towards the end of that year. Later he spent a further period of approximately 16 years at the Marais, playing Cliton in **Corneille**'s *Le Menteur* (*The Liar*, 1643) and the eponymous lead in several farces written especially for him, notably *Jodelet, ou le Maître-Valet* (*Jodelet, or the Master-Servant*, 1645) by **Scarron** and *Jodelet Prince* (1655) by **Thomas Corneille**. Capitalizing on his naturally comic appearance, with a large mouth, long snout-like nose and bushy eyebrows, he had only to walk on stage to provoke gales of laughter which his nasal speaking voice then served to redouble. **Molière**, doubtless intent on securing the collaboration or neutralizing the competition of a rival comedian who was already the favourite of Paris audiences, persuaded Jodelet to join his company soon after their arrival in the capital in 1658 and wrote for him the part of the Vicomte de Jodelet opposite his own Marquis de Mascarille in *Les Précieuses Ridicules* (*The Affected Ladies*, 1659). Similarly the title role in *Sganarelle, ou le Cocu Imaginare* (*Sganarelle, or the Imaginary Cuckold*, 1660) might well have been played by Jodelet, had it not been for his death. His brother François (?–1663), also an actor under the name of L'Espy, remained a close companion throughout his career.   DR

Jodelle, Etienne (1532–73) French dramatist and poet of the Pléiade group, who is of greater interest as pioneer of an indigenous literary drama of classical inspiration than for the indifferent quality of his achievement. Only three plays of his are extant, two of them – the tragedy *Cléopâtre Captive* and the comedy *Eugène* – dating from 1552 when they were performed before Henri II by the young Jodelle and his friends, and a further tragedy entitled *Didon Se Sacrifiant* (*Dido Sacrificing Herself*) from 1558. Both tragedies are excessively literary in the Senecan manner, with no development of character, little action and lengthy soliloquizing and narration of events and are more acceptable as lyric verse than as writing for the stage.

A prologue to *Eugène* vaunts it as an original work which has turned its back on medieval forms and accommodated the classical dramatic tradition to present-day taste and expectations. In fact its subject – adultery and the complaisant cuckoldry of a stupid husband – owes much to medieval farce and the play is at its best when commenting with satirical verve on aspects of contemporary life.   DR

Joffré, Sara (1935–) Peruvian playwright and director. After travel and study abroad, she returned to Lima to found Homero, Teatro de Grillos (Homer, Cricket Theatre) in 1963. Author and director of six published one-act plays for adults, Joffré is primarily known for her work with children's theatre in Peru.   GW

John F. Kennedy Center for the Performing Arts 1701 Pennsylvania Ave, Washington DC [Architect: Edward Durrell Stone]. A national cultural centre had been created by law in 1958 under the presidency of Dwight D. Eisenhower, but did not get started until it was deemed a fitting monument to the assassinated president, John F. Kennedy. It opened in 1971 on the banks of the Potomac and encompassed three theatres: the Eisenhower with 1,140 seats for dramatic presentations, the Concert Hall with 2,670 seats and the Opera House with 2,200 seats. The entire complex has been guided since its inception by **Roger Stevens**, president of the Centre since 1961. In 1978, a fourth theatre was added, the Studio Playhouse, on the roof terrace level, and seats 500 for films, dance concerts, experimental productions and children's theatre. Some productions originate at the Centre, but many others are booked in.   MCH

John Golden Theatre 252 West 45th St, New York City [Architect: Herbert J. Krapp]. In 1927, as part of their chain, the Chanin construction interests built the Theatre Masque with only 800 seats and intended it for the presentation of intimate or experimental plays which may not have been able to survive on Broadway at the time. Unfortunately, the playhouse was destined to pass from their control in the early 1930s. In 1934, the **Shuberts** bought it and promptly leased it to producer John Golden, who assigned his own name to the theatre. It is considered ideal for one-person and small cast plays and such performers as Victor Borge, Yves Montand, **Comden** and **Green**, **Nichols** and May, Bob and Ray, **Cornelia Otis Skinner** and **Emlyn Williams** have presented shows of their own creation on its stage. In 1956, **Samuel Beckett's** *Waiting for Godot* appeared at the Golden, marking the first (and only) time a Beckett play has appeared on Broadway. Apart from two years when it was leased as a movie theatre, the playhouse has seldom been closed. It remains a Shubert house.   MCH

John Street Theatre 15–21 John Street, New York City. The third and most substantial theatre to be built in New York by **David Douglass**, the playhouse in John Street served the city until 1798, when it was replaced by a new theatre afterward known as the **Park**. There were three periods in the John Street's history. The first, prior to the Revolution, consisted of two long seasons beginning in 1767; the second com-

menced in 1777, when the British troops took it over, renamed it the Theatre Royal and presented plays as an antidote to tedium in their long occupation; and the last and most important period began in the summer of 1785 with the return of **Lewis Hallam** the younger, who began with 'entertainments', which blossomed into full-scale productions. Hallam established a permanent resident company and was joined by actor **John Henry** in its management, but both were replaced by **John Hodgkinson** and **William Dunlap** in its final years.

No iconography exists of the John Street. William Dunlap described it as 'principally of wood, an unsightly object, painted red'. It contained two tiers of boxes, a pit and a gallery with dressing rooms and a greenroom located in a shed nearby. A description of the interior was included in **Royall Tyler**'s *The Contrast* (1787), which premiered at the theatre. When it was closed, it was annexed to a feed-and-grain store next door.   MCH

Johnson, J. Rosamond see **Cole, Bob**

Johnson, Dr Samuel (1709–84) Having known **Garrick** in Lichfield, he walked with him to London in 1737. In 1746 he began work on the *Dictionary*. He was invited by Garrick to write the prologue for the opening of Garrick's management of **Drury Lane** in 1747 and formulated Garrick's managerial policy in the couplet 'The Drama's laws the Drama's patrons give,/ For we that live to please must please to live.' His only play, *Irene*, was produced by Garrick in 1749. Much of it had been written before he came to London; a sterile tragedy it survived for nine nights through Garrick's advocacy. In 1756 Johnson published his proposals for an edition of **Shakespeare**. The edition, published in 1765, contains his remarkable preface as well as notes of acute critical perception, if vulnerable scholarship. Many of his *Lives of the Poets* (1779–81) are studies of dramatists, written with great sensitivity.   PH

Johnston, (William) Denis (1901–84) Irish playwright of a well-to-do Dublin family, Johnston had a remarkably varied career: barrister, actor, warcorrespondent, pre- and post-war producer for BBC radio and television, critic, teacher. His *Nine Rivers from Jordan* (1953) is an impressionistic account of his wartime experiences. *In Search of Swift* (1959) is a controversial examination of Swift's relationship with Stella and Vanessa. *The Brazen Horn* (1977) speculates around a personal mystical philosophy.

Johnston's first play, rejected by the **Abbey** (hence its title, *The Old Lady Says 'No!'*, 1929), is a sparkling expressionist satire of Ireland after independence, superbly produced by the **Gate** at the Peacock. Johnston followed it with *The Moon in the Yellow River* (1931), a wryly tragic version of the same theme, realist in manner. Of his subsequent plays, only two use expressionist techniques, *A Bride for the Unicorn* (1933), a modernized Morality, and *The Dreaming Dust* (1940), in which seven actors from a Masque of the Seven Deadly Sins explore the enigmas of Swift's life. His other plays include two intelligent *pièces à thèse*, *The Golden Cuckoo* (1939) and *Strange Occurrence on Ireland's Eye* (1956). Based on law cases, they subject the law's inadequacies to witty and searching scrutiny. Johnston's last play, *The Scythe and the Sunset* (1958), is a treatment of the Easter Rising, blending farce and tragedy, as its title suggests, a counterpart to **O'Casey**. It illustrates again Johnston's ability to push realist theatre beyond its normal boundaries, ranging from prose to economically deployed verse.

Until recently, Johnston's work was undervalued, partly because of a maverick quality that resisted categories. His plays command both traditional and very independently experimental forms. They mix prose and verse, combine human scepticism with a visionary consciousness, salute and deride the mythology of the new Ireland. Though a relatively small body of work – Johnston was an inveterate reviser – Johnston's theatre is now rightly judged in the company of **Synge** and O'Casey. Indeed, although not to **Yeats**'s taste, it almost epitomizes Yeats's declared aims for an Irish drama.   DM

Jolly, George (*fl.* ?1630–73) English actor-manager. He started acting before the Civil War but from 1648 he continued the old tradition of touring Germany with a troupe of English actors performing in English and German. In 1651 the company contained actresses and used changeable scenery, long before such innovations had been used on the professional stage in London, using **Salisbury Court** and the **Red Bull Theatre**. In 1662 he temporarily signed the licence over to **Davenant** and **Killigrew** and took a group of actors on tour in East Anglia. Davenant and Killigrew convinced the King that the licence had been sold to them outright and Jolly was prevented from performing in London. As a scant recompense, they allowed him to run the nursery theatres in Hatton Garden in 1668 and subsequently at Vere Street, Bun Hill and the Barbican.   PH

Jolson, Al (1886–1950) American singer and comedian. After spending his early years in circuses, minstrel shows, and vaudeville, Jolson made his stage debut in *La Belle Paree* (1911). In *The Whirl of Society* (1912), he first played the blackfaced servant Gus, a character he was to impersonate in a series of loosely plotted musicals, including *Robinson Crusoe, Jr* (1916), *Bombo* (1921), and *Big Boy* (1925). The use of blackface, a common practice in the minstrel shows where Jolson had received his early training, gave racist overtones to much of the humour in his productions. Most spectators came to Jolson's shows to hear him sing his repertoire of hit songs, and on many occasions he obliged them by stopping the performance, dismissing the other actors, and spending the rest of the evening singing directly to the audience. After his motion picture debut in *The Jazz Singer* (1927) Jolson moved to Hollywood. His only other Broadway appearances were in the revue *The Wonder Bar* (1931) and in the musical comedy *Hold on to Your Hats* (1940). Possessed of a good baritone voice, Jolson was a charismatic performer whose energy, good humour and emotional singing style made him the most popular musical comedy performer of his day.   MK

Jones, David (Hugh) (1934–) British director, who started as a television producer on the pioneering BBC arts programme, *Monitor*. He had acted at Cambridge University in some **Peter Hall** productions and in 1962, Hall invited him to direct Boris Vian's *The Empire Builders* in an experimental season at the Arts Theatre Club. This was his first professional stage production, but it was not until 1964 that he joined the **Royal Shakespeare Company**, primarily in an administrative capacity. In 1968, he became a co-director of the RSC's operations at the Aldwych and 1975 to 1977, he was the director of the Aldwych Theatre, responsible for the London wing of the RSC's programmes. Although he directed a wide variety of plays for the RSC by such writers as **Brecht**, **Günter Grass**, **David Mercer** and **Sean O'Casey**, he was best known for introducing the plays of **Maksim Gorky** to British audiences. From 1979–81, he was the artistic director of the Brooklyn Academy of Music Theatre Co. in New York. His strengths as a director lie in the clear dramatic expositions, the encouragement of sensitive performances from his casts and his awareness of European theatrical traditions. In 1982, his first full-length feature film appeared, of **Harold Pinter**'s *Betrayal*.   JE

Jones, Henry Arthur (1851–1929) English playwright who was put to work in a draper's shop at the age of 12. He 'improved' himself by reading Herbert Spencer, Ruskin and, above all, Matthew Arnold, whose moralized view of culture Jones loosely translated into earnestness. He had his first play staged in 1878 and his first success when **Wilson Barrett** staged a sensationally effective melodrama, *The Silver King* (1882), written in collaboration with Henry Herman. *Breaking a Butterfly* (1884), another collaboration with Herman, was a version of **Ibsen**'s *A Doll's House*, which solemnly distorted the point of the original by having Flossie (Nora) decide to stay with her husband. In the plays of his mid-career, Jones found a place for Ibsenite idealists, battered and sometimes broken by narrow-minded religiosity. *Saints and Sinners* (1884), *The Middleman* (1889), *Judah* (1890), *The Dancing Girl* (1891), *The Crusaders* (1891), for which Jones leased the Avenue Theatre, commissioned William Morris to design the sets and on which he lost £4,000, and *Michael and His Lost Angel* (1896) belong to this period. They dramatize the war of flesh and spirit with some vigour, but without much subtlety, and are a marked improvement on the melodramas Jones had continued to write for Wilson Barrett until 1886. He was, however, an opponent of the Shavian 'theatre of ideas', and his dialogue, though often urbane, exposes moral polarities without challenging them. It was his urbanity that attracted **Charles Wyndham**, whose interest launched Jones into producing his finest work, *The Case of Rebellious Susan* (1894), *The Liars* (1897) and *Mrs Dane's Defence* (1900). He had still 20 plays to write, none of them outstandingly successful, though his standing in the USA was higher than in England. His health began to fail in 1912, and his last years were marred by several rancorous outbursts against **George Bernard Shaw**. Having flirted with socialism in his youth, Jones ended up a diehard Tory.   PT

Jones, Inigo (1573–1652) English architect and scene-designer who introduced to the English Court the artistry and sophistication of Renaissance staging practices from the continent, above all from Italy. Having been appointed to the household of Prince Henry in 1604, Jones supervised the design and construction of almost all the notable Stuart masques from then until the dissolution of the Court at the outbreak of the Civil War. He introduced perspective scenery for **Jonson**'s *The Masque of Blackness* (1605), having already followed the example of **Serlio** by building a raked stage. Because perspective scenery demanded masking, he developed decorated sides for the proscenium – golden statues for *Hymenaei* (1606), pilasters for *Hue and Cry after Cupid* (1608) and giant figures of Neptune and Nereus linked by a frieze for *Tethys' Festival* (1610). The proscenium arch framing the stage picture owed its dominance of the English stage to the triumphant practice of Inigo Jones. Visits to Paris in 1609 and to Italy in 1613–14 extended the range of his ideas. To the classical *periaktoi*, he added the neoclassical devices of the *scena versatilis* (a front-piece which swivelled to reveal a different scene on the reverse side) and the *scena ductilis* (a scene painted on shutters, which could be pulled apart to reveal another scene behind). *The Masque of Queens* (1609) achieved the effects of coloured lighting by placing candles behind bottles filled with tinted liquids. For **Thomas Campion**'s *Lords' Masque* (1613), Jones provided the first of his many relief scenes, further elaborated by a two-tiered design. The Banqueting House at Whitehall, which he designed (1619–22), was equipped with unprecedented mechanical facilities, enabling the raising and lowering of whole scenes. It was scarcely surprising that Jonson grumbled about the displacing of poetry by spectacle. Their collaboration ended in 1631, shortly after Jones had completed his clever conversion of the **Cockpit-in-Court**. Later masques, designed to illuminate **William Davenant**'s text, showed no diminution of inventiveness, and Jones's enthusiasm for the form was expressed in his last great architectural project, the Masquing House at Whitehall (1637). Always dependent on Court favour, Jones died in poverty during the Interregnum. A collection of his drawings and designs survives in Chatsworth House, underlining his place as England's first scene-designer. PT

Jones, James Earl (1931–) Afro-American actor. Son of the actor Robert Earl Jones, James Earl trained at the University of Michigan, the American Theatre Wing and with **Lee Strasburg** before making his 1958 Broadway debut in *Sunrise at Campobello*. He soon attracted attention winning several acting awards for performances in **New York Shakespeare Festival** productions (1960–6) as well as in *Moon on a Rainbow Shawl* (1962) and *Baal* (1965) Off-Broadway. Jones was unforgettable as the despised prizefighter Jack Jefferson in *The Great White Hope* (1968), a role that earned him the Tony Award. An actor of magnetic physical presence and vocal power, he appears frequently in non-black roles. He has played King Lear, Macbeth, Coriolanus, Lopahin in *The Cherry Orchard* (1973), Hickey in *The Iceman Cometh* (1973) and Lenny in *Of Mice and Men* (1974). He gave a memorable performance in the monodrama *Paul Robeson* (1978), despite the controversy surrounding the production, and he won further acclaim for his Othello to **Christopher Plummer**'s Iago on Broadway in 1982.

Recently he has appeared in several of **Athol Fugard**'s South African plays under the direction of Lloyd Richards. EGH

Jones, Joseph S[tevens] (1809–77) American actor, manager and playwright, was associated with Boston theatre. Beginning with *The Liberty Tree* (1832), he may have written as many as 150 plays; he could not remember. In many, however, he infused his heroes with the qualities of individuality, personal conviction and freedom of spirit that identified Jacksonian America. For his good friend and Yankee actor, **George H. Hill**, he wrote *The Green Mountain Boy* (1833) and *The People's Lawyer* (1839), a favourite with several Yankee actors. Melodramas such as *The Surgeon of Paris* (1838) and *The Carpenter of Rouen* (1840) were popular, but his most lasting play was *The Silver Spoon* (1852) in which **William Warren** acted until 1883. A thoroughly professional man of the theatre who supported copyright protection and adequate recompense for playwrights, and provided the spectacles audiences demanded, Jones was also a medical doctor (Harvard, 1843) and was advertised in theatres as 'the celebrated Dr Jones'. WJM

Jones, Margo (Margaret Virginia) (1913–55) American director and producer whose major contributions were made in her home state of Texas, where she managed a theatre in Dallas dedicated to the production of new plays. Her New York credits included the co-direction, with **Eddie Dowling**, of *The Glass Menagerie* (1945), Maxine Wood's *On Whitman Avenue* (1946), **Anderson**'s *Joan of Lorraine* (1946), *Summer and Smoke* (1948), and Owen Crump's *Southern Exposure* (1950), the latter two first presented in Dallas. The Dallas theatre opened as Theatre '47 (with yearly name changes until Jones's accidental death when it became the Margo Jones Theatre). During its 12 seasons 133 plays were presented, 86 of which were new plays, including **Inge**'s *The Dark at the Top of the Stairs*, **Williams**'s *Summer and Smoke*, and **Lawrence** and **Lee**'s *Inherit the Wind*. Jones's theatre became the most celebrated home of arena staging in the United States and a pioneer in the decentralization of the American theatre, others emulating her example in part as a result of her book, *Theatre-in-the-Round* (1951). DBW

Jones, Robert Edmond (1887–1954) American set and costume designer. Jones's 1915 design for *The Man Who Married a Dumb Wife*, directed by **Harley Granville Barker**, is generally considered the beginning of the New Stagecraft in America. Rebelling against the romantic realism of **David Belasco** and other producers of the late 19th century, Jones evolved a style of simplified sets that were suggestive, rather than a reproduction of the real world. Having travelled in Europe and observing **Max Reinhardt** for a year at the **Deutsches Theater**, Jones returned to the USA with an appreciation for the power of symbolic or emblematic elements. Paraphrasing a line from *Hamlet*, Jones wrote 'Stage designing should be addressed to [the] eye of the mind.' He advocated a style of design that elicited an underlying feeling for the play, not one that eliminated the imagination. For director **Arthur Hopkins**, Jones designed the sets for several **Shakespeare** plays in the early 1920s. The

Set by Robert Edmond Jones for Eugene O'Neill's *Desire Under the Elms*, Greenwich Village Theatre, 1924, with Mary Morris as Abbie, Walter Huston as Cabot and Charles Ellis as Eben.

designs employed unit sets – then, virtually unknown – and a strong use of light and shadow in the style of **Appia**. For *Macbeth*, the three witches were portrayed by three large masks hanging over the stage. Jones was also an early member of the **Provincetown Players** and designed most of **Eugene O'Neill**'s plays including *Anna Christie*, *The Great God Brown*, and *Mourning Becomes Electra*. From 1923 to 1929 Jones served as a producer with Kenneth MacGowan and O'Neill of the Experimental Theatre, Inc. – the successor to the Provincetown. Perhaps as important as his revolutionary design was his writing – most notably the book, *The Dramatic Imagination* – in which he expressed his visionary ideas which made him an inspiration to theatre artists in the next generation.   AA

Jongleur see Juggler

Jonkonnu Jamaican Christmas custom, documented since the 18th century, in which costumed characters such as Cow Head, Horse Head, Jack-in-the-Green, Actor Boy, Devil, Policeman and Belly Woman process through the streets accompanied by 'fife and drum music'. The actors, all male, do not remove their masks in public, and, if they speak at all, do so in heavily disguised voices. The custom appears to be a synthesis of European mumming and West African masquerade.   AEG

Jonson, Ben[jamin] (1572–1637) English playwright and poet, probably born as well as educated in Westminster, where his schooling, under the remarkable William Camden, was thorough. Jonson may have gone on to work with his stepfather, a master bricklayer, before serving as a mercenary in Flanders. We do not know how, nor precisely when, he entered the acting profession. Entries in **Henslowe**'s *Diary* confirm that he was employed as both actor and writer by 1597, the year in which the *Isle of Dogs* furore threatened the whole future of London's theatres. The already controversial Jonson was probably co-author (with **Thomas Nashe**) of this lost play, whose vigorous satire provoked action against the public theatres and probably led to the imprisonment of Jonson and several of his fellow-actors. Never a man to tread warily, Jonson was again in trouble in 1598, when he was arrested for killing another actor, **Gabriel Spencer**, in a duel. He escaped execution by pleading benefit of clergy. The combative independence that was a leading characteristic was already unmistakable.

Jonson thought little enough of his earliest surviving play, *The Case Is Altered* (c. 1597), to omit it from his own collected works in 1616, but its immediate successor, *Every Man in His Humour* (1598) turned him into a celebrity at the same time as it established the brief vogue for the comedy of humours. He followed it, less successfully, with *Every Man out of His Humour* (1599) and *Cynthia's Revels* (1600), satirical comedies which displayed his classical scholarship and his delight in formal experiment. Jonson's quickness to give and take offence made him a leading participant in the **war of the theatres**, in which **Marston** and **Dekker** were his chief adversaries and to which *The Poetaster* (1601) was his unattractive major contribution. His decision to portray himself there as **Horace** indicates his admiration for the Latin poet whose *Art of Poetry* he translated. It was to Roman history that he turned for his next play, the tragedy *Sejanus, His Fall* (1603). That he laboured hard on the composition of this classically disciplined play is over-evident in the text, though Jonson tells us that the published version differs from the one performed by the King's Men. He was probably surprised to find himself in trouble again, brought before the Privy Council to answer charges of 'popery and treason', but he had made no secret of his prison conversion to Roman Catholicism, and it was at least tactless for a Catholic to risk writing about conspiracy and assassination at Court during the tense first months of James I's reign. Undeterred, the truculent Jonson was briefly imprisoned in 1604, when the anti-Scottish jokes of *Eastward Ho*, which he wrote in collaboration with **Chapman** and his erstwhile enemy Marston, offended the King. It is all the more surprising that, in 1605, he should have begun a long association with the Stuart Court by collaborating with the designer, **Inigo Jones**, on *The Masque of Blackness*. Jonson's masques are far more numerous than his plays, and they contain some of his loveliest poetry. For *The Masque of Queens* (1609), he introduced the discordant anti-masque, which remained an exuberantly grotesque feature of his subsequent work in the genre. Increasingly disenchanted by the displacement of his poetry by the ingeniously spectacular scenery of Jones, Jonson complained and quarrelled and finally abandoned masque-writing in 1634.

The plays on which Jonson's enduring reputation is based are all comedies and all written in the ten years from 1605–14. They are *Volpone* (1605), *Epicoene: or, The Silent Woman* (1609), *The Alchemist* (1610) and *Bartholomew Fair* (1614). It is here that Jonson's stagecraft is at its most brilliant. The incidents and episodes are artfully controlled and yet preserve an air of

David Garrick as Abel Drugger in Jonson's *The Alchemist*.

improvisatory spontaneity. The characters, though strictly defined by their names, seem able to command the freedom of the stage. The cutting edge of Jonson's comedies is sharp. They are peopled with deceivers and dupes, and the virtuous intelligent have an unusually small part to play. The 'image of the times', promised in the Prologue to the revised *Every Man in His Humour* (1616), is an uncomfortable one. It is an age of usury, in which human folly gives living room to moral outrage. In such an ethos, it is not surprising that the junior devil Pug, permitted a day of earthly malpractice in *The Devil Is an Ass* (1616), finds himself outmanoeuvred by humans more devious than he. The comparative failure of *The Devil Is an Ass* may have discouraged Jonson. It was nine years before his next comedy, *The Staple of News* (1625), was staged, and his effective dramatic output is completed by *The New Inn* (1629) and *A Tale of a Tub* (1633). But Jonson was never inactive. His stubborn belief in his own superior talent is represented by the unprecedented publication, in folio, of his dramatic and poetic *Works* (1616) and by his continuing provision of masques for the Stuart Court. He was rewarded with a royal pension and appointment as Poet Laureate. The songs and poems in the masques, together with the collected verse of *Epigrams* and *The Forrest* (both 1616) and *Underwoods* (1640), explain his hold over younger contemporaries, the self-styled 'tribe' or 'sons' of Ben. His prose style, founded like his poems on classical precedent, is memorably recalled in the published notes of William Drummond of Hawthornden (1632), based on conversations held during Jonson's visit to Scotland in 1618–19. Jonson's profound knowledge of London life was rewarded by his appointment as City Chronologer in 1628, the year in which he suffered a severe stroke. Many of the friends who remained loyal to him during his difficult last years attended his funeral in Westminster Abbey and contributed to the collection of memorial elegies, *Jonsonus Virbius* (1638). One of them, the forgotten Jack Young, inscribed the words 'O rare Ben Jonson' on his gravestone.   PT

Jordan, Dorothy (1761–1816) English actress. Born Dorothy Bland, she made her debut in 1779 in Dublin and acted with **John Philip Kemble** at Smock Alley Theatre in 1781–2. After an affair with the manager,

Richard Daly, she fled to England, pregnant. She auditioned for **Tate Wilkinson** successfully and he recommended a change of name ('You have crossed the water so I'll call you Jordan'). She reached the London theatres by 1785 and, after a slow start, became a huge success in breeches and hoyden roles like Peggy in **Garrick**'s *The Country Girl* and Priscilla Tomboy in *The Romp*. She had three children by Richard Ford, a barrister, and in 1790 became mistress of the Duke of Clarence by whom she had ten children. She continued to star successfully, even though no longer able to play the same roles: as **Hazlitt** commented, 'her person was large, soft and generous like her soul'. She was highly praised as Viola and Ophelia, particularly for her delivery of verse so that, as **Lamb** said, 'it was no set speech'. A devoted mother and an extravagant spender, she worked extremely hard as an actress both on stage and in her negotiations with managers: her daughters had dowries of £10,000 each. In 1811 she separated from the Duke. In 1815, swindled out of a large sum of money, she fled to Paris fearing arrest and died there in poverty.   PH

Joris, Charles (1935–) Swiss director and actor. Studied French literature at Neuchâtel University and trained as an actor in Strasbourg (Centre Dramatique de l'Est, 1958–61), under Hubert Gignoux. In 1961, he founded the Théâtre Populaire Romand, the first professional French-speaking theatre ensemble in Switzerland. The TPR tours all linguistic regions of the country and neighbouring France. In its 25 years, the TPR has produced over 50 plays, mostly Swiss or world premieres. The style of presentation is scenographically highly inventive and relies on sophisticated acting skills (acrobatics, free improvisation). The TPR pursues a conscious community policy (youth theatre,

Dorothy Jordan as Viola in *Twelfth Night*.

courses for amateur companies, open workshops, summer festivals in Neuchâtel and La Chaux-de-Fonds) and performs in towns and villages which have never seen professional theatre before. In 1975 Joris was awarded the Reinhart-Ring, the highest Swiss distinction for work in the theatre. The TPR's most notable *mises en scène* include: Bernard Liègme's *Les Murs de la Ville* (*The City Walls*, 1961) and *Le Soleil et la Mort* (*Sun and Death*, 1966), Henri Deblüe's *Le Procès de la Truie* (*The Sow's Trial*, 1962), **Brecht**'s *Man is Man* (1968), **Shakespeare**'s *Lear*, **Arden**'s *The Workhouse Donkey* (1978), **Handke**'s *Through Towns and Villages* (1984), **Beckett**'s *Godot* (1985). cls

Joseph, Stephen (1927–67) British director, lecturer and pioneer of theatre-in-the-round in England. Son of actress Hermione Gingold and publisher Michael Joseph, he founded, in 1955, the Studio Theatre Company in Scarborough with which he toured theatre-less towns in the north of England for several years, exploring at the same time the potential of performances 'in the round'. This venture together with experience of theatres-in-the-round in the USA convinced him of the potential of this staging form and he began to advocate its practice with increasing passion. With minimal financial support he set up the country's first permanent such theatre in Stoke-on-Trent in 1962 as a home for his company: the **Victoria Theatre**. In 1961 he was appointed Fellow in Drama at the newly created Drama Department of Manchester University. His books include *New Theatre Forms* and *Theatre in the Round*. The Stephen Joseph Theatre in the Round at Scarborough was opened in 1976 as a memorial to his work. AJ

Jouvet, Louis (1887–1951) French actor and director. Like **Dullin**, Jouvet joined **Copeau**'s first company at the **Vieux-Colombier** but left in 1922 to found his own company. At first he was Copeau's technical and lighting director only gradually revealing his qualities as a star actor. In 1923, at the Comédie des Champs Elysées, he scored a hit with a new play *Dr Knock or the Triumph of Medicine* by **Jules Romains**. In 1927 he was a co-founder of the **Cartel** and in 1928 he produced the first play by **Giraudoux**. His productions of Giraudoux's plays over the next 17 years involved a large measure of collaboration and rewriting in rehearsal. When the Popular Front Government offered him the directorship of the **Comédie-Française** he suggested instead a group of directors. He spent the war years on tour with his company in Latin America and returned to produce Giraudoux's last play, *The Madwoman of Chaillot* (1945), and **Genet**'s first, *The Maids* (1947). He died while working on **Sartre**'s *The Devil and the Good Lord* in 1951. Since 1934, when he took over the Athénée theatre, he had often worked with the designer **Christian Bérard** whose self-consciously picturesque style fitted Jouvet's theatrical performances. In the cinema, Jouvet was able to tone down his performance style admirably to suit the camera. He wrote several books about the art of actor and director. DB

Judic (Anne-Marie-Louise Damiens) (1850–1911) French actress and singer, who began playing comedy as soon as she graduated from the Conserva-toire. She was an immediate hit at her music-hall debut at the Paris Eldorado in 1869, because of her superb diction and talent for innuendo, which won her the nickname 'The School for Mimes'. Later she made a brilliant career in comic opera, especially in Offenbach, touring the United States. Her last appearance as a singer was at the **Folies-Bergère** in 1900. LS

Juggler The art of balancing objects, tossing and catching them in different rhythms, may be the oldest performance skill, known in ancient Egypt, Assyria, China, Greece, and Rome. Roman jugglers were usually denominated by their specialities, as *ventilatores* (knife throwers) and *pilarii* (ball-players), whereas the medieval Latin term *joculator* referred more broadly to the lower level of strolling entertainer. Hence its derivatives, 'juggler' in English, *jongleur* in French, *guillare* in Italian, *Gugelleute* in German, bore pejorative connotations, suggesting deception for criminal purposes. The Spanish 'malabarist' came to mean an illusionist who also juggles. The first named juggler was Pierre Gringore (b. 1475).

On the 19th- and 20th-century variety stage a distinction is made between strength jugglers and salon jugglers. The former juggle heavy objects, including human beings, occasionally work on horseback or unicycle, and catch cannon-balls on the back of their necks; the most celebrated have been Karl Rappo (1800–54), Paul Conchas (Huett, d. 1916) and John Holtum (b. 1845). The latter juggle billiard balls, cigar boxes, diabolos and similar paraphernalia, sometimes with their mouths; among the most adroit have been **Paul Cinquevalli**, **Ernesto Rastelli**, Kara (Michael Steiner, 1867–1939), and **W. C. Fields**.

A music-hall speciality was the restaurant scene, originated by Agoust and perfected by the Charles Perzoff Troupe (1890–1910) in which waiters and customers juggle a complete five-course meal; a variation was the plate-breaking number of Carl Baggessen (?1868–1931). Once a staple in the repertory of every itinerant performer, juggling is now a common item in the curriculum of drama schools, used to train agility and coordination. LS

See: K. H. Ziethen, *4,000 Years of Juggling*, 2 vols., Cauvigny, 1981.

Julia, Raul (1940–) American film and stage actor, born in Puerto Rico. His New York debut was as Astolfo in *Life Is A Dream* in Spanish. Principal stage appearances include classical roles at the Delacorte and the **Vivian Beaumont** in New York. In 1982 he starred in *Nine* as Guido Contini, in which critics referred to him as 'a standout' and 'childishly wise, boyishly insincere, and totally right'. For *Nine* he was nominated for an Antoinette Perry (Tony) Award, as he was for *The Threepenny Opera* (1976), *Where's Charley* (1974), and *Two Gentlemen of Verona* (1971). SMA

Juvarra, Filippo (1676–1736) Italian architect and scene designer. Having studied architecture under Carlo Fontana in Rome, he won the prize of the Concorso Clementino and became a member of the Academia di San Luca in 1705. In 1706 he became assistant to designer Giuseppe Capelli at the San

Bartolomeo opera house in Naples. At this time he adopted the use of angled perspective or *scena per angolo*. Under the patronage of Cardinal Ottoboni from 1708 to 1714, he designed and built the theatre at the Palazzo della Cancelleria and created the scenic effects for its productions. At the same time, in 1713, he designed elaborate opera sets for the private theatres of both Prince Capricanica and the Queen of Poland. By 1714 he became chief architect at the Savoy court in Turin.

His style is characterized by the use of curvilinear settings which draw the observer's eye in a circle and then to the foreground. The effect is accomplished with the use of free-standing units and a permanent foreground with changing vistas. Draperies, tropical foliage and Near Eastern architecture are his hallmarks. AJN

Juvenile drama see **Toy theatre**

K

Kabuki The most important urban Japanese theatre form between its beginnings c. 1600 and the early 20th century. *Kabuki*, the noun form of the verb *kabuku*, off-centre, meant unorthodox, strange, new. The scandalous nature of early performance is clear from the fact that *kabuki* was commonly written with the ideographs song (*ka*), dance (*bu*), and prostitute (*ki*) (in response to the tuts of Victorian moralists in the late 19th century, the ideograph meaning skill replaced the ideograph meaning prostitute).

Because *kabuki* depended on a popular audience, it was always up-to-date, adapting its plays, music, dance, acting, and staging styles to the taste of the times and always striving to be new and fashionable. Throughout *kabuki* history, plays and performing techniques have been borrowed from **nō**, **kyōgen**, and **bunraku**. As a consequence the Meiji period scholar Tsubouchi Shōyō called *kabuki* a multi-headed monster. It is notable that even a wildly successful play was never revived intact. It was always rewritten, often so drastically it was like a new play (hence scores of texts exist for important plays like *Wait a Moment!*). *Kabuki* was a contemporary theatre; history plays, though set in distant times, were imbued with the spirit of the present. New plays and new acting, music, dance, and staging styles were constantly being created. Actors made their fame by being different not by merely repeating the style of their predecessors. The ideal performer was one who carried on the acting traditions of his family (*ie no gei*) while at the same time adding his own creativity to that style. (A brief history of the actors who have held the **Ichikawa Danjūrō** name indicates this very clearly.) Only within the past half century or so has *kabuki* become a 'classical' theatre, repeating a known repertory in a relatively fixed fashion.

In early *kabuki*, actors sang, danced, and acted, but by the late 17th century, singing was given over to specialist singers who accompanied the actors from offstage or, in dance scenes, onstage. Actors thereafter concentrated on dancing and spoken elocution. Actors of female roles displayed their charm and skill through solo dances (*shosagoto* or *keigoto*) that playwrights worked into plays of all types. Actors of male roles developed skills in bravura poses (*mie*). It is characteristic of *kabuki* acting to freeze in tableau at climactic points, thus prolonging moments of high dramatic tension. A high level of energy in the actor sustains these silent, motionless moments. They also mastered demanding vocal techniques. Intricately written speeches that included involved verbal puns were delivered in a melodious style (*yakuharai*) that is said to have come from Buddhist chanting. Sukeroku's name-saying speech (*nanori*) requires a machine-gun like

tempo of speech parsed out in exceptionally long phrases (*ippon chōshi*). In later plays (mid-19th century), passages of antiphonal dialogue composed in lines of 7 and 5 syllables (*shichigochō*) demanded a rhythmic style of delivery that is a delight to hear.

Nō and *bunraku* each have a single style of music; but *kabuki* has many musical styles to match its many styles of drama and performance. Three basic types of instruments combine in *kabuki*. The *nō* ensemble of drums and flute (*hayashi*) (seen in paintings of Okuni's performances in Kyoto, c. 1600–10) combine with large drums, gongs, bells, and other sound effects instruments, to make up *kabuki*'s percussion ensemble (*narimono*). The plucked lute (*shamisen*) is seen in paintings of *kabuki* performance of the period 1610–20. Today, percussion, *shamisen*, and singers make up *kabuki*'s basic musical grouping. Seated offstage right (*geza*, lower seat), they perform *nagauta* (long song) style music and provide sound effects. Their music is ubiquitous throughout a performance: instrumental *shamisen* melodies (*aikata*) set an appropriate mood for a scene, following the tempo that the actors establish; patterns beaten on the large barrel drum (*ōdaiko*) indicate rain, snow, wind, ocean waves, or the time of day; *shamisen* and song accompany exits and entrances of characters along the rampway through the audience. More than 500 melodies and rhythms, as well as special gong and bell sounds, are part of the offstage musical repertory.

A dance play is accompanied by a musical ensemble seated onstage. This may be an *nagauta* ensemble, or an ensemble of *shamisen* players and singers performing in *tokiwazu*, *tomimoto*, or *kiyomoto* style. The music of these last three styles was created in the 18th century specifically for *kabuki* dance plays; they do not use percussion or flute and hence are softer and more romantic than *nagauta* music. The puppet theatre's *gidayū shamisen* and singing style was brought into *kabuki* in the 17th century (and renamed *takemoto*). *Takemoto* music accompanies puppet plays taken into the *kabuki* repertory (*maruhonmono*) and is used in some dance pieces, as well. The *takemoto* duo of chanter and *shamisen* player appears by the left proscenium; other ensembles appear at the rear or one side of the stage proper. The musical ensembles, dressed in formal Tokugawa period costume, that sit on stage during dance plays and dance scenes are a deliberate part of the spectacular stage picture. Complex dance plays call for more than one ensemble – *nagauta* and *tokiwazu* in *The Zen Substitute*; *nagauta*, *takemote*, and *tokiwazu* in *The Maple Viewing*, for example – to match the changing mood of the play.

The bravura acting style of heroic figures (*aragoto*), developed by the Ichikawa Danjūrō acting family of the city of Edo (Tokyo), is often considered synonymous with *kabuki*. The exaggerated costumes and properties and the bold red and black lines of makeup (*kumadori*) of this style are familiar through actor portraits in wood-block prints. Yet other styles are equally important.

Comic-erotic acting (*wagoto*) is appropriate for playing gentle good-for-nothing heroes of domestic plays of the Kyoto-Osaka area. Both *aragoto* and *wagoto* acting often occurs in a play, balancing each other. When puppet plays were brought into the *kabuki* repertory, actors mimicked the actions of the puppets to a certain extent; speaking style especially has been greatly influenced by *bunraku* chanting style. In dance plays actors may move stiffly, like puppets, for comic effect. The overall style of dance in *kabuki*, called *shosa*, showing-the-body, fuses rural and urban dances (*odori*) of the common people, characterized originally by lively leaping, and *no*'s characteristic turning or pivoting dances (*mai*). Actors of female roles (*onnagata*) developed over three centuries a highly stylized art that suggests femininity but is wholly unlike a flesh and blood woman. The *onnagata* is a 'third sex' in which the strength of a man and the delicacy of a woman are fused.

A *kabuki* performance is structured to provide constantly evolving moods and emotional states over time. On a macro scale, the annual season consisted of six productions timed to open two months apart: the 1st, 3rd, 5th, 7th, and 9th lunar month productions matched the Five Annual Festivals of the lunar calendar (the 11th month production was the season opening, *kaomise*). The nature of the play matched the season: love in spring, martial vigour on Boy's Day (5th month), lament for the spirits of the dead in the summer, for example. A day's performance began before dawn and ended 10 to 12 hours later at dusk. Through the day the bill progressed from casual 'practice' plays (*jobiraki* and *futatateme*), through formal history and legendary pieces (*jidaimono*), to pieces about commoners in contemporary situations (*sewamono*), concluding in a felicitous dance finale (*ōgiri*). This structuring is widely followed in *kabuki* programmes today. The intended progression in mood from easy-going, to formal, to emotional, to celebratory, is analogous to the *jo-ha-kyū* structure of **bugaku** and *nō* performance.

On a micro scale, actors worked within identifiable forms or patterns (*kata*) of acting that were perfected over generations. These *kata* were as well known as the words of the text, and an actor was understood to 'own' the acting form, to have a copyright on it, in the same sense that an author owns the right to his or her written creations. *Kata* were not, however, frozen or absolute. Succeeding generations of actors altered the inherited *kata* and created new *kata* when they wished to. Today, the process of change has significantly slowed; only the most original actors go beyond the *kata* they have learned from their elders.

The Tokugawa government limited the number of large *kabuki* theatres to nine through most of the Edo period: three in Edo, three in Kyoto, and three in Osaka. A drum tower over the theatre entrance signified the owner held a licence to produce *kabuki*. Licensed theatres could use the striped draw curtain, the revolving stage, and other *kabuki* symbols. Small, unlicensed *kabuki* houses, numbering from three to six

in each city, could not. In the fall the theatre owner signed for one-year contracts a troupe actor-manager (*zagashira* or *zamoto*), a leading female impersonator (*tate onnagata* or *tate oyama*), a house playwright (*sakusha*), and a company of 50 to 70 supporting writers, actors, musicians, singers, costumers, wig-makers, and technicians. In addition, the house staff of a large theatre, like the Nakamura Theatre in Edo, would include as many as 150 barkers, ticket sellers, doormen, ushers, food vendors, cushion vendors, bouncers, and the like. Theatres were restricted by government decree to a single district in each city, usually no larger than two or three city blocks. Side-by-side, *kabuki* and *bunraku* puppet theatres engaged in heated competition for the same audience.

A special theatre structure evolved for playing *kabuki*. It is an oblong box in which the audience and stage are physically part of the same space. The stage pushes forward into the auditorium, two-storey boxes surround the sides of the stage, and when the house was full cheap standing room was sold behind the acting area. A rampway or *hanamichi* carried the stage space through the left portion of the audience nearly to the back of the house. *Hanamichi*, flower path, probably meant 'gift path' in the late 17th century, flower being a euphemism for a gift. The *hanamichi* provides a means for the actor to walk through the audience when entering and exiting, and deliver a major speech and dance while standing in its midst. A second *hanamichi* ran through the right portion of most *kabuki* houses until this century. A common feature of late *kabuki* plays (e.g.: *The Scarlet Princess of Edo*) is a scene in which two separated characters, one on each *hanamichi*, speak alternate speeches over the heads of the audience, a technique not unsimilar to cinema montage. By mid-18th century *kabuki* theatres were equipped with floor-level revolving stages (often one within another) for moving scenery and actors, one hundred years before Lautenschläger in Europe. Because performance occurred during the daytime, the stage was lit by opening and closing sliding panels under the house eaves and by placing lighted candles along the front of the stage. One of the functions of the black-robed stage assistant (*kōken* or *kurogo*) was to light a star's face with a candle held out on a flexible pole (*tsura akari*, face light).

Major changes have occurred in staging *kabuki* during the 20th century. Cavernous new theatres were constructed for *kabuki*, modelled in part on European opera houses. Their auditoriums and stages were as much as three times the size of the traditional theatre – the present Kabuki-za in Tokyo has a 93-foot wide stage and it seats 2,600. The effects have not been good: the actor, who used to stand out on the traditional small *kabuki* stage, is dwarfed by the theatre's dimensions; acres of painted scenery fill the stage and compete with the actor for attention; spectators in the overhanging balconies can no longer see actors on much of the *hanamichi*. The transformation of *kabuki* from a plebeian, popular, even despised, theatre into a classic art has been accompanied by the phenomenon of gigantism in theatre architecture. One must go to older, smaller theatres in Osaka and Kyoto to find an appropriate relationship between *kabuki* performance and stage space. JRB

**Kachalov (pseudonym of Shverubovich),
Vasily Ivanovich** (1875–1948) Soviet-Russian
actor, who began his professional career in A. S.
Suvorin's Theatre of the Literary Artistic Society in St
Petersburg (1896–7) and in 1900 joined the **Moscow
Art Theatre** (MAT), where from 1900 to 1948 he
played 55 roles. An intelligent actor, he excelled at
impersonating idealists, humanists and leading-man
types, including: the original Tuzenbach and Trofimov
in *The Three Sisters* (1902) and *The Cherry Orchard*
(1904), respectively, as well as the title role in **Chekhov**'s *Ivanov* (1904); the Baron in the premiere of
Gorky's *The Lower Depths* (1902) and Protasov in the
same author's *Children of the Sun* (1905); Julius Caesar in
Shakespeare's tragedy (1903); Chatsky in **Griboedov**'s *Woe from Wit* (1906 and 1914); Don Juan in
Pushkin's *The Stone Guest* (1915); **Ibsen**'s *Brand*
(1906); and Hamlet in the famous **Gordon Craig–
Stanislavsky** collaboration (1912). He also appeared as
the definitive thinking man, Ivan Karamazov, in
Nemirovich-Danchenko's famous 1910 production
of Dostoevsky's *The Brothers Karamazov*. Kachalov's
career continued unabated after the October Revolution on the concert stage, in theatre, radio and film in a
full complement of roles from the classical repertory,
including that of Chatsky in the 1938 *Woe from Wit*
revival. He also appeared in the new Soviet drama,
e.g., as Vershinin in **Vsevolod Ivanov**'s *Armoured
Train 14–69* (1927). In 1936 he was named a 'People's
Artist of the USSR'. SG

Kaduma, Godwin (1938–) Tanzanian playwright. He has two plays, both in Swahili, one
published, the other not: *Dhamana* (*Pledge*, 1980), on
the proper use of education, and *Mabatini* on the
frustrations of the poor peasantry. Godwin Kaduma is
Director of Culture in the Ministry of Culture, Youth
and Sports. PML

Kainz, Josef (1858–1910) Austrian actor. As a young
man Kainz acted with the **Meininger** (from 1877 to
1880) and with the Munich Court Theatre (from 1880
to 1883). He was hired in 1883 by **Adolph L'Arronge**
to become a founding member of the company of the
Deutsches Theater, Berlin. Here his emotional interpretation of the title role in *Don Carlos* brought him
national fame. Kainz remained the leading actor of the
Deutsches Theater until 1899, when he joined the
Vienna **Burgtheater**. Here he remained until his
death. He was undoubtedly the most popular actor of
his day due to his aristocratic appearance, his phenomenally flexible and accurate voice, and his unusual
physical dexterity. His technique has been described as
'impressionist' and in his day his acting was compared
to that of **Sarah Bernhardt**, **Coquelin**, and **Eleonora
Duse**. A common feature in his interpretation of the
tragic roles of **Shakespeare**, **Goethe**, **Schiller**, and
Grillparzer, was his representation of them as victories of the human spirit over adversity, rather than
defeats. During the last decade of his life, these
interpretations became darker and his acting revealed
reserves of violent passion in the characters. Most
famous among his several celebrated roles were
Romeo, Hamlet, Mark Antony, and Torquato Tasso,
not to mention his masterpieces of comic characterization in the plays of **Molière** and **Nestroy**. SW

Kainz as Hamlet.

Kaiser, Georg (1878–1945) German dramatist,
author of over 60 plays in a wide variety of styles and
genres. After early satiric treatments of mythical or
biblical subjects – themes that he returned to in his final
plays – he gained international recognition with *The
Burgers of Calais* (1914, performed 1917). Although set
in a historical context, the anti-militarism and self-sacrifice for the benefit of humanity that the action
celebrates link this to his modern Morality Play *From
Morn to Midnight* produced the same year. This portrays
the pilgrimage of a bank clerk, from an automaton-like
existence through the rejection of materialism to a
search for spiritual values. The action is dream-like and
distorted, and his suicide following the discovery that
even religion has become corrupted is portrayed as a
crucifixion. These elements, which had a decisive
influence on later expressionism, are extended in his
most ambitious work, the trilogy of *The Coral* (1917),
Gas I (1918) and *Gas II* (1920). Here the expressionist
'new man' emerges, the Son of the Billionaire owner of
a plant producing the gas that fuels modern industrialization and makes the dehumanizing of man possible.
His rejection of the capitalist ethos reforms the father
who represents it, but the succeeding plays dismiss the
hope of meaningful change. An explosion which
destroys the plant offers an opportunity for social
regeneration, but the Son's refusal to rebuild it
causes a riot among the workers, who have earlier
been given cooperative ownership. As a consequence the plant comes under state control, and when
the grandson discovers that it is being used to manufac-

ture poison gas he sets off a bomb that destroys the whole human race. The melodramatic plots, simplified characters and abstraction in this key expressionist work make the flaws of this dramatic style all too obvious. But thematically it is also a rejection of the expressionist outlook, and by 1923 Kaiser had discarded its techniques though the same sort of statement recurs in a late play like *The Raft of the Medusa* (1943, performed 1963). CI

Kamban, Gudmundur (1888–1945) Icelandic playwright and director. Like **Sigurjónsson** he wanted to break the isolation of Icelandic letters, writing mostly in Danish, although his best plays, *Marble* (1918) and *We Murderers* (1920), are set in New York. His neoromantic *Hadda-Padda* (1914) made his name in Iceland and Denmark. Mainly treating modern urban society, Kamban frequently deals with moral dilemma. Thus in *Marble* he questions the basis of the Western legislation regarding crime and punishment, while the debate in *We Murderers* is whether crime is the victim's responsibility. Another important play is the historical tragedy *Skálholt* (1934). Kamban's plays were seen in Scandinavia and Germany in the 1920s and 1930s and are still performed in Iceland. Kamban, an active director in Copenhagen and Germany during the 1920s, staged his own work and plays by **Björnstjerne Björnson**, Knut Hamsun and others. He was the first Icelandic film director. AI

Kamińska, Esther Rachel (1862–1930) (Polish actress) and **Ida** (1899–1970) Variously known as 'The Jewish Duse' and 'Mother of the Yiddish Theatre', Esther Rachel Kamińska began as an actress in 1892 and achieved fame particularly in the fine series of female roles of the **Jacob Gordin** plays, her most notable being that of *Mirele Efros*, with her young daughter Ida playing her stage daughter. In 1921 the Warsaw Yiddish Art Theatre (VYKT) was formed by the Kamińska family, all of whom were actors, performing in the highest traditions of European realistic theatre. In 1950 the Polish Jewish State Theatre was formed, housed in the specially built E. R. Kamińska Theatre in Warsaw, and Ida Kamińska, who had inherited her father's administrative ability and her mother's acting talent, became its artistic director, a role she filled with distinction as actress, producer, translator and teacher, until her death. AB

Kamiriithu The Kamiriithu Community Educational and Cultural Centre at Limuru in Kenya was formed in 1976. An 'emergency village' during the Mau Mau War of independence, it became after independence a labour reserve for nearby plantations and industries. Disillusioned workers and peasants in collaboration with **Ngugi wa Thiong'o**, Ngugi wa Mirii, an adult educator and research worker at the University of Nairobi and other intellectuals collectively formed the Centre to embark upon a programme of 'integrated rural development', including theatre. *Ngaahika Ndeenda* (*I'll Marry When I Want*) was its first production.

Democratically devised, it was a powerful attack on the betrayal of the Kenyan masses by local *comprador* classes and their alliance with exploitative 'foreign interests'. This it presented with great cultural richness,

the peasants and workers themselves making the major contribution on language, traditional ritual, song and dance. Moreover, the theatre production became the focus of many other collective activities in the life of the community. An open-air theatre was constructed by a 'Harambee of Sweat' – i.e. – self-help and labour. The actual performance was 'a play of the people . . . for the people by the people' (*Sunday Nation*, Nairobi). After seven weeks it was banned. Shortly afterwards Ngugi wa Thiong'o was detained. On his release a year later he returned to Kamiriithu and the community began a new play, *Maitu Njugira* (*Mother Sing To Me*), focusing on the resistance to colonial oppression of the various Kenyan nationalities. The authorities closed the centre, refused to allow performances of the play at the National Theatre and destroyed the open-air theatre. Nevertheless thousands of Kenyans saw 'rehearsals' at the University of Nairobi. The Kamiriithu experience became an inspiration to artists and cultural workers in neo-colonial African countries. RK

Kampuchea Kampuchea, formerly Cambodia, is a South-East Asian nation which boasts a refined heritage of performance dating back at least 1,700 years. The country of six million borders on Laos, Thailand, Vietnam, and the Gulf of Siam. Ethnic Khmer make up 93% of the population and their performance traditions predominate, though arts of the minority Chinese, Vietnamese, Cham, and the ethnically related but culturally distinct hill tribes (called Khmer Loeu) are also found. Theraveda Buddhism has been the predominant religion since the 13th century, but Hindu, Mahayana Buddhist and, recently, socialist thought have had an impact on the performing arts.

The first reports of performance are Chinese court records which note that musicians from Funan, an early kingdom in this area, were part of an embassy to the Chinese emperor in AD 243. Performance under temple and royal patronage flourished during the Angkor period with Indian and Indonesian influences apparent in the repertoire and performance system. Cambodian dance practice was adopted by Thai and Lao rulers seeking to replicate Angkor's glory in the period after 1431 when the sack of Angkor by the Thai began the gradual decline of Khmer power in the area. In the 19th century Thai performers were brought in to help restructure Cambodian court performance. This Thai–Khmer tradition was further modified in this century as palace performance developed until the end of the monarchy in 1970. Under the socialist regime, lyrics were sometimes altered as the arts adjusted to the new age. Overseas, former court performers who fled the chaos wrought by the South-East Asian conflict have regrouped in Paris and the United States attempting to maintain the classical tradition.

Khmer arts can be conceptually divided into three categories: (1) traditional village performance (2) classical court forms, and (3) modern popular genres. The village and court forms are part of a single continuum, while the more recently developed popular genres have borrowed significantly from Thai, Malay, and Vietnamese models of the last 100 years.

Traditional village performance Village performance corresponds to a general South-East Asian pattern in which the arts are used for entertainment, social integration, and spirit propitiation, sometimes serving more than one of these functions simultaneously. For example, *ayay* is a kind of folk chant inspired by legends, which provides both entertainment and courting opportunities. Young men and women form two groups and sing dialogues to the tune of a two-stringed fiddle or zither. Improvisation and satirical comment are encouraged in the form, and simple dance movements are executed. The music quickens as the verbal jousting intensifies.

The *trott* (stag dance) is a form which has both entertainment and ritual functions. Dancers impersonating deer and hunters accompanied by musicians go house to house dancing and collecting payment in the area around Siamreap (Angkor) and Battambang. The dance, it is believed, helps end drought and brings luck at the beginning of the new year. The deer is conceived of as a demonic creature, related to the ogre who assumes the guise of a golden deer in the *Ramayana*.

Some performance specialists occur at village level. These include blind musicians and wandering singers, who reinterpret legends to the accompaniment of a *cha pei*, a long-necked lute; and female dancers, who perform at a village shrine as an invitation to spirits who then possess the village spirit medium. Though none of these village performances represent drama in which an actor impersonates a character in a sustained narrative, all of these forms contain mimetic elements and probably contribute features that were elaborated in the court tradition.

Classical court forms Classical court forms include the female dance drama (*lakhon kbach boran*), shadow play (*nang sebek*), and the mask dance (*lakhon khol*). These forms are comparable to Thailand's *lakon fai nai*, *nang yai*, and *khon*, respectively, though research has yet to clarify whether Thai shadow play and masked dance were, like the female dance form, first developed in Cambodia. The confusion on this question is exacerbated by the fact that the current Cambodian variants on the ancient arts are only about 150 years old, and were influenced by Thai models in the 19th century. Although indigenous, Indian and Indonesian influences were probably important in the creation of these arts a millennium ago, a significant break occurred with the fall of Angkor.

Indigenous elements probably contributed to the ritual importance of performance in Khmer courts. As early as the 7th century, dance was a feature of the funeral rites of kings – a tradition continued into this century. A dance–ritual, the ceremonial salutation to teachers and spirits, performed in the palace each Thursday was thought to promote good luck. More elaborate performances might be staged to promote rain and fertility, *Buong Suong* (paying respect to heavenly spirits) performances were enacted to promote rain. Such rites show the link between performance and communication with the supernatural which seems indigenous to South-East Asia.

Indian influence is seen in the importance of the *Ramayana* in the repertoire and the primary importance of female dancers. The preference for *Ramayana* materials shows Vaishnavite influence which may have come via Indonesia or Bengal. The Indian temple dancers (*devadasi*) who were ritually married to temple idols and, in Vaishnavite practice, became associated

with god-kings, probably formed a model for the court dancers. The references to female dancers in Cambodia begin as early as AD 611 when there are reports of female dancers being dedicated to Hindu temples. The practice of dedicating performers to temples was continued after Buddhism became the state religion, and in the time of Jayavarman VII (1181–?1219) over 3,000 dancers were so dedicated.

Indonesian practices are believed to have been introduced in 802 when Jayavarman II, the founder of the Khmer kingdom and the *devaraja* ('god-king') cult, reportedly returned from Sriwijaya, a kingdom in the Malay archipelago. The fact that the major Khmer court arts all have clear counterparts in the Malay world, bolsters the belief in this venerable connection. The Javanese semi-ritual court dance (*bedaya*), the shadow play (*wayang kulit*), the mask dance (*topeng*) are, like the Khmer court arts, modern versions of ancient forms that linked the ruler with the world of ancestors and spirits, ensuring him godlike power.

Similarly, the Cambodian *pinpeat* orchestra shares many structural features with the *gamelan* ensembles indigenous to the Malay world, probably as a result of borrowing in past ages. It is, however, difficult to prove when and how this interchange occurred, for trade contacts with the Malay Archipelago and Malaysian mainland have persisted over an extended period, and the incorporation of Malay principles could have come after 802. It seems likely than an early infusion may have been reinforced by subsequent borrowings. Perhaps some of the later Malay/Indonesian impact came via the Thai, whose dramatic arts were heavily influenced by Malay kingdoms on its southern frontier (see **Thailand**).

Though the exact nature of ancient Khmer performance is obscure, scholars feel that non-dramatic dances by large groups of women were part of the repertoire, as were couple dances by pairs of women with one lady in each couple impersonating a prince and the other a princess. One 13th-century inscription, cited by Cravath, indicates that a *jataka* (Buddhist birth-story) was played by female performers, but such reference to dance drama is rare in the Angkor period. Written evidence for shadow play and masked dance is completely lacking. This leads some scholars to feel that narrative drama was not highly developed during the Angkor period, indeed, to the present, genres that are thought to be the oldest female dance forms of the Malay/Indonesian courts are largely non-dramatic.

It is possible that the common dramatic repertoire of the Khmer and Thai arts largely evolved in the more secular environment of the Thai courts after Angkor's decline beginning in 1431. Many of the tales currently in the repertoire may first have come from Thai sources.

Information known about Khmer court arts ceases with the 15th century and only resumes in the mid 19th century, when, according to the oral tradition, King Ang Duong (1796–1859) directed a reformation of the arts. The practice of court performers prior to that time is said to have been close to village dance, as in *ayay*, described above. The King, who had spent time in the Thai court, directed that the movement, especially of male dancers, be made more rounded and less jerky. Elbows that were held stiffly at shoulder level were lowered. Meanwhile, costumes were modelled on those of the Thai court. Whether these refinements were, as Cambodian oral tradition reports, a return to the past or the expropriation of Thai models can be debated. The innovations do, however, explain the close similarities between Khmer and Thai arts in the present era. Current performance of female dance drama, puppetry, and mask dance derives from this period.

The *lakhon kbach boran*, the dance of the palace ladies, is the most important of the court arts. The performers were wives, concubines, or relatives of the ruler. A new troupe normally would be organized at the beginning of each ruler's reign, under the direction of a lady appointed by the king. The women would be trained for a single role – male, female, monkey, or ogre – according to their body type. Prior to the last generation, men would not be allowed to appear with the ladies. Exceptions to this rule were the man who played the hermit role and had certain ritual functions in training and graduating dancers, and the men who played clown roles. This female troupe with male ritual specialists and clowns is comparable to Thai *lakon fai nai*, and Malaysian *mak yong*.

Floor patterns in the female dance tend toward circles and lines, and the hand gestures are, like most South-East Asian systems, abstract rather than the gesture of language of Indian *mudras*. The repertoire of the female court dance, which came to be known in the West as the Royal Cambodian Ballet, is currently composed of about 60 *robom*, pure dance pieces, and 40 *roeung* (dance dramas). As previously noted, the pure dance pieces are considered the oldest part of the repertoire.

In the dance dramas, actresses mime the action as an offstage chorus of female singers delivers the text to *pinpeat* musical accompaniment. This ensemble customarily includes a *samphor* (horizontal drum), *skor thom* (a pair of barrel drums), a *kong touch* and *kong thom* (gong chimes), a *roneat ek* and *roneat thung* (high and low pitched xylophones), a *sralai* (oboe), and a *ching* (pair of small cymbals). The stories performed include episodes from the *Ramker*, the Cambodian version of the *Ramayana*; the Javanese *Panji* cycle; the tale of *Anrudh* (a grandson of Krishna); *jataka* stories including the tale of the bird-woman, *Manora*, and the conch prince, *Preah Sang*; and local legends. The tales typically focus on the struggle of the noble hero with an ogrely villain for the love of a woman, who is often associated with images of fertility. An episode of great popularity is the story of *Sovann Macha*, a fish queen who is courted by Hanuman, the monkey general leading Rama's troops. Cravath interprets these stories as models of how the rightful ruler must unite with the female principle to promote prosperity in the realm. Traditionally, performances might last for four days with the tale being danced for two four-hour periods each day. The ladies trained and performed in the palace, dancing when required by the king, and commoners would not normally be allowed to view presentations. But the traditional system has been modified considerably in the last generations.

The history of the dance in the last 100 years is an abstract of the struggle for royal autonomy during the colonial era. The kings strove to maintain the female dance during the French protectorate, inaugurated in 1863, but found the allowances accorded the monarch were not sufficient to support the 500 dancer troupe of former times. By 1904, 100 dancers remained and about half accompanied King Sisowath to Europe to perform at the Marseilles exhibition in 1906. European acclaim followed, but the decay in numbers continued as dancers left the palace to go to school or marry. Frenchmen like George Groslier, who as Art Director of the colony pleaded for support for the troupe, became significant in fostering the dance. In 1928 the Palace administration and French proponents agreed to place the troupe under the Ecole des Beaux Arts. During the 1930s the French authorities gave support to a non-court troupe organized by a former dancer, Say Sangvann, whose dancers, unlike the royal troupe, were willing to appear in French salons. The teaching and performance of the dance outside the palace were a sign of the times: the magico-religious significance of the art as a symbol of the potent ruler united with the chthonic forces of female fertility were on the wane and kings were forced to quibble about allowances for dance costumes with French civil servants.

Yet the politics of the period were, in a sense, reflective of the tradition of female dance – in Cambodia, he who controlled the dance controlled the nation. When the king was no longer powerful enough to support his dancers and prevent performance outside the palace, his arts were expropriated by the new powers. Symbolically, the French ability to expropriate the dance was a kind of validation of their reign.

The former queen mother, Kossamak, was instrumental in a renaissance of the court troupe which flourished during the reign of King Norodum Sihanouk, her son who ascended the throne in 1941 and reigned until he was set aside by the Lon Nol government in 1970. She regained control of the dance and effectively revamped the programme, venues, and costuming. She streamlined the programme to fit the short time period a modern, Western audience finds appropriate for performances. Instead of long dramas, excerpts became the norm and a presentation typically included a group dance, a short dance drama selection, and a group dance as a finale. Performances at Angkor and abroad as well as in the palace were frequent during the queen mother's administration of the troupe. For some choreographies, she replaced the Thai influenced costumes with garments modelled on the carvings in Angkor temples. The queen mother made the royal dancers a significant feature in emerging culture politics of the modern Cambodia.

In the 1960s Sihanouk's daughter Bopa Devi was the major dancer in the group, and, following Kossamak's innovations, the Royal Cambodian Ballet performed at capitals around the world on cultural missions and for visiting heads of state in Cambodia. The 254 members of the troupe (2 masters, 17 dancing mistresses, 6 prime dancers, 25 corps de ballet, 160 pupils, 30 attendants (dressers, costumers, jewellery persons, makeup artists), 10 singers, and 4 clowns) in 1962 show that in this era, the *lakhon kbach boran* was again an important attribute of the Khmer king's power.

Of lesser significance to the Khmer court were the two male forms, the shadow play and the masked dance. *Nang sbeck* is the shadow play which involves 10 dancers dancing with large leather panels portraying multi-person scenes in front of and behind a white screen 30 feet long and 10 feet high. The performance is under the direction of two narrators and accompanied by a *pinpeat* ensemble. The panels, which are about 4½ feet high, usually show multiple characters in a scene from the *Ramayana*. The two narrators using narration and dialogue alternate in delivering episodes from the epic story of Rama. The iconography of the 150 puppets in the set corresponds to dance drama figures in both role types and distinguishing headdresses. In addition to providing entertainment and edification, some performances might be done to promote rain or cure epidemics.

The form has had little support in the present generation, and a single troupe was operating in Siam Reap in the early 1970s, playing from 8 pm to 1 am, and taking 7 nights to do the Rama story. The form corresponds to the Thai *nang yai* and the curative powers of performance, the use of a percussive orchestra, the strategy of mixing humour and heroic action in a theatre of character types link it to the *wayang* tradition of Indonesia and Malaysia.

The mask dance *lakhon khol* is believed to have developed from the shadow play, as puppeteers exchanged their leather panels for masks. The footwork of the dancers is derived from the dance of the puppet manipulators. The dramatic and musical repertoire correspond to the shadow theatre.

In 1970, King Sihanouk was deposed, and the court arts are understandably in a period of transition. In the wake of the Khmer Rouge triumph in 1975, and the subsequent take-over of the country in 1979 by a Vietnamese-backed government, the classical dance style has been adapted to present socially relevant themes. Training in classical dance has been carried out in refugee camps in Thailand, and what was a palace prerogative may be reaching new segments of the Khmer population as a result. The mass emigration from Cambodia during this troubled decade has resulted in troupes being set up abroad: in Paris a group operates under Bopha Devi's direction and a Maryland-based group in the United States toured that nation in 1984. But though the outer form may survive, the Khmer court dance which has been developed and refined as a prerogative and a proof of royal power is struggling to redefine itself in this new epoch.

Modern popular forms The Cambodian popular forms are heavily influenced by genres that have emerged in other countries, and adapted to suit Khmer tastes. These arts include *yike*, *lakon bassac*, *nang kalun*, and spoken drama.

Yike developed in response to tours by Malay *bangsawan* troupes in the late 19th century. The art parallels the Thai *likay* in its mixture of classical and modern features. The introduction of wing and drop scenery, the rough approximation of classical dance for entrances and exits, and the humorous burlesques of classical legends or the introduction of new plots coupled with witty improvisation by performers helped *yike* gain wide popularity among the populace. Performances were even staged at court.

Lakon bassac is a form which combines elements borrowed from Vietnamese theatre with indigenous techniques. The form developed in the 19th century in the Bassac river region in Vietnam where Khmer peoples live, and spread to Cambodia. It mixes traditional Cambodian features and elements of the Chinese-influenced Vietnamese theatre. Brandon notes

that *pinpeat* music may play in one scene, and a Chinese two-stringed fiddle in the next, while one costume will seem fit for a classical Khmer dancer, the next resembles a Chinese opera outfit.

A third popular form is *nang kalun* or *ayang*, a shadow puppet theatre related to the *nang talung* of Thailand. Like the Thai theatre it probably has grown up in emulation of the Indonesian/Malay *wayang kulit* (leather shadow puppet) tradition, but differs from that model in its use of multiple puppeteers. Stories from the *Ream Ker* and *jataka* tradition can be presented, and the buffoonery of the clown endears the form to the peasant audience.

A final form that has developed in the 20th century is spoken Western drama, based on French models. King Sihanouk, himself, wrote and produced plays in this genre. The fate and the future of all these popular arts, like the court and folk forms, awaits stabilization of the country. As the Khmer recover from the traumas of war, revolution, defoliation, mass emigration, and famine, they will surely perpetuate a tradition of art that is long and strong.   KF

See: E. Blumenthal, 'The Court Ballet: Cambodia's Loveliest Jewel', *Cultural Survival* (Summer 1990); J. Brandon, *Theatre in Southeast Asia*, Cambridge, Mass., 1967; J. Brunet, *Nang Shek*, Berlin, 1969; and 'Nang Sbek', *World of Music* 9/4 1968 (18); G. Coedes, *The Indianized States of Southeast Asia*, ed. W. Vella, trans. S. Cowing, Honolulu, 1968; P. Cravath, 'Earth in Flower', Ph.D, Univ. of Hawaii, 1985; and 'Origins of the Classical Dance Drama of Cambodia', *Asian Theatre Journal* 3, 2 (1986); B. Groslier, 'Danse et musique sous les rois d'Angkor', *Felicitation Volumes of Southeast Asian Studies Presented to His Highness Dhaninivat Kromamun Bidyalabh Bridhyakorn*, vol. 2, Bangkok, 1965 and *Danseuses cambodgiennes anciennes et modernes*, Paris; A. Leclère, *Le théâtre cambodgien*, Paris, 1911; S. Thierry, *Les danses sacrées*, Paris, 1963; Tran Quang Hai, 'Kampuchea', *New Grove Dictionary of Music and Musicians*, ed. S. Sadie, 1980; *Royal Cambodian Ballet*, Phnom Penh, 1963; X. Zarina, 'Royal Cambodian Dancers', *Classical Dances of the Orient*, New York, 1967.

Kantor, Tadeusz (1915–90) Polish scene designer, director and visual artist, who graduated from the Cracow Academy of Fine Arts in 1939. During the

A scene from Kantor's *The Dead Class*, 1975. Kantor is designer, creator, director and performer.

Nazi occupation he founded the underground Independent Theatre, staging **Słowacki**'s *Balladyna* (1943) and **Wyspiański**'s *Return of Odysseus* (1944). After the war he created avant-garde stage designs for the Teatr Stary in Cracow, including *Saint Joan* (1956), and for the Teatr Ludowy in Nowa Huta, notably *Measure for Measure* (1956). Dissatisfied with institutionalized avant-garde, he organized his own theatre in 1956 with a group of visual artists, calling it Cricot II, to mark continuity with the painters' theatre Cricot from the 1930s. In the 1960s Kantor produced happenings, exhibited widely, and travelled with his company, creating an autonomous theatre in which actors are used as props and manikins, and the text (usually by **Witkiewicz**) exists as an object on a par with other components of the production. In the 1970s he developed 'The Theatre of Death', where time, memory and the interpenetration of life and death hold sway, and Kantor himself appeared as a master of ceremonies at the seance. Major productions were *The Cuttlefish* (1956), *In a Small Country House* (1961), *The Madman and the Nun* (1963), *The Water Hen* (1968), *The Green Pill* (1973), *The Dead Class* (1975), *Wielopole, Wielopole* (1980, created in Florence), *Where Are the Snows of Yesteryear?* (1982), *Let the Artists Die* (1985, created in Nuremberg). DG

Kapnist, Vasily Vasilievich (1757–1823) Ukrainian dramatist and lyric poet whose satirical play *Chicane* (1793) was the only 18th-century Russian comedy to approach **Fonvizin**'s work in skill and ferocity. Its tone is suggestive of **Griboedov**'s later *Woe from Wit* and its subject, judicial corruption in a provincial town, foreshadows **Gogol**'s *The Inspector General*. Although the author's preface stresses the pastness of these abuses, Kapnist's play was refused permission for production and publication until after the death of Catherine the Great (1798), when it was performed for a brief time before being removed from the repertoire. It was revived in 1808 and again in 1812. Kapnist also translated **Molière**'s *Sganarelle* (1780, revised 1806), reflecting the penchant of Russia's most talented dramatists for the works of their French counterpart. SG

Karagöz (Karaghioz, Karagheuz, Kara-Goze; Turkish, lit., Dark Eyes) The comic character in Oriental shadow-plays of Turkish origin, said to have been invented by a sheikh Kishteri. An entertainer named Karagöz may have lived in the 13th century, but from the mid-17th century, the characterization was heavily influenced by Persian and Chinese puppet plays. Karagöz is the quick-witted, impudent young roisterer, endowed with a huge phallus, who is constantly misconstruing Hacivat (Hadj'Iwâz), the older, more pretentious showoff, and his wife Lachampiyya, in a series of bawdy, scatological dialogues. Secondary characters, usually racial stereotypes, were added later. The Karagöz plays were first performed only at nightfall during Ramadan in coffee-houses. They greatly influenced puppet drama throughout the Islamic world: in North Africa he pops up as Karagush or Karogheuz, a kind of Priapic picaroon with a flexible leather member. The Greek version Karaghiosis emerged from the 1821 revolution as an exemplary

spokesman for freedom and morality, who travelled the countryside accompanied by musicians.   LS

Karatygin, Vasily Andreevich (1802–53) Famous Russian tragedian, born of an acting family, considered along with **I. I. Sosnitsky** to be one of the best St Petersburg performers of his time. He was a former student of **Shakhovskoi**, with whose instruction he became disaffected, and later of Katenin, who compared his acting to **Talma**'s. He took a premeditated and declamatory approach to acting which created a coldly technical and unsurprising, if often heroic, impression. In this he was abetted by a good education, native intelligence, a handsome figure and *basso* voice. These virtues proved more than sufficient for the neoclassical, melodramatic and historical-patriotic roles he was mostly called upon to play in the works of **Ozerov**, **Kukolnik** and **Polevoi**. Although he was a court favourite, experts and literati such as **Shchepkin**, **Pushkin** and Belinsky preferred the more impassioned, albeit inconsistent, performances of his Moscow counterpart, **Mochalov**. Karatygin was the original Chatsky in **Griboedov**'s *Woe from Wit* (1831), Don Juan and the Baron in Pushkin's 'little tragedies', *The Stone Guest* (1847) and *The Covetous Knight* (1852), respectively and Arbenin in **Lermontov**'s *Masquerade* (1852). His wife, A. M. Kolosova, was also a noted actress. SG

Kariyala (India) Also *Kariala*. This is the rural theatre form once popular among the Hindu villagers of Himachal Pradesh in northern India. Like **Bhand Jashna**, another form of rural theatre popular in the mountainous areas of the country, *Kariyala* is also performed during the day, as well as at night.

The performance space or arena (*akhara*) is located between hillocks, permitting all the spectators to see the action. Musicians sit at one side of the playing area and the actors make a slow procession through the spectators from the dressing room to the playing area. As is typical in many rural settings, the men sit together on mats (*durees*) on one side and women huddle on the other. The children usually crowd close to the playing area where they may get a good view of the action. Many of them fall asleep during the all-night performances and are carried home or join their parents in the early hours of the morning. Costumes are usually contemporary local dress to which brightly coloured headdresses and cloth pieces are added allowing them to stand out from the local people.

Performances begin when a clown and a female character dance and pantomime as the chorus sings songs of praise to the deities. The plays are loosely structured, simple stories built around character-types and their acts (*swangs*). Satire and the reinforcement of well-known moral lessons characterize most of the works. Stories about money-lenders, village policemen, shepherds, religious medicants (*sadhus*) and old men who marry young wives are popular fare. FaR

Kasoma Kabwe (*fl.* 1970s) Zambian playwright, whose published work includes *The Black Mamba* trilogy of plays on Kenneth Kaunda and the struggle for independence (*African Plays for Playing 2*, ed. M.

Etherton, 1975). Kasoma is director of the University of Zambia dance troupe and Centre for the Arts.   RK

Kasper, Kasperl, Kasperle Clown in the old Viennese folk comedy who became the **Punch** of the Austro-German puppet play. He was originally created by stout Johann Laroche (1745–1806), leading player at the Leopoldstadt Theatre, Vienna, from 1781; for 40 years, audiences rejoiced to hear his beery voice call 'Auwedl' ('Deary me') from the wings. When Metternich forbade the good-natured dunce to speak, he cultivated his pantomime, giving rise to the Viennese expression, 'To laugh as if you were watching Kasperl'. The name was adopted by a hand-puppet, descending from the Meister Hämmerlein of the 16th century, who wielded a wooden bat; his partners were Gretel, Grandmother, Policeman, Death, the Devil and the crocodile. In Munich Count Franz von Pocci (1807–76) and the puppeteer Josef Leonhard Schmid (1821–1912) tried to refine the dialect-speaking figure into the more literary Kasper Larifari, and early 20th-century educators used Kasperl as a spokesman for programmes of enlightenment. In the late 1920s, Max Jacob (1888–1967) developed a sardonic Kasperl, a displaced person given to officious preachments. The most popular puppet in the German-speaking world, Kasper has become a standard term for any puppet.   LS

Kataev, Valentin Petrovich (1897–   ) Respected Soviet prose writer and dramatist, who survived Stalinism and is best known for his upbeat romantic social comedy of the New Economic Policy period, *Squaring the Circle* (1928), a tale of mismatched newlywed couples – one staunchly communist, the other quasi-bourgeois – thrown together in a Soviet housing shortage, who eventually swap mates. It premiered at the **Moscow Art Theatre** under **Nemirovich-Danchenko**'s direction and played successfully in New York and London. Most of his plays are comedies, vaudevilles and adaptations of his own novels and are characterized by a generosity of spirit combined with acute satire. *The Embezzlers* (1928), from his best-known novel, is a NEP adventure story with satirical overtones. *The Vanguard* (1930) is one of the first plays about collectivization. *A Lonely White Sail* (1937), describing the picaresque adventures of two young boys during the 1905 Revolution, was adapted from his novel (1936) for stage and screen. It, along with the war-time dramas *The Soldier at the Front* (1937), *The Blue Scarf* (1943) and *Son of the Regiment* (1945), reflect the author's sensitivity to young adults, children and sentimental themes. The drama *Time Forward!* (1932), a socialist realist First Five Year Plan drama inspired by **Mayakovsky**'s poem 'March of the Shock-Brigades', optimistically posits its theme of social progress through industrialization. Among his many produced comedies and vaudevilles are: *The Road of Flowers* (1934), *Day of Rest* (1946) and *The Case of a Genius* (1955). Kataev was one of the few Soviet writers who successfully and acceptably coaxed comedy and even farce from sobering reality.   SG

Kathakali (India) *Kathakali* is a form of dance–drama popular in the state of Kerala, south India, which has gained a considerable international reputation in recent years for its vigorous masculine style of physical movement, bold superhuman characterizations and dance. It is a blend of dance, music and acting which dramatizes stories, most of which are adaptations from the Indian epics – *Ramayana*, *Mahabharata* and the *Puranas*.

Kathakali emerged in the 17th century, borrowing heavily from various theatre and dance forms of a region rich in cultural traditions. Perhaps *Kathakali*'s ritual elements and emphasis on elaborate facial and eye expressions and hand gestures were adapted from **Kutiyattam**. Its devotional character, style of dance, movement and music may have been borrowed from the **Krishnattam**. *Kathakali*'s direct predecessor was *Ramanattam*, a form of theatre in which plays were composed from events adapted from the *Ramayana*. It is a popular belief that *Ramanattam* was created because the Maharaja of Kottayam was jealous of the popularity of *Krishnattam* and developed his own form of theatre as a form of competition and self-aggrandisement.

Soon it became apparent that the fledgeling form of theatre needed a broader base for stories than the *Ramayana* provided, and so the enthusiastic playwrights and patrons who came forward to create dramas to be enacted in the form chose a canvas which included a wide range of popular epic material. *Ramanattam* then became known as *Kathakali*, which literally means 'story play'.

Kathakali's patrons included rulers and rich landowners and, like the founders of *Krishnattam*, the actors were Nairs, a caste of individuals trained in the martial art techniques, popular in Kerala, used to develop soldiers to engage in ritual battle. Today, the actors hail from many different castes and communities, although many of the *Kathakali* actors are Nairs.

Actor training is a long and arduous process, often taking from six to ten years to complete. Like many of the world's great art forms it takes a lifetime to achieve greatness. Generally, training begins at a very young age usually between 10 and 14. Originally, training followed the traditional method – the sons of actors were trained in the art by their fathers, near relatives or trusted teachers employed by a company or by those employed by schools subsidized by the government or private sources.

The selection of potential candidates is a difficult task because so much time and energy is invested in the student once he is selected to participate in a programme that the teachers must have a keen eye for spotting potential talent in the very young. Once selected, the student undergoes extensive body training to develop flexibility and stamina to endure the long hours of performance.

Stress is placed on eye and facial exercises, as well as mastery of an elaborate code of about 600 hand gestures.

Training normally begins in the early morning before dawn and extends until just before midnight. During a typical day dance sequences that are suited to specific plays are taught and choreographic sections are committed to memory in which gestures, facial expressions and movements are integrated. The texts of the *Kathakali* (attakatha) plays are also learned by heart. During all stages in the student's development, the rhythm and tempo of the action must be ingrained.

Since the ideas of a play are conveyed by actors almost entirely through hand-gestures, facial and body expressions, precision and size of expression are crucial. The text of the plays is chanted by two singers who stand behind the actors and provide the basic tempo and rhythm of the music. The leading singer (*ponnani*) holds a heavy brass-bell gong struck with a curved stick made of banana root. The second singer plays large bell-brass cymbals. The singers interweave their voices throughout the show moving systematically through individual verses and dialogue portions of the text in a style of singing known as *sopana*. Three chief drums accompany the entire dramatic action. The large horizontal drum (*maddalam*) is carried across the waist of the drummer. It provides flexibility of pace and intonation. The vertical drum (*centa*) is used during battle scenes and scenes with special sound effects and high drama. The small hour-glass shaped drum (*itekka*) has a delicate sound and is especially effective when female characters take stage. A harmonium provides the basic notes necessary to keep the singers on pitch and the conch shell (*sanka*) is used when gods or important ritual events are at hand. Since performers require the text to be used by individuals who are not actors and the gestures are performed by non-singers, a close bond must be established between the musicians and the actors in order to create a unified dramatic effect.

Performances usually begin around nine or ten at night after an elaborate percussion overture followed by preliminaries danced by young apprentices. The proceedings take about two to three hours to complete.

Any spot is considered appropriate for a *Kathakali* performance – be it in a temple compound, in a family home, a large hall or on a proscenium arch stage. Although the performance seems designed to be played on a rectangular space, 20 to 30 feet square demarcated by four poles, audiences prefer to gather at the front, near the bell-metal lamp, opposite the musicians. No matter how the audiences organize themselves, the actors still play to one side.

The atmosphere of a *Kathakali* is charged with excitement, with children and women relegated to the front and to one side of the house and the men arranged on the other.

Troupes of actors, musicians and backstage technicians and costumers are often commissioned to choose a play at short notice from a whole repertory of plays. The exact play may not be decided until several hours before the show begins, just in time for the actors quickly to wear the appropriate costumes and makeup.

A show may include selected and favourite scenes from various *Kathakali* plays or it may be an entire play performed from beginning to end. In village performances, shows conclude around 6 am often with a band of enthusiastic devotees awake to the very end who trudge wearily home with the sound of drums still ringing in their ears. FaR

Kathputli The string puppets of Rajasthan, India, are known as *Kathputli*; *Katha* means 'story' and *putli* means 'puppet'.

The puppets are doll figures, usually not more than two feet tall, manipulated by a puppeteer who stands above and works the puppets by strings connected to the head, waist and hands. Usually the puppets do not have legs and feet because the lower part of their bodies is covered by a long colourful skirt.

The puppeteers carve the heads and trunk of the body from mango wood patterning the figures after traditional designs, many of which may be seen in traditional Rajput paintings. The figures wear colourful turbans and crowns to identify their social status and they sport painted beards and moustaches corresponding to their station in life. Women too have a special iconography.

The puppet arms are stuffed with cloth to give them a human appearance. Sometimes properties, such as swords and shields, are stitched to the hands.

Popular animal figures used in the shows are camels and horses. Except for the neck of a beast, there are generally no movable parts and the figures are stuffed so that they are hard and durable.

Today, the puppet figures have become a popular tourist item in government sales emporia throughout the country, and special puppets and dolls are now being mass-produced only to satisfy the tourist trade and not for use in the puppet theatre.

Puppeteers come from the Bhatt community and are known as *Nat Bhatt*, those who perform plays. They lead nomadic lives travelling from village to village to entertain the public and earn a meagre livelihood. Troupes of puppeteers consist of the main puppeteer (*sutradhar*), an assistant, usually one of his brothers or sons, a narrator–singer (*bhagavat*) and musicians, including a drummer, cymbal player and harmonium player. The puppeteer's wife also may sing during a performance.

An unusual instrument which accompanies the Rajasthani puppets is the shrill, reed-like bamboo vibrator which attracts attention to the vigorous movements of the puppets and helps to sustain interest during a show.

The themes of the plays centre on the heroic deeds of Amar Singh Rathor, a Rajput warrior king, Prithvi Raj Chauhan of Ajmer and Delhi and King Vikramaditya of Ujjain. The events from the lives of these famous individuals provide ample material for the puppeteers to demonstrate their expert skill with the puppets, such as juggling, tumbling, horseback riding, swordsmanship and dancing. Through clever manoeuvres of the strings the puppeteers endow the little figures with life.

The stage may be arranged anywhere there is room to stand two wooden cots (*charphoys*) on end and stretch cloth masking to create a proscenium arch. Among the puppeteers the proscenium is known as the 'Taj Mahal'. A dark curtain about three feet high is stretched about 18 inches upstage of the proscenium to mask the puppeteers who stand above and behind the curtain to work the puppets. Electric lights, torches or coconut oil lamps are used to illuminate the acting area.

Today, although *Kathputli* is among the best-known of India's puppet forms, it has deteriorated to little more than a side show entertainment. Hardly more than an hour is taken to demonstrate the various tricks of the little figures. Unfortunately, the dramatic urge has been replaced by sheer entertainment to satisfy the cravings of the spectators. FaR

Katona, József (1791–1830) Hungarian playwright, born in Kecskemét, became attracted to the theatre while studying law in Pest. He wrote *Bánk Bán* in 1815 for a competition held by the theatre in Kolozsvár, which never acknowledged the play. Discouraged,

Katona had it published in 1821, and wrote no more for the stage. He died without realizing that *Bánk Bán* would eventually be considered the greatest Hungarian play of the century. Set in 13th-century Hungary, this tragedy details the psychological undoing of Bánk, an honourable palatine, who is placed in a situation where his loyalties to his country, his king, and his wife become irreconcilable. The 1845 production of *Bánk Bán* at the National Theatre made clear not only its dramatic merits, but also its political implications: the play treats the issue of foreign exploitation of the nation.   EB

Kaufman, George S[imon] (1889–1961) American playwright and director. A Founding Father of the American popular theatre, Kaufman enjoyed a long and extraordinarily productive Broadway career. On his own he wrote only one play, a satire of the theatre called *The Butter and Egg Man* (1925); in collaboration he wrote 40 plays, more than half of them certified hits. His partners included **Marc Connelly** (*Dulcy*, 1921, and *Beggar on Horseback*, 1924); Edna Ferber (*The Royal Family*, 1927, *Dinner at Eight*, 1932, and *Stage Door*, 1936); Morrie Ryskind (*The Cocoanuts*, 1925, and *Animal Crackers*, 1928, two **Marx Brothers** vehicles, and *Of Thee I Sing*, which won the Pulitzer Prize in 1931); and **Moss Hart** (*Once in a Lifetime*, 1930, and the 1936 Pulitzer Prize winner *You Can't Take It With You*, and *The Man Who Came to Dinner*, 1939). While his partners were stronger on plot contrivance, Kaufman's speciality was dialogue, which he enlivened with witty, sarcastic rejoinders: the fabled Kaufman wisecrack. He was a born satirist whose targets included not only his own beat, the New York theatre world, but also Hollywood, big business, politics, and provincialism (although Kaufman himself was accused of being parochial in his subject matter). His subjects were drawn from life but his artificial, well-made plots were manufactured for the theatre. Kaufman's dry wit earned him a seat at the Algonquin Round Table, and his instinctive abhorrence of romance, sentiment, and melodrama provided a counterbalance to his less cynical collaborators. Though his tone was captious and ironic, Kaufman was never so abrasive as to offend the large popular audience his bread and butter depended on; at the finale he tempered his sting with forgiveness.

Kaufman began his directing career in 1927 with a jumpy, frenetic production of *The Front Page*. Like a terse Kaufman script, a Kaufman-directed show had remarkable precision. Swift timing was his trademark; he had no patience for analysis or introspection, and when a solemn actor once made the mistake of asking about motivation, Kaufman snapped 'Your job'.   FH

Kawadwa, Byron (c. 1940–77) Ugandan playwright. Founded Kampala City Players and Uganda Schools Drama Festival. Creative Writing Fellow, Makerere University, and Director, Uganda National Theatre, 1973–7. A staunch royalist, his two most important works, in collaboration with musician Wassanyi Serukenya, have palace themes. *Makula ga Kulabako* (1970) tells the love story of princess Kulabako and a commoner. It always plays to full houses and has been made into a film. *Oluimba lwa Wankoko* (1971) tells of the attempt to oust the rightful heir by an ambitious politician. This was Uganda's entry to FESTAC in Lagos and is said to have caused Kawadwa's murder. In both plays music matches words and theme, and is both original and Ugandan, and other writers have learned the techniques.   MMAC

Kazan, Elia (1909–) American director. **Group Theatre** member and co-founder of the **Actors Studio**, Kazan has long been considered America's leading director of actors for both stage and film. His stage productions of *A Streetcar Named Desire* (1947), *Death of a Salesman* (1949), *Cat on a Hot Tin Roof* (1955), and *Sweet Bird of Youth* (1959), and his films, *Streetcar* (1951), *On the Waterfront* (1954), and *East of Eden* (1955), have earned him the reputation of the pre-eminent Method director whose overheated, naturalistic style is synonymous with the work of the Actors Studio. A Kazan-directed performance is excitingly high-strung, notable for its depth and intensity of feeling, its verbal stammers and backtracking, its emotional ambivalences, and its sexual vibrancy. Based on **Stanislavsky** and on **Lee Strasberg**, Kazan's method depends on personal contact with his actors. A shrewd judge of character, he takes actors off to the side, his arm draped casually over their shoulders, to whisper some private confidence or observation. Although he has rarely directed, in films or theatre, since he resigned in 1964 as co-director of the **Vivian Beaumont Theatre**, he remains a revered figure among New York actors.   FH

Kazantzákis, Nikos (1884–1957) Greek playwright. Better known for his novels and the long epic *Odyssey* (a sequel to Homer), Kazantzákis was also a prolific author of plays, some of them in verse and most of them on subjects derived from Greek myth and history. *It Is Dawning* (1906) was praised at a drama contest but was refused the prize because of its passionate, anti-conformist character. The one-act tragedy *Comedy* (1908) has been likened to **Sartre**'s *Huis Clos* and **Beckett**'s *Waiting for Godot*. *The Master Builder* (1910) and all subsequent dramas show a Nietzschian influence with the Buddhist credo as a counterpoint: *Christ* (1921), *Odysseus* (1922), *Nikiphóros Phokás* (1927), *Mélissa* (1937), *Julian the Apostate* (1939), *Prometheus* (1943), *Capodistria* (1944), *Sodhom and Gomorha* (1948), *Koúros* (1949), *Christopher Columbus* (1949), *Constantine Paleológhos* (1951), *Buddha* (1922–56). Disappointed by the reaction of critics and the public to his plays, Kazantzákis wrote his dramas with little attention to the practicalities of the stage, stressing the poetic and philosophic elements in them, tackling important existential issues. Several of Kazantzákis's dramas were staged in Greece and other countries after his death.   GT

Keach, Stacy (1941–) American stage, film and television actor. Keach gained critical attention in the title role of *MacBird!* Off-Broadway in 1967, as Buffalo Bill in **Kopit**'s *Indians* at the **Arena Stage** and on Broadway in 1969, and as Jamie in *Long Day's Journey into Night* (Off-Broadway 1971 revival). He has thrice played Hamlet, most recently in Los Angeles's **Mark Taper Forum** (1974).   DBW

Kean, Charles (1811–68) English actor and theatre manager, the son of **Edmund Kean**, beside whom

Charles Kean as Leontes with Ellen Terry as Mamillius in *The Winter's Tale*, 1856.

Charles looks even more of a prig than he actually was. He had been sent to Eton, and the lingering effect was to make him a gentlemanly actor and a pedagogic manager. He made his debut at **Drury Lane** in 1827, playing young Norval in **Home**'s *Douglas* to mixed notices, and it was his name as much as his acting prowess that sustained him in leading roles in Britain and on American tours in 1830, 1840 and 1845–7 prior to his significant move into management at the **Princess's Theatre** in 1850. With a judicious mixture of **Shakespeare**, **Byron** and **Boucicault**, Kean made the Princess's a centre of fashion. The admiration of Queen Victoria, who appointed him director of her private theatricals at Windsor in 1848, was a particular feather in his cap. Kean's productions of classical plays were researched with a meticulous eye for historical accuracy. For *Macbeth* (1852) he sought advice on pre-Norman building from the architectural historian, George Godwin. For the revival of Byron's *Sardanapalus* (1852) he instructed his scene painters to consult Layard's recent account of his excavations, *Nineveh and its Remains* (1849). Each production was accompanied by a nearly book-length documentation of historical sources, a labour of love for which Kean was rewarded by election as a Fellow of the Society of Antiquaries in 1857. He was concerned also to light his sets appropriately and was the first person to deploy focused limelight effectively. The stubborn fact remains that he was a rather wooden actor. It is for the care he lavished on the look of his stage that Kean deserves to be remembered. Together with his wife, the actress Ellen Tree (1806–80), he exercised the Victorian virtue of thrift, and so could retire with a secure fortune in 1859. PT

Kean, Edmund (1789–1833) English actor who embodied the spirit of the romantic movement at its most turbulent. He was the illegitimate son of a minor actress who exploited his precocious talent. Probably resentful of the role of 'infant prodigy', Kean broke away from his mother in c. 1804 and spent ten years as a struggling provincial actor, during which time he married and had two sons, the elder of whom died in infancy. Small, wiry and swarthy as a gypsy (which he was sometimes believed to be), Kean was also a skilful acrobat and mime, capable of playing the dumb **Harlequin** as well as speaking roles in the stock companies of Irish and English towns and cities. He had already gathered a reputation for riotous living when he was culled from Exeter to London by **Robert Elliston**. Confusion over contracts, together with some sharp practice, led to his making his debut at **Drury Lane** instead of at Elliston's **Olympic**. Drury Lane was at a point of crisis, and it was the miracle of Kean's triumph that saved its shareholders. He opened as Shylock, defying tradition by wearing a black beard in place of the established red and playing the Jew as a monster of energetic evil. The date was 26 January 1814 and it marked a turning point in the fortunes of Drury Lane as well as of Kean. Before the end of that first season, he added to Shylock his finest role, Richard III, as well as Hamlet, Othello, Iago and Luke Frugal in **Massinger**'s *The City Madam*. It was already evident that demonic passions would be his *forte*. It was in the frenzy of Othello, as it would be in the final throes of Sir Giles Overreach in Massinger's *A New Way to Pay Old Debts* (1816), that he found his focus. Coleridge's famous observation that 'To see him act is like reading **Shakespeare** by flashes of lightning' contains an important pointer to Kean's method. It was not on the sustained character study of a **John Philip Kemble** that he relied, but on the making of startlingly indicative 'points'. His admired transitions, those sudden shifts from 'high' to 'low', were inspirational in the days of his greatness and became mechanical only in the long years of his decline. That decline was all too rapid. After the years of struggle, Kean succumbed quickly to the headiness of adulation. **Hazlitt** perceived a loss of concentration as early as his second season at Drury Lane (1814–15), when he added a controversial Macbeth and an often inert Romeo to his Shakespearian roles as well as restoring the neglected *Richard II* to the stage. Timon (1816), King John (1818), Coriolanus (1819), Lear (1820), Cardinal Wolsey (1822), Posthumus in *Cymbeline* (1823) – **Irving** would later have the wisdom to prefer Iachimo – and a dismal fiasco as Henry V (1830) complete the catalogue of Kean's Drury Lane Shakespeare, but there was as much drama behind the scenes as on the stage. Frequently stupefied by drink, often in the company of Elliston with whom he had become dangerously reconciled, Kean lost all sexual restraint. Matters came to a head in 1824, when his affair with Charlotte Cox, wife of a member of the Drury Lane committee, was discovered. Kean was taken to court in January 1825 and booed throughout the playing of *Richard III* on 24 January. Bowing to public opinion, he paid a second visit to the USA (the first was in 1820), and, although accepted on his return, he was only intermittently fit to perform. He made his last appearance in March 1833, as Othello to the Iago of his son, **Charles Kean**, but collapsed on stage and died a few weeks later. The supreme example of the charismatic actor, he had burned himself out by 1821, but there can be no doubt that for seven years he gave a lovely light. PT

Keane, John Brendan (1928–   ) Irish playwright. Most of Keane's score of plays have been locally produced. The **Abbey** gave *Hut 42* (1962). Set on a building site in northern England, it differs from most of his plays, which in contemporary local settings revive the traditional themes of land-hunger, made marriages, and emigration. The most notable are *Sive* (1959), *The Year of the Hiker* (1963), *The Field* (1966), *Big Maggie* (1970; revived, New York 1984). DM

Keeley, Mary Ann (née Goward) (1806–99) English actress, extremely popular in farce and low comedy. She made her debut as a singer in 1825, but her fame was based on her playing of below-stairs characters. She was the ideal pert maid in melodrama as well as farce, not least because of her ability to transform herself from soubrette to waif when the occasion arose. Two of her most successful parts required male impersonation. They were the title roles in **Buckstone**'s *Jack Sheppard* (1839) and Edward Stirling's *The Fortunes of Smike* (1840). She married Robert Keeley (1793–1869) in 1829, and from then on they always acted together. He was a chubby, round-faced comedian, who specialized in female impersonation, a famous Sarah Gamp in Stirling's *Martin Chuzzlewit* (1844) and the first actor to carry **Douglas Jerrold**'s Mrs Caudle (1844) from *Punch* onto the stage. The Keeleys retired in 1859, though they continued to make occasional appearances thereafter. Managers considered them the safest 'draw' in the London theatre. PT

Keene, Laura (Mary Frances Moss) (1826–73) English-born American actress and manager. While facts about her origins, training, and name are disputed, Laura Keene apparently made her London debut in 1851, a year before **James W. Wallack** hired her as leading lady for his company in New York. Her grace and charm as well as her comic ability endeared her with New York audiences in her favourite roles of Lady Teazle, Lady Gay Spanker, and Beatrice in *Much Ado*. After a year with Wallack's company, she spent the next two seasons in Baltimore and San Francisco before touring Australia with young **Edwin Booth**. In 1855 she returned to New York and opened her own Laura Keene Varieties Theatre. From 1856–63 she managed and acted in her Laura Keene's New Theatre which became known for its lavishly mounted comedies. She encouraged the production of new American plays and closely supervised an excellent company which included **E. A. Sothern**, **Joseph Jefferson III**, Kate Reignolds, **W. J. Florence**, **Agnes Robertson**, John T. Raymond, and Charles W. Couldock. She returned to touring in 1863, and was performing in *Our American Cousin* at **Ford's Theatre** in Washington, DC, when President Lincoln was assassinated. During her career, she became closely identified with the emotional drama (e.g., *Camille*). TLM

Keith, Benjamin Franklin see **Vaudeville, American**

Kellar, Harry (Heinrich Keller) (1849–1922) American magician who acted as assistant to the Fakir of Ava (I. Harris Hughes) and the Davenport Brothers, before striking out on his own. Kellar tended to appropriate and refashion tricks conceived by others. A master of publicity, he won fame with **Buatier de Kolta**'s 'Vanishing Birdcage'; from **Maskelyne**, he derived the disappearing act 'The Witch, the Sailor and the Monkey' and his supreme illusion 'The Levitation of the Princess Karnac' (1904). After touring the world in 1880, he resettled in the United States where he set a record of 323 consecutive performances at Philadelphia's Egyptian Hall (1884) and 179 at the Comedy Theatre, New York (1886–7). He retired on a well-invested fortune in 1908, naming **Howard Thurston** as his successor. LS

Kelly, Frances Maria (1790–1882) Anglo-Irish actress and singer, niece of the musician and singing star, Michael Kelly (1762–1826). It was possibly he who brought her into the **Drury Lane** chorus for the production of **George Colman the Younger**'s *Blue Beard* (1798), for which he was composer and musical director, and it was at Drury Lane that her adult career later took shape. She was a regular member of the company from 1810–33, playing leads in the ephemeral musical pieces that were a required part of the long evenings' entertainment. 'Fanny' Kelly owes her immortality to **Charles Lamb** rather than to her own skills. He adored her 'divine plain face', wrote a famous essay about her under the deceiving title 'Barbara S——' and proposed marriage to her in 1819. Her delicate refusal of the proposal is evidence of an interesting independence. Fanny Kelly was unprepared to dwindle into a wife. The madman who took a shot at her during a performance of **O'Keeffe**'s *Modern Antiques* in 1816 was another rejected suitor, and she further asserted the rights of women by promoting the all-female *Belles without Beaux* (1819), an anonymous piece which she may have helped to write. In 1833, she established a Theatre and Dramatic School at the Strand Theatre, boosting the income derived from pupils by performing a one-woman show of *Dramatic Recollections*, and transferring it in 1840 to a 200-seat theatre, built at the back of her house in Soho. She took her teaching seriously, and was proud of such famous pupils as **Boucicault** and **Mrs Keeley**, but the venture had nearly bankrupted her by 1849, and she spent her last years in modest retirement in what was then the village of Feltham. PT

Kelly, George (1887–1974) American playwright. A member of the famed Philadelphia Kellys and uncle of Princess Grace, Kelly had three major Broadway successes in the twenties: *The Torchbearers* (1922), a satire of little theatre enthusiasts; *The Show-Off* (1924), a comedy of provincial manners about the battle between a commonsensical mother and braggart son-in-law; and *Craig's Wife* (which won the Pulitzer Prize in 1925), an exposure of an American ice maiden whose immaculate home is more important to her than her husband. Although he was a practical man of the theatre – he began his career in 1912 as an actor on the vaudeville circuit – Kelly did not want to be labelled as a popular entertainer, and he insisted on directing each of his plays to preserve their distinctive rhythms. In later work such as *The Deep Mrs Sykes* (1945) and *The Fatal Weakness* (1946), he deliberately muted comic elements. Kelly thought of himself as a moralist whose satires were designed to instruct and improve as well as to amuse; his work gains its idiosyncratic stamp from the targets he chose: bossy, smug suburban matrons, untalented would-be actors and playwrights, and freeloaders. While Kelly worked within a conventional range of modest domestic settings, seemingly dictaphonic dialogue, and characters and situations drawn from middle-class American life, his writing achieves a unique voice, tart, scolding, droll, and delightfully eccentric. FH

Kelly, Hugh (1739–77) Irish playwright. He moved to London in 1760 and began writing, including essays on theatre for *The Babbler* and a satire on actors, *Thespis* (1766). *False Delicacy* (1768) was produced to capitalize on the success of **Goldsmith**'s *The Good Natured Man* at **Covent Garden** and proved more immediately popular than its rival. *A Word to the Wise* (1769) closed after riots against Kelly for being a government apologist. Though often damned as a writer of sentimental comedy, Kelly's plays, particularly *The School for Wives* (1773), mock the absurd excesses of sentimentalism while appealing to feeling in pursuit of a moral argument. PH

Kemble, Charles (1775–1854) English actor, the youngest brother of **Sarah Siddons** and **John Philip Kemble**, who were playing the leads in *Macbeth* when he made his London debut as Malcolm in 1794. His finest Shakespearian roles were Mercutio and Faulconbridge in *King John*, though, unlike his better known siblings, he was effective also in comedy – as Benedick, Orlando and Charles Surface in *The School for Scandal*. Intelligent, like most of the Kembles, Charles was a student of acting, but one who rarely excited audiences when he put his studies into practice. His reign as manager of **Covent Garden** (1822–32) was uneasy. From the start, he was outmanoeuvred by **Elliston** at **Drury Lane**, losing his best actors to the higher salaries of the rival house. The production of *King John* in 1823, with its pioneering devotion to historically accurate costumes (the research was done by **J. R. Planché**), was an isolated triumph until the record-breaking production of Weber's *Der Freischütz* (1824). By 1829, the position was critical and Kemble, reluctantly, cajoled his daughter into a profession from which he had hoped to spare her. **Fanny Kemble**'s appearance as Juliet (1829) began a slow recovery, completed by a highly profitable tour of Philadelphia and New York (1832–3). Father and daughter played their favourite parts to more acclaim than they received in England. On his return home, Kemble was appointed Examiner of Plays (1836–40), a post which he resigned to his son. Despite increasing deafness, he played a final season at Covent Garden in 1842. PT

Kemble, Frances Anne (1809–93) English actress, daughter of **Charles Kemble**. More ambitious to write than to act, she made her debut as Juliet in 1829 in a bid to rescue her father from financial disaster at **Covent Garden**. Welcomed by a public that was curious to see the latest of the Kembles, she continued at Covent Garden until the end of the 1831–2 season,

performing many of the parts from the repertoire of her aunt, **Sarah Siddons**, in addition to Portia, Beatrice and Lady Teazle. She also acted in her own tragedy, *Francis I* (1832), which required the audience's indulgence as well as her father's, and created the part of Julia in **Sheridan Knowles**'s popular success, *The Hunchback* (1832). The restoration of Charles Kemble's fortunes was completed by a tour of theatres in New York and Philadelphia (1832–3) in which he shared star-billing with Fanny. When the tour was over she remained in Philadelphia to marry Pierce Butler (1834). The marriage turned out to be a battle of wills, finally foundering on the issue of slavery. Fanny was a vehement abolitionist, her husband a slave-owner. She left him in 1845 (he divorced her in 1849) and, after a year of rest with her sister in Rome, she reluctantly returned to the English stage. Grown stout and already looking middle-aged, she was reduced to touring the provinces in *The Hunchback* for most of 1847, and her Lady Macbeth to **Macready**'s Macbeth in London (1848) was not a success. But she was never easily deterred. For 26 years (1848–74) she financed herself by public readings from **Shakespeare**, which became famous on both sides of the Atlantic. In retirement, she wrote three volumes of autobiography (1878, 1882 and 1890) and a novel, *Far Away and Long Ago* (1889). PT

Kemble, John Philip (1757–1823) English actor, manager. Born in Lancashire, the son of Roger Kemble, a theatre manager, he travelled with his father's company acting as a child. Intended for the priesthood he trained at Douai, leaving there in 1775 to become an actor. After some successes in Liverpool he wrote to **Tate Wilkinson** for work listing 126 roles in his repertory. At this stage in his career he also wrote a number of poor plays. He slowly built a substantial reputation and his acting was marked by careful preparation, studying other actors' work. He made his London debut at **Drury Lane** in 1783 as Hamlet and was highly praised for his gentleness and aristocratic grace, though there were already signs of the stiff and artificial technique and idiosyncratic pronunciation that marked his later work. His performance as Jaffier in **Otway**'s *Venice Preserv'd* was too cold: his sister **Mrs Siddons** complained that 'his sensibilities are not so acute as they ought to be for the part of a lover'. In 1786 he published *Macbeth Reconsidered*, an erudite literary study focusing on Macbeth's courage and defining his later approach to the role. In 1787 his performance as Lear was praised for its tremendous grandeur while his Othello was too studied and insufficiently passionate. In 1788 he took over the management of Drury Lane, inaugurating a series of spectacular productions like *Henry VIII* and *Coriolanus* with an original interest in antiquarian realism and a disciplined classicism. His own noble acting style reached its peak with Roman roles such as Coriolanus. The limitations of his approach were glaringly apparent as Charles Surface in **Sheridan**'s *The School for Scandal* which, played as a serious role, was 'as merry as a funeral and as lively as an elephant'. Drury Lane was declared unsafe in 1790 and demolished and Kemble opened the new theatre with its huge stage and vastly increased capacity in 1794. By the following year he was suffering severely from gout and asthma. In 1796, he left Drury Lane after wrangles with Sheridan and moved to **Covent Garden**

John Philip Kemble as Coriolanus.

with a repertory of classical and Shakespearian revivals. He allowed the **Master Betty** hysteria to take its course but was nearly bankrupted when Covent Garden was destroyed by fire in 1808 and was underinsured. The new theatre opened in 1809 but arguments about prices led to the Old Price Riots which lasted 67 nights and disillusioned Kemble. Mrs Siddons retired in 1812 and Kemble was seen as old-fashioned when **Kean** made his triumphant debut in 1814. He retired from the stage in 1817 to Lausanne. He accumulated a massive library of plays and playbills. His own many adaptations of earlier plays were published as *British Theatre* in 1815. His acting style of cultivated classicism was the result of sustained intellectual effort rather than genius, creating a performance that both was and appeared studied and lacking in spontaneity. Part of the deliberateness was the result of the asthma. His rare successes in new roles were in romantic melodramas like Penruddock in **Cumberland**'s *The Wheel of Fortune* (1795). Often regarded as progenitor of the director, his productions had aesthetic unity as well as atmospheric scenery and massive processional tableaux. He was the greatest English classical actor.   PH

Kempe (or Kemp), Will[iam] (d. c. 1603) English clown, the popular successor to **Richard Tarlton**, whom he may have replaced in the company of **Leicester's Men** as early as 1583. Kempe is known to have acted in France, the Netherlands and Denmark at around this time, and his popularity there suggests that his routines had a strong visual element. This is further confirmed by a speech in the anonymous *The Pilgrimage to Parnassus* (1597): 'Clowns have been thrust into plays by head and shoulders ever since Kempe could make a scurvy face . . . Why, if thou canst but draw thy mouth awry, lay thy leg over thy staff, saw a piece of cheese asunder with a dagger, lap up drink on the earth, I warrant thee they'll laugh mightily.' The stage business which made Kempe's appearance in a post-play jig so popular is easily inferred. After a period with **Strange's Men**, Kempe was a sharer in the newly-formed **Lord Chamberlain's Men** from 1594–9. He played Peter in *Romeo and Juliet* (presumably on the promise of a chance for something better in the jig) and Dogberry in *Much Ado About Nothing*. It is a reasonable guess that he also featured as Lancelot Gobbo and Bottom in *The Merchant of Venice* and *A Midsummer Night's Dream*, though we have no evidence of that. It may be that **Shakespeare** had Kempe in mind when he had Hamlet complain of clowns who speak 'more than is set down for them'. Whatever the reason, Kempe left the Chamberlain's Men either just before or just after they had moved from the **Theatre** to the **Globe** in 1599, taking his gift as a self-publicist into his fantastic morris-dance from London to Norwich. His pamphlet-account of this trip, *Kempe's Nine Days Wonder* (1600), is almost the last we hear of him, though it is thought that he went on a short visit to the continent before joining Worcester's Men in 1601.   PT

Kendal, Margaret Sholto (1848–1935) English actress, the youngest of 22 children, of whom the playwright **T. W. Robertson** was the eldest. (This, at least, is what is always said, although there were only 19 years between them. The confusion is not lessened by 'Madge' Kendal's autobiography (1933), in which she says not only that she was 30 years younger than Robertson, but also that there was a gap of several years between the birth of the 21st child and her own.) Having acted as a child, most significantly in the Bristol circuit of James Henry Chute, she made her London debut in 1865, as Ophelia at the **Haymarket**. It was at this 'home of comedy' under **Buckstone** that she established her reputation, above all in society comedy. Her partnership with W. H. Kendal (1843–1917), whom she married in 1869, was broken only by his death. It was as 'the Kendals' that they continued to star at the Haymarket – in *The Rivals* (1870), *As You Like It* (1875), *She Stoops to Conquer* (1875) and a notable sequence of **W. S. Gilbert** premieres, *The Palace of Truth* (1870), *Pygmalion and Galatea* (1871), *The Wicked World* (1873), *Charity* (1874) – and at **John Hare**'s **Royal Court** (1875–9). They were joint managers with Hare of the **St James's** from 1879–88, where they were adventurous and prosperous. They remained much in demand, at home and abroad, until their retirement in 1908. But Madge Kendal, even during her management, was less notable as an actress than as a theatrical *grande dame*, the sort who inaugurates charity benefits, unveils plaques and opens fêtes. She was widely admired for taking up the case of John Merrick, the Elephant Man, in 1888 and lived to a ripe old age as the acme of respectability. She was appointed DBE in 1926.   PT

Kennedy, Adrienne (1931–) Black American playwright who blends symbols, historical figures, racial images and myths to create surreal, highly personalized one-act plays. *Funnyhouse of a Negro*, which won an Obie in 1964, depicts the final moments before the suicide of Sarah, a mulatto psychically torn by an inability to reconcile herself to her mixed racial heritage. *The Owl Answers* (1969) portrays another mulatto woman caught in a hallucinatory nightmare of confused racial identity in which biographical and historical characters emerge, dissolve and metamorphose. Kennedy's other plays include: *A Rat's Mass* (1966), a fantasy of war and prejudice; *In His Own Write* (1967), an adaptation of musician John Lennon's autobiographical writings; and *A Lancashire Lad* (1980), a children's play based on the early life of Charlie Chaplin. FB

Kennedy, Arthur (1914–) American film, stage, and television actor. He began acting with the **Group Theatre** and made his debut on Broadway as Bushy in *Richard II* (1937). Later successes were Chris in *All My Sons* (1947), Biff in *Death of a Salesman* (1949), and John Proctor in *The Crucible* (1953). Awards include a Tony for Biff (1949), the New York Film Critics Award for *Bright Victory* (1951), and a Golden Globe Award for *Trial* (1955). SMA

Kennedy, Charles Rann (1871–1950) Playwright from England who became an American citizen in 1917. An advocate of Christian principles, which he dramatized with more ardour than theatrical effectiveness, Kennedy helped bring the Social Gospel movement to the American stage. In *The Servant in the House* (1907), his best-known play, he presented a Christ-figure who reveals the hypocrisy of organized religion. Later plays, many written for his actress wife, Edith Wynne Matthison, include *The Idol Breaker* (1914) and *The Terrible Meek* (1912), a daring anti-war play. Leaving Broadway, the Kennedys became associated with Bennett College where he continued to write plays and direct Greek plays. WJM

Kenya The population of Kenya is estimated at about 20 million people, inhabiting 225,000 square miles, two thirds of which is scarcely suitable for habitation. Formerly a British colony, Kenya achieved its independence in 1963 after many years of struggle and open war waged by the Mau Mau Land Freedom Army between 1952 and 1960. Since independence Kenya has developed a form of free enterprise capitalism which has divided the society into two worlds – that of a small class of Kenyans together with their foreign business partners and the broad masses of the people, a state of affairs depicted in the 1979 play *Thi Ni Igiri (There Are Two Worlds)*, which will be referred to later.

As to be expected in a colony with a significant settler population, theatre before independence was dominated by a tradition of 'Little Theatre' which functioned to provide its audiences with an opportunity to escape from reality and the increasing challenge of the anti-colonial forces, who themselves were using theatre as a means of mobilizing opposition to the colonial regime.

In 1952 at the height of the struggle for independence the colonial government opened a cultural centre which also houses the National Theatre. Many of the productions performed there served to entertain and inspire the British soldiers who came to Kenya. They also served the settler community, white colonial administrators and industrial top management, as well as the educated Kenyan African petit-bourgeoisie which had accepted colonial culture.

Apart from the dramatic forms of the pre-colonial society, indigenous Kenyan drama first developed within the colonial education system and ultimately gave rise to the Kenya Schools Drama Festival, at which the set pieces, the adjudicators and the criteria were all foreign. In the late 1940s the Nairobi African Dramatic Society was formed, a group which was to initiate the idea of taking theatre to the people by performing in Machakos, Kiambu, Thika and Nakulu, all not far from Nairobi.

In 1955 the Nairobi African Dramatic Society entered the white-dominated National Drama Festival with the play *Not Guilty* by Graham Hyslop, and won awards. Subsequently the development of indigenous theatre in Kenya was characterized either by acceptance of the junior partner tag or the struggle to find its own voice and direction. At first most activity was very much an extension of the 'Little Theatre' movement and the 'civilizing mission' of the mission schools. Comedians such as Athmani Suleiman (Mzee Tamaa) and Kipanga, who were trailblazers in the art of popular comedy, 'graced' the stage of the National Theatre and were much enjoyed by settler audiences for their slapstick and *kisetla kiswahili*. They were to continue amusing people in live shows and radio and television broadcasts after independence to set a tradition which has found worthy successors in such modern television programmes as *Vitimbi*.

At independence, the Kenya National Theatre, like the economic and other spheres of national life, was not democratized. It continued to serve foreign interests, now widened to include the tastes of those from other European countries. Plays and musicals of no relevance to the cultural life of the majority of Kenyans were performed.

In the years that followed more and more black schools entered the National Drama Festival, at first performing published European set books but later, as African plays began to be published, their entries changed in character. At the University of Nairobi too, African plays such as **Soyinka**'s *Kongi's Harvest* and Lewis Nkosi's *The Rhythm of Violence* were produced and acted by people such as Arthur Kemoli, Ben Chahilu and David Mulwa. A National Drama School was set up by the National Theatre, which produced artists such as **Kenneth Watene**, Titus Gathwe, Sese Njugu and Frank Kimotho. In the meantime **Ngugi wa Thiong'o**, who had been active at Makerere, writing and publishing his early plays, had joined the then Department of English at the University (a name which he and others fought to change to Department of Literature). In addition John Ruganda, **Francis Imbuga** and later Waigwa Wachira were developing drama there, in particular the Free Travelling Theatre, which annually toured the country performing in schools and market places.

It was in the 1970s that the social contradictions created by neocolonialism became clearly visible. The increasing political and social polarization expressed itself in the arts, nowhere more clearly than in the novels and plays of Ngugi, in particular his collaborative drama with **Micere Mugo**, *The Trial of Dedan*

Kimathi, which along with Imbuga's *Betrayal in the City*, Kenya's entries for FESTAC in 1976, was performed at the National Theatre to a predominantly working-class audience. Both form and content were inspiring and created an atmosphere of communal song, dance and solidarity which served to highlight the role a truly national theatre could play and therefore exposed the exclusiveness of the so-called National Theatre. The question of who controlled the art facilities in the country raised the more fundamental question of who controlled the economy. However, participants in this new and dynamic theatre were not ideologically united.

It is within the context of this quest for a national theatre that the performance of *I'll Marry When I Want* by Ngugi wa Thiong'o and Ngugi wa Mirii in 1977 should be seen – in its use of the Gikuyu language, the participation of workers, peasants and intellectuals of different nationalities bringing town and rural areas together and the move away from the National Theatre building into a more organically national context, the **Kamiriithu** Community Educational and Cultural Centre at Limuru. The potential of the Kamiriithu phenomenon to usher in a new, independent community-based theatre is best illustrated by the interest aroused by the play's performance and its being able to tap and release an inexhaustible flow of creativity from ordinary people.

The Kenyan government however moved to suppress the play. Its licence was withdrawn and subsequently Ngugi wa Thiong'o was detained without trial and Ngugi wa Mirii lost his job at the University. The same centre again in 1982 was denied a licence to perform a play by Ngugi wa Thiong'o entitled *Mother Sing To Me*. The government further publicly announced the deregistration of the centre on 11 March 1982, thus banning all the centre's educational and cultural activities and sent the police to raze the open-air theatre built by peasants and workers and the unemployed youth of Kamiriithu village.

By the 1980s Kenyan theatre was characterized by three trends: the colonial theatre, the 'African theatre' patronized by Western cultural missions and the political national theatre symbolized by Kamiriithu. There was however a growing tendency towards more populist activity sometimes of a militant nature, exemplified by Tamaduni Players' collectively evolved sketches on the life of the 'parking boys' in Nairobi, and their Swahili performance of *The Trial of Dedan Kimathi* to working-class and student audiences. Independent drama groups proliferated in most townships and working-class suburbs, laying the foundations for a community-based theatre movement, e.g. Capricorn Theatre Group and Wanamtaa. An itinerant street theatre group with preachers, jokers and charlatans came into existence, performing at the Jeevanjee Gardens in Nairobi. In 1986 these groups came together to organize a four-day festival at the City Hall. The above developments signal an increased working-class cooption of theatre as an art form which can serve their interests.

In the face of the efforts of Kenyan artists to develop an independent and relevant theatre, the Kenyan government has repeatedly acted to suppress and distort its development. In 1979 Riara Mission School outside Nairobi entered the schools festival with the play entitled *There Are Two Worlds*, referred to earlier. The school was raided soon after by the Special Branch and the teacher in charge interrogated. In March 1982, officials tried to nullify the decision of the school drama festival judges to award a prize to the play and it was only after a fierce struggle and because of the firm stand taken by the audience that they were forced to recognize the judges' decision. In April the government banned a school play and in October another. During the Teachers Training Colleges Drama Festival the Ministry of Education banned one of the entries, harassed the actors and the authors and confiscated the manuscript. The Chief Adjudicator at the festival commented that this intimidation was preventing young Kenyans from thinking about national issues which affected the majority and suppressed not only creativity but also free democratic thinking in their everyday life.

Every theatre group must register with the government and performance licences are only granted after rigorous security checks and after each script is read and approved by the administration. Theatre in Kenya now struggles to develop in a situation of growing confrontation between two worlds and intensifying state repression and harassment.   KG NWaM

See: E. Gachuka and K Akivaga (eds.), *The Teaching of Literature in Kenya Secondary School* (East African Literature Bureau, Nairobi, 1979) – includes a section on drama in Kenya; R. Kidd, 'Popular Theatre and Popular Struggle in Kenya', in *Theatrework*, 2, 6 (Sept – Oct 1982); C. D. Killam, *An Introduction to the Writing of Ngugi* (London, 1980); L. Mbughuni, 'Old and New Drama from East Africa', in *African Literature Today*, 9 (1976); M. Mugo and G. Wasambu-were, *A New Approach to the Teaching of Literature in Kenyan High Schools* (Nairobi, forthcoming) – includes a section on drama in Kenya; Ngugi wa Thiongo, *Detained* (London, 1981); C. B. Robson, *Ngugi wa Thiongo* (New York, 1979).

Kern, Jerome (1885–1945) American composer. After studying musical composition, Kern began his theatrical career as a house composer for producer **Charles Frohman** in London. Returning to America, he worked as a song-plugger and rehearsal pianist. Individual songs by Kern were interpolated into several Broadway musicals before he was given his first opportunity to compose a complete score, *The Red Petticoat* (1912). In 1915 Kern was asked by producers F. Ray Comstock and Elisabeth Marbury to write the score for a modest musical that would be appropriate to the tiny, 299-seat Princess Theatre. The result, *Nobody Home*, enchanted critics and audiences with its personable cast, contemporary setting, and lively score. An even greater success was the second Princess Theatre musical, *Very Good Eddie* (1915). With librettist **Guy Bolton** and lyricist **P. G. Wodehouse**, Kern created *Have a Heart* (1917), *Oh, Boy* (1917), *Leave It to Jane* (1917), and *Oh, Lady! Lady!* (1918). By replacing the mythical kingdoms and stilted language of European operetta with recognizable characters, believable dramatic situations, and American musical idioms, these shows strongly influenced the direction in which American musical comedy was to evolve in the 1920s.

After writing a number of successful, if conventional, musicals in the first half of the 1920s, Kern again pioneered a new style of musical theatre with his score for *Show Boat* (1927). Conceived as a musical drama, *Show Boat*, with book and lyrics by **Oscar Hammerstein II**, proved that shows with serious librettos and songs that grew naturally out of the dramatic action could be successful. Kern's shows of the 1930s, although containing many fine songs, were more traditional operettas and musical comedies. His last complete score for Broadway was *Very Warm for May* (1939). Kern is remembered as an innovator whose scores for the Princess Theatre musicals and *Show Boat* were landmarks in the evolution of the modern musical. MK

Kerr, Walter (1913–) American drama critic, playwright, lecturer, teacher, and director. Kerr was educated at Northwestern University before beginning in 1938 an 11-year career as teacher of drama at Catholic University. There he wrote or co-wrote and directed a number of new scripts, four of which reached Broadway. With his wife Jean, he collaborated on several shows including the musical comedy, *Goldilocks* (1958). In 1950, Kerr began reviewing for *Commonweal*. The following year, he replaced Howard Barnes as drama critic for the *New York Herald Tribune*, a post he held until that paper's demise in 1966. The *New York Times* then hired Kerr as chief critic for the Sunday edition, a position he held until his retirement in 1983. Regarded as the most perceptive critic reviewing the Broadway theatre during the 1960s and 1970s, Kerr brought intelligence, insight, knowledge, and a graceful style to his work. He believed that a play's truths must be perceived by an audience intuitively rather than intellectually and that a play must touch a group consciousness so that there is a 'single unified response'. His views are expressed in *The Decline of Pleasure* (1962), *The Theatre in Spite of Itself* (1963), *Tragedy and Comedy* (1967), *Journey to the Centre of the Theatre* (1979). He won a Pulitzer Prize for Dramatic Criticism in 1978. TLM

Kerz, Leo (1912–76) German-American theatre and film set designer. Born in Berlin, Kerz studied with **Bertolt Brecht** and Laszlo Moholy-Nagy, and from 1927 worked as an assistant designer to **Erwin Piscator**. These influences remained with him throughout his career and his sets tended toward sweeping proportions and emblematic scenic elements. Like Piscator, he also incorporated film and projections into many of his designs. He left Berlin soon after Hitler assumed power and worked in London, Amsterdam and Prague before founding the Pioneer Theatre in Johannesburg, South Africa. Kerz came to the USA in 1942, assisted **Jo Mielziner**, Watson Barrett, and Stewart Chaney and resumed his work with Piscator. Kerz made his Broadway debut in 1947 with the **Katharine Cornell** production of *Antony and Cleopatra*. He is best known for his opera designs for the Metropolitan and New York City Operas, among others, and for his work at the **Arena Stage** from 1969 to 1971. He also designed for television and film including the controversial *Ecstasy* with Heddy Lamarr in 1934. AA

Kessler, David (1860–1920) Star actor of the American Yiddish theatre. Graduating from the Goldfaden Company, he became a leading exponent of the plays of **Jacob Gordin** in America achieving such fame that in 1909 the Second Avenue Theatre was built for him. Amongst many notable roles were *Yankel Boyle* in Leon Kobrin's play of that name and Yekl Shapshovitch in *The God of Vengeance*. AB

Khmelnitsky, Nikolai Ivanovich (1789–1845) Russian dramatist. An early skilled practitioner of vaudeville and *haute comédie*, adapted from French salon comedy as a reaction against the moralizing tendency of Russian drama. Wit took precedence over didacticism in Khmelnitsky's plays which were above all noteworthy for the simplicity, pliancy and native vitality of their dialogue and which advanced Russian comedy in the manner perfected by **Griboedov**, with whom he was friendly and whose *Woe from Wit* (along with **Pushkin**'s and **Gogol**'s work) he probably influenced. His works include: *The Chatterbox* (1871), adapted from the comedy *Le Babillard* by Louis de Boissy, and perhaps his best play; *Castles in the Air* (1818), his longest running play; a dozen or more additional vaudevilles; two historical dramas from the 1840s, a tragedy based on the life of a famous ancestor who led a Cossack Rebellion against Polish rule in 1648 and a treatment of Peter the Great's reign; and translations of **Molière**'s *School for Wives* (1821) and *Tartuffe* (1828) that were said to be superior to those of his predecessors. SG

Khyal (India) Also known as *Khyala*. A popular form for village theatre in the northern state of Uttar Pradesh and in the western state of Rajasthan. *Khyal*'s history is uncertain but there is some evidence to suggest that it existed at least as early as the 18th century and that the city of Agra was its home.

Various styles of *Khyal* exist and are known by the city, such as Jaipuri *Khyal*; the community, such as Gadhaspa *Khyal*; the acting style, such as Abhinaya *Khyal*; and the author of the work, such as Alibaksh *Khyal*. Subtle differences among the various styles are determined by the music and language of performance, as well as the staging techniques.

Khyal stages are generally more elaborate than most village acting areas in north India. The audience sits on three sides of an arena. On one side of a platform, three to four feet high, white sheets are spread out on the ground to demarcate one of the acting areas. Sometimes, instead of the sheets, a stage lower in height than the main stage is erected, called the *laghu* or 'little stage'. At the four corners of the main stage platform, trunks of banana trees are placed in the ground and decorative flags are strung between the four pillars to provide a festive appearance. Behind the main platform stage is a balcony-like structure 12 to 20 feet tall which is erected on poles or perhaps partially supported by the roof of a nearby house. The balcony is just wide enough to hold a few actors and is curtained at the sides and back. The high platform stage is connected to the main stage by a wooden ladder. Thus, *Khyal* performances use three distinct acting areas to achieve a dramatic effect. Petromax lanterns, strategically placed at the corners of the pillars and at the front of the balcony, give off a harsh undirected white light which illuminates the acting areas and the audience alike. Originally, cloth rolls dipped in oil cast a flickering yellow light over the acting area. Today, electric and fluorescent lights are fast replacing the petromax lamps as sources of illumination destroying the mystery of the performance.

Prior to the building of the stage, there is a ceremony in which a pole is installed at the performance site, perhaps an ancient reminder of ritual practices found in the Sanskrit drama.

Plays begin with prayers to Ganapati, the elephant-headed god, and include invocations to other gods and goddesses, as well. This is followed by comic antics by clowns. The plays that are performed are mythological, semi-historical or fanciful.

The accent on melodrama and the evocation of moods of romance, valour and pathos are typical of *Khyal*. Like so many other rural theatre forms, the performances include musical accompaniment played on the *nagara* or *dholak* drums, bell-metal cymbals and the harmonium. The human voice provides a strong melodic line and the drums set the various tempos of the action.

Male actors play all the roles. Depending on the wealth of the company, their costumes are elaborate and derived from historical periods and styles which have long since vanished. The action is carefully controlled by the director–producer (*ustad*) who sits in a chair on the main stage following the sequence of events carefully in his prompt script. FaR

Portrait of Thomas Killigrew, by W. Sheppard.

Kiesler, Frederick (1890–1965) Austrian-American architect and designer. Very little of Kiesler's visionary theatre was ever fully realized, yet his plans and projects exerted a strong influence on the development of mid-20th-century theatre architecture and on the emergence of environmental theatre. Most of his projects were variations on the co-called 'Endless Theatre' – a futuristic theatre of ramps and spirals within an ellipsoidal shell projected to hold 10,000 or more spectators. Kiesler's main concept was a theatre that created continuous – rather than segmented – space that allowed performance and spectator spaces to blend. He called it 'integrated space'. Expanding on the Appian idea of placing the performer within three-dimensional space, Kiesler wanted the audience to experience the space as well. His more practical projects included flexible theatres capable of changing size and configuration, and 'space stages', which were essentially non-scenic architectural stages. He was head of design for the 1924 Vienna Music and Theatre Festival. Other significant designs include *The Emperor Jones* (Berlin, 1923) and *Francisca* (Berlin and Vienna, 1925). He came to the United States in 1926 with the International Theatre Exhibit – the first look many Americans had at new European design – and stayed, but he never achieved the prominence he had known in Europe. Despite many projects, the only significant theatre fully realized in the USA was the Eighth Street Cinema in New York (1930). AA

Killigrew, Thomas (1612–83) English playwright, theatre manager. He began acting as a child, playing devils at the **Red Bull Theatre** in order to see the plays free. Though lacking a formal education, he had established himself as a courtier by 1633. His first plays were produced at the Phoenix Theatre and were tragicomic romances based on French models. His best play, *The Parson's Wedding* (c. 1640), is an energetic and bawdy comedy. During the Interregnum he went into

exile with the King, travelling throughout Europe and gaining further preferment from Charles. Some of his experiences were transmuted into his long roman-ticized dramatic semi-autobiography, *Thomaso the Wanderer* (written c. 1654). He wrote a number of closet dramas during his period of exile, all extremely long and virtually unperformable. In 1660, with **Davenant**, he secured a monopoly patent to set up a theatre company and established the King's Company, using the patent to close down all other companies except Davenant's. Killigrew's company was built around actors who had been players before the Civil War, particularly **Hart**, Mohun and **Lacy**. He took over Gibbon's Tennis Court in Vere Street and converted it into a theatre much like pre-war private theatres without scenery. Claiming descent from the earlier King's Men, Killigrew took the rights for his company to the major part of the earlier drama but he lacked the foresight to encourage new writers for the company. In May 1663 the company moved to the Theatre Royal in Bridges Street. He established a Nursery Theatre for the training of young actors in 1667. Though Killigrew boasted to **Pepys** of his achievements as manager (wax-candles, an orchestra of ten violinists, civil behaviour among the audience, visits from royalty and the provision of a prostitute for the company's younger actors), his lack of experience and good business-sense prevented him from being financially successful or efficient. By the early 1670s he had pawned most of his interests in the company, having handed over management to his son Charles in 1671, and by 1676 was no longer directly involved in the company. He was Master of the Revels from 1673 to 1677. PH

Kilroy, Thomas (1934–) Irish playwright. His novel *The Big Chapel* (1971) won a number of Irish and

English awards, but outside his academic pursuits Kilroy has been primarily a dramatist: *The Death and Resurrection of Mr Roche*, a success at the 1968 **Dublin International Theatre Festival**, then in London; *The O'Neill* (1969); *Tea and Sex and Shakespeare* (1976); *Talbot's Box* (1977). The first and the last are unquestionably the most impressive.

In *Mr Roche*, strange events – a spontaneously open door, a piano accompaniment where there is no piano – permeate a seedy Dublin flat and an all-male drinking party with otherworldly anticipations. Mr Roche, a middle-aged, homosexual Jew, is immured, dies, revives: mistaken diagnosis, trick, or miracle. Whichever, the encounter undermines the revellers' desperate self-deceptions, though probably not their ability to renew them. In *Talbot's Box*, kaleidoscopic, stylized scenes enact the life and agonized death of Matt Talbot, Dublin's 'workers' saint', searching the mystery of his frenzied devotion and its corruption by lay and clerical power-seekers.

These two plays are most accomplished theatre, absorbing their slums and flats into an unforced symbolism of the struggle between spirit and circumstance.   DM

Kim U-jin (1897–1927) Korean director, producer, and playwright. Born in south-west Korea of a well-to-do family and educated at Waseda University in Japan. In 1921 he led the Tongwuhoe Group for which he was financially responsible, and introduced the realistic drama. The subjects of the plays produced by the group largely dealt with the freedom of man and the principle of self-determination. He wrote five plays in which he experimented with realism, naturalism, and expressionism – the first attempt by a Korean playwright. The plays are about the conflict between old ethics and new ideas, and the suffering of women. The list of his plays includes *Yi Yŏng-nyŏ Nanp'a* (*The Shipwreck*), and *Sandoeji* (*The Boar*).   OKC

Kinet or **Kinet Gwadd** Ethiopian revolutionary performing groups established by the mass organizations in accordance with the 'Art for Revolution' slogan. Kinets are to be found amongst the urban dwellers, peasants, youth and women's associations, in factories and the armed forces. They work at provincial levels e.g. the Lalibela of Wello, Gishe Abbay of Gojjam and Yelelew Liyunet (No Discrimination) of Gama Gofa; Andinet Kinet is also made up of previously despised *azmareewoch* (professional entertainers and musicians). Dramas are devised democratically by the group, free use is made of popular performing media such as music, song and mime, staging is simple and flexible and the audience helps with instruments, props, costumes etc., participating vigorously in performance by commenting, accompanying songs with clapping, dancing with the actors etc. Plays are political and developmental in intention.   RK

King, Dennis (1897–1971) American actor and singer. Born in England, King began his career as an actor with the **Birmingham Repertory Theatre**. After his arrival in New York in the early 1920s, King appeared in the **Theatre Guild** production of *Back to Methuselah* and as Mercutio in *Romeo and Juliet*. His fine baritone voice and his training as an actor made King the ideal leading man for operetta. In 1924 he appeared as Jim Kenyon in *Rose-Marie*, and his success in that role was followed by critically acclaimed performances as François Villon in *The Vagabond King* (1925), and as D'Artagnan in *The Three Musketeers* (1928). From the 1920s on, King concentrated on acting in straight plays, returning to the musical stage on rare occasions, most notably to create the role of Willie Palaffi in **Rodgers** and **Hart**'s *I Married an Angel* (1938).   MK

King's Men see **Lord Chamberlain's Men**

Kingsley, Sidney (1906–) American playwright. Kingsley made his reputation with realistic social melodramas. *Dead End* (1935), concerned with the effect of slum life near New York's East River on a group of kids, is his most memorable success, but *Men in White* (1933), about a young doctor's experiences in a hospital, won him a Pulitzer Prize. His anti-war play, *Ten Million Ghosts* (1936), failed, and *The Patriots* (1943), contrasting the political theories of Thomas Jefferson and Alexander Hamilton, was a weak effort. Returning to realistic and vivid melodrama, but without the detail that distinguished his early work, he wrote *Detective Story* (1949), featuring a conscientious police detective whose emotional involvement drives him to sadism, and a dramatization of Arthur Koestler's novel *Darkness at Noon* (1951). Later plays, a farce entitled *Lunatics and Lovers* (1954) and *Night Life* (1962), a murder melodrama with overtones of labour and politics, suggest the diminishing quality of his work.   WJM

Kipphardt, Heinar (1922–) German dramatist, whose work provides the first example of fully developed documentary theatre. Trained as a medical doctor, in 1951 he became dramaturge at the **Deutsches Theater** in Berlin, where he wrote a number of conventional plays including *Wanted Urgently: Shakespeare* (1954), a call for writers to deal with major contemporary issues which he answered himself with *In the Matter of J. Robert Oppenheimer* (1964). Originally written for television, like most of his mature plays, it was developed for the stage by **Piscator** and set new standards for the objective treatment of factual material. The action is based directly on transcripts of the US Atomic Energy Commission hearing in which the physicist responsible for developing the nuclear bomb was indicted for treason, and it uses media techniques – film, tape-recording, news clips, headlines – to give an impression of reportage. It attracted considerable international attention, running in London (1966) and New York (1969), and was followed by *Joel Brand – The History of a Deal* (1965), The transaction in question was the Nazi proposal to exchange a million Jews for 10,000 trucks, turned down by the Allies, but despite the controversial subject the play was unsuccessful. Kipphardt withdrew from the stage, even being dismissed for his political views from his position of dramaturge at the Munich Kammerspiele in 1971.

However, recently he has been responsible for a revival in documentary drama with *The Life of the Schizophrenic Poet Alexander März* (1981 – adapted from an earlier television script) and *Brother Eichmann* (1983). Possibly his most significant play, this retrospective biography of a mass murderer shows his attitudes as typical of the average citizen and establishes parallels to the present nuclear strategy of NATO. CI

Kiralfy Hungarian family of dancers and impresarios. After a distinguished career in German theatre, the three brothers **Imre** (1845–1919), **Arnold** (d. 1908) and **Bolossy** (1848–1932) came to New York with their sister **Haniola** (d. 1889) as dancers in **G. L. Fox**'s *Hiccory Diccory Dock* (1869). They soon branched out on their own, staging lavish spectacles. Arnold and Bolossy claimed the United States as their territory, building the Alhambra Palace in Philadelphia (1876). Imre, who had organized his first exhibition in Brussels in 1868, produced *Around the World in 80 Days*, *The Fall of Babylon*, an open-air spectacular with 1,000 performers, and, with **Barnum**, *Columbus* (1890) in the United States. He then settled in London, where his projects included *Venice in London* (1892), a reconstruction of the Earl's Court exhibition hall (1893), *India* (1896), the Victorian Era Exhibition (1897), the Military Exhibition (1901), *Paris in London* (1902), and the Coronation Exhibition (1912). The Kiralfys were distinguished by their magnificent deployment of extras, their innovative use of electricity, and their inability to get on with one another. LS

Kirshon, Vladimir Mikhailovich (1902–38) Today regarded by the Soviets as one of the founders of their modern dramaturgy, Kirshon's staunch advocacy (along with **Afinogenov**) of social and psychological realism as opposed to romantic monumentalism as the basis for the new drama encountered strong opposition from playwrights **Vishnevsky** and **Pogodin** and in official circles. His plays attempt to balance clearly individuated characters against melodramatic situations and ideological themes without severely tipping the balance toward the latter. His first major play, *Konstantin Terekhin* (co-written with Andrei Uspensky; 1926), which deals with the problems of post-revolutionary Soviet youth, was produced under the title *Red Rust* by New York's **Theatre Guild** (1929) with **Lee Strasberg**, Luther Adler and Franchot Tone in the cast. His most important play, *Bread* (1930), deals with the suppression of the *kulaks* – the prosperous peasant class – during the years of the First Five Year Plan. In an episodic structure with interpolated songs and musical themes and calling for a revolving stage, Kirshon warns against oversimplification and idealization in confronting social problems, much as he did in relation to art. His other plays include: *The Rails are Humming* (1927), one of the first Soviet dramas to portray heroic labour; *City of the Winds* (1929), a revolutionary drama from which Kirshon created the libretto for the Knipper opera *Northern Wind* (1930); *The Court* (1932), concerning the Social Democrats in Germany; *The Miraculous Alloy* (1934), an extremely popular social comedy about youth; and *A Great Day* (1936), about life in the Soviet army. Kirshon was arrested and executed on the charge of 'Trotskyism' during the Stalinist purge trials. SG

Kishon, Ephraim (1924–) Israeli satirist and playwright. Born in Budapest, he survived the Holocaust and immigrated to Israel in 1949. He arrived in Israel without a word of Hebrew, but three years later he produced his first Hebrew play, *His Name Goes*

Kkoktu kaksi, traditional Korean puppet theatre.

Before Him (1952). He brought to the Hebrew stage a background of Central European culture and humour. For many years he wrote a daily satirical column. Kishon's plays and books have been widely translated and some have become international best-sellers, although he is less appreciated at home. Among his plays: *Black on White* (1955), on racism amongst mice, *The Marriage Contract* (1961), *Plug It Out, the Water's Boiling* (1966), an attack on modern art and its upholders, *Oh, Julia* (1973), about Romeo and Julia in their forties. HAS

Kkoktu kaksi Traditional Korean puppet theatre or play depicting humans and animals. Largely humorous, dealing with the corruption of Buddhist monks, domestic problems, and satire against immoral officials. OKC

Klein, Charles (1867–1915) American playwright. Emigrating from London aged 16, he had a brief career as a juvenile actor. His first play was *By Proxy* (1891), and he wrote another 15 strong domestic melodramas, the best of which was *The Music Master* (1904), produced by **David Belasco** and starring **David Warfield**. He then wrote six social plays in the muckraking manner of Ida Tarbell and Upton Sinclair. Typical of these were *The Lion and the Mouse* (1905), which exposed legislative corruption at the hands of big business, and *The Third Degree* (1909), which dramatized police brutality. DMCD

Kleist, Heinrich von (1777–1811) German playwright. During his relatively brief life, which was terminated by suicide, Kleist found neither acceptance in the military or civil service nor recognition as writer. Today, however, his plays are regarded as being among the greatest achievements of a time when German culture was being enriched by both classicism and romanticism in art and literature. Kleist's plays do not fit easily into either category. Although it failed when first staged by **Goethe** at Weimar in 1808, *The Broken Jug* has since been accepted as one of the greatest comedies in the language, especially because of the Falstaffian central figure, the corrupt judge Adam. *Amphitryon* (1807) offers in the development of its central situation a striking example of romantic irony. Among the later plays, *Penthesilea* (1808) is a remarkable portrayal of sexual frenzy, while *Das Käthchen von*

Heilbronn (1810) is a deeply moving tale of love and devotion in a knightly, medieval environment. Kleist's final play, *The Prince of Homburg* (1811), is his masterpiece; in it, Kleist reveals his profound attachment to and yet strong antipathy for Prussian militarism. Virtually unknown during his lifetime, a fact that no doubt contributed towards his suicide, Kleist's plays were later produced through the agency of, among others, **Ludwig Tieck**. SW

Kline, Kevin (1947–) American actor. Born in St Louis and educated at Indiana University, Kline studied acting at the Juilliard School, graduating in 1972. As a founding member of the **Acting Company**, he played numerous roles including: Charles Surface in *The School for Scandal*; Vaskal Pepel in *The Lower Depths* (1972); Vershinin in *The Three Sisters*, MacHeath in *The Beggar's Opera* (1973), and Jamie Lockhart in *The Robber Bridegroom* (1975). Kline won recognition as Bruce Granit in *On the Twentieth Century* (1978) and Paul in *Loose Ends* (1979) followed by critical acclaim as the Pirate King in *The Pirates of Penzance* (1980), which established him as a star, and as Bluntschi in a 1985 revival of *Arms and the Man*. Frank Rich (1981) thought that Kline had 'all the ingredients for conventional leading man stardom – big voice, dashing good looks, infinite charm – and . . . the grace and timing of a silent-movie clown'. Kline's film appearances include *Sophie's Choice* (1982), *The Pirates of Penzance* (1983), and *The Big Chill* (1983). In 1986 Kline played Hamlet at the Public Theatre, New York. TLM

Klingemann, Ernst (1777–1831) German director and playwright. Klingemann directed two theatres in Brunswick, including the Court Theatre. Here he staged the first performance of **Goethe**'s *Faust Part 1* in January 1829. Klingemann was moderately successful as a playwright, writing his own stageworthy version of the Faust legend. His travel volumes *Art and Nature* (1819–29) are an invaluable source for the theatre historian. SW

Klischnigg, Edward see **Animal impersonation**

Klotz, Florence (c. 1920–) American costume designer. Klotz, by her own admission, became involved in design almost by accident. Through the 1960s she designed several light contemporary comedies. In 1971 she teamed up with director **Harold Prince** to design *Follies* which had 140 costumes ranging from rags to lavish show costumes spanning half a century. She subsequently designed several Prince–**Stephen Sondheim** musicals, each with a distinctly different style and period. Her costumes manage to combine contemporary sensibilities with period style. AA

Knipper-Chekhova, Olga Leonardovna (1868–1959) Soviet-Russian actress, who upon completing **Nemirovich-Danchenko**'s course at the Music and Drama School of the Moscow Philharmonia (1896–8) joined the original company at the newly-formed **Moscow Art Theatre** (MAT, 1898). In the premiere season she played Tsaritsa Irina in **A. K. Tolstoi**'s historical tragedy *Tsar Fyodor Ioannovich* and the actress Arkadina in **Chekhov**'s *The Seagull*. The latter led to a personal and professional association with Chekhov. She married him in 1901 and played leading roles in all his major plays staged at MAT: Elena Andreevna, *Uncle Vanya* (1899); Masha, *The Three Sisters* (1901); Anna Petrovna, *Ivanov* (1904); and Ranevskaya, in *The Cherry Orchard* (1904), a role she laid claim to well into her old-age. She was Nastya in the original MAT production of **Gorky**'s *The Lower Depths* (1902) as well as the theatre's Anna Andreevna in *The Inspector General* and Natalya Petrovna in **Turgenev**'s *A Month in the Country* (1909). She was named a 'People's Artist of the USSR' in 1937 and awarded a State Prize in 1943. SG

Knowles, James Sheridan (1784–1862) Anglo-Irish playwright, Knowles was born in Cork, the son of a lexicographer, but moved with his family to London in 1793 and studied medicine at the University of Aberdeen. After early practice as a doctor, he became an actor in 1808, a schoolmaster in 1811, an actor again from 1832–43 and an evangelical preacher after 1844. His decidedly sanctimonious *Lectures on Dramatic Literature* (2 vols., 1873) are pulpit pieces, written with the brief authority of a former playwright, considered in his time a rival to **Shakespeare**. Almost forgotten today, Knowles is a victim of his own inflated reputation. Much of that reputation was owed to the actor, **William Macready**, whose moving portrayal of suffering fatherhood in Knowles's *Virginius* (1820) brought the playwright into prominence. Later paternal tragedies included *William Tell* (1825) and *John of Procida* (1840). Written, like all his 23 plays, in overregular blank verse, they are too mawkish to survive 20th-century appraisal. The romances, modelled on **Fletcher** rather than Shakespeare, are more successful. They include *The Beggar's Daughter of Bethnal Green* (1828), revised as *The Beggar of Bethnal Green* (1834), and the understandably popular *The Hunchback* (1832). Best of all, though entirely neglected because of Knowles's claims as a writer of tragedies, are the comedies, *The Love-Chase* (1837) and *Old Maids* (1841). PT

Knyazhnin, Yakov Borisovich (1742–91) Son-in-law of the influential Russian man of letters **A. P. Sumarokov**, whom he succeeded as a writer of tragedy after the French neoclassical models of **Racine** and **Voltaire**. His chief literary rival, **I. A. Krylov**, satirized Knyazhnin's tendency to plagiarize the French via the character Rifmokradov ('Rhyme Thief') in his play *The Bombastics* (1787). The latter also contains a reference to Knyazhnin's conviction for embezzling government funds. While his career in public service faltered, however, his literary accomplishments earned him election in 1783 as one of the 30 charter members of the Russian Academy. His seven tragedies, beginning with *Dido* (1769) and extending through to his best-known and most controversial plays, *Rosslav* (1784) and especially *Vadim of Novgorod* (1789), are characterized by intricate plotting and dramatic stage effects but are short on originality, genuine historical detail and richly imagined characters. His heroes and villains are designed to argue for what Knyazhnin and Sumarokov believed to be the theatre's role, to propagate liberalism and civic responsibility. *Vadim*, which contrasted the virtues of republicanism and monarchism, so threatened Catherine the Great in the wake of the French Revolution that she ordered it burned. Although its complete text was not published until 1914, the play influenced Decembrist dramaturgy in the 1810s and resulted in a version by **Pushkin**. Knyzahnin was a far better comic writer. His talented verse comedies (earlier Russian comedies were largely written in prose) satirize the abuses of serfdom and the corrupt nobility's pursuit of title and rank, Gallomania, reliance on foolish and fraudulent foreign tutors and '*valet-philosophes*'. His comic operas feature highly actable characters, richly aphoristic language and ample local colour. The comedies include: *The Unsuccessful Mediator* (1785); *The Braggart* (1786), based on du Brieux's *L'Important* (1723) and featuring a prototype for **Gogol**'s Khlestakov; and *The Odd Fellows* (1790), based on **Destouches**'s *L'Homme Singulier* (1764). His comic operas are highly successful: *The Mead-Seller* (1784), music by Byulant; and his best single work, *Misfortune from a Carriage* (written 1772, produced 1779), music by V. A. Pashkevich, which offered **Shchepkin** one of his earliest roles. Knyazhnin's, like Sumarokov's, popularity was eclipsed by the Russian romantic writers of the early 1880s. SG

Koch, Heinrich Gottfried (1703–75) German actor. Major actor of the 18th century who worked with **Caroline Neuber** and **Johann Schönemann**. He took over the leadership of the Schönemann troupe when **Ekhof** was still a member, but the two had differences, especially over Koch's tendency to improvise, so Ekhof left to join the **Ackermann** troupe. Koch's troupe continued to travel in the Leipzig area until his death. SW

Kochergin, Edward Stepanovich (1937–) Russian stage designer. Schooled under Soviet artists Bruni and **Akimov**, Kochergin became Head of Design of the Leningrad Theatre of Drama and Comedy in 1963. In 1966, he was appointed Head Designer of the Kommissarjevskaya Dramatic Theatre. He was later promoted to chief artist of the Gorky Theatre in Leningrad. Kochergin has refined a style which has been compared to **Grotowski**'s 'poor theatre' productions. His sparse, textured, yet simple settings have been integral to such Gorky Theatre productions as *Hamlet* (1972), *Boris Godunov* (1973), and **Nikolai Gogol**'s *Notes of a Madman* (1978). Among the many other productions which he designed for the Gorky Theatre are Shukshin's *Energetic People*, **Roshchin**'s *Valentin and Valentina*, **Vampilov**'s *Last Summer in Chulimsk*, **Bulgakov**'s *Molière* and **Gorky**'s *Summer Folk*. His design for Lev Dodin's production of *The House* (from Fyodor Abramov's family chronicle) at Leningrad's Maly Dramatic Theatre consisted of five wooden horses (used metaphorically) of the sort which traditionally decorate rural Russian houses. In 1975 Kochergin designed the striking set for the highly popular dramatization (by Mark Rozovsky) of **Lev Tolstoi**'s *The Story of a Horse* (*Kholstomer*) at the Gorky. Here the audience is seated inside the horse, looking into its worn flesh which tears open to reveal paisley-lined flaps for actors' entrances and exits. Kochergin's design for **Lyubimov**'s *The Inspector's Recounting* (based upon Gogol's works) at the Taganka made similar use of a textured background, a huge

piece of felt representing the famous overcoat of Gogol's Akaky Akakyevich which is being stitched together on numerous machines operated by *chinovniki* (clerks). The felt contained openings through which performers could make sudden appearances and cast various parts of their bodies (including nude knees representing noses). A series of small elevator platforms used for spectral ascents and descents completed the set. For Rozovsky's *High* (about **Mayakovsky**) at the Mayakovsky Theatre, Kochergin designed a suprematist environment after Kazimir Malevich. Kochergin is generally considered to be one of the Soviet Union's greatest living scene designers. SG TM

Kokoschka, Oskar (1886–1980) Austrian painter and dramatist, whose works were the earliest examples of expressionism with their direct externalization of subconscious states. *Sphinx and Strawman* (1907) became one of the influences for dadaist theatre, while *Murderer, the Hope of Women* (1907), staged in 1918 and 1919 and as an opera with music by Hindemith in 1922, was a forerunner of **Artaud**'s 'Theatre of Cruelty'. CI

Kolam Kolam is a form of folk theatre that was once popular along the southern coastal region of Sri Lanka. The word *Kolam* in Sinhalese means either an appearance, an impersonation, or an assumed guise, usually one that is comic and exaggerated so as to provoke laughter. Since full face masks are used to identify the various characters, *Kolam* includes a wide range of at least 50 stock character types many of whom are introduced through a ritual prologue and some of whom assume importance in the dramatic action which follows. Among the characters that appear in the dramas are the king and the queen, the king's herald, his wife, a policeman, a washerman, the washerman's wife and a paramour, a village dignitary, plus various celestial beings, demons and animals. Despite the large range of possible characters which compose a drama, fewer than a dozen plays were written in the form.

After ritual dances and chants in honour of the presiding deities and preceding the dramatic action of the plays, there is a colourful and elaborate ritual entrance of each character which is accompanied by the chanting of the verses of the musicians who outline the history of each character. The entrance of the characters is highlighted by dances appropriate to his or her station in life. The masks do not seem to have been designed for singing or speaking; therefore, in the dialogue portions of the play, the masks are rarely worn.

Performances usually take place in any open space in a village and begin around nine in the evening and conclude about sunrise.

Although the exact origin of *Kolam* is not known, according to one of the dramas, a certain queen, big with child, suffered from a pregnancy craving for dances and amusements which the king ultimately satisfied by ordering performances of *Kolam*. This tale along with other stories dealing with fertility, suggests that *Kolam* may well have arisen as an ancient pregnancy rite. FAR

Koltai, Ralph (1924–) German-born British stage designer, who is noted for his bold imagery and

Ralph Koltai's design for *Much Ado About Nothing*, Royal Shakespeare Company, 1982.

conscious sense of style in the service of a production concept. Suggesting the art of sculpture and architecture, his designs usually centre on highly expressive forms and constructions that often employ untraditional scenic materials such as plexiglass, styrofoam, steel, and fibreglass. Primarily a freelance designer, almost half of whose work has been in opera, Koltai has also had extensive association with both the **Royal Shakespeare** and **National** Theatres. The artistry of his work has frequently led to prizes and exhibitions. From 1965 to 1973 he was head of the theatre design programme at London's Central School. Notable productions have included *Doctor Faustus* (1964), *Back to Methuselah* (1968), the opera *Taverner* (1972), **Wagner**'s *Ring* (1970–3), *Brand* (1978), *Much Ado About Nothing* (1982), *Othello* (1985).   JMB

Komissarzhevskaya, Vera Fyodorovna

(1864–1910) A mystical, poetic actress of spiritual essences, Komissarzhevskaya captured the restiveness and yearning of pre-revolutionary Russia's artistic elite. With her extreme nervosity and sensitivity, her virginal tenderness and sincerity, her luminous, otherworldly presence and an inner angst which seemed to play itself out via her roles, she became the perfect icon for the Russian symbolists – **Blok**, **Bely**, **Briusov**, **Kuzmin**, **Sologub**, Georgy Chulkov – a useful conduit for **Meyerhold**'s directorial ideas and a possible model for characters in **Evreinov**'s plays. The daughter of a noted opera tenor, she possessed a hypnotic, deeply resonant, 'inwardly musical' voice, which her contemporaries likened to a Stradivarius violin. She began her amateur acting career in St Petersburg in 1891 and shortly thereafter joined the amateur Moscow Society of Art and Literature run by her father, **Stanislavsky** and A. F. Fedotov. By the time she joined Petersburg's Aleksandrinsky Theatre company, she had appeared in well over 60 roles in two separate professional theatres, mostly as ingenues and in musical vaudevilles. At the Aleksandrinksy she originated the role of Nina in the disastrous first production of *The Seagull*. She was the only company member who appreciated the play and remained **Chekhov**'s favourite interpreter of the role. She left this theatre in 1902 and after two years touring founded the Dramatic Theatre of V. F. Komissarzhevskaya in St Petersburg. It immediately became a haven for symbolist artists and progressive students, who saw in her the social commitment of a latter-day **Ermolova**. Her attraction to new ideas and to authoritarian figures led her to appoint Meyerhold as the theatre's artistic director and to become close to Briusov, who translated **Maeterlinck**'s *Pelléas and Mélisande* for their production in which she played the title role (1907). To her admirers' chagrin, she subordinated her talent to Meyerhold's master plan, which at this time called for extreme stylization, scenic flatness, immobility and puppet-like actors intoning in strangely rhythmic cadences. Excellent at playing victims, sufferers and visionaries – all touched by unreality – she here appeared as Maeterlinck's Sister Beatrice (1906) and as a bizarrely vampirish Hedda Gabler in the director's notorious, colour-coded production of **Ibsen**'s play. This was a great act of faith for an actress who saw Ibsen as her special calling and who had been memorable as Nora in *A Doll's House* and as Hilda Wangel in *The Master Builder*.

It also reflected her theatre's commitment to innovative stage design by symbolist painters such as Nikolai Sapunov and Serge Soudeikine (Sergei Sudeikin). In 1908 she replaced Meyerhold with Evreinov and her half-brother, **Fyodor Komissarzhevsky**, in an effort to reclaim authority for the actor, but she continued to perform Meyerhold's symbolist play choices. She even approved Evreinov's frankly erotic production of **Wilde**'s *Salome* with Kalmakov's set design resembling huge female genitalia, which the Holy Synod banned in 1908. A falling-off in attendance and a personal psychological crisis led to her closing the theatre in 1908 and planning a school for the human development of actors with Andrei Bely. However, while on a fund-raising tour of Tashkent, she contracted smallpox and died.   SG

Komissarzhevsky, Fyodor Fyodorovich

(1882–1954) Russian director, teacher, theorist, half-brother of noted actress **Vera Komissarzhevskaya**, whose theatre he headed with **Evreinov** following **Meyerhold**'s dismissal (1908). Here he staged **Andreev**'s *Black Masks* and **Ibsen**'s *The Master Builder* (1907–9) and during a company hiatus (1909) co-produced with Evreinov a programme of light fare on the premises, which they re-dubbed 'the Merry Theatre for Grown-up Children'. From 1910 he worked in Moscow, staging productions at the Maly (1913) and at Nezlobin's Theatre of **Ostrovsky**'s *Not a Kopek and Suddenly a Rouble* (1910), **Molière**'s *The Bourgeois Gentleman* (with exotic set and costume designs by Sapunov, 1911), **Goethe**'s *Faust* (1912) and Dostoevsky's *The Idiot* (1913). Between 1910 and 1918 he directed productions at his own studio, including: **Ozerov**'s *Dmitry Donskoi* (1914), *Lysistrata* and plays by **Sologub**, Andreev and **Kuzmin**. In his many opera productions at the Bolshoi Theatre and elsewhere – *The Golden Cockerel* (1917), *Lohengrin* (1918), *Boris Godunov* (1918), etc. – he tried to realize his concept of a cultured, synthetic theatre, philosophically romantic in tone, created around a universal actor-singer-dancer. Following a year of directing a new studio theatre, he emigrated (1919), continuing in London, Stratford-upon-Avon, Rome, Paris, New York and Vienna to design and direct 'synthetic' productions of **Shakespeare**, **Pirandello**, Crommelynck and especially, Russian classical dramas – by **Gogol**, **Turgenev** – and operas – by Mussorgsky, Borodin. He also directed films in England and wrote the books, *The Actor's Creative Work and Stanislavsky Theory* (1916), *Theatrical Preludes* (1916), *Myself and the Theatre* (1929), *Costume of the Theatre* (1931), and *The Theatre and a Changing Civilization* (1935).   SG

Kong Shangren

(1648–1718) Chinese dramatist. A native of Shandong he was a descendant of Confucius in the 64th generation and an authority on ancient rites and music. A semi-recluse until his mid-thirties he lived in the mountains of his ancestral territory. Between 1684 and 1699 he held a series of official posts following the Emperor's recognition of his talents and erudition. In 1699 he published his play *The Peach Blossom Fan* (*Taohua shan*). A long piece in 40 scenes written in southern style, it is still considered a masterpiece of poetic composition by the Chinese today. It records the treachery and intrigue which facilitated the Manchu seizure of power with the fall of the Ming dynasty in 1644. The characters are based on real personalities and central to the theme is one of the great love stories of Chinese literature. The play won immediate popularity but resulted in the playwright's dismissal from office by the Manchu authorities. Kong was considered one of the two great masters of his day, the second being **Hong Sheng**.   ACS

Kongelige Teater (Copenhagen) Denmark's national theatre, located on Kongens Nytorv since 1748, actually comprises four related organizations, performing on several stages: the theatre company, the Royal Opera, the Royal Danish Ballet and the Royal Orchestra. Its present building dates from 1874; the recently restored 'Old Stage' is used almost exclusively for opera and ballet, with spoken drama relegated to the adjacent but unsatisfactory 'New Stage' and to studio theatres elsewhere in the city. The theatre company rightly claims its origins in the first Danish-speaking theatre founded in Lille Grønnegade street in 1722. Traditionally, a peak in its history was the mid-19th century, when a company of fine actors were assembled around the **Heibergs**. In the 20th century, it has nurtured actors of undisputed genius, such as Bodil Ipsen, **Poul Reumert**, Bodil Kjer and **Mogens Wieth**, and enjoyed a period of particular success under Peer Gregaard's management in 1966–75.   HL

Kopit, Arthur (Lee) (1937–) New York born and Harvard educated playwright who has had a distinguished place in the American theatre as a serious and inventive writer for more than 20 years, though he has rarely gained popular acceptance. He first received international attention with *Oh Dad, Poor Dad, Mama's Hung You in the Closet and I'm Feelin' So Sad* (1960), a brilliant parody of the Oedipus complex. Since *Oh Dad* he has written a number of plays that experiment with dramatic form, most notably *The Day the Whores Came Out to Play Tennis* (1964), a comic portrayal of social-climbing country-clubbers, *Indians* (1968), a study of genocide of the Indians by white Americans, *Wings* (1978), a portrait of a stroke victim, and *The End of the World* (1984), a dark comedy about nuclear proliferation.   DBW

Korea Korea is a nation on a peninsula in far Eastern Asia, with approximately 60 million people who speak a single language, Korean. Since 1948, the nation has been divided into two republics: Seoul is the capital of South Korea and P'yŏngyang the capital of North Korea. For the past several hundred years, Korean folk theatre has existed in several geographical regions, but modern Korean theatre, heavily influenced by the West, was limited in large part to Seoul until the end of the Second World War. Since 1948 the South's theatre has been largely concentrated in Seoul, and the North's in P'yŏngyang. Regional theatre companies began to emerge in the South in the 1980s.

Folk theatre The precise origin of Korean theatre is unknown. The beginnings of Korean theatre may be traced back to a number of ancient ceremonies, folk observances, and shamanistic rites. Some civic observances which were believed to have included primitive theatrical elements took place more than 2,000 years

ago. The most important ones were the *ch'ŏngun*, *much'ŏn*, and *yŏnggo*. They were mainly performed for two purposes: for heaven worship and for appeasement of ancestral spirits. Presumably these rituals required the performers to sing and dance as well as wear masks.

During the 7th century, the *kiak*, originally consisting of music and dance, was imported to Korea from China. This was performed as a kind of simple masked dance drama at the Buddhist temple for an audience. And it is believed that the *kiak* became the genesis of today's **sandae-gŭk**.

During the Silla period (57 BC–AD 935), the *kŏmmu*, *muaemu* and *ch'ŏyongmu* were the important dance forms containing some theatrical elements. The *kŏmmu*, originating in the story of the death of a young warrior who killed an enemy king, was a masked sword dance, while the *muaemu*, performed for the promulgation of Buddhism, was a dance done without masks. Of these three, the *ch'ŏyongmu* – based on the story of the legendary Ch'ŏyong, a son of the Dragon King of the East Sea, was the most grotesque and pungent early type of masked dance drama of Korea.

During the Koryŏ period (918–1392) in which civilization was heavily influenced by Buddhism, there were no important amusements except for religious festivals such as the *p'algwanhoe* and *yŏndŭnghoe*. The former, produced mostly in midwinter, was a festival performed in honour of the earthly deity, while the latter, held in the first lunar month, was a Buddhist mass. Although the purpose of the events differed, preparations for both of the activities were strikingly similar; numerous lanterns of different sizes and colours were hung and a temporary high stage adorned with bright colours was built. Included in the programmes were somersaults, a tight-rope display, acrobatic dance on the top of a bamboo pole, puppet plays, and the *sandae-japgŭk*, or various impure forms of masked dance drama.

Another activity in this period was the *narae* which was performed in uncertain times to chase the evil spirits out of the palace. But the purpose of this event soon changed; later it was performed for the public by professional actors, called the *kwangdae*, probably the first actors in the history of Korean theatre who made their living by performing.

Some actors of this period belonged to the court, and they could be called upon to perform at any given time. In addition, there were a considerable number of actors who maintained their living by entertaining the merchant class people. All actors, considered social outcasts, kept separate residential areas apart from the main stream of society. When they were not performing, they engaged in such lowly professions as butchery, hunting, and wickerwork.

The cultural activities of the Chosŏn court (1392–1910) were heavily influenced by the Confucianists who openly defied Buddhism. But it was this period in which popular literature, fine arts, and theatre blossomed, gaining increasing support from the commoners, mostly the merchants and craftsmen.

The anti-Buddhistic Chosŏn court refused to perform the religious festivals of Koryŏ. From past dynasties, however, they inherited performances of the *narae* and of the *sandae-japgŭk* which eventually developed into the *sandae-gŭk*. Also there were other forms of entertainment whose performance did not require the use of masks. It is believed that they were comic-satirical dramas in which perverse high officials and tyrannical rulers became the targets of ridicule. This type of theatre was referred to as the *chaphŭi*, meaning a variety of impure drama, or the *paewuhŭi*, plays performed by actors as distinguished from the *sandae-gŭk* or masked dance drama.

The **p'ansori**, a one-man operetta performed by the *kwangdae* actor accompanied by a *pug* (double-headed barrel drum), was developed during the latter part of the Chosŏn period. The origin of this art is not clear. Some scholars suggest that it began with a number of short songs sung by the shamans in their rituals of the early 18th century. But it was the itinerant **kwangdae**, in search of material with which to entertain, who took it over as a performing art. It is believed that the *kwangdae* replaced the short lyrics with the more popular songs derived from well-known stories. There had been no written text of the *p'ansori* until the 19th century when Sin Jae-hyo (1817–84) made a permanent record of the 12 existing repertoires.

The staging of the *p'ansori* is simple, requiring only a single singer, a drummer, and a small mat. This simplicity enabled a performance to take place anywhere for any size audience and is responsible for *p'ansori* being one of the most popular entertainments for people of all classes for the past two centuries. During the performance, the singer, called *kwangdae*, usually stands while the drummer, *kosu*, sits. The singer's performance must include three theatrical elements: *sori* (singing), *aniri* (dialogue/narration), *ballim* (acting/pantomime restricted to emotional expression of joy). He may also employ some gestures, called *ch'umsae*. Of these elements, singing is regarded as the most important. The songs are interspersed with dialogue so that the singer need not sing continuously throughout the performance which lasts several hours.

The early *p'ansori* singer was the kindred of shamans who belonged to the lowest class in society. If any member of that class was talented and possessed the appropriate vocal qualities, he was given training to become a *p'ansori* singer. These singers were required to have a heavy hoarse vocal timbre which was acquired after long arduous training, necessitating frequent shouting in remote areas. If he had no talent vocally, he learned how to play musical instruments to become an accompanist. Anyone lacking musical talent became a tight-rope walker or an acrobat.

Today *p'ansori* is frequently performed, including being broadcast on television and radio for the mass audience, and is still popular.

There are two classifications of Korean masked dance drama: the *purakje* (village festival) plays and the *sandae-gŭk* plays (the theatre which was once controlled by the court). The first category includes the Hahoe *pyŏlsin-gut*, *kwanno*, *pŏm-gut*, and *t'al-gut* of the east central region of the country. The second category embraces the rest of all major forms of the known masked dance drama: the *pyŏlsandae* plays of Yangju and Songp'a; the *t'alch'um* plays of Pongsan, Ŭnyul, and Kangnyŏng; the *ogwangdae* plays of T'ongyŏng, Kosŏng, and Kasan; the *yaryu* plays of Tongnae and Suyŏng. Their performances took place in different regions.

Of the *purakje* plays, the Hahoe *pyŏlsin-gut* was the most well-known. Performances of this play, occur-ring every ten years as part of the village festival, took place on the 15th day of the first lunar month.

Twelve masks were required for the performance of the Hahoe *pyŏlsin-gut*. But only nine of the original wooden masks – the most refined among the Korean masks – remain today. No one knows the whereabouts of the remaining three. When they were not in use, the masks were traditionally kept in the village shrine. The task of mask making in the village was supposedly related to the divinities; it is said that they were made only by a man instructed by divine message in a dream. Both the maker and the date of the remaining masks are unknown today.

Being an orally transmitted play, no complete script of the Hahoe *pyŏlsin-gut* play remains. A knowledge of the characters and main action of the play has been preserved by the villagers. In the play there is no single central plot; instead, the play is made up of a number of independent scenes. But the play gives the impression of being held together by means of a common theme running through all the scences: the monks guilty of transgression, the corrupt aristocrats, and the insensi-tive local officials.

During the early period of the Chosŏn dynasty, the *sandae-gŭk* drama was performed under the sponsor-ship of the *sandae-togam* (Master of Revels), an office of the court, for a number of purposes: to entertain the Chinese envoys; to get rid of evil spirits; and to welcome the newly appointed provincial governors. When official support was withdrawn with the aboli-tion of the *sandae-togam* in 1634, this theatre, a public event in an earlier period, gradually developed into a folk drama during the last half of the Chosŏn period. The repeal of official support for this theatre also resulted in the branching out into a number of regional forms by itinerant *kwangdae* troupes. Among these some differences do exist, but there still remain many similarities.

The performance of all *sandae-gŭk* requires dance, singing, music, pantomime, the exchange of witti-cisms, and dialogue. Of these elements, the prime emphasis is placed on three: dancing, singing, and music. None of these outdoor theatres necessitates the use of a formal stage, curtain or stage settings. The visual elements of the production are achieved by the grotesque masks and colourful costumes intensified with light from the blazing torchlights at night.

The movement patterns of the dances employed in the *sandae-gŭk* drama, which number more than a dozen, are complicated and difficult to decipher. In particular, the production of the Yangju *pyŏlsandae* demands a wide variety of dances. Some of the frequently performed forms in the production are the *yŏdaji*-dance, *kopsawi*-dance, and *kkaeki*-dance. The *yŏdaji*-dance, for example, requires forward move-ments; the player places both hands on the upper front of his body and, extending them forward, pantomimes the opening of his chest while his feet kick forward. Some dances are used for a humorous purpose; for example, the *hŏrijapi*-dance, which requires the lifting of the player's leg, while resting his hands on his waist, is performed to tease the other player.

The performance of all *sandae-gŭk* plays, with the exception of a few roles, requires the use of masks which are made with either dried gourds or paper. Traditionally, they were burned at the end of each performance. The masks of the Yangju *pyŏlsandae*, for example, are made with dried gourds. Around the edge of the mask a dark cloth called *t'alpo* is attached to cover the back of the head; dark strips of cloth are also used to tie the mask around the player's neck.

The performance of all *sandae-togam-gŭk* plays calls for musical accompaniment usually supplied by six instruments referred to as *samhyŏn-yukkak*: one *chŏttae* (transverse flute), two *p'iri* (fife), one *haegŭm* (two-stringed fiddle), one *changgo* (hourglass-shaped drum), and one *puk* (barrel drum). In addition, one *kkwaenggwari* (small gong) may be added. Three tunes are played most frequently: the *kutkŏri*, *t'aryŏng*, and *yŏmbul*. The *kutkŏri* is a flowing tune of a twelve-beat pattern, while the *t'aryŏng* has a twelve-beat pattern with an accent on the ninth beat. The *yŏmbul* is a six-beat rhythmic pattern. The songs which are interlaced with dance and dialogue in the plays are mostly derived from popular folk songs and shamanistic ravings of the Chosŏn period. Often the contents of the songs, oddly enough, have no bearing on the plot of the subject of the scene at all.

The costumes worn by the players of the *sandae-gŭk* drama are important in terms of theatrical spectacle. In particular, the costumes worn by the servants and the female of questionable morality appear to be gaudier than those of the others.

Being collaborative works and transmitted orally, not a single author of the *sandae-gŭk* plays has been identified. Only recently have they been recorded and published. Thus the performance of each play – relying on a rough synopsis of the plot – depended on the spontaneous improvisations of the actors. All plays are devoid of organic structure. A typical example can be drawn from the Yangju *pyŏlsandae*. For example, Act I is about Sangjwa, a monk, while Act II is nothing more than an exchange of nonsensical dialogue between two characters. The transgression of a Buddhist monk is the subject of Act V. Interestingly, some characters are introduced in certain scenes and never appear again. Unlike the Pongsan *t'alch'um* which is full of poetic expression, the language of this play, which is often very frank, is typified by the everyday colloquial conversation of the common people. In almost all of the plays, four types of privileged people become major targets of satire: the corrupt local official who steals someone else's woman; the apostate Buddhist monk who engages in lascivious intemperance with women; the aristocrats who blindly excercise their power; the tyrannical husband who mistreats his wife.

For example, traditionally the performance of the Yangju *pyŏlsandae* took place in Yangju, a town roughly 15 miles north-east of Seoul, on a number of different occasions during the year. Of these, the one which was performed on the 8th day of the fourth lunar month (Buddha's Birthday, also called the Lantern Festival) was the most splendid. For the performance, the entire town was lit up with colourful lanterns. The performance took place at night and lasted until dawn. Like all the other *sandae-gŭk* plays, however, recently this play has been performed during the day-time. Traditionally, the players of this drama were made up of the local farmers and the petty town officials.

The performing area for the Yangju *pyŏlsandae* could be set up easily. The costume room called *kaebokch'ŏng*

was installed on one side of an open field, usually at the foot of a hill, while the musicians took their positions at one end of the circular playing area. Then the audience either stood or sat, facing the musicians, across the playing area. The costume room had two doors through which the players made their entrances and exits. Neither a curtain nor an artificial scenic background was necessary. To indicate a change of scene a moment's pause was all that was required.

Another branch of the *sandae-gŭk* was the traditional puppet theatre, called **kkoktu kaksi**, which was believed to be introduced into Korea by wandering players from the Asian continent to the west during the 7th century. Traditionally, this art was performed by itinerant players, known as the *namsadang* (troupes of song-and-dance people), who have been credited with the preservation of this theatre. Being nomads and social outcasts, like the *kwangdae*, they never belonged to the main stream of society.

The Korean puppet, in a strict sense, does not belong to any of the most familiar puppet categories; that is, it cannot be classified as either a hand puppet, a rod puppet, or a marionette. It combines aspects of all of these. The body of the puppet, the main stick, is held by the hand, which is reminiscent of the hand puppet, its arms, somewhat like the marionette, are manipulated by strings below, and the stiff arm movements remind the audience of the rod puppet. The Korean puppet, called *kkoktu*, is easy to construct. Into the carved wooden or papier-mâché head, the main stick of the puppet, a piece of one-by-three-inch light wood, is wedged. A rectangular main body frame of light wood is attached a few inches below the neck of the puppet. The upper horizontal bar of the frame forms the shoulders to which arm sticks are loosely bolted, enabling them to be manipulated from below by strings attached to the upper portion of the arms. Appropriate costumes are then fitted to the puppet. During the performance a puppeteer, who also delivers the dialogue and sings songs to the accompanying music, manipulates a single puppet at a time.

There exist a number of different orally transmitted versions of the play – ranging between seven and ten scenes – according to the troupes. But all of them deal with the same subjects in a humorous comic way: satire against the apostate monk; the triangular relationship between husband, wife and concubine; the unethical high official; the corrupt upper-class citizen. Generally, a different subject is treated in each scene. But the structure of this drama is more tightly organized than the *sandae-gŭk* plays due to the appearance of the main character in every scene, serving as the narrator.

Until the beginning of the 20th century, both the masked dance drama and the puppet theatre satisfactorily entertained their audiences. For the modern audience, however, these art forms contained some shortcomings: first, the performing time was too long; second, being an outdoor theatre, the audience complained about the unintelligible lines delivered by the players behind their masks; third, it was regarded as old-fashioned to be entertained by means of masks and puppets. In addition, these folk arts were faced by a stronger enemy, the occupying Japanese military, who were determined to wipe out the entire Korean culture. Consequently, no performances of the masked dance drama or the puppet theatre worthy of mentioning took place between 1930 and 1945.

Since the end of the Second World War, the folk theatre of Korea has not only been resurrected but also revitalized through performance, study, and publication of the plays. Furthermore, the government of South Korea has been actively supporting these efforts by designating these art forms as Important Intangible Cultural Properties. In North Korea, unfortunately, they do not seem to flourish. The North Korean government, virtually forbidding its theatre to resemble past forms, discourages the performance of folk theatre. They regard the masked dance drama and the puppet theatre as backward and not sufficiently revolutionary.

Modern theatre At the beginning of the 20th century, two types of modern drama were introduced into Korea: the *shinp'a*, an imitation of sentimental melodrama; and the *shingŭk*, the realistic drama of Western influence. For a time, the folk theatre coexisted with these modern forms. But soon the popularity of the folk theatre began to decline.

The people of the folk theatre who were the first to respond to the influx of modern theatrical forms were the performers of the *p'ansori* who established the first indoor theatre, the Hyŏpyul-sa, in 1902. They managed to reform the performance of the *p'ansori*, and called this theatre the *ch'anggŭk*, a kind of music drama. The important difference between the *p'ansori* and the *ch'anggŭk* was that the performance of the latter required more than two singer-actors. Despite these changes, the *ch'anggŭk* lost its popularity due to a limited repertoire, although it was able to continue performing mainly because of its sentimental lyrics and music which appealed to the emotions of an audience.

At the beginning, the *shinp'a* theatre was heavily influenced by the Japanese theatre of the same genre. Among the *shinp'a* plays three types were predominant: military plays; detective plays; domestic plays. In the military plays the patriotic soldiers who defend the nation against the invading enemy were glorified as national heroes. The young policeman who relentlessly pursues the robber, disregarding personal wounds, to restore law and peace in the community became the most popular character in the detective plays. In domestic drama, the soap opera of the time, love, hatred, injustice, revenge, filial piety, and the conflicts between legitimate and illegitimate children were the most frequently dealt with subjects. Soon the domestic plays became the predominant category of the *shinp'a* drama. Typically in the domestic plays the national suffering, caused by the Japanese occupation, was heavily utilized as the root of individual hardship. For example, in *Arirang-goge* by **Pak Sŭng-hi** the lovers are forced to part because of family bankruptcy due to Japanese exploitation. The Korean audience of the time responded enthusiastically to productions of this type of drama because they were able to relate their own personal sufferings resulting from the national tragedy to the misfortune of the dramatic characters in the plays.

An early prominent *shinp'a* company was the Hyŏksin-tan led by Im Sŏng-ku (1887–1921). Some of Im's performances and productions were popular, but he was unable to raise the quality of the *shinp'a* theatre.

Not only did he simply imitate the third-rate touring Japanese counterpart but also his productions depended too heavily upon improvisation. The true furtherance of the *shinp'a* theatre is credited to *Pak Sŭng-hi* (1901–64), a prolific playwright, who led the noted Towŏl-hoe Group for approximately 20 years. Pak was the first person to use completely developed play scripts for his productions.

The *shingŭk* was at last introduced into Korea in 1921 by the Tongwuhoe (Society of Comradeship), organized by a group of students studying in Tokyo. During summer vacation, the group toured extensively in Korea under the leadership of **Kim U-jin** (1897–1927) producing such popular new plays as *Kim Yŏng-il ŭi chugŭm* (*The Death of Kim Yŏng-il*) by Cho Myŏng-hi. The plays produced by the group mainly dealt with the principle of self-determination and freedom of man, the ideas newly advocated by Woodrow Wilson after the First World War. For the first time, they produced the plays of **Ibsen**, **O'Neill**, **Čapek**, and **Pirandello** for Korean audiences. But the group was soon forced to dissolve after only 40 productions by the Japanese police. Despite its short existence, the Tongwuhoe made some notable contributions to Korean theatre: it served as the pioneer for the *shingŭk* which stood in contrast to the *shinp'a*; it forced many other companies to raise their production quality; it demonstrated that the theatre can be utilized as an educational tool to teach new ideologies by producing certain plays.

Despite the efforts of the Tongwuhoe and Kim U-jin, realistic drama failed to emerge as a strong theatrical movement in Korea during the 1920s. There was neither a single notable playwright of realism, nor sufficient audience, which was so deeply influenced by the *shinp'a*, ready to accept this new theatre. It was not until 1931 when a group of young intellectuals organized the Kŭgyesul Yŏnguhoe (Theatre Arts Research Society) that realistic drama came into its own. Members of this group engaged in a wide variety of activities such as performance, playwriting, criticism, audience education, and the translation of foreign plays. On their experimental stage, they produced the plays of **Chekhov**, Ibsen, **Gogol**, **Galsworthy**, etc. At the same time, Korea saw the emergence of some notable young playwrights under the influence of realism and naturalism. In their plays they began to expose the reality of the suffering Koreans under the harsh measures taken against them by the Japanese military. *T'omak* (*The Earthen Hut*) by **Yu Ch'i-jin** (1905–74), for example, depicts the misery of an aged farmer whose sole hope for regaining his farm ends in anguish when he learns that his only son is killed by the Japanese police while engaging in the national independence movement.

During the 1930s Korean theatre was largely divided into two camps: the popular commercial theatre represented by the *shinp'a* and the nationalistic *shingŭk* of realism and naturalism. Sadly, the *shingŭk* theatre could not last long. The censorship and oppression directed against it by the Japanese military which began in the early 1920s became even harsher as time passed. Those active in the nationalistic theatre movement became the subject of frequent arrest, torture, and detention. Under these adverse circumstances, the Kŭgyesul Yŏnguhoe managed to exist for eight years until it was finally forced to dissolve in 1939. With the suppression of this group, Korean theatre was once again dominated by the *shinp'a* drama for a short period until it too was suppressed. The Japanese military seeing the possibility of using the theatre to serve their militaristic policy proposed to organize a single theatre in 1941. Only nine groups were allowed to join this theatre while the rest of the companies and individuals were banned from performing. The playwrights too were forced to write plays in which Japanese military policy was glorified.

The liberation of Korea from Japanese domination at the end of the Second World War brought the division of the nation into two parts, North and South, and the splitting of the theatre people into the two vehemently opposing camps – the leftist and rightist factions. They were ideologically as widely apart as the politicians of the time. To some of them, especially the leftist group, the theatre became a tool for political propaganda. The majority of the left-wing theatre people came from the *shinp'a* groups, while the right-wing theatre was organized by the nationalistic theatre people of the *shingŭk*. When the government of South Korea was established in 1948, a large number of the left-wing theatre people went to the North where they became the nucleus of North Korean theatre.

Since the end of the Second World War, the theatre of North Korea has been utilized for political propaganda. Until 1950 the dominant subject of drama was the struggle against the Japanese during the 1930s led by General Kim Il-sung, the present leader. The plays of this period were written with a single purpose: to broadcast the political message. During the 1950s, after the political purge, the so-called 'great revolutionary works' emerged. In fact, they were nothing new; they were still the same kind of political propaganda plays in the style of the *shinp'a* with greater emphasis on spectacle.

Since the 1970s three types of theatre have been dominating the stage in North Korea: The 'revolutionary opera'; the 'music and dance drama'; the 'epic drama of music and dance'. The major characteristics of the 'revolutionary opera' are songs, chorus, music, exaggerated scenic settings, and colourful costumes. The difference between this theatre and the 'music and dance drama' is that the latter places a heavier emphasis on dance. In the 'epic drama of music and dance', the epics containing political messages are performed in the form of dance, song, chorus, and music. Almost all the theatrical productions presented on the major stages in P'yŏngyang today place great emphasis on spectacle with large casts, numbering up to several thousands, overly elaborate scenery, colourful costumes, and dazzling lighting. To accommodate this type of production, the government of North Korea has built some large-scale theatres whose stages are big enough to hold several thousand actors at one time.

In these plays only a few familiar themes recur again and again: the struggle against Japanese imperialism in the 1930s; the war against United States imperialism and the South Korean puppet government; commendation of land-reform; the glorious life in North Korea. Somehow these themes are invariably related to Kim Il-sung. Thus the theatre in North Korea is utilized to glorify, praise, and idolize Kim. To this day these types of productions dominate the stage in North Korea.

This history of the theatre in South Korea for the next five years after the Second World War was marked by two events: the organization of the Kŭgyesul Hyŏphoe (Theatre Arts Association) in 1947 and the establishment of the National Theatre in 1950. The former was organized to counter the left-wing theatre. The National Theatre was created with two purposes: the promotion of the nationalistic theatre; the advancement of the theatrical arts exchange with foreign nations. To this theatre two performing groups, the Shinhyŏp and Kŭghyŏp, were attached as the resident companies. But the promising theatre which attracted more than 50,000 people for the opening production of *Wŏnsulrang* by Yu Ch'i-jin was forced to take refuge in Taegu with the outbreak of the Korean War – less than two months after its opening.

During the Korean War most of the theatrical groups barely continued to perform. With the end of the war in 1953 the theatre returned to Seoul and resumed performance. By this time a number of new groups were organized. But the dominant troupe was the Shinhyŏp, which broke away from the National Theatre; it kept the theatre alive in the war-ravaged capital, performing the plays of **Miller**, **Williams**, and **Inge**, and a few new works by the Korean authors. Another notable event was the opening of the Wŏngaksa Theatre in 1958, a small theatre with 306 seats, constructed by the government to promote the little theatre movement. Unfortunately, this theatre burned down in 1960.

In the early 1960s the dominance of the Shinhyŏp was beginning to be challenged by a number of new groups. The strongest attack was made by the Silhŏmkŭgchang (1960) whose opening production was **Ionesco**'s *The Bald Prima Donna*, an obvious rebellion against the Shinhyŏp whose realistic production style dominated in the 1950s. When the Korean theatre was still at a low ebb, the ambitious Drama Centre, by Yu Ch'i-jin, with 450 seats, provided with initial funding from the Rockefeller Foundation, was opened in 1962 with the great expectation that it would revive the declining Korean theatre. From the beginning, however, it was plagued by controversies. Contrary to its stated purpose, five of the first six productions were foreign plays. Many other factors were also at the root of its troubles: financial strains; lack of audience; the influx of foreign movies; migration of able theatre people to television. Thus the venture of the Drama Centre failed within a year.

If the 1950s were marked by the production of contemporary American drama, the 1960s were the period in which the plays of the modern European authors such as **Dürrenmatt**, **Frisch**, **Anouilh**, and **Beckett** were introduced. A number of new playwrights also began to write their plays on different subjects: the contemporary economic-political systems; satires on modern society; the problems of modern life. Some notable authors of this period were O Yŏng-jin, Ch'a Pŏm-sŏk, and Yi Kŭn-sam.

Since the 1970s some experiments both in playwriting and in production have been carried out. A few playwrights sought their dramatic subjects in legends, shamanistic rites, and classical literature. Some of them even attempted to include the old folk songs in their plays of modern subjects. They are yet to prove successful in their attempts. The list of authors in this period includes Yun Tae-sŏng, O T'ae-sŏk, and Yi Jae-hyŏn.

In this period a number of young directors also emerged such as Kim Chŏng-ok, Im Yong-ung, and Yu Tŏk-hyŏng. By this time a score of plays belonging to the theatre of the absurd were produced on Korean stages, but they were unable to cast off completely the realistic approach to productions. The basic mode of directing and acting largely depended upon the often misunderstood **Stanislavsky** method. These directors, beginning with Yu in 1969, attempted to apply the production techniques of the total theatre.

Since 1980 a few new initiatives have been seen in Korean theatre: an experimentation with surrealism; the attempt to update the puppet theatre to meet the demands of today's audience; the infusion of Brechtian epic theatre in playwriting; the attempt to modernize the old *gut* (exorcism) as theatre. It appears that Korean theatre practitioners will continue to experiment in the future in search of a new direction, a formidable task. okc

See: Oh-kon Cho, *Korean Puppet Theatre: Kkoktu Kaksi*, East Lansing, Mich., 1979; Sang-su Choe, *A Study of Korean Puppet Play*, Seoul, 1961; Korean ITI, *The Korean Theatre: Past & Present*, Seoul, 1981; Korean National Commission for UNESCO, *Traditional Performing Arts of Korea*, Seoul, 1975.

Kornblĭt, A. Y. see **Tairov**

Korneichuk, Aleksandr Evdokimovich (1905–72) Prolific and administratively highly placed Ukrainian dramatist, whose optimistic and heroic socialist realist melodramas made him extremely popular with the government and earned him honorary Russian status among Soviet historians, officialdom and the theatregoing public. His plays – with the exception of *The Truth* (1937), which offers one of the first dramatic depictions of Lenin on the Soviet stage, *Bogdan Khmelnitsky* (1939), a paean to the Ukrainian people's courage in repelling invaders, and several war plays featuring Ukrainian characters and settings – eschew regional for national issues. His most famous plays include: *The Wreck of the Squadron* (1933), a historically based, monumentalist account of heroic Red seamen during the Revolution; *Platon Krechet* (1934, revised 1963), which offers a dedicated young surgeon as a symbol of the intelligent and humane new Soviet man; and *Front* (1942), an extremely popular, patriotic drama, growing out of the Soviet Union's early defeats in the Second World War, which argued that the old guard in the military must be replaced by younger officers with the necessary training to fight and win a modern war. Korneichuk's *Why the Stars Smiled* (1957) and *Where the Dnieper Flows* (1960) are more intimate, comic and romantic treatments of the trials and entanglements of parents and their offspring, better suited to the climate of the post-1953 'Thaw' period in Soviet culture. sg

Körner, Theodor (1791–1813) German playwright. Körner's promising career was cut short by his death while fighting in the Napoleonic wars. His most successful play was the tragedy *Toni* (1812). Körner was briefly official dramatist to the **Burgtheater**. sw

Kornfeld, Paul (1889–1942) Czechoslovakian dramatist, whose tragedies *The Seduction* and *Heaven*

and Earth (both produced 1920) marked the high point of German expressionism, while his essays provided a theoretical basis for the movement. In his later plays he turned to social comedy, and died in a concentration camp. ci

Kortner, Fritz (1892–1970) Austrian actor and director, who established his reputation as the leading interpreter of expressionism with his 1919 role in **Toller**'s *Transfiguration* and, under **Jessner**, in *Wilhelm Tell*, *Richard III* and **Wedekind**'s *The Marquis of Keith*. After his return to Germany in 1948 he directed in Munich, Berlin and Düsseldorf where his meticulous productions of the classics were particularly influential, though he also introduced **Beckett**'s *Waiting for Godot* to the German stage. ci

Koster and Bial's Music Hall 116–117 West 23rd St, New York City. Built in 1869 as the 23rd Street Opera House, it was leased to Dan Bryant and his minstrels the following year. After Bryant's death in 1875, it passed to other managers and eventually to the partnership of John Koster and Albert Bial in 1879. Replacing the stage with a small platform, enlarging the building and adding outdoor gardens, the partners transformed it into Koster and Bial's Music Hall, a concert saloon which dispensed alcoholic beverages with variety entertainment. They were able to skirt existing laws against serving both in the same establishment by using a giant fan as a curtain, which fell apart to reveal the performers. But when the laws were tightened, they abandoned the enterprise and fell in with Oscar Hammerstein to create Koster and Bial's New Music Hall on West 34th Street. The old theatre struggled along for a few more years and was torn down in 1924, but the newer theatre had an even shorter life and was eventually razed to become part of Macy's Department Store in 1901. mch

Kotopoúli, Maríka (1887–1954) Greek actress who was virtually born into the theatre, as both her parents were actors. Kotopoúli's range was wide, for she could play tragic roles as well as vaudeville parts. For more than 30 years she managed her own theatrical group, Elefthéra Skiní (Independent Stage, or Theatre), after a successful start at the Greek Royal Theatre (1901–8), hosting a variety of plays from classical and modern theatre. Towards the end of her career, Kotopoúli helped revive ancient Greek drama by playing Electra, Clytemnestra, and other heroines of tragedy. She was likened to **Sarah Bernhardt** and her bust guards the entrance of the Theatrical Museum of Athens. gt

Kott, Jan (1914–) Polish theatre critic. His book *Shakespeare, Our Contemporary* (1964) argues exactly that, and many directors – **Peter Brook** among them – have taken Kott's ideas about the power of the fool in periods of change into the dimension of theatrical action. mb

Kotzebue, August von (1761–1819) German playwright. Although Kotzebue spent much of his life in the political service of the Russian Tsars, he was also an extraordinarily prolific writer. His early work, *Misanthropy and Repentance* (1798), was adapted by Benjamin Thompson as *The Stranger* (1798) to become one of the most popular plays of the 19th century in England. Equally popular in Germany were *The Two Klingsbergs* (1801) and *The Small-Town Germans* (1803), plays that might still receive the odd revival today. Several of Kotzebue's widely performed plays had historical settings. His work, which was deliberately written to appeal to as broad a cross-section of the populace as possible, reflects the transition from sentimentalism to melodrama.   SW

Kraus, Karl (1874–1936) Austrian critic and dramatist. The publisher of the radical journal *Die Fackel* (*The Torch*) from 1899 to 1936 and the first to promote **Wedekind**, his plays *The Last Days of Mankind* (1919) and *The Unconquerable Ones* (1928) present a satiric panorama of the era.   CI

Krishnattam (India) Only one company of performers practises this unique form of dance-drama, that of the famous Guruvayur Temple, located in a pilgrimage town of the same name among the lush paddy fields and palm trees of a coastal region of Kerala state, south India. The form was conceived by a Zamorin king, Raja Manaveda, in the mid-17th century as a means of glorifying the name of Krishna, one of Lord Vishnu's most beloved incarnations. Coupled with *attam* which means 'story' in Malayalam, the form implies 'the dramas of Krishna'.

A legendary tale about its origin says that Manaveda was a devout follower of Krishna. One day he heard that a holy man had gone into trance and seen Krishna at the Guruvayur Temple. He, too, wanted to experience the miracle of seeing the god, so Manaveda went to the temple and fervently prayed. To his amazement Krishna appeared before him as a small boy playing under a tree in the temple courtyard. In his excitement, Manaveda reached out to touch the boy and the vision vanished leaving behind a peacock feather that he had seen Krishna wear in his hair. The feather was said to have been used in the crown of generations of actors who portrayed Krishna until it was destroyed by fire which devastated part of the temple several decades ago.

Inspired by his miraculous vision, Manaveda wrote *Krishnagita* incidents from the life of Krishna, which are based on the *Bhagavata Purana* and which serve as the basis for the eight plays which comprise the entire dramatic repertory of the form.

Given the fact that Kerala possesses a long history of notable forms of theatre, such as the **Kutiyattam** and **Kathakali**, it is not surprising tht *Krishnattam* shares many features with them, and yet has its own peculiar characteristics.

Like the *Kutiyattam* and *Kathakali*, the dancer–actors perform the text employing a highly sophisticated code of gesture-language to interpret the plays. Preliminary studies reveal that the meaning of many of the gestures and their execution is different from that of all the other Kerala performing arts. The dance movements closely resemble those of *Kathakali* but they have their own definite character which stresses a lyrical, feminine quality of group movement rather than the masculine vigour of *Kathakali* or the more abstract angularity of *Kutiyattam*.

The makeup patterns of the various mythological characters – humans, demons and animals – reveal striking similarities to those of *Kathakali* but display their own particular flair. To a sophisticated theatregoer, the makeup, costumes and ornaments, although seemingly the same as those of *Kathakali*, have shapes and patterns which could only belong to the *Krishnattam*.

The actors of the troupes, all of whom are male, are devotees of the god. Many of them were offered in grateful service to god and the temple when they were small boys in exchange for a boon that was granted to their parents. Others came freely to devote their lives to the service of god. Although not apparent to laymen the level of devotion of the participants runs high and is echoed by the religious fervour of the pilgrims who watch the performances.

Traditionally, performances are commissioned by pilgrims from all over India who pay the temple authorities to have a *Krishnattam* performed as a part of their ritual sacrifice. The devotee may choose any of the eight stories to be enacted. Favourite stories are associated with requests for particular boons. The play which includes Krishna's marriage is thought particularly auspicious for a devotee celebrating a marriage in his family, the story which depicts Krishna's miraculous birth is thought to ensure the birth of a male child to barren parents; and, the story which shows the destruction of the wicked King Kamsa is thought to ward off the evil eye. If all eight plays are performed in sequence, they must be followed by the reenactment of the first night's play showing the birth of Krishna because it is thought inauspicious to end a sequence with Krishna's death.

Performances are generally held in the courtyard of the temple, north-east of the main shrine; however, a special proscenium arch stage has been constructed outside the temple compound so that non-Hindus who have a desire to see *Krishnattam* may do so. In recent years, *Krishnattam* has been played in towns and cities elsewhere in India and in several international engagements in Europe and the United States. Any open space about 15 feet square with plenty of open room around it for spectators to sit may serve as an appropriate place for a *Krishnattam* performance. Scenery is not used and only a simple stool symbolizes a throne, a mountain, a bench or whatever the drama requires. A four-foot high bell-metal oil lamp fed with wicks of cloth provides a flickering glow to the performance. In the proscenium house, two scoop lamps situated on the floor to the right and left of the oil lamp illuminate the space but tend to deaden and flatten out the costumes and ornaments which were designed to be seen under lamp light.

Performances take place between 9 pm and 3 am. They may only be presented after the temple rituals are concluded and before the doors of the *sanctum sanctorum* have been opened for the morning prayers. The reason for the strict time frame stems from a charming story: Many years ago, when the doors of the temple shrine were inadvertently left open, the effigy of Krishna was so moved by the music that it came to life and danced with the actors causing considerable dismay to the temple priests. Care is now taken not to allow the same incident to happen again.

The texts of all the plays are sung by two chief singers in the soprano style of singing popular in Kerala. The actor–dancers do not speak, except perhaps to use grunts and groans when demanded by their character. The basic rhythmic patterns for the dance-drama are provided by two *maddalam* drums struck at both ends and suspended around the waist of the drummers, an hour-glass drum (*idakka*) played at the drummer's side and bell-metal cymbals. A harmonium provides the pitch around which the singers weave their intricate melodies. A conch shell is played during auspicious dramatic action.

In recent years, owing to the continual flood of pilgrims that come to the temple to perform austerities, *Krishnattam* is usually performed every night of the year. Unionization of the players has led the management to restructure the companies so that there are enough actors to make up two groups and thus no one is exploited. Experts complain that the death of the older generation of artists has led to a serious decline in the quality of *Krishnattam*. The performance of the same material over and over again has led to a lethargy among many of the artists whose work has become routinized. No new work may be added to the repertory, however. Only on rare occasions is the full cycle of plays performed.   FaR

Krleža, Miroslav (1893–1981) Yugoslav playwright. Born in Zagreb, Croatia, where he spent most of his life. Educated in military schools of the Austro-Hungarian Empire, in whose army he fought in the First World War. An early supporter of the idea of a Yugoslav state, and of socialism. As an embattled intellectual and modernist, Krleža belongs to the same Central European orbit as **Kraus**, Musil, **Horváth** and Canetti. His early plays, written in symbolist and expressionist manner – *The Legend* (1913), *Salome* (1913), *Kraljevo* (1915), *Christopher Columbus* (1917), *Michelangelo Buonarroti* (1918), *Adam and Eve* (1922) – were initally considered unstageable and, if published at all, were largely ignored. They were successfully staged in Yugoslav theatres only after 1955. Between the two world wars, Krleža was editor of several leftist literary reviews, a productive novelist, poet, essayist and polemicist. As a playwright, he became established only after a gradual transition to realism, as marked by *Vučjak* (1923) and his trilogy *The Noble Glembays, In Agony* and *Leda* (1928–31). Isolated from the left for his early critique of Stalinism, and persecuted by the right for his leftist ideas, Krleža was a lonely figure from the late 1930s until Yugoslavia's break with Stalin in 1948; then he emerged as the towering figure of the domestic cultural scene, instrumental in rejecting socialist realism and inaugurating aesthetic pluralism. In the last three decades of his life he established and led the Yugoslav Lexicography Institute in Zagreb; edited the *Encyclopaedia Yugoslavica*; revised and published many of his old manuscripts, especially essays and diaries; and wrote a long novel and only one new play – *Aretheius* (1958), a gloomy portrait of the collapse of European civilization. Krleža's plays, often loaded with the author's erudition and marked by vibrant intellectual discourse, have been translated into all the Slavic languages, as well as German, French and Hungarian. They have been performed in Central and Eastern Europe, but remain practically unknown in the English-speaking world.   DK

Kroetz, Franz Xaver (1946–) German dramatist, who is the most significant exponent of the contemporary **Volksstück** (Folk Play). Introduced to **Horváth** and **Fleisser**'s work by **Fassbinder**, who directed his first play *Wild Game Crossing* (*Wildwechsel*, 1969), his typical themes are the brutalized existence of the proletariat, moral repression and linguistic deprivation. *Homework* and *Stiffnecked*, dealing with emotional degradation, casual sex and abortion in harshly realistic terms that denied the conventional sentimental image of peasant life, provoked riots at their premiere in 1971. But the most complete example of the genre comes in the double play *Dairy Farm* (*Stallerhof*) and *Ghost Train* (1972). The under-age, mentally retarded daughter of a farmer runs away to keep her child, joining the elderly labourer who seduced her, only to kill the baby in desperation when the social services commit it to an orphanage after he dies of cancer. The simplicity of the action, the minimal dialogue that reflects the inarticulacy of the characters, a concentration of the minutiae of daily activities and the objective depiction of basic bodily functions are characteristic, but the range of social analysis is extended in *Oberösterreich* (1972) or *The Nest* (1975). Here the accepted ideals that the action reveals as illusory are those of the consumer economy, and the 'folk' are average urban workers, whose standard of living falls below the poverty-line when a working wife becomes pregnant or whose children are injured by industrial pollution. Cultural values are also exposed as sentimental in *Maria Magdalena* (1973) where **Hebbel**'s 19th-century classic is parodied in a contemporary adaptation.

The violence in these plays – suicide, child abuse, murder – tends to melodrama, as in the sexually motivated duel-to-the-death of *Men's Business*, which Kroetz prohibited from performance after its 1972 premiere and has subsequently rewritten in four different versions. Possibly because of this, later work like *Neither Fish nor Flesh* (1981) is far more stylized. As with Jochen Ziem and other contemporary *Volksstück* authors, his approach is in conscious contrast to **Brecht** and this is recognized by his most recent play *Fear and Hope in the FRG* (1984, derived from *Fear and Misery in the Third Reich*, 1938).   CI

Krog, Helge (1889–1962) Popular Norwegian dramatist and essayist, author of 16 sometimes playful social problem plays that owe at least an initial debt to **Ibsen** and **Gunnar Heiberg**. A recurrent theme is the unliberated position of women in modern society, especially in his strongest plays *The Conch Shell* (1929) and *Break-Up* (1936). Krog is particularly admired for the wit and subtle dexterity of his dialogue, which may owe something to **Shaw**, and the ironic (even satirical) tone that qualifies his treatment of human nature.   HL

Kruchonykh, Aleksei Eliseevich (1886–1969) Soviet-Russian futurist poet, dramatist and theorist, an extremist and 'the father of *zaum*', or transrational, universal language based solely upon expressive sounds and bypassing cognitive poetic thought. This marked an attempt to jettison Russia's romantic poetic past (e.g. **Pushkin**), to forestall the philosophical influence of symbolism and to capture directly the confused sensory impulses of the moment, which was a cornerstone of futurist poetics. Along with his fellow futurists, Kruchonykh exploded grammar and syntax, invented new words, made purposeful omissions of phrases and punctuation, played with typography and 'textures' to stress certain words and sounds and generally cultivated dissonance and 'primitive coarseness' in his art. He became attached to cubo-futurism in 1912, co-signing with painter David Burlyuk and **Vladimir Mayakovsky** the manifesto *A Slap in the Face of Public Taste* and participating in the poetic groups Hylaea (1910–13), 41° (1918–19) and Mayakovsky's Lef (The Left Front of Art group) (1923–5). His work, which was strongly erotic, drew upon folk and children's art and the overall primitivist trend. He was librettist for the first and only pre-revolutionary futurist opera *Victory Over the Sun* (1913) – music by Mikhail Matyushin, sets by Kazimir Malevich, prologue by Velimir Khlebnikov – which alternated over four nights (2–5 December 1913) with Mayakovsky's 'tragedy' *Vladimir Mayakovsky* at the Union of Youth in St Petersburg's Luna Park. The libretto, representing 'a complete break between concepts and words', and the music, suggesting 'a distorted Verdi', combined with the abstract sets, 'inept chorus', hastily assembled and rehearsed amateur actors, pausing after every syllable as per Kruchonykh's instructions, and the out-of-tune piano to create the desired anti-aesthetic effect and elicit a satisfactory outpouring of hisses, hurled fruit and laughter. At the play's end the futurist 'Strong Men' 'are victorious over the sun of cheap appearances and have lit their own inner light', thus assuring the continued progress of futurism beyond the earth's demise. SG

Krylov, Ivan Andreevich (1769–1844) Best-
known as the greatest Russian fabulist, a conservative middle-class philosopher noted for his masterful aphoristic language and his pointed satirical barbs aimed at political and literary enemies, the arrogantly stupid and self-satisfied inept of all classes and professions. Prior to the period in which the majority of his nine volumes of *Fables* were written (1809–20), Krylov was a dramatist and satirical journalist of some note. His malicious but largely accurate portrayal of rival dramatist **Ya. B. Knyazhnin** as an embezzler and plagiarist and his wife, **Sumarokov**'s daughter, as an adulteress kept his coarse comedy *The Bombastics* (written 1787, produced 1793) from the stage until after Knyazhnin's death. In his comedies Krylov also attacked: the Russian literary vogue for sentimental heroines perpetrated by Karamzin (*The Pie*, 1802); Russian classical tragedy's weakness for depicting enlightened monarchs (*Trumpf* or *Podshchipa*, a mock tragedy, 1799); and the abuses of serfdom, but in something of a common sell-out, via the person of an overseer rather than a landowner (*The Fortune-Teller*, a Knyazhnin-like comic opera, 1783). His prose comedy *The Fashionable Boutique* (1805) captures the growing anti-French feeling following Louis XVI's execution and Russia's breaking off of diplomatic relations. On the other hand, his most popular play *A Lesson to Daughters* (1806) reflects **Molière**'s continued influence on Russian comic dramatists, extending from situations and devices such as disguisings to play titles. Despite his nationalist sympathies and his great contributions to the creation of a highly colloquial national literature, Krylov's satirical comedies and comic operas received no public performances in St Petersburg, the seat of the government, during his lifetime. SG

Kuchipudi (India) Kuchipudi is the name of a village in the Krishna river delta of Andhra Pradesh, south India. The word has come to refer to a form of classical dance-drama performed by Brahmin citizens of the village. More recently, it has come to refer to any dance in this particular style. Therefore, it is both the dance-dramas of Kuchipudi village and the classical dances presented on the concert stage of India's cities.

The village of Kuchipudi was granted to performers who tell religious stories. Abdul Husan Qutab Shah, the Muslim Nawab of Golconda, is responsible for patronizing these Hindu players when he issued the village to them by inscription on a copper plate sometime between 1672 and 1687. The earliest reference to the Brahmin artists is 1505–9, when we know that they performed before King Vira Narasimha Raya of the Vijayanagar Empire. Some authorities claim that the *Kuchipudi* form dates earlier in history because it is similar to *Bharata Natyam*, the oldest surviving form of Indian classical dance described in the *Natyasastra*. But we may only be certain that Siddhendra Yogi, who lived during the 17th century, was regarded as the father of modern *Kuchipudi* because he composed dance-dramas for the players and required all the Brahmin families of the village to take an oath to perform the role of Satyabhama, Krishna's jealous wife, in his drama *Bhamakalapam*, at least once during their lifetime. The practice continues, even today.

Some authorities conjecture that Siddhendra Yogi learned the **Yakshagana** of Mysore state during the 20 years he studied Madhava philosophy at Upidi, the centre of *Yakshagana* in south Kanara region. The argument runs that he returned to Andhra Pradesh after an intense religious experience and taught this form of *Yakshagana* to the Bhagavatulu of Kuchipudi. But no one has yet proved whether Siddhendra Yogi learned *Yakshagana* and took it back to Andhra or whether he taught *Kuchipudi* to the people of south Kanara. In any case, authorities continue to seek documentary proof of their contentions and the issue has not yet been resolved. However, the Brahmin men and boys of Kuchipudi village families who still practise the art are believed to be the direct descendants of those who were the beneficiaries of Siddhendra Yogi's instruction many centuries ago.

Kuchipudi is the best-known 'classical' form of dance-drama in the Telugu language. Like **Bhagavata Mela**, the stories are drawn from sources which deal with the incarnations of the god Vishnu. The following dance-dramas are part of the *Kuchipudi* repertory: *Prahlad Charitram*, *Usha Parinayam*, *Sashirekha Parinayam*, *Mohini Rukmangada*, *Harishchandra Nataka*, *Gayopakhyanam*, *Rama Natakam* and *Rukmini Kalyanam*. The dramas of *Bhamakalapam* and **Gollakalapam** have become so popular that they are now regarded as separate performance forms.

Kuchipudi is very nearly like *Bhagavata Mela* but is performed with more sophistication and attention paid to the classical hand-gestures described in the *Natyasastra*. *Kuchipudi* also exhibits considerable feats of physical skill in dance. In one of the items, a dancer performs on the sharp edge of a metal plate holding a round-bottom water pot on his head and executes intricate rhythmic patterns by manipulating the plate using difficult hand-gestures correctly and all without spilling a drop of water.

Kuchipudi troupes are, and have always been, touring companies. Usually, they improvise an acting area in an open space before a temple, such as that of the Ramalingeshwara Temple of Kuchipudi village. Four poles are firmly planted at the four corners of the playing area and a thatched roof is stretched overhead. The spectators sit around the area and witness performances all night. A curtain is used for entrances of characters and illumination is provided by torches fed by castor oil and held by village washermen (*dhobis*). Resin powder is thrown on the torches to produce spectacular flashes of light to accentuate entrances of important characters.

Performances begin with a prayer to the goddess Amba. Following this, a young boy enters carrying the flagstaff (*jarjara*) of Indra, a practice in direct imitation of one of the preliminaries described in the *Natyasastra*. Then the lamp and incense are carried on and a dancer performs sacrifices. Another dancer follows carrying sacred water in a pitcher used to sprinkle and sanctify the acting area. The stage manager (*sutradhara*) enters carrying a crooked stick (*kuttilaka*) and announces the title of the play. He joins the musicians and accompanies them by playing cymbals during the show.

Stage attendants hold a curtain behind which a dancer enters wearing a mask of Ganapati, the elephant-headed god of good fortune. The curtain is removed and a dance follows. The curtain is brought forward once again and the chief character enters and makes an elaborate dance entrance using the curtain to tease the audience. Eventually, he casts it aside and is fully exposed to the anxious spectators. Special dances (*patra pravesha daru*) follow. These dances are characterized as abstract dances emphasizing form and style and those requiring elaborate gesture-language coordinated with the precise meaning of the songs.

Dialogue in Telugu mixes with humorous and witty remarks. Songs and dances are sprinkled throughout the evening to give variety and emphasize dramatic moments.

Music is set in the classical Karnatic style and played on classical instruments, such as the *mridangam* drum, the violin played in the south Indian manner, traverse bamboo flute, *tutti*, brass cymbals and the harmonium, a small keyboard instrument played by bellows.

Rich costumes and ornaments are characteristic of the form. Except when the artists attempt to incorporate wing and drop settings, not originally part of the tradition, performances take place without scenery and properties allowing for total focus on the performers and permitting the free play of the spectator's imagination.

Should a particular performer excel, he is rewarded by being garlanded with necklaces of fresh flowers. Enthusiastic spectators intrude on the progress of the dramatic action by stepping into the playing area and honouring a favourite artist.

On the concert stage, dances are adapted from the dance-drama repertory and performed as solo items. Master-teachers have also choreographed items using themes from a variety of sources but retaining the fundamental characteristics of the form.

Owing to its popular reputation as a branch of classical Indian dance, few members of urban audiences are aware that the form is still practised as a full-scale dramatic performance in the villages of Andhra Pradesh. In addition, they are not aware of the close association with the religious convictions of rural exponents and the ritual significance of the dance-drama in village life.   FaR

Kugel, Aleksandr Rafailovich (1864–1928) Russian literary and theatrical critic (under the pseudonym 'Homo Novus', editor of the influential journal *Theatre and Art* (1897–1918), member of the directorate of St Petersburg's Theatrical Club (1908), dramatist and co-founder with his wife, Z. V. Kholmskaya, of the Crooked Mirror Theatre, where he served as director and *de facto* spokesman (1908–28). A knowledgeable man with strong opinions, Kugel argued in his articles and editorials for an actor's theatre to counter the directorial dominance of **Meyerhold** and **Evreinov** and the 'anarchic individualism' of the new dramatists. Although he at first criticized **Moscow Art Theatre** realism and embraced the primitivist trend of his day, supporting in theory if not always in practice Evreinov's experiments at the Ancient Theatre, and although he hired Evreinov to become artistic director at the Crooked Mirror (1910), he was opposed to extremism in the arts. Evreinov later hired Kugel to help stage the grotesque buffoonery of the bourgeoisie and the Provisional Government in the Soviet mass spectacle *The Storming of the Winter Palace* (1920). After 1920 Kugel briefly headed the Petrograd People's Theatre, which during his tenure produced historical plays, and published some notable books, including: *Affirmation of the Theatre* (1923), *Literary Reminiscences* (1923), *Theatrical Portraits* (1923), *Shadows of the Theatre* (1926), *Leaves from Trees* (1926), *Profiles of the Theatre* (1929) and *Russian Dramatists* (1933).   SG

Kukolnik, Nestor Vasilievich (1809–68) Perhaps the best-known Russian reactionary romanticist writer of patriotic historical plays during the reign of Tsar Nikolai I. His contemporary, dramatist-critic F. A. Koni, likened Kukolnik to **Alexandre Dumas** *père* who relied on 'overinvolved plots, affectation, historical colouration, interpolated scenes and horrible theatrical effects'. His characters are unchanging declamatory figures who deliver themselves of rhetorical eulogies of king, country and the good old days. Nevertheless, they served as colourful starring vehicles for two of the great actors of Kukolnik's day, **V. A. Karatygin** and **P. S. Mochalov**. His most famous blank verse historical epic was *The Hand of the Almighty Has Saved the Fatherland* (1833), set during the election of the first Romanov to the throne (1613) and given an elaborate staging for its monarchist sympathies. Critical and popular response to this play became an acid test of loyalty to the state, and it was revived even in the succeeding reign to reawaken patriotic feeling. The title and its author have become synonymous in the annals of Russian drama with artist compliance to state demands. Kukolnik's other historical plays with Russian settings and themes include *Prince Mikhail Vasilievich Skopin-Shuisky* (1835), *Ivan Ryabov, and Archangel Fisherman* (1839) and *Prince Daniil Vasilievich Kholmsky* (1841). At the same time, Kukolnik composed a series of dramatic verse 'fantasies', most notably *Torquato Tasso* (1833) and *Giulio Mosti* (1833) which treated the theme of the suffering artist with which he perhaps could or at least imagined he could identify.   SG

Kundhei Nata (India) Also known as *Gopa Lila*. This is a form of glove puppet theatre found in Orissa State in north-eastern India. The form is in a serious state of decline. The content of the stories centres on the love of Radha and Krishna. The puppets are constructed of wood and paper and clothed in long flowing skirts. A party of two usually makes up the troupe, one person manipulates the puppets and the other plays the drum, sings and narrates the dialogue.   FaR

Kunqu The name of a 16th-century Chinese musical style which gave rise to a theatre genre taking the parent name. *Kunqu* originated in the Kunshan area dominated by the town of Suzhou in Jiangsu province. The singer-composer **Wei Liangfu** and his collaborators transformed the original music into a more refined and sophisticated style by drawing upon other current regional modes which were contributory to the southern musical mainstream. The new style created a trend. Liang Chenyu, who had worked with Wei, used it as the structural basis for a play he composed entitled *Washing the Silk Yarn (Huansha ji)*. It was widely acclaimed and marked the debut of a literary–musical genre destined to have a significant effect on the future course of Chinese theatre. Early developments in stage performance became manifest in two schools of thought concerning dramatic composition. One led by Shen Jing (1553–1610), a theorist first and playwright second, sought to codify a theory of prosody in relation to rhyme, tone and their correlation with the sung text. The second was dominated by the playwright **Tang Xianzu** who advocated poetic licence and free rein to the imagination at the expense of rigid musical theory. The intellectual climate arising from these two points of view marked acceptance of *kunqu* as the preoccupation of scholarly writers during the 17th and 18th centuries.

In its elemental form *kunqu* is performed as chamber music accompanied by a seven-holed horizontal bamboo flute (*dizi*), wooden clappers and a small hardwood drum slung on a tripod. On stage, string and percussion instruments are added and singing is synthesized with dance, gesture, song and speech. Monody and monologue are common devices. The pitches of the seven-holed flute, a key instrument in the *kunqu*, set the tonics for keys and modalities which animate the versification and general structure of a play. Solo song passages are characterized by extremely intricate ornamentation and some of the lengthiest melismatic effects to be heard on the Chinese stage. Dance movements have great fluency of line extended through airy control of sleeve movements in their spatial context of the actors' dance gestures. Plays are predominantly romantic and tend to emphasize the situations and dilemmas of young love.

Primarily appealing to the aesthetic awareness of a literary elite *kunqu* began to lose ground in the late 18th century and by the early 19th century was passing into decline as a nationally supreme genre. The occupation of the Jiangsu area by the Taiping revolutionaries in mid-century was a disaster from which this fountainhead of *kunqu* activity never recovered. By the end of the 19th century it had been superseded in popularity by the more robust theatricality of the **jingxi** which drew considerable artistic nourishment from the stage practices of the older form.

There have been two major phases of *kunqu* revival in the present century. The first was in the 1920s when a school was set up in Shanghai producing a number of talented performers some of whom are teachers today. In 1961 the *kunqu* students of the Shanghai School of Dramatic Art made their stage debut after eight years of training under veteran actors and the leadership of **Yu Zhenfei**. The critics predicted a new era but everything was brought to a halt with the Cultural Revolution. Today continuity has been reestablished and *kunqu* is being sponsored and promoted for contemporary audiences. Individual artists are being given recognition as in the past and praised for raising *kunqu* to new heights.   ACS

Kunst, Johann Christian (d. 1703) A leading German actor-director of his time who was approached in 1701 by an emissary of Peter the Great to found the first national public theatre in Moscow as part of the tsar's overall cultural programme. Accepting the charge in 1702, Kunst and a company of seven German actors undertook the training of Russian performers and presented three comedies at the palace of General Lefort in Moscow's foreign quarter. Before a separate wooden theatre in Moscow's Red Square facing the Kremlin could be completed for the company, Kunst died. He was succeeded by another German, Otto Fürst, who continued to draw upon the native population for actors. On 31 May 1706 the company, which since its conception had encountered some opposition, was disbanded and the theatre itself dismantled owing to obstreperous behaviour on the part of the audience and performers. The theatre's failure has been attributed to the absence of Russian plays in its repertoire and of a literary language into which foreign plays could be translated. The 450-seat theatre averaged 25 admissions per performance.   SG

Kuravanji (India) The words *Kuram* and *Kuluva Natakam* are also used to refer to this form of theatre which derives its name from the *Kuravas* and *Chenchus*, nomadic clans of hunters classified as tribals. The hunters inhabit the hilly regions of Andhra Pradesh and their women are said to be excellent fortune tellers. The term *anji* refers to the dances (*adavus*) performed by these people.

Kuravanji originated in the 17th century and the exact details of its origin are as yet uncertain. It may be that *Kuravanji* was an off-shoot of the entertainments in dance and song presented by bands of actors during festival seasons at holy shrines in Andhra Pradesh.

In Tamil Nadu the form follows its own particular pattern. The preliminaries begin with a procession in praise of Sri Vighneswara, the elephant-headed god. Then the clown (*kattiakaran*, also a character in **Therukoothu**) announces the gist of the story to be enacted. During the proceedings, the heroine appears with her maids and, after being announced, she dances to depict her yearnings and sufferings. We come to know that the young girl is pining for her lover, who never makes an appearance in any of the plays. Her companions, usually spritely maidens, tease her as she tries to persuade them to convey her love messages. She even implores the clouds, the wind, birds and the moon to act as intermediaries, but to no avail. Then a gypsy woman (*kuratthi*) appears and, after an elaborate description of the country from which she comes, boasts of her expertise. At the request of the young heroine she reads her palm. The heroine denies that she is in love but eventually admits that she is. The gypsy is richly rewarded for her efforts. Then a hunter (*kurava*) enters the scene in search of his wife, the gypsy. She accuses him of infidelity but he convinces her of his innocence. The play comes to a happy conclusion.

The form was cleverly used by the Maharaja Serfoji II (1798–1833) to teach world geography to students who spoke Marathi, the language of the ruling class of that time. The Maharaja set about accomplishing his aim by transferring a major portion of the dialogue to a gypsy who through song and dance presented the material in an entertaining way. S. D. S. Yogi, a distinguished modern poet of Tamil Nadu, composed a *Kuravanji* only a few years ago entitled *Bhavani*. The play centres on the gifts of the river Bhavani after the construction of a dam.   FaR

Kutiyattam

Kutiyattam Perhaps *Kutiyattam* is India's oldest continuously performed theatre form and one of the oldest surviving art forms of the ancient world. *Kutiyattam* is unique to the state of Kerala, a lush tropical region located on the south-western coast of the Indian subcontinent. Historical evidence points to the existence of *Kutiyattam* as early as the tenth century AD when it is said to have been reformed by King Kulashekara Varman. The high stage of its development, at this early point in its history, suggests that it may well have originated at a somewhat earlier date thus linking it directly with the traditions of the ancient Sanskrit theatre.

Kutiyattam preserves a tradition of performing plays in Sanskrit, the classical language. Some of the plays were composed by well-known classical playwrights. Plays by Bhasa, Harsha and Mahendra Vikrama Pallava are among those which are popular in the repertory. The actors of *Kutiyattam* also use the Prakrit language and an old form of Malayalam, the regional language of Kerala, to convey the contents of the plays, much as ancient actors are thought to have used various regional dialects in their shows.

The artists who are responsible for preserving this unique theatre form for so many centuries are the few, but dedicated, members of a sub-branch of temple servants. Traditionally, the actors are members of the Cakyar caste, whose duty has been to perform *Kutiyattam* in selected temples as a ritual sacrifice to the chief deity and to entertain the spectators who assemble there to pay their homage. The Cakyar actors are accompanied in this ritual duty by the *nambiars*, a sub-caste of drummers who play the *mizhavu*, a large pot-shaped drum peculiar only to *Kutiyattam*. The *Nanyars*, women of the Nambiar community, normally act the female roles, as well as play the small bell-metal cymbals which sustain the basic tempo of every production. Although *Kutiyattam* has been the exclusive province of these three caste groups, members of other castes have studied *Kutiyattam* in modern times

Entrance of Ravana, centre, the demon king of Lanka, with his minister (right) and charioteer (left), in a *Kutiyattam* version of a Sanskrit play.

and regularly appear on stage, although they may not act in temple performances because it violates agreements made between the temple authorities and the hereditary artists.

The unique contribution of *Kutiyattam* to world theatre architecture has been the development of permanent theatres (*kuttampalam*). About nine theatres have been built in various temples in Kerala since the 16th century, the largest and most impressive of which is located in the Vatukumnathan Temple of Trichur. The interior of this impressive structure is about 72 x 55 feet and, like all of the remaining structures, it is rectangular in shape. According to traditional practice, the theatre building is a separate structure located in the walled compound of the temple and situated in front and to the right of the main shrine housing the chief deity. From the solid base of the building, pillars support a high central roof. The stage of the Vatakumnathan Temple is a large, square, raised, stone platform, the front edge of which divides the whole structure in half. Clusters of three pillars extend upward from each of the four corners of the stage to support an interior roof reminiscent of those used for nō stages of Japan. A back wall separates the dressing room from the stage. The wall has two narrow doors. The door upstage left is normally used for entrances and that upright is reserved for exits. Downstage, between the doors, the large pot-shaped drums are suspended in heavy wooden stands. The surface of the stage, in all but a few of the theatres, is convex which allows easy drainage of the stage after washing. Intricate wooden carvings of decorative floral motifs, deities and mythological characters are all but obliterated to the spectators who watch the performance, usually seated in front of the stage under the flickering but weak light of a large bell-metal lamp placed squarely downstage centre.

Kutiyattam performances are rarely seen today, owing to the decline in interest in temple based arts and the fluctuating fortunes of the large temple complexes. However, the Vatukumnathan Temple generally schedules at least one show a year, as does the Irinjalagauda Temple located in a neighbouring town. Measures have been taken by the state and national government and private institutions and individuals to support *Kutiyattam*. Performances of *Kutiyattam* have been arranged in theatres outside the temple compounds, in various towns and cities in Kerala and elsewhere in India, as well as tours to Western countries, where non-Hindus may see performances of this ancient art form.

Instruction in the art is provided in at least three schools in Kerala – at the famous Kerala Kalamandalam School of Cheruthuruthy village, that run by Mani Madhava Cakyar in his village home at Likkadi and the school run by Madhavan Cakyar at Irinjalagauda. Although much effort has been made to bring local, national and international attention to *Kutiyattam*, its importance to the history of theatre has still not been fully realized.

A typical *Kutiyattam* performance is generally quite long, extending over a period of several days. During the first few days of the performance sequence, the characters are introduced to the audience and historical incidents about them are explored in considerable detail. On the final day of the performance the entire act of the play is performed in chronological order, from beginning to end, just as it was written. Although this may seem to violate the intention of the playwright to present all of the events of a play in one performance, it is characteristic of the *Kutiyattam* to explore selected events of the character and the dramatic action in considerable detail. Performances begin around 9 pm, after the final rituals have been performed before the deity in the *sanctum sanctorum* of the temple. Segments of the performance usually finish around midnight and generally no later than 3 am, just before the morning rituals are performed in the *sanctum*. On the last day, the show lasts until 5 or 6 am.

Elaborately dressed actors with fantastical makeup and headdresses perform the various roles of mythological characters, gods and demons using an elaborate code of gesture-language, chanted speech and exaggerated facial and eye expressions. Although there is little dance in *Kutiyattam*, much of the action is accompanied by the *mizhavu* drums, small bell-metal cymbals, a small hour-glass shaped drum (*idakka*), a wind instrument resembling an oboe (*kuzhal*) and a conch shell (*sankha*).

Ritual actions occur throughout all performances and even in the dressing room owing to the sacred character of the performance and the great respect for religion shown by the actors. Ancient manuals of instruction are consulted by the actors in order to ensure that correct procedures are followed.   FaR

Kuwait see **Middle East**

Kuzmin, Mikhail Alekseevich (1875–1936) Dandyish, decadent aesthete, Russian symbolist and later acmeist (clarist) poet, prose writer, composer and dramatist, who played a diverse and significant role in the cabaret and theatre of small forms scene in pre-revolutionary St Petersburg. Educated in music by Rimsky-Korsakov, well-travelled, an avowed homosexual and a supreme ironist, Kuzmin embodied many of the ideas and tendencies of his day: a transcendental-sensual aesthetic; an attraction to paradox and taboo, exoticism and eroticism; a sense of life as tragic *balagan* (puppet show) and self-created work of theatricalist art and of art as festive, transformative ritual. His period of major output, 1907–21, includes: contributions to the symbolist journal, *The Scales* (1904–9); unofficial membership in **Vyacheslav Ivanov**'s Tower apartment literary circle (1905–7); controversial poetry and prose on homosexual themes – *Wings* (a novella, 1907), 'Alexandrian Songs' (poem cycle, in *Nets*, 1908), *Lakes in Autumn* (poetry collection, 1912); and his multi-faceted work in the theatre. The last category included: early attempts to realize a Wagnerian *Gesamtkunstwerk* combining music, dance, poetry and the visual arts, galvanized by World of Art aestheticism; an epic quest-for-truth play, the 'dramatic poem' *The History of the Knight d'Alessio* (his first published work, 1905); music for **Meyerhold**'s production of **Blok**'s *Puppet Show* (1906), which influenced Kuzmin's thinking about puppet theatre; numerous divertissements – pantomimes, operettas, comic operas, mimic and mythological ballets, children's plays, puppet shows, pastorales and masquerades, some written for Meyerhold's 'Doctor Dapertutto' experiments around St Petersburg (c. 1910) and others for the Stray Dog cabaret; three lyrical 'mysteries', which are variants on the voguish harlot–saint theme – *The Comedy of Alexis, Man of God, The Comedy of Eudoxia of Helipolis*, which Blok called the most perfect Russian lyrical drama, and *The Comedy of Martinian* (1908); and his major play, *The Venetian Madcaps* (1912; produced 1914), a dark *commedia* piece on a temptress's destruction of a male friendship, possibly influenced by Meyerhold's production of **Lermontov**'s *Masquerade* (1911) for which Kuzmin composed the original music. Despite the appealing theatricality of his plays and even though Meyerhold named him one of the dramatists who had created the 'new theatre' in Russia (1911), Kuzmin continues to be known primarily as a poet.   SG

Kwangdae Traditionally low-class Korean entertainer who performed all forms of entertainment such as **p'ansori**, tumbling, dance, etc.   OKC

Kyd, Thomas (1558–94) English playwright, remembered for a single masterpiece, *The Spanish Tragedy* (c. 1589). The details of Kyd's life are obscure, and even his authorship of this immensely popular play is in some doubt. His association with **Marlowe** seems to have led to his arrest for heresy in 1593, and he died not long after his release from torture and imprisonment. *The Spanish Tragedy* adapted several features of Senecan tragedy for the more visual taste of the Elizabethan stage. It was a primary influence in the development of revenge tragedy, but it is far too good a play to be thought of primarily as a predecessor of *Hamlet*. Kyd's other known play, *Cornelia* (c. 1594), is a version from the French of **Robert Garnier** and the ascription to him of a lost *Hamlet*, used as a source by

Shakespeare, is the product of scholarly specu-lation.   PT

Kynaston, Ned (Edward) (c. 1640–1706) English boy actor, who specialized in women's roles – probably the last of his profession. He was a favourite on the Restoration stage, and after he had grown beyond female portrayal, played effectively in other roles.   MB

Kyōgen A traditional Japanese theatre genre consist-ing of a repertory of some 260 short plays, celebratory and usually comic, that are performed by specialist *kyōgen* actors on a **nō** stage normally as part of a joint *nō-kyōgen* programme. *Kyōgen* humour arises in part from poking fun at human foibles – greed, lust, chicanery, cowardice. Characters are not idealized as they are in *nō*. Their social weaknesses are shown: a priest is ignorant or useless (*Mushrooms, The Crow*), a wife is domineering (*Fortified Beard*), a servant dishon-est (*Poison Sugar*), a demon witless (*Head-pulling, Spring Evening*), and so forth. Humour comes from punning, onomatopoeia, and physical action. Plays such as *Monkey Quiver* begin seriously – a lord plans to kill a pet monkey to make a quiver from its hide – but conclude in felicitous celebration. As in many Shintō-derived arts, *kyōgen* plays are fundamentally joyous and affirm the goodness of the natural order.

Language is vernacular prose of the 15th and 16th centuries and readily understood by today's audiences.

Actors perform with a high energy level in controlled, clearly articulated vocal and movement patterns which, while stylized, are derived from daily speech and actions. *Kyōgen* is one of the few traditional theatre genres in Asia that is primarily spoken. Unaccompan-ied songs may be sung at the climax of a play, which has the effect of lifting characters out of their particular, plebeian circumstances and transporting them into a universal state of 'rapture'. In a small number of plays, especially those which parody *nō*, songs are accom-panied by the drums and flute of the *nō* musical ensemble (*hayashi*) and a chorus (*ji*) sings while the actor dances. Masks are worn for animals and special characters, but usually the actor performs without mask or makeup. Costume is based on the real clothing people wore in medieval times and is plain in compari-son with the gorgeous and expensive silk brocades worn in *nō*. Tarōkaja, the stock servant character, wears large-checked under-kimono, sleeveless vest, bold patterned bloused trousers, and yellow socks. A landowner is characteristically identified by his trailing trousers and sword.

Today *kyōgen* actors, while formally affiliated with the Ōkura or the Izumi 'school' (*ryū*), tend to work within a smaller family group. The most active groups today are the Nomura and Miyake familes (Izumi school) and the Yamamoto, Shigeyama, and Zenchiku families (Ōkura school). The actors live in Tokyo, Kyoto, and Nagoya and they perform in *nō-kyōgen* programmes throughout the country.   JRB

L

L'Arronge, Adolph (1838–1908) German director, playwright, and musician. A successful writer of light comedies, L'Arronge is best known as a founding member of the **Deutsches Theater** in Berlin and as its first director, from 1887 to 1894. SW

La Chaussée, Pierre-Claude Nivelle de (1692–1754) French dramatist and man of letters who after a life of dissipation turned to producing edifying material for the theatre. Although he wrote other plays, he was most successful in his day and is still associated above all with his 'comédies larmoyantes', tearful comedies in which the influence of the contemporary sentimental novel is manifest. In them pathos is all-pervading to the virtual exclusion of comic elements and the audience are invited to sympathize with the domestic misfortunes and agonies of their recognizable counterparts on stage, particularly in the field of conjugal relations. While the proposed moral uplift is estimable enough, the emotions tapped are disproportionate to the situations created, characterization is woefully simplistic and tears have to be jerked by rhetorical artifice and stock theatrical devices. *Mélanide* (1741) is commonly regarded as his best play, but two others on the subject of unhappy marriage, *La Fausse Antipathie* (*The False Antipathy*, 1733) and *Le Préjugé à la Mode* (*The Fashionable Prejudice*, 1735), are worthy of note, as is his adaptation of Richardson's novel *Paméla* (1743). They were widely translated in their day and as symptoms of 18th-century sensibility and forerunners of the 'drame bourgeois' or fully-fledged domestic drama they retain a precise historical value. He was elected to the Académie-Française in 1736. DR

La Grange (Charles Varlet) (1635–92) French actor, friend and devoted assistant of **Molière**, whose company he joined in 1659 soon after their arrival in Paris and never left. A good-looking man of refined manners, he played the young lover in most of the repertoire, though his creation of parts like Don Juan and Acaste in *The Misanthrope* (1666) suggests that he was more than a simple jeune premier. In 1667 he took over from Molière as company 'orator', responsible for the formal address to the audience and announcement of the forthcoming performance. He was also its secretary and archivist and kept a daily register of all plays performed, together with a record of takings and comments on other company matters, which is an invaluable source of information. After Molière's death he was instrumental in rebuilding the company and ensuring its survival and he became the first orator of the newly constituted **Comédie-Française** in 1680. In 1682 he brought out the first collected edition of Molière's plays, to which he contributed a prefatory *Life* of the author. His wife Marie, daughter of the pastrycook-actor Cyprien Ragueneau, acted with him after their marriage in 1672. DR

La Mama (USA) Off-Off Broadway theatre founded in 1962 by Ellen Stewart, a Cajun who arrived penniless in New York in 1950 and became a successful fashion designer. With her earnings, she began Café La Mama in a cramped, decrepit Manhattan basement and moved several times before settling on East 4th Street in 1969 where the theatre now operates two large performance spaces and a cabaret. The Café became La Mama ETC (Experimental Theatre Club) and Stewart still functions as artistic director, fundraiser, tour manager, and maternal spiritual guardian. Having produced more than 1,000 plays, La Mama introduced important American playwrights and directors like **Rochelle Owens**, **Megan Terry**, Jeff Weiss, **Sam Shepard**, **Harvey Fierstein**, H. M. Koutoukas, **Lanford Wilson**, Julie Bovasso, **Adrienne Kennedy**, and Tom O'Horgan. In addition, La Mama has brought to America such artists as **Jerzy Grotowski**, **Andrei Serban**, **Peter Brook**, **Eugenio Barba**, and **Tadeusz Kantor**. In 1980 La Mama established the Third World Institute of Theatre Arts and Studies (TWITAS). AS

La Rue, Danny (Daniel Patrick Carroll) (1928–) British actor, born in Ireland, who has made his reputation in cabaret, pantomime (*Queen Passionella and the Sleeping Beauty*, 1968) and variety shows (*Danny La Rue at the Palace*, 1970) as the leading female impersonator. CI

La Taille, Jean de (c. 1535–c. 1608) French dramatist and poet. Of his two tragedies on biblical subjects, *Saül le Furieux* (*Saul Enraged*), published in 1572, and its sequel *La Famine, ou les Gabéonites* (*The Famine*, 1573), the first is the more effective in dramatic terms and is prefaced by a treatise on the art of tragedy which, in recapitulating the observations of **Aristotle** and **Horace**, stressing the importance of the three unities and condemning the presentation of violence on stage, offers a convenient résumé of the dramatic theory of 16th-century humanist scholars. In *Les Corrivaux* (*The Rivals*, 1574) La Taille wrote the first French comedy in prose. DR

Labiche, Eugène (1815–88) French dramatist. Labiche was one of the more prolific authors of the 19th century and, like many of those who saw themselves essentially as entertainers, generally worked with a collaborator, the most important of these being Marc

Michel. Of his 175 plays, 57 were published in his *Complete Plays*. The majority of these are light comedies, or *vaudevilles*, but a few are more serious comedies of manners. The *vaudeville* itself – generally a one-act comedy with some songs – was the most popular form in the 19th-century theatre. Labiche turned initially for his craft to the master of the *vaudeville*, **Eugène Scribe**, but gradually transformed the genre itself into the 'French farce' that **Feydeau** would bring to perfection. Labiche's heyday was the Second Empire, and his plays were written for the entertainment of the bourgeoisie of that period. This same bourgeoisie forms the basic subject matter for all the plays and is closely observed and constantly caricatured by Labiche in the tradition of Henri Monnier and Honoré Daumier. Labiche's career as a dramatist began in 1838, with his first real success in 1848, *Un Jeune Homme Pressé (A Young Man in a Hurry)*, for which he defined *vaudeville* as 'the art of making the girl's father, who first said no, say yes'. *An Italian Straw Hat* (1851) was one of his most popular plays (and survived into the 20th century with René Clair's classic film). A full-length play, it takes a popular device of farce and melodrama, the chase, but instead of keeping it for the end of the play, uses it as a leit-motif running throughout, as the hapless hero is pursued by an entire wedding party. The play abounds in wickedly accurate observations of the bourgeoisie, and moves at breakneck speed from situation to situation and misunderstanding to misunderstanding. *Le Voyage de Monsieur Perrichon (Monsieur Perrichon's Holiday*, 1860) showed a more developed sense of characterization, its hero being the epitome of the Second Empire bourgeois. Much of the action hinges on the simple psychological mechanism that we are much more grateful to those we help than to those who help us. In *Célimare le Bien-aimé (Célimare the Beloved*, 1863), a play that seems to anticipate the work of **Anouilh**, the hero causes consternation to two husbands he has cuckolded when he decides to get married. This theme of the ménage à trois, previously thought of more as the subject for a drama, was fully developed by Labiche in one of his last plays, *The Happiest of the Three* (1870), in which the husband is the happiest (and ultimately prefers domestic bliss with the wife's lover rather than the wife). In 1864 Labiche was accepted into the **Comédie-Française** with his harsh comedy about an egotist, *I*, but this was not one of his more successful pieces. *Three Cheers for Paris (La Cagnotte*, 1864) is the *Italian Straw Hat* in a darker vein, bringing a group of provincials to Paris, where they experience a variety of discomforts. Labiche was admitted to the French Academy in 1880 and spent his last years on the estate he had purchased with the proceeds of his plays.   JMCC

Lackaye, Wilton (1862–1932) American actor who began his professional career in 1883 as Lucentio in **Lawrence Barrett**'s revival of **Boker**'s *Francesca da Rimini*. During a very active career he played hundreds of roles for many managements. In 1886 he supported **Fanny Davenport** at the **Union Square Theatre**. In 1906 he adapted **Hugo**'s *Les Misérables* into the play *Law and the Man* in which he played Jean Valjean and M. Madeline. He is remembered, however, as the original Svengali in **Du Maurier**'s *Trilby* (1895), which he revived frequently. A devout Catholic, he founded the Catholic Actors' Guild and assisted with the organization of the American Actors' Equity Association.   DBW

Lacy, James (1696–1774) English actor and manager who began acting in 1724 but soon realized that his talents were as a theatre manager. Arrested in 1737 for attempting to evade the Licensing Act, in 1744 he joined the partnership running **Drury Lane** and in 1747 persuaded **Garrick** to take a half-share in the company. Drury Lane had been in severe decline but the huge success of the Lacy–Garrick partnership enabled them to recoup their investment within four years. Lacy played a major part in the success through his great determination and good business sense, though inclined to try to lord it over Garrick.   PH

Lacy, John (1615–81) English actor and playwright. Apprenticed as a dancer, he was acting in the 1630s. At the Restoration he joined **Beeston**'s company at **Salisbury Court** and then the King's Men, playing Ananias in **Jonson**'s *The Alchemist*. He was a major shareholder in the building of the Theatre Royal in Bridges Street and was soon co-managing the company for **Killigrew** with Mohun and **Hart**. In 1667 he was arrested for mocking the court in his role as a rustic in *The Change of Crowns*. He was a brilliant clown, particularly famed as Teague, an Irish footman, in Sir **Robert Howard**'s *The Committee*, in the title role in his own *Sauny the Scot* and as **Molière**'s Sganarelle. His own plays included farces like *The Old Troop* and adaptations of **Shakespeare**. He was painted in three of his roles, commissioned by Charles II.   PH

Ladipo, Duro (1931–78) Nigerian musician, dramatist and performer; a notable composer of Yoruba folk opera, and founder of the Duro Ladipo Theatre. Born in Oshogbo in what was then the Western Region of Nigeria, Ladipo discovered his theatrical inspiration in the oral tradition of Yoruba history, and in the Oshogbo masquerades and festivals, which rubbed against the grain of his stern Christian upbringing. He

A scene from Ladipo's *Oba Ko So*.

established the Mbari-Mbayo Centre (1962) in Oshogbo, with a performance of his first opera *Oba Moro* (published as a text in 1964). Aided by Chief Ulli Beier and Suzanne Wenger, Mbari-Mbayo became a hothouse for young Yorubas, talented in the Arts, some of whom went on to achieve international fame as painters, sculptors and performers. Ladipo's most famous opera, *Oba Ko So* (1964), concerns the religio-mythic figure of Sango, God of Lightning, in the Yoruba pantheon. The opera, with Ladipo as Sango, remained in the repertory of his Company for more than 12 years and was performed in many parts of the world, always with great success. Other operas which appealed to Yoruba audiences and achieved critical acclaim were *Oba Waja*, based on an incident in Nigeria's colonial period when a British District Officer tried to stop a sacred ritual suicide; *Moremi*, based on the legend of a Yoruba woman who allowed herself to be captured so that she might learn the secret of the success of her people's enemy; and *Eda*, his adaptation of *Everyman*. Ladipo also composed sketches for television, and made a series, *Bode Wasinmi*. He was a gifted musician; and this talent was enhanced by the further gift of a strong visual sensibility. His work derived from Yoruba history, and indeed his art was more concerned with a specifically Yoruba aesthetic, as part of a wider Nigerian theatre aesthetic. His early death was a tragedy for Nigerian theatre. ME

Lafayette Players (1915–32) An Afro-American stock company organized by the actress Anita Bush to provide dramatic entertainment for the Harlem community in place of minstrel and vaudeville shows that often ridiculed black folk. On a weekly schedule the company presented at the Lafayette Theatre abridged versions of popular Broadway comedies and melodramas hoping to demonstrate that black actors could play dramatic roles as well as song-and-dance clowns. As these productions gained popular support, the Players formed road companies for touring. In 1928 they moved to Los Angeles where they played successfully to mixed audiences, compiling a production record of 250 plays over 17 years before becoming a casualty of nation-wide financial depression. Among well-recognized former players are **Charles Gilpin**, Clarence Muse, 'Dooley' Wilson, Inez Clough, Evelyn Ellis and Abbie Mitchell. EGH

Lagerkvist, Pär (1891–1974) Swedish playwright, novelist and poet, winner of the Nobel Prize for Literature. Best known in the English-speaking world as a novelist, he was also recognized in Scandinavia as an innovative dramatist who relentlessly explored new dramatic forms. His concern with form was proclaimed in his essay 'Modern Theatre: Points of View and Attack' (1918), in which he dismissed naturalism (especially **Ibsen**'s plays) as untheatrical and applauded the theatricalism of **Strindberg**'s later plays. His own plays are exploratory variations on a single theme, that of evil as an abstract force in life and as an irrepressible instinct in the individual mind. His early plays, especially the one-act trilogy *The Difficult Hour* (1918) and the short *The Secret of Heaven* (1919), are grotesque expressionistic fantasies, showing humanity trapped within and poisoned by a meaningless, ferocious world. In the 1920s, his faith in humanity seemed to

increase, as in *He Who Lived His Life Over* (1928), but with the rise of fascism in the 1930s, his plays focused with increasing urgency on the dangerous religion of brutality, often contrasting it with some feminine figure representing motherly protection. Certainly his most forceful and imaginative play of the period was *The Hangman* (1933), given productions all over Scandinavia by **Per Lindberg**, Lagerkvist's most understanding director. His most popular play in the theatre was his most accessible, the moral parable *The Philosopher's Stone* (1947), which uses the story of a medieval alchemist to examine the complexities of faith. HL

Lahr, Bert (Irving Lahrheim) (1895–1967) American comic actor. After an apprenticeship in juvenile vaudeville acts, Lahr broke into burlesque as a Dutch comedian. His first feature part, a punch-drunk fighter in *Hold Everything* (1928), won him critical acclaim and starring roles in musical comedies *Flying High* (1930), *Hot-Cha!* (1932) and *The Show is On* (1936). Lahr's stock-in-trade included a grimace like that 'of a camel with acute gastric disorder' and a laryngeal bleat 'like a lovesick ram'. His style was too broad for film, although he is immortalized as the Cowardly Lion in *The Wizard of Oz* (1938). He returned to Broadway in *Du Barry Was A Lady* (1939). Lahr considered the turning-point in his career to be Estragon in *Waiting for Godot* (1956). This association with the avant-garde brought him roles in **Shaw**, **Molière** and **Shakespeare** (Bottom). He enlivened five roles in S. J. Perelman's *The Beauty Part* (1962). Lahr never retired but died during the shooting of *The Night They Raided Minsky's*. LS

Lahr, John (1941–) American drama critic and author. Born in Los Angeles, Lahr studied at Yale and Oxford University. He worked as a dramaturge for the **Guthrie Theatre** (1968) and for the Repertory Theatre of Lincoln Center (1969–71). He has served as contributing editor of *Evergreen Review*, theatre editor of *Grove Press*, and drama critic of *Village Voice*. Lahr asks that theatre be socially responsible and forge new images to 'revitalize the imaginative life of its audience'. Such theatre, he feels, must be 'shocking, violent, and unpredictable'. Lahr is the author of at least ten books, including a biography of his father, the comedian **Bert Lahr** (*Notes on a Cowardly Lion*, 1969). TLM

Lamarche, Gustave (1895–1987) French Canadian playwright, director and poet. A Catholic priest, his collected works comprise 34 plays in six volumes. In the 1930s and 40s the plays which he wrote and directed, generally staged outdoors, attracted huge crowds, sometimes estimated at more than 100,000 spectators for a single performance. They are vast pageant-plays, medieval in format and inspiration, usually based on biblical themes. Best known are *Jonathas* (1935), *La Défaite de l'Enfer* (*Hell Defeated*, 1938), *Notre-Dame-des-Neiges* (*Our Lady of the Snows*, 1942), and *Notre-Dame-de-la-Couronne* (*Our Lady of the Crown*, 1947). In conjunction with Father **Emile Legault**, Lamarche succeeded in making theatre, long suspect to the Catholic church in French Canada, a respectable and worthwhile occupation. LED

Lamb, Charles (1775–1834) English essayist and critic, a long-term employee of the East India Company and an inveterate theatregoer. He included many theatrical subjects in his *Essays of Elia*, helping in particular to preserve the memory of Joseph Munden, **Robert Elliston** and **Fanny Kelly**, for whom he cherished an unrequited love. His influential *Specimens of English Dramatic Poets who lived about the time of Shakespeare* (1808) raised awareness of the great age of English drama, and the *Tales from Shakespeare* (1807), written with his sister Mary, was a children's classic. Lamb was far from being the gentle angel of posthumous portraits, though he is rightly admired for his lifelong protection of his brilliant but unbalanced sister. His theatrical criticism was robust. He was, for example, a vigorous opponent of the greedy taste for vast theatres, in which broad effects ousted subtlety and which he considered inappropriate for the performance of **Shakespeare**'s plays. When his own farce, *Mr H — —* (1806), was hissed off the **Drury Lane** stage, he covered his chagrin by joining in the hissing. He was the author also of a remorse-laden tragedy, *John Woodvil* (published 1802), which **John Kemble** declined to present, though it is no worse than some that he did.   PT

Lang, Matheson (1879–1948) British actor–manager, born in Canada, who toured in **Frank Benson**'s company and with **Lillie Langtry** and **Ellen Terry**, before appearing in **Granville Barker**'s productions of **Ibsen** and **Shaw** at the **Royal Court Theatre**. From 1910 he toured Australia, South Africa and India with his own company, until 1913 when he returned to London in *Mr Wu* – a melodramatic part he became identified with, which he revived repeatedly all over the world – and in 1914 he directed and acted in the first **Shakespeare** season at the **Old Vic**.   CI

Lange, Harmut (1937–) German dramatist, who escaped to the West after early work like his ironic verse celebration of collective-farming *Marski* (1963 – first performed 1968) was banned in the DDR. His best-known play *The Countess of Rathenow* (1969) attacks German traditionalism, but his characteristic style is political allegory (*Hercules*, 1968; *The Murder of Ajax*, 1971).   CI

Langner, Lawrence (1890–1962) One of the most enlightened producers in American theatre history, Langner grew up in London and studied to be a patent lawyer. In 1911 he emigrated to New York and established himself as a patent attorney, later heading a large international firm. In 1914 he helped organize the **Washington Square Players** and wrote several one-act plays for the group. After it disbanded because of the war (1917), he brought together members of the group in late 1918 to form the **Theatre Guild**. The most important of these was **Theresa Helburn** who together with Langner managed the organization throughout much of its active life. They pursued artistic aims and built a subscription audience of 25,000 by 1925. The success of their second production, *John Ferguson* (1919), established them artistically and commercially. Langner encouraged the production of foreign plays including works by **Toller**, **Kaiser**, **Molnar**, and **Pirandello**. He obtained for the Guild,

Shaw's *Heartbreak House* in 1919, *Back to Methuselah* in 1921, and *St Joan* in 1923. And he persuaded the Guild to stage **O'Neill**'s *Strange Interlude* in 1928. With his wife Armina, Langner built the Westport County Playhouse in 1931 and formed an acting company. And in the early 1950s he founded the **American Shakespeare Festival** at Stratford, Conn. Called by **Brooks Atkinson** 'one of the most articulate men alive', Langner brought an able business mind to bear upon the American theatre for almost 50 years.   TLM

Langtry, Lillie (1853–1929) English actress and society beauty, born in Jersey, of which her father, the Very Reverend William le Breton, was Dean. She made her London social debut in 1877, three years after her marriage to an Anglo-Irish landowner, and her theatrical debut under the **Bancrofts** at the **Haymarket** in 1881, when she played Kate Hardcastle in a charity matinee performance of *She Stoops to Conquer*. Her amorous conquests had, by then, included the future Edward VII and Prince Louis of Battenberg, and her notoriety had been enhanced by Millais's portrait of her, holding a Jersey lily. It was as 'the Jersey Lily' that she continued to draw audiences in England, South Africa and, most of all, in the USA until her retirement in 1918. At best a competent actress and a shrewd company manager, she numbered Rosalind in *As You Like It* and Lady Teazle in *The School for Scandal* among her most effective roles, but it was in **Sydney Grundy**'s *The Degenerates* (1899) that she tempted and scandalized her public by offering glimpses of autobiographical sin in high society. Lillie Langtry was part-author, with J. Hartley Manners, of an unsuccessful play called *The Crossways* (1902). She also wrote a novel

Millais's portrait of Lillie Langtry, 'The Jersey Lily'.

(as Lady de Bathe, her title by a second marriage), *All at Sea* (1909), and an evasive autobiography, *The Days I Knew* (1921). She died in her villa in Monte Carlo.   PT

Languirand, Jacques (1931–   ) French Canadian playwright, essayist and producer. Much influenced by the dramatists he met and the plays he saw during his studies in Paris, 1949–53, he became on his return Canada's most important exponent of the European theatre of the absurd. Several of his dramatic texts were performed on radio before his first stage play, *Les Insolites* (*The Unusual Ones*), was awarded the prize for best Canadian play at the Dominion Drama Festival in 1956. The same year *Le Roi Ivre* (*The Drunken King*) was performed with success in Montreal, followed by his best-known work, *Les Grands Départs* (*Great Departures*), televised in 1957 and staged in 1958. Languirand continued to write and produce plays for the next dozen years, principally *Les Violons de l'Automne* (*Violins of Autumn*, 1961), the multi-media *Man, Inc.* (1970) and the musical comedy *Klondyke* (1970), but despite performances in France and Great Britain, his work has had little appeal for Canadian audiences. Since 1970 he has abandoned the theatre in favour of philosophic essays.   LED

Lao She (pen name of Shu Qingchung) (1899–1966) Chinese playwright and novelist. He was born and educated in Beijing. After various posts in the educational field he left for England in 1924. There he taught at the London School of Oriental Studies for five years and began to write. He returned to China an acknowledged comic novelist with a keen sense of character. His masterpiece, *Xiangzi the Camel* (*Luotuo Xiangzi*), a story of the corruption and tragic fate of a good natured Beijing rickshaw puller, brought him international fame through an unauthorized English edition with a changed conclusion. The original Chinese version was first published in serial form during 1936–7. Lao She spent the war years in Chongqing where he began to write plays and work with theatre groups. In 1946 he was invited to the United States, remaining there for three years. After returning to China he began writing plays again and participated in literary committees and organizations under the new government. In 1951 he wrote *Dragon Beard Ditch* (*Longu gou*), a play concerning the successful rehabilitation of a Beijing slum area which earned him the title of People's Artist. In 1957 he published *Teahouse* (*Chaguan*) a three-act play in which he demonstrated his skilful command of the colloquial and a sensitive insight on a changing society. A much admired writer his death was reportedly due to suicide following ill treatment by Red Guards.   ACS

Laos The population of this South-East Asian country bordering on Thailand, Cambodia, Burma, and Vietnam is composed primarily of Lao peoples who are closely related to the Thai. The artistic traditions of the three million Lao, which are largely shared by the 13 million Lao of northern Thailand, can be divided into three kinds of performance: (1) proto-theatrical, indigenous forms (2) court forms which since their 14th-century inception have emulated Khmer-Thai models, and (3) modern, popular genres created during the 20th century by combining folk forms with ideas borrowed from Thai popular theatre forms, especially *likay*.

Proto-theatrical, indigenous forms   The indigenous, folk forms can roughly be divided into three categories according to the functions they serve: (1) story-telling (2) courting (3) curing. The format of the performance and personnel needed devolve from the function.

Sung story-telling, *lum pun*, is an old tradition which is now seldom encountered. In it a single male singer is accompanied by a musician playing a *kaen* (a bamboo mouth organ) as he sings *jataka* (tales of Buddha's previous lives), local epics or historical tales. One popular story is the defeat of the Lao kingdom of Wiangjun by the Thai in 1827. The stories, told over one to three nights, are in *glawn* poetry. *Glawn* verse has four lines to a stanza, seven or more syllables to a line, and uses specific tones from the tonal Lao language for set words. The singer is called *mawlum* (*Maw*, an expert; *lum*, a melody derived from word tones). This solo, male singer of tales sometimes acts out all the parts, changing his costume and movement for each character: in this case the genre is called *lum luang*. Other performance forms, comparable to the story-telling model, are *an nungsu* (reading a book) in which men read tales from palm leaf manuscripts during wakes, and the sung recitation of *jataka* or the delivery of sermons, *tet*, by Buddhist priests. All these are solo, male genres which tell a story.

It takes two to flirt; hence, the forms that relate to courting customs involve a male–female dialogue. *Pa-nyah* is a courting game in which boys and girls engage in a sung poetic dialogue, testing each other's wit and skill. A more theatrical form which alternates a male and female voice is the popular *lum glawn*. *Kaen* playing accompanies two professional singers who use memorized passages of poetry, improvising the order, according to the needs of the presentation, or compose new verses in performance guided by the constraints of the poetic tradition. This *lum glawn* presentation which is popular at temple festivals and family celebrations begins about 9 pm as the male singer praises the beauty and expresses his longing for the woman; it intensifies as she admits a reciprocal attraction tinged with fear of betrayal; and it concludes shortly before dawn when the pair must sorrowfully part. Rhythm and musical scale as well as content of the poetry help create the different moods of the 'affair', and dance interludes (*fawn*) break up the singing. The charismatic singers may address the suggestive verses to audience members of the opposite sex, rather than their partner. Real courting poems (*glawn gio*) have contributed heavily to the repertoire of the *lum glawn*.

Performers customarily learn their art by studying music and poetry with a *mawlum* or a Buddhist monk. Many performers come from families that have a tradition of excellence in singing. The form may be called by a different name in each area of the country, but the pattern and personnel are constant. A variation on courting themes is *lum ching choo* (competing for a lover) in which two males seek the hand of one lady. The courting forms customarily involve a member of each sex, and a contest of wits characterizes the subtle, procreant struggles of the sexes.

Curing is the aim of *lum pee fah* (sky spirit singing) which is performed by old women who contact this powerful, benevolent spirit to counteract illnesses caused by lesser sprites. Ecstatic dance, spirit possession, and oracular statements about the identity of the disease-producing spirit are customary. Predominance of females in this form may be evidence of the importance of women as spirit mediums in pre-Buddhist, indigenous ritual, a pattern which may be related to Burma's model of the *nat kadaw* (spirit wife, i.e. female trance dance medium). Men are the story-tellers and initiators in performance forms, but women are especially significant in divination, healing, and spirit possession.

Court forms The court forms are imported traditions, established as Lao kings copied the customs of power-ful neighbouring monarchs. Tradition holds that Khmer court dance, along with the *Ramayana* and *jataka* repertoire were introduced to Laos by Prince Fa Nguan in 1353. During the 14th century the Lao kingdom of Lan Sang ('Million Elephants') was an important force in the area, where the Khmer mon-archs with their troupe of female wife-dancers were the epitome of potent kingship. Keeping up with the Khmer meant establishing the female dance. The courts of the Lao kings were never as rich as their prototype at Angkor. Nor could the Lao compete with the 15th-century newcomer, the Thai ruler who himself fol-lowed Khmer practice, first at Ayutthaya and, in later centuries, in Bangkok (see **Kampuchea** and **Thai-land**). If Lan Sang in the early period aped Angkor, the small princedoms of Luang Prabang, Wiangjun, and Chapassak, established by a partition in 1700, followed Thai models: Thai female court dance *lakon fai nai*, male masked dance drama *khon* and shadow play *nang yai* became the court genres. The Lao did little to naturalize the forms: the Royal Lao Ballet of the 1960s in Luang Prabang included only female dancers, the best of whom had trained in Bangkok. Rather than staging full dance dramas like the Thai and Khmer, this smaller court favoured solo and small group dances.

Modern popular forms Drama which involves mul-tiple performers playing characters in an extended narrative is largely a phenomenon of the last 60 years, occurring first in the Lao areas which have become part of Thailand. Thai *likay* troupes began touring to these northern provinces in the 1920s, and soon local Lao groups started emulating features of *likay*, integrating them with indigenous ideas. From *likay* came flashy costumes, wing and drop scenery, repertoire, and stock character types; from *lum pun/luang* came *kaen* playing and *mawlum*-style singing. This mixed genre came to be called by different names, including *likay lao* (Lao-style *likay*), *mawlum moo* (group *mawlum*), *mawlum plun* (spontaneous *mawlum*), *lum moo* (group singing) and *lum luang* (sung story).

The two major variants that Miller found popular in the 1970s are *mawlum plun* developed in 1950 in Ubon province using the Thai story of *Gaeo na mah* (*The Horse-faced Girl*), and *mawlum moo* which developed about 1952 when a group became noted for playing *Nang Daeng-awn*, the story of a crocodile maid. Miller saw *mawlum plun* distinguished from *mawlum moo* by the latter's less serious mood, its use of more instru-ments than *kaen* (in the early period a lute called a *pin* was incorporated, more recently Western-style drums are added), and the break-neck pace of singing. The repertoire for both forms consists of *jatakas*, Thai legends, and Lao historical tales.

Performances generally take place on raised outdoor stages about 30ft x 15ft. Electric bulbs hang above the stage providing light for the nightlong performance. Scenery mounted on bamboo poles represents general locales such as a court, a forest, or a town. Immovable microphones, which make the singing audible to the audience, are the focal points of the performance. The slight staging of action that is attempted never takes the actors far from them.

A troupe averages some 20 members who play stock types: a hero (*pra ek*) and heroine (*nang ek*), secondary male and female characters (*pra rawung*, *nang rawung*), a king/father (*paw payah*), a queen/mother (*mae payah*), a villain (*poo rai*), and a clown (*dua dalok*). To these roles servants, monkeys, ogres, hermits, soldiers, ghost, etc. are added as the particular plot demands. Thousands of performers are part of such troupes in north-east Thailand. In the 1970s these forms were increasingly showing the impact of Western popular culture – rock music and mini-skirted go-go girls were increasingly noticeable in performances.

A Thai shadow theatre, *Nang talung*, has been adapted by Lao living in Thailand to create *nang daloong*. This new shadow theatre appeared in the north as early as 1926, when amateurs began perform-ing the Thai version of the *Ramayana* to the accompani-ment of xylophones, finger cymbals, and drums. Current troupes perform Lao tales as well as stories from the Thai repertoire and incorporate *kaen* playing and *mawlum*-style singing to win local audiences. Although the form derives from the *wayang* tradition of Malaysia and Indonesia, multiple manipulators have replaced the single *dalang* (puppet-master) of the *wayang* and the ritual import of the theatre is gone. Some 17 *nang daloong* troupes were active in the Chi River area in the late 1970s.

In Laos proper, which tends to be more conservative than the Thai influenced south, it is still the proto-theatrical, folk forms which prevail. Theatre proper is almost non-existent. The court forms, however lovely, have never blended with these indigenous strains. It is in those areas where Lao arts have freely interacted with Thai theatrical stimuli that a Lao theatre has emerged in the last 50 years, and even in these recent forms singing skill remains the prime requisite for a good performer, and acoustics, rather than dramatic factors, govern the staging. What is heard, not what is seen, still matters most to Lao theatre-goers. KF

See: J. Brandon, *Theatre in Southeast Asia*, Cambridge, Mass, 1967; R. de Berval, *Kingdom of Laos*, Saigon, 1959; C. Compton, *Courting Poetry in Laos*, DeKalb, 1979; T. Miller, 'Kaen Playing and Mawlum Singing in Northeast Thailand', Ph.D. diss., Indiana Univ., 1977, and 'Laos' in S. Sadie (ed.), *New Grove Dictionary of Music and Musicians*, London, 1980; S. J. Tambiah, *Buddhism and Spirit Cults in Northeastern Thailand*, London, 1970.

Larivey, Pierre de (c. 1540–1619) French dramatist of Italian descent, his name being a French pun on the family name of Giunti. Inspired by the performances of itinerant **commedia dell'arte** players visiting France, he wrote a number of comedies based on Italian models but transposed to a French milieu, of which six were published in 1579 and a further three in 1611. Employ-ing the type characters and familiar plot devices of *commedia*, they abound in imposture, deceit, seduction and other characteristic forms of unscrupulous behaviour and derive additional comic thrust from the racy, colourful idiom in which they are written and the opportunities they provide for stage business. They were widely performed and republished several times in his lifetime, infusing the French comic tradition with transalpine vitality. The most interesting, *Les Esprits* (*The Ghosts*, 1579), was adapted from an original by Lorenzo de' Medici which itself was indebted to **Plautus** and **Terence**, and strong echoes of it can be found in plays by **Molière** and **Regnard**.   DR

Larochelle, Henri (1827–84) French theatre manager. Larochelle (born Boullanger), studied as an actor at the Conservatoire, played with **Séveste**'s troupes and was accepted by the **Odéon** in 1848. In 1850 he became manager of the Théâtre Montmartre for the Sévestes and in 1851 he bought the ailing Théâtre Montparnasse, followed by the Théâtre de Grenelle. In 1851 Larochelle ran four troupes and actors often had to commute between theatres in the course of the evening. Within a short time he found himself in control of some eight or ten suburban theatres. In 1856 he rebuilt Montparnasse, increasing its size to 700 seats, and in 1866 opened a new theatre in Paris, the Cluny, where he aimed at a repertoire of higher quality, often doing plays rejected by other managements, such as Erckmann–Chatrian's *Le Juif Polonais* (*The Polish Jew*, in England, *The Bells*). In 1869 he built the Théâtre des Gobelins, to replace the Théâtre Saint Marcel, and invited an unknown sculptor called Rodin to provide statues for the facade. After 1870 he turned his attention to larger theatres. Montparnasse was taken over by Hartmann in 1874, and rebuilt in 1886 (it was this theatre that was used for some of the Théâtre Libre performances, including **Tolstoi**'s *The Power of Darkness* (1888) and the Théâtre d'Art of Paul Fort also performed there in 1891 and 1892). Larochelle became director of the Porte-Saint-Martin in 1872, mounting **Hugo**'s *Marie Tudor*, with the aged **Frédérick Lemaître**, *Les Deux Orphelines*, **Dennery** and Cormon's *The Two Orphans*, and the vastly successful *Around the World in Eighty Days*. In 1877 he took on the direction of the Ambigu. In 1878 he 'retired', taking up the management of the Gaîté, where one of his most spectacular productions was Paul Meurice's adaptation of Victor Hugo's *Quatre-vingt-treize* (*Ninety-three*).   JMCC

Lateiner, Jacob see **Hurwitz, Moishe**

Laterna Magika Devised by the Czechs Alfred Radok and **Josef Svoboda**, it is a system that integrates live performance with film projections of the performers themselves on multiple screens. It premiered in the Czechoslovakian pavilion at the Brussels Expo in 1958. Subsequently it degenerated into tourist entertainment, but occasionally its principle appeared in serious drama: e.g. *The Last Ones* (1966), a Radok-Svoboda collaboration. Svoboda has continued to explore scenographic applications of the system, as in the large-scale spectacle of *The Odyssey* in 1987.   JMB

Latin America To deal with the theatre of Latin America as a unit is to presuppose that a homogeneity exists with certain common denominators. As with all generalizations, this one contains both truth and fiction. The Spanish conquest began with Columbus's arrival in 1492, and the Portuguese explorers who claimed the territory of Brazil followed soon after. The geographic size and population diversity render a comprehensive term somewhat unsatisfactory, but despite its limitations, 'Latin America' acknowledges common historical, linguistic and cultural developments.

Theatre, or at least theatrical forms, existed in the Americas before the arrival of the Spanish and Portuguese. For the most part, these manifestations were not well documented by the conquerors; in fact, from the perspective of a religious conquest of the New World, their 'heretical' nature generally caused them to be suppressed. Some indigenous forms are described in the early Spanish chronicles, but the only authentic non-European work to survive is the **Rabinal Achí** of the *maya-quichés*. *El baile de El Güegüence* and **Ollantay** are both cited as early plays with indigenous flavour, but both are of dubious origin and have European characteristics.

Early religious plays in the colonies, at a time that the Spanish theatre itself was still rudimentary, often drew on local traditions and customs to facilitate comprehension by the Indians. Performed in the church atriums and plazas, these plays soon shared time with more secular manifestations dramatizing important events in the colonies, such as the arrival or departure of a viceroy, or the saint's day of an important personage. Traffic between Spain and Portugal and their colonies was constant throughout the colonial period, and the advanced state of development of peninsular theatre during the Siglo de Oro (Golden Age), dominated by **Lope de Vega** and **Calderón de la Barca** and their respective schools, contributed to the early transfer of theatrical interest from Spain and Portugal to Latin America. Both **Juan Ruiz de Alarcón** (born in Mexico) and **Tirso de Molina** spent periods of time in the colonies, but neither had a significant impact on the development of national dramaturgy, in spite of critics' claims to the contrary. By the end of the 17th century, Mexico had produced one great playwright, the extraordinary nun Sor Juana Inés de la Cruz.

Throughout the colonial years the theatre tended to be either an imported phenomenon or an artistic form that paralleled closely the prevailing modes of the mother countries. During the 17th century the aesthetic trends ranged from early Renaissance to baroque characteristics in tone, language and form. The **autos sacramentales** popular during the 17th century were banned by Charles III in 1765 as religious drama became increasingly corrupted.

The period of independence in Latin America lasted from 1810 to 1825, but political independence did little to ensure cultural independence. Neoclassic and romantic plays characterized the first half of the 19th century with strong influence of both French and Spanish literature and thought. Even though realism and the psychological theatre marked the latter half of the 19th century in Spain, a second wave of romantic influences impeded the development of a realistic, autochthonous theatre in the New World, and romanticism continued to prevail in many countries until about 1910.

Only in the 20th century did theatre in Latin America begin to find its own expression. The Golden Decade (1900–10) in Argentina sprang from the popular traditions of the circus and gaucho. From the late 1920s forward, the development of a vast movement of experimental and independent theatres, attuned to the latest techniques of staging, lighting, diction and direction in the European theatre – not to mention theatre architecture and construction – brought about a theatrical renovation and revolution in Latin America. These independent/experimental theatres paved the way for the introduction of serious, committed theatre from the 1950s forward, in contrast to the frivolous costumbristic comedies that had often dominated the professional stage.

Massive problems continue to plague the development of theatre in Latin America. Censorship, social injustices, the lack of dramatic arts schools for the training of theatre professionals (directors, actors, and technicians), impoverished and inadequate theatre structures poorly equipped to deal with modern plays – all are manifestations of wrenching socio-political and economic problems. In fact, much of the recent theatre reflects the deep-seated problems within the various societies, and with pedagogical intention it serves as a vehicle for ideological change. New forms of popular theatre can be found both in traditional theatre spaces and in manifestations of street theatre where a revolutionary spirit often prevails, invoking a process of change. The theatre in Latin America is responsive to world currents and at the same time it continues to develop its own themes and forms. In spite of the problems, therefore, the theatre continues to be a vital and dynamic medium of artistic expression in Latin America. Detailed information on each country is found under appropriate listings.   GW

See: J. J. Arrom, *Historia del el teatro hispanoamericano: época colonial*, Mexico, 1967; P. Bravo Elizondo, *Teatro hispanoamericano de crítica social*, Madrid, 1975; F. Dauster, *Ensayos sobre el teatro hispanoamericano*, Mexico, 1975; *idem*, *Historia del teatro hispanoamericano: siglos XIX y XX*, Mexico, 1973; W. K. Jones, *Behind Spanish American Footlights*, Austin, 1966; G. Luzuriaga, *Popular Theatre for Social Change in Latin America*, Los Angeles, 1978; L. Lyday and G. Woodyard, *Dramatists in Revolt: The New Latin American Theatre*, Austin, 1976; E. G. Neglia, *Aspectos del teatro moderno hispanoamericano*, Bogota, 1975; G. Rojo, *Orígenes del teatro hispanoamericano contemporáneo*, Valparaíso, 1972; A del Saz Sánchez, *Teatro hispanoamericano*, 2 vols., Barcelona, 1963–4; C. Solórzano, *El teatro latinoamericano en el siglo XX*, Mexico, 1964; J. Villegas, *La interpretación de la obra dramática*, Santiago, 1971.

Laube, Heinrich (1806–84) German playwright and director. As a young journalist, Laube was closely associated with the Junges Deutschland (Young Germany) movement and was briefly imprisoned for his writings in 1837. After his release, he turned to playwriting, producing several dramas in the fashion of **Scribe**, who was then enjoying an immense vogue in Germany. Among Laube's most frequently performed plays were *Monaldeschi* (1841), *Rococo* (1842), *Struensee* (1845), *Gottsched and Gellert* (1845), and *The Karlschüler* (1846). Despite his liberal views, in 1849 Laube was appointed director of the **Burgtheater** where, over the next 18 years, he developed the ensemble style of the

company to its zenith. After his resignation in 1867, Laube took over the direction of the Leipzig Town Theatre. He returned to Vienna in 1871 to found a Town Theatre there, which he directed until 1880. Laube's memoirs on his career and his histories of German theatre are major sources for the historian.   SW

Lauder, Harry (Henry MacLennan) (1870–1950) Scottish music-hall performer, who worked in a flax mill and coal mines for 10 years, before playing in concert parties as an Irish comic. His London debut in 1900 as an extra turn made him a star overnight, and he soon became the highest paid British performer of his time. His repertory originally contained a whole gallery of Scottish types, but eventually he settled into a cosy, chuckling caricature of the canny Scot, invariably singing 'I Love a Lassie' and 'Roamin' in the Gloamin' '. He made 22 tours of the USA between 1909 and 1932, organized the first front-line entertainment units during the First World War and was knighted in 1919. He was also the most prolific recording artist of the music-hall.   LS

Laughton, Charles (1899–1962) British-born actor who became an American citizen with his actress wife Elsa Lanchester in 1950. His first professional role in *The Inspector General* (1926) was followed by parts including Hercule Poirot in *Alibi* and William Marble in *Payment Deferred*, the latter also marking his 1931 New York debut. At the **Old Vic** (1933–4) he played in seven productions, including leading roles in *The Cherry Orchard*, *The Tempest*, and *Macbeth*. As the first

A photomontage showing Harry Lauder as 'the Tailor's Wife' and 'the Saftest o' the Family'.

English actor to perform at the **Comédie-Française** (1936), he appeared in *Le Médecin Malgré Lui*. After a decade of film work, he returned to the stage in 1947 with *Galileo*, adapted with **Brecht** and first performed in Los Angeles. For several years he toured the USA reading from the Bible, **Shakespeare**, and modern classics. As director and the Devil in **Shaw**'s *Don Juan in Hell* (1951) he earned critical acclaim. He played Bottom in *A Midsummer Night's Dream* and King Lear at Stratford-upon-Avon (1959). DBW

Laurents, Arthur (1918–) American screenwriter, director and dramatist, revealed his dramatic skills and insight into human nature in his first success, *Home of the Brave* (1945), concerned with a Jewish soldier's wartime problems. In *The Time of the Cuckoo* (1952), *A Clearing in the Woods* (1957) and *Invitation to a March* (1960) he wrote about women whose psychological problems drive them towards disaster. *The Bird Cage* (1950) builds upon the sexual frustrations of a vicious night club owner. Laurents is celebrated for writing the book for the musicals *West Side Story* (1957) and *Gypsy* (1960) and such screenplays as *Anna Lucasta* (1949) and *Anastasia* (1956). A playwright of substance and imagination, believing in character development, language and clear optimism, Laurents's later work – *The Enclave* (1973) and *Heartsong* (1974) – was less successful in contemporary theatre. WJM

Lawler, Ray (1921–) Australian playwright. As an actor in Melbourne he achieved fame when *Summer of the Seventeenth Doll* (1955), depicting two Queensland cane-cutters' annual holiday with their city girls, gained Australian and international success. After living in Britain and Ireland he returned to Australia in 1975, becoming literary adviser to the Melbourne Theatre Company. His plays include *The Piccadilly Bushman* (1959), *The Man who Shot the Albatross* (1971), and *Kid Stakes* (1975) and *Other Times* (1977), depicting the characters of *The Doll* in earlier years and completing *The Doll Trilogy*. MW

Lawrence, D[avid] H[erbert] (1885–1930) British author, whose notoriety for the sexual explicitness of his novels prevented his plays from reaching the public stage until 1967–8, though a biblical epic (*David*) was performed by the **Stage Society** (1927), as was *The Widowing of Mrs Holroyd* (1926). This, like *A Collier's Friday Night* (written 1906), *The Daughter-in-Law* based on the coal strike of 1912, or *The Fight for Barbara* reflecting his own relationship with a married woman, superimposed the class struggle on the struggle of the sexes. Written from personal experience as the son of a miner and more starkly realistic than the plays of a contemporary like **Galsworthy**, these were well received when revived in repertory at the **Royal Court Theatre** in 1965–7, leading to performances of Lawrence's other social plays, *The Merry-Go-Round* (1973) and *Touch and Go* (1979). CI

Lawrence, Gertrude (1898–1952) British actress and dancer, a musical comedy star (*Oh, Kay!*, 1926; *The King and I*, 1951), who played opposite **Noël Coward** in his plays *Private Lives* (1930) and *To-night at 8.30* (1936). CI

Lawrence, Jerome (1915–) and **Robert E[dwin] Lee** (1918–) American playwriting team. This pair of Ohio-born dramatists joined in formal partnership in 1942 and have since written dozens of plays, many produced in New York and most extremely popular with regional and amateur groups. Perhaps their best received effort was *Inherit the Wind* (1955), a faithful, flashy, dramatic retelling of the story of the famous Scopes 'monkey trial'. Also extremely popular was their adaptation of *Auntie Mame* (1956) and the subsequent musical version, *Mame* (1966), for which they wrote the libretto. Their play, *The Night Thoreau Spent in Jail* (1970), a standard for several years with amateur groups, was an early offering of the American Playwrights' Theatre. This versatile and prolific team has also been responsible for many one-act operas, screenplays, television plays, and radio programmes. LDC

Lawson, John Howard (1895–1977) American playwright. In the theatre of the twenties Lawson was an anomaly, a dramatist of fiery left-wing convictions. Striking out against the convention-bound commercial theatre on the one hand and the ivory tower art theatre on the other, he attempted to forge a new theatrical style which he called political vaudeville. His most successful experiment was *Processional* (1925), a staccato, fragmented series of sketches set in a West Virginia town during a coal strike. In 1926 he was a co-founder of the short-lived, politically radical New Playwrights' Theatre, for which he wrote a strident satire of political campaigning called *Loud Speaker*. Lawson changed his style in the thirties, replacing extravagance with a richly idiomatic realism that had a strong influence on **Clifford Odets**. The eloquently embittered working-class anti-heroes of his *Success Story* (1932) and *Gentlewoman* (1934) speak a racy urban poetry. An active screenwriter (*Blockade*, *Action in the North Atlantic*) and a president of the Screen Writer's Guild, Lawson was imprisoned in 1948 for defending the Bill of Rights against the inquisition of the House Un-American Activities Committee. In 1949 he published a now standard work, *Theory and Technique of Playwriting and Screenwriting*. FH

Laya, Jean-Louis (1761–1833) French dramatist. Laya's reputation rests mainly on his political comedy, *L'Ami des Lois* (*The Friend of the Laws*, 1793), which was staged at the Théâtre de la Nation (the **Comédie-Française**) and vigorously attacked political extremists, in particular Marat and Robespierre. Laya ended up in prison and the play was hotly attacked by the Commune on the grounds that it could cause disturbances. It became a rallying point for former aristocrats and the trial of Louis XVI was interrupted to discuss whether it should be banned. The play continued to be regarded as subversive well after the Revolutionary period. In 1819 Laya wrote a pamphlet on the abuses of theatre censorship. His son Leon Laya (1809–72) was also a dramatist, best-known for *Duke Job* (Comédie-Française, 1859). JMCC

Lazarenko, Vitaly Efimovich (1890–1939) Russian clown, son of a coal-miner and a seamstress. He began in Kotlikov's circus as a trapeze gymnast at the age of eight; in Nikitin's circus in Moscow (1914), he developed a vein of satiric comedy, influenced by **Anatoli Durov** and Richard Ribot, and established a world record by leaping over three elephants. After the Revolution, he came into his own as a proletarian star, playing in many satirical pantomimes, including two pieces written for him by **Vladimir Mayakovsky**: 'The Universal Class Struggle Championship' and 'ABC'. He performed for soldiers at the Western front in 1918 and 1921 and at the Eastern front in 1938. His proletarian costume of overalls impressed **Meyerhold**, who cast him as the devil in his second staging of Mayakovsky's *Mystery-Bouffe*.   LS

Lazzo (plural, **Lazzi**; possibly a corruption of *l'azione*, action) An important constituent element in improvised Italian **commedia dell'arte**. A lazzo may be a play on words, a *quid pro quo*, a piece of comic business, a sleight-of-hand trick, or a pantomimic joke, usually intended to prompt laughter independent of the plot. Often sadistic and scatological, employing clysters and razors, some lazzi became traditional, such as **Harlequin**'s fly-catching or **John Rich**'s hatching from an egg. Latterly, the more extended version, the *burla*, did serve a dramatic function, as with the dinner scene in **Goldoni**'s *Servant of Two Masters*.   LS

Le Fartere, Roland (Rolland le Pettour) In c. 1250 he is recorded as holding land in Hemmingstone, Suffolk (England), on condition that he appear before the king every year on Christmas Day to perform the jump, whistle and fart ('unum saltum et unum siffletum et unum bumbulum'). Farting is well attested as an amateur performing art to the present day, and artists such as **Le Pétomane** have occasionally achieved success with it on the commercial stage; in the Middle Ages it seems to have belonged to the repertory of skills of the professional minstrel, whom, no doubt, Roland was emulating in a ritual of abasement – though the nickname which stuck as his surname suggests a recognition of his skill which puts it outside the realm of the semi-professional.   AEG

Le Gallienne, Eva (1899–1991) Best known as an actress, Le Gallienne participated in every aspect of American theatre. She had her New York debut in *Mrs Boltay's Daughter* (1915), but her first big success was as Julie in *Liliom* (1921). For the next 60-plus years Le Gallienne played most of the major female roles in Western drama, receiving critical acclaim for performances in plays by **Ibsen**, **Chekhov** and **Shakespeare**, Queen Elizabeth in **Schiller**'s *Mary Stuart*, and Elizabeth in *Elizabeth the Queen*.

Le Gallienne's contribution to American theatre includes more than her considerable acting skill. She introduced audiences throughout the country to Ibsen, Chekhov and French playwrights through her translations and productions of their plays. A lifelong believer in repertory theatre, Le Gallienne founded the Civic Repertory Theatre (1926–33). There she produced, directed and starred, offering quality theatre at bargain ticket prices. The Civic presented 1,581 performances of over 30 plays, including many of the classics, **Glaspell**'s *Alison's House*, *Peter Pan* (in which Le Gallienne was the first actress to 'fly'), and *Alice in Wonderland* (written by Le Gallienne and Florida Friebus). In 1946, Le Gallienne, **Cheryl Crawford** and

Margaret Webster founded the **American Repertory Company**, which lasted only one season.

Most recently, Le Gallienne directed and acted for the National Repertory Theatre (1961–6); acted in a revival of *The Royal Family* (1976), *To Grandmother's House We Go* (1981), a revival of *Alice in Wonderland* (1983), and a film role in *Resurrection* (1980). She has also published her translations of Ibsen and Chekhov, a biography of **Eleonora Duse**, and two autobiographies – *At 33* (1934) and *With a Quiet Heart* (1953). In addition, she has garnered most of the major awards in American performing arts, including Woman of the Year (1947), ANTA (1964), a special Tony (1964), and an Emmy (1978).   FB

Leach, Wilford (1929–88) American director, teacher, playwright, and designer. Born in Virginia, Leach attended William and Mary, and the University of Illinois (PhD) before teaching at Sarah Lawrence College (1958–). From 1970–7 he was artistic director of **La Mama ETC**. Since 1977 he has worked mainly for the **New York Shakespeare Festival**, designing as well as directing productions. His major credits include: *Mandragola* (1977); *All's Well* and *The Taming of the Shrew* (1978); *Othello* (1979); *Mother Courage* (1980); *The Pirates of Penzance* (1980); *The Human Comedy* (1983); *La Bohème* (1984); and *The Mystery of Edwin Drood* (1985). Leach's highly original style draws on vaudeville, film, animated cartoon, opera, and puppet theatre.   TLM

Lebanon see **Middle East**

LeCompte, Elizabeth (1944–) American director and playwright and, since 1979, artistic director of the experimental theatre collective known as the Wooster Group. With **Spalding Gray** and other members of the group, she co-wrote and directed *Sakonnet Point* (1975), *Rumstick Road* (1977), and *Nayatt School* (1978), a trilogy called *Three Places in Rhode Island*. In 1979 LeCompte and the Group created an 'epilogue' (without dialogue) to this trilogy called *Point Judith*. She was also instrumental in the creation of *Route 1 & 9* (1981) and *L. S. D.* (1984). In 1984 she was appointed Associate Director of the American National Theatre (under **Peter Sellars**) at the **John F. Kennedy Centre for the Performing Arts**. In the 1980s she has been a leader in the nourishing of a sometimes radical avant-garde theatre in New York.   DBW

Lecoq, Jacques see **Mime**

Lecouvreur, Adrienne (1692–1730) French actress, the outstanding tragedienne of her day. She first attracted attention with an amateur company in Paris and then spent some years in the provinces before making her debut at the **Comédie-Française** in 1717 in the title role of **Crébillon**'s *Electre*. Its success rapidly won her the position of *sociétaire* and with it a series of leading roles in the classical repertoire of **Corneille** and **Racine** as well as contemporary tragedy. Though not a great natural beauty she was an instinctive performer with an imposing stage presence and the power to move an audience deeply. Owing to a frail constitution her vocal range was limited but this was turned to advantage by the control and emotional nuance of her delivery, which appeared to subsume the actress within the character played. Indeed, contemporary reports credited her, as they did **Mlle Clairon** a generation later, with an altogether simpler, less declamatory style of playing and an innovative regard for propriety in stage costume. After a fêted career she died suddenly in somewhat mysterious circumstances and the church's refusal of Christian burial followed by the disposal of her body in open ground under cover of darkness prompted **Voltaire** to write an angry lament deploring the hypocrisy of current attitudes to the acting profession. A century later, in 1849, she became the subject of a play by **Scribe** and Legouvé which afforded a prime role for **Rachel** and subsequently **Sarah Bernhardt**.   DR

Lee, Canada (1907–52) Afro-American actor. Born Leonard Canegata whose successful boxing career was halted by an eye injury, Lee's fighting spirit was manifested in several memorable roles. He played Blacksnake in the 1934 revival of the anti-lynching drama *Stevedore*, Banquo in the **Federal Theatre**'s 'voodoo' *Macbeth* (1936), and the emperor Christophe in *Haiti* (1938). His finest performance was as Bigger Thomas in Richard Wright's *Native Son* (1941). Lee played Caliban in **Margaret Webster**'s 1945 production of *The Tempest* and a white-face Bosola in *The Duchess of Malfi* (1946). He was a powerful actor of animal-like grace who was committed to a theatre of social relevance.   EGH

Lee, Eugene (1939–) American set designer. Lee is unique among American designers in both concept and execution. Approaching each production without preconceived ideas, he treats the whole space of the theatre – not only the stage – as a place to be designed. From the late 1960s onward he was resident designer for the **Trinity Square Repertory Company** in Providence, RI, and together with director Adrian Hall created iconoclastic, often environmental, settings. He brought environmental design to Off-Broadway and Broadway with *Slaveship*, *Alice in Wonderland*, and *Candide*. Even with more conventional productions his sets tend to be large, use moving parts, and use real materials. Lee has worked with **Peter Brook** in Shiraz and Paris and with **Harold Prince** on several shows including *Sweeney Todd*. He also designed television's *Saturday Night Live* from its inception to 1980 and several television specials as well as rock concerts.   AA

Lee, Gypsy Rose (Rose Louise Hovick) (?1914–70) American burlesque artist and writer. After performing a child-act with her sister June in vaudeville (1922–8), she starred in Minsky's Burlesque by the age of 17. Her act comprised more 'tease' than 'strip', tantalizing with suggestive silk stockings, lace panties and a rose-garter tossed into the audience as a coda. H. L. Mencken coined the term 'ecdysiast' to label her speciality, and her sophisticated songs were parodied in the musical *Pal Joey* (1940). Seen in the *Ziegfeld Follies of 1936*, nightclubs, fairs and carnivals, she was the first celebrity stripper. Her writings include a play *The Naked Genius* (1943), some murder mysteries, and a memoir *Gypsy* (1957), turned into a popular musical comedy (1959).   LS

Lee, Ming Cho (1930–) Generally considered the current doyen of American set designers. His style and technique have significantly influenced the look of opera and theatre design since the mid-1960s. Lee was born in Shanghai and studied Chinese watercolour before emigrating to the USA in 1949. In 1954 he became an assistant to **Jo Mielziner**. The spare, minimalist, emblematic style that became Lee's trademark was, in part, a response to the poetic realism of Mielziner. It is best exemplified in the 1964 production of *Electra* at the **New York Shakespeare Festival**. Lee is usually associated with pipe-work scaffolding, textured surfaces, and collage. But since the late 1970s, his work has turned to detail and ultra-realism as in the production of *K2* in which he created a mountain on the stage. He is constantly working with new materials and new approaches. Despite his importance he has designed little on Broadway. Much of his work has been with the New York Shakespeare Festival and regional theatres, as well as opera – most notably, the New York City Opera. Lee also heads the design programme at the Yale School of Drama.   AA

Lee, Nathaniel (c. 1650–92) English playwright. After graduating from Trinity College, Cambridge, he moved to London in 1671. A brief career as an actor led to his beginning to write plays. *Nero* was performed in 1674. *The Rival Queens* (1677) was a substantial success and its brilliance as a vehicle for two actresses playing Roxana and Statira ensured its frequent revival. In 1678 Lee collaborated with **Dryden** on a version of *Oedipus* of spectacular bloodthirstiness. *Lucius Junius Brutus* (1680), a careful study of ideological conflict and tyranny and the best political play of the Restoration, was banned after a brief run. In its intensity and restraint it is remarkably unlike the verbal and visual extravagances of his other work with their frequent scenes of torture and speeches of ranting passion. Lee's only comedy, *The Princess of Cleves*, turns the calm feeling of Mme de la Fayette's novel into a vicious satire on the sexual excesses of Restoration society. In 1684 Lee went mad and spent the next four years in an asylum. He died in obscurity.   PH

Legault, Emile (1906–83) French Canadian director, playwright and essayist. A Catholic priest, he studied theatre briefly on a bursary in Paris, and on his return to Montreal in 1937 assumed direction of Les Compagnons de Saint-Laurent, making of it the most influential stage company in French Canada for the next 15 years. Initially a college troupe providing basic instruction in theatre arts, Les Compagnons evolved from an early emphasis on religious theatre towards a more eclectic, contemporary repertoire, in the process training the actors, directors and theatre professionals that would provide leadership over the next three decades. Legault also composed dramatic texts such as *Premiers Gestes* (*First Deeds*, 1954) and *Kermesse des Anges et des Hommes* (*Church-fair for Angels and Men*, 1960), but his reputation rests mainly on his role as director and manager.   LED

Leicester's Men The first of the great Elizabethan household companies was formed in 1559, enjoyed a period of high prosperity from c. 1570–83, and had already dwindled into comparative insignificance by the time the Earl of Leicester died in 1588. The fluctuation owed something to Leicester's favour, or lack of it, at Court, something to the new spirit of professionalism in London following the opening of the **Theatre** in 1576 and much to the challenge of **Queen Elizabeth's Men**, which commandeered many of the country's best-known performers on its foundation in 1583. **James Burbage**, who built the Theatre, and **Will Kempe**, who became its star attraction, were both members of Leicester's Men in the early stages of their very different careers.   PT

Leigh, Mike (1943–) British director and playwright. His distinctive contribution to the British stage (and television) has been the devised plays which he has created together with the actors involved. Leigh's technique is to offer actors a basic idea and to encourage them to develop characters and situations which he then shapes into the final product. Significant successes have included *Abigail's Party* (1977) and *Goose-Pimples* (1981). For television his credits are longer. The strength of his group-created plays is in their acute observation, the weakness in the tendency of that observation to become petty and malicious.   MB

Leigh, Vivien (Vivian Mary Hartley) (1913–67) British actress, married to **Laurence Olivier** with whom she played in a number of striking Shakespearian performances – in *Hamlet* at Elsinore (1937), *Romeo and Juliet* in New York (1940), *Antony and Cleopatra* in London (1951), *Titus Andronicus* at Stratford-upon-Avon (1955). Her success in *The Doctor's Dilemma* (1942) prompted **Shaw** to suggest she play Cleopatra in the film of *Caesar and Cleopatra* (also staged with Olivier, 1951), and it is as a film actress that she is perhaps best remembered for her roles in *Gone With the Wind* and *A Streetcar Named Desire* (re-creating her acclaimed 1949 theatrical performance). The sensitivity and precision of her acting was widely admired, and after touring with the **Old Vic** and in **Giraudoux**'s *Duel of Angels*, she gave her final performance with **Gielgud** in **Chekhov**'s *Ivanov* (New York, 1966).   CI

Leipzig style A formal, wooden style of acting of the early 18th century, encouraged by **J. C. Gottsched** in an effort to elevate the way in which tragic drama was acted. It was practised initially by the **Neuber** troupe. Although such acting was highly unsubtle, based as it was on misconceptions of classical gesture and French tragic acting, it was for many a suitable alternative to the rough improvisation that, until the time of the Neubers, was standard on the German stage. The Leipzig style remained the dominant style of acting until the rise of the *bürgerliches Trauerspiel* required a quieter realism.   SW

Leis, Raúl (1947–) Panamanian playwright, journalist, sociologist, essayist, poet, and popular educator. In addition to several children's plays, author of *Viaje a la Salvación y otros países* (*Journey to Salvation and Other Countries*, 1973) and *Viene el sol con su sombrero de combate puesto* (*The Sun Comes Up with its Combat Helmet On*) dealing with sovereignty issues over the canal. *María Picana* (1979) captures the inherent violence in Latin

A street performance of Raúl Leis's *Viaje a la salvación y otros países*, Panama, 1982.

America through a woman torturer, metaphorically raised as a child by animals. *El nido de Macúa* (*The Nest of the Macúa*, 1981) treats syncretism and magic in Panamanian social issues. Recent works include *Lo peor del boxeo* (*The Worst of Boxing*), *Primero de mayo* (*First of May*), and *El señor Sol* (*Mr Sun*, 1983).   GW

Lekain (Henri-Louis Kain) (1729–78) French actor who was first noticed and encouraged by **Voltaire**. In 1750 he made his debut at the **Comédie-Française**, where despite the enmity of his professional relationship with **Mlle Clairon**, he gradually established himself as the company's foremost tragedian. His modest stature and bow legs were more than compensated for by a majestic bearing and forceful, passionate playing, a quality well suited to the plays of Voltaire, many of whose tragic heroes he was the first to portray. The thoughtful, responsible attitude that he took to his profession was reflected in his rejection of the tradition of conventional stage costume, a process he began by adopting an approximation to ancient Greek dress as Oreste in **Racine**'s *Andromaque* and some hints of *chinoiserie* in Voltaire's *Orphelin de la Chine* (*The Chinese Orphan*). His encouragement of movement on stage and contempt for the long cherished practice of delivering big speeches downstage centre was of a piece with his campaign for the removal of audience seating on the stage, a century-old institution favoured by fashionable theatregoers which was finally abolished in 1759 to make room for the introduction of changeable scenery occupying the entire playing area. He also drew up plans for an acting school associated with the Comédie-Française, for which royal patronage was obtained with the accession of Louis XVI in 1774, though failing health compelled him to relinquish its direction. Perennially in financial difficulties, he undertook many provincial tours to supplement his income and these may well have undermined his delicate constitution and contributed to his premature death. He was widely admired by contemporary critics and often likened to **Garrick**, but perhaps the most eloquent testimony to his theatrical genius was provided by Voltaire's epigram that it was not he but Lekain who had created his tragedies.   DR

Lemaître, Frédérick (1800–76) French actor. Arguably the greatest, and certainly the most flamboyant and colourful actor of the century, Frédérick began his career humbly at the tiny Variétés Amusantes of Boulevard du Temple in 1815 in a lion skin in a pantomime, *Pyrame et Thisbé*. He graduated to the nearby **Funambules** where he performed in harlequinades and, in 1816, was noticed, recommended for the Conservatoire, and offered work in the mimodrames of the **Cirque Olympique**. He stayed there from 1817–20, playing Mallorno (alias Iago) in their version of *Othello* in 1818. Accepted by the **Odéon** in 1820 to play minor roles, he was dismissed in 1823 and moved to the Ambigu, where he replaced Frénoy in the part of Vivaldi in **Pixérécourt**'s *L'Homme à Trois Visages* (*The Man with Three Faces*). The turning point in his career came in 1824 when, together with the actor **Firmin**, he sent up a particularly pathetic melodrama, *L'Auberge des Adrets*, turning it into a hilarious parody of the genre and creating the unforgettable silhouette of Robert Macaire with a costume picked up from rag and bone merchants. The subversive quality of the performance did not go unnoticed, and after 85 performances the piece was suddenly banned. The character of Robert Macaire took on an independent existence, especially through broadsheets and the lithographs of Daumier, and later became a means of attacking the government and society of Louis Philippe. Lemaître remained at the Ambigu until the fire of 1827, playing some 25 parts. He went to the Porte-Saint-Martin, which he saw as the new temple of romanticism, and found one of his greatest roles (one which he would play for over 40 years), that of Georges de Germany in *Thirty Years of a Gamester's Life*. At the Porte-Saint-Martin, he also met an ideal partner in **Marie Dorval**. He was tempted back to the Ambigu, with offers of both an actor and a stage-director's salary, and thus lost the opportunity of playing the original Marino Faliero (the part was taken by **Ligier**, but Lemaître obtained it in the revival). In 1830, he joined **Harel** at the Odéon, playing **Dumas**'s Napoléon, Ambrosio in *The Monk*, and Concini in *La Maréchale d'Ancre*. From 1831–3 he was back at the Porte-Saint-Martin, which Harel had now acquired, and here he created Dumas's *Richard Darlington* with enormous success, following it with Gennaro in **Hugo**'s *Lucrèce Borgia* (**Mlle George** played Lucrèce and Hugo was delighted with his interpreters). After a row he left the Porte-Saint-Martin and went on tour. On returning to Paris in 1834 he took a new piece, *Robert Macaire* by the same team of authors as *L'Auberge des Adrets*, though he claimed to be the sole author, to the Folies Dramatiques (Harel had managed to shut the doors of most of the theatres to him). This satirical piece of indulgent buffoonery became the fashionable play to see, and Lemaître, ever extravagant, bought himself a country house out of the profits. In 1836, this time at the Variétés, he had another triumph, in a play which seemed almost tailor-made for him, Dumas's *Kean*. In 1838 Victor Hugo finished writing *Ruy Blas* for him – yet another success – and this was performed at the Renaissance. In 1840 he gave the first performance of Balzac's *Vautrin* at the Porte-Saint-Martin, and the play was immediately banned (possibly because Lemaître made himself up to look like the king). He went from theatre to theatre, playing **Bouchardy**'s made-to-measure role, *Paris le Bohémien* (*Paris the*

Frédérick Lemaître as Robert Macaire.

Gypsy) in 1842, Jacques Ferrand in the stage adaptation of Sue's *Mysteries of Paris* and Don César de Bazan in 1844, **Pyat**'s *Le Chiffonnier de Paris* (*The Rag-picker of Paris*, 1847) and *Toussaint l'Ouverture* and *Paillasse* in 1850. All the time he was touring. In 1852, the re-establishment of the censorship hit his major roles, including Robert Macaire and Ruy Blas. During his last years he revived his earlier successes. In 1862 he gave the second performance of *Vautrin*, which was a flop. By the 1870s he was in a state of near destitution, playing the suburban theatres, and he died in 1876.   JMCC

Leñero, Vicente (1933–   ) Mexican playwright and novelist, born in Guadalajara, trained as a civil engineer at the UNAM (1958), winner of various literary prizes and a Guggenheim Fellowship, his first serious novel, *Los albañiles* (*The Bricklayers*, 1964), was a major contribution to the 'boom' in Latin American letters. His introduction to the theatre is *Pueblo rechazado* (*Rejected Town*, 1968), a controversial documentary piece based on a Cuernavaca monastery that promulgated psychoanalysis for its monks instead of slavish attention to prayer. Most of his subsequent plays are also documentaries: *Compañero* (*Companion*, 1971), based on Che Guevara; *El Juicio* (*The Trial*, 1971), on the trial of the assassin of Mexican President-elect Obregón in 1928; *Los hijos de Sánchez* (*The Children of Sánchez*, 1972), on the Oscar Lewis socio-anthropological study of a Mexican village; plus several others including *El martirio de Morelos* (*The Martyrdom of Morelos*, 1981), about the Mexican national hero. His *Vivir del teatro* (*Life in the Theatre*) recounts the vicissitudes of staging his several plays.   GW

Leno, Dan (George Galvin) (1860–1904) Generally regarded as the greatest British variety artist. In a short lifetime, which ended in mental and physical collapse, he brought to maturity the achievements of his predecessors in music-hall and pantomime.

The son of minor London music-hall artists, by his own testimony he first went on stage at the age of three, and long before he reached manhood had acquired an impressive range of skills – contortionist, clog-dancer, Irish comedian, character vocalist – and a veteran's experience of the exhausting provincial tour and the challenging performance conditions of the minor halls. To the end of his days he employed the attention-grabbing entrance described by fellow-comedian Harry Randall as 'a quick run down to the footlights, a roll like a drum with his feet, his leg raised, and brought down with a loud clap from the foot'; after which he would relax into an attitude of confidential friendliness to create a colourful character-sketch, deliver a tortuous monologue or patter-song, and impart the latest gossip of his fictitious neighbour Mrs Kelly.

His solo London debut came in the East End in 1885. He was an immediate hit with his first recorded appearance in drag as a 'Dickensian nurse-maid' who was 'off to get milk for the twins', rapidly transferred to the West End, and got his first London pantomime engagement as dame in 'Jack and the Beanstalk' at the Surrey the following year – the beginning of an illustrious run of Christmas shows, including 15 consecutively at **Drury Lane** from 1888. By 1897, when he made his first American appearance, he was billed hyperbolically as 'the funniest man on earth', and in 1898 Milton Bode wrote the burlesque revue 'Orlando Dando' specifically as a vehicle for his talents. In 1901, after a command performance at Sandringham, he was presented with a diamond cravat-pin of the royal monogram, and became known (to the press at least) as 'The King's Jester'. It was the nearest he got to the honour bestowed on his younger contemporaries **Harry Lauder** and **George Robey**. Leno's studio sound-recordings are disappointing, for he lacked the vocal strength and subtlety of **Merson** and Robey. But some elements of his genius can be defined. Observers paid tribute to his infectious energy, and he had been trained in physical techniques since he could walk; it seems likely that he applied these to the creation of the multitude of vivid caricatures which throng his career. These imply, too, a fertile imagination, manifest again in his peopling the stage with non-existent characters with whom he conducted a one-sided dialogue. Finally, **Marie Lloyd** noticed the distressing effect of his eyes, large and deep-set beneath steeply arched brows (and she might have mentioned his mouth, which in repose turned down slightly at the corners), and there are hints in his script (mainly written for him by Herbert Darnley) of the laughter that fights back tears. Physical objects take on a life of their own – an egg is 'awfully artful' and a cake may look as if it has 'an extremely obstinate nature'. Human relationships are predatory: landladies advertise 'Young men taken in and done for', and even friends meeting at Christmas are probably wondering who is going to stand the first drink. 'You can't get away from facts', Leno was fond of saying; inescapably, his ambiguous comic vision was of a recalcitrant physical world inhabited by unreliable people.

The burlesque autobiography, *Dan Leno, Hys Book*, is now known to have been ghosted by T. C. Elder.   AEG

Lenormand, Henri-René (1882–1951) French playwright. Lenormand's work became associated with the **Pitoëff** company who performed many of his plays between the wars. They employed techniques pioneered by **Chekhov** and **Pirandello** to convey the psychological life, drawing on the insights of Freudian psychoanalysis. His plays have not been revived since the war but his *Confessions d'un Auteur Dramatique* (*Confessions of a Playwright*, 1952) gives insight into both the period and the profession of playwright.   DB

Lenz, Johann Michael Reinhold (1751–92) German playwright. Among the most prominent of the **Sturm und Drang** dramatists, Lenz is best known for his comedies of contemporary life. *The Tutor* (1774) and *The Soldiers* (1776), which are among the first German plays of genuine quality to exhibit the influence of **Shakespeare**. His essay 'Observations on the Theatre' (1774) is among the most perceptive documents of the important German Shakespeare criticism of the 18th century. Lenz's creative career was cut short by a severe decline in his mental faculties, which led to his early death.   SW

Leonard, Hugh (pseudonym of John Leyes Byrne) (1926–) Irish playwright. The **Abbey** produced Leonard's first two long plays, *The Birthday Party* (1956) and *A Leap in the Dark* (1958). Shortly afterwards he joined Granada television, writing original plays, many adaptations, and a farcical series, *Me Mammy*. Leonard is knowledgeable in farce. He has adapted **Labiche**'s *Célimare*; his *The Patrick Pearse Motel* (1971) and *Time Was* (1976) use the genre to satirize Dublin's fashionable outer suburbs.

Da (1973), enormously successful in New York, is a serio-comic treatment of the same location: *revenants*, re-enacting a writer's Dalkey childhood, confuse his flippant self-confidence. *A Life* (1976) retraces Mr Drumm's path to his desiccated marriage, accounting for, perhaps disturbing, his defensive reserve.

Technically highly proficient, inevitably suspected of glibness, Leonard in these experiments with time creates his suburban deceptions and despairs with a fulness that may dispel the reservations.   DM

Leonardo da Vinci (1452–1519) Italian artist, scientist and stage designer. Little is known of his work for the theatre, but extant designs suggest a keen interest in scenic decoration and stage machinery; from these several attempts have been made to construct models of the machinery and stages he intended, like those for Isabella of Aragon's entry into Milan (1489), and the scene and revolving stage prepared for Poliziano's *Orfeo* (c. 1495).   KR

Leonov, Leonid Maksimovich (1899–) A prolific, Lenin Prize-winning Soviet novelist and dramatist, important for his efforts to make psychological and social realism the bases for the new Soviet literature. His work, which tends to be symbolic and even in places allegorical, consciously evokes Dostoevsky, **Chekhov**, **Gorky** and other predecessors in its treatment of the moral, emotional and psychological crises precipitated in individuals of various social classes, especially the 'little man', by societal change. His 13 plays include dramatizations of two of his novels, *The Badgers* (1927) and *Skutarevsky* (1934). The former, like his first original play, *Untilovsk* (1928), employs a Siberian setting. The latter, a character study of an old-guard scientist converted to Bolshevism, reflects the familiar Soviet conflict between 'altruism and egoism, self-sacrifice and self-love', i.e., between service to the collective and to the individual, a question about which Leonov is more philosophical than dogmatic. His best-known play, *The Orchards of Polovchansk* (1938), embodies a Chekhovian sense of place, milieu and history – society on the brink of change. Written during the purges of 1936–8, it was transformed by its author under official pressure from a psychological character study to a socio-political tale with a clearly identifiable anti-Soviet villain. His most popular play, *Invasion* (1942), like *Lyonushka* (1943), is a patriotic picture of wartime heroism. It is notable for demonstrating the character-building potential of war. SG

Léotard, Jules (1838–70) French aerialist, son of a gymnastics instructor; he abandoned his law studies to become a trapeze artist, winning almost immediate success on his debut at the Cirque Napoléon, Paris, 12 Nov. 1859. Léotard perfected the trapeze act, inventing the *salto mortale* through the moving apparatus; lending his name to the tight-fitting garment he wore; and, after an engagement at the London Alhambra, inspiring the song 'The Daring Young Man on the Flying Trapeze'. His career was an unbroken series of triumphs, and in 1959 a commemorative plaque in his honour was dedicated at the Cirque d'Hiver. LS

Lermontov, Mikhail Yurievich (1814–41) Russia's greatest romantic poet after **Pushkin**; a somewhat lesser novelist and dramatist in the same vein. He wrote under the influence of **Shakespeare**, **Byron**, **Schiller**, Pushkin, **Griboedov**, Scott and **Hugo**, as well as at the promptings of a melancholic, self-dramatizing, rebellious temperament. His career as an artist and military man described a cycle of sin, redemption and willed death which he achieved in a duel with a former schoolmate. His five dramas palely reflect his life. *The Spaniards* (written 1830, published 1880, produced 1924) employs the romantic locale of Spain during the Inquisition as a metaphor for the repressive reign of Tsar Nikolai I. It is replete with poisonings, abduction, pathos, frenzy and a semi-autobiographical protagonist at odds with himself and society who murders the thing he loves. His best play, *Masquerade* (written 1836, censored production 1852, uncensored production 1862), is a Russian *Othello* by way of Pushkin which combines romanticism and social realism. The languor of its 'superfluous man' protagonist Arbenin masks a tormented soul, much as the court society which victimizes him and his wife masks cruelty and hypocrisy with gaiety and fashion. The play received an opulent mounting at the Aleksandrinsky Theatre in 1917 by **Meyerhold** with sets by Golovin and music by Glazunov. Lermontov's remaining plays include: *Men and Passions* (written 1830, published 1880); *The Strange Man* (written 1831, published 1860), a rewritten version of the former; and *The Two Brothers* (written 1836, produced 1915), which he reworked as the psychological novel *Princess Ligovskaya*. His celebrated novel, *A Hero of Our Time* (1840), features the fatalistic hero Pechorin, whom **Chekhov** spoofs via Solyony in *Three Sisters*. As a dramatist Lermontov continued the progressive romantic tendencies begun by Pushkin, mixing extreme subjectivism with a socially minded anti-tyrannical stance. His eccentric social satire suggests Griboedov, and his grotesque social realism,

Sukhovo-Kobylin. His theatricalized fatalism, dandyism and eroticism, primarily in *Masquerade*, has something of the flavour of the symbolist-influenced dramatists of the early 20th century, especially **Andreev**, **Sologub** and **Kuzmin**. SG

Lerner, Alan Jay (1918–86) and **Frederick Loewe** (1904–88) American lyricist and composer. Loewe, a classically trained composer born in Vienna, and Lerner, who had studied at Juilliard and Harvard, collaborated on their first musical score, *What's Up*, in 1943. Four years later the team had its first major success with *Brigadoon*, a fantasy set in a magical Scottish village. Their next show, *Paint Your Wagon*, achieved a modest run. In 1956, Lerner and Loewe wrote the score for *My Fair Lady*, a musical version of **George Bernard Shaw**'s *Pygmalion*. One of the most successful musical comedies ever produced, *My Fair Lady*'s score was a perfect blending of Loewe's operetta music with Lerner's pseudo-Shavian lyrics. Their next show, *Camelot* (1960), was generally conceded to be inferior to its predecessor. Lerner and Loewe collaborated on only one other Broadway musical, a 1973 adaptation of their film *Gigi*. After Loewe's retirement Lerner worked with other composers on a number of shows.

Loewe's music successfully combined the older operetta tradition with more modern Broadway musical idioms. Lerner's versatility as a lyricist was demonstrated in songs whose styles ranged from the sophisticated verbal trickery of **Lorenz Hart** to the simple treatment of **Oscar Hammerstein II**. MK

Lesage, Alain-René (1668–1747) French novelist and dramatist. A near-penniless orphan in his teens, he subsequently supported himself and his own family by his pen alone. His earliest plays, based on Spanish models, were unremarkable but it was a Spanish romance that inspired his first truly original work, *Le Diable Boiteux* (*The Devil on Two Sticks*, 1707), a novel painting a realistic picture of contemporary French society and social types. The same year saw his first theatrical success with the comedy *Crispin Rival de Son Maître* (*Crispin Rival of his Master*), which reflects a similar impulse to depict the true manners of the age in its portrayal of an opportunistic valet who impersonates his master in order to usurp the marriage settlement to which he considers himself no less entitled and who acquits himself so well as almost to succeed. In his next play, *Turcaret* (1709), the central character, a financier or tax-farmer who is exploited by the fashionable people of his circle as mercilessly as he exploits others, is clearly drawn from contemporary life and Lesage takes a sardonic view of a society motivated entirely by greed and self-interest. The play met with fierce opposition from financial quarters and despite its success at the **Comédie-Française** was withdrawn after only seven performances, though it has remained in the classic repertoire until the present day. Thereafter Lesage devoted himself almost entirely to the fair theatres and between 1712 and 1744 when he left Paris to live in Boulogne he produced over 100 *vaudevilles*, comic operas, 'pièces à écriteaux' (placard plays) and suchlike, many of them in collaboration with **Fuzelier**, d'Orneval and **Piron**. His best-known work, however, is the picaresque tale of *Gil Blas de Santillane*, published in 12 books between 1715 and 1735, which profoundly influenced the evolution of the European novel. Despite his disapproval two of his sons became professional actors, the eldest, René-André (1695–1743), with some distinction under the name of Montménil.   DR

Lescarbot, Marc (?1570–1642) French historian, poet and playwright, author of the first dramatic text composed and performed in French in the New World, the verse-play *Le Théâtre de Neptune en la Nouvelle-France* (*The Theatre of Neptune in New France*), enacted on the waters before Port Royal, Acadia (today's Annapolis Royal, Nova Scotia) in November of 1606. It portrays Neptune and his Tritons, who along with four Amerindians welcome the colony's leaders on their return from a dangerous exploration, ending with an invitation to all present to share a celebratory banquet. Replete with neoclassical allusions, this slender text, first published in 1609, is a good-humoured example of the dramatic sub-genre known in France as a *réception*, a form that would long remain popular in French Canada. It was performed again on the same spot in 1956, marking the 350th anniversary of the birth of the theatre in North America.   LED

Leslie, Fred (Frederick Hobson) (1855–92) English actor, the greatest star of early musical comedy. He made his professional debut in 1878, but it was a musical version of **Boucicault**'s *Rip Van Winkle* at the Comedy Theatre in 1882 that made him into a star. Employed by **George Edwardes** at the **Gaiety** in 1885, he played opposite **Nellie Farren** in the burlesque *Little Jack Sheppard* (1885) and *Monte Cristo, Jr* (1886) as well as in his own *Ruy Blas and the Blas and the Blasé Roué* (1889), and it was he above all who sustained the fortunes of the Gaiety in the aftermath of Nellie Farren's retirement in 1891. His untimely death of typhoid robbed the English theatre of a remarkable talent.   PT

Lesotho see **Botswana**

Lessing, Gotthold Ephraim (1729–81) German playwright and critic. Although Lessing's career in the theatre might seem to be lacking in stature, because he so frequently deprecated his own work, his writings were in fact crucial to the German theatre at an important phase in its development. As a journalist, critic, and dramaturge during the short-lived Hamburg National Theatre project, his essays consistently brought to his contemporaries' attention the shortcomings of the French drama, still widely admired and imitated in Germany. Lessing was also among the first to recognize the strengths of **Shakespeare** and the English dramatic tradition, in particular for the warm humanity expressed in their plays. In the *Hamburg Dramaturgy* (1768) especially, Lessing attempted to rid the German stage of its dependence on the French and in so doing engaged in radical interpretation of **Aristotle**, focusing in particular on the nature of pity and fear. The end of drama, as conceived by Lessing, is compassion; by arousing compassion, the drama fulfils its important social function, as the audience becomes more aware of the humanity of those around it. Lessing wrote several plays, the most notable of which are *Miss*

Sara Sampson (1755), a domestic tragedy, highly popular in its day, that owed much to **George Lillo** and the novels of Samuel Richardson, *Minna von Barnhelm* (1767), widely regarded as the first major comedy in the German language, *Emilia Galotti* (1772), a tense, disturbing, and theatrically effective tragedy that contains much criticism of the egoism and venality of the rulers of contemporary petty states, and *Nathan the Wise* (1779), a moving and noble plea for religious tolerance. Though Lessing claimed that he did not create with the spontaneity of the true artist, these four plays were among the first works of enduring quality written for the German stage.   SW

Levene, Sam[uel] (Levine) (1905–80) American character actor. One of the more durable figures on the New York stage for over 50 years, Levene specialized in roles that capitalized on his dour expression and his prominent New York accent, frequently New York Jewish types. He is best remembered for Patsy in *Three Men on a Horse* (1935), Gordon Miller in *Room Service* (1937), Sidney Black in *Light Up the Sky* (1948), Nathan Detroit in *Guys and Dolls* (1950), Al Lewis in **Neil Simon**'s *The Sunshine Boys* (1972), and Oscar Wolfe in the revival of *The Royal Family* (1975), his last major appearance. Adept in vehicles that ranged from popular farce to the more serious, Levene also appeared notably in *The Last Analysis*, *The Devil's Advocate*, *Heartbreak House*, *Dinner at Eight*, and the London production of *The Matchmaker* with **Ruth Gordon**.   DBW

Levin, Hanoch (1943–) Israeli satirical playwright. The thesis of all his plays has been defined as: 'I humiliate and/or am humiliated, therefore I am.' His plays depict petit-bourgeois life in Tel-Aviv as the antithesis of the idealism of the pioneers. His irreverent and pessimistic debunking of society has earned him the reputation of a misanthrope and a decadent writer. But he has won recognition and popularity for his unflinching naturalism of speech and his satirical barbs. In the greatest of his plays, *The Passion of Job* (1981), he created the Jewish equivalent of the Gentile myth. Among his other plays: *You and I and the Next War* (1969), *Queen of the Bath* (1970), *Hefetz* (1972), *Yaacobi and Leidental* (Working Title) (1972), *Vardaleh's Youth* (1974), *Shitz* (1975), *Krum* (1975), *The Patriot* (1982), *The Suitcase Packers* (1983). Although admired at home, Levin's plays have not found favour with audiences abroad, perhaps because of the highly local idiom of his satire.   HAS

Lewes, George Henry (1817–78) English critic and playwright, the grandson of an actor. Lewes was a man of many parts – philosopher, linguist, actor, dramatist, novelist, biographer and dabbler in the law, business and medicine. He had 14 plays, mostly adaptations from the French, performed in his lifetime, the most successful of which, *The Game of Speculation* (1851), provided **Charles James Mathews** with one of his best parts, that of Affable Hawk. Lewes's dramatic criticism has lasted better than his plays. The earliest examples were written for the *Leader* (1850–4), of which he was joint-editor with **Leigh Hunt**'s son, Thornton. The campaign he conducted there against **Charles Kean** was extended into the longer essays, written for the *Pall Mall Gazette*, some of which were collected in *On*

Actors and the Art of Acting (1875). There is very little finer writing on the art of the actor than Lewes's essays on **Edmund Kean**, **Rachel** and Charles James Mathews. They are eloquent and penetrating. Lewes was one of the many distinguished amateurs who delighted to act for **Charles Dickens** at Tavistock House – he had had some professional experience in Manchester in 1849. It is a pity that his own distinction as a writer has been engulfed by interest in his long liaison with George Eliot.   PT

Lewis, Leopold (1828–90) English playwright whose single claim to fame was his adaptation as *The Bells* of *Le Juif Polonais* by Erckmann and Chatrian. The role of the guilt-stricken Mathias was superbly played by **Irving** in 1871. Lewis was a solicitor, volatile to the point of instability. Of three later plays staged in London, none succeeded.   PT

Lewis, Robert (1909–   ) American director, producer, and actor. Lewis first appeared with the Civic Repertory Theatre during the 1929–30 season. From 1931 to 1941 he worked with the **Group Theatre**, for whom he directed the road company of *Golden Boy* in 1938. He made his first appearance in London in the same year. After the war he directed extensively on Broadway; among his hit productions were *Brigadoon* (1947) and *Teahouse of the August Moon* (1953). With **Elia Kazan** and **Cheryl Crawford**, he founded the **Actors Studio** in 1947. As well, Lewis has appeared in many films. He has taught acting and theatre at Sarah Lawrence College and Yale and is the author of *Method – or Madness?*, an explication of the **Stanislavsky** System of acting. In 1984 he published his autobiography, *Slings and Arrows*.   SMA

Leybourne, George (1842–84) British music-hall star, born in Stourbridge. As a 'buffo vocalist' under the name Joe Saunders he honed his skills at Tyneside concert-rooms and made his London debut around 1863 working with a mechanical donkey. Imposingly tall (6 ft 4 in) and handsome, Leybourne perfected the image of the 'lion comique', the free-spending, hard-drinking sport. His most famous number was *Champagne Charlie*, a persona he carried into private life, treating all and sundry. He was rivalled by Arthur Lloyd, Alfred Vance and G. H. Macdermott, but he excelled them all in the breadth of his repertory and the magnetism of his personality. Alcoholic, debilitated and impoverished, he was still at the top of the bill when he made his final appearance in 1884, at the Queens, Poplar.   LS

Li Yu (1610–80) Chinese dramatist and theatre practitioner. Born in Jiangsu he failed in the provincial examinations for imperial office and abandoned a political career. He ran his own theatre troupe of actresses whom he trained and directed, travelling round the country to perform at the homes of high officials. He was a talented and versatile playwright, author and critic. His work revealed a profound knowledge of stage practices and dramatic composition based on first-hand experience. He rejected the stigma laid upon theatre by his contemporaries. His book on dramatic theory *A Temporary Lodge for My Leisure Thoughts* (*Xianqing ouji*), published in 1671, is the most outstanding work of its genre written in 17th-century China.   ACS

Libya see **Middle East**

Lifshits, A. M. see **Volodin**

Lighting see **Stage lighting**

Ligier (1796–1872) French actor of large voice, small stature and a considerable talent for makeup, he made his debut at the **Comédie-Française** in 1820 as Néron in *Britannicus*. In 1824 he was allowed to play heavies. His argumentative temperament led to his departure from the Comédie for the **Odéon**. In 1829 he created **Delavigne**'s *Marino Faliero* at the Porte-Saint-Martin, following this with parts in the new repertoire at the Odéon, notably in **Dumas**'s *Christine ou Stockholm et Fontainebleau* and **Vigny**'s *La Maréchale d'Ancre*. Admitted to the Comédie-Française as a *sociétaire* in 1831, he continued his line of sinister historical figures with *Louis XI* (1832), created Triboulet for the one performance of *Le Roi S'Amuse*, Glocester in *Les Enfants d'Edouard*, Savoisy in *Charles VII et Ses Grands Vassaux*, Caligula (1837) and, one of his greatest roles, Frédéric in **Hugo**'s *Les Burgraves*. His last role was that of Antoine in *Caesar's Will* (*Le Testament de César*, 1847). He retired in 1851, but continued to appear at the Porte-Saint-Martin for a time, then returned to his native Bordeaux.   JMCC

Lillie, Beatrice Gladys (Constance Sylvia Munston) (Lady Robert Peel) (1894–1989) Canadian comedienne, who appeared in variety as a child. Her debut in London revue came in *Not Likely* (1914), singing lachrymose ballads, and she did not find her niche as a comic until André Charlot's revues of 1917 and 1924. The latter brought her to the United States; her New York successes include *This Year of Grace* (1929) with **Noël Coward**, *The Show Is On* (1936) with **Bert Lahr**, *Set to Music* (1939) when she introduced Coward's 'I've Been to a Mahhhvelous Party', and *Inside USA* (1948). Lillie was the consummate revue performer, wielding the slapstick with a raised pinky, puncturing her own poses of sophisticated grandeur with lapses into raucous vulgarity. She performed in a one-woman show *An Evening with Beatrice Lillie* (1952), a revival of *The Ziegfeld Follies* (1957), as *Auntie Mame* (1958) and as the medium Mme Arcati in *High Spirits* (1964). She also wrote an autobiography, *Every Other Inch a Lady*.   LS

Lillo, George (?1691–1739) English playwright. Very little is known of his life. He worked as a partner in his father's jewellery business and seems to have died a fairly wealthy man. He began writing plays in 1730. His reputation is based on two works: *The London Merchant* (1731) and *Fatal Curiosity* (1736). The former, also known as *The History of George Barnwell*, is a rare example of English domestic tragedy, recounting the fall of an apprentice lured to steal from his master by his passion for an evil woman. The genre's antecedents in Elizabethan forms like **Arden of Feversham** (which Lillo also adapted) are turned by Lillo into drama much more dominated by pathos. The apprentice as tragic hero was highly influential in the development of European 'bourgeois' tragedy by **Rousseau**, **Diderot** and **Lessing**, all of whom praised Lillo's play highly. *Fatal Curiosity*, set in Cornwall and recounting an impoverished old couple's desperate decision to murder a wealthy stranger who turns out to be their long-lost son, is far more fatalistic and profoundly affected the development of German **Schicksaltragödie**.   PH

Lincoln's Inn Fields Theatre (London)

In March 1660 Sir **William Davenant** leased Lisle's Tennis Court and enlarged it for use as a theatre. It opened in June 1661 with performances of his play *The Siege of Rhodes*, the first production in England to use changeable scenery in a permanent professional theatre. Davenant's company used it until November 1671 when they moved into **Dorset Garden**. In January 1672 a fire gutted the Theatre Royal at Bridges Street and **Killigrew**'s company, the King's Company, moved into Lincoln's Inn Fields in February, opening with a performance in the presence of the King with the company 'discovered on stage in melancholic postures'. They used the theatre until March 1674 when they moved to the rebuilt Theatre Royal. It reverted to use as a tennis-court until 1695 when **Betterton**'s company, seceding from the United Company, refurbished it and opened there in April 1695 with **Congreve**'s *Love for Love*. From 1705 until 1714 it was not used but **John Rich** then relicensed it and rebuilt it into a theatre with a capacity of 1,400. His company used it until 1732 and it was in occasional use until 1744.   PH

Lindau, Paul

(1839–1919) German journalist, playwright, and director. Lindau's comedies enjoyed some success in his lifetime. In 1895 he directed the **Meininger** company, after it had concluded its tours. In 1904, he was briefly director of the **Deutsches Theater** before **Max Reinhardt** took it over.   SW

Lindberg, August

(1846–1916) Swedish actor and manager, highly influential in the breakthrough of naturalism in 19th-century Scandinavian theatre. Impatient with the outmoded and commercial principles of most established theatres of his time, he toured Scandinavia with companies that were often compared to the **Meininger** for their ensemble playing. A relentless champion of **Ibsen**, he directed the European premiere of *Ghosts* (1883) and the Norwegian premieres of *Brand* (1895) and *John Gabriel Borkman* (1897). As an actor, he excelled in such diverse Ibsen roles as Oswald, Peer Gynt, Solness and Borkman, giving them an emotional complexity that also distinguished his Hamlet and Richard II. Late in life, he won acclaim for his overseas tours reading *The Tempest*, *Peer Gynt*, *Faust* and *Oedipus the King*.   HL

Lindberg, Per

(1890–1944) Swedish director, who introduced to Scandinavia the non-illusionistic principles of such modernists as **Craig**, **Reinhardt** and **Meyerhold**. He also fought to establish a broadly based People's Theatre, based on German and Soviet models. With the designer Knut Ström he made an early impact at the Lorensberg Theatre, Gothenburg (1918–23), with theatricalistic productions of **Shakespeare**, **Strindberg** and contemporary European dramatists and also tried to create a People's Theatre, based on a socially relevant repertoire, inexpensive subscription schemes and the physical unification of stage and auditorium. These ideas were later pursued in Stockholm at the huge Concert Hall Theatre (1926–7 and 1931–2) and the Club Theatre he created at **Dramaten**. During the 1930s, Lindberg's work was increasingly dominated by his fight against fascism, especially in his productions in Bergen (1934) and Oslo (1935) of *The Hangman* by **Pär Lagerkvist**, with whom he shared a long and close collaboration.   HL

Lindsay, Howard

(1889–1968) American playwright, director, actor, and producer. Born in Waterford, New York, Lindsay attended Harvard University for one year and the American Academy of Dramatic Arts for six months before launching his acting career in 1909. Numerous stage appearances followed in vaudeville and burlesque; on tour with McKee Rankin; and as a member of **Margaret Anglin**'s Company (1913–18). After military service in the First World War he returned to the stage, and in 1921 directed as well as acted in *Dulcy*. In the 1920s Lindsay established himself on Broadway as both a director and actor. He married the actress Dorothy Stickney in 1927, and starred with her in *Life with Father* (1939), a play he co-wrote with **Russel Crouse**. Other collaborations with Crouse included: the book for *Anything Goes* (1934); *State of the Union* (1945), which won the Pulitzer Prize; the book for *Call Me Madam* (1950); *The Great Sebastians*, which featured **Alfred Lunt** and **Lynn Fontanne**; and the books for *The Sound of Music* (1959) and *Mr President* (1962). Lindsay's most popular role, Father in *Life with Father*, drew praise from **Brooks Atkinson** for its 'rare taste and solid heartiness'. He was a craftsman more than an artist, able to 'pull together' stageworthy theatrical pieces with his collaborators.   TLM

Linney, Romulus

(1930–) American director and playwright. Trained at the Yale School of Drama, Linney's career has been nurtured primarily by the non-profit professional theatre outside New York and by Off-Broadway, as well as repertory theatres of Great Britain, Canada, Germany, and Austria. His over a dozen critically acclaimed plays include *The Sorrows of Frederick* (1967), *The Love Suicide at Schofield Barracks* (1972), *Holy Ghosts* (1976), *Childe Byron* (1978), *Tennessee* (1979; Obie award, 1980), *Laughing Stock* (1984), and *Woman Without a Name* (1985). Martin Gottfried has called Linney 'one of the best kept secrets of the American theatre, a playwright of true literacy, a writer in the grand tradition'. In 1984 he received the Award in Literature from the American Academy and Institute of Arts and Letters.   DBW

Liston, John

(1776–1846) English comic actor, born in London and an early specialist in 'cockney' parts. Liston made his undistinguished debut in London in 1799, but earned his reputation in the provinces before returning to star at the **Haymarket** in 1805. His first major success was as Caper in J. T. Allingham's *Who Wins?* (1808). Vanity, stupidity and cowardice were traits of Caper and of many of Liston's later successes, among them Apollo Belvi in Theodore Hook's *Killing No Murder* (1809) and Lubin Log in James Kenney's

Love, Law and Physics (1812). Snub-nosed, red-cheeked, enormously broad-bottomed, Liston provoked laughter by his very appearance as well as by the shrewd way in which he costumed himself to heighten the comic effect. He was a low comedian, given to extempore gags, but also to exploiting a contrast between the extravagance of his appearance and the comparative restraint of his performance-style. That the management of **Covent Garden**, where he acted from 1805–22, wished to keep him a buffoon is implicit in the Shakespearian parts he was allotted – Ophelia in **John Poole**'s *Hamlet Travestie* (1813), Bottom (1816), Pompey Bum (1816), Cloten (1817), Dromio of Syracuse (1819), Sir Andrew Aguecheek (1820) and Launce (1821). It was at the Haymarket that Liston created his greatest role, that of Paul Pry in Poole's play of that name (1825). Liston had left Covent Garden for **Drury Lane** in 1823. There he became an established star, the most highly paid comic actor in the history of English theatre. His own hankering for more subtle performance led to the surprise move to the **Olympic** under **Madame Vestris** (1831–7), and it was there that he spent his last active years, acknowledged as one of the greatest of the age's many 'personality actors'. He retired in 1837.   PT

Little Theatre movement

Little Theatre movement (USA) Thespian societies and parlour theatricals were common in America long before the advent of the Little Theatres. In 1901 Jane Addams and Mrs Laura Dainty Pelham organized the Hull-House Players in Chicago because they believed that good plays performed by amateurs could have 'a salutary influence on the community'. The big movement came a decade later with The Players (1909) in Providence, Rhode Island, Thomas H. Dickinson's Wisconsin Dramatic Society in Madison and Milwaukee (1911), Mrs Lyman Gale's Boston Toy Theatre (1912), Alfred Arvold's Little Country Theatre in Fargo, North Dakota (1912), and Maurice Brown's Chicago Little Theatre (1912). The sudden and simultaneous flowering of Little Theatres can be attributed to: the visit of **Lady Gregory**'s Irish Players (1911), **Percy MacKaye**'s call for 'constructive leisure' in his book *The Civic Theatre* (1912), the founding of **The Drama League** (1909), **George P. Baker**'s 'Workshop 47' at Harvard (1912), the numerous articles about the European art theatres, dissatisfaction with the offerings of the commercial theatre, and a passionate belief, if sometimes ill-founded, that the arts and crafts of the theatre could be grasped by enthusiastic and ambitious amateurs eager for 'self-expression'.

The pioneers were quickly joined by Samuel Eliot's Little Theatre in Indianapolis (1915), **Sam Hume**'s Arts and Crafts Theatre in Detroit (1916), Frederick McConnell's **Cleveland Play House** (1916), Gilmore Brown's **Pasadena Playhouse** (1918), and Oliver Hinsdell's Dallas Little Theatre (1920). By 1920 there were more than 50 groups scattered across the country (e.g. Cincinnati, Duluth, Galesburg, Rochester, Baltimore, Ypsilanti) who found further support for their endeavours from **Gordon Craig**'s *Toward a New Theatre* (1913), Hume's exhibition of the New Stagecraft (1914), New York's **Provincetown Players** (1914) and **Washington Square Players** (1915), from *Theatre Arts Magazine* (1916, later **Theatre Arts**)

Monthly) and from Constance D'Arcy Mackay's *The Little Theatre in the United States* (1917).

They performed in improvised quarters (family mansions, livery stables, churches, community centres) on temporary platforms framed by proscenium openings of fifteen feet or less and with accommodation for fewer than a hundred spectators most of whom were season subscribers. They specialized in bills of one-act plays which required minimal scenery, few rehearsals, and offered less demanding roles to more members. The more ambitious attempted the plays of **Shaw**, **Ibsen**, and **Strindberg**, and at one time or another (in the 1920s) most took a turn at laughing at themselves with **George Kelly**'s *The Torchbearers*. They also sponsored lectures, play readings, and classes in theatre arts and crafts.

Little Theatres (now numbering more than 5,000) have become an integral part of the cultural life of their communities, and many have built their own theatre complexes. A 1984 survey by the American Community Theatre Association found nearly a hundred which have been in continuous operation for fifty years or more. Some have been transformed into regional professional theatres (e.g. Cleveland, Houston, Washington, Dallas), and even those that have maintained their amateur (or semi-amateur) status can hardly be called 'Little'; they operate on budgets approaching a million dollars and present full seasons of major plays, both old and new.   RM

Little Tich (Harry Relph)

Little Tich (Harry Relph) (1867–1928) Diminutive English character-comedian, patter-singer and eccentric dancer. Initially a nigger minstrel (billed as Little Tichborne after the notorious claimant), in which role he perfected the big boot dance which became his trademark, he went solo in 1884, and made his pantomime début in Glasgow the following year. One of the most internationally minded and linguistically gifted of British variety artists, he worked with great success in the USA and Europe, particularly in France where he played the Olympia and the **Folies-Bergère** – to such effect that in 1910 he was made an officer of the Académie-Française for his service to French theatre. A master of surrealistic patter, his caricatures of the Territorial, the Gas Inspector, the Ballerina, and others, trod a delicate line between the realistic and the bizarre. He appeared in the first Royal Command Charity Performance, at the Palace Theatre in 1912, along with **Cinquevalli**, **Lauder**, **Robey**, **Tate**, **Tilley** and others, and was an important influence on Chaplin.   AEG

Littler, Prince

Littler, Prince (1901–73) and **Emile** (1903–) Two brothers who became the leading impresarios in popular theatre after the Second World War. Prince Littler began by staging major pantomimes in the West End, such as *Jack and the Beanstalk* at **Drury Lane** in 1936, and continued for more than 20 years with light entertainment, bringing over musicals like *Brigadoon* (1950) and *Carousel* (1951) from the USA. His great talent, however, lay as a business man, who became Chairman and Managing Director of Stoll Theatres Corporation, Chairman of Moss Empire and, through Prince Littler Consolidated Trust, came to own or control nearly half the West End theatres and 57 of the main out-of-London touring theatres. When Prince

Littler turned his attention and diverted some of his assets into commercial television in 1955, the effect was to cause a major slump in regional theatre. His younger brother, Emile, who was knighted in 1974, was a more orthodox impresario who had worked his way through the profession from being **Barry Jackson**'s Assistant Stage Manager at the **Birmingham Rep** in the 1920s to his debut as a producer in 1934. He excelled in comedies, pantomimes and musicals, producing *Annie Get Your Gun, Son of Norway, Zip Goes a Million* and many other hits. From 1964 to 1967, he was President of the Society of West End Theatre Managers and a governor of the **Royal Shakespeare Company**, until he retired in 1973. From 1946 to 1983, he controlled the Palace Theatre in London, where many of his successes were staged.   JE

Littlewood, (Maudie) Joan (1914–   ) British director, who was the driving force behind the establishment of the Theatre Workshop company at the Theatre Royal, Stratford, East London. Although she trained at the Royal Academy of Dramatic Art, she was always contemptuous of West End theatrical values and accordingly left London to go to Manchester as a radio producer. In 1935, she met the folk-singer and playwright, Ewan MacColl (Jimmy Miller), whom she married and together they founded an adventurous, left-wing, touring company, Theatre Union. This became a pioneering example for the fringe companies of the 1960s, using agit-prop techniques borrowed from German theatre and compensating for the lack of technical resources by the vigour of performance. In 1953, after years on the road playing in village halls and community centres, Littlewood brought her small company to a decaying music hall in London's East End. The ambitiousness of her programmes, combining contemporary documentary drama with classic productions of little known plays, attracted interest from the **Edinburgh Festival** in 1955, where her productions of **Arden of Feversham** and **Ben Jonson**'s *Volpone* were hits. The next five years saw the Littlewood's work and energy at the Theatre Workshop, Stratford. New plays (**Brendan Behan**'s *The Quare Fellow* and *The Hostage*, **Shelagh Delaney**'s *A Taste of Honey*), new musicals (**Frank Norman** and **Lionel Bart**'s *Fings Ain't Wot They Used T'Be*) and, above all, new character actors and actresses came from her theatre, often to the despised West End. Despairing at the inadequacy of her grants and her inability to keep her team together against the financial lures elsewhere, she tried to launch a 'fun palace' in Lea Valley, which never reached even the trial stage. After visits to Tunisia, more receptive initially to her schemes, Littlewood returned to Theatre Workshop in 1963 to direct her greatest success *Oh, What A Lovely War!*, a documentary satire about the First World War, set within a seaside concert party framework. Subsequently, although she directed the successful *Mrs Wilson's Diary* (1967) and *The Marie Lloyd Story* (1967) at the Theatre Workshop, of which the first transferred to the West End, she lost her old energy and passion for people's theatre. Her last Stratford production was *So You Want To Be in Pictures?* (1973), but her influence on other British directors and companies has been profound.   JE

Liverpool Playhouse Britain's oldest continuously operating repertory theatre (excluding war years). Inspired by the achievements of the **Gaiety** company in Manchester, theatre-enthusiasts in Liverpool organized a trial session in 1911, the success of which led to the setting up of a company, financed by 900 shareholders from the city, which in turn bought the old Star Theatre and reopened it later that year as the Liverpool Repertory Theatre (from 1916 known as the Playhouse), with **Basil Dean** as artistic director. Perhaps less adventurous than its sister theatres in Manchester and Birmingham, it has had a more stable history than either, benefiting from the consistent support of its shareholders and audiences, a more cautious choice of plays, the long stays of director William Armstrong (from 1922 to 1940) and general manager Maud Carpenter (1923–62) and the reputations of the actors it has nurtured (such as Robert Donat, **Michael Redgrave** and **Rex Harrison**). Improvements and extensions to the theatre (including a studio theatre) were made in 1966–8. A marked change of course occurred in 1981 with the appointment of four writers as joint artistic directors (Alan Bleasdale, Chris Bond, Bill Morrison and **Willy Russell**) and a consequent emphasis upon new and recent writing.   AJ

Living Newspaper Although antecedents can be identified, this term most frequently is associated with the **Federal Theatre Project** (USA). A documentary methodology was used, defining a problem and then calling for specific action. Bringing together both unemployed newspaper men and theatre personnel, presentations were written on such varied problems as housing, health care, labour unions, public utilities, cooperatives, natural resources, Negroes, and even the motion pictures. Six examples were produced by the New York unit, although the first, *Ethiopia*, on the war in Abyssinia, was cancelled under pressure from the United States State Department. The three most successful attempts were by Arthur Arent: *Triple-A-Plowed Under* (the need for farmers and consumers to unite for improved incomes and cheaper food) was a great success in 1936; *Power* (1937), a plea for public ownership of utilities; and *One-Third of a Nation* (1938), an exposé of urban housing conditions. Less successful were *1935*, a satire of the public's indifference to social issues, and *Injunction Granted* (1936), an account of labour's treatment in the courts. Units in other cities developed living newspapers on local problems, though few were produced. The techniques have been applied to more contemporary didactic theatre, such as the so-called Theatre of Fact begun in the 1950s.   DBW

Living picture or **Tableau vivant** A mute, immobile arrangement of performers to reproduce a scene from art, literature or the imagination. Displayed by the medieval church on the Feast of the Resurrection to reproduce episodes from the Gospels, such pictures were often borne in procession on a float; similar, allegorical tableaux were staged at Renaissance banquets. In 1760 **Carlo Bertinazzi** recreated Greuze's painting *The Village Betrothal* in *Les Noces d'Arlequin*, and shortly before the French Revolution Mme de Genlis used *tableaux historiques*, arranged by the painters David and Isabey, to instruct the children of the Duc d'Orléans. The *tableau*, as a device enabling the spectator to take in clearly visible signs of emotional and moral states, was promoted as an important dramatic device by **Diderot** and became a component fixture of the melodrama, especially at the ends of acts.

The *pose plastique*, in which the performer purports to imitate classical statuary, introduced a sensual note, originating in Naples with Lady Emma Hamilton, and, throughout the 19th century, was an allegedly artistic means of exhibiting nudes. Such shows provided finales at the song-and-supper rooms of Regency London and the Judge-and-Jury Society revels organized by 'Chief Baron' Renton Nicholson, as well as the private gatherings of courtiers at the Tuileries and Fontainebleau under Napoleon III. More respectable showings included The Court of Beauties, arranged at the **Olympic** in 1835 by **Mme Vestris**, based on portraits by Peter Lely, and the Operatic Tableaux Vivants to be seen at the Royal Victoria Coffee Music Hall (**Old Vic**). The European troupes that toured England, like the Rudolphs and the Kellers, were highly respectable and often played at private parties, but the tinge of immorality still clung and their audiences were exclusively male. The *pose plastique* as 'living statuary' found a home in turn-of-the-century music-halls, its exponents, like La Milo (Pansy Montague), whitened down with pearl powder. The spectacular revue made much of sumptuous tableaux, such as those arranged by Ben Ali Haggin for the *Ziegfeld Follies*.

As Martin Meisel has recently demonstrated, the principle of the living picture underlay much 19th-century staging, and paintings by Wilkie and Frith were enacted as climactic moments in melodrama. The 'picturesque' quality was pursued in the productions of **Charles Kean**, the Duke of Saxe-**Meiningen**, **Henry Irving** and the young **Stanislavsky**, as a primary responsibility of the director. The most noteworthy recent artistic employment of the *tableau vivant* has been in **Stephen Sondheim**'s musical *Sunday in the Park with George* (1983), in which Seurat's 'Sunday on the Isle of La Grande Jatte' gradually comes to life on stage.   LS

See: J. W. McCullough, *Living Pictures on the New York Stage*, Ann Arbor, Mich., 1979; M. Meisel, *Realizations: Narrative, Pictorial and Theatrical Arts of the Nineteenth Century*, Princeton, NJ, 1983; N. Miller, 'Mutmassungen über Lebende Bilder', in *Das Triviale in Literatur, Musik und Bildenden Kunst*, ed. H. de la Motte-Haber, Frankfurt, 1972.

Living Theatre (USA)

When Julian Beck and his wife, Judith Malina, founded the Living Theatre in 1948, they inaugurated the experimental Off-Off Broadway movement in New York. With one of the most influential and long-lasting avant-garde companies in American history, the Becks became the prophets of the burgeoning theatrical experimentation that was to explode during the 1960s.

From the very beginning, the Living Theatre sought the marriage of a political and aesthetic radicalism. 'We insisted,' Beck said, 'on experimentation that was an image for a changing society. If one can experiment in theater, one can experiment in life.' This principle took a variety of shapes as the LT developed, but the Becks' anarchist-pacifist viewpoint remained a constant.

The Theatre began producing plays by Paul Goodman, Gertrude Stein, **García Lorca**, **Pirandello**, **Cocteau**, and **Brecht**, seeking an anti-realism that could match the contemporary fervour in the visual arts and music. The group did not find a permanent performance space until 1959, and they lost it four years later when the Internal Revenue Service evicted them for non-payment of taxes. Early landmark productions before being closed were profoundly influenced by **Artaud**'s *The Theatre and Its Double* including Jack Gelber's *The Connection* (1959) about heroin addicts awaiting a promised fix, Brecht's *Man is Man*, and Kenneth Brown's *The Brig* (1963). This detailed documentary of daily brutal routine in a US Marine Corps brig in Japan was the company's last New York production; having defied IRS orders to leave its building, the LT gave its final performance of *The Brig* in a padlocked theatre. The audience had to enter by climbing in the windows.

From September 1964 until August 1968, the LT performed only in Europe, concentrating on works made up of exercises and improvisations, and created collectively. This experimentation culminated in *Paradise Now* (1968), a 'spiritual and political voyage for actors and spectators'.

A tour to the USA in 1968 helped convince the Becks that they no longer wanted to perform for a middle-class audience, but preferred to work in the streets with the people. After a brief return to Europe, the company went to Brazil in 1970 and stayed 13 months experimenting with collective creation before returning to the USA to work with coal miners and steel mill workers in Pittsburgh. They went back to Europe for further exploration of dramatic form and acting.

In 1984 the LT settled once again in New York. Since Julian Beck's death in 1985, the company has continued under the direction of Judith Malina and Hanon Reznikov.

The Becks' works and ideas are described in Beck's 1972 book, *The Life of the Theater*, and Malina's *Diaries 1947–57* (1984).   AS

Livings, Henry

(1929–) British dramatist, who was an actor with **Joan Littlewood**'s Theatre Workshop company. The anarchic cheerfulness of his plays, the sympathy with the underdog and his feeling for North Country towns, perhaps in his native Lancashire, were all aspects of his writing encouraged by the Littlewood style. His first play, *Stop It, Whoever You Are* (1961), was staged at the Arts Theatre Club during a new plays season and featured Wilfred Brambell as a downtrodden lavatory attendant in a factory who plots revenge against the bosses, including his wife. The heroes of his comedies are all underdogs, Stanley the television mechanic in *Big Soft Nellie* (1961), the cook in *Nil Carborundum* (1962) and Valentine Brose in *Eh?* (1964), although Kelly in *Kelly's Eye* (1963) is a fighter who believes in punching first to teach the others a lesson. Behind the farcical plotting and the caricatures, Livings retained a bleak estimate of man's inhumanity to man, clearly seen in *The Little Mrs Foster Show* (1966), which tells the story of a white mercenary in Africa through the framework of a stage show. His underdogs are often presented as mildly sub-normal and their successes are minimal kicks against the system, amusing but sadly ineffectual. A prolific writer, Livings has television and radio plays to his credit and more than 30 stage plays. Although at one time he was criticized for the vulgarity of his themes and language, these objections have dated more rapidly than have his plays. Of his naturalistic plays, *Nil Carborundum* set in a RAF camp has a compassionate understanding of those individuals who, despite the title, were ground down by military life.   JE

Lizárraga, Andrés (1919–82) Argentine playwright and television writer. Although he wrote more than 20 plays, Lizárraga is known primarily for his historical plays that used national themes to speak to contemporary issues. In 1960 *Tres jueces para un largo silencio* (*Three Judges for a Long Silence*), *Santa Juana de América* (*Saint Joan of America*) and *Alto Perú* (*High Peru*) constituted a 'May trilogy', based on moments and figures of the Revolution and Counter-Revolution. The Brechtian techniques fit well with the development of social themes throughout his dramatic production.   GW

Lloyd, Marie (Matilda Alice Victoria Wood) (1870–1922) 'Our Marie', most legendary of English music-hall stars. Born in Hoxton, the daughter of a waiter, she made artificial flowers before her debut in 1885 at the Royal Eagle in City Road, as Bella Delmare. After choosing the name Marie Lloyd (from 'Lloyd's Newspaper'), she rose to prominence at the Star Music Hall, Bermondsey, with Nelly Power's song 'The Boy I Love Is Up in the Gallery'. As early as 1888, she was known for saucy songs, such as 'Then You Wink the Other Eye' and 'She'd Never Had Her Ticket Punched Before' delivered with an assortment of winks, ogles and chuckles. Soon she was earning £600 a week, but was so carelessly charitable that she was seldom solvent. She married three times, unhappily, and it was her reputation for bawdiness and her divorce from coster comedian Alec Hurley (1911) that kept her from being invited to the first Royal Command Variety Performance of 1912; on the other hand, she was active in the Music-hall War against the managers, and entertained troops and factory workers during the Boer War and the First World War. Ageing rapidly, she switched her stage persona from knowing clothes-horse to cheerful harridan, in such numbers as 'Don't Dilly Dally' and 'One of the Ruins that Cromwell Knocked About a Bit'. Max Beerbohm named her, with Florence Nightingale and Queen Victoria, one of the three greatest women of the age, and **T. S. Eliot** praised her as a true voice of the people; at least three unmemorable musical comedies have been based on her life.   LS

Lloyd Webber, Andrew (1948–) British theatre composer, whose first major success came when he was only 20, with *Joseph and the Amazing Technicolour Dreamcoat*, with lyrics by **Timothy Rice**. *Jesus Christ Superstar* (1970), *Evita* (1976), *Cats* (1981), *Song and Dance* (1981) and *Starlight Express* (1984) provided an unparalleled sequence of hit musicals, which not only established him as the leading theatre composer of his time, against some competition from such American composers as **Stephen Sondheim**, but also transformed the respective roles of London and New York as centres for musicals. In the 1980s, London became the major centre for new musicals, greatly aided by **Trevor Nunn**'s direction of *Cats*, *Starlight Express* and other non-Lloyd Webber musicals, such as *Les Misérables*. Lloyd Webber's gift for lilting tunes provided one ingredient of his success but he is also an astute business man and producer, responsible for such West End productions as *Daisy Pulls It Off*.   JE

Loa A short theatre piece, normally with music, common in Spain and Latin America during the years of conquest and colonization. Of sacred origin, the principal object was to praise high-level officials on special occasions. These pieces were popular with audiences and served to introduce full-length works.   GW

Loesser, Frank (1910–69) American composer and lyricist. After contributing songs to *The Illustrators' Show* (1936), Loesser spent twelve years in Hollywood writing the lyrics for numerous motion picture musicals. He returned to Broadway with the score for *Where's Charley?* (1948), a musical version of *Charley's Aunt*. Two years later Loesser wrote his most memorable songs for *Guys and Dolls*, a musical based on Damon Runyan's short stories about tough but soft-hearted New York gamblers and their girl friends. Loesser then devoted four years to writing the score for *The Most Happy Fella* (1956), an ambitious musical whose thirty songs ranged from operatic arias to typical Broadway speciality numbers. After a failure with *Greenwillow* (1960), Loesser wrote his last Broadway score for *How to Succeed in Business Without Really Trying* (1961), a satire on corporate politics and chicanery. Loesser also operated a musical publishing house through which he furthered the careers of several young composers.   MK

Loewe, Frederick see **Lerner, Alan Jay**

Logan, Cornelius A[mbrosius] (1806–52) American actor and playwright. A popular comedian, mainly in the West and South, Logan also defended the theatre with a vigour later displayed in the work of his daughter Olive Logan. As a playwright, Logan wrote a few successful Yankee vehicle plays. He wrote *The Wag of Maine* (1834) for **James Hackett** and revised it as *Yankee Land* (1842) for **Dan Marble** who portrayed Deuteronomy Dutiful, a talkative country bumpkin, in Logan's *The Vermont Wool Dealer* (1838). Joshua Silsbee acted Lot Sap Sago in Logan's *The Celestial Empire; or, The Yankee in China* (1846). Logan wrote and acted successfully in *Chloroform* (1849), his last play.   WJM

Logan, Joshua (1908–) American director, producer, and playwright. Logan has been associated with many of Broadway's most successful plays and musicals as director, co-producer, or co-author. Frequently as all three: *South Pacific* (1949) for which he and co-author **Oscar Hammerstein** received the Pulitzer Prize (1950); *The Wisteria Trees* (1950), based on **Chekhov**'s *The Cherry Orchard* and written by Logan; *Wish You Were Here* (1952); and *Fanny* (1954). He was director and co-producer of *John Loves Mary* (1947), and *Picnic* (1953). *Mister Roberts* (1948) was directed by him and written with Thomas Heggen. Other plays and musicals exhibited Logan's skill as an inventive director: *On Borrowed Time* (1938), *Knickerbocker Holiday* (1938), *Mornings at Seven* (1939), *Charley's Aunt* (1940), *By Jupiter* (1942), *Annie Get Your Gun* (1946), and *Happy Birthday* (1946). He also directed motion pictures: *Bus Stop* (1956), *South Pacific* (1958), and *Camelot* (1967).

His apprenticeship began with the Triangle Club at Princeton and continued with the University Players. He is married to Nedda Harrigan and has written two volumes of autobiography: *Josh* (1976) and *Movie Stars, Real People, and Me* (1978).   RM

Lohenstein, Daniel Caspar von (1635–83) German baroque dramatist. Lohenstein's plays contain much overt violence and are written in an extremely florid style. They have rarely been performed.   SW

Lomonosov, Mikhail Vasilievich (1711–65) The lawgiver of Russian literature, a true Renaissance man of the peasant class and among the best educated and most influential men of his generation. Trained primarily at the Imperial Academy of Sciences in St Petersburg, where he later taught, and in Germany by philosopher-mathematician Christian Wolff and others, Lomonosov mastered the disciplines of classic and modern literature, literary criticism and translation, grammar, rhetoric and language theory, chemistry, physics, astronomy, geology, mining and metallurgy, mathematics and philosophy. He published a major study of Russian grammar (1757), virtually defined the high, middle and low styles of Russian literary language and set forth the principles of the syllabotonic system of versification which has more or less dominated Russian poetry since the 18th century. In his two verse tragedies for the stage, *Temira and Selim* (1750) and *Demophon* (1752), he made significant adjustments in the courtly classical style of **Sumarokov**. He transformed the classical opposition of love versus duty into a politico-moral consideration of the natural man forced to endure unnatural forms such as tyranny. Sumarokov attempted unsuccessfully to spoof the more original artist. Lomonosov is also noteworthy for having helped to found Moscow University (1755) which today bears his name.   SG

Londemann, Gert (1718–73) Danish actor, the leading comedian of the 'Danish Playhouse' (later the **Kongelige Teater**), opened in Copenhagen in 1747. The supreme Danish **Harlequin** of his era, he was an expert clown, juggler and acrobat, admired for his spontaneity and quicksilver improvisations. He specialized in playing charming but cunning servants, such as **Holberg**'s Henrik (especially in *The Political Tinker*) and **Molière**'s Sganarelle. Londemann was particularly successful when he partnered Niels Clementin, whose dry, refined style was an excellent foil for his exuberance.   HL

Long Wharf Theatre (New Haven, Connecticut) Founded in 1965 by Jon Jory and Harlan Kleiman, this non-profit resident theatre is now under the leadership of artistic director Arvin Brown (since 1967) and M. Edgar Rosenblum. Known as an actor's theatre, Long Wharf, with two intimate performance spaces in the New Haven Meat and Produce Terminal, emphasizes the production of new and established, home-grown

and foreign works that explore human relationships. Although transference to New York is not a priority at LWT, many important productions have made the move virtually intact, including *Shadow Box, Streamers, The Changing Room, Sizwe Banzi is Dead, The Gin Game, Quartermaine's Terms*, and revivals of *A View From the Bridge* (1982) and *American Buffalo* (1984). LWT has won praise and numerous awards, including a special Tony Award in 1978, for the quality of its productions as well as the stability of its organizational structure.   DBW

Longacre Theatre 220 West 48th St, New York City [Architect: Henry B. Herts]. Built by H. H. Frazee, a baseball magnate who liked to dabble in play production, the compact Longacre is ideally suited for small musicals and intimate comedies and dramas, which indeed have been its regular fare. Seating just over 1,000, it was leased to the **Shuberts** during the depression and has since passed to their ownership. From 1944 to 1953, the theatre was used as a radio and television playhouse, but was returned to play production and has remained a legitimate house since then. Among its noteworthy tenants have been *Paradise Lost* (1935), *On Borrowed Time* (1938), *Rhinoceros* (1961), *Ain't Misbehavin'* (1978) and *Children of a Lesser God* (1980).   MCH

Lonsdale, Frederick (1881–1954) British dramatist, who began his career with a series of librettos for musical comedy including *The Maid of the Mountains* (1917). After *Madame Pompadour* in 1923 he turned to social comedies dealing ironically with polite manners and modern marriage, which at the time were compared with **Maugham**. Epigrammatic wit and neatly constructed, near-farcical situations made his work highly successful, and the best of his eleven plays, *The Last of Mrs Cheney* (1925) where the maid in a gang of burglar-servants gives up her criminal career to marry into the aristocracy, still retains its popularity.   CI

Loos, Anita (c. 1888–1981) American actress, screenwriter and playwright, noted for her satiric comedies. Loos, who wrote some 200 scripts for both silent and sound movies, created the art of writing film captions, beginning with D. W. Griffith's silent films, such as *Intolerance* (1916). In 1926 she and her husband, John Emerson, dramatized her successful novel, *Gentlemen Prefer Blondes*. Noted for Lorelei Lee, the stereotypical 'dumb blonde', the play was made into a musical in 1949 by Loos and Joseph Fields. Throughout her career Loos wrote plays – *Happy Birthday* (1946); and screenplays – *San Francisco* (1936) and *The Women* (1939); adapted French plays into hit American shows – *Gigi* (1951); and wrote witty, gossipy memoirs of her career in Hollywood – *A Girl Like I* (1966) and *Kiss Hollywood Goodbye* (1974).   FB

Lope de Vega see **Vega Carpio, Lope Felix de**

López, Willebaldo (1944–) Mexican playwright, TV producer, actor and director. After studies in theatre in the Mexican Institute of Fine Arts, López held a fellowship in the Mexican Writers' Centre in 1971–2. Many of his plays have dealt with problems of Mexican youth – adolescents facing multiple problems of drugs, sex, unemployment, and social pressures. His *Los arrieros con sus burros por la hermosa capital* (*The Muleteers with their Animals in the Beautiful Capital*, 1967) is a study in provincial/urban prejudices; *Cosas de muchachos* (*Kids' Things*, 1968) dramatizes the ubiquitous tensions and frustrations of adolescence. Other major works include *Yo soy Juárez* (*I am Juárez*, 1972), *Pilo Tamirano Luca* (1973) and *Vine, vi y mejor me fui* (*I Came, I Saw, and I Should Have Gone*, 1971). López has won major prizes for his plays. GW

Loquasto, Santo (1944–) American set and costume designer. Loquasto is able to deal equally well with detailed realism and conceptual or theatricalist productions. His early Broadway and regional theatre successes such as *That Championship Season* and *American Buffalo* were often typified by clutter and detail. At the same time, his work with the **New York Shakespeare Festival**'s outdoor productions led him to work with towering sets and to employ constructivist and emblematic designs. His sculptural design and angularity create a strong sense of three-dimensional space. He designs frequently for dance, especially for choreographer Twyla Tharp. His costumes possess the same detail, sense of colour and texture as his sets. For dance he often designs costumes alone. Since the late 1970s Loquasto has worked frequently on films, notably with Woody Allen. AA

Loranger, Françoise (1913–) French Canadian playwright and novelist. She began writing for radio in the 1930s, and for national television from its inception in 1952. Her first stage play, *Une Maison. . . un Jour* (*One House. . . One Day*, 1965), was well received at home and abroad. A psychological drama, it was followed by *Encore Cinq Minutes* (*Five More Minutes*, 1967), one of the first Canadian plays to raise feminist concerns. The author's growing political commitment is evident in *Le Chemin du Roy* (*The King's Highway*, 1968) and *Médium Saignant* (*Medium rare*, 1970). The former, a savage satire written in collaboration with Claude Levac, depicts, in the guise of a violent hockey game between Quebec and Ottawa, the diplomatic fiasco resulting from President de Gaulle's provocative behaviour on his 1967 visit to the province; the latter focuses on the struggle for francophone rights in the atmosphere of Quebec's controversial Bill 63, which attempted to legislate those rights. *Double Jeu* (*Double Game*, 1969) reverts to her earlier psychodramas, but in an experimental vein that requires audience participation in the resolution of its romantic plot. LED

Lorca see **García Lorca**

Lord Chamberlain's Men The finest of Elizabethan theatre companies was founded in 1594 under the patronage of the Lord Chamberlain, Lord Hunsdon. Most of its senior members had been previously together in **Strange's Men**, and it is likely that friendship as well as financial interest united the men who agreed to share the risks and profits of the enterprise. The original sharers were Cuthbert and **Richard Burbage**, Thomas Pope, **Augustine Phillips**, **John Heminges**, **William Kempe** and **William Shakespeare**. The Chamberlain's Men took up residence at **James Burbage**'s **Theatre** and quickly gained

a highly prized access to the Court. Of the 20 recorded royal commands from 1594–7, 13 went to them and 7 to the **Admiral's Men**. When the theatres of London were threatened with closure in the wake of the *Isle of Dogs* scandal of 1597, these two companies were specifically exempted by the Privy Council. Licensed to 'use and practise stage plays', the Chamberlain's Men faced the threat of homelessness when the lease on the Theatre expired in 1597. James Burbage died in the February of that year, bequeathing the problem to his son Cuthbert. To his other son, Richard, he left his interest in the indoor **Blackfriars**. But the company's access to the Blackfriars was blocked by a residents' petition, which included their new patron among its signatories. (Lord Hunsdon died in 1596, passing his title, his office and his theatre company to his son.) Using the **Curtain** as a stop-gap home, the Chamberlain's Men sought out and purchased a new site, south of the river and close to the Admiral's Men at the **Rose**. The building of the **Globe** was completed in 1599, and it was there that the Chamberlain's Men confirmed their supremacy in a repertoire that included work by **Jonson**, **Webster**, **Tourneur**, **Middleton**, **Marston**, **Beaumont**, **Fletcher** and the finest of Shakespeare's plays. They continued to use the Globe after the delayed occupation of the Blackfriars was at last complete in 1608–9. Their theatrical leadership had been openly acknowledged in 1603, when the new King, James I, adopted them as the King's Men, and they maintained it throughout the reigns of the first two Stuart kings. With the exception of Kempe, who left the company and sold his share before the opening of the Globe, and Shakespeare, who seems to have retired in c. 1613, all the leading actors of the King's Men remained active members until death or the 1642 closure of the theatres halted them. Having carried the major responsibilities of management from c. 1611 until his death, Heminges was succeeded by **Joseph Taylor** and **John Lowin**. Shakespeare's place as 'ordinary' playwright was taken successively by Fletcher and **Massinger**. The company's hold at Court, though sometimes challenged, was never surrendered. It was probably largely for their use that Charles I authorized the conversion of the **Cockpit-in-Court**. PT

Lorde, André de see **Grand-Guignol**

Lortel, Lucille (1902–) American producer. Born in New York, Lortel attended the American Academy of Dramatic Arts (1920) before studying in Germany with Arnold Korf and **Max Reinhardt**. After a year in stock (1924), she made her Broadway debut in a minor role. Upon her marriage in 1931, she gave up the stage until 1947 when she offered her Westport, Conn., barn for a dramatic reading. After two seasons of readings, she remodelled the White Barn Theatre into a functioning theatre which served as a showcase for new talent. Lortel acquired the Théâtre de Lys in 1955 to move worthy White Barn productions into New York. Her first Théâtre de Lys production, *The Threepenny Opera*, ran for seven years. In 1956 she began offering a Matinee Series, which continued for 20 years. At both theatres she has presented lesser known plays by **Brecht**, **Ionesco**, **Genet**, Mario Fratti, and **Athol Fugard**. The more successful presentations at the

Théâtre de Lys include: *Dames at Sea, A Life in the Theatre, Buried Child, Getting Out, Cloud Nine*, and *Woza Albert*. In 1981 the theatre was rechristened the Lucille Lortel Theatre in her honour. She is the co-founder of the **American Shakespeare Festival** and a recipient of the Margo Jones award for her dedication to new plays.   TLM

Louis, Victor (1731–1802) French theatre architect, the most influential of the late 18th century. His Bordeaux theatre, generally considered the finest in France, opened in 1780. It is known for its grand staircase, which **Garnier** would borrow a century later for the Paris opera house. With its 12-column façade, the Grand Theatre is a magnificent piece of urban landscaping. Louis used a circular auditorium, slightly opening out towards the stage, with a ceiling held up by four massive columns, two of them framing the stage. The proscenium was shallower than that of previous 18th-century theatres and the auditorium had indirect lighting rather than the conventional chandelier. In 1781, after a fire at the Opéra, the Duke of Orleans commissioned Louis to build a new Opéra in his palace. By the time the theatre was built (1790) it was not needed for this purpose and was taken over by two theatrical entrepreneurs, Gaillard and Dorfeuille, who ran it briefly as the Variétés Amusantes. In 1799, this became the permanent home of the **Comédie-Française**. Louis had to cope with a more limited site than at Bordeaux. He solved this problem by supporting the auditorium on 32 columns in the ground-floor vestibule. The auditorium was longer than Bordeaux, with parallel sides, which allowed for a wider proscenium (also imitated by Garnier). In 1791, **La Montansier**, who had a small theatre (originally built for puppets) in the **Palais-Royal**, asked Louis to transform this, which he did in a matter of two weeks, increasing the seating to 1,300 and doubling the stage dimensions to make the staging of tragedies, dramas and even operas possible. In 1792, La Montansier acquired a site opposite the Bibliothèque Nationale and commissioned Louis to built her a theatre. The Théâtre National de Montansier was completed in 1793. Less monumental externally, it had a magnificent auditorium, with a stage 75 feet square and 100 high. There were no stage-boxes, which emphasized the growing separation between actor and audience. The Opéra engineered the arrest of La Montansier and took over the theatre where it remained until 1820, when the Duke of Berry, heir to the throne, was assassinated there and the theatre had to be demolished. Louis's much admired auditorium was reconstituted for the new Opéra in the rue Lepeletier.   JMCC

Lowell, Robert (Traill Spence, Jr) (1917–77) Pulitzer Prize-winning American poet and playwright considered by many the best English-language poet of his generation. He is best known for the trilogy of plays adapted from Nathaniel Hawthorne and Herman Melville titled *The Old Glory* (*Benito Cereno*; *My Kinsman, Major Molineux*; and *Endecott of the Red Cross*), first performed at the **American Place Theatre**, New York, in 1964. *Benito Cereno*, most successful of the trilogy, was seen in 1967 at London's Mermaid. Lowell also adapted **Racine**'s *Phèdre* (publ. 1960) and **Aeschy-**

lus' *Prometheus Bound* (1966), the latter seen at the Mermaid in 1971.   DBW

Lowin, John (1576–c. 1659) English actor, who probably abandoned the trade of goldsmith for the stage. He is first heard of with Worcester's Men at the **Rose** in 1602, and from 1603 until the closure of the theatres was a member of the King's Men, for whom he may have become business manager after the death of **Heminges**. Among the parts Lowin is known to have played are Falstaff, Volpone, Morose in **Jonson**'s *Epicoene* and Bosola in **Webster**'s *The Duchess of Malfi*. His longevity made him an important link in the evolution of acting styles. In *Roscius Anglicanus* (1708), Downes claims that Lowin advised **Davenant** on **Shakespeare**'s ideas for the playing of Henry VIII and that Davenant then instructed **Betterton**. After some years as landlord of the Three Pigeons in Brentford, Lowin died in poverty.   PT

Ludlam, Charles (1943–87) American actor, director and playwright. Ludlam was an early member of John Vaccaro's Play-House of the Ridiculous, an Off-Off Broadway theatre which presented his *Big Hotel* (1967) and *Conquest of the Universe* (1967). Splitting with Vaccaro in 1967, Ludlam started his own theatre, The Ridiculous Theatrical Company, where his plays have included *Bluebeard* (1970), *Camille* (1973), *Stageblood* (1975), *Professor Bedlam's Punch and Judy Show* (1975), *Der Ring Gott Farblonjet* (1977), *Le Bourgeois Avant-Garde* (1982), and *The Mystery of Irma Vep* (1984). These plays combine popular and high art forms, mixing colourful staging, scatological humour, and female impersonation with plots and styles drawn from dramatic and operatic literature. But Ludlam's treatments of *Hamlet*, **Wagner**'s *Ring*, or *Camille* transcend mere spoofing; his depth of involvement, he explains, gives rise to independent works that transcend parody. One of the first New York theatres to deal explicitly with homosexual themes, the Ridiculous Theatrical Company often features Ludlam in female roles – which he doesn't necessarily play campily. In 1984 Pittsburgh's American Ibsen Theatre invited Ludlam to play Hedda Gabler.   AS

Ludlow, Noah Miller (1795–1886) American actor-manager, who with **Sol Smith** brought the legitimate theatre to the Ohio and Mississippi valleys. First employed by **Samuel Drake** in 1815 to barnstorm in Kentucky, Ludlow formed his own company, playing New Orleans and remote corners of the south and west. In 1828 he joined **T. A. Cooper** as manager of the **Chatham Theatre** in New York, but failed financially. With Smith, Ludlow formed the American Theatrical Commonwealth Company from 1835 to 1853, building and operating theatres in Mobile, New Orleans, St Louis, and other cities, engaging many of the leading stars of the day. The partnership dissolved in hostility; Smith's journals never mention his partner. Ludlow's autobiography, *Dramatic Life as I Found It* (1880), although bitter in condemnation of Smith, offers an unequalled factual account of the frontier theatre in America.   SMA

Ludwig, Otto (1813–65) German playwright and theorist. Ludwig was prevented by ill-health from achieving the eminence he coveted as a dramatist. Furthermore, he had a theoretical rather than a creative bent. Nevertheless, *The Hereditary Forester* (1850) is an effectively melodramatic tragedy, while *The Maccabeuses* (1852), a romantic verse tragedy set in ancient Rome, has some power. Ludwig's most durable writings are probably his *Shakespeare Studies* (published 1871). SW

Lugné-Poe, Aurélien (1869–1940) French actor and director (real name Lugné). Remembered as the leader of the symbolist reaction against naturalism, Lugné started as an actor under **Antoine**, but soon moved to Paul Fort's Théâtre d'Art, becoming its director in 1893 and renaming it Théâtre de l'Oeuvre. The characteristic style of Oeuvre performances was a stylized or abstract décor, artificial intonation of dialogue and a pervasive dream-like atmosphere. Here he produced **Ibsen** (e.g. *Brand, Rosmersholm*), **Maeterlinck**, **Hauptmann**, **D'Annunzio**. Forced to close by financial pressures in 1899 he reopened the theatre in 1912 with **Claudel**'s *The Tidings Brought to Mary* and continued, with interruptions, to direct work of a symbolist tendency until he withdrew in 1929. He is remembered especially for *Ubu Roi* (1896) which he produced against his better judgement and had only two performances. His *Cocu Magnifique* by Crommelynck (1920) was influential. DB

Lully, Jean-Baptiste (1632–87) Italian musician, dancer and composer whose entire career was spent in France and who was naturalized French in 1661. Appointed composer to Louis XIV in 1653 and superintendent of music at court eight years later he came to dominate French musical life for three decades. Apart from arranging and conducting instrumental concerts he acted as impresario/composer for all court entertainments of a theatrical nature and collaborated with leading playwrights in their preparation, notably with Benserade on ballets, with **Molière** on 'comédies-ballets' and with **Quinault** on operas or 'tragédies en musique'. In 1672 control of the French Opéra, which had been founded by letters patent from the crown three years earlier, was transferred to Lully under the title of 'Académie royale de musique' and he continued to direct it successfully until his death, inducing other dramatists (**Thomas Corneille**, **Campistron**) to take advantage of the opportunities it afforded for spectacular scenic presentation. An able if autocratic administrator, Lully enjoyed the zealous favour of the king and amassed a considerable personal fortune as well as a title. DR

Lunacharsky, Anatoly Vasilievich (1875–1933) The intelligent, cosmopolitan and humane Soviet First People's Commissar for Education (1917–29) as well as a dramatist and critic involved largely with repertory questions, Lunacharsky's enthusiasm for the theatre (he was married to an actress) helped to save a good many artists and institutions in the years following the October Revolution. A revolutionary from 1897 and a Bolshevik from 1904 with a record of arrests and exile for Party activity and an on and off relationship with Lenin, he helped to create the 1919 decree of the Council of People's Commissars (Sovnarkom), which nationalized all theatres in regions under Bolshevik

control. He proceeded cautiously in his official capacity, moving to preserve what was best in Russian and European culture while the new Soviet culture was evolving. At the same time he was actively involved in giving Soviet art the opportunity to develop without undue pressure or overreaction. Thus, he was generally fair-minded and in some cases even protective of artists as diverse as **Stanislavsky**, **Meyerhold**, **Vakhtangov** and **Tairov** (although he was decidedly ambivalent toward Meyerhold and Tairov), but he never confused tolerance for the avant-garde with loyalty to the Party or to the spirit of the Revolution. He proclaimed 'Back to October!' (1923) in protesting directorial corruption of the classics, urged the theatres to adopt the new Soviet drama, championed realism and proletarian art and encouraged new theatres built since the Revolution, including the First State Theatre for Children (Moscow, 1920), which he directed. He opposed Meyerhold's plan as head of the Theatre Section of the People's Commissariat for Education (1920) to 'revolutionize' the **Moscow Art Theatre** and closed the director's R.S.F.S.R. Theatre No. 1 over his radical production of Emile Verhaeren's symbolist play *The Dawns* (1920), which had dissatisfied Lenin's wife. Lunacharsky was the author of 14 somewhat fustian plays in which historical or legendary themes were contemporized so as to gain revolutionary resonance. These included: *Faust and the City* (1918), *Oliver Cromwell* (1920), *Foma Campanella* (two-thirds of a trilogy, 1921) and *The Liberated Don Quixote* (1921). His historical plays were attacked by Marxist extremists, who saw his dimensionalized character portraits as emphasizing the role of the individual in history. SG

Lunt, Alfred (1892–1977) and **Lynn Fontanne (Lillie Louise)** (1887–1983) American actors. Alfred Lunt became a star as the oafish lead in **Booth Tarkington**'s *Clarence* in 1919. Lynn Fontanne's first major role was as a dizzy matron addicted to clichés in **Kaufman** and **Connelly**'s 1921 satire, *Dulcy*. But it wasn't until they appeared together, two years after their marriage, in the **Theatre Guild**'s sparkling 1924 production of *The Guardsman*, **Molnár**'s droll comedy of sexual intrigue, that their reputations and the future course of their career were assured. From then on they were known as the Lunts, and until their farewell in *The Visit* in 1958 they had what was probably the most successful acting partnership of the 20th century. Audiences, critics, and fellow actors were delighted by the charged intimacy of their dual performances; their good friend **Noël Coward** quipped that they were really one person. Though every gesture and fraction of a pause was scrupulously intentioned, the Lunts created the illusion of spontaneity. To later generations they came to represent an outmoded stylized tradition, over-deliberate and genteel, but in their heyday they were thought to have introduced a new American style. They broke with old-fashioned Broadway acting techniques by playing comedy in a conversational way, their love scenes were startlingly physical, and their overlapping method of speaking their lines – at times they seemed to be talking simultaneously – surprised audiences in the twenties.

Individually, each had a few notable achievements in dramas – Fontanne was the original Nina Leeds in *Strange Interlude* (1928), a role she professed not to understand, and Lunt was memorable when cast against type as a tough-talking bootlegger in **Sidney Howard**'s *Ned McCobb's Daughter* (1926) – but it was in a high comedy that they excelled. Their favourite playwrights, **Robert E. Sherwood** and **S. N. Behrman**, provided them with vehicles in which the war between the sexes is a duel of wit and sly, charming manipulation. Highlights of their career include Behrman's *The Second Man* (1927), *Amphitryon 38* (1937), and *I Know My Love* (1949); Sherwood's *Reunion in Vienna* (1931), *Idiot's Delight* (1936), and *There Shall Be No Night* (1940); Sil-Vara's *Caprice* (1928); a rollicking *Taming of the Shrew* (1935) noted more for its vaudevillian spirits than for its poetry; *The Seagull* (1938); and Coward's *Design for Living* (1933). They became so closely identified with cosmopolitan comedy that producers as well as audiences were reluctant to let them try anything else, and at the end of their career the Lunts expressed regret that they hadn't been asked to do such plays as *Death of a Salesman* and *Long Day's Journey into Night*.

The Lunts were renowned among actors for their dedication – they were known to hold rehearsals for minor adjustments on the last day of a run – and for their career-long devotion to 'the road'. They played more one-night stands in remote towns than any other stars. They were also remarkable for their lack of greed. Unlike other stage stars, they resisted Hollywood except for one unhappy venture in 1931 when they made a film of *The Guardsman*. And when they could have commanded higher salaries from independent producers they maintained their loyalty to the Theatre Guild.   FH

Lunt–Fontanne Theatre 205 West 46th St, New York City [Architects: Carrere and Hastings]. Producer Charles Dillingham achieved the hallmark of success when he was able to build a theatre for his own productions in 1910. Originally known as the Globe, the Renaissance-style structure also housed his offices and apartments where he could entertain his stars and backers. In 1931, Dillingham lost his theatre, which was bought by a movie chain. It was reclaimed in 1958 by new owners, who completely renovated it and renamed it the Lunt–Fontanne for the famous husband-and-wife acting team. The entrance, which was originally on Broadway, was diverted to West 46th Street. The first production in the restored house was the American premiere of **Friedrich Dürrenmatt**'s *The Visit*, starring the Lunts. The theatre is now owned by the **Nederlander** Organization.   MCH

Lupino Family of English performers and designers. Historians have been unable to substantiate the family's claim to descend from an Italian puppeteer who settled in London in the reign of Elizabeth I. The first member of the tribe to make a mark in the theatre was George Richard Estcourt Luppino (*sic*) (1710–87) who, according to tradition, played in pantomime with **John Rich**, designed scenery and costumes for Galuppi's opera *Enrico* (1743) and was a ballet-master in Dublin and Edinburgh. His son Thomas Frederick (1749–1845) painted pantomime scenery at the King's Theatre (1784–5) and **Covent Garden** (1786–9, 1792–1803), a trade carried on by his son Samuel George (d. 1830). The modern branch of the family, which shortened the

name to Lupino, is descended from Samuel's son (possibly adopted) George Hook Luppino (1820–1902), a **Harlequin**. Of his progeny, George (1853–1932) was the best clown, a stalwart of the Britannia Theatre pantomimes, who allegedly is depicted in Frith's painting *Derby Day*; Henry Charles (1865–1925), an eccentric dancer, married into the Lane family that managed the Britannia; and Arthur (1864–1908) created the role of Nana in *Peter Pan* (1904).

George's sons Barry (1882–1962) and **Stanley** (1893–1942) both entered the theatre as children, and were stalwarts in pantomimes and musical comedies for many years. Barry specialized in dame roles and wrote over 50 musical comedies, making his last appearance in *Dick Whittington* (1954). Stanley was seen in *So This Is Love* (1928), *Love Lies* (1929), and *Room for Two* (1932), as well as in numerous plays of his own composition; his daughter Ida (1914–), after graduating from RADA, became a Hollywood star. Their cousin Lupino Lane (Henry George Lupino, 1892–1959) made his debut in infancy as Nipper Lane, and later created Nipper Productions to film his routines; he toured widely in music-hall, musical comedy and pantomime before enjoying his greatest success as Bill Snibson in *Me and My Girl* (1937) in which he introduced the Lambeth Walk; he also popularized the songs 'Chase Me, Charlie' and 'Knees Up, Mother Brown'. An expert tumbler, he was often seen with his brother Wallace (1897–1961) and his son Lauri, who went into film.   LS

Lupino, Stanley (1893–1942) British comedian and dramatist, who like his brother Barry and his cousin Lupino Lane specialized in pantomime and revue. He starred in several works co-written with Arthur Rigby, one of which he also directed (*Room for Two*, 1932), and in a series of his own plays, the most popular of which was *Crazy Days* (1937).   CI

LuPone, Patti (1949–) American actress. Born in Northport, New York, LuPone studied acting at the Juilliard School, graduating in 1972. A founding member of the **Acting Company**, she demonstrated her versatility in a variety of roles: Lady Teazle in *The School for Scandal*, Kathleen in *The Hostage* (1972); Irina in *The Three Sisters*, Lucy Lockit in *The Beggar's Opera* (1973); and Rosamund in *The Robber Bridegroom*, Kitty in *The Time of Your Life* (1975). LuPone's portrayal of the title character in *Evita* (1979) won a Tony and praise from **Walter Kerr** for 'rattlesnake vitality'.   TLM

Lyceum Theatre, London The first building on the site in Wellington Street, just off the Strand, was intended as an Exhibition Hall by the architect, James Payne, who erected it in c. 1765. It was probably first used for live entertainment by **Charles Dibdin** and, a little later, by the ubiquitous **Philip Astley**, and it was the musician, Samuel Arnold, who converted it into a theatre in 1794. There followed a period of struggle against the patent theatres, during which freak shows, exhibitions, concerts, Madame Tussaud's first waxwork display (1802) and lectures alternated with occasional performances. Arnold was clearly stating his own preferences by calling it the English Opera House. As long ago as 1765, he had been the chief composer for *The Maid of the Mill*, **Bickerstaffe**'s popular challenge to the Italian opera. But the new name was not endorsed until 1810, under the management of Arnold's son, and then only because the **Drury Lane** company had used it for a season after the burning of their own theatre. The younger Samuel Arnold was granted a licence for summer performance, and in 1815–16 he rebuilt the theatre to Samuel Beazley's design, incorporating an elegant saloon 72 feet long and 40 wide. **Fanny Kelly** made her London reputation here in 1816, the year before gas was installed on the stage and two years before **Charles Mathews** presented the first of his annual *At Homes*. The building was destroyed by fire in 1830 and rebuilt, again to Beazley's design, in 1834. Under the **Keeleys** (1844–7) and **Madame Vestris** and **Charles James Mathews** (1847–55), the renamed Lyceum established its place in a London scene freed from restrictions by the 1843 Theatres Act. **Charles Fechter** attracted adulation and controversy during his seasons of management (1863–7), but it was not until **Henry Irving** made his first appearance in *The Bells* (1871), under the management of **Hezekiah Bateman** (1871–5) that the Lyceum entered on its period of unique greatness. Under Irving's inspired management (1878–99), it became virtually a national theatre, the standard of dramatic excellence in Britain. Forced by financial losses to enter into a syndicate in 1899, Irving made his last Lyceum appearance in 1902, still with **Ellen Terry** at his side, and the theatre fell into disuse. It was demolished in 1904. A new theatre, designed by Bertie Crewe for use as a music-hall, opened later the same year. Under the management of the brothers Walter and Frederick Melville (1909–38), it was known as a home for melodrama and pantomime. It was scheduled for demolition in 1939 and **John Gielgud** presented six performances of *Hamlet* there as a symbolic farewell, but the war intervened, the London County Council changed its plans and the Lyceum became a Mecca dance-hall in 1945. The late 1980s hold promise for its re-emergence as a theatre.   PT

Lyceum Theatre New York City theatre at 149 West 45th Street, designed by the architectural firm of Herts and Tallant for manager **Daniel Frohman**. Originally known as the New Lyceum to distinguish it from Frohman's earlier playhouse on Fourth Avenue and 23rd Street, the theatre was opened on 2 November 1903, with a performance of *The Proud Prince*, starring **E. H. Sothern**. Under Frohman's management, the Lyceum was the home of first-class productions. The theatre suffered a serious decline during the depression, however, and was in danger of being torn down in 1939 when it was purchased by a group of investors that included playwrights **George S. Kaufman** and **Moss Hart**, and producer Max Gordon. The investors sold the Lyceum in 1945 and the theatre is presently owned by the **Shubert Organization**. During the late 1960s it was leased to the APA-Phoenix Repertory Company. The Lyceum seats approximately 900 and contains the most extensive complex of scene shops of any Broadway theatre, as well as an elaborate penthouse apartment. The penthouse is presently the home of the Shubert Archive, a collection of materials related to the history of the Shubert Organization. The Lyceum, which is the oldest Broadway theatre still in operation, was declared a landmark in 1975.   BMCN

Lyly, John (c. 1553–1606) English playwright, whose entry into Court circles after periods of study at both Oxford and Cambridge was facilitated by the patronage of the influential Burleigh family. Lyly made his literary reputation with the prose romance, *Euphues* (1578), which set a fashion for ornate English and donated the word 'euphuism' to the language. His plays were all written for **Boys' Companies**, and had in mind a sophisticated audience, familiar with the pinciples of rhetoric and with classical mythology. His use of prose in refined comedy was innovatory, although it is the verbal display that is more likely to impress or fatigue a modern reader. Lyly became formally involved in the management of the **Boys of St Paul's** by 1584, the probable year of performance of his first two plays, *Campaspe* and *Sappho and Phao*. It may be that the original audience was dissatisfied with the allusiveness of his third, *Galathea* (c. 1585), and that the choice of an English folk-theme in *Mother Bombie* (c. 1587) was intended to soften opposition. Lyly's best-known play, *Endimion* (c. 1588), includes a transparently flattering portrait of Elizabeth I as Cynthia. We can assume that contemporary audiences were alert to Lyly's allegorical references to figures and incidents at Court. He was a vocal supporter of the established church and the author of a pamphlet which took the episcopal side in the Marprelate Controversy. When he involved the Paul's Boys in the debate, probably by allusive costuming, Archbishop Whitgift was among those alarmed by the vulgarizing of the issues, and the theatrical activities of London's choristers were halted. Lyly's work was already old-fashioned in the fast-moving theatre and his last play, *The Woman in the Moon* (c. 1593), may never have been performed.   PT

Lyric Theatre, Belfast The Lyric Players Theatre, inaugurated in 1951 by Mary and her husband Pearse O'Malley at their Lisburn Road home, Belfast, it moved with them in 1952 to Derryvolgie Avenue where they converted a room into a small theatre. A Trust since 1960, since 1968 it has occupied a new 300-seat, well-equipped theatre, now subsidized by the Northern Ireland Arts Council, and has consolidated a stock of local players.

The Lyric has presented world theatre from **Aristophanes** to **Stoppard**, and all the major Irish dramatists, maintaining its commitment to poetic drama, **Yeats**'s particularly, and more recently appointing resident dramatists to foster new writing. The Lyric publishes the periodical *Threshold*.   DM

Lyric Theatre, Hammersmith (London) Originally the Lyric Opera House, opened in 1890 and specializing in melodrama and pantomime, in 1918 it was taken over by Nigel Playfair, who had previously acted with **Frank Benson**, **Beerbohm Tree** and **Granville Barker**. With **Arnold Bennett** and the designer Lovat Fraser, Playfair established a distinctive style of simplified realism, stylized gesture and formalized composition in a brilliant series of elegant productions, in many of which he also performed together with young actors of the stature of **Gielgud** or **Edith Evans**. Although it opened with **A. A. Milne**'s first play, *Make Believe*, a Christmas entertainment especially written for Playfair, the production that really established the theatre's reputation was his revival of **Gay**'s *The Beggar's Opera*. Its unprecedented run of 1,463 performances reawakened interest in Restoration and 18th-century drama; and it was followed by other Ballad-Operas by Gay and **Bickerstaffe**, together with outstanding revivals of **Congreve**, **Farquhar**, **Sheridan** and **Goldsmith**, as well as classic productions of **Chekhov** and **Wilde** and contemporary light comedy by A. P. Herbert or **Clifford Bax**. Knighted in 1928, Playfair left the theatre in 1933, after which it declined. Despite a period of renewed popularity with further revivals by the Company of Four after 1945, **Peter Brook**'s production of *The Brothers Karamazov* (1946) or a season under Gielgud (1952–3), the theatre closed in 1966. It was demolished in 1972, although the name was transferred to a new, smaller theatre built nearby.   CI

Lytton, Edward Bulwer, Lord see Bulwer, Edward

Lyubimov, Yury Petrovich (1917–) Soviet

director. Until his firing as artistic director of the Moscow Theatre of Drama and Comedy on Taganka Square ('The Taganka') in April 1984 and his subsequent expulsion from the USSR, Lyubimov was perhaps the greatest and certainly the most controversial and socially important contemporary Soviet director. Called 'the theatrical conscience of his nation', Lyubimov is a moral artist in the 19th-century tradition of **Gogol**, **Tolstoi** and Dostoevsky and a theatricalist innovator in the Meyerholdian vein. Born in the year of the October Revolution, there has always been a strong agit-prop element in his work, an attempt to bridge the gap between stage and audience and to address the issues of his day. He was trained at the Second Moscow Art Theatre Studio until its closing in 1936 and then at the Vakhtangov Theatre School, graduating into the war and thereafter into the Vakhtangov Theatre's acting company. His celebrated production of **Brecht**'s *The Good Person of Setzuan* with his third-year acting class at the Shchukin Theatre Institute, where he was teaching (1962), earned him the artistic directorship of the moribund Taganka Theatre (1964). For the next 20 years with **Meyerhold**, **Stanislavsky**, **Vakhtangov** and Brecht as his spiritual guides, Lyubimov eschewed Soviet drama for the more imaginative worlds of poetry and narrative fiction, which he dramatized, and the classics, which he broke apart, reconstituted and presented from a pronounced critical perspective. His carefully orchestrated *mises en scène* are masterfully focused in mobile, tactile and transformative scenic metaphors, Meyerholdian 'machines for acting', most often co-created with his brilliant designer **David Borovsky**. Lyubimov's productions feature: a complex lighting plan which he designs; detailed, precisely-timed music and acoustic sound scores; interpolated poetry and songs, performed by a highly musical company; direct audience address and

presentational play, which often originates and culminates in the theatre lobby. His productions include: John Reed's *Ten Days That Shook the World* (1965), an exercise in Eisensteinian agit-prop, cinematic montage produced through a light curtain; Chernyshevsky's *What Is To Be Done?* (1971), performed on a tracking, 19th-century tiered wooden school seating unit; Boris Vasiliev's sentimental patriotic tale of female heroism in the Second World War, *And Here the Dawns are Silent* (1971), realized via a wooden military transport which transforms into showers, rafts, trees, walls and coffins. His poetry-based 'recital' presentations extend from Andrei Voznesensky's and Evgeny Evtushenko's impressions of their visits to America, *Antiworlds* (1965) and *Under the Skin of the Statue of Liberty* (1972), respectively, to meditations on the lives of the poets themselves: *Listen!* (1967), in which five **Maya-kovsky**s cavort upon out-sized children's alphabet blocks; *Comrade, Believe!* (1973), in which an overhead tracking black leather carriage and an opulent stationary carriage illustrate five **Pushkin**s' flight from tsarist persecution; the rarely produced *Death of a Poet* (*Vladimir Vysotsky*), commemorating the Taganka's leading actor and legendary folk singer who died in 1980, performed in a white-shrouded theatre auditorium mock-up. Among his socially minded productions are: two adapted from Yury Trifonov novellas, *The Exchange* (1976), on urban moral blight evoked via an overstuffed apartment collage of real objects, and the controversial Stalinist guilt memory piece *The House on the Embankment* (1980), in which a glass 'wall of silence' separating stage from audience reveals the inner workings of Soviet life; and Boris Mozhaev's *Alive*, banned since 1968, on the errors committed in 1930s collectivization by bureaucrats who in performance literally descend via lighting battens into the pristine clarity of a birch-pole forest. Representative radical stagings of the classics include: *Tartuffe* (1969) on **Molière**'s play in crisis, under attack by church and state performed before a puppet king and cardinal through life-size character portraits; *Hamlet* (1974), featuring a huge mobile woven rope curtain, representing a redemptive theatrical life force; **Bulgakov**'s *The Master and Margarita* (1977), composed from recycled theatrical props and scenic pieces, including the *Hamlet* curtain and a large pendulum from Ezni Stavinsky's *Rush Hour* (1969) which swings between Christ and the Devil; *The Inspector's Recounting* (1978), in which the **Gogol** oeuvre is presented phantasmagorically through holes in a giant overcoat being stitched on machines which sound like clerks' abacuses and atop spectrally moving elevator-platforms; Dostoevsky's *Crime and Punishment* (1983), in which a murderous Raskolnikov, rather than the Soviets' victimized proto-revolutionary hero, is pursued by a blood-stained door. Lyubimov has recently staged this as well as Dostoevsky's *The Possessed* abroad and has written an autobiography, *The Sacred Fire*.   SG

M

Maach (India) Very little written material in English is available concerning this form of folk theatre popular in the villages of central India. *Maach* is thought to be about 300 years old. Its native home is said to have been Rajasthan, although today it is found principally in the villages of Madhya Pradesh, especially in Malwa. *Maach* was introduced to Malwa by Sri Gopalji Guru who is reputed to have composed several *Maach* plays and who served as the first of a long line of rural playwrights.

Originally, *Maach* was associated with the holiday festivals surrounding *Holi*, a spring celebration. Today, it may be performed on any festival occasion.

Village performances are usually held on any open space in a village on one end of which is a three-foot raised stage approximately 15 x 12 feet. A curtain at the back serves as the only scenery and a one and a half foot wide border stretches across the front of the stage, masking the feet of the actor-dancers.

Although some dialogue has been introduced into *Maach* today, it has always been a sung drama. Well-known performers earned their reputations because of their excellent singing voices. The principal musical instruments are the *sarangi*, the classical north Indian stringed instrument, *dhol* drum and harmonium.

Folk dances occur throughout performance to add spice and variety. Traditionally, men play all the roles but there are a few notable exceptions in which women distinguish themselves in the female parts. Performances usually begin around 10.30 or 11 pm and continue until dawn.

Performances traditionally begin with the *bhisti raag* which, like similar ritual overtures in other theatre forms, is meant to sanctify the proceedings. Today, the *bhisti* is danced rather than sung and serves to call the villagers to the playing area. Following this is the *bhisti-farrasan samvad*, a set of preliminary activities in dance and song which provide an overture to the drama.

Among the important characters is the *bidhab* or *shermarkhan*, adviser or consultant to the chief character, who is frequently a king. This clown character serves to enliven the show, helping to knit together all the various threads of the complicated plots of the plays and converting the songs into dialogue, interpreting their meaning to the spectators. The plays may be categorized into historical, social and religious groups and seem to satisfy the taste of village audiences for romantic sentiment charged with strong morals. FaR

Mabou Mines A collaborative, experimental American theatre company. Mabou Mines was founded formally in 1970 after years of collaborative work among its founding members **JoAnne Akalaitis**, **Lee Breuer**, and Ruth Maleczech in San Francisco, and later in Europe with Philip Glass and David Warrilow. The company has developed a formal performance style that synthesizes traditional motivational acting, narrative techniques, and mixed media – revealing the influence of the group's regular collaboration with painters, sculptors, video artists, film-makers, and composers. Though this distinctive acting style is always evident in Mabou productions, the group's directors leave their own particular stamps. Breuer's *The Red Horse Animation* (1970), *The B-Beaver Animation* (1974), and *The Shaggy Dog Animation* (1978) are theatrically clever and inventive, funny, and self-reflexive as opposed, for instance, to Akalaitis's ironically romping *Dead End Kids* (1982) or her hyper-real production of **Kroetz**'s *Through the Leaves* (1984). In addition to creating original works, Mabou is considered one of the foremost interpreters of **Samuel Beckett**; its influential productions of *The Lost Ones*, *Play*, *Come and Go*, *Cascando*, and *Company* combine narration and elaborate visual spectacle. In residence for three years at **La Mama**, Mabou has performed at the **New York Shakespeare Festival** since 1975. AS

McCabe, Eugene (1930–) Irish playwright, educated at University College, Cork. The subjects of McCabe's work range from his *Swift*, another attempt to illuminate Swift's complex nature, to a television trilogy about the present Northern violence (*Cancer, Heritage, Siege* 1976). His first stage play remains most impressive. Bringing today's rural Ireland into a view of its past, *The King of the Castle* (1964) makes remarkably coherent the domestic tragedy of Scober – the King – public hard man, ageing husband privately, the dispersed peasantry whose vagabond contemporary heirs we see, and the Big House vandalized by Scober's improvements. DM

McCarthy, Lillah (1875–1960) British actress and theatre manager. After touring with **Ben Greet** and **Wilson Barrett**'s companies, she became closely associated with **Shaw**'s work, playing in the first productions of *Man and Superman* (1905), *The Doctor's Dilemma* (1906) and *Androcles and the Lion* (1913) under her first husband **Granville Barker**, for whom she also created the title role in **John Masefield**'s *The Tragedy of Nan* (1908). In 1911 she took over the Little Theatre, playing a repertoire of **Ibsen**, Shaw and **Schnitzler** under her own management, and after repeating some of her most famous roles in New York she became manager of the Kingsway Theatre in 1919. CI

Macauley, Barney (1837–86) American actor, manager. Beginning his career as an actor in Buffalo, New York (1853), he became a leading actor in the Ohio Valley in 1861, and made his New York debut opposite **Matilda Heron** during 1864–5. He entered management in partnership with John Miles of Cincinnati (1868–72), and in 1872 assumed solo management in Louisville, where he had always been popular. He built his own theatre there (1873). In 1878 he turned the management over to his brother, John, and spent the rest of his career as the star of his own combination playing a rural melodrama, *The Messenger from Jarvis Section.* DMCD

McClintic, Guthrie (1893–1961) American actor, director, and producer. Born in Seattle, McClintic studied acting at the American Academy of Dramatic Arts before making his first stage appearance in 1913, and his New York debut a year later. During the 1915–16 season, he appeared in numerous roles with Grace George's Company at the Playhouse, followed by a ten-year association with the producer, **Winthrop Ames**. McClintic began his career as a director and producer in 1921 by presenting **A. A. Milne**'s *The Dover Road*. In the same year he married the actress **Katharine Cornell** and began a long professional association with her as the director of her major successes. Recognized as one of the most distinguished directors in the American theatre, McClintic staged more than 90 productions including the Pulitzer Prize-winning *The Old Maid* (1935) and *Winterset* (1935) which won the New York Drama Critics' Circle Award. His other major credits include: *The Barretts of Wimpole Street* (1931); *Yellow Jack* (1934); *Ethan Frome* and *The Wingless Victory* (1936); *High Tor* and *Candida* (1937); *No Time for Comedy* and *Key Largo* (1939); *The Doctor's Dilemma* (1941); *You Touched Me* (1945); *The Playboy of the Western World* (1946); *Antony and Cleopatra* (1947); *Life with Mother* (1948); *Medea* (1949); *The Constant Wife* (1951); and *Bernadine* (1952). He was known for casting his shows wisely and knowing how to get the most out of his actors. **Brooks Atkinson** called McClintic 'one of our most accomplished directors, especially for plays that depend on taste and elegance'. TLM

McCowen, Alec (Alexander Duncan) (1925–) British actor, who played in reps in Birmingham and York from 1943–50, before his first major London appearance as Daventry in *Escapade* (1953). He played Claverton-Ferry in **T. S. Eliot**'s *The Elder Statesman* (1958) and joined the **Old Vic** company in 1959. In the early 1960s, he became an established actor with major classical companies and also appeared in contemporary plays in the West End; but his first major international success came in Peter Luke's *Hadrian VII* where he played the man-who-would-be-pope with an unforgettable irony and wit. Sheer intelligence was a feature of his acting, shining through his Hamlet in Birmingham in 1969, and it led him towards roles of intellectuals and academics, notably in **Christopher Hampton**'s *The Philanthropist* (1970), as Alceste in *The Misanthrope* and Dysart in **Shaffer**'s *Equus* (two outstandingly successful **National Theatre** productions) and Higgins in the 1974 West End revival of **Shaw**'s *Pygmalion*. In 1978, he devised his remarkable solo performance of St Mark's Gospel, with which he toured widely in Britain and the States. He returned to the National Theatre to play Crocker-Harris in the revival of **Rattigan**'s *The Browning Version*, and in 1984, devised a new solo production as *Kipling*. His autobiographical writings include *Young Gemini* (1979) and *Double Bill* (1980). In 1972, he was awarded an OBE. JE

McCullough, John (1832–85) American actor born in Ireland. He made his stage debut at the **Arch Street Theatre** in Philadelphia in 1857 in *The Belle's Stratagem*. He subsequently toured with **E. L. Davenport** (1860–1) and **Edwin Forrest** (1861–5). A tall, classically handsome man in the heroic mould, McCullough's volatile, physically robust acting style resembled Forrest's. After the latter's death in 1872, he assumed several of Forrest's major roles, including Spartacus in *The Gladiator*, Virginius, and Jack Cade. He also excelled as Othello, King Lear, Coriolanus and Mark Antony. From 1866 to 1877 he managed the California Theatre in San Francisco for the first four years in association with **Lawrence Barrett**. A heavy financial loss forced his retirement from management and he spent the rest of his career as a successful touring star. In 1881 he made a brief starring engagement at **Drury Lane** in London appearing as Virginius and Othello. In 1883, his health declined. In the summer of 1885, he was placed in a mental institution. DJW

McCullough, Paul see **Clark, Bobby**

MacDonagh, Donagh (1912–68) Irish playwright. MacDonagh wrote three verse plays: *Happy as Larry* (1946), *God's Gentry* (1951), and *Step-in-the-Hollow* (1957). Rather in the manner of **John Gay**'s *Beggar's Opera*, MacDonagh combines song and street ballads with an easily spoken, at times doggerel, verse. In its period his work was associated with the supposed revival of verse drama represented by **Fry** and **Eliot**. DM

MacDonald, Christie (1875–1962) American singer and actress. She began her career in a summer theatre in Boston, and by 1892 was singing supporting roles in the **Francis Wilson** Opera Company. Her first starring role was in *Princess Chic* (1900), after which she appeared in a succession of comic operas, including *The Toreador* (1902), *The Sho-Gun* (1904), *The Belle of Mayfair* (1906), *Miss Hook of Holland* (1907), and *The Prince of Bohemia* (1910). MacDonald made her greatest success in *The Spring Maid* (1910). In 1913 she starred as Sylvia in the operetta *Sweethearts*, which **Victor Herbert** had composed with her in mind. She was also seen in a revival of *Florodora* (1920). Possessed of a sweet, delicate, slightly weak singing voice of impressive range, MacDonald captivated audiences with her vivacious, unaffected personality and her nimble dancing. MK

McGee, Greg (1950–) New Zealand playwright who achieved immediate prominence with his first play, *Foreskin's Lament* (1980), a treatment of violence and cultural obtuseness, ostensibly within the context of rugby football. Various television plays have followed, as well as two notable stage plays: *Out in the Cold* (1983) and *Tooth and Claw* (1982).   HDMCN

McGrath, John (Peter) (1935–) British dramatist and director who founded the adventurous left-wing 7:84 Theatre Company in 1971. McGrath's early plays, *Events While Guarding the Bofors Gun* (1966) and *Bakke's Night of Fame* (1968), were written in a conventional social drama idiom, showing his sympathies with the underdogs of society, and produced in mainstream 'new plays' theatres, such as **Hampstead Theatre**. After 1968, with the new spirit of revolution which entered British theatre, McGrath developed a style of popular theatre which introduced songs, music-hall gags and dances into a loose 'epic' play structure. The most successful of these were written for his company, 7:84, which owed its odd name to the statistic that 7% of the British population owned 84% of the national wealth. *The Cheviot, The Stag and the Black, Black Oil* (1973), *Little Red Hen (1975) and The Imperial Policeman* (1984) are distinguished by their liveliness, conviction and popular fervour. In 1973, 7:84 divided into two geographically defined companies, for the North of England and Scotland, McGrath staying with the Scottish company.

In addition to many plays for stage and television, poems, songs and scripts for several feature films, McGrath has written the book *A Good Night Out* (1981), in which he argues the case for a theatre that is both socialist and popular, reaching working-class audiences in their own venues and helping to articulate the need for social change.   JE AJ

Machiavelli, Niccolo (1469–1527) Italian political theorist, historian, military strategist and dramatist. Born into the Florentine nobility, he served in that city's state diplomatic service within and beyond Italy until the return to power of the Medici family in 1512 forced him into premature retirement. Most of his writings, including *Il Principe* (*The Prince*, 1513) and *I Discorsi* (*The Discourses*) were a product of that retirement, as probably were versions he made of **Terence**'s *Andria*, **Plautus**' *Aulularia*, and the play by which he is best remembered, *La Mandragola* (c. 1518), generally considered to be the finest comedy of the Italian Renaissance. A witty, sharp, cold-eyed view of the more provincial aspects of Florentine society, it has been variously interpreted as a social comedy exposing the hypocrisy of pseudo-Christian values, a light *jeu d'esprit* expressive of the high summer of Renaissance confidence, and a deep, cunning and admonitory political allegory. It was first produced in Florence in 1521, and was accorded an elaborate scenographic setting out which, along with its observance of the unities of time, place and action, Machiavelli mocked in his prologue. In 1524 he wrote his last play, *La Clizia*, closely based on Plautus' *Casina*. An early piece, based on **Aristophanes**' *The Clouds*, and apparently written about 1504, is now lost. His classical adaptations and emulations nicely reflect the humanistic preoccupations of his age, but in *La Mandragola* he transcended classic models, and working as much from the example of Boccaccio and the *novelle* tradition, produced a work richly of its own time and place and neatly expressive of the amoral pragmatism more rigorously formulated in *Il Principe*. That work, if more by repute and the

vulgarization of its ideas, than any considered understanding of its arguments in context, exerted considerable influence on foreign, particularly Elizabethan and Jacobean, dramatists' conceptions of Italian court life and political intrigue, the devious Machiavellian schemer becoming a stock figure in many plays.   LR

MacIntyre, Tom (1933–) Irish playwright. In MacIntyre's early plays, relatively realistic in manner, groupings and lighting suggest rather than depict the detail of scene and action. *Eye-Winker, Tom-Tinker* (1972) dissects the inertia and the self-absorbed rhetoric of a vacillating Irish revolutionary. Words are paramount. Since then MacIntyre has turned increasingly to mime, gesture, visual and aural effects, as in his highly acclaimed adaptation of Patrick Kavanagh's *The Great Hunger* (1983). *The Bearded Lady* (1984) similarly enlarges its text with visual effects developed from *Gulliver's Travels*, Yahoos and Houhynhmns as metaphors of Swift's own tormented psychology.   DM

MacKaye, James Morrison Steele (1842–94) American actor, playwright, teacher, architect, and inventor. A brilliant, if erratic, dreamer, MacKaye's innovations in stage mechanics, his crusade for realism in acting and for 'true-to-life' dialogue marked him as 'the most unsuccessful sucessful figure in the American theatre'.

His early dreams of becoming an actor and artist, supported by unrestricted family funds, permitted him to study painting with George Inness and acting with François Delsarte (in Paris, 1869), and to found a 'school of expression' in New York (1871) for propagating the Delsartian system. He made his professional debut as actor, playwright, and manager with *Monaldi* (New York, 1872), played Hamlet in London (Crystal Palace, 1873), and then achieved success as a playwright with *Rose Michel* (1875) and *Won At Last* (1877). Of his thirty plays, *Hazel Kirke* (1880), presented in his **Madison Square Theatre**, was the best. It ran for over a year, was repeatedly revived during the next two decades, but unwittingly MacKaye's contract assigned the profits to his financial backers, the Mallory brothers.

The Madison Square Theatre, MacKaye's first venture into architecture, had an elevator stage which changes scenes in two minutes, a lighting system devised by Edison, folding seats, and an ingenious ventilating system. His second theatre, to be combined with a hotel, never progressed beyond the blueprint stage. His third, the **Lyceum** (1885), incorporated new stage machinery, fire-fighting equipment, an orchestra pit on an elevator, and quarters for America's first dramatic school.

His ultimate theatrical dream, a Spectatorium (480 feet long, 380 feet wide, and 270 feet high) for the Chicago World's Fair (1893) to house his chronicle of Columbus's adventures, 'The World Finder', was disrupted by the national financial panic and was reduced to a scaled-down Scenitorium.

His son, the playwright **Percy MacKaye**, has written a detailed account of his life and work (*Epoch*, 1927).   RM

MacKaye, Percy (1875–1956) American playwright. His grand dramatic visions resembled those of his father, **Steele MacKaye**: *St Louis Masque* (1914), celebrating the 150th anniversary of the city's founding; *Caliban by the Yellow Sands* (1916, in Central Park), to commemorate the tercentenary of **Shakespeare**'s death; and his tetralogy, *The Mystery of Hamlet* (1949), exploring 30 years of the Hamlet saga prior to Shakespeare's play.

His best known plays were *The Scarecrow* (1909) adapted from Hawthorne's *Feathertop*, and *Jeanne D'Arc* (1906). He crusaded for 'a theatre for the people' in *The Playhouse and the Play* (1909), *The Civic Theatre* (1912), and *Community Drama* (1917), wrote 13 other plays and seven masques, six volumes of stories and poems, and an opera, *Rip Van Winkle* (1919, music by **Reginald De Koven**). RM

McKellen, Ian (Murray) (1939–) British actor, whose first London appearance in **James Saunders**'s *A Scent of Flowers* (1964) led to a season at the **National Theatre** and major roles in Donald Howarth's *A Lily in Little India* (1966) and **Alexei Arbuzov**'s *The Promise* (1967). He first emerged as a major classical actor, however, through the Prospect Theatre Company and his twin performances as **Shakespeare**'s Richard II (1968) and **Marlowe**'s Edward II (1969) established his reputation as one of the most sensitive and intelligent actors in Britain. He was a founder member of the touring acting cooperative, the Actors' Company, playing both leading and small character parts with equal panache. He joined the **Royal Shakespeare Company** in 1974 where, despite several major roles in the main theatre, he will be best remembered for an outstanding studio Macbeth with **Judi Dench** as Lady Macbeth. He led the small-scale touring RSC company in 1978 playing major roles in *Three Sisters* and *Twelfth Night*. In 1979, he appeared as one of two homosexuals imprisoned in a Nazi concentration camp in Martin Sherman's *Bent*, which transferred to the West End, and in 1980 took the part of Salieri in the New York production of **Peter Shaffer**'s *Amadeus*. In 1984, he joined the National Theatre as an Associate Director, playing Coriolanus in a major **Peter Hall** production. JE

McKern, Leo (Reginald) (1920–) Australian actor. Initially a Sydney actor, he appeared with the London **Old Vic** in 1949 and has since played many classical and modern roles at the Old Vic, in Stratford-upon-Avon, and the West End, including Peer Gynt, Iago and Toad of Toad Hall; he directed the London production of *The Shifting Heart* (1959). He returned to Australia with the 1952–3 Shakespeare Memorial Theatre tour, and to play in Douglas Stewart's *Ned Kelly* (1955) and **Ray Lawler**'s *The Man who Shot the Albatross* (1971). His best-known television role is as the BBC's 'Rumpole of the Bailey'. MW

Macklin, Charles (1699–1797) Irish actor, manager and playwright. After an apprenticeship touring, Macklin began to establish himself in London in the 1730s. In 1739 he was convicted of the manslaughter of an actor after a quarrel over a stage wig. In 1736 he scored his first major success as Peachum in **Gay**'s *The Beggar's Opera*. He was at this stage a remarkably versatile actor with a massive repertory. In 1740 he played Shylock, turning him from the comic character of tradition into a fierce, harsh and powerful figure, while keeping the stock costume of red hair, hooked nose and *pantalone* costume. It was a huge success, even though played opposite **Kitty Clive**'s Portia: Pope praised it, 'This is the Jew / That Shakespeare drew'. By 1742 he was widely involved in the teaching of actors, helping **Garrick** learn King Lear. The following year when the actors revolted against the management, the terms of the agreement specifically excluded Macklin who could not forgive Garrick for his part in it. When Garrick took over **Drury Lane** in 1747, Macklin's Shylock opened the first season. His increasing reputation as a teacher and an unsettled relationship to the companies led him to retire in 1753 to run a coffee-house and school of oratory but bankruptcy led him back to the stage. In 1759, his seventh play, *Love A-la-mode*, gave him his first success as a playwright. When he returned to play Macbeth in 1774 he was unable to persuade the company to adopt an authentically researched ancient Scots setting but his own costume was 'the old Caledonian habit'. In his eighties he starred as Sir Pertinax Macsycophant in his own play *The Man of the World* and finally retired in 1789 when he realized that his memory was failing. His plays are marked by an uncommon recurrent attempt at colloquial dialogue and realistic detail as well as a recurrent fascination with the nature of dramatic illusion. His own acting style and his influence as a teacher were heavily weighted towards a restrained naturalism. PH

Mackney, Edmund William (1825–1909) The first important English blackface performer; of a theatrical family, he made a debut in pantomime at the age of nine. Mackney commenced in London variety at the Royal Standard, Pimlico, offering a one-man show in the style of **T. D. Rice**, accompanying himself on piano, banjo, bones, guitar and violin, the last providing farmyard imitations. However, he was better at ballad parodies and topical songs than as an interpreter of Negro life and only after many vicissitudes as a burnt-cork comedian and tavern-keeper did he achieve success, when he was booked by **Charles Morton** at Canterbury Hall. Thereafter he divided his time between the music-halls and touring the provinces with his own concert party at town halls and mechanics' institutes for a public that regarded theatres as immoral. He retired in early middle-age to devote himself to rose-growing but returned to the stage after suffering financial reversals. LS

MacLeish, Archibald (1892–1982) American poet and playwright whose dramatic reputation rests chiefly on the success of one script, *J. B.* Educated at Harvard and Yale, MacLeish had twice won the Pulitzer Prize for Poetry (1932, 1953) and had written a few unsuccessful scripts before the 1958 production of *J. B.*, a 20th-century version of the book of *Job*. Besides the Pulitzer Prize for Drama in 1959, *J. B.* won the Antoinette Perry Award for the same year. Of it, **Brooks Atkinson** said, 'it portrays in vibrant verse the spiritual dilemma of the twentieth century'; other critics were mixed in their reactions. MacLeish's other verse dramas did not succeed, nor did *Scratch* (1971), based on Benét's 'The Devil and Daniel Webster'. SMA

McMahon, Gregan (1874–1941) Australian director. Initially an actor with Robert Brough, in 1911 he founded the Melbourne Repertory Theatre to stage serious drama and promising Australian works. Throughout his career he moved between commercial and amateur theatre, working with the **J. C. Williamson** and Tait managements, and establishing the Sydney Repertory Society in the 1920s, and the semi-professional Gregan McMahon Players in the 1930s, both known for high standards and a serious repertoire; but an attempt to create a professional repertory theatre under Tait sponsorship proved unsuccessful. McMahon was awarded a CBE in 1938.   MW

McNally, Terrence (1939–) American playwright. His first produced script was *And Things That Go Bump in the Night* at the **Tyrone Guthrie Theatre** in 1964 and on Broadway the following year. *Bad Habits*, a double-bill of *Ravenswood* and *Dunelawn*, was produced Off-Broadway and moved to Broadway in 1974. Other Broadway productions include *The Ritz* in 1975 and *Broadway* in 1979. McNally has also written drama for television and radio. *Where Has Tommy Flowers Gone?*, produced in 1971 at the Eastside Playhouse in New York, is often considered McNally's best script. His subject matter involved the major concerns of the late 1960s and early 1970s, assassination, the Vietnam War, rebellion, and the sexual revolution. Beginning as an angry and outraged playwright, his more recent work is in sharp contrast more lyrical and positive.   SMA

MacNamara, Gerald (Harry Morrow) (1866–1938) Irish playwright and actor in the **Ulster Literary Theatre**, MacNamara wrote two popular comedies. *Thompson in Tir nan Og* (1918) deposits an Orangeman in the Gaelic Land of Youth; the title of *The Mist that Does Be on the Bog* (1909), a parody of the **Abbey** peasant play, gave a phrase to the language.   DM

Macready, William Charles (1793–1873) English actor, the son of the well-known manager of the Bristol theatrical circuit. Sent to Rugby and intended for the law, Macready had to leave school at 15 on his father's sudden bankruptcy and imprisonment for debt. Reluctantly, he plumped for the immediate financial prospects of the stage and made his debut as Romeo in Birmingham in 1810. The bitterness remained close to the surface throughout his 40-year career, emerging often in the angry, fascinating *Diaries* he kept from 1833–51. (A pruned selection was first published in 1875.) In 1816, with **John Kemble** newly retired and **Edmund Kean** reigning supreme at **Drury Lane**, Macready was hired as a new attraction at **Covent Garden**. Poorly used there, he made little impact until 1819, when he risked all in a part that was virtually the property of Kean, Richard III, and was the first Covent Garden actor to be summoned for a curtain-call by an enthusiastic audience. He followed up his success with the first of many parts in which he could display his skill in the portrayal of a favourite 19th-century emotion, paternal love. This was **Sheridan Knowles**'s *Virginius* (1820) and it marked the beginning of a mutually advantageous link between playwright and actor. Not until 1834 did Macready first play Lear, **Shakespeare**'s paternal tragedy and, by some accounts, Macready's

finest role. Industrious and observant rather than charismatic, he aimed always to make passion intelligible. Knowles was the first of many contemporary playwrights through whom Macready hoped to raise the standards of the English drama. Others were Talfourd, Barry Cornwall, **Dickens**, Browning and, more successfully, **Bulwer**, whose most effective plays he helped to create. If the stage was to be his life, he was determined to make it worthy of him, and there is some pathos in his growing fury at others' refusal to measure up to his high standards. Well enough established to confine his London appearances to Covent Garden, Drury Lane and (in the summer) the **Haymarket**, Macready also made regular tours to provincial theatres and three to the USA (1826, 1843 and 1848), the last of which was scarred by the enmity of **Edwin Forrest** and the tragic conclusion of the Astor Place riot. His spells as manager of Covent Garden (1837–9) and Drury Lane (1841–3) had, for all their high endeavour, left him bankrupt, and he spent his last years on the stage saving towards his retirement. He took his farewell in 1851, in his favourite part of Macbeth, concluding his diary with the exclamation 'Thank God!'.   PT

McVicker, James Hubert (1822–96) American actor and theatre manager. He first achieved national recognition as an actor of 'Yankee' characters in the 1850s. In 1857 he settled in Chicago and built his own theatre which he managed successfully until his death. Although the theatre was destroyed in the great Chicago fire of 1871 and burned again in 1890, it was rebuilt on both occasions in less than a year. McVicker was a highly regarded manager, noted for the quality of his stock company and for his carefully mounted revivals of *The School for Scandal*, *A Midsummer Night's Dream* and *The Tempest*. His adopted daughter Mary Runnion McVicker married **Edwin Booth** in 1869 and McVicker managed one of Booth's starring tours, including an engagement at the **Lyceum Theatre** in New York in 1876.   DJW

McVicker's Theatre Madison Street, Chicago [Architect: Otis Wheelock]. Built in 1857 by actor-manager **James H. McVicker**, the theatre was a commodious clapboard version of an Italianate palazzo and the best theatre in the west. Although he maintained a stock company, McVicker presented a succession of stars from **Sarah Bernhardt** to **Eddie Foy**. At his death in 1896, the house passed to Jacob Litt, who tried to retain first-rate legitimate fare in the face of competition from vaudeville and the movies. In 1913, the house was surrendered to first one, then the other. During its history, it was rebuilt four times. In 1871, after a remodelling, the theatre was consumed by the Chicago fire and was rebuilt. In 1885, McVicker engaged Adler and Sullivan to remodel it and in 1890, after it burned for a second time, it was again resurrected. In 1922, it was razed and a new house for movies was erected on the site. It, too, was demolished in 1984.   MCH

Madách, Imre (1823–64) Hungarian dramatist. His masterpiece, the dramatic poem *The Tragedy of Man*, written in 1860, is a panoramic, epic statement about mankind's destiny, in the genre of **Goethe**'s *Faust*,

Byron's *Cain*, and **Ibsen**'s *Peer Gynt*. It rejects Hegel's view of history as linear progress, and anticipates Spengler's view of history as cyclical. In a dream Lucifer leads Adam through episodes in human history, past and future, culminating in the demise of civilization and of life itself. The work ends with an enigmatic affirmation of faith in the need to struggle on against all odds. Its unity derives from the alternation of scenes pitting individual rights against collective ones and vice-versa, and from the fact that Adam, Eve, and Lucifer play the historical figures throughout. Madách's scepticism can be traced to the collapse of the traditional religious world outlook, induced by advances in the natural sciences, and to the defeat of Hungary's War of Independence (1848–9). *The Tragedy of Man* was premiered in 1883 at the National Theatre, and remains one of Hungary's most enduring theatrical successes. It has been translated into more than 20 languages, produced numerous times in Germany, Austria, and Czechoslovakia, and broadcast as a radio play in France and Switzerland. EB

Maddy, Yulisa Amadu (1936–) Sierra Leonean playwright, theatre director and novelist; founder of the Gbakanda Afrikan Tiata. Maddy was educated in Freetown and also at the Rose Bruford College of Speech and Drama, England. He has made a powerful impact on theatre in Sierra Leone, where he has been imprisoned, as well as in other African countries. He also promotes black theatre and African performing arts during lengthy sojourns in Denmark, Britain and the USA. Although he is an imaginative and experimental director – his production of Alem Mezgebe's *Pulse* at the **Edinburgh Festival** in 1979 won a Fringe award – his greatest contribution to African theatre is probably as a playwright.

Maddy comes out of the urban Creolized context of Freetown. Increasingly, he writes in Krio, an urban language suitable for a theatre depicting the West African urban milieu, and bases his dramas within a class analysis. He has always written about the oppressed and their sense of a collectivity within communities which have lost hope. The humanist overview within the plays is always a complex one. The characters rarely find easy solutions to their oppression as they struggle towards a fairer society within the scope of their limited resources. An early play, *Yon Kon* (published 1968), is about a criminal who is the 'boss' of the other prisoners in the jail. Inside and outside of the prison an amoral world is deliberately created through the language of conventional morality. The drama is developed through a series of short scenes to its ironic conclusion. Another early play is *Life Everlasting*, in which some recognizable Sierra Leonean types arrive, dead, in Hell, and are organized by 'Big Boy'. The play has Sartrean overtones. An anthology of his plays (1971) includes *Obasai* and *Gbana Bendu*. *Obasai* is a quasi-naturalistic play with emotive songs and some vivid theatrical images. It is about community renewal being spear-headed by the least likely people in that community. Again there are no easy solutions, and again the play ends ironically. *Gbana Bendu* is experimental, breaking new theatrical ground. It enters into the penumbra of the masquerade and the secret cult in order to explore the contradictory paths to social justice. It is obviously difficult to write this play onto the page because it is a wholly integrated piece of total theatre.

Maddy's artistic and political ambitions are effectively realized in his two recent Krio plays: *Big Breeze Blow*, a satire on family planning amongst other things, and *Big Berrin*, for which he was imprisoned in Sierra Leone. This play is set in a compound of multiple occupancy among the urban poor. It explores the secret desires of its occupants; relates these desires, surrealistically, to the hegemony of the State; and, in a highly ironic ending, shows the immoral implications of this individual materialism. The play confirms Maddy's commitment to his independent social and theatrical vision. The title of his published novel, *No Past, No Present, No Future* (1973), perhaps indicates his dilemma. He does not have, in Creole Freetown, the ancient performance traditions which can compel new dramatic forms and a new vision – as do, for example, the Akan in Ghana. Nor has he been able to be part of the new political drama discourse in Nigeria, or in Zambia (he has tried to work in both these countries). He is, none the less, a unique and important voice in African theatre. ME

Madison Square Theatre West 24th St, between Broadway and Sixth Avenue, New York City. When the **Fifth Avenue Theatre** burned and its manager **Augustin Daly** moved to another theatre, the house was not immediately rebuilt. Four years later, in 1877, it was resurrected to become Minnie Commings's Drawing Room with an open stage. In 1879, backed by the Mallory brothers, **Steele MacKaye** gutted and redesigned the house, installing his famous double stage, experimenting with atmospheric lighting, relocating the orchestra above the stage and improving the comfort of his patrons with his invention of the folding chair. The theatre was renamed the Madison Square. In 1880, he had his greatest triumph with *Hazel Kirke*,

The interior of the Madison Square Theatre, 1880.

which brought about a falling-out with the Mallorys and MacKaye left the playhouse. In 1884, **A. M. Palmer** was asked to take over and his businesslike methods and his policy of presenting stars in imported and stageworthy plays brought great prosperity to the house. In 1891, **Charles H. Hoyt** secured the lease to showcase his own plays and eventually changed the name to Hoyt's Theatre. On his death, it was rented on a run-of-the-play basis but in 1908, obsolete and too far downtown, it was razed to make way for an office building.   MCH

Maeterlinck, Maurice (1862–1949) Belgian poet, playwright, essayist and Nobel Prizewinner (1911). This Fleming wrote in French and reached international fame through plays like *La Princesse Maleine* (1889), *Les Aveugles* (1890), *L'Intruse* (1890), and *Pelléas et Mélisande* (1892; performed in Paris by **Lugné-Poe**; this play inspired Debussy's opera of 1902). Maeterlinck represents the victory of symbolism over naturalism. He was fascinated by dimensions that make life elusive, such as mysterious forces and blindness. Only through contemplation, absolute silence, and inactivity could these be made visible. His plays are characterized by their lack of action or conflict, and by their suggestive force. Especially his early work made him, in the eyes of some, a precursor of absurdism. The mysterious forces evoke an atmosphere resembling early **Pinter**. Later work included three 'drames pour marionnettes' (1894: *Alladine et Palomides*, *Intérieur*, *La Mort de Tintagiles*), a 'classical' tragedy *Monna Vanna* (1902), a theatrical fantasy *L'Oiseau Bleu* (1908, first performance in Moscow and filmed several times), and *La Princesse Isabelle* (1935), *L'Ombre des Ailes* (1937), *L'Autre Monde ou le Cadran Stellaire* (1941) and *Jeanne d'Arc* (1943).   MG   WH   HS

Maffei, Francesco Scipione (1675–1755) Italian dramatist and antiquarian. Of aristocratic birth and Jesuit educated, he spent most of his life in his home town of Verona dedicated to the study of its antiquities and publishing extensive materials on the subject, including the important *Verona Illustrata* (*Verona Illustrated*, 1732). His verse tragedy *Merope* (1713) ranks as one of the major Italian plays of the century and was admired and imitated by **Voltaire** and **Alfieri**, but was indifferently received when staged by **Luigi Riccoboni** as part of his attempt to reform, and raise the standards of, the Italian literary theatre.   LR

Magaña, Sergio (1924–91) Mexican playwright, achieved early success with his popular *Los signos del Zodíaco* (*Signs of the Zodiac*, 1951), a play with sometimes simultaneous action in various settings of a lower-class neighbourhood. Later plays include *Moctezuma II* (1953) with its view of pre-Hispanic Mexico and an Emperor destined to fall and *Los argonautas* (*The Argonauts*, 1967), which presents a jaundiced view of Cortés and the conquest of Mexico.   GW

Maggi, Carlos (1922–) Uruguayan playwright, novelist, and lawyer. One of Uruguay's best, he has utilized absurdist techniques to uncover the social and political problems of the national situation. His black humour, sharp dialogue and inventive techniques were evident in his earliest plays: *La trastienda* (*The Backstore*,

1958), *La biblioteca* (*The Library*, 1959) and *Esperando a Rodó* (*Waiting for Rodó*, 1961), the latter an obvious play on **Beckett**'s title but with Maggi's particular vision of national corruption that foiled the great Uruguayan essayist's dream of an American utopia. *Las llamadas* (*The Calls*, 1965) decried the loss of national identity through the dehumanizing effects of television, with a resulting imbecilic language. *El patio de la Torcaza* (*The Patio of the Torcaza*, 1967) is a complex analysis of the disintegration of the national welfare state.   GW

Magic In the guise of sleight-of-hand, magic had long been a fairground and street amusement before it entered the theatre in the mid-18th century: Isaac Fawkes or Faux worked the Bartholomew and Southwark Fairs and was succeeded by Christopher Pinchbeck. During the Enlightenment, conjurers often used the paraphernalia and ambience of the Egyptian Rites of Freemasonry, founded by Alessandro Cagliostro; the American **Jacob Philadelphia** and the French optical illusionist **Robertson** played on these associations and this style had its effect on Mozart's *Magic Flute*, itself a forerunner of the Austrian *Zauberposse* or magical farce, so popular in the 19th century. (Much spectacular theatre of the period was predicated on technical magic, the instantaneous transformations of scenery and the tricks of the harlequinade.) Many magic acts posed as scientific demonstrations, like those of the quack Katterfelto, or centred on ingenious automata that played chess and performed lightning calculations.

With the peace that followed Napoleon's defeat, solo conjurers criss-crossed Europe, among them the great cup-and-ball artist Bartolomeo Bosco (1793–1863), Ludwig Leopold Döbler (1801–64) who caught a chosen card from a flung pack on the tip of a sword, and **Prof. J. H. Anderson** 'the Great Wizard of the North'. This school generally performed surrounded by the detritus of witchcraft, using flowing robes and intricate draperies for concealment. It was **Robert-Houdin** and Wiljalba Frikell (1816–1903) who first worked on a stage denuded of apparatus and supernatural frills, lending their acts the respectable charm of a drawing-room entertainment.

A fresh impetus was given by the spiritist movement that gained popularity in the 1860s. Mediums like the Davenport brothers (Ira Erastus, 1838–1911, and William Henry, 1841–77) claimed to effect miraculous escapes from knots and locked cabinets with the aid of ectoplasmic assistants; in turn, debunkers like **John Nevil Maskelyne** made an evening of demonstrating how such tricks could be accomplished naturally. Although exclusive magic theatres such as those of Robert-Houdin and **Henri Robin** in Paris and Maskelyne's Egyptian Hall in London offered a full performance of a carefully structured series of illusions, the rise of variety required conjurers to dazzle an audience in 20 minutes. Once again, touring magicians like Robert Heller (William Henry Palmer, 1826–78) and the Herrmanns (Carl or Compars, 1816–87, his brother Alexander, 1843–96, Alexander's widow Adelaide Scarcez, 1853–1932, and his cousin Leon, 1867–1909) won international reputations. Innovations such as mentalism or mind-reading (invented by the Chicago newspaperman John Randall Brown and later performed over the radio by Joseph Dunniger) arose, and there were vogues for Chinese or Hindu conjurers, not uncommonly Europeans in masquerade, such as the Great Lafayette (Sigmund Neuberger, 1871–1911) and William Ellsworth Robinson known as Chung Ling Soo (1861–1918) who was killed in his own catch-the-bullet act. Since card tricks and simple prestidigitation did not carry over well in *fin de siècle* palatial music-halls and variety theatres, flashy and gigantic illusions, vanishing acts and mid-air transformations became popular as devised by **Buatier de Kolta**, **David Devant**, P. T. Selbit (Percy Thomas Tibbles, 1879–1939), **Kellar**, **Thurston**, and **Horace Goldin**. Not untypically, **Harry Houdini** began as a card and coin manipulator before gaining fame as an 'escapologist', capable of keeping an audience in suspense for several minutes as it watched a static tank in which he was encased.

Ironically, cinematic trickery which seemed to outdo the feats of stage magicians was introduced by the stage conjurer **Georges Méliès**, and, with the decline of live variety entertainments, the more lavish acts folded. There were still flamboyant throwbacks like the Dane Dante (August Harry Jansen, 1883–1955), who updated the spirit cabinet routines, and Harry Blackstone (1885–1959) who perpetuated and perfected classic illusions like levitation and sawing a woman in half. Magicians continued to play wherever variety shows were offered; the German Kalanag (Helmut Ewald Schreiber, 1893–1963), the Bengali Protul Chandra Sorcar (Sarcar, 1913–71), and the Russian Kio (Emil Renard, 1900–65) maintained an international stardom; but in America, conjurers often drifted into chautauquas (lecture meetings of an educational or religious nature), circuses and fairgrounds. Television provided a new arena for old techniques, and there was a stage resurgence of sorts in the 1970s. Broadway, which had proved cool to Houdini in 1926 and Dante in 1940, warmed to the musical *The Magic Show* (by Bob Randall and Stephen Schwartz, 1974) in which the Canadian Doug Henning (1947–   ) performed Houdini's water torture cell in blue jeans and T-shirt and vanished a tiger; he and colleagues like David Copperfield have invigorated the magic act with 'show biz' glamour and cunning lighting techniques. Cabaret and casinos are now a common venue for conjurers: the Las Vegas-style revue makes a congenial setting for the wild-beast illusions of Siegfried (Fischbacher) and Roy (Horn).

The fantastic aspects of the magical tradition have influenced much avant-garde theatre, particularly the surrealist obsession with the *insolite*: **Cocteau**'s *Orphée* (1926) is a knowing adaptation of illusionism to a poetical conceit. **John Vaccaro**'s transvestite production *The Magic Show of Dr Ma-Gico* (by Kenneth Bernard, **La Mama**, 1973) exploited the structure of the magic act for anarchic audience-bashing, a technique more subtly and amiably wielded by **Jérôme Savary**'s Grand Magic Circus shows.   LS

See: M. Christopher, *The Illustrated History of Magic*, NY, 1973; E. A. Dawes, *The Great Illusionists*, Newton Abbot, 1979; T. Frost, *The Lives of the Conjurers*, London, 1876; H. Houdini, *The Unmasking of Robert-Houdin*, NY and London, 1908; D. Price, *Magic: A Pictorial History of Conjurers in the Theatre*, NY and London, 1985.

Magnani, Anna (1908–73) Italian actress. In the 1930s and 40s she worked in both the 'straight' and

revue theatres, notably in the early 1940s with the comedian **Totò**, developing too a career in cinema that increasingly kept her from the stage, but brought her international status, first in Italian neorealist films like Rossellini's *Roma Città Aperta* (*Rome, Open City*, 1945) and *Amare* (1948), then in **Visconti**'s *Bellissima* (1951) and Renoir's *La Carosse d'Or* (*The Golden Coach*, 1952). In 1955 she won an Oscar for her performance in the Hollywood-made *Rose Tattoo*, from **Tennessee Williams**'s play. Of her later film work, perhaps most memorable was the role she played in Pasolini's *Mamma Roma* (1962), a characteristically witty, volcanic and engaging performance in which she transcended the kind of 'woman of the people' typecasting that too much of her later film work confined her to. She made occasional stage appearances post-war, notably in **O'Neill**'s *Anna Christie* (1945) and **Verga**'s *La Lupa* (1965).   KR

Mahelot, Laurent Resident designer and machinist of the Comédiens du Roi at the **Hôtel de Bourgogne**, who compiled a manuscript *Mémoire* listing all 71 plays in the company's repertoire in the early 1630s. The document also gives an often detailed description of the scenery, machinery and other effects required for their performance, together, in 47 cases, with a sketch of the resultant stage setting. The scenic pieces illustrated, which include palaces, fortresses, prisons, shops, fountains, forests, grottos, mountains and hermitages, are sometimes practicable and clearly derive from the tradition of multiple staging associated with medieval religious drama, though arranged in a semi-ellipse around a central acting area to fit the shape of an indoor stage. Mahelot's use of perspective foreshortening and concern for symmetry, however, betray a debt to the influence of Italian Renaissance scenography and his designs therefore mark an interesting transition between two distinct staging traditions. The *Mémoire*'s index was continued by another hand, giving the titles of plays in the repertoire in the mid-1640s, and two further supplements, added by Michel Laurent and others, contain a list and brief description of the décor of plays performed by the company in the late 1670s and by the **Comédie-Française** in the 1680s. As a whole the manuscript represents a unique record of 17th-century stage practice.   DR

Maillet, Antonine (1929–   ) French Canadian playwright and novelist, the leading voice of francophone Acadia. Her career as dramatist began with performances of her unpublished texts *Entr'acte* (*Intermission*, 1957) and *Poireâcre*, which won first prize in the 1958 Dominion Drama Festival. The play *Les Crasseux* (*The Unwashed*, 1968) and her scripts for Radio-Canada led to her greatest success, *La Sagouine* (*The Slattern*, 1971), performed in French and English on national television and in theatres across Canada. In 16 monologues, the titular character, an unlettered Acadian washerwoman, reflects philosophically on the injustices she and her people have suffered. She does so in the archaic dialect of New Brunswick. *La Sagouine*'s themes and language return in most of Maillet's subsequent works such as *Gapi et Sullivan* (1973), *La Veuve Enragée* (*The Mad Widow*, 1977), *La Contrabandière* (*Smuggler Woman*, 1981), but most notably in her other critical and popular success, *Evangéline Deusse*

(*Evangeline The Second*, 1976), in which she sets out to replace Longfellow's tragic heroine, too long the symbol of a passive Acadia. A major novelist, her *Pélagie-la-Charette* was awarded France's prestigious Prix Goncourt in 1979.   LED

Mairet, Jean (1604–86) French dramatist who occupies a significant place in the evolution of 17th-century tragedy. His early work, written in the irregular vein then current, is unremarkable (if successful in its day), but in *Silvanire* (1629) he created a pastoral tragicomedy which faithfully observed the three unities and went on to advocate their universal application in a preface to the published text. His tragedy *Sophonisbe* (1634) was a model of classical regularity and decorum and its success contributed substantially to the acceptance of classical rules. Predictably he took part in the critical attack on **Corneille**'s *Le Cid* in 1637, though his later work adopted a cavalier attitude to his own professed criteria. He enjoyed the favour of **Richelieu**, being one of the five dramatists commissioned to write plays for him, and was attached for some years to **Montdory**'s company at the **Marais** before abandoning the theatre for a diplomatic career in 1640.   DR

Majestic Theatre 245 West 44th St, New York City [Architect: Herbert J. Krapp]. The Majestic was the last of the Chanin-built houses in the theatre district and like the 46th Street Theatre, it was designed with a rising orchestra floor somewhat like an amphitheatre. Intended for operetta and musical comedy, it had an original seating capacity of 1,700 which was later increased to make it one of the largest of the Broadway theatres. In 1934, it was taken over by the **Shubert brothers** and has remained a Shubert house ever since. During most of its early history, it presented a less than notable series of musicals and operettas except for the **Gilbert** and Sullivan revivals, but during its later history, it could boast of four **Rodgers** and **Hammerstein** musicals, beginning with *Carousel* (1945) and continuing with *Allegro* (1947), *South Pacific* (1949) and *Me and Juliet* (1953). In 1957, *The Music Man* took its stage only to give it up to *Camelot* in 1960. Because of its large seating capacity, musicals which become hits at other theatres are frequently moved to the Majestic to take advantage of the extra seats. A case in point is the musical *42nd Street*, which originated at the **Winter Garden** and continued its run at the Majestic.   MCH

Malawi If judged by the published script, there is little theatre activity in Malawi. Information on what is actually going on is hard to come by. But in fact there is a great deal of theatre activity in the country, particularly in the schools, on the radio and in the major towns and cities.

In the rural areas there is what one might call 'indigenous' theatre, existing as part of some ceremony, ritual or village celebration and serving the following functions: entertainment, education or therapy. Those of the Nyau, Vimbuza, Mashawe and Malombo are typical examples of this kind of theatre.

The development of the 'indigenous' theatre tradition was arrested by Christian antagonism and colonial attitudes, according to which it was either obscene and heathen or not 'civilized'. It was left to the colonial community to introduce 'civilized arts amongst the

An outdoor production of Steve Chimombo's *Wachiona Ndani*, Malawi.

natives' and as early as 1910, ten years after the country had been declared a British Protectorate, they introduced amateur European theatre in clubs exclusively for themselves.

While such activity went on, the African watched closely and started to imitate the colonial life style. Malawian indigenous recreation patterns became fused with alien ones to give us what are now popularly known as *Beni* and *Malipenga* or *Mganda* dance-dramas, which expressed not only an imitation but also a criticism of the colonial experience. While such forms started in the urban areas they then moved to the countryside where they are now looked upon as part of the country's indigenous theatre. They still include

We shall Sing for the Fatherland, Malawi.

comment on contemporary experiences, albeit in a veiled way.

It was the mission schools that introduced Western drama, not for its own sake but as a way of inculcating Christian ideas, teaching hygiene or new methods of agriculture or even as a way of encouraging Africans to drink tea. Alongside this didactic theatre of the stage came radio drama, introduced in the early 1950s. Radio drama was improvised and equally didactic – a tradition that is still in existence today in the form of two weekly programmes, *Kapale-pale* and *Pa Majiga*. The Ministries of Agriculture and Health have extension services which employ puppet and stage drama in their work.

Contemporary theatre With time the government took over the running of education from the missionaries and a more liberal attitude became possible. European literature was made available to Malawians. Through this they were formally introduced to the theatre of **Shakespeare**, **Shaw** and others. It is no surprise therefore to find David Rubadiri producing *Macbeth* at Dedza Secondary School in 1957 and Malawians beginning to write their own plays, Paliani leading the way in Chichewa and Rubadiri and Kachingwe following with radio plays in English.

The late 1950s were the peak of political upheaval in colonial Malawi. The people who might have spearheaded the evolution of contemporary theatre in the country found themselves at the centre of the political struggle. Theatre work had to wait until after independence in the 1960s when the schools, the university and the Malawi Broadcasting Corporation became the major forces in the development of theatre.

The Association for Teachers of English in Malawi started an annual National Schools Festival. The university, mainly at Chancellor College, started a travelling theatre company modelled on those of Ibadan in Nigeria and Makerere in Uganda. In addition the Malawi Broadcasting Corporation started a weekly drama programme of Malawian plays in English, Theatre of the Air, which is still running. Playwrights like James Ng'ombe, Steve Chimombo, Innocent Banda, Owen Mbilizi, Thonyi Gondwe, Chris Kamlongera and Du Chisiza have all had some association with at least one of them.

Since 1981 the Chancellor College Travelling Theatre has extended its work to include theatre for development (see **Third World popular theatre**). This meant a shift from English to Chichewa plays created through improvisation and collective research. This resulted in a mushrooming of drama groups throughout the country producing plays in local languages through improvisation. The role of the playwright is thus giving way to that of the creative artist. This development has led to the growth of a theatre that is owned by the people and not just an elite minority. In the future an exciting marriage of this more recent theatre practice and the indigenous theatre traditions may become a possibility.   CK

See: Anon., 'Introduction', in *Nine Malawian Plays*, Limbe and Lilongwe, 1976; C. Kamlongera, 'Theatre for Development: The Case of Malawi', in *Theatre Research International 7, 3* (Autumn 1982).

Malaysia This South-East Asian nation has a population of 14 million people of Malay, Chinese, Indian and Negrito heritage. The small Negrito population has music, dance, and trance performance, but no developed theatre practice. The Malays have had a lively performance tradition for at least the last 500 years, and their theatre shows a distinctive reworking of pan-South-East Asian patterns. Chinese glove and shadow puppet plays; Hokkien, Teochew, and Cantonese opera; and spirit mediumship are strong among the Chinese. South Indian *bharata natyam* dance, carnatic music, and the yearly Thiapusam festival, in which Hindu devotees pierce their body with metal skewers and dance in processions, are among notable performance events of the Indian community. Yet the overseas communities from China and India seem to have largely transplanted practices from their homelands after the British colonial rule began in 1824, and performances may be better understood in the context of those cultures. The Malay genres, discussed here, fall into four categories: (1) proto-theatrical customs (2) Hindu–Islamic folk and court genres (3) popular, urban theatre of the last century (4) modern drama developed since the Second World War.

Proto-theatrical customs As throughout South-East Asia, proto-theatrical customs, including epic recitation, poetry games, and spirit mediumship, contributed to theatrical development. The singing of epics, *penglipur lara*, is still found. Stories are based on the *Ramayana* and Malay legends, *hikayat*. In a variant called *awang batil*, the performer plays the accompaniment on a brass bowl, and in *awang selampit*, on a *rebab* (bowed lute). Such story-telling traditions may have paved the way for the shadow puppet tradition.

Songs and games may involve dialogues that become a base for folk theatricals. *Pantun* singing is poetry in which singers present memorized or newly composed octosyllabic lines in quatrains, with the first two lines creating a sound pattern and the final lines revealing the true message. Similar poetry is associated with courting games throughout the Malay world.

Kuda kepang horse dance performers of Malaysia and Indonesia may eat lightbulbs while in a trance.

Call and response singing also forms a base for more recently evolved Muslim theatricals: for example, *dikir barat* is a village entertainment, originally based on sufi chanting. Two teams of men present improvised texts: a leader inaugurates the song, and the group repeats his line. Verses can be satiric or obscene, and mimed interludes are included.

Though epic and poetic traditions may generate the techniques, the deep need for theatre may rise from the use of performance to communicate with spirits. Music, dance, and drama are generally found in the context of seasonal ceremonies and rites of passage when spirits must be placated, and, hence, most shows open with mantra addressed to the spirits. Perhaps the clearest link with spirits occurs in trances in which dancers become the medium for spirits. In *ulek bandul*, a dance of seven girls and two boys, the featured female dancer communicates with the rice spirit; in *ulek meyang*, a man holding an areca-nut root enters into a trance to the chant of a male chorus; while *tari labi labi* summons a turtle spirit into the dancer. *Kuda kepang* is a possession rite of Johore and Selangor in which men possessed by horse spirits perform amazing feats, while in *dabus* performers may dance *silat* the martial arts dance, then pierce their skin with knives, without pain or lasting wounds.

Probably the most important of these trance related forms is *main puteri*, which supposedly receives its name – 'play of the princess' – from the legend that it was first established to cure a melancholic princess. In performances, which are found in Kelantan and Trengganu, two male curers (*bomoh*), using trance dances, diagnose and then treat patients, usually females. Since illnesses are believed to be caused by spirits, the main shaman, the *to'puteri*, allows the spirits to enter his body. His assistant, the *to'mindok*, plays the *rebab*, facilitating the trance with the musical tune, and converses with the spirits who speak through his partner to reveal the cause of the illness. Clownish, refined, and rough spirits may alternate in the medium's body making the form a lively entertainment. Once the illness is identified the cure may be effected by a performance of the related female dance drama, *ma'yong*, discussed below.

Likewise, some major celebrations which involved various performances were needed to keep good relations with the spirits: *puja pantai* ('ritual of the Shore') was a three-day ceremony involving various performances meant to placate sea spirits. *Berjamu* were exorcisms whereby those in danger of angering spirits could regain favour. For example, puppetmasters in the *wayang siam* (shadow theatre in 'Siamese' style) or *ma'yong* dancers might require such rituals every few years. Although such ceremonies are particularly focused at a spirit audience, any performance genre created prior to the last century aimed to entertain spirits as well as men.

Folk and court theatricals It seems likely that the basis for traditional folk or court theatre developed in the old Malay states, like Patani, that existed in what is now Thai territory. Hindu and Buddhist thought affected these kingdoms via Indian, mainland South-East Asian, and Indonesian currents, hence the *Ramayana* and Buddhist birth tales are standard stories. The Indonesian current seems to be especially important for

Malaysian *wayang siam* figure sporting modern dress.

understanding theatrical developments in Malaysia. Currently scholars hypothesize that the similarities in story patterns and theatre genres in island and mainland South-East Asia and variance of these from standard Indian models is due to the influence of the Indonesian Sriwijaya kingdom over both areas from approximately the 7th–13th centuries. Sriwijaya's power declined, but its arts including female dance and puppet theatre prevailed in the courts of the new states emerging on the mainland. Islamicized reinterpretations of dance and puppetry may have again flowed from Indonesia in the 15th–16th century, carried by the network of Muslim traders and Sufi mystics. More recent emigration from Indonesia has established Javanese, Sumatran, and Bugis communities in Malaysia with their arts intact. The centuries of intercommunication have created similar, but distinctive theatre genres in Indonesia and Malaysia today.

The puppet tradition and the female dance drama remain relatively strong in the northern part of Malaysia in states that bordered on what was the Malay kingdom of Patani (now Thai territory). The *nang talung*, shadow puppet theatre of southern Thailand, and the *manora*, the masked dance drama, developed in the Patani area, perhaps as early as the 12th century, and a tradition of female court dance was active in 1611–13, when the European traveller Peter Flores visited there. From Patani *wayang siam* (shadow theatre) was supposedly brought to Kelantan by a female *dalang* (puppetmaster), about 400 years ago, and court dance and female dance drama in Kelantan and Trengganu developed under similar influence.

Three types of shadow puppet performance are found in Malaysia today: *wayang siam*, *wayang malayu* (or *jawa*), and *wayang gedek*. *Wayang siam*, despite its Siamese name and origin, is the unique Malay tradition, and with about 350 *dalang* (puppetmasters) in current Kelantan it is probably the most important traditional theatre genre. *Wayang malayu* is a local variant of Javanese *wayang kulit purwa* of Indonesia, and *wayang gedek* is a Malay variant of current shadow theatre (*nang talung*) of Thailand. The *wayang siam* is a shadow form in which a single performer manipulates all the puppets, presents the dialogue, and controls a *gamelan* orchestra composed of musicians playing six drums (two *gedang*, two *gedombak*, two *geduk*), two large hanging gongs (*tetawak*), two small horizontal gongs (*canang*), oboe (*serunai*) and metal clappers (*kesi*).

Performances are based on the South-East Asian versions of the *Ramayana*, called *Cerita Maharaja Wana* (*The Story of Maharaja Ravana*), but most performances will be invented episodes, called 'branch stories', that improvise new events around the givens of this central story. Tales from the Panji epic and local histories are sometimes presented. Major characters' Thai head-dresses and opening incantations, containing mixed Javanese–Thai–Malay vocabulary, recapitulate the apparent migration of the form. The troupe performs inside an enclosed stage-house while the audience watches the front of the 8ft x 12ft screen. Puppets which average about 2 ft tall are stuck into a banana log resting along the screen bottom when not dancing or fighting. The performance opens with a musical prelude, then come the set scenes of the *dalang muda* ('young dalang') section which allow apprentice performers to gain expertise needed for improvising within the constraints of the genre. The student will also need to gain magical skills to attract audiences before his master initiates him. Only fully trained *dalang* ordinarily perform the later part of the performance, where the story of the evening is presented. Of special significance is the clown puppet, *Pak Dogol*, a local variant of the pan-South-East Asian god-clown. Legends hold that *Pak Dogol* first brought the shadow play to men from heaven, and puppeteers treat this figure with special ceremony.

Traditions are changing in current *wayang siam*. The puppets are traditionally made of water buffalo hide, but translucent plastic is now sometimes used. Performances traditionally took place all night, but are now generally given from only 8.30 pm to 12.30 am. Kerosene or electric lamps replace flickering flames of old. Formerly performances were given in the context of life cycle ceremonies and were paid for by a single sponsor, but most current performances are played for a paying audience that comes specifically to attend the show. The added importance of clowning is highlighted in the proliferation of new clown characters in current performances. Wright noted two major groupings of *dalang* in the late 1970s – those who tend toward more traditional practice, as represented by Hassan Omar and Ghani Jambul, and those who incorporate new clown characters, puppets in modern dress, and tunes from pop music, as represented by Abdullah Baju Merah and his emulators.

Scholars debate the age and origin of the female dance drama *ma'yong* which thrived in the Kelantan palace in the first quarter of this century. It appears that the form originated in the folk tradition, was elevated to a court art by a princely patron, and returned with newly acquired polish to the folk sphere after his death. From 1912 to the 1920s the Prince in Kota Baru, Temenggong Ghaffar, had a *ma'yong* troupe which carried out performances as we currently know them.

Female performers and two clowns act out a repertoire of about 12 stories. The major roles are the *ma'yong* (queen), *ma'yong muda* (princess), *pa'yong* (king) and the *pa'yong muda* (prince). Ogres, hermits, and attendants round out the tale. Presentations start with opening rituals (*buka panggung*), followed by a tune for the lead actress, which culminate in the first dance ('Honouring the Rebab'). Then a scene in a palace will define the problem which takes the hero questing in the wilds. Major plays are *Dewa Muda*, and *Dewa Pechil* named after their heroes, and the Thai *The Conch Shell Prince* story, called *The Child of Raja Godang*. The orchestra includes the featured *rebab*, two *gendang* drums, gong (*tetawak*), and sometimes oboe (*serunai*) and horizontal gongs (*canang*). About 30 tunes are found in the repertoire, and are associated with specific types of character or action, while dialogue is improvised within set constraints. Though lacking in its former glory, *ma'yong* is currently preserved by troupes like Seri Temenggong, named after the noted patron.

The form corresponds to the female dance drama of Thailand and Cambodia. Three sources probably contributed to its genesis: *nora*, female court dance, and trance medium rites. The Thai *nora* thrived in Patani and is still found to an extent in Kelantan. Though *nora* supposedly began as a three-person male genre, similar stories, character types, and auras of magic power animate it and *ma'yong*. Likewise, *ma'yong* relates to the female court dance adopted by Malay kingdoms, perhaps in emulation of ritual court dancers of the Indonesian archipelago. *Asik*, the graceful female dance of the Patani palace, shared movement, costume, and dance features with the *ma'yong*. The clearest connection is, however, with trance medium forms: *ulek bandel* with its configuration of seven women and two men calls for similar personnel and *main puteri*, which today sometimes recommends *ma'yong* as the cure for illness, is a form which is clearly related. Current *ma'yong* clowns often double as the shaman-like *bomoh* of *main puteri*, recommending the patient play out the hero's part in a *ma'yong* story with the assistance of experienced actresses as part of the cure.

Perhaps drama therapy is the original impulse behind the South-East Asian female dance drama forms. Women who had healed themselves under the guidance of *bomoh*-clowns, turned their experience to curing and entertaining others. Since the forms were ways of communicating with powerful spirits, aristocrats might have desired groups of medium-wives who could maintain a firm connection with the other world. Such a model may lie behind these forms and explain the evolution of female drama in Burma, Cambodia, and Thailand.

Popular theatre Modern genres are developments of the more economically developed west coast of Malaysia which has largely abandoned traditional theatre for more Western entertainments. *Bangsawan* developed at the end of the 19th century in emulation of touring performances of Indian Parsi theatre, which played Indian, Arabian, and Shakespearian tales in the 1870s. By 1885 in Penang Mohammed Pushi created the first local troupe on this model calling the genre *bangsawan*. *Bangsawan* was the first urban-based theatre which played for commercial audiences, and the sexes for the first time mingled freely on the stage. Groups found audiences everywhere, touring to Indonesia and influencing Thailand.

The female star was the main performer, though hero, clown and the evil genie were also major roles in the 30- to 60-member troupes. Stories could last throughout a single night or be shown in shorter segments over several evenings. Indigenous musical ensembles gradually incorporated piano and saxophone. Proscenium stages with realistic wing and drop sets and spectacular effects were the norm. The clever improvisations of actors (especially clowns) from the scenario, the lavish costumes, and interludes by lovely female dancers packed the houses. The decline of *bangsawan* came with the Second World War, and post-war fighting with communist insurgents prevented groups from reforming. Only in 1972 was a government-sponsored troupe recreated, and still later PESBANA (National Bangsawan Art Organization) was founded.

As *bangsawan* passed, a new more Westernized theatre appeared. *Sandiwara*, popular into the 1950s, for the first time used a written script, amateur actors, and a director. Arising first in schools, it appealed to the Westernized educated viewers. Historical and contemporary themes were treated by authors: Shararom Husain wrote major historical plays like *The Hunchback of Tajong Puteri* (1956) about a pirate who opposed the British take-over of the country, and Kalam Hamidy, author of *To keep alive the Maize in London before Cooking the Rice*, looked at the inter-cultural problems of a Malay foreign student in love with an English girl. Though more realistic in content and production values than *bangsawan*, such plays still appeared on a mixed bill with dance dramas, and pantomimes.

Modern drama (see also **Asia, South-East (Modern)**) Modern drama has been the major theatre genre of the last 20 years, and includes scripts like *For Wiping away the Tears* (1963) by Awang Had Salleh and *Tiled Roof, Thatched Roof* (1963) by Mustafa Kamil Yassin. In the 1960s realism was the major thrust as sets showed contemporary Malay homes. Plays examined the workings of this world, and single plays replaced varied programmes of *sandiwara*. More diversity arose in the 1970s as some writers and directors followed Western experimental trends and others delved into traditional theatre for new, yet indigenous approaches. Innovative directors like Krishen Jit of the University of Malaysia, and researchers into traditional theatre like Gulam-Sawar Yousof of the University of Science in Penang took the lead. Writer Nooridin Hassan borrowed eclectically from traditional forms, *dikir barat* in *Five Braided Pillars* (1973), and *bangsawan* in the 1982 version of *Don't Kill the Butterflies*. Syed Alwi explored the life of a local medicine seller *Tok Perak* (1973) using film, slides, and shadow figures. Current theatre is struggling to keep pace with social change: traditional theatres are rapidly modifying performances to meet the needs of the changing rural population, while the urban artists are seeking roots in tradition and hoping to expand their audiences past the educated elite. The success of these endeavours is yet to be judged.   KF

See: K. Jit, 'Toward an Islamic Theatre for Malaysia: Nooridin Hassan and *Don't Kill the Butterflies*', *Asian Theatre Journal* 1, 2 (1984) 127–47; 'Malaysia', *New Grove Dictionary of Music and Musicians*, ed. S. Sadie, London, 1980; N. Nanney, 'An Analysis of Modern Malaysian Drama', Ph.D. diss. Univ. of Hawaii, 1983; M. T. Osman, ed., *Traditional Drama and Music of Southeast Asia*, Kuala Lumpur, 1974; M. Sheppard, *Taman Indera: A Royal Pleasure Ground*, Kuala Lumpur, 1972; P. L. A. Sweeney, *The Ramayana and the Malay Shadow Play*, Kuala Lumpur, 1972; P. L. A. Sweeney, 'Professional Malay Storytelling: Some Questions of Style and Presentation', *Studies in Malaysian Oral and Musical Traditions*, VIII, Ann Arbor, 1974, 47; B. Wright, 'Wayang Siam', Ph.D. Yale Univ., 1980; Gulam-Sawar Yousof, 'The Kelantan Mak Yong Dance Theatre', Ph.D. diss. Univ of Hawaii, 1976.

Male impersonation Unlike female impersonation in the theatre women dressing as men has had little sanction from ancient religion or folk tradition; it has usually been condemned as a wanton assumption of masculine prerogative. When women first came on the Western stage, costuming them in men's garb was simply a means to show off their limbs and provide freedom of movement. This was certainly the case during the Restoration, when **Pepys** remarked of an actress in knee-breeches 'she had the best legs that I ever saw, and I was well pleased by it'. **Nell Gwyn**, Moll Davis and others took advantage of these 'breeches roles', but few could, like **Anne Bracegirdle**, give a convincing portrayal of a male. Often, the part travestied was that of a young rake – Sir Harry Wildair in *The Constant Couple* and Macheath in *The Beggar's Opera* – providing a thrill from the pseudo-lesbian overtones of the plot's situations.

The leading 'breeches' actresses of the early 19th century, **Mme Vestris** and **Mrs Keeley**, noted for their delicacy, made an impression less mannish than boyish. The same holds true for the first 'principal boys' in English pantomime, and as Aladdins and Dick Whittingtons became more ample in flesh throughout the Victorian period, no real effort was made to pretend they were men. **Jenny Hill** on the music-halls and

The American impersonator Ella Wesner (1841–1917) as the dude Captain Cuff in her variety act.

Jennie Lee as Jo in various adaptations of *Bleak House*, Vernet in Paris and Josefine Dora and Hansi Niese in Vienna, represented the proletarian waif, a pathetic or cocky adolescent, not a mature male.

True male impersonation was first introduced on the American variety stage by the Englishwoman Annie Hindle (b. c. 1847) and her imitator Ella Wesner (1841–1917) in the guise of 'fast' young men, swaggering, cigar-smoking and coarse. They performed in the English music-hall as well, but there an edulcorated portrayal aimed at a more genteel audience was affected by Bessie Bonehill. With her mezzo-soprano voice, she blended the coarse-grained fast man with the principal boy into a type that could be admired for its lack of vulgarity. Her example was followed by the celebrated **Vesta Tilley**, whose soprano voice never really fooled any listener; her epicene young men-about-town were ideal types for the 1890s, sexually ambiguous without being threatening. Even so, at the Royal Command Performance of 1912, Queen Mary turned her back on Tilley's act.

After the First World War, with radical changes in dress and manners, the male impersonator became a relic, although the tradition persisted in **Ella Shields** ('Burlington Bertie from Bow'), Hettie King and, in Negro vaudeville, Gladys Fergusson. Ironically, contemporary feminist theatre groups have revived the type for political reasons, as in Eve Merriam's revue *The Club* (1976), Timberlake Wertenbaker's *New Anatomies* (ICA Theatre, 1981), and German ensembles like Brühwarm. In a work like **Caryl Churchill**'s *Cloud Nine* (1979), sexual cross-casting is an important aspect of the play's inquiry into sexual identity.

Another aspect of male impersonation is the assumption of Shakespearian men's roles by actresses. It was long a practice to cast women as such children as Mamillius, the Princes in the Tower, and Prince Arthur, as well as supernatural beings like Puck and Ariel. More ambitious was the usurpation of leading parts. The powerful American actress **Charlotte Cushman** played Romeo to her sister's Juliet and later aspired to Cardinal Wolsey. Women have undertaken Shylock and Falstaff on occasion, but Hamlet has proven to be irresistible. The most distinguished female Dane was **Sarah Bernhardt**, who, according to **Mounet-Sully**, lacked only the buttons to her flies, but according to Max Beerbohm, came off *très grande dame*. In our time, Dame **Judith Anderson** and Frances de la Tour have tried the experiment, but this has proved less acceptable to a contemporary audience than the all-male *As You Like It* attempted by the **Royal Shakespeare Company**.

Both as a legacy from 18th-century *castrato* singing and for reasons of vocal balance, breeches parts have persisted in opera, and it takes little time for an audience to adjust to sopranos impersonating libidinous youths like Cherubino and Octavian. Less successful are antiquarian attempts to revive past dramatic practices: although Christopherl the apprentice in **Nestroy**'s *Einen Jux will er sich machen* (1842) is always played in the German-speaking world by a woman (**Elizabeth Bergner** did it for **Reinhardt**), Felicity Kendal was sadly adrift in **Tom Stoppard**'s version *On the Razzle*. On the other hand, *Peter Pan* (1904), incarnated from its premiere by a series of formidable actresses including Pauline Chase, **Maude Adams** and **Mary Martin**,

benefited in the **National Theatre** revival of 1981 by being conferred on a young man.   LS

See: A. Holtmont, *Die Hosenrolle*, Munich, 1925; L. Senelick, 'The Evolution of the Male Impersonator on the 19th Century Popular Stage', *Essays in Theatre* (1982).

Mali Known as the Soudan during the colonial period, Mali has since its independence in 1960 been ruled by a strongly socialist government which has encouraged and also directly influenced the development of the theatre in that country. Interest in modern theatre did, however, precede independence; students from the Soudan wrote and performed plays at the Ecole Normale William Ponty in Dakar in the thirties, launching a taste for historical themes which has continued into independence because of the didactic and nationalistic emphasis they can carry. The Ponty play *L'Entrevue de Samory et du Capitaine Péroz* (*The Meeting of Samory and Captain Péroz*) has been followed by other plays about great African leaders, such as M. M. Diabaté's *Une si Belle Leçon de Patience* (*Such a Good Lesson in Patience*) (about Samory) (1972), S. Konaké's *Le Grand Destin de Soundjata* (*The Great Destiny of Soundjata*, 1973) and above all S. Badian's highly successful *The Death of Chaka* (1965) which is frequently performed throughout French-speaking Africa. Because of its moralistic character, allegory is also favoured, for example in G. Diawara's *L'Aube des Béliers* (*The Dawn of the Sheep*, 1975) and D. and A. Kaba's *Les Hommes du Bakchich* (*The Men of Bakshish*, 1973). The Somonobozo tribe's practice of strangling its king every seven years provides two writers with a theme that contains great dramatic potential while allowing for a heightened presentation of the moral problems posed by some African traditional values and practices: A. Kaba, *Mourir pour Vivre* (*Die to Live*, 1976) and A. Koné's *De la Chaire au Trône* (*From Chair to Throne*, 1975). The practice of child sacrifice is similarly exploited in another of Koné's plays, *Le Respect des Morts* (*The Respect for the Dead*, 1980). G. Diawara has, however, made the most significant contribution to the Malian theatre, not only as a playwright but also as a director and as the head of the drama section of the Institut National des Arts. He has made good use of his theatre training in Moscow and of a period spent working with the **Berliner Ensemble**, and has sought to draw on the traditional Malian *koteba* (dance and mime) theatre, making it, for instance, an essential element in his own second allegorical play *Moriba Yassa* (which means 'the goat's dance') (1983). In the immediate pre-independence period there were some 20 theatre companies of various sorts in Mali; just before independence these were amalgamated into the Troupe Nationale Soudanaise which, after independence, became the Théâtre du Mali.   CW

See: M. Banham with C. Wake, *African Theatre Today*, London, 1976; R. Cornevin, *Le Théâtre en Afrique Noire et à Madagascar*, Paris, 1970; G. Diawara, *Panorama Critique du Théâtre Malien dans son Evolution*, Dakar, 1981.

Malina, Judith see **Living Theatre**

Malleson, Miles (1888–1969) British actor and dramatist, one of Playfair's company at the **Lyric Theatre** who made his name in Shakespearian and

Restoration comedy, and after 1950 helped to win popularity for **Molière** on the English stage in his own adaptations. CI

Malmö City Theatre Opening in 1944, this large Swedish theatre was an attempt to realize the ideal of a People's Theatre. Inspired by **Reinhardt**'s Grosses Schauspielhaus, its fan-shaped auditorium seats up to 1,695 people, around a shallow thrust stage, backed by an enormously wide proscenium. Movable walls allow changes in its capacity, including a 500-seat 'intimate' format, but in practice this cumbersome system is rarely used, with spoken drama increasingly relegated to the Intimate and New theatres, leaving the main stage to opera, musicals and ballet. One of the few to use it successfully for spoken drama was **Ingmar Bergman**, who made it one of the most important Scandinavian theatres during the 1950s. Particularly acclaimed were his productions of **Strindberg**'s *The Crown Bride* (1952) and *The Ghost Sonata* (1954), **Ibsen**'s *Peer Gynt* and **Molière**'s *The Misanthrope* (both 1957) and **Goethe**'s *Ur-Faust* (1958). HL

Mamet, David (1947–) American playwright, one of the most important and highly regarded dramatists to emerge from the 1970s. Mamet first attracted attention with such one-acts as *Sexual Perversity in Chicago* and *Duck Variations*. The 1977 production of *American Buffalo* marked his Broadway debut. This script involves three thugs plotting to steal an especially valuable American buffalo nickel, which they never accomplish. Traditional plot is minimal; subtle character development emerges in its place. A similarly minimal script, *A Life in the Theatre* (1977), presents an elderly and a youthful actor, both on and back stage, contrasting their different attitudes toward their work. While many traditionalists have been hostile toward or bewildered by Mamet's work or offended by his liberal use of profanity and sexual language, the 1983–4 London and New York productions of *Glengarry Glen Ross* led to the Pulitzer Prize for Drama for Mamet. SMA

Mamoulian, Rouben (1897–1987) Russian-born American director. While preparing for a law career at the University of Moscow, Mamoulian attended **Vakhtangov**'s Studio Theatre. After graduation he went to London, and in 1922 successfully staged *The Beating on the Door* at the **St James's Theatre**. In 1923 he was invited to Rochester, New York, by George Eastman, and for the next three years headed the Eastman Theatre. In 1926 he became a teacher at the **Theatre Guild** in New York, and a year later made his Broadway directing debut with *Porgy*, gaining a reputation for integrating music, drama, and dance into a rhythmic whole. He staged six plays in 1928 including **O'Neill**'s *Marco Millions*; two plays in 1929 including **Karel Čapek**'s *R. U. R.*; and four in 1930 including *Month in the Country*. Dividing his time between Hollywood and New York during the 1930s, his theatrical output declined. His other outstanding stage credits include: *Porgy and Bess* (1935); *Oklahoma!* (1943); *Carousel* (1945), which won him a Donaldson Award for best director; and *Lost in the Stars* (1949). His sixteen films include *Applause* (1929), *Dr Jekyll and Mr Hyde*

(1932), *Golden Boy* (1939), *Blood and Sand* (1941), and *Silk Stockings* (1957). TLM

Manhattan Theatre Club, USA Off-Broadway company founded by A. E. Jeffcoat, Peregrine Whittlesey, Margaret Kennedy, Victor Germack and Joseph Tandet in 1970 to develop new work. Under its Artistic Director (since 1972) Lynne Meadow, MTC is 'committed to presenting the provocative work of the world's best writers' of drama, opera, poetry and music. MTC's premieres or significant productions include **McNally**'s *Bad Habits* (1973–4), **Medoff**'s *The Wager* (1974), Jacker's *Bits & Pieces* (Obie, 1975), **Fugard**'s *The Blood Knot* (Obie, 1976), **Storey**'s *Life Class* (1976), **David Rudkin**'s *Ashes* (Obie, 1976 – with **New York Shakespeare Festival**), the Fats Waller musical *Ain't Misbehavin'* (Tony, 1978), **Beckett**'s *Play*, *That Time* and *Footfalls* (1978), Bill C. Davis's *Mass Appeal* (1980), **Henley**'s *Crimes of the Heart* (Pulitzer Prize, 1981) and *The Miss Firecracker Contest* (1984), and **van Itallie**'s new translations of **Chekhov**'s *The Seagull* (directed by **Joseph Chaikin**, 1975) and *The Three Sisters* (1982). Operas MTC presented include **Brecht** and Weill's *Little Mahagonny* (1973) and Apollinaire and Poulenc's *The Breasts of Tiresias* (1974). MTC received a 1977 Obie for 'Sustained Excellence'. REK

Mani–Rimdu Mani-Rimdu is a form of dance-drama popular among the Sherpa people of Nepal. Performances are presented as seasonal three-day rituals held in the confines of Buddhist monasteries, such as those of Thami and Tengpoche, in the Khumbu valley of north-eastern Nepal. Monks serve as the actors, and the spectators, who often assemble from nearby villages to participate in the ceremony, number hardly more than 500.

The main purpose of the Mani-Rimdu is to reinforce traditionally held beliefs in Buddhism and to depict the superiority of the religion over the ancient Bon religion, the tenets of which are denigrated in numerous ways during the performance. Performances are held in the month of May at Thami and in November at Tengpoche.

Mani-Rimdu is a colourful outdoor spectacle which is remarkable for the grandeur of its backdrop, Mount Everest and the high valleys and peaks which surround it. It is thought to have had its origins in Tibet which is considered the ancient homeland of the Sherpas, and may have been inspired by the Cham and Lha-ma dance-dramas, relatively obscure forms of performance of that remote region.

The open space of the courtyard (*cham-ra*) which is about 30 feet square, located in front of the temple (*gomba*), is used for the acting area. A flagpole with ritual objects at its base stands at the centre of the area. Dignitaries and ecclesiastic authorities are provided with special seats apart from the laity. The temple and monastic buildings are used for the dressing room and for entrances and exits.

The first day of performance is known as the 'Life-Consecration' rite and is intended to bless the entire ceremony. Festivities of the opening ceremony begin around 1 pm. Ritual acts and prayers are accompanied by special music and activities which have symbolic significance but little entertainment value.

The second day is regarded as the most enjoyable and significant part of the drama from the point of view of the laymen who dress in their finest apparel for the occasion. The performance is divided into 13 separate units consisting of simple group dances and two short improvised comic dramas. The events are punctuated by distribution of ritual foods and rice beer. Usually each of the events lasts for approximately 20 minutes, partially because of the breathlessness of the dancers who tire easily under the strain of wearing the heavy masks and costumes. The second day begins around 10 am and continues until early evening.

The monks who dance and act the Mani-Rimdu wear a variety of colourfully painted and designed masks representing various deities, mythological characters and human beings. The masks are larger than life size and weigh about five pounds each. The colour and cut of the costumes and ornaments have symbolic meaning. The language of the performance is somewhat obscure which enhances the other-worldly quality of the event.

Musicians accompany the performers and play a very important role in the progress of the action. Depending on the structure of the monastery, the musicians sit near the acting area or on the balcony above it. Ten-foot long brass horns are among the more unique musical instruments. A trumpet fashioned from a human thigh bone, brass trumpets, cymbals and drums are also part of the musical ensemble.

At the end of the second day the spectators gather in the courtyard to dance and sing folk songs until the early hours of the morning.

On the third day, rituals are performed to symbolize the final destruction of evil forces in the Khumbu valley. The chief abbot of the monastery presides over the rituals and his presence helps to ensure the sanctity of the Mani-Rimdu and to symbolize the supremacy of Buddhism as a means of protecting the laity from harm during the coming months until the next public festival is held. FaR

Manitoba Theatre Centre Canadian regional theatre founded in 1958 through the union of the long-established amateur Winnipeg Little Theatre and **John Hirsch**'s newly formed professional Theatre 77. Building upon firm roots in the community and developing audiences through its theatre school and touring children's programmes, the MTC under John Hirsch soon became a model for and an inspiration to similar regional theatres across Canada and the United States. For several years in the 1960s it served as an unofficial winter home for much of the **Stratford Festival** company. The opening of its new home in 1970 emphasized its permanence and importance in the community. Although it has not been able to retain its initial pre-eminence, the MTC remains a major Canadian institution. JA

Mannheim Court Theatre The most important years of the Mannheim Court Theatre were its initial ones when, under the direction of Baron Heribert von Dalberg (1750–1806), it exercised much influence on the development of German theatre. Dalberg hired many of the actors from the Gotha Court Theatre after **Ekhof**'s death in 1778. Among them was **Iffland**. For the next 12 years Dalberg encouraged them to develop a moderate, idealized realism in acting that became known as the Mannheim style. He also developed a wide repertoire and insisted on his actors being educated and capable of playing together in a unified whole. SW

Mansfield, Richard (1854–1907) American actor-producer. Hailed by many as America's answer to **Henry Irving** after the death of **Edwin Booth**, this strong personality generated critical controversy whenever he performed. He played his first important role of Baron Chevrial in *A Parisian Romance* in 1883 after a series of minor roles in England and the USA. In 1886 he launched a production with himself as the star in the title role of *Prince Karl*. With this role, he began his successful career as a star and producer. Each year, Mansfield would arrange to occupy theatres in New York and on the road where he would present a repertory consisting of one or two new characters and revivals of his more successful previous vehicles. A compelling, intense actor and skilful producer, his notable roles and productions included the dual role *Dr Jekyll and Mr Hyde* (1887); *Richard III, Henry V*, **Clyde Fitch**'s *Beau Brummell* (1890); Bluntschli in *Arms and the Man*, the first production of **Shaw** in the USA (1894); Napoleon Bonaparte (1894); Dick Dudgeon in Shaw's *The Devil's Disciple* (1897); *Cyrano de Bergerac* (1889); **Booth Tarkington**'s *Beaucaire* (1901); and *Peer Gynt* (1907). Mansfield also produced, but did not play in, *A Doll's House* in London (1888) and in New York (1889) with Beatrice Cameron (whom he was to marry in 1892) as Nora. His productions were characterized by lavish spectacle and a meticulous attention to realistic detail. Although he utilized a more contemporary repertory and staging techniques, Mansfield was an autocratic actor–manager. MR DJW

Mantell, Robert Bruce (1854–1928) Scottish-born American actor. Mantell trained in England under some of the leading late 19th-century practitioners of 'classical' acting such as Barry Sullivan and **Samuel Phelps**. He came to America in 1878 as a member of **Helena** Modjeska (**Modrzejewska**)'s touring company. He returned to England, but came back to play in support of **Fanny Davenport** in *Fedora* in 1883. In 1886 he made his first star appearance in *Tangled Lives*, a modern domestic melodrama. A series of starring tours in modern heroic melodramas outside of New York were only limited successes until he began to incorporate the tragedies of **Shakespeare** and the 'classical' romances of **Bulwer-Lytton** into his repertory in the 1890s. In 1904 he made a triumphant return to New York and established himself as the last remaining representative of a robust, passionate 'old school' of tragic acting in America, generating much discussion over the merits of this system. Amongst his more celebrated roles were Othello, Shylock, King John, King Lear, Macbeth, Richard III, Richelieu and Louis XI. MR DJW

Mantle, (Robert) Burns (1873–1948) American dramatic critic and annalist. Trained as a printer, Burns Mantle turned to dramatic criticism in 1898 for the *Denver Times*, moved to the *Denver Republican* in 1901, and during the same year left for Chicago and a six-year stint as critic for the *Inter-Ocean* (1901–7). In 1907 he spent a year as reviewer for the *Chicago Tribune* before becoming that paper's Sunday editor. In 1911 he accepted the dramatic post for the *New York Evening Mail*, and changed jobs one last time in 1922 when he moved to the *Daily News* (1922–43). A strong supporter of the American drama, Mantle wrote in a bright and newsy style. His *Best Play* series, which he edited from 1919 until 1947–8, remains his most enduring contribution to the American stage.   TLM

Manzoni, Alessandro (1785–1873) Italian novelist and dramatist whose best-known novel, *I Promessi Sposi* (*The Betrothed*, 1840–2), has several times been adapted for stage and screen. He wrote two plays, *Il Conte di Carmagnola* (*The Count of Carmagnola*, 1815–19) and *Adelchi* (1820–2), both essentially literary works in the tradition of romantic poets like Shelley and **Byron**; they are rarely performed today, although versions of the second have been given interesting stagings by **Vittorio Gassman** (1960) and **Carmelo Bene** (1984), the last in the style of an oratorio. Manzoni was much influenced by **Shakespeare** and helped to establish the English dramatist's reputation in Italy in the early decades of the 19th century.   LR

Maori Theatre The culture of the pre-European population of New Zealand was rich in ritualized performance, generally without using impersonation. This century, Maori theatre retains a strong collective tradition, sometimes aggressively agit-prop, as in the touring Maranga Mai ('Wake Up', 1980). Many individual playwrights have recently emerged, including Rore Hapipi, Riwia Brown, Hone Tuwhare, Selwyn Muru, Rangimoana Taylor, Samson Samasoni, Rena Owen, and John Broughton. Much of their (often bilingual) work has been fostered by Wellington's Depot Theatre, which has served as a base for Te Ohu Whakaari (Young Maori in Performance) and was in 1991 re-named Taki Rua ('weaving two threads', biculturalism)   HDMCN.

Marais, Théâtre du Originally built as an indoor tennis court in the rue Vieille-du-Temple, it was rented, like other covered courts, by itinerant actors visiting Paris until a company led by **Montdory** and Charles Le Noir settled there permanently in 1634 and acquired a reputation with their performances of **Corneille**'s plays which threatened to eclipse the Comédiens du Roi at the **Hôtel de Bourgogne**. It was destroyed by fire in 1644 but reconstructed as a fully-fledged theatre and reopened in the same year, subsequently serving as a model for structural improvements at other playhouses. It was larger than most, with a raked stage offering a playing-area of approximately 38ft by 32ft, a smaller upper stage and a well appointed auditorium capable of holding an audience of up to 1,500. After the departure of **Floridor** in 1647 its fortunes declined somewhat and were sustained only by the perennial popularity of **Jodelet** in comedy and farce and by a fashion for plays with elaborate machinery and spectacular scenic effects. In 1673 the leading actors from the Marais were amalgamated by royal decree with the rump of **Molière**'s former company and moved to a theatre in the rue Guénégaud before a further fusion with the Hôtel de Bourgogne in 1680 gave birth to the **Comédie-Française**.   DR

Marble, Danforth (1810–49) American actor, started a successful career in 1832 telling Yankee stories. In competition with **George H. Hill** and **James H. Hackett**, Marble developed a distinctive Yankee character with broad American idiosyncrasies. His vehicles included *The Forest Rose*, *The Vermont Wool Dealer*, *Yankee Land* and *The Backwoodsman; or The Gamecock of the Wilderness*, but his particular success was as *Sam Patch; or, The Daring Yankee* (1836). The real Sam Patch made a career of jumping from high places. His last jump was from the top of the Genesee Falls in 1829, a distance of 125 feet. Marble made his jumps in theatres as spectacular as possible. A consummate teller of tales and strikingly costumed, he enjoyed a successful visit to England in 1844, playing before the King and Queen; he sponsored a playwriting contest for new material in 1845 and toured America extensively. He died of cholera on the night of his benefit – the play, *A Cure for the Cholera*.   WJM

Marceau, Marcel (1923–) The most influential and best-beloved of modern mimes, a student of **Decroux** and **Dullin**, Marceau made his debut in 1947 at the Théâtre de Poche, Paris. Inspired by both silent-film comics and the **commedia dell'arte**, his character Bip, recognizable by his striped jersey, whiteface and the red rose in his top hat, was adaptable to all kinds of pantomime. Starting with simple stylistic exercises ('The Tug of War', 'Chasing Butterflies'), he moved on to such philosophical and elliptical mimo-dramas as 'The Cage' and 'The Mask Maker', and with his company (1948–60) could even expand into an

Marcel Marceau in his dressing-room in the 1950s. On the make-up table is a portrait of Deburau.

adaptation of **Gogol**'s 'The Overcoat'. Marceau's international standing was confirmed at the Berlin Festival of 1951, where he won the friendship of **Brecht**, and tours of 66 countries disseminated his abstract style throughout the world. In 1974 he presented a retrospective of his work and in 1978 founded the Ecole de mimodrame de Paris.   LS

March, Fredric (Frederick McIntyre Bickel) (1897–1975) American actor. Educated at the University of Wisconsin, March made his theatrical debut (under his real name) in 1920 in **Sacha Guitry**'s *Deburau*, and followed it closely in **George Ade**'s *Country Chairman* (1921). His first major role was in **William A. Brady**'s production of *The Law Breaker* (1922). After an assortment of juvenile leads, he performed in **Molnár**'s *The Swan* in Denver with the actress **Florence Eldridge** (1926). They were married a year later and worked together for the rest of their careers. After spending most of the 1930s in Hollywood, March returned to the stage in 1938, co-starring with his wife in *Ye Obedient Husband*. Working in both media, he created for the stage roles of Mr Antrobus in *The Skin of Our Teeth* (1942); Major Victor Joppolo in *A Bell for Adano* (1944); Nicholas Denery in *The Autumn Garden* (1951); and James Tyrone in *Long Day's Journey into Night* (1956), which won him a Tony. He appeared in 69 films including starring roles in *Dr Jekyll and Mr Hyde* (1935) which won him an Oscar; *Les Misérables* (1935); *A Star Is Born* (1937); *The Best Years of Our Lives* (1946), which won him an Oscar; *Inherit the Wind* (1960); and *The Iceman Cometh* (1973). March considered the role of James Tyrone his finest work. **Brooks Atkinson** wrote: 'As the aging actor who stands at the head of the family, Fredric March gives a masterly performance that will stand as a milestone in the acting of an **O'Neill** play.'   TLM

Marcos, Plínio (1935–) Brazilian playwright. Of humble beginnings, lacking formal education but trained in the world by experiences as a manual labourer and soccer player, Marcos entered the theatre world as actor and administrator and eventually became a playwright. *Dois perdidos numa noite suja* (*Two Lost Men in a Dirty Night*, 1966) scandalized the São Paulo public for its brutally realistic treatment of the marginal society of two 'bums' who attempt to victimize society as they have been victimized, and eventually destroy each other. *Navalha na carne* (*Knife in the Flesh*, 1967) shows the brutal world of a prostitute, a pimp and a homosexual, a subculture elevated in lyrical terms through human suffering and psychological understanding. Other plays include *Homens de papel* (*Paper Men*), *Quando as máquinas param* (*When the Machines Stop*, 1967), *Jornada de un imbécil até o entendimento* (*Journey of an Imbecile to Understanding*, 1968), and *Balbina de Iansã* (1970), the latter dealing with *umbanda* (São Paulo style voodoo). Marcos experienced serious problems with censorship during the 1970s, although he continued to write, and returned to the stage as political restrictions were lifted in the 1980s.   GW

Marcus, Frank (1928–) British actor, director, dramatist and critic, who was born in Germany and emigrated to Britain in 1939. His German background

helped him to produce a thoughtful translation/adaptation of **Arthur Schnitzler**'s *Reigen*, produced in London as *Merry-Go-Round* (1952), and some traces of Schnitzler's cool analysis of sexual behaviour appeared in his first West End success, *The Formation Dancers* (1964), and in *Cleo* (1965), which is like a female version of Schnitzler's *Anatol*. *The Killing of Sister George* (1965) established his reputation as one of Britain's leading writers of serious comedies, describing how the BBC got rid of a leading radio star because of her lesbian proclivities. His subsequent plays which include *Mrs Mouse, Are You Within* (1968) and *Notes on a Love Affair* (1972) were less successful and, from 1968 until 1980, Marcus was best known as the perceptive theatre critic of the *Sunday Telegraph*.   JE

Maréchal, Marcel (1937–) French actor and director. Maréchal became known as the director of the avant-garde Théâtre du Cothurne in Lyon in the 1960s when **Planchon** had moved to Villeurbanne. His productions of **Audiberti** and **Vauthier** gave new life to these dramatists who had been associated with the Parisian absurdist theatre of the 1950s. In 1968 he inaugurated the Théâtre du Huitième with *La Poupée* (*The Doll*) by Audiberti and also commissioned a new play by Vauthier *Le Sang* (*Blood*) first performed in 1970. He has also produced work by **Brecht**, **Weisss**, **Beckett**, **Yacine** but is best known for an exuberant style well exemplified in *The Three Musketeers* (1980). In 1975 he became director of the new Théâtre National de Marseille.   DB

Margalit, Meir (1906–73) Hebrew actor. Born in Poland, he came to Palestine as a pioneer in 1922, where he joined the Ohel Theatre. His performance as the brave soldier Schweik in Hasek's play (1936) established him as the greatest comic actor in the country. The play was performed over 800 times. Margalit is especially remembered for the lead roles in **Molière**'s *L'Avare*, *Le Bourgeois Gentilhomme* and *Le Malade Imaginaire*, and Falstaff in *The Merry Wives of Windsor*.   HAS

Marinetti, Filippo Tommaso (1876–1944) Italian poet, dramatist and polemicist. Founder and most active publicist of the futurist movement, he was active for some time in the French literary world, publishing one of his first plays in Paris, *Le Roi Bombance* in 1905, and announcing the principles of the new art he championed, with 'The Futurist Manifesto', in *Le Figaro*, 20 February 1909. Three years later his ideas were further developed in 'The Technical Manifesto of Futurist Literature'. Indeed he pioneered a new literary form, the manifesto, and in the next few years many of these poured from his pen, concerned with all the arts futurism embraced, including theatre, on which the most important were *Il Teatro di Varietà* (*The Variety Theatre*, 1913) and *Il Teatro Sintetico Futurista* (*The Synthetic Theatre*, 1915); later manifestos, prepared alone or with others, amplified early ideas or extended into new areas, like *Il Teatro della Sorpresa* (*The Theatre of Surprise*, 1921), *Il Teatro Anti-psicologico Astratto di Puri Elementi e Il Teatro Tattile* (*The Manifesto of Tactilism*, 1924), and *Teatro Totale per Masse* (*Total Theatre for the Masses*, 1933).

Marinetti's dramatic output was basically of two

kinds: the syntheses, which were among the movement's best, and full-length plays, including *Poupées Electriques* (*Electric Puppets*, 1909) later adapted under various titles, *Il Tamburo di Fuoco* (*Fire Drum*, 1922), *Luci Veloci* (*Rapid Light*, 1929) and *Simultanina* (1931), the last three of which combine spectacular effects with an empty verbosity. A champion of scientific modernity, Marinetti was interested too in the possibilities of radio and television, issuing futurist pronouncements on both in the early 1930s. The futurist exaltation of machines and technology, of man dominating the natural world through science, had latent fascist elements in it from the beginning and these came to the fore with the rise to power of Mussolini. In 1924 Marinetti lauded the new political nationalism in *Futurismo e Fascismo* (*Futurism and Fascism*), became a propagandist for fascist values and remained true to the regime even in its last stage, the Republic of Salò. In the post-war years his work was understandably neglected, but in the late 1960s and 70s was rediscovered and exerted a brief, general influence. LR

Marionette A type of puppet hanging from a crosspiece or stick, whose articulated limbs are worked from above by strings or wires. The name may derive from medieval French: *mariotes*, *mariettes*, *mariolettes*, little statues of the Virgin Mary; it is used that way in the 13th-century pastoral play *Le Jeu de Robin et de Marion*. Marionettes were known as well to the ancient Greeks as *neurospasta*, wooden figures on strings; Xenophon cites a Syracusan puppeteer performing at a banquet of Kallias, and **Aristotle** refers to them as a metaphor for the methods of a supreme being. According to Athenaeus, the puppeteer Potheinos, a contemporary of **Euripides** (485–406 BC), was so popular that the archons made the theatre of Dionysus available for his performances.

During the Middle Ages, marionettes recurred both as playthings and as performance tools. The 12th-century *Hortus Deliciarum* shows two knight-dolls manipulated by cords across a table. The church employed marionettes to illustrate Bible stories, especially the nativity, and in Spain they played an important part in religious processions. The Council of Trent (1563) banned their use in church, but to little effect. In Italy in c. 1500 the *magatelli* are said to 'play, fight, hunt, dance, blow the trumpet and cook very skilfully'; in the next century, the term became *fantoccini*. In Sicily, the prolonged *opera dei puppi*, adventures of the Paladins drawn from **Ariosto**'s *Orlando Furioso*, require 300 characters, nearly life-size figures, and go on for weeks; they have been successfully transferred to New York by the Manteco family. Between the 17th and 19th centuries marionettes enjoyed their most widespread popularity in Europe, often replacing live actors. Each major Italian city had its own theatre devoted to the favourite local character: Cassandrino in Rome, Girolamo in Milan, Gianduja in Turin. Ambulant showmen used lightweight and easily portable booths. The Teatro Fiando in Milan specialized in fairy plays and even operas. In Spain the *títeres* dramatized saints' legends and chivalric romances, as in the case of Maese Pedro, whose Saracenic display was devastated by Don Quixote.

Marionettes appeared in Germany as early as the 10th and 12th centuries as *Tokkespill*, animated statuettes employed by itinerant minstrels. German and Dutch marionettes were greatly influenced by the **Englische Komödianten** (English Comedians) who toured in the 16th and 17th century, mingling them with live actors. The influence was mutual; a German chapbook of the life of Dr Faust by Johann Spiess (1587) inspired **Christopher Marlowe**, and his *Dr Faustus* (c. 1589), played in Germany by the English Comedians, was in turn adapted as a marionette show, which was seen by the young **Goethe** in Frankfurt-am-Main. After travelling through Saxony, Bohemia, South Germany, and Austria (where **Kasperl** would become the leading comic figure) marionettes came to court. In 1669 Johann Peter Hilverding, chamberlain of the Archbishop of Salzburg, performed 50 comedies and operas with figures about one metre long, and this tradition was maintained well into the 20th century. Joseph Haydn wrote music for five puppet operas (1773–8) on classic themes, sung at the court of Prince Esterházy. Such technical perfection inspired **Heinrich von Kleist**'s essay on marionettes (1810), wherein the puppet's judgement is praised for being never distorted by human prejudice.

A well-established marionette theatre existed in Paris c. 1590, around which time the classic characters Polichinelle and La Mère Gigogne were created. During the early reign of Louis XIV, the leading impresario was Jean Brioché (Giovanni Briocci) on the Pont-Neuf, who was paid 1,365 livres for a performance before the Dauphin, and had the honour of being attacked from the pulpit by Bossuet; his son François known as Fanchon kept up the business. The legitimate theatre found the competition too great and in 1710 statutes forbade marionettes to sing; they gradually removed to the fairs, where **Lesage** wrote for them.

The usual terms in England were *mammet* and *puppet* for the figure, and *motion* and *drollery* for the show. From 1562, marionettes performed all sorts of plays, from *The Prodigal Son* to *Julius Caesar* in fairground showbooths, and managed to escape the proscription of the playhouses in 1642 and 1647; when the theatres reopened they sought (1675) the closure of the puppet-shows, unsuccessfully. The leading exhibitors were Martin Powell, whose **Punch** show (1710–13) became a byword; Pinkethman, who portrayed the gods of Olympus; and Crawley, who staged the Creation of the World with a very wet Deluge.

Marionettes were somewhat displaced in popularity during the 19th century, for many of the local types – Punch, **Guignol**, Kasperl – could be readily performed in the streets by hand-puppets. A revival occurred in artistic circles in the early 20th century. Kurt Schmidt experimented with them at the Bauhaus and many famous writers and musicians created especially for marionettes. A specially American renaissance was promoted by Tony Sarg and Remo Bufano, and later by Bil Baird. The Czech Josef Skupa (1892–1957) invented the character Spejbl, a naive, prejudiced man-in-the-street; Gustav Nosek developed his alert and active son Hurvinek; the two puppets became vehicles for anti-Nazi satire, even appearing in concentration-camp pyjamas, leading the Gestapo to confiscate the original figures. The Nazi regime also put a temporary end to UNIMA (Union Internationale des Marionettes), founded in Prague in 1929; it resumed in 1959, and since 1960 has been a member of ITI.

Czechoslovakia has remained in the forefront of developments, led by Jan Malik and Jiri Trncka.

In modern stage aesthetics, marionettes have played an influential role. **Maurice Maeterlinck**'s propaganda in their favour was followed by **Gordon Craig**'s desideratum of an *Über-Marionette* as the ideal actor. **Jarry**'s *Ubu* cycle was conceived as a marionette spectacle, **Antonin Artaud** prescribed gigantic marionettes for his Theatre of Cruelty, and **Michel de Ghelderode** and **García Lorca** (in the tradition of **Gozzi**'s *Love of Three Oranges*) composed plays specifically for them. On the contemporary scene, **Dario Fo** has suggested marionettes as agents in the proletarian revolution, Takuo Endo has applied them to performance art, and the allegorical figures of the **Bread and Puppet Theatre** can be seen as a logical extension. LS

See also: **Burma**
See: A. Altherr, *Marionetten*, Zurich, n.d.; J. Chesnais, *Histoire générale des marionettes*, Paris, 1947; G. Le Bolzer, *La Marionette*, Paris, 1958; Jan Malik, *Les Marionettes tchécoslovacques*, Prague, n.d.; 'The Marionette' special issue of *Theatre Arts Monthly* (NY, July 1928).

Marivaux, Pierre Carlet de Chamblain de (1688–1763) French playwright, novelist and versatile man of letters. After studying law in Paris he turned to writing and became an habitué of salon and café society, where he associated particularly with La Fontenelle and **Houdar de la Motte** and seconded their staunch advocacy of the 'Moderns' against the 'Ancients' in that lingering aesthetic debate. His earliest published works were novels and magazine articles, but in 1720 he produced three plays, two comedies, *L'Amour et la Vérité* (*Love and Truth*) and *Arlequin Poli par l'Amour* (*Harlequin Refined by Love*), for the **Comédie-Italienne** and a tragedy, *Annibal* (*Hannibal*), for the **Comédie-Française**. Thereafter he divided his time between writing for both these theatres and active journalism, becoming editor of several literary-cum-philosophical periodicals. It was for the Italian players that the greater part, and certainly the best, of his dramatic output was provided, presumably because he found them more responsive to the nuances of his dialogue, in which young love and the self-discovery it occasions are analysed so sensitively, often obliquely through subtle changes in linguistic register, betraying an emotional sub-text, especially in the female roles. 'Marivaudage' was the term coined, at first pejoratively, for these delicate exchanges between young lovers by spectators who found the turgid sentimentality of **La Chaussée**'s *comédie larmoyante* more to their liking, but unlike the latter Marivaux has survived and is now widely performed. Amongst his most successful Italian plays were *La Surprise de l'Amour* (*The Surprise of Love*, 1722), *La Double Inconstance* (*The Double Inconstancy*, 1723), *Le Prince Travesti* (*The Prince in Disguise*, 1724), *Le Jeu de l'Amour et du Hasard* (*The Game of Love and Chance*, 1730), *Les Fausses Confidences* (*The False Confessions*, 1737) and *L'Epreuve* (*The Test*, 1740), while *La Seconde Surprise de l'Amour* (*The Second Surprise of Love*, 1727) and *Le Legs* (*The Legacy*, 1736) were well received at the Comédie-Française. He published further novels in the 1730s and was elected to the Académie-Française in 1743. DR

Mark Hellinger Theatre 237 West 51st St, New York City [Architect: Thomas W. Lamb]. In the early years of the depression, many theatres which became unprofitable for their owners were turned into movie houses, but the Hollywood Theatre, built by Warner Brothers to showcase their most important movies, appeared to have reversed the trend. Opening in 1930, it switched to legitimate fare in 1934, but from then until 1949, when the film company disposed of it, it changed name and policy frequently. Even the entrance was diverted from Broadway to West 51st Street in 1936. In 1949, its name became the Mark Hellinger in honour of the Broadway columnist and so it has remained. In 1956, the theatre received its most illustrious tenant in its lacklustre history when *My Fair Lady* opened and held its stage until 1962. Since then, with the exception of the rock musical *Jesus Christ Superstar* (1971) and *Sugar Babies* (1979), which introduced Mickey Rooney to Broadway, there have been few outstanding productions at the theatre. The Hellinger is now controlled by the **Nederlander** Organization. MCH

Mark Taper Forum Theatre 135 North Grand Ave, Los Angeles [Architect: Welton Beckett]. Rising from the centre of a cultural mall in downtown Los Angeles is the giant concrete mushroom-shaped Mark Taper Forum, the home of Gordon Davidson's Centre Theatre Group, which grew out of a professional company attached to the University of California at Los Angeles. Opening in 1967, the theatre and its company are dedicated to producing new and old musicals and dramas and to introducing new works with a West Coast flavour. The playhouse is named after a Los Angeles financier-philanthropist, who was instrumental in planning and building the Los Angeles Music Centre, of which the 740-seat Mark Taper Forum is part. Davidson operates two other theatres in Hollywood, from which he sometimes transfers productions into the Mark Taper. MCH

Marks, Josephine Preston Peabody (1874–1922) American writer, was the author of three noteworthy poetic dramas. Her first full-length play, *Marlowe* (1901), an idealized view of the poet-dramatist as revealed in his 'passionate shepherd' poem, was unsuccessful. *The Wolf of Gubbio* (1913) dramatized the influence of St Francis of Assisi. Marks's greatest work *The Piper* (1910) impressed **Otis Skinner** and won the Stratford Competition. Her piper was a 'fanatical idealist' in whom the forces of love, greed and the supernatural present a universal human struggle as cynical bitterness battles with self-denying love. Marks's success in poetic drama was outstanding; unfortunately, she wrote nothing else of merit. WJM

Marlowe, Christopher (1564–93) English playwright and poet, born to a Canterbury shoemaker and educated at Cambridge University. He may still have been an undergraduate when he first worked as an agent for Francis Walsingham, Elizabeth I's scheming minister. Certainly Thomas Walsingham, Francis's brother, was Marlowe's patron at a time when the cult of friendship was strong at Court. We have no knowledge of secret missions undertaken by Marlowe, and it is only speculation that links his violent death in a Deptford tavern with his activities as an agent. What is known is that he took his BA in 1584, his MA, after some hesitation from the University authorities, in 1587, and that almost at once he changed the course of English drama by presenting the still-emergent professional theatre of London with the startlingly original first part of *Tamburlaine the Great* (1587). There is presumptive evidence that the play was first performed by the **Admiral's Men**, with **Edward Alleyn** in the title role. It certainly became, together with Marlowe's later plays, a popular feature of that important company's repertoire. Its rhetoric, the self-proclaimed 'high astounding terms', were superbly handled by Alleyn, and the second part (1587) matched the success of the first. Marlowe had probably already collaborated with **Nashe** in writing *Dido, Queen of Carthage* for the **Children of the Chapel Royal** – the chronological order of his work cannot be precisely established – but it was *Tamburlane* that made him famous. The notoriety of his private life, which led to accusations of atheism, blasphemy, subversion and homosexuality, added spice to his reputation. Certainly he was freethinking and indiscreet. But *Dido*, for all its shortcomings, demonstrates a serious application to the playwright's craft. Like the translation of Lucan's *Pharsalia* (published 1600, but possibly completed at Cambridge) and of Ovid's *Elegies* (published 1595, but probably also student work), it shows a careful apprenticeship in the classics. Whilst the play is drawn mainly from Book Four of Virgil's *Aeneid*, it suggests a confident familiarity with the whole poem.

After *Tamburlane*, Marlowe continued to dramatize the careers and aspirations of overreaching heroes whose titanic defiance of social, political and religious taboos commands admiration at the same time as it invites condemnation. *The Jew of Malta* (c. 1589), described as a tragedy on the title-page of its first edition (1633), is better understood as a grotesque comedy, in which murderous excess and inflated rhetoric parody statesmanship and the posturings of Christian authority, but we do not know how much Marlowe's text had been revised by a later hand, perhaps that of **Thomas Heywood**. As in *Tamburlane*, interest (and most of the best lines) centres on the utterly unscrupulous villain-hero, Barabas. *The Massacre at Paris* (c. 1589), which has survived in a manifestly corrupt text, is similar in tone. Its central figure, the Duke of Guise, adopts with gusto a self-conscious villainy not unlike Barabas's. That the horrific St Bartholomew massacre of 1572 should be treated so sardonically in the theatres of Protestant England must have been shocking to contemporary audiences. So, in a different way, was Marlowe's most accomplished play, *Edward II* (c. 1592), in which the defeat and eventual murder of a homosexual king by powerful barons is depicted with a new plainness of style. *Edward II* carried the crude chronicle play a long step towards its sophistication in the mature history plays of **Shakespeare**. It is a tragedy, in which the focus shifts subtly from Edward to his lover Gaveston, to his Queen Isabella and to her lover Mortimer. Whilst each of these characters provokes fate by defying propriety, the Marlovian overreacher comes to what, in retrospect, seems to be a logical conclusion in the title-role of *Doctor Faustus*, and this sense of logic has contributed to the belief that this is the last of Marlowe's plays. It survives in two unsatisfactory texts

(1604 and 1616), each of which shows the marks of playhouse accretion and adaptation, but Faustus himself and his increasingly symbiotic relationship with Mephistopheles remain magnificently unaffected. The poetry of Faustus's despair as the Devil is about to claim him is particularly fine. *Doctor Faustus*, even more than *Tamburlane*, *The Jew of Malta* and *Edward II*, has proved its power in many 20th-century revivals.   PT

Marlowe, Julia (1866–1950) American actress. When **E. H. Sothern** and Julia Marlowe first appeared together in 1904, until her retirement in 1924 American theatre-goers identified **Shakespeare** with Sothern and Marlowe. They were an established team even before their marriage in 1911. The roles of Rosalind, Viola, Juliet, Ophelia, and Portia became her property, and she captured the critics who praised her feminine loveliness, magnetic warmth, and admirable grace. When they appeared in England in 1907, Arthur Symons wrote: 'No actors on the British stage could speak English verse so beautifully.'

Marlowe had a long and steady apprenticeship. Her family migrated from England when she was five and settled in Cincinnati where she appeared with a juvenile company and was tutored in the 'classic' repertoire by Ada Dow, a retired actress. In 1884 Miss Dow brought her to New York, secured touring engagements for her

Julia Marlowe, 1896.

in roles such as Lady Teazle and Miss Hardcastle, and (in 1986) as Lydia Languish with **Joseph Jefferson**'s touring company. Her first New York triumph came in 1899 in the title-role in **Clyde Fitch**'s *Barbara Frietchie*. RM

Marmion, Shakerley (1603–39) English playwright and poet, educated at Oxford. After serving as a soldier in the Netherlands, he settled in London, where he enjoyed the patronage of **Ben Jonson** and the friendship of **Sir John Suckling**. Marmion wrote three plays, the first two for Prince Charles's Men at the **Salisbury Court Theatre** and the third for Queen Henrietta's Men at the **Phoenix**. The chivalric main plot of *Holland's Leaguer* (1631) is less interesting than the scenes depicting Elizabeth Holland's notorious Southwark brothel. *A Fine Companion* (1633), like his first play, is a Jonsonian comedy of humours, less effective than *The Antiquary* (c. 1635), in which the follies of old age are wittily displayed. PT

Marowitz, Charles (1934–) American-born director and critic who directed his first London production in 1958, after which he worked with **Peter Brook** on a series of productions. These included *King Lear* (1962), an experimental 'Theatre of Cruelty' season based on **Artaud** and **Genet** (1964), and the first of his 'collage' versions of **Shakespeare** (*Hamlet*, 1965 – followed by *Macbeth*, 1970; *Othello*, 1972; *The Taming of the Shrew*, 1973; and *Measure for Measure*, 1975). In 1968 he founded the Open Space Company, introducing avant-garde drama by contemporary North American writers (John Herbert, *Fortune and Men's Eyes*, 1968; **Sam Shepard**, *The Tooth of Crime*, 1972) as well as his own plays (*Artaud at Rodez*, 1975) and adaptations (*Woyzeck*, 1973; *Hedda*, 1980); but their London stage closed in 1979, and the company disbanded in 1981. CI

Marqués, René (1919–79) Puerto Rican director, playwright, short story writer, and novelist. Born in Arecibo, he studied agronomy, a career he abandoned after studying literature in Madrid. On his return to Puerto Rico, he founded a little theatre group in Arecibo. A Rockefeller Foundation grant in 1949 allowed him to study at Columbia University and in **Piscator**'s Dramatic Workshop; a Guggenheim in 1957 was used to write a novel. In 1951 he helped establish the Teatro Experimental del Ateneo in San Juan and directed the group for three years. Devoted to maintaining the Hispanic traditions of Puerto Rico, he actively opposed the USA economic and cultural invasion of the island, favouring independence instead of the commonwealth status. His plays reflect great experimentation, ranging from realism/naturalism (*La carreta, The Cart*, 1952) to the absurd (*El apartamiento, The Apartment/Alienation*, 1964) to a biblical trilogy including *Sacrificio en el Monte Moriah* (*Sacrifice on Mount Moriah*, 1970). His best are *Los soles truncos* (*The Fanlights*, 1958) and *Un niño azul para esa sombra* (*A Blue Child for that Shadow*, 1970), both complex psychological works on Puerto Rican identity problems. GW

Marron, Hanna (1923–) Israeli actress. Started acting at the age of four in her native Germany. Immigrated to Israel at the age of ten and grew up in Tel-Aviv. Trained at the **Habimah** studio. Joined the British army in 1941 and later performed in army troupes. One of the founders of the Cameri Theatre. She lost a leg in the 1970 terrorist attack in the Munich airport, but returned to the stage. Among her famous roles are the leading roles in **Ibsen**'s *Ghosts* (1990), *Hedda Gabler* (1966) and *A Doll's House* (1959), Leah Goldberg's *The Lady of the Manor* (1948), Moshe Shamir's *He Walked the Fields* (1948), **Seneca**'s *Medea*, **Shaw**'s *Pygmalion* (1954), and Arkadina in **Chekhov**'s *The Seagull*, Winnie in **Beckett**'s *Happy Days* and Queen Elizabeth in **Schiller**'s *Mary Stuart* (1961). HAS

Mars, Mlle (Anne Françoise Hippolyte Boutet) (1779–1847) French actress. Daughter of the actor Monvel, she made her first appearance at Versailles as a child, then followed **La Montansier** to Paris. At 16 she was part of the troupe of the **Comédie-Française** at the Théâtre Feydeau, and with the reunification of the troupe, she was admitted with ⅜ of a share. Physically an ugly duckling she had an attractive voice and good eyes. She attracted attention in the role of a deaf mute in *L'Abbé de l'Epée* because of the simplicity of her expression, and this led to a series of *ingénue* roles, especially those of **Molière**. By the age of 30 she had become really attractive. She managed to bring back **Marivaux** to the Comédie-Française repertoire, being an incomparable Sylvia in *The Game of Love and Chance* and it was at her instigation that all of Molière's great comedies were brought back to the stage. From 1795 to 1839, she created 109 roles at the Comédie-Française, including a number of romantic ones: the Duchesse de Guise in *Henri III et Sa Cour* (1829), Desdémone in *Le More de Venise* and, not without some resistance, Dona Sol in *Hernani*. Her later roles included Clarisse Harlowe, Elisabeth in *Les Enfants d'Edouard* (1833), Tisbé in *Angelo* (1835), Mademoiselle de Belle Isle (1839) – her last new part, created at the age of 60. Mars became the model of fashion for Parisian ladies for 30 years. In her final illness the Comédie-Française published a daily bulletin. When she died, she lay in state for three days and 50,000 people attended her funeral. JMCC

Marsh, Ngaio (1895–1982) New Zealand director. Educated as a Fine Arts student at Canterbury University College, she began a notable series of student **Shakespeare** productions there with *Hamlet* in 1943, continuing to work with her students and ex-students until *Henry V* in 1972. An attempt at a more ambitious touring professional company in 1951, the British Commonwealth Theatre Company, failed. Marsh also achieved an international reputation as a writer of crime fiction. HDMCN

Marshall, Norman (1901–80) British director, theatre manager and critic, who joined **Terence Gray** at the Cambridge Festival Theatre in 1926. After managing the company in 1932, when he staged the first English production of **O'Neill**'s *Marco Millions*, he took over the **Gate Theatre** in London, where he directed a series of new and to some extent experimental plays. After 1942 he formed his own repertory company in association with **CEMA**, touring Europe and India for the British Council from 1949 to 1951, and in 1952 directed *Volpone* for the Cameri Theatre in

Israel. As Head of Drama for Associated-Rediffusion (1955–9) he encouraged the development of theatrical programming for television, and later played an active role in planning the **National Theatre**. CI

Marston, John (1576–1634) English playwright, the son of a Shropshire lawyer. Marston entered the Middle Temple after graduating from Oxford, but abandoned the law after his father's death. He made his literary debut with acerbic verse satires, and much of his dramatic work expresses his combative anger at a world in moral disorder. Marston's talent for the unpredictable is already evident in his first plays, written for the **Boys of St Paul's**. The dark comedy of *Antonio and Mellida* (1599) is followed with wilful logic into the hysterical violence of its sequel, *Antonio's Revenge* (1599–1600). *Jack Drum's Entertainment* (1600) and *What You Will* (c. 1601), also written for the Paul's Boys, are comparatively good-humoured satires of the follies of contemporary would-be gallants. But Marston became embroiled, as **Ben Jonson**'s adversary, in the ill-tempered '**war of the theatres**', reworking an unknown author's play, *Histriomastix*, to include a mocking portrait of Jonson, and perhaps sharing with **Dekker** in the clumsy *Satiromastix* (1601). In *Poetaster* (1601), Jonson gave rather better than he got. Within a few years, the volatile Marston had dedicated his finest play, *The Malcontent* (published 1604), to Jonson, and collaborated with him and **Chapman** in the lively and controversial parody of citizen comedy, *Eastward Ho* (1605). The central figure of *The Malcontent*, Malevole, is a usurped and alienated Duke, whose bitter commentary on courtly corruption is eloquently representative of contemporary disaffection. *Parasitaster; or, The Fawn* (c. 1604) is no less outspoken and probably more directly critical of James I and his court, as was *Eastward Ho*. *The Dutch Courtesan* (c. 1604), a more exuberant comedy, is nonetheless censorious. For reasons unknown, Marston was imprisoned in 1608, and on his release he renounced the theatre and took holy orders. PT

Marston, John Westland (1819–90) English playwright and dramatic critic whose best-known play, *The Patrician's Daughter* (1842), was one of many verse tragedies promoted and performed by the actor **William Macready**. Marston's intelligent theatrical reviews for the *Athenaeum* in the 1860s and his retrospective book *Our Recent Actors* (1888) are substantial contributions to theatrical literature. PT

Martin, Karlheinz (1886–1948) German director, who founded the Tribune in Berlin, where he staged **Toller**'s *Transfiguration* in 1919, and the Proletarian Theatre, which influenced **Piscator**. He is best known for his film of **Kaiser**'s *From Morn to Midnight* (1920), and for a cycle of 'revolutionary classics' produced in the Grosses Schauspielhaus constructed by **Reinhardt**, with whom he worked after 1921. CI

Martin, Mary (1913–90) American singer and actress. Martin made her Broadway debut in *Leave It To Me* (1938), in which she stopped the show with her teasing rendition of 'My Heart Belongs to Daddy'. Her first starring role was as a statue come to life in *One Touch of Venus* (1943). Three years later, she played the faithful wife in *Lute Song*, a musical version of a traditional Chinese play. In 1947 she headed the national company of *Annie Get Your Gun*. Martin had the greatest success of her career as Nellie Forbush, a native nurse from Little Rock, Arkansas, in **Rodgers** and **Hammerstein**'s *South Pacific* (1949). Among the songs she introduced in the show were 'A Cockeyed Optimist', 'I'm Gonna Wash That Man Right Outa My Hair', and 'I'm In Love with a Wonderful Guy'. The role was ideally suited to her sunny temperament and buoyant singing style, and also gave her an opportunity to demonstrate her skill as an actress during the show's more serious scenes. In 1954 she appeared in a musical version of **James M. Barrie**'s *Peter Pan*, a role she repeated in two television versions of the show. Although rather mature for the part of a young novice, Martin's performance in *The Sound of Music* (1959) was a favourite with audiences. Her next show, *Jennie* (1963), was a failure. Martin starred in the London company of *Hello, Dolly!* before appearing with Robert Preston in *I Do! I Do!* (1966), a two-character musical that followed a couple through 50 years of married life. In most of her musical theatre roles Martin portrayed a warm-hearted idealist who ultimately triumphs over the problems she faces. Her clear singing voice, winning personality, and high spirits contributed greatly to the success of the shows in which she appeared. Her autobiography was published in 1974. MK

Martin Beck Theatre 302 West 45th St, New York [Architect: G. Albert Lansburgh]. Built in 1924 as a monument to its owner, the 1,300-seat playhouse was named after Martin Beck, a leading vaudeville producer of the era. Located west of 8th Avenue on the edge of the theatre district, the theatre was thought to be too far away to attract productions and audiences, but the sceptics were confounded. Opening with an operetta, it has subsequently housed a mixture of large and small productions, musical and non-musical, and did not endure long periods of inactivity. Its most noteworthy tenants have included productions by the **Theatre Guild**, the Irish Abbey Players and the D'Oyly Carte Company and plays by **Eugene O'Neill**, **Robert E. Sherwood**, **Lillian Hellman**, **Maxwell Anderson**, Philip Barry, **Edward Albee** and **Tennessee Williams**. The theatre was a special favourite of **Katharine Cornell** and **Guthrie McClintic**, who booked the house for their repertory. Two Pulitzer Prize-winners opened at the Martin Beck: *The Teahouse of the August Moon* (1953) and *A Delicate Balance* (1966). When Martin Beck died in 1940, his widow continued to operate the theatre, but in 1966, she sold it to the Jujamcyn Organization. MCH

Martin-Harvey, John (1863–1944) English actor-manager, one of the last of his kind. After an extended apprenticeship in **Irving**'s **Lyceum** company (1882–96), during which his only real opportunities came when Irving was away on tour, he played Pelléas to **Mrs Patrick Campbell**'s Mélisande in **Maeterlinck**'s poetic drama (1898) to moderate notices and Sydney Carton in a commissioned version of *A Tale of Two Cities* at the Lyceum during another of Irving's tours (1899). Hacked out of the novel by two forgotten clergymen, *The Only Way* became Martin-Harvey's staple diet for 40 years (he made his farewell tour in it in 1939), though it was not until his second provincial tour in it that he began to make money. He established his own company around it and, like many actor-managers, made his fortune in the provinces (and in Canada) rather than in London. Like Irving, on whom he modelled himself, Martin-Harvey was less interested in drama than in theatre. *The Breed of the Treshams* (1903), written under the pen-name of 'John Rutherford' by two Bostonian ladies, is histrionic hokum as surely as was *The Bells*, and it became another stock piece in a company repertoire that also included *Hamlet, Richard III, Henry V* and *The Taming of the Shrew*. Martin-Harvey's critical reception might have been better if his wife, Nina de Silva (1869–1949), had been as good an actress as he thought she was. His Oedipus, in **Reinhardt**'s spectacular production of *Oedipus Rex* (1912), gave full value to **Gilbert Murray**'s translation. It played for three weeks at **Covent Garden** in 1912 and was the finest thing he ever did. Knighted in 1921, Martin-Harvey held on to his Victorian vision, risible to some and magnificent to others, until the eve of the Second World War. PT

Martinelli Family of Italian actors. **Drusiano** (d. 1606/8), a famous Arlecchino, brought the first important **commedia dell'arte** troupe to England (1577–8), and travelled to Spain in 1588. His wife Angelica Alberigi or Alberghini (*fl.* 1580–94) had her own company, the **Uniti**. As an actor Drusiano was overshadowed by his brother **Tristano** (c. 1556–1630), the most famous Arlecchino before **Biancolelli**, who boasted of numbering kings and queens among his 'gossips'. Owing to his domineering pugnacity, he shifted from company to company, appearing with the **Accesi** in 1601, and in Paris with the **Andreini** (1611–13) who accused him of undermining their authority. His business acumen was as exceptional as his wit and acrobatic skill, and he was able to leave considerable property to his heirs. LS

Martínez, José de Jesús (1929–91) Panamanian playwright, director, poet, and professor of philosophy and mathematics at the University of Panama. Born in Managua, Nicaragua, and educated in Mexico, Madrid, and Germany, he held Panamanian citizenship. His first works included *La mentira* (*The Lie*), *La perrea* (*The Doghouse*) and *La venganza* (*The Vengeance*), all published in Spain in 1954. His doctoral work in metaphysics clearly influenced these plays as well as *El juicio final* (*Final Judgement*, 1962), a monologue of contemporary human anguish. *El mendigo y el avaro* (*The Beggar and the Miser*, 1963) questions the false aspects of charity. *Segundo asalto* (*Second Assault*, 1968) and *Cero y van tres* (*Zero and There Go Three*, 1979) are penetrating studies of personal domination and destructiveness. In *La guerra del banano* (*Banana War*, 1974), he attacked capitalistic intervention into the banana industry with a play constructed on meta-theatrical and collective techniques. GW

Martínez Queirolo, José (1931–) Ecuadorian dramatist and poet. Winner of various national prizes for his theatre. In addition to adaptations and translations of several works (**Cervantes, Oscar Wilde, Mrozek** and others), he has written more than twenty

plays. His principal works are *Réquiem por la lluvia* (*Requiem for the Rain*, 1960), a dramatic monologue, *Los unos vs. los otros* (*Some Against Others*, 1968), designated as a 'sensational open-air encounter' in which socio-economic family differences are disputed within a boxing match environment, and *Q.E.P.D.* (*R.I.P.*, 1969) with its descriptions of death and burial by two participants. GW

Marx Bros (their preferred billing) American comedy team. The first to perform were **Gummo** (Milton, 1897–1977) and **Groucho** (Julius, 1895–1977), with material written by their uncle Al Shean of Gallagher & Shean; **Chico** (Leonard, 1891–1961) and **Harpo** (Adolph, 1893–1964) joined later. Shean wrote their act 'Fun in Hi Skool' (1912) with Groucho as a Dutch-accented schoolmaster, and 'Home Again' (1914), directed by their formidable mother Minnie Palmer. When Gummo was drafted into war service, **Zeppo** (Herbert, 1901–79) stepped in. By the time they topped the bill at the **Palace** in 1920, they were commanding 10,000 dollars a week for their hilarious mayhem. By then, their distinctive characteristics were in place: Zeppo the handsome, bemused straight-man; Harpo the uninhibited curly-headed mute, honking his horn, goosing show-girls and taking every metaphor literally; Chico, the saturnine Neapolitan, interrupting his con-games only to crack bad puns and play ragtime piano; and Groucho with his greasepaint moustache and eyeglasses, stooping lope and unflagging cigar, confuting reason on every plane. They played London in 1922, but tiring of vaudeville moved to revue with *I'll Say She Is* (Casino, 1924), with its famous Napoleon scene in which Groucho ordered the band to strike up 'The Mayonnaise'. Their next shows, *The Cocoanuts* (Lyric, 1926) and *Animal Crackers* (44th St, 1928), were co-written by **George S. Kaufman**, who, with S. J. Perelman, was largely responsible for perfecting their verbal style. With the filming of these productions, the brothers moved successfully to Hollywood, although during their MGM period, they continued to make stage appearances to try out the comic scenes in their screenplays. Not so much satirists as anarchists, they flouted normality whenever they confronted it. Their film career petered out in the 1940s; Groucho became the star of a television quiz programme and did a one-man show at Carnegie Hall. LS

Masefield, John (1878–1967) British poet laureate, dramatist and novelist, whose verse tragedies progressed from depictions of social alienation in contemporary settings (*The Campden Wonder*, 1907; *The Tragedy of Nan*, 1908) and historical subjects (*The Tragedy of Pompey the Great*, 1910; *Philip the King*, 1914), to biblical themes (*Esther*, an adaptation of **Racine**, 1921; *A King's Daughter*, based on the story of Jezebel, 1923) and religious affirmation (*The Trial of Jesus*, 1927; *Easter: A Play for Singers*, 1929). Relying on verbal imagery rather than dramatic action, they indicate some of the difficulties in finding appropriate theatrical forms for modern poetic drama, which led Masefield to experiment with Japanese models (*The Faithful*, derived from **kabuki**) and older European traditions (*The Empress of Rome*, based on a French miracle play, 1937). CI

Maskelyne A dynasty of English magicians. **John Nevil** Maskelyne (1839–1917), trained as a watchmaker, was an expert plate-spinner; he gained celebrity by exposing the psychic phenomena of the spiritualist Davenport Brothers as tricks that could be replicated. With his aide George Alfred Cooke, he staged exhibitions of illusionism at the Crystal Palace and the St James Theatre (1867, 1873) that were so successful that he took over Egyptian Hall, making it England's first 'home of magic' (1873–1904). His sketch 'Will, the Witch and the Watch', using a 'cabinet of Proteus' to effect lightning transformations and disappearances, played over 11,000 times. An ingenious mechanic, Maskelyne invented the coin lock, the automatic ticket dispensing machine, a keyboard typewriter and a cash register, as well as air-driven automata, the whist-playing 'Psycho' and the sketching 'Zoe'. His wife **Elizabeth**, sons **Archie** and **Nevil** (d. 1924), and grandsons **Clive** (1895–1928), **Jasper** (1903–73), **John** and **Noel** carried on the tradition.   LS

Mason, Bruce (1921–82) New Zealand playwright and actor whose early experience at Wellington's amateur Unity Theatre led him into realistic one-act plays which caustically analysed New Zealand society. Association with Richard Campion led him to write a series of mostly full-length plays on Maori themes: *The Pohutukawa Tree* (1957), *Awatea* (1965), *Swan Song* (1967), *The Hand on the Rail* (1967), and *Hongi* (1968). Mason also achieved celebrity with his solo works for his own performance, notably *The End of the Golden Weather* (1959), *Men of Soul* (1965), *Not Christmas but Guy Fawkes* (1976), and *Courting Blackbird* (1976). Mason's last major work was *Blood of the Lamb* (1980); several television plays have been premiered since his death.   HDMCN

Mason, Marshall W. (1940–) American director and a co-founder and the current artistic director of the **Circle Repertory Company** in New York. Trained at the **Actors Studio**, Mason specializes in the production of new American plays, especially those of **Lanford Wilson** (most notably *The Hot l Baltimore*, 1973; *Fifth of July*, 1978; *Talley's Folly*, 1979; and *Angels Fall*, 1983). In 1985 his award-winning Circle Rep production of William M. Hoffman's *As Is*, one of the first American plays to deal with the disease AIDS, was transferred to Broadway. He is the recipient of an Obie Award for Sustained Achievement.   DBW

Masque It is not difficult to trace the derivation of the English masque from the rituals devised to celebrate the presence of welcome visitors in a resident community. Such rituals involved the ceremonial distribution of gifts and concluded with a dance in which guests joined with their hosts. Already formalized in the elaborate disguisings of the 15th- and 16th-century courts, these rituals became increasingly the pretext for display, in which music and dance were punctuated by florid speeches and rivalled by lavish costume and inventive masks. During the latter half of the 16th century, these masks were sufficiently notable to give their name to the ceremonies they adorned. It was not, however, an idle whim of **Ben Jonson**'s to prefer the French spelling, 'masque', to the English, since the court entertainments which he and **Inigo Jones** provided for

James I owed much to the continental precedent. It was from his travels in France and Italy that Jones developed an interest in the scenes and machines which distinguished his work on Jacobean and Caroline masques. The famous collaboration of Jonson and Jones lasted, despite differences, from 1605–34, and included *The Masque of Blackness* (1605), *Oberon, the Faery Prince* (1611) and *Pleasure Reconciled to Virtue* (1618) among its particular splendours. The musician Thomas Campion was another notable exponent of the masque, as, after Jonson's angry severance from Jones, were **Shirley** and **Davenant**. Charles I and his Queen were greater devotees even than James I, and it was for them that Jones designed the Whitehall Masquing House (1637). The court masque, still characterized by dance, music, lavish costume and measured poetry, was embellished at the Stuart court by Jones's perspective scenery (viewed perfectly only from the monarch's central throne) and varied by the excitement of his mechanical scene changes, movable shutters and occasional scenes in relief. For *The Masque of Queens* (1609), Jonson introduced the boisterous contrast of anti-masque, in which the urgent need for harmony was signalled by the enactment of disharmony. The public theatres could not rival the splendours of the court masque, but there are many examples of masques used as devices within plays, often to startling effect, as in **Kyd**'s *The Spanish Tragedy* (c. 1589), **Tourneur**'s *The Revenger's Tragedy* (c. 1606) and **Middleton**'s *Women Beware Women* (c. 1625). The English court masque was brought to a sudden end by the outbreak of the Civil War, and its significant influence is recognizable only in such scenic innovations as the proscenium arch, changeable scenery and the further deployment of stage machinery.   PT

Massey, Raymond Hart (1896–1983) Canadian-born actor and director who became a United States citizen in 1944. From 1922, when he made his debut in London as Jack in **O'Neill**'s *In the Zone* at the Everyman Theatre, until 1931, when he made his Broadway debut in **Bel Geddes**'s unorthodox production of *Hamlet*, he acted in England in several dozen plays and directed numerous others. Subsequently his career, largely limited to the United States, ranged from **Shakespeare**, **Strindberg**, **Shaw**, **O'Casey** and O'Neill in the theatre, to a wide range of villains and heroes in films (over 70), and the role of Dr Gillespie in the television series *Dr Kildare*. His most memorable role was Lincoln in **Robert Sherwood**'s *Abe Lincoln in Illinois* (1938), which suited his imposing presence, craggy handsomeness, and vibrant voice. Other notable roles included: Ethan Frome in an adaptation of the novel (1936), Harry Van in *Idiot's Delight* (1938), Sir Colenso Ridgeon in *The Doctor's Dilemma* (1941), James Morell in *Candida* (1942), Higgins in *Pygmalion* (1945), Mr Zuss in *J. B.* (1958), and Tom Garrison in *I Never Sang for My Father* (his return to the London stage in 1970). Massey was the author of two autobiographies, *When I Was Young* (1976) and *A Hundred Different Lives* (1979). His children Daniel and Anna, born in England, have had successful careers in the theatre.   DBW

Massinger, Philip (1583–1640) English playwright, uncommonly prolific both collaboratively and singly.

Massinger's father was an agent to the Earl of Pembroke, prosperous enough to send his son to Oxford, which he left without a degree. He settled in London in 1606 and may have earned his living as an actor. The first reference to his writing – in **Henslowe**'s *Diary* – dates from 1613, and his earliest known plays, *The Queen of Corinth* and *The Knight of Malta* (both c. 1617), were collaborations with **Fletcher** and **Nathan Field**. He was to work with Fletcher regularly until the latter's death in 1625. About 15 of the plays once ascribed to **Beaumont** and Fletcher are, in fact, the work of Fletcher and Massinger. They include *The Custom of the Country* (c. 1619), *Sir John Van Olden Barnavelt* (1619), *The False One* (c. 1620), *The Double Marriage* (c. 1621), *The Spanish Curate* (c. 1622), *The Beggar's Bush*, *The Sea Voyage* and *The Prophetess* (all 1622). These were written for performance by the King's Men, with whom Massinger had a nearly continuous association from 1613–40. He was a man of strong views, savage against the new rich of the city and bold enough to risk sympathetic portraits of Catholics in *The Virgin Martyr* (c. 1620), a collaboration with **Dekker**, and, most notably, in *The Renegado* (1624). *The Maid of Honour* (c. 1621) dared to attack the Elector Palatine and *The Bondman* (1623) satirized the powerful Duke of Buckingham, whilst the anti-Spanish *Believe As You List* (1631) was licensed only after considerable cosmetic alterations. Massinger's own favourite among his works was *The Roman Actor* (1626), an ambitious tragedy about the Emperor Domitian, which has proved less durable than *A New Way to Pay Old Debts* (c. 1621), a comedy based on **Middleton**'s *A Trick to Catch the Old One*, and *The City Madam* (c. 1632), a reworking of *Eastward Ho* whose original authors, **Chapman**, **Jonson** and **Marston**, had infuriated the newly crowned James I. Both plays gain their peculiar power from Massinger's creation of central characters, respectively Sir Giles Overreach and Luke Frugal, whose monstrous appetites threaten to divert comic harmony into tragic chaos. Overreach was brilliantly played in the 19th century by **Edmund Kean** and in the 20th by **Donald Wolfit**.   PT

Master of the Revels This title for the official of the Royal household responsible for the King's entertainment was first used in 1494, under Henry VII of England. The first permanent Master was Sir Thomas Cawarden (1545–59), under whom the office became formally concerned with censorship. The notoriously idle Sir Edmund Tilney, Master from 1579–1610, enjoyed the revenue for reading new plays and licensing theatres, respectively 7 shillings per text and £3 per month by 1600, and was, in effect if not in effort, the controller of London's theatrical life. He was succeeded by his nephew, Sir George Buck (1610–22), who took the job more seriously than his uncle. It was he who banned the publication of **Chapman**'s *Byron* plays, eliciting from the playwright an angry complaint about 'Illiterate Authority' that 'sets up his Bristles against Poverty'. After Buck's death, Sir Henry Herbert (1596–1673) thought the Mastership of the Revels worth a purchase-price of £150. Herbert was an intelligent and ambitious man. His office-books have been lost, but collected passages were published in 1917, and they provide important information about the conduct of the theatre during his 50 years (broken by the Interregnum) as Master of the Revels. Herbert received £2 for each play he licensed (£1 for a revival) as well as regular payments from the managers of London's theatres. He retained formal responsibility for entertainments at Court and no theatre would willingly risk his displeasure. After the restoration of Charles II, Herbert failed in his attempts to maintain the power of his office. He was succeeded, after his death, by **Thomas Killigrew**, already a manager of one of London's two patented companies and therefore occupationally committed to the restraint of rival theatres. It was the activity of an unlicensed theatre that brought about the Licensing Act of 1737, which lodged with the Lord Chamberlain the responsibility for the censorship of the drama and effectively terminated the Mastership of the Revels.   PT

Mathews, Charles (1776–1835) English actor who owed most of his contemporary fame to his gift for mimicry. He made his professional debut in Dublin in 1794 and was a leading low comedian with **Tate Wilkinson** on the York circuit from 1798–1802, after which he was engaged by **George Colman the Younger** for the **Haymarket** in London. Less troubled than Wilkinson had been by Mathew's lopsided mouth, Colman wrote parts to suit his new comedian. His double-act with **John Liston** was particularly popular – Mathews playing the rapid, quick-thinking comic and Liston the slow, gullible one. He was already popular enough to take his pick of **Covent Garden** or **Drury Lane** in the winter months, using the summer to play at the smaller Haymarket or tour the provinces, when he decided to test out the idea, learned from Jack Bannister, of a one-man entertainment. *The Mail Coach Adventure* (1808), in which his second wife played a small part, was tried out in Hull and repeated on provincial tours for the next two seasons. From 1811–12, he toured a second show, *The Travellers*, this time with the singer Charles Incledon, and then, from 1813–17, a reshaped *Mail Coach Adventure* for himself alone. This evolved into the famous series under the title *Mr Mathews At Home* which were an annual feature of his acting year from 1818 until his last months, the lameness resulting from a coaching

Charles Mathews Sr as the Old Scotch Lady.

accident in 1814 notwithstanding. A combination of mimicry, story-telling, quick-change artistry, comic songs and improvisation, they were equally popular in England and the USA, which Mathews toured in 1822–3 and 1834.   PT

Mathews, Charles James (1803–78) English actor, the son of **Charles Mathews**. He trained as an architect and became an actor only after his father's death. Having written some of the material for his father's *At Homes*, he wrote, or helped to write, over 30 dramatic pieces, of which *Patter versus Clatter* (1838) was the most successful. It allowed him to express his versatility as an actor in five contrasting parts. He had made his debut at the **Olympic** in 1835 and quickly became a popular member of the excellent company there. The manager was **Madame Vestris**, whom Mathews married in 1838, the year in which they toured the theatres of New York and Philadelphia. Together they managed **Covent Garden** (1839–42), where **Boucicault**'s *London Assurance* (1841) provided Mathews with one of his most characteristic parts as the light-tongued Dazzle. He was a new style of gentleman-comedian, relaxed and urbane, who spoke his lines without the conventional histrionic pauses. Contemporary audiences heard it as a rapid rattle and named it 'patter' after the character in which he regularly appeared. Boucicault would later provide him (though Mathews claimed the credit for much of the writing) with another favourite part, as Sir Charles Coldstream in *Used Up* (1844). The Covent Garden management ended in bankruptcy and a brief imprisonment for debt. The story at the **Lyceum** (1847–55) was similar. Madame Vestris died in 1856, a few days after her improvident husband's release from a second term of imprisonment. He found his salvation in a second American tour (1857–8), which culminated in a second marriage, this time to a woman of means. Mathews combined acting with

Charles Mathews Jr as Sir Charles Coldstream in *Used Up*.

writing and travelling for the rest of his life. His autobiography was completed and edited by Charles Dickens Jr (1879).   PT

Matkowsky, Adalbert (1857–1909) German actor. Matkowsky began his career in 1877 at the **Dresden Court Theatre**; then, after a few years spent in Hamburg, he was hired in 1889 by the **Berlin Royal Theatre**. He stayed here until his death. Matkowsky had a herculean stage presence that best suited roles such as Coriolanus, Macbeth, and Karl Moor. He was widely regarded by contemporaries as the last 'romantic' actor.   SW

Matthews, (James) Brander (1852–1929) American educator, scholar, critic, and playwright. Born in New Orleans to wealthy parents, Matthews grew up in New York and was educated at Columbia University. He entered Law School in 1871 but became more interested in French drama, and in writing novels and plays. From 1875 to 1895, he wrote for the *Nation*; in 1878 he penned his first original play, *Margery's Lovers*; and from 1891 until his retirement in 1924, he taught drama at Columbia. In 1902 he was given the title of Professor of Dramatic Literature, the first such post in American universities. His wide knowledge of French, English, and American theatre is reflected in his 24 books; the best known are *The French Dramatists of the Nineteenth Century* (1882); *Development of the Drama* (1903), and *Principles of Playmaking* (1919). His position that a play is intended primarily to be performed rather than read, brought credibility to theatre as an academic subject.   TLM

Maugham, (William) Somerset (1874–1965) British novelist and playwright. Qualified as a surgeon, his early light comedies from *Marriages Are Made in Heaven* (staged in Berlin, 1899) and *A Man of Honour* (produced by the **Stage Society**, 1903) to *Caroline* (performed as *The Unattainable*, 1916) reflect his view that drama was a craft on the order of woodcarving or dancing, rather than an art. Designed to appeal to a wide audience, their tight construction, wit and unpretentious absence of any serious theme was so successful that in 1908 he had four plays running simultaneously in London: *Lady Frederick*, *Mrs Dot*, *Jack Straw* and *The Explorer*. With *Our Betters* (1917), in which adultery reveals apparent upper-class respectability as an empty facade, Maugham's comedy began to focus on social issues; and his masterpiece *The Circle* (1921) deals with repeated behaviour patterns over two generations, setting up expectations in the satiric depiction of manners and using ironic reversal to expose the gap between conventional morality and personal fulfilment. The combination of cynicism and polished wit in these plays has been not unjustifiably compared to **Wycherley** and **Congreve**. However, this serious commentary on sexual relationships, continued in *The Constant Wife* (1926) or *The Breadwinner* (1930), was extended into less comfortable and unconventional areas like miscegenation (*East of Suez*, 1922) or arguments for euthanasia (*The Sacred Flame*, 1928). His work became increasingly didactic, and after the failure of *Sheppey* (1933), which portrays the martyrdom of a common man who is condemned as insane when he attempts to live according to Christ's teaching,

Maugham abandoned drama in disgust at the public response to his plays. Although his reputation as a dramatist may have declined, the serious comedies of his middle period are frequently revived since **Gielgud**'s production of *The Circle* in his outstanding 1944–5 season at the **Haymarket Theatre**.   CI

Maunder, Paul (1945–) New Zealand playwright, actor, and director. Amamus Theatre, founded by Maunder and others in 1971, specialized in group-developed scripts and, touring from Wellington through the 1970s, was the major force in New Zealand group theatre. The major achievement of its last years was *Song of a Kiwi* (1977) which, like much Amamus material, was developed over several years. Amamus has since evolved into Theatre of the Eighth Day, also directed by Maunder, staging *Electra* (*Thoughts during the Tour*) in 1982 and in 1984 the bilingual *Encounter at Te Puna*, dealing with Maori reactions to the first Europeans.   HDMCN

Mauritius Mauritius, independent since 1968, is situated in the south-west of the Indian Ocean, about 500 miles east of Madagascar. During French rule (1722–1810) slaves were brought in from Africa and when slavery was abolished (1834) under British rule (1810–1968) indentured labourers were brought in from India. The population (1 million) is multi-ethnic and multi-lingual. English is the official language, French is semi-official; there are several ancestral languages of Asian origin and Creole is the national language.

Formal and non-formal theatre has always been an integral part of the cultural scene. The slaves from Africa brought with them a type of happening known as *Sega*, the immigrants from India came with their folk drama, and the Europeans at a very early stage of settlement showed their interest in formal theatre. According to the historian, Antoine Chelin, the first theatre building was fitted up in 1754. From then onwards theatrical activities with a heavy bias towards lyrical drama, performed by French artists for a francophone elite, thrived. Although Mauritius was formally ceded to Britain in 1814, the first English play was staged in 1823. It is only in 1932 with the founding of the Mauritius Dramatic Club that theatre in English really started to develop.

Zozef ek so palto larkansiel, a Creole adaptation of *Joseph and the Amazing Technicolour Dreamcoat*, Mauritius, 1982.

We have to wait for the late 1930s to see the emergence of notable Mauritian performing artists like Amédée Poupard, Max Moutia, Yves Forget and others. During the Second World War, as a result of shortage of films from India, a new form of entertainment in Hindustani was created: 'Natak' (Dance drama).

The post-war and pre-independence period saw the development of new trends. Firstly several local writers tried their hands at play-writing in French and Hindi. Secondly, since the organization of the first Youth Drama Festival in 1951, the interest in theatre activities substantially increased to reach a much wider audience and to motivate young talents. Another boost came with the founding of the Société des Metteurs en Scène (1966).

In the post-independence period local writers in different languages now reach an even wider audience through the stage, radio and television. The Youth Drama Festival which originally accepted only entries in English is now open to all languages of Mauritius. The most spectacular event is perhaps the rise of Creole as a powerful vehicle of dramatic expression.

Non-formal theatrical activities are still very much alive on important occasions such as weddings, anniversaries, campings, end of the year parties.

Formal theatrical activities are today a very dynamic element of Mauritian cultural life thanks to the contributions of, to mention only a few, Guy Lagesse, Gérard Sullivan, Serge Constantin, Harry Saminaden, Siva Appasamy, Azize Asgarally, Henri Favory, Dev Virahsawmy, Raj Bumma, Abhimanyu Unnuth, the Natraj Group, the Mauritius Drama League.   DV

See: A. Chelin, *Le Théâtre à l'Ile Maurice*, Mauritius, 1954; G. A. Decotter, *Le Plaza*, Rose-Hill, Mauritius, 1983.

Mayakovsky,   Vladimir   Vladimirovich (1893–1930) Grandiloquent Soviet futurist poet and dramatist, the self-dramatizing 'loud-mouthed Zarathustra' of his day. His noisy hooliganism and eccentric individualism served an intellectual anarchism which hopefully forecast a new age of freedom. A Georgian by birth and a Bolshevik from 1908, Mayakovsky co-signed the futurist manifesto *A Slap in the Face of Public Taste* (1912) with his 'real teacher', painter-poet David Burlyuk, and launched his literary career. In his poetry, which includes *Me* (his first collection, 1913) and the narrative poems *A Cloud in Trousers* (1915), *The Backbone Flute* (1915), *War and Peace* (1916) and *Man* (1917), he cultivated a concrete, unpoetic, dissonant style of writing, consisting of staccato rhythms and coarsely colloquial speech. This was meant to counteract the refinement of the previous generation's symbolism and to embody the Russian futurist poetic. The poems likewise manifested soon-to-be familiar Mayakovskian themes: love's pain and disappointment; the poet's loneliness and alienation from the bourgeois world; the concordance of art, religion and revolution. Although he never officially joined the Communist Party, never read Lenin's works (Lenin in turn found his art to be incomprehensible) and was on easy terms with **Gorky**, Mayakovsky, in his *Directive to the Army of Art* (1918), called for futurism to join forces with Bolshevism. In the latter he saw the faith in man as conqueror of history and nature, the breakage with the

Set design by K. S. Malevich for Mayakovsky's carnivalesque political allegory, *Mystery–Bouffe*, 1918/21. Pictured is the earth, and the proletarian (Unclean) and bourgeois (Clean) survivalists who have fled it.

past and sense of moment which the futurists extolled. Throughout the 1920s Mayakovsky created effective propagandist art: verse-captioned cartoons (*Windows of the Russian Telegraph Agency*, 1919); poetry (*Left March*, 1919; *Vladimir Ilyich Lenin*, 1924); advertising jingles for state stores (1923–5); the avant-garde journals *Lef* (1923–5) and *New Lef* (1927–8); and a series of plays and playlets mixing Russian folk idioms and Party slogans, moving-poster imagery, farcical and circus techniques – *And What If? ... May First Daydreams in a Bourgeois Armchair*, *A Small Play About Priests who Do Not Understand What Is Meant by the Holiday*, *How Some People Spend Time Celebrating Holidays*, *The Championship of the Universal Class Struggle* (all written 1920) and *Moscow Is Burning* (1930). His major dramatic works embody Mayakovsky's preoccupation with time and its effects on personality (primarily his own), socio-political structures and the fate of the human race. *Vladimir Mayakovsky, A Tragedy* (1913), which he produced and acted in (on a programme with the futurist opera *Victory Over the Sun*), is a monodrama depicting the transformation of the author as solitary artistic genius into saviour of the people. It reflects the recurring Mayakovsky-as-Christ theme, the author's interest in cinema (he wrote 13 film scenarios) and the influence of **Evreinov**. *Mystery-Bouffe* (1918, revised version 1921) is a neo-mystery-fantasy-satire in which the people establish paradise on earth. The premiere production was co-directed by Mayakovsky and **Meyerhold** and designed by Malevich. His two greatest plays, *The Bedbug* (1929) and *The Bathhouse* (1930), are Gogolian social satires which sharply criticize the petty bourgeoisie and the communist bureaucracy and grotesquely parody the promised future utopia, while expressing nostalgia for the romantic revolutionary past. Both plays were given coolly-received theatricalist stagings by Meyerhold at his Moscow theatre, a fact which may have contributed, along with the author's disappointment in love and in the course that the Revolution had taken, to Mayakovsky's suicide in 1930. Stalin's rehabilitation of the poet in 1935 led to the republication of work banned since 1930. Until 1954 he was glorified as the 'drummer of the Revolution', but since de-Stalinization he has been admired for his artistic merit.   SG

Mayfest Mayfest (1983 to the present day) presents a programme of international popular music and drama in Glasgow during the first two weeks of May each year.   LM

Mayne, Rutherford Pseudonym of Samuel Waddell (1878–1967), a successful **Ulster Literary Theatre** actor and playwright. Except for *Peter* (1930), the action largely its protagonist's dream, Mayne's plays are much of their period, influenced by his experiences with the Land Commission. *The Troth* (1909) and *Red Turf* (1911) turn on landlordism and land rivalry. *The Drone* (1908) was probably the most popular Ulster comedy of its time.   DM

Mayo, Frank (1839–96) American actor and manager. Born and educated in Boston, Mayo made his stage debut in 1856 at the American Theatre in San Francisco; served as leading man at Maguire's Opera House from 1863–5; took a similar position at the Boston Theatre from 1865–6. He was competent in roles such as Hamlet, Iago, Othello, and Jack Cade but garnered critical and popular acclaim for his Badger in *The Streets of New York*. While he made his New York debut in 1869, Mayo remained an outsider, touring as a star in his own company. In 1872 he first acted the frontiersman, Davy Crockett, a part he would perform over 2,000 times. He wrote several plays in the 1880s but none were successful. In 1895 he adapted Mark Twain's *Pudd'nhead Wilson* for the stage and played the title role to popular acclaim until his death the following year. In his day he was thought a 'natural' actor because he underplayed the emotional scenes. While a versatile actor, Mayo found success only in roles which promoted Yankee individualism or the myth of the American frontier.   TLM

Mayol, Félix (1872–1941) French music-hall performer, originally from Toulon. He attained stardom at the Paris Scala 1902, with 'Viens poupoule'. Mayol's distinctive blond quiff, lily-of-the-valley buttonhole and eloquent, if over-illustrative, hand gestures were widely publicized and imitated. He ennobled the *caf'conc'* (*cafés-concerts*) style by substituting gesticulatory mime for the usual frenetic movements, and his repertory was extensive, ranging from gooey sentimentality to sly innuendo. He managed his own Concert Mayol from 1909 to 1914; it remained an important venue for singers until it was turned into a porno cinema and then closed in 1979. Mayol aged into a self-caricature who staged seven farewell appearances and finally retired in 1938.   LS

Mazurier, Charles-François (1798–1828) French acrobatic mime and dancer; already a star in Lyon when he made his Parisian debut at the Porte-Saint-Martin (1824) in *Polichinelle vampire*, which presented the French **Punch** as a greedy, hyperactive, ebullient type. His masterpiece was *Jocko or The Brasilian Ape* (1825), a grotesque amalgam of pantomime, knockabout and melodrama; audiences in Paris and London wept copiously over the death of a monkey. Mazurier's performances influenced the **Ravels**, the Prices, the

Hanlon-Lees, and the **Kiralfys** who preserved his repertory to 1893. When he died of consumption aggravated by fatigue, his body was denied Christian rites. LS

Mbogo, Emmanuel (1947–) Tanzanian playwright. He has two published plays in Swahili, *Giza Limeingia* (*The Dawn of Darkness*) on the advantages of *Ujamaa* villages, and *Tone la mwisho* (*The Last Drop*, 1985), on the liberation struggle in Zimbabwe. Mbogo is a Research Fellow in the Institute of Kiswahili Research at the University of Dar es Salaam. PML

Medebach, Girolamo (1706–90) Italian actor and manager. An actor from his early teens, in his thirties he entered a company of rope dancers led by Gasparo Raffi, married Raffi's actress daughter, Teodora, took over the direction of the company, trained its performers in the methods of the 'straight' theatre, and established them in the little San Moisè Theatre in Venice. In 1748 he signed up **Carlo Goldoni** as house dramatist to his troupe at Venice's Sant' Angelo theatre: the playwright was contracted to write eight comedies and two operas a year, for 450 ducats. The bargain ensured Medebach an important place in Italian theatrical history, for while with Medebach Goldoni drove through his reform of the Italian comic stage and wrote some of his most enduring plays, the actor–manager creating the lead male roles in many of them, like Don Marzio in *La Bottega del Caffe* and the Cavaliere di Ripafratta in *La Locandiera*. His wife similarly benefited from the Goldoni connection, and was, according to Goldoni's account in his *Memoirs*, an excellent if temperamental actress. A sharp businessman, Medebach claimed the publication rights to Goldoni's work, and when the dramatist left him for the rival San Luca theatre in 1752, he replaced him with his arch-rival, the Abate **Chiari**. In the late 1750s he joined the service of the Duke of Mantua as master of the court theatre. KR

Medicine shows The North American descendants of the mountebanks of Renaissance Europe: working from caravan wagons, itinerant pedlars of patent medicines enlivened their sales-pitch with variety acts, ranging from simple card tricks and banjo solos to the elaborate powwows and war dances of the turn-of-the-century Kickapoo shows. To meet competition from vaudeville, the medicine show began to offer an idiosyncratic form of variety only occasionally broken by a commercial message. The performances, often changed nightly, were dominated by a blackface comedian generically called Sambo or Jake, a hybrid of minstrel endman and hobo clown. The shows themselves, a mixture of ventriloquism, chalk talks, burlesque comedy, prestidigitation, and banjo-picking, usually lasted two hours, the eight or ten numbers interrupted by a few lectures with their medicine 'pitchs'. The afterpiece, an audience favourite, was a chaotic farce involving a sheeted ghost. Certain medicine men like Fred Foster Bloodgood and Tommy Scott continued to play their routes well into the late 20th century, and in 1983 *The Vi-Ton-Ka Medicine Show*, a reconstruction with original performers, was staged at the **American Place Theatre**, New York. LS

See: B. McNamara, *Step Right Up*, Garden City, NY, 1976.

Medieval drama in Europe In thinking about drama in Europe in the Middle Ages, it is worth remembering that the period in question – over 600 years – is far longer than that of modern drama, but that until the 14th century there is insufficient evidence to give an overall idea of the forms and shapes that drama took. We are dependent upon what has happened to survive and what happened to be recorded. The sections which follow (except for Eastern Europe) are divided by country, but these headings should be taken in a very general sense of areas where a language or a group of related languages were spoken, since boundaries were often not fixed until very much later, or varied over the course of the period.

Much of the drama that has survived was written to teach; that is to familiarize people with the stories of the Bible and apocrypha (Old and New Testaments) as well as to inculcate Christian doctrine and encourage moral behaviour. But medieval playwrights, whether writing for the church in Latin or in the vernacular for towns or private patrons, were as aware as anyone of the need to entertain in order to teach. Entertaining in the Middle Ages often means spectacle, entertaining the eyes, but not exclusively so; comedy, satire, knock-about horse-play, music, acrobatics, dancing, all have their part to play.

The earliest recorded drama in all the countries of Western Europe is the liturgical drama of the church. Ecclesiastical prohibitions suggest the presence of other forms, and there is no doubt that mimes, jugglers, acrobats, illusionists and dancers existed; but how widespread or exactly what their activities were is unknown since they have left almost no records. Equally it is likely that early folk drama existed, but again there is no evidence. The earliest liturgical drama (and this includes texts and a description of the action) is mid-10th century; the earliest indication of folk drama is 12th century. Though it is right to stress the early appearance of liturgical drama, however, it would be wrong to see it as the source of all later drama. It remains largely itself, influencing in some cases but by no means directing the course of the later vernacular plays. PM

Liturgical drama The ceremonies and texts which, in the last hundred years, have been extracted from medieval service books and anthologized as 'liturgical drama' would not have been generically and formally distinguished from the liturgy at the time of compilation and performance (c. 10th–16th centuries). Medieval concepts of drama are obscure, but it is clear that these ceremonies, most of which are associated with Easter, were customarily regarded as part of the liturgy, the official public worship of the church, and textually and in performance did and do appear almost indistinguishable from the liturgical context in which they are imbedded. It is from the Easter liturgy, the most important feast of the Christian year, the celebration of the Resurrection of Christ, that the following dialogue of an early 'play', possibly one of Europe's earliest recorded textually based plays, comes. It is a trope, that is a verbal expansion of a part of the liturgy proper:

Interrogatio:
Quem queritis in sepulchro, Christicole?

Responsio:
Jesum Nazarenum crucifixum, o caelicolae

Non est hic, surrexit sicut predixerat; ite, nuntiate quia surrexit de sepulchro.

[*Question*:
Whom do you seek in the sepulchre, followers of Christ?

Answer:
Jesus of Nazareth who was crucified, O heaven-dwellers.

He is not here, he has risen as he had foretold; go, announce that he has risen from the sepulchre.]

(St Gall *Quem queritis* c. 950)

Like all liturgical drama it is sung, not spoken, and the kind of music demonstrates incontrovertibly its dependence upon the liturgy. Although sung by monks, for a monastic congregation, with no purpose-made costume or staging, this is a 'play'. This dialogue is found at the core of some thousand texts of ceremonies associated with the Easter liturgy from all parts of what is now Western Europe, and from the 10th to the 16th centuries. The elaborated versions of the *Quem queritis*, usually called the *Visitatio Sepulchri* (Visit to the Sepulchre), include such incidents as the buying of the ointment to anoint Christ's body, the appearance of Christ to Mary Magdalene, the running of Peter and John to the sepulchre. Many of them utilize the vestments, sacred objects and church furnishings, including the altar itself, which were normally available for worship; as is clear from the *Visitatio* in the *Regularis Concordia*, a work compiled in England in the 10th century to coordinate the various monastic rules. It is a measure of the frequency and importance of these celebrations that in many churches permanent structures were built to serve as sepulchres; in others curtained enclosures were set up at Easter each year. No comprehensive pattern of derivation and influence encompassing these thousand texts is discernible. Public worship changes and is changed by cultural, social and political forces, and it is in the 9th-century Carolingian renaissance, although in no simple way, that the origins of what we recognize as modern European drama are to be found.

The liturgy comprises some of the essentials of drama whilst remaining a fundamentally different activity: both are communal, not individual activities; liturgically this is manifest most obviously in anti-phonal singing, in which the two sides of the choir, or two choirs, sing alternate verses. This depends upon the disciplined, rehearsed cooperation of a group of people in the public rendition of textually based material. A repertoire of fixed, formalized movements, ways of walking, especially processionally, and stand-ing and sitting; the symbolic evaluation of space within the church, as in the location and use of the altar, nave, and in the orientation of the church itself; the dedication of times of the year as holydays or holidays; role playing; the use of crucifixes, thuribles and other furnishings, and of vestments: – these are all character-istics of drama. The liturgy as a whole, and ceremonial most of all, could be, and was, elaborated and simpli-fied, simplified and elaborated, from time to time and place to place throughout the Middle Ages: there was emphatically neither uniformity nor unilinear historical 'development'.

There was some dramatic elaboration at the other great festival season, Christmas, when a *Quem queritis* trope developed around the Shepherds' visit to the stable. Unlike the Easter trope, this does not become the centre of development, but instead parts of the Christmas season produce their own dramas: the visit of the Magi (including the first appearance of the Herod figure), the Slaughter of the Innocents, and the *Ordo Prophetarum* (The Play of the Prophets), derived ulti-mately from the pseudo-Augustinian sermon of the prophecies concerning Christ's birth. Developments independent of Easter and Christmas took place at various times; such as the play of the *Presentation of Mary in the Temple* by Phillipe de Mézières (late 14th-century); Old Testament plays of Isaac and Rebecca (? Austria, late 12th-century), and Daniel (two versions, both 12th-century, one by Hilarius and one from Beauvais); plays of St Nicholas; and eschatologi-cal plays, the *Sponsus* and *Antichrist*. Many contain extensive stage directions for performance (and indeed some have been successfully performed in modern times). All are still part of the sung Latin drama of the church, though some by their length alone can no longer be seen as part of the liturgy. Nothing, how-ever, matched the number, range, diversity in details and historical persistence throughout the period of the Easter ceremonies.

Ceremonial and ritual alike were curbed by the Reformation and Counter-Reformation: by then lit-urgical drama had become an archaism. The monastic communities which had nourished it in the 10th and 11th centuries had by the 16th century been radically transformed or dis-established. PFM

Eastern Europe Medieval drama in the eastern half of Europe developed in two quite different ways depend-ing in the first place on whether the region was converted to Christianity by missionaries from the Latin or the Greek churches, and in the second on the frequency and nature of the invasions and dynastic changes which continued to disrupt the area right through the period. The dichotomy is exemplified in two of the countries which make up modern Yugo-slavia: in Croatia, which was Catholic and closely linked with the Holy Roman Empire in the north, and with the Italian states, especially Venice, to the west, both liturgical and vernacular drama flourished; while in Orthodox Serbia, invaded by the Turks in the 14th century when vernacular drama was emerging in the towns of England or France or Croatia, there is no medieval dramatic tradition at all.

In the countries of the Catholic group, Poland, Hungary, Croatia, and Bohemia (western Czechoslo-vakia), Latin and Old Church Slavonic manuscripts of the traditional liturgical Christmas and Easter plays have survived in considerable numbers, while vernacu-lar drama developed in different ways. In Bohemia it was short-lived: there are four liturgical plays in mixed Latin (sung) and Czech (spoken) and a few fragments of 14th-century vernacular plays including two versions of an incomplete farce, *The Quackdoctor*, featuring the merchant from whom the Three Maries buy their spices. The speeches of the Maries are, like the liturgical plays, partly in Latin. The complete lack of later vernacular plays in Bohemia may be attributed to the importance of the Hussite movement in encouraging the supersession of German by native Czech culture in the early 15th century: Hus, like Wyclif in England, was opposed to all kinds of popular entertainment as being causes of immorality.

Poland possesses a considerable number of vernacular religious plays dating mainly from the 16th and 17th centuries. The most notable is the *History of the Glorious Resurrection* of 1590, which includes some information about performance. It is possible also that the traditional Polish puppet-plays of the Nativity, performed for several centuries to an accompaniment of Christmas carols in Polish and which often include contemporary satirical characters, have medieval roots.

Hungary, despite the threat from the pagan Tartars to the east and pressure from the German-speaking Holy Roman Empire to the west, managed to create and maintain a national identity and express it in vernacular drama, though the surviving evidence is mainly in the form of performance records rather than texts. The earliest plays were similar to the Italian *laude*, and there are also many references in the 15th century to the presentation of plays linked with sermons and preaching. A number of morality plays are also extant, mainly debates of allegorical figures (cf. the Italian *Contrasti*) or based on the theme of the Dance of Death. A short Latin morality dialogue of c. 1388 is painted on the wall of a church in Zseliz. **Hrotsvitha**'s newly rediscovered *Dulcitius* was adapted into Hungarian at the very end of the 15th century, with a Turkish ruler replacing the Roman seducer of the 9th-century original. In some of the religious plays, as well as in the court festivals and the performances of the travelling minstrels or *regös*, there are elements of secular and satirical humour or folk traditions such as the three birds, eagle, owl and peacock, who greet the new-born Christ in the fourth part of the Bucsu *regös* mystery, which combines survivals of pagan winter rites with the Christmas story and a legend of the founder king of Hungary, St Stephen.

Croatia's vernacular drama was first performed by religious confraternities in the Italian tradition, though with some texts written in Glagolitic. Later a separate national drama was developed whose major surviving text, the *Muka (Sufferings)*, is a Passion play some 3,500 lines long, dating from the end of the 15th century and extant in several manuscripts including one in Glagolitic. The growing domination of the Dalmatian coast by Venice produced in the 16th century a renewed Italian influence on the Croatian drama, both religious and secular.

The development of drama in the countries christianized from the Greek-speaking Byzantine church follows a very different pattern. The elaborate ritual of the Orthodox liturgy and the eremitical nature of much Eastern monasticism did not encourage the sense of community celebration and festival which nurtured the earliest Latin drama. Moreover, since there is no substantial difference between the Greek of the liturgy and of the laity, the Western European distinction between Latin and vernacular drama is hardly applicable. However, although the evidence for church drama in the Eastern Empire is uncertain and inconclusive it is not wholly lacking. Early this century an Italian scholar put forward the theory that a group of homilies (preserved in 9th–11th-century manuscripts) which contain dramatic scenes and dialogues, especially on the Annunciation, the Baptism of Christ and the Harrowing of Hell, represent the relics of an early and substantial Byzantine liturgical drama.

The main group of such Byzantine sermon-plays are those on the Annunciation, which include dialogues between Mary and the Angel or Mary and Joseph. In the former, the Virgin treats Gabriel as a youth who threatens her reputation and warns him not to incur her husband's wrath. Joseph too is outspoken on the subject: 'Expose the plotter against my house. Bring into public view the one who has disordered it that I may take off his head with my craftsman's knife because he has dishonoured my grey hairs . . .' It is interesting, and may be significant, that Abramio of Sousdal, in his description of the Florentine *Annunciation* play which he attended in 1439, describes a very similar scene in which Mary rebukes the angel: 'Go away, young man, so that Joseph does not see you speaking to me in my house and cut off your head with his axe.' No parallel to this threat of violence by Joseph is extant in Western drama, either Latin or vernacular, and the Russian visitor to Florence may be drawing on his own Orthodox heritage rather than reporting actual words used on the stage.

Whatever the purpose of these homilies – dramatic, liturgical or didactic – the combination of drama and sermon is found in many countries of both Eastern and Western Europe, while the pseudo-Augustinian sermon (perhaps originally composed in Greek) is an acknowledged source of the Latin prophet-plays. Moreover, the reality of Greek drama, outside the extant homiletic form, is attested by two Passion plays, both surviving in 13th-century manuscripts though one may be much older.

Christ's Passion (Christos Paschon) is attributed in the earliest manuscript (c. 1260) to the 4th-century Greek Father, Gregory of Nazianzus. Critical opinion on this attribution – which would make the play the oldest Christian drama in Europe – has been divided ever since it was first questioned in the 16th century. The play – a cento of the tragedies of **Euripides** – narrates the events of Good Friday from the point of view of the Mother of God. The text comprises the lamentations of the Mother, St John and a chorus – in the classical Greek style – of wailing women, while the action is narrated by a Messenger. This pattern is broken by the central dialogue between the Mother and the Son while he hangs on the cross. There are no stage directions but the play is certainly susceptible of performance.

In contrast, the other surviving Passion play, a 13th-century text from Cyprus, is a director's copy with detailed instructions for performance and only the opening words of the speeches. An important prologue spells out the director's duties and responsibilities for the preparation and rehearsal of the actors, including warnings against allowing either gestures or costumes which might give rise to laughter. The writer (*grapheus*) of the manuscript and probable author of the play, Konstantinos Euteles, was an Orthodox monk, serving as Chief Notary under the rule of the Latin King of Cyprus. The island had been taken over by the Western church after the conquest of Constantinople, but there is no real evidence that the play was influenced by Latin drama.

In the 16th century another island, Crete, produced a Greek play of the *Sacrifice of Abraham* which shows affinities with the medieval versions of the subject in French and English, though the closest analogue is the Italian *Lo Isach* by the Venetian, Groto, published in 1585.

The relationship between the Eastern and Western churches, especially in the Mediterranean, makes it very difficult to determine how far their drama was mutually influential, but the closest links would certainly seem to have been through Italy which, by trade and travel, linked the eastern Mediterranean with the more northerly areas of the west. LRM

England, Scotland and Ireland; Cornwall and Wales It

is customary to think of the English medieval theatre in terms of liturgical drama, mystery plays (civic cycles), saints' plays, moralities, and interludes, and though the actual variety is far greater than this implies, it is convenient to use these terms as a starting point.

The liturgical dramas centring on Easter which are found in the *Regularis Concordia* (c. 965–75) are amongst the earliest in Europe. They are of particular importance because they consist of descriptions and texts of the Good Friday ceremonies of laying the cross in the sepulchre, and of an extended *Quem queritis*, or visit of the Maries to the sepulchre, on Easter Day. All the parts were performed by monks of the monastery; costume and props (all liturgical), movement and gesture, impersonation and surprise discovery are all touched upon. After this time there are very occasional texts and a large number of references to sung Latin drama in churches (mainly at Easter) from a variety of places up until the Reformation, the most important of which is the Barking Easter ceremony of the later 14th century. This was the work of Katherine de Sutton, abbess at the nunnery of Barking, and was aimed not only at the nuns but was intended to stir the devotions of the people. It consisted of an elaborate Easter ceremony, including a Harrowing of Hell, performed by the priests serving the nunnery and the nuns themselves.

A variety of plays performed in churches are recorded (e.g. plays of the Magi, the Annunciation, the Pilgrims to Emmaus, as well as saints' plays) but it is not normally possible to be sure whether they are liturgical or extra-liturgical, whether in Latin or the vernacular, whether sung or spoken, or who performed them. Associated with the church too are the semi-dramatic Boy Bishop and Feast of Fools celebrations of the Christmas season of misrule, and the more serious representations of the prophets (including Caiaphas) during the Palm Sunday procession. Two rather unusual texts have survived from the drama of the church. The Shrewsbury fragments (15th-century manuscript) are a single actor's part from three plays, Shepherds, *Quem queritis*, and Pilgrims, with sung and spoken Latin as well as spoken English texts. They are clearly in some sense liturgical, and are thought to come from Lichfield, though one of the English stanzas from the Shepherds' play is taken from the York Shepherds' pageant. The other unusual text is a pair of English plays, the *Burial* and *Resurrection of Christ* (early 16th-century manuscript). They deal with the events of Good Friday and Easter Day and are strongly devotional in tone. They appear to come from a Carthusian

monastery and to be part of the vernacular teaching work of that order.

Plays based on the Bible and the apocrypha, especially on the life of Christ, non-liturgical and in the vernacular, survive from early in the period, if the 12th-century Anglo-Norman *Adam* and *La Seinte Resurreccion* are English plays. If not, there is only the reference to a performance of a Resurrection play at Beverley (c. 1220), played in the churchyard by masked actors, to indicate early development. The earliest surviving text of an English play of this sort is the fully-fledged York Mystery Cycle, the first records of which date from 1376 and the text from 1463–77. This is one of the four extant plays of this type: York (over 13,000 lines), Chester (over 11,000), Towneley (over 12,000) and N.town (nearly 11,000). York and Chester are closely linked in many ways. Both provide the whole story of mankind from Creation to Last Judgement (as do Towneley and N.town); both were civic plays; both plays were divided into a number of shorter 'pageants', performed by different craft guilds or companies; both were performed on wagons or carriages (the Chester term) at a series of 'stations' or stopping-places around the city. There are, however, also considerable differences. The York text is divided up into 48 pageants (some less than 100 lines in length), Chester into 24; York was played on a single day, Corpus Christi (the first Thursday after Trinity Sunday), Chester on three, the Monday, Tuesday and Wednesday of Whitsun week; and the subject matter does not exactly match. Chester has, for example, pageants of Abraham and Melchisadek, Balaam and his ass, and two relating to Antichrist immediately before the Last Judgement. York has none of these but has one on Moses and Pharaoh and a very much fuller series depicting the Passion. York also had four pageants on the later life of Mary (three survive), Chester only one.

Information about the staging of the York play is derived from the civic archives and from two series of guild records: the Mercers', by far the most extensive, and the Bakers'. The guild records provide information about repairs to the wagon and about props and costumes; but without the recently (1974) discovered Mercers' indenture of 1433 there would be remarkably little certainty about the appearance, costuming or props of a York pageant. Even with that we know only about one wagon. The civic archives provide very full information about the route and stations of the play, its earlier (1415) content, the organization by mayor and council, and the varying responsibilities of the guilds for pageants. The Chester records are in some ways very different. The route and stations are far less well documented but there is far more about such things as rehearsal, props and especially actors – their names (in some cases) and their wages. Whereas the Mercers' records at York, however, begin in the early 15th century, for none of the Chester companies are there records earlier than 1546.

Towneley (manuscript of the late 15th or early 16th century) is in many ways similar, being a series of separate pageants with the same time-span. Moreover it includes six pageants which are the same as, or based on, York ones (Pharaoh, Doctors, Harrowing of Hell, Resurrection, Last Judgement, and the *Talents*, probably based on the lost York Millers' pageant). It lacks, however, the backing of any civic or guild records. It is associated with Wakefield but even if this can be taken as certain the town records add little information about its staging. It has been suggested that it would lend itself to 'place and scaffold' rather than wagon or 'processional' staging, but the same might be said of Chester if the city records did not prove the reverse. The Towneley cycle contains the plays of the so-called Wakefield Master, a playwright with a remarkable dramatic range (especially clear in the second of the Shepherds' pageants), and a strong line in ranting tyrants. His work represents one of the many examples of revision apparent in the cycles.

The N.town group of plays (late 15th-century manuscript) stands apart from the cycles. It contains a number of pageants, but also two unique plays: a play on the early life of Mary (c. 1,600 lines) and a two-part Passion play (c. 3,000 lines). The stage directions in both groups, pageants and plays, which are unusually full, suggest place and scaffold staging, and the Proclamation for the pageants, leaving space for the insertion of the place of performance, hints at performance by a group of smaller towns and villages (therefore not a civic play) and indicates Sunday as the day of performance (and therefore not a feast day). The subject matter is also unusual, not only in the presence of the early life of Mary (unique to English drama), but also in including such episodes as the Trial of Mary and Joseph, the death of Lamech, and a Jesse tree of prophecies of Christ's birth.

Of the surviving fragments of cycles (Coventry, Newcastle and Norwich), Coventry is by far the most important, since though only two pageants survive its records surpass those of York and Chester. In other places similar plays once existed. There is a list of pageants from Beverley, and enough evidence survives to show that it once possessed a similar cycle of pageants to that at York. At Hereford, Ipswich, or somewhere like Louth in Lincolnshire, however, the records are too scanty to allow certainty about the form or performance of the 'Corpus Christi play'.

The wagon-staged or processional cycles tend to dominate the picture of English vernacular theatre, but it is important to remember that besides the extant N.town Passion there are quite full records of a Passion play on fixed stages at New Romney in Kent in the 16th century, and of what sounds like place and scaffold staging of a full-scale civic play at Clerkenwell in London; quite apart from all the recorded performances about whose staging we know nothing. The London play, first recorded in 1384, was performed over a number of days (from three to seven) like the great French Passions, but it covered the same time-span as the English cycles, Creation to Last Judgement. There are no records of the play after 1410–11.

The N.town Mary Play may well have been written for a religious guild or a parish celebration, and other short plays may have had the same purpose. Certainly the Killing of the Children (566 lines) was intended as one in a series of New Testament plays performed each year in honour of St Anne. Plays were also staged as fund-raisers for the church. The epilogue for such a play is preserved in the 15th-century commonplace book of Richard Reynes of Acle in Norfolk. Far larger were the two religious guild plays from York: the Creed and Paternoster plays. The former was the property of the Corpus Christi guild and the latter of the Paternoster guild. No texts survive but since both were sometimes played instead of the York cycle play, and were apparently staged in a similar way, they were clearly of considerable extent. The Paternoster Play is first heard of in 1388 and the Creed Play in 1446.

Equally possible as guild, church or town celebration are the saints' plays. References to saints' plays occur from all over England, from the single early 12th-century example of St Katharine at Dunstable to the multifarious 15th-century ones. They are not, however, as varied or as numerous in their survival as the French, and there are only two extant texts to give an idea of the genre: Mary Magdalen (2,139 lines), and The Conversion of St Paul (662). Both are late 15th or early 16th century and come from East Anglia. Mary Magdalen can be roughly divided into two parts: the first skilfully interweaves her life with that of Christ, and the second, totally apocryphal, deals with her conversion of Marseilles and her death. Like the N.town plays it has a series of full stage directions which indicate place and scaffold performance and various special effects, like the collapsing idol, the burning of the temple, and the constantly voyaging ship. St Paul, like the N.town Mary Play, and the Killing of the Children, is introduced and the episodes linked by an expositor (in this case Poeta). He emphasizes its truth to the Bible though the play also contains devil scenes and dances. The two plays suggest something of the variety of possibility within the saints' play genre.

Like the saints' plays, the moralities are enormously varied. What they have in common is the presentation, usually through allegorical figures, of the struggle of good and evil for the soul of man. Apart from the fragmentary Pride of Life (15th-century manuscript but perhaps written as early as the beginning of the 14th century), the earliest morality to have survived is also the one with the largest scope, the Castle of Perseverance (3,700 lines; 15th-century manuscript). It opens before Mankind's birth and closes after his death. It contains a wide range of allegorical characters, including the seven deadly sins, the seven virtues, the three enemies of mankind – the World, the Flesh and the Devil, each with his own scaffold – but the plot is single-minded in its concentration on the depiction of the life of man. The play is perhaps best known for its stage plan showing the scaffolds of the three enemies, Covetousness and God on the perimenter of a circle and the castle itself at the centre. The words 'place' and 'scaffold' both appear on the plan, and as a whole it gives the clearest indication of a possible lay-out for this type of staging that there is. Like the N.town Proclamation, that of the Castle leaves space for the insertion of the name of the town or village where the play is to be performed. It is not therefore to be assumed that it is a play belonging to a travelling company – it is far too complex a production for that – but that the manuscript could be used at different times in different places. Of the other surviving moralities, two appear in what is now the same manuscript as the Castle, though written much later. Wisdom is a dignified but spirited depiction of the corruption of the facets of the soul and their ultimate purification. It includes three sets of dances. Mankind contains exuberant and linguistically inventive comedy while still depicting the struggle of good and evil (here represented by Mercy on the one hand, and Mischief supported by New Guise, Nowadays and Nought, and the devil Titivillus, on the other) for man's soul. There is also the Latin 'moral play' from Oxford, Thomas Chaundler's *Liber Apologeticus de Omni Statu Humanae Naturae* (c. 1460).

Everyman (first printed c. 1510–25), the best-known today of all the moralities, is a translation from the Dutch play *Elckerlijc*. It is not so much a presentation of the struggle for man's soul as a picture of a man's realization in the last moments of his life of what is necessary for salvation. Earlier than *Everyman* but printed at about the same time, was **Henry Medwall**'s *Nature*, a morality still on the universal medieval pattern. **John Skelton**'s *Magnyfycence*, also printed at about the same time, shows the beginning of the shift towards a more specific satirical purpose which finally gives rise to the polemical moralities of religious controversy.

The term 'interlude' is often used of any short play, especially of the early 16th century. Its use in the Middle Ages is both varied and vague. The earliest surviving interlude is *The Clerk and the Girl* (*Interludium de Clerico et Puella*; early 14th-century manuscript). Its plot is close to that of *Dame Sirith*, a dramatic monologue of a secular, comic and amorous nature (late 13th-century), and the interlude is the nearest play in English to a French farce. *Dame Sirith* may give some slight idea of one side of the minstrel's repertoire – marginal letters in the manuscript indicate different speakers, perhaps for a change of voice by the reciter. The word 'interlude' is frequently used in records of the 14th and 15th centuries; it can refer to indoor or outdoor performance, in church, churchyard or hall, or more often in an unspecified location. It is sometimes associated with minstrels and sometimes not. It is clear that something dramatic existed that was conveniently labelled in this way, but what it was is unclear. We are on safer ground with Medwall's *Fulgens and Lucres* (c. 1495) in as much as the text has survived. It was almost certainly written for performance in Cardinal Morton's hall in Lambeth Palace. It is also amorous and secular but the comedy is mainly confined to the sub-plot. Its main subject is a debate about the true source of nobility. It is in many ways a remarkable play, not least for its use of the comic sub-plot echoing the serious one and for its use of the audience. The debate or dialogue dominates the two plays from a 15th-century manuscript, *Lucidus and Dubius* and *Occupation and Idleness*, though the latter injects considerable vitality into it. It seems almost certain that they are school or college plays. After the turn of the century the word 'interlude' embraces all the variety of the short plays of the early Tudor period.

Confusingly the word 'miracle' is used of plays in general in the Middle Ages in England, not simply to describe plays specifically concerning miracles. The only true miracle play surviving is the *Croxton Play of the Sacrament*, dealing with the attempted desecration of the eucharistic wafer by a group of Jews and the consequent manifestation of its miraculous powers. The play includes an interpolated quack doctor scene similar in many ways to those of the later folk plays.

Whether by chance survival or frequency of performance, certain areas stand out for their theatrical activities. East Anglia is the source of extant texts of every kind of play: mystery, saints, miracle, liturgical. Yorkshire was the home of at least three mystery cycles. Equally striking is the survival of Celtic drama from Cornwall. Not only is there probably the earliest mystery play manuscript surviving from Britain, the *Ordinalia*, but also a full-scale saint's play, *Beunans Meriasek* (*The Life of Meriasek*; manuscript 1504), and the first part of another mystery play, *Gwreans an Bys* (*The Creation of the World*; manuscript 1611). *Meriasek* and the *Ordinalia* both contain circular staging diagrams similar in many ways to that of the *Castle of Perseverance*, and in this case interestingly related to the Cornish 'rounds' or 'playing-places' (*plen-an-gwary*) examples of which still survive at St Just and near Perranporth. The *Ordinalia* were performed over three days: the first, Old Testament including the legend of the cross; the second, Passion, and the third, Resurrection and Ascension. All the Cornish plays contain extensive stage directions in Latin or English.

The only other Celtic plays to have survived are some Welsh biblical and morality plays and fragments of the late 15th and early 16th centuries, and a late 16th-century play of *Troelus a Chresyd* (*Troilus and Cressida*) partly based on **Chaucer**.

From Ireland and Scotland there are records and some extant texts of liturgical plays and plays in English. Dublin, capital of the English Pale, had a *Quem queritis* (14th-century manuscript), and there are lists of pageants for Corpus Christi and St George's Day from the 15th century. Kilkenny may have had earlier plays, but records survive only from the second half of the 16th century: **John Bale**'s productions in 1553 of his Protestant polemical plays, and Corpus Christi and Midsummer plays from 1580. The *Pride of Life*, the earliest English morality, may stem from Ireland or have been copied there. Scotland has a great variety of records from the 16th century, including a surprising number of **Robin Hood** entertainments. The only town with a record of theatrical activity stretching back to the early 15th century is Aberdeen, with its *Play of the Holy Blood*, the abbot of Bonaccord, pageants of Candlemas and Corpus Christi; but Edinburgh, with Sir David Lindsay's morality, *A Satire of the Three Estates* (first version performed in Linlithgow, 1540), is the only city whose drama is represented by a text. *The Three Estates* was given an elaborate open-air performance in Edinburgh in 1554. The city also had its royal entries and court disguisings. Perth, St Andrews and other places have isolated early references. There is in fact no reason to suppose that the variety of theatrical activity was any less in Scotland than in England in the later Middle Ages.

It is impossible to tell when most of the plays mentioned ceased to be performed. Only the civic cycles have sufficiently regular records and frequency of performance for the effect of the Reformation to be traced, sometimes in some detail. At first the effect was small. In York the plays on the life of Mary were not played in the 1540s, and, no doubt for the same reason, the Chester Assumption pageant has not survived in any of the manuscripts. It was not until quite late in Elizabeth's reign (after a brief late-flowering under Mary) that the plays finally succumbed to government and ecclesiastical pressure. The same year as the abortive pro-Catholic Rising of the Northern Earls, 1569, saw the last performance of the York Play. The Chester one survived until 1575, despite injunctions from the Archbishop of York to prevent its performance. Coventry was 'brought forth' for the last time in 1579. Various substitutes were tried. At Coventry the costly *Destruction of Jerusalem* still used the guild organization and their individual pageants, but it was certainly performed only once, in 1582. At York one of the other medieval plays, the Paternoster Play, was performed in 1572, but not again. At Chester the emphasis seems to have shifted to the Midsummer Show, and at Lincoln the play of *Tobit*, performed over two days in 1564, replaced the old St Anne's Day show and its pageants. All this time records of the visits of groups of travelling companies attached to a nobleman's household increase in frequency.

The rather more formal dramatic pieces that have so far been described need to be seen in their context of theatrical and semi-dramatic entertainments and celebrations throughout the latter part of the period. Civic and religious processions, especially that of Corpus Christi, were an opportunity for display, and there is little doubt that the 'processional' performance of the cycle plays had its origin there. Tournaments, which from at least the late 13th century combined armed combat with costumed display; triumphal entries to celebrate the visit of nobility or royalty to a town or city – particularly a development of the 15th century but recorded in England from the late 14th century; mummings and disguisings, again a largely 15th-century development but whose heyday was in the early 16th century; *pas d'armes* and entertainments at feasts; folk celebrations and entertainments – Robin Hood and St George plays, summer games, crying Christmas, plough plays; all these hint at a wealth of theatrical activity. Occasionally a fuller record illuminates the hint. Payments to St George or for refurbishing the dragon appear at York, Newcastle upon Tyne and Norwich; elaborate descriptions of tournaments and disguisings appear in chronicles such as Froissart's and Hall's, eked out by the details of the royal household accounts of the late 15th and early 16th centuries, and by the descriptions and texts of the 15th-century monk and court poet, John Lydgate. Royal entries are sometimes described and the speeches recorded, as at York in 1486 or Coventry in 1474. A summer game may be more fully described because of a court case involving the 'queen', as at Wistow in Yorkshire in 1469; or the text of a crying of Christmas survive, as at Lincoln or York in the 16th century. Despite the hundreds of references to Robin Hood only one fragment of a Robin Hood play survives from the late 15th century to give an idea of the entertainment sometimes attached to his name; but even this cannot recreate the context of its performance.   PM

France Medieval drama in France differs from that of its European neighbours not only in the survival of some very early texts, but also in its richness and variety. Though its origins are no doubt the same as those of the drama of the rest of Western Europe, and reflect the influence of Latin liturgical drama and of popular dramatic modes, it is difficult to prove that the earliest religious plays derive directly from Latin liturgical dramas, since in the case of France complex religious plays in the vernacular precede, or at least are simultaneous with, the complex Latin church dramas.

The earliest examples of these latter plays are the two 12th-century versions of the story of Daniel, one from

Beauvais and the other by the wandering scholar, Hilarius, who also wrote plays on the Raising of Lazarus and a Miracle of St Nicholas. A 13th-century manuscript from St-Benoît-sur-Loire, known as the Fleury Play-book, contains ten plays. Six of these are biblical: plays of the Magi and the Slaughter of the Innocents, the Raising of Lazarus, a *Visitatio* and a Pilgrims to Emmaus, and a unique play of the Conversion of St Paul. Four miracles of St Nicholas (the only post-biblical saint to feature in early Latin drama) complete this unusual and important collection. Two elaborate Easter plays also survive; one from Tours, and one from the convent at Origny-Sainte-Benoîte which has a Latin text and French rubrics. All these plays are in Latin and intended to be sung, and are therefore liturgical in mode if not in context of performance.

Two of the three earliest vernacular plays are clearly linked to the liturgy. The *Sponsus* of the late 11th century, a 100-line sung drama in stanzas of varied metres, some in Latin and some in French, is a dramatization of the parable of the Wise and Foolish Virgins; though not part of the liturgy proper, the play was probably associated either with Advent or with the Easter Vigil ceremonies, dealing as it does with the arrival of Christ and the Day of Judgement. The *Ordo Representationis Ade*, usually known as the *Play of Adam* (*Le Jeu d'Adam*), and dating from the 12th century, is in effect a dramatized sermon based on the responses in the Septuagesima liturgy; it consists of the Creation and Fall of Adam and Eve, the Cain and Abel story, and a series of Old Testament prophecies of the coming of the Redeemer. After the reading of the first chapter of Genesis, the choir sings the responses, each of which is followed by a loose translation and expansion in dramatic form in Anglo-Norman verse. The Play of Adam is a remarkable achievement; it is unique in its structure and composition, and its anonymous author's sense of the dramatic and his penetrating psychological insight, especially in the Temptation scenes, prove that the oldest medieval plays are often among the best. The third play, the incomplete Anglo-Norman *Seinte Resurreccion*, though dealing with the Burial and Resurrection of Christ, and thus based on the same material as the expanded *Visitatio Sepulchri* ceremonies, has no connection with the liturgy; its dramatic form and writing are more typical of later Passion plays.

The most striking feature of the six surviving 13th-century plays is that all but one were composed near Arras, then a thriving city, in north-east France. The two plays dating from the beginning of the century both present a religious message in a partly comic guise. *Courtois d'Arras* takes the parable of the Prodigal Son and places it in the realistic setting of 13th-century Artois, whereas Jehan Bodel's 1,500 line *Jeu de Saint Nicolas*, the first French miracle play, dramatizes the legend of the saint's supernatural power to protect treasure entrusted to him, in the anachronistically juxtaposed worlds of Arras taverns and Saracen battlefields, the result being a totally original blend of low comedy and Christian commitment. Towards the end of the 13th century Adam de la Halle, equally well known as a composer of music and as a lyric poet, wrote two contrasting secular, comic plays. The *Jeu de la Feuillée* is a kind of student review in which satire on contemporary religious and political issues springs from discussion of the author's wish to leave Arras for Paris. It is unique in that the characters on stage include not only the author's inventions, but also real people (and indeed the author himself) presumably acted by themselves. The *Jeu de Robin et de Marion*, often described as the first musical, is a dramatization of the lyric genres of the *pastourelle* and the *bergerie* (in the same way as his other play dramatizes the *congé*), in which the contrast between courtly and peasant cultures is demonstrated in a series of scenes interspersed with popular songs.

The 14th century sees not only the earliest French Passion play, the 2,000-line *Passion du Palatinus*, but also the further development of the miracle play, attested by the *Miracles de Nostre Dame par personnages*, a collection of 40 plays whose lengths vary between 1,000 and 3,000 lines, preserved in one illuminated manuscript now in Paris. These plays were performed annually at the meetings of the Paris Guild of Goldsmiths between 1339 and 1382. All the texts take the form of an action in which the dramatic tension is resolved by the miraculous intervention of the Virgin Mary; however this formula is but a framework within which the playwrights contrive to dramatize a vast range of narrative material which often has nothing miraculous or even religious about it. Thus the collection contains 'miracle plays' based on secular romances and *chansons de geste*, as well as saints' lives, the Nativity of Christ and true Marian miracles. Although comedy is rare in the *Miracles de Nostre Dame*, it is clear that, during the 13th and 14th centuries the divisions between religious and secular, comic and serious are not strictly observed, and that the labels attached to plays, both then and now, may be misleading.

This appears to be less true in the following centuries. From the beginning of the 15th century, and especially after the end of the Hundred Years War, there was a great expansion in dramatic activity, attested not only by the large numbers of texts that have survived, but also by other archival documentation which reveals wide-spread and frequent performances. The expansion is reflected moreover in a clearer differentiation in the types of play – mystery plays, morality plays, farces, *sotties* – and, most notably, in the increasing length of religious plays. Although texts between 1,000 and 2,000 lines are still written, by the middle of the 15th century many plays exceeded 10,000 lines and their performance, of necessity, spread over three, four or more days ('journées'). By the early 16th century, plays of 50,000–60,000 lines had been written, their performance extending over 30 or 40 days. Even the major Passion plays of the mid-15th century were often 30,000 lines long and took four full days to perform. And these texts were not broken down into small easily manageable units, as was the case in England.

The texts of over 150 mystery plays have survived, mostly in manuscript form, though from the late 15th century many early printed editions were published. The manuscripts are extremely varied in nature and function; though some are elegantly written and illuminated, clearly items of luxury, most are hastily written records of the text, with frequent stage-directions, marginal additions and corrections. There are also a few examples of actors' roles (long strips of paper sewn together vertically, containing the lines of just one actor, which were wound around the actor's finger during rehearsals) such as those found at Fribourg and of producers' texts, like that used for the Passion performed at Mons in 1501, where the stage directions are numerous, but where only the first and last line of each speech is given.

Mystery plays were in essence historical plays, in that they recreated on stage events that were perceived by the audience as being historically true. Virtually all mystery plays had religious subject matter, and one can break them down into two groups: those based on the life of a saint and those based on biblical material, in particular the life of Christ, commonly referred to as Passion plays.

The earliest Passion plays date from the 14th century, the *Passion du Palatinus* and the 4,500-line *Passion Nostre Seigneur* in the Paris Sainte Geneviève Library; these early texts are limited to the events of Passion week. Later Passion plays cover much more – the childhood of Christ, the life of John the Baptist and the Virgin Mary, Old Testament episodes, etc. The sources of these plays are not only the Bible or the Canonical Gospels, but also the many apocryphal Gospels and other Christian legends that circulated widely during the Middle Ages in non-dramatic literature and in contemporary art. The earliest Passion plays were based on the narrative *Passion des Jongleurs*, which is a 3,000-line conflation of a number of sources, relating in a lively manner the events of Holy Week. But later Passion plays drew on much wider and more learned sources.

Although hundreds of Passion play performances took place, new texts were not written for each occasion. Obviously, many original texts were composed, but more often than not, when a Passion play performance was planned, an existing text was adapted – lengthened, shortened, modified, restaged – to suit the circumstances. The effect of this is that the surviving texts can be grouped into loose families, often attached to a particular region or province of France. For example, the *Passion du Palatinus* can be linked to several other texts which are associated with Burgundy including the 9,000-line *Passion de Semur*; there are two manuscripts of Passion plays originating from Auvergne. All members of these families have certain distinctive features in common, e.g. length, external structure, order of episodes, absence or presence of certain characters' names. The two best-known French Passion plays illustrate this state of affairs. Arnoul Gréban's *Mystère de la Passion*, composed probably in Paris around 1450, dramatizes not only the life of Christ but also some Old Testament material as well. Its 35,000 lines, mostly octosyllabic but containing occasional stretches of more complex versification, are divided into four days. The first day starts with an abbreviated version of the Creation, then jumps to the Annunciation and continues up to the episode of Jesus among the Doctors; Day 2 takes us from the coming of John the Baptist to Peter's Denials; Day 3 contains the Passion up to the Entombment; Day 4 deals with the Resurrection and the Appearances. The success of this play is attested not only by the fact that it survives in several virtually identical manuscripts – very unusual for a play – but also by how much it was used by other *fatistes* (mystery play adapters). The second and third days of this play were copied and greatly expanded by

Jehan Michel in his equally famous play, printed in 1486; another revision survives in the *Passion de Troyes* produced in Troyes c. 1490. It was also used in parts of the Passion plays performed at Mons in 1501 (along with Michel's text) and in the *Mystère du Viel Testament* of the early 16th century. Yet many critics maintain that Gréban himself was greatly indebted to the *Passion d'Arras*, a play composed in Arras around 1420–30 probably by Eustache Marcadé; this play too was in four days, 25,000-lines long, and contained most of the subject matter later appearing in Gréban.

The mystery plays based on the lives of saints were less subject to this continual adaptation, since the saints chosen were often those whose cult was limited to a particular area or town or group of people. For example, in the mid-15th century, the shoemakers of both Paris and Rouen produced the same play on the lives of their patron saints Crespin and Crespinien; Saint Martin plays were performed in Burgundy and Maurienne, and at least two different plays were devoted to each of saints Barbe, Christofle, Fiacre, Laurent, Louis and Sébastien. Almost 40 such plays have come down to us, from all corners of France.

Though the Passion plays and saints' plays have the primary religious function of illustrating and reinforcing the beliefs of the audience, it would be wrong to see them as uniformly serious in tone. Indeed, it is the great contrasts in register that disturbed many churchmen during the Reformation and critics in the 19th century. Next to solemn scenes like a sermon or the Crucifixion, the audience would witness action which was vulgar and violent, comic and scabrous. The best mystery plays catered for all tastes and all moods; they were microcosms of the real world.

The real world – at least that of the peasant and the bourgeois – appears to be reflected in the farces, of which over 150 survive, mostly in one of the four main collections. Typically, these are short (300–400 lines) comic plays involving three or four characters and based on the device of some sort of trick or deceit, played by one character on another; frequently the action concludes with a reversal, so that the outcome shows the deceiver deceived. The setting is often the *ménage à trois*, or the world of commerce or of law; the characters are given real names and a lifelike setting. However the realism is more apparent than real, owing to the stylization of the genre. The careful symmetry of the plots, the often very self-conscious use of language, the stereotyped characters and action are artificial features, but the very features that make the farces so amusing. This is well proven in the case of *Maistre Pierre Pathelin*, which is usually held to be the masterpiece of the genre, in spite of its untypical length and complexity.

Closely linked to the farce was the *sottie*, which was also a short comic play; indeed some surviving texts were entitled *Farce et sottie . . .* But the typical farce is clearly different from the typical *sottie*. The characters in the *sotties* were unsually unnamed 'sots' or fools, and often wore the identifying costume of cap with ass's ears, parti-coloured dress and staff with bells. Many *sotties* had no real plot, but just consisted of lively exchanges of banter based on word-play and misunderstandings, as well as acrobatics and slap-stick comedy. The titles of the following examples reveal the nature of the *sottie*: *la Sottie des Menus Propos*; *la Sottie des Sots Triumphants Qui Trompent Chascun*; *la Sottie des Sots Fourrés de Malice*; *la Sottie des Sots Ecclesiastiques Qui Jouent Leur Benefice au Content*. The aim was to produce riotous laughter, and the means was often satirical allegory directed at social, political or religious abuses. In this latter respect at least, the *sotties* resembled the morality plays, which also survive in great numbers (about 70) from the later 15th and early 16th centuries.

Traditional criticism views the morality plays as a comic genre, but their fundamental aim was undoubtedly didactic, even if their method was to 'instruire en amusant'. In their scope the morality plays were much closer to the mystery plays, in that some were as long as 20,000 lines, and most of the best-known were of considerable length. The essence of the morality play is the illustration of a lesson by means of a dramatic action enacted by a number of allegorical characters. The vices attacked may be gluttony (as in *La Condamnation des Banquets*), poverty (*Moralité de Charité*), blasphemy (*Les Blasphémateurs du Nom de Dieu*). The characters may represent vices or virtues, social groups, institutions, or 'moral types', e.g. the Sinner, the Rich Man. In addition to the more usual moral allegories, there were also a small number of political morality plays, like the *Concile de Basle*. The 15th- and 16th-century comic plays were usually composed and performed by societies set up for the purpose. Groups of professional entertainers, often called Les Enfants sans soucy, appeared all over France; one especially famous group was the Basochiens, a society of law clerks, originally attached to the Paris high court.

All of these genres, mystery play, farce, morality and *sottie*, flourished well into the middle of the 16th century. Mystery plays were performed as late as the 17th and 18th centuries in some of the distant southeastern provinces. Even in Paris the 1548 Edict of the Paris Parlement forbidding the performance of *mystères sacrés* was not immediately respected. Thus, in France, for many years in the middle of the 16th century 'medieval' plays were performed at the same time as 'Renaissance' plays. It was the former which appealed more to the general, uneducated public.

The staging of drama in medieval France has given rise to much controversy, sometimes because evidence is lacking, sometimes because it is ambiguous. This is especially the case with religious plays. Of course, some plays, such as the *sotties* and the short morality plays required no special theatre or stage; an open space, indoors or outdoors, was all that was needed. And our knowledge about farce performances is supported by iconographical evidence, such as the Brueghel painting of the *Village Festival*; many farces were performed out-of-doors in a village square by a small travelling troupe, using a stage of planks placed on trestles or barrels, at head-height to the spectators. The stage area was divided by a curtain into two halves, lengthwise, the front half being used for the acting, the rear part serving as the 'wings', for changing and for the prompter.

The real problems arise in the case of the early religious plays and the mystery plays. One feature which critics agree is common to all such plays is the system of simultaneous staging; this is shown clearly in the prologue of the 12th-century Anglo-Norman *Seinte Resurreccion*, where a description is given of the stage just before the action begins. All the sets and actors needed for the play are present on the stage from the very start. Moreover, this prologue also seems to imply two different types of item on the stage: areas (*lieux*) where groups of actors wait, and constructed sets (*mansions*). This distinction between places for actors and sets (also called *eschaffaults* (scaffolds)) seems to obtain throughout the medieval period. More controversial is the shape of the stage used for any given play and, for the earlier plays, whether the stage is indoors or not. For example, whereas it is certain that the *Miracles de Nostre Dame* was performed in the Guild of Goldsmiths' Hall (which thus limited the number of sets used in all 40 plays to no more than six or seven), critics are divided about the staging of the *Jeu d'Adam*, some seeing it staged outside the west end of a church, others preferring a production inside the church, more in keeping with the traditions of liturgical drama.

The main controversy surrounding 15th- and 16th-century mystery plays focuses on whether stages were linear or in-the-round. Until recently, critics unhesitatingly accepted the notion that these plays were performed outdoors on vast linear stages, on which the numerous sets were placed side-by-side, with the action taking place in front of the sets. The audience stood or sat in front of this stage. It is undoubtedly the case that performances of this sort did take place. Evidence for this is not only reconstruction, but also documents like carpenters' contracts and, especially, Hubert Cailleau's miniature of the 1547 *Passion de Valenciennes*. However, it would be wrong to see this as a model for all mystery play stages, since many were performed in theatres in the round, or at least on stages where the audience watched from three or four sides. Again, this type of stage can be proved to have existed by archive documents supported by the famous miniature by Jehan Fouquet dated about 1450 apparently showing a performance of a play on the life of Saint Apollonia. It seems that medieval producers had no preconceived notion of the shape of a theatre, and simply made the best use of the space available. What is certain is that no permanent theatres existed; theatres were made especially for a particular performance and then dismantled afterwards. They were 'one-off' affairs, which was often the case with the texts of the plays themselves. However, towards the end of the Middle Ages, the famous – but unique – Confrérie de la Passion in Paris did regularly rent rooms at the Hôtel de la Trinité and later at the **Hôtel de Bourgogne**, for its performances of mystery plays.

Producing plays was expensive and time-consuming and required the financial and personal commitment of patrons. In France the type of patron seemed to evolve along with the plays themselves. The early religious plays obviously owed much to the church authorities; but the Arras plays, some saints' plays and the *Miracles de Nostre Dame* were commissioned and financed by religious confraternities and trade guilds. Mystery plays, being the most complex of all, needed the support of whole towns and cities, and were usually planned and subsidized by the local authorities. Although most performances of mystery plays sprang from religious convictions, several were clearly designed to be lucrative in themselves, or even 'loss-leaders' attracting trade to the town. In France, there is only one example of an individual who financed large numbers of plays, both farces and mystery plays, and that is the pleasure-loving but spend-thrift René d'Anjou.

There is little doubt that the theatre in medieval France was the most popular of all the 'literary genres'. Not only did it reach beyond the literate public and appeal to the masses, but it flourished and evolved rapidly from the 11th to the 16th centuries in all parts of France; this is attested not only by the vast numbers of recorded performances, but also by the survival of over 500 texts reflecting the widest possible range of dramatic experiences. GAR

Germany, Switzerland, etc. The medieval theatre of the German-speaking countries divides clearly into 'religious' and 'secular', with separate origins and relatively little cross-fertilization between the two.

Religious theatre includes plays in Latin, in German and in a mixture of the two languages. Beyond the incontrovertible basic fact that the Easter and Christmas plays derive in some way from the Latin Easter and Christmas celebrations associated with the Mass for these festivals, details of the process of development are entirely unclear. The most recent scholarship in this area rejects the notion of a straightforward line of development from Latin to mixed to German plays. At least some of the mixed Latin–German plays are now seen not to fit chronologically into such a scheme, and are now regarded rather as a late development confined to specific contexts, where the clergy perceived a need to bring plays back closer to their ecclesiastical origins and purposes. Whereas the original celebrations were part of 'divine service' offered as praise to God, the vernacular plays are concerned with teaching the people the Christian message of salvation through faith in Christ's death and resurrection. Such non-liturgical plays are to be found in the German-speaking area from the 13th century onwards, reaching their peak in the 15th and early 16th, with isolated examples surviving into the early 17th century.

Of all the extant texts and the performances about which evidence – but no text – survives, over two-thirds are in some way related to the Easter story. (Included in this total are the relatively few plays dealing with the Virgin Mary, '*Planctus*' and 'Assumption' plays; also Ascension and Whitsuntide plays.) The majority deal in some way with the Easter story itself. What scholars today refer to as 'Easter plays' (German *Osterspiele*) were in the Middle Ages often called 'Resurrection plays' (*spil von der urstend*) and as that title implies, began with Easter morning; what are now called 'Passion plays' (*Passionsspiele*) were often called 'Easter plays', though the word '*passion*' (masc. gender) does occur, and these included scenes from the whole of Christ's life and ministry besides in many cases a number of Old Testament scenes, especially those thought to have a prefigurative significance for the New Testament action. These Passion plays and the 'Corpus Christi plays' (*Fronleichnamsspiele*) which deal with the same material but differ in the manner of presentation, occur only later in the Middle Ages, from the 13th century onwards. Amongst the best-known of the earlier Passion plays is the *Benediktbeurer Passionsspiel* (*Benediktbeuern Passion Play*) of c. 1120, which like the *Carmina Burana* poems from the same manuscript contains both Latin and German text. The *Künzelsauer Fronleichnamsspiel* (*Künzelsau Corpus Christi Play*) from Künzelsau in Württemberg was performed at least between 1479 and 1522.

The remaining one third of the plays are spread fairly evenly between the four groups: Nativity plays; saints' plays, eschatological plays and moralities. Nativity plays in German, with the sole exception of the *St Galler Kindheit Jesu* (*St Gall Childhood of Jesus*) c. 1330, occur only in the 15th and 16th centuries. Amongst saints' plays only those concerning St Catherine, St Dorothy and St George occur in significant numbers. Eschatological plays include plays on the Wise and Foolish Virgins (*Zehnjungfrauenspiele*) surviving in late 15th- and early 16th-century versions; Antichrist plays, of which the only true extant text, the Latin *Ludus de Antichristo*, belongs to the 12th century and the only other two surviving examples occur in a form close to the Nuremberg **Fastnachtspiel** (see below); and Judgement plays, the commonest of these sub-groups. The morality play occurs far less frequently in the German-speaking area than in the westernmost European countries and belongs almost exclusively to the Low German-speaking north and west of the area, closest to those countries where this genre occurs most frequently.

Confusingly the great majority of medieval German plays are known by titles which relate to the place where the manuscript was found rather than to the area in which the play was performed. Therefore recent scholarship refers to 'The Rhenish-Hessian Passion Play from Berlin manuscript' rather than as previously to the 'Berlin Passion Play' (manuscript dated 1460). It has nevertheless long been recognized that the extant texts, where they are numerous enough to allow broader comparison, i.e. especially among the Easter, Passion and Corpus Christi plays, seem to belong to a number of areas where such plays were more common than elsewhere. Most notable are the Hessian group, for which several texts associated with Frankfurt/Main (see also below) and Friedberg are known, even though the precise relationships between the actual extant texts are less easy to determine; and the South Tyrolean group from the area south of the Brenner Pass around the towns of Bolzano (formerly Bozen) and Vipentino (Sterzing) which though historically German-speaking is now part of Italy. However, it may well be that such ideas of concentration of medieval religious drama in a number of areas are illusory, based on no more than the chances of the origins of the surviving manuscripts. Recent work by B. Neumann reveals a much wider set of references for performances of all kinds of plays than had hitherto been supposed.

The Easter and Christmas celebrations, by virtue of their liturgical origins, were sung and performed in church by clergy wearing vestments; few significant details regarding the staging are recorded.

The Passion plays, which sometimes lasted several days, were staged in the open air using 'simultaneous staging'; all those involved in the day's performance entered together and took up their basic positions in fixed locations called 'house' or 'stall' (*domus* or *hof*) allocated to their group. They remained there throughout the performance, for up to 12 hours, seated except when involved in the action. The actors, all men, sit when performing only if they are rulers, e.g. Herod or Caiaphas, or in very special cases such as participating in one of the meals recorded in the New Testament, most notably in the Last Supper, which includes Christ's washing of the Apostles' feet.

This single large location, occupying the principal square of the town, allowed spectators to be all around, behind the stalls of the performers. This involved both the construction of spectator 'stands' and the use of the frontages of surrounding houses and other buildings to provide vantage points. These structures required for both performers and spectators were a major expense and records show they were regularly paid for by the local town or city council. There is however no evidence from the German-speaking countries of admission charges to the plays.

Corpus Christi plays differed in that they were processional, allowing performances at a number of locations along a route, and incorporated *tableaux vivants* as well as dramatic scenes. The surviving material, including texts, from Freiburg im Breisgau shows the transition from procession to dramatic performance and while the older surviving documents from Künzelsau call the director *rector processionis*, in the later ones he is called *rector ludi*.

Open-air performance to large audiences of both Passion and Corpus Christi plays allowed little subtlety in acting style, when some of the audience were inevitably seeing the actors' backs and others were up to 50 yards away. This presumably fitted well with the fact that all the actors were amateurs, members of the local community who vied with one another to obtain a part. Lists of actors' names are known from Alsfeld, Bozen, Sterzing, Lucerne and Zurzach and show participation by a wide range of social groups, though members of the local administration are particularly well represented – town councillors, magistrates, mayors, town clerks and lesser officials. Participation also cost money, since each actor provided not only his own costume but also small props associated with it or with the scene (e.g. at Lucerne the actor playing the Virgin Mary was responsible for providing the requisites for the Annunciation). There is also some evidence of a further cash levy towards costs being made on a sliding scale according to the importance of the part to be played, cash to be handed over before the actor received the separate text of his part. A note also survives from Lucerne that nobody worthy of a part should be omitted if genuinely unable to pay.

The Passion plays do not divide properly into separate acts or scenes, though the term *Actus* is used in some plays; the simultaneous staging allows the possibility of one scene with dialogue going on at the same time as a piece of mimed action elsewhere on the acting area, e.g. at Lucerne Barrabas's murder of a pedlar to account for his imprisonment is mimed during a genuine New Testament scene. The action is often interspersed with music, which can either further the action or serve to fill in a pause in speech; music also often accompanies the walking about which signifies moving between locations. Such music was largely vocal but included instrumental music; paid musicians were indeed the only participants from outside the local community involved in such a performance.

Such plays were almost invariably anonymous. The clergy had a significant role as censors of the theological soundness of the doctrines incorporated into the text and may often have been authors. Names of directors/producers (*Regent/regens ludi . . .*) are recorded more frequently; we know of Benedikt Debs (d. 1515) in Bozen, Vigil Raber (d. 1552) in Sterzing, and in

Lucerne during the 16th century of Hans Salat, Zacharias Bletz and Renward Cysat.

Details of the staging of such Passion play performances are known from various kinds of document. First, some textual manuscripts especially those which served as the director's prompt copy (e.g. the surviving first quarter of the 1583 Lucerne Passion Play manuscript, Cysat's copy) contain details of how stage effects were achieved. A similar purpose lies behind documents such as the *Frankfurter Dirigierrolle* (Frankfurt Director's Roll), dating from the early 14th century, a series of incipits and explicits plus a certain number of stage directions on a series of seven pieces of parchment glued together to form a narrow roll 436 cm. long. Various details about staging and performance matters, e.g. costume, appear in other extant documents, sometimes fortuitously but occasionally by deliberate effort, as at Lucerne where Cysat, director of the last performances (that in 1616 was postponed from 1614 when he died), not only collected his own notes and materials but also those of his predecessors, so that they remain in considerable quantity in local archives today.

To him we owe also the most detailed and most famous stage plans from the medieval German theatre, which he drew for the 1583 Lucerne performance and used again for the next performance in 1597. These show the positions all round the Lucerne Weinmarkt occupied by the groups associated with the various important characters. There is also the usual opposition between 'Heaven', half-way up the facade of the building at the upper end of the square, the Haus zur Sonne, and 'Hell', with the opening Hell's Mouth, in the bottom corner of the platea, alongside the scaffold for actors and audience built over the fountain which occupied the middle of the square. But even these plans, like those from Alsfeld and Villingen, are not unambiguously clear in all the details they appear to state and must be read with more understanding of all the known details concerning the relevant performances than has sometimes been the case in the past. In particular they do not give details of the relationship between the stalls for performers, the grandstands for spectators and the buildings behind them.

The great flowering of religious drama in the German-speaking countries comes right at the end of the medieval period. It ended with the Reformation in the areas which became Protestant and in areas which remained Catholic it continued throughout the 16th century and in sub-literary folk theatre even longer (see **Oberammergau**).

There is an unjustified tendency to label all medieval secular drama in German *Fastnacht(s)spiel* (Shrovetide Play or Carnival Comedy). Though this label is valid for the majority of extant plays and those known about, it is not applicable to all.

One small group is made up of the plays of demonstrably literary origin representing the clash between Spring and Autumn (*Mai und Herbst* in the titles). These represent ultimately the clash between courtly elegance and refinement and uncourtly excess and self-indulgence.

The Neidhart Plays (*Neidhartspiele*) attach themselves to the historical poet Neidhart von Reuental (about 1190–1245) whose works reveal his aristocratic hatred of *nouveau riche* peasants who ape aristocratic fashion and knightly behaviour at best only in their externals. Some of the manuscripts and the *Sterzinger Szenar* (Sterzing Scenario), which is akin to the *Frankfurter Dirigierrolle*, contain elaborate stage directions. These plays are however critical not only of the peasants but also of the degenerate effete nobility. The concern of their plots with faeces and the provocation of a fight bring them close to the *Fastnachtspiel*, in which form two texts survive.

Since the medieval term *vasnachtspil* covers all kinds of pre-Lenten entertainment and performance as well as the actual dramatic *Fastnachtspiel* it is difficult to make accurate statements about the extent and frequency of *Fastnachtspiel* as a dramatic genre. The largest corpus of texts, contained mainly in a handful of 15th-century manuscript compendia, comes from Nuremberg, where the origin of the genre seems to be in the telling of bawdy and scatological tall stories in turn in a limited verse form of two or three rhymed couplets per speaker. In these *Reinhenspiele* or Revue pieces each speaker starts afresh and only by the implicit seeking to outdo the others does each speech refer indirectly to what has preceded it. The narrated exploits of these grotesquely unsuccessful lovers are often presented in the mouths of peasants, establishing the possibility of connection with the personnel of the *Neidhartspiele*.

The *Fastnachtspiel* is, like the religious drama, an urban genre. Its performers were apparently the journeymen members of the guilds who during this time of celibacy imposed on them by guild regulation relieved themselves of tensions at Shrovetide by at least verbal sexual excesses. Small groups went about between houses and inns during the days of pre-Lenten festivity, making a space for their performance on the floor amidst the other revelries – many texts begin with a call for silence and a claim on the attention of those present. Similarly the ends of these plays pass the action back to the wider celebration, often incorporating a request for a drink from the host before they depart or involving the performers and members of the audience in a closing dance.

Whilst the simplest Revue pieces were scarcely dramatic and are only just emerging from the sub-literary folk culture, as the 15th century develops plays incorporating a plot, *Handlungsspiele*, begin to appear, often relating to tales known in contemporary German *Mären* and French *fabliaux*. The only known authors of these *Fastnachtspiele* are Hans Rosenplüt (mid-15th century) and Hans Folz (c. 1440–1513). This material brings into German drama for the first time the notion of stock comic characters, e.g. the unpleasant old woman, the cunning maid, the wise fool, as well as for the first time introducing the concept of dramatic intrigue. These plays like the associated *Lügenmärchen* (tall stories) do not represent reality but use the licence of Shrovetide to turn contemporary society topsy-turvy and present it as these texts might well say 'arse over tits'. The effect is not merely intended *pour épater les bourgeois* but more subtly to remind the audience that the world is not as it should be. If we bear this strand of concern in mind, it is less surprising to find the Nuremberg *Fastnachtspiel* in the 16th century in the hands of Hans Sachs reduced to mild didactic moralizing. A small number of the 15th-century *Fastnachtspiele* from Nuremberg show clear tendencies to social criticism as the citizens of the Free Imperial City rail at the shortcomings of territorial princes and high-ranking clergy and the venality of secular and clerical office-bearers.

Other centres with a known tradition of Shrovetide Plays were Eger (now Cheb in Czechoslovakia) with 25 known performances between 1442 and 1522, from which no texts survive; and South Tyrol where Vigil Raber (see above) copied over 20 pieces, probably from Nuremberg, as well as acting in these and other plays. A series of performances also took place in Lübeck between 1430 and at least 1537. Though no texts survive we have a list of titles of the plays which were performed in the open air by a patrician society, the Zirkelbruderschaft. They are quite different from the South German *Fastnachtspiele* in having a serious moralizing purpose. Themes from classical antiquity and medieval European epic literature (Arthur, Charlemagne, old Germanic heroes) predominate early in the period; later, moralizing satirical criticism of contemporary society went alongside plays presenting the virtues desired of good citizens. An incomplete Basel manuscript dated 1434 also contains parts of a serious Shrovetide Play involving social criticism; a scene involving Lucifer sending out his devils into the world provides one of the few clear points of interrelationship between religious and secular drama.   JET

Italy The earliest Italian drama, the sung Latin liturgical plays, comprises traditional representations of the Nativity – including both Shepherds and Magi – Annunciation, Purification and more than a score of Resurrection plays as well as a number of more unusual and interesting subjects. The oldest extant manuscript of a Passion play, the 12th-century Latin text from Montecassino is unfortunately incomplete at the beginning and the end: scenes of the Betrayal, Arrest and Trials of Christ lead up to the Crucifixion and the manuscript then breaks off after three lines of a vernacular *Planctus* (Lament) of the Virgin Mary. The 317 lines of the text are interspersed with directions for movement and action but there is no indication of the location or time of the performance as there is in the 14th-century *Planctus Marie et aliorum in die Parasceven* (*Lament of Mary and others on Good Friday*) from Cividale, in which each of the Maries and Disciples lamenting round the Cross has prescribed gestures written – in a smaller script – above nearly every line of the sung text.

A reference to the Passion being '*rappresenta*' (represented) in Siena in 1200 unfortunately only survives at secondhand and there is no way of knowing if the people who – paid by the town – '*facevano tali figure*' (created such figures) were model-makers, actors or participants in a tableau. There is, however, a definite record of performance of a play in Padua in 1244 when the Passion and Resurrection were staged out of doors, at Easter, '*solemniter et ordinate*' (in a solemn and orderly way). The Padua text has not survived but the same events – from the Arrest of Christ to the Crucifixion – are included in a 14th-century manuscript from Sulmona of the role – speeches and cues only – of the Fourth Soldier (*Quartus Miles*). Although many lines in this actor's copy are identical with lines in the 12th-century Montecassino play, it is unlikely there was a direct association between the two texts: such borrowings were very common.

Very few Latin Old Testament plays have survived

apart from a 16th-century version from Salerno of the Pseudo-Augustinian Sermon (on which the *Procession of Prophets* was based) in which the text is not read as a lection at Matins but recited in dramatic form, with individualized speakers, at the end of the first of the three Masses of Christmas. This version may well have been in use for a considerable time before it was printed in the 1594 service book. Evidence of a Creation play in the 13th century is provided by performances recorded from Cividale in 1298 and 1303. In both years the plays were staged on Whitsunday and the two following days, by the city clergy in the courtyard of the episcopal palace in the presence of ecclesiastical and civic dignitaries. The *Representation of the Play of Christ* in 1298 comprised only the Passion, Resurrection, Ascension, Pentecost and Last Judgement, but in 1303 these episodes were preceded by scenes of the Creation, Annunciation, Nativity 'and many others'. A play of Antichrist was also added making a sequence – Creation to Judgement – very similar to that of the English cycle plays. The Cividale texts have not survived but it seems probable, given the strongly clerical nature of the occasion, that they were performed in Latin. However, sung plays in the vernacular including all the Old and New Testament incidents represented at Cividale were already being composed and performed in Italy by the end of the 13th century.

The impetus for the creation of a sung vernacular drama closely linked with the liturgical year was given by the flagellant movement which arose in Umbria in the second half of the 13th century when groups of laymen – inspired particularly by the preaching of Joachim of Fiore – banded together to do public penance of behalf of the sinful world and alternated the singing of praises (*laude*) to God with periods of self-flagellation (*disciplina*). The first company of *disciplinati* under a certain Raniero Fasano was formed in Perugia whence the movement spread rapidly throughout Umbria; appropriate *laude*, based on a secular verse form, the *ballata*, with a soloist and chorus, were composed for the different Sundays and Feastdays of the church calendar, some of them merely lyrical, others in simple dramatic form. The most famous of the early *laude* is the *Donna del Paradiso* (*Queen of Heaven*) by Jacopone da Todi, a vernacular development of the Latin *Planctus* in which the weeping Virgin speaks in turn with Christ, John and finally, the Cross itself. Of lesser poetic stature but considerable importance in the history of Italian drama are the texts of the *Libro de Laode* or *Laudario* (*Book of Praises*) from Perugia which introduced in the dramatic *laude* the use of a six-line stanza sung to a solemn (*passionale*) melody for the penitential seasons – Advent, Lent and Holy Week – while retaining the old *ballata* eight-line stanza to a joyful (*pasquale*) melody in the *laude* for Christmas, Easter and other festivals. The performance of these texts was genuinely theatrical as can be seen from the records of costumes and properties belonging to the Confraternity of Saint Augustine in Perugia whose *Libro di Prestanze* (*Book of Loans*) lists cloaks, masks for devils and death, curtains, painted cloths and so on.

By the end of the 14th century, the *laude* had passed through a series of changes, the most important being that from sung to spoken drama. The plays, now called *laude*, *devozioni* or even *rappresentazioni* interchangeably, used a mixture of verse forms including six- and eight-line stanzas as well as quatrains, triolets and even whole sonnets. The subject matter is also more varied and less closely tied to the liturgical year: the Orvieto *Laudario* includes a play on the Creation and Fall of the Angels and Man which demands both choral movement and singing; at the end, the Devoti (members of the confraternity) pray to God to save Man in a scene reminiscent of the Trial in Heaven and suggestive of a link with the season of Advent.

Both the Franciscan and the Dominican friars were influential in the development of this vernacular drama; the former used stanzas and scenes from the Holy Week *laude* (including the *Donna del Paradiso*) to illustrate their sermons as well as creating semi-dramatic presentations like the *Passio Volgarizzata* (*Vernacular Passion*) from Abruzzo which combines the '*Dic et tu*' (Now you speak) technique of the pseudo-Augustinian Sermon with the practice of dramatizing the Passion lections on Good Friday and Holy Saturday. The Dominicans used plays as a means of more general instruction: their 14th-century *Laudario* from Aquila contains a long and elaborate three-day dramatization of the life of their fellow Dominican, St Thomas Aquinas, involving numerous scene changes, a large cast and much realistic detail in the presentation of secular life in court and castle. Both these theatrical forms, the Passion play and the biographical saint's play, were to be developed further in the 15th century, which in Italy, as in other parts of Europe, was the golden age of the medieval drama.

The most celebrated of the many Passion plays recorded is probably that performed annually from 1460 by the Gonfaloniere di Santa Lucia (Bannerbearers of St Lucy) in the Coliseum in Rome. The surviving text and records suggest a conflation of a number of short plays covering incidents from the Ministry, Passion and Resurrection, using multiple staging and performed, according to the German pilgrim Arnold von Harff who watched it on Good Friday morning 1494, 'by young gentlemen of good family'. After 1500 the performances became less regular and the play was finally banned by the Pope in 1539.

Among the many imitators of the Gonfaloniere was the Confraternity of St John in Velletri who, lacking a ready-made Coliseum/theatre, constructed early in the 16th century a permanent stone-built stage (the *palcoscenico*) for their Passion play. Set against the city walls, it occupied the whole of the west side of the Piazza San Giacomo so that there was shade for the afternoon performance. The stage was raised up six feet and access was through two doors in the front of the structure from which steps led up a passageway for the actors behind the facade whose archways were adorned with Corinthian columns and pediments. The Passion was staged there until 1563 and the structure was finally demolished in 1765 by order of the Town Council though fortunately not before Cardinal Stefano Borgia had had an engraving made of it.

It was probably on a multiple stage, perhaps similar to that at Velletri, that the community of the Alpine town of Revello presented their three-day Passion play in the French style in 1494. Other notable performances include those in Ferrara under the Este family. In 1481, the Duke had the Passion performed in the palace chapel on a stage specially constructed over the altar,

with a wooden serpent's mouth which opened and closed, for the scene of the Harrowing of Hell. In Holy Week of 1489, scaffolds for both performers and spectators were erected in the main square of Ferrara (leaving access to the houses and shops) where the events of Maundy Thursday and Good Friday were re-enacted on the appropriate days. These plays, sung by the choir from the ducal chapel, were in Latin except for four scenes in the vernacular, including the Lament of the Virgin Mary.

Although plays were performed in many different towns and communities, the outstanding contributor to the later religious drama is undoubtedly Florence. In the early 15th century plays were presented in many Florentine churches for the liturgical feasts, some of them with complex machinery, music and lights: **Vasari** describes a Paradise and angels designed by Brunelleschi and elaborate flying and lifting machinery is recorded by the Russian patriarch, Abramio of Sousdal, who watched plays of the Annunciation and Ascension during his visit to Florence for the Ecumenical Council of 1439. The extensive surviving manuscript records of performance and staging details are only now being studied and published, and many plays are also unedited including a 16th-century manuscript of a huge Passion play compilation, described as *alcuni misteri* (some mystery plays). The subject matter runs from the Prophets to Pentecost – including the Trial in Heaven and an Interlude of the Seven Deadly Sins – followed by miracles of SS Peter, James and Ignatius and the Invention of the Holy Cross. The sequence from the Betrayal to the Entombment of Christ, alone, is more than five thousand lines.

Florence also had processional drama. A Greek visitor to the Ecumenical Council has described the magnificent array of mounted and walking figures, biblical, legendary and fantastic, with which the Florentines celebrated the Feast of their patron, St John the Baptist. In 1439 and in 1454 the St John's Day procession included a series of wagon-plays. Similar mixtures of processions and plays are recorded from other towns and the extant text from Bologna includes plays on the Temptation of Adam, the Trial in Heaven and the Nativity as well as lists of walking characters – saints, Old Testament figures and religious orders.

The special contribution of Florence to the religious drama, however, was the *sacra rappresentazione*, a development of the later, spoken *lauda* but written by an individual and performed on any suitable occasion outside the liturgical calendar. The earliest known writer is Feo Belcari (1410–64) who wrote a number of these plays for the youths of the Company of St John the Evangelist, the *Vangelista*, whose principal patron, Lorenzo da Medici himself, wrote for them a play on *SS Giovanni e Paulo*. More than a hundred *sacre rappresentazioni* have survived in manuscripts or printed texts; all are Florentine in origin though many were subsequently reprinted and perhaps performed in other towns and regions throughout the 16th century. Subjects appropriate to the mainly youthful performers predominate in these plays: stories of Isaac, Ishmael (an example to be shunned), Joseph and the Prodigal Son. Each play has a prologue or *Annunziazione* (probably so-called because it is usually spoken by an angel) which outlines the plot and the relevant moral as well as giving the traditional appeals for silence and attention.

At the end the angel gives the audience leave (*Licenzia*) to depart. The didactic force of the plays is sometimes enhanced by a framework of contemporary scenes involving youthful characters: a group of good and bad boys, a father with a good and a bad son etc. Many details of production and staging can be gleaned from these scenes which may even show their characters talking to the performers of the main play. There are also quite frequent stage directions in the body of the text. Not all the *sacre rappresentazioni* were written for boys; many do not specify performers or audiences, while some appear to be written for religious houses. The version of the play of *Santa Teodora* (*St Theodora*) printed in 1554 was probably designed for a convent since the framework scenes show the nuns arguing about their roles, costumes and the number of lines they have to learn. (Satirical plays of the period claim that on these occasions the nuns dressed up as men, with cloaks and swords and breeches, but there is no independent evidence of this.) A few of the framework sequences were printed independently of their centrepiece under the name of *frottole* (comic dialogues) thus forming a kind of bridge between the religious and secular theatre.

A link of a different kind is provided by the early Latin work known as the *Cena Cypriani* (*Cyprian's Feast*). Originally composed in Latin prose and attributed to the 3rd-century St Cyprian, bishop of Carthage, this popular comedy was remodelled in verse in the 9th century by John the Deacon who describes it as a satirical play (*satiram ludam*). Joel, an eastern king, invites many biblical figures to a wedding feast at Cana. The humour derives mainly from the use of apt biblical allusions in describing the seating arrangements (Eve is under a fig-tree, Samson on a pillar); the clothes (Lazarus is given a shroud as a wedding garment); and the food (Elisha is served bear's meat and Abel gets lamb). The work was probably written in Italy (the wines served are all Italian) and the references to 'seeing' and 'hearing' in the prologue suggest that it was performed in the style of the ancient Roman mimes, with a narrator reciting the text and accompanying dumb-shows. The large cast, many costumes and great variety of properties needed for this 'pantomime' make it appropriate for performance, as John the Deacon suggested, as an entertainment for the papal or imperial court.

Comic scenes are rare in Italian religious drama and there is not a great deal of humour in the medieval secular plays either, though some of the semi-dramatic debates, *contrasti*, have an element of visual comedy such as the mock battle in the *Debate of Carnival and Lent*. Dialogues (*frottole*) between stereotype characters – a husband and wife or a blonde and a brunette – together with a few genuine farces make up the brief tally of humorous 'medieval' theatre. Nor is this paucity surprising in a period when the classical comedies of **Plautus** and **Terence** were already inspiring the new generation of renaissance dramatists. The semi-dramatic *giostre* (Jousts) which like the English tournament or the French *pas d'armes* were often the occasion for pageants and maskings as well as combats also show classical influence: the printed text of the *Giostra di Giuliano da Medici* consists of a series of verses followed by the *Festa di Orpheo* (*Play of Orpheus*), the first neoclassical drama of the end of the 15th century.

Examples of serious secular drama are the Florentine plays on the stories of *Santa Uliva* or *Regina Rosana*. Although as Miracles of the Virgin they technically belong with the religious theatre, yet in subject matter and treatment they owe more to the biographical romances than to hagiography, for scenes of everyday life (such as were used in the *lauda* of St Thomas) alternate with marvellous adventures, while in the *Santa Uliva* the action is divided by interludes involving mythical and allegorical figures. Like all the Florentine plays, these romantic dramas were continually reprinted throughout the 16th century so that on paper at least the medieval drama in Italy survived long after it had been effectively superseded by the new genres of tragedy and comedy. LRM

The Low Countries   The development of drama in the Low Countries ran parallel to that in the surrounding countries, especially France, and the range of religious and secular drama was as extensive. Town and church accounts contain many references to dramatic events such as pageantry or processions with *tableaux vivants* or to drama proper with action and speech, often with music as an essential element as in liturgical drama, or as an incidental element as in other dramatic genres.

Much of the evidence comes from the Southern Netherlands, from the wealthy provinces of Flanders and Brabant with their powerful trading towns, but the Northern Netherlands, in particular the provinces of Holland, Zeeland and Utrecht, had their share of drama and of literature in general too, much more than has often been supposed.

Judging from the many references to Easter, Christmas and Epiphany plays, liturgical drama was important and widespread. Two 12th-century Utrecht antiphonaria contain the *Quem queritis* trope, with roles for the women and for the Angel, sung and performed by priests. Slightly more elaborate is the 13th-century Haarlem Easter Play, which ends with the *elevatio* accompanied by the singing of 'Christus Dominus surrexit' and 'Deo gratias', then the *Te Deum*. The role of the ointment-seller, here called *physicus* (doctor), survives from an Easter Play performed in Delft in 1496 and 1503. The properties and the helpers needed are recorded in the church accounts and show it to have been an elaborate affair: clothes, a crown, a *sudarium*, a psalter, nails, pins, thread, weapons for the Pharisees, paint for the grave, wood for the stage, crucifixes for the two murderers, payment for the writing out of the various roles, to Jan the organ pumper, to the carpenter, to Jan the bellringer, the cost of beer and wine. The most extensive surviving church drama, the Maastricht Easter Drama of c. 1200, was performed annually in the Church of Our Lady in Maastricht on the first day of Easter. There are nine roles: Christ appears as gardener, as deacon and as pilgrim, there are two angels, three women, two disciples dressed as pilgrims and the ointment-seller. The manuscript contains many stage directions and various locations in the church had special functions.

The largest collection of early vernacular plays is that in the Van Hulthem manuscript (c. 1410). It contains more than 200 literary texts, most important amongst which are four serious, secular plays, the *Abele Spelen*, and six farces or *Sotterniën*. The plays are not all grouped together but each of the four serious plays is followed by a farce; the two remaining farces, incomplete due to a missing leaf, follow each other. The *Abele Spelen* each treat of love. The first three, *Esmoreit*, *Gloriant* and *Lanseloet van Denemarken*, are romances, the fourth, *Vanden Winter ende Vanden Somer* (*Of Winter and Summer*), is an elaborate debate. The six farces too are variations on a theme: that of the wicked woman – a standard character in many farces and other genres, such as the narrative *fabliau*.

The serious plays and their accompanying farces were not conceived as a unity, but grouped together gradually, perhaps selected for their thematic similarities. By the time they were incorporated into the manuscript, the plays had been welded together, *Abel spel* to farce, by additions and changes in the prologues, the epilogues and the rhyme. The Van Hulthem manuscript was probably used in a *scriptorium* as a collection from which customers could choose pieces. There is no record of the performances of these plays, except for a mention of the play of Lanseloet being performed in Aachen on 14 August 1412 by the Company of Diest, a town in Brabant. The plays could be performed by a small company, and there is a slender chance that amongst groups of minstrels, such as those employed, for example, by the Count of Flanders in 1378, there were not only musicians who sang and recited but also performers of plays. The *Abele Spelen* and the farces are probably much older than the Van Hulthem manuscript; *Esmoreit*, indeed, may date from as early as c. 1340.

We have no indication of what stage directions once existed, or indeed what development in staging took place between the time the plays were written and first performed and their appearance in the manuscript, or when they were given later performances. We must remember though that a medieval playwright would not normally write a play without the certainty that it was going to be performed.

There is no evidence that the *Abele Spelen* and *Sotterniën* were included in the repertory of a Chamber of Rhetoric until 1720, when the 's-Gravenpolder Chamber commissioned the copying of a 'Play of Lanseloet'; a sure sign that they meant to perform it and once more evidence of the longevity of the tradition of the Chambers of Rhetoric as well as of the circulation of medieval texts.

It is impossible to discuss any of the drama produced in the 15th century without giving some attention to the Rederijkerskamers (Chambers of Rhetoric), whose presence is first recorded in the early years of the century and which were to become such a dominant feature in the literary life of the Low Countries, in particular towards the end of the 15th and during most of the 16th century. These amateur literary guilds were in origin not a special feature of the Low Countries. Non-aristocratic brotherhoods, *confréries* or guilds, made their appearance in Western Europe in many places as a third class of traders, merchants and craftsmen began to conceive of themselves as a separate and valuable part of society. The origins of the Chambers of Rhetoric go back in part to secular devotional brotherhoods which sometimes acted as an aid to the clergy in religious processions and drama. Some brotherhoods became converted into Chambers of Rhetoric. The element of mutual social and economic aid, so strong in the craft and religious guilds, can be perceived in the Chambers too, for instance in the care they took to ensure that their members were given proper funerals. Whereas in spirit, the Chambers long retained the devotional element of the religious brotherhoods, in their organization they were very akin to the Archers' Guilds. These were common in the Low Countries, originally formed as local defence guilds by the fortified towns. The Chambers developed and made independent an element that was already present in such Guilds, that of dramatic activities. Important archery competitions, for instance, were accompanied by other festive events such as the performance of drama or the antics of Fools, and some members of an Archers' Guild could become an independent organization. Rhetoricians are also known to have accompanied the Archers to competitions.

In their activities the Chambers of Rhetoric resemble societies which were numerous in the French-speaking provinces in the Burgundian Netherlands before the Chambers of Rhetoric appear, the so-called Puys. Poetry and drama, specifically in honour of Our Lady and the Saints, were their main activities and there was a strong competitive element, just as in the case of the Chambers of Rhetoric. In the Flemish-speaking provinces similar societies spread like wildfire. In the 15th century about 60 Chambers were established and the number grew to about 180 in the 16th century. They varied in size, from about 16 to 150 members.

Their dramatic activities consisted of the writing and the production of plays, religious and secular, serious and comic. The Rhetoricians also played an active part in all manner of pageantry and processions. In religious processions, often held on an important feast day such as Palm Sunday, Easter, Corpus Christi or Shrove Tuesday, they often organized *tableaux vivants* or wagon-plays with biblical or historical subject matter, some of these very elaborate, with all manner of music as well as marvels such as giants, fire-breathing dragons, and Trees of Jesse with small children on every branch. On secular occasions, too, the Rhetoricians had important contributions to make and indeed were expected by their town to add lustre to such occasions as the celebrations of a peace, royal or ducal Entries, weddings, coronations, funerals of their immediate overlords or members of the ducal or royal family. A very specific item on such occasions was the triumphal arch, the development of which influenced the stage facades of the Rhetoricians. Instead of the simple platform with a curtained-off booth, 16th-century pictures show architectural facades with elaborate classically inspired decoration, with a number of entrances and compartments behind the screen, which could be incorporated into the available acting space in a number of different ways. The triumphal arches and the facades were often made by members of the painters' guilds and the pooling of these artistic resources resulted in very elaborate decorations and staging.

An important part of the Rhetoricians' activities was their participation in local or regional literary competitions. A competition was an occasion which involved and affected the whole town. Special provisions had to be made for the intake of many people. The streets had to be cleared, decorations had to be made and put up. Everything was turned into spectacle, from the festive entry of all the Chambers into the host town and their welcome by the resident Chambers, to the presentation of their heraldic emblems; from the decoration of the inns where they lodged, to the *tableau vivant* on a wagon depicting a prescribed subject, such as Peace, and the solemn procession to church. Then there was the declamation of the Prologue on a set theme, and the actual plays: the *esbatement*, the *spel van sinnen* and the *factie*, a short comic piece of street theatre. Prizes were given for all these parts of the competition as well as for the best actor, the best Fool, and the most splendid celebration afterwards.

Strict rules were laid down for the length and subject matter of the entries, and in particular for the allegorical *spelen van sinnen* (moralities). Bound as they were to answer particular moral, religious, social or ethical questions, they are often somewhat stiff and stilted. The *esbatementen*, however, were often comic and possessed verve and lively dramatic action. They were not printed, but used as exchange material and were copied out by other Chambers and played again, sometimes till well into the 18th century.

The *spelen van sinnen*, the moralities, were the most distinctive form to be created by the Rhetoricians, but from the beginning of the 15th century there is evidence to indicate that the Guild members were involved in religious drama very akin to that in for instance France. The Low Countries had their mystery and miracle plays and the few surviving texts are witnesses to what must have been a lively and fully-developed tradition. In fact, it is not easy to find 15th- and 16th-century drama in the Low Countries without implicit or explicit involvement of the Rhetoricians.

The Chambers of Rhetoric produced a great deal of religious drama and they are connected with the performing of the only surviving mystery plays. *The First Joy of Mary* (*Die Eerste Bliscap van Maria*) and *The Seventh Joy of Our Lady* (*Die Sevenste Bliscap van Onser Vrouwen*) are the only remnants of a cycle of seven plays and they relate respectively the events leading up to the Annunciation and to the Death and Assumption of Our Lady. The first recorded performance of *The First Joy* took place in Brussels in 1448, the last known performance of *The Seventh Joy* occurred in 1566. In 1556 *The Fourth Joy* was staged, as we know from an eyewitness account by a member of the retinue of the Emperor Charles V. These mystery plays were part of the celebration of a local legendary event linked with Our Lady, which was commemorated by a very elaborate procession or *ommeganc*. It took place on the Sunday before Pentecost and its organization was in the hands of the Guild of the Crossbowmen who, possibly aided by members of the Chambers of Rhetoric in the town, also took part in the organization and performance of the mystery plays.

Much more is known about this procession, due to the meticulous description given by the same courtier mentioned above, than about the mystery plays. It took place in the morning and the mystery plays followed in the afternoon, one *Joy* every year, until the cycle was completed. In 1559 and 1566 the Chamber of Rhetoric called the Cornflower was responsible for the performance of the *Seventh Joy* and the two manuscripts of the *First* and the *Seventh Joy* are both annotated by the producer, the town poet of Brussels. The stage on that occasion was built 'in the form of the Coliseum'. *The First Joy* contains a list of players, including two women, and shows that the players sometimes had more than one role. The plays have a number of stage directions. One frequently used is that of *pausa*, a moment when the stage is empty, although action in some cases is implied behind closed curtains and often music is played. A similar expression *selete* indicates another moment when the stage is empty or the actors are silent or miming. It can also indicate a change of characters or a shift to a different location, and on such occasions music often had an important place.

The Play of the Holy Sacrament of Nyeuwervaert (*Het Spel vanden Heilighen Sacramente vander Nyeuwervaert*) is the oldest surviving miracle play in the Low Countries. Its author is unknown; its date of origin must have been shortly after 1463, when a Brotherhood of the Holy Sacrament of Nyeuwervaert was founded in Breda, to honour the miracles performed by a Host found in a marsh in a village in the same diocese as Breda. The only known performance was organized by the Breda Chamber of Rhetoric on 24 June, St John's Day, in 1500. A Sacraments Procession on the Sunday before St John's Day was a regular feature in Breda which continued into the 16th century, and it may be that the play was performed for a number of years in the same week. The procession was accompanied by various dramatic events and dancing; possibly *tableaux vivants* are indicated by 'a play of St Hubert, of St George, of St Barbara, of Herod, a Shepherd's play, a play of the Four Sons of Aymon versus the King of France' and there were sword-dancers and a savage.

The performance of the play took place on a stage in or in front of an inn in the market square in Breda, and needed only six players. It is no more than a description of the discovery of the Host and its miraculous property of bleeding as soon as it is touched by anyone else but a priest. The miracles it performs are reported. The play required a hell-mouth and is set in three different places, one of which, Nyeuwervaert with its church and its immediate surroundings, occurs five times. The liveliness and the dramatic tension are entirely due to the *sinnekens*, devilish tempters of Mankind.

Possibly dating from the end of the 15th century is the only other surviving mystery play in the Low Countries, the *Play of the Five Wise and the Five Foolish Virgins* (*Het Spel van de V Vroede ende van de V Dwaeze Maeghden*). Both the Old and the New Testament, and the parables in particular, became very popular subject matter in the drama of the Rhetoricians, especially in the 16th century. Another characteristic feature in the *Play of the Virgins* is its allegorical nature and didactic emphasis. The Foolish Virgins, for example, have names symbolic of Man's forgetfulness of the Day of Judgement: Waste of Time, Recklessness, Pride, Vainglory, Foolish Chatter.

The stage directions concern mainly action and movement; the most elaborate occurs when the Wise Virgins are admitted to God's Glory. The play is distinguished from its French and German counterparts, the *Sponsus* and the *Zehnjungfrauenspiel*, in two scenes in particular: first the waffle-eating feast of the Foolish Virgins, and second the very original devil scene when the Foolish Virgins are dragged into Hell. There are no *sinnekens* in this play but two of the devils have names very typical of these characters: Sharp Investigation and Evil Counsel. The play has a processional ending; the only one extant in Dutch drama.

The true and very miraculous history of Mariken van

Nieumeghen who lived more than seven years with the devil shows its problematic status already in its title. In form it hovers between narrative and dramatic text. It survives as a printed book (c. 1515) in which the dramatic dialogues are interspersed with elaborate descriptive chapter-headings in prose. Whether the unknown author wrote it originally as a play is not at all clear. It has become a classic in Dutch literature and is, ironically, the most often performed medieval Dutch 'play' in modern times.

It is an extraordinarily rich text, this *exemplum* of Mariken who was the devil's paramour. It has a great deal to offer of historical, political and topical interest as well as of dramatic craft. Particularly interesting from a theatrical point of view is Mariken's moment of true insight into her situation and her repentance, which occurs when she watches a play on a wagon performed in her native town Nijmegen in which Our Lady pleads for forgiveness for Mankind from God and succeeds notwithstanding strong opposition from Masscheroen, the Devil's advocate. This play-in-a-play is not unique in the drama of the Low Countries in so far as a number of Rhetoricians' plays have inner and outer plays but this is a particularly effective example of that and of a Trial in Heaven. No stage directions survive.

The Mirror of the Bliss of Everyman (Den Spieghel der Salicheit van Elckerlijc) has gained fame in world literature in its English translation *Everyman*. Its author and date of origin are unknown. It survived in three printed versions (oldest 1495) and one manuscript (c. 1595). Whether the printer, who introduced this text as 'a beautiful booklet made in the manner of a play or short play', left out any stage directions is uncertain; the four surviving versions do not contain any. One of its Latin translations, *Homulus*, claims that *Elckerlijc* was performed at a competition of Brabant Chambers of Rhetoric in Antwerp where it won the first prize. Though *Elckerlijc*'s allegorical presentation is entirely in keeping with the Rhetoricians' didactic mode there is no evidence to corroborate this statement.

For a survey of the many surviving Rhetoricians' plays, c. 600, one must turn to W. M. H. Hummelen's invaluable *Repertorium van het Rederijkersdrama, 1500–c. 1620*. To give some idea of the treasure trove of 16th-century drama in the Low Countries, a division according to subject matter, rather than genre, is more informative. There are plays with classical and mythological material, legendary and historical subjects, both ancient and contemporary, Old and New Testament plays as well as those with a wide range of theological and religious, social, political and economic topics. Many of these plays are allegorical and moralistic. They are not very long; farces vary from 300 to 600 lines, dinner plays from 200 to 300, serious plays from 1,000 to 1,500 lines. Some 280 plays are printed, the rest are in manuscript.

Individual playwrights have made names for themselves; the best known of these are the Bruges poet and playwright Anthonis de Roovere (c. 1430–82); the Brussels poet Jan Smeken (c. 1450–1517); and the Flemish Rhetorician Matthys Casteleyn (1485–1550), poet, playwright, composer and author of the first extensive *art poétique* in Dutch *De Conste van Rhetoriken (The Art of Rhetoric)*, written 1548, published 1555. The only survivor of his plays, reputedly numbering 106, is the delightful *spel van sinnen Pyramus and Thisbe*, which presents the Ovidian material in an orthodox Catholic and moralistic manner.

The Bruges playwright Cornelis Everaert collected his own 35 plays, written between 1509 and 1538, in a manuscript, possibly because no one else would pay much attention to his work. Reactionary in nature, his work reflects the social issues of his time.

The work of the Zeeland Rhetorician Job Gommersz, writing c. 1565, yields much information about staging.

Jan van den Berghe (d. Brussels 1559) must be mentioned for his *spel van sinnen Voluptuous Man (De Wellustighe Mensch)* in which the sybaritic main character, tempted into great excesses by the *sinnekens* Carnal Lust and Bad Faith, repents ultimately and is forgiven through God's Grace.

The work of the Haarlem poet Louris Jansz shows him to have been a typical humanist and liberal, tolerant, stressing the importance of Reason as a guiding force in Man's existence and with an eye for the evils in society, especially those brought about by war.

The influence of the Renaissance is clearly noticeable in the work of the Antwerp poet Willem van Haecht (c. 1530) who uses classical and mythological material. He also wrote three plays called *The Acts of the Apostles (Dwerck der Apostelen)* remarkable for their staging and their stage directions, using a facade stage with three or four openings in an extraordinarily flexible manner, showing numerous locations and a complete shipwreck.

The Antwerp poet and translator Cornelis van Ghistele (b. 1510) was an important interpreter of classical culture to his contemporaries. He was the *factor* or poetic leader of one of the three Antwerp Chambers of Rhetoric, The Marigold. Two of his plays were performed in May 1552 in Antwerp with the title of 'Eneas and Dido, two amorous plays'. Together the two plays form a continuous narrative which is an excellent example of the richness of Rhetoricians' theatre both conceptually and dramatically.   ES

Spain Since the reconquest of Spain from the Moors was a gradual process, taking several centuries, the liturgical drama in the Peninsula developed first in the north-east, in Catalonia, the earliest province to return to Christian rule. For more than two hundred years after the introduction there of the Roman-French rite, the Catalan dioceses were placed under the metropolitan see of Narbonne. Liturgical drama was widespread and popular in Catalonia as in France, the oldest surviving texts (early 12th-century) being from the monastery of Ripoll, which had close links with St Martial de Limoges. In addition to numerous texts of Christmas and Easter plays (the merchant scene in the *Visitatio* from Ripoll is the earliest known) the Catalan material also includes dramatizations of the prose, *Victimae Paschale*, within the Mass, found in the Customaries from Gerona and Mallorca, that from the latter being in the vernacular.

A small number of liturgical texts is found in the provinces of northern Spain – Aragon, León, and Galicia – carried there perhaps by pilgrims en route to the shrine of St James at Compostella. Castile, however, has almost no liturgical texts apart from a handful of *Quem queritis* tropes. It is generally accepted that this dearth resulted from the fact that after the expulsion of the Moors in the 12th century, Castile came under the influence of Cluniac monks and liturgical drama was almost unknown in Cluniac houses.

Church drama is also unknown in Portugal with the solitary exception of a brief shepherds' play of the 14th century from the monastery of Coimbra which from its foundation in 1132 followed the customs of Avignon.

The only religious dramatic ceremony found widely and uniquely in the Peninsula is the Monologue of the Sibyl on the Fifteen Signs of Judgement. Scenes of performances are recorded from all the provinces but it is unknown outside Spain except as part of a prophet play.

The *Auto de los Reyes Magos* (*Play of the Royal Magi*), probably dating from the end of the 12th century, is the only pre-15th-century extant Castilian vernacular play. The manuscript itself bears no title. The play covers the meeting of the three Kings, their decision, on seeing the star, to go to Bethlehem and, by offering gifts to the new-born child, to try to discover if he is man, king or God. We see their visit to Herod and his consultation with his own wise men, who quarrel and are unable to decide on the significance of Christ's birth. The manuscript breaks off here, and the suggestion has been made that it originally ended with the three Kings' visit to the Christ child, who would have accepted all three gifts. Some scholars, however, have recently advanced the view that the play is complete in itself. The 147-line *Auto* makes much use of typology when treating the relationship between the Old and the New Testament; the rabbis are shown as denying the advent of Christ and in consequence being unable fully to interpret the Old Testament texts. Many critics have advanced the *Auto de los Reyes Magos* as evidence of a pre-existing tradition of religious drama in the vernacular. More recent investigation, however, has pointed to the probability of Gascon authorship, and it has been suggested that it may have been written by a Gascon priest who intended it for the Epiphany services in Toledo. Strong evidence for this view is the similarity of motifs between the *Auto* and French narrative poems on the infancy of Christ and the fact that some words which do not rhyme in Castilian would do so if given Gascon pronunciation. If this view is accepted, the *Auto* cannot be taken as evidence of an earlier dramatic tradition in Castile.

Few other vernacular texts are known before the 14th century, but from then on biblical pageants were included in the Corpus Christi processions in Barcelona and Valencia and details from the accounts in Valencia in 1414 indicate how the floats – *rocas* or *entramesos* – were refurbished year by year; the cost of building, adorning and storing these pageant wagons was shared between the religious houses and the trade guilds. A description of the Barcelona procession from 1424 suggests the presence of mimed action but the earliest evidence of full dramatic plays with dialogue comes from the island of Mallorca in 1442. One of the major surviving play manuscripts in Catalan is also from the island – the 49 plays, written in the 16th century, were performed in and staged by the cathedral in Palma. Variously referred to as *consuetas*, *representaciós* and *misteris*, they depict incidents from the Old and New Testaments and saints' lives. Many of them have elaborate staging directions indicating that they were performed on scaffolds (*cadefals*), from three to five in

number, set in the crossing of the cathedral, with action taking place on and between the different locations. Special effects and machinery for raising and lowering are also described. This use of multiple staging in the French mode is also found in some of the mainland plays, such as those from Valencia, which were, however, normally performed out of doors. An exception to this practice is the group of Assumption plays of the 16th century found in a number of towns, including Valencia and Prades, and usually presented in a cathedral or large church where the *ara-celi*, the machine used to lower actors from Heaven to Earth and raise them again, is often described. In the Elche play, still performed regularly today, the *ara-celi* and its machinery were built into the structure when the church was reconstructed after a fire in the 18th century.

By the end of the 15th century, Corpus Christi processions with floats and tableaux are found in many parts of Spain: the records from Toledo are particularly detailed and interesting. Although the trade guilds were involved in these celebrations, they never achieved the dominant position in play production of, say, England; the Feast and its activities, processional and theatrical, remained very much in the hands of the church. Details of the tableaux of the floats, which were carried on the shoulders of men hidden by the side curtains (not pulled by man or beast as in other countries), and of the numerous walking figures, allegorical, biblical and fantastic, show some similarities to Italian practice.

Sacred and secular themes overlapped frequently in religious processions and Royal Entries; dancings and disguisings, jousts and processions were common in the different courts: the first use of the name *entramesos* for the floats occurs in 1373, and the accounts of the coronation of Martin I at Saragossa in 1399 show sieges, battles and hunting scenes being enacted on such wheeled floats between the tables at the banquet.

Both music and dance were a regular part of plays: in some, especially the Mallorcan texts, the dialogue was sung rather than spoken and, despite the frequent Councils forbidding dancing inside the church, dance-plays remained a very popular part of Spanish religious festivals as can be seen from the 1540 contract from Seville for a danced representation of the Magi in the Corpus Christi procession or the 16th-century play of the Nativity by Suárez de Robles in which the action is danced throughout.

The *momos* (mumming) played an important part in court entertainment, with ever more elaborate machinery being employed. Many references to *momos* can be found from the middle of the 15th century onwards, and in all parts of Spain and Portugal. Mock battles also play a part in court entertainment of the time. No clear distinction can be drawn between aristocratic entertainment and religious drama; there is evidence that religious plays were performed at court, and in the 1460s Christmas and Epiphany Gospel scenes were arranged for performance in Jaén (Granada) by Miguel Lucas de Iranzo.

From the second half of the 15th century come four dramatic texts from Castile by Gómez Manrique; one of these was written for the nuns of the convent of Calabozanos, where the author's sister was abbess. Two of the plays are *momos*; one, composed in honour of the 14th birthday of Prince Alfonso in 1467, has a prologue in prose and shows the court ladies conferring virtues and talents on the prince. The other celebrates the birth of the author's nephew and follows the same pattern, except that the service is carried out for the child by the four cardinal and three theological virtues. Another short piece consists of speeches by the Virgin Mary and St John and is largely based on the *Planctus Mariae* (*Mary's Lament*). In the case of both this and the preceding two *momos* we cannot be sure if performance or reading was intended; however, the fourth of Gómez Manrique's dramatic works, the *Representación del Nacimiento de Nuestro Señor* (*Representation of the Nativity of Our Lord*), is clearly written for perform-ance. Based on the *Officium Pastorum* (*Shepherds' Play*), it adds an opening scene in the medieval tradition of St Joseph as a comic figure, in which he is rebuked by an angel for his excessive suspiciousness: 'O old man of many days and few brains!' Mary meditates on the birth of her child and foresees the events of the Crucifixion; *momos* follow, where symbols of the Passion are presented to the baby, and the play ends with a lullaby in *villancico* form. The *Representación* has sometimes been compared, to its detriment, with the *Auto de los Reyes Magos*; it has been argued that it is inferior because less dramatic. This view, however, fails to take into account the very different techniques employed to achieve different ends; in the *Auto* the argument proceeds in a direct line from beginning to end, whereas the *Representación* consists of a series of tableaux-like scenes, largely amplifying the Gospel narratives. It is clear that Manrique was familiar to some extent with liturgical drama, and he combines the techniques of this genre with those of the *momos* to illustrate the essential link between the Nativity and the Crucifixion. The figure of Manrique stands alone and, despite his apparent knowledge of a liturgical Christ-mas drama, he does not form part of a Castilian dramatic tradition. Despite the existence of some plays, there is no evidence of a strong vernacular tradition before the second half of the 15th century.

Awareness of a dramatic tradition, although this need not, of course, be a Spanish vernacular one, is shown by Diego de San Pedro in his *Pasión trobada* (*Minstrels' Passion*), and there is evidence that this was in fact staged on one occasion in the 16th century. Dramatic qualities have also been noted in the work of Francisco Imperial and in the *Vita Christi* (*Life of Christ*) of Inigo de Mendoza. Debate-poems also contain dramatic possibilities, and the *Diálogo entre el Amor, el Viejo y la Hermosa* (*Dialogue between Love, the Old Man and the Beautiful Girl*) contains several lines suggesting that it was intended to be staged.

The production of plays for both court and church festivities continued throughout the 16th century with professional writers and producers becoming ever more involved in their preparation. **Autos sacramen-tales** (sacred plays) were composed on a wide variety of religious subjects, many of them including scenes of allegorical or typological significance such as the 16th-century *Farsa del Santísimo Sacramento* (*Play of the Most Holy Sacrament*) which describes the Feast of Corpus Christi itself. The use of the term *Farsa* even for a serious play is typical of the intermingling of the different strands of drama, religious and secular, which in the Iberian Peninsula, unhindered by Reformation or Puritanism, continued to evolve smoothly into the 17th-century drama of the Golden Age of Spanish theatre. PN LRM

Staging in the Middle Ages The wealth and variety of dramatic and theatrical activity in Europe in the Middle Ages is echoed in its staging. Everywhere was potenti-ally a theatre: the street, the private hall and the guild hall, the church, the open field, the market square, the churchyard. Evidence, however, like that for theatrical activity is variable in its frequency and its fullness. Information comes from a variety of sources besides texts and stage directions: church, guild and city accounts, carpenters' and other workmen's contracts, stage plans, descriptions, pictorial representations. These suggest a broad division into multiple and single-focus staging. The most important sources of evidence for multiple staging are stage plans, especially those of Lucerne (though late 16th century) and the *Castle of Perseverance*. The information contained in the Lucerne plans is supported and extended by the remarkable collection of notes and descriptions made for and by the director, Renward Cysat, and by the surviving texts and stage directions. The *Castle* plan is important as the centre of a cluster of information drawn from plays with apparently similar staging (*Mary Magdalen* and the *N.town Passion*), from the stage plans of the Cornish plays, and from the Fouquet miniature of the martyrdom of St Apollonia. Though it should be stressed that the stage plans are specific to their own plays and their own times, nevertheless they can be used to clarify the often brief and enigmatic references that appear elsewhere.

Basically both sets of evidence show an open central area surrounded by a number of specific locations. In the case of the *Castle* these are all apparently raised as in the Fouquet miniature, but unlike the miniature and like *Mary Magdalen* and the *Passion*, action takes place on these 'scaffolds' as well as in the 'place'. At Lucerne the locations are divided between those which are merely 'stalls' or waiting-places for the actors, and those in which part of the action occurs, e.g. Heaven, Hell, the Temple, Mount Sinai. Some are raised (e.g. Heaven, the Nativity Hut), some are at ground level (e.g. most of the stalls, the Temple, Hell). In the *Castle*, there is a central fixed scaffold, the castle itself, and similarly in one of the plans for the Cornish *Beunans Meriasek* there is a central chapel; at Lucerne there are a number of scaffolds or stage properties which are moved in, around or out of the *platz* either during the day's performance (the sacrifice scaffolds) or between the two days (Moses' water rock, the Pool of Siloam). Mount Sinai is shifted across the upper end of the square to become the Mount of Olives on the second day.

The vocabulary used to describe multiple staging varies somewhat from play to play, though there are recurrent words, mainly everyday ones given a specific application. To what extent these were felt to be technical terms it is difficult to say. 'Place' (Eng.), *platea* (Lat.), *place, champ, parc* (Fr.), *platz* (Ger.) are all used with some frequency for the open playing area; *domus* (Lat.), *lieu, mansion* (Fr.), *hof* (Ger.), for the surround-ing locations. When no plan or supporting docu-mentation exists it is hard to be sure what these terms mean, and it is possible that in some cases they are merely intended as indicators of a general mode of staging: the open playing area and the individual waiting or playing locations. On occasion the individual location will be decorated or will become a structure, perhaps a raised one (words like the English 'scaffold', French '*eschaffaut*' and Spanish '*cadafal*' imply this). Often such a structure will be called what it represents – Heaven, Hell, Paradise, the Temple – but it is only through the description of the staging structure or from the financial accounts of their construction that we can be sure what form they took, as for example from Mons (1501) and Romans (1509), in France, and from Lucerne in Switzerland.

This kind of staging is adaptable in shape and size, from the semi-circle to the square and from the dimensions of a church to those of a city square. It can adapt itself to a quarry (as at Shrewsbury) or an amphitheatre (as at Bourges) or the Coliseum in Rome, and it offers scope for the most spectacular effects, like the Flood at Mons. The 'place' can be ground surface, as at Lucerne, or a raised stage, as at Mons or Romans. Structures can remain fixed around the edge or in the middle, as apparently with the *Castle*, or be movable, as with the scaffold for Abraham's sacrifice at Lucerne. The structures can be merely scaffolds, as shown in the Fouquet miniature, or elaborately decorated sets, like the Paradise of *Adam* with curtains and silk cloths, foliage and flowers, or the Hell at Mons, plastered, painted and stuck with stumps of willow trees.

The multiple set arranged in a straight line – the linear stage – is represented by the Cailleau miniature of the 1547 Valenciennes *Passion*, and perhaps also by the stage specially built for the Passion at Velletri. In the former the individual structures appear as representative buildings, from the tumble-down castle of Hell and Limbo, to the classical lines of the palace and the temple.

The single-focus set also has its variants in the Middle Ages: e.g. movable: the pageant-wagon, or fixed: the booth stage. With the pageant-wagon the levels of the place and the scaffold are maintained through the use of wagon floor and street, but the wagon is used as a visual focus for the most significant action. The booth stage appears to restrict the action to the stage structure itself. The Rhetoricians' stages of the Low Countries in some ways resembled the booth stage, but they made considerable use of different levels and of inner stages behind the elaborate facades. Though these are sometimes divided into three separate 'compartments' at stage level, almost becoming mini-Valenciennes stages at times, they are still best considered single-focus sets since the divisions were not permanent and the three could very easily be merged into a single inner stage. Despite problems of movement in narrow streets, and possibly of non-steering wagons, the pageant could become very elaborate. No illustrations of performing pageant-wagons survive but the wagons of the *ommeganc*, or procession, of the Low Countries reveal how spectacular processional wagons could be, ranging from the house on wheels for the Nativity or the Annunciation, to the fully rigged ship, to the astonishing Tree of Jesse with its child prophets and kings perched precariously in its branches (as shown in the van Alsloot paintings of Brussels in 1615), and to the towering structures of the late 16th-century *ommeganc* at Leuven; though late in date, the pictures show

structures which survive from an earlier period. In Spain an agreement for the renovation of floats shows that the Creation at Barcelona (1453) contained a heaven of clouds on top of pillars, with two angels and a throne for God, while suspended beneath was an elaborately decorated revolving globe, and at floor level a 'revolve' on which four singing angels stood while four more stood and sang at the feet of the pillars. The Bethlehem float was divided into two structures, each roof supported by four pillars with angels on top and a vaulted heaven spanning the inner four pillars. There was clearly a common tradition of elaborate wagon and float decoration. The 1454 description of the St John's Day pageants at Florence confirms that the elaboration extended to wagons intended for performance.

The Rhetoricians' stages too appear from the many surviving illustrations to have been often highly decorative, though the decoration is concentrated on the facade. They may well have been influenced in the first place by the complex scaffolds of the royal entries which were at their most splendid in the Low Countries of the late 15th century. Nothing is known of the more ordinary booth stages beyond what can be deduced from pictures such as the Brueghel *Village Festival*. The stage is above the heads of the spectators, usually rests on large barrels or trestles, and sometimes has what appears to be a protective barrier around it (cf. the railings attached to some fixed stages e.g. Romans, and wagons e.g. Alcalá, 1568). In many cases the purpose was no doubt purely decorative, but that there was sometimes need for protection is shown by the performance in Florence (1454) when the actor playing the emperor Octavian was seized and flung down from his wagon by an apparently enraged German who had clambered up from the street.

Both fixed and movable forms of staging frequently made use of complicated machinery. Possibly the most remarkable of all was the revolving heaven peopled with angels, constructed by the architect and designer Brunelleschi in the roof of the church of San Felice in Piazza in Florence for an Annunciation play. Some idea of the effect of this church machinery can even now be gained from the play of the Assumption of the Virgin still annually performed in the church at Elche in south-eastern Spain, where the most striking effect is the opening of the leaves of the 'pomegranate' to reveal the angel inside, all within a few feet of the ceiling of the dome. Raising and lowering of figures, real and artificial, to and from the ceilings of churches and halls (cf. the unfortunate accident attending the raising of the royal jester in Saragossa in the early 15th century) was a common spectacle. Such raising devices were used also in outdoor performances: at Bourges (1536) a mechanism was required for 'flying' Simon Magus and also the apostles. Here, as almost inevitably elsewhere, this is associated with clouds; no doubt for appropriately concealing the mechanics. Even on pageant-wagons some kind of raising mechanism was required for certain episodes (e.g. the Ascension or the Assumption), though the only documented one is that for the Mercers' pageant of the Last Judgement at York (1433).

The fixed stages frequently made use of the space underneath for surprise appearances and disappearances through trap-doors, and for removing actors altogether whose parts were over or who were changing roles. At Bourges, St Matthew moves to a position near a trap-door so that a dragon can appear near him spouting fire and be subdued by him. Characters are frequently said to 'vanish' and 'go underground' to re-appear in another part of the stage. At Lucerne many of the dead are buried in the 'general burying place' to re-emerge later as other characters. Stages set up in a town square allowed not only scaffolds to be used but also the buildings around the square. The movement of the star and the dove representing the Holy Spirit at Lucerne was controlled by one of the stage crew from an upper room in the Haus zur Sonne at the upper end of the square. The eclipse of sun and moon at Christ's death were also controlled from there. Musketeers were stationed on the roofs of certain houses to echo the divine thunder. At Mons the roofs were used to set up large barrels from which leaden pipes carried the waters of the Flood before they descended upon the stage below. The town walls and the walls of surrounding buildings were also used to support scaffolds (Alençon, 1520) or a covering awning (Romans).

The large multiple set created considerable problems of control for the director (indeed made an overall director a necessity). Cysat at Lucerne made endless notes of the positioning and timing of processions, crowd scenes, the doubling of parts, entries and special effects, even at times making a note to be there himself – the famous 'Director, go to hell'. At Mons the thunder-makers had separate cue-sheets to which they were urged to pay close attention so that they stopped when Christ said to the storm: 'Peace, be still!' A strong sense of the complexities of such a play in action is given simply by the cues in the director's copy. For instance, in the middle of the Transfiguration, 258 lines and a considerable amount of complicated action before he is due to appear with smoke and explosions, the devil Fergalus is warned to go to the trap-door beneath the Canaanite woman from whom he is to burst.

At Lucerne and at the large-scale French plays the most elaborate provision for audiences is found, though clearly the windows of surrounding houses where they existed were still the most prized viewing places. At Romans, stands with rows of separate lockable rooms were constructed with safety railings in front and privies at the ends of the rows. At Autun (1516) an 'amphitheatre' was made with all the seating covered by awnings as a protection against the sun, as in Romans. The provision of spectator-scaffolds was a feature of tournaments from a very much earlier period, though nothing as complex as those for the plays is recorded. Here besides the audience's comfort there is some concern with being able to see; but even so it must frequently have been difficult both to see and hear in an open space like the Weinmarkt at Lucerne. To some extent in other types of staging this is overcome by having a mobile audience, thereby making sight-lines the individual concern of each spectator. But this in itself could cause problems with the more adventurous: the boy who fell from the triforium at Beverley (c. 1220), or the roof collapsing at Bautzen in 1413 because of the weight of spectators on it. Sometimes the audience was conducted from stage to stage, as in the *Conversion of St Paul*. The advantage for the organizers of a play of fixed audience accommodation was the revenue. There is considerable evidence from France of a concern with financial success or at least

with making as little loss as possible (e.g. Valenciennes, Mons, Issoudun); but these were one-off performances, not regularly recurring ones. There is no evidence of organized payment of this kind in England, though certain enterprising York citizens took advantage of the pageants stopping outside their houses to set up scaffolds and charge for access to them, and later the city council too made house-owners pay for the privilege of having the pageants stop outside. None of this was direct recouping of the expenses of the play however. The civic cycles were financed by members of the guilds with no hope of return.

One of the most costly and cherished features of many of the French plays were the *feintes* or special effects. The list for the Bourges *Acts of the Apostles* (1536) fills several pages of the printed account. The provision for the Flood at Mons has already been mentioned. There also the stage was turfed over and contained a Sea of Galilee (perhaps like the sea in the Cailleau painting) upon which real boats floated, as well as the usual series of trap-doors for a variety of appearances and disappearances. Firework effects were the work of experts who were called in specially to organize them. This is evident in the contract for the Modane *Anti-Christ* play (1580), but was clearly also true very much earlier (e.g. Mons). Special effects were varied and ubiquitous. There is the polished bowl used to reflect the sun onto Christ's white robes for the Transfiguration at Revello (1483), the painting of the bloody sweat onto Christ's face as he prostrates himself on the Mount of Olives by a painter concealed underneath (Lucerne and Revello), Balaam's talking ass at Chester, or the extraordinary illumination of the church at Florence for the Annunciation play of 1439.

Other forms of special effects were the exotic animals, giants and other figures that were made mainly for processions but which were also used in plays. Representations of such creatures survive in, for example, the paintings by van Alsloot of the Brussels *ommeganc* or the *Liber Boonen* sketches from Leuven (late 16th century). Those referred to in Chester were made for the Midsummer Show, those in Valencia for the Corpus Christi procession (including lions, an eagle and dragons), while those in Lucerne (camel, elephant and dromedary) were for the entry of the three kings in the Easter play. In France the *monstre*, or pre-performance parade, often included elaborate floats and figures (Bourges).

A frequent feature of these and all other displays and entertainments is the use of elaborate masks which fulfil a variety of purposes: in the courtly mumming (the early Revels accounts abound in mask references) for tantalizing concealment, in all mummings as a manifestation of the exotic or the frightening, or in plays symbolically to show disease or to express attributes of a character, especially extremes. The golden face of God or the hideous head of the devil recur throughout Europe. The golden mask was not only a feature of God in glory but also of Christ in his manhood on earth, mingling masked with unmasked actors in a single theatrical context. A symbolic effect of a similar kind is also created by certain kinds of costuming. Characters will be marked for what they are by a symbol: the young Mary with a crown to show that she is also Queen of Heaven, the apostle Peter with keys to show his later saintly and papal role. Only later in the period is there a move towards a semi-historical costume (e.g. Aaron in the Lucerne play dressed as an Old Testament priest). If there is symbolic there is also literal detail: the painting on of Christ's bloody sweat in the garden of Gethsemane, or, in props, the use of real birds, animals and fish in the Creation (as at Mons).

Realism did not extend as a rule to the playing of women by women on the public stage, though it could clearly happen in nunneries (e.g. Barking and probably the *Sta Teodora* play from Italy). There are examples in France (at Romans, a few roles at Mons, and Valenciennes, Françoise Buatier at Grenoble, 1535, etc.) but, except perhaps as dancers, they do not appear elsewhere – or perhaps it would be more accurate to say that the available evidence points to the playing of female roles by men and boys. Understandably realism did not extend to nudity, only to body-stockings (*lybkleidern* at Lucerne). Some directors clearly had trouble even making costume appropriate, since there are prohibitions on people wearing the best costumes available regardless of what role they are playing.

At Lucerne there is concern with finding the right actor for the part, in York there is concern for the general proficiency of all available players. Nowhere is there the suggestion of a casual attitude to the final effect, whether it is the skill of the actor, the efficiency of the stage staff, or the ability of the painter or mechanist. The notes made by Cysat, the Lucerne director (and also Town Clerk), show the painstaking care that went into the smallest details. Cysat was an 'amateur' and almost all the plays referred to in the course of this section were performed by 'amateur' actors. The 'professional' – in the sense of someone who earns his living solely by acting – seems to put in an appearance only during the late 15th century. Some actors were paid for their performances (at Chester for example), some had to pay to perform (at Lucerne). They were drawn from all walks of life – the idea of medieval drama as the working-man's drama is a totally false one. The only real 'professionals' were the musicians, brought in for their specialist training. Certainly music played an important part in the plays. It could echo or emphasize the magnificence of Heaven, establish or symbolize through the singing of angels or mortals the harmony of Heaven or earth, or simply accompany a movement or a pause in the action (in France and elsewhere both *silete* and *pause* came to be music cues).

It is almost impossible to posit any one acting-style for a drama as varied as that of the Middle Ages. Even in church drama there is a wide range of possibility, from the ritual movements of the Maries to the horseplay of Herod hurling spears down the church and beating the choir with a bladder (Padua, 13th century). It is sometimes said that a carrying voice, broad gesture and movement are essential elements and for many plays this must have been true. But there is no reason to suppose that a medieval actor was unable to adapt himself to a more confined space such as a hall or narrow street might offer. Where evidence exists it points to a rhetorical style of broad gesture and open speaking but it would be wrong to rule out other styles suggested by the text. The fixed tiered seating of many of the big civic plays must have distanced the audience to some extent, whereas a mobile standing audience could be used as a crowd to hide in, move through,

attack or harangue almost as a part of the action. In a formal way involvement with the audience was the essence of mummings, which often ended with the exotic good-luck visitors dancing with their 'audience'. Though use of the audience seems likely in the plays, there is not a lot of evidence of it. There are forays by the devils in *Adam* (perhaps like the devils in the van Alsloot paintings); there is the concealment of *Bien Naturel* (Natural Goodness) in the audience in Jean Parmentier's *The Assumption of Our Lady* (1527); but more relevant to a style of acting is the presence of servants A and B in the audience of *Fulgens and Lucres*. By far the most common actor–audience contact is direct address; that of A and B is intimate and colloquial, but still verse. Audience address is common in a wide variety of plays for a wide variety of purposes and with a comparable variety of tone: teaching, making a collection, gaining sympathy or simply chat. At all levels it is one of the most effective devices for involving the audience in the meaning and emotions of the play.

Plays in the Middle Ages were part of a broad use of drama and theatre which penetrated every level of society and grew within a wide variety of non-theatrical events. Interaction was not just among dramatic and theatrical activities themselves but between them and the semi-theatrical, like tournaments, and the non-theatrical, like feasts and festivals. The church liturgy produced its own drama, and its music and ritual as well as some of its texts influenced the vernacular plays. The tournaments provided a model for audience provision and outdoor performance, as well as providing an opportunity for display and costumed role-playing. The mumming exploited the use of masks in the winter feasts and festivals in hall; royal entries enriched the single-focus stage of the streets; processions revealed the possibility of movement combined with elaborate staging and provided the occasion for it. Theatrical forms interpenetrated each other. How much awareness of the tradition of one country influenced that of another is very difficult to tell. It is hard to believe that an Englishman present at one of the great French Passions would remain unimpressed, but being impressed is not necessarily followed by imitation. For a final suggestive piece of evidence we come back to Cysat at Lucerne. In worrying about the smoke at the Ascension and Pentecost he notes: 'In Milan they have artificial fire in the plays which goes up quickly, produces much smoke, and yet neither burns nor stinks.' Did he discover the secret and use it at Lucerne?

The 20th century has seen a notable revival of interest in medieval theatre. Individual scholars in many countries have turned back to the records of performance, and in some cases whole projects have been set up for the purpose, like that of Records of Early English Drama (REED) in Toronto. There has also been practical experiment in the form of historical reconstructions of the staging of a number of the plays, e.g. processional staging on pageant-wagons of the York and Chester cycles at Leeds (1975 and 1983) and Toronto (1977 and 1983); fixed, 'place and scaffold' staging of the Cornish *Ordinalia* in St Piran's Round (1969), and the *Castle of Perseverance*, the *N.town Passion* and the Towneley cycle in Toronto (1979, 1981 and 1985), and *Mary Magdalen* at Durham (1982). Impetus was given to these historical reconstructions by the many productions of individual plays and groups of plays which began early in the century in many parts of Europe. A professional company, The Medieval Players, exists in Britain devoted to the performance of medieval and renaissance plays, and the **National Theatre** in London has had enormous success with its promenade adaptation by Tony Harrison of the cycle plays, *The Mysteries* (1985). In 1977 an international society was formed for the study of medieval theatre, the Société Internationale pour L'Etude du Théâtre Médiéval. PM

Medieval Drama in Europe
See: *Lateinische Osterfeiern und Osterspiele*, ed. W. Lipphardt, 6 vols. to date, Berlin and New York, 1975–; *Medieval Drama*, ed. D. Bevington, Boston, 1975; *The Revels History of Drama in English*, vol. I, *Medieval Drama*, ed. Lois Potter, London, 1983; K. Young, *The Drama of the Medieval Church*, 2 vols., Oxford, 1933.

Liturgical Drama
See: *Anglo-Saxon Easter* (recording of music from Winchester), Archiv: 413546-1 (record) 413546-4 (tape).

Eastern Europe
See: *The Cyprus Passion Cycle*, ed. A. C. Mahr, Notre Dame, Indiana, 1947; Grégoire de Nazianze, *La Passion du Christ*, ed. A. Tuiler, Paris, 1969; *Essays in Medieval Drama (Proceedings of the SITM's 3rd International Colloquium at Dublin 1980)*, ed. A. J. Fletcher, Farmington (Maine), forthcoming.

England, Scotland, Ireland, Cornwall and Wales
See: E. K. Chambers, *The Medieval Stage*, 2 vols., London, 1903; I. Lancashire, *Dramatic Texts and Records of Britain to 1558*, Toronto, 1984; A. J. Mill, *Medieval Plays in Scotland*, St Andrews Publications 24, Edinburgh and London, 1927; *Records of Early English Drama* – York, Chester, Coventry, Newcastle upon Tyne, Norwich, Cumberland/Westmorland/Gloucestershire, and Devon, University of Toronto Press, 1979, 1979, 1981, 1982, 1984, 1986 and 1986; *Revels History of Drama in English* Vols. I and II, London, 1983 and 1980; *Medieval English Theatre*; Malone Society Collections volumes; especially VII, VIII and XI, Oxford, 1965, 1969, 1980/81; *Records of Early English Drama Newsletter*.

France
See: M. Accarie, *Le Théâtre Sacré de la Fin du Moyen Age: Etude sur le sens moral de la Passion de Jehan Michel*, Genève, 1979; J.-Cl. Aubailly, *Le Théâtre mediéval profane et comique*, Paris, 1975; J.-Cl. Aubailly, *Le Monologue, le Dialogue et la Sottie: Essai sur quelques genres dramatiques de la fin du Moyen Age et du début du XVIe siècle*, Paris, 1976; R. Axton, *European Drama of the Early Middle Ages*, London, 1974; R. Bossuat, *Manuel Bibliographique de la littérature française du Moyen Age*, Paris, 1951, and supplements; G. Cohen, *Histoire de la Mise en Scène dans le théâtre religieux francais du Moyen Age*, Paris, 1951; G. Frank, *The Medieval French Drama*, Oxford, 1954; *Grundiss der Romanischen Literaturen des Mittelalters* (forthcoming), vol. XII (Theatre); tome I: Partie Documentaire; tome II: Partie Historique; H. Lewicka, *Bibliographie du théâtre profane français des XVe et XVIe siècles*, 2nd edn Paris, 1980; 'Medieval French Drama: a Review of Recent Scholarship' in *Research Opportunities in Renaissance Drama*, vols. XXI–XXIII (1978–80); L. Petit de Julleville, *Les Mystères*, Paris, 1980; L. Petit de Julleville, *Répertoire du Théâtre Comique en France*, Paris, 1986; C. Stratman, *Bibliography of Medieval Drama*, 2nd edn revised and enlarged, New York, 1972.

Germany, Switzerland, etc.
See: R. Bergmann, 'Spiele, Mittelalterliche geistliche' in *Reallexikon der deutschen Literatur*, Band 4, pp. 64–100, Berlin & New York, 1979; D. Brett-Evans, *Von Hrotsvit bis Folz und Gengenbach*. 2 vols. (Gundlagen der Germaniskit 15 & 18), Berlin, 1975; M. B. Evans, *The Passion Play of Lucerne: An Historical and Critical Introduction*, New York & London, 1943; reprint 1977; H. Linke, 'Das volkssprachige Drama und Theater im deutschen und niederländischen Sprachbereich' in *Neues Handbuch der Literaturwissenschaft. Band 8: Europäisches Mittelalter* Wiesbaden, 1978; W. F. Michael, *Das deutsche Drama des Mittelalters*, Berlin & New York, 1971; B. Neumann, *Zeugnisse mittelalterlicher Aufführungen im deutschen Sprachraum*. Teil 1, Cologne, 1979; B. Neumann, *Geistliches Schauspiel im Zeugnis der Zeit*. 2 vols. (Münchner Texte und Untersuchungen 84 & 85), Zurich & Munich, 1987.

Italy
See: A. D'Ancona, *Origini del teatro italiano* 2 vols., 1891; rpt. Rome, 1966; V. De Bartholomaeis, *Origini della Poesia drammatica italiano*, 2nd edn Turin, 1952; A. Cioni, *Bibliografia delle Sacre Rappresentazioni*, Florence, 1961 – includes MSS, early printed editions and modern collections of texts by D'Ancona and De Bartholomaeis; *Johannis Diaconi Versiculi de Cena Cypriani*, ed. Karl Strecker, Monumenta Germaniae Historica, Poetarum Latinorum medii aevi IV, fasc II, Berlin, 1923, pp. 857–98.

Low Countries
See: W. M. H. Hummelen, *Repertorium van het Rederijkersdrama, 1500–c. 1620*, Assen, 1968; W. M. H. Hummelen, 'Tekst en toneelinrichting in de Abele Spelen', in *De Nieuwe Taalgids*, 70 (1977) 3, 227ff; W. M. H. Hummelen, 'Types and Methods of the Dutch Rhetoricians Theatre' in *The Third Globe. Symposium for the Reconstruction of the Globe Playhouse, Wayne State University 1979*, edited by C. W. Hodges, S. Schoenbaum and L. Leone, Detroit, 1981; G. R. Kernodle, *From Art to Theatre. Form and Convention in the Renaissance*, Chicago, 1944; J. J. Mak, *De Rederijkers*, Amsterdam, 1945; J. A. Worp, *Geschiedenis van het drama en het toneel in Nederland*, Gronigen, 1904.

Spain
See: R. B. Donovan, *The Liturgical Drama in Medieval Spain*, Toronto, 1958; N. D. Shergold, *A History of the Spanish Stage*, Oxford, 1967.

Staging
See: E. Konigson, *L'Espace Théâtral Médiéval*, Paris, 1975; P. Meredith and J. Tailby (eds.), *The Staging of Religious Drama in the Later Middle Ages: Texts and Documents in English Translation* (EDAM Monograph Series 4), Kalamazoo, 1983; H. Rey-Flaud, *Le Cercle Magique*, Paris, 1975; W. Tydeman, *The Theatre in the Middle Ages*, Cambridge, 1978; G. Wickham, *Early English Stages 1330–1660*, vols. I and II, London, 1959 and 1963; *Medieval English Theatre*; *Research Opportunities in Renaissance Drama*.

Medina, Louisa (c. 1813–38) American, unique in her day as a successful woman dramatist, Medina is credited with 34 plays between 1833 and 1838; however, only 11 have been documented and only 3 have survived. All of her plays were written for Thomas S. Hamblin, manager of the **Bowery Theatre** and possibly her husband, and probably all were dramatizations of historical and adventure novels. Medina's talent for increasing the dramatic and spectacular elements of the novels made her plays successful and profitable melodramas, the staple of the Bowery. Her dramatization of **Robert Montgomery Bird**'s *Nick of* *the Woods* had 29 performances in 1838 – the longest run on a New York stage to that date. Other successes include *The Last Days of Pompeii, Rienzi, Norman Leslie* and *Ernest Maltravers*.   FB

Medoff, Mark (1940–) American playwright, director, and actor. Medoff first won success Off-Broadway with *When You Comin' Back, Red Ryder?* in 1973 and *The Wager* in 1974. *Children of a Lesser God* ran 887 performances in 1980–1, winning Medoff a Tony Award for Best Script. *Children* concerns an instructor for the deaf who marries a deaf student. Fear of having a deaf child contributes to the marriage's destruction. After *Children* Medoff worked primarily in film and television, but in 1985 the American Conservatory Theatre staged his *The Majestic Kid*.   SMA

Medwall, Henry (*fl.* 1500) English playwright. His interlude, *Fulgens and Lucres* (c. 1495), shows a lively sense of theatre in the context of its presumed presentation as a diversion at a banquet. He is also known to have written a morality play, *Nature*. He becomes, therefore, a collectors' item in tracing the development of the English theatre of his period.   MB

Mei Lanfang (1894–1961) Chinese dan actor. Born into a traditional Beijing theatre family he was trained in the women's roles like his father and grandfather before him. His name became a household word in China and he was idolized by the theatre-going public as a supreme master. Mei's professional contributions to traditional stage art were many sided. He created new dance plays based on historical literary themes which gave new dimensions to the repertoire. Roles in which song, dance and combat techniques were combined in solo performance were another of his innovations. Mei was active in breaking down the prejudices against women on the traditional stage. He took them as pupils and a talented body of actresses became his disciples. Until 1931 he collaborated with Qi Rushan (1876–1962) a theatre scholar who became his adviser-impresario-playwright and had a deep influence on Mei's artistic development. Mei was the first actor of artistic stature to introduce Chinese theatre to Western audiences through his tours to America in 1930 and Russia in 1935. In Moscow he gave an acting demonstration which was seen by **Brecht** with significant consequences for the German playwright's ideas on theatre. Mei refused to perform during the Japanese occupation of China, remaining secluded in Shanghai. After 1949 he remained active on the stage and in teaching carrying out an extremely heavy programme urged upon him by the new government. His former home in Beijing has been made into a commemorative museum in honour of his achievements.   ACS

Meilhac, Henri (1831–97) and **Ludovic Halévy** (1834–1908). French dramatists. Although they did some work alone or with other collaborators, the names of Meilhac and Halévy are firmly linked as entertainers of the Second Empire and, above all, as librettists for the work of Jacques Offenbach. Meilhac began his career as a caricaturist, later transferring this skill into the creation of amusing dramatic figures. From 1855 he had a series of *vaudevilles* staged at the Gymnase. In 1861 he collaborated for the first time with Halévy on a piece for the Variétés, *Le Menuet de Danae* (*Danae's Minuet*) and would continue to work with him for most of his career. In 1883 he and Philippe Gille wrote *Mam'zelle Nitouche*, a delightful musical comedy about a respectable school music teacher who also writes naughty operettas. In 1888 he was elected to the French Academy. Halévy, son of the dramatist Léon Halévy, worked as a librettist, his first great success being *Orpheus in the Underworld* (1861). He also wrote novels and was elected to the Academy in 1884. Together Meilhac and Halévy provided librettos for Offenbach's *La Belle Hélène* (1864), *Bluebeard* (1866), *The Grand Duchess of Gerolstein* (1867) with the talented Hortense Schneider (this show was the first thing the Emperor Alexander wanted to see when he visited Paris for the Great Exhibition), and *La Périchole* (1868). There are some parallels to be drawn between their work and that of **W. S. Gilbert**. Meilhac and Halévy also wrote one of the most successful light comedies of the Second Empire, *Froufrou* (1869), which would later provide a popular role for **Sarah Bernhardt**. Meilhac was more given to the fantastic and the grotesque, whereas Halévy preferred realistic detail and close observation of contemporary life and mores.   JMCC

Meiningen company German court theatre. During the last decades of the 19th century, the Meiningen Court Theatre was possibly the most widely admired and imitated company in Europe. It was developed out of the existent Meiningen Court Theatre by Georg II, Duke of Saxe-Meiningen (1826–1914), his wife Ellen Franz (1839–1923), and the director Ludwig Chronegk (1837–91). It was financed by the Duke's private money. In 1874, during their first guest appearance in Berlin, the Meininger achieved national prominence with their performances of *Julius Caesar, Twelfth Night*, and other plays. From then until 1890, the company performed both in Meiningen and on tour in 38 German and European cities. One of the most arresting aspects of their productions was the extreme accuracy with which the historical sets and costumes were designed. The actors were also directed with a meticulous eye for the whole stage picture. The company was celebrated for the individuality of its crowd members. A rigorous standard of ensemble was constantly striven for. Although some critics felt that the plays suffered from overproduction, too much attention being paid to the physical elements of the stage, it was the Duke's ambition that each production should provide only sufficient means to support the dramatic text effectively. The Meininger were seen on tour by **André Antoine** and **Konstantin Stanislavksy**, both of whom claimed that the company had a profound influence on their own work.   SW

Melanesia see **Oceania**

Méliès, Georges (1861–1938) French conjurer and film-maker, the first showman to conceive of the importance of cinema as entertainment. He took over the Théâtre Robert-Houdin in 1888, giving a series of 'fantastic evenings'. This illusionism led to lantern-slide *féeries*; he transformed the theatre into a projection room and founded the first film studio (1896), Star-Film, using music-hall singers and underpaid chorus girls from the Théâtre du Châtelet, since legitimate actors refused at first to appear in such a low medium. Between 1895 and 1910 he produced 4,000 reels of standard pantomime subjects and cinematic trickery, the most famous being *A Trip to the Moon* (1902). Méliès is also important for taking the first live-action films in a theatre; using 30 arc-lamps he captured **Paulus** in his act. LS

Mélingue, Etienne Marin (1807–75) French actor. One of the most attractive, picturesque and original of the Boulevard, his career was particularly associated with the great cloak and dagger parts of **Dumas** *père*. Having studied drawing and sculpture at Caen, he made his stage debut at Belleville in 1829. In 1832 he was a *grand utilité* at Rouen, where **Dorval** noticed him and introduced him to Alexandre Dumas. He was taken on at the Porte-Saint-Martin, where he played lead roles until 1840, when he moved to the Ambigu, creating **Bouchardy**'s *Lazare le Pâtre* (*Lazarus the Shepherd*), and built his reputation with the plays of **Soulié**. In 1847 he joined Dumas at his newly-opened Théâtre Historique, where one of his great parts was Edmond Dantès in *Monte Cristo* (1848). After the collapse of Dumas's venture, Mélingue was not attached to any one theatre. His most popular roles included Fanfan-la-Tulipe and Benvenuto Cellini. As the latter he had to carve a statuette on stage every night (Napoleon III gave him a gold snuff-box set with diamonds for one of them). In the last 15 years of his career he mainly revived earlier parts. His last major role was that of Don César de Bazan in the 1872 revival of *Ruy Blas* (**Odéon**). Mélingue was the idol of popular audiences, extremely handsome and gifted with a very powerful voice. He paid great attention to details of costume and makeup in preparing his parts. His wife, Mlle Théodorine, was also an actress and was chosen by **Hugo** for the role of Guanhumara in *Les Burgraves* (1843). JMCC

Melodrama Like farce, melodrama is a popular form of theatre which has been denigrated by critics, so that it is associated with sensationalism and implausibility. These features make for lively theatre, however, and they sustain the mass media today. The word melodrama comes from France, where **Rousseau** coined it for his *Pygmalion* (1766) in which music served as background for dialogue (in contrast to opera, where music is joined to dialogue). Since the **Comédie-Française** had a monopoly on plays with spoken dialogue, the new genre in many variants was seized upon by other theatres along the Boulevard du Temple, and became the staple fare of the appropriately named Théâtre de l'Ambigu-Comique. There, at the convenient date of 1800, *Coelina* by **Guilbert de Pixérécourt** was performed, in which innocent young lovers suffer at the separation engineered by a scheming villain. All ends well, with assistance from a tell-tale scar, a conspiracy overheard, and a helpful comic. Within two years, in that pre-copyright age, the play crossed the Channel as *A Tale of Mystery* by **Thomas Holcroft**, the first English play to be labelled melodrama. In the rapidly industrializing capitals of London, Paris, and Berlin, melodrama played triumphantly in large theatres to illiterate audiences. Necessarily, it was a *large* genre with spectacular settings, large casts gestur-

ing broadly, and loud music to accompany the predictable emotions. Each of the major European capitals sported its playwright of melodrama – Pixérécourt in Paris, **Kotzebue** in Berlin, and **Boucicault** in London (and New York). These three men led such melodramatic (adventure-filled) lives that they may well have thought they were inventing realism in their plays, were it not that they so often stole their action-filled plots, usually from novels. By mid-century, melodrama was less formulaic: crime was popular on both sides of the Channel, so that the Paris theatre row was called Boulevard du Crime; patriotism was exhibited in battles on stage; social protest took the harmless form of equating poverty with nobility and virtue; the dastardly villain (the choice role) persecutes the defenceless heroine, who is rescued by an intrepid hero aided by a benevolent and colloquial comic, against increasingly spectacular dangers. Coelina had merely to survive a raging storm, but her progeny gasped through near drowning, burning, devouring by wild beasts – all thrillingly palpable in the large theatres packed with thousands of spectators. Boucicault especially had a gift for 'sensation scenes' designing prison escapes, avalanches, explosions, but his colleagues soon introduced icebergs, air balloons, speeding trains. With technical sophistication came more sophisticated plots; innocence does not triumph in **Uncle Tom's Cabin**, and virtue is tainted in *East Lynne*. By the turn of the 20th century melodrama merged into realism in England and France, but American melodrama was revitalized by **David Belasco**, who insisted on careful writing for a basic plot of poor heroine facing assorted calamities, weak hero, resourceful comic who was the star of the show, and a sequence of heavies who kept the plot speeding along. After the First World War agit-prop plays adopt the structure, but no longer the settings, of melodrama.

Historians of melodrama stress its democratic and humanitarian substratum. **Eric Bentley** in *The Life of the Drama* (1964) and Robert Heilman in *The Iceman, The Arsonist, and The Troubled Agent* have both defended melodrama as a different genre from tragedy, which should be evaluated by its own attributes. Bentley finds melodramatic elements in most great tragedies of the anglophone tradition, and he dubs **O'Neill** a successful melodramatist rather than tragic playwright. Heilman distinguishes between the divided protagonist of tragedy and the whole protagonist of melodrama; the first contributes to his own undoing, whereas the second is crushed by external forces. This necessitates reclassifying some classical tragedies as melodramas – *Romeo and Juliet*, *The Duchess of Malfi*. On the other hand, the righteous-victim-triumphant of socialist realism and of Chinese Opera (revised to support the Revolution) abjure the name of melodrama but adopt its all-or-nothing ethic. RC

Mélodrame Not to be confused with the English word 'melodrama', which refers to plays of a sensational type, nor with the Italian *melodramma*, often merely a synonym for 'opera', *mélodrame* signifies one of the many ways of manipulating speech and music in the service of drama. Spoken words are uttered either unaccompanied during intervals between instrumental movements or against a background of instrumental music. A most influential and perhaps the most famous *mélodrame* is *Pygmalion* (1770) with text by **Jean-Jacques Rousseau** (1712–78) and music by Horace Coignet (1735–1821). This text was also set in 1779 by Georg Benda (1722–1821) who composed several *mélodrames*, notably *Ariadne auf Naxos* (1775) to words by **Johann Christian Brandes** (1735–99) and *Medea* (1775) to words by Friedrich Wilhelm Gotter (1736–97).

The *mélodrame* never established itself as an independent form, but passages of *mélodrame* are to be found in many operas, a notable example being in the dungeon scene of Beethoven's *Fidelio*. Brief snatches of spoken dialogue in otherwise completely sung operas (e.g. the few words of Ellen and Balstrode in Benjamin Britten's *Peter Grimes*) can only be pedantically referred to as *mélodrame*.   GH

Menander (c. 342 – c. 291 BC) The most celebrated poet of the Athenian New Comedy (see **Greece, ancient**). He wrote over 100 plays (the first probably performed in 321), but won first prize only eight times. After his death, however, he became one of the most popular and influential of all Greek poets.

Until this century, knowledge of his work rested only on the numerous lines quoted by later authors, generally for their edifying content, and on the fact that three plays by **Plautus** and four by **Terence** were known to be adaptations of Menandrean originals. The position has been transformed, however, by the publication of ancient texts, generally on papyrus, which have been excavated in Egypt. These publications began in 1905 and still continue. We now have one virtually complete play, *Dyscolus* (*The Bad-Tempered Man*, performed in 316 BC, published in 1959), more than three acts of *Samia* (*The Girl from Samos*), substantial portions of *Aspis* (*The Shield*), *Epitrepontes* (*The Men who Went to Arbitration*), *Perikeiromene* (*The Girl who Had her Hair Cut*), *Sicyonius* (*The Sicyonian*) and *Misoumenos* (*The Bête Noire*), and smaller fragments of several others.

While some of Menander's characters and themes have precedents in Old Comedy, his is a very different world from that of **Aristophanes** – a world of bourgeois families and their servants, striving to act decently according to their lights (except for the occasional villain, like the wicked uncle Smicrines in *Aspis*), their lives bounded by the same laws of nature and the same social conventions as the Greeks of Menander's audience. Unity of place and time are carefully observed. Dramatic illusion can be toyed with, through sly references to comedy or tragedy, but is not broken, except by the formal 'prologue speech', in which a character or god addresses the audience directly to explain the situation. This is a convention borrowed, not from earlier comedy, but from the tragedy of **Euripides**, who also provides precedents for the aside, the moralizing soliloquy and the recognition scene (which often involves foundlings recognized by tokens, as in Euripides' *Ion* and some lost tragedies). There are five acts, usually in a single metre, with little music or singing (except between the acts, in choral performances that are not part of the text). Language, though colloquial, is never indecent.

Plots were ingeniously worked out, with the audience well able to predict the essentials of the denouement but kept in suspense as to how it could be accomplished. The plot of *Dyscolus* is simple enough – the resolution comes when the misanthropic Cnemon, who has refused to let his daughter marry her wealthy suitor, is made to repent by being rescued after falling down a well. But this was an early play, and evidently the complexities were greater elsewhere.

There is a limited range of stock character-types – stern fathers, lovesick youths, innocent girls, worldly courtesans, fawning parasites, cunning slaves, clownish cooks, and so forth – though there is room for variation within each type, and the dramatist can play with the expectations which the types create. Plot-motifs too are drawn from a fairly restricted repertory of deceptions, misunderstandings, estrangements and recognitions, and the happy ending often depends on a coincidence that would be highly unlikely in real life. All this has made it difficult for some modern critics to discern the realism for which Menander was famous in antiquity. But by ringing the changes on his types and motifs Menander is able to confront his characters with any number of socially delicate situations, and the realism, as well as the humour, lies largely in their reactions to these. And it is because he works on a relatively small canvas that such subtleties can capture the audience's attention.

The moral sentiments which take up so much of Menander can often be seen, when the context is known, to be ironically undercut by the situation in which they are spoken. While he doubtless intended them to be remembered and quoted for their wisdom and elegant expression, he ensures that they always contribute to the comedy, never interrupt it.   ALB

Mengistu Lemma (1925–) Ethiopian poet and playwright. After an Orthodox Church education, he studied in England and joined the Imperial Diplomatic Corps. His first two plays were comedies in Amharic, *Marriage By Abduction* (performed 1963) and *The Marriage of Unequals*. In 1980 his *Anti-Colonialist*, a play on the Italian occupation, was performed. He has also translated into Amharic works by **Chekhov**, **Priestley** and Tawfīq al-Hakīm. He is at present on the staff of the Theatre Department at Addis Ababa University.   RK

Menken, Adah Isaacs (Adele McCard) (1835–68) American actress and poet, born near New Orleans; after the deaths of her stepfather and her first husband, Alexander Isaacs Menken, a conductor, she supported herself as a dancer and circus rider, before making her acting debut at Shreveport as Pauline in *The Lady of Lyons* (1857). A bigamous marriage to the pugilist John Neenan (1859) ended in scandal, which she topped by appearing in flesh-coloured tights and minimal drapery, bound to a 'wild horse of Tartary' in Milner's melodrama *Mazeppa* (Green St Theatre, Albany, 1861). This role, which she performed throughout America, won her renown as the 'Naked Lady' and made her a star. A marriage to R. H. Newell ('Orpheus C. Kerr') brought her popularity with New York's Bohemia, and a tour to San Francisco repeated this with the literati of the Far West. In London, at **Astley**'s (1864), she played *Mazeppa* and *The Child of the Sun* for £500 a performance, the highest salary yet earned by an actress, and was lionized by **Dickens**,

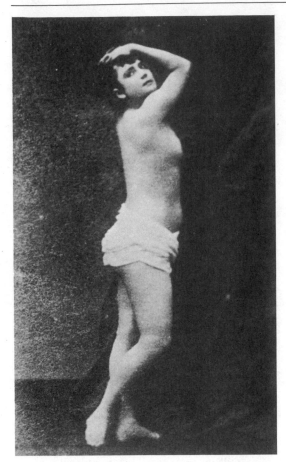

A pin-up of Adah Isaacs Menken in her 'Naked Lady' guise.

Rossetti and Swinburne. After a fourth marriage, the last phase of her career took place in Paris, in a silent equestrian role in *The Pirates of the Savannah* (Gaîté); she was rumoured to have had an affair with **Dumas** *père*. Her last performance was at **Sadler's Wells**, 1868, before her sudden death from peritonitis. LS

Mercer, David (1928–80) British dramatist, who wrote prolifically for the stage, television and films during the 1960s and early 1970s. Throughout his life, he retained an individualistic Marxist faith which he tried to reconcile with the circumstances around him as a writer from Northern working-class roots who became successful in the middle-class South. That was the theme of his first West End play, *Ride a Cock Horse* (1965), in which the successful writer, Peter, reverted to infantilism. Madness, usually but not invariably caused by social circumstances, was the subject of his screenplay, *A Suitable Case for Treatment* (1965), and *In Two Minds* (1967), while Mercer's plays also featured rebellious eccentrics, such as Flint the agnostic vicar who runs away with a pregnant Irish girl in *Flint* (1970). This eccentricity could be caused by the tug of loyalties between love and economic necessity, between class backgrounds or other factors; but Mercer's heroes are usually in retreat from societies which appal them. In *After Haggerty* (1970), a critic dislikes the new world of theatre almost as much as he rebels against the narrow-minded fundamentalism of his father's generation, while in *Cousin Vladimir* (1978) a refugee from Soviet Russia finds himself appalled by the degeneracy of modern Britain. Mercer's dialogue was usually witty, handling profound ideas and complicated themes with energy and grace; but his more abstract style of writing, as in *Duck Song* (1974), worked less well in the theatre. JE

Mercier, Louis-Sébastien (1740–1814) French dramatist, critic and man of letters, deputy to the revolutionary Convention of 1792. As befitted a friend and disciple of **Diderot** and an admirer of contemporary English authors, the bulk of Mercier's work for the stage consisted of domestic dramas and comedies, with characters and incidents drawn from everyday middle-class life but often unduly sentimental or declamatory in tone, earnest and moralizing in their espousal of social issues. Notable are *Le Déserteur* (*The Deserter*, 1770), a remonstrance against war, and *La Brouette du Vinaigrier* (*The Vinegar-man's Barrow*, 1775), which through a mésalliance between a rich girl and a boy from the working class presents a plea for equality and the dignity of labour. He was also the author of historical dramas and adaptations of **Shakespeare** which domesticated Lear's troubles and gave Romeo and Juliet a happy ending. His critical writing not only reiterated Diderot's arguments for an extension in the normal subject matter of drama but anticipated the attack on classical values mounted by the romantics and some of their preoccupations. DR

Mercury Theatre (London) A small 150-seat theatre opened by **Ashley Dukes** in 1933, the combination of poetic drama and dance in its first production (*Jupiter Translated*, an adaptation of **Molière**'s *Amphitryon* with an interpolated ballet by Rupert Doone) marked the two lines that have characterized the work presented there. From the beginning it served as the London base of the Ballet Rambert, while its early successes included **Martin Browne**'s 1935 production of **Eliot**'s *Murder in the Cathedral* (originally intended as part of a Poets' Theatre season that was to have included works by **Yeats** and **Auden**) and the 1937 premiere of *The Ascent of F6* by Auden and **Isherwood**. Its reputation for verse drama was re-established by the Pilgrim Players' 1945–7 seasons under Browne's management, with productions of contemporary religious plays – Norman Nicholson's *The Old Man of the Mountains*, Ronald Duncan's *This Way to the Tomb*, Anne Ridler's *The Shadow Factory* – which were followed by two popular poetic comedies, **Christopher Fry**'s *A Phoenix too Frequent* and **Donagh MacDonagh**'s *Happy as Larry*. Although used solely as a studio for the Ballet Rambert from 1952 to 1966, its suitability for avant-garde work, demonstrated by the London premieres of **Saroyan**'s *The Beautiful People* (1947) or **Genet**'s *The Maids* (1952), has more recently made it a base for visiting companies like the International Theatre Club, the Café **La Mama** or the Other Company. CI

Mercury Theatre, The A repertory company established in New York in 1937 by **Orson Welles** and **John Houseman**. The brief but historically significant two-year history, from the Welles–Houseman withdrawal from the **Federal Theatre Project** over the denial by Washington bureaucrats to produce Marc Blitzstein's proletarian drama with music *The Cradle Will Rock* to the final production of *Danton's Death* (1938), is told vividly in Houseman's *Run-Through* (1972). The other imaginative productions were: *The Shoemaker's Holiday*, *Heartbreak House*, and a modern-dress *Julius Caesar* intended as an anti-Fascist tract, though in fact Welles's cutting of the text led to confusion. The ensemble included Norman Lloyd, Joseph Cotton, Martin Gabel, Vincent Price, Ruth Ford, Hiram Sherman and **Geraldine Fitzgerald**. The Mercury Theatre of the Air was responsible for the infamous broadcast of *The War of the Worlds* (1938) and many of the company members appeared in Welles's film *Citizen Kane* (1940).   DBW

Merman, Ethel (1909–84) American singer and actress. Merman made an auspicious stage debut in *Girl Crazy* (1930), where her renditions of two **Gershwin** songs, 'I Got Rhythm', and 'Sam and Delilah', stopped the show nightly. She was soon typecast as a brassy, big-hearted nightclub singer, a role she played, with slight variations, in *Take a Chance* (1932), *Anything Goes* (1934), *Red, Hot and Blue* (1936). Although she appeared in secondary roles in these shows, Merman was often given the best songs to sing because of her powerful voice and exemplary diction. She received her first solo star billing for *Panama Hattie* (1940), in which she again portrayed a nightclub singer. After a change-of-pace role as a defence worker in *Something for the Boys* (1943), Merman appeared in **Irving Berlin**'s *Annie Get Your Gun* (1946). The part of western sharpshooter Annie Oakley gave Merman a rare opportunity to portray a character that differed significantly from her own personality. Four years later Merman was back in another Berlin show, *Call Me Madam*, in which she portrayed a Washington hostess who is appointed ambassador to a tiny European kingdom. Her next musical, *Happy Hunting* (1956), gave her a similar role as a Philadelphia socialite seeking a husband for her daughter. In 1959 Merman capped

Ethel Merman in Annie Get Your Gun.

her career with her performance as Rose, the quintessential stage mother, in *Gypsy*. Both her singing and her acting received superlative reviews from the critics. A decade later Merman made her last Broadway appearance when she took over the title role in *Hello, Dolly!*

Although most of the shows she appeared in were haphazard assemblages of stale musical comedy formulas, their major appeal lay in Merman's electrifying interpretations of songs by such important musical comedy composers as the Gershwins, **Cole Porter**, and Irving Berlin. She published her autobiography in 1955.   MK

Merrick, David (1912–) American producer. Beginning with his first success in 1954, *Fanny*, Merrick produced or co-produced over 70 plays, including many imported foreign hits. Some of his more successful have included *The Entertainer* (1958), *Gypsy* (1959), *Becket* (1960), *Stop the World – I Want to Get Off* (1962), *Luther* and *One Flew Over the Cuckoo's Nest* (1963), *Oh What a Lovely War!* and *Hello, Dolly!* (1964), *Marat/Sade* (1965), *I Do! I Do!* (1966), *Rosencrantz and Guildenstern Are Dead* (1967), *Play It Again, Sam* (1969), *Travesties* (1975), and *42nd Street* (1981).

Merrick's publicity stunts for his shows are legendary on Broadway. To publicize *Fanny*, Merrick commissioned a nude statue of Nejla Ates, the show's belly dancer, and had it placed in Central Park, opposite a bust of **Shakespeare**. *Life* covered the story, and *Fanny* ran for 888 performances. Of such stunts, Merrick said 'Other things being equal, using promotion stunts would allow me to get ahead of my competitors. I'd say that's been a big factor in my success.'

On 13 February 1983 Merrick suffered a stroke which rendered him incapable of administering his $50–70 million estate, but in 1985 the New York Supreme Court ruled him sufficiently recovered to manage his affairs.   SMA

Merry (née Brunton), Anne (1769–1808) British-born actress and manager noted for appearances on the American stage, where, according to her biographer Gresdna Doty, she was the artistic pacesetter. Daughter of John Brunton, provincial English actor-manager, she followed her successful debut at Bath in 1785 with an engagement at **Covent Garden** for the next season, remaining there until her retirement in 1792 after her marriage to minor poet Robert Merry. Soon Merry lost his money and Anne accepted an offer in 1796 from **Thomas Wignell** to join the **Chestnut Street Theatre** company in Philadelphia. Widowed four years, she married Wignell in 1803. When he died seven weeks later, she co-managed the Chestnut Street. In 1806 she married **William Warren**; two years later she died in childbirth at 39. As an actress she was known for her excellence in tragic roles and especially for the sweetness of her voice, her gentleness, simplicity, and grace on stage. Her brother John and sister Louisa were also actors.   DBW

Merson, Billy (William Thompson) (1881–1947) English pantomime and variety artist. Chiefly remembered as composer and singer of 'The Spaniard that Blighted my Life', this versatile Nottingham-born performer illustrates neatly the range and skill of the music-hall professional. After an apprenticeship as half of a double act, working under various pseudonyms as Irish comedian, eccentric equilibrist, and circus clown, he went solo under his best-known billing in 1908. A successful career in musical comedy culminated in 1925 in his creation of the role of Hard Boiled Herman in *Rose Marie* at **Drury Lane**. His craft is perhaps best appreciated from a recording of 'The Night I appeared in *Macbeth*'. Studio recording was an unkind medium to many variety artists, including some of the greatest such as **Dan Leno**, because it deprived them of the relationship with their audience that was at once structure and nourishment. Merson transcends it, conveying through the recording not only his finely controlled natural baritone, impeccable diction, and delicate use of *Sprechstimme*, but also his ability to create instantly a rich characterization. His interpretation of an ageing and unsuccessful thespian of the old school – 'They made me a present/of Mornington Crescent,/ They threw it a brick at a time' – is a classic example of the music-hall comedian's ability to evoke laughter and sympathy simultaneously.   AEG

Meskin, Aaron (1898–1974) **Habimah**'s greatest actor. Born in Russia, the son of a poor shoemaker, he joined the collective in 1918 and remained with it all his life. Of a big stature and deep voice, his most famous role was that of the man of clay in Leivik's *The Golem* (1925). Acted Willy Loman in **Arthur Miller**'s *Death of a Salesman* (1951) and the father in **O'Neill**'s *Anna Christie* (1957). Noted for his characterizations of Othello (1950), Macbeth (1954), King Lear (1955), and especially Shylock (1936, 1959).   HaS

Messel, Oliver (1905–78) British stage and film designer, and artist. Messel started his career designing for **C. B. Cochran**'s annual *Revues* from 1926 to 1931. Known as a colourist who frequently employed classical rules of perspective in his designs, Messel designed for the ballet such works as Frederick Ashton's and Ninette Valois's *Sleeping Beauty* (1946), and Ashton's *Homage to the Queen* (1953). His efforts in play design are highlighted by *A Midsummer Night's Dream* (1938), *The Lady's Not for Burning* (1949), and *Roshomon* (1959). Messel's versatility is exemplified in his designs for such films as *Caesar and Cleopatra* and *Suddenly Last Summer*. In addition Messel is the author of a text on scene design titled *Stage Designs and Costumes* (London, 1934).   TM

Metastasio, Pietro Pseudonym of Pietro Trapassi (1698–1782) Italian poet, dramatist and librettist. Of modest social background, his literary gifts were early recognized and he was given an intensive private education in which study of classical literature and theory was prominent and left a lasting influence on his writing. Prolific of verse and plays from his youth, in his mid-twenties he found his true *forte*, the opera libretto, his first *opera seria*, *Didone Abbandonata* (*Dido Forsaken*), being performed in Naples in 1724. Among composers who later set this sentimental drama, drawn from Virgil's *Aeneid*, was Handel, and to his music it quickly achieved a European-wide celebrity. Metastasio became the most popular and successful opera librettist of his age, enjoying a European-wide reputation as a major poet. Vivaldi, Albinoni and Mozart were among the scores of composers eager to set his

work. In 1729 he was called to Vienna, where he remained official court poet for the rest of his life. Most of his subject matter was taken from Graeco-Roman history, mythology and literature, and his later critical writings indicate the extent to which he deliberately sought to emulate the austerity and elevation of Greek tragedy, while eschewing its elemental realism in favour of a formality, dignity and pathos more in tune with his temperament and acceptable to his age. Benefiting from the turn of the century reform of Italian *opera seria*, he wrote at a time when music was still subordinate to text, and thus his work could enjoy a literary status *sui generis* and influence writing for the non-musical stage. His strengths lay in his instinct for the theatrically effective, his ability to produce fluent and mellifluous verse, and his consummate skill at wedding the needs of dramatic action and character delineation on the one hand, with those of music, vocal delivery and stage spectacle on the other. In large measure his reputation passed as his subject matter (and even more the social and moral assumptions underpinning his treatment of it) ceased to appeal. But in recent years his theatrical skills and the extent of his influence on the drama of his age have come increasingly to be appreciated.   KR

Mexico With the longest sustained tradition in all of Latin America, the theatre in Mexico has passed through many stages of development. Hernán Cortés led his band of *conquistadores* against the flourishing culture of the Aztecs in 1519 and despite overwhelming odds was able to defeat Moctezuma. Using as a point of departure the Aztecs' natural inclination toward music and dance that was evident in their own dramatic productions, the early missionaries used drama to convert the indigenous peoples to Catholicism. These pieces later showed refinements but the initial purpose of the theatre was closely related to religious instruction. A secular theatre was not long in developing in the New World for the diversion of those accustomed to the delights of the continental theatre. With regular routes of communication established with Spain, the influence of the Madrid theatre made itself apparent throughout the region. A developing creole theatre emphasized local themes. Juan Pérez Ramírez (1545–?) is considered to be the first dramatist born in America; his contemporary Fernán González de Eslava (c. 1534–c. 1601) arrived in Mexico at an early age and wrote *coloquios*, *entremeses* and **loas**, pieces with a strong religious orientation and graceful style that overcame their dramatic defects.

During the 17th and 18th centuries, the Mexican theatre continued to reflect the literary traditions of the continent. **Juan Ruiz de Alarcón** (1581–1639) was born in Mexico but made his most significant contributions to the Spanish theatre. Known as the moralist of his age, he valued human dignity in his works, combining the didactic with the entertaining. His best plays, *Las paredes oyen* (*The Walls have Ears*, 1617) and *La verdad sospechosa* (*The Doubtful Truth*, 1621), presented the vices of inherent character faults with dramatic formulae adopted later by **Corneille** and **Molière**. The other important writer of the period was Sor Juana Inés de la Cruz (1651–95), the inimitable and precocious nun whose poetry, essays and theatre rivalled in quality the European masters. Unequalled in the American baroque, her theatre corresponds to the cycle of **Calderón**. *El divino Narciso* (*The Divine Narcissus*, c. 1680) was a prime example of the **auto sacramental** destined for the festivities of Corpus Christi. *Amor es más laberinto* (*Love is a Greater Labyrinth*, c. 1668) was a typical cloak and dagger play and *Los empeños de una casa* (*The Obligations of a Household*, c. 1680) parodied the title of Calderón's play, *Los empeños de un acaso* (*The Obligations of Chance*).

By way of contrast, the 18th-century theatre, born in Spain and in Mexico, overshadowed by the earlier Golden Age masterpieces, produced a derivative and exaggerated style. In Mexico, the secular theatre competed unsuccessfully with the dominant church as a locus for public meetings and as the vehicle for transmitting ideas and customs. Spanish plays that had already proved themselves in the peninsula were favoured over local dramatic productions. The century in Mexico is represented primarily by Eusebio Vela (1688–1737), the impresario of the insolvent 'Coliseo de México' (Mexican Colosseum). Only three of his plays have survived, all of which show the baroque taste which mark him as one who tried to sustain the traditions of **Lope de Vega** and Calderón de la Barca.

During the first quarter of the 19th century the disruptive influence of the wars of independence produced a general state of decay in the Latin American theatre. In Mexico the famous 'Cry of Dolores' rang out on 16 September 1810, the day recognized as Independence Day when Father Hidalgo led the charge against the Spanish. Fighting continued until 1821, but even after that date the cultural bonds with the mother country remained strong. The neoclassical tendencies in vogue in Spain at the time continued to dominate, although romanticism was by then prevalent in the rest of the continent. Joaquín Fernández de Lizardi (1776–1827), known as the 'Mexican Thinker', captured the picaresque tradition in the first novel written in Spanish America, *El periquillo sarniento* (*The Itchy Parrot*, 1816), but his theatre was less innovative and also less moralizing, with plays ranging from allegorical and religious topics to contemporary historical events. The major playwright of the period is Manuel Eduardo de Gorostiza (1789–1851), who was born and died in Mexico but was educated and spent most of his life in Europe during the height of romanticism. He was not induced to follow the romantic currents, however, and his masterpiece, *Contigo pan y cebolla* (*Bread and Onion with Thee*, 1833), presented first in Madrid and shortly after in Mexico, satirized the exaggerations of the movement. Gorostiza used a mildly didactic tone to ridicule excessive sentimentalism and the idealization of standards.

Romanticism was nourished primarily by themes and techniques of Europe. The indigenous elements lacked a coherent expression, although some writers turned their attention to local matters which gave rise to the **costumbrista** theatre. Also the awakening of national consciousness coincided with independence and the new political and literary freedom generated innumerable works barely worthy of mention. The principal exponent of Mexican romanticism was Fernando Calderón (1809–45) whose dramas portrayed a desire to escape temporal and spatial boundaries in search of European themes, especially chivalrous themes of the Middle Ages. His only play with a Mexican setting is *A ninguna de las tres* (*None of the Three*, 1839), a satiric comedy written as a reply to **Bretón de los Herreros**'s *Marcela o ¿a cuál de las tres?* (*Marcela, or Which of the Three?*, 1831). The works of Ignacio Rodríguez Galván (1816–42) reflected his romantic existence, but unlike his contemporary Calderón, instead of seeking inspiration in the tales of medieval Europe, he looked to the traditions and legends of the New World. His dramatic production is scanty because of his premature death, but one play *Muñoz, Visitador de México* (*Muñoz, Inspector General of Mexico*, 1938) was an early historical drama. Later in the century, as realistic and naturalistic aesthetics signalled the advent of a technological, scientific, and psychological society, a post-romantic momentum controlled the theatre with little sign of evolution. José Peón y Contreras (1843–1907) has been compared with Lope de Vega for his prolific production and with the Spanish romanticist **Zorrilla** for his facile verses. *El pasado* (*The Past*, 1872), a play with monologues and asides, reserved a place in Mexican theatre history for its young author, Manuel Acuña (1849–73), who committed suicide. Manuel José Othón (1848–1906), a classical poet of some renown, reflected the romantic influence of **José Echegaray** in two important works, *Después de la muerte* (*After Death*, 1883) and *Lo que hay detrás de la dicha* (*What's beyond Happiness*, 1886). The first pieces of children's theatre appeared during this period, works by José Rosas Moreno (1838–83), a melancholic poet and playwright whose *Sor Juana Inés de la Cruz* (1882) dealt with the apocryphal love of the illustrious nun for the Count of Mancera. At the end of the century, there was a great deal of theatre activity, although the quality was uneven at best.

20th century   The peace, order and economic progress proclaimed by Porfirio Díaz during the early part of the century did little to foment the development of Mexican theatre which was still closely tied to the Spanish tradition. The outbreak of the Mexican Revolution in 1910, following by exactly 100 years the wars of independence, brought some insignificant political drama, but for the most part, the period was little more than a prolongation of the previous century. Many travelling foreign companies stopped in Mexico, where they helped the efforts of such playwrights as Federico Gamboa (1864–1939), Marcelino Dávalos (1871–1923) and Antonio Mediz Bolio (1884–1957).

After the constitutional consolidation at the end of the Revolution, coinciding with the end of the First World War, the nationalist current became stronger, and the period of the 1920s was characterized by a desire for reconstruction and reforms. Popular customs of local life and colour were captured in the light forms of the *sainete* and **zarzuela**. The Teatro Folklórico (Folkloric Theatre) (1921) and the Teatro del Murciélago (Theatre of the Bat) (1924) fostered typically indigenous dances, songs, and ritual ceremonies from all of Mexico. The struggling Sociedad de Autores Dramáticos (Playwrights' Society) founded in 1902 was re-established in 1923 as the Unión de Autores Dramáticos (Playwrights' Union) to organize the reading of plays and translations. This impetus prepared the way for the formation of the more important Grupo de los Siete Autores (Group of Seven Authors) in 1925, whose members were Francisco Monterde, José Joaquín

Gamboa, Carlos Noriega Hope, Víctor Manuel Díez Barroso, Ricardo Parada León and the brothers Lázaro and Carlos Lozano García. This group started the process of modernization by discarding some quaint procedures such as asides and by accepting Mexican Spanish instead of Madrid Spanish for stage dialogue, tendencies also adopted by the Comedia Mexicana (Mexican Comedy) (1927). Carlos Díaz Dufóo's *Padre mercader* (*Father Merchant*, 1929), a realistic social play about the dismal economic situation of a Mexican family, was the first Mexican play of the century to achieve 100 performances.

The renovation lacking in the professional companies was fostered by a series of experimental groups. In 1928 **Xavier Villaurrutia** and **Salvador Novo** established the **Teatro de Ulises** (Ulysses Theatre) under the patronage of Antonieta Rivas Mercado. This vanguard theatre experiment lasted only two seasons but it presented six plays, all foreign, to counteract the out-moded influence of the Mexican Comedy. Other groups followed, of which the most influential was the **Teatro de Orientación** (Theatre of Orientation) (1932–4; 1938–9), founded by **Celestino Gorostiza** with government sponsorship. These groups relied on intimate settings, and the most recent concepts of European directors and artists – **Craig**, **Reinhardt**, **Stanislavsky**, **Piscator**, and others – to achieve the greatest plasticity. With translations of plays by the world masters – **Shakespeare**, Molière, **Lenormand**, **Chekhov**, **Ibsen**, **Shaw**, **O'Neill**, to name a few – they brought new concepts to the Mexican theatre, which in turn stimulated national works. Julio Bracho and the Escolares del Teatro (Theatre Scholars) produced the first play in the new movement in 1931, *Proteo* (*Proteus*) by Francisco Monterde. Although the play did not have long-range influence, it was important for the director to take responsibility for balancing multiple aspects of a performance. These groups also encouraged the construction of small theatres with a capacity of 200 or less. Seki Sano, the Japanese director trained in Stanislavsky techniques, arrived in Mexico in 1939 and participated in actor training and the creation of new groups, including Proa (1942), La Linterna Mágica (The Magic Lantern) (1946), Teatro de Arte Moderno (Modern Art Theatre) (1947) and his own group, the Teatro de la Reforma (Theatre of Reform) (1948). The major writers included Xavier Villaurrutia (1903–50), a brilliant poet who wrote short philosophical and intellectual plays such as the *Autos profanos* (*Profane Pieces*, 1933–7) and other works dealing with generational conflicts and the Mexican middle class. Salvador Novo (1904–74) and Celestino Gorostiza (1904–67) both made major contributions to theatre over many years as directors, critics and playwrights. The exceptional case was **Rodolfo Usigli** (1905–79) who criticized Mexican reality in family and class relations but without moralizing. Usigli was a diplomat, theatre historian, and prolific playwright; two of his plays have become modern classics. *El gesticulador* (*The Impostor*) is a complex, provocative examination of hypocrisy in Mexican life portrayed by a history professor who adopts the identity of a Revolutionary general. *Corona de sombra* (*Crown of Shadow*, 1943) revises history to study the ill-begotten empire of Maximilian and Carlota in Mexico (1864–7) and to penetrate the lessons imparted by Carlota's long years

of madness. The play is part of his *Corona* trilogy that also focused on Cuauhtémoc and the Virgin of Guadalupe. Usigli was a major experimenter in the Mexican theatre although he did not affiliate with any experimental group. Among other features, the nationalistic movement of the 1920s focused new interest on the rising middle class, a new source of dramatic conflict, with plays implicitly or explicitly critical of social situations and revealing an increased interest in psychological examination.

The experimental cycle begun in 1928 ended in 1947 with the demise of the Teatro de México (Theatre of Mexico), and a new era of professionalism was marked that year by the formation of the Instituto Nacional de Bellas Artes (National Institute of Fine Arts). The INBA was established to foment national art through actor training, professional theatre seasons, and practical courses for theatre personnel in artistic centres. Annual drama festivals were sponsored by INBA with prizes for new plays. For the most part, the post-Second World War theatre in Mexico concerned with psychological or character studies developed along two lines: a realistic tendency of the *costumbristic theatre*, and the fantasy tendency of an expressionistic theatre. Of this generation **Emilio Carballido** (b. 1925) was the most prolific and innovative. His theatre was marked by the dual inclinations towards both the realistic and the fantastic, the former in provincial settings such as *Rosalba y los Llaveros* (*Rosalba and the Llavero Family*, 1950), a play that penetrates the psychological contrast between a young city girl and her provincial cousins, and the fantastic in such plays as *La hebra de oro* (*The Golden Thread*, 1955), *Yo también hablo de la rosa* (*I Too Speak of the Rose*, 1965) or *Las cartas de Mozart* (*Mozart's Letters*, 1974). Carballido's creative spirit led to innovative forms in psychological, ontological and even political issues. In addition, he promoted a younger generation of writers through classes in directing and playwriting, and through the publication of a major theatre journal, *Tramoya*, and various editions of plays by the younger generation. His contemporary, **Luisa Josefina Hernández** (b. 1928), inherited Usigli's position as professor of theatre history at the National University; her plays showed careful structure and solid character development, always tempered by a Mexican reality. Other major writers of the period included Federico S. Inclán, Luis G. Basurto (1920–90), **Sergio Magaña** (b. 1924), Wilberto Canton (1925–79), Jorge Ibargüengoitia (1928–84) and Hugo Argüelles (b. 1932). Héctor Azar (b. 1930) promoted theatre training through CADAC, his centre for actor training and for performing his own plays and adaptations. A number of women writers were particularly active, Margarita Urueta (b. 1913), María Luisa Algarra (1916–57), Maruxa Vilalta (b. 1932), and Pilar Campesino (formerly Pilar Retes); the most outstanding internationally is **Elena Garro** (b. 1922), whose poetic works bordering on fantasy were promoted by **Poesía en Voz Alta** (Poetry Out Loud). **Carlos Solórzano** (b. 1922) was born in Guatemala but as a theatre director, critic, historian, and playwright, his career belonged to Mexico. Affiliated with Camusian existentialism, the main currents in both his short plays as well as his full-length plays – *Doña Beatriz* (1952), *El hechicero* (*The Wizard*, 1954) and *Las manos de Dios* (*The Hands of God*, 1956) – were aspects of individual freedom.

During the period of the 1950s the theatre in Mexico was strongly realistic in conception, design and staging. Both the INBA and the theatre programme of the National University staged translated plays by such authors as **Arthur Miller** and **Tennessee Williams**. Between 1956 and 1963, Poetry Out Loud sought to bring a new intellectual and imaginative dimension to the Mexican theatre. Comprising Mexico's leading poets and most creative people, the mainsprings in the initial years included Juan José Arreola and Octavio Paz. In the eight programmes of its eight years of existence, the group presented plays ranging from Greek and Spanish classics to modern contemporary works, always with the intention of uplifting and renovating the theatre. The critics were often hostile to what was perceived as an elitist movement, and fiscal support was difficult, but many talented actors and directors contributed and thrived from the association. Héctor Mendoza, Juan José Gurrola, José Luis Ibáñez, Nancy Cárdenas, and Julio Castillo were principal directors whose work continued to show the influence of Poetry Out Loud long after the group's demise. The group constituted an interesting chapter in Mexico's theatre history.

In the late 1960s a new generation of authors, many of them the products of Carballido's theatre workshops, began to emerge in spite of the difficulties of staging new plays by unknown authors. **Oscar Villegas** challenged theatrical conventions with thematically and technically daring pieces: *La paz de la buena gente* (*The Peace of the Good People*, 1967), *Marlon Brando es otro* (*Marlon Brando is Another*, 1967) and his major play, *Atlántida* (*Atlantis*, 1976). **José Agustín**, an engaging novelist as well, also helped set the tone of a generation influenced by rock music with his *Abolición de la propiedad* (*Abolition of Property*, 1969), an experimental work incorporating technological elements (closed circuit TV, tape recordings, slides, etc.) and reflecting thematically the ontological uncertainty of the generation. Felipe Santander (b. 1934) arrived late but with a huge success: *El extensionista* (*The County Extension Agent*). The young writers reflected the problems of their age; specifically, the political, social, and economic issues facing Mexico, and the interpersonal relationships of her youth. The generation included **Jesús González Dávila**, Tomás Espinoza (b. 1943), Willebaldo López (b. 1944). Damte del Castillo (b. 1946), Oscar Liera (1944–90), Carlos Olmos (b. 1947), Gerardo Velázquez (b. 1949), Victor Hugo Rascón Banda (b. 1950), Antonio Argudín (b. 1953), Sabina Berman (b. 1953), Alejandro Licona (b. 1953), Miguel Angel Tenorio (b. 1954) and one major provincial dramatist from Monterrey, **Guillermo Schmidhuber de la Mora**. Two novelists who have enjoyed great success in the theatre are **Carlos Fuentes** and **Vicente Leñero**. Leñero was particularly attracted to the documentary which he exercised with plays on Che Guevara, Morelos and other figures from the Mexican past. Fuentes, after two plays in 1970, returned to theatre in 1982. *Orquídeas a la luz de la luna/Orchids in the Moonlight* was written simultaneously in Spanish and English, and deals with the changing values and realities in the world of two ageing Mexican film stars.

Following on the heady years of the 1960s and 70s which featured such directors as Ignacio Retes and Julio Prieto, and a brilliant group of actors, including Ignacio

López Tarso and others, the López Portillo regime sponsored an ambitious theatre project through the Social Security agency. Called Teatro de la Nación (National Theatre) and organized by Carlos Solórzano, the project consisted of five cycles (classical, Mexican, theatre of the Americas, experimental and lyrical) plus invited companies. The recent government has been less supportive for economic and cultural reasons. Although some serious work is being done, the current theatre fare in Mexico is dominated by light comedy and bedroom farce, a source of disillusionment to serious playwrights and directors who strive to strengthen the state of the art. Talent is not lacking, but public taste is fickle. GW

See: A. De Kuehne, *Teatro mexicano contemporáneo (1940–62)*, Mexico, 1962; A. Magaña Esquivel, *Medio siglo de teatro mexicano (1900–61)*, Mexico, 1964; R. S. Lamb, *Breve historia del teatro mexicano*, Mexico, 1958; J. B. Nomland, *Teatro mexicano contemporáneo (1900–50)*, Mexico, 1967; C. Solórzano, *Testimonios teatrales de México*, Mexico, 1973; R. Unger, *Poesía en Voz Alta in the Theatre of Mexico*, Missouri, 1981; R. Usigli, *México en el teatro*, Mexico, 1932.

Meyerhold, Vsevolod Emilievich (1874–1940)

The genius among Soviet-Russian theatricalist directors, his career describes the full trajectory from idealistic aestheticism through revolutionary experimentalism to prescriptive socialist realism that spans one of modern theatre history's most significant chapters (c. 1898–1939). Born Karl Theodor Kasimir Meyerhold, the future director trained in music and law before entering **Nemirovich-Danchenko**'s drama course at the Moscow Philharmonia (1896–8). He and classmate **Olga Knipper** were invited to join the newly founded **Moscow Art Theatre** (MAT, 1898), where he first played the roles of Treplev and Tuzenbach in **Chekhov**'s *The Seagull* and *The Three Sisters*, respectively. In 1902 he and other MAT company members formed the 'Fellowship of the New Drama', which toured the provinces for two years in typical realistic MAT fare. His growing interest in symbolist drama – **Maeterlinck**, Przbyszewski, **Andreev**, **Blok** – coincided with **Stanislavsky**'s, and the latter invited him to test new staging methods at the MAT Studio on Povarskaya Street (1905). Like **Gordon Craig**, **Georg Fuchs** and the Oriental theatre masters, Meyerhold came to believe in the primacy of movement in the theatre and in the essential difference between the rhythms of drama and life. This resulted in what Stanislavsky considered to be puppet-like acting in Meyerhold's stagings of Maeterlinck's *Death of Tintagiles* and **Hauptmann**'s *Schluck und Jau*, which Stanislavsky refused permission to open. The following year Meyerhold became artistic director of **Vera Komissarzhevskaya**'s Theatre (1906–7), where his experiments with stylized methods – bas-relief, rhythmic movement and intonation – applied to such symbolic and symbolist plays as **Ibsen**'s *Hedda Gabler*, Maeterlinck's *Sister Beatrice*, Andreev's *The Life of Man*, Blok's *The Puppet Show* (with innovative designs by Sudeikin and Sapunov) combined with the under- and misuse of his lead actress–employer again led to his dismissal. His official work as director at St Petersburg's Imperial opera and drama theatres (1908–18), which included sumptuous mountings of **Molière**'s *Don Juan* (1910) and **Lermontov**'s *Masquerade* (1917) (both designed by Golovin), was paralleled in time by experimental work at various small theatres and studios – the St Petersburg House of Interludes, Tower and Strand Theatres – under the pseudonym 'Dr Dapertutto'. He continued the **commedia dell'arte** research begun with *The Puppet Show* in his production of **Schnitzler**'s *Columbine's Scarf* (1910), the first important event in the area of theatrical pantomime, and in his journal *Love for Three Oranges* (1914–16) in which were published scenarios and related articles. Meyerhold was developing his theory of the actor-*cabotin*, a combination singer-dancer-juggler-tumbler, whose precise physicalization and mask-like presence would unite primordial and contemporary forms in a new, universal theatre. His experiments in scenic reconstructivism (paralleling **Evreinov**'s), begun with *Sister Beatrice*, *Tristan and Isolde* (1909) and *Don Juan*, continued with his staging of **Calderón de la Barca**'s *The Adoration of the Cross* (Tower Theatre, 1910). Meyerhold embraced Bolshevism and with the rallying cry 'Put the October Revolution into the Theatre' (1920) initiated a personal programme to make his art accessible to political themes and to the new proletarian audience. **Lunacharsky** named him head of the Theatre Division of the People's Commissariat for Education (1920). His productions at the Theatre of the Revolution (1922–4) and at the Meyerhold Theatre (1923–38) fall into two categories. The first discovered new forms for old and old-style plays, beginning with his production of Crommelynck's *The Magnanimous Cuckold* (1922), which utilized the first pure constructivist set (by **Popova**) – a 'machine for acting' – and biomechanics, his system of kinetic, reflexive acting derived from sports, circus acrobatics, Pavlovian association and industrial time–motion studies. He composed complex and exact 'directorial scores' based upon a playful and grotesque ('the schematization of the real') musical and rhythmic restructuring of space, text and perspective for **Sukhovo-Kobylin**'s *Tarelkin's Death* (with a famous design by **Stepanova**, 1922), **Ostrovsky**'s *The Forest* (1924), **Gogol**'s *The Inspector General* (1926) and **Griboedov**'s *Woe from Wit* (which he retitled *Woe to Wit*, 1928). His agit-prop-derived political productions include: **Mayakovsky**'s *Mystery-Bouffe* (1918, 1921), Verhaeren's *The Dawns* (1920), **Sergei Tretyakov**'s *Earth Rampant* (1923) and *Roar, China!* (1926) and M. Podgayetsky's *D. E.* (1924). He also staged impressive productions of such new Soviet plays as Mayakovsky's *The Bedbug* (1929) and *The Bathhouse* (1930), **Erdman**'s *The Mandate* (1925) and *The Suicide* (closed at dress rehearsal, 1932), **Olesha**'s *A List of Blessings* (1931) and Tretyakov's *I Want a Child* (refused permission to open, 1927–30). Accused of formalism, Meyerhold lost his company and the 'total theatre' that was being built for him. After some opera stagings including a stint at the Stanislavsky Opera Theatre in Moscow (1938–9), Meyerhold's anger and frustration over his situation and the influx of untalented socialist realism into the Soviet theatre led to a brave but futile tirade at a theatrical congress (1939), which sealed his fate. He was immediately arrested and either executed or died in a labour camp (probably 1940). His wife and lead actress Zinaida Raikh was butchered in their apartment, and Meyerhold officially became a 'nonperson'. He was

rehabilitated in 1955 and since then has exerted a tremendous influence on Soviet and Western directors, most notably on **Yury Lyubimov**, the Taganka Theatre's former artistic director.   SG

Micere Mugo (1942–   ) Kenyan educationist and writer, co-author with **Ngugi wa Thiong'o** of *The Trial of Dedan Kimathi*. Also published – *The Illness of Ex-Chief Kiti* (1976) and a radio play *Disillusioned* (1976). Now lives in exile.   RK

Michell, Keith (1928–   ) Australian actor. After acting in Adelaide, he joined the **Young Vic** Company in 1950, and has since played many leading roles at Stratford-upon-Avon, the **Old Vic**, and in the West End and New York. He was Artistic Director of the **Chichester Festival Theatre** 1974–8, and has appeared in Australia with the Shakespeare Memorial Theatre tour of 1952–3, in *The First Four Hundred Years* (1964), *Othello* (1978), and *La Cage aux Folles* (1985), and acted with the Queensland Theatre Company (1982). His most famous television role is Henry VIII in the BBC's *The Six Wives of Henry VIII* (1970).   MW

Mickery-theater   The Mickery-theater in Amsterdam is the Dutch institution which consistently chooses to present and produce theatrical productions from abroad that stand for new developments and trends in theatre. The Mickery-theater was founded in 1965 by Ritsaert Ten Cate. Performances were held in Ten Cate's farmhouse in Loenersloot, a village close to Amsterdam. After having been a private enterprise for five years Mickery received subsidy for the first time in 1970 and moved to Amsterdam. Their building there (a former cinema) has no fixed area for either audience or actors.

Mickery-theater wishes to give new impulses to Dutch actors and theatre. In cooperation with foreign companies, Mickery stimulates and develops theatrical initiatives that are difficult to stage elsewhere. There are a few 'regulars' amongst the companies, whose developments are followed with particular interest: **Traverse Theatre** (Edinburgh), **La Mama** (New York), The Pip Simmons Theatre Group (London), Tenjo Tsukiji (Tokyo) and the People Show (London).

Projects produced by Mickery itself show an increasing interest in the relationship between the theatre and reality, and between theatre and audio-visual means. Quite spectacular has been the use of movable cubicles, which, supported by air-cushions, lead the audience in various orders past several scenes. The following projects were realized by making use of these cubicles: *Fairground* (1975), *Cloud Cuckooland* (1979, with Tenjo Sajiki), *Outside* (1979), and *Fairground '84* (produced for the Holland Festival). During the seasons of 84–5 and 85–6, research into the relationship between the theatre and video/television took a central place in the initiatives undertaken by Mickery-theater, for instance in Pip Simmons's *La Ballista*.   MG   HS

Mickiewicz, Adam (1798–1855) Polish romantic poet and playwright who from 1823 lived in Russia, Germany, Italy and France as a political exile dedicated to the cause of Poland's freedom. His visionary work on the suffering and messianic destiny of Poland, *Forefathers' Eve* (1823, 1832; fully staged 1901), is the national sacred drama, dreamlike in structure. His ideas for a monumental theatre based on Greek tragedy, medieval mysteries and primeval folklore have had enduring influence on Polish directors.   DG

Micronesia see Oceania

Middle East It has long been assumed that theatre is a recent import to the Middle East and North Africa from the Western world. Modern scholarship is rapidly demonstrating that this is a misconception. While it is certainly true that Western plays and production styles were imported to most urban areas of the region from Europe for the first time in the late 19th and early 20th century, earlier indigenous theatrical traditions have existed in the Middle East continuously for many centuries. The richness and importance of these earlier traditions, which have played an important role in the cultural life of the region for centuries, has only recently begun to be appreciated. According to some theorists, Middle Eastern traditional theatre may even have influenced the development of theatre in the West, particularly comic theatre.

The rediscovery of traditional theatre in the Middle East has become an important cultural feature of the overall development of art in the region as playwrights and writers attempt to develop new modes of artistic expression which move away from imitation of Western tradition, and attempt to develop new theatre which speaks to the cultural roots of modern Middle Eastern peoples.

Most of these historical forms of Middle Eastern and North African theatre escaped the attention of orientalist scholars because they existed primarily as folk theatrical tradition with little in the way of formally recorded text. Today it is not possible to reconstruct the exact forms of the earliest historical traditions. Researchers must rely on comparisons of existing folk traditions, and historical accounts by travellers and local chroniclers to come to an understanding of the earliest theatrical forms.

The ancient past Evidence exists which suggests that dramatic performances were held in Pharaonic Egypt in temple settings. Ancient Pharaonic texts dating to as early as 2500 BC exist which suggest dialogue, stage directions and dramatic conventions. Particularly notable are the coronation 'dramas' of ancient Egypt, which were enacted in processional style, each scene being presented at a separate station along the route. Another well-known text, the Memphite Creation Drama, deals with the death and resurrection of Osiris, and was probably enacted on the first day of spring.

These early works suggest that ancient Egyptian drama probably consisted of enactment of legends and religious stories which were well known by spectators. No attempt seems to have been made to produce 'catharsis' or emotional reaction in the audience. Nevertheless, comic dialogues also exist which show that humour was present in these early performances.

Theodore Gaster, in his comprehensive study, *Thespis: Ritual, Myth and Drama in the Ancient Near East*, suggests that ritual and drama have a common religious origin in the Near East. He deals not only with the ancient Egyptian texts mentioned above, but also with ritual poems and texts from Canaanite, Babylonian and Hittite sources. While many of the sources cited by Gaster are not written in contemporary dramatic form, these mythological texts were probably enacted in ritual context before a public audience.

From Alexander to the Moghul empires There is little mention of indigenous theatrical activity in the Middle East during the period from the 3rd century BC to the establishment of the great Moghul empires throughout the region in the 13th century. What is known about traditional theatre can only be surmised from indirect evidence.

Greek and Roman civilization penetrated into most areas of Mesopotamia, Asia Minor and North Africa during the early centuries of this period on the heels of the conquests of Alexander the Great, and through the establishment of the Eastern Roman Empire at Byzantium. The ruins of ancient theatres and colosseums are found throughout North Africa, in Syria, and as far East as the central part of present-day Turkey, and it must be presumed that Greek and Roman spectacles, including dramatic presentations, were performed in them.

It is also undoubtedly the case that performance traditions of the Indian sub-continent were known in parts of the Middle East, particularly in the Sassanian Empire of Iran (c. AD 225–652). Numerous historical sources document the migration of Gypsies across the Iranian plateau during this period. The Iranian poet Ferdowsi, in his epic, *Shāhnāmeh*, notes that Bahrām-Gur (AD 420–38), the legendary Sassanian king, ordered the importation of ten thousand musicians, dancers, and performers from India to Iran during his reign. Another Sassanian ruler, the grand patron of the arts Khosrow Parviz (AD 591–628), is likewise said to have supported performers in his court.

The Islamic conquest of the region beginning in the 7th century AD marks a period with little mention of any dramatic or theatrical activity. Orthodox Islam tended to view dramatic presentation as suspect, since it involved the depiction of personages who were imaginary or deceased. Thus the most conservative religious officials labelled it idolatry, an illicit attempt to create an alternative reality to that created by God. Just as images of human beings and animals were banned from plastic and pictorial arts under Islam, human images were banned from depiction in public performance.

Nevertheless, the verbal arts of poetry, story-telling, and recitation continued to be practised widely throughout the Islamic world. Many of these arts, such as the public recitation of epic poetry or of religious stories, took on the quality of dramatic art. These practices continued down to modern times, and served as the basis for the development of more modern theatrical forms.

Several forms of Middle Eastern traditional performing arts probably came into being in the centuries between the advent of Islam and the great 16th-century empires. These were (1) Puppet drama, particularly shadow puppet drama (2) Narrative drama and dramatic story-telling (3) Religious epic drama (4) Comic improvisatory drama.

Shadow puppet theatre similar to that found today throughout East and South-East Asia was probably introduced to the Middle East at the time of the Mongol invasion in the 13th century. Even before this time a rotating magic lantern with shadow figures propelled by hot air generated by the light inside the lantern was known in the region. Omar Khayyām (?1021–1122) mentions it in one of his quatrains, calling it *fanus-e khayāl*, 'lantern of fantasy' or 'lantern of dreams'.

Shadow puppets are found from Japan to Greece, and vary little in their basic form of manufacture. Their method of manufacture helped them deal with basic orthodox Islamic objections to their existence. Shadow puppet makers were able to circumvent these objections by pointing out that since the figures were perforated with holes, they no longer represent animate beings. Even so, tradition dictates that angels cannot enter houses with these questionable images. Therefore during religious holidays it is desirable to hold performances in gardens or courtyards.

Although there is very little record of shadow puppet drama in Iran, it was known throughout the Turkish, Greek and Arabic world first as *Khayāl az-zill*, then by the Turkish word **Karagöz**, or *'ara-'uz* in Arabic, 'black-eye' in reference to the chief comic character, who had a black eye.

Other forms of puppet drama are also certainly very old in the Middle East. Khayyām mentions them in his quatrains:

> We are the puppets (*lo'bat*)
> and destiny is the puppeteer.
> We play on the spread of life
> and go again into the trunk of death.
> (after Gaffary 1984:365)

The poet Farīdu'd-dīn 'Attar (d. 1221) also deals at length with the puppet theatre in his *Oshtor Nāme (Book of the Camel)*. The poet Nezami also mentions puppets in his *Makhzen ul-Esrār (Treasure-house of Secrets, 1165/6)*.

Metin And, the renowned Turkish folklorist, maintains that shadow puppet theatre first appeared in the Middle East as a borrowing from Indonesia. Arabic traders brought the entertainment to Egypt during the medieval period where it was first witnessed by the Ottoman sultans in the 16th century. Adopted by the Ottoman court, it soon assimilated themes from human and puppet drama already in existence.

Narrative drama may have originated in religious preaching, but it also has pre-Islamic precedent in the Parthian story-telling practice known as *gōsān*. The epic folk tale is very ancient throughout the Middle East, and is found in all languages. The episodic organization of long epics such as the *Thousand and One Nights* suggests the story-teller's art may have served as the principle of their organization. Already at the end of the 9th century, a celebrated Arabian story-teller, ibn al-Magazili, had begun to introduce dramatic elements and characterization into his performances. By the 11th century it had crystallized into a literary genre, the *maqāma* ('assembly'), at the hands of Badī 'az-Zamān al-Hamadāni, and expanded by al-Harīri.

Whatever its origin, it is certain that narrative drama was given impetus by the sermons and public recitations occasioned by Islam. It was a natural step for eulogizers and panegyrists to begin recitation of popular drama. The fact that these narratives became associated with the Islamic month of religious fasting, Ramazan, gives further support to the idea that they may have had a religious origin. In the Ottoman world narrative drama was known as *Meddah*, 'eulogy'. In Iran it came to be known as *naqqāli*, 'recounting', for coffee-house recitation of secular epics, such as Ferdowsi's *Shāhnāmeh pardeh-dāri*, lit., 'screen-keeping' for narration of religious stories with large illustrated screens which contained visual images of the stories being presented; and *rowzeh-khāni* for recitation of the events surrounding the events of the death of the 7th century AD Shi'a martyr, Imam Husain (d. 680).

Religious epic drama was limited to Shi'a communities, and, like *rowzeh-khāni*, concerned the events surrounding the death of Imam Husain. Known variously as *Shabih* (simulation) or *Ta'ziyeh* (mourning), religious epic drama may also have had its origins in pre-Islamic practices of mourning for the legendary prince Siyāvosh, a blameless hero, killed unjustly by his father-in-law. These mourning practices were noted in the 10th century by the historian Narshakhi, as having taken place for many centuries in the city of Bukhara. They were still practised in some parts of Iran until as recently as 1974.

Present-day *Ta'ziyeh* probably grew out of public mourning ceremonies for Imam Husain which were seen as early as the Buyyid Empire (c. AD 940–76). These ceremonies began as processions and later took on enactment of the story in dramatic form.

Comic drama was known throughout the Middle East generically as *taqlid* (also *taklid* or *taklit*), 'imitation'. However, in local areas it became better known by specific names. In the Ottoman Empire it was *orta-oyunu*, 'play in the middle' referring to the open square, or *meidan* where it was usually performed. In many Arab countries itinerant players presented *fuṣul mudḥika* (comic scenes). In Iran the same dramatic form came to be known by many names, but one common appellation in modern times is *ru-howzi* or *takht-e howzi* theatre, referring also to the place of performance: *ru* 'on' the *howz* 'pool', referring to the pool commonly found in the courtyards of large homes, over which a platform (usually a plank bed – a *takht*) was often placed for the performance.

In eastern Afghanistan, in and around the city of Herat, Magadi theatre, named after the social group which performs it, the Magads, is directly related to *orta-oyunu* and *ru-howzi* traditions. Many theatrical forms of the Indian sub-continent, such as *Bhavai* in Gujarat, *Bhand Pater* in Kashmir, *Khiyal* in Rajasthan and *Sang* in Uttar Pradesh, are clearly related to these forms as well, suggesting a long history of migration for the traditions. Indeed, the traditions are almost certainly also linked to European **commedia dell'arte** raising the possibility that this European form may once have had Asian roots. *Orta-oyunu* performances were first recorded during the Seljuq dynasty (11th–12th century AD) in the city of Konya. Similar performances are not noted in Iran until several centuries later. Nevertheless given its extraordinarily wide distribution throughout South and South-West Asia, it is likely that improvisatory comic theatre was performed in Iran on a regular basis long before it was first recorded in historical accounts.

Traditional theatre from the 16th to 19th centuries

Following the Mongol invasion, two great empires arose in the Middle East – the Ottoman, centred in Istanbul (1498–1926), and the Safavid in Iran (1501–

1723). The Safavids were succeeded after a short interim by the Qājar dynasty (1779–1924). Except for extreme North-western Africa, all of the present-day Middle East was contained under the reign of these empires until the First World War.

Court life dominated the wealthy classes, and all manner of entertainments were found in the capitals of the empires. For the most part the shahs of Iran and the sultans of the Ottoman Empire were interested in patronizing the arts. They maintained performers, including actors and artists, in their courts despite general Islamic disapproval of these entertainments. At the same time, the theatrical arts flourished on a popular level outside court settings, although the historical record of these more popular forms is much less complete.

Puppet drama fared better in the Ottoman Empire than in Iran, where shadow puppet drama seems to have disappeared completely, the last vestigial performance recorded in 1926. *Karagöz* by contrast spread throughout the Ottoman Empire and adjacent lands. It was found at its peak in Egypt, Syria, Morocco, Algeria, Bosnia-Herzegovina and Greece, as well as throughout Asia Minor.

The Ottoman Sultans were great patrons of *karagöz*. The form first flourished under the reign of Bayazid Yildirim (1389–1402), especially at the hand of one of the Sultan's servants, one Kör Hasan. Shadow puppetry was especially encouraged by Selim I, who was greatly impressed by a performance he witnessed in Egypt in 1517. Under Suleiman the Magnificent (1520–66) shadow puppet theatre was shown on ceremonial days, such as celebrations of the circumcision of royal princes. The plays were called haial (compare Persian and Arabic khiyāl, 'dream, fantasy') and the puppeteers, haialdji, the suffix -ji signifying a practitioner of any trade.

The 17th-century Turkish traveller, geographer and historian Evliya Chelebi describes *karagöz* extensively in his *Siyahet Name* or *Book of Travels*. In this he describes the artist Kör Hasan Zade Mehmed Chelebi, descendant of Kör Hasan, the famous puppeteer who served under Bayazid Yildirim. Mehmed Chelebi gave performances twice a week in the court of Sultan Murad IV (1623–40). Most of the characters were those of modern *karagöz*, and many of the plays presented are still known today.

By the reign of Sultan Ibrahim (1640–8) puppet drama had reached unprecedented popularity. It was at the Sultan's coronation on 23 February 1640 that the first European, the French traveller Thévenot, witnessed the shadow theatre, which he called 'Carageuz'.

Numerous famous haialdjis dot Ottoman cultural history. Of particular note were Hafiz Bey in the reign of Selim III (1789–1807); Said Efendi (1808–39). Royal patronage continued unabated until the early 20th century. By this time, *karagöz* was being performed in coffee-houses throughout Constantinople and was a lucrative form of popular entertainment among the masses as well as in the court.

Although shadow puppetry never was widespread in Iran during this period, glove puppets and marionettes gained a degree of popularity. The German traveller Adam Oléarius provides an account of a strolling puppeteer in Iran in the first half of the 17th century. It is interesting in Iran that puppeteers traditionally used glove puppets during the day, and marionettes during the evening when their strings would be less noticeable. Puppet drama in Iran was commonly called *kheimeh shab-bāzi (tent-play in the night)*. There is no historical record of royal patronage, though individual strolling players existed up until the revolution of 1978–9.

Narrative drama was well established by the 13th century among the Arab populations of the Middle East. At this time the story-tellers of Baghdad organized themselves into a guild headed by a sheikh.

Story-tellers were already popular at the beginning of the Ottoman Empire. They were greatly revered in the Ottoman court, and are mentioned continually in accounts of the reigns of the Sultans from Bayazid Yildirim in the 15th century down to the First World War. *Meddahs* (eulogizers) in the Ottoman Empire were ingenious parodists and satirists. Because of their tendency to burlesque political affairs, they were subject to rigorous censorship, particularly in the 19th century. They could not use the word 'Sultan' nor mention riots, revolutions or insurrections, even those of other countries. They were also prohibited from mocking the clergy.

The *meddahs* performed most often in coffee-houses in large cities. Financial arrangements varied. Occasionally tickets were sold, and the coffee-house owner was paid rent for the use of the room. Often the proprietor would be content with the additional income brought in by the large number of customers attracted by the performance.

The Iranian *naqqāl* operated in a similar fashion, working from coffee-houses, or occasionally from private homes. His stock in trade was almost exclusively Ferdowsi's *Shāhnāmeh (Book of Kings)*, although he would occasionally narrate other epics for the pleasure of the crowd. The art of the *naqqāl* was codified in a 17th-century work, *Tarāz al-Akhbār (The Adornment of Narrative)*. One unusual setting for the Iranian story-teller even today is the *zurkhāneh* (house of strength), a traditional athletic club. In this setting, a professional chanter, called a *murshed*, accompanies the traditional athletic exercises with drum beat, and recitations of deeds of bravery from Ferdowsi's epic.

The history of *pardeh-dāri* (screen-keeping) is lost to us. Similar narrative techniques exist throughout Asia and the Middle East, however, suggesting great antiquity. The *pardeh-dar*'s episodes from Islamic religious drama were illustrated using a giant rolled screen which was often handed down from father to son. The *pardeh-dars* would ply their trade in public markets and bazaars collecting money as free-will public offerings for their stories. They most often would recite the events of the martyrdom of Imam Husain at Kerbala, and are occasionally seen even today.

Rowzeh-khāni would not be called entertainment by strictly religious persons in Iran, but it was so classified in Safavid and Qājar Iran. The *rowzeh-khāns* even had a guild at one time. These reciters of the events of Kerbala are often Islamic clergymen, but they need not be. They receive fees for their services when reciting outside normal prayer services at public mosques, at funerals, private family memorial services, or occasionally as private devotions. Since Safavid times on principal Shi'a religious holidays, the most famous *rowzeh-khāns* were in heavy demand. Many became both rich and famous for their performances. In recent years, their recitations were even sold as audio tape cassettes. *Rowzeh-khāni* is noteworthy as the one narrative tradition open to women, but only for consumption by all-female audiences.

Religious epic drama in Iran most likely evolved under the patronage of the Safavid shahs. They themselves had origins as a religious brotherhood, and were particularly interested in encouraging religious ritual. Mourning ceremonies for Imam Husain were patronized by them on a grand scale. During their reign enormous processions of mourners in groups, called *dasteh*, would congregate in the streets during the first ten days of the Islamic month of Muharram, scourging themselves with chains, and cutting themselves with swords and knives while they chanted rhythmic dirges of mourning. As the size of the processions grew, they became more elaborate with depictions of the events of the martyrdom enacted by players on 'floats' situated at intervals among the mourners.

Early travellers noted these processions. The first fully-fledged account was given by the English traveller William Francklin in 1787, though the Russian voyager Gmelin noted the ceremonies and used the word 'theatre' to describe them in 1770, and two other travellers, Salamons and Van Goch, had seen the processions without calling them 'theatre' sometime between 1722 and 1735.

By the 19th century, *ta'ziyeh* was being performed as a fully-fledged dramatic form. Adrian Dupré, who was attached to the scientific body accompanying the French Mission to Persia in 1807–9, gives an account which is essentially a description of the dramatic form as it is seen today. Manuscripts of *ta'ziyeh* dramas held privately in Iran date from the late 18th century suggesting that the form was already well established when Dupré saw it.

The form was lavishly patronized by the Qājar shahs. Huge open-air arenas called *tekiyeh* were built for royally patronized performances featuring thousands of actors and an equally large number of live animals. Members of the foreign community were regularly invited to attend, and Naser od-Dīn Shah (1848–96) had a *ta'ziyeh* 'director' as part of his royal household. Gradually the dramas began to be performed nearly all year, not only in the court, but in cities and villages throughout the country. Shi'a communities in Lebanon and Bahrain also enacted *ta'ziyeh* though not on such a grand scale. The processional form of the mourning ceremony continues today in Shi'a communities in India and Pakistan.

Comic improvisatory theatre was also supported by the courts. Shah 'Abbās of Iran (1588–1629) had a famous jester, Kal 'Enāyat (Bald Enāyat), who performed comic entertainments in court. A miniature painting by Soltan Mohammad Naqqāsh from this period (1621) shows performers entertaining in what seems to be a court setting. One of the clowns is wearing a tall hat, and others are clothed in goat-skins. Bezā'i reports that musicians from this period used to give comic performances when called on to entertain in the homes of the wealthy.

Entertainers in *taqlid* would normally imitate the accents and personal characteristics of well known people in the towns and villages in which they performed. These people would be seen meeting and greeting each other. After a short while they would fall to arguing and making fun of each other's accents and behaviour, and the story would end with the two characters fighting and chasing each other. (Bezā'i 1965:55)

Orta-oyunu was active throughout the duration of the Ottoman empire, and served as an important form of social protest. In true *taqlid* style (*taklid* in Turkish), performers in *orta-oyunu* would imitate the attitudes and accents of persons of different trades and nationalities and make fun of them. The Sultan maintained a troupe at court which performed on Imperial holidays, such as the birth of a prince, his circumcision, coronations, and other state occasions. A band of actors accompanied the Sultan into war where they served to divert him from the difficulties of battle. Bands of actors also accompanied ambassadors, provincial governors and foreign legations, thus spreading theatrical practice into the provinces and other lands where Ottoman influence was felt. Local nobles in Egypt, Walachia, Moldavia and other provinces wishing to imitate the Sultans likewise organized theatrical performances.

The advent of Western theatre During the 19th century, the Qājar and Ottoman empires began to come under the influence of European culture. Although many European travellers had journeyed to Middle Eastern lands in the 16th and 17th centuries, it was only in the 18th century that Middle Easterners began to tour Europe with any regularity. Most cultured travellers were greatly impressed with European theatre. It was at this point that European-style drama began to be performed.

It is difficult to ascertain who staged the first Western-style drama in a Middle Eastern language, but a strong claim may be made for Marūn Mikhail al-Naqqāsh, a Maronite Christian with musical and literary talents born in Sidon in 1817. He was trained as a book-keeper and, as a member of the Beirut Chamber of Commerce, travelled throughout the Ottoman empire. In 1846 he travelled to Italy where he was greatly struck with the theatre. On returning to Beirut, he determined to stage a theatrical performance with his friends, and mounted an original drama in Arabic heavily inspired by **Molière**'s *L'Avare*, titled *al-Bakhil* (*The Miser*), in 1847.

The play was produced in Naqqāsh's home, and was enthusiastically received, prompting him to stage another play, *Abū al-Hasan al-Mughaffal o Hārūn al-Rashīd* (*Abū al-Hasan the Gullible or* [*the Caliph*] *Ha'rūn al-Rashīd*), a story adapted from the *Thousand and One Nights*, in 1849. Many notables of the city were invited. The British traveller David Urquhart witnessed this performance in 1850, and declared it technically weak, but successful in an artistic sense.

These successes encouraged Naqqāsh to stage a third drama, after obtaining permission to build a stage adjacent to his home. The third production was staged in 1851, *Al-Salīt al-Hasūd* (*The Impudent and Jealous One*). This drama is almost entirely original, but Naqqāsh borrows from Molière in places, particularly from *Tartuffe*. He also includes the famous passage from *Le Bourgeois Gentilhomme* where M. Jourdain discovers to his surprise that he has been speaking prose all his life.

Unfortunately, Naqqāsh died of a fever in 1855, but he had inspired a number of younger men. His nephew Salīm later took his theatrical troupe to Egypt, where *Abū al-Hasan al-Mughaffal* was staged in Alexandria in 1876.

The first Western-style Arabic production in Cairo was not that of Naqqāsh, but rather the play *Operette* by Ya'qūb Sanū', staged in 1870 in the garden of a coffee-house at Azbakiyah park, which had been built, along with the Cairo Opera House, by Khedive Isma'īl who had an interest in transforming Egypt into a Europeanized state.

Sanū', also known as James Sanua, was a Cairene of Italian-Jewish parentage. Brought up in Italy, he taught at a government college in Cairo. His 1870 production was the first of a long number of humorous musical sketches produced by his company. The Khedive at first loved the productions given by Sanū', dubbing him the 'Molière of Egypt', but the plays produced in Sanū''s theatre continued to follow the satirical *orta-oyunu* style, criticizing court corruption and morals, and even satirizing a failed Egyptian military adventure in Ethiopia. The Khedive then closed the theatre himself, leaving Sanū' to the publication of written satire.

Salīm Naqqāsh's productions in Alexandria were highly successful, developing some remarkable actors, including Yūsuf Khayyāt. When Naqqāsh himself became embroiled in political controversy through his journalistic writings in 1878, Khayyāt moved the troupe to Cairo, where the sturdy *Abū al-Hasan al-Mughaffal* was once again produced with success before the Khedive. Another play, Salīm al-Naqqāsh's *Hifz al-Widād aw al-Zulūm* (*Preserving Friendship, or Dislike*), angered Isma'īl, and forced the troupe to perform in Alexandria and other provincial towns, where it enjoyed enormous success. Khayyāt was himself responsible for introducing a number of excellent actors to the stage, including the entertainer Salāma Hijāzī, an outstanding singer and actor.

Sulaymān al-Qardāhī was another player in Khayyāt's troupe who went on to found his own company. Al-Qardāhī's troupe was established in 1885 during the British occupation of Egypt. He toured Egypt, Syria, Europe, and North Africa, where he eventually settled in Tunis until his death in 1909. Al-Qardāhī is credited with introducing the first Western-style theatre produced in Arabic to North Africa.

The first professional theatre in Syria after the amateur productions of Marūn Naqqāsh was established by Ahmad Abū Khalīl al-Qabbānī (1836–1902), born in what is present-day Turkey, and raised in Damascus. Al-Qabbānī first produced his own amateur plays, including Salīm Naqqāsh's Arabic adaptation of Verdi's *Aida*. Government officials in Damascus, bent on modernization, supported al-Qabbānī, and ordered construction of a theatre, but religious officials, objecting to the theatre, forced the troupe to leave the country in 1884 for Cairo.

In Cairo al-Qabbānī achieved enormous success, employing the best performers of the period. Unfortunately a fire in his Cairo theatre ruined him financially, and he lived out his days in Damascus on a government stipend. One of his actors, Iskandar Farah, formed yet another troupe, which was reputedly even better than

al-Qabbānī's. Farah's troupe achieved such renown that it was able even to attract the famous actor Salāma Hijāzī. Farah was notable in that he commissioned a number of new plays in Arabic from promising writers of the day.

Further to the east another early pioneer of Western-style theatre was Mirzā Fath 'Ali Ākhundzādeh (1812–78). Though living in the Russian Caucasus, Ākhundzādeh wrote in Āzeri Turkish, the dialect of Āzerbāijān. He composed six plays between 1850 and 1855: *Mollā Ibrāhim Khalil Kimiyāgar* (*Mullah Ibrahim the Alchemist*); *Musir Jordān, Hakim-e Nabātāt* (*Monsieur Jordan the Botanist*); *Vizir-e Khān-e Sarāb* (*The Vizier of the Khān of Sarab*); *Khers-e Qoldorbāsān* (*The Thief-catching Bear*); *Sargozasht-e Mard-e Khasis* (*The History of a Miser*); *Vokalā-ye Morāfe'e-ye Tabriz* (*The Rich Lawyers of Tabriz*). He translated some of these plays into Russian and performed them in large cities of the Caucasus. A collection of these works, *Tamsilāt* (*Proverbs*), was published in Āzeri Turkish in 1859 and later became the first Western-style dramatic literature published in Persian in a translation by Mirza Mohammad Qarāje-dāghi in Tehran (1974).

The first original plays in Persian were written by Mirzā Āqā Tabrizi, a literary government bureaucrat who visited Constantinople and came in contact with Ākhundzādeh's writings. Ākhundzādeh asked Mirzā Āqā to translate his works into Persian, but the latter preferred to write original works. His comedies, *Ashraf Khān Hokzumat-e Zamān Khān* (*The Rule of Zamā Khān*), *Kerbalā Raftan-e Shāh Qoli Mirzā* (*The Pilgrimage to Kerbalā of Shāh Qoli Mirzā*) and *'Āsheq Shodan-e 'Āqā Hāshem* (*Āqā Hāshem's Love Affair*), are extremely amusing and surprisingly modern. Until recently many of Mirzā Āqā's works were attributed to Malkām Khān, a literate, rebellious politician who lived abroad. Because of the satirical nature of many of the plays, Mirzā Āqā may have been content to allow this mistake to stand.

Western-style theatre in Istanbul was first established by the Armenian community, who had closer ties to Europe than the Muslim Turks. The father of Western-style theatre in Turkish was Agop Vartovyan, later known as Güllü Agop, an Armenian who later converted to Islam. Agop established the Ottoman Theatre Company at Gedikpaşa Theatre in Istanbul. The first play produced there was *César Borgia*, a translation from French to Turkish, in April 1868. This was not a success, and Güllü Agop in 1869 produced a tragedy by Mustafa Efendi based on the well-known Middle Eastern romance *Leylā ve Mecnun*. This was a success and fostered much original Turkish theatre in the decade to come.

The Grand Vizier Ali Paşa granted Güllü a ten-year monopoly on all theatrical productions in Istanbul in 1870, which somewhat limited the growth of Turkish theatre. Would-be producers started in cities in the provinces: Adana, Trabazon and Bursa being the most prominent. Ahmet Vefik Paşa, who founded the theatre in Bursa, translated nearly all of Molière into Turkish and trained his own company of actors.

Orta-oyunu actors claimed exemption from Güllü Agop's monopoly and challenged him for audiences in Istanbul. The result was a revived *orta-oyunu* tradition that stood somewhere between Western-style theatre and the traditional improvisatory styles.

Popular theatre in the 20th century Traditional theatre forms have declined greatly in the 20th century, but have continued to influence theatrical development in all countries in the Middle East and North Africa. An assessment of their form today is also a key to understanding something of their artistic structure in the past.

Puppet drama Although marionette and glove-puppet theatre has nearly disappeared in the Middle East, shadow-puppet theatre, *karagöz*, is still actively performed in Turkey, Greece and several of the Arabic-speaking countries.

The stage for *karagöz* consists of a frame covered with white, translucent cloth. The puppets are constructed of fine, thin leather, traditionally camelskin through which light can shine. They range between 25 and 35 centimetres in height, with some special figures ranging to nearly 60 centimetres. The leather is coloured, so the figures likewise appear in colour on the screen. The puppets differ from Oriental shadow puppets in that they are held by a horizontal rod extending at right angles from the back of the puppet, as compared with the vertical rods used by East Asian puppeteers. The puppets are hinged, and have a second rod which allows the puppeteer to manipulate the body parts. Other devices allow the puppets to swivel, or allow more than two puppets to be held against the screen at one time. Some puppets contain special devices, such as second heads, which can be flipped up by the puppeteer for special effects.

There are three parts to a *karagöz* performance: the prologue (*mukaddeme*), dialogue and interlude (*muhavere* and *muhaveresi*) and the main story (*fasil*). Like in Asian shadow-puppet drama, a screen ornament appears against the cloth before the drama actually begins.

A whistle, *nareke*, introduces the prologue. One of the main characters, *Hacivat*, appears first, and often gives a religious invocation and a long speech. Then *Karagöz* himself appears and has an argument with *Hacivat*, where he is beaten. He in turn hits *Hacivat* every time he appears on stage.

The dialogue which then ensues may have nothing to do with the main plot of the performance. It may be a humorous battle of wits, or a trading of insults in 'duelling rhyme' form, something also practised by children on the streets of Turkey, and thus greatly appreciated by them.

The main story unfolds involving many ethnic and linguistic types of people, including women both young and old; a juvenile character, *Çelebi*, who is always in love with a princess or girl of high family; various odd characters, such as an opium addict, dwarf, or drunkard; and numerous ethnic types, Persians, Jews, Balkans, Greeks, Armenians, Kurds and Arabs.

Much of *karagöz* involves parody of various occupations or ethnic groups. One stock plot involves Çelebi falling in love with a young girl of good family and having various obstacles put in his way before being allowed to marry her. In this, *Karagöz* and *Hacivat* are always implicated in some manner.

There are dozens of stock stories presently performed by puppeteers. These have been passed down for generations, and are largely improvisatory in nature, although over time some of the scripts have been transcribed. Among some of the better known are: *Kanli Kavak* (*The Bloody Poplar*), *Timarhane* (*The Madhouse*), *Yazici* (*The Public Scribe*), *Kanli Nigâr* (*Bloody Nigâr*).

Throughout the 19th and 20th centuries, *karagöz* has served not only as entertainment, but also as a focus for political protest. In Greece, where *karagöz* was established as an art form in 1860 by John Vrahalis, *karagöz* performances ironically served as the meeting place for anti-Turkish revolutionary leaders. In the Greek shadow theatre, *Karagöz* becomes *Karaghiozis*, and *Hacivat*, *Hatziavatis* but it is clear that these characters originally come from Turkish tradition.

Improvisatory comic theatre The two principal forms of comic improvisatory theatre in the Middle East, *ru-howzi* and *orta-oyunu* theatre, are very similar, and probably related historically. In the 20th century they still bear a clear resemblance to each other, sharing many common features.

Comic improvisatory troupes in both *ru-howzi* and *orta-oyunu* traditions are generally actors and musicians. All members of the troupe generally play one or more musical instruments, and are able usually to perform a full musical programme in addition to, or in lieu of, a theatrical performance. Many troupe members, especially those who specialize in women's roles, also are adept as dancers.

Troupes have largely hereditary recruitment patterns. That is, most troupe members are recruited from the families of other members. They tend to 'grow up in the tradition', taking minor roles when young, and graduating to major roles such as 'clown' or 'king' when older.

In the past, troupes were highly itinerant. They would at times leave home for months on a performance circuit that would take them hundreds of miles from home. In the past it was possible for performers to support themselves entirely from their work as performers. Troupes also existed in urban areas throughout Iran and Turkey performing in commercial theatres.

Troupes handle their financial arrangements using division according to importance of role in the total performance. The total proceeds obtained by the troupe for an evening are divided into shares. Major performers and principal musicians receive more shares than minor performers. Also equipment, such as the costume trunk or amplification equipment, may receive a 'share'. Proceeds for a performance are typically divided after the performance. The troupe leader may be morally obliged to support members of the troupe during slack seasons, or to loan them money to be paid back when the troupe is working.

Performers use a 'secret language' with a number of vocabulary items in Romany (Gypsy), mixed with disguised speech (on the model of pig-Latin) known primarily to musicians in many cases.

All comic traditions in South and South-West Asia emphasize the clown as a central figure, and *ru-howzi* and *orta-oyunu* are no exceptions. He may be thought of as the central figure around whom the 'text' of the performance is constructed. In *ru-howzi* the clown has no fixed name, but 'Rajab' seems to be a common personal name assigned to him, especially when he is cast in the role of a servant. He is dressed in blackface, and so is regularly referred to by performers as the 'Siah' or 'Black'. Similarly, playing the clown is called *siah-bāzi*, or 'black-playing'. In *orta-oyunu* the clown is called *Pişekiar*. He is dressed in a yellow gown and red trousers, with a multi-coloured cap. He is often called 'Tosun Efendi'. There is always a second principal figure in both *ru-howzi* and *orta-oyunu*. In *ru-howzi*, it is the *hajji*, an elderly merchant who represents conventional morality and respectability. In *orta-oyunu* the second figure may often be a merchant, but he is also often a companion of *Pişekiar*. He is called *Kavuklu*, 'large hat', and is often called by the name 'Hamdi'. He often wears a turban or fez.

The performance also depends on stock characters in addition to the clown. The most important of these are the juvenile 'dandy', called *Zampara* in *orta-oyunu*, female figures, nobles, court figures, and a whole range of ethnic characterizations. Parallels here with *karagöz* are very clear, and have led to speculation that live comic improvisatory drama may have developed from puppet drama.

Performances are not entirely improvisatory. Perhaps they would better be characterized as semi-improvisatory. Although in *orta-oyunu* texts have been recorded, in *ru-howzi* there is no written text. In both traditions, stock plots are most commonly transmitted through rehearsal and oral transmission and learned by troupe members. These plays are refined over years of performance, and acquire slightly different realizations for each individual troupe.

One important feature of performance is that the individual play storylines are interlaced with set comic routines – *schtiks*, or, using a term from *commedia dell'arte*, *lazzi*. These routines are 'set pieces' often involving pratfalls, acrobatics, visual or verbal humour. Many involve satirizing other groups and dialects, and skill as a performer is often linked to the ability to mimic other language and ethnic groups.

Performance is expandable or contractable at will. Troupes can perform the same play in half an hour, or three hours depending on necessity.

The active repertoire of troupes consists of from 10 to 20 pieces. Many more are known by troupe members, but are not in active use. These can be resurrected if requested by patrons.

Plays given by *ru-howzi* troupes bear a close relationship to the concerns of the patrons they serve. They involve a great deal of satire, and they favour broad mockery of groups and individuals typically seen as oppressive of the communities served by the performing troupes. Thus there are many authority figures who are mocked in the performances.

Another important source of humour is based on sexual reference. In this regard troupes are able to approach topics which are extremely sensitive in society at large.

The clown is typically the vehicle for approaching the sensitive topics of authority and sexuality. By serving as a surrogate for the audience, the clown is able to provide that audience with a vicarious method of dealing with these vital areas of their own life. His use of paradox, mockery, and distortion to create humour makes these potentially dangerous areas of social life manageable. He is able to dispel their danger in laughter.

The performance in both traditions has a fixed form.

Following music and a dance by all members of the troupe except the two principal comic figures, the clown enters. He engages in comic dialogue with the musicians, exits, and the performance begins, often with a dialogue between the two comic characters. Then the comic story begins in earnest. Many plots are common to both traditions. A few follow:

1 A master has a girlfriend, and doesn't want his wife to know about it, so he persuades his servant, the clown, to sleep in his place so his wife will not detect that he is gone to his girlfriend's house. The wife discovers the ruse, and decides to teach both the master and the clown a lesson by pretending to make sexual advances to the clown.

2 Two thieves, one quick-witted, one slow-witted, proceed to rob a house in the dark. They divide the spoils, which turn out to be a large number of ridiculous or sexually suggestive objects. The quick-witted clown manages to get the best booty for himself.

3 A clown persuades his companion, a merchant, to balance a bowl of yoghurt on his head as a cure for an ailment. The yoghurt eventually ends up all over the companion's head and face.

4 A master suspects his wife of being unfaithful. His servant the clown persuades him to pretend to be dead to see what his wife will do. Her lover immediately arrives on hearing of the master's death, and puts on his clothes, talks about using his money to go abroad, etc. The clown then resurrects the master from the dead to scare the couple.

A second set of plots are based on literary, historical and legendary events which are illustrated through performance. Here, actual historical figures, such as Harun-al-Rashīd or Moses, are seen, as well as legendary figures drawn from epics such as Ferdowsi's *Shāhnāmeh*, or other literary works such as the *Haft Peikar* of Nezami.

Some examples:

1 The Three Riddles. The king's daughter declares that she will only marry a clever man, so each suitor must answer three riddles. The hajji, his son and the clown all go to the court with the purpose of obtaining the princess for the son. On seeing the princess, the hajji decides he wants her for himself, as does the clown. They bandy words with court officials, and finally give silly answers to the riddles. The son gives the correct answers, and the hajji and clown are admonished to seek more suitable wives.

2 Moses and the Pharaoh. The clown is servant to Moses, and harasses the Pharaoh in the traditional story of the Children of Egypt.

3 Rostām and Sohrāb. The clown is servant to Rostām, and is present at the famous epic unwitting battle between father and son. He manages to make fun of all and sundry, as well as the event itself, finally announcing to the hapless Rostām, 'Oh, now you've done it – you shouldn't have killed that poor boy, you know.'

Religious epic theatre Religious epic theatre, *ta'ziyeh* or *shabih* continues to be performed in areas of the Middle East with large Shi'a populations: Iran, Iraq, Southern Lebanon and Bahrain. Nevertheless, the most elaborate, full-blown performaances of *ta'ziyeh* continued to be performed in Iran.

Performances of *ta'ziyeh* are given both by 'professional' troupes of players and by villagers in amateur performances. Many small towns and villages have erected special buildings – *hoseinieh* – specifically for the performances of mourning ceremonies during the month of Muharram. It is most often in these buildings that *ta'ziyeh* is performed, although an open-air playing space may also be constructed to accommodate large crowds, live animals and dozens of players, some on horseback.

Whether the performers are hired for the occasion, or amateur, the staging of *ta'ziyeh* is a community affair, with cooperative funds committed for the purpose. Performances may be long or short, but they often take place all day, particularly on the ninth and tenth days of the Islamic month of Muharrām, called *Tasuā* and *Ashurā* respectively, the latter being the day of the martyrdom of Imam Husain. A noon meal may be provided for spectators, and the performance may be preceded or followed by communal mourning ceremonies, consisting of processions, religious chanting, and self-flagellation. Often persons leave a bequest in their wills to contribute to the annual support of these rituals.

Participants and spectators do not view *ta'ziyeh* as theatre, but rather as part of ritual mourning. Nevertheless it has many theatrical conventions. The players do not, by convention, memorize their roles (though many have them memorized through years of repetition), they rather read them from strips of paper held in their hands. The parts are not welded together in a common script, but are maintained as separate scripts with cuelines, for each role. The 'good' characters, on the side of Imam Husain, chant their lines in classical Persian musical modes, and wear the colour green. The 'bad' characters declaim their lines in stentorian tones and wear the colour red. Women's roles are taken by men, who wear black, and veil their faces. The performances have a number of roles for children, played by young boys, who are also dressed in black, but are unveiled.

Several forms of staging exist, but most observe the convention of having one area for the camp of Imam Husain, and another area in the same open playing space for the camp of the enemies. A third space may represent Damascus, the seat of the governor Yazid, who ordered the death of the martyrs. A fourth area usually contains props.

When characters are not 'on stage' they often do not leave the playing area, but merely retire to their playing space, drink tea, and converse. When moving in the playing area, spaces traversed in circles or arcs represent long distances, straight lines are short distances.

Each of the first ten days of Muharrām is the occasion for the staging of a different performance depicting the death of each of the relatives and supporters of Imam Husain. Typically on the day of *Ashurā* a synoptic performance is given where all of the martyrs' deaths are presented in a single recounting.

Over the years a number of 'secular' *ta'ziyeh* performances developed around other religious or even political themes, including events preceding or following the martyrdoms at Kerbālā, and also other religious or even secular themes including Moses and the Pharaoh, and Solomon and the Queen of Sheba. These included even 'comic' *ta'ziyeh* performances, such as 'The Binding of the Thumbs of the Demon' which has

a masked figure playing the demon's role. All of these performances eventually turn back to the events of Kerbālā however.

Ta'ziyeh performances have suffered a decline in the 20th century. Immensely popular, they are none the less suspect both from a religious and political standpoint. Religious officials were always uncomfortable with the depiction of actual historical figures on stage. Political officials did not like huge gatherings of people mourning injustice. Nevertheless, the performances continue unabated in many parts of the Shi'a world.

The influence of these traditional forms is deeply felt in the modern theatrical tradition of the Middle East. Despite the importation of Western-style theatre to the region in the 20th century, when native writers have attempted original work, the most successful productions always contain elements of these traditional performance genres.

The 20th-century rise of national theatres The great 19th-century empires came to an end with the First World War. The Ottoman Empire was split into a dozen small states, and modern Iran emerged under the leadership of Mohammad Rezā shah Pahlavi. All of the resulting new nations looked toward Europe and the United States as models for development. The theatre was no exception. Traditional theatre forms declined rapidly in favour of Western-style theatre. Film and later television became important entertainment media, further speeding the decline of traditional performance forms.

For the most part the national theatres arising in 20th-century Middle Eastern nations have been pale imitations of Western theatre. It has only been in the last 20 years that new experimentation combining traditional forms of past centuries with modern directorial and acting styles has yielded a revitalized theatre in the Middle East.

Turkey, Egypt, Syria, the Maghreb, and Iran have remained central in theatrical development in the 20th century. A brief review of principal trends for each nation follows.

Turkey Theatre in Turkey in the 20th century continued the trend toward political commentary and satire present in traditional *karagöz, meddah* and *orta-oyunu*. In the last days of the Ottoman Empire, a number of writers turned to political drama as a means of expressing new feelings of protest. Namik Kemal (1840–88) felt that drama could be used as a means of awakening people and inspiring them to greater political sensibility. His play *Vatan yahut Silistre (Fatherland or Silistre)* was produced at the Gedikpaşa theatre in 1873, and was partially instrumental in the theatre's closing the next year. Popular sentiment against the Sultan aroused by the play was so great that Namik Kemal was put in prison, and the play censored. Abdülhak Hamit (1852–1937), a diplomat and poet, wrote some 20 plays which circulated as literature, but were never produced during his lifetime because of their political content. Social reform was also represented in the works of a number of playwrights. Ahmet Mithat (Efendi) railed aginst polygamy and superstition in his plays *Eyvah (Alas,* 1873) and *Çengi (Dancing Girl,* 1884).

After the Young Turk revolution of 1908, the National Theatre, called the Darülbedaye (Academy of Fine Arts), was established. It began to function as a training school for young artists. In 1918 the first female student was admitted. Audiences would not accept women on the stage at first, but gradually their reticence was overcome, and by 1923 actresses were seen regularly on the Turkish stage.

The father of modern Turkish theatre, Muhsin Ertuğul, began his stage career in 1908. In 1920, following a period acting and stage managing in the German film industry, he was appointed head of the Darülbedaye. In 1925 he studied in Russia with **Stanislavsky** and **Meyerhold**, and returned to reform acting and production in Turkey.

Ertuğul gradually introduced the latest techniques in staging and direction. He promoted the production of Western classic plays alongside original Turkish productions by new playwrights, such as Müsahipzade Celâl (1870–1959), Vedat Nedim Tör (b. 1897) and Nazim Hikmet (Ran) (1902–63).

Many private companies began to develop starting in 1930, including the Milli Sahne (The National Stage), Türk tiyatrosu (The Turkish theatre), Türk Akademi Tiyatrosu (The Turkish Academy Theatre). Following the Second World War many other small theatres opened. In 1951 Ertuğul himself resigned from the state theatre and opened a small art theatre, Küçük Sahne (The Little Stage). Other similar ventures followed, until by the mid-1970s there were six municipal theatres and over 20 private municipal theatres in Istanbul alone.

The principal trend in Turkish theatre in the post-1945 period has been toward the production of more native Turkish drama. Nearly 200 new plays in Turkish have been produced in the years following the war on an enormous variety of themes and styles.

Traditional theatre has served as the inspiration for much of the most modern period. The trend toward theatre integrated with music and dance has been very strong in recent years, particularly in the emergence of a form known as *operet*, a form of musical theatre, before the Second World War. Two of the most popular writers in this style were Ekrem Reşit Rey (librettist) and Cemal Reşit Rey (composer), whose popular pieces included *Uç Saat* (*Three Hours*, 1932), *Deli Dolu* (*Crazy*, 1934) and *Lüks Hayat* (*High Life*, 1934). The Rey brothers paved the way for highly successful musical theatre in the 1960s and 1970s.

Although the development of the Turkish film and television industry has slowed the growth of theatre somewhat, the future seems very good for a rigorous modern Turkish theatre tradition.

Egypt Egypt has dominated the theatre of the Arabic-speaking world for the entire 20th century. The foundation for this domination was laid in the 19th century with the establishment of a number of successful theatrical troupes, within which actors of excellent quality developed, who then established their own troupes. Theatre was additionally aided by the talents of a number of prominent literary figures who directed a significant part of their energy to writing for the stage.

For the first 20 years of the century the most important troupe was that established by Jurj Abyad, born in Beirut, and trained at the Paris Conservatoire in acting under a government scholarship. Abyad first appeared in Cairo in 1910 as head of a troupe of French

actors. He was encouraged by the Minister of Education to stay and form an Arabic-speaking troupe, drawing from the actors of the troupes of al-Qardāhī and Farah which had begun to decline. Abyad was an excellent dramatic actor, and specialized in both comedy and tragedy. He performed both original Arabic works and a number of European works in translation, such as Molière's *Tartuffe* and **George Bernard Shaw**'s *Caesar and Cleopatra*.

In 1914 he joined forces with Salāma al-Ḥijāzī, who had formed his own troupe. Al-Ḥijāzī's skills as a singer and dancer complemented Abyad's dramatic skills, and the resulting troupe was an enormous critical and financial success.

Abyad and al-Ḥijāzī's troupe, in typical fashion, engendered yet other troupes, such as those of Yūsuf Wahbī, Fātima Rushdī, and Naguib al-Rīḥānī (1892–1949).

Al-Rīḥānī was born in Cairo. He acted with Abyad's troupe in 1914 having worked earlier with a small troupe in Alexandria. He became employed with a Greek *karagöz* theatre, the Abbaye des Roses, in 1916 and there developed his most famous character, Kishkish Bey, a turbaned village chief – pompous, wily and yet likeable. Plays involving Kishkish Bey had a stock plot. He would invariably be tricked by Europeanized city-slickers, but would always outsmart them in the end. A whole series of stock characters accompanied him, making Kishkish Bey dramas a strong depiction of an Egyptian everyman in his natural social setting.

Al-Rīḥānī later turned to the development of more serious satire. The struggle was long and difficult, since the public only wished to see more of Kishkish Bey, but finally in the 1930s and 1940s, he was able to achieve success with his more serious comic work, such as *Al-Gīney al-Miṣrī* (*The Egyptian Pound*, 1931), and *Hukm Qarāqūsh* (*Qarāqūsh's Rule*, 1935). He also toured extensively and appeared in films, making his popularity greater than ever, before his death in 1949.

The development of dramatic literature in Egypt has paralleled the development of theatrical institutions. Although the number of dramatic writers has increased continually in the 20th century, four individuals can be singled out for their outstanding contributions to playwriting. These are Aḥmad Shauqī, Tawfīq al-Hakīm, Nu'man 'Ashūr and Rashad Rushdy.

Aḥmad Shauqī (1868–1932) achieved success first as a poet and only secondarily as a playwright. Nevertheless he succeeded in writing six historical dramas, five of them in verse, and one comedy. He was heavily influenced by an early education in law in France, where he wrote his first tragic drama, '*Ali Bek al-Kabīr* (*Ali Bey the Great*). His other dramas include *Majnūn Lailā*, his own version of the Leila and Majnun story, *Masra' Kliūpātrā* (*The Fall of Cleopatra*), a tragedy dealing with Cleopatra borrowing somewhat from **Shakespeare**; *Qambīz*, a historical version of the story of Cambyses; *Amīrat al-Andalus* (*The Princess of Andalusia*), a story of a princess in early Islamic Spain; '*Antara*, a play about the pre-Islamic poet, Antara b. Shaddād; and the largely ignored comedy *al-Sitt Hudā* (*Lady Huda*).

Shauqī was considered a fine versifier, and paid great attention to historical detail. He was less successful in the construction of character and plot. Almost all of his characters are killed by the end of his tragedies, a feature which at times seems strained and artificial. He adopted the innovative device of changing the poetic metre to accord with the character and the subject. While acknowledging his contribution to Arabic drama, critics generally have found him to be a better poet than playwright.

Tawfīq al-Ḥakīm has been called the father of modern Egyptian drama. Like Shauqī he was trained in France in law in the 1920s. Through this he developed a close acquaintance with European literature and cultural life. Among European writers, he admired George Bernard Shaw greatly.

Al-Ḥakīm was a prolific and varied playwright. He completed more than 70 literary works, 40 of them plays written in a number of different styles.

His work divides into three periods. The first consists of works written during his schooling in France, such as 'Ali Baba, which now seem to have been lost. After his return to Egypt from France in 1927 he wrote a number of popular dramas drawing from historical or religious subjects which he termed 'plays of the intellect'. During this time he was employed first as a court prosecutor in Alexandria, and from 1929 with the Ministry of Education in Cairo. From this period, his 1933 play Ahl al-Khaf (People of the Cave) achieved great success. The play presents a Qu'ranic legend concerning three Christians who awake from a cave after 300 years' sleep to a newly Islamicized world. The sleepers cannot accept the changed world, and return to the cave to die. The play was the first to be performed by the Egyptian National Troupe, formed in 1935.

Many of Al-Ḥakīm's 'plays of the intellect' indeed seemed to have been written more to be read than produced. His 1936 play on the life of Mohammad, Muhammad, may be the longest play ever written in Arabic, and it is doubtful that he ever intended it to be performed on stage.

The third period is al-Ḥakīm's modern period after the overthrow of the Egyptian monarchy. He engages in gentle social criticism in plays such as Al-Aidī al-Nā'ima (Soft Hands, 1954) and Al-Sultān al-Ḥā'ir (The Sultan who Could Not Make Up His Mind, 1960). He also shows traces of the theatre of the absurd as in his 1962 play Yā Tāli' al-Shajara (The Tree Climbers). In this, as in all of his plays, al-Ḥakīm emphasizes the conflict between opposing forces: compromise and heroism; tradition and modernization; idealism and realism. Whether pursuing these ideas in classical or absurdist dramatic format, his work has been continually provocative and influential.

Mahmūd Taymūr (1894–1973) is another contemporary playwright who has had extensive influence on Arabic drama. Taymūr has been a remarkably prolific literary figure, writing poetry, short stories, and literary criticism in addition to a dozen plays of varying quality. Like al-Ḥakīm, Taymūr's plays seem to work better as literary efforts than as stage productions. He has sought to reflect everyday society in Egypt, and was indeed the first playwright of note to use colloquial Egyptian Arabic on the stage as the principal vehicle for dialogue. His plays are largely comic in nature, but with an overlay of social criticism.

One of his more important works is Al-Makhba' Raqm 13 (Shelter Number 13, 1941) which deals with a mixed group of people caught in an air-raid shelter, who steadfastly maintain their social differences despite the danger surrounding them. This play is noteworthy because it was written twice – once in classical Arabic as a literary work, and once in colloquial Arabic for stage production.

Another of his plays, Haflat Shāi (A Tea Party, 1946), is a heavily satirical look at the snobbism and affectation of the emerging Egyptian middle classes, who ape foreign customs, while forgetting essential elements of human interaction.

Nu'man 'Ashūr deals also with Egyptian social themes, and with explorations of human foibles and frailty. Unlike his French-influenced contemporaries, 'Ashūr was most heavily influenced by the work of **Anton Chekhov**. His well-known plays, Al-Nās illi Taḥt (The People Upstairs, 1956) and Al-Nās illi Fauq (The People Downstairs, 1958), deal with the difficulties of reconciliation between socio-economic classes. The drama Bilad Barrah (Abroad, 1966?) treats society a decade after the revolution which overthrew the Egyptian monarchy. The older generation are seen to have fully adapted to the revolution, having returned to old corrupt ways, leaving the next generation bereft of the fruits of revolution.

In contrast to al-Ḥakīm and 'Ashūr, Rashad Rushdy gives heavy emphasis in his work to creating drama of high quality. His works are eminently suitable for the stage and not meant just to be read. A leading critic and literary scholar Rushdy was able to survive censorship during the Nasser era largely because of the excellence of his work. His plays range from explorations of Egyptian social institutions and human foibles (Al-Farāsha (The Butterfly), 1959; The Game of Love, 1961) to direct political and social criticism (Journey Beyond the Fence, 1964?; Egypt My Love, 1967).

Other notable writers for the stage in the 1960s and 1970s include Yūsef Idrīs, whose drama Al-Farāfir ('Small-Fry' translated into English as Flipflap and his Master, 1963), a direct satire on the Egyptian leadership, was even presented on television; Salāḥ 'Abd al-Sabbūr (Ma'sāt al-Hallāj (The Tragedy of Hallaj), 1965) and 'Ali Salīm ('Afārit Miṣr al-Jadīda (The Ghosts of New Egypt, 1968), which ridiculed government spies and informers).

The years following the 1967 war with Israel and the assassination of Anwar Sadāt in 1981 were not good for the development of Egyptian theatre. Difficult economic conditions during the war years were followed by an upsurge in Islamic religious fundamentalism which made stage productions difficult. During this period television and film became more prominent as vehicles for dramatic art. The growing market for Egyptian television soap operas and frothy films throughout the Arabic-speaking world gave these dramatic vehicles an economic and artistic prominence which eclipsed the stage. It is to be hoped that this is a temporary situation, and that live dramatic art will once again assume the importance it once had in Egyptian cultural life.

Iran The first Western-style playing space in Iran was not constructed until 1886 at the Dār al Fonun secondary school. Because of religious opposition, performances there of translations of Molière and other European authors were only patronized by the court. It was not until after the establishment of the Teātr-e Melli (National Theatre) in 1911 and the constitutional revolution of 1912, that the first Western-style theatre was presented. A number of writers began to translate European stage works, and a few original plays were produced.

Ahmad Mahmudi Kamāl al-Vezāreh (1875–1930) wrote a number of dramas, including *Ostād Nowruz-e Pineduz* (*Ostād Nowruz, the Cobbler*, 1919) in which the colloquial Persian of south Tehran was used for the first time. Mirzādeh Eshqi (1893–1925) wrote six historical patriotic works including *Rastākhiz-e Salātin-e Irān* (*The Resurrection of Iranian Kings*, 1916) which conjures up the spirits of the pre-Islamic Achamenian kings of Iran. Hasan Moqaddam (1896–1925) wrote a mocking satire, *Ja'far Khān az Farang Amadeh* (*Ja'afar Khān Returns From Europe*, 1923) which makes light of Europeanized Iranians.

Rezā Shāh Pahlavi's reign from 1925 to 1941 proved difficult for the Iranian theatre because of heavy censorship. Few writers of fiction turned their talents to the stage, although the famous novelist Sādeq Hedāyat did write two plays: *Parvin Dokhtār-e Sāsān* (*Parvin, the Daughter of Sāsān*, 1928) and *Māzyār* (1933), both concerned with the Arab invasion of Iran in the 7th century AD. During the reign of Rezā Shāh women appeared on the Iranian stage for the first time.

It was only after the end of the Second World War that Western-style theatre became established on a fully professional basis. 'Ali Nasiriān and 'Abbās Javānmard began to stage productions in a small theatrical company, the Goruh-e Honar-e Melli (National Art Group), brought into being by Shāhin Sarkissiān (1912–66). Both Nasiriān and Javānmard later worked with the Office of Dramatic Arts of the Ministry of Culture and Arts after its establishment in 1964. In its early days the Goruh-e Honar-e Melli produced stage adaptations of Hedāyāt's stories, including *Mohallel* (*The Temporary Husband*, 1957), and *Mordeh Khorhā* (*Eaters of the Dead*, 1957). Nasiriān was the first serious Iranian writer to be inspired by traditional performance forms in writing for the modern stage. He has written several successful plays including *Afi-ye Talā'i* (*The Golden Serpent*, 1957) and *Bolbol-e Sar-gashteh* (*The Wandering Nightingale*, 1959). The latter, based on a folktale, was the first Iranian play to be produced in Europe (Paris, 1960); he also wrote *Siyāh* (*The Black One*, 1962?), a play depicting the deep sadness of the blackfaced clown of *ru-howzi* comedy, and *Bongāh-e Theatrāl* (*The Theatre Company*, 1974), a straight scripted version of a *ru-howzi* comedy.

The finest dramatic writer of the post-war years was also one of Iran's greatest novelists and short-story writers, Gholam Hoseyn Sa'edi (1935–85), who often wrote under the pen name Gohār Morād. Like many Iranian writers, Sāedi avoided censorship by couching his work in heavy symbolism. His play *Chub-be-dasthā-ye Varazil* (*The Club-wielders of Varazil*, 1965) told the story of villagers threatened by hunters who first befriend them. The villagers eventually take refuge in an Islamic shrine. Several of his plays were published together as *Panj Namayeshnāmeh az Enqelāb-e Mashrutiyat* (*Five Plays of the Constitutional Revolution*, 1966). Of his other plays, perhaps the best known are *Āy bi Kolāh, Āy bā Kolāh* ('*A' Without a 'Hat', 'A' With a 'Hat'* (Referring to the 'long A' in the Persian alphabet, which has a stroke, or 'hat' over it), 1967); and *Vāy bar Maghlub* (*Woe to the Vanquished*, 1971).

Bahrām Bezā'i (b. 1938) has had a varied career as a theatre scholar, film director and playwright. His study *Namāyesh dar Iran* (*Performance in Iran*, Tehran, 1965) remains the definitive historical work on Iranian traditional theatre. His plays are highly symbolic, and often draw on folkloric sources. The puppet theatre inspired his *Ghorub dar Diyāri Gharib* (*Sunset in a Strange Land*, 1963) and *Qesse-ye Māh-e Penhān* (*Tale of the Hidden Moon*, 1963). Traditional Iranian wrestling forms the backdrop of *Pahlavān Akbar Mimirad* (*Akbar the Champion Dies*, 1965). *Marg-e Yazdigerd* (*The Death of Yazdigerd*, 1979) deals with the last Sassanian king before the Islamic conquest of Iran in the 7th century.

Several institutions formed the backdrop for dramatic work in Iran in the 1960s and 1970s as the regime of Mohammad Rezā Pahlavi attempted to develop the arts along European lines. A School of Dramatic Arts was founded, and a major national theatre, the 25th of Shahrivar Hall, was opened with a regular theatre season in both the main theatre, and a smaller studio space. A good deal of experimental theatre work was produced here.

National Iranian Radio-Television also served as a major source for support of theatre. The Kār-gāh-ye Namāyesh (Performance Workshop) was opened in 1969, and served as a training school for a number of actors. Within this framework a number of plays were also written and given outstanding productions by a group of talented young writers and directors. Arby Ovanessian (b. 1942) produced several plays by 'Abbās Na'lbandiān (b. 1947), including *Pazhuheshi Zharf* (*Profound Research*, 1968) a surrealist drama in **Beckett** style about a number of persons waiting for an 'answer', and *Nāgāhān* (*Suddenly*, 1972) concerning the murder of an 'outsider' by a group of fanatics. Bizhan Mofid wrote *Shahr-e Qesseh* (*A City of Tales*, 1968) mocking Iranian society using actors in the guise of animals, and using traditional story-telling methods and music, and *Jān-Nessār* (*Soul-sacrificer*, 1972), a hilarious satirical farce which preserves the style of traditional *ru-howzi* comedy. Esmā'il Khalaj wrote several plays dealing with village life, including *Hālet Chetowr-e Mash Rahim* (*How are you, Mash Rahim*, 1977) and *Goldune Khānom* (1977). Ashurbanipal Bābella's *Emshab Shab-e Māhtāb-e* (*Tonight is Moonlight*, 1974) is a *ru-howzi* inspired satire.

The most important contribution of National Iranian Radio-Television to theatrical life in Iran was perhaps the establishment of the Festival of Arts in Shiraz. Under the direction of the writer and film-maker, Farrokh Gaffary, the Festival was a major international showcase for avant-garde Western drama, and of the traditional performance arts of Asia, Africa and Latin America.

All major post-war Iranian actors and directors produced works at the Festival. Additionally, the major avant-garde directors of the world during this period also appeared to produce new works, including **Peter Brook**, **Jerzy Grotowski**, **Robert Wilson**, Shuji Teriyama, Peter Schuman, **Tadeusz Kantor** and **André Gregory** among others. One important consequence of the Festival was the artistic cross-fertilization it produced. Iranian actors and directors had the opportunity to see daring new works, such as Brook's *Orghast* (1971) and Wilson's *Ka Mountain and GUARDenia Terrace* (1972). These directors in turn had the opportunity to be exposed to traditional performing arts, such as *ta'ziyeh* and *ru-howzi* theatre, both of which were produced extensively at the Festivals. *Ta'ziyeh* was first produced at the 1967 Festival by director Parviz Sayyād in conjunction with theatre scholar Kojasteh Kiā. Sayyād had presented an earlier production in Tehran in 1965. In 1976 a series of ten *ta'ziyeh* performances were held at the Festival under the direction of actor, director and theatre researcher Mohammad Bāgher Ghaffāri.

Ru-howzi was presented in several 'modernized' forms during the 11 years the Festival was in existence. In 1977, Mohammad Bāgher Ghaffāri assembled existing traditional troupes from throughout the country for a series of highly successful performances held in a garden in Shiraz.

The revolution of 1978–9 stopped much of the theatrical activity that had taken place under the Pahlavi regime, making the future of theatre much less certain. Theatrical training schools and regular performances in public virtually ceased in Iran. National Iranian Radio-Television, its name changed to 'The Voice and Vision of the Islamic Republic of Iran', produced dramas on revolutionary themes for television on occasion, but stage drama was viewed with great suspicion. Sa'id Soltānpur, a leftist writer, staged *'Abbās Āqā Kārgar* (*'Abbās Āqā, Worker*) in 1980 but was executed by the authorities in 1981. Many Iranian actors and directors emigrated, and continued to work producing works in Persian abroad. Director Parviz Sayyād toured the United States with two successful plays, *Khar* (*The Donkey*, 1983), and *Samad be Jang Miravad* (*Samad goes to War*, 1984), both dealing with Iran after the revolution, and a number of revivals of pre-Revolutionary drama were presented both in the United States and Europe. Interestingly, sturdy *ru-howzi* theatre seems to have survived the revolution, by turning its satire on the former Pahlavi regime.

Other Middle Eastern countries Significant theatrical development has taken place in other Middle Eastern countries, particularly following the First World War. Three principal areas can be singled out: North Africa, Syria and Lebanon, and Iraq. Some theatrical activity has also been seen in recent years in Kuwait.

In Tunisia, Algeria and Morocco before the First World War the court traditions of the Ottoman Empire, including *karagöz* and *orta-oyunu* performances, were supported. Although a Viennese troupe visited Tunis in 1826, and many foreign language performances of plays took place throughout the 19th century, the first Western-style play presented in Arabic in North Africa was *Al-'Ashiq al-Muttaham* (*The Accused Lover*) presented by the Egyptian troupe of Sulaymān al-Qardāhī in Tunis in 1908. Al-Qardāhī then settled in Tunis until his death a year later.

Shortly thereafter two Tunisian troupes were formed, Al-Khahama (Pride) and al-Ādāb (Literature). This second troupe presented, on 7 April 1911, the first piece in Arabic by a native company, *Salah ad-Dīn* (*Saladin*) by Najīb Haddad. The two troupes joined together in 1922. From them and the actors associated with them a number of smaller companies formed and grew, proliferating until 1954 with the creation of al-Firqa al-Baladiya, the Municipal Troupe of Tunis. During this earlier period most productions were translations of European works, or productions of plays by Egyptian playwrights. But the creation of the Municipal Troupe marked the beginning of real professional theatre in Tunisia.

In the 1960s and 1970s the Municipal Troupe was widely identified with Aly Ben Ayed, a talented director who mounted a number of successful productions which toured in Europe and in festivals in the Middle East. His death in 1972 was a great blow, but the troupe continued under a series of equally able directors. The first permanent regional company was started by Moncef Souissi in Kef in 1967. By the end of the 1970s there were eight permanent professional troupes throughout Tunisia, a number of festivals, and a healthy audience for theatre.

Algeria, of all North African countries, was most widely influenced by *karagöz* and *orta-oyunu* which was performed in colloquial dialect. Serious stage drama had difficulty becoming established because of the disparity between the classical Arabic of the stage and the language understood by the audience. Even visiting Egyptian troupes had difficulty being accepted. Eventually two troupes were formed which emphasized comedy performed in native Algerian dialect, the troupes of Rashīd Ksentīnī (1887–1944), and Bāshtarzī Muhī'l-Dīn. Ksentīnī produced farces in the provinces starting in 1926, but later wrote comic plays which attracted urban crowds as well. Muhī'l-Dīn produced musical theatre, weaving simple plots with songs. Later he wrote more complex plays, including adaptions of Molière and Shakespeare. **Kateb Yacine** (see also **French-speaking North Africa**) ranks as one of the principal literary figures of Algeria, having composed a number of compelling dramas, although he wrote in French. Today, theatre is active in Algeria, but the film industry is more important, and serves as the basis for employment of most actors.

Theatre in Morocco and Libya is the least developed in North Africa. Libya is small in population, and theatrical activity is restricted by the fundamentalist Islamic orientation of its government. Amateur theatre troupes exist in several Moroccan cities, dating from the independence movement in 1956. In 1959 a centre for dramatic research was established where actor training took place, but it was closed in 1962. Nevertheless, sporadic productions continue to be produced by directors such as Tayyeb Seddiki, Ahmad Tayyeb Laalj, 'Abd al-Samad Dīnia and others. Many productions are in French. Much of Moroccan theatrical effort has become absorbed in television production.

Syrian theatre underwent a strong upsurge in the 1960s which died back under the regime of Hafiz al-Assad. The members of the Thought and Art Society, a group of intellectuals largely trained in Europe, began to present amateur theatrical productions of European playwrights, and some works by Egyptian writers, such as Tawfiq al-Hakīm. The government founded the National Theatre troupe in 1961 drawing on members of the Thought and Art Society, including Rafiq al-Saban, and Hani Snobar. Other actors trained at the Institute of Dramatic Art in Cairo joined the troupe. During the next decade the National Theatre produced five or six plays a year to small audiences. The private 'Liberal Theatre', which started in 1956, proved more adventurous. The troupe has been successful by producing works exclusively written by Arab writers, and in a highly popular vein.

Among other works, they produced a number of popular works by the Syrian playwright Sa'adallah Wannūs, including his very successful *Haflat Samar min Ajli 5 Huzairān* (*An Evening Party for the 5th of June*, 1967), which reflects the bitterness of the Arab defeat in the Arab-Israeli war, and *Mughamarat Ra's al Mamluk Jabīr* (*Adventure of the Head of Jabir the Slave*, 1971). The Popular Theatre Troupe of Aleppo was founded in 1968 and enjoys popularity by concentrating on Arabic writers.

Theatre in Lebanon has suffered greatly in the post-1945 years. One theatre, the Masrah Fārūq in Beirut, was little more than a night-club with some dramatic sketches presented between rounds of belly-dancing, before the civil conflict that consumed the country throughout the 1970s and 1980s. During this period some amateur theatrical performances were given, particularly in university settings. One important writer, Sa'īd Taqī al-Dīn, emerged during this period. His widely praised play, *Al-Manbūdh* (*The Outcast*, 1953), proved prophetic in detailing the social strife that would later emerge in the 1970s. Antoine Moultaqa, who directed the Lebanon University theatre, presented several productions abroad, including an appearance at Nancy. Ḥasan 'Alā' al-Dīn produced popular satires in his own theatre. The Festival of Arts at Baalbek, which emphasized music, eventually had a theatre troupe associated with it, led by Mūnir Abū Dibs, producing European drama. One pioneering experimental work, *Li-Tamut Desdemona* (*Let Desdemona Die*) produced by Raymond Jabara using university students as actors, was seen by a small audience in 1970, but demonstrated the limited appeal for the avant-garde even among the sophisticated citizens of Beirut in that year.

The first professional company in Iraq was founded in 1927 by Haqqī al-Shiblī, who also founded the Department of Theatre in the Baghdad Fine Arts Institute. al-Shiblī had acted with Jurj Abyaḍ's troupe in Cairo. Theatre was lively in the 1930s with works by Egyptian playwrights being shown with regularity. A few Iraqi playwrights began to emerge as well, including Muhammad Mūsā al-Shābandar, whose play *Waḥida* was produced with great success in 1930. More recently, Iraqi playwrights have emphasized social inequalities and the need for reform. Yūsuf al-'Ani is one writer of distinction whose plays have achieved widespread popularity.

A few productions have been seen in Kuwait in recent years. 'abd al-'Azīz al-Sarī' has written plays expressing social dilemmas which have been widely produced in the Arab world, including *Dā'a al-Dīk* (*The Cock is Lost*) which deals with an English-educated man with a Kuwaiti father looking for his family roots. **WOB**

See: M. H. al-Khozai, *The Development of Early Arabic Drama 1847–1900*, London, 1984; 'Ali al-Ra'i, *Funun al-kumidiya* (*The Craft of Comedy*), Cairo, 1971; 'Adel Abu-Shanab, *Karakūz*, Damascus, Ministry for the Preservation and Promulgation of Antiquities, n.d; M. And, 'Origins and Early Development of the Turkish Theater', *Review of National Literatures*, 4 (1973), 53–64; and *A History of Theatre and Popular Entertainment in Turkey*, Ankara, 1963–4; and *Karagöz, Turkish Shadow Theatre*, Istanbul, 1979; Badr el din Aroudiki, 'Theatre in Syria', *Lotus: Afro-Asian Writings*, Cairo, 19 (1974), 74–93; L.

Awad, 'Problems of the Egyptian Theatre', in R. C. Ostle, *Studies in Modern Arabic Literature*, Warminster, England, 1975; Hafiz Baghban, 'The Context and Concept of Humour in Magadi Theatre', PhD thesis, Indiana University, Bloomington, Indiana, 1977; Turgay-Ahmad Bedi, 'Modern Turkish Theater', *Review of National Literatures*, 4 (1973), 65–81; O. W. Beeman, *Culture, Performance and Communication in Iran*, Tokyo, Institute for the Study of Languages and Cultures of Asia and Africa, 1982; and 'A Full Arena: The Development and Meaning of Popular Performance Traditions in Iran' in E. Bonine and N. R. Keddie, eds., *Modern Iran: The Dialectics of Continuity and Change*, Albany, 1981; and 'Why Do They Laugh? An Interactional Approach to Humour in Traditional Iranian Improvisatory Theater', *Journal of American Folklore* 94(374) (1981), 506–26; Hamadi Ben Halima, *Un Demi-siècle de Théâtre Arabe en Tunisie (1907–1957)*, Tunis, 1974; Bahrām Bezā'i, *Namāyesh Dar Irān* (*Performance in Iran*), Tehran, 1965; Issa J. Boullata, ed., *Critical Perspectives on Modern Arabic Literature*, Washington, DC, 1980; P. J. Chelkowski, 'Bibliographic Spectrum' in P. Chelkowski, ed., *Ta'ziyeh: Indigenous Avant-Garde Theater of Iran*, New York, 1979; E. Drioton, *Le Théâtre Egyptien*, Cairo, 1942; Farrokh Gaffary, 'Evolution of Rituals and Theater in Iran', *Iranian Studies* 17(4), 361–90; T. H. Gaster, *Thespis: Ritual, Myth and Drama in the Ancient Near East*, 2nd edn, New York, 1959; Abdel-Aziz Hammouda, 'Modern Egyptian Theatre: Three Major Dramatists', *World Literature Today* 53(4) (1979), 601–5; Georg Jacob, *Geschichte des Schattentheaters in Morgen-und Abenland*, Hannover, 1925; Abu al-Qāsem Jannati-Atā'i, *Bonyād-e Namāyesh dar Irān* (*The Institution of Performance in Iran*), Tehran Chāp-e Mihan, 1955; Ahatanel' Krymsky, *The Persian Theatre: Its Origin and Development*, Kiev, 1925; J. Landau, *Studies in the Arab Theatre and Cinema*, Philadelphia, 1958; I. Lassy, *The Muharram Mysteries among the Āzerbāijān Turks of Caucasia*, Helsingfors, 1916; Hassan Mniai, 'Connaissance du Théâtre Marocain', *Europe: Revue Littéraire Mensuelle*, 602–3 (1979), 158–62; Matti Moosa, 'Naqqāsh and the Rise of the Native Arab Theatre in Syria', *Journal of Arabic Literature* 3 (1972), 106–17; R. C. Ostle, ed., *Studies in Modern Arabic Literature*, Warminster, England, 1975; L. Pelly, *The Miracle Play of Hasan and Hussein*, 2 vols, London, 1879; Medjid Rezvani, *Le Théâtre et la Danse en Iran*, Paris, 1962; S. E. Siyavuşgil, *Karagöz, Its History, Its Characters, Its Mystic and Satiric Spirit*, Ankara, 1955; A. Tietze, *The Turkish Shadow Theatre and the Puppet Collection of the L. A. Mayer Memorial Foundation*, Berlin, 1977; N. Tomiche and C. Khaznadar, eds., *Le Théâtre Arabe*, Paris, 1969.

Middleton, Thomas

Middleton, Thomas (c. 1580–1627) English playwright, the son of a master bricklayer. He may have spent some time at Gray's Inn in London after leaving Oxford University. He is first identified as a working playwright in **Henslowe**'s *Diary* in 1602. His earliest known play, *The Phoenix* (1603–4), was written for the **Boys of St Paul's**, as were the citizen comedies, *A Trick to Catch the Old One* (c. 1604), *Michaelmas Term* (c. 1605) and *A Mad World, My Masters* (c. 1605). *Your Five Gallants* (1607) was produced by the rival **Children of the Chapel Royal**. It says much about Middleton's industry that he should, at the same time, have been providing material for Henslowe and the adult **Admiral's Men**. Two collaborations with **Dekker**, both superior catchpenny comedies, frame the plays written for boys. They are *The Honest Whore* (1604) and

The Roaring Girl (c. 1610). In common with Middleton's own comic masterpiece, A Chaste Maid in Cheapside (1611), these collaborative works rely on the ingenious interweaving of multiple plots, but Middleton's individual voice, objective and quizzical, is discernible. His moral observations on mercantile values and manners are strangely uncorrective. A similar ambivalence marks the collaborations with **William Rowley**, A Fair Quarrel (c. 1616), The World Tossed at Tennis (c. 1619) and the extraordinary tragicomedy, The Changeling (1622), one of the most fluent and unerring of Jacobean plays, and The Spanish Gipsy (1623). Middleton was an unfussy poet, with a fine ear for dialogue. That he was also tough-minded is suggested by the steady control of his insistently unsentimental plays, and by the professional opportunism that dictated his choice of themes in such plays as The Witch (c. 1612), More Dissemblers Besides Women (c. 1615) and the controversial anti-Spanish satire, A Game at Chess (1624). Middleton was certainly admonished and may have been imprisoned as a result of this play. His appointment as City Chronologer of London (1620–7) would not have protected him, though it did reward his achievements as a writer of masques and pageants. His last known play is the remarkable tragedy Women Beware Women (c. 1625), which concludes mischievously in an almost-comic scene of slaughter. It is not surprising, in view of this piece, that Middleton is seen by many critics as a more likely author for The Revenger's Tragedy than **Tourneur**.   PT

Mielziner, Jo (1901–76) The most dominant figure in American set and lighting design from the mid-1920s until his death. Mielziner created the sets for virtually every major American drama and musical in the 1930s, 40s, and 50s. As such he exerted a great influence not only on the field of design, but on the plays themselves. Dramas such as A Streetcar Named Desire and Death of a Salesman were in part shaped by his designs, and their success was to some degree dependent upon them. His use of scrims and a painterly style created a visual counterpart to the poetic realism of the plays of the period, notably the works of **Tennessee Williams**. The scrims together with fragmented scenic units allowed a cinematic transformation from one scene to the next through the manipulation of light – not by shifting scenery. This was in keeping with the trend in playwriting toward a cinematic structure. He was equally capable of realism as demonstrated by his set for Street Scene in 1929 in which he recreated the facade of a tenement and a New York City street. His designs for musicals such as Carousel, Annie Get Your Gun, and Guys and Dolls captured the vibrancy of the American musical at its peak. The power of Mielziner's designs is demonstrated by the fact that some of his designs have outlasted the plays or are integrally entwined with them. His design for **Maxwell Anderson**'s Winterset – a soaring panorama of the Brooklyn Bridge receding into the fog – is better remembered than the play itself; designers today trying to recreate Death of a Salesman must compete with the ghost of Mielziner's set. Mielziner also lit most of his own plays in order to control light, mood and colour. Working together with Edward F. Kook, he was responsible for many improvements in lighting instruments. Mielziner also worked as a theatre designer and consultant on many theatres, including the somewhat controversial **Vivian Beaumont Theatre** in New York.   AA

Mikhoels, Solomon (1890–1948) Leading actor and later director of the **Moscow State Jewish Theatre**, and one of the favourite actors of the Soviet public until his death in mysterious circumstances immediately after the enforced closure of his theatre in 1948. His greatest roles were King Lear, for which he received international acclaim, Reb Alter in An Evening of Sholom Aleichem, Benjamin in Mendele Mocher Sforim's The Voyage of Benjamin III and Hostmach in **Goldfaden**'s The Witch.   AB

Miles, Bernard (James) (1907–91) British actor and director. His career as an actor flourished from the 1930s onward, but it is as the founder of the Mermaid Theatre, London, that he made his greatest contribution to the British theatre. Miles had always wished to establish a resident theatre company within the City of London, and after several temporary 'Mermaids' had tested the ground, the permanent building, created largely through the enthusiasm and effort of Miles and his wife Josephine, opened on the north bank of the River Thames at Puddle Dock in May 1959. The first production was Miles's own adaptation of **Fielding**'s Rape upon Rape, called Lock Up Your Daughters – a rumbustious play with music. At the Mermaid Miles built a repertoire of classics and directed and performed in many of them. In more recent years the theatre has come under financial pressure, but in 1987 the **Royal Shakespeare Company** made it the London base for productions created at the Swan Theatre in Stratford-upon-Avon. Bernard Miles also appeared in a large number of British films and created a radio character whose monologues of rural life made him a nationally known figure even before the Mermaid venture. He was knighted in 1969.   MB

Miller, Arthur (1915–) American playwright. Following the death of **Tennessee Williams** in 1983, and in spite of the paucity of his own recent output, Arthur Miller remains relatively unchallenged as America's greatest living playwright. His first play, The Man Who Had All the Luck (1944), was a consummate failure, but All My Sons (1947) proved that Miller could create powerful scenes and believable characters. His next play, Death of a Salesman (1949), won him both the Pulitzer Prize and the Drama Critics' Circle Award. Shifting neatly between realism and expressionism, this piercing study of an ageing drummer (commercial traveller) elicited highly praised, prize-winning efforts from the entire original production company and has subsequently been performed all over the world. His adaptation of **Ibsen**'s An Enemy of the People (1950) was a thematic prelude to The Crucible (1953), a drama of the Salem witchcraft trials written in passionate response to Senator Joseph McCarthy's investigations of accused subversives. This spellbinding drama of real conflict and impassioned action has outlived the immediacy of its inception and may yet prove to be Miller's finest work. A View from the Bridge (1955), which played in New York the same year Miller married Marilyn Monroe, continued his exploration of the tragedy of the common man. This time his hero is a hard-working Sicilian longshoreman who is killed because he breaks the community's law of silence about some illegal immigrants. Miller's stage voice was silent for the next eight years, during which time he divorced Marilyn Monroe (1961) and married photographer Ingeborg Morath (1962). He returned to the stage in 1964 with *After the Fall*, apparently a highly personal play based on his life with the beautiful film star, Monroe. *Incident at Vichy*, an examination of the Nazi–Jewish conflict during the Second World War, followed in the same year. *The Price* (1968), a heart-wrenching confrontation between two brothers, managed a run of 429 performances and became the last Miller play to achieve anything like a popular success. *The Creation of the World and Other Business* (1972) and *The American Clock* (1980) failed and were hastily withdrawn. Throughout his career Miller produced a rich collection of essays about the craft of playwriting, especially the nature of modern tragedy. These pieces, published as *The Theatre Essays of Arthur Miller* (edited by Robert A. Martin, 1971), remain the closest thing to a complete 'poetics' yet written by an American playwright.   LDC

Miller, Gilbert Heron (1884–1969) American producer, director, theatre manager, son of the actor **Henry Miller** and actress Bijou (Heron). Miller produced over 100 productions in London and New York during a half-century career. He was known for his elegant staging of high comedy by such writers as Philip Barry, **Somerset Maugham**, and other masters of literate dialogue. He introduced to the American stage such British actors as **Charles Laughton**, **Alec Guinness**, and Leslie Howard. From 1918 until its demolition in 1958 he owned the **St James's Theatre**, London; from 1929 until his death, the **Lyric Theatre**, London; and from 1926 until 1968 the Henry Miller Theatre in New York. His greatest success was *Victoria Regina* (1936) with **Helen Hayes**. Other significant productions included: Maugham's *The Constant Wife* (1927), **Sherriff**'s *Journey's End* (1928), **Eliot**'s *The Cocktail Party* (1950), and **Thomas**'s *Under Milkwood* (1957).   DBW

Miller, Henry (1859–1925) American actor and manager. Born in London, he emigrated with his parents to Canada, where he made his debut in 1876. He quickly became a juvenile leading man in America opposite a variety of young actresses, including Bijou Heron, whom he married in 1883. In 1893 he became leading man of **Charles Frohman**'s new **Empire Theatre** Stock Company. from 1905 to 1908 he and **Margaret Anglin** starred under their own management, notably in *The Great Divide* by **William Vaughn Moody**. Though he continued to act until after the First World War, Miller's principal occupation after 1908 was as a producer for others. He launched the career of **Alla Nazimova**, and became manager and producer for **Walter Hampden**, Laura Hope Crewes, and Ruth Chatterton, among others. As an actor, Miller personified the American ideal of honest, sympathetic, taciturn masculinity.   DMCD

Miller, Joaquin (Cincinnatus Hiner Miller) (1839–1913) American writer. His early life among the miners and Indians of California and Oregon is confused by his autobiographical embroidery. In 1863 he

settled as a newspaper editor in Oregon. When his early poems and stories were favourably received, he moved to San Francisco (1870), but his Byronic appearance, behaviour, and writing were most popular in England. His best works were *Songs of the Sierras* (1871) and *Life Among the Modocs* (1873). He also wrote four plays, and *The Danites in the Sierras* was performed in a heavily revised version by McKee Rankin (1877–81).   DMCD

Miller, Jonathan (Wolfe) (1934–) British actor and director, who was part of the original *Beyond the Fringe* team which added, in 1960, a new note of political satire to intimate revue. He qualified as a doctor at Cambridge University and his career has combined medical research with his contributions to stage and television. In 1962, he was invited to direct **John Osborne**'s one-act play *Under Plain Cover* at the **Royal Court** and subsequently worked as a director in New York, at the Mermaid Theatre in London and elsewhere. His 1969 production of *King Lear* with **Michael Hordern** introduced a scientific understanding of the ageing process and established him as a director of originality and insight. He was invited by **Laurence Olivier** to direct at the **National Theatre**, notably *The Merchant of Venice* with Olivier as Shylock, which led to an eventual appointment as Associate Director from 1973–5. His relationship with **Peter Hall**, who succeeded Olivier at the National Theatre, was less happy and he left to direct a season of 'family' plays, including *Hamlet* and *Ghosts* at Greenwich Theatre in 1974, and subsequently free-lanced among several regional repertory theatres, including the Yvonne Arnaud Theatre in Guildford where he directed a memorable production of **Chekhov**'s *Three Sisters*. Miller preferred to work within relaxed conditions where no large sums of money or national prestige were at stake and where he could develop his remarkable gifts at encouraging actors to pursue accurate interpretations. Miller has also directed opera with great success including a remarkable *Rigoletto* for the English National Opera in 1984, set among the Sicilian Mafia in New York during the 1930s.   JE

Miller, Marilyn (Marilynn) (1898–1936) American dancer and singer. As a child she appeared in vaudeville, and was dancing in a London club when she was discovered by **Lee Shubert**. She made her Broadway debut in *The Passing Show of 1914*. Miller was a featured performer in two editions of *The Ziegfeld Follies* (1918, 1919). In *Sally* (1920), she was given her first starring role as a poor dishwasher who becomes a star of the *Ziegfeld Follies*. Critics found her performance enchanting, complimenting her on her graceful dancing, her delicate beauty, and her buoyant personality. After a long run and national tour in *Sally*, Miller returned to Broadway in *Sunny* (1925). Her weekly salary for *Sunny* was reported to be $3,000, making her the highest-paid musical comedy performer of the 1920s. Her next shows, *Rosalie* (1928) and *Smiles* (1930), were not as successful as *Sally* and *Sunny*. In 1933 she made her final Broadway appearance in *As Thousands Cheer*, a revue with a score by **Irving Berlin**. Although her singing voice was so weak as to be inaudible at times, Miller's radiant beauty and elegant dancing made her the reigning queen of musical comedy in the 1920s.   MK

Miller, Max (Thomas Sargent) (1895–1963) The most celebrated British comedian of the heyday of variety. 'The Cheeky Chappie'. Born in Brighton, he began work as a motor-mechanic, but soon took to popular entertainment, initially with amateur concert-parties in his home town, then professionally with the original Billy Smart's Circus. Although his circus career was interrupted by the outbreak of the First World War, he was drafted into an army entertainments unit in which he seems to have got his first solo experience. After demobilization, three years touring provincial venues was followed by his London debut in 1922. Though not an overnight success, by 1924 he was working steadily under his subsequently famous solo billing, and by 1926 was top of the bill at the Holborn Empire, a position he maintained for three decades until his retirement.

A brashly colourful figure in white trilby, two-tone shoes, kipper tie and multi-coloured plus-four suit, he was accurately summed up by a reviewer as 'vulgar, loud, earthy and blue'. Though his act was mainly concerned with sex, and was generally regarded by contemporaries as rather daring, his material was no bawdier than that of many comedians before and since. What made it seem so was his stage-persona, and his relationship with his audience.

The dandified appearance, preening gestures and physical display – which so easily imply effeminacy – expressed total sexual confidence, the more so as his numerous asides were invariably addressed familiarly to ladies. Further, his stories were often in the first person. Finally, Miller told everybody that he was dirty, and drew them into complicity. 'I'm filthy with money', he confided, flashing his gross dress-ring, and adding as an afterthought, 'I'm filthy without it.' Complimenting himself on the quality of his suiting, he would invite a lady in the front row to have a feel. To draw the whole house into his conspiracy, he would display the White and Blue Books which allegedly contained clean and dirty jokes, and make them choose. Hobson's choice. Thereafter, the audience were looking for trouble even when none existed, and of course they always found it, encouraged by the comedian's simple but beautifully handled technique of not completing his punch-line or omitting the end-rhyme of his mildly saucy ditties. The inevitable laughter would be punctuated by pained appeals of 'Here, listen' (a proletarian version of **George Robey**'s injunction to 'desist'), challenges to the audiences to 'make something of that', and his famous complaint, 'You're the kind of people who'll get me a bad name.' They did, they would, and they were. His handling of an audience (there for all to hear in a 1957 recording of one of his last bookings, at the Metropolitan, Edgware Road) was masterly. His timing was superb; his ability to prompt laughter and encourage it to grow by saying virtually nothing was unrivalled; above all, he exuded personal and professional self-confidence, while approaching his audience (not to mention the band-leader) with a relaxed and conversational intimacy. While Miller was on stage, they were all 'pals'. AEG

Mills, John (Lewis Ernest Watts) (1908–) British actor and director, who first appeared on the stage in 1929. A popular actor in the 1930s, who appeared in light comedies and musicals, and played a season at the **Old Vic** in 1938, Mills became best known as a film-star during the 1940s and 1950s, appearing in many patriotic war films as well as such epics as *Scott of the Antarctic*, *The Colditz Story* and *Around the World in Eighty Days*. For at least two generations of film audiences, Mills represented the figure of a cheerful, stocky Englishman whose fundamental decency could always be relied on, especially in a crisis. He took few unsympathetic or character roles. His stage career, however, indicates an acting range beyond that of his films. He appeared in the New York production of **Rattigan**'s *Ross* (1961) and in **Charles Wood**'s *Veterans* at the **Royal Court** in 1972, a satire on ageing film actors on location. His roles in the musical version of *The Good Companions* (1974), in *Separate Tables* (1977) and *Goodbye Mr Chips* (1982) can be regarded as within his familiar range, but he astonished audiences at the **National Theatre** in 1986 with his performance as General Sir Edmund Milne in Brian Clark's *The Petition*, an elderly right-wing hawk distressed to find that his wife after many years of marriage is a dying dove. Mills is an actor who has a wide emotional range, from light comedy to tragedy, within an apparently limited stage and film personality. His autobiography, *Gentlemen Please*, was published in 1980. He received the CBE in 1960 and was knighted in 1976. JE

Milne, A[dam] A[lexander] (1882–1956) British children's author and dramatist. Of his many light comedies written after 1918, his satiric demolition of conservativism *Mr Pim Passes By* (1919), or *The Dover Road* and *The Truth About Blayds*, in which run-away couples are brought to realize that escape to Paris is not the path to happiness and a revered poet is discovered to be a fake (both 1921), all became popular repertory pieces. Their whimsical fantasy and sentimental humour mark Milne as the successor to **Barrie**, and his best-known play *Toad of Toad Hall* (1929 – based on Kenneth Grahame's *The Wind in the Willows*) is still revived almost every Christmas in London. CI

Mime and Pantomime. These two terms have altered in meaning and become confused over the centuries. Today they are used interchangeably to signify wordless, gestural performance; but in classical times they referred to distinct and different phenomena. *Mime*, from the Greek *mimos*, originally meant a form of comic folk play and then the actor who performed it (see **Greece, ancient**). Dorian or Megaran in origin, the plays at first parodied mythological characters, but later were sketches of contemporary life; the two or three characters were masked and phallephoric and featured a gluttonous slave. Epicharmus (c. 530–c. 440 BC) packed his mimes with puns; Herodas turned out vignettes of everyday life, introducing the schoolmaster, the inveterate shopper and the quack doctor as standard types. Sophron of Syracuse (c. 430 BC) brought the genre to a literary pitch that influenced the idylls of Theocritus and Moschus.

Among the Romans, the mime changed in both form and content (see **Rome**). It gradually usurped the popularity of the Atellan farces, and could be distinguished from regular comedy by the fact that women (*mimae*) performed, and masks and cothurnoi were not worn. Homogeneous companies of various sizes were led by an *archimimus* or *archimima*, an actor–manager who played the lead role. The comic types usually included the *stupidus*, a bald-headed, soot-smeared lout, and the *sannio* or face-maker; a common item of costume was the *centunculus*, a variegated cloak which some scholars have seen as an ancestor of **Harlequin**'s piebald jacket. In the tradition of the Floralia when prostitutes appeared naked, the *mima* was often required to undress before the public. Officially, mimes were on the lowest rung of the social ladder, but their popularity was such that many of their names have been preserved, and in time they toppled tragedy and comedy from their pedestals. Their plays were slices of life, often highly satirical and earthily obscene, with an emphasis on adulteries, swindles, and rough-housing. Political satire which thrived under the Republic was less independent under the Empire: the most popular and frequently revived mime between AD 30 and 200 was *Laureolus* by Quintus Lutatius Catullus, which demonstrated by the fate of its bandit-hero that the government knows best. (The emperor Domitian replaced the actor with a condemned criminal in the final scenes, so that the audience might enjoy genuine torture and execution.) Comic Christians were a frequent butt, with much byplay made of the rite of baptism. In the late classical period, mimes of a high literary quality were written by Decimus Laberius (106–43 BC) and his contemporary Publilius Syrus. But the greater the mime's popularity, the less important the written script became; actors gesticulated and improvised their own dialogue, while the **Grand-Guignol** recourse to real bloodshed increased.

The Roman *pantomime*, on the other hand, whose name derives from the Greek for 'imitating every-thing', was a male dancer who single-handedly inter-preted classical literature, especially tragedies, to the accompaniment of chanted recitation and flute music, and by changing masks. These one-man shows were supported by factions and associated with court intrigue, subject to imperial favour or displeasure by turns. The most famous were Pylades (c. 20 BC), who introduced a large choir in place of the solo singer, and Bathyllus whose racy performance of *Leda and the Swan* was mentioned by Juvenal. They too were censured for lasciviousness.

Mimes and pantomimes alike composed the bridge that brought the tradition of professional acting into the medieval world, although condemned by church coun-cils and outlawed by monarchs. The mime thrived in Byzantium, and certain ecclesiastics like Gregory of Nazianzus (?33–?390) tried to adapt it to sacred sub-jects. Choricius (6th century AD) defended the mimic performer as an imitator of life, but these proponents were in the minority. Eventually, the excommunicated *mimi* were lumped with all itinerant jugglers, minstrels and showmen, and renamed *ioculatores*, Goliards or **vagantes**. The miscellaneous nature of the mime's performance is clear in the description Theodoric, King of the Visigoths, made of the mime he sent to King Clovis of France: 'a skilful man who joins the art of expressing feelings by gestures and facial movements to the harmony of voices and sounds of instruments'. This all-purpose entertainer excelled at farce and was employed to interlard more serious presentations with 'dainty morsels' of his fooling: in French, *entremets*; in Spanish *entremeses*.

One curious cognate is the Elizabethan 'dumb show', best remembered for its appearance in *Hamlet*. Descended from the allegorical 'mummings' on festive occasions, it was never used as an interlude but always related to the play in which it was inserted. It served both to prefigure action to come and to endow that action with a more symbolic meaning. Besides **Shake-speare**, **Marston**, **Middleton** and **Webster** all used it to pungent effect.

The preservation of the mimic tradition in continen-tal Europe devolved upon the **commedia dell'arte**, whose comedy was physical but also highly verbal. The association with mute expressiveness may result from the first introduction of Italian troupes into France: not knowing French, they fell back on the universal language of gesture.

Modern mime and pantomime emerged in the 18th century from French fairgrounds and minor theatres, where the dramatic monopoly constrained 'illegit-imate' performers to avoid dialogue and develop a primarily physical means of expression. At the Saint-Germain fair in 1710, Pierre Alard (d. 1721), whose troupe was forbidden to speak, played 'pièces à la muette', in which the actors mimed to scrolls pulled out of their pockets and, later, signboards let down from the flies. Such mimic shows, accompanied throughout by music, were brought to London, and soon became acclimated as the **English pantomime**, which developed its own idiosyncratic conventions.

Diderot, vexed by the static nature of conventional acting, argued for gestural action to be made equal to the words in legitimate drama; and Marmontel in the *Encyclopédie* deemed pantomime especially necessary for 'the most impassioned movements of the soul . . . There it seconds the words, or takes their place entirely.' Mimic gesture became an important principle of late 18th-century acting theory: Johann Jakob Engel (1741–1802) in his *Ideas towards a System of Mimicry* (1785–6) suggested that mimic gesture in rituals func-tioned as natural signs, as colour does in painting; but the actor had to provide the strongest, most animated expressiveness to jolt the audience's awareness of what was imitated. Ultimately, he concluded, mime was imperfect because it had to convey both ideas and feelings.

The *philosophes* were seeking a primal universal language, but the fairground *pantomimes dialoguées* and *pantomimes historiques*, cross-pollinating the increas-ingly popular *ballets d'action*, evolved in other ways. Pre-romantic ballet was dominated by fairground performers like Grimaldo Nicolini, who was approved by **Lessing**, and the line between dance and panto-mime was hard to draw. After the French Revolution, for a newly proletarian audience, gestural acting became a dominant partner of dialogue in melodrama, while *mimodrame*, as practised at the **Cirque Olym-pique**, eschewed language altogether.

Throughout the 19th century, the spectacular panto-mime was subjugated to the style of its leading actors. **Mazurier** bequeathed his acrobatic style to the immen-sely popular **Ravels** who popularized pantomime in the United States. **Jean-Gaspard Deburau** made **Pierrot** the indispensable pivot of the pantomimes at Paris's **Théâtre des Funambules**, a whey-faced Everyman whose loose smock garbed historical char-acters and modern types, no matter what the plot; this tradition was upheld by his son Charles and by the more robust Paul Legrand (1816–98). The whiteness of costume and makeup put attitudes, gestures and facial expressions in relief. However, since this form of pantomime dispensed with words and used music only as an auxiliary, it required a conventionalized dramatic subject. Charles Nodier, **Jules Janin** and **Théophile Gautier** all wrote scenarios for it, but the chief purveyor was Champfleury.

This genre declined as its favourites died out, and was replaced in popularity by the violent, so-called American pantomimes of the **Hanlon-Lees**. But the older style enjoyed a brief and fashionable revival with the foundation of the amateur Cercle Funambulesque in 1888, when music played a preponderant role: Paul Margueritte's *Pierrot Assassin de sa Femme*, Catulle Mendès's *'Chand d'Habits* and *L'Enfant Prodigue* by Michel Carré *fils* (1890) were widely performed, not to popular audiences but to a middle-class public in quest of novelty. The great mimes of this period are Louis Rouffe and his student Séverin, noted for refinement, delicacy and precision. In *Mains et Masque*, the latter reduced Pierrot to a silent mask and eloquent hands.

In the 20th century, the silent film's ability to present a convincing representation of reality compelled the theatre to reexamine its own roots in search of inspiration. François Delsarte had already tried to classify and categorize the possibilities of emotional expression by the human body. **Gordon Craig** with his concept of the *Über-Marionette* (1905, 1911), **Yeats** with his demand for an aristocratic Western **nō** theatre, and other anti-realists called for symbolic gesture. The dance reforms of Isadora Duncan and the eurhythmic exercises of Jacques-Dalcroze were regarded as potential sources for a new theatrical art. **Jacques Copeau**, who had always seen the *commedia dell'arte* as a fountainhead of the actor's art, founded a school in 1921 where exercises with masks worked to isolate the body as a tool of expression in preparation for the spoken drama.

What had been a means for Copeau became an end in itself for his student **Etienne Decroux**. Decroux formulated 'pure mime' or 'pantomime de style', an independent art form whose (usually solo) performer creates a circumambient world and its objects wholly through movement. Hand gestures were reduced to a minimum, the face to a neutral mask, and narrative elements discarded in favour of an abstract distillation of a symbolic essence. Decroux viewed man as a struggling worm, with a right to unhappiness. This aspect of his teaching was emphasized by his disciple **Jean-Louis Barrault**, whose mimodramas usually depicted a struggle against time and death. Jacques Lecoq (b. 1921), who studied mask work with Copeau's son-in-law **Jean Dasté**, founded a school in 1956, whose two-year course deliberately excluded this austerity to embrace more psychological situations, theatrical styles, sound, colour and lighting effects.

Decroux's teaching was in part widely popularized by yet another student **Marcel Marceau**. As early as 1947, Marceau's character Bip of the white face and striped jersey appeared at the Théâtre de Poche, Paris, a sophisicated throwback to Deburau's Pierrot. Although fascinated by death, Marceau diluted his melancholy with wistful comedy and did not disdain to tell a story. His influence has been phenomenal, not only on such professionals as the Israeli Samy Molcho, the Czech **Ladislav Fialka**, and (in opposition) the American Adam Darius, but also on the cohorts of street performers who perpetuate his exercises of the cage and walking against the wind *ad infinitum* and *ad nauseam*.

A new direction in mime was taken by the Pole Henryk Tomaszewski, who founded the Wroclaw Pantomime Theatre in 1956. Distrustful of the sterility of 'pure mime', Tomaszewski creates elaborate ensemble pantomimes inspired by painting, sculpture, architecture and Oriental theatre, and based on such cultural archetypes as Gilgamesh, Dionysus, Hamlet, Faust and Woyzeck. Offering an 'absurdist' view of the universe, his sumptuous mélange of mime and dance raises questions about human existence but leaves the meaning sufficiently ambiguous to force the spectator to interpret the dreamlike and sensuous spectacle.

Contemporary mime has also been invigorated with injections of choreography and clowning. The German *Ausdruckstanz* or expressive dancing of the 1920s had given rise to **Valeska Gert**, whose dance-pantomimes explored the type of the whore; in America, Angna (Anita) Enters (b. c. 1907) practised a similar art with avatars of the Madonna. Gert's work was carried on by the grotesque Lotte Goslar, and, recently, a resurgence of this dance-pantomime can be discerned in the work of Pina Bausch and her Wuppertal Tanztheater.

Bausch's exploration of sexual roles indicates the more serious ends to which modern mime has been adapted. The San Francisco Mime Troupe split from the Actors' Workshop in 1959 to play *commedia dell'arte* scenarios in public parks; its broadly humorous collective creativity has always served radical political ends. The same holds true of the **Bread and Puppet Theatre**. A more Jungian approach is taken by the Swiss trio Mummenschanz (literally, Game of Chance), founded in 1972 by Andrés Brossard, Bernie Schürch and Floriana Frassetto. Its use of masks made of vacuum-cleaner hoses and toilet rolls creates a nightmarish, abstract and chilling view of the human predicament, reminiscent of the paintings of Paul Klee. The most recent experiments in mime have been omniclusive, admitting words and whatever might prove expressive to expand its potential. LS

See: J. Dorcy, *The Mime*, London, 1975; M. Felner, *Apostles of Silence: The Modern French Mime*, London, 1985; P. Hugonnet, *Mimes et Pierrots*, Paris, 1889; D. Mehl, *The Elizabethan Dumb Show*, Cambridge, Mass., 1966; A. Nicoll, *Masks, Mimes & Miracles*, London, 1931; R. Rolfe, ed., *Mimes on Miming*, Los Angeles, 1982; M. H. Winter, *The Pre-Romantic Ballet*, London, 1974.

Mime see **Greece, ancient**

Mimodrame see **Mime**

Mimus see **Mime**

Minskoff Theatre 1515 Broadway, New York City [Architect: Robert Allan Jacobs]. Like the **Gershwin Theatre** to the north, the Minskoff resides within the lower floors of a commercial office building and is reached by banks of escalators. The building stands on the site where the Hotel Astor formerly stood and the playhouse is named after its original owners and builders. A large house seating more than 1,600, it is best suited for musicals and opened with a successful revival of *Irene* (1973). Since then, its fare has been a succession of original musicals and revivals, the most notable being the **New York Shakespeare Festival** Company's adaptation of **Gilbert** and Sullivan's *The Pirates of Penzance* (1981) and a revival of the musical *Sweet Charity* (1986). The **Nederlander** Organization share the management of the theatre with Jerome Minskoff.   MCH

Minstrel show An American medley of sentimental ballads, comic dialogue and dance interludes, ostensibly founded on Negro life in the Southern USA. Its origin is attributed to **T. D. Rice**, who copied the eccentric mannerisms of an elderly black in Baltimore in 1828 and adopted blackface and banjo to produce the wildly popular 'Jim Crow'. At first a solo act, minstrelsy grew to four performers of violin, banjo, bones and tambourine with the Virginia Minstrels, founded by Dan Emmett (1842–3); despite the burnt cork, their repertoire drew heavily on traditional English choral singing and lugubrious parlour ballads. The same held true with the troupe of E. P. Christy (d. 1862) who invented Mr Interlocutor the white-faced master-of-ceremonies and the semi-circular arrangement of performers; his troupe had 30 members and gave 2,500 performances in New York in a single year. By the early 1850s Christy had evolved what was to be the standard tripartite programme: in the first part, the performers would enter in the 'walkround' until told, 'Gentlemen, be seated'. Vocal numbers, both lively and sentimental would be sung, interspersed with comic chat from the 'endmen' (in England, 'cornermen'), Mr Tambo and Mr Bones. Part Two, the olio, was a fantasia of speciality acts before the drop curtain; these included the stump speech, perfected by James Unsworth, and the wench impersonation, originated by George N. Christy (Harrington). Part Three comprised a sketch, either a plantation scene with dancing darkies or burlesques of Shakespearian plays and melodramas. Originally most of the performers and composers were white Northerners who like Stephen Foster had little first-hand acquaintance with Southern life; consequently the blacks they portrayed were extravagant fictions, like Zip Coon the urban dandy, and blackface comprised a theatrical mask not unlike **Harlequin**'s.

After the Civil War, competition from other popular forms, especially variety and musical comedy, compelled the minstrel show to expand and change its homely character. In 1878 J. H. Haverly combined four troupes in his United Mastodon Minstrels with his slogan, 'Forty – Count 'Em – Forty'. Sumptuous costumes and lavish scenery became the rule. Primrose and West even omitted the blackface and dressed their minstrels in 18th-century court dress. From 1880 the traditionalists complained loudly about such changes. A more significant change was the entry of blacks themselves into the form, first with Haverly's Coloured Minstrels. By adopting such stereotypes as the loyal uncle, warmhearted mammy, and shiftless lazybones, and by adding female performers, they perpetuated the notion that such caricatures were true to life.

Nevertheless, the minstrel show was one of the few truly indigenous American entertainments and made a

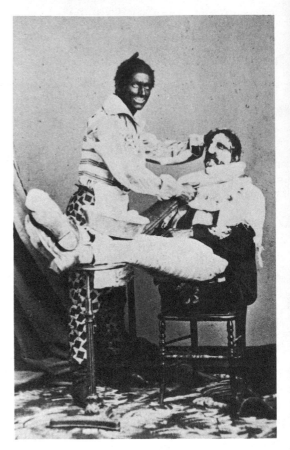

Dan Bryant, a blackface Figaro, shaving Eph Horn in an American minstrel act of the 1860s.

profound impression world-wide. American popular music and theatre remained influenced by it; many outstanding performers, such as **Eddie Cantor**, **Al Jolson** and **Bert Williams**, received their training in it. Great Britain rapidly took to minstrelsy, sending its own troupes as far afield as India and Australia. St James's Hall, Piccadilly, was the capital of English minstrelsy 1859–1904; and Moore and Burgess, the Mohawks, and Sam Hague's the principal troupes. It bequeathed blackface artists like **G. H. Chirgwin**, Eugene Stratton and G. H. Elliott to the music-hall and the seaside pier, where the stereotypes were even more remote from Afro-American reality.   LS

See: H. Nathan, *Dan Emmett and the Rise of Early Negro Minstrelsy*, Norman, O, 1962; H. Reynolds, *Minstrel Memories*, London, 1928; R. Toll, *Blacking Up. The Minstrel Show in Nineteenth Century America*, London, 1974; C. Wittke, *Tambo and Bones*, Durham, NC, 1930.

Mira de Amescua, Antonio (1574–1644) Spanish playwright of the school of **Lope de Vega**, showing developments towards the drama of **Calderón**. Of Andalusian origin, he became a priest and later held a chaplaincy at Granada, but spent rather more time in literary circles in Madrid. He wrote religious and historical plays with a moral seriousness in some ways reminiscent of **Alarcón**, but inferior in construction. His verse style is between the clarity of Lope de Vega and the cultured style of Calderón.

His best play is *El esclavo del demonio* (*The Devil's Slave*, before 1612), foreshadowing Calderón's *El mágico prodigioso*. Equally fine in the two-part *La próspera y la adversa fortuna de don Alvaro de Luna* (*The Rise and Fall of Alvaro de Luna*), a **comedia de privanza** on the 15th-century favourite.

He also wrote a number of fine comedies, such as *La fénix de Salamanca* (*The Phoenix of Salamanca*).   CL

Miracle plays see Medieval drama in Europe

Mirren, Helen (1946–   ) British actress who was discovered through the **National Youth Theatre** for whom she played, at the age of 19, a fiery Cleopatra in *Antony and Cleopatra*. She joined the **Royal Shakespeare Company** where she was chosen for such roles as Cressida in *Troilus and Cressida* and **Strindberg**'s Miss Julie, which demanded her voluptuous good looks and capacity to convey a wayward temperament. She was, however, too intelligent to be easily typecast as a temptress and in 1972 joined **Peter Brook**'s International Centre of Theatre Research, touring North African desert villages in a mainly improvised story, *The Conference of Birds*. She returned to the RSC to play Lady Macbeth in 1974, while her first major part in a contemporary play came when she played an alcoholic lead singer in **David Hare**'s *Teeth 'n' Smiles* (1975). She also appeared in **Ben Travers**'s *The Bed Before Yesterday* (1975) and **Brian Friel**'s *The Faith Healer* (1981), but her maturity as an actress has been distinguished by her performances in major classic roles for a variety of companies, in the title role in **Webster**'s *The Duchess of Malfi* (1980) for the **Royal Exchange Company** in Manchester, as Cleopatra in the RSC's studio *Antony and Cleopatra* (1983). She has appeared in many films.   JE

Mistinguett (Jeanne-Marie Bourgeois) (1873–1956) Fabled queen of the Parisian music-hall and revue, who escaped her middle-class upbringing by going on the stage, first as Miss Helyett, then Miss Tinguette, and finally Mistinguett. Her debut at the Trianon-Concert (1885) was followed by a long tenure at the Eldorado (1897–1907). Her double-jointed mimicry made up for her thin voice, as she moved from singing to eccentric comedy to revue. The success of the 'valse chaloupée', danced with **Max Dearly** at the **Moulin-Rouge** (1909), made her a star, and she confirmed her status with the 'valse renversante' (1912) with **Maurice Chevalier**, who was for a time her partner, lover and model for all her subsequent leading men. From 1919 to 1923 she flourished in tours of both Americas, introducing 'My Man'. When she appeared in *Ça c'est Paris* (1926), Colette called her a 'national treasure' and **Cocteau** described her 'poignant voice' as the symbol of Paris. Her shapely legs and buck teeth were godsends for caricaturists, and even at the end of her long career, audiences gladly accepted her in the role of a little flower girl.   LS

Mitchell, Julian (1854–1926) American director. After an early career as a performer, Mitchell served as assistant director on several of **Charles Hoyt**'s farce comedies. He directed a number of burlesques for **Weber** and **Fields**, after which he turned to the staging of elaborate comic operas such as *The Wizard of Oz* (1903) and *Babes in Toyland* (1903). From 1907 through 1914 he directed the *Ziegfeld Follies*, and is credited with creating the chorus of beautiful, lively, and individualized girls that became the hallmark of those shows. He continued to be in demand as a director of musicals up to the time of his death.   MK

Mitchell, Langdon Elwyn (1862–1935) American playwright. Son of the eminent physician and novelist Silas Weir Mitchell, he is principally known for one play, *The New York Idea* (1906). This witty satire on easy divorce and easy marriage, defined as 'three parts love and seven parts forgiveness of sin', prompted critics to call him 'the American **Shaw**'. 'What I wanted to satirize', Mitchell once wrote, 'was the extreme frivolity of our American life.' Written for **Minnie Maddern Fiske**, it was revived by Grace George (1915), and was produced by **Max Reinhardt** in Berlin (1916).

He also wrote *In the Season* (1893), *Betty Sharpe* (1899), an adaptation of *Vanity Fair* and a vehicle for Mrs Fiske, *The Kreutzer Sonata* (1906), an adaptation from the Yiddish of **Jacob Gordin**, *The New Marriage* (1911), and *Major Pendennis* (1916), adapted from Thackeray's novel.

Mitchell was educated at St Paul's, studied in Dresden and Paris, attended law school at Harvard and Columbia, was admitted to the New York bar in 1886, and in 1892 married the English actress Marion Lea who appeared in *The New York Idea*.   RM

Mitchell, Loften (1919–   ) Afro-American playwright and theatre historian. Mitchell studied playwriting with John Gassner and had three of his early plays produced in Harlem before gaining recognition with *A Land Beyond the River* (1957), a drama based on the life of the Rev. Dr Joseph DeLaine who fought to end discrimination in public schools. Mitchell co-wrote the book for *Ballad for Bimshire* (1963) and the freedom pageant *Ballad for the Winter Soldiers* (1964). Alone, he wrote the television documentary *Tell Pharaoh* (1963), dramatized the **Bert Williams** story in *Star of the Morning* (published 1971), and also wrote the successful *Bubbling Brown Sugar* (1976). His informal history *Black Drama* (1967) and *Voices of the Black Theatre* (1975) chronicle the experiences of Afro-Americans in the American theatre.   EGH

Mitchell, William (1798–1856) English-born actor, playwright and theatre manager. A distinguished comedian from London and English provincial theatres since 1831, Mitchell appeared first at the National Theatre in New York in 1836. His particular achievement was his management of **Mitchell's Olympic** in New York from 9 December 1839 to 9 March 1850, the year of his retirement. Advertising the production of 'Vaudevilles, Burlesques, Extravaganzas, Farces, Etc.', Mitchell made the Olympic a popular success when other theatres were failing. As an actor Mitchell was a favourite as Vincent Crummles in a farce created from **Dickens**'s *Nicholas Nickleby* entitled *The Savage and the Maiden*. A staff of actor–playwrights – Henry Horncastle, Charles Walcot, Alexander Allen, **Benjamin A. Baker** – provided him with novelties. *1840; or, Crummles in Search of Novelty* was repeated in *1841* and *1842*. Catching the topic of the day was the clue to Mitchell's success. When **Boucicault**'s *London Assurance* came to New York, Mitchell responded with *Olympic Insurance*; he burlesqued Dickens's visit in *Boz* and the **Edwin Forrest–William Macready** feud in three sketches; he starred in and wrote *Billy Taylor*, a local extravaganza. The greatest event at Mitchell's Olympic, however, was Baker's *A Glance at New York*, 1848, with Mose the fire b'hoy.   WJM

Mitchell's Olympic 442–4 Broadway, New York City [Architect: Calvin Pollard]. In 1837, Willard and Blake opened the Olympic patterned after **Madame Vestris**'s famous London **Olympic** both in physical structure and policy. They presented comedies, farces, vaudevilles and musical pieces. Since the city was surfeited with theatres and entertainment, they quickly lost their theatre. In 1839, despite hard times, **William 'Billy' Mitchell** revived the fortunes of the house with a combination of his own talents and managerial prowess. His reduced prices and his diet of light comic entertainment and burlesques made it the most popular theatre in town. When he retired in 1850, the playhouse passed to other managements and was used briefly as a minstrel hall and a German-language theatre. In 1852, it was converted to business uses and two years later, the structure burned to the ground.   MCH

Mitterwurzer, Friedrich (1844–97) German actor. An unusually restless man, Mitterwurzer was hired on three different occasions by the Vienna **Burgtheater** – 1871 to 1874, 1875 to 1880, and 1894 to 1897. He was renowned for his ability to play what **Laube** called 'broken characters'. His staccato acting, which revealed inconsistencies in characters, went against the general idealist interpretation of classic roles, but was eminently suited for **Ibsen**. Mitterwurzer was a celebrated Consul Bernick, Hjalmar Ekdal, and Alfred Allmers. Some historians claim his acting foreshadowed expressionism.   SW

Mnouchkine, Ariane (1934–) French theatre director known for her successful use of *création collective* (collaboratively devised productions) and shared responsibility within her theatre group the **Théâtre du Soleil**. After studies at the Universities of Paris and Oxford, where she was involved in student theatre, she travelled to the Far East, returning to found the Soleil in 1964. Inspired by the ideas of **Copeau** and the work of **Vilar**, she sought to extend research into the theatrical resources and implications of a people's theatre. Like **Artaud** she wanted to use the whole range of expressive means available to theatre but like **Brecht** she wanted to develop an idiom appropriate for dealing with social process as well as private drama. The choice of **Wesker**'s *Kitchen* (1967) was a first move in this direction but it was only after the upheavals of 1968 that she felt the group must create its own plays. Her influence was strongly evident in the recourse to popular clown traditions in *The Clowns* (1969). But she felt this had been essentially a set of individual creations. She wanted a *collective* creation, something the company achieved in *1789* (1970), *1793* (1972) and

L'Age d'Or (*The Golden Age*, 1975). After this, she drew on her father's experience as a film director to make a remarkable film of **Molière**, in which she confronted the problems of how a theatre company can live and work together. She returned to theatre production with her adaptation of Klaus Mann's *Mephisto* (1979) and then embarked on a cycle of **Shakespeare** plays: *Richard II* (1981), *Twelfth Night* (1982) and *Henry IV Pt 1* (1984). These were followed by an epic play about Cambodia by Hélène Cixous: *Norodom Sihanouk* (1985) in which similar production methods to those employed for the Shakespeare plays, in particular a strong influence of oriental theatre, were brought to bear on contemporary reality.   DB

Mochalov, Pavel Stepanovich (1800–48) The son of a former serf actor, he became the 'Russian **Kean**', the greatest Russian tragedian of the early 19th century. In the debate over the question of genius versus craft, his inspired but uneven performances at Moscow's Maly Theatre were favoured by merchants, students and literati such as **Shchepkin**, **Pushkin**, Herzen, Belinsky and **Semyonova** over those of his St Petersburg rival, the coolly technical tragedian **Karatygin**. He was hindered in his career by a lack of discipline engendered in part by his father, a tendency to play to his audiences at the expense of the role, and by a shrewish wife who drove him to alcoholism and self-destructiveness. He paid little attention to costumes and makeup, relying instead upon the power of his imagination and his physical attributes to transform him. Although melodrama and neoclassical tragedy by **Kotzebue**, **Voltaire**, **Ozerov**, **Polevoi** and **Kukolnik** were staples of his repertoire, he succeeded in the roles of **Schiller**'s Don Carlos (1829), Karl and Franz Moor (1828 and 1844) and Mortimer (1835) and as **Shakespeare**'s Othello (1837), Lear (1839) and Richard III (1839). The high and low ends of this spectrum were his romantic Hamlet (1837), much praised by Belinsky, in Polevoi's translation and Romeo which he played at the age of 41. He thought himself miscast as Chatsky in the original Moscow production of *Woe from Wit* (1831). Mochalov was a revolutionary romantic icon, much loved and admired by the people, in the reactionary Nikolayen era. His tours helped to promote Shakespeare and Schiller in the provinces. He also wrote a romantic drama, *The Circassian Girl* (produced 1840), some lyric poetry and a theoretical treatise on acting (published 1953).   SG

Modena, Gustavo (1803–61) Italian actor whose career is inextricably linked with the Italian struggle for independence. After studying law at Bologna he worked in a number of acting troupes before forming his own company, in association with his father Giacomo, in 1829. Political events obliged him to leave Italy in 1832, and he spent several years in exile in Switzerland, France, Belgium and England. In London, under the patronage of Mazzini, and to advance the national cause, he gave a public reading from Dante's *Divina Commedia* at the Queen's Theatre. In 1843, after his return to Italy, he formed a company of young actors that included **Tommaso Salvini** and **Luigi Bellotti-Bon**, and through them his insistence on a natural, unemphatic style and uncluttered scenic decoration profoundly affected stage presentation in

Italy for several decades. He was a champion too of using the stage as a means of debating social and political issues. Off stage his social commitment involved him in the 1848 Risorgimento. The acting roles with which he was best associated were the stock pieces in the mid-19th-century Italian actor's repertoire: **Alfieri**'s Saul, **Delavigne**'s Louis XI and **Dumas**'s Kean. He made an unsuccessful attempt, in a much adapted version, to introduce Italian spectators to **Shakespeare**'s Othello; the failure of this venture in 1847 led him to abandon his plan to do *Hamlet*.   LR

Modjeska, Helena see Modrzejewska, Helena

Modrzejewska, Helena (1840–1909) Polish, and later, as Modjeska, American actress known for Shakespearian roles. She began her professional career in 1865 with touring companies. Recognized as a major talent in *Adrienne Lecouvreur* (**Scribe**/Legouvé), she became a star with the Warsaw Theatre (1869–76). Exceptional beauty and ability to move audiences brought her international success. In 1876 she emigrated to the United States, and from 1877 toured in America and England with her own company, returning to Poland for guest appearances. Throughout a career lasting until 1907, she played 260 roles, including **Schiller**'s Maria Stuart, **Dumas** *fils*'s Marguerite Gautier, and Nora in *A Doll's House*, which she introduced in America in 1883. Her autobiography is *Memories and Impressions* (1910).   DG

Moeller, Philip (1880–1958) American director, producer, and playwright. Born in New York, Moeller graduated from Columbia University and joined the **Washington Square Players** in the winter of 1914. His one-act plays, *Two Blind Beggars and One Less Blind* and *Helena's Husband* were produced by the group and attracted critical attention. But Moeller made his reputation as a director and was regarded by **Lawrence Langner** as one of the most brilliant directors of comedy in this country. A founder and director of the **Theatre Guild**, he staged their first production, *Bonds of Interest*, in 1919. He was especially adept in directing the plays of **Eugene O'Neill**. His Guild credits include: *Strange Interlude* (1928), *Dynamo* (1929), *Mourning Becomes Electra* (1931), and *Ah, Wilderness!* (1933). **Brooks Atkinson** called his direction of *Strange Interlude* a 'tremendous achievement' because he found a way to distinguish between the speeches and the asides. Atkinson also praised Moeller for finding the 'exact tempo and style' in *Mourning Becomes Electra*. Moeller thought of himself as an inspirational director. After directing films for RKO Radio in the early 1930s, he went into virtual retirement.   TLM

Mogulesco, Sigmund (*fl.* 1880–90) Rumanian-born actor of the Yiddish theatre who started his career with **Goldfaden**'s company before moving to America in 1886. A natural clown, he specialized in comic roles besides being an accomplished musician.   AB

Moiseiwitsch, Tanya (1914–) British set and costume designer noted for her collaborations with director **Tyrone Guthrie** and the bold thrust stage and innovative auditorium she designed for the Shakespeare Festival Theatre in Stratford, Ontario (1957) and the similar **Guthrie Theatre** in Minneapolis (1963). Moiseiwitsch began her career in London in 1934. The following year she went to the **Abbey Theatre** in Dublin where she designed over 50 productions through 1939. She subsequently designed for the **Old Vic** beginning in 1944 and at the Shakespeare Memorial Theatre in Stratford-upon-Avon from 1949, as well as commercial theatre in London and theatres in Italy, the USA and Australia. She is most closely associated with the plays of **Shakespeare**, but notable productions include *Oedipus Rex* at Ontario (1954; film 1957), and *The House of Atreus* in Minneapolis (1968) both of which contain what is perhaps the most successful use of masks in the 20th century. Beginning with her work at the Abbey, Moiseiwitsch's designs have been typified by simple, direct, presentational sets that embodied the visual metaphor of the play. Since she generally designed costumes as well there was a strong visual unity to her productions. With the polygonal, stepped stages at Ontario and Minneapolis that jutted into the steeply banked auditoriums, Moiseiwitsch was able to eliminate most scenery and provide a space in which her highly textured costumes could be sculpted by light.   AA

Moisiu, Aleksandër (Alexander Moissi) (1879–1935) Albanian actor, born 2 April 1879 in Trieste, the youngest child of émigré Albanian forwarding agent Moissi Moisiu and his Italian-Albanian wife Amalia (née De Rada). He had his first speaking role in Prague in 1902, and in 1904 he joined **Max Reinhardt**'s company in Berlin, where he quickly distinguished himself for his deep, psychologi-

Aleksandër Moisiu as the Beggar (*The Salzburg Great Theatre of The World* by Hofmannsthal).

deep, psychological interpretations of the roles he played, for his expressive, melodious voice, and for his mobile features and body. He normally performed without makeup. Fluent in English, French, German, Greek, Italian and Spanish, he attained international fame, performing in Argentina, Austria, Britain, Czechoslovakia, Egypt, France, Germany, Greece, Holland, Hungary, Italy, Japan, Mexico, Rumania, Russia, Sweden, Switzerland and the United States. He also appeared between 1910 and 1935 in 12 films, including three sound films. He was the author of a play about Napoleon, *The Prisoner*, first performed in Hamburg. His most famous stage roles were those of **Shakespeare**'s Hamlet and Othello, **Goethe**'s Faust, **Ibsen**'s Oswald (in *Ghosts*), **Shaw**'s Dubedat (in *The Doctor's Dilemma*) and **Tolstoi**'s Fedya (in *The Living Corpse*). He married in 1919 the German actress Johann Terwin (1884–1962). Becoming an Albanian citizen in 1934, he died in Vienna 22 March 1935. In 1962 he was posthumously awarded the highest Albanian decoration in the artistic field, that of 'People's Artist'; a theatre in Durrës (Albania) is named after him.   WBB

Molander, Olof (1892–1966) Swedish director, who accomplished far-reaching reforms in his country's perceptions of direction, scenography and acting style, particularly during his leadership of **Dramaten** during the 1930s. Compared with those of his contemporary **Per Lindberg**, his innovations were more carefully considered and ultimately long-lasting. An early admirer of **Edward Gordon Craig**, he stressed the importance of the director's serving the text by coordinating scenography and acting around its central idea. Molander established the predominant mid-century Swedish approach to **Strindberg**, particularly such late plays as *A Dream Play*, *The Ghost Sonata* and *The Great Highway*, by rejecting **Reinhardt**'s forcefully expressionistic style in favour of a blend of fantasy and selective realism that stressed the plays' autobiographical content. Dramaten's international reputation in the staging of **O'Neill** (including several European and world premieres) owed much to Molander's powerful productions of *Mourning Becomes Electra*, *The Iceman Cometh* and *A Moon for the Misbegotten*.   HL

Molière (Jean-Baptiste Poquelin) (1622–73) French actor-manager and dramatist, one of the theatre's greatest comic artists. Well-educated son of a prosperous Paris merchant, he forsook the family's upholstery business at the age of 21 to throw in his lot with a group of friends and young professional actors and found a new theatre company, the Illustre-Théâtre. Unable to compete with the established **Hôtel de Bourgogne** and **Marais**, it went bankrupt within two years and in 1645, after a short spell in debtor's prison, Molière left Paris with **Madeleine Béjart** and other erstwhile colleagues to join an itinerant company led by the actor Charles Dufresne. There followed almost 13 years of constant peregrination in the southern provinces, a period of strenuous but invaluable apprenticeship which allowed him to discover and refine his gifts as a comic actor and to develop into a resourceful company leader. During this period he also wrote his first plays, *L'Etourdi* (*The Blunderer*, 1653), and *Le Dépit Amoureux* (*Lovers' Quarrel*, 1656), and the brief, partly improvised farces *La Jalousie du Barbouillé* (*The Jealousy*

of Barbouillé) and *Le Médecin Volant* (*The Flying Doctor*), inspired by the work of *commedia* troupes encountered on his travels and tailormade for his fellow actors.

In 1658 he brought them north and through the patronage of the king's brother secured a command performance before Louis XIV comprising **Corneille**'s *Nicomède* and his own farce *Le Docteur Amoureux* (*The Doctor in Love*). The young king was so amused by the latter that he granted Molière the use of the **Petit-Bourbon** in alternation with the *commedia* company of **Fiorilli** and it became the scene of his first successes with the Parisian public, *Les Précieuses Ridicules* (*The Affected Ladies*, 1659) and *Sganarelle, ou le Cocu Imaginaire* (*Sganarelle, or The Imaginary Cuckold*, 1660). Following its demolition Molière was installed at the refurbished **Palais-Royal**, where in 1661 the failure of his 'heroic comedy' *Dom Garcie de Navarre* was quickly redeemed by *L'Ecole des Maris* (*The School for Husbands*) and by his first 'comédie-ballet', *Les Fâcheux* (*The Bores*), initially performed at Fouquet's residence at Vaux. In the following year the 40-year-old Molière married the teenage **Armande Béjart** and produced his first great comedy of character, *The School for Wives*, a reflection on the role of women and the incompatibility of youth and age. So huge a success did it enjoy both in Paris and at court that it provoked accusations of immorality from churchmen and its author found himself scurrilously pilloried in the plays of jealous rivals. Molière counter-attacked vigorously and amusingly in *La Critique de l'Ecole des Femmes* and *L'Impromptu de Versailles* (both 1663) and emerged from this first skirmish with his enemies more securely placed than ever, the king even agreeing to act as godfather to his firstborn in 1664. The same year brought commissions for royal entertainments, *Le Mariage Forcé* (*The Forced Marriage*) at the Louvre and *La Princesse d'Elide* at Versailles, while in 1665 as a tangible mark of this favour Molière's company was awarded a regular pension from the crown and took the title of the 'Troupe du Roy'. Thereafter Molière, with **Lully**, became the accredited purveyor of divertissements to the court: *L'Amour Médecin* (*Love's the Best Doctor*, 1665), *Mélicerte* (1666), *La Pastorale Comique* (1667), *Le Sicilien, ou l'Amour Peintre* (*The Sicilian, or Love Makes the Painter*, 1667), *Monsieur de Pourceaugnac* (1669), *Les Amants Magnifiques* (*The Magnificent Lovers*, 1670), *The Bourgeois Gentleman* (1670) and *La Comtesse d'Escarbagnas* (1671), mostly couched in the form of 'comédie-ballets', and *Psyché* (1671), a 'tragédie-ballet' written in collaboration with Corneille and **Quinault**, were all initially performed at royal *fêtes* before being transferred with modifications to his public theatre in Paris.

Meanwhile the comedies intended for the Palais-Royal had encountered a mixed reception and in some cases powerful opposition. His study of religious hypocrisy, *Tartuffe*, after its premiere at Versailles in 1664 was withheld from public performance until a revised version was acted once in 1667, only to be denounced for its impiety by the church and proscribed by the Parlement, the ban not being finally lifted until 1669. *Don Juan* (1665), too, doubtless because it was considered to present its cynical, free-thinking hero in too favourable a light, was abruptly withdrawn despite public success and never re-staged in Molière's lifetime. *The Misanthrope* (1666) was received with only cool interest, while *The Miser* (1668) was an outright failure and *Les Fourberies de Scapin* (*The Tricks of Scapin*, 1671) little more. Contrariwise, there was an enthusiastic response to *A Doctor in Spite of Himself* (1666) and *Amphitryon* (1668), though of the later comedies of character only *The Learned Ladies* (1672) could be accounted an unequivocal success. At the same time Molière's over-exertion was taking its toll, illness having already forced him to give up acting for several months in 1667. His last play proved to be *The Imaginary Invalid* (1673), another 'comédie-ballet' evidently designed for presentation at court but actually created at the Palais-Royal, presumably in the wake of some fall from royal grace. During the fourth performance Molière, ironically playing the hypochondriac Argan, was seized with a genuine coughing fit and died later that night.

In the course of 14 years of ceaseless activity in Paris as performer and playwright Molière transformed French comedy. His comic method, mastered during the preliminary years of touring, is an intensely physical one in that it has little recourse to technical resources and gives full scope to the prowess of the actor, aided only by costume, an almost emblematic use of personal properties and a skilful patterning of dialogue which encourages specific movement and visual display on stage. With these deceptively simple means Molière's text breathes new life into the traditional situations of French farce and the stock masks and devices of the Italian *commedia*, by which he was so deeply impressed, to produce a satiric commentary on the society of his time and a penetrating exploration of eternal human foibles and obsessive attitudes of mind. In his hands their absurdity never ceases to amuse but equally their potential for mischief and harm is clearly perceived by a comedian of genius whose view of life is imbued with a sense of philosophical resignation. DR

Molina, Tirso de (1580–1648) (Gabriel de Téllez) Spanish playwright of the Golden Age, ranking behind only **Calderón** and **Lope de Vega** in this period. Little is known of his life, and nothing of his parentage or birth. He joined the Mercedarian Order in 1600, and presumably received his education from them. He spent some time in Toledo, two years in the West Indies, and lived in Madrid from 1621 to 1625. His best plays were probably written from about 1612 to 1625, very few being written after this date. In 1625 he was exiled by his order to their remote house at Trujillo, and forbidden to write plays. He returned to Toledo and to Madrid in 1634 after being promoted in the Order, where he published four volumes of plays in two years. In 1640 he was again banished, this time to Soria, where he was made prior in 1645, dying at Almazán three years later.

Tirso claimed to have written 300 plays by 1621, but about 80 remain today. He wrote many fine plays, well constructed with powerfully drawn characters. In particular he is noted for his portrayal of strong-minded heroines. These ladies are remarkably frank and outspoken for the period in their attitudes to love, often relentlessly pursuing the man who has abandoned them after seducing them on the promise of marriage. In other cases they are man-hating Amazons who are eventually tamed by love.

Amongst many high-spirited, rather unbridled comedies, two set in the Court are *Don Gil de las calzas verdes* (*Don Gil in Green Breeches*) and *El vergonzoso en palacio* (*The Shy Man at Court*). He also wrote numerous *capa y espada* plays, including *Marta la piadosa* (*Pious Martha*) whose heroine feigns an attack of piety in order to avoid an unwelcome match and continue seeing her lover, and *Por el sótano y el torno* (*Through Basement and Hatch*) in which a lady tries to preserve the honour of her brazen sister.

Tirso wrote few plays dealing with the theme of adultery and honour, apart from *El celoso prudente* (*Jealous but Prudent*) in which the protagonist learns just in time that his wife is innocent. Among his freely treated historical plays is a trilogy on the fortunes of the Pizarro family, and in these and other plays he is critical of authority, apparently making veiled attacks on Philip IV's favourite Olivares in *Tanto es lo de más como lo de menos* (*Too Much is as Bad as Too Little*), which may have led to his exile in 1625. Another fine historical play, *La prudencia en la mujer* (*Prudence in Women*) portrays the efforts of a young widowed queen to keep the throne for her young son.

Tirso wrote several serious plays based on Old Testament stories including *La venganza de Tamar* (*Tamar's Vengeance*) and *La mujer que manda en casa* (*The Woman who Rules the Roost*) on the story of Jezabel.

Perhaps his most important play is *El burlador de Sevilla y convidado de piedra* (*The Trickster of Seville and the Stone Guest*), the first great treatment of the Don Juan Tenorio legend, without the comic or sympathetic treatment of later versions. Equally fine and showing the other side of the coin is *El condenado por desconfiado* (*Damned for Lack of Faith*) which contrasts a great sinner saved by last-minute repentance and a saintly hermit who despairs and becomes a brigand, and is damned when he refuses to repent. CL

Molloy, Michael Joseph (1917–) Irish playwright. Abandoned training for the priesthood through illness, then farmed near his birthplace. His foremost works are his first play, *The Old Road* (1943), *The Visiting House* (1946), *The King of Friday's Men* (1948), *The Wood of the Whispering* and *The Paddy Pedlar* (1953).

The King of Friday's Men has claims to greatness. Set in western Ireland in 1787, it mourns the passage of a feudal *modus vivendi*, freshly evoking a bygone world, ignoring neither the landlord's careless autocracy nor, among the peasants' thriving folkways, the savage sport of mass shillelagh fights.

Molloy deals less certainly with the contemporary residue of those folkways, but *The Visiting House* effectively dramatizes the dying institution where country districts were regaled with songs and stories, real life in the play having to compete with the Master's beguiling games and eccentric accomplices. Molloy's dialect speech at its fluent best carries his often knotty plots. Though more restricted by his region than either **Synge** or **Fitzmaurice**, Molloy is the last remarkable exponent of their folk drama. DM

Molnár, Ferenc (1878–1952) Hungarian playwright, born in Budapest. He gained an international reputation for his plays which exhibit technical mastery and sophisticated dialogue, and which depict the minor pitfalls that threaten but never seriously damage the bourgeois morality of his characters. His use of light and clever satire is tempered by sincere sentiment and pathos. Many of his plays, including *The Devil* (1907), *Liliom* (1909), *The Guardsman* (1910), *The Swan* (1920), and *The Play's the Thing* (1926), were produced in Vienna, London, Paris, and on Broadway, as well as in Hungary. In 1928 a volume, *Twenty-five Plays*, by Molnár appeared in English. *The Play's the Thing* is continually revived the world over, and the famous musical *Carousel* (1945) by **Rodgers** and **Hammerstein** is based on *Liliom*. EB

Moncrieff, Gladys (1892–1976) Australian musical comedy star. As a child in Queensland she sang with her parents' travelling picture show, and later in suburban vaudeville. She appeared in musicals with the **J. C. Williamson** management, first starring in *Katinka* (1918), and until 1959 appeared in numerous musicals and operetta, including *The Maid of the Mountains* (1921), the London production of *The Blue Mazurka* (1926), *Rio Rita*, in which she toured Australia in 1928–30, the Australian musical *Collit's Inn* (1933), and various productions of *The Merry Widow*. To her Australian public she was affectionately known as 'our Glad'. MW

Moncrieff, William Thomas (1794–1857) English playwright and theatre manager, lessee at various times of the Queen's, **Astley**'s Amphitheatre, the Coburg, Vauxhall Gardens and the City Theatre. Moncrieff was a hack writer who turned out plays to suit the time. Adaptations of novels by Scott, **Bulwer** and **Dickens** were entrusted to him by managers eager to cash in on the latest vogue. *The Lear of Private Life* (1820), from a novel by Mrs Opie, has some interest as a 19th-century domestication of **Shakespeare**. *The Shipwreck of the Medusa* (1820) exploited the excitement created by Géricault's picture, which was being exhibited in Bullock's Egyptian Hall in 1820 (nearly 50,000 people paid· to see it). *Tom and Jerry* (1821) was a particularly zestful adaptation of Pierce Egan's documentary novel, *Life in London*. *The Cataract of the Ganges* (1823) was the sensation of its season at **Drury Lane**, less for the script than for the use of David's horse troupe and the lavish sets (there was real water in the cataract for the finale) of **Clarkson Stanfield** and David Roberts. Moncrieff, who wrote over 100 plays, was evidently willing to accept the modest standing of contemporary playwright. PT

Monk, Meredith (1942–) American choreographer, composer, performance artist, and leading innovator in the so-called 'Next Wave' since the mid-1960s and her association with the Judson Dance Theatre (New York City). Her dances have evolved into multimedia, nonverbal theatre pieces, such as *Vessel* (1971–2) and *Quarry* (1975–6), both termed 'opera epics'. In the early and mid-70s she also created several chamber theatre works: the 'travelogue' series (*Paris, Chacon, Venice/Milan*) in collaboration with Ping Chong and the 'archaeology' pieces (*Small Scroll, Anthology, The Plateau Series, Recent Ruins*). In the late 1970s she began to concentrate on musical composition and performance, having begun to 'distrust the theatre a little bit', although by the early 1980s two multimedia theatre pieces had been added to her canon: *Specimen Days* (1981) and *The Games* (1983), the latter commissioned by **Peter Stein**'s Schaubuhne repertory theatre in West Berlin, with its USA premiere at the Brooklyn Academy of Music's Next Wave Festival the following year. DBW

Montansier, Mlle (Marguerite Brunet) (1730–1820) French actress who forsook the boards to pursue a long and colourful career in theatre management. Having opened a playhouse at Versailles in 1777 she was invited to present performances at court and, with the help of her able business-manager and devoted lover Neuville, another ex-actor, proceeded to widen her base by acquiring a chain of provincial theatres before establishing herself in Paris in 1790 at a theatre in the **Palais-Royal**, to which she gave her own name. After the Revolution she presided over a salon frequented by literary and theatrical personalities and built a large new theatre under the name of the Théâtre National. Always suspect for her previous Royalist associations, she was finally denounced in 1793, imprisoned and narrowly missed the guillotine. Despite this and severe financial setbacks she persisted, opening the Salle Olympique in 1801 and the celebrated Théâtre des Variétés on the boulevard Montmartre in 1807 while running her Palais-Royal theatre as a house for acrobats and puppeteers. Predictably her resilient career was later to become the stuff of several popular plays. DR

Montdory (Guillaume Des Gilberts) (1594–1653/4) French actor-manager, the most powerful tragedian of his day. First heard of as a member of **Valleran**'s company in 1612, he spent more than a decade touring the northern provinces and Holland in the plays of **Hardy** before bringing a new company to Paris, where he played in a number of tennis court theatres in succession but settled for good at the **Marais** in 1634, thanks to the munificence of **Cardinal Richelieu**. It was here, playing the central role of Don Rodrigue, that he presented *Le Cid* with huge success in January 1637, having already created *Mélite* and other early plays of **Corneille**, but his triumph was to be short-lived for in August of that year he was seized by a partial paralysis of the body and tongue while playing Herod in **Tristan**'s *La Mariane* (*Mariamne*) and was obliged to retire from the stage, whereupon Richelieu awarded him a handsome pension. This mishap suggests that there was an element of rant or physical exaggeration in his playing, but with his strong voice and well-proportioned physique he must have possessed an impressive presence on stage for no less a critic than **d'Aubignac** called him 'the greatest actor of our time'. DR

Monteiro, Luís de Sttau (1926–) Portuguese playwright. Also a left-wing journalist and novelist, Sttau Monteiro came to the theatre in 1961 with *Felizmente Há Luar* (*Luckily We Still Have the Moonlight*) to attack contemporary abuses and institutions in a historical drama based on the Portuguese people's struggle against the 'liberating' English rule of Beresford in the period immediately after the Peninsular War campaigns in Portugal. *A Estátua* (*The Statue*, 1966) ridicules the hero-worship sought by and accorded to Salazar, while the *Auto da Barca do Motor Fora da Borda*, of the same year, updates **Vicente**'s *Auto da Barca do Inferno* by providing the boat with an outboard motor and redirecting the satire against latter-day capitalists. LK

Montez, Lola (Maria Dolores Eliza Rosanna Gilbert) (1818–61) Irish adventuress, who, when her first marriage failed, went on stage as a dancer (London, 1843), performing in Europe, America and Australia. Her beauty and charm compensated for her lack of talent and musical sense. Her liaison with Ludwig I of Bavaria (1847–8) culminated in his forced abdication, and she came to the United States, making her New York debut (1851) in *Betley the Tyrolean*; a biographical play, *Lola Montes [sic] in Bavaria* by C. P. T. Ware (1852), capitalized on her sensational past. She toured to the Gold Rush country, performing a spider dance that shocked San Francisco audiences, and took the child actress **Lotta Crabtree** under her tutelage. After 1856, she appeared as a spiritualist and lecturer, speaking on fashion, gallantry and Roman Catholicism. She underwent a religious conversion and became a recluse after 1859.   LS

Montfleury (Zacharie Jacob) (c. 1600–67) French actor who first appeared at the **Hôtel de Bourgogne** in about 1638 and remained there until the end of his career, excelling both in tragedy and comedy, according to **Chappuzeau**. Despite this testimony, his excessive corpulence and capacity for mannered, self-indulgent acting attracted the wicked jibes of Cyrano de Bergerac and more particularly **Molière** in *L'Impromptu de Versailles* (1663), where he is described as 'roaring' his lines and signalling when the audience is to applaud. This provoked a bitter exchange with Molière, whom he publicly accused of having married his own daughter. In reality Montfleury may have been guilty of no more than an exaggeration of the rhetorical delivery then associated with tragedy, but he certainly seems to have been a physically assertive performer to judge by the reputed manner of his death, occasioned by bursting a blood vessel while playing Oreste in **Racine**'s *Andromaque* (1667). In his one play, *La Mort d'Asdrubal* (*The Death of Hasdrubal*, 1647), he wrote an inferior tragedy with a leading part for himself.   DR

Montherlant, Henry de (1896–1972) French writer. Montherlant came to the theatre late in life, his first big success being *La Reine Morte* (*The Dead Queen*) at the **Comédie-Française** in 1942. This was inspired by Guevara's *Reinar depués de morir* and was the first of a number of plays in which Montherlant attempted to celebrate the values of the Spanish Golden Age. A great literary stylist, as his novels show, Montherlant was never interested in theatre production, seeing drama as above all literary and psychological. His better plays attempt to deal with religious subjects along French neoclassical lines, e.g. *Le Maître de Santiago* (1948), *Port-Royal* (1954). His one generally acknowledged masterpiece is *La Ville dont le Prince est un Enfant* (*The Town whose Prince is a Child*). This semi-autobiographical play was written in 1951 but he did not allow a production until 1967 (directed by Michel). It depicts the passionate relationships between boys and priests in a Catholic seminary with considerable truthfulness, restraint and force.   DB

Monti, Ricardo (1944–) Argentine playwright. As a participant in the vanguard theatre of the 1970s, he sought new forms for exposing old problems of the bourgeoisie through symbols and allegories. For the Laboratory Theatre he wrote *Una noche con el señor Magnus e Hijos* (*A Night with Mr Magnus and Sons*, 1970) and for the Payró Theatre in 1971, *Historia tendenciosa de la clase media argentina* (*Tendentious History of the Argentine Middle Class*). Later plays include *Visita* (*Visit*, 1977) and *Marathón* (*Marathon*, 1980). As a workshop director Monti has had a major influence in forming a new generation of Argentine playwrights.   GW

Montigny, Adolphe Lemoine (?1812–80) French actor, dramatist and theatre manager. Montigny began his career as an actor at the **Comédie-Française** in 1829. Conscientious rather than gifted, he moved to the boulevard theatres, scoring a success in an adaptation of Balzac's *Les Chouans* at the Nouveautés and moving on to play more important parts at the Ambigu. He became a director of the Gaîté, with Meyer, in 1841, and in 1844 took over the ailing Gymnase, which he brought back to fashionable popularity with the talents of his wife, Rose Chéri, and the repertoire of **Eugène Scribe**. He ran the Gymnase for over 30 years and achieved official recognition in 1865, when he was decorated. A very able theatre manager and play director, he specialized in the French equivalent of 'cup and saucer' drama and moved the French theatre strongly in the direction of a more intimate naturalism. In the 1830s he wrote a number of *vaudevilles* and dramas usually in collaboration; these include *Le Doigt de Dieu* (*The Finger of God*, 1834), *Amazampo; ou la Découverte de Quinquina* (*Amazampo, or the Discovery of Quinine*, 1836), *Zarah* (1837), *Samuel le Marchand* (*Samuel the Merchant*, 1838), *Le Fils* (*The Son*, 1839). In 1847, Montigny published his *Observations on the Théâtre Français and the secondary theatres*, in which he attempted to diagnose the current ills of the Comédie-Française.   JMCC

Moody, William Vaughn (1869–1910) American dramatist. Born in Indiana, he took a degree in English at Harvard (1893) and taught there and at the University of Chicago (1895–1902). He co-wrote a standard history of English literature, and was widely regarded as the best lyric poet of his generation. With Harriet Brainard, whom he married (1909), he was active in Donald Robertson's New Theatre. He experimented with two verse plays, but turned to prose when he dramatized a story about a woman kidnapped by a band of drunken cowboys. *The Great Divide* was premiered by **Henry Miller** and **Margaret Anglin** at a matinee in Chicago (April 1906). It was easily the finest American play of its time, successfully blending realistic motivation with poetic treatment of the national myth. His last play, *The Faith Healer* (1909), was a failure in performance, and Moody died of a brain tumour soon after.   DMcD

Moore, Dora Mavor (1888–1979) One of the founders of modern Canadian theatre. Born in Scotland she came to Toronto with her father, Professor James Mavor. Abandoning University for the theatre she became the first Canadian student at RADA, and made her professional acting debut in Ottawa in 1912. She joined **Ben Greet**'s touring company in New York State, played on Broadway, and in 1918 became the first Canadian to act at the **Old Vic**, playing Viola for Ben Greet.

Following the war she returned to Toronto to teach and direct, first founding the Village Players to tour **Shakespeare** to the schools, and later to present summer seasons which included works by **Lorca** and **Brecht** as well as new Canadian plays.

In 1946 the Village Players became fully professional as the New Play Society, inspired by the example of the **Abbey Theatre**. An impromptu revue, *Spring Thaw* (1948), became an annual Canadian institution for almost 20 years. In 1950 the NPS opened a school to provide high-level professional theatre training. The school closed in 1968, and the NPS was dissolved in 1971 after having trained and inspired a whole generation of theatre practitioners.

As well as being a remarkable teacher-director, Dora Mavor Moore was instrumental in bringing **Tyrone Guthrie** to Canada to direct the first **Stratford Shakespearian Festival**. The annual Toronto Theatre awards are called 'Doras' in her honour.   JA

Moore, Edward (1712–57) English playwright. He turned to writing plays when his business as a linen-draper failed. His first play, *The Foundling* (1748), was a serious and sentimental comedy, full of feeling and devoid of humour. He adapted **Lesage**'s *Gil Blas* in 1751 as an energetic disguise comedy. His major contribution was a domestic tragedy heavily influenced by **Lillo**, *The Gamester* (1753), where the hero, overwhelmed with gambling debts, commits suicide moments before he would have heard he had inherited a fortune. The play was adapted by **Diderot** and was a strong influence on the development of the *drame bourgeois*.   PH

Moorehead, Agnes (1906–74) American stage, film, and television actress. She appeared in summer stock aged ten and spent four years with the St Louis Municipal Opera. Moorehead earned a doctorate in literature at Bradley University, taught dramatics at the Dalton School, and began to appear on Broadway in such shows as *Marco Millions*. During the depression, she turned to radio, appearing on 'The March of Time' and the suspense classic, 'Sorry, Wrong Number'. She was a charter member of the **Mercury Theatre** and made her movie debut in *Citizen Kane* with **Orson Welles**. In 1951 Moorehead appeared with the highly acclaimed First Drama Quartet. She made about 100 films, winning five Academy Awards nominations, but was best known to modern audiences as Endora in the television comedy, *Bewitched*.   SMA

Moratín see **Fernández de Moratín**

Moresca Dance-drama of the eastern Adriatic, the northern Mediterranean littoral and some of the islands, Iberia, and Central America. Sometimes associated with carnival, sometimes with a local feast (as on Korčula, where it is performed in July, largely to tourists), it reflects the political and commercial interplay between Christian and Muslim (in Spain it is explicitly entitled *Cristianos y moros*). Though its form varies little – a spoken prologue, sometimes with character-interaction, to a spectacular sword-dance –

aetiological legends, inside or outside the text, frequently refer it to a particular local event. The name may have given us Morris Dance; there is otherwise no resemblance.   AEG

Moreto y Cabaña, Agustín de (1618–69) Spanish playwright of Italian parentage, born in Madrid, and living there and in Toledo where he held a benefice in minor orders and later became head of a charitable fraternity. The best of the disciples of **Calderón**, he had some success with serious plays, but is best known for his fine comedies. His poetry is not exceptional but his dialogue is always witty and unaffected, and his command of dramatic structure impeccable.

Amongst Moreto's refined court comedies is his masterpiece *El desdén con el desdén* (*Disdain Conquered by Disdain*, published 1654) in which a nobleman wins a cold princess by feigning complete indifference. It was the model for **Molière**'s *La Princesse d'Elide*. He also wrote many fine *capa y espada* plays. *El lindo don Diego* (*Don Diego the Dandy*, published 1662) is to some extent a **comedia de figurón** whose comic character, a narcissistic fop, is diverted from the unwilling heroine by the hope of marrying a countess. *No puede ser el guardar una mujer* (*Impossible to Guard a Woman*, 1659–61) is a witty thesis play demonstrating that a lady will only be chaste if she wants to, not through force. Here, as generally in Moreto, the heroine is a model of propriety who firmly but gently defends her rights.

Of his serious plays, *Antíoco y Seleuco* (published 1654) follows **Lope de Vega**'s *El castigo sin venganza* in its theme of a son who falls in love with his father's intended bride, but with a happy ending when the father allows the son to marry her.

Moreto's light but decorous style retained its popularity with audiences well into the 18th century.   CL

Morley, Robert (1908–   ) British actor and playwright, who has made a reputation playing eccentric extroverts like **Oscar Wilde**, a part he first played under **Norman Marshall** at the London **Gate Theatre** in 1936 and later repeated in a film version of Wilde's life, Professor Higgins in **Shaw**'s *Pygmalion* at the **Old Vic** in 1937, or Sheridan Whiteside in *The Man Who Came to Dinner* by **George S. Kaufman** and **Moss Hart**, which he played for two years after his first appearance in the part in 1941. As the author of several light comedies, including *Edward, My Son* (with Noel Langley, 1947), *Hippo Dancing* (adapted from André Roussin, 1954), *Hook, Line and Sinker* (1958) or *A Ghost on Tiptoe* (with Rosemary Sisson, 1974), he has specialized in roles written by himself as well as appearing in farces by Peter Ustinov, **Alan Ayckbourn** and **Ben Travers**.   CI

Morocco see **French-speaking North Africa; Middle East**

Morosco, Oliver (Mitchell) (1876–1945) American manager and producer. Born in Utah, Morosco moved to San Francisco at an early age and appeared as an acrobat in the troupe of Walter Morosco. After adopting his mentor's name, he managed several theatres in the Bay area, later acquiring on his own at least six theatres in Los Angeles. He began producing in 1909, and later offered in New York *The Bird of Paradise*

(1912), and *Peg O' My Heart* (1912), both starring **Laurette Taylor**; and in 1915, *The Unchastened Woman* with Emily Stevens. The **Shuberts** built and named a theatre for him in New York (1917) which he opened with his own play, *Canary Island*. Notable productions to appear at the **Morosco Theatre** include *Beyond the Horizon* (1920) and *The Bat* (1920). The author of numerous plays, all undistinguished, Morosco went bankrupt in 1926 in a scheme to build a motion picture settlement in California. TLM

Morosco Theatre 217 West 45th St, New York City [Architect: Herbert J. Krapp]. The Morosco was the first of many theatres to be designed for the **Shuberts** by Herbert J. Krapp, a talented young architect who had served his apprenticeship with Henry B. Herts, an earlier favoured Shubert architect. Built in 1917, it was intended as a showcase for the productions of **Oliver Morosco**, a successful West Coast producer. An intimate, 1,000-seat one-balcony house, it was well suited to realistic dramas and intimate musicals. On its stage was launched the Broadway career of **Eugene O'Neill**, whose first full-length play, *Beyond the Horizon* (1920), was presented at a matinee performance. In 1936, the Shuberts were forced to relinquish the theatre, which changed hands several times before it was razed in 1982 to make way for a new hotel. In addition to O'Neill, its stage had proved kind to such American playwrights as **Thornton Wilder**, **Tennessee Williams**, **Arthur Miller**, **Robert Anderson** and **Arthur Kopit**. MCH

Morris (Morrison), Clara (1846/8–1925) American actress, possibly born in Canada of a bigamous union, who received her early training in **John A. Ellsler**'s stock company in Cleveland (1861–9). For years she sustained a reputation as one of America's greatest emotionalistic actresses, although her career is one of incongruities. In the 1870s she was praised as realistic, though by the 80s she was denounced by many as the queen of spasms and the mistress of the tricks of the acting trade. In 1870 she began her New York career as a member of **Augustin Daly**'s company, excelling in plays like *Man and Wife*, *Divorce*, and especially Daly's *Article 47*, in which she played Cora the Creole. She left Daly in 1873 and spent most of her remaining career as a travelling star appearing in popular roles such as Camille and Miss Moulton (in a version of *East Lynne*). Although she attempted classical roles, she was always more successful when playing pathetic girls in melodrama that allowed her to use her 'tearful' voice and to loose a veritable flood of emotion on her audience. She appeared in vaudeville in the 1900s and made her last appearance in Washington, DC, in 1906. She wrote three unreliable autobiographies (1901–6). DBW

Morris, Mary (1895–1970) American actress. At Radcliffe College she performed in **George Pierce Baker**'s 'Workshop 47', but left to gain practical theatre experience. After a year as an unsalaried prompter, she made her professional debut in *The Clod* with the **Washington Square Players** in 1916. In 1918 she toured *Alexander Hamilton* with **George Arliss** whom she credited with teaching her the most about acting.

For two years (1924–6) she played Abbie in *Desire Under the Elms*. She appeared with numerous stock companies, on Broadway, and in two films. In 1937 she made her London debut. She taught and directed at Carnegie Institute of Technology (1939–60) and at the **American Shakespeare Festival** and Academy (1961–2). FHL

Morton, Charles (1819–1904) English waiter and publican who rose to become 'The Grand Old Man of the Music Hall'. Around the age of 21, he opened a small tavern in Pimlico that featured 'harmonic meetings', and in 1849 the 'Old Canterbury Arms' in Westminster Bridge Road. His elegant Canterbury Hall (1852, rebuilt 1854) was the first music-hall to appeal to a broad middle-class public with its mixture of classical and popular music. A master of publicity, Morton initiated music-hall advertising in *The Times* and presented Sunday evening performances. He later managed the Oxford, the Philharmonic Theatre and the **Gaiety**, expanding into comic opera and minstrelsy; his longest tenure was at the Alhambra (1877–81, 1883–90) and on his retirement he was dubbed, somewhat inaccurately, 'The Father of the Music Hall'. LS

Morton, Thomas (1764–1838) English playwright, born in County Durham, but orphaned at the age of four and brought up by an uncle in London. He was sent to Lincoln's Inn, but showed no interest in the law, preferring cricket and the theatre. His first play, *Columbus* (1792), like most of the other 25, was staged at **Covent Garden**, though he owed his first successes to the patronage of **George Colman the Younger** at the **Haymarket**. These were the sentimental operetta *The Children in the Wood* (1793) and the preposterous *Zorinski* (1795). There followed a sequence of five-act comedies for Covent Garden, of which the best are *The Way to Get Married* (1796), *A Cure for the Heartache* (1797), *Secrets Worth Knowing* (1798) and the splendid *Speed the Plough* (1800), avowedly a comedy but embodying many of the features of later domestic melodramas. *Speed the Plough* deserves to be remembered for much more than the invention of **Mrs Grundy**, a character who never appears, but whose possible disapproval clouds the Ashfield home. As famous in Morton's lifetime, largely by virtue of **John Emery**'s comic mastery of the Yorkshire dialect, was the character of Tyke in *The School of Reform* (1805). Towards the end of his active writing life, Morton became successively Reader of Plays for Covent Garden and **Drury Lane**. His son John Maddison Morton (1811–91) was a prolific writer of short farces, many of them adroitly adapted from French originals. The best known began as *The Double-Bedded Room* (1843), was rewritten as *Box and Cox* (1847) and transformed, by the addition of Sullivan's music, into *Cox and Box* (1867). PT

Moscow Art Theatre (MAT) Soviet Russian theatre's original 'house of art', a realistic ensemble based upon a homegrown system and paralleling European models (the Meininger troupe, Théâtre Libre, **Freie Bühne**), dedicated to aesthetic and social idealism. On 21 June 1897 **Konstantin Stanislavsky**, an amateur actor-director with the Moscow Society of

Art and Literature, and **Vladimir Nemirovich-Danchenko**, a playwright-teacher at the Music and Drama School of the Moscow Philharmonia, joined contrasting backgrounds (industrialist's son and nobleman by marriage), temperaments, skills (theatrical and literary) as well as acting pupils – **Olga Knipper**, **Vsevolod Meyerhold**, **Ivan Moskvin** – to form a theatre based upon new principles. These included: a conscious, craft-like realistic approach to acting to counter the lazy and artificial 19th-century conventions that still reigned – artificial declamation and falsely inspired emotions; a harmonious ensemble dedicated to art and not themselves or the idea of a 'star system'; the blending of the new acting style with a scenic approach, newly and fully conceived for each individual drama, utilizing in-depth research into historical detail; a lengthy and systematic rehearsal to allow the actors to realize the essence of the play; education of the public to appreciate the new art and the theatre as 'temple of art' via the elimination of the footlights, taking a unified, sober approach to the theatre's décor, barring latecomers from entering the auditorium until intermission, dispensing with curtain calls until the play's end. MAT (originally the Moscow Art Accessible Theatre) took its role as social educator seriously and hoped to take the pulse of contemporary Russian life. The company opened on 14 October 1898 at the Hermitage Theatre on Carriage Row with a production of **A. K. Tolstoi**'s history play *Tsar Fyodor Ioannovich*, which proved to be an exercise in archaeological reconstruction featuring **Meiningen**-like crowd scenes. The theatre wing took on **Chekhov**'s *The Seagull* (1898), which gave the company its logo and identity and began a legendary association with the playwright – *Uncle Vanya* (1899), *The Three Sisters* (1901), *The Cherry Orchard* (1904). V. A. Simov's textured, varied realistic settings and Stanislavsky's innovative staging – including actors with their backs to the audience and a detailed sound score – helped to realize the 'theatre of mood'. In 1902 MAT began its long association with **Gorky**, after whom the theatre would be named in 1932. His *The Lower Depths* together with **Lev Tolstoi**'s *The Power of Darkness*, both produced in 1902, brought the inner lives of the lower classes to the stage and testified to the theatre's social consciousness. MAT was aesthetically more committed to lyrical realism than to naturalism and even made tentative forays into symbolism, as its varied and significant work of the next 30 years would prove: productions of **Ibsen**, **Hauptmann**, Hamsun, **Maeterlinck**, **Andreev** and **Shakespeare**; production and studio work by anti-realist directors Meyerhold, **Vakhtangov**, **Michael Chekhov**, K. A. Mardzhanov, **A. N. Benois** and **Gordon Craig** (the famous 1911–12 monodramatic *Hamlet*); innovative design work by Benois, M. V. Dobuzhinsky and N. K. Roerikh. This anti-realistic approach proved unpopular with the public and with Stanislavsky, who reapplied himself to developing an acting system, the first results of which were seen in his 1909 production of **Turgenev**'s *A Month in the Country*. Nemirovich-Danchenko's more mystical stagings of Dostoevsky's *The Brothers Karamazov* (1910) and *Nikolai Stavrogin*, from *The Devils* (1913), elicited the charge of negativism from Gorky. Overall the theatre's aesthetic and ideological profile was moderate. MAT survived the ravages of the October Revolution and

Civil War – company attrition due to voluntary defections abroad and involuntary detainment by White Guard troops – and was named an academic theatre (1920) largely through the good offices of Lenin and **Lunacharsky**. While the theatre publicly committed itself to reinforcing Bolshevik themes in its work, its directors privately disagreed philosophically over what artistic course it should follow. The first post-revolutionary production, **Byron**'s *Cain* (1920), was politically anomalous. Anti-realistic experimentation continued under Vakhtangov at the Third Studio (1920) and at the Fourth Studio (1931). Stanislavsky applied his acting techniques at the Bolshoi Theatre's opera studio, while Nemirovich-Danchenko opened his Musical Studio at MAT. Simultaneously, the theatre produced the new Soviet drama. **Bulgakov**'s *The Days of the Turbins*, despite its White sympathies, proved a favourite of Stalin's and thus was successful as was **Vsevolod Ivanov**'s *Armoured Train 14–69* (1927) and **Valentin Kataev**'s comedy, *Squaring the Circle* (1928). The 1920s also saw influential MAT tours of Europe and the United States (1922–4) and richly visualized productions (sets by Golovin) of **Ostrovsky**'s *The Ardent Heart* (1926) and **Beaumarchais**'s *Marriage of Figaro* (1927). In the 1930s new productions of Russian classics by **Gogol** and Lev Tolstoi were staged, Chekhov's *Three Sisters* was ideologically reworked (1940), socialist realism (1934–53) was solidified and more of the new Soviet drama produced (**Afinogenov**, **Kirshon**) and Stanislavsky died (1938). The Thaw (1954–6) was the training period for a new generation of directors, including Nemirovich-Danchenko's former student and Sovremennik Theatre head **Oleg Efremov**, who in 1972 reluctantly became MAT's new artistic director. As founder of the Sovremennik Theatre (1958), the Soviet theatre of the 1960s, Efremov and his young company had tried to speak for and to their generation via new drama and styles. While his initial attempts to revitalize MAT failed, the 1980s have seen the theatre prosper. In 1973 MAT moved to its new, modernly equipped, 1,370-seat facility on Tverskoi Boulevard, complete with an updated 'seagull' act curtain and prompter's box, while running productions concurrently in the original and filial theatre buildings. Successes of the Efremov era have included two widely divergent productions by the brilliant controversial **Anatoly Efros**: a fairly orthodox staging of **Mikhail Roshchin**'s patriotic war play *Troop Train* and a Marx (Brothers)-inspired rendering of **Molière**'s *Tartuffe* (1981) on MAT's filial stage. SG

Moscow State Jewish Theatre

Moscow State Jewish Theatre Founded as the Jewish Theatrical Studio in 1919 under the leadership of Alexander Granowski. After a period of intensive training of a young company, including Marc Chagall and Nathan Altman as designers and Alexander Krein as composer, and actors like **Solomon Mikhoels** and Benjamin Zuskin, the company soon created a unique style and was designated a State Theatre. The problem of finding plays reflecting both the company's ethnic quality and its political fervour was solved by ruthlessly adapting the classic Jewish plays of **Sholom Aleichem**, Mendele Mocher Sforim, **Goldfaden** etc. The company was particularly successful with **Shakespeare**'s plays and *King Lear*, directed in 1935 by Sergei

Radlov with Mikhoels as Lear and Zuskin as Fool, was a triumph. The theatre was closed down by an edict of Stalin in 1948 along with all Jewish theatres.   AB

Moskvin, Ivan Mikhailovich (1874–1946) One of the best Soviet-Russian character actors of his generation, who specialized in portraying native types from the sub-class of the 'insulted and the injured'. Following stints with **G. N. Fedotova**'s (**Stanislavsky**'s teacher) touring company, at Z. A. Malinovsky's theatre in Yaroslav (1896), where he played 77 roles in one season, and at Korsh's Theatre in Moscow (1897–8), Moskvin was invited to become a charter member of the **Moscow Art Theatre** (1898). There he was reunited with **Vladimir Nemirovich-Danchenko**, who had been his acting teacher at the Moscow Philharmonia (1893) and who now helped secure him the title role in MAT's premiere production, **A. K. Tolstoi**'s historical drama *Tsar Fyodor Ioannovich* (1898). From this success Moskvin went on to play a wide variety of roles at MAT, where he spent his entire professional career. These included Luka in **Gorky**'s *The Lower Depths* (1902), Epikhodov in **Chekhov**'s *The Cherry Orchard* and Snegiryov in Nemirovich-Danchenko's dramatization of Dostoevsky's *The Brothers Karamazov* (1910). He was noted for the deft comic touch and the sharply individualized idiosyncratic detail, betokening a richly imagined inner life, which he brought to his roles. In the Soviet period he appeared in the dramas of **Trenyov**, **Korneichuk** and Kron and played a leading role in **Pogodin**'s *Kremlin Chimes* (1942) about Lenin. His career also extended to film acting and stage directing. He helped stage the MAT productions of **Maeterlinck**'s *The Blue Bird* (1908), **Gogol**'s *The Inspector General* (1908) and **Turgenev**'s *A Month in the Country* (1909). In 1943 he was appointed director of MAT.   SG

Mostel, Zero (Samuel Joel) (1915–77) American actor. Trained as an artist, he became an immensely talented comic actor, noted for his sagging jowls and large paunch but dancer's grace, acrobat's control, and enormously expressive face. After appearing in sketches at a Greenwich Village night club in 1942, he made his Broadway debut the same year in *Keep 'Em Laughing*. Subsequent roles of note included Shu Fu in *The Good Person of Setzuan* (1956), Leopold Bloom in *Ulysses in Nighttown* (1958; 1974), Jean in *Rhinoceros* (1961), Pseudolus in the musical *A Funny Thing Happened on the Way to the Forum* (1962), and his greatest popular triumph, Tevye in *Fiddler on the Roof* (1964; 1976). He died in Philadelphia rehearsing Shylock in **Wesker**'s *The Merchant*. His memoirs appeared in 1965.   DBW

Moulin-Rouge, Bal du In 1889, a former butcher named Charles Zidler, with Joseph Oller, opened a dance-hall-cum-*café-concert* in the Place Blanche, Paris, intending to convey the boisterous cancan of the amateur music-halls to more respectable premises. The entrance was surmounted by a giant windmill designed by Willette and a hollow stucco elephant stood in the garden to house intimate performance. The *quadrille naturaliste* with its *porte d'armes* (the uplifted ankle held by the dancer's hand) and *grand écart* (splits), as danced by **La Goulue** and her squalid colleagues, and the

insinuating songs of **Yvette Guilbert** gave the house a reputation that enhanced the erotic prestige of Montmartre. The dance-floor was reduced in 1903 to make way for a music-hall stage; after the building burned in 1915, it reopened to offer dinner shows of cancan and ballet. Between 1925 and 1929, Jacques-Charles revived the old glories with eight spectacularly novel revues; then it was converted to a cinema and not reopened as a place of live entertainment until 1953.   LS

Mounet, Paul (1847–1922) French actor. Like his more celebrated brother, **Mounet-Sully**, Paul Mounet came to the theatre relatively late, making his debut at the **Odéon** in 1880 as the young Horace in **Corneille**'s play. He joined the **Comédie-Française** in 1889, appearing as Don Salluste in *Ruy Blas*. He excelled in older and character parts and his deep and resonant bass voice suited him not only for tragic roles, but also for more sinister ones such as Iago. Other memorable parts were in *Le Juif Polonais* (*The Polish Jew*) and as an imposing Hercules in *Alkestis*. In 1908 he appeared, with **Sarah Bernhardt**, in a silent film of *La Tosca*.   JMCC

Mounet-Sully, Jean (1841–1916) French actor. The major tragic actor of the late 19th century, Mounet-Sully originally trained to be a Protestant pastor. He left the Conservatoire in 1868 and managed to find work at the Montmartre theatre, where he was noticed by **Chilly** who needed an actor with a strong voice for the **Odéon**. He added Sully to his name and first appeared there as Cornwall in *King Lear*. After the 1870 war he joined the troupe of the **Comédie-Française**, making his debut in 1872 as Oreste in *Andromaque*, followed by Rodrigue in *Le Cid*. Like **Rachel** in 1838, he was immediately seen as the perfect actor for the classical repertoire, audiences being overwhelmed by his passion, conviction and sheer dramatic power. His greatest roles were Hamlet, Oreste and Oedipus. His vocal and physical means and his majestic attitudes made him the definitive Oedipus of the period (1881). His range included the 19th-century repertoire, notably the plays of **Victor Hugo**: his Didier in *Marion de Lorme* (1873) led to his becoming a *sociétaire* and he played a particularly fine Hernani opposite **Sarah Bernhardt**. In 1889 he was decorated with the Légion d'Honneur. In 1909 he appeared as Jesus in a silent film, *The Kiss of Judas*.   JMCC

Mowatt (Ritchie), Anna Cora Ogden (1819–70) American playwright and actress. Although now best known for *Fashion* (1845), a satire on the nouveaux-riches who make themselves ridiculous by aping foreign manners, in her own time she was also known as a public reader and actress. Encouraged by Longfellow, she began her readings in Boston (1841) and the following year in New York. After the success of *Fashion*, she toured for 200 nights as Lady Teazle, Juliet, and Pauline in **Bulwer-Lytton**'s *The Lady of Lyons*, toured again in 1852, and performed in England (1847 and 1851). As an actress she was admired for her grace, her radiant smile, and her naturalness, which Edgar Allan Poe found 'so pleasantly removed from the customary rant and cant'.

Her second play, *Armand* (1847), was also well received, and she wrote two vivid accounts of theatrical life: *Autobiography of an Actress* (1854) and *Mimic Life, or Before and Behind the Curtain* (1856).

She had read all of **Shakespeare** by age 10, at 14 translated, staged, and acted in **Voltaire**'s *Alzire* in the family parlour, wrote her first play, *Pelayo*, when she was 17, and became a regular contributor to *Graham's Magazine* and *The Columbian*.

She married James Mowatt when she was 15, and after his death (1851), married William F. Ritchie.   RM

Mrożek, Sławomir (1932–) Polish playwright, essayist, cartoonist and author of comic stories, who has lived in Italy and France since 1963. Using slapstick techniques of vaudeville and cabaret, he transforms concepts into model theatrical situations. Early one-act parables – *Out at Sea* (1960), *Striptease* and *Charlie* (1961) – reveal the mechanisms of power by pushing absurd premises to logical extremes. Using satire and the grotesque, he mocks national myths and parodies different theatrical styles and genres, notably the Polish romantic tradition. *Tango* (1964) traces European civilization from liberalism to totalitarianism in the form of family drama. *Emigrés* (1974) is an ironic view of exiles confronting freedom. Other plays include *The Police* (1958), *Vatzlav* (1970), *The Ambassador* (1981), *Alpha* (1984).   DG

Muhando, Penina (Mlama) (1948–) Tanzanian playwright and director. All her published plays are in Swahili and include *Hatia* (*Guilt*, 1972), *Tambueni Haki Setu* (*Recognize Our Rights*, 1973), *Heshima Yangu* (*My Respect*, 1974), *Pambo* (*Decoration*, 1975), *Talaka si mke wangu* (*I Divorce You*, 1976), *Nguzo Mama* (*Mother the Main Pillar*, 1982), *Harakati za Ukombozi* (*Liberation Struggles*, 1982), with **A. Lihamba** and others, and *Lina Ubani* (*There is an Antidote for Rot*, 1984). As with other Tanzanian playwrights, Mlama deals with the problems of the struggle for liberation and a just society as in *Tambueni Haki Zetu*, *Harakati za Ukombozi* and *Lina Ubani*. She also explores more personal problems, as in her treatment of the effects of divorce on children in *Talaka* and hypocrisy in *Heshima Yangu*. As a woman she is concerned with women's rights and her *Nguzo Mama* shows the conflicts and contradictions in the Tanzanian struggle for the liberation of women. She also takes an active part in the theatre for development (see **Third World popular theatre**) movement. Penina Mlama heads the Department of Art, Music and Theatre at the University of Dar es Salaam.   PML

Müller, Heiner (1929–) German playwright, whose work falls into three contrasting categories: naturalistic plays dealing with the means of production and the creation of a socialist society like *Tractor* (1961) or *Cement* (1972 – both first performed in 1975); re-workings of mythical or literary material using subjects and characters from antiquity to discuss general political and philosophical problems (*Hercules 5*, 1966, *Hercules 2 or the Hydra*, 1974) together with translations and adaptations, such as *Macbeth* (1972), *Hamlet-Machine* (1979, first performed in France, 1982) or *Depraved Shore* (*Verkommenes Ufer*, based on **Euripides**' *Medea*, 1982); and plays focusing on German history. Marked by a fragmentary and open-ended dramaturgy presenting highly politicized collages of violence and fantasy, the most ambitious of these is

Germania – Death in Berlin (1971 – first performed 1978). *Quartet* (1982), a psychological study of social dominance in sexuality and aggression, marks a new departure. His 'historical pessimism' was heavily criticized in the DDR and his work censored during the 1960s, but since 1976 he has been recognized as one of its leading playwrights.   CI

Munday, Anthony (1560–1633) English playwright, pamphleteer, actor and government agent, engaged in anti-Catholic espionage. Munday was a prolific journeyman-writer and translator, who could turn his hand as readily to anti-theatrical tracts as to writing plays for the public theatres or pageants for the city of London. Francis Meres, in *Palladis Tamia* (1598), surprisingly calls him 'the best for comedy' and 'our best plotter'. For the Elizabethans, the latter skill defined the dextrous division of a given story into appropriate dramatic episodes. It is not particularly evident in Munday's extant plays, *Fedele and Fortunio* (c. 1584), *John a Kent and John a Cumber* (1594) and the two parts of *The Downfall* and *The Death of Robert, Earl of Huntingdon* (1598), written with **Henry Chettle**. However, his collaborative skills may have been appreciated by fellow-writers in many lost plays as well as in the revisions of *Sir Thomas More* (c. 1596) and in Part One of *Sir John Oldcastle* (1599).   PT

Munford, Robert (c. 1737–83) American playwright and politician. An influential member of Virginia's elected representatives, both before and after the Revolution, Munford wrote two plays which are outstanding examples of America's early comic drama and its interest in satire. *The Candidates; or, The Humours of a Virginia Election* (1770) satirizes the methods by which politicians win elections. *The Patriots* (1779) attacks half-hearted and hypocritical patriots as well as Tory and Whig politics. Not a serious playwright, Munford wrote mainly to air his views, showing some skill in contriving plots and creating amusing scenes with stereotypical characters. Both plays were published in 1798.   WJM

Muni, Paul (1896–1967) American actor who started in the Yiddish theatre at the age of 12 as Muni Weisenfreund, playing old men parts, quickly establishing himself as a superb character actor and master of makeup. After 18 years as a leading Yiddish actor he moved to Broadway in English-speaking roles and then to a distinguished career in Hollywood.   AB

Munk, Kaj (1892–1944) Danish writer and Lutheran pastor, author of some 35 plays vigorously exploring such moral issues as faith, the human will and the discovery of identity through courageous action; his debt to Kierkegaard and **Ibsen** is frequently clear. Some early plays betray a fascination with 'strong leaders', such as Herod in *An Idealist* (1924) and Henry VIII in *Cant* (1931), anticipating his brief but real attraction to Nazism's apparent promise to lead mankind to a new age of faith. Very different views emerge in the explicitly anti-Nazi *He Sits at the Melting Pot* (1938) and in the parable of Danish resistance *Niels Ebbesen* (1940–2); its suppression began a process that ended with his murder by the Gestapo in 1944. His most enduring play is *The Word* (1925), about the power of faith and the will to free humanity from prejudice. HL

Murdoch, Frank (1843–72) American actor and playwright. An actor of juvenile and comedy parts, Murdoch spent his entire career with **Louisa Drew's Arch Street Theatre** Company in Philadelphia. Of his four plays, *Davy Crockett* (1872) was written for **Frank Mayo** who worked on it, after its early discouraging reputation, and created a popular play for a generation of theatre-goers. Murdoch died of meningitis after the failure of *Bohemia; or, The Lottery of Art* (1872), a satire on critics. WJM

Murdoch, James Edward (1811–93) American actor. He made his debut in 1829 at the **Arch Street Theatre** in Philadelphia as Frederick in **Kotzebue**'s *Lover's Vows*. In 1833, he supported **Fanny Kemble** during her appearance at the **Chestnut Street Theatre**. For the next decade, he appeared in various theatres in New Orleans, Mobile, Pittsburgh, Philadelphia, New York and Boston. For two years, he retired from the stage and lectured on Shakespearian characters and 'The Uses and Abuses of the Stage' and gave elocution lessons. He returned to the stage in 1845 and for the next 15 years, he established a reputation as both a tragedian and a light comedian. In 1856, he appeared at London's **Haymarket Theatre** for 110 nights and was also engaged briefly in Liverpool. He retired again in 1861 and 1879, but appeared intermittently until 1889. Among his more acclaimed roles were Hamlet, Charles Surface in *The School for Scandal*, Benedick, Orlando and Mercutio. His reminiscences *The Stage; or, Recollections of Actors and Acting from an Experience of Fifty Years* were published in 1880. DJW

Murphy, Arthur (1727–1805) Irish playwright. Dissatisfied with his career as a clerk in a banking house, he turned to journalism as a columnist in *The Gray's Inn Journal* in 1752. He began writing plays in 1753, through friendship with **Samuel Foote** but, resisting **Garrick**'s attempts to improve his play, he rewrote it as *The Apprentice* (1756). He was an actor briefly from 1755, playing Othello, but recognized that he would never be particularly successful and returned to journalism as well as training in law, where he practised as a barrister until 1788, and continued to write plays. He translated **Voltaire**'s tragedy *The Orphan of China* (1759) but his best work was in comedy, including a study of married life and its attendant boredom in *The Way to Keep Him* (1760) and the more sentimental *Know Your Own Mind* (1777), after disputes over his tragedy *The Grecian Daughter*, his later plays being presented at **Covent Garden**. He retired both from the law and the theatre in 1788 and was given a royal pension in 1803. PH

Murphy, Thomas Bernard (1935–) Irish playwright. Murphy's first play, *A Whistle in the Dark*, produced at Stratford East in 1961, concerns an Irish immigrant family in Coventry whose despairs find outlet in brutal violence. After *A Whistle* Murphy lived in London, writing television and film scripts, returning to Ireland in 1970. Outstanding among his subsequent plays are *Famine* (1968), *A Crucial Week in the Life of a Grocer's Assistant* (1969), *The Morning After Opti-*

mism (1971), *The Sanctuary Lamp* (1975), *The Blue Macushla* (1980), *The Gigli Concert* (1983). They explore various modifications of the straight realist stage of *A Whistle*.

A Crucial Week has a tight, surrealistic structure, calling for subtle effects of light, blending John Joe Moran's dream and waking lives, full of Joycean wordplay. Unusually among Murphy's characters, John Joe reaches a fairly satisfying resolution of his frustrations 'on this corpse of a street' in a provincial town. In *The Morning*, a whore and a pimp are the shadows and finally the murderers of two idealized lovers in a debased Forest of Arden.

The Sanctuary Lamp peoples its stage with three grotesque derelicts whose pathetic companionship in an empty church neither the secular world nor the Church, 'a poxy con!', can consolidate. *The Blue Macushla*, in a stunning night club setting, is a satire of seamy Irish politics, its metaphor, lovingly developed, the gangster films of the 1930s. In *The Gigli Concert* an Irish businessman who in his depressions aspires to sing like Gigli 'consults' an English 'philosophical dynamatologist'. The deadpan zaniness of the situation and its bravura comic setpieces accommodate the characters' genuine quest into themselves on the margins of art and therapy.

Murphy's is a secular world where the theological symbolism of innocence, guilt and forgiveness persists, rendered in a language of great complexity which fully retains its theatrical function. In **Brian Friel**'s account of it, it bespeaks an 'antic' imagination, 'capable of great cruelty and great compassion'; and a mitigating inseparable humour. DM

Murray, (George) Gilbert Aimé (1866–1957) British classical scholar, philosopher and dramatist, who provided **Shaw** with the model for Cusins in *Major Barbara*. After writing two original plays, *Carlyon Sahib* (1889) and *Andromache* (1900), he turned to verse translations of Greek tragedy which had a significant influence in the first decades of the century. His versions of **Euripides** were staged by **Granville Barker** for the **Stage Society** at the **Royal Court Theatre** (*Hippolytus*, 1904; *The Trojan Women*, 1905; *Electra*, 1906) and at the Savoy Theatre (*Medea*, 1907), while his translation of **Sophocles**' *Oedipus Rex* was staged by **Reinhardt** at **Covent Garden** in 1912. He later turned to comedy with adaptations of **Aristophanes** and the first reconstructions of **Menander** – *The Rape of the Locks* (*Perikeiromenê*, 1914); *The Arbitration* (*Epitrepontes*, 1945). CI

Murray, Thomas Cornelius (1873–1959) Irish playwright. With **Lennox Robinson**, one of the 'Cork realists', in the **Abbey**'s early years, whose work determined the theatre's characteristic style. In *Birthright* (1910), his first play, a father's jealous care for the disposition of his land becomes a mortal issue between his two sons. It is a theme typical of Murray's sombre vision of a small-farming society obsessed by ownership of their harsh land, 'with more o' the rock, an' the briar, an' the sour weed than the sweet grass'. Marriage and careers come equally under its sway.

Murray's most successful later plays are *Aftermath* (1922), *Autumn Fire* (1924), and *Michaelmas Eve* (1932). In none of them does anyone win: the mother of an idealistic young teacher forces him into a 'practical' marriage with a woman who could 'buy and sell them that talk like angels'; an ageing man marries a young girl who falls in love with his son. In a society bound by strict Catholic teaching, which Murray approved, his characters must simply endure within the restrictions. From the tension between extreme emotional conflicts and their enforced suppression, Murray's plays derive their intense, claustrophobic atmosphere.   DM

Murrell, John (1945–   ) Canadian playwright, born in the USA but raised in Canada. As a teacher he wrote and produced plays with his students, then turned full-time to the theatre. *Waiting for the Parade* (1977), a sensitive portrayal of the lives of five women waiting for their men to come home from the Second World War, has been widely produced in Canada, and in London and New York. *Memoir* (1977), depicting the last days of **Sarah Bernhardt**, was first produced at Canada's Guelph Spring Festival with the Irish actress, Siobhan McKenna, as the Divine Sarah. It has been produced in more than 20 countries in 15 languages, including a lengthy run in French translation in Paris with Delphine Seyrig in the title role. He has also produced notable translations of the classics, bringing a contemporary Canadian tone to such works as *Uncle Vanya*, *The Seagull* (both for the **Stratford Festival**), *Mandragola*, and *Bajazet*.   JA

Musco, Angelo (1872–1937) Italian actor and company manager. Beginning in the Sicilian marionette theatre, he later joined the company of **Giovanni Grasso** as an actor in the 'straight' theatre. Although eventually established in Milan and elsewhere with his own company, much of his most important work looked back to his Sicilian roots; **Capuana**'s *Il Paraninfo* (*The Marriage Arranger*, 1915) was an early success, and he was a noted interpreter of **Pirandello**'s plays, like the one act piece *La Giara* (*The Jug*), and the full-length *Pensaci, Giacomino!* (*Think, Giacomino!*) and *Liolà*.   LR

Music Box Theatre 239 West 45th St, New York City [Architect: C. Howard Crane]. The Music Box was named by **Irving Berlin**, one of its three original owners, who also lent the name to a series of revues which opened the house in 1921 and continued annually until 1925. With a seating capacity of 1,000 its presentations have alternated between musicals and plays, but more recently it has housed non-musical productions or intimate, small-cast musicals. Irving Berlin continues as half-owner of the theatre with the **Shubert Organization**. During the depression years, one of its tenants, *Of Thee I Sing* (1931), not only became the first musical to win the Pulitzer Prize but also helped to save the theatre for its owners. During its history, not quite a dozen of the **George S. Kaufman** collaborations appeared on its stage.   MCH

Music-hall English Victorian term for variety theatre, with earlier analogues (so-called 'music-halls' had opened in Bolton and Manchester in 1832). Under the patents system, minor theatres had perforce to offer musical entertainments, but music was available elsewhere: the public-house bar parlour or 'free-and-easy' with its weekly sing-songs (the Georgian catch or Comus clubs), performed by amateurs, with a chair-

man and some professionals; the assembly-room entertainments at hotels; and the suburban London tea-garden, a middle-class version of the pleasure-gardens, where aristocratic patronage had fallen off by 1830, and which exhibited singers on a small stage. All three forms were licensed under the liberally interpreted Music and Dancing Act of George II. These places of mixed entertainment, smoking and light refreshment included the Britannia in Hoxton, the Bower in the Lower Marsh, and the Grecian in the City Road, whose pleasure-garden was also known as the Eagle Tavern, described by **Dickens** in *Sketches by Boz*.

The Theatres Act of 1843, which distinguished sharply between legitimate playhouses under the Lord Chamberlain's control where no smoking and drinking was allowed in the auditorium, and Tavern Concert-Rooms under the jurisdiction of local magistrates where such practices were allowed, compelled many of the lesser resorts to make an evolutionary choice. Saloon theatres opted either to go legitimate or carry on as miscellaneous entertainments with no permission to stage plays. Typically, the Mogul tavern in Drury Lane transmuted into the Middlesex or 'Old Mo' music-hall and eventually became the grandiose Winter Garden theatre.

The old bohemian singing-rooms in night-cellars gradually disappeared, among them the Cyder Cellars in Maiden Lane and the Coal Hole in the Strand. These had been all-male resorts, featuring hearty suppers and strong drink, bawdy songs and blood-curdling performers like W. G. Ross as 'Sam Hall'. Evans's in Covent Garden, the last to go, survived by turning into a respectable music-hall that admitted ladies (1854). Respectability was the touchstone for success with many early 'halls: **Charles Morton** the intelligent manager of the Canterbury Hall in Lambeth (1852) opened it to ladies at all times and presented the first English performance of Gounod's *Faust* as an oratorio, although bookmakers still shouted odds on the premises. Morton's Oxford near St Giles's Circus, the London Pavilion in Piccadilly Circus and the Tivoli in the Strand were other important West End houses.

At first, music-hall programmes copied the repertory of the 'Harmonic Meetings', mingling madrigals and glees with lengthy burlesque ballads, such as **Sam Cowell**'s 'Villikins and his Dinah' and 'The Rat-catcher's Daughter', **Sam Collins**'s Irish ditties, and **E. W. Mackney**'s 'Ethiopian' delineations. In the 1860s, the type of the *lion comique*, a free-spending swell, was made popular by **George Leybourne**, 'The Great Vance' (Alfred Peck Stevens) and Arthur Lloyd, while women excelled at dramatic renditions. **Jenny Hill**, the 'Vital Spark', was typical in coming from a background of poverty, achieving fame and fortune, and retiring early because of ill health and exhaustion. Drawn from the working classes, performers shared common experience with their audiences who were boisterous, fond of joining in the chorus and 'giving the bird'.

In 1878, the Metropolitan Board of Works required a Certificate of Suitability, which caused some 200 halls, unable to meet new standards, to close. In reaction, stock companies formed to float luxurious, well-appointed houses, designed by outstanding architects like Frank Matcham. The first palatial hall was the Great Variety Theatre in Leicester Square, whose transport and improved street-lighting that made it safer to venture out at night. Prominent managers who sponsored changes were, in London, **Oswald Stoll**, Edward Moss and Richard Thornton; the Livermore Brothers and James Kiernan in Liverpool; Joseph Smith in Rochdale; and William Morgan in Bradford. The Empire and Alhambra in Leicester Square and the Palace in Cambridge Circus became the models for halls all along the new circuits organized by agents and managements.

The average single turn seldom lasted more than 20 minutes, enabling popular performers to play several halls a night. However, to pay the increased costs, Henry de Frece in Liverpool and George Belmont in London instituted the notorious 'twice-nightly' arrangement (1885). These costs now included star salaries, for the 1890s was the heyday of the music-hall star. **Marie Lloyd** with her artful innuendo, **Albert Chevalier**, a legitimate actor who excelled at coster impersonations, **Little Tich** the eccentric pygmy, **Dan Leno**, greatest of the comedians of humble life, **Harry Lauder** with his Scottish ballads, the male impersonator **Vesta Tilley**, blackface artistes **G. H. Chirgwin** and Eugene Stratton, **George Robey** of the outraged eyebrows and outrageous *double entendre* were expensive performers to maintain.

This period of consolidation also saw some last-ditch assaults on the institution. Prostitution on the premises had always been an outrage to reformers, and Mrs Ormiston Chant attacked the London Empire for its flagrant promenade in 1895. In Manchester a combination of reform groups opposed the licence for the new Palace, and in Liverpool disputes over licensing were conducted along class lines. In the wake of the Local Government Act of 1888, anti-music-hall forces were backed by newly elected town councils, bodies more susceptible to public pressure than local magistrates had been. Another attack came from the Lord Chamberlain's office as sketches began to play a prominent part in the music-hall bill. Parliamentary commissions of 1866 and 1892 both recommended more liberal changes in licensing, but these were not followed up until 1912, when half-an-hour of dialogue was permitted. One result was the appearance of legitimate stars like **Beerbohm Tree** on the variety stage.

The old intimate relationship between the performer and audience began to disappear as colossal halls like Moss's London **Hippodrome** with its water-tank for aquatic spectacles and the Stoll **Coliseum** with its triple revolving stage were built. Programmes became filled with acrobats, trained seals and elephants, living statuary, 15-minute melodramas, mentalists, and adagio dancing, edging out though not entirely displacing the solo comedian and singer who had been the music-hall's staple. In 1906, the Variety Artists Federation, a trade union, was formed and the next year held a strike for paid matinees and abrogation of the 'barring clause' that prevented contracted performers from appearing at neighbourhood houses after a term of contract ended. The strike resulted in a compromise.

A token but important recognition of the music-hall came with the Royal Command Performance in 1912. A kind of resurgence occurred in the 1920s with the introduction of American jazz and ragtime and singers like **Sophie Tucker**, who were already known to the public through their recordings. But it could not

Harry Tate in his sketch 'Golfing'.

neo-Moorish building burnt down and rebuilt as the Alhambra Palace under E. T. Smith became famous for its ballets, managing to survive a law-suit citing them as dramatic performances. Variety theatres continued to advance in number and importance, with improved ventilation, comfort and decoration, as well as higher prices. Admission rose from 1s at the London Tivoli in the 1860s to 3s in the 1890s; the top price at the Liverpool Palace was 5s. Soon every London neighbourhood had its local, and the journalist F. Anstey could discern four distinct levels of quality and audience in London alone: the aristocratic variety theatre in the West End, the small West End house, the large bourgeois music-hall in the outlying areas and suburbs, and that of the poor and squalid districts. In the provinces, most halls clustered in the centres, even in Manchester, Liverpool and Glasgow.

From 1879, the infusion of music-hall stars into pantomime accustomed the family audience to variety material and persuaded it to attend. The middle classes took to visiting halls as the managers strove successfully to dispel the public-house image, banning sales of drinks in the auditorium, replacing tables with rows of seats, cleaning up artistes' material and taking measures to control audience behaviour. The chairman, a holdover from the singing-room, eventually disappeared, replaced by numbers slotted into the proscenium arch, and cued to a printed programme. Since sanitation, elegance and safety were totems of the middle-class ethos, the music-hall sought to embody them. It was aided by new access through public compete with the talking pictures, the wireless, or the wartime air raids that made going to the theatre a danger. The music-hall was still capable of fostering such talents as **Max Miller** and **Gracie Fields** and throve at the Palladium till 1961. But television put paid to the process of diminution by featuring most of the surviving music-hall types on its variety programmes and the microphone reduced the camaraderie between performer and public. Most of the extant buildings were wantonly demolished or restored for other purposes. Ironically, the tavern concerts that spawned the music-hall thrive as working-men's clubs in industrial areas, whereas ersatz 'olde-tyme' music-halls forcibly demonstrate the obsolescence of the original form.

But the spirit long infused British drama, not only thematically as in **John Osborne**'s *The Entertainer* (1957) and **Trevor Griffiths**'s *Comedians* (1975), but in the dialogue rhythms in **Beckett**, **O'Casey**, **Pinter** and **Peter Nichols**, as well as in performance style. A comedian like **Max Wall** excelling in *Krapp's Last Tape* is a perfect example of this cross-fertilization.   LS

See: D. Cheshire, *Music Hall in Britain*, Newton Abbott, 1974; U. Schneider, *Die Londoner Music-Halls und ihre Songs 1850–1920*, Tübingen, 1985; H. Scott, *The Early Doors*, London, 1946; L. Senelick, D. Cheshire and U. Schneider, *British Music Hall 1840–1923: A Bibliography and Guide to Sources*, Hamden, Conn., 1981; C. D. Stuart and A. J. Park, *The Variety Stage*, London, 1985.

Music-hall, French see **Café chantant; Revue**

Musical see **American musical theatre**

Musical comedy Writing about *A Gaiety Girl* (1893) **William Archer** commented, 'There is no doubt that this class of play has become a social institution, the history of which will one day form a curious study. This is the real New Drama . . .' Archer applauded the usurpation of burlesque by musical comedy, a term whose limits are somewhat indefinite and a phenomenon that was probably at its height between the 1890s and 1918.

From the providers' point of view musical comedy was a matter of showbusiness, from the consumers' a thrilling, titillating, amusing, tuneful affair making little call on credibility. What was hoped would be a box office success was cobbled together by a story deviser, a lyric writer and a composer, often with collaborators. The original material was frequently much altered during rehearsals, dialogue changed, musical numbers dropped or added, and characters eliminated or introduced. Even after the opening night, alterations were made from time to time according to audiences' reactions. *The Lucky Star* (Savoy 1899) was advertised as 'Founded on a French original by Leterrier and Vanloo, adapted by J. Cheever Goodwin and Woolson Morse, with new dialogue by Charles H. Brookfield and new lyrics by Adrian Ross and Aubrey Hopwood, the whole revised and assembled by H. L., and with music by Ivan Caryll.' No mention was made of the fact that some of the music was borrowed from the 'French original'. A couple of months after the show opened, the *Monthly Musical Record* observed, 'The libretto has been brightened up on every page and Mr François Cellier has done wonders in touching up

the music.' Such tinkering was the true but often unacknowledged fate of most musical comedies.

The books of musical comedies were strung together by writers who had an eye to what would keep a far from intellectual audience attentive throughout. This included a simple central feature such as the love of the highly placed for the humble (who often turned out to be not so humble after all) or luck arising from a windfall, and there had to be plenty of occasions for laughter and for the admiration of elegant females, everything set, if possible, in a modern context. The lyrics were often platitudinous and sometimes sheer nonsense. Catch phrases were eagerly sought after. Nevertheless some of the rhymesters displayed considerable talent, notably Adrian Ross (1859–1933) who, in Archer's opinion, was 'easier and more fluent' than **W. S. Gilbert**. Adrian Ross was the pseudonym of Arthur Reed Ropes who had distinguished himself as a scholar at Cambridge and who wrote both musical comedy lyrics and serious literature. Musical comedy was full of pseudonyms, many of which plumbed the depths. James Davis (1854–1907) called himself 'Owen Hall' which was complemented by Arthur Roberts's (1852–1933) assumption of 'Payne Nunn'.

The music of each work was newly written by one or two composers, but this did not prevent the later interpolation of previously written numbers either by these or other composers. This music was calculated to have an immediate appeal and was hoped to have a hit tune in it somewhere. The composers were often highly trained musicians whose craftsmanship was of a high order and whose facility guaranteed an instant response to a request for a new number.

The cult of 'the girl' in musical comedy is obvious from the very titles of the works. A short selection from the years 1893 to 1913 (with the number of performances each achieved on its first appearance) could include *The Casino Girl* (196), *The Circus Girl* (497), *A Country Girl* (729), *The Earl and the Girl* (371), *A Gaiety Girl* (413), *The Girl from Kay's* (432), *The Girl from Utah* (195), *The Girl in the Taxi* (385), *The Girl in the Train* (340), *My Girl* (183), *The Pearl Girl* (254), *The Quaker Girl* (536), *The Shop Girl* (546), *The Sunshine Girl* (336), *A Runaway Girl* (593). (A similar list could be made for the USA, e.g. *The Motor Girl*, *The Yankee Girl*, *The Wall Street Girl*, *The Charity Girl*, etc.) Although 'the girl' appears so frequently, the tendency was to emphasize 'the lady'. In contrast to the tights and short skirts of Victorian burlesque, costumes were expensive and elegant. This elegance, and sometimes a studied simplicity, is well illustrated in the mass-produced photographs eagerly purchased by the public. The ladies of musical comedy are picture postcard beauties *par excellence*. Not infrequently their lives had outcomes like their roles. The Baroness Churston, the Countess of Dudley, the Countess of Drogheda, Countess Poulett, the Marchioness of Headfort and others were recruited to the peerage from the musical comedy stage.

The promoters of musical comedy aimed at long runs and big profits. The performance figures noted above are not exceptional. It is true that some shows did not achieve 183 performances, but others exceeded 729, notably *A Chinese Honeymoon* (1901) with 1,075 and the remarkable *Chu-Chin-Chow* (1916) with 2,238. As well as these initial runs there were frequent revivals and there were touring versions playing not only in Britain but in America and Australia as well. **George Edwardes** (1852–1915), whose principal London theatres were the **Gaiety** and Daly's, is regarded as the prime architect of musical comedy – if someone whose sole gift seems to have been spotting what would keep the paybox busy can be called an architect. He is said to have had as many as 16 touring companies roaming Britain. The distinctions between musical comedy and operetta on the one hand and revue on the other are often very blurred. A European operetta that was transmogrified into a most successful English musical comedy was *The Merry Widow* (Daly's 1907) by Franz Lehar (1870–1948). This was followed by further adaptations of Lehar and he was only one of the Continental composers upon whom English musical comedy fastened. But the years after the First World War saw the gradual decline of musical comedy of the distinctive Edwardian kind. The cinema began to vie with the theatre in spectacle, the cult of the film star replaced that of the picture postcard beauty, up-to-the-minute references became the province of revue, and the somewhat effete melodiousness of the old music was challenged by jazz. These influences were markedly American. America and England had had a musical comedy import–export relationship. Now America was growing in independence. Composers such as **Jerome Kern** (1885–1945) and **George Gershwin** (1898–1937) added lustre to the musical theatre, and native American librettists adopted an increasingly contemporary American outlook. In England the old style was a long time a-dying, but after the Second World War the influence of the vitality, coherence, wit, seriousness and even political awareness to be found in American musical theatre had an overwhelming effect and the old kind of musical comedy was gone, replaced by what was merely called 'the musical'. Musicals such as *Cabaret* (1966) and *Evita* (1978) belong to the same family as musical comedies such as *A Gaiety Girl* (1893) and *The Belle of New York* (1897), but their relationship is not the closest, nor is it free of the bar sinister. GH

Musser, Tharon (1925–) American lighting designer. Musser began her career as designer and stage manager for the Jose Limon Dance Company and made her Broadway debut with the premiere production of *Long Day's Journey into Night*. By the late 1960s she was probably the dominant lighting designer on Broadway. Her versatility is apparent from her credits which include several seasons with the **American Shakespeare Festival**, all of **Neil Simon**'s plays since *Prisoner of Second Avenue* (1971), and musicals such as *Mame*. Since 1975 she has teamed up with designers **Robin Wagner** and **Theoni Aldredge** and director **Michael Bennett** to design *A Chorus Line*, *Dreamgirls* and several others. Her style ranges from flashy production numbers to painstakingly researched recreations of specific light qualities and moods. AA

Musset, Alfred de (1810–57) French poet and dramatist. For a long time thought of as a poet, Musset's stature as a dramatist has increased steadily since the beginning of the 20th century. His earliest plays appeared in a volume of verse, *Tales of Spain and Italy* (1830). After the failure of his first performed work, *La Nuit Vénitienne* (**Odéon** 1830), he published his plays as armchair theatre. In 1837 his one-act dramatic proverb *Un Caprice* was performed in St Petersburg by a French actress, and the play entered the repertoire of the **Comédie-Française** in 1847. From this date Musset wrote with the theatre directly in view, and created new stage versions of earlier plays, published in editions of his work after 1851. After his death his brother Paul also reworked some of the plays. Musset's main creative period extends from 1833 to 1837 with *André del Sarto* and *Les Caprices de Marianne* (1833), *Fantasio*, *On Ne Badine Pas Avec l'Amour* (*Love is not to be Trifled With*) and *Lorenzaccio* (1834), *La Quenouille de Barberine* (*Barberine's Distaff*) and *Le Chandelier* (1835), *Il Ne Faut Jurer de Rien* (*Nothing is Certain*, 1836) and *Un Caprice* (1837). This period corresponds largely with his traumatic relationship with George Sand, and its aftermath. The best of his later plays are *Il Faut qu'Une Porte Soit Ouverte ou Fermée* (*A Door must Either be Open or Shut*, 1845) and *Carmosine* (1850). Most of the plays, especially the dramatic proverbs, concern conflicts between the sexes, with detailed psychological observation and an emphasis on sub-text. Musset's women are usually idealized or regarded as false and heartless. The young Musset stated that he wanted to be **Shakespeare** or **Schiller**. The structure of his plays, not written with specific production in mind, has a fluidity reminiscent of the Elizabethans, with a number of short scenes focusing on different groups of characters, rather than the traditional French construction in long unbroken acts. *Lorenzaccio*, often called the French *Hamlet*, has 34 scenes and an army of characters. Here the emphasis is on the identity of the central figure who ceases to be able to distinguish between his 'real' self and the mask he wears (the double is a favourite Musset theme). The morality of Musset's plays worried the censors – the end of *André del Sarto* had to be re-written, and *Le Chandelier* had to be taken off at the **Comédie-Française** in 1852. *Lorenzaccio*, with its overt attacks on the monarchy of Louis Philippe and on the bourgeoisie, was unperformable in the 1830s, forbidden under the Second Empire, and only reached the stage, much adapted and reduced, with **Sarah Bernhardt** in 1896. Since then a number of actresses have tried the role of the hero, including Maguerite Jamois in **Baty**'s famous production of 1945, which, played with properties against a black background, restored the original rhythm and fluidity of the play. It became an established classic of the *théâtre populaire* repertoire with **Gérard Philipe**'s more muscular performance at Avignon in 1952. Musset was particularly interested in the actress **Rachel**, to whom he dedicated an important essay on tragedy, and for whom he wrote an abandoned play, *La Servante du Roi* (*The King's Handmaid*). JMCC

Mystery plays see **Medieval drama in Europe**

Nadagama *Nadagama* is a form of folk theatre that is said to have been introduced to Sri Lanka by Catholic missionaries from south India in the early 19th century. Although its original intention seems to have been to proselytize the religion, it soon added non-religious stories to its repertory and thrived along the whole western coastal region of the island, from the extreme north to the deep south. The plays, many of which are available in script form, are long and episodic often dealing with the exploits of heroic characters who encounter numerous dramatic challenges in love and war. Tamil and Sinhalese mix freely in the works indicating that they were particularly popular among the Tamil-speaking minority of the region.

Phillipu Sinno is regarded as the author of many of the works and the legendary father of *Nadagama*. Little is known about the man except that he was a popular versifier and a blacksmith born in Colombo. No less than 13 plays are attributed to him.

Nadagama performances take place in the village and are acted on a raised platform, semi-circular in shape. A roof shelters the acting area and painted scenery separates the acting area from the dressing room. No front curtain is used. Entrances are made from the side of the stage near which the Presenter (Pote Gura) stands and sings verses to introduce each character. The Presenter is joined by two other musicians who serve as a chorus, repeating each line of the song. Seated on the floor at the opposite side of the stage are two drummers and the Horana and cymbal players. In recent times, a violin and a harmonium have been added to the musical ensemble. The audience gains entrance to the performance area by paying a small price for seating space on the ground or a slightly higher price to sit in a chair.

A performance usually begins when the Presenter chants introductory stanzas paying homage to the deities and asking their protection for a successful performance. Then, he describes the plot of the story and craves the audience's indulgence. Next, he introduces the stock characters, one by one, beginning with the jester. Punctuating the jester's dances, the Presenter asks questions which provoke humorous responses from the jester. The next character to be introduced is the Sellan Lama, a wise man, learned in the 64 arts and sciences. Then come the Desanavadi, two characters who foretell the future, and by doing so give insight into the story to be enacted. Next, the drummers employed in the royal court enter and announce in a declamatory tone the arrival of the king. Last the king's criers enter making way for the king who summons various characters of his court who make ceremonial entrances in dance and song. Finally, the dramatic action gets underway.

A traditional *Nadagama* play takes a week to enact, beginning every evening with the presentation of the stock characters which goes on from about 9 pm until midnight. A unique feature of the *Nadagama* is the use of musical techniques adapted from south India and later from the more popular Hindustani music of north India. FAR

Naluyuks Eskimo Twelfth Night mummers of northern Labrador, literally 'heathens'. Groups of masked young men, disguised in bear skins of sacking, visit houses where there are children, interrogating them on their behaviour and distributing presents. In return, the children are required to sing a Christmas carol. Formal behaviour inside turns to boisterousness outside: spectators are chased and harassed, special attention being devoted to social undesirables, with the encouragement of the crowd. The tradition has both indigenous and European elements. AEG

Nansen, Betty (1873–1943) Danish actress and director, who in 1917 transformed a small Copenhagen playhouse (renamed the Betty Nansen Theatre) into an art theatre specializing in **Ibsen**, **Bjørnson**, **Strindberg** and contemporary European and American drama. She introduced **Pirandello**'s *Six Characters in Search of an Author* to Denmark, as well as plays by **Toller**, the **Čapeks**, **O'Neill** and **Shaw**; she also presented new Danish plays rejected by other theatres, such as **Kaj Munk**'s *The Word*. As an actress she had authority and edge, but was limited by a technique that echoed the 19th-century grand manner. Among her major roles were Hedda Gabler and Mrs Alving, which she also played in Paris. HL

Napier, John (1944–) British stage designer primarily associated with the **Royal Shakespeare Company**, who studied sculpture in art school before receiving theatre design training under **Ralph Koltai** at London's Central School. Rejecting decorative, pictorial design conventions, his early work revealed highly selective realism and a sculptor's sense of space. More recently, he has become known for art and pop-art assemblages with which he creates unusual stage environments frequently involving complex mechanisms and basic reconstructions of stage and auditorium. Representative productions include *Twelfth Night* (1978), *Nicholas Nickleby* (1980), *Cats* (1981), and *Les Misérables* (1985). JMB

Naqal (India) Also *Naqqal* and *Nakkal*. Virtually nothing of consequence has been written in English about this form of rural entertainment, once popular

John Napier's design for *Cats*, 1981.

but now in a serious state of decline in certain areas of north India – in Uttar Pradesh, Punjab and Kashmir. It may have its origins among the lower social classes of Muslims who peopled the streets during the Mugal era. The leader is known as the *khalifa*.

The form stressed farce, thus the clowns are among the more important characters, mercilessly satirizing the audience and providing fast paced entertainment through their witty words and actions. Men play all the roles and perform for weddings and other household celebrations in towns and villages. Any open space in the house, yard or street may suffice for the players who work in and among the crowd, confronting the spectators at close range.   FaR

Nash, 'Jolly' John (1830–1901) English music-hall artist. Former Gloucestershire metal-worker, billed as 'The Laughing Blacksmith'. An early protégé of **Charles Morton** he appeared at the Oxford Music Hall in 1861, was the first music-hall artist to perform at royal command, and one of the first British variety performers to tour the USA, in 1874. A musician and specialist in silly walks, his act centred on laughing songs such as the famous 'Little Brown Jug'.   AEG

Nashe, Thomas (1567–c. 1601) English pamphleteer and playwright, known as one of the **University Wits** and associated with **Lyly**, **Greene** and **Marlowe**, with the last of whom he collaborated on *Dido, Queen of Carthage* (c. 1587). The vigour and exuberance of Nashe's prose are splendidly displayed in the pamphlet, *Pierce Penilesse* (1592), and the picaresque tale, *The*

Unfortunate Traveller (1594). His surviving play, *Summer's Last Will and Testament* (c. 1593), is comparatively subdued. It is a courtly entertainment, probably presented before Archbishop Whitgift. The punning title refers, not only to summer's yielding to autumn, but also to Henry VIII's famous jester, Will Summers. Evidently more characteristic of the combative Nashe was *The Isle of Dogs* (1597), a collaboration with **Ben Jonson**. This lost play so offended the authorities when performed at the **Swan** that a Privy Council order for the destruction of all London's theatres was issued. For unknown reasons, the order was not obeyed, but neither the Swan nor Pembroke's Men, who had performed the play, ever recovered.   PT

Nathan, George Jean (1882–1958) Born of wealthy parents in Fort Wayne, Indiana, Nathan graduated from Cornell University in 1904, and studied abroad for a year at the University of Bologna (1905). In 1906 he worked as a reporter for the *New York Herald*, after which he reviewed plays for *Outing* and *The Bohemian*. He became drama critic of *Smart Set*, in 1909 joining H. L. Mencken who had been hired in 1908 to review books. The two served as co-editors from 1914 to 1924, and made *Smart Set* a cult publication among young intellectuals. Their irreverence and iconoclasm seemed to epitomize a generation attempting to rid itself of the Genteel Tradition. They founded the *American Mercury* in 1923 but quarrelled in 1924, with Nathan continuing only as drama critic until 1932. He founded and edited the *American Spectator* (1932–5), then reviewed for numerous publications including *Newsweek*, *Theatre*

Arts, Saturday Review, and *Esquire.* Influenced by **James Huneker** and **George Bernard Shaw**, Nathan wrote in a lively, impressionistic style and fought for a drama of ideas. He became a champion of **Eugene O'Neill**, publishing his early plays in *Smart Set*, and arranging for professional productions of his work. He reviewed musical revues noting that 'Good drama is anything that interests an intelligently emotional group of persons assembled together in an illuminated hall.' His reputation declined after his death in 1958 because his 'hot' impressionistic style cooled with age, and many of his opinions after 1930 proved to be erroneous. Nathan reworked his criticism into books which appeared almost every year from 1915 until 1953. From 1943 until 1951 he published a *Theatre Book of the Year.* In 1955 he married the actress, Julie Haydon, and in his will left a provision for the George Jean Nathan Award for Dramatic Criticism to be given annually.   TLM

National Theatre (Britain) The long struggle to establish a national theatre began in the 18th century with calls from **David Garrick**, but only received widespread support in 1848 with the appearance of a Proposition from the publisher, Effingham Wilson, for a theatre and drama school to be built at Stratford-upon-Avon in the name of **Shakespeare**, 'the world's greatest moral teacher'. This proposal won the support of the dramatist-MP, **Bulwer Lytton**, **Henry Irving** and Alfred Lyttelton, the father of the National Theatre's first Chairman, Oliver Lyttelton (Lord Chandos). Matthew Arnold was converted to the cause when in 1879 he saw the **Comédie-Française** for the first time. His essay 'The French Play in London' in the magazine, *Nineteenth Century,* concluded with a much-quoted clarion call, 'The theatre is irresistible, organise the theatre!'

The first serious attempts to establish a national theatre, however, came in 1907 with the publication of a detailed Scheme, with financial estimates, prepared by the critic, **William Archer**, and **Harley Granville Barker**, then at the height of his influence as a director and dramatist. This led to the formation of a Shakespeare Memorial National Theatre committee with broad support within the acting profession which raised £100,000 in five years. A Private Member's bill was introduced into the House of Commons in 1913 to 'crown' this sum with money from the public exchequer – and was passed, though not with a sufficiently large majority to make it effective. A site was bought in Bloomsbury, but all future plans were halted by the First World War.

Between the wars, the cause was upheld by the **British Drama League** through the efforts of its General Secretary, Geoffrey Whitworth, and its President, Granville Barker. The Bloomsbury site was sold and another bought in Kensington. Sir Edwin Lutyens designed an imposing building which would have faced the Victoria and Albert Museum. But the funds were never forthcoming, either from private or public sources, and supporters of the **Old Vic**, including **Lilian Baylis**, actively opposed the SMNT campaign. During the Second World War, a reconciliation took place between Geoffrey Whitworth of the SMNT committee and Sir Reginald Rowe of the Vic–Wells Trust, which cleared the way for eventual LCC and

parliamentary support. A bill was passed in 1948 which allocated one million pounds from public funds to build a national theatre on the south bank of the Thames. A design was commissioned from a fresh architect, Brian O'Rorke, and in 1951, in a third ceremonial laying of a foundation stone, Queen Elizabeth, deputizing for King George VI, laid a trough of mortar in what afterwards turned out to be the wrong place.

These plans were for various reasons delayed, until **Laurence Olivier** lent his support to the cause. He was appointed the National Theatre's first Director and it was decided to form a National Theatre company which could operate at the Old Vic until its new theatre building was completed. The National Theatre opened at the Old Vic with a production of *Hamlet* in 1963 and the first seasons were triumphantly successful, with Olivier's Othello, **Peter Shaffer**'s *The Royal Hunt of the Sun* and **Farquhar**'s *The Recruiting Officer* providing highlights. Meanwhile, a new architect, Denys Lasdun, was chosen to design a major new complex which contained three theatres, the open-stage Olivier, the proscenium arch Lyttelton and the experimental 'black-box' Cottesloe, together with large foyers, workshops, restaurants and dressing rooms. The sophisticated stage technology was considered to be in advance of its time.

The costs rose beyond those anticipated by parliament and the delays were considerable. The new National Theatre complex eventually opened piecemeal in 1976–7. Olivier had given way as director to **Peter Hall** in 1973 and the company found itself surrounded by controversies. Some issues were short-lived, occasioned by the high costs of running the new building. Others were more fundamental, in that high subsidies to the National Theatre were regarded with envy by grant-aided regional managements and with distrust by West End commercial companies. Furthermore, the National Theatre had deviated from the original intention of providing a classic repertoire along the lines of continental theatre companies and was venturing into deals with commercial theatre companies. The bulk of the profits from the Peter Shaffer hit, *Amadeus*, launched at the National Theatre in 1979, went to the **Shubert Organization** in the United States, which owned the rights. This was far from the original scheme proposed by Archer and Granville Barker. Despite some loss of the original idealism, Hall managed to bring together a talented team of writers, directors and designers to work at the National Theatre, including **Peter Gill**, **David Hare** and **Bill Bryden**, and although the artistic achievements in recent years have not matched those of the 1960s, the National Theatre has retained its foremost place among British companies, rivalled only by the **Royal Shakespeare Company**.   JE

National Theatre 1321 Pennsylvania Ave North, Washington, DC [Architect: McElfatrick, 1885]. In 1834, the first National Theatre opened its doors through the financial support of six Washington businessmen, who decided that the city needed a new place of entertainment. Fires destroyed the house in 1845, 1857, 1873 and 1885 and all but obliterated the early features in the rebuilt versions. In 1885, the theatre was completely redesigned and is the structure which still stands. The fortunes of the National followed the pattern typical of the 19th-century playhouse, which began with a resident stock company and ended as a theatre for booked-in performances. During long periods in the 20th century, the house was not used. Now owned by the Pennsylvania Avenue Development Corporation, it was renovated in 1984 and reopened for touring attractions.   MCH

National Theatre School Montreal, Canada. Founded in 1960 with the guidance of **Michel Saint-Denis**, it offers intense, co-lingual training in acting, production and design, and recently playwriting, to a select group of students drawn from all parts of the country. Much of the instruction is carried out by working theatre professionals brought to the school for short engagements. It is supported by the federal Canada Council and by granting agencies in all ten provinces, making it a truly national institution. One of its important contributions has been the raising of the standards of professionalism in Canadian theatre production.   JA

National Youth Theatre (Britain) The actor, novelist and schoolmaster, Michael Croft (d. 1986), founded this organization in 1956 primarily to give his young school actors a chance to take part in a **Shakespeare** play during the summer holidays, which would be directed to professional standards. At first the actors came from Alleyn's School where Croft taught and Dulwich College nearby, but after the NYT successes at the **Edinburgh Festival** and in London, students from all over Britain came to audition. During the 1960s, the NYT summer seasons which were held in various London theatres, such as the Jeannetta Cochrane in Holborn, began to include contemporary plays. The NYT produced **David Halliwell**'s *Little Malcolm* in 1965 and with spectacular success, gave the premiere of **Peter Terson**'s *Zigger Zagger* in 1967, in which the songs of the football terraces mingled with a gentle warning against soccer hooliganism provided the structure for the most popular school play which has yet been written. Terson wrote several other plays for the NYT, as did Barrie Keefe in the 1970s; but the fortunes of the company were changed when they moved into the Shaw Theatre in Marylebone Road, owned by Camden Council. They launched the Dolphin Company, a professional group which played in the theatre when it was not wanted for the NYT seasons. In 1981, when the NYT's small grant from the Arts Council was withdrawn, the NYT received sponsorship from the oil company, Texaco. Among the many famous actors to have emerged from the ranks of the NYT, **Derek Jacobi** and **Helen Mirren** were shortly to be seen at the **National Theatre** and the **RSC**.   JE

Nationale Scene (Bergen) The National Stage, founded in 1876, one of Norway's three major theatres, with traditions beginning with the Norwegian Theatre of 1850, where **Ibsen** was resident playwright and stage director. Although the company struggled on in the antiquated Comedy House until 1909, it was from the start aggressively innovative, premiering important plays before they were seen in Oslo: *The Wild Duck* (1885), *Rosmersholm* (1887), *The Master Builder* (1894) and *Little Eyolf* (1895). Traditionally it has also been an important training ground for future stars, such as **Johanne Dybwad**, **Egil Eide**, Ingolf Schanche and **Tore Segelcke**. Among its many inspired artistic directors have been **Gunnar Heiberg** (1884–8), **Hans Jacob Nilsen** (1934–9), Knut Thomassen (1967–76) and Kjetil Bang-Hansen (1982–6). Nilsen especially, with his remarkable productions of controversial plays, briefly made Bergen the centre of theatrical Norway. In 1967 the Little Stage opened, and in 1982 the Small Stage, both to house some of the company's most innovative work.   HL

Nationaltheatret (Oslo) Norway's National Theatre opened in 1899, the result of the gradual Norwegianization of its predecessor, the originally Danish-speaking Christiania Theatre, founded in 1827. Its first director, **Bjørn Bjørnson**, had fought for its construction and assembled a first-rate company, despite the theatre's uncertain economic basis; it remained an unsubsidized private company until 1927, but is now 90% government-subsidized. Among its more important directors have been Halfdan Christensen (two terms between 1910 and 1933), Knut Hergel (1946–60) and Arild Brinchmann (1967–78). The intimate Amphitheatre Stage opened in 1963 and in 1977 the suburban Theatre in Torshov, where some excellent, innovative work has been done, especially under the direction of Stein Winge. From Autumn 1986, Nationaltheatret's director was Kjetil Bang-Hansen.   HL

Naturalism Although naturalism and realism are often assumed to be synonymous, it is useful to distinguish between them, and in this enterprise such practitioners as **Strindberg** and **Zola** are unhelpful. The words realism and naturalism entered the English language through philosophy. Naturalism emphasized the natural as opposed to the supernatural, and, by the 19th century, the scientific as opposed to the mystical.

Although naturalism in the arts shares the mimetic mode with realism, it takes more explicit cognizance of environment, not merely as a setting but as an element of the action of drama. In an essay on English naturalism (*English Drama: Forms and Development*, 1977) Raymond Williams summarizes: 'In high naturalism the lives of the characters have soaked into their environment . . . Moreover, the environment has soaked into the lives.' The theatricalization of that environment is coloured by the ideas of Darwin, Bernard, and Marx. If the key play of realism is **Ibsen**'s middle class *Ghosts*, that of naturalism is **Tolstoi**'s peasant *Power of Darkness*, forbidden in Russia but played in Paris in 1886.

Among the plays often heralded as classics of naturalism are *The Selicke Family* of **Holz** and Schlaf, **Hauptmann**'s *Weavers*, **Gorky**'s *Lower Depths*, the minetown plays of **D. H. Lawrence**, and the sea plays of **Eugene O'Neill**. These dramas depict a group protagonist in a hostile environment that is visible and sometimes palpable on stage; the group belongs to a distinctly less fortunate class than the usual bourgeois audience.

Although such plays continue to be written e.g.

Caryl Churchill's *Fen*, the adjective 'naturalist' has fallen into disuse, replaced in English by 'kitchen-sink drama', in French by *théâtre du quotidien*, in German by 'new realism'. RC

Naughton, Bill (1910–) British dramatist, who started to write novels and short stories in the 1940s, after earning his living as a lorry driver and weaver in Lancashire. His upbringing in Bolton provided the background for two gentle, ironic, domestic comedies, *All in Good Time* (1963) and *Spring and Port Wine* (1964). He became the natural successor to the writers of the Manchester school, **Houghton**, **Brighouse** and later Walter Greenwood. But his range was wider than that of Lancashire comedy, for *Alfie* (1963), which provided **John Neville** with one of his best roles, concerns a Cockney 'wide boy' with a gift for 'pulling the birds'. Alfie's philandering was presented not in a spirit of moral censoriousness, but with a cool sense of tragic waste. Naughton has also attempted Orwellian satire, *He Was Gone When We Got There* (1966), and wrote his autobiography, *Pony Boy*, in 1966. JE

Naumachia (Greek, *naval battle*) A mimic sea combat, devised by the ancient Romans as a spectacular entertainment, staged by constructing basins in amphitheatres which were then flooded. The first on record was presented by Julius Caesar on a lake in the Campus Martius (46 BC), as a fight between a Tyrian and an Egyptian fleet, involving 2,000 combatants and 4,000 rowers; the brutality was striking. The Emperors Augustus and Titus also patronized such diversions, and under Claudius (AD 52) a crew of 19,000 gladiators and condemned criminals, costumed as Rhodians and Sicilians, fought and manoeuvred to their deaths. In later efforts, volunteers took part and crocodiles were employed for special effects. During the Renaissance, the *naumachia* was revived both for popular festivals and noble divertissements, especially at weddings. The marriage of Cosimo II Medici (1608) was celebrated by an *Argonautica* staged on the Arno; and a production of **Seneca**'s *Hercules Furens* at Düsseldorf in 1585 was enhanced by such a show. One final efflorescence can be seen in the aquatic dramas produced by **Charles Dibdin** the Younger at **Sadler's Wells**, London (1804–17). LS

Nautanki (India) Until recently this was one of the most beloved and popular forms of theatre along the heavily populated central Indo-Gangetic plain of north India, primarily found in the villages and towns of Uttar Pradesh, Punjab, Rajasthan, Hariyana and Bihar. Although the exact derivation of the term is questionable, there is a musical play which bears the name *The Story of Princess Nautanki* (*Shehzadi Nautanki*). It may be that the form came to be known by the name of the play's popular heroine. The origin of the form is also unclear. It was certainly popular in the 19th century and there is evidence to suggest that it was closely related to the **Svanga**, thought to have been performed as early as the 16th century, and the **Bhagat**, a form of religious theatre in the cities of Agra, Mathura and Vrndavan, which may be traced to at least the early 19th century. *Nautanki*'s popularity is due in part to the strong singing voices of its actors who train to reach crowds of

spectators sometimes numbering thousands and the catchy rhythms produced on the kettle drums (*nakkaras*). Indeed it is said that spectators make up their minds to attend a *Nautanki* performance based on the reputation of the singers and the drummers. The play holds less appeal for them than does the virtuosity of its artists.

Nautanki may take place virtually anywhere, in an open space of a village, in a farmer's field, in the courtyard of a patron, in an enclosed proscenium theatre or under a tent (*shamyana*). Whenever it is performed, it is organized to celebrate some special occasion – a wedding, birth of a male child, festival occasion or fair. A raised stage of three to four feet high is erected. Should additional playing space be needed, the actors commandeer the balcony or veranda of a nearby house or any raised space, even that surrounding a tree in the village. In early times, the site was demarcated by a special post of wood inserted with great ceremony by the company head, several days before the stage was erected.

The plays usually stress the melodramatic and romantic and are drawn from a variety of sources – mythology, history, semi-history, popular folklore and original sources. Their structure is either epic or narrative in form. A typical company consists of 10 to 12 actors. The stage manager (*ranga*) acts as a bridge linking diverse elements of the plot together. Following the preliminary rituals, he informs the spectators that they are going to see a particular story and the dramatic action follows, accordingly.

Music is provided by small and large drum (*nakkara*). The pitch of the large drum is controlled by a damp cloth which the musician applies to the head of the drum throughout the performance. The head of the small drum is warmed over hot coals conveniently located near the musicians who sit on a lower platform in front of the acting area. The *dholak* drum, bell-metal cymbals and the harmonium are additional and less important musical instruments. The wooden *sarangi*, the classical north Indian stringed instrument, is no longer popular in the musical ensemble and wind instruments, such as the clarinet, have been introduced in recent years by some parties owing to the popularity of film music. *Nautanki* music is a blend of classical, folk and film music. Its lusty appeal has kept it competitive but the influence of film songs has resulted in enormous changes in its style in recent years. Although the actors are generally Hindus of various lower castes, the musicians are Muslims. Songs dominate the plays but some dialogue is used occasionally to break up the action and simple dances incorporating film and folk elements are performed for the sake of variety. Improvised comic skits are also used to relieve the tension of the dramas which are usually serious and highly moralistic in tone.

With the introduction of women as performers in many of the companies after the 1930s, the predominantly male audiences have demanded actions and dances which are somewhat more provocative. In traditional companies, young boys always play the female roles. Whatever the sex of the players, enthusiastic patrons are permitted, and even encouraged, to make donations of money to the singers during the show. The women take the welcome gift and stick it in their blouses and repeat the song or dance to please the adoring follower. More discriminating companies have the stage manager take the money and name the donor out loud to the public indicating how much he gave to the player.

Today, *Nautanki* players find it difficult to survive in a society in which films have dominated the public imagination and where television is on the verge of becoming readily accessible to millions of rural patrons who once supported traditional art forms. Troupe leaders usually hold odd jobs and assemble available players when commissioned to give a performance. The failure to hold a company together for an extended period of time has eroded the quality of a once great art form.

Two styles of *Nautanki* dominate today – that of the city of Hathras and that of Kanpur – although there are other regional styles as well, such as those of Mazaffarnagar, Saharanpur and Kanauj. The two dominant styles differ in various essential respects. The Hathras style is regarded as the older and was popularized by Indarman and his pupil Natharam in the 19th century. They established a training centre (*akhara*) for disciples. The leader of the group (*khalifa*) served as the central authority on questions of artistic standards and the training process. As a result of their strict discipline and attention to detail, the master-teachers exercised enormous control over the form and through the enterprise of Natharam, who printed and distributed *Nautanki* scripts to the voracious reading public of peasants and lower caste townspeople, the style gained a wide popular following. The artists of the Hathras style sing in a high pitch and elaborate and ornate their notes. Performers work on simple raised platform stages with little or no scenic decorations, inviting the audience to use its imagination.

The Kanpur style was originated by Sri Krishna Pahalvan who entered the profession in about 1913. His goal was to crack the tight *akhara* system which admitted no one other than those who adhered to the dictates of its teachers. Instead of the traditional prayers to gods and teachers, the choral beginning of the style requires the entire cast to sing in a simple metre. This proved to be popular with audiences. Individuals were admitted to the profession on the strength of their imagination, and not according to their years of training. Thus, it did not require that a performer begin to study in his youth but that he demonstrate promise and inspiration in his singing ability. Kanpur *Nautanki* stresses a lower singing pitch and the dramatic story line is emphasized over vocal ornamentation. Typically, the style incorporates greater scenic detail. Wings and drops are used to set locales on a raised platform. 'The garden' and 'the court' are typical stock set pieces used as background for the dramatic action. This has forced audiences into a frontal juxtaposition to the acting area, virtually abandoning the three-sided or arena performance spaces with their neutral acting area so typical of the Hathras style.   FAR

Nazimova, Alla (Alla Yakovlevna Leventon)

(1879–1945) Russian actress. She studied with **Vladimir Nemirovich-Danchenko**, acted with the **Moscow Art Theatre**, and became leading lady of a St Petersburg theatre. She toured Europe and America in 1905. In New York in 1906 she presented, in English, matinee performances of *Hedda Gabler*, *A Doll's House*, and *The Master Builder*. She appeared different from the popular personality actresses of the day since she could transform herself externally into different characters. She remained in America, but by 1918 her fame had faded, and she was considered another personality actress capitalizing on her sensuous exoticism. After ten years starring in Hollywood films such as *Camille* and *Salome*, she performed with the Civic Repertory Theatre and the **Theatre Guild**. In 1935 she directed and starred in her own version of *Ghosts* after which she returned to film-making.   RAS

Ndao, Cheik Sidi Ahmed Aliou

(1933–) Senegalese playwright. Ndao was educated at the Ecole William Ponty at Thiès (near Dakar, the capital of Senegal) and at the universities of Grenoble in France and Swansea in Wales. He returned to the Ecole William Ponty as a teacher of English. Although French is his main medium of literary expression, Ndao also writes in English and especially in his mother tongue, Wolof. His first play *Le Marabout* was performed in 1961, but has never been published. He is best known as the author of *L'Exil d'Albouri* (*The Exile of Albouri*), which was performed at the Daniel Sorano Theatre in Dakar in 1968 before going on to win the first prize for drama at the Pan-African Festival in Algiers in 1969. Like his other plays it has been performed in various parts of French-speaking Africa. Ndao's reputation as a playwright in Africa derives largely from his ability to dramatize the often intractable and inherently tragic dilemmas encountered by Senegal's 19th-century rulers when confronted by the territorial ambitions of French colonialism. Other plays deal with the theme of racialism in the United States and the failures of military dictatorship. None of Ndao's plays has yet been translated into English. They are: *L'Exil d'Albouri* (*The Exile of Albouri*) and *La Décision* (*The Decision*, 1967), *Le Fils de l'Almamy* (*The Almamy's Son*) and *La Case de l'Homme* (*The Man's House*, 1973), *L'Ile de Bahila* (*The Island of Bahila*, 1973) and *Du Sang pour un Trône* (*Blood for a Throne*, 1983). Ndao has also published volumes of poetry, novels and stories.   CW

Nederlander, James

(1922–) American producer and theatre owner, born in Detroit, Michigan. Nederlander was a member of the Air Force staff producing *Winged Victory* in New York in 1943. One of the major forces in the Broadway theatre, Nederlander owns the **Palace**, **Brooks Atkinson**, and Uris Theatres in New York, as well as theatres in Detroit, Minneapolis, Chicago, San Francisco, San Diego, Los Angeles, and London. Only the **Shubert Organization** controls more theatres in the United States. Among his more successful productions are *On a Clear Day You Can See Forever* (1967), *Applause* (1970), *Abelard and Heloise* and *The Effect of Gamma Rays on Man-in-the-Moon Marigolds* (1971), as well as engagements of leading solo artists. In 1979 Nederlander produced *Whose Life Is It Anyway?* and a revival of *Peter Pan*.   SMA

Nederlander Theatre

208 West 41st St, New York City [Architect: William Neil Smith]. Built as the National in 1921 by Walter C. Jordan, a leading

theatrical agent, it stands today as the only commercial Broadway theatre below 42nd Street. With about 1,200 seats, it can be used both for musicals and dramas. In 1927, the **Shuberts** added it to their chain, then sold it in 1934, bought it back in 1944, only to be forced to relinquish it again in 1956 to satisfy a court-mandated consent decree. In 1958, it was acquired by Billy Rose, who reopened it after extensive renovation under his own name the following year. In 1979, it was bought from his estate by the Nederlander Organization, which renamed it briefly the Trafalgar, then the Nederlander after the founder of the theatrical dynasty. Among its noteworthy tenants have been **Ethel Barrymore** in *The Corn Is Green* (1940) and **Katharine Cornell** in *Dear Liar* (1960), which ended her long career. In 1981, Lena Horne took its stage with a one-woman show for a limited engagement, which stretched out to more than a year.   MCH

Negro Ensemble Company (1967–) Established in racially troubled times with a generous Ford Foundation grant, the predominantly Afro-American company inhabited the Off-Broadway St Mark's Theatre. Under **Douglas Turner Ward**'s inspired leadership, it began an ambitious programme of training young theatre aspirants and producing plays relevant to black Americans. The company was initially criticized for locating outside the black community and producing foreign plays, but its successful nurturing of black writers, performers, directors and technicians, and the sustained excellence of its productions have brought it national and international renown. In 18 successive seasons it has presented over 40 major productions and given twice that number of workshop presentations and staged readings. It has undertaken six national tours and performed abroad in London, Rome, Bermuda, Munich, and on tour in Australia. Among its many awards are the 1982 Pulitzer Prize for *A Soldier's Play*, two Tony Awards for 'special achievement' and *The River Niger* (1973), and 13 Obie Awards for outstanding new plays, performances, and productions such as *Dream on Monkey Mountain* (1971), *The First Breeze of Summer* (1975), and *Eden* (1976). In 1980 the company relocated its offices in New York's theatre district and its productions to Theatre Four on West 55th Street.   EGH

Neighbourhood Playhouse, The Like the **Provincetown Players** and the **Washington Square Players**, the Neighbourhood Playhouse (1915–27) was a pioneering Off-Broadway theatre. Remote both geographically and temperamentally from the commercial theatre, the Playhouse, located on New York's Lower East Side, was an experimental outpost connected with the Henry Street Settlement House, a social agency for the area's immigrant population. The Playhouse's major interest was in exploring through folk drama the theatre's ritual, lyric, mystical roots. Among its celebrated offerings were an ancient Hindu comedy entitled *The Little Clay Cart* (1924), *The Dybbuk* (1926), a 14th-century French mystery, a **nō** drama, a dance drama based on Celtic legend, a Norse fairy tale, and a medieval interlude as well as more conventional fare such as **Galsworthy**'s *The Mob* (1920), **O'Neill**'s *The First Man* (1922), **James Joyce**'s

Exiles (1924), and five editions of a musical revue called *The Grand Street Follies*.

Organized as an educational and philanthropic enterprise, the Playhouse achieved a renown its amateur patrons Alice and Irene Lewisohn had never envisaged. **Ellen Terry**, **Yvette Guilbert**, **Ethel Barrymore**, and Richard Boleslavski, among others, offered their services. The theatre provided an important impetus to Martha Graham and to scene designers **Aline Bernstein** and **Donald Oenslager**, and it generated both the Neighbourhood Playhouse School of the Theatre, begun in 1928 and still flourishing (for the past 50 years under the direction of Sanford Meisner), and the Costume Institute of the Metropolitan Museum, founded in 1937. In 1959 Alice Lewisohn Crowley published *The Neighborhood Playhouse: Leaves from a Theater Scrapbook*, a modest and charming memoir.   FH

Neil Simon Theatre 250 West 52nd St, New York City [Architect: Herbert J. Krapp]. As the Alvin Theatre, the 1,400-seat playhouse on the outer fringe of the theatre district had enjoyed a spectacularly successful history under the management of its two founders, Alex Aarons and Vinton Freedley, who combined the first syllables of their names to give it its name. They opened it in 1927 to house the highest forms of musical comedy and until 1932, when they lost control of the house, they fulfilled their promise by presenting works by the **Gershwins**, **Rodgers** and **Hart** and **Jerome Kern**. In 1934, a young **Ethel Merman** made her debut on its stage and in 1964, the veteran **Beatrice Lillie** bade her farewell from its stage. Under a succession of owners, the Alvin has presented non-musical fare as well, *Mr Roberts* (1948), *The Great White Hope* (1968) and *No Time for Sergeants* (1957), but nothing to equal its musical triumphs which continued with *Lady in the Dark* (1941), *A Funny Thing Happened on the Way to the Forum* (1962), *Company* (1970) and *Annie* (1977). The one musical production presented on its stage which should have been successful but was not at its introduction was *Porgy and Bess* (1935). In 1983, the theatre was renamed the **Neil Simon** by the **Nederlander** Organization in honour of the playwright.   MCH

Neilson, Adelaide (Elizabeth Ann Brown) (1848–80) English actress. Born in Leeds, she ran away to London under the name Lizzie Ann Bland and worked as a **Shakespeare**-reciting barmaid near the Haymarket. She played Julia in *The Hunchback* for her stage debut at Margate in 1865; and Juliet for her London debut that same year and for her New York debut in 1872. A highly regarded Juliet and Viola, she was praised for her intelligent conception of the role as well as her genuine acting talent, fresh beauty, and 'deliciously musical' voice. Slender, dark-eyed, and 'ravishingly pretty', she projected a commingling of gleeful childlike vitality and deep womanly pathos. Her other outstanding roles were Shakespeare's Rosalind, Beatrice, and Isabella; and Amy Robsart in *Kenilworth* and Rebecca in *Ivanhoe*. She played return engagements in America in 1874, 1876, and 1879–80. She was only 32 at the time of her sudden death in Paris.   FHL

Nelson, Rudolf (Lewysohn) (1878–1960) German variety manager. He began as a child prodigy pianist, and by 1904 was running the elegant cabaret 'Roland von Berlin'. Later he founded the German 'Chat Noir' (1907) and the Metropol-Kabarett (1910), both supplanted by the Nelson-Kunstlerspiele (1919). A gifted Offenbachian composer, he wrote the music for several operettas, and toured with his troupe 1926–32. The rise of the Nazis exiled him to Amsterdam, where he founded 'La Gaieté' (1934). After the war, he returned to West Berlin and undertook experimental revues. Nelson was instrumental in providing a style of cabaret that was not particularly satiric or political, but had sophistication and high-tone.   LS

Nemirovich-Danchenko, Vladimir Ivanovich (1858–1943)

Soviet-Russian dramatist-teacher-director and co-founder with **Stanislavsky** of the **Moscow Art Theatre** (MAT, 1897), where as its literary manager and dramaturge, he manifested a superior sensitivity to playwrights and their plays. In 1877 he began contributing theatre criticism to various journals and in 1881 initiated his career as a writer of narrative fiction. He wrote 11 plays, mostly conventional light comedies and melodramas, which achieved popular success in productions at the Aleksandrinsky and Maly Theatres. His *The Worth of Life* (1896) won the prestigious Griboedov Prize as the season's best play, an honour he felt should have gone to **Chekhov**'s innovative *The Seagull*, which had been savaged by actors, critics and audience in its Aleksandrinsky Theatre premiere. From 1891 to 1901 he taught in the Music and Drama School of the Moscow Philharmonia, whose prize acting students – **Olga Knipper**, **Vsevolod Meyerhold** and **Ivan Moskvin** – he took with him to the Moscow Art Theatre (1898). On MAT's behalf he coaxed permission from Chekhov to revive *The Seagull* and enlisted **Gorky** to write *The Petty Bourgeoisie* and *The Lower Depths* (1902), even assisting in their creation. With Stanislavsky he co-directed *The Lower Depths* and Chekhov's plays, save for *Ivanov*, which he staged alone. As a dramatist he was especially sensitive to realizing the author's intentions and the play's essence and sought to educate Stanislavsky, who was prone to sentimentality and extraneous detail in his staging, in Chekhov's special lyricism. A number of his MAT productions reflect his penchant for poetry and mysticism: **Ibsen**'s *When We Dead Awaken* (1900), *Pillars of Society* (1903), *Rosmersholm* (1908) and *Brand* (1906); **Shakespeare**'s *Julius Caesar* (1903); **Andreev**'s *Anathema* (1909), *Ekaterina Ivanovna* (1912) and *Thought* (1914); Dmitry Merezhkovsky's *There Will Be Joy* (1916); and especially, his productions of Dostoevsky – the two-evening long *The Brothers Karamazov* (whose pessimism was protested at by Gorky, 1910) and *Nikolai Stavrogin* (from the novel *The Devils*, 1913). In 1919 he organized MAT's Musical Studio, which in 1926 became the Vl. I. Nemirovich-Danchenko Musical Theatre. He brought MAT principles of performance to his opera work, replacing the conventional singer with the 'singing actor', rethinking the role of the chorus and striving to capture the music's essence as he did a play's. One of his most important productions was of Dmitry Shostakovich's *Lady Macbeth of Mtsensk District* (*Katerina Izmailova*, 1934). He was named a 'People's Artist of the USSR' in 1936 and became sole director of MAT following Stanislavsky's death in 1938. His book *My Life in the Russian Theatre* (1937) offers personal opinions about and memories of MAT's halcyon days.   SG

Nestroy, Johann Nepomuck (1801–62)

Austrian actor and playwright. After several years as an opera singer and then as an actor in various provincial theatres, Nestroy made his debut in Vienna at the Theater an der Wien in 1831. From then until his retirement in 1860, he was consistently the most visible and controversial figure of the Viennese theatre, as improvisational actor, as actor–manager, and as playwright. His penetrating wit and fearless attitude towards the Viennese censor ensured that he was continuously in conflict with authority, which occasionally landed him in gaol. Nestroy wrote over 80 plays: these indicate a shift of interest in the Viennese **Volksstück** from magic to consistently secular matters. Of them, the most enduring are the *The Evil Spirit Lumpazivagbundus* (1833), *Zu ebener Erde und im ersten Stock* (*On the Ground Floor and the First Storey*, 1835), which employs a split stage to demonstrate class differences, *The Talisman* (1840), *The Girl from the Suburbs* (1841), *Einen Jux will er sich machen* (*He Will Go On A Spree*, 1842), best known to English audiences in **Thornton Wilder**'s adaptation, *The Matchmaker*, *Der Zerrissene* (*The Torn One*, 1844), and a political satire that borders on greatness, *Freedom in Krahwinkel* (1848). Nestroy was also a master of parody; *Judith and Holofernes* (1849), a travesty of **Hebbel**'s *Judith*, is his masterpiece in this genre. Although Nestroy's reputation went into steep decline after his death, the 20th century has seen a vigorous and probably permanent revival of interest in his work. This was initiated by **Karl Kraus**, who enthusiastically brought his work to public attention. However, this interest is likely to remain confined to the German-speaking world as, due to Nestroy's dependence on Viennese dialect and his extraordinarily complex verbal play, his comedies are almost impossible to translate accurately.   SW

Netherlands, The

The origins of Dutch theatre are generally assumed to lie in the liturgy of Catholic worship at the beginning of the 12th century. It is presumed that ritual drama, spoken in the vernacular, developed from here. Although no definite statement can be made, it seems likely that a parallel tradition grew from rituals that marked the beginning of a new season and from festivities held at annual fairs. Thus far, theatrical development in The Netherlands bears close resemblance to that of other Western European countries. (See **Medieval drama in Europe**.)

The 17th century is The Netherlands' Golden Age of dramatic art. Under the influence of the classics, the distinction between tragedy and comedy became of renewed importance. The master of Dutch comedy is **Gerbrand Adriaansz Bredero**, who wrote a number of farces. They stand out for the way in which they faithfully reproduce everyday life in 17th-century Amsterdam, particularly where the language is concerned, as for instance in *The Farce of the Cow* and *The Spanish Brabanter*.

The outstanding representative of Dutch 17th-century baroque is **Joost van den Vondel**. His

Gijsbrecht van Aemstel marked the opening of the municipal theatre of Amsterdam, the **Amsterdamse Schouwburg**, in 1638. Next to Vondel, **P. C. Hooft** occupies a special place. Going back to the classics, notably **Seneca**, Hooft developed his individual, self-assured Dutch neoclassicist style.

The 18th century marks the transition from a declamatory style of acting to a relatively realistic style, which, measured by modern standards, can still be considered rather artificial. Jelgerhuis (1770–1836), who was an actor, graphic artist, and painter, has left us a text-book on the art of acting, the instructive illustrations of which give an impression of the standards and style of 18th-century acting.

In the 19th century, it is mainly 'vaudevilles' that are performed, in which the comic element is predominant. Towards the end of the century, a group of interested citizens reacted by taking the initiative to start a drama school in 1874, a drama magazine, and a theatrical company, all with the aim, similar to that of the **Comédie-Française**, to reestablish drama as an art. To this end, De Koninklijke Vereeniging Het Nederlandsch Tooneel (The Royal Dutch Drama Society) was founded. Acting with this company, Louis Bouwmeester (1842–1925) as Shylock, and his sister Theodora Mann-Bouwmeester (1850–1934) gave highly acclaimed performances. Its director, Willem Pieter de Leur, was a disciple of **Meiningen**'s.

After 1870, in imitation of the Théâtre Libre and the **Freie Bühne**, the Nederlandsche Tooneelvereeniging (Dutch Drama Society) was founded, under the leadership of Louis Henry Crispÿn (1854–1926), who produced plays by **Ibsen**, **Hauptmann**, and **Maeterlinck**.

Around 1900, **Herman Heijermans** appeared before the footlights as a playwright and producer of distinction. He wrote his realistic plays, which show a deep concern and solidarity with the poorest in society, for the Nederlandsche Tooneelvereeniging.

In the age of literary naturalism, Eduard Verkade (1878–1961) and Willem Royaards (1867–1929) stepped forward as theatrical leaders. They opposed the literary taste of their time. Royaards appreciated the aesthetic innovations and, being a student of **Reinhardt**'s, set out to visualize poetic language through theatrical means. He managed to realize his aesthetic ideals in performances that were defined by a refined and immaculate taste for colour, style, and costumes, set against a spacious and sober background. It was a prerequisite that the actors worked together as an ensemble. Verkade, on the contrary, strove, inspired by **Edward Gordon Craig**, for stylization and symbolism, which occasionally was seen as clashing with the theatrical requirements of a performance.

Van Dalsum (1889–1971) and Defresne (1893–1961), both taught by Verkade and Royaards, bear witness to a humanitarian sense of life. In their productions truth prevails over beauty. *De Beul* (*The Hangman*, 1935) by **Pär Lagerkvist** has a clear anti-fascist moral, and was interfered with by the NSB (the Dutch equivalent of the German NSDAP). The action by the NSB and the reaction of the government, which clung convulsively to a political course of neutrality, point to a changing climate, even to such an extent, that during the Second World War the development of drama reached a temporary standstill. The Kultuurkamer (Chamber of Culture), established by the Germans, led to a controversy amongst actors. To become a member, one was to sign a declaration that stated one was an Aryan (a non-Jew). The actors that signed in actual fact entered German employment. Others refused on principle. Plans were designed in secret, in preparation for the period after the war. It was then that Van Dalsum, Sternheim, and Defresne, actors who had all gone underground, were given as a matter of course free access to the municipal theatre. Those actors who had played through the war were, where deemed necessary, hit by punitive measures, issued by a committee which was established especially for that purpose.

After the war, the government became directly involved in the theatre by supplying subsidies. In the big cities, repertory companies were formed that received a guaranteed subsidy on the condition that they perform outside their own theatres as well. The aim was to reach a wide audience throughout the country. In practice, this meant that the companies had to travel a great deal.

Just after the war, it was Sjaroff, a student of **Stanislavsky**'s, who, as a guest-director, left his mark upon performances of plays by **Ostrovsky**, **Gogol**, and **Chekhov**. Through Sjaroff, Stanislavkian acting-methods became known in The Netherlands.

During the sixties, much attention was given to Dutch playwrights; their plays, however, differed widely in quality, and thus failed to provide a solid basis for a tradition of playwriting. In the seventies the repertory company Centrum (1961– ; director Peter Oosthoek) devoted itself to producing new Dutch plays (e.g. plays by Gerben Hellinga, Gerard Lemmens, Ton Vorstenbosch, Wim Schipper).

Also during the sixties, new locations were tried out in search of an alternative for the proscenium arch theatre. Notably, the **Mickery-theater** and, somewhat later, the Shaffy-theater were in the forefront of new developments.

In the late sixties, **Aktie Tomaat** (The tomato campaign) created a considerable stir in the Dutch theatre world. It was a fierce campaign against traditional repertory drama, attacking it for its lack of any form of social involvement; moreover, it formed a protest against the authoritarian status of the director. This resulted in a reformation within repertory companies from 1970 onwards. Some disappeared altogether, and new companies emerged. This development created the (financial) space for the establishment of new small companies like the Onafhankelijk Toneel (1974–) (Independent Theatre), an organization in which plastic arts work jointly with theatre producers, the Appel (1972–) (director Erik Vos) which tried to give new form to classical repertory (**Aeschylus**, *Oresteia*; **Shakespeare**, *King Lear*), and the **Werkteater**, which was set up as a kind of laboratory for practical theatre research. Yet, repertory theatre had its controversial performances, too, notably those directed by Gerard-Jan Rijnders for Globe. The political **Vormingstoneel** (educational drama), which makes use of drama to educate and to emancipate its audience, flourished: companies like Sater and Proloog (1967–83) were part of the official theatre circuit.

Outside the official circuit, 1975 marks the birth of the Festival of Fools. An initiative taken by 'fool' Jango Edwards, it is intended to be held every other year. Run virtually without subsidy, the Festival of Fools provides a stimulus to fringe theatre, performed in regular theatres and in the streets of Amsterdam as well. The 'fool' stands for the basic idea behind the festival: he is the jester, who comments upon life and draws attention to its ironies.

In the eighties, the heyday of official theatre seems to have come to an end; many little companies however perform very often without subsidies. Their repertory varies from the very traditional to performances in which new environments are explored, (e.g. in warehouses or in locks (Hollandia's performance *La Paloma*, 1986). Cuts in subsidy seem to form a serious impediment to new developments. Nevertheless, immigrant theatre does form a new development. Immigrant workers, who have started entering the country ever since the fifties, brought their cultural heritage with them. Since 1983, the Stagedoor-festival has been held annually. Here migrant theatre companies from Surinam, Morocco, Turkey, and other countries, are offered the opportunity to present themselves to an audience. MG WH HS

See: B. Albach, *Helden, draken en comedianten. Het Nederlandse toneelleven voor, in en na de Franse tijd*, Amsterdam, 1956; B. Albach, *Duizend jaar toneel in Nederland*, Bussum, 1965; E. Alexander, 'For Holland a new beginning: Royaards (1867–1929) and Verkade (1879–1961)', in *Theatre Research/Recherches théâtrales*, x, 2 (1969), 82–6; H. Becker, 'Divine Love as the unifying principle in Vondel's Lucifer', in *Modern Language Review*, 54, 3 (1959), 384–90; A. Brine, 'Amsterdam. Europe Newsletter', in *Plays and Players*, xvi, 1 (1968), 66–7; B. Gascoigne, 'The Low Countries and Amsterdam', in B. Gascoigne, *World Theatre*, London, 1968; W. M. H. Hummelen, *Repertorium van het rederijkersdrama 1500 – ca. 1620*, Assen, 1968; B. Hunningher, 'The Nederlandish Abele Spelen', in *Maske und Kothurn*, 10 (1964), I, 244–53; J. Jelgershuis, *Theoretische lessen over de gesticulatie en mimiek*, Reprint edn, 1827, Amsterdam, 1970: Summary 17–28; G. R. Kernodle, *From Art to Theatre: The Rederijkers Stage in the Netherlands*, Chicago, 1944, 111–29; P. King, 'The sacramental Thought in Vondel's Drama', in *Modern Language Review*, 51, 2 (1956), 203–14; H. H. J. de Leeuwe, 'Das Theater in den Niederlanden', in M. Hürlimann (ed.), *Das Atlantisbuch des Theaters*, Zurich, 1966; J. J. Mak, *De Rederijkers*, Amsterdam, 1944; J. M. Manly, 'Elckerlijc-Everyman: The Question of Priority', in *Modern Philology*, VIII (1910), 269–77; G. Rekers, 'Avant-Garde theatre in the Netherlands', in *International Theater Informations*, 1971, 3–9; J. G. Riewald, 'New light on the English actors in the Netherlands, c. 1590 – c. 1660', in *English Studies*, XLI (1960), 1–28; B. Stroman, *De Nederlandse toneelschrijfkunst: Poging tot verklaring van een gemis*, Amsterdam/Antwerp, 1973; H. Traver, 'Religious implications in the Abele Spelen of the Hulthem manuscript', in *Germanic Review*, XXVI, New York (1951), 35; G. J. de Voogd, *Facetten van vijftig jaar Nederlands toneel: 1920 – 1970*, Amsterdam, 1970; J. A. Worp, *Geschiedenis van het drama en van het tooneel in Nederland*, Groningen, 1904, 1908 (2 vols.); W. Zweers and L. Welters, *Toneel en Publiek in Nederland*, Rotterdam, 1970.

Nethersole, Olga (1870–1951) British actress and manager. Born in London, she made her first stage appearance in Brighton, England, at age 17, and performed for 26 years, touring Britain, America, Australia, and France. Her 1888 London debut was in *The Union Jack*; she first appeared in America in 1894 in Chicago in *The Transgressor*. In 1895 she visited the USA with *The Wife of Scarli*, and returned in 1899 with *The Second Mrs Tanqueray*. For the next six years she toured America. Later successes included *Mary Magdalene* and *Camille*. In 1900 she excited considerable controversy with a production of *Sappho*, which was closed by the New York police as immoral. The courts cleared Nethersole; she took the show to London for a huge success. Upon the outbreak of the First World War, she retired and became a nurse, appearing only for a single performance in 1923 in London. SMA

Neuber, Caroline (1697–1760) German actress. With her husband Johann (1697–1756), Caroline Neuber served as leader of the most successful troupe of travelling players in Germany during the 1720s and 1730s. In cooperation with **Gottsched**, she attempted to raise the standards of contemporary theatre by abolishing improvisation and by introducing into the repertoire 'regular' tragic drama, translated from or modelled on French tragedy. She had much initial success, though her fortunes declined after breaking with Gottsched in 1741, and her final years were spent in obscurity. As an actress Neuber was most successful in comedy, to which she brought much personal grace. SW

Neville, John (1925–) British actor and theatre director. After some years in repertory he achieved national distinction at the **Old Vic** (1953–9) as an actor in the classical mould, giving memorable performances as Romeo, Mark Antony and (alternating with **Richard Burton**) Othello and Iago. In 1961 he joined the Nottingham Playhouse and, in 1963, at the opening of the new Playhouse, became its artistic director. After five energetic years there in which he firmly placed the theatre in the forefront of regional theatres (aiming at creating a 'national theatre' for the area), he resigned amidst a controversial dispute with the **Arts Council** and the Theatre Board over matters of funding and artistic control. While at Nottingham he had demonstrated the range and depth of his acting in roles as diverse as Oedipus and the homosexual barber in Charles Dyer's *Staircase*. Neville eventually moved to Canada where he was appointed director of the Citadel Theatre, Edmonton, in 1973 and artistic director of the Neptune Theatre in Halifax in 1978. AJ

New Amsterdam Theatre 214 West 42nd St, New York City [Architects: Herts and Tallant]. When it was built in 1903 by Klaw and Erlanger, it was intended to be their premier theatre for musical productions and spectacles. From 1913 to 1937, **Florenz Ziegfeld**'s annual editions of the *Follies* were presented on its stage, but in 1937, it was sold to motion picture interests and became one of the 'grind' (continuous show) movie houses lining 42nd Street. In 1982, as part of the reclamation programme, it was taken over by the **Nederlander** Organization to be reconstructed and renovated as a legitimate house, but work on it has not been completed. Almost as famous as the ornate 1,700-seat auditorium is the Roof Garden above the theatre, which dispensed light entertainment and refreshment to after-theatre crowds for many years. In

1930, it was rented first as a radio studio, then as a television studio. In recent times, it has served as a rehearsal hall. It is in the process of reconstruction as a small theatre.   MCH

New Dramatists (1949–) American service organization for playwrights. Founded in New York by Michaela O'Harra with assistance from **Robert Anderson**, **Richard Rodgers**, and **Howard Lindsay**, New Dramatists exists to 'encourage and develop playwriting in America'. After a screening process, accepted members are provided a cast and director for readings of their plays. A critique session with other playwrights and professionals gives the writer a frank evaluation and suggestions for rewriting. Members also may be assigned to review a Broadway production from beginning rehearsal to opening. New Dramatists informs members about current writing opportunities; provides classes on the craft of writing; solicits tickets to current theatre productions; maintains a library of current periodicals and trade journals; and provides loans for members with plays in production. Successful alumni include: **John Guare**, **Lanford Wilson**, **William Inge**, **Ed Bullins**, **Megan Terry**, **Maria Irene Fornes**, **Paddy Chayefsky**, Horton Foote, and **Rochelle Owens**.   TLM

New Play Centre Canadian theatre company that grew out of a play-reading service for local writers established in Vancouver in 1970 to encourage the development of original plays for all media. Under the direction of Pam Hawthorne it became a major force in Canadian drama. As many as 25 new works are given workshops each year, with 3–5 of them having major public productions. Among the important playwrights who have benefited from its services are **Sharon Pollock**, Sheldon Rosen and Betty Lambert. A 1978 visit by the literary manager of the **Stratford Festival** resulted in a close relationship between the two organizations, bringing both the Centre's director and its playwrights to the attention of eastern audiences. The New Play Centre provides an alternative way for writers to see their work on stage and it has helped make the west coast a remarkably fertile ground for the development of new playwrights.   JA

New Theatre (New York) (1909–11); **The Century** (1911–30) New York's first major art theatre (Central Park West at 62nd Street, a stone's throw from the present Lincoln Center complex) had an auspicious dedication ceremony (6 November 1909) with speeches by J. Pierpont Morgan, Woodrow Wilson, **George Pierce Baker**, **W. D. Howells**, Thomas A. Edison, and **William Archer**, preceding the performance of *Antony and Cleopatra* with **E. H. Sothern** and **Julia Marlowe**.

The idea for the New Theatre originated with Heinrich Conried, director of the Metropolitan Opera; funds were subscribed by 30 wealthy opera patrons to build an elegant Italian Renaissance structure with magnificent staircases and lobbies, a roof garden, a spacious orchestra pit, the latest stage equipment including the first electrically operated revolving stage, and **Winthrop Ames** from Boston's Castle Square Theatre was appointed director.

The New got off to a poor start. The production was not ready, the house seating 2,500 was too large, the acoustics were abominable. Clearly the plan to stage operas and plays in the same theatre had been a mistake. In two seasons only **Galsworthy**'s *Strife*, **Edward Sheldon**'s *The Nigger*, and Mary Austin's *The Arrow Maker* could properly be called 'new'. The lessons from its brief life were clear. An art theatre could not be bought with dollars. The new theatre movement demanded intimate quarters.

The **Shubert brothers** acquired the building and renamed it. As the Century, it housed an assortment of musicals by **Victor Herbert**, Offenbach, Romberg, and Oscar Strauss, Morris Gest's production of **Reinhardt**'s *The Miracle* (1924) for which **Norman Bel Geddes** transformed the theatre into a massive Gothic cathedral, and, that same season, **Eleonora Duse** in eleven matinees of five plays including *Lady from the Sea* and *Ghosts*. It was demolished in 1930 and replaced with the Century Apartments.   RM

New York Shakespeare Festival (USA) New York's busiest company, founded in 1954 by **Joseph Papp** 'to encourage and cultivate interest in poetic drama with emphasis on . . . Shakespeare . . . and to establish an annual summer Shakespeare Festival'. Forming the Shakespearian Theatre Workshop in a Lower East Side church, Papp believed 'theatre with the highest professional standards can and should reach a broadly based public'. Every summer, Papp produces two free productions in Central Park's Delacorte Theatre, built for NYSF in 1957. Bernard Gersten joined NYSF in 1960 as Associate Producer, and, in 1967, they renovated the East Village's Astor Library for their headquarters, the Public Theatre. In 1973, Papp became director of Lincoln Center's **Vivian Beaumont** and **Mitzi E. Newhouse Theatres**, but financial difficulties forced departure in 1977; Gersten left NYSF the next year. In 1980, after another crisis permitted only one Delacorte production – a hugely successful modernization of **Gilbert** and Sullivan's *The Pirates of Penzance* – New York City awarded NYSF a permanent subsidy. In 1982, Papp established the Festival Latino de Nueva York, and in 1983, NYSF adopted the Young Playwrights Festival, started in 1981 by **Circle Repertory**.

Apart from Shakespeare, NYSF stages new American plays, including Gerome Ragni, James Rado and Galt MacDermot's *Hair* (1967), **Charles Gordone**'s

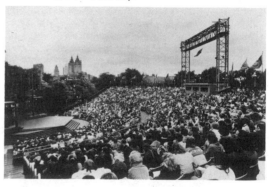

The New York Shakespeare Festival's Delacorte Theatre in Central Park, New York City.

No Place to Be Somebody (Pulitzer Prize for Off-Broadway, 1969), MacDermot's musical Two Gentlemen of Verona (Tony, 1971), **Rabe**'s Sticks and Bones (Tony, 1971), Jason Miller's That Championship Season (Tony and Pulitzer, 1972), **Bennett**'s A Chorus Line (Tony, 1975 – and Broadway's longest-running show), **Ntozake Shange**'s For Colored Girls Who Have Considered Suicide/When the Rainbow is Enuf (1976), David Henry Hwang's The Dance and the Railroad (1981), Elizabeth Swados's The Haggadah (1982) and **Durang**'s The Marriage of Bette and Boo (1985). NYSF also hosts visiting companies and artists, such as **Mabou Mines, Meredith Monk, Richard Foreman, Joseph Chaikin** and **Andrei Serban**, and produces American premieres of European and South American works, including **Václav Havel**'s The Memorandum (1968), Roberto Athaye's Miss Margareda's Way (1977), **David Hare**'s Plenty (1983), **Caryl Churchill**'s Top Girls (1983) and Fen (1984) and Louise Page's Salonika (1985). In 1983, Papp established an exchange with London's **Royal Court Theatre**. REK

New Zealand Pioneer theatres, mostly hotel annexes, began to appear with systematic European colonization (1840–), and the gold rush economy of the 1860s saw the establishment of substantial theatres in most towns. Until the turn of the century, these generally housed touring professional companies covering the Australasian circuit, although resident stock companies also occurred. A few locally written melodramas were presented, including George Darrell's Transported for Life (1876) and The Pakeha (1890) and George Leitch's The Land of the Moa (1895), only the last of which has survived. Just as a national railway system began to facilitate touring, which had previously depended on coastal shipping, the advent of motion pictures effectively destroyed it; a vacuum was created, to be partially filled by 'Repertory' theatres (large amateur groups, sometimes with a professional director) in most cities in the late 1920s. A New Zealand branch of the **British Drama League** was established in 1932, coordinating an extensive amateur movement that was now reaching smaller towns with festivals and playwriting competitions. One-act plays by Alan Mulgan, J. A. S. Coppard, Eric Bradwell, and **Ngaio Marsh** were thus promoted, while full-length works by expatriates such as Merton Hodge, Austin Strong, and Reginald Berkeley were also seen. Tours by various **J. C. Williamson** professional companies (operating from Australia since 1881) continued intermittently after the War, generally presenting musicals and polite comedy, but the only comparable New Zealand companies to achieve a significant duration were the **New Zealand Players** and the **Community Arts Service Theatre**. A few idiosyncratic amateur groups encouraged local scripts, notably Unity Theatre, Wellington (1944–78), Elmwood Players, Christchurch (1949–), and the Globe Theatre, Dunedin (1961–); **Bruce Mason, James K. Baxter**, and Craig Harrison were major playwrights who emerged through this context. However, the main stimulus for local dramatic writing in the late 1950s and early 1960s was the national radio (NZ Broadcasting Service, later Corporation, now Radio NZ). Government subsidy on a significant scale came with the Queen Elizabeth II Arts Council's foundation in 1964; this has supported

various professional and semi-professional companies, most of which also engage in limited touring: the Southern Comedy Players (Dunedin, 1957–71), Central Theatre (Auckland, 1962–76), **Downstage Theatre** (Wellington, 1964–), Mercury Theatre (Auckland, 1968–), Four Seasons Theatre (Wanganui, 1970–), The Court Theatre (Christchurch, 1971–), Gateway Theatre (Tauranga, 1972–7), Fortune Theatre (Dunedin, 1973–), Theatre Corporate (Auckland, 1973–), Centrepoint Theatre (Palmerston North, 1974–), and Circa Theatre (Wellington, 1976–). The Association of Community Theatres (ACT) represents most of these theatres and workshops and distributes New Zealand plays through Playmarket; the New Zealand Drama School, also supported by the Arts Council, offers a two-year course which trains many of the actors entering these theatres. In the 1960s, Downstage was prominent as the patron of local writers, producing Bruce Mason, Peter Bland, Robert Lord, and Joseph Musaphia, but in the 1970s other theatres became equally important: **Mervyn Thompson** was first produced at the Court, and **Greg McGee** at Theatre Corporate, which in 1982 premiered Outside In, a prison play by Hilary Beaton, one of the country's most interesting feminist playwrights. Unquestionably the most popular recent drama has been the satirical comedy of Roger Hall, initially at Circa (Glide Time, 1976, Middle Age Spread, 1977). The establishment of the community theatres in the 1970s has stimulated alternative forms such as **Maori theatre** and the collectives of Francis Batten and **Paul Maunder**. Also, the vitality of contemporary New Zealand theatre has attracted numerous writers already established in other genres, including Alistair Campbell (When the Bough Breaks, Downstage, 1969), Vincent O'Sullivan (Shuriken, Downstage, 1983), and Maurice Shadbolt (Once on Chunuk Bair, Mercury, 1982); the last two are war plays with a documentary basis which, produced in the country's major theatres, indicate a growing audience acceptance of intellectually complex scripts. HDMCN

New Zealand Players Touring professional company founded by Richard and Edith Campion in 1953, in association with another graduate of the **Old Vic** Theatre School, the designer Raymond Boyce; G. H. A. Swan was administrator. Touring the major centres from Wellington several times a year, the Players offered a repertoire popular enough to compensate for the lack of subsidy, until economic factors conflicted with their elaborate style, leading to collapse in 1960; a quartet touring schools continued through the 1960s. Boyce and the Campions have made notable contributions to other Wellington theatres, such as **Downstage** and Unity, particularly in mounting New Zealand plays (few of which were done by the Players). HDMCN

Ngahyoma, Ngalimecha (fl. 1970s) Tanzanian playwright, working with the Audio-Visual Institute in Dar es Salaam. He has published two Swahili plays, Huka (1973), which portrays the problems of a young schoolgirl trapped and destroyed by the evils of city life, and Kijiji Chetu (Our Village, 1975), which deals with some of the social problems arising from the creation of Ujamaa villages. PMl

Ngugi wa Thiong'o (1938–) Kenyan novelist, playwright and polemicist. His plays in English include *The Black Hermit* (1962), *This Time Tomorrow* (1968) and *The Trial of Dedan Kimathi* (with **Micere Mugo**). With Ngugi wa Mirii he wrote the draft script of **Kamiriithu** Community Educational and Cultural Centre's Gikuyu play, *I'll Marry When I Want*, and following that, also in Gikuyu, *Mother Sing To Me*. Ngugi's work is characterized by a consistent development of early nationalist positions into an anti-imperialist commitment to the cause of peasants and workers in Kenya today. His work in theatre shows a parallel development – from individual authorship to collective authorship in Gikuyu and other Kenyan languages. Ngugi was detained by the Kenyan government from 1977 to 1978 and now lives in exile.   RK

Niblo's Garden Northeast corner of Broadway and Prince St, New York City. A tavern keeper, William Niblo, leased the Columbian Gardens from the Van Rennselaer family and turned it into a summer retreat for New Yorkers. In 1828, he converted a stable into a summer theatre named the Sans Souci. He later added a proper theatre as a year-long enterprise and presented regular dramatic fare. From then on, it simply became known as 'Niblo's Garden'. When the complex was levelled by fire in 1846, Niblo retreated to his country estate, a millionaire, but was induced to rebuild it a few years later. The Van Rennselaers built the Metropolitan Hotel on part of the same site and the theatre was entered through the hotel lobby. During its long history, every kind of entertainment and most of the reigning stars appeared on its stage, but none more popular than the Ravel family of comedians and *The Black Crook*, which opened in 1866 and ran for 16 months. Another fire in 1872 destroyed the theatre, but it was rebuilt and survived until 1892, when both the hotel and the theatre were razed.   MCH

Nicaragua Nicaragua's early claim to drama lies in *El baile de Güegüence* (*The Dance of the Old Man*), a folkloric piece combining ballet and dialogue whose origins belong to the Nahuatl pre-Columbian period. By the time it was recorded, certain Spanish elements had been integrated into the story of an old man, el Macho Ratón, in a family exchange with the regional governor. Less pure than the **Rabinal Achí**, the maya-quiché play from the Guatemalan region, it nonetheless conserves vestiges of the indigenous dramatic tradition.

The colonial years left few traces of theatre in Nicaragua. Through the 19th century some travelling companies visited the country and several expatriate writers, such as the Cuban–Dominican Alejandro Angulo Guridi (1826–1906) and the Salvadoran Francisco Gavidia (1864–1955), settled in Nicaragua. Rubén Darío (1867–1916), Latin America's modernist poet *par excellence*, presented two plays in Managua, one comedy and one tragedy, but both texts are lost.

20th century Sporadic theatre activity continued in the 1900s. Santiago Argüello (1871–1940), Marcial Ríos Jerez (b. 1897) and Hernán Robleto (b. 1893), who spent most of his life in Mexico, tried varieties of tragedy mixed with religious and romantic dramas, but without great aesthetic success. It was the creation of

the literary journal *Vanguardia* (*Vanguard*) in 1928, followed by a homonymous theatre group in 1935, that began to bring to Nicaragua a sense of world styles and techniques. Joaquín Pasos (1915–47) and José Coronel Urtecho (b. 1906) exaggerated the popular figures of Nicaraguan folk tales into grotesque caricatures with popular poetry in their *Chinfonía burguesa* (*Bourgeois 'Chymphony'*) (written in 1932 as a poem, rewritten as a dramatic farce in 1939). **Pablo Antonio Cuadra** (b. 1912) also utilized traditional and popular religious forms. His major play *Por los caminos van los campesinos* (*Along the Roads Go the Peasants*, 1937) focused on a farmer's struggle to retain his land and his dignity in the face of adversity, aggression and injustice. Other plays of psychological bent are *El árbol seco* (*The Dry Tree*) and *El avaro* (*The Miser*). Other playwrights include **Rolando Steiner** (b. 1935), whose major works are *Judit* and *La puerta* (*The Door*), and Alberto Ycaza (b. 1945), the author of surrealistic plays based on a pre-Hispanic tradition, such as *Ancestral 66*.

Nicaragua has one of the most modern theatre buildings in all of Latin America, the Rubén Darío Theatre, completed in 1969 and located on the shores of Lake Managua. Its 1,300-seat main stage and a small experimental theatre below (named for Edgar Munguía) offer attractive space both for local productions and visiting troupes. Before the fall of the Somoza dynasty in 1979, several amateur theatre groups were operational, including Jaime Alberdi's Teatro Experimental de Managua (Managua Experimental Theatre). With the advent of the Sandinista Revolution (1979), these groups were displaced by a new revolutionary theatre based largely on the Cuban model. Socorro Bonilla made the transition with the Comedia Nacional de Nicaragua (Nicaraguan National Comedy) established in 1965. Under the direction of the Ministry of Culture, this movement generated new groups throughout the provinces that concentrated on popular theatre with liberationist themes embedded in folkloric music and dance. With only rudimentary props and costumes, the people used theatre to express their culture, their joys and sorrows, and the process of change in a revolutionary society. Groups include the Nixtayolero, Teatro Investigación de Niquinohomo, Xipaltomal and others. Hernán Robledo and Alan Bolt are primary writers and directors in this movement which is reinforced by the annual festivals, and meetings sponsored regularly by the government.   GW

See: O. Ciccone, 'Il Muestra Nacional de Teatro (Managua)', *Latin American Theatre Review* 16,2, Spring 1983, 67–71; N. Miller, 'II Encuentro de Teatristas Latinoamericanos y del Caribe (Nicaragua, 1983)', *Latin American Theatre Review* 17,2, Spring 1984, 85–8; C. Morton, 'The Nicaraguan Drama: Theatre of Testimony', *Latin American Theatre Review* 17,2, Spring 1984, 89–92; O. Rodríguez Sardiñas, C. M. Suárez Radillo, *Teatro contemporáneo hispanoamericano*, Madrid, 1971; C. Solórzano, *Teatro breve hispanoamericanao*, Madrid, 1970.

Nichols, Anne (c. 1891–1966) American playwright who wrote numerous forgettable plays, vaudeville sketches and musicals before and after the phenomenal success of her record-breaking *Abie's Irish Rose*. The story of the mixed-up marriage between a Jewish boy and an Irish girl, the play ran for 2,327 consecutive nights on Broadway (1922–7). Although critics attacked it as a cliché-ridden, ethnic burlesque, the play made a fortune for its author–producer. Called 'the million dollar play' it was revived in 1937 and 1954, filmed in 1928 and 1946, became a radio show in the 1940s and served as the basis of a 1970s TV sitcom, *Bridget Loves Bernie*.   FB

Nichols, Mike (Michael Igor Peschkowsky) (1931–) American actor, director, and producer. Born in Berlin, Nichols fled to New York with his parents to escape the Nazis. He attended the University of Chicago for two years after which he studied with **Lee Strasberg** at the **Actors Studio**. He began his professional career in Chicago performing with a comedy group which included Elaine May. In 1957 Nichols and May developed their own act which included regular satirical sketches and improvisations. They gave two New York concerts in 1959, followed by *An Evening with Mike Nichols and Elaine May* on Broadway in 1960, establishing both performers as major stars. Nichols turned to directing in 1963 with **Neil Simon**'s *Barefoot in the Park*, followed by *The Knack* (1964); *Luv* (1964); *The Odd Couple* (1965); *The Apple Tree* (1966); *Plaza Suite* (1968); and *The Prisoner of Second Avenue* (1971). His comic inventiveness made him one of the most sought after directors in New York. In the 1970s and 1980s, Nichols has turned to more serious fare, including *Streamers* (1976); *Comedians* (1976); *The Gin Game* (1977); *The Real Thing* (1983); and *Hurlyburly* (1984), demonstrating skill and vitality in shaping complex dramatic works. Richard Schickel (*Time*) praised his 'uncanny sense of modern body language' in communicating the shapeless lives in **David Rabe**'s *Hurlyburly*. Nichols produced the musical *Annie* (1977) and *The Gin Game*. His major films include: *Who's Afraid of Virginia Woolf?* (1965); *The Graduate* (1968); *Catch 22* (1970); *Carnal Knowledge* (1971); and *Silkwood* (1983). Winner of 5 Tonys and 1 Oscar, Nichols remains one of the most successful American directors of the contemporary theatre.   TLM

Nichols, Peter (Richard) (1927–) British dramatist, who worked as an actor and schoolteacher, before starting to write television plays in the early 1960s. His first stage success came in 1967 with *A Day in the Death of Joe Egg*, about how two parents coped, or not, with their spastic child, a 'vegetable'. This early play demonstrated Nichols's ability to take a painful theme, to handle it with a directness that does not exclude comedy and to write powerful acting parts. Nichols's plays fall, perhaps deceptively, into two categories. There are his broad, expansive plays about social or historical themes, written in spacious manner, with interludes, songs and sometimes music-hall routines. These would include *The National Health* (1969) set in a hospital ward for incurables, *The Freeway* (1974) about a Britain choked up by a vast traffic jam, *Privates on Parade* (1977) about an army concert party in Malaya after the war which also describes the decline of British colonialism and *Poppy* (1983) about the opium wars in China, which Nichols conceived as a tatty Victorian panto and was given a wholly inappropriate production by the **RSC**. The second category consists of domestic plays, tightly, often ingeniously, written, naturalistic and exact in details, such as *Chez Nous* (1974), *Born In The Gardens* (1980) and *Passion Play* (1981) in which the *alter egos* of the partners in an adulterous marriage are given a chance to speak. Nichols is a liberal moralist in that all his plays are directed towards a consideration of ethical and social issues without stridently imposing solutions. Although his work has mainly been staged in the **National Theatre** or at the RSC, it also reaches out to wider audiences and an apparently slight, nostalgic play such as *Forget-me-not Lane* (1971) has proved popular with British repertory theatres.   JE

Nicolet, Jean-Baptiste (1728–96) Parisian showman who inherited his father's puppetshows at the fairs of St Germain and St Laurent, and soon added live actors, playing the roles of **Harlequins** and bankers himself. In 1759 he removed to a building in the Boulevard du Temple, amplifying his offerings of pantomimes with comic opera and pieces from the repertory of the **Comédie-Italienne**. He made an instant success, and for 30 years had to placate the jealousies of the legitimate theatres and the scrutiny of police inspectors. Outside, the theatre performed *scènes à la Momus*, farcical skits; inside, saucy plays were interspersed with acrobats, ropedancers and trained animals: the ape Turco made all Paris laugh with his parody of the indisposed Molé. In 1772 Louis XV was amused by the troupe and dubbed it the 'Théâtre des Grands Danseurs du Roi'. Deemed by his rivals illiterate and churlish, Nicolet managed by his intuition of popular taste to amass a fortune and could boast a company of 30 actors, 60 dancers, 20 musicians and 150 works in his repertory. 'To go from strength to strength as at Nicolet's' became a proverb. After the Revolution he renamed his house the Théâtre de la Gaité and added classics, enjoying a huge success with **Molière**'s *Georges Dandin*.   LS

Nietzsche, Friedrich (1844–1900) German philosopher and aphorist. Nietzsche's most substantial contribution to the theatre, his essay *The Birth of Tragedy* (1872), argues that Greek tragedy came about through the eruption of irrational, Dionysian forces into the serenity of Apollonian culture. Tragedy declined, Nietzsche argued, when it was reduced in scope by **Euripides** and clarified by Socratic rationalism. Nietzsche's version of Greek drama has often been questioned and may more correctly be regarded as an argument in support of **Richard Wagner**'s music drama, which, to Nietzsche's mind, exercised a 'Dionysian' influence in the modern 'Socratic' world. Later, Nietzsche was to repudiate both Wagner and the ideas expressed in *The Birth of Tragedy*.   SW

Nigeria Nigeria, with more than 70 million people, is the most populous country in Africa. It became independent from Britain in 1960, within boundaries created by European rivalry during the 19th century which ignored existing African societies. After the civil war (the so-called Biafran War) had failed to break up the country at the end of the 1960s, Nigerians through their oil wealth were able to create a number of States within the Federation, which generated both spectacular consumption and a dynamic internal market. One aspect of this State spending which encouraged the development of drama was the establishment of institutions which would foster the unique cultural identity of each State: Arts Council, University, TV channel.

These State institutions tried to create a cultural affiliation for their people which fulfilled a need that the wider social formation of Nigeria did not, while still being economically dependent on the latter. Thus, although the States are dependent on central government they are important for the direction of development in drama and theatre. They have established the means of production for live and televised performance: by 1980 there were Arts Councils with purpose-built theatres, colour television channels based in nearly every State capital, twenty-three universities (in 1985) at least a quarter of which offered undergraduate and postgraduate degrees in Theatre Arts, Performing Arts or Drama (the Universities of Ibadan, Jos, Ahmadu Bello, Ifé, Calabar, Ilorin, Benin and Nsukka) and a few fully professional theatre companies and performance troupes paid for by the universities and/or the Arts Councils. This demonstration of public funding for theatre and drama is a massive national commitment by any criteria. However, since the early 1980s, the drastic reduction in oil revenues and therefore in Nigeria's GNP has arrested the development and even the consolidation of this establishment.

There are regional variations to this general picture of substantial commitment to theatre from the Nigerian public purse. While all the States, without exception, are conscious of their heritage in the traditional performing arts, contemporary theatre is more vigorously encouraged by the southern States, and is most vigorous in the largely Yoruba States (Ondo, Oyo and Kwara). Nevertheless, theatre is neither weak nor necessarily retarded in the largely Muslim Hausa and Fulani States in the north. Traditional performance there is dynamic and complex, though different to the southern masquerade traditions; modern drama is developing in rural villages in innovative and political ways; and some young northerners are notably channelling their dramatic talents into film-making and television. And States like Benue, whose peoples are not part of the large groupings (Hausa, Yoruba, Igbo), have supplied a disproportionately large number of talented drama graduates who have become actors, teachers and recorders of rich performance traditions which have thus received recognition nationally.

Traditional performance The States within the Nigerian Federation have not entirely taken over the patronage of traditional performance. Many traditional rulers still remain the ultimate authority for seasonal and religious rituals and cults. Nevertheless, the sponsorship by each State of a regional cultural identity has created the conditions for contemporary drama to grow out of traditional performance, because dances, music, masquerades, festivals, story-telling, minstrelsy – all part of the oral tradition – have survived the years of colonial rule to offer now a richer historical view than that drawn from written colonial records. This forms the basis of both discourse and aesthetic in the emerging Nigerian theatre. For example, J. A. Adedeji's pioneering study of *Alarinjo* Theatre in the Oyo Yoruba empire shows how that theatrical art evolved in the 14th century out of the *Egungun* masquerade, becoming eventually both Court Masque and professional popular travelling theatre. This important theatre research is complemented by other studies of *Egungun*, exploring, for example, the mim-

etic satire of the *Gelede* masquerade which imposes animated wooden puppetry upon the mask. *Egungun* is given a complex metaphysical significance by the playwright **Wole Soyinka** both in his writing and in his aesthetic theory. In fact, many Yoruba playwrights, writing either in Yoruba or in English, find both content and style in *Egungun*.

The *Ozidi* saga (Ijọ) is an example of a full-scale dramatic performance within the tradition which is still performed today. It takes a number of years to rehearse and three nights and days to perform. It engulfs the whole village in which it takes place (**J. P. Clark**). Similar in dramatic scope is the drama *Ekong* (Ibibio) which takes six years to rehearse and involves in the enactment of its narrative every aspect of performance (J. Messenger). Scholars like Adelugba, Amankulor, Echeruo, Nzewi have variously and extensively researched and analysed the relationship between theatre and drama on the one hand and trance, festivals, masquerades and rituals on the other, for example, the Igbo *Ekpe* dance-drama which occurs in December at the close of the *Ekpe* cycle within the religious-ritual year (J. Amankulor). These ancient traditional performances can still extend their scope and are able to represent modern Nigeria; an example of a vividly contemporary yet traditional theatrical display is the *Kwagh hir* of the Tiv in Benue State, which consists of highly complex animated puppets, either in tableaux on mobile platforms depicting modern Tivland, or as giant bestiary and shamanesque masks. They are non-affective; and are presented in a night of competition between villages. Each village's puppet team is backed up by a chorus of women singers and a large orchestra of traditional instruments. The judgement, by a team of judges, is an aesthetic one and seeks to relate the depiction of modern Tivland to established traditional aesthetics, especially in song and music. At the other end of the spectrum from this public spectacle and dazzling technical accomplishment is the domestic and informal story-telling performance, such as *Ocha Oocha* (Idoma, Benue State) (O. Abah).

In the north there are some nascent theatrical elements in the grand spectacle of the Fulani Emirs' *Sallah* processions on the high feast days of Islam. Hundreds, sometimes thousands, of people take part in each *Sallah*, either on caparisoned horses and camels or on foot, costumed and in armour. In the midst of this pomp, and often ridiculing it, are the *'yankama*, whose entertainment, *'yankamanchi*, is made up of satirical skits, songs and scurrilous surrealism. The *'yankama* are travelling minstrels who entertain both at the Emir's court and in the market place. They are in guilds, and are sometimes protected and patronized by an Emir; they are an accepted part of the cultural life of the Emirates (E. Kofoworola, C. G. B. Gidley). Not so *Bori* (researched variously by D. Adelugba, A. Horn, M. Onwuejeogwu) which is an ancient Hausa ritual possession cult, pre-Islamic, by women who live sequestered within their own compound. *Bori* has an affective healing context with access to the spirit world; it also has a pure entertainment mode, the enjoyment of which derives from a complex aesthetic. *Bori* is not acceptable to Islam, or to the traditional rulers. Yet another sort of traditional performance among some Hausa villages is a 'Lord of Misrule' festival, an example of which is *Kalankuwa* in Zaria, Kaduna State, organized by the young male farmers. There is a strong contemporary satire in the mimetic role play, with people in naturalistic costume acting out national and local rulers and bureaucrats, in the context of 24 hours of total licence within the village.

New drama and theatre The years of the struggle for independence were accompanied by a flowering of dramatic talent at all levels in society which has not abated in the twenty-five years since independence. Inspiration comes from many directions, though the traditional arts are dominant. The main legacy of performance traditions to new Nigerian drama is a concept of total theatre. This applies whether the play is performed in English, or, say, Yoruba, or in Pidgin, or even in a mixture of languages and language registers. The linguistic dimension is itself a part of total theatre which also includes significant non-naturalistic idioms: masks, masquerades, music, dance, rhythm and movement, incantation and word-play. Many of these elements are fused to create surrealist physical imagery. Plays which vividly demonstrate total theatre are the Yoruba operas developed in the 1950s by people like **Hubert Ogunde** and at the Mbari Clubs at Oshogbo and Ibadan where **Duro Ladipo**'s great success *Oba Ko So* (1964) was created. Other important examples of total theatre are Soyinka's *A Dance of the Forests* and Wale Ogunyemi's *Langbodo* (directed by Dapo Adelugba for FESTAC in 1977 and revived for a European tour in 1985).

Some playwrights deal with the supernatural as content, but avoid its meaning through symbolism in the style of the play. Oti's *The Old Masters* (1977) deals naturalistically with the clash between church and cult; and the brilliant actor E. K. Ogunmola in his adaptation of Tutuola's *Palm Wine Drinkard*, retreats from Tutuola's surrealism. Some plays, however, promote a serious debate on Nigeria's social formation by moving deeply into traditional modes of performance, for example, in a play about a farmers' revolt which simultaneously depicts a class analysis and a sacrificial masquerade in order to engage an audience with the significance of the past in the present. Plays like Kole Omotoso's *The Curse* (1975), Bode Sowande's *Farewell to Babylon* (1978) and Akanji Nasiru's *Our Survival* (1982) are notable examples, as are the plays of **Osofisan**.

Writers and performers are influenced by naturalism, on television and in the cinema (which shows predominantly 'Kung Fu' and Indian love movies) as well as in the theatre. A direct presentation of contemporary life on stage appeals to actors as well as to audiences who take pleasure in the acute observation of human behaviour at a time of extensive social change. Naturalistic drama is exemplified in the successful plays of James Ene-Henshaw, such as his *Dinner for Promotion* (1967). Plays concerned with personal morality in sexual and social relationships among socially upwardly-mobile Nigerians tend also to be crafted and performed naturalistically: Meki Nzewi's *Two Fists in One Mouth* (1976); Laolu Ogunniyi's television plays, like *Candle in the Wind* (1977); and Rasheed Gbadamosi's *Echoes from the Lagoon* (1972) all exemplify this. Naturalism, though still present, is less obvious in a number of theatrically effective historical dramas, like *Ovonramwen Nogbaisi*, by **Ola Rotimi**, as well as in

some recent Pidgin plays, like 'Segun Oyekunle's *Katakata for Sufferhead* (1978) about a group of petty criminals who, in the jail, act out the poverty and petty theft of the latest convict to join them. Tunde Lakoju's *Moonshine Solidarity* (1980) which is a political satire on the 1979 civilian government elections in Nigeria and uses the newspaper cartoon-strip character, Pappy Joe, is read naturalistically by Nigerian audiences – as are Pidgin adaptations of **Brecht**.

If there is an underlying aesthetic in contemporary Nigerian theatre it is the way in which quite disparate styles are effortlessly combined in performance. Life is presented on the stage, directly; but it is mediated by symbolic representations of a further or 'other' reality. This may be as a result of performing to eager audiences with eclectic tastes. Many playwrights forged their art in the context of establishing a performance company: Soyinka and the Orishun Theatre, Rotimi and the Ori Olokun Theatre in Ife; Osofisan with the Kakaun Sela Kompany in Ibadan; Oyekunle and Lakoju worked in the Mud Studio Theatre in Zaria; Kalu Uka and Meki Nzewi at the Oak Theatre in Nsukka.

Finally, in the development of a new drama, playwrights have drawn on quite diverse models from world theatre: Ladipo's *Eda* from **von Hofmannsthal**'s *Jederman* (*Everyman*); 'Zulu Sofola's *Wizard of Law*, from *Pierre Patelin*; the Zaria Performing Arts Company's *Lawal Kung Fu Kaduna*, from **Udall**'s *Ralph Roister Doister*; Rotimi's *The Gods Are Not To Blame*, from **Sophocles**' *King Oedipus*; Osofisan's *Who's Afraid of Solarin*, from **Gogol**'s *The Inspector General*; Oyekunle's *Man Pickin*, from Brecht's *The Good Person of Setzuan*. All these examples have become distinctively Nigerian plays. Their audiences neither know nor care about the originals; they receive the plays as yet further contribution to the rich texture of Nigerian theatre today.   ME

See: M. Banham and C. Wake, *African Theatre Today*, London, 1976; E. Clark, *Hubert Ogunde: the Making of Nigerian Theatre*, London, 1979; J. P. Clark, *The Ozidi Saga*, Ibadan, 1977; B. Crow, *Studying Drama*, London, 1983; M. Etherton, *The Development of African Drama*, London, 1982; B. Jeyifo, *The Truthful Lie: Essays on a Sociology of African Drama*, London, 1985; B. Jeyifo, *The Yoruba Popular Travelling Theatre of Nigeria*, Lagos, 1984; O. Ogunbiyi (ed.), *Drama and Theatre in Nigeria: a Critical Source Book*, Lagos, 1981; W. Soyinka, *Myth, Literature and the African World*, Cambridge, 1976.

Nilsen, Hans Jacob (1897–1957) Norwegian director and actor, crucial in the development of modern Norwegian theatre; Director of the **Norske Teatret** (1933–4 and 1946–50), the **Nationale Scene** (1934–9) and the Folketeatret (1952–5); during the war he joined the Free Norwegian Stage in Sweden. An associate of **Per Lindberg** and Halfdan Christensen, Nilsen wanted a people's theatre that was theatricalistic and socially committed. Among his major achievements were productions of important (often controversial) new plays, such as **Grieg**'s *Our Power and Our Glory* (1935) and the **Čapeks**' *Insect Play* (1939) and perceptive revaluations of classics, such as his 1948 'anti-romantic' *Peer Gynt* and his 1934 spirited, cartoon-like *Jeppe of the Hill*. As an actor he achieved particular success as Hamlet, Peer Gynt and Masterbuilder Solness.   HL

Nō A serious and subtle dance drama that evolved in Japan in the 14th century out of earlier songs, dances, and sketches. It was originally performed by priest-performers attached to Buddhist temples. In *nō* performance movement, music, and words create an ever-shifting web of tension and ambiguity. A *nō* text (*utaibon*, song book) contains prose (*kotoba*) and poetry (*utai*) sections. Prose is delivered in a sonorous voice that rises gradually and evenly in pitch, then drops at the end of a phrase. This typically repeating pattern is heard in all plays and varies only slightly by character type. No attempt is made by the male actors to reproduce the female voice. Poetry sections are sung (indicated by the musical term *fushi*, melody) by the Doer (*shite*), Sideman (*waki*), or Chorus (*ji*); they make up the bulk of the text. The voice moves flexibly, with many melismas and slides, on and around a few basic pitches (three in soft song style, *yowagin*, and five in strong song style, *tsuyogin*). The most common verse form is in lines of 12 syllables, each line divided into a first phrase of 7 and a second phrase of 5 syllables, known as normal rhythm (*hira nori*). This is the metre of the central, narrative module of a play (*kuse*), in which the major character dances a crucial event from his or her past to a song sung by the Chorus. The vocal pattern of 7–5 syllables is overlaid on an 8-beat rhythm played by the hip drum (*ōtsumi*), shoulder drum (*kotsuzumi*), and a bamboo flute (*nōkan*), producing constant syncopation and internal tensions in the sound. In contrast, 8-syllable lines of verse (*ō nori*) and 16-syllable lines (*chū nori*) used for strong dances at the climax of a play are congruent with the 8-beat rhythm; usually a stick drum (*taiko*) joins the musical ensemble (*hayashi*) to add to the rhythmic effect. Even here, however, voice, action, and music are not precisely matched. That would be bare and uninteresting. Tempo is constantly in flux, within a play, a scene, or a phrase of movement or sound, following the basic Japanese aesthetic principle of *jo-ha-kyū* (beginning, break, fast). Each strand of the performance can be perceived separately; the spectator senses a continual advancing and receding of one performance element *vis-à-vis* the others. The well-known finesse of *nō* performance rests on the Buddhist view that the world is in a state of continual flux, a view that is carried out through the performance characteristics just described.

Acceptance of change underlies the admonition that the *nō* actor must always seek newness or freshness (*hana*, flower) in performance. The actor should never do what is expected, but rather, by analysing the performance situation – the audience, the season, the time of day, previous plays on the bill – he should choose a play and an interpretation that will elicit audience interest by being unexpected, new, fresh. There is no single correct way of acting, the actor-playwright-theorist Zeami Motokiyo wrote in *The Way of the Flower*; there are only more or less appropriate ways of interesting audiences under specific circumstances. It is possible to be interesting by harmonizing the performance with the situation (a celebratory play in the New Year season), but juxtaposing opposites – the Chinese theory of *yin* and *yang* – is more highly recommended: a strong demon role should be acted with a degree of gentleness, when the day is gloomy choose a lively piece. Following this theory, a male actor playing a female role in *nō* is inherently interesting because of the always perceptible contrast between the actor's masculinity and the character's femininity. In all cases, says Zeami, audience approval is the aim of the actor.

The dramatic development of a play can also be analysed according to *jo-ha-kyū* structure (with the middle *ha* also divided into *jo-ha-kyū*): Sideman's entrance (*jo*), Doer's entrance (*jo of ha*), conversation between Doer and Sideman (*ha of ha*), beginning of the Doer's narrative (*kyū of ha*), and conclusion of Doer's narrative (*kyū*). Each of these scenes is made up of several structural modules (*shōdan*, small scene), identifiable by dramatic function or music/dance form. For example, a typical play would consist of opening music and Chorus song (*shidai*), Sideman's self-introduction speech (*nanori*), travel song (*michiyuki*), and arrival speech (*tsukizerifu*), Doer's arrival song (*issei*), Doer–Sideman conversation, spoken (*mondō*) or sung (*kakeai*), Doer's opening narrative song (*kuri* and *sashi*) leading into Doer's narrative dance while the Chorus sings (*kuse*), interlude by Villager (*ai kyōgen*), Sideman's song waiting for Doer's return (*machi utai*), and Doer's final dance (*mai*) and Chorus song (*kiri*). High-pitched songs (*age uta*), low-pitched songs (*sage uta*), Doer–Chorus songs (*rongi*), and other modules are used where needed.

The *nō* stage, which took numerous forms before 1600, became standardized around that date. It consists of a raised dancing platform about 19 feet square. The floor of polished cyprus wood is covered by a temple-like roof that is supported by pillars at the four corners. The roof protects the outdoor stage from the elements and, with the pillars, demarks the performance area visually, thus helping to focus audience attention on the performance. A bridgeway (*hashigakari*) 20–40 feet long runs from upstage right diagonally back to the dressing room and serves as an entrance and exit passage. It serves the same function as the passage for the deities in *kagura*: it connects the 'other world' from which the performer comes to the space set before a human audience where the performance takes place.

Role types have conventional locations on the stage. The Sideman sits beside the Sideman pillar, down left, while the flutist is next to the flute pillar, up left, and the Doer tends, when not at centre, to be next to the Doer pillar, up right. Players of the interlude (*kyōgen kata*) sit where the bridgeway adjoins the stage, musicians (*hayashi kata*) sit at the rear centre (*ato za*), stage assistants (*kōken*) wait behind them stage right, and the Chorus sits in two rows of four or five singers on the side stage (*waki za*). A Chorus was a relatively late development in *nō* (apparently after Zeami's death) and a separate area was added to the stage to accommodate it, marked by its separate roof.

Outdoor, free-standing *nō* theatres are found in the grounds of many temples and shrines. They are used once or several times a year at festival times, when performances are given either by local troupes – now increasingly rare – or by city-based troupes invited out to the countryside for the festival. The typical *nō* theatre in Japan today, however, is a conventional stage placed within a modern building. It is used daily for training and several days a week for public performances. Major *nō* theatres in Tokyo include the Kanze, Hōshō, Umewaka, Tessenkai, and Kita theatres owned and run by traditional *nō* families or 'schools' and the National

Noh Theatre, funded by the national government, in Kyoto the Kanze and Kongō theatres, and in Osaka the Yamamoto theatre.   JRB

Noah, Mordecai M[anuel] (1785–1851) American playwright. Noah was an active Zionist, sought his livelihood in politics (surveyor of the Port of New York, judge of the Court of Sessions), in journalism (New York *Enquirer, The Commercial Advertiser, The Times and Messenger*), and his diversion in the theatre. He was an inveterate theatre-goer, an intimate of the managers (**Price**, Simpson, **Dunlap**, and **Sol Smith**), and an occasional playwright. His ardent patriotism was reflected in his documentary-like plays: *She Would Be a Soldier, or the Plains of Chippewa* (1819), based on the Battle of Chippewa (1814) and written for Catherine Leesugg; *The Siege of Tripoli* (1820), the piratical menace with which Noah had first-hand experience as Consul to Tunis; *Marion, or The Hero of Lake George* (1821), the battle of Saratoga; *The Grecian Captive* (1822), the Greek Revolution; *The Siege of Yorktown* (1824), the Revolutionary War. *She Would Be a Soldier* became a popular patriotic piece for national holidays for over 40 years.   RM

Noble, Adrian (Keith) (1950–) British director, who studied at Bristol University and the Drama Centre in London, before becoming an Associate Director of the **Bristol Old Vic** (1976–9). He was a guest director at the **Royal Exchange Theatre, Manchester**, in 1980–1, where his productions of *The Duchess of Malfi* (1980) (with **Helen Mirren**) and *A Doll's House* (1981) won critical acclaim, particularly when they transferred to the Round House in London. From 1980–2, Noble was resident director with the **Royal Shakespeare Company**, becoming an Associate Director in 1982, where his productions of *King Lear* (1982) and *Henry V* (1984) attracted particular attention within a range of other ambitious Shakespearian and Jacobean works. Noble is an imaginative, original director, whose weaknesses are related to his strengths. To present Lear and the Fool, played by **Michael Gambon** and **Anthony Sher**, as a Beckett-like couple from a Shakespearian *Waiting for Godot*, was a bold gamble which nearly worked at Stratford, but to offer a version of *Mephisto* (1986), without much in the way of a devil, was less happy. Noble has also directed *Antony and Cleopatra* (1982), *The Comedy of Errors* and *Measure for Measure* (1983), *The Winter's Tale* (1984) and *As You Like It* (1985) for the RSC; and *Don Giovanni* for Kent Opera.   JE

Noguchi, Isamu (1904–) American sculptor and designer. Although he designed almost solely for dance, his abstract design and use of objects, and his ability to focus the cubic volume of the stage space had a significant effect on mid-20th-century design. Born in Los Angeles, Noguchi moved to Japan with his Japanese mother at the age of 2 and remained until 1917 before returning to the USA. In 1926 he went to Paris where he was an assistant to the sculptor Brancusi. His first theatre work was also in 1926 when he designed

masks for actress Itō Michio for **Yeats**'s *At the Hawk's Well*. In 1935 choreographer Martha Graham asked him to design a set for *Frontier*. It was the first set she had ever used and it began a collaboration that lasted until 1966 including *Appalachian Spring* (1944) and *Seraphic Dialogue* (1955). Noguchi described his first theatre work as an attempt 'to wed the total void of theatre space to form and function'. Drawing on the tradition of **nō** and the vocabulary of his own sculptures, his designs were simple distillations of images creating psychological rather than literal space. Noguchi has also designed for George Balanchine (*Orpheus*, 1948), Erick Hawkins, Merce Cunningham, and the **Royal Shakespeare Company** (*King Lear*, 1955).   AA

Nondi Natakam (India) The term *nondi* means 'one who limps'. *Natakam* refers to a play. The form is also known as *Ottraikkaal Natakam* (a play enacted by a one-legged person). Although *Nondi Natakam* was created in the late 17th or early 18th centuries in Tamil Nadu, a state in south India, its precise origin is uncertain. The story is narrated by an actor who impersonates a thief who jumps about on one leg. The other leg is firmly tied behind his back. The thief sings about his escapades with a courtesan for whom he develops an infatuation. She takes all his earnings and persuades him to replenish his funds by stealing. His obsession with debauchery is insatiable. Finally, he travels to a distant town ruled by a local chieftain. He impresses the ruler as a man of means but at night attempts to steal one of the royal horses. Caught in the act, the thief is brought to the ruler who orders the amputation of one of his hands and legs, a common practice for thieves in medieval India. The cruel sentence is carried out. After a time, a saintly person finds the poor thief and takes pity on him by relieving his pain with soothing balms. He also offers spiritual counsel. The thief accepts his advice and goes to the temple to express his devotion. At last, his prayers are answered. God appears and restores his hand and leg leaving no trace of mutilation. Obviously the play centres on the theme of forgiveness and devotion. But rustic, humorous vulgarities are sprinkled liberally throughout. The form is popular in the region around the city of Madurai.   FaR

Norén, Lars (1944–) Swedish playwright and poet, currently one of Scandinavia's most widely performed dramatists. His plays explore with disturbing frankness the perversions in relationships that have become brutal struggles for self-preservation. A recurrent motif is the child, emotionally stunted by parental neglect and therefore incapable of healthy adult relationships. Significant plays are *Demons* (1982), *Communion* (1985) and two trilogies: one of contemporary life (1981–3), consisting of *A Terrifying Joy*, *When They Burned Butterflies on the Small Stage* and *The Smile of the Underworld*; a second (1978–84) consists of the partly autobiographical plays *The Courage to Kill*, *Night is the Mother of Day* and *Chaos is a Neighbour of God*.   HL

Norman, Frank (John Frank) (1930–) British dramatist, who was brought up in a Dr Barnardo's home from 1937–46. He worked as a farm labourer and with a travelling fair; and served several short prison sentences for minor crimes. His two autobiographical accounts of prison life, *Bang to Rights* (1958) and *Stand on Me* (1961), were published by Secker and Warburg, earning him a reputation as an authority on low life and cockney slang. With Lionel Bart, he wrote the successful musical, *Fings Ain't Wot They Used T'Be* (1959), set in Soho, which was produced by **Joan Littlewood** at the Theatre Royal, Stratford East, and had a long run in the West End. Further musicals with Joan Littlewood's company followed, *A Kayf Up West* (1964, with music by Stanley Myers), and *Costa Packet* (1972, with Lionel Bart and Alan Klein); but they were less successful. In 1969, his play *Insideout* was produced at the **Royal Court Theatre**; but since the early 1970s, he has mainly written novels, reminiscences and studies of London's underworld.   JE

Norman, Marsha (1947–) American playwright whose realistic characters confront some devastation in their past to determine whether and how to survive. *Getting Out* (1978) reveals the internal conflict of a woman parolee in her choice for a new beginning – dramatized by two actresses who simultaneously portray her violent, younger self and her present, numbed self. In 1983 Norman won the Pulitzer Prize for *'night, Mother*, a wrenching enactment of the last night in the life of a hopeless young woman as she prepares herself and her mother for her suicide and of the mother's desperate attempts to prevent it. Other works include: *Third and Oak: The Laundromat* (and) *The Pool Hall* (1978), *The Holdup* (1980), and *Traveler in the Dark* (1984), as well as television plays and several unpublished screenplays.   FB

Norske Teatret (Oslo) The Norwegian Theatre, one of the country's three most significant companies, is devoted to performance in Nynorsk ('New Norwegian'), one of two official forms of the language. Derived from provincial dialects, in contrast to the Danish-derived Norwegian of the capital, it remains part of an ongoing movement to strengthen indigenous culture. Founded in 1913, thanks to the efforts of Arne and Hulda Garborg, the theatre established traditions in addition to those of language, including commitments to touring and new drama. It became one of the most avant-garde in Scandinavia, despite its inadequate facilities. From the start, it attracted superb actors: Lars Tvinde, Edvard Drabløs, Alfred and Tordis Maurstad, Liv Ullman. Important directors have included Agnes Mowinckel, **Hans Jacob Nilsen** and Tormod Skagestad; for more than 40 years its scenographer was the gifted Arne Walentin. Since 1985, it has occupied one of Europe's most modern theatres, with several stages, huge workshops and advanced equipment.   HL

Norton, Thomas see **Sackville, Thomas**

Norton, (William) Elliot (1903–) American drama critic. Born in Boston, Norton attended Harvard University where he studied with George Lyman Littredge and **George Pierce Baker**. After graduation in 1926, he worked as a reporter for the *Boston Post*, taking over as drama critic when Edward Harold Crosby retired in 1934. With the demise of the *Post* in

1956, he switched to Hearst's *Record American*. Norton acquired the reputation of being honest and reliable about new shows that were Broadway-bound. **Mike Nichols** and **Joshua Logan** thought that he had a 'smell for the public' and for 'what the public is feeling'. He was not a great stylist nor did his reviews break new critical ground. But New York producers respected his opinion and made changes in their shows based upon his reviews. He received the first George Jean Nathan award for dramatic criticism in 1964, and a special Tony in 1971.   TLM

Norway Although Norway has had theatre for at least four centuries, its first permanent playhouses, using Norwegian actors, were not established until the 1800s. The Union of Kalmar (1397) united Norway with Denmark until 1814 and Danish became the language of government, learning and literature. Norway's greatest dramatist before **Ibsen**, **Ludvig Holberg**, received his major education in Copenhagen and became a founding figure of the Danish theatre.

Although the Sagas suggest the presence of court entertainers as early as the 12th century, the earliest firm evidence of acting comes after the Reformation in 1539. Nevertheless, it is commonly assumed that there were medieval liturgical plays at Epiphany and Easter and Epiphany plays that survived to this century in Bergen may have derived from them. (See **Medieval drama in Europe**.) By the mid-16th century, Bergen certainly had humanist school dramas, such as the 1562 *Fall of Adam*, by a cathedral schoolmaster, Absalon Beyer; a 1617 city ordinance encouraged school plays, to teach good behaviour. Then, in the mid-17th century, German touring companies arrived, with their popular **Haupt- und Staatsaktionen** plays, followed by Danish companies offering similar fare. By 1771, the German actor Martin Nürenbach considered Christiania (now Oslo) ready for a permanent company and obtained permission to present Danish plays with Norwegian actors; the venture rapidly folded. Much more successful were the amateur dramatic societies that flourished between 1780 and 1830, many with permanent playhouses, such as the Bergen Comedy House (1800) and the Trondhjem theatre (1816). Their success increased the audience for professional touring companies and in 1825 Johan Peter Strömberg founded the first Norwegian acting school and then in 1827 opened the Christiania Theatre, the first permanent playhouse with professional Norwegian actors. However, they were so scornfully criticized that the theatre rapidly replaced them with Danes, beginning Christiania Theatre's 'Danish Period'. The playhouse itself burned in 1835, to be replaced by a new building on Bank Square, which housed the company until its move in 1899 to the present **Nationaltheatret**.

The future of Norwegian theatre was a central issue in the 19th-century struggle between the so-called 'Danomanes', led by the poet J. S. Welhaven, and the nationalistic 'Patriots', led by Henrik Wergeland. The nationalists' first achievement in the theatre was Ole Bull's founding of the Norwegian Theatre, Bergen, in 1850; Henrik Ibsen joined the company in 1852 as resident playwright and stage director. Meanwhile, Christiania Theatre had accepted its first two Norwegian-born performers and in 1852 Christiania's

Norwegian Theatre opened with a completely Norwegian-speaking company. It struggled on against impossible problems until 1862, with Ibsen leading it for the last five years. His colleague **Bjørnstjerne Bjørnson** had meanwhile organized and led a campaign against Danish domination of Christiania Theatre and in 1863 the two theatres combined, with a predominantly Norwegian company. Bjørnson himself directed it from 1865–7, creating distinguished productions of **Shakespeare**, Holberg, Ibsen and his own social-problem plays such as *The Newly Married*.

Bergen's Norwegian Theatre had folded in 1863, but was revived as the **Nationale Scene** in 1876. Christiania Theatre achieved new high standards under the leadership of the Swede Ludvig Josephson in 1873–7; his many premieres of Norwegian plays included the first *Peer Gynt* (1876), with Grieg's music. Both theatres entered crucial periods in the 1880s, with **Gunnar Heiberg** in Bergen (1884–8) and **Bjørn Bjørnson** in Christiania (1885–91), both determined to achieve naturalistic acting and staging for the new plays they were directing: *The Wild Duck* in both theatres, 1885; *Rosmersholm* in Bergen, 1887; *The Lady from the Sea* in Christiania, 1889. While actors trained in the older declamatory style found the transition difficult, new actors like **Johanne Dybwad** emerged to lead the way. At the close of the century, several new playhouses opened: Stavanger Theatre (1883); the Central Theatre, Christiania (1897); and in 1899 the present Nationaltheatret, led by Bjørn Bjørnson. The fine, new ensemble he built indicated how rapidly Norwegian acting had developed: Johanne Dybwad, Sophie Reimers, Ragna Wettergren, **Egil Eide**, August Oddvar, Halfdan Christensen, to be joined by Ingolf Schanche and many more. Despite its precarious finances (for it was a private, unsubsidized theatre until 1927), Bjørnson's Nationaltheatret gave an impressive series of fine premieres (including Ibsen, Bjørnstjerne Bjørnson and Gunnar Heiberg) until he resigned on health grounds in 1907.

By 1913, the development of Nynorsk ('New Norwegian'), one of the country's two official language-forms, was sufficient to enable Arne and Hulda Garborg to found the **Norske Teatret**, devoted to performance in Nynorsk. From the start, it also emphasized touring and attracted major actors, such as Edvard Drabløs and Lars Tvinde, to be joined by Agnes Mowinckel, **Hans Jacob Nilsen** and Tordis and Alfred Maurstad. The demand of playwrights for a stage dedicated to new drama led to the opening of the New Theatre (1929); in 1959 it was combined with the Folketeatret, to become the popular Oslo New Theatre, owned by the city. With Nazism on the rise in Europe, Norwegian theatres became increasingly politically conscious in the 1930s. In Bergen, the brilliant Hans Jacob Nilsen made the Nationale Scene Norway's major theatre, with his productions of **Pär Lagerkvist** and **Nordahl Grieg**. During the German occupation (1940–5), audiences boycotted Nazi-run theatres, while actors fought to escape their contracts or fled to the Free Norwegian Stage in Sweden. With the Liberation came the Studio Theatre (1945–50), run as a Stanislavskian ensemble to do important plays. The Norske Teatret entered an important period under Hans Jacob Nilsen, highlighted by his 1948 'anti-romantic' production of *Peer Gynt*. Trøndelag Theatre

in Trondheim (1937) became increasingly ambitious, joined by Stavanger's Rogaland Theatre (1947). Riksteatret, the national touring theatre (1949), began by sending out other theatres' productions but later produced its own. For several decades its centrality to Norwegian theatre life attracted major actors and directors, but with the development in the 1970s of regional and group theatres, its future is now controversial.

The contemporary situation The 1960s was a period of growth and consolidation. Tormod Skagestad confirmed the avant-garde role of the Norske Teatret with innovative programming (such as Norway's first production of **Euripides'** *Medea*, 1963) and major foreign directors like Peter Palitzsch and Henryk Tomaszewski. Under Erik Pierstorff, Trøndelag Theatre became an important training ground for key directors of today, such as Stein Winge and Kjetil Bang-Hansen. The 1970s brought both increased expansion and politicization. Five subsidized regional theatres opened, in Tromsø (1971), Molde (1972), Skien (1975), Forde (1977) and Mo i Rana (1979). Important free groups sprang up, such as Musidra (1971), Saltkompagniet and Perleporten (1975), and Grenland Friteater with its close links to Denmark's **Odin Teatret** (1976). By 1977, there were sufficient free groups to form the Theatre Centre, a lobbying and administrative organization with about 20 member groups. There were also group projects within Nationaltheatret, such as Stein Winge's production of Klaus Hagerup's satire *Alice in the Underworld* and the documentary group creation *The Black Cat*, about the bankruptcy of a cellulose company. Out of this activity evolved the Theatre at Torshov (1977), an experimental stage in an Oslo suburb, where many feel Nationaltheatret's best work has been done.

The 1980s have brought harsh economic conditions, felt most keenly by the free groups, although new ones have emerged, such as Bikuben Music Theatre, Theatre Beljash and the Sami theatre Beaivvas in Kautokeino. In 1985 the Norske Teatret opened one of the most modern theatre-complexes in Europe. The shortage of good new Norwegian plays is still discussed, although there are several fine dramatists: Cecilie Løveid, Edvard Hoem, Klaus Hagerup; sadly, Sverre Udnaes died in 1982. There are excellent directors, such as Stein Winge, Kjetil Bang-Hansen and Janken Varden, and a few gifted scenographers, such as John-Kristian Alsaker and Helge Hoff Monsen. Norway continues to have many superb actors, including Espen Skjønberg, Ella Hval, Liv Ullman, Sverre Anker Ousdal, Lars Andreas Larsen, Frøydis Armand and Jon Eikemo. HL

See: F. J. and Lise-Lone Marker, *The Scandinavian Theatre*, Oxford, 1975; M. Meyer, *Henrik Ibsen*, London, 1971; *Modern Nordic Plays: Norway*, intro. E. Eide, New York, 1974; S. H. Rossel, *A History of Scandinavian Literature 1870–1980*, Minneapolis, 1982; *Theatre in Norway 1979*, Oslo, 1979; C. R. Waal, *Johanne Dybwad, Norwegian Actress*, Oslo, 1967; *20th Century Drama in Scandinavia*, ed. J. Wrede, Helsinki, 1979.

Nouvelle Compagnie d'Avignon French theatre company which has worked together in the Théâtre des Carmes at Avignon since 1963 under the influence of its director André Benedetto, who writes many of its plays. Its work employs a broad range of techniques from the traditions of farce, and open air performance. Its stance is extremely radical, challenging not only political orthodoxies but cultural ones as well and identifying with problems of the Occitan community. DB

Novelli, Ermete (1851–1919) Italian actor and company manager who began acting at 17 and rose to prominence in the company of **Bellotti-Bon** in the early eighties before establishing his own companies from 1884. Very much a 'personality' player, his repertoire consisted largely of stock-pieces, in which he showed the wide range of his talent, from plays by **Goldoni** to those by **Dumas**. It was for his versatility, indeed, that he was perhaps most noted. He occasionally attempted **Shakespeare**, most successfully with *King Lear* and *The Merchant of Venice*, and toured widely in Europe and South America. Involved in turn of the century attempts to raise the standards of Italian theatre by the establishment of *teatri stabili*, his own semi-permanent company, 'The Casa di Goldoni', based at the Valle Theatre in Rome in 1900, met with little success and he soon returned to regular touring. LR

Novo, Salvador (1904–74) Mexican playwright, instrumental in founding the **Teatro de Ulises** with his friend **Xavier Villaurrutia**, thereby launching the independent theatre movement in Mexico in 1928. A serious director, actor and critic, Novo held important positions in the Mexican Institute of Fine Arts and wrote several major plays, many of them based on classical Greek or Mexican characters. Of special note are *Yocasta, o casi* (*Jocasta, or Almost*, 1961), *Ha vuelto Ulises* (*Ulysses Has Returned*, 1961), *In Pipiltzintzin o La guerra de las gordas* (*The War of the Large Ladies*, 1963) and *In Ticitezcatl o El espejo encantado* (*The Enchanted Mirror*, 1965). GW

Nowra, Louis (1950–) Australian playwright. His plays, often with exotic or historical settings, depict the private worlds of illusion, obsession and madness under pressure from external power structures, and are characterized by episodic construction, heightened language and powerful, even lurid, theatrical effects. They include two radio plays *Albert Named Edward* (1975) and *The Song Room* (1980), *Inner Voices* (1977), *Visions* (1978), *Inside the Island* (1980), *The Precious Woman* (1980) and *Sunrise* (1983), and a television drama, *Displaced Persons* (1985). MW

Nudity on stage For prurient effect nudity on stage was already common in the Roman pantomime or *mimus* which provided undressing scenes for female performers. In the presentations of the Floralia the *mima* was often shown naked by the end of the performance, and Apuleius describes a nude *Judgement of Paris*. The *mimus* also preserved the leather phallus of Greek comedy as late as the 5th century AD, long after it had lost its religious significance.

Christianity was scandalized by both nakedness and the theatre, and the emperor Justinian imposed drawers on all mimes, tumblers and acrobats. The medieval church banned public nudity, so that the Adam and Eve of the mystery plays were clad in form-fitting doeskin.

Yet, according to Marc de Montifard, the cleavage was so deep on the three Marys in one Passion Play that, gazing down from the cross, Christ suffered a conspicuous erection. Princely pageants were exempt from the ecclesiastical strictures: at the entry of Charles VII into Paris in 1437 three naked girls swam in an ornamental fountain; when Louis XI entered Paris in 1461 several unclothed beauties portrayed mermaids. Allegorical nudes occasionally turned up in the festivals and masques of the Renaissance.

With the common acceptance of women as actors, the exposure of breasts and legs became a popular allurement, and was equated by the authorities with full nudity. The French church censured the Italian **Gelosi** troupe for emphasizing the female bosom in its pantomimic business, but many plays of the 17th century made the denuding of the bosom a climactic moment in the denouement. After Mme de St Huberty appeared as a nymph in 1783 with one bared breast and naked legs, the government forbade her appearance. Yet 'historical accuracy' demanded looser draperies on dancers, so tights (invented by the Opéra milliner Maillot) became *de rigueur* c. 1780, soon to be followed by trunks and the tutu (conceived by Duponchel). The Pope allowed such garb on the Roman stage, provided the tights were sky-blue rather than pink.

In the early 19th century a static display of female nudity was available in 'The Hymns to Nature' and 'Living Statuary' to be seen at The Hall of Rome in London. These developed into **'living pictures'** and *'poses plastiques'*, in which several naked or semi-clothed women would hold an artistic pose for some moments, often in imitation of a well-known painting or sculpture. **Frédéric Soulié** applied the principle of static nudity to drama in *Christine à Fontainebleau* (**Odéon**, 1829) by showing a naked woman on a dissecting table, a gimmick twice repeated in Naples, but soon abandoned owing to the hostility of the audience. The accepted definition of nudity was elastic and not infrequently ballet-dancers with brief skirts or 'leg show' performers who wore tights without skirts would be accused of brazenness. The fleshings of **Adah Isaacs Menken** won her the billing of 'The Naked Lady' and **Lola Montez** created a scandal by omitting tights during her dances. But most of what passed for flesh on stage was cunningly dyed fabric: Cassive in **Feydeau**'s *The Lady from Maxim's* (1899) appeared in bed in flesh-coloured tights under a corset and still managed to scandalize.

The strip-tease, a ritual wherein various garments are serially discarded leaving the performer more or less totally undressed, was, according to legend, first performed by a certain Mona at an art students' ball at the **Moulin-Rouge** on 9 February 1893. It was definitely exhibited by Mlle Cavelli at Le Divan Fayouau on 13 March 1894 in a sketch entitled 'Le Coucher d'Yvette'; this was much imitated and even repeated at the World's Fair by Renée de Presles in 'Le Coucher de la Parisienne'. In America legend related that it was introduced by the trapeze artist Charmian, who inadvertently lost her tights during a performance; by 1920 it had become a burlesque attraction offered by Millie de Leon, and was later perfected as a 'dance' by **Gypsy Rose Lee** and Ann Corio. Originally, at the climax a blackout or fall of the curtain supervened; certain wardrobe items, the 'pasties' that covered the nipples, would often be flung to the audience, but the *cache-sexe* or G-string usually stayed in place. Later the performers at such tourist-traps as Paris's Crazy-Horse Saloon (opened 1953) would leave nothing to the imagination.

Five stark naked beauties were seen at a revue at the Variétés (1901); Colette Willy appeared stripped to the waist in the pantomime *La Chair* (1907); and an undressed dancer first appeared at the **Folies-Bergère** in 1912. The music-hall dancer Maud Allan and her imitators were censured for their abbreviated Salome costumes, but the biblical theme was the chief cause for objection. After 1918, in reaction to pre-war prudery, taboo-breaking and voyeurism combined to produce the *Naktballett* that originated in Berlin. It was first danced by Celly de Rheydt (Cäcilia Schmidt) in 1919, to be immediately rivalled by a naked Salome ballet; by 1922, it had become widespread throughout Germany, its principal star the notorious Anita Berber (1899–1929). Influenced by Isadora Duncan, the physical culture movement and sports, undraped dancing based on classical art remained popular in cabarets until about 1927. Sally Rand's (Hazel Gould Beck, 1904–79) fan-dance first seen at the Chicago Exposition in 1933 became a byword.

In the Anglo-Saxon world, however, stage nudity was permissible only if it was inert as in the lavish tableaux Ben Ali Haggin staged for **Ziegfeld**. The Lord Chamberlain's ruling on the Revuedeville at the Windmill Theatre, London, in 1931 – 'If it moves, it's rude' – became a guiding principle followed by the theatre's wartime manager Vivian van Damm (1889–1960) who could boast, 'We never closed.'

In the 1960s, nudity became a tactical weapon of the alternative theatre, a direct assault on middle-class sensibilities and an alignment with 'Nature'. 1968 was its *annus mirabilis*, when the rock musical *Hair* displayed its unclad cast frontally; the **Living Theatre**'s players were arrested in San Francisco for disrobing ('We can't take off our clothes in public', was one of their opening plaints, until, at the London Round House, an audience member undressed to confute them); and Sally Kirkland became the first New York dramatic actress to appear fully nude throughout an entire play, in **Terrence McNally**'s *Sweet Eros*. The commercial theatre was quick to adopt this licence in *Oh, Calcutta!* (1969), whose company, male and female, shed its bathrobes in the first moments. Soon full-frontal nudity could be seen in London in **Dürrenmatt**'s *Meteor*, in Paris in Panizza's *Council of Love* and in Frankfurt in **Handke**'s *Self-Accusation*. German directors have been particularly active in defoliating their lead actresses. That male nudity, at least in motion and at a state theatre, still had the power to shock was clear from the flustered over-reaction to **Howard Brenton**'s *The Romans in Britain* (1980). LS

See: F. Des Aulnoyes, 'Histoire et philosophie du Strip-Tease', *Music-Hall*, Paris, 1957; G. Normandy, *Le Nu à l'église, au théâtre et dans la rue*, Paris, 1910; G.-J. Witkowski and L. Nass, *Le Nu au théâtre depuis l'antiquité jusqu'à nos jours*, Paris, 1909.

Nuevo Grupo, El (The New Group) Venezuelan theatre group created in 1967 and headed by a triumvirate, **Isaac Chocrón**, **Román Chalbaud** and **José Ignacio Cabrujas**. Instrumental in establishing the standards for the contemporary theatre movement in Venezuela, the group operates two theatres and provides regular programming of the best international and national plays. Alternating as authors, directors, and actors, this 'Holy Trinity', as they are called, has been at the forefront of the new theatre. GW

Núñez, José Gabriel (1937–) Venezuelan playwright. Born in Carúpano, trained as an economist, he has been an active force in Venezuelan theatre and television since he began to write in 1967. With more than 25 original plays and various adaptations, he has won several prizes. He also writes for literary reviews and regular columns. Principal works are *Parecido a la felicidad* (*Similar to Happiness*, 1969), *El largo camino del Edén* (*The Long Road to Eden*, 1970), *Madame Pompinette* (1981), and *María Cristina me quiere gobernar* (*María Cristina Wants to Govern Me*, 1984). GW

Nunn, Trevor (Robert) (1940–) British director, who started to direct plays with the Marlowe Society at Cambridge University. After a spell as a trainee director with the Belgrade Theatre, Coventry, he joined the **Royal Shakespeare Company** in 1965 and succeeded **Peter Hall** as the RSC's artistic director in 1968. In 1978, he became Chief Executive and joint artistic director with **Terry Hands** at the RSC, which helped him to take some time away from the company to direct in commercial theatre, where in 1981, he staged the hit musical, *Cats*, and in 1984, *Starlight Express*. Nunn can be regarded without too much challenge as the best all-round director currently working in British theatre. His first RSC success came with **Tourneur**'s *The Revenger's Tragedy* in 1966 which, with **Alan Howard** as Lussurioso, exactly captured the play's voluptuous yet macabre obsessions. His range of classical productions at the RSC is unequalled for its richness and variety – **Shakespeare**'s 'Roman' plays in 1972, his musical version of *The Comedy of Errors* (1976), the studio *Macbeth* (1976) and his Edwardian *All's Well That Ends Well* (1981). In 1980, he collaborated with John Caird, **David Edgar** and the RSC company to bring together *Nicholas Nickleby* in two substantial evenings, which presented a vivid picture of **Charles Dickens**'s London and paraded the wealth of acting talents at the RSC. Nunn possesses most directorial skills. He works well with individual actors, encouraging them to explore new possibilities in the text, but he is also excellent with large companies. He has a fine eye for scenic pictures on the stage, a sound instinct for style and historical appropriateness. He is sensitive to music, dancing and has rivalled American directors at their prized skills in staging musicals. He has proved to be an excellent administrator of the RSC. He is not, however, an intellectual's director, unlike **Peter Brook**, nor can he be regarded, in European terms, as an innovator. Under his guidance, however, the RSC became the leading company in Britain and ranked as one of the world's major theatres. JE

Nurseries Under the Patents granted to Sir **William Davenant** and **Thomas Killigrew** in 1660 they acquired the right to establish in London 'nurseries', training companies for young actors. The precise location and span of existence for these companies are unclear but there were at least three. One was established by Killigrew in 1667 in Hatton Garden and operated until 1669. One was set up by Lady Davenant, Sir William's widow, in the Barbican in 1671. One was run by John Perin at Bun Hill in Finsbury Fields in 1671. It was a site of trouble, the Secretary of State warning the King that 'If the nurseries be not taken away in a year, expect a disorder.' At various times **George Jolly** was involved in the running of the nurseries. Few of their actors appear to have graduated to the professional adult stage.   PH

Nusic, Branislav (1864–1938) Yugoslav playwright whose comedies have been part of the national repertory for almost a century. Born and educated in law in Belgrade, Nusic had his career as a humorist interrupted by imprisonment for writing an antidynastic poem at the time of his first theatrical success, *A Suspicious Person* (1887). Later, he served as a Serbian consular officer in the territories, and as a ministry official and head of theatres in Belgrade and other cities. His patriotic historic tragedies and his heavily moralistic domestic dramas remained completely overshadowed by his popular comedies in which figures of patriarchal Serbian mentality are shown in transition from an agrarian, oriental state towards urban and European aspirations. Nusic is rarely and only marginally a satirist, and his humour is mostly verbal. His incompetent bureaucrats, corrupt politicians, town gossips and con-men, newly enriched merchants and their quasi-Westernized offspring, have served as most effective vehicles for generations of comic actors. Recent attempts to transcend in staging the realistic pattern of Nusic's plays have usually failed. Often performed in the Slavic world and in Germany, Austria and Hungary, Nusic's main plays are *The Cabinet Minister's Wife* (1929) and *The Bereaved Family* (1934).   DK

O

Oberammergau When, following a severe outbreak of the Black Death in 1633, the inhabitants of this Upper Bavarian village vowed to perform a Passion play every ten years if they were spared from further deaths, the late medieval Passion play tradition in the south of the German-speaking area was still alive. Their original play was based on the 15th-century manuscript from Augsburg known as the 'Augsburg Passion Play' and on the Passion play by Sebastian Wild from the same city. The version of the text currently used was written originally for the 1810 performance by the Benedictine priest Othmar Weis from the nearby Ettal monastery and the music was composed at the same time by the village schoolmaster Rochus Dedler. The text has been revised several times since; recently this has involved removal of anti-Jewish statements. The current version consists of two sessions each of some three hours duration performed in the morning and in the late afternoon and includes 17 *tableaux vivants* of the Glorified Christ.

The regular performance in 1980 was followed by a 350th anniversary production in 1984 when performances on five days per week ran from late May to the end of September. Several major roles, most notably Christ, Virgin Mary, Prologue, Peter, John, Judas, were played at alternate performances by two actors; unmarried women played all the women's roles.   JET

Obey, André (1892–1975) French playwright associated with the work of **Copeau**'s disciples who formed the **Compagnie des Quinze** and commissioned and staged five of his plays at the **Vieux-Colombier** theatre. These included his first and best play *Noah* (1931), later staged with equal success by the group's director, **Michel Saint-Denis**, when he moved to London (1935). Other plays included a new version of the Don Juan story, twice rewritten and staged by Copeau in 1937 as *Le Trompeur de Séville* and by the **Comédie-Française** in 1949 as *L'Homme de Cendres*. He was director of the Comédie-Française for one year 1946/7. His plays combine mythical archetype with modern setting in a manner reminiscent of **Giraudoux**, his contemporary, but with less verbal preciosity and more sense of what is effective in performance.   DB

Obraztsov, Sergei Vladimirovich (1901–) Russian actor and puppeteer. After studying painting, Obraztsov made his acting debut at the **Moscow Art Theatre** Musical Studio in 1922, and only the next year appeared as a solo puppeteer. He alternated careers until 1931, when he became artistic director of the newly founded State Central Puppet Theatre, Moscow,

premiering with *Jim and Dollar* (a new building was opened in 1970). He has staged more than 50 puppet plays, made documentary films, and written several books, including *The Actor and the Puppet* (1938). He tried to introduce Javanese rod-puppets to the West in 1945, and toured Europe (1950/51, 1966, 1970), demonstrating his virtuosity with satirical sketches and magical fantasies.   LS

O'Casey, Sean (1880–1964) Irish playwright. O'Casey was the youngest child of a lower-middle-class Protestant family, severely impoverished when his father died in 1883. He worked as a labourer, interesting himself at nights in Irish culture, and active in the Republican and Labour movements. Disillusioned by the shift from socialism to Catholic nationalism, O'Casey withdrew acrimoniously from political and militant organizations, separating himself particularly from Padraic Pearse's cult of violence. He remained a life-long 'proletarian Communist'.

Afflicted by poor eyesight, O'Casey read omnivorously: **Shakespeare** and the Elizabethans, Shelley and **Shaw**; and shared the working-class folklore of patriotic oratory, ballads, the poems of Burns, Tom Moore's songs. He appeared occasionally in amateur theatricals, when he could afford it attended plays, and submitted his own work to the **Abbey**.

In 1923 the Abbey accepted *The Shadow of a Gunman*. Its period is the Anglo-Irish war which led to the 1921 Settlement. *Juno and the Paycock* (1924), set in the Civil War after the Settlement, and *The Plough and the Stars* (1926), an anti-heroic version of the 1916 Rising, completed his 'Dublin trilogy'. *The Shadow* and *Juno* were popular successes and repaired the Abbey's rocky finances. *The Plough* attracted riotous abuse. 'You have disgraced yourselves again', **Yeats** told the audience, alluding to a similar response to **Synge**'s *Playboy*.

In 1928 the Abbey directors refused *The Silver Tassie*, O'Casey's pacifist play about the First World War, objecting unpersuasively to its expressionist second act, its distance from O'Casey's own experience, the absence of strong comic characterization. Yeats's distaste for the War as a subject may have been influential. Disturbed by the reception of *The Plough* O'Casey, now living in England, was outraged by the rejection. He broke with the Abbey and despite some fragile reconciliations never established a permanent relationship with it or any other theatre.

O'Casey's later work is in its attitudes didactic, informed by his Communist beliefs, and in its forms symbolic, stylized, experimental: *Within the Gates* (1934), *The Star Turns Red* (1940), *Red Roses for Me* (1943), *Purple Dust* (1945), *Oak Leaves and Lavender*

(1947), *Cock-a-Doodle-Dandy* (1949), *The Bishop's Bonfire* (1955), *The Drums of Father Ned* (1958) (dates of first production).

A common judgement has been that O'Casey's Dublin trilogy is his masterpiece, which he never equalled. However one may censure the plays – for structural disunities, conventional plotting – they refute complaint by their brilliant comic invention; above all by their world of music-hall knockabout and rhetorical extravagance, where moments of tragic, often brutal, action collaborate with farce.

Of the later plays only *Red Roses* is set in Dublin. Though it exemplifies O'Casey's uncertainty with 'fine writing', and overplays the vernacular, it movingly evokes the 1913 Lockout, effectively using song, dance, mime – a populist version of Yeats's prescriptions. *The Star* (placed in a heavily symbolic Dublin), *Gates*, and *Dust* are political allegories, restlessly seeking form appropriate to 'message'. *Bonfire*, *Cock-a-Doodle* and *Father Ned* return to Irish villages. The two latter are symbolic celebrations of the Life-Force, sexual, liberated, defeating clerical oppression. Abbey productions of the 1970s and 80s showed that the latter plays, despite their reputation, can have a vigorous stage presence.

Although O'Casey also wrote (1939–54) a remarkable autobiography, he was primarily a dramatist. His plays, embodying his disputatious scepticism and great warmth for the antic human pageant, establish his place among the major Irish dramatists. DM

Oceania The Pacific region is customarily divided into three groupings, Melanesia, Micronesia, and Polynesia. Though linguistic, ethnic, and cultural features make the distinction useful, certain features bind together the performance of this area. Firstly, a combination of music, dance and poetry and improvised comic skits are, traditionally, more significant arts than theatrical pieces in which actors take on another persona in an extended narrative. Secondly, although the expertise of artists is high, most earn their livelihood by other work in these small, geographically isolated communities. Thirdly, performance often takes place in the context of festivals, life-cycle ceremonies, or communal feasts which celebrate the social life of the community and often involves large groups of dancers, most often of a single sex. Hundreds of dancers may join in a running dance at a New Guinea *sing-sing* (communal feast), long lines of women or rows of men perform unison dance movement in a Fijian *meke*, a Hawaiian *hula* or an *ur* on the Micronesian island of Ifaluk. This tendency is not new: in the 1790s, just 16 years after the first European landfall, George Vancouver described a Hawaiian performance in which 200 women danced in astounding unison.

The talents of singing and dancing are often thought to be common to all rather than reserved to a few. Though some solo forms do exist, the precision and uniformity of the group is generally more cultivated than the self-expression of the individual performer. Even the composer–choreographer's songs are often thought to be the gift of the spirits, communicated in dream or vision. Performance is more important as the activation of group cohesiveness than individual expressivity.

The social change wrought by contact with the West and Christianization in the 19th and early 20th centuries was profound. Traditional arts, deprived of their former contexts and attacked by early missionaries, often fell into disuse. In some cases the indigenous language was largely replaced by that of the colonial power and understanding of both text and context of traditional performance lost to the general audience. Only in the last 30 years due to altered church policy and growing political awareness have religious festival and government holidays increasingly become a venue for what remains of traditional performance. Performances were often recast to suit the expectations of a tourist audience, and retailored to fit the changing tastes of the indigenous peoples. Music, dance, and dramatic performance maintain traditional elements, but acculturation includes, for example, the adaptation of European musical instruments, modification of themes, and movements once indigenous to a specific island can be found throughout the region. Often performances have changed from out-of-doors, nightlong, torchlit entertainments for communal feasts into two-hour presentations on electrically lit, proscenium stages. Current attempts to create 'professional' companies, with full-time, paid performers, and emphasis on individual creativity or solo dancing have also come in the wake of Western influence and urbanization. Also apparent is the need to articulate an ethnic image to both a national and an international audience, via the creation of national companies in places like Papua New Guinea, the Cook Islands, and Fiji.

Though the stated aim of some current performers is to recreate the pre-European contact models, the arts of the current period are post-traditional. Current performance is best viewed as a modern political statement documenting the search for alternatives to the pop culture and mass media of the First World. These exciting experiments show that dance and drama are still important modes of integrating the societies concerned.

A brief survey of the three major areas can help clarify some of the variations and reveal the continuity or disjuncture with the past. Two strains of performance can be noted: first forms which develop out of indigenous music and dance or mime traditions and, second, forms which derive more strongly from Western models. The former include dances and dance-mimes of the past. The latter include religious plays presented by the Christian churches and modern drama which has been introduced through the schools. The growing tendency of religious and modern drama to reintegrate traditional music, dance, and themes shows the current blending of these two strains.

Melanesia Melanesia includes Papua New Guinea, Irian Jaya, Vanuatu (New Hebrides), New Caledonia, and the Solomons. Though linguistic and cultural features vary, these islands are largely inhabited by people who cultivate democratic societies in which leadership is achieved rather than inherited. Leaders, called 'big men' in Pidgin, traditionally held feasts involving mass killings of pigs (which represented wealth) with concomitant public donations/hand outs to bind supporters to them. Performances of music, dance, and clowning were a regular part of such feasts. Dance-mimes are common throughout the Melanesian area. While Micronesians and Polynesians often act out fishing or hunting from the human viewpoint, the Melanesian tends to show the perspective of the prey. Masks and other performing objects are common through the region, and are often thought to represent spirits. The ingrained mimetic bias makes drama an important feature of Melanesian society to the present.

The relative autonomy of ethnic groups until the present century has resulted in a wealth of distinctive artistic choices. For an understanding of the implications of the individual performance systems, readers should refer to specific group practices recorded in anthropological literature. This brief survey of selected genres can only hint at the creative usage of elements like time, space, and costuming in the region.

One performance that used time expansively was documented by F. E. Williams in the 1930s when the Orokolo of Papua conducted a now-defunct cycle of ceremonies that took decades to enact and culminated when huge masks were danced amid general rejoicing from the men's club house to the sea. The demise of the ceremonial cycle came with modernization and social change that enervated the men's organizations by undercutting their myths. The performance systems of many other Melanesian groups have also been substantially altered by the changes in religion and social practices that have ended initiation rites, traditional warfare, and secret societies.

The elaborate feather headdresses, penis coverings, leaf or tapa coverings, body painting, and tattooing that are found in Melanesian performance show the human body in unique splendour. Masks of wood, gourds, bark-cloth and other natural materials are often activated in performance and ritual. The spatial usage is often striking: societies which use trees as stages (as in a New Ireland form of women's song) and allow masked images suddenly to materialize in front of a hut from the surrounding jungle (as in *duk-duk* dances of the Tolai of New Britain) show impressive use of the environment. In Vanuatu's Pentecost Island men dive from high platforms only to be caught by vines attached to their feet in a performance which commemorates how a woman foiled a persistent suitor by sending him plummeting to death while she saved herself by this ruse.

The entire village is often involved in a performance in such a way that the line between audience and performers is blurred. In a Papua New Guinea *sing-sing*, the whole community may join in the night-long dancing. Perhaps as a result of this, the dance steps tend to be rather simple, consisting perhaps of a running hop-step or, in some areas, a side to side swing for women. But, though participation is wide, some divisions between performers are significant. Men and women often dance in separate groups, reaffirming the importance of sex differentiation, and only a few performers tend to take central roles, often by wearing the masks that are the centrepieces of the event.

Exactly who takes the central roles varies significantly, but in New Guinea it is often initiated men. Many performance objects – bull-roarers, gongs, masks – are the property of a village men's club. The method of using these objects is learned during the initiation period while boys are separated from their mothers and tested for manhood. In such instances, it is via this performance training that initiated men come to activate their superiority to women and children who are told the figures they enact are spirits.

In New Guinea these performers often gain the prime roles by making certain sacrifices. Among the Umeda Gell noted that the wearing of the main masks of a bowman and cassowary (a running bird) necessitated undertaking difficult fasts. In other areas, bloodletting ceremonies or beatings might be inflicted at the time of learning songs or steps which accompanied mask dances. Brought with pain, the song–dances were apt to be remembered. Suffering has a part in the *gisaro* performance of the Papuan Kaluli peoples; singers try to make the audience members cry by making songs that remind people of their dead. The emotionally aroused audience members then seize torches and brand the singer, and the skilled performer is known by his wealth of burns the morning after a presentation. Such performers who suffer can, perhaps, be compared to 'big men' within the political sphere. Though performance is democratic in that everyone can participate, those who sacrifice more gain the admiration of the community.

Performance in Melanesia often serves a recognized social function. The conical masks of the *duk-duk* society of New Britain's Tolai people are 'spirit' manifestations, played by initiated members of the group to frighten and control those who flout social mores or gain members' anger. Funeral rites in New Ireland, the buying of a higher grade in a secret society in Vanuatu, the dedication of slit gongs in the Solomon Islands, or the marking of male initiation ceremonies or a killing in battle in traditional Papua New Guinea all require performances. In each case, something irreversible happens and the performance marks the new status.

In this century church theatricals introduced by missionaries absorbed some of the energy of earlier men's house mimesis in the form of plays about martyrdom of early missionaries. Choirs and marching bands were first widely introduced, though present practice encourages more traditional dance and music in the context of church events. Other attempts to assimilate pre-Christian practices into the new order are also apparent in practices of the newly emergent educated elite. Michael Somare, the sometime Prime Minister of Papua New Guinea, underwent a modified initiation ceremony of his ethnic group, while in Vanuatu some city-dwellers in the late 1970s returned to pig-killing ceremonies for wedding celebrations. But these events are modified to suit the constraints of a modern life-style.

Modern drama has been an innovation of the late 1960s and the 1970s, introduced by European teachers and reworked by local artists to inculcate social change. A whole group of students at the University of Papua New Guinea studied creative writing under German Ulli Beier in the late 1960s. The course was aimed at creating political and cultural awareness through literature, and students wrote plays which agitated for independence and portrayed the conflict of traditional values and those inculcated by Western education. Early plays like Leo Hannet's *Ungrateful Daughter* placed emphasis on text, and lent themselves to realistic staging. It showed an adopted Papua New Guinea girl rejecting the values of her European parents in favour of indigenous standards. Produced in Port Moresby and abroad, this play gained sympathy for the independence movement which culminated in the end of colonial rule in 1975. Other works like John Kasaipwalova's *Kanaka* showed the problems a villager encounters returning to his hamlet from a sojourn in the city. John Kaniku's *Scattered By the Wind* dealt with the disruptions that Christianity, modern schooling and government regulations introduced into village life. The writers, a number of whom were subsequently to take prominent posts in the Papua New Guinea government, found writing was a way to make political statements with relative impunity. As Leo Hannet who became a leader of the Bougainville province government noted in 1977, 'Writing was a catharsis, you could make statements and no one could throw rocks at you.'

In New Caledonia modern drama was also a seedbed for political activism. The first modern theatrical experiment was *Kanaka*, given at an exhibition entitled Melanesia 2000 in 1975. The text drew on pre-Christian ceremonies as recorded by the missionary-anthropologist, Maurice Leenhardt. The performance presented by actors/dancers moving to a pre-recorded tape showed the invasion of the islands by missionaries, slavers, and merchants as Kanak tribesmen struggled to carry out death ceremonies for the old chief and prepare for the election of a new leader. The performance – created by Jean Marie Tjibaou, who then spearheaded the anti-colonial activism, and George Dobbelaere – was a rehearsal for Kanak attempts to reassert control over the nickel rich French colony.

As independence has come to some areas of Melanesia, more experimentation with traditional models has begun. Recent work in Papua New Guinea de-emphasizes text and initiates more lyrical, myth-based presentations which involve music, traditional dance, and masks. These tendencies are evident in the work of Arthur Jawadimbori, head of the Papua New Guinea National Theatre in Port Moresby, and the work of the Raun Raun Theatre in Garoka whose work has been influenced by Greg Murphy, an Australian director. These troupes have been funded by the Papua New Guinea government since 1975. In 1980 the former group presented *Eberia*, a play by William Takaku, and the latter a performance based on John Kasaipwalova's *Sail the Midnight Sun* at the Pacific Arts Festival, a quadrennial event which since its inauguration in 1972 has prompted some of the best theatre productions in the pan-Pacific area. Each play takes indigenous myths and explores new theatrical avenues – the first the rock opera genre, the latter a free mixing of dance, mask, and musical elements from different ethnic groups. The sound-movement emphasis of these productions may be a sign that the text-based modern drama of the 1970s is returning to more indigenous mime for a base.

Satire is also a developing genre in Papua New Guinea: indigenous clown traditions have been evoked by the Raun Raun players who play improvised comedies in open air performances at village gatherings, and political satire exploited by Nora Vargi Brash, author of *Which Way Big Man* (1977) which mocks the pretensions of the new government elite in the young nation. Radio drama is another lively outlet for writers in Papua New Guinea, which leads the Pacific in modern theatrical activity.

Micronesia Micronesia is composed of the Federated States of Micronesia (Yap, Truk, Ponape and Kosrae – formerly the Carolines), Mariana Islands, Marshall Islands, Beleu (Palau), Kiribati (formerly Gilbert Islands), and Nauru. The people are related to the Malays and speak Austronesian languages. Societies acknowledge hereditary chiefs, but differentiation in status is less extreme than in the Polynesian area. Matrilineal patterns can be seen in traditional society and this may contribute to the importance of girls and women as performers. Research and documentation of the performing arts of this region has not been extensive, but based on the information currently available, the following generalizations seem to hold true.

Though mimesis is sometimes evident in the performance of this area, its importance is de-emphasized. For the Micronesian the beginning is the word: song texts are considered the most important element in a presentation. Songs are usually presented in conjunction with group or solo dances, and most gestures are abstractly decorative. Even in present practice, poetry, as represented in the writings of Micronesian authors published in *Mana*, a journal of arts issued by the University of the South Pacific in Fiji, is a livelier genre than drama.

The impersonation that does occur tends to be (1) representation of creatures, often a frigate bird or iguana; (2) mimes of fishing, canoeing, battling or lovemaking; and (3) possession trances in which a spirit enters a performer. Though possession is the exception rather than the rule, the nature of some dance movements – the quivering movements of the frigate bird impersonation and the convulsive movements of some iguana dances (both animals associated with old religious practice) – is possibly evidence of a venerable link between possession and the dance of this area.

Dances may be sitting or standing. Canoe paddles or sticks may be used as props. Musical instruments are traditionally few and the human voice the major accompaniment. In the normal group dances one or two dancers may parody the movements of the group, adopting a clown persona. Performances may be in village assembly halls, but are often outside, where they might traditionally be part of religious worship, female initiation rites, welcoming ceremonies for visitors on the beach, lovers' trysts, performance contests between villagers, entertainments at village feasts, etc.

Islands such as Beleu, Guam, and Ponape, which have been capitals for the colonial governments, exhibit few of the traditional performance practices that were noted by early European visitors, and marching bands, church choirs, and 'Micronesian' dances of relatively recent vintage are more common. More removed islands, like Ifaluk and Kiribati, have more conservative performance practice. On both islands danced poetry dealing with themes like the sea, spirits and love remains of great significance.

In Kiribati the composer–choreographer role has shamanic overtones, for he often receives songs from the spirit world in trance and then teaches these *ruoia* (dance-songs) to villagers.

One or two dancers may clown during performance, thereby distinguishing themselves from the group. A woman is often the dance leader, a practice which may come from older sitting dances called *te bino*, which feature a female and have movements said to be

Dance postures of the Micronesian performers in a Kiribati *ruoia* emulate the flight of the frigate bird, an old religious symbol.

inspired by the flight of birds. In *ruoia*, some performers may suddenly cease the group dance and emulate a frigate bird. Small girls have prominence in some dances, and the special status of pre-pubescent performers in societies as distant as Bali and Kiribati makes some scholars wonder if this was a feature of archaic Malayo-Polynesian groups.

On Ifaluk, as Burrows reports, old religious chants tend to be dances like the *gapengpeng* where the single-sex, seated chorus calls on the god to take possession of a dancer, or the *ur*, a group standing dance done by either sex in which individuals again emerge from the group 'becoming' a frigate bird. Women are notable performers on this island, too, but their compositions, called *bwarux*, are primarily solo dance-songs meant for the male lover as sole audience. The association of these songs and female fertility may explain their performance on other occasions, including female initiation ceremonies which mark a girl's first menstruation, honouring male visitors from other islands, and welcoming schools of fish to the harbour.

Performance in Micronesia generally promotes group solidarity under the direction of the composer-choreographer, who may himself be thought to be directed by spirits. Performers may emerge from the group, but often this occurs only when the signs of the old god – possession or bird impersonation – are with them. One does not seize the group focus for self-expression, but to act out the spirit world. Individual love songs, in theory at least, are for the ears of the loved one alone.

Polynesia Polynesia is divided by specialists into two separate groups: West Polynesia includes Tonga, Samoa, Uvea (Wallis), Futuna, Niue, Tuvalu (Ellice), Tokelau, Fiji; and East Polynesia includes the Society Islands (Tahiti), Marquesas Islands, Austral Islands, Mangareva, Tuamotu Islands, Cook Islands, Easter Island, New Zealand, and Hawaii. In the Eastern area, as Kaeppler notes, the movement of the lower body, especially hips and knees, is a strong feature of dance, while the Western area does not emphasize this part of the body. Performance in Polynesia traditionally involved music and dance which interpreted poetic texts often rich in metaphor and allusion. Rather than decorative dance, as in Micronesia, the Polynesian tends to use the hands and arms to signify selected words of the text via an elaborate gestural language. Movements of the legs and hips are more abstract, relating to the rhythm of the music. The dancer is a story-teller, but one who customarily delivers the story in his own persona rather than by becoming the characters in the text. More mimetic interludes might come between these poetic dance-songs: short skits in which performers, usually men or sometimes older women, use spoken dialogue improvised on pre-arranged themes, usually satirical in nature, have been part of many Polynesian cultures.

The Polynesian societies were traditionally class-stratified ones in which genealogy determined rank and power. Texts often were in praise of important individuals and many performances were at events which reiterated the power of the aristocracy, who had the resources and influence to mount large scale performances which needed extensive rehearsal. Performance specialists included composer–choreographers and dancers trained under them.

Kaeppler notes that performances were largely a reaffirmation of social structure: large groups of men, women, or occasionally men and women might perform dances in unison with the choreography directed toward the most important viewers, i.e. – the chief and his guests. Placement of dancers in the configuration might also reflect the hierarchy of rank and age, and obedience to the composer–choreographer was likewise strict. Satirical interludes seem to have served as a release from these customary constraints, and impromptu dialogue and the free use of space, language, and subject matter delighted the audiences. A brief consideration of some Tahitian, Samoan, and Fijian performance gives examples of traditional and contemporary performance in Polynesia.

Perhaps the most elaborate performance system reported by early European visitors was that of Tahiti, where the Arioi, a guild of performers, was found. This was a group that worshipped Oro, the god of fertility, and as part of his service became specialists in dance-chant in which the poetry was the major factor. Clowning and dramas enacting serious myths and including female actors, are reported, though it is difficult to assess the parameters of pre-contact practice based on the fragmentary evidence remaining. The 'lewd' dance which included much hip and pelvis articulation, the raising of skirts, and facial contortions distressed Europeans. The sexual licence of society members who did not marry and were normally required to kill any children that they might bear caused the missions effectively to outlaw the sect.

In current Tahitian practice as reported by Moulin, hip movement is still important, but even the churches now foster the dance as a mode of bringing the congregations together. But, as in Hawaii where the indigenous language has been largely replaced by a European tongue, the emphasis on poetry is greatly diminished and the gestural language is more limited. In contrast to the past where groups predominated, virtuoso solo or couple dances receive focus. These are indications that the current societal values may vary significantly from former ones. Emphasis on decor and spectacle was noted by Victor Carrell in recent Bastille

Day competitions. Since their inauguration at the end of the last century Bastille *fêtes* have become the major dance event in Tahiti, and the audience is apt to be treated to innovations such as that prepared by Coco, a major troupe leader, who had his dancers fall on their stomach and mime swimming in the ocean in a 1985 piece that departed freely from traditional dance.

One group which presents a more traditional version of the dance of this general area is the Cook Islands National Theatre under Ota Joseph. The group is traditional in its preference for precision, group dancing, but the theatricalization of folk culture is evident in their work. In addition to traditional group standing and sitting dances, mimes of kite flying, and coronation ceremonies, dance dramas such as one exploring the coming of the Bible to the Cook Islands may be done. These works, based on careful research, are conscious attempts to recycle traditional material in modes that will suit modern audiences.

Examples of how the comedy works in the total context of Polynesian traditional performance can still be seen in Samoa. There performers of *fale aitu* (house of the spirit) are called *fa'aluma*. Traditionally a chief might take a pair of these clowns as part of his dance group when he went travelling to other islands. Supposedly, spirits (*aitu*) could be invoked by the best performers, and, under the protection of these ghosts, the *fa'aluma* might be allowed to mock the highest chief in skits presented between dance-chants by the larger ensemble of dancers. Performances that mix group dance by 50–200 performers and such clowning are now usually presented at church fairs. Skits show traditional comic figures, such as transvestites or homosexuals and Europeans; or explore Samoan economic difficulties. Petelo, from Western Samoa, is probably the most noted exponent of this form.

In Samoa, church theatricals on religious themes are also popular, especially on children's day, White Sunday, and experiments in biblical opera, such as Ueta Solomona's *Jeptha* presented at the 1972 Pacific Arts Festival, are products of this tradition. In recent years there has been some experimentation in Samoa in modern spoken drama, but the tradition is confined to a rather small segment of the population.

Fiji culturally and ethnically lies on the border of Melanesia and Polynesia. It exhibits the strengths to be derived from each of these strains *vis-à-vis* its theatrical arts – both dance-songs and dramatic enactments thrive. Traditional dance and the highly formalized *kava* drinking ceremony are to be found at church fairs. The traditional *meke* (dance-songs) include war, club, spear, fan and other standing and sitting dances. The most important member of a group is the composer (*dau ni vucvu*) who may receive inspiration from the sprite-like *veli*, spirits who teach dances with quick unpredictable movement, or stillborn children, who teach more sedate songs, though other tunes are composed without such spirit helpers.

One innovative group working in Fiji is the Dance Theatre of Fiji under Manoa Rasignatale, a former pop star who began researching his island heritage after the 1972 Pacific Arts Festival. But rather than presenting only humorous sketches as performed between traditional dances, the performances of the Dance Theatre of Fiji re-enact village life. Top-spinning contests or the spirit-inspired creation of a *meke* may be acted out. This

Iolani Luahine, the greatest exponent of Hawaiian *hula* of this generation.

theatrical presentation of indigenous practices is comparable to the choices of Cook Islands National Theatre and conforms to folkloric theatre-dance companies that have emerged in many Third World countries. The Dance Theatre has found popularity both at home and abroad.

Modern drama is written and presented at the University of the South Pacific in Fiji by Joe Nacola. In Hawaii, too, university theatre programmes have resulted in a wealth of modern spoken drama and given rise to groups like the professional Honolulu Theatre for Youth, which plays to child audiences, and the Kuma Kahua players who are dedicated to the production of new plays by playwrights who live in Hawaii.

It is notable that in Polynesia, as in Melanesia, spoken drama is being utilized to vent criticism of Western culture or remoulded to reflect the cultures that make up the multi-ethnic and multi-talented population of the Pacific basin where universities have choirs that perform traditional dance-chant (University of the South Pacific) and give degrees for courses of study that focus on Asian Theatre or Pacific Dance (University of Hawaii). The excitement that permeates the annual Merrie Monarch *hula* competition in Hawaii, Bastille Day performances in Tahiti, and the pan-Pacific fervour that erupts as each island prepares to send dances and dramas to the South Pacific Arts Festival that occurs every four years shows that the arts are changing, but remain vital to the peoples of Oceania.   KF

See: U. Beier, *Voices of Independence: New Black Writing from Papua New Guinea*, New York, 1980; M. Browning,

Micronesian Heritage: Dance Perspectives 43 (Autumn 1970); E. Burrows, *Flower in my Ear: Arts and Ethos of Ifaluk Atoll*, Seattle, 1963; B. Dean, *South Pacific Dance*, Sydney, 1978; N. Emerson, *Unwritten Literature of Hawaii: The Sacred Songs of the Hula*, Washington, 1909; A. Gell, *Metamorphosis of the Cassowaries: Umeda Society, Language and Ritual*, London, 1975; T. Henry, *Ancient Tahiti*, Honolulu, 1948; A. Kaeppler, 'Movement in the Performing Arts of the Pacific Islands', in *Theatrical Movement: a Bibliographical Anthology*, ed. R. Fleshman, London, 1986; G. and S. Koch, 'Kultur der Gilbert Inseln', *Encyclopaedia cinematographica*, Gottingen, 1969; J. Layard, *Stone Men of Malekula*, London, 1942; J. Moulin, *The Dance of Tahiti*, Papeete, 1979; D. Oliver, *A Solomon Island Society*, Cambridge, Mass., 1955; S. Sadie, ed., *New Grove Dictionary of Music and Musicians*, London, 1980, entries on 'Melanesia', 'Micronesia', 'Pacific Islands', 'Polynesia'; E. Schieffelin, *The Sorrow of the Lonely and the Burning of the Dancers*, New York, 1976; A. and M. Strathern, *Self-Decoration in Mount Hagan*, London, 1971; V. Tausie, *Art in the New Pacific*, Suva, 1980; C. Thompson, 'Fijian Music and Dance', *Fijian Society Transactions and Proceedings*, 11: 14–21; F. E. Williams, *The Drama of Orokolo*, Oxford, 1940; Sister Francis Xavier, 'Dancing and Singing in the Gilbert Islands', *Mana* 1, 2 (Dec. 1976), 43–9.

October group French agit-prop theatre company working between 1933 and 1936. Many of its short plays were scripted by Jacques Prévert and were distinguished by a combination of playful wit and biting satire. An example is *The Battle of Fontennoy* (1933) which presented the First World War as a spectator sport in which lives were sacrificed in the name of hypocritical idealism while the population (the spectators) bayed for blood. The group's work was supported by the French Worker's Theatre Federation, which selected them to represent France at the Moscow Theatre Olympiad of 1933, where they won first prize. As Prévert began to work as a film script writer, many members of the group followed him and can be seen at their best in Renoir's *The Crime of Monsieur Lange* (1935).   DB

Odéon (France) 1,900-seat theatre in the Latin quarter of Paris constructed by the architects Peyre and Wailly to house the **Comédie-Française** in 1782. It was the first to introduce benches into the pit. **Beaumarchais**'s *Marriage of Figaro* was first produced there in 1784. In 1789 the more revolutionary members of the troupe, including **Talma**, moved to the Théâtre de la République, which became the Comédie-Française in 1799. From 1794–7 the theatre closed, then opened under the name Odéon. Burnt in 1799, its actors rejoined the rest of the troupe at the 'new' Comédie-Française. It reopened in 1808, suffered another fire in 1818, when it became the Second Théâtre-Français. Here the first plays of **Casimir Delavigne** were performed. Under **Harel** (1829–32) this 'Siberia' of dramatic art saw productions of **Augier**'s *Le Ciguë* (*Hemlock*) and a move towards realism with George Sand's *François le Champi*. **Musset**'s *Une Nuit Vénitienne* had its disastrous first night there in 1830, and his *Carmosine* was shown there for the first time in 1865. In 1866 **Sarah Bernhardt** became one of the leading actresses of the theatre, notably with the role of Zanetto, the young

musician in François Coppée's *The Passer-by* (1869), and during the siege of Paris in 1870 she turned the theatre into a field hospital. In 1872 she played the queen in a very successful revival of **Victor Hugo**'s *Ruy Blas* (banned during the Second Empire). Major managers were La Rounat (1872–80) and Porel (1884–92). Duquesnel turned resolutely to more ambitious *mise-en-scène*, his production of Newsky's *Les Danicheff* (1878) providing the longest run in the history of the theatre. Porel made a success of Alphonse Daudet's *L'Arlésienne* (1885), with a chorus and orchestra of 150 and Bizet's music. He also staged a number of **Shakespeare** plays, with much attention to music and spectacle, kept in touch with the naturalist movement (in 1887 he produced the Théâtre Libre play, *Jacques Damour*). Porel left the theatre thriving. He introduced electric lighting in 1888 (one of the last theatres in Paris). In 1896, **André Antoine** became director of the Odéon for the first time, in collaboration with Paul Ginisty. 17 days after the opening of the new directorate, Antoine resigned; the more conservative Ginisty remained in control for a decade. In 1906 Antoine returned as sole director, installing an up-to-date lighting system and getting rid of the old chandelier which had remained lit throughout performances. In the years leading up to the First World War his company set new standards of truth to life and quality of ensemble playing. The next major figure at the Odéon was **Firmin Gémier**, who took over in 1921 and used his position as director in his campaign to establish an effective National People's Theatre. Gémier had steps installed joining the stage to the auditorium so that actors could enter through the audience. Towards the end of the 1920s Paul Abram became co-director and, from 1930, sole director, a post he retained till the occupation of Paris by the German army. Abram continued Gémier's policy of trying to present a repertoire of broad appeal with a judicious mixture of classic revivals and new plays; for a while Saint-Georges de Bouhélier was resident dramatist. In 1946 the theatre was annexed by the Comédie-Française and became its second house, used particularly for modern works, while the classics remained at the Salle Richelieu. In 1959 this arrangement was cancelled by André Malraux, minister of culture under de Gaulle, who installed the Renaud-**Barrault** company there instead. Here they performed some of the key plays in the recent history of French theatre, including *Rhinoceros* by **Ionesco** (1960) and *The Screens* by **Genet** (1966), an event which provoked riots both inside and outside the theatre. From 1967 to 1970 the performances of the **Théâtre des Nations** were given at the Odéon and it was after one of these, on 15 May 1968, that the theatre was occupied by students. They used it as a debating forum until they were expelled on 14 June. Barrault was dismissed by Malraux for having displayed too much tolerance in dealing with the occupation. From 1971 onwards, the company again came under the administration of the Comédie-Française. Companies of the **decentralization movement** also use it as a Paris showcase for their best productions.   JMCC DB

Odets, Clifford (1906–63) American playwright. In the entire sweep of American theatre history, Odets is the one true company playwright. In the early days of the **Group Theatre**, as he listened to **Harold Clurman**'s orations and followed **Lee Strasberg**'s formulations of the basic principles of Method acting, Odets was absorbing the elements of a theatrical style that erupted on 14 January 1935, when the Group presented *Waiting for Lefty*, his incendiary play about taxi drivers driven to call a strike. In a series of short, jabbing scenes and in language alive with the rhythms and inflections of urban folk idiom, Odets expressed the fury and passion and sorrow of the dispossessed working class. With this play the Group discovered its voice: *Lefty* released the full potential of the new realistic acting style that its members had been investigating for four years.

Later in the same year the Group produced two other Odets plays, *Awake and Sing!* and *Paradise Lost*, family dramas whose contemporary but archetypal Jewish sufferers speak in a language of their own, a dense idiom of metaphor and incantatory repetition alternating irony with exultation and brief, stabbing sentences with longer speeches of operatic intensity. When Odets left for Hollywood at the end of his triumphant year, his Group colleagues felt betrayed. As if in compensation, Odets presented them with a new play, *Golden Boy* (1937). In it, his hero's hard choice between being a violinist and a prize fighter expresses Odets's own conflict about whether to serve art or commerce. Though this central premiss is spurious, the play proved to be the Group's biggest moneymaker. Odets's final work for the Group, *Rocket to the Moon* (1938) and *Night Music* (1940), is diminished in its thematic scope and vitality. By 1940, when the Group itself had lost its focus, Odets had also apparently

reached a creative impasse. Despite their ripe language and strong conflict, Odets's four remaining dramas – *Clash by Night* (1941), *The Big Knife* (1949), *The Country Girl* (1950), and *The Flowering Peach* (1954) – don't have the same sense of occasion as even the least of the Group efforts. To accomplish his most vibrant work Odets seemed to require a depression background; he is now regarded as the quintessential thirties playwright, who transmuted working-class pressures into timeless theatrical eloquence.   FH

Odin Teatret (Nordisk Teaterlaboratorium for Skuespillerkunst – Nordic Theatrical Arts Laboratory) International theatrical community founded in Oslo in 1964 by the expatriate Italian **Eugenio Barba**, who had just returned from three years with **Grotowski** in Opole. The company's first production, *Ortofilene*, toured Scandinavia with such success that the town of Holstebro, Denmark, invited them to create a permanent theatre there. Since 1966 this has been the company's base, though it also tours extensively. The Holstebro company opened in September 1967 with *Kaspariana* (based on the strange life of Kaspar Hauser, 1812–33) and followed this in 1969 with *Ferai*, scripted by Peter Seeberg on the basis of Scandinavian mythology and **Euripides**' *Alcestis*. Shown at the **Théâtre des Nations** in Paris, it brought them the international reputation which they have enjoyed ever since. These early productions were strongly Grotowskian, and his ideas and training methods remain central to the company's work: a community of actors living under a strict regime of taxing physical and vocal exercise, and at the same time involved in policy and organization;

Odin Teatret performing *Anabasis* in Peru, 1978.

creating performances which arise from their personal confrontation with source-materials, techniques and each other; appearing before the public, often to deliberately small audiences, only when they feel that they have something to show. This notion remains fundamental. At the same time, during the early 1970s, Barba began to mistrust the fetichistic devotion to skills within a highly protected environment; and partly as a result of experiencing less reverential and more vocal audience responses while touring Sardinia with *Min Fars Hus* (*My Father's House* – based on the life and work of Dostoevsky), the company began to mount clown shows, street parades, and improvised musical performances, and developed its 'barter-principle', whereby, instead of paying in cash for a performance, the audience offer in return their own performance, or a commitment to some local project. AEG

Oehlenschläger, Adam (1779–1850) Danish poet and dramatist, whose early work reflected his enthusiasm for the ideals of Jena romanticism. His poem 'The Golden Horns' (1803) proclaimed a renaissance of ancient Nordic culture and mythology, which provided the subject matter for many of the plays he wrote in imitation of **Goethe** and **Schiller**, including *Hakon Jarl* and *Baldur the Good* (both 1807), *Staerkodder* (1812) and *Hagbarthe and Signe* (1815). However, in the theatre only the much more fanciful *Midsummer Night's Play* (1803) and *Aladdin* (1805) have continued to be staged into the 20th century. His creativity seems to have been in decline by about 1811 and in the 1820s his reputation suffered even more seriously from the well-argued criticisms of **Johan Ludvig Heiberg**. HL

Oenslager, Donald (1902–75) American set designer and educator. His influences include **George Pierce Baker**, the work of **Appia** and **Craig** which he saw in Europe in 1921, and **Robert Edmond Jones** whom he assisted in the early 1920s. Oenslager designed some 250 productions including *Anything Goes, You Can't Take It with You*, and *The Man Who Came to Dinner*. Although he emphasized the need to find the proper style for each play, his designs were frequently decorative and elegant. His greatest influence, however, was as a teacher – he was a professor of design at Yale University for nearly 50 years (1925–71) and many of the major figures in American design were trained by him. He is author of *Scenery Then and Now* and *Four Centuries of Theatre Design* which was illustrated with drawings from his extensive private collection. AA

Off-Broadway (USA) The term, coined in the 1950s, for both New York City productions or theatres outside the so-called 'Broadway' area surrounding Times Square and an (American) Actors' Equity Association contract for theatres with 100–299 seats. Some theatres that house Off-Broadway plays are the **Astor Place**, **Lucille Lortel** (formerly Théâtre de Lys), Orpheum, Westside Arts, Perry Street, Collonades Theatre Lab, Minetta Lane and several houses along **Theatre Row**, a renovated block of mid-town New York devoted to Off- and Off-Off Broadway theatre.

Off-Broadway is also a movement with roots in the early 1900s. Reaching its most productive period in the 1950s, Off-Broadway began as the 'Little Theatre movement' among New York's intelligentsia. Offering artistically significant plays in an inexpensive, non-commercial atmosphere, groups such as the **Washington Square Players** and the **Provincetown Players** staged, in small, out-of-the-way theatres, plays Broadway producers ignored. Other early companies included the **Neighbourhood Playhouse**, Cherry Lane Theatre, Civic Repertory Company and **Group Theatre**. Many were not only experimental but amateur as well, lasting only a few years despite artistic successes. Often they were victims of that success, as playwrights, actors, directors, and designers parlayed artistic triumphs into jobs in commercial theatre and, later, Hollywood. After the Second World War, however, Off-Broadway attracted critical attention. Several successes transferred to Broadway, beginning with New Stages' production of **Sartre**'s *The Respectful Prostitute* in 1948.

In the 1950s and early 1960s, several new companies had a major impact on American theatre. With untried, non-commercial, or experimental plays or productions, using then-unknown talent and shoe-string budgets, Off-Broadway became an artistic magnet. Serious attention started with the 1952 revival of **Tennessee Williams**'s *Summer and Smoke* by the infant **Circle in the Square** which launched the careers of director **José Quintero** and **Geraldine Page**. Such companies as the **Living Theatre**, Circle in the Square, Phoenix Theatre, **New York Shakespeare Festival**, **American Place Theatre**, **Negro Ensemble Company**, Roundabout Theatre Company, Chelsea Theatre Centre, **Circle Repertory** and **Manhattan Theatre Club** presented premieres and revivals of neglected plays or plays that failed on Broadway. Over the years, Off-Broadway theatres premiered such works as **Beckett**'s *Endgame* and *Play*, **Albee**'s *The Zoo Story*, Gelber's *The Connection*, Jones and Schmidt's *The Fantasticks* (America's longest-running play, opening in 1960), **Genet**'s *The Blacks*, **Orton**'s *What the Butler Saw*, Bernard Pomerance's *The Elephant Man*, **Charles Fuller**'s *A Soldier's Play* and **Caryl Churchill**'s *Cloud 9* and *Fen*. Other writers for Off-Broadway included **Kopit**, Schisgal, LeRoi Jones (**Amiri Baraka**), **van Itallie**, **Lanford Wilson**, **Guare**, **Bullins**, Vonnegut, **Rabe**, **Mamet**, **Zindel**, and **Innaurato**.

The talent in these productions included directors Quintero, **Schneider**, **Grotowski**, O'Horgan and **Grosbard** and actors **Jason Robards, Jr**, **Colleen Dewhurst**, **George C. Scott**, **James Earl Jones**, Barbara Harris, **Dustin Hoffman**, **Meryl Streep**, **Kevin Kline**, **Stacy Keach**, **Ruby Dee**, Jack McGowran, **Claire Bloom**, and **Al Pacino**. Off-Broadway is also a place for established actors to try unfamiliar roles, including that of director. Recent productions have been directed by actors **Geraldine Fitzgerald** (*Mass Appeal* and an all-black *Long Day's Journey Into Night*) and George C. Scott (*Present Laughter* and *Design for Living*). In 1955, the *Village Voice* established the Obie (for Off-Broadway) Awards to recognize accomplishments in this arena.

After the 1960s, Off-Broadway became a smaller version of Broadway, leaving the experimentation and discovery mostly to Off-Off Broadway. Today, Off-Broadway concentrates on commercial revivals of classics or older standards, and a few new works by established, but younger playwrights. Unknown artists look to the store-front or loft houses of Off-Off Broadway. Recently, some of the early Off-Broadway excitement has been generated by regional repertory companies across the country.   REK

See: S. W. Little, *Off-Broadway: The Prophetic Theater*, New York, 1972; J. S. Price, *The Off-Broadway Theater*, New York, 1962.

Off-Off Broadway (USA) The term coined in the early 1960s to distinguish professional, commercial theatre (Broadway and Off-Broadway) from non-commercial theatre presented in coffee houses, churches, lofts, and storefronts in New York's Greenwich Village and Lower East Side. Technically, the term also refers to productions that fall under the American Actors' Equity Basic Showcase Code for performances with limited runs that feature unsalaried union actors in non-contractual theatres of not more than 100 seats.

Often perceived as a movement, Off-Off Broadway encompasses a wide spectrum of theatrical activity so diverse in impulse, conception, method, and intent that no common objective characterizes it; Off-Off Broadway has spawned works of numerous types and terms to go with them: Experimental, **Collective**, Alternative, Environmental, Radical, Guerilla, and Theatre of Images.

Off-Off Broadway is usually considered an alternative theatre grounded in exploration and experimentation, and questioning the limits of performance. The initial impulse was to generate new approaches and methods in a climate free from the demands of popular taste that inform commercial theatre artistically and economically. Frequently, though, Off-Off Broadway plays are mounted to test commercial viability. When used as an avenue to commercial success, Off-Off Broadway productions mirror commercial theatre values and standards.

Caffé Cino became the first Off-Off Broadway theatre when Joe Cino began to present plays in his one-room coffee house in 1959. By 1965 there were several small producing organizations. The major ones include Judson Poet's Theatre formed in 1961 by Al Carmines; Café **La Mama** founded by Ellen Stewart in 1962; and Theatre Genesis founded in 1964 by Ralph Cook. Devoted primarily to producing work of new American playwrights, these houses mounted plays by writers like Julie Bovasso, **Ed Bullins**, **Rosalyn Drexler**, Tom Eyen, **Maria Irene Fornes**, Paul Foster, **Israel Horowitz**, **Adrienne Kennedy**, H. M. Koutoukas, Ruth Krauss, **Charles Ludlam**, **Terrence McNally**, Leonard Melfi, **Rochelle Owens**, **Sam Shepard**, Ronald Tavel, **Megan Terry**, John Vaccaro, **Jean-Claude van Itallie**, Jeff Weiss, and **Lanford Wilson**.

Theatre groups like the **Open Theatre**, **Performance Group**, Wooster Group, Manhattan Project, **Mabou Mines**, Play-House of the Ridiculous, Ridiculous Theatrical Company, Spiderwoman Theatre, and **Bread and Puppet Theatre** are also considered Off-Off Broadway, as are individual writers, directors, and actors who mount their own productions, like Jack Smith, **Richard Foreman**, **Robert Wilson**, Michael Kirby, **Spalding Gray**, and Stuart Sherman.   AS

Ogilvie, George (1931–) Australian director. An actor in the 1950s, he first directed with the Union Theatre Repertory Company, Melbourne, before studying at the Le Coq mime school in Paris and becoming a tutor at the Central School of Drama, London; he also conducted workshops for the **Royal Shakespeare Company**. Returning to Australia in 1966, he has directed with several major companies, including the South Australian Theatre Company, Melbourne Theatre Company, the Australian Opera and the Australian Ballet, as well as for television.   MW

Ogunde, Chief Hubert (1916–) Nigerian playwright and musician, founder of the Ogunde Theatre; and founder of the Association of Theatre Practitioners of Nigeria (with a membership of over 100 professional travelling theatre companies). Ogunde is sometimes described as the father of Nigerian theatre, or the father of contemporary Yoruba theatre. His work is mainly in Yoruba, and reveals some largely Yoruba influences: the traditional *Alarinjo* Theatre which came out of the *Egungun* masqueraders, the Lagos Concert Parties, and the (Lagosian) Church of the Lord. Nevertheless, for nearly 40 years he has travelled the length and breadth of Nigeria. He developed this national view in the years before independence. He began his theatre career in 1944, while being a poorly paid policeman, with his first folk opera *The Garden of Eden and the Throne of God*, to raise money for his Church. The following year he resigned from the police to start his own professional travelling theatre company. During the next 35 years he composed over 50 operas, plays and melodramas. During a full life he has taken titles, reputedly become a millionaire, and is now a film-maker and arts entrepreneur. His productions over the years are a record in performance of a popular perception of all the major events in Nigeria's recent history. Between 1946 and independence in 1960 he identified closely with the political struggle, and his plays were banned by the colonial authorities: *Tiger's Empire* (1946), *Strike and Hunger* (1946), *Bread and Bullet* (1950). He was commissioned to write a play for the independence Celebrations, *Song of Unity* (1960). These almost agit-prop operas were interspersed with other folk operas based on myths and love stories. After independence he became embroiled in the political turbulence in the Western Region, as the country began to slide towards civil war, and his most famous political play, *Yoruba Ronu!* (*Yoruba Awake!*, 1964), resulted in his being banned from performing in the Western Region. He produced *Otito Koro* (*Truth is Bitter*) '. . . as a biting answer to this ban' (Ebun Clark). He composed and produced an opera, *Muritala Mohammed*, in 1976 after the traumatic assassination of that Nigerian Head of State.

He has always worked hard to remain in touch with popular sentiment; and he has subjected himself as well as his company to gruelling touring schedules, even when it was no longer necessary for either himself or his company to reach so many distant audiences. In turn he has always sought to increase a national awareness among his largely Yoruba audiences. He is a superb entertainer: able to catch the mood of an audience and then suddenly heighten it – thus transforming rather bland tales of love, heroism and evil politicians into exciting theatrical performances which are observant, witty, and full of meaning for their enraptured audiences. Ogunde has recently made two successful feature films, *Aiye* (1980) and *Jaiyesimi* (1981); and film-making is a likely development for his company. ME

O'Keeffe, John (1747–1833) Irish playwright. Born in Dublin, he began acting in 1764, working with companies touring Ireland as actor, singer, writer of pantomimes and plays. His first plays were produced in Ireland from 1767 including *The Shamrock*, later successful as *The Poor Soldier* (1783). From 1777, through friendship with **George Colman the Elder**, he began to establish a reputation as a playwright, particularly with *Tony Lumpkin in Town*, and moved to London in 1781. Most of his plays of this period depend heavily on songs and incidental music, turning them into a form between musical farce and comic opera, for example *The Castle of Andalusia* (1782). By far his best play, *Wild Oats*, an often sentimental and genial farce with a brilliant portrait of a strolling player, Rover, was produced in 1791. Though he continued to be prolific, writing more than 60 plays, a long series of failures in the 1790s left him withdrawn and reserved. He retired in 1798, publishing his collected plays. In 1803 he sold the copyrights for all his plays in return for an annuity and settled in Sussex, writing his energetic autobiography, *Recollections* (1826). PH

Okhlopkov, Nikolai Pavlovich (1900–67) Postrevolutionary Soviet actor-director, important primarily for his cinematic productions at the Realistic Theatre in the 1930s, in which he experimented with flexible stage–auditorium configurations. The success of his 1921 mass spectacle, *The Struggle between Labour and Capital*, which he staged with a cast of 30,000 Siberians in his native Irkutsk, and his 1922 Youth Theatre production of **Mayakovsky**'s *Mystery-Bouffe*, propelled him to Moscow and the State Institute of Theatrical Art (GITIS). Here he studied with **Meyerhold**, at whose theatre (1923) he became the ideal biomechanical actor, in full control of his body. Meyerhold taught him about **commedia dell'arte**, **kabuki** and **nō** theatre techniques, about ancient and folk theatres, **Appia** and **Fuchs**. Theatrical co-worker Sergei Eisenstein, who would direct Okhlopkov in *Aleksandr Nevsky* (Okhlopkov was a film actor from 1924), helped teach him about cinematic montage. This was reinforced by Okhlopkov's work as a film director, following his departure from Meyerhold's Theatre (1926) in a disagreement over the actor's role. His productions at Moscow's smallest theatre, the Realistic, of which he was artistic director (1930–7), embodied the stage dynamism, strong emotionalism, cinematic, improvisatory and eastern techniques he had absorbed. Replacing the stage with mobile platforms and rearranging audience seating for each new production, he brought the immediacy of the outdoor theatre indoors. For Stavsky's *The Start* (1932), he utilized arena staging, a ramp half-surround of the audience and overhead circular bridge. For **Gorky**'s *The Mother* (1933), he affected montage via light shifted among small square platforms surrounding the audience. For Serafimovich's *The Iron Flood* (1933), he replaced the stage with a landscape, as he would in his 1953 production of **Ostrovsky**'s *The Thunderstorm* at the

Moscow Theatre of Drama, in which the mountains actually moved. His production of **Pogodin**'s *The Aristocrats* (1935) drew upon Oriental staging techniques and pointed towards the full-scale carnivalization of **Rostand**'s *Cyrano de Bergerac* (1943), which featured giant, silent puppets as choral presences and the milling audience as a Parisian crowd. The latter was Okhlopkov's second production for the Vakhtangov Theatre, following his departure from the Realistic, which had been forcibly merged with **Tairov**'s Kamerny Theatre in 1938. His famous *Hamlet* (1954) at the Mayakovsky Theatre (formerly the Moscow Theatre of Drama) was set in and around a huge pair of iron gates, symbolizing the prison that Denmark and the world had become. In both A. P. Shtein's war play, *Hotel Astoria* (1956), and **Arbuzov**'s *Irkutsk Story* (1960), Okhlopkov employed variants on the Japanese bridge or *hanamichi*. For his production of **Euripides**' *Medea* (1961), in which the protagonist was presented as a social victim, the director made over the interior of the Tchaikovsky Concert Hall (originally built as Meyerhold's theatre) to resemble a Greek amphitheatre. Since Okhlopkov's death, Soviet critics have judged rather harshly his post-1930s work and his insistence on cultivating multiple perspectives in the theatre. SG

Old Tup, the A traditional British comic balladdrama, centred on the slaughter of its eponymous animal hero, first recorded c. 1845, though the ballad as such is documented earlier, and a proverbial reference may indicate its existence as early as 1739. It is impossible to know whether the play is a dramatization of a pre-existing song or the song derived from the play. Performed by teenage boys and girls during the Christmas and New Year period, generally in pubs and clubs, its distribution is largely restricted to an area bounded by Chesterfield, Mansfield and Sheffield. It is a very lively and popular tradition: fieldwork during the 1970s (*Folk Music Journal*, 3, 1979) located 41 groups of actors from 14 communities, collecting substantial sums for their performances. AEG

Old Vic Theatre, London Built on the unfashionable south bank of the Thames, not far from Waterloo Bridge, the Old Vic was originally called the Coburg. It opened in 1818. Derided as the home of vulgar 'transpontine' melodrama by critics who preferred the smarter and safer theatres north of the river, it played to packed houses when most other London theatres were struggling to make ends meet. After extensive redecoration in 1833, the Coburg was renamed the Royal Victoria and was soon affectionately familiarized as the Old Vic. By mid-century it had declined into a notoriously rough house, was closed in 1871, reopened as the New Victoria Palace, closed again in 1880 and bought by a temperance reformer called Emma Cons. Having supervised the reconstruction of the interior, Emma Cons opened it as a concert hall in late 1880 under the indicative name of the Royal Victoria Hall and Coffee Tavern. She was joined in 1898 by her niece, **Lilian Baylis**, who took over and transformed the enterprise in 1912. Lilian Baylis was an eccentric, whose first love was opera and who was utterly unafraid of big schemes. The first such scheme led to the presentation at the Old Vic (1914–23), at popular prices, of all the plays in the **Shakespeare** First Folio. From 1915, **Ben Greet** was the director of most of these productions and **Sybil Thorndike** the star. Extensive repairs and refurbishing were needed in 1927, but from then on and throughout the 1930s, the Old Vic remained a centre of excellence. **Gielgud, Olivier, Wolfit, Laughton, Ashcroft, Richardson, Edith Evans,** and **Flora Robson** were among those who acted there and **Tyrone Guthrie** and **Michel Saint-Denis** among the directors. Lilian Baylis died in 1937, having run the Old Vic and **Sadler's Wells** in tandem since 1931, and the war closed the theatre in 1939. Damaged by bombs in 1941, it was not fully repaired until 1950, though it housed the influential Old Vic School, under Michel Saint-Denis, from 1947–52. Michael Benthall, as artistic director of the renovated Old Vic, repeated the achievement of presenting plays in the Shakespeare First Folio as part of an announced five-year plan (1953–8). In 1963, after further extensive alterations, the Old Vic became the first home of the **National Theatre** Company under Laurence Olivier. Among its outstanding productions during this period were *Othello* (1964), **Peter Shaffer**'s *The Royal Hunt of the Sun* (1964) and *Equus* (1973), **Stoppard**'s *Rosencrantz and Guildenstern Are Dead* (1967) and *Jumpers* (1972), **Seneca**'s *Oedipus* (1968), directed by **Peter Brook**, and **Trevor Griffiths**'s *The Party* (1973), which brought Olivier's management to an end. **Peter Hall** became director in 1974 and led the company to its new home in 1976. After a spell as the London base of the touring Prospect Theatre Company (1977–81) was brought to an end by cutting of **Arts Council** subsidy, the Old Vic was left empty until 1983, when it was bought by a commercial speculator, and embarked on a programme of repertory. PT

The tin man from the original production of Yuri Olesha's *The Conspiracy of Feelings*, 1929.

Oldfield, Anne (1683–1730) English actress. She is said to have been discovered by **Farquhar** who overheard her reading aloud. **Vanbrugh** introduced her to Christopher Rich who employed her at **Drury Lane** in 1692. She began to take new roles from 1700 but her career was slow to reach success. In 1703 her worth was recognized by **Cibber** who cast her in *The Careless Husband* and that ensured her reputation. As a result **Mrs Bracegirdle** retired and Mrs Oldfield triumphed over her rival Mrs Rogers. Farquhar was in love with her but she did not marry. She was frequently cast in star roles by Cibber and **Rowe**, and she proved equally good in comedy and tragedy, e.g. Andromache in **Philips**'s *The Distressed Mother*. She continued acting until her death and was buried in Westminster Abbey, though with no monument because of her two illegitimate children. PH

Olesha, Yury Karlovich (1899–1960) Soviet novelist, short story writer, poet, dramatist, essayist, journalist, translator and film scenarist, in whose work was manifested the fatal ambivalence of the intelligentsia toward the communist regime. The son of Polish Catholic monarchists, Olesha embraced Bolshevism, enlisting in the Red Army (1919), but grew disillusioned with the curtailments of artistic freedom under the new order. He wrote satirical verse (published collections, 1924, 1927) for the Moscow railway newspaper *Gudok*, whose writing staff included **Bulgakov**,

Ilf and Petrov and **Valentin Kataev**. He transformed his famous novel *Envy* (1927) into the play *The Conspiracy of Feelings* (1928) at the suggestion of the Vakhtangov Theatre, where it received a controversial expressionist staging by Sergei Eisenstein (1929). Here Olesha externalized his conflicting feelings via two brothers – a pro-Soviet rational pragmatist and a retrograde, impractical dreamer, who fails in his attempt to destroy him. Olesha's one original play, *A List of Blessings* (1931), was staged by **Meyerhold** (whom the author admired) at his theatre as a contemporary Soviet tragedy. An egotistical Russian actress, celebrated for her Hamlet, is ambivalent about Soviet society's treatment of the artist, until exposure to the crass materialism of Parisian society leads her belatedly to embrace and martyr herself to the communist cause. Meyerhold's wife, Zinaida Raikh, played the actress, said to be based on **Michael Chekhov**, whose interpretation of Hamlet as victim of his own and society's ills aroused the ire of the communist press (1924–5). At **Stanislavsky**'s and **Nemirovich-Danchenko**'s suggestion, Olesha adapted his fairy-tale *The Three Fat Men* (1922) for the stage, and it became a Soviet classic, spawning opera, ballet and film versions. It depicts the overthrow of the titular autocrats by a band of circus performers-revolutionaries. *The Stern Young Man* (1934), a short scenario for a film by Abram Room that was never released into general circulation, *The Black Man* (1932), a fragment featuring another divided self,

Play on an Execution Block, a 'little drama' in rhymed alexandrines, and dramatizations of **Chekhov**'s short story 'Late-Blooming Flowers' and of Dostoevsky's novel *The Idiot* (1958) round out the author's writing for the stage.   SG

Olivier, Laurence (Kerr) (1907–) British actor, director, and manager, who was a matinée idol in the 1930s, regarded as the finest classical actor of his generation in the 1940s, a patron of new wave theatre in the 1950s, the first Director of the **National Theatre** in the 1960s and the first actor to receive a life peerage in 1970. At school, Olivier proved to be a fine, natural actor and **Sybil Thorndike** described his performance as Katharina in *The Taming of the Shrew* when he was only 14 as 'the best Kate I ever saw'. He joined **Barry Jackson**'s **Birmingham Rep** in 1926, then the best training ground for acting talent in the country, and gave up the chance to play Stanhope in **R. C. Sherriff**'s *Journey's End* (1928) in the West End, a part he created, for the chance to star as Beau Geste in a commercial version of P. C. Wren's story, which turned out to be a glossy failure. This lapse of judgement can nonetheless be seen as characteristic in that Olivier excels in dashing, adventurous roles and seems temperamentally less suited to the quieter, monochromatic qualities of Sherriff's play. After playing second fiddle to **Noël Coward** in *Private Lives* (1920), impatiently but fruitfully for it brought him his first experience of success in London and Broadway, he joined **John Gielgud** at the New Theatre to alternate with him the parts of Romeo and Mercutio in *Romeo and Juliet* (1935). The fascinating duel, in a production directed by Gielgud which also offered **Peggy Ashcroft**'s Juliet and **Edith Evans**'s Nurse, immediately began to upset conventional theories about the correct playing of **Shakespeare**. Gielgud's Romeo was a superbly controlled, musical performance, but Olivier's had more daring and virility, though his verse-speaking was considered rough. He joined the **Old Vic** in 1937 where under **Tyrone Guthrie**'s direction, he played Hamlet, Sir Toby Belch, Macbeth and Henry V in his first season, and Iago (to **Ralph Richardson**'s Othello) and Coriolanus in his second. In 1939, he went to Hollywood where, through such films as *Wuthering Heights* and *Lady Hamilton*, he became an international film star, and he married another star, **Vivien Leigh**, at the height of her fame from *Gone With the Wind*. Despite the glamour of their life in Hollywood, Olivier returned to England in 1941 to enlist in the Royal Navy Volunteer Reserve, but his patriotism was indispensable on the screen. His films, *The Demi-Paradise* (1943) and *Henry V* (1944), which he also directed, encouraged a national pride without lowering artistic sights. In 1944–5, he joined Ralph Richardson to lead the Old Vic company at the New Theatre; and those seasons in which he played Richard III, Hotspur and Justice Shallow, Oedipus and Astrov in *Uncle Vanya* have entered into the legends of British theatre, acting of the finest quality to be seen in a London ravaged by the blitz. The Old Vic after the war contained the elements of a National Theatre, with an acting school attached to a heroic company; but in a grotesque miscalculation, the Old Vic governors decided not to renew the contracts of Olivier and Richardson, while they were away on tour in Australia. For a few years, Olivier made films with Vivien Leigh and entered into theatrical management in London. But his marriage was deteriorating, and Olivier quickly realized that the theatre of the 1930s was no longer suitable in post-war Britain. After appearing in **Peter Brook**'s production of *Titus Andronicus* (1956) with Vivien Leigh at Stratford-upon-Avon, which was taken on a triumphant European tour, he returned to films, partly to escape from a theatre in which he no longer believed. In 1957, he allied himself with the new wave of British dramatists, which was then barely a ripple, by appearing in **John Osborne**'s *The Entertainer* as the seedy comic, Archie Rice, and in the following years, he played Berenger in **Ionesco**'s *Rhinoceros*, Becket and then Henry II in **Anouilh**'s *Becket* and Fred Midway in David Turner's satirical comedy, *Semi-Detached* (1962). His marriage to Vivien Leigh was dissolved in 1960 and he married **Joan Plowright**, his third wife, whom he had met at the **Royal Court**, in 1961. He was appointed the director of the first **Chichester Festival** in 1962, which he partly used to prepare a repertoire for the newly formed National Theatre company which opened at the Old Vic in 1963. His years as the first director of the National Theatre were courageous, in that he battled against building delays, state parsimony, cancer and other major illnesses; and still managed to offer such daring acting performances as his Othello (1964), Edgar in *The Dance of Death* and James Tyrone in *Long Day's Journey Into Night* (1971). In 1970, he was created a Life Peer, Baron Olivier of Brighton. In 1971, the governing board of the National Theatre decided to approach **Peter Hall** as Olivier's successor without consulting him and it was several months before he heard of their decision. In 1973, he resigned as Director two years before the new National Theatre complex opened on the south bank, with an auditorium that bears his name. Since then, he has appeared in films and on television, notably as King Lear in 1984.   JE

Ollantay A Quechua language play from Peru that vies with the **Rabinal Achí** as an authentically pre-Columbian work. Padre Antonio Valdés directed a performance around 1780 near Cuzco in the presence of Tupac Amaru II, the Inca chieftain who rebelled against the Spanish. The dispute centres on whether Valdés wrote the play down as the oral tradition dictated, or whether he constructed it out of the myths and legends that existed from pre-Columbian times. Its Golden Age structure favours the latter interpretation. The post-Second World War period has produced adaptations by César Miró and **Sebastián Salazar Bondy**, as well as a translation by José María Arguendas.   GW

Olympia, The (music-hall and theatre) Broadway between 44th and 45th Sts, New York City [Architect: J. B. McElfatrick and Co.]. In 1895, Oscar Hammerstein crossed 42nd Street to build his pleasure palace, where for the price of one admission, patrons could find their diversions from among concerts, plays, vaudevilles, Turkish baths, billiards, bowling, cafés, restaurants and a roof garden. Like his many ventures, the Olympia never fulfilled his vision and in 1899, the two theatres included in it were leased to separate managements under the names New York and Criterion Theatres. In 1907, the roof garden Jardin de Paris introduced the prototype of **Florenz Ziegfeld**'s *Follies*. After conversion to vaudeville and movies, both theatres were razed in 1935. MCH

Olympic Theatre, London

Olympic Theatre, London Situated in the meanness of Wych Street, off Drury Lane, the Olympic was one of London's most successful minor theatres during the 19th century. The first theatre on the site was erected by **Philip Astley** in 1805, chiefly from the wood of a French warship. Because of its tent shape, it came to be known as the Olympic Pavilion. Finding it too small for effective hippodrama, Astley sold it to **R. W. Elliston** in 1813. The flamboyant Elliston installed gas there in c. 1815, rebuilt it in 1818 and, in 1819, bought the lesseeship of **Drury Lane** on his profits. A lean period in the theatre's fortunes was ended by the brilliant management of **Madame Vestris** (1830–9), who made the Olympic the genteel home of tastefully presented light entertainment, with **Planché** as her resident dramatist and with an unrivalled company of comic actors, including **Liston**, the **Keeleys** and, after 1835, **Charles James Mathews**. When Madame Vestris left, the Olympic soon lost its fashionable audience, briefly recalled by Gustavus Brooke's sensational playing of Othello (1847), and was destroyed by fire in 1849. Walter Watts, having rebuilt it to seat 1,750 and reopened it within nine months, was found, three months later, to have embezzled money for the venture (he hanged himself rather than face transportation), and the comedian William Farren took over as manager (1850–3). It was under Farren that the extraordinary **Frederick Robson** made his first Olympic appearance in 1853, but it was under the next manager, Alfred Wigan (1853–7), that Robson became a star attraction, making the Olympic famous again in a sequence of bizarre burlesques. Robson was joint-manager (with John Emden) of the Olympic from 1857 until his death in 1864, during the run of **Tom Taylor**'s *The Ticket-of-Leave Man* (1863). Subsequent managers included Horace Wigan (1864–9), Henry Neville (1873–9), **Geneviève Ward** (1883) and **Wilson Barrett** (1890–1), for whom the theatre was rebuilt to accommodate 3,000, but the Olympic had, by then, a reputation as an unlucky house. It closed in 1897 and was demolished in 1904. PT

Ombres chinoises

Ombres chinoises see **Shadow puppets**

O'Neil, Nance

O'Neil, Nance (1874–1965) American actress. She joined the Arthur McKee Rankin company in San Francisco in 1893, and he soon built her into a star. He booked her into several national tours and in 1900 sponsored her world tour of *Magda*, *Fedora*, *La Tosca*, and *Camille*. In 1903 she added **Ibsen**'s *Lady Inger of Ostrat* to her repertoire and played it in San Francisco and Boston. Two years later she began performing *Hedda Gabler* and eventually took it to New York. Billed as the great tragedienne, she was usually considered to stand in the shadow of other great emotional actresses. RAS

O'Neill, Eliza

O'Neill, Eliza (1791–1872) Irish actress, who was greeted on her **Covent Garden** debut as Juliet in 1814 as a second **Mrs Siddons**. Other successes during her remarkable five-year career at Covent Garden included Lady Teazle in *The School for Scandal* and the title-role in Richard Lalor Shiel's tragedy, *Evadne* (1819). Shelley wrote *The Cenci* with her in mind, as well as **Edmund Kean**. She retired in 1819 to marry a Mr (later Sir) William Becher. PT

O'Neill, Eugene Gladstone

O'Neill, Eugene Gladstone (1888–1953) The first US playwright of major talent, the only one ever to win the Nobel Prize for Literature (in 1936), and still universally regarded as America's finest. Also, having written his autobiography not only in *Long Day's Journey Into Night* but piece-meal, under less or greater disguise in most of his works, he is among the most subjective of dramatists. Probably only **Strindberg**, whom he called his mentor, was as obsessed with his own life and family history. The son of actor **James O'Neill** (1846–1920), Eugene used to deride the sentimental and melodramatic theatre of his father's day, yet he stood on his father's shoulders in attaining his pre-eminent position. Immersed in a theatrical milieu from birth, he unconsciously absorbed, as though by osmosis, the basics of stagecraft and playwriting. In youth and early manhood, however, there was virtually no indication that he would ever, in any field, amount to much; it appeared, rather, that he, like his self-destructive older brother, would become a hard-drinking wastrel.

Perhaps the main key to understanding him is that he suffered from lifelong feelings of guilt, born apparently of the fact that his mother, a shy, devout Catholic, innocently became a drug addict as a result of his birth. Recalling how wretched he felt on learning of her morphinism and of his role in her downfall, he says through his counterpart in *Long Day's Journey*: 'God, it made everything in life seem rotten!' Turning against his ancestral faith, the apostate began to question all orthodoxies, all authority. Despite his familiarity with the ancient Greeks and **Shakespeare**, his sense of tragedy grew from his own life, not from the classics. He was an emotional haemophiliac whose family-inflicted wounds never healed. Here, then, we find the original of his sombre outlook on life, the major source of the power and anguish pounding throughout his writings.

After an unimpressive record at Catholic and secular schools, he, intent on experiencing 'real life', sought the lower depths. He went to sea, drifted on the waterfronts of Buenos Aires and New York, and once became so depressed that he attempted suicide. O'Neill often said that he never thought of being a writer till his health broke down, in his mid-20s, confining him to a TB sanatorium for months. While recuperating, he 'really thought' about his life for the first time and resolved to become a playwright. After his recovery in 1913, plays began to pour out of him, most of them tales of the sea and of the underside of life. What, in other words, had seemed mis-spent years, proved to be a major part of his working capital as a writer.

In a move beneficial to both parties, Eugene in 1916 joined a group of amateur playmakers on Cape Cod, who became known as the **Provincetown Players** on moving to Greenwich Village, with O'Neill as their most imaginative and gifted writer. When he made his Broadway debut in 1920 with *Beyond the Horizon* (written in 1918), a story of defeat on a farm with the sea beckoning in the background, most of the critics, though faced with something novel in their experience – an American tragedy – were enthusiastic; but several complained that the play was too long, while another criticized its many changes of scene. The harsher critics failed to realize that the author, who eventually would ignore most stage conventions, was determined to hack out his own course. The play enjoyed a good run for so sombre a work and won for O'Neill the first of his four Pulitzer Prizes. The others were for *Anna Christie* (written in 1920), *Strange Interlude* (1926–7) and *Long Day's Journey Into Night* (1939–41).

A veritable Proteus of the drama, O'Neill kept changing his style. Starting as a realist, with occasional returns to the genre, he also wrote expressionistic works (*The Emperor Jones*, 1920, and *The Hairy Ape*, 1921), costume drama (*The Fountain*, 1921–2, and *Marco Millions*, 1923–5), Strindbergian views of marriage (*Welded*, 1922–3), biblical fables (*Lazarus Laughed*, 1925–6) and even a comedy (*Ah, Wilderness!*, 1932). As though set on avenging his father's bondage to plays pandering to popular taste, he made demands on his audiences with extra-long works, namely *Strange Interlude*, nine acts; *Mourning Becomes Electra* (1929–31), a trilogy in 13 acts, and *The Iceman Cometh* (1939), twice the standard length. He also, testing what the public would accept, wrote *The Great God Brown* (1925), a bewildering work in which the characters constantly mask and unmask; *All God's Chillun Got Wings* (1923), a poignant story ahead of its day about a white girl married to a black, and *Desire Under the Elms* (1924), a drama of greed, incest and infanticide. In writing some 30 long works and nearly a score of short ones in so many different styles, O'Neill almost exhausted the stage's non-verbal resources through his use of song, pantomime, dance, masks, imaginative scenic devices and novel sound effects. In the end, though, after all his imaginative flights, realism proved his forte, as was demonstrated by *The Iceman Cometh* and *Long Day's Journey Into Night*, his masterpieces.

In the 1930s he worked for years on his most ambitious project, a cycle entitled 'A Tale of Possessors Self-Possessed' that would span a large part of the American past in dramatizing highlights in the history, generation after generation, of a 'far from model' family. In the work, first envisioned as five plays, then seven, next nine and, for a time, eleven, O'Neill aimed to show that materialism and greed had corrupted America. Unfortunately, a number of factors, particularly ill health and his despair as the Second World War loomed, prevented him from achieving his goal. After he had destroyed most of his cycle writings, all that survived was one finished play, *A Touch of the Poet* (1935–42), and, by chance, a rough draft of another, *More Stately Mansions* (1935–40), which was staged posthumously in truncated form. LSH

O'Neill, James (1846–1920) Irish-American actor. Despite his great popularity in the late 19th century, he is primarily remembered today as the father of **Eugene O'Neill**. For a time, appearing opposite such stars as **Charlotte Cushman**, **Adelaide Neilson**, and **Edwin Booth**, it appeared that he would attain similar stature, that he would become Booth's successor. His promise faded, however, particularly after he had, as his son

said, 'the good bad luck' to find a gold mine in **Charles Fechter**'s dramatization of **Dumas**'s *The Count of Monte Cristo*. Initially O'Neill, who had suffered a hungry childhood, rejoiced in his prosperity as the Dumas hero, but as the decades piled up and the audiences flocked to see him only when he played Edmond Dantès, the role became a straitjacket that gradually diminished his talent. Fragments of his history are woven into his son's devastating family portrait, *Long Day's Journey Into Night*. LSH

Onnagata see **Female impersonation**

Open Theatre (USA) An experimental Off-Off Broadway acting company from 1963–73. **Joseph Chaikin** left the **Living Theatre** after playing Galy Gay in **Brecht**'s *Man is Man* to establish a study group for exploring new styles of acting. This collection of actors, writers, and dramaturges came to be known as the Open Theatre. Chaikin believed that the creative intervention of the performer could lead to a new dramatic expression, and he developed a technique based on the ideas of presence – focusing on the performer, not the character – and transformation – the actor changing from one role to another before the audience's eyes. This approach is described in Chaikin's book, *The Presence of the Actor*. Open Theatre workshops combined vigorous physical, vocal, breathing and improvisational exercises with discussions led by critics Gordon Rogoff and Richard Gilman. Gradually the group began to work on ensemble creations shaped by a single writer, resulting in *Viet Rock* by **Megan Terry** (1966), *The Serpent* by **Jean-Claude van Itallie** (1968), and *Terminal* by Susan Yankowitz (1969). The Open Theatre gave these works full productions and then created some chamber works, including *The Mutation Show* (1971) and *Nightwalk* (1973). But as the Open Theatre edged away from being an acting workshop toward becoming a producing company, it decided to close; in Rogoff's words, it was 'doomed to succeed'. AS

Opera In order to avoid speculation about such early and such exotic examples of music-drama as could by some highly debatable definition be considered to be opera, and about very recent examples of music-drama that may be reaching beyond the limits of what is generally called opera, the following has been made consistent with John Drummond's statement, '*Opera* is, strictly speaking, one particular child in the family of music-drama. Born in Western Europe at the end of the sixteenth century, it is now, according to some, fast approaching its demise. It is essentially a regional art-form, although it has been exported along with other trappings of Western civilization to many parts of the globe.' (*Opera in Perspective*, London, 1980)

An opera is not, as many rough and ready definitions claim, a play with music, nor is it a play set to music or a sung play. Opera is a form of theatre in which music provides a dramatic and aesthetic predicate to the situations in which the characters find themselves. The words, supplied by the libretto, that are sung in opera are usually in themselves of rudimentary dramatic and of slight aesthetic significance. If they had such significance in any marked degree they would resist musical setting; it would be a case of gilding refined gold or painting the lily. The words indicate a focus for the feelings aroused in the audience by the music, or, the music arouses the feelings that are to be fused with the import of the words. The gaiety or the melancholy aroused by a passage in a Mozart symphony are general. The gaiety is not specifically that of a child at play nor the melancholy that of someone bereaved, yet either could be the case. In a Mozart opera such feelings are part of an organic whole whose other elements are particular characters in particular situations. **Wagner**'s image of male and female creating a child is very apt. The words are the male element, the music the female, and opera the child. Both male and female are autonomous beings. They come together and the result is a child which is not the mere addition of male and female but a creation from them. Features of both father and mother will be discernible in the child, who nevertheless will itself have a distinct identity. Although Wagner's image arose in a particular 19th-century context, the central idea is applicable to all opera, the nature of its applicability varying at different periods of opera's history.

Music, with its immediate sensuous appeal, affects the feelings. The effect on the feelings of the two bars during which the hero sings 'Venere splende' ('Venus is shining') at the end of the first act of Verdi's *Otello* is not merely due to the information conveyed by the two words in the context of what has happened so far in the opera. It is also due to the effect of the music, both of the orchestral accompaniment and of the singing. An actor in a play both supplies information and affects feelings by means of spoken words. He chooses his manner of utterance according to one of the several possible interpretations of his part. Although the score cannot specify his utterance with absolute precision, the actor in opera is much more restricted. His pitch, his inflections, his emphases, his pauses are under the rigorous control of the composer.

Theatre is an art that exists in time. One of its more important characteristics is its exploitation of time in the form of rhythm. Much of the impact of a play is due to the rhythm of its performance, the changes of pace in utterance and movement. Although the speeds at which various sections of a play are performed may not be wholly determined by the director and the actors, under the influence of a particular audience, they are largely so. The paces of the various sections of an opera are very much less at the discretion of the director, the conductor and the performers, or under the influence of the audience. Again, the score does not rule with absolute authority, but it exercises great control. The composer indicates whether a passage is to be delivered quickly or slowly. He specifies the rhythm of the words, indicating the location of pauses and their lengths and indicating the relative lengths of syllables. When, in the second act of **Shakespeare**'s *A Midsummer Night's Dream*, Helena says 'O wilt thou darkling leave me? Do not so,' the performer may speak the line at any one of various speeds, give the syllables various relative emphases, introduce various pauses, make various inflections. The utterance chosen will accord with one of the several legitimate interpretations of the play as a whole. Although it cannot be said that there is a unique legitimate interpretation of Benjamin Britten's opera *A Midsummer Night's Dream*, the performer

singing the same words as Helena is by no means as free as the actress in Shakespeare. The speed at which she is to sing is indicated by a metronome marking. The relative lengths of the syllables are set down: e.g. the proportions of the first five syllables are 2, 3, 1, 2, 2. There must be a substantial pause after 'darkling' and another of equal length after 'me'. The voice at the end of the line has to be a major third lower than it was at the beginning. Music's fundamental control of pace, pitch and emphasis may, from one point of view, be restrictive: from another it is liberating. In a particular situation in a play several characters may simultaneously be reacting quite differently but equally forcibly. They cannot be allowed equal status in the expression of their reactions. All cannot speak at once and be individually understood. Usually one speaks and the others are restricted to movements and gesture. If all speak at the same time a significant feature in the unfolding of the drama will occur – confusion. Opera is at an advantage. It is a commonplace for several lines of music to be clearly perceptible when sounded simultaneously, and for their simultaneity to produce a further clearly perceptible effect. Several characters in an opera can express forcible and sustained yet distinct reactions at the same time, and if the manner of expression is not absolutely equal for all of the characters it is very much more nearly so than could ever occur in a play. This is admirably illustrated by the famous quartet to be found towards the end of Verdi's *Rigoletto*. The Duke and Maddalena are in a room in Sparafucile's lair. Gilda and Rigoletto are outside. We hear the Duke protesting his love and at the same time, to quote Ernest Newman, 'Maddalena laughing it all off ironically, Gilda bemoaning her lover's perfidy and her own sad lot, and Rigoletto assuring her with grim persistence that she shall soon be avenged. **Victor Hugo**, when he heard the opera (which after all is derived from his own play *Le Roi S'Amuse*) commented wistfully on the advantages music sometimes has over poetry or prose, opera over spoken drama: 'what would the ordinary dramatist not give', he asked, 'to be able to make four people animated by different sentiments speak all at the same time, each in character, and each fully intelligible to the audience!' (*More Opera Nights*, London, 1954)

It is often objected that opera is essentially ridiculous. Particular manifestations of it may be so; but this is true of any activity, theatrical or otherwise. The English have a long tradition of scoffing at opera. Although guilty of travesty of meaning and misattribution of source, they frequently claim that **Dr Johnson** defined opera as 'an exotic and irrational entertainment'. Such sentiments have always had wide popular approval. In **Planché**'s burletta *The Deep, Deep Sea* (1833) Perseus exclaims,

> Run – fly – the dreadful sacrifice delay
> Till my arrival. I will only stay
> To sing a song – as opera heroes choose
> Always to do, when they've no time to lose.

In 1874, 18 years after Verdi's *La Traviata* had been first performed in England, a critic writing in the *Athenaeum* referred to that opera's heroine as 'the consumptive lady, who coughs *pianissimo* and sings *fortissimo* in her death scene'.

Theatre is not actuality. Even in a play by **Zola** the actors do not live their lives on the stage: they act. Objects are not there to serve the actors but to serve the characters, and whether or not the objects are those of everyday life is a matter of style, not of essence. It has been well pointed out that actors do not need to consume real food during a meal in a play. Their responsibility is to act, not to eat. And such actuality as is introduced by drinking glasses of real wine is immediately confounded when characters are required to take poison. Opera is exotic, at least in origin, as far as the English are concerned. It is also irrational in the way that plays are irrational, dealing with personae divorced from persons. Dr Johnson was right when, in his *Preface to Shakespeare* (1765), he claimed, 'It is false, that any representation is mistaken for reality; that any dramatic fable in its materiality was ever credible, or, for a single moment, was ever credited.' Planché was right in noting that a character in opera who has no time to lose may sing at length. The dramatic objective of the singing will be the anguish that the character feels in his harassed situation. The *Athenaeum* critic's comment must be similarly interpreted. *La Traviata* is not concerned to present a clinically accurate simulation of the heroine's death. It conveys the feelings that are appropriate to the character desperately aware of imminent death. In real life a consumptive lady *in extremis* may be capable of no more than a faint whisper. The intensity of her feelings may call for powerful expression. It is with these feelings that opera is concerned.

Opera, like all forms of art, requires the acceptance of convention. Many people are quite unable to cope with the convention of opera. People do not pause to sing when they are beset by hostile pursuers. Frail people do not sing loudly at the point of death. In fact people do not carry out their lives in song at all. If you cannot accept the fundamental conventions of opera you can have no access to it. There is no point in someone who cannot understand Chinese dismissing a book written in Chinese as rubbish, and anyone who thinks that a portrait must be as closely as possible identical with a colour photograph will be cut off from much art. Opera gives access to experience that cannot be had otherwise, an experience in which the main elements are feelings integral to situations. Like all conventions, the convention of opera is a means and opera, like all art, requires the means to be as unobtrusive as possible. The convention is the blind man's stick. The blind man does not pay attention to his stick, but to what his stick reveals to him, information to which he would have no access were it not for his stick. Different kinds of stick will give access to different kinds of information and the effective use of any kind of stick must be learned. Opera is a particular kind of stick and its use must be learned.

The music in opera is not confined to the performers on the stage. Much of it may be located in the orchestra pit, and the contribution of the orchestra may have a considerable effect on the drama. The orchestra may act as commentator or as dramatic memory. While a character expresses his overt reaction to a particular situation, the orchestra may introduce irony, pathos or other feelings as it plays passages heard earlier in the work that set what is now being uttered on the stage in the context of past happenings or feelings. It was in relation to this possibility that **Appia** commented that a character can leave the orchestra to express his suffering while he himself expresses what his situation immediately calls for. The matter had been noted a century earlier by the Belgian composer Grétry: 'I soon grasped that music has resources that declamation alone certainly has not. For example, a girl assures her mother that she is ignorant of love, but while she affects indifference by means of a simple and monotonous melody, the orchestra expresses the torment of her amorous heart.' (*Mémoires: ou Essais sur la Musique*, Paris, 1789)

Music is essential to opera, but so are words. An opera libretto is on its own incomplete. It requires music for its completion. If a libretto were merely performed in speech and movement it would make a bad play. Considerable skill is needed to write a good libretto. The librettist must not try to write a play, yet inability to write a play is by no means a guarantee of skill as a librettist. The rhythm of an opera, in detail and overall, is dictated by the music. The feelings evoked by opera are at the behest of the music, not of the words. Unlike words, music cannot cope with elaborate factual information. Music has its own formal structure to which words must submit. **Bernard Shaw** has pointed out that however impressive words may be when read silently, they are unsuitable for a play unless they can be spoken effectively. Similarly, words are unsuitable for opera unless they can be sung effectively. Wagner claimed that the ideal situation occurs when composer and librettist are the same person, a combination achieved by himself and certain others. Many composers have not provided their own librettos. Some have worked to a libretto they have been presented with. Some have been fired by a play, a novel, a historical incident, and have required a writer to base a libretto on it. Many composers have insisted on the revision of the structure of librettos with which they have been presented, and many have insisted on verbal alterations. How an opera came to have a particular libretto is of interest; but how good an opera results from the fusion of libretto and music is the essentially important matter.

Many operas are based on plays, and frequently not on the best plays. Verdi's *La Traviata* originated in *La Dame aux Camélias* by **Dumas** *fils*, **Puccini**'s *Tosca* in **Sardou**'s *La Tosca*. Both of these plays are highly melodramatic. Melodrama is a kind of theatrical puppetry. It is when music infuses feelings into the characters and the situations of melodramatic plays that the works cease to be theatrical manipulation and become drama. Of course, some operas, Verdi's *Otello* for instance, are not based on inferior plays; but examination always shows marked differences between the librettos and the original plays. It is because *Otello* and *Othello* are both great theatrical works that audiences attribute to them a degree of similarity greater than is justified by sober comparison. Whilst the foregoing is almost universally true, two exceptions must be noted. Berg's opera *Wozzeck* and Britten's *A Midsummer Night's Dream* are settings of the almost unaltered plays by **Büchner** and Shakespeare.

Othello was written in English, the libretto of *Otello* in Italian. The music of *Otello* is as accessible to an English audience as are the words of *Othello*: the words of *Otello* are not. The English audience has no difficulty with the music of Wagner's *Ring* cycle, but it has with the original words. Audiences ignorant of Russian attend performances of Mussorgsky's *Boris Godunov*. Those with no familiarity with Central European languages patronize operas by Smetana and Janáček. Such people are in danger of treating operas not as dramas but as concerts in costume. Short of requiring audiences to learn several languages, what is to be done? The obvious answer is to provide translations. But faithful translation, difficult in any event, is notoriously difficult in opera. As well as being faithful to the import of the original words, the translation of a libretto must make as accurate a fit as possible with the music, and this was written in conjunction with totally different words. To consider the matter at the simplest level it is sufficient to remember that in different languages words of equivalent meaning frequently differ in their numbers of syllables. For example, an English monosyllabic word common in opera, 'hope', becomes in Italian, French and German, 'speranza', 'espoir', 'Hoffnung'. The Italian, French and German vocal lines may have different notes for each syllable. How are these notes to be managed if a monosyllabic translation is attempted? Accuracy in detail in libretto translation is virtually impossible, especially in view of the fact that a great number of opera books, as they are sometimes called, are in rhyming verse. In Verdi's *Aïda* the words 'Numi pietà' are in one translation rendered as 'Merciful gods' and these words fit the music; but in the original mercy is not attributed to the gods, it is sought from them, and the sustained note for the fourth syllable emphasizes 'pity' not 'gods'. The most successful libretto translations provide words that make a good fit with the music and that express the import of the original as closely as this fit will allow. When in Mozart's *The Magic Flute* Tamino gazes at the medallion-portrait of Pamina, he sings, 'Dies Bildnis ist bezaubernd schön', literally, 'This likeness is enchantingly beautiful.' Edward Dent has rendered this as 'O loveliness beyond compare', not achieving accuracy in detail but commendable fidelity in general. Translations do not only reduce the risk of operas becoming concerts in costume. As Dent put it in his address to the Musical Association in 1935, '. . . translation is a necessity if opera is to receive any popular encouragement'. It will have been noted that *Aïda* and *The Magic Flute* have been referred to, as is common, as Verdi's and Mozart's and not as Ghislanzoni's and Schikaneder's, the writers of the librettos. This is a sharp illumination of the status of the libretto in comparison with the music of an opera.

The foregoing has been a broad description of matters relevant to opera in general. Particular operas, especially those written at different historical periods, exhibit certain features more vividly than others. The earliest operas are distinguished by their preoccupation with classical subjects. This arose because opera originated in deliberate attempts by Florentine *camerate* (groups of noblemen, musicians and men of letters) to re-create what they assumed ancient Greek theatrical performance to have been. The first of all operas was *Dafne*, with words by Ottavio Rinuccini (1562–1621) and music by Jacopo Peri (1561–1633). It was played in 1597 to a private audience in the palace of Jacopo Corsi, who may have contributed some of the music. Unfortunately the score has disappeared, except for a couple of fragments. The earliest opera whose music we still have is *Euridice*. Its libretto is by Rinuccini and there are two settings, one by Peri and one by Giulio Caccini (?1545–1618). Peri's version was first performed in the Pitti Palace in 1600. Caccini's had to wait another two years. In the early operas, again because of their aim of reproducing Greek drama, the words tend to dominate the music, and the music's form is very much what is known as recitative. This state of affairs was much altered by Claudio Monteverdi (1567–1643) whose *Orfeo* was produced in 1607 and his *L'Incoronazione di Poppea* in 1642. As Donald Jay Grout has written, 'The doctrines of the Camerata had emphasised poetic values at the expense of music. Monteverdi, by means of organising the recitative, deepening its content, and introducing arioso or aria forms at critical points in the action, had made the music an equal partner with the text . . .' (*A Short History of Opera*, New York, 1947). Opera henceforth sees constant attempts to integrate words and music, both of which aspire to self-sufficiency, into a unity whose justification is dramatic effectiveness, and it falls under a new influence with the establishment of public as against private performances. The words and music are disposed in such a manner that information-giving is accommodated by recitative and feelings by arias and ensembles.

Opera spread from the Italy of its origins to other countries in Europe and fell under the spell of already existing activities, e.g. in France the ballet, in England the masque. Italian opera had always been associated with spectacle. Association with ballet and masque reinforced the tie. Gradually the river from the Italian spring divided into many streams. As Italian, French, German and English music and spoken drama took on particular identities, so did their styles of opera; and by the end of the 19th and beginning of the 20th centuries there were recognizably Russian and Czech opera.

The history of opera, especially from the 18th century, has been treated exhaustively in many authoritative and readily available books. There is not space to summarize it adequately here. Nevertheless mention should be made of a few very significant figures. **Christoph Willibald Gluck** (1714–87) reinvested opera that was tending towards the purely decorative with powerful drama, purity and nobility. Wolfgang Amadeus Mozart (1756–91) demonstrated a high degree of perfection in the various styles – formal, relaxed, comic, serious – that had emerged by the second half of the 18th century. Giacomo Meyerbeer (1791–1864) was, in spite of his Italian-German name, responsible for French Grand Opera, which exploited purely theatrical values to the full. Richard Wagner (1813–83) was more seriously concerned with and more thoroughly understood theatrical effectiveness in the service of powerful drama than any other creator of opera. He claimed to write 'music dramas' rather than operas, was his own librettist and wrote extensively on the nature of opera and of the theatre. He abandoned the practice of recitative and aria, writing works of close bound unity that follow an uninterrupted dramatic flow and in which the orchestra plays an equal, not subordinate, part. Originally adulated by some composers and audiences and vilified by others, his work split the world of opera into Wagnerians and anti-Wagnerians. The passage of time has shown Wagner's operas to be of intrinsic worth and to have had profound influence on the general development of opera. The operas of Giuseppe Verdi (1813–1901) have the distinction of enjoying more performances than those of any other composer. They range from traditional Italian style works in which vocal considerations take precedence to intensely romantic operas in which both voices and orchestra are used equally powerfully. It has been said that the two greatest of all love operas are Wagner's *Tristan und Isolde* (1865) and Verdi's *Otello* (1887), and indeed in many ways these works typify the musical-dramatic achievements of their composers. In the 20th century, various types of opera have emerged, some developments of Wagner, some of Verdi, some experimental under the influence of twelve-tone music or of naturalist, surrealist or expressionist drama, some arising from renewed interest in old forms. Most recently there have been manifestations of what is called 'music theatre' which attempts to bring theatre into the concert hall or use the concert hall as a kind of theatre.

A note on opera in England is called for. Italian opera did not establish itself as firmly in England as it did in France and Germany. Henry Purcell (1659–95) wrote a very fine *Dido and Aeneas*, but in spite of its title it is not Italianate. From the early part of the 18th century the Italianate operas of George Frederick Handel (1685–1759), a German who became a naturalized Englishman, were much patronized in London, and the cultivation of foreign opera by the aristocracy became both a fact and an object of satire, lasting until the early years of the 20th century. It was assumed that only foreign musicians were of any worth and that Italian was the only language suitable for opera; hence the assumption of foreign names by English singers and performances of, say, *Die Zauberflöte* neither in its original German nor in the English spoken by the audience, but in Italian as *Il Flauto Magico*. The ridiculous situation was made fun of by many English writers and was most effectively satirized in *The Beggar's Opera* (1728) by **John Gay** (1685–1732) and John Pepusch (1667–1752) in which songs are sung to well-known tunes, there is much spoken dialogue, the characters are contemporary and from the gutter not from the palace, and references are made to contemporary manners not to eternal verities. The 19th century saw many attempts by British composers and librettists to write operas comparable in achievement to those of Continental works, but the composers produced at best imitations of Italian and German models and they succumbed to publishers' demands for 'shop ballads', that is detachable songs that could be sold to amateurs over the counter, rather like the 'hit songs' of 20th-century musicals. Some composers sold detached numbers from operas they were yet to compose. The librettists churned out drivel that was frequently nonsensical. In spite of sustained efforts no English composer was significant in the field of opera until Benjamin Britten (1913–76). Only the comic works of Arthur Sullivan (1842–1900) to librettos by **W. S. Gilbert** (1836–1911) achieved both immediate and lasting success.

Opera is European in origin. Countries outside Europe tended to enjoy opera to the extent that they were settled by Europeans concerned to preserve the ways of life of their original countries. As immigrants and natives forged a new nation, characteristic music and drama, and hence opera, slowly emerged. In the United States, for example, English, French, Italian and German operas were presented in the 18th and early 19th centuries, and American operatic activity was much like that in European countries. The first work by a Native American to be acknowledged as a 'real' opera was *Leonora* (1845) with music by William Henry Fry (1813–64) who was not a professional musician. *Leonora* resounded with European echoes. In later years American operas were written by very professional musicians and the European echoes became fainter but were still clearly audible. The influences of Negro and Latin American cultures and of the social, political and economic climates have all contributed to the emergence of American opera. *Treemonisha* (1911) by Scott Joplin (1868–1917) is historically significant, although it was not performed during the composer's lifetime. *Porgy and Bess* (1935) by **George Gershwin** (1898–1937) has proved a lasting characteristically American opera. The works of Marc Blitzstein (1905–64) exhibit social and political awareness and those of Gunther Schuller (b. 1925) are notable for their jazz. Many Americans have written many operas, but not many have created truly American operas. This may in part be due to the great success of the American musical which the United States seems to find a more vital form than opera – although where on the musical-theatrical continuum opera ends and the musical begins is highly debatable. Such successful works as *West Side Story* (1957) by **Leonard Bernstein** (1918–90) and *Sweeney Todd* (1979) by **Stephen Sondheim** (b. 1930 seem to be as much operas as, say, *The Beggar's Opera*.

Australasia is further than the United States from Europe and it has not been so subject to direct influences. Isaac Nathan (1790–1864), who went to Australia from London, promoted opera of the old-world type. Neville George Barnett (1854–95), born in London, wrote an opera *Pomare* 'on a Tahitian legend' which was performed privately in Auckland. Australians who have written operas have not tended to produce anything characteristically Australian, e.g. Arthur Benjamin (1893–1960), Malcolm Williamson (b. 1931).

Since the middle of the 20th century opera composers outside Europe have been subjected to two powerful influences: that of the music and manners of their countries, which gives rise to individuality, and that of a world shrinking because of advances in communications, which tends to produce a marked uniformity.

Operas are not an undifferentiated collection. They are usually assigned to a variety of types, although accurate classification is often difficult and frequently pointless. The following should be noted.

Opéra Bouffe This term denotes a form of opera that was extremely popular during the Second Empire in France and that was vigorously exploited by Jacques Offenbach (1819–80). Farcical, rather than comical, and often satirical, it included spoken dialogue, stage spectacle and both gay and sentimental music of immediate appeal. Its librettos and manner of performance were thought by the Victorian English to be indecent – markedly so in comparison with Gilbert and Sullivan.

Opera Buffa This, a form of comic opera, had its heyday in 18th-century Italy. It included no spoken dialogue. In contrast to those of Opera Seria its characters were distinguished by ordinariness and truth to life, and its action tended to be bustling rather than restrained.

Opéra Comique This, in spite of its name, is not necessarily comic. Derived from 18th-century French *vaudevilles*, its characteristic is having spoken dialogue. The comicality from the *vaudevilles* declined, the speech remained. *Carmen* (1875) by Georges Bizet (1838–75), a far from comic work, is an authentic Opéra Comique.

Opera Seria Literally 'serious opera', this is the term applied to 18th-century opera of great stylistic formality. Its subjects are drawn from mythology and ancient history. It is closely associated with the librettos of **Pietro Metastasio** (1698–1782) which were widely set, some achieving musical treatment by upwards of 20 different composers.

Operetta Although the word means 'little opera', an Operetta is distinguished by its tone rather than by its length. Any seriousness tends towards sentimentality and the overall effect is one of pleasantness, if not of unalloyed gaiety. An Operetta's construction may vary from a close resemblance to that of a full-blown opera to a close kinship with a play enhanced by songs. Spectacular staging is almost inevitable. The expression Light Opera is often used as an alternative to Operetta which, in turn, is often extended to include Opéras Bouffes and musical comedies.   GH

Opéra Bouffe see **Opera**

Opera Buffa see **Opera**

Opéra Comique see **Opera**

Opera Seria see **Opera**

Operetta see **Opera**

Opitz, Martin (1597–1639) German writer. Opitz translated Latin and Italian plays and wrote a book of poetics, published in 1624. His work helped turn the German theatre towards classicism, which was to dominate it until the middle of the 18th century.   SW

Oregon Shakespeare Festival (1935–   ) The Festival was founded by Angus L. Bowmer in Ashland, Oregon, to produce **Shakespeare**'s plays in an Elizabethan-style setting. Beginning on a rough, wooden platform, the Festival built the present stage in 1959, in the style of the **Fortune Theatre**. With a seating capacity of 1,173 and standing room for 115, the Festival offers a three-play repertory summer season of mainly Shakespeare. In 1970 the Festival opened the new 601-seat indoor Angus Bowmer Theatre to house modern works; and in 1977 the 138-seat Black Swan for more experimental productions. Noted for a house style which emphasizes the clarity and beauty of the text, the Festival has completed the Shakespeare canon twice: for the first time in 1958 with *Troilus and Cressida*; and for the second time in 1978 with *Timon of Athens*. The 1985 budget of $5.1 million supports 11

productions for 643 performances in the three theatres before an audience of over 300,000. Artistic Directors have included Angus L. Bowmer (1935–71) and Jerry Turner (1971–   ).   TLM

Örkény, István (1912–79) Hungarian playwright, has been called 'master of the grotesque'. He was sent to the Russian front, and returned to Hungary in 1947 after four years as a prisoner of war. He at first depicted this dehumanizing experience in naturalistic stories. By the mid-1960s his grotesque style emerged. His plays document life in 20th-century Hungary, with a keen sense of the absurdities of modern life. Plays, e.g., *Stevie in the Bloodstorm* (1969), *Blood Relations* (1974), *Keysearchers* (1975), and *Screenplay* (1979), have enjoyed great acclaim in Hungary, and the success abroad of *The Toth Family* (1967) and *Catsplay* (1966) established his international reputation. He was awarded several Hungarian literary prizes.   EB

Orton, Joe (1933–67) British dramatist, who specialized in high camp comedy, whose excesses were expressed in a delicate verbal wit. His first stage play, *Entertaining Mr Sloane* (1964), caused a *succès de scandale* when it was first produced at the Arts Theatre Club. A violent young man is blackmailed into becoming the sexual pet of a respectable brother and sister whose father he has murdered. *Loot* (1966) is like an updated black farce from the 1950s – with a comic detective who will stop at nothing, the corpse of a recently deceased mother, and tons of money. His funniest play, *What the Butler Saw* (1969), succeeds on several levels – as a French farce, a burlesque on psychiatry and as an Edwardian comedy with the same dandified use of language. A one-act play, *Funeral Games* (1970), and two short plays, *The Ruffian on the Stair* (1967), originally written for radio, and *The Erpingham Camp* (1967), complete the short list of Orton's stage works, although his television play, *The Good and Faithful Servant* (1964), was performed at the King's Head, Islington. In 1967 Orton was brutally murdered by his homosexual friend, Kenneth Halliwell, who then committed suicide.   JE

Osborn, Paul (1901–   ) American playwright. Educated at the University of Michigan and Yale, Osborn's best remembered plays are *On Borrowed Time* (1938) and *Morning's at Seven* (1939). The former was a touching study of an old man's attempt to cheat death. The latter, although praised by some critics after its brief original production and kept alive in anthologies, had to wait until a 1980 revival to achieve wide acclaim. It took a nostalgic and sometimes bittersweet look at the life of four sisters in an American small town. Most of Osborn's works to reach Broadway were adaptations of novels, such as *A Bell for Adano* (1944), *Point of No Return* (1951), and *The World of Suzie Wong* (1958). His plays provide a *mélange* of characters drawn with skill and affection.   LDC

Osborne, John (James) (1929–   ) British dramatist and actor, who started as an actor playing in northern reps. He sent his third play, *Look Back in Anger*, to the newly formed English Stage Company at the **Royal Court Theatre** where it received its premiere on 8 May 1956, a date often taken to signify the start of the post-war British theatre revival. The central character, Jimmy Porter, came from a working-class background but had been educated at university without afterwards finding a job to match his self-esteem. His tirades against British society led to the phrase, 'angry young man', which was afterwards applied not just to Osborne but to almost all new writers who criticized the system. *Look Back in Anger* was the English Stage Company's first outright success. In 1957, he wrote *The Entertainer* which provided **Laurence Olivier** with the splendidly tatty part of Archie Rice, the forlorn comic of touring nude revues. Osborne's major plays have all been distinguished by their central roles which offer major opportunities to the actor. *Luther* (1961) has a loosely written second act, but the first, which tells of Martin Luther's novitiate and the events leading to his stand against the Church, is subtle and powerful. **Nicol Williamson** as the hard-pressed solicitor in *Inadmissible Evidence* (1964) and Maximilian Schell as Reidl in *A Patriot for Me* (1965) took full advantage of the robust, truthful language and insights into the characters which Osborne had provided. These plays have all been successfully revived. The death of **George Devine**, who had done much to nurture Osborne's career, came as a deep personal loss, and Osborne's subsequent plays lacked some of the original flair, partly perhaps because there was no longer a management on whom he could completely rely. His adaptation of **Lope de Vega**'s *La fianza satisfecha* (*A Bond Honoured*, 1966) provided a scrappy half to a **National Theatre** double bill; and although *Time Present* (1968) and *Hotel in Amsterdam* (1968) were well-balanced plays, they had little of Osborne's forcefulness. *West of Suez* (1971) was an untidy but vivid lament for the old British certainties, a play where Osborne expressed a kind of reborn conservatism. His later plays all mourn the loss of past values, coupled with a wholesale attack on the present: *A Sense of Detachment* (1972), *The End of Me Old Cigar* (1974) and *Watch It Come Down* (1976).   JE

Osofisan, Femi (1946–) Nigerian playwright, novelist and critic. Osofisan was born in Iloto Ijebu-Ode, Ogun State. He studied French at Ibadan University, and then pursued postgraduate studies at the universities of Dakar and Paris. He took his doctorate at Ibadan University, and after lecturing there, was appointed Professor of Theatre Arts at the University of Benin in 1983. His critical writing reflects his exposure to some of the Marxist criticism and structuralist philosophy in French intellectual circles in the 1960s and 70s. With fellow Nigerian playwrights, like Kole Omotoso, and left-wing critics, like Biodun Jeyifo, Osofisan has helped shape a new discourse which places contemporary political class analysis at the centre of the literary and theatrical enterprise. This has involved a critique of the work of established writers like **Soyinka** and **J. P. Clark**: a rejection of their metaphysics and of what is regarded as their unreconstructed view of myth and African history. Soyinka, in turn, refers to this group as Nigeria's 'leftocrats'. Osofisan's own vigorous analysis of mat-culture in Africa appeals to many Nigerian students and young writers in the post-oil-boom 1980s. In the later 1970s the discourse was publicly extended in the periodical *Positive Review*, and Osofisan was part of the editorial collective. Taking up where Soyinka's *Ch'Indaba* (formerly *Transition*) left off, it attempted to situate art, history and literature in a class-based analysis of Nigeria's social formation. Performances of Osofisan's plays on Nigerian university campuses have reinforced his popularity among radical students and intellectuals. First was *Red is the Freedom Road* (1969; formerly titled *You Have Lost Your Fine Face*); followed by the publication of a satirical novel *Kolera Kolej* (1975; later dramatized and produced at Ibadan by Dexter Lyndersay); and then by a widely performed satirical Nigerian version of **Gogol**'s *The Inspector General*: *Who's Afraid of Solarin* (1978). In 1976 the first of the three plays for which he is admired, *The Chattering and the Song*, was successfully performed in Ibadan. It is about an underground farmers' revolutionary movement and the relationship of a number of intellectuals towards the movement – and towards each other as their affiliations emerge. This was followed in 1978 by the first production of *Once Upon Four Robbers*. The play is an attack on the Nigerian Military, both government and soldiery: 'The play revolves around a magnificent irony: the real armed robbers [the soldiers] are those set to catch the four robbers' (Niyi Osundare). In 1979, his most ambitious work to date, *Morountodun*, was premiered in Ibadan. The play combines the myth of Moremi with the 1969 uprising of farmers in the west of Nigeria. The synthesis is made in the context of an enactment of the latter by a 'Theatre Director' and 'Actors', in order to show 'the urgent necessity to deploy the energies of the past to struggle against and defeat the forces of oppression and injustice that ensnare our people in the purgatory of poverty and insecurity' (*Positive Review*). Osofisan's satirical flair was shown again in *Midnight Hotel*, his adaptation of **Feydeau**'s farce, *Paradise Hotel*. With the publication of his plays his work is receiving increasing critical attention. A view expressed is that his considerable talent for theatre has not yet meshed with his socialist aims – 'a sense of technique riding free of function' (Dunton). However, the recurring theme 'that the machinery of oppression in human society is created by man and man is capable also of demolishing it' (Osundare) has established an eager audience in Nigeria for his plays.   ME

Ostrovsky, Aleksandr Nikolaevich (1823–86) Russian dramatist and administrator at the Maly Theatre, who charted the course of 20th-century Russian stage realism, based upon questions of social class, environment and ethics. A native Muscovite and son of a government clerk turned merchant-lawyer, he became Russia's most prolific painter of mercantile society and the common people, writing well over 50 plays, mostly comedies, for the stage. His first comedy, *The Bankrupt* (1847), later revised as *It's a Family Affair – We'll Settle It Ourselves* (1849), exposed fraudulent business practices for which it was banned from production for 11 years. His best-known comedy in the West, *Diary of a Scoundrel* (or *Enough Stupidity for Every Wise Man*, 1868), dealt with a double-dealer in the tradition of **Gogol**'s Khlestakov and **Sukhovo-Kobylin**'s Krechinsky. While he translated plays by **Plautus**, **Terence**, **Shakespeare**, **Cervantes**, **Gozzi**

and **Machiavelli** for his own education as a dramatist, Ostrovsky saw his chief role to be the furthering of a native dramatic tradition. He embraced a less dogmatic Slavophilism and aligned himself with publisher M. P. Pogodin's *Moskvityanin* circle of journal editors and associates (poet-critic Apollon Grigoriev, actor **Prov Sadovsky**, dramatist **A. F. Pisemsky**, etc.), which conducted ethnographic and historical inquiries into Russian folk poetry and ritual. This folk quality can be found in the most famous of his three tragedies, *The Thunderstorm* (1859). Derived in part from information gathered while on a literary tour of the Volga in 1886, Ostrovsky here dramatized in characteristic fashion the struggle between oppressor and oppressed, and the corruption of innocence, with nature participating as an agent of fate in the outcome. His dramatic fable, *The Snow Maiden* (1873), drew upon his knowledge of Russian folk songs, proverbs and popular poetry, blending romanticism with realism. These plays, *An Ardent Heart* (1869) and others furnished Russian actresses with strong roles through which to further their craft. He created characters with specific performers in mind, rewriting roles to suit the individuals cast while in rehearsal, often as the play's director. While **Shchepkin** had difficulty realizing these roles, Sadovsky and a new generation of actors built their careers upon them. His understanding of the actor's world is reflected in such comedies as *The Comedian of the Seventeenth Century* (1872), on the founding of the first Russian theatre in Moscow, and *The Forest* (1871), which features a pair of itinerant performers. The latter received a controversial non-realistic staging by **Meyerhold** in 1924. Ostrovsky was less sympathetic towards the nobility and fashionable society whom he ridiculed as idlers, hypocrites and petty tyrants. This made him popular in progressive circles and throughout the nation after the 1917 Revolution, when he became the most frequently performed classical Russian dramatist. He founded and was president of the Society of Russian Dramatic Writers and Opera Composers (1874) which awarded the Griboedov Prize for playwriting and secured for its members production royalties. In 1882 he helped to break the monopoly of the Imperial Theatres, beginning with the establishment of the Korsh Theatre in Moscow, which set tradition for the **Moscow Art Theatre** to follow in 1897. In 1885 he was appointed director of the artistic department of the Moscow Imperial Theatres and head of the Moscow Theatrical School. Ostrovsky the dramatist tended toward the sentimental and melodramatic; his plotting was often structurally weak and his endings contrived. He lacked **Griboedov**'s and Gogol's talent for abstraction and mastery of language. What he had was a genius for concreteness – a clear sense of environment conditioning behaviour, idiomatic expression tailored to individualized characters and a broad view of the social stratification, socio-economic relationships and native traditions which contribute to the formation of a national consciousness. SG

O'Toole, Peter (1932–) British actor, born in Ireland, who made his reputation with the **Bristol Old Vic** from 1955 to 1958. He was spotted by London managements at the **Royal Court Theatre** in *The Long and the Short and the Tall* (1959). He joined the Shakespeare Memorial Company in 1960, where he

was a memorable Shylock and Petruchio; and played Hamlet in the inaugural production of the **National Theatre** company at the **Old Vic** in 1963. Increasingly, however, he was drawn towards films, and starred as Lawrence in the epic, *Lawrence of Arabia* (1962). His stage appearances became infrequent, although he appeared as the novelist Peter in **David Mercer**'s *Ride a Cock Horse* (1965) and in Dublin as Jack Boyle in **O'Casey**'s *Juno and the Paycock* (1966). His blond hair, gaunt face and idiosyncratic vocal delivery could be compelling in the right part, but his screen career seemed to magnify his mannerisms when he returned to the stage. He was unfortunate enough to appear in a disastrous *Macbeth* for Prospect Company at the Old Vic in 1980, although he redeemed his reputation with a forceful John Tanner in a West End production of *Man and Superman* two years later. JE

Otto, Teo (1904–68) German stage designer. Educated at the Academy of Fine Arts, Kassel, and at the Bauhaus, he began designing agit-prop plays for the Proletkult Kassel in 1926. Otto Klemperer engaged him in 1927 for the Kroll Opera, Berlin. In 1931 he became chief designer at the Berlin State Theatre where he worked until he emigrated to Switzerland in 1933. His association with the Schauspielhaus in Zurich led to a collaboration with **Brecht** on the premiere productions of *Mother Courage* (1941), *Galileo* (1943) and *The Good Person of Setzuan* (1943). Also in Zurich he designed premiere productions of plays by **Dürrenmatt** and **Max Frisch**. During the 1950s his designs could be seen in major opera houses and theatres in Austria and Germany. The most important of these productions was **Gründgen**'s revival in Hamburg of *Faust, Part I and Part II* (1957) which was brought to New York's City Centre in 1961. While in New York he designed productions of *Nabucco* and *Tristan und Isolde* (1960) for the Metropolitan Opera. Professor of Stage Design at the Academy of Fine Arts in Dusseldorf until his death, he wrote two books on design theory: *Nie wieder* and *Meine Szene*. His designs were noted for economy of architectural detail, sparse and symbolic use of properties, decorative screens and atmospheric lighting. AJN

Otway, Thomas (1652–85) English playwright. Educated at Winchester and Oxford, he moved to London, failing as an actor when, as the King in **Aphra Behn**'s *The Forced Marriage*, he suffered badly from stage-fright. His first play, *Alcibiades* (1675), gave a leading role to **Mrs Barry**, with whom Otway became hopelessly and unrequitedly in love. He followed *Alcibiades'* success with further heroic tragedies, *Don Carlos* (1676) and *Titus and Berenice* (1676), a version of **Racine**'s *Bérénice*, performed with his adaptation of **Molière**'s farce *The Cheats of Scapin*. Realizing his talent for bitter comedy, he wrote *Friendship in Fashion* (1678). At about this time he served briefly in the Duke of Monmouth's regiment in the Netherlands, making some use of his experience as a soldier in his comedy *The Soldier's Fortune* (1680) and its sequel *The Atheist* (1683). He also adapted **Shakespeare**'s *Romeo and Juliet* as *The History and Fall of Caius Marius* (1679). But Otway's enormous reputation in the 18th century was based on the two tragedies that led to his being praised as 'next to Shakespeare': *The Orphan* (1680) and *Venice*

Preserv'd (1682). *The Orphan* is a tearful tragedy of the innocent woman caught between love for two men, both equally virtuous. *Venice Preserv'd* combines a similarly pitiable love with a remarkable analysis of a conspiracy to overthrow the corrupt Venetian state and containing a vicious mockery of Shaftesbury's sexual tastes in the caricature of Antonio. Otway died in penury. PH

Ouellette, Rose-Alma ('La Poune') (1903–) French Canadian actress, comedian and theatre manager. She began her stage career as a child singer in variety shows, then as a comic in early American-style burlesque. In the 1920s she worked with Oliver Guimond ('Ti-Zoune'), then considered the outstanding practitioner of the art. In a genre that required great improvisational ability and little or no prepared text, 'La Poune' rapidly became the best-known stage personality of her day. She directed Montreal's Cartier Theatre, 1928–36, and the National, 1936–53, during what is called the Golden Age of Burlesque in Canada.

When television brought burlesque into disfavour she moved easily into the new medium, playing in TV dramas and serials such as *Dix sur Dix*, *Rue des pignons*, and *Les Coqueluches*. She is author of a book of memoirs. LED

Owen, Alun (Davies) (1926–) British dramatist, who began his stage career as an actor with the **Birmingham Rep** (1943–4). A prolific writer for television and radio, Owen adapted his first play, *The Rough and Ready Lot* (1958), for the stage from the original radio script. It concerned four soldiers of fortune in South America after the end of the American Civil War, and illustrated Owen's easy command of dialogue and his gift of characterization. *Progress to the Park* (1959) was a vivid portrait of his birthplace, Liverpool, and given a characteristically lively production by **Joan Littlewood** at the Theatre Workshop, Stratford. *A Little Winter Love* was produced in Dublin in 1963 and in London two years later; and he collaborated with the songwriter, Lionel Bart, in an ambitious musical about a Liverpool legend, *Maggie May* (1964). Owen's stage plays never matched the popular success of his television writing, partly because his stories seem to lose their shape when extended to a full evening. At best, his language has a poetic quality of its own, combining unforced imagery, a keen ear for dialect and a love of the unusual phrase. JE

Owens, John Edmond (1823–86) American actor and manager. Born in Liverpool, he came to Philadelphia in 1828, began as a supernumerary at Burton's National Theatre (1841), quickly graduated to speaking roles, and then played in all the principal American cities and in London (1865). He bought and managed the Baltimore Museum (1849–52), made his New York debut (1850) as Uriah Heep in **John Brougham**'s *The People's Lawyer*, the role for which he became best known and which prompted the critics to speak of his 'merry temperament, his exuberant and incessant glee'. RM

Owens, Rochelle (1936–) American playwright who creates her own cultural anthropology complete with myths, ritual, chants and symbols in her experi-mental, Off-Off Broadway plays. Her first highly controversial play, which won an Obie Award, was *Futz* (1967), a tragicomedy relating the sexual love of a man and his pig and the violent, demented response of his repressed neighbours to his sodomy. Owens continued to explore perversity, violence and sexuality as responses to the conflict of individual primal impulse with a self-righteous society in such plays as *Belcch* (1967) – an example of Theatre of Cruelty with its depiction of savagery and depravity; *Istanbul* (1965); *Kontraption* (1970); *He Wants Shih* (1975); *Chucky's Hunch* (1981); and two surreal historical biographies – *The Karl Marx Play* (1973) and *Emma Instigated Me* (1977). FB

Oyônô-Mbia, Guillaume (1939–) Cameroonian playwright. Born at Mvoutessi, near Sangmélina, which provides the rural setting that features in his plays. Educated at the Collège Evangélique, Libambu, and at the University of Keele, England (1968–9). On his return to the Cameroons, he joined the English department of the University of Yaoundé as a lecturer, and was for a time (1972–5) head of the Cultural Affairs division of the Ministry of Information and Culture. Equally at home in French or English, Oyônô-Mbia always translates his plays himself into the other language; all but one of them (*Our Daughter Must not Marry*) have two versions. Three of his plays were initially written for the radio for performance by the BBC and the French ORTF and have won prizes in that medium. Oyônô-Mbia's plays have been performed widely in Africa, especially in the Cameroons, and have also been produced in France and England. They owe their success largely to a combination of the author's sharp awareness of the comic conventions of the theatre and his ability to use them to portray social behaviour at a time of fundamental change in African society, particularly in the key realms of education, marriage, wealth and social status. Oyônô-Mbia's four plays are: *Three Suitors: One Husband* (1964), *Until Further Notice* (1970), *Notre Fille Ne Se Mariera Pas* (*Our Daughter Must not Marry*, 1971), *His Excellency's Special Train* (1979). The date given is that of the publication of the first version, whether it was in French or English; all of Oyônô-Mbia's plays received their first performance before publication. Oyônô-Mbia has also published three volumes of stories portraying characters and situations resembling those found in his plays. CS

Ozerov, Vladislav Aleksandrovich (1769–1816) Russian dramatist who wrote neoclassical tragedy which in the conventions of its form imitated **Corneille**, **Racine**, **Voltaire**, but which in its linguistic style and heightened subjectivism pointed toward the developing sentimental and pre-romantic schools of playwriting. As opposed to his contemporaries, **A. P. Sumarokov** and **Ya. B. Knyazhnin**, Ozerov adopted a more conversational tone and posited more complex psychological motives and more realistic limitations for his heroes. Nevertheless, his plays were still largely contrived, and the declamatory acting style and emotional demands which they required made them favourites of such star performers as **A. S. Yakovlev**, **E. S. Semyonova**, Ya. E. Shucherin and **V. A. Karatygin**. The plays which followed his initial, strictly classical tragedy *Yaropolk and Oleg* (1798) enjoyed a brilliant albeit shortlived success for the cleverness with which their author drew parallels between historical and contemporary political events. *Oedipus in Athens* (1804), a reworking of *Oedipus at Colonus*, was based on a French rather than the original Greek model which accounts for its relatively restrained happy ending. *Fingal* (1805) was inspired by the Ossianic poems. *Dmitry of the Don* (*Donskoi*, 1807) was by far his most popular work, bolstering Russians' patriotic spirit during their struggle with Napoleon by reminding them of their stirring victory over the Tartars in 1380. The play, which became even more popular after 1812, was not highly regarded by Ozerov's peers any more than was the author himself in general. **Griboedov** penned a parody entitled *Dmitry of the Trash* (*Dryanskoi*) and **Pushkin** would say 'I dislike Ozerov not because I envy him but because I love art.' Ozerov's best play *Polyxena* (1809), which dramatized the eponymous heroine's tragic love for Achilles, met with some opposition from the censor and was not a success. Depression over financial matters, partly relating to the poor box-office performance of this play, prompted Ozerov to destroy the manuscript of his last complete tragedy, *Medea*, and to sink into an irreversible state of paralysis and catatonia.   SG

P

Pacino, Al (1940–) American actor. A devoted student of **Lee Strasberg** and a member of the **Actors Studio**, Pacino made a strong impression on stage in the late sixties playing jittery, violent low-life New Yorkers. Off-Broadway he was a demented pan-handler in *The Indian Wants the Bronx* (1968), and in his Broadway debut he was a drug addict in *Does a Tiger Wear a Necktie?* (1969). His naturalistic style, the flickering, hungry eyes that are often the only signs of life in his masklike face, and the promise of thunder in his voice and gestures, proved ideal for film (*The Godfather, Serpico, Scarface*). In his periodic returns to the stage Pacino has tried with limited success to overcome the typecasting of his films. His *Richard III* (1973) was brave though unavoidably contemporary. He was more comfortable as **Tennessee Williams**'s Everyman in the 1970 Lincoln Center revival of *Camino Real*; and as a wheezing, shuffling, pinch-voiced crook with a battery of tics in a revival of **David Mamet**'s *American Buffalo* (1982), he was at full blaze. FH

Page, Geraldine (1924–87) American actress. Born in Missouri, Page attended the Goodman Theatre Dramatic School (1942–5) in Chicago before making her New York debut in the Blackfriar's Guild produc-tion of *Seven Mirrors* (1945). **José Quintero** cast her as Alma in the Off-Broadway production of *Summer and Smoke* at the **Circle in the Square** (1951–2) to rave reviews, establishing her career. Her Broadway debut as Lily in *Midsummer* (1953) again received critical acclaim; Wolcott Gibbs in *The New Yorker* praised her 'charm and pathos and almost matchless technique'. Her later work included Lizzie in *The Rainmaker* (1954); Alexandra del Lago in *Sweet Bird of Youth* (1959); Olga in *Three Sisters* (1964); Baroness Lemberg in *White Lies* and Clea in *Black Comedy* (1967); Marion in *Absurd Person Singular* (1974); and Mother Miriam Ruth in *Agnes of God* (1982). From 1983 she was a member of the Mirror Theatre Company. Her husband was actor Rip Torn. While Page appeared too often in neurotic roles, she was a versatile actress capable of a wide emotional range. Her Alexandra del Lago provoked **Brooks Atkinson** to eloquence: 'Loose-jointed, gang-ling, raucous of voice, crumpled, shrewd, abandoned yet sensitive about some things that live in the heart, Miss Page is at the peak of form in this raffish characterization.' Her numerous film appearances include *Summer and Smoke* (1961) and Woody Allen's *Interiors* (1978). In 1986 she won an Academy Award for her portrayal of Carrie Watts in *The Trip to Bountiful* (her eighth Oscar nomination). TLM

Pak Sŭng-hi (1901–64) Korean director, producer, and playwright. He led the Towŏl-hoe Group which largely produced the *shinp'a* plays (see **Korea**). Born of a well-to-do family and educated in Japan. For this theatrical venture he exhausted his inheritance. He was responsible for the upgrading of the *shinp'a* theatre. Nearly 200 new plays and adaptations have been credited to him, but most of them have not sur-vived. OKC

Pakhomuhka Russian folk-farce, performed by young men or women at village parties, or during collective sedentary work such as sewing-bees. It concerns the humped and fanged idiot Pakhomuhka and his sexually frustrated wife Pakhomikha. The hero's attempt to find a bride among the girls in the audience develops into a burlesque marriage and wedding-night, and finally into a farce of cuckoldry and revenge. Organization and performance are infor-mal: roles are distributed and costumes and props improvised on the spot, by-play between actors and audience is the norm. AEG

Pakistan The history of the theatre of Pakistan is the history of the Urdu theatre which started in 1853 with the composition of Mirza Amanat's *Inder Sabha* per-formed at the court of Wajid Ali Shah of Oudh in the city of Lucknow in north central India. Owing primar-ily to the fact that Pakistan is an Islamic state and like neighbouring countries of the Middle East has not, for religious reasons, condoned or encouraged the produc-tion of plays, it is not surprising that theatre in this region of the subcontinent and among the communities concerned has been relatively slow in developing and only recently became a part of the cultural heritage of the people. In Pakistan, there was no classical tradition on which a theatre could be built and what folk heritage there may have been is obscure, except for perform-ances of the **Bhands** of the Punjab, recitation of dramatic poetry and the puppet theatre.

Inder Sabha was not intended to be a landmark production but was designed to satisfy the cravings of a lavish court life ruled by an extravagant composer-king. The play is in verse with musical accompaniment and dance and requires elaborate costumes to be fully realized. In 1856 the kingdom of Oudh came to an abrupt end when the British deposed the Shah and exiled him to Calcutta. However, for at least two generations after that, actors and musicians of Oudh sang the songs of *Inder Sabha* and kept alive the potential of an Urdu theatre.

The next major dramatic activity in Urdu occurred in an entirely different region of the Indian subcontinent when some Parsi entrepreneurs of Bombay, motivated no doubt by economic gain, set about developing a form of theatre in Urdu which was to captivate the public imagination, not only in the whole of India but even in Sri Lanka and parts of South-East Asia, as well. Producers, such as Pestonji Framji and Khurshidji Balliwalla, developed a popular form of theatre known as the Parsi musical. In 1870, assisted by several Muslim munshis, they composed Urdu plays which were set to music. Then, after 1880, plays were commissioned and the Muslim authors were given credit for their effort. Raunaq Banarsi, Mian Zarif, Vinayak Prasad Talib, Ahsan Lucknowi, Narain Prasad Betab, and Agra Hashr Kashmiri are among the better known writers of the Parsi musicals of the Victoria Theatrical Company, the Alfred Company and the New Alfred Company.

The plays were designed exclusively to entertain and thus satisfy the taste of audiences of the day. Themes of romantic love, chivalry and generosity were popularized out of a wide array of literary sources – classics, history and legends. Even some of **Shakespeare**'s plays were reassembled and the characters provided Indian names while the dialogue was set to Urdu verse. Two distinct plot lines emerged – one humorous and the other serious. These were made to correlate and interweave, even if the results did not seem to make much sense.

From the very outset, dancing girls were a part of every show. This led to an expression of outrage in 1914 when the New Alfred Theatrical Company visited Lahore to stage Betab's *Mahabharata*, based on the Hindu epic of the same name. The audience reacted negatively to characters with religious names such as Rukmini and Draupadi when they were played by women whom they considered of questionable morals. As a consequence, the company did not present the show.

Although the main goal of the Urdu theatre of the Parsi companies was to make money through entertainment, some authors of the time demonstrated a social consciousness by attacking social evils of the day, such as child marriage and the rigidity of the purdah system. Others expressed an interest in political subject matter by addressing issues such as the controversy over the formation of Punjab state and border disputes with the Japanese.

With the development of the film industry in the 1930s, the audience quickly shifted its allegiance to the cinema and many of the most successful companies closed their doors for good and their personnel went into the film industry. Only the smaller groups and minor companies remained as a testament of a very active past.

The modern states of Pakistan and India were created in 1947. Pakistan was composed of East Bengal and West Pakistan separated by more than 1,000 miles of Indian territory. In 1971 the modern state of Bangladesh, formerly East Pakistan, came into being.

In West Pakistan, scattered activity in theatre began soon after independence with the formation of dramatic clubs in colleges and universities, such as that of the Government College of Lahore. The dramatic club of the Government College was managed by students under the supervision of interested staff members. At first both Urdu and English plays were presented. The

Urdu plays were mostly translations from Western dramas. Some of the plays staged between 1951 and 1957 were *Swan Ran Ka Sapana*, a Punjabi version of Shakespeare's *A Midsummer Night's Dream*, an Urdu version of **Gogol**'s *The Inspector General* and adaptations of one-act plays by **Molière**. Many of the students who were part of this early activity have now entered the professional field of films and television.

In 1956, the Pakistan Arts Council opened a small theatre in the council building and invited productions by Government College students and for the next three years the citizens of Lahore found an alternative theatre outside the college environment. Among the better-known productions were **Priestley**'s *An Inspector Calls* and **Ibsen**'s *A Doll's House*, both of which were presented in Urdu. After 1960, the production of comedies drew larger and more regular theatre-going audiences.

In 1964 the Arts Council attempted to turn the Alahamra Theatre into a year-round theatre rather than an occasional place for performance. By 1966 plays were running on a regular basis and a campaign was begun to produce original plays in Urdu. In 1967 the theatre in Lahore was broad-based and had gained considerable momentum.

After independence, the theatre in Karachi still clung to the old theatrical traditions inherited from Bombay and Calcutta. Then, in 1950-1, the Osmania University Old Boys produced Khwaja Moinuddin's *Zawal-e-Hydrabad*, a tense drama portraying the conditions of the Kashmiris under Indian Army rule. The play had touching lyrics and music which helped to make it a popular success. Another of the plays by the same author, entitled *Naya Nishan*, was produced in the same year and gained even greater public recognition, so much so that it was banned by the government for probing a sensitive political issue when the Indian and Pakistan governments were attempting to negotiate a treaty over Kashmir.

In 1953, Khwaja Moinuddin wrote *Lal Qile Se Lalukhet* which revolved around the trials of a family that had to migrate to Pakistan from India after partition. It was produced in the K. M. C. Stadium and the four-hour drama set a record attendance by drawing nearly 10,000 people. It was later staged in Karachi at the Katrak Hall and ran for 140 performances. Later, it played in Lahore, Hyderabad and Mirpurkhas and was revived in 1956 in Karachi and Lahore.

Numerous productions were produced by various groups formed in Karachi between 1952 and 1955. Some of these were supported by the oil companies that encourage dramatic activity under their welfare programme for the benefit of their employees. Throughout this entire period the British Amateur Society of Karachi, better known as the Clifton Players, produced a number of drawing room comedies.

In 1956 the Karachi Theatre was formed which originated from the Theatre Group of the Arts Council headed by Sigrid Nyberg Kahle, German wife of a diplomat, the playwright Khwaja Moinuddin and the actor Zia Mohyeddin, whose work in the film *A Passage to India*, and more recently in *The Jewel in the Crown*, gained him world-wide recognition. Productions included Molière's *School for Wives*, *Gas Light*, *Our Town*, *Antigone*, and Khwaja Moinuddin's *Lal Qile Se Lalukhet*, among others.

When Ms Kahle left the group to go abroad, the Avant Garde Arts Theatre came into being presenting Urdu versions of **Gorky**'s *The Lower Depths*, Molière's *Perfect Gentleman*, **Beckett**'s *Waiting for Godot* and **Coward**'s *Hay Fever*. Much of the success of the group was due to the work of Meherji and Pervez Dastur, who broke away from the AGAT and formed The Seekers.

In 1967–8, many of the theatre organizations in Pakistan's cities began to tour the country, much as groups do in India, in order to sustain their activities through revenues earned in the smaller towns of the countryside. During this period, theatre came to the attention of the central government when it exempted plays from paying a small but annoying entertainment tax. During the time, state awards by the president of Pakistan helped to bring greater national recognition to theatre. Then, too, the period saw many plays published in Urdu. And finally, a number of small semi-professional theatre companies formed, and there was an increase in the number of men and women interested and skilled in theatre, television and film. FaR

Pala (India) This form of theatre is performed either by parties of players who sit (*baithaki*) or stand (*thhia*). Groups that stand require six players dressed in royal attire. The chief player (*gayaka*) holds a yak's tail fly whisk and plays small bell-metal cymbals. The other players (*palias*) form a chorus. The form honours Satyapir, a deity worshipped by Hindus and Muslims of Orissa state in eastern India. The preliminary rituals of the form are said to closely resemble those described in the *Natyasastra*. The *Thhia Pala* has a high literary level. Humour is provided by one of the party. The chief player explains passages of singing in a language that the people may understand. Any open space may be used for a performance. Sometimes two groups of *Pala* compete for prizes. FaR

Palace Theatre, New York The legendary Mecca for vaudeville performers, it was built by Martin Beck, who then had to turn over 75% of the stock to Edward Albee for permission to use Keith Circuit acts; Albee in turn paid Oscar Hammerstein 225,000 dollars for the rights to offer Keith acts in that neighbourhood. Located at Broadway and 47th St, the theatre, which seated 1,800, opened on 25 March 1913, and, after a slow start, gained popularity with the booking of **Sarah Bernhardt**. 'Playing the Palace' was the ambition of every American variety act, although names did not go up in lights until 1928. The record bill was for a nine-week teaming of **Eddie Cantor** and George Jessel in 1931. On 7 May 1932, the Palace became a four-a-day theatre, the live performance mingled with newsreels and cartoons, and on 16 November turned into a five-a-day cinema; this date marks the official death of vaudeville as a dominant entertainment form. After a period as a burlesque house and a brief revival of vaudeville in 1950, the Palace was converted into a theatre for musical comedy in 1965. LS

Palais-Royal, Théâtre du Originally known as the Palais-Cardinal, it was built by the architect Jacques Lemercier as a small private playhouse in **Richelieu**'s

palace and inaugurated in January 1641 with a performance for Louis XIII. Designed to emulate the aristocratic theatres of Italy, it boasted a permanent proscenium arch and drop curtain, machinery for scene changes and an elegant auditorium with two balconies at either side and 27 rows of tiered seating in the centre. Reverting to the crown after Richelieu's death, it was occasionally used for court entertainments, Luigi Rossi's opera *Orfeo* being mounted there in 1647 by **Torelli**, who demolished the existing stage walls to accommodate more sophisticated machinery. In 1660 it was made available to **Molière**'s company following the loss of the **Petit-Bourbon** and substantially refurbished and re-equipped in 1670 for the presentation of spectacular 'machine-plays'. After Molière's death it was acquired by **Lully** as a home for his 'Académie royale de musique' and with further structural modifications by **Vigarani** it remained in use as an opera house until 1763 when it was destroyed by fire and rebuilt. A further fire in 1781 caused the whole site to be re-developed and a number of theatres were subsequently built there under this name. DR

Palitzsch, Peter (1918–) German director, trained in the **Berliner Ensemble**, who introduced **Brecht**'s theatrical methods to the West German stage when he left the DDR in 1960. He extended and modified the principles of epic theatre in productions of the classics, particularly his adaptation of **Shakespeare**, *The Wars of the Roses* (Stuttgart, 1967) which became an anti-illusionistic study of the dialectics of history, and has been instrumental in promoting contemporary German drama with influential productions of the first major plays by **Walser** (*The Black Swan*, 1964), Jochen Ziem (*The Invitation*, 1967) and **Dorst** (*Toller*, 1968). CI

Palladio, Andrea, pseudonym of Andrea di Pietro Monaro (1509–80), Italian architect. Most of his work was done in Venice and Vicenza, where he was a member of the Accademia Olimpica, founded by his patron, **Trissino**. One of the greatest of Italian Renaissance architects, his work was rooted in a close study of Roman remains and the writings of **Vitruvius**, and in the ideas of Alberti on the correspondences between architectural and musical forms. In execution, however, his work was profoundly original in the fluency, purity and harmony of its lines, and his influence throughout Europe in the 17th and early 18th centuries was considerable. In 1561 and 1562 he built theatres within the hall of the Basilica at Vicenza, the second being used for the production of Trissino's *Sofonisba*. His most famous theatre is the Teatro Olimpico at Vicenza, begun in the year of his death and finished by **Scamozzi** in 1585 essentially on the basis of his plans. It represents the triumph of Renaissance academicism, a beautifully conceived and completed structure for all that its Roman *scaenae frons* had by the time of its conception been made obsolete by the development of the proscenium stage with changeable settings. KR

Pallenberg, Max (1877–1934) Austrian actor, a leading figure in **Reinhardt**'s theatre between 1911 and 1919, who won extraordinary popularity for his comic fantasy. His range can be indicated by his two most

One of Pallenberg's most famous roles was as Schweik in Piscator's 1928 production. Parallel conveyor belts on the stage carry Schweik and the Officer-marionette past each other.

famous roles – the title character in **Piscator**'s production of *Schweik* (1928), and Mephisto in Reinhardt's *Faust* (1933).   CI

Palme, Ulf (1920–) Swedish actor, whose physical authority and intellectual energy made him a key member of **Dramaten**, from about 1945. He was a celebrated Stanley Kowalski and one of this century's most powerful interpreters of Jean in *Miss Julie*, both on stage and in **Alf Sjöberg**'s film; other important **Strindberg** roles have been Erik XIV and Edgar in *The Dance of Death*. His most celebrated performance was undoubtedly that of Jamie in the world premiere of **O'Neill**'s *Long Day's Journey Into Night* (1956). Since the mid-1960s, Palme has directed **Shakespeare**, Strindberg and numerous contemporary plays and has also been active in radio drama.   HL

Palmer, Albert Marshman (1838–1905) American theatrical manager. He first entered the theatre as co-manager with Sheridan Shook of the **Union Square Theatre** in 1872. Although trained as a lawyer and without theatrical background or experience, he established a reputation as one of the leading managers of his time with a keen business sense and cultivated theatrical tastes. During his ten-year tenure at the Union Square, he improved both the quality of the acting company and production standards. He also fostered the production of contemporary drama, particularly American drama, often commissioning new plays, translations and adaptations. In 1883, following a dispute with Shook, he left the Union Square. However, he subsequently managed the **Madison Square Theatre** from 1884 to 1891. In 1888, he secured control of **Wallack's Theatre**, renaming it Palmer's and in 1891 he moved his famous Madison Square stock company to this theatre. Unlike **Daly** and **Frohman**, he was not a 'star-maker', but he did promote the careers of numerous actors and actresses, including Agnes Booth, **Richard Mansfield**, **W. H. Crane**, **Maurice Barrymore**, **Clara Morris**, and **James O'Neill**. Among his more notable productions of American plays were **Bronson Howard**'s *The Banker's Daughter* (1878), **Bartley Campbell**'s *My Partner* (1879), **Clyde Fitch**'s *Beau Brummel* (1890), **James A. Herne**'s *Margaret Fleming* (1891) and **Augustus Thomas**'s *Alabama* (1891). He also produced plays by **Henry Arthur Jones**, **Oscar Wilde**, **W. S. Gilbert**, and a popular dramatization of **Du Maurier**'s *Trilby* (1895). Palmer was also among the first American managers to pay foreign authors royalties for the performance of their plays, and he was a major force in the founding of the Actor's Fund of America in 1882.   DJW

Palsgrave's Men see **Admiral's Men**

Panama The possibility of constructing a canal across Panama to facilitate traffic between the oceans surfaced during the years of the conquest, but the Panama Canal did not become a reality until 1914. In the intervening years, the territory of Panama was assigned first to the viceregency of Peru, later to New Granada (Colombia), and finally became a separate nation in 1903 when the United States interests in building the Canal supported the insurgents' claim to independence. Panamanian interests and economics during the 20th century have been closely related to the Canal.

Cultural life in the colony and even into the 19th century was quite limited. The first play written and performed in Panama was by Víctor de la Guardia (1772–1824); his *La política del mundo* (*World Politics*, 1809) was a classical Roman play with references to the Napoleonic invasion of Spain. References to other performances in the 19th century are infrequent, and no plays of substance have survived, although the indigenous populations and country folk traditionally developed popular theatrical forms that mixed their customs and religious elements.

20th century The economic boom produced by the construction of the Canal permitted Panama to build the National Theatre in 1920, which has served to house visiting troupes. In 1937 the poet **Rogelio Sinán** (pseudonym of Bernardo Domínguez Alba, b. 1904) launched a children's theatre movement with a musical farce *La cucarachita mandinga* (*The Impish Little Cockroach*) a trend followed later by Eda Nela, among others, who wrote *La fuga de Blanca Nieves* (*Snow White's Flight*) in 1950. Plays deriving from Panamanian folklore, myths and legends became popular in the 1940s during the regime of the fascist president Dr Arnulfo Arias. Some of these plays had a moralizing message designed to improve living conditions for poor peasants. In 1942 the government established the Ricardo Miró award to stimulate national interest in fiction and poetry. The competition was extended to theatre in 1952, and Renato Ozores (b. 1910) won the first award with *Un angel* (*An Angel*). Daniel Guigui established the Teatro de Arte (Art Theatre) in 1953 and the University Theatre was created in 1959. Other major writers from this period include Mario Augusto Rodríguez, Mario de Obaldía (1891–1951), Moisés Castillo (b. 1899) and Juan O. Díaz Lewis (b. 1916).

In the post-war period the theatre began to acquire higher levels of social commitment. Mario Riera Pinilla (1920–67) advocated peasant revolt in *La montaña encendida* (*The Burning Mountain*, 1952). The Nicaraguan-born **José de Jesús Martínez** (1929–91), long-time Panamanian citizen, has been a major force in the theatre as playwright, director and organizer of theatre programmes for underprivileged areas. His early plays, such as *La mentira* (*The Lie*, 1955) and *El juicio final* (*Final Judgement*, 1962), reflected his doctoral training in philosophy and metaphysics. The urgency of individual freedom turned towards social concerns in his later plays such as *La guerra del banano* (*The Banana War*, 1974). The cultural impetus generated by the nationalist period of Omar Torrijos, and the anti-imperialistic struggle of the Panamanian people brought forth another major voice, that of **Raúl Leis** (b. 1947). An outspoken revolutionary, author of such plays as *María Picana* (1979) and *El nido de Macúa* (*The Nest of Macúa*, 1981), he writes plays that intercalate folklore and magic with political protest and even violence. Since 1981 Danny Calden, a director and actor, has sponsored an intense project of popular theatre and collective creations in the poorer regions of the country. A popular theatre group, Oveja Negra (Black Sheep), directed by Ileana Solís Palma, presented its first collective work, *El gran circo requeterrojo* (*The Big Red Circus*) in 1982.   GW

P'ansori Korean folk operetta performed by a single singer, or *kwangdae*, with the accompaniment of a *puk*, a double-headed drum. The subjects are largely drawn from well-known novels.   OKC

Pantomime see **Mime**

Pantomime, English

Pantomime, English A form of entertainment so indigenous that its conventions have to be interpreted to non-Britons. It originated in the early 18th century under the influence of French fairground performers, who put on 'night scenes' with **commedia dell'arte** characters in London. John Weaver, a dancing-master, copied these in short ballets staged at **Drury Lane** in 1716, and was in turn imitated by **John Rich** at Lincoln's Inn, with *A New Italian Mimic Scene between a Scaramouch, a Harlequin, a Country Farmer, his Wife and others*. Rich played **Harlequin** under the name Lun, and in Weaver's *The Cheats of the Tavern Bilkers* (22 April 1716) transferred the action to a contemporary setting, thus creating a truly native 'pantomime'. His first outstanding success was *The Necromancer or Harlequin Dr Faustus* (1723), which prompted imitations at Drury Lane and the **Haymarket**. Soon pantomime settled into its customary format; the opening was drawn from classical mythology and, following a transformation of characters into the types of Harlequin, Pantaloon, Columbine etc., the second half devolved into a knockabout harlequinade. Rich was lavish with mechanical devices, such as a coiling serpent, and his own mimic agility became proverbial. When theatrical censorship was applied to the spoken word in 1737, there was more recourse to pantomime; even **Garrick** had to comply with the popular taste, featuring Henry Woodward as his Harlequin. In *The Genius of Nonsense* (1780), **George Colman** effectively altered the mythological opening to a fairy tale, which became standard.

By the early 19th century, these afterpieces had swollen to fill the major portion of a bill and accrued a number of traditions: the 'dame' roles were played by men, the old Harlequin costume had been transformed by James Byrne into a skin-tight suit of spangled lozenges, and the entertainment predominated at Christmas and Easter. **Carlo Delpini** had already shifted the comic emphasis from Harlequin to **Pierrot**, and this moved to Clown via the genius of **Joseph**

George Graves as Mrs Halleybut and Arthur Conquest as Priscilla the Cow in the pantomime *Jack and the Beanstalk*, Drury Lane, 1910–11.

Grimaldi. Grimaldi came to prominence in Thomas Dibdin's *Harlequin Mother Goose or The Golden Egg* (**Covent Garden**, 1806), a panto which also set a pattern with its 'big heads' masking the characters in the opening prior to their transformation. 'Joey' the Clown with his introductory cry of 'Here we are again!', his singing of 'Hot Codlins' and 'Tippiti-witchet', his tricks of construction turning household utensils into animated figures, his greediness and exuberance were Grimaldi's legacy to future generations, who faithfully imitated his costume, makeup and behaviour (Tom Matthews added the frills, but allowed a stand-in to perform the acrobatics). This style of panto was carried to America by Charles Parsloe in 1831, but it enjoyed only a limited period of popularity, culminating in **George L. Fox** at the **Bowery Theatre**, New York (1850–67), and his *Humpty Dumpty* (1868).

In the Victorian age, pantomime, as scripted by **J. R. Planché** and E. L. Blanchard, was alloyed with elements from the French *féerie*, the burlesque and the operetta; the hero became the 'principal boy', played by a woman in tights (**Mme Céleste** may have been the first in 1855) and backed up by a stockinetted chorus line. Certain stories proved to be worth repeating, such as *Cinderella*, *Puss in Boots*, *The Babes in the Wood*, *Dick Whittington* and *Aladdin*, and standard characters like the Widow Twankey (first seen in **H. J. Byron**'s burlesque *Aladdin*, 1861), Baron Hardup and Buttons in *Cinderella* (a descendant of Dandini in Rossini's opera by way of the Dandy Lover in Regency pantomime), the Broker's Men, and Whittington's Cat were carried over from year to year. It became exclusively a Christmas-time amusement aimed primarily at a juvenile audience, a seasonal source of employment for minor craftsmen, performers and children used to play fairies and animals. Some theatres, like the Britannia, Hoxton, and the Grecian, City Road, were famous for the excellence of their pantos. Elaborate trickwork, utilizing traps, hinged properties, instantaneous transformations dazzling with Dutch metal and gilt, were expected at the climactic moments.

The second half of the 19th century beheld the rise of the spectacular pantomime with its sumptuous processions, ballets and flying corps, the star status of the principal boy, and the decline of the harlequinade. It became a speciality of actor-clans like the **Conquests**, the **Lupinos**, and the Vokeses who monopolized it at Drury Lane (1869–80) with their indefatigable high-kicks. But they were ousted by Augustus Harris, Jr (known as Druriolanus), who was eager to attract middle-class audiences who attended only pantomime by familiarizing them with the stars of the less respectable music-hall and burlesque. Hence, from 1879, the introduction of Fannie Leslie, Herbert Campbell, Arthur Roberts, **Marie Lloyd** and **Dan Leno**, causing critics to complain of non-juvenile gagging and topical songs, as well as speciality acts imported from vaudeville which held up the action.

After the First World War, pantomime was banished from Drury Lane by musical comedy until 1929, and from Covent Garden by opera and ballet until 1938. It survived as 'rep-theatre panto' domesticated and formulaic with its obligatory kitchens, schoolroom and dressing-for-the-ball scenes, and such audience-participation devices as the 'Oh, no, it isn't – Oh, yes, it is' interchange, the shouts of 'Look behind you', and the sing-along chorus. It was reinstituted at the Palladium (1948–60); in 1961 Norman Wisdom played principal boy, an innovation repeated for a decade with male pop and rock stars until Cilla Black resumed the female prerogative in 1971. The substitution of **Rodgers** and **Hammerstein**'s 'book musical' *Cinderella* at the **Coliseum** (1957) was an ill portent, which had no serious after-effects. The conventional pantomime returned to favour, albeit with some curious alterations, such as the Dame taking centre stage as a glamorous drag queen (**Danny La Rue**) and the **National Theatre** adding panto to its repertory in 1983. In 1984–5, there was only one West End panto, but 30 in the London suburbs, 70 in the provinces and 22 in Scotland, Wales and Ireland. On the dramatic stage, the conventions of the panto have often been adopted for special effect: in *The Fairy's Dilemma* (1904), **W. S. Gilbert** staged a topsy-turvy transformation scene; **G. B. Shaw** (not a fan) brought Harlequin and Columbine on in the last act of *Misalliance* (1910); and **Peter Nichols**'s *Poppy* (1983) attacked imperialism through a pantomime about the Opium Wars.   LS

See: G. Frow, *'Oh, Yes It Is!' A History of Pantomime*, London, 1985; R. Mander and J. Mitchenson, *Pantomime: A Story in Pictures*, London, 1973; D. Mayer, *Harlequin in His Element*, Cambridge, Mass., 1969.

Pantomimus see **Mime**

Papp, Joseph (Papirofsky) (1921–91) American director and producer whose interest in bringing theatre to everyone led him to found the **New York Shakespeare Festival** in 1954. Starting as a stage manager on Broadway and at CBS-TV (1952–60), Papp began the Shakespearian Theatre Workshop on New York's Lower East Side in 1953. Since then, he has devoted himself to NYSF's many activities. Beginning as a director with *Cymbeline* (1954) and *The Changeling* (1956), Papp still occasionally directs for NYSF. His productions include *Twelfth Night* (1958, 1963 and 1969), *Hamlet* (1964, 1967, 1968 and 1983), **Rabe**'s *Boom Boom Room* (1973), Babe's *Buried Inside Extra* (1983) and *Measure for Measure* (1985). For television, he directed *The Merchant of Venice* (1962), *Antony and Cleopatra* (1963) and *Hamlet* (1964). From 1973 to 1977, Papp served as director of Lincoln Center's **Vivian Beaumont** and **Mitzi E. Newhouse Theatres**.

In 1958, Papp received an Antoinette Perry (Tony) Award for Distinguished Service to the Theatre. The same year, the (USA) House Committee for Un-American Activities asked him to reveal names of theatre artists involved in left-wing politics; he refused. A few years later, when he proposed to take NYSF productions into New York City schools, that action returned to haunt him. The plan was ultimately approved, but not without a struggle. A producer who frequently takes great artistic chances, he has been an advocate of creative freedom, and Off- and Off-Off Broadway theatre. Papp is the subject of Stuart W. Little's biography, *Enter Joseph Papp* (1974).   REK

Paraguay The territory of Paraguay was largely ignored during colonial times after the capital city, Asunción, was founded in 1537, and the Spanish barely protested when Paraguay declared independence in 1811. In the interim, the Jesuit missionaries were active in education, religion and agriculture from their arrival in 1588 until expulsion in 1767. In addition to the occasional travelling company that brought Spanish classical fare, the Jesuits promoted local productions in both Spanish and Guaraní, the two dominant languages of the area.

Since independence Paraguayan politics have been marked by a series of repressive dictatorships. The cruel regime of Francia was followed by that of Carlos Antonio López, who contracted with the Spaniard Ildefonso Antonio Bermejo (1820–92) to bring journalism, education and theatre to Paraguay. His productions of Larra, **Zorrilla** and Ramón de la Cruz brought more acclaim than his own plays. The Marshal Francisco Solano López continued his father's tradition during his brief term (1862–70), and even started work on a theatre modelled after Milan's La Scala, but construction was interrupted by the devastating War of the Triple Alliance (1865–70) with Brazil, Argentina and Uruguay which left Paraguay and its male population nearly decimated.

20th century Until the War of Chaco with Bolivia (1932–5) somewhat restored Paraguay's shattered image, theatre in the capital and outlying parts consisted primarily of visiting Spanish and Argentine troupes and an occasional local play. Writers such as Alejandro Guanes (1872–1925), Leopoldo Centurión (1893–1922), Eusebio Aveiro Lugo and Leopoldo Ramos Jiménez were the 20th-century pioneers, writing works with historical and social themes that suffered generally from melodramatism and flamboyancy. With so little importance given to local productions, many plays were actually lost during a period when the general public preferred the movies or imported plays. Julio Correa (1890–1953) is the major playwright, director and actor of the period. With his own company he traversed the provinces with psychological plays in

Guaraní that dealt directly but gracefully with the problems of the country folk or the lower class who suffered social, economic or psychological disruption during the period after the wars. Two *émigrés*, Arturo Alsina (b. 1897) from Argentina and **Josefina Pla** (b. 1909) from the Canaries, brought talent to their adopted country. Pla is a prolific writer, Paraguay's best known playwright outside the country. She often collaborated with Roque Centurión Miranda who established the Municipal School of Dramatic Art in 1948. José María Rivarola Matto (b. 1917) is known for rural social plays and his work as a critic.

Without state support the Paraguayan theatre struggles for survival in modern times. Paraguay's artistic subservience to Argentina has tended to eclipse local talent, and a repressive dictatorship has forced many intellectuals into exile. Groups have been stimulated to some extent by the national theatre festivals and participation in international festivals, although the scarcity of theatre space (the century-old Municipal Theatre is the only decently equipped house) obliges groups normally to rent space or perform in the open air. Censorship continues to be a major concern.

In spite of a host of problems, both professional companies and independent groups continue to promote the theatre. One of the most stable traditional companies is Ernesto Baez's group which normally presents rural or provincial theatre. The Ateneo Paraguayo (Paraguayan Atheneum), one of Paraguay's oldest, stages Greek, French and Paraguayan fare. The de los Ríos family promotes high quality international and national theatre as well. Although more than 20 independent theatre groups exist, the movement is ephemeral. The short-lived Tiempoovillo used collective techniques in staging collages and national works, and the Aty Ne'e (Assembly) has been promising since its formation in 1975. The Paraguayan–American Centre has the best technical equipment available in Asunción. Other groups include the Teatro Latino, La Farándula, Arlequín and the company of Teresita Pesoa.

The currently active Paraguayan writers continue to deal with the massive problems that confront present-day Paraguay: social injustices, class differences, discrimination, censorship and repression. The younger generation of writers includes Ramiro Domínguez (b. 1930), Alcibiades González Delvalle (b. 1936), Ovidio Benítez Pereira (b. 1939), Tadeo Zarratea (b. 1947), and Néstor Romero Valdovinos. The Guaraní theatre is a major force, and plays in Guaraní and Spanish are often translated into the other language. Mario Prono and Antonio Pecci are important directors; Pecci is also an impresario and critic who promotes theatre through festivals and anthologies. Josefina Pla in 1984 won the Ollantay Prize, offered by CELCIT in Venezuela, for her research on four centuries of Paraguayan theatre. Paraguayan theatre is still largely concentrated in the capital city of Asunción, although sporadic activity exists in provincial areas. GW

See: A. Pecci (ed.), *Teatro breve del Paraguay*, Asunción, 1981; J. Pla, *Cuatro siglos de teatro en el Paraguay*, Asunción, 1966.

Parigi, Giulio (1580–1635). Italian architect and scene designer. He was a student and assistant to **Buontalenti** whom he succeeded in 1608 as architect at the Medici court. Like his mentor, he became responsible for the decor for court festivities, the most important of which he designed in 1606, 1608, 1615 and 1616. In addition to influencing the work of German architect **Josef Furttenbach**, he became the teacher of the English designer **Inigo Jones**, thus disseminating the technology of stage machinery and movable scenery to Germany and England. His most important designs included *Il Guidizio di Paride* (1608), a pastoral with intermezzi and *naumachia* in honour of Prince Cosimo's marriage to Archduchess Maria Magdalena; *Eros and Anteros* (1613); *The Liberation of Tyrrhenus* (1616), an intermezzo performed at carnival time before the Medici court; and *La Guerra d'Amore* (1616), an equestrian ballet for which a wooden amphitheatre had to be constructed. In 1620 he was replaced as designer for the Medici by his son Alfonso (d. 1656). AJN

Park Theatre 21–25 Park Row, New York City [Architect: Joseph Mangin]. In 1795, tired of the deteriorating and déclassé **John Street Theatre**, a group of prominent New Yorkers subscribed money to erect a new theatre in an area which promised to become the heart of the early 19th-century city. Three years later, it opened as the New Theatre in an unfinished state. The unattractive exterior belied a comfortable and handsome interior, which was designed continental-style with three tiers of boxes overhanging a U-shaped pit with a gallery above the highest tier. The first managers were actors **John Hodgkinson** and **Lewis Hallam**, who moved their John Street company into the new house. **William Dunlap** was added to the management and he suc-

Interior of the Park Theatre, New York, 1822.

ceeded them as sole manager for several years until he was forced into bankruptcy in 1805. The house, now known as the Park, was bought by John Jacob Astor and John Beekman, who eventually leased it in 1808 to **Stephen Price**. Credited with introducing the 'star system' to American theatre practice, Price bolstered flagging box office receipts by importing English stars and managing their tours. In 1810, he brought over **George Frederick Cooke** and in 1820, he lured **Edmund Kean** to America. Because he spent so much time in England, Price left actor Edmund Simpson in charge of the theatre during his absences. In 1820, the Park burned to its exterior walls, but was rebuilt the following year. For more than a decade, the Park established itself as the first theatre in the land with an outstanding resident company. In addition to English stars, it helped to create such American stars as **Edwin Forrest** and **Charlotte Cushman**. In its last decades, the high status of the Park was eclipsed and Simpson was forced to place meretricious fare on its stage. In 1848, fire again consumed the house and the Astor heirs replaced it with commercial buildings.   MCH

Parker, Louis Napoleon (1852–1944) Dramatist, composer and pageant-master, born in France, whose light comedies, melodramas and historical plays were staple popular fare for the English stage between 1890 and 1919. Between 1892 and 1905 he regularly had as many as four plays produced in London during a single year, and he also wrote specifically for the American stage (*The Mayflower*, 1897; *The Woman and the Sheriff*, 1911). The popularity of his plays was largely due to the strong acting parts they offered, the best of which, *Disraeli* with **George Arliss** in the title role, was revived several times and had a long run in New York. In addition he gained a reputation as a deviser and producer of civic pageants throughout England as well as in the Lord Mayor's procession (1907, 1908) and on patriotic themes in London during the First World War, culminating in *The Pageant of Drury Lane* at the **Drury Lane Theatre** in 1918.   CI

Parker, Stewart (1941–88) Irish playwright. His *Spokesong* (1975) is an entertaining satire, with music, on the North's history of sectarian dispute. *Catchpenny Twist* (1977), somewhat resembling the Auden–Isherwood plays of the 1930s, views the present North of bombs and assassinations through the career of two aspiring pop musicians. From a mélange of conjuring, fairy and mystery tale, *Nightshade* (1980) presents illusion as a way of life. *Northern Star* (1984) composes a pastiche of Irish writers as part of its commentary on the 1798 rebellion. Parker's plays enunciate his 'instinct for play itself . . . a quintessentially ludicrous theatre'.   DM

Parody Burlesque, parody, and satire are often treated as synonyms for ridicule through distortion, but it is useful to suggest distinctions between them. None of the three words refers exclusively to drama; yet all have been applied to drama. In point of time, parody is the first to enter European languages, deriving through the French from the Greek, where it means a song by the side, or a mocking of another song. Setting **Aeschylus** against **Euripides**, **Aristophanes** parodies both of them in a famous scene in his comedy

The Frogs. Since parody caricatures a particular figure or work, it rarely embraces a whole play. Recently, parody has been analysed by Linda Hutcheon (*Theory of Parody*, 1984) as a technique of ironic inversion, which spans all the arts, and which is embedded in art rather than life. Though few of her examples are drawn from drama, she does mention **Brecht**'s *Threepenny Opera* and *Arturo Ui*.   RC

Parsons, Estelle (1927–) American actress. Best known for her brash Academy Award-winning performance in *Bonnie and Clyde* (1967), Parsons prefers theatre, which she considers an actor's medium, to film, which she feels belongs to directors and editors. With her sharp nasal voice and lived-in face, Parsons sounds and looks refreshingly real; and though she was trained in **Lee Strasberg**'s method of psychological realism she has eagerly sought work in other styles, from **Shakespeare** to musical theatre. Dedicated to acting and indifferent to money or prestige, she says she will go anywhere for a challenging role. Her richest parts on Broadway have been as **Tennessee Williams**'s dotty, good-natured stripper in *The Seven Descents of Myrtle* (1968), as the alcoholic title character in *And Miss Reardon Drinks a Little* (1971), in the Public Theatre's *Pirates of Penzance* (1981), and as the caustic, deranged, dictatorial schoolteacher in Roberto Athayde's *Miss Margarida's Way* (1977), a virtuoso one-woman show in which she fenced improvisationally with the audience, exchanging quips and issuing reprimands. Her experiments Off-Broadway and regionally include **Brecht**'s *Mahagonny* (1970), June Havoc's *Tintinnabulation of the Bells* at the **Actors Studio** (1975), Lady Macbeth at the University of Hawaii (1980), and another one-woman extravaganza, **Dario Fo**'s *Orgasmo Adulto Escapes from the Zoo* (1983).   FH

Pasadena Playhouse Founded in 1917 by Gilmour Brown and incorporated in 1918, the Pasadena Playhouse grew into an important theatre institution. Brown depended upon amateur talent and volunteer help. He built a new theatre in 1925, added a school for training actors in 1928, and an intimate Playbox Theatre in 1929. Premieres of new works, including **O'Neill**'s *Lazarus Laughed* (1928), and revivals of seldom-produced classics made the Playhouse famous. Beginning in 1935 it offered a series of Midsummer Drama Festivals which attracted wide attention. The theatre gained a reputation as a showcase for aspiring film actors with Randolph Scott, **Tyrone Power**, and Robert Young among those stars discovered. Brown served 31 years as President and retired as director of the Playhouse in 1959. In decline, the Playhouse closed and its properties were sold in 1970.   TLM

Páskándi, Géza (1933–) Hungarian playwright. As a member of the Hungarian minority in Rumania, he studied at Bolyai University in Kolozsvár, and was imprisoned for political reasons (1957–63); he has lived in Budapest since 1974. His coinage, 'absurdoid', characterizes his drama, in which absurdity is presented as an *aspect* of life: as the creation of his characters, or as something that unexpectedly visits itself upon them. In historical dramas, e.g., *Sojourn* (1970), *The Hiding Place* (1972), and *Residents of the Windmill* (1981), Páskándi seamlessly combines psychological realism with the absurdity elicited by external and internal constraints. His plays have been performed in theatres throughout Hungary, including the National. His *oeuvre* includes poetry, short stories, and essays. His work has appeared in seven other languages.   EB

Pasku Pasku is a Roman Catholic Passion play which originated in the Catholic areas of Jaffna in northern Sri Lanka in the late 19th century and migrated to the Sinhalese-speaking Catholic regions of the western coastal region shortly thereafter. Traditionally, it began in Passion Week and lasted for the entire Holy Week. In some congregations, the actors are replaced by life-size statues depicting the central characters in the episodes of Christ's death and resurrection. The statues move and create stage pictures above and behind six-foot-high temporary walls. Painted scenes ascend to nearly 20 feet behind the figures. A reciter stands between the audience seated on the ground, and the statues interpreting each scene of the well-known biblical stories. In some locales live actors enact the drama wearing historical costumes of the period. Whether statues or live actors are used, performances incorporate Christian church music and sometimes even Western musical instruments, such as the organ, are employed as accompaniment.

Several notable plays were written and produced by K. Lawrence Perera of Boralessa whose ambition was to imitate the famous **Oberammergau** Passion Play. He created the Shridhara Boralessa Passion Play in 1923 which drew together unschooled actors from among local village folk from virtually every humble profession of the area. Over a hundred performers participated to create the epic. The stage consisted of five sections arranged like the **Rukada** puppet theatre with a central acting area and side wings stretching out to the right and left. A sensation occurred in 1939 when it was announced that all the female roles would be played by women. The Archbishop of Colombo banned the performance on the grounds that it violated the decorum of the country for women to act on the same stage with men. Although they were not pleased, the actors gave in to church pressure.   FaR

Paso see **Género chico**

Pastor, Tony (Antonio) (1837–1908) American variety performer and manager, called 'The Father of Vaudeville'. The son of a theatre violinist, he made his professional debut in 1846 as an infant prodigy at **Barnum**'s Museum. He later travelled as a circus clown, minstrel and ballad-singer, with a repertory of some 1,500 songs, arranging concerts in small towns. He first booked variety into the rowdy American Theatre, at 444 Broadway, New York (1861) and, determined to attract a respectable audience, took over the Volksgarten at 201 Bowery in 1865. Renaming it the Opera House, Pastor advertised it as 'The Great Family Resort' and invited women and children to special matinees, but even door-prizes of turkeys, hams and barrels of flour were insufficient to attract a Godfearing public. The fat man with the waxed moustache and mincing step moved his clean bill of variety to 585 Broadway in 1875, where he introduced the theatre check-room, and then to 14th Street in 1881.

There he finally succeeded in promoting clean vaudeville to a family audience, paving the way for Keith and Albee; performers he sponsored include **Nat Goodwin**, **Lillian Russell** and **Weber** and **Fields**. A devout Catholic who kept a shrine backstage, he continued to pay low salaries, lost his stars to sharper managers and died a relatively poor man.   LS

Pastoral The pastoral form found its way into drama by way of poetry. Theocritus and Virgil provided a classical precedent, carried into renaissance Italy not least in the dramatic work of Poliziano and Beccari. **Tasso**'s *L'Aminta* (1573) is generally regarded as the first true pastoral play, but the genre is not easily defined. Pastorals generally depict the happy outcome of faithful love in a removed, rural setting. **Guarini**'s *Il Pastor Fido* (1596) influenced one of the finest English examples, **Fletcher**'s *The Faithful Shepherdess* (1608). **Lyly**'s *Love's Metamorphosis* (c. 1589) looked to Spanish as well as Italian models. **Philip Sidney**'s influential prose romance, *Arcadia* (published 1590), was avowedly inspired by the Spanish Jorge de Montemayor's *Diana* (c. 1560), and itself became the source of **James Shirley**'s play *The Arcadia* (c. 1630). In much the same way, **Shakespeare** built *As You Like It* out of Thomas Lodge's pastoral romance *Rosalynde* (1590). The rudimentary dramatic form of the dialogues that comprise Spenser's *The Shepherd's Calendar* (1597) is a closer formal model for **John Day**'s *The Parliament of Bees* (written c. 1595), which was intended for recitation rather than theatrical performance, but which indicates the ease with which the charms of pastoral poetry could be accommodated in the language of the court masque. Pastoral plays had a longer life in the French theatre, above all in the work of **Jean Mairet**, than they did in England, though Milton's *Comus* (1634) belongs to the genre as securely as had **Peele**'s masterpiece, *The Old Wives Tale* (published 1595), and **Ben Jonson** left an unfinished pastoral, *The Sad Shepherd*, at his death.   PT

Patrick, John (1905–   ) American playwright. This prolific writer has been a favourite among American regional theatres, dinner theatres, and amateur groups. His two best remembered Broadway successes both grew out of the Second World War. *The Hasty Heart* (1945) told the touching story of an obstreperous Scottish soldier dying in a field hospital filled with a comic group of recuperating soldiers, representing most of the Allied armies, tended by a sympathetic nurse. *The Teahouse of the August Moon* (1953) pictured the foibles of an attempt to Americanize an Okinawan village. Regional and amateur groups also continue to revive *The Curious Savage* (1950) and *Everybody Loves Opal* (1961). Patrick lives in the Virgin Islands where he writes two or three plays a year for companies seeking light, entertaining comedies.   LDC

Paulding, James Kirke (1778–1860) is significant in American theatre for two reasons. Writing about 'American Drama' for the *American Quarterly Review* (1827), he urged a carefully supported 'National Drama'. His play, *The Lion of the West* (1830), won a prize from **James H. Hackett** and, after revisions by **John Augustus Stone** and William Bayle Bernard, opened at **Covent Garden** in 1833 as *The Kentuckian*.

Hackett enjoyed considerable success in the role of Colonel Nimrod Wildfire, a genial imitation of Davy Crockett.   WJM

Paulus (Paul Habans) (1845–1908) One of the earliest stars of the French music-hall, the first to earn a huge salary (400 francs a night in 1888) and to rely heavily on publicity. His career was a series of ups and downs in Paris and Marseilles, quarrels with managers, broken contracts and attacks by the censors. Then, in 1886, he won glory by adding a topical verse about General Boulanger to the song 'En revenant de la revue', which became epidemic. A strenuous performer with a stentorian voice, he founded and edited *La Revue des Concerts* (1887) as a vent for his vindictiveness; toured to London and America (1891–2); and managed the Ba-ta-clan and the Marseilles Alhambra unsuccessfully, before retiring in 1903.   LS

Pavai Kathakali (India) This is a unique form of glove puppet theatre in which dolls with wooden heads and hands are designed and decorated to imitate various characters in the repertory of the **Kathakali** dance-drama of Kerala state, south India. The figures are about one to one and a half feet tall and are operated by a manipulator who sticks his middle finger into the head of the figure. His thumb and little finger operate its hands. A cloth skirt resembling that of the *Kathakali* dancers masks the manipulator's arm halfway to the elbow.

The stories are drawn from the *Mahabharata* and follow the *Kathakali* pattern of organization. Musical accompaniment is played by bell-metal cymbals and the *cenda* drum. The manipulation is done by at least four puppeteers standing behind a curtain stretched between poles. They hold the glove puppets above their heads to perform.

The artists come from the village of Kavadi Parambu in Palghat district and are relatively secretive about their art form which is rarely seen today, and generally only on religious occasions.   FaR

Pavai Koothu (India) In Thiruchendoor, a city in Tamil Nadu, *Pavai koothu*, a glove puppet theatre form which may have originated in the 16th century, is performed. The language of performance is Tamil. *Pavai* means 'woman' and *koothu* means a 'play'.

Puppets are about a foot tall. Heads and arms are made of papier mâché. Costumes are simple, constructed of cloth and garlanded with coconut fibre or paper. The stories centre on Vali, a female attendant of Shiva, and her love for Subramanya, one of Shiva's sons. On Shiva's advice Vali was born to a deer in the forest. A hunter found her and he and his wife reared her. Seeing the beautiful maiden one day in the forest, Narada, divine trouble maker, hastened to tell Lord Subramanya about the fetching beauty. Infatuated by Narada's description, Subramanya disguised himself as an old bangle seller and came to the hunter's cottage in the forest. Through a ruse, he took Vali far from her home and then revealed himself to her in his heavenly form. They embraced and received the blessings of Ganesha, who appeared to them in the form of an elephant, an auspicious sign.

To manipulate the puppets, the thumb and little finger are inserted in the arms of the puppet and the middle finger works the head. The performance is given by a single manipulator who sits cross-legged behind a simple wooden box, just large enough to mask him from view. He is accompanied by an *idakka* drummer and a singer who keeps the time with bell-metal cymbals. Popular tunes are sung, liberally borrowing from folk melodies of the region.   FaR

Pavaikuthu (India) Also called *tholpavaikuthu. Pava* means 'figure of a shadow' and *kuthu* means 'play'. The *Pavaikuthu* is the shadow puppet theatre of Kerala state, south India. The form relates the stories drawn from a Tamil version of the *Ramayana* called *Kambar Ramayana*, named after Kambar, its author, and written for a Chola king in the 9th century AD. The origin of the form is not certain but it has unique characteristics which distinguish it from other forms of shadow puppet theatre in south India, including the fact that the people of the region in which the performance takes place speak Malayalam not Tamil, which is the language of the drama. *Pavaikuthu* is usually performed near the *sanctum sanctorum* of Kali temples as a ritual form of entertainment for the goddess. Processions and general celebrations are part of every programme.

The puppets are short, stout silhouettes as small as 4 inches and as large as 36 inches tall, made of antelope doe skin, thought to be holy. They are often called *ola pava* which refers to the thickness of the skin. Because of their thickness the puppets are not translucent, a marked deviation from the shadow puppets found elsewhere in India. Indeed, the silhouettes projected on the screen are only outlines of the figures created by shapes with minimal perforations made in the leather to delineate costume and ornament. The puppets are held against the screen by a short strip of bamboo attached to the trunk of the puppet by string. They are pressed tightly against the screen by a thorn pin or spike. The shadows are articulated by movable heads, arms and hands. Puppets with no movable parts are usually less important characters. In general, the *ola pava* are not nearly as refined as the Javanese *wayang* of either the *Jojga* or *Solo* styles and they are probably more closely related to the Malaysian shadows.

Performances are held in specifically constructed enclosures called *kuthumadom* which are about 42 feet long, 9 feet deep and about 4 feet above ground level. These special stage houses are placed at an elevated end of a broad stretch of temple compound. The shadows usually face south, though the practice varies depending on the direction that the deity faces. The long narrow opening in the *kuthumadom* is completely draped to create a screen about 18 feet long and 5 feet high, the upper portion of which is white and the lower portion black.

Below the white screen a long strip of bamboo is stretched horizontally in which grooves are cut, and coconut halves or small earthen vessels are placed in the holes to serve as lamps. Wicks are made from bits of rag tightly wrapped and fed by coconut oil. These lamps are the only source of illumination.

In *Pavaikuthu*, manipulators squat below the white portion of the screen masked by the black curtain and operate the puppets from behind a row of lamps. The position minimizes the chance that their shadows will fall on the screen.

A performance usually begins when drums are played and a wick from the *sanctum sanctorum* of the Kali temple is brought in procession to the *kuthumadom* to light the wicks of the oil lamps behind the screen. This ritual is called *kotti kayattam* which means 'installing the puppets to the sound of the drums'. Next, a special ritual sacrifice is offered to Ganapati, the elephant-headed god of success and beginnings. After the installation ceremony, all but two of the puppets are removed from the screen.

Gangayati Patter and Muther Patter, the remaining characters, praise the gurus of *Pavaikuthu*, past and present, invoke the blessing of specific gods and, if patronized by a family, bless the household. Then, they provide a summary of the previous night's story which serves as a prologue to the events about to take place. The episodes of the local version of the *Ramayana* are enacted in sequence.

The conclusion to the story is the grand coronation of Rama. The sacrifice to Ganapati is again performed and the *kirita pava* (clown) performs a ritual of his own, after which Rama appears wearing his crown. At this point, the show is over. The night of the coronation scene is enlivened by a procession beginning from the innermost part of the temple to the *kuthumadom* to pay homage to Rama whose spirit is worshipped in the puppet. FaR

Pavlovsky, Eduardo (1933–) Argentine playwright, actor and director. Also a medical doctor, specialist in psychoanalysis. Studied in New York, and in Buenos Aires founded a specialized theatre group. Protesting the absurd political situation, he considers himself a representative of what he calls 'exasperated realism'. From the psychoanalytic position of early plays, such as *La espera trágica* (*Tragic Wait*, 1964), he turned to more committed socio-political plays with *La mueca* (*The Grimace*, 1971), *El Señor Galíndez* (*Mr Galíndez*, 1973), *Telarañas* (*Spiderwebs*, 1976), and *El Señor Laforgue* (*Mr Laforgue*, 1982). *Galíndez* and *Laforgue* are particularly outspoken about brutality, torture and repressive political actions in Argentina and Haiti, respectively. GW

Pavy, Salathiel (Solomon) (c. 1590 – c. 1603) English boy-actor, who may have begun with the **Boys of St Paul's** before joining the **Children of the Chapel Royal**, for whom he acted in **Jonson's** *Cynthia's Revels* (1600) and *Poetaster* (1601). It is to Jonson's touching Epitaph that Pavy owes his immortality. Though 'scarce thirteen' when he died, he was, Jonson claims, the 'stage's jewel' for 'three fill'd zodiacs', so skilled in the playing of old men that even sophisticated spectators thought him one. PT

Payne, Ben Iden (1881–1976) British director, whose experience as an actor with **Frank Benson's** company and as stage director at the **Abbey Theatre** in Dublin directly contributed to the success of Miss **Horniman's** repertory company in Manchester, which he managed from its inception in 1907 until 1911. From 1913 until 1934 he was active in American theatre – directing in Chicago and New York, appointed Artistic Director of the Little Theatre, Philadelphia (1914), and of the **Goodman Theatre**, Chicago (1926). In charge of the School of Drama at the Carnegie Institute from 1919, he directed for the **Theatre Guild** in 1928–9, and in 1934 became Director of the Shakespeare Memorial Theatre at Stratford-upon-Avon. Returning to America in 1943, again at the Carnegie Institute and the Theatre Guild, he inaugurated a summer Shakespeare Festival in San Diego (1949–52) and directed productions of **Shakespeare** at the Oregon Festival (1956 and 1961) and in Alberta (1958–60 and 1962), being given the Rodgers and Hammerstein Award for distinguished services to the theatre in 1962. CI

Payne, John Howard (1791–1852) American actor and playwright. Now remembered for the lyrics to 'Home, Sweet Home!' (music by H. R. Bishop) in his *Clari, or the Maid of Milan* (**Covent Garden**, 1823), he wrote or translated and adapted from the French some sixty plays. Among the best known are *Brutus, or the Fall of Tarquin* (with **Edmund Kean**, **Drury Lane**, 1818 and with **Edwin Forrest** in New York, 1829); *Thérèse, or the Orphan of Geneva* (Drury Lane, 1821 and with Forrest in New York, 1829); *Clari*; and two collaborations with Washington Irving, *Charles II, or the Merry Monarch* (Covent Garden, 1824); and *Richelieu* (Covent Garden, 1826). In spite of close friendships with Irving, Coleridge, and **Lamb**, and in Paris with **Talma** who encouraged him to translate French melodramas, and his occasional appearances as an actor and one season as manager of **Sadler's Wells** (1820), Payne's years abroad (1813–32) were marked by financial distress. Twice he was confined to debtor's prison.

He made his acting debut as Young Norval in **Home's** *Douglas* (New York's **Park Theatre**, 1809), appeared as Hamlet and Romeo, quickly became known as 'Master Payne, the American **Roscius**' and was favourably compared with 'Master **Betty**'.

His writing debut came earlier with little magazines: *The Fly* (co-edited with **Samuel Woodworth**, 1804); *Thespian Mirror* (1805); and his first play *Julia, or The Wanderer* (1806).

In 1842 President Tyler appointed Payne Consul at Tunis (a reward for his crusade on behalf of the Cherokee Indians) where he served until 1845 and again from 1851 until his death. RM

Peele, George (1558–96) English playwright, son of a salter. Having graduated from Oxford, Peele became associated with other **University Wits**, **Greene**, **Nashe** and **Marlowe** among them, in the uncertain world of professional writing. Two civic pageants survive from an unknown number as well as several interesting examples of court-ceremonial verse. Peele's earliest extant play, *The Arraignment of Paris* (1581–4), was written for performance by the **Children of the Chapel Royal** before the Queen. It is a lifeless debate-play, distinguished only by the beautiful songs so characteristic of Peele. *The Battle of Alcazar* (c. 1598) provided **Edward Alleyn** with a role reminiscent of Marlowe's Tamburlane. *Edward I* (c. 1593) deploys historical characters in apocryphal adventures. *The Love of King David and Fair Bethsabe* (c. 1594) is much more unified in style and moral purpose, but Peele is better remembered for *The Old Wives Tale* (published 1595), a unique play which combines good-hearted parody of contemporary dramatic styles with a lyrical delight in story-telling. PT

Pekin Theatre (1904–12) Situated in Chicago's black district, the Pekin was opened for vaudeville entertainment by Robert T. Motts as part of his saloon and restaurant business. Within a year Motts had hired an all-black stock company of young actors, singers and dancers, a producing staff, resident orchestra, writers and composers, and gave nightly performances of original musical comedies with a new show every two or three weeks. Rebuilt after a 1906 fire, the Pekin seated 900 on floor, gallery, and in 30 private boxes reserved for whites. It was 'scrupulously clean, neat and tasteful' and in its finest season, 1907, produced 25 original musicals. The departure of its star comedian Harrison Stewart, the growing popularity of 'picture shows', stiff competition from rival vaudeville houses, and the early death of its gifted director–playwright–actor J. Ed Green in 1910 and of Motts in 1911 led to the theatre's decline and eventual closing.   EGH

Pene du Bois, Raoul (1914–85) American set and costume designer who began his career at the age of 14 designing some costumes for the *Garrick Gaieties*. From the 1930s on he designed many shows and musicals ranging from *DuBarry Was a Lady* and *Jumbo* to *Wonderful Town* and *No, No, Nanette*. He also designed for films, ballets, ice shows and the Rockettes. His designs are typified by a strong sense of colour, and a certain whimsicality of line.   AA

Penny gaff see **Penny theatres**

Penny theatres Cheap minor playhouses which arose in Regency London and which allowed amateurs, on payment of a fee, to play roles of their choice; **Dickens** penned a classic description of them in *Sketches by Boz*. First known as 'dukeys', the earliest was an unnamed booth at the back of the Westminster Theatre in the Broadway; it was copied by Hector Simpson's Vine Yard, Tooley Street, which specialized in dog drama, and Bryant's Varieties, New Road, Sloane Square, where Richard III cost a fiver and the Lord Mayor six shillings to enact. Performing without a licence, these houses were frequently closed: the Bower Saloon, Stangate, which presented a pantomime three times daily was suppressed in 1838. But the Theatres Act of 1843 spawned a spate of low-priced professional houses; their emphasis on gruesome true-crime melodramas like *Maria Marten* was another nuisance to the authorities, who put down the Dust Hole in Tottenham Court Road in 1858 for its staging of *The Bloodspot or The Maiden, the Miser and the Murderer*. Legally, spoken dialogue was not permitted, but the statute was honoured more in the breach than the observance.

Henry Mayhew, who visited several 'penny gaffs', as they had come to be known, in the early 1860s, found them a crude descendant of the fairground booth, pandering to a juvenile public with obscenity and horseplay. The Rotunda in the Blackfriar's Road was the largest, seating 1,000, and giving two performances an evening at a top-price of threepence; but the average might offer six performances of 'flash' singing and dancing in a converted warehouse.

The New York equivalent was the Grand Duke's Opera House, located in a Baxter St cellar and operated by street boys, with tallow candles as footlights, wash-tubs as private boxes, and a six-cent admission fee. Throughout the 1870s, it was a favourite Bohemian resort, and **Weber** and **Fields** got their start there.   LS

See: P. Sheridan, *Penny Theatres of Victorian London*, London, 1981.

People's National Theatre (London) Founded in 1930 by the actress Nancy Price, who had begun her career with **Frank Benson**'s company in 1899, it was based on similar ideas to the Scottish National Theatre Society or the New York **Theatre Guild**. Its first production was a revival of Anstey's *The Man from Blankley's* at the **Fortune Theatre**, and in 1932 a permanent home was found at the Little Theatre, a 309-seat house until then mainly identified with **Grand–Guignol** and Revue. There was an extensive programme of non-commercial drama was presented ranging from **Euripides** to **Pirandello**, though Price also staged (and acted in) Mazo de la Roche's *Whiteoaks* which ran for two years. The venture came to an end when the Little Theatre was destroyed in 1941.   CI

Pepper's Ghost A theatrical effect, whereby an actor standing at a 90° angle in the orchestra-pit below the level of the stage is lit so that his reflection is cast on a sheet of glass mounted between the audience and the stage, thus producing the impression of a phantom. The illusion was invented by a retired civil engineer named Henry Dircks, who sold it, as the Ætheroscope, in 1862 to John Henry Pepper, director of the

Henri Robin menaced by his own version of the Pepper's Ghost illusion.

Polytechnic Institution, London. It was first used there for a dramatic reading of **Dickens**'s *The Haunted Man* on Christmas Eve of that year, and the many theatres that pirated it were soon forced to pay Pepper a royalty, so that 'Pepper's Ghost' became current as the term for any trick-effect in raising stage spectres. It was introduced to the United States by Harry Watkins in a melodrama, *True to the Last*, **Wallack**'s Theatre, New York (1863), and for the next two months New York managers presented horror shows teeming with ghosts. The illusion eventually was superseded by the use of back-lit scrim.   LS

Pepys, Samuel (1633–1703) English diarist. He began writing his great Diary in 1660 as a rising young civil servant working in the Navy Office. He gave it up in 1669 believing that he was going blind. Throughout its nine years, Pepys recorded his impressions of his great love, the theatre, providing the earliest English account of regular play-going. If some of his critical comments are notoriously dogmatic, e.g. announcing that *A Midsummer Night's Dream* was 'the most insipid ridiculous play that ever I saw in my life', his tastes were broad and his pleasure in theatre is infectious. In his numerous comments on the players, the scenery, the other members of the audience and the plays he vividly records the Restoration theatre.   PH

Peretz, Isaac Loeb (1852–1915) Polish-born playwright who directed the Hazomir Group in Warsaw. The most notable of his plays are *The Sisters* (1904) dealing with the extreme poverty of the Jews in Poland, and *Night in the Old Market*, an eerie, atmospheric,

Michal Swejlich as the Rabbi in Isaac Loeb Peretz's *Night in the Old Market*.

poetic fantasy first produced by Alexander Granowski for the **Moscow State Jewish Theatre** (1925) and offering a challenge to Art Theatres ever since.   AB

Performance Group, The One of the most controversial and visible of the environmental theatre groups of the 1960s and 70s, formed in New York City in 1967 by Richard Schechner, critic, director, and former editor of *The Drama Review* (a post resumed in 1985). Although in practice the work of the Group often seemed amateurish and self-indulgent, Schechner broke through traditional barriers of a text and stage-bound theatre with productions such as *Dionysus in 69* (1968), *Makbeth* (1969), *Commune* (1970), and *The Balcony* (1979). Schechner's ideas were codified somewhat in his book on *Environmental Theatre* (1973). Though only partially successful, Schechner's group, performing in the Performing Garage in Wooster Street, was notable for its risk-taking, its concern with social issues, and, with some direct influence from **Grotowski**, an investigation into ritual and the use of other cultures in the development of a new performance art. Schechner left the Garage in 1980 and the Group, renamed the Wooster Group, has continued under the nominal leadership of **Elizabeth LeCompte**.   DBW

Performing Arts Company of the Centre for Nigerian Cultural Studies (CNCS) Nigerian professional performing arts company, based in Zaria in northern Nigeria, is subsidized by the Cultural Institute of Ahmadu Bello University (ABU). The company is loosely connected through its personnel to the ABU Studio Theatre – the 'Mud Theatre' – purpose-built by traditional Hausa craftsmen in the style of a Hausa compound, with decorated mud and thatch, as a facility for African theatre research.

The CNCS Performing Arts Company travels within Nigeria and abroad. It has its own Training School which exports talent and expertise around Nigeria and which has acted as a catalyst in establishing the performing arts all over northern Nigeria. Dexter Lyndersay established the Company in Kano; he was succeeded by Andrew Horn who with Peter Badejo, the dancer and choreographer, created the dance-mime *Fadakarwa* in 1976 which achieved notable success. The CNCS Performing Arts Company also included the brilliant actor and playwright Kasimu Yero, whose weekly television plays in Hausa which he devised through improvisation with a group of actors had huge ratings in the seventies. Other actors were absorbed into film-acting, like the late Umaru Ladan who starred in the film of his own play *Shehu Umar*. In the 1980s the choreography of Peter Badejo has combined with the Nigerian music experiments of jazz musician Yusuf Lateef to create balletic pieces which greatly extend a Hausa-Fulani and partly Islamic performance aesthetic.

The 'Mud Theatre' has enabled Drama students from all over Nigeria to develop a Pidgin drama for the Nigerian cities. The plays of 'Segun Oyekunle (who has now branched into film-making) and of Tunde Lakoju were premiered in the theatre in the late 1970s.   ME

Perkins, Osgood (1892–1937) American stage and film actor, noted for his versatility and polish. He graduated from Harvard in 1914 after having participated in some of the **George Pierce Baker** plays. He served in the First World War, then formed the Film Guild, a cinematic production company, and appeared in several of its productions. **Winthrop Ames** then cast him as Homer Cady in *Beggar on Horseback*, his Broadway debut. **Jed Harris** then hired him for *Weak Sisters*; Perkins later appeared as Walter Burns in *The Front Page*, 1928, and Astroff in *Uncle Vanya*, 1930. He also appeared in films such as *Scarface* and *Madame Du Barry*. He was described as 'wiry, nervous, [and] unerring in his attack'. Perkins's son, Anthony, has enjoyed a highly successful stage and film acting career. SMA

Peru Accounts of the legendary riches of the Incas reached the Spanish even before the Spanish reached Peru. Atahualpa filled rooms with silver and gold but was nonetheless betrayed by his conqueror Pizarro, an act that symbolized the treachery of the Spanish in dealing with these cultured Indians. The Inca Garcilaso de la Vega (1539–1616) wrote in his chronicles both of tragedies and comedies performed by the Indians as well as the *tarquis*, ritual festivals set to music representing nature's sacred cosmovision. As early as 1546, Cuzco, then the capital, was the usual site of the religious and secular works offered on feast days of the church or in celebration of a secular event (the crowning of a king, the arrival of a viceroy). The first theatre building constructed in Lima in the late 16th century served for performances of the Golden Age plays in vogue as well as an occasional local work. Arequipa, located on the route from Lima to Potosí, also boasted early theatrical productions, but Lima, as the major cultural centre in all of South America, fomented the most theatre. The early writers included the satirical poet Juan del Valle y Caviedes (1652–94), who wrote **loas** and *entremeses*, as did Lorenzo de las Llamosas (1665–1705) and others. The major figure was Pedro de Peralta Barnuevo (1664–1743), who wrote historical plays with French and Greek motifs, as well as folkloric works with prototypes of colonial society. An internationally-known actress of the time was Michaela Villegas, known as La Perricholi, who captivated Lima with her talents (and apparently the heart of the Viceroy Amat as well, a man fascinated with French encyclopaedism).

The tempo of dramatic activity increased in the latter part of the 18th century, even though the century was not on the whole a productive time for the arts. Around 1780 the growing resentment with Spain produced rebellions led by Tupac Amaru II, the great Inca leader whose exploits and heroism were recaptured in 19th- and 20th-century drama. In his presence Padre Antonio Valdés directed a performance near Cuzco of the **Ollantay**, an allegedly pre-Columbian play in Quechua that recounts love and war among the Indians before the arrival of the Spanish.

After General San Martín withdrew to the south in 1822, Bolívar imposed independence on Peru in spite of the lack of enthusiasm of the local citizenry. The theatre during the 19th century was dominated by two major playwrights whose styles are quite different from each other. Felipe Pardo y Aliaga (1806–68), perhaps because his formative years were spent in Spain, followed the Hispanic tradition, writing elevated,

lightly satirical pieces such as *Frutos de la educación* (*The Fruits of Education*, 1830), considered to be the first dramatic work of independent Peru. With a neoclassical posture and technique, the play examined the value of education. Pardo's counterpart, Manuel Ascencio Segura (1805–71), on the other hand, was more lively and spontaneous in his efforts to capture local colour and life in a popular vein. His *Ña Catita* (1856), the portrait of a Lima matchmaker, is still the best known most played Peruvian work.

20th century The early part of the century witnessed a continuation of the romantic and costumbristic theatre of the previous century. Among others, José Chioino (1898–1960) was representative of this period in which few plays were written and few groups were active. In 1938 the creation of the Asociación de Artistas Aficionados (Association of Amateur Artists) as a private institution dedicated to the promotion of the arts, including ballet and music, was a first major step in renovating the moribund theatre. Bernardo Roca Rey (1918–84) developed as its principal director, and the AAA theatre now carries his name.

In the years immediately following the Second World War, when a new excitement about the world community was growing in Lima, several events helped the theatre to prosper. The Compañía Nacional de Comedias (National Drama Company) was created in 1945, and the ENAE (Escuela Nacional de Arte Escénico, National School of Dramatic Art) was formed the same year, later reorganized as the Instituto Nacional de Arte Escénico (National Institute of Dramatic Art). The ubiquitous Margarita Xirgú toured Peru with her exciting versions of **García Lorca**, and three new playwrights appeared in response to the national theatre contest of 1946–7: Percy Gibson Parra (b. 1908) wrote *Esa luna que empieza* (*That Crescent Moon*), a successful poetic and metaphysical play. Juan Ríos (b. 1914) with *Don Quixote* and **Sebastián Salazar Bondy** (1924–65) with *Amor, gran laberinto* (*Love, the Great Labyrinth*) launched overlapping careers with different styles. Ríos followed a more traditional and universal tradition while Salazar Bondy, more experimental and nationalistic, established a sense of a new Peruvian drama, and became Peru's best known playwright on an international scale. **Gregor Díaz** (b. 1933) collaborated with the Club de Teatro (Theatre Club) and wrote strong social protest plays such as *La huelga* (*Strike*, 1966). *Collacocha* (1958) by **Enrique Solari Swayne** (b. 1915) set the tone for high-level national tragedy in its treatment of a civil engineer defeated by the powerful forces of nature. Other major writers of the period include Julio Ramón Ribeyro (b. 1929), Edgardo Pérez Luna (b. 1928) and Víctor Zavala (b. 1932), who deals especially with problems of peasant classes. Two exiled playwrights took university positions in the United States: Julio Ortega (b. 1942), author of 18 short plays including the documentary/drama *Mesa pelada* (1972), and **Alonso Alegría** (b. 1940), former director of the Teatro Nacional Popular (National Popular Theatre) and author of *El cruce sobre el Niágara* (*Niagara Crossing*, 1969), a prize-winning rendition of existential values predicated on the 19th-century French tightrope artist, **Blondin**. Peru's internationally known novelist of the 'boom', Mario Vargas Llosa (b. 1936), turned to theatre

Pilar Nuñez in Mario Delgado's *Retazos*, Lima, Peru, 1981.

in 1981 with *La señorita de Tacna* (*The Girl from Tacna*), an excellent play dramatizing the process of storytelling, followed in 1983 by *Kathie y el hipopótamo* (*Kathie and the Hippopotamus*).

Although Peru has produced important writers and some major plays, the theatre has not developed as an organic, cohesive national phenomenon. The government is unable and/or unwilling to patronize the arts, and the 20 or more theatre groups that operate in and around Lima maintain a precarious existence. Theatre fare is sparse for a city of four million inhabitants, and young playwrights do not receive much encouragement or support. Theatre groups appear and disappear. One of the oldest is the TUSM (Teatro de la Universidad de San Marcos, San Marcos University Theatre), originally established in 1941. Directed by Guillermo Ugarte Chamorro since 1968, it sponsors an active season and maintains an ambitious publication programme devoted to all aspects of theatre. The most significant and transcendent group is the Club de Teatro (Theatre Club), established by Salazar Bondy in 1953 with the Argentine Reynaldo D'Amore (b. 1923), who introduced the **Stanislavsky** system. The Club inaugurated the first school of independent theatre art in Peru and gave respectability to the independent theatre movement. Histrión, established soon after, promoted high quality work during its lifetime (1956–77). **Sara Joffré**, creator of Homero, Teatro de Grillos (Homer, Cricket Theatre) directs, writes and publishes, especially in children's theatre. Efforts by Miriam Reátegui and Ernesto Ráez, editors of *Creart*, a monthly newsletter about cultural events in Lima, to organize the disparate groups and coalesce the Peruvian theatre movement coincide with the sponsorship of an international festival of children's theatre held in Lima in 1985. Jorge Chiarella's *Alondra* (Lark) is another major group.

In recent years the depletion of Peru's rich natural resources (mines, guano, fisheries, to name a few) and a depressed economy have encouraged the development of revolutionary theatre groups, although some contend that the popular theatre forms scattered throughout the Peruvian provinces – the famous Devils of Cajabamba, the fiestas of Buldibuyo, or the Magi plays of Huavlillas – are the true antecedents of the recent impetus. The ideological positions expressed by such groups as Cuatrotablas (Four Sides) and the TIT (Taller de Teatro, Theatre Workshop) speak to the urgency of social reform. Yuyachkani (1971) is a lively musical group with an ideological position that has achieved an international reputation for its vibrant popular theatre. Ensayo, Asociación de Estudio y Producción Teatral (Rehearsal, Theatre Study and Production Association) was established in 1983 by graduates of the Catholic University theatre programme: Alberto Isola, Jorge Guerra and Luis Peirano. The Muestras Nacionales (National Showcases), the first four of them organized by Homero, provided exposure for several playwrights, directors and groups, and a major festival in Ayacucho in 1978 attracted international participation on revolutionary themes. Street theatre is popular in Lima, also, especially in the poorer districts, while most conventional theatre is now located in the suburban areas of Miraflores, San Isidro and Barranco.

After Quechua was recognized as an official language in Peru in 1975, the TUSM sponsored the first national contest for dramatic works written in Quechua. Nevertheless, Quechuan theatre is not yet a major force, in comparison with the importance of the Guaraní theatre in Paraguay, for example. Even so, many Peruvian plays written in Spanish deal with themes and figures from the indigenous national past, such as Tupac Amaru, Ayar Manko and Ollantay. GW

See: R. J. Morris, *The Contemporary Peruvian Theatre*, Lubbock, Texas, 1977; C. M. Suárez Radillo, 'Poesía y realidad social en el teatro peruano contemporáneo', *Cuadernos Hispanoamericanos*, No. 269, November 1972.

Peruzzi, Baldassare (1481–1536) Italian painter and architect. Important in theatre history as a pioneer of stage perspective and decoration, and for his use of original research on the archaeology of classical theatre buildings. **Vasari** devotes on of his *Lives* to him, and in that indicates the range of his contribution to the early development of stage settings, theatrical machinery, and the devising and execution of festival entertainment and triumphs. His designs probably provided the models for **Serlio**'s influential tragic, comic and pastoral settings. KR

Peshkov, A. M. see **Gorky, M.**

PETA see **Asia, South-East (Modern)**

Petit-Bourbon, Salle du A lofty, well-appointed hall in the former palace of the Dukes of Burgundy, adjacent to the Louvre and frequently used for court entertainments in the 16th and 17th centuries. Equipped at either side with balconies divided into boxes, it was long enough to accommodate a spacious stage, approximately 50ft square, at one end while the flat floor afforded a convenient space for court ballets and masques. Over the years it was temporarily occupied by a variety of visiting companies from Italy and Spain and in 1645 the backstage area was reconstructed by the designer-machinist **Torelli** for his productions of Italian opera. In 1658, following his successful command performance before the young Louis XIV, **Molière** was given use of the theatre in alternation with the **commedia** troupe of **Tiberio Fiorilli** already established there and it became the scene of his earliest successes with the Parisian public. Two years later it was demolished, **Vigarani** appropriating the scenery and stage machinery installed by Torelli, and Molière being allowed to take the boxes and other fittings with him to his new base at the **Palais-Royal**.   DR

Petitclair, Pierre (1813–60) French Canadian dramatist, author of the first published play (apart from political drama appearing in newspapers) by a native French Canadian, *Griphon, ou La Vengeance d'un Valet* (*Griphon: or a Valet's Revenge*, 1837), a three-act comedy with strong farcical elements, visibly influenced by **Molière**. This work was never performed, but was followed by two others staged with repeated success: his two-act *La Donation* (*The Legal Donation*, 1842), the first French Canadian melodrama, with some allusions to contemporary politics, and *Une Partie de Campagne* (*A Country Outing*, 1857), an engaging comedy of manners, portraying the dangers of mimicking British speech and customs. This latter play is also remarkable for its authentic use of rural Québécois speech. Like all Canadian writers of his day, Petitclair was obliged to earn his living by other means, in his case as a private tutor to a family in Labrador, which kept him away from the cities and the stage he loved so well.   LED

Petito, Antonio (1822–76) Italian actor and dramatist. Born into the profession, he worked mainly in Naples, and although he early acted in a wide variety of drama, including playing Iago in an adaptation of *Othello*, he was best known for his performances in the mask of Pulcinella, and the un-masked character Pascariello, in Neapolitan farces, many of his own devising. He first acted Pulcinella at Naples's San Carlino Theatre in 1853, and later wrote many pieces for the farce player, **Scarpetta**.   LR

Pétomane, Le (Joseph Pujol) (1857–1945) French music-hall artist, whose billing means 'the man mad about farts'. A star at the **Moulin-Rouge** (1906–10), he earned 20,000 francs by vibrating his sphincter to imitate the characteristic eructations of a mother-in-law, various animals, and a bride on her wedding night. He also used it to smoke a cigarette, produce music on the ocarina and blow out a candle at a distance of 20 centimetres.   LS

Petrolini, Ettore (1886–1935) Italian actor, entertainer and playwright. Began his career in the *caffè-concerto* world of Rome when in his late teens, specializing in comic patter and songs and acquiring wide experience abroad too in the Americas. Although established nationally before the First World War, after it his art matured and took new directions, becoming sharper, more bitter and satirical, in a series of self-devised sketches, including *Nerone*, *Romani de Roma*, *Mustafà* and *Gastone*. He formed his own company specializing in his sketches and improvisations, adaptations of comedies by dramatists like Testoni and Novelli, and embracing one-act pieces by **Pirandello**; some critics have found a Pirandellian influence in his caustic, questioning humour.   LR

Peymann, Claus (1938–   ) German director, who established both **Handke** and **Bernhard** on the stage with the first productions of all their earlier plays (*Offending the Audience*, 1966; *Kaspar*, 1968; *A Feast for Boris*, 1970; *The Ignoramus and the Madman*, 1972; *The Ride Across Lake Constance*, 1973) and has since gained a reputation for radically unconventional interpretations of the classics.   CI

Pezzana, Giacinta (1841–1919) Italian actress. She first appeared on the stage in 1859, rising quickly to become lead actress in the company of Cesare Dondini, playing opposite **Ernesto Rossi** in a wide variety of drama, from romantic stock-pieces to **Shakespeare**. From 1870 she led her own company, touring abroad to South America, Egypt and Russia. She achieved a notable success as the mother in **Zola**'s *Thérèse Raquin* (1879) at the Teatro dei Fiorentini in Naples, acting with **Emanuel** and the young **Duse**.   LR

Phelps, Samuel (1804–78) English actor whose career as a leading Shakespearian began during the supremacy of **Macready** and ended during the supremacy of **Irving**. He was, in fact, more devoted to **Shakespeare** than either of his more illustrious fellows. He made his debut in the York circuit in 1826 and his first London appearance as Shylock at the **Haymarket** in 1837. This challenge to the memory of **Edmund**

Samuel Phelps as Henry IV.

Kean was sustained throughout his Haymarket engagement, when he appeared exclusively in parts that Kean had favoured – Hamlet, Othello, Richard III and Sir Edward Mortimer in the younger **Colman**'s *The Iron Chest*. Playing opposite Macready at **Covent Garden** (1837–8) taught Phelps a lesson about theatrical rivalry. After playing Iago to Phelps's Othello, Macready relegated his new employee to minor parts. Only at the Haymarket and in the provinces could he play leads. His opportunity came with the abolition of the Patent monopoly in 1843. He became joint-lessee of the highly unfashionable **Sadler's Wells**, where, from 1844–62, he staged all but four of Shakespeare's plays. Not only that; he also showed a rare respect for the text. His was the first serious production of *Antony and Cleopatra* (1849) for over two centuries and the first London *Pericles* since the Restoration. Temperamentally austere, Phelps was the finest Lear of his generation, and although not at ease in comedy, widely admired as Bottom, Falstaff and, less surprisingly, Jacques in *As You Like It*. After leaving Sadler's Wells, he continued to act, making his last appearance as Cardinal Wolsey in the year of his death.   PT

Philadelphia, Jacob (Jacob Meyer) (1721–c. 1800) American conjuror, the son of Polish Jews. He acted as a scientific jester for William Augustus, Duke of Cumberland, performing mathematical and physical experiments. After the Duke's death in 1765, he went public, travelling through Europe billed as 'An Artist of Mathematics', and played before Catherine the Great, Sultan Mustafa III, and Frederick the Great, who was very fond of him. Philadelphia, the member of a secret Rosicrucian society and anti-monarchical, was eventually expelled from Berlin. Meanwhile he had gained the reputation of a true sorcerer who could pass through doors, grow a second head and read minds.   LS

Philipe, Gérard (1922–59) French actor who made his name in the title role of **Camus**'s *Caligula* (1945), followed by numerous film roles. In 1951 he played Rodrigue to **Vilar**'s Don Diègue in *Le Cid* at the **Avignon festival**. After this he joined the **TNP** team and until his death played leading roles e.g. Lorenzaccio, Friedrich Prince of Hamburg. He was unique among French actors in achieving at one and the same time acclaim from the theatre critics and adoration from young theatre-goers who reacted to him with the kind of hysteria normally reserved for pop stars.   DB

Philippines (see also **Asia, South-East (Modern)**.) In this South-East Asian island nation of 55 million, the tribes that follow indigenous religion have remnants of performance traditions which probably were widespread in pre-colonial times. The 5% of the population who are Muslim have traditions related to Malaysia and Indonesia, and the 90% who are Christian have practices developed under Hispanic and American colonial influence. The major performance categories are (1) proto-theatrical forms (2) Islamic dances (3) Hispanic-influenced theatre genres, and (4) American-influenced forms, including modern drama.

Proto-theatrical forms Scholars have turned to the performance of the tribes that have not accepted the Christian or Islamic religion, in attempts to reconstruct the parameters of early Filipino entertainments. Though performances themselves may have changed in the hundreds of years that Muslim and Christian influences have dominated the lowland areas, the categories have probably remained stable. Spirit mediumship, epic recitation, dances, games involving improvised poetry, are so widespread in South-East Asia that they seem part of the common heritage of the Malay peoples. The first European reports noted such forms in the 16th and 17th centuries.

Music and dance are traditionally used for curing, courting, entertainment, and rites of passage ceremonies. Though many dances are abstract, mimetic dance is also common. Examples include the honey gathering dance of the Negritos, and the boar hunting dance of the Igorots. Courting and war dances are widespread. The *pinanyo-wan* ('veiled'), for example, is a wedding dance of the Bontok, in which a boy and girl dance with the boy's foot movements emulating a cock attracting a hen. The *tchugas* (exorcism) of the Kalinga is a victory dance over ghosts of a slain enemy in which two young men and a priestess re-enact a war dance, whereupon the priestess asks the ancestral spirits to give her the names of glorious headhunters.

Rituals were undertaken by local shamans, called *babaylan* among the Visayan peoples and *catalonan* among the Tagalogs. Performances were frequently part of curing, and possession trance was common. A present-day example is the Tagbanwa female shaman who, in trance dance, communicates with spirits and may be possessed by them.

The singing of epics is found in all layers of Filipino culture, and it may be that Muslim and Hispanic variants are cultural adaptations that allowed older oral narrative practices to continue with a new content.

Reynaldo Alejandro, a scholar-artist of Filipino dance, presenting a theatrical version of an indigenous tribal dance.

Epics might be sung for one to three nights in celebration of a wedding, at gatherings for guests, or as entertainment for villagers. Among the Mandaya, Mansaka, and Bagobo, heroes like Agyu, Tuwaang and Ulahingan may be praised. *Tutol* are the epic songs found among the Muslim Magindanao and tell of the exploits of heroes like Radya Indara Patra, a noble who flies to the palace of the clouds and fights mythical monsters to save his people. Epic singing may also be seen as related to the singing of the *pasyon*, a chanted narrative of the Passion and other biblical events sung during Lent, and metrical romances, including the duodecasyllabic line *awit* and octosyllabic *corrido*. The latter are Filipino narratives, based on European tales, written in quatrains and published in the early 19th century, which gave rise to corresponding folk theatricals.

Games involving dialogues between two or more voices are another indigenous theatrical impulse. One common form has a singer sing in a set verse form, showing skill by improvised riddles and allusions. While the chorus repeat the last lines the singer must prepare for his next line. Among the Ibaloi the *badiw* has this structure, and it is the principal vocal form. During the ceremonies for the dead the singer might invite spirit relatives to drink rice wine, praise the host, or comment on the properties of the deceased. Another dialogue game is *kaharian*. A king or *hari* makes an accusation (e.g. – 'You stole the roses from my garden!') and the accused must improvise a defence or accuse another in quatrains full of riddles and poetic devices. The player who fails to provide an acceptable response is found guilty as charged. Frequently the dialogue games involve a male and a female voice and may be part of ancient courting practices. As early as 1668 the Jesuit Alzina reported that the Leyte-Samar Visayans had *bikal*, verbal jousts in song with two boys and girls amusingly finding fault with each other. In the rather functional *pamanhikan* – asking for a girl's hand in marriage – one singer represents the groom and the answering voice sets out the demands of the girl. Although remaining in game framework, these sung dialogues form the substructure of indigenous drama, and show that Filipino performance relates to a pan-South-East Asian pattern of courting games and verbal jousts.

Islamic dances Muslim performance, believed to have come to the southern Philippines via Borneo, shows similarity to dance and music traditions of Islamic peoples of Indonesia and Malaysia. Theatrical aspects, however, are not as developed. Dances are generally performed to the *kulintang*, a gong chime ensemble related to the Indonesian gamelan. The subtle grace of dancers who may impersonate princesses and slave girls and the curving gestures of the lower arm correspond to the movement of refined characters in Indonesian dance drama. There is some evidence that Muslim sword dances, probably related to Indonesia's horse trance dance and *dabus*, contributed to the evolution of the Christian *moro-moro* folk theatricals, but no evidence links the Filipino *carillo*, the shadow theatre using rough cardboard figures, with the intricately developed shadow theatre of the Malay world, the *wayang*. Shadow puppetry only seems to appear in the Philippines in 1879, inspired, perhaps, by then current European experiments which were themselves only shadows of Asian models.

Hispanic-influenced genres The major theatre traditions that developed after Spanish colonization and Christianization continue, in some form, to the present. These include (1) religious spectacles (2) the *moro-moro* or *komedya*, and (3) the **zarzuela**. Though Spanish influences were significant, indigenous elements are apparent.

Religious customs with dramatic aspects were introduced by the Spanish in an attempt to displace folk rituals. Popular performances included the Lenten play (*senakulo*), Christmas theatricals (*panunuluyan*), the digging for the true cross by St Helena (*tibag*), and the lives of the saints. The *senakulo*, for example, takes its name from the cenacle where the Last Supper took place. Produced during Holy Week all over the Philippines, these plays, which re-enacted the death of Christ, may have evolved the *pasyon* narrative singing. Plays are in verse, and major religious figures maintain slow, decorous movement and declamation. Peter, ageing and absent-minded, added comic touches, while Mary Magdalene, dancing and seducing her soldier, helped make the action more stimulating. Self-flagellations and real crucifixions of devotees, undertaken in fulfilment of vows; tableaux; and processions made performances powerful events in the community life. *Senakulo* continue to the present, but scholars note diminution of fervour in urban centres.

From religious plays based on Spanish models, the major genre of the 17th to the 20th centuries, the *komedya* is believed to have developed. In 1598 a priest, Vincente Puche, wrote a Latin play presented by schoolboys in Cebu. In 1609 the first play in the vernacular concerning St Barbara reportedly prompted many conversions in Bohol. By 1619 there were five-day programmes with plays on Old and New Testament events and more recent themes, like the martyrs in Japan, presented for church celebrations by the sons of the native aristocracy.

The most famous play was supposedly written in 1637 – celebrating a victory of the local Christians over the Muslim leader Kudarat (Corralat). The event was probably first played out in Cavite province by boys and the one playing the Muslim leader was actually wounded. Fr Jeronimo Perez saw the enactment and was inspired to write on this theme, creating the first *moro-moro* or *komedya*. These are plays, affected by Spanish *comedia* models and centred on the struggle of Christians and Muslims.

The typical plot involves a Muslim prince or princess in love with a Christian ruler of the opposite sex. After love scenes, escapes, battles, magical episodes, some clowning, perhaps a death and a miraculous resurrection, the lovers unite with the conversion of the Muslim partner. Alternatively, they are doomed to separation should death or different religions continue to divide them. Story material is related to the sung epics, the *corrido* and *awit*, and some see the genre as growing largely from these oral narratives.

Speeches were in quatrains of 8-, 10- or 12-syllable lines. The style of the presentation was broad: bombastic speech, stylized battles using *arnis*, the martial arts system; open air performances running three to five hours a day for up to 30-day fiesta periods were characteristic. A brass band played three major pieces in variable tempi; dignified marches sounded for Christians but double time played for Moors. Rowdy audiences at Ilocano performances might even demand the repeat of favourite battle scenes or love encounters.

Noted exponents of the *komedya* include Jose de la Cruz (1746–1829) better known as 'Huseng Sisiw' (Chicken Joe) who could create a *komedya* in a day. He is credited with such titles as *The Civil War of Grenada* and *The Enchanted Queen* or *Forced Marriage*. He was critic–censor of the *komedyas* at the Tondo theatre. Francisco Baltazar ('Balagtas') (1788–1862) is credited with over 100 titles. In 1841 his *Almanzor and Rosalina* was staged for 12 consecutive days from 2.30 pm to dusk.

Although most scholars trace the form to European models, some counter-arguments should be noted. The fight of the boys inspiring the first author could have been a hobby horse dance, related to the *kuda kepang* dances of Indonesia – trance dances involving a stylized battle with self-mutilation. This argument is strengthened by the fact that some sources cite furious battle dances by six Muslim soldiers at the baptism of a Sultan of Jolo in 1750 as the true source of *komedya*: such dances sound like *dabus*, martial dances still found in sufi sects of the Malay area. Evidence becomes more convincing if we consider that plots which may involve princesses and princes marrying after a ritual battle and resurrection are commonly found after Muslim influence appears in areas as far apart as England, Spain, East Java, and the Philippines. The persistence of the name – *moro-moro* (play of the Moors), morris dance, morisco – is notable. It is possible that Eurocentric biases are blinding scholars to a significant drama that grew from dances of sufi mystics and entered the Philippines and other areas with Islamic, as well as Christian influences.

Likewise, the use of set characters, stylized movement, the popularity of *pusong* (clown), the open air production scheme and the enactment in the context of a fiesta are features that relate to widespread South-East Asian theatre practice, not just European models. The belief that the omission of a *komedya* presentation might cause rain and trouble is reminiscent of South-East Asian use of performance to placate supernatural powers. Perhaps even the puzzling lack of scripts prior to the 19th century may hint that like most South-East Asian performance, scenario, rather than text was the generative principle, and indigenous rhyming improvisation games paved the way for actors to create dialogue.

With the rise of middle-class, educated Filipinos came the birth of a more literary focused theatre. Indoor proscenium theatres lit by gaslight appear from the beginning of the 1800s, but only become numerous around the end of the century. The Zorrilla theatre (1893) with 400 orchestra seats and 52 boxes was the most noted of these structures. Spanish genres, such as *entremés* (interlude) and *sainete* (short comic piece written in octosyllabic verse), and Italian operas caught the audiences' attention.

In the 1880s a Spanish actor Alejandro Cubero, 'Father of Spanish Theatre in the Philippines', and his mistress, actress Elisea Raguer, brought the Spanish *zarzuela* to the fore. These musical plays on contemporary themes first appeared in the mid 18th century, but Spanish remained the language medium until the

United States took over the colony in 1898. In September 1900 came *The Patcher*, the first vernacular *zarzuela*, written by Mariono Proceso Palaban in Pampango vernacular. By turn of century *komedya* had retreated to the *barrios*, and Severino Reyes (1861–1942), a Tagalog playwright, wrote a *zarzuela*, *RIP* (1902), showing actors burying the old form and taking up the new, more realistic genre.

Reyes's *Without a Wound* (1902) was a stringent attack on Spanish dominance and characterized the nationalistic flavour of these plays. *Zarzuela* replaced foreign heroes and locales with scenes of Filipino domestic life. Though most plays were melodramatic entanglements where true love eventually triumphed, the use of indigenous characters and scenes was considered a commitment to nationalism and realism. The wing and drop scenery and contemporary costuming were prized, and the songs became hits of the period. Atang de la Rama was the most noted of performers. As 'Queen of Zarzuela', she achieved national acclaim in this form which prevailed to the 1930s.

American-influenced genres Vaudeville, called *bodabil* or *vodavil*, made its debut around American bases by 1916, but it was Louis Borromeo, who arrived from the United States in 1921, who made the genre important. Troupes included torch singers like the noted Katy de la Kruz, clowns like the Chaplinesque Canuplin, and rockette-like chorus girls. During the Japanese occupation of the Second World War *bodabil* shows, which had long included skits, expanded to include plays. The Barangay Theatre Guild under Lamberto Avellana, one of the foremost groups currently presenting modern drama, began working in this format. *Bodabil* itself later evolved into burlesque-like girlie shows.

Modern spoken drama rose in conjunction with the *zarzuela*, beginning 1878 with the didactic domestic drama *The Ideal Woman* by Cornelio Hilado written in Iloilo vernacular. Being prose works in which songs were de-emphasized, drama was considered appropriate for serious themes. By 1903 actors were slanting anti-colonial criticism against the American government. *I Am Not Dead* by Juan Matapang Cruz, *Golden Chain* (1903) by Juan Abad (1872–1932), and *Yesterday, Today, and Tomorrow* (1903) by Aurelio Tolentino (?1867–1915) were labelled anti-American and the authors were arrested. In the so-called 'seditious' plays of this period, actors' costumes might be coloured so that when they moved into the correct configuration the outlawed Philippine flag was formed.

The first English-language play *A Modern Filipina* by Jesus Araullo and Lino Casillejo was written in 1915, but only after 1945, when English became a major language of the educated, did English dominate the dramatic scene. Nick Joaquin's *The Portrait of the Artist as Filipino* (1951) was the most popular script of this movement of the 1950s–60s. In the 1970s the theatre returned to the vernacular. First American plays were translated into Tagalog and some like *Our Town* were reset in the *barrio*. As groups like PETA (Philippine Educational Theatre Association), founded in 1967 by Cecile Guidote, emerged from university modern drama groups, interest in earlier traditions surfaced. *Komedya* and *zarzuela* were researched and performed in modern theatres such as the Philippines Cultural Centre. Dance troupes like Bayanihan (founded 1958) and Filipinescas were, simultaneously, researching indigenous dances and re-choreographing them as dance dramas for modern, urban audiences.

After martial law was imposed in 1972, drama took on an increasingly Filipino perspective and political issues became central. As vernacular language became the major mode, playwrights looked for indigenous content and forms. Historical plays on Filipino rebels against tyranny, docu-dramas showing current social injustices, street theatre performance–demonstrations, and plays using the model of earlier genres, especially religious plays and *zarzuela*, proliferated. Even traditional Lenten religious plays regained some of their impassioned flagellations. The message, that the martyrdom of the meek continued, was clear and the 'seditious' voices of modern theatre artists urged the fall of Ferdinand Marcos's regime.   KF

See: R. Alejendro, 'Sayaw Silangan: Dance in the Philippines', *Dance Perspective* 51, 1972; R. Banas, *Philipino Music and Theatre*, Quezon City, 1969; D. Fernendez, 'From Ritual to Realism: Brief Historical Survey of Philippine Drama', *Philippine Studies* 28 (1980), 389–419; and 'Contemporary Philippine Drama: the Liveliest Voice', *Philippine Studies* 31 (1983), 5–36; T. Hernandez, *The Emergence of Modern Drama in the Philippines (1898–1930)*, Philippine Studies Working Paper 1, Honolulu Asian Studies Program, 1976; J. Maceda, L. Goquingco, L. Kasilag, 'Philippines' in S. Sadie (ed.), *New Grove Dictionary of Music and Musicians*, New York 1980; F. Mendoza, *The Comedia (Moro-Moro) Rediscovered*, Manila, 1976; L. Mendoza, 'Lenten Rituals and Practices: The Philippines', *The Drama Review* 21 (1977), 21–32; T. Muoz, 'Notes on Theatre: Pre-Hispanic Philippines (Religion, Myth, Religious Ritual)', in Antonio Manuud (ed.), *Brown Heritage*, Quezon City, 1967, 648–67.

Philips, Ambrose (1674–1749) English playwright. Educated at St John's College, Cambridge, where he became a Fellow, his *Pastorals* were first published in 1706. In 1712 his first play, an adaptation of **Racine**'s *Andromaque*, retitled *The Distressed Mother*, was extraordinarily successful, a surprisingly good neoclassical tragedy. It continued to be popular through most of the 18th century. His later plays, *The Briton* (1722) and *Humphrey, Duke of Gloucester* (1723), were less noticed and he gave up writing plays when he became an Irish MP, in 1727. He was nicknamed 'Namby-Pamby' by Swift, undeservedly.   PH

Phillips, Augustine (d. 1605) English actor, one of the original sharers in the **Lord Chamberlain's Men**, with whom he remained from 1594 until his death. From the slender surviving evidence, we can guess that Phillips was a social centre of **Shakespeare**'s company of players, that he was a musician and an athlete as well as an actor and that he was the performer as well as the author of his own *Jig of the Slippers* (1595). In his will he left 30 shillings to Shakespeare and **Condell** and silver bowls worth £5 to **Heminges**, **Sly** and **Richard Burbage**. These were not negligible bequests.   PT

Phillips, Stephen (1864–1915) English playwright and poet, who acted in his cousin **F. R. Benson**'s **Shakespeare** company from 1885–92. His *Poems*

(1898) earned him the prestige of a literary prize and there was briefly an extravagant vogue for his sonorous poetic dramas. **Tree** staged *Herod* (1900) and *Ulysses* (1902) at **His Majesty's** and **Alexander** produced the pick of the bunch, *Paolo and Francesca* (1902), at the **St James's**. But *Nero* (1906) and *Faust* (1908) limped at His Majesty's and *Iole* (1913) and *The Sin of David* (1914) failed without the theatrical flair of Tree or Alexander to back them. Having made and squandered fortunes, Phillips died destitute.   PT

Phiri, Masautso (*fl.* 1970s) Zambian artist, active in theatre since 1963, co-founded Bazamai (Travellers) Theatre Group in 1970 while a student and Tikwiza Theatre in 1975. Written and directed a number of plays, a trilogy on Soweto, for instance, also novels and poetry.   RK

Phlyax Play see **Greece, ancient**

Phoenix Theatre, London The first theatre of this name is better known as the **Cockpit**. A second, on the corner of Charing Cross Road and Phoenix Street, was opened in 1930.   PT

Phrynichus (6th–5th centuries BC) An older contemporary of **Aeschylus**, and his most prominent rival. He is chiefly remembered for two tragedies on historical subjects: the *Capture of Miletus*, which according to Herodotus so upset the Athenians that Phrynichus was heavily fined, and the *Phoenician Women*, which influenced Aeschylus' *Persians*. Few fragments survive.   ALB

Piaf, Edith (Edith Giovanna Gassion) (1915–63) French singer and song-writer. The daughter of street performers, she began singing in the streets at 12 and, by 17, already a mother, was well ensconced in the Pigalle milieu of whores and pimps. In 1935 she was hired to sing at a chic club by Louis Leplée who dubbed her 'la môme Piaf' (Kid Sparrow). An appearance at the ABC in 1937 made her a star, not least because of the way she used emotion and emotion used her. The brassy voice blaring out of the frail, black-clad body sang of hopeless love and intense suffering, and sounded as if it meant it. With her best numbers, 'L'Accordéoniste' and 'La Vie en rose', she became the darling of the intellectuals, their emblem of tormented devotion. Successful tours of the United States (1949, 1955) and a triumphal return to France in 1956 with 'Milord' and 'Je ne regrette rien' were vitiated by her increasing reliance on drugs. Her addiction and ill health grew until she collapsed during a concert in 1959. After surviving three hepatic comas, she died in 1963. **Jean Cocteau**, who had written the monologue *Le Bel Indifférent* for her, succumbed the following day. A biographical play by **Pam Gems**, *Piaf* (1980), enjoyed a good run in London and New York.   LS

Picard, Louis B. (1769–1828) French dramatist, actor, theatre director, best known as a writer of comedies during the Empire and Restoration. His first play, *Le Badinage Dangereux (Dangerous Trifling)*, was staged at the Théâtre de Monsieur in 1789, and *Encore des Menechmes (The Nephew as Uncle*, 1791) established him. He appeared as an actor at the Feydeau and

Louvois theatres in 1796 and at the **Odéon** in 1798, excelling in the roles of comic valets. His play *The Parasite* (*Médiocre et Rampant*), a comedy of manners, was performed at the Louvois in 1797 after the burning of the Odéon. In 1799 he made a huge success playing the lawyer, Pavaret, in his own play *Le Collatéral*. In 1801 he set up his company at the Théâtre Louvois and became known for casting actors according to their physical qualities and defects, rather than according to stock *emplois*. Picard himself tended to shout on stage, and his actors also. However, his plays themselves were praised for their lively sense of observation. In 1805 he staged *Bertrand et Raton*, and in 1806 *Les Marionettes*, considered one of his best plays. In 1807 he gave up acting, and was made director of the Opéra, which he left in 1815 for the Odéon. He continued to write for the Louvois company, which was not doing very well, but after 1815 he had a series of successes at the Odéon, notably *Les Deux Philibert*, *Le Capitaine Belronde*, *Une Matinée d'Henri IV*, *Vaugelas* and *La Maison en Loterie*. With the Odéon fire of 1818 he moved temporarily to the Favart. In 1820 he retired and in the same year his *Les Deux Ménages* (*Two Households*) was successfully staged at the Odéon, and subsequently taken into the **Comédie-Française** repertoire. His last play, written in conjunction with Mazères, *L'Enfant Trouvé* (*The Foundling*), was also put on at the Odéon in 1824.   JMCC

Picasso, Pablo (1881–1973) Spanish painter and sculptor; worked primarily in France. Picasso, of course, was perhaps the most significant figure in 20th-century art. Although much of his early work included theatrical motifs, he did not turn to theatre design until his cubist period when he was asked by Serge Diaghilev, probably at the suggestion of **Jean Cocteau** and Leonide Massine, to design the Ballets Russes production of *Parade* (1917). Over the following eight years he designed seven more ballets and a play including *Le Tricorne* (1919), *Pulcinella* (1920), and *Mercure* (1924). In all of these he sought to find a means of combining the thematic aspects of the dance with his artistic aesthetics. *Parade*, for example, combines a colourful, whimsical act-curtain reminiscent of his early work, and the cubistic costumes of the Managers that were intended to connect the three-dimensionality of the dancers with the non-illusionist images of the decor. This tendency reached its peak with *Mercure*. Picasso continued to provide designs for the stage as late as 1962 (Honneger's *Icare*) but the later works were generally backdrops or simple scenery adapted from existing drawings. He also wrote two plays: *Desire Caught by the Tale* (1941) and *The Four Little Girls* (1965).   AA

Piccolo Teatro see **Strehler, Giorgio**

Picon, Molly (1898–   ) Impish musical comedy actress of the American Yiddish theatre, later successful on Broadway and in the cinema.   AB

Pierrot Probably a 17th-century avatar of Pedrolino, he appears first with the Italian comedians in Paris, played by Giuseppe Giratoni, who is shown in an engraving of the 1670s in the characteristic loose white clothing, ruff and soft hat, with unmasked, whitened

Fred Pullan's Yorkshire Pierrots, a typical Pierrot troupe, photographed in 1909.

face. Though Giratoni may have naturalized the character in terms of sentimental comedy, there is some slight evidence in the earlier Italian scenarios that Pedrolino was already one of the gentler and more romantic of the **zanni**. Regularly included in scripted plays and pantomimes of the 18th century, and popularized in England by **Delpini**, Pierrot took on in the 19th century the piquant blend of comedy and pathos now generally associated with him, in the work of the gifted French mime artist **Jean-Gaspard Deburau**. Imitators such as Paul Legrand at the Folies-Dramatiques further emphasized the lyrical and sentimental attributes of the role at the expense of the comic.   AEG

Pierrot shows English seaside entertainment which at the turn of the 20th century successfully supplanted the 'nigger minstrels' who had hitherto dominated the sands. Around 1890 small groups of concert singers from London would perform at houseboat parties in masks; in 1891 Clifford Essex introduced a song-and-dance group costumed as Pierrots in loose blouses with ruffs and pompons in Southern Ireland and the Isle of Wight. These innovations were rapidly taken up, the leading entrepreneurs being Carlton Frederick (Weymouth, 1894), Will Catlin (Scarborough, 1894) and Edwin Adeler (Southport, 1898). In a later format, the Pierrot costumes would be exchanged in the second half for blazers, boaters and holiday attire. The Pierrots' freshness and exuberance were conveyed to the West End by H. G. Pélissier's revue *The Follies* (Apollo Theatre, 1908, 1910) and the 'Pierrot entertainment' *The Co-optimists* (Royalty Theatre, 1921–7). Ben Popplewell's 'Good Companions' at Bradford inspired **J. B. Priestley**'s eponymous novel, and several popular comedians, such as Arthur Askey, Fred Emney, Leslie Henson, and Elsie and Doris Waters, served their apprenticeships on the piers. By the time **Joan Littlewood** ironically costumed the players of her antimilitaristic revue *Oh, What a Lovely War!* (1963) in Pierrot costumes, the conventions of the seaside show were regarded as fey and antiquated.   LS

Pike Theatre Club (Dublin) Established in 1953 by Alan Simpson and Carolyn Swift. Its 12 ft square, ingeniously lighted stage held the premiere of **Brendan Behan**'s *The Hostage* (1954) and shared the London premiere of **Beckett**'s *Waiting for Godot* (1955) – adventurous presentations in the Irish theatre of the time. In 1957 Simpson gave **Tennessee Williams**'s *The Rose Tattoo* for the **Dublin Theatre Festival** and was charged with 'presenting for gain an indecent and profane performance'. Although he was eventually acquitted, legal costs and the blow to the theatre's morale were an insuperable setback. DM

Piñera, Virgilio (1912–79) Cuban playwright, poet and fiction writer. Studied in the University of Havana and lived in Argentina from 1946–58. His first play, *Electra Garrigó* (1948), set off a heated scandal for its bold Cuban treatment of a classical myth. His theatre is characterized by the absurd, black humour and a depiction of reality in intellectual and on occasion abstract terms. On the other hand, his *Aire frío* (*Cold Air*, 1962), considered a classic Cuban play, is a totally realistic vision of a middle-class family before the Revolution. Among his most significant works are *El flaco y el gordo* (*The Thin Man and the Fat Man*, 1949), *Jesús* (1950), *El filántropo* (*The Philanthropist*, 1960) and *Dos viejos pánicos* (*Two Old Panics*), the latter a recipient of the Casa de las Américas prize in 1968. GW

Pinero, Arthur Wing (1855–1934) English playwright, born in London and frugally educated there, Pinero left his father's law office to become an actor in 1874. He had written 15 plays before 1884, when he abandoned acting to commit himself wholly to authorship, and the work that established him as the leading playwright of his period post-dates that critical decision. He was successful in two distinct styles, that of farce and that of the social 'problem' play. Of the first kind are *The Magistrate* (1885), *The Schoolmistress* (1886) and *Dandy Dick* (1887). *The Cabinet Minister* (1890) is less sure-footed. Pinero had, by the time he wrote it, established a new reputation as a writer of comedy with the outrageously sentimental *Sweet Lavender* (1888) and risked that reputation with *The Profligate* (1889), controversial in its time simply because its plot hinged on seduction. Without radically criticizing contemporary moral values, Pinero proceeded to write a succession of social dramas highlighting the plight of women in an unforgiving world. They include the sensationally successful *The Second Mrs Tanqueray* (1893), with its unctuous ending in the wayward heroine's socially expedient suicide, *The Notorious Mrs Ebbsmith* (1895), *The Benefit of the Doubt* (1895), *Iris* (1901), *Letty* (1903), *His House in Order* (1906), *The Thunderbolt* (1908) and *Mid-Channel* (1909). A preparedness to examine, if not quite to challenge, conventional morality is present also in two effective comedies, *The Princess and the Butterfly* (1897) and *The Gay Lord Quex* (1899). Pinero's best comedy, *Trelawny of the 'Wells'* (1898), is a nostalgic celebration of the mid-Victorian theatre, already lost in the era of the long run. Pinero was knighted in 1909. He continued to write plays for the rest of his life, seeking to maintain a hold in a theatre that changed too fast for him. PT

Pinski, David (1872–1959) American humanist writer of Jewish plays which, in almost poetic form, search for the eternal meanings and true values of life,

particularly for the poor. From over 60 plays the most notable are *Isaac Sheftel* (1899), *The Family Zevi* (1904), *The Eternal Jew* (1906) and *The Treasure* (1906). AB

Pinter, Harold (1930–) British dramatist and director, who once acted under the stage name of David Baron. His early plays, *The Room* (1957) and *The Birthday Party* (1958) which received a very short London run, were condemned by most critics as obscure, although Harold Hobson and J. C. Trewin recognized that he was 'a natural dramatist'. He clearly possessed an acute ear for dialogue and his plays undeniably contained suspense, even if they did not seem to lead anywhere. Pinter was labelled a writer of the absurd and placed in that loose category with such dramatists as **N. F. Simpson**, **Eugène Ionesco** and **Samuel Beckett**. In fact, Pinter's only affinity was with Beckett, whose novels and plays he absorbed with an intuitive understanding. Pinter's one-act play, *A Slight Ache* (1959), has marked similarities with the second part of Beckett's novel, *Molloy*, while the tramp Davies in Pinter's *The Caretaker* (1960) has more than rags in common with the tramps in *Waiting for Godot*. The studied ambiguity of Pinter's writing can also be compared with the self-contradictions of Beckett's creatures, although at this point the similarities begin to peter away. Beckett is trying to establish a sense of metaphysical isolation in which nothing is or can be precisely known. Pinter is more influenced by the naturalistic tradition and particularly by his Jewish childhood in Hackney at a time when fascist demonstrations were causing trouble. The bullies, Goldberg and McCann, in *The Birthday Party* who terrorize Stanley, are not abstract creations but closely observed tormentors. The settings in *The Caretaker* and *The Homecoming* (1965) are precisely evoked and belong to unfashionable London. But Pinter likes (if not exactly to confuse) to allow his themes to accumulate layers of possible meanings. *The Homecoming* is ostensibly about a don who returns from a civilized university campus in the United States to his childhood home in North London, bringing his wife Ruth to meet his working-class father, uncle and brothers. But Ruth also brings a feeling of home to the all-male household, while her internal sexual fantasies are aroused by the surrounding longings. Thus she too comes 'home' to her instincts and while the play's final scene still provides a shock, where Ruth accepts the life of a Soho prostitute, at least Pinter gives us plenty of clues during the course of the action. Other plays are less complex, such as *The Lover* (1963), and Pinter wrote some delightful sketches for intimate revues. As his idiom became more familiar to his audiences and the term 'Pinteresque' was invented to describe anything menacing and enigmatic, Pinter seemed to tire of his former themes and territory. He started to play with ideas of time, as in *Landscape* and *Silence* (1969), a double bill first produced by the **Royal Shakespeare Company**, which also produced his memory play, *Old Times* (1971). His long association with **Peter Hall** which began with *The Homecoming* continued when Hall went to the **National Theatre**, where Pinter became an Associate Director. Hall directed **John Gielgud** and **Ralph Richardson** in *No Man's Land* (1975) and in 1982, a triple bill which included *A Kind of Alaska* (1982) which described, unusually for Pinter, a particular illness, sleeping sickness, from which the patient can recover through the drug, L-Dopa. Another short play, *One for the Road*, describes an inquisition from an agent of a totalitarian regime; and illustrates the change in Pinter's style, towards the less enigmatic and more direct form of story-telling, a process which began with his retrospective look at how an adultery started, *Betrayal* (1978). As a director, Pinter has been particularly associated with the plays of **Simon Gray**. JE

Pirandello, Luigi (1867–1936) Italian dramatist, novelist and short-story writer, who was born into a prosperous middle-class Sicilian family, and after studying at the Universities of Palermo and Rome, and taking a doctorate in philosophy at Bonn, settled into a comfortable, mildly Bohemian literary life in Rome's cafe society of the 1890s. During that decade he published several volumes of poetry, wrote short stories, and in 1893 produced his first novel, *L'Esclusa* (*The Outcast*). In 1894 he married, and in the mid and late nineties his wife, the daughter of his father's business partner, bore him three children. But the comfort and equanimity of his domestic and literary life were shattered when the family sulphur mines in Sicily were destroyed by floods, leaving his father and father-in-law bankrupt. Hitherto financially dependent on them, now in order to support himself and his family Pirandello was dependent upon a university lecturing post. His wife's mental health gradually deteriorated, and she became prey to suspicions and rages which led eventually to her being confined to an asylum. Pirandello gave up teaching only in 1922. By that time he had begun to acquire international status as a dramatist.

Pirandello turned to playwriting late in his career, after establishing his reputation in Italy with novels, short stories and two critical works, *Arte e scienza* and *L'umorismo* (both 1908). His *Weltanschauung* was sceptical, pessimistic and emotionally deep-rooted, and his fraught domestic life may well have reinforced it. Perhaps the most important of his novels, *Il Fu Mattia Pascal* (*The Late Mattia Pascal*) appeared in 1904, and treated of themes he was later to explore in his plays: the elusiveness of personal identity, the relativity of all values, the dependence of the individual on social forms and conventions for self-definition, and the relationship between art, characterized by its fixity, and life, subject to constant flux. Such motives recur too in the short stories, some 28 of which Pirandello later adapted into plays.

It was his plays which first won for Pirandello an international reputation. Encouraged by the Sicilian actor **Angelo Musco**, shortly before and during the First World War he wrote a number of one-act pieces for Sicilian dialect companies, then followed these with a series of full-length plays crafted for Italian bourgeois audiences including *Pensaci, Giacomino!* (*Think, Giacomino!*, 1916), *Liolà* (1916), *Così è, (Se Vi Pare)* (*It Is So, if You Think So*, 1917), *Il Piacere dell'Onestà* (*The Pleasure of Honesty*, 1918), and *Il Giuoco delle Parti* (*The Rules of the Game*, 1918), plays which made contemporary critics associate him with the theatre of the grotesque. By the end of the war his national reputation as a playwright was secure. Perhaps the most influential of all his plays, *Sei Personaggi in Cerca d'Autore* (*Six Characters in Search of an Author*, 1921), provoked

uproar when first performed in Rome, but quickly came to be recognized as seminal, expressing the early 20th-century crisis in bourgeois social and cultural values and encapsulating the 'modernist' assault on traditional theatre forms. It was the first of his three so-called 'theatre in the theatre' plays which all explored the relationship between appearance and reality, life and the theatre, private accommodations and social role-playing. The other two, *Ciascuno a Suo Modo* (*Each in His Own Way*, 1924) and *Questa Sera Si Recita a Soggetto* (*Tonight We Improvise*, 1929), have never enjoyed the success or influence of *Sei Personaggi*, the **Pitoëff** production of which in 1924 made an impact in Paris comparable to that of **Beckett**'s *Waiting for Godot* in the early 1950s.

Throughout the 1920s and 30s Pirandello was remarkably prolific, although the quality of his work was uneven. Among the best-known plays are *Vestire gli Ignudi* (*To Dress the Naked*, 1922), *Enrico IV* (1922), *La Vita che ti Diedi* (*The Life I Gave You*, 1923), the one-act *L'Uomo dal Fiore in Bocca* (*The Man with the Flower in his Mouth*, 1923), *Diana e la Tuda* (*Diana and Tuda*, 1926), *Bellavita* (1927), *La Nuova Colonia* (*The New Colony*, 1928), *Lazzaro* (*Lazarus*, 1929), *Trovarsi* (*To Find Oneself*, 1932), *Quando si è Qualcuno* (*When one is Somebody*, 1933), *Come Tu Mi Vuoi* (*As You Desire Me*, 1936), and *I Giganti della Montagna* (*The Mountain Giants*, posthumously 1937). Some of these were written for, and were performed by, Pirandello's own company, the Teatro d'Arte, established in 1925 with Marta Abba and **Ruggero Ruggeri** as lead players, and with which he travelled extensively throughout Europe and Latin America. The company was formed with financial support from the new Mussolini-led government, and many commentators have felt that Pirandello's later years were unhappily compromised by his association – real, but fluctuating and often uneasy – with the Fascist regime, notwithstanding his own attempts to divorce writing from politics by insisting on the irreconcilability of the aims of art and propaganda, and by cultivating – some would say retreating into – a mythological dimension in some of his later work. In 1934 he was awarded the Nobel Prize for Literature, and two years later died in Rome.

Together with **Ibsen** and **Brecht**, Pirandello has been one of the most influential of modern dramatists, yet the extent of his achievement remains peculiarly hard to calculate. A prolific writer, the sheer range of his output – plays, novels, short stories, critical and theoretical writings – has militated against any easy classification and assessment; again much of what was once strikingly innovative in his work has now been so thoroughly assimilated as to leave the plays themselves historically stranded: even in his most overtly experimental 'theatre in the theatre' plays, his mockery of directorial authoritarianism and the conventions of bourgeois drawing-room naturalism is now rather jarringly *passé*, for all that the objects of his mockery are still evident in much contemporary theatre. His plays dominate the repertory today in Italy and several regularly hold the stage internationally. Yet when revived, outside Italy at least, they invariably provoke a mixed critical response. One problem is that even the finest, like *Sei Personaggi* and *Enrico IV*, can today appear irritatingly prolix, marred by excessive discussion and explanation, and by an overly insistent irony.

Pirandello questioned received assumptions about individual personality, the nature of 'reality', the status of theatrical illusion and the relationship between art and life. By stripping away what he saw as self-constructed deceptions he sought to expose the essential 'nakedness' of man in a condition of things subject to constant flux. He opened up the abyss of the absurd. But he never wholly escaped from the pull of the traditions he rejected as he sought to turn the drama of middle-class drawing rooms, character psychology and domestic conflict to serve his 'modernist' perceptions. Striking as many of his theatrical situations are, he still tends to trust verbal discourse more than the theatrical image. Of course, as far as English response is concerned translation has proved a problem: not all the plays have yet been made available, nor has much of his occasional writing, letters and such like, been translated. Again, the validity and pertinence of his quasi-philosophical arguments remain contentious, generating suspicions that he traffics meretriciously in melodrama and showmanship. Yet the sheer theatrical power of his best work, in its bitter humour, emotional drive and story-telling power, is undeniable and Pirandello, like **Strindberg**, can disturb and persuade in ways not readily definable by critical explication. Like Strindberg he remains challengingly elusive and a still potent force.   LR

Pires, José Cardoso (1925–) Portuguese playwright and novelist. The first of two plays to date, *O Render dos Heróis* (*Relieving the Heroes*, 1965), deals with a historical event, a reactionary peasant revolt of the 1840s that failed, showing it up as an illusory or mythical episode that was marginal to the machinations of those in real power. The approach and techniques employed are highly 'Brechtian', with 'alienating' cutting from scene to scene, the mix of 'real' named characters with stock characters as old as drama, e.g. Coronel Matamundos (Col. Kill-'em-all), a blind man who signifies when he wishes to be blind and when he does not by turning over a placard with the appropriate labelling hung round his neck. *Corpo-Delito na Sala de Espelhos* (*Body of Evidence in the Hall of Mirrors*, 1979), Brechtian and absurd, with more than a touch of the **Genet** of *Le Balcon*, brings the nightmare of the PIDE (Salazar's secret police) to the boards frighteningly and unforgettably.   LK

Piron, Alexis (1689–1773) French dramatist and poet. His first success came as a regular purveyor of *vaudeville* and operatic parodies to the Paris fair theatres in the 1720s before he turned to the legitimate stage with a series of plays for the **Comédie-Française**. Of these, *Gustave Wasa* (*Gustavus Vasa*, 1733), a historical tragedy, and *L'Ecole des Pères* (*The School for Fathers*, 1728), a tearful middle-class comedy, are of some interest, but it is for *La Métromanie* (*Metromania*, 1738) that he is justly remembered. This is a lively, original comedy on the subject of poetry and poets and has as its central character a young provincial poet with recognizable affinities to Piron himself. He was also famous as the author of witty epigrams directed against contemporary literary figures, especially **Voltaire** of whom he was a persistent antagonist.   DR

Pisarev, Aleksandr Ivanovich (1803–28) In his short career he became known as the best Russian vaudeville dramatist, combining farcical situations with effective characterization and even some early social criticism. **Gogol** condemned the vaudeville for 'its light mockery at the funny sides of society without a glance at the soul of man'. However, during the reactionary reign of Nikolai I when freedom of speech and the press was largely curtailed, the disarming medium of the vaudeville became one of the few avenues for superficial criticism into which the audience could read its own deeper meanings. In spite of his talent for vaudeville and verse comedy, most of Pisarev's 23 plays were translations or adaptations of French neoclassical models. Basically a conservative in literary matters, Pisarev aligned himself with the classically minded **Shakhovskoi** circle in its attack of *Moscow Telegraph* editor **N. A. Polevoi** and with Shakhovskoi and **I. A. Krylov** founded the classicist (anti-romantic) journal *The Diplomatic Courier* (1808). **M. S. Shchepkin**, the father of Russian realistic acting, took a serious approach to the playing of roles in Pisarev's vaudevilles *The Tutor and the Pupil* (1824) and *The Busybody* (1825), although he preferred to play in the comedies of **Molière** which also formed part of the standard repertory. *The Tutor and the Pupil* is also noteworthy for its satirical portrait of a stupid pedant named Schelling, a topical reference to the vogue in certain circles of Russian society for the German philosopher of the same name. Two of Pisarev's works, *The Caliph's Amusements* (1825) and *The Magic Nose, or the Talisman and the Dates* (1825), were dubbed 'vaudeville-operas', indicating a greater emphasis on spectacle-scenic transformations, costumes and dances which was well-suited to their Oriental stories. The first play also offered some criticism of judicial corruption.   SG

Piscator, Erwin Friedrich Max (1893–1966) German director, whose concept of political theatre formed one of the most significant creative forces in German drama during the 1920s as well as in the 1960s. Founding the Tribune (1919) in imitation of the expressionist director **Karlheinz Martin**, whom he succeeded as director of the Proletarian Theatre, Piscator developed a form of agit-prop suited to the German context which culminated in a historical revue *Despite All!* (1925). The latter presented a polemic panorama of events between the outbreak of war in 1914 and the deaths of Liebknecht and Rosa Luxemburg in a simultaneous montage of authentic speeches, news-extracts, photographs and film sequences. His dramatic aims were utilitarian, to influence voters or clarify Communist policy, and the standards of authenticity and contemporaneity carried over into his productions for the **Volksbühne**. Dismissed in 1927 after incorporating film into Ehm Welk's *Storm over Gottland*, overlaying the 14th-century plot with the Russian Revolution, he founded the Piscator-Bühne in opposition to the Volksbühne. There he mounted a series of striking multi-media productions designed to present complex economic and social forces in concrete terms. **Toller**'s *Hurrah, We Live!* (1927) was performed on a four-storey structure, onto which filmed scenes were projected, and Piscator's technological staging was extended to its fullest by *Rasputin*, later the same year. This used a revolving hemisphere – symbolizing both the globe and mechanization – with scenes played within its opening segments, film and photographs inegrated with the action, and texts or dates projected on screens flanking the stage. One element could comment on another, gaining an effect of objectivity or linking cause and effect. Although the technology was too ambitious to be financially viable, it provided a model of epic theatre that influenced **Brecht**, who collaborated on the *Rasputin* production and that of *The Adventures of the Good Soldier Schweik* (1928), as well as containing all the techniques of the modern documentary drama. It also influenced the Theatre Workshop of **Joan Littlewood** in England and the **Living Newspaper** productions of the **Federal Theatre Project** in the USA through his book on *The Political Theatre* (1929).

After teaching at the Dramatic Workshop in New York during the war, where he first staged his adaptation of *War and Peace* (1942), he returned to Germany and became director of the new Freie Volksbühne in 1962. There he was instrumental in developing the documentary plays of **Hochhuth** (*The Representative*, 1963 and *Soldiers*, 1966), **Kipphardt** (*In the Matter of J. Robert Oppenheimer*, 1964) and **Weiss** (*The Investigation*, 1965). CI

Pisemsky, Aleksei Feofilaktovich (1821–81) Russian writer-dramatist (non-ideological, sceptical, realistic-naturalistic) who, with his friend **Ostrovsky**, brought the common people on to the Russian stage. His play *A Bitter Fate* (1859) is sometimes called the first Russian realistic tragedy. Antecedent in plot, character and theme to **L. N. Tolstoi**'s *The Power of Darkness*, Pisemsky's dramatization of a provincial ménage à trois with fatal consequences is largely devoid of Tolstoi's moral didacticism. It was preferred by such knowledgeable critics as **I. F. Annensky** and D. S. Mirsky. His later plays were mostly historical melodramas and satires on incipient capitalism in the 1860s and 1870s (e.g., *Baal*, 1873), the latter suggesting **Sukhovo-Kobylin**'s *The Case* in theme and intensity. An unallied spokesman for the objective representation of reality, his narrative works include the novels *The Muff* (1850), *A Thousand Souls* (1858) and *Troubled Seas* (1863). He continued the Gogolian tradition of exposing the baser side of humanity and shared with this author a malady that was the subject of his first stage comedy, *The Hypochondriac* (1852). SG

Pitoëff, George (1884–1939), **Ludmilla** (1895–1951), **Sacha** (1920–   ) George and Ludmilla Pitoëff left Russia, where they had known **Stanislavsky** and **Meyerhold**, for Switzerland (1915–21) and then Paris, where his productions were some of the most significant of the inter-war period. George, a member of the **Cartel**, was an outstandingly inventive director in spite of having to work with constant financial difficulties. He is particularly remembered for his productions of **Pirandello** (*Six Characters in Search of an Author*, 1923) and **Chekhov**, but his repertoire was enormously wide-ranging and thoroughly international. He was important in bringing both **Lenormand** and **Anouilh** to public notice. Ludmilla, his wife, was an outstanding actress and something of a mystic. As well as in Chekhov, she triumphed in **Shaw**'s *St Joan* (1925) and in **Claudel**'s *L'Echange* (1937 and 1946). Their son,

Sacha, set up his own company in 1949, which excelled in productions of Pirandello and Chekhov. A powerful actor, who exudes a sense of mystery, he has also performed in films, notably Resnais's *Last Year at Marienbad* (1961). DB

Pix, Mary (1666–1709) English playwright. Her first plays appeared in 1696, a tragedy *Ibrahim* and a lively farce *The Spanish Wives*. By the following year she had become well enough known to be mocked with other female playwrights in *The Female Wits*. Her fast-paced comedy *The Deceiver Deceived* (1698) was plagiarized by the actor George Powell for his play *The Imposture Defeated* performed by the rival company. Her friendship with **Congreve** began in 1700. In all she wrote 12 plays, tragedies of heroic sentiment and comedies of witty intrigue; all her work displays a similar concern to defend the independence of her heroines. PH

Pixérécourt, René Charles Guilbert de (1773–1844) French dramatist. Pixérécourt, son of a noble family, destitute at the Revolution, turned to the theatre to make a living, his first performed play being *Selico; ou les Nègres Généreux* (*Selico; or The Generous Negroes*) (Nancy, 1796). Within a few years he had become the acknowledged father of the newly emergent genre, the melodrama. He also wrote *vaudevilles* and comic operas, but the most successful of his 120 works were melodramas, some of which ran for hundreds of performances. He generally directed his own plays, attaching much importance to the *mise-en-scène*. From 1825–35 he managed the Gaîté. His last play, *Bijou; ou L'Enfant de Paris* (*Bijou or the Parisian Child*), was performed in 1838. Pixérécourt's triumphal career began with a work originally intended for the Opéra Comique and adapted from the popular novelist Ducray-Duminil (whose novels provided sources for many early melodramas), *Victor; ou L'Enfant de la Forêt* (*Victor or the Child of the Forest*, 1797). The play, with its theme of a virtuous youth discovering his father to be a brigand, shows clearly Pixérécourt's fondness for sententious moralizing and his view of the theatre as a school for virtue for the popular classes. *Coelina; ou L'Enfant du Mystère* (1800 – adapted into English by **Holcroft** as *A Tale of Mystery*) set the pattern for melodrama. It exploits the idea of a mutilated 'hero', has an innocent persecuted heroine, a good comic role, an exciting chase and conflict above a ravine, and the final triumph of virtue. It also exploits the pathetic fallacy, the mood of the action being reflected in the scenery and the behaviour of nature. *L'Homme à Trois Visages* (*The Man With Three Faces*, 1801), with its Venetian setting, conspiracies, and hero who is obliged to play three different roles, established another much-followed pattern in the early melodrama. *Tékéli* (1803) was one of Pixérécourt's favourite plays, and one of his most heroic. *Robinson Crusoe* (1805) owed little to Defoe, made much of the noble savage theme, and borrowed Birnam wood from *Macbeth*. *The Forest of Bondy; or, The Dog of Montargis* (1814) owed its appeal to the use made of a dog to prove the innocence of the hero about to be falsely executed. *Christophe Colomb; ou la Découverte du Nouveau Monde* (*Christopher Columbus*, 1815) had an interesting move in the direction of local colour with its savages speaking a language from a dictionary of Caribbean. Over a dozen stage adaptations were made of d'Arlincourt's best-seller novel, *The Solitary*. One of the better versions was Pixérécourt's one for the Gaîté, *Le Mont Sauvage; ou le Solitaire* (*The Wild Mountain; or, the Solitary*, 1821) with its striking scenic effects by Gué, including a famous vision scene. His *Le Château du Loch Leven; ou la Captivité de Marie Stuart* (*Castle of Loch Leven, or the Captivity of Mary Stuart*, 1822) managed to have a happy ending. After 1830 he joined in the flood of napoleonic pieces now permitted with *Malmaison et Sainte Hélène*. His last major play, and one of his most important, *Latude; ou Trente-cinq Ans de Captivité* (*Latude or Thirty-five Years of Captivity*, 1834), was based on a real event, an unjust imprisonment, and the action illustrated well the episodic nature of many melodramas. Pixérécourt had an excellent sense of theatre, but his dialogue was little more than a support for the action, and after his death most of his plays rapidly disappeared from the repertoire. Pixérécourt was one of the founders of the Committee of Authors and did much to ensure the payment of proper royalties.   JMCC

Pla, Josefina (1909–) Paraguayan dramatist. Born in the Canary Islands, but Paraguayan resident since 1927, later naturalized. Also a poet, journalist, and critic. More than 40 plays, some written in collaboration with Roque Centurión Miranda, with whom in 1948 she created the Municipal School of Dramatic Art in Asunción. Best-known play is *Historia de un número* (*Story of a Number*, 1949), an expressionistic, sentimental farce; other plays range from local themes, written in Guaraní, to classical tragedies such as *Alcestes*.   GW

Placide family A famous family of American actors, less known but equal in American theatrical importance to the **Booths** or **Jeffersons**. The USA Placides begin with **Alexander Placide** (?–1812), a French rope dancer and pantomimist of some distinction, who fled from France during the Revolution. He emigrated to the United States, and first appeared in America at the **John Street Theatre**, New York, in 1792. He married a Miss Wighten, the daughter of a celebrated London actress. For a time, Placide managed theatres in Charleston and Richmond, and was announced for a benefit on 26 December 1811, the day of a disastrous Richmond fire.

Of Placide's many children, the best known was **Henry Placide** (1799–1870), considered one of the finest character actors of the American stage. After appearing as a child actor in 1814, he made his debut in 1823 at the **Park Theatre** as Zekiel Home-spun. He remained at the Park for 20 years, acting more than 500 roles, 200 of which he created. He attempted one London engagement, unsuccessfully. American audiences considered him best in traditional English comedy, Sir Peter Teazle being among his most successful parts.

Henry Placide's older sister **Caroline** (1789–1881) married **William Rufus Blake**, and his siblings **Eliza** (?–1874) and **Thomas** (1808–77) both had theatrical careers, Thomas managing the Park Theatre for some years. **Jane** (1804–35), another sister, made her debut in Norfolk, Virginia, in 1820, and in 1823 she appeared in New Orleans, Louisiana, playing there almost exclusively for a decade. At that time she appeared as a singer, as well as a dramatic and comic actress. She was said to be the most polished actress in the South in her time and was referred to as the 'Queen of the Drama in New Orleans', her Lady Macbeth and Cordelia being especially admired. She appeared at **Covent Garden** in 1834 and died shortly after her return to the USA.   SMA

Planché, James Robinson (1795–1880) English playwright, antiquarian and musician whose autobiographical *Recollections and Reflections* (1872) is uniquely informative about 19th-century theatre practice. Planché had his first play produced in 1818, but it was an adaptation from the French of *The Vampire* (1820) at the **Lyceum** that brought him into prominence, not least for its introduction of the 'vampire trap'. For **Charles Kemble** at **Covent Garden**, he designed accurate historical costumes for a revival of *King John* (1823), and his research in this field culminated in the publication of *The History of British Costume* (1834). Almost single-handed, Planché had transformed the theatre's view of 'wardrobe'. Already a Fellow of the Society of Antiquaries (1829), he became a member of the British Archaeological Association in 1844 and a Somerset Herald in 1866. All these activities had outlets in his theatrical practice. Planché wrote over 150 plays and librettos. His libretto for Weber's *Oberon* at Covent Garden (1826) contributed to the opera's phenomenal success. It was written during his year as director of music at Vauxhall Gardens. Planché's most original dramatic work, however, was written for **Madame Vestris** at the **Olympic** from 1830–9. *Olympic Revels* (1830) was the first of a rich sequence of charming extravaganzas, tailor-made for the talented and ambitious actress-singer. Wittily rhymed and prettily costumed, these extravaganzas, based on classical mythology, significantly altered the development of English pantomime. Planché maintained the style after Madame Vestris had left the Olympic. In 1845, he embellished her **Haymarket** season with one of his best, *The Golden Fleece*, and ten years later, he matched the very different genius of **Frederick Robson** with the part of Prince Richcraft in *The Discreet Princess*. Planché stands as an exemplary figure of the 19th-century British theatre – a man of high standards only too prepared to lower them.   PT

Planchon, Roger (1931–) French director, actor, playwright. Planchon is of working-class origins and largely self-educated in the theatre; all his work is marked by the originality and vigour of the young man discovering the great theatre classics for himself, not through the classroom. His first company was founded when he was 21 in a disused printing works in Lyon. In this small (110-seat) auditorium he alternated ebullient musical comedies (mostly scripted by himself and his company) with avant-garde plays by **Adamov** and **Ionesco**. One of the first directors to produce **Brecht** in France (*The Good Person of Setzuan*, 1954), he and Adamov together evolved a Marxist theatre style of great social and theatrical complexity. He coined the term *écriture scénique* (scenic writing) to express the importance of the director's work which should complement that of the author which he called dramatic writing. His first production to be shown in Paris was Adamov's *Paolo-Paoli* (1957) which divided the critics, some praising its brilliant mix of theatricality and social

Gérard Guillaumat as Cléante in Planchon's 1973 production of *Tartuffe*. Sitting on the bench is a statue of Christ.

detail, others complaining at the demystification of the *belle époque* in this production which made the French capitalism of the period look both ludicrous and murderous. In 1957 he moved to the large municipal theatre in Lyon's workers' suburb of Villeurbanne, where he has remained ever since. Here his work has been particularly characterized by Marxist reinterpretations of plays by **Shakespeare** (*Henry IV*, 1957, *Troilus and Cressida*, 1964, *Richard III*, 1966), **Molière** (*George Dandin*, 1958, *Le Tartuffe*, 1962 and 1973 (new version), *Dom Juan*, 1980), **Marivaux** (*La Seconde Surprise de l'Amour*, 1959) and **Racine** (*Bérénice*, 1966, *Athalie*, 1980). Since 1962 he has written over a dozen plays of his own, many of which he has directed and performed in, notably *La Remise* (1962), *Bleus Blancs Rouges ou les Libertins* (1967), *L'Infâme* (1969), *Le Cochon Noir* (1973), *Gilles de Rais* (1976). These often present images of peasant life in which clashing ideological concepts are dramatized in realistic scenes of great theatrical force. In 1972 Planchon's theatre received the title **Théâtre National Populaire** and so the mantle of **Vilar** passed to him. His style is much richer than Vilar's and he does not share Vilar's vision of culture as a uniting force, but by remaining in Villeurbanne he has placed a similar emphasis on making the best of modern theatre available to working-class audiences. Much of his success is due to his ability to retain a small group of fine actors together, notably Jean Bouise, Isabelle

Sadoyan and Claude Lochy who also wrote the music for the company's productions. René Allio designed most of his productions in the 1960s and he has worked regularly with others e.g. André Acquart, Luciano Damian and Ezio Frigerio. He has also encouraged other directors and helped them to establish themselves e.g. Jacques Rosner, **Patrice Chéreau** and Georges Lavaudant. DB

Plater, Alan (Frederick) (1935–) British dramatist, born in County Durham, who became in 1970 a co-founder of the Hull Arts Centre. He began writing television plays, several of which he adapted for the stage. *A Smashing Day* (1965) received a brief London run in 1966 and concerned the problems of a young man who did not know what he wanted to do with his life or whom he should do it with. *See The Pretty Lights* (1970) is a tender love-story between a middle-aged man and a teenage girl. But Plater's true vitality as a writer only emerged when he started to work with songwriters such as Alex Glasgow and in a style of regional 'epics' which owed much to **Joan Littlewood**, combining songs, music-hall sketches and comedy gags into what were often serious social themes. The most successful of these local documentaries was *Close The Coalhouse Door* (1968), based on stories by Sid Chaplin, which described the history of coalmining as seen through the eyes of the Milburn family. JE

Platt An Elizabethan theatrical term for the outline or 'plot' of a play. The Elizabethan platt was not an abstract but a concrete reality. Because plays had to be prepared in haste and performed in repertoire, the book-keeper was entrusted with the task of writing out the detail of the plot and hanging it where it could be consulted by actors and stage-hands. A few such platts have survived. Written on foolscap, divided into two columns, with marginal notes on properties and sound effects, they generally noted the names of the actors as well as the characters they were to impersonate against the episodes in which they were to appear. The platts were then pasted on to a thin wood pulp board, pierced at the top for hanging. PT

Plautus (d. c. 184 BC) The first Roman dramatist to specialize solely in comedy, and the first whose work survives. The legends concerning his life are of little value, though it could be true that he worked as a stage-hand or actor before starting to write plays. Not even his name is certain; it is usually given as Titus Maccius Plautus, but all three names may be nicknames.

Nor do we know how many plays he wrote. After his death there were said to be 130 circulating in his name, but Roman scholars were agreed that many were spurious. The scholar Varro drew up a list of 21 that were universally regarded as authentic, and these doubtless correspond to the 21 preserved, completely or partly, in medieval manuscripts. The authenticity of all of these is accepted by most modern scholars.

Of the 21, one (*Vidularia*, *The Wallet Play*) is a mere fragment. Only two are firmly dated, *Stichus* to 200 BC and *Pseudolus* to 192. The others are *Amphitruo*, *Asinaria* (*The Ass Play*), *Aulularia* (*The Jar Play*), *Bacchides* (*The Bacchises*), *Captivi* (*The Prisoners*), *Casina*, *Cistellaria*

(*The Casket Play*), *Curculio, Epidicus, Menaechmi* (*The Menaechmuses*), *Mercator* (*The Merchant*), *Miles Gloriosus* (*The Braggart Soldier*), *Mostellaria* (*The Spook Play*), *Persa* (*The Persian*), *Poenulus* (*The Wretch from Carthage*), *Pseudolus, Rudens* (*The Rope*), *Trinummus* (*Threepence*), and *Truculentus*. All are adapted from Greek originals: three by **Menander**, two by Diphilus, two by Philemon, one probably by Alexis, one by a certain Demophilus, the rest by unknown authors.

There has been much scholarly discussion of the extent to which Plautus departed from these originals. Our increased knowledge of Menander's work has made this easier to assess, but brings dangers, for Menander had a distinctive style of his own which was not simply representative of New Comedy; and there is evidence that some character-types which to us seem peculiar to Roman comedy (such as the braggart soldier) were deliberately avoided by Menander, not unknown to him.

Certainly Plautus' style is far more jokey than that of his models, being full of puns, alliteration, coinages, bizarre imagery, and other tricks of language. Even the more serious figures are allowed to come out of character for the sake of a joke, though more often it is the slaves and other low-life figures who joke at their expense. The role of the Cunning Slave – a likeable rogue who solves all his master's problems with his trickery – is built up enormously, and this character may give his name to a play (*Epidicus, Pseudolus, Stichus*), as he never does in Greek. Obscenities and topical allusions are not particularly common, but are far more so than in Greek New Comedy. Address to the audience is frequent, especially from the Cunning Slave; sometimes this is thinly disguised as soliloquy, but Plautus is quite prepared to break the 'dramatic illusion' altogether by acknowledging the audience's presence. The pathos and moral delicacy of Menander are abandoned or undercut, as the cynicism and deceitfulness of the Cunning Slave prevails over all (though there is some moral edification in *Captivi*). Metres are far more varied than in Menander, large sections of most of the plays being written for musical accompaniment.

Names of persons and places are Greek (or sometimes a comic parody of Greek), but Greek institutions and customs are generally Romanized – sometimes merely to avoid puzzling the audience, but sometimes to create deliberate incongruity. *Amphitruo* is the only ancient comedy to survive on a mythical theme, but even here the focus is on intrigue and deception and the characters are familiar Plautine types.

In some plays, such as *Aulularia* and *Menaechmi* (the source of **Shakespeare**'s *Comedy of Errors*), the plot is well sustained and more or less consistent; in others, such as *Stichus*, it is ragged and unimportant beside the element of farce and slapstick. No doubt the former plays are closer to their Greek models than the latter. The only case in which we can make a direct comparison, however, is that of *Bacchides*, adapted from Menander's *Dis Exapaton* (*The Double Deceiver*), of which a fragment has been discovered. Here it can be seen that Plautus has altered the structure considerably, amalgamating two speeches, which were separated by an act-division, into one. Sometimes, however, the positions of act-divisions in the original remain obvious in the adaptation.

The formal prologue, which Menander had used to set the scene, is sometimes abandoned altogether (and some of the prologues we have are probably not by Plautus himself). When it is retained, it not only sets the scene but attracts the audience's attention by means of jokes and direct advertisement of the play's merits. Sometimes it is delivered by an anonymous person who has no other function, rather than by a god or a character in the ensuing action.

Plautus can have had no conception (unlike **Terence**, perhaps) that he was writing literature, to be studied by readers who would criticize the loose ends of his plots, the incongruity of his jokes, and the repetitiveness of his farcical scenes. He was writing scripts for theatrical performance, and it is obvious that he knew his theatre and his audience intimately, and provided exactly what was wanted.   ALB

Plavilshchikov, Pyotor Alekseevich (1760–1812)

Russian dramatist, actor and teacher, who helped to forge the Russian national theatre envisioned by Lukin. After graduating from Moscow University in 1779, he taught history, literature and rhetoric and then embarked on an acting career in Moscow and St Petersburg (early 1780s). As a former student of the famous actor-teacher **Ivan Dmitrevsky**, he continued the tradition of coolly reasoned playing. Added to this were athletic good looks and a noble countenance which made him ideally suited for the impersonation of positive heroes, kings and moralizers in tragedy. His search for original ideas in everything he assayed may have been responsible for the assortment of tricks which he employed in such roles as Oedipus in **Ozerov**'s tragedy, lurching and freezing, shrieking and whispering all of a sudden for effect. His real talent was expressed in roles drawn from bourgeois drama and *bytovoi* (daily life) comedies. Here he manifested a degree of simplicity, naturalness and sincerity of feeling and expression which in a sense belied his training but revealed his instincts. These works were closer in style and tone to his own bourgeois dramas and doleful comedies on Russian historical, patriotic and colloquial themes. He rejected Lukin's compromise method of transforming foreign plays to a Russian context and regarded the unities as inconsequential. His comic opera, *The Miller and the Mead-Seller as Rivals* (1782), a sequel to **Knyazhnin**'s *The Mead-Seller* and Ablesimov's comic opera *The Miller*, favours the miller for his more total Russianness. His comedy, *Kuteikin's Agreement* (1789), is a sequel to **Fonvizin**'s classic Russian national comedy, *The Minor*. *The Landless Peasant* (1790), on the other hand, violates Fonvizin's fiercely satirical spirit by sentimentally depicting the relationship between master and serfs. *The Shopman* (1804) offers a satirical treatment of the Russian merchant class in a state of moral decline under French influence which foreshadows **Ostrovsky**'s comedies of the latter half of the 19th century. Plavilshchikov was also a man of great administrative talents. In 1781 he succeeded Dmitrevsky as supervisor of the Russian theatre in St Petersburg. Leaving for Moscow two years later as a result of a contract dispute with Prince Yusupov, he taught declamation at the Noblemen's Boarding School and trained companies of serf actors, one of which was acquired by the directorate of the Imperial theatres. Everywhere he worked he tried to enhance the standard repertory with new dramatic offerings. In a case of life imitating art, he died in 1812 in a remote province while fleeing the French invaders.   SG

Play Play is central to the health and the growth of individual and community. Through play human beings both celebrate and shape their world. It is a dynamic which permeates culture; more a process, a relationship, and an attitude than a thing in itself. Play is a free activity, intrinsically self-motivated and non-utilitarian, where attention is voluntarily limited. For the player, absorption may lead to an altered sense of time and/or space, a fusion of action and awareness, and an enhanced feeling of competence, energy, and discovery. The activity is often felt to be different, set apart, from everyday life, and in Protestant cultures this division has been rigidified in the opposition of work and play. The uselessness of play is an irritant to a moralistic work ethic and this rigidity has nurtured a considerable anti-theatrical prejudice.

In many languages the word or words used to express play are at root associated with swift movement, with leaping, dancing, joking. Motion through space and time, fun and make-believe, the flow of appearance and experience, are constituent elements of theatre, and from an early period in England the Anglo-Saxon words *pleg* and *gamen* were used to describe theatrical events of all kinds. Throughout medieval and Tudor times the live performance, that unique meeting between actor and spectators, was known in the vernacular as a play or a game. For this sport, a 'play-ground' or 'play-house' was required and usually, along with other 'play-stuff', a 'play-book' (sometimes with separate 'rolls' for individual players). Many of the artifacts needed for the practice of theatre took on terms related to the central activity. A play in the sense of a literary text is a late and special use of the word.

A play as a script can take many forms. It may be a record written down after the event, like numerous British folk-plays transcribed in the 19th and 20th centuries by enthusiastic collectors. It may be an elaborate narrative written down, after a period of oral transmission, in order to stabilize the story but with little concern for the way it is staged, like the manuscripts of Tibetan Harvest Festival dramas. It may be a schematic aid to performance – outlining plot, characters, entrances and exits, and the disposition of 'props' – like the scenarios or *canovacci* of the **commedia dell'arte**. Or it may be a literary composition in dialogue form with either implicit and explicit instructions for the players or, as with **Shaw** and **O'Neill**, lengthy novelistic stage directions intended primarily for the reader. This preparation of a text for a reading public alongside the principal aim of notation for performance creates a double focus. Rules and conventions alien to the play as event shape the play as script. For example, the notion of the division of playing time into five acts comes from the world of reading. The performances of **Plautus** and **Terence** were continuous. In England, the Renaissance interest in this pattern at first affected the printing, far more than the playing, of plays. However, the development of scenic illusion, and the gradual division of actors and audience into separate acoustic spaces, meant that act-structure became a substantive part of the play as experienced.

This double focus can lead in literate societies to an undue emphasis on 'interpretation', to a conviction that the play is in essence literature, and, more seriously, to a division of labour which excludes the living writer from direct involvement in theatre-making. Early records in Britain refer to 'devisers', 'doers', and 'makers' of plays and games. These unnamed creators share with most great dramatists, many of whom were actors, a common interest and involvement in the actual activity of play. A playwright is one who works play. That is both the craft and the essence of theatre.   LSR

Playhouse Theatre 137 West 48th St, New York City [Architect: Charles A. Rich]. In 1911, Broadway producer **William A. Brady** built the small Playhouse for his own productions, which often starred his wife Grace George. With an auditorium seating fewer than 1,000, the theatre also contained his own offices and those of other producers, press agents and the League of New York Theatres and Producers. At the age of 81, Brady sold his theatre, which eventually passed to Rockefeller real estate interests in 1967. A year later, it was demolished. Its most notable tenants included the first Broadway production of *Major Barbara* (1915), the Pulitzer Prize-winning *Street Scene* and *The Miracle Worker* (1959). On its stage, **Laurette Taylor** played her last and greatest role, Amanda Wingfield, in *The Glass Menagerie*.   MCH

Playwrights Horizon (1971–) American writer's theatre. Founded in New York by Robert Moss, Playwrights Horizon exists to develop and produce new scripts. Working in two small theatres on **Theatre Row** (West 42nd Street) the organization through readings, workshops, and full-scale productions has presented more than 200 new plays including *Kennedy's Children*, *Gemini*, *Sister Mary Ignatius Explains It All For You*, *The Dining Room*, and *Sunday in the Park with George* (TCG). Andre Bishop (artistic director) and Paul S. Daniels (managing director) work with a stable group of nine resident playwrights which has included **Christopher Durang**, **A. R. Gurney Jr**, **Albert Innaurato**, Ted Tally, and **Wendy Wasserstein**.   TLM

Pleasants, Jack (1874–1923) English comedian, 'the Bashful Limit'. *Ne plus ultra* of the shy comedian, the beauty of whose act lies in the spectacle of one so ostensibly ill-at-ease and tongue-tied exhibiting himself solo before a packed house (at the other end of the spectrum lies the brash persona of a **Max Miller**). Discovered at the Scarbrough Taps, Leeds, then the talent-spotting venue for the City Varieties (both still exist, though there is no longer a business connection between them), he opened his professional career at the Varieties in 1884. Following a big success in pantomime at the Theatre Royal in his native Bradford, in 1906, he expanded his career outside his northern stamping ground to become a nationally known dialect comedian. He 'wore a costume suggestive of the charity boy who had outgrown his clothes', and carried or sported in his buttonhole his whimsical trade-mark, a large white daisy. Remembered chiefly for the naive gaiety of 'Twenty-one Today' and the sexual gaucheness of his key-note song 'I'm Shy, Mary Ellen, I'm

Shy', he contributed to the long-standing and questionable tradition of regional gormlessness on the English stage. AEG

Pleasence, Donald (1919–) British actor, who made his first stage appearance in Jersey in 1939. After serving with the RAF during the war, and after being shot down and taken prisoner, he returned to the theatre in 1946, playing in *The Brothers Karamazov* at the **Lyric, Hammersmith**, and in *Huis Clos* at the **Arts**. He joined the **Birmingham Repertory Theatre** (1948–50) and the **Bristol Old Vic** in 1951; and in 1953, wrote and appeared in his play, *Ebb Tide*, which transferred from the **Edinburgh Festival** to the **Royal Court**. His voice, soft and expressive, and his slightly plump appearance brought him into demand as a character actor throughout the 1950s, in plays by **Anouilh** and **Pirandello** which received respectable reviews and London runs; but it was not until he played the tramp in **Harold Pinter**'s *The Caretaker* (1960), alternately cringing and sinister, that he became a star, repeating his London success in New York. Two other major roles followed, in Anouilh's *Poor Bitos* and as Eichmann in Robert Shaw's play, *The Man in the Glass Booth* (1967), for which he won the London Variety Award for Stage Actor of the Year (1968). His film and television appearances have been numerous, often playing sinister German officers in war dramas or master-criminals; and this stereotyping has tended to conceal the range of his acting abilities, which are now too rarely seen on stage. JE

Plowright, Joan (Anne) (Lady Olivier) (1929–) British actress, who trained at the **Old Vic** Theatre School in the late 1940s and joined **George Devine**'s original English Stage Company in 1956. Despite her successes as Margery Pinchwife in **Wycherley**'s *The Country Wife* and as the Old Woman in **Ionesco**'s *The Chairs* (1957), she emerged as a leading actress of her generation when creating the part of Beatie in **Wesker**'s *Roots* in Coventry and London in 1959. She met **Laurence Olivier** at the **Royal Court** and played Daisy in Ionesco's *Rhinoceros* (1960), opposite Olivier's Berenger, in an English Stage Company production, directed by **Orson Welles**. She joined the **National Theatre** company when it was formed in 1963, playing a variety of major roles there in subsequent years, including Joan in **Shaw**'s *St Joan*, Hilde in **Ibsen**'s *The Master Builder* and Portia in *The Merchant of Venice* (1970). Her particular quality lay in down-to-earth directness showing few mannerisms and little fuss, but good technical control and much emotional warmth, assets which were particularly helpful in two plays by **Eduardo de Filippo**, *Saturday, Sunday, Monday*, produced at the National Theatre in 1973, and *Filumena*, which opened in the West End in 1977. She appeared in **Ben Travers**'s last comedy, *The Bed Before Yesterday* (1975) and in **Alan Bennett**'s *Enjoy* (1980). She married Laurence Olivier in 1961. JE

Plummer, (Arthur) Christopher (Orme) (1929–) Toronto-born actor who, after playing nearly 100 roles with the Canadian Repertory Theatre, beginning in 1950, made his New York debut in 1954. In the 1950s and 60s his speciality was **Shakespeare**, appearing at the **American Shakespeare Theatre**

(1955), the Stratford Ontario Shakespeare Festival (1956, 1957, 1960, 1962), and with the **Royal Shakespeare Company** (1961). Roles included Mark Antony, Henry V, Hamlet, Sir Andrew Aguecheek, Benedick, Leontes, Mercutio, and Richard III. In 1981 he returned to the American Shakespeare Theatre as Iago and in the title role and Chorus in *Henry V*. He was Nickles in **MacLeish**'s *J. B.* (1958), Pizarro in *The Royal Hunt of the Sun* (1965), won the Tony Award as best actor in a musical (version of *Cyrano de Bergerac* with music) in 1973, and played Chekhov in **Neil Simon**'s *The Good Doctor* (1973). In London he played King Henry in *Becket* (1961). He joined the **National Theatre** at the New Theatre, London, in 1971. DBW

Plymouth Theatre 236 West 45th St, New York City [Architect: Herbert J. Krapp]. In 1917, backed by the ubiquitous **Shuberts**, producer-director **Arthur Hopkins** built the Plymouth as the theatrical home for himself and his productions. A man of quiet daring, Hopkins tended to produce the unusual play during his lifetime. At his theatre, he brought **John** and **Lionel Barrymore** on stage in *The Jest* (1919), the anti-war *What Price Glory?* (1924) and Sophie Treadwell's *Machinal* (1927). Unfortunately, the depression years tempered his activities and he was forced to relinquish his 1,000-seat, one-balcony house to the Shuberts after 1935. In its history, the Plymouth has had many notable tenants, none more extraordinary than the **Royal Shakespeare Company**'s production of *Nicholas Nickleby* (1981), which ran for eight hours with a dinner intermission and a ticket price of $100. The theatre has remained a Shubert house. MCH

Plyuchek, Valentin Nikolaevich (1909–) Soviet director, he was one of **Meyerhold**'s pupils in the latter's experimental studio (1926–9) and worked as an actor at the Meyerhold Theatre (1929–32), while simultaneously organizing a Theatre of Young Workers (TRAM). In 1939 he co-founded with **Aleksei Arbuzov** an experimental Moscow studio where, in 1940, a production entitled *A City at Dawn* was co-created by Arbuzov and the studio's students and directed by Plyuchek. In 1941 the studio became a front-line theatre, and in 1942 Plyuchek was made director of the Theatre of the Northern Fleet. He directed the Moscow Touring Theatre (1945–50) and staged plays at the Moscow Theatre of Satire (1950–7), where he has been artistic director since 1957. Founded in 1925 on the former site of **Baliev**'s 'Bat' cabaret, the Theatre of Satire at first duplicated that organization's variety-sketch format. Its search for good domestic satirical comedies, difficult enough in the 1920s, became even harder for its artistic director N. M. Gorchakov during the period of socialist realism (1934–53), when satire was regarded with suspicion. Plyuchek's arrival at the theatre coincided with the 'Thaw', the new order being announced by his productions of **Mayakovsky**'s now classic satires, *The Bathhouse* (1954, with Nikolai Petrov and Sergei Yutkevich), *The Bedbug* (1955, with Yutkevich) and *Mystery-Bouffe* (1957). Plyuchek's controversial constructivist stagings à la Meyerhold remained in the repertory, thanks largely to Mayakovsky's rehabilitated reputation. Plyuchek became a specialist in staging the hyperbolic satirical grotesque and has produced plays by Russian

satirists Ilf and Petrov, poet-editor Aleksandr Tvar-
kovsky, **G. B. Shaw**, **Beaumarchais**, **Brecht** (who
received the Stalin Prize in 1954 and thereafter became
'performable' in the Soviet Union), **Ostrovsky**, Aleksandr Shtein, **Erdman** and **Rozov**. In 1964 Plyuchek
was named a 'People's Artist of the RSFSR'.   SG

Poel, William (1852–1934) English actor and director and pioneer polemicist of the return to the bare
Elizabethan stage. Pole (Poel was a stage name) abandoned office work in 1875 to follow his idol, **Charles
James Mathews**, into the theatre. It was the beginning
of a strangely obsessive and initially piecemeal career.
In the early days, he was, for a while, manager for
Emma Cons of what became the **Old Vic** and, during
the first half of 1884, **F. R. Benson**'s stage manager.
But his real direction was already evident in his staging
of the bad quarto of *Hamlet* on a bare platform in
London's St George's Hall (1881). It was an isolated
and, with Poel himself as Hamlet, probably an excruciating event, but it heralded a lifetime's challenge to
rescuing **Shakespeare** and his contemporaries from
the restrictions of the picture-frame stage. An 1893
production of *Measure for Measure* was plain and
impressive, and Poel's work for the Elizabethan Stage
Society (1895–1905) was not only original in itself but
also immediately influential on **Harley Granville
Barker** and, through him, on theatrical ideas through
the 20th century. Beginning with *Twelfth Night* (1895),
and including a notable production of *Everyman* (1901)
as well as neglected work by **Ford**, **Marlowe**,
Fletcher, **Jonson**, **Middleton**, and even **Calderón**,
Coleridge and Swinburne, this unique venture ended
with *Romeo and Juliet* (1905). It was not in theatres, but
in halls, lecture-rooms and courtyards that the Elizabethan Stage Society performed. Critical recognition

might have been swifter if Poel had not added to his
love of austerity some quirkily fanatical views on voice
production. Too often the outcome was risible and
Poel increasingly barricaded himself behind his ideas.
His voluminous writing is fairly represented by the
selection in *Shakespeare in the Theatre* (1913) and his
startling combativeness by his rejection of a knighthood, proffered in 1929, because 'it was inconceivable
to me that my name could be added to the long list of
theatrical Knights not one of whom was in sympathy
with an Elizabethan method of presentation'.   PT

Poesía en Voz Alta (Poetry Out Loud) Mexican
theatre group (1956–63), founded by Juan José
Arreola, Octavio Paz, Juan Soriano and Leonora
Carrington, all writers and painters, an experimental
and controversial theatre project dedicated to the
importance of language and poetry in the theatre. Its
eight programmes in eight years, with total or partial
support from the National University, conceptualized
theatre as a game. Despite its stormy trajectory, the
movement inspired experimentation in other formats,
and produced a new generation of talented directors,
including Héctor Mendoza.   GW

Poetomachia see **War of the theatres**

**Pogodin (pseudonym of Stukalov), Nikolai
Fyodorovich** (1900–62) Soviet journalist and prolific (almost 30 plays) and much decorated (Stalin and
Lenin Prizes, etc.) conformist playwright, who
embraced socialist realism and myth-making monumentalism as opposed to psychological and social
veracity. His unabashedly schematic, 'conflictless'
plays demonstrate the inevitable conversion of recalcitrant types to the noble cause of 'socialist construction'.

William Poel's 1893 production of *Measure for Measure* attempted a reconstruction of the Elizabethan Fortune stage within the
proscenium arch of the Royalty Theatre.

They reflect his own experiences as a labourer and *Pravda* correspondent (1922–30), who travelled to construction sites throughout the USSR. *Tempo* (1929), his first play, attempts via earthy humour and the use of a sympathetic American engineer protagonist to depict the inspiring construction work of the First Five-Year Plan (1928–33). *Aristocrats* (1934), produced by **Okhlopkov** at the Realistic Theatre, depicts the reclamation for Soviet society of prison camp inmates, who become inspired by their work on the Baltic–White Sea Canal project. Part of Pogodin's creative programme to glorify and humanize the Soviet leadership is his Lenin cycle – *The Man with a Gun* (1937), *The Kremlin Chimes* (1942), *The Third, Pathétique* (1959) – of which the middle drama is the best. Set during Lenin's drive to electrify Russia, it shows the sensitive leader's effect on a disaffected Jewish engineer, who finally agrees to repair the chimes so that they will again play the 'Internationale'. Pogodin's most atypical play, *A Petrarchan Sonnet* (1957), concerns the corruption of a platonic affair by hypocritical busybodies and broaches the subject so relevant under Stalin of the individual's right to the privacy of his emotional life. Its theme, its call for humanism and attack on the 'new philistinism' and its open-ended conclusion – the antithesis of socialist realism's 'happy endings' – identify this as a drama of the 'year of protest' (1956). SG

Poisson, Raymond (c. 1630–90) French actor and playwright, founder of a minor theatrical dynasty. After some years as a provincial actor in the 1650s he made his debut at the **Hôtel de Bourgogne** under the stage name of Belleroche in about 1660 and remained there until 1680, whereupon he became a member of the first **Comédie-Française** company until his retirement in 1685. He was renowned above all for developing the character of Crispin as a comic type, using his considerable bulk, his large mouth and even his tendency to stutter to advantage, and he became a great favourite of Louis XIV. He was also the author of a number of farcical comedies, the most interesting of which, *Le Baron de la Crasse* (1661), concerns a performance for an audience of country gentry given by some itinerant actors whose leader has been taken to be a caricature of **Molière**. Of the six children he had by his actress wife, no fewer than four took to the stage, notably his elder son Paul (c. 1658–1735), who inherited his father's roles when he entered the Comédie-Française in 1686, even preserving the speech defect, while two grandsons also became actors, the elder soon retiring to write plays, and one granddaughter a dramatist. DR

Polaire (Emilie-Marie Bouchard) (1877–1939) French actress and singer, born in Algeria. Her singing career began in Paris at the age of 14, and her minuscule waist, doe's eyes and bobbed hair (20 years ahead of its time) caught the public's attention. She introduced 'Ta-ra-ra-boom-deay' to France, and was taken up by Colette whose *Claudine à Paris* she played (1906). She was also seen in London and New York (1910), billed cruelly as 'the ugliest woman in the world'. After the First World War, she devoted herself exclusively to acting. LS

Poland Theatre in Poland has always occupied a special place in the life of the nation. Constant threats to

The Polish Theatre (Teatr Polski) was established by Arnold Szyfman in Warsaw in 1913. Its opening production was Krasiński's *Iridion* (a play written in 1833–6, but only previously performed, by Teatr Zjednoczony, Warsaw, in 1912).

its very existence have made theatre the guardian of national consciousness. In the unending struggle against censorship and political controls, Polish theatre remains a vital institution. Denied other outlets for the discussion of national issues, Poles find in theatre a public forum where, in response to poetic metaphor and allusion, they may express their feelings and reassert their sense of identity as a people. Even though there has been little Polish political drama, all theatre in Poland becomes political because of the expectations of audiences who look to the stage for what they can find nowhere else. For Polish artists, creating theatre in opposition to the powers that be, under circumstances of adversity, in exile, or underground, has often been a common fate.

The earliest form of Polish theatre was liturgical drama in Latin growing out of the Easter Mass and performed by the clergy. By the 16th century these ritual dramas had already been replaced by mystery plays dealing with the life of Christ and other biblical stories, written in the vernacular and performed in marketplaces by guild members and paid student actors. Two celebrated Polish mysteries are *The Story of the Most Glorious Resurrection of Our Lord* (1570) by Mikołaj of Wilkowiecko, a Pauline monk, and *The Life of Joseph* (1545) by the Calvinist poet Mikołaj Rej. Combining music, pageantry and spectacular stage effects, the mystery plays often contained farcical episodes and extraneous folk materials, and reflected contemporary manners and dress. Nativity plays spread throughout Poland and served as the basis for the *szopka*, a popular form of puppet theatre presented at Christmas time, which survives today.

Under the influence of Renaissance humanism, the Polish school theatres in the 16th century introduced the plays of **Seneca**, **Plautus** and **Terence**, which were given at the court and by University of Cracow students, in both Latin and vernacular adaptations. Jesuit school theatre flourished for over two hundred years – from 1566 to 1773 – staging plays in Latin,

Greek and Polish, and using drama as propaganda in the battle against Protestantism.

Court theatre produced a masterpiece in *The Dismissal of the Greek Envoys*, a humanist tragedy by the greatest Polish Renaissance poet, Jan Kochanowski (1530–84). The play was performed by amateur actors for a royal wedding in 1578. Divided into five acts (although only slightly over 600 lines), and with a chorus and messenger, Kochanowski's blank-verse tragedy dramatizes portions of Book III of *The Iliad*, but is actually concerned with topical political issues addressed to the audience of the time.

Companies of actors were established at the court theatres, where Italian opera and **commedia dell'arte** enjoyed a vogue and foreign plays, particularly French works, were translated, adapted and performed. Italian, French and German companies played at the Polish court throughout the 16th century; and in the private theatres of the leading nobles, the lords and ladies themselves, their guests, and the servants and serfs (who became the earliest professional actors in Poland) took part in performances on festive occasions.

By the early 17th century, strolling players and buffoons gave public performances in marketplaces and at fairs, and foreign troupes toured the country. In 1611 a company of English comedians led by John Greene came to Poland with **Shakespeare**'s plays. Native itinerant theatre produced a popular form of drama known as *komedia rybałtowska*, which gave a satirical picture of manners and morals and featured typical characters such as priests, bailiff, merchant and beggar. A good example of the genre is *Peasant Turned King*, written in 1637 by Piotr Baryka.

The evolution of the Polish theatre was disrupted in the mid-17th century by the decline of town life and the middle class, and by the Swedish invasion. It was not until 1765 that Stanisław August Poniatowski, the last king of Poland, founded the National Theatre in Warsaw and created the first professional company acting in Polish for the general paying public.

Under **Wojciech Bogusławski**'s directorship from 1783 to 1814, the National Theatre achieved a high level of excellence and began to develop a repertory of original Polish plays. Because of his prestige as a nobleman, Bogusławski was able to change the status of the actor and make the profession respectable. His leadership of the National Theatre came at the time of Poland's loss of independence due to the three partitions – in 1722, 1793 and 1795 – at the hands of Russia, Prussia and Austria, resulting in the country's total disappearance from the map until 1918. Bogusławski's plays reflect his involvement in the patriotic cause of resistance. Because of its sympathetic portrayal of peasants and mountaineers, *The Cracovians and the Mountaineers* – a national comic opera with music by Jan Stefani – was stopped by the occupying powers in 1794 on the eve of Kościuszko's insurrection against the Russians. After the suppression of the revolt, the National Theatre was closed, and Bogusławski forced to flee to Lwów.

In the course of the 19th century, unsuccessful uprisings – against Russia in 1831, Austria and Prussia in 1846, and Russia again in 1863 – were suppressed and followed by harsh reprisals. Yet the theatrical life continued even under conditions of material and political duress. In fact, Polish theatre acquired new impor-tance for its role in maintaining the cultural, national and linguistic identity of a people which had lost all its own institutions.

Although theatres in all sections of the divided country were subject to censorship and under constant surveillance, the level of cultural repression in the three occupied zones differed markedly. In the first half of the 19th century, conditions were least favourable in the Prussian-ruled western territory, where a programme of Germanization was in effect and no permanent Polish theatre was allowed. Under Tsarist domination, which encompassed over half the country, including Warsaw, and brought about the closing of Polish universities, some Polish theatre was permitted under severe restrictions. New plays were often forbidden and old ones drastically cut to remove any episodes that might excite thoughts of rebellion. Authors, actors and audiences grew skilful at the game of allusions, and even the most oblique references to Poland, the fatherland or persecution were greeted with applause.

The southern portion of the country, under Austrian rule, known as Galicia and containing the provincial cities Cracow and Lwów, enjoyed more cultural freedom, and it was there that the most interesting theatrical developments occurred. Poland's major comic dramatist, **Aleksander Fredro** (1793–1876), came from Galicia and wrote many of his finest works for the theatre in Lwów. His plays bring to perfection the genre of verse comedy that evolved from Polish neoclassical comedy and the French tradition going back to **Molière**.

The most significant event for the future course of Polish theatre was the November Uprising in 1830, begun by Polish army officers. As a result of its defeat more than 10,000 Poles – leaders in politics, the military and the arts – left the country in the Great Emigration. Among those seeking refuge in the West were Poland's two outstanding romantic poet-playwrights, **Adam Mickiewicz** and **Juliusz Słowacki**, who wrote their dramas in exile without a thought for the practicalities of the stage, knowing that they could not be performed for political reasons.

Romantic drama characteristically exists outside the reigning conventions of performance; modelled after **Goethe**'s *Faust* and **Byron**'s *Manfred*, the plays of Mickiewicz and Słowacki – and of their politically conservative contemporary Zygmunt Krasiński – share certain traits with the 'dramatic poems' of the 19th-century European literary tradition. Polish romantic drama differs from its counterpart in the West in the power and originality of its theatrical form and in the resonance of its social and political vision. These seemingly unstageable works have in the 20th century become the classics of the Polish repertory and the basis of modern theatrical practice and innovation.

Writing as seers about martyred Poland's messianic destiny as the Christ of nations, the Polish romantic poets were able to create an imaginary stage that transcended the narrow conventions of the 19th-century playhouse. In his 16th lecture at the Collège de France in 1843, on the future of Slavic drama, Mickiewicz forecast a theatre that would encompass the various arts, appeal to all classes, emulate the medieval mysteries and draw on primeval rites, and yet utilize the most modern scenic techniques of Italian opera and the Parisian **Cirque Olympique**.

The masterworks of Polish romantic drama – Mickiewicz's *Forefathers' Eve* (1832), Słowacki's *Kordian* (1834) and Krasiński's *The Undivine Comedy* (1833) – were called forth by the November Uprising, the first in a long series of lost causes in which Poles have fought unsuccessfully to regain their freedom. In *Forefathers' Eve*, Mickiewicz draws upon ancient Lithuanian folklore and primitive religion, and fulfils two of the principal goals of modern theatre: the return to myth and ritual and the creation of a total spectacle. Słowacki intended *Kordian* as a counterstatement to *Forefathers' Eve* in an ongoing debate about the role of the artist-intellectual in the struggle for Poland's freedom; it thus introduced what would become a characteristic procedure in the Polish dramatic tradition: response to an earlier work as a springboard for new creativity (an artistic practice not unlike **Brecht**'s *Gegenstück*). *The Undivine Comedy*, written when Krasiński was 21, theatricalizes the dynamics of violent class revolution (conceived in almost Hegelian terms) in an unspecific European setting, rather than in the context of Polish history, making it a work of universal and prophetic application.

In partitioned Poland, a hidebound theatre lagged behind the other arts and produced results on a par with Western Europe only in ballet and opera. The National (a dangerous word) Theatre, which became the Warsaw Theatre on orders from the Russian government that financed it, was known for its drama school and high standard of acting; the repertory was mediocre, consisting mainly of translations, adaptations and imitations of French melodrama. The Tsarist censor was reluctant to allow any plays of social significance, or even Shakespeare's dramas, which showed too many crimes in high places and conspiracies and rebellions. In retaliation the Polish theatres (run by Poles but administered by a Tsarist official) refused to present Russian plays, and guest appearances by Russian companies from Moscow and St Petersburg were boycotted by the Polish public.

Only in the second half of the 19th century, under the influence of the French well-made play and the trend to realism, was there a change toward the portrayal of manners and character types. High comedy became the dominant genre, and Warsaw attracted many celebrated actors and actresses, such as **Helena Modrzejewska**. The cult of the performer and intense public interest in the art of acting were encouraged by the authorities in order to fill the vacuum left in the absence of any political life. Despite the visit in 1885 of the **Meiningen** Theatre, the Warsaw stage remained an old-fashioned actor's showplace in which the role was more important than the play or production.

The situation was different in Austrian-ruled Galicia, where a semi-independent Polish administration made possible an advanced repertory, including many plays forbidden by the Prussian and Russian occupations. **Wagner** and **Ibsen** were first performed in the late 1870s in Lwów, the capital of the province, where a new audience of bourgeois intellectuals with progressive political views was receptive to innovations. Always a centre of the fine arts, Cracow, with its small elite public, developed a distinct visual approach to stage production, which it has retained to the present; noted painters such as Matejk and Kossak worked on settings and produced elaborate historical reconstructions.

Throughout much of the 19th century, Polish-language companies toured and sometimes found permanent homes in Lithuania, Belorussia and the Ukraine, and at the same time foreign-language theatres competed for different audiences within Polish society. A German-language stage existed in Cracow, Jewish theatre in Yiddish enjoyed success in both Galicia and the Russian sector, and an Italian opera company played for several months each year in Warsaw.

Modern Polish theatre begins with the movement in the arts known as Young Poland, which flourished in Cracow and Lwów from the early 1890s until the outbreak of the First World War. Drawing upon Western European naturalism and symbolism, the Polish modernist movement in theatre was a brilliant adaptation of foreign influences to the Polish tradition of romantic drama, which finally became realizable on stage. A quieter, more nuanced acting style permitted subtle characterization and revelation of inner life; electric lighting, a painterly approach to design, and a strong directorial hand, led to the creation of harmonious stage pictures and powerful scenic effects. All subsequent Polish theatre is the result of an alliance between a nationalistic romantic movement and modernist stagecraft and design.

Polish modernism attracted poets, novelists and artists to the theatre. Stanisław Przybyszewski (1868–1927) revealed the torments of the naked soul in lurid dramas of the battle between the sexes; **Gabriela Zapolska** (1857–1921) introduced naturalism to the Polish stage in biting comedies and brutal melodramas. The most exciting Polish theatrical figure at the turn of the century was **Stanisław Wyspiański** (1869–1907), a painter and playwright who continued the work of the Polish romantics and anticipated the ideas of **Appia** and **Craig**. Designing costumes, properties and sets for the theatre in Cracow, Wyspiański worked on the staging of his own and others' plays, including the first complete production of *Forefathers' Eve* in a condensed version presented in 1901.

Using Greek theatre and Wagner's music-drama as his models, and drawing upon folk arts, village customs, popular ceremonies, processions and the *szopka*, Wyspiański created a total theatre uniting many arts. The production of his play *The Wedding* (1901) ends with an extended wordless scene, characteristic of Polish theatre at its best. At dawn the drunken wedding guests, weary of waiting for the great revolution that never comes, put down the scythes with which they have armed themselves and begin a slow, somnambulistic dance, a striking theatrical image of stagnation and hopelessness that will be taken up again and again by later Polish writers, film-makers and directors. Because of Russian censorship, *The Wedding* could not be performed in Warsaw, although there were clandestine stagings in private apartments.

After the Revolution of 1905 brought some liberalization to the Russian sector, the authorities allowed private entrepreneurs to establish new theatres. When Arnold Szyfman opened the Teatr Polski in Warsaw in 1913, it was the most modern and best-equipped stage in Poland, with an excellent acting ensemble and directors. Audiences for theatre constantly expanded. To meet the need, state-supported theatre for the urban lower classes was provided, but under strict police control. Regional amateur theatres in the countryside, devoted to preserving local customs and language, specialized in staging huge pageants for mass audiences. Cracow was the inspiration for all the provincial theatres in the period before 1914; it also gave birth to 'The Green Balloon', a cabaret (modelled on the Parisian Chat Noir) which functioned as a miniature satirical theatre and drew upon the traditions of the *szopka* and its puppets. During the First World War actors from the different sectors were scattered throughout Europe and established Polish theatres in Vienna, Kiev and Moscow.

From 1918, when Poland regained her independence, until 1939, Polish theatre enjoyed a brief but unstable interlude in which it tried to stand on its own feet. Because the government was too poor to subsidize the arts, the burden of financing fell on the cities, but the economic crisis of 1929 made the situation increasingly difficult. Censorship and government interference in the arts continued, but were now directed against anything suspected of being Bolshevik or anarchist, which included almost all forms of artistic experimentation. Writers were harassed and arrested, magazines confiscated and theatres raided.

Despite the general mood of hostility to innovation in the arts, avant-garde theatres sprang up in the inter-war years. In 1919 Juliusz Osterwa, an actor recently returned from Moscow where he had become acquainted with **Stanislavsky**'s work, founded the actor's studio Reduta, which was to be an outpost in the battle against theatrical falsity and conventionality. The company's guiding principles were monastic dedication to truth in art, scrupulous psychological realism and communal effort.

The representative man of the theatre in the inter-war years was **Leon Schiller** (1887–1954), who began his career as a proponent of Wyspiański's theatre, made his reputation as a reinterpreter of the Polish classics, and survived war and imprisonment to become the teacher of a new generation of directors. The Ateneum, established by actors from the Reduta, including Stefan Jaracz (1883–1945) who managed the theatre in the 1930s, was known for its repertory of modern plays on social issues. Attempts to establish a revolutionary workers' theatre in Poland in the 1920s ended in disaster. Witold Wandurski (1891–1937), known for *Death on a Pear Tree* (1925), and Bruno Jasieński (1901–37), author of *Ball of the Mannequins* (1931), fleeing persecution and arrest, escaped to the Soviet Union where they perished in concentration camps during Stalin's purges.

The most colourful and controversial figure in the Polish avant-garde between the wars was **Stanisław Ignacy Witkiewicz** (1885–1939), whose plays and theories enjoyed little success until after 1956. Another writer who suffered neglect was Stanisława Przybyszewska (1901–35), author of a trilogy about the French Revolution, of which only *The Danton Case* was staged in her lifetime. Innovative Polish dramatists did not find encouragement in the inter-war years from theatres, public or critics.

With the outbreak of the Second World War in September 1939, Poland was again divided and threatened with extinction. Theatre continued to exist in Lwów under Soviet rule until all of Poland came under German occupation in 1941. Collaborationist light entertainment persisted, but most Polish actors refused to appear publicly. Instead, clandestine performances (as during the partitions) were given in private homes, actors secretly trained and theatres set up conspiratorially, most notably, in Cracow, **Tadeusz Kantor**'s Independent Theatre (1942–4) and Mieczysław Kotlarczyk's Rhapsodic Theatre (1941–67), in which Karol Wojtyła (later Pope John Paul II) appeared. (He also wrote plays – *Our God's Brother* (1950), *The Jeweller's Shop* (1960) – and essays on theatrical theory.) Wartime theatre also existed in military units and Prisoner of War and concentration camps.

The first period in post-war theatre under the new Communist government (1945–9) was devoted to reconstruction. Not a single theatre had been left standing in Warsaw; devastation elsewhere was great. No centralized control yet existed to impose ideological conformity. The repertory consisted of Polish classics, including some Słowacki (although no *Kordian*, *Forefathers' Eve* or *Undivine Comedy*), Shakespeare and recent Western drama.

Once power was consolidated by the Communist Party, Stalinism descended on Poland. In January 1949, at the Congress of the Polish Writers' Union in Szczecin, socialist realism was proclaimed as the only style for all the arts. At the end of the year a festival of Russian and Soviet plays (in which 47 Polish theatres took part) was organized to teach Polish playwrights how to portray 'the building of socialism', and young artists and intellectuals made an effort to adopt the new dogma. In 1951, at the New Theatre in Łódź, Kazimierz Dejmek – whose career has mirrored all the vicissitudes of modern Polish theatre – staged a productivity play, *Grinder Karhan's Team* (by the Czech Vašek Kářa), in which an entire factory was faithfully reproduced.

Soviet-dictated socialist realism proved so alien to the Polish tradition of metaphoric, poetic drama that even Leon Schiller, now an active party member, resigned from the directorship of the Teatr Polski in 1951 because he was denied the possibility of staging the national romantic repertory. In late 1954, when the abuses of Stalinism were about to be exposed, Dejmek presented **Mayakovsky**'s *Bathhouse* at the New Theatre as a scathing attack on bureaucracy. In 1955 *Forefathers' Eve* – always a talisman of incalculable power – returned to the stage at the Teatr Polski in Warsaw, attracting audiences from all over the country.

With the thaw in 1956 allowing more cultural autonomy, the great period of modern Polish theatre began. The avant-garde became the mainstream, officially sanctioned and lavishly subsidized, with no restrictions on form, although censorship of content continued, ruling out truthful presentation of everyday social reality, criticism of the USSR and its relations to Poland, and treatment of religious or sexual issues that might offend the Catholic hierarchy and upset the delicate church–state balance. Given these limitations, the repertory was immense and varied, consisting of 400 new productions a year, the majority contemporary foreign plays.

Beckett, **Ionesco**, **Dürrenmatt**, **Frisch** and the entire Western avant-garde were quickly assimilated and widely performed, after being first published in translation in the new drama magazine *Dialog*. There were also the triumphal stagings, often for the first time, of Polish works from the inter-war years, such as **Witold Gombrowicz**'s *Ivona* in 1957, and especially the plays of Witkiewicz, although censorship kept his most political drama, *Shoemakers*, from being publicly performed until 1970. Among new playwrights in the later 1950s, **Sławomir Mrozek** and **Tadeusz Róze-wicz** have proved the most enduring, dominating the Polish stage for the past 25 years.

After 1956 theatres became municipally financed and controlled (by local planning committees), with general supervision by the Ministry of Culture and Art. Different functions, audiences and repertories are assigned to each theatre, which presents two or three plays a week, with a yearly offering of eight to ten works which may stay in the repertory four or five years. The artistic director of the theatre chooses the repertory in consultation with his literary manager and board of actors. Actors from major theatres appear in television drama. Theatre reviews in newspapers have no effect on the success or failure of a play.

Among the outstanding directors are Aleksander Bardini, Erwin Axer, **Josef Szajna**, Andrzej Wajda, Jerzy Jarocki, Zygmunt Hübner, Janusz Warmiński, Wanda Laskowska, Konrad Swinarski, Adam Hanusz-kiewicz, Kazimierz Dejmek, Kazimierz Braun, Jerzy Grzegorzewski and Janusz Wiśniewski. Leading theatres are the Stary in Cracow, the Contemporary in Wrocław, the Ludowy in Nowa Huta, the Nowy in Łódź, and the Ateneum, Dramatic, Studio, Polski, Powszechny, Contemporary and National in Warsaw. Landmark productions include Mickiewicz's *Fore-fathers' Eve* (1973) by Swinarski, Dostoevsky's *Possessed* (1971) by Wajda, and Witkiewicz's *Mother* (1964 and 1972) by Jarocki at the Stary; Mrozek's *Tango* (1965) by Axer at the Contemporary (Warsaw); *Replica* (1972), about the Holocaust, created by Szajna at the Studio; Przybyszewska's *Danton Case* (1975) by Wajda at the Powszechny; *The Story of the Glorious Resurrection* (1962) and *Forefathers' Eve* (1967) by Dejmek at the National, the latter stopped by the authorities for inciting anti-Soviet demonstrations and resulting in Dejmek's dismissal as manager of the theatre.

Other professional theatres of a special nature include the Wrocław Pantomime Theatre, directed by Henryk Tomaszewski since 1955, and the Warsaw Jewish Theatre, from 1955 to 1968 led by **Ida Kamińska** (whose parents **Esther** and Aleksander headed a Jewish theatre from 1913 to 1939). Puppet theatres such as the Groteska in Cracow, Lalka in Warsaw and Marcinek in Poznań, draw on both folk and avant-garde sources.

Two outstanding theatre artists, **Jerzy Grotowski** and Tadeusz Kantor, moved outside the official struc-ture in the 1950s, established their own theatres, trained their own actors and created their own texts or radically reshaped existing ones. By the late 1970s both were working abroad. Other alternative forms of theatre have played a role in developing an artistic medium independent of state financing and supervision. The poet Miron Białoszewski set up 'A Theatre Apart' in his apartment, where from 1953 to 1961 he and his friends performed his radical linguistic experiments.

Polish student theatres have been a powerful force for freedom and renewal, leading the struggle against socialist realism in the early 1950s. Part of the univer-sity system and financed by student organizations,

early groups such as STS, Stodoła and Hybrydy in Warsaw, Pstrąg in Łódź, Bim-Bom in Gdańsk and Kalambur in Wrocław, were not connected to the regime's cultural apparatus and could offer spontan-eous commentary on social issues. Some staged plays (including works banned elsewhere); others worked with cabaret, poetry or song. A semi-independent world of culture grew up around the student theatres, with competitions, festivals, workshops, galleries and actors' studios. In the 1970s the Ministry of Culture gave professional status and financing to groups of long standing, so that they could be more effectively controlled. Principal companies are Teatr STU (Cra-cow), Teatr 77 (Łódź), the Academy of Movement (Warsaw), playing in the streets of urban centres; Gardzienice (near Lublin), recovering folk culture in rural communities; and Theatre of the Eighth Day (Poznań), utilizing the methods of Grotowski's Lab-oratory (largely ignored by the professional theatre).

During the triumph of Solidarity (1979–81), official theatre was not able to keep pace with the changes taking place in society, although there were staged readings of previously censored poetry. After the military takeover and martial law in December 1981, all theatres were closed. When they reopened in spring 1982, some managers lost their jobs in reprisal for association with Solidarity, and because of the boycott of television theatre the actors' union was dissolved. Censorship, greatly relaxed during Solidarity, was reinstated. Having tasted greater freedom, many artists were not content with the return of restrictions and performances outside the sanctioned theatres became common.

In March 1982, with the curfew still in effect, Jarocki staged **Eliot**'s *Murder in the Cathedral* at St John's Cathedral in Warsaw, the Four Knights armoured like Polish security forces. Clandestine theatre by profes-sional actors using banned texts appeared in homes and apartments. In the spring of 1985, Wajda presented a biblical drama by Ernest Bryll in a Warsaw church, when it was forbidden by the censor for its political allusions. The Theatre of the Eighth Day, denied official status in 1984, now gives performances in churches. In times of crisis, Polish theatre has reverted to traditions of underground performance established during the partitions and occupation, and has even gone back into the church, attesting to its resilience and attachment to national roots. DG

See: Edward Csató, *The Polish Theatre*, Warsaw, 1963; Witold Filler, *Contemporary Polish Theatre*, Warsaw, 1977; Daniel Gerould, 'Introduction', *Twentieth-Century Polish Avant-Garde Drama*, Ithaca, 1977; August Grodzicki, *Polish Theatre Directors*, Warsaw, 1979; August Grodzicki and Roman Szydłowski, *The Theatre in People's Poland*, War-saw, 1975; Tadeusz Kudliński, *Rodowód polskiego teatru*, Warsaw, 1974; Stanisław Marczak-Oborski, *Teatr czasu wojny 1939–1944*, Warsaw, 1967; Stanisław Marczak-Oborski, *Życie teatralne w latach 1944–1964*, Warsaw, 1968; Konstanty Puzyna, 'Prologue', *Theatre in Modern Poland*, Warsaw, 1963; Zbigniew Raszewski, *Krótka historia teatru polskiego*, Warsaw, 1977; Harold B. Segel, 'Introduction', *Polish Romantic Drama*, Ithaca, 1977; Małgorzata Semil and Elżbieta Wysińska, *Słownik współczesnego teatru*, Warsaw, 1980; Zenobiusz Strzelecki, *Współczesna scenografia polska/ Contemporary Polish Stage Design*, Warsaw, 1984; Bolesław Taborski, 'Poland', *Cromwell's Handbook of Contemporary*

Drama, New York, 1971; *Teatry studenckie w polsce*, Warsaw, 1968.

Polevoi, Nikolai Alekseevich (1796–1846) A self-educated son of the Russian merchant class, he brought an unjaded eye but sometimes erring and paradoxical sensibility to his roles as editor-critic of the progressive journal *The Moscow Telegraph* and contributor to the 'officially nationalistic' drama of the Nikolayen era which glorified the oppressive rule he otherwise opposed. He undervalued two of the century's most significant plays, **Pushkin**'s *Boris Godunov* and **Gogol**'s *The Inspector General*, although in fairness they were equally misunderstood by liberals and conservatives in their time. His translation of *Hamlet*, staged in 1837 in Moscow and St Petersburg with **P. S. Mochalov** and **V. A. Karatygin** in the title role in the respective productions, was praised by many but attacked by some for its sentimentalism. The charge of 'Kotzebuism' or plagiarized sentimentalism was levied against virtually all of the 38 plays which he hastily composed over the last eight years of his life. Of these negligible works, which enjoyed audience and official popularity to match their critical disfavour, the most characteristic was *The Grandfather of the Russian Fleet* (1838). This specimen of time-serving reactionary romanticism was of the same type as **Kukolnik**'s *The Hand of the Almighty Has Saved the Fatherland* (1833). Ironically, Polevoi's savaging of the latter helped lead to the closing down of his journal in 1834. While his art was attacked from such diverse quarters as the liberal critic Belinsky and the vaudeville playwright **Pisarev**, his politics were applauded by Herzen, Chernyshevsky and Belinsky as well. SG

Poliakoff, Stephen (1952–) British dramatist, who started to write plays as a teenager and contributed to *Lay-By* (1971), a group play about pornography and rape. Three plays produced by the **Bush Theatre**, *The Carnation Gang* (1973), *Hitting Town* (1975) and *City Sugar* (1975), together with *Heroes* (1974), established him as a prolific, original playwright with an instinct for powerful contemporary metaphors. He was appointed the writer-in-residence to the **National Theatre** in 1976–7, during which time he wrote *Strawberry Fields* (1977), but *Shout Across the River* (1978), produced by the **Royal Shakespeare Company**, revealed a new dimension to his work. The story concerned a mother, suffering from agoraphobia, who tries to protect her delinquent daughter from the horrors of big city life, curing herself but not saving the young girl. In a succession of short scenes, Poliakoff conveyed a panoramic view of life in a concrete jungle. *Favourite Nights* (1981) about a girl addicted to gambling was less successful and revealed Poliakoff's main weakness as a dramatist, a looseness of construction which demands a firm directorial hand. In *Breaking the Silence* (1984), produced by the RSC with **Alan Howard** in the cast, he came close to fulfilling his early promise in a compelling story about the early days of the Russian Revolution, prompted by the experiences of his grandfather. JE

Polichinelle see **Punch**

Polin **(Pierre-Paul Marsalès)** (1863–1927)

French music-hall performer, for 20 years a favourite comic singer at the Paris Scala. He popularized the type of the ingenuous private, his cap at a rakish angle, and his songs 'Ah, Mademoiselle Rose' and 'La Petite Tonkinoise' became classics. The originality of Polin's technique lay in standing still, using only a checkered handkerchief to make his effects, and to slur his words to compel the audience's attention. His subtle style had a great effect of Raimu and Fernandel. After the First World War, he appeared on the legitimate stage, playing *The Imaginary Invalid* at the Opéra in 1922. LS

Pollock, Sharon (1936–) Canadian playwright, actress and director. *Walsh* (1974), an epic retelling of the treatment accorded Chief Sitting Bull in Canada after his defeat of General Custer, had its premiere at Theatre Calgary, and was staged at the **Stratford Festival** in 1974. Despite the historical settings, Pollock's commitment to important social issues was clear, and it was again demonstrated in *The Komagata Maru Incident* (1978), condemning Canada's racist immigration policy, and *One Tiger to Kill* (1980), based on a contemporary prison hostage-taking incident. *Blood Relation* (1980), her version of the famous Lizzie Borden story, marked a shift to a more sophisticated exploration of personal issues, which continued in her admittedly autobiographical *Doc* (1984). JA

Polynesia see **Oceania**

Ponnelle, Jean-Pierre (1932–) French opera director and designer. Ponnelle studied philosophy and art history at the Sorbonne, music at the Paris Conservatory, and painting with Fernand Léger. He began his design career with Hans Werner Henze's opera *Boulevard Solitude* (1952), and continued to design ballets and operas in Europe and in San Francisco for the next decade. His 1962 production of *Tristan and Isolde* in Dusseldorf marked the start of a dual career as director and designer of opera. Together with **Franco Zeffirelli**, Ponnelle is now considered one of the foremost director–designers of opera in the world. Some prominent examples of his work include *Il Barbiere di Siviglia* (Salzburg, 1968), *La Cenerentola* (San Francisco, 1969), *Pelléas et Mélisande* (Munich, 1973), *Le Nozze di Figaro* (Salzburg, 1976), and *Lear* (San Francisco, 1981). His design style is metaphoric and suggests the historical context as the internal mood of the operas. This is perhaps best typified by his controversial *Tosca* at the San Francisco Opera in which the showy facades of the church were shown as unfinished shells. AJN

Ponsard, François (1814–67) French dramatist. At a time when romantic drama was going out of fashion, Ponsard was seen as a champion of the revival of neoclassical tragedy with *Lucrèce*, inspired by Mlle Rachel, but staged at the **Odéon** in 1843. In 1846 *Agnès de Méranie* returned to more fashionable medieval themes and in 1850, with *Charlotte Corday*, often regarded as his best work, he was accepted by the **Comédie-Française**. The play explores different approaches to the Revolution. In 1853 and in 1856 he produced two important satirical comedies on contemporary life, *L'Honneur et L'Argent* (*Honour and Money*) and *La Bourse* (*The Stock-Exchange*). The first of these ran for nearly a hundred performances at the Odéon and opened the doors of the French Academy to its author. *Le Lion Amoureux* (*The Lion in Love*, 1866) returned to the Revolutionary period and was an attempt to write a new 'scientific' tragedy.   JMCC

Poole, John (1786–1872) English playwright, whose first dramatic work, the *Hamlet Travestie* (1811), established a fashion for burlesque versions of **Shakespeare**. Only with *Paul Pry* (1825) did Poole again rise above the journeyman-level of other hack-dramatists, and the credit for that play's extraordinary success must be shared with the actor **John Liston**, who played the name-part.   PT

Popov, Oleg Konstantinovich (1930–) Russian clown, who, after mastering acrobatics and juggling, excelled at parodies of circus acts and naive spectators. His type embodies the simple-minded booby Ivanushka of Russian folklore with his blond Dutch-boy haircut and checkered cap. Although adept at satiric sketches, he prefers to fill the pauses between acts, rather than create elaborate numbers.   LS

Popova, Lyubov Sergeevna (1889–1924) Innovative Soviet-Russian scene and costume designer who, for **Meyerhold**'s production of Crommelynck's *The Magnanimous Cuckold* (1922), designed what is considered to be the first pure constructivist stage set. Influenced in her early career by the mystical Russian painter Mikhail Vrubel and by Renaissance art, her commitment to modern art was strengthened and focused at Vladimir Tatlin's studio (1912–15). She progressed through several creative phases prior to constructivism in which she confronted the problems of form (cubism), movement and colour (futurism), abstraction of the object, 'displacement' or 'shift' (related to futurist 'transrationalism'), construction of form and line (post-cubism) and colour (suprematism). Her talent for thinking austerely, concretely and three-dimensionally led to a series of 'plastic paintings' (1915), reliefs, graphics and linocuts (1920–1) in which she explored the creative function of space in art and anticipated her *Magnanimous Cuckold* design. The latter was a configuration of moving wheels – one large black wheel, bearing the letters 'CR-ML-NK', and two small red and white wheels – ramps, slides, ladders, stairways and platforms, which interpreted the actions in the script kinetically in keeping with Meyerhold's 'biomechanics' approach to the acting. This design greatly influenced **Varvara Stepanova**'s for the Meyerhold production of *Tarelkin's Death* (1922) and Aleksandr Vesnin's for G. K. Chesterton's *The Man Who Was Thursday*, directed by **Tairov** at the Kamerny Theatre (1923). Popova's less successful design for **Sergei Tretyakov**'s *Earth Rampant* (1923), also directed by Meyerhold, was an agitational mass spectacle-inspired montage of real objects – modes of transport, weapons, telephones, a screen, on which were projected slides and films, etc. – all set against a huge gantry crane and illuminated by searchlights. Popova's other theatrical designs include: costumes for a children's puppet play at the Theatre of Marionettes (1919) and for **Lunacharsky**'s play *The Locksmith and the Chancellor* (Korsh Theatre, 1921); fantastic pictorial sets and costumes for Tairov's *Romeo and Juliet* (Kamerny Theatre, 1921) of

which the director disapproved, replacing her with Aleksandr Vesnin; and an unrealized collaborative design with Meyerhold and Vesnin for the mass spectacle *Struggle and Victory* (1921).   SG

Pornographic theatre Participants graphically depict sexual acts, combining exhibitionism with voyeurism (technically known as scopophilia). It is only when eroticism has been divorced from any religious, poetic or symbolic significance (or American law's 'redeeming social value') that a performance can be deemed truly pornographic, though moralists have tried to apply that label to erotic manifestations in the theatre throughout history. The Romans of the Empire solicited such exhibitions from their mimes, and the Byzantine empress Theodora gave public displays of genital acrobatics during her early days as a circus girl (5th century AD).

Although the Restoration stage has enjoyed a reputation for licentiousness, its one wholly pornographic play, *Sodom or The Quintessence of Debauchery* (c. 1684), a medley of fornication, buggery and incest couched in heroic couplets and attributed erroneously to John Wilmot, Earl of Rochester, was probably never staged. Throughout the 18th century brothels were the usual arenas for sexual exhibition in London: the Rose Tavern in Russell St offered 'posture women' who posed naked on a large platter manipulating a lighted candle (the preparations can be seen in the third plate of Hogarth's *Rake's Progress*). Mrs Charlotte Hayes in King's Place, Pall Mall, invited clients to see a facsimile of a Tahitian fertility rite performed by 12 'beautiful nymphs' and 12 'athletic youths'. Similar shows were provided in Berlin by Mme Schwitz and at De Fontein in Amsterdam. The first exclusively pornographic theatre may have been that run by the Parisian brothelkeeper Lacroix in 1741, but private erotic theatres soon became a fad of the French nobility and their actress mistresses.

The Regent, Philippe d'Orléans, opened one in Montmartre in 1749, where, following the tradition of fairground *parades*, the smut was purely verbal. The best was that of Duc d'Hénin, whose stars were Sophie Arnould and the Comte de Grammont; the realistic *Priapées* of the house-dramatist Delisle de Sales (Jean B. C. Isoard, b. 1745), known as 'the Sade of the drama', required sexual athletes to perform them, and included *L'Air de Mirza*, staged in the actress's bathroom. Other such theatres were the primarily scatological playhouse built by Grandval *fils* for Dumesnil; and those in Paris and Auteuil managed by Geneviève and Marie Verriers (Riteau), the latter the greatgrandmother of George Sand. The Prince de Soubise built a superb secret theatre for Marie-Madeleine Guimard, the Opéra dancer and patron of the painter David; the pornographic plays of Collé were cast from ballet-girls and directed by the choreographer Dauberval. In Russia, a rougher equivalent were the erotic shows put on by dissolute landowners in their serf theatres.

Times of social upheaval are particularly ripe for this sort of exhibition, and in 1791, after the outbreak of Revolution, a pair of so-called savages did the deed of kind in the **Palais-Royal** as a public show. (Similarly in Berlin in 1919 a married couple staged a *Schönheitsabend*, performing the sex act behind a muslin curtain.)

But the 19th century returned such displays to the brothel, where Guy de·Maupassant's obscene play ambiguously titled *A la feuille de rose, Maison Turque* (*At the Sign of the Rose Petal, Turkish House*) was performed for the Goncourts and Flaubert, who remarked, 'Mon Dieu, this *is* entertaining.' The Theatron Erotikon or Théâtre érotique de la rue de la Santé founded by Henry Monnier and Albert Glatigny in 1862 was a puppet-show playing smutty one-acts for a similarly select gathering. In England, such plays were circulated *sub rosa* but not put on; *The Sod's Opera*, once attributed for no good reason to **Gilbert** and Sullivan, and the cod pantomime *Harlequin Prince Cherry Top and the Good Fairy Fairfuck*, jokingly advertised as produced at the Theatre Royal Olimprick in 1879, remained closet reading in an age when **Ibsen**'s *Ghosts* was attacked by conservatives as pornographic.

Secret erotic theatres sprang up in Germany after the First World War as part of the black market, but it was not until the so-called 'Sexual Revolution' of the 1960s that ordinary titillation was augmented by programmatic exploitation of 'deviant' practices. **Fernando Arrabal** used taboo-breaking simulation of sadism and *bestialité érotique* to rouse audiences from their torpor, and the works of Sade himself were dramatized. Michael McClure's play *The Beard* (1967) which ends with Billy the Kid performing cunnilingus on Jean Harlow was merely a tame prelude to Lennox Raphael's *Che!* (1969) featuring a nude Uncle Sam whose involvement in oral sex and sodomy caused the whole cast to be arrested by the New York police. Much of this blatant sexuality was done in the name of theatrical experimentation and dadaism, much in protest, as with Tuli Kupferberg's anti-war spectacle *Fuck Nam*. But a good deal was purely commercial, like the clubs that sprang up in West Germany to show simulated sexual acts, while the real thing was offered in United States nightspots. **Kenneth Tynan**'s revue *Oh, Calcutta!* (1968) garnered contributions from **Beckett**, Gore Vidal, **Jules Feiffer** and others in its celebration of copulation; imitations like *Let My People Come* had less pretence to wit. The boundary-lines between Underground and Establishment were entirely effaced with orgies a commonplace in grand opera, as in **Peter Hall**'s production of Schoenberg's *Moses and Aaron* (**Covent Garden**, 1969) and Swinarski's production of Penderecki's *Devils of Loudon* (Stuttgart, 1969); but the buggering of a naked druid in **Howard Brenton**'s *The Romans in Britain* (**National Theatre**, 1980), though meant as a metaphor for imperialist rape, proved too literal for many. Some sort of climax was reached with the happenings of Austrian Otto Muehl, who slaughtered a pig over the body of a naked woman and then proceeded to abuse her in other less imaginative ways. The prevalence of pornography in film and videotape has somewhat reduced its allure in the live theatre, freeing playwrights to use the sexual act or leave it alone as dramatic need arises. LS

See: A. M. Rabenalt, *Mimus Eroticus*, 5 vols., Hamburg, 1965; A. M. Rabenalt, *Theater ohne Tabu*, Emsdetten, 1970; A. M. Rabenalt, *Voluptas ludens*, Emsdetten, n.d.

Porter, Cole (1891–1964) American composer and lyricist. Born into a wealthy midwestern family, Porter abandoned his plans for a legal career to study at the Harvard University School of Music. He contributed songs to the Broadway musical *See America First* in 1916. After a stint with the French Foreign Legion, Porter lived in Europe for most of the 1920s. At the end of the decade he wrote songs for two Broadway shows with French settings: *Paris* (1928) and *Fifty Million Frenchmen* (1929). In the 1930s Porter wrote the scores for a series of frothy musical comedies, including *The Gay Divorce* (1932), *Anything Goes* (1934), *Red, Hot and Blue!* (1936), *Leave It to Me!* (1938), and *Du Barry Was a Lady* (1939). His songs for these shows, generally characterized by ingenious lyrics and unusual rhythms, placed him in the forefront of musical comedy composers.

After his legs were crushed in a riding accident in 1937, Porter's creativity seemed to wane. His shows of the early 1940s were financially successful but artistically undistinguished. However, in 1948 he created what many consider to be his most theatrically effective and versatile score, *Kiss Me, Kate*, a musical version of **Shakespeare**'s *The Taming of the Shrew*. During the 1950s Porter wrote his last two hit shows: *Can-Can* (1953) and *Silk Stockings* (1955).

For most of his career Porter was content with providing sophisticated songs for shows with trivial librettos. As a consequence, although his songs still remain popular few of his shows are revived in their entirety. MK

Portugal There are no extent texts of works written expressly for performance before **Vicente**'s 1502 *Monólogo do Vaqueiro*. There are many references to performers over the medieval period, probably strolling players; and to miming and mimics, dating from 1193, where the Latin word *arrimidilum* – *arremedilho* in Portuguese – seems to indicate a playlet or 'turn' in which the actors poked fun at people, often no doubt at butts indicated for them by their royal employers.

Far better documented are the *momos*, a genre linked to the French *momerie*, the Venetian *momarie* and English *mummery*, at least in the emphasis on dumbshow. The Portuguese term is wide, embracing fairly simple pieces with a handful of masked actors and highly elaborate and luxurious costumes, staging and special effects. The court was the principal patron and the ambient for these productions. We have reference to a princess bequeathing her mask to a brother in 1276, a 1413 reference to the existence of a permanent corps of court tailors and weavers specially for such spectacles. There are detailed descriptions of many of the more famous *momos* associated with royal weddings, major feastdays of the church and royal entries into such cities as were perforce the temporary hosts of the highly peripatetic court. There was little authentic dialogue in the *momos*: the overwhelming pageantry was accompanied at best by stilted speeches of a formal or diplomatic nature and emblematic and allegorical content. The *momo* developed into much more of a play in the hands of Vicente, who injects life into the dialogue and allegory to produce masques which are highly readable (if too expensive to stage) today, e.g. *As Cortes de Jupiter* (*Jove's Parliament*, 1521), put on for a royal wedding. Apart from *arremedilho* and *momo*, there was a slender tradition of medieval debate and poetic contest, including improvisation, which whiled away many a *serão* (soirée) in the long evenings at court, with the

Teatro Nacional D. Maria II, Lisbon.

occasional pieces to be found in the anthologies which can be considered as embryonic dramatic monologues or duologues.

For lack of texts from these early four centuries, Gil Vicente, court playwright from 1502 to about 1536, is usually taken to be the father of the Portuguese theatre. His plays, created at a historical and cultural turning point, put everything on stage, in a repertoire that comprises a summation of European medieval theatre and the first Renaissance theatre in the country: saint plays, mystery and morality, dramatized chivalresque episode, elaborate allegories on real ceremonial events, *farsas* which are far closer to **Molière** than his models, the Italians and the Spaniard **Torres Naharro**, *tragicomédias* which are the truest inspiration for Spanish Golden Age theatre, and *pastoril* (shepherd) plays in which the early abysmally unlettered shepherds evolve into sophisticated pastoral characters versed in the casuistry of love.

The resources upon which Vicente could call were considerable, and there is much internal evidence of elaborate sets for some plays. There is none, surprisingly, whether internal or secondary, to suggest the building of a permanent theatre within any of the royal palaces or houses, as happened in the courts of other countries. Nor is there any stage direction anywhere to suggest there existed a raised platform, even though many plays cry out for separate stage levels.

On the death of Vicente, court theatre died too. Vicente, with his genius and strong political position at court, overshadowed those of his contemporaries and successors known collectively as 'The School of Gil Vicente'. There are indications that he protected his post jealously, even over-zealously, from possible competitors. He had no successor as court playwright. The increasing puritanism of the court and the growth in power of the Inquisition in the middle and late 1500s

militated against the emergence of a robust theatrical tradition. Nevertheless, some of the obvious disciples of Vicente had considerable flair. Anrique da Mota (dates not known, alive still in 1544) wrote a number of proto-playlets, of which the *Trovas do alfaiate* (*The Tailor's Tale*) is the most dramatic. António Prestes (? – 1587) wrote about legal affairs, as in the *Auto do procurador* (*The Attorney's Play*, post-1563) and the *Auto do desembargador* (*The High Court Judge's Play*); but also, importantly, transferred theatrical interest to the four walls of a bourgeois domestic setting. Jerónimo Ribeiro (dates unknown), with four plays surviving, is best remembered for his *Auto de S. Aleixo* (*Saint Alexius*, published 1537) – the story of a nobleman who for love of Christ forsook home and kin and returned as a beggar to die at his family's door, told with a moving dignity and poignancy. With António Ribeiro Chiado (? – 1591), the theatre effectively goes public, finding its audience in the squares of Lisbon (one of the most central is named for him). Two plays with *Prática . . .* (*Conversation . . .*) in their titles evince his enormous talent for creating character linguistically; the *Auto das Regateiras* (*The Fishwives' Play*) is racy lower-class comedy – mothers scheming to marry off their daughters, who then, like Vicente's Inês Pereira, give free rein to their sensuality with a variety of suitors. The *Auto da Natural Invençao* (*The Play of Native Wit* – Chiado's – performed between 1545 and 1557) depicts the antics of a band of the by-then familiar travelling theatricals. They put up at a boarding house, whose landlord rashly decides to have them put on a show and even pay them for the performance. He repents too late . . .

A neoclassical school, initiated by the poet Sá de Miranda (?1481–1558) on his return from Italy in 1527, naturalized the new comedy in Portuguese. *Os Estrangeiros* (*The Foreigners*, 1528) and *Os Vilhalpandos* (a family name, 1538) were both given first performances in Coimbra. They are five-acters, respect the three unities and have a deal of wit, but not quite the verve of Vicente. Sá de Miranda's lead in the comedy was followed by **António Ferreira** in two plays: *A comédia do Franchono* (also, perhaps, more commonly known as *O Bristo*, 1564), about two friends, rivals in love, and two braggart soldiers who owe much to **Plautus'** *milites gloriosi*; and *O Cioso* (*The Jealous Man*), a **Terence**-like treatment of a twice-cuckolded husband.

The neoclassical tragedy was a genre cultivated at the University, and largely the province of humanists and men of letters. A version of the *Electra* dates from 1537, to be followed by a spate of versions of Greek and Roman plays, with some originals, from 1547 onwards at Coimbra University. The high point in this theatre is António Ferreira's *Castro*, a tragedy on national history, with a Christian dimension of free will and action that depends less on fatality than on the clash of individuals' options – a formula that was not to be used again with such success until **Racine**.

Luís de Camões (1525–80), the country's greatest epic and lyric poet, created three hybrid plays in which the classical plot and theme, faithfully followed, are set in contemporary Portugal and couched in a language closer to Vicente and the colloquial usage. *O auto dos Enfatriões* (performed between 1543 and 1549 at Coimbra) is one of the worthiest plays from the long line stretching from Plautus' *Amphitruo* to **Giraudoux**'s *Amphitryon 38*. *El-Rei Seleuco* (*King Seleucus*, also

1543–9) also deals with a classical episode, from Plutarch. *Filodemo* (*Philodemus*), a pastoral drama on love themes, had its first performance in Goa in 1555 and would stand revival, at least before an academic audience.

With the Philippine (Spanish) annexation of the Portuguese state from 1580 to 1640, and increasingly harsh Inquisition censorship, the theatre went into almost total eclipse. The Jesuits monopolized the national stage with their doctrinal expositions of biblical, dogmatic and classical themes, characterized by an excess of rhetoric and a corresponding lack of dramatic dialogue and contact with real life; this from the late 1500s to the late 1700s! Lacking in dramatic vigour, these plays were strong on spectacle, and do provide a link between the lavish *momos* and the richly spectacular Italian opera which came to dominate taste in the 1700s. Both needed large amounts of money for their staging: a 1619 play about the discoveries in the East featured 300-odd actors and over 5,000 precious stones adorned the principals in homage to Philip II (III of Spain); the 18th-century Brazilian bonanza permitted Lisbon to become one of opera's most munificent patrons.

The only 17th-century play worth (and well worth) revival is the comedy-farce *O Fidalgo Aprendiz* (*The Apprentice Nobleman*, 1646), in which D. Francisco Manuel de Mello (1608–66) brings together the tight construction of the Spanish cloak and dagger drama and the native tradition. A boorish minor provincial nobleman comes to Lisbon and, the better to get embroiled in amorous intrigue, takes lessons from a *maître d'armes*, a dancing master and a versifier. A transparent (if unproven) model for *Le Bourgeois Gentilhomme*, the play not only exploits specific situations, with comedy of movement as well as of language, but also delivers a swingeing attack on those aspects of Portuguese society life – most – that Mello found wanting. The 18th century too is fairly devoid of truly dramatic activity. Opera ruled, and the common people had to be content with puppet theatre. But they had their own venues, theatres in Lisbon's Bairro Alto, and commissioned their own plays. The best writer of these plays, **António José da Silva** (1705–39), used puppets, interpolated operatic arias and used weird and wonderful stage machinery for 'magic' effects. The dialogue is fanciful and incisively witty. Silva's successors wrote more for the reader than for the playgoer, combining their own armchair theatre with the conscientious translation of French plays and dramatic criticism, Racine and **Boileau** more particularly, and later the Italians. Self-titled Arcadians, their theatre was academic.

The man who made the leap between, or more properly combined neoclassical and romantic was **João Baptista de Almeida Garrett**, first director and resident dramatist of the National Theatre inaugurated in 1846. After him, reacting to outside influence, the native bent of the Portuguese for satire found a voice in the theatre of the **revista** (from 1859 to the present), a pantechnicon genre eschewing little but strictly legitimate theatre. Drama went somewhat morbidly naturalistic and vaguely socialistic in thesis or problem plays, especially those of Gomes de Amorim (1827–91), with give-away titles like *Ódio de Raça* (*Race Hatred*, 1854) and *Aleijões Sociais* (*Society's Deformities*, published 1870, previously performed as *A Escravatura*

Branca, White Slavery). Mendes Leal (1818–86) was the most successful of these dramatists, but even his best work, e. g. *Pobreza Envergonhada* (*The Shame of Poverty*, 1864), is oversentimental, unconvincing in psychology and points a doubtfully valid moral.

At the turn of the century, we find dramatists of greater refinement. Júlio Dantas (1876–1962) attracted much personal opprobrium, seen as he was as the regime's official author and playwright, but his 20-odd plays were extremely popular, especially *A Ceia dos Cardeais* (*The Cardinals' Supper*, 1902). Three cardinals, one Italian, one French and one Portuguese, meet for supper in the Vatican, and over a pheasant stuffed with truffles, discuss the amours of their youth, and in so doing portray their national way of being madly in love. Nostalgic, anodyne, it was, and is, nevertheless a marvellous vehicle for virtuoso acting, an important factor in the play's long success. More substantial as a middle-class dramatist was D. João da Câmara (1852–1908), who, starting by writing somewhat romantic historical dramas, then graduated through a poetic realism to tentative essays in symbolist and verse drama. His best-known play, *Os Velhos* (*The Old Folk*, 1893), set in 1874, deals with the expropriation of the peasants' land for the spreading railway network, but concentrates more on the loving portrayal of character than on the happenings. His later plays were ahead of public taste.

Legitimate theatre became esoteric in the First World War years and in the 1920s, with much experimentation by poets open to the European influences, futurism, dada for example. None of these major lyric poets, however – Eugénio de Castro (1869–1944), Fernando Pessoa (1888–1935), Mário de Sá-Carneiro (1890–1916) – left a lasting mark on the theatre.

Alfredo Cortez (1890–1946), no poet, is one of three writers with a truly theatrical talent. With 11 plays to his credit, he more than any contemporary brought new theatrical experiences to his public. His *Zilda* (1921) is a portrayal of a self-willed, narcissistic and essentially empty woman, a free agent in the **Ibsen** mould, or amoral according to the eye of the beholder and, simultaneously, the unmasking of a society that has lost its bearings. Another play, *Gladiadores* (*Gladiators*, 1934), is a 'caricature of the age in which we live', using techniques learned with **Pirandello** (ten male and ten female characters reacting fluidly to successive situations), and from surrealism and expressionism. **Raúl Brandão** (1867–1930), also ahead of his time, wrote of cripples, physical and social, and grotesques in existential dramas that allowed him great scope for arousing compassion and understanding in his audience. **José Régio** (1901–69), like Cortez, underwent the strong influence of Pirandello, sharing the Italian's questioning of reality and appearances, and has an affinity with the 'spiritual' theatre of such writers as **Claudel**. These three are the founders of contemporary Portuguese theatre, and their influence has been as strong as their individual achievements.

The Salazar regime (1928–74) dealt very repressively with theatre and intellectual freedom, suspecting theatre, rightly, of being subversive – the *revista* often cocked a snook at government shortcomings. Serious theatre, when not overtly concerned with social and political matters, survived, but the censorship of police closure or the self-censorship of theatre managers denied wide public airing of any politically motivated drama attacking the regime. Nevertheless, there were plays mounting frontal attacks, usually closed down rapidly. The would-be audience would just as rapidly buy copies of the play before the police circulated the booksellers. A prime example of this overt activist theatre, **Bernardo Santareno**'s *A Traição do Padre Martinho* (*Father Martin's Treason*, 1969) depicts a priest disciplined for attempting to apply principles of Catholic social justice and charity. His superiors, abjectly supporting the New State, ordain his transfer. The people rally to him, the situation gets tenser and the para-military police eventually fire on a demonstrating crowd, killing a young girl. The audience is drawn into the action because the order to disperse comes from behind them. More often, though, authors resorted to the time-honoured devices of using historical situations to treat of the present – the case of **Cardoso Pires**'s *O Render dos Heróis* (*Relieving* [as of sentries] *the Heroes*, also, punningly, *The Surrender of the Heroes*, 1960) and **Sttau Monteiro**'s *Felizmente Há Luar* (*Luckily We Still Have the Moonlight*, 1961); and a 'fabular' method of distancing in space, e.g. Sttau Monteiro's *A Estátua* (1966) is ostensibly *any* dictator's statue. In Alves Redol's (1911–69) *O Destino Morreu de Repente* (*Destiny Died all of a Sudden*, 1967), the action is supposed to take place and to be played in a circus arena. The audience is swept in imagination to the Land of Destiny. The ringmaster cracks the whip and all the cast have to jump to it. Things go desperately wrong because there is a vast bureaucracy between whip-crack and jump which ensures that they do. Destiny of this imposed kind is itself doomed to collapse when faced by the human longing for freedom.

Since the 1974 coup, there has been a great expansion of interest in the theatre. Lisbon had 15 theatres in 1984 instead of 10 in 1974, Oporto seven instead of one, and all over the country semi-professional and amateur groups have sprung up. The most radical theatres have probably been the Lisbon Teatro da Comuna (The Commune) and A Barraca (literally The Shed, but also 'The Flop'). Portuguese theatre as a whole has continued to revive classics, and present foreign plays, as well as giving recognition to the plays suppressed prior to 1974 and welcoming new experimental plays by established and new authors. Productions are lively, imaginative, original, and the audience grows, and grows to appreciate all kinds of theatrical experience. LK

See: (review) *Bulletin d'histoire du théâtre portugais*, Lisbon, 1950–4; L. W. Keates, *The Court Theatre of Gil Vicente*, Lisbon, 1962 (Portuguese trans., Teorema, Lisbon, 1987); F. Mendonça, *Para o Estudo do Teatro em Portugal, 1946–1966*, Assis (Brazil), 1971; L. S. Picchio, *Storia del Teatro Portoghese*, Edizioni dell'Ateneo, Roma, 1964; C. Porto and S. T. de Menezes, *10 Anos de Teatro e Cinema em Portugal, 1974–84*, Caminho, Lisbon, 1985; L. F. Rebello, *História do Teatro Português*, Europa-America, Mem Martins, 1967.

Pose plastique see **Living picture; Nudity on stage**

Potier, Charles (1774–1838) French actor. One of the great comic performers of the 19th century, he has been called a major actor in a minor genre. Of noble

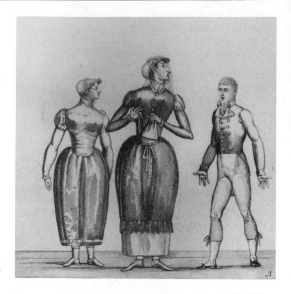

Brunet and Potier (centre) in *Les Anglaises pour rire* (*English Ladies for a Joke*), a very popular comic piece typical of the repertoire at the Variétés during the Restoration.

origin, he first appeared on the stage of the Délassements, then worked in the provinces, including Bordeaux. He drew maximum advantage from a weak voice and an emaciated build. His debut at the Variétés in 1809 led to his becoming that theatre's chief comic actor. In 1812, he showed he could appear in three different plays in the same evening, and give the impression of three different actors. He brought all Paris to the Variétés in such plays as *Les Anglaises Pour Rire* (*English Ladies for a Joke*, 1814). In 1818 he moved to the Porte-Saint-Martin, where he created the role of le Père Sournois in *Les Petites Danaïdes* (*The Little Danaides*). In 1825 he returned to the Variétés, in 1826 he spent two months in England, and in 1827 his health forced him to give his farewell performance. In 1829 he was invited to the new Nouveautés, where he showed his versatility once more in *Antoine, ou Les Trois Générations*. One of his most popular roles was in *Le Ci-Devant Jeune Homme* (*The Young Man from the Old Regime*, 1812). JMCC

Potter, Dennis (1935–) British television playwright. Although he has written for the stage (and adapted some of his television plays) it is as a television playwright that Potter is distinguished. From *Vote, Vote, Vote for Nigel Barton* (1965) to *The Singing Detective* (1986) Potter has created a body of work that has used the medium with ingenuity and imagination. *Son of Man* (1969) was a bold portrayal of a 'human' Christ anguished by self-doubt; *Pennies from Heaven* (1978) anticipated *The Singing Detective* by an extraordinary use of popular songs to form, divert and generate the action. *Blue Remembered Hills* (1979) cast adults as children, giving their games played in the context of the Second World War a rare fantasy. Potter's television and stage output is well over 20 plays, or extended plays (as often the pieces are devised in episodes), and his work always excites an anticipation of innovative use of the medium. MB

Poulsen, Emil (1842–1911) Leading Danish actor at the **Kongelige Teater**, where he played some 250 roles, including **Shakespeare**, **Molière**, **Holberg** and **Ibsen**. His astonishingly wide range accommodated such lyrical roles as Romeo as well as the inner torment of Shylock, Macbeth and Ibsen's Bishop Nicholas. He had some success in comedy (especially as Tartuffe) and from the late 1870s regularly appeared in Danish premieres of Ibsen: Consul Bernick, Torvald Helmer (in the world premiere of *A Doll's House*, 1879), Dr Stockmann, Hjalmar Ekdal, Ejlert Lovborg, Alfred Allmers, Dr Wangel, Masterbuilder Solness and John Gabriel Borkman. His brother Olaf was a Holberg specialist in the same company and his sons Adam and **Johannes** were actors and directors. HL

Poulsen, Johannes (1881–1938) Danish actor, son of **Emil Poulsen** and with the **Kongelige Teater** from 1909. He was a forceful actor, rather than subtle; dark-voiced and able to establish a character in a few vigorous strokes. His successes included comic roles by **Shakespeare** and **Holberg**, **Oehlenschläger**'s Aladdin, **Ibsen**'s Peer Gynt and Bishop Nicholas, and **Kaj Munk**'s Henry VIII. As a director he countered naturalism with a form of spectacular theatricalism partly imitative of **Reinhardt**, as in his 1914 *Everyman* (revived in Hollywood in 1936) and a revival of Oehlenschläger's *Aladdin* that swamped the text with oriental extravagance. His most unusual initiative was to engage **Edward Gordon Craig** to design his 1926 revival of Ibsen's *The Pretenders*. HL

Powers, the A family of Irish actors, most of whom spent large portions of their careers in the United

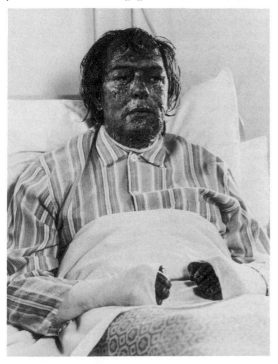

Michael Gambon as Philip Marlow in Dennis Potter's six-part television serial *The Singing Detective*, BBC TV, 1986.

States. The first, **Tyrone Power** (1795–1841), successfully played stage Irishmen in London and wrote a number of comedies until 1840, when he went to the United States. A great success there, he returned often and was drowned at sea on a transatlantic trip. His 1836 *Impressions of America* offer a sympathetic and detailed view of the American theatre at the time. Power's son **Maurice** (?–1849) was an actor, and another son, Harold, sired **Frederick Tyrone Edmond** (1869–1931), a leading man and member of **Daly**'s company, with whom he appeared in London. He first appeared successfully with **Madame Janauschek**. For a time he appeared with **Minnie Maddern Fiske**, his Lord Steyne in *Becky Sharp* being especially well received. In later life, he appeared almost exclusively as major support in Shakespearian revivals.

In turn, his son **Tyrone** (1914–58) was for some time on the stage, but won his most substantial reputation as a film actor. He made his debut as Benvolio in **Katharine Cornell**'s production of *Romeo and Juliet*. After his film career he appeared in *John Brown's Body* and *The Dark Is Light Enough*. In the 1980s his son, **Tyrone, Jr**, has also become an actor. SMA

Praga, Marco (1862–1929) Italian dramatist and critic. After a modest success with *La Moglie Ideale* (*The Ideal Wife*, 1891), in which **Duse** appeared, he was prolific of pieces in the 1890s, written either alone or in collaboration, treating middle-class psychology and manners and more particularly the woman with a past. His work is marked by considerable technical skill and some mordant social comment, but his morality was too conventional seriously to question the values of the society he depicted in plays like *L'Innamorata* (1894), *La Crisi* (*The Crisis*, 1905), *La Porta Chiusa* (*The Closed Door*, 1914) in which Duse scored a great success, and *Divorzio* (1915). His theatrical criticism in *L'Illustrazione Italiana* was highly influential. LR

Prahlada Nataka (India) Numerous villages in the district of Ganjam in the state of Orissa in eastern India preserve a unique style of performing *The Play of Prahlada* which demonstrates the faith of a little prince who worships the name of Vishnu despite the evil machinations of his wicked father-king. The play is thought to have been adapted from a classical text popularized by Raja Ramakrishna Deva Chotterai, a local ruler of the mid-19th century. Some 40 village companies still enact the play on special festival occasions. A special mask, thought to be endowed with great power, is used by the actor who plays Narsimha, the man–lion incarnation of Lord Vishnu who ultimately destroys the wicked king. Performances take place in an open field with a bleacher-like platform on which the actors pose and dance. Music is provided by *mridangam* drums, harmonium, wind instruments (*mukha veena*), cymbals and conch shells. At the climax of the dramatic action, when an actor dons the mask of the man–lion, he becomes possessed and must be forcibly restrained by attendants who prevent him from inflicting harm on the person of the actor playing the king. Symbolically, the king is killed and order is restored to the universe by Vishnu. FaR

Prampolini, Enrico (1894–1956) Italian painter, sculptor, stage designer and director. An early member of the futurist movement, with **Marinetti** he wrote many of its major manifestos, and advanced the movement through the many exhibitions he organized, and the journals he edited like *Noi* and *Stile Futurista*. From 1921 he was particularly active in theatre, designing scenes and costumes first for the Teatro Sintetico Futurista, then collaborating with **Bragaglia**'s Teatro degli Indipendenti. The grand and visionary range of his ideas for art work outside the theatre is well seen in his *Manifesto dell'Aeropittura* (1929). Avoiding many of the political associations futurism had in the 1920s and 30s, he remained committed to its artistic principles throughout his life.   LR

Prehauser, Gottfried (1699–1769) Austrian actor, who inherited and cultivated the role of **Hanswurst**. He made his debut in 1716 with an itinerant troupe in the Viennese suburbs, and in 1720 first played Hanswurst in Salzburg. **Stranitzky** acknowledged him as his successor and Prehauser became the Hanswurst of the Vienna Kärntnertortheater from 1725, refining the type into a polished Viennese gallant. According to **Eduard Devrient**, he was a better comic and mimic than his predecessor: 'His caricatures always remain recognizable human beings and never sink to burlesque.'   LS

Preston, Thomas (? 16th century) English playwright. His tragicomedy *Cambyses King of Persia* illustrates the bridge in English drama from the medieval to the Elizabethan periods, offering a historical tale rather than a morality. That play was written around 1569 and Preston wrote others, but details are unreliable. Certainly he wrote with a flourish that gave this play contemporary popularity.   MB

Prevelákis, Pantelís (1909–86) Greek playwright. Like his mentor **Kazantzákis**, Prevelákis was a versatile author who also wrote for the theatre, besides translating into Greek a number of Spanish, Italian and French dramas. He displays a concern for ethical issues. His main characters are people with existential questions, in search of their better identity. The early and the late plays are set in Greece and the time is the present, while the trilogy 'The Sickness of the Century' (referring to the moral crisis of Western Civilization) combines biblical, renaissance and modern settings and times. In the first part of the trilogy, *The Holy Sacrifice* (1952), the protagonist Juliano dei Medici walks to his death knowingly in order to purge, through his sacrifice, both himself and those around him. *The Hands of the Living God* (1952) treats a theme drawn from Dostoevsky. The play leads again to a catharsis. *Lazarus* (1954), which concludes the trilogy, was meant to recall, structurally, an ancient Greek tragedy and delves deeply into the spiritual aspect of a physical miracle. *The Volcano* (1962) develops a heroic theme from Crete's struggle of liberation from Turkish yoke. Prevelákis shows good knowledge of the practical side of theatre and aims at a classical type of expression.   GT

Prévost, Robert (1927–82) French Canadian set and costume designer, considered by critics the outstanding practitioner of these arts in Quebec. His career began with Les Compagnons de Saint-Laurent under **Emile**

Legault in the early 1940s. After that troupe disbanded in 1952 he worked professionally for the television department of Radio Canada, and in Montreal with the **Théâtre du Nouveau Monde**, La Nouvelle Compagnie Théâtrale and Le Rideau Vert, with Les Grands Ballets Canadiens, the Montreal Symphony Orchestra (notably for its 1967 performance of Gounod's *Faust*), the Royal Winnipeg Ballet, the **Stratford (Ontario) Festival** and CBC Television. Renowned for his original settings for classical works, particularly those of **Molière**, he designed costumes and sets for major Canadian plays as well, notably those of **Marcel Dubé**.   LED

Price, Stephen (1783–1840) The first successful American theatre manager who was neither a playwright nor an actor. Price began gaining control of the **Park Theatre** in New York in 1808 and in 1810 began importing English stars. This practice gradually destroyed the resident repertory tradition in America. Price, with Simpson, managed to keep the Park open during the war of 1812 and after the war went frequently to London to recruit new talent. In 1816 he imported Mrs John Barnes from **Drury Lane**, marking the beginning of an especially prosperous period for the Park. From 1826 to 1830 Price managed the Drury Lane Theatre in London, gaining a monopoly over English stars, forcing other American managers to deal with him for their services. This power caused Washington Irving to refer to Price as 'King Stephen'. Price drained the London stage of its talent to supply visiting stars for the Park; other American managers were forced to employ his visiting stars on Price's terms in order to compete. Price was shrewd, even unscrupulous in his dealings, with the arrogance of the self-made man, but he gave audiences what they would pay for on both sides of the Atlantic.   SMA

Priestley, J[ohn] B[oynton] (1894–1984) British dramatist, novelist and critic. After the success of the dramatization of his best-selling novel *The Good Companions* (1931, adapted with Edward Knoblok), a sentimental comedy about an acting troupe, Priestley began to develop his characteristic themes in *Dangerous Corner* (1932). The idea of relativity, encapsulated in two alternative sequences of events following from the same incident, was transferred to time in two 1937 plays contrasting hopes for the future and the actualities of 20 years later (*Time and the Conways*) or presenting actions as conditioned by unconscious patterns established in previous incarnations (*I Have Been Here Before*). Though viewed as strikingly original at the time, the concepts are used as dramatic devices, rather than posing serious intellectual questions. In 1938 he took over the Westminster Theatre with his own company, the London Mask Theatre, which performed his more experimental works like *Music at Night* and the modern morality play, *Johnson over Jordan* (both 1939), four-dimensional dramas using expressionistic techniques. During the same period he wrote a series of comedies, such as *Laburnum Grove* (1933) satirizing middle-class suburbia or *When We Are Married* (1938) bordering on farce, and in 1943 a socialist allegory *They Came to a City*. After the war, during which he became a popular radio broadcaster, he continued the same mixture of dramas based on relativity and the spirit world (*An Inspector Calls*, 1946) or exploring political attitudes (*The Linden Tree*, 1947), experimental works (*Dragon's Mouth*, 1952, a play for voices written with Jacquetta Hawkes) and comedy. One of the last of his 49 plays, a dramatization of Iris Murdoch's novel *A Severed Head* (written in collaboration with her, 1963), ran for two years in the West End and his work has continued to be a staple of English repertory theatre. CI

Prince, Harold (1928–) American producer and director. Launching his career as a producer in partnership with Robert E. Griffith and Frederick Brisson, Prince had immediate success with *The Pajama Game* (1954) and *Damn Yankees* (1955). With Griffith he produced *West Side Story* (1957) and *Fiorello* (1961), and on his own produced *Fiddler on the Roof* (1964). Beginning with *She Loves Me* (1963), he served as both producer and director of a number of successful musicals. Prince's most notable contribution to the musical stage was the series of 'concept musicals' which he produced and directed in conjunction with composer-lyricist **Stephen Sondheim**: *Company* (1970), *Follies* (1971), *A Little Night Music* (1973), *Pacific Overtures* (1976), *Sweeney Todd* (1979), and *Merrily We Roll Along* (1981). He directed *Phantom of the Opera*, New York, 1986. His autobiography, *Contradictions*, was published in 1974. MK

Prince Henry's Men see **Admiral's Men**

Prince of Wales's Theatre, London Built in 1772 as a Concert Room, this small theatre in Tottenham Court Street had so declined that, by the mid-19th century it was familiarly known as the 'Dust Hole'. Determined on management, **Marie Wilton**, a popular star of burlesque at the Strand, bought it in 1865. Having completely redecorated it and made it the most comfortable theatre in London, she renamed it, with royal permission, the Prince of Wales's. By a mixture of luck and good judgement, she proceeded to bring to the theatre 15 years of unparalleled prosperity. Marie Wilton had intended, in partnership with **H. J. Byron**, to provide a mixed fare of burlesque and comedy, but it was the series of plays by **T. W. Robertson**, beginning with *Society* (1865), that made her fortune and that of the actor, **Squire Bancroft**, whom she married in 1867. They were already rich by 1880, when they left the Prince of Wales's for the **Haymarket**. Two years later, the theatre was found to be structurally unsound, and ended up as a Salvation Army hostel. It was demolished in 1903, except for the portico, which became the stage-door of the Scala, an undistinguished theatre which was itself demolished in 1972.

Another theatre, originally the Prince's, but renamed the Prince of Wales's in 1886, was built in Coventry Street in 1884. It was demolished in 1937 and replaced by the present building in the same year. PT

Princess's Theatre, London The original building opened in Oxford Street in 1828, when it housed a diorama by **Clarkson Stanfield** and David Roberts. It was adapted as a theatre in 1836 and named the Princess's in 1840. Its most distinguished period was that of **Charles Kean**'s management (1851–9), during which it became London's most fashionable theatre.

Kean mixed gentlemanly melodrama with grandly pictorial productions of **Shakespeare** and **Lord Byron**. The subsequent management of Augustus Harris (1859–63) was most notable for the unsuccessful London debut of **Henry Irving** and the phenomenally successful one of the French actor, **Charles Fechter**. The rest of the theatre's history is patchy. It was at the Princess's that Charles Warner gave his startling version of the physical effects of alcoholism in **Charles Reade**'s *Drink* (1879) and in the rebuilt and enlarged house (1880) that **Wilson Barrett** had his most successful years in London management (1881–6). The Princess's ceased to be used as a theatre in 1902, stood empty for several years and ended its life as a warehouse. It was demolished in 1931. PT

Principal boy see **Pantomime, English; Male impersonation**

Pritchard, Hannah (1711–68) English actress, who was a leading member of **Garrick**'s company at **Drury Lane** from 1748 almost to her death. Her most acclaimed performance was as Lady Macbeth to Garrick's Macbeth. Before then she had mainly been associated with comedy roles, and contemporary reports indicate an actress of charm and gentleness, wit and intelligence. They also unkindly draw attention to her stoutness, against which she fought a losing battle in her later years. MB

Private theatres The indoor playhouses of Elizabethan, Jacobean and Caroline London were, and still are, sometimes called 'private theatres' to distinguish them from the open-air public theatres. The title embodies a fiction which was a useful defence against interference from the civic authorities. They were, in fact, open to the public on the payment of an admission charge which was generally higher than that of the public theatres. But the first actors to use private playhouses were choristers, and it was convenient for their managers to claim that what the public witnessed were private rehearsals of plays in preparation for presentation at Court. The title stuck long after it had lost all conviction. The main private theatres were the unknown home of the **Boys of St Paul's** (c. 1575), the first **Blackfriars** (1576), the second Blackfriars (1600), the **Whitefriars** (1605–8), the **Cockpit** or Phoenix (1616) and the **Salisbury Court** (1629). More genuinely private were the Court theatres. PT

Producer In the professional theatre (as in television and film) the producer brings together the financial and artistic resources that are necessary to create a production. The producer may have the original idea for a production, or commission others to develop an idea. In amateur theatre the term is often used to describe the function of the person more correctly known as the director. MB

Prokopovich, Feofan (1681–1736) Ukrainian clergyman and classical humanist who, via his brilliant sermons and orations, historical and literary-theoretical treatises (*De arte libri tres*, written 1705, published 1786) and political school dramas, championed Peter the Great's enlightenment programme of reform against reactionary obscurantism. Educated at the Kiev Academy, then in Poland and Rome, he brought a mastery of theology, philosophy, classical literature and poetics, mathematics and the natural sciences back with him to the Ukraine where he assumed monastic orders. He became a teacher at, then rector of, Kiev Academy (1710), bishop of Pskov (1718), archbishop of Novgorod (1720) and vice-president of the Synod, co-organizer of St Petersburg's Academy of Sciences and from 1715 ecclesiastical adviser to Peter's reform programme. His tragicomedy *Vladimir, Duke and Ruler of Slavic Russian Lands Led by the Holy Ghost from the Darkness of Unbelief to Evangelical Light, in the Year 988 After the Birth of Christ* (1705), a 13-syllable verse drama on the introduction of Christianity into Old Russia, is actually allegorical propaganda glorifying the valiant struggle of the reform-minded Tsar Peter (who is praised in the prologue) against unenlightened opposition. Prokopovich introduced into his play comic characters, musical interludes, more natural dialogue and satirical commentary on daily life in an effort to secularize the school drama. His satirical treatment of the priestly caste was borrowed from the folk theatre, where this was commonplace. This marks another early unsuccessful attempt to devise a dramatic literature for a national theatre. SG

Provincetown Players (USA) Led by George Cram Cook, an enthusiastic visionary from Iowa who revered the ancient Greek drama. In the summer of 1915 a band of amateurs staged several of their own plays in Provincetown, Massachusetts. The following year, after **Eugene O'Neill** joined the group and contributed the outstanding work *Bound East for Cardiff*, Cook, backed by O'Neill and journalist John Reed, among others, decided to move their playmaking to Greenwich Village, New York City. Launched in a brownstone at 139 Macdougal Street on 3 November 1916, the Provincetown Players initially featured short works, with O'Neill and **Susan Glaspell** as their leading writers. After two years, the Players moved into larger quarters at 133 Macdougal Street. Though Cook gave unstintingly of himself for O'Neill's writings, most notably for *The Emperor Jones* (1920), he himself had literary ambitions and envied the other's growing fame. In 1922 he and his wife Susan Glaspell sailed for Greece, where he died two years later. After a hiatus (1922–3), the Players were headed by a triumvirate of O'Neill, Kenneth Macgowan and **Robert Edmond Jones**, who in turn were succeeded by James Light as director. A casualty of the stock market crash and the depression, the Players folded in 1929. LSH

Prowse, Philip (19?–) British designer–director affiliated with the **Glasgow Citizens' Theatre**. Trained in Theatre Design at the Slade School of Art, he subsequently gained experience as a design assistant at **Covent Garden** before moving on as stage designer at Watford (1967–9) and Glasgow (since 1969). Although primarily a designer of plays he has also worked in opera and ballet with other companies and abroad. Prowse's stage settings are marked by their highly expressive, architectonic character. Rather than merely indicate the place where action occurs, his sets tend to function dramatically during the course of the action. Since the mid-1970s he has combined designing

Philip Prowse's design for Webster's *The Duchess of Malfi*, National Theatre, London, 1985.

with the direction of his own productions, notable examples being *Phèdre* (1984) and *The Duchess of Malfi* (1985), both of which were produced in London. JMB

Pryce, Jonathan (19?–) British actor. Repertory at Liverpool Everyman Theatre and Nottingham Playhouse established his reputation as one of Britain's most exciting younger actors. At Nottingham he played Gethin Price in **Trevor Griffiths**'s *Comedians* (1975), a production that went on to tour internationally. His Hamlet at the **Royal Court** was made remarkable by the manner in which Pryce also played the Ghost as a regurgitated voice from within Hamlet, and his Macbeth for the **RSC** (1986) gave further evidence of Pryce's fierce power. He has worked in film, television and as a director. MB

Prynne, William (1600–69) English campaigning Puritan and pamphleteer, whose long *Histriomastix* (1632) is one of the most famous of anti-theatrical tracts. Because it was seen by Archbishop Laud to contain attacks – albeit veiled – on the King and Queen, Prynne was fined, pilloried, had his ears cut off and was sentenced to life imprisonment. Freed by the Long Parliament in 1640, he became a leading Puritan and a vigorous Member of Parliament. PT

Public theatres The open-air theatres of Elizabethan, Jacobean and Caroline London were, and still are, sometimes called 'public' playhouses to distinguish them from the equally public but more exclusive indoor 'private theatres'. They are, in approximate chronological order, the **Theatre** (1576), the **Curtain** (1577), a theatre of unknown name in Newington Butts (c. 1580), the **Rose** (c. 1587), the **Swan** (1595), the **Globe** (1599), the **Boar's Head** (c. 1599), the **Fortune** (1600), the **Red Bull** (1605), the second Globe (1614), the **Hope** (1614) and the second Fortune (1623). PT

Puccini, Giacomo (1858–1924) Italian composer. Born into a musical family, the first of his pieces to attract attention was the one-act *Le Villi*, which the librettist **Arrigo Boito** was instrumental in getting produced at Milan in 1884. His mature work, beginning with *Manon Lescaut* (1893), is characterized by powerful, if at times sentimental melodic lyricism and a highly developed theatrical sense, particularly in the depiction of character psychology and the handling of *arie*. Several of his finest operas were taken from stage plays, and indeed have survived triumphantly on the stage as the plays themselves have not: *Tosca* (1900) from **Sardou**, and *Madame Butterfly* (1904) and *La Fanciulla del West* (1910) from the American dramatist, **David Belasco**. His *Turandot*, begun in 1921, was unfinished at his death.   KR   LR

Puerto Rico Until the 19th century only sporadic theatre activity existed on this eastern island in the Antilles chain. From the time of the Spanish conquest, the rivalries among the Spanish, French, English and Dutch for possession of the Caribbean islands resulted in invasions and raids that left little time for cultural development and entertainment. Through the 18th century the scant records showed the performance of an occasional Golden Age or religious play to mark special occasions. Although researchers have documented some 130 plays during the 19th century, few are of transcendental value. For the most part the century was still dominated by foreign imports. Spanish, Italian, Mexican and Argentine travelling companies staged operas, operettas, **zarzuelas** and plays from the classic Spanish repertory or the romantic pieces of **José Zorrilla**, for example. The principal themes of the emerging Puerto Rican theatre ranged from the fanciful, escapist works following the romantic model to regionally-oriented works with historical or socio-political overtones. The acknowledged founder of the Puerto Rican theatre, Alejandro Tapia y Rivera (1826–82), was censured for trying to humanize the English royal family in *Roberto D'Evreux* (1854). Other plays dramatized historical figures, and his *La cuarterona* (*The Quadroon*, 1867) dealt with racial issues on the island. *La parte del león* (*The Lion's Share*, 1880) anticipated later concerns about woman's role in the society. The other important 19th-century author is Salvador Brau (1842–1912) whose romantic play *La vuelta al hogar* (*Return Home*, 1877) teemed with pirates and adventures, but is only one of his many successful plays. Carmen Hernández de Araújo (1832–77) was the island's first woman playwright, and Eugenio Astol (1843–1904) was Puerto Rico's outstanding actor of the romantic period. In the final decades of the century, the costumbristic theatre also gained importance through plays such as *El jíbaro* (*The Farmer*, 1878) by Ramón Méndez Quiñones (1847–89).

Before the first theatre houses were built, it was customary to arrange provincial sites to present plays in the model of the Spanish *corral*. In 1823 the Teatro de Amigos del País (Friends of the Country Theatre) staged several plays, and in 1834 the first theatre opened in Puerto Rico, not with a theatre itself but with operatic performances, an indication of the importance of music in the local culture. (The municipal theatre was subsequently remodelled and renamed the Tapia Theatre in 1950 (in honour of Tapia y Rivera) and restored in the 1970s to its colonial grandeur.) Throughout the century the strong hand of the church and an active censorship programme discouraged free expression, but was not able to suppress the construction of new theatres in San Juan, Ponce, Mayagüez, Arecibo and other towns scattered across the island.

20th century In the War of 1898, Spain ceded control of

Puerto Rico to the United States. Until the Commonwealth was created in 1952, Puerto Rico was governed by a series of American-imposed governors. The changes resulting from this new political status did little to promote theatre on the island, although *El grito de Lares* (1914) by Luis Lloréns Torres (1878–1944) signalled the first of a long series of plays that examined and protested American intervention. The stimulus for new theatre came in 1938 when **Emilio Belaval**, as president of the Ateneo Puertorriqueño (Puerto Rican Atheneum), called for the creation of a national dramaturgy. The three plays honoured in the contest sponsored by the Ateneo were by Manuel Méndez Ballester (b. 1909), author of *El clamor de los surcos* (*Cry of the Land*), Gonzalo Arocho del Toro (1898–1954), with *El desmonte* (*The Clearing*) and Fernando Sierra Berdecía (1903–62), whose *Esta noche juega el jóker* (*Tonight the Joker Plays*) broke new ground in dealing with the painful issue of the Puerto Rican immigrant in New York.

Belaval's theatre group, Areyto, created in 1939, lasted only two seasons but succeeded in establishing the basis for other groups and for a new sense of identity in the Puerto Rican theatre. **Francisco Arriví**'s Tinglado Puertorriqueño (Puerto Rican Stage) (1944) captured the same spirit and was followed by **René Marqués**'s Teatro Nuestro (Our Theatre) (1950) and the Ateneo's Experimental Theatre (1951), both in conjunction with José Lacomba (b. 1924). The Puerto Rican Cultural Institute, established in 1955, sponsored its first Puerto Rican theatre festival in 1958, an unparalleled event for encouraging new playwrights and fostering theatre in Puerto Rico. The University of Puerto Rico, unable to present Puerto Rican plays from 1944 (Enrique Laguerre's *La resentida*) to 1956 (Arriví's *El murciélago* and *Medusa en la bahía*) because of political compromises, contributed to the training of new directors, actors, designers and technical crew.

Belaval, Arriví and especially René Marqués (1919–79) set the standards for the new theatre. Their plays dealt with life and death, philosophical and political issues; Arriví's works were often lyrical and metaphysical, such as *María Soledad* (1947). René Marqués experimented with social commitment, absurdism and biblical motifs, all within vanguard techniques incorporating light and sound. His *Los soles truncos* (*The Fanlights*, 1958) is still the classic Puerto Rican play because of the effective combination of its theme of psychological, cultural and political distress with techniques of poetic staging. The common denominator throughout Marqués's plays is his opposition to American encroachment on Hispanic values.

Some of the later generation of writers such as Myrna Casas (b. 1934) followed Arriví's lyrical patterns. Others echoed the socio-political commitment of Marqués, especially **Luis Rafael Sánchez** (b. 1936) in *La pasión según Antígona Pérez* (*The Passion according to Antígona Pérez*, 1968). Piri Fernández (b. 1925), working for the Institute of Puerto Rican Culture, wrote and staged plays such as *De tanto caminar* (*So Much Walking*, 1960), depicting with double planes of action the religious doubts of a nun.

Between 1966 and 1975 collective theatre achieved new levels of popularity and influence, as seen in such groups as El Tajo del Alacrán (The Scorpion's Sting) (1966), headed by Lydia Milagros González (b. 1942),

Ruben Figueroa in Carlos Canales's *Maria del Rosario*, Puerto Rico, 1985.

Unamu, Teatro de Guerrilla (Guerrilla Theatre) (1969), Morivivi (1972), and others, all with the function of raising the consciousness of political theatre of protest. Jaime Carrero (b. 1931) dealt with the Vietnam War and the Puerto Rican in the United States in his plays *Flag Inside* (1966) and *Pipo Subway no sabe reír* (*Pipo Subway Does Not Know How to Laugh*, 1971). Pedro Santiliz (b. 1938) arranged works especially for street theatre. The younger writers include José 'Papo' Márquez (b. 1950), Abneil Morales (b. 1958), and others who struggled against bourgeois influences in the theatre. The best of this generation may be **Roberto Ramos-Perea** (b. 1956) whose plays are brutal and closely tied to a contemporary Puerto Rican reality.

In addition to the festival sponsored by the Puerto Rican Cultural Institute (1985 was the 26th), other events raised the level of theatre consciousness. The International Theatre Festival (created in 1956) staged the best foreign plays. In the 1970s the Muestras (Showcases) sponsored by the Spanish-born Luis Molina promoted a consciousness of third-world theatre and provoked a political storm, testing allegiances among theatre groups vying for funding. A host of independent theatre groups was formed in the 1960s and 70s, some of them short-lived: El Cemí, Teatro Yukayeke, Teatro La Máscara, Cimarrón, Proscenio, Nuestro Teatro and others. Teatro del Sesenta has functioned for more than 20 years and owns the Sylvia Rexach Theatre. Travelling groups such as Teatro Rodante and Farándula Universitaria generate interest in the theatre across the island. Ironically, the oldest existing theatre group is still the English-speaking Little Theatre, created in 1931.

The mixture of Anglo and Hispanic culture on the island remains anomalous. In spite of programmes like Operation Bootstrap designed to encourage the Puerto Rican economy, New York has lured millions of Puerto Ricans over the years, although many have returned disillusioned to the island. Political positions in Puerto Rico range from independence to statehood, with the present Commonwealth status in the middle. The threat of annexation by the United States provokes groups such as the Comité de Defensa de la Cultura Puertorriqueña (Puerto Rican Cultural Defence League) to use theatre as a weapon for defending the Hispanic identity. GW

See: F. Arriví, *Areyto Mayor*, San Juan, 1966; J. A. Collins, *Contemporary Theater in Puerto Rico*, San Juan, 1979; *idem*, *Contemporary Theater in Puerto Rico: The Decade of the Seventies*, Río Piedras, 1982; N. González, *Bibliografía de teatro puertorriqueño (siglos XIX y XX)*, Río Piedras, 1979; A. Morfi, *Historia crítica de un siglo de teatro puertorriqueño*, San Juan, 1980; E. J. Pasarell, *Orígenes y desarrollo de la afición teatral en Puerto Rico*, Santurce, 1969; J. B. Phillips, *Contemporary Puerto Rican Drama*, New York, 1972.

Pulcinella see **Punch**

Punch The most celebrated of English puppets; the name is short for Punchinello, itself from the Italian *Policinella*, whose etymology is disputed. The character's hooked nose and hump may derive from the Maccus of the Roman Atellan farces, although these attributes are more invariable with the Northern European puppet than with the Neapolitan **commedia dell'arte** figure, Pulcinella. The latter, according to some claims, was invented by the actor **Silvio Fiorillo** and then perfected by Andrea Calcese, alias Ciuccio (d. 1656). His Pulcinella was a peasant of Acerra, shrill, cowardly, oafish and given to mischief and sententiousness. At the Teatro San Carlino, Naples, the character became acclimated as a kind of **Harlequin** clad in a loose white smock and black half-mask, and was a constant participant in all public ceremonies there and in Venice.

The French Polichinelle first appears as a marionette in the 17th-century show of the tooth-drawer Jean Brioché; cleverer than his Italian counterpart, this 'little wooden Aesop, moving, turning, spinning, dancing, laughing, talking, farting', as he was described in *Le Combat de Cyrano de Bergerac* (1649), was soon adapted to political satire. A puppet Polizinell crops up in Nuremberg in 1649 and a Don Cristóval Pulichinella in Spain of the same period. The flesh-and-blood Polichinelle played in an intermezzo to **Molière**'s *Imaginary Invalid* (1673), but **Gherardi** dropped the character from the Théâtre Italien for being too scurrilous a villain. After a lapse in popularity, the early 19th century saw a Polichinelle revival: the dancer **Mazurier** imitated the puppet and the mime Vautier made him a major character at the **Théâtre des Funambules**.

The English Punch probably came over during the Restoration, for the word was in common use by 1669 to describe something short and thick. **Pepys** and Evelyn both witnessed a marionette Punch and as early as 1678 **Otway** in *Friendship in Fashion* mentions Punch's characteristic voice, later produced by the 'swazzle' or 'swatchel', a device of metal and silk held in the showman's mouth. The English Punch inherited many of the traits of the medieval Vice and was linked up with all sorts of traditional themes: he took part in the creation of the world (Bartholomew Fair, 1703), the Deluge (1709) and, as the hero of Martin Powell's puppet-show at **Covent Garden** (1710), associated with paladins and danced a minuet with a pig.

By 1780, the glove-puppet Punch had become a familiar street show, played in a curtained booth either solo or with a commentator and 'bottler' who collected the audience's coins. A conventional scenario had taken shape: Punch, a kind of anarchic Falstaff, lying, bragging and bullying, in a series of confrontations with representatives of the social order – wife, beadle, doctor, executioner, devil – wins out by sheer egoistic brazenness. His dog Toby, first wooden, then real, is a silent observer of the mayhem. The first 'swatchel omi', as Punchmen are known in street performer slang, to be taken up by the literati was Giovanni Piccini (d. 1835), whose script was published by John Payne Collier with engravings by George Cruikshank in 1828. Percy Press is the best-known of the modern showmen, though other dynasties, like the Maggs and the Codman, still thrive, playing chiefly at seaside resorts. In 1962, the 300th anniversary of Punch's advent in England (dated from Pepys's diary entry) was celebrated at St Paul's Cathedral, London; but of late he has been under attack by feminists and educationists for his wife-beating and child abuse.   LS

See: R. Leach, *The Punch and Judy Show,* London, 1985; G. Speaight, *Punch and Judy,* London, Boston, 1970.

Puppets A type of performance in which a doll or figure imitates human behaviour, often in a parodic or alienated manner. Live manipulators animate the figures dexterously to produce an impression of life upon the spectators; the paradox is that the puppeteer remains hidden or obscured, while his creation takes centre stage as a vivid individual. The art may have arisen out of masked religious ceremonials, and the use of miniature human figurines for magical purposes. The earliest to develop were the stringed puppets or marionettes, which appear to have been known to the early Egyptians, Hindus and Greeks. Other common types are hand or glove puppets, shadow puppets and rod puppets.

Hand puppetry, in which the puppeteer cannot see the public's reaction, is portrayed as early as 1340 in the Oxford MS *Li romans du bon roi Alexandre* by the Fleming Jehan de Grise, but is probably much older. Three, rarely five, fingers are used, and the stage concealing the manipulator is a booth with three walls, known in the Romance languages as *castelet, castillo* and *castello.* The 'motions' of Elizabethan and Jacobean England, reproduced in **Ben Jonson**'s *Bartholomew Fair* (1614), presented anachronistic legends, chock-full of slapstick, violence and bawdry. Hand puppets were a favourite instrument of the Russian **skomorokhi**, being easily portable and wielded by one man, and devolved into the popular figure Petrushka. Indeed, the most enduring national types of puppet – **Punch** in England, **Guignol** in France, **Kasperl** in Germany and Austria – were portrayed most commonly by hand puppets. The leading 20th-century performer is **Sergei Obraztsov**.

Rod puppets, more characteristic of the Orient, may

have been created in Bengal and, with the spread of Hinduism, became the popular *wayang golek* of Java and Sunda. In China, the *tiexian kuilei* are first mentioned at a mourning service during the Tang Era (618–906), but gained popularity during the Sung Dynasty. The three leading types are the Big Heads from Sichuan, the medium-sized from Hunan, Shanxi and Beijing; and the miniature variety from Shandong. Except for the clowns, most have no feet and the faces are painted in the style of Beijing Opera, the colour combination indicating the complexity of the character. Occasionally, in an intricate action like a swordfight, the puppeteer will use his hands as well as the rods.

In Japan, the **bunraku** is a separate genre of the drama, with its own repertory. The large but lightweight figures are moved by a principal operator, assisted by two hooded auxiliaries, by means of a control stick and various levers manipulating arms, fingers, eyes, eyebrows, mouth, and so on, The voices are provided by a *joruri* reciter, who spins the narrative to samisen accompaniment. This style arose in the early 17th century and flourished during the Tokugawa period (1727–47), by which time it had the masterpieces of Chikamatsu Monzaemon to perform.

In the 19th century, puppets engaged the imagination of the literary world. George Sand created a Théâtre des Amis for hand puppets at her estate at Nohant; Henry Monnier opened a pornographic puppet theatre in 1862; and Count Franz Pocci, intendant of the Munich court theatre, composed plays for Kasperle. The notion of the actor as puppet gained ground among the European avant-garde. In 1888, Henri Signoret opened a Petit Théâtre des Marionettes, which presented **Aristophanes**, **Cervantes** and **Shakespeare**. **Maurice Maeterlinck** wrote three plays for puppets in 1894 (*Alladine et Palomides, Intérieur, La Mort de Tintagiles*), claiming that actors were too obtuse to convey his metaphysical concerns. The Russian symbolist **Fyodor Sologub** (Teternikov) argued that actors should simply perform what the playwright reads aloud, thus emblematizing the relationship of the helpless human being to fate. **Jarry**'s *Ubu Roi* was performed at a Théâtre des Pantins in 1898 with puppets of the painter Bonnard, and **Gordon Craig** hoped in 1905 and 1911 that the actor would acquire the technique and ego-less grace of an *Über-Marionette.* **Erwin Piscator** staged *The Adventures of the Good Soldier Schweik* with figures devised by George Grosz (1928). Such oversized manikins became a popular agit-prop device, taken to heights of ingenious creativity in the United States during the anti-Vietnam War protests by the **Bread and Puppet Theatre**.   LS

See: M. Batchelder, *The Puppet Theatre Handbook,* NY, 1947; S. Benegal, *Puppet Theatre around the World,* New Delhi, 1961; M. Byron, *Punch in the Italian Puppet Theatre,* London, 1983; J. Buch and A. Lehmann, *Das Puppentheater,* 4 vols., Leipzig, 1923–31; P. McPharlin, *The Puppet Theatre in America: A History 1524–1948, with a supplement by M. B. McPharlin,* NY, 1969; G. Speaight, *The History of the English Puppet Theatre,* London, 1955.

Purim play Purim, a Jewish festival held on Adar 14 and 15 (late March and early April), celebrates the thwarting of Haman's planned massacre of the Jews in Persia under Artaxerxes (Ahasuerus) by Esther and Mordecai. From earliest times, it constituted a Jewish equivalent to carnival, with masquerades and cross-dressing. At first, Haman was burnt in effigy and the story retold in the bosom of the family; by the late 15th century, jesters and mummers were performing more public enactments and selecting a 'King of Purim'. This gave rise to the only true Jewish folk-drama. Significantly, the first Judaeo-Spanish play is *Esther* by Solomon Usque and Lazara Gratiano (1567); and an anonymous comedy of *Haman and Mordechai* was published in Leyden in 1699. *Purimspiele* were of long standing among the German Jews; a *Spil von Tab Jaklein mit Sein Weib* was performed every Purim in Tannhausen throughout the 16th century. The first of these to be published was *Ahasweroshspiel* (Frankfurt, 1708). The Rabbinical authorities frequently forbade performances and burnt the texts, because they parodied serious portions of the ritual.

The *Mekirat Yosef*, a recounting of the tale of Joseph and his brethren by Baermann of Limburg (c. 1711), was enacted by Jewish theological students of Prague and Hamburg with the author as their stage-manager. It created a sensation, but was banned as soon as Christians began to attend. (It could be seen in Minsk as late as 1858.) An *Esther and Ahasuerus* acted in Prague by rabbinical students in 1774 was later rewritten by Itsik Manger in the 1920s, with the action translated to a small Eastern European village; this version played both in America and Tel Aviv. Ephraim Lauter's 1925 Purim play initiated the first Yiddish theatre in the Ukraine. By this time, it had become a vehicle for the *badchen*, the improvising master of ceremonies of Jewish weddings and celebrations; the term 'Purim play' had become synonymous with crude Yiddish productions and 'Purim author' with a hack playwright.   LS

See: Steinschneider, *Purim und Parodie*, Berlin, 1902; Z. Zylbercweig, *Lexikon fun yiddish Theater*, NY, 1959.

Purimspiel see **Hebrew theatre; Purim play**

Purvis, Billy (c. 1781–1853) British showman, clown, conjuror, dancer and virtuoso of the Northumbrian pipes. Though born near Edinburgh he was brought up in Newcastle upon Tyne, where he became a call boy at the Theatre Royal. In 1818 he established a fit-up company (subsequently and grandly known as the 'Victorian Theatre') which toured the fairs and races of the north of England and lowland Scotland presenting 'pantomime plays full o' reed an' blue fire', melodramas and cut versions of **Shakespeare**; interspersed with local songs, dances and music, and introduced by Billy himself, grotesque in clown's pantaloons, skull cap and round glasses, who would invite the public to walk up across the forestage of his booth, or, if they proved diffident, to 'get in by Billy's backside' (the rear entrance). At his death his former employee **Ned Corvan** penned an affectionate elegy which refers to a number of Billy's skills and gags, notably his routine of 'stealing the bundle', a simple **lazzo** with improvised asides to the audience in which the clown robbed an unsuspecting bumpkin of his possessions.   AEG

Pushkin, Aleksandr Sergeevich (1799–1837) Russia's greatest national poet and formulator of her literary language who, despite his admiration for the verse comedies of **Fonvizin, Knyazhnin, Shakhovskoi, Khmelnitsky** and **Griboedov**, pioneered the historical, romantic, pre-realistic drama in opposition to the prevailing French neoclassical model. His dramatic output, while not large and somewhat diffuse, is ambitious, novel and experimental, progressive and even revolutionary technically and ideologically. He drew upon contemporary parlance, literary sources and native folklore to forge a purposely hybrid Russian literary language suitable to comic and tragic scenes and character-specific for individuals of every class and profession. His inspiration for this was **Shakespeare** whom he read in the translations and criticisms of **A. W. Schlegel** and François Guizot. The direct result was his dramatic magnum opus, *Boris Godunov* (written 1825, produced 1870), an episodic blank verse tragedy about the Time of Troubles patterned after Shakespeare's historical chronicle plays. It illustrates Pushkin's thesis that the object of tragedy is 'man's fate and the people's destinies'. Ever watchful of Boris, the Slavic Macbeth, are the people 'always clandestinely leaning towards sedition', in what is the most celebrated instance of the collective hero in Russian drama. Here, as elsewhere in his work, Pushkin reveals insight into the poignant, seductive and above all tragic relationship between ruler and ruled, the struggle against tyranny and the yielding to power. A publication and performance ban together with a long-standing myth concerning its unstageability has kept the play from assuming a place in the dramatic repertoire equal to that occupied by Moussorgsky's operatic treatment (1873). In his *Little Tragedies* (written 1823–30, published 1832–9), Pushkin presents history writ small via a series of short, self-contained character sketches of familiar European literary types – the miser (*The Covetous Knight*), the artistic genius and his rival (*Mozart and Salieri*), and the legendary Don Juan as a tragic romancer (*The Stone Guest*). These dramatic variations on three of the deadly sins together with an allied piece, *The Feast in Plague-Time* (after John Wilson), are seldom performed. The **Moscow Art Theatre**, recognizing the opportunities afforded in them for psychological realism, presented a programme of all save *The Covetous Knight* in 1915 with sets by **Benois**, and with **Stanislavsky** and **Kachalov** in major roles. Pushkin's *Rusalka* (1831), a revenge tragedy on a fairy tale theme which provided tragedienne **M. N. Ermolova** with an artistic success, and *Scenes from the Age of Chivalry* (1835), an unfinished historical-dramatic meditation on peasant rebellion and the impoverished nobility, round off his playwriting career. He was also a noteworthy dramatic theorist. Several theatres in Moscow and Leningrad today bear his name.   SG

Putul Nautch (India) The term means 'dancing dolls' and refers to the form of rod puppet theatre only found in Bengal state in eastern India. The puppets vary from two to three feet in height and were originally made of bamboo covered with a plaster made of hay and rice husks covered by banana leaves to give shape to the different parts of the body. Nowadays, the dolls are carved from wood, which is hollowed out to reduce the weight and allow rods and strings to pass through the body.

The manipulators work the dolls from below. To their waistband they tie a cup in which they support a long rod which goes through the centre of the puppet to its head. Through a system of strings connected to the various parts of the figure, they manipulate the puppets. By dancing, the puppeteers give life to the figures.

Today, shows are rarely seen in the rural areas and when they are presented they are held in connection with fairs and festivals. The stories centre on events drawn from the *Mahabharata* and from local folk tales, such as that of Manasa, the snake goddess sister of Sesha, the serpent-king, and those concerning Radha and Krishna.   FaR

Pyat, Félix (1810–89) French journalist and dramatist. A prominent utopian socialist, hostile to the government of Louis Philippe and later to Napoleon III (during most of whose reign he had to remain in exile), he became an important figure in the Commune of 1871 and was obliged to return to exile for a further ten years. He made three brief incursions into government in 1848, 1871 and 1888. Pyat saw himself as a socialist dramatist and as having a role to play in the creation of a popular theatre. He subscribed to the moral virtues of the melodrama and most of his ten principal plays, with the exception of *Diogène* (1846), are cast in this form. *Ango*, written in collaboration with Auguste Luchet in 1835, was a virulent attack on the monarchy in the person of François I. The censors demanded modifications after the first performance, and the play was definitively banned a few days later following the Fieschi attempt on the life of the king. With *Les Deux Serruriers* (*The Two Locksmiths*, 1841) and *Le Chiffonnier de Paris* (*The Rag-Picker of Paris*, 1847), starring **Frédérick Lemaître**, he turned to a drama of modern society where the villains are bankers and where it is clearly shown that there is one law for the rich and another for the poor. *Le Chiffonnier de Paris* was his most popular work and contains the common opposition between poverty and virtue in a garret and wealth and corruption in an affluent drawing-room. The tone is at times close to that of the novels of Eugène Sue, whose *Mathilde* he had dramatized in 1841.   JMCC

Q

Q Theatre (London) Opened by Jack de Leon in 1924, it gained a reputation for try-outs of new plays, among which were **Terence Rattigan**'s earliest work *First Episode* (1934) and **Priestley**'s *Bright Shadow* (1950), as well as for the number of actors who made their first appearance on its stage, who included Max Adrian, **Anthony Quayle** and Dirk Bogarde. The death of de Leon in 1956 ended a campaign for funds to modernize the building, which had been refused a performance licence a year earlier, and it was demolished in 1958.   CI

Quayle, (John) Anthony (1913–) British actor and director, who was a stalwart member of the **Old Vic** company in the 1930s without ever becoming one of its stars. He joined the Royal Artillery during the war and when he left in 1945, he took a leading part in the reconstruction of British theatre in the post-war years. He succeeded **Barry Jackson** as the director of the Shakespeare Memorial Theatre at Stratford-upon-Avon and stayed there for eight years, during which time he had built up its financial resources and earned the company an international reputation with such productions as *Titus Andronicus* (1956), directed by **Peter Brook** and starring **Laurence Olivier**, in which he played Aaron. His Stratford policy was criticized for being too star-orientated, but under difficult conditions, he nevertheless provided a succession of worth-while Shakespearian productions and acted in many of them himself, notably as Falstaff in *Henry IV Parts 1 and 2* (1951), *Coriolanus* (1952) and *Othello* (1954). On leaving Stratford in 1957, he was in continual demand as an actor in contemporary plays, and scored a personal triumph in François Billetdoux's *Chin-Chin* (1960), playing opposite Celia Johnson. He appeared as Sir Charles Dilke in *The Right Honourable Gentleman* (1964), as Galileo in **Brecht**'s play in New York in 1967 and directed Dostoevsky's *The Idiot* (1970) for the **National Theatre**. He appeared in numerous films, usually in major supporting roles, and his normally restrained acting style is not one which commands centre-stage attention. With **Peggy Ashcroft** as his partner, he provided a memorable account of **Aleksei Arbusov**'s *Old World* in 1978. In 1978, he joined the Prospect Theatre Company to direct *The Rivals* and play King Lear, and when Prospect eventually collapsed as Britain's major touring classical company, he formed an unsubsidized alternative, Orbit, in 1981 which brought leading actors in classical productions to many regional theatres.   JE

Queen Elizabeth's Men It was a sign of the growing power of the theatre in England when Elizabeth I granted the patronage of her name to a new company, formed primarily for the purpose of performing at Court, in 1583. That it had a bias towards comedy and extempore entertainment is suggested by the prominence in it of **Richard Tarlton** and **Robert Wilson**. The company's best days ended with Tarlton's death in 1588, and it was disbanded in 1594.   PT

Quesnel, Joseph (1746–1809) French Canadian playwright, poet, musician and composer. Born to a prosperous French merchant family, he settled permanently in Canada in 1779 after his ship, carrying contraband to the Americas, was impounded by the British. Soon active in amateur theatricals, he is the author of the first operetta composed in North America, *Colas et Colinette, ou Le Bailli Dupé* (*Colas and Colinette: or The Bailiff Confounded*), first performed in Montreal in 1790 and printed there in 1808. A light, humorous work set in rural France, it was followed by two satirical plays which, although unpublished and probably unplayed until the 20th century, circulated widely in manuscript: *Les Républicains Français* (*The French Republicans*), a biting attack on the excesses of the French Revolution, written about 1801; and, in 1803, *L'Anglomanie, ou Le Dîner à l'Anglaise* (*Anglomania: or Dinner, English-Style*), a good-humoured attack on those French Canadians who had begun to ape English ways.   LED

Questors Theatre (Ealing, West London) A leading amateur theatre group in Britain since its foundation in 1929, its tireless leader for the first 40 years of its existence was Alfred Emmet (d. 1991), who distrusted commercial theatre and wanted to present intellectually stimulating plays in competent productions. From 1933 until the late 1950s, the company used a disused chapel in Mattock Lane, but it acquired the site and built a new 400-seat theatre, adaptable in its staging, although its best configuration is as an open stage, with the audience sitting on three sides. Questors Theatre has facilities beyond the range of most amateur companies; but it also has a proud reputation in discovering new plays and dramatists, **James Saunders** being perhaps the best known. For 17 years, from 1960 to 1977, it ran an annual Festival of New plays. It is also internationally known, a founder-member of the International Amateur Theatre Association (IATA) in 1952, and has acted as the host to amateur companies from Europe, North America and the Third World. Alfred Emmet retired in 1969, leaving behind a professionally run administration, a membership of 3,000 and a training school for actors in the West London region, in addition to Questors Theatre itself. Right up to his death he remained actively involved, as other members of his family still are. Questors has proved a sympathetic training ground for actors, writers and directors for half-a-century. JE

Quin, James (1693–1766) English actor, known as 'Bellower Quin'. Contemporary records show that in matters of costume and vocal projection Quin favoured the grand style. As an actor at **Lincoln's Inn Fields** from 1718 to 1732 he played the major Shakespearian tragic heroes. He remained working in London, at **Covent Garden** and finally **Drury Lane** until 1751, his manner of playing becoming less and less fashionable but a powerful reminder of the heroic tastes of the Restoration Theatre. MB

Quinault, Philippe (1635–88) French dramatist and librettist. From a humble background, he went into service with **Tristan l'Hermite** who encouraged his natural ability and helped him make his way in literary and fashionable society. He was only 18 when he adapted *Les Rivales* (*The Rivals*) from a comedy by **Rotrou** and went on to produce a series of plays for the **Hôtel de Bourgogne** and the **Marais**, all cleverly contrived and popular with the public, though occasionally owing more than a little to the work of other writers. The most successful were the tragedy *Astrate, Roi de Tyr* (*Astrates, King of Tyre*, 1664) and the comedy *La Mère Coquette* (*The Flirtatious Mother*), which opened at the Hôtel de Bourgogne in 1665 in direct opposition to **Donneau de Visé**'s play of the same name at the Marais. Writing the libretto for **Lully**'s court *divertissement La Grotte de Versailles* in 1668 enabled him to discover his most distinctive talent and with the foundation of the Paris Opéra in 1672 he became Lully's accredited collaborator, producing librettos for a dozen large-scale works which delighted Louis XIV and were to dominate operatic tradition for many years. He also collaborated with **Molière** and **Corneille** on the lyrics for the 'tragédie-ballet' *Psyché* in 1671, the year after his election to the Académie-Française. DR

Quiñones de Benavente, Luis (?1593–1651) Spanish playwright, born in Toledo. The greatest exponent of the *entremés* (see **género chico**), his name became so linked with the genre that many are falsely attributed to him, though his output must be counted in hundreds. He began writing about 1609 and had stopped by 1645 when his friend Manuel Vargas published a collection of his playlets. These have been divided into the realistic, taking the form of a miniature **comedia**, and the fantastic, usually sung. A frequent character is Juan Rana, a comic doctor, lawyer or mayor, played with enormous success at the time by the actor Cosme Pérez. CL

Quintero, José (1924–) Panamanian-born American director specializing in the plays of **O'Neill**. Having begun directing in 1949 at the Woodstock (NY) Summer Theatre, Quintero and Theodore Mann launched **Circle in the Square** in Greenwich Village, New York, in 1951. First drawn to theatre for its passion, 'the essence of all life', Quintero demands 'depth of feeling and commitment' from his collabor-

ators, and an 'inflexible, deep-rooted belief that . . . the collective product [is] more important than any individual contribution'. For Circle, which he left in 1964, and others, his O'Neill productions include the definitive *The Iceman Cometh* with **Jason Robards, Jr** (1956 – Vernon Rice Award), *Long Day's Journey into Night* (premiere, Broadway, 1956 – Tony), *A Moon for the Misbegotten* (Festival of Two Worlds, Spoleto, Italy, 1958; Broadway, 1973 – Tony and Drama Desk Award; Oslo, 1975), *Strange Interlude* (for the **Actors Studio**, 1963) and *A Touch of the Poet* (Broadway, 1977). Awarded the 1981 O'Neill Birthday Medal 'for enhancing the understanding' of the playwright's work by the Theatre Committee for Eugene O'Neill, of which he is a director, Quintero directed a 1985 touring revival of his famous *Iceman* with Robards.

Other Quintero productions include the famous Circle revival of **Tennessee Williams**'s *Summer and Smoke* (1952), **Behan**'s *The Hostage* (1954) and *The Quare Fellow* (1958), Leoncavallo's *I Pagliacci* and Mascagni's *Cavalleria Rusticana* (Metropolitan Opera, 1966), **Jules Feiffer**'s *Knock Knock* (1976) and **Cocteau**'s *The Human Voice* (1978, Melbourne, Australia; 1979, Broadway). After the Broadway failure of Tennessee Williams's last play, *Clothes for a Summer Hotel* (1980), and other disappointments, Quintero left New York for Los Angeles, where, as Artistic Director, he is forming the Chaplin-O'Neill Theatre. In 1983, he was named Artistic Director of the Springold Theatre of Boston's Brandeis University, where he ran a student directing programme. He directed television versions of **Euripides**' *Medea* (1959), **Wilder**'s *Our Town* (1959) and *Moon for the Misbegotten* (1975), and the film *The Roman Spring of Mrs Stone* (1961). Quintero's autobiography, *If You Don't Dance, They Beat You*, was published in 1974. REK

Quotidien, Théâtre du Name given to a style of theatre influenced partly by German-language playwrights e.g. **Fassbinder, Kroetz, Sperr, Handke** and pioneered in the 1970s by the Comédie de Caen and the Théâtre National de Strasbourg. The plays characteristically show inarticulate people in everyday situations presented with a heightened realism so that powerful theatrical images express, often brutally, the desires and needs which they are unable to express in spoken language. Behind the ordinariness of these people's lives the hidden violence of modern European social structures emerges with great force. Plots are fragmentary and characters are often controlled by language that is imposed upon them from outside e.g. the language of the sports business in René Kalisky's *Skandalon* (1970) about a champion racing cyclist, controlled entirely by the interests of others. Georges Michel is often seen as the first of these playwrights, though his success *La Promenade du Dimanche* (*The Sunday Walk*, 1966) also owes much to the absurd. Michel's work was encouraged by **Sartre**, who published his first play, *Les Jouets* (*The Toys*), in *Les Temps Modernes* in 1963. He has since written several more plays on the theme of alienation in the consumer society of which the best is *Un Petit Nid d'Amour* (*A Little love Nest*, 1970). The major Quotidien playwrights of the 1970s were Michel Deutsch and Jean-Paul Wenzel. During this period Deutsch worked as dramaturge for the Théâtre National de Strasbourg under **Jean-Pierre Vincent** and some of his plays were commissioned for that theatre e.g. *Convoi* (*Convoy*, 1980) depicting the relationship between a young Jewish girl and the old French peasant woman who tries to shelter her during the Occupation. Their relationship becomes a battle-ground for conflicting ways of articulating experience, mirroring the larger national conflict. Wenzel has directed the work of Deutsch as well as writing his own plays, the most successful being *Loin d'Hagondange* (*Far From Hagondange*), partly thanks to a brilliant production by **Patrice Chéreau** at the TNP (1977).   DB

Quyi The vocal arts. A generic description for the different styles of Chinese story-telling and balladry. There are said to be some 350 forms extant today. They flourish in every provincial region where local dialectical usage conditions their individual appeal. Performers sing or recite to the accompaniment of drums, wooden clappers or stringed instruments. They may be self-accompanied or work with a small musical ensemble. The unadorned appeal of their vocal skill may be sufficient in itself or else reinforced with dramatic gesture and mime. Chinese story-tellers are superb mimics. Repertoires are based on the classical epics and romantic novels of China's past but there is an extensive range of contemporary material. It ranges from comic skits to social commentary enlivened with sly digs and allusions. In the past the story-tellers worked the street pitches, market places and tea-house-theatres. In contemporary China they hold a prestigious position in the hierarchy of performing arts. Television seems likely to enhance their calling although nothing can substitute for the live presence of these popular artists. They were forced into silence during the Cultural Revolution but are back in full force today.

The texts used to propagate Buddhist sutras, such as those discovered at the Dunhuang caves from 1899, the patter and foolery of the jesters at the Han courts in the 2nd century and the comic dialogues of the early *zaju* or variety play, have all been cited as distant sources linked to the history of the vocal arts. The Song dynasty (960–1279) was a period which saw a great flowering of story-telling as a public entertainment. All story-telling performers in China rely on a meticulous control of prescribed rhythmic patterns and aural devices no less than the actor. Both their crafts share a long history of interrelationship and common sources.   ACS

R

Rabb, Ellis (1930–) American actor, director, and producer; founder and artistic director of the **Association of Producing Artists** (APA) in 1960. In 1964 it joined with the Phoenix Theatre to become APA at the Phoenix. Until its dissolution in 1970, Rabb directed most of this company's productions and acted in many as well. Prior to the APA he was with the Antioch Arena Theatre, Yellow Springs, Ohio (1952–7) and spent a season at the **American Shakespeare Festival** (1958). Since 1963 he has also directed at the **American Shakespeare Theatre**, the Old Globe in San Diego, and the Kansas City Opera. Of his most recent New York productions, most notable have been *Twelfth Night* at Lincoln Center (1972), *The Royal Family* (1975), *Caesar and Cleopatra* (1977), and *Anatol* at **Circle in the Square** in 1985. A flamboyant and stylish actor and director Rabb has made significant contributions to the American theatre in both areas and has been recognized with numerous awards, including the Obie and Vernon Rice Awards for his Off-Broadway season with the APA, 1962–3, and the Tony Award for direction in 1976. To Rabb's credit he has worked diligently throughout his career to bring true repertory to the American stage. DBW

Rabe, David (1940–) American playwright. One of the few dramatists to write with conviction and success about the Vietnam War, Rabe is among the most promising of the young, contemporary playwrights. He is a product of **Joseph Papp**'s **New York Shakespeare Festival** Public Theatre, where he won both an Obie Award and a Tony Award for his first two plays, *The Basic Training of Pavlo Hummel* and *Sticks and Bones* (both 1971). *The Orphan* (1973) and *In the Boom Boom Room* (1973) failed to generate the excitement of his first works, but he successfully returned to the subject of Vietnam with *Streamers* (1976). Rabe was born in Iowa and educated at Loras College and Villanova, where he has been playwright in residence. LDC

Rabemananjara, Jacques (1913–) Malagasy playwright. Born at Maroantsetra. After an education in Catholic mission schools, Rabemananjara joined the colonial administration. He was in Paris at the outbreak of the Second World War; he returned to Madagascar in 1946 to enter active politics. His alleged involvement in an uprising against French rule in 1947 led to imprisonment then exile in France. In 1960 he returned to hold a ministerial post in the country's first post-independence government. Following a coup in 1972 he again went into exile in France. Rabemananjara had a close association with the negritude writers of his generation, particularly the Senegalese poet Léopold Sédar Senghor. His own reputation as a writer derives mainly from his large output as a poet, but he has also written three substantial plays based on the legend and history of Madagascar. Their style owes much to the French tradition of classical drama which accords well with the heroic emphasis in Rabemananjara's plays. In spite of their undoubted power, they are not often performed because of their length and their essentially literary quality, nor have they been translated into English: *Les Dieux Malgaches* ('The Malagasy Gods', 1942), *Les Boutriers de l'Aurore* ('The Boats from the East', 1957), *Agapes des Dieux-Tritriva* ('The Feast of the Gods', 1962). CW

Rabinal Achí The only indisputably authentic dramatic work of the pre-Colombian New World. (The **Ollantay** of Peru and the *Güegüence* of Nicaragua have later influences.) Created as the *Dance of Tun* by the maya-quiché Indians, it shows no European influence. Music and spectacle are integral to the repetitious, stylized dialogue involving two primary characters, the Quiché Warrior and the Rabinal Warrior, engaged in ceremonial battle over death with honour. Preserved through oral tradition, the play was first recorded in 1850, subsequently translated into French, Spanish and English. A part of the rich folkloric tradition of Guatemala, the play is still performed annually at the end of January in the city of Rabinal. GW

Rachel (1820–58) French tragic actress. The greatest in France in the 19th century, Rachel (born Elisa Felix) was the daughter of a pedlar. In 1836 she joined the Conservatoire for a few months but then was taken on at the Gymnase, where she appeared in **Scribe**'s *Le Mariage de Raison* (*Marriage of Reason*). In 1838 she was discovered by the actor **Samson**, who took her into his class at the Conservatoire and found that she could wear classical costume as if it were made for her. In June of that year she made her debut at the **Comédie-Française** as Camille in **Corneille**'s *Horace*. By September audiences were flocking to that theatre. Rachel rapidly became extremely demanding, prompted by a family who were not slow to exploit her. The rest of the troupe had to put up with her caprices and, as the years went by, her increasingly frequent absences on personally lucrative tours. In 1849 she had her contract as a 'sociétaire' annulled, and then had herself re-employed at a salary of 42,000 francs as a 'pensionnaire' (which gave her six months leave a year). She had visited England in 1841, 1843 and 1846, when the Comédie-Française had refused to prolong her leave. In 1850 she spent four months touring, in 1851 six months. In 1855 she resigned from the Comédie-Française, paid a final visit to England, went to New York with her own troupe in August, but began to suffer from tuberculosis and had to dissolve her troupe in January 1856. Rachel's greatest roles were in the classical repertoire and in 1838 she played Hermione in *Andromaque*, Emilie in *Cinna*, and Roxanne in *Bajazet*. **Alfred de Musset** became one of her lovers in 1841 (others were Véron, who included her in his harem at the Opéra, the Prince de Joinville, and Napoleon's son, Count Walewski, and nephew, Prince Napoleon). He wrote a review of Rachel's first season, which is virtually a manifesto for a new type of tragedy on neoclassical lines using themes from French history. Musset also wrote a celebrated description of a visit to Rachel, *A Supper at Rachel's*. Rachel was an inspired natural performer, with an ability to give to the text a strong human quality and to make it sound as if it were being heard for the first time. She also had very clear diction, a sense of musical rhythms and an economy of gesture (particularly striking at a period when the larger gestures of melodrama were the norm). Although she was to play Bérénice (1844), Athalie (1847) and, less successfully, Agrippine in *Britannicus* (1848), her greatest triumph in the Racinian repertoire was as Phèdre, first performed in 1843, when it ran for an unprecedented 74 successive performances. Rachel also appeared with some success in the modern repertoire in Scribe's *Adrienne Lecouvreur*, but her last new part in his *The Czarina* at the Comédie-Française in 1855 was a failure. In her later years, when her talent was declining, Rachel was often compared unfavourably to the Italian actress **Ristori** by those who preferred a more romantic style.   JMCC

Racine, Jean (1639–99) French poet and dramatist, the most gifted tragedian of his century. Orphaned as a child, he received an outstanding classical education at the Jansenist schools of Port-Royal, where he wrote some early religious verse. Having vainly sought an ecclesiastical living through his uncle's influence, he opted for the worldly pleasures of Paris and endeavoured to make a career in literature, dedicating verse to likely patrons and becoming friendly with La Fontaine and **Boileau**. He also made the acquaintance of **Molière**, who agreed to present his first play, *La Thébaïde, ou les Frères Ennemis* (*The Thebaïd, or The Enemy Brothers*, 1664). When a second tragedy, *Alexandre le Grand* (*Alexander the Great*, 1665), again premiered by Molière at the **Palais-Royal**, proved successful, he promptly transferred it to Molière's competitors at the **Hôtel de Bourgogne**, who were the recognized performers of tragedy. Further evidence of his ambition and lack of scruple was provided by an offensively personal attack on Pierre Nicole, his erstwhile teacher at Port-Royal, for the latter's condemnation of dramatic authors. Racine may also have engineered the defection from Molière's company of his current mistress, the talented tragic actress Mlle du Parc, in order to play the lead in his next tragedy *Andromaque* at the Hôtel de Bourgogne. It was a triumph there in 1667 and was followed by a period of intense creativity for Racine. In addition to the comedy *Les Plaideurs* (*The Litigants*, 1668), derived partly from the *Wasps* of **Aristophanes**, he produced six tragedies in only ten years, all of them masterpieces. *Britannicus* (1668),

Bérénice (1670), *Bajazet* (1672), *Mithridate* (1673), *Iphigénie en Aulide* (1674) and *Phèdre* (1677).

It was also a period of growing antagonism with the ageing **Corneille**, whose *Tite et Bérénice* was presented by Molière only one week before Racine's version at the rival theatre and whose reputation as a tragic dramatist Racine was soon acknowledged to have outstripped. His Bérénice, and new mistress, was **Mlle Champmeslé**, who scored some of her greatest successes in this and the following plays. Having now reached the pinnacle of his career, he could count on protection in the highest places, above all from the king, and he was elected to the Académie-Française in 1673. But inevitably he had made enemies and in 1677 an organized cabal ensured not only that a tragedy entitled *Phèdre et Hippolyte* by Pradon opened in direct opposition to his own play on the subject but also that it was more favourably received. This experience may have contributed to his abrupt decision to retire from the theatrical scene, as must assuredly his appointment as historiographer-royal in the same year. He married, became reconciled with Port-Royal and took his duties as courtier seriously enough to be made a secretary to the king. He subsequently relented only to write a court divertissement to music by **Lully**, *Idylle Sur La Paix* (*Idyll on Peace*, 1685), and, at Mme de Maintenon's request, two tragedies on biblical subjects, *Esther* (1689) and *Athalie* (1691), for performance, with music, by the young ladies of the school she had founded at Saint-Cyr. Although different in inspiration and form, they have since taken their place alongside his earlier work in the classic French repertoire. Other spiritual writings occupied his last years, when his ties with Jansenist circles grew even closer.

Racine's *oeuvre* offers a vindication of the principles of neoclassical dramaturgy, but in observing its constraints he transcended them. In his hands tragedy became a highly refined, sophisticated vehicle for the expression of tragic feeling which is all the more powerful and poignant for being confined within a defined emotional spectrum, a precise convention of language and a fairly rigid structural form. Decorum and the unities combine to displace the centre of interest from the incidents of a story towards their effect on the characters, from physical action towards what goes on in their weak or vacillating minds, and this begets a remorseless exploration of profound psychological depths, most of all in his female roles, which have attracted leading actresses of every generation, though difficulties of translation have conspired to deny Racine his due attention in English-speaking countries.   DR

Radio City Music Hall West 50th St and Ave of the Americas, New York City [Architects: Feinhard and Hofmeister, Hood and Foulihoux and Corbett, Harison and MacMurray]. Built in 1932 by S. L. 'Roxy' Rothafel with Rockefeller money, the 6,200-seat, Art Deco theatre was originally intended to present popular-priced vaudeville, but the policy and leadership changed quickly. The new formula of showing a movie in combination with a stage show highlighted by the Rockettes, a precision tap-dancing chorus, endured for many years. When the supply of 'family-type' films fell off and the attraction of the stage show wore thin, the theatre seemed doomed. But in 1979, it

was declared a landmark and was thoroughly renovated to reopen as a showplace for large spectacles and
star appearances. MCH

Radio drama If radio comes, can drama be far
behind? Immediately after the end of the First World
War, radio began to establish itself internationally as a
medium of mass communication, and its potential for
drama was quickly appreciated by the pioneers of
broadcasting. Indeed, some theorists of the media
believe that it is in the nature of both radio and
television to aspire to the condition of drama. What this
means is that much more of the non-musical output of
radio is 'dramatic' than would be the case if this word
were thought to designate only productions emanating
from drama departments. For one thing, fiction is not
the preserve of these departments: what is labelled
'light entertainment' includes a considerable amount of
material that is essentially dramatic and that descends
from popular theatre, such as the English music-hall
and American vaudeville traditions, involving stand-
up comedians and humorous sketches. Comedy series
and sitcoms, including such major BBC ones as
Tommy Handley's *ITMA* in the 1940s, *Hancock's Half
Hour* and *The Goon Show* in the 1950s, and the more
recent *Dad's Army* and *Yes, Minister*, are undoubtedly
dramatic in their employment of narrative and character creation. Several students of radio have argued that
The Goon Show has claims to be one of the most
dramatically innovative programmes in the history of
sound broadcasting since it exploits the representational possibilities and limitations of radio to the full.

If, as Martin Esslin (a former head of BBC Radio
Drama) has argued, theatre is what happens when
exhibitionists confront voyeurs, 'theatre' encompasses
an enormous range of performances from strip and sex
shows to productions of the *Oresteia* and *King Lear*.
Similarly, radio drama, like Walt Whitman, contains
multitudes, and academic attempts to reserve the term
for the more serious and highbrow end of the radio-
drama spectrum soon founder on the impossibility of
clear-cut demarcations when analysing a popular mass
medium reaching millions. Is the BBC's long-running
daily serial in fifteen-minute instalments, *The Archers*,
radio drama or not? If not, what is it? During the
inter-war years, a substantial amount of fictional
programming on American radio took the form of
serialized soap operas, and to separate the 'soaps'
(together with comedy series) from 'radio drama'
would be to reduce the American experience to a
marginal rump. But the problem of definition is not
restricted to manifestly fictional output, from dramatized readings, through comedy series and thriller
serials, to new one-off plays and productions of stage
classics. If radio really does have in-built tendencies
towards the dramatic, this would apply to factual or at
least non-fictional areas of broadcasting as well as to
what would be widely acknowledged to be variants of
drama proper. The most obvious case is documentary,
which slides very easily into what has become known
as docudrama, but quiz programmes, confrontational
discussions and interviews, actuality reportage, and
even illustrated accounts of yesterday's proceedings in
parliament (a non-stop theatre with a cast of hundreds)
or language-instruction programmes with interpolated
episodes of typical conversational situations do develop

dramatic momentum and tension, helping to sustain
listeners' interest.

The history of British radio is particularly relevant to
the problem concerning the boundaries between fact
and fiction and between the dramatic and non-
dramatic. From the 1930s, the Features Department of
the BBC existed alongside the Drama Department
before they were eventually merged in the mid-1960s,
and credit for exploring the unique dramatic potential
of radio during the 1930s, 1940s and early 1950s is
rightly accorded to Features, under the brilliant leadership of Laurence Gilliam, rather than to Drama,
which in its earlier days concentrated on conventional,
theatre-like plays. The word 'feature' suggests a factual
basis as opposed to an entirely fictional construct, but in
practice the BBC Features Department blurred any
clear-cut distinction between fact and fiction. Long
before the word 'faction' was coined to describe a mode
of writing in which the techniques of fiction were
applied to real-life stories (non-fiction novels such as
Truman Capote's *In Cold Blood* and Thomas Keneally's
Schindler's Ark, and documentary drama of the kind
associated with **Peter Weiss** and various South African
groups), this is precisely what Features specialized in,
although it did other things too. Among the principal
writer-producers of radio features were a number of
poets, notably Louis MacNeice, and 'highly imaginative' is the best way of describing their work, whether
documentary or non-documentary. Some of the most
famous and seminal productions by Features, including
D. G. Bridson's *The March of the '45* (1936) and
MacNeice's *Christopher Columbus* (1942), resemble
Elizabethan chronicle history plays in existing as both
dramatized history and poetic drama, documentary
and fiction. Yet Features also produced entirely fictional work, including two of the most renowned radio
plays in the history of broadcasting, MacNeice's *The
Dark Tower* (1946) and **Dylan Thomas**'s even more
revered *Under Milk Wood* (1954). Such works were the
province of BBC Features rather than Radio Drama
because they totally violate conventional ideas of
well-made realistic drama and accord with the free,
radiogenic form of the feature. MacNeice shapes his
work as a poetic, saga-like quest with rapid shifts from
episode to episode, while Thomas uses a narrative
structure with dramatized inserts involving numerous
characters.

Although broadcasting organizations and their
histories differ widely from nation to nation, and what
happened at the BBC has not been exactly paralleled
elsewhere, the fluidity of 'radio drama' and the concomitant problem of fixing frontiers has been an almost
universal phenomenon. In some countries, such as
Australia, this indeterminacy is virtually institutionalized in the official nomenclature: the ABC has a Radio
Drama and Features Department, a name simultaneously acknowledging a distinction and closely linking
the two modes under one umbrella, with the same
production staff. The most famous American radio
broadcast ever – and probably in the world – illustrates
radio's uncertainty principle in a way that remains
startling nearly 50 years later. At Hallowe'en in 1938,
one of the Columbia Broadcasting System's radio-
drama series, Mercury Theatre on the Air, put out an
adaptation by **Orson Welles** of H. G. Wells's novel,
The War of the Worlds. Not only did this occupy a

regular drama slot that should have established it as fiction; it was also science fiction, a fantasy about a Martian invasion of the Earth. Yet millions of Americans reacted to it as though it were actually happening; there was widespread mass hysteria, and people fled from their homes and cities in panic and terror. The truth proved to be much stranger than the totally fabricated and far-fetched fiction that caused it, a fiction interpreted by many listeners as fact. Although a newcomer to radio, Welles grasped the actuality techniques characteristic of American radio drama in the 1930s, which were designed to promote realism and conviction, and were identical to those employed in radio journalism and other factual investigations; in *The War of the Worlds* he employed them to give as much authenticity as possible to a highly improbable story. Welles and his colleagues did not for a moment imagine that the broadcast would have the extraordinary effect it did, and many books and essays have been written by students of the media, social history, and mass psychology to account for what happened, but the Mercury Theatre production demonstrates how powerful an illusion of reality radio can create, and how different radio drama is from drama with a visual dimension, whether stage, television, or big screen. None of these media could have produced an equivalent response; in Welles's hands, the 'blindness' of radio turned out to be its greatest asset.

This much-discussed 'blindness' is the most significant factor in distinguishing radio drama from any other dramatic form. Historically, most drama from the Ancient World onwards has been intended for performance in visual as well as aural terms. Some poets, including Milton, Shelley, and Matthew Arnold, have written works in dramatic form aimed at the silent reader, not the stage, but such dramatic poems are exceptions. **Seneca** has been claimed as a forerunner of radio drama because his plays were performed by readers as sound plays, not by actors as stage plays, but in this respect Seneca had no significant predecessors or successors until 20th-century technology made possible the widespread dissemination of sound plays. As a former head of BBC Radio Drama, Val Gielgud, liked to point out, we do not talk of going to hear or listen to plays but to see them. Indeed, in the recent past a number of influential theorists stressed the visual side of theatre at the expense of other elements, which has in turn provoked other theorists to reassert the primacy of language. If the extreme case that drama is an essentially visual medium were true, mime would be far more central and popular than it is, and the 'talkies' would not have supplanted the silent – more precisely, speechless – cinema as easily as they did. Nevertheless, the everyday use of 'show' as a synonym for 'theatrical presentation' emphasizes an experience for the eye, although the fact that radio-drama producers use the same word to refer to what they are creating is a reminder that 'showing', or ostension (to use the technical term), can be an entirely aural experience and, except for totally silent mime, always involves the ear, however lavish the visual spectacle may be. On radio, ostension is achieved largely through language, which is why radio drama is thought of as more of a writer's medium than theatre itself: somewhere between an entirely verbal form, such as the novel, and stage drama. It is possible for

radio drama to dispense with speech altogether and rely solely on sound effects, as in Andrew Sachs's pursuit play *The Revenge*, which caused a considerable stir when broadcast by BBC Radio 3 in 1978; but however interesting an occasional experiment of this kind is, its self-imposed limitations as a narrative consisting of nothing but noises make it a curiosity, not a feasible model for further development.

The sightlessness of radio makes impossible a number of elements we take for granted in drama on stage: in addition to scenery, costumes, lighting, and visual symbols, there are proxemics and kinesics – the positioning and movement of actors as well as their physical gestures and facial expressions. Stereophonic and quadrophonic productions on radio can create some illusion of space, but they do so at the price of sacrificing monophonic radio's symbolic reality (its spacelessness, its sense of being located in the listener's head rather than 'out there') for an imaginatively impoverished iconic one. In the very early days of radio, attempts were made to broadcast live stage performances, from both 'straight' theatre and music hall, but these were disastrous because in unadapted form they proved to be very difficult to follow or even downright incomprehensible without visual definition. On radio, settings, including the time of day, have to be conveyed principally through language; without a verbal context, the usefulness of sound effects is severely restricted owing to their inherent imprecision and ambiguity. The notorious BBC seagull implies water but does not, in itself, tell us whether the setting is on land or at sea, a beach or a small sailing boat, a dockside or a luxury liner. Even a clock chiming twelve can mean midday or midnight, so that speech or a qualifying sound effect (a traffic jam, an owl hooting) is needed to clarify the exact time. This is why Elizabethan and Jacobean drama, with its verbal scene painting and other descriptive devices necessitated by the theatrical conventions of the time, transfers to radio much more easily than some stage plays in the naturalistic and expressionistic traditions, which rely heavily on visual presentation.

An actor on radio is a voice – no more, no less – and identification by an audience is entirely aural. This makes it difficult to mount plays with large casts on radio, especially if there are a number of equally important characters using roughly the same linguistic register, because the unaided ear (at least in sighted people) cannot recognize and keep track of more than a few voices, unless there are frequent and possibly awkward reminders in the form of name dropping, either by the characters themselves or by an intrusive narrator. Effects entirely natural to the stage, such as the counterpointing of words and actions, are not feasible on radio, which accounts for the notorious difficulty experienced in adapting **Chekhov** for the medium. Whereas a silent character on stage can have a powerful visual presence, a silent character on radio is an absence and simply does not exist. 'I speak, therefore I am', is the appropriate neo-Cartesian formulation for radio. Pauses and hesitations can be extremely expressive in stage plays (Chekhov, **Beckett**), but only because we can see the characters. On radio, an unfilled break in the dialogue is more likely to be interpreted as a fault in transmission than a meaningful silence.

There are a number of ways in which radio obviously

cannot compete with the stage, television, or cinema as a medium for drama, but the comparison is by no means to its disadvantage. Marshall McLuhan, who was fond of perverse paradoxes, described television as a tactile medium because it appeals to the sense of touch, and radio as a visual medium because it stimulates the inward eye by denying the eye itself anything to hold its attention. Much has been made of the imaginative possibilities of radio and of listeners' active involvement in creating a fictional reality from the acoustic information provided by a broadcast play. In this respect, the process more closely resembles the reading of fiction than the viewing of drama in any of its visual forms, although listeners, like members of a theatre or cinema audience and unlike readers of the printed page, have to respond to the spoken word and a variety of other acoustic signals, sometimes including music as well as effects. Radio's stage is in the mind, and each listener, like each reader of a novel, constructs his or her own imaginary world without having it fixed, as in any visual form, by the physical appearance of the actors, the decor, and the sequence of images decided by the director. It is easy to overlook how imaginatively restricting theatrical productions can be, which explains why many people find reading such open texts as the great dramatic classics (*King Lear*, *Hamlet*) a more satisfying and complete experience than seeing them, however heretical this may be at a time when orthodoxy decrees that *on stage* the play's the thing. There is a sense in which all productions of *Hamlet* and all interpretations of the prince himself by actors, whether good, bad or indifferent, original or stale, illuminating or perfunctory, are reductive, since certain possibilities are necessarily developed at the expense of others. A reader, on the other hand, is not dictated to by visual presentation, and is more capable of holding a multiplicity of interpretations than a captive audience in a theatre. In a radio play, unlike a novel, narration and dialogue are, of course, fixed aurally through the actors' voices – direct speech really is speech – but the human ear is much less of a tyrant than the eye and does indeed leave a lot to the imagination.

Early producers of radio in the 1920s soon realized its positive advantages as an imaginative medium, and how important the difference is between drama *on* radio and drama *for* radio, a distinction disguised by the term 'radio drama'. The German word *Hörspiel*, stressing the mode of sensory apprehension (hearing) rather than the mode of transmission (radio), is more exact in designating a work written for the medium, but unfortunately there is no English equivalent: the word 'earplay', coined by the outstanding Canadian producer Fletcher Markle as a radio-drama series-title for American National (Public) Radio in 1978 as part of the attempt to revive the form in the USA during the 1970s, comes very close, but like **Tyrone Guthrie**'s much earlier term 'microphone play' it has not entered the critical vocabulary. *Hörspiel* is *le mot juste* for the first play written for the new medium to be broadcast by the BBC, Richard Hughes's *Danger* (1924), which is set in total darkness, a coalmine following an accident that has literally put out the light. Because there is nothing to see, *Danger* is unstageable: it is 'a play for voices', to use the phrase Dylan Thomas attached to *Under Milk Wood*, which can be staged though never without a considerable degree of awkwardness (even more than Chekhov on radio). Unlike *Danger* and *Under Milk Wood*, many broadcast plays fall into the category of 'drama on radio' (stage plays and plays written in the hope of stage and television production but not achieving it), but there is also a considerable body of 'drama for radio', exploiting its ability to go places and do things either impossible or unsatisfactory in live theatre or even the more visually flexible media of film and television. *Danger*, about trapped miners in a blacked-out pit, is a good example, but Andrew Crisell has recently drawn attention to a single BBC effects track that illustrates, in a particularly startling and succinct way, radio's ability to enter places with zero visibility. Called 'premature burial', this presents the experience of a supposedly dead person inside a coffin returning to consciousness after an interment ceremony and attempting to escape in a state of extreme panic. Being totally 'blind', this piece of Poe-like Gothicism would be impossible to convey visually but can be vividly evoked in sound. 'Premature burial' is an extreme case, but sound effects can suggest with great ease, compared with any visual medium, such events and experiences as large-scale catastrophes (the destruction of Pompeii, the fire-bombing of Dresden) and, at the other end of the scale, inner states of mind such as mental anguish (noises in the head). In comedy, too, invisibility can be a great help rather than a hindrance, especially when it comes to sound effects. The surreal humour of *The Goon Show*, which perfected this technique, depends on hilarious patterns of sound that have no exact visual analogues and could function in no other medium.

In discovering what was radiogenic and what was not, early producers were influenced, strangely enough, by the methods of the silent cinema. For a short time in the 1920s, drama in a new medium that could be seen but not heard coincided with drama in an even newer medium that could be heard but not seen. Radio writers borrowed from cinema many of the techniques that distinguished it from theatre, including montage and superimposition, and adapted them to suit a presentation in sound alone. The visual flexibility of cinema, moving from scene to scene with a single cut, sliding between past and present with a dissolve, and placing characters in situations impossible in theatre (Charlie Chaplin in the precariously balanced hut in *The Gold Rush*), has its counterpart in the aural flexibility of radio. Even moving from long shot to close-up can be paralleled in sound since radio can create a sense of distance and also enter the minds of characters, the latter much more readily than any visual medium. Such devices as the soliloquy and aside are, of course, entirely satisfactory in small doses on an Elizabethan thrust stage, however clumsy they may appear in a proscenium-arch picture frame, but radio focuses very naturally on the interior workings of consciousness and can relay mental processes at length without any sense of strain. The invisibility of the radio actor makes the dramatic convention of speaking thoughts aloud particularly appropriate to the medium, in a way that it is not in cinema, television, and realistic stage plays; since we do not see the actor speaking, the words seem to come straight from the mind, not the mouth. This accounts for the great intimacy of radio drama, the paradoxical sense of immediacy and proximity produced by actors physically at a considerable distance from the listener.

Arguably the best of the three 'microphone plays' Tyrone Guthrie wrote within a couple of years while working for the BBC, *The Flowers Are Not for You to Pick* (1930), exemplifies how gifted writers in the early days of radio seized on a cinematic method that could readily be adapted for radio, while also indulging to the full the new medium's novelistic ability to render the inner lives of people. Guthrie's play is all in the mind of its central character, who as a drowning man in the middle of an ocean is located realistically in a position unrealizable in the theatre, except in a highly stylized way. To capture the man's dying review of his entire life, Guthrie employs a sequence of flashbacks, a collage of memories involving fast transitions in time and place. The result is unstageable drama but seminal radio. Even more unstageable are the contemporary 'radiophonic' experiments by Lance Sieveking, notably *Kaleidoscope I* (1928), a decidedly original montage of speech and sound owing little to theatrical tradition but indebted to the principles of cinematic editing. What makes the achievement of these avant-garde figures so remarkable is that their complex works were broadcast live without benefit of magnetic tape, in conditions and using equipment that now seem primitive.

An important feature of radio drama that seems to be completely uncinematic is narration, a method largely eschewed by film and television and relatively rare in Western theatre, in spite of the importance of the chorus in Greek tragedy and **Brecht**'s influence on recent drama. What makes narration so natural on radio is, as with some other aspects of the genre, the invisibility of the speaker. Excessive reliance on narration in radio drama did lead to a reaction against it by the new writers of the 1950s and 1960s, such as **Giles Cooper** and Samuel Beckett, but abuse of an essentially radiogenic technique does not invalidate it, and it has been making a strong comeback since the heyday of the absurdists. Narration can certainly be an over-easy way of solving problems, but handled with skill, as in *Under Milk Wood*, it functions as a verbal camera, suggesting another, though oblique and unexpected, cinematic analogue. On radio, a narrator can establish with a few words a fictional reality that might cost a fortune to provide visually: mention Ancient Rome or an elaborate sci-fi supercity in space, add appropriate effects, and they exist in sound. In his enormously popular radio-drama serial, *The Hitch-Hiker's Guide to the Galaxy* (1978), which acquired cult status and seduced the young into thinking of radio as a source of something other than non-stop pop music, Douglas Adams made brilliant use of narration. This self-reflexive cosmic fantasy, accommodating a major character with two heads, numerous time warps, visits to a number of bizarre planets, a variety of weird life forms, not to mention chatty computers, presented radio with marvellous opportunities rather than problems. Such is life today, however, that its triumphant success led to a television adaptation, which was vastly inferior to the point of embarrassment, not because it was badly done, but because what was imaginatively stimulating on radio inevitably became gauche when translated into visual images. Perhaps the ultimate comment on the hazards inherent in converting radio codes into visual ones is a famous joke from *The Goon*

Show: Bloodnok asks Eccles to climb on his shoulders and then reach down and pull him up, to which Eccles replies with devastating acuteness as he performs this physically impossible but radiophonically simple task, 'I'd like to see them do this on television.'

Radio excels in creating fantasy and symbolic worlds, indeterminate characters who may or may not be real, and interior monologue. Although Mervyn Peake was a gifted painter and his prose is strongly visual, a dramatic adaptation of his grotesque *Gormenghast* novels into theatrical or filmic terms would be fraught with near-insoluble difficulties, whereas the recent BBC radio version is among the Drama Department's triumphs of the 1980s. John Huston's famous film of *Moby Dick* is far from contemptible, but it reduces the allegorical dimensions of Melville's novel to a thin realism, the white whale being no more than a white whale, an artificial one to boot. Henry Reed's 1947 radio adaptation, on the other hand, is among the masterpieces of radio. Among the imaginary worlds that radio has no problem in establishing are the ones giving speech to voiceless things, whether animate or inanimate: in Don Haworth's *On a Day in a Garden in Summer* (1975), for example, the speakers or 'characters' are plants. The nearest visual equivalent would almost certainly be whimsically twee and his serious purpose completely subverted. The ghosts of Elizabethan and Jacobean tragedy, such as Hamlet's father and Banquo, present a radio producer with none of the hard decisions a stage director has to make about whether they should be represented physically, even if through a glass darkly or as electronic flickerings. Similarly, Macbeth's hallucinatory dagger, made visible in Polanski's film although normally invisible on stage, is, on radio, what Macbeth says it is, 'a dagger of the mind'. A celebrated example of a character having an uncertain existence on radio is the mute matchseller in **Harold Pinter**'s *A Slight Ache* (1959). In stage productions, the matchseller has either to be shown (in which case he exists independently) or not shown (in which case he exists only in the minds of the two 'real' characters). Radio does not have to make this choice and can sustain an uneasy ambiguity without, to cite Keats on Negative Capability, 'any irritable reaching after fact and reason'. Pinter's matchseller may lack body and consciousness, but disembodied consciousness might be called 'the stuff of radio', to borrow the title of Lance Sieveking's pioneering study of the medium (1934). Because it presents six disembodied consciousnesses rather than six characters, Virginia Woolf's most abstract work of fiction, *The Waves*, probably defies transformation into a visual medium more than any major novel apart from *Finnegans Wake*, but her six voices might almost have been designed for radio, as MacNeice's celebrated adaptation reveals.

The fate of radio drama in different countries during its short history of only two-thirds of a century has depended on their vastly different broadcasting structures as well as on internal and external political pressures. In various parts of Europe, radio got off to an enterprising start during the 1920s, but with the spread of totalitarian regimes, both right and left, it increasingly became a propaganda tool and an instrument of state control. As a mass-medium art form, radio drama inevitably suffered badly. Germany was in the forefront of radio-drama development during the post-

First World War Weimar period, but Hitler's rise to power in 1933 put an end to this momentum and stifled experiment. It was some time after the Second World War before German radio recaptured something of its early imaginative energy, by which time it was under pressure from television. Today, Germany is one of the main producers of radio drama, and the *Hörspiel* probably has a higher artistic status there than radio drama does in any other country, including Britain, but Germany is one of a number of countries conspicuously lacking in the so-called Golden Age of radio (including drama) in the anglophone world, the period from the early 1930s to the early or mid-1950s. This Golden Age in such nations as Australia, Britain, Canada, and the USA, depended on the stability and continuity of democratic institutions, something denied to Continental Europe except for non-combatant Sweden and Switzerland. Ironically, the Second World War was a crucial factor in the making of the Golden Age since it effectively postponed the domination of television for more than a decade. Television transmissions began in the 1930s, well before radio had even come of age, but the war curtailed these experimental broadcasts, and in Britain, for example, the television audience did not overtake the radio audience until the televising of Elizabeth II's Coronation in 1953, an event that encouraged millions of people to buy television sets. In some countries, radio drama did not have to compete with television for considerably longer because the introduction of the latter was delayed for political reasons. This explains why radio drama remains a viable form in South Africa whereas in the USA it is again on the extreme edge of extinction after receiving a temporary reprieve in the 1970s.

The ability of radio drama to withstand the assault of television varied according to the broadcasting system involved. From the beginning, the American system was based on commercial sponsorship, and the bulk of radio drama was unashamedly popular: soap operas, variety series, mystery and detective series. What happened with the advent of television was that all such forms deserted radio for the newer medium, leaving a vacuum to be filled by pop music. Although the output of serious radio drama in the USA was relatively small, the work of the three directorial giants of the 1930s and 1940s, Norman Corwin, Arch Oboler, and Orson Welles, was of a consistently high quality and was widely appreciated. Nevertheless, even in the Golden Age, serious drama led a fairly embattled existence, with worthwhile series being set up and dropped almost at whim, and there was no structure to save it from the tidal wave of television. American radio drama did limp on throughout the 1950s, but was apparently laid to rest about 1960, only to be tentatively resurrected by Elliot Lewis and a few others in the mid-1970s. This was heralded as a new dawn, but could also be interpreted as a last gasp or a final flicker, and the omens in the 1980s are not good.

The American experience of a rapid rise and an equally rapid decline in the fortunes of radio drama has been partly paralleled in countries such as Australia and Canada where commercial sponsorship has had an important, sometimes dominant, role in broadcasting alongside a public-service sector akin to the BBC (in Australia, the ABC; in Canada, the CBC). It has been estimated that fewer than one in ten of the Australian

population ever tune in to an ABC radio broadcast; the CBC, however, commands considerably greater loyalty from Canadians. In both Australia and Canada, television arrived later than in the USA, its spread was slower, and consequently its impact was not so immediately overwhelming. Indeed, Howard Fink has argued that the Golden Age of radio drama in Canada did not begin until the mid-1940s, when television arrived in the USA, and lasted until the mid-1960s, by which time American radio drama was little more than a memory. Yet despite the commitment of both ABC and CBC to maintain drama as a presence on radio, output has declined steadily although not dried up altogether. Audiences have shrunk, and in enormous countries with small populations this absence of listeners is more conspicuous than in much smaller European countries with much larger populations, such as Britain and Germany. The conditions that encouraged the poet Douglas Stewart, a New Zealander by birth but Australian by adoption, to write in verse one of the finest radio plays ever broadcast, *The Fire on the Snow*, first produced by the ABC in 1941, no longer appertain. Yet some young writers in Australia and Canada have been attracted to radio during the 1970s and 1980s, partly as a reaction against television. The celebrated intimacy of radio and its existence as spoken language still have appeal for literary artists, and the ABC and CBC continue to provide a limited outlet for them.

The reasons for Britain's pre-eminence in radio drama should now be clear: on the one hand, political stability, continuity, and openness; on the other, the BBC's monopoly in nationwide broadcasting as a public-service institution. Whereas commercial television began transmissions in 1955 on a national basis, commercial radio stations were not allowed to operate until 1973, and then only to serve strictly circumscribed localities. Proposals for national commercial radio are currently under discussion, but such a development, if permitted, would belong to the 1990s. During the 1960s and 1970s, it was fashionable to sneer at the Reithian doctrines enshrined in the theory and practice of the BBC from the 1920s to the 1950s as elitist and patronizing, but it is now obvious that without such commitment to excellence in all areas of broadcasting and to disseminating high culture as well as popular entertainment the BBC would not enjoy its international reputation as, arguably, the most reliable and most imaginative broadcasting institution in the world. The idea of radio being a national theatre of the air, in the absence of a bricks-and-mortar national theatre, developed early in BBC history: radio could bring the theatre to the people in their homes, making available the masterpieces of world drama from **Aeschylus** to **Ibsen** to millions who either had no access to live theatre or lacked the theatre-going habit, especially when it came to the classics. The BBC has undergone several major reorganizations since the Second World War, but its policy for serious radio drama, as opposed to light-entertainment drama, has survived more-or-less intact; although audiences have declined considerably, output has remained remarkably buoyant. Plenty of stage classics and adaptations of classic novels are still broadcast, as are plenty of new plays. Radio-drama production may be relatively expensive by the standards of radio, but it is absurdly cheap by the standards of television, and radio can therefore take risks and attempt experiments that would be totally out of the question in television.

The BBC's strong tradition of radio-drama and feature production has been a vital factor in enabling these forms to survive so well in the television era, despite all the talk about a dying art during the past 25 years. One crucial change, following the recommendations of audience research, has been to move drama away from prime-viewing times (previously peak listening times) to afternoon and early evening slots, and even morning and late-at-night ones. Yet developments in drama itself helped to give radio a new lease of life as a dramatic medium when television was taking over as *the* mass medium in the 1950s. Several critics have argued that radio is the natural home for the theatre of the absurd, and there was something approaching a revolution in radio drama between the mid-1950s and the mid-1960s, with Giles Cooper, Samuel Beckett, Rhys Adrian, Frederick Bradnum, Harold Pinter, **James Saunders**, Barry Bermange, **Joe Orton**, and **Tom Stoppard**. Until this time, there was a tendency for some of the best radio writers to compensate for its blindness by providing rich verbal textures, colours for the ear, as in *The Dark Tower* and *Under Milk Wood*. The new writers demonstrated that radio drama could function just as well without such compensation, that minimalism could be as radiogenic as the work of poets such as MacNeice and Thomas. Indeed, radio proved to be the training ground for a new generation of British playwrights, who subsequently made their names in the theatre, television, and film. Radio continues to do this, but the momentum of the 1960s is now something to be recollected in tranquillity. Yet plays of the stature of **David Rudkin**'s *Cries from Casement As His Bones Are Brought to Dublin* (1973) and **John Arden**'s *Pearl* (1978) are reminders that, if radio is a dying or dead art in some countries, it is still thriving in others, notably in Britain and Germany. There, at least, it is dying by millimetres if it is dying at all.   PL

See: D. G. Bridson, *Prospero and Ariel: The Rise and Fall of Radio*, London, 1971; A. Crisell, *Understanding Radio*, London and New York, 1986; J. Drakakis, *British Radio Drama*, Cambridge, 1981; A. P. Frank, *Das Hörspiel*, Heidelberg, 1963; V. Gielgud, *British Radio Drama 1922–1956*, London, 1957; P. Lewis (ed.), *Papers of the Radio Literature Conference 1977*, Durham, 1978; P. Lewis (ed.), *Radio Drama*, London and New York, 1981; D. McWhinnie, *The Art of Radio*, London, 1959; H. Priessnitz, *Das englische 'radio play' seit 1945: Typen, Themen und Formen*, Berlin, 1977; H. Priessnitz (ed.), *Das englische Hörspiel: Interpretationen*, Düsseldorf, 1977; I. Rodger, *Radio Drama*, London, 1982; L. Sieveking, *The Stuff of Radio*, London, 1934.

Radlov, Sergei Ernestovich (1892–1958) Soviet-Russian director, a leader in the post-revolutionary movement to unite folk theatrical forms with modern 'urban eccentrism' in order to create a new popular theatre. His techniques derived primarily from **commedia dell'arte**, circus and silent screen comedy and demonstrated his belief that the actor's art consists of 'pure sound + pure movement + pure emotion – correctly disposed in time and space'. He received his early training from **Meyerhold** during the latter's *commedia* period at the Studio on Borodinskaya Street and on the journal *Love for Three Oranges* (1913–17). As part of two projects sponsored by the People's Commissariat for Education – the mobile First Communal Troupe, which played the Civil War front, and the Petrograd Theatre-Studio (with K. Tverskoi and K. Landau, 1918–19) – Radlov worked with improvisation, children's and puppet theatre. In 1920 he co-directed with Nikolai Petrov, Vladimir Solovyov and Adrian Piotrovsky the mass spectacle *Towards a World Commune* and founded with Solovyov the Theatre of Popular Comedy, which operated until 1922. The latter utilized circus performers, as had **Yury Annenkov** in his 1919 production of *The First Distiller*, in a series of 'circus-comedies' and 'circus pantomimes' on anti-capitalist themes: *The Corpse's Bride* and *The Monkey Who Was an Informer* (1919), *The Sultan and the Devil* and *The Adopted Son* (1920), *Love and Gold* (1921). Drawing upon the speed and ingenuity of American popular forms such as detective and adventure serials, Radlov experimented with multiple and simultaneous staging in order to create a sense of continuous flow. He employed similar means to contemporize and dynamize comedic classics – **Molière**, Hans Sachs, **Calderón de la Barca**, **Labiche** and especially **Shakespeare**. In 1922 Radlov opened the Laboratory for Theatre Research and thereafter directed at a series of theatres and studios in Petrograd (1929–42) and in Latvia (1953–8). He staged a number of notable productions of Shakespeare in the 1930s – *Romeo and Juliet* (1934, 1939), *Othello* (1932, 1935), *Hamlet* (1938) and his most celebrated, *King Lear* (1935) at the Moscow State Jewish Theatre, designed by Aleksandr Tyshler and starring the great **Solomon Mikhoels**. Radlov also taught (1922–35) and wrote *Ten Years in the Theatre* (1929) and several works on staging Shakespeare.   SG

Radrigán, Juan (1937–) A late bloomer in the recent Chilean theatre, Radrigán is affiliated with theatre of the marginal classes. His plays are brutal and violent portrayals of contemporary society, written in the vernacular but with poetic imagery. Since he burst on the theatre scene with *Testimonios sobre la muerte de Sabina* (*Testimonies on the Death of Sabina*) in 1979, he has become one of Chile's most prolific writers. Other major plays are *Viva Somoza* (*Long Live Somoza*) written in collaboration with Gustavo Meza in 1980, *El loco y la triste* (*The Crazy One and the Sad One*, 1980), *Hechos consumados* (*Accomplished Deeds*, 1981), *El toro por las astas* (*The Bull by the Horns*, 1982), and *Las voces de la ira* (*Voices of Anger*, 1984).   GW

Radzinsky, Edvard Stanislavovich (1938–) Soviet dramatist of the post-war generation, whose plays present the philosophical dilemmas of the native intelligentsia past and present and of youth in conflict with the values of their elders. The son of a well-known man of letters, Radzinsky graduated from the Moscow State Historical-Archival Institute in 1960. The author of 14 plays, his first popular success was the bittersweet romance *104 Pages about Love* (1964), one of five of his works staged by the youth-oriented director **Anatoly Efros**. A largely comic play with an unexpected tragic ending and representative of the trend toward personal dramas in the 1960s, it has been staged in 120 Soviet theatres, made into a ballet and a film. *Making a Movie* (1965) deals with a no longer young film director's difficulties in maintaining his integrity in art, love and life. This theme is broadened and deepened considerably in Radzinsky's historical plays of conscience – *Conversations with Socrates* (1975), *Lunin* (1977, about a Decembrist conspirator) and *Theatre in the Time of Nero and Seneca* (1980). Utilizing all manner of theatrical devices from ancient Greek masks and *cothurni* to *tableaux vivants*, romantic prison house metaphor and hallucinatory visions, Radzinsky focuses on teacher–pupil/master–servant relationships and suggests various sources and traditions vying for pride of place in the collective memory of the Russian intelligentsia: **Chekhov**'s meditations on the price of survival and the pathos of extinction; Gogolian and Bulgakovian theatrical grotesque to render the former's sense of Russia's moral failure and the latter's crisis of freedom in the thrall of patrimony and the nightmare of exile; Western metafictional heroes – Hamlet, Quixote and Robinson Crusoe – as free creators; **Diderot** and the *encyclopédistes* as symbols of national inquiry and honest discourse. Radzinsky's heroes struggle to escape the mythmaking apparatus which rewrites history in the manner of the Soviets to conform to a prescribed end (e.g., the path to the October Revolution). In *The Seducer Kolobashkin* (1968) and *Don Juan Continued . . .* (1979), he employs the idea of time travel to suggest the eternal flight of the creative persona from false and banal reality. With the highly popular *She, in the Absence of Love and Death* (1980), Radzinsky returned to the difficulties of the young in reconciling their ideals and fantasies with contemporary reality bereft of the great romantic 19th-century literary themes. SG

Raikin, Arkadi Isaakovich (1911–) Soviet Russian clown, who began his career as an actor and mime with the TRAM group, and in 1938 shifted to cabaret, becoming the director of the Leningrad Theatre of Miniatures. There he combined drama, operetta, variety and pantomime into an idiosyncratic style. Despite the bluntness of his satire and his Jewish ancestry, Raikin managed to avoid persecution because of his immense popularity. His range extended from full-length shows such as *Around the World in 80 Days* (1951) to one-man quick-change concerts. He was seen in London in 1964. LS

Raimund, Ferdinand (1790–1836) Austrian actor and playwright. After an unsuccessful start as a tragic actor, Raimund won acclaim in the comic roles that he played at Vienna's Theater in der Josefstadt in 1814. After moving to the Theater in der Leopoldstadt in 1817, he started to write plays that represented a sustained attempt to employ the Viennese **Volksstück**, especially in the *Zauberstück*, to express serious romantic themes. They represent the high point of that Austrian dramatic tradition, originating in the Jesuit drama, that explored the interrelationship of spiritual and secular spheres of being. Of the nine plays Raimund wrote, *The Peasant as Millionaire* (1826), *The King of the Alps and the Misanthrope* (1828), and the ambitious, serious comedy written after his retirement from the Theater in der Leopoldstadt, *The Spendthrift* (1834) have proved to be remarkably durable, though

Raimund as Aschenmann.

with his contemporaries his earlier, lighter comedies were more popular. Raimund shot himself as he believed he had contracted rabies after being bitten by a dog. It has been speculated that his suicide may have been caused by his apprehension at the growing reputation of **Nestroy**, whose caustic wit and social satire were more to the public taste than his own poetic style. SW

Rajatabla Venezuelan theatre group, subsidiary of the Ateneo de Caracas (Caracas Atheneum), created in 1971 and headed for years by Carlos Giménez, Argentine director long established in Venezuela. A major force in experimenting with vanguard theatre in Caracas. GW

Rame, Franca see Fo, Dario

Ramlila (India) Celebration through the depiction of dramatic episodes from the life of Rama, hero of the Sanskrit epic *Ramayana*, is an all-India phenomenon. At no time is it more prevalent than in the months of September, October and November and nowhere is it celebrated with greater verve than in north India. Activities leading up to the destruction of evil, symbolized in the effigies built for the *Dassahra* Festival, provide the opportunity for the Hindu community to express its renewed faith in the restoration of world order. Following soon after *Dassahra* is *Devali*, the Festival of Lights, which welcomes Rama home from his self-imposed exile from Ayodhya, his kingdom and his home. Millions of tiny oil lamps that decorate the exteriors of countless village homes throughout the north symbolically light Rama's path along the way. This great public outpouring of faith over a three-month period is accomplished by public performances of *Ramlila*, the name of a form of theatre popular in villages and cities in the north. Although the performances all share the same subject matter, they differ considerably in the manner of their execution and length.

Ramlila is a generic term describing dramatic events performed on festival occasions that centre around Rama's life and which applies to a variety of different theatre activities, primarily in the north. Literally translated, *Ramlila* means the 'play of Rama'. *Ramlila* may have originated in ancient India. Clear historical evidence for its beginning is not found until the early to mid-17th century when a version of the story was staged, based on a Hindu version of the *Ramayana*, entitled *Ramcharitmanas*, composed by Tulsidas who is credited with popularizing the story of Rama among the villagers of north India.

Some centres for large-scale *Ramlilas* are the cities of Ramnagar, Allahabad, Mathura and Delhi. There are many organized performances in these places, attracting thousands of spectators each. In Ramnagar alone, the public spectacles attract over a million pilgrims to the vast processions and performances organized by the Maharaja Udit Narain Singh (commonly known as the Maharaja of Benares) and supported by a grant of public money which helps the upkeep of the temples in the great pilgrimage city of Varanasi, across the river from the Maharaja's palace.

The usual procedure for establishing small-scale versions of the *Ramlila* begins with the formation of committees, often democratically elected, by the constituents of an area of a town or city. Although members of the *ksatriya* caste are thought to dominate the committees in many areas, in Mathura and Allahabad, members of the merchant community control the organization. Obviously, besides expressing their religious devotion through public service on the *Ramlila* committee, merchants might reap profits from the festival occasions, especially since people purchase new clothing and prepare special sweets and foods, as well as increase their charitable contributions at this time of year. The bulk of the money to support festival activities is normally raised by small subscriptions collected from thousands of eager patrons.

Ramlila falls within the province of amateur performers drawn from the community. In some areas, actors have been taken from the same Brahmin families for centuries. It is customary for the roles of the five chief characters – Rama, Sita, his wife, Lakshmana, Bharata and Satrugna, his three brothers, to be played by Brahmin boys who have not yet reached the age of puberty. Normally the youths are required to live in the house of the head of the *Ramlila* committee prior to the opening of the performance because they are thought to take on the aspects of the gods they represent, to become *svarups*, the embodiments of divinities.

The person who trains the boys and who heads the entire *Ramlila* performance is called the *liladhari*. He inherits the right to instruct the amateur players in the proper stage deportment, to lead the singing and to make sure that the correct procedures are followed in the preparation of the scenery, costumes, makeup and music.

The approach to the stage space varies depending on the city where a performance is held and the community that prepares the festivities. In Ramnagar, which literally means 'Rama's city', 30 days are assigned to the

Ramlila, each with its own particular events and activities organized to take place in various locations of the city and surrounding area. The Maharaja often travels from one event to another in his own horse-drawn carriage or rides atop his elephant better to see the activities. During the great battle scenes between the monkey soldiers of Rama and the demon soldiers of Ravana, the symbolic representation of evil, hundreds of youths take part. The spectacle ends in the burning of the effigies of Ravana and his demon brothers. The effigies are four to five storeys tall. At the conclusion of the evening they are shot with burning arrows and they burst into flames and explode with fireworks falling in a heap at the feet of the actor playing Rama, as the crowd fervently chants 'Victory to Rama'.

In some villages an earthen platform three to four feet off the ground topped by a colourful canopy serves as the stage on which all the dramatic events are enacted. Processions of floats (*chaukis*), separate chariots designed for Ravana and Rama and processions of elephants and camels represent various events in the action. Microphones and loudspeakers are used to convey the songs, music and dialogue in some performances. In other places, the actors must project their voices valiantly in open spaces but are rarely heard by the thousands of participants who jam the area just to be a part of the ritual occasion.

People from many walks of life participate in the *Ramlila* – Hindus, Muslims, Christians, Sikhs, Parsis – rich and poor alike, maharajas and beggars, whoever comes to witness the events may participate. Those who consider the events sacred often reverently touch the feet of Rama and Sita when they draw near.

Costumes differ considerably among the various groups. Because hundreds of actors typically participate in the major performances, costume houses in the area specialize in *Ramlila* costumes which are rented out for the duration of the season. The makeup of the five central characters is usually a pinkish-white base over which stencil designs in the shapes of flowers and stars are drawn. Sequins and mica are added to provide a glittering, colourful and unrealistic appearance. The moment the actors wear their crowns they are thought to be invested with the spirit of the god–man they portray.

The actor who plays Ravana wears a mask depicting the ten heads that the demon-king was supposed to have had. His brothers usually have various distorted and deformed features, as do his demon hordes, many of whom smear black makeup on their faces to symbolize their evil nature.

The music of *Ramlila* follows the folk music tradition of the area but religious tunes are mixed in, as well as some classical pieces. Bell-metal cymbals, drums and harmonium are the chief musical instruments used for accompaniment. Chanting of the whole of the *Ramcharitmanas* is a part of the ritual activities in many areas and priests capable of excellent recitation regard this as a ritual obligation, no matter what the hour of the day or night.

In Andhra Pradesh State there is a popular form of presenting the *Ramayana*, called *Chiratala Ramayanam*. The actors, mostly amateurs from different communities, wear makeup and costumes appropriate to the characters they portray and gather in any open place for the celebration. They stand in a circle and dance, keeping time with *kartal*, a pair of wooden pieces with small metal disks held in the hand and struck against each other. The *kartal* are associated with devotional music (*bhajans*). The *tabla* drums and the harmonium accompany the performers. The musicians sit in the centre of the circle. When a passage of music is used for dance the clown, who keeps a whistle in his mouth, blows it in time to the rapidly accelerated music. He acts almost like a referee at a football match. He governs the performance and moves the action forward. Boys act all the roles and the general quality of their improvisation is rather weak.   FaR

Ramos-Perea, Roberto (1956–) Puerto Rican playwright, essayist, short story writer. Born in Mayagüez, he studied in Mexico and Puerto Rico, and has been an actor and director in several Puerto Rican theatre groups. In addition to *Los 200 no* (*The 200 No*, 1983), a violent encounter between a university student and professor, and *Ese punto de vista* (*That Point of View*, 1984), his work includes a major historical trilogy: *Revolución en el infierno* (*Revolution in Hell*), based on the Ponce massacre of 1937; *Módulo 104 (Revolución en el purgatorio)* (*Module 104, Revolution in Purgatory*), based on the Puerto Rican penal system during the years 1980–2; and *Cueva de ladrones (Revolución en el paraíso)* (*Thieves' Cave, Revolution in Paradise*), based on the radical student movement.   GW

Rana, Juan see **Quiñones de Benavente**

Randolph, Thomas (1605–35) English playwright and poet, who owed his contemporary esteem to the work he produced while at Cambridge University. The facility with which he wrote is well illustrated by 'An Ode to Master Anthony Stafford', which is a charming poem in praise of country life. His pastoral play, *Amyntas* (1630), is enlivened by its comic scenes, but his other full-length piece, *The Jealous Lovers* (1632), is dramatically insipid. Randolph was better suited to the writing of dramatic sketches. *Aristippus: or The Jovial Philosopher* (c. 1626) proposes that study of the philosophy of drinking should be added to the university syllabus, a theme pursued with variations in *The Drinking Academy* (c. 1626). *The Conceited Pedlar* (1627) is an ephemerally witty monologue. *The Muses' Looking-Glass* (1630), in which an actor out-argues Puritan opposition to the theatre, is Randolph's most interesting work. It reflects the influence of **Ben Jonson**, of whom Randolph was a favoured 'son'.   PT

Rasdhari (India) About 160 years ago, the **Raslila** of Mathura was introduced to Rajasthan when the Braj artists performed at the Shrinathji Temple at Nathdwara, a principal centre of pilgrimage for the followers of Krishna. Initially, the form appealed to the Vairagis community which developed its own version of the form in the late 19th century, principally in the Phulera area of the state and primarily in Rojdi village. From the very beginning, the companies which formed in imitation of the Braj *Raslila* were professional troupes. Before long, they developed performances around Vaishnava shrines throughout the state, such as those of Kishangarh, Jaipur, Bharatpur, Kota, Nathdwara and Kankroli.

Two types of groups came into being – those that were devotional in character but which, unlike their Braj brethren, did not cast Brahmin boys who had not yet reached puberty to play the leading roles of Krishna and Radha, and those that were less religiously oriented and which adapted stories from a wide variety of mythological and historical sources. The latter groups also allowed individuals from different communities to participate in their activities. Those individuals who originally organized the *Raslila* performances in Rajashan were known as *Rasdharis* and eventually the word came to indicate the theatre form, with its own unique features and characteristics.

Today, village productions by itinerant troupes of actors and musicians take place in any open meeting area in the village. Spectators generally ring the performers in a close packed crowd. It is not uncommon for spectators to lean out of the doors or windows of surrounding houses, to settle into a comfortable fork of a nearby tree or to rest on any raised space where they may better view the show. Since the acting area is the open space ringed by the audience, the actors must constantly keep on moving to provide variety and allow for adequate visibility to all the individuals who come to see an all-night show. Musicians sit among the spectators and entrances and exits are negotiated by the actors through the crowd, when necessary.

No stage scenery is needed to relate the stories. Vivid word pictures in speech and song help the spectators to visualize the action in time and place. If a simple prop is needed, it is easily obtained from a nearby household.

The songs and musical accompaniment of the musicians are borrowed from other styles of music and theatre popular in the region and do not have their own unique character. Improvisation is freely used in dialogue and song as the actors test the interest of the audience in particular themes or dramatic action. Dance too is improvised. Although to outsiders the form may seem completely devoid of distinctive features, the fast-paced, energetic performances and volume of the players create a strong positive rapport between artists and spectators which makes it very popular.

Costumes are the local dress of the spectators and the manner and behaviour of mythological characters imitate those of local inhabitants. The simplicity of the form allows considerable latitude in interpreting and altering the classical stories and reinforcing moral behaviour.   FaR

Raslila This is a generic term used widely throughout India to describe various dances and dance-dramas which have a particular theme. It takes on special significance in several regions as a form of theatre. The term *ras* refers to Lord Krishna's joyous, melodious, circular dance with the wives of Brahmin cowherds of Vrindavan, a holy city in north India, described in mythological sources. *Lila* means 'play' and implies more than just dramatic literature but refers to god's playful tryst with man and earthly beings.

Perhaps the *Raslila* of Vrindavan is the best-known form of *Raslila* in all of India. There are also other forms of *Raslila*, such as those of Manipur, the **Krishnattam** of Kerala and the **Ankiya Nat** of Assam. The *ras* dances of Gujarat and those of other states have not been included here because they do not have a significant dramatic structure.

Raslila of Vrindavan, the Braj region along the Jumna River of north India (a 90-mile square locality south of Delhi), is a devotional dance-drama. Although the precise date of its origin is uncertain, the present form probably came into being in the 16th century due to the popularity of the devotional (*bhakti*) movement which swept this part of north India to celebrate Lord Vishnu's incarnations, principally Krishna, the centre of the faith.

Krishna is thought to have been born in the city of Mathura, a few miles distant from Vrindavan, the place where he spent his childhood and youth. Thus, the whole area is considered holy ground and the enactment of the dance-drama is an extension of the religious fervour of the inhabitants and the hundreds of thousands of pilgrims who flock to the area every year to join in the holy day celebrations and to walk the very ground which Krishna is reputed to have trod. To witness *Raslila* is tantamount to experiencing *darshan* (revelation of god).

Understandably, the performances centre on Krishna and aspects of his earthly life and the miraculous experiences of lovers and devotees in association with him. The first part of any performance begins with Krishna seated enthroned with Radha, his beloved and chief consort (*sakhi*), seated to his left. Less important *sakhis* are arranged on lower steps of a platform to his right and left. The tableau is called *jhanki*. The chief singer and other musicians reverently touch the feet of the divine couple, for at that moment they are regarded as the incarnations of god and must be paid due respects. Ritual prayers are sung in praise of them and of various heavenly deities. A tray with a lighted lamp is waved in a circular motion in front of them (*arati*), the same ritual which is performed in the temple before idols. The next major item in the show is the *Nitya Ras*, a series of dances, some of which are performed by Krishna and Radha alone or accompanied by the *sakhis*. Songs emphasizing different rhythmic patterns, and designed slowly to raise the level of religious fervour of the spectators, accompany the dances. When particular sections are well executed the spectators shower verbal praise on the gods, not on the artists. Sometimes fervent devotees are moved by an action or moment in the performance and stand and sway to the infectious rhythms or make their way to the playing area and reverently bow down and touch their heads to the ground in front of the actors.

At the end of the dances the couple sit enthroned in sumptuous fabrics on the platform. A short discourse may be delivered by Krishna which is then followed by songs. After a short interval, the second part of the *Nitya Ras* begins in which songs dominate the action and dance plays a secondary role. Group singing involves the spectators in the emotional fervour which climaxes in a duet sung by Krishna and Radha, particularly relished by the crowd. Then Krishna, Radha and the *sakhis* perform a final group dance which culminates in a tableau. At this point in time, many devotees surge forward, touch the feet of the divine couple and leave gifts of money after they have prostrated themselves before the god-actors. During this devotional section, the musicians sing popular hymns. At the end of the *Nitya Ras*, curtains are closed masking the tableau and a short interval follows.

The final part of the evening's performance is a short play (*lila*) expanding on an episode in Krishna's life. The plays are composed primarily of dialogue and song. Relatively little dance is woven into the action. Nearly 150 *lilas* are said to have been composed from which the company may choose only one a night to perform, due to time constraints. Often the choice is dictated by the particular audience, the season of the year thought appropriate for the enactment of the story, and the particular holiday season at hand. Plays concern episodes connected with Krishna's birth, his mischievous childhood, his sport with the young milkmaids of Vrindavan and his adult life. At the conclusion of a *lila*, the devotees shout 'Victory to Krishna of Vrindavan!' and the show and the rituals end.

Performances usually take no more than two and a half hours to complete. Unlike many forms of rural theatre, *Raslila* must be completed before midnight. Since it is regarded as a religious ritual and not just an entertainment to pass the time of the pilgrims, certain etiquette must be followed by the spectators. Shoes are to be removed outside the immediate performance area, as a sign of respect. Spectators are requested to sit on the ground and not sit on chairs or presume to sit or stand above the heads of the actors who play Radha and Krishna; smoking and talking are strictly forbidden.

The proper place for *Raslila* performances is in a temple, a private garden, a bungalow or holy resting place for travellers. It is not considered appropriate to perform such a sacred event in the street.

The *Raslila* performance area is a circle (*mandal*), echoing the circle dance of the *Nitya Ras*. A throne is placed at one side with several platform steps leading down to the ground. A curtain strung on wire masks the platform from the view of the spectators sitting opposite. A rectangular area (about 15 x 20 ft) is marked out on the playing area in front of the throne. To one side of the playing area, facing the throne, the musicians (*samajis*) arrange themselves. The musical party consists of two singers, each of which has his own harmonium, a *tabla* drummer and a cymbal player. The musicians act as a chorus and the chief singer (*rasdhari*) takes the lead and controls the progress of the performance.

A *Raslila* party consists of from 10 to 18 individuals, all of whom are male. Boys who have not yet reached the age of puberty play the *sakhis*. The roles of Radha and Krishna are carefully chosen from among traditional families of Brahmins of Braj. When the young actors reach puberty they may no longer play the divine couple or any of the *sakhis* but may become musicians. When the young actors wear the crowns of Krishna and Radha they are thought to be the gods and are treated with great deference. They are carried on the backs of the troupe leader to the playing area so that their feet do not touch the ground. Adults who have distinguished themselves for their playing skill take the roles of adults in the *lilas*.

The young boys study with a teacher (*swami*) who serves as the leader of the troupe. Standards of the troupe and the skills of the players differ widely, as do those of the musicians. The text of the songs and the *lilas* is taught verbally to those who are not literate. In a full-scale performance, actors often seem to drop out of character, staring at the audience indiscriminately. No standard of excellence exists, even though the companies are professional. The religious fervour of the experience seems to outweigh any aesthetic consideration.

The chief singer (*samaji*) acts as the prompter during the performance and may correct the actors or jump in to aid them to speak a line properly or to support them when they fall out of character or forget a particular section of dance.

The high season for *Raslila* performances in Vrindavan is the monsoon season and the holy days connected with Krishna's birth and special events in his life. FAR

Rastell, John (c. 1475–1536) English playwright. Brother-in-law of Sir Thomas More, father-in-law of **John Heywood**, Rastell is regarded not as a particularly good writer, but as an important one in terms of the movement of English drama away from moralities to more secular themes. Plays believed to be by him include *The Nature of the Four Elements* (c. 1517) in which the leading character is offered the benefits of the new Renaissance education, despite alternative temptations, *The Dialogue of Gentleness and Nobility* (c. 1527), and *Calisto and Melibea* (c. 1527), taken from **de Rojas**'s *Celestina*. Rastell and his son William were printers, and published the interludes of other writers including Heywood. MB

Rastelli, Enrico (1896–1931) Italian juggler, born in Samara, where his circus family was on tour. He trained for the slack-rope, trapeze and acrobatics, for his father had forbidden him to juggle; but he practised in secret and made his debut at the Circo Gatti in 1922, breaking a world record by juggling ten rubber balls in one hand and ten table mats in the other. Unequalled for accuracy and number in balancing spheres, he usually performed in football shorts and ended his act with a one-man soccer game that sent the balls into the audience. A victim of leukaemia, he hastened his death by over-rehearsal. LS

Rattigan, Terence (1911–77) British dramatist. Although his early output was somewhat uneven, he established a reputation for light comedy with *French Without Tears* (1936), which ran for more than 1,000 performances, *While the Sun Shines* (1943) and *Love in Idleness* (played by the **Lunts** 1944, and in New York as *O Mistress Mine*, 1946). However, the autobiographical play about his wartime experiences *Flare Path* (1942) began to introduce serious themes, which became the key-note of social dramas that made him the leading playwright of the immediate post-war period. These ranged from dramatizations of notorious miscarriages of justice – *The Winslow Boy* (1946) dealing with the Archer-Shee trial where a schoolboy was accused of theft, or *Cause Célèbre* (1977) based on a murder case – and provocative moral issues – *Ross* (1960) dramatizing homosexuality through the life of T. E. Lawrence, or *A Bequest to the Nation* (1970) on the relationship between Nelson and Lady Hamilton – to sensitive studies of psychological domination in *The Browning Version* (performed together with *Harlequinade* under the title of *Playbill*, 1948) and *Separate Tables* (1954). He

also continued to write comedy, with *The Sleeping Prince* (1956), and contributed a number of successful film scripts.

By the time Rattigan was knighted in 1971, his works were already being criticized as conventional 'problem play' treatments catering to unsophisticated popular taste – the 'Aunt Ednas' of his prefaces – but his skilful craftsmanship and subtle characterization have been recently recognized in revivals of *Playbill* (at the **National Theatre**, 1980) and *Separate Tables* (at the Ontario **Stratford Festival**, 1984). CI

Raucourt, Françoise (Marie Antoinette Josephe Sancerotte) (1756–1815) French actress. Endowed with a fine voice, noble bearing and considerable beauty, she made her debut at the Théâtre-Français in 1772 in the role of Dido. Her popularity with the public was mitigated by her strong masculine tendencies and scandals associated with her private life. In 1776 she made a fine appearance as the statue in **Rousseau**'s *Pygmalion*, and then spent some time in Russia, returning to the **Comédie-Française** in 1779. She played roles of mothers and queens and was magnificent as Athalie or Cléopâtre (*Rodogune*), but less good in roles requiring the depiction of motherly love. An ardent royalist, she was imprisoned, and nearly executed in 1793. In 1796 she grouped together a company for a second Théâtre-Français at the Théâtre Louvois. This company included Molé, **Picard**, **Larochelle** and other more conservative elements. With the closure of the Louvois in 1797, she moved to the **Odéon** in 1798, and rejoined her former colleagues in 1799. In 1807, Napoleon gave Raucourt the task of organizing a French company for Italy, performing in Milan, Turin, Genoa and Venice, which lasted until 1814. One of her last roles was Cathérine de Médicis in *Les Etats de Blois* (*The Parliament at Blois*, 1814). 15,000 people attended her funeral, but the curé of the Eglise Saint Roch would not accept her body into the church until the king gave orders that she receive full Christian burial. JMCC

Raupach, Ernst (1784–1852) German dramatist. Referred to by **Laube** as 'the **Shakespeare** of triviality', Raupach was by far the most popular and fertile dramatist of his day. He wrote several melodramas, but was most celebrated for his skilfully constructed history plays, of which the 16-play cycle, *The Hohenstaufens* (1837), was the best known. SW

Ravana Chhaya One of three forms of shadow puppet theatre in India, *Ravana Chhaya* struggles to survive in Orissa State in eastern India. The date of its origin is lost in antiquity. The term *Ravana* refers to the demon-king of Lanka who is a principal character in the epic *Ramayana*. *Chhaya* means 'shadow'. Scholars have struggled to explain how a theatre form could have been named after a demon-king, especially since the story of the epic centres primarily on the exploits of the epic hero Rama. The puppet of Ravana is much more interesting and larger in size than that created for Rama. Some scholars believe that the influence of the Jain religion and Buddhism tempered the desire of the creator to name the form after the central hero of the epic which is a major Hindu work. In the Jain version of the *Ramayana*, Ravana assumes considerable dignity.

Perhaps it is Ravana's enhanced reputation in the Jain epics that convinced the creators to name the form as they did, or it may be their hesitance to speak of Rama as a shadow, when he is in fact the incarnation of Vishnu, a popular and important figure of worship and respect.

Whatever the reason, the form has only one story in its repertory – that concerning the life of Rama and his struggles with Ravana. The episodes are drawn from the *Vichitra Ramayana* of Viswanath Khuntia, who is believed to have composed his work between 1692 and 1720. The Oriyan version of the Sanskrit epic is one of 50 versions of the region, albeit the best known.

The puppets used to illustrate the story are simple figures between six and eight inches tall. About seven hundred puppets are required to perform all seven nights of the *Ramayana*. Sometimes one character requires more than one puppet to depict its various moods. Besides the characters of the epic, there are the stock characters of the village barber and his grandson, and numerous properties and scenic items which lend interest to the progress of the story.

The puppets are made of deer skin mounted between strips of bamboo. Unlike other shadow figures found elsewhere in India, those of *Ravana Chhaya* do not have movable parts. Life is breathed into them after they are created through a simple ritual sacrifice. When they are no longer used, due to excessive wear, they are symbolically cremated and reverently disposed of in a nearby river. Besides spending their lives on the screen, they make their home in the puppeteer's basket, normally kept in his bedroom.

Performances are simple affairs and may be arranged at any convenient location where two poles may be fixed in the ground about six to seven feet apart between which a white curtain about four feet wide may be stetched, outlined by a frame of straw mats threaded together to provide masking for the puppeteer who squats behind the screen. A simple oil lamp fixed to the top of a pole about three feet high burns throughout the long hours of the night.

Besides the dialogue and songs of the puppeteers, music accompanies the performance blending Oriyan folk and classical melodies set to lively rhythmic patterns.

Performances begin when a coconut is broken and a sacrifice (*puja*) is performed invoking the blessings of the elephant-headed god Ganapati and Rama. The leader of the troupe steps to the side of the acting area in full view of the audience and offers a prayer to Rama. Then he introduces the story in a prose narrative. The village barber and his grandson enter on the screen and the narrator speaks their lines in character voice. He takes the parts of all the characters, joined only by two singers who perform the songs.

Although the action is limited by the static construction of the puppets, the evening is heightened by the religious atmosphere of the event and the magical transformation of the screen coupled with poetic language and musical background to suit the occasion. FaR

Ravel A family of French mimes and dancers, arguably the most popular and influential performers in early 19th-century America. **Gabriel** (1810–82), an excellent pantomimist and rope-dancer, was the chief businessman of the troupe; **Jérome** (1814–90) wrote such durable scenarios as *The Green Monster, Mazulme or The Night Owl, Pongo the Intelligent Ape*, and *Raoul or The Magic Star*. The other siblings were **Angélique** (1813–95), **Antoine** (1812–82) and **François** (1823–81). After training in Italy, they earned fame in Paris by 1828 and created a furore at **Drury Lane** in 1830 with pantos, inspired by **Mazurier**, that combined skilled acrobatics, graceful dance, and advanced trick-work. They appeared at the Park Theatre, New York, 1836–7, and then became a fixture at **Niblo's Garden**, 1842–6, 1849–50, and 1857–60, where they were much admired by the boy Henry James. In 1850 the troupe divided with Jérome and Antoine touring the United States and François and Gabriel playing in Europe; throughout their career they were closely associated with the Martinettis, the Marzettis, the Lehmans, the Zanfrettas, **Léotard**, and the dancers Paul Brilliant and Josephine Bertin. They returned to France to retire in 1866. Angélique's children Marietta (Mrs Martin Hanley) and Charles Winter Ravel preserved the family tradition for many years, and the pantomimes were revived by the **Kiralfys** in spectacular versions. LS

Ravenscroft, Edward (1643–1707) English playwright. He followed his father, a successful barrister, in becoming a member of the Inner Temple in 1659 and Middle Temple in 1667 but with the success of his first play, an adaptation of **Molière's** *Le Bourgeois Gentilhomme* as *The Citizen Turned Gentleman* (also known as *Mamamouchi* in its revivals) in 1672, he gave up the law for a career in the theatre. Ravenscroft tried most genres, including one of the first plays to use characters from **commedia dell'arte** in England, *Scaramouche a Philosopher* (1677), and a good farce, *The Anatomist* (1697), a favourite play of **Garrick**, as well as a **Shakespeare** adaptation, *Titus Andronicus* (1686). By far his most successful play, *The London Cuckolds*, a bawdy mockery of the sexual ambitions of citizens, proved to be so popular with the citizens themselves that it became traditional to perform the play on the Lord Mayor's Day every year until Garrick stopped the practice at **Drury Lane** in 1751. PH

Reade, Charles (1814–84) English playwright and novelist, most often remembered as the author of the historical novel, *The Cloister and the Hearth* (1861). Reade managed to combine a cloistered life as a Fellow of Magdalen College, Oxford, with a vigorous and often litigious career as a social campaigner. Fascinated by the theatre, he wrote plays before he wrote novels. Early performed work included *The Ladies' Battle* (1851) at the **Olympic** and a highly successful collaboration with **Tom Taylor** on *Masks and Faces* (1852) at the **Haymarket**. He based his first novel, *Peg Woffington* (1853), on the latter. The relationship was reversed in the case of *It Is Never Too Late to Mend*, which Reade published as a novel in 1856 and dramatized in 1868. It is a typically pugnacious criticism of the brutality of the British penal system. *Foul Play* (1868), a collaboration with **Boucicault**, and *Griffith Gaunt* (1867) were other works to appear as both novels and plays, the latter under the preferred title of *Kate Peyton*. Reade's adaptation of **Zola's** novel, *L'Assommoir*, as *Drink* (1879) provided the actor Charles Warner with a virtuoso role as a man drawn into alcoholism. *The Lyons Mail* (1854), an effective adaptation from the French, passed from the repertoire of **Fechter** to that of **Irving** and on to **Martin-Harvey**. A lifelong bachelor, Reade was a close companion of the actress Laura Seymour and a friend of **Ellen Terry**, whom he persuaded back to the professional stage in 1874, to take over a part in his play, *The Wandering Heir* (1873), a story based on the celebrated case of the Tichborne claimant.   PT

Realism Although realism and naturalism are often assumed to be synonymous, it is useful to distinguish between them, and in this enterprise their practitioners are unhelpful. In his art criticism of the 1860s, for example, **Emile Zola** wrote ardently and indiscriminately of impressionism, realism, and naturalism. With arguments often advanced for realism, **Strindberg** defends naturalism in his preface to *Miss Julie*.

What realism and naturalism share is an allegiance to an art of representation or imitation of unheroic everyday contemporary life. Zola, the main spokesman for realism, was attracted to the 'real' in realism, but it is now clear that realism is a style, no closer to reality than the several movements that rose in reaction against it, each claiming to approach reality more closely. The 19th-century novel is a bastion of realism, but its techniques entered the theatre gradually. Toward the middle of the 19th century came real objects on a stage that resembled a room with the fourth wall removed – the so-called picture-frame stage. **Tom Robertson** introduced real bread and real tea to the London stage of the 1860s, but Zola's dramatization of his novel *Thérèse Raquin* is usually cited as the first realist play. **André Antoine** founded the Théâtre Libre in Paris in 1887, where he provided authentic settings for slice-of-life dramas that eschewed the tight suspenseful structure of the well-made play. Inspired by him, **Otto Brahm** founded the **Freie Bühne** in Berlin in 1889, and J. T. Grein his Independent Theatre Society in London in 1891. For these three avant-garde theatres, **Ibsen**'s *Ghosts* was the key realistic play. Variously ill-received in their day, the realistic plays of these theatres are now acknowledged as the beginning of the modern repertory. After Danchenko and **Stanislavsky** founded the **Moscow Art Theatre** in 1898, an understated, psychologically-based style of acting accommodated realistic plays; through **Strasberg**'s 'Method' adaptation of Stanislavsky, such acting now dominates film. Realism is the dominant style of modern drama, recognizable in verisimilitude of setting, coherence of character, modernity of problems, and prosaic quality of dialogue.   RC

Reaney, James (1926–) Canadian poet and playwright. Taught English at the University of Manitoba 1949–60, where he came to know **John Hirsch**, and where he published two award-winning volumes of poetry. In 1960 he moved to the University of Western Ontario, near his birthplace just outside the city of Stratford. His first play, *The Killdeer* (1960), established most of the themes and methods that permeate his more than 30 theatre works: a focus on local settings and local myths, childish play, the movement from innocence to experience, an almost surrealistic approach to realistic stories, a kaleidoscopic, fragmen-

ted style, a dense symbolic structure, and rich poetic imagery often expressed in incantatory chanting. They are found in *Listen to the Wind* (1966) and in *Colours in the Dark* (1967) produced at the **Stratford Festival** by John Hirsch.

With *Sticks and Stones* (1973) Reaney's plays moved from the poetic to the historic. It is the first play in a trilogy entitled *The Donnellys* about a bitter blood-feud that climaxed in 1880 in the mass murder of an entire Irish immigrant family just a few miles from Reaney's birthplace. *Sticks and Stones* and the other two plays, *St Nicholas Hotel* (1974) and *Handcuffs* (1975), were developed in workshops – a favourite Reaney method – by Keith Turnbull and the NDWT Company, and first produced at Toronto's **Tarragon Theatre**. In the fall of 1975 they were taken on a cross-country tour, climaxing in a day-long presentation of all three plays in Toronto. Reaney's later plays have continued to explore southern Ontario history and myth, though none as successfully as *The Donnellys*. Idiosyncratic and highly imaginative (or, in his own words, 'quirky, odd, weird') James Reaney's plays have brought a strong poetic voice to Canadian drama, but one inextricably tied to live performance.   JA

Recitative Operas, like plays, involve passages that convey necessary information about the action and passages that express characters' states of feeling. Recitative copes with the first, aria with the second. Recitative approximates to the rhythms and inflections of ordinary speech. In the style known as *recitativo secco* ('dry' recitative) the voice is accompanied only by a harpsichord and string basses that provide a kind of punctuation by means of fairly infrequent chords and arpeggios. In *recitativo stromentato* or *accompagnato* ('instrumented' or 'accompanied' recitative) the accompaniment is orchestral. Rather than strictly following the composer's indication of the length of notes in recitative, singers have always allowed themselves some discretion, on the grounds that they are coping with a quasi-speech that cannot be accurately notated. Once recitative became accompanied by the orchestra its musical significance increased and the singer's discretion decreased. This, together with the increased flexibility of the aria and the growing concern for the organic rather than the aggregative work of art, ultimately resulted in operas in which there is a continuous flow of music rather than a number of arias connected (or separated) by recitative. In the 20th century some opera composers have used '**Sprechstimme**' as a device for the effective utterance of the words.   GH

Red Bull Theatre, London One of the many London inns used for occasional theatrical productions, the Red Bull was converted into a distinctive theatre by Aaron Holland in 1605. It was situated on St John Street in Clerkenwell, close to the site of the modern City University. The yard was almost certainly square, surrounded by galleries on all four sides. Dimensions are not known, but the Red Bull was reputed to be 'big'. During the significant years of its occupation by Queen Anne's Men (1605–19) it was certainly notorious for the boisterousness of its audiences and for its ready recourse to specious effectiveness and to the popular appeal of jigs and drolls. **Thomas Heywood**

provided much of the most successful material. After the death of Queen Anne in 1619 and the defection of **Christopher Beeston**, the Red Bull housed a number of companies. Renovations in 1625 did little either to raise its status or deter its audience. Even during the Interregnum, the Red Bull could attract people to illegal productions and to puppet-plays. After the Restoration it quickly lost its place and seems to have been demolished in 1665. PT

Redgrave, Michael (Scudamore) (1908–85) British actor from a long-established theatrical family, who worked as a schoolmaster before joining the **Liverpool Playhouse** company in 1934, where he met and married the actress, Rachel Kempson. In 1936, they went to the **Old Vic**, then under the direction of **Tyrone Guthrie**, where Redgrave played such roles as Orlando in *As You Like It*, Horner in **Wycherley**'s *The Country Wife* and Laertes in *Hamlet*. He was a member of **John Gielgud**'s repertory company at the Queen's Theatre in 1937 and played Harry in **T. S. Eliot**'s *The Family Reunion* in 1939, his first major part in a contemporary play. His handsome presence, polite but somewhat studious manner and gentle speaking voice was equally well suited to the stage and screen; and in the 1940s, he starred as Charleston in Robert Ardrey's *Thunder Rock* (1940), a wartime hit, and in Alfred Hitchcock's comedy-thriller, *The Lady Vanishes*. He joined the Royal Navy during the war, but also appeared in several discreetly patriotic wartime films. He created the part of Crocker-Harris in **Terence Rattigan**'s *The Browning Version* (1948) and joined the Shakespeare Memorial Company in 1951, playing Richard II and starting an association with that company which led to notable performances as Prospero, Hotspur, Antony and King Lear. In 1959, he appeared in his own adaptation of Henry James's *The Aspern Papers*. In 1962, he joined **Laurence Olivier**'s company in the first Chichester Festival season, playing the title role in *Uncle Vanya*, a production which entered the first repertoire season of the **National Theatre** at the Old Vic. Subsequently, he played Hobson in *Hobson's Choice* and Solness in *The Master Builder* at the National Theatre, before ill-health forced him to leave the company. He returned in 1972 to play the silent ageing academic in **Simon Gray**'s *Close of Play*, but he suffered in later years from fears about memory lapses. Redgrave's two books on acting, *The Actor's Ways and Means* (1955, revised 1979) and *Mask or Face* (1958), reveal his intelligent, almost too self-aware, approach to his craft; and he was knighted in 1959. The repertory theatre in Farnham, Surrey, was named after him in 1965 and he was appointed the artistic director of the Yvonne Arnaud Theatre, Guildford, for a season. His autobiography, *In My Mind's Eye*, was published in 1983. His three children, **Vanessa** (b. 1937), Corin (b. 1939) and Lynn (b. 1943), all became successful actors, as are two of his grandchildren by Vanessa Redgrave (Richardson). JE

Redgrave, Vanessa (1937–) British actress, daughter of **Michael Redgrave** and Rachel Kempson, who first appeared in the West End with her father in **N. C. Hunter**'s *A Touch of the Sun* (1958). Her Rosalind in **Michael Elliot**'s production of *As You*

Like It (1961) at Stratford-upon-Avon was acclaimed and she appeared in other Elliot productions including Ellida in *The Lady from the Sea* (1982). She played Nina in *The Seagull* (1964), directed by Tony Richardson who was then her husband, and in 1966 achieved a triumphant success as Miss Brodie the Scottish schoolmistress in the stage version of Muriel Spark's novel, *The Prime of Miss Jean Brodie*. In recent years, her membership of the WRP (Workers' Revolutionary Party) and her passionate advocacy of political causes have attracted much publicity; but her dedication and sincerity, two outstanding qualities also of her acting, have rarely been questioned. Her tall, willowy appearance, expressive voice, and, not least, her marvellous comic sense have made her one of the leading actresses of her time internationally as well as nationally. JE

Régio, José (1901–69) Portuguese playwright. With only four dramas and three further one-act plays to his credit, Régio is nevertheless his country's greatest dramatist of the mid-century. His theme is essentially the same as that explored in his non-dramatic writing, and recurs poetically and dramatically over the 20 years between the mystery *Jacob e o Anjo* (*Jacob and the Angel*, 1941, performed 1952 in Paris) and the one act *Mário ou Eu-Próprio-o Outro* (*Mário/or/Myself-the Other Person*, 1957): the theme of duality, either of identity, or that of living in a dualistic world between spirit and matter, between God and the Devil, which in turn leads to conflicts of conscience or ambiguities in the apprehension of reality. Régio's protagonists are characteristically 'fools' in the Erasmian sense, or Pirandellian, believing in an ideal or an illusion that sets them apart from their fellows; but possessed nevertheless of an otherworldly lucidity and higher understanding. Often criticized for being too 'literary', Régio's works have in fact been well received in performance; one in particular, *A Virgem Benilde* (*The Virgin Benilde*, 1947), has recently (as *A Virgem-Mãe – Benilde, the Virgin Mother –* 1974) been filmed by the Leone de Oro director Manoel de Oliveira, with great lyrical and dramatic impact. LK

Regional theatre (Britain) The history of regional theatre this century has been dominated by two main trends: the decline of the commercial touring circuit from its peak in the Edwardian period, and the growth of the repertory movement from campaigns and experiments at the turn of the century to its establishment now as the major provider of theatre in the regions. Recent years have seen interesting and lively variations of the pattern: the partial revival of the touring circuit with the help of public subvention, and the emergence of small-scale community theatre touring to non-theatre venues.

The touring theatre At the beginning of the century dramatic entertainment outside London – in the towns, cities and suburbs – was provided mainly by theatres that were part of a complex series of touring circuits: the larger, more opulent and more strategically placed houses able to attract the finest companies, the smaller attracting the lesser, second, third and even fourth rate companies. The rapid expansion of road and rail links in the second half of the 19th century had allowed the actor-managers to transport complete productions –

elaborate sets and entire acting companies – with relative ease, and in the face of such competition the old resident 'stock' company had all but disappeared. Long-running, well-proven West End productions (mostly of melodramas, musical comedies and variety with some leavening of **Shakespeare**) could thus be seen in their original spectacular form in Manchester, Newcastle and Glasgow. Likewise new plays could be tried out in the regions before transferring (if successful) to the West End. There were too the companies devoted wholly to touring, with repertories ranging again from melodrama to Shakespeare (**Frank Benson**'s company being the most notable example of such a troupe exclusively dedicated to the classics).

The confidence in, and profitability of, the touring system was evidenced in the boom in new theatre building that occurred between the mid-1890s and 1914. Frank Matcham, that most prolific of theatre architects, was responsible during this period for almost 100 new or rebuilt provincial theatres. By 1914, Liverpool was able to boast seven theatres (of varying size and status) and Birmingham five, while the increasingly popular seaside resorts such as Blackpool and Brighton equally found new theatres a profitable investment. Only in the late twenties, with the arrival of the 'talkie' to boost still further the rise of cinema in the public's affections, did theatre building virtually cease. Thereafter the impact of cinema upon the touring system was profound. In 1914 there had been 170 or so touring companies; 20 years later there were less than 40. The old actor-manager system was by this time almost a thing of the past: **Donald Wolfit**'s company (started in 1937), touring Shakespeare and the classics, was one of the few exceptions to the rule.

Another symptom of the sea-change undergone by the commercial theatre during these early decades was the marked shift in the patterns of theatre ownership. Although this had begun before the First World War it became most noticeable in the post-1918 years and undoubtedly was to contribute further to the wane of touring. Wartime profits from the entertainment industry had led business combines to take control of many of the London theatres and the suburban and regional theatre circuits likewise increasingly became 'chains' run by a small but powerful number of commercial enterprises. Artistic control both of the buildings and of the products staged inside them passed steadily out of the hands of actors and into those of business managers representing limited liability companies. Later, in the face of stiff competition from cinema, 'business sense' by and large dictated a policy of hasty retreat from the risks of live, large-scale theatre.

The decline of touring continued unabated after the Second World War, the next blow being the rapid growth in the fifties of television and especially, with the inauguration of commercial television in 1955, of the sheer range of entertainment it offered. The touring houses themselves shrank in number during the fifties and sixties through demolition or conversion to cinemas and later bingo halls. By 1970 the number of touring and variety theatres had been reduced from 130 in 1930 to about 30. The quality and availability of shows for tour had likewise dwindled. Actors were increasingly loathe to leave London as work opportunities in television multiplied; and the actor whose aspirations lay primarily in the field of live theatre was more likely to find fulfilment in the subsidized regional or national companies than on tour. In fact more and more of the touring product that was available had originated within the subsidized sector – the **Arts Council**-sponsored tour of *Oklahoma!* (in 1980) for example, and the national tours of the major opera, ballet and theatre companies. While there was still a need for the touring theatre, at least in key geographical areas of the country, it became increasingly clear during the early 1970s that the commercial sector was now so entwined with the subsidized that complete separation was no longer feasible nor desirable. In order that the large, costly and mostly antiquated buildings could go on providing the kind of service that the repertory theatres could not, rejuvenation was essential. With Arts Council encouragement and financial support, the big city municipalities – and a number of smaller ones too – actively sought business sponsorship and public subscription and themselves invested considerable sums in renovating and rebuilding. As a result there now exists a greatly reduced but healthier network of restored and vastly improved touring theatres in such towns and cities as Nottingham (the Theatre Royal), Buxton (the Opera House), Leeds (the Grand Theatre and Opera House), Manchester (the Palace), Newcastle (the Theatre Royal), Glasgow (the Theatre Royal) and Belfast (the Grand Opera House) – all serving large populations and capable of receiving a wide variety of dramatic and musical productions. This in turn has helped to generate an increase in both the quality and quantity of touring shows compared with the situation in the early 1970s, and audience figures have risen correspondingly.

The repertory movement It was primarily against the commercial touring system and all that went with it that the early pioneers of repertory rebelled. The actor-managers, the 'stars', the long runs, the domination of London, the priority of profit over experiment and new work – all these features were seen as stultifying and a hindrance to the healthy development of theatre as a social force. Looking back to the days of the resident 'stock' companies and abroad to the accomplishments of the well-endowed national and state theatres (the **Comédie-Française** in particular), men such as **Harley Granville Barker** and **William Archer**, during the early years of the century, argued forcefully for the establishment of a National Repertory Theatre in London, to be followed later by regional theatres on similar lines if smaller in scale. In its ideal form, a Repertory Theatre would offer to the public a wide variety of the very best of drama, old and new, British and foreign, popular and minority interest. Commercial considerations ought not to govern the repertoire and for this reason, it was claimed, the theatre would need to be well-funded, either by private benefactors or, preferably, by national or local government (just as were museums and libraries). A large stock of productions would be maintained and presented on a regular, rotating basis by a permanent, resident company of actors able to play as an ensemble and to keep plays fresh in performance, freed from the deadening constraints of the long run. Barker's famous seasons at the **Royal Court Theatre**, 1904–7, were an early attempt to put some of the ideas to the test and certainly inspired others to carry the movement forward. But with London entrenched in the very system that repertory was endeavouring to oppose, it was in cities outside the capital that the establishment of full scale repertory companies was to come. The repertory movement was henceforward essentially *regional* in character and in philosophy.

Within a space of just seven years, five repertory ventures had been initiated: at Manchester in 1907 (**Miss Horniman**'s company, which based itself in the refurbished **Gaiety Theatre** from 1908); at Glasgow in 1909 (under Alfred Wareing); at Liverpool in 1911 (the first such theatre to be run by a Trust rather than a wealthy patron); at Birmingham in 1913 (under **Barry Jackson**); and briefly, at Bristol in 1914. These early repertory companies set the pattern for future growth, successfully building reputations for their high quality ensemble playing, for their provision of a varied repertoire and for their encouragement of new writers (**Houghton**, **Brighouse** and Drinkwater to name only a few).

After the First World War, the movement in many respects lost momentum. It diversified: in many towns and seaside resorts small *commercial* repertories were started as were a number of *touring* repertories – both contradictions in terms, both playing only the most easily digestible of repertories (farces and thrillers in the main) and giving rise to the common association of repertory with the third-rate. At the other end of the spectrum there was the adventurousness of **Terence Gray**'s Cambridge Festival Theatre (1926–33) and his experiments in 'presentational' stage design. Birmingham and Liverpool however continued to be the twin beacons of the movement and provided the inspiration for the founding of a dozen more genuine repertory theatres across the country. It was the work of the handful of outstanding companies – in Bristol, Oxford, Cambridge, Sheffield and Northampton especially, in addition to Birmingham and Liverpool – that helped to ensure a firm (if uncoordinated) basis on which could be built the stronger national network of repertory theatres after the Second World War.

The massive process of renewal of towns and cities which began in 1945 was accompanied by new attitudes to the role of the arts at both national and local government level. The whole idea of civic theatres, for so long an objective of Barker, Jackson and others, now grew in official acceptability, evidenced by the schemes that emerged, slowly at first but surely, for new repertory theatre buildings at Coventry, Nottingham, Birmingham and elsewhere – to be heavily financed by the local authorities often with additional money from the Arts Council and public subscription. Coventry's Belgrade Theatre (1958) was the first purpose-built repertory theatre for 20 years. By 1980 some 40 new theatres (or major conversions of pre-existing buildings) had been completed, most of which were designed for regional repertory. The buildings were often prestigious in character, sometimes too large (and costly to run) but sometimes imaginative and exciting in design: Sheffield Crucible Theatre's thrust stage and the **Manchester Royal Exchange**'s in-the-round auditorium are good examples. Arts Council money, though it was eventually made available for capital building projects, was first channelled into an even

more pressing cause – the freeing of companies from the tyranny of 'weekly rep' (the dominant practice of weekly changes in the bill to maximize box-office income). With the help of subsidy more and more theatres were able to change to two- and then three-weekly runs, increase rehearsal time and so improve their standards. At the same time ticket prices could be kept at reasonable levels and new or experimental work risked more frequently. The common causes, from the 1960s onwards, were less to do with opposition to the commercial theatre that, in the provinces at least, was on its knees, and more to do with the very survival of a vital regional theatre in the face of television and a fast-changing increasingly complex urban society. Subsidy helped, but even more crucial has been the imagination, energy and enterprise of dozens of directors, actors and administrators and, not least, the moral and financial support of many theatre trusts. Of special note have been the seasons directed by **John Neville**, Stuart Burge and **Richard Eyre** at the Nottingham Playhouse (between 1963 and 1978); Peter Cheeseman's series of local documentaries at the **Victoria Theatre**, Stoke-on-Trent; and the unique, assertively theatrical style pursued at the **Citizens' Theatre**, Glasgow, since 1970.

The repertory concept had, by the mid-sixties, begun to widen out to take on a more strategic, 'audience-centred' significance – less associated now with providing a varied selection of plays for regular, traditional theatre-goers, more with the function of *regional* theatres serving a multiplicity of interests and tastes, communities and age groups, and in a multiplicity of ways, inside and outside the building, on the main stage and in studio theatres – and as such claiming and earning public subsidy for a public service. Community touring and theatre-in-education units made significant strides in bringing theatre to new audiences while the buildings themselves became more accessible and pleasing venues as befitted the theatres' own changing perceptions of their role in society.

Not all the aims of the original proponents of repertory have been achieved. The permanent acting company can rarely be afforded by theatres other than the **National** and **Royal Shakespeare** Theatres, and rarely are plays presented in 'true repertory' (i.e. on the rotational basis): companies are usually held together now for two or at most three productions in succession, and 'short runs' are the norm. Nonetheless, since the war, artistic standards have undoubtedly been raised, the repertoire broadened, much new work generated, the principle of subsidy (if not its correct level) agreed and a decentralized network of some 60 regional theatres firmly established. But, having become the establishment, it was inevitable, in the cycle of things, that they should be challenged and alternatives sought.

Community theatre Whereas in the USA 'community theatre' usually refers to amateur theatre, in Britain the term refers essentially to professionals, based in and working for and with the local community. With roots in the work of some of the more locality-minded repertories (notably Cheeseman's Victoria Theatre in Stoke), in **Littlewood**'s Theatre Workshop, Stratford East, and in **Wesker**'s Centre 42, community theatre emerged in the late 1960s and early 70s alongside the political and young people's theatre movements and the growth of 'community arts'. The first of the community theatre groups (as distinct from political and general 'fringe' companies) was Professor Dogg's Troupe formed by Ed Berman as part of his **Inter-Action** community arts schemes in 1968 in north London. The group performed in the streets and on play sites, ran play-schemes for children and was soon joined by OATS (Old Age Theatre Society) and the Fun Art Bus, all part of the same overall operation and all aiming to involve different sections of the community in activities beyond the actual performances: helping for example parents and others to create and run their own play-schemes and perform their own plays. OATS was shortlived but in every other respect Inter-Action has expanded, moving into its new centre in Kentish Town in 1977 which houses some 14 different community projects. Its success in becoming part of, and a stimulus within, its locality was unquestionable, and Inter-Action has provided a model for many similar if smaller-scale ventures elsewhere.

Community theatre since has tended to be of three main kinds: (1) the companies whose primary role is *performance*, usually of original plays written with the locality in mind which are toured to non-theatre venues *within a distinct geographical area* – to community centres, schools, play-schemes, trade union clubs, etc. Often such companies combine this work with theatre-in-education or children's theatre. Examples are: Theatr Powys in mid-Wales, Pit Prop Theatre in Wigan, Medium Fair in south and east Devon, Solent People's Theatre in Hampshire and North West Spanner in Manchester and Salford, the latter specializing (until the early 1980s) in taking plays into factories and labour clubs. Some repertory theatres also have attached community theatre units, such as Theatre About Glasgow (based at the Citizens' Theatre); (2) the *community arts* companies who see the theatre as just one part of a larger operation in which 'animating' the community, getting people to become involved in a whole range of activities, from drama to silk-screen printing or video-making, is just as important as the group's own performances. Such groups are Inter-Action, Hoxton Hall Theatre Project (London) and Contact Theatre's Community Drama Project (Manchester). Also deserving of attention here are **Ann Jellicoe**'s experiments in large-scale community productions in Devon and Dorset involving professionals and amateurs, adults and schoolchildren; (3) companies who gear themselves less to geographical areas than to serving specific 'communities of interest' – women's groups, racial minorities, gays, etc. – and who will often tour nationally. Such companies are the Women's Theatre Group, the Asian Tara Arts Group, the Black Theatre Cooperative, Graeae Theatre Company (of and for the disabled) and Gay Sweatshop. (See **Fringe theatre**.)

Despite their manifold differences of purpose and strategy, all of these companies (of which there are now over 50) tend to operate within communities that are theatre-less and in other ways under-privileged. Almost without exception, too, their work is underpinned by a concern for social improvement and a belief in the power of theatre to help effect change: the work is often openly socialist. Their repertoires can be as much celebratory as critical and the best companies have succeeded in creating theatre that is at once entertaining, directly relevant to the concerns of its audiences, challenging, un-patronizing and, in its standards of performance, easily comparable to (if it does not surpass) most mainstream theatre.   AJ

Regnard, Jean-François (1655–1709) French playwright, son of a wealthy merchant, who after an adventurous youth devoted to pleasure and travel took up writing largely as a leisure pursuit. His first efforts were farces and light comedies, some written in collaboration with Dufresny, for the **Comédie-Italienne** which he always admired. Appropriately, his later, more substantial comedies for the **Comédie-Française** retain the same Italianate spirit laced with some palpable echoes of **Molière**. *Le Joueur* (1696), concerning an incurable gambler, and above all *Le Légataire Universel* (*The Residuary Legatee*, 1708), in which love and the finer feelings are all subordinated to a naked profit motive, are particularly interesting in their refusal to moralize about the most callous, unsavoury behaviour. Regnard's detached, uncomfortably realistic view of human nature is saved from an indigestible cynicism only by the sheer verve of his writing and some buoyant comic plotting.   DR

Rehan, Ada (Crehan) (1860–1916) American actress. Her family migrated to Brooklyn from Ireland when she was five. She made her debut at age 13, and at 15 became a member of **Mrs Drew**'s **Arch Street Theatre** company in Philadelphia. In 1877 when **Augustin Daly** spotted her in Albany and engaged her to appear in New York in his own play *Pique* (1878), he was so impressed with her talents that he persuaded her to join him permanently, and from then until his death (1899) she was his leading lady.

During her 31 years on stage in the United States and in England, she played over 200 roles ranging from the title role in Daly's *Odette* (1882), Lady Teazle in *The School for Scandal* (1894), to a host of Shakespearian roles: Katherina, Rosalind, Viola, Beatrice, Miranda, and Portia. She appeared in London at Toole's Theatre (1884), played Katherina at the Shakespeare Memorial Theatre (1888), opened Daly's Theatre (just off Leicester Square) as Viola (1893), made a cross-country tour of the United States (1896), and finally after Daly's death toured again with **Otis Skinner** in *The Taming of the Shrew* (1904–5).

Critics called her 'sweetly reckless', 'ardently impetuous', and 'piquantly alluring'. **Ellen Terry** described her as 'the most lovely, humorous darling I have ever seen on the stage'.   RM

Reicher, Emanuel (1849–1924) German actor. After several years acting in Vienna, Munich, and Hamburg, in 1887 Reicher was hired by the Berlin Residenztheater. Here his performance as Pastor Manders in *Ghosts* established him as a leading naturalistic actor. From 1895, he acted under **Brahm** at the **Deutsches Theater**. Here he was celebrated for the minute psychological accuracy of his roles, especially in **Ibsen**'s plays. From 1917, he directed the Garden Theatre in New York.   SW

Reid, J. Graham (1945–) Irish playwright. Reid's first two plays, *The Death of Humpty-Dumpty* (1979) and *The Closed Door* (1980), tell equally harrowing stories of victims on the periphery of terrorist violence, and the widening circle of loss. He has since written a successful trilogy, *Billy* (1982), and two stage plays, *The Hidden Curriculum* (1982) and *Remembrance* (Lyric 1984), all, in **Stewart Parker**'s phrase, pungent with 'the thick and acrid' air of Belfast. DM

Reid, Kate (1930–) Canadian actress of international stature noted for her work in roles demanding intense emotional energy. Trained at **Hart House Theatre**, she appeared there, in summer stock, and at Toronto's Crest Theatre before making her London (England) debut in the title role of *The Stepmother* (1958). She returned to Canada to appear at the **Stratford Festival** from 1959–62, playing Emilia in *Othello*, Lady Macbeth, and Katharina in *The Taming of the Shrew* among other roles.

In 1962 she went to New York to play Martha in the matinee cast of **Edward Albee**'s *Who's Afraid of Virginia Woolf?* (1962), and in 1964 was nominated for a Tony Award for her performance opposite Sir **Alec Guinness** in *Dylan*. She co-starred in **Tennessee Williams**'s *Slapstick Tragedy* (1966) and spent almost two years in **Arthur Miller**'s *The Price* in New York and London. For the American Shakespeare Festival she played Gertrude in *Hamlet* in 1969 and, in 1974, the Nurse in *Romeo and Juliet* and Big Mama in *Cat on a Hot Tin Roof*. In 1985 she played opposite **Dustin Hoffman** in a major revival of *Death of a Salesman*.

In Canada she played Madame Ranevskaya in *The Cherry Orchard* at Stratford in 1965 and returned to the Festival in 1970 and 1980, primarily in modern plays. Other important Canadian appearances were in *Mrs Warren's Profession* at the Shaw Festival in 1976 and Clytemnestra in the National Arts Centre's 1983 production of the *Oresteia*. She has also had a successful film and television career, primarily in the USA. JA

Reinhardt, Max (1873–1943) Austrian director. Reinhardt's early years in the theatre were spent as an actor, mainly of old men's roles, first at the Salzburg Town Theatre, then at the **Deutsches Theater** in Berlin under the direction of **Otto Brahm**. In 1903, he gave up acting to concentrate on directing, and over the next decade became the most celebrated stage director in Europe. Although Reinhardt was able effortlessly to absorb the latest developments in scenic design, employing designers such as **Edward Gordon Craig** and Ernst Stern (1876–1954), and fully to exploit advances in actorial training and technique, he always maintained an illusionistic stage. This illusionism is the unifying element in his work that otherwise appears to be unusually eclectic, ranging from intimate chamber drama through vivid productions of **Shakespeare** and the classics, to vast spectacles staged in arenas throughout Germany and Europe. During these years Reinhardt was director of the Deutsches Theater in Berlin, a post he kept until 1933. From 1917 on, he was closely involved with running the newly established Salzburg Festival; here he employed both theatres and extra-theatrical settings such as churches and the cathedral square for his productions. During the 1920s, his style

of theatre came to seem slightly dated due to the rise of an anti-illusionistic stage, especially in Berlin. Because of this and for political reasons, Reinhardt's career increasingly became centred on Salzburg and Vienna, where he was, for several years, director of the Theater in der Josefstadt. In 1933, with the coming to power of the Nazis, Reinhardt gave the Berlin theatres he owned and directed to the German people. While he kept a foothold in Salzburg, from then on more and more of his time was spent in the USA, where he worked both in Hollywood and on Broadway. His most significant work in these later years was his film of *A Midsummer Night's Dream* (1935). He died in New York. SW

Réjane (1856–1920) French actress. Born Gabrielle Réju, the daughter of a refreshment-seller at the Ambigu, Réjane, after a difficult beginning, became one of the most brilliant actresses of the Boulevard. If she excelled in light and polished comedy, her range included much broader popular roles, such as **Sardou**'s Madame Sans-Gêne (1893) or the carefully observed naturalism of her interpretation of the pathetic and grotesque servant, Germinie Lacerteux, based on the Goncourt novel (1888). She was associated with a number of theatres, but the most important period of her career was spent at the Vaudeville, whose director, Porel, she married in 1893 (they divorced in 1905). The Porel management opened with the triumph of *Madame Sans-Gêne*, which was followed by Réjane in **Becque**'s *La Parisienne*. In the following year she was the first French Nora in **Ibsen**'s *Doll's House*. One of her greatest parts was in Paul Hervieu's *Course au Flambeau* (1901). In 1905 she left the Vaudeville and in 1908 she took on the Théâtre Nouveau and baptized it the Théâtre Réjane. It was here that she staged *John Gabriel Borkman*. She was also involved in the making of films, notably *Madame Sans-Gêne* and, a few weeks before her death, *Miarka, la Fille à l'Ours* (*Miarka, the Girl With a Bear*). JMCC

Remizov, Aleksei Mikhailovich (1877–1957) Russian modernist writer. A superb literary craftsman known variously as the 'sacrist' and **Picasso** of the Russian language, his novels, stories and plays reflect his interest in ancient rituals and folklore, children's games and fairy tales, dreams, etymology and Old Russia. Although attracted to symbolism, his work embodies a more individual tragic sense of life's mysterious causality and man's incomprehensible suffering, balanced by a mischievous and at times blasphemous playfulness in tone and literary devices. He served as literary manager of **Meyerhold**'s 'Fellowship of the New Drama' in Kherson, South Russia (1903–4), and wrote several plays. These are contemporary stylizations of ancient legends and forms, reflecting his belief in theatre as 'a cult, a mass, in the mysteries of which perhaps the Redemption is concealed'. *The Devil Play* (1907) is a modernization of a medieval Kievan legend, featuring commentary, stylized gestures and the onstage transport via serpent of a newly extracted soul to hell. Although it may come closest of all the Russian symbolist neo-mysteries to capturing the spirit and style of the original, Remizov was booed off the stage when the play was produced. *The Tragedy of Judas, Prince of Iscariot* (1909) combines an apocryphal Judas legend, the Oedipus myth and Russian folkloric imagery and stylization. *Tsar Maximilian* (1919) is Remizov's version of a well-known and much re-written Russian folk drama. His prose works formed the bulk of his writing and include a major critical work on Russian literature, *The Fire of Things* (1954). He emigrated to Berlin in 1921 and to Paris in 1923.   SG

Rene, Roy ('Mo') (1892–1954) Australian com-edian. Born Harry van der Sluys in Adelaide, as 'Master Roy' he sang and appeared in pantomime, and later in suburban minstrel shows, from which he adapted 'Mo''s characteristic black-and-white makeup. Part-nered from 1916–28 by Nat Phillips ('Stiffy'), he dominated Australian vaudeville in the 1920s–30s with a distinctive earthy humour and outrageous innuendo; his catch-phrase 'Strike me lucky!' became a household term. In the 1940s he appeared in the radio comedy series McCackie Mansions; his last stage appearance was in *Hellzapoppin'* in 1949–50.   MW

Rengifo, César (1915–80) Venezuelan playwright, director, professor, historian, politician, and journalist. Another career took him into painting and muralism. Author of more than 60 plays (from 1942), Rengifo wrote trilogies on Venezuelan history and the petro-leum industry. Chronologically, these periods are the conquest, pre-independence, the wars of Federation, and the petroleum period. A revisionist historian, he made strong critical statements about injustices in contemporary society. His leftist political orientation led him to experiment with Brechtian techniques, balancing aesthetics against ideology to avoid outright propaganda. His *Manuelote* (1952) is widely known; other major plays include *El vendaval amarillo* (*Yellow Wind*, 1959), *Lo que dejó la tempestad* (*What the Storm Left*, 1961) and *Las torres y el viento* (*Towers and Wind*, 1970).   GW

Repertory theatre, Britain see **Regional theatre, Britain**

Resident non-profit professional theatre in the USA This movement, which gained its greatest momentum in the 1960s, has variously been called the regional, repertory, or resident theatre movement, though its most current nomenclature is 'resident' so as not to exclude not-for-profit theatres in New York City, although the initial impetus for the movement was to create an alternate, decentralized theatre net-work in the United States outside of New York. Its non-profit status is significant in that box office profit is not of prime concern; rather the focus is on the art of the theatre, the development of theatre artists, craftsmen and administrators dedicated to establishing a new American theatre, and the production of classical and innovative contemporary drama. Most resident theatres have a set season with subscribers and are established in their own building. From a handful of theatres two decades ago today there are more than 250 theatres playing to about 15 million people annually, forming a complex network and comprising the near-est thing in the United States to a national theatre institution. Today these theatres are the chief origina-tors and producers of significant theatre in America. According to a 1983–4 survey of 230 theatres made by Theatre Communications Group, more than 23,000 artists, administrators, and technical and production personnel are currently employed by these theatres. Surviving on the basis of both public and private subsidy, these theatres have been in jeopardy since the mid-1980s due to the erratic pattern of contributed support that has failed to close the growing gap between income and expenses. Since 1980 almost 30 theatres, including at least two that have existed for more than a decade, have ceased operation. Nonethe-less, as a result of this movement, most major Ameri-can cities, such as Chicago, Los Angeles, San Francisco, and Seattle, today are important centres of theatre activity.

Claiming as antecedents the amateur **Little Theatre movement** of the 1920s, the **Group Theatre** of the 1930s, and the **Federal Theatre Project** of the depres-sion, the movement most frequently marks its begin-ning with the founding of the **Cleveland Play House** in 1915, still in existence, although its impetus and inspiration is credited to **Margo Jones** who in the 1940s devised the prototype for the regional theatre with her Theatre '47 in Dallas, Texas. In her book on arena staging (1951), which was the manifesto for the movement for many years, she proposed a network of regional theatres. Following Jones's lead, Nina Vance founded Houston's **Alley Theatre** in 1947 and Zelda Fichandler co-founded in Washington, DC, the **Arena Stage** in an old moviehouse in 1950. With Jones and Vance deceased, Fichandler is now considered the prime representative of the movement's beginnings and a visionary voice for its future. From these beginnings others followed in quick succession: the Milwaukee Repertory Theatre and the **New York Shakespeare Festival** (1954); the **Dallas Theatre Centre** (1959); Baltimore's Centre Stage, the **Seattle Repertory Theatre**, Washington, and the **Guthrie Theatre** in Minneapolis, Minnesota (founded by **Tyrone Guthrie**, Olivier Rea and Peter Zeisler, the latter is the only major regional theatre that chose its city rather than the city evolving the theatre) (1963); **Actors Theatre** of Louisville, the **American Place Theatre**, Hartford Stage Company and the O'Neill Theatre Centre (both in Connecticut), South Coast Repertory (Costa Mesa, California), and **Trinity Square Repertory Company** (1964); San Francisco's **American Conservatory Theatre** and **Long Wharf Theatre** in New Haven, Connecticut (1965); New Haven's **Yale Repertory Theatre** and the Arizona Theatre Company (1966); Los Angeles's **Mark Taper Forum** and San Francisco's Magic Theatre (1967); and Atlanta, Georgia's Alliance Theatre and New York's **Circle Repertory Company** (1969). During the decade of the 1970s the number of theatres established increased appreciably, only to ebb during the 1980s. Early in its history the movement was helped exten-sively by the Ford (under the dynamic leadership of W. McNeil Lowry) and Rockefeller Foundations and later by the National Endowment for the Arts, though under the administration of President Ronald Reagan the latter souce of support has failed to increase as it had during the 1960s and 70s.

As theatres associated with specific communities, these institutions have attempted to serve their specific areas in terms of individual needs and profiles. In addition to preserving the classics as exciting living theatre for their patrons, potentially these theatres can achieve ensemble acting possible only in companies that work together in numerous productions over many years; they can be educational resources for their communities (as well as creating professional theatre training programmes); and, perhaps their major mission, they can develop new texts without the restrictions of theme and content, as is often not true of the commercial theatre. Indeed, the number of playwrights who owe allegiance to the resident theatre is impressive, though not as extensive as it could be. For example, Chicago's **Goodman Theatre** (founded in 1925) has devoted much of its energy to the development of plays by **David Mamet** (who previously worked extensively at Chicago's now defunct St Nicholas Theatre) and **John Guare**. Jon Jory's Actors Theatre of Louisville has demonstrated an intense interest in new plays with an annual new play festival. Playwrights such as **Marsha Norman** and **Beth Henley** have emerged from this programme. Writers as diverse as **Sam Shepard**, **Lanford Wilson**, and **Charles Fuller** have been nurtured by the non-profit theatre. It is significant that nine consecutive Pulitzer Prizes (through to 1984) premiered in non-profit theatres before being transferred to commercial theatres on Broadway, although such a trend predates 1976 (one of the first was Arena Stage's 1968 production of Howard Sackler's *The Great White Hope*) and continues today. Indeed, the non-profit theatre has been accused of becoming nothing more than a tryout institution for the commercial theatre, a charge that ignores the natural desire to prolong the life of and give greater visibility to significant plays. It is, therefore, noteworthy that David Mamet's *Glengarry Glen Ross* (1984 Pulitzer) began at Goodman, that Marsha Norman's *'night, Mother* (1983 winner) came to New York from the **American Repertory Theatre**, and that a play like **Mark Medoff**'s *Children of a Lesser God* originated at the Mark Taper Forum or **August Wilson**'s *Ma Rainey's Black Bottom* was developed at the Yale Repertory Theatre. Other examples of plays first presented in the regions include **Fugard**'s *A Lesson from Aloes* and *Master Harold and the Boys* (Yale), **David Rabe**'s *Hurlyburly* (Goodman), Herb Gardner's *I'm Not Rappaport* (Seattle Rep), and Lyle Kessler's *Orphans* (Chicago's Steppenwolf Theatre). In 1984 *A Chorus Line*, produced on Broadway by the non-profit New York Shakespeare Festival, significantly celebrated its 10th anniversary. This transference, and others, and the considerable profits accrued as a result, has allowed **Joseph Papp** to produce dozens of less profitable or more risky plays and musicals.

Unquestionably, in today's non-profit resident theatre there is a true danger of allowing artistic product to take second place to an institution, of creating a regional theatre that moves away from indigenous needs to a more traditionally commercial, conservative, and safe product that appeals to a mass audience and guarantees the box office needed to supplement other sources of income for survival. It is certainly a fact that little avant-garde or true experimentation, with notable exceptions, has taken place in the regions. However, as long as the American resident theatres allow strong personalities to operate these theatres with vision and sensitivity they will remain more individual than similar. In this regard, however, it is significant that a true network is beginning to emerge that perhaps stresses important similarities of goals and aspirations. For example, one of the most popular resident theatre plays of the 1980s, Sam Shepard's *Fool for Love*, originated at San Francisco's Magic Theatre before it played at New York's Circle Repertory Company, both non-profit theatres. Michael Cristofer's *The Shadow Box* (1977) went from the Mark Taper to New Haven's Long Wharf to Broadway. Several seasons ago **Christopher Durang**'s *A History of the American Film* was staged in different productions at the Hartford (Connecticut) Stage Company, the Arena Stage, and the Mark Taper Forum before it was presented in New York. Emily Mann's *Execution of Justice* (about political assassination) was seen at the Arena Stage in 1985 after an earlier production at the Actors Theatre. Such a pattern of movement within the regional network is becoming more commonplace.

The non-profit theatre network in the USA is served by dozens of organizations, although two are of special importance. Theatre Communications Group, founded in 1961, serves as a communications network for its institutional members and individual artists. Among their goals is 'to foster cross-fertilization and interaction among different types of organizations and individuals that comprise the profession'. One of TCG's services is the annual publication of *Theatre Facts* which provides a statistical guide to the finances and productivity of the non-profit professional theatre in America. Recent reports underscore the increasing number of large deficits of major institutions since 1980 and the ominous news that 'the costs of doing business have grown faster than available income' and that long-range planning efforts 'are increasingly hampered by the shifting philanthropic terrain'. The second vital organization, the League of Resident Theatres (LORT), represents about 80 non-profit professional theatres, is active in labour relations, and concerns itself with the artistic and management needs of its members.

What seems clear from all available evidence is that the non-profit professional theatre is being forced to reexamine its structure and product in order to assure stability throughout the 1980s and into the 1990s. Thus far action has included reducing the number of plays produced in a season, making administrative cuts and changes, and frequently seeking a balanced season that both restricts the size and scope of productions while minimizing changes in artistic integrity and vision. DBW

See: G. M. Berkowitz, *New Broadways: Theatre Across America 1950–1980*, Totowa, New Jersey, 1982; M. Jones, *Theatre-in-the-Round*, New York, 1951; J. Novick, *Beyond Broadway: The Quest for Permanent Theatres*, New York, 1968; L. Ross (ed.), *Theatre Profiles 6*, New York, 1984; J. L. Zeigler, *Regional Theatre: The Revolutionary Stage*, Minneapolis, Minnesota, 1973.

Reumert, Poul (1883–1968) Danish actor, who began at the Dagmar and New theatres, where his speciality included operetta, before beginning a long and glorious career at the **Kongelige Teater**, most of it in a legendary partnership with Bodil Ipsen. He specialized in complex tragicomic roles, contrasting well with her exuberant, provocative style; they were especially successful as Edgar and Alice in *The Dance of*

Death and Ill and Madame Zachanassian in *The Visit*. Perfectly fluent in French, Reumert had a special affinity to the plays of **Molière**, whose *Précieuses Ridicules* he translated. An outstanding Scapin, a very sensual Tartuffe and a controversially grave Alceste, he acted Molière throughout Scandinavia and in Paris, where he also lectured at the Sorbonne.   HL

Reutter, Otto (Otto Pfützenreuter) (1870–1931) German music-hall singer and songwriter; after a commercial education, he gained experience as a walk-on at minor theatres and as a folk-singer, before launching his real career at Berlin's Apollo Theatre in 1895. Basically a minstrel of the proletariat, conservative and patriotic, occasionally topically satirical, he displayed a wit and feeling in his reflections on the workaday world that taught volumes to more sophisticated songwriters. He played all the major music-halls in Germany, and wrote the words and music to thousands of numbers, the most famous being 'Ick wundre mir über gar nischt mehr' ('Nothing Surprises Me No More') and 'In fünfzig Jahren ist alles vorbei' ('It'll All Be Over in Fifty Years').   LS

Revenge tragedy The fashion for revenge tragedy in Elizabethan and Jacobean England was sparked off by the success of **Kyd**'s *The Spanish Tragedy* (c. 1589). Strictly speaking, a revenge tragedy begins with the appearance of the ghost of a wronged and/or murdered man to a still-living descendant or associate. Having heard the ghost's story, the listener assumes the role of avenger and the play pursues the story through to the completion of the revenge. Rarely adherents of strict form, the Elizabethan playwrights incorporated those features that best suited them whilst re-ordering or abandoning others. **Shakespeare**'s two revenge tragedies, *Titus Andronicus* (c. 1592) and *Hamlet* (c. 1601), exhibit almost the full range of their kind. Other notable examples come from **Tourneur** – *The Revenger's Tragedy* (c. 1606) and the clumsy *The Atheist's Tragedy* (published 1611); **Webster** – *The White Devil* (c. 1612) and *The Duchess of Malfi* (c. 1613); **Middleton** – *The Changeling* (1622) and *Women Beware Women* (c. 1625); **Marston** – *Antonio's Revenge* (1600) and **Shirley** – *The Traitor* (1631). But the theme of revenge so dominated the tragedies of the period that the list could be vastly prolonged.   PT

Revista The Portuguese *revista* is somewhat wider in definition than its immediate translation 'review' would suggest, ranging from intimate sketch to mini-musical. Characteristically, it has played in the larger theatres, more particularly in Lisbon. The first *revista*, an imitation of the early 19th-century revue, *Fossilismo e Progresso* (*Fossil-Worship and Progress*, 1859), started a tradition of one annual *Revista do Ano* (*Review of the Year*), which was just that. Initially with no real plot, just a series of brief sketches, they were the theatrical equivalents of lampoon and caricature: the queen might be depicted squawking out a *fado*, the government furtively picking the lock of the Treasury. By the end of the century, the *revista* had acquired the framework of a story, usually mythological in theme, for its political satire, a chorus line and orchestra; and could have long runs: *Sal e Pimenta* (*Salt and Pepper*, with the actress

Palmira Bastos at the beginning of a half-century's career in the lead) ran for more than 200 performances.

The satire was often vitriolic and usually near to the bone. It was fired against the dictator Franco in the first decade of the new century, and against over-heavy policing under the Republic. The *revista* gained great popularity and importance under the Estado Novo (Salazar's corporatist regime, c. 1928–74) because, in spite of having somehow to accommodate the rigours of censorship, it was the only political theatre with any continuity in the nation's life. In the five decades following 1920, there was a high of 122 new shows in the 30s and a relative low of 68 in the 60s.   LK

Revue An episodic programme of songs, comedy sketches, mime, dance and instrumental music, ostensibly organized around topical and satirical subject matter, occasionally connected by a single theme or a master of ceremonies. Topical humour is as old as **Aristophanes** and elements of revue may be discerned in Adam de la Halle's *Jeu de la Feuillée* (c. 1262), but the term first appears at a French fairground theatre with *La Revue des Théâtres* by Romagnesi and Dominique (1728). The end-of-year survey became an annual Parisian feature at the Théâtre de la Porte-Saint-Martin 1828–48 (*L'An 1841 et l'an 1941* by the brothers Cogniard is an early example of the contrast-structure), and Berlin continued the tradition at the Metropol-Theater, 1903–14. In London, **J. R. Planché** experimented with allegorical entertainments (1838–55) and **John Brougham** staged a revue in New York in 1869, but these bore no fruit. The small-scale topical revue was later absorbed into cabaret and chamber-theatre.

At the turn of the century, the spectacular revue arrived, a dance-dominated form that substitutes nostalgia, sentimentality and visual effects for satire. The *revue à grand spectacle* is built on cumulative effects and sensual contrast, each tableau contributing to an overwhelming sense of glamour. The first was *Place aux Jeunes* (1886) at the **Folies-Bergère**, Paris, which became a leading purveyor of this form, ever increasing in splendour: by 1906, the show boasted 18 tableaux and 600 costumes; by 1928, 80 tableaux, 500 performers, 1,200 costumes. Other Parisian theatres making it a speciality were the Casino de Paris, Bobino, Alhambra, and Ba-ta-clan.

In Germany and Austria, the revue became the second half of variety programmes and occasionally transmuted into operetta. Eric Charrell and James Klein were its leading producers there, and jazz bands, nude women and light shows regular features after the First World War. The form's loose-knit structure attracted the theatrical avant-garde. **Max Reinhardt**'s pantomimic spectacles *Sumurun* (1910) and *The Miracle* (1911) owed much to it, and **Erwin Piscator**'s *Revue Rote Rummel* (1924), which employed hundreds of lay actors, effectively adapted to leftist political ends, inspiring **Ernst Toller**'s *Trotz Alledem* (1925) and the agit-prop 'Red Revues' of the German Communist party. **Brecht** in Berlin, **Mayakovsky** and **Meyerhold** in Moscow, **Voskovec** and **Werich** in Prague, and Constantin Tanase in Bucharest also took it as a structural model.

Despite earlier attempts like *Under the Clock* by **Seymour Hicks** and Charles Brookfield (1893), the revue did not catch on in England until 1912 with Albert de Courville's *Hullo, Ragtime*; the wartime thirst for light entertainment confirmed its success, when **Oswald Stoll** imported French revues to the Hippodrome. The impresarios André Charlot and **C. B. Cochran** specialized in more intimate showcases for such talents as **Noël Coward, Beatrice Lillie** and **Gertrude Lawrence** (*Cheep*, 1917; *London Calling*, 1923; *Charlot's Revue*, 1924; *On with the Dance*, 1925; *Words and Music*, 1932, etc.). The basic unit became the 'black-out' sketch, a short comic scene ending with a punchline and a rapid lights-out. The smart West End revue flourished well into the 1960s and proved to be a nursery for comedians, singers and dancers whose personalities admirably suited the cosily saucy style of the genre: Binnie Hale, Cicely Courtneidge, Jack Hulbert, Cyril Ritchard, Hermione Gingold, Dora Bryan, Max Adrian and **Joyce Grenfell**. Eventually it succumbed to television and a blacker brand of satire, more akin to cabaret.

In New York some 200 revues opened between 1900 and 1930, often originating in the after-hours roof gardens of legitimate theatres. These included both the spectacular – the *Ziegfeld Follies* (1907–31, 1933, 1936, 1943), the **Shubert** Brothers' *Passing Show* (1912–34), **George White**'s *Scandals* (1919–29, with music by **George Gershwin** and Paul Whiteman; 1931, 1936, 1939), and Earl Carroll's *Vanities* (1923–32); and the intimate – *Greenwich Village Follies* (1919–28), *Music Box Revue* (1921–4, with music by **Irving Berlin**), *Garrick Gaieties* (1925). *As Thousands Cheer* (1933) was the first revue to feature a female black star, **Ethel Waters**, in a white cast. The decline of the intimate revue is due in part to the disappearance of a homogeneous audience, that is reliably *au courant*, shares similar tastes, and possesses a certain level of urbanity.

After 1945, the spectacular revue diversified into night club shows (Las Vegas, or the Paris Lido), floor shows, strip-tease (The Crazy Horse Saloon, Paris), ice shows, and fashion shows. Much of its function had already been usurped by the revue film, exemplified by the work of Busby Berkeley. The topical revue became a feature of television, while the intimate revue was narrowed to a survey of a single composer's work (*Oh, Coward!*, 1972; *Side by Side by Sondheim*, 1976). In the 1960s, revue techniques once more inspired experimental theatre, while writers like **N. F. Simpson** and **Harold Pinter** provided sketches for commercial revues (*Pieces of Eight, One to Another*, both 1959). Poland's **Laterna Magika**, **Joan Littlewood**'s *Oh, What a Lovely War!* (1963), **Peter Brook**'s *US* (1966), **Jean-Louis Barrault**'s *Rabelais* (1968), **Luca Ronconi**'s *Orlando Furioso* (1969) and **Ariane Mnouchkine**'s *1789* (1970) have drawn on the revue format; much contemporary radical street and alternative performance (e.g., Bloolips) is organized as a deliberate perversion of the revue's more outmoded traditions. LS

> See: R. Baral, *Revue*, NY and London, 1962; J. Damase, *Les Folies du music-hall de 1917 à nos jours*, Paris, 1960; London, 1962; F.-P. Kothes, *Die theatralische Revue in Berlin und Wien 1900–1938*, Wilhelmshaven, 1977; R. Mander and J. Mitchenson, *Revue: A Story in Pictures*, London and NY, 1971.

Reyes, Carlos José (1941–) Colombian play-

wright and director. After his initiation to theatre with the Independent Theatre Club, he joined El Buho (The Owl) from 1959 to 1962 as a member of the governing board, directing **García Lorca**, **Eliot**, and his own children's theatre. Affiliated with several other groups (Experimental Theatre of the Industrial University of Santander, the Popular Art Theatre and others), he collaborated with **Santiago García** to establish the Casa de Cultura de Bogotá, later the Teatro La Candelaria. He has operated his own theatre, El Alacrán, which merged in 1984 with the Popular Theatre of Bogotá. A committed writer, he has a wide range of plays, including many pieces of children's theatre and extensive historical dramas written exclusively for Colombian television. Among his major plays are: *Soldados* (*Soldiers*, 1967), a gripping account of Colombian violence based on a chapter of Alvaro Cepeda Zamudio's novel, *La casa grande* (*The Big House*). *Los viejos baúles empolvados que nuestros padres nos prohibieron abrir* (*The Dusty Old Trunks our Parents Forbade Us to Open*, 1968), and *Variaciones sobre la Metamorfosis* (*Variations on Metamorphosis*), a play structured around Kafka's work *Metamorphosis*, are later examples. GW

Ribeyro, Julio Ramón (1929–) Peruvian novelist and playwright. Principally known for *Santiago, el pajarero* (*Santiago, the Bird Dealer*, 1970), inspired by a *tradición* of Ricardo Palma, the play criticizes governmental systems in an 18th-century setting. His other plays include *El sótano* (*The Basement*, 1959), *Fin de semana* (*Weekend*, 1961), *Los caracoles* (*The Snails*, 1964), and *Atusparia* (1979), a work based on an indigenous revolt in 1885. GW

Ribman, Ronald (1932–) American playwright. Born in New York and educated at the University of Pittsburgh, Ribman attracted critical attention in 1965 with his *Harry, Noon and Night* at the **American Place Theatre**. During the following year, his *The Journey of the Fifth Horse* won an Obie. Other major dramatic works by Ribman include: *The Ceremony of Innocence* (1965), *Passing Through from Exotic Places* (1969), *Fingernails Blue as Flowers* (1971), *A Break in the Skin* (1972), *The Poison Tree* (1973), and *Cold Storage* (1977), a Dramatist Guild Award-winning comedy about the function of death. More respected than loved, Ribman's plays deal with man's entrapment by a universe he can't change. TLM

Riccoboni Family of Italian actors. The founder of the dynasty **Antonio** (*fl.* 1655–95) was seen in London as Pantalone in 1679. His son Luigi Andreas, known as **Lélio** (1676–1753), sought in 1699 to establish a theatre in the French taste in northern Italy, in opposition to a decadent **commedia dell'arte**; in 1716, under the protection of the Duc d'Orléans, he reopened the **Comédie-Italienne**, which, ironically, he gallicized to suit the taste of Paris and where he won acclaim for his expressive acting, especially in **Marivaux**'s plays. He toured to London 1727–8; served as a majordomo at the court of Parma 1729–31; and returned to Paris in 1733. His works include a history of the Italian theatre (Paris, 1728, 1731), a study of European acting (1738); and calls for theatre reform (1738, 1743) in support of sentimental comedy. He married (1) Gabriella Gardellini, known as Argentina; and (2) Elena Balletti (1686–1771), known as Flaminia.

His son Antoine-François-Valentin, known as Lélio *fils* (1707–72), worked with the Comédie-Italienne 1726–50 as first lover, dancer and choreographer; his acting was judged to be cold and pretentious, and he quit because the Duc de Richelieu insulted him during the **Favart** affair. He wrote several comedies, a discourse on parody (1746) promoting opera over tragedy, and *L'Art du théâtre* (1750), which raised questions of the actor's emotional involvement in his role. His wife Marie-Jeanne de La Boras, known as Mme Riccoboni (1713–92), was a friend of **Diderot** and wrote comedies in the style of Marivaux.   LS

Rice, Dan (1823–1900) American clown, son of a New York grocer. He led a chequered career as a jockey, strong man, blackface minstrel and, at one time, agent for the Mormon leader Joseph Smith, before commencing as showman in 1841 with Lord Byron 'the most sapient of pigs'. His debut as clown was made in Galena, Illinois, in 1844, and he was soon a favourite for his native American humour with its heavyhanded satire of local politicians. His red-and-white striped costume, top hat and chin-whiskers later became attributes of Uncle Sam. Rice popularized the term 'one-horse show', originally an insult flung at him by a journalist, and as the 'Great Shakespearian clown', bandied mangled quotations with his audience. He was half-seriously nominated for President in 1868; alcoholism undermined his abilities and his last public appearances were as a temperance lecturer in the 1870s,

though it was said the water pitcher on the podium contained gin. A forerunner of **Will Rogers**, Rice exemplified an authentic folk strain in popular performance.   LS

Rice, Elmer (Reizenstein) (1892–1967) American playwright. Rice's career started in 1914 with *On Trial*, an experimental play using a courtroom scene for flashbacks into aspects of the crime being tried. A New Yorker who graduated from law school before becoming a playwright, Rice used his legal knowledge in several plays, in various disputes with theatres and in causes he served – from Marxism in the 1930s to the American Civil Liberties Union. A fearless and talented man, Rice wrote with fortitude and wisdom on both popular and unpopular subjects. When his valued efforts with the **Federal Theatre Project** were threatened with government censorship, he was outraged, and resigned. Responding to the high-handed methods of the **Theatre Guild**, he and four other playwrights – **Robert Sherwood**, **S. N. Behrman**, **Sidney Howard**, **Maxwell Anderson** – founded the Playwrights' Company in 1938. He vigorously opposed Senator Joseph McCarthy's attacks on theatre artists.

Rice's plays reflect the man – his interest in experimentation, realism, protest and comedy. His best work is *The Adding Machine* (1923), an expressionistic play about the dehumanization of man. Further experiments – *The Subway* (1929) and *Dream Girl* (1945), a slight but successful fantasy – were not impressive. Man's condition fascinated and angered Rice who exclaimed through a character in *Street Scene* (1929): 'Everywhere

A scene from Elmer Rice's *Street Scene*, 1929.

you look, oppression and cruelty!' *We, the People* (1933), a bitter attack on depression times, ended in an agit-prop call for democratic ideals. In *Judgment Day* (1934) Rice scourged Nazi fascism, and in *Between Two Worlds* (1934) contrasted the political systems of Russia and America. Finally, in *American Landscape* (1938) Rice, disillusioned with both Marxism and American commercial theatre, supported American traditions. War was approaching. Post-war theatre gave Rice little satisfaction. *The Grand Tour* (1951), *Winners* (1954) and *Cue for Passion* (1958) did little for his reputation. Always a liberal idealist, Rice preached individual freedom from all tyranny.   WJM

Rice, Thomas Dartmouth 'Daddy' (1806–60)

American blackface performer ('Ethiopian delineator') considered the 'father of American minstrelsy'. Between 1828 and 1831 Rice, according to tradition, observed a crippled Negro stableman, possibly in Louisville, Kentucky, sing a refrain and dance with a jerky jump, thus 'Jump Jim Crow', after the slave's name. From this single song and dance Rice developed full-length entertainments called 'Ethiopian operas'. He toured the British Isles in 1836, 1838, and 1843, leaving his stamp on the English stage. In 1858, he played the title role at the **Bowery Theatre** in **Uncle Tom's Cabin** (1850), though generally Rice remained a solo entertainer throughout his career.   DBW

Rice, Tim[othy] (Miles Bindon) (1944–)

British lyricist and author, who teamed up with **Andrew Lloyd Webber** while still at school to write

T. D. Rice as the original Jim Crow, c. 1830.

Joseph and the Amazing Technicolour Dreamcoat, which was eventually seen in London in a professional production in 1968. Rice is a skilful if unconventional lyricist, whose off-rhymes and unusual rhythms contributed to the success of two further Lloyd Webber musicals, *Jesus Christ Superstar* (1970) and *Evita* (1976); but *Blondel* (1983), written with Stephen Oliver, received only a short run at the Aldwych Theatre. *Chess* (1986) with music by Benny Andersson and Björn Ulvacus told a love story against a background of cold-war politics in sport; and like *Evita*, revealed an earnest if somewhat raw world outlook. He has written lyrics for such composers as Paul McCartney and Marvin Hamlisch; and written and edited books on cricket, including the *Lord's Taverners Sticky Wicket Book* (1979). He is also well known in Britain as a TV presenter.   JE

Rich, John (?1682–1761)

English actor and manager. He was the son of Christopher Rich, the unscrupulous manager who had secured the Patent for **Drury Lane Theatre** and, when expelled, took over the **Lincoln's Inn Fields Theatre**. Christopher Rich died before the theatre was ready to reopen but his son inherited the Patent and opened in 1714 with a cast of actors from Drury Lane. In 1716 he began producing pantomimes with extraordinary success, starring himself as **Harlequin**, under the stage-name of John Lun. The tradition of the annual pantomime continued until his death. In 1728 he was persuaded to accept **Gay**'s *The Beggar's Opera* which made 'Gay rich and Rich gay'. In 1730 he raised money by subscription to open a new theatre in **Covent Garden** and he used it intermittently until 1732 when it began to be fully used by his company. Illiterate and with the affectation of never remembering names, he used his business acumen to ensure the commercial profitability and popularity of his theatres.   PH

Richardson, Ian (1934–)

British actor, born and trained in Scotland. His substantial reputation rests on his Shakespearian work. He played Hamlet at **Birmingham Repertory Theatre** in the 1958–9 season, and then, in 1960, went to the Shakespeare Memorial Theatre (later the **RSC**) in Stratford-upon-Avon. For the next 15 years he performed across the range of the repertoire, including Sir Andrew Aguecheek (1960), Oberon (1962), Edmund (in **Peter Brook**'s *King Lear*, 1964), Chorus in *Henry V* (1966), Richard II (1973), Richard III (1973). He also had notable successes in *The Duchess of Malfi* (Count Malatesti, 1960) and **Weiss**'s *Marat/Sade* (1965). He has also worked extensively in film and television, and developed his work as a director of **Shakespeare** and modern classics.   MB

Richardson, John see Richardson's Show

Richardson, Ralph (David) (1902–83)

British actor, who joined the **Birmingham Repertory Company** in 1926 where he made his early reputation, playing the Stranger in **Sophocles**' *Oedipus at Colonus* (1926). In 1930, he joined the **Old Vic** company, where he showed his versatility as an actor in roles which ranged from Caliban in *The Tempest* to Henry V. He was not, however, ideally suited to the major classical parts, having neither the exceptional musicality of

John **Gielgud** nor the dynamic sex appeal of **Laurence Olivier**, his two great contemporaries. Richardson's qualities emerged through his performances in contemporary plays, by **Maugham** (*For Services Rendered*, 1932, and *Sheppey*, 1933) and **J. B. Priestley** (*Eden End* 1934, and *Cornelius*, 1935). As Johnson in Priestley's *Johnson over Jordan* (1939), he gave a memorable performance as a modern Everyman, recollecting at the moment of death the vagaries of his life. Richardson excelled as the ordinary man with a natural decency and even innocence; and his Othello (1938), partnered by Olivier's homosexual Iago, was a notable example of miscasting. He joined the Fleet Air Arm during the war but was invited to lead a revitalized Old Vic company at the New Theatre in 1944. With Olivier, he provided four outstanding Old Vic seasons, in which his personal successes came as Peer Gynt, Falstaff and Inspector Goole in J. B. Priestley's *An Inspector Calls*. He was knighted in 1947, but with Olivier was shabbily treated by the Old Vic governing board in 1948. But his career did not suffer from the uncertainties and sharp changes of direction which characterized that of Olivier. In the 1950s, he continued to play major roles at the Shakespeare Memorial Company, such as Prospero in *The Tempest* (1952) and Volpone, and at the Old Vic as Timon in *Timon of Athens* (1956); while also finding suitable starring roles in contemporary West End successes, such as Cherry in **Robert Bolt**'s *Flowering Cherry* (1957). He was not fully in tune with the new wave of British drama and was notably ill-at-ease in **Joe Orton**'s *What The Butler Saw* (1969); but where the writers were taking notice of his particular skills, he became a fine interpreter. For **William Douglas Home**, he became a latter-day A. E. Matthews, enjoying a bumbling eccentricity in *Lloyd George Knew My Father* (1972) and *The Kingfisher* (1977). With John Gielgud, he starred in **David Storey**'s *Home* (1970) and in **Harold Pinter**'s *No Man's Land* (1975), in which he played the elderly wealthy writer, Hirst, for **Peter Hall**'s **National Theatre** production. As a member of the National Theatre company, he played in *The Wild Duck* and the title role in *John Gabriel Borkman* (1975), but his last major role came as the elder statesman contemplating his political career without much affection in David Storey's *Early Days* (1980). JE

Richardson's Show English fairground theatre most responsible for spreading popular drama beyond London in the early 19th century. A former workhouse boy, itinerant actor and publican, John Richardson (1766–1836) opened his first showbooth at Bartholomew Fair in 1798 with scenery from **Drury Lane** and three blind Scotsmen as musicians. At its zenith, the widely touring show consisted of a large booth with an elevated platform lined at the back in green baize; the interior stage boasted crimson curtains. The attenuated, narrow theatre (100 feet long by 30 feet wide) was said to contain 1,500 lamps and a thousand spectators. The average offering presented an overture, a melodrama (with three murders and a ghost, according to **Dickens**), a pantomime, a comic song and incidental music in the space of 25 minutes. James Barnes the Pantaloon and the young **Edmund Kean** both worked there at one time. Taciturn but charitable Richardson tried to auction off his show in 1826, but owing to low

bids carried on until his death, when it was taken over by Nelson Lee, who finally sold the property in 1853. LS

Richelieu, Armand-Jean du Plessis, Cardinal de (1585–1642) Chief minister of Louis XIII and generous patron of the arts who exerted a strong influence on 17th-century French literature. From the circle of writers and scholars with whom he surrounded himself he formed the Académie-Française in 1634, whose prescribed role as guardian of French language and culture led to the dissemination of their prestige throughout Europe. His patronage extended particularly to the theatre, on which he doted: in 1634 he helped to establish **Montdory**'s company on a permanent footing at the **Marais** and in 1641 was the inspiration behind a royal decree authorizing the legal 'rehabilitation' of professional actors upon certain conditions. He also commissioned a group of five dramatists (Boisrobert, Colletet, **Pierre Corneille**, Claude de l'Estoile and **Rotrou**, all but the last sometime academicians) to write plays at his suggestion and to the greater glory of the French stage, perhaps intending them ultimately for performance in the well-equipped private theatre he built within his palace, later to be known as the **Palais-Royal**. It opened in January 1641 with *Mirame*, a tragicomedy by Desmarets de Saint-Sorlin in which Richelieu himself is reputed to have had a hand. DR

Ridley, George (1835–64) English (Gateshead-born) performer and composer of comic songs, notably 'Blaydon Races', who took to the stage after a serious accident in the pit. In his naturalistically costumed and highly characterized performances he belonged to the new and growing tradition of the music-hall; his penny songbooks, effectively chapbooks (complete with crude woodcut), look back to an older tradition of ballad publication. AEG

Rigg, Diana (1938–) British actress, who joined the Shakespeare Memorial Company in 1959 and remained with the company until 1964, by which time it had become transformed into the **Royal Shakespeare Company**. She became a popular television star through *The Avengers* series in which she played Emma Peel, returning to the stage in 1966 to appear as a memorable Viola in the RSC's *Twelfth Night*. She joined the **National Theatre** in 1972, to appear in **Tom Stoppard**'s *Jumpers* (1972), as Lady Macbeth to Denis Quilley's Macbeth and with particular success in **Molière**'s *The Misanthrope* (1973), updated to the court of de Gaulle's France by Tony Harrison, where she played Célimène to **Alec McCowen**'s Alceste, directed by **John Dexter**. The same Rigg–McCowen–Dexter team appeared in a West End production of *Pygmalion* (1974), while in 1975, she returned to the National Theatre in another Harrison modernization, this time of **Racine**'s *Phèdre, Phaedra Britannica*. A strikingly attractive actress, Rigg excels in roles which bring out her gifts for ironic comedy, usually understressed, revealing a natural gift for timing. In 1978, she starred in Tom Stoppard's play, *Night and Day*. JE

Ringelnatz, Joachim (Hanns Bötticher)
(1883–1934) German poet and cabaret artist, formerly a
sailor, shop clerk and window-dresser before entering
the Munich cabaret Simplicissimus as 'House Poet' in
1909. The hard-featured Bohemian was renowned as a
reciter at Berlin's Schall und Rauch during the 1920s,
performing his poetry, particularly the scurrilous
exploits of the mythical seaman Kuttel Daddeldu. His
style lies somewhere between nonsense verse and
topical satire, and influenced **Brecht**. In 1933 his
performances were declared 'undesirable' by the Nazis
and he died the following year of tuberculosis. LS

Ringwood, Gwen Pharis (1910–84) Canadian
playwright and teacher, born in the USA. She studied
at the University of Alberta where she came under the
influence of noted teacher, Elizabeth Sterling Haynes,
who had studied under Roy Mitchell at **Hart House**.
Her first play, *The Dragon of Kent*, was produced at the
Banff School of Fine Arts in 1935. In 1937 she went to
the USA to study at the University of North Carolina
where she naturally became involved with the Carolina
Playmakers as a writer and actress. Four of her plays
were produced by the Playmakers including her classic,
Still Stands the House (1938). From 1939 she taught
playwriting at the University of Alberta and continued
to write. Her prairie tragedy, *Dark Harvest* (1945), was
produced at the University of Winnipeg. Many of her
plays were based on local history. Her later works
became more socially conscious but still dealt with local
concerns. However, her move to a remote town in
British Columbia in 1953 removed her from the
mainstream of Canadian drama, though she continued
to write and work in community theatre. The theatre in
her town of Williams Lake, BC, was named after her in
1968. JA

Ristori, Adelaide (1822–1906) Italian actress, who
was born to the profession and appeared on the stage at
an early age, entering the major Compagnia Reale
Sarda at the age of 15 and in a few years becoming its
leading actress. In the 1840s she was *prima attrice* to
many of the prominent actor–managers of the day, like
Domeniconi and Coltellini, before retiring for several
years following her marriage to an Italian nobleman.
To this point her reputation had been won largely in
native Italian drama, from **Goldoni**, through **Alfieri**
to contemporary writers and adapters of French plays.
In 1853 she returned to the stage again with the Reale
Sarda, and the mid-fifties saw her established as an
actress of international standing: in 1855 she triumphed
in Paris, benefiting from French critical hostility to the
waning star, **Rachel**: this success she repeated in 1856,
adding Lady Macbeth to her repertoire. In 1857 she
appeared for the first time in London, winning acclaim
for her powerfully 'realistic' interpretation of
Legouvé's Medea and **Shakespeare**'s Lady Macbeth,
notwithstanding that the latter role dominated a much
truncated version of the play. She was now launched on
a long international career as 'star' actress and company
manager, which took her to North and South America,
North Africa and most of Europe. The plays in her
repertoire were likewise international, including
Alfieri's *Mirra*, **Schiller**'s *Maria Stuart*, **Racine**'s *Phèdre*
and **Giacometti**'s *Elisabetta Regina d'Inghilterra*, as well
as the roles of Medea and Lady Macbeth. After first

performing the sleep-walking scene from *Macbeth* in
English as a finale to her London performances of 1873,
in 1882 she undertook the whole part in English with
commendable success for so ambitious a venture
(elsewhere she did the sleep-walking scene in French
and Spanish, as well as in Italian). Her great strength lay
in her combination of classical appearance, pose and
deportment, and acute psychological realism. In common with her younger contemporary, **Tommaso
Salvini**, she studied her parts in depth, developing a
subtle, emotionally powerful characterization through
the accumulation of small but significant detail: her
extant prompt books for the sleep-walking scene show
how meticulous was her working out of moves,
gestures and delivery. Her memoirs and occasional
writings on theatre reveal the seriousness of her
approach to her art, and her comments on the strengths
and weaknesses of her contemporary rivals, like those
for example on **Duse**, are measured and perceptive. KR

Ritchard, Cyril (?1897–1977) Actor and director,
born in Sydney, Australia. He made his debut as a
chorus boy in a Sydney musical in 1917 and went to
America in 1924 to appear in New York in *Puzzles of
1925*. He is best remembered for Captain Hook in *Peter
Pan* (1954) and leading roles in *Visit to a Small Planet*
(1957) and *The Roar of the Greasepaint, the Smell of the
Crowd* (1965). Ritchard directed both for the theatre
and opera and appeared in films. His awards include a
Tony for Captain Hook and two Donaldson Awards
for Hook on television in 1955. SMA

Rites of passage Ritual to celebrate and effect the
transition of an individual from one social position to
the next. Naming ceremonies, puberty rites, weddings
and funerals are typical and virtually universal examples, but occupational rituals such as degree ceremonies
and the transformation of an apprentice into a craftsman are also included. Their structure is invariably
tripartite: the separation of the individual from his/her
existing network of relationships, a liminal period
during which he/she stands outside normality, and
his/her incorporation into a new network of rights and
obligations. AEG

Rittner, Rudolf (1869–1943) German actor. The
naturalistic actor who most completely fulfilled **Otto
Brahm**'s conception of acting. He created many of
Hauptmann's leading roles under Brahm's direction
at the **Freie Bühne**, the **Deutsches Theater**, and the
Lessingtheater in Berlin. He retired in 1907 to take up
farming. SW

Ritual Ever since Jane Ellen Harrison's classic studies
of ancient Greek religion, the relationship between
ritual and theatre, and even the derivation of the latter
from the former, has been one of the keystones of
theatre history and dramatic analysis, and an important
element in certain forms of 20th-century dramatic
practice as diverse as the work of **Grotowski** and
Welfare State. There is undeniably a danger in
pressing the relationship to the point where the two
become synonymous, and in the related process of
treating a relationship of analogy as one of chronological and generic evolution. The latter, all too common in

theatre history, is seen at its clearest in the analysis of folk drama, where every manifestation of traditional working class theatrical activity, especially if rural in provenance, is likely to be seen, not as a phenomenon with its own – possibly quite brief – history, but as a corrupted remnant of an ancient religious or magical act. At the same time, there is lasting value in Harrison's Aristotelian observation that both ritual and drama are 'the things done', which places the emphasis, in both, on the action rather than the agent, and directs our attention to the concrete and actual rather than the metaphysical and putative.

At bottom, both drama and ritual deal with social relationships, and both do so in the most direct way possible, through the enactment of those relationships by living people. God may be held by believers to be present in the wafer and wine; everyone can agree immediately that a priest holding a chalice is present as a focus of attention. Similarly, it may be a matter of endless debate whether or not the spectator in a theatre suspends his/her disbelief, willingly or otherwise, and what exactly that might mean; it is not a matter of debate that an actor representing a murderer mimics the assassination of an actor representing a victim. Further, in both modes, social relationships are given very high definition. As the anthropologist Edmund Leach has observed, the very notion of 'social relationships' is an abstraction; they are not something that can be observed. What we observe are forms of greeting, expressions of deference, gestures of affection. Most of these, if not all of them, are 'ritualistic' in the sense that their form and meaning are culturally determined and inherited, not spontaneously generated. This fact is not altered merely because we take them for granted: one function of cultural determinism is precisely to get things taken for granted. However, even the simplest of routine actions will shift its meaning according to context. In Western cultures, to hold a door open and let somebody pass through is, at its simplest, merely a routine courtesy, and, where total strangers of the same sex and similar age are concerned, who holds the door depends on nothing more significant than who gets there first, or which has the more commitment to good manners. If, however, one is a man and one a woman, whether they are acquainted or not, a different significance is present which derives from a whole bundle of notions about the roles of men and women and which puts on the man a quite strong obligation to hold the door. Finally, if the woman is also the Queen of England, it is virtually unthinkable that the man would not give her precedence. Here, status is involved as well as sex. Both ritual and drama take these routine acts and their contextually determined meanings, the small change of social currency, exaggerate them, stylize them, refine them, and set them into a pattern of expressive sequences of visual and auditory symbols.

There, however, the identity between them stops; the means they have in common are applied to divergent ends. Overlap is likely to remain in practice as well as principle – community theatre companies invoke the notion and structures of communal celebration in framing their performances, and the professional Balinese **shaman** offers his trance-dance as an entertainment for tourists – but ritual and theatre lie at the opposite poles of a functional continuum. While theatre confines itself to saying things about social

relationships, ritual also does things with them; and what it does is to reinforce or change them.

This function, and the distinction between theatre and ritual, is clearly seen in the rite of passage, such as the wedding ceremony. The young woman who dresses in ceremonial clothes to play Hippolyta in the final act of *Midsummer Night's Dream* is clearly an actress representing a bride, and she will do so repeatedly during the run. Enactment is infinitely replicable (and as such is a useful laboratory for the inspection of social relationships). The young woman who dresses in ceremonial clothes on the morning of her wedding day *is* a 'bride', from that moment, and will remain so until she and her 'groom' are pronounced 'man and wife'. Nor, in principle, is her action replicable. The change in status and role which has been effected by the ritual of marriage cannot be reversed. A legal or ecclesiastical nicety may define the ritual itself as having been invalid, thus in effect not to have occurred; otherwise a woman whose husband dies becomes a 'widow', and a woman whose marriage is dissolved becomes a 'divorcée'. No woman who has participated in a valid ritual can revert to the status of 'maiden' or 'spinster'. The linguistic and social embarrassments suffered by the divorced are a powerful indicator of the ritual's ability not merely to describe a change in status and role, but to constitute it. 'With this ring I thee wed' is not a descriptive but a performative utterance. Further, not only the bride and groom are involved in an event which changes their relationship to each other, so, if less radically (and without any necessary accompanying status-change), are their kinsfolk, and even their friends. Not just two individuals but two extended families are conjoined in a relationship not previously existing, and certain obligations will follow (even if they are subsumed in a conveniently symbolic exchange of Christmas cards). Even 'friendship' (that ultimate in voluntary and loosely defined associations) may find itself subject to obligation, as the accidental welding of two individuals into a new social unit necessitates meeting and mixing with acquaintances not of one's own choosing.

The interest of such a ceremony is that it creates new social arrangements in an actual sense (real people are redeployed and redefined within the social network) while reinforcing an existing structure of relationships (a woman is 'given' by one man to another, a 'son' and 'daughter' take on the additional, publicly recognized roles of 'husband and wife', the nature of their new relationship is defined in traditional terms); and that it does this by theatrical means. For it is crucial to the event, and its constitutive power, that there be not merely protagonists and a master of ceremonies, but an audience, whose presence as witnesses ratifies the validity of the ceremony and the specific redeployment that is taking place. Further, just as in the theatre the audience contracts to accept a fiction, so in the wedding ceremony the congregation condones *en masse*, both by its silence and by its vocal participation when called upon, not merely the particular act but a whole framework of values within which it exists. A liberal agnostic wedding congregation witnessing the enactment of a marriage through the English *Book of Common Prayer*, agrees that marriage was ordained for the procreation of children, to be brought up in the fear of the Lord; that it is a permanent and metaphysical state not subject to human dissolution; that a man may endow a woman with all his worldly goods but not vice versa; and so on. Very little of which the average wedding-guest, as an individual, is likely to believe. Yet, as a congregation, whether they suspend their disbelief or not, they silence it, and their silence gives consent. This it is that makes ritual such a powerful conservative force, even while it effects pragmatic change.

Ritual is never an unambiguously progressive force. Its effectiveness depends on the public acceptance of a status quo, whatever the participant's private reservations may be; its symbols, though often complex and diffuse, are never avant-garde (a dual consideration which might give pause to exponents of 'ritual' theatre). The Kwakiutl Indian, Quesalid, who set out to expose witch-doctors as fraudulent and to his surprise achieved fame as a practitioner, did not become a shaman because he was a skilled healer; he became a skilled healer because he was a shaman. His patients were unimpressed when he disclosed the tricks of the trade; they had never taken them wholly seriously anyway. Their concern was that they were ill and he was able to cure them. Prestidigitation with pebbles and bloody feathers was merely a technique through which the end was achieved. Similarly, a Queensland Kanaka who sickens and even dies as a result of a sorcerer's bewitchment does not get ill because a bone has been pointed at him – a merely indicative action – but because he believes in the sorcerer's power to damage him. The effects either way, for healing or harming, are broadly psychosomatic and medical attempts have been made to explain them, with some success. The symbolism is no more than a trigger-mechanism which releases powerful psycho-social forces to work on the organism.

This should not surprise us. For all man's long history of evolving cultural systems which adapt, harness, and even over-ride nature, still men and women are biological organisms and subject to the same internal rhythms as other living things. This is one of the things which life-cycle rituals celebrate, and which the magician can exploit for good or ill. It is a commonplace that rituals are often tied to seasons and cycles whether those of the natural world or of the many sacred and secular calendric calibrations of it; harvest celebrations depending for both their content and their timing on season and weather spring readily to mind, as does, from a calendric point of view, the pre-Lent festival of carnival. But the idea of seasonality is more deeply embedded in culture, and specifically in its ritual expression, than these simple examples show. Annual festivities mark out time as signposts and fences mark out space; their recurrence, usually in a form which changes only slowly and gives the impression of not changing at all, at once lends a comforting air of continuity to human life and reminds participants that their own time is passing. Laid over this inexorable terrestrial rhythm is the changing of the human seasons, the movement from the cradle to the grave celebrated in the life-cycle rituals. The two kinds of seasonality come together in the fact that, although it is in itself no rite of passage, any annual festivity may involve people not previously present (the baby's first Christmas, the first involvement in masquerade of a newly initiated age-grade), and suffer the absence, through death, of former participants. It is important to note here a further distinction between ritual and theatre: whereas the latter almost always sets its action in fictional time, the action of the former always exists in real time, and it is arguable that it would otherwise lose its point.

These, then, are the two axes at whose intersection the ritual act stands: the passage of time, both terrestrial and human, and the cyclic recurrence of crucial biological events within it; and the interplay of the human group through its inevitable losses and replacements and necessary redeployments, as manifest in the actions of ritual protagonists and the bearing witness of, in principle, the whole reference group (or, in practice, enough members of it to constitute an undefined but recognizable quorum). In any given ritual, one axis may be the more strongly marked but the other is there vestigially, and shows a tendency to claim greater prominence even when the immediate function of the ritual seems not to require it.

This is clear in those rituals concerned with the administration of justice. Certain 'ritualistic' elements in court proceedings have often been noticed: the elaborate formal courtesies, the use of a specialized language, the stylization of the presentation of evidence into a **flyting** between 'prosecution' and 'defence', the vital role of the citizenry – as represented by 12 good men and true – in redefining the status of the 'accused', who occupies a liminal position for as long as he or she bears that name. Clearly, the event is structured so as to declare the accused to be or not to be a fit person to retain his or her position in society. Less frequently noted is the element of time. In English courts this is manifest in the partly archaic dress worn by the legal specialists. Just as a priest's vestments give him an identity beyond the personal one, going back in mythological terms to Melchizedek, so the robes and wigs of judge and counsel declare them to be representatives of the Law, an abstract value and an institution whose existence stretches back beyond their birth (and by implication forward beyond their death) and which pre-empts any personal views they may have on the matter in hand. And this is important; for the evidence which counsel presents, and the judgement given by the judge on the basis of the jury's finding, will result in an atomization of the accused's time: to be left untouched if not guilty; if guilty, a series of carefully graduated sentences, up to and including the judgement that on a given day the condemned criminal will have no more time left.

The latter sentence is an extreme example of ritual's ability to manage social time and space; and it is no surprise that, until a growing distaste for public violence and a concern for the discreet management of public order led to their abolition, the public execution was a popular and complex event all over Europe. As Dr Johnson said, in a famous objection to the abolition of public hangings, 'If they do not draw spectators they don't answer their purpose'; and vast crowds flocked to witness the 'morality play' of public justice, in which the crimes of the condemned were re-enacted on his own body, in which public confessions (sometimes in verse) were given from the scaffold (and ballad-sellers distributed their substance at a penny a sheet), and the condemned might be harried beyond death in the ghastly practices of quartering and decapitation. The gibbeted body or the head displayed on a spike would remain as an eerie puppet-like image of the consequences of wickedness. At the same time, the event has a strangely festive air, and not merely because the throngs of spectators, ballad-singers, street-vendors, pick-pockets and colourfully uniformed military made it look a cross between a grand parade and a chartered fair. In 18th-century London, a condemned man would often dress as a bridegroom for his final ride to Tyburn, and, depending on public sentiment concerning himself and his offence, might find himself the recipient of nosegays rather than brickbats. **Gay**'s 'The youth in his cart hath the air of a lord/And we cry, "There dies an Adonis"' was no mere literary conceit. A condemned man might indeed be a hero to a proletarian populace suffering under increasingly draconian property laws; and if, doubtless in most cases, the popular view was more ambiguous than that, still he was a hero in the theatrical sense, and the events of the day the last act of his tragedy. His white-trimmed garments declared him to be about to be wedded to death, and ironically evoked the idea of human seasonality explicit in the rite of passage.

Less extreme in its effect on the individual, but in consequence even clearer as evidence of the force of the ritual imagery, is the widespread juridical ritual of the **charivari**, organized not by the state but by the community, and applied not to criminal offences but to anti-social acts such as sharp practice in trade, marital disharmony, or unsuitable marriages such as that between an old widower and a young virgin. Characteristically the community or its representatives (often the peer-group of young adult males, no doubt encouraged by their elders) would express their disapproval by a procession with rough music (the beating of pans and kettles etc.) to the dwelling of the wrong-doer, usually early in the morning or late at night so as to cause maximum uproar and publicity of the offence, and maximum embarrassment to the offender. In more elaborate forms, the procession would include an effigy of the offender, riding backwards on a donkey or mounted on a pole, which would subsequently be hanged or burned. The offender had two choices: either to correct his or her behaviour, or, if this was impossible (e.g. the old widower) to buy the rough musicians off – effectively a fine or even, in this case, financial compensation for their loss of a potential bride. Either way, re-incorporation into decent society would follow.

Usually a charivari would occur as occasion demanded; but not infrequently we find it associated with seasonal festivities such as 5 November in England (in Horsham, Sussex, the effigy, known as the 'Crispin', would be displayed between 25 October, St Crispin's Day, and Bonfire Night, when it was carried in procession and ceremonially burned on a public bonfire) and, in continental Europe, Carnival. Again, a clear expression of the tendency of ritual to locate social relationships and values in time, as conventionally defined.

To ritual, convention is all. Though a crowd at a public execution may express sympathy with the condemned through floral tributes, that very expression is conventional, even though the sentiment expressed be unorthodox, as far as the State's rulers are concerned. The unconventional act would be to rescue the condemned, or to rescue the corpse before it was mutilated or displayed. Both happened; and both disrupted the ritual as surely as if a wedding guest were to stand up and show just cause. There are rituals which invert status – the common practice of army officers' serving a celebratory dinner to other ranks is a simple case – or turn normal values inside out in a more comprehensive sense – the 12 day Christmas period of Misrule in medieval and early modern Europe springs to mind. But in both examples normality reasserts itself as soon as the defined period of licence comes to an end. Carnival, because more open-ended in its time-span and its expressive activities, and because by definition it involves large numbers of people the worse for drink, has sometimes got out of hand; so that over the six centuries which separate *böse Fastnacht* in Basel from Notting Hill Carnival in the 1970s, participants have tried to make a reality out of the idea of the world turned upside-down. But without exception Lent returns and triumphs; the authorities, temporarily shaken, reassert their control, break a few heads, jail a few ringleaders, and clear the streets of broken glass. And what happens is not revolution, but a reversion to status quo for another year. Misrule may be subversive as an idea; as a practice, there is no evidence that it has ever done other than provide a safety-valve for the pressure on existing arrangements. AEG

See: W. B. Cannon, '"Voodoo" Death', *American Anthropologist*, 44, 1942; M. Foucault, *Discipline and Punish*, London, 1977; M. Gluckman (ed.), *Essays on the Ritual of Social Relations*, Manchester, 1962; E. R. Leach, 'Ritual' in D. Sills (ed.), *International Encyclopedia of the Social Sciences*, Vol. XIII, 1968; R. Rappaport, 'Obvious Aspects of Ritual', *Cambridge Anthropologist*, 1, 1974; A. Smith, *The Seasons*, London, 1970; V. Turner, *The Ritual Process*, London, 1969; A. Van Gennep, *The Rites of Passage*, London, 1960.

Ritz Theatre 219 West 48th St, New York City [Architect: Herbert J. Krapp]. Built by the **Shuberts** in 1921, the Ritz was rushed to completion in 66 days. With slightly under 1,000 seats, it was a frequently booked house during the 1920s and 1930s and was leased by the **Federal Theatre Project** from 1936 to 1939. From 1939 to 1964, it was used as a radio, then television studio. Thereafter, it entered a rocky period when it served as a theatre, a pornographic movie house and massage parlour, and briefly as the Robert F. Kennedy Children's Theatre. In 1983, after a complete renovation, it has returned as a legitimate playhouse owned by the Jujamcyn Organization. MCH

Rivel, Charlie (José Andreu) (1896–1983) Spanish clown, born into an old circus family. In 1929 he won world fame at the London Olympia and the Cirque d'Hiver, Paris, in a parody of Charlie Chaplin on the flying trapeze. At the age of 61, he joined two of his brothers; with the Three Rivels as the traditional 'august' his standard outfit was an ankle-length, sleeveless red jersey, a bald pate, and a square red nose. Like **Grock**, a musical-acrobatic clown of few words, he emitted at regular intervals the cry: 'Akrobat – schööööön!' He inspired some clown dynasties, e.g., the Charlirivels. LS

Riverside Studios (London) Arts centre in Hammersmith, occupying premises beside the Thames which were once television studios belonging to the BBC. It was founded as an independent trust in 1975 with **Peter Gill** as its first artistic director and for ten years, under Gill, Jenny Stein and David Gothard, it was the most adventurous centre of its kind in Britain, bringing over avant-garde companies from abroad (such as **Tadeusz Kantor**'s Cricot 2) and providing a London venue for such British touring companies as Joint Stock. Gill staged several notable productions in the main studio, of *The Changeling*, *The Cherry Orchard* and *Measure for Measure*, but when he moved to the **National Theatre** in 1980, the Riverside Studios came under threat from the local authorities. David Lefeaux joined David Gothard in 1982 and directed several ambitious plays there, including **Eugene O'Neill**'s *A Moon for the Misbegotten*, which transferred to Broadway, but in 1984, their long rearguard campaign to protect the Studios from the twin evils of shortage of funds and interference from the local authorities came to an end with their departures. JE

Rix, Brian (1924–) British actor–manager, under whom the Whitehall Theatre established a reputation for farce between 1950 and 1967 that rivalled the Aldwych farces of the 1930s. The first of these, Colin Morris's *Reluctant Heroes* (previously toured with his own company and with Rix in the lead role), ran for four years, as did *Dry Rot* (1954), which was followed by *Simple Spymen* (1958, both by John Chapman), and by Ray Cooney's *One for the Pot* (1961) and *Chase Me, Comrade* (1964). After a further series of successful farces at the Garrick and Cambridge Theatres, he left the stage for charity work with the mentally handicapped in 1980. CI

Robards, Jason, Jr (1922–) American actor, praised for his rich voice and intense characterizations. He made his debut as Nick in the American Academy of Dramatic Arts production of *Holiday* (1946). His Broadway debut was in D'Oyly Carte's *Mikado* (1947), after which he stage-managed for a time. He attracted considerable attention as Hickey in a now-legendary production of *The Iceman Cometh* (1956) at the **Circle in the Square**. Robards secured his stardom as James Tyrone in *Long Day's Journey into Night* (1956), in which he was noted as 'an actor of tremendous dynamic skill'. Another triumph was as Quentin in **Arthur Miller**'s *After the Fall*, for which critics lauded him as 'brilliant', 'magnificent', and 'beyond praise'. His distinguished film and television career included *Long Day's Journey* and *A Thousand Clowns*, as well as film scripts in which he played various curmudgeons and outcasts. SMA

Robbins, Carrie (1943–) American costume designer. Robbins began her professional career in the late 1960s and has become one of the busiest designers in the theatre. Although she has done contemporary costumes, her best work is detailed, yet theatrical, period costumes such as the 1971 *Beggar's Opera* or lavish operatic ones such as *Samson et Dalila* for the San Francisco Opera which combined a 19th-century sensibility with a biblical epic style. Her work is typified by rich textures and bold lines and her sketches are detailed and almost frenetic – creating a sense of energy and

movement. She has frequently collaborated with set designer Douglas Schmidt, notably on *Grease* and *Frankenstein*. AA

Robbins, Jerome (1918–) American choreographer and director. Trained in the techniques of classical ballet, Robbins joined the American Ballet Theatre in 1940 and danced in several of its programmes. In 1944 he choreographed *Fancy Free*, a ballet with music by **Leonard Bernstein**. Later the same year Robbins repeated his role as choreographer when *Fancy Free* was transformed into the Broadway musical *On the Town*. In 1947 Robbins created a hilarious Keystone Kops ballet for *High Button Shoes* that remains one of the few masterpieces of comic choreography in the American musical theatre. Among his other memorable dances of the period was the 'Small House of Uncle Thomas' ballet for *The King and I* (1951). For the teenage gang members of *West Side Story* (1957), Robbins created a restless, explosive, yet balletic style of movement. He directed and choreographed two other acclaimed musicals: *Gypsy* (1959), and *Fiddler on the Roof* (1964). MK

Robert-Houdin (Jean-Eugène Robert) (1805–71) French conjurer who utterly transformed the performance of magic. Wed to the daughter of a watchmaker named Houdin, he built automata, created surgical and optical instruments and the first pneumatic clock, while privately practising illusionism. In 1845 he gave up watchmaking and opened the Théâtre des soirées fantastiques de Robert-Houdin, in the Palais-Royal, Paris, where for seven years he played to full houses. There he turned what had been a fairground amusement into a salon entertainment by doing away with obvious fakery, macabre decorations and verbose commentary. He is also said to have invented the matinee performance. During the conquest of Algeria, the French government employed him to overawe the rebels and diminish the prestige of the marabouts with his Invincible Man act, in which he seemed impervious to bullets. In 1853 he moved his theatre to the Boulevard des Italiens and retired; the building survived until 1925 when it was demolished. LS

Robertson, Agnes (1833–1916) An English actress who appeared often in the United States and was called 'The Pocket Venus'. Born on Christmas Day in Edinburgh, she made her debut aged ten and later appeared with **Fanny Kemble** and **Macready**, winning some renown as a singer and dancer, being the first to dance the polka in Dublin. **Charles Kean** brought her to London. She shortly thereafter married **Dion Boucicault**, with whom she shared a brilliant career, appearing in many of his scripts, such as *The Colleen Bawn*, *The Octoroon*, and *The Shaughraun*. Four of their children, Dion, Aubrey, Eve, and Nina, were active in the theatre. Robertson was a great favourite of Queen Victoria. SMA

Robertson (Etienne-Gaspard Robert) (1763–1837) French illusionist, the first to present animated projections using the 'fantascope', a magic lantern on wheels (1798). Starting in Paris at the Pavillon de l'échiquier, he moved to a deconsecrated Capuchin monastery (where Franconi's first **Cirque Olympi-**

que would be installed in 1807). There he terrified audiences with 'supernatural' evocations of François Villon, William Tell, **Voltaire**, **Rousseau** and Marat who seemed to approach and withdraw. The atmosphere was thickened by fake bats, clouds forming on the ceiling and performers in white sheets and masks surging through the hall lit by hidden lamps. Shadow-puppet techniques allowed Robertson to give the illusion of legs moving and other rudimentary actions.   LS

Robertson, T[homas] W[illiam] (1829–71) English playwright, the eldest of 22 children born into a family of provincial actors. Robertson travelled the Lincoln circuit with his parents and siblings, acting, writing and making himself useful about the stage. He was 16 when *The Chevalier de St George* (1845) was staged at the **Princess's** in London, to be followed by *Noémie* (1846), both adaptations from the French, but this gives a misleading impression of precocious success. It was by drudgery and industry that Robertson made his scanty living in London after the collapse of his uncle's Lincoln-based company in 1848–9. Until 1864, when the personality-actor, **E. A. Sothern**, chanced to select the previously unperformed *David Garrick*, a perfunctory adaptation from the French, for performance at the **Haymarket**, Robertson was known, if known at all, as a journalist, prolific contributor to, among many other journals, the *Illustrated Times*, which housed the bitter comedy of his gallery of 'Theatrical Types', and *Fun*. After prolonged struggles as a bit-player, prompter and stage manager, during which **Samuel Phelps** and **Madame Vestris** were among his employers, he had retired from the theatre in c. 1859. It was probably Robertson's friend, the playwright **H. J. Byron**, who persuaded **Marie Wilton** to stage *Society* (1865) at the **Prince of Wales's**, where her adventurous management had just begun. The content of *Society* would have been familiar enough to contemporary theatregoers, but the detail of its conduct, under Robertson's own meticulous supervision, had the freshness of revelation. The production saw the birth of what came to be known as 'cup-and-saucer drama', the faithful-seeming reproduction on stage of the indoor customs of Victorian England. It is, by any reckoning, extraordinary that a playwright as conventional and intellectually drab as Robertson was should have had so radical an influence on the English theatre, and some credit must be given to the innovative ensemble playing of the company, but it was Robertson who perceived the potential purchase on the public imagination of a style of writing and acting that would replace the blatantly theatrical with the persuasively accurate. The making of a roly-poly pudding in *Ours* (1866), immediate successor to *Society* at the Prince of Wales's, is a brilliant domestic adaptation of the melodramatic sensation scene supremely exploited by Robertson's chief rival among mid-century playwrights, **Boucicault**. The tea-and-sandwiches of Act I of *Caste* (1867) are a comic *tour de force* in the genre. In his brief remaining lifetime, Robertson never matched *Caste*, though *Play* (1868), particularly *School* (1869) and *M.P.* (1870) all had successful runs at the Prince of Wales's, and Robertson's modest innovations admitted a new realism to the writing and acting of plays in the last decades of the 19th century. Historians of early

20th-century theatre, whilst celebrating **Shaw**, **Craig** and the **Royal Court** seasons of 1904–7, have overlooked the remarkable summer season of 1910, when the impresario Robert Arthur staged eight of Robertson's comedies in repertoire at the Coronet Theatre, Notting Hill.   PT

Robeson, Paul (1898–1976) Afro-American actor. A Columbia Law School graduate, Robeson opted for a stage career and gained prominence in 1924 when he appeared in the **Provincetown Players**' revival of *The Emperor Jones* and as Jim Harris, the black lawyer who marries white in **O'Neill**'s controversial play, *All God's Chillun Got Wings*. Robeson took the lead in *Black Boy* (1926), played Crown in *Porgy and Bess* (1927), and was Joe in the London performance of *Show Boat* (1928) in which he sang 'Ol' Man River', the song he refashioned into a life-long protest against oppression. With a commanding physique, deep, resonant voice, and humane spirit, Robeson was a magnificent Othello, a role he played three times: in London (1930), in New York for a record-breaking run (1943), and at Stratford-upon-Avon (1959). He was also renowned as a concert artist and film actor. Robeson's outspoken opposition to racial discrimination, his embrace of leftist causes world-wide and his communist sympathies led to professional ostracism at home and the withdrawal of his passport. In failing health, he retired from public life in the 1960s. His life was dramatized in the 1978 monodrama *Paul Robeson* by Philip Hayes Dean.   EGH

Robey, George (George Wade) (1869–1954) 'the Prime Minister of Mirth'. English comedian, London-born son of a civil engineer, he spent his teens in Germany, and attended the universities of Leipzig and

Paul Robeson in the title role of O'Neill's *The Emperor Jones*, 1939.

Cambridge, though he came away from both without a degree. When family difficulties forced him to leave Cambridge, he worked on the construction of Birmingham's cable tramway, and began to appear at the city's smoking concerts. His rise to stardom was rapid: a first London appearance in April 1891, at a minor hall, was followed by his West End debut at the Oxford in June of the same year; by the end of 1892 he was top of the bill and there he stayed through a long and varied career in music-hall, variety, pantomime, revue, operetta and musical comedy. At the age of 66 he tried his hand at **Shakespeare**, appearing to critical acclaim (including **Laurence Olivier**'s) as Falstaff in *Henry IV, Part 1* at **His Majesty's**. In addition to live theatre, he worked extensively in radio and television, played Sancho Panza opposite Chaliapin in Pabst's 1932 film of *Don Quixote*, and made a brief retrospective appearance as the dying Falstaff in Olivier's film of *Henry V*. He was still touring in musical comedy at the age of 82.

His solo work pursued two music-hall traditions: that of the buffo vocalist's unchanging persona (though for the classic frock-coat Robey substituted a simple black costume suggesting rather than representing the clerical, with bowler hat and swish cane); and the newer mode, associated with **Dan Leno** and **Jenny Hill**, of character-monologue and patter-song, in which he ranged widely from the Prehistoric Man to contemporary figures such as the District Nurse.

Fundamentally a high-status comedian, he employed an orotund but crystal-clear middle class diction, eschewed the egalitarian matiness of a **Chirgwin** and the low-status bashfulness of **Jack Pleasants**, and constantly ordered his audience to 'desist' from laughing – an injunction utterly undermined by his exaggerated air of dignity, his mobile face, and his famous raised eyebrows.

His superb handling of a song, his impeccable diction and timing, and his ability to lend dignity to cheap material, are manifest in the well-known recording, with Violet Loraine, of 'If you were the only Girl in the World'.   AEG

Robin, Henri (Henrik Joseph Donckel) (1811–74) Dutch illusionist.

As early as 1847, he displayed a 'Living Phantasmagoria' in Paris, using the plate-glass principle to conjure up phantoms which he fought; this well-established trick later prevented **'Pepper's Ghost'** from getting a French patent. Robin performed in England 1850–3 (with a command performance at Windsor Castle) and in 1861 gave the first full evening's show of magic at the Egyptian Hall, London. He managed his own theatre in the Boulevard du Temple successfully 1862–9. His famous illusion here was 'The Medium of Inkerman', a drum on a tripod which, allegedly beaten by the spirit of a slain drummer, tapped out answers to questions from the audience.   LS

Robin Hood plays Popular dramatizations of episodes from the life of the great English outlaw, related to and possibly derived from ballads about him, and associated with May Games. Allusions to the playing of Robin Hood exist in the 15th and 16th centuries, and two (possibly three) texts are extant, 'Robin Hood and the Friar' (c. 1560), which may be an amalgamation of two plays, and the fragmentary 'Robin Hood and the

Sheriff' (c. 1475). References cease at the end of the 16th century: later 'Robin Hood plays' are ecotypes of the **Hero-Combat**.   AEG

Robinson, Bill (1878–1949) American dancer and singer. After many years as a star of vaudeville, Robinson made his musical theatre debut in *Blackbirds of 1928*, where his seemingly effortless tap dancing helped the show become a hit. Robinson was next seen in *Brown Buddies* (1930), *Blackbirds of 1933*, and *The Hot Mikado* (1939), a jazz version of the **Gilbert** and Sullivan classic. Unlike the 1920s, when a number of black musicals had been successful on Broadway, the shows of the 1930s were unable to garner long runs, even when featuring popular stars like Bill Robinson. In the 1940s, he appeared in two other failures, *All in Fun* (1940) and *Memphis Bound!* (1945), the last a jazz adaptation of Gilbert and Sullivan's *HMS Pinafore*. Although few of Robinson's shows were big successes, his performances were uniformly praised for the matchless ease and grace of his tap dancing.   MK

Robinson, (Esmé Stuart) Lennox (1886–1958) Irish playwright. The year after his first play – *The Clancy Name* (1908), a gloomy exercise in the 'Cork realist' manner – Robinson became the **Abbey**'s playdirector. Disagreements with **Lady Gregory** and an unprofitable American tour led to his resignation in 1914. Reappointed in 1919, he founded the **Dublin Drama League**, and was the Abbey's main playdirector until 1934, when **Hugh Hunt** succeeded him. Joining the Abbey Board of Directors in 1923, he remained until his death.

Robinson was a skilful, at times a facile, craftsman. His early plays are unremittingly cheerless, as he acknowledged: *Harvest* (1910) manages to turn a situation promising comic development into bitter despair. His talent was in fact for satiric comedy, as he demonstrated in *The Whiteheaded Boy* (1916) and *Drama at Inish* (1934). Yet he ranged widely: *The Big House* (1926) movingly chronicles the fortunes of an Ascendancy family; *Church Street* (1934) draws effectively on **Pirandello**, as a young Irish dramatist invents plots for his family's lives.

Though much criticized in the 1940s and 50s for the Abbey's doldrums, Robinson served the theatre well, as administrator and one of its liveliest writers.   DM

Robinson, Richard (c. 1598–1648) English actor, one of the few known to have made a successful transition from boy to adult in the Jacobean theatre. Robinson may have been apprenticed to **Richard Burbage**, whose widow he married, when he first appeared with the King's Men in c. 1611. In that year he played the Lady in *The Second Maiden's Tragedy* and possibly Fulvia in **Jonson**'s *Catiline*. Jonson praises his female impersonation in *The Devil Is an Ass* (1616), but he had probably by then graduated to male roles. He is known to have played the Cardinal in a revival of **Webster**'s *The Duchess of Malfi* and to have remained with the King's Men until the closure of the theatres in 1642.   PT

Robson, Flora (1902–84) British actress. A consistently fine actress who – whilst never dominating the great female roles – was always offering sensitive, witty and intelligent portrayals in a wide range of styles. For the **Old Vic** in 1933 she played Gwendoline in **Wilde**'s *The Importance of Being Earnest* and over 30 years later, in 1968, played Miss Prism in the same play in London's West End. She worked extensively in America (including Hollywood), playing Lady Macbeth in New York in 1948, a part she had previously played in 1933. Her Shakespearian roles were few, but for **John Gielgud**'s production of *The Winter's Tale* (1951) she created what many critics describe as her best performance, typically in a 'supporting' role, Paulina. Her full list of credits is impressive and her status in the British theatre was confirmed when she was made a Dame of the British Empire in 1960. She effectively retired from the stage in 1969.   MB

Robson, Frederick (1821–64) English actor, born Thomas Brownbill, whose years at the **Olympic** (1853–63) were among the most astonishing success stories of the 19th-century theatre. Robson was only five feet tall and had no choice but to make his lack of inches a feature. **J. R. Planché**, for example, wrote for him the title role of Gam-Bogie in *The Yellow Dwarf* (1854), exploiting both his diminutiveness and his unrivalled ability to combine comedy and terror. It was Robson's sudden transitions from hilarity to horror that delighted Olympic audiences. **Tom Taylor** provided him with an ideal vehicle in *A Blighted Being* (1854) as the suicidal Job Wort, who swallows what he believes to be poison and only then discovers, to his consternation, that he is in love and enjoying life. Playing for laughs at first, Robson would suddenly silence spectators by betraying Job Wort's anguish. This trick of grounding extravagant comedy on a base of pathos was Robson's source of power, but it had discomforting parallels in his private life. Having trained as an engraver, he had made his first theatrical appearances (1842–4) as a singer of comic songs, and was a regular performer at the Grecian from 1844–50 before 'coming out' as an actor in Dublin in 1850. It was his singing of 'Vilikens and his Dinah' in the character of Jem Bags in Henry Mayhew's revived *The Wandering Minstrel* that turned him into a star at the Olympic in 1853. Until then, he had been considered a burlesque actor merely – a comically inappropriate Macbeth and an exaggeratedly Jewish Shylock in Talfourd's travesties (1853). From early on, and increasingly, acting was an ordeal for Robson, and he drank to give himself courage. Critics frequently alluded to the Dickensian quirkiness of his character creations, but Robson was more like the dying clown of *Pickwick Papers* than they knew.   PT

Robson, Stuart (Henry Robson Stuart) (1836–1903) American actor. He made his stage debut as Horace Courtney in *Uncle Tom's Cabin as It Is*, a dramatic retort to **Uncle Tom's Cabin**, at the Baltimore Museum in 1852. Subsequently he appeared with numerous stock companies, including those of **Laura Keene**'s Theatre in New York, **Mrs John Drew**'s Theatre in Philadelphia, and the Globe Theatre in Boston. From 1877 until 1889, he teamed with **W. H. Crane** starring in such farces as *Our Bachelors*, and *Our Boarding House*, but also in *A Comedy of Errors*, as the two Dromios, and *The Merry Wives of Windsor*, as Falstaff (Crane) and Slender (Robson). **Bronson**

Howard's *The Henrietta* was especially written for them. After 1890, Robson starred on his own, most notably as Tony Lumpkin in *She Stoops to Conquer*.   DJW

Rodgers, Richard (1902–79) American composer. After studying music and writing scores for amateur musicals, Rodgers teamed up with lyricist **Lorenz Hart** in 1919. Their songs were heard in *A Lonely Romeo* (1920) and *Poor Little Ritz Girl* (1920). After their first successful score for *The Garrick Gaieties* (1925), they created an almost unbroken stream of hit musicals, including *Dearest Enemy* (1925), *The Girl Friend* (1926), *Peggy-Ann* (1926), and *A Connecticut Yankee* (1927). In the early 1930s Rodgers and Hart wrote the songs for several Hollywood musical films, then returned to Broadway to create some of the most popular scores of the late 1930s and early 1940s, including *Jumbo* (1935), *On Your Toes* (1936), *Babes in Arms* (1937), *I'd Rather Be Right* (1937), *I Married an Angel* (1938), *The Boys from Syracuse* (1938), *Too Many Girls* (1939), and *By Jupiter* (1942). *Pal Joey* (1940), a musical chronicling the adventures of an amoral nightclub owner, was initially unpopular with critics and audiences, but more successful in its 1952 revival.

In 1943 Rodgers initiated his partnership with lyricist-librettist **Oscar Hammerstein II**. Their first show was *Oklahoma!*, one of the most popular and influential of all American musicals. The Rodgers–Hammerstein partnership was responsible for some of the longest running shows of the 1940s and 1950s, including *Flower Drum Song* (1958), and *The Sound of Music* (1959). Their shows were noted for the care with which music and dance were integrated with the libretto.

After Hammerstein's death in 1960, Rodgers served as his own lyricist for *No Strings* (1962), then collaborated with other lyricists on *Do I Hear a Waltz?* (1965), *Two by Two* (1970), *Rex* (1976), and *I Remember Mama* (1979). His autobiography, *Musical Stages*, was published in 1975.

Early in his career Rodgers composed bouncy, jazz-influenced music that complemented the clever lyrics of Lorenz Hart. After demonstrating that he could compose on a grander, more sweeping scale with the 'Slaughter on Tenth Avenue' ballet for *On Your Toes*, Rodgers wrote dramatic, emotionally expansive scores for his 'musical plays' of the 1940s and 50s.   MK

Rodrigues, Nelson (1912–81) Brazilian playwright. Known for sensational and provocative topics, his first major success, *O vestido de noiva* (*Wedding Gown*) in 1942, was the play that marked the renovation of the contemporary Brazilian theatre through an ingenious staging by Zbigniew Ziembinski, a Polish émigré director whose knowledge of European vanguard expressionistic staging enabled him to capture the three levels of a complex play. His plays often range through taboo topics such as incest, homosexuality and adultery, with melodramatic treatments, seen in *Album de família* (*Family Album*), *Anjo negro* (*Black Angel*), *Toda desnudez será castigada* (*Nudity will be Punished*) and *O beijo no asfalto* (*Kiss on the Pavement*). Now Brazil's most widely staged playwright, the 1981 production of *O eterno retorno* (*The Eternal Return*) by Antunes Filho triggered a resurgence of interest in professional productions of his works. GW

Rogers, Will (William Penn Adair Rogers)

(1879–1935) This warm, gum-chewing American folk hero began in **Wild West** shows billed as 'The Cherokee Kid, the wonderful Lasso-Artist', making $20 a week. At the St Louis World's Fair in 1904 he dazzled audiences by circling a horse and rider with a lasso in each hand. He made his first appearance in New York in 1905 with a trick roping and riding company (Madison Square Garden) and gradually evolved his technique of commenting drolly on current events in his slow Oklahoma drawl while he played with his lariat. His stage personality, which used no makeup or comic properties, was basically an extension of his own, winning the audience's trust and affection. Rogers appeared in musicals, the *Ziegfeld Follies* of 1916, 1917, 1918, 1922 and 1924, on the vaudeville stage and in 24 films. In 1934, he played the father in **O'Neill**'s *Ah, Wilderness!*, and the next year was lost flying over Alaska with the aviator Wiley Post. LS

Rojas Zorrilla, Francisco de

(1607–48) Spanish playwright of the School of **Calderón**. Born in Toledo, he lived in Madrid from 1610 apart from studies at Salamanca. He was admitted to the Order of Santiago in 1645. Of more than 80 plays ascribed to him only about 30 are certainly his, including comedies, serious plays and Senecan revenge tragedies.

His best known play is *Del rey abajo ninguno* (*None but the King*, published 1650), on the dilemma of a peasant who believes that the king, on whom he cannot avenge himself, is attempting to seduce his wife. In *Cada cual lo que le toca* (*To Each His Just Deserts*), a woman raped before marriage restores her husband's honour by killing the attacker herself – a solution which aroused the hostility of the contemporary audience. The Senecan tragedies include *Morir pensando matar* (*Killers Turned Victims*) (published 1642) and *Lucrecia y Tarquino* on the Rape of Lucretia.

His comedies have received less attention though they are considered superior by some critics. They include the *comedia de figurón Entre bobos anda el juego* (*A Fool's Game*, 1638) and *capa y espada* plays. CL

Rolland, Romain

(1866–1944) French novelist and playwright, he was one of the first to advocate *le théâtre populaire*. His essay on *Le Théâtre du Peuple* (1903) was a major reference point for subsequent practitioners and he also attempted to put theory into practice with plays about the French Revolution, notably *Danton* (1900) and *Le 14 juillet* (1902). But these melodramatic and rather worthy dramas did not have the same force as *Le Théâtre du Peuple*. DB

Romains, Jules

(1885–1972) French novelist and playwright, influenced by unanimism, but whose most important plays were social satires on the theme of imposture, propaganda and trickery. His unanimist play *Crommedeyre le Vieil* (*Old Crommedeyre*) was produced by **Copeau** in 1920 but **Jouvet** acted and produced his most successful play *Dr Knock ou le Triomphe de la Médicine* (*Dr Knock or the Triumph of Medicine*) in 1923, a comedy satirizing the mystificatory tendencies of medicine with a verve that recalls **Molière**. He also adapted **Jonson**'s *Volpone* (from Stefan Zweig's version), one of **Dullin**'s major successes, and wrote a series of plays based on a self-important Professor Le Trouhadec, the first of which were also produced by Jouvet. DB

Roman theatres and amphitheatres

(see also **Theatre buildings**) The earliest Roman theatres were temporary wooden constructions, erected when needed at the different sites of the various festivals. The scenic resources required by the plays of **Plautus** and **Terence** are very simple: the stage has merely to be backed by a building with up to three doors, representing entrances to different houses. Plautus' *Amphitruo* shows that it was possible to climb to the roof of the building. Similar resources were presumably used in tragedy and farce.

The first stone theatre at Rome was the Theatre of Pompey, opened in 55 BC. Others followed in the time of Augustus, and under the emperors theatres became widespread throughout most of the Empire. Those which survive are among the most impressive of all Roman monuments; there are particularly well-preserved examples at Aspendus in Turkey, Orange in France, and Sabratha and Leptis Magna in North Africa. It comes as a disappointment to realize that all these were built at a time when comedy and tragedy had been largely replaced by mime and pantomime; indeed there is no proof that any surviving Roman play was ever performed in any surviving theatre. Often the theatres must have been used merely for public assemblies or (in place of amphitheatres) for gladiatorial contests and wild-beast shows; one writer complains that even the Theatre of Dionysus at Athens has been subjected to this indignity.

In a Roman theatre the *scaena* (scene-building) rises to the full height of the *cavea* (seating) or higher, and is integrally connected to it. Thus the *parodoi* leading to the *orchēstra* from outside consist of vaulted passages. While Greek theatres had to be built against hillsides, the engineering skills of the Romans enabled them to build free-standing theatres on level ground. The stone-floored *orchēstra*, no longer used for dancing, was reduced to a small semicircle, and might be occupied by additional seating. The wood-floored stage was broader, deeper and lower than that of Hellenistic Greece. Behind it rose the imposing facade, the *scaenae frons*, richly ornamented with pillars, niches and statues.

The theatre at Aspendus, Turkey.

The interior of the Colosseum, Rome.

A stage curtain was commonly used. Though the evidence is confusing, it appears that the normal arrangement was to lower the curtain for the duration of the performance, storing it in a slot at the front of the stage, and to raise it at the end. There might be a roof over the stage, and an awning might be spread over the entire theatre. Small theatres, called odea, were completely roofed, and were housed in rectangular buildings.

Vitruvius, an architectural writer of the Augustan period, gives instructions for the design of a Roman theatre, distinguishing it from the Greek type. These instructions were closely studied by **Palladio** and other theatre-builders of the Renaissance. He also describes painted scenery, with perspective effects, for tragedy, comedy and satyr play (see **Greece, ancient**). Certain wall-paintings in houses at Pompeii and Boscoreale may be inspired by scenery of the same kind. Vitruvius and the later Greek writer Pollux describe various scenic devices such as *periaktoi* – prism-shaped wooden constructions painted with three different scenes, any one of which could be turned to face the audience. It is unclear, however, in what theatres these were actually used.

Amphitheatres were used for gladiatorial contests and wild-beast fights, and some could be flooded to accommodate mock sea-battles. They consisted of an oval arena (beneath which there might be concealed pits to house equipment and animals) completely surrounded by seating. Thus, as the name implies, the shape was roughly that of two theatres facing each other (but the story that there once existed two theatres which could *actually* be combined to form an amphitheatre is surely fictional). Greatest of all was the Flavian Amphi-

theatre or Colosseum at Rome, which was built in the first century AD and could seat about 45,000 spectators.   ALB

> *See*: W. Beare, *The Roman Stage*, 3rd edn, London, 1964; M. Bieber, *The History of the Greek and Roman Theater*, 2nd edn, Princeton, 1961.

Romans Town on the Isère, 50 miles west of Grenoble, which provides our best documented example of a carnival which became assimilated to social conflict, and ended in bloodshed. In 1580, against a complex background of economic and political tensions, the town's patricians and plebeians mobilized the traditional carnival societies as paramilitary power-bases, and transformed the processions into political demonstrations. In what they afterwards represented as a pre-emptive strike, on the evening of *lundi gras* the bourgeois party murdered the moderate craftsmen's leader, Jean Serve (whose worst proven offence was to sit in Council wearing a zoomorphic costume), and arrested and hanged the 'ringleaders' of an alleged popular uprising. The intricate behaviour of both parties before the masks came off and the weapons out shows clearly that, under the *ancien régime* at least, symbolism may be disingenuous but is rarely innocent.   AEG

Rome

1 Origins of drama Patriotic Romans such as Livy and **Horace** liked to claim that Rome possessed an indigenous dramatic tradition, which had developed from certain religious ceremonies and from the ritual abuse ('Fescennine verses') which accompanied them. It is difficult, however, to relate these claims to the types of drama actually known to have existed in Republican times. Certainly the festivals of the Roman calendar, at which aristocratic magistrates vied with each other to finance shows that would win the favour of the electorate, provided good opportunities for drama to develop and flourish. From an early date, however, Rome was in contact with the Greek colonies of southern Italy, and these colonies (notably Tarentum) had a thriving tradition of drama, both literary and sub-literary. And even the most popular and informal types of drama at Rome seem to have had non-Roman origins.

These types were the mime and the Atellan farce, both of which were established at Rome by the late 3rd century BC. The mime was a Romanized version of a widespread Greek form (see **Greece, ancient**) – a vulgar, often improvised low-life episode performed by a small group of unmasked actors. The Atellan farce (*fabula Atellana*) was believed to be an import from the Oscan town of Atellae in Campania, which would itself have had close connections with the Greek colonies. It was a boisterous entertainment performed by a stock troupe of masked clowns – Maccus, Pappus, Bucco, Dossenus and others – somewhat reminiscent of the **commedia dell'arte**.

Literary drama at Rome probably dates from 240 BC, when the Romanized Greek Livius **Andronicus** first produced a Latin adaptation of a Greek play at the Ludi Romani (one of the annual festivals). Such adaptations became popular, and the conventions of Roman drama were quickly established. Andronicus and his immediate successors, Naevius and **Ennius**, differed from the Greek dramatists in writing both tragedy and comedy, as well as non-dramatic works.

2 Tragedy, historical drama and pantomime We possess only fragments and play-titles from the work of the great tragedians of the Roman Republic – the 3rd-century pioneers Andronicus and Gnaeus Naevius, and the 2nd-century classics Quintus Ennius, Marcus Pacuvius and Lucius Accius. Tragedies were almost always based on Greek originals, though Accius may occasionally have taken his material direct from epic poetry, showing the same degree of originality as the Greek tragedians themselves. The plays of **Euripides** were especially favoured as models, and there was a general preference for warlike and melodramatic themes. The interest in the supernatural (ghosts, dreams and portents) and in madness, which is prominent in **Seneca**, can be traced back to this period. Though the Greek mythical settings were retained, the values expressed and celebrated – courage, endurance and piety, especially in the service of the state – were distinctively Roman; and Stoic philosophy became influential at an early date. Above all, Roman tragedy was strongly rhetorical, and increasingly so as it developed; and the rhetoric, clothed in elaborately ornate diction, seems to have aimed more at solemn grandeur than at the intellectual stimulation and provocation found in the best work of Euripides.

The metre of spoken dialogue, the iambic senarius, was adapted from the main dialogue metre of Greek tragedy, but was less strict. Large sections of the actors' parts, however, were sung, chanted or declaimed to the accompaniment of the pipe or *tibia* (the Greek *aulos*). The Chorus was retained, but no attempt was made to imitate the complex metres of Greek choral songs.

From the time of Naevius onward, the tragedians occasionally wrote plays on subjects from Roman history, whether legendary or recent. These *fabulae praetextae* (plays performed in the *toga praetexta*, the bordered toga of Roman magistrates) had a precedent in Greek historical tragedies such as **Aeschylus'** *Persians*, but the plots naturally had to be freely invented by the Roman dramatists.

In the 1st century BC, revivals of existing Latin tragedies continued to be popular, but we hear less of the composition of new works for the stage – perhaps largely because the subjects which appealed to Roman taste had already been treated. At the same time poets started to write tragedies merely as literary exercises, intended for declamation (like other Roman poetry), not for staged performance. The *Thyestes* of Varius Rufus, performed in 29 BC, is the last tragedy known to have been produced on stage; the *Medea* of Ovid (43 BC to AD 17) was evidently not produced. By the time of Seneca the stage was regarded with contempt by respectable Romans, but the word 'tragedy' had a lofty sound and the form was one in which the contemporary taste for blood, rhetoric and melodrama could be indulged to the full.

One reason for the decline of staged tragedy was doubtless the rise of the pantomime, which was introduced in the reign of Augustus. This was a performance in dumb-show by a masked dancer (the *pantomimus* himself) to the accompaniment of a kind of cantata sung by a chorus. The subject was normally taken from Greek myth, but the libretto was unimportant; what mattered was the grace of the dancer and his skill in mimicking the actions described. Sometimes the *pantomimus* used more than one mask in the course of his performance, and sometimes two or more *pantomimi* might perform together. This curious form of entertainment was despised by the best-educated Romans, but remained extremely popular as long as the Western Empire lasted, and survived in the East well into the Byzantine period. We also hear of performances by solo singers (including the Emperor Nero) on tragic themes; references to 'tragedies' acted in late Imperial and Byzantine times probably mean performances of this type.

3 Comedy, farce and mime The most admired writers of Roman comedy were **Plautus**, Caecilius Statius and **Terence**. Like Livius Andronicus, Naevius and Ennius, they adapted their plays from the New Comedy of 4th-century and 3rd-century Greece (unless Plautus' *Amphitruo* is adapted from Middle Comedy). The characters' names and the nominal settings were Greek, and comedies of this kind are known as *fabulae palliatae*, plays performed in the *pallium* or Greek cloak. The action usually takes place in a city street, and always in front of one, two or three houses, each with a visible door.

The Greek plots were handled with considerable freedom, although the *kind* of freedom varied from one dramatist to another. The complexity of the intrigue was often increased by Terence, often reduced or casually treated by Plautus. The Chorus, already vestigial in **Menander**, was dropped altogether (though a trace remains in Plautus' *Rudens*). This meant that the action of each play was continuous, and, while the act-divisions of the Greek originals are sometimes easy to detect, they are sometimes concealed (the act-divisions in our texts are an editorial addition). Those Greek institutions and customs which would have puzzled the Roman audience are either Romanized (especially in Plautus) or played down (especially in Terence). The Prologue may serve to advertise the coming play as well as (Plautus), or instead of (Terence), setting the scene. The practice of adding scenes or characters from one Greek original to a play mainly based on another is particularly associated with Terence, but he himself claims (in the Prologue to *Andria*) to have precedents for this in the work of Naevius, Plautus and Ennius. Plautus constantly enlivens his plays with jokes, puns, topical allusions, audience address, and vulgarities of various kinds (but not political satire, which was restricted by libel laws, and for which Naevius had been prosecuted). These elements, however, were perhaps reduced by Caecilius, and certainly much reduced by Terence.

The verse-forms are much more varied than those of Greek New Comedy, and similar to those of Roman tragedy, showing that large sections of each play were accompanied on the *tibia*. The accompanied passages are usually referred to as 'recitative' (blocks of a single iambic or trochaic metre) or 'song' (in varied metres), though the actual modes of delivery are uncertain. Even the 'songs' (which are rare in Terence) are not divided into stanzas, and contribute to the action in much the same way as 'recitative' and unaccompanied dialogue.

The writing of *palliatae* continued for a time after the death of Terence, but came to an end with the work of Sextus Turpilius, who died in 103 BC. Revivals of the old plays remained popular in Cicero's day (mid-1st century BC), but are not heard of thereafter.

The increased refinement and Hellenization of the *palliata* at the hands of Terence left room for a more popular form of comedy that would inherit the more boisterous and Roman side of Plautus' work. Hence, probably, the *fabula togata*, or drama in Roman dress, of Titinius, Afranius and Atta. This was set among the lower classes in Italian towns, but otherwise the fragments suggest that the plays resembled Plautus', with much vulgar abuse between the characters and with plot-motifs of love, intrigue and misunderstanding borrowed from the *palliata*. The writing of *togatae* seems to have come to an end with Atta, who is said to have died in 77 BC, though we hear of later revivals.

In the late Republican period attempts were made to give literary form to the Atellan farce and the mime. Atellans were written in the early 1st century BC by Pomponius and Novius, and mimes were written rather later by Decimus Laberius and Publilius Syrus. Both forms seem to have been used as tailpieces after more serious plays. The authors borrowed verse-forms, and perhaps plot-motifs, from the *palliata*, but the plays evidently retained the crude and simple character of their subliterary prototypes. Atellan titles such as *Maccus as Soldier*, *Bucco as Gladiator*, *The Pig*, *The Farmer*, show how the stock troupe of clowns could be put to various uses, and evoke the plays' homely and rustic settings. Adultery was a frequent theme of the mime, which by now employed actresses

as well as male actors; and mime-actors might also indulge in ribald political satire, which could not be risked in respectable types of drama.

Though the literary farce and mime were short-lived, their improvised counterparts continued. Atellans survived until the 1st century AD, while the mime survived into and through the Byzantine period, persisting even after Justinian's official closing of the theatres in the 6th century. Its vulgarity was constantly denounced by moralists, especially after the rise of Christianity, and no doubt many mimes consisted simply of pornography, but the type was too informal and popular to be suppressed.

4 Shows and spectacles From the earliest times the Romans used shows of various kinds to mark the annual religious festivals, as well as special events such as triumphs and important funerals. Dancing, acrobatics and gymnastic contests must always have existed, but in 264 BC such harmless entertainments were supplemented by the introduction of gladiatorial fights from Etruria. Gladiators were prisoners, condemned criminals or otherwise desperate men, who, having nothing to lose, were prepared to fight to the death in the hope of winning fame and popularity if they survived. Various kind of specialized equipment were used to lend variety and excitement to the spectacle. As early as Terence we read (in the prologues to *Hecyra*) of audiences being distracted from watching comedy by the rival attractions of tightrope-walkers, boxers and gladiators.

By the end of the Republic the main types of spectacle were well established: the gladiatorial fight, the wild-beast show (all manner of exotic animals being pitted against men or against each other), the mock sea-battle and the chariot race. As the population of Rome grew, as wealth flowed in from wars of conquest and an expanding empire, and as struggles for power among the nobility grew more and more desperate, greater and greater sums were spent on buying the favour of the Roman mob. Under the emperors this expenditure continued, since the largely unemployed populace of Rome and other cities had to be kept quiet by being given the entertainments which it had come to expect.

Such spectacles might be performed in the theatres themselves (see **Roman theatres and amphitheatres**), and dramatic performance was inevitably influenced by the public taste for lavish expenditure and crude realism. We hear of a *fabula togata* of Afranius, concerning a fire, being revived in the time of Nero for the sake of showing a building burnt to the ground on stage. Less reliable, perhaps, are the claims of salacious Roman writers that condemned criminals might be executed on stage as part of a dramatic performance.

5 Actors and musicians The usual word for 'actor', *histrio*, apparently derives from an Etruscan word for a masked dancer. The earliest Roman dramatists are said to have acted in their own plays, like the earliest Greek ones. By the time of Plautus and Terence, however, there were permanent troupes of professional actors, each led by an actor-manager, and a dramatist had to win the patronage of one of these if his plays were to be staged. Plautus sometimes alludes to one of these actor-managers, Titus Publilius Pellio, and some of

Terence's prologues are written to be delivered by another, Lucius Ambivius Turpio, in his own person. Turpio is presented as a man proud of his artistic calling and of his discernment in championing the unpopular work of Terence, as he earlier championed that of Caecilius Statius. He and Pellio had aristocratic names, and were evidently men of consequence. They in their turn had to win the favour of the aediles (magistrates responsible for the administration of the festivals), by whom they and their fellow-actors were paid.

There is no evidence for any restriction on the number of actors in any one play. Plautus' *Poenulus* requires six actors on stage at once; other plays could be performed with four or five, given some doubling. The *tibia*-player was evidently an important figure, for many of the surviving production-notices give us his name and tell us what kind of *tibia* he used. The plays were delivered to an audience of both sexes and all social classes, and production-notices often tell us whether a play 'pleased' or not, though it is unclear how this was judged.

At the end of the Republic acting was still a respectable enough profession for Quintus Roscius Gallus, a famous actor who performed in both tragedy and comedy, to be the friend and protégé of Cicero. In the next generation, however, Livy writes contemptuously of actors, apparently thinking mainly of performers in mimes and pantomimes, who were always of low social class. But this did not prevent successful *pantomimi* under the Empire from winning all the wealth and adulation accorded to stars of opera and ballet today.

6 Masks and costumes   Some Roman writers claim that masks were not worn on the Roman stage until the time of Roscius, but it is generally agreed that this must rest on a misunderstanding and that they were worn from the first (except in the mime), as they had always been in Greece. Surviving representations and descriptions of actors and masks date only from the time of the late Republic and Empire, but indicate that the Romans followed, or exaggerated, the practice of the Hellenistic Greek theatre.

Thus tragic actors had their height increased by means of raised soles to their boots (*cothurni*) and a raised forehead (*onkos*) on the mask, and wore padding under their robes so that their build was proportional to their height. The mask of the *pantomimus* had a closed mouth. Comic actors wore the costume of everyday life, whether Greek (for the *palliata*) or Roman (for the *togata* – which cannot often have required actual togas – and the *Atellana*). Masks of slaves, old men and other figures of fun had gaping mouths and comically exaggerated features, while those of young men and maidens were more realistic.

Representations of tragic and comic actors and, in particular, masks continue to be common in painting, sculpture and mosaic throughout the Imperial period. The masks are often grotesquely distorted for comic or horrific effect. It is uncertain, however, how much these representations owe to contemporary dramatic performances (for which there is little other evidence) and how much to artistic convention.   ALB

See: W. G. Arnott, *Menander, Plautus and Terence (Greece & Rome New Surveys in the Classics* 9), Oxford, 1975; W. Beare, *The Roman Stage*, 3rd edn, London, 1964; R. L. Hunter, *The New Comedy of Greece and Rome*, Cambridge, 1985; E. J. Kenney and W. V. Clausen (eds.), *The Cambridge History of Classical Literature*, II, Cambridge, 1982; D. Konstan, *Roman Comedy*, Cornell, 1983; F. H. Sandbach, *The Comic Theatre of Greece and Rome*, London, 1977.

Romeril, John (1945–) Australian playwright. Initially a writer for La Mama and the Pram Factory, Melbourne; his plays, often with strong political or social content, range from the surreal absurdity of *I Don't Know Who to Feel Sorry For* (1969), and realism of *Bastardy* (1972) to cartoon-like expressionism in *Chicago Chicago* (1971) and *The Floating World* (1974), and the musical adaptation of a novel, *Jonah Jones* (1985).   MW

Romero, Mariela (1949–) Venezuelan playwright and essayist. Her major plays include *El juego* (*The Game*, 1977), the bifurcated experiences of two characters named Ana. *Rosa de la noche* (*Rose of the Night*, 1980) takes place in the seedy Caracas underworld of pimps and prostitutes. In *El vendedor* (*The Salesman*, 1981), the world of a lonely woman without love is invaded by an aggressive type pretending to be a salesman.   GW

Ronconi, Luca (1933–) Italian actor and director. After drama school training he acted with a number of major companies before turning to direction with a version of **Goldoni**'s *La Buona Moglie* (*The Good Wife*) in 1963. In the course of the mid and later 1960s, he evolved a distinctive and highly theatrical production style with mountings, particularly, of Renaissance drama, including **Shakespeare**'s *Measure for Measure* and *Richard III*, Bruno's *Il Candelaio* (*The Candle Maker*) and **Tourneur**'s *The Revenger's Tragedy*. Perhaps his most ambitious work of the 1960s was an inventive and stunningly spectacular stage treatment in 1968 of **Ariosto**'s epic poem *Orlando Furioso*, which he co-scripted with the poet Eduardo Sanguinetti. The range of his work in the 1970s and 80s has been considerable, including productions of **Aeschylus**' *Oresteia*, **Middleton**'s *A Game at Chess* and **Ibsen**'s *Ghosts*, plays which reflect an apparent preference for classic or neglected drama, of a kind both intellectually challenging and likely to permit the highly imaginative stage reorchestration that is a hall-mark of his work. He has had a distinguished career too in the lyric theatre, his work there including productions of Gounod's *Faust*, **Wagner**'s *Siegfried* and **Gluck**'s *Orpheus and Eurydice*.   LR

Roscius Gallus, Quintus (c. 120–62 BC) Roman actor. His reputation in plays by **Plautus** and **Terence** was of the highest, and it is suggested that he took great care in the preparation of his roles. His name has been conferred as an accolade of virtuosity on a number of more recent actors, not always with good cause. For instance **Sam Cowell** was dubbed the Young American Roscius, and **Ira Aldridge**, the black American actor, the African Roscius.   MB

Rose, George (Walter) (1920–) English-born actor. Although to many Rose is the archetype of the British character actor, he has lived in New York City since 1961, the year he played The Common Man in *A Man for All Seasons*. Rose joined the **Old Vic** Company in 1945. At the Shakespeare Memorial Theatre, his Dogberry in **Gielgud**'s 1959 production of *Much Ado About Nothing* established him as a first-rate Shakespearian clown. Since settling in New York City, he appeared prominently in *The Royal Hunt of the Sun* (1965), *My Fair Lady* (Doolittle in 1968 and 1976 revivals), the musical *Coco* (1969), *My Fat Friend* (1974), *The Kingfisher* (1978), *Peter Pan* (Captain Hood and Mr Darling in a 1979 revival), *The Pirates of Penzance* (Major General Stanley in the **New York Shakespeare Festival**'s 1980 revival), the 1983 revival of *You Can't Take it With You*, and *The Mystery of Edwin Drood* (1985).   DBW

Rose Theatre, London The building of the Rose, in the liberty of the Clink on the south bank of the Thames, was a commercial speculation of **Philip Henslowe**'s. That the speculation was successful is evident from the 1989 excavations of the site. The original 1587 structure was significantly extended in 1592, presumably to increase the capacity (from c.1,950 to c.2,400). It was polygonal, probably fourteen-sided and plastered and painted to look round, Even after enlargement, it was significantly smaller than the **Globe**, with a stage about 18 ft deep and tapering from c.37 ft at the tiring-house to c.28 ft at the front. We can reasonably assume that a three-tiered gallery surrounded the open yard and that the structure was topped by a thatched roof. It was here that **Strange's Men** presented **Shakespeare**'s Henry VI in 1592. From 1594 to 1600, the Rose was the home of the **Admiral's Men**. **Marlowe**'s plays were regularly revived there. But in 1600, perhaps outshone by the **Chamberlain's Men** at the nearby Globe, the company moved to the **Fortune**, leaving the Rose to Worcester's Men. The playhouse was demolished in 1605–6.   PT

Rosencof, Mauricio (1933–) Uruguayan playwright, journalist and short story writer. His first play was presented by the theatre group El Galpón in 1960, but it was *Las ranas* (*The Frogs*) in 1961 that brought him public attention for its realistic presentation of the human misery that permeates a lower class neighbourhood. In a brief incursion into children's theatre he also dealt with social themes, and *La valija* (*The Suitcase*, 1964) has been frequently anthologized and translated. His major work is *Los caballos* (*The Horses*, 1967) in which he follows the formal and stylistic realism of his earlier plays but experiments with elements of fantasy with considerable success. During the period of military repression in Uruguay in the 1970s–80s, Rosencof was imprisoned for his writings and activities.   GW

Rosenthal, Jean (1912–69) American theatre, architectural and industrial lighting designer. Rosenthal virtually invented the field of lighting design. When she began working with **Orson Welles** and **John Houseman** in the **Federal Theatre Project** there were no lighting designers; the job was done by the set designer or electrician. In 1938 she began working for Martha Graham as lighting and production supervisor (and continued until her death). Because dance is so dependent on light, Rosenthal was able to develop the new art of lighting design. A common element in all her designs is an evocative sense of mood. Critics and directors commented on her apparent ability to work magic with her effects. Rosenthal's hundreds of theatre designs include *West Side Story* and *The Sound of Music*. She also designed the architectural lighting for theatres and projects ranging from airline terminals to hotels. Her ideas and techniques are presented in her book, *The Magic of Light*.   AA

Roshchin, Mikhail (1933–) A member of the post-war generation of Soviet playwrights which includes **Radzinsky** and **Vampilov** and a practitioner of the 1960s 'new lyricism' applied to personal romantic themes by **Rozov**, **Volodin** and **Arbuzov**. Roshchin lived a peripatetic early life as a result of dislocation caused by the war, the need to support his family at age 16 following his father's death and his job as an editor of the journals *The Banner* and *New World* during the 1950s and 1960s. He published his first book at age 23 and his first play, *The Seven Feats of Heracles*, on the cleaning of the Augean Stables, seven years later. In 1968 he wrote both the very popular *A Rainbow in Winter* (1968) and the more problematic *The Old New Year*. The latter, the first Soviet satire in some time, was produced at the **Moscow Art Theatre** in 1973, largely owing to the success of Roshchin's 1971 youth play, *Valentin and Valentina*, which has been performed in some 60 Soviet theatres and in America at San Francisco's **American Conservatory Theatre** (1977), where it failed. A contemporary Soviet *Romeo and Juliet*, which utilizes 1950s and 1960s theatricalist devices, the young lovers are here not so much star-crossed as impeded by abandoned mothers and a divorced older sister (representing different social classes) who discourage young marriage; crowded living conditions which permit no privacy – the spatial logistics of three generations of family living together reinforcing the theme of generational conflict; a society which has overlooked personal problems in favour of social ideology and productivity; youth's own confusion over the possibility and proper place of romantic love in contemporary life; the lack of paternal guidance, many fathers having been lost in the Second World War. *Echelon* (1975), Roshchin's emotional commemoration of the 30th anniversary of the Second World War and of his mother's personal experience aboard a crowded troop train, is noteworthy for its cast of almost entirely female types, its creation of environment via a box-car setting and stage effects and its deeply felt tone. It was successfully staged by **Anatoly Efros** at the Moscow Art Theatre and at the Sovremennik by Galina Volchyok, who was brought to Houston's Alley Theatre in 1978 to replicate her Moscow production. Other plays by Roshchin include: *Husband and Wife*, a *Valentin and Valentina* update on the problems of young marrieds; *The Galoshes of Happiness*, a censored adaptation of Hans Christian Andersen's tale of a man who encounters unhappiness and similar problems in the past, present and future; *Mother of Pearl Zinaida*, a satirical comedy about a writer named Aladdin; *Hurry to Do Good*, and an adaptation of **Tolstoi**'s *Anna Karenina*, all of which were being prepared for production in the early 1980s.   SG

Rossi, Cesare (1829–98) Italian actor and company manager. A solid player of the middle rank, in the 1850s and 60s he rose slowly through the profession acting with many leading companies, including those of **Ernesto Rossi** and **Luigi Bellotti-Bon** until in the mid-seventies he formed his own company, attempting to establish it on a semi-permanent basis in Turin. Perhaps his most sustained and distinguished period as a company manager was that between 1881 and 1884 when his troupe included the young **Eleonora Duse** and her leading man Flavio Andò. In association with Duse, Rossi made a tour of Latin America in 1885–6. Never himself an outstanding player, but sound in second rank roles, a model of careful study and an excellent manager, many younger players, like Duse and **Zacconi**, learned much from their work with him. KR

Rossi, Ernesto (1827–96) Italian actor–manager who began his career in companies run by the leading players of the period, **Gustavo Modena** and **Adelaide Ristori**, with the last of whom he made his first appearances outside Italy when she played in Paris in 1855. From the 1860s to the end of his career he acted mainly with his own companies in a large repertoire that included the major Italian stock pieces of the century. **Shakespeare** figured prominently in his list of lead roles, including Othello and Hamlet, of which he gave the first textually significant performances in Italy in 1856. His other Shakespearian roles included Macbeth, King Lear, Richard III, Shylock, Romeo and Coriolanus. He translated and adapted *Julius Caesar* for his own stage interpretation, and had some knowledge of English stage versions of the other Shakespeare plays he staged. In the manner of 19th-century 'star' actors he spent much time performing abroad, travelling to North and South America and throughout Europe. In 1876 he took several of his Shakespeare productions (including those of *Hamlet*, *King Lear* and *Macbeth*) to London where he was in the main well received, particularly as Romeo, but he never enjoyed the same success as his contemporary **Salvini**, and a return visit in 1882, when he performed King Lear in Italian with English players acting the rest of the play in English, was a disaster. This experiment he had attempted the previous year in New York, during the last of his visits to the United States, with no greater success. When he first toured there in 1865, Henry James noted his reliance on tricks and technique, and while acknowledging his great histrionic skill, thought him, and perhaps with justice, not an actor of the first rank. His contribution in the area of direction (or, more properly, stage-management), and in acclimatizing Shakespeare to the Italian stage, is perhaps rather underrated, in part perhaps because he himself makes too much of the last in his informative, if somewhat pompous, memoirs. Of solid, rather stocky appearance, and of limited vocal range, he had a lively, demonstrative mode of playing that well suited him to romantic roles, and a fondness for interpolating engaging, if often extraneous, stage-business. Sensibly, he was not reluctant to adapt Shakespeare to the tastes of his Italian audiences; a practice that won him contemporary success in the theatre, and the lasting suspicion of academe. KR

Rostand, Edmond (1868–1918) French dramatist. At a time when naturalism was the dominant ortho-

doxy, Rostand's plays seem to look back to the romantic period in spirit. At the same time, a part of their appeal lay in their explicit or implicit patriotic sentiment, most noticeable in *Cyrano de Bergerac* (1897) and *L'Aiglon* (1900). A one-act play, *Les Deux Pierrots*, was turned down in 1891 by the **Comédie-Française**, but the same theatre accepted his charming comedy *The Fantasticks* (*Les Romanesques*, 1894), which had many of the qualities of the comedies of **Alfred de Musset**, notably a light and witty dialogue. *La Princesse Lointaine* (*The Distant Princess*, 1895) provided a role for **Sarah Bernhardt**, as Melissinde, the princess of its poet hero's idealized dream. Sarah again played the lead role in *La Samaritaine* (*The Woman of Samaria*, 1897), a biblical piece based on the meeting of Christ and the Woman of Samaria. *Cyrano de Bergerac*, created by **Coquelin** at the Porte-Saint-Martin, was his most popular play, combining nostalgia for the 'Grand Siècle' (scenes include a reconstruction of the 17th-century **Hôtel de Bourgogne** theatre in Paris) with swashbuckling heroism and panache and a strongly romantic theme of a love which can never express itself to its object. Audiences loved its swordsman-poet hero and were carried along by the strongly lyrical quality of Rostand's verse. *L'Aiglon*, a play about the Duke of Reichstadt, son of Napoleon, was less strong, but depended even more heavily upon stirring up patriotic fervour, and offered another major role to Bernhardt as the sickly prince. Rostand's career was cut short by ill health, but he did write one other major play, *Chantecler* (1910), with Lucien Guitry in the role of the cock. It was based on the *Roman de Renart* and the actors wore cumbersome costumes as farmyard animals. Like **Victor Hugo**, Rostand was often more poet than dramatist, but his romanticism was always tinged with a streak of clear-sighted realism, whether in the character of Cyrano or in the satirical comment on contemporary politics and literature contained in *Chantecler*. JMCC

Rostovsky, St Dmitry (Danylo Savych Tuptalo) (1651–1709) Ukrainian ecclesiastic poet and dramatist, appointed metropolitan of Rostov by Peter the Great although he neither supported (like **Feofan Prokopovich**) nor opposed his reforms. His popular school dramas, based on medieval mystery and morality plays, mixed biblical and allegorical characters with low comic types and demonstrated his gift for poetic and dramatic language. These include: *Nativity Play* (produced 1702, Rostov), *The Dormition Play*, *Esther and Ahasuerus*, *The Resurrection of Christ* and *A Sinner's Repentance*. The last, performed at court by **Fyodor Volkov**'s company (1752), featured the future famous actor **Ivan Dmitrevsky**. This established Volkov's Yaroslavl troupe in Petersburg, an important step in the development of the formal Russian theatre. Tuptalo was canonized in 1757. SG

Rote Sprachrohr, Das 'The Red Megaphone', the first and most important agit-prop troupe in Weimar Germany, was founded in 1927 by M. Valletin, using members of communist youth groups. It performed choral works, didactic plays and revues at workers' gatherings. *Hallo, Kollege Jungarbeiter* (*Hello, Young Colleagues*, 1928) depicted workers struggling against exploitation in episodic scenes, and a choral piece *Dritte*

Internationale (*Third International*, 1929), with songs by Hanns Eisler, toured the USSR. After 1930, the group moved towards Epic Theatre techniques with *Song of the Red United Front* and *General Strike* (both 1931). Several brigades continued to perform for a few weeks after the Nazi seizure of power, but their members either were arrested or emigrated.   LS

Rotimi, Ola (1936–) Nigerian playwright and theatre director. Born in Sapele, in the Niger delta, in what is now Bendel State. Rotimi went to Boston University and Yale University in the USA. He returned to Nigeria to a Research Fellowship at Ife University, where he founded the Ori Olokun Acting Company (later the Ori Olokun Players). The popularity of this theatre in the late 1960s and early 70s was the result not only of the talents of Rotimi as writer and director, but also of the considerable musical talents of the composer Akin Euba. Rotimi began writing plays in America. *Our Husband Has Gone Mad Again* was premiered at Yale, directed by Jack Landau, in 1966 (although it was only published in 1977, after Rotimi had made his theatrical reputation in Nigeria). It is a comedy, set in a Nigeria in the throes of a general election. It concerns a retired Nigerian Army major who has latterly made money in cocoa farming, and is now determined to get himself and his Party elected to power – so that he can make more money. The comedy arises mainly out of his marital condition: he has two Nigerian wives about whom he has failed to tell his 'abroad' wife. She unexpectedly flies into Lagos as the election is in progress. The play has an earthy wit, often appropriately communicated through Pidgin phrases. This play is especially interesting in the light of Rotimi's play, *If*, which was first performed in Port Harcourt, Nigeria, in 1979 (published in 1983). In *If* the action takes place in the middle of a general election. Unlike *Our Husband . . .* of 13 years before, *If* has a serious political intent and is wholly concerned with a group of ordinary working class Nigerians. The electoral candidate is their oppressive landlord and is seen only at the beginning and end of the play. He is depicted as an evil figure against whom good people struggle and fail. The racy dialogue in this play again reflects the linguistic texture of Nigeria as it does in *Our Husband . . .* However, the difference in tone between the two plays could not be more divergent. The transition is perhaps an indication of Rotimi's disillusionment with the political processes in Nigeria and the increasing politicization of his dramatic art. However, the play has a number of elements characteristic of Rotimi's craft as a playwright: a strong theatricality combined with elements of melodrama (such as the death of the little boy from asthma, and the use of music to heighten emotion) which builds to a tragic climax.

One of Rotimi's best-known plays is *The Gods Are Not To Blame*, a Nigerian version of **Sophocles**' *Oedipus the King*. It was the first production of the Ori Olokun Acting Company in 1968, and published in 1971. In a subsequent interview Rotimi hinted that the play was an allegory of the Nigerian Civil War: the ethnic pride of Nigerians, and not Fate or 'The Gods', was responsible for the slide into civil war in 1966. Its first performance during the Civil War might well have been read in this way; its later success comes from its appealing theatricality.

A scene from Rotimi's *The Gods Are Not To Blame*, Mary Kingsley Theatre, Freetown, Sierra Leone.

After this, Rotimi turned to creating Nigerian history on stage, and from a Nigerian perspective. *Kurunmi* (premiered by Ori Olokun in 1969; published in 1971) depicts an aspect of the internecine wars amongst the Yorubas in the middle of the 19th century and creates an Aristotelian tragic hero out of the Yoruba commander, Kurunmi. This was followed in 1971 by *Ovonramwen Nogbaisi*, enacting the sack of Benin by the British in 1897 and the exile of the eponymous Oba. Again, the playwright's vision is tragic, though historically the central figure, the Oba, is less susceptible to this heroic treatment.

Rotimi moved from Ife to Port Harcourt, to become Head of Drama in the University there; and he formed a new company of players to stage his work. *If* was premiered here; it was preceded by *Holding Talks: An Absurdist Drama* (published in 1979) which was popularly received. *Hopes of the Living Dead*, produced in Ibadan in 1985, is based on the life of Ikoli Harcourt-Whyte who was a leper from the age of 19: 'Leprosy . . . is a grand metaphor for a social, political and psychological disease which though daunting and stigmatising can be tackled . . .' (Osundare). Rotimi's work probably falls somewhere between the academic theatre of the campuses and the theatre of the popular Yoruba-language folk operas. Perhaps because of this his work has received less critical attention than it deserves.   ME

Rotrou, Jean de (1609–50) French dramatist, contemporary of **Corneille** and his only serious rival in stature. His first play was produced at the **Hôtel de Bourgogne** when he was only 19 and he seems to have become the theatre's resident playwright in succession to **Hardy**: certainly many of his plays were in its repertoire in the early 1630s and their staging requirements were noted by **Mahelot** in his *Mémoire*. Rotrou's total output may have been well in excess of the 35 plays that survive, of which the majority are good examples of the free-wheeling tragicomedy then popular, compounded of multiple incident and an almost total disregard for the unities. One of them, *La Bague de l'Oubli* (*The Ring of Forgetfulness*, 1629), which is a translation from **Lope de Vega**, reflects an interest in Spanish literature which he shared with Corneille. He also wrote a number of comedies, the best of which is a version of the Amphitryon story entitled *Les Sosies* (*The Doubles*, 1636), and several tragedies, amongst them *Hercule Mourant* (*Hercules Dying*, 1634), which along with the work of **Mairet** and Corneille helped to introduce a more regular neoclassical form of tragedy. He was sufficiently esteemed by **Richelieu** to become one of the group of five dramatists who wrote plays under the Cardinal's aegis, though his most mature work was produced in the last decade of his life after he had returned to take up a post in his native Dreux. It included the tragicomedy *Venceslas* (1647), the regular tragedy *Cosroès* (1648) – both of which continued to be performed for many years, the former until the 19th century – and his most imaginative tragedy *Le Véritable Saint Genest* (1645), also derived from Lope de Vega, which depicts the conversion of the Roman actor Genesius while playing the part of a Christian martyr and his own condemnation to martyrdom in consequence. DR

Rousseau, Jean-Jacques (1712–78) Philosopher and man of letters of Swiss birth and French culture. Although the author of several operatic works, notably *Le Devin du Village* (*The Village Soothsayer*, 1753), and *Pygmalion* (1770), and a comedy *Narcisse* (1752), presented at the **Comédie-Française**, Rousseau condemned the theatre in his philosophical writings, seeing it as a baleful social influence. In his *Lettre à d'Alembert* (1758) challenging the proposal to establish a playhouse in Geneva, he widens the argument into a general indictment of the theatre, whose aim is solely to please, not to instruct, and far from stimulating moral sentiments exploits them in the service of mere diversion. Both tragedy and comedy are equally guilty of interesting us in characters who, in their excessive heroism, villainy or foolishness, are disproportionate to our own experience; both give an undue prominence to love and often present vice in an attractive or sympathetic light, thus exciting our sensibilities unhealthily. Moreover, theatregoing itself encourages a taste for extravagance and indolence, while the very company of actors, whose art depends on dissembling and flouts natural modesty, is suspect. In essence his ideological position is the direct antithesis to that of **Diderot**. DR

Roux, Jean-Louis (1923–) French Canadian director, playwright and actor. He studied theatre in Paris, 1947–50, and on his return helped found Montreal's enduring **Théâtre du Nouveau Monde** (1951),

becoming its Artistic Director in 1966 and guiding it towards a modern, diversified repertoire. Since 1981 he has been director of the Ecole Nationale du Théâtre. His brilliant career as an actor has included major stage, radio and television plays. He has adapted many works for Quebec audiences, notably **Shakespeare**'s *Julius Caesar* (*Jules César*, 1971), and is the author of *Rose Latulippe* (1951), dealing with a popular Canadian legend, and *Les Bois-brûlés* (*Halfbreeds*, 1967), a historical drama dealing with the armed revolt of French-speaking Western-Canadian Métis under Louis Riel against federal authority in 1885. LED

Rovina, Hanna (1889–1980) Russian-born First Lady of the Hebrew stage. Together with **Nahum Zemach** and Menahem Gnessin, founded the original **Habimah** Studio, immigrated with it to Palestine in 1931 and remained an active member of the Habimah theatre all her life. Her dedication to her art and to the collective was absolute: 'My family is the Habimah.' The role that brought her international fame was that of Leah, the possessed bride in *The Dybbuk*. She played memorable mother roles in *The Eternal Jew* by **David Pinski** (1923), *The Mother* by **Karel Čapek** (1939), *Mirele Efros* by **Jacob Gordin** (1939), *In the Wastes of the Negev* by Yigal Mossinson (1949), and *Hanna Szenes* by Aaron Megged (1958). Among her great roles were also **Euripides**' *Medea* (1955) and the Old Lady in **Dürrenmatt**'s *The Visit* (1959). HAS

Hanna Rovina in the original Habimah production of *The Dybbuk*, 1922.

Rovinski, Samuel (1932–) Costa Rican playwright whose motivation derives from a sense of justice and the need to raise the consciousness of those responsible for intolerable situations. His plays focus on social and political issues, for the most part, and include: *Gobierno de alcoba* (*Bedroom Government*, 1971), *Las fisgonas de Paso Ancho* (*The Busybodies of Paso Ancho*, 1971), a caricature of a wide variety of social ills, *Un modelo para Rosaura* (*A Model for Rosaura*, 1974), and *El martirio del pastor* (*Pastoral Martyrdom*, 1984), which dealt with the assassination in El Salvador of Monsignor Romero.   GW

Rowe, Nicholas (1674–1718) English playwright and actor. He gave up law on inheriting the family estate in 1692 and began writing plays. His first play, *The Ambitious Stepmother* (1700), established his serious neoclassical style, larded with political allegory in *Tamerlane* (1701) which celebrated William III. He adapted **Massinger**'s *The Fatal Dowry* as *The Fair Penitent* (1703) and began to write in a style much influenced by the 'she-tragedies' of **Banks** centring the drama on the plight of a virtuous woman and aiming at pathos and tears. His best play in this form, *The Tragedy of Jane Shore* (1714), was explicitly written 'in imitation of **Shakespeare**'s style' and combines *Richard III* with a more Restoration style of political and pathetic tragedy. His drama of pity and moral warning was markedly unsentimental. In 1709 Rowe published his edition of Shakespeare in six volumes. The first serious attempt to edit Shakespeare since the First Folio (1623), the edition attempted to remove textual corruption and add scene and stage directions, as well as regularizing act and scene divisions and act numberings according to Rowe's belief in neoclassical five-act form. For all its indications of the gulf between Rowe and Shakespeare it is significant for inaugurating the work of editing Shakespeare afresh.   PH

Rowley, Samuel (c. 1575–1624) English actor and playwright, who was a leading member of the **Admiral's Men** from at least 1597 to 1613. As an 'attached playwright' to his company, Rowley probably agreed not to publish his work. The only known survival, *When You See Me, You Know Me* (1603), is a rambling chronicle play about Henry VIII. His name is associated with the lost *The Taming of a Shrew* (c. 1589), which **Shakespeare** knew, and **Henslowe** records a payment to him in 1602 for 'additions' to **Marlowe**'s *Doctor Faustus*.   PT

Rowley, William (c. 1585–1626) English actor and playwright, who was a leading member of Prince Charles's Men and, on occasions, of the King's Men from 1610–25. To judge from the parts he is known to have played – Plumporridge in **Middleton**'s *Masque of Heroes* (1619), the Fat Clown in his own muddled tragedy, *All's Lost by Lust* (c. 1620), the Fat Bishop in Middleton's *A Game at Chess* (1624) – Rowley made comic capital out of his size. He was a force in the Jacobean theatre, not only as actor and writer, but also as a company manager after the fashion of **John Heminges** with the King's Men. Best remembered as a playwright for his collaboration with Middleton on *The Changeling* (1622), Rowley worked with Middle-

ton on several other plays and was much influenced by him in his own citizen comedies, *A New Wonder: A Woman Never Vexed* (published 1632) and *A Match at Midnight* (published 1633). He collaborated with **Dekker** and **Ford** on *The Witch of Edmonton* (1621) and with **Fletcher** on *The Maid in the Mill* (1623).   PT

Royal Court Theatre, London. The present theatre, extensively renovated after bomb damage in 1940, opened in 1888 to replace a Chelsea theatre demolished for road-widening. After an undistinguished decade, it staged a major hit in **Pinero**'s *Trelawny of the Wells* (1898), and made its most distinctive early contribution to the advance of the English theatre under the joint management of **J. E. Vedrenne** and **Harley Granville Barker** (1904–7). It was these seasons that established **Shaw** as a major force and introduced the English public to recent work by the continental avant-garde. Its location, away from London's theatreland, and its modest capacity (642 when first opened) made management of the Royal Court a financial hazard and, after challenging post-1918 seasons under **J. B. Fagan**, **Barry Jackson** and, for three Shaw-filled years, the Madonna Players, it was converted into a cinema in 1932. It was not in regular use as a theatre again until 1952. A second great period in the history of the Royal Court began in 1956, when the English Stage Company appointed **George Devine** as its artistic director. His commitment to the staging of new, and if necessary controversial, plays was triumphantly vindicated by the success of *Look Back in Anger* (1956), which introduced **John Osborne** to a startled public and involved the previously disengaged drama in the abrasive cultural spirit of the times. That the Royal Court was much more than a home for 'angry young men' was amply illustrated by a repertoire that stretched from **Brecht** to **Ionesco** by way of **Wesker**, **N. F. Simpson** and **John Arden**. Devine died soon after the renovations of 1964 had been completed, but the Royal Court maintained its leadership of the 'new' drama under his successor, **William Gaskill** (1965–72). Under Gaskill, in regular association with **Lindsay Anderson**, the theatre gave prominence to plays by **David Storey** and **Edward Bond** as well as reviving the neglected work of **D. H. Lawrence** and it has maintained its challenging lead under Oscar Lewenstein (1972–7), Stuart Burge (1977–9) and Max Stafford-Clark. The additional provision of the Small Theatre Upstairs in 1969 has enabled the staging of low-budget new plays, sustaining the hopes for London performance of many young playwrights. Still no stranger to controversy, the Royal Court notably raised hackles in 1987, first by determining to stage Jim Allen's *Perdition*, a play proposing the historical complicity of certain Zionist Hungarian Jews in the Holocaust, and then by withdrawing it at the eleventh hour.   PT

Royal Exchange Theatre, Manchester. One of the premier regional theatres in Britain. The building itself is a remarkable piece of theatre design: a theatre-in-the-round built of steel tubing and glass suspended within the vast hall of Manchester's old Royal Exchange – a unique combination of new and old. The company began life as the 69 Theatre Company, based

The Royal Exchange Theatre, Manchester, an example of theatre-in-the round, was constructed within the old Exchange building.

in the Manchester University Theatre 1968–73, and eventually, with a change of name, transferred to the new theatre when it opened in 1976. High quality productions especially of the classics and modern classics, often with star names in the cast, have been the hallmark of the policy, notable productions including *The Rivals* (1976), *The Duchess of Malfi* (1980), *The Dresser* (1980) and *The Three Sisters* (1985). There has never, apart from one season, been a resident acting company, but continuity is provided by the multiple artistic directorship which has included **Michael Elliot**, Braham Murray, James Maxwell and Casper Wrede.   AJ

Royal Shakespeare Company (RSC)

Royal Shakespeare Company (RSC) The first Shakespeare Memorial Theatre at Stratford-upon-Avon was opened in 1879 and destroyed by fire in 1926. The present building, designed by Elizabeth Scott, opened in 1932. It was renamed the Royal Shakespeare Theatre in 1961. The present theatre incorporates the surviving elements of the first theatre; it has a 29-foot proscenium stage and can accommodate 1,500 spectators. The transformation of what had been a seasonal festival theatre at Stratford-upon-Avon, the Shakespeare Memorial Theatre, into the home for Britain's first *de facto* national theatre company can be largely credited to the determination of two men, Fordham Flower and **Peter Hall**. Fordham Flower was a member of the family of Stratford brewers who had been the chief patrons of the theatre from the beginning. His great uncle, Charles Flower, had raised the money and launched the theatre in 1879, and appointed **F. R. Benson** as the first director of its festival seasons. Fordham Flower followed his father, Archibald, and his grandfather, Edgar, as Chairman of the Board, a post which he held from 1944 until his death in 1966.

Fordham Flower led the theatre through the difficult post-war years to its comparative prosperity and expansion during the 1950s. In 1946, he appointed Sir **Barry Jackson** as director, in an attempt to graft new

ideas on to what had previously been regarded as an unadventurous tradition, and Jackson had responded by introducing such young directors and actors as **Peter Brook** and **Paul Scofield**. When Jackson retired in 1948, he turned to **Anthony Quayle**, the actor–director, who brought in stars from London, such as the Oliviers. Quayle exploited the relative decline in the fortunes of the **Old Vic**; and such spectacular successes as Peter Brook's *Titus Andronicus*, with **Laurence Olivier** as Titus, in 1955 established the Stratford theatre as a mecca for Shakespearian production. When Quayle resigned in 1957, to be succeeded briefly by Glen Byam Shaw who had joined him in the leadership of the company in 1953, the Shakespeare Memorial Company was comparatively wealthy, with many gifts and assets at Stratford (apart from the theatre) and with a useful surplus in the bank.

In 1958, while the company was on tour in Leningrad, Fordham Flower discussed the company's future with Peter Hall, then 28 years old, who had successfully directed *Love's Labour's Lost* (1956), *Cymbeline* (1957) and *Twelfth Night* (1958) at Stratford. They shared the same vision of a theatre modelled along the lines of the major European repertory companies, with resources and a permanence previously unknown in Britain. Hall was appointed to succeed Shaw as director in 1960, but even before he took over, some of his radical proposals were being widely discussed. These included establishing a large semi-permanent company, with actors on two- or three-year contracts, who would be encouraged to stay with what was then a provincial company by the prospect of also playing in a second theatre in London, the Aldwych Theatre eventually being chosen. The Stratford programmes would concentrate on the work of **Shakespeare** and his contemporaries, while those at the Aldwych would include modern plays from Britain and abroad, together with transfers from Stratford. Not least among the assumptions was that the days of private patronage were over and that the new company should actively pursue state support at a level appropriate to its planned national status. To that end, the old pious but somewhat funereal title was dropped and replaced in 1961 by the Royal Shakespeare Company, and the royal charter of 1925 was amended to this effect.

This dramatic transformation was praised, but also criticized, by Brook among others for putting expansion of the company before the raising of its standards and by some members of the board for gambling away the company's hard won resources. The company's trading position revealed that following the start of the RSC's residency at the Aldwych Theatre in 1960 a small surplus in 1959–60 had become a deficit in 1960–1, and despite the first annual subsidy from the **Arts Council** in 1963, the deficits and the grants continued to grow in future years. By the time of Peter Hall's departure in 1968, however, the audiences had trebled and in addition to running its two theatres, the RSC ran experimental seasons at smaller theatres, such as the influential Arts Theatre season in 1962 and the 'Theatre of Cruelty' collage at LAMDA in 1964. The company's reputation had soared, led by such Peter Brook productions as **Peter Weiss**'s *The Marat/Sade* (1964) and *US* (1966) and by the Hall–**John Barton** adaptation of Shakespeare's early history plays, *The Wars of the Roses*

(1963). A rivalry developed between the RSC, regarded as a 'director's theatre' and the newly formed **National Theatre** under Laurence Olivier, an actor's theatre with higher subsidies.

Like the National Theatre, the RSC sought a new London theatre as its metropolitan home, which eventually opened in 1982 as part of the Barbican Arts Centre. Hall, frustrated by the delays and dispirited by the death of Fordham Flower whom he regarded as 'a second father', handed over the RSC's directorship in 1968 to **Trevor Nunn**, who was as young as Hall had been when originally appointed. In 1978, **Terry Hands** became with Nunn joint Artistic Director, a post made necessary by the continuing expansion of the company. Notable among Nunn's achievements was the establishment of two studio theatres in London and Stratford, where vigorous programmes of new and experimental productions could be pursued. In London, the studios were at The Place, then at the Donmar Warehouse and then, after the move into the Barbican, the Pit; while at Stratford, a converted store and rehearsal room became known as The Other Place (1974). Despite the record of new plays by **Edward Bond**, **Howard Barker** and Dusty Hughes among other contemporary writers, the studio productions of *Hamlet* (1975) and *Macbeth* (1976) were particularly memorable and reflected a growing dissatisfaction with over-decorated versions of Shakespeare. In 1977, the RSC opened a six-week season at Newcastle upon Tyne, part of its growing regional responsibilities which also included small-scale touring productions; and the Newcastle seasons became an established feature of the RSC's annual programme. The RSC also became internationally known for the bold scale of its ventures, such as the cycle of Roman plays directed by Trevor Nunn in 1972, the *Henry VI* trilogy directed by Terry Hands in 1977 and the collective efforts at historical reconstruction reflected in *Nicholas Nickleby* (1982) and *Les Misérables* (1985).

In 1986 an anonymous benefaction made possible the opening of a third theatre in Stratford, The Swan – an open-stage theatre in the shell of the auditorium of the old Memorial Theatre. Formally opened before Queen Elizabeth II with **Heywood**'s *The Fair Maid of the West*, directed by Trevor Nunn, The Swan is dedicated to exploring the work of Shakespeare's contemporaries.

Late in 1986 Trevor Nunn stepped back from the leadership of the RSC team, and his colleague Terry Hands assumed that role.   JE MB SS

Royale Theatre 242 West 46th St, New York City [Architect: Herbert J. Krapp]. Built as one of a chain of six theatres by the Chanin brothers, the Royale opened early in 1927. The Chanin control did not survive the depression and all of their theatres passed to other interests. The **Shuberts** became part owner of the house but did not directly control it until 1940. With 1,100 seats, the playhouse has presented both musical and non-musical fare. When it was leased by John Golden from 1934 to 1936, it was briefly named after him and served for his own productions. It was also used (1937–40) as a CBS radio studio during this era. It has housed two Pulitzer Prize-winners, *Both Your Houses* (1932) and *The Subject was Roses* (1964). Other memorable productions on its stage have included *Diamond Lil* (1928), *The Boy Friend* (1954), *The Match-*maker (1955) and *A Day in Hollywood, A Night in the Ukraine* (1981). It remains a Shubert theatre.   MCH

Royce, Edward William (1841–1926) English actor and dancer, who was the least obtrusive of the famous **Gaiety** Quartette (**Nellie Farren**, **Kate Vaughan**, and **Edward Terry** were the others) from 1876–83. He had been trained, and made his London debut, in ballet, but it was as what was known as a 'character dancer' that he achieved his brief fame. After a breakdown in health, Royce returned to the theatre and remained active as a choreographer as well as an actor long after the rest of the Quartette was dead.   PT

Rozenberg, Lev S. see **Bakst, Léon**

Rozenmacher, Germán (1936–71) Argentine playwright who dealt with Jewish values and traditions in such plays as *Réquiem para un viernes a la noche* (*Requiem for a Friday Night*, 1964). He collaborated with **Cossa**, **Somigliana** and **Talesnik** in the creation of *El avión negro* (*The Black Airplane*, 1970), a play that in various scenes anticipated Perón's return to Argentina.   GW

Różewicz, Tadeusz (1921–90) Polish playwright, poet and prose writer, who fought in a guerilla unit during the Nazi occupation. Judging both traditional and avant-garde drama as obsolete, Różewicz considers himself a poetic realist who creates plays out of fragments of daily life, newspapers and conversational clichés, as collages from the refuse heap of modern civilization. Practising open dramaturgy in which director and actors are invited to collaborate, he mixes genres and creates extensive stage directions that are arguments with the theatre. Major plays are *The Card File* (1960), *The Old Woman Broods* (1968), *White Marriage* (1974), *The Trap* (1982).   DG

Rozov, Viktor Sergeevich (1913–) Extremely popular and prolific Soviet social dramatist who, despite a penchant for conventional and sentimental plotting, is important as part of the movement beginning in the late 1950s to demythologize and rehumanize the Soviet theatre by focusing on real, often anti-heroic contemporary personalities and their problems. A student at **Meyerhold**'s school affiliated with the Moscow Theatre of the Revolution (1934–8), Rozov acted and directed at the front until he was wounded. His first play, *Her Friends* (1949), written in the year he entered Moscow's Gorky Literary Institute, initiated a long association between the author, the Central Children's Theatre and the director **Anatoly Efros**. The majority of his plays deal with the painful necessity of taking stock of one's life, making legitimate compromises and divesting oneself of unrealizable dreams, while maintaining personal integrity, moral strength and a belief in the power of love. His characters' successes are measured on the basis of personal fulfilment rather than in terms of professional advancement or ideological correctness which means that some of society's ostensible losers are actually winners in his plays. Rozov often focuses upon a single family or an organizing social device – a wedding, a reunion – to provide a theatrical microcosm of the world at large. Some of his many plays which conform to these themes and models are: *Good Luck!* (1954), *On the Wedding Day* (1964), *The Reunion* (1967) and *From Night to Noon* (1969). *Alive Forever* (1956), a revised version of his 1943 play *The Serebrisky Family*, treats the small-scale human dramas which occur around the edges of war and extols the sensitive and committed individual and the sustaining force of Russianness without embracing ideological positions. It was the opening production and remains the signature piece of Moscow's Sovremennik Theatre (1957) and was made into the popular and critically acclaimed film *The Cranes are Flying*. His 1979 family drama, *The Nest of the Woodgrouse (Meet My Model Family)*, is a generational conflict play, which confronts the problems of careerism and moral decay among top-level bureaucrats, the collision of material, social and spiritual values, precipitating a sense of longing and renewed religious consciousness, especially among the young. Originally denied permission to be produced in Moscow, it was eventually staged at the Moscow Theatre of Satire (1981) and later at the **New York Shakespeare Festival**'s Public Theatre. Rozov continued this somewhat tougher trend in his playwriting with *The Back of Beyond* (1983), based on an actual incident, in which the corrupt officials of a small town not far from Moscow out of self-interest covered up a father's murder of his son. SG

Rudkin, (James) David (1936–) British dramatist, whose first play, *Afore Night Come* (1960), revealed an instinct for high tragedy and myth. The story concerned an itinerant Irish tramp who is murdered by a gang of fruit-pickers on a Midlands farm, but the heightened language evoked themes of ritual slaughter, infertility and the suppression of the imagination (and Ireland) by British imperialism. The relationship between Ireland and England is the subject of *Cries from Casement as his Bones are Brought to Dublin* (1973) and *Ashes* (1974), his best-known play, about a Belfast couple whose infertility is mysteriously linked to the struggle in Ulster. In *Sons of Light* (1976), Rudkin moves away from a specific political situation towards an allegorical assessment of contemporary man, part-fable, part-science fiction, in which science, materialism and the lust for political power drives all human instincts into a furtive animality. Rudkin has written extensively for radio and television, is an accomplished linguist and musician whose translation of the libretto to Schoenberg's *Moses and Aaron* was performed in 1965 and who also adapted **Euripides**' *Hippolytus* (1978) for the **Royal Shakespeare Company**. JE

Rudman, Michael (Edward) (1939–) American born theatre director who came over to Britain to study at Oxford and was President of OUDS from 1963–4. After gaining experience as an associate director at the Nottingham and Newcastle Playhouses (1964–8) and at the **Royal Shakespeare Company** (1968), he became artistic director of the influential **Traverse Theatre Club** in Edinburgh from 1970–3, where his international outlook and championship of such Scottish dramatists as **Taylor** and **Eveling** became a major feature of the annual **Edinburgh Festival**. He moved to a London theatre club of similar size, Hampstead, in 1973 where he stayed for five years, producing and directing such plays as **Handke**'s *Ride*

across Lake Constance, Taylor's *The Black and White Minstrels* and Eveling's *Union Jack (and Bonzo)* (both previously seen at the Traverse), **Frayn**'s *Clouds*, *Alphabetical Order* and *Donkey's Years*, and **Pam Gems**'s first play, *Dusa, Fish, Stas and Vi*. He joined the **National Theatre** in 1979, being appointed director in charge of the Lyttelton Theatre, where he directed *Death of a Salesman*, *Measure for Measure* and *The Second Mrs Tanqueray*. Other National Theatre productions include *Watch on the Rhine*, a black *Measure for Measure* and *On the Razzle*, the **Tom Stoppard** version of a **Nestroy** comedy. He also directed a revival of *Camelot* in the West End, but Rudman's gifts for nurturing new talents were more obvious at the Traverse Theatre and Hampstead than in his later career. JE

Rueda, Lope de (?1509–65) Spanish playwright and one of the first actor-managers of the Golden Age. Born in Seville, he toured with his company throughout Spain, acting in inn-yards, squares and palace-halls. **Cervantes** praised his comic acting and his poetry, though his description of Rueda's company exaggerates the simplicity of the performances.

Four of his **comedias**, showing strong Italian influences, and two pastorals were published in 1567, as well as seven prose *pasos* or *entremeses* under the title of *El deleitoso (The Delightful)*. Rueda's short works are very witty and far superior to his longer plays. CL

Rueda, Manuel (1921–) Born in Monte Cristi, Dominican Republic, poet, musician, playwright, fiction writer and critic, he is considered one of the most important writers of his country. His play *La trinitaria blanca (The White Flower)* won the National Prize in 1957, and was anthologized in 1968 along with *Vacaciones en el cielo (Vacations in Heaven)*, *La tía Beatriz hace un milagro (Aunt Beatriz Works a Miracle)*, and *Entre alambradas (Inside Fences)*, the latter a work dealing with the USA occupation of the Dominican Republic in 1965. Rueda's theatre is characterized by his balance in form, poetic language, humour and dramatic action. *El rey Clinejas (King Clinejas)* won the National Prize for Theatre in 1979 and as an example of popular theatre, has enjoyed good public reaction for its poetry and fantasy. GW

Ruggeri, Ruggero (1871–1953) Italian actor. He first appeared on the stage in 1888 and had a long professional career working with many of the major players of his day including **Novelli**, Talli and Grammatica. A forceful actor with a striking presence, he is best remembered for his acting in the plays of **Pirandello**, playing lead roles in, among others, *Il Giuoco delle Parti (The Rules of the Game*, 1918), *Enrico IV* (1922) and *Sei Personaggi in Cerca d'Autore (Six Characters in Search of an Author*, 1925). A member of the company Pirandello took to Paris in 1925, he there acted with spectacular success the lead role in *Enrico IV*. LR

Rukada Rukada is the doll puppet theatre of Sri Lanka. Although no date has been assigned to its origin, it must have developed after the **Nadagama**, since those who practise the form were formerly practitioners of the Nadagama folk theatre of the state.

The art seems to be practised exclusively in the city of Ambalangoda, on the south-western coast of the island. Three- to four-foot-high puppets are manipulated by strings from above. Performances are presented on an acting area divided into three sections. The central area occupies the back of a raised platform. Side stages extend out towards the audience to the right and to the left. The centre stage symbolizes the audience chamber of the king. All three divisions have dark back curtains and drops. A front curtain is used to mask scene changes while one of the acting areas is in use. The puppeteers stand on a ledge above the stage and manipulate the puppets below.

The orchestra is composed of a harmonium player, a violinist and a *tabla* drummer who sit facing the stage with their backs to the audience. The songs and stories are adapted from the Nadagama and set to Hindustani tunes rather than in the more traditional Karnataka musical style of south India. FaR

Rumania Thracian tribal ceremonials, classical Greek drama, Roman gladiatorial contests, Slavic funeral rites, and Byzantine mimes mark the history of theatrical performance in the Rumanian lands – Wallachia, Moldavia and Transylvania – from antiquity to the early Middle Ages, when the structural elements of the Rumanian folk theatre – its masks, symbolic accessories, mimetic dances, and pantomime scenes – are believed to have taken shape. In the following centuries, these elements gave rise to a number of noteworthy late medieval folk plays including the *căluşarii* (in modern form the most celebrated of all Rumanian folk dances) in which transvestite, male, magical dancers carried naked swords at Whitsuntide, and the *turca* or *brezaia* (which became the still-popular winter goat pageant *capra*) whose protagonists were a mythical beast and a droll old man.

Considering such performances an undesirable pagan tradition, the Rumanian Orthodox Church tried either to suppress them, or to graft them on to its own theatrical forms, of which the most important was the two-part pageant of the *viclem*. Performed between Christmas and Epiphany from the beginning of the 19th century until well into the 20th century, this pageant began with the *irozii*, a vivid dramatization of biblical and apocryphal stories about Herod and the three Magi, and it ended with the *jocul papuşilor*, a farcical puppet show in which the puppets, coarsely carved in wood and colourfully dressed, were made to enact plotless plays on the candle-lit miniature stage of the *chivot*, a portable chest in the shape of a church and richly adorned with Nativity scenes. To build up these plays, the puppeteer, accompanied by a fiddler, brought to life a wide range of such diverse episodes as the amorous misadventures of Vasilache the Gypsy and his jealous wife Gagiţa, or of the Gallicized lady Mariţa, or the beheading of the Turk by the Cossack (an echo of the Russo-Turkish wars), or the naive song of a mouse who ends up being eaten by a cat. Much of the humour of these puppet shows, whose uninhibited satire sometimes prompted local authorities to prohibit them, resulted from the hilarious use of picturesque and foreign words, a technique which was to have notable reverberations in the Rumanian literary establishment. If the *irozii* was most probably an adaptation of a Transylvanian German mystery play, the puppet theatre of the *viclem* owed much to *hayali zil*, the Turkish shadow show which was so popular with

Rumanians that to this day the word *caraghios* (ludicrous) is descriptive of attributes of the farcical Turkish character **Karagöz**.

First mentioned in 1652 as a court entertainment, the shadow show remained a favourite with the Rumanian aristocracy until well into the 18th century, when Western observers expressed astonishment at its lack of decorum. For most of the late Middle Ages, which in Rumania lasted into the 19th century, a taste for low comedy characterized the court and the boyars (nobles), whose chief theatrical divertissements included *măscărici*, jesters who could be killed by anyone with impunity, *pehlivani*, travelling acrobats who, joined by the *măscărici*, performed circus numbers at wedding ceremonies, and *soitari*, gaudily dressed retainers who, in the vein of Turkish *orta-uyunu* farces, enacted resourceful, topical, and obscene improvisations in Rumanian, Turkish, and Greek. But, in the late 18th century and especially in the first quarter of the 19th century, a period in which an increasing number of foreign troupes – French, Italian, German, Russian, and Polish – came to the Ottoman-dominated Principalities of Wallachia and Moldavia, preferences changed rapidly in favour of Western theatrical forms.

In Bucharest, the capital of Wallachia, the beginnings of legitimate theatre are linked to the activities of the Hetairia, a Greek secret society seeking national emancipation. To spread their anti-despotic ideas, the Hetairists encouraged student representations in Greek of Greek, French, and Italian plays – I. R. Nerulos, **Voltaire**, and **Alfieri** were favourite authors. These pioneer theatrical endeavours proved successful and, in 1818, their influential patron, Ralu, the youngest daughter of Prince Ioan Caragea, provided the first permanent theatre building in Wallachia, located at Cişmeaua Roşie, for the enthusiastic actors – exclusively men at the beginning, but later women also acted. In 1819 this theatre had its first Rumanian-language production: emulous Rumanian students staged *Hecuba* by **Euripides**. The performance opened with a memorable Prologue by Iancu Văcărescu which, urging the implementation of the moral, educational, and patriotic functions of theatre, gave quintessential expression to the overriding concerns of the early Rumanian theatrical promoters and practitioners, members of the intelligentsia for the most part.

In 1833, with a view to training actors and musicians for the much-desired national theatre, Ion Heliade Rădulescu and Ion Cîmpineanu founded the first conservatory in Wallachia, the Philharmonic Society. Its initial repertory relied largely on plays by **Molière** and Voltaire which, however, were soon to yield to plays by **Kotzebue**, the favourite author of the time. Under the guidance of Costache Aristia, their professor of declamation, the students performed, alternately with German players of opera, at the Momolo Theatre, built by an Italian cook and entrepreneur in 1833; but when political suspicion and rowdy personal disputes put an end to the Philharmonic in 1837, the first generation of Rumanian actors disbanded. Their staging and often fiery acting style were for the most part a response to an eclectic body of French ideas about theatre, which included those of **Boileau**, Voltaire, and **Hugo**. Of the former students the only one who pursued a theatrical career was Costache Caragiale. His activities as an actor, impresario, and playwright reinforced the general wish for a state-subsidized theatre in Bucharest on the model of those in other European capitals and, when the 1,000-seat Great Theatre opened in 1852, he assumed the leadership of the Rumanian troupe which was to share the facilities with an Italian opera company. By that time a number of Wallachian plays, chiefly satiric comedies, had been published, of which some were also successfully performed (notably Costache Bălăcescu's *A Good Education*, 1845, and Costache Caragiale's *A Soirée in Suburbia*, 1847), but, written in the spirit of Ion Heliade Rădulescu's famous dictum 'write, boys, just write', they are now of only historical interest.

Theatrical developments in Jassy, the capital of Moldavia, differed from those in Bucharest in few, but significant, respects. While in Jassy student representations were less important, the participation of the aristocracy in the theatre arts produced superior results; it also imprinted a characteristic Bohemian quality on the theatrical life of that city. Although young boyars had begun to perform plays in Rumanian in their parents' manor houses as early as 1816, it was only in 1834 that a Moldavian production took place on a public stage, that of the elegant Théâtre des variétés, built in Jassy in 1832 for the French Fouraux troupe. There, amateur actors played *The Moldavian Shepherds' Festival*, a historical pastoral by Gheorghe Asachi, Moldavia's distinguished theatrical promoter. Other occasional performances followed, and, in 1836, the Philharmonic Dramatic Conservatory was established. Its activities were similar to, yet less intense and more conservative than those of the Philharmonic Society. It closed in 1839 owing to financial difficulties, but Rumanian-language theatre revived during the sojourn in Jassy of the Wallachian Costache Caragiale. In 1840, the successful Rumanian troupe he had assembled was united with the French troupe under a single subsidized directorship to which, in 1846, Prince Mihail Sturza offered his houses at Copou for Moldavia's Great Theatre. Official theatrical patronage, however, was hardly magnanimous and censorship was ironhanded – the playwright Alecu Russo and three leading actors ended up in monasteries to fast, pray, and repent for the political liberties they had taken in the production of *Provisioner Vadră* (1846), a satire on the popular violent melodramas of the day. Yet, that eventful period saw the glory of Moldavian drama – the *vaudevilles*, farces, and comedies of Vasile Alecsandri, a French-educated aristocrat, whose plays about the adventures of Chirița, an upstart provincial lady who has many of the traits of the puppet lady Marița, still fill the theatres in both Rumania and Soviet Moldavia (the eastern half of Moldavia). Essential to Chirița's success was the interpretative art of that comic master of women's parts, Matei Millo, a boyar who became Moldavia's foremost actor. Trained in Paris, he brought a new, more natural style to Rumanian acting, and his rising star soon eclipsed that of Costache Caragiale. Millo also wrote plays: his 'operetta-witchery' *Hîrca, the Old Hag* (1848) was probably the single most successful Rumanian play in the 19th century.

After Wallachia united with Moldavia to form Rumania in 1859, Bucharest, the capital and largest city, emerged as the theatrical centre of the new country. Led by prominent *literati* and politicians, the Great Theatre of Bucharest, renamed the National Theatre in 1875, operated as a subsidized concessionary enterprise until 1877, when the Rumanian Parliament voted to reorganize it on the model of the **Comédie-Française**. Similar changes were subsequently made for the theatres of Jassy and Craiova. Thus, at the beginning of the 20th century there were three state-subsidized theatres in Rumania, the only ones allowed to bear the name of National Theatre. In addition to these, there were numerous private and municipal theatres. There, as well as in hotels and outdoor cafés, itinerant troupes produced melodramas, operettas, vaudevilles, comedies, and revues, along with a few serious dramas. Despite some attempts by Rumania's first director, Paul Gusty, an admirer of **Otto Brahm**, to implement naturalist production methods at the National Theatre of Bucharest, rigidly conservative practices and regulations threatened to freeze this foremost Rumanian theatre in outmoded traditions. To address this problem, Alexandru Davila, who led the National Theatre of Bucharest between 1905–8 and 1912–13, introduced a series of reforms aimed at modernizing stagecraft and at allowing more room for contemporary plays, chiefly French. Davila also founded the first important Rumanian private acting company in 1909 – it played at the Modern Theatre.

Although Rumanian acting, having by now established its own traditions, was rapidly raising its standards, it was also losing some of the éclat it had had at the end of the 19th century. The greatest names among the actors of that period are Grigore Manolescu, the most celebrated Rumanian Hamlet; Aristizza Romanescu, renowned for her 'silver bell' voice; and Constantin I. Nottara. Trained in Paris, these star performers, all of the National Theatre at Bucharest, were also influenced by their older colleague Mihail Pascaly, Rumania's chief romantic actor. An important Rumanian actress who acquired international fame was Agatha Bârsescu, a stately tragedienne who played in Austria, Germany, and the United States.

Encouraged by officials and drawing on the talent of a number of literary figures, Rumanian drama flourished between the Union of the Principalities (1859) and the First World War. Even though it generally echoed trends in the playwriting of the day, it achieved considerable originality, at least in spirit if not necessarily in form, in the brilliant dramatic work of **Ion Luca Caragiale**, Costache Caragiale's nephew, whose caustic farcical comedies present, in a style reminiscent of **Labiche**'s, a grotesque picture of hopelessly degraded and ridiculous humanity – their characters, without exception, are both amoral and, in one way or another, mentally defective. Other enduring plays of the period are for the most part historical pieces, especially attractive in a country whose national identity had long been denied (Rumania proclaimed its independence from the Ottoman Empire only in 1877). It was Bogdan Petriceicu Hașdeu who gave the Rumanian theatre its first important historical play, and probably its best romantic verse drama, *Răzvan and Vidra* (1867), in which a medieval Gypsy brigand, Răzvan, spurred by Vidra, the so-called Rumanian Lady Macbeth, ascends to and dies tragically on the throne of Moldavia. The same Hugo-inspired spirit marks *Prince Despot* (1879) by Vasile Alecsandri, who, in a new burst of creativity, went on to write two gracefully sensual and melancholic 'Roman plays', *The Fountain of Blandusia*

(1883) and *Ovid* (1885). More in line with the romantic tradition of Rumanian historical drama are Alexandru Davila's sober and gripping verse play *Prince Vlaicu* (1902) about an obscure episode at the beginning of Wallachia's history, and the monumental (over 100 characters) prose trilogy *Sunset* (1909), *The Storm* (1910), and *The Morning Star* (1910) by Barbu Ştefănescu Delavrancea. Naturalistic touches serve as a counterpoint to the lyrical tone of the best part of the trilogy, *Sunset*, which centres on the figure of the ageing Stephen the Great, Moldavia's most famous medieval ruler. While I. L. Caragiale, Haşdeu, Alecsandri, Davila, and Delavrancea have come to be considered Rumania's classic dramatists, other playwrights popular at the time are no longer in fashion. These include: Vasile Urechiă, most successful as an author of historical melodramas (*Minister Bucioc*, 1867); Grigore Ventura, of note for his topical and colourful war melodrama *Curcanii* (1878); I. Bengescu-Dabija, whose melodramatic verse tragedy *Pygmalion, the King of Phoenicia* (1886) was highly praised by contemporary critics; Haralamb Lecca, a leading writer of Ibsenite bourgeois dramas (*The Card Players*, 1899, *The Dogs*, 1902); and Ronetti Roman, a talenţed Rumanian-Jewish playwright who, in his compelling *Manasse* (1900), a *pièce-à-thèse* about inter-racial marriage, addressed the controversial issue of the integration of Jews in Rumanian society. More enduring in popularity has been Mihail Sorbul, the author of the naturalistic drama *The Red Passion* (1916). Also deserving of mention are the early 20th-century symbolic verse plays *The Gossamer Legend* (1907) by Şt. O. Iosif and Dimitrie Anghel; *String Yourself, Pearl!* (1911) and *The Black Rooster* (1913) by Victor Eftimiu; *The Red Roses* (1915) by Zaharia Bârsan; and *Zamolxes* (1921), a 'pagan mystery' in blank verse by Lucian Blaga.

In 1918, following the dissolution of the Austro-Hungarian Empire, Rumania acquired Transylvania, a province where large Hungarian and German minorities had been politically and culturally dominant since the early Middle Ages. The pre-eminent Hungarian-language theatre (founded in 1792) was at Cluj (Kolozsvár), and the principal German-language theatre (founded in 1787) was at Sibiu (Hermannstadt). Partly because of cultural oppression, partly because of frequent tours by professional troupes from Rumania, the Rumanians in Transylvania (the majority of the population) did not develop a significant theatre of their own until 1919 when Rumania's fourth National Theatre was established at Cluj.

The period between the wars saw a considerable and fruitful diversification of Rumanian theatrical life, due largely to the rapid expansion of the commercial theatre. In Bucharest, which remained the theatrical centre of the country, the foremost private acting company was the Bulandra, led by a team of actors of whom Tony Bulandra, his wife Lucia Sturza Bulandra, and Ion Manolescu were the most important. Among the other great Bucharest actors of the period were George Calboreanu at the National Theatre, Maria Filotti at the Sărindar, and Constantin Tănase, the undisputed master of Rumanian revue, at the Cărăbus. Eclectic for the most part, Rumanian directing was best represented by the work of Aurel Ion Maican; of the non-conformist Ion Sava, whose 1946 production of *Macbeth* with masks made history on the stage of the

National Theatre in Bucharest; of the exigent Victor Ion Popa; and of Soare Z. Soare, a disciple of **Max Reinhardt**. Another distinguished director was Iacob Sternberg, who, together with scene designer M. H. Maxy, painter Marcel Iancu (Tristan Tzara's former collaborator and one of the founders of dadaism), and others, championed the avant-garde theatre movement in Bucharest in the 1920s. Sternberg was also the chief promoter of Bucharest's Yiddish theatre, which he led back to the variety tradition begun by Avram (**Abraham**) **Goldfaden**.

Of the important and often revived dramatists of the period Camil Petrescu is notable for his intellectual dramas *The Fairies' Dance* (1919) and *Danton* (1925); George Mihail Zamfirescu (also known as a director) for his 'tragic comedy' with songs *Miss Nastasia* (1927), a masterpiece which blends melodrama, naturalism, and expressionism; George Ciprian for the mystic comedy *The Man with the Jade* (1927); Alexandru Kiriţescu for his comedy of manners *The Jays* (1930); Tudor Muşatescu for *Titanic Waltz* (1932) and . . . *Escu* (1933), two satirical comedies; Victor Ion Popa for *Take, Ianka, and Cadîr* (1933), a comedy on racial prejudice; and Mihail Sebastian for the lyrical comedies *The Nameless Star* (1943) and *Stop News* (1945).

After the Second World War the Rumanian stage entered a period of increased material prosperity brought about by the nationalization of the theatres in 1948. For a time the prescriptions of Socialist Realism, the official artistic doctrine, were strictly followed, but, in the later 1950s, a number of young directors and scene designers, of whom the most influential was **Liviu Ciulei**, began to call for a theatre of visual metaphor and allusion, more in tune with current Western theatrical trends. This movement for the 're-theatricalization' of stagecraft gained ground in the 1960s and led to an internationally acclaimed flowering of Rumanian theatrical art. Among the leading directors of the period are Liviu Ciulei, **Lucian Pintilie**, Radu Penciulescu, David Esrig, Dinu Cernescu, and Lucian Giurchescu, all also known outside their country and noted for their ability to find contemporary resonances in classic plays; among the scene designers Liviu Ciulei, Ion Popescu-Udriste and Radu Boruzescu (whose wife Miruna is a prominent costume designer); and among the actors Toma Caragiu, Radu Beligan, Gina Patrichi, Irina Petrescu, and George Dinică, who was outstanding in David Esrig's 1968 version of **Diderot**'s *Rameau's Nephew* at the Lucia Sturza Bulandra Theatre in Bucharest. Other theatres in the capital include the Mic, Foarte Mic Nottara, National, and Comedy. There is also a popular variety theatre, the Constantin Tănase, and an excellent puppet theatre, the Ţăndărică. Major provincial theatres are at Jassy, Cluj-Napoca, Piatra Neamţ, and Tîrgu Mureş.

In contemporary Rumanian drama, which has ranged from Socialist Realism to the abstract, but has eschewed such themes as eroticism, violence, or alienation, well-known playwrights are Aurel Baranga, whose *The Rabid Lamb* (1954) is a satire against bureaucracy; Horia Lovinescu, the author of *The Boga Sisters* (1959), in which, unlike in its model, *The Three Sisters* by **Chekhov**, poetic justice prevails; Ecaterina Oproiu, whose popular romantic comedy *I Am Not the Eiffel Tower* (1965) signalled a movement away from Socialist Realism; and Marin Sorescu, who wrote a number of innovative plays including *Jonah* (1969), a symbolic monodrama, and *The Third Pale* (1978), a metaphorical historical drama about the medieval Wallachian prince Vlad the Impaler (Dracula).

A recent development in the theatrical life of the country has been the establishment of the national festival 'Singing Rumanian'. This mass artistic competition, which in the early 1980s came to play an increasingly important role in Rumanian culture, consists primarily of amateur performances of song and dance, agit-prop, and short plays.   BM

> *See*: S. Alterescu (ed.), *An Abridged History of Romanian Theatre*, Bucureşti, 1973; S. Alterescu (ed.), *Istoria teatrului în România*, 3 vols., Bucureşti, 1965–73; T. T. Burada, *Istoria teatrului în Moldova*, Bucureşti, 1975; G. Călinescu, *Istoria literaturii române*, Bucureşti, 1982; I. Massoff, *Teatrul românesc*, 5 vols., Bucureşti, 1961–74; A. Mititelu, *Teatro romeno*, Milan, 1960; D. C. Ollănescu, *Teatrul la români*, Bucureşti, 1981.

Russell, Annie (1864–1936) English-born American actress. Two years after her New York stage debut in 1879, Annie Russell established her career with a brilliant portrayal of the title character in *Esmeralda*. Ill health forced her from the stage for three seasons (1891–4), but she returned to regain her popularity and

Annie Russell.

invite comparison with **Eleonora Duse** for her simplicity and naturalism. She was effective especially in emotional and comic roles. In 1905 she created **Shaw**'s heroine in *Major Barbara*, and gave memorable performances of Puck in *A Midsummer Night's Dream* (1906), Viola in *Twelfth Night* (1909), Beatrice in *Much Ado* (1912), and Lady Teazle in *The School for Scandal* (1914). Her charming stage presence made her the ideal ingenue. She retired from the stage in 1918 to head the dramatic programme at Rollins College, Winter Park, Florida.   TLM

Russell, Henry (1812–1900) English entertainer and songwriter, of Jewish descent; after studying music with Rossini and Bellini, he descended to being an organist and choral director in Rochester, New York. In 1837, he made a debut as a ballad singer at the Brooklyn Lyceum; in a short time he became a hugely popular performer, offering the first solo vocal programmes in America, aimed at the common man. He not only sang in a pleasant baritone and accompanied himself on the piano, but composed his entire repertory. This included such warhorses-to-be as *Cheer, Boys, Cheer!*, *Woodman! Spare That Tree*, *A Life on the Ocean Wave*, and *The Old Armchair*, as well as temperance, anti-slavery and humanitarian ballads. His appearance in London at the Hanover Square Rooms, 1842, was a triumph; he performed in England and America until the early 1860s.   LS

Russell, Lillian (née Helen Louise Leonard) (1861–1922) American singer and actress whose name is synonymous with one of her show titles, *An American Beauty*. Rising from obscurity in Clinton, Iowa, she became a much sought after star in comic opera, burlesque, vaudeville, and drama. **Tony Pastor** billed her as 'The English Ballad Singer' at his Broadway variety theatre in 1880. Cross-country tours and engagements in New York and England followed. She was applauded for her physical and vocal charms in such vehicles as *The Pie Rats of Penn Yan*, Pastor's burlesque of *The Pirates of Penzance*; *The Snake Charmer*; *The Sorcerer*; *The Princess of Trebizonde*; *Iolanthe*; and *The Princess Nicotine*. With **Weber** and **Fields**'s celebrated troupe she enjoyed five seasons, 1899–1904. Roles in *Lady Teazle* (musical version of *The School for Scandal*), *The Butterfly*, and *Wildfire* furthered her already flourishing reputation. She died in Pittsburgh, survived by her fourth husband and a daughter.   DBW

Russell, Willy (William Martin) (1947–   ) British author and dramatist, who was born and educated in Liverpool, and took many jobs, including being a hairdresser, before becoming a full-time writer in 1971. His first three short plays, *Blind Scouse*, appeared in 1971–2; but his first success came with a musical biography of the Beatles, *John, Paul, George, Ringo and Bert* (1974), which transferred to London. The cheerful humour of his comedies, *Breezeblock Park* (1975), *One for the Road* (1976) and *Stags and Hens* (1978), brought him popularity as an observer of Liverpudlian life; but *Educating Rita* (1979) proved to be much less parochial in its appeal, a study of a pupil–teacher relationship where the attractive intelligent student eventually takes control. Russell, who composes songs for the guitar, writes casual, informal musicals, such as *Blood Brothers* (1983) and *Our Day Out* (1984), far removed in style from the glittering show-business creations of the West End and Broadway. He is the author of several television plays and plays for schools.   JE

Russia and the Soviet Union Despite Russian Orthodox Church opposition and that of the absolutist tsar, the largely illiterate general populace and the affected, unsympathetic aristocracy, Russian theatre and drama developed from a pagan, animistic, oral base into a fully-fledged institution by the 18th century, a good deal later than their European counterparts. Russia's earliest semi-professional entertainers were the **skomorokhi**, itinerant and from 1572 court-attached jesters–musicians–singers–story-tellers, who often performed with bears and puppets. Their performances, the profane evolution of what may have been priestly rites prior to 988 (when Russia converted to Orthodox Christianity), were too shocking and their presences too charismatic – the people credited them with magical powers – to be tolerated by the church and state, and they were officially proscribed by Tsar Aleksei Mikhailovich in 1648. They died out as a profession in the late 18th century. Not so easily suppressed was a tradition of seasonal and occasional theatrical plays which included: fairs (*gulyaniya*); Christmas and Shrovetide carnivals, featuring animal-human transformations and impersonations and a schedule of games, feasts, revels and processionals; birth and puberty rites with mimetic dances (*igrovye*); and 'performed' weddings with a town-wide participation in 'scenes' and interludes, clowning, mock battles and round dances (*khorovody*). These rituals inspired parodic folk plays which often satirized the ignorant and corrupt rural clergy. Non-ritual folk dramas, offering socio-political commentary and protest, developed by the 17th century, the most popular of

A 17th-century Russian woodcut, showing clowns.

Jesters in Ladoga, 1636–9.

which were *The Ship* (*Lodka*) and the scenic assemblage *Tsar Maksimilian*, which dealt with the pagan ruler's conflict with and murder of his Christian son, Adolph. These were performed in the late 18th century in temporary wooden structures called *balagany* (from the Persian *balakhan* – an upper chamber or balcony), originally built at markets and fairs during Shrovetide and Easter week, and most often associated with comic interludes and harlequinades. Puppet theatre, especially the Ukrainian *vertep*, performed on a medieval-type, two-tiered, trapped stage, may also have influenced the live folk theatre tradition from the 17th century.

The origins of Russian theatre and drama were then folkloric and not liturgical, although the church exerted considerable positive and negative influence on their early development. Russian bishop Avraamy of Suzdaal left an enthusiastic written account of the spectacular stage effects achieved in performances of two *sacre rappresentazioni* in Florence, Italy (1437–9). A church-produced 'Fiery Furnace' show, in which townspeople-Chaldeans burned three choirboy-impersonated Israelite youths in a pulpit-cauldron, was staged in Novgorod prior to 1548. School dramas, designed to teach Latin and religion via stories about the Nativity, the Resurrection of Christ and Lives of the Saints and Martyrs, entered Russia from Poland via the Kiev (Mohyla) Academy (1615, 1632), established to counter Polish attempts to convert Russia to Catholicism during and after the Time of Troubles (1604–13). Theological students tailored these dramas to popular tastes by converting them to the vernacular and Church Slavonic and by introducing comic interludes which eventually toured independently. Three clerics associated with the Kiev Academy – Simeon Polotsky, Danylo Tuptalo (Metropolitan Dmitry of Rostov) and **Feofan Prokopovich** – helped establish a formal Russian dramatic repertory in the late 17th and early 18th centuries with their plays on biblical and historical themes, expressing pro-tsarist sympathies and incorporating realistic elements, songs and dances.

The Russian court theatre was founded in 1672 under reformed theatre-hater Tsar Aleksei Mikhailovich, who invited Lutheran Pastor **Johann Gottfried Gregory** of Moscow's foreign quarter to stage a play in honour of his son and heir's (the future Peter the Great's) birth. The ten-hour presentation of *The Comedy of Esther, or The Play of Artaxerxes*, featuring a cast of 64, mainly merchants' sons, led to the development of a dramatic repertory composed of biblical and adapted Elizabethan dramas and tragicomedies for a theatre which remained open only until the tsar's death in 1676. Peter I ('the Great', reigned 1682–1725), introduced to theatre while abroad and cognizant of its propaganda value, sponsored the first secular public theatre, under the leadership of German actor-manager **Johann Kunst**, and encouraged attendance via several methods: introducing the ceremonial spectacle, a musical and special effects extravaganza on mythical and allegorical themes expressing partisan politics; staging performances in Russian as well as in German, which only the court spoke; eliminating road taxes on performance days; offering free admission; issuing imperial decrees. The theatre lasted only from 1702 to 1706, and although comic interludes remained popular, a formal theatrical tradition had yet to be established. During the reigns of Empresses Anna (1730–40) and Elizabeth (1741–61), visiting Italian artists introduced: opera (Francesco Araia); **commedia dell'arte**, whose masks were absorbed into the Russian interludes accompanying the *vertep* and the school dramas; perspective scenery techniques (Giovani Buon); and an acrobatic form of ballet (Antonio and Giulia Fusano), which was replaced by a more graceful style devised by Frenchman Jean Baptiste Landet. German actress **Caroline Neuber**, a disciple of **Johann Gottsched**, established classical tragedy at the Russian Court (1739–40). Unfortunately, the lavishness of theatrical spectacle, much of it the work of foreigners, reinforced the Russians' sense of theatre as being something alien to their culture.

The first permanent professional public theatre in Russia was founded in 1756, at the behest of Empress Elizabeth, by the Yaroslavl actor **Fyodor Volkov**, his brother Grigory and director–dramatist **Aleksandr Sumarokov**, Russia's first professional man of letters. His Russified neoclassical Voltairian tragedies – e.g., *Khorev* (1747) and *Dmitry the Pretender* (1771) – written for Russia's first great tragedian, **Ivan Dmitrevsky**, and his **Molière**-based comedies helped free Russian theatre of its dependency upon translations of foreign works and remained repertory staples for the next two decades. This lustreless neoclassical tradition was continued by Sumarokov's son-in-law, **Yakov Knyazhnin**, and by Vasily Maikov, Aleksei Rzhevsky, Nikolai Nikolev, Mikhail Kheraskov and the father of Russian science, **Mikhail Lomonosov**.

Empress Catherine II ('the Great', reigned 1762–96) regarded the Russian theatre as a 'national school' and herself – the author of forgettable historical plays, satirical comedies and comic operas aimed at her enemies, the Freemasons and the Theosophists – the senior teacher. While theatrical enterprises multiplied, the drama remained didactic, and Catherine's liberality waned following the French Revolution (1789). During Catherine's reign, German manager Karl Knipper and English circus performer Michael Maddox founded short-lived theatres. More importantly, in 1771 Catherine ordered the building of the Petersburg Bolshoi Theatre and in 1779 added the Imperial Theatre School for the training of Russian actors, singers and dancers. Catherine's 1762 charter freeing the nobles from many of their state obligations led to the beginning of the serf theatre, a microcosm of tsarist patriarchy in which indentured performers were treated as

The Serf Theatre of Sheremetiev at Ostankino.

gifted children and had bestowed upon them monetary and amorous favours alternating with torture and public humiliation. Eventually numbering 173 venues, the serf theatres of Prince Yusupov, **Nikolai Sheremetiev** and others were the best-equipped and most lavishly appointed facilities in the land. In the 1840s the combination of rising Imperial municipal theatres' fortunes and falling rural landowners' profits brought their closure or absorption into professional and amateur provincial touring companies, the latter precipitating the birth of the provincial repertory system. The spectre of serfdom, abolished in 1861, haunts **Chekhov**'s plays and the lot of the provincial actor is well described by **Ostrovsky**.

From 1710 to the late 1740s (the advent of Russian neoclassicism), the chivalric romance play, adapted from French and Italian poetic sources and produced by Princess Natalya (Peter the Great's younger sister) at her private theatre, was the most popular form of secular drama in Russia. By the end of the century, the Russian aristocracy, following Europe's lead and desirous of casting a glow of moral goodness around the status quo, embraced sentimentalism and especially the work of **August von Kotzebue**, who became the most frequently performed foreign dramatist in 19th-century Russia. Dramatist **Nikolai Polevoi** became the leading Russian theorist of Kotzebuism and Nikolai Ilyin its most influential interpreter with his popular ballad opera *Liza, or the Triumph of Gratitude* (1802). Like Vasily Fyodorov's highly successful *Liza, or the Consequence of Pride and Seduction* (1803), it derived from Nikolai Karamzin's sentimental novella *Poor Liza*. The ballad and comic opera (*opéra comique*), the bourgeois drama (*drame*) and the sentimental comedy (*comédie larmoyante*) – all part of an effort to democratize the stage via satire and moralizing in the manner of **Destouches**, **Diderot**, **Beaumarchais**, **Lillo** and **Lessing** – were exceedingly popular in early 19th-century Russia. Comic opera authors included: actor **Pyotr Plavilshchikov**; former serf Mikhail Matinsky; minor journalist Nikolai Lvov; Aleksandr Ablesimov, whose *The Miller, the Magician, the Deceiver and the Matchmaker* (1779) was a popular success; and Vladimir Lukin, whose campaign to Russify the stage was reinforced by intensified anti-French feeling after the French Revolution and during Napoleon's reign. While Lukin's call for a people's theatre was not immediately heeded, sentimental drama – e.g., Nikolev's *Rozanna and Lyubim* (1776) and Mikhail Popov's *Anyuita* (1772), the first Russian comic opera – extolled the people's moral values and aroused empathy for the difficult conditions of the peasant serf's life without actually questioning the institution of serfdom itself. Sentimentalism was also applied to neoclassical tragic formulas to produce the patriotic, tsarist–propagandist history plays in mythological and historical settings of **Vladislav Ozerov** (*Oedipus in Athens*, 1804; *Dmitry of the Don*, 1807) and **Nestor Kukolnik** (*The Hand of the Almighty Has Saved the Fatherland*, 1833). **Denis Fonvizin**'s *The Brigadier* (1769) and *The Minor* (1781) established the Russian satirical comedy of manners, which although neoclassical in form, constituted the first step toward a national comedy of social realism with its native character, linguistic and topical elements. **Vasily Kapnist**'s *Chicanery* (1789), which satirized judicial corruption, deepened Russian comedy's social role while synthesizing the earlier prose comedy conventions of Lukin and Fonvizin. However, it was the vaudeville genre, adapted from the French prototype and from Russian comic opera, commencing with **Prince Aleksandr Shakhovskoi**'s *The Cossack Poet* (1812) and intensifying during the reactionary reign of Nikolai I (1825–55) which offered the most pointed social commentary. Its Russian practitioners included: **Aleksandr Pisarev**, its 'father'; poet Nikolai Nekrasov; Nikolai Khmelnitsky, who elevated its social setting; Pyotr Karatygin, the great tragedian Vasily's brother; Mikhail Zagoskin; theatrical journalist Fyodor Koni; Dmitry Lensky, author of the extremely popular *Lev Gurych Sinichkin*; and Russia's greatest moral fabulist, **Ivan Krylov**, who invented 'Aesopian language' (a term later coined by **Saltykov-Shchedrin**), i.e., the allegorical, circumlocutory expression of satirical and ironic criticism of and commentary on the status quo which became the currency of Soviet drama after 1917. **Aleksandr Griboedov**'s comic verse masterpiece *Woe from Wit* (1824) became the basis for Russian national comedy and the most commonly quoted Russian literary source. Griboedov refined and complicated plot and psychological character, streamlined exposition and introduced philosophical content, relating to the Decembrist movement. His protagonist, Chatsky, an inveterate truth-teller and victimized, uncompromising spirit imprisoned in a soulless society, became a variously interpreted paradigm in Russian and Soviet drama.

The first two decades of the 19th century saw the Imperial Theatre Directorate gaining a monopoly over the Moscow and St Petersburg stages which lasted until 1882. The first censorship law (1804) led to Imperial censorship control over all provincial and capital theatres in 1842 and to the hegemony of Nikolai I's secret committee after 1848. The acting profession ascended in craft and prestige during this century, despite the overall weakness of the repertory, the limitations of *emploi* and the general lack of enlightenment among administrators, audiences and actors themselves. In the first third of the century, Dmitrevsky and Shakhovskoi trained many of the best actors: Moscow's craft-conscious Y. E. Shusherin; the more emotional and incipiently realistic **A. S. Yakovlev** and **E. S. Semyonova**, **Pushkin**'s favourite; coolly technical Y. G. Bryansky; and the great Petersburg tragedians **V. A. Karatygin** and **I. I. Sosnitsky**. The Imperial Maly Theatre became 'the house of the actor', and former serf actor **Mikhail Shchepkin**, that theatre's and Russian realism's patriarch. His pupil and **Stanislavsky**'s teacher, **Glikeriya Fedotova**, the popular **Mariya Ermolova**, romantic tragedian **Pavel Mochalov** and Ostrovsky specialist **Prov Sadovsky** all helped earn the Maly the mantle of 'a second Moscow University'. Directing lagged behind in the Russian theatrical consciousness, with the protean Shakhovskoi receiving credit as being the first régisseur. Although stage scenery followed the lead of the 'natural school' of the 1830s–50s and the box set and specialized décor for opera and ballet were developed, dramatic productions relied on a handful of stock sets and the designer's role was ill-defined and ill-appreciated until the advent of the **Moscow Art Theatre** and the World of Art group in the late 1890s.

Russian romanticism (1815–40), adapted from English, French and German sources (especially from fabulist **E. T. A. Hoffmann**) and from native folkloric, historical and traditional sources, initiated linguistic experimentation and genre cross-fertilization, as well as several themes – man's and reality's doubleness, woman's infernality, urban paranoia – which resonated primarily in poetry and secondarily in drama until 1917. Its leading exponent and Russia's national poet, Aleksandr Pushkin, attempted to found a school of national tragedy with *Boris Godunov* (1825), a sprawling, misunderstood and seldom-staged account of the Time of Troubles, embodying the influences of **Shakespeare**, **Khmelnitsky** and Griboedov, whose final image of the strong but silently suffering People fired the Bolsheviks' imagination nearly a century later. His four psychological miniatures, collectively entitled *The Little Tragedies* (1830), were reclaimed by the Moscow Art Theatre in 1915 and were made into operas by Dargomyzhsky, Rimsky-Korsakov and Rakhmaninov. Pushkin's literary criticism included useful commentary on dramatic genres and the educational purpose of dramatic repertory, but the most important 19th-century Russian literary criticism, written by Vissarion Belinsky, Nikolai Chernyshevsky and Nikolai Dobrolyubov, was socially utilitarian. The great lyric poet, **Mikhail Lermontov**, wrote several Byronic dramas, of which only the *Othello*-inspired *Masquerade* (1836) is remembered and that owing more to the sumptuously designed (by Aleksandr Golovin), **Meyerhold**-directed Imperial Aleksandrinsky Theatre production (1917) than to the intrinsic merit of the play. Despite the significant anti-aristocratic, popular biases of Griboedov's, Pushkin's and Lermontov's plays, they were banned in their own day and did not exert nearly the influence of **Nikolai Gogol**'s *The Inspector General*, Russia's greatest comic masterpiece since *Woe from Wit*. A brilliantly eccentric mix of a traditional premiss suggested by Pushkin – a town duped by its own avarice and paranoia in the form of a self-dramatizing non-entity – the *vertep*, *commedia dell'arte*, Plautine farce, medieval allegory and apocalyptic tale – it has been variously interpreted as social satire, moral parable and pure theatrical hyperbole. Gogol, who publicly disapproved of farce and vaudeville, wrote several, as did **Ivan Turgenev**, although the latter is remembered for *A Month in the Country* (1850), a psychological study of 'superfluous' gentry lives, redo-

The bribery scene from Gogol's *The Inspector General*,
Meyerhold Theatre.

lent with proto-Chekhovian ambiance. Disgraced
nobleman **Aleksandr Sukhovo-Kobylin**'s dramatic
trilogy – *Krechinsky's Wedding* (1854), *The Case* (1861)
and *Tarelkin's Death* (1869) – combined the Gogolian
satirical grotesque with the author's personal experience of bureaucratic hell to evoke the sense of imminent
dehumanization, vampirism, loss of faith and innocence that awaited the Comtean-Darwinian world of
the future and the modernist art that followed. Monstrous merchant and peasant milieux were depicted in
satirist Mikhail Saltykov-Shchedrin's *Pazukhin's Death*
(1857) and in **Aleksei Pisemsky**'s *A Bitter Fate* (1859),
respectively, the latter antecedent to **Lev Tolstoi**'s
better-known but less-skilled peasant tragedy *The
Power of Darkness* (1888) and part of the realistic peasant
drama tradition initiated by Aleksei Potekhin's plays of
the 1850s–70s. The so-called first Russian tragedy, *The
Thunderstorm* (1859), was written by 19th-century
Russia's consummate professional dramatist, Aleksandr Ostrovsky, best known for creating the quotidian (*bytovaya*) drama of merchant life, beginning with
Don't Get into Another's Sleigh, the 1853 Maly Theatre
production of which established his reputation and
solidified his relationship with this producing organization. Ostrovsky also wrote historical dramas, as did:
L. A. Mei, whose *The Tsar's Bride* (1849) and *The Maid
of Pskov* (1859) were transformed into operas by
Rimsky-Korsakov; D. V. Averkiev; I. Lazhechnikov;
and above all, **Aleksei Tolstoi**, whose trilogy – *The
Death of Ivan the Terrible* (1866), *Tsar Fyodor Ioannovich*
(1868), *Tsar Boris* (1870) – provided the Moscow Art
Theatre with psychologically detailed, strongly contrasting characters (the rapacious Ivan and Boris; the
gentle Fyodor) to realize.

Konstantin Stanislavsky's and **Vladimir
Nemirovich-Danchenko**'s Moscow Art Accessible
Theatre, as it was originally called, was the culimi-
nation of a century's progress toward realism. Inspired
by the Russian tours of the **Meininger** troupe (1885
and 1890) and by the new dramaturgy of **Ibsen**,
Hauptmann and **Maeterlinck**, it increased the
public's theatrical awareness, elevated the acting profession and set new production standards, largely
through its collaborations with successful short story
writer and previously failed dramatist Anton Chekhov

and with self-made prose writer and social icon **Maksim Gorky**, after whom MAT was named in 1932. In
his comedies of uneventful, stunted lives – *The Seagull*
(1896), *Uncle Vanya* (1899), *The Three Sisters* (1901),
The Cherry Orchard (1904) – Chekhov deconstructed
the artificially closed and logical structure of the
well-made play and the orderly world it reflected,
recycled 19th-century farce-vaudeville types and conventions and achieved a world of concrete mystery
related to symbolism, but with greater humour and less
pretence. The majority of Gorky's dramas, which
marginally resemble his mentor Chekhov's, embody
his ingrained sense of class distinctions and social
inequities and his hatred for the self-satisfied philistinism of the intelligentsia and the bourgeoisie. His
best-known play in the West, the somewhat atypical,
philosophically ambiguous tramp drama *The Lower
Depths* (1902), is drawn from his own early life
experience. Gorky encouraged both realistic writers –
Evgeny Chirikov, Semyon Yushkevich, Sergei Nai-
dyonov – and anti-realists **Blok** and **Andreev** through
his publishing house Znanie (Knowledge, 1900), as
well as protecting countless others after the Revolution
from his unequalled position of cultural eminence. Aid
came as well from the sympathetic First People's
Commissar for Education, **Anatoly Lunacharsky**, a
theatre aficionado and author of politically conceived
historical dramas.

The anti-realist movement began in the 1890s with
the cultural aestheticism of the World of Art group
painters – **Alexandre Benois**, **Léon Bakst**, Mstislav
Dobuzhinsky, Nikolai Sapunov, Serge Soudeikine, *et
al.* – whose decorative work graced their own highly
refined journal (founded 1898), the related Ballets
Russes productions of Sergei Diaghilev and numerous
theatre projects by Stanislavsky, Meyerhold, Evreinov
and others. They were particularly important to the
Petersburg-based cultural retrospectivism movement,
centred in Evreinov's and Baron Nikolai Drizen's
Ancient Theatre, and to the cabaret-theatre of small
forms – e.g., the Bat, the Crooked Mirror Theatre, the
Stray Dog, the Comedians' Rest – specializing in
literary and theatrical parody, harlequinade, panto-

A scene from Sukhovo-Kobylin's *Tarelkin's Death*, showing
Vavana Stepanova's constructivist set for the third and most
grotesque play in that author's dramatic trilogy. Pictured are
various torture devices used by police for purposes of
interrogation.

mime and variety acts, in the capital cities. Low art, which gained sustenance from primitive and folkloric forms, entered the official theatres primarily via Meyerhold and bridged the gap between pre-revolutionary decorative aestheticism and post-revolutionary dynamic functionalism, in which vaudeville, circus and cinema were employed in mass actions and agit-prop presentations. The 'high art' of Russian symbolism (1890–1917) combined the philosopher Vladimir Solovyov's apocalyptic theories, **Friedrich Nietzsche**'s ideas on the Dionysian origins of the drama, **Richard Wagner**'s *Gesamtkuntswerk*, Baudelaire's theory of correspondences, and the philosophical–symbolic, folk and subjectivist dramatic visions of Ibsen, Maeterlinck, Hauptmann and **Strindberg**. The Russian symbolists' erudite, static and visionary dramas, beginning with Nikolai Minsky's *Alma* (1900), reflected their self-dramatizing personalities and ruling concepts, including: Dmitry Merezhkovsky's and his wife the poetess Zinaida Gippius's God-seeking; **Vyacheslav Ivanov**'s theatre of congregate action; **Valery Briusov**'s *uslovny* (self-conscious, conventional) theatre; **Andrei Bely**'s neo-mystery plays; **Innokenty Annensky**'s and **Aleksei Remizov**'s mythic and Russian folkloric themes; **Fyodor Sologub**'s fatalism and author-centred 'Theatre of One Will'; and **Mikhail Kuzmin**'s darkly dandyish *commedia*. The greatest symbolist dramatist, Aleksandr Blok, posited theatricalism as an alternative faith to symbolist mysticism in his epochal harlequinade *The Puppet Show* (1906), so too did such marginally symbolist writers as **Nikolai Evreinov**, in his mono-dramas and in his major play *The Chief Thing* (1921), and Leonid Andreev, in his Poe-like romantically horrific, allegorical meditations on death's proximity and life's vacuity (e.g., *He Who Gets Slapped*, 1915). While the symbolists faltered as aesthetic saints, the most talented of their director-contemporaries – Evreinov at the Ancient Theatre and the Crooked Mirror, Meyerhold, **Tairov** and **Vakhtangov** – succeeded as theatricalist visionary showmen. Vsevolod Meyerhold's career embraced all of the foregoing aesthetic trends, as well as constructivism, his 1922 constructivist-designed production of Crommelynck's *The Magnanimous Cuckold* coinciding with Aleksei Gan's manifesto stating that 'art is dead'. The 'new machine art' of constructivist designers **Lyubov Popova**, Vladimir Tatlin, **Aleksandra Ekster**, Aleksandr Rodchenko, Vladimir Stenberg and others, derived in part from cubo-futurism and modelled on industrial design, posited a new, demystified, scientific basis for art, the glorification of proletarian man and the 'truth' and organization of materials. This new democratization of the stage was opposed by Aleksandr Tairov at his aesthetically elitist Kamerny (Chamber) Theatre (founded 1914), which featured balletic, cubist- and *commedia*-influenced productions (e.g. **Racine**'s *Phaedra*, 1922; Hoffmann's *Princess Brambilla*, 1920) and aspired to the ideal of musical sculpture and a complete synthesis of the arts. Evgeny Vakhtangov synthesized the Stanislavskian and Meyerholdian theatrical approaches in his 'fantastic realism', whereby he alternately carnivalized (*Princess Turandot*, 1922) and ritualized (*The Dybbuk*, 1922) the stage and sounded a note of harmonious creation in the final days of 'War Communism's' (1917–22) optimistic experiments.

This period saw a theatrical explosion – over 3,000 professional troupes in Russia alone, the nationalization of all theatres in regions under Bolshevik control (1919) and attempts by the innovators Meyerhold, Evreinov, **Sergi Radlov**, **Yuri Annenkov**, Sergei Eisenstein to create a uniquely Soviet popular theatre of montage-like mass spectacles and agit-prop presentations, performed by circus artistes, gymnasts, military personnel and participants in the actual historical events being dramatized. These tendencies were continued by the Proletkult (1917–23) and Blue Blouse movements (1923–8), the latter numbering 484 professional and 8,000 amateur companies nation-wide in its final year of operation. Its 'montage of attractions' approach – film, animated poster, agit-prop cabaret, etc. – owed much to Italian futurist **Marinetti**'s 'Variety Manifesto' of 1913. The advent of the New Economic Policy (NEP, 1921–8) engendered a Soviet brand of satirical grotesque which focused upon careerists and financial speculators, as well as a theatre, the Moscow Theatre of Satire (founded 1924), at which to perform them. The futurist poet **Vladimir Mayakovsky**, whose neo-mystery *Mystery-Bouffe* (1918) has been called the first Soviet play, summarized and transformed NEP satire in *The Bedbug* (1928) and *The Bathhouse* (1929), which projected anti-utopian images drawn from cartoons, cinema and science fiction. This pessimistic experimentalism was countered by the 'factographic' melodramas of **Sergei Tretyakov** and by the Civil War paeans of **Vladimir Bill-Belotserkovsky**, **Vsevolod Ivanov**, **Konstantin Trenyov**, **Leonid Leonov** and Boris Lavrenyov, whose *The Break-up* (1927), in a not unfamiliar scenario, was rewritten at Stalin's direction. From these followed the epic, romantic monumentalist plays of the 1930s – **Vsevolod Vishnevsky**'s *An Optimistic Tragedy* (1933), **Aleksandr Afinogenov**'s *Fear* (1931), **Aleksandr Korneichuk**'s *Platon Krechet* (1934) and **Nikolai Pogodin**'s Lenin trilogy, beginning with *The Man with a Gun* (1937). The best plays of the 1920s–40s were branded 'formalist' and went largely unproduced until after Stalin's death. The dramas of **Mikhail Bulgakov** – *The Days of the Turbins* (1926), *Flight* (1927), *A Cabal of Hypocrites* (*Molière*, 1930), etc. – **Nikolai Erdman** – *The Mandate* (1925) and *The Suicide* (1928) – and **Yury Olesha** – *The Conspiracy of Feelings* (1928) and *A List of Blessings*

The finale to Meyerhold's production of Ostrovsky's 1871 comedy, *The Forest*, 1924. The acting, like the set, embodied a strong sense of rhythm.

(1931) – presented common-man dreamers, artistic 'egoists', 'class enemies' and 'former people' alienated from the Soviet ideal of progress and the new personality-less society. The Serapion Brothers (1921–9) – **Evgeny Zamyatin**, *et al.* – and the OBERIU (The Association for Real Art, 1927–30), led by Aleksandr Vvedensky and Daniil Kharms, rejected ideological art in favour of modernist, allegorical, neo-futurist and proto-absurdist forms whose impact did not register until the 1960s. The children's theatre movement, whose flagship institution, the Moscow Central Children's Theatre (its name after 1936), was founded in 1920 by Natalya Sats, and which was compelled to stage Stalinist parables in the 1930s, produced one dramatic master of Aesopian language, **Evgeny Shvarts** (*The Naked King*, 1934; *The Shadow*, 1940; *The Dragon*, 1943). (See also **Soviet children's theatre**.)

In 1934 a Party spokesman and 'culture specialist' Andrei Zhdanov, speaking at the First All-Union Congress of Soviet Writers, proclaimed the doctrine of 'socialist realism', resulting in the greying out of Soviet art and literature until after Stalin's death in 1953. Finding recent precedents in the policies of the First Five-Year Plan (1928–32), it fused Russia's belief in its messianic mission, the mission of its proletariat and its penchant for separating the 'useful' from the 'superfluous'. History was reconceived as the inexorable path to revolutionary communism, whose material accessibility made it a suitable spiritual replacement for Christian paradise. Scientists were dubbed 'soldiers of the mind' and artists 'engineers of the soul' in the war against egoism, mysticism and self-doubt, and in the ideological transformation and education of workers. The implicit moral superiority and final victory of communism led Nikolai Virta to posit the theory of 'conflictless drama', which featured the 'positive hero', new slogans like 'party spirit' (*partinost*) and 'national character' (*narodnost*) and pursued a new mythic egalitarianism which glorified labour and produced common-denominator art – 'plays about whether to plant wheat or to plant corn' (Viktor Rozov). The patriotic war plays of **Konstantin Simonov**, Kornei-

A scene from Lyubimov's production of *Rugachyov*, 1967. Adapted from dramatist and 'peasant poet' Sergei Esenin's lyrical tragedy, it tells of an abortive 18th century peasant rebellion, claimed by the soviets as a forerunner of the 1917 Revolution.

chuk and Leonov, the anti-capitalist dramas of Simonov and Lavrenyov and the historical rewrites of **A. N. Tolstoi** and Vishnevsky put these themes into practice.

Stalin's death and Krushchev's de-Stalinization speech at the 20th Party Congress (1956) ushered in the 'Thaw' period in the arts, which precipitated a 'new lyricism' and 'rehumanization' in the theatre. The first generation of post-Thaw dramatists – **Viktor Rozov**, **Aleksandr Volodin** and **Aleksei Arbuzov** – created a new form of intimate play of conscience and crisis, presented in a diversified theatricalist style composed of interpolated music, songs, dances, pantomime and poetry, choruses, flashbacks, split focus and montage, borrowed in part from the 1920s. While the results in drama were sometimes overly schematic and sentimentally monumentalist, these experiments suited a new generation of stage directors seeking to dramatize narrative fiction and to revitalize and gain critical perspective on classic and contemporary plays. **Yury Lyubimov** made the *mise en scène* the star at the Taganka Theatre, whose direction he assumed in 1964, and perfected a style which combined agit-prop, minstrelsy and revisionist historical and cultural criticism. The equally controversial and peripatetic **Anatoly Efros** sought in his productions to capture the essence of contemporaneity by internalizing the *mise en scène* in the actor as iconographic feeling man. **Georgy Tovstonogov**, since 1956 director of Leningrad's Bolshoi Dramatic Theatre, brought a more sober but humanitarian sensibility to his productions. He has also helped to popularize and adapt the American musical, along with younger directors Vladimir Vorovyov and Efim Padve (his former students), Gennady Yudenich, Vyacheslav Spesivtsev, Mark Rozovsky and Mark Zakharov. **Oleg Efremov**'s youth-oriented Sovremennik (Contemporary) Theatre embodied the first flush of post-Thaw optimism and self-criticism, some of which was directed at the moribund 'realism' of the Moscow Art Theatre, which Efremov now heads. The Sovremennik's production of Chingiz Aitmatov's and Kaltai Mukhamedzhanov's *The Ascent of Mount Fuji* (1973), within a month of the 20th anniversary of Stalin's death, symbolized the new standard for self-

A scene from Yury Lyubimov's 1965 adaptation of John Need's *Ten Days that Shook the World*. Despite accusations from the Soviet press and officialdom of irreverence toward the Revolution, this became one of Lyubimov's longest running productions at the Taganka. It is a characteristic (for him) cinematic montage of light, shadow, carnival mask and grotesque in the service of revolutionary agit-prop.

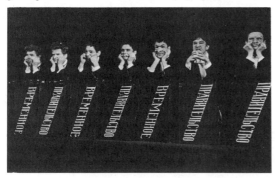

criticism, not only in its subject matter – collective guilt over compliance with Stalinist tyranny – but in its materials, drawn from the biographies of poet-folksinger Bulat Okudzhava and dissident novelist Aleksandr Solzhenitsyn, and its means – a reunion and the 'truth' game from Dostoevsky's *The Idiot*. While Arbuzov reinvented the 19th-century farce-vaudeville, **Andrei Amalrik** updated OBERIU drama to modern absurdism, **Vasily Aksyonov** reclaimed NEP satire and **Edvard Radzinsky** extended the Gogolian-Bulgakovian line of satirical grotesque and philosophical inquiry to expose the mythic fallacy of Soviet history, Soviet drama closed out the 1960s and entered the 1970s and 1980s on a youthful note. By the time of his accidental death at the age of 35, **Aleksandr Vampilov** had become the voice of his generation, and with his play *Duck Hunting* (1967), he initiated the genre of the 'urban grotesque' – i.e., realistic dramas in claustrophobic, modern urban settings. Practised by older writers such as Arbuzov, Volodin, Rozov and the late Yury Trifonov, whose work Lyubimov adapted for the Taganka stage, it has become the preserve of such younger playwrights as Semyon Zlotnikov, Mark Rozovsky, Viktor Slavkin, Aleksei Kazantsev and especially, Lyudmila Petrushevskaya. Her hyper-realistic, small-cast plays – *Music Lessons, Smirnova's Birthday, Cinzano* (all 1973), *Love* and *Come into the Kitchen* (both 1979) – are rendered with purposeful

'Acting machines' at the Taganka Theatre. The clock pendulum from Ezi Stavinsky's *Rush Hour*, directed by Lyubimov, 1969.

non-theatricality and ambiguity and encourage an informal actor–audience relationship well-suited to the small studios and amateur theatres in which they were first performed. What began in the late 1960s – with Arbuzov, Volodin, Rozovsky and others – as an effort to transcend the bureaucratic red tape and Party policy restrictions on the professional theatre repertory and in response to the theatres' stunted growth (the Sovremennik and the Taganka are the only two Moscow theatres built since the Second World War) has in the 1980s, with the help of Party directives in 1976 and 1977, become a fully-fledged movement of enlightened amateurs and innovative and often controversial theatre professionals. While government policy toward the theatre has been conservative since Brezhnev's death in 1982, there have been some encouraging developments: the proliferation of the aforementioned venues, together with second stages that are today attached to many professional theatres; the increased sharing of actors and directors among established theatres; and the appearance of new, young and critical dramatists and directors, many of whom gained experience and continue to work in studio and amateur theatres, as well as on various main and second stages. The 'new' directors include: dramatists Mark Rozovsky and Aleksei Kazantsev, Roman Viktyuk, Lev Dodin, Valery Fokin, Kama Ginkas, Genrikh Cherniakhovsky, Genrietta Yanovskaya, Anatoly Vasilyev and Vladimir Portnov. Since the 1970s dramatists have been treating the problems of youth, the family and social relationships progressively more realistically, and even clinically. Teenage pregnancy, alienation, brutality, rebellion and failure at personal commitment, often in the light of the negative examples set by their elders, are being closely and objectively examined by Alla Sokolova, Andrei Kuternitsky, Olga Kuchkina-Pavlova, Galina Shcherbakova, Nina Pavlova, Lyudmila Razumovskaya, Viktor Slavkin, as well as by: Aleksandr Gelman, who with Ignaty Dvoretsky had helped promulgate the industrial plays of the 1970s; Radzinsky who, in *She, in the Absence of Love and Death* (1980), has returned to the intimate scale of his 60s plays; Arbuzov and Rozov, whose *Cruel Games* (1978) and *The Nest of the Woodgrouse* (1979) respectively are their most controversial plays in recent years. In January 1985, after more than a decade of struggle, **Edward Albee**'s corruscating *Who's Afraid of Virginia Woolf?* premiered at the Sovremennik Theatre, which in 1973 had produced **David Rabe**'s devastating 'family play' *Sticks and Bones* under the title *As Brother to Brother*. Finally, youth's voice has been heard in the Soviet version of the American rock musical, which although long on passion, is short on song and dance speciality skills. Most inventive and eclectic in this sphere has been Mark Zakharov, a graduate (along with Mark Rozovsky) of Sergei Yutkevich's Student Theatre at Moscow University, and since 1973, artistic director of Moscow's Lenin Komsomol Theatre. His productions of *Auto City XXI*, *Til* (from Charles de Coster's 'Til Eulenspiegel' novel), *The Stars and the Death of Joaquin Murieta, the Chilean Bandit Who Was Brutally Murdered in California on July 23, 1853* (from Pablo Neruda, 1976) and *Juno and Avos* (from Andrei Voznesensky, 1981) have proved to be extremely popular and reflect the influences of Western cinema (e.g., Fellini) and of Soviet theatre of the 1920s, especially Vakhtangov and Meyerhold. Since the scale of Soviet theatre is so enormous – 600 professional theatres (300 dramatic), serving some 110 million spectators in 40 languages, many attending exciting national theatres outside Russia (especially in Estonia, Latvia, Lithuania and Georgia) – these are matters of some consequence. SG

English language sources
See: Alexander Bakshy, *The Path of the Modern Russian Stage and Other Essays*, London, 1916; A. Bates, *The Drama: Its History, Literature, and Influence on Civilization*, Vol. 18: *Russian Drama*, London, 1903; John E. Bowlt, *Russian Stage Design. Scenic Innovation, 1900–1930* from the Collection of Mr and Mrs Nikita D. Lobanov-Rostovsky, Jackson, MS, 1982; John E. Bowlt, *The Silver Age: Russian Art of the Early Twentieth Century and the 'World of Art' Group* Newtonville, MA, 1982; W. E. Brown, *A History of Seventeenth-Century Russian Literature*, Ann Arbor, MI, 1980; W. E. Brown, *A History of Eighteenth-Century Russian Literature*, Ann Arbor, MI, 1980; M. A. S. Burgess, 'The Early Theatre' and 'The Nineteenth- and Early Twentieth-Century Theatre' in Robert Auty and Dimitri Obolensky (eds.), *An Introduction to Russian Language and Literature*, Cambridge, 1977, 231–70; Huntly Carter, *The New Spirit in Russian Theatre 1917–28*, London, 1921; H. W. L. Dana, *Handbook on Soviet Drama*, New York, 1938; René Füllöp-Miller, and Joseph Gregor, *The Russian Theatre*, New York–London, 1968; George Gibian (trans.), *Russia's Lost Literature of the Absurd*, Ithaca, 1971; Nikolai Gorchakov, *The Theatre in Soviet Russia*, New York, 1957; Leo Hecht (ed.), *Newsnotes on Soviet and East European Drama and Theatre*, Fairfax, VA, 1981–5, in progress; Norris Houghton, *Moscow Rehearsals*, New York, 1936; Norris Houghton, *Return Engagement*, New York, 1962; C. V. James, *Soviet Socialist Realism: Origins and Theory*, New York, 1973; George Kalbouss, *The Plays of the Russian Symbolists*, East Lansing, MI, 1982; Simon Karlinsky, *Russian Drama from Its Beginnings to the Age of Pushkin*, Berkeley, CA, 1985; Janet Kennedy, *The 'Mir iskusstva' Group and Russian Art 1898–1912*, New York–London, 1977; Alma H. Law, and C. Peter Goslett (comp. and ed.), *Soviet Plays in Translation. An Annotated Bibliography*, New York, 1981; Christina Lodder, *Russian Constructivism*, New Haven, CT, 1983; Vladimir Markov, *Russian Futurism: A History*, 1968; Herbert Marshall, *The Pictorial History of the Russian Theatre*, 1977; D. S. Mirsky, *A History of Russian Literature*, New York, 1973; Carl and Ellendea Proffer (eds.), *The Silver Age of Russian Culture: An Anthology*, Ann Arbor, MI, 1975; Spencer E. Roberts, *Soviet Historical Drama: Its Role in the Development of a National Mythology*, The Hague, 1975; 'Russian Issue', *The Drama Review* 17 (March 1973); Harold B. Segel, *The Literature of Eighteenth-Century Russia*, 2 vols., New York, 1967; Harold B. Segel, *Twentieth-Century Russian Drama from Gorky to the Present*, New York, 1979; Laurence Senelick, *Russian Dramatic Theory from Pushkin to the Symbolists*, Austin, TX, 1981; Marc Slonim, *Russian Theatre from the Empire to the Soviets*, New York, 1962; Andre van Gyseghem, *Theatre in Soviet Russia*, London, 1943; B. V. Varneke, *History of the Russian Theatre*, New York, 1951; Elizabeth A. Warner, *The Russian Folk Theatre*, The Hague–Paris, 1977; L. Warner, *Russian Folk Drama*, The Hague, 1978; David J. Welsh, *Russian Comedy 1765–1823*, The Hague–Paris, 1966; Peter Yershov, *Comedy in the Soviet Theatre*, New York, 1956; Russell Zguta, *Russian Minstrels. A History of the Skomorokhi*, Pittsburgh, 1978.

Russian language sources
See: A. A. Anikst, *Teoriya dramy v Rossii ot Pushkina do Chekhova*, Moscow, 1972; B. N. Aseyev, *Russkii dramaticheskii teatr XVII–XVIII vekov*, Moscow, 1958; P. N. Berkov, *Russkaya narodnaya drama XVII–XX vekov*, Moscow, 1953; A. O. Boguslavsky, and V. A. Diev, *Russkaya sovetskaya dramaturgiya*, 3 vols., Moscow, 1965–8; A. O. Boguslavsky, and V. A. Diev, *Russkaya sovetskaya dramaturgiya 1917–35. Osnovye problemy razvitiya*, Moscow, 1963; A. O. Boguslavsky, V. A. Diev and A. S. Karpov, *Kratkaya istoriya russkoi sovetskoi dramaturgii*, Moscow, 1966; V. Churakov (ed.), *Dramaturgiya Znaniya*, Moscow, 1964; N. N. Chushkin, *et al.* (eds.), *Moskovskii khudozhestvennyi teatr*, vol. 1, *1898–1917*, Moscow, 1955; S. S. Danilov, *Ocherki po istorii russkogo dramaticheskogo teatra*, Moscow–Leningrad, 1948; S. S. Danilov, and M. G. Portugalova, *Russkii dramaticheskii teatr XIX veka*, 2 vols., Leningrad, 1974; O. Z. Derzhavina, K. N. Lomunov and A. N. Robinson (eds.), *Rannaya russkaya dramaturgiya XVII-pervoi poloviny XVIII v.*, 5 vols., Moscow, 1972–6; V. Frolov, *Zhanry sovetskoi dramaturgii*, Moscow, 1957; *Istoriya russkogo dramaticheskogo teatra*, 7 vols., Moscow, 1977– in progress; A. R. Kugel, *Russkie dramaturgii*, Moscow, 1923; Lydia Lotman, *et al.* (eds.), *Istoriya russkoi dramaturgii XVII–pervaya polovina XIX veka*, Leningrad, 1982; P. A. Markov, *O teatre*, 4 vols., Moscow, 1976; S. S. Mokulsky, *et al.* (eds.), *Teatralnaya entsiklopediya*, 5 vols., Moscow, 1961–7; Y. Osnos, *Sovetskaya istoricheskaya drama*, Moscow, 1947; M. Paushkin (ed.), *Strarii russkii vodvil 1819–1849*, Moscow, 1937; *Pesy sovetskikh pisatelei*, 6 vols., Moscow, 1972–5; V. F. Pimenov (ed.), *Pervye sovetskie pyesy*, Moscow, 1958; V. Pimenov, *Sovetskie dramaturgi o svoyom tvorchestve. Sbornik statei*, Moscow, 1967; Mark Polyakov (ed.), *Russkaya teatralnaya parodiya XIX-nachala XX veka*, Moscow, 1976; *Rossiiskii teatr* 43 vols., St Petersburg, 1786–94; K. Rudnitsky, *Portrety dramaturgov*, Moscow, 1961; *Russkaya dramaturgiya XVIII v.*, 2 vols., Moscow–Leningrad, 1959; *Russkie dramaturgi XVIII–XIX vv. Monograficheksie ocherki*, 3 vols., Moscow, 1959–62; T. Shantarenkov (ed.), *Russkii vodvil*, Moscow, 1970; *Sovetskaya dramaturgiya 1917–1947*, 6 vols., Moscow–Leningrad, 1948; L. Tamashin, *Sovetskaya dramaturgiya v gody grazhdanskoi voiny*, Moscow, 1961; *Teatr. Kniga o novom teatre*, St Petersburg, 1908; V. Vsevoldsky-Gerngross, *Istoriya russkogo teatra*, 2 vols., Leningrad, 1929; V. Vsevolodsky-Gerngross, *Russkii teatr ot istokov do serediny XVIII v.*, Moscow, 1957; V. Vsevolodsky-Gerngross, *Russkii teatr votoroi poloviny XVIII v.*, Moscow, 1960; M. O. Yankovsky (ed.), *Stikhotvorenaya komediya kontsa XVIII-nachala XIX v.*, Moscow–Leningrad, 1964; A. Z. Yufit (ed.), *Sovetskii teatr: Dokumenty i materialy 1917–67*, Leningrad, 1968; E. A. Znosko-Borovsky, *Russkii teatr nachala 20 v.*, 2 vols., Prague, 1925; David Zolotnitsky, *Zori teatralnogo oktyabrya*, Leningrad, 1976.

Ruzzante or **Ruzante, Il** (The Chatterbox) (Angelo Beolco) (?1502–43) Italian amateur actor, whose plays in the Paduan dialect paved the way for the **commedia dell'arte**. The head of a travelling company, which performed chiefly in Padua but also at Venice and Ferrara at carnival time from 1520, he incarnated the type of a garrulous, grumbling peasant, pungently criticizing princes, citizens and war. The members of his ensemble which spoke the vernacular always impersonated the same characters: M. A. Alvarotto as Menato, G. Zanetti as Vezzo. Ruzzante's comedies united the experiments of court theatre such as the pastoral eclogue and the Terentian comedy with the indigenous *momarie* of urban Venice and the *mariazi* of the Paduan countryside. In his own time, his reputation as an actor overwhelmed his fame as a playwright, for his sensual, surly, anti-idealistic Ruzzante was a striking natural. He has been rediscovered at regular intervals in the 20th century: **Jacques Copeau** revived his *Ancontana* (1522?) in 1927; the Teatro Stabile of Turin staged his *Moschetta* (1528) in 1960; and in England *Il Reduce*, his caustic anti-war monologue, has occasionally been revived.   LS

Ryga, George (1932–   ) Canadian playwright, poet and novelist who applies surrealistic techniques to powerful and realistic stories of injustice and oppression. *The Ecstasy of Rita Joe* (1967), his most successful work, is a grim indictment of Canada's treatment of its native people. It has been widely produced across Canada, in Britain and the USA, and even turned into a ballet. *Grass and Wild Strawberries* (1969) explores the generational conflicts of the 1960s. *Captives of the Faceless Drummer* (1972) depicts the kidnapping of a diplomat by revolutionaries, and bore such obvious reference to actual events in Canada in 1970, that it provoked a storm of controversy and its initial production was abandoned. Since that time Ryga's stern polemics have not been successful, and much of his recent work has been in television and the novel.   JA

S

Sabbattini, Nicola (1574–1654) Italian architect and engineer and author of *Pratica di Fabricar Scene e Machine ne' Teatri* (1638). Sabbattini was born and died in Pesaro and for many years was architect for the Duke of Urbino. Although most of his work was on civil and military projects, he also designed and built theatres – which at the time meant transforming great halls – and scenery. The one theatre specifically attributed to him is the Teatro del Sol at Pesaro in 1637 for the production of *L'Asmondo*. His importance lies in his book which documents the theatre machinery and technology of the day with special reference to perspective and *intermezzi*. It was widely read and influenced theatre practice throughout Europe. AA

Sacco or Sacchi, Giovanni Antonio (1708–88) A famous Truffaldino, he travelled with his **commedia dell'arte** troupe throughout half of Europe (1738–62). In Venice he played at the Teatro Sant'Angelo, where, at his urging, **Goldoni** wrote for him *The Servant of Two Masters* (1745), *Truffaldino's 32 Mishaps* (1738–40) and *Truffaldino's Son Lost and Found* (1746). **Gozzi** followed suit with *The Love of Three Oranges* (1761), an enormous success. **Garrick** and Casanova spoke highly of Sacchi's talents, especially in improvised comedy. LS

Sackville, Thomas (1536–1608) English playwright. With Thomas Norton he wrote *The Tragedy of Gorboduc* (1561). This is usually considered the first English tragedy, drawing upon classical precedent in some respects (chorus, reported action) but otherwise showing an inclination to freer form and to political comment that was to be a feature of classic Elizabethan tragedy. MB

Sadler's Wells Theatre (London) Sadler (there is dispute about whether his first name was Dick or Thomas) was a Surveyor of Highways by profession and a theatrical impresario by inclination. He opened a Musick-House in 1683 on a site in Finsbury, aiming to provide cheap entertainment in the northern fringes of London. The discovery of a medicinal spring on the same site – either just before or just after the opening of the Musick-House – turned the gardens of Sadler's Wells into a popular resort, but the prestige of both Hall and gardens had sunk by 1746, when the lease was bought by Thomas Rosoman. Under Rosoman, the old wooden Hall was replaced by a brick theatre in 1764–5 (capacity 2,600) and Sadler's Wells was recognized as one of London's effective 'minor theatres', a home for pantomime and illegitimate drama in addi-

tion to music and acrobatic displays. Tom King, who had made his name as an actor at Smock Alley and **Drury Lane**, was the active lessee from 1772–85. Under his shrewd control, the theatre earned a fashionable reputation for patriotic spectacle, musical innovations (particularly through the work of **Charles Dibdin**) and good wine. The infant **Joseph Grimaldi** began his long association with Sadler's Wells in 1781 and his precocious dancing was one of many bids to preserve for the theatre its reputation for novelty over the next 60 years of its history. King and his managerial successors would try anything, from dancing dogs to feats of arms and even a staging of the storming of the Bastille (August 1789). From 1799–1819, the driving force was the enterprising and ambitious Charles Dibdin the Younger. He it was who exploited the theatre's aquatic potential in 1803 by installing a large water tank (90 ft x 25 ft) on the stage, but the opening success of *The Siege of Gibraltar* (1804) proved hard to follow. It was above all Grimaldi who sustained Sadler's Wells during the difficult years from 1807, when panic following a false alarm of fire caused 18 deaths, until his retirement in 1828. By then, melodrama was the rage and, having lost its confidence in novelty, Sadler's Wells followed the lead of other minor theatres. A thorough renovation in 1838 failed to halt the slide. It was **Samuel Phelps**'s decision, in the wake of the Theatres Act of 1843, to take a lease on Sadler's Wells that raised the theatre to new heights. Between 1844 and 1862, Phelps staged a classical repertoire, including 31 of **Shakespeare**'s plays, and attracted by far the most discerning audience in London. The supremacy of Sadler's Wells did not survive his retirement and by 1878 the theatre was virtually derelict. After a full interior reconstruction, it was reopened in 1879 by Mrs Bateman, former lessee of the **Lyceum**, and struggled on in a variety of guises until 1906. Despite the pleas of conservationists, London's oldest surviving theatre was allowed to deteriorate, and it was in a new building on the site, designed by F. G. M. Chancellor to seat 1,550, that **Lilian Baylis** opened her north London operations, in association with the **Old Vic** in south London, in 1931. The original plan was to alternate productions at the two theatres, but by 1934 Sadler's Wells was devoted almost exclusively to opera and ballet. The policy continued after wartime closure (1940–5) until the ballet company moved to **Covent Garden** in 1956 to provide the nucleus of the Royal Ballet. In 1968, the opera company, under similar financial pressure, moved to the Coliseum as part of the English National Opera. After a period of uncertainty, the theatre became the home of the Sadler's Wells Royal Ballet in 1977. PT

The interior of Sadler's Wells Theatre, showing the water tank, c. 1809.

Sadovsky (pseudonym of Ermilov), Prov Mikhailovich (1818–72) Russian actor. Scion of a century-old family of actors at the Maly Theatre, he was the primary interpreter of **Ostrovsky** and succeeded **Shchepkin** in developing naturalness, simplicity and psychological veracity as the cornerstones of Russian realistic acting. Shchepkin discovered, advised and promoted the provincial actor, arranging for his Moscow debut in 1839. Although he appeared in foreign melodramas and vaudevilles and acted with some success in **Molière**'s comedies, he was most believable playing Russians or characters like the gravedigger in *Hamlet* whom he could transform into earthy Russian types. Apart from the 29 roles in 28 plays which helped to establish Ostrovsky on the Russian stage, he performed works by **Gogol**, D. T. Lensky, **Pisemsky**, **Turgenev** and **Sukhovo-Kobylin**. The latter rejected Sadovsky's interpretation of Rasplyuev in *Krechinsky's Wedding*, in spite of its popular success, as being too vulgar. This very commonness made Sadovsky's Osip in *The Inspector General* (1845) so believable that observers thought he had become the role. Sadovsky, along with Ostrovsky, belonged to Pogodin's Slavophile *Moskvityanin* circle of journal editors and associates, which championed native culture over Western influences.   SG

Sainete see **Género chico**

St Charles Theatre St Charles St between Poydras and Gravier, New Orleans [Architect: Antoine Mondelli]. Built by **James H. Caldwell** in 1835, the St Charles was the largest, handsomest and probably the most expensive theatre built in America to that date. The original stock company included **Charlotte Cushman** and **James E. Murdoch**. In 1842, it burned to the ground and was replaced by a lesser structure, which eventually passed to the management of Caldwell's rivals, **Noah Ludlow** and **Sol Smith**. During its highwater years, most American and English stars played at the theatre and the last known performance of **J. B. Booth** occurred on its stage. In 1899, it burned again and was rebuilt in 1901 as a vaudeville house, which changed to movies in the movie era. For a number of years, it served as a rehearsal hall for the New Orleans Symphony Orchestra because of its excellent acoustics, but was torn down in 1966.   MCH

St James Theatre 246 West 44th St, New York City [Architects: Warren and Wetmore]. Intended to be a personal monument to its builder, Abraham Erlanger, a partner in the infamous **Theatrical Syndicate**, the theatre was named the Erlanger for the first five years of its existence. Opening in 1927 with a lesser **George M. Cohan** musical, the theatre reverted to the Astor estate in the early depression. It was then leased to a succession of producers until it was bought by the **Shuberts**, who were later forced to relinquish it to comply with the terms of a consent decree limiting the number of theatres in their control in 1957. It was bought and has remained a property of the Jujamcyn Organization. Built as a musical house with more than 1,600 seats, Broadway history has been made on its stage. In 1943, the **Rodgers** and **Hammerstein** musical *Oklahoma!* held its stage for five years. In 1951, *The King and I*, another Rodgers and Hammerstein production, opened and did not close for three years at the theatre. Their *Flower Drum Song* followed in 1958. Other notable musicals have included *Hello Dolly!* (1964), *Barnum* (1980) and *My One and Only* (1983). MCH

St James's Theatre, London Designed by Samuel Beazley for the famous tenor, John Braham, this theatre opened close to Piccadilly in 1835 and earned itself a reputation as an unlucky house. Despite occasional successes, like the appearances of the French actress, **Rachel**, between 1846 and 1855, this reputation held good until 1879, when it was taken over by **John Hare** and the **Kendals**. After renovations the house held 1,200 in unrivalled comfort. Hare and the Kendals tempted fashionable society with comedies about fashionable society, including several of **Pinero**'s early plays. They left in 1888. **Lillie Langtry** took the St James's for a season in 1890, but its most brilliant years began in 1891 with the management of **George Alexander**. Until his retirement in 1917, the theatre and Alexander were identified. His best known productions include Pinero's *The Second Mrs Tanqueray* (1893), **Wilde**'s *The Importance of Being Earnest* (1895), **Henry James**'s *Guy Domville* (1895), **Stephen Phillips**'s *Paolo and Francesca* (1902) and Pinero's *His House in Order* (1906). Alexander was an excellent manager and his choice of plays appealed to the intelligent middle-class audience of his day by its judicious mixture of audaciousness and reassurance. Alexander was succeeded in management by Gilbert Miller, an American impresario whose method was to sub-let the St James's to interested, and often interesting, companies. **Laurence Olivier** and **Vivien Leigh** took it in 1950-1, opening with **Christopher Fry**'s *Venus Observed* and then alternating *Antony and Cleopatra* with **Shaw**'s *Caesar and Cleopatra*. **Barrault** and **Renault** presented a fine season of French plays in 1951. **Rattigan**'s *Separate Tables* (1954) broke the theatre's long-run record. All was in vain. Despite a vigorous campaign, the St James's was closed in 1957 to be replaced by an office-block. PT

Saint-Denis, Michel (1897–1971) French director. The nephew of **Copeau**, Saint-Denis's first directing work was with **La Compagnie des Quinze**, a group of Copeau's former pupils. In 1935 he left France to direct **Gielgud** in an English version of the Quinze's success: *Noah* by **Obey**. He stayed on in London to found the London Theatre Studio, a theatre school modelled on Copeau's ideas. Out of this he hoped to develop an art theatre similar to those of the Paris **Cartel**, but the venture failed. However, his production of **Chekhov**'s *Three Sisters* in 1939 is still remembered. During the war he worked for the BBC and then helped, with **Hugh Hunt** and **George Devine**, to revive the **Old Vic** and establish its theatre school. Disagreements with the governors led to his departure

in 1951 and in 1952 he became director of one of the new decentralized theatres, the Comédie de l'Est. He founded the first theatre school outside Paris and moved both theatre and school to Strasbourg in 1953, where both have since acquired an international reputation. In 1957 he went to America to advise on theatres and theatre training, later becoming co-director of the Juilliard School at the Lincoln Center, New York. He also served as artistic adviser to the **Royal Shakespeare Company** and to the Canadian **National Theatre School**. In 1960 he published *Theatre: a Rediscovery of Style* in which methods and approaches derived from Copeau are set out. DB

Saint-Subber, Arnold (1918–) American producer. Born in Washington, DC, and educated at New York University, Saint-Subber began his theatrical career in 1938 as assistant stage manager for *Hellzapoppin*. He then served as assistant to **John Murray Anderson** for numerous productions including the *Ziegfeld Follies of 1943*. His close association with playwright **Neil Simon** established him as an important name on Broadway in the 1960s. Of the more than 25 shows he has produced or co-produced, the more notable are: *Kiss Me Kate* (1948), *The Grass Harp* (1952), *My Three Angels* (1953), *Dark at the Top of the Stairs* (1957), *The Tenth Man* (1959), *Barefoot in the Park* (1963), *The Odd Couple* (1965), *Plaza Suite* (1968), *Last of the Red Hot Lovers* (1969), *The Prisoner of Second Avenue* (1971), *Gigi* (1973), and *1600 Pennsylvania Avenue* (1978). TLM

Sakhi Kundhei (India) Also known as *Sakhi Nata*, *Kundhei Nata* and *Gopa Lila*. The *Sakhi Kundhei* is a form of string puppet performance found in Orissa state in eastern India. The terms refer to doll dance. There are two types of puppets – one type is about one and a half feet tall and, like their Rajasthani counterparts, they have skirts. The other type has legs as well as arms. The puppet heads and hands are made of light wood and paper. Their dress follows that of the **Jatra** actors of the region, especially in the well-known character roles. Animal puppets are also found in the form, especially tigers, elephants, goats and horses.

The stage is like that of the **Kathputli** of Rajasthan and may be decorated with colourful cloth pieces of the region, depending on the wealth of the players. Families of four or five itinerant individuals work fairs and festivals in the region, collecting what they can in donations from the villagers. Stories centre on events surrounding the life of Lord Krishna.

Musicians sing folk tunes and adaptations of film songs to narrate the story. A cymbal player, *pakhavaj* drummer and harmonium player provide the basic rhythm for the narrator/singer. FaR

Saks, Gene (1921–) American director and actor. Born in New York City and educated at Cornell University (1939–43), Saks studied acting at **Actors Studio** and Dramatic Workshop. He made his New York debut in 1947 as Joxer in *Juno and the Paycock*. During the next decade he appeared mainly in supporting roles before attracting critical attention in 1962 as Leo Herman in *A Thousand Clowns*. He turned to directing in 1963, establishing himself as one of Broadway's premier directors of comedy, known for his inventiveness and attention to detail. His major directing credits include: *Nobody Loves an Albatross* (1963); *Generation* (1965); *Mame* (1966); *Sheep on the Runway* (1970); *How the Other Half Loves* (1971); *Sometime, Next Year* (1975); *I Love My Wife* (1977); *Supporting Cast* (1981); *Special Occasions* (1982); *Brighton Beach Memoirs* (1983); and *Biloxi Blues* (1984), for which he received a Tony. He is married to the actress Beatrice Arthur. Numerous films include *Barefoot in the Park*, *The Odd Couple*, *Last of the Red Hot Lovers*, and *Mame*. TLM

Salacrou, Armand (1899–) French playwright who made a small fortune in advertising but sold up to devote himself to writing. His first success was *Patchouli* produced by **Dullin** in 1930 and Dullin was to direct many of his subsequent plays, notably *Atlas-Hotel* (1931) and *La Terre est Ronde* (*The World is Round*, 1938). He was influential in the late 1940s, partly because of **Barrault**'s fine staging of *Les Nuits de la Colère* (*Nights of Anger*) in 1946, a play about Resistance and Collaboration which was chosen by **Strehler** the year after to open his Piccolo Teatro. *L'Archipel Lenoir* (*The Lenoir Archipelago*) (directed by Dullin 1947) satirized the bourgeoisie and *Boulevard Durand* (directed by Reybaz 1961) was a documentary drama about Jules Durand, a trade union activist of Le Havre sentenced to death in 1910 for a murder he did not commit. Salacrou was a fine craftsman, using the well-tried devices of plot and character. Some of his plays explore themes later developed by **Sartre** and his *L'Inconnue d'Arras* (*The Unknown Woman of Arras*, 1935) has been seen as a source for *In Camera*. He anticipated the social drama that flourished in the **decentralization movement** after the Second World War, but his work was neither so bold theatrically nor so clear politically as that of **Brecht** and his successors who became the mainstay of those theatres. His major contribution to the movement was *Boulevard Durand* performed in Le Havre by the Centre Dramatique du Nord in 1961. His earlier plays show men and women who cover their sense of the meaninglessness of life with a commitment to action, however futile. DB

Salazar Bondy, Sebastián (1924–65) Peruvian playwright and poet. Studied in the University of San Marcos, later at the National Conservatory in Paris. Founded the Club de Teatro (Theatre Club) in Lima in 1953 with Reynaldo D'Amore. Obtained first prize in national theatre contest in 1947 for his first play, *Amor, gran laberinto* (*Love, the Great Labyrinth*), that revealed his affinity for satirical farce. *Rodil* (1952) and *Flora Tristán* (1958) dealt with aspects of Peruvian social history. *El fabricante de deudas* (*The Debt Arranger*, 1962), inspired by Balzac, used humour and Brechtian techniques to uncover bourgeois economics. His masterpiece was *El Rabdomante* (*The Diviner*, 1965), a play that incorporated his earlier techniques of satire, social commentary and humour into an absurdist mould. His several one-act plays, which he called 'games' and 'toys', are also important. GW

Salisbury Court Theatre, London This indoor theatre, built of brick and stone, was the last to be erected before the Civil War. It was opened in 1630 as a home for the Children of the King's Revels under the management of an actor-playwright, Richard Gunnell,

and with the King's **Master of Revels** as a shareholder. An **Inigo Jones** drawing at Worcester College, Oxford of a previously unidentified theatre may be his design for the Salisbury Court. It housed a semi-circular stage in a rectangular frame 53 ft by 37 ft, a typically intimate 'private' Caroline theatre. Prince Charles's Men and Queen Henrietta's Men were among prominent companies to play there before the closure of the theatres. During the Interregnum, the lease of the Salisbury Court was purchased by **William Beeston**, perhaps for surreptitious performance by a children's company which provoked a military raid in 1649. The dismantled theatre was refurbished by Beeston in 1660 and continued to house plays until its destruction in the Great Fire of 1666. PT

Salle des Machines A large theatre in the Tuileries palace, built by the architect Le Vau and lavishly equipped by **Gaspare Vigarani** for the entertainments arranged to celebrate the marriage of Louis XIV in 1660. It remained in use for many years for court performances, notably of opera and similar spectacles, under the successive direction of the younger Vigarani, **Berain** and ultimately **Servandoni**. It housed the Opéra between 1763 and 1770 and the **Comédie-Française** for a short period after 1770. DR

Saltykov-Shchedrin, Mikhail Evgrafovich (pseudonym: N. Shchedrin) (1826–89) Russian satirist, novelist, dramatist and radical journalist, who exposed hypocrisy, petty tyranny, spiritual and moral bankruptcy at all levels of tsarist society. A long-time civil servant and one-time provincial governor, he became a colleague in the liberal press of Chernyshevsky, Dobrolyubov and Nekrasov, writing for *The Contemporary* and editing its successor, *Notes of the Fatherland*. His major narrative works include: *Provincial Sketches* (1856), an anti-bureaucratic satire; *History of a Town* (1869), a parody of Russian history and attack on tsarist tyranny via the study of a mythical town named 'Stupidville'; *The Golovlyovs* (1880), a gloomy chronicle of a family's gradual self-destruction; and *Fables* (1869–86), which employs the traditional Russian device of Aesopian language to criticize the status quo. His writings, rich in dialogue and character sketches, were staged during his lifetime not always to the author's satisfaction. His two plays met with somewhat more resistance. *Pazukhin's Death* (1857), which depicts another monstrous family, received its provincial and Moscow premieres in 1889 and 1893, respectively. It was revived by **Nemirovich-Danchenko** at the **Moscow Art Theatre** in 1914. *Shadows* (1862–5), another satire on the world of clerks and bureaucrats, was first staged in 1914. Saltykov's satire has been tentatively embraced by the Soviet regime, blessed by **Gorky** as an indictment of the past and staged in recent years by **Tovstonogov**, Lev Dodin and others. SG

Salvini, Tommaso (1829–1915) Italian actor-manager. Born into the profession he acted professionally from an early age, and was a prominent member of the new young company formed in 1843 by **Gustavo Modena** whose stage reforms in favour of simplicity, naturalness and psychological truth greatly influenced his development. By his late teens he was playing lead

Salvini as Othello.

roles opposite the principal actresses of the age, including **Ristori**. In 1856 he gave one of the first significant performances of a **Shakespeare** play in Italy when he acted Othello at Vicenza (**Ernesto Rossi** undertook the part at about the same time); shortly afterwards he did Hamlet. His repertoire was never large and these roles (to which he later added Macbeth, King Lear and Coriolanus), along with a handful of Italian parts, like Corrado in **Giacometti**'s *La Morte Civile* (*Civil Death*) and the title role in **Alfieri**'s *Saul*, formed the cornerstone of his later foreign touring repertoire. He became the most internationally celebrated actor of his age, enjoying a triumphant histrionic progress, from 1869 onwards to his retirement, through North and South America, Western Europe and Russia. The opening performance of his Othello at the Boston Conservatoire in 1873 was an unqualified triumph, and that success he repeated two years later in London, where the gradually unleashed savage animality of his Moor astonished critics and public alike. Endowed with rich physical attributes – a powerful, sonorous voice, striking and muscular figure, stage presence, and perfect command of gesture and movement – he brought intelligence and imaginative perception to his preparation and execution of roles, on occasions retiring from the stage for months at a time in order to study

a new piece. Although none of his Shakespearian roles equalled his Othello in public favour, all commanded admiration in part or in whole, particularly his Hamlet, which **G. H. Lewes** thought the most satisfying interpretation he had ever seen. Critics and practitioners, from Henry James and **Théophile Gautier** to **Bernard Shaw**, from Ristori to **Bernhardt** to **Stanislavsky**, were unanimous in his praise. The success of his British tour in 1876 through a dozen provincial cities is witness to the spell he could exercise on spectators wholly ignorant of the language in which he performed. For all that his productions were meticulously thought out and respectably, if simply, mounted, his performance was always the dominant attraction: he was perhaps the consummate 'star' actor of the century.   KR

Sam S. Shubert Theatre 225 West 44th St, New York City [Architect: Henry B. Herts]. In 1913, **Lee** and **J. J. Shubert**, their position as producers and theatre owners assured, bought a site which ran through the block from West 44th to West 45th Street behind the Hotel Astor. There they built two theatres, one of which they named after their brother Sam S. Shubert, who had been killed in a railroad accident in 1905. It was to become the flagship of the Shubert enterprises and their headquarters, which it has remained. Ultimately, with the **Booth Theatre**, it formed the western wall of Shubert Alley. For most of its history, the Shuberts have presented their own brand of musical drama and comedies. In 1975, **Joseph Papp** moved *A Chorus Line* to the Shubert, which has since broken all standing records as the longest running production on a Broadway stage.   MCH

Samson, Joseph Isidore (1793–1871) French actor. Samson's career was particularly associated with the **Comédie-Française**, of which he became *doyen* in 1840. Admitted to the Conservatoire in 1810, he was advised to try comedy rather than tragedy because of his nasal voice and undistinguished appearance. He worked in the provinces, especially Rouen, until **Picard** brought him to the reconstructed **Odéon** in 1819. In 1826, the Comédie-Française, using a right granted it in 1818, co-opted him. In 1831 he moved to the **Palais-Royal** for a brief period, but was forced to return to the Théâtre-Français, where he had his first successes in the repertoire of **Scribe**, with Bertrand de Rantzau in *Bertrand et Raton* (1833) and the doctor in *L'Ambitieux* (*The Ambitious Man*, 1834). He wrote a number of plays, of which the most successful was *La Famille Poisson* (1845). Together with Baron Taylor, he founded the Society for Dramatic Artistes. His major later roles included André in *Le Chandelier* (*The Candleholder*, 1852) and the marquis in *Mlle de Seiglière* (1851), a role in which he was unequalled. He had a particularly fine reputation as a teacher at the Conservatoire, and **Mlle Rachel** was one of his pupils and protégés.   JMCC

Sánchez, Luis Rafael (1936–) Puerto Rican playwright, novelist and professor. Influenced by **Ionesco** and by his compatriot, **René Marqués**, in early stages, his *Sol 13, Interior* (*Sol 13, Inside*, 1961) consisted of a suite, *La hiel nuestra de cada día* (*Our Daily Gall*) and *Los ángeles se han fatigado* (*The Angels are Tired*), plays thematically linked in contemporary lower class Puerto Rican settings to classical motifs. *O casi el alma* (*Or Almost the Soul*, 1964) posits Christ in a theological discussion of Puerto Rico. *La pasión según Antígona Pérez* (*The Passion according to Antígona Pérez*, 1968) is an 'American chronicle' of Latin American revolution using Brechtian techniques and the Antigone dilemma. *Quíntuples* (*Quintuplets*, 1984) is a series of poetic dialogues.   GW

Sandae-gŭk (or **sandae-togam-gŭk**) A generic term of Korean masked dance drama which embraces all today's known regional forms. The term is derived from *sandae-togan*, an office of the Chosŏn court, which controlled all entertainment forms.   OKC

Sandow, Eugen (Friedrich Müller) (1867–1925) German strong man, the first stage Hercules to parlay his physique into a commercial property. As a boy he was influenced by classical statuary and developed a system of body-building through attention to individual muscle groups. At his London debut at the Royal Aquarium (1889), he wrestled the champion Samson and lifted weights, including, later, a 312 lb dumbbell and a 600 lb cart-horse (1891). At the Chicago Columbian Exposition of 1893, **Florenz Ziegfeld** glorified him with spectacular publicity, abbreviated costumes and such stunts as having him lift his pianist with the grand piano. Sandow advertised products like corsets and health oils and promoted several physical culture magazines. He retired in 1907 and died trying to lift a car out of a ditch.   LS

Eugen Sandow in a typical pose which led contemporaries to debate how the fig-leaf was kept on.

Sangallo, Bastiano da, called Aristotile (1481–1551) Italian architect and stage designer and a crucially influential figure in the evolution of perspective staging and scenic effects. Both **Buontalenti** and **Vasari** were his pupils and learned much from him, although few examples of his scenic work have survived.   KR

Sanger, 'Lord' George (1827–1911) English showman, who began as a child spieling outside his father's showbooth. He created a sensation using naphtha lamps in the Mile End Road, and moved on to limelight with lantern shows in the Midlands. His first circus opened at Charter Fair, Kings Lynn, and in 1860 he originated the first three-ring circus at Plymouth Hoe, but finding it did not pay, reverted to one ring. In 1871 he bought **Astley**'s Amphitheatre, enlarged it and opened it as Sanger's Grand National Amphitheatre with the pantomime *Lady Godiva*. There and at Royal Agricultural Hall he staged mammoth spectaculars that earned him a fortune. In 1893 he let the Ecclesiastical Commissioners pull down Astley's, but carried on his gigantic tenting show until 1905. The dapper bald man with the handlebar moustache was married to the lion-tamer Ella Chapman and, in 1911, was murdered by a berserk farmhand wielding an axe.   LS

Sanquirico, Alessandro (1777–1849) Italian scene designer. From 1817 to 1832 Sanquirico was the sole designer and chief scene painter for La Scala in Milan. He designed operas by Bellini, Donizetti, Mozart, Meyerbeer, and Rossini thus exerting great influence on the development of grand opera. Among the hundreds of operas and ballets designed for La Scala, the most important included the premieres of Rossini's *La Gazza Ladra* (1827), Bellini's *Norma* (1831), and Donizetti's *Lucretia Borgia* (1834). His settings were on a vast scale, using a richly decorated architectural foreground and opening out to a broad landscape view painted with a single-point perspective. He used the qualities of gas lighting to create the correct atmosphere against his painted scenery. His designs epitomized the 'grand opera' style and became published and circulated, creating a standard for opera design in Italy and elsewhere in the mid-19th century.   AJN

Santana, Rodolfo (1944–   ) A prolific Venezuelan playwright, Santana has written more than 50 plays, most of them performed and/or published. An early period was dominated by metaphysical, absurdist and science-fiction plays. In a later period he used Kafkaesque techniques to examine cruelty, violence, sex and revolution in contemporary society: *La muerte de Alfredo Gris* (*The Death of Alfredo Gris*, 1968) and *El sitio* (*The Siege*, 1969) are examples. A third more eclectic period included experimentation with historical materials (*Barbarroja*, 1970) as well as socio-political issues. Santana's plays have won prizes in many of the national drama festivals. Recent works include the monologue *La empresa perdona un momento de locura* (*The Company Allows a Moment of Madness*, 1979), *El animador* (*The MC*, 1980) and the boxing *Fin del Round* (*End of the Round*, 1981).   GW

Freddy Pereira and Carlota Sosa in Santana's *La empresa perdona un momento de locura* (*The Company Allows a Moment of Madness*), 1981.

Santareno, Bernardo (1920–80) *Nom-de-guerre* of Dr Antonio Martinho do Rosario. Portuguese playwright. Driven by *saeva indignatio* against all forms of exploitation and injustice, Santareno was the dramatist most closely and constantly in touch with the most intimate and passionately cherished aspirations of the people in the Salazar era. In the theatre he developed a highly naturalistic and compelling dramatic construction and dialogue, from *A Promessa* (*The Promise*, 1957), over most of the 18 plays he wrote up to the unpublished *O Punho* (*The Fist*). *A Promessa* was first performed in the Teatro Experimental do Porto; many subsequent plays were banned or withdrawn after short runs. His *Crime de Aldeia Velha* (1959) shows superstition, rural backwardness and mass hysteria leading to a 'witch' trial and burning, every bit as powerfully as **Miller** in *The Crucible*. *O Judeu* (*The Jew*, 1966) is a harrowing reconstruction of the infamous Inquisition trial of the 18th-century dramatist **Silva**, and of the society which could countenance such an institutional crime.   LK

Saqui, Madame (Marguerite-Antoinette-Sévère Lalane) (1777–1866) Greatest rope-dancer of her age, the daughter of gymnasts. As 'la belle Nini', she played juvenile roles and at 15 made a thunderous debut at the **Cirque Olympique**. In 1809 she married the acrobat and impresario Saqui. Her exploits included vaulting over 24 armed soldiers and dancing on a cord stretched between the towers of Notre Dame. When she performed before Napoleon, she was set ablaze by the fireworks. In 1816, she performed quick-change roles in her own booth on the Boulevard du Temple, which she maintained till 1830. Penniless, she returned to touring, amassing 32,000 francs which were stolen by highway robbers when she was 75. She came back to Paris and could be seen in the Champ de Mars pushing a child in a wheelbarrow across the tightrope.   LS

Sarcey, Francisque (1827–99) French critic. Sarcey began his career as a teacher, but was dismissed for his liberal beliefs. In 1860 he gave public lectures at literary matinees at the Athénée and Gaîté theatres. Under various pseudonyms he contributed to a number of newspapers. From its foundation in 1860 he was drama critic for *L'Opinion Nationale* and in 1867 he took on Sainte-Beuve's Monday column in *Le Temps*, which he continued until his death. His criticisms were published by Adolphe Brisson as *Quarante Ans de Théâtre* (1900–2). Sarcey was much respected by actors, who knew him as 'uncle' Sarcey, and noted for his impartiality. His tastes were basically conservative and he placed great emphasis on common sense and professionalism. He believed that the critic should go with the current of popular opinion and try to shape it, rather than offer absolute principles, that the voice of the critic was that of the audience and that a play should be judged according to its own conventions.   JMCC

Sardou, Victorien (1831–1908) French dramatist. Like **Scribe**, to whom he is often compared, Sardou was a master-craftsman of the theatre. He developed the well-made play, using a wide arsenal of effective devices. Like much popular, but secondary, 19th-century dramatic writing, his work depends on the exploitation of successful formulae. It was this aspect of his work that led **G. B. Shaw** to coin the term 'Sardoodledom' (he refers to the Napoleon of Sardou's *Madame Sans-Gêne* as 'nothing but the jealous husband of a thousand fashionable dramas, talking Buonapartiana'). Sardou had a good sense of stage business. Every exit and entrance had a distinct purpose for the development of the plot. The dialogue is basically naturalistic, avoiding long monologues and generally slipping exposition into casual remarks. Sardou ranks with **Augier** and **Dumas** *fils* as one of the successful dramatists of the Second Empire and Third Republic, despite the frequently meretricious quality of his plays. The major areas exploited by Sardou are the large-scale historical play and comedies reflecting French society towards the end of the Second Empire. His first play, *La Taverne des Etudiants* (*The Students' Tavern*, 1854), was a failure, and he could not get another play staged until **Virginie Déjazet** put on his *Les Premières Armes de Figaro* (*Figaro's First Arms*) at her theatre in 1859. *A Scrap of Paper* (*Pattes de Mouches*, 1860), at the Gymnase, established his reputation as a master of stagecraft, this comedy being a very clever piece of skilfully manipulated intrigue. He is at his best in his comedies, notably in early works such as *La Famille Benoîton* (1865) and *Nos Bons Villageois* (*Our Good Villagers*, 1866), in the hard-hitting political satire of *Rabagas* (1872) or in the extremely amusing *vaudeville*, *Let's Get a Divorce* (1880). He embarked on the large-scale historical drama with *Patrie* (*Fatherland*, 1869) and *La Haine* (*Hatred*, 1874). These plays are partly an excuse for an imposing *mise-en-scène* and generally involve a mixing of dramatic genres. Characterization is schematic and the more serious of these plays leave a sense of melodrama with pretensions. This is particularly true of a series of plays written as vehicles for a star, **Sarah Bernhardt**: *La Tosca* (1887), *Cléopâtre* (1890) and *Gismonda* (1894), or his historical comedy *Madame Sans-Gêne* played first by **Réjane** in 1893. The latter illustrated how much more at home he was in historical comedy than in more serious works, where the hollowness of the psychology is only too evident. Two of his late plays, *Robespierre* (1899) and *Dante* (1903), were written to be staged by **Irving**. *L'Affaire des Poisons* (1907) was his last play and exploited a particularly seamy side of the court of Louis XIV. JMCC

Saroyan, William (1908–81) American playwright. This Californian Armenian made his debut as a playwright with *My Heart's in the Highlands* (1939). Both the **Group Theatre** and the **Theatre Guild** had a hand in its production, and although most playgoers were baffled by its loose allegorical form, the play received enough critical acclaim to establish Saroyan as the leading avant-garde playwright of the day. His next play, *The Time of Your Life* (1939), solidified his critical reputation by winning the Pulitzer Prize and the Drama Critics' Circle Award (the first time the two groups ever agreed on a choice). Saroyan rejected the Pulitzer Prize on the grounds that material awards were debilitating to the recipient. Now a modern American classic, *The Time of Your Life* not only is revived periodically in New York but also has appeared on the bill of almost every professional regional theatre, pleasing audiences with its originality, imagination, wit, humanity, and local San Francisco colour. Continuing to write for the stage through the late 50s, Saroyan never again achieved the success of his first two plays, although amateur groups everywhere have produced his uncharacteristically conventional one-act play, *Hello Out There* (1942). *The Beautiful People* (1941), directed by the playwright, and *The Cave Dwellers* (1957) found a brief audience and are occasionally revived, but his other works including *Love's Old Sweet Song* (1940) and *Get Away Old Man* (1943) were quick failures. Much of Saroyan's later years were spent writing novels and autobiographical remembrances. LDC

Sartre, Jean-Paul (1905–80) French philosopher, novelist, playwright. Sartre rejected psychological theatre, defining his as a 'theatre of situations' in which characters are defined not by their psychological states, but by their choices and actions. Sartre's existentialism posits a world of inter-personal relations in which each person struggles to control the other and this makes for exciting dramatic situations especially well exemplified by *Huis Clos* (*In Camera*, 1944) which has become an acknowledged masterpiece of the modern theatre. Sartre's career as a playwright began with *Les Mouches* (*The Flies*) (directed by **Dullin**, 1943) a modern version of the Electra story which was seen in occupied Paris as a call to resistance. His reputation was high throughout the late 1940s, when he wrote many plays, several of which were performed at the Théâtre Antoine which otherwise specialized in boulevard comedy. These included *Les Mains Sales* (*Dirty Hands*, 1948) about political expediency and *Le Diable et le Bon Dieu* (*The Devil and the Good Lord*, 1951) which **Jouvet** had been directing when he died. In 1954 he made a successful adaptation of **Dumas**'s *Kean* in which Pierre Brasseur scored a big success but *Nekrassov* (1955) was a failure with the boulevard public because of its caustic anticapitalist satire. In *Les Séquestrés d'Altona* (*The Condemned of Altona*, 1959) he came nearest to writing a tragedy of modern times with the story of a young German whose attempts at free choice during the Hitler period were falsified by the subsequent turn of historical events. In 1965 he wrote a fine adaptation of **Euripides'** *Trojan Women* (directed by Cacoyannis, **TNP**). Despite his lifelong interest in Greek Tragedy, Sartre's imagination was essentially melodramatic. The model for his dramaturgical practice was Alexandre Dumas, whose work he so brilliantly adapted. Like **Salacrou**, he attempted to articulate themes of existential despair and political commitment without ever elaborating a fully adequate dramatic form. DB

Sastre, Alfonso (1926–) Spanish playwright and dramatic theorist who has made an important contribution to the theatre with his plays of social awareness, influenced by such authors as **Camus** and **Pirandello**. Born in Madrid, he studied philosophy and literature there, co-founding the student theatre group Arte Nuevo (1945–8). His first plays date from this period, and he went on to found Teatro de Agitación Social in 1950, publishing his ideas on socially committed theatre as an instrument of reform in *Drama y sociedad* (1956). In 1956 he founded the Grupo de Teatro Realista, performing his own works and those of others.

Sastre's plays are not outspoken or overtly political, making their point rather by suggestion and symbolism, a necessary concession during the Franco regime (1939–75). But though their publication was permitted, few were performed other than by his own theatre groups, and several have been banned. These include *Escuadra hacia la muerte* (*Death Squad*, 1953), a play set in a bunker 'during the next war', and *En la red* (*In the Web*, 1961) inspired by the Algerian war. Other plays from this period are *Prólogo patético* (*Pathetic Prologue*, 1949) about the morality of terrorist action, *El cuervo* (*The Raven*, 1957) a 'time-slip' play of suspense and *La Cornada* (*Death Thrust*, 1960) describing the last hours of a bullfighter and his exploiting manager.

Later plays include *El banquete* (*The Banquet*, 1965), *La taberna fantástica* (*The Fantastic Inn*, 1966), *Crónicas romanas* (*Roman Chronicles*, 1968) *Ejercicios de terror* (*Exercises in Terror*, 1970) *Las olas magnéticas* (*Magnetic Waves*, 1972) and *El escenario diabólico* (*Diabolical Scenario*) a play of terror written in 1958 and published in 1973. After this he turned to the novel, but returned to the theatre with *Ahola no es de leil* (*It's No Laughing Matter*, 1979) and most recently *Tragicomedia de la gitana Celestina* (*Tragicomedy of the Gypsy Celestina*, 1984). CL

Satire Burlesque, parody, and satire are often treated as synonyms for ridicule through distortion, but it is useful to suggest distinctions between them. None of the three words refers exclusively to drama; yet all have been applied to drama. Although sometimes confused with the Greek satyr-play, the word satire is of Roman origin, meaning a dish of mixed fruit, and the long poems first called satires mixed several literary techniques. Satire as ridicule with a meliorative intention did not, however, await the invention of the Latin word, for the technique of satire is virulently evident in the comedies of **Aristophanes**. Sometimes claimed as a genre distinct from comedy, satire can vary from the gentle mockery of **Shakespeare** or **Molière** to the bitter thrust of **Marston** or **Lesage**. Perhaps the most celebrated modern satirist is **Shaw**, but **Brecht** also draws upon its long tradition in such plays as *Man is Man*.   RC

Satyr play see **Greece, ancient**

Satz, Ludwig (1895–1944) Much-loved leading 'star' comedian of the American Yiddish theatre from 1918 until his death in 1944. Billed as 'the man who makes you laugh with tears and cry with a smile', he was a master of characterization, improvisation and makeup.   AB

Saunders, James (1925–) British dramatist, whose early plays were influenced both by English poetic drama and the French absurdists. His **Ionesco**-inspired duologue, *Alas, Poor Fred*, was produced in Scarborough in 1959, and in London seven years later, but his first stage success came with *Next Time I'll Sing To You* (1963), produced within a season of new plays at the Arts Theatre Club. It was suggested by the life of an Essex hermit, Jimmy Mason, but the actors, who discuss the recluse, act little episodes from his life and sometimes wonder self-consciously what they are supposed to be doing, are themselves presented as lonely individuals, not essentially different from Mason himself. Loneliness is also a theme in *A Scent of Flowers* (1964), about a young girl who died from lack of love. Literary experiment is a feature of James Saunders's prolific output with frequent echoes from **Pirandello**, **Beckett** and even **Beaumont** and **Fletcher** (in *The Borage Pigeon Affair*, 1969). He collaborated with Iris Murdoch in adapting her novel, *The Italian Girl* (1968), for the stage, and adapted **Heinrich von Kleist**'s story, *Michael Kohlhaus* (1973), which was produced at Greenwich Theatre. Saunders has worked primarily among the smaller theatres around London with occasional transfers to the West End, of which the most successful was *Bodies* (1978), about two middle-aged couples facing various crises. Saunders has written extensively for radio and television, and has been a strong supporter of the amateur **Questors Theatre** in Ealing.   JE

Savary, Jérôme (1942–) French actor, director, dramatist. Savary's theatre career began with the writing and production of a 'musical tragedy' in 1965 and the founding (with **Arrabal**) of the Grand Théâtre Panique. This became the Grand Magic Circus in 1968 and produced a series of highly successful shows, part cabaret, part social satire, usually performed in unconventional theatre spaces. In 1981 he applied his irreverent performance techniques to **Molière**'s *Le Bourgeois Gentilhomme* and in 1982 he was given the post of director of a new Maison de la Culture at Béziers. He has directed Offenbach in Germany and made several films.   DB

Savits, Jocza (1847–1915) German director. Savits pioneered the 'Shakespeare-stage' in the Munich Court Theatre between 1888 and 1906. With this stage Savits attempted, without much success, to recreate the non-illusionistic playing conditions of the Elizabethan theatre. Despite the incompleteness of his achievement, Savits's experiments predated those of the Englishman **William Poel** and also influenced **Georg Fuchs** in his founding of the Munich Artists' Theatre.   SW

Savoy, Bert (Everett Mackenzie) see **Female impersonation**

Saxe-Meiningen, Duke of see **Meiningen company**

Scamozzi, Vincenzo (1552–1616) Italian architect and stage designer. From the school of **Palladio**, on the latter's death he completed the Teatro Olimpico at Vicenza (1585), and was himself responsible for the Teatro Olimpico at Sabbioneta, completed in 1590. His work on both theatres shows his original and imaginative borrowing from classical models, and both theatres are supreme examples of late Renaissance theatrical architecture, for all that they look back, rather than forwards to theatre and stage structures determined by developments in stage scenography and mechanics.   KR

Scarpetta, Eduardo (1853–1925) Italian actor and dramatist. At an early age he rose to fame in the Neapolitan theatre with a farce character type, Don Felice Sciosciammocca. Engaged by the San Carlino Theatre, he there met the actor–writer **Antonio Petito**, who for the next few years worked closely with him on writing and staging pieces in Neapolitan dialect. After Petito's death he formed his own company performing in several Neapolitan theatres, but based particularly at the San Carlino from 1881, producing work like *Lo Scarflietto* (1881), *Il Romanzo di un Farmacista Povero* (1882) and, particularly, *Miseria e Nobilità* (1888). Although much of his work was a Neapolitanization of French farce, he did much to reform the theatre by eliminating the gratuitous **lazzi** of the old tradition and rooting comedy in recognizable local life. He retired in 1914, having dominated the Neapolitan stage for some 40 years. His successor as a master of Neapolitan comedy, **Eduardo De Filippo**, was a member of his company in its last years.   LR

Scarron, Paul (1610–60) French dramatist and man of letters whose long disablement by rheumatism gave him a capacity for self-mockery and an amused view of the world. Literary recognition came initially with the publication of collections of burlesque verse and a similar manner informed his first play, *Jodelet, ou Le Maître-Valet* (*Jodelet, or the Master-Servant*), a vehicle for the comedian of that name and a great success at the **Marais** in 1645. More comedies in the same vein followed, some of them adapted from Spanish originals, including *Don Japhet d'Arménie* (1647), which was often revived by **Molière** and is regarded as his best work for the stage, and *L'Ecolier de Salamanque* (*The Student of Salamanca*, 1654), which popularized the character of Crispin later associated with members of the **Poisson** family. Nowadays their mixture of verbal wit and stylistic incongruity makes them more difficult to appreciate and he is best known for *Le Roman*

Comique (*The Comical Romance*), a long picaresque romance in two parts (1651 and 1657), which recounts the adventures of a troupe of strolling players and tempers its fantasy with some realistic details of theatrical and provincial life.   DR

Schembartläufer Masked figures of the Bavarian and Austrian carnival, particularly associated with Nuremberg. Their name, as well as denoting obvious attributes of their appearance and behaviour (they are bearded, and 'run' through the streets), also suggests that they are phantoms. Their masks, though always bearded, are female as well as male, they carry staves or lances, and their behaviour is wild and threatening. They are recorded as throwing ashes, and sometimes burning embers, into the crowd.   AEG

Schicksaltragödie ('Fate Tragedy') A form of play, popular in Germany during the romantic period, that represents *in extremis* the Sophoclean concept of fate as an inescapable force. The most celebrated *Schicksaltragödie* was **Zacharias Werner**'s *The 24th of February* (1810), which owed much to **George Lillo**'s *Fatal Curiosity* and itself influenced **Albert Camus**'s *Le Malentendu*. Werner's play was also widely imitated in its time, most notably by Adolf Müllner (1774–1829) in *The 29th of February* (1815). **Grillparzer**'s first play *The Prophetess*, though of a far higher standard than most *Schicksaltragödien*, owed its success partially to its affinity with some popular plays of this genre.   SW

Schikaneder, Emanuel (1751–1812) Austrian actor and singer. Schikaneder, a highly successful impresario in the Viennese popular theatre, is best known today as the librettist for Mozart's *The Magic Flute* (1791). Partly due to the immense popularity of this opera, he was able to build the Theater an der Wien.   SW

Schiller, Friedrich (1759–1805) German playwright, historian, and aesthetician. Schiller's contribution to the development of German drama is equal in quality and importance to that of **Goethe**, with whom Schiller was closely associated during the last nine years of his life. Schiller's first play, *The Robbers* (1781), written while he was a deeply disaffected recruit in the military academy in Württemberg, must be considered to be among the greatest of all first plays. Though dependent on **Shakespeare** and imitative of the **Sturm und Drang** movement of the previous decade, in its depiction of the Moor brothers, one of whom is a monster of malice, the other of titanic disaffection, *The Robbers* has a unique power. Of his next two plays, written while he was house dramatist at Mannheim, *Fiesko* (1781–2) and *Love and Intrigue* (1782–3), the latter is still stageworthy because Schiller's intense sense of outrage at the injustice of the class system can be viscerally felt, despite the play's strident tone. *Don Carlos* (1787) took Schiller several years to write, which is reflected in the unwieldy and complex plot and in a radical change in tone halfway through the play. While the first part of the play, involving Don Carlos's fear and hatred of his father Philip II, belongs to *Sturm und Drang*, the second part, with its ironic view of the idealist Posa and the surprisingly humane characterization of Philip, elevates the tragedy to a more complex plane. The next ten years Schiller devoted to the study of history, philosophy, and aesthetics, in 1789 becoming professor of history at Jena University, close to Weimar. When he returned to the drama with his trilogy on the Thirty Years War general, Wallenstein – *Wallenstein's Camp*, *The Piccolomini*, and *Wallenstein's Death* (all 1799) – Schiller produced a tragedy on the strength and fallibility of the tragic hero that belongs to the rank of world drama. His next play, *Maria Stuart* (1800), he labelled a 'romantic tragedy' possibly because of the disquieting appeal of his beautiful heroine and his dispassionate portrayal of the political forces to which she falls victim. His next major play, *The Bride of Messina* (1803), was a deliberate revival of Greek tragedy. His final completed work, the ever-popular *Wilhelm Tell* (1804), while demonstrating a thorough knowledge of current romantic philosophies and a fine grasp of romantic dramaturgy, in fact throws doubt upon the viability of the romantic personality as embodied in the enigmatic figure of Tell. Schiller possessed a surer understanding of the practical stage than Goethe, and his tragedies, in which the influence of Greek, Shakespearian, and French neoclassical forms can be found, have proved more durable than much of Goethe's dramatic work. As a result, Schiller is widely regarded as being the national dramatist of Germany.   SW

Schiller, Leon (1887–1954) Polish director, manager, composer, author and teacher. As a young man he came under the influence of **Gordon Craig**, whose views he assimilated into the Polish tradition of **Mickiewicz** and **Wyspiański**. He began directing in his mid-30s, staging old Polish nativities and mysteries. He founded the Bogusławski Theatre (1924–6), where he developed a monumental style based on the Polish romantic repertory and combining elements of expressionism, constructivism and cubism with the use of large crowds, **Piscator**'s technique of montage, and revolutionary themes. In the 1930s he moved to radical political theatre and neorealism. After the war, he created the State Theatre Institute. Major productions are Miciński's *Revolt of the Potemkin* (1925), Wyspiański's *Achilleis* (1925), Krasiński's *Undivine Comedy* (1926), **Brecht**'s *Threepenny Opera* (1929), Słowacki's *Kordian* (1930), Mickiewicz's *Forefathers' Eve* (1932), **Tretyakov**'s *Roar, China* (1932).   DG

Schlegel, August Wilhelm (1767–1845) German literary historian and translator. Schlegel's work did much to familiarize the public with the ideas of the romantics. In particular, his *Lectures on Dramatic Art and Literature*, first delivered in Vienna in 1808, covered the whole field of Western drama, creating an awareness of how genuinely popular the theatre had been in past ages. The ideal of such a theatre was shared by many romantics. Schlegel was also a translator of genius, and his versions of 17 of **Shakespeare**'s plays, published between 1797 and 1810 (the series was completed by Dorothea Tieck and Wolf von Baudissin in 1833), are regarded by some as being as close in quality as can possibly be to the original. Schlegel also adapted **Euripides**' *Ion*, which was produced by **Goethe** at Weimar in 1802.   SW

Schlegel, Johann Elias (1719–49) German playwright and aesthetician. Although he was associated with **Johann Gottsched**, Schlegel had a strong appreciation of **Shakespeare** and of how his works were an alternative to the neoclassical tradition. However, as a playwright, Schlegel is known as 'the German **Racine**'. Of his several neoclassical tragedies, *Canute* (1746) is possibly the most original. sw

Schlemmer, Oskar (1888–1943) German sculptor, painter, and designer and head of the Bauhaus stage workshop from 1923 to 1929. Like many designers of the era, Schlemmer sought to unite the human figure with the three-dimensional space of the stage but he approached it from the standpoint of making the human form abstract. Based upon mathematical analysis of the geometric shapes that the body or parts of the body made as it moved through space, Schlemmer created masks and costumes that suggested, in Walter Gropius's words, 'moving architecture'. Schlemmer also sought to create a modern vocabulary of visual symbols. These explorations were best realized in his *Form Dance*, *Gesture Dance*, and *Space Dance*. The most complete integration of his ideas was achieved in the *Triadic Ballet* (1912–22), a highly structured and schematized series of dance scenes. His work with the Bauhaus was not only an influence on post-war design but on modern dance. Schlemmer also designed for the commercial theatre and dance – notably the **Kokoschka**–Hindemith opera, *Mörder, Hoffnung der Frauen* – creating settings in the style of the expressionist painters with broad swaths of rich and subtly shaded colours. AA

Schmidhuber de la Mora, Guillermo (1943–) Mexican playwright. With degrees in engineering and business, this young writer has for years managed the Alfa Technological Museum in Monterrey. In a country where theatre activity tends to concentrate in the capital, he continues to write diligently and to win national prizes. Major works include *Los herederos de Segismundo* (*Segismundo's Heirs*, 1981) with its attribution to **Calderón**'s *Life is a Dream*. GW

Schneider, Alan (Abram Leopoldovich Schneider) (1917–84) Director known as **Beckett**'s American interpreter. Born in Kharkhov, Russia, Schneider made his debut as a director with **Saroyan**'s *Jim Dandy* (Catholic University of America, Washington, DC, 1941) and as an actor in **Maxwell Anderson**'s *Storm Operation* (Broadway, 1944). His New York directing debut was Randolph Goodman and Walter Carroll's *A Long Way from Home* (Broadway, 1948). Leaving Catholic University in 1952, he worked regularly at Washington's **Arena Stage** (Artistic Director, 1952–3; Acting Producer, 1973–4), New York's **Neighbourhood Playhouse** and elsewhere across the United States. Before turning to theatre, Schneider was a reporter (1936–9), radio announcer (1939) and public relations agent (1940). Drama critic for *The New Leader* until 1965, he also contributed to *Saturday Review*, **Theatre Arts** and *New York Times*.

Schneider directed premieres of, among others, Beckett's *Waiting for Godot* (Miami, Florida, 1956), *Endgame* (1958), *Happy Days* (1961), *Play* (1964) and the movie *Film* starring Buster Keaton (1964). He received Antoinette Perry (Tony) and Off-Broadway (Obie)

Awards for *The Pinter Plays* (*The Collection* and *The Dumbwaiter*, 1962) and a Tony for **Albee**'s *Who's Afraid of Virginia Woolf?* (1963). He was nominated for Albee's *Tiny Alice* (1965) and *A Delicate Balance* (1967) and **Robert Anderson**'s *You Know I Can't Hear You When the Water's Running* (1968). REK

Schnitzler, Arthur (1862–1931) Austrian playwright and short-story writer. Schnitzler's training as a doctor is often considered to have influenced fundamentally his attitude as a dramatist. His plays are for the most part stringently ironic analyses of life in contemporary Vienna. *Anatol* (1893) and *La Ronde* (1900), both cycles of one-act plays that disclose the anxieties lying behind the gracious appearance and easy sexual mores of the city's life, are best known internationally. But Schnitzler's greatest achievement probably lies in his full-length plays, in the moving and tragic **Volksstück** *Liebelei* (*The Game of Love*, 1895), the melancholy drama *The Lonely Way* (1904), the bitterly satirical survey of Viennese society *The Vast Country* (1911), and the powerful play on anti-semitism in Vienna, *Professor Bernhardi* (1912). Though he was only slightly acquainted with Freud, there is a remarkable concordance between Freud's and Schnitzler's perceptions of the human condition, one Freud himself acknowledged. sw

Schönemann, Johann Friedrich (1704–82) German actor. Schönemann took over the leadership of the Neuber troupe after **Caroline Neuber** had broken with **Gottsched**. He continued for several years to perpetuate the **Leipzig style** of acting, though his preeminence in the profession declined due to the rise of realism in acting, associated with **Ekhof**. Schönemann's mismanagement of his finances eventually led to his early retirement in 1757. sw

Schönherr, Karl (1867–1943) Austrian playwright. Schönherr was best known for his grim and powerful realistic dramas about peasant life in the Tyrol. Among the most successful of his plays are *The Picture Carvers* (1900), *Midsummer-Day* (1902), *Carnival People* (1905) and *Faith and the Homeland* (1910). sw

Schreyvogel, Josef (1788–1832) Austrian director. From 1815 until close to his death, Schreyvogel was artistic director of the **Burgtheater**. During this time he established the famous ensemble style of the company, translated and produced important Spanish plays, and introduced the plays of **Grillparzer**. sw

Schröder, Friedrich Ludwig (1744–1816) German actor and playwright. The stepson of **Konrad Ackermann**, Schröder spent most of his childhood and adolescence as a comic, improvisational actor in Ackermann's troupe. He took over the leadership on his stepfather's death in 1771. In 1776, he established the troupe on a permanent basis at the Hamburg Town Theatre. In 1780, he left to join the Vienna **Burgtheater**, where he stayed until 1784. Then he returned to Hamburg to direct his old theatre until his retirement in 1798. As an actor, Schröder was famous for his unvarnished realism, powerful climaxes, and distinct characterization, which embraced a broad emotional compass. Such acting was referred to as the

Schröder as Falstaff.

success and founded the **Yiddish Art Theatre** in 1918 at the Irving Place Theatre in New York where his carefully selected company included **Celia Adler**, **Jacob Ben-Ami**, **Bertha Gerstein**, Anna Apfel and **Ludwig Satz**, and where he set the highest standards in play selection, production values and acting. From a long sequence of great roles, his *Yoshe Kalb*, Shylock and Tevye stand out. His company appeared several times on Broadway in both Yiddish and English and toured the world.   AB

Scofield, (David) Paul (1922–) British actor. His first substantial work was developed at the **Birmingham Repertory Theatre** under the direction of Sir **Barry Jackson**, where Scofield went after a period in local repertory in 1942. He followed Jackson to Stratford-upon-Avon and the then Shakespeare Memorial Theatre in 1946, and this brought Scofield a series of Shakespearian roles in which he has distinguished himself over the years. These have included one of his most renowned performances, Lear in **Peter Brook**'s production of *King Lear* in 1962 (subsequently filmed, 1969) for the **RSC**, and portrayals of Macbeth (RSC, 1967), Prospero in *The Tempest* (Leeds Playhouse, 1974), Othello (**National Theatre**, 1980) and Oberon (National Theatre, 1982). But he has not been limited to Shakespearian roles. His Sir Thomas More in **Bolt**'s *A Man For All Seasons* (Globe Theatre, London, 1960, filmed 1966) remains one of the great performances in post-war British theatre, and work in plays by contemporary playwrights (**Osborne**'s *Hotel in Amsterdam* (1968), **Hampton**'s *Savages* (1973), **Shaffer**'s *Amadeus* (1979) for instance) has given evidence of Scofield's power, range and versatility.   MB

'**Hamburg style**', and was later regarded as antithetical to **Goethe**'s **Weimar style**. In Hamburg, he introduced to the stage several **Sturm und Drang** plays and, most importantly, many of **Shakespeare**'s works: some of his adaptations of Shakespeare enjoyed wide popularity in Germany until the early 19th century. His production of *Hamlet* in 1776, with **Brockmann** as Hamlet and himself as the Ghost, was a landmark in the introduction of Shakespeare to the German stage. Schröder was a skilled playwright and adapted the work of several other English dramatists, including **Sheridan**, for German audiences. As leader of the Hamburg Town Theatre, he accumulated an unprecedentedly large stock of sets and costumes, doing much to improve the quality of physical production. Schröder was the original for the figure of the actor–manager Serlo in Goethe's novel *Wilhelm Meister's Apprenticeship*.   SW

Schröder, Sophie (1781–1868) German actress. The most important years of Sophie Schröder's career were between 1815 and 1829 when she was a leading actress at the **Burgtheater** under **Schreyvogel**. Here she gave the first performance, in 1818, of **Grillparzer**'s Sappho, and, in 1821, of his Medea. In these and in classic roles, her acting was regarded as the epitome of romanticism.   SW

Schwartz, Maurice (?1890–1960) Dominant figure as actor, director and playwright in the New York Yiddish theatre. Starting in 1906, he soon achieved

Scotland Scotland has a rich, lively theatrical tradition, which has played a significant part in the country's cultural development, but which has been sorely neglected for a number of rather complex reasons. One complicating factor is that in the past Scots themselves have sometimes refused to acknowledge their indigenous theatre tradition. As late as 1932, Murray McClymont bewailed the fact that 'theatrically we are and have been for four hundred years a conquered nation'. Moreover, Scots have laboured under the misapprehension that they are not (as a nation) theatrically inclined. **William Hazlitt** first expressed this view when he contrasted the Irish and Scottish temperament in terms of their general adaptability and theatricality.

McClymont's views are perfectly understandable, for the Scottish theatre tradition has developed in an irregular and intermittent fashion, in the face of considerable opposition, and this irregularity has made it extremely difficult for succeeding generations to see themselves working within a discernible tradition. Similarly, Hazlitt's views are explicable on the grounds that they were formed during one of Scottish theatre's low points. Yet, neither view is ultimately borne out by the facts, least of all Hazlitt's, for the Scottish people have at all times retained a basic, native love for popular forms of theatrical and musical entertainment, notably the ballad opera, the ceildh, the Burns Supper and the village concert. Moreover, at various times, recourse to these forms has even assisted Scottish theatre's further development.

Another complicating factor lies in the fact that

Scottish theatre historians have not only denied and belittled the Scottish theatre tradition, they have also tended to look at it somewhat askance, placing too much emphasis on Scottish drama (as opposed to other forms of theatrical entertainment) and, in the 20th century, on professional and conventional drama at the expense of amateur, popular or working class drama.

Scottish drama has a long, but intermittent history. During the past four hundred years, periods of intense activity have been followed by long years of inactivity. There are three main eras in which Scottish drama has developed apace. The first of these is the period from the mid-15th to the 16th century, when travelling players performed a series of morality plays, which were highly critical of the pre-Reformation Church. The high point of their theatrical achievement came with Sir David Lindsay's *Ane Satyre of the Thrie Estaites*, which was performed before King James V of Scotland at Linlithgow Palace in 1542.

The second period of growth came in the 18th century in the wake of the Scottish Enlightenment. At this time, the first theatres were built in Scottish cities and towns – notably, Edinburgh, the Athens of the North – and new Scottish plays were written and performed, including Allan Ramsay's *The Gentle Shepherd* (1725) and **John Home**'s *Douglas* (1756). The latter caused great controversy: it was condemned by the Kirk, but enthusiastically received by its audience, one member of which was heard to give vent to Scottish theatre's celebrated battle-cry 'Whaur's yer Wullie Shakespeare noo?'

These periods of growth were followed by periods of decline in the 17th and 19th centuries. Such lapses are difficult to account for in full, though many theories have been put forward. The Scottish dramatic tradition's decline in the 17th century can be attributed both to the loss of patronage following the removal of James VI and I's court to London and the artistic, cultural and moral rigidity imposed by the Scottish Reformation, the spread of Calvinism and Presbyterianism. Scottish drama's subsequent decline in the 19th century can, likewise, largely be attributed to English cultural dominance in the British Empire's heyday, during which time the Scottish arts withdrew into celtic myth, the Kailyard and tartanry.

It is important, before moving on to look at subsequent developments, to take a closer look at Scottish theatre in the 19th century. During this period of English cultural hegemony, Scottish cities and towns became largely dependent on English, actor-manager, touring companies for their dramatic fare, while Scottish villages depended on the pennygeggie's Victorian melodramas, such as *Burke and Hare*. At the same time, the Scottish music-hall came to the fore, offering annual pantomimes and weekly variety programmes, starring Scottish comedians such as **Harry Lauder**, Will Fyffe, Harry Gordon, Tommy Lorne, Tommy Morgan and George West to name but a few. These pantomimes and variety programmes (as **Lewis Casson** first pointed out) formed the national theatre of Scotland, in the absence of a native drama tradition. Their legacy has been mixed for – like the Kailyard novels of the 19th century – they lapsed into Scottish sentimentality and tartanry. At the same time, many modern theatre companies – notably 7:84 Scotland – have made extensive use of the variety theatre's format

and technique, and many reputable actors from Duncan Macrae to Bill Paterson have readily acknowledged their debt to music-hall and pantomime.

Scottish drama's third and latest period of development came in the early 20th century in the wake of the Scottish Literary Renaissance. Its development since that time has been rapid, continuous and sustained. Scottish drama has, in fact, developed not one but two, often complementary traditions. Firstly, there is the Scottish conventional theatre tradition, which was founded by the Scottish Repertory Theatre (1909–14) and revived after the First World War by the Scottish National Players (1921–48). Its further development in the inter-war years was assisted by two early repertory theatres, Perth and Dundee; a series of little theatres, including the Curtain Theatre (1930–9), the Tron Theatre Club (1931–2), the MSU Theatre, Rutherglen (1939–44) and the Byre Theatre, St Andrews; as well as the small, conventional, amateur theatre clubs which took part in the Scottish Community Drama Association's Annual Festivals, including Torch Theatre Clubs to name but a few.

These early theatre companies prepared the way for Scotland's war-time and post-war repertory theatres, including **James Bridie**'s **Citizens' Theatre** (1943 to the present day); John Stewart's Park Theatre (1940–9) and Pitlochry Festival Theatre (1951 to the present day); the Gateway Theatre, Edinburgh (1953–65); and the Royal Lyceum Theatre Company (1965 to the present day). The same pre-war theatre companies also prepared the way for the post-war theatre clubs, which specialized in a more intimate theatre. These include the Traverse Theatre Club (1963 to the present day); the Close Theatre Club (1965–73); and the Glasgow Tron Theatre Club (1981 to the present day).

At the same time, the early 20th century saw the emergence of Scottish popular, political, working class theatre companies in the urban, industrial centres of Scotland, notably Glasgow and the mining villages of Ayrshire, Fife, Lanarkshire and Lothian. Some of these theatre companies were formed as Scottish branches of two British theatre movements, the Workers Theatre Movement (the WTM) and Unity Theatre Society. Many more were formed independently by local socialist and other working class organizations – local branches of the Communist, Labour and Independent Labour Parties; the Scottish Labour College; the Clarion Society; Co-operative Societies and Socialist Sunday Schools; as well as Burns Clubs and Miners Welfare Institutes. There were literally hundreds of these theatre companies – too many to list them all by name. The most important ones include the Bowhill or Fife Miner Players (1926–31); the Glasgow Workers Theatre Group (1937–40); the Glasgow Jewish Institute Players (1936–63) and Glasgow Unity Theatre (1941–51). Moreover, these popular, political, working class theatre companies – like their conventional counterparts – provided precursors for modern, popular, political, theatre companies, such as 7:84 Scotland and Wildcat Stage Productions.

Scottish drama's development in the 20th century has been influenced by a number of factors, not least the country's geography. Scotland has a small population, spread over a relatively wide area, concentrated in large cities and towns, but otherwise scattered in remote, rural communities. Consequently, Scottish theatre companies – from both traditions – have demonstrated a strong interest in touring their productions. During the early 20th century, the Scottish National Players and Scottish popular, political, working class theatre companies – notably the Fife Miner Players and Glasgow Unity Theatre – set a precedent. Today, modern theatre companies – notably the Scottish Theatre Company, 7:84 Scotland, Borderline and Wildcat – continue to tour extensively.

During the post-war era, Scottish drama's development has also been assisted and influenced by the state's financial aid. During the Second World War, the Citizens' Theatre Company received help from **CEMA**. During the post-war years, Scotland's other conventional, repertory theatres received support from the Scottish Committee of the **Arts Council of Great Britain** (1947–67), though their popular, political counterparts – notably Glasgow Unity Theatre – were less fortunate. During the 1970s the balance was restored, many more theatre companies – including professional, popular, political theatre companies – receiving welcome financial assistance from the Scottish Committee of the Arts Council of Great Britain's more autonomous successor.

Scottish drama's development has been dominated by two major concerns. Firstly, there is the concept of the Scottish National Theatre, the Scots' urge to create a native dramatic tradition, which is matched by a simultaneous desire to assert their independence of English theatrical development. This has led Scottish playwrights, directors, designers and performers to turn inward to their national culture and experience and outward to alternative, international models for inspiration. The Scottish National Players turned to the **Abbey Theatre** in Dublin; while the early Scottish popular, political, working class theatre companies turned to international theatrical models, such as the American **Federal Theatre Project** and a wide range of international, socialist authors, including **Odets, O'Neill**, and **Elmer Rice, Gorky, Lorca, O'Casey** and **Ernst Toller**. During the post-war era, the **Edinburgh International Festival** of Music and Drama (1947 to the present day) and Giles Havergal's policy as Artistic Director of the Citizens' Theatre (1970 to the present day) ensured that Scottish theatres and theatregoers would continue to be brought into close, regular contact with contemporary, international developments.

Secondly, there is the matter of Scottish playwriting. At the turn of the century, it was possible to count all the Scottish plays of note on one hand. During modern times, Scots have therefore been peculiarly conscious of the need to produce a body of dramatic literature. This has led to a proliferation of playwrights and plays. Indeed, many Scots writers in other literary forms – poetry and the novel – have attempted to write plays. These include Hugh MacDiarmid, Neil Gunn, Sydney Goodsir Smith and many others.

It is important, before moving on to look at the patterns of playwriting which have evolved, to take a brief look at **J. M. Barrie** and James Bridie, who remain the two most celebrated Scottish playwrights of the 20th century. Barrie and Bridie stand in a rather odd relation to Scottish drama's overall development, largely because their best-known plays were first performed in London, not Scotland. Consequently, neither has strongly influenced modern Scottish playwriting.

The Scottish Repertory Theatre was the first Scottish theatre company to encourage Scottish playwrights. During the inter-war years, its mantle was taken up by the Scottish National Players (1921–48), the Scottish Community Drama Association (1926 to the present day), and other conventional, amateur theatre clubs of the day, notably the Curtain Theatre (1930–9). These companies promoted two kinds of plays, both of which were deeply flawed. Firstly, there were Scottish historical dramas. These included intelligent, exploratory plays like Robert McLellan's *Jamie the Saxt* (first performed by the Curtain Theatre in 1936), but they also included a great many inadequate and insubstantial, historically vague and sentimental dramas about well-worn topics, notably the '45 and Bonnie Prince Charlie's flight to Skye.

Secondly, there were Kailyard dramas, such as Graham Moffat's *Bunty Pulls the Strings* (1906). These Kailyard dramas came into vogue in the 19th century, but remained very popular in the 20th. They were rural romances and comedies, concerning minor events in the lives of rather two-dimensional, Lowland, village folk, notably the minister, the Elders of the Kirk or the schoolmaster: they were parochial (in the worst sense of the word) and sentimental. The Scottish National Players – inspired by the Scottish Literary Renaissance and the Abbey Theatre – set out to create a new, native drama, but merely succeeded in extending the scope and territory of the Kailyard. They presented plays about Highland, rather than Lowland folk, but their plays remained firmly attached to rural domestic life and were as couthy and sentimental as their predecessors. The Scottish Community Drama Association further extended the scope of the Kailyard, introducing the 'Kitchen comedy', plays which portrayed domestic incidents in the lives of working class people in rural and industrial contexts in a similarly comic, not to say banal, fashion.

It was only the Scottish popular, political, working class theatre companies which offered a credible alternative in the early 20th century. During the 1920s, 30s and 40s, they produced plays about contemporary, urban, industrial, working class living and working conditions. These included Joe Corrie's *In Time O' Strife* (first performed by the Bowhill or Fife Miner Players in 1927), Robert McLeish's *The Gorbals Story*, Ena Lamont Stewart's *Men Should Weep* and Benedick Scott's *The Lambs of God*, first performed by Glasgow Unity Theatre in 1946, 1947 and 1948 respectively.

Today, Scottish playwrights write about an increasingly broad range of subjects and these are not necessarily confined to issues which directly concern their country. The Scottish playwrights who choose to write about Scotland certainly like to think that the Kailyard tradition has finally been laid to rest. Some writers continue to draw on Scottish history: **John McGrath**, for instance, drew most productively on the history of the Highland Clearances in his play *The Cheviot, The Stag and the Black, Black Oil* (first performed by the 7:84 Scotland Theatre Company in 1973). At the same time, a great many writers continue to explore Scottish urban, industrial, working class experience, past and present. The large majority address this subject in a genuinely exploratory way. Nonetheless, there is an underlying danger that this preoccupation will lapse into a new, alternative 'industrial Kailyard', in which the values of Scotland's urban industrial, working class people of 60 years ago become as over-simplified and sentimentalized as the values of Lowland ministers and schoolteachers were sentimentalized in the 19th century.

Scottish drama has dominated Scottish theatre's development. However, the 20th century has also witnessed Scottish contributions to opera and ballet. Today, Scottish Opera presents a wide international repertoire, including some new Scottish work. Scottish Ballet (1970 to the present day), which traces its origins back to Margaret Morris's Celtic Ballet (1947–58) and the Scottish National Ballet (c. 1960), has likewise been immensely active. LM

Pre-20th century
See: P. Baxter, *The Drama in Perth*, Perth, 1907; Walter Baynham, *The Glasgow Stage*, Glasgow, 1892; Frank Boyd, *Records of the Dundee Stage from the Earliest Times to the Present Day*, Dundee, 1886; John Malcolm Bulloch, *The Playhouse of Bon-Accord: A Short Survey of the Actor's Art in the City of Aberdeen*, Aberdeen, 1906; J. C. Dibden, *Annals of the Edinburgh Stage*, Edinburgh, 1888; R. Lawson, *The Story of the Scots Stage*, Paisley, 1917; D. MacKenzie, *Scotland's First National Theatre: A History of the First Theatre Royal, Edinburgh*, Edinburgh, 1963; Alec Robertson, *History of the Dundee Theatre*, London, 1949.

20th century
Winnifred Bannister, *James Bridie and his Theatre*, London, 1955; David Hutchinson, *The Modern Scottish Theatre*, Molendinar Press, Glasgow, 1977; W. Isaac, *Alfred Wareing*, London, 1951; Linda Mackenney, *The Directory of Scottish Theatre Collection*, Scottish Theatre Archive, Glasgow University Library; Linda Mackenney, *Scottish Popular Theatre, 1900 to 1950*, 7:84 Publications, Autumn 1986; Helen Murdoch, *Travelling Hopefully: The Story of Molly Urquhart*, Paul Harris Publishing, Edinburgh, 1981.

Scott, George C. (1927–) American film and stage actor and director, noted for a strong artistic integrity and intense acting style. His first stage appearance was at the University of Missouri after the Second World War. After playing some 150 roles in stock companies, Scott made his New York debut as Richard III in the **New York Shakespeare Festival** (1957). He received excellent response to *Children of Darkness* (1958). Alternating stage work with an outstanding film career, he appeared as Ephraim Cabot in *Desire Under the Elms* (1963). More recent successes on Broadway include *Sly Fox* (1976), based on *Volpone*. Although noted for his dramatic intensity, Scott directed and starred in **Noël Coward**'s *Present Laughter* in 1982 and directed *Design for Living* in 1984. He refused in 1971 to accept the Academy Award for Best Actor in the title role of *Patton*. Scott has also appeared with the New York Shakespeare Festival playing Antony and Shylock. SMA

Scribe, Auguste Eugène (1791–1861) French dramatist and librettist. One of the most prolific writers of the 19th-century theatre, Scribe is generally thought of as the creator of the 'well-made play'. A master of his craft he was much imitated by his successors, notably by **Labiche** and **Sardou**. Scribe's favourite genre was the *vaudeville* (nearly 250 pieces,

accounting for well over half of his total output). His primary material was the bourgeoisie of his day, which he observed with great accuracy. Again and again he showed, especially in the one-act *vaudeville*, how something could be made of nothing. His characters are not highly developed, but are sustained by the sheer force of the dramatic action. Each play is built around a central situation, but in addition to this there is normally a 'situation' in every scene. Scribe understood the art of preparing a situation, prolonging it, and finally sorting it out, and it is this very neatness that has always impressed. Initially trained for the law, Scribe had his first play performed at the Variétés in 1810. He tried his hand at almost every genre, but the *vaudeville* was that in which he excelled. His first success came in 1815 with *Une Nuit de la Garde Nationale* (*A Night of the National Guard*), written in collaboration with Delestre Poirson. A large part of his writing would be in collaboration, a widespread 19th-century practice. His popular *vaudeville*, *L'Ours et le Pacha* (*The Bear and the Pacha*, 1820), added a proverbial expression to the French language. In 1820, the Théâtre de Madame, which would become the Gymnase, opened as a 'fashionable' boulevard theatre, patronized by the Duchess of Berry. The repertoire of this theatre was to be light comedies and *vaudevilles*. Scribe was contracted as a house dramatist to the Gymnase in 1821 and, over the next ten years, alone or in collaboration, turned out some 150 plays for it. *L'Héritière* (*The Heiress*, 1823), written with G. Delavigne, became one of the classics of the Gymnase repertoire. *Bertrand et Suzette; ou le Mariage de Raison* (1826), whose theme is that of a girl turning her back on the man she loves in favour of a mercenary marriage, created a scandal, but it is one of the best plays. He explored this theme further in a play for the **Comédie-Française**, *Le Mariage d'Argent* (*The Mercenary Marriage*, 1827), where the hero sacrifices his own happiness in order to keep his fortune. The play, which refused to idealize society, was poorly received, but remained in the repertoire. It is often felt that Scribe's best work was produced for the Gymnase, but the Comédie-Française represented a form of consecration, and it was for this theatre that his major plays were written (usually without collaborators). He developed a new type of political-historical comedy, often based on the thesis that great effects are the result of trivial causes. In the plays for the Comédie-Française greater attention is given to characterization than in the *vaudevilles*. These plays include *The School for Politicians* (*Bertrand et Raton; ou l'Art de Conspirer*, 1833), *La Camaraderie* (1837), *La Calomnie* (1840), *The Glass of Water* (1840), *Une Chaîne* (1841), *Adrienne Lecouvreur* (1849), specially written for **Rachel**, and *The Ladies' Battle* (1850). Scribe was also librettist for some 28 operas as well as nearly 100 *opéras-comiques*. Amongst these are *La Dame Blanche* (1825), *Masaniello; or The Dumb Girl of Portici* (1828), *Fra Diavolo* (1830), *Robert the Devil* (1831), *The Jewess* (1835), *The Huguenots* (1836), *The Black Domino* (1837), *La Favorite* (1840), *The Crown Diamonds* (1841) and *The Prophet* (1849). When he died in 1861 he was working on the libretto for Meyerbeer's *L'Africaine*. JMCC

Scudéry, Georges de (1601–67) French dramatist and poet who after service as a soldier, on which he subsequently capitalized, laid down the sword in favour of the pen and in 1629 began to frequent the Paris salons, publishing books of verse and providing a quantity of plays to both established theatre companies, at the **Hôtel de Bourgogne** and the **Marais**. Tragedies, tragicomedies and comedies, irregularly constructed, stronger on rhetorical eloquence than characterization, and full of extravagant or violent incidents, they hold little interest now, with the exception of *La Comédie des Comédiens* (*The Actors' Comedy*, 1635) which presents on stage the company of actors under **Montdory** who performed it. In 1637 he initiated the influential literary controversy over **Corneille**'s *Le Cid* by publishing his adverse comments on the play. Later he collaborated with his sister Madeleine in the composition of her successful romances and was elected to the Académie-Française in 1649.   DR

Seaside entertainment see Pierrot shows

Seattle Repertory Theatre

An American regional theatre, founded in Seattle, Washington, in 1963 by Stuart Vaughn in a building erected for the 1963 World's Fair. The company met financial difficulties in its early days; by 1969–70 their deficit was over a quarter of a million dollars. W. Duncan Ross was appointed Managing Director at that time; six years later the company had 22,000 season subscriptions.

In 1974 they leased a second building, called the 2nd Stage, to house a second season of five plays. In 1979 Ross accepted a position elsewhere and was replaced by Daniel Sullivan; two years later Sullivan became Artistic Director. Sullivan continued previous policy, but added a New Plays workshop and began to employ more local actors.

In 1983 the company opened the 850-seat Bagley Wright Theatre at the Seattle Centre, which also contains a 250-seat PONCHO Forum for new works. The Wright Theatre annually presents a six play season, balancing classics, contemporary works, and premieres of new plays.   SMA

Sedaine, Michel-Jean

(1719–97) French dramatist and poet, a former stonemason by trade and largely self-educated. He became a friend of **Diderot** and seems to have shared his views on widening the subject matter and social range of contemporary drama. In *Le Philosophe Sans Le Savoir* (*A Philosopher Without Knowing It*), his most progressive play, Sedaine wrote a good example of Diderot's projected genre of the serious bourgeois comedy, with adequate touches of domestic realism to leaven the prevailing sentiment and special pleading and certainly better than Diderot's own attempts to dramatize his theory. The play was well received at the **Comédie-Française** in 1765, as was his engaging one-act comedy *La Gageure Imprévue* (*The Unforeseen Gamble*, 1768), but the bulk of his output consisted of *opéras-comiques*, or comedies with songs and musical accompaniment, which he wrote in collaboration with Grétry, Monsigny and other composers for performance at the **Comédie-Italienne** and the theatres of the Paris fairs.   DR

Segelcke, Tore

(1901–79) With her colleagues Gerd Egede Nissen and Aase Bye, this remarkable Norwegian actress dominated the female repertoire at **Nationaltheatret** from the 1930s to the 1950s. Specializing in roles demanding both inner strength and emotional spontaneity, she was particularly successful in **O'Neill** (Nina Leeds, Lavinia Mannon and Josie Hogan) and **Ibsen**. Her Nora was admired for its clear through-line and she was an especially strong Agnes in *Brand*. Among her later successes were Mrs Alving and the title role in **Brecht**'s *The Mother*. She was much acclaimed during her 1956 tour of the USA.   HL

Seibel, Beatriz

(1934–   ) Argentine critic, director and playwright. She has had success with children's theatre, *De gatos y lunas* (*Of Cats and Moons*, 1965) and with adult theatre such as *Siete veces Eva* (*Seven Times Eve*, 1982) and *Canto latinoamericano* (*Latin American Song*, 1985). A serious researcher, she often incorporates historical and literary items into her theatre.   GW

Seldes, Marian

(1928–   ) American actress, director, and teacher; daughter of Gilbert Seldes. A member of the theatre and dance faculties at the Juilliard School since 1969, Seldes, an award-winning actress trained in her teens at the **Neighborhood Playhouse**, appeared in the complete Broadway runs of *Equus* and *Deathtrap*. Originally a dancer, the tall, regal, articulate Seldes is considered an actor's actor. Most recently starring in *Painting Churches* (1983–4), she is the author of an unusual theatre memoir, *The Bright Lights* (1978; new edition 1984), a superb analysis of the chemistry of acting.   DBW

Sellars, Peter

(1958–   ) One of the USA's youngest artistic directors of a major theatre, Sellars, who had directed over 100 productions by the age of 27, first came to prominence as a Harvard undergraduate when he directed *The Inspector General* for the **American Repertory Theatre** (1980–1). After one year as artistic director of the Boston Shakespeare Company (1983–4), Sellars became head of the American National Theatre Company at the **Kennedy Centre** in Washington, DC, a post which he left, perhaps temporarily, in 1986. Among Sellars's ambitious and controversial productions have been Handel's *Orlando* (1982), **Brecht**'s *The Visions of Simone Marchard* (1983), a **Gorky–Gershwin** melange at the **Guthrie** called *Hang On to Me* (1984), and *The Count of Monte Cristo* (1985) for the ANT in Washington. After being fired as the original director of Broadway's *My One and Only* in 1983, he received the same week an unsolicited grant for $136,000 from the MacArthur Foundation.   DBW

Semyonova, Ekaterina Semyonovna

(1786–1849) The greatest Russian actress of her day, a favourite with **Pushkin** and Decembrist youth, often compared to **Mlle George** whose singsong, declamatory delivery she emulated in a rich contralto voice. The daughter of a landowner and one of his female serfs, Semyonova was trained by the heroic, neoclassical actor **Dmitrevsky** and beginning in 1803 excelled in the roles of tragic heroines to which she brought sincerity and ardent emotionalism. Her career is closely linked with those of **Prince Shakhovskoi** and dramatist-translator N. I. Gnedich, who advised her professionally, and with that of 'the unfortunate **Ozerov**' whose plays Pushkin said she 'ennobled' in the 1810s. Although she played Sofia in the original St Petersburg cast of *Woe from Wit* (**Griboedov** also translated Barthe's *Feigned Infidelity* for her), her career suffered when classical tragedy gave way to romantic drama on the Russian stage. She and her famous fellow St Petersburg company member **A. S. Yakovlev** straddled the line between two acting traditions – one artificial, the other more realistic. During 1820–2 she temporarily retired from the stage. In 1826 she married Prince S. Gagarin, thereafter using her power to terrorize her enemies and rivals, especially young actresses. Her notable roles include **Racine**'s Clytemnestra and Phaedra, **Voltaire**'s Merope and **Schiller**'s Mary Stuart. SG

Semzaba, Edwin (1951–   ) Tanzanian playwright. He has two published plays in Swahili, *Tendehogo* (*Dates and Cassava*, 1984), based on the old slave caravans, and *Hesabu iliyo-haribika* (*The Ruined Census*, 1976), on the conflict between urban and rural values and the generation gap. PML

Seneca (c. 4 BC–AD 65) Lucius Annaeus Seneca, 'Seneca the Younger'. He won fame as an orator and Stoic philosopher, and, after a period of exile, was made tutor to the young Nero. When Nero became Emperor in AD 54, Seneca remained his adviser, and was able for some years to exercise a benign influence on him, while amassing immense wealth for himself. He retired from public life in 62, and in 65 was accused of complicity in the Conspiracy of Piso and forced to commit suicide.

Ten plays are ascribed to Seneca in medieval manuscripts. The ascription has been doubted, but is now generally accepted, except for two plays thought to be by a later hand. The probably authentic plays are *Hercules Furens*, *Troades* (*Trojan Women*), *Phoenissae* (*Phoenician Women*), *Medea*, *Phaedra*, *Oedipus*, *Agamemnon* and *Thyestes*. *Oedipus* is based on **Sophocles** (*Oedipus Tyrannus*), *Agamemnon* on **Aeschylus**, *Thyestes* on an unknown (perhaps Latin) source, the rest on **Euripides**. The adaptation, however, is always free, as Seneca selects only those scenes of the original plays which suit his purpose, and makes many additions and rearrangements.

Of the plays considered spurious, one, *Hercules Oetaeus*, is merely a ponderous imitation of Senecan tragedy, but the other, *Octavia*, is of interest as the only surviving *fabula praetexta*, or play on a historical subject (see **Rome**). It concerns events in AD 62, when Nero divorced his wife Octavia and then ordered her execution, and was evidently written after Nero's death, which it prophesies.

It is disputed whether the plays were written for stage performance or merely (like most *non*-dramatic Latin poetry) for recitation to a small private audience. They contain nothing that *cannot* be staged, given a theatre with some stage-machinery (see **Roman theatres and amphitheatres**) and an audience with some imagination. But dramatic realities are persistently neglected; often, for instance, it is impossible to determine when a character enters, as he turns out to be present only when he starts to speak. It is anyway probable that the haughty and wealthy Seneca would have thought it beneath his dignity to write for the theatre. Passages of rapid dialogue could not easily have been delivered by a *single* reciter, but it is possible to imagine a small group of reciters, and perhaps some kind of semi-staged performance.

Certainly Seneca's main concern is with the rhetoric of speeches. He portrays the most heightened extremes of passion throughout, while striving at the same time for neatness and cleverness in his epigrams and rhetorical conceits. These purpo.es work against each other, giving, to modern tastes, an extremely artificial effect, and eliminating all possibility of subtle characterization. The epigrams and conceits are often striking and memorable; but every idea, whether striking or banal, is invariably flogged to death, often with a long list of mythical or geographical examples.

Each of the tragedies has five acts. Between the acts the Chorus utters general reflections loosely inspired by the action, but it hardly seems to occupy the same world as the characters, and is itself barely characterized. From *Phoenissae*, as we have it, choral songs are for some reason missing.

Stoic ideas are sometimes expressed, and the plays in general are Stoic in their portrayal of the evils stemming from passion and ambition. But evil always prevails, and there is no sign that human beings can ever attain the wisdom of the ideal Stoic sage.

Every tragedy builds up to a violent climax, related in a messenger-speech towards the end. The violence, like everything else, is evoked in the most extravagant terms, and to read some of these messenger-speeches requires a strong stomach, even by today's standards.

Senecan tragedy came into its own in the Renaissance, when the plays were assumed to be meant for performance, and were sometimes performed at universities. Among the tragedies of Elizabethan and Jacobean England Senecan influence is most obvious in inferior plays, such as **Shakespeare**'s *Titus Andronicus*; but without that influence, the tragedy of the period could not have existed at all. ALB

Senegal Of all the French-speaking countries in Africa, Senegal has had the longest contact with France; French presence began to build up in the 18th century and in the 1850s France undertook to extend its authority over more and more of what is now known as Senegal. The remainder of French-speaking Africa only came under the colonial influence of France and, in the case of present-day Zaire, Belgium, from the late 19th century. The result is that Senegal has been more deeply affected by cultural contact with France than the other French-speaking countries, an influence which could only be even more deeply implanted when Dakar became the capital of the federation of French West African colonies at the turn of the century. Thus it was that European theatre in French-speaking Africa was launched from the Ecole Normale William Ponty in Senegal in the early 1930s – the Ponty school was the one institution of secondary education in the whole federation and was attended by pupils from all the constituent territories.

Resources, never very lavish in French colonial Africa, were more readily available in Senegal. Even so, it was some years after the Second World War before the territory acquired its first theatre, the Théâtre du Palais, which opened in 1954. There was nothing very grand about this essentially basic building, but it immediately became an important centre for theatrical activity in French-speaking Africa, putting on French plays and adaptations of French plays, along with traditional African dramatic performances. There were as yet no Senegalese playwrights writing in French, but there were the stories of Birago Diop, drawn from the African story-telling tradition; a dramatization of one of them, *Sarzan*, was staged with great success in 1955. In 1965, a few years after Senegal gained its independence, the Théâtre du Palais was demolished and a new, rather more elaborate theatre erected in its place, named after the celebrated French actor Daniel Sorano, who had been born in Senegal. Maurice Sonar Senghor, the President's nephew, became its first director. This was in time for the World Festival of Black Arts held in Senegal in 1966. For the occasion, a group of actors calling themselves the Compagnie du Toucan performed **Aimé Césaire**'s *La Tragédie du Roi Christophe* (*The Tragedy of King Christophe*). There is no doubt that the presence of a large number of visiting African theatre companies performing in the Théâtre National Daniel Sorano during the festival provided a valuable stimulus to theatre in Senegal. The French director, Raymond Hermantier, who visited Senegal on two occasions, in 1965 and 1967, and the Haitian director and playwright, Gérard Chenet, who has settled in Senegal, have contributed their own considerable energy and talent to this development. After independence, the creation of the Ecole des Arts (School of Arts) provided a facility for training actors and directors, although there has been some criticism that even at their most innovative, methods have tended to follow European fashions rather than focusing on the exploration of traditional African dramatic techniques. The traditional tale and the traditions of story-telling, especially among the griots, are strong in Senegal and it is felt that their inherently dramatic features should be fully used in the creation of an indigenous theatre for Senegal.

The National Theatre draws its repertoire from the whole range of plays written in French-speaking Africa and the West Indies, as for example in Raymond Hermantier's production of **Shakespeare**'s *Macbeth*, and in the production of **Molière**'s plays, to which African audiences are readily receptive. There are, however, disappointingly few plays being published by Senegalese writers: of some 30 plays that it is possible to list to date, all but one or two belong to the 1970s and 1980s with little sign so far that the overall number for the 80s will exceed that of the 70s. There is only one writer who regards the theatre as a normal medium of expression, and that is **Cheik Aliou Ndao**, who has published six plays since 1967. His first play,

A scene from Diop's *L'Os de Mor Lam*, Senegal, 1967.

L'Exil d'Albouri (*The Exile of Albouri*), won the first prize for drama at the Pan-African Festival in Algiers in 1969 and has been frequently performed since then both in Senegal and elsewhere in French-speaking Africa.

Half of Ndao's plays so far are historical tragedies, and the historical play is by far the most popular among the country's authors (they amount to some 55% of the total). Most of these historical plays portray the Senegalese rulers who resisted French military expansion in the 19th century, although Ndao's are more subtle than most in that they tend to deal with the way these heroes handled the difficult moral and political problems with which their situation confronted them. Apart from Ndao's plays, the best known are Thierno Bâ's *Lat Dior* (1970), Mamadou Mbengue's *Le Procès de Lat Dior* (*The Trial of Lat Dior*, 1972), Amadou Cissé Dia's *Les Derniers Jours de Lat Dior*, (*The Last Days of Lat Dior*) and *La Mort du Damel* (*The Death of the Damel*, 1978), Ousmane Goundiam's *Le Procès du Pilon* (*The Trial of the Pestle*, 1980) and Alioune Badara Beye's *Le Sacre du Cedo* (*The Enthronement of the Cedo*, 1982). The reason for the popularity of the historical play probably has something to do with Senegal's long association with France, as a result of which the memory of a long period of military conquest has become fixed in the people's memory and the undermining of Senegalese culture by the culturally aggressive French has produced a deep-seated reaction – expressed by some in the shape of negritude – in favour of the African tradition and especially the exemplary heroes of the past.

Not all Senegalese plays are, however, based on historical themes. In some respects the most truly outstanding Senegalese dramatist is Abdou Anta Ka, who published four plays together in 1972 under the title *Théâtre*. Three of these are adaptations of other literary texts, including Ka's own version of the Chaka story originally told by the Sotho writer Thomas Mofolo. The fourth play – and the most interesting – is entitled *Pinthioum Fann* ('pinthioum' is a Wolof word meaning 'public gathering'); it deals with life in a mental hospital in Senegal and is based on the author's own experience. There is a quality of human insight in Ka's plays, and a sense of the theatricality of language, which place these rather difficult plays at a higher level of creative achievement than those of his fellow Senegalese playwrights, including Ndao. M'Baye Gana Kebe has entered two plays for the annual French radio play competition held in Africa: *L'Afrique a Parlé* (*Africa has Spoken*, 1972) and *L'Afrique Une* (*Africa One*, 1975) – these are both allegories pointing to eventual harmony between Africa and Europe; the former won the Listeners' Prize in the competition. CW

See: M. Banham with C. Wake, *African Theatre Today*, London, 1976; R. Cornevin, *Le Théâtre en Afrique Noire et à Madagascar*, Paris, 1970.

Serban, Andrei (1943–) Rumanian born and educated American director who made his debut in the United States at Ellen Stewart's **La Mama** in 1970. Unconventional and imaginative, Serban, whose greatest influence has been **Peter Brook**, soon became one of the prominent figures in contemporary American theatre. Among his most notable productions were a controversial comic interpretation of *The Cherry*

Orchard and *Agamemnon* at Lincoln Center in 1977; *The Ghost Sonata* at the **Yale Repertory Theatre**, where he worked between 1977–8; *The Marriage of Figaro* at the **Guthrie Theatre** in 1982; *Uncle Vanya*, with **Joseph Chaikin**, at La Mama in 1983; and *The King Stag* at the **American Repertory Theatre** in 1984. Operas he stage-directed include Tchaikovsky's *Eugene Onegin* (Welsh National Opera, 1980), Verdi's *La Traviata* (Juilliard American Opera Centre, 1981), Handel's *Alcina* (New York City Opera, 1983). BM REK

Serlio, Sebastiano (1475–1554) Born in Bologna, he worked as painter and architect before going to Rome in 1525 to work with **Baldassare Peruzzi**. Before going to Paris in 1541 to work on the palace at Fontainebleau, he designed a temporary wooden theatre in Vicenza, said at the time to be the world's largest, the only specific theatre architecture Serlio is known to have done. *Architettura* (1537–51), Serlio's seven-volume commentary on Vitruvius' *De Architectura*, was probably the most influential and significant Renaissance work on architecture. Book II of his treatise, published in 1545, contained a short section on theatre architecture and design which formed the basis for theatre practice throughout Europe for the next two centuries.

Serlio's significance lies in the way he combined his study of antiquity with Renaissance aesthetics and technology, thereby creating the foundation for the development of the proscenium stage and illusionistic scenery. His theatre plan included a long narrow stage and semicircular arrangement of seats taken from the classical Roman theatre. But he also assumed that the theatre would be contained in a rectangular space so that the seating plan was truncated. More importantly, the stage was backed by a deep, raked, scenic stage that contained stock perspective scenery on flat frames enhanced by 'wooden relief'. The three scenes were the tragic, comic, and satyric. The first, which bore a striking resemblance to Peruzzi's 1514 scene for *La Calandria*, contained a street with stately houses, statuary and the like. The comic was a street containing houses of ordinary citizens and was to include a tavern, courtesan's house, and a church. And the satyric depicted a pastoral setting. By 1620 his writings on theatre were translated into five languages. When François I died in 1547 Serlio fell into disfavour and became destitute. He spent a few years in Lyon but was able to return to Paris before he died. AA

Serreau, Jean-Marie (1915–73) Having trained with **Dullin**, Serreau became one of the directors responsible for the success of the theatre of the absurd, directing plays by **Adamov**, **Genet**, **Ionesco** and **Beckett**. But he also directed one of the first plays by **Brecht** to be performed in France (*The Exception and the Rule*, 1947) and in the 1960s became identified with the post-Brechtian political theatre of writers such as **Césaire** and **Yacine**. In reality the consistent guiding thread in Serreau's work was an experimental approach and in the 1960s he conducted a series of experiments in multi-media performance, attempting to find a synthesis between science and poetry. His widow, Geneviève Serreau, also works as a theatre producer and adapter and wrote one of the best accounts of the

theatre of the absurd: *Histoire du Nouveau Théâtre* (1966). DB

Serulle, Haffe (1947–) Dominican Republic fiction writer and playwright with a socially-committed tendency. Two historical plays: *Duarte* (1975) and *El hatero del Seybo* (Pedro Santana, 1976). His other plays denounce a variety of secular evils: *La danza de Mingó* (Mingó's Dance, 1977), *Prostitución en la casa de Dios* (Prostitution in God's House, 1978), *Testimonio de un pueblo oprimido* (Testimony of an Oppressed People, 1980), *Miriam la buena* (The Good Miriam, 1982) and *Bianto y su señor* (Bianto and his Master, 1984). GW

Serumaga, Robert (c. 1940–81) Ugandan playwright. Educated at Trinity College, Dublin, he had overseas theatre and radio experience. On return to Uganda, 1966, he founded the semi-professional Theatre Ltd, largely with expatriates, and later the Abafumi Players with school-leavers whom he trained as professional performers and with whom he travelled widely. He held the senior Creative Writing Fellowship at Makerere University for one year and was briefly Minister of Commerce under Y. K. Lule in 1979. He returned to the Abafumi, now based in Nairobi, where he died. His published plays are *A Play* (1967), *The Elephants* (1970), and *Majangwa* (1971), which he took to the Third World Theatre Festival in Manila. Later he moved into dance drama. MMac

Servandoni, Giovanni Niccolò (Jean Nicolas Servan) (1695–1766) Italian architect, painter and stage designer who came to Paris in 1724 and subsequently spent most of his working life in France. From 1728 he was principal designer at the Opéra and was frequently commissioned to devise the decorations for official court functions and those of the aristocracy. Between 1738 and 1742 and again in the 1750s he mounted at the **Salle des Machines** a number of performances with non-speaking actors which were little more than a pretext for displaying spectacular changeable scenery, machines and lighting effects to a scenario written by himself. In later years he worked in several other European capitals. In 1749 **Covent Garden** imported him to paint scenes for their operas and plays and in 1763 he was hired for one year by Duke Karl Eugen as a scene painter for the court at Wurttemberg. Servandoni's designs, with their impressive perspectives and diagonal vistas, mark the high-point of illusionistic scenery as an autonomous element in the stage picture. DR AJN

Settle, Elkanah (1647–1724) English playwright. Educated at Westminster and Trinity College, Oxford, he began writing plays in 1666. His tragedy *The Empress of Morocco* (1669) was the first play published in England with illustrations of the performance. It was burlesqued by Thomas Duffett for the rival company and fiercely attacked in a pamphlet by **Dryden**, **Crowne** and **Shadwell**. He wrote numerous heroic tragedies, including *The Female Prelate* (1680), a play on Pope Joan, and adaptations of earlier plays before turning to operatic spectacle. His adaptation of *A Midsummer Night's Dream* as *The Fairy Queen* with music by Purcell was first performed in 1692 and contains spectacular scenes of music and dancing for monkeys and Chinamen. In 1679 his comedy *The World on the Moon* was performed with the most extravagant machine effects yet tried in England. From 1683 onwards Settle also wrote drolls, shortened comic versions of his own and others' plays, for performance in booths at Bartholomew Fair and Southwark Fair. He may have acted in these as well. In 1691 he became city poet and produced city pageants for London until 1708. From 1718 until his death he lived in Charterhouse, a poorhouse.   PH

Séveste, Pierre-Jacques (1773–1825) French theatre manager. A former dancer and actor in the boulevard theatres, Séveste set up one of the first dramatic agencies in France c. 1810. With the Restoration of the monarchy he acquired special favour by helping to find the burial place of Louis XVI and Marie Antoinette, and was granted a licence to erect theatres in the suburbs in 1817, and to perform plays which had recently been performed at the theatres in Paris. His first theatre was the 348-seat Théâtre Montparnasse (1819), and this was followed by the larger Théâtre de Montmartre (1822). His actors were usually badly paid, and often of semi-amateur status. After the death of Pierre-Jacques, his widow and sons Edmond and Jules continued the business, adding the theatres of Belleville (1827) and Grenelle (1830), and taking over, with compensation, the Batignolles theatre, 'illegally' built by Souchet in 1830. The Séveste monopoly of suburban theatres in a rapidly expanding city was the subject of much jealousy and opposition. They maintained it, without making their fortune, until 1851. The most important of the theatres was Montmartre, built largely from the demolished Château de Cramagel (from whence came much of the original scenery), and which was described as 'ideal for a provincial town of 8–10,000 inhabitants'. Prices at Montmartre ranged from 2frs. to 0.50c in 1845 and by the mid-century these theatres were becoming the real 'popular' theatres of Paris.   JMCC

Sewell, Stephen (1953–) Australian playwright. His plays, written from a Marxist perspective, share an episodic structure, powerful theatrical effects and a preoccupation with the tension between political commitment and private emotion. They include *The Father We Loved on a Beach by the Sea* (1976), *Traitors* (1979) (staged at **Hampstead Theatre Club**, London, in 1980), *Welcome the Bright World* (1982), *The Blind Giant is Dancing* (1983), *Dreams in an Empty City* (1986) and a television drama, *The Long Way Home* (1985).   MW

Seydelmann, Karl (1793–1843) German actor. One of the greatest virtuosi of the 19th century, Seydelmann acted in companies in Prague, Kassel, Darmstadt, Stuttgart (from 1828 to 1837), and, during the final years of his life, at the **Berlin Royal Theatre**. Chronic sickness and nervous disorders meant that he was a lonely and difficult man. His interpretation of classic roles, especially Carlos in *Clavigo*, Mephistopheles, King Philip in *Don Carlos*, and Shylock, were distinguished for the dryness and individuality of his approach. For some of his critics, Seydelmann acted with little attention to the role's context within the play; for others he was the epitome of the 'thinking' intellectual actor. His letters and occasional writings are an invaluable source for the theatre history of the time.   SW

Seymour, William (1855–1933) American actor, director, stage manager. A child actor in New Orleans until 1865, when he went to New York. He served as a callboy at **Booth's Theatre** and performed with **Edwin Booth**, **Joseph Jefferson**, **Charlotte Cushman** and **Edwin Forrest**. Among Seymour's many management positions were the **Union Square Theatre**, the **Madison Square Theatre**, the Metropolitan Opera House, and **Charles Frohman**'s **Empire Theatre** in New York, and a decade (1879–88) at the **Boston Museum**. In 1882 he married May Davenport, daughter of **E. L. Davenport** and younger sister of **Fanny Davenport**. His theatrical memorabilia and personal library form the nucleus of the extensive theatre collection at the Princeton University Library.   FHL DJW

Shadow puppets, Shadow theatre A form of entertainment in which flat figures of a non- or semi-transparent material reflect stylized shadows against a screen, and are moved to music or chant. All Oriental shadow theatres began as illustrations to narration. In Indonesia (Java and Bali) the figures of the *wayang* (i.e. silhouette) theatre are usually of water-buffalo hide: the *wayang klitik* figures are flat with movable arms; those of the *wayang golek* are three-dimensional with movable heads and arms. The forms of the characters are traditional, the difference in size indicating their type. Some tales of gods, heroes and demons are drawn from south Indian myth and ritual, with an admixture of topical and sexual matters. The *dalangs* or showman-reciters perform only by invitation and are used to spread religious and dynastic propaganda; they now present 'drawing-room versions' of traditional plays. The play is performed on a screen 4 metres long and 1.5 metres high set up in an inner verandah; it begins at sundown after a long musical introduction, and goes on into the night (in Bali up to 1 a.m., in Java until 4 or 5 a.m.). It is a common diversion for the night after a wedding.

The Thai version, *nang*, still performed by a few troupes, is not technically a shadow play since the leather puppets which can represent a single character or a whole scene are in direct view. They are moved according to the choreography of the Siamese dance, and a troupe may comprise 10 to 20 players.

The *piyingxi* of China is a form of miniature opera. The translucent figures of coloured parchment (or leather in Sichuan) cast coloured shadows in this synthesis of painting, song, music and manual choreography. The technique originated in the Song Era (960–1279) as depictions of the folkloric tales *shuo-shu*, but soon evolved a distinct repertory of historic and Buddhist themes. It declined after 1911, but in the 1930s Tang Jiheng proposed its revival as competition for the Western cinema. During the Japanese occupation, it was used for Resistance propaganda, and during the Korean War, the Communist government exploited it in training soldiers. For a short period in the 1950s, it was influenced by the American comic strip, but has reverted to the traditional love stories, criminal cases and battles.

Oriental shadow puppets first came to Central Europe in the 17th century, as an auxiliary to the use of the magic lantern. In France they became known as *ombres chinoises*, especially as popularized by Dominique Seraphin (1747–1800) and were later sophisticated by Henri Rivière at the Parisian cabaret Chat Noir (after 1887) with crowd scenes, incandescent colour shifts and scored music. They greatly influenced the Austrian artist Richard Teschner (1879–1948), whose Golden Shrine Theatre (1912) featured a synthesis of Indonesian and Viennese Secession elements. Alexander von Bernus also brought it to a high degree of artistry in his Schwabing Shadow Plays (1907–12). In the early 1920s Lotte Reiniger (b. 1899) brought shadow puppets to the screen in her classic animated films, such as *Prince Achmet* (1926). LS

See: W. Grube, *Chinesische Schattenspiele*, Munich, 1915; R. Long, *Javanese Shadow Theatre*, Ann Arbor, 1982; I. C. Orr, 'Puppet Theatre in Asia', *Asian Folklore Studies* 33 (1974); J. Pimpaneau, *Les Poupées à l'Ombre*, Paris, 1977; J. and P. Remise and R. Van de Walle, *Magie lumineuse*, Tours, 1979.

Shadwell, Thomas (c. 1642–92) English playwright. Most famous as the target of **Dryden**'s satire *MacFlecknoe* (1678), an attack revenged when Shadwell succeeded Dryden as Poet Laureate and Historiographer Royal after the Revolution of 1688. He was educated at Caius College, Cambridge, and at the Middle Temple and began writing plays with an adaptation of **Molière**'s *Les Fâcheux* as *The Sullen Lovers* (1668). Shadwell quickly defined himself as the inheritor of the style of **Jonson** in *The Humorists* (1670) and *Epsom Wells* (1672). He transformed Dryden and **Davenant**'s version of **Shakespeare**'s *The Tempest* into an opera in 1674 as well as adapting Molière's *The Miser* (1672), and collaborating with William Cavendish, Duke of Newcastle, on *The Triumphant Widow* (1677). Of his original plays, the best of his satiric comedies are *The Virtuoso* (1676) which incorporates mockery of the pseudo-science of the Royal Society, *The Squire of Alsatia* (1688) with a virtuoso display of the language of the criminal underworld and *Bury Fair* (1689) exploring provincial aping of London manners. His dark comic version of the Don Juan story, *The Libertine*, was performed in 1675 and his version of Shakespeare's *Timon of Athens*, in part turned into a contemporary political satire, in 1678. PH

Shaffer, Peter (Levin) (1926–) British dramatist, who worked as a coalminer, librarian and music critic before his early play, *Five Finger Exercise*, was successfully produced in 1958. This, like his two one-act plays, *The Private Ear* and *The Public Eye* (1962), suggested that Shaffer was a natural successor to **Terence Rattigan** with command of the skills of drawing-room comedies and drama. His television plays, *The Salt Land* (1955) and *Balance of Terror* (1957), revealed an imagination drawn toward religious and philosophical themes. The first stage play which fully combined his flair for craftsmanship with his wider preoccupations was *The Royal Hunt of the Sun* (1964), about the destruction of the Inca civilization in Peru by the Spanish conquistadores led by Pizarro; and the contrast between the Inca god-king, Atahuallpa, and Pizarro anticipated future moral conflicts, personified by two warring men, in later plays. *The Royal Hunt of the Sun* demanded unusual mime and vocal disciplines from the **National Theatre** company, but proved triumphantly successful, the first NT hit in a contemporary play. An amusing farce, *Black Comedy* (1965), in which the stage characters grope around apparently in pitch darkness while the audience watches them in full light, was another NT hit, and later matched with *White Lies* (1968), to form a double bill in the West End. Although *The Battle of Shrivings* (1970) was less successful in a commercial production in London, Shaffer's two subsequent plays, *Equus* (1973) and *Amadeus* (1979), both produced at the National Theatre, were acclaimed as masterpieces. In *Equus*, a weary psychoanalyst attempts to grapple with the mysteriously Dionysian faiths of a delinquent youth, Alan Strang, while in *Amadeus*, the composer Salieri bitterly watches the progress of his divinely inspired rival, Mozart. Both plays contrast reason with faith, materialism with inspiration, and constitute the core works in Shaffer's output. *Yonadab* (1985) echoes some of these themes without providing so powerful a myth. Shaffer's twin brother, Anthony, is also a dramatist and a novelist, and they have collaborated on three detective novels, published in the early 1950s. JE

Shakespeare, William (1564–1616) In a flamboyant age and a notoriously flamboyant profession – he was an active member of a theatre company for at least 20 years – Shakespeare was abnormally reticent. As a result, researchers have had painstakingly to piece together the story of his life from surviving scraps of evidence.

He was born in the market town of Stratford-upon-Avon, where his father was a prosperous glover and one of the town's 14 principal burgesses. In 1565, John Shakespeare was promoted to the rank of alderman, and he became Chief Alderman in 1571. It is a reasonable assumption that such a man would send his son to the local grammar school, though there is speculation that the boy did not complete his course there, owing to the decline in his father's fortunes after 1576. The years before Shakespeare's marriage to Anne Hathaway in 1582 are blank. Within six months of the wedding, the couple had a daughter. She was the Susanna who later married John Hall, a local physician, and lived prosperously in Stratford. The family was completed with the birth of twins, Judith and Hamnet, in 1585. Hamnet died in 1596 and was buried in Stratford, where Judith remained until her death in 1662.

Virtually nothing is known of Shakespeare's life from 1585 to 1592. It may be that he left home and family to tour with a group of London players. Certainly his name was sufficiently familiar in the London theatres by 1592 to invite **Robert Greene**'s jibe at him as an 'upstart crow'. Greene was one of the university men who resented the rivalry of the new breed of professional playwrights, and he had probably in mind Shakespeare's part in the writing of the three *Henry VI* plays. This early collaboration suggests that

Shakespeare served his apprenticeship alongside some of the growing number of dramatic aspirants seeking advantage in the demand for plays from the emergent professional theatre. Other surviving texts from the 1590s, however, suggest that Shakespeare preferred to work alone. Only in *Sir Thomas More* (c. 1595) has his collaborative hand been confidently detected. We do not know how Shakespeare came by the money to purchase a share in the newly formed **Lord Chamberlain's Men** in 1594. His likeliest patron, Henry Wriothesley, Earl of Southampton, was in financial straits of his own at this time, but he cherished the role of Maecenas and may have helped the young man who had already dedicated to him his narrative poem, *Venus and Adonis* (1593). By 1594, Shakespeare had also written at least three comedies, *The Comedy of Errors*, *The Two Gentlemen of Verona* and *The Taming of the Shrew*, and two corpse-laden tragedies, *Titus Andronicus* and *Richard III*, the latter of which provided a brilliantly original conclusion to the three parts of *Henry VI*, as well as a second narrative poem, *The Rape of Lucrece*. The Lord Chamberlain's Men must have perceived in him, not simply an actor, but also a potential resident writer for their London base, the **Theatre** in Shoreditch.

Living close to Bishopsgate and the Theatre, Shakespeare continued to write plays at the rate of approximately two per year. The period 1594–8 may have seen the first productions of *King John* (sometimes dated as early as 1589), the middle comedies, *Love's Labour's Lost* (scholars continue to argue about *Love's Labour's Won*, ascribed to Shakespeare by Francis Meres in *Palladis Tamia* (1598)), *A Midsummer Night's Dream* and *The Merchant of Venice*, the outstandingly popular tragedy *Romeo and Juliet* and the cycle of English history plays comprising *Richard II*, the two parts of *Henry IV* and *Henry V*. That Shakespeare also had aspirations as a gentleman, and sufficient means to support them, is apparent in the application, on his father's behalf, for a coat of arms. The award was made in 1596. In the following year, Shakespeare bought New Place, one of the finest houses in Stratford. Early in 1598 he made a small investment in malt (malting was Stratford's principal industry). The London theatres were under threat of permanent closure at this time, and Shakespeare may have been contemplating the life of a country gentleman. If so, the plan was shelved when, at the end of 1598, the company responded to the landlord's threat of eviction from the Theatre by transporting its timbers to the south bank of the Thames and re-erecting them as the **Globe**.

Shakespeare wrote most of his greatest plays during the first decade (1599–1608) of his company's occupation of the Globe. They include the mature comedies, *Much Ado About Nothing* (which may shortly pre-date the move), *As You Like It* and *Twelfth Night*, the darker comedies, sometimes called 'problem plays', *All's Well that Ends Well*, *Measure for Measure* and *Troilus and Cressida*, a pot-boiler, *The Merry Wives of Windsor*, written in response to demands for more of Falstaff, and the major tragedies, *Julius Caesar*, *Hamlet*, *Othello*, *King Lear*, *Macbeth*, *Antony and Cleopatra*, *Coriolanus*, and *Timon of Athens*. It was a period that saw the Lord Chamberlain's Men honoured by the new monarch with the title of King's Men and confirmed in their ascendancy at Court. Shakespeare had moved his London lodgings to Southwark, in closer proximity to the new theatre, and maintained his financial interests in Stratford. A small investment in land (1602) was followed by a larger one (1605). He may have feared the continuing insecurity of his profession, threatened by authority, by the regular outbreaks of plague and by the faddish interest in boy actors. Facile younger dramatists, **Beaumont** and **Fletcher** in particular, were challenging his supremacy by the readiness of their response to Jacobean taste for sensation and spectacle. It was a taste more easily satisfied in the indoor **Blackfriars**, which the King's Men added to the outdoor Globe in 1608. Shakespeare's last plays, *Pericles, Prince of Tyre* (on which he collaborated, probably with George Wilkins), *Cymbeline*, *The Winter's Tale* and *The Tempest*, take account of the revived interest in romance, magic and improbable resolutions whilst giving scope to a new 'indoor' fondness for scenic spectacle. At the end of his career, Shakespeare returned to the collaborative composition with which he had begun, working with Fletcher on *Henry VIII*, *The Two Noble Kinsmen* and the lost *Cardenio*. By 1613, when the Globe was destroyed by fire, his hold on the London theatre was slipping. He had just purchased the upper floor of one of the Blackfriars gatehouses and may not have wished to contribute more to the rebuilding of the Globe. It is possible, though not certain, that he relinquished his share in the old theatre, now under reconstruction, and spent his last years in Stratford.

Texts Less than half of Shakespeare's plays were published during his own life, and this is not at all surprising. Not only were plays held in low esteem as literature, but also acting companies were unwilling to make their possessions available to others and to the public at large. The single known example of a playwright's contract, **Richard Brome**'s with Queen Henrietta's Men at the **Salisbury Court Theatre** (1635), specifies that Brome shall publish none of the plays written for the company. Authorized publication of plays often followed unauthorized, 'pirated' publication of unreliable texts, like the famous 'bad' Quarto of *Hamlet* (1603). It was, then, an act of singular homage when two of the King's Men, **John Heminges** and **Henry Condell**, oversaw the publication in lavish Folio form, of 36 plays by their late colleague. The First Folio (1623, reprinted 1632, 1664 and 1685) includes 20 plays which might otherwise never have been published. It was, by any reckoning, a remarkable printing achievement. Various facsimiles have been subsequently published. Subsequent editors, even of the 16 plays published in earlier Quartos, have always to refer to the Folio. The first critical edition was that of **Nicholas Rowe** (1709), who used the Fourth Folio as his authority. Himself a playwright, Rowe respected Shakespeare's text more than was common in the theatre of his time, but he sought to regularize the plays' division into scenes and acts in a way that the Folio editors had considered unnecessary. Later 18th-century editors, including Alexander Pope (1725), **Lewis Theobald** (1734), **Samuel Johnson** (1765) and Edmond Malone (1790), followed Rowe's pattern.

Malone's exemplary scholarship is commemorated in the reprints of dramatic texts and documents by the Malone Society (founded 1907). Modern editors are served, not only by the textual studies of W. W. Greg and his successors, but also by the Variorum editions pioneered by H. H. Furness in 1871. Reliable single-volume collections include those edited by Peter Alexander, W. J. Craig and C. J. Sissons. Untroubled by the anxieties that led Thomas Bowdler to produce an expurgated 'Family Shakespeare' (1818), 20th-century editors seek to establish as perfect a text as possible, explaining their decisions in copious notes. Even so, discrepancies remain, and no two editions of the same play will ever be identical. Outstanding among 20th-century series are the variously edited Arden, New Cambridge, Penguin and Oxford Shakespeares.

Shakespeare in performance There can be little certainty about the conditions in which Shakespeare's plays were first performed. We know that **Richard Burbage**'s acting was greatly admired and that he played Richard III, Hamlet, Lear and Othello, but we do not know how he played them, nor even how well he knew his lines. There is some contemporary evidence, particularly in the case of comic roles, that Elizabethan actors sometimes substituted their own words for the playwright's. We cannot assume that Shakespeare's own company performed his plays 'straight' and word-perfect. What we can say is that the actors walked out onto the platform to deliver their part of a story, since it was as a story-telling art that the drama made its bid for audiences. It is a mistake of which many scholars have been guilty to suppose that there was a single style of playing – formal and rhetorical, say some, natural and direct, say others. On the contrary, the variety of verbal styles in which the best Elizabethan plays were written indicates the expectation of a variety in the acting. Play-days in the open-air theatres were probably boisterous and certainly colourful – an extravagant delight in clothes was shared by actors and audiences. Rich gowns turned boy-actors into acceptable women, one of many conventions on which effective staging relied. The Elizabethan theatre was not a haven for purists, and the more 'correct' taste of the late 17th century found fault with it. Even Shakespeare's admirers, like **Davenant** and **Dryden**, admitted the need to improve him. From the early days of the Restoration theatre until well into the 19th century, it was normal practice to hack, reshape and plunder Shakespeare's texts to suit prevailing tastes or to ease the task of leading actors. **Nahum Tate**'s *King Lear* (1681) and **Colley Cibber**'s *Richard III* (1700) are only the best remembered of the cobbled versions in which the plays reached Restoration audiences. **Thomas Betterton**, whose playing of such contrasting parts as Hamlet and Falstaff brought Shakespeare's name into a new prominence, did his own doctoring of the texts, setting a precedent which would be followed by later actor-managers from **David Garrick** through **John Philip Kemble**, **William Macready**, **Charles Kean**, **Henry Irving** to **Beerbohm Tree** and the 20th century. The manifest leader of his profession, Betterton unwittingly established the rule that the greatness of English actors

would be measured by their achievement in Shakespearian roles. His versions had to take account of the new delight in changeable scenery, a sophistication which ran counter to the fluidity of scene changes on the bare Elizabethan stage. The reordering of scenes may not be the most offensive of the alterations of Shakespeare, but it is one of the most enduring. The director of the **Royal Shakespeare Company**'s 1977 revival of the *Henry VI* trilogy, **Terry Hands**, for example, laid stress on the decision 'not to do even our own usual reshaping of a few corners'. A programme note for the same company's 1974 *King Johan* confessed that 'the text for this production incorporates lines from *The Troublesome Reign* and **Bale**'s *Kynge Johan*, and some additions by John Barton'. It would be a mistake for 20th-century audiences, confident of the respect in which Shakespeare's text is now held, to neglect the continuing theatrical urge to bend what cannot easily be made to fit.

Betterton's formally cadenced delivery of Shakespeare's lines was copied by **James Quin**. They stood, probably firm-footed and facing front, on the proscenium in the full light of the candelabra, enacting through gesture the passions expressed in their lines. Garrick's memorable debut as Richard III (1741) was an energetic, and eventually decisive, challenge to the old-school conventions, as, earlier in the same year, was **Charles Macklin**'s vividly serious Shylock. But Shakespearian acting was changed also by external forces. The increasing size of the major London theatres throughout the 18th century demanded a broader style. Only a presence as imposing as that of **Sarah Siddons** or as charismatic as that of **Edmund Kean** could command an audience of over 3,000. With the development of gas-lighting during the second decade of the 19th century came another significant change. The greater visibility allowed actors to play inside, rather than in front of, the scenery. One significant outcome was the increasing hold of 'pictorial Shakespeare', to which designers contributed almost as much as actors. The various regimes of Macready, **Madame Vestris**, Charles Kean, Irving and Tree brought the visual elements of Shakespearian production into parity with the aural. The splendour of the crowded 19th-century stage was a new convention which few actor-managers – **Samuel Phelps** outstandingly at **Sadler's Wells** (1844–62) – were bold enough to challenge before **William Poel** began his sequence of bare-stage productions for the Elizabethan Stage Society in 1894.

It is the replacement of the actor-manager by the director that distinguishes 20th-century Shakespearian production. **Granville Barker**'s innovatory work at the Savoy (1912–14) demonstrated how the text could be released by the clearing of the cluttered stage. The new approach was further strengthened during **Lilian Baylis**'s years at the **Old Vic**, where the young **Tyrone Guthrie** was one among many directors who dared radically to reinterpret Shakespeare's plays. At the rebuilt Shakespeare Memorial Theatre (opened 1932), Komisarjevsky (**Komissarzhevsky**) offended purists with a series of unconventionally designed productions (1933–9), bringing Stratford into new prominence as a centre of Shakespearian performance.

That prominence was firmly established by 1960, when **Peter Hall** became the managing director of the newly-named Royal Shakespeare Company. Most of the major English actors and directors have worked at Stratford, or at the company's London bases, the Aldwych (1960–82) and the Barbican (since 1982). The conventions of modern Shakespearian production – that the director should discover the leading idea or ideas of a play and reinforce them through design and costume on a stage that permits the free flow of scenes – have been authorized by the Royal Shakespeare Company. PT

Shakespearian Festivals in the United States

In the United States, the modern idea of a 'festival' of Shakespearian plays seems to have been initiated by Angus L. Bowmer, who founded the **Oregon Shakespeare Festival** in 1935, still the oldest surviving American Shakespearian festival. The San Diego National Shakespeare Festival can also trace its origins back to 1935, although it did not offer a summer festival of plays until 1949. In the 1950s and 1960s several other important North American Shakespearian festivals were founded, including the **American Shakespeare Theatre** Festival in 1955, the **New York Shakespeare Festival** in 1961, and the Great Lakes Shakespeare Festival in 1962. Although initially confined to a summer season most of the major festival theatres have gradually extended their seasons and expanded their operations. The Oregon Shakespeare Festival, for example, went from a two-month summer season to a virtually year-round operation. In 1970 the modern, indoor Angus Bowmer Theatre was built adjacent to the outdoor Elizabethan Theatre modelled after John Cranford Adams's Globe reconstruction. The present Elizabethan Theatre opened in 1959, replacing two earlier outdoor theatres. Typically, the Oregon festival also operates a small 'studio' theatre named the Black Swan. In the late 1960s and 1970s, the San Diego and New York festivals also expanded into additional theatres and longer seasons. In 1984, the Alabama Shakespeare Festival moved into a new two theatre multi-million dollar complex in Montgomery. With such expansion, these major festival theatres have also stretched their repertoires well beyond Shakespeare's plays. A typical season will now include not only two or three Shakespearian plays, but also revivals of international classics and productions of contemporary comedies, dramas, and musicals. As an indication of its less restricted repertoire, the Great Lakes festival has recently dropped 'Shakespeare' from its name. Although Shakespeare's plays present producers with formidable artistic and financial challenges, a Shakespearian festival remains an attractive concept, particularly for theatres operating mainly in the summer. Almost every American region has at least one summer Shakespearian festival. Among the principal ones are the Berkeley Shakespeare Festival, The Theatre at Monmouth (Maine), Shakespeare & Company at Lenox, Massachusetts, the Shakespeare Festival of Dallas, the Three Rivers Shakespeare Festival in Pittsburgh, The Colorado Shakespeare Festival, The Shakespeare Festival (Vermont) and The Globe of the Great Southwest in Odessa, Texas. The quality of presentation can vary widely from festival to festival and season to season, but the various festivals do offer thousands of theatregoers the opportunity to experience Shakespeare on stage. Moreover, they also provide Shakespearian performance and production opportunities for numerous aspiring and accomplished American actors, directors, and designers. Festival productions are usually reviewed on an annual basis in issues of *Shakespeare Quarterly*. Glen Loney and Patricia MacKay's *The Shakespeare Complex* (New York, 1975) provides an excellent if somewhat out of date overview of both year round and summer festivals. DJW

Shakhovskoi, Prince Aleksandr Aleksandrovich (1777–1846)

An indefatigable force in the 19th-century Russian theatre: conservative Director of the repertory section of the Imperial Theatre (1802–26); author of over 100 plays, including tragedies, melodramas, vaudevilles, opera librettos, patriotic historical dramas, and most notably, satirical comedies of manners; a demanding acting teacher, whose famous pupils included **E. S. Semyonova**, **V. A. Karatygin** and **I. I. Sosnitsky**; translator-adapter from French, German and English (**Shakespeare** and Walter Scott); one of Russia's first serious régisseurs; member of the Russian Academy (1810). Physically unprepossessing and vocally limited – fat with a long, pointed nose and unable to pronounce 'r' and 'sh' – Shakhovskoi forged an acting style in part from his observations of Monvel and **Talma** while in Paris to engage a French company (1803). He began writing plays under the influence of **Molière** and at the instigation of the actor **Dmitrevsky**, *A Woman's Jest* (1796) being his first and the comedy of manners *The New Sterne* (1805) making him famous. He was engaged in several conservative literary enterprises, including A. S. Shishkov's 'Forum of the Friends of the Russian Language' (1811–16), which attempted to preserve old forms, and, along with **I. A. Krylov** and **A. I. Pisarev**, publication of *The Dramatic Courier* in which neoclassicism was defended against the onslaught of sentimentalism and early romanticism. These last two trends, together with Gallomania and the 'neo-*philosophes*' (*umniki*), were ridiculed in his most controversial comedy, *Lesson for Coquettes, or The Lipetsk Spa* (1815) via a character said to have been modelled on the poet V. A. Zhukovsky. This was also the first five-act Russian play to set its entire action out of doors. Shakhovskoi eventually embraced romanticism, co-authoring a comedy *All in the Family, or the Married Fiancée* (1817) with **Griboedov**, whose early work he had influenced, and **Khmelnitsky**. He also freely adapted Shakespeare's *The Tempest* (1827), brought **Pushkin**'s 'Queen of Spades' to the stage (1836) and was the author of 'magical' comedy-ballets, replete with spectacular stage effects. In *Seigneurial Pursuits, or Home Theatre* (1808) Shakhovskoi characterized the serf theatre and introduced the stage type of the upstart landowner, reprised in his *Tranchirin's Boast* (1822) which marked the acting debut of **Mikhail Shchepkin**. Shakhovskoi's *The Cossack Poet* (1812) is generally considered to be the first Russian vaudeville. His longest running play, *The Bigamous Wife* (1830), was an early attempt to portray the merchant class on stage. While not a superior playwright, the suppleness of his verse, the naturalness of his dialogue and the individualism of his characters helped prepare the way for Griboedov, who in *Woe from Wit* (1824) transformed the Russian satirical comedy of manners into truly social comedy. SG

Shaman Tungus word now in general use to mean a witch-doctor, medicine man, cunning person or professional sorcerer. His (less frequently her) skills are various: human and veterinary medicine, the location of lost goods and people, the identification of witches and counter-measures against them, the ability to harm an enemy magically. The method of work is usually a ritual performance employing literary, musical, dramatic or choreographic techniques. Typically, the shaman is one whose own affliction has been cured by a shamanic ritual. AEG

Shange, Ntozake (1948–) Afro-American playwright. Born Paulette Williams in Trenton, New Jersey, Barnard College graduate Shange's first play *For Colored Girls Who Have Considered Suicide When The Rainbow is Enuf* (1976) brought immediate acclaim to an exciting and innovative playwright. The play called for seven women in individual recitations to recount life experiences. More conventional was *A Photograph: A Study in Cruelty* (1977), followed by *Spell #7* (1978), an extended choreopoem of character revelations using poetry, song, dance, and masks, and by *Boogie Woogie Landscapes* (1980). Shange's free-form theatre pieces give her a distinctive voice on the contemporary stage. EGH

Shank, John (d. 1636) English actor, who was a member of several companies before joining the King's Men at some time between 1613 and 1619. His links with an older tradition of gagging clowns are supported by his liking for jigs, at least one of which, *Shank's Ordinary* (1624), he wrote. He is known to have maintained, and perhaps trained, several apprentices during his membership of the King's Men. The most provocatively interesting of the parts allotted to him is that of the waiting-woman Petella in a revival of **Fletcher**'s *The Wild Goose Chase*. We do not know how often a company would exploit the broad comic potential of the clown in female roles. PT

Sharaff, Irene (1910–) American theatre and film costume designer. Sharaff began as an assistant to **Aline Bernstein** and by the early 1930s was designing major Broadway plays and, primarily, musicals such as *As Thousands Cheer* and *On Your Toes*. Through the 1960s she designed many significant musicals including *The King and I* and *West Side Story*. Her Hollywood career began in 1944 with *Meet Me in St Louis* and later included *An American in Paris*, *Cleopatra* and *Who's Afraid of Virginia Woolf?* Although the latter demonstrated her ability to create pedestrian costumes, she is best known for stylish design and her use of colour. She also had the unusual ability to translate stage productions into film. AA

Sharman, Jim (1945–) Australian director. Graduating from NIDA in 1965, he was based in London in the early 1970s, working at the **Royal Court Theatre** and directing large-scale productions, including *Hair*, *Jesus Christ Superstar* and *The Rocky Horror Show* in London, America and Japan. Returning to Australia in 1975, he specialized in staging **Patrick White**'s work and has directed with several major companies, including the South Australian Theatre Company, the Sydney Theatre Company and the Australian Opera. He was director of the Adelaide Festival in 1982. MW

Shaw, George Bernard (1856–1950) Irish-born playwright, critic and polemicist. Shaw's uneasy childhood and youth were spent in Dublin, which he left in 1876 to accompany his mother, a singer, to London. There he developed his largely self-taught interest in the arts and in politics, declaring himself a socialist in 1882 and joining the Fabian Society in 1884. He was already writing prolifically and the pull of the theatre is evident in the serialized novels of the early eighties, from *Immaturity* to *Cashel Byron's Profession*. It was, however, as music critic for the *Star* (1888–90) and the *World* (1890–4) that he began to develop the witty iconoclasm that was to characterize his finest writing. Shaw had abandoned novel writing by the time he undertook to provide J. T. Grein's Independent Theatre with a play. The work began as a collaboration with **William Archer**, whose interest in **Ibsen** Shaw shared and had quirkily expressed in *The Quintessence of Ibsenism* (1891), but Shavian social analysis was too overwhelmingly individualistic for the well-intentioned Archer. *Widowers' Houses* (1892), by its diagnosis of slum-landlordism, exposes the collaboration of aristocracy and the 'respectable' bourgeoisie against labour, announcing, however clumsily, the dramatic intentions of the fledgeling playwright whose mental agility was to disturb the placid surface of the English theatre for 50 years.

Not only Shaw's themes, but also the jesting stance he took towards the craft of playmaking, made it virtually impossible for the contemporary theatre to accommodate his work. He had to rely on readings, private productions and publication to mount his attack on the entrenched actor–managers and the traditional deceits of the received drama. Shaw's combativeness is exemplified in the titles he chose for the three published collections of his first ten plays. *Plays Unpleasant* (1898) contained *Widowers' Houses*, the much more proficient and highly controversial *Mrs Warren's Profession* (first performed 1902) and *The Philanderer* (first performed 1905). More palatable, though rich with tongue-in-cheek challenges to conventional dramatic values, were the *Plays Pleasant* (1898), *Arms and the Man* (1894), *Candida* (1897), *The Man of Destiny* (1897) and *You Never Can Tell* (1899). The *Three Plays for Puritans* (1901), *The Devil's Disciple* (1897), *Captain Brassbound's Conversion* (1900) and *Caesar and Cleopatra* (1907), are often-impish illustrations of the Shavian dictum that 'decency is indecency's conspiracy of silence'. These early plays are all fed by Shaw's perception of the intellectual flabbiness of the English 19th-century theatre and can usefully be read alongside the dramatic criticisms he contributed to the *Saturday Review* (1895–8), collected in *Our Theatre in the Nineties* (3 vols., 1932). Incisive, irreverent and always suspicious of anything normally taken for granted, Shaw's writing on drama has the liveliness and eye-opening rhetoric of the published *Prefaces* to his plays (collected in a single volume in 1934, with revisions and additions in 1938 and 1965). Throughout his long life, he sustained his mischievously boyish delight in outstripping the ponderous intellectual establishment, which responded by underrating him as effectively as it could manage. But the stifling or misrepresentation of Shaw's talent was brought to an end during the seasons at the **Royal Court Theatre** (1904–7) under **Harley Granville Barker** and **J. E. Vedrenne**. They not only revived several of the earlier plays, but also mounted the first performances of major new plays in which Shaw's genius for dramatizing debate on social and political issues of national importance was fully revealed. *John Bull's Other Island* (1904) drew attention to the persistent Irish question. In *Man and Superman* (1905), a socialist hero can outmanoeuvre all his political adversaries but surrenders to the rival life-force of a woman. *Major Barbara* (1905) displays Shaw's debating talents at their most dazzling, pitting social conscience against conscienceless social reform. Two decades later, this play would excite **Bertolt Brecht** to call Shaw a 'terrorist' and to complement Shaw's original with his own *Saint Joan of the Stockyards*. Beside *Major Barbara*, *The Doctor's Dilemma* (1906) seems barrenly clever.

Shaw's hold on the London theatre was maintained, though not greatly enhanced, by further discussion plays like *Getting Married* (1908) and *Misalliance* (1910) as well as by the controversy aroused when the Lord Chamberlain banned performances of *The Shewing Up of Blanco Posnet* (1909) on the grounds of blasphemy. Shaw was no stranger to the risks involved in contrasting Christian forms with the substance of Christ's teaching, and conversion is a major theme in his plays from *Candida* to *Androcles and the Lion* (1913) and beyond, but it was the satirical account of a thoroughly secular conversion that brought him his first and greatest popular triumph, *Pygmalion* (1914). Staged by one of the last great actor–managers, **Herbert Beerbohm Tree**, and starring **Mrs Patrick Campbell** as the flower seller who conquers society through elocution, *Pygmalion* established Shaw as England's leading playwright. It was a reputation soon tarnished amid the jingoism of 1914 by the publication of the brilliantly rational essay *Common Sense about the War* (1914).

Between the outbreak of the First World War and his death in old age, Shaw would write upwards of 30 new plays, but only a few of them have established a place in the theatrical repertoire. They include his most complex discussion play, *Heartbreak House* (1920), the extraordinary and eccentric philosophical 'pentateuch', *Back to Methuselah* (1922), the startlingly original historical tragedy, *Saint Joan* (1923), three plays which he termed 'political extravaganzas', *The Apple Cart* (1929), *Too True to Be Good* (1932) and *Geneva* (1938), and a frequently underrated comedy, *The Millionairess* (1936). There has been a recent revival of interest in *In Good King Charles's Golden Days* (1939), 'a true history that never happened', but Shaw's command of the English-speaking theatre has significantly weakened in recent years, not least because of the birth of a modern political drama to reinforce what used to be his lonely voice. Scholars have come increasingly to recognize the contribution he made to the developing art of the director and to the serious study of acting, of which there is much evidence in the many selections from his voluminous correspondence.   PT

Shchepkin, Mikhail Semyonovich (1788–1863) The former serf actor who became the acknowledged father of Russian realistic acting and a major influence upon **Stanislavsky** via the education of the latter's teacher, **Glikeriya Fedotova**. Shchepkin's professional career, which began in the provinces in 1805 and later moved to Moscow (1822) and the Maly Theatre (1824), was partially shaped by amateur actor Prince P. V. Meshchersky and Slavophile writer-critic S. T. Aksakov. The former demonstrated natural stage speech in opposition to the declamatory approach exemplified by **Dmitrevsky**. The latter improved his tastes in foreign literature, translating **Molière**'s *The Miser* for him to perform, and encouraged the development of a more intelligent native drama. A political conservative and 'closet democrat', Shchepkin counted a wide assortment of artist-intellectuals among his social equals and personal friends, a situation unheard of since Dmitrevsky's day. These included radical writer-critics Herzen, Belinsky and Nekrasov, as well as dramatists **Griboedov**, **Pushkin**, **Turgenev**, **Sukhovo-Kobylin** and especially fellow Ukrainian **Gogol**. Shchepkin supplied these inventors of the modern Russian drama with anecdotes that were incorporated into their plays and served as the models from which a number of their characters were conceived. This collaboration helped to end the hegemony of foreign comedies, farces, tragedies, melodramas and operettas on the Russian stage, and to educate the Russian critics and audience, especially the intelligentsia, to accept and appreciate Russian plays. Shchepkin, whose squat, rotund physiognomy, large head and natural exuberance targeted him from youth for the 'comic old man' *emploi*, applied his natural warmth and humour, facility with verse, simplicity and emotional expressiveness, profound humanity, personal dignity and moral strength to the social satires and dramas of the 'little man' which began to appear. By the 1840s he had won acclaim as Famusov in *Woe from Wit* (1830) and the Mayor in *The Inspector General* (1836). By the 1860s, however, the 'House of Shchepkin', as the Maly was called, became the 'House of **Ostrovsky**', in honour of the dramatist whose brand of photographic realism achieved great success via the performances of a new generation of actors headed by **Prov Sadovsky**. In 1897 the Shchepkin legacy passed to the **Moscow Art Theatre** in the form of the following ideas: the sacredness of theatrical art and the selflessness of acting in a role as part of an ensemble; the need for extensive rehearsals; strict discipline, careful observation, self-knowledge, imagination and emotion as the cornerstones of the actor's craft. The systematizer of these tenets, Stanislavsky, was born the year of Shchepkin's death.   SG

Sheldon, Edward (Brewster) (1886–1946) American playwright. A graduate of **George Pierce Baker**'s Workshop 47 at Harvard College, Sheldon was an early proponent of social realism in America with *Salvation Nell* (1908), in which a girl avoids a repulsive 'profession' by joining the Salvation Army; *The Nigger* (1909), concerned with the struggle of a southern governor who discovers that his grandmother was an octoroon slave; *The Boss* (1911), a drama of labour-management conflicts. His romantic conclusions in these plays, however, suggested his true interests as revealed in *The High Road* (1912), a search for beauty, and *Romance* (1913), as an American clergyman explains his love for an Italian diva. When poor health essentially incapacitated Sheldon, he collaborated with such dramatists as **Sidney Howard** (*Bewitched*, 1924) and Charles MacArthur (*Lulu Belle*, 1926). Although none of his later works was outstanding, Sheldon remained a source of inspiration and help on dramaturgical problems for a number of prominent dramatists. WJM

Shepard, Sam (Samuel Shepard Rogers)

(1943–) American playwright who, though lacking a major commercial Broadway success, is arguably the most critically acclaimed, if the most obscure and undisciplined United States dramatist of the past 15 years. *New York Magazine* called him 'The most inventive in language and revolutionary in craft', as well as the 'writer whose work most accurately maps the interior and exterior landscapes of his society'. Uniquely American and contemporary in his subject matter, ranging from myths of the American West, American stereotypes, the death or betrayal of the American dream, the travail of the family, to the search for roots, Shepard defies easy classification. Influenced by rock and roll, the pop and counter-cultures beginning in the 1950s, the graphic arts and dance, the West of Hollywood, hallucinatory experiences, and a dozen other eclectic forces, his path as a writer is hard to plot. Richard Gilman suggests that it is best to accept the volatility and interdependence of Shepard's plays – 'they constitute a series of facets of a single continuing act of imagination'. Of his more than 40 plays, 11 of which have received Obie Awards, beginning with the Theatre Genesis (New York City) productions of *Cowboy* and *The Rock Garden* in 1964, the following are major works: *La Turista* (1966); *The Tooth of Crime* (1972), a rock-drama written during a four-year period in London; *Curse of the Starving Class*, written in 1976 and produced first in 1978 at the **New York Shakespeare Festival** with a successful New York revival in 1985; *Buried Child* (1978), for which he won the 1979 Pulitzer Prize; *True West* (1980) and *Fool for Love* (1979), both originally staged at the Magic Theatre in San Francisco where he was playwright-in-residence for several years; and *A Lie of the Mind* (1985). A film actor and screenwriter as well, Shepard has appeared in several successful films, including his own *Fool for Love*, and for his screenplay *Paris, Texas*, won the Golden Palm Award at the 1985 Cannes Film Festival. DBW

Sher, Antony

(1951–) South African born, British actor. He trained in London and Manchester, and after a period in repertory established his reputation with a series of roles between 1975 and 1981, especially as Klestakov in **Gogol**'s *The Inspector General* (Edinburgh 1975), and Muhammad, the confused Arab businessman, in **Mike Leigh**'s *Goose Pimples* (1981). He joined the **RSC** in 1982 and his Fool in *King Lear* was the first of his brilliantly theatrical creations of Shakespearian characters. Richard III in 1984 and Shylock in 1987 were others. He is a truly exciting actor to watch in action, taking risks that are usually triumphantly vindicated. MB

Sheremetiev, Count Nikolai Petrovich

(1751– 1809) Owner of the largest and most sumptuous serf theatres in Russia, which set the standard for others to follow. Educated at the University of Leiden, he spent the period 1769–73 familiarizing himself with theatre in England, Switzerland and the Netherlands. Upon his return to Russia, he inherited his father Count Pytor Sheremetiev's serf company on his estate at Kuskuvo, a Moscow suburb. What had been the site of occasional entertainments honouring state visits and the like, hosting as many as 30,000 persons, became under the son a fully-fledged theatrical enterprise rivalling St Petersburg's court theatres and far surpassing Moscow's public theatres. Sheremetiev imported leading Moscow actors such as **I. A. Dmitrevsky** and **P. A. Plavilshchikov** to instruct his company of serf actors which numbered as many as 95. Senior musicians were imported from abroad to train his serf orchestra. A scenic designer and translator were on staff. Ballets, comedies and vaudevilles were staged, but operas were the favourite and received the most attention. This was especially true after 1801 when the Count married his leading lady, the serf actress Praskovya Ivanovna, to whom he gave the stage name Zhemchugova ('The Pearl'). In order to remove his new wife from her serf environment, he moved his company to the Moscow suburb of Ostankino. There, based on the latest information on theatre architecture secured from abroad, two serf architects erected a theatre with a seating capacity of 300, a removable parquet floor to allow for balls and banquets and a large stage equipped with trapdoors, *periaktoi*, flying machines and all manner of special effects. The Count treated his serf actors better than those belonging to other landowners and far better than his other serfs. His wife, around whom his productions were built, died in 1803, 20 days after giving birth to their son. SG

Sheridan, Richard Brinsley

(1751–1816) Irish playwright and theatre manager. Born in Dublin, educated at Harrow, he lived in Bath with his family, his father running a school of elocution. After marriage to a singer he moved to London and in 1775 his first three plays were produced. *The Rivals* made brilliant use of Sheridan's experiences of Bath as a setting for a tangled plot contrasting mockery of sentimentalism in Lydia Languish against apparent admiration for it in the serious lovers, Faulkland and Julia. Sheridan's verbal dexterity is at its best in his creation of Mrs Malaprop. The other two plays of 1775 were a farce, *St Patrick's Day*, and a very successful comic opera, *The Duenna*. In 1776 he took over as principal manager of **Drury Lane Theatre**, though his ambitions, his difficulties in dealing with his colleagues and successive financial crises never made him a success as manager. In 1777 his adaptation of **Vanbrugh**'s *The Relapse* as *A Trip to Scarborough* appeared as well as his best play, *The School for Scandal*. Sheridan's attack on scandal-mongers returns to the satiric methods of Restoration comedy while finding in the reconciliation of the Teazles, after Lady Teazle's flirtation with adultery, a distinctive optimism. His affectionate but sharp mockery of the foolishness of much contemporary drama, *The Critic* (1779), continues the tradition of **Buckingham**'s *The Rehearsal*. In 1780 he became an MP, was appointed Secretary to the Treasury in 1783 and was extremely active in the parliamentary proceedings in the impeachment of Warren Hastings. He was still closely involved in running Drury Lane, opening the rebuilt theatre in 1794, though he wrote few plays other than adaptations of **Kotzebue**. He finally gave up management not long after the disastrous fire that destroyed Drury Lane in 1809, a fire that he watched in an armchair in the street, 'by his own fireside' as he said. PH

Sherriff, R[obert] C[edric] (1896–1975) British dramatist and novelist, whose bitterly realistic depiction of the pressures on front-line soldiers in a dug-out preparing for an attack, *Journey's End*, was performed by the **Stage Society** in 1928 and had a wide international impact. It still provides an effective anti-war statement, but the conventional naturalism of his later work has dated. Although providing impressive roles for an actor like **Ralph Richardson** and dealing with similar psychological themes, the immediacy and public commitment was missing in historical subjects like the last years of Roman Britain or Napoleon (*The Long Sunset*, 1955; *St Helena*, 1935), a study of amnesia (*Home at Seven*, 1953) or a rustic comedy about village cricket (*Badger's Green*, 1930). CI

Sherwood, Robert E[mmet] (1896–1955) American dramatist, screenwriter, essayist, historian and propagandist, was a man of strong emotions and good will who preached simplistic solutions to complicated problems. His career started with *The Road to Rome* (1927) and continued with such plays as *Reunion in Vienna* (1931), both sentimental and frivolous comedies about emotional problems. With *The Petrified Forest* (1935), a story of frustrated idealism, *Idiot's Delight* (1936), an anti-war play, and *Abe Lincoln in Illinois* (1938) Sherwood won three Pulitzer Prizes. During the 1930s he wrote screenplays, served as president of the Dramatists Guild and helped found the Playwrights' Company (1938).

Sherwood changed with the advent of war in Europe. Having complained that his plays always started with a message and ended with good entertainment, he wrote *There Shall Be No Night* (1940), a militant condemnation of American isolationism, trumpeted across the land by actors **Lunt** and **Fontanne**. Soon he became a speech-writer for President Roosevelt who appointed him director of the Overseas Branch of the Office of War Information. Sherwood's post-war plays – *The Rugged Path* (1945) and *Small War on Murray Hill* (1957) – were failures. Only in his history of *Roosevelt and Hopkins* (1948) did he show again his considerable writing skills. WJM

Shields, Ella (1879–1952) American (Baltimore-born) singer, comedienne and male impersonator. Initially a coon singer, in which role she began a twenty-five-year career on the British variety stage in 1904. She rapidly moved into pantomime, and in 1910 at the London Palladium made her first appearance in top hat and tails, à la **Vesta Tilley**. Many of her songs became popular classics, notably 'If You Knew Susie' and the celebrated 'Burlington Bertie from Bow', written by her husband William Hargreaves. AEG

Shiels, George (1886–1949) Irish playwright. Permanently crippled in a railway accident in Canada in 1913, Shiels returned to Ballymoney and took to writing. His earliest plays (one-acters), written under the name George Morshiel, were produced by the **Ulster Literary Theatre**. The **Abbey** presented his first full-length play, *Paul Twyning* (1922). Thereafter Shiels supplied the Abbey with a string of box-office successes whose popularity owed much to the theatre's broadly farcical interpretation of them. They include *Professor Tim* (1925), *Cartney and Kevney* (1927), *The New Gossoon* (1930), *The Passing Day* (1936), *The Old Broom* (Group 1944), *Tenants at Will* (1945), *The Caretakers* (1948).

Even the first two Abbey plays, where the comic machinations are lighthearted, take place in a deceitful world with 'happy endings' not so happy as the characters imagine. *Tenants at Will*, called 'a comedy in three acts', is a tragedy of 19th-century peasant miseries. In *The Passing Day*, memorably directed by **Tyrone Guthrie** at the 1951 Festival of Britain, a dying man manipulates and is manipulated by his family and business circles. The characters appeal to whatever codes of behaviour may suit their purpose, with no sense of the contradictions between them, nor from the dramatist any moral judgement – 'not the playwright's business'. Feelings – friendship, love – are professed but not felt, envisaged in an underlying vocabulary of mortgages, bank loans, coalitions.

Shiels's plays have their funny, indeed their farcical, scenes, but the laughter does not conceal the ironic reserve noted and disliked by **Yeats**. The plays occasionally contrive sentimental endings, though any justice involved is more rough than poetic. Although his range is narrow, with recurring situations and characters, contemporary Northern Irish settings, and a prose holding close to common speech, Shiels's dispassionate observation of human meanness and folly conveys unsettling but not depressing truths. DM

Shirley, James (1596–1666) English playwright, born in London and educated at the Merchant Taylors' School and the Universities of Oxford and Cambridge. Shirley took holy orders, and in 1623 was appointed headmaster of the grammar school in St Albans, a post which he forfeited in 1625 by his conversion to Roman Catholicism. He returned to London to make money by writing and had completed at least 36 plays before the closure of the theatres in 1642, at which time he had few rivals as the leading working dramatist in London. Having sided with the Royalists during the Civil War, Shirley could count himself lucky to find a post as a schoolmaster during the Interregnum. He did not long survive the Restoration, dying of exposure in the Great Fire of London. Shirley was an uncomplicated writer, an admirer of **John Fletcher** whose fondness for contrivance he emulated in the multiple plots of such comedies as *The Witty Fair One* (1628), *Hyde Park* (1632), *The Gamester* (1633), *The Lady of Pleasure* (1635), *The Imposture* (1640) and *The Sisters* (1642). The social values and witty dialogue anticipate elements of Restoration comedy. Shirley's tragedies look rather to the past, bringing revenge tragedy to a moral end. They include *The Traitor* (1631), *The Politician* (c. 1639) and *The Cardinal* (1641). A few of Shirley's masques survive, among them *The Triumph of Peace* (1634), one of the showiest of its kind, as well as a modest volume of *Poems* (1646). PT

Sholom Aleichem (Solomon Rappaport)

(1859–1916) The most treasured of Yiddish writers whose homely plays, filled with lovable philosophical comic characters, provided artistic and financial successes for theatre companies all over the world. *Tevye the Milkman* (made into the American musical *Fiddler on the Roof*) is probably the best known. *200,000*, a most amusing play sometimes called *The Big Win*, is nevertheless filled with social significance, whilst in *Hard to Be a Jew*, two students, one Jewish and one not, change places for a year to find out whether it is indeed hard to be a Jew. Other plays include *Scattered and Dispersed*, about the dissemination of the Jewish people at the turn of the century, and many dramatizations of his novels. AB

Showboats

From the early 19th century, flatboats, then steamers and paddlewheelers plied the Mississippi and Ohio rivers, offering entertainment to the residents along the banks. Although **Noah Ludlow**, **Joseph Jefferson** and **Sol Smith** dabbled in such amusements, the first intentionally designed showboat was that of William Chapman Sr, launched at Pittsburgh in 1831. The Chapman family in their 'Floating Theatre', a rude shed set on a barge and poled downriver, soon became a familiar sight, making annual tours of the major waterways with a repertory of **Kotzebue**, **Shakespeare** and musical farces. Before Chapman's widow sold out in 1847, they had set the style of similar enterprises, although imitators tended to song-and-dance and lecture entertainments and sometimes lacked the respectable domestic veneer of the Chapmans. The crafts ranged from ramshackle scows to grandiose arks. Circus boats, led by Spalding and Rogers's Floating Circus Palace (1851), were capable of seating up to 3,400 spectators and offered minstrel shows and a museum of curiosities in addition to sawdust acts.

After the disastrous hiatus of the Civil War, a new period of prosperity came to the showboat. The leading entrepreneur was Augustus Byron French, a riparian **Barnum** who operated five boats from 1878 to 1901; he pioneered the use of marching bands on shore to advertise his lavish variety bills and launched both the apt term and the luxurious vessel, the 'floating palace'. His double-decker 'Sensation No. 2' sat 759, but the

Spalding and Rogers's Floating Circus Palace.

only full-length drama ever offered was **Uncle Tom's Cabin**. French's main rival was E. A. Price, whose press agent Ralph Emerson came up with sensational innovations in publicity, using calliopes, billboards and postcards to herald the boat's arrival.

The reliance on variety was challenged by the Eisenbarth-Henderson Temple of Amusement, which purveyed drama exclusively; these 'moral amusements', which included *Faust*, were lit by electricity. As 'The Cotton Blossom' under Emerson's management, it featured Broadway hits and spectacular melodramas until 1931. Drama was also the fare provided by Norman Thom, 'the **John Drew** of the Rivers', the first actor since Chapman to own a boat; for 'The Princess', he shrewdly chose plays of regional interest. The Bryants specialized in lurid melodrama, offered in direct competition to the rival silent pictures.

There were 26 showboats (as they had come to be known) active in 1910, 14 in 1928, and 5 in 1938. The last recorded by Philip Graham was 'The Goldenrod', tied up in St Louis in 1943. The decline can be attributed to the closure of the frontier; unable to compete with the urban entertainments that sprang up in the wake of civilization, the owners suffered greatly from the depression of 1929. Behind the fashion even in their heyday, the boats became a nostalgic artifact, and imitations were much in use by society promoters in the 1930s. It was **Jerome Kern**'s and **Oscar Hammerstein**'s musical adaptation of *Show Boat* (1927), a novel by Edna Ferber, that simultaneously immortalized the phenomenon and encased it in an aura of quaintness. Once a unique product of westward expansion, showboats are now adjuncts of tourism and municipal festivals. LS

See: B. Bryant, *Children of Ol' Man River*, NY, 1936; P. Graham, *Showboats. The History of an American Institution*, Austin & London, 1951.

Shubert family

American theatre owners and producers. The family business was founded by three brothers – **Sam S.** (1879–1905), **Lee** (1875–1953), and **Jacob J.** (1880–1963) Shubert – who began their careers in Syracuse, New York, in the late 19th century. The brothers moved to New York City in 1900 and began producing and acquiring theatres, including the Herald Square and the **Casino**. Among the stars who worked in Shubert shows during the early years were **Richard Mansfield**, **Sarah Bernhardt**, and **Lillian Russell**. Sam Shubert died in a train crash in 1905, but his brothers continued to operate the business on an increasingly lavish scale, often coming into conflict with the **Theatrical Syndicate**, a rival group of theatre owners and managers which dominated American theatrical activity in the early 20th century. By 1916, however, the Shuberts had broken the Syndicate monopoly and had themselves become the nation's most important and powerful theatre owners and managers. During the teens and twenties, the Shubert brothers built many of Broadway's theatres, including the **Winter Garden**, the **Sam S. Shubert**, and the **Imperial**. In addition, they came to own or operate more than 100 theatres across the country and to book more than 1,000 others. Among their major stars of the period were **Al Jolson** and **Eddie Cantor**, both of whom were great successes at the Winter Garden. The

Shuberts were especially well known for their productions of operettas by Sigmund Rombert, among them *Maytime* (1917), *Blossom Time* (1921), and *The Student Prince* (1924). They were also known for their popular annual revues – *The Passing Show*, which appeared regularly from 1912 through 1924, and *Artists and Models*, which was produced in a number of editions from 1923 to 1943. Although the Shuberts' business was badly hurt by the depression, they continued to produce throughout the 1930s and 1940s, presenting a number of well-known musicals and revues, including the later editions of the *Ziegfeld Follies*, **Cole Porter**'s *You Never Know* (1938), and Olsen and Johnson's *Hellzapoppin'* (1938), as well as such popular straight plays as *Ten Little Indians* (1944) and *Dark of the Moon* (1945). During the 1950s the US government brought an anti-trust suit against the Shuberts, who were forced to divest themselves of a number of their theatres in 1956. During the 1950s and early 1960s the company was run by J. J. Shubert's son **John** (1909–62), and after his death by a great-nephew of the founders, **Lawrence Shubert Lawrence, Jr** (b. 1916).   BMCN

Shubert Organization Theatrical real estate and producing company founded in the late nineteenth century by the **Shubert family**. Since 1972 its chief operating officers have been two former Shubert lawyers, Gerald Schoenfeld and Bernard B. Jacobs. Jacobs serves as President of the Shubert Organization and Schoenfeld as Chairman of the Board. In addition, they are respectively President and Chairman of the Shubert Foundation, a related philanthropic institution which provides support to many non-profit theatre and dance producing groups. The Shubert Organization currently owns and manages 16 of the operating Broadway theatres, including the **Ambassador**, the **Ethel Barrymore**, the **Belasco**, the **Booth**, the **Broadhurst**, the **Broadway**, the **Cort**, the **John Golden**, the **Imperial**, the **Longacre**, the **Lyceum**, the **Majestic**, the **Plymouth**, the **Royale**, the **Sam S. Shubert**, and the **Winter Garden**. In addition, the company has a half interest in the **Music Box** Theatre. Outside New York City, the Shubert Organization owns and operates the Shubert and Blackstone in Chicago, the Forrest in Philadelphia, and the Shubert in Boston. It leases and manages two other theatres, the Shubert in Los Angeles and the **National** in Washington, DC. Although the company was not active in theatrical production during the 1950s and 1960s, in recent years it has once again become involved in Broadway producing. Some of its recent productions have included *Sly Fox* (1976), *Gin Game* (1977), *Ain't Misbehavin'* (1978), *Dancin'* (1978), *Amadeus* (1980), *Children of a Lesser God* (1980), *Dream Girls* (1981), *Nicholas Nickleby* (1981), *Cats* (1982), *Glengarry Glen Ross* (1984), and *Sunday in the Park with George* (1984). The Shubert Organization has also produced a highly successful Off-Broadway show, *Little Shop of Horrors* (1982). The company has been influential in the revitalization of the Times Square theatrical district and has pioneered a number of innovative theatre business practices, among them the introduction of telephone and charge ticket sales and a computerized ticketing system.   BMCN

Shund theatre ('Shund' = rubbish) Term used to describe the popular sentimental and melodramatic Yiddish theatre in America, designed to please the mass audience of unsophisticated immigrants from 1890 onwards.   AB

Shvarts, Evgeny Lvovich (1896–1958) Soviet dramatist, writer of witty and wise adult fairy-tales that were transparent yet evocative socio-political satires, absolutely unique during the period of socialist realism (1934–53). The son of liberal Jewish intellectuals in Kazan, Shvarts's legal studies at Moscow University were interrupted by his father's conscription during the war. He toured as an actor with P. K. Veysbrem's amateur theatre troupe from Rostov-upon-the-Don (1917–22) and eventually settled in Leningrad, where he built his life and career. His work for the publishing house and children's magazines *Canary* and *Hedgehog* of writer-poet-editor-translator Samuil Marshak led to Shvarts's producing his first short story, 'The Tale of the Old Balalaika' (1925), and his first play, *Underwood* (1929), about a witch who steals a typewriter and the orphan who retrieves it. In the late 1920s he became friendly with the Serapion Brothers and the Oberiuty, whose work ranged from the realistic to the absurd and whose formalist experiments appealed to Shvarts as did the fairy-tale which was then also regarded with suspicion. Shvarts was influenced by fabulists Hans Christian Andersen, **E. T. A. Hoffmann** and Charles Perrault, as well as by the symbolists, who believed in life's doubleness and in the possibility of creating a philosophical drama, and by **Vakhtangov**, whose 'fantastic realism' manifested a joyful theatrical dualism. Shvarts eschewed the straight allegory, preferring to mix or texture his sources to achieve a rich ambiguity. While these plays have had a troubled production history, they were not condemned outright for two main reasons. First, they are written in 'Aesopian language', making their exact satirical meanings somewhat flexible – thus, Shvarts's studies in militarism, tyranny, racism, xenophobia, the humanness of animals and the bestiality of man could be applied as easily to Hitler (as Shvarts openly did), who invaded Russia in 1941, or to the Soviets' recalcitrant capitalist allies, as they could to Stalin. Second, Shvarts wisely balanced his fantasy output with realistic, patriotic plays extolling the courage and resourcefulness of the Russian people, which as a civil defence warden during the Nazi blockade of Leningrad, he knew about firsthand. Such plays include: *The Treasure* (1933); *Brother and Sister* (1936); *Our Hospitality* (1939) which went unproduced, because it showed a plane penetrating Soviet borders; *One Night* (1941), about the bombing of Leningrad; and *Far Land* (1943), dedicated to the Leningrad children separated from their parents during the evacuation. The first of his major fairy-tale satires, *The Naked King* (1934), drawn from several Andersen stories, exposes the pettiness and fakery in all dictators and was banned from the stage until 1960 when the Sovremennik Theatre produced it. His best and most philosophical play, *The Shadow* (1940), based on Andersen's 'Peter Schlemeil', contemplates man's doubleness, his capacity for good and evil, his repressed power fantasies, the relativity of truth and reality which makes simple solutions unwise if not impossible and the precariousness of life, art and even history which as in several of Shvarts's plays is transformed into a fairy-tale. There are even veiled references in the play to recently 'rehabilitated' Soviet writers. The play was beautifully realized by designer-director **Nikolai Akimov** in 1940 at the Leningrad Theatre of Comedy. *The Dragon* (1944), his most political play, is based on Perrault's legend of Lancelot and attacks the conspiracy to tyranny between ruler and ruled. Like Shvarts's work in general, it posits the need for constant vigilance of self and society, thus rejecting the traditional happy ending of fairy-tales and socialist realist literature. Staged by Akimov in 1944, it was banned until 1960, the same year in which *The Naked King* and *The Shadow*, which had been removed from the stage shortly after their premieres, were revived. *An Ordinary Miracle* (1956), Shvarts's *The Tempest*, about a senior magician who learns that love is the real magic, also was staged by Akimov in 1956. Shvarts's remaining work includes: the fairy tale plays *Adventures of Hohenstaufen* (1932), *Little Red Riding Hood* (1937), *The Snow Queen* (1938) and *Two Maples* (1954) which preach the value of the collective and the dangers of capitalism; screenplays, including *Cinderella* (1947), which has been adapted for the stage, and *Don Quixote* (1957), based on the 1938 **Bulgakov** adaptation and filmed by Kozintsev with Nikolai Cherkasov in the title role; and a number of puppet plays.   SG

Shverubovich, V. I. see **Kachalov**

Sibenke, Ben (1945–   ) Zimbabwean playwright and actor, founder member of the People's Company, and author of, among other plays in both English and Shona, *My Uncle Grey Bhonzo*, a comedy on the need for cultural roots, and *Chidembo Chanhuwa* (*The Polecat Stank*), a play set in the rural areas after independence.   RK

Siddons, Sarah (1755–1831) English actress, probably the greatest English actress in tragedy. The eldest child of Roger Kemble, a touring theatre manager, she was educated on the road and was soon acting as a child star, an infant phenomenon. Arguments over her love for William Siddons, a young actor, led to her being sent away as a lady's maid but she married him in 1773. In 1775 she was engaged by **Garrick** to play at **Drury Lane** but she failed completely and left the company. She learnt her art in Manchester, touring on **Tate Wilkinson**'s circuit in Yorkshire and in Bath, returning to London to triumph on her debut as Isabella in Garrick's version of **Southerne**'s *The Fatal Marriage* in 1782. Her declamatory delivery was offset by the eloquence of her face so that, as Davies noted, 'her eye is so full of information that the passion is told from her look before she speaks'. She was instantly admired for the unremitting concentration of her performances. In 1784 she was painted by Sir Joshua Reynolds as 'The Tragic Muse'. She toured to Dublin and Edinburgh with equal success and returned to London where her brother **John Philip Kemble** was now acting. In 1785 she played Lady Macbeth for the first time, perhaps her greatest role. By 1790 she had left Drury Lane, acting there only occasionally until she moved to **Covent Garden** in 1801. In June 1812 she retired, playing Lady Macbeth in her last performance, the play stopping after the sleep-walking scene, though she appeared occasionally thereafter at charity performances. She found retirement difficult. Apart from *Macbeth*, she

was famous as Jane Shore in **Rowe**'s play, Belvidera in **Otway**'s *Venice Preserv'd* and other classical English roles. Wilkinson's tribute to her dignity exemplifies her style: 'If you ask me "What is a queen?" I should say Mrs Siddons.'   PH

Sidney, Philip (1554–86) One of the outstanding figures of Elizabethan England, Sidney died too young to witness the golden age of drama, and his doubts about the status of plays as literature are evident in *The Apology for Poetry* (c. 1580), which nonetheless provides important evidence of the cultured scepticism soon to be challenged by the work of **Marlowe** and the **University Wits**.   PT

Sierra Leone Sierra Leone, in West Africa, has been independent since 1961. Its capital, Freetown, had in fact been established in 1792 for blacks in America and the Caribbean who had been free for some time: Christian with European acculturation. They later inter-mixed with much larger numbers of men and women whom British anti-slavery patrols freed from the illegal slave-ships of the 19th century. Together, these black settlers came to be known as the Creoles. They acquired formal education, while developing in commerce a common language of oral exchange, Krio. The drama of Sierra Leone inevitably reflects the urban black settler culture of the Freetown Creoles. There is, first of all, a less secure base in the traditional roots of drama than there is, for example, in Ghana. There is, of course, a traditional culture among the up-country indigenous groups. The Mende, for instance, have a vigorous story-telling performance tradition (extensively researched by Cosentino). However, the character of the independence struggle precluded the emergence of the traditional culture as the means of expressing black aspirations. A Europeanized Creole culture was already in place.

A moralizing critique of post-independence Creole society is presented by the plays of the Freetown medical practitioner, R. Sarif Easmon: the prize-winning *Dear Parent and Ogre*; and *The New Patriots* (1965). The plays explore the private lives of the new black rulers. The love affairs, the corruption, and matters of state are combined in tight plots with obvious moral lessons. A high art reaction against what might be seen as a limiting naturalism is reflected in Gaston Bart-Williams's *The Drug*, an experimental drama first broadcast on West German radio in 1972, which owes something to the influence of **Peter Weiss**'s contemporary experimentation in German theatre. The dramatists and playwrights who spearheaded an alternative, class-based Krio theatre were Dele Charlie and **Yulisa Amadu Maddy**. Charlie founded the Tabule Experimental Theatre in 1968. This group was responsible for the popular new play *Titi Shine Shine* (1970) and the even more successful *The Blood of a Stranger* which was performed more than 20 times between 1975 and 1977 and was entered for FESTAC in 1977.

Maddy was responsible for the founding of Gbakanda Tiata in Freetown in 1969, but, because he then went to Zambia to train the new Zambian National Dance Troupe, it did not really get going until he returned to Freetown in 1974. He and his theatre have a stormy relationship with the Sierra Leonean government. He was head of Radio Drama before going to Zambia; and acting Director of Arts and Culture on his return in 1974. He was later imprisoned for his political plays in Krio. Latterly he has remained abroad, in Nigeria, in the USA, Denmark and Britain. His mantle may have fallen on the playwright, John Kargbo, as seen in his Krio play *Poyohtown Wahalla*. In 1981, Parliament decreed that all plays for performance should be censored. ME

See: D. Cosentino, *Defiant Maids and Stubborn Farmers: Tradition and Invention in Mende Story Performance*, Cambridge, 1982.

Sieveking, Alejandro (1934–) Chilean playwright and director. After initial studies in architecture at the University of Chile, Sieveking studied acting and presented his first play, *Encuentro con las sombras* (*Meeting with Shadows*), at an amateur festival in 1955. An accomplished writer and director, his work tends towards realistic psychological drama, as in *Mi hermano Cristián* (*My Brother Christian*, 1957), presenting the case of a man victimized by his invalid sibling. *Parecido a la felicidad* (*Akin to Happiness*, 1959) was a successful tour show about intimate personal relations, a pleasant touch before the violence of *La madre de los conejos* (*Mother Rabbit*, 1961), a family study in sibling rape with two suicides. During the 1960s Sieveking continued to explore folkloric and poetic tendencies in *Animas de día claro* (*Fair Weather Souls*, 1962), a successful musical *La remolienda* (*The Carousing*, 1965), and *La mantis religiosa* (*The Praying Mantis*, 1971). Like his contemporaries, he has also dealt with socio-political issues as in *Tres tristes tigres* (*Three Sad Tigers*, 1967). A versatile and prolific writer and director, Sieveking normally works within a realistic framework. From 1974–84 he and his wife, Bélgica Castro, the lead actress for whom he often writes, maintained the Teatro del Angel in San José, Costa Rica, during the post-Allende period of Chile. GW

Sigurjónsson, Jóhann (1880–1919) Icelandic playwright, internationally acclaimed just before the First World War. His first success came with the 1908 production in Reykjavík of *The Hraun Farm*, which marks the beginning of an era of Icelandic playwriting. Subsequent plays, originally staged by the Royal Theatre, Copenhagen, were written simultaneously in Icelandic and Danish, as Sigurjónsson wanted to reach a bigger audience than he could find in Iceland. His masterpiece, the neo-romantic tragedy *Eyvind of the Mountains* (1911), was produced in 12 countries both sides of the Atlantic, ranking him with major playwrights of the period. The play was filmed by Victor Sjöström as *The Outlaw and His Wife* (1917). The heroic-poetic *The Wish* (1914), based on an Icelandic Faustian legend, could have been as successful as *Eyvind of the Mountains*, but the war prevented its getting outside Scandinavia. Sigurjónsson's last play, *The Liar* (1917) based on *Njal's Saga*, was commissioned by the Royal Theatre, but failed to regenerate interest outside Denmark. Sigurjónsson is today considered the classic Icelandic playwright. AI

Silva, António José da (1705–39) Portuguese playwright, probably the most noteworthy between **Vicente** and **Ferreira** and the 19th-century figure of **Garrett**, who was burned by the Inquisition for his

being allegedly a practising Jew, an iniquitous event dramatized in **Santareno**'s *O Judeu* of 1966. His seven plays made great use of stage machinery and effects and incorporated quasi-operatic arias. The first, *Vida do Grande D. Quixote e do Gordo Sancho Pança*, had the knight, his squire and the supporting cast played by puppets. The best, *As Guerras do Alecrim e da Manjerona* (*The Wars of Rosemary and Marjoram*), contrasts the preciousness of the higher classes with the racy earthiness of the common people and is finely observed. LK

Simeon Polotsky (Samuil Emelyanovich Petrovskii-Sitniyanovich) (1629–80) Russia's first court poet-playwright and founder of its didactic, civic-minded school drama. A native of White Russia, he graduated from the Kiev Academy in 1650, entered a monastery and having settled in Moscow became tutor to Tsar Aleksei Mikhailovich's children. He revised **Johann Gregory**'s dramatic repertoire and in the 1670s wrote two plays of his own, ostensibly on biblical themes after the Jesuit school drama, *The Comedy-Parable of the Prodigal Son* (published 1685) and *Of Nebuchadnezzar, the Golden Calf, and the Three Youths Who Were Not Burned in the Furnace*, a new version of the fiery furnace show which was said to have entered Moscow from the West via Novgorod. The first play employed ecclesiastical trappings to criticize the contemporary practice of young nobles travelling abroad to secure an education and giving themselves over to drinking, carousing and sometimes expatriation. In the second play a wise and just king, meant to resemble Aleskei Mikhailovich, opposes a tyrant, who is the cause of national suffering. Simeon Polotsky was not above enlivening his plays with music, dancing and scenic effects. SG

Simon, John (1925–) American drama and film critic. Born in Yugoslavia and educated at Harvard (PhD, 1959), Simon has been regarded as a brilliant stylist who demands that the theatre be intelligent and articulate. He has written about the drama for *Hudson Review* since 1960; about films and drama for *New York Magazine* since 1969; and about films for the *New Leader* since 1962. He is author of at least eight books, including *Singularities: Essays on the Theater, 1964–73* (1976). Simon believes that the critic is responsible first to himself then to his audience; and that a piece of criticism should be both pleasurable to read and philosophical in nature. A penchant for invective and harsh personal comments, however, has put him at odds with the theatre community and his colleagues. TLM

Simon, (Marvin) Neil (1927–) American playwright. Critical acclaim has come slowly for Simon who has more smash hits than any other American playwright. Even with almost a hit a year since 1961, he fights a reputation of being a gag writer who caters to the moral hangups and material greed of middle-class America. Born in New York, Simon learned his craft by writing comic material for radio and television personalities. With his brother Danny, he wrote sketches for Broadway shows, *Catch a Star* (1955), and *New Faces of 1956*. His first full-length comedy, *Come Blow Your Horn* (1961), was a hit followed closely by the musical farce, *Little Me* (1962), with Cy Coleman and Carolyn Leigh. After *Barefoot in the Park* (1963), he penned one of the funniest and wisest plays in 1965, *The Odd Couple*; and a year later added the musical *Sweet Charity*, and *The Star-Spangled Girl*. With four shows running simultaneously on Broadway, Simon was the most successful playwright of the 1960s. He added *Plaza Suite* to his list of smash hits in 1968 together with the musical, *Promises, Promises* (with Burt Bacharach and Hal David). After *Last of the Red Hot Lovers* (1969), Simon wrote *The Gingerbread Lady* (1970) which attempted to deal honestly with alcoholism. While audiences rejected it, the playwright seemed more willing to attempt serious themes, and two bittersweet comedies followed: *The Prisoner of Second Avenue* and *The Sunshine Boys* (both 1972). Following the death of his wife in 1973, he reached a low point in his career with two failures: *The Good Doctor* (1973), adapted from short stories by **Anton Chekhov**; and *God's Favorite* adapted from the Bible (1976). But a move to California resulted in another hit, *California Suite* (1976), a Beverly Hills version of *Plaza Suite*. His marriage to the actress Marsha Mason resulted in *Chapter Two* (1977), regarded by some critics as his finest play to date. His fourth musical, *They're Playing Our Song*, proved popular in 1979 but his next three efforts were not successful: *I Ought To Be in Pictures* (1980); *Fools* (1981); and a revised version of *Little Me* (1982). Simon then returned to his own past for a charming *Brighton Beach Memoirs* (1983) and the Tony Award-winning *Biloxi Blues* (1984). And by recasting the two major roles in *The Odd Couple* for women, Simon found himself with three hits in 1985, and new respect from the critics.   TLM

Simonov, Konstantin (Kirill) Mikhailovich

(1915–79) Soviet prose writer, poet and dramatist who survived Stalinism, achieved international repute and a long list of government posts and prizes ('Hero of Socialist Labour', six Stalin Prizes, one Lenin Prize) by composing patriotic war stories and anti-capitalist partisan tales, strong on romance, heroism, sentiment, and strict adherence to the Party line. His prolific literary career began in 1934, and in 1938 he graduated from Moscow's Gorky Literary Institute. A second career in journalism, begun in 1939, included stints as: a war correspondent for *Red Star*; editor-in-chief of *New World* (1946–50, 1954–8), where he replaced the condemned Aleksandr Tvardovsky and proposed a more flexible reading of socialist realist doctrine; and editor of *The Literary Gazette* (1938, 1950–3). His romantic poetry and novels – *Comrade in Arms* (1952) and the trilogy consisting of *Days and Nights* (1943–4), *The Living and the Dead* (1959–71) and *Soldiers Are Not Born* (1963–4) – all relate to the war and were of great importance to the Russian people during the 1940s and 1950s. The same can be said of his 10 plays which include: *A Fellow from Our Town* (1940–1), a Stalin Prize-winner about a tank driver; *Wait for Me* (1942), a dramatization of one of his romantic poems about a Russian pilot shot down behind enemy lines trying to return to his beloved wife; his best-known war play, *The Russian People* (1942), whose message of solidarity among Russians and the heroic potential of ordinary people appealed to **Clifford Odets**, who prepared an American acting edition for New York's **Theatre**

Guild; *Under the Chestnut Trees of Prague* (1945), a post-war play demonstrating the necessity of Soviet guidance in the democratization of its satellite countries; and *The Russian Question* (1947), an anti-capitalist piece set in New York City which argues that the inherent goodness and Soviet sympathies of the American people are being undermined by corrupt Wall Street speculators. Simonov served as secretary of the Union of Soviet Writers and as a Deputy of the Supreme Soviet.   SG

Simonson, Lee

(1888–1967) American set designer; a founding member and director of the **Theatre Guild**. Simonson studied for three years in Paris and, like **Robert Edmond Jones**, returned to the USA with great excitement about the New Stagecraft. He advocated simplified realism – while creating sets that were based in realism, he stripped away all scenic elements that were unnecessary for mood or information. As resident designer for the Theatre Guild he designed over half their productions including *Heartbreak House*, *Liliom*, and *Green Grow the Lilacs*. His designs for *The Adding Machine* were among the most successful examples of expressionism on the American stage.   AA

Simpson, N[orman] F[rederick]

(1919–) British dramatist. His most successful plays were written in the late 1950s (*The Resounding Tinkle*, 1957, *The Hole*, 1958, and *One Way Pendulum*, 1959) and were staged at the **Royal Court Theatre**. These plays were seen as peculiarly British versions of the absurd, distinguished by anarchic comedy. Later work (*The Cresta Run*, 1965, *Playback 625* – in collaboration with Leopoldo Maler – 1970, and *Was He Anyone*, 1972) failed to make the impact of the earlier plays, but Simpson continued a writing career in television and film.   MB

Sinán, Rogelio

(1904–) (Pseudonym of Bernardo Domínguez Alba.) Panamanian poet, playwright, and fiction writer. Revolutionized Panamanian poetry with his vanguardist collection, *Onda* (*Wave*, 1929). Author of such children's plays as *La cucarachita mandinga* (*The Impish Little Cockroach*) and *El desquite de Caperucita Roja* (*The Revenge of Little Red Riding Hood*). *Lobo Go Home* (*Wolf Go Home*, 1978) deals with the political, economic, cultural and military intervention of the USA in Panama through a retelling of the Little Red Riding Hood story.   GW

Sinden, Donald (Alfred)

(1923–) British actor. His distinctive vocal qualities and broad style have emphasized Sinden's reputation as a fine comedy actor, though this has sometimes meant that he has worked in plays of slight merit. But as a classical actor he has produced exciting and often adventurous performances, as, for instance, in his role as Richard Plantagenet in **John Barton**'s *The Wars of the Roses* (**RSC**, 1963). He has played Lear and Othello for the RSC (1977 and 1979 respectively) as well as creating witty character studies in such roles as Lord Foppington (**Vanbrugh**'s *The Relapse*, RSC, 1967) and Sir Peter Teazle (**Sheridan**'s *The School for Scandal*, 1983). His skills in demanding naturalistic roles have been shown in appearances as Vanya in **Chekhov**'s *Uncle Vanya* (1982) and Doctor Stockmann in **Ibsen**'s *An Enemy of* *the People* (1975). A keen theatre historian, Sinden has been a strong advocate and worker for the establishment of the British Theatre Museum (which opened in London's Covent Garden in 1987). MB

Singapore see **Asia, South-East (Modern)**

Singspiel A popular form of musical drama that arose in Germany during the mid-18th century as a result, it has been argued, of the popularity of **Gay**'s *Beggar's Opera* (1728). Most *Singspiele* have a popular setting and comprise light, tuneful songs connected by dialogue that is spoken, not sung. Several dramatists wrote *Singspiele*, most notable among whom is **J. W. Goethe**, but the most consummate achievements in the genre are Mozart's *The Abduction from the Seraglio* (1782) and *The Magic Flute* (1791). The operetta of the 19th century evolved in part from the *Singspiel*. SW

Sissle, Noble (1889–1975) and **Eubie Blake** (1883–1983) American lyricist and composer. Pianist and composer Eubie Blake met singer lyricist Noble Sissle in 1915. For several years they performed in vaudeville in an act featuring their own songs. In 1921 they joined with the vaudeville comedy team of Flournoy Miller and Aubrey Lyles to create the first black musical to play a major Broadway theatre during the regular theatrical season, *Shuffle Along*. With a book by Miller and Lyles, who also starred in it, *Shuffle Along* was a big hit both in New York and on tour. Critics and audiences delighted in the vitality of the score and the lively dancing of the chorus.

Sissle and Blake went on to write the scores for several other musicals, including *The Chocolate Dandies* (1924), and *Shuffle Along of 1932*, but without the success that had been achieved with *Shuffle Along*. On his own, Blake wrote the music for several other shows. A revival of *Shuffle Along* in 1952 was a failure, but with the rediscovery of ragtime in the 1960s and 1970s Sissle and Blake songs were again heard on Broadway in *Doctor Jazz* (1975), *Bubbling Brown Sugar* (1976), and *Eubie* (1978). MK

Sjöberg, Alf (1903–80) Swedish director, whose 50-year career at **Dramaten** was a decisive force in modern theatre. He combined a belief in the moral and intellectual function of theatre in a confused, unjust world with an impressive mastery of modern stage technology. He is best known for his productions of **Shakespeare**, **Strindberg** and modern European dramatists such as **Claudel**, **Ionesco**, **Brecht**, **Gombrowicz** and **Witkiewicz**. Typically he balanced analysis of a play's historical context with a focus on its relevance to modern ideas. An accomplished designer, he made light and space particularly vital elements in his fluid staging. Some of his most inventive work, such as his adaptations of C. J. L. Almqvist's novels *Amorina* and *The Queen's Jewel*, was done within the limited resources of Dramaten's Little Stage. HL

Skelton, John (c. 1460–1529) English poet and playwright, about whom exact facts are difficult to establish but who wrote comedies and morality plays including the only extant one *Magnyfycence*. This was printed (by **John Rastell**) in 1530 and would have been performed probably some time before then. The play

deals – as a good morality should – in the conflict between good and bad counsel, with the good triumphing. MB

Skinner, Cornelia Otis (1901–79) American actress, monologuist, humorist and author, daughter of actor **Otis Skinner**, with whom she made her professional debut in 1921 in *Blood and Sand*. She established her reputation as a fine actress beginning in the 1920s touring the United States and Britain in monodramas she wrote and staged herself. These included *The Wives of Henry VIII* (1931), *The Empress Eugenie* (1932), *The Loves of Charles II* (1933), and *Paris '90* (1952). In more traditional theatre she appeared in *Candida* (1939), *Theatre* (1941), *Lady Windermere's Fan* (1946), and *The Pleasure of His Company* (1958), the latter co-authored with Samuel Taylor. She also wrote memoirs, light verse, essays, and two critically acclaimed theatrical biographies, *Madame Sarah*, a life of **Sarah Bernhardt** (1967), and *Life with Lindsay and Crouse* (1976). She is probably most remembered for the 1942 travelogue she co-wrote with Emily Kimbrough titled *Our Hearts Were Young and Gay*. DBW

Skinner, Otis (1858–1942) American actor. One of America's most versatile actors, by his own account Skinner played over 140 roles between 1877 and 1879 with the resident companies of the Philadelphia Museum and the **Walnut Street Theatre**. Between 1879 and 1892, Skinner played in the companies of **Edwin Booth**, **Lawrence Barrett**, **Augustin Daly**, **Helena Modjeska** (**Modrzejewska**), and **Joseph Jefferson III**, and occasionally starred as romantic hero, classical tragedian, comedian, and character actor. From 1892, Skinner was a confirmed and popular star who continued to play a varied repertory. In his own time and for later generations, he was best remembered for the role of Hajj, the beggar, in *Kismet* which he created in 1911, played exclusively for three years, and preserved in two film versions. Skinner, and his actress daughter, **Cornelia Otis Skinner**, were both prolific authors. MR

Skomorokhi Itinerant players of old Russia. The Byzantine chronicler Theophanes mentioned Slavs playing guzlas as early as 583, but the first clear reference was a condemnation of them by the Primary Chronicle in 1068. Musicians, boxers and dancers with long hair and tunics had been portrayed in the frescos of the Sophia Cathedral in Kiev in 1037; however, the church opposed them as anti-ascetic vestiges of paganism and propagandists for immorality. Their antics at Easter with made-up faces and old clothes, and their disguises as women or animals on New Year's Eve proclaimed the *skomorokhi*'s heathen origins. By the late 16th and early 17th centuries, they had become hugely popular, some troupes consisting of over 100 men. They dressed in ordinary peasant clothing, ornamented with ribbons, and excelled as puppeteers, bear-leaders, dog and rat trainers, and story-tellers. The most famous, Foma and Erema, entered folklore. Following an uprising in Moscow, Tsar Aleksey Mikhailovich, first of the Romanovs, banned them 'and all manner of devilish sports' (1648); this ban was strictly enforced and they were exiled to the northern hinterlands, where the traditions were long upheld. Some became private jesters, some entertainers at weddings and parties. They exercised an immeasurable influence on the Russian puppet theatre and the fairground booth, and, through them, Russian circus and variety.   LS

> See: R. Zaguta, *Russian Minstrels: A History of the Skomorokhi*, Pittsburg, 1978.

Słowacki, Juliusz (1809–49) Polish romantic poet and playwright who from 1831 lived in political exile in Switzerland, Italy and France. He wrote over 20 verse dramas dealing with European and Polish history and legend, folklore and fairy tale, which blend the mystical and cruel, the cosmic and grotesque, in loose, fragmentary scenes. Major works are *Maria Stuart* (1832), *Kordian* (1834), *Beatrix Cenci* (1839), *Balladyna* (1839), *Mazeppa* (1840), *Fantazy* (1841).   DG

Sly, William (d. 1608) English actor, first heard of in 1590, when he was with **Strange's Men** in **Tarlton's** *The Seven Deadly Sins*. After a spell with the **Admiral's Men**, he joined the **Lord Chamberlain's Men**, perhaps from the company's foundation in 1594, becoming a sharer after the death of **Augustine Phillips**. A surviving portrait in the Dulwich library shows a dark, strong face, turned slightly sinister by the curl of the lips. It is not known what parts Sly played, though he may have served an apprenticeship with Phillips and inherited his role as actor-athlete in the company.   PT

Smith, Albert Richard (1816–60) English writer and entertainer, Smith was already a popular humorist and journalist, with some theatrical success accruing to his extravaganzas and dramatizations of **Dickens**, when in 1850 he presented his panorama-lecture *The Overland Mail*, studded with songs, anecdotes and impersonations at Willis's Rooms, London. Aided by his brother Arthur (1825–61), the bluff, bearded Smith took over the Egyptian Hall for the entertainment, *The Ascent of Mont Blanc* (1852), complete even to the sound effects of popping champagne corks. It was one of the greatest hits of the Victorian amusement scene and ran for 2,000 performances, shocking the German actor **Ludwig Barnay** that a gentleman should so exhibit himself. It was followed by *Mont Blanc to China* (1858–9). In 1859 Smith married a daughter of the comedian Robert Keeley.   LS

Smith, Harry B. (1860–1936) American librettist and lyricist. Smith's first connection with the theatre was as a dramatic and musical editor for a Chicago newspaper. For composer **Reginald De Koven** he created the libretto and most of the lyrics for the most beloved American comic opera of the late 19th century, *Robin Hood* (1891). Although much of his writing was mediocre by modern standards, Smith's ability to adapt to changing styles and tastes in musical theatre ensured him a long and prolific career in the course of which he was reported to have written some 300 librettos and 6,000 lyrics. His autobiography appeared in 1931.   MK

Smith, Maggie (Mrs Margaret Natalie Cross) (1934–) British actress, who appeared briefly in the New York revue, *New Faces*, before starring with Kenneth Williams in the Bamber Gascoigne revue, *Share My Lettuce* (1956). Her attractive wit and lively personality gave her a considerable West End success; but she wisely chose not to stay with intimate revue but to gain experience as an actress elsewhere. She joined the **Old Vic** company for the 1959–60 season, playing in *As You Like It* and *Richard II*; and then appeared in **Anouilh**'s *The Rehearsal* (1961) and **Peter Shaffer**'s *The Private Ear* and *The Public Eye* (1962), two parts in a double bill which brought her the *Evening Standard*'s 'Best Actress' Drama Award for 1962. She was invited to join **Olivier**'s **National Theatre** company for the opening seasons, playing in *The Recruiting Officer*, *Miss Julie*, *Hay Fever* and memorably as Desdemona to Olivier's Othello. She began her film career in 1963 mainly playing light comedy parts, but with *The Prime of Miss Jean Brodie* (1968), which won her an Oscar, she became a major film star. Her sensitive face, husky voice and ironic delivery helped her to excel in comedies of manners from all periods, in **Noël Coward**'s plays (*Design for Living* 1971, *Private Lives* 1972) or in **Congreve**'s *The Way of the World* as Millamant (1984), which brought her her sixth major acting award. Her skills as a tragic actress, however, have been questioned, although her Hedda Gabler (1970) was much admired. In 1976, after her first marriage to the actor **Robert Stephens** was dissolved, she joined the Stratford, Ontario, company in Canada, where she stayed for several seasons, giving the premiere performance there of *Virginia*, a study of the life of Virginia Woolf, which was later seen in London (1981). In 1970, she was awarded the CBE and in 1982, became a director of United British Artists. In 1975, she married the playwright, Beverley Cross.   JE

Smith, Oliver (1918–) American set-designer and theatrical producer. Smith has designed some 400 theatre, dance, opera, and film productions since 1941. He also served as co-director of American Ballet Theatre from 1945 to 1981. He began his career designing for dance, notably *Rodeo* and *Fall River Legend* for **Agnes de Mille**, and *Fancy Free* for **Jerome Robbins**. Starting with the 1944 production of *On the Town* (which he also co-produced), Smith designed a steady stream of long-running musicals including *My Fair Lady*, *West Side Story*, and *Hello Dolly!*. Smith believes that scenery for musicals should be bright, entertaining, and change quickly and unobtrusively. He has talked about scenery in terms of choreography. In *Fall River Legend*, the scenery is, in fact, an integral part of the choreography. In terms of style he frequently mixes painterly backgrounds with sculptural scenic elements. He also has an almost formulaic approach to the arrangement of scenic elements and space which meshed well with the musicals of the 1940s and 50s and contributed to his prodigious output.   AA

Smith, Richard Penn (1799–1854) One of many American intellectuals who wrote fiction and poetry and edited journals, created some 20 plays, five of them staged in 1829. Of these, *The Eighth of January* celebrated Andrew Jackson's victory, while *William Penn* reveals Smith's talent for comedy. *Caius Marius* (1831), a scholarly tragedy based on the Roman Marius's love of his country, was selected as a Prize Play by **Edwin Forrest**. Although Smith enjoyed some success, his interest in the theatre was momentary.   WJM

Smith, Solomon Franklin (1801–69) American theatre manager and actor, especially noted for his pioneering work on the frontier. He began his theatrical career in Vincennes, Indiana, in 1819 and by 1823 had organized his own company, which he managed for four years. He then toured the Mississippi valley with **J. H. Caldwell**, and in 1835 entered into a partnership with **Noah Ludlow**. They dominated the frontier theatre of their time, but ended the partnership in 1853.

As an actor, Smith, affectionately known as 'Old Sol', was particularly effective as a low comedian in such roles as Mawworm in *The Hypocrite*. He eventually went into law and became a Missouri state senator. His three autobiographical volumes, *Theatrical Apprenticeship* (1845), *The Theatrical Journey-work and Anecdotal Recollections of Sol. Smith* (1854), and *Theatrical Management in the West and South for Thirty Years* (1868), are flawed but valuable insights into theatrical conditions of the time.   SMA

Smith, William Henry Sedley (1806–72) American playwright, actor, and stage-manager. Smith's *The Drunkard, or The Fallen Saved* (Boston, 1844; New York, 1850) was the first successful temperance drama and the most enduring. The play depicted the path of Edward Middleton (first played by Smith) from his first glass to the torment of delirium tremens and finally to his reformation. After the initial 100-performance runs in Boston and New York, the play blanketed the country, and as late as 1953 concluded a 20-year stand in Los Angeles.

Born in Wales, Smith began acting with the Theatre Royal, Lancaster (1822), joined Philadelphia's **Walnut Street** company (1827), the **Tremont Theatre** in Boston (1828), and the **Boston Museum** (1843) where he remained as stage-manager and actor.   RM

Smithson, Harriet Constance (1800–54) English actress, born in Ireland, where her father managed theatres. She made her debut at **Drury Lane** in 1818, but her impact on London audiences was slight. In Paris, by contrast, where she played Juliet, Ophelia and **Nicholas Rowe**'s Jane Shore in the company of **Charles Kemble** in 1827, she was a sensation. The frantic adulation of youthful Frenchmen, including Sainte-Beuve, Gautier, **Dumas** *père* and **Hugo**, contributed to the rise of the French romantic theatre. Extravagantly courted by Berlioz, Smithson eventually married him in 1833. She retired from the stage in 1836 and spent the rest of her life in increasingly brandy-soaked isolation and misery as the neglected Madame Berlioz.   PT

Sokari *Sokari* is regarded as one of the oldest, if not the oldest, forms of theatre in Sri Lanka. It is performed after the Sinhalese New Year in the months of Vesak and Poson which end around September as a votive offering to the goddess Pattini, chief among the deities who are worshipped through ritual as a means of blessing human undertakings and granting immunity from disaster. Performances are confined to the remote hilly regions of the state and the performers, who are all male peasants, undergo training by elder performers in preparation for their devotional duties. Any open spot in the village, usually the threshing ground, is used for an all-night show. Dancing and music punctuate the lively events and full face-masks are used by some, if not all, of the performers.

Like so many ritual performances, there is only one story which is enacted, the story of *Sokari*. The story differs in various details from group to group and place to place, with some performers even integrating popular music to enliven the original story line.

In essence, the episodic events centre around the following story: Guru Hami, a north Indian, and Sokari, his wife, along with Paraya, their comic servant, are disenfranchised, build a boat and sail to Sri Lanka where they experience various comic adventures. Sokari, who is young and seductive, elopes with, or is seduced by, a local doctor who has been summoned to treat Guru Hami for a dog bite. Eventually, Sokari returns and delivers a child. The ending, along with the recurrent sexual symbolism and obscenities that appear throughout the performance, suggest that *Sokari* may be a dramatic elaboration of an archaic fertility ritual.

Among its unique features, *Sokari* makes elaborate use of mime in which the players depict the various activities which are described in song.   FaR

Solari Swayne, Enrique (1915–) Peruvian playwright, studied in Germany, professor of psychology at the University of San Marcos in Lima. Known primarily for *Collacocha* (1955), a play that epitomized the tragic struggle of an engineer, Echecopar, to conquer the forces of nature. *La mazorca* (*The Corn*, 1964) echoed similar telluric concerns in a Peruvian jungle plantation setting. *Ayax Telemonio* (1969) used a classical motif to criticize current national sociopolitical issues.   GW

Soleil, Théâtre du French Theatre company founded in 1964 by **Ariane Mnouchkine** and a group of friends who had worked together in university theatre. They adopted a cooperative structure, sharing all the jobs of running the theatre and taking decisions collectively. After starting with a repertoire typical of the decentralized theatres, including *The Kitchen* (1967), the first **Wesker** to be performed in France, they became committed to the system of *la création collective* or collaborative devising of productions after taking part in the political upheavals of 1968. Their most famous production *1789* (1970) was devised by a combination of historical research and improvisation. It told the story of the French Revolution from the point of view of the people, employing a wide mixture of theatre styles. Its scenic inventiveness (it was performed in a large open space on stages placed around the audience, who were free to move about) contributed to the atmosphere of festivity and celebration which made the production so successful with audiences eager to pursue ideas thrown up in 1968. The company set up home in a disused *cartoucherie* (cartridge-warehouse) at Vincennes and the very remoteness of the location contributed to the excitement of audiences. *1789* was followed by two further collective creations *1793* (1972) and *L'Âge d'Or* (*The Golden Age*, 1975). Both productions were attempts to press further the political lessons of *1789* while continuing to search for an appropriate performance style. *L'Age d'Or* owed much to **Meyerhold** and the tradition of the **commedia dell'arte**. In 1976 the company disbanded and a splinter group was formed under Jean-Claude Penchenat: the **Campagnol**. A film *Molière ou la Vie d'un Honnête Homme* employed the energies of Mnouchkine and some company members until they regrouped for *Mephisto* in 1979, a dramatization of Klaus Mann's novel. This was followed in the early 1980s by a cycle of **Shakespeare** plays, *Richard II*, *Henry IV, Pt 1* and *Twelfth Night*, performed in a style giving maximum opportunity to physical expressiveness while also suggesting the remote, hieratic quality of Shakespeare's nobles by borrowings from Oriental theatre styles, costumes etc. The purpose of the Shakespeare cycle was to permit the company to develop a contemporary play about South-East Asia, *Norodom Sihanouk*, which opened in 1985.   DB

Sologub, Fyodor (pseudonym of Fyodor Kuzmich Teternikov) (1863–1927) Russian decadent poet, novelist, short story writer and dramatist preoccupied with the following concomitant themes: Platonic Idealism and perverse sensualism; the possibility and impossibility of communion between the real and ideal worlds; beauty and banality; love–death as preferable to life–suffering; art as transcendent medium; and the artist as insensitive, unsuccessful discoverer of life's hidden beauty ('the uncrowned Dulcinea'). A repressed, obsessive pessimist bordering on nihilism, Sologub envisioned an inverted cosmos in which God rules an evil world of matter and desire, while Satan governs a calm realm of beauty and death. Although man's inner world is good, its commerce with the outer world via naive projection precipitates the romantic irony of life. Sologub's art, in the manner of the symbolists, remythologizes ancient legends, transforming them into highly private scenarios which in his case revolve around sex, sadism and the humiliation of the very beauty he seeks. His idea of theatre, as expressed in the essay 'The Theatre of One Will' (1908), is similarly contradictory and self-referential as well as vaguely suggestive of **Evreinov**'s theory of monodrama. Via the self-conscious, subjective expression of the author's 'I', theatre may achieve the focused spirituality of the Russian icon and affect a congregant mystery between stage and audience. Although he advocated a bare stage and presentation of the text by the author or a single reader, Sologub's 18 plays offer theatrical levels and devices, interesting shifts in perspective, focus and pacing, which attracted theatricalist directors. **Meyerhold** achieved a rare success for symbolist drama with his Craigian-set staging of *The Triumph of Death* (1907), his last production at Vera Komissarzhevskaya's Theatre. An ironic, quasi-Maeterlinckian treatment of a medieval tragedy involving cruel romantic deception, suffering and death, Sologub wrote a special prologue for Meyerhold as the Poet to deliver, which was meant to parody the symbolist mystery's pretentiousness. Meyerhold's symbolic-realist staging of *The Hostages of Life* (1912) – a mystical variation of **Ibsen**'s *The Master Builder* – marked the first production of a symbolist play at a traditional theatre, the Aleksandrinsky. Evreinov presented *Nocturnal Dances* (1908), with choreography by

Mikhail Fokine, at his Merry Theatre for Grown-up Children (1909). A fairytale-based, tragicomic rendering of Sologub's 'Poet as blind defiler of beauty' theme, the play's central image of princesses ecstatically dancing suggests the author's attraction to Isadora Duncan's 'frolic dance' as metaphor for the non-cognitive, transformative potential of art. Sologub and Evreinov were both less successful with *Vanka the Lackey and Jean the Page*, at Vera Komissarzhevskaya's Theatre (1909), a rapidly shifting, self-highly stylized presentation of parallel tales of seduction in medieval Russia and France. Of his other dramatic 'remythologizations', Sologub's *Gift of the Wise Bees* (1907) treats the Laodamia legend also assayed by **Annensky** and **Briusov**. Sologub's most popular play was a dramatization of his novel *The Petty Demon* (1907) for Nezlobin's Theatre (1910).   SG

Solórzano, Carlos (1922–) Guatemalan-born playwright, critic, professor, Mexican resident since 1939, where he studied architecture and literature, received a doctorate at the National University of Mexico with a thesis on Miguel de Unamuno. With a Rockefeller grant he spent 1948–50 in Europe, where he met **Albert Camus**, **Michel de Ghelderode** and existentialism. In Mexico he was named artistic director of the Professional University Theatre and later professor at the National University. His major plays are *Doña Beatriz* (1952), *El hechicero* (*The Sorcerer*, 1954) and his masterpiece, *Las manos de Dios* (*The Hands of God*, 1956), plus several one-act plays. He actively fomented theatre and theatre criticism with several books on Latin American theatre and a weekly column in a major Mexican journal. During the regime of López Portillo (1976–82) he served as executive director of an ambitious project under Social Security to organize the Teatro de la Nación (Theatre of the Nation).   GW

Somigliana, Carlos (1932–) Argentine playwright, also lawyer and journalist. A figure in the realistic generation of Argentine theatre of the 1960s, his major plays include *Amarillo* (*Yellow*, 1965), *El avión negro* (*The Black Airplane*, 1970), written in collaboration with **Cossa**, **Rozenmacher** and **Talesnik**, and short plays for **Teatro Abierto** in 1981 and following years.   GW

Sommi (or Somi, Leone Di, or Sommo) de' Portaleone, Yehuda Leone de' (1527–92) Jewish Italian author of the first Hebrew play (see **Hebrew theatre**), *A Comedy of Betrothal* (c.1550, Eng. tr. 1988), a typical Renaissance comedy with a racy Hebrew flavour. The main plot, based on the Midrash, tells the story of a young man Shalom, whose father died far away bequeathing all his possessions save one to his slave. Shalom may claim any one of them as his. On the advice of the wise Rabbi, the young man chooses the slave, thus obtaining the full inheritance. This tale is intertwined with a conventional romantic plot. The play was rediscovered by modern scholarship and produced first by a university group and in 1968 by the Haifa Municipal Theatre.

De' Sommi was a prolific writer of poetry and plays in both Italian and Hebrew, but most of his work was destroyed by a fire in 1904. Apparently he produced plays for the Duke of Gonzaga at Mantua. He wrote an important theoretical treatise, *Four Dialogues on Scenic Representation* (English translation by Allardyce Nicoll, 1937). HAS

Sondheim, Stephen (1930–) American lyricist and composer. After an apprenticeship with **Oscar Hammerstein II** and some early writing for television, Sondheim created the lyrics for *West Side Story* (1957) and *Gypsy* (1959). In 1962 he received his first opportunity to write both music and lyrics for *A Funny Thing Happened on the Way to the Forum*. After a failure with *Anyone Can Whistle* (1970), Sondheim startled the musical theatre world with the scores for a series of highly experimental shows. *Company* (1964) was a collage of musical vignettes about married life in contemporary New York. *Follies* (1971) used a reunion of musical comedy performers to examine the effects of middle age on love and marriage. *A Little Night Music* (1973) had a score written entirely in three-four time. *Pacific Overtures* (1976) employed the conventions of Japanese **kabuki** theatre and an all-Oriental cast to tell of the opening of Japan to the West. *Sweeney Todd* (1979) adapted Victorian melodrama to modern sensibilities by suggesting the tormented soul behind the 'demon barber of Fleet Street'. *Merrily We Roll Along* (1981) examined the myth of the American success story by tracing the lives of its central characters backwards from middle age to youth. *Sunday in the Park With George* (1984) explored the process of artistic creation by bringing to life the work of French painter Georges Seurat. With his brilliant, often cerebral lyrics and driving, unsentimental music, he is generally considered the most distinguished composer-lyricist in musical theatre today. His most recent works include *Into the Woods* (1987) and *Assassins* (1991). MK

Sonnenfels, Josef von (1733–1817) Austrian critic. Strongly influenced by **Gottsched**, Sonnenfels's *Letters on the Viennese Stage* (1768) attacked the local, improvised comedy and advocated a more decorous, scripted theatre. Although he did not succeed in dislodging the popular theatre, Sonnenfels had considerable influence on the founding of the **Burgtheater** and on the development of its ideals of ensemble. SW

Sophocles (c. 496–406/5 BC) Sophocles the tragedian came from Colonus, near Athens. As a boy he is said to have led the singing of a paean to celebrate the Greek victory at Salamis (480). He produced his first set of plays in 468, and won first prize (see **Greece, ancient**) although he was competing against **Aeschylus**. He is said to have given up acting in his own plays because of a weak voice, but had a remarkably long and successful career as a dramatist. He is said to have produced 132 plays (we know the titles of over 110) and never to have been placed third in the competitions. He probably won 18 victories at the Great Dionysia (making 72 victorious plays) and others at the Lenaea. It is doubtful whether any of his plays belonged to connected tetralogies; certainly most did not. He is said to have been responsible for introducing the third actor (though this is also attributed to Aeschylus) and for increasing the size of the tragic chorus from 12 to 15. He took an active part in public life, and his offices included

a generalship (an elective one-year post) in 440/1 as a colleague of the statesman Pericles. In later times he had a reputation for piety, illustrated by various anecdotes.

The chronology of the seven surviving plays is uncertain. There is evidence dating *Antigone* to c. 442, and some reason for thinking that *Ajax* and *Trachiniae* (*Women of Trachis*, concerning the death of Heracles) are earlier than this. *Oedipus Tyrannus* (*King Oedipus*) perhaps dates from the 420s. *Philoctetes* is securely dated to 409, and *Electra* may not be much earlier. *Oedipus at Colonus* was not produced until 401, after Sophocles' death. Thus even the earliest surviving plays may not have been written until Sophocles was in his 50s, and he seems to have written the latest – still assured masterpieces like the rest – when well into his 80s. We also possess about half of a satyr play, *Ichneutae* (*Trackers*, concerning the childhood of Hermes), and various shorter fragments.

Any reader of the seven plays senses common themes and purposes running through them. One constant factor is a concern with plot, regarded as a complete and coherent sequence of events, linked together by principles of cause and effect and of plausible human motivation. While critics have found problems in the construction of some of the plays – notably *Ajax*, *Trachiniae* and *Antigone*, in all of which a central character dies some time before the end – the importance of plot as a shaping and unifying principle is certainly greater than in Aeschylus or **Euripides** (hence the admiration which Sophocles inspired in **Aristotle**, who regarded *Oedipus Tyrannus* as the ideal tragedy). With this goes the importance of prophecy: by the end of a play it generally turns out that the prophecy of an oracle or seer has been fulfilled, in a way that at least some of the characters did not expect or intend. This concern is paralleled in the work of the historian Herodotus, whom Sophocles probably knew, and no doubt reflects the dramatist's actual beliefs; but it also helps to shape the plays by making the denouement seem inevitable, and to make possible the pervasive dramatic irony.

Each of the plays is concerned with death (at least the possibility of it, though in *Philoctetes* no one actually dies); with human suffering (sometimes acute physical suffering, evoked in harrowing detail); and with abrupt changes of fortune, whether for good or ill (the mutability of fortune being a staple theme of Sophoclean moralizing). There is a fruitful tension between this grim material and the harmonious form of the plays. While the effect of death, suffering and change is not softened by any real compensation or consolation, these things are seen to form part of a pattern; and this pattern reflects the working of the gods in human affairs. The gods do not act justly in any human sense (indeed the characters may complain bitterly of their injustice, notably at the end of *Trachiniae*); nor do they act arbitrarily and unintelligibly. Their perfect knowledge is set against the inevitably limited knowledge of mortals, who may bring disaster on themselves while acting with the best of motives (*Trachiniae*, *Oedipus Tyrannus*), and may deceive each other with lying messenger-speeches that are as plausible as any truthful ones (*Trachiniae*, *Electra*, *Philoctetes*).

Schematic attempts to make each play centre on a single 'Sophoclean hero' have not been successful (in *Trachiniae*, *Antigone* and *Philoctetes* they have led to sterile arguments as to who 'the hero' is). Nevertheless, each play contains a major character who, while he may be less attractive morally than those around him, wins our respect by his uncompromising adherence to some purpose, whatever opposition and whatever the cost. Thus Ajax insists on suicide, Heracles on making outrageous demands on his son (though this case is rather different from the rest), Antigone on burying her brother, Oedipus *Tyrannus* on learning the truth about the killing of Laius and his own identity, Electra on opposing her father's murderers, Philoctetes on refusing to come to Troy, Oedipus *at Colonus* on remaining at Colonus and on cursing his sons. When this intransigence is set against the forces of change and illusion, the result is often the death of the 'hero'; but, as he remains morally undefeated, his courage attains a paradoxical value which transcends death itself. There is further paradox in the fact that two of these characters are women (the defiance of Antigone and Electra must have startled the Greek audience) while two others are destitute outcasts (Philoctetes and Oedipus *at Colonus*), who are granted power over other men's lives through the will of the gods, and whose inner strength enables them to resist manipulation by those men.

Characterization is always strong enough to provide a criterion by which actions may be judged plausible, but does not extend to psychologically detailed portraiture. The Chorus, while less central than in Aeschylus, is resourcefully used for various puposes. It often draws a moral lesson from the action that it witnesses, but such lessons are there for the sake of the play, not as ends in themselves; and, as it always remains within the framework of the drama, it often contributes to the dramatic irony by sharing the misapprehensions of the characters. In the choral odes Sophocles' style can be almost as ornate and elaborate as that of Aeschylus; in dialogue it is simpler, combining dignity and elevation with great suppleness and vigour.   ALB

Sorge, Reinhard Johannes (1892–1916) German dramatist and poet, whose visionary play *The Beggar* (1912, staged by **Reinhardt** in 1917) was the first fully developed work in the 'ecstatic' line of expressionism. Its subjective intensity, episodic structure and portrayal of the spiritual regeneration of mankind through the poet-hero's murder of his technologically obsessed father, became typical elements in the movement.   CI

Sorma, Agnes (1865–1927) German actress. A woman of quite extraordinary grace and beauty, whose poetic style on stage complemented exactly the acting of **Josef Kainz**, with whom she was a colleague at the **Deutsches Theater** from 1883 to 1899. Later she worked with **Max Reinhardt**, specializing both in classical and contemporary leads. Her last years were spent in the United States. She died on her ranch in Arizona.   SW

Sosnitsky, Ivan Ivanovich (1794–1872) Along with **Karatygin**, one of the two leading St Petersburg (Russian) actors of his day. Trained by **Dmitrevsky** and later **Shakhovskoi**, he was an attractive, elegant, charming and popular actor, who often paid more attention to polish than to feeling. He excelled as lovers, officers, rakes and dandies in light comedies and vaudevilles and was noted for his skill in playing multiple roles in a single play via external transformation. **Shchepkin** helped turn him into a more serious realistic actor with the result that he inherited some of the 'old man' roles that had been his friend's staple since youth. Sosnitsky and Shchepkin each played the role of the Mayor in *The Inspector General* in the St Petersburg and Moscow premieres, respectively. The latter's portrayal was realistic, whereas the former's was in the spirit of vaudeville. The rivalry undermined their friendship. Other rogues in his gallery included Figaro, Tartuffe and Repetilov (*Woe from Wit*).   SG

Sothern, E[dward] A[skew] (1826–81), and **E[dward] H[ugh]** (1859–1933) American actors. Beginning his career as an eccentric comedian on English stages, the elder Sothern made his American debut as Dr Pangloss in *The Heir-at-Law* in 1852. He achieved sudden star status with **Laura Keene**'s company when he assumed the role of Lord Dundreary in **Tom Taylor**'s *Our American Cousin* in 1858 for an uninterrupted run of five months. In 1861, after 400 consecutive performances, Londoners indulged in frequent 'Dundrearyisms' and his distinctive sidewhiskers, known as 'Dundrearies', became popular. Other Sothern roles included Dundreary's Brother Sam in the play of that name (1862), and the title roles in

E. A. Sothern as Lord Dundreary in Tom Taylor's *Our American Cousin*.

T. W. **Robertson**'s *David Garrick* (1864) and **H. J. Byron**'s *The Crushed Tragedian* (1878). Excelling in original comic business, the British-born actor remained popular on both sides of the Atlantic and died in London. In 1879, Sothern provided the opportunity for his American-born son, E. H. Sothern, to make his debut in New York in a small role in *Brother Sam*. Playing in England and America, the younger Sothern gained experience in the companies of **John McCullough**, Helen Dauvray, and others. In 1887 **Daniel Frohman** engaged Sothern for the newly formed company at the **Lyceum Theatre**. Sothern quickly established himself as a dashing romantic hero in such roles as Prince Rudolph in *The Prisoner of Zenda* (1895). Still under Frohman's management, Sothern broadened his range to poetic drama in 1900 as the hero in **Hauptmann**'s *The Sunken Bell* and as Hamlet. Under the management of **Charles Frohman**, Sothern first appeared with **Julia Marlowe**, whom he married in 1911, in *Romeo and Juliet* in 1904. Together, until Marlowe's retirement, they reigned for a decade as America's foremost Shakespearian players. Sothern retired in 1927.   MR

Soulié, Frédéric (1800–47) French dramatist and novelist. Soulié's reputation as a dramatist rests on the plays written during the 1840s. His early plays, written for the **Odéon**, were mostly historical with some literary pretension. An adaptation of *Romeo and Juliet* (1828) was the first to be performed, followed by a disastrous *Christine à Fontainebleau* (1829), which had to be replaced by **Dumas**'s rather more successful play on the same theme. His interest in a more socially committed type of drama could be seen in *L'Homme à la Blouse* (*The Man in a Smock*), at the Porte-Saint-Martin (1832). In the later thirties he published a series of novels, most of them in *feuilleton* form, which he subsequently adapted for the theatre. The short-lived Renaissance Theatre (1838–41), which aimed at a 'quality' repertoire under the direction of Antenor Joly, with the collaboration of **Hugo** and Dumas, was temporarily saved from closure by the success of Soulié's *Diane de Chivri* (1839), which together with *Le Fils de la Folle* (*The Son of the Madwoman*) and *Le Proscrit* formed a trilogy on French history from the Revolution to the reign of Louis Philippe. The melodrama theatres gave Soulié the outlet he really needed. Starting with *Le Proscrit* (*The Workman*, 1840), he wrote a series of highly profitable plays for the Ambigu-Comique. The populist appeal was strong, with villains, robbers and virtuous workers amongst the dramatis personae. With *Gaetan, Il Mammone* (1842) he turned to a complex Neapolitan plot and provided an excellent role for the popular boulevard actor, **Mélingue**. *Eulalie Pontois* (1843), was pure melodrama, heavily dependent upon complicated plot and gothic castles. *Les Amants de Murcie* (1844) was a rather more romantic Spanish version of *Romeo and Juliet*. *Les Talismans* (1845) exploited a contemporary fashion for the diabolical, and the cast included good and bad angels in a variety of guises. His much lighter piece, *Les Etudiants* (*The Students*, 1845), anticipated Henri Murger's presentation of student life. Soulié's last, and major, work was *La Closerie des Genêts* (1846), adapted by **Boucicault** as *The Willow Copse*, which contained material from two of his novels, *The She-Tiger of Paris*

(*La Lionne*) and its sequel *The Countess of Monrion*. The play ran for hundreds of performances and took five hours to play. It is often regarded as one of the best plays of the reign of Louis Philippe. Its interest is in the wide range of carefully studied social types and in the interaction of different traditions in post-Napoleonic France. The complicated plot looks seriously at social attitudes to illegitimacy and also introduces a particularly unpleasant villainess, Leona, with an unsavoury past, anticipating such characters in the plays of the latter half of the century.   JMCC

Sound in the theatre

Sound effects In the days before microphones, gramophone records and tape recorders, sound in the theatre depended on mechanical and live effects. The creation of these was a great art and was usually the domain of the property department. Even in the mid-fifties, although gramophone records had very much taken over, live effects were still employed. Rather than hire expensive sound equipment and records, producers would insist, say, that mechanical wind or wave machines, clock chimes or metal thunder sheets be used.

Certain sounds will always be more convincingly produced 'live' or manually. For example, a pistol shot is most effective with a real gun and a blank cartridge. And the sounds of door bells, phone bells, door chimes and door knockers are usually more easily achieved live. Glass and crockery crashes are better with the real thing.

One of the most famous of all sound effects was for *The Ghost Train* by Arnold Ridley. First produced at the St Martin's Theatre in London in 1925, it is still a firm favourite with repertory and amateur companies. The stage directions in the original script call for an assortment of tubular bells, garden rollers, galvanized iron tanks, thunder sheets, drums, air cylinders, whistles, milk churns, mallets and wire brushes, and require six carefully rehearsed stage-hands to create the various train sounds.

During the late 1940s and into the 1950s the use of 78 rpm sound effects discs was prevalent. The sounds were selected from specialist libraries and transferred to lacquer disc. Usually only two or three items were recorded on each single-side to allow for maximum

A 'panatrope' in use during the 1950s.

Taped sound effects at the Theatre Royal, Drury Lane, London, 1957.

flexibility during replay. Music was still obtainable on 78 rpm commercial discs since the new long playing record (at that incredibly low speed of 33⅓ rpm) was only introduced in the mid-fifties.

The turntable units were rugged affairs, incorporating large valve (or tube) amplifiers and loudspeaker switching. Each pick-up arm had a lowering device and some form of patent groove-locator. In Britain, these large gramophones were called 'panatropes' and instead of 'sound cues' stage managers used to write 'Pan cues' in their prompt scripts. A selection of sound effects discs was very convenient during rehearsals because the director could call for any combination, sequence and balance of effects *in situ*. It is interesting to note that the BBC and other broadcasting authorities, with their fast turnover of programmes, still use sound effects discs for drama because of this flexibility.

The first major production in London to use tape machinery was *My Fair Lady* which transferred from Broadway to the **Theatre Royal, Drury Lane**, in 1957. American theatre had been a few years ahead of Britain with the transition from disc to tape. But from around this period most theatres have employed open reel tape machines for the playback of music and effects.

Cassette tape recorders have not proved very successful because of the difficulty to 'cue-in' accurately and the impossibility of editing. However, tape cartridge recorders are growing in popularity because they are compact, mechanically silent and extremely accurate in operation. These machines were developed particularly for use in radio stations for the convenient handling of jingles and commercials; and they are

sometimes used in theatres where a separate cartridge is employed for each effect.

It is not possible to rewind cartridges fast and the relatively slow forward wind to return to the start of the recorded effect plus the difficulties of editing can be drawbacks.

Most of the everyday sounds of weather, traffic, birds, animals, aircraft, bells, people, etc. can be obtained on commercial recordings. However, these recordings are limited both in the range of available sounds and in the duration of the tracks. With portable recording equipment many natural sounds can be captured. But it can be very time consuming and sometimes impossible to record the wanted sound devoid of other background noises; and in the theatre it is essential to have clean sound effects. It is often, therefore, preferable to simulate effects in front of a microphone where extraneous noises can be eliminated altogether.

Sound effects are used in the theatre for a variety of reasons:
1   To establish (a) locale (b) time of year (c) day or night (d) weather conditions.
2   To evoke atmosphere.
3   To link scenes.
4   As an emotional stimulus.
5   To reproduce physical happenings: cars arriving, babies crying, clocks striking etc.

Because one is usually putting a single sound on to a loudspeaker, theatre recordings are more often than not monaural. But there are exceptions. For example, in most cases music is enhanced by stereo. Stereo can also be useful for providing breadth and perspective to crowd, battle, traffic, sea effects, etc. Moving sounds like cars, aeroplanes, and trains can, of course, be recorded in stereo, but will be fixed in their timing. It is much more flexible to have the same mono sound on twin tracks fed separately by two loudspeakers. Then, by adjusting the relative gains, the effect can be moved from one loudspeaker to the other at will. Twin tracks may also be used for two different continuous effects of indeterminate length: e.g., rain on one track and wind on the other. This would leave a second tape machine free for superimposing other effects.

Sound reinforcement and public address   Public Address systems were originally, as implied, functional systems for addressing the public where quality of sound was secondary to the clear transmission of information.

A significant improvement in quality did not come about until the explosion of the pop music scene during the 1960s. A new breed of high performance sound equipment was developed so that recording artists like the Beatles and the Rolling Stones could present themselves in concert to vast audiences. With a Sound Reinforcement system the microphone is not necessarily near the performer and the aim is to present the listener with an amplified yet natural sound.

Modern musicals more often than not call for a combination of the close and distant microphone techniques to produce louder than natural sound – in other words a cross between Reinforcement and Public Address. This requirement has arisen because on the one hand audiences, having become used to the electronic sound of broadcasting, films and pop concerts, are less prepared to concentrate in the theatre than was once the case. And on the other hand modern equipment and techniques have made it possible to provide a bigger sound for a live performance.

Another factor is that composers, knowing that a sound system will be available, feel freer to write orchestration which once would have been appropriate only in a recording studio. It also has to be said that the style of acting has changed: a large percentage of actors have either lost the art of projection or are content to rely upon the sound system to reach the audience at the back of the room.

During the period from the 1930s to the late 1960s a theatre speech reinforcement system would normally consist of a set of microphones on raised stands along the front edge of the stage, two or four (probably column) loudspeakers on the proscenium driven by one or two power amplifiers and a simple mixer with rotary master volume and treble and bass controls. The operating procedure was to turn the master control up for the songs and down for the dialogue. This is a far cry from the sophisticated mixing desks that are now installed in theatres where the balance engineers often have to control 40 or more microphones. The first musical in London to use a recording studio style of mixing desk was *Company*. This musical by **Stephen Sondheim** was first produced on Broadway in 1970 and later that year transferred to London. It is interesting to note that the Broadway production employed a number of the old style rotary fader mixers.

Around this period it became the practice to site the mixing desk within the body of the auditorium for balancing the sound of musicals. Before this, microphone controls plus a disc and tape playback would be located somewhere on the side of the stage where the sound operator could only guess at what the audience was hearing.

Loudspeakers Whether we are dealing with Reinforcement or PA somewhere has to be found for the loudspeakers, and their positioning and angling are critical. The basic requirements are that they should be sited as near to the stage as possible to maintain the illusion of the sound coming from the actors; they should be on the audience side of the microphones to minimize acoustic feedback; and they should be angled to provide direct sound to every seat in the house.

In theory a single sound source in the centre above the proscenium will give the 'cleanest' sound, as the number of sound paths and therefore the chances of unwanted reflections have been reduced to a minimum. Furthermore, the sound source is not in close proximity to any one section of the audience. One of the drawbacks to this solution is that often there is a sightline cut-off from overhanging balconies. If there are seats in the house where it is not possible to see the top of the proscenium the people sitting there will not receive direct sound. And, of course, these are the areas which normally require the most help from a sound system. A solution might be to add some small loudspeakers to 'fill-in' the dead areas. But if this is attempted it will be necessary to incorporate some form of electronic time delay; otherwise, because electricity travels faster than airborne sound, the audience at the back would hear the sound from the nearer 'fill-in'

loudspeakers a fraction of a second before the main loudspeakers and the natural sound from the stage. This can be a disconcerting effect, certainly destroying the realism and often actually hindering intelligibility. The delayed sound can be surprisingly loud (up to 10dB louder than the source at the listening point) without sacrificing realism because the human brain always registers the initial sound received as being the source.

Acoustic feedback **or** *Howlround* is caused by the signal from a loudspeaker being picked up by a microphone going round through the system and out of the loudspeaker again *ad infinitum*. Sound reflecting off walls, ceilings and balcony fronts back to the microphone can be a prime cause of feedback. For this reason we tend to use loudspeakers with directional characteristics so that the sound is delivered to where it is required and reflections back to the microphones from walls and balcony fronts are kept to a minimum. So an overhead loudspeaker array in an auditorium might consist of one or a number of bass units (which will not be very directional) plus some mid and high frequency reproducers which will have directional properties.

Sometimes additional loudspeakers are installed at the sides of the proscenium in order to cater for stereo music reproduction and, perhaps, to bring the 'image' of the sound down from the overhead loudspeaker array. Where a central loudspeaker position is not suitable or not desired, then the side proscenium locations become the prime source.

Microphones In a reinforcement system where the requirement is for maximum pick-up with minimum potential feedback we deal almost exclusively with directional, or cardioid, microphones.

The most obvious and usually the most important position for Reinforcement microphones is along the front edge of the stage, being directly in the firing-line between the actors and the audience. We call microphones in this position 'foot mics' or more commonly in Britain 'float mics'. (This is because all theatres once had lights in this position called 'footlights', which were originally known as 'floats' because they consisted of lighted wicks floating in wax.)

It used to be the object of every sound engineer to raise the float microphones as near as possible to the source of sound; that is, the actor's head. But in the late 1960s some American engineers were testing out a large installation and discovered that one of the microphones appeared to perform more efficiently than all the others. Upon closer inspection they were surprised to find that the microphone in question had fallen from its stand and was resting on the floor.

Subsequent experiments with test equipment produced the explanation that when a microphone is raised in the air it will receive direct sound plus reflections from the floor, and these reflections will not only make for a less clean sound but the short time-lag will mean that certain groups of frequencies will arrive at the microphone out of phase with those of the original signal. This produces a cancelling effect in those frequencies. Thus the quality of sound is impaired. If the microphone is placed at floor level the direct and reflected sound waves arrive at the microphone at almost the same instant producing a tighter sound with no audible cancellation effect. And there are additional benefits in that not only does the floor act as a radiator but the microphone in this low position is more shielded from the sounds emanating from the orchestra pit.

Transmitted foot noise is checked by correct shock mounting to isolate the microphone from floor vibrations. Shock mounts especially designed for float microphones are now available.

If the action takes place at some distance from the front of the stage or upon raised platforms, it might be necessary to employ overhead microphones. These will normally be of the very directional 'shotgun' variety.

It has become common practice for leading performers in musicals each to be equipped with a wireless microphone. The kit comes in two or three parts: the microphone and transmitter, which can be separate or integrated, and the receiver. The receiver with its aerial (or antenna) simply plugs into an input on the mixer like an ordinary microphone. With the separate microphone the transmitter pack, tuned to the same frequency as the receiver, is secreted somewhere in the actor's clothing. The associated microphone should be fixed so that it remains in a central position, approximately 4 in. (100cm) below the chin. It is vital to ensure that the head of the microphone is completely exposed or, at most, covered by only a thin piece of material.

The microphone will be of the omnidirectional variety, providing a general pick-up to cope with all the head movements. Since it is so near the source of sound there are unlikely to be serious feedback problems.

For the cabaret or concert performer and for some musicals hand-held microphones are called for. They may be either wireless systems or conventional microphones with trailing leads. If the musical backing is on stage it will be necessary to use a very directional microphone (hyper-cardioid) and one which is designed to be used close to the mouth. Both of these factors will help exclude the orchestral sounds and allow the voice to predominate. This type of microphone will have a built-in 'windshield' or 'pop-gag' to stop explosive breath sounds. Other microphones designed for close work under less stringent conditions – either on a stand or in the hand – will be straightforward cardioids with, perhaps, optional windshields for use as necessity dictates. Some performers find a very directional microphone difficult to handle because one can so easily move 'off-mike'.

Amplifying musical instruments There are different techniques for amplifying musical instruments, but most of these employ a directional microphone placed as near the source of sound as possible; e.g. near the bridge of a violin, the bell of a wind instrument, the struck surface of a drum or cymbal, the loudspeaker of an electric guitar or organ, and so on.

There are available contact microphones which are actually attached to the sounding boards of instruments like pianos, harps and double basses, where the microphone reacts to the vibrations of the sounding board. The main advantage is the exclusion of pick-up from other instruments.

With electronic instruments there is an excellent way of ensuring a 'clean' sound. This is with the use of a little plugging unit called a direct injection box. This box accepts the feed at the preamplifier stage from the guitar or keyboard and splits it two ways: one into the instrument's own amplifier in the normal way, and the other straight into the mixer. So a microphone is not used at all because the signal is directly injected into the mixer. Some instrument amplifiers incorporate suitable output for sending direct signals to the mixer.

There are also microphone inserts of different types especially designed to be inserted into various wind instruments. The object is to obtain as clean a sound as possible.

The control position It is as important for the sound technician to hear what the audience is hearing as for the lighting switchboard operator to see what the audience is seeing. It can even be argued that with a complicated sound balance it is much more important. For, whereas lighting levels when plotted will remain the same for every performance, sound levels will vary. The number of people in the auditorium, even the clothes they are wearing (whether lightweight or heavy and absorbent) will have an influence. The amount of humidity in the air also has an effect. When one is working with microphones the changes can be quite dramatic. Every performance will need a slightly different balance. A particular performer may be 'giving' more or less or may be at a different distance from the microphone; or the orchestra may be playing louder or softer, and so on.

It is therefore of the utmost importance that a permanent sound control position is centrally placed within the auditorium. Ideally, it should be a room at the centre rear of the main floor or first tier. (The central position is particularly vital for balancing stereo.) It should be soundproofed to the auditorium but have a very large window, which opens easily and quietly, with an unrestricted view of the stage and orchestra pit. The control room should have a space for the mixing desk, one or two turntables, two or more tape machines and a certain amount of storage. There should also be adequate silent ventilation.

For balancing a multi-microphone set-up it is essential for the operator to be within the acoustic environment of the auditorium where the sound from the stage combined with the sound from all the loudspeakers plus the natural reflections from walls, ceilings and other surfaces can be assimilated. An alternative plug-in point in the auditorium with all the necessary microphone lines and tie-lines to power amplifiers, etc. will facilitate the movement of a portable mixer from the control room as required.   DC

See: D. Collison, *Stage Sound*, London, 1976.

South Africa Political relations in a racially heterogeneous population of 30 million people have produced fundamental cultural tensions in South Africa. These are expressed in a multiplicity of theatrical forms and traditions. As a result of colonization and subsequent control of the means of production and distribution of resources, nearly five million 'white' people of European descent have wielded political power over the rest of the population, of whom nearly 20 million are disfranchised 'blacks' of African descent. This latter group comprises descendants of the Bantu-speaking peoples whose performance traditions pre-date the arrival of European colonizers in 1652.

These early Africans of the pre-colonial period practised various forms of dramatic enactment in, for example, songs and story-telling narratives. Some of these, like the Xhosa *intsomi* and the Zulu *inganekwane*, would be invoked by later dramatists as important models for 'authentic' African theatrical dialogue and action. In addition, the Nguni *izibongo* tradition in praise poetry employed mimetic narrative and dance in a form which incorporated oral communication as well as broadly gestural visual enactment. Religious rituals and military and political ceremonies were other occasions for dramatic enactment through movement, speech and singing. The *function* of such performance was a major determinant of form and theme: the pieces were related to contemporary contingencies such as reinforcement of the tribal social structure or the invocation of religious or historical precedent. These traditions are by no means archaic forms, but are still constantly being recreated, changing in theme and style in relation to historical developments. They have continued into the present in two ways. Firstly, the most obvious arena for their contemporary performance is the mining compound, where tribal groupings are maintained (as part of white political strategy). In some cases traditional forms have undergone metamorphosis in accordance with the changed circumstances of the migrant labourer. One such

contemporary form of oral poetry is *sefela*, which enacts the life and experience of the migrant labourer temporarily uprooted from his rural home. Secondly, some of the aspects of visual and oral communication derived from narratives and praise poetry have been incorporated into contemporary theatrical forms. Many plays currently in performance rely in great measure on the traditions of narration and solo enactment that have their roots in the early indigenous forms. Apart from these modes of performance amongst the Bantu-speaking peoples, there is evidence of other modes in the games and ceremonies of the nomadic Bushman communities which roam over vast areas of semi-desert terrain in the Cape province. There are therefore many roots of African performance which were in existence before the arrival of Europeans.

As part of the strategy to maintain white hegemony, authoritative accounts of South African cultural history have largely ignored these indigenous African traditions and have focused instead on the European influence. Thus a performance of **Beaumarchais**'s *The Barber of Seville* given in 1783 by French troops at the military barracks in Cape Town (which was at that time an important refreshment station on the sea route to the East) is commonly considered to be the earliest recorded example of theatrical performance in South

The Market Theatre Company's production of Mbongeni Ngema's *Asinamali (We have no Money)*. The prisoners' story is related through a kaleidoscope of song, dance and mime.

Africa. From this event it is possible to trace the growth and development of a European tradition in South African theatre, although alongside this tradition there were always alternative indigenous and syncretic forms – one of the earliest of which was the Anglicized Dutch dramatic poem *Kaatje Kekkelbek* in the first decade of the 19th century. The dominant cultural influence from the first years of the century coincided with British political rule over the Cape Colony. After the founding in 1801 of the first theatre – The African Theatre in Cape Town – visiting professionals and entrepreneurs imported European plays and players. Actor–managers and impresarios arriving from England and other European countries developed theatre under the influence of English theatrical taste. Then the discovery of diamonds in 1867 and of gold in 1886 brought an influx of immigrants, which in turn determined the growth of amateur theatre in many different European languages to cater for the needs of a new cosmopolitan audience. By the end of the century, Afrikaans drama appeared. The first Afrikaans play, S. J. du Toit's *Magrita Prinslo*, was produced in 1897. After the Anglo-Boer War of 1902 Afrikaans nationalism found expression in a wave of patriotic writings such as C. J. Langenhoven's drama *Die Hoop van Suid-Afrika* in 1912, and in numerous Afrikaans plays which were toured by companies to the rural areas – at that time dominated by Afrikaans farming communities. By the beginning of the 20th century the large cities boasted numerous well-equipped theatre buildings modelled on London's West End theatres, and during the first quarter of the century both Afrikaans and English companies had established an infrastructure for professional theatre in both languages. In addition, in both these languages there was a thriving amateur theatre industry. European political dominance, therefore, was reinforced by cultural policies in which the theatre played an important role.

While the second quarter of the 20th century witnessed the consolidation of this process, important developments were taking place in theatre amongst black communities. In 1927 the first publication of Xhosa drama was G. B. Sinxo's *Debeza's Baboons*, and in 1935 H. I. E. Dhlomo became the first black person to publish a play in English with his drama about the Xhosa legend, *The Girl Who Killed to Save: Nongqause the Liberator*. The black middle class began to assert a taste for theatre based on European models of dramatic literature, and elitist clubs were formed, such as the Johannesburg Bantu Dramatic Society in 1932. Meanwhile, however, a popular form of theatre amongst working-class black people began to make an impact. Mthethwa's Lucky Stars was founded in Natal in 1927 as the first professional black troupe, and toured the country with plays based on Zulu legends and customs, performing in the vernacular to popular appeal. During the 1930s and 1940s the urbanization of Africans, gathered in slumyards and communities in and near the big cities, produced syncretic forms of music and theatre. The synthesis of tribal performance traditions with Western models of performance, especially from America, would lead eventually to an important event when in 1959 the black musical *King Kong*, about the rise and fall of a heavyweight boxer, brought African musicians and actors to the attention of theatre-goers in Johannesburg, London and New York. Meanwhile

English and Afrikaans theatre profited in the second quarter of the century by a number of developments. The growth of professional and amateur theatre until the end of the Second World War was rapid but eclectic, and some cohesion was necessary. In 1938 a nation-wide coordination of amateur theatre groups was achieved when P. P. B. Breytenbach founded the Federation of Amateur Theatrical Societies of South Africa. Then in 1947 the National Theatre Organization was founded, and Breytenbach soon became Chairman of this first state-funded body for professional theatre. During the 1950s the NTO provided important training and experience for a new generation of actors and directors, and in 1963 the process of consolidation was crystallized with the formation of provincial Performing Arts Councils.

This event coincided with the entrenchment of rigid racial segregation in theatres, and a consequent international playwrights' boycott. As it came of age, the state-funded theatre found itself symbolizing the political system which had plunged South Africa into international disrepute. In opposition to this theatre alternative forms of theatre emerged amongst practitioners determined to defy government policies with regard to racial segregation. One important group was Union Artists, which coordinated activities on behalf of black musicians and actors. This was the group which produced *King Kong*. It also gave encouragement to an important generation of theatre practitioners. Two of these were **Athol Fugard** and Gibson Kente. Both were to forge independent careers in the 1960s and 1970s – Fugard with a reputation as a white liberal exploring on stage the relationships of South Africans frustrated by social and political pressures, and Kente as a black entrepreneur creating popular musicals about life in the black townships.

While Afrikaans theatre existed almost exclusively within the Performing Arts Councils from 1963 until the 1980s, some English writers emerged to present their work in fringe theatres, but none achieved the sustained success of Fugard's work. Far more important for English-language theatre after 1963 was the training and experience of a number of actors and directors in the Performing Arts Councils. These practitioners of the theatre would make an important contribution in the 1970s. At the same time, an important development occurred with the growth of black nationalism. The Black Consciousness movement began in the universities and quickly spread to other sectors of the black populace. Black Consciousness led to radical changes in black politics, and 'black' cultural expression became one way of asserting an alternative, black, hegemony. Militant political theatre emerged from groups like People's Experimental Theatre and the Theatre Council of Natal. Both of these groups were cited in the charge sheet at a trial under the 'Terrorism Act' for their involvement in the dissemination of 'subversive' plays and literature. Significantly, the groups involved in what was defined as 'black' theatre in the 1970s comprised, in addition to Africans, the other population groups categorized by the state as 'Indian' and 'Coloured'. Throughout the country theatre became, amongst all three population groups, a means to reassert black nationalism. Even Gibson Kente introduced a more pronounced political theme into his musicals, and the title song of his play

How Long? attained a symbolic importance in the revolutionary action which developed amongst schoolchildren in the townships in 1976. The wave of black political militancy also influenced white theatre practitioners, and in the 1970s important fringe groups emerged, producing plays about South African politics and race relations. The Market Theatre in Johannesburg and The Space Theatre in Cape Town were two of the most innovative groups, both providing venues for many of Fugard's works as well as works by a number of young writers and directors. The extraordinary international success of John Kani and Winston Ntshona, the actors who created *Sizwe Bansi is Dead* with Fugard, inspired many groups to adopt improvisatory methods in the creation of theatre, and by the end of the decade South African theatre had rejected many of its European and American models and discovered its own voice. In the 1980s one of the most successful plays to emerge was *Woza Albert*, created in workshop by director Barney Simon with actors Percy Mtwa and Mbongeni Ngema. Two other developments were related to the developing political crisis in the 1980s. Firstly trade union workers' theatre emerged as various black trade unions introduced plays about working conditions and union solidarity as one way of educating black workers about these important issues. Secondly, the township musical, which remained the dominant form of theatre in the townships in the hands of people like Kente, began to be supplemented by political plays. Major exponents of black political township drama were Mzwandile Maqina, Matsemela Manaka and Maishe Maponya.

Apart from politically committed theatre there also existed a popularly supported commercial theatre. In the 1970s African musicals, backed by white capital and marketing strategies, enjoyed lengthy runs both in South Africa and abroad. Though popular with audiences, these were often criticized as inauthentic 'tribal musicals' exploited for commercial ends. Most prominent of the genre was the musical *Ipi-Tombi*, while Welcome Msomi's *Umabatha*, a Zulu adaptation of *Macbeth*, achieved critical acclaim at the 1972 World Theatre Season in London. White commercial theatre also flourished in South Africa's major cities, despite (and perhaps partly because of) the inauguration of broadcast television in 1976.

In the 1990s South African theatre enjoys an impressive infrastructure. Political theatre and theatre based on the country's unique history of apartheid-related problems have given birth to a new identity. The Eurocentric models have been abandoned, and writers and practitioners use all the indigenous languages to create plays about South Africans learning to live in a post-apartheid society. Commercial success has led to the establishment of many independent professional managements. Training facilities proliferate as the universities and training colleges offer courses in all aspects of the performing arts. The relatively young film and television industries provide further opportunities for employees, and each of the major cities can boast impressively equipped theatre buildings.   IS

See: Anon., 'Black Theatre in South Africa', Fact Paper on South Africa by the International Defence and Aid Fund for Southern Africa, London, 1976; D. Coplan, *In Township Tonight! South Africa's Black City Music and Theatre*, London and New York, 1985; S. Gray, *Athol Fugard*, Johannesburg, 1982; T. Hauptfleisch and I. Steadman, *South African Theatre: Four Plays and an Introduction*, Pretoria, 1984; R. Kavanagh, *South African People's Plays*, London, 1981; and *Theatre and Cultural Struggle in South Africa*, London, 1985; S. Roberts, 'South African Bilingual and Multilingual Drama of the Seventies', in *Canadian Drama* 6 (i), 134–50. See also special issues of the journals *Theatre Quarterly* 28, 1978 and *Critical Arts* (Johannesburg) 1 (iii) 1980, and 2 (i) 1981.

Southerne, Thomas (1660–1746) Irish playwright. Educated at Trinity College, Dublin, he entered the Middle Temple in London in 1680. After writing two plays, *The Loyal Brother* (1682) and *The Disappointment* (1684), he joined the army as an ensign in 1685 rising to captain in 1688 when he turned back to the theatre. Between 1690 and 1696 he wrote five plays and, though he continued to write plays infrequently until 1726, none of his later work was as successful. *Sir Anthony Love* (1690) gave Susanna Mountfort a virtuoso role in a **breeches part** as the disguised woman playing at being a rake. *The Wives' Excuse* (1691), Southerne's best play, is a large-scale depiction of the intrigues of society, placing at its centre a serious depiction of the unfortunate wife who refuses to take the easy option advocated by Southerne's subtitle, 'cuckolds make themselves', as revenge of her foolish husband's treatment of her. In its representation of the complex interconnections of events in a closely-knit community, the play is extraordinary. *The Maid's Last Prayer* (1693) is a similar though even more vicious satire on some women's pursuit of 'any, rather than fail', this play's subtitle. Southerne's two tragedies from this period were both long-lasting successes and both based on novellas by **Aphra Behn**: *The Fatal Marriage* (1695) from *The Nun* points forward to a more sentimental form of tragedy; *Oroonoko* (1695) is a fine example of the sentimental noble savage play, combining noble actions with exotic locations. Throughout his career Southerne was admired by all other writers and gained a particular reputation for his attempts to help younger dramatists with their first plays.   PH

Southwark Theatre South St between 4th and 5th Sts, Philadelphia. In 1766, **David Douglass** erected America's first substantial theatre just outside Philadelphia's city limits to avert official interference. It was to remain active for 51 years. On its stage, Douglass presented the first play by a native American, Thomas Godfrey's *The Prince of Parthia* (1767). Closed by the Continental Congress in 1774, it was used briefly as a hospital, then reopened by British occupation troops for entertainments to benefit widows and orphans. A drop curtain attributed to Major John André continued to be used until the theatre closed. The playhouse was 2½ storeys high, painted red, brick in its lower storey and surmounted by a cupola. In 1784, **Lewis Hallam** the younger reoccupied the theatre skirting the laws against play-acting by presenting 'moral lectures'. In 1789, the ban was lifted and the Southwark was in full operation. Outmoded as newer theatres were built and better companies were assembled, the playhouse closed its doors in 1817. When the structure was damaged by fire a few years later, a brewery was built on its foundations and survived until 1912.   MCH

Soviet children's theatre A child of the October (1917) Revolution, sired by the director-dramatist Natalya I. Sats (b. 1903) and the director-theorist Aleksandr A. Bryantsev (b. 1883) and assorted members of the intelligentsia, with the support of Soviet First People's Commissar for Education **Anatoly V. Lunacharsky**, acting in the name of Lenin. Today there are some 50 Children's Theatres and Theatres for Young Spectators (TYUZs) in the 15 Soviet republics. They account for 400–500 plays annually in the various national languages, encompassing traditional and modern fairy tales, Russian, ethnic and foreign classics, historical and psychological dramas, comedies, musicals, melodramas and dramatizations of poetry, biography and other narrative forms. The Soviet children's theatre presently constitutes the most ambitious and successful enterprise of its kind in the world. Audience growth (23 million in 1974) has far outstripped new theatre construction, with the result that adult companies must include a certain percentage of children's theatre productions in their repertoires or lose their government subsidies. It has not always been so.

Russia has a rich folkloric heritage. School dramas and children's literature were introduced in the 17th and 18th centuries (the former by Simon Polotsky and **Feofan Prokopovich**). However, the scattered attempts to create professional children's theatres prior to 1917 stalled due to lack of commercial success. Children's theatrical fare, with rare exceptions like the **Moscow Art Theatre**'s productions of **Ostrovsky**'s *The Snow Queen* (1900) and **Maeterlinck**'s *The Blue Bird* (1908), were mainly relegated to matinées in the adult theatres. Few adult actors specialized in children's or 'travesty' roles, and adolescents were perceived as being 'first-draft' adults. The government's decision to invest in children's theatres after 1917 was largely political. Lenin's wife, Nadezhda K. Krupskaya, saw them as a means of making youth sensitive to the beauty of the new society's ideals and the unprecedented act of creative imagination that building such a society necessitates. **Stanislavsky** called for a children's theatre independent from and superior to the adult theatre, what Bryantsev named a 'theatre of special commitment'. Children's writer Kornei I. Chukovsky counselled that the child's emotional education was paramount. What evolved was a children's theatre aesthetic balanced precariously between fantasy and reality, classical humanism and revolutionary idealism.

In 1918 the Commissariat for Education organized mobile children's theatre performances in Moscow, Petrograd and Saratov. The Moscow venture became permanent in October 1918, the first anniversary of the Revolution, under the direction of N. I. Sats (daughter of Moscow Art Theatre composer Ilya A. Sats), N. Ya. Efimov, V. A. Favorsky, composer A. N. Aleksandrov and balletmaster K. Ya. Goleizovsky. The theatre presented puppet shows, concerts and ballets. The First State Children's Theatre was opened in 1920 (renamed the State Central Theatre for Young Spectators in 1931) under Lunacharsky's direction. He was succeeded by G. M. Paskar, Yu. M. Bondy and G. L. Roshal. Here the first Soviet plays for children on contemporary themes were presented. Bryantsev founded Petrograd's TYUZ in 1921 which since 1963 (as Leningrad TYUZ) has been directed by Zinovy Korogotsky. In 1936, Moscow's Central Children's Theatre (founded 1921), under the direction of N. I. Sats, moved to Sverdlov Square, near the Bolshoi Theatre. Here Sats pioneered 'synthesized theatre' – a combination of music, dance, acrobatics, drama and multi-media – which has become a dominant style of children's theatre production.

Children's theatres opened in the republics during the Civil War (1918–21) and thereafter. The Ekaterinodarsky (Krasnodar) Children's Theatre (1920–4) became the first to develop its own children's dramatic repertoire, featuring the plays of poetess Elena N. Vasilyeva and influential children's writer and children's literature publisher Samuel Ya. Marshak. The Kharkov Children's Theatre (founded in the early 1920s as 'Fairy Tale'; now the Lvov TYUZ) was the first and is now the oldest continuously existing Ukrainian children's theatre. Ukrainian TYUZs were later created in Kiev – Russian (1924) and Yiddish (1928) – and in Odessa (1930). Important children's theatres also opened in Riga (Latvia), Tbilisi (Georgian and Russian, 1927–8), Alma-Ata (Kazakhstan), Tashkent (Uzbek and Russian) and throughout the Central Asian republics (1938–40). By the beginning of the Great Patriotic War (the Second World War, 1941–5), there were 71 children's theatres (and 120 puppet theatres) in the Soviet Union, drawing an audience of five million. By the war's end, only 20 children's theatres remained, but 21 were rebuilt, and new theatres were created. The war years saw a preponderance of children's plays on historical and contemporary patriotic themes. Overall, the period of socialist realism (1934–56) shifted the balance in children's theatres' dramatic repertoires towards realism. Natalya Sats disappeared into a labour camp for 26 years. The 'Thaw' (1956) brought the character of Lenin to the stages of Moscow's TYUZ (M. F. Shatrov's *In the Name of the Revolution*, 1957) and Central Children's Theatre (*Popov's Family*, 1960). **Viktor Rozov** introduced the adolescent as a viable stage character in *Her Friends* (1949), *A Page from Life* (1953) and in a succession of plays directed by **Anatoly Efros** at the Central Children's Theatre, including *Good Luck!* (1954), *In Search of Happiness* (1957), *Unequal Battle* (1960), *Before Supper* (1962) and *On the Day of the Wedding* (1964). The 1960s saw the founding in Moscow of the First State Museum of Children's Theatre (1964) and the first State Children's Musical Theatre (1965), both under the direction of Natalya Sats, as well as of the Soviet Centre of the International Association of Theatre for Children and Youth (ASSITEJ, 1965). Since 1966, the Centre, which is governed by representatives from all the republics, has sponsored trips by Soviet children's theatres to international festivals, and since 1968, it has hosted children's theatre practitioners from abroad.

'The stage for young audiences', Bryantsev had stated, 'must be a collaboration between artists who think like educators and teachers with the perceptions of artists'. The task of introducing and conditioning the child to the theatre is approached scientifically by each theatre's pedagogical department (headed by a trained teacher, the Chief Pedagogue), which: meets with teachers, parents and Komsomol (Young Communist) organizations; advises on script selection and production style appropriate to particular age groups (7–10, 11–14 and 15–18) – unambiguous and highly theatrical fare for the youngest, more complex and real material for the oldest; consults at rehearsals and on script rewrites; observes audience members and tracks them for a time after the performance to gauge the psychological effects of theatrical productions; sponsors production-related art and essay contests; provides class study guides; visits classrooms; and ensures that the theatre's repertory reflects what is being studied in the schools. Among the more famous pedagogues are: N. N. Bakhtin, S. Ya. Gorodisskaya and N. A. Litvinovich.

The first dramatic literature staged in the children's theatres consisted of adaptations of fairy tales and popular children's stories with romantic subjects and heroic protagonists by such authors as Longfellow, **Hugo** and Jack London. In the 1920s and 1930s there developed a body of contemporary Soviet plays for young spectators by S. G. Rozanov, N. I. Sats, S. A. Auslender, S. S. Zayaitsky, V. A. Selikhova, N. Ya. Shestakov and Aleksandra Ya. Brushtein, Bryantsev's collaborator at Leningrad's TYUZ. Today, these theatres perform Russian and Soviet classics by: **Fonvizin, Pushkin, Gogol,** Ostrovsky, **Lev** and **Aleksei N. Tolstoi, Chekhov, Gorky, Mayakovsky, A. N. Afinogenov,** A. A. Kron, **K. M. Simonov, K. A. Trenyov, V. N. Bill-Belotserkovsky,** A. A. Fadeev, **V. P. Kataev, A. N. Arbuzov,** V. S. Rosov, **M. Roshchin, L. G. Zorin,** I. V. Shtok, L. A. Kasill, G. Mamlin, A. Aleksin, M. F. Shatrov and others. Leading authors of fairy tales written for or adapted by the children's theatres include: Pushkin (*The Fisherman and the Little Goldfish, The Golden Cockerel*); S. Ya. Marshak (*Carousel; The Luckless One; Twelve Months*); **E. L. Shvarts** (*The Two Maples; The Snow Queen*); A. N. Tolstoi (*The Little Golden Key,* adapted from *Pinocchio*); V. P. Kataev (*The Seven-Petal Magic Flower*); L. E. Ustinov (*The City without Love*); P. P. Ershov (*The Little Humpbacked Horse*). Foreign authors represented in the children's theatre repertoire include: **Shakespeare, Cervantes, Gozzi, Molière,** Hugo, **Goethe, Brecht,** Maeterlinck, **Karel Čapek, Dickens, Shaw, Kipling,** Jules Verne, Hans Christian Andersen, Charles Perrault, Mark Twain, Harriet Beecher Stowe, Poe, Faulkner, and **Lillian Hellman.** Among the leading artists from adult theatres who have worked in the children's companies are: (actors and directors) I. V. Ilyinsky, N. K. Cherkasov, M. O. Knebel, A. D. Diky, R. N. Simonov, **G. A. Tovstonogov,** B. V. Zon, Yu. P. Kiselev, G. L. Roshal, A. Ya. Shapiro, K. Ya. Shakh-Azizov, **O. N. Efremov** and A. V. Efros; (designers) V. F. Ryndin, N. A. Shifrin and I. V. Shtenberg; (composers) D. B. Kabalevsky, Krennikov and M. R. Rauthverger; and the puppeteer **Sergei V. Obraztsov.**

Among the most innovative and controversial Soviet children's theatre productions of the 1970s and 1980s were several by Vyacheslav Spesivtsev, who, in *Stenka Razin*, showed young actors engaged in violence, drunkenness and debauchery, and in *Romeo and Juliet* featured multiple actors in the roles of the two protagonists à la **Lyubimov**'s Taganka Theatre productions for which he once staged mime. Spesivtsev's production of *The Train of My Memory*, adapted from

Gadarev's novel, took place on board an actual train in transit. In 1983 he lost his artistic director's position. Recently, E. Nekroshus has filled houses and set off mass hysteria with his punk-rock musical on the Romeo and Juliet theme, *Love and Death in Verona*, at the Vilnius (Lithuania) Youth Dramatic Theatre.   SG

English and other language sources
See: M. Goldberg, 'The Pedagogue in the Eastern European Children's Theatre', *Educational Theatre Journal*, 24 (March, 1972); H. Marshall, *The Pictorial History of the Russian Theatre*, New York, 1977; M. Morton (ed. and trans.), *Russian Plays for Young Audiences*, Rowayton, CT, 1977; M. Morton (ed. and trans.), *Through the Magic Curtain: Theatre for Children, Adolescents and Young Adults in the U.S.S.R.*, New Orleans, 1979; H. Pascar, *Mon théâtre à Moscou*, Paris, 1930.

Russian language sources
See: V. F. Ashmarin, M. E. Koltsov, A. Y. Tairov, Y. V. Pisarenko, *Natalya Sats: Desyat let sredi detei*, Moscow, 1928; A. Bryantsev, *Khudozhnik v teatr dlya detei*, Leningrad, 1927; S. N. Lunacharskaya, *Teatr dlya detei kak orudie kommunisticheskogo vospitaniya*, Moscow, 1931; L. Makarev, *Gosudarstvenny teatr yunykh zritelei*, Leningrad, 1929; N. Sats, *Deti prixodyat v teatr*, Moscow, 1960; N. Sats, *Nash put: Moskovsky teatr dlya detei i ego zritel*, Moscow, 1932; N. Sats and S. Rozanov, *Teatr dlya detei*, Leningrad, 1925; L. Shpet, *Sovetsky teatr dlya detei*, Moscow, 1971; E. Vasilyeva and S. Marshak, *Teatr dlya detei*, Krasnodar, 1922.

Soya, Carl-Erik (1896–1983) Danish dramatist and novelist, author of some 35 plays, including several suites of shorter plays. Popular in the 1930s, Soya uses the theatre to juggle fancifully with major ideas, whose magnitude he often contrasts with human pettiness. Several plays, including *Pieces of a Pattern* (1940) and *Two Threads* (1943), explore the possibly deterministic nature of existence. Others, like *Who Am I?* (1932) and *Purpose, Faith and Point of View* (1938), deal with individual identity and guilt. The popular *Lion With a Corset* (1950) looks sceptically at the roots of aggression and war. While Soya's tone is persistently playful, it also frequently intimates an underlying despair.   HL

Soyinka, Wole (1934–) Nigerian playwright, poet, novelist. Generally recognized as Africa's greatest living playwright; considered by some critics as one of the foremost writers of his generation. Soyinka was born in Aké, Abeokuta, in what was then the Western Region of Nigeria, the son of a Canon in the Anglican Church. Soyinka has recreated his childhood in a reminiscence, *Aké: the Years of Childhood* (1981). The tensions between the Christian home, and the Yoruba Egungun masqueraders among the people, have helped create the dynamic of his poetic vision. He treated the conflict many years before in a radio play about an adolescent emerging into a tense world of confused adults, *Camwood on the Leaves*, broadcast on Nigerian radio in 1960 and on the BBC World Service in 1965. *Aké. . .* is more the sustained recollection of the writer's youth in his maturity.

Soyinka went to University College in Ibadan, and then to Leeds University in England in 1956. He became involved in the new drama at the **Royal Court**

Theatre, London, where he became a play-reader in 1959/60. He developed three experimental pieces there with a company of actors whom he had brought together. While Soyinka was still in England two of his plays were produced in Nigeria: *The Swamp-Dwellers*, about the moral realignment necessary to make the land productive and the community whole in rural Nigeria; and *The Lion and the Jewel*, a comedy in which a village chief and the school teacher vie with each other for the hand of the village belle. Soyinka returned to Nigeria in 1960 and founded The 1960 Masks, which presented his first major play, *A Dance of the Forests*, for the independence celebrations. The play was not what was expected. It offered a critique of pre-colonial history whilst diminishing the cultural significance of the colonial period. Many of the themes of Soyinka's later plays are present in this complex play: the notion of three parallel and interlocking worlds of the past, the present and the future (the dead, the living and the unborn); Nature, conceived metaphysically in a romantic vision of the moral imperative laid upon the questing hero; the need for sacrifice; the role of the artist in society; the presence of the god, Ogun.

The theatre company The 1960 Masks acted as an umbrella, administratively, for the younger, fully professional Orisun Theatre Company whose actors Soyinka personally trained between 1962 and 1965. The Company premiered two series of sketches with some pungent political satire: *The New Republican* and *Before the Blackout*. During these years some of his major plays appeared in print, following performances in Nigeria; their publication acted as a spur to young dramatists in other countries in anglophone East and West Africa: *The Trials of Brother Jero*, a satirical comedy recounting the adventures, sexual and otherwise, of a mendicant Christian preacher on Lagos's Bar Beach; *The Strong Breed*, an ironical exposition of the context for human sacrifice today; and *The Road*, also concerned, metaphysically, with sacrifice, but in the context of wanton death on Nigeria's roads and the rubbishing by society of a lumpen working class. *The Road* suggests that in modern Nigeria the Egungun masquerade can offer a Nigerian audience a more contemporary discourse than can a naturalistically presented materialism. The mask can discover a meaning for those at the base of society for their wasted lives and random deaths – even though the class-based nature of their oppression remains 'hidden' in the play (Jeyifo).

In 1965, Soyinka published his first novel, *The Interpreters*, about, again, meaning in the lives and deaths of a group of young Nigerian artists and intellectuals. He also had two plays broadcast on the BBC, London. Then, in October, he was arrested for allegedly seizing the Western Region radio studios and making a political broadcast disputing the published results of the recent elections. He was acquitted in December. His next play, *Kongi's Harvest*, about the abuse of power and the tyrant's ability to corrupt a whole people, was performed at the Dakar Festival of Negro Arts in 1966. It was published in 1967; so was his collection of poems *Idanre and Other Poems*.

Nigeria slid into civil war. In August 1967, Soyinka was detained without trial and only released in October 1969. He made notes during this period of incarcer-

ation, secretly, and was able to publish them on his release under the title *The Man Died* (1972) – 'The man dies', he wrote, 'in all who keep silent in the face of tyranny.' This book forms a quartet with his next major play, *Madmen and Specialists* (premiered in Connecticut, USA, 1970); with another collection of poems, *A Shuttle in the Crypt* (1971) and with the novel, *Season of Anomy* (1973). *Madmen and Specialists* is set in the civil war, also known as the Biafran War, and is an intensely moral play about man's responsibility to his fellow men, in his control both of his own nature and of an external Nature. The whole quartet shows how Soyinka's intense vision of people corrupted and debased by power-play transcends any single genre and moves vividly through them all. After his release in 1969, Soyinka went into exile. He became editor of the cultural and political magazine, *Ch'Indaba* (formerly *Transition*) which he intermittently edited from Ghana between 1970 and 1975. He was appointed Professor of Comparative Literature at the University of Ifé but was not able to take up the position. He wrote for the (British) **National Theatre** in London a version of *The Bacchae of Euripides* (the actual title of the play) which was performed in London in 1973. He had a Visiting Professorship at Sheffield University and a Fellowship at Churchill College, Cambridge University. Out of his reaction to the latter experience came a collection of essays, *Myth, Literature and the African World* (1976), a theorizing of African aesthetics. This important text develops, amongst other things, the relationship of myth to performance today. He has a vision of the transformation of the physicalities of space and time in the act of performance. In particular, he explores the significance of Ogun in the Yoruba pantheon. Ogun is the God of Iron, War and creative fire. He is seen by Soyinka as the embodiment of contradiction; he is the original sacrifice, the one who dares chaos and the abyss. In connection with the concept of the co-existence of the three worlds of the dead, the living and the unborn, Soyinka emphasizes the importance of the masquerade for a new moral consciousness: through the rites of passage there is 'a movement of transition' between these worlds, which open upon each other. The mask – and, by extension, the modern actor – can actualize this metaphysic.

Whilst at Cambridge Soyinka also wrote *Death and the King's Horseman* (1975). This play reworks a moment in Nigeria's colonial past from inside the Yoruba metaphysic: it is about the halting of the ritual suicide of the equerry of the Alafin of Oyo by the local British District Officer, in 1946. The incident had already been handled in an opera by **Duro Ladipo**. The play in performance is the praxis of Soyinka's theory. Together, theory and drama are a summation of his work up to his return to Nigeria. Many of the plays of this period require the dialogue to carry the burden of the playwright's meaning. The writing is dense and Soyinka has been criticized for the overloading of the language, through his play on words, control of rhythm and assonance, and with metaphor piled on brilliant metaphor. His sensibility often seems to outstrip his audience's sensibilities.

Soyinka returned to Nigeria, to Ifé, in 1976. After directing a production of *Death and the King's Horseman* there in 1976, he set about generating a new drama:

through a new oeuvre, a new Theatre Company – the Guerilla Theatre Unit – and through film. This drama seeks to confront post-independence tyranny and corruption in African states directly, rather than through metaphor and metaphysics. In December 1977 he produced *Opera Wonyosi*, a Nigerian version of both **Gay**'s *The Beggar's Opera* and **Brecht**'s *Threepenny Opera*. The play is a full-frontal satirical attack on Bokasa, the self-crowned emperor of the short-lived Central African Empire; and, in the context of this, an attack also on the values of the Nigerian petit bourgeoisie who benefit materially from such tyrants. The attack was continued in his next play, *A Play of Giants* (1985). Using **Genet**'s *The Balcony* as a model, Soyinka parodies some of Africa's worst modern tyrants, in particular, Idi Amin of Uganda. The play also attacks the Superpowers and the United Nations, which he sees as sanctioning the megalomania and butchery of these dictators. These plays, and the work of the Guerilla Theatre Unit, are complemented by Soyinka's film *Blues for a Prodigal* (1985) in which he attacks the power play and corruption of the civilian government of Shehu Shagari. Banned in Nigeria, the film was screened privately in London in 1985 on the occasion of his Herbert Read Memorial Lecture at which Soyinka reaffirmed his commitment to a political praxis in his dramatic art.

Soyinka is a political playwright; but, rather than being didactic, his work demonstrates the dialectic within the term 'political art'. He thinks politically, and can see no other way of thinking as an artist in Africa today. Thus, the greater Soyinka's commitment is to his art, the more political it becomes; and the greater his commitment to praxis, the more artistically compelling are the plays which come out of his experience. Soyinka was awarded the Nobel Prize for Literature in 1986. ME

Spain Spain's period of greatness as a political power in the 16th and 17th centuries was matched by a Golden Age in literature and the arts which produced a rich contribution to world drama. From the end of the 17th century, however, dramatic production in Spain, though continuous, has never regained its earlier heights.

As in England, but unlike France, there was no clean break with the theatre of the Middle Ages in the 16th century. Though in close contact with Italy and classical drama, the typical Spanish play of the period, the **comedia**, resisted the classical model to create a form that was popular, dynamic and unique in many ways. The legacy of the Middle Ages is clear in the work of playwrights of the early 16th century – **Encina**, **Torres Naharro** and **Gil Vicente**. Encina visited Italy and was influenced by Renaissance themes; Torres Naharro lived there and wrote plays on themes that were to become classics of the Spanish theatre. Gil Vicente, working in isolation in Portugal and Castile, wrote chivalric plays and short religious scenes in both languages.

These dramatists wrote works for noble patrons to be produced in palaces, not for a public. By the middle of the 16th century, however, a public, commercial theatre had developed, and companies of paid actors toured Spanish cities and towns. No great authors

emerged in this period, though the actor-manager **Lope de Rueda** achieved some success. In the latter half of the 16th century several elements and influences combined to produce the climate in which the *comedia* was to develop. Frequent visits by Italian **commedia dell'arte** troupes influenced public taste and playwrights. Religious drama continued to develop, with an increasing use of allegory, and learned elements were introduced through the plays written for students by university teachers. Dominated by the Jesuits, these plays formed part of the education of all the great dramatists of the period.

So far very little classical tragedy had been produced in Spain. Authors like Bermúdez and Virués began to write such plays in the later part of the 16th century, the influences being, as in England, Senecan rather than Greek, and the plays tending to be rather novelesque. **Juan de la Cueva** had greater success by creating a more 'national' tragedy based on episodes from the rich Spanish ballad tradition. **Cervantes**, too, wrote numerous full-scale plays, but achieved little success in the theatre.

The controversy between the supporters of classical precepts in drama and those favouring the national hybrid form continued into the early years of the 17th century. With it went a furious row over the morality of the theatre, led by the Jesuits, who attacked the immoral life of performers and the incitement to sin in the material. The theatre remained immensely popular, however, especially after the establishment of fixed public theatres, known as *corrales*, in all major cities. Profits from these theatres went to maintain charitable institutions, which came to rely on this source of revenue. As a result, closures of the theatres during periods of royal mourning were usually kept to a minimum.

While the one-act short comedy, called *paso* or *entremés*, continued to flourish, the establishment of the full-length *comedia* was due largely to the enormous talent of **Lope de Vega**. He perfected the *comedia* in three acts using verse of varied rhythms, with many changes of rhyme in each act. The logical three-movement form of exposition, development and resolution made for a theatre of action rather than character-drawing. As in England, there was no strict separation of comedy and tragedy, and little classical material was used before the age of **Calderón**. Sources used were

Corral de Comedias, Almagro, Ciudad Real, Spain.

Spanish history, legends and ballads, and the Italian *novelle*. Lives of the saints, biblical stories and other religious material were also greatly used. Stock characters included an aged father, pairs of noble lovers and comic servants, especially the *gracioso*, who had all the best lines. There was often also a foolish old servant, or *escudero*, but older women and mothers were rarely depicted.

The great themes of drama in this period were Religion, Honour, and Love. Religion in Spain meant of course the Roman Catholic faith, and its dramatization was naturally totally orthodox. However, the secular values of society and individual status, expressed in terms of a code of honour, dominated other forms of drama. The Spanish view of honour, as in other Mediterranean countries, made not only rank, wealth and reputation essential criteria, but also the chastity of the female members of one's family. Hence a small group of plays deal with the murder of wives suspected of adultery, and in plays of the *capa y espada* type, honour obliges the parent or guardian of an unmarried woman to keep her from contact with men, obliging lovers to court secretly. In these comic plays, the problem is resolved when the lovers agree to marry. The theme of love pervades almost every play of the period, even the *comedia de santo*. Love at first sight is common, and freedom of choice in marriage almost always defended. The reduction of independent or man-hating women by the power of love is a popular theme.

Within Lope's lifetime many playwrights followed his lead to supply the *corrales*, since there was a very rapid turnover of plays. Amongst many talented authors, Montalbán and Vélez de Guevara are worthy of mention. **Alarcón y Mendoza** wrote comedies of social criticism attacking the vices of Spanish society, and **Mira de Amescua** wrote more exuberant if less careful plays. Regional centres were also important, **Guillén de Castro** leading a thriving Valencian school, while the genius of **Tirso de Molina** places him only a little behind Lope and Calderón.

From the 1620s the attacks of the moralists and the evolution of public taste brought a demand for a more responsible and moral theatre. From this time *refundiciones*, the reworking of old plots, became common, both because of the difficulty of finding new themes and the feeling that many old ones could be improved artistically and morally. Hand in hand with these trends went a more elevated, baroque style of language. The author who excelled at this later form of the *comedia* was Calderón de la Barca, a genius as great as Lope. Where Lope was spontaneous and natural, Calderón impresses with his intellect, and frequently his moral instruction, though he was equally renowned for his witty comedies. After 1640 Calderón wrote increasingly for the new royal theatre, the Coliseo, which though similar in plan to the *corrales* had a proscenium arch, wings, backcloth and painted scenery introduced from Italy by Cosme Lotti, who worked in Spain till 1643. It also had more elaborate stage machinery for special effects.

Of the followers of Calderón, the best were undoubtedly **Moreto**, who excelled in comedy, and **Rojas Zorrilla**, who made his name in Senecan tragedy. Other playwrights of the period were Cubillo de Aragón, Solís y Ribadeneyra, Coello y Ochoa, and

Bances Candamo, the last notable dramatist of the age. In effect by the death of Calderón the great days of Spanish theatre were long over.

The accession of the Bourbon dynasty after 1700 did not immediately bring about a change in dramatic styles, but a lack of talented authors meant that few plays of note were written at this period. Golden Age plays continued to be performed, though often mutilated to suit the changing taste of the times. The use of *tramoyas* (spectacular stage machinery) was now essential to' the success of a play. Only Cañizares and Antonio de Zamora wrote works in any way memorable, with a new variety of verse-forms and greater use of music.

Misgivings about the trivial nature of many plays of this period and the influence of French taste led to a new interest in classical forms, first expressed by Ignacio de Luzán in his *Poética* of 1737. Luzán's concern for public morality and reason led him to a move towards classical tragedy. His friend Montiano was the first to attempt the form, though the elder **Moratín**'s tragedies were better both in structure and use of verse-forms. Other authors of the 1760s and 1770s include Cadalso, López de Ayala and García de la Huerta, using Spanish as well as classical subjects, while the essayist Jovellanos wrote a few plays with a tendency towards the French *comédie larmoyante*. At the same time the comic theatre was also developing. The *sainetes* of Ramón de la Cruz, parodying tragic formulae or depicting the low-life of Madrid, were very popular. The full-length comedy was transformed by **Leandro Fernández de Moratín**, son of the tragedian, whose neoclassical comedies on Enlightenment values and social questions set the tone for comic writing for the next 50 years.

In the early years of the 19th century a few tragedies on patriotic themes were still being written, but spectacle still dominated the stage. Of the few notable playwrights before the romantic period, Martínez de la Rosa wrote comedies, political plays and heroic tragedies with romantic trappings, while Angel Saavedra, later Duque de Rivas, preferred Moorish or Medieval settings. With the full tide of romanticism sweeping through Spain after 1833, historical drama became the mode. Worthy of mention are García Gutiérrez, **José Zorrilla**, and Hartzenbusch, son of a German immigrant, whose work in editing Golden Age plays was as important as his tragedies of doomed historical lovers. The decline in European theatre between the end of the romantic period and the rise of Russian and Scandinavian drama in the 1870s was particularly marked in Spain. The prolific output of Bretón de los Herreros and Ventura de la Vega did little to halt this decline, though the latter paved the way for new developments. Historical drama dragged on in debased form until the end of the century in the melodramas of **Echegaray**, but the **zarzuela**, moribund for 150 years, now came into vogue again as a form of light operetta. When reform and renovation came in the theatre, it was in a very timid form, that of the *alta comedia*, dealing with social problems of the high bourgeoisie. Two playwrights worthy of mention in this genre are **Tamayo y Baus** and López de Ayala. The apparent revival was short-lived, however, and the domination of the end of the century by Echegaray demonstrated the essential decadence and mediocrity reigning in the theatre, which was now patronized almost entirely by the upper middle classes who liked to be moved to tears or indignation but would not tolerate any questioning of the social order. Thus Galdós's dramatizations of his novels, though sometimes fine plays, were never popular. The fragmentation of styles and lack of a genius to please all sections of society were the essential problems.

The essayists of the literary generation of 1898 all tried their hand at playwriting, but had no immediate effect on drama in the early 1900s. The most interesting developments henceforth would be mainly outside the commercial theatre. The *alta comedia* was improved somewhat by the sharply satirical but shallow plays of **Benavente**. Other forms popular in the early years of the century were the one-act *costumbrismo* plays, depending on local colour and traditional types, typified by the large output of the brothers **Alvarez Quintero**. The chief exponent of the *zarzuela*, Carlos Arniches, also wrote *costumbrismo* plays, occasionally adding an element of degradation and indignation which anticipated the **esperpento**. Poetic drama was also popular, Martínez Sierra's examples, written in collaboration with his wife, being less important than his work as director of the Teatro Eslava in Madrid, where he introduced a wide range of European drama, as Gual had done at the Teatro Intim in Barcelona from 1903. **Valle-Inclán** also tried poetic drama and various forms of comedy and farce before developing the *esperpento*, a bitter scathing satire using a form of alienation effect, and the first to break out of the old forms.

Few other playwrights of the period are noteworthy apart from **Jacinto Grau**, who had more success with his serious drama abroad than in Spain. Only **García Lorca** had belated and indeed posthumous success with his peasant tragedies and other plays. The Republican government (1931–6) sponsored touring companies to bring theatre back to the people, the Teatro del pueblo, directed by **Casona**, and the Teatro Universitario, known as La Barraca, run by García Lorca and others.

The disasters of the Civil War (1936–9) resulted in death or exile for many playwrights and a heavy censorship for those who remained. The safe, comfortable plays of Benavente continued to pour out with no evident development or originality. Casona continued to work outside Spain, and López Rubio and Ruiz Iriarte followed his precepts in what became known as *teatro de evasión*, on the theme of the need for escapism, though often only hinting at a serious message. Writers such as Mihura and Laiglesia continued the absurd comic traditions of **Jardiel Poncela**, while Calvo Sotelo concentrated on political and moral themes from a conservative, Catholic viewpoint.

In the 1950s and 60s **Buero Vallejo** achieved a respectable reputation with symbolic tragedies and social dramas, his work in the latter field being continued by Carlos Muñiz, Ricardo Buded and Lauro Olmo in their plays on working class poverty and degradation. **Alfonso Sastre**, working outside the commercial theatre in university drama groups, wrote a socially committed drama which, though seldom outspoken, was rarely permitted to be performed, though it was published. The seeds of change were sown in the late 1960s with the establishment of independent theatre groups, such as Tábano and El Búho, founded by Juan Margallo, Los Goliardos, founded by Angel Facio, and Els Joglars and Els Comedians in Catalonia. Seeking a different mode of expression from the heavily censored conventional theatre, they combined techniques such as ritual, mime, acrobatics, grotesque masks and music to form a total theatrical experience, often with a satirical or anti-establishment element, collective creation being more common than texts by individual authors.

The death of Franco (1975) and the restoration of democracy (1977) brought about a relaxation of censorship and, in the political sphere, a degree of autonomy for the principal Spanish regions, which began to encourage their own cultures and languages once again. National, regional and local sponsorship of the theatre has greatly increased, Drama Centres have been set up, and an impressive number of festivals established, the most important being those of Almagro (founded 1977 in the restored *corral*), Madrid, and Barcelona. The Independent theatre groups have become more stable with government support, and playwrights such as Fermín Cabal and Alonso de Santos are recognized as the most important voices of the contemporary theatre. A broad range of European theatre can now be seen and opera, *zarzuela* and cabaret are buoyant. With so much enthusiasm and vitality, the Spanish theatre still has to capture a wider audience if momentum is to be maintained. CL

See: G. G. Brown, *The Twentieth Century (A Literary History of Spain)* ed. R. O. Jones, London, 1971; N. Glendinning, *The Eighteenth Century (A Literary History of Spain)* ed. R. O. Jones, London, 1972; D. L. Shaw, *The Nineteenth Century (A Literary History of Spain)* ed. R. O. Jones, London, 1970; N. D. Shergold, *A History of the Spanish Stage from Medieval Times until the End of the 17th Century*, Oxford, 1967; E. M. Wilson, *Spanish Drama of the Golden Age*, Oxford, 1969.

Spencer, Gabriel (d. 1598) English actor, who joined the **Admiral's Men** after the dissolution of Pembroke's Men in 1597. There is no record of the parts he played, though **Henslowe** is known to have valued him. Spencer is remembered only for his death, 'slain in Hogsdon fields by the hands of Benjamin Jonson bricklayer', as Henslowe wrote to **Edward Alleyn**. In 1596 Spencer had killed a man who attacked him with a candlestick. We do not know the cause of his quarrel with **Jonson**. PT

Sperr, Martin (1944–) German dramatist, whose first play *Hunting Scenes from Lower Bavaria* (1966) provides the earliest example of the contemporary **Volksstück**. Using village life as a microcosm of social attitudes, it focuses on the persecution of a homosexual. Influenced by **Edward Bond**, whose play *Saved* Sperr translated for **Peter Stein**'s 1967 production in Munich, his extreme realism is designed as 'shock theatre'. As with **Wolfgang Bauer**, his use of sex games and sadism results in sensationalism and made his plays notorious. But the ironically idyllic endings of *Tales from Landshut* (1967) or *Munich Freedom* (1971), showing capitalism as literally murderous or suicidal, owe more to **Horváth**. CI

Sprechstimme The possible relations of music with words have always preoccupied composers of opera. (See **recitative** and **mélodrame**.) *Sprechstimme* (literally 'speech voice') has been used in the 20th century to bring the singer's utterance closer to speech than was the case with traditional recitative. The rise and fall of the voice is indicated, but there is no precise pitch indication. There has always been a tendency for singers to move towards *Sprechstimme* at intense moments during the action of an opera: e.g. Tosca's last words at the end of Act II of **Puccini**'s opera. Notable use of *Sprechstimme* proper occurs in *Wozzeck* (1925) and *Lulu* (1937) by Alban Berg (1885–1935) and *Moses and Aaron* (1957) by Arnold Schoenberg (1874–1951). Sometimes a distinction is made between *Sprechstimme* and *Sprechgesang* (literally 'speech song'), but essentially both signify singing that approaches speech.   GH

Spurling, John (1936–) British dramatist, whose innovative plays sought to examine historical themes from several points of view. *MacRune's Guevara* (1969) which was produced by the **National Theatre** gives an account of the life of the Bolivian revolutionary hero, Che Guevara, as interpreted by the dead Scottish artist, MacRune, a marxist, and the narrator who deciphers MacRune's drawings, Edward Hotel. This multi-viewpoint approach allows Spurling to discuss the nature of political myths; and *In the Heart of the British Museum* (1971) extends this technique into the consideration of three kinds of cultural revolutions, in China during the 1960s, in Ovid's Rome and in the Aztec empire, when Quetzalcoatl was succeeded by Texcatlipoca as god. *The British Empire, Part One* (1980), which was staged in the studio theatre of the **Birmingham Rep**, vividly contrasted different episodes of British colonial history by placing them on side platforms, with a promenade audience. Spurling has likened his ideal theatre to an art gallery. A witty and sophisticated writer, Spurling has trouble in conveying information to audiences who are less well-informed than he is: and his plays, which include *Shades of Heathcliff* (1971), *Death of Captain Doughty* (1973), *Coming Ashore in Guadaloupe* (1976) and *Antigone Through a Looking Glass* (1979), have been staged mainly in studio and fringe theatres.   JE

Squarzina, Luigi (1922–) Italian director and playwright. Trained at the Academy of Dramatic Art in Rome, since the late 1940s he has been one of the most active and versatile directors in the Italian theatre for both classic and modern drama. Between 1962 and 1976 he was artistic director of the Teatro Stabile in Genoa, and from 1976 to 1983 of the Teatro Stabile in Rome. His work on classic texts, in particular those of **Goldoni**, **Pirandello** and **Shakespeare**, has been marked by an intelligent and sensitive orchestration that both serves and illuminates the text. He was one of the first to re-explore the stage possibilities of **D'Annunzio**'s plays after their post-war neglect. Among his most recent work may be noted *Measure for Measure* (1976), *Timon of Athens* (1983, only the second time the play had been given a professional production in Italy), and Pirandello's *Ciascuno a suo Modo* (*Each in His Own Way*, 1984). He has written a number of plays on political themes and is a notable commentator on the condition of the contemporary Italian stage.   KR

Sri Lanka The theatre of Sri Lanka originated in the various rituals and ceremonies of the folk religions that are practised throughout the island. Unlike India – the dominant culture of the region, which had a classical tradition of drama on which to build – the Sinhalese writers had no classical model, except that provided by the Sanskrit tradition. The only possible explanation for the absence of a classical tradition of drama of Sri Lanka is that the Buddhist monks were the principal writers in ancient times and considered drama a taboo art form and so confined their efforts to poetry and narrative stories.

The elaborate ceremonies connected with the worship and propitiation of the numerous folk deities of the island seem to have inspired the dramatic impulse. In form alone, the rituals have a strong dramatic character, even though they cannot be considered theatre. For example, the *Rata Yakuma* ceremony, which is performed to ensure the safe delivery of a child, to protect the child in the womb, ensuring the health of the infant already born, or to make a barren woman conceive, has the following dramatic action: first, a sacrificial altar is constructed from bamboo stems and coconut leaves. Inside the altar are seven smaller altars dedicated to the Seven Barren Queens. The ceremony begins with evening offerings consisting of chanted invocatory stanzas accompanied by drumming and dancing. Then three exorcists approach the site of the ceremony dressed in female attire. They are questioned by the chief exorcist or a drummer in order to reveal the purpose of the ceremony. Then the exorcist chants the legend of the Seven Barren Queens. Next, an exorcist wraps a white cloth around his head and after chanting verses spreads the cloth on the altar and throws incense on the flames of a torch which causes the whole altar to seem to burst into flames. This is an enactment of the legend of the demons' birth. Then follows the Twelvefold Ritual in which the seven daughters present a cloth to the Dipankara Buddha and thus attain permission to cause illness to human beings and eventually, through sacrificial offerings are willing to relinquish their control.

At the conclusion of the Twelvefold Ritual, the exorcist depicts in mime how the Barren Queens wore a cloth to be offered to the Dipankara Buddha. During the action which follows a man comes forward and the exorcist leads him around the performance area and mimes the Origin of the Mat, a symbolic fertility rite. Through song and mime, the exorcist relates the birth and swaddling of a child. Eventually, he symbolically places the child in the arms of the parent and pronounces blessings on the mother and later presents the child to the relatives of the parent, as well as other individuals gathered to watch the ceremony and, in turn, he receives presents from the family.

Ceremonies, such as these, often require the 'patient' himself or an exorcist to dress in the supposed likeness of the 'afflictor', wearing elaborate makeup or masks and costumes and brandishing various weapons. In the process of introduction which may include dancing to musical accompaniment, the patient or performer may become possessed and speak in the voice of the demon communicating with the priest who asks numerous questions. These transitions occur which begin with rituals and end with rituals and closely resemble dramas in the structure of the acts that occur between them. During the ceremonies, offerings are made to appease the demon, sometimes in the form of a cock whose blood is either symbolically or actually shed or in the form of human sacrifices depicted through effigies, dolls or their symbolic representations. Ceremonies usually begin in the evening and continue the entire night without reaching a conclusion until midday.

In some ritual events, dramatic interludes using mime and comic dialogue have been added to entertain the audience and occasionally for ritual purposes. These interludes break up the tedium of the long hours of the ceremonies and serve to entertain the participants.

Perhaps one of the most interesting and popular of these interludes is that of the Brahmins from the Port of Vadiga which occurs in a ritual intended to dispel evil influence that may accrue to a person who is suspected of having evil charms performed against him.

The interlude depicts the arrival in Sri Lanka of some Brahmins who are versed in the ritual. When they enter they see a ceremony being performed and begin to question what is going on. Because they cannot speak Sinhalese they have trouble communicating with the exorcist, a situation which results in a great deal of humour. Finally, it is discovered that the Brahmins speak Pali, which is understood in Sri Lanka, and a dialogue commences between them and one of the exorcists in a kind of pseudo-Pali which is considered very amusing. At the conclusion of the ritual, they dance, bless the patient and exit, allowing the ritual ceremonies to proceed.

Among the specific forms in which ritual and drama are almost equally balanced are the **Sokari** and the **Kolam**. Both forms use striking and colourful masks. The date of their origin has not yet been determined. In contrast, the **Nadagama** is a full-scale form of folk theatre with a considerable body of dramatic literature and a specific history beginning in the early 19th century. The **Rukada** puppet theatre sprang from the *Nadagama*, although the exact date of its origin cannot be traced.

In the late 19th century, the **Pasku**, or Passion play, was born and popularized among a segment of the population.

Modern theatre Modern drama, designed to appeal to urban audiences, did not get a start until the last decade of the 19th century in Colombo. It was inspired by the immense success of a touring troupe from Bombay – Baliwallas's Elphinstone Dramatic Company which appeared in the 1880s. The style of theatre that so struck the imagination of Colombo audiences of the time was the Parsi musical. It combined popular Hindustani music with techniques borrowed from the amateur English theatre of India – proscenium arch stages, painted changeable scenery, elaborate costumes, declamatory acting and Western-style seating within an enclosed building designed exclusively for the purpose of performance. The popularity of the Parsi musical prompted Colombo writers to imitate the Parsi models with Sinhalese dialogue and songs set to Hindustani tunes. The resultant form was known as *Nurti*, or new drama, which gained in popularity soon ousting the *Nadagama* music. Drama became a popular medium of expression and low cost play editions soon became available. Among the best-known writers was John de Silva (1857–1922) whose popularity eventually led to the construction of a theatre named in his honour. He borrowed ideas from the Sanskrit drama and combined them with those of the Parsi musicals. His plays were staged by the Arya Subadha Natya Sabha and later by the Vijaya Ranga Sabha. The first Sinhalese *Nurti* was C. Don Bastian's *Romeo and Juliet* staged in 1884 and published in 1885. The play was not a translation of **Shakespeare**'s work but was based on an adaptation by D. J. Wijesingha.

With the *Nurti* women were introduced to the stage for the first time. This caused a reluctance of the educated middle class among people of Colombo to patronize the theatre. *Nurti*'s real popularity was realized among the working-class people of the smaller towns and cities and it is still preserved today by bands of amateur theatrical organizations which present performances during the major Buddhist religious festivals. Although these activities are not called *Nurti*, they maintain the same amalgam of melodrama and comedy, song and declaimed dialogue and loose episodic structure as *Nurti*. The performances are enacted on high stages and are given free for sightseers who throng the streets during festival nights. In Colombo, *Nurti* declined and disappeared with the advent of the films in the 1930s. Symbolically, its death knell was sounded with the conversion of Colombo's Tower Hall to a cinema.

During the 1920s and 1930s the *Nurti* was replaced by a brand of playwriting known by an actor who made the plays successful – Eddie Jayamanna. *Jayamanna* plays satirized the middle and upper middle classes of Colombo. They maintained a pretence of using literary language in which the characters sometimes burst into song. Besides the acting of Eddie Jayamanna, the plays are also remembered for the singing of Rukmini Devi. Eventually, the *Jayamanna* plays were adapted into the films and have long since disappeared from the stage.

In the 1940s and 1950s straight plays were composed in prose dialogue and colloquial language written by students of the Sinhalese Society of the University College, Colombo, which is now the University of Ceylon. The plays were Sinhalese translations and adaptations of modern Western classics by **Molière**, **Wilde** and **Chekhov**. They were written by the intelligentsia for the intelligentsia.

In 1956 Ediriweera Sarachchandra's dramatization of a Buddhist Jataka tale, entitled *Maname*, broke new ground by attempting to formulate an indigenous style of writing using the *Nadagama*, *Sokari*, *Thovil* and folk dance music coupled with a serious theme meant for intellectuals. This led to a split among the writers into those favouring realism and those opposed to it. By the mid-1960s the paths of the writers began to converge.

Today, modern theatre in Sri Lanka is still a part-time occupation for almost all those engaged in it. Short-term workshops and symposia provide the only training for practitioners except for their own performances. By custom, playwrights usually serve as directors and producers and groups of actors in urban centres generally disband after a show has been completed. Theatre facilities are minimal, except in Colombo. But a large and loyal following for modern theatre has developed outside the urban centres as a result of touring companies who carry their lighting equipment and scenery with them and who set up their shows in makeshift facilities in cinema houses and schools.

Interest in drama has been prompted by the young in island-wide drama competitions conducted by the Ministry of Cultural Affairs through the Department of Cultural Affairs which showcase young talent. Drama and theatre have recently been adapted as part of the school curriculum and training of drama teachers has proved quite successful at the University of Sri Lanka. FaR

Stage lighting Stage lighting, particularly in the 100 years since the first use of electricity in the theatre, has had a profound effect upon staging, scenery, styles of production and acting, and even upon the shape of the theatre building itself. But its impact must be seen against a continuum that takes us back centuries.

Sophisticated electric lighting now employs computers and precisely focused lighting instruments subtly to control the composition, intensity, and colour of light. Such control allows atmospheric light to fill the theatrical space, to reveal the living actor and unify him with his stage environment. Its development has encouraged a new, specialist profession of the lighting designer.

Theatre has always used the technology of its period. Stage lighting did not begin with electricity. Its important role in the theatre has been recognized since the 16th century. During the days of candle, oil lamp and gas, great ingenuity was employed to illuminate the stage and provide atmosphere and effects. Many principles concerning the placement of lighting, the basic types of instrument and even the intentions of the lighting designer were conceived a surprisingly long time ago.

Theatre began outdoors: God said 'Let there be light' and he liked what he saw. Jehovah, Apollo, Osiris – all religions have recognized light as a fundamental element, the one which enables us to see. From the most ancient times, light and its primeval influence on our every thought, emotion and action has been seen as a harbinger of things to come, as a messenger from the supernatural and as a constantly changing companion that shapes all life on earth.

The theatre evolved from religious ritual. The moving of the sun across the sky, the waxing and waning of the moon, the wheeling firmament of stars, the seasons, all played an important role in the life of early man. Primitive theatre used this natural light. As the open-air theatres of ancient Egypt, Crete and Greece developed and became more formalized, the cycle of natural light would play a part.

The more comfort-loving audiences of ancient Rome were protected from the weather by coloured awnings that could be drawn over the semicircular auditorium. Presumably daylight was still the predominant light source, although after dark, torches, braziers, fires and oil lamps were put to theatrical use, for they were the only means of dispelling darkness. (Nero's 'concert lighting' became the stuff of legends.)

The earliest custom-built theatres of England were also open to the elements and natural light. These theatres had a flexible, but usually thrust-shaped stage, surrounded by the audience. The stage roof space concealed the hoisting machinery for the descent of gods and visions, and the ceiling was painted to represent the heavens. (Light was also represented in this way in the surprisingly similar forms of theatre across the world in China.) The beauty of light has never been more exquisitely described in words than by **Shakespeare**, but perhaps even he used flame to illuminate a gloomy winter matinee performance, or to enhance the drama.

In *Seven Deadly Sins of London* (1606), **Thomas Dekker** described a shuttered city 'like a private playhouse, when the windows are clampt down, as if some nocturnal or dismal tragedy were presently to be acted'. Indoor performances must also have taken place, and perhaps had done so since the cave dwellers. No doubt, light was admitted or shuttered and artificial light kindled or put out, according to the show, the time of day and the ingenuity of the ancient organizers.

The church was very organized indeed. Religious ceremony has always employed the symbolism of light, but the 15th century marks a significant beginning to the employment of artificial light: a Russian bishop describes a performance by Brunelleschi (1377–1446) in the church of San Felice, Florence, of *The Annunciation*. From a revolving globe, surrounded by circles of light, illuminating translucent clouds, which supported eight cherubim, was lowered another, internally lit globe, containing the Angel Gabriel. This could be darkened by remote control as he stepped out to speak to Mary. As the angel returned and rose into the air, the light blazed forth again. Other descriptions of the period reveal more spectacular effects, with over 1,000 oil lamps, diagonal and tracking movements of tableaux and lighting, rays of fire, glistering fireworks and glowing clouds – all recreating in three dimensions the wonders of Renaissance painting and pointing the way to the stagecraft that was soon to come.

But in the open-air mystery plays of more northern Europe, how was light evoked? The mansion or wagon depicting hell's mouth probably belched out real flame and smoke. But a stage direction of 1501 in the Mons Passion reads 'See to it that the painter goes to Paradise to paint Raphael's face red.' In the same play, Christ is described with gold hands and feet and 'let there be a big sun behind him'. Painting the features, metal reflective haloes or even a brightly polished basin to reflect the sunlight were used, some indications of which are to be found in the Revello Passion of 1483.

The Italian Renaissance theatre became the cradle of stage lighting. Artificial light must have possessed great power over people's imagination. For most of the population, darkness, that began as the sun set each day, was only occasionally broken by flame, torch or guttering smoky candle.

The courts of 16th-century Italy provided the opportunity. First in 1514 is a description of **Peruzzi**'s design of *La Calandria*, one of the earliest views of the use of perspective on the stage. 'One cannot imagine how in so narrow a space he could build up so many palaces . . . with great knowledge he also arranged the sources of light, the inner light that increases the perspective illusion'. In 1580 we have the author **Guarini**, extolling the virtue and economy of good lighting for his plays: 'Without artificial lighting, the scene will be deprived of its beauty . . . besides expenses will be reduced . . . for the beauty that can be created by light can be made up only by great expense in adorning devices'.

A pupil of Peruzzi, **Serlio** (1475–1554), built a theatre in Vicenza during the 1530s, and in 1545 published *Architettura* which describes contemporary theatrical methods. His drawings of a semicircular theatre with shallow perspective scenes are part of theatre history. His lighting descriptions, which are less well known, bring his woodcut renderings to life. He describes 'General stage light', which lights the whole stage, 'Decorative light', ornamenting the perspective picture, and 'Mobile light' that often simulates the sun or moon moving across the sky.

General light is achieved by torches and chandeliers hung above and to the front of the stage, but the chandelier has reflective glass vessels filled with liquid to aim the light toward the stage. 'It is better to illuminate the scene from the middle because of the greater power of a light hanging in the centre' he states, but he also mentions 'A large number of lights are placed leaning at the front of the scene' – the first mention of footlights?

The first recorded stage lighting instrument was the *bozze*. This was a glass vessel of various convex and concave shapes, filled either with oil and wick when used as a lamp, or with coloured liquids as a colour medium, lens or reflector. These, fixed to boards behind holes in the scene, lit up the windows of the street or the many coloured silk transparencies of the pastoral scene.

When a strong light is needed 'you put a torch behind a glass and behind, a barber's basin well burnished'. Thus the spotlight had also arrived. The stage, glowing with multi-coloured, flickering light, shining with encrusted and translucent scenery and costumes that shimmered with jewels, must have been an astonishing and lovely spectacle.

In about 1565, **Leoni Di Sommi** (1527–92), a dramatist and stage designer of Mantua, anticipated **Gordon Craig** by 350 years and wrote *Four Dialogues on Scenic Representation* in which his protagonists discourse upon mood and atmosphere. From a stage expressing joy, brightness and life with brilliant and glowing colours, they discuss the onset of tragedy with much of the lighting dimmed or put out. 'This created a profound impression of horror . . . and won universal praise.'

Di Somi pointed out that the coloured lens-like *bozze* not only coloured the light effectively but also reduced glare. He recommended the use of mirrors to amplify the lights, but also to allow them to be placed further from the stage, hidden from view behind the wings, to reduce obnoxious smoke. Smoke and heat were severe problems for hundreds of years.

Finally Di Somi championed the darkened auditorium: 'A man in the shade sees more distinctly an object illuminated from afar.' Further: 'you obviate smoke fumes and render the seeing clearer'. Lastly: 'you save the Duke fifty ducats in respect of the torches usually set'.

Truly, stage lighting has begun!

Angelo Ingeneri (1550–1613) was the scene designer for the famed Teatro Olimpico in Vicenza in 1585. He described lighting in 1598 as 'one matter of supreme theatrical importance'. He also said 'The darker the auditorium, the more luminous seems the stage.' He wanted light sources concealed and was concerned that the actors' faces must be well lit. To this end he proposed the first flown lighting position over the front of the stage: 'A valance . . . on the inner side fitted with lamps having tinsel reflectors'. Ingeneri described the use of gauze to give an effect of mystery and he stressed the creative use of light and darkness to enhance the drama.

Also in Italy, **Bernardo Buontalenti** (1536–1608) worked on a stage at Uffizi, which used about 100 oil lamps with four wicks each, including footlights behind an ornamental balustrade. The lighting crew were told to take great care in trimming the wicks and refilling the lamps.

Stage lighting was becoming systematized and **Sabbattini** (1574–1654) in his *Manual for Theatrical Scene and Machines* (1638) describes that system in words and drawings. He evaluates the merits and problems of oil lamps and candles and sketches the fittings. He illustrates a method of remote dimming by lowering tin cylinders on cords over each light. He describes proscenium lights, footlights and sidelights behind the wings ('lights must be strongly fixed so they do not shake during the dances'). Sabbattini started a discussion on the problems of footlights that was to last over 300 years. 'The disadvantages outweigh the advantages. You believe that you make the stage brighter, but it actually becomes darker. Heat, dazzle and smell force the actors backward, their legs and costumes are brighter than their pale and haggard faces and a haze of smoke creates a barrier to clear vision.' Sabbattini also mentions a concealed upstage row of lamps, parallel to the footlights, to light ground rows and backcloths. A German who studied in Italy, **Josef Furttenbach** (1591–1667), and published *Architectura Recreationis* in 1640, gives a detailed description of lighting, which includes *bozzi* with reflectors in a seven-foot-deep upstage pit, as well as, for the first time, rows of lamps overhead 'between the clouds'. This completed the repertoire of Renaissance lighting that created precedents for patterns of thought and practice that still pertain today.

As the Renaissance transformed itself into the elaborations of the Baroque, Italian influence spread across

A candle-snuffer trimming the footlights.

Europe, with each country emphasizing one aspect or another according to their own theatrical tradition.

In England, **Inigo Jones** (1573–1652) bought and used some *bozzi* in 1609. He opened English theatre to Italian-style spectacle and employed multi-coloured lights in profusion. He vividly used translucencies and produced extraordinary effects of nature, but his more old fashioned flambeaux torches, used in the Whitehall Banqueting Room, damaged the ceiling paintings and theatrical performances there were stopped.

The Puritan Revolution brought English theatre to a halt, but the future King Charles II, living in France, saw much of theatrical development in the French court. In 1660, Richard Flecknoe in *A Discourse of the English Stage* said 'We in England are only scholars and learners yet . . . especially not knowing how to place our lights, for the more advantage and illuminating of the scenes.'

With the English Restoration, London theatres were built and restored, but were now indoors. The **Cock-pit** (1660) had two chandeliers and five pairs of sconces. In the Hall Theatre (1665) tin lanterns and reflectors are described, but a few years later these were supplanted by 130 candlesticks with reflectors. Footlights too are described in February 1670. The frontispiece to *The Wits*, 1672, shows an indoor stage but with an almost Elizabethan thrust, lit with chandeliers and footlights.

In France, the court led the way to innovation. In 1581 the *Balet Comique de La Reine* was performed. The famous sketch of this production shows a courtyard space with audience on three sides, but the settings are simultaneously spread through parts of the hall, like medieval 'mansions'. Detailed descriptions tell of scenery glittering with gold and jewels, shining in the light of many lamps. Gauzes and glowing translucencies, transparent coloured glasses – all the techniques of Renaissance lighting must have made a magical spectacle, which sadly only comes to us today through an inadequate black and white engraving.

In 1641 in Paris, Cardinal **Richelieu** began the horseshoe-shaped **Palais-Royal** theatre, where **Molière** was later to perform. The width of the proscenium was only 9.5 metres and the stage depth 17.55 metres. In 1687, Nicodemus Tessin, a Swedish architect touring Europe, describes the lighting. Footlights with 50 lamps, each with 5 flames, supplemented candles on vertical lighting poles at either side of the stage and chandeliers in the auditorium. The French theatre blazed with light throughout, unlike the Italian, where more frequently the auditorium was darkened to increase the impact of the stage.

Tessin also wrote of his experiences in the Italian theatre. In Venice he visited the San Giovanni Grisostomo. The lighting is developed from the principles of Sabbattini. The chandeliers at the front of the auditorium are hoisted out of sight to darken the auditorium and the footlights may be gradually raised or lowered. Side lighting is now on turnable poles to enable the brightness to be varied and portable lighting strips may be attached to wing trolleys or set pieces.

The Italian stage rapidly grew in width and depth. A scene could be created up to 40 metres in depth. Wings, sliding in grooves, could be swiftly changed and backcloths could be flown in to vary the depth of the stage. Machines could move huge tableaux with performers and lights up and down and diagonally.

Mirrors, glass and translucency made spectacular effects.

Contrasts of light and shade enhanced the sense of depth of the stage and increasingly asymmetry and oblique perspective scenery became popular. **Ferdinando Bibiena** (1657–1743) and his family led the movement that produced astonishing vistas on the stage. Asymmetrical scenery with great columns or trees in the middle of the stage, behind which lights could be hidden, must have greatly improved the possibility of lighting the darker middle of the backcloth.

An Italian, who worked extensively in Paris, **G. N. Servandoni** (1695–1766), developed further the use of distorted perspective and transparencies to create the impression of vast distances and spectacle. In 1738 he opened his 'Spectacle d'optique' in the **Salle des Machines**, Paris, with a stage 40 metres deep. From a darkened auditorium, spectators watched performances depicting mythological events, which used live and painted figures in gigantic settings. 'A large number of lamps were so well arranged that it all resembled a tableau of a perfectly arranged chiaroscuro' and 'that which is perfectly arranged is daylight' were two complementary observations. Servandoni himself observed that 'expenses for the lighting had been no less than 10,000 francs, but that the admission-fees had yielded nearly 20,000 francs'. Outside the conventional theatre, such spectacles, under the direction of leading stage designers such as **De Loutherbourg** (in 1781) and Daguerre (in 1822), proved their popularity time and again. Their value as a place of experiment, which returns benefit to the theatre, has parallels for today, where high budget, industrial theatre or rock and roll spectacle provide a similar opportunity for development.

England's great actor and director, **David Garrick** (1717–79), travelled to the Continent in 1765 and returned determined to modernize lighting at his **Theatre Royal, Drury Lane**. A friend, Jean Monnet of the Paris Opéra-Comique, sent samples of stage lighting equipment to London. They were a success: 'The public were agreeably surprised to see the stage illuminated with a strong and clear light, and the rings removed that used to supply it.' Garrick introduced wing and footlights with reflectors and removed the overhanging chandeliers. Garrick's great scene designer was P. J. De Loutherbourg (1740–1812), a master of the creation of atmosphere who used colour-changing silks on his side lighting. In 1772 he wrote to Garrick assuming that he was to be responsible for lighting his designs at Drury Lane. At the **Comédie-Française**, a designer, Ferdinando Quaglio, stated that he needed one whole day to arrange the scenery and lighting: 'The illumination should be to my taste and regardless of expense, particularly during the first two or three nights.' He also stipulated his desire for billing on the posters. The management were grudging. They might provide billing, but the lighting would be arranged by the theatre 'as was habitual'. However M. Quaglio 'could have access to the stage, provided no other performance was jeopardized'.

In 1790 George Saunders wrote *A Treatise on Theatres*. He recommends placing 'reverberators' on the front of the near-stage boxes and mentions these front of house spotlights being used successfully at several theatres including Blenheim.

The Warsaw Court Theatre, 1791. The stage, auditorium and orchestra pit are all lit by candles.

Stage lighting was continually growing brighter. At the Comédie-Française in 1719, 48 tallow candles were used in the footlights. In 1783 there were 128 of the more efficient, but more expensive wax candles. In 1784 the Argand lamp was developed. This was an oil lamp but, for the first time, with a chimney. It was as bright as about a dozen wax candles. Used with reflectors it created new conditions on the stage, which contributed toward the reduction of makeup, new styles of costume and, most importantly, encouraged another step toward more naturalistic acting.

In 1803, the **Lyceum Theatre**, London, was the scene of a historic demonstration: lighting by gaslight. It was not until 1817 that the stage of the same theatre was to be the first lit in England by the new substance. A month later the stage of Drury Lane blazed with the new light, but across the Atlantic, the **Chestnut Street Theatre**, Philadelphia, installed gas the year before. The owners 'flatter themselves that its superior safety, brilliance and neatness will be satisfactory'.

Gaslight was burnt with a bare flame, for the mantle was not invented until the end of the 19th century. Dependent on the quality of the gas, it was brighter and whiter than even the Argand lamp. It burnt without changing intensity and required no trimming of wicks, but most vitally, it was easier to control. The brightness could be varied by regulating the gas supply and a 'gas table', that allowed control of separate parts of the stage, became the first 'stage switchboard'. At the Paris Opéra in 1822, the former ballet-master wrote 'This light is perfect for the stage. One can obtain gradation of brightness that is really magical.' But there were problems. The smell of gas could be offensive and the danger from heat was more serious than ever. Bare gas jets next to wood and canvas presented a major hazard. Our aforementioned Chestnut Street Theatre, Phil-

adelphia, disappointed its owners and was one of the first of hundreds of theatres to be burnt down.

As the use of gas became more widespread, it was principally used to replace the former oil lamps and candles. Perhaps the only significant change in lighting positions was the increase of overhead battens of light. It was easier to light a row of gas jets than a great quantity of candles high in the air. But brightness again increased and opened up new possibilities. *The Corsair* at **Her Majesty's Theatre**, London, in 1856 removed the customary wings and employed a panoramic cyclorama. Once again styles of acting, scenery, costumes and makeup that had seemed acceptable under murky candle and oil lamp now seemed overblown, vulgar and garish.

Gaslight could not provide a beam or shaft of light any better than its predecessors. But in 1826, a new light source, limelight, was invented. **Charles Macready** tested it in his pantomime *Peeping Tom of Coventry* at **Covent Garden** in 1837. Limelight used a block of quicklime heated by a flame of oxygen and hydrogen to provide an intense point source that could be installed in a hand operated spotlight. This, for the first time, was used to provide strong accents of light across the stage.

The practice of darkening the auditorium during the performance was introduced by Sir **Henry Irving** (1838–1905), who was a great innovator in stage lighting. He said 'stage lighting and groupings are of more consequence than the scenery'. He further explored the subtleties of colour mixing and sought to enhance his productions with the imaginative use of light and shade. Bram Stoker his lighting assistant said 'It became an easy matter to throw any special part of the stage into greater prominence.' Irving had extensive lighting rehearsals without actors, but attended by the staff, which included his 30 gasmen and eight limelight operators. In 1889 the French director **Antoine** wrote of his admiration for Irving's lighting.

In 1857, Charles Garnier's new Paris Opéra opened. It contained a lighting system with 28 miles of piping, feeding 960 gas jets from a gas table of 88 stopcocks. A Parisian lighting catalogue of 1877 contains details of many types of instrument, including carbon-arc spotlights which ranged from the largest that could flood the whole stage, to small hand held follow spotlights. A multitude of special effects and projection apparatus was used and the climax of the age of gas certainly employed massive resources often to spectacular effect.

In 1881 the Savoy Theatre in London opened with an electric lighting installation. 1,158 incandescent lamps were used, of which 824 were on the stage, controlled by six dimmers. Richard D'Oyly Carte appeared before the curtain and demonstrated the new safety of electricity by smashing a lit lamp wrapped in muslin. This was greeted with tumultuous cheers.

The electrical revolution quickly spread across the world. **Belasco** states that the first theatre in the USA to be equipped with electricity was the California in San Francisco.

However for many years electric light was only used to replace the gas jets that preceded it. Footlights, battens and vertical strips at the side of the stage were converted to the new electricity. It was brighter, had no smell and was much safer. (A Captain Shaw noted that the temperature in the Grid of the Savoy was 68 degrees

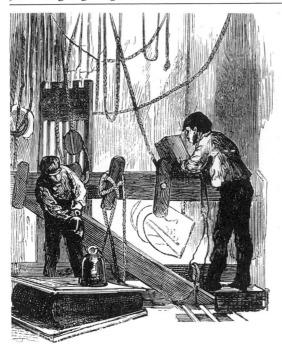

Limelight men operating in the gallery, 1874.

while at the Alhambra, with gaslight, it was 105 degrees Fahrenheit.) It has been estimated that the electric lamp was perhaps a third brighter than the gas jet. Despite frequent criticism of excessive, harsh brightness, theatres rapidly increased the number of lamps used. By 1902, the Prinzregententheater in Munich had a four-colour system using 1,542 onstage lamps in footlights, battens and wings, 770 lamps in movable standards (floor stands) and lengths (strip lights) and 12 arc lamps.

Despite being cumbersome, flickering and often noisy, arc lights were still required to give accent. It was many years before the spotlight, coupled to the dimmer, began to offer new opportunities. Even today the arc lamp is still in use as the brightest long range follow spot, although newer light sources such as Xenon increasingly replace the carbon arc.

Meanwhile, in reaction against the flat glare of early electric light, two men, Gordon Craig (1872–1966) and **Adolphe Appia** (1862–1928), dreamt of a new stage lighting. Both rejected the increasingly realistic scenery of their time, and both, inspired by the beauty and evocative power of natural light, imagined a stage with the actor within an environment unified by being filled with three-dimensional light. Appia said 'Light is to space what sounds are to time.' Craig wrote of a 'master of the art and science of the theatre', the stage manager, who would unify all the arts of theatre into a harmonious whole.

Craig and Appia were more influential by their writings than by their all too few productions. Others, although perhaps without realizing it, took up the challenge that their inspiration posed.

In the USA, David Belasco (1859–1931) was the first director of the 20th century to pay great attention to lighting. Lighting rehearsals for his productions could take weeks and he established a lighting laboratory to plan the lighting in advance. His lighting engineer was Louis Hartmann, who for 28 years worked with him and was responsible for the development of the first incandescent spotlights. They also introduced indirect overhead lighting by shining spotlights into reflective silver-coated bowls, which produced a soft, naturalistic impression of light from the sky. Today, a multiplicity of carefully focused spotlights creates an equally soft and potentially naturalistic impression, but with the advantage of precise control.

Hartmann, a great innovator, was truly a man of theatre. 'Why should we suppose that a radical change is necessary in the theatre', he wrote. 'The glory of a sunrise or sunset is just the same today as when the first human beheld it. Our emotions have not changed. Let us use our modern devices to enhance the value of the text; and "hold, as 't were, the mirror up to nature".'

In 1917 Hartmann's baby spotlights were first brought to England by the director, **Basil Dean** (1888–1978). He, like Belasco, was intensely concerned with stage lighting and also introduced German equipment, such as the Acting Area flood. In 1923 he installed a Schwabe cyclorama system at the St Martin's Theatre, London, and in *R. U. R.* used scene projection in England for the first time. In 1939, he directed **J. B. Priestley**'s *Johnson Over Jordan*, devising with his electrician, Bill Lorraine, an English version of Hartmann's reflected light.

A giant of the German theatre, who also shared his conviction about the importance of lighting, was the director **Max Reinhardt** (1873–1943). His versatility

The electric switchboard of the Paris Opéra, 1887.

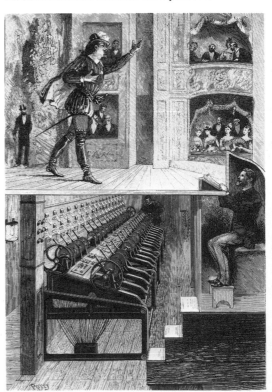

made him a master of the stage, in the tradition spoken of by Gordon Craig, with productions that ranged from the vast and spectacular like *The Miracle* to the most intimate, such as his work at the Redoutensaal recital room in Vienna. 'Lighting must replace the decorations', he wrote in 1901.

German theatres, since the mid 19th century, had been lavishly appointed, aided by substantial funding from the court or state. The practice of repertoire, with a different performance every night, led to large stages equipped with bridges hung over the stage to carry the lighting, which could thus be readily reached and reset by electricians. Equipment was large but finely engineered. High quality optics and spacious stages encouraged developments in large scale scene projection. Linnebach, Haseit and other German engineers developed a pattern of stage lighting, which from the twenties was to remain largely unchanged for many years. Meanwhile in the USA and later in England, lighting that at first was electric lamps in rows of battens (or X-rays) and footlights, imitating the soft overall lighting of the age of gas, began to change.

The oldest specialist stage lighting manufacturer is Kliegl Bros of New York, founded in 1896. Siemens of Germany and Clemançon in Paris are early pioneers, but counted the stage as only one of many activities. In England, Strand Electric was founded in 1914 and remained the leading British company in the field for over fifty years. Innovation was largely under the direction of Frederick Bentham (b. 1911). He led the development of English instruments, but his major achievement was in the field of lighting control.

Intensity control of electric light was achieved with dimmers, variable resistances or auto-transformers, the movement of which was synchronized by increasingly sophisticated mechanical linkage systems. A grand master control allowed dimmers to be connected via shafts and clutches to a central lever or wheel. Bentham, inspired by a life-long enthusiasm for 'colour music', mixing light to music, conceived that lighting should be controlled in a way that was analogous to music. He developed the light console, which employed a console, derived from the cinema organ, driving remote motor driven dimmers. An alternative way of miniaturizing lighting control, with multiple presets, was developed using thyratron valves. These were later replaced by Silicon Control Rectifiers (SCR). A skilled operator was able to play the lighting in a remarkably fluid manner. One man instead of many could control several hundred dimmers. This led to remote control systems being installed by West End commercial managements a decade before such systems were adopted by Broadway in the USA. The emerging, and wealthy, TV industry in England adopted the principle of dimmer control for each light and installed similar control systems. The advent of the computer led to the first memory control.

In the USA, Ed Kook founded Century Lighting. He developed the compact ellipsoidal spotlight, often colloquially named the Leko, after himself and his partner Levy. More significantly, Kook supported the emergence of the new profession in the theatre, the Lighting Designer. While in England between the wars, lighting was the province of the director, with men such as **Terence Gray** and **Norman Marshall** working with their electrician Harold Ridge; in the

USA, lighting remained the designer's responsibility. **Lee Simonson**, **Norman Bel Geddes**, **Robert Edmond Jones**, **Donald Oenslager** and **Jo Mielziner** all extended the use of lighting as an integral part of their scene designs.

In 1925, Stanley McCandless was appointed to teach stage lighting at Yale University. In *A Method of Lighting the Stage* he formulated a structured approach to the new lighting. Specialists in lighting design, Abe Feder, Peggy Clark and **Jean Rosenthal** (1912–69) emerged and began to establish a professionalism around the lighting process.

In England in the late thirties, Joe Davis (1912–84) was an electrician with leading theatrical producers, H. M. Tennent. His lighting for hundreds of productions demonstrated a rare sensitivity and his work reproducing American productions which transferred to London in the fifties demonstrated the advances that had been effected by the professional lighting designer in the USA.

Richard Pilbrow founded Theatre Projects in 1957. He introduced American methods of preplanning lighting and equipment from America and Germany. He developed a team of lighting designers, which included Robert Ornbo, Robert Bryan, John B. Read and David Hersey, who established the profession in England. As Theatre Consultant to the **National Theatre** of Great Britain, Pilbrow designed Lightboard, a control that developed Bentham's 'playability', with new freedom to mix lighting images, now made possible by computers. It established a standard for many of the control systems that followed.

In the USA, unlike England, the universities increasingly offered training in stage lighting design. Outstanding designers such as **Tharon Musser**, Jules Fisher, **Jennifer Tipton**, Roger Morgan, John Gleason, Ken Billington and Marc Weiss lead a profession rich in numbers and talent. Just as designers of the 18th century took their work outside the theatre, so today the lighting designer's skills find a wider audience. Designed lighting in architecture has received significant impact from theatre practitioners, as has lighting for television. The fields of rock and roll concert lighting and industrial theatre and exhibitions have been fruitful areas of operation for the designer, which have also offered opportunity for experiment.

English and American techniques have increasingly merged in the 1980s. Lighting is achieved with a multiplicity of spotlights (largely ellipsoidal or profile spots that allow the beam of light to be shaped at will), which may be coloured with a choice of hundreds of different shades of plastic colour media. Accent light is provided by low voltage beam projectors or PAR (parabolic reflector sealed beam) reflector lamps. Instruments are still usually positioned overhead on pipes in rows across the stage and vertically at the side. Swings of theatrical fashion seem to dictate whether or not the lighting should be hidden from the sight of the audience, or incorporated into the scenic design. Production lighting schemes increasingly echo the 'mobile light' of Serlio and are designed to incorporate moving batteries of light. In the fifties, probably 200 instruments were commonplace, but in 1986 over 600–1,000 units are found, of an average power of 1,000 watts.

Instrument design has advanced little since the principles were established in the thirties. In England,

Sutherland Studio Theatre's *Oedipus Rex*, 1984; lighting by David I. Taylor.

CCT first developed profile spots with a variable zoom beam angle. Low voltage has long been seen as a means of achieving compactness and efficiency in the incandescent lamp. The use of new light sources is continually investigated, but the theatre's need to have smooth dimming from full brightness to black out is presently a considerable restraint. Highly efficient discharge lighting sources using mechanical shutters to fade or black out the light are used especially in Germany.

In 1986, despite the sophisticated computer control over intensity that man possesses, he still requires access by stepladder or from a bridge to change the focus position of a spotlight. Many spotlights with motorized focusing and colour change have been developed, but usually at considerable cost. The world of rock and roll began using remotely resettable spotlights successfully and this will spread rapidly into the theatre. The future will allow fluid control over not only the intensity of light, but also its movement about the stage and its colour, all capable of sudden or subtle change as the live action unfolds.

The centuries old argument over footlights and the need for light from the front and above the actor is long over. Front of house spotlighting was first mounted on the front of the balconies, then invaded the audience boxes and now hundreds of instruments may be used. New theatres make elaborate provision, with bridges in the ceiling and slots in the walls, to allow light to reach the stage with the greatest possible freedom of angle.

In Europe and even Germany, lighting design has generally not made such creative advances, except in the work of some exceptional artists. **Wieland Wagner** (1917–66), in directing his grandfather's operas at Bayreuth, has created memorable images with light. **Josef Svoboda** (b. 1920), the Czech scenographer, has, with light (often low voltage) and projection, opened new vistas. But many theatres of Europe still regard lighting as only an aid to creating stage pictures and illumination and not as the 'unifying element' dreamt of by Craig and Appia.

Jean Rosenthal in her book *The Magic of Light* wrote, 'Light is quite tactile to me. It has shape and dimension. It has an edge. It has quality and it is an entity. It is the one miracle of creation without which, to me, the others would be meaningless.'

Today the stage is a space that can be filled with any shape, pattern, texture, feeling or atmosphere of light that the performance requires. Opera, ballet, dance, musicals, drama, popular music, each make particular demands on theatrical lighting. Each can be well or poorly lit. That judgement must be a summation of how expressively and purposefully light has been used to illuminate the stage appropriately, how the performers are three-dimensionally revealed, the composition of the lighting within the overall visual intent of the scenic picture and finally the degree to which the stage is charged with the correctly evocative atmosphere. Each of these qualities will stem from the content and intended style of the production.

Each step of progress in lighting, candle to oil lamp, oil lamp to gas, and gas to electricity, has brought change. More light, safety, greater facility for control have been achieved and yet always accompanied by complaints of over-brightness. Each step has been followed by changes in acting technique, and ever more subtle and often more realistic scenery, costumes and makeup. By the 1980s the 20th century has seen the passing of many styles of production. Realism has given way to many other -isms and the wheel of style continues to revolve. But the new lighting, the ability to fill stage space with light of character, remote from its source, has had an effect that is perhaps more profound than ever before.

The scenic environment surrounding the actor has become more three dimensional. Physical thickness, depth and texture, used with light, have replaced much of the painted detail of previous ages. Often scenic elements have become larger and backstage areas have had to accommodate consequently bulkier scenery.

But the most significant change has been in the theatres themselves and in the relationship between the actor and the audience. Throughout most theatre times the players performed amongst their audience and both were lit throughout the performance. As we have seen, every period produced innovators who wished to darken the auditorium, but only in the late 19th century did this become the norm. The desire for increased naturalism and audience concentration on the stage made dimming the houselights the symbol of the play's commencement. The actor had to perform upstage of the proscenium lighting in order to be seen and a gulf grew between him and the darkened audience. Almost immediately visionary directors realized that this broke the fragile bond of communication that lay at the heart of live theatre, which is the live interplay between performer and spectator.

The coming of the spotlight, which illuminated space from a distance, not only allowed the actors' faces to be lit from the auditorium, it allowed the actor to work in lit space that could be placed within the audience. So a reexamination of antique and new forms of theatre began. Theatre-in-the-round, thrust, transverse, environmental, open stages all became legitimate means of theatrical expression. All were enabled by lighting to place actor and audience in the same space, but allowed the proper focus of attention to remain with the performer. Once more the actor is able to be at the heart of his audience. Once more he can be seen as a live, three-dimensional human being in intimate communication with his living audience. At a period of theatre history where new, electronic means of story-telling challenge the live theatre as never before, this rediscovered intimacy, this living contact, continues to give theatre its uniqueness in a world of ever more dazzling media.

Lighting, as an element in the theatre, has had a long and often unrecognized history. Just as stained glass in a gothic cathedral brought wonder to the beholder, so since the Renaissance, lighting has played its part in bringing magic to the stage. Today the lighting designer has at his fingertips computer-controlled intensity and, potentially, movement and colour. These things were imagined by our theatrical ancestors, but electricity has brought them within our grasp. The speed of technological change is still accelerating. The challenge of the future must be to match technical development with a creativity that is always sensitive to the theatre's essentially human needs, so that lighting plays its appropriate role in the service of the living theatre. RP

See: W. F. Bellman, *Lighting the Stage: Art and Practice*, New York and London, 1974; F. P. Bentham, *Art of Stage Lighting*, London, 1980; G. M. Bergman, *Lighting in the Theatre*, New Jersey, 1977; S. McCandless, *A Method of Lighting The Stage*, New York, 1958; R. H. Palmer, *The Lighting Art: The Aesthetics of Stage Lighting Design*, New York, 1979; W. O. Parker and H. K. Smith, *Scene Design and Stage Lighting*, New York, 1979; R. Pilbrow, *Stage Lighting*, London, 1979; T. Rees, *Theatre Lighting in The Age of Gas*, London, 1978; F. Reid, *Stage Lighting Handbook*, London, 1982; J. Rosenthal and L. Wertenbaeker, *The Magic Of Light*, New York, 1972; H. D. Sellman and M. Lessley, *Essentials of Stage Lighting*, New York, 1982; T. Streader and J. A. Williams, *Create Your Own Stage Lighting*, London, 1985; W. B. Warfel, *Handbook of Stage Lighting Graphics*, New York, 1974.

Stage Society, The Incorporated, London. The successor to Grein's Independent Theatre Club, this was founded in 1899 to produce modern plays that had been refused a licence for public performance, in professional stage conditions on Sunday nights when the theatres were otherwise closed. It was the first to produce **Shaw**'s early plays, opening with *You Never Can Tell* and successfully asserting its freedom from stage censorship with *Mrs Warren's Profession* (1902). As well as opening the theatre to other new English works like **Granville Barker**'s *Waste* (1907), it introduced a whole range of major European dramatists from the naturalism of **Hauptmann**, **Gorky** and **Tolstoi**, to forerunners of expressionism like **Kaiser** and **Wedekind**. It provided the impetus for the influential 1904–7 **Royal Court** seasons of **Vedrenne** and Granville Barker, who gained his experience as an actor and director in early Stage Society productions. It also initiated the Phoenix Society. This was formed to continue the revivals of Restoration Comedy that had been started in 1915, and was instrumental in bringing early English drama back to the public stage with a series of productions ranging from **Marlowe** and **Jonson** to **Dryden** and **Wycherley** between 1919 and 1925.

In the inter-war period the Stage Society continued its function of championing new and unlicensed works – including the plays of James Joyce, **D. H. Lawrence**, John Van Druten and **R. C. Sherriff** as well as drama by **Pirandello**, **Cocteau**, **Odets** and **Lorca** (*Blood Wedding* being its final production in 1939) – although by that time it was no longer unique and its role had been largely taken over by the **Group Theatre** or by Peter Godfrey and **Norman Marshall** at the **Gate Theatre**. CI

Stainless Stephen (Arthur Baynes) (1892–1971) English (Sheffield-born) comedian and ex-schoolteacher who built into his act both his regional identity – stainless steel shirt front and bowler hat band – and his former professional pedantry – through the technique of speaking the punctuation of his script (not to mention his own stage-directions) as if giving dictation. He is included here by special request of the editor, whose childhood he greatly influenced. AEG

Stanfield, Clarkson (1793–1867) English scene-painter, responsible during a long and varied career for over 550 recorded scenes. Stanfield's father, an actor and former seaman, apprenticed his son to a heraldic painter, but the boy was at sea from 1808–15. Seascapes remained a feature of his later painting. His first engagement was as a scene-painter at the East London Theatre in 1815 and, after a spell at the Coburg, he was added to **Elliston**'s team of painters at **Drury Lane** in 1823. Elliston's object was to challenge the supremacy of the **Grieve** family at **Covent Garden**. Stanfield remained at Drury Lane until 1834, dividing his time between theatre work and easel painting on his own behalf. Admired as a marine and landscape artist, even compared by some to Turner, he was elected to the Royal Academy in 1835. **Macready**, who was a personal friend, persuaded Stanfield to paint scenes for him at Covent Garden, the 1839 diorama for *Henry V* being particularly famous. Among the finest of Stanfield's many dioramas, spectacles in their own right though used to enliven Drury Lane pantomimes, were his Plymouth Breakwater (1823) and his Venice (1831). He had no rival in the depiction of the subtle textures and colourings of water. His last theatrical work was an 1858 act-drop for the New **Adelphi Theatre**, a service to another friend, **Benjamin Webster**. PT

Stanislavsky (pseudonym of Alekseev), Konstantin Sergeevich (1863–1938) Soviet-Russian actor-director-teacher, creator of the most influential 'system' of acting in the Western world. The son of enlightened progressive art patrons – the rich industrialist Alekseev and his wife, descended from the French actress Varley – Stanislavsky (he adopted this stage name in 1885) was quickly introduced to ballet, theatre and Italian opera. This instilled in him a sense of plastique and musicality and aversions to fustian stage conventions and disrespectful audience behaviour. His amateur theatrical career began at home (1877) with the 'Alekseev Circle's' productions of farces and operettas and continued at the Moscow Society of Art and Literature (1888), which he co-founded with **Shchepkin**'s pupil **Glikeriya Fedotova** and three others. Here Stanislavsky played a variety of roles from the Russian and European repertoire and in so doing recognized the limitations of his craft – a poor memory, the result of rote training at school, a somewhat random approach to acting and artificial playing. However, his self-critical temperament, physical endowments – height, handsomeness and grace – and

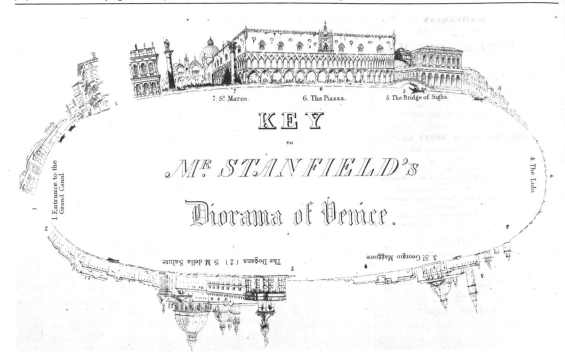

Stanfield's Diorama of Venice.

good role models – the opera star Fyodor Shaliapin and actors **Tommaso Salvini**, Fedotova, etc. – would eventually combine to create a first class character actor. **Vladimir Nemirovich-Danchenko**, a popular playwright and teacher at the Moscow Philharmonia, was impressed with Stanislavsky's first directorial effort for the amateur Society, **Tolstoi**'s *The Fruits of Enlightenment* (1891) with future star **Vera Komissarzhevskaya** in the cast. In 1897 a lengthy discussion of common goals led to the founding of the **Moscow Art Theatre**, dedicated to the highest ideals of ensemble art, good citizenry and public education. The bases of the company's approach were naturalness, simplicity, clarity, the end to the actor's traditional *emploi*, the alternation of large and small roles and the detailed and individuated realization of the essence and world of the play. With staff director A. A. Sanin and designer V. A. Simov in tow, the company opened with an antiquarian-set, naturalistically staged production of **A. K. Tolstoi**'s historical drama *Tsar Fyodor Ioannovich* (14 October 1898), which featured sensitive acting and a rich overlay of sound, lighting and scenic effects deemed necessary by Stanislavsky and extraneous and counter-productive by **Chekhov**. Stanislavsky's wife (since 1887), Mariya Petrovna Perevoshchikova, née Lilina, and Chekhov's future spouse, **Olga Knipper**, scored personal triumphs as Masha and Arkadina, respectively, as did Stanislavsky as Trigorin. Stanislavsky excelled in all of Chekhov's plays for MAT – Astrov in *Uncle Vanya* (1899), Vershinin in *The Three Sisters* (1901), Gaev in *The Cherry Orchard* (1904) – as well as in the roles of: Dr Stockmann in **Ibsen**'s *An Enemy of the People* (1900); Satin in **Gorky**'s *The Lower Depths* (1902), which helped launch a long association between the theatre

and that author; Famusov in **Griboedov**'s *Woe from Wit* (1906); Argan in **Molière**'s *The Imaginary Invalid* (1913); and in many others requiring in-depth preparation and total transformation of his physical appearance. He became interested in the new symbolist-decadent drama, which he as a director felt ill-equipped (despite attempts) to realize, and in the possibility of finding alternative methods of staging the classics. He invited **Gordon Craig** to design-direct *Hamlet* (1912), **Aleksandr Benois** to perform the same tasks for Molière and **Goldoni** (1913–14) and **Vsevolod Meyerhold** to stage **Maeterlinck**'s *The Death of Tintagiles* (1905), a production which, owing to the stylization of the acting, Stanislavsky refused to let open. Stanislavsky's frustration with these alternative approaches led to a reaffirmation of his own instincts, which he tested together with Leopold Sulerzhitsky at MAT's First Studio (1912), where the 'system' was developed and the theatre enjoyed its first post-revolutionary success – *Twelfth Night* (1917). While new Soviet dramas – e.g., **Bulgakov**'s *The Days of the Turbins* (1926) and **Vsevelod Ivanov**'s *Armoured Train 14–69* (1927) – were produced by younger company members, Stanislavsky sidestepped the effects of the Revolution by working at the Bolshoi Theatre's opera studio, continuing to supervise experimental studio work and administering MAT's European and American tours (1922–4). His productions of **Ostrovsky**'s *The Ardent Heart* (1926) and **Beaumarchais**'s *The Marriage of Figaro* (1927) embraced the grotesque even as he began to record the tenets of his realistic acting system. To publicize the American tour he hastily and somewhat carelessly assembled the autobiographical *My Life in Art*, which he revised in 1926 and 1936. While recuperating from a heart attack (1928), he worked on the first part of his text *The Actor's Work on Himself*, completed in 1937, at which point he began the second part. While housebound, Stanislavsky also continued to coach singers and opera singers, his last directing work being on Molière's *Tartuffe* (1935). He was named a 'People's Artist of the USSR' in 1936 and save for occasional lapses in popularity, his system has remained the basis of Russian acting. Stanislavsky advocated a balance between the actor's inner experiencing of the role (*perezhivaniye*) and its precisely attuned physical and vocal expression. Using the imaginative 'magic if' and 'affective memory' (adapted from the French experimental psychologist Théodule Armand Ribot) as bridges between actor and character realities, the 'circle of attention' for focusing the actor's powers, 'the through-line of action', broken into units and objectives, to score the role, the system offers a clear and precise groundplan. The confused publication history of Stanislavsky's acting text in the United States and Americans' penchant for self-analysis and self-expression led to the psychologically and emotionally based, physically and vocally underfed 'Method' approach of New York's **Actors Studio** which has been mistaken for the original system.   SG

Stapleton, Maureen (1925–) American actress who made her New York debut as Sara Tansey in *Playboy of the Western World* (1946). Among her outstanding roles has been Serafina in *The Rose Tattoo* (1951), Flora in *27 Wagons Full of Cotton* (1955), Lady Torrance in *Orpheus Descending* (1957), and Carrie in *Toys in the Attic* (1960). For Eva, the alcoholic performer in **Neil Simon**'s *The Gingerbread Lady* (1970), she won the Tony as Best Actress with a performance described as 'remorselessly honest'. Stapleton has appeared in a number of feature films and many television programmes. As Carrie, critics described Stapleton as 'comic, discerning, awkward and pathetic', and 'splendid . . . gabby, open-hearted'. In 1969 the actress received a National Institute of Arts and Letters Award.   SMA

Starr, Frances (1886–1973) American actress. She made her debut in her hometown stock company (Albany, New York, 1901), and for the next four years worked in similar companies in San Francisco, Boston, and New York City. **Belasco** hired her as a replacement for the ingenue during the run of *The Music Master*, and then starred her as Juanita in *The Rose of the Rancho* (1906) and as Laura Murdock in *The Easiest Way* by **Eugene Walter** (1909). In the latter role she personified the dilemma of the modern woman, morally liberated but economically enslaved. She continued to act until 1940.   DMCD

Steele, Richard (1672–1729) Irish dramatist. Educated at Charterhouse, where he met **Joseph Addison** with whom he so often collaborated as essayist, and Oxford, he became a soldier in 1694, writing his pious tract, *The Christian Hero* (1701), as an aid to fellow-soldiers. His plays were the most consistent attempt to respond to the criticisms of **Jeremy Collier** by producing a drama that was both entertaining and moral. *The Funeral* (1701) was a farce mocking undertaking but *The Lying Lover* (1703) and *The Tender Husband*

(1703) were serious, almost pious, studies of the success of virtue in a comic world. With their advocacy of repentance and their lack of realism in dramatic form they were strong influences on the development of sentimental comedy. But the plays were not successful and Steele began editing a series of periodicals, including *The Tatler* (1709–11), *The Spectator* (1711–12), *The Guardian* (1713), *The Englishman* (1713–15), *Town Talk* (1715) and *The Theatre* (1720), which were all frequently concerned to discuss theatre and drama, advocating new plays and new genres and satirizing staging and acting. In 1715 he was knighted and also took on the management of **Drury Lane Theatre**. His fourth and last play, *The Conscious Lovers* (1722), was a fully-fledged sentimental comedy, influential in the establishment of *comédie larmoyante* in Europe, a serious and unfunny play founded on middle-class morality and using **Terence**'s *Andria* as source.   PH

Stein, Peter (1937–) German director, whose collective productions at the Berlin Schaubühne since 1970 have provided some of the most interesting work in contemporary German theatre. Highly political – his staging of **Weiss**'s *Vietnam Discourse* at the Munich Kammerspiele (1969) ended with a collection for the Viet Cong – his approach has been based on meticulous research into the social and political context of a text. This creative rehearsal method has culminated in independent performances exploring the ethos of an era, such as *Dream of the Poor Heinrich Kleist of Prince Homburg* (1972) or the double-evening 'Total theatre' spectacle *Shakespeare Memory* (1966), which presented the background material for the ensemble's staging of *As You Like It* (1977). It is the basis for strikingly objective interpretations of the classics (**Ibsen**'s *Peer*

Elke Petri as Phoebe in Peter Stein's production of *As You Like It*.

Gynt, 1971; **Gorky**'s *Summer Folk*, 1974; **Aeschylus'** *Oresteia*, 1980; **Chekhov**'s *Three Sisters*, 1984) which expose the contemporary relevance of historical attitudes. CI

Steinbeck, John (Ernest) (1902–68) American Nobel Prize-winning (1962) novelist who wrote 24 works of fiction but only three plays, each adapted from a novel. The first, *Of Mice and Men* (1937), a tragic fable of the strong and the weak, was dramatized with **George S. Kaufman** (a musical version was produced in 1958). *The Moon Is Down* (1942), an anti-Nazi play, followed; *Burning Bright* was adapted in 1950. *Tortilla Flat*, about California Mexican-American peasants, was dramatized by Jack Kirkland in 1938, and in 1955 **Oscar Hammerstein** adapted Steinbeck's novel about Cannery Row, *Sweet Thursday* (1954), into the musical *Pipe Dream* (music by **Richard Rodgers**). DBW

Steiner, Rolando (1935–) Nicaraguan playwright, journalist and critic. Studied in Spain (1963–5) and returned to Managua to work for *La Prensa*, the major newspaper. His three one-act plays, *Judith, Un drama corriente* (*An Ordinary Drama*) and *La puerta* (*The Door*), were collected under the title *La trilogía del matrimonio* (*The Matrimonial Trilogy*) and published in 1970. GW

Steinsson, Gudmundur (1925–) Icelandic playwright whose tragicomic *A Brief Respite* (1979) broke box-office records at Iceland's National Theatre, subsequently going on European tour. It has since been produced in eight countries, including Japan. Essentially a critique of consumer society mentality, the play depicts an average urban family caught in the rat-race, where there is no time for anything, not even for death. Another popular play is the farcical *Viva España* (1976), which describes holidaymakers in Spain, their boredom, alienation and sexual frustration under a veneer of marital bliss. Steinsson often deals in highly stylized satire with alienation and self-deception, while some of his plays are large-scale allegories about man's self-inflicted fate. Important plays include *Matthew* (1975), *The Garden Party* (1982) and *The Wedding Portrait* (1986). AI

Stepanova, Varvara Fyodorovna (1894–1958) One of the original group of Soviet-Russian constructivist designers who, although overshadowed by colleagues **Lyubov Popova** and husband Aleksandr Rodchenko, is remembered for her distinctive work on **Meyerhold**'s production of **Sukhovo-Kobylin**'s *Tarelkin's Death* (24 November 1922). Indebted to Popova's design for *The Magnanimous Cuckold* (1922), which it tried to outdo (according to Meyerhold), the *Tarelkin* set consisted of a series of booby-trapped, white-painted wooden 'acting machines', each individually conceived – chairs with false spring seats, a stool that detonated a blank cartridge, a table whose legs collapsed, a tall box that served as a human jack-in-the-box and, most prominently, a large, barred cage and wheel resembling a meat grinder. Whereas Popova had designed the entire space, Stepanova simply inhabited hers with designed objects. Ironically, Stepanova complained that it was the director's and actor's insistence on playing through themselves rather than through the objects which had made the latter appear illusory and decorative, the exact opposite of what constructivist design intended. Stepanova's complaint ended her association with Meyerhold. Still, the single production with its baggy costumes resembling prisoners' uniforms (also designed by Stepanova), its knockabout action, role reversals and carnivalesque tone is representative of the 'eccentrist' trend of the day, begun with **Annenkov**'s production of *The First Distiller* (1919), and of Meyerhold's circus phase. SG

Stephens, Robert (1931–) British actor, who started his career with Caryl Jenner's Mobile Theatre before appearing at the **Royal Court Theatre** in *The Crucible* (1956) with the English Stage Company. He became a familiar member of **George Devine**'s acting team, playing in **Osborne**'s *The Entertainer* (1957) and *Epitaph for George Dillon* (1958); and he was often cast as a smooth young man, perhaps untrustworthy. He appeared in the West End in *Look After Lulu* (1959) and *The Wrong Side of the Park* (1960) and appeared in the film version of *A Taste of Honey* (1962); but the range of his talents was not recognized until after **Laurence Olivier** invited him to join the **National Theatre** company in 1963. He appeared in the NT's *Hamlet, St Joan* and *The Recruiting Officer*, but his first great success came as Atahuallpa in **Peter Shaffer**'s *The Royal Hunt of the Sun* (1964). Through arduous physical training and brilliant vocal and mime control, Stephens transformed himself into an image of the Sun God of the Incas. Other major roles followed in such NT productions as *Armstrong's Last Goodnight, Trelawny of the 'Wells', A Bond Honoured* and *The Dance of Death*. He continued his NT career under **Peter Hall**, appearing in *The Cherry Orchard* (1978) and *Brand* (1978), but by the mid-seventies, he was equally well-known as a television and film star. While Stephens has not so far become a major star, either in Britain or the States, the versatility and professionalism of his acting strengthened two leading companies in post-war British theatre, Devine's Royal Court and Olivier's National Theatre, and it is perhaps as a company actor that his work is best respected. JE

Sternheim, Carl (1878–1942) German dramatist, whose cycle of eight comedies under the title of *Scenes from the Heroic Life of the Middle Classes* have become modern classics. Sometimes listed as a forerunner of expressionism, his work is more in the tradition of **Molière**, although the closest German counterpart is the satiric sketches of George Grosz. Chronicling the rise of the 'Maske' family over three generations from *The Underpants* (1911) to *1913* and *Tabula Rasa* (1915), this cycle portrays the moral anarchy of a soulless society in figures who have no core of personality behind their materialistic obsessions and whose language is fragmented cliché, transforming the commonplace into the grotesque. In some ways anticipating absurd drama beneath their naturalistic surface, the plays were repeatedly banned – under the monarchy (performance of *The Underpants* being forbidden for 'immorality'), during the First World War (as threatening 'internal order') and under the Nazis – but *The Snob*, originally produced by **Reinhardt** in 1914, was the first play to be staged in Berlin when the theatres reopened after 1945. CI

Stevens, Roger Lacey (1910–) American producer, born in Detroit, Michigan. Since producing *Twelfth Night* on Broadway in 1949, Stevens has worked steadily with great distinction in the American theatre and has been associated with many of the leading theatrical groups of the USA: The Producers Theatre, the Phoenix Theatre, the American National Theatre and Academy, the Metropolitan Opera Company, the **Actors Studio Theatre**, the **American Shakespeare Festival** and Academy, the New Dramatists Committee, and the **John F. Kennedy Centre for the Performing Arts**. Stevens chaired the National Council on the Arts, 1964–9.

While Stevens was a member of the Playwrights Company (1951–60), that organization produced or co-produced 38 Broadway plays, including *The Fourposter* (1951), *Tea and Sympathy* (1953), *Ondine* and *The Bad Seed* (1954), and *Cat on a Hot Tin Roof* (1955).

As head of the John F. Kennedy Centre for the Performing Arts in Washington DC, Stevens has produced 30 productions which went on to other theatres. In 1957 he received the Sam H. Shubert Foundation Award for the outstanding producer on Broadway and in 1971 was given a special Antoinette Perry (Tony) Award. His productions have won numerous New York Drama Critics Awards, Tonys, and Outer Circle Awards. SMA

Stewart, Nellie (Eleanor) (1858–1931) Australian actress. Daughter of the actress Theodosia Yates (Mrs Guerin), she appeared aged five with **Charles Kean** in Melbourne, and in childhood toured internationally in *Rainbow Revels*, written for the Stewart family. She first starred in the pantomime *Sinbad* in 1880, and was identified with many musical roles, including Griolet in *La Fille du Tambour Major*, Sweet Nell of Old Drury, and Cinderella. Her lifelong companion George Musgrove managed her career in Australia, England and America. An enchanging performer even in old age, she played Romeo in the balcony scene shortly before her death. MW

Stoll, Oswald (Gray) (1866–1942) English manager, born in Melbourne, Australia. He began by sharing the management of the Parthenon Music Hall, Liverpool, with his mother, and after various provincial successes, took over the London **Coliseum** (1904), which in his hands became a home for giant circuses, gargantuan musicals and **Max Reinhardt**'s epics. Other theatres under his control were the Hackney, Shepherd's Bush and Ardwick Empires, the Croydon and Manchester Hippodromes and the Leicester Palace. In 1911 he left Moss Empires and joined Walter Gibbons's Variety Theatres Consolidated, thereby gaining 29 halls with a capitalization of two million pounds. A knighthood came in 1919. A follower of Herbert Spencer, Stoll was known as a cold and formal employer, and a shrewd dealer. LS

Stone, John Augustus (1800–34) American playwright and actor. Stone's *Metamora, or the Last of Wampanoags* (1829) was the winner over 13 other entries in **Edwin Forrest**'s first playwriting contest (judged by W. C. Bryant, William Leggett, Prosper Wetmore, *et al.*). The play became Forrest's property and his 'war-horse' piece with over 200 performances.

The Stone–Forrest Indian chief epitomized the natural goodness of the 'noble savage'. He was brave, chivalrous, gentle towards his squaw, and imbued with an unfaltering trust in the Almighty Manitou. At the opening Wetmore spoke the prologue: 'Tonight we test the strength of native powers,/Subject and bard and actor, all are yours.'

Stone made his debut as Old Norval in *Douglas* (1820) and through most of his career played eccentric comics or 'rough and bluff' old men. He wrote nine other unsuccessful plays, among them: *The Demoniac* (1831), *The Ancient Briton* (1833), and *The Knight of the Golden Fleece* (1834). RM

Stoppard (Straussler), Tom (1937–) British dramatist, who was born in Czechoslovakia. His family emigrated via Singapore to Britain, where they settled in 1946. After working as a journalist on the *Western Daily Press*, Stoppard began to write plays for television and radio, and his first television play, *A Walk on the Water* (1963), was later adapted for the stage as *Enter a Free Man* (1968). He also adapted Sławomir Mrożek's *Tango* (1968) for British audiences, and in much of his later work, the influence of Polish and Czech 'absurdist' writers can be felt. His first major success, however, came with *Rozencrantz and Guildenstern are Dead* (1966), which was originally produced by the Oxford Theatre Group on the **Edinburgh Festival** fringe, but bought and staged six months later by the **National Theatre**. The story of *Hamlet* is seen through the eyes of two attendant courtiers who simply do not know, to the point of their deaths, what is going on; and through Stoppard's wit and technical virtuosity, this sad farce about the human condition became a powerful myth for British audiences in a world increasingly dominated by events (such as the war in Vietnam) over which they had no control. The professor of moral philosophy, George, in *Jumpers* (1972) is similarly out of touch with the politics of a brave new world, while Henry Carr in *Travesties* (1974) is a minor British consular official in Zürich in 1917, a town visited by Lenin, James Joyce and Tristan Tzara, of whose significance Carr is sublimely unaware. Stoppard's political agnosticism and his sympathy with the underdog led to a concern for those imprisoned by totalitarian regimes, in his play (with music by André Previn), *Every Good Boy Deserves Favour* (1977); and his liberal scepticism permeates *Night and Day* (1978) about politics and Western journalism in an African state. But Stoppard is also adept at generating an atmosphere of sheer fun, as in his Whitehall farce, *Dirty Linen* (1976), *Dogg's Hamlet* and *Cahoot's Macbeth* (1979) – and his adaptation of a play by the Austrian playwright, **Johann Nestroy**, *On The Razzle* (1981). His serious comedy about adultery, *The Real Thing* (1982), was equally successful in the West End and on Broadway. JE

Storey, David (Malcolm) (1933–) British dramatist and novelist, whose early novels (including *This Sporting Life*, 1960) describe the Yorkshire working-class background which permeates his later plays. He conceived his first play, *The Restoration of Arnold Middleton*, in 1959, but the first London production came at the **Royal Court Theatre** in 1967; and its study of a provincial schoolmaster, driven to madness in an unhappy marriage but also through homesickness for his lost Northern childhood, expressed eloquently Storey's understanding of class alienation. Although it transferred to the West End, *Arnold Middleton* was a somewhat clumsy play with brilliant individual tirades in the Jimmy Porter manner. When Storey teamed up with his sympathetic director, **Lindsay Anderson**, his plays gained in sharpness and dramatic effect. *In Celebration* (1969) ironically contrasts the life-styles of two generations of the Shaw family, indicating that material and social success do not bring happiness. Storey's observation of working environments provided the framework for *The Contractor* (1969) in which a large wedding marquee is raised and lowered on stage, *The Changing Room* (1971) about a rugby team, *The Farm* (1973) and *Life Class* (1974), but Storey cleverly selects the details to reveal the emotional complexities of individual lives. *Home* (1970), in which **John Gielgud** and **Ralph Richardson** appeared, ostensibly describes a rest home for the near-senile, but Storey hints that this place could be a model for Britain itself. This satirical, allegorical vein appears in *Cromwell* (1973), the curious black sex farce *Mother's Day* (1976) and *Sisters* (1978); but *Early Days* (1980) provided Ralph Richardson with a fine near-solo role as an elder statesman contemplating his past life, in a striking **National Theatre** production. JE

Strachan, Alan (Lockhart Thomson) (1946–) British director, who joined **Bernard Miles**'s Mermaid Theatre in 1970 as Associate Director. This gave him the opportunity not just to direct such plays as *John Bull's Other Island* (1971) but also to devise useful, small-scale musical shows, such as *Cowardy Custard* (1972) and *Cole* (1974), based on the songs of **Noël Coward** and **Cole Porter**. His sensitive, practical approach to the theatre stood him in good stead as a freelance director (1975–8), when he directed several West End successes, including *A Family and a Fortune* (1975), based on the novel by Ivy Compton Burnett, **Alan Ayckbourn**'s *Confusions* (1976) and *Just Between Ourselves* (1977). In 1978, he was appointed the artistic director of Greenwich Theatre, where his blend of popular classics and intelligent new plays won high attendance figures for a London suburban repertory theatre whose audiences were always in danger of being drawn away by the West End. Several Coward plays transferred from Greenwich to central London, but Greenwich Theatre also became known as the theatre where Ayckbourn's plays were tried out before their London runs. JE

Strange's Men This prominent Elizabethan household company was active in the provinces before its first recorded appearance at Elizabeth I's Court in 1582. Its patron was the son of the Earl of Derby, who had a household troupe of his own, and the two companies caused confusion among contemporaries as well as later scholars. As was the case with all the early Elizabethan groups of players, Strange's Men often amalgamated with actors from other companies when performing in London's public theatres. They were with the **Admiral's Men** at the **Theatre** in 1590–1 and at the **Rose** in 1592–3. A playhouse synopsis of the second part of **Tarlton**'s *The Seven Deadly Sins*, which Strange's Men performed in London between 1590 and 1592, names

the actors of this lost play. Among many prominent players are **Richard Burbage**, **William Sly**, and **Augustine Phillips**. Although **Shakespeare** is not named, his imminent association with these three in the formation of the **Lord Chamberlain's Men** in 1594 adds credibility to the claim that his early plays were in the repertoire of Strange's Men. When Lord Strange became Earl of Derby on his father's death in 1593, his company was touring the provinces, driven out of London by a virulent plague epidemic. On their return to London, they formed the nucleus of the incomparable Chamberlain's Men, of which Shakespeare was indubitably a member. PT

Stranitzky, Josef Anton (1676–1726) Austrian comic actor, creator of the character **Hanswurst**. He is first heard of in 1699 as an itinerant comedian in southern Germany, before he moved in 1705 to Vienna, where he set up as a tooth-drawer. Acting with Johann Baptist Hilverding's troupe at a fairbooth in the Vienna marketplace around 1705, he developed the part of a Salzburg peasant, which became a leading role when he took over the company in 1706 and moved it to the new Kärntnertor Theatre in 1711. It was there that Lady Mary Montagu saw him in 1716 and was shocked by his smutty jokes and the dropping of his trousers. Stranitzky's Hanswurst was earthy and foul-mouthed, improvising irreverently even in the lofty **Haupt- und Staatsaktionen** whose themes were drawn from Italian *opera seria*. He made a fortune and, as actor-author, founded a tradition that would descend to **Nestroy**. LS

Strasberg, Lee (1901–82) American director and acting teacher. Strasberg studied at the **American Laboratory Theatre**, acted with the **Theatre Guild** and in 1931 helped found and directed for the **Group Theatre**, espousing the work of the Russian director, **Konstantin Stanislavsky**. Among his directorial successes were *The House of Connelly*, *Night over Taos*, *Men in White*, and *Clash by Night*.

In 1950 he became a director for the **Actors Studio** and emerged as the leading exponent of the Method, based on the Stanislavsky System. In 1965 he directed a highly controversial *Three Sisters* which played at the **Aldwych Theatre** in London during the World Theatre Season. A great many of America's leading film and stage actors studied with Strasberg, either privately or at the Studio, among them **Marlon Brando**, whose internal style as Stanley in *A Streetcar Named Desire* became popularly associated with Method acting. Among his more famous students were Montgomery Clift, **Ann Bancroft**, Shelley Winters, Paul Newman, and Joanne Woodward.

Although his methods and results excited great controversy, little doubt remains that Strasberg had a major effect on modern acting. SMA

Stratford Festival (Canada) An annual summer festival in Stratford, Ontario, Canada, and the leading classical repertory theatre in North America.

In 1952 a group of Stratford citizens invited **Tyrone Guthrie** to help them establish a summer **Shakespeare** Festival. Guthrie was happy to accept because it gave him the opportunity to continue his experiments in open staging. He and designer **Tanya Moiseiwitsch** created an architecturally complete apron stage and then built a theatre round it, initially under a canvas roof. The daring of the concept and the high standards of production made the Festival an immense critical and popular success from the opening night of *Richard III* on 13 July 1953.

Guthrie's flair and originality maintained the excitement over three seasons before he handed control to Michael Langham who began his term astutely in 1956 with a bi-cultural production of *Henry V* starring **Christopher Plummer** with the French roles played by actors from Montreal's **Théâtre du Nouveau Monde**. Over the next ten years Langham consolidated Guthrie's achievements and built the company into a superb acting ensemble. In 1957 a remarkable permanent building replaced the earlier tent, and the Festival soon took over the Avon Theatre, a vaudeville-turned-movie house with a conventional proscenium, as its second stage.

Jean Gascon, founder of the Théâtre du Nouveau Monde, succeeded Langham in 1968, sharing the post with **John Hirsch** for the first 18 months. The Gascon era was a time of ambitious expansion. The repertoire grew to include not only **Molière** and European classics, but also **Jonson**, **Webster**, and the less familiar Shakespeare such as *Cymbeline* and *Pericles*. In 1970 Gascon established the smaller Third Stage for new and experimental works. The Festival company toured extensively in Canada, the USA, Europe, the USSR, and Australia, and in 1969–70 briefly found a winter home in Ottawa's newly opened National Arts Centre, but it proved financially untenable.

When Gascon resigned in 1974, the young English director, Robin Phillips, was appointed to succeed him, releasing a storm of nationalist outrage. Phillips relied heavily on imported stars such as **Maggie Smith** and Peter Ustinov to sell his seasons, and control was centralized to such an extent that his resignation in 1980 provoked a dangerous crisis.

Initially a committee was to take over the directorship, but their efforts to plan a 1981 season were frustrated. After many months of turmoil, bitterness, accusations of betrayal on all sides, and government intervention, John Hirsch was finally asked to become Artistic Director and reluctantly accepted.

Raising the tent over the Stratford Festival Stage, Ontario, June 1953.

During Hirsch's tenure, the Festival never fully recovered from the unseemly debacle. Many leading actors boycotted Stratford in protest, the company was demoralized, much of the public was alienated, and artistic crises were replaced by financial ones. Only the announcement that **John Neville**, who had emigrated to Canada in 1972 and proved himself at Halifax's Neptune and Edmonton's Citadel theatres, would succeed Hirsch in 1986 suggested the possibility of reconciliation and recovery.

The Stratford Festival's importance to world theatre lies in the influence of its stage and staging techniques. In London, Chichester, and Sheffield; in New York and Minneapolis, new theatres have been consciously modelled after it though none has been as successful. However, as the biggest and most important of the open stages, the Stratford Festival has contributed a great deal to the loosening of the grip of the proscenium arch in modern theatre architecture everywhere.

The Stratford Festival's importance to Canadian theatre is two-fold. Initially it provided training and inspiration for a generation of theatre artists and established the highest production standards for the emerging professional theatre. In more recent years it has provided an irresistible target for the attacks of the 'alternate theatre movement' which, in some measure, grew out of a reaction against Stratford and all that it represented. Past attempts to try to bring the Festival back into what has become the mainstream of Canadian theatre have not been notably successful. It remains to be seen whether it is destined always to remain a thing apart.   JA

Strauss, Botho (1944–) German dramatist and critic, co-editor of *Theater Heute* from 1967–70, then dramaturge for the Berlin Schaubühne under **Peter Stein**, for whom he adapted **Ibsen**'s *Peer Gynt*, **Kleist**'s *Prince of Homburg*, and **Gorky**'s *Summer Folk*. After quasi-absurd exercises, like *The Hypochondriacs* (1971), he gained international acclaim with *Three Acts of Recognition* in 1976, which questions the relationship between art and experience. *Great and Small* (1978) added a political dimension, which is extended in *Kalldewey Farce* (1982), where the incongruity of tragic values in contemporary society is set beside neo-fascist revanchism.   CI

Streep, Meryl (1949–) American film and stage actress. She made her New York debut as Imogen in *Trelawny of the 'Wells'* (1975). For the Phoenix she next played Flora in *27 Wagons Full of Cotton* and Patricia in *A Memory of Two Mondays* in 1976, also appearing in *Secret Service*. Over the next two years she played Katharine in *Henry V*, Isabella in *Measure for Measure*, Dunyyasha in *The Cherry Orchard*, Lillian in *Happy End*, which she played on Broadway, and Katharina in *The Taming of the Shrew*. Streep soon after began a brilliant film career, during which she has won two Academy Awards. Of her, **Joe Papp** has said 'I'm convinced we haven't yet begun to see the richness of her talent.' Equally at ease in drama or farce, Streep is noted for meticulous preparation, a wide-ranging intellect, and intense truthfulness in her acting.   SMA

Strehler, Giorgio (1921–) Italian director, and one of the major figures in post-Second World War theatre in Italy. Although he began his career as an actor he soon emerged as a leading director, and in Milan, jointly with Paolo Grassi, established in 1947 the first fully-fledged Italian *teatro stabile*, the Piccolo Teatro. A subsidized theatre, with an acknowledged public service purpose, it tried to reach a socially more heterogeneous audience than had traditional urban theatre. Save for a period between 1968 and 1972, when the events of May encouraged Strehler to form the Gruppo Teatro e Azione, and explore a more politically engaged theatre, it is at the Piccolo that he has been mainly based, although in the 1980s he has been equally involved in the work of the Théâtre de l'Europe for which he has directed plays like **Brecht**'s *The Threepenny Opera*.

Strehler's work has been massively wide-ranging, running to more than 200 productions in the musical and regular theatre. He has brought a questing, lively intelligence and brilliant theatrical flair to so many and very different kinds of drama, that his career does not readily divide into clear periods. The early work, however, of the late 1940s and early 1950s, may be seen as exploratory mainly of the European classical and modern repertory, a focus reflective perhaps of the artistically uncertain bearings of post-war theatre as a whole. A seminal influence was the work of Brecht's **Berliner Ensemble** and its European tour of 1956. Strehler later mounted important Italian productions of *The Threepenny Opera*, *The Good Person of Setzuan*, *The Good Soldier Schweik* and *Galileo* and Brechtian influence is felt in his work on other plays, like **Shakespeare**'s *Coriolanus* (1957). Shakespeare indeed has been an on-going interest, from 1948 when he mounted *The Tempest* in the Boboli Gardens in Florence, through the 1950s when he staged a number of the history plays like *Richard III* (1950), *Henry IV* (1951) and *Julius Caesar* (1953), through to the exploratory metaphysical and poetically evocative productions of *King Lear* (1972) and *The Tempest* (1978).

Strehler's work on the Italian repertoire has included notable reorchestrations and rediscoveries, among them Ferrari's 19th-century piece *Goldoni e le Sue Sedici Commedia Nuove* (*Goldoni and His Sixteen New Comedies*, 1958), turn of the century plays by **Praga** and **Bertolazzi**, an influential revival of **Pirandello**'s *I Giganti della Montagna* (*The Mountain Giants*, 1951), and a string of plays by **Goldoni**: *Gli Innamorati* (*The Lovers*, 1950), *L'Amante Militare* (*The Military Lover*, 1951), *La Trilogia della Villegiatura* (*The Villeggiatura Trilogy*, 1954), *Le Baruffe Chiozzote* (*The Chioggian Squabbles*, 1964) and several re-workings of *Arlecchino, Servitore di Due Padrone* (*Arlecchino, Servant of Two Masters*, from 1947). In his productions of this last play he has sought to recuperate the masked tradition of the *settecento* for modern audiences; his work on several of the late Goldoni plays has brought out a note of melancholy to underscore the passing of a culture and its values. Strehler's fascination with the mid-18th century is evident too in his many productions of Mozart's operas, and the lighter comic pieces of Piccinni and Cimarosa. His current work straddles activity in Paris and Milan and points the European, indeed international, emphasis of his engagement with the theatre. LR

Strindberg, August (1849–1912) Swedish playwright, novelist and essayist, who began by trying to succeed as an actor. Two of his first plays, *In Rome* (1870) and *The Outlaw* (1871), were staged by **Dramaten**; both were indebted to **Oehlenschläger**'s history plays. Paradoxically, the same theatre rejected his first major play, the remarkable *Master Olof*, which had to wait until **August Lindberg**'s six-hour production in 1881, Strindberg's real breakthrough in the Swedish theatre. Meanwhile, in the 1870s he had abandoned a university education, married his first wife Siri von Essen and written his first novel *The Red Room* (1879). His plays were more frequently staged in the 1880s; Dramaten produced *The Secret of the Guild* and Ludvig Josephson's New Theatre staged *Master Olof*, *Sir Bengt's Wife* and *Lucky Per's Journey*. Always eager to be at the forefront of new trends, Strindberg was quick to respond to **Zola**'s call for naturalism in the theatre, albeit in a typically personal way. *The Father* (1887) employed a naturalism that baffled Zola, but which Strindberg claimed was the French naturalists' real goal: 'the great naturalism', larger than real life, focusing on extraordinary, major conflicts, 'the struggles between natural forces'. While he gives his naturalistic plays a psychological basis, explained in the two essays 'On Psychic Murder' (1887) and 'On Modern Drama and the Modern Theatre' (1889), Strindberg points psychology to a level of symbolic, elemental action. *Miss Julie* (1888), especially in its 'Preface', seems an eloquent celebration of the tenets of naturalism, with its emphasis on heredity and environment, its vacillating characters and meandering, non-sequential dialogue. However, its schematic patterns and mythic references lift it beyond the literal to the symbolic.

Strindberg's dream of having his own theatre was briefly realized in Copenhagen in 1889, with the 'Scandinavian Experimental Theatre', modelled on **Antoine**'s Théâtre Libre. The Danish censor having banned *Miss Julie* (performed privately a few days later), the theatre's single programme consisted of *Creditors* and two of his better *quart d'heure* plays, *The Stronger* and *Pariah*. Strindberg spent much of the 1890s in Berlin (where he met his second wife Frida Uhl), Austria and Paris, devoting himself obsessively to scientific experiments and occult studies. Between 1894 and 1896 occurred what is called the Inferno Crisis, a sequence of at least five psychotic episodes, culminating in his hospitalization and eventual return to Sweden. His recovery was partly aided by his discovery of the 18th-century Swedish mystic, Emmanuel Swedenborg, who provided a religious explanation of his sufferings and a rationalization of apparently chaotic phenomena as 'correspondences' of a higher, coherent reality. Determined to be 'the Zola of the Occult', Strindberg assembled masses of esoterically connected phenomena in his *Occult Diary*; they provided much of the detail in his semi-fictional accounts of the crisis, *Inferno*, *Legends* and *Jacob Wrestles*, and his post-Inferno plays. Revivals of earlier plays persuaded him to resume dramatic writing, beginning in 1898 with Part One of *To Damascus*, the first of a new type of drama, exploring mankind's spiritual progress in a divine context. The 34 plays that followed in the next 14 years are remarkable for their diversity and innovation. Some, like the *Damascus* trilogy and *The Great Highway* (1909), are large psycho-spiritual pilgrimage dramas with dream-like settings and action. Others, such as *A*

Dream Play (1902), use dream-structure to reformulate experience. Strindberg also resumed writing history plays, producing 11 on Swedish topics and several plans for *The Saga of Mankind*, an ambitious world-history cycle, of which four were actually completed.

From 1907, Strindberg was actively involved in running the tiny Intimate Theatre, which he had opened with the actor August Falck, in imitation of **Reinhardt**'s Kammerspielhaus. For it he wrote special 'chamber plays', attempting to create the dramatic equivalent of chamber music, 'intimate in form; a simple theme treated with thoroughness; few characters; vast perspectives'. Four of these – *Storm Weather*, *The Burned House*, *The Ghost Sonata* and *The Pelican* – explore the encounter with death as a kind of painful awakening from a life of sleep-walking illusion. As a practising painter, he had an acute sense of the visual in theatre and used the Intimate Theatre's tiny stage to experiment with ways to 'dematerialize' settings. Projected scenery had been tried for productions of *To Damascus* (1900) and *A Dream Play* (1907) and had failed. Now he tried other solutions: drapery and tapestry settings; formal stages derived from the study of theatre history; coloured lighting. His entire career was marked by the urge to experiment and redefine. He exploded the narrow limits of Zola's naturalism; his history plays established a new kind of relationship between background events and the personal drama in the foreground; and his dream and fantasy plays anticipated and paved the way for surrealistic, expressionistic and absurdist theatre.   HL

Strip-tease see **Burlesque show, American; Nudity on stage**

Strittmatter, Erwin (1912–) German dramatist and novelist, one of the 'working writers' of the DDR, whose experience as a baker and farm labourer forms the material of his work. Under the influence of **Brecht**, *Katzgraben* (produced by the **Berliner Ensemble**, 1953) was transformed from a naturalistic dispute about the construction of a road into a dialectical analysis of social change over the decade from 1945, but later plays like *The Blue Nightingale* (1972) show a movement towards utopian fantasy which is not uncommon in East German drama.   CI

Stubbes, Philip (c. 1555–91) English printer and minor poet who is best known for his colourful attack on London's immorality in *The Anatomy of Abuses* (1583). Only a small portion of Stubbes's invective is directed against the public theatres, but it was on this portion that **Nashe** concentrated in his answering *The Anatomy of Absurdity* (1589). Stubbes's book is ironically treasured for the information it gives on popular entertainments in Elizabethan England.   PT

Stukalov, N. F. see **Pogodin**

Sturm und Drang ('Storm and Stress') Term used to denote the work of certain German dramatists and writers of the 1770s. *Sturm und Drang* drama represents a reaction to the rational drama of the Enlightenment. It was written under the influence of **Rousseau**'s natural philosophy and of the plays of **Shakespeare**, which at that time were being translated into German and, very gradually, introduced onto the stage. In *Sturm und Drang* drama, the rights of the individual are often unequivocally expressed, focus is frequently centred upon those aspects of personality and character that render the individual unadjusted to ordered society, and heroes may well be luminescent personalities who attract a following by the sheer force of their personality. Themes of the *Sturm und Drang* dramatists are often sensational, as they deal with incest, infanticide, extreme suffering, and radical disaffection with the world. Dramaturgically their plays are indebted to the 'epic' form of Shakespeare rather than to the carefully composed work of playwrights such as **Lessing**. **J. W. Goethe** was a leader among these writers in the first half of the 1770s, his *Götz von Berlichingen* being one of the most accomplished and characteristic specimens of this type of drama. The plays of **Lenz** are also among the most durable works of *Sturm und Drang*. Other prominent writers in the movement were Heinrich Leopold Wagner (1747–79), who wrote two plays of considerable power, *Repentance After the Deed* (1775) and *The Child Killer* (1776), and Friedrich Klinger (1752–1831), who was known for *The Twins* (1776) and the play that has been used to give the movement its name, *Storm and Stress* (1776). The plays of the young **Schiller**, *The Robbers*, *Fiesko*, and *Love and Intrigue*, although written in the 1780s, show many of the characteristic features of the movement. Several of the plays were given their first performances either by **Döbbelin** in Berlin or **Schröder** in Hamburg. The acting of Schröder was especially suited to the jagged, harsh characterizations in these plays.   SW

Suassuna, Ariano (1927–) Brazilian playwright from the north-east (Pernambuco). His *Auto da compadecida* (*The Rogue's Trial*) in 1957 vaulted him into national prominence in Rio and São Paulo for its aesthetic and ingenious mixture of popular, religious and folkloric elements from the Brazilian north-east. Other plays in similar vein, although less successful, are *O arco desolado* (*The Desolate Arch*), *O casamento suspeitoso* (*The Suspicious Marriage*), and *O santo e a porca* (*The Saint and the Pig*), the latter a treatment of the classical miser, borrowed freely from **Plautus** and **Molière** but with a uniquely Brazilian flavour.   GW

Sudermann, Hermann (1857–1928) German playwright. At the height of his fame over the turn of the century, Sudermann was regarded by many as a playwright equivalent in stature to **Ibsen**. His naturalistic dramas *Honour* (1889), *Sodom's End* (1890), and *Heimat* (1893 – *Homeland*, known in English as *Magda*) were celebrated, the last mentioned because the powerful central role appealed to the prominent actresses of the time. As the naturalist movement ebbed, Sudermann moved unsuccessfully into poetic drama. Despite his dramaturgical expertise, Sudermann's plays, though occasionally revived, are dated, due to his almost total dependence on Ibsen and the well-made play.   SW

Sukhovo-Kobylin, Aleksandr Vasilievich (1817–1903) Wealthy Russian noble, trained primarily in Hegelian philosophy, whom fate helped make a dramatist. Falsely indicted for the murder of his estranged French mistress, he was dragged through the tsarist court system for seven years before being acquitted. His experiences of this period resulted in the writing of the dramatic trilogy which is his sole but major claim to fame. Published in 1869 under the collective title *Tableaux of the Past*, each of the three plays is written in a distinct style, furthers a sequential course of events and revolves around an interlocking set of characters. The monstrous petty bureaucrats, romantic deceivers and mercenary thieves herein depicted are reminiscent of **Gogol** and **Saltykov-Shchedrin**. The plays describe a movement from apparent truth to blatant falsehood, from naive idealism to degenerate amoralism via concentric philosophical, social and dramatic structures. *Krechinsky's Wedding* (written in prison, 1854) is a Scribean 'well-made play' whose romantic contrivance symbolizes an innocent world about to be corrupted. A Khlestakov-like gambler-poseur deceives a young girl and her family and is unmasked. *The Case* (1861) grimly chronicles the spiralling events that trap and ruin the girl and her father when they are dragged into the bureaucratic beehive of the tsarist legal system. Here the tone is harshly satirical, the structure, language and environment more realistic. *Tarelkin's Death* (1869) is a phantasmagoria featuring two petty-bureaucratic vultures who, having disposed of the hapless family in the previous play, now attempt to cheat one another. Here all is sham, including disguisings, feigned death and the charge of vampirism. This is fittingly the most self-consciously theatrical of the three plays, rooted in the tradition of the Gogolian grotesque and foreshadowing the theatre of the absurd. While *Krechinsky* premiered in 1855, *Case* was not staged until 1882 as *Bygone Times* (stressing its 'pastness') and *Tarelkin* until 1900 as *Rasplyuev's Merry Days*. The entire trilogy was performed in 1901 on succeeding evenings. The most famous single production was **Meyerhold**'s *Tarelkin* in 1922, which featured the director's experiments in biomechanics and circus play utilizing constructivist sets by **Varvara Stepanova**. Both *Krechinsky* (in the 1970s) and *Tarelkin* (in the 1980s) have been transformed into musicals in Leningrad. Sukhovo-Kobylin was elected to the Russian Academy of Sciences in 1902. SG

Sumarokov, Aleksandr Petrovich (1717–77)

Russia's first modern tragic and comic dramatist, a poet, critic, 'the Russian **Boileau**', whose 'Epistle on Poetry' (1748) was the rough equivalent of 'L'Art poétique'. He was for his time an enlightened noble and humanist, sensitive to the abuse of power by the tsar and other hereditary nobility, dedicated to the concept of *noblesse oblige* and convinced of the theatre's importance as an agent for social and moral education. He was one of the first graduates of St Petersburg's Noble College of Land Cadets (1740), where his best tragedy, *Khorev* (1747), was played under his direction. This was the first Russian neoclassical play to be performed by Russians and like his eight other tragedies adhered to the three unities, the five-act play structure, the rhetorical language and heroic tone of the French models. Of some interest are his *Hamlet* (1748), based on French

translations, and *Dmitry the Pretender* (1771), which previews the historical events treated by **Pushkin** in his superior *Boris Godunov*. His 12 comedies of character and situation, inspired by **Molière**, attack the commonly depicted vices of his day: Gallomania, judicial corruption, ignorant and self-serving *philosophes*, dandyism, the idleness and cruelty of landowners, the abuses of serfdom and the problem of education. Of these, *The Odd Fellows*, *Nartsiss* and *Tresotinius*, all from 1750, are characteristic. Although his situations were largely borrowed and his characters undeveloped, his comedies as well as his tragedies remained highly popular until the advent of sentimental comedy, bourgeois drama and **Fonvizin**'s more original and refined comedies of manners. Still, Sumarokov provided the necessary first step in introducing native elements and cultured language where before there had been only translations and adaptations. In 1756 he was appointed director of St Petersburg's Russian Patent Theatre, the first permanent Russian professional public theatre, at which **Fyodor Volkov** and **Ivan Dmitrevsky** performed. In 1761 he was relieved of his position and replaced by Volkov. Upon his death, the theatre passed over to the imperial household, thus initiating the tradition of the Russian Imperial Theatres. SG

Surrealism

After rejecting the word 'surnaturalism', the poet Guillaume Apollinaire in 1917 invented the word 'surrealism' in the preface to his play *The Breasts of Tiresias*: 'When man wanted to imitate walking, he created the wheel, which does not resemble a leg. He thus made surrealism without being aware of it.' And he – Guillaume Apollinaire – thus founded an art movement, without being aware of it.

The seed, as opposed to the name, of surrealism was planted in neutral Zurich in 1916. Young artists, refugees from the First World War, viewed all art with a jaundiced eye and voiced their disapproval raucously – especially in unmatrixed performances at the Café Voltaire. Rumanian Tristan Tzara not only participated in these manifestations; he also established correspondence channels with a rebellious avant-garde among the futurists in Italy and the cubists in Paris. Apparently choosing their name 'dada' by opening a dictionary at random, the temperamentally theatrical artists opposed dada to art, process to product. Nevertheless, Tzara penned a play, *The First Celestial Adventure of M. Antipyrine*, which was first performed in Zurich, and four years later in Paris, when Tzara moved to that bastion of the avant-garde.

Paris had not only seen Apollinaire's *Breasts* in 1917, but the **Picasso–Cocteau**–Diaghilev *Parade*, and the publication by André Breton and Philippe Soupault of their *Magnetic Fields*, a dialogue obtained by automatic writing. Chance, spontaneity, deliberate shock were the tactics of the year 1920, with more or less collective participation. By 1924, the rivalry of Tzara and Breton was irremediable, and the latter, seizing upon the neologism of Apollinaire, 'the patron saint of surrealism' (dead in 1917) published the movement's first Manifesto. An heir of symbolism in its opposition to reason and realism; a sibling of dada in its espousal of the unconscious, the erotic, the shocking; surrealism was more ambitiously a life style that sought through images to pierce to man's deepest centre. Programmatically hostile to theatre, Breton expelled **Artaud** and **Vitrac**. If we exclude dada performances and the unreconstructed dadaist Georges Ribemont-Dessaignes, there were scarcely a dozen surrealist performances, but the emphasis upon spontaneity and imagery nevertheless was a lasting legacy of surrealism to the theatre. Above all, surrealism's impact on the theatre came through the mediacy of its first director of research, Antonin Artaud. RC

Sutherland, Efua Theodora (1924–) Ghanaian playwright, director, researcher. Born in Cape Coast and educated in England and Ghana, Efua Sutherland has dominated Ghanaian theatre since independence and has made an incalculable contribution to the development of drama in Ghana over 30 years. As a playwright she has written and devised a wide range of plays in Akan and English; as a director she has staged many kinds of performances, from the traditional community music to modern experimental drama. She has also devoted her energies to the social production of dramatic art in Ghana. She has, for example, inspired the innovative *Kodzidan* ('The Story House'), built by community effort in rural Atwia as a centre for musical and dramatic performances. She has established the Ghana Drama Studio in Accra, which she helped design and for which she raised funds, and she has explored the scope of research into traditional performance, in the Institute of African Studies in the University of Ghana. Through her position of influence she found the means to set up a programme of experimental theatre (1958–61); and subsequently to explore new plays for children, e.g. her 'Rhythm Plays' *Vulture! Vulture!* and *Tahinta* which she later published as a text with photographs. She later developed *Anansegoro* (drama extensions of *Anansesem* – story-telling performances of Ananse, the spider man). *Anansegoro* were performed by a number of groups, mainly in Akan; an English text of Sutherland's own *The Marriage of Anansewa* (1975) was published together with a brief introduction to the theory and practice of the new dramatic form. Her own earlier stage plays, *Foriwa* (1962) and *Edufa* (1962), show an eclecticism and an interest in Western dramatic modes. The economic problems in Ghana constantly postpone the realization of a National Theatre for Ghana which Sutherland has consistently promoted. ME

Sütő, András (1927–) Hungarian playwright, born in the Mezőség region of Transylvania. He is the leading writer of the Hungarian minority in Rumania. Sütő's dramas probe the duty of the individual, confronted by arbitrary authority, to preserve his dignity and identity even at the cost of his life. *The Palm Sunday of a Horse Dealer* (1974), *Star at the Stake* (1975), and *The Wedding Feast at Susa* (1981) are historical dramas; these and *Cain and Abel* (1977) have had numerous productions in Hungary and Transylvania. Their success is due as much to the lyrical beauty of Sütő's language as to their subject matter. Sütő is also well known for prose works, and his writings have appeared in ten other languages. He was awarded the 1979 Herder Prize (Vienna). EB

Sutro, Alfred (1863–1933) British dramatist, whose more than 50 works made him one of the most popular

exponents of the 'well-made play' after **Pinero**, though he was also responsible for translating **Maeterlinck**'s plays. CI

Suzman, Janet (1939–) British actress, who was born and educated in South Africa, the niece of a leading political opponent of apartheid, Helen Suzman. She came to London to study drama at the London Academy of Music and Dramatic Art, which staged an experimental season in 1963 with the newly formed **Royal Shakespeare Company**. Suzman joined the RSC, playing Joan la Pucelle in *The Wars of the Roses* (1963–4) and for the next 15 years, came to play major classical roles with the company, including Rosalind and Portia (1965), Ophelia (1965–6), Cleopatra (1972), and Clytemnestra and Helen in **John Barton**'s cycle, *The Greeks* (1980). Her most notable achievements, however, have come in more recently written plays, an outstanding Hedda in *Hedda Gabler* (1972), Masha in **Jonathan Miller**'s production of *Three Sisters* (1976) and Hesta in **Athol Fugard**'s *Hello and Goodbye* (1973). She has been equally successful in films and television, notably in *The Draughtsman's Contract* (1981) and the TV serial *Clayhanger* (1975–6). Strikingly tall and attractive, Suzman nevertheless commands attention as an actress more through the subtlety of her voice inflexions and the intelligent ironies of her interpretations. JE

Svanga (India) Also known as *Swang* and *Sang* and sometimes referred to as *Sangeet*. This is a rural theatre form found in Harayana, Uttar Pradesh and Punjab, all states of north India. *Svanga* is thought to have originated in the late 18th century and to have spread to urban, as well as rural areas. Hindu festivals and family celebrations, especially marriages and the birth of a son, provide the occasion for a *Svanga*. Performances centre on the conflicts between rival forces found in popular ballads and semi-historical tales. Stories of love, honour and duty abound.

Performances take place in an open space of the village or on the veranda of a patron's house. The actors, who are all male, wear costumes which are simple village garments with exaggerated headdresses and brightly coloured cloth pieces, false hair and beards which 'theatricalize' the performance to satisfy village tastes.

An evening's entertainment begins with songs in praise of Hindu deities, especially Ganapati, the elephant-headed god of good fortune. A strong plot line emerges in which characters express their feelings in the dialogue of the region and punctuate their emotions with songs which have a strong poetic line.

The term *Svanga* also refers to the acts of **Kariyala**, the rural theatre of Himachal Pradesh, and a popular play of *Svanga* is called **Nautanki**, which is also a popular form of rural theatre elsewhere in north India. FaR

Svoboda, Josef (1920–) Czech scenographer. Educated in Prague as an architect, he was for nearly thirty years chief designer and head of technical operations in the National Theatre; since the early 1980s he has been head of the **Laterna Magika** operation, now a branch of the National Theatre. Svoboda's work is based on a metaphoric rather than realistic approach to

Svoboda's set for Mozart's *Idomeneo*, Ottawa National Arts Centre, 1981.

design, on the premiss that stage setting and lighting form an organic, dynamic component of production rather than a static indication of place, and on the use of the widest range of contemporary equipment, materials, and techniques in the creation of the total scenography for a given production concept. Outstanding among his more than 500 productions have been *Hamlet* (Brussels 1958), *Romeo and Juliet* (Prague 1963), *Carmen* (New York 1972), Wagner's *Ring* (London 1974–6, Geneva 1975–7), *Idomeneo* (Ottawa 1983), *Partage de Midi* (Louvain 1984), **Goethe**'s *Faust* (Milan 1989). JMB

Swan Theatre, London This undistinguished theatre, built in c. 1595 by the parsimonious Frances Langley, is given a peculiar significance by the chance preservation of a sketch of its interior, made in 1596 by a visiting Dutchman, Johannes de Witt. Published in 1888, shortly after its discovery, this sketch, the only substantial visual evidence of the inside of an Elizabethan playhouse, caused a radical revision of assumptions about Elizabethan staging. De Witt shows us a round, or more probably polygonal, building with three galleries surrounding an open yard. An almost-square stage, supported by stout timbers, occupies half of the yard. Access for actors is provided by two double-doors, and the unadorned platform is backed by a gallery and partly roofed. The pillars which support the roof effectively break the stage into sections. The Swan, built on the south bank of the Thames, was not a lucky theatre. A performance of *The Isle of Dogs* there in 1597 was largely responsible for a Privy Council ban on the performance of plays in London. One of the authors, **Jonson**, was imprisoned, another, **Nashe**, fled to the continent, Pembroke's Men, who staged the play, disbanded and the Swan itself sank into obscurity. It was used for amateur performances as well as, occasionally, by professional companies and promoters of prize-fights. The only surviving play known to have been staged there is **Middleton**'s *A Chaste Maid in Cheapside* (c. 1611). Probably disused after the death of James I in 1625, the Swan was already 'fallen to decay' by 1632, when Nicholas Goodman described it in his pamphlet, *Holland's Leaguer*.

In 1986 the **Royal Shakespeare Company** opened a new Swan Theatre, designed with an open stage, at Stratford-upon-Avon. This new Swan has, as its policy, the presentation of plays by Shakespeare's contemporaries and the playwrights of the Restoration stage. PT MB

Swanston, Elliard (Eyllaerdt) (d. 1651) English actor who was a leading member of the King's Men from 1624 until the closure of the theatres in 1642. As well as creating many of **Massinger**'s main roles, Swanston is known to have played Othello, Richard III and **Chapman**'s Bussy d'Ambois in revivals. In **Shadwell**'s *The Virtuoso* (1676), he is remembered as 'a brave roaring Fellow, who would make the House shake'. Swanston was, unlike most actors, on the parliamentary side in the Civil War, and is said to have turned jeweller during the Interregnum. PT

Swaziland see **Botswana**

Sweden While there may have been acting in Sweden from the 6th century, the earliest clear evidence is of 13th-century liturgical drama, a genre cut short by the Reformation in 1521 (see **Medieval drama in Europe**). However, Epiphany and Resurrection plays survived outside the churches until the 17th century, augmented by miracle and morality drama. The Lutheran Church encouraged play-acting in schools, to improve morals and manners, not only **Terence** and **Plautus** but indigenous hybrids like *The Play of Tobias, The Play of Judith and Holofernes* and *Rebecca*. The 17th century witnessed increasing secularization, as in the

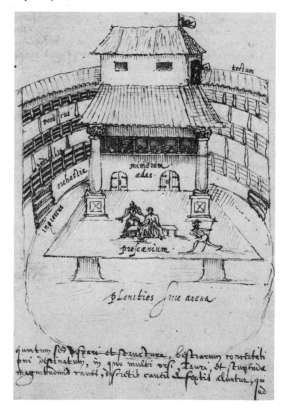

Johannes de Witt's sketch of the Swan Playhouse, 1596, as copied by Arend van Buchel.

burlesque interludes (undoubtedly imitative of the farces played by itinerant German actors) included in the morality *Judas Redivivus* (1614). Significantly, when an Uppsala professor, Johannes Messenius, decided to write a cycle of 50 plays, he decided not to employ biblical matter but Swedish history.

School drama gradually declined in the 17th century, as royal patronage began its long domination of the Swedish stage. In 1628, Gustav II Adolf engaged the finest permanent court troupe, but it was Christina (1632–54) who encouraged really rapid growth: elaborate temporary theatres, with complicated changeable scenery; foreign opera and **commedia dell'arte** troupes; and *ballets de cour* and pageants for royal amateurs. Under her successors, theatrical activity continued to thrive. In 1667 a disused palace lion-house was equipped in imitation of the Amsterdam Schouwburg, serving as court theatre for 30 years. Charles XII (1697–1718) engaged a permanent troupe of French actors, led by Claude Rosidor, and the Royal Tennis Court was converted into a theatre in the French style, with Parisian scenery by **Jean Bérain**. They were followed by a French opera company and then, in 1737, by the first Swedish troupe under royal patronage, 'The Royal Swedish Stage', performing a mixture of French and Swedish plays and Harlequinades. This company, containing the germ of the present-day **Dramaten**, lasted until 1753, when Queen Lovisa Ulrika had them replaced with yet another French company. It was she, with her passion for French drama and Italian opera, who commissioned the **Drottningholm Court Theatre**. The present building, with its decorated auditorium and elaborate stage machinery, is the best-preserved baroque court theatre in the world; it opened in 1766, replacing an earlier building destroyed by fire.

Royal patronage reached a peak in the reign of Gustav III (1771–92), not only at Drottningholm, where summer opera and ballet seasons included open-air pageants such as *The Conquest of Galtar Rock* (1779), but also in the refurbished Tennis Court and the new Opera House (1782). Gustav hired leading designers, such as **Carlo Bibiena** and Louis Jean Desprez; he engaged the French actor 'Monvel' to train rising Swedish stars like **Lars Hjortsberg**; he himself wrote and promoted indigenous drama, both lyric and spoken. He revived the Royal Dramatic Theatre (Dramaten), to perform original Swedish drama, albeit in the French neoclassical style. Gustav's relentless efforts make him very much the father of the Swedish stage and his murder in 1792 brought a temporary halt to such activity. However, while Drottningholm gradually fell into neglect, Dramaten reopened, in the converted Royal Arsenal, with Gustav's last play *The Jealous Neapolitan*, whose gothic atmosphere signalled a trend away from French taste toward German and English. Indeed, **Shakespeare** was finally to reach Dramaten in 1819, with a production of *Hamlet*; however, the most popular playwright in Stockholm at the time was, as in other countries, **Kotzebue**. Swedish romantic poets, such as Stagnelius and Atterbom, had no direct impact on the theatre and not until the 1840s, with the popular comedies of F. A. Dahlgren and August Blanche, did Swedish drama become significant. When the Arsenal burned in 1825, Dramaten began an unsatisfactory shared tenancy of the Opera House, whose mere size may have influenced the popularity of spectacular historical dramas, glorifying the Nordic past. Stockholm's first private theatre, the New, opened in 1842 and by the 1880s under Ludvig Josephson's direction, became Sweden's major progressive theatre, staging **Bjørnson**, Ibsen and **Strindberg**, who achieved his first success with *Master Olof*, in **August Lindberg**'s superb production. The end of the century brought other new theatres (many owned by the 'Theatre King' Albert Ranft) and new stars, such as August Palme, Anders de Wahl, **Emil Hillberg**, Harriet Bosse and Gerda Lundequist. Dramaten, however, was in crisis, deprived temporarily of its subsidy and attacked for its conservatism.

Although Dramaten did in fact premiere several of Strindberg's later plays, he was increasingly dissatisfied by the cluttered realism employed and eagerly collaborated in the moderately experimental work of the Intimate Theatre (1907–10), for which he wrote his Chamber Plays. Paradoxically, the breakthrough of modernism was to occur after Strindberg's death, prompted by visits from the **Reinhardt** and Michel Fokine companies and realized in Sweden by the innovative theatricalism of **Per Lindberg** and Knut Ström at the new Lorensberg Theatre in Gothenburg. Lindberg's erratic but seminal work reached its climax in his productions of **Pär Lagerkvist** in the 1920s and 30s. He was Sweden's major proponent of the 'people's theatre' concept and fought to realize it in the huge Concert Hall theatre in the 1920s, in the People's Parks theatres and on radio. Overlapping with his career was that of **Olof Molander**, under whose leadership Dramaten achieved particular success in the 1930s. In his influential productions of Strindberg, **O'Neill** and the classics, Molander did much to develop the restrained, psychological acting style for which Dramaten was to become renowned, especially in its world premieres of several of O'Neill's plays in the 1950s. Also at Dramaten from the 1930s was **Alf Sjöberg**; before his death in 1980, he directed some 130 productions, constantly exploring new styles and finding new social relevance for the plays he directed. At mid-century, the company could boast a superb acting company, including **Lars Hanson**, **Inga Tidblad**, **Tora Teje**, **Anders Ek**, and Allan Edwall.

Regional theatre in Sweden became progressively important, with the opening of such new city theatres as those in Helsingborg (1921), Gothenburg (1934), **Malmö** (1944) and Uppsala-Gävle (1951). Another innovation in 1934 was Riksteater (the national touring theatre), still very active and still partly controlled by its member organizations. The city theatres' importance has varied enormously, depending on artistic leadership; for example, **Ingmar Bergman**'s early career seemed to cause a wave of creativity as he moved from one provincial theatre to another. In 1963, Bergman took over Dramaten, at a time when theatre was undergoing extraordinary and complex growth. He himself contributed, not only with superb productions, but by giving actors a voice in artistic policy, raising their salaries and opening rehearsals to the public. Among the many small, experimental theatres springing up was one large one, the Stockholm City Theatre, destined seriously to challenge Dramaten with its several companies, including the impressive young people's theatre, Young Klara, led by Suzanne Osten.

In addition to a proliferation of new theatres, the 1960s and 70s saw new State Theatre Schools established in Stockholm, Gothenburg and Malmö, new regional ensembles within the national touring theatre and a growing politicization of theatre in general, as productions increasingly reflected the major political and social controversies of the day. Group projects developed within established theatres, such as Dramaten's *Gypsies* (1968) and the controversial steelworks documentary *N.J.A.* (1969), performed by the group which eventually became the important Free Pro Theatre. This kind of activity had begun at the **Gothenburg City Theatre** in a series of social and political parables directed by Lennart Hjulström, beginning with Kent Andersson's *The Raft* (1967) and followed by *The Home*, *The Sandbox* and *The State of Affairs*. Partly group created, these plays use metaphorical settings (a drifting raft, an old people's home, a mental hospital) to explore a Swedish welfare state that allegedly encourages intolerance and complacency and ignores injustice.

The contemporary situation In 1967 the collectively organized Norrbottens Theatre opened, serving Sweden's most northern county; its desire to treat local issues in its work was reflected in *The Play of Norrbotten* created with local amateurs in 1970. Meanwhile, in 1965 Sweden's first 'free group', Narren, had formed, soon to spawn Fickteatern, which specialized in provocative children's drama like *A Play About School* (1968). By 1969 there was need for a Theatre Centre to coordinate and promote the free groups (today it has more than 60 members) and new ones followed: Theatre 9 (1969); the music theatre Oktober (1972); Skånska Teater (1973), famous for remarkably fresh treatment of the classics and its 1982 trilogy of Rudolf Värnlund's plays; the laboratory theatre Schahrazad (1976); Earth Circus (1977), known internationally for its political street theatre; and then the two remarkable suburban branches of the Gothenburg City Theatre, Angereds Ensemble (1978) and the Backa children's theatre (1982). Meanwhile, older groups like the Pistol and Free Pro theatres continued to be central in Swedish theatre. Two special projects highlighted the theatre's political activism in the late 70s: *The Storm* (1978), in which all Dramaten's resources were committed to a multi-activity presentation about nuclear energy, and the 1977 'Tent Project', *We Are Thousands*, in which about 100 performers toured Sweden for four months, performing a musical documentary about the Swedish labour movement in a circus tent. More recently, in Jokkmokk on the Arctic Circle, the Sami have created a theatre group called Dalvadis.

Adverse economic conditions have hampered growth in the early 80s, especially for the free groups, but progressive institutional theatres like the Stockholm City and the Gothenburg People's theatres have maximized their resources in especially creative ways. Much is hoped for from Sweden's newest major theatre, the People's Theatre in Gävle, led by the director Peter Oskarson. Other important directors are Ingmar Bergman (reunited in 1985 with Dramaten), Suzanne Osten, Lennart Hjulström and Per Verner-Carlson. Outstanding among scenographers are Gunilla Palmstierna-Weiss and Sören Brunes. Sweden remains a country of remarkable but diverse actors,

A scene from the Pistol Theatre's production of Molière's *Les Femmes Savantes* (*The Learned Ladies*), Stockholm, 1984.

including Max von Sydow, Toivo Pawlo, Percy Brandt, Bibi Andersson, Sven Wollter, Stina Ekblad and Stellan Skarsgård. Like other Nordic countries, it faces a dearth of major playwrights, with the exception of **Lars Forssell** and the controversial **Lars Norén**. HL

See: A. Gustafson, *A History of Swedish Literature*, Minneapolis, 1961; G. Hilleström, *The Drottningholm Theatre – Past and Present*, Stockholm, 1956, and *Swedish Theatre During Five Decades*, Stockholm, 1962; F. J. and Lise-Lone Marker, *The Scandinavian Theatre*, Oxford, 1975; and *Ingmar Bergman. Four Decades in the Theatre*, Cambridge, 1982; M. Meyer, *Strindberg. A Biography*, London, 1982; *Modern Nordic Plays: Sweden*, intro. H. Lang, New York, 1973; T. J. A. Olsson, *Facts About the Royal Dramatic Theatre*, Stockholm, n.d.; H. Sjögren, *Stage and Society in Sweden*, Stockholm, 1979; D. K. Weaver (ed.), *Strindberg on Stage*, Stockholm, 1983.

Switzerland The geo-political situation of Switzerland, turntable of Europe, has exerted a profound influence on its cultural life. On the one hand Switzerland enjoys rich and varied theatrical activity, on the other it lacks a distinctive national drama.

Middle Ages and Renaissance (see also **Medieval drama in Europe**) The Abbey of Saint-Gall, early in the 10th century, staged a Latin Easter Play which is at the origin of the flowering of the tradition of Passion plays performed throughout Europe to the end of the 16th century. Early in the 13th century the first dramatic text in German appeared in Muri: *Osterspiel von Muri* (anon.). Lausanne staged its first Passion play in 1453 and the same year saw the beginning of the famous tradition of the Osterspiele on the Weinmarkt in Lucerne. During the 16th century, theatre was used to further the aims of Swiss political independence (*Urner Tellenspiel*, Altdorf, 1511–12), of the Reformation (Théodore de Bèze, *Abraham Sacrifiant*, Geneva, 1550), and of the Counter-Reformation (Jesuit Drama in Lucerne, Fribourg, Sion and, particularly, in Einsiedeln).

17th–18th centuries Theatre under attack: autocratic governments banned plays in Lucerne (1616), Geneva (1623), and Zurich (1624). In 1692, the reformed city of Berne banned a play attacking Louis XIV's persecution of the Huguenots after a complaint from the French envoy. In the 18th century, the only activities in German as well as in French Switzerland were foreign tours of German, French and English companies, and shows put on by aristocratic amateur societies. The first permanent theatres were built in Baden (1673), Lucerne (1741), Solothurn (1755), and Geneva (1783). The most important event during the 'Enlightenment' was the controversy opposing **Voltaire** and **Rousseau**: in his *Lettre à d'Alembert* (1758) Rousseau accused the theatre of immorality and of frivolity and his intervention led to a total ban in Geneva. But the ruling families of the city flocked to Voltaire's house in Ferney (a few kilometres away, but in French territory) to applaud comedies ridiculing their philistinism and religiosity. Rousseau's letter, however, also had a positive effect: it reminded its readers of the lost medieval tradition of religious popular festivals and called for the active creation of open-air civic festivities staged by the entire community for its own wholesome delight and true enlightenment. It so happened that the *Tellspiel* was revived at the end of the century in German Switzerland and that the wine-harvest feast of Vevey grew into a theatrical event, two developments which will bear fruit in the 20th century.

19th century A new freedom entered Swiss theatre with the arrival of Napoleon's armies. A call was heard for the creation of a National Theatre, comprising two companies, one German, one French. In 1837, Berne awarded the first (modest) official grant to a municipal theatre, and by the middle of the century Zurich was regarded as an important centre of German theatre.

Popular theatre The end of the 19th and the beginning of the 20th centuries witnessed a strong resurgence of an amateur and semi-professional theatre movement, creating new or reviving ancient festivals or *Festspiele*. The theme of these huge popular pageants was the commemoration of glorious events of Swiss history or folklore, or the celebration of the agricultural year, especially the harvest (grain or grape). Actors were, and still are, members of local choirs, sport societies, amateur drama companies. The *mise-en-scène* of the *Festspiele* consists of lavish and colourful sets, a profusion of rich and historically accurate costumes, many favourite country dances, music, songs and breathtaking crowd scenes. The renowned *Fête des Vignerons de Vevey* began modestly in the 17th century. It celebrates the four seasons and glorifies Bacchus. It is now staged every 25 years. For the *Fête* of 1977, Charles Apothéloz directed over 4,000 unpaid amateurs, a small cast of professionals and an army of technicians. The production cost over 17 million Swiss francs and attracted 200,000 spectators. **Schiller**'s *Wilhelm Tell* is performed every two years in Altdorf since 1899 (Tellspielhaus) and annually, in the open, in Interlaken since 1912. In 1924 Einsiedeln harked back to its medieval past, presenting – at irregular intervals – **Calderón**'s *The Great Theatre of the World* (*Das Grosse Welttheater*). Romansh and Italian theatre in Switzerland deserve a passing mention here as Tschlin (in Engadine) organizes a popular festival, and in Ticino, Mendrisio perpetuates a 17th-century tradition by staging a religious procession, the *Sacra Rappresentazione*, during the holy week. René Morax, author of the libretto of the *Fête des Vignerons* of 1905, created in 1908

the Théâtre du Jorat, dreaming of uniting nature, culture and society by setting a theatre in the middle of the countryside (Mézières). Inside the building, Morax abolished the separation between auditorium and stage with the addition of stairs linking the two. His best play, *King David*, was set to music by Arthur Honegger.

20th century On a smaller scale, but with the same aim of reaching a popular public, the novelist C. F. Ramuz wrote *The Soldier's Tale* (*L'Histoire du Soldat*, 1918) which Stravinsky set to music. Two other Russians, **Ludmilla** and **George Pitoëff**, passed briefly through Switzerland (1915–21). In Lausanne and Geneva they performed new authors: **Ibsen, Pirandello, Shaw** and, obviously, **Chekhov**, and were part of an avant-garde comprising the creator of eurhythmics Jacques-Dalcroze and the far-seeing designer **Appia**. Unfortunately the burghers of Geneva failed to see their luck: the Pitoëffs settled in Paris in 1921, never to return. Similarly Appia, who rejected painted flats and naturalistic sets in favour of suggestive architectural construction and the use of atmospheric lighting adapted to the inner spirit of the work of art, was ignored, not only in Geneva but throughout the theatre world. The first decades of the 20th century saw the establishment of municipal theatres in every major town: Basle, Zurich, Berne, Lucerne, Bienne, Lausanne, Geneva . . . These theatres are used for plays, ballets, operas and operettas and host mainly touring companies, especially in French Switzerland where, until the 70s, most professional shows were provincial tours of Parisian commercial successes. Only Basle and Zurich and, to a lesser extent, Berne had a resident company. **Oskar Wälterlin** was outstanding as a director in Basle, where he invited Appia in the 20s to design **Wagner**'s *Ring*, and then at the Zurich Schauspielhaus which he established as the main centre of German theatre from the 30s to the 60s. In 1938, returning from Frankfurt, he attracted to Zurich actors and directors fleeing Hitler's persecutions. Under his direction Leopold Lindtberg premiered **Brecht**'s *Mother Courage* (1941) to be followed by *The Good Person of Setzuan* (1947) and *Galileo* (1947). It was Wälterlin also who revealed the two foremost Swiss authors to the public of the Schauspielhaus: **Frisch** and **Dürrenmatt**. Basle (under Werner Düggelin) and Zurich (under Kurt Hirschfield) have retained their excellence, even if the true driving force is now to be found in the 'small theatre movement' and in regional touring companies. 'Pocket theatres' (*théâtres de poche*) are permanent amateur or semi-professional companies, specializing in new avant-garde and 'alternative' plays. In Lausanne, Les Faux-Nez, under Apothéloz, presented **Ionesco** and **Beckett** in the early 50s, plays by local authors, cabarets and street-theatre. Similar organizations sprang up, in the 60s, in Berne, Basle, Zurich, Bienne, Aarau, Neuchâtel . . . New authors emerged: Adolf Muschg, Hans Mühlethaler, Heinrich Henkel in German; Henri Deblüe, Walter Weideli, Bernard Liègme in French: they are regularly performed in Switzerland, and write mainly about the difficulty of being Swiss, although no author has yet emerged to challenge Frisch and Dürrenmatt. In the mid-80s, Swiss theatre people speak of a profound crisis. The established theatres fail to attract new spectators and the little theatres have lost their early

A spectacular view of the arena and the performance space, backed by Lake Geneva and the French Alps, *La Fête des Vignerons*, Vevey, Switzerland, 1977. (Photo: Marcel Imsand, Lausanne)

impetus. The arrival of **Benno Besson** in Geneva (1982), welcome as he is, highlights the malaise: commentators of the Swiss cultural scene were quick to predict that his appointment would transform the situation for the better, ignoring that the two most important theatres, the Théâtre Populaire Romand (TPR) under **Charles Joris**, and Das Theater für den Kanton Zürich (TZ) under Reinhart Spörri, are struggling for their survival and wasting a lot of their energies fighting bureaucracy instead of creating plays. These two theatres, founded respectively in 1961 and 1971, tour extensively and perform a rich mixture of world classics and indigenous plays (in the case of TZ often in German Swiss dialect). Both theatres fulfil an important social as well as cultural role, taking their plays outside the main centres and encouraging theatrical activities in the communities. The TPR pursues the task of permanent training inside the company which is of vital importance, as Switzerland has no policy of theatrical education and lags behind other European countries. The overall picture is not bleak (popular festivals, municipal theatres, amateur companies provide a large variety of performances), but it will be very bland if new developments are stifled for lack of official support. CLS

Symbolism Symbolism in theatre is probably as old as theatre itself, but the widely symbolic must not be confused with the self-styled French symbolists of the last decade of the 19th century. These poet–playwrights admired a man of the theatre, **Richard Wagner**, and a philosopher (of theatre, among other matters), **Friedrich Nietzsche**. The major symbolist poet and thinker was Stéphane Mallarmé, who viewed

Hamlet as a drama of the mind, and who urged the creation of a new drama that would reflect the mental or spiritual life, rather than the crude world of the senses. Through Mallarmé the symbolists viewed art not only as expression, but primarily as a mode of cognition.

Disdaining everyday reality and the realism that reflected it, symbolism came to the theatre in reaction against **Antoine**'s Théâtre Libre (whose repertory was not exclusively realist). 18-year-old poet Paul Fort founded his Art Theatre in 1890 and committed it to symbolism the following year, notably with the production of **Maeterlinck**'s *Intruder* (death) and *The Blind* (who are blind to death) – short, static plays in which the interior life is conveyed mainly through atmospheric effect. Fort was fortunate in securing the services of actor **Aurélien Lugné-Poe** (the Poe affixed in admiration for the American poet), but the young theatre manager was unable to sustain his symbolist theatre, which he dissolved before producing *Axel* by the recently deceased Villiers de l'Isle Adam. This operatic work introduced sensitive aristocrats in a Gothic landscape of forest, moonlight, and castle, which would also be found in the work of such symbolist playwrights as **Hofmannsthal**, early **Yeats**, and, with modifications, **Paul Claudel**. When Fort retired at age 20, Lugné-Poe raised the symbolist banner over his Théâtre de l'Oeuvre, which lasted till 1929. Although symbolist plays are rarely seen in contemporary production, the *fin de siècle* symbolist theatre is noteworthy as the first modern Western theatre to look beyond the stage to occult powers – what Baudelaire in a famous sonnet called 'Correspondences' between the natural and the supernatural, the visible and the invisible, the material and the mystical. RC

Syndicate, Theatrical The origins of the Syndicate lay in the combination system of producing. The expansion of railroads after the Civil War made it possible to tour a production anywhere in America. This proved more profitable than the previous system of resident companies hosting visiting stars. Consequently, by 1885 nearly all the first class stock companies had been replaced by combinations from New York City, and both producers and regional theatre owners had opened booking offices there to arrange these tours. In 1896 the producer **Charles Frohman** joined the booking agency of Marc Klaw and Abraham Erlanger in a partnership with Alfred Hayman, who leased the most important theatres in the west, and with Fred Nixon and Fred Zimmerman, who controlled Philadelphia and the mid-Atlantic region. This arrangement was called The Theatrical Syndicate. By 1903 it governed first class theatrical production in America. The source of its power was its insistence upon exclusive representation. Its clients had to agree to do business only with it, taking the attractions, routes, and dates it specified, and paying the fees it levied.

Its monopoly was broken not by rebellious clients, but by even more ruthless monopolists. The brothers **Sam**, **Lee**, and **Jacob Shubert** were regular clients of the Syndicate, operating some 30 theatres in the north-east. In 1905, concerned about potential rivalry, the Syndicate ordered them to stop acquiring theatres.

Instead, they secured bank financing and declared war. By 1913 they controlled twice as many theatres as the Syndicate. The last Syndicate agreement expired in 1916; and the Shuberts retained a national monopoly on theatres until 1930, and a Broadway one until 1950.

The Syndicate was a means of maximizing profit, not a vehicle for artistic innovation or social welfare. Consquently, it was ruthless in its methods and rapacious in its charges. However, monopoly was the accepted way of doing business in the 19th century, and the Syndicate was only doing in theatre what Standard Oil, United States Steel, and American Telephone and Telegraph were doing in their industries. Furthermore, the Syndicate was only one theatrical monopoly. The so-called 'popular price' theatres were monopolized between 1900 and 1911 by the firm of Edward D. Stair and John Havlin. In 1900 B. F. Keith and Edward Albee organized their United Booking Office, which monopolized all of vaudeville; and Samuel Scribner's Columbia Amusement Exchange virtually monopolized burlesque after 1905.   DMCD

Synge, John Millington (1871–1909) Irish playwright. From 1895 he lived mainly in Paris, regularly visiting home. His permanent return in 1903 had been preceded by his journeys to the Aran islands, beginning in 1898, the last in 1902. In the west he also travelled through Mayo and Kerry, in the east in remote parts of Wicklow. But as **Yeats** had foreseen, when the two met in Paris in 1896, these awesome scenes were the inspiration which Synge's rather aimless pursuit of an artistic vocation had lacked.

The last seven years of Synge's life were intensely productive. In 1902 he wrote *In the Shadow of the Glen* (staged by Frank and Willie Fay, 1903), *Riders to the Sea* (Irish National Theatre Society, 1904), and drafted *The Tinker's Wedding*, whose anti-clericalism frightened the **Abbey**. (It went unproduced until 1971.) *The Well of the Saints* was produced in 1905, *The Playboy of the Western World*, which occasioned riots, in 1907, and his last play, *Deirdre*, posthumously in 1910.

Synge was robust, and a force in the Abbey directorate from 1905, but his body harboured Hodgkins disease, which killed him. David Greene, his biographer, ascribes Synge's fascination with death to a family disposition, and his mother's evangelical religion. Intellectually, he was estranged from his family and his class: landowning, clerical, bourgeois Protestant. He abominated the organized churches; his life acquired a Bohemian aura: Paris, the study of music, of Irish, his love for the Abbey actress Marie O'Neill. Synge was introspective, sometimes shy even with his friends, on his rural travels convivial.

These travels prompted his creative urge. He scorned the experimental drama of **Ibsen** and **Maeterlinck**, but responded to a tragic joy in the endurance of the Aran islanders. The Aran experience precipitated Synge's private suffering into the healing lament of his tragicomic art, a delight in an almost pantheistic nature, elating and dangerous.

Synge's characters assert their destinies. Deirdre exalts her death into 'a story will be told forever'. In *The Well of the Saints* the blind and outcast Douls see in their 'own minds . . . lakes, and broadening rivers, and hills are waiting for the spade'. The tramp's 'fine bit of talk' in *The Shadow* entices Nora from her husband's small-holding – 'each day and it passing you by' – to 'the south wind blowing in the glens' – and 'the cold and the frost'. Off they go together – to the outrage of the play's first audiences.

Berated for defaming the purity of Irish morals, Synge was also attacked on the grounds that his language travestied and coarsened Irish speech. He defended its authenticity, but his aim was not faithful transcription. Synge's achievement was the greater one of forging a dramatic rhetoric from imaginative fidelity to its source. It is a splendid convention, as artificial as **Shakespeare**'s blank verse. The speech of Synge's plays invests their realist stage with a poetry both lyrical and mocking.   DM

Syria see **Middle East**

Szajna, Josef (1922–) Polish director, scenographer, and artist. Szajna's theatrical activities started in Nowa Huta at the People's Theatre in 1955 where he designed such plays as *Princess Turandot* (1956), and *Of Mice and Men* (1956). He eventually became its director from 1963 to 1966. After moving to Warsaw, Szajna worked on many productions, the best known of which was for **Grotowski**'s revival of **Wyspiański**'s *Acropolis* (1966). In 1971, Szajna became director-designer for the Studio Theatre in Warsaw. A total theatre artist in the spirit of **Edward Gordon Craig**, Szajna has been a playwright and dramaturge, developing scripts from sections of literary texts by such authors as Dante, **Goethe**, and **Shakespeare**. His work in this realm includes productions of *Faust* (1971), *Dante* (1974), *Cervantes* (1976), as well as *Macbeth* (1963, England). Szajna taught scenography at the Academy of Fine Arts in Cracow, published works on the subject, and lectured and toured such productions as *Death on a Pear Tree* (1978), throughout Europe and North America. In 1982, he retired to confine his activities to directing and designing.   TM

Tabarin (Antoine Girard) (c. 1584–1626) French clown and farce-player about whose career the surviving evidence is scant and rather confused. After some provincial activity he settled in Paris where in about 1618 he set up a booth stage in the Place Dauphine (and perhaps the adjacent Pont-Neuf) in company with his brother Philippe, who played the quack-doctor Mondor, and a few other performers. There the passing crowd were regaled with a free entertainment of cross-talk routines, comic monologues and short knockabout farces, designed to alternate with and promote the profitable business of selling nostrums and medicaments. Tabarin's stage-name presumably derived from the short cloak (or *tabar*) which he wore over a belted smock and baggy, calf-length trousers, together with a wooden sword or slapstick and his most famous prop, a floppy felt hat capable of any number of metamorphoses for comic effect. So successful had he become by 1622 that rival publishers brought out two separate collections of his material, much of it probably improvised in performance after the manner of **commedia**, to which he was clearly indebted, and characterized by the most uninhibited, frequently scatological humour. Unlike other booth performers such as Jean Farine and **Bruscambille**, who also published anthologies of his original material, Tabarin appears never to have acted with an orthodox theatre company, but he fired the popular imagination sufficiently to bequeath his name to the language in the sense of street-performer and in the expression 'faire le tabarin' (to play the fool). DR

Tableau vivant see **Living picture**

Tairov (pseudonym of Kornblit), Aleksandr Yakovlevich (1885–1950) Soviet-Russian director, founder with his actress-wife Alisa Georgievna Koonen of the Moscow Kamerny (Chamber) Theatre (1941), a venue for highly sophisticated 'synthetic theatre' productions structured around the master-actor, composed along musical and rhythmic lines and featuring innovative cubist and constructivist designs. Tairov began his acting career in Kiev (1905), joining Vera Komissarzhevskaya's Theatre in St Petersburg for the 1906–7 season. Disillusioned with the artistic director **Meyerhold**'s idea of the actor, he quit and signed on with P. P. Gaideburov's touring company (1907–9) for which he directed *Hamlet* and *Uncle Vanya* (1908) as well as other plays. In 1913 he completed law school and staged *Yellow Jacket* and the **Schnitzler**-Donani musical pantomime *The Veil of Pierrette* for Konstantin Mardzhanov's (Mardzhanishvili) Free Theatre. The Kamerny Theatre, which he founded next, owed much to the production work of Mardzhanov, who went on to create the modern Georgian theatre. Tairov's theatre was dedicated to the connoisseur, to theatrical art as self-contained reality and to the creation of beauty. If Meyerhold's theatre often resembled a circus – purposely crude and gymnastic – Tairov's consistently suggested ballet – controlled, exquisite, lacking in rough edges. While Meyerhold sometimes made the actor anonymous in proletarian dress, Tairov geared his entire theatre to the actor's three-dimensionality, clothing him in dramatic, dynamic costumes which fit like a 'second skin'. As with **Appia** and **Jessner**, sets for Tairov were 'keyboards for the actor's playing', rhythmic assemblages of ramps, steps and platforms. All movement was choreographed, dialogue intoned. The acting was neither strictly representational nor presentational but expressive. Rejecting Stanislavskian emotion memory and transcending *perezhivaniye* (emotional experiencing), Tairov called for 'emotional saturation', i.e., for the refilling of beautifully crafted actions with emotions generated during performance. Overall, the theatrical presentation was to strive to equal the purity of music. While the Kamerny's opening production, the Pavel Kuznetsov-designed *Shakuntala* (1914), failed to realize Tairov's vision, **Aleksandra Ekster**'s cubist-designed *Thamira, the Cither Player* (1916) by **Annensky** and Aleksandr Vesnin's severely constructivist *Phaedra* (1922) came closer. Tairov's contention that theatrical action hovers between two poles – the mystery and harlequinade (he discounted the primacy of literature in the theatre) – was reflected in the Kamerny production of **E. T. A. Hoffmann**'s *Princess Brambilla* (1920), adapted by L. Krasovsky. Designed by Georgy Yakulov in a harlequin's motley of swirling colours, boldly defined shapes, 'dynamic décor' (moving banners and scenic pieces) and expressionist lighting effects, which helped create a subjective, dream-like perspective, this 'capriccio for the theatre' embodied the pure joy of creativity. With music by Henri Forterre and choreography by Antonia Shalomytova, one of the Kamerny dancers, this approached Tairov's synthesis of theatrical elements and forms. Yakulov went on to design the highly successful, circus-like *Giroflé-Girofla* (1922) for the Kamerny. The theatre also helped introduce Western classics to the Soviet stage, including: **Wilde**'s *Salome* (1917), whose premiere at Vera Komissarzhevskaya's Theatre (1908) had been banned; G. K. Chesterton's *The Man Who Was Thursday* (1923) with a Vesnin constructivist design; **Shaw**'s *St Joan* (1924); **O'Neill**'s *The Hairy Ape* and *Desire Under the Elms* (1926) and *All God's Chillun Got Wings* (1929). Tairov's productions of Soviet plays ranged from **Bulgakov**'s *The Crimson Island* (1928) and Semyonov's *Natalya Tarpova* (1929), anti-establishment works which were quickly removed from the repertoire, to **Vishnevsky**'s orthodox, romantically monumentalist *An Optimistic Tragedy* (1934), which helped win the director the honour 'People's Artist of the USSR' (1935). Tairov's ability to serve the state and his theatre earned him the Order of Lenin (1945) but is better dramatized by the fact that the Kamerny, despite periods of government intervention and supervision, remained open until shortly before the director's death. Tairov's *Notes of a Director*, chronicling his theatrical work and ideas, was published in 1921. SG

Taiwan Taiwan is a mountainous island of 13,885 square miles in the South China Sea, about 90 miles off the Chinese coast. The Chinese took control of Taiwan in the late 1600s and administered it as part of China. In 1895 Japan gained control of the island as a result of the first Sino-Japanese War. China regained Taiwan after the Second World War. In 1949 the Chinese Communists defeated Chiang Kai-shek's Nationalist forces and took control of the mainland. Chiang moved the government of the Republic of China to Taiwan in December of that year. The population of Taiwan in 1986 was around 20 million.

The native theatre form of Taiwan is the Taiwanese Opera or *Gozai Xi*, a regional Chinese drama that first flourished in the southern Fujian province. The Taiwanese Opera is similar to the Peking Opera in its basic patterns of staging such as movement, costumes, makeup, and the percussive accompaniment, but musically the two forms are entirely different. *Gozai Xi* literally means 'the drama of songs', the singing element is therefore most important. Most of the songs consist of rhymed lyrics of seven words to each line. At first *Gozai Xi* was performed at street corners or country fairs without a stage; later a make-shift, open-air stage was provided. Finally, when this local opera was well accepted by the audiences, it was moved into theatre structures with the added element of scenery, lighting, and special effects. During the Japanese occupation of the island *Gozai Xi* was banned by the authorities. After the Second World War it gradually regained its popularity. It is without doubt the most popular form of theatrical entertainment in Taiwan today, with Yang Li-hua reigning supreme as the most celebrated actress. Other forms of Taiwanese theatre consist of the tribal dances of the Aborigines and puppet theatres of various kinds. The glove-puppet theatre, called the *Budai Xi*, is especially popular among peasants and fishermen on the island.

Although the mainlanders comprise but one-tenth of the Taiwan population, their theatrical taste – mainly the appreciation of the much refined Peking Opera – has affected theatre development in Taiwan in the last half-century. The first visit of a Peking Opera troupe to this island was a Shanghai troupe which had a two-week run in Taipei in August 1909. Ever since, a good number of mainland troupes have visited the island with varying degrees of success. The most important visit, which had a lasting effect on the Taiwan theatre scene, was a troupe led by a talented young actress Ku Cheng-ch'iu. She and 60 of her colleagues came to the

island in December 1948 and performed at the Yung Lo Theatre in Taipei. Her talent quickly won the approval of the Taiwan audiences, including a large number of wealthy mainlanders who had fled to the island to avoid the Communist take-over. By the end of 1949 the Communists had taken over the entire Chinese mainland. Ku and her colleagues were forced to remain on the island and kept performing. The run at the Yung Lo Theatre continued for four and a half years – a record length in the history of the Chinese theatre. While Ku and her Company were enjoying this long run a number of other Peking Opera troupes also made their exodus to Taiwan to avoid the Communists on the mainland. Some of these troupes were associated with the armed forces, most notably the Ta P'eng Peking Opera Troupe of the Chinese Air Force. The Commander-in-Chief at that time, General Wang Shu-min, happened to be an avid theatre lover. Under his patronage the Ta P'eng Troupe became the best and largest Peking Opera company in Taiwan. A training school was later added to the Troupe, which in the next 30 years trained a good number of talented young actors many of whom are still performing on the stage today.

There are five major Peking Opera troupes performing in Taiwan at present: the Ta P'eng troupe associated with the Air Force, the Lu Kuang troupe with the Army, the Hai Kuang troupe with the Navy, the Ming T'ou troupe with the Armed Forces Logistics Command, and the Fu Hsing troupe associated with the National Fu Hsing Dramatic Arts Academy – the leading training institution for Peking Opera actors, musicians, and backstage personnel on the island. These five troupes take turns performing at the Armed Forces Cultural Activities Centre, a modestly equipped 950-seat theatre in Taipei. Matinee performances on Sunday mornings are given by training school students for student audiences free of charge – a government sponsored project to cultivate a young audience for this traditional art form. Peking Operas and Taiwanese Operas are also featured on television quite frequently as another means to develop a wider audience. Paid attendance at regular Peking Opera performances, however, has been declining steadily.

Two Peking Opera actresses in contemporary Taiwan deserve mention. The first one is Hsu Lu, a skilled performer of female roles with a superb singing voice who was the first graduate of the Ta P'eng training school. Between 1960 and 1980 she was the most popular Peking Opera actress in Taiwan, having made eight tours to South-East Asia, Europe, and South America. She had over 100 roles in her repertoire and has been equally versatile in the roles of 'virtuous woman', 'coquette', and 'female warriors'. Another noted actress is Kuo Hsiao-chuang (b. 1951), a later graduate of the Ta P'eng training school who is known for her beauty and charm in the performance of the 'coquette' roles. After a successful career on the stage, including two United States tours in 1973 and 1974, she became a star on television and in cinema which widened her audience appeal. In 1979 she formed her own company the Ya Yin (Elegant Music) Opera Ensemble whose aim was to present Peking Opera with a contemporary spirit by utilizing modern stage-craft and a more sophisticated orchestration. A typical

Ya Yin production would take a long, arduous period of rehearsals and preparation, involving top playwrights, composers, and designers on the island or from abroad. The result has been much polished productions adorned by enthusiastic young audiences who usually don't attend Peking Opera performances. Kuo Hsiao-chuang and her Ya Yin Opera Ensemble represent a new force in contemporary Taiwan to revive a fading interest in the traditional theatre.

The modern theatre, called the **huaju** or the 'spoken drama', had a much less important position in Taiwan, although its earliest performance activity could be traced to 1911 when a Japanese director came to stage several productions with local actors. Most of the actors recruited were ruffians in town, hence the earliest type of modern drama in Taiwan was called the 'ruffian drama'. In the next twenty years quite a number of local drama troupes were organized, staging popular works by mainland playwrights as well as those by local authors dealing with Taiwan themes. The most noted theatre figure during this early period was Chang Wei-hsien, a local director and acting teacher who studied dramatic arts in Tokyo in the 1930s. The amateur theatre activities in Taiwan had the first chance of improvement in 1949 when Chiang Kai-shek's nationalist government moved to the island. Among the 1.5 million mainland refugees, there were some playwrights, directors, and actors of the modern 'spoken drama'. Most of these theatre artists were associated with the entertainment units of the armed forces. They became the main core of specialists who mounted productions and trained the next generation of theatre workers. They also helped the development of the film and television industries on the island. Among people in the pre-1980 Taiwan modern drama scene the woman playwright Li Man-kuei deserves mention. Li was responsible for a brief Little Theatre Movement in Taiwan in the early 1960s. In 1962 she organized the Committee on Spoken Drama Appreciation which was for years the major producing agency of modern dramas in Taiwan. Over 120 productions were presented between 1961 and 1969 under the auspices of Li's Committee. This Committee also started a World

Lan Ling Ensemble's 1979 production of *Ho Chu's New Match*, a free mixture of Peking Opera conventions and contemporary theatre elements.

Drama Festival in 1967, presenting foreign plays in the original languages by language students in local universities. In 1968 the Committee created a Youth Drama Festival presenting plays by local playwrights performed by university students in the Chinese language. These two festivals are still in existence today and are instrumental in the development of school drama in colleges and universities on the island.

Judged on the international scale, the modern theatre in Taiwan is rather insignificant. Performance quality is low, even compared with its Asian neighbours such as mainland China, Japan, Korea, and Hong Kong. As of 1986 Taiwan still does not have a full professional theatre company with paid actors offering high-quality 'spoken dramas' on a regular, year-round basis. Theatre facilities used to be poor and scarce; the first adequately equipped theatre auditorium (the Chung Hsing Hall in Taichung) was not built until the mid-1970s. Although there has long been a degree-granting theatre department in a Taipei college (now the University of Chinese Culture), full-scale training programmes for students of modern drama did not start until the establishment of the National Institute of the Arts in 1982. Among the semi-professional and amateur 'spoken drama' theatre groups in Taiwan, the best known one is the Lan Ling Ensemble, an experimental theatre group founded in 1980 by Wu Chin-chi, a psychology professor who had worked and trained at the **La Mama** Theatre Company in New York. Wu and his actors, who all have other occupations, rehearse three evenings a week and present an average of three productions a year to an enthusiastic young audience. The Lan Ling productions are noted for their free adaptation of Chinese materials, the simplicity of staging devoid of scenery, and the use of actor's voice and movement rather than the dialogue as their chief means of communication. One of their early works, *Ho Chu's New Match* (1979), is a free adaptation of a Peking Opera utilizing many conventions of the traditional theatre often in a hilarious fashion.

In recent years the government of Taiwan started a few ambitious projects which, upon completion, should advance the progress of the modern theatre on the island. The first one is the construction of the National Theatre and Concert Hall Complex in the heart of Taipei. The projected date of completion is October 1987. This cultural complex plus a few other district theatres under construction will provide international-standard performance spaces which will help the improvement of production quality of modern dramas on the island. Another major project is the establishment of the National Institute of the Arts. This Institute has four departments: music, fine arts, theatre, and dance.   DSPY

See: J. R. Brandon, *Brandon's Guide to Theatre in Asia*, Honolulu, 1976; Huang Mei-shu, 'Taiwan huaju de huigu yu zhanwang' (The past and future of the spoken drama in Taiwan), *Muqien muhou, taishang taixia* (In front and behind the curtain, on and off the stage), Taipei, 1980, 104–11; Li Fu-sheng, *Zhonghua guoju shi* (History of the national opera), Taipei, 1969; Lu Su-shang, *Taiwan dienyin xiju shi* (A history of cinema and drama in Taiwan), Taipei, 1961; A. C. Scott, *Literature and the Arts in Twentieth Century China*, New York, 1963; Selected brochures, pamphlets, and souvenir programmes of the theatre companies and institutions cited.

Talesnik, Ricardo (1935–) Argentine playwright, actor and director. After an auspicious beginning in television, he wrote *La fiaca* (*The Doldrums*, 1967), a dramatization of the lack of individual freedom experienced by a man suffering from Monday morning 'blah's'. The play was an instant success, was staged throughout Europe and Latin America and filmed in 1968. Major later plays include *Cien veces no debo* (*A Hundred Times I Ought Not*, 1970) and *Los japoneses no esperan* (*The Japanese Don't Wait*, 1973), both with anti-bourgeois postures. Talesnik has experimented with musical comedy, pantomime, and one-person shows, and was a collaborator with **Rozenmacher**, **Somigliana** and **Cossa** in *El avión negro* (*The Black Airplane*, 1970), a play based on myths regarding Perón's proposed return to Argentina. GW

Talli, Virgilio (1858–1928) Italian actor and company manager. An able rather than an outstanding actor, his importance as an actor–manager lay particularly in his contribution to stage-management, in which his activities prefigured those of the director in the Italian theatre in concern for the unity of a production and insistence on subordinating the personality playing of lead actors to the requirements of the play in production. From 1885 he managed a number of fine companies and was responsible for the first stagings of plays like **Giacosa**'s *Come le Foglie* (*Like the Leaves*, 1900) and **D'Annunzio**'s *La Figlia d'Iorio* (*Iorio's Daughter*, 1904). LR

Talma, François Joseph (1763–1826) French actor. Talma was Napoleon's favourite actor. He contributed to a revival of interest in neoclassical tragedy which accorded with Napoleon's own attempt to create an Empire inspired by ancient Rome. More importantly, Talma, whose early years had been spent in England (where he trained to be a dentist), was interested in reforms in stage costume which he had seen there and introduced to France. In 1789, playing a small part in **Voltaire**'s *Brutus* at the **Comédie-Française**, he delighted his audience and scandalized his colleagues by appearing in authentic Roman dress, with bare arms and a toga (instead of a periwig and breeches), designed by the painter David, and this led to a rapid costume revolution at the Comédie-Française. Talma, who had been one of the first pupils of the newly founded Conservatoire in 1796, studied under the actors Molé and Dugazon. From Molé, who did not believe in the romantic idea of the actor being guided by nature, he received a firm grounding in technique. Dugazon, much interested in *pantomime*, trained him in the expressive use of his face and taught him to act when not actually speaking. His own experience of the English theatre led him towards a more natural style of delivery than the traditional declamation normally reserved for tragedy. His attention to detail in the preparation of his roles, costume and makeup was unusual for the period. Talma made his debut at the Comédie-Française in Voltaire's *Mahomet* in 1787. In 1789 he played *Charles IX* in Marie-Joseph Chénier's violently anti-monarchical and anti-clerical play. He took the part because no one else wanted it, and it allowed him to show his skill at portraying the darker passions of fury and despair,

which he would use to advantage in the **Ducis** adaptations of *Othello*, *Hamlet* and *Macbeth*, as well as Néron in **Racine**'s *Britannicus* or Oreste in *Andromaque*. *Charles IX* was the occasion of a split in the Comédie-Française. Talma, although never really active in politics, espoused the revolutionary cause in what was a fundamentally royalist institution, and finally left with a group of other dissidents to take up residence at the former Variétés Amusantes, the Théâtre de la République (the present Comédie-Française) in 1791. It was at this period that he came to know Napoleon, of whom he became a fervent admirer and who had a considerable interest in the theatre and a taste for neoclassical plays (notably those of **Corneille**, whose Cinna was to be one of Talma's great roles, being played by command before the famous parterre of kings at Erfurt in 1808). Talma once more became part of the Comédie-Française when the various factions were brought together in 1799. From 1802 to 1811 he frequently toured and was often attacked for this by the critic Geoffroy (with whom he finally had a punch-up in a box at the Comédie-Française in 1812). One of the few parts in which Geoffroy had liked him was as Manlius in Lafosse's *Manlius Capitolinus* (1806), Talma's most popular role after Oreste in Racine's *Andromaque*. In 1815 he left the Comédie-Française and continued to tour for the next few years. In 1816 the king renewed the pension that Napoleon had granted him. In 1819 Talma was the one person to vote for the admission of **Frédérick Lemaître** to the **Odéon**. He did not return to the Comédie-Française until his last role, significantly another historical role. Talma was almost a symbol of the Empire. He was also the actor who made the bridge between neoclassical tragedy and the romantic drama, to which his temperament and style of playing clearly drew him. It is significant that **Victor Hugo** had Talma in mind as he worked on *Cromwell* (1827), whose central part was tailor-made for him. JMCC

Tamasha Of India's many forms of rural theatre, few stress humour as a dominant feature of their content as extensively as does *Tamasha*. *Tamasha* satirizes and pokes fun at contemporary society, often at the expense of politicians and businessmen, priests and prophets, clothing its barbs in the guise of historical or mythological stories. Indeed, it is a major form of rural theatre in the state of Maharashtra, in west central India. Rough estimates suggest that approximately 10,000 artists from around 450 *Tamasha* troupes service a population base of about 62 million people. In sheer numbers alone, this makes *Tamasha* among the more popular forms of rural theatre in India.

Although the precise date of its origin is uncertain, evidence suggests that it developed in the 16th century as a bawdy form of entertainment to please the Mogul armies that occupied the Deccan plain and among the insurgent Maratha forces determined to free their people from their oppressors. The term itself is a Persian word meaning 'fun', 'play', and 'entertainment' and was probably introduced to the area by the Urdu-speaking soldiers of the Mogul armies sent by the Delhi sultanate to maintain its authority over the region between the 14th and the 16th centuries. The form that we call *Tamasha* today is probably the amalgam of many different influences which may be traced back over many centuries, ideas that were adapted by rural artists to suit their own needs. Some scholars have suggested that *Tamasha* developed out of the decaying remnants of two short forms of classical Sanskrit entertainment – the *prahasana* and the *bhana*. Just how this transpired is not certain. Still other scholars suppose that diverse pieces of musical, dance and dramatic entertainment coalesced and eventually produced the *Tamasha* sometime in the 16th century. There were certainly plenty of forms of entertainment available from which artists might draw an inspiration – the classical *Kathak* dance of north India, with its infectious rhythms and sensuous appeal; the *kavali* and *ghazal* songs designed to assault the ear with rich melodies and exotic rhythm; the **Dashavatara** musical plays and *Bharud* dramatic poetry recitals; the *Lalit* religious play and *Gondhal* religious songs; the *kirtan* one-man musical sermon and the *Kal Sutri* puppet shows.

The diverse elements of a typical *Tamasha* performance suggest its borrowing from different elements of the forms mentioned above. All *Tamashas* open with a *gan*, or devotional song in praise of the deities, lustily sung by the chief male singer and musicians. Following this is the *gaulan*, a dramatic segment in which Krishna and his clown attendant waylay milkmaids on their journey to market. Their conversation with the milkmaids and their old aunty provides considerable cause for mirth. In this section, songs and dances intervene to punctuate the raucous humour. Following this is the *vag*, a short dialogue play drawn from historical and mythological sources, laced with satirical incidents and broad slapstick humour. After the *vag* were introduced to *Tamasha* in the 19th century, they quickly became the soul of the art form.

The pattern, described above, typifies the performance process of the *dholki-baaris* folk drama troupes which are distinguished as one variety of *Tamasha* performance. Perhaps the older varieties of companies are the *sangeet-baaris*, or song troupes, which emphasize song and dance in their work and do not use the *vag* as part of their entertainment.

The *sangeet-baaris* troupes are relatively small in size, consisting of half a dozen dancers and singers and several instrumentalists. The *dholki-baaris* troupes get their name from the popular drum used in *Tamasha*, the *dholki*, and consist of a leading male actor, half a dozen male actor–singers, one or more female dancer–singers and several instrumentalists. The clown character (*songadya*), whose improvised humour is so integral to the success of all *Tamasha* troupes, is common to both varieties of *Tamasha*.

Tamasha's popularity is also partially due to the popularity of the love-songs (*lavani*) which are interpreted through singing and dancing. *Lavani* entered the form during the Peshva period of Maharashtra's history (1707–1818). The songs were sung by male singers dressed as women until the end of the 19th century. Today, the songs are sung by professional dancing girls whose physical charms, as much as their vocal abilities, help to sell a song. Enthusiastic patrons pleased with a particularly brilliant *lavani* or perhaps taken with the beauty of the singer are encouraged to go to the performance area and offer a token of their esteem to the singer in the form of a rupee note. These special requests (*daulat-jadda*) are often honoured by the singer

who repeats the song again to the enchanted enthusiast. Poetic dialogues coupled with mime (*chakkad*) are also honoured in this way. The songs themselves have provided the inspiration for many popular Hindi and Marathi film songs and vice versa, thus feeding the mutual support of the entertainment business throughout the full spectrum of audiences in rural and urban areas.

In addition to the *dholki* drum, *Tamasha* musicians play the *tuntuni*, a single-string drum instrument; the *manjeera* cymbals; the *daf*, a large tambourine-like instrument with a single leather surface; the *halgi*, a small version of the *daf*; the *kade*, a metal triangle; the *lejim*, an instrument resembling buttons strung like beads on a wooden rod, producing jangling sounds; and, the harmonium, a box-like accordion. The many strings of *ghungrus*, or ankle bells, worn by the dancers also help to accentuate the rhythmic aspects of the music.

Tamasha dance is an amalgam of Kathak classical dance technique and indigenous folk dance ideas, broadly described as 'filmic' by some local critics.

Historically, *Tamasha* has been linked with two untouchable communities of Maharashtra – the Kolhatis and the Mahars. Training has largely been kept within the confines of family units associated with the art. With the introduction of female dancers in the late 19th century however, the general public assumed that the artists were little more than prostitutes; and, consequently they have continued to be the subject of ridicule by puritanical and conservative forces of Maharashtrian society.

For much of *Tamasha*'s history the poet–singers (*shahirs*) have left their mark. During the 18th century these individuals were chiefly responsible for raising the artistic level of the narratives and love-songs to great heights. As company leaders, they gained an enviable reputation with the rulers of the day and helped to raise the reputation of the Tamasha artists somewhat above that of prostitutes and outcasts. This tradition of *shahirs* continued throughout the independence movement in 1947 and brought the idea of freedom from British rule to the heartland of India. As political differences began to emerge in the 1930s and 1940s, some popular *shahirs* became associated with Communist causes. In recent years, the influence and reputation of the *shahirs* has diminished, perhaps owing to the availability of various forms of mass communication and the rise in the literacy rates. Their role in *Tamasha*'s history and future was discussed in 1969 when they formed an association of *shahirs* to discuss ways to revitalize interest in their work and in *Tamasha*.

Historically, *Tamasha* has been performed almost anywhere that there was an open space providing room for the actors, dancers and musicians to work and plenty of room for the audience. Throughout most of the year, performances have been presented out of doors, but during the heavy monsoon rains indoor performances have been given in certain urban, proscenium arch theatres in Bombay, Pune, Nagpur, Nasik, Aurangabad and elsewhere in the state. Troupes that perform in these theatres are regarded as 'raw' *Tamasha* and are admitted to facilities in the working-class districts.

Another type of company has grown up in recent years to attend to the taste of urban sophisticates who demand wholesome family entertainment cleansed of some of the obscene remarks and actions typical of the rural companies. The companies which have developed to please this element of society are known as *loknatya*, or people's theatre. These companies perform in expensive urban playhouses frequented by patrons who can afford to pay the relatively high-price admission. Both types of groups have experienced the vicissitudes of unscrupulous impresarios who have often manipulated them into a debtor's status. Government schemes introduced in the 1960s have attempted to restore solvency and dignity to the companies and to educate the humble women performers, as a means of protecting them from exploitation, but the job has been difficult in the face of long-standing traditions and complicated social entanglements.

Like other forms of rural theatre, *Tamasha* has served as a source of inspiration to modern urban directors and actors. Several prominent productions have been developed in imitation of *Tamasha* technique. Among the most prominent in recent years have been Vijaya Mehta's Marathi versions of *The Caucasian Chalk Circle*, *The Little Clay Cart* and Girish Karnad's *Hayavadana*; Vijay Tendulkar's *Ghashiram Kotwal* directed by Jabbar Patel; and *Teen Paishacha Tamasha*, also directed by Jabbar Patel and adapted from **Brecht**'s *Threepenny Opera* by P. L. Deshpande.   FAR

Tamayo y Baus, Manuel (1829–98) Spanish playwright, whose attempts to halt the decline of the theatre between romanticism and realism led to the establishment of the *alta comedia*. After adapting French and German plays he had his first original success with *Virginia* (1853), a tragedy in the manner of **Alfieri**. He tried historical dramas in verse and prose, then changed to thesis plays of social morality with *La bola de nieve* (*The Snowball*, 1853) attacking the vice of jealousy. Similarly, *Lances de honor* (*Affairs of Honour*, 1863) attacks duelling. His best play is generally considered to be *Un drama nuevo* (*A New Play*, 1867), depicting the hidden passions among actors of **Shakespeare**'s company rehearsing a new play by the master.   CL

Tandy, Jessica (1909–) English actress who in 1954 became a naturalized American citizen. She studied at the Ben Greet Academy of Acting and made her professional debut as Sara Manderson in *The Manderson Girls*, London, 1927; the next year she joined the **Birmingham Repertory** Company, first appearing as Gladys in *The Comedy of Good and Evil*. Her first appearance in London was as Lena Jackson in the 1929 production of *The Rumour*. Tandy made her debut on Broadway as Toni Rakonitz in 1930 in *The Matriarch*. Among her later outstanding roles were Ophelia to **John Gielgud**'s *Hamlet* (1934) and Blanche Dubois in *A Streetcar Named Desire* (1947). As Blanche she won rave reviews and achieved Broadway stardom; a critic called the role 'deeply moving . . . acted gloriously . . . one of the most arresting and moving performances you are likely to thrill to in many a semester'.

In 1942 Tandy married **Hume Cronyn**; since then she has appeared in six Broadway productions with him: *The Fourposter* (1951); *The Physicists* (1964); *A Delicate Balance* (1966); *Noël Coward in Two Keys* (1974); *The Gin Game* (1977); and *Foxfire* (1982). Tandy and Cronyn appear regularly in American regional theatres, chief among them the **Guthrie Theatre**, which they appreciate for having longer rehearsal periods and better facilities than Broadway theatres. At the Guthrie, Tandy has played such roles as Linda in *Death of a Salesman*, Gertrude in *Hamlet*, and Madam Ranevskaya in *The Cherry Orchard*.

Tandy has appeared in numerous British and American television programmes, first appearing on British television in 1939.   SMA

Tang Xianzu (1550–1616) Chinese dramatist. A native of Jiangxi he passed the imperial examinations in 1583 and entered government service. Conspicuously unsuccessful in an official career he abandoned it in 1598 to devote himself to his writing. Tang was a romantic and an individualist who sidestepped the rigid rules of orthodox metrical usage in favour of a freer, more sensual, use of diction and poetic expression. His contemporary and rival Shen Jing (1553–1610), in contrast, adhered strictly to the traditional forms of metrical composition. Each man acquired his own following representing two main schools of thought which contributed to the greater development of **kunqu** as a dramatic form. Tang's major bequest to the repertoire was a quartet of plays with a dream motif. One of these, *The Peony Pavilion* (*Mudan ting*) in 55 scenes, is one of the longest of its kind. The theme of romantic love expounded in a supernatural context had a great emotional impact on the audiences of the day. It remains outstanding to the Chinese for the excellence of its poetic style. Excerpts from this play have been constantly performed on the traditional Peking stage.   ACS

Tanzania Tanzania is located on the East African coast. Over 90% of the 20 million inhabitants subsist on agriculture. The 123 ethnic groups are linguistically united by Kiswahili, the national language, which has greatly influenced the growing nationalist theatre movement, especially after the adoption of *Ujamaa* (socialism) in 1967.

The theatre of the pre-colonial times was a conglomeration of many theatre forms derived from a variety of pre-capitalist production modes and their resultant cultures. These can be broadly categorized into four types: ritual theatre, especially relating to initiation; celebration dances related to some social event with the basic aim of reinforcing social values e.g., *Nindo* (Wagogo), *Mkwajungoma* (Wazaramo), *Maseve* (Wangoni), *Selo* (Wazigua) and *Hiari ya Moyo* (Wanyamwezi); story-telling e.g. *Simo* (Wagogo) and *Haditi* (coastal groups); and heroic recitations.

Colonization by the Germans and later the British brought about significant changes. Though the British by means of the missionaries, colonial educators and administrators discouraged or prohibited traditional theatre performances as 'barbaric' and 'uncivilized', most forms stubbornly survived. In 1948 however colonial policy changed and traditional theatre performances were encouraged at agricultural exhibitions and trade fairs as well as colonial festivals such as Empire Day to ensure wider publicity and to distract the people from their discontent with the colonial situation. This resulted in the formation of more than 58 dance associations in the urban areas by 1954.

The colonialists also encouraged certain new dances

that were considered 'appropriate' for 'enlightened natives' e.g. *Beni*, whose movement, costuming and music borrowed from colonial military bands, and *Mpendoo*, which was devised especially to distract the Christian and 'educated' Wagogo from their traditional *Nindo* and *Msunyunho* dances. Later, however, the colonial government again discouraged these traditional dance groups because of their subversive potential.

Western theatre was introduced in the early 1920s and by 1952 almost all schools were staging the plays of **Shakespeare**, **Shaw**, **Gilbert** and Sullivan etc. In 1957 the British Council launched a school drama competition to foster British culture and to emphasize correct and proper English speech. Because of the exposure to exclusively British bourgeois theatre, the Tanzanian colonial elite came to look upon this kind of theatre as the one and only one.

Vichekesho is an offshoot of the Western theatre and was very popular in the schools alongside the imported Western drama. Based on improvised sketches, directed and performed by students, *vichekesho* sought to 'cause laughter' among the audience by making fun of the 'uncivilized' and 'uneducated' masses for not being able to use such items of 'civilized' life as a fork, a springbed or a mirror.

Expatriate theatre was established in the form of two 'Little Theatres' – the Dar es Salaam Players (1947) and the Arusha Little Theatre (1953) and they remain to this day completely oblivious of any theatre tradition inside or outside Tanzania other than that of Broadway and the West End. As a result they have exerted no influence on the development of Tanzanian theatre.

The attainment of political independence in Tanzania did not usher in much change in the theatrical scene. The formation of the Youth Drama Association in 1966 under the patronage of expatriates and Tanzanian elite resulted in the emergence of original Swahili plays by Tanzanian playwrights e.g. *Mukwava wa Uhehe* (*Mukwava of the Hehe People*) by M. Mulokozi. *Vichekesho* continued but the content changed from laughing at the 'uncivilized' to rebuking the educated for looking down on their own people e.g., *Zabibi* (*The Raisin*), a radio play, and *Martin Kayamba* by G. Uhinga.

More significant changes came with the Arusha Declaration, the blueprint for *Ujamaa*, in 1967. Plays by foreign dramatists were discouraged and theatre in Kiswahili gained the upper hand. All 20 published Tanzanian playwrights emerged during this period. The plays of 1967–77 portray a general enthusiasm and support for the policy of socialism though they also point out hurdles in its implementation. Examples of such plays are *Kijiji Chetu* (*Our Village*) by **N. Ngahyoma**, *Hatia* (*Guilt*) by **P. Muhando**, *Mwanzo wa Tufani* (*Beginning of the Storm*) by K. Kahigi and A. Ngemera and *Giza Limeingia* (*The Dawn of Darkness*) by **E. Mbogo**.

Plays produced after 1978 present a more critical analysis of the socialist construction process, portraying the disillusion and helplessness of the masses in the face of mounting corruption and exploitation by members of the ruling class e.g. *Kaptula la Marx* (*Marx's Capital*) by E. Kezilahabi, *Nguzo Mama* (*Mother the Main Pillar*) and *Lina Ubani* (*There is an Antidote for Rot*) both by Muhando, *Harakati za Ukombozi* (*Liberation Struggles*) by **A. Lihamba** and others and *Ayubu* by

the Paukwa Theatre Association. *Vichekesho* continued, to become the core of workers' theatre.

Another theatre form developed in the period was *Ngonjera*, which was based on traditional poetic forms and constituted a recital accompanied by dramatic movement and gesture, costumes and props. Commonly performed at Party functions, national festivals and other official occasions, *Ngonjera* answered President Nyerere's call for poets to 'go out and publicize *Ujamaa*'. *Ngonjera* troupes now exist in all schools and it is one of the most popular theatre forms.

Traditional dance too has transformed itself into an appropriate carrier of new messages of the *Ujamaa* era. Over 30 dance troupes, some of which are professional, exist in Dar es Salaam alone. These groups also engage in slapstick improvised drama.

The search for a Tanzania-based theatre has been the preoccupation of the University of Dar es Salaam Department of Art, Music and Theatre, the Bagamoyo College of Art and the Butimba Arts College of Education. Drawing from traditional and contemporary local resources as well as foreign theatre traditions, they have produced performances and writings both based in Tanzanian cultural reality and of contemporary relevance e.g. *Shing'weng'we*, *Harakati za Ukombozi* and *Nyani na mkia wake* (*The Monkey and its Tail*) by the University, *Tunda*, *The Challenge and the Gap* and *Chakatu* by Bagamoyo and *Azota na Azenga* (*Azota and Azenga*) by Butimba. The same trend is apparent in the writings of those produced by these institutions – Muhando, Lihamba, **Hussein** – and in the work of the amateur theatre groups such as Paukwa and Sayari as exemplified in the former's *Ayubu* and *Chuano*.

In the 1980s the theatre for development (see **Third World popular theatre**) movement came into existence in Tanzania, spearheaded by the University's Department of Art, Music and Theatre. Long-term projects and short-term workshops have been conducted in Malya (Mwanza), Msoga (Bagamoyo) and Bagamoyo villages. PMl

See: E. Hussein, 'On the Development of Theatre in East Africa', PhD thesis, Humbolt University 1975; A. Lihamba, 'Politics and Theatre in Tanzania After the Arusha Declaration, 1967–1984', PhD thesis, Leeds 1985; L. Mbughuni, 'Old and New Drama from East Africa', in *African Literature Today*, 8, London, 1976; P. Muhando (Mlama), 'Traditional African Theatre as a Pedagogical Institution', PhD thesis, UDSM 1984 and 'African Theatre – the Case of Tanzania', UDSM, unpublished paper; M. Rugyendo, 'Towards a Truly African Theatre', in *Umma*, 1,2 (Dar es Salaam, 1974), pp. 63–76.

Tarkington, Booth (1869–1946) American novelist and playwright. Although better known as a novelist, Tarkington was the author of 21 produced plays. He liked to write for actors – *Monsieur Beaucaire* (1900) for **Richard Mansfield**, *Master Antonio* (1916) for **Otis Skinner**, *Poldekin* (1920) for **George Arliss**. His most successful play, *Clarence* (1919), showing the disruption of a normal household by a handsome, bumbling hero, was written for **Alfred Lunt** and **Helen Hayes**. After their success with *The Man from Home* (1907), Tarkington and Harry Leon Wilson collaborated on nine plays. Seldom satisfied with his reception, Tarkington distrusted the theatre as a place for serious art or thought.   WJM

Tarlton (or Tarleton), Richard (d. 1588) English clown, who became a legend in his own lifetime. He is first heard of in 1570, as the supposed author of a ballad, and the Stationers' Register lists among his lost work *Tarlton's Toys* and *Tarlton's Tragical Treatises* (both 1576) and *Tarlton's Device upon this unlooked for great snow* (1579). The manuscript of *Tarlton's Jig of a horse loade of Fooles* is now assumed to be one of John Payne Collier's many forgeries, but Tarlton was almost certainly the author of the popular play, *The Seven Deadly Sins* (1585), of whose second part an outline plot (or **platt**) survives. It was performed by **Queen Elizabeth's Men**, which Tarlton joined on the company's formation in 1583. He had probably been one of **Leicester's Men** prior to that date. There is every indication that Tarlton was more suited to solo or extempore performance than to the faithful recitation of other men's lines. The spirit, though not the letter, of his comic routines is probably present in the posthumously published *Tarlton's Jests* (1611), an important source-book of biographical information. Tarlton specialized in the jigs, which were a popular feature of the playhouse programme. He was also a Master of Fence and a skilled musician. The well-known drawing by John Scottowe shows him in a buttoned cap and short boots, playing a pipe while beating a tabor. It is the image of a rustic clown, with curly hair, broad nose, flattened and bent, and simple suit, probably russet. The squint to which he confessed is not evident. That Tarlton's fame outlived him is not surprising. He was the finest popular entertainer of his generation as well as a favourite at Court. It is something more than sentiment that reinforces claims that **Shakespeare** had him in mind when he wrote Hamlet's reminiscence of Yorick.   PT

Tarragon Theatre The most solidly established of Toronto's so-called alternate theatres, Tarragon, under the direction of its founder, Bill Glassco, was a major source of new work in the 1970s, particularly the plays of **David French**. It acquired a reputation for realistic drama despite the fact that it also introduced the work of **Michel Tremblay** to English Canada and provided a stage for the epic poetry of **James Reaney**'s *Donnelly* trilogy. Its name was chosen in a deliberate attempt to 'avoid anything with workshop, studio or lab in it', but despite the avoidance of experimentation it has managed to be both an artistic and a commercial success and, more than any other theatre, has succeeded in bringing Canadian drama into the mainstream of Canadian theatre. Since 1983 it has been directed by Urjo Kareda, a former drama critic, dramaturge and briefly co-artistic director of the **Stratford Festival**. While still maintaining a commitment to new Canadian works it has considerably broadened its repertoire.   JA

Tasso, Torquato (1544–95) Italian poet and dramatist. Most of his dramatic writing was done for court entertainment, celebrations, festivals and like theatricals. Among the many kinds of dramatic writing he produced two plays are particularly important: *Re Torrismondo* (*King Torrismondo*, 1578, but written ear-

lier), a quasi-baroque verse tragedy in emulation of **Sophocles** that treats of the disastrous consequences ensuing from an illicit passion, and *Aminta*, the most celebrated and influential dramatic pastoral of the Renaissance, first performed at Ferrara in 1573 by the **Gelosi** company. One of the most admired of Italian poets abroad, his influence was strongly felt in the work of many English 16th- and 17th-century writers.   LR

Tate, Harry (Ronald Macdonald Hutchinson) (1872–1940) Scottish comedian, on the British music-halls 1895–1939. As the man who was 'always in control of the situation', he possessed the superb capability of reducing his environment to utter chaos. At golf, billiards, motoring, fishing, flying or broadcasting, he was invariably defeated by the malice of objects, including his recalcitrant moustache, and obstructive fellow-creatures like his obnoxious son and mute, staring little boys. His sketches became classics and made catchphrases of 'Good-byeeee' and 'Isn't it annoying, Papaaaa!' His influence on **W. C. Fields** was patent.   LS

Tate, Nahum (1652–1715) Irish playwright. Born in Dublin and educated at Trinity College, he graduated in 1672. His poems began to be published in 1676. He began having his plays performed in 1678. In 1680 his adaptation of **Shakespeare**'s *Richard III* was banned for its study of usurpation and abdication: Tate disguised it as *The Sicilian Usurper*. In 1681 Tate's version of *King Lear* was performed and, itself adapted, effectively kept Shakespeare's play off the stage until 1838. Tate's work is endlessly vilified for its elimination of the Fool, the introduction of a love-plot between Edgar and Cordelia and its happy ending with Lear restored to the throne but his changes are the result of an honest attempt to combine new conventions of probability and decorum with a work that he admired. Tate adapted Shakespeare again in the same year, turning *Coriolanus* into *The Ingratitude of a Commonwealth*. His farce, *A Duke and No Duke*, was performed in 1684; the second edition (1693) contains an important defence of farce by Tate. Tate wrote the libretto for Purcell's *Dido and Aeneas* (1689). In 1692 he was appointed poet laureate and in 1702 historiographer royal.   PH

Taylor, Cecil P[hilip] (1928–81) British dramatist, who once described his career as 'a gradual scaling down of ambition'. Throughout his life he kept faith with the socialism of his Glasgow Jewish childhood, but the revolutionary flavour of his early plays, such as his first *Aa Went to Blaydon Races* (1962), gave way to the warm humour of such plays as *Allergy*, a one-act comedy about the downfall of a Trotskyist paper within a very small circulation, or *The Black and White Minstrels* (1972) which came from Edinburgh to the **Hampstead Theatre Club** in London. Taylor was a prolific dramatist, adapting plays by **Sternheim** and **Ibsen**, as well as writing for the stage and television; and for many years, he stayed with regional companies in Newcastle, Liverpool and in Scotland, producing scripts for their needs rather than for the more financially rewarding theatres in the South. His *Schippel* (adapted from a Sternheim comedy) was seen as *The Plumber's Progress* (1975) in London with Harry Secombe, while *Bread and Butter* (1966), *Bandits* (1977)

And a Nightingale Sang . . . (1979), and his last play, *Bring me Sunshine, Bring me Smiles* (1982), had brief London runs. His most successful play, *Good*, about a liberal German professor in the 1930s whose moral cowardice leads to a military career and a job in Auschwitz, was first staged by the **RSC** at the Warehouse in 1981 and later transferred to the West End, staring **Alan Howard**. Taylor's energy and charm were present in all his writing, giving life to even apparently casual scripts; but he sometimes lacked the disciplined concentration to ensure that his many talents lived up to their promise. JE

Taylor, Joseph (1586–1652) English actor, already famous in London when he joined the King's Men, probably to replace **Richard Burbage**, in 1619. After the death of **Heminges** in 1630, Taylor shared with **Lowin** the business management of the company, as well as creating many of **Massinger**'s leading roles and playing Hamlet, Iago, and Ferdinand in **Webster**'s *The Duchess of Malfi*. The fact that Burbage is known to have created Hamlet and Ferdinand strengthens the belief that Taylor was his successor as the company's leading tragedian. But he was versatile enough to be an outstanding Mosca in a revival of **Jonson**'s *Volpone*. PT

Taylor, Laurette (Cooney) (1884–1946) American actress who made her first appearance as a child in Gloucester, Massachusetts, then went in 1903 to the Boston Athenaeum. She first appeared in New York

the same year in *From Rags to Riches*. Her first substantial success came in 1910 in *Alias Jimmy Valentine*, but she achieved stardom in the title role of *Peg O' My Heart* in 1912, a script by J. Hartley Manners, who married Taylor in 1911.

Later roles included Nell Gwynne in *Sweet Nell of Old Drury* and Rose Trelawny in *Trelawny of the Wells*. After her husband's death in 1928, Taylor retired from the stage, but returned as Mrs Midgit in the 1938 revival of *Outward Bound*. She co-starred in 1945 in *The Glass Menagerie*, a smash hit which made her once more the toast of Broadway. SMA

Taylor, Tom (1817–80) English playwright, journalist and art critic whose phenomenal energy allowed him to cram several careers into less than 63 years. Taylor was born near Sunderland and educated at the Universities of Glasgow and Cambridge, at the latter of which he taught for two years before moving to London in 1844. He was Professor of English in the University of London from 1845–7, during which time he was called to the Bar and had eight plays staged at the **Lyceum**. After practice as a barrister on the northern circuit from 1847–50, he was appointed Assistant Secretary to the newly created Board of Health in London, continuing to serve the Board in various capacities until 1871, by which time he had written a further 60 plays (there were at least nine more to come), published a three-volume biography of the painter Benjamin Haydon (1853), and established himself as art critic of *The Times*, regular writer of leaders for the

Laurette Taylor (second from left) in her famous role as Peg in *Peg O' My Heart*, by her husband John Hartley Manners, Court Theatre, New York, 1912.

Morning Chronicle and the *Daily News* and popular contributor to *Punch*, of which he became editor from 1874 until his death. Add to all that the fact that he was virtually house-dramatist for the Wigans at the **Olympic** from 1853–65 and for **Buckstone** at the **Haymarket** from 1859–61 and some estimate of his productivity can be made. It is not surprising that most of Taylor's plays have proved as ephemeral as his journalism. He gratified the taste of the time with burlesques, pantomimes, even a hippodrama (*Garibaldi*, 1859), and, like most contemporary playwrights, he was a shameless thief of French plots. His most famous melodrama, *The Ticket-of-Leave Man* (1863), is from the French, as is his probing moral comedy, *Still Waters Run Deep* (1855), whilst two of his best comedies, *The Contested Election* (1859) and *The Overland Route* (1860), are certainly derivative, though not tied to a particular source. Taylor's most ambitious work for the theatre was the succession of history plays, some in blank verse, which began with *'Twixt Axe and Crown* (1870) and ended with *Anne Boleyn* (1876). They have survived no better than *Our American Cousin* (1858), the outstanding popular success of Taylor's lifetime, which owed much more to the inventiveness of the creator of Lord Dundreary, **E. A. Sothern**, than it did to Taylor. There is finer stuff among Taylor's collaborative work, *Masks and Faces* (1852) with **Charles Reade** and *New Man and Old Acres* (1869) with Augustus Dubourg, for example. It is a fair summary of Taylor's dramatic career to say that he took the styles he found – farce, comedy, melodrama, history play – and, without ever trying very hard, improved on them. **PT**

Tchelitchew, Pavel (1898–1957) Russian-American theatrical designer and artist. Tchelitchew studied abstract art and stage design under **Aleksandra Ekster**, and in 1918 became an assistant to soviet designer Isaac Rabinovitch. But Tchelitchew eventually renounced his Cubist style and moved to Berlin in 1921 where he designed the opera *Le Coq d'Or* and met Serge Diaghilev. In Paris in 1923 he embraced a neoromantic style and developed his controversial technique of multiple perspectives. This technique gave his representational painting a surrealistic quality and brought him to the attention of Gertrude Stein. In 1934 he designed **Louis Jouvet**'s production of *Ondine* in Paris, and subsequently moved to the United States where he eventually acquired citizenship. His designs for ballet included *Nobilissima Visione* (1938) and *Balustrade* (1940) for George Balanchine. By the 1940s Tchelitchew became disillusioned with stage design and he refused **Agnes de Mille**'s offer to design the ballet *Rodeo* (1942), suggesting instead that she use **Oliver Smith**. Tchelitchew's works were frequently shown in galleries in Paris, the Museum of Modern Art in New York, and elsewhere. **TM**

Teatro Abierto (Open Theatre) Argentine theatre phenomenon organized by **Osvaldo Dragún** and others in 1981 in response to an oppressive political regime. Designed to revitalize a stagnant stage, the first promotion in 1981 resulted in 20 new one-act plays by as many authors, staged by 20 directors, in a seven-day cycle with three plays each night (with one missing). The Teatro Picadero mysteriously burned at the end of a week, but the fierce determination of the group,

coupled with great public enthusiasm for the event, caused them to continue in the Teatro Tabarís almost immediately. The 1982 cycle was overshadowed by the Falklands (Malvinas) War and by a diminished quality of the 51 new scripts. Events scheduled for subsequent years have become less impelling because of the Alfonsín election of 1983 and the return to democratic procedures in Argentina. **GW**

Teatro Campesino, El (The Farmworkers' Theatre) Theatre company founded by **Luis Valdéz** in 1965 to support Filipino and Mexican-American strikers against the grape-farmers of the San Joaquin valley, California. Initially an agit-prop group tailoring its *actos* (short plays) to the issues and needs of the moment, in a style at once cartoon-like, comic, and realistic, the company took on a wider political involvement – though still focusing on Chicano concerns – during the period of maximum opposition to the Vietnam War. In the 1970s, disillusion with the growing violence of Chicano politics, together with a need to develop artistically, prompted a change of direction. El Centro Campesino Cultural was created on 40 acres of farmland at San Juan Bautista, south of San Francisco, for Valdéz and his people to research Indian myth and ritual as a basis for life and theatre. In performance, the early *actos* were replaced by *mitos* ('myths') such as *El baile de los gigantes* (*The Dance of the Giants*, 1974), though the basic principle of a bi-lingual theatre using a vivid physical style remained the same. **AEG**

Teatro de Orientación (1932–4 and 1938–9). With objectives similar to those of the **Teatro de Ulises**, this Mexican theatre group was established with a governmental subvention under the direction of **Celestino Gorostiza**. **GW**

Teatro de Ulises (1928–9) Mexican theatre group co-founded in 1928 by **Xavier Villaurrutia** and **Salvador Novo** with the patronage of Antonieta Rivas Mercado, the group broke with the old traditions of Castilian accent, the prompter's box, and full attention on the star of the show in order to stress the overall coordination of the director. The objectives were a poetic, universal, conceptual theatre. New lighting and staging techniques were adopted from the European masters, **Craig**, **Reinhardt**, **Stanislavsky**, **Piscator** and others. Defunct by 1929, the group presented six plays, mostly French translations, and managed to give new impetus to the renovation of Mexican drama, and new spirit to Mexican playwrights and directors. **GW**

Teatro del grottesco The name given to a body of plays by Italian dramatists of the second and third decades of the 20th century. Never a movement, the Theatre of the Grotesque sought an anti-naturalistic renewal of the bourgeois theatre by the development of ironic, parodistic and grotesque situations, the use of an author's spokesman or *raisonneur*, and by emphasis upon the public and private face of dramatic characters. The best-known plays of this theatre included the widely translated and performed *La Maschera e il Volto* (*The Mask and the Face*, 1916) by **Luigi Chiarelli**, and Rosso di San Secondo's *Marionette che Passione!* (*Puppets, What Passion!*, 1918). **Pirandello** is considered by many to have written some of his early plays in this vein, and his essay on humour, *L'Umorismo* (*Humour*, 1908), was a seminal influence.   LR

Teatro Nacional D. Maria II The Portuguese National Theatre is the most visible result of a very deliberate decision taken in 1836 of a newly formed and fragile Liberal regime and administration to further the dramatic and theatrical arts in the country. The locale eventually chosen was the premier site in the capital, at the head of the Rossio, the most topographically central and historically important square in Lisbon.

The first director, **Almeida Garrett**, concurrently Inspector-General of Theatres, supervised its building, provided its first successful plays, transformed the professional training of actors, set up the theatrical archives associated with the building and generally launched it as the 'decent home for the national drama' it was intended to be. As was true of many national theatres, it was and is the goal of most aspiring dramatists and actors. Even during the Salazar regime, under the management of the actors Amélia Rey-Colaço and Robles Monteiro (1929–64), it strove to maintain high standards. Portuguese and foreign classics alternated with foreign moderns from **Anouilh** to **Valle-Inclán** and native playwrights who, in revival or first performance – achieved often enough through one laudable subterfuge or another – were remembered or introduced to the capital's and the country's theatre-going public. The prestige and imaginative direction of the company in the latter years enabled it to soar above the crasser censorship and conformist social pressures, even if it tended to play safe.

Garrett's beautiful theatre was gutted by fire in 1964; but arose, like a phoenix from its ruins, to be reopened in 1978. To the more traditional main auditorium, it has now added a *sala experimental* (workshop theatre). The theatre as a whole is extremely elegant and well-appointed, but disappoints some by continuing to be too 'discreet' with its repertoire and montages. The criticism applies far less to the workshop theatre, where the contributor saw the first production of 1986, a telling performance, in translation, of Edna O'Brien's *Virginia*.   LK

Teje, Tora (1893–1970) The major Swedish tragedienne of her times, noted for her vocal musicality (occasionally overexploited) and her physical authority and expressiveness. From the 1920s to the early 50s, she was **Dramaten**'s natural choice for such roles as Medea, Phèdre and Queen Margaret in *Richard III*. Among her important **Strindberg** roles were Indra's Daughter in **Olof Molander**'s revolutionary 1935 production of *A Dream Play* and Alice in *The Dance of Death*. She was admired for her early work in **O'Neill** (Nina Leeds in *Strange Interlude* and Abbie Putnam in *Desire Under the Elms*), but was not part of the O'Neill wave that swept Dramaten in the 1950s.   HL

Television drama More people all over the world are being exposed to more drama than ever before. The drama they watch is not mainly that of the theatre or even the cinema: it comes to them on the television screen in their own homes or – sometimes in the case of the Third World countries – in communal venues.

Television may be no more than a means of transmission of preexisting material. The simplest form of electronic drama is that resulting from putting one or more cameras in front of a stage. At a more ambitious level, a theatre play may be adapted for the interpretative possibilities of the medium. **Shakespeare** has proved to be effective on the small screen in many countries; indeed, the BBC has presented the entire canon in a six-year project begun in 1978. In France, the **Comédie-Française** has performed **Molière, Marivaux, Beaumarchais** and other classics on TV; in Greece Channel ERT 1 has recorded some of the drama of antiquity, including all the plays of **Aristophanes** and **Euripides**, in the theatres of Epidaurus and Herodes Atticus. Japan's public-service network NHK televises not only **kabuki** plays but also items from the most esoteric **bugaku** and **nō** repertoire.

Television may also be, and frequently is, a channel for broadcasting films originally intended for the cinema.

Now it would be doctrinaire to object categorically to recordings or adaptations of stage plays or to the transmission of cinema films: the reaching out for wider audiences for these is a worthwhile undertaking. But television has its own dramatic potential although plays written for the medium, some pre-war experiments apart, did not emerge until the late forties and early fifties. At that time TV plays were exclusively produced in the studio. The difference between film and television studio production was that, whereas for film a single camera would take each shot discontinuously to be edited afterwards, for television two, three or more cameras would shoot the action from different angles in an unbroken run. TV plays, normally set indoors, would go out 'live', i.e. they were seen at the actual moment of performance. Exterior scenes if needed had been filmed beforehand and were fed into the transmission. In other words television drama had much in common with theatre, notably the element of 'real time' untouched by any editing process.

The coming of videotape in 1958 was to change all that: plays could now be recorded and edited, making more cinematic construction possible. Indeed in the sixties many television writers and directors turned directly to the film camera in order to break out of the studio. The fact that in the eighties light-weight video cameras have increasingly replaced film cameras does not affect the issue: television drama retains its visual mobility and its structural flexibility. From the viewers' standpoint a more obvious innovation was the introduction in the sixties and seventies of colour (PAL, SECAM or NTSC according to the prevailing system). So television drama, even in the strict sense of a medium-specific form, can draw on a range of techniques: studio and/or location, monochrome and/or colour, film (of different gauges) and/or videotape (of different formats).

It follows that the defining characteristic of television drama is not so much any one mode of production as the mode of reception. Even here it is as well not to be dogmatic. But it is a valid generalization to say that the viewer does not go out to see a play with any sense of occasion; it is offered to him in the distracting conditions of his home. He has the choice at any time to switch over or off. Screen size and image resolution make the viewing experience less overwhelming than that of the cinema. A television play then has to grab the viewer quickly to retain his attention; the response is rarely going to be the enthralled one of a crowd in the theatre or the cinema. TV drama speaks to spectators as individuals or as members of small groups; it may even be felt to be something of an intruder in the home with its various family taboos.

But perhaps the significant point is not so much the impact of any one play as such but that of television drama as a whole. Embedded in a continuous stream of electronic information (news, weather reports etc.) it forms part of the viewer's alternative world, an extension or even a partial replacement of first-hand experience. Is this enriching or enfeebling? That will of course depend on the overall context of programming, the sense of social reality it conveys. Even the advertising messages on commercial channels that punctuate plays will colour them subliminally. The sheer quantity of television drama available for consumption in itself becomes problematic: in 1979 the average American family spent six hours and twenty-six minutes daily in front of the 'box', with drama a substantial part of the fare.

It is said that viewing conditions favour the close-up as against the long shot, the actor as against the environment, a narrow domestic vision as against the social insight. But technical circumstances are contingent; the coming of high definition television (with a standard of 1,125 lines) can drastically change picture quality; larger screen sizes may enhance image impact. The programming context might alter too. We must therefore see the medium's seeming preference for domestic naturalism as a conditional rather than an unchallengeable fact. What will remain constant is the smallness of the domestic audience and the discourse arising from this premiss.

TV drama in different countries varies according to differing socio-economic, technological and cultural/political conditions. Some Third World countries cannot as yet afford television. Others are so poor, with thin network coverage and few sets in private ownership, as to make television – drama or whatever – a negligible influence. For instance in India, with as few as 1.5 receivers per 1,000 head of population in 1979, the impact of TV drama cannot begin to compare with that of the flourishing film industry.

The cultural climate cannot fail to be a major factor in the tone and quality of television drama. In the Socialist countries political considerations take priority in broadcasting; there are, however, differences in programming policy between various countries. Yugoslavia and Hungary, for instance, screen far more Western TV drama than the Soviet Union – though when the BBC's *Forsyte Saga* was shown on Soviet television in 1971 it was well received. Much of Soviet television drama is derived from stage plays. Official guidelines frown on scenes of sex, violence and racism. In China during the Cultural Revolution, TV drama was largely confined to the few Peking Operas of which Mme Mao approved. Recently, more topical plays have been broadcast.

Elsewhere different factors influence television drama. In Thailand, Channel 7 which is run by the Army has used the traditional operatic form of *mau-lum* for anti-communist propaganda. West German TV has from time to time broadcast plays that try to come to terms with the Nazi past. Non-political elements, too,

will colour a nation's TV drama output: Hong Kong is addicted to kung-fu as Japan is to samurai epics. In Italy the cinema tradition has been so strong that Radio Televisione Italiana (RAI) has commissioned films from leading directors (e.g. Bertolucci's *The Spider's Stratagem* or Fellini's *The Orchestra Rehearsal*) for showing on the small as well as the large screen – proving incidentally that the requirements of these two media, while different, may well converge.

The actual organization of broadcasting institutions is bound to be crucial. Commercialism as in the United States; a state-run service as in Cuba or Czechoslovakia; a duopoly, partly public service and partly commercial, as in Great Britain; or any of the possible variants of the above all make for very different kinds of drama.

The world's largest producer of TV drama, chiefly of the 'entertainment' variety, is the United States. The domestic strength of the industry makes it the leading exporter, able to offer its programmes abroad at irresistible prices. An oligopoly of three networks – ABC, CBS and NBC – dominates the numerous local stations which get 70% of their material from the Big Three. There is a solid home market: in 1979, 98% of the population owned a set; in 30 million homes there were two, and in 10 million homes three or more sets. Since the purpose of commercial television is to sell airtime to advertisers, the criteria of success are 'ratings' (i.e., viewer numbers) or at a more sophisticated level 'demographic profiles' (i.e., the socio-economic section of the market reached). The networks, which produce only a fraction of their own material, buy in telefilms from six major Hollywood studios (Columbia, Paramount, MGM, 20th Century Fox, Universal and Warner Brothers) or large independent TV film production companies (such as MTM Enterprises and Lorimar) as well as a number of smaller independents. The bulk of these productions comes from the West Coast; their style and ethos is that of Hollywood. Production values count for a great deal, cultural prestige hardly at all. In the ceaseless competition for a slice of the market, the principle of Least Objectionable Programming (an upmarket version of the Lowest Common Denominator) is held in high regard. The Public Broadcasting Service which transmits quality work hardly affects the overall picture: it only reaches 2% of American viewers.

But at times propaganda considerations supplement or replace purely commercial ones. ABC's 8-part, 12-hour serial *Amerika* (1987) – a fantasy of a Soviet take-over of the USA set in the near future – provoked protests at home and abroad against such deliberate 'warnography'. The fact that the ABC/Capital Cities board has close links with the defence industries is not irrelevant here.

In Britain where the BBC, guided by the Reithian public-service ethos, used to enjoy a monopoly of the air, television drama tended at first to be little more than televised theatre. But in the early fifties attempts were made to ginger things up; Nigel Kneale's science-fiction tale, *The Quatermass Experiment*, caused a stir in 1953. The coming, after a vigorous debate, of commercial television in 1955 opened up British broadcasting to more popular tastes.

The United States has shown the way. The American networks, originally broadcasting from New York, had encouraged a spate of fresh TV playwriting, probably in order to persuade people in the higher income brackets to buy receivers. The competition between 'The Philco Playhouse' (NBC) and 'Studio One' (CBS) in the late forties and early fifties brought on what in retrospect glowed like a golden age of television drama. Writers like Gore Vidal, N. Richard Nash and Reginald Rose made their mark. **Paddy Chayefsky**'s *Marty* (NBC 1953) depicted an unglamorous butcher's longing for love with wry affection; other plays of his such as *The Catered Affair*, *The Bachelor Party* and *Middle of the Night* all revelled in what he called 'the marvellous world of the ordinary'. A similar outburst of creativity took place in Canadian television around that time.

In seeking out more popular material, Britain – both the BBC and the drama-oriented independent company ABC – bought in a large number of North American scripts. ABC's 'Armchair Theatre' (derided as 'Armpit Theatre' for its gritty realism) changed the tone of drama on the small screen; writers like **Alun Owen**, Clive Exton and **Bill Naughton** began to give it a contemporary and British accent. Associated Television, ATV and Granada also promoted original TV playwriting. In 1964 the BBC started 'The Wednesday Play', a title changed in 1970 to 'Play for Today'; this became a platform for innovative (and to some timid souls, alarming) drama, presenting the work of **Michael Frayn**, Rhys Adrian, **Simon Gray**, **Peter Terson** and many others who either were already or were destined shortly to become well known. **David Mercer**'s *In Two Minds* (1967) questioned the conventional wisdom about schizophrenia. In *The Big Flame* (1969) Jim Allen looked at casual dock labour from a revolutionary perspective. One of the instant hits was Jeremy Sandford's *Cathy Come Home* (1966), brilliantly directed by Ken Loach. This story of young Cathy and Reg, filmed on location in cinéma-vérité style, not only brought the plight of the homeless close to millions of viewers but also implied, in the author's words, that 'our State is needlessly cruel'. The verisimilitude of *Cathy* and other documentary dramas (an ill-defined category that runs all the way from the biopic via any lifelike story whatever, to out-and-out journalism) gave rise to some anxiety: would viewers be fooled into thinking the play was *real*? Curiously enough such fears were only aroused by plays with a radical thrust. Royal lives or the depiction of unrest in Poland, like Granada's *Three Days in Szczecin* (1976), seemed to cause no alarm.

It is not to underrate the contribution made by directors, actors and designers to say that it was above all the writers that raised the prestige of British television drama in the sixties and seventies. Established literary figures like **Terence Rattigan** and **J. B. Priestley** were attracted to the new medium. Authors like **John Osborne**, John Mortimer and **Tom Stoppard** were all to write for it. The success on the domestic screen of *A Night Out* (ABC 1960) gave **Harold Pinter** a wider public hearing than his first stage plays had commanded. John Hopkins's quartet, *Talking to a Stranger* (BBC 1966), was described as 'the first authentic masterpiece written directly for television'. **Dennis Potter**, eager to break away from the limitations of naturalism, was to make his name as a television playwright before becoming a Hollywood screenwriter. The politically committed author **Trevor Griffiths**, who has also written for the stage and the cinema, favours the TV screen as giving him the widest possible audience. **Mike Leigh**, *animateur* rather than playwright, has transferred his improvisational playmaking technique to television. The novelist William Trevor has produced a large number of TV plays, variations on the theme of loneliness. Elaine Morgan has shown great skill in dramatized biographies. **Alan Plater**, inspired by Paddy Chayefsky's respect for ordinary life, has used his North Country background to create regional characters and regional speech of great authenticity.

This literary flavour contrasts with American television where a script like **Arthur Miller**'s harrowing Auschwitz story, *Playing for Time* (CBS 1980), is the exception. In Britain the single play has been held to be the key to dramatic innovation; whenever that is in danger of being crowded out by the series, however excellent that format may be at times, all the alarm bells start to ring. It was precisely in this field that the BBC's freedom from commercial pressures allowed it to take risks and thus to set standards that the independent companies had to acknowledge and follow. Even so, there were unstated limits as to how far drama might go. Peter Watkins's *The War Game* (1965), an unsensational vision of how Britain might fare in a nuclear war, was banned on the grounds that 'it had the power to produce unpredictable emotions'. If over the years the BBC was to slide into less enterprising postures, the creation in 1982 of Channel 4 with a brief to commission rather than to produce programmes has given British television drama a new fillip, a number of production companies springing up to fill the programme gap.

West German television presents yet another organizational picture. Authority in the first channel (ARD) is vested in the regional (Länder) governments; the second channel (ZDF) is jointly controlled by Federal Government, Länder and various interest groups. This arrangement leaves an occasional space for delving into controversial areas. In the early seventies the regional station EDR screened a number of telefilms dealing sympathetically with working-class topics, such as Klaus Wiese and Christian Ziewer's *Dear Mother, I'm OK* and *Snowdrops Bloom in September*, as well as Ingo Kratisch and Marianne Lüdke's *Wages and Love*. **R. W. Fassbinder**'s five-part series *Eight Hours Don't Make a Day*, which examined the link in working-class life between work, home and leisure, managed to antagonize critics both right and left. A regular platform for experimental telefilms has been provided by ZDF's weekly slot, *Das kleine Fernsehspiel* (The Little Television Play) which puts out work of minority interest.

Once American television play production had moved to the West Coast, the series replaced the single play. Commercially the change-over made sense: cast, location and sets can be used repeatedly, and captive audiences 'delivered' to advertisers with a high degree of certainty. A 'wasteland' (in the words of the Chairman of the Federal Communications Commission) followed the era of creativity. But a crude ratings approach gave way in the early seventies to demographic considerations: in order to retain upmarket viewers, networks had to provide something better than what one critic called 'mind candy'. Standards improved without actually departing from a broad consensus of taste.

Like Hollywood movies, series quickly took on genre patterns. The Western proved to be as popular on TV as it had in the cinema. *Wagon Trail* (NBC) began its long, largely studio-bound career in 1957, some of its episodes improbably inspired by *Pride and Prejudice* and *Great Expectations*. Owen Wister's 1902 novel, *The Virginian*, had spawned some films for the cinema; now NBC was to run a series under that title (1962–9), with guest performers like **George C. Scott**, Bette Davis and Robert Redford. *Bonanza* (NBC 1959–71) was a sort of Western soap opera.

In the movies, crime had been depicted largely from the gangster's perspective; on television it is policemen or detectives who carry the action: long-term identification has to be with the side of law and order. The policemen Columbo, McCloud and Madigan were the eponymous heroes of the 'Mystery Movie' cycle made by Universal for NBC (1971–7); *Kojak* (CBS 1973–7) fought crime while licking a lollipop; *Hill Street Blues*, started by NBC in 1980, has taken a disenchanted look at a police station in a deprived East Coast city: law officers have drinking problems, their daughters are raped, urban warfare prevails.

The British version of the genre was at first more benign. *Dixon of Dock Green*, a cosy sort of cop show (BBC), ran from 1955 until 1976, by which time its avuncular lead Jack Warner was well beyond retirement age. *Z Cars* (BBC 1960–78) gave a more down-to-earth picture of police work; Thames TV's *The Sweeney* (1974–8) portrayed Scotland Yard's Flying Squad in action-packed mid-Atlantic terms.

The detective – private eye or member of the force – is a television hero in many countries. Robert Taylor, his boyish good looks long since gone, starred in ABC's *The Detective* (1959–61). In the French series *The Last Five Minutes* (ORTF 1958), Inspector Bourrel always solved his case just in the nick of time. In the late fifties the BBC's *Maigret* series, based on Simenon's famous sleuth, conjured up a satisfyingly French atmosphere; many of the scripts were by **Giles Cooper**. Indeed villainy has a world-wide appeal: a series on Radio Television Hong Kong dramatizing real crimes enjoyed the collaboration of the police; East German Television's crime series, *The Prosecutor Takes the Floor* and *Police Call 110*, had a very long run indeed.

The medical show, too, had a well established Hollywood history. MGM, which had made as many as nine films between 1938 and 1947 on Dr Kildare, a young intern under the mentorship of a crusty old doctor, went on to make a television *Dr Kildare* series for NBC (1961–6). In Britain *Emergency – Ward 10* (often misread as *Emergency Ward 10*) kept ATV viewers tranquillized from 1957 onwards; with *Call Oxbridge 2000* followed by *General Hospital*, the treatment continued for an almost uninterrupted 21 years.

The most important of the lighter sorts of television drama is situation comedy (sitcom for short). Its format is based on the need to spin (often initially an unpredictable number of) episodes out of a more or less constant situation. Its ancestor is radio comedy with its weekly instalments rather than any theatrical genre, other than the **commedia dell'arte** with its kaleidoscopic variations. In a sitcom a group of people assembled within a fixed framework are made to strike sparks from each

Tony Hancock as the Blood Donor, BBC TV.

other: the performers' personality is the key to success. Though normally close to reality (with some inevitable stereotyping), it may well verge on farce; John Cleese's misadventures as the manic hotel owner of *Fawlty Towers* (BBC 1975–9) were pure latter-day **Feydeau**.

American sitcoms have often been built around a female character. CBS starred the effervescent and indestructible Lucille Ball in *I Love Lucy* (1951–5), *The Lucy Show* (1962–8) and *Here's Lucy* (1968–73). The *Mary Tyler Moore Show* (CBS 1970–4) focused on a bachelor girl working in a TV station newsroom and produced two more woman-based series – *Phyllis* and *Rhoda* – among several spin-offs.

In Britain sitcom had its first flowering in the prickly (and alas, self-destructive) Tony Hancock. *Hancock's Half Hour*, scripted by Alan Simpson and Ray Galton, produced notable delights on radio as well as BBC television between 1954 and 1961; *The Blood Donor* (1961) is a fondly remembered classic. From the same co-authors' *Steptoe and Son* (BBC 1964–73), in which a rag-and-bone man bickered incessantly with his adult son and partner, to Antony Jay and Jonathan Lynn's *Yes, Minister* (BBC, from 1980), a keyhole view of the Whitehall corridors of power, British sitcom has covered a wide social spectrum. In Johnny Speight's *Till Death Us Do Part* (BBC 1966–74), the preposterous views of Alf Garnett, a working-class reactionary impersonated by Warren Mitchell, were held up to ridicule. Significantly Archie Bunker, his counterpart in the American adaptations *All in the Family* (CBS 1971–9), was equally foul-mouthed but more of a wisecracker.

A subdivision of sitcom found on both sides of the

Atlantic is the military comedy. *You'll Never Get Rich* (CBS 1955–8) featured Phil Silvers as the tireless schemer Sgt Bilko; Jimmy Perry and David Croft's *Dad's Army* (BBC 1967–77) poked gentle fun at an ineffectual but lovable Home Guard platoon in the Second World War.

*M*A*S*H* (CBS 1972–83), a medical-cum-army sitcom, was set in a Mobile Army Surgical Hospital during the Korean War. That war lasted three years; *M*A*S*H* ran for eleven. When the last of its 251 episodes went out in the United States it was watched by 125 million viewers. Robert Altman, the maker of the film on which the series was based, disapproved of it as 'the most insidious kind of propaganda'. However, *M*A*S*H* did manage at times to go beyond mere blood-and-guts comedy: the episode 'Dreams' was haunted by truly disturbing nightmares.

A genre of American derivation but universal appeal is the soap opera, so called because its radio predecessor in the thirties was mainly sponsored by soap powder firms. Its hold on the American public is such that addicts can read a 'Soap Opera Digest' or dial a 24-hour 'Soap by Phone' service to bring themselves up to date on any episodes they have unhappily missed. In 1979 there were as many as 12 soaps a day on tap. This type of group narrative (family, community, workplace) has a beginning but no end, and hence no middle: **Aristotle** would not have approved. A soap opera dies of inanition rather than for any dramaturgical reasons. Its tone is a mixture of the melodramatic and the mundane. Viewer identification is essential, hence narrative time and viewing time generally coincide: when it is Christmas in the story it is actually Christmas-time. A common feature is the interweaving of several narrative strands in any one instalment so as to keep track of the group as a whole. Cliffhanger endings characterize not only the end of episodes but even the moment before the commercial breaks: the viewer must not be let off the hook.

With their Hollywood gloss, American soaps have lathered their way into the hearts of (much of) mankind. Though put out as entertainment, they carry a host of unacknowledged ideological messages. Perhaps none has had a greater impact than *Dallas*, made by Lorimar for CBS (1978–82), with an international audience of some 300 million viewers. The feuding among the Texan super-rich keeps the telemasses spellbound, unmoved by *Variety*'s judgement, 'Basically it has all the trashy elements people want from this kind of fare.'

In Britain, too, soap opera had its roots in radio – serials like *Mrs Dale's Diary* (1948–69) and *The Archers*, broadcast daily ever since 1 January 1951. British soap opera keeps some grip on social and regional realities. While the suburban lower-middle-class *Grove Family* (BBC 1953–6) led the way, quite the greatest success among British soap operas (though its makers reject the label) has been *Coronation Street*, the Granada serial in a Lancashire working-class setting. Launched on 9 December 1960, it was originally scheduled to run for a mere 13 weeks – but it just never stopped. The Rovers Return must be the best known pub in the country; the fame of Bet Lynch, Elsie Tanner and Hilda Ogden rivals that of royalty. The biographies of the saga's characters are chronicled by an archivist for the benefit of succeeding generations of scriptwriters. Studiously

contemporary in external detail, *Coronation Street* plays on nostalgia for older, more settled values.

Crossroads (ATV/Central 1964–87) also counted its followers in millions; they more than half believed in the real existence of the characters whose lives intersected in this symbolically named Midlands hotel. Lower in production values, *Crossroads* never enjoyed the critical esteem of *Coronation Street*. *Emmerdale Farm* (Yorkshire TV, since 1972) combines studio work with location shooting in the country. Scottish Television joined the chorus in 1980 with *Take the High Road*. Merseyside Television's *Brookside*, broadcast on Channel 4 since 1982, has a topical look. Shot on location on an actual housing estate near Liverpool, it has confronted problems of the day such as unemployment. *EastEnders* (BBC, from 1985) is the most recent success in this genre.

Soap opera is not confined to the English-speaking world. In Japan, NHK puts out 15-minute instalments of soap for breakfast television. *O-Shin* (1983) was not perhaps classical soap opera in that it was set in the Meiji era rather than in the present; but this melodrama of a woman from a poor farming background who achieves success after countless tribulations became a national obsession quite in the manner of soap opera. (It is only fair to add that NHK also features culturally ambitious and socially questioning telefilms such as *A Family* and *All the Way Home*, prize winners in 1979 and 1980 respectively at the Monte Carlo TV Festival; the former dealt with the plight of the elderly against the background of the country's changing values, the latter with that rare creature, a liberated Japanese woman living in the countryside.)

A soapy flavour is found in much of Egypt's TV drama. The more popular programmes are known as 'street cleaners' because crowds tend to disappear off the streets during transmission times. Though the Egyptian state broadcasting company ERT takes a good deal of foreign, chiefly American, material it also turns out or commissions from local independent producers a large volume of TV drama. Egypt, the first country in Africa to have colour TV which was introduced in 1971, enjoys a great advantage: there has been a fully established film industry there since well before the Second World War, and television can therefore draw on a pool of creative and technical talent. Being far and away the strongest producer of

O-Shin, second from left, in a scene from the popular Japanese television drama.

TV drama in the Arab world, it exports a great many programmes to other Arabic-speaking countries – including Saudi Arabia which, itself inactive in the field of TV drama production, is careful only to screen what fits in with its religious outlook. Egyptian soap operas pose no political or moral challenges. In addition to tales of everyday life, ERT also presents plays with a patriotic or religious thrust; for several years it filled the screens during the month of Ramadan with 30-part serials on the lives of the prophets, ending the cycle with a lavishly mounted biography of Mohammed himself.

TV plays fulfil different social functions according to a given country's level of development: in some places soap opera may be more than mere entertainment. *Cockcrow at Dawn*, broadcast by the Nigerian Television Authority since 1980, tells the story of the Bello family, country folk who fail to adapt to city life and return to the land where they settle down as small farmers. Without being overtly didactic, the serial slips in practical hints about modern farming methods.

Televisa, the major private network in Mexico, has used the Latin American parallel to soap opera, the *telenovela*, for educational purposes. *Come with Me* (1974–5) conducted a literary campaign in story form; *Join with Me* (1977–8) advocated birth control, apparently with tangible results. Other Mexican telenovelas have dealt with the status of women in a macho society and with teenage sex education.

To be precise, a telenovela is not quite a soap opera; though it invites viewer identification and tends to be very long, it is not necessarily as open-ended as the true continuous serial. Initially Mexico was the chief producer of these, exporting them to other Latin American countries; in the seventies Brazil was to sprint into the lead. TV Tupi, a São Paulo station that has since gone out of business, launched *Beto Rockefeller* in 1968, the tale of a poor young man who makes his way to the top. Fantasies of social climbing were to be a major ingredient of the genre, a feature perfectly acceptable to Brazil's military government. Telenovela authors became national figures; the funeral of one of the best known of these, Janete Clair, was a great public occasion watched by millions on television. The length of telenovelas is prodigious: Dias Gomes's *The Well Beloved*, a saga of politics in a town in Bahia, ran for 177 episodes, Gilberto Braga's *Dancin' Days*, which was set in a discotheque, for 174.

The chief provider of telenovelas in Brazil is the Globo network; broadcasting since 1965, it interlocks with a communications empire that comprises newspapers, a publishing house, radio stations and a recording company. With a TV drama output more than equivalent to making two feature films a day, Globo is not indifferent to quality: it employs leading writers, directors, actors and musicians. Its serials achieve viewing figures of up to 50 million per programme. A degree of political liberalization in Brazil has enabled Globo to turn out somewhat less escapist material. *Gabriela*, a feminist story based on a Jorge Amado novel, proved enormously popular not only at home but also in Portugal where a bishop denounced it for subverting the family. *The Woman Malu* showed a middle-class divorcee who comes to question many of society's dominant values. The fact that Globo exports its telefilms to more than 80 countries (including

The priest on a mule in a scene from *Gabriela*, Brazilian TV.

China) suggests that US preponderance in the world market for TV drama is not an immutable fact of life.

Undeniably television drama is a significant social phenomenon; but is it aesthetically significant? The bulk of it is trivial to be sure; but then no one year sees the production of hundreds of theatrical or cinematic masterpieces either. A critical problem is that popular and minority tastes, regrettably perhaps, tend to diverge (which is not to say that either is wholly good or wholly bad). Both levels have their separate justification; both should, ideally, be catered for in a mass medium such as TV drama.

Once in a while a single play, a series or a serial will transcend this divide. Let us take two British examples. *The Jewel in the Crown* (Granada 1984), a 14-episode adaptation by Ken Taylor of Paul Scott's 'Raj Quartet', was partly shot on location in India. This splendidly directed super-production glittered with stars of the first rank. It tackled a delicate subject, the last days of British rule in India, with a complexity and wealth of narrative detail impossible in the cinema: here the spaciousness of the serial was essential. Dramatic adaptation, a practice familiar in the theatre from Shakespeare to **Brecht**, justified itself on the television screen.

Equally notable though in a wholly different key was Alan Bleasdale's *The Boys from the Blackstuff* (BBC 1982). In this angry, compassionate study of a group of

Art Malik and Tim Pigott-Smith in Granada Television's *The Jewel in the Crown*.

unemployed Liverpool workers and their families, each man in turn came to the fore in each of the five episodes. The style moved from naturalism to something almost surreal in its desolate picture of society in the eighties. The death of the militant worker George Malone while being pushed in a wheelchair through the ruins of Liverpool's dockland sounded a requiem for a whole era.

Television drama may well be in danger of becoming socially enervating by its very quantity which creates a distracting dream world for the viewer. Its essentially individualistic domestic appeal may be stripping dramatic performances of their sense of festive occasion. On the other hand, plays that enter virtually every home can, in ideal circumstances, have the power to move a whole nation at once. Television drama deserves to be taken seriously as a potential art as well as a social fact. Able to speak to each viewer in an intimate voice, to articulate private hopes and fears and to show, in Hamlet's words, the very age and body of the time his form and pressure, it will – worthily on occasion – join its elder dramatic sisters.   GWB

> See: G. W. Brandt (ed.), *British Television Drama*, Cambridge University Press, 1981; R. Dyer (et al.), *Coronation Street*, London, BFI Publishing, 1981; J. Ellis, *Visible Fictions/Cinema: Television: Video*, London, Routledge & Kegan Paul, 1982; J. Feuer, P. Kerr & T. Vahimagi (eds.), *MTM, 'Quality Television'*, London, BFI, 1984; S. Kalter, *The Complete Book of M*A*S*H*, Bromley, Columbus Books, 1984; I. Shubik, *Play for Today: The Evolution of Television Drama*, London, Davis-Poynter, 1975; R. W. Stedman, *The Serial*, University of Oklahoma Press, 1977.

Téllez, Gabriel de see Molina, Tirso de

Templeton, Fay (1865–1939) American actress, a favourite of the musical comedy stage at the turn of the 20th century. Born in Little Rock, Arkansas, on Christmas Day, she appeared on stage as a child. She toured extensively with her parents, then joined **Weber** and **Fields** for four seasons, making a hit of the song, 'Rosey, You Are My Posey'. In 1905 she appeared in **Cohan**'s *Forty-five Minutes from Broadway* as Mary, singing 'Mary Is a Grand Old Name', a huge success. She later appeared in **Gilbert** and Sullivan, and retired from the stage in 1931 after appearing in *HMS Pinafore*. She lived for a time in the Actors Fund Home in Englewood, New Jersey, and died in San Francisco.   SMA

Tennyson, Alfred, Lord (1809–92) English poet who, if his teenage fantasy *The Devil and the Lady* is discounted, completed his first play at the age of 65. This was *Queen Mary*, staged at the **Lyceum** in 1876, with **Irving** as Philip of Spain. A second historical verse drama, *Harold*, remained unperformed until 1928, when **Laurence Olivier** took the title role in a production by the **Birmingham Repertory** Company at the **Royal Court** in London. A third, *Becket*, was in rehearsal at the Lyceum when Tennyson died. It opened early in 1893, and the part of Becket remained in Irving's repertoire until the night of his death in Bradford, scarcely an hour after the curtain had rung down on Tennyson's play. Irving also provided *The Cup*, a short play that is too long just the same, with a lavish Lyceum production in 1881, but Tennyson's remaining three plays were staged in lesser theatres, the one-act *The Falcon* by William and **Margaret Kendal** at the **St James's** in 1879, the domestic tragedy in prose, *The Promise of May*, at the **Globe** in 1882 (the production was a fiasco) and *The Foresters* in a production by **Augustin Daly** at his own New York theatre in 1892. Only **Byron** among 19th-century poets had a stage life to rival Tennyson.   PT

Tent show An American style of theatrical presentation in which plays or variety shows are trouped from community to community and staged under canvas. One of the earliest entrepreneurs was Fayette Lodowick 'Yankee' Robinson, whose touring company performed in the river towns of Iowa and Illinois in 1851; prosperity led him to switch from drama to circus. By the late 19th century, travelling troupes with repertories extensive enough to provide a week's worth of entertainment had become popular in the summer, when local opera houses were too poorly ventilated to attract the public. The influence of the Chautauqua circuit (lecture meetings of an educational or religious nature) with its portable theatres lit by naphtha lamps was strong after 1904; its tents were brown to distinguish its educational purpose from the white tops of the circus. In France, **Firmin Gémier** had commissioned an elaborate canvas structure to house the tours of the Théâtre Antoine in 1911, but the average American show-tent was limited to a width of 50 or 60 feet, with bare benches or bleachers and a platform stage designed for portability.

The earliest repertories were imitations, often pirated, of the standard dramatic fare, primarily melodrama; but as these grew stale and copyright laws stricter, tent showmen composed their own plays, carpentered to a limited company and the familiar themes of rural life. The standbys of this repertory include Charles Harrison's *Saintly Hypocrites and Honest Sinners* (1915) and W. C. Herman's *Call of the Woods*, which pitted homespun virtue against urban corruption. The comic character **Toby**, developed c. 1911, became the popular hero of these works, often partnered with the tomboy Susie and the eccentric known as the G-string character, a sage descendant of the stage Yankee.

After the First World War, motor vehicles replaced rail transport, and tent shows proliferated, doubling their rate to 1 dollar admissions. Some 400 shows were travelling through the United States by 1927, playing to an estimated audience of 78 million. But the catastrophic effect of the depression and dust-storms on the agricultural population led to a decline in the 'rag opries'. Price cutting and unionization, the competition from local cinemas and inability to organize were also contributory factors to the closure of hundreds of long-standing companies in the 1930s. The **Federal Theatre Project** absorbed many of these entertainers and in the 1950s only some dozen troupes survived. In 1976 a revival of the Harley Sadler Show, one of the most prosperous in its time, was staged at Texas Tech University, which houses a Tent Show Collection.   LS

> See: C. Ashby and S. D. May, *Trouping through Texas. Harley Sadler and his Tent Show*, Bowling Green, O., 1982; W. L. Slout, *Theatre in a Tent. The Development of a Provincial Entertainment*, Bowling Green, O., 1972.

Ter-Arutunian, Rouben (1920–) Armenian-American set and costume designer; born in Russia, educated in Berlin 1927–43, emigrated to the USA in 1951. In addition to theatre and opera, Ter-Arutunian designed for television in the 1950s. His work falls primarily into two categories: 'decorative' (or painterly) such as his famous *Nutcracker* for the New York City Ballet; or sculptural such as *Riceracare* for American Ballet Theatre. He prefers the latter style which allows him to create space around a minimal amount of scenery. He says that he designs 'visual counterpart to drama, poetry, music and movement . . . with simplicity, clarity, and a certain element of mystery'. AA

Terence (c. 184–159 BC) Publius Terentius Afer, Roman comic dramatist. A number of alleged biographical details are preserved, but they must be treated with caution. He is said to have been a freed slave from Carthage; to have associated with aristocratic and cultured philhellenes in the circle of Scipio Aemilianus; and to have been killed in his 25th (or 35th) year on a journey to Greece or Asia.

The six plays which survive appear to be all he ever wrote. They are *Andria* (*The Girl from Andros*, 166 BC); *Hecyra* (*The Mother-in-Law*, performed unsuccessfully in 165, then once unsuccessfully and once successfully in 160); *Heauton Timoroumenos* (*The Self-Tormentor*, 163); *Eunuchus* (*The Eunuch*, 161); *Phormio* (161); and *Adelphoe* (*The Brothers*, 160). *Hecyra* and *Phormio* were adapted from plays by Apollodorus of Carystus, a follower of **Menander**, the others from plays by Menander himself.

The broad and farcical humour which **Plautus** had introduced into his plays was largely eliminated by Terence, who sought to bring Menandrean restraint and refinement to Roman comedy. While *Eunuchus* and *Adelphoe* contain farcical scenes, and *Phormio* has a clever trickster as its central character, the humour of Terence's work is generally a subtle consequence of the interplay of character and situation. *Hecyra*, indeed, is a largely serious and realistic exploration of domestic difficulties, with little, apart from the happy ending, to qualify it as a comedy at all.

Terence was not a mere translator, however, but tried in various ways to improve on his Greek models. For one thing, he dispensed with the expository Prologue which Menander had used to set the scene. Thus some details of the initial situation are not revealed at all (so that the element of suspense and surprise is increased, at the expense of dramatic irony), while others are revealed through dialogue. All the plays do in fact possess prologues, but these were not always written for the first performance, and stand entirely outside the drama (two, indeed, are explicitly written for delivery by the actor-manager who championed Terence's work, Lucius Ambivius Turpio). They serve the special purpose of explaining Terence's aims, complaining of the audience's past failure to appreciate his work, and replying to the attacks of a jealous rival, one Luscius Lanuvinus. The prologues are thus of great interest as revealing a new artistic self-consciousness and affording a glimpse of the theatrical conditions of the period.

Luscius had alleged that Terence's style was thin; that he had plagiarized other Latin plays; that he had

received help from aristocratic friends; and that he had 'spoiled' many Greek comedies by inserting scenes or characters from one into a play otherwise based on another. Terence's reply to the last charge is surprisingly defensive: in mixing his sources he is doing no more than Naevius, Plautus and **Ennius** had done (see **Rome**), and he prefers their 'carelessness' to pedantic fidelity to his source. The actual extent of the mixing has been much debated, for Terence's plays are certainly not the scissors-and-paste work which his prologues might suggest; and it is now generally agreed that the four Menandrean plays, at least, have been substantially reworked. A simple case, where Terence's motive is clear, is that of *Andria*: the play concerns a young man's efforts to marry the girl he loves instead of the wife his father intends for him, but Terence (unlike Menander) provides the latter girl with a suitor of her own, so as to give the play a rudimentary sub-plot and ensure a happy ending for all.

While self-conscious moralizing is avoided, the plays as wholes have a distinctly high-minded tone. Most characters try to act for the best; their problems are held up for sympathy rather than ridicule, and their foibles are exposed with genial tolerance. Terence shows insight and understanding in his portrayal of women, and has a particular interest in relations between fathers and sons. The 'humanity' for which he is famous can now be seen to be largely an inheritance from Menander, but it is at least an inheritance which he preserved intact, to be passed on to such admirers as **Molière**.

Unlike Plautus, Terence has perhaps had more success with readers than with audiences. The wholesomeness of his plays and the purity of his Latin ensured that he was a favourite author for school use, both among the Romans and in more recent times. A commentary by the 4th-century grammarian Donatus preserves useful information about Terence's sources. ALB

Terriss, William (Charles James) (1847–97) English actor (born William Lewin), the son of a barrister. He made his professional debut in Birmingham in 1868 and was briefly with the **Bancrofts** at the **Prince of Wales's** in 1869. Terriss found it difficult to choose between the stage and an outdoor life (he had been briefly a merchant seaman and a tea-planter in Assam), and from 1869–71 he was a sheep-farmer in the Falkland Islands, where his daughter, the actress Ellaline Terriss (1871–1971), was born. The rest of his life belongs to the English stage, where his first significant success was as Squire Thornhill to **Ellen Terry**'s Olivia in **W. G. Wills**'s sentimental dramatization of **Goldsmith**'s *The Vicar of Wakefield*. He repeated the part at the end of his five-year engagement with **Irving** at the **Lyceum** (1880–5), during which he also played Cassio in *Othello*, Laertes in *Hamlet*, Mercutio in *Romeo and Juliet* and Orsino in *Twelfth Night*. He returned to the Lyceum in 1892 to play the King in Irving's lavish production of *Henry VIII*. But Terriss found his natural home at the **Adelphi**, where, after 1885, he featured in a succession of muscular melodramas, beginning with *The Harbour Lights* (1885), by George R. Sims and Henry Pettit. Terriss's swashbuckling athleticism earned him the nickname of 'Breezy Bill' and there was no subtlety about his acting. He was, however, immensely popular and widely mourned when a deranged fellow-actor stabbed him to death outside the stage-door of the Adelphi.   PT

Terry, Edward O'Connor (1844–1912) English actor, who worked in the provinces from 1863–7 and who made his London reputation in burlesque at the Strand from 1869–76. **John Hollingshead** brought him to the **Gaiety** in 1876, and from then until 1883 he was **Nellie Farren**'s rival as the leading member of the Gaiety Quartette (**Kate Vaughan** and **Edward Royce** were the others). In 1888, he opened Terry's Theatre in the Strand, creating there the part of the good-hearted drunkard Dick Phenyl in **Pinero**'s immensely popular (and immensely sentimental) *Sweet Lavender* (1888). Terry was an eccentric comedian, famous for his self-transformations through makeup. Having sold his theatre for conversion to a cinema in 1910, he spent his last active years on a world tour in his most famous comedy and burlesque roles.   PT

Terry, Ellen (Alice) (1847–1928) English actress, the second daughter of a theatrical family. Hurried into the theatre – she played Mamillius for **Charles Kean** at the **Princess's** in 1856 and toured in a programme of sketches with her elder sister Kate in 1859–61 – she was also jostled into an unfortunate marriage with the artist George Frederick Watts in 1864. A contemporary photograph by Julia Cameron gives surer evidence than such canvases as Watts's 'Choosing' of her extraordinary beauty (an unusual mixture of innocence and opulence) at this time. Sadly at odds with Watts, she returned to the theatre, playing, among other parts, the 'shrew' to **Irving**'s Petruchio at the Queen's (1867). Irving considered her charming but frivolous. She was already contemplating a liaison with the married architect E. W. Godwin, a deeper relationship than she achieved in any of her three marriages. They lived together in the Hertfordshire countryside from 1868–75 and had two extraordinary children who came to be known in the theatre as **Edith Craig** and **Edward Gordon Craig**. Their different effect on Ellen Terry's life is a story in itself. Her return to the theatre was

Ellen Terry, 1864, photographed by Julia Margaret Cameron.

negotiated by **Charles Reade**, who needed a replacement for **Mrs John Wood** in his Tichborne claimant play, *The Wandering Heir* (1874). In 1875, Terry made her first major Shakespearian appearance, as Portia in the **Bancrofts**' production of *The Merchant of Venice*. The apparent spontaneity of her verse-speaking, a natural ability to record the processes as well as the product of reflection, would continue to charm audiences for 50 years. In 1878, having just seen Terry playing the sentimental title-role in **W. G. Wills**'s *Olivia* (this version of **Goldsmith**'s *The Vicar of Wakefield* was still in her repertoire 30 years later), Irving hesitantly invited her to join him at the **Lyceum**, where she remained for 25 years and was recognized as the leading actress of the English stage. She was Irving's Ophelia (1878), Portia (1879), Desdemona (1881), Juliet (1882), Beatrice (1882), Viola (1884), Lady Macbeth (1888), Queen Katharine (1892), Cordelia (1892), Imogen (1896) and Volumnia (1901), but never his Rosalind, since *As You Like It* had no satisfactory part for him. It was this unbalance, her agreement to play second fiddle, that antagonized **George Bernard Shaw** and that underlay his long and loving correspondence with Terry (published in 1931). She would eventually play the part Shaw wrote for her as Lady Cicely Waynflete in *Captain Brassbound's Conversion* (1906). By then, Irving was dead, and Terry herself had tried a spell of management in her own right, at the Imperial, where she staged **Ibsen**'s *The Vikings* (1903) in sets designed by her son, Gordon Craig. The production was a costly failure. Partly to recoup her losses and partly to keep the improvident Craig in pocket, Terry played Hermione for **Beerbohm Tree** at **His Majesty's** (1906). It was her last Shakespearian role. In her retirement home in Smallhythe, she completed an autobiography, *The Story of My Life* (1908), and prepared the series of lectures on **Shakespeare**'s heroines that became a regular part of her programme from 1910–21. She also appeared, unflatteringly, in five silent films between 1916 and 1921. In 1925, when the Godwin scandal had died away, and four years after **Geneviève Ward** had been the first actress so honoured, Terry was appointed DBE. Few stage personalities have ever been so loved.

Benjamin Terry (1818–96) fathered a veritable theatrical dynasty. Three of Ellen's sisters, Kate (1844–1924), Marion (1852–1930) and Florence (1855–96), had distinguished stage careers, as did her brother Fred (1864–1932) and a multitude of great-nephews, -nieces and grandchildren, of whom **John Gielgud** is the best known.   PT

Terry, Megan (1932–   ) One of the most important playwrights of the avant-garde, Off-Off Broadway theatre of the 1960s, Terry wrote plays reflecting important political, social and sexual issues. In her association with the **Open Theatre** from 1963 to 1968, she helped develop many techniques introduced by that group, such as audience contact, experimental staging, and 'transformation', whereby characters, place, time and action change rapidly, and actors switch roles, often regardless of gender. Terry achieved international acclaim with *Viet Rock* (1966), a collaborative effort which was the first rock musical and the first protest play about the Vietnam war. Other plays by

Terry include *Calm Down Mother* and *Keep Tightly Closed in a Cool Dry Place* (1965); *The People vs. Ranchman* (1967); *Hothouse* (1974); and *Approaching Simone* (1970) – an Obie-winning chronicle of the brief, heroic life of Simone Weil. Since 1974, Terry has produced numerous plays as playwright-in-residence at the Omaha Magic Theatre. FB

Terson (Patterson), Peter (1932–) British dramatist, who worked as a teacher for ten years before his first play, *A Night to Make the Angels Weep* (1964), was produced at the **Victoria Theatre, Stoke-on-Trent**. This play, together with *The Mighty Reservoy* (1964), revealed him to be an amusing observer of life in the Midlands and the North of England, with the instinctive ability to seize on a symbolic idea which raised his naturalism towards myth. He became resident dramatist at Stoke-on-Trent in 1966 and wrote prolifically for that company, collaborating with Joyce Cheeseman to adapt **Arnold Bennett**'s novel, *Clayhanger*, for the stage in 1967. Several of these plays transferred to small London theatres, although his appealing play, *Mooney and his Caravans*, about the bullying proprietor of a caravan estate who intimidates an inoffensive couple, was first seen on television in 1966 before its stage premiere at the **Hampstead Theatre Club** in 1968. His first major success in London came with the **National Youth Theatre**'s production of *Zigger Zagger* (1967), about football fans and hooligans, which offered a moral tale against a background of football songs from packed terraces. Terson wrote other NYT successes such as *The Apprentices* (1968), *Spring Heeled Jack* (1970) and *Good Lads at Heart* (1971). His work always has retained its background in regional, local and community situations, which may have restricted its appeal to national audiences; although *Strippers* (1984), describing the life of women in high areas of unemployment who take to stripping in pubs for pocket money, received a worthy, if controversial, London run. JE

Tesfaye Gesesse (1937–) Ethiopian playwright, actor and director. Studied drama in the United States and then worked at the Haile Selassie I Theatre in Addis Ababa University. He was director of the Ethiopian National Theatre until 1983. In addition to short stories he has written a number of plays in Amharic on a variety of themes, including *Moresh* (1979) and *The Verdict is Yours* (1984). RK

Teternikov, F. K. see **Sologub, F.**

Thailand Thailand (formerly Siam) is a South-East Asian country bordering on Malaysia, Burma, Laos, Cambodia and the Gulf of Siam. Its population is a mixture of hill tribes and lowlanders. Malays of the southern provinces have been significant in moulding Thai dramatic practice, while Lao peoples in the north-east and Chinese Thais enjoy performances comparable to those found in Laos and southern China respectively.

Religion and political developments have influenced drama. Theraveda Buddhism was adopted by the early Thais, and this belief is mixed with indigenous animism and Brahmanism-Hinduism is held by 95% of the population. Dance and dramatic performances may first have evolved in conjunction with this religious practice at the village level, and rural performances continue to be a regular part of religious festivals. The emergence of Thais as a political force on the peninsula began in the 13th century, but artistic ascendency came only after the capture of the Khmer kingdoms of Angkor in 1431, an event which cemented the Thai predilection for adopting Khmer arts. The expertly trained musicians and harem lady-dancers of the Khmer king's household were carried into exile. This ready-made performance tradition was developed by Thais of the next generations, with many monarchs and princesses becoming accomplished performers or poets of dance drama texts. This expanded tradition became, in turn, the model for the Burmese court theatre, when the Burmese seized the Thai court lady-dancers and musicians during the sack of Ayutthaya, the Thai capital, in 1767. Later the Thais returned the Cambodian loan of artistry with interest, for much of the repertoire which the Khmer adopted in the 19th century for court performance may have been borrowed from the Thai court models.

The theatrical impact of Indian and island South-East Asian prototypes is recognized by the Thais. Indian influences are felt by Thais to have come via the Khmer who were, in turn, affected by the Indonesian versions of Indian materials. More research is required to establish whether the route of Indian influence on mainland South-East Asian performance was more direct, possibly via Bengal. In any case, the current music, performance practice, and repertoire of the Thai theatre are related to pan-South-East Asian patterns, and clear historical relationships with Cambodian and Malay theatres exist. The major theatre types are (1) village animist-influenced performances (2) court forms (3) modern popular genres, and (4) modern spoken drama.

Village animist-influenced performances Dance offerings to the spirits have probably been carried out from the early period of Thai history. Even in the modern Bangkok of today one can find temples where dancers regularly carry out performances commissioned by donors in thanks for some boon granted. Current dancers attempt to emulate the costume and dance style of the court forms. Though pure dance is more often seen than dramatic episodes, scenes and whole plays may be presented. A mixture of animistic, Hindu, and Buddhist influences seems to underlie these practices. Although most performances discussed hereafter are for audience entertainment rather than such ritual purposes, it is significant that much theatre continues to be presented in the context of temple festivals on temple stages, a result perhaps of these old associations.

The earliest known drama in Thailand may have originated in village performances connected with animist–Buddhist practice in the ethnically Malay south and around the 14th century. This early form, *Nora* or *Manora*, is still extant in the area around Nakhon Sri Thammarat where Ligor, a Malay Buddhist kingdom taken over by the Thai in the 14th century, was situated. The form, sometimes called *lakon jatri*, seems to have evolved practices that affected later theatrical genres.

The traditional troupe was composed of three actors – a hero-prince, a heroine-princess, and a clown. The clown, wearing masks, assumed all the other roles – hermits, ogres, monkeys and birds. The teacher of the dancers was the head of the troupe and the group was completed by an orchestra of musicians, who played a double reed (*pi*), two vase drums (*thon jatri*), a barrel drum (*klong jatri*), and a pair of small horizontal gongs (*khong khu*). Performance, as described in this century, began with a musical prelude, followed by a ritual incantation which described the origin of the *nora*. Then came a series of solo dances of the main characters, songs, skits, and, finally, a play.

The legendary origin of the form hints at a possible relationship with female spirit mediums: a Thai princess, Nuensamli, was possessed by a god, and her crazed activity caused her family to cast her out. She gave birth to a son, who learned dance by watching *kinnari* (mythical bird-women); the son magically created a clown from a rock; and a god became incarnate to become the third performer of the genre. The story, believed to be the only one presented in the early period of the form, may be further evidence of the relationship with spiritually empowered women. Manora is a bird-woman (*kinnari*) who takes off her wings to bathe, and has them stolen by a hunter, Bun. He takes her to the prince, Suton, who marries her, but true love is complicated when a minister turns the people against her in the prince's absence. As Manora is to be executed, she borrows her wings for one last dance, and thus escapes to her mountain home. Her faithful husband follows her there, proving his devotion. This tale, conceived of in mainland South-East Asia as a *jataka* (a tale of a previous life of the Buddha), is known in many cultures, but its pattern gains greater significance when seen in relation to later plots, such as *Rothasen*, in which a young prince strives to find a cure for his mother's blindness. He marries the step-daughter of an ogress, who teaches him the cure, but then abandons the love-stricken maid to return home. She dies cursing him to be the lovelorn one when they meet in a future life.

Both plot patterns and origin myth associate men with women who are possessed, powerful, or semi-divine. They may be evidence that *nora* was originally a male performance form that evolved from female spirit-medium dances of divination. Such dances are still found in Burma, where two princes emulating female mediums in the 1400s are the alleged origin of Burmese drama. The two reports may be variants on a theme: female mediums' trance rites become the model for male artists' performance practice.

In times past, troupe heads were felt to have great spiritual power and were called on for exorcisms, ordinations, and other ceremonies. It is said these sorcerers would enchant their audiences so that viewers would follow from performance to performance. Though magic still creates an aura around the form, changes have occurred. Current performers may be of either sex, more than three actors are used, and a vaudeville format prevails. By 1972 this genre had been transformed: singers in Western costume crooned romantic lyrics to Western band accompaniment with skits and comic routines interspersed.

If the tradition dies out, it will be the end of an art which may explain patterns which underlie human drama in Thailand. The three-person configuration may be the source of the role types that dominate Thai theatre. The male (*phra*), the female (*nang*), ogre (*yak*) and monkey (*ling*) are the types into which all traditional roles are divided. The first two correspond to the hero and heroine of the *nora*, and the last two in court dance are always masked, resulting, perhaps, from the fact that in *nora* they were performed by a single person using masks. More research might clarify, too, how *nora* relates to other mask dance genres of the South-East Asian area and to what extent the significance of type characters in the region may be linked to these masked dance forms.

A theatre form which developed out of the *nora* and pleased audiences up to the first decades of this century is the *lakon nok* (literally, 'outside [the palace] play'). It originated in the same southern area, and was introduced in the Bangkok region. An expanded cast and orchestra, and more secular emphasis, characterized the form. As in *nora*, dance and music were components, but in *lakon nok* the dialogue, action, and comedy gained in significance. The rough performance style, scatological humour, and lively improvisation of the performers pleased the village audiences. Eventually the *lakon nok* repertoire of Buddhist birth stories, local histories, and legendary tales was to effect the more stylized courtly performance.

Initially *lakon nok* troupes were all-male, but by the mid-19th century females began playing female roles as women from the palace tradition were allowed to perform in public. *Lakon nok* is now defunct, and though performances in *lakon nok* style are occasionally staged by the National Theatre in Bangkok the refinement of the technique when played by the exquisitely trained dancers of that company seems close to the court forms. For a sense of the rough and ready *lakon nok* of former days one must, perhaps, look to the popular genres of today, rather than these studied recreations.

Court forms Court performance, consisting of *nang yai* (large leather puppets), *khon* (mask dance drama), and *lakon fai nai* (female dance drama), is derived from Cambodian court arts of the 15th century, but scholars debate the extent of Khmer impact. Cambodia (now Kampuchea) currently boasts equivalents of all three forms, and may have had all in 1431, when the Thai captured Angkor. But many scholars feel that what was taken differed substantially from current practice, that the close similarity of the Thai and Khmer classical theatre in the current era results from Thai innovations introduced to the Cambodian courts in the 19th century.

It seems reasonable that the Khmer equivalent of *nang yai*, called *nang sbek*, was already in existence, even though the 1458 Thai Palatine Law is the first extant reference to the mutually shared form, for the Khmer were influenced by Indonesia where shadow puppetry, masked dance, and female non-dramatic dance were venerable court traditions. Hence, it seems likely that the Khmer who were strongly influenced by Indonesia around 800 and kept subsequent trade contacts with the Malay world might be expected to have had similar court arts prior to 1431. Female dance drama does, however, seem to have been a major innovation that has no clear Indonesian precedent.

Nang yai is a shadow and silhouette play performed with large, incised, two-dimensional leather puppets manipulated in front of and behind a wide white screen 30 feet long and 10 feet high by dancing puppeteers. Two narrators called *khon pak* recite an episode from the Thai version of the *Ramayana*, the *Ramakien*, to the accompaniment of the *piphat* orchestra, composed minimally of a double reed (*pi*), xylophone (*ranat ek*), barrel drum (*klong that*), cymbals (*ching*), gong chime (*khong wong yai*), and another type of barrel drum called *taphon*. Eventually, other stories were presented using *nang yai* technique, but these stories did not rival the popularity of the Rama material, which was put into literary form by Thai kings such as Rama I, who ruled 1782–1809.

Each performance begins with a ritual invocation which is followed by a standard scene in which a pale and a dark monkey battle. Then the chosen episode from the Rama cycle, customarily one that presents battle scenes, will be enacted. The main outline of the story follows the Indian epic in which Rama, an incarnation of the god Vishnu, with the assistance of monkey warriors wins back his wife Sita who has been kidnapped by the demon king Ravana (the Thai Tosakanth), who desires her. Variations from Indian material are, however, apparent: for example, Sita is Ravana's daughter, abandoned as a child, and many new episodes are interpolated. Especially popular in the repertoire are dramatizations of these new episodes that deal with the amorous and martial exploits of Hanuman, the Rama's monkey general. Typically Hanuman meets and marries some demon's beautiful daughter.

Similarities in story patterns link the *nang yai* to the Indonesian *wayang* (shadow theatre), though Bengali versions of the *Ramayana* may be the ultimate source of the story materials used by both. The similar centrality of a narrator or story-teller, the mode of introducing satire via the clowns, and the function of the orchestra within the performance make the Indonesian and Thai theatres comparable. But many techniques have no Indonesian parallel: the Thai–Khmer court tradition uses five by four foot puppets which dwarf the one to three foot shadow puppets of Java. The depiction of multi-character scenes in a single puppet, and the need for multiple puppeteers who dance on both sides of the screen with a single figure is also divergent from the solo, stationary puppeteer mode of Indonesia, and leads some scholars to look for Indian models. In south India, puppet forms are found in which multi-character scenes are represented, and multiple puppeteers are common. However, the aesthetic which allows the dancing puppeteers to emerge from behind the screen has no known Indonesian or Indian precedent, and must be attributed to indigenous ingenuity.

The figures are impressive, being the largest shadow figures in Asia and perhaps the world. The iconography of the puppets corresponds to images on temple walls, and most figures sport the distinctive crown-type headdress (*chada*) that is worn by classical dancers. The fine carving emulates the delicate patterns of the cloth of gold and the jewel inlay of dance drama costumes – outfits into which court dancers were sewn before each performance. Unfortunately, performances of *nang yai* are rare today, but at least two temples maintain this tradition that fell into disarray when court support lapsed in the 1930s. Troupes of about ten dancers, two narrators, and ten musicians are needed for performances, which are now held for temple festivals.

The *khon* is a masked dance drama enacted by a male cast to the chanted narrative of a *khon pak* (narrator) which alternates with the accompaniment of a *piphat* orchestra. Dancers mime the action of the text, normally excerpted from literary versions of the *Ramakien*. The *khon* was supposedly first presented in the Thai court in 1515 when King Rama Thibodi II celebrated his 25th birthday, though it too may stem from a Khmer model. The original dancers are said to have been manipulators of the *nang yai*. The techniques of *khon* with the basic, square stance of the dancers, its tendency to flatten the dimensions of the dancer to two and construct visual friezes as they assume poses, correlates well with the style of manipulation that enhanced the figure of the large puppet against a screen. Because of the puppet origin of the form, scripts are divided into 'sets' (for the set, *chut*, of puppets used in the *nang yai* episode) rather than scenes.

Once more, parallels with Indonesian theatre are apparent; there, too, mask dance is conceptually the next step after puppetry toward the maskless dance drama, and dance technique is believed to draw on puppet manipulation for its aesthetic. The *khon luang* (royal *khon*) was supported by the Thai rulers, and early performances seem to have emphasized fight sequences and the recitation (*kampak*) of the narrator, making it close to the puppet theatre. In later periods, characters playing refined males and females have ceased to wear masks, and non-battle scenes and song have become more significant. The movement away from all-masked, martial theatre has probably come as a result of the popularity and impact of the female dance drama tradition, for females have increasingly taken over these refined roles and have rarely worn masks in Thai theatre.

The supposed origin of the female dance tradition is the carrying of the Khmer court dancers into Thailand in 1431. However, it seems likely that the Thai may have emulated the Khmer custom of coupling the role of queen or royal concubine and dancer prior to this date. Though it is difficult to pinpoint exactly when the custom originated and trace precisely when drama rather than abstract dance became the focus, the female court drama is clearly the most significant and innovative of Thai court arts. The *lakon fai nai* (literally, 'inner court play') is the most refined, poetic, and slow moving of the dance dramas. Female performers dance-act a story accompanied by a *piphat* orchestra and a chorus. Texts are poetic and attributed to members of the nobility. Though some dialogue may be taken by performers, much of the text is sung by the offstage singers. Clowns who improvise their own dialogue are, traditionally, the sole male performers.

The name of the form comes from the fact that it is performed by the ladies of court and, hence, only inside the palace. Dancers would traditionally be under the direction of one of the queens and serve as performer and king's lady for the duration of a reign. Upon the death of a king, this group would disband, and the new monarch would appoint one of the former king's dancers to teach his own group. Provincial lords would eventually emulate this practice, but few groups could compete with the training, grace, exquisite costuming, and delicate singing of the king's troupe. Other terms for the form are *lakon nai* and *lakon phuying*.

The *lakon fai nai* evolved from the early, non-dramatic dances of the Khmer court ladies, which served a semi-ritual purpose of linking the ruler with chthonic forces of earth and fertility (see **Kampuchea**). The tradition of female group dances that ritually celebrate the union of the ruler and divine power is found in Javanese, Balinese and Malay court performances, and may have been adopted by the Khmer from these southern courts. The Thai secularized this ritual function, and allowed the form to become more dramatically oriented. Scholars debate whether the transition from non-dramatic dances to full-scale dramas first took place in Cambodia or Thailand – only one 12th-century inscription in Cambodia refers to ladies enacting a drama, though many references to non-dramatic dance occur. It is, of course, possible that a Malay court introduced the custom. Nonetheless, though it is possible that in Khmer ladies enacted some scenes during court entertainments prior to 1431, it is certain that the Thai expanded the repertoire significantly, often incorporating material from the Malay regions of Thailand.

It is certain that Thai court dancers were presenting drama in day-long performance episodes in the late 1600s when the Frenchman de la Loubère visited Thailand. After this date more information is available. An advance in the use of court dancers to present dramatic episodes occurred around 1760 when two of the royal princesses learned the Prince Panji story (called *Inao* in Thailand) from a Malay maid and wrote their own versions as a basis for a dance drama. Though the princesses' versions were later superseded by the version of Rama II, who reigned 1809–24, their choice of subject was apt. The amorous exploits of this Javanese prince, creeping unbeknownst to fathers, husbands, and rightful suitors into the bedchambers of his beloveds, must have had resonance for the ladies of the king's entourage, who were themselves given to forbidden affairs. It became the favoured subject of the dance drama.

The languorous, graceful dance style of the ladies fit these episodes, and, though some of the women were trained for the ogre and monkey roles needed for the *Ramakien* material, the emphasis in the *lakon fai nai* remained on feminine concerns and female characters. Hence, episodes like 'Surpanakha's Pangs of Jealousy', which showed the hopeless love of Ravanna's sister for Rama, and the 'Abduction of Sita', which depicted the helpless wife of Rama carried off by the ogre king, were preferred to the battles and monkey exploits presented in male *khon* and *nang yai*. Other stories were introduced over time, including *Unaruth*, which tells of the loves of a grandson of Krishna, and episodes from the repertoire of the Malay-influenced *lakon nok*.

Rama II is said to have introduced six *lakon nok* stories in the female drama, including the popular *jataka* of *Sang Thong* about the prince born as a conch shell. The strange birth results in mother and shell being cast out of the palace. Later the conch prince steals magic accoutrements from his adoptive mother, an ogress, and disguises himself as a negrito. Despite his disguise, a princess marries him, braving persecution by her mortified family. Another popular story that may have originated in the south is *Suwanna-hongse*, which tells

how Prince Suwanna-hongse climbs a kite string to find the princess of his dreams, an ogre king's daughter, but is killed by her sisters. The princess disguises herself as a brahmin and, with the aid of an oafish clown-ogre, restores the prince to life. This last tale seems to have come to the *lakon nok* from the previously mentioned *nora*. Its presence in the repertoire may hint at some link with the female court dance drama of Malaysia, the *mak yong*, for the story is a version of the most significant and sacred story in the *ma'yong* repertoire, *Dewa Muda*, or *The Magic Kite*.

It seems significant that both the Panji story and the *lakon nok* tales come to the female dance drama from the Malay south. Further research into the past dramatic practice of the southern provinces might clarify whether the importance of women as actors in a court dance drama could have been stimulated by practices of this area as well, perhaps in the court of Patani where a visiting European, Peter Flores, attended a 1613 banquet given by the queen and saw, 'A commedye all by women, to the manner of Java, which were apparelled very antikly, very pleasant to beholde'.

The development and innovation in the *khon* and *lakon fai nai* traditions have continued in the last century, first under royal direction and then under the government Department of Fine Arts (Krom Silpakon). From the reign of Rama IV, King Mongkut (1851–68), division of sexes in theatre forms disintegrated, as males were allowed to dance with the royal ladies and female dancers were allowed to perform and teach outside the court. Today women play in virtually all forms and may even play the refined hero roles. Men customarily play ogres, clowns and monkeys and, perhaps, refined male roles. As a result the clear distinctions between genres have blurred: *khon* has become more refined in its dance style and *lakon nai* with male ogre and monkey dancers probably lacks the delicate ambience of times past. Most often the two forms are nowadays intermingled and the combined genre termed *khon*.

Extensive experimentation has characterized the 19th and 20th century. Puppet performances of classical plays were performed both in and outside the court with three-dimensional puppets, *hun*, which probably were inspired by Chinese rod and string puppet theatres. *Lakon dukdamban* was an innovation of Rama V's (King Chulalongkorn's) reign (1868–1910), in which actors sang their own lines, and the off-stage chorus and elaborate, descriptive passages characteristic of earlier court drama were eliminated. During the reign of Rama VI – King Vajiravudh – (1910–25) experiments proliferated. The king wrote *Savitri*, the story of the faithful Indian wife who wins her husband back from death, as a *lakon rong* (literally, a sung drama), an all-female opera form developed in the 19th century. He also wrote spoken dramas, based on Western models. Meanwhile Prince Naradhip adapted plots from English musicals and European operas to present in Thai classical dance style.

The sponsorship of theatrical activities was assumed by the government Department of Fine Arts following the transition to a constitutional monarchy in 1932. In 1934, a training school for music and dance was founded under the department's direction, and this institution eventually became the College of Dance (Witthayalai Natasin). Since 1971, seven new branch

Colleges of Dance, training students in *khon, lakon fai nai*, and traditional music, have been established outside Bangkok. There students are still groomed for one of the four major roles, studying carefully the 66 gestures (sometimes said to be 68) of the classical dance technique which were established as early as the reign of Rama I (1782–1809) in the *Text for the Training of Dancers*. Outstanding graduates may become members of the National Theatre Company housed in the Western-style stage of the National Theatre in Bangkok. There the forms which a hundred years ago were played only to an invited few in a hall of the royal palace are performed for a ticket-purchasing public of thousands. The company presents most of the previously noted genres, *khon, lakon fai nai, lakon dukdamban, lakon nok* and *lakon phantang* (mixed genre experiments). The latter form may combine local legends from the *sebha*, a rhymed story-telling tradition, with classical dance presentation to create a new drama.

Still, few performers can maintain themselves by performing classical arts. Performers at the National Theatre receive only token payment, and most turn to tourist performance for income. The artistic satisfactions of tourist performance are, however, few. Other outlets are limited: Thammasat and Chulalongkorn Universities stage student productions of classical dramas, but these are amateur productions. The puppet performances, in particular, are extremely rare. *Nang yai* players are mostly aged, with few students to take over when they die. The last rod puppet troupe retired in 1975, and only an amateur group under the Bangkok painter, Chakrapand, does occasional performances.

Popular forms The most popular theatrical entertainments at present, *nang talung* and *likay*, both trace their origins to the Malay south from whence *lakon jatri* and *lakon nok* came in generations past.

Little is known of the origin of *nang talung* (literally, shadow theatre of Pattalung province), a form which is related to the *wayang siam* of Malaysia, but it is likely that the form has long been a feature of the Malays of south Thailand. A single performer, called a *nang nai*, manipulates the translucent, leather puppets whose iconography is derived from the costumes of the classical dance drama. Through dialogue and narration,

Likay, the modern urban theatre of Thailand.

the *nang nai* presents the story which may be based on Ramayana-derived stories, local histories, or legends. The *nang nai*, accompanied by an orchestra of five musicians, performs in a raised enclosed stage set up for the occasion, as audience members watch from outside, lounging and eating as the performance continues.

Performances of *nang talung* parallel Indonesian *wayang* in that they continue all night, are performed for festive occasions in the life of the individual or village, use 40–50 of up to 200 puppets in the set in a single episode, feature the witty and obscene satire of the clown character, and combine entertainment and instruction. The form seems to be the source of related genres found in north-east Thailand, Kampuchea and Laos. Literature to date downplays the ritual aspects of this theatre, which would separate it from the norm of *wayang* performance in South-East Asia. Further research may discover if the secularization is inherent in the genre or a recent development.

Meanwhile the *nang talung* continues to thrive: in the 1970s contests between as many as 27 troupes might be arranged by an entrepreneur in a provincial capital, with a substantial prize for the troupe that won the largest audience share. Troupes were commissioned by the American government during the Vietnam war to carry anti-communist messages: a sign of the significance of the genre as a mass medium.

Likay, while also of southern origin, is an innovation of the last hundred years. Remnants of court performance and current rock-and-roll meet in this popular, commercial drama that utilizes many elements of traditional forms, including dance, singing and piphat music, yet has adapted these elements to suit the tastes of the middle-class housewives who form its prime audience. Performances may be outside on simple, temporary stages or permanent temple ones. In the rainy season troupes may utilize an available movie theatre. Unlike the traditional theatre which uses no scenery, *likay* uses drops and wings for throne room and forest scenes. Prior to the show the troupe member in charge of stories will outline the plot to the actors, who must remember the order of events. The backstage story-teller will then signal the orchestra to play the entrance and exit music for each character, after speaking some linking narration. Performers are types – hero, heroine, villain, mother – and each actor improvises his own dialogue and song lyrics, after entering in pseudo-classical dance style. Comedy, flashy costumes partly derived from traditional models, skilful improvisation and striking plot devices have replaced court refinements. Modern stories as well as classical tales can be found in the repertoire. If the female court dancer was the mistress of times past, the *likay* hero, kept by his middle-aged patroness, is the man of the present. The tastes of the bourgeoisie, rather than the courtier, create the style.

The *likay* developed from the *dikay*, a form of Islamic singing in the southern provinces. Buddhist chanting for funerals, known as *suat phramalai*, may also have influenced the form in its early stages. But as presently acted, it seems far from these sources. In its combination of classical, rock, and Indian popular singing and dancing it represents the mixture of influences that appeal to the current audiences. Its popularity far surpasses the esoteric appeal of the court-derived and modern spoken drama (*lakon phut*) forms. It shows the drama which is sung and danced remains the preferred theatre of the Thai.

Other popular forms which exhibit some of the same flexibility as *likay* have maintained audiences outside Bangkok. *Mohlam luong* in the north-east Lao area uses Lao language and a Lao mouth organ, called a *khen*, rather than *piphat* accompaniment, but costumes, dancing and stories parallel *likay* (see **Laos**). Some 3,000 troupes were active in 1975. *Lakon saw* is found in northern Thailand: like *mohlum*, it is derived from a local story-telling tradition, that has expanded into improvised theatre, perhaps in emulation of the *likay* model. Chinese opera is another genre which draws audiences from among the Chinese Thai population.

Spoken drama   Spoken drama, *lakon phut*, originated in theatre experiments of Thai aristocrats. Prince Vajiravudh produced the first spoken drama in 1904 in a 100-seat theatre he had built upon his return from study in Europe. The form has only appealed to the intelligentsia, and has tended to echo European trends towards realism or away from it. Spoken drama is taught and produced in universities and by amateur groups, but playwrights usually support themselves by other professions. An example is Somopop Chandaraprapa, author of *Noresuan the Great* (1973), who earns his living as an engineer.

Different genres of Thai theatre enjoy varying popularity at present. In general, folk forms remain the most vigorous, yet even these forms do not promise a comfortable level of living to most performers. Though there is little sign that the varied tradition of Thailand will soon vanish, it cannot be denied that the court and community support of times past was stronger than the government or box-office support of the present.   KF

See: J. Brandon, *Theatre in Southeast Asia*, Cambridge, Mass., 1967; Prince Dhaninivat and Dhanit Yupho, *The Khon*, Bangkok, 1962; F. Ingersoll, trans., *Sang Thong: A Dance Drama from Thailand*, Rutland, Vt, 1973; D. Morton, *The Traditional Music of Thailand*, Berkeley, 1976; M. Rutnin, ed., *The Siamese Theatre*, Bangkok, 1975, and 'The Development of Theatre Studies at the University Level', *Journal of the National Research Council of Thailand*, 14, 2 (July–Dec. 1982); S. Virulrak, 'Likay: A Popular Theatre in Thailand', PhD, Univ. of Hawaii, 1980; D. Yupho, *The Khon and Lakon: Dance Dramas Presented by the Department of Fine Arts*, Bangkok, 1963; *The Preliminary Course of Training in Thai Theatrical Art*, Bangkok, 1955; and *Thai Musical Instruments*, Bangkok, 1960; X. Zarina, *Classical Dances of the Orient*, New York, 1967.

Theatre, The   This first purpose-built public playhouse in England was situated in Shoreditch, outside the city walls of London. Opened in 1576, as a bold commercial project, by **James Burbage**, it became the favourite home of the **Lord Chamberlain's Men** and provided the first stage for many of **Shakespeare**'s plays. When Burbage's lease ran out in 1597, the Theatre was hastily dismantled and its timbers carried over the Thames to provide building material for the **Globe**. It is from this evident compatibility that scholars have concluded that the otherwise unrecorded Theatre was, like the Globe, a polygonal building, with three galleries surrounding an open yard. Since James Burbage would have wanted his arena to be suitable for the popular spectacle of animal-baiting, we can reasonably assume that its scaffold-stage was removable.   PT

Theatre Arts Monthly (1916–64) United States Theatre journal. Established as a quarterly by Sheldon Cheney in 1916, and published in Detroit by the Arts and Crafts Society, *Theatre Arts* proclaimed its intention to 'develop the creative impulse in the American Theatre' and to eliminate the speculator. Cheney moved the magazine to New York in 1917 when a photograph of a German theatre upset war-sensitive Detroit. Edith J. R. Isaacs, Kenneth Macgowan, and Marion Tucker joined Cheney in 1919, with Isaacs assuming the editorship in 1922. As publisher and editor, she expanded *Theatre Arts* into a monthly in 1924, and hired Rosamund Gilder as associate editor. Gilder served with distinction until 1948, the last two years as editor. As the magazine became more international in scope, **Ashley Dukes** became English editor. Essays on **Adolphe Appia**, **Gordon Craig**, the **Federal Theatre**, **Eugene O'Neill**, and other topics of current interest raised the intellectual tone, especially when compared with the gossipy quality of its competitors. Contributors included **Robert E. Sherwood**, **Louis Jouvet**, Hallie Flanagan, **Robert Edmond Jones**, **Ray Bolger**, **Thornton Wilder**, and **John Gielgud**. Both visionary and practical, *Theatre Arts* transmitted new ideas about theatrical art to a new generation of artists and audience. In 1948 it combined with *The Stage*, ending, for all practical purposes, the original publication.   TLM

Theatre awards, American   Numerous awards for excellence in the various aspects of the theatre are given annually in the USA. Among the most important are those listed below.

1 American Academy of Arts and Letters Medal for Good Speech. Founded 1924 to recognize correct utterance in the use of language on the stage and in radio and television.

2 The American Shakespeare Festival Theatre Shakespeare Awards. Founded in 1954 'in recognition of works which stimulate appreciation of **Shakespeare** and the classical theatre'.

3 The American Theatre Association annually gives an Award of Merit for distinguished service to the educational theatre, the ATA Citation for Distinguished Service to the Theatre, and the ITI World Theatre Award.

4 The American Theatre Wing Antoinette Perry Awards (Tonys), begun in 1947, are given annually for 'Distinguished Achievement in the Theatre', awards being given for each of the several aspects of production.

5 Barter Theatre of Virginia Awards, founded 1939, honour an outstanding contribution to the theatre by an American during the current season.

6 Brandeis University Creative Arts Awards, begun in 1957, recognize outstanding artistic contributions during a lifetime of distinguished achievement.

7 Clarence Derwent Awards, founded 1945 by **Derwent**, recognize the best actor and actress appearing in non-featured roles.

8 Donaldson Awards, established in 1944, discontinued 1955, for various categories of production.

9 The Drama League of America annually awards the Delia Austrian Medal for 'the most distinguished performance of the season'.

10 The Dramatists Guild annually awards the Elizabeth Hull–Kate Warriner Award to a playwright dealing with a controversial subject.

11 John Simon Guggenheim Memorial Foundation Fellowships include Fellow in Drama since 1928 and Fellows in Stage Design and Production since 1926.

12 Kelcey Allen Awards were awarded from 1955 to 1968.

13 The Margo Jones Awards, established 1961, are given annually to 'the producing manager of an American or Canadian theatre whose policy of presenting new dramatic works continues most faithfully in the tradition of **Margo Jones**'.

14 Maharam Theatrical Design Awards, established 1965, honour scenic and costume design in Broadway and Off-Broadway shows.

15 The George Jean Nathan Awards, begun in 1959, honour the author of 'the best piece of drama criticism published during the previous year'.

16 The New England Theatre Conference Awards, founded 1957, annually honour outstanding creative achievement in the American theatre.

17 The New York Drama Critics' Circle Awards, established 1936, annually honour outstanding productions.

18 The Newspaper Guild of New York Awards in Theatre (Page One Awards), begun in 1945 for theatrical achievement, were discontinued in 1965.

19 Outer Circle Awards, begun 1950, annually honour outstanding achievement in the professional theatre.

20 Pulitzer Prizes for Drama, founded in 1917–18, honour the best 'original American play performed in New York'.

21 **Shubert** Foundation Award, since 1945 annually recognizes 'the most outstanding individual contribution to the New York theatrical season'.

22 The Theatre Library Association since 1968 annually recognizes a published work in the field of theatre in the USA.

23 The Daniel Blum *Theatre World* Awards, founded in 1945, recognize 'promising personalities who have appeared throughout the season'.

24 The Annual *Variety* New York Drama Critics Poll, begun in 1939, annually recognizes outstanding achievement in a variety of categories.

25 The *Village Voice* Off-Broadway Awards (Obies), founded in 1956, recognize theatrical achievement in the Off-Broadway theatre. SMA

Theatre buildings Theatre buildings are not essential for theatre performances. The roots of drama lie in the interaction between actor and audience, and there are regular pleas to return to these roots. But a common slogan of the fundamentalists – Two Planks and a Passion – includes recognition of some of the basic reasons for organizing theatre space. Planks assist the actor to project passion by enhancing visibility and audibility. And they also help to delineate the acting area.

The Greeks To improve visibility and audibility as the size of the audience increases, the options are to raise the actors or the audience or both. Early drama discovered

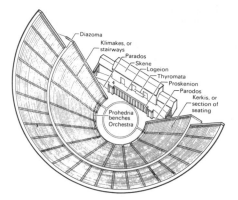

Features of the early Greek theatre.

the usefulness of performing on a hillside and this became the normal positioning for the Greeks (see **Greece, ancient**) who developed the first permanent theatres for their drama which had originated in temples and market-places. Temporary timber seating gave way to durable stone carved into the hillside. The need to get large numbers of audience close to the actors led to the adoption of a semicircular arena format with seating on an arc exceeding 180° focused on a circular stage. This produced a strong actor–audience relationship and also, by making the audience aware of each other, helped to promote a bond between individuals in the way that makes an audience respond corporately as more than the sum of its parts. This is essential to the whole concept of a theatre experience.

Carving such an auditorium from a hillside and lining it with stone results in a favourable acoustic, something of whose success we can still experience in the remains of the ancient theatres. Unfortunately the only parts of the Greek theatres to survive in a completely understandable form are the auditorium and circular *orchéstra* for chorus movement at the focus of the audience sightlines.

Our knowledge of the raised stage that developed behind the orchestra for the speaking actor, the dressing room arrangements and the facilities that later allowed simple machinery and decorations, is based upon comparative analysis of fragmentary remains in relation to documentary evidence, particularly from vases, mosaics and wall paintings. Continuous development ensured that there was no really typical Greek theatre. Experiments with seating produced the frustration which has been the basis of a continuing debate ever since: reduction of side seats to improve frontal sightlines places more audience further away from the stage. The production methods began to use increased technology. The *skene* that backed the actors on their shallow raised *proskenion* above the chorus in the circular orchestra grew more elaborate with a series of entrances and upper levels with hoists for the elevation of the deities who resolved the plot. Three-sided *periaktoi* offered changeable indications of scene. But thin evidence coupled with continuous development makes it difficult to extract a neat consensus from the necessarily speculative analyses of the researchers.

Rome (see also **Roman theatres and amphitheatres**) By the time that the Greek theatre was evolving into the Roman model there had been incorporated all the basic features of every subsequent theatre including those of today. Sight and sound are enhanced by raising both actor and audience whose respective areas are shaped to maximize contact between them, yet clearly delineating the acting area. Once seating is provided within a structure, it is possible to control the audience by selective admission and selective seating – with an option of charging for tickets. After regulating the performance spaces for actor and audience, facilities like dressing rooms and foyers follow, the productions become more elaborate and stage technology grows. This growth is often towards decadence: either long term as accompanied the decline and fall of the Roman Empire, or short term as in today's continuing cycles of reactionary return to the simplicities of the street where success triggers an escalation into the provision of ever more elaborate planks for projecting the passion.

Under the Romans the *cavea* contracted to an exact semicircle of 180°, matching the orchestra which reduced from a full to a half circle. The principal acting area became a deepened *proscenium* behind which arose a permanent architectural background, the *scaenae frons*, of monumental proportions. While the tradition of utilizing the site of a hillside continued, particularly in theatres that were adapted from existing Greek models, the Romans found that it could be increasingly effective to build on a level site. With the *scaenae frons* rising to the same height as the perimeter of the *cavea*, it was possible to cover the entire structure with a ceiling awning or *velarium*. Technology included a front curtain, lowering into the orchestra, and curtains to cover parts of the *scaenae frons* behind the actors. The increasing relegation of the orchestra, now enclosed by a parapet, to a place for gladiatorial display or even water ballets is just one example of what pure drama lovers might classify as a move towards decadence. But it was in the *Anfiteatro*, a huge, tiered, oval, multipurpose arena with encircling audience of more than 20,000, that the real spectaculars were mounted. Racing chariots, combating gladiators and persecuted

Christians were deployed on a scale unknown between the fall of Rome and the rise of Hollywood.

Something like ten centuries spanned the period from the emergence of the Greek theatre until the collapse of Rome. It would be another ten centuries before dramatic performances would again require permanent purpose-built theatres – at least in the West. In India and the Orient, performances had a very formal structure but, being more intimate, could be housed in less ambitious buildings. Nevertheless, the proportions of the respective areas for actor and audience were meticulously specified and development continued throughout the thousand years when Western drama moved haphazardly towards its renaissance.

The Middle Ages The elaborate forms of organized drama may have disappeared during the Middle Ages but the art and craft of the actor survived. The mimes, minstrels, acrobats, conjurors and ballad singers performed wherever the need arose – this was largely a time of passion without planks. Liturgical drama found an obvious home in the churches, often developing quite complex productions, moving through, and involving the audience in the action. Occasionally, complex machinery, as extant at Elche in Spain, was installed to lower angels from the heavens at climactic moments. But the most organized medieval dramas were the mysteries for which a sequence of 'mansions' appropriate to each episode were built on temporary platforms arranged formally or scattered around a market square. Alternatively, as in most of the English mysteries, the episodes could be built on wagons and moved from station to station around the town.

The Renaissance During the 16th century with the general cultural Renaissance came that surge of interest in drama which stimulated a simultaneous revival of theatre building throughout Europe. In Italy the desire of the humanists to restore to the stage the classical dramas of the ancients resulted in an attempt to revive the architectural forms of the theatres of antiquity. Renaissance Italians, combining a study of the architectural books of Vitruvius with their observations of the remains of the Roman theatres, created temporary open air theatres in courtyards on the Roman model. Permanent indoor theatres followed, and in Vicenza we still have **Palladio**'s Teatro Olimpico with its monumental *scaenae frons* backing an acting stage facing an orchestra and an audience *cavea* whose semicircle has been flattened to fit the site. Beyond the five openings in the *scaenae frons* still stand the perspective street scenes designed by **Scamozzi** for the opening performance in 1585 of **Sophocles**' *Oedipus Tyrannus*. These represent the other line of Italian renaissance development – the concept of perspective scenery developed by **Serlio** whose illustrated writings on theatre architecture, published in French (1545) and English (1611), as 'The Second Book of Architecture', were probably the most influential source for renaissance theatre builders.

Outside Italy there was less concern to seek inspiration from the ancient world and the new theatres were designed to accommodate the growth of indigenous drama. The surge of theatre growth that began in Elizabethan England and continued until the Commonwealth embargo in 1642, bred two forms of theatre building. Outdoor theatres such as the **Curtain**,

The Theatre of Marcellus, Rome, 13–11 BC.

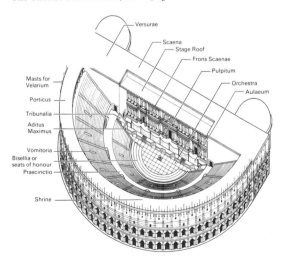

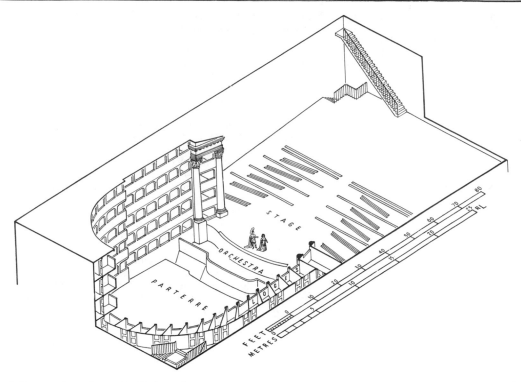

The Italian opera house has retained its basic form since the Teatro SS Giovanni e Paolo, Venice, of 1639, up to the present day.

Swan, **Globe** and **Fortune** developed out of the methods used for temporary staging in inn yards and bear-baiting pits. A thrust stage in an encircling courtyard was surrounded for some 300° by an audience in galleries and on the ground. This was the theatre that **Shakespeare** wrote for – a theatre based on the passion of words delivered from planks that might support some furniture and simple mechanics but virtually no representational scenery. The indoor theatres such as the **Cockpit** had a Palladian inspired *scaenae frons* resulting from **Inigo Jones**'s 1613 visit to Vicenza's Teatro Olimpico. Jones as designer of temporary stagings for the Court Masques in Whitehall was also heavily influenced by Serlio and developed a scenic style of wings and back shutters opening to reveal 'relieves', vistas in three-dimensional relief. Following the Restoration, the Jacobean theatres therefore tended to combine the two styles, utilizing an elaborate frontispiece which did not merely back the actors but framed a scenic stage.

Meanwhile the shape of theatres outdoors in Madrid and indoors in Paris had been developing in a form much closer to that which would be standard for a long period as the English Playhouse and even longer as the Italian Opera House. The first Spanish permanent theatre since the Romans (whose theatre in Merida still stands) was the 1582 Corral Príncipe in Madrid with a stage set squarely across the end of a rectangular auditorium galleried all around and with rows of seats at ground level. Whereas the Spaniards had adapted the configuration of an inn yard, the French fitted their early theatres into the space of a tennis court. In 1548 a roofed rectangular theatre had been built on the site of

the **Hôtel de Bourgogne** to house mystery plays, and the development of indoor courtyard theatres can be traced through its successive alterations. Although the Bourgogne auditorium remained much the same in spirit, if not in finer detail, its stage in the mid-16th century was a simple end platform supporting the 'mansions' of the medieval mysteries; in the 17th century it had the angled perspective wings of Serlio, and by the early 18th century sliding wings of painted changeable scenery.

Italian concern with a revival of the ancient Roman dramatic traditions was short lived: the growth of opera in the 17th century moulded theatre building in the same basic form that was emerging everywhere – the proscenium framed scenic stage facing a galleried auditorium. Indeed auditorium shape across Europe, and in those countries colonized by Europeans, became relatively stabilized throughout the 18th and much of the 19th centuries. There were many variations in the geometry of the balconies (mostly boxed) that lined the walls, which were occasionally straight, but mostly curved on every possible inspiration from the bell to the horseshoe. English actors continued throughout the Georgian period to play in something of a residual tradition of the ancient theatre and its early renaissance revival, by acting on an apron stage, thrust forward through a proscenium arch flanked by 'doors of entrance' and framing a background of changeable scenery. Although this forestage was gradually cut back, it lasted well into the 19th century, when public taste for a more spectacular entertainment forced the actors somewhat reluctantly back into a scenic environment. Throughout the 18th and early 19th centuries the

British playhouse remained relatively simple in structure and unadorned in decoration, with its architectural roots in the concept of a simple shell building furnished by a carpenter. Elsewhere in Europe however, particularly in Italy and Germany, theatre auditoria became places for artists like the **Bibienas** to lavish the grandeurs of the baroque and the elegances of the rococo. Sometimes this spilled over into the foyers, but elsewhere, as in the extant Margrafentheater in Bayreuth, the approaches were kept very simple indeed in order to increase the stunning effect of the auditorium. The simplicity of British theatres resulted partly from their being predominantly dramatic rather than lyric, entrepreneurial rather than court or civic, and in a country generally less committed to art than central Europe.

Financial considerations led in the latter part of the 19th century to a further drifting apart between Britain and much of the rest of Europe. British theatre was to remain unsubsidized until the mid-20th century whereas in central Europe a grid of court theatres developed into municipal theatres, supported financially as civic amenities. Proscenium theatres are most successful when the balconies remain shallow with preferably only two or three, but certainly not more than four or five, rows of seats. In Britain financial pressures forced the balconies to deepen until their overhangs produced a tunnel effect that broke contact between actor and audience. When cantilever engineering made supporting pillars redundant, deep balconies became ever more popular.

Return to sightlines In the mid-19th century **Richard Wagner** reacted strongly against the virtually universal Western concept of a theatre audience hung on every available wall space, irrespective of its view of the stage. The Graeco-Roman concept of a single raked seating area had never been entirely lost – there are particularly magnificent examples of such 18th-century court theatres extant in Gripsholm (Sweden) and Potsdam (Germany) – but this system of the ancients, revived briefly at the Renaissance, had mostly given way to the curved courtyards with tiers of boxes covering the walls and extending to the proscenium arch. Wagner called for universally perfect sightlines from every seat to a scenic stage, and in 1876 built his Bayreuth Festspielhaus with a single wedge of raked seating. Blank side walls can be a problem in such a theatre but at Bayreuth this was solved with a success that has eluded many later architects. Here they were broken up by a series of short pillared walls at right angles to the side walls, deepening towards the stage and focusing on it so that the actual proscenium seemed unstressed and less of a barrier than many a conventional frame. The result was excellent when applied to the new music drama deploying singers, orchestra and scenery on a particularly large scale to perform works dealing with themes of epic grandeur. However it was less satisfactory for more intimate music theatre or for drama, even when scaled down. Nevertheless preoccupation with sightlines became an increasing feature of the debate, particularly as the role of theatre in society became more and more a matter for philosophic agonizing. The suggestion that boxes enabled the audience to be seen rather than to see was an obvious battlecry for those who sought a new serious role for

the drama and pursued a democratic theatre based on purity of sightline from all seats.

Technological influences Meanwhile theatre technology was advancing. In nearly two centuries there had been only one really major development in the backstage area: the full height flying towers that became standard in the second half of the 19th century. Most scenery had continued to move in one plane, parallel to the front of the stage – whether it came down from the flies, up through sloats (slotes) or traps in the floor, or slid on from the sides. Here again there were differences between British practice and the rest of Europe, mostly attributable to their respective traditions of subsidized opera or commercial drama. In central Europe the scenic wing flats were simultaneously changed by elaborate carriage systems running on rails in the basement under slots in the stage, whereas British wings moved in simple wooden grooves fixed to the stage and suspended from the flies. Towards the end of the 19th century a number of factors produced a shift away from perspective painting towards solid three-dimensional scenery. One was the introduction of electricity which was less sympathetic to painted scenery than the soft gaslight that preceded it (even gas had seemed hard after the shimmering haze from candles and oil lamps, but this had been a difference that could largely be compensated for by painting techniques) (see also **Stage lighting**). But perhaps more important was that three-dimensional scenery was more appropriate to a new drama that pursued realism rather than rhetoric.

The growth in the use of three-dimensional scenery required new methods to change it. Complex technologies were developed in Germany particularly. First the turntable stage enabled a sequence of scenes to be revolved towards the proscenium opening (first installed for *Don Giovanni* at Munich's Cuvilliestheater in 1896). Then came wagon stage systems whereby full-sized stage areas could be slid on from left, right or rear to fill the proscenium. Although a few revolves were installed in Britain, scene changing mainly remained a labour intensive exercise involving breaking down the set into small elements which could be stored as flat as possible against the walls or in a small 'dock' alongside. But Britain's Victorian theatre expansion had abandoned the repertoire system of its early Georgian growth phase and based its organization on 'runs' or performances of the same play. This was unlike most of Europe where the repertoire system remained, requiring sophisticated changing, storage, rehearsal and production manufacturing facilities of all kinds. The Italians stood aside from all this continuing with simple stages and a system of scenery based on painted canvas stored in rolls and temporarily battened out on simple timber framing when required for a performance. However because opera was (and still is) a matter of popular importance in Italy, the public areas were as extensive as in Germany and other countries where a theatre was an important civic building. Indeed, in comparing plans of British and other European theatres in the late 19th century, the ratio of auditorium space to the rest of the building is very telling.

European concepts of theatre architecture were carried forth into the new world by colonists who sought, at least initially, only to create a theatre in the image that they knew. In the intensely colonized areas such as the Americas and the Antipodes, there was little indigenous drama, it was not organized to the point of requiring special housing, and settlers were more likely to suppress than to encourage it. Available resources tended to restrict theatres to the more simple models although there were exceptions – Manaus, isolated up the Amazon, built an opulent opera house to demonstrate the wealth of its rubber economy to the world. The earliest American theatres were firmly based on the British Georgian playhouse, but by quite early in the 18th century the basic form was already showing signs of the widening of stage and auditorium that would in the early 19th and 20th centuries give a characteristic shape to Broadway and the road houses across America, which were fed with tours from the New York base. This configuration brought a higher proportion of audience closer to the stage by adopting a short, wide, format, rather than the long, narrow, shape more common in Europe. Colonization of the Antipodes came later, and so their early theatre tended to reflect the approach that was standard for much of the great surge of British theatre building during the later decades of the 19th century. These had deep galleries with two or three token side boxes to break up the side walls.

The 19th century Today, most of Britain's remaining stock of 'old' theatres dates from this period which came to an end in the years leading up to the First World War. Outside London's West End, with its open-ended runs of the same play, these theatres were intended for a touring system of plays and musicals based on a weekly run (or multiples of one week) in each town. Their stage arrangements lacked storage and workshops while their seating capacities were geared to a commercial system whereby a couple of reasonable houses on Friday and Saturday could comfortably clear the costs, leaving the rest of the week as profits. This required the sort of capacities (1,000 was small) which could only be achieved by making the balconies deep and steep. Sightlines to the stage were often clear (after cantilevers had removed the need for pillars) but the view could be from far away and often funnelled by the overhang of the balcony above. The commercial basis of such theatres also required that they be built on a minimum site area and the most prolific architect of the period, Frank Matcham, was renowned for his skill in extracting maximum usage from small irregularly shaped sites. He was also adept at contriving the rich decorative treatment which a popular theatre needed to offer as an escape from the social conditions of a rapidly developed industrialization.

The 20th century Art centuries rarely tally with neat spans of a hundred years: the 20th century for theatre architecture got under way in the 1920s and was, inevitably, heavily influenced by the cinema. Boxes on the side walls disappeared altogether or became so vestigial that they were intended as decoration rather than for audience. Out went the plasterer's excesses of Victorian and Edwardian quasi-baroque and in came the new clean lines of modernity. The plasterer's art was redeployed to form coves in which the colour symphonies of the concealed indirect lighting replaced the earlier traditions of the Georgian painters and their

successors who pursued their art in gilt and plush. A single rake of auditorium seating with the possible addition of not more than one deep balcony became the norm. Everyone could see from seats which became cheaper as the stage became ever more distant. Outside the majority of theatres built on this norm, there were many exceptions. Everywhere that **Max Reinhardt** went, an interesting theatre seemed to emerge: in Berlin the Grosses Schauspielhaus wrapped its 3,000 audience around a huge arena stage thrusting forward from a restrained proscenium; in London, Olympia became a cathedral while in Salzburg the cathedral square became a theatre, as did the 17th-century rock-hewn riding school. On a smaller scale, **Copeau** in Paris and **Terence Gray** in Cambridge were amongst those who thrust through the proscenium arch and discarded it totally. Visionaries such as **Gropius** and **Norman Bel Geddes** produced exciting schemes which were rather too advanced to build – and by the time that their philosophies were adopted some 50 years later, a reaction had already set in. However developments in lighting, particularly the limitless spatial backgrounds of Fortuny's cyclorama, helped to realize a stage design revolution sought by **Appia** and **Craig**, whose visual concepts had initially been frustrated by the available technology.

By the time that the Second World War loomed, the age of agonizing was well established – it had been started by Wagner and gathered momentum until by the mid-20th century it had become a major conference topic. No magazine was complete without an article on adaptable theatres or the actor–audience relationship, and the correspondence columns were alive with anarchy. It even bred a new occupation, probably always in existence, but now formalized as theatre consultancy whose members endeavoured to establish the purpose of a proposed theatre and rationalize that purpose against the various current theories. Theatre Consultants, although aiming for objectivity, tended to be people with strong, rather subjective, ideas and therefore they became a major influence, often sharing at least equal responsibility with the architect for the theatrical form of the building.

In 1945 Europe was devastated with many theatres destroyed or disabled. In Germany particularly the rebuilding began almost immediately with performances restarting in improvised theatres. (German opera house stages were so large that it was often possible to contrive an interim theatre of stage, orchestra pit and auditorium for more than 600 on the old stage, if the fire curtain had saved the backstage area.) In Britain, old theatres temporarily saved by the wartime surge in demand for entertainment now entered a downward spiral of decreasing quality, increasing costs and lack of maintenance. But the repertory movement, slowly established between the wars, now blossomed with **Arts Council** funding and there was a growing demand for new theatres with their own resident acting companies in every town of consequence. In the USA the universities were developing drama faculties which needed housing, and each campus became the focus for a regional theatre movement that first complemented and then began to replace the old touring houses in all but the biggest centres of population. In the Antipodes the old theatres were coming down to be replaced within new commercial developments, and there was a growing demand for major opera house sized theatres in the major centres. Third World countries gaining independence often regarded a National Theatre as a desirable acquisition. Even Great Britain once again revived its long smouldering **National Theatre** ambitions.

But what was to be the shape of the new theatres? Today's building techniques and regulations bring an inflexibility unknown to earlier theatre builders who 'fitted out' a theatre by furnishing a shell which could expect to house a series of different fashions during a century of its lifetime. But concrete has finality, and

this has helped to fuel demand for an adaptable theatre which can cope with every style of production from intimate drama to grand opera, from proscenium via thrust to fully encircled theatre-in-the-round, and to audiences of widely varying sizes. A 1961 international conference in London on 'Adaptable Theatres', launching the new Association of British Theatre Technicians, appeared to reach a consensus that adaptability was a strictly limited concept: if a theatre tried to do too many things, it ended up doing none of them well. Nevertheless experiments in flexible theatre have continued from time to time, often using complex expen-

The Ziegfeld Theatre, New York (1926), combines an auditorium influenced by the cinema with a cyclorama to exploit the new developments in stage lighting.

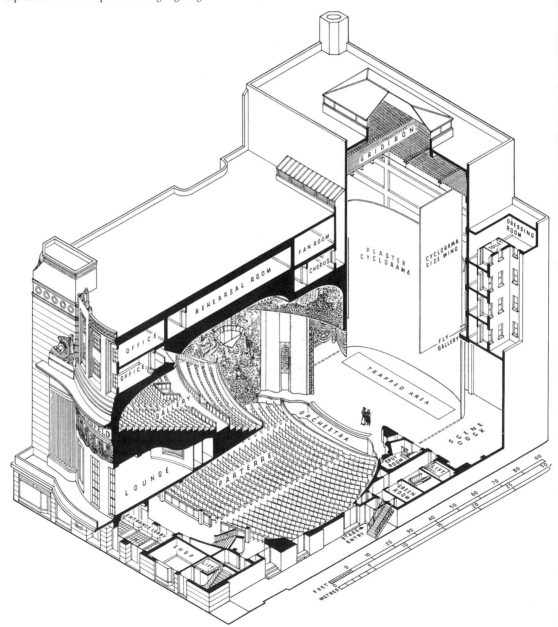

sive engineering to produce variations that were either nominal or, if significant, had become unfashionable by the time the theatre opened. More successful were the small theatres where flexibility could be achieved manually – but unfortunately frequently so expensively in terms of money and/or time that such theatres soon found their most comfortable format and stayed that way.

The new German opera houses generally opted to hang the audience on the walls, but adopted a fan-shaped auditorium so that the ascending tiers of boxes faced the stage. The main proscenium was often unstressed but standardized technology produced an inner black-clad structure of bridge and towers to carry the lighting equipment. This provided a frame, adjustable in width and height, for the huge wagons and elevators for moving scenery. Most Grosses Haus had a Kleines Haus attached and this tended to be a more flexible space, increasingly moving towards the neutral black box concept that represented an ideal for many people in the 1960s and 70s. In the USA, mainstream theatres got bigger and bigger: perfect sightline was supreme. Australia built, in Sydney's Opera House, the only new theatre to be instantly recognizable by everyone across the world, whether or not they ever went to a theatre. During the fitting out of this magnificent shell, some unfortunate decisions led to the

actual performance space being considerably less than ideal. The rest of the main Australian cities then built simple large theatre complexes which are probably the best of the world's pure sightline theatres. In Britain the new theatre building was almost entirely regional playhouses with seating in the 350–650 bracket, usually with a studio attached for about 100 people – the wedge-shaped single tier being the most popular and at its most effective capable of up to about 500 seats. The proscenium was unstressed, being formed by the natural termination of the walls and ceiling. It became standard to have a flexible area in front of the stage which could be optional forestage, flat floor or sunken orchestra pit. The old theatres and their touring circuits were allowed to die away in the 1960s but several (often ones that had been preserved by use as Bingo Halls) were refurbished during the 1970s to provide a national grid for opera, dance, musicals and star performers of all kinds. The National Theatre was finally built. Its largest auditorium, showing considerable resonances with pre-war Bel Geddes concepts, was the culmination of a growth in thrust staging that started with **Tyrone Guthrie**'s improvised stage at the **Edinburgh Festival** in the late 1940s, continued by him in North America, and by the **Chichester Festival Theatre** and the Crucible in Sheffield. Its second auditorium was a straightforward proscenium house, serviceable but not

The Forum Theatre, Billingdon (1968), is an example of a current return to 'papering the walls with people', acknowledging the importance of audience togetherness which can be lost in a theatre designed purely for good sight lines.

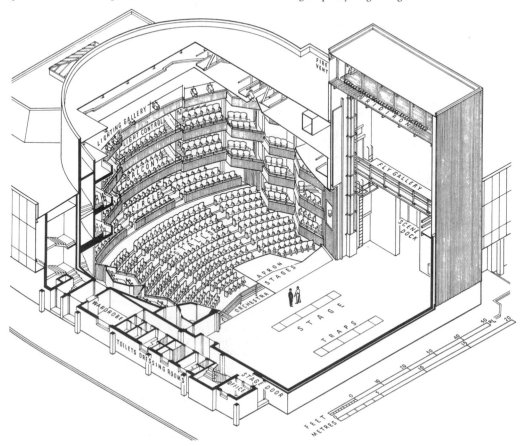

particularly distinguished. However it is the third and smallest that has caught most imagination and stimulated an almost inevitable rediscovery of what has been labelled as the courtyard form.

The courtyard revival is a response to the isolation that can be experienced by an individual member of the audience in a theatre designed to give everyone a direct clean uninterrupted view of the stage. Indeed it almost follows from defining a pure sightline that an individual will not be aware of fellow members of the audience. Hang some on the walls, and those in the central seats will be aware, out of the corners of their eyes, of the response of those hanging over their balcony rails to see the stage. This may not be an ideal in a theatre with democratic aims, but many would hold that, for the cheaper seats, close contact is more important than a view that is clear but remote. Consequently an increasing number of theatres are being built to concepts against which Wagner started the reaction.

The future So where does theatre architecture go next? As we stand at the end of the 1980s, a particularly hectic 50 years of intensive theatre building has slowed down. The post-war renewal and development phase is complete and economic stagnation has concentrated diminishing resources on maintaining performances on existing stages rather than creating new ones. When new theatres arise, they tend to be adaptations of existing non-theatre buildings, often organized in a very simple spatial way. The clue to the future may lie in the way in which alternative theatres, setting out as a reaction against the established theatre, become absorbed by it. This becomes a cycle of rediscovery: a theatre building and its technology grow until a reaction provokes allegations of decadence and demands for a return to the simplicities of street theatre. But success in the street builds an audience, and planks are again required to project the passion – the beginning of another escalation that will eventually provoke a reaction. In today's theatres there are so many overlapping cycles that all forms from the simplest to the most sophisticated coexist. There is no reason to suppose that this will change. A whole series of stylistic options for realizing a text in performance will require a similarly wide series of architectural options. Or is the adaptable theatre possible? Technology, which in its rigid systems of elevators and hydraulics seemed to offer only an option of fixed variables which turned out to be more restrictive than an empty space, is now offering, through the air castor, the possibility of moving huge chunks of building around on the hovercraft principle without tracks or other preconceived movement paths. Perhaps this will return architecture to the flexibility of the age of the carpenter.

Meanwhile, simple or complex, we would do well to bear in mind the definition that has been offered by John Orrell: 'The essence of theatre design is to bring players and audience together in a fruitful collaboration, never allowing the two elements to become remote from each other, nor yet so mingling them together that the audience loses its capacity for wonder.'   FR

Théâtre des Nations Name given to a festival of international theatre held for two months of each year in Paris between 1957 and 1968. It had a strong influence on the development of European theatre styles, especially in France, where new discoveries are sometimes hailed with exaggerated enthusiasm. It had begun as the Festival de Paris in 1954, when the visit of the **Berliner Ensemble**, giving its first performance in the West, struck many with the force of a revelation. Other companies who visited were Theatre Workshop, the Piccolo Teatro and the **Living Theatre**. Since 1968 being the work of Krejca, **Grotowski**, **The Bread and Puppet Theatre**, **Wilson** and **Kantor**, but the Théâtre des Nations has become peripatetic and is managed by the **International Theatre Institute**.   DB

Theatre design While the necessary ingredients for a theatrical event vary depending upon the needs and expectations of particular societies in particular eras, there are only two elements essential for theatre to occur: a performer and a spectator. But a performance must occur *somewhere*, and if there is space there is, inherently, design.

The design may range from a circular piece of ground surrounded by standing spectators – as in much street theatre, ritual performances, and, probably, pre-Aeschylean Greek dance and dithyrambs – to the lavish settings and computerized mechanisms of grand opera performed for spectators surrounded by Baroque splendour. In both cases someone has made decisions about the space, about its delineation, about the relationship of the performer to the space and the space to the spectator, and about the role the space plays in the spectators' responses. All of this is design, and no theatre exists without it. Indeed, it can be argued that design is as essential to theatre as the performer. Theatre is, after all, a visual medium and the size, shape, colour, texture, arrangement, and style of the sets, costumes, and lights frequently determine the movement and rhythm of a performance and, in conjunction with the theatre space, significantly affect the spectators' responses, even if subliminally. (See also **Theatre buildings**.)

While there are periods in theatre history in which it is possible to talk about scenic design separately from stage architecture – the painterly style of, say, the romantic scenic artists, or the distorted and exaggerated sets of the German expressionists – in most cases there is an indivisible connection between the stage, the overall space of the theatre, and the elements that comprise the scenic design. And in most of the classic periods of theatre history – ancient Greece and Rome, the 15th-century **nō** of Japan, Elizabethan England, 17th-century France and Spain – there is little scenery *per se*, but formal, architectural stages instead; platforms on which to act. Scenery, by which we normally mean some sort of stage decoration, tends to be either illusionistic – pretending to be something it is not, such as a room or a forest – emblematic, or evocative. Formal stages emphasize their own theatricality, constantly reminding the audience that what they are seeing is taking place in a theatre. Such stages also throw focus onto the performers and the language.

Theatre architecture or space is generally classified according to the relationship of the stage to the audience. Scenic design is usually categorized by its style. There are two broad categories of staging: frontal and environmental. In the former, the audience sees a performance directly in front of it; in the latter, the audience is surrounded to some degree by the performance space. Most theatre, of course, is frontal and this category can be broken down to end stage – usually a raised stage at one end of a rectangular theatre, directly facing an audience; thrust – a stage surrounded on three sides by audience; and arena – a stage completely surrounded by the audience. Needless to say, there are many variants on this arrangement, most notably the booth or trestle stage generally associated with popular entertainment and certain forms of medieval staging. It consists of a raised stage, usually with a curtain or scenic backdrop at the rear creating a 'backstage' area for costume changes, storage, and entrances. It differs from an endstage only in that it is most frequently used outdoors or as a temporary structure in spaces not normally used for theatre.

It might be noted that outdoor theatre (which includes most theatre throughout approximately the first 2,000 years of both Occidental and Oriental theatre history) tends to blur the distinction between frontal and environmental staging. Many plays and theatre structures in such surroundings incorporate natural events and topography into the design and production in a way that indoor theatres rarely do, leading the spectator to perceive him or herself surrounded by the 'design'.

Design is broadly categorized as presentational or representational. Representational theatre tries to create an illusion of reality. Presentational theatre emphasizes theatricality and acknowledges the theatre as theatre – there is no illusion. Just as in the history of art, there are many individual styles too numerous to list here. There are, however, three general classifications that are worth noting: architectural, sculptural, and painterly. Architectural stages – such as those of ancient Greece and Rome, Elizabethan England, and most of the permanent stages of classic Indian, Chinese, and Japanese theatres – are the result of a marriage between design and architecture. The features of the stage – arches, platforms, doors, steps, etc. – are permanently built into the stage space. While specific scenery and set pieces may be used within a production to transform the stage into a specific place, the designer and performers are limited by the basic architecture.

Sculptural settings see the stage space as a cubic volume and, like sculptures, emphasize the fact by organizing the space around itself. It emphasizes three-dimensionality of the stage space (rather than creating an *illusion* of depth) by the use of three-dimensional forms and the sculpting of space with light. This is largely a 20th-century phenomenon and is typified by the use of geometric forms, abstract structures, platforms and steps. It is sometimes referred to as a structural stage.

Painterly, as the name suggests, relies on painted images, usually to create an illusion of place, or to evoke a particular mood or sensibility. Painterly designs of one style or another dominated much Western theatre design from the Renaissance until fairly recently.

Greece The method of presentation of Greek theatre apparently evolved from the dancing circle or *orchéstra* upon the threshing floor of the Agora. (See also **Greece, ancient**.) When the first Theatre of Dionysus was built on the hillside of the Acropolis a more formal orchestra was created by levelling part of the slope. Very little is known of the physical aspects of the early Greek theatre. The earliest version of the Theatre of Dionysus probably presented the spectators – who were seated on the hillside or perhaps on wooden benches – with no more than the orchestra and a view of the Temple of Dionysus behind it and the sea in the distance. All the extant plays prior to about 460 BC take place in the open countryside or barren place; there are no references to buildings of any kind. In levelling the hillside, an embankment of some six feet was created at the rear of the orchestra. **Aeschylus** probably took advantage of this in *Prometheus Bound* and had Prometheus sink behind the embankment as if into the earth, presumably to rise again at the start of the second play of the trilogy, the fragmentary *Prometheus Unbound*.

This being an outdoor theatre, lighting, of course, came from the sun. But even so, the playwrights learned to utilize natural phenomena in the design. The performances commenced at dawn, and several plays incorporate the sunrise into the script. In Aeschylus' *Agamemnon*, for example, the play begins with the Watchman waiting for a beacon that will announce the capture of Troy. In his speech he refers to the waning stars, the morning dew, and, if the timing were accurate, the sunrise. 'Oh hail, blaze of the darkness,' he cries, 'harbinger of the day's shining'. [Trans. Richmond Lattimore.] Similarly, the opening of **Euripides**' *Iphigenia at Aulis*: 'That light / Shows the approach of morn, the harbinger / Of the sun's fiery steeds.'

Sometime in the mid-5th century a *skene* or scene building was introduced. The evidence is so minimal that scholars cannot agree on its size or shape. In its earliest versions it was probably a temporary wooden structure which later became more elaborate and permanent. But whatever its form, the *skene* provided playwrights and performers with greatly expanded possibilities. About two-thirds of the extant tragedies occur before a temple or palace which could, of course, be represented by the *skene*. The door (perhaps three doors by the end of the 5th century) allowed for exits and entrances, and the possibility of concealment and surprise. The roof of the *skene* provided a raised stage for certain scenes, particularly the appearance of gods. Through the next century the emphasis shifted from the chorus to the actor and hence the size of the orchestra shrank as the stage was raised higher.

Scholars have debated fiercely about the use of painted scenery in conjunction with the architectural stage. In the *Poetics* **Aristotle** claims that **Sophocles** introduced *skenographia* which has generally been taken to mean 'scene painting'. There is, however, no evidence or reference to scene painting, or to specific, illusionistic, or changeable scenery in any other source except the writings of the Roman architect **Vitruvius**. Writing in the 1st century BC he says that Agatharchus first created scenery, but he implies that this was a permanent image depicting architectural perspective – in other words, a decoration or generic scene. Those who have tried to make a case for play-specific decor tend to be influenced by the general use of literal and realistic scenery of Western theatre in the 19th and 20th centuries. The Greek theatre was a theatre of convention; locale, by and large, was suggested through dialogue and actions in front of a bare facade or an unchanging stylized background as in the Japanese *no* theatre.

There is evidence, however, for at least two mechanical scenic devices. One is the *mechane* or 'machine', probably a crane-like device for flying gods, chariots, and the like – hence the phrase '*deus ex machina*' or god from the machine. There is no evidence that Aeschylus or Sophocles used the device but it was used frequently by Euripides (and was parodied by **Aristophanes**); the phrase came to signify a contrived ending.

The other device is the *ekkyklema*, a rolling platform or wagon that was wheeled out through the door of the *skene* to display a tableau or scene such as the end of *Agamemnon* in which Clytemnestra is discovered with the bodies of Agamemnon and Cassandra. The fact that an 'interior' scene now intruded upon what had been an 'exterior' scene apparently did not trouble Greek audiences. The unities of time and place, so rigidly demanded by Renaissance interpreters of Aristotle, were unnecessary in a theatre of suggestion, imagination, and convention.

It should be noted, however, that as Greek theatre evolved through the 5th century, there was an increasing tendency toward greater naturalism. Thus, in the plays of Euripides it is no longer sufficient to say that it is night; the performers must also carry torches. By the 4th century BC there were very likely more scenic devices such as the *pinakes* or painted panels set in niches or between supporting columns. Vitruvius suggests that these were made of wood and functioned as sound resonators as well as decoration. Vitruvius also speaks of *periaktoi* – prism-shaped scenic pieces with scenes painted on each of their three sides. By rotating the *periaktoi* a change of scene could be suggested.

Rome The great period of Roman playwriting, the period of **Plautus** and **Terence**, occurred in the 2nd century BC, but this was before the building of the first permanent theatres in Rome. (See also **Rome**.) The theatre of Pompey was not constructed until 80 BC. In Rome itself theatre was performed on temporary platform stages; elsewhere it could be done in existing Greek and Graeco-Roman theatres. Virtually all the extant comedies are set on a street in front of three houses, suggesting that even in the 2nd century the stage was probably a bare platform with three doors in the facade behind the stage. When Roman theatres were finally constructed the Greek *skene* became the *scaenae frons*, a three-tiered facade of pillars, niches, and statuary with three doors (and one door at either side of the stage). The Romans also used two kinds of curtains: the *aulaeum*, a front curtain, possibly decorated, that *lowered* into a trough in front of the stage; and the *siparium* which was a relatively small painted drop or backcloth that covered part of the *scaenae frons* and was raised and lowered somewhat in the manner of a Venetian blind. The *siparia* were clearly used to suggest more specific locales, yet, ironically, the extant Roman plays tend to be less specific in their identification of place than the Greek.

A major difference between the Roman theatre and the Greek resulted from the Roman's architectural use of the arch. This device allowed free-standing structures of great size and the theatre no longer had to be built into a hill. The *cavea* or auditorium of the Roman

theatre was architecturally unified with stage or *proscenium*. (And the *cavea* was probably at least partially covered by a *velarium* or awning.) For the spectator this meant being enclosed within a unified space, separated from the world outside. This differed from the Greek experience of a play as religious festival which was intrinsically set within the natural and religious surroundings. The early Greek theatre was, in a sense, able to incorporate the physical world within the experience of the play. The Roman experience was one of escapism; the Greek, at least prior to the Hellenistic period, was one of communion.

Legitimate theatre atrophied in the period of the Empire. But the spectacles and paratheatrical events which supplanted theatre, such as *naumachia*, gladiatorial games, and *venationes*, also employed scenery ranging from the epic (Caesar's man-made lake and replicas of warships for *naumachia*) to the simple and suggestive that was used to give a sense of narrative story to many of the bloodthirsty events at the Colosseum.

What survived the fall of Rome was the popular entertainer, the one constant throughout theatre history. Obviously, there is little information on such performances, but the little evidence and documentation that does survive indicates that the presentation has remained virtually unchanged from Greek times to the present. Performers who presented plays or skits (as opposed to simple circus skills) used a platform stage with a painted backcloth. It is this stage that became the basic scenic element of medieval theatre.

Medieval theatre Certain staging concepts predominated in the Middle Ages that may seem alien to modern audiences used to a more-or-less realistic approach to design. (See also **Medieval drama in Europe**.) Of greatest significance were the ideas of *simultaneous setting* and *emblematic* design. Simultaneous setting (or multiple staging) involved the depiction of several discrete locations simultaneously, rather than sequentially which is more common in contemporary theatre. In some cases the spectators moved from one scene to the next; but the scenes could also exist side by side on a raised stage. Emblematic design involves the suggestion of a place or idea by use of an image or device. For example, in certain medieval productions Jerusalem was depicted simply by a gate, and Hell by an open-mouthed monster head spewing fire and smoke.

Liturgical drama developed within the church and it was to a great extent the architectural elements of the church, the balconies, aisles, tombs, altar, that provided the theatrical design. The basic arrangement and use of space is what has come to be called *mansion* and *platea* or (with raised *mansions*) place and scaffold. The *mansion* was an emblematic structure suggesting a location, person, or idea (i.e., Bethlehem, Herod, Paradise); the *platea* was the neutral space in front of or surrounding the mansion. From the earliest records it is evident that the *mansion* could involve the making of a separate structure but it is also clear that even in the 16th century some churches still simply used altar, rood screen or other pre-existing structure for performance. The most elaborate structures within churches for which descriptions survive are the Italian ones of the early 15th century (e.g. those of Brunelleschi, 1377–

1446) where the *platea* appears to have become something akin to a raised stage and the older distinction between *mansion* and *platea* in many ways no longer exists.

Information about the early outdoor place and scaffold staging is very limited. There are the often detailed descriptions of the elaborate scaffolds and indications of *platea* action in the *Jeu d'Adam* (12th century), which is

A miniature by Jean Fouquet (15th century) of the Martyrdom of St Apollonia, presented as if it were a place-and-scaffold play.

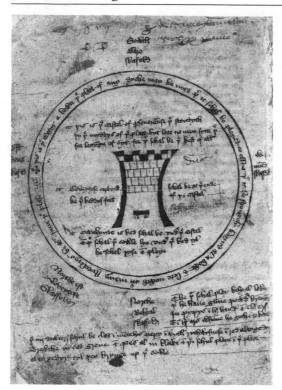

The ground-plan for the staging of *The Castle of Perseverance*, c. 1425.

generally thought to be designed for outdoor performance, but most of the information comes from very much later: the booth stages (in the paintings of Brueghel and others), the Dutch rhetoricians' stages, the Easter Play from Lucerne, the *Passions* from Mons and Valenciennes, all are from the 16th century.

Most medieval theatres used some variant of the *mansion* and *platea* idea. The pageant wagons of English and Spanish mystery cycles were essentially rolling *mansions* with the street or square as *platea*. The raised stage and simultaneous setting of the mystery play at Valenciennes, for example, was a frontal version of the *mansion* and *platea*. Likewise, the presentation of secular farces at innyards, palaces, and market squares, and the 'in-the-round' staging of plays in the Cornish 'rounds' all employed the concept of *mansion* and *platea*.

The *mansions* (or *pageants*, as the wagons were often called) were not intended to contain the action, as the stage direction from Coventry shows: 'Here Herod rages in the pageant and in the street also.' By the act of stepping out of a *mansion* the actor transformed all the space through which he moved into an extension of the *mansion* even if he performed in front of another scenic unit. The *platea* could also function metaphorically. The movement of performers or audience through the *platea* to another *mansion* functioned as a movement through time and space. A walk of a few yards could transport the spectators from Rome to Jerusalem; from Noah's Ark to Egypt.

In terms of the scenic elements, the medieval produc-

tions employed a seemingly contradictory mixture of realistic and emblematic devices. There are accounts of actors playing Christ or Judas who had to be removed from their respective crosses or nooses because they had nearly died in reality. Yet the parting of the Red Sea, not easily achieved on a rolling pageant, might be suggested by parting a red cloth which was subsequently draped over the 'Egyptians' to indicate their being swallowed up by the Sea. As with simultaneity, medieval audiences saw no contradictions in this style.

The Renaissance The road to naturalistic design – the attempt to create an illusion of reality or verisimilitude – began in the Renaissance; and at the same time theory, design, and architecture combined radically to alter the relationship between the stage and the auditorium. The three most significant developments in this period were the relocation of the theatre indoors, the discovery of techniques for creating perspective sets, and the evolution of changeable scenery.

The physical theatre of the period evolved as Renaissance scholars became aware of Vitruvius' *De Architectura* which contained descriptions of Greek and Roman theatres, but no illustrations. **Sebastiano Serlio**, the most significant designer and theatre architect of the period, first addressed the problems of design and architecture in his treatise, *Architettura* (1545). Synthesizing the ideas of Vitruvius and others, he set forth a plan for a classical style theatre, but one that would be temporary and housed in existing spaces – usually the rectangular great halls of palaces. As Serlio and others interpreted Vitruvius they inevitably devised a classical theatre that was informed by the technology, sensibilities, and aesthetics of the Renaissance.

This can be seen in the early attempts at staging the rediscovered plays of Terence and Plautus for which mansions were placed on a raised end stage – the so-called Terence stages. Illustrations from that period, however, suggest that the mansions were placed side-by-side and architecturally unified; the mansions were more like curtained sections of an arcade screen than the free standing mansions of the Middle Ages or the doors of the *scaenae frons*. Whereas the medieval stage allowed the juxtaposition of seemingly incongruous scenery, and symbolic movement through time and space, the Renaissance sensibility moved toward unification and rationality in its attempt to maintain the ideal of verisimilitude.

The Teatro Olimpico at Vicenza, designed by **Andrea Palladio** and **Vincenzo Scamozzi**, opened in 1585, is the most stunning example of the combination of classical and Renaissance ideas, as well as being the first permanent theatre of the Italian Renaissance. The theatre had to fit into an existing space and thus the auditorium became elliptical, rather than semicircular. But the long narrow stage was backed by an elaborate *scaenae frons* with three arched openings and a doorway at either side. Behind the three arches, however, were five 'streets' lined by buildings constructed in perspective style, thus adding contemporary practice to classical design. This theatre, though, was unique and had little impact on the subsequent development of theatre architecture.

Another Teatro Olimpico, this one at Sabbioneta, was designed by Scamozzi alone. Opened in 1588, it was essentially a permanent adaptation of Serlio's design in which a scenic stage – a stage constructed for the purpose of displaying scenery – rather than an architectural stage was used. This small theatre was the true precursor of modern theatre architecture.

The rules of perspective – the ability to paint an object or scene which, when viewed from a particular point, achieved mathematically correct spatial relationships – were developed in the early 15th century. The first-known use of perspective scenery was for **Ariosto**'s *La Cassaria* at Ferrara in 1508, designed by Pelligrino da Udine. The chief proponent of perspective design in the 16th century was **Baldassare Peruzzi** whose work and ideas were enhanced and disseminated by Serlio, his student. The development of perspective design was facilitated by its use in the *intermezzi* or spectacle performances often staged by the Medicis and others, and for whom **Bernardo Buontalenti** was chief architect, designer, and machinist (inventing the machines that created the special effects).

Perspective scenery made possible the illusion of real space onstage. Now, rather than looking at discrete units of emblematic scenery, the audience saw a view of the stage that appeared to be a continuation of the auditorium – a vista of a street, perhaps, that seemed to disappear into the distance just as a real street would. Of course, the illusion was totally successful only from a fixed point in the auditorium directly opposite the stage.

Serlio, working from Vitruvius, devised three generic perspective scenes – one tragic, one comic, one satyric – that were to be used for all plays. The first two were city streets with buildings on either side that appeared to recede into the distance upstage, the tragic showing columns, pediments, and stately buildings; the comic showing private residences, shops, and balconies. The satyric showed trees, caverns, and rustic dwellings. The illusion was to be created through perspective-painted book flats diminishing in size on either side of a raked stage, converging toward a central vanishing point on a perspective-painted backcloth or back shutter at the rear of the stage.

Several things become apparent in considering these scenes. First, the offstage sides had to be concealed in order for the illusion to be believable; second, actors could not move within the scenic stage without destroying the illusion – they would be significantly larger than the scenery as they moved upstage; and third, there was no easy way to alter the location without disrupting the performance.

The problem of masking the wings was solved by framing the stage. The Teatro Farnese, built in 1618 and designed by **Giovanni Battista Aleotti**, is the first-known example of a proscenium arch theatre. The proscenium – in essence an architectural picture frame – hid not only the offstage side of the flats, but the increasingly elaborate stage machinery being developed in order to change the scenes or create special effects. More significantly, the frame had a perceptual effect; it psychologically distanced the spectator, making the audience more of a voyeur than participant. The irony of the Renaissance theatre was that once the audience was architecturally separated from the stage by the proscenium arch, it was pictorially unified with it through perspective illusion.

It is worth noting at this point that scholars have debated the origin of the proscenium arch, attributing it variously to an expansion of the unifying frame of the Terence stages, triumphal arches erected for public processions, the central arch of the Teatro Olimpico of Vicenza, and the method of framing paintings in that time. While these undoubtedly contributed to the general perceptions of art and performance, and may have provided a subliminal inspiration, the framing of the stage seems to be a logical response to the exigencies of presentation and the Renaissance ideal of unity.

The second problem, that of the actor, was solved by keeping the performance space in front of the scenery. Serlio's 1545 plan for a temporary theatre shows a semicircular orchestra used primarily as a seating area for distinguished spectators, a raised, relatively shallow stage, and a raked, fairly deep scenic stage. In this arrangement, the performers could go no farther upstage than the first wing. In many of the early court theatres in Italy and elsewhere, however, the orchestra was replaced with an extremely deep thrust stage surrounded by a horseshoe-shaped auditorium with a raised scenic stage at the rear. The result was a theatre divided into three discrete sections: the auditorium, the performance stage, and the scenic stage.

During the 16th to the 18th centuries, the Baroque and Rococo period, theatre architecture was dominated by the Italianate ideal and the trend was towards ever deeper scenic stages that allowed more splendid and spectacular design while allowing the actors to step further and further into the scene. It was not until the mid-19th century, however, that the actor was totally enveloped within the environment of the proscenium stage. It is important to note that even with increasing depth, the full perspective illusion still worked only for that part of the audience seated directly opposite the stage.

Although neoclassical theoreticians interpreted Aristotle as demanding the unities of time, place and action – arguing whether a play could unfold in several locations or had to be confined to a single room – the audiences delighted in spectacle, and changeable scenery emerged to cater to this taste. Early attempts at changing scenes tended to be awkward and it was suggested in all seriousness that the audience be momentarily distracted by staging a fight or blowing horns at the rear of the auditorium. In the early 17th century Aleotti developed a system of flat wings that could be slid on and off the stage in grooves. While this greatly simplified and improved changes it was still inefficient and **Giacomo Torelli**, probably the most important designer of the 17th century – called 'il gran stregoni' (the great wizard) – developed the chariot-and-pole system at the Teatro Novissimo in Venice in the 1640s. By cutting slots in the stage floor, flats with rods descending through the slots to rolling wagons all attached to a single winch could be smoothly and easily shifted. Overhead borders were shifted in the same way. The changing of scenes, which created an impression somewhat like cinematic dissolves, became so fascinating that totally unnecessary shifts were made during the course of a production for the pure delight of seeing it.

While the performances of neoclassical drama tended to be played in front of an unchanging scene, intermezzi – allegorical scenes presented between the five acts of

the drama or as part of court spectacles and performances – developed in Italy into lavish and wondrous
displays of scenic technology. By the mid-1600s audiences could be awed by the sight of choruses of angels
descending from the deepest recesses of the stage on
cloud machines (scenic elements that looked like clouds
and would unfold to reveal often scores of performers);
gods arriving in flying chariots; rocky grottoes transforming into stormy seas complete with ships. Thus,
by the 17th century an audience at such a spectacle was
treated to the experience of a tragedy or comedy in five
acts in front of a single setting that was transformed at
the close of each act into an allegorical scene of fantasy
and splendour. Although the scenes depicted in the
intermezzi were fantasy, they were done in perspective
illusion – a sort of fantastic realism.

The design and technology of the intermezzi affected
the development of opera in the 17th century. The
ability easily to transform scenes – to travel through
time and space – allowed the scenes of the opera to
occur anywhere. The librettist was no longer confined

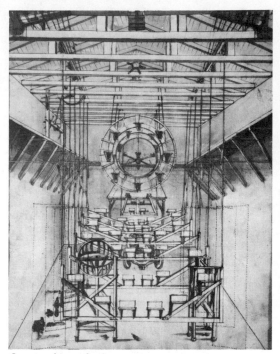

Stage machinery for the same, 1675.

A 'Glory' on stage at San Salvatore Opera House, Venice,
1675.

by the limitations of a single setting. Also, the work of
Torelli and his contemporary, Alfonso **Parigi** led to an
increased ability to control light through the use of
reflectors and lens-like devices. The theatre moved
indoors in the Renaissance and developments in lighting control made it possible not only to illuminate the
stage, but to contribute to the illusion and mood and
enhance the effects of changeable scenery. Costumes
for the opera tended to be lavish and embroidered in
gold and silver – a perfect surface for the reflection of
light that added even more spectacle.

While these developments occurred in Italy and had
their greatest impact on the development of opera
design and architecture, the theatre in England, France,
and Spain developed in somewhat different directions.

Although English culture and scholarship turned to
Italy for inspiration, the English theatre of the Renaissance emerged organically out of the strong traditions of
medieval theatre. The physical theatre combined the
trestle stages and presentational style – mansion and
platea – of liturgical and popular theatre; the architecture of the great halls of manors and castles (generally
rectangular rooms with an arcade screen against one
end containing one to three doors and a balcony above)
commonly used for the presentation of interludes; and
existing structures such as bull- and bear-baiting arenas
and courtyards. Concrete evidence is frustratingly
lacking, but the generally accepted view is that most of
the thriving Elizabethan theatres were circular or
polygonal three-tiered structures with audience galleries or boxes in each tier, a trestle-style stage thrusting
into the arena or 'pit', behind which were one to three
doors leading into the backstage area known as the
tiring house, a roof over the stage supported by two
columns, and, perhaps, the second gallery continuing

through this back wall to be used as a balcony if necessary (as in *Romeo and Juliet*) or for spectators at other times, thus creating an arena stage. The pit contained standing patrons. Scenery was minimal; existing records suggest some generic props including chairs, tables, thrones, rocks, trees and the like. There may have been some mansion-like scenic pieces, but these would have to have been placed upstage so as not to hamper sightlines. Thus, while the Italianate ideal of complex and illusionistic changeable scenery was spreading throughout Europe, English popular theatre achieved the same rapid changes of locale through language and imagination.

In the court theatre of James I and Charles I, however, the Italian style thrived. In the masques designed by **Inigo Jones**, who had spent time in Italy and been influenced by the work of Palladio as well as the scenic artists, perspective illusion and clever machinery created lavish spectacle. But while the court and public theatres coexisted, there was little, if any, scenographic influence of one upon the other until the Restoration.

The Italian ideal spread more rapidly in Paris. Through the mid-1630s staging was essentially medieval with simultaneous, mansion-like settings on a raised end stage. Many illustrations of these settings are preserved in a volume by the designer **Laurent Mahelot**. The illustrations suggest that certain scenes, especially those on the backcloth, may have been painted in perspective. The mansions, too, may well have bridged the two eras as many of Mahelot's illustrations suggest that the mansions were painted on flats along either edge of the stage, thus combining a medieval concept with Italian techniques.

It was Cardinal **Richelieu** who first brought Italian staging to Paris. The Palais Cardinal (**Palais-Royal** after Richelieu's death in 1642) was designed by Le Mercier, and was the first French theatre to have a permanent proscenium arch and employ painted-perspective wings. It was built in a rectangular space with galleries along each side; the king and his special guests were seated in the orchestra or *parterre* section while the majority of spectators sat in the galleries facing each other and the king, rather than the stage. The theatre opened in 1641 with *Mirame* designed by Georges Buffequin.

Cardinal Mazarin brought Torelli to Paris where he grudgingly designed for the **commedia dell'arte** troupe but also remodelled the **Petit-Bourbon** as a chariot-and-pole theatre and staged *La Finta Pazzi* there in 1645. The opera was a huge success and firmly established Italianate staging in France. The marvels of the new scenography became so popular, in fact, that a genre emerged known as 'machine plays' which consisted essentially of a minimal plot that could be used as an excuse for scenographic wonders – opera without singing. **Gaspare Vigarani**, brought to Paris by Mazarin in 1659, built the **Salle des Machines** on the site of the former Petit-Bourbon. When opened in 1662 with the opera *Hercules in Love*, it was the largest theatre in Europe, with a stage depth of 140 feet (42.67 m), a proscenium opening of only 32 feet (9.7 m), and a cloud machine capable of flying 300 people.

The French public theatres of the time, the **Hôtel de Bourgogne**, the **Marais**, and others were long narrow theatres with raised end stages. The theatre form was determined to some extent by the royal tennis courts in which makeshift theatres were erected from time to time. The tennis courts had a seating gallery along one side – ideal for viewing the back-and-forth action of a tennis game, but singularly unsuited for theatre. Nonetheless, existing architecture and economics won over common sense.

Many of the etchings from the time showing productions by **Molière**'s troupe or the earlier farces at the Hôtel de Bourgogne depict what appears to be a very shallow architectural stage, sometimes with a single chair or throne as sole scenic element. In actuality, the 'architectural' facade was constructed scenery, but was placed in the first wing position, creating a very shallow stage and functioning as an architectural setting would. Many of the plays of Molière and his contemporaries adhered fairly well to the unity of place and the action was frequently set in a single room – a generic room whose specificity was unimportant. Acting in 17th-century Paris generally consisted of standing near the centre of the stage, rather estranged from the scenic background; the scene provided entrances and places of concealment and a vague suggestion of place. Even the tragedies were presented in front of stock scenes: the *palais à volonté* and a *chambre à quatre ports*. This isolation was reinforced by spectators who sat on the edges of the stage, essentially creating a thrust stage. Thus the scenery functioned as a medieval mansion – a suggestion of locale – with the stage as platea.

Although the size and complexity of Parisian theatres grew through the 18th century, the basic arrangement – rectangular auditorium, seating along sides of a *parterre*, and scenic end stage – remained constant.

The English theatre of the Restoration became a strange amalgam of the Elizabethan thrust stage and the continental scenic stage that became familiar to English royalty and theatre practitioners exiled in Paris. As in France, the early Restoration theatres were built in converted tennis courts. In the early 1670s two theatres were built: **Dorset Garden** and **Drury Lane**, both designed by Christopher Wren. The theatres were sometimes identified by the auditorium arrangement of 'box, pit, and gallery'. The gallery was the open seating of the upper balcony, the boxes were the private compartments along the sides and back of the theatre, and the pit was the floor level which in this case was filled with rows of benches. With the building of Drury Lane in 1674, Wren created a fan-shaped auditorium which has been the basis of much theatre architecture ever since.

The acting area consisted of a deep, raked stage in *front* of the proscenium. The upper tier of boxes extended along the side of this stage and entrances were made by doors – two on either side, and referred to as proscenium doors – beneath the boxes. Behind the proscenium were sliding wing-and-groove, perspective scenes (chariot-and-pole was seldom used in England). Somewhat as in the French theatres, the actor was thus isolated from the scenery. Entrances and exits were generally made through the proscenium doors, regardless of dramatic location; a door could lead to 'another part of the forest' as easily as to a palace room. Scenery tended to be stock scenes of rooms, palaces, parks, etc., and, of course, the perspective illusion allowed for little interaction between actor and scenery. The result was that the performers were intimately connected to the audience – surrounded on three sides by them and sharing the same architectural space – while the scenery was architecturally separated from the performers and spectators by the proscenium. Audience onstage, until removed by **David Garrick** in 1762, also contributed to the isolation of the performer.

Lighting also contributed to the use of and perception of space. (See also **Stage lighting**.) The auditorium remained lighted by chandeliers; and the lighting on the scenic stage was generally not as bright as that on the forestage. But through the 18th century, the control and brightness of light increased so that it was possible to illuminate the scenery more brightly than the forestage. This, in combination with increased skill at perspective scenery and the desire of the managers to make more money by creating space for more spectators, led to the slow, but ineluctable shrinkage of the forestage as the actors retreated into the scenery.

While Italy's importance to the world of drama rapidly declined through the 17th century, it still dominated design until well into the 18th century. The main reason for this was the work of a remarkable family of designers and architects beginning with Giovanni Maria **Galli da Bibiena** and continuing through four generations to the end of the 18th century. Their work dominated court spectacle, performance, opera, and ballet throughout Europe from St Petersburg to London. The work of the Bibienas is the epitome of the triumphant and grandiose style of the Baroque.

Ferdinando Bibiena is usually credited with the next major innovation in stage design, the *scena per angolo* or multipoint (angled) perspective in 1703. But evidence suggests that this technique was used as early as 1694 by Marcantonio Chiarini in *La Forza della Virtu* at Bologna. Until this time, all perspective scenery had a single vanishing point – for a spectator seated in an ideal position, the scenery seemed to disappear at a single point in the distance. Because of this, the scenery appeared to be an extension of the auditorium; it was in the same scale as the spectators. Multipoint perspective, as the name implies, could have several vanishing points. The effect of this, apart from more varied possibilities, was to free the stage from the auditorium. The scene behind the proscenium no longer had to conform to the scale of the spectators; it could be larger than life. There was no need for symmetry; a scene could be shown from any point of view. The designs of the Bibienas in the 18th century were marked by soaring splendour as seemingly vast rooms and colonnades disappeared in the heights above the proscenium and divergent corridors seemed to dissolve into the far depths of the stage. Now, not only did the proscenium create an architectural separation between spectator and performance, but the setting, too, depicted not merely a different time and place, but a different world.

Apparently, the Bibienas used the *scena per angolo* in conjunction with the standard sets of wings on either side of the stage, at least for the first decade or so of the 18th century. But an important step was taken by **Filippo Juvarra** who enhanced the perspective illusion by placing flats anywhere across the stage, though still parallel to the proscenium. This allowed a greater freedom to designers and laid important groundwork for the scenography of the 19th century.

The 18th century   By the middle of the 18th century most of the elements of modern theatre were in place or were being developed. Most major cities had opera houses whose tiers of boxes resembled the interior of a beehive. Although the orchestra seating was still not the place of choice, neither was it the domain of groundlings or musketeers as it once was. Orchestra pits were placed in front of elaborate proscenium arches; many opera houses experimented with devices for enhancing acoustics; a curtain across the proscenium would part at the start of the performance. The scenery was done in painted perspective on flats, drops, overhead borders, and shutters arranged so as to recede upstage, although some decor employed scene pieces at other positions. Depending on the theatre, the scenery might either be new and specific for the performance, or part of the theatre's stock. In most continental opera houses the scenery was shifted by the chariot-and-pole method. The use of *scena per angolo*, improved lighting technology, and other techniques allowed the performers further and further back into the setting, thus emphasizing the separation between auditorium and stage. The smaller public theatres that presented dramatic fare were generally rectangular with a proscenium end stage. The basic arrangements, technology, and decor were essentially the same as at the opera houses, though on a smaller scale.

By the middle of the 18th century, a trend towards both realism and exoticism was apparent, as a fascination with history and distant cultures developed. Just as in the world of art, neoclassicism and a burgeoning romanticism vied for dominance. The neoclassicism manifested itself in terms of simplicity, symmetry, and formal style as opposed to the lavish and complex decor of the Baroque and Rococo, while romanticism was apparent in terms of a fascination with nature, historical accuracy, local colour, and mood.

Already, by the end of the 16th century, Italian designer **Leone di Somi** was calling for the use of historically accurate costumes in tragedy. In 1741, German actor-manager **Caroline Neuber** attempted such costumes in one of her productions but was laughed off the stage. The great French actor **Talma** met with derision from his fellow actors at the **Comédie-Française** as late as 1789 when he recreated a Roman costume with help from the painter David for his small part in *Brutus*. But in England, at least, audiences and performers seemed more accepting of these trends. The actor **Charles Macklin** created detailed costumes for Macbeth and Shylock in the mid-1700s, while Garrick did the same for Lear in 1776.

Interest in antiquarianism, as it was called, was sparked off by the discovery and early excavation of Pompeii which led to an 18th-century fascination with ruins. In terms of design this manifested itself in dark and moody scenes of ancient ruins, Gothic architecture, and pastoral settings. One of the strongest influences at the time was the painter and designer Gian Battista Piranesi whose sketches of prisons and ruins were suffused with shadows, dark recesses, and a general sense of mystery. By the early 19th century, German designer Karl Friedrich Schinkel declared that a designer could no longer be a mere perspective artist but must also be an architect, archaeologist, sculptor, and historian.

The most significant designer from this period was

Philip James De Louterbourg, brought to London by Garrick in 1771. De Louterbourg, in his stage designs and in the designs for his miniature theatre, the Eidophusikon, made important advances in lighting technology and scenic placement that allowed for greater detail and transformation than had ever been available before. His theatrical reproductions of actual places stimulated the vogue for 'local colour' in design; and through the use of silk screens, gauze curtains, and other means of controlling the amount and colour of light – including the introduction of overhead lighting battens – he was able to suggest weather and the passage of time. A scene might begin in morning sunlight, transform into a thunderstorm, and finally transform from afternoon into night. By breaking up the stage with ground rows and free standing set pieces he was able to achieve a greater sense of depth and reality while avoiding the symmetricality of the wing-and-groove system. The invention of the Argand lamp at this time also made it possible to intensify the brightness and colour of light behind the proscenium and contributed to the retreat of the actors into the scenic stage.

Romanticism By the beginning of the 19th century, a standard design for historical dramas tended to consist of a scene in the foreground – constructed with flats, ground rows, set pieces, and the like – that seemed to frame an accurate and detailed vista of a foreign or historical locale painted on a drop or shutter at the rear. Schinkel's design for *Die Jungfrau von Orleans* at Berlin in 1817, for instance, included an accurately reproduced vista of the cathedral and city of Rheims which was seen through the Gothic arches of a vaulted terrace during Joan of Arc's soliloquy.

In England, designer **William Capon** convinced actor–manager **John Philip Kemble** to begin using historically correct costumes and scenery in his productions of **Shakespeare**. This concept was carried further by **James Robinson Planché** in his work with **Charles Kemble**, and in the work of **William Charles Macready**. It would be more than half a century, however, before the antiquarian approach became consistent. Because new scenery cost money, and because performers were responsible for their own wardrobes, it was not unusual for a production to have one accurate set while the rest of the scenes were played in front of the stock scenery, or for one character to be dressed in historical costume while the other performers were dressed in contemporary finery. In the 1860s George II, Duke of Saxe-Meiningen, sometimes considered the first modern director, imposed a consistent visual style based on painstaking historical and cultural research. As his theatre company toured Europe in the 1870s it had a profound influence on the development of theatre production and design.

However, it was neither theory nor romantic sensibilities that determined the course of theatre as much as economics. As the general public began attending the theatre in increasing numbers, it quickly became apparent to managers that larger theatres meant larger profits. In England, as the forestage was chipped away, the rest of the auditorium was expanded. By 1810, the Theatre Royal, **Covent Garden** and the Theatre Royal, Drury Lane each held well over 3,000 spectators and the farthest spectator might be 100 feet away. Under such circumstances, subtlety was utterly useless

and a broad style of acting and a reliance on spectacle became dominant.

Spectacle could simply be the use of gimmicks, such as the 1820 production of *King Lear* at Drury Lane, in which the trees in the heath scene bent in the wind. Certainly it was apparent in the rising melodramatic theatre which regularly depicted earthquakes, water falls, erupting volcanoes, shipwrecks and the like. Etchings and paintings of the productions as seen from the audience's perspective show marvels and wonders. Backstage sketches, however, suggest relatively simple and crude devices dependent on cut-outs, ground rows, free standing set pieces, and even street urchins hired to create a stormy sea by crawling about under a blue ground cloth. More complex means, of course, were used and included stages divided into sections, each capable of rising above or sinking below stage level, special traps to allow for the sudden appearance or disappearance of a character, and fairly sophisticated devices such as **Pepper's Ghost** – a means of suggesting an apparition by projecting an image from the orchestra pit onto a piece of tilted glass situated onstage. The same principle is still in use – perhaps a bit more sophisticated – in Disney World.

Just as the late Renaissance theatre of France culminated in the creation of the Salle des Machines, so English melodrama achieved a technological, if not aesthetic, peak with two early 19th-century theatres: **Sadler's Wells**, with a water tank beneath the stage, and **Astley**'s Amphitheatre that included a circus ring where the orchestra seats or stalls would normally be in addition to the proscenium stage. Equestrian melodramas were shown at Astley's – plays whose plots included a horse race or chase, or in some way incorporated equestrian acts. Sadler's Wells saw sea battles, mythological and allegorical scenes, and anything else that might conceivably make use of water.

By the mid-19th century, historical accuracy was often a euphemism for spectacle and pageantry. Processions, lavish weddings and feasts, elaborately staged battles, as well as natural disasters were incorporated to 'illustrate' the texts. On the Continent this was best exemplified in the designs of **Alessandro Sanquirico** at La Scala in Milan. In England it reached a pinnacle of sorts with the mid-century productions of Shakespeare at the **Princess's Theatre** by actor–manager **Charles Kean** who worked with designers Thomas Grieve, Frederick Lloyds, H. Cuthbert, and William Telbin (who founded a family of scene painters that worked into the 20th century). Kean became known as the 'illustrator' of Shakespeare because he frequently cut Shakespeare's descriptive passages and replaced them with spectacle, processions, lavish feasts, and pantomime. Examples included the workshop of Quince the Carpenter in *A Midsummer Night's Dream*, and Bolingbroke's triumphal entry into London in *Richard II*.

As theatre moved in this direction, however, much of the scenery, rather than becoming more realistic in design and execution, turned towards painted images. The designer in the mid-19th century became more of a scene painter than a scenographer. The French poet **Théophile Gautier** declared that the 'age of purely visual spectacles [had] arrived'. The painted scene was well suited for creating the ethereal images of untrammelled nature and exotic locales that so typified the romantic era. The romantic atmosphere was further enhanced by the warm glow of the newly introduced gaslight (1816 in Philadelphia, 1817 at Covent Garden and Drury Lane, 1822 at the Paris Opéra). While much of the legitimate theatre of the period was devoted to melodramatic spectacle, the ballet became the home for the romantic scene painter. Nowhere was this better demonstrated than at the Paris Opéra in the designs of **Pierre Ciceri** for such ballets as *La Sylphide* and *Aladin ou la Lampe Merveilleuse*.

Illustrations from the theatre of this period suggest a stage that was almost a parody of the Serlian perspective. Rather than a series of wings receding upstage toward a painted perspective backshutter, the action, frequently, was brought downstage and a painted drop hung directly behind. While the drop itself may have been expertly rendered, the image came to an abrupt end where the bottom of the drop hit the undisguised stage floor. While this may not have been entirely obvious to patrons in the orchestra seats, it certainly was to the denizens of the boxes and galleries.

The quest for ever greater realism while maintaining a sense of visual interest led, by the last quarter of the century, to gimmicks now associated with films. Scenery would revolve or move to create the equivalent of reverse angles, tracking, and dolly shots. A prime example was **Dion Boucicault**'s *Arrah-na-Pogue* in which a character is shown escaping from a tower prison. He is first seen within the tower climbing out the window. The scene then revolved to show him climbing out from an exterior point of view; climbing down the vine-covered wall was then achieved by having the scenery rise toward the flyspace as he descended. It is no mere accident or coincidence that films were invented at the time that drama reached a realistic pinnacle. Earlier in the century the daguerreotype was invented in part as a result of Louis-Jacques Daguerre's attempts to create more realistic images in theatre design. Now, theatre seemed to have gone as far as it possibly could in terms of illusion – the film was the only possible solution.

While romantic drama of the period used some of this technology to create castles, mountain fortresses, ships at sea, etc., the melodrama was becoming increasingly sophisticated. The so-called 'gentlemanly melodrama' shied away from a reliance on visual and spectacular effects and substituted instead realistic depictions of middle- or upper-class life with tasteful effects such as the vision scene in Boucicault's *The Corsican Brothers* in which one brother sees his twin dying – achieved by use of a scrim allowing a scene to become visible upstage.

The primary development associated with this form was the *box set* – a depiction of a room with three walls and a ceiling, the fourth wall supposedly removed so that the audience could see in. The introduction of the box set is frequently attributed to **Mme Vestris** who worked with Planché at the **Olympic Theatre** in London from 1831 to 1838. However, something like a box set may have been achieved as early as 1642 in Venice by Torelli with the production of *Il Bellerofonte*. Painted perspective borders created an illusion of a ceiling and it is possible that he also placed panels between the wings to achieve continuous walls. And by the early 18th century, the free placement of flats and the enclosure of space downstage practised by the

Bibienas created at least the illusion, if not the actuality, of a box set. By the late 18th century box sets were not unusual, at least on the Continent. Through the middle of the 19th century the box set became increasingly realistic as actual furniture, rugs, book shelves, wall sconces, knick-knacks, and the like were added to create the aura of the real world.

In order for the 'fourth wall' concept to work, the set and the performer had to be completely contained within the proscenium. While the proscenium doors of the London theatres were eliminated by the 1820s, the apron persisted. Beginning in 1867 at the **Prince of Wales's Theatre**, the theatrical managers **Squire Bancroft** and **Marie Wilton** strictly adhered to the fourth wall demarcated by the proscenium arch, and when they assumed the management of the **Haymarket Theatre** in 1880 they extended the gilded proscenium arch across the bottom of the stage. The metaphoric picture frame was now a literal reality. The so-called peep-show stage had arrived.

The obvious concession to theatricality, of course, was that all action and all the furniture had to be placed so as to face the audience. Also, as more and more real props, furniture and set pieces were added, the more unbelievable became theatrical devices, props, or scenic pieces. As late as 1888, well into the modern period, playwright **August Strindberg**, in his Preface to *Miss Julie*, complained of canvas walls that shook when doors were slammed, and painted pots and pans on the walls instead of real ones.

The rise of realism in the 19th century culminated with the birth of naturalism in the 1870s, led by **Emile Zola**. In terms of scenographic practice, it was **André Antoine**'s Théâtre Libre in Paris that took naturalism to its logical end. Antoine was one of the many theatre practitioners of the era to see and be influenced by the work of the **Meininger Troupe**. In rehearsal Antoine would place the furniture and props as they would be in a real room and only later decide which wall was to be removed. Thus, even though the spectators saw a box set with an imaginary fourth wall, blocking and scenery made relatively few compromises to sightlines and visibility. Antoine also sought to have actual props and set pieces onstage. In his production of *The Butcher*, set in a butcher's shop, real sides of beef hung from hooks on the stage.

This approach was continued by **Konstantin Stanislavsky** at the **Moscow Art Theatre** in conjunction with such designers as Viktor Simov, Konstantin Korovine, Alexander Golovine, Mstislav Dobuzhinsky, and others. Although the MAT, at least in the first decade of its existence, was associated with realism, the settings showed strange inconsistencies. While a room in a house was entirely decorated by furniture and props taken from an actual home, the exterior scenes often were created with obviously painted two-dimensional trees and a painted backdrop.

What became obvious to many within a few years of Zola's manifesto was that absolute realism was unattainable on a stage – the moment anything is framed (actually or metaphorically) on a stage, it loses its 'reality'; it becomes part of the theatricality of the performance. Further, the use of real items inevitably focused attention on the unreality of a stage performance. A prime example comes not from naturalism but from melodrama. In Boucicault's play, *The Colleen Bawn*, there is a scene in which a character jumps into a lake to save a drowning woman. In the original production in 1860, the lake was created by strands of silk cloth set at about waist height and surrounded by cut-out scenery, ground rows, and papier-maché rocks. The soft gaslight shimmering on the silk created an easily accepted illusion of waves as the actors moved through, apparently immersed in the water. Because all the scenery was of a single style, there was, in Coleridge's famous phrase, a suspension of disbelief – the audience accepted the convention readily. In the 1890s, however, there was a revival of the play in which a lake containing real water was created. The actors, naturally, created real ripples and splashes and emerged dripping wet. Yet, because the audience knew, of course, that it was not a real lake, and because it was so obviously inconsistent with the scenery round it, the illusion, rather than be enhanced, was completely shattered.

Modern At the same time that realism in the theatre was moving into its ultimate phase of naturalism there were already movements in a different direction. The most significant theorist was the opera composer **Richard Wagner** who fundamentally altered the theatre auditorium and whose writings inspired future generations. Wagner's concept of *Gesamtkunstwerk* or 'total work of art' was based on the idea that all the elements of a production must be unified. While such an idea seems obvious, it was a radical notion in the mid-19th century when, as noted, there was generally no overriding artistic control over sets and costumes.

To house his operas Wagner had a new theatre constructed at Bayreuth. Designed by Gottfried Semper, Wilhelm Neumann, Otto Bruckwald and others, the opera house opened in 1876. The major innovation was in the auditorium with its 'democratic' seating; the box, pit, and gallery arrangement that had dominated theatre architecture for over two centuries was abandoned. There were no side boxes or central aisle. Rather, there were thirty rows of seats in the raked auditorium, each leading to a side exit. The auditorium was fan-shaped, approximately 50 feet wide at the front and 115 feet at the rear. There was a large box at the rear over which was a small balcony. The orchestra pit was hidden under the apron of the stage so that the illusion of the stage picture would not be broken. Wagner talked about a 'mystic chasm' between the stage and auditorium, created by a double proscenium, by which the 'ideal' world of the stage was to be separated from the everyday world of the spectators. The goal was, by means of the production and mythic elements of the opera, to create a communal experience that would unite the audience.

The most lasting contribution apart from the seating plan, however, was the darkening of the auditorium. For the first time in history it was possible to plunge the audience into darkness while illuminating the stage. Taken for granted today, the effect wrought profound changes upon the experience of theatre. The social interaction that had been as much a part of the theatrical experience as the play itself, and the sense of unity with the performers, if not the scenic stage, was now eliminated. The separation of the stage and auditorium, begun with the invention of the proscenium arch and continued through the development of the *scena per angolo*, was now complete.

Ironically, for all his innovations, Wagner was strongly rooted in the scenography of the 19th century; his ideal was to be reached through total illusion. His productions, rather than forging new ground were, in a sense, the epitome of romantic staging. It was the symbolists, inspired by Wagner's theoretical writings, who were to begin the reaction to naturalism in the late 1880s.

The symbolists' battle cry was 'de-theatricalize the theatre'. What they meant by this apparently contradictory aesthetic was a desire to bring the theatre back toward its original roots and impulses by stripping away the accumulated bulk of the naturalistic stage and replace it with an evocative theatre more dependent on the imagination and subconscious response.

The symbolist theatre emerged in the Théâtre d'Art founded by Paul Fort in 1890 which evolved into the Théâtre de l'Oeuvre in 1892 under the leadership of **Aurélien Marie Lugné-Poe** whose motto was 'the word creates the decor'. The decor was certainly far simpler than that of the concurrent naturalist and melodramatic theatres, but they did not forsake scenery altogether. Scrims were a common aspect of the productions, frequently hung several deep across the stage, creating a soft-edged ephemeral image. Medieval and Gothic iconography were common in their attempt to create a 'forest of symbols' whose effect was evocative but non-specific. The symbolists also experimented with synaesthesia, trying to relate sounds with colours and even smells. Among those who contributed to the theatre were future famous painters such as Edouard Vuillard, Maurice Denis, Pierre Bonnard, Odilon Redon, and Henri Toulouse-Lautrec.

Although many of the productions at these theatres were radically avant-garde and are little known today outside scholarly circles, symbolism quickly spread into mainstream theatre. Many of the visual ideals were furthered by the writings and works of Swiss designer **Adolphe Appia** and British designer **Edward Gordon Craig**. Attacking both the naturalistic and the pictorial approaches, these two men stripped the stage of its illusionistic clutter and detail and provided instead evocative masses of light and shadow, and three-dimensional forms, objects and masses. Their design harked back to the architectural stages of ancient Greece and the formal stages of the Orient.

Appia was strongly influenced by Wagner's writings but felt that Wagner's staging of the operas did not coincide with his theories. Appia set out to resolve this contradiction. He saw a fundamental problem in 19th-century staging that juxtaposed the moving, three-dimensional actor with two-dimensional painted scenery, and the flat, non-illusionistic stage floor. Beginning with the concept that the actor was the primary aspect of the theatre, Appia's solution was to create a plastic stage environment of suggestive scenery – including the stage floor – enhanced by a sculptural form of lighting. Appia was one of the first to realize the potential and possibilities of electric light which had begun to be introduced in theatres in the 1880s. He realized that the appearance of three-dimensionality is created by the sculptural use of light and shadow and described one scene, for instance, as 'Siegfried bathed in light and flickering shadow.'

Appia's sketches, generally done in shades of black, white, and grey, were suggestive (but still recognizable) scenes bathed in moody and evocative light, but light, nonetheless, that clearly defined the sculptural space of the stage. He also saw light as the visual counterpart of music which needed to be orchestrated to coincide with the moods of the play. These ideas led him toward a structural stage setting. For the music school of Emile Jacques-Dalcroze at Hellerau, whom he met in 1906, Appia created 'rhythmic' scenic units – steps, platforms, ramps – that were to function as the visual equivalent of the rhythm of the text. Appia's approach to lighting became the basis for much 20th-century lighting practice, and his structural stage became the basic vocabulary for much 20th-century reaction to naturalism.

Edward Gordon Craig also moved the stage setting away from literalism. But whereas Appia created suggestive but generally recognizable scenes, Craig developed an approach dependent on movable screens that created a theatrical space. By the movement of screens (in essence flats), the stage space would be constantly redefined – closed in or expansive, cramped or soaring. Although some of Craig's sketches are vaguely suggestive of location – his sketch for a scene in *Macbeth*, for instance, shows a staircase winding around a massive column issuing up from some cavernous Gothic palace – basically, his sets emphasize their own theatricality.

Craig was attacked by some contemporary designers and critics as being impractical. And indeed, many of his designs, if built, could not fit into the space of any existing theatre. Furthermore, there was no technical means of creating the transformation of space smoothly; the screens were not meant to slide back and forth on parallel tracks as in the Renaissance, but to move gracefully and cinematically in any direction, including vertically. Those designs Craig was able to execute seldom possessed the grandeur or kinetic energy of his sketches. Nonetheless, they served as inspiration for much 20th-century design ranging from German expressionism of the 1910s to the musicals of Broadway.

Alternatives to the proscenium Except for court theatres in which vast sums of money could be spent to entertain an individual for perhaps a single time, theatre architecture, like all aspects of theatre, is public and must compromise with the dictates of economics (and the even more mundane dictates of public safety). Allardyce Nicoll has pointed out how, at the same time that reactions to the illusionistic stage were blossoming, the proscenium arch became even more structurally entrenched in turn-of-the-century theatres because of laws requiring fire walls and fire curtains between the stage and auditorium.

But many felt that with the encapsulation of the actor and setting within the proscenium, a sense of intimacy and communion that had once been an essential part of theatre was lost. They now sought to recapture that experience and as early as the 1840s there was a definite movement toward other forms. In Germany, **Ludwig Tieck** and **Karl Immermann** both advocated an open stage based upon their understandings of Shakespearian staging. Tieck adapted the open-stage idea to the proscenium and the result, not surprisingly, was very similar to the English Restoration stage. Immermann's stage for an 1840 production of *Twelfth Night* resembled the Teatro Olimpico in many ways. These were, nonetheless, significant movements away from the pictorial realism of the proscenium stage that dominated at the time.

In the second half of the 19th century, a greater interest and knowledge of Oriental theatre developed that reinforced this trend. One of the first elements borrowed from the East was the revolving stage of the **kabuki** theatre which was first used by Karl Lautenschläger in Munich in 1896. Ironically, it was put to use to speed up and simplify scene changes required by the detailed naturalism of the period. But the *nō* and *kabuki* of Japan also used thrust stages: runways into the audience; simple, stylized, and emblematic scenery; a starkly presentational style; and a formal, minutely prescribed theatre architecture. Whether this had any direct effect on symbolist staging is not clear, but it most definitely influenced the major theoreticians and practitioners of 20th-century design and staging.

The reaction against the proscenium went in several directions. The most successful involved thrust stages and architectural stages (sometimes the two combined), but there were also fanciful projects involving annular stages, revolving auditoriums, stages or spectators suspended in the centre of spherical theatres and so on. Most of the latter, of course, were never built, but detailed plans and even models exist for such projects as **Walter Gropius**'s Totaltheatre, The Spherical Theatre of his Bauhaus colleague Andreas Weininger, **Frederick Kiesler**'s Endless Theatre, and the several projects of **Norman Bel Geddes**. Of the theatres that were constructed, the most notable and influential were **Max Reinhardt**'s Grosses Schauspielhaus and the Redoutensaal, and **Jacques Copeau**'s **Vieux-Colombier Theatre**.

The Grosses Schauspielhaus in Berlin was adapted by Hans Poelzig from an existing circus in 1920. It was, in essence, a modern version of the Teatro Farnese. 3,500 spectators sat in a U-shaped auditorium surrounding a thrust stage some 60 feet deep, behind which was a scenic stage with a revolve. The audience and the performers on the thrust, therefore, were architecturally united. The theatre worked well for Reinhardt's spectacles, but was totally inappropriate for more intimate fare.

The Redoutensaal, converted from an 18th-century palace ballroom in Vienna in 1922, was also an architecturally unified space but, like Appia's theatre at Hellerau, enveloped the audience in a single intimate surrounding. The stage was a raised platform with an architectural-style setting of curved screens and a balcony.

But it was the architectural stage of the Vieux-Colombier that had the biggest influence on design and architecture in the post-First World War era. Copeau first simplified the proscenium stage of the converted music-hall in 1913, with the idea that the bare essentials of scenography would focus attention on the actors. In 1919 he renovated it again. The proscenium was eliminated and a concrete stepped arch was built at the back. The basic idea of the spare, non-illusionistic scene, architecturally united with the auditorium – traceable from Tieck and Immermann through the symbolists, Appia and Craig, and Reinhardt – seemed

V. Hofman's design for Sophocles' *Oedipus*, Prague National Theatre, 1932.

to have triumphed. But while the open stage gained popularity, the architectural stage was found to be too limiting. Even with the use of curtains, and scenic pieces that could plug into the arches and doorways of the stage, the basic groundplan and limited access could never be completely overcome and Copeau abandoned the theatre in 1924. But the open thrust stage slowly began to emerge, and by the 1950s the architectural thrust stage and the pictorial thrust stage (a combination of a scenic end stage with a thrust) seemed to be the standard for all new theatre spaces.

Most of the various art movements of the early 20th century found counterparts in the theatre, but in terms of design there was little true innovation. Artists working in two-dimensional forms were rarely successful in translating these into the three-dimensional scenery of the stage. Most notably, **Picasso**, who designed several dances for the Ballets Russes, seemed unable to find a vocabulary that allowed cubism to transform from a two-dimensional exploration of planes to the requirements of the stage. His sets were frequently painted backdrops – beautiful as works of art, but hardly innovative – and his costumes, as in *Parade*, seemed to mimic the look of cubism without actually achieving it.

Some artists, however, were successful at developing a painterly style for the theatre that was bold, striking and stimulating. At the same time that stage designers were moving toward simplification of the image, Serge Diaghilev, director of the Ballets Russes, brought artists such as **Léon Bakst**, **Natalya Goncharova**, and Mikhail Larionov to design for him. Bakst employed Byzantine and Oriental splendour notable for its vivid use of colours and line. In contrast to the monochromatic and moody images of Craig and Appia, Bakst used rich colours in startling combinations, grotesque exaggeration of form, and a stark, theatrical false perspective. Goncharova and Larionov carried this a step farther, virtually eliminating perspective, and painting, instead, flat images in the style of primitive painters and medieval icons. The result was the adaptation of the painterly style to the non-illusionistic stage. But for all the excitement this created

when the Ballets Russes first performed in Paris in 1909, there was no form of dramatic theatre for which this style of design seemed appropriate. The immediate effect was to reinforce the movement away from realism toward theatricality, but by and large, stage design turned to non-painterly approaches.

Some of the most notable anti-illusionistic movements also came from Russia and were associated with the dynamic avant-garde art movements of the first three decades of the century. The most significant figure was director, actor, and theoretician **Vsevolod Meyerhold**. Strongly influenced by Appia in his early years, Meyerhold was a central figure of futurism and constructivism in the theatre but worked in many styles. Artists and designers who worked with him included Kazimir Malevich, Aleksandr Vesnin, **Lyubov Popova**, Georgii and Vladimir Stenberg, and El Lissitzky. Constructivism emerged about 1920, and was clearly influenced by futurism and cubism. This movement sought an art based on 'space and time' and using 'kinetic and dynamic elements'. This was manifested in skeletal sets of wood and metal with platforms, ramps, steps and various kinetic elements, often on stages otherwise stripped bare. Meyerhold called these sets 'machines for acting'.

Constructivist design was also the predominant form at the Kamerny Theatre of **Aleksandr Tairov**, although the sets by **Aleksandra Ekster**, his primary collaborator, were seldom as stark or 'homemade'-looking as most constructivist design. Tairov also worked with Georgii Yakulov, Goncharova, Larionov, and Vesnin. Other avant-garde artists who designed for the theatre at some time included **Yury Annenkov**, Aleksandr Rodchenko, and Vladimir Tatlin. As with so many other 'isms', pure constructivism in stage design lasted only briefly (although variations on the idea can be seen to this very day), but it was a major contributor toward theatricality over illusion and was especially notable for settings that sat like islands in the midst of the stage with no connection, literally or metaphorically, with the wings or flyspace.

The most dominant theatrical force during the early decades of the century was expressionism. Clearly influenced by Appia, expressionist design frequently reduced the stage to its bare essentials, often little more than a few scenic elements and black drapes on an otherwise bare stage. Light became the most important aspect of design. The movement of light reinforced the stream-of-consciousness imagery of many expressionist plays, and allowed the smooth transition through episodic scenes. The light frequently cut a swath through the dark void of black-curtained stages. The contrast of light and shadow, unusual angles, and unrealistic colours of light contributed to the nightmare quality of the productions. Images were distorted and exaggerated; walls tilted at precarious angles; oversized set and prop pieces and bold blocks of colour wrenched the image out of objective reality into a subjective view of the world. Expressionist design is frequently associated with the work of director **Leopold Jessner** who, working primarily with designer Emil Pirchan, created architectural/structural settings of steps and platforms that changed through the use of lights and curtains. Jessner's reliance on this formula led to cliché and quickly became known as *Jessnertreppen* (Jessner steps).

In the years before and after the First World War, many American designers and directors went to Europe and studied with these designers, or observed productions. The various ideas were distilled through American sensibilities and production needs and the result became known as the New Stagecraft. Led by designers **Robert Edmond Jones**, **Lee Simonson**, and Norman Bel Geddes, the practitioners of the New Stagecraft revolted against the 'Belasco realism' (so called because of director **David Belasco**'s highly detailed, realistic productions) in favour of simplification and abstraction. Although examples of constructivism, expressionism, and other specific movements cropped up on the American stage, most American theatre remained firmly rooted in realism and the new design substituted simplicity and suggestion – sometimes called selective realism – for naturalism.

This has remained, albeit with some changes, as the most dominant style of American design. The second generation of these designers, led by **Jo Mielziner**, evolved a style sometimes known as 'poetic realism' that relied on painterly images often rendered in a soft-edged, almost dream-like style, a style enhanced by Mielziner's use of scrim which accommodated transitions from outside reality to scenes of memory and subjective experience typical of plays by **Arthur Miller**, **Tennessee Williams**, and others.

The 20th century The closer one gets to one's own time, the harder it becomes to separate the small details from the overall developments. Several major directions in 20th-century design, none of which are mutually exclusive, can be identified. These include (1) a continuation of the trend already discussed – simplified

David Warfield in Belasco's *The Return of Peter Grimm*, New York, 1911, showing the scenic naturalism.

or selective realism (2) new directions in pictorial design (3) sculptural design (4) multi-media design (5) environmental theatre; and (6) conceptual design.

The bulk of modern drama, especially in the English-speaking world, has remained realistically based, although much of it has included flashbacks, memory scenes, dream sequences, subjective perception, poetic imagery, cinematic transformations from scene to scene and other 'non-realistic' devices. Clearly, a purely naturalistic approach to design for such conventions would be cumbersome and inappropriate. Thus, fragmentary images, scrims, washes of coloured light, emblematic or exaggerated set pieces, isolated details, or fragmentary sets placed in the midst of a theatrical void are some of the devices that designers have used to meet this challenge. Although the terms 'selective' or 'poetic realism' are the most common, the struggle between the forces of realism and theatricality is perhaps best captured in the term 'magic realism'.

The second movement of the modern era was a continuation of the painterly style which was still thriving. In the 20th century this was typically lyrical and fantastic depictions of scenes. It is most evident in the mid-century designs for ballet and its roots can be traced to **Alexandre Benois**'s sets for Diaghilev. Some of the finest examples can be seen in the work of **Christian Bérard**, **Eugene Berman**, George Sheringham, **Oliver Messel**, Leslie Hurry, Nicholas Georgiadis, Lucien Coutaud, Gianni Polidori, and **Cecil Beaton**.

The third style, sculptural design, deals with new conceptions of space on the stage. From the Renaissance until the end of the 19th century design was essentially pictorial – a two-dimensional image creating the illusion of depth or volume. Building upon the foundations of Appia and constructivism, however, many designers rejected any form of realism for sculptural design. The images themselves varied greatly. Geometric masses, architectonic structures, fanciful versions of classical columns, ramps, platforms and steps intersecting on a multitude of planes, scaffold-like structures all found their way onto the stage. The work of **Tanya Moiseiwitsch**, Nadine Baylis, Ming Cho Lee, **Santo Loquasto** and others typify much of this aesthetic.

The fourth tendency is the incorporation of technology, primarily in the form of film and projections. From a theoretical viewpoint, it was a logical extension of contemporary practices. Since it was impossible ever to recreate the outside world fully onstage, the argument went, why not acknowledge the fact while still using the image? In other words, project a picture of the real thing. The stage could become any place in the world at the push of a button. It was a photographic equivalent of the Renaissance–Baroque scenic stage – an image that existed behind and separate from the performer and that functioned as a visual reference point for the audience. The evolution of the projected scenery was somewhat more pedestrian than the theory. It was essentially **Erwin Piscator**'s response to necessity; his need to present performances on a limited budget on makeshift stages for factory workers. Projected images, of course, became a major element in **Bertolt Brecht**'s subsequent epic theatre, and they reached their pinnacle in the work of Czech scenographer **Josef Svoboda** in the 1960s and 70s.

There was, however, a reaction to this and to the poetic realism of the Americans. Building upon the ideas of constructivism and sculptural design, designers in the 1960s began to reject any form of illusion. This reaction began with stripping away the 'content' of scenic structures, leaving skeletal frameworks instead. Structures were dismembered, leaving fragments. A favourite device was to 'perforate' settings, thus allowing the 'reality' of the stage to penetrate the illusion of the decor. This was followed by settings composed of scaffolds, tubing, fabrics, and 'real' objects and materials such as raw wood, erosion cloth, and metal. Collage settings – frequently including photo blowups, junk, and fabric sculptures – became popular. Significantly, the designers creating these new settings were using the vertical space of the stage in a way that had rarely been attempted before.

In some cases the stage was stripped down to bare essentials – planks, platforms and ramps with little or no objective scenery. The circle, in a sense, was completed: the designers of the 1960s and 70s had returned to the open stage of ancient Greece and Elizabethan England; to Molière's 'two boards and a passion'.

One manifestation of this response was environmental theatre. The concept of the spectator and performer sharing the space of the theatre, or the inclusion of the spectator within the performance space, had been current since at least the Middle Ages, but the term was coined by American director and theoretician Richard Schechner. The roots of modern environmental theatre can be traced to the productions in the 1930s of Szygmunt Tonecki in Poland and **Nikolai Okhlopkov** in the USSR. The most significant examples in the post-war era are the works of **Jerzy Grotowski** (and his sometime collaborator, **Josef Szajna**) in Poland, **Ariane Mnouchkine** at the **Théâtre du Soleil** in Paris, **Luca Ronconi** in Italy, and Schechner's **Performance Group** in the USA.

Related to this is the movement in the 1970s and 80s often termed 'conceptual design' or 'theatricalism'. Primarily a European development, these tend to be designs for classical plays and operas created either by a director working closely with a designer, or a single individual assuming both roles, such as **Franco Zeffirelli** or **Jean-Pierre Ponnelle**. In either case, one individual is generally responsible for all aspects of design, not just sets, and from this comes the term 'scenographer' which implies a more unified and far-reaching involvement than the term 'designer' does. Typically, the setting is a single image – or a single basic setting that can transform into variations of the single image – that embodies the central concept of the production. These are most often productions in which the directorial concept is more significant or more pronounced than the playwright's script if, indeed, one exists. The impulse for this approach is traceable to Reinhardt and Meyerhold and the practices of Brecht. The productions of the **Berliner Ensemble** have been an acknowledged influence on many contemporary designers.

Although such designs may, of course, take any of the forms listed above, theatricalism has rediscovered the proscenium, as it were, and the designs tend to enclose the cubic space of the stage. Theatricalist sets are frequently distinguished by high walls that soar into the flyspace and seemingly overwhelm the performers; and by overwhelming images or emblems whose visual power suffuses the sets and costumes. Examples can be found in the work of Karl von Appen, Achim Freyer, **André Acquart**, **John Napier**, **John Bury**, **Ralph Koltai**, **Eugene Lee**, **Wieland Wagner**, and in the productions of **Benno Besson**, **Giorgio Strehler**, **Patrice Chéreau**, **Liviu Ciulei**, **Andrei Serban**, **Peter Stein**, **Robert Wilson**, and **Richard Foreman**.

Thus, by the 1980s, theatre design seemed to be heading in two antithetical directions: conceptual design with its strong images, metaphorical use of line and space, and celebration of the stage on the one hand; and on the other a rejection of standard or formal theatrical spaces altogether. The latter seems to be fading, however. Through the 1970s performance moved out of theatres and into streets, beaches, public spaces, city rooftops, old factories, ancient ruins, and almost any conceivable 'found' space. The major anthologies of design for those years, *Stage Design Throughout the World Since 1960* and *Stage Design Throughout the World 1970-1975*, exalted the revolution in production and the rejection of the bourgeois theatre.

But at the same time that this was happening, opera directors and designers were reclaiming the stage. In both East and West Germany, and to a lesser extent elsewhere, the idea of scenography was coming to fruition. As opera and avant-garde theatre began to merge – at least in the area of design – money for new productions allowed for spectacles of greater size and technology than had been possible previously. Moreover, many of the new theatre festivals, which often commissioned new works, were being held in proscenium-style opera houses such as the Next Wave Festival at the Brooklyn Academy of Music.

There is no question that the Western and even some Eastern theatre is still dominated by forms of realism, painterly design, and the kinetic stages of musical theatre. But, ironically, just as the scenic practices of the burgeoning opera of the 17th century helped shape the style and technology of theatre design throughout the 19th century, it may be doing so again, at a time when many thought opera was dying.   AA

Théâtre du Nouveau Monde The most respected and influential of existing companies in French Canada, founded in Montreal in 1951. Under **Jean Gascon** it began staging French classics, especially works of **Molière**; by the end of the decade it was offering at least one Canadian play each season, notably the works of **Marcel Dubé**. The TNM has collaborated with the **Stratford (Ontario) Festival** and toured successfully in Europe. In 1966 Gascon was replaced by **Jean-Louis Roux**, under whose direction it has moved towards a more varied repertoire, including experimental plays and musical revues. A subsidiary troupe, Les Jeunes Comédiens, trained many of the theatre professionals now active in Quebec. The economic difficulties of the later 1970s and the 80s have had serious effects upon the TNM, circumscribing its ability to experiment. It appeared, in 1984-5, that this prestigious troupe would disappear; that threat has now receded, with the provision of additional government funding and the prospect of new, permanent quarters.   LED

Theatre for development see **Third World popular theatre**

Theatre Guild, The In 1915, a group of young actors and writers dissatisfied with the conventions of the commercial theatre organized the **Washington Square Players**. For three seasons they presented a series of one-act plays distinctly modern in both content and form. After the war, in 1919, a patent lawyer and sometime playwright named **Lawrence Langner** restructured the Players as the Theatre Guild. Langner and his Board, which included **Philip Moeller**, who was to become the Guild's leading director, **Theresa Helburn**, a play reader soon to be made Executive Director, actress Helen Westley, banker Maurice Wertheim, and scene designer **Lee Simonson**, were determined to shed their amateur downtown status and to present challenging full-length plays on Broadway. In its first few years the Guild's notable achievements were with European expressionism (**Kaiser**'s *Man and the Masses*, 1924) and with the world premieres of several plays by **Shaw** (*Heartbreak House*, 1920; *Back to Methuselah*, 1922; *Saint Joan*, 1923; and *Caesar and Cleopatra*, 1925). Although the Guild was criticized for neglecting American writers, two American plays that it presented early in its history, **Elmer Rice**'s *The Adding Machine* (1923) and **John Howard Lawson**'s *Processional* (1925), testify to the influence its productions of European plays had on native experiment. Later in the twenties, and for the following three decades, the Guild produced the work of major American dramatists including **Sidney Howard** (*They Knew What They Wanted*, 1924, and *The Silver Cord*, 1926); **S. N. Behrman** (*The Second Man*, 1927, and *Biography*, 1932); **Robert E. Sherwood** (*Reunion in Vienna*, 1931, and *Idiot's Delight*, 1936); and **Maxwell Anderson** (*Elizabeth the Queen*, 1930, and *Mary of Scotland*, 1933). In 1928, with *Strange Interlude* and *Marco Millions*, the Guild began regularly to produce **Eugene O'Neill**'s plays.

If in the twenties the Guild had the lustre of an experiment conducted by idealistic upstarts, by the early thirties it had begun to acquire the reputation of a theatrical dowager. In 1931 some of its younger members defected to form the **Group Theatre**, whose agenda of knitting systematically trained actors into a true ensemble and encouraging the development of socially relevant plays highlighted two areas where the Guild had failed. Throughout the thirties and forties, as it produced popular shows like *Philadelphia Story* (1939) and musicals like *Oklahoma!* (1943) and *Carousel* (1945), and depended over and over again on its in-house stars, the **Lunts**, to rescue it from a financial abyss (thereby violating its original policy of starring the play rather than the player), the Guild became little different from a commercial producer. Despite its lack of success in maintaining a repertory set-up or in developing a company of actors, despite its concessions to popularity and its literary shortcomings – its predilection for airy comedies and stodgy historical romances – the Guild's record is unique in the history of the American theatre. Through its subscription policy and its extensive national tours the Guild brought more worthwhile, well-produced plays to a greater number of people, and over a longer period of time, than any other theatrical organization. FH

Theatre-in-Education **(TIE)** see **Young People's Theatre (Britain)**

Théâtre National Populaire (TNP) French National People's theatre founded by **Firmin Gémier** in 1920 after years of campaigning by **Rolland** and other advocates of *le théâtre populaire*. Despite Gémier's success in persuading Parliament to acknowledge the TNP as a State-subsidized venture, he was given only a theatre (see **Chaillot**) and not the means to run a producing company. His achievement was thus limited and after his death in 1933 the TNP remained moribund until the appointment of **Vilar** in 1951. He brought to the enormous theatre (rebuilt 1937) the company and production style pioneered at the **Avignon festival**, abolishing footlights, front curtain and painted scenery, making use of bold movement, lavish costume and complex lighting. Under Vilar's administrator, Jean Rouvet, the normal Parisian theatre-going ritual was simplified: evening dress and tipping were abolished, performances began on time with latecomers excluded, and the text of the play was sold in place of glossy programmes. Rouvet pioneered a network of supporter groups through trade unions and student organizations, which was soon copied by the decentralized theatres. The repertoire combined vigorous productions of French classics, in a fluent style not frightened of heroics, with **Shakespeare**, the German romantics and other world classics unfamiliar in France of the 1950s. Vilar directed some of the first **Brecht** to be seen in France: *Mother Courage* (1951) and *Arturo Ui* (1960) as well as modern classics such as **T. S. Eliot**'s *Murder in the Cathedral*, but was not successful in his attempts to introduce contemporary plays. Actors of the highest calibre were attracted to the TNP e.g. **Gérard Philipe**, **Maria Casarès**. One of these, Georges Wilson, succeeded Vilar in 1963. Wilson tried to follow the same policies as Vilar but was overtaken by a rapidly polarizing political situation in the late 1960s: young and committed audiences were looking for new formulae and Wilson's audience figures dropped disastrously. In 1972 the TNP crisis was solved by the expedient of transferring the title to **Planchon**'s company in Lyon. The new title meant increased subsidy and touring obligations but not a change of artistic direction for Planchon and his new co-director **Chéreau**. Their company continued its policy of adventurous revivals and new plays, often of a demanding nature. Against Gémier's view of the TNP as a place of commission and Vilar's as a 'public service', Planchon considers it must constantly remind people of the violent cultural divide in modern French society: 'our job is to keep the wound open'. In 1986 Georges Lavaudant succeeded Chéreau as co-director. DB

Theatre of the absurd Literally meaning 'out of harmony', absurd was **Albert Camus**'s designation for the situation of modern humanity, a stranger in an inhuman universe. Recognizing such strangers in stage characters of the 1950s, the critic Martin Esslin in 1961 published his influential *Theatre of the Absurd*. He defined plays of the absurd as those that presented man's metaphysical absurdity in aberrant dramatic style that mirrored the human situation. Never a formal movement, the playwrights of the absurd were centred in post-war Paris, but they soared to international fame with the unexpected success of **Beckett's** *Waiting for Godot*. Journalists soon seized upon the label, confusing it with the everyday meaning of absurd as outrageously comic. Esslin's main absurdists are Beckett, **Adamov**, **Ionesco**, and **Genet**, with less attention paid to **Albee** and **Pinter**.

Almost every non-realistic modern dramatist has had this label affixed thereafter. Certain absurdist techniques have, nevertheless, established themselves in the contemporary theatre, and it is in this formal sense, rather than in a philosophical one, that the idea of 'theatre of the absurd' has been maintained in critical currency. Among these techniques are the rejection of narrative continuity and character coherence and of the rigidity of logic, leading to ridiculous conclusions; scepticism about the meaning of language, bizarre relationship of stage properties to dramatic situation. Such techniques have occasionally resulted in memorable stage images. RC

Theatre of the Ridiculous In 1967 the Play-House of the Ridiculous opened on Off-Off Broadway with *The Life of Lady Godiva*, written by Ronald Tavel, directed by John Vaccaro, and featuring **Charles Ludlam** as actor. Though these three men did not stay together long, they independently continued their 'ridiculous' work – a self-consciously wild dramaturgy full of witty word-play, sexual double entendre, theatrical flamboyance, sexual ambiguity, and bad taste. Tavel left the Play-House within a year to pursue a writing career, and in 1967 Vaccaro directed two Ludlam works, *Big Hotel* and *Conquest of the Universe*, before Ludlam left to become actor–manager of his own company. Vaccaro toured Europe with the Play-House and then operated it out of **La Mama** until 1972 when he closed his theatre. At the Ridiculous Theatrical Company, Ludlam went on to write, direct and perform in plays such as *Turds in Hell* (1968), *Camille* (1973), and *Der Ring Gott Farblonjet* (1977). AS

Théâtre Libre see **Antoine, André**

Théâtre Ouvert Organization set up in France by Lucien Attoun in 1971 at the 25th **Avignon theatre festival** to promote new work by playwrights. Attoun's formula involved presentation through rehearsed readings with the possibility of broadcast on the radio programme he produced. In 1974, the *Gueuloir* was introduced, a chance for an author to give a free public reading of his play and in 1975 the possibility for an author to work on his play with actors was added. In 1978 *tapuscrits* were introduced: cheaply produced duplicated typescripts of new works to be circulated among theatre professionals. Gradually activities were extended to Paris and other parts of France. In 1981 the organization moved into a permanent studio theatre at the Winter Garden in Montmartre. Here authors are given a chance to try out plays with actors in a laboratory context which may or may not lead to public performance. Many new authors have benefited and Théâtre Ouvert has been a significant force in encouraging new writing. DB

Théâtre populaire de Lorraine One of a number of groups which formed in France in the 1960s as part of the **decentralization movement** influenced by the ideals of *théâtre populaire*. This company began with performances by **Adamov** and 19th-century classics, then, like the **Soleil**, changed to *création collective* for a play about local steel mining *Splendeur et Misère de Minette la Bonne Lorraine* (1969). Since 1970, many of its plays have been written by its artistic director Jacques Kraemer. DB

Theatre Row West 42nd St between 9th and 10th Aves, New York City. In 1975, when Robert Moss, the director of **Playwrights Horizon**, an Off-Off Broadway group, found himself without a theatre, he rented a building on West 42nd Street amid a neighbourhood of pornographic shops, burlesque houses and massage parlours, and transformed it quickly and cheaply into a performing space. His success signalled the development of an alternative theatre district a few blocks west of Broadway for Off-Off Broadway companies. A quasi-governmental agency, the 42nd Street Redevelopment Corporation was persuaded to buy the block from 9th to Dyer Avenues to begin Phase I of the transformation. The created spaces were then rented out to companies, which accepted the responsibility to rebuild them into theatres and offices. In 1978, amid much official fanfare, Theatre Row was opened and comprised ten working companies. All were to be operated on a non-profit basis and represented diverse artistic goals as well as ethnic backgrounds. Phase II, which encompasses the block between Dyer and 10th Avenues, has added four other members and the development has not ended.

In 1982, most of the original companies found themselves struggling to survive under the weight of mortgages and escalating operating expenses and decided collectively to rent their theatres when they were not being used by themselves. The formula worked and all are back on a firm financial footing.

The theatres and companies utilize a collective box office, Ticket Central, to serve their patrons and offer a variety of entertainment at relatively low cost. Theatre Row provides a testing ground for actors, directors, playwrights and designers, many of whom move their activities to Broadway, Off-Broadway and regional theatre. The presence of restaurants, shops and Manhattan Plaza, a subsidized housing complex for performing artists, has stabilized and revitalized the surrounding area.

The theatres and companies comprising Theatre Row number 15: Samuel Beckett Theatre, Manhattan Punch Line, Actors and Directors Lab, Harold Clurman Theatre, Playwrights Horizon, Intar Hispanic American Arts Centre, Harlem Children's Theatre Company, **The Acting Company**, Lion Theatre Company, South Street Company, Nat Horne Musical Theatre, Raft Company, Image Theatre and Studio, Douglas Fairbanks Theatre and the John Houseman Theatre Centre. MCH

Theatrical training in the United States Till the late 19th century, most American actors learned their craft in some form of apprenticeship, similarly to English actors. **Edwin Forrest**, for example, studied elocution, took part in amateur theatricals, then began his professional career in small roles, touring the frontier. **Edwin Booth** and **Joseph Jefferson III** learned the theatrical profession by travelling with their fathers. **Charlotte Cushman** trained as an opera singer, ruined her voice by straining it, then became a tragedienne. Talent and industry could cause an actor to emerge from supernumerary or small parts and eventually lead him to the top of the profession. Most American actors had similar beginnings.

At present, apprenticeship remains a viable entry to professional acting. Apprentice positions are available from LORT (League of Resident Theatres) or from summer theatres, usually associated with URTA (University/Resident Theatre Association), which holds annual auditions for non-Equity actors.

A second avenue into the profession is commercial or professional training programmes. In the last quarter of the 19th century, need became apparent for a more systematic training in acting. In the 1870s **Steele MacKaye** began teaching formally the Delsarte System, which he had studied in Paris. In the next decade **Dion Boucicault**, in connection with **A. M. Palmer** and the **Madison Square Theatre**, offered classes in acting to train the performers in Palmer's road companies.

Today dozens of commercial training programmes are available to the student actor. Mostly located in New York and Los Angeles, a collection of teachers and schools teach acting and other theatrical disciplines for fixed fees. Over 40 such programmes exist in New York; some 24 offer similar training opportunities in Los Angeles. Among the most respected in New York are the **Neighbourhood Playhouse** School of the Theatre and the HB (**Hagen-Berghof**) Studio, or in Los Angeles the Film Actors' Workshop. The **Actors Studio**, espousing the philosophies of **Lee Strasberg**, has schools in both cities. The Goodman School of the Drama in Chicago has also been well received, as has the Juilliard School in New York.

The vast majority of American actors, however, received their first training in colleges and universities. (For the development of the American academic theatre, see **Academic theatre in the United States**.) A typical pattern might be for a student to pursue a Bachelor of Arts degree in theatre, possibly followed by a Master of Fine Arts, then move to a metropolitan area to continue study with a commercial school or teacher. In some cases, apprenticeships and academic credit may be combined.

In the past few decades regional theatres and universities have sought to combine forces, offering the student the best of both worlds. The **Tyrone Guthrie** Theatre in Minneapolis and the University of Minnesota, for example, and Florida State University and the Asolo Theatre of Sarasota, offer joint programmes.

Some American students seek the more classic training of the Royal Academy of Dramatic Art or the London Academy of Music and Dramatic Art, both of whom hold annual auditions in the United States. SMA

Theatrum mundi A mechanical theatre, whose figurines are moved horizontally by means of strings along a track in a flat wing-and-border set by a single performer or, in German, *Mechanikus*. This forerunner of the newsreel recreated current events, such as natural disasters, battles or scenes from everyday life. Brown's

Theatre of Arts toured British fairs (1830–40) with miniatures of Napoleon's campaigns, while Clapton's featured Grace Darling's heroic rescue. **Goethe** owned such a theatre, and that in Berlin's Luisenstrasse in 1848 displayed 'The Battle of Genoa', 'The Battle of Schleswig-Holstein' and 'Bombardment by the First German Fleet'. LS

Theobald, Lewis (1688–1744) English playwright and critic. Trained as a lawyer, he undertook in 1714 a large and unfinished project to translate Greek drama. His adaptation of **Shakespeare**'s *Richard III* (1719) was not a success but he wrote a number of innovative and entertaining pantomimes for **John Rich** throughout the 1720s, e.g. *Harlequin Sorcerer* (1725). In 1726 he attacked Pope's edition of Shakespeare in *Shakespeare Restored*, the first book ever published on Shakespeare alone. Though mocked, Theobald's attempts to emend and restore the text of Shakespeare's work were intelligent and effective. His own edition of Shakespeare was published in 1734. In 1727 his play *The Double Falsehood* was performed. Theobald claimed that it was an adaptation of Shakespeare's lost play *Cardenio* (written with **John Fletcher** and performed in 1613) but it seems unlikely. He adapted **Webster**'s *The Duchess of Malfi* as *The Fatal Secret* (1733). He was appointed Poet Laureate in 1730. PH

Thérésa (Eugénie Emma Valadon) (1837–1913) First star of the French music-hall. Daughter of a tailor, she made her stage debut in Paris in 1856 at the Théâtre de la Porte-Saint-Martin. Fame arrived in 1863 at the Alcazar; already known for sentimental ballads, she decided to parody one with a comic yodel and was cheered to the echo. For almost 30 years, this scrawny (later stout), swarthy woman with a mouth 'large enough to swallow the conductor' kept audiences in stitches with such favourites as 'Nothing is Sacred to a Sapper' and 'The Bearded Lady'. She also appeared in *féeries* and comic operas (*La Reine des Halles*, 1881) before her retirement in 1893. LS

Therukoothu (India) *Theru* means 'street' and *koothu* is a play. As the name suggests, the *Therukoothu* has a rustic origin. Although no one knows quite where it came from and when it began, it is popular among the lower class urban population and rural people of Tamil

Dancers in a *Therukoothu* production.

Nadu, south India. Some scholars suggest that it was inspired by the **Yakshagana** of Mysore state. Others think it comes from the **Kathakali** of Kerala. Little has been done to prove any of these assertions. One thing seems clear, *Therukoothu* is not like any other form of traditional theatre in south India.

It is usually performed by members of the Koothadi community and is most frequently seen in north and south Arcot and Chingleput districts of Tamil Nadu. Very few companies remain today. The one most highly praised is the Raghava Thambiran Company named after its organizing member who hails from the village of Purisai. The company is now headed by the founder's two nephews, Natesa and Kanna.

Several popular companies play in and around the slums of Madras city but they have long since abandoned the use of traditional costumes and have resorted to using film music to attract people to their shows.

The players come from the lower strata of society. They perform in any open space in a village. Four tall posts of bamboo or wood are fixed in the ground bounding the acting area. A large banner proclaiming the company name hangs above the musicians who assemble in the space upstage centre. Colourful banners are strung overhead between the remaining posts. The dressing room is any improvised space, such as a room or a shed near the performance area. A simple oil lamp provides the only illumination for the makeup and costume preparations of the players. The makeup of central characters is bright blue and red accentuated with white and black lines. Heavily waxed moustaches accentuate the virility of the heroic characters of the epics and *Puranas*. Colourful wooden ornaments decorate their chests and arms and impressive crowns accentuate their heads. Special short grass skirts are used under the outer cloth skirts. In some respects, the makeup and ornaments resemble those of the *Yakshagana* of Andhra Pradesh and south Kanara and the skirts seem to be a modification of the large *Kathakali* skirts of the Kerala actors.

As part of large-scale ritualistic events of a village, the actors parade through the streets of the village along with the temple deities. Following an all-night show, they participate in the symbolic destruction of evil under the watchful eye of the temple effigies and thousands of enthusiastic villagers who participate in the ceremony which concludes when they walk across beds of hot coals to prove their faith in god.

Among the popular fun-loving figures in *Therukoothu* is the *kattiakaran*, a clown figure who combines the function of the fool with that of the stage manager.

Traditional *Therukoothu* music is a blend of classical and folk music of the area. All of the melodies are sung by the actors who sing a line or two which is then repeated by the other musicians singing in chorus. About half of all the performances are made up of songs. The other half is improvised prose dialogue spoken in Tamil. *Therukoothu* songs characteristically require a high shrill pitch demanding sustained vocal power for a nine-hour performance.

The musicians' space is called the *pin pattu*, or 'back song'. When an actor is not in character, he joins the musicians and sings from the *pin pattu*. The harmonium provides the basic pitch for the songs. A wind instrument like an oboe (*kurukuzhal*) provides melodic background. Small hand drums played on both ends

and bell-metal cymbals complete the musical ensemble.

The dance steps are simple, violent movements. Dance is little more than a circular movement with quick turning leaps. There is no symbolic code of hand gestures. If anything, dance provides an element of fast paced spectacle demonstrating the emotional state of the character or as part of a battle scene.

Therukoothu plays centre primarily on stories drawn from the epic literature and surround events in the lives of famous epic characters.   FaR

Thespis (6th century BC) The earliest tragedian whose name was known to ancient scholars (see **Greece, ancient**). He is said to have won a victory with a play produced c. 534 and to have been the first to introduce an actor (the dramatist himself) conversing with the Chorus. He is also credited with inventing the mask. Since none of his plays was preserved for posterity, no authentic fragments survive, and it is impossible to assess the value of the traditions concerning him.   ALB

Thimig Distinguished Viennese family of actors. **Hugo** (1854–1944) was a leading comic actor at the **Burgtheater**. His daughter **Helene** (1889–1974), a versatile actress, was married to **Max Reinhardt**; she did much to perpetuate her husband's method of training actors. Hugo's two sons, **Hermann** (b. 1890) and **Hans** (b. 1900), also acted with the Burgtheater.   sw

Third World popular theatre Theatre used by oppressed Third World people to achieve justice and development for themselves. There are now thousands of organized groups of landless peasants, workers and threatened minorities, in Africa, the Americas, Asia, who use drama and theatre to confront the political, economic and social problems in their lives. These initiatives occurred quite separately in the late 1970s all over the Third World as economic and social conditions worsened for the very poor. Some indigenous activists came to despair of any solutions to the growing misery by conventional development and political strategies. The despair focused on the 'top-down' nature of these 'solutions', seen to be located in Super-Power rivalry, a one-world economy, and the nuclear and conventional arms race. Theatre provided those at the base of society with their own voice. Drama, as a process of collective improvisation using existing cultural forms of expression, could offer the means of creating an analysis by very poor people of their material and cultural conditions. Subsequently, these drama and theatre initiatives were discovered to have many objectives and strategies in common. Various local, regional and international networks were established during the 1980s, including the International Popular Theatre Alliance. However, this networking remains tenuous except at local levels. Regional and international workshops in the early 80s, funded by some aid agencies responding to grass-roots Third World initiatives for radical development alternatives, exchanged drama and organizational skills at village level, and discussed new perspectives and insights. Since the essential characteristic of this grass-roots theatre is that it enables those making the drama to form their own analysis and strategies, a distinction is drawn between this drama for collective awareness and other political and popular theatre in the Third World which adopts a 'top-down' approach. This includes agit-prop and sloganizing theatre; professional theatre companies used by governments and development agencies to put across specific messages (for example, encouraging people to dig pit latrines); and popular theatre which, because of commercial objectives, is unwittingly articulated into the hegemony of the ruling elites. Instead, the theatre grows out of collective thought, and the dramatic process carries that thinking further. It is also concerned with cultural identity among minorities threatened with the complete destruction of their societies: Native populations in the Americas (for example, the Inuit in Canada; the Caribbs in Dominica), and Aboriginal peoples in Australasia. Therefore, despite the common perspectives and intentions of these organized groups, there are also considerable differences resulting from the cultural and political forces of the particular region.

The following examples may indicate the scope of this Third World popular theatre.

In Latin America, some groups, like Teatro Nixtayolero in Nicaragua, have developed among rural peasant farmers; others, like the theatre workshops of TAREA, a popular education support group in the *barrios* of Lima, Peru, have emerged among the dispossessed and landless peasants who have drifted into the cities. Some are Indian or Inca groups, like the Ayni Ruway, an indigenous people's movement in the Cochebamba Valley of Bolivia among the Aymara and Quechua people, whose spontaneous theatre at festivals and markets is part of their fight for justice and material improvement within their own historical identity. The cultural problems and material contradictions of colonialism and neo-colonialism in the region are reflected, for example, in the work of a gifted (black American) Panamanian dancer-actor, Danny Calden, who rejected his career and his background to work politically and artistically alongside Native Indians, the most ignored and deprived group in Panama. They draw on his skills and artistic expertise to help them work out for themselves possible strategies for survival.

In the Caribbean a quite different project is the theatre company of a group of working class women in Kingston, Jamaica: Sistren. This group of women have found a means through drama of enabling the most oppressed class of women in the Third World to articulate to large audiences of other classes, male and female, their growing consciousness and confidence. This brilliant theatre enterprise is now internationally known through tours of their plays, and more especially through workshops amongst black female workers in, for example, Canada and Britain.

In Africa, in the wake of destruction of life at the base of society by dictatorial regimes inheriting the independent African state, there have been a number of attempts to involve peasant farmers in articulating a new order, using drama and theatre. Perhaps the most notable was the drama project of the people of Kamiriithu in Kenya. This involved the Kenyan playwright **Ngugi wa Thiong'o**. The government imprisoned him, banned the plays and bulldozed the theatre. However, drama initiatives in Africa tend to lose momentum through a lack of wider organizational structure.

In parts of Asia, the scale of popular theatre is linked to successful economic and political organizations among the oppressed. The thousands of theatre groups in Mindanao, southern Philippines, have emerged through the church and popular education organizations, and in turn gave focus and momentum to the opposition to the oppressed of the Marcos regime in that country. The theatre groups have used the Catholic feast days and liturgical processions to communicate their thinking and growing confidence. Karl Gaspar, actor, poet, artist and lay-secretary of the Church Conference in the area, was among many imprisoned without trial in 1983 for participating with these theatre groups.

In Bangladesh there are now hundreds of groups of landless wage-labourers in remote rural areas who have formed themselves into economic organizations and who use drama as a means to action against local injustice. Such is their growing confidence that they have asked members of the student theatre company Aranyak to leave Dhaka, live with them in their poverty and contribute their drama skills as animateurs in the wider organizations.

It is in India, however, that popular theatre is most diverse and effective. A significant example is the work among Harijans (so-called 'Untouchables') in Tamil Nadu by the Association for the Rural Poor and the Integrated Rural Development Society. These organizations, founded and run by Harijans, use drama to analyse issues, think through stategies thoroughly, and 'rehearse' a particular line of action, which has then been carried out successfully.

These examples indicate a growing Third World theatre which is subordinate to effective new social and economic initiatives amongst the very poor. It reflects the use of their culture by the people themselves to develop their own thinking and analysis. ME

Thoma, Ludwig (1867–1928) German playwright and novelist. Thoma wrote several comedies about life in rural Bavaria. The most popular is *The Local Train* (1902), which is still revived. SW

Thomas, Augustus (1857–1934) American playwright. Thomas always dealt with well-documented

The climactic scene of Augustus Thomas's *The Witching Hour*, 1907.

American scenes in such plays as *Alabama* (1891), *In Mizzoura* (1893), and *Arizona* (1899). *The Copperhead* (1918), which made **Lionel Barrymore** a star, details the story of an Illinois farmer who, at the request of President Lincoln, pretends to be a sympathizer with the Confederacy. Many plays explored contemporary issues: capital and labour in *New Blood* (1894); politics in *The Capitol* (1895), hypnotism in *The Witching Hour* (1907); and mental healing in *As a Man Thinks* (1911). Even his farces, *The Earl of Pawtucket* (1903) and *Mrs Leffingwell's Boots* (1905), had a distinctively American flavour.

The prefaces to many of his more than 60 plays provide a lively and intimate account of the dramatist at work.   RM

Thomas, Dylan (Marlais) (1914–53) Welsh poet and dramatist, at one time an actor in repertory theatre, whose expressionistic radio 'play for voices' *Under Milk Wood* (first staged in 1953) has gained a wide reputation.   CI

Thomas, (Walter) Brandon (1856–1914) English actor and playwright, born in Liverpool, where he first attempted to make a career as a journalist, supplementing his income by writing and performing coon songs in music-halls. He made his London debut as an actor in 1879–80, and was a prominent member of the **Hare/Kendal** company at the **St James's**. Shaw, who saw him as Sir Lucius O'Trigger in an 1895 revival of *The Rivals*, thought he played the part 'agreeably and even with dignity, mainly by not doing what is expected of him', a characteristic which Thomas had significantly displayed in the writing of *Charley's Aunt* (1892), an immensely popular farce which describes the escapades of three Oxford undergraduates, the most vacuously obliging of whom is cajoled into playing the part of a rich woman in order to advance the marital ambitions of the other two. It is for *Charley's Aunt* alone that Thomas is remembered, though he is credited with at least a dozen more plays.   PT

Thomashevski, Boris (Thomashefsky) (1886–1939) Flamboyant actor-manager and matinee idol of the New York **Shund theatre**, who, though large and fat, played romantic hero parts in musical comedy and melodrama, though occasionally aspiring towards the better plays for brief periods.   AB

Thompson, Denman (1833–1911) American actor, playwright. Raised in New England, he became a specialist in ethnic and eccentric comedy. He first played his sketch featuring Uncle Josh Whitcomb in 1875. By 1877 it had become a three-act play, and in 1886, with George Ryer, he completely revised it as *The Old Homestead*, which he played until 1910. A derivation of temperance melodrama, *The Old Homestead* was the epitome of sentimental rural Americana.   DMCD

Thompson, Lydia (1836–1908) English actress. Fair-haired and sprightly, she had already made a name for herself as a dancer and comedienne in London, the English provinces and Germany when she brought her troupe of British Blondes to New York (1868). Heralded by a barrage of publicity, her production of *Ixion*,

Lydia Thompson as Robinson Crusoe in H. B. Farnie's burlesque of that name, 1877.

or *The Man at the Wheel*, the first modern burlesque in more than one act, did not so much introduce burlesque to America as combine it with pulchritude in tights to create the 'leg show'. A strict taskmistress to her underlings and a shrewd businesswoman, Thompson was the first actress to horsewhip a libellous newspaper editor. Teamed with Willie Edouin, for a while, she toured the United States several times (1868–71, 1877–8, 1886, 1888–9, 1891), retaining her popularity on both sides of the Atlantic. Her last appearance was with **Mrs Patrick Campbell** in *A Queen's Romance* (Imperial Theatre, London, 1904).   LS

Thompson, Mervyn (1936–) New Zealand playwright and director. Co-founder of the Court Theatre, Christchurch, Artistic Director of **Downstage Theatre**, 1975–6, senior lecturer in drama, University of Auckland, 1977–89. Major plays: *O! Temperance!* (1972), *First Return* (1974), *Songs to Uncle Scrim* (1976), *A Night at the Races* (1977), *Songs to the Judges* (1980), *Coaltown Blues* (1984). Thompson's unique form of 'songplay' is fully developed in *Judges*. He has also written a theatrical autobiography, *All My Lives* (1980).   HDMCN

Thompson, Sada (1929–) American actress who trained at the Carnegie Institute of Technology. She made her professional debut in *The Beautiful People* in 1947, and she first appeared in New York in a reading of *Under Milkwood* in 1953.

Among her best received efforts have been *The Misanthrope* (1956), Valerie Barton in *The River Line*

(1957), Dorine in *Tartuffe* (1964–5), Beatrice in *The Effects of Gamma Rays on Man-in-the-Moon Marigolds* (1970), and Ma in *Twigs* (1971), for which she received a Tony. Of her work in *Twigs*, it was said that Thompson 'has long since demonstrated a depth of acting technique and a variety of performing outputs while working the range of dramatic literature'. SMA

Thompson, Sam (1916–65) Irish playwright. A shipyard painter, Thompson began writing for BBC radio. The soberly observed realities of *Over the Bridge* (1960), denouncing mob bigotry and murder, outraged the Unionist establishment in the **Group**'s directorate. It was independently produced by James Ellis in Belfast, Dublin, Scotland and England. *The Evangelist* (1963), whose butt is commercialized religion, was very effective theatre in Hilton Edwards's Belfast Opera House production. In a posthumously discovered MS, *The Masquerade*, three characters act out Nazi fantasies in a London basement. Thompson's political and social themes were clearly encouraging him to new forms of expression. DM

Thorndike, (Agnes) Sybil (1882–1976) British actress, who joined Miss **Horniman**'s company in 1908 after touring America with **Ben Greet** in an extraordinarily wide variety of Shakespearian roles, male as well as female. She made her name in a number of modern plays – **Maugham**'s *Smith* (New York, 1910), **Granville Barker**'s *The Madras House* and **Houghton**'s *Hindle Wakes* (London, 1910 and 1912), or **St John Ervine**'s *Jane Clegg* (Manchester, 1912) – before joining the **Old Vic**, where she not only played Shakespearian and Restoration heroines but also Prince Hal in *Henry IV, Part 1*, Ferdinand in *The Tempest*, the Fool in *King Lear* and Launcelot Gobbo in *The Merchant of Venice*. She extended her range still further with a repertoire of **Claudel** and **Gilbert Murray**'s translations of **Euripides** (1919–20), and a season of **Grand-Guignol** (1920–2), but her major successes in the inter-war period were in the title roles of **Shaw**'s *Candida* (1920), *St Joan* (a part written specifically for her, 1924), and a revival of *Major Barbara* (1929). She also worked with the Phoenix Society, acted in several films and gave striking performances in plays by John Van Druten, **Emlyn Williams** and **Priestley**.

During and after the Second World War she toured widely with the Old Vic company for **ENSA**. In the later part of her career she frequently appeared with her husband, **Lewis Casson** (notably in Priestley's *The Linden Tree*, 1949; **John Home**'s *Douglas* at the **Edinburgh Festival**, 1950; **Clemence Dane**'s *Eighty in the Shade*, specially written for them, 1959; **Coward**'s *Waiting in the Wings*, 1960, and **Chekhov**'s *Uncle Vanya* at the first **Chichester Festival**, 1962). She was appointed DBE in 1931, CH in 1970, and her final performance in 1966 inaugurated a new theatre in Surrey named after her. CI

Throckmorton, Cleon (1897–1965) American set designer. Throckmorton began his career with the **Provincetown Players** and designed many of **Eugene O'Neill**'s early plays including *Emperor Jones* and *The Hairy Ape*. In the same way that O'Neill was experimenting with expressionism, Throckmorton employed stylized settings in the manner of various

European movements. He designed several plays for the **Theatre Guild** including *Porgy*. AA

Thurston, Howard Franklin (1869–1936) American magician. The son of a carriage-maker, he began as a card manipulator, playing at **Tony Pastor**'s 14th St Theatre, New York, but developed into a specialist in spectacular illusions. In his acts, he would make vanish an Arabian horse, a girl playing a piano, a Whippet automobile; in 'The Triple Mystery' he made a girl materialize in a nested box, suspended her in a mummy case above the stage, and then caused her to appear in a roped trunk above the spectators' heads. He was held over at the London Palace for six months in 1900, purchased **Harry Kellar**'s show in 1907, and introduced his version of the Indian Rope Trick in 1926. Having lost millions, he toured a ghost play *The Demon* (1929), finally retiring in 1935. LS

Tibetan drama A form of theatre popular in Tibet and among other Tibetan communities, including those in Sichuan, Qinghai and Yunnan provinces in China and India.

The origins of a real and developed drama in Tibet go back to the Buddhist monk Tang-ston rgyal-po (flourished 15th century), who formed a company of singers and dancers in which individual performers impersonated characters to relate stories based on Buddhist sutras. It was not until the 17th century that Tibetan drama became split from religious ritual.

Tibetan drama is a highly integrated art form in which singing, dialogue, dance, acrobatics, mime and extremely colourful costumes all play a part. Musical accompaniment is confined to percussion instruments, drums and cymbals, and a chorus. Makeup is simple, but masks are an important feature. In the unreformed traditional Tibetan drama there is no scenery and no more than simple properties. The performance may take place in a square or any open space, with the spectators on three or all four sides of the action. Sometimes a temple is an appropriate venue.

There are three sections of a Tibetan drama. The first is the prologue, a masked dance explaining the plot. Then comes the core, the drama itself. Finally a farewell blessing is given, bearing no relation to the plot. It enables the company to seek donations from the audience.

Tibetan drama was, and to some extent remains, an oral tradition. Many items were not written down and varied greatly from troupe to troupe and time to time. Over a dozen survive today. They concern Tibetan history and mythology, kings, queens, and beautiful women. Several are based on Indian literary works. The characterization tends to be stark, with the positive and negative character clearly delineated. The elements of love, magic, religion and comedy are strong. Most of the dramas were long and performed in the day-time only, extending over one or several days.

A well-known and popular item is *The Historical Drama of King Srong-btsan-sgam-po*. The great Tibetan king of the title, a real historical figure (d. AD 650), sends an ambassador to China to seek marriage with the Princess Wencheng. Through great integrity he performs difficult tasks set him by the Chinese emperor and wins his king the bride. In contemporary China the story is considered to promote 'the unity of the nationalities'.

In the past, performers held a very low social status. Usually it was men who played female roles. Fully professional companies existed, but most were semi-professional only, their members being mainly male peasants serving overlords. These troupes stayed together only part of the year. In the summers, late in the sixth month and early in the seventh according to the old lunar calendar, 12 famous troupes were selected from among the semi-professional folk groups to gather in Lhasa for a competitive drama season.

The Tibetan Drama Troupe of Tibet was set up in Lhasa in 1960 just after the 1959 rebellion against Chinese rule. As of the mid-1980s it is the only state-run professional Tibetan drama company in Tibet. It performs mainly traditional items which occupy only two or three hours. Though somewhat reformed, these retain the traditional dance, costumes, singing style, offstage chorus, and masked dance of the prologue, as well as the main elements of the older stories. The accompanying orchestra has been much enlarged to include wind and string instruments, not only Tibetan, but also Han Chinese and Western. Professional companies perform in a theatre with a stage, properties and scenery. In Tibet in the 1980s there are also numerous semi-amateur folk troupes, which perform traditional dramas completely unchanged from the past, except that women play female roles. The custom of gathering troupes in Lhasa for a summer festival was revived in 1984. There is a Tibetan Institute of Performing Arts in Dharamsala in the northern Punjab, India, which studies and performs the traditional Tibetan drama.   CPM

Tidblad, Inga (1901–75) Major Swedish actress of the mid-20th century, particularly admired for roles in Shakespearian comedy (Rosalind, Viola, Beatrice and Portia) to which she brought depth and subtlety. She never played major classical tragedy, but specialized increasingly in **Strindberg**, **Ibsen** and **Eugene O'Neill**. Her Miss Julie (which she played in New York at 61) and Queen Christina were greatly admired for their poise and complexity, as were her roles in world premieres of O'Neill: Mary Tyrone in *Long Day's Journey Into Night* (1956) and Deborah in both *A Touch of the Poet* (1957) and *More Stately Mansions* (1962).   HL

Tieck, Ludwig (1773–1853) German playwright, novelist, and essayist. One of Tieck's earliest loves was the theatre, and his interest in it was sustained throughout his extremely fertile career as a writer and editor. His plays exhibit the same failings as those of other early romantic writers. While they are wonderfully inventive, and often idiosyncratic, they defy effective staging, though his comedies *Puss in Boots* (1797) and *The World Upside Down* (1798) have done well in modern revivals. However, his vast dramatic fantasy, *Emperor Octavian* (1804), cannot be properly represented on stage. Throughout his life, Tieck was profoundly interested in **Shakespeare** and the Elizabethan playwrights. He translated some of the plays, notably *The Tempest* (1795), and was involved in the completion of **A. W. Schlegel**'s translations of Shakespeare. In his critical writings, he explored more thoroughly and richly than previous critics Shakespeare's imaginative world. As a result of a visit to

England in 1817 to collect materials on the Elizabethans, he became interested in the physical arrangement of the Elizabethan theatre. In 1836, with the help of the architect Gottfried Semper, he reconstructed on paper the **Fortune Theatre**. In 1843 he produced *A Midsummer Night's Dream* in Berlin, utilizing many features of the Elizabethan stage. Earlier, in 1824, he had been appointed dramaturge of the **Dresden Court Theatre**, where he laboured, not always with success, to improve standards of diction and to create, especially in the classics, a simpler approach to staging than the one then current. His writings on the theatre are collected in the four volumes of *Critical Writings* published in 1848.   SW

Tilley, Vesta (Matilda Alice Victoria Powles) (1864–1952) The most popular male impersonator of the English music-hall, she made her stage debut at the Gloucester Theatre Royal at the age of three or four, and first appeared in trousers as the 'Pocket Sims Reeves'. Her first London appearance was in 1878 at the Royal Holborn. Although she was a celebrated principal boy in pantomime, famous for her waltz-tempo songs, her chief contribution was as an elegant young man-about-town, singing such numbers as 'Following in Father's Footsteps' and 'The Midnight Son'. Her natty masculine attire, specially tailored for her, set fashions, and her transvestism was made palatable for a newly genteel audience by the fact that the visual illusion was undermined by her soprano voice. During the First World War, she won greater

Vesta Tilley as a bank-clerk on a spree.

popularity and some opprobrium for her aid in recruiting (dressed as a Tommy, she sang 'The Army of Today's All Right'). She retired in 1920 after her husband, the manager Walter de Frece, was knighted, and devoted the rest of her life to charity work.   LS

Tingeltangel Generic term for a lower class music-hall in Berlin; it derives from a song the comedian Tange sang at the Triangel Theater. Ten or 20 female singers and a few comedians would sit on a small stage and come forward to deliver their numbers, accompanied solely by a piano. The verses were usually ribald and called for the almost exclusively male audience of artisans, small tradesmen and students to join in the chorus and goose-step round the platform. At the end of the 19th century the most famous were Moors Academy of Music, the Silberhalle and Elysium, the Kuhstall, Klosterstiebel and the Singspielhalle.   LS

Tipton, Jennifer (19??–   ) American lighting designer. Tipton's early interest in dance led to an appreciation of the potential of light, and its uses and impact on performance. She studied with lighting designer Tom Skelton and began her career designing for choreographer Paul Taylor and since 1965 has designed every production by choreographer Twyla Tharp. In theatre she has designed frequently for the **New York Shakespeare Festival**, the **Goodman Theatre** and many regional theatres. Her preference for more 'abstract' theatre has led to collaboration with **Mabou Mines**, **Robert Wilson** and **Andrei Serban**. Tipton's work is typified by a sense of sculptured and textured space.   AA

Tireman The tireman (wardrobe master) was an important member of Elizabethan theatre companies, since costume was the most costly and colourful element in contemporary styles of performance. Whilst leading actors possessed their own costumes, the tireman would probably have checked their appropriateness as well as supplying women's clothes for the boys and fitting the hired men. What could not be supplied out of stock, he would have to make or order, and we can assume that it was his task to maintain and replenish the wardrobe store in the tiring house.   PT

Tiring house The name given to that section of Elizabethan theatre buildings directly behind and giving access to the stage is derived from one (the most important in a clothes-conscious age) of its many functions. It was there that the actors 'attired' themselves for performance. But the tiring house must also have accommodated a wardrobe and property store, the collection of plays in the care of the book-keeper and meeting-rooms for the company and privileged visitors. Its facade served as the upstage wall of the platform, so that actors entered directly from the tiring house onto the stage.   PT

Toby The principal character of the North American **tent show**, a redhaired, freckle-faced farmboy. He appears to derive from the rustic low comedians of 18th-century farce; accepted tradition is that Fred Wilson of Horace Murphy's Comedians combined all his 'silly kid' roles under the blanket name Toby around

1909. His dramatic function resembles that of the 'comic man' in melodrama, providing laughs while contributing to the happy ending. Wilson's Toby was still recognizable as a farmhand in his checked shirt and boots, but the character grew more grotesque. Harley Sadler turned him into a Texas cowpoke in woolly chaps and a phallic pistol and Neil Schaffner into an awkward dude, whose large freckles and blacked-out front teeth constituted a kind of *commedia* mask. The female equivalent was Sis Hopkins, created by Rose Melville c. 1898, an 'Indiana jay' in pigtails and a pinafore; the type became known as Susie. The growing predominance of Toby and his antics to the detriment of the dramas in which he appeared has been cited as a factor in the declining popularity of the tent show.   LS

Toller, Ernst (1893–1939) German dramatist and poet, whose life was characterized by radical political commitment. The founder of a pacifist organization after being invalided out of the army in 1917, he was arrested for his involvement in a munitions strike in 1918, becoming president of the first short-lived Bavarian Soviet Republic then commander of its Red Army. Sentenced to five years' imprisonment after its fall in 1919, he subsequently campaigned for judicial reform and, in 1938, for refugee relief. His plays, which are among the most significant works of expressionism, reflect this experience yet transpose it to a universal level where the world becomes a projection of the mind. *Transfiguration* (staged by **Karlheinz Martin**, 1919) presents graphic images of war in following the protagonist's conversion from patriotism to militant pacifism, but realism alternates with dream sequences and his example alone is sufficient to bring about the spiritual regeneration of humanity. *Masses and Man* (1920) and *The Machine Wreckers* (1922) deal with revolution through strike action and the Luddite destruction of the factories that enslave the workers, but each stresses the gap between idealistic leaders and the proletariat, who can only be converted to non-violence by their deaths. In *Hinkemann* (1923), which shares the same returning soldier theme as **Brecht**'s *Drums in the Night*, and *Hurrah, We Live!* (staged by **Piscator**, 1927), where a revolutionary is released after several years in prison, the discrepancy between the grotesque reality the protagonist finds and the ideals for which he has suffered leads to suicide.

Wotan Unchained (1923) satirizes the forces that produced fascism and drove him into exile in 1933, where he produced *Draw the Fires*, a protest against the coming war based on a 1917 naval mutiny, in Manchester (1935). He worked on film scripts with Sidney Kaufman in Hollywood, including the adaptation of his last play *Pastor Hall* (1939), and committed suicide on the outbreak of war. His artistic predicament, the gap between idealistic drama and political actuality, is characteristic of the expressionists, and forms the subject of **Tankred Dorst**'s play *Toller* (1968).   CI

Tollu Bommalu Also spelled *tholubommalatta*. This is one of the best-known forms of puppetry in India and one of the marvellous and varied examples of the shadow puppet theatre of Asia. It is found in several regions of Andhra Pradesh, a state in south India. *Tolu* means a 'doll' and *bommalu* means 'leather'. According to the oral tradition, the form originated in 200 BC when it is said to have been patronized by the rulers of the Satavahana dynasty. However, it is clear from manuscripts that it existed at least in the 16th century under the reign of King Kona Reddy, a ruler of the Vijayanagar Empire. Under his patronage a Telugu manuscript entitled *Ramayana Ranganathana* was composed specifically for the shadow theatre. Besides providing a text of the famous epic story, the manuscript includes instructions for the construction and decoration of the shadow puppets. Unfortunately, families of puppeteers prevent scholarly research by jealously guarding copies of the manuscripts.

Most of the *Tollu Bommalu* shadow puppets are cut from hide of goats that is processed in a special manner. Some puppets are made from deer and buffalo hide as well. A relationship is said to exist between the kind of skin used and the character that the puppet portrays. Typically, humans and saints are made of goat skin. Demons are made of buffalo hide and gods and heroes are cut from deer skin. Puppets are generally large, translucent and multi-coloured. Depending on the area of the state in which the puppets were produced, they are relatively large or small in size. For example, those from Madnapalli district are generally around four feet tall and those from Kakinada may be as tall as five feet.

The puppets are wedged between a bamboo strip split down the middle and are tied along the length of the cane from the head to the crotch to provide support. More than one puppet may be used to represent the same character, depending on the different emotional states he depicts in the story. Puppets are even constructed incorporating a scenic environment around the figure. For example, Rama's wife Sita, who pines for him under the Ashoka tree during her captivity in the evil King Ravana's garden, represents this type of puppet.

Many puppets have movable parts, especially hands and legs. Some even have movable heads and necks. Thin strips of bamboo are joined to the hands by a knot of yarn to allow physical action. The legs of a puppet are usually allowed to dangle from the trunk of the puppet. And the skirt of a dancing girl is hinged to her waist and, through a clever device contrived with strings and knots, she may even turn her head from side to side, pertly whisking her hair plait behind her as she does so.

In general, refined characters have a delicate physiognomy, whereas demons have exaggerated and gross features revealing their excessiveness and crudity. Some puppets are delicately carved with traceries of fine perforations revealing the subtle artistry of their makers. The basic colours used to dye the skin are black, red and green and combinations derived of these colours. Yellow is a dominant colour for female figures and sages.

The colourful shadows are cast on a wide, white screen made of sturdy cotton *saris* or cloth pieces stitched together. The screen is stretched between two poles temporarily fixed in the ground about 6 to 12 feet apart. The total height of the screen depends on the size of the puppets used and may range from 5 to 7 feet. The stage behind the screen is raised about half a foot above the ground and encased by thatch matting to provide privacy for the party of performers and their families during the long hours of the show.

About 11 inches above the bottom of the screen a rope is stretched on which the puppets may be rested when they are on stage. Puppets are pinned in place on the screen by thorn pins from the acacia bush which grows wild in the rural areas of Andhra. Oil lamps and torches fed with castor oil were traditionally used to cast a flickering mellow glow to produce the shadows on the screen. Nowadays companies have resorted to the pressures of modernization and use petromax lamps which give off a harsh blue-white glow, distorting the true colour of the images. The petromax lamps hang from a length of bamboo stretched across the frame supporting the screen, above the heads of the puppeteers. The chief manipulator stands pressing the large puppets firmly against the screen. With his free hand he manipulates the arms of the puppet. When big puppets are used for fight sequences, two people manipulate each puppet. Puppets are passed from hand to hand when they are moved across the wide screen. The manipulator wears a set of bells on one of his ankles which he uses to accentuate the dance steps. A loose elevated board on the floor of the performance booth provides additional sound effects when struck with his foot.

A typical troupe of between six and ten people is composed of manipulators, singers, dancers and instrumentalists. Women always speak the female parts and the stage manager manipulates the shadows during the dance numbers.

Only the songs have a written text. Dialogue sections are improvised and continue as long as the puppeteers think the audience is interested. The musical company is composed of a *mridangam* drummer. Bell-metal cymbals are used to keep the rhythm. A metal barrel, one end of which serves for a drum head, is played by long thin sticks. A piece of leather provides special sound effects when slapped by the hand. A harmonium and *mukavina*, an oboe-like wind instrument, are sometimes used. Folk and classical melodies are integrated. Even film music has crept in because of its popularity.

During performance the puppeteers chant and speak their dialogue to each other rather than through the puppets. The puppets seem to act only as symbols of the characters portrayed to which the manipulators add their own highly effective emotional reactions.

Special effects are sometimes achieved to the delight of the audience. For example, when a character is shot with an arrow during a battle, a whizzing noise is produced by a small whistle as a leather arrow on a rod is whisked across the screen. When it strikes its victim severing his head, the puppet head is detached quickly by a string and made to roll across the screen. The drummers accentuate the action with loud thuds. The action is usually accompanied by wild applause from the spectators.

Among the more popular characters are the clowns – Katikayata, the drunken lecher and womanizer, and Bangavaka, his fat, scandal-mongering wife. The pair provide comic interludes throughout a showing breaking the monotony of the familiar epic stories which are drawn from the *Ramayana*, the *Mahabharata* and the *Puranas*. Normally, a company has between half a dozen and a dozen plays in its repertory which each take four to eight hours to perform.

Lord Shiva is regarded as the patron saint of the puppeteers. During Shiva's birthday in May, some companies perform special nine-night programmes in his honour outside the temples of the region. This tends to be one of their most lucrative engagements. The playing season usually extends between the monsoons which strike Andhra Pradesh twice a year.

Performances begin when the puppet of Ganapati, the elephant-headed god, is placed on the screen and songs of praise are sung in his honour. Then Saraswathi, goddess of learning, appears and is praised.

A comic interlude takes place between the husband and wife. Jokes are made about the local spectators. Then the stage manager introduces the subject of the play. Nearly two hours are devoted to preliminaries and introduction of characters. Finally, the drama begins, following the particular sequence of events of whatever epic story is presented. About sunrise performances end with songs of thanksgiving. FAR

Tolstoi, Aleksei Konstantinovich (1817–75) Diplomat, poet, novelist and major Russian historical dramatist of the 19th century. He began his literary career in 1841 with one of three vampire tales which may have provided source material for **Sukhovo-Kobylin**'s *Tarelkin's Death*. From 1853 to 1863 he published nonsense verse, satirical prose and theatrical parodies with his cousins the Zhemchuzhnikovs in the person of pseudonymous author 'Kozma Prutkov', an arrogant clerk with literary pretensions. 'His' work influenced Vladimir Solovyov, Count Vladimir Sollogub and **Nikolai Evreinov** in the late 19th–early 20th centuries. Tolstoi also wrote well-regarded satirical and lyrical verse and ballads under his own name, some of which have been set to music by Tchaikovsky, Mussorgsky and Rimsky-Korsakov. His popular romantic historical novel, *Prince Serebryany* (1862), based largely on Karamzin's *History of the Russian State* (1818–26), is set during the reign of Ivan the Terrible. His reputation as a dramatist rests on his popular blank verse historical trilogy on three of Russia's feudal monarchs (1533–1605): *The Death of Ivan the Terrible* (1864), *Tsar Fyodor Ioannovich* (1868) and *Tsar Boris* (1870). In each of these self-contained dramas, Tolstoi humanizes history à la **Schiller** by focusing upon the personal psychological and moral ramifications of the ruler-protagonist's political crisis. The first play received a lavish, antiquarian staging in 1867 at St Petersburg's Aleksandrinsky Theatre, owing to the author's court connections, but failed with a comic actor miscast in the title role. The second drama premiered in 1898 in St Petersburg and then at the **Moscow Art Theatre**, whose production established the play in Russia's permanent dramatic repertoire. The role of gentle, naive Fyodor is a favourite of actors and has been interpreted memorably by **Ivan Moskvin** at the MAT premiere and by Innokenty Smoktunovsky at the Maly Theatre in the 1970s. SG

Tolstoi, Aleksei Nikolaevich (1883–1945) Soviet novelist, short story writer and dramatist, in that order of significance, whose works have become official classics. A nobleman by birth and an anti-Bolshevik at the time of the Revolution, Tolstoi, later known as the 'Red Count', accommodated himself totally to the new regime and became an apologist for Stalin following an interlude in Parisian exile (1918–23). Prior to 1917 he produced symbolist poetry and some talented novels

and short story collections. He wrote 28 plays, beginning in 1908. His pre-revolutionary plays are farces and comedies satirizing the landed gentry and the merchant class. Seven received Moscow stagings, and his dramatic fairy tale *The Sorcerer's Daughter and the Enchanted Prince* was produced at **Meyerhold**'s theatre of small forms, The Strand (1908). In the 1920s Tolstoi was the co-author of three historical dramas with historian P. E. Shchegolev, the science fiction play *The Revolt of the Machines* (1924) and the first part of his Peter the Great trilogy – *On the Rack* (1929), rewritten as *Peter the First* (first version, 1935; second version, 1939) – which parallels his unfinished three-part historical novel *Peter the First* (1930, 1934, 1945), recipient of the 1941 Stalin Prize and thought by some to be exemplary of its genre. Tolstoi's evolving presentation of Peter as tyrant, modernizer and finally national hero reflects the shift in official perspective which was interested in likening Peter to Stalin. His two-part historical play *Ivan the Terrible* (*The Eagle and Its Mate*, 1944; *The Difficult Years*, 1946), which won him a third, posthumous Stalin Prize in 1946, is a somewhat idealized view of the tsar which Soviet critics consider to be his best dramatic work. SG

Tolstoi, Lev Nikolaevich (1828–1910) A titled noble, one of Russia's greatest novelists and a social dramatist, Count Tolstoi rejected his class and justified art solely as a means of inculcating Christian doctrine and virtue and of changing the status quo. Following the success of his autobiographical writings of the 1850s, he turned to educational reform, founding a school for his serfs' children, studying European educational theory and practice and publishing his findings in the 1860s and 1870s. In 1878, following the completion of his masterful novels *War and Peace* (1869) and *Anna Karenina* (1877), he underwent a celebrated spiritual crisis, resulting in his rejection of Orthodox Christianity in favour of a partially self-devised code of nonresistance to evil. This ethical philosophy manifests itself in all of his remaining work – three religious treatises (1880–3); social polemics exposing the inequalities of the class system, the evils of alcohol, tobacco, war and patriotism; aesthetic essays; and dramas. About the latter, he had decidedly mixed feelings. He rejected theatre's sham and self-indulgence but embraced its potential for educating and uplifting a popular audience. He was particular as to how and by whom his plays were performed. His earliest plays – *A Contaminated Family* (1864), *The Nihilist* (1866) and *The First Distiller* (1886) – two satires and a moral fable, treated such contemporary evils as women's rights, nihilism and alcoholism. In *What is Art?* (1897–8), 'On **Shakespeare** and the Drama' (1903–4) and other aesthetic and critical works, Tolstoi distinguished between true and counterfeit art. True Art is universal, moral, affective but not excessive in emotional and scenographic detail. False art, which includes the works of Shakespeare, **Goethe**, **Hugo** and others, violates these criteria and those relating purely to craft. Tolstoi condemned his own naturalistic peasant tragedy, *The Power of Darkness* (1886), for wallowing in extraneous detail, but it remains a powerful indictment of the inhumanity and moral degeneracy brought on by the ignorance and squalor of Russian peasant life. Based upon a contemporary criminal case and echoing **Pisemsky**'s *A Bitter Fate*, it relates a tale of adultery and infanticide and features a typically meek Tolstoyan raisonneur and climactic confession-conversion. Originally written for performance in the 'popular theatres', it was banned from the Russian stage until 1895, premiering instead at **Antoine**'s Théâtre Libre in 1888. *The Fruits of Enlightenment* (1889) satirized the unenlightened attitude of the Russian landed nobility towards the peasantry, despite the abolition of serfdom in 1861. *The Living Corpse* (1900), like *Power*, was based on an actual court case and, like *Fruits*, exposed the inadequacy of secular laws, this time governing marriage and divorce. *The Light Shines in the Darkness* (1900) is an unfinished autobiographical tale of an aristocrat whose adherence to a transparently Tolstoyan ethic puts him at odds with his family and society. *The Cause of It All* (1910) is another anti-alcohol tract. While the plays suffer somewhat from the author's moral didacticism, they benefit from the emotional intensity generated by his convictions. His vision and the veracity of his language and characters align Tolstoi somewhat more closely with **Griboedov**'s and **Gogol**'s psychological realism than with **Ostrovsky**'s contrived ethnographic realism. Much of his narrative writing has been adapted for the stage, including most recently the short story 'Kholstomer' by playwright Mark Rozovsky and director **Georgy Tovstonogov** at Leningrad's Gorky Theatre (1975-6). This version was further adapted and produced as *Strider. The Story of A Horse* in New York at the Chelsea Theatre Centre in 1979 and later on Broadway and in regional theatres. SG

Tomaszewski, Henryk see **Mime**

Toole, John Laurence (1830-1906) English actor, the foremost low comedian of the 19th century's last decades. Toole made his professional debut in Dublin in 1852 and his London debut later in the same year. His famous friendship with **Henry Irving** began in Edinburgh in 1857 (Toole was the Artful Dodger and Irving Monks in a deplorable adaptation of *Oliver Twist*, which might have tested Dickens's fondness for Toole had he seen it) and blossomed into lifelong intimacy when they acted together in London in 1867. The relationship was a gift for cartoonists, the squat extrovert comedian and the gaunt introverted tragedian, but their performances together in their years of fame were limited to benefits. Toole was the first to win public favour as a star of **Adelphi** farces and burlesques from 1859-67. Like **Frederick Robson**, whom he admired, Toole was at his best in roles combining eccentric comedy and pathos. Caleb Plummer in **Boucicault**'s *Dot* (1862) and Michael Garner in **H. J. Byron**'s *Dearer than Life* (1868). For **John Hollingshead** at the **Gaiety** (1869-73), he revived *Paul Pry*, in conscious emulation of the great **John Liston**. In 1879, Toole bought the lease of the Charing Cross Theatre, which he rechristened Toole's Theatre in 1882. He was the first English actor confident enough of his standing with the London public to name a theatre after himself (it was not until 1888 that **Edward Terry** became the second). He proved a shrewd manager, though his choice of plays (H. J. Byron and F. C. Burnand dominated the repertoire) was generally predictable. He was, however, the first to present **J. M. Barrie**'s plays – *Ibsen's Ghost; or, Toole Up-to-Date* (1891) and *Walker, London* (1892).

Toole retired in 1895 and left a fortune when he died. PT

Topol, Haim (1935–) Israeli actor, now residing in England. His great roles in Israel were Azdak in **Brecht**'s *The Caucasian Chalk Circle* (1962) and Sallah Shabbati in the film of that name (1964) by **Ephraim Kishon**. In London he rose to fame with his portrayal of Tevye in the musical *Fiddler on the Roof* (1967), based on **Sholom Aleichem**'s Yiddish novel. HAS

Torelli, Giacomo (1608–78) Italian architect, engineer and stage designer whose innovations became a standard part of continental theatre practice. He was responsible for developing the chariot-and-pole system of changeable scenery which consisted of attaching wing flats through slits in the stage floor to rolling wagons in the cellar beneath: by an arrangement of pulleys and ropes wound on a common drum all the flats could move smoothly and simultaneously under the control of a single stagehand, while overhead borders were similarly operated by counterweights. The result was a swift, magical transformation of one scene to the next, creating an illusion akin to a cinematic dissolve which had a profound effect not only on design but on the evolution of theatrical forms, notably opera and intermezzi. Torelli is said to have been a pupil of **Aleotti** at the Teatro Farnese but he first became prominent in Venice where he designed the Teatro Novissimo and several of its earliest operatic productions, including *La Finta Pazza* (1641), *Bellerofonte* (1642) and *Venere Gelosa* (1643). Their use of machinery was so impressive that he was dubbed 'the great sorcerer'. Summoned to Paris by Mazarin in 1645, he re-equipped the **Petit-Bourbon** where his designs for the performances of Italian opera, for **Corneille**'s 'machine-play' *Andromède* (1650) and subsequently for a series of court ballets earned him an equal reputation with French audiences. In 1659 the arrival in France of his fellow-countryman **Gaspare Vigarani** soon ousted him from royal favour and shortly after supervising the staging of **Molière**'s *Les Fâcheux* (*The Bores*) for Fouquet in 1661 he was forced to return to his native Fano, where he continued to work until his death and produced some of his most interesting designs. With the demolition of the Petit-Bourbon the machinery he had installed there was removed and destroyed by the jealous Vigarani, but his drawings survived and were later reproduced in **Diderot**'s *Encyclopédie* (1772) under 'Machines de Théâtre'. Torelli's achievement in revolutionizing French *mise en scène* established an Italianate tradition of spectacular staging for opera and ballet which was to be maintained by Vigarani, **Berain** and **Servandoni**. AA DR

Toronto Workshop Productions The oldest of Toronto's alternate theatres. It was founded and is still directed by George Luscombe, who had studied with **Dora Mavor Moore**'s New Play Society and worked with **Joan Littlewood** in England. In 1959 he established an acting studio and theatre workshop in a small factory building; it grew gradually, becoming a year-round professional company in 1963. In 1967 the company moved to its present home in downtown Toronto.

TWP's two guiding principles have always been

group creation and a strong leftist political orientation, but both ideals have been coloured by the dominant controlling personality of its founder, a self-confessed political showman and master of theatrical tricks. His first success, *Hey Rube* (1960), was virtually a miniature circus, and *Mr Bones* (1968), a political minstrel show, shared the billing with *Che Guevara* when the TWP represented Canada at the 1969 Venice Biennale. *Chicago 70* (1970), the TWP version of the Chicago conspiracy trials, has been made into a film and *Ten Lost Years* (1974), an evocation of the depression years in Canada, toured the country twice and was seen in Europe and the British Isles before being recreated for television.

TWP and George Luscombe did much to popularize the idea of collective creation, though with a strong guiding hand (usually playwright Jack Winter's), an approach further developed by many other companies across the country, particularly Toronto's Théâtre Passe Muraille and Saskatoon's Twenty-fifth Street House. In the defiantly artificial theatricality of its production style it provided a needed counterpoint to the realistic domestic dramas seen on so many Canadian stages in the 1970s. JA

Torres Naharro, Bartolomé de (c. 1485–c. 1520) Spanish playwright who wrote most of his plays in Italy. After a varied career he reached Rome about 1508, where he published a collection of plays and verse, the *Propalladia*, in 1517. He returned to Spain, and added further plays to later editions. The work was banned by the *Index* of 1559, but an expurgated edition was published in Madrid in 1573. His nine plays are (except for one) in five acts with an introduction, using one verse form throughout. In *Prohemio* he gives his views on the Theatre, discussing classical theory and types of plot. His plays influenced later writers, especially *Himenea* with its plot foreshadowing that of the typical *capa y espada* play. CL

Totò Stage name of Antonio de Curtis (1898–1967), Italian comedian and actor. After an early career as a club entertainer he entered the 'straight' theatre, eventually becoming an actor–manager, specializing in comedy and revue which exploited his mimic genius, perfect timing of lines, and skill with frenetic stage 'business'. Often compared to screen comedians like Chaplin and Keaton, he was a brilliant improviser whose impact was more visual than verbal, not least thanks to his expressive face and hand gestures. In the 1950s, he rapidly became established as one of the most popular Italian film comedians in films like *Napoli Milionaria* (*Affluent Naples*, 1950), *Guardie e Ladri* (1951) and *L'Oro di Napoli* (*The Gold of Naples*, 1954), a reputation he enjoyed until his death. LR

Tourneur, Cyril (c. 1575–1626) Tourneur's is the extraordinary case of a writer whose name is celebrated for a single play, *The Revenger's Tragedy* (c. 1606), that is, in the view of many scholars, more likely to have been the work of **Middleton**. The details of his life are obscure. He was probably, at various times, in the service of the Earl of Essex, the Veres and the Cecils, dying in Ireland as a result of wounds or illness after Sir Edward Cecil's ill-starred expedition against Cadiz. Tourneur is known to be the author of a lost play, *The*

Nobleman (c. 1607), and *The Atheist's Tragedy* (published 1611), a dismally mechanical revenge tragedy. It is difficult to believe that the same man could also have written the sombrely ironic *The Revenger's Tragedy*. PT

Tovstonogov, Georgy Aleksandrovich (1915–) Soviet director, part of the wave of new artists to emerge from the Thaw period (1954–6), who since becoming artistic director of the Bolshoi Dramatic Theatre (BDT or the Gorky) in 1956 has transformed it into the best theatre in Leningrad and its company – especially its mature actors – into perhaps the best in the Soviet Union. He began his career in Tbilisi as an actor and assistant director (1931) and after completing the Moscow State Theatrical Institute (GITIS) in 1938 became artistic director of the Tbilisi Russian Theatre (the Griboedov Theatre, 1938–46). From 1946 to 1949 he directed the Moscow Children's Theatre, and between 1950 and 1956 he was chief director of Leningrad's Lenin Komsomol Theatre, where he developed the successful policy of mixing Soviet dramas, Russian classics and Western literature, which he took with him to the Gorky. A **Stanislavsky**-based craftsman with a lush, romantic pictorial style, Tovstonogov does not so much radically reinterpret as carefully texture literature with new values. His orthodox Soviet productions include: stagings in the later 1950s and 1960s of works by Dvoretsky, **Korneichuk**, Shtein, Sholokhov and Rakhmanov; Aleksandr Gelman's *Minutes of a Meeting* (1976), one of four plays by the author on industrial themes, whose static conference-table format Tovstonogov relieved by revolving the set periodically to force new perspectives; and V. Tendryakov's *Three Sacks of Wheat Tailings* (1974), a good collective farm chairman versus corrupt Party official drama, staged to celebrate 'Thirty Years of Victory Over Fascism', which for some time was watched closely by Moscow officials before formally being admitted into the theatre's repertoire. Tovstonogov has staged a number of examples of post-Thaw 'new lyricism' and intimate, human drama: **Volodin**'s *Five Evenings* (1959) and *My Elder Sister* (1961); **Arbuzov**'s *Irkutsk Story* (1960) and *Happy Days of an Unhappy Man* (1968); and **Rozov**'s *The Reunion* (1964). Best are his tastefully different readings of classical texts, justly celebrated for their brilliant ensemble play: Dostoevsky's *The Idiot* (1957; London, 1966) with the exceptional Innokenty Smoktunovsky as Myshkin; **Griboedov**'s *Woe from Wit* (1962), featuring another charismatic performer, Sergei Yursky, as an atypical Chatsky; **Chekhov**'s *The Three Sisters* (1965), a production which has been favourably compared to the **Moscow Art Theatre**'s; **Gorky**'s *The Petty Bourgeoisie* (1967), which has become the theatre's longest-running production; **Shakespeare**'s *Henry IV, Parts 1 and 2* (1969), condensed into a single evening and another repertory standard; **Gogol**'s *The Inspector General* (1972), featuring a nightmarish 'Inspector' in dark glasses en route throughout the production as a manifestation of the Mayor's and contemporary Soviet paranoia, which has been compared with some exaggeration to **Meyerhold**'s landmark production; *The Story of a Horse* (adapted from **Tolstoi**'s narrative 'Kholstomer' by co-director Mark Rozovsky, 1975), an alternately ebullient and touching treatment of the man's-inhumanity-to-man theme from the perspective of a horse, beautifully enacted by Evgeny Lebedev, one of the theatre's stalwarts, and with folk-influenced songs and dances and a richly weathered-looking set by Edvard Kochergin. The play's immense popularity extended to America, where it has been produced on Broadway and in university and repertory theatres. In 1984 Tovstonogov premiered a musical version of **Sukhovo-Kobylin**'s *Tarelkin's Death*. He has also been responsible for producing such modern Western classics as: Dreiser's *An American Tragedy* (at the Lenin Komsomol, 1951); **Brecht**'s *Arturo Ui* (directed by Erwin Axer, 1963); **Steinbeck**'s *Of Mice and Men* (1966) and the **Bernstein–Laurents–Sondheim** musical *West Side Story* (1968), student productions at the Leningrad State Institute of Theatre, Music and Cinematography, where he trained Vladimir Vorovyov and Efim Padve, who have continued their musical theatre experiments as artistic directors of the Leningrad Theatre of Musical Comedy and the Leningrad Youth Theatre, respectively; **Arthur Miller**'s *The Price* (1968); and **O'Neill**'s *A Moon for the Misbegotten* (1968). The recent defection to other theatres of actors Yursky and Oleg Borisov and the seniority of others such as Lebedev, V. I. Strzhelchik, Oleg Basilashvili and Tovstonogov himself, make the theatre's continued artistic dominance uncertain. Tovstonogov's book *The Profession of the Stage Director* (1965) has been published in English (1972). In 1957 he was named a 'People's Artist of the USSR'. SG

Towse, John Ranken (1845–1933) American drama critic. Born in England and educated at Cambridge, Towse came to New York in 1869 as a reporter for the *Evening Post*. In 1874 he was given the drama desk, a position he held until his retirement in 1927. Regarded as a scholarly and trustworthy critic, Towse fought to maintain Victorian tastes in drama, and 19th-century standards in the theatre. Like his contemporaries, **William Winter** and **Henry Austin Clapp**, he could not accept realism, especially the plays of **Ibsen**. His book, *Sixty Years of the Theatre* (1916), provides a detailed account and analysis of 19th-century actors. TLM

Toy theatre Otherwise known as Juvenile Drama, toy theatre originated in early 19th-century London with the full-length coloured theatrical portraits of Robert Dighton. Possibly influenced by engraved pages of characters and scenery for the use of provincial managers issued by a French concern in 1806, sheets of characters from current London productions, 'a penny plain and tuppence coloured', began to appear. In line with earlier cut-out story books and turn-up harlequinades, sets of sheets providing all the major poses, scenery and properties, along with a book of words, enabled children to recreate the stage of their time. The images were cut out, pasted on cardboard, mounted on wire slides, and manipulated in miniature wooden playhouses, lit by candles or small oil-wicks. Often the characters' costumes would be ornamented with gilt and tinsel. The early sheets are of great historical importance, preserving the look of Regency melodrama, operetta and pantomime; the most popular and frequently reprinted plays were M. G. Lewis's *Timour*

A typical tuppence-coloured toy theatre sheet, representing the leading characters in a Victorian harlequinade.

the Tartar (1811), an equestrian spectacle, and Isaac Pocock's *The Miller and his Men* (1813), with its climactic explosion of gunpowder stores. Since the publishers were highly conservative, these were copied again and again, lending what had once been authentic an aura of quaintness: **W. S. Gilbert** clothed the buccaneers in the first production of *The Pirates of Penzance* (1880) in garb appropriate to the toy theatres of the audience's childhood.

The leading publishers, beginning in 1811, were William West, J. K. Green, J. H. Jameson, and Hodgson and Co.; they were followed by Martin Skelt, W. G. Webb, Green's successor J. Redington, and Redington's son-in-law Benjamin Pollock. Germany was a late starter in the 1830s, but by mid-century dominated the English market with elegant sets, based on fairy-tales and operas, designed by Trentsensky of Vienna. France, Spain and Denmark also produced toy theatres, but their repertory was not drawn from actual stage productions; the USA, with Seltz's American Boy's Theatre, was content to copy English models. A minor artistic revival of the form took place in the early 20th century with plays written and/or illustrated by Jack Yeats and Albert Rutherston. Alan Leen and George Speaight revived Pollock's business, and under Marguerite Fawdry, it became the Toy Museum in Monmouth St, then in Scala St, and presently maintains a shop in Covent Garden. LS

See: G. Speaight, *The History of the English Toy Theatre*, London, 1969.

Tracy, Lee (1898–1968) A commercially successful American actor for over 50 years, Tracy, noted for his exuberance and excitement on stage, is best remembered for his Roy Lane, the hoofer in *Broadway* (1926), and Hildy Johnson, the newspaperman in *The Front*

Page (1928). From his New York debut in *The Show-Off* to his last major role as the ex-President in *The Best Man* (1960), he appeared in a steady stream of forgettable plays, although his London debut as Harry Van in *Idiot's Delight* (1938) and his Australian debut as Queeg in *The Caine Mutiny Court Martial* (1955) are noteworthy. DBW

Tragedy Almost every culture offers an audience pleasure – paradoxically – through an art based on human suffering. In Western culture a significant form of such art is tragedy, a word whose meaning changes with time and place of text or performance. Through the centuries, too, the very word 'tragedy' has acquired a valorizing resonance, which is unique for an art form. Ancient and modern critics have contrasted tragedy with comedy; and more recently with melodrama. Early critics – pre-eminently **Aristotle** – focused on tragic action, whereas recent critics dwell on tragic vision. After centuries of commentary on Greek elements of tragedy, more recent approaches have shifted to abstruse semiotics and ideological codes of tragedy.

Tragedy (*tragōidia*) means goat-song, but there is no caproic trace in what we know of Greek tragedy. Performed annually to celebrate the god Dionysus, Attic tragedy of the 5th century BC was based on Greek myth. Formally, each tragedy was a verse exchange between a chorus and a small number of actors (usually three). The episodes of the plot were punctuated by choral songs, and the ending was not necessarily unhappy. Of the three Greek tragic playwrights whose works are extant, only **Aeschylus** wrote tetralogies, i.e. three sequential tragedies followed by a satyr play. Between Aeschylus and **Euripides** the scope of tragedy narrowed from cosmic moral questions to more personal passions.

In was Aristotle in the 4th century BC who first praised tragedy as the highest form of poetry. Preferring **Sophocles** to other dramatists, and *Oedipus* to other tragedies, Aristotle began the comparative evaluation of works, which has since become a major tool of criticism. Although Aristotle was descriptive rather than prescriptive, he bequeathed to posterity terms that today elude exact definition – *hamartia* (error), *catharsis* (purgation), *mimesis* (imitation), as well as the more familiar pity and fear.

Aside from criticism, later homage to Greek tragedy was seen in imitation. Roman **Seneca** accomplished this so sensationally that his nine plays became the strongest influence upon subsequent European tragedy. To him later tragedy is indebted for the five-act structure, the violent catastrophic ending, and the clash of characters speaking *stichomythia* (under emotional stress, each character utters a line that is rhythmically matched to the one preceding it).

In the medieval dearth of theatre, tragedy came to mean the downfall of a person of high degree. During the Renaissance, this bleak fate entered the drama as *de casibus* tragedy. With the Renaissance, tragedy gained importance both in theory and practice. Italy and especially France looked back and up to the pagan classics. Senecan imitation (in Latin) began in the 14th century, but after the defeat of Constantinople in 1453, Greek tragedy gradually became the model, and a misunderstood Aristotle the rule. Thus **Giraldi**, who proclaimed the superiority of Seneca to the Greeks, in 1543 set forth the unities of time and action; Scaligero in

1561 added that of place. The architect **Serlio** in 1545 distinguished between tragic, comic, and satyric settings. Italian Renaissance tragedy, as opposed to comedy, is of only scholarly interest, and not until **Alfieri** in the 18th century did Italy produce a playable tragedy.

France took a similar path a century later, with **Mairet** in 1630 prescribing the three unities. Other dramatists voluntarily donned this straitjacket. Since **Corneille**'s *Cid* violated the unities, it gave rise to the 'Querelle du Cid', which was terminated when the French Academy laid down the rules of tragedy. Self-consciously noble, neoclassical verse tragedy with its strict decorum dominated not only French but continental drama for the next 150 years.

In England and Spain, however, popular traditions outweighed the learned, encouraging 'impure' tragedy. Although the first English tragedy *Gorboduc* is sternly regular, **Marlowe** and **Shakespeare** soon rattled the stage with their action-packed tragedies, towering protagonists, ironies, images, and final catastrophes. **Kyd**'s *Spanish Tragedy* is usually cited as the first revenge tragedy, a self-explanatory subgenre, of which *Hamlet* is the crowning achievement.

When James I succeeded Elizabeth, the tragic genre grew darker and more sceptical. Good and Bad Angels underline the moral conflict of Marlowe's *Dr Faustus*, but **Webster**, **Tourneur**, and **Chapman** question the very basis of moral judgement in tragedy. Moreover, alongside these dramas of the unfortunate mighty, a few so-called domestic tragedies dramatized the suffering of common people, and this departure from the tragic tradition was to culminate in the 18th-century *London Merchant* (**Lillo**) a source of middle-class drama throughout Europe, so that noble tragedy suffered an eclipse. Before then, however, during the court-centred theatre of the Restoration, English tragedy briefly adapted the French form into heroic tragedy, a violence-filled struggle between Love and Honour, neatly encapsulated in couplets.

With romantic bardolatry, tragedy returned loquaciously but untheatrically to literature, since almost every romantic poet of every European country tried his (left) hand at verse tragedy. Along with these efforts came a resurgence of theory, in the works of the **Schlegel** brothers, **Lessing**, and **Hugo**'s preface to his *Cromwell*, with its blatant rejection of decorum. During the same period the philosopher Hegel enunciated his view of tragedy as 'the collision of equally justified ethical claims'. Towards the end of the 19th century, **Nietzsche** rejected a moral approach to tragedy, and instead he praised the Dionysian irrational element that paralleled the spirit of music. Realists refused to limit tragedy to privileged protagonists, and the director **Antoine** found nothing incompatible between realism and tragedy, while **Strindberg** called his *Miss Julie* 'a naturalistic tragedy'. Whether or not they were preoccupied with genre, several modern playwrights have been labelled tragic – **Ibsen**, **Chekhov**, **O'Neill**, **Lorca**, **Beckett**.

In the voluminous 20th-century literature on tragedy, two major questions recur: (i) Is tragedy possible in our anarchic age that lacks a community of belief? (ii) Is the ordinary individual a fitting subject for tragedy in our democratic age? Perhaps the most resounding negative reply to the first question is George Steiner's *Death of Tragedy*, whereas **Arthur Miller** has uttered as resounding an affirmative answer to the second question. Although contemporary dramatists may care little about genre designations for their plays, tragedy is still of deep concern to many contemporary critics – not only those of drama.   RC

Tragicomedy The word conjures a mixture of sadness and merriment, but the genre has meant different mixtures at different periods in the Western theatre. The word was coined by **Plautus** in the Prologue to his *Amphitryon*; spoken by the god Mercury, it high-handedly designates a new genre in which kings (who frequent tragedy) mix with slaves (who frequent comedy). Another fissure of classical decorum had earlier been noted by **Aristotle**, in the happy endings of several tragedies by **Euripides** (seven extant to our time), but these plays were not called tragicomedies until the Renaissance, when Italian playwrights turned critics to justify their practice.

From late classical to late medieval times, genre terminology was loose, and we cannot recapture today the meaning of such sporadic labels as *tragicomoedia*, *comoedotragoedia*, and *comoedia tragica*. Often unlabelled, popular drama mixed the funny and the sad, the common and the divine. The seriocomic *Second Shepherd's Play* was contemporary with Latin school plays of serious main plot and comic subplot. These different mixtures – neoclassical and popular – flourished indiscriminately in the playing spaces of England, France, and the Low Countries, but Italian playwright–critics tried to systematize the amorphous practice. **Giraldi Cinzio** spurned the word tragicomedy for his tragedies with happy endings, preferring 'mixed tragedy'. It was, however, **Guarini** whose pastoral tragicomedy *Il Pastor Fido* (1590) and critical defence *Compendio della Poesia Tragicomica* (1601) raised a lively little storm. As playwrights, both men evolved labyrinthine plots that twisted their way to a happy and romantic ending, but those of Cinzio were solemn, whereas Guarini sounded an occasional comic note in such figures as a satyr. Both playwrights voluminously defended their respective practices, citing a host of classical authorities to justify the breach of classical decorum. The genre proved eminently exportable, and in the early 17th century tragicomedy (for the most part removed to court from pasture) bloomed happily in England, France, and Spain, counting among its practitioners **Fletcher**, **Shakespeare**, **Heywood**, **Marston**, **Massinger**, **Shirley**; **Garnier**, **Hardy**, **Mairet**, **Corneille**, **Rotrou**; **Lope de Vega**, **Tirso de Molina**, and **Zorrilla**.

Renaissance tragicomedy, in verse form, was set exotically, plotted suspensefully, and resolved satisfactorily; as the 17th century rolled on, the violent action of tragicomedy departed more and more from the inner thrust of tragedy, while more or less comic elements provided entertaining distraction. Although lacklustre dramatists tried to prolong its life into the 18th century, prose popular theatre soon displaced it. The ghost of tragicomedy nevertheless infiltrated into Gothic melodrama of the 19th century.

Modern tragicomedy derives from a minor attribute of the Renaissance variety–comic elements in the basically serious action. There is, however, no clean lineage; there rarely is in theatre. If one seeks a history of a merry–melancholy genre, much depends on the mixture. Almost all English Renaissance tragedies have a comic component, but the mixture became programmatic in the romantic movements of France and Germany. Melodrama, the mass medium of the time, thrived on a comic character who helped the hero defeat the villain. Throughout the 19th century, English verse drama tended toward solemnity, and perhaps for that reason rarely reached a theatre, but in prose and verse, comic notes sound increasingly loud in plays by Germans **Lenz**, **Grabbe**, **Büchner**, and even **Kleist**.

With the advent of realism in the late 19th century, classical genre designations were all but forgotten, and most serious plays supported a comic component, without reducing it formulaically, as in melodrama. **Shaw** recognized: 'Ibsen was the dramatic poet who firmly established tragicomedy as a much deeper and grimmer entertainment than tragedy.' Although neither Shaw nor Ibsen (who designated *The Wild Duck* as tragicomedy) defines the modern genre, it overlaps with such terms as irony, humorism, the grotesque, and the absurd. Ironists and humorists tend to dramatize contradictions within a realistic world, whereas playwrights of the grotesque and the absurd tend to disorientate the spectator to the frontier of fantasy. Ibsen, **Strindberg**, Shaw, **Chekhov**, and **Pirandello** are masters of the first group; the second is larger, embracing the Spaniards **Valle-Inclán**, **Lorca**, and **Arrabal**; Flemish **Ghelderode** and Rumanian Tzara; Swiss **Dürrenmatt** and **Frisch**; and most prolifically the Paris-centred playwrights of the 1950s, **Adamov**, **Beckett**, **Genet**, **Ionesco** and Pinget. Dürrenmatt and Ionesco have reverted to the Italian Renaissance habit of rationalizing their practice with theory of tragicomedy, but the critic **Eric Bentley** in *Life of the Drama* most instructively classifies modern tragicomedy into (i) tragedy transcended (as opposed to Renaissance 'tragedy averted'), for example Strindberg's *Dream Play*; and (ii) comedy with an unhappy or indeterminate ending, for example Beckett's *Waiting for Godot*. Contemporary dramatists tend to express their tragic vision with comic devices, creating tragicomedy that is funny without being foolish, serious without being solemn.   RC

Travers, Ben (1886–1980) British dramatist and novelist, who made his reputation with the ten 'Aldwych farces', a label given to his plays because they occupied the stage of the Aldwych Theatre continuously from *A Cuckoo in the Nest* (1925), *Rookery Nook* (1926) and *Thark* (1927), to *Dirty Work* (1932) and *A Bit of a Test* (1933). Combining absurdly improbable situations, eccentric characters and broad humour with social satire, his work has stood the test of time well. Film versions, for which he provided the scripts, have helped to spread its popularity, and in 1970 he adapted seven of his farces for television. In 1976 there were three of his plays on the London stage: a revival of *Plunder* (1928) at the **National Theatre**; a revival of one of his later farces *Banana Ridge* (1938) with **Robert Morley**; and his last play *The Bed Before Yesterday*, which opened in 1975 with **Joan Plowright** as an outspoken middle-aged woman who belatedly discovers the joy of sex. His autobiographies, *Vale of Laughter* (1957) and *A-Sitting on a Gate* (1978), provide many insights into the technical craft of farce.   CI

Traverse Theatre, Edinburgh Britain's first Studio Theatre, the Traverse (so called because its audiences were seated either side of the stage) was started in 1963 with the aim of providing an experimental theatre club offering creative opportunities for theatre artists the whole year round and not merely during the **Edinburgh Festival**. Its founder was Jim Haynes, an American director who subsequently went on to start the Arts Lab in London. His policy was to present new plays and explore new styles of performance and in the early years he was responsible for introducing to the British stage many of the plays of such international writers as **Arrabal**, **Mrożek**, **Weiss**, **Kroetz**, Bellow and **Shepard**, and quickly established a reputation for commissioning new work from British playwrights. This policy remains central to the club's work. In 1969 the club moved to new premises and now operates two auditoria, one seating 100 and the other 70. New work recently premiered at the Traverse includes Jimmy Boyle's and Tom McGrath's *The Hardman*, Clare Luckham's *Trafford Tanzi*, C. P. Taylor's *Bread and Butter* and **Steven Berkoff**'s *East*.   AJ

Travesty role (sometimes called 'trouser role' or 'pants part') A male character in opera written for and sung by a woman's voice. It is to be distinguished from male parts originally written for castrati but nowadays sometimes sung by women. The currently most frequently heard travesty roles are Siebel in *Faust* (1859) by Charles Gounod (1818–93), Nicklaus in *Tales of Hoffmann* (1881) by Jacques Offenbach (1819–80), Prince Orlofsky in *Die Fledermaus* (1874) by Johann Strauss II (1825–99), Octavian in *Der Rosenkavalier* (1911) and the Composer in *Ariadne auf Naxos* (1916) both by Richard Strauss (1864–1949).   GH

Tree, Herbert (Draper) Beerbohm (1853–1917) English actor and theatre manager, the half brother of Max Beerbohm. He made his professional debut, against stern parental opposition, in 1878. His first success was as the Rev. Robert Spalding in Charles Hawtrey's *The Private Secretary* (1884), a farce whose popularity went unchallenged until the appearance of *Charley's Aunt* (1892). Acting on his own principle that 'everything comes to him who doesn't wait', Tree entered into management in 1887, briefly at the Comedy Theatre and then at the **Haymarket** (1887–96). The authority gave new scope to his flair for showmanship. Tree was no more a literary purist than **Irving**. He liked plays with plenty of action and knew the value of a dash of scandal. **Henry Arthur Jones**'s *The Dancing Girl* (1891), **Wilde**'s *A Woman of No Importance* (1893) and a matinée production of the still-shocking **Ibsen**'s *An Enemy of the People* (1893) all endowed Tree's Haymarket with one or the other. His *Hamlet* (1892) was probably mistaken and anyway belittled by **W. S. Gilbert**'s widely quoted view that it was 'funny without being vulgar'. (No one broadcast the comment more than Tree.) But the outstanding Haymarket productions were the last two, Paul Potter's dramatization of *Trilby* (1895), with Tree as Svengali, and *Henry IV, Part 1* (1896), with Tree as Falstaff. He was one of the great makeup artists – like Irving before him – and a shameless dominator of the stage. His larger-than-life personality dominated and became identified with **His Majesty's Theatre**, of which he was manager from 1897–1915. He had planned the theatre himself, from foyer to private penthouse, and, with 14 productions during his tenure, he earned for it a reputation as the home of lavish Shakespearian productions, the last surviving monument of pictorial Shakespeare. The repertoire contained little else of note. It was at His Majesty's that the stock of **Stephen Phillips** rose (*Herod*, 1900; *Ulysses*, 1902) and fell (*Nero*, 1906), that Tree created in Fagin another of his great costume-roles (1905) and, supremely, that **Shaw**'s *Pygmalion* (1914) opened, with Tree as Henry Higgins partly obliterated by **Mrs Patrick Campbell**'s Eliza Doolittle. An Edwardian, even during the reign of Victoria, Tree was a witty and humane man, whose commitment to the theatre was rarely untouched by humour. Despite his major role in the foundation of the Royal Academy of Dramatic Art (1904), he was less a student of acting than a brilliant opportunist. He was knighted in 1907.   PT

Tremblay, Michel (1942–) French Canadian playwright and novelist. He first achieved national prominence with *Les Belles-soeurs* (*The Sisters-in-Law*) in 1968, transposing to the stage the profound frustrations of Montreal's urban proletariat of which he is himself a product. In this play, set in one tawdry flat, his characters, all female, express their individual and collective despair in pure *joual*, the impoverished popular idiom of Quebec (the word itself is symbolic, a deformation of Standard French *cheval*: 'horse'). Yet this stark setting and starker language are infused with great poetic feeling, enhanced by stylized monologues and choreographed choruses which transform a seemingly banal plot into poignant tragedy. The influence of this play has been remarkable, a whole generation of young dramatists following Tremblay's lead in the use of *joual* without, however, attaining his dramatic and poetic intensity.

In nine plays composed over the next decade he continued to portray Montreal's microcosm of social and economic despair, peopled by transvestites, homosexuals and misfits. Some characters reappear, in works such as *En Pièces Détachées* (*Broken Pieces*, 1969); *À Toi Pour Toujours, ta Marie-Lou* (*Forever Yours, Marie-Lou*, 1971); *Hosanna* (1973); *Sainte Carmen de la Main* (*Saint Carmen of Main Street*, 1976) and *Damnée Manon, Sacrée Sandra* (*Damned Manon, Holy Sandra*, 1977). Tremblay's own literary and financial success has generally been used to explain the end of this first period, underlined by his move to Outremont, an affluent section of Montreal. But the election of an independent Parti Québécois government in 1976 has also been an important factor in his personal evolution. A fervent separatist, he appears to avoid embarrassing the government which, nominally at least, represents his cause. Plays such as *L'Impromptu d'Outremont* (*The Impromptu of Outremont*, 1980) deal with middle-class concerns, and his most recent, *Albertine en Cinq Temps* (*Albertine in Five Times*, 1984), already considered by many to be his finest work, is timeless, portraying brilliantly the universal problem of ageing.

His theatre has been performed successfully in France, Belgium and Switzerland and, in translation, The Netherlands, Great Britain, the USA and Japan. Only after 1976 did he permit its performance in English in his native province. Tremblay is French Canada's outstanding dramatist to date.   LED

Tremont Theatre 76 Tremont St, Boston [Architect: Isiah Rogers]. In 1827, although they were hardly able to support the **Federal Street Theatre**, Bostonians were presented with a second theatre, a handsome and elegant edifice built through the largesse of a group of wealthy and prominent citizens. For the next 16 years, the house struggled to survive as stars were lured to its stage and an excellent stock company was assembled. It was never able to pay for itself and its managers resorted to a succession of novelties to keep it afloat. In 1835, **Charlotte Cushman** made her first appearance on stage as a singer in *The Marriage of Figaro*. In 1843, the theatre was sold to the Baptist church and transformed into the Tremont Temple. Nine years later, it burned down and was rebuilt as a church. MCH

Trenyov, Konstantin Andreevich (1876–1945) Soviet short story writer and dramatist who helped create the post-revolutionary Soviet drama. His playwriting, which began in 1907 with some **Gorky**-influenced one-act plays, only became a career with the **Moscow Art Theatre** production of *Pugachyov Times* (1924). This monumentalist play was made controversial by the author's unexpectedly harsh depiction of the popular hero of the 18th-century peasant revolt. His classic Civil War drama, *Lyubov Yarovaya* (1926), offered a gallery of clearly individuated characters on both sides of the conflict set against an epic historical backdrop. The play's titular heroine, a strong-minded schoolteacher who sacrifices her beloved White Russian husband for her Bolshevik beliefs, became a prototype for Revolutionary women in Soviet dramas (e.g., the lady commissar in **Vishnevsky**'s *An Optimistic Tragedy*). Produced at Moscow's Maly Theatre (1926) and at the Moscow Art Theatre following a Stalin-induced revision (1936), it returned to the stage in its original form after 1956. Trenyov's remaining plays were primarily anti-bourgeois satires and Soviet problem plays grounded in psychological realism. *On the Banks of the Neva* (1937), set during the Revolution, marked an early appearance by Lenin on the Soviet stage. His final play, *The Commander* (1945), about General Kutuzov, hero of the War of 1812, represented Trenyov's return to the epic historical drama. SG

Tretyakov, Sergei Mikhailovich (1892–1939) Soviet poet, journalist, translator and dramatist, best known for his post revolutionary agit-prop theatrical collaborations with **Meyerhold** and the latter's pupil Sergei Eisenstein. An ego-futurist from just before the Revolution, Tretyakov became an aggressive spokesman for utilitarian, 'factographic' (agit-prop documentary) art and constructivist design and poetics as a member of **Mayakovsky**'s journals *Lef* (1923–5) and *Novy Lef* (*New Left*, 1927–8). His first theatrical work with Eisenstein (at the Proletkult Theatre) was their 'annihilation' and 'circusization' of **Ostrovsky**'s *Enough Stupidity for Every Wise Man* (1923), staged as a 'montage of attractions' – an episodic, politically satiric revue featuring clowning, acrobatics, caricature and film clips. Eisenstein's production of Tretyakov's *Gas Masks* (1923), about a German factory revolt, was actually staged in a Moscow gas-works, an extreme example of the contemporary trend to merge the factory and the theatre. Tretyakov's *Earth Rampant* (1923), an adaptation of Marcel Martinet's play *Night*, was a laconically and episodically conceived, constructivist-designed (by **Lyubov Popova**) 'military-revolutionary action' dedicated to the Red Army and its leader Lev Trotsky on the fifth anniversary of its founding (23 February 1923). Staged by Meyerhold at his theatre on Sadovo-Triumfalnaya Street, it incorporated all of the elements of the mass spectacle – military transports and weaponry spilling out into the audience, propaganda slogans projected onto a screen (a 'machine-photo-poster'), declamatory acting and grotesque characterizations of priests, the tsar and his generals. Often performed in the open air, it played to an audience of 25,000 at the Fifth Congress of the Comintern in Moscow (June 1924), enlisting the participation of infantry and horse cavalry. *Roar, China!* (1926), a great success at Meyerhold's theatre, was based on a real incident known to Tretyakov from his 1924 stint as a lecturer in Russian literature at Peking University. Meyerhold offered a naturalistic staging of colonialist brutalization of the Chinese, humanizing the victims and caricaturing the exploiters. Its effectiveness as a propaganda vehicle led to productions throughout Europe and in New York by the **Theatre Guild** in 1930. The author's *I Want a Child* recommended socially based eugenics to achieve perfect proletarian children in Soviet society, a thesis which he sought to make more palatable by first presenting in episodic fashion the sordidness of the worker's life – a technique later employed by Mayakovsky in *The Bedbug*. Meyerhold's production (1927–30), designed by El Lissitzky (pseudonym of Lazar Markovich Lisitsky), was denied permission by Glavrepertkom (The Main Repertory Committee), which considered the play to be ahead of its time. **Brecht**, who met Tretyakov on the 1930 *Roar, China!* tour in Berlin, called him 'my teacher', found the factographic approach to be useful to his concept of epic theatre and adapted *I Want a Child* for the German stage, where it never played. Tretyakov translated Brecht's *St Joan of the Stockyards*, *The Measures Taken* and *The Mother* into Russian (1936). Arrested and executed in 1939, Tretyakov was rehabilitated in the 1960s, when the influence of his collaboration with Meyerhold could be seen in **Yuri Lyubimov**'s staging of *Ten Days that Shook the World* and in other productions at Moscow's Taganka Theatre. SG

Triana, José (1931–) Cuban playwright, studied in Santiago de Cuba, wrote poetry in Spain and returned to Cuba to espouse Revolutionary programmes. His first plays, *Medea en el espejo* (*Medea in the Mirror*, 1960) and *La muerte del ñeque* (*Death of the Strong Man*, 1963), both contain elements of classical Greek tragic figures integrated into a lower-class Cuban environment, where violence and criminality prefigure the game symbolism in his later theatre. His masterpiece and Cuba's best known play internationally is *La noche de los asesinos* (*The Night of the Assassins*, 1965), a brutal play with metatheatrical techniques that involves three adolescents in the myth, ritual and exorcism of killing their parents. No other plays appeared until Triana defected on a trip to Paris in 1980. *Ceremonial de guerra* (*War Ceremony*), written over the period 1968–73, and *Diálogo de mujeres* (*Women's Dialogue*, 1979–80) are both set in Cuba at the turn of the century. The **Royal Shakespeare Company** staged his *Worlds Apart* – a study of Cuba in the period 1894–1914 – in 1986, at Stratford.   GW

Trinidad Carnival In its 200-year history the pre-Lenten Trinidad Carnival has encompassed many theatrical forms. Essentially an annual parade of original costumes worn by bands of masked revellers, the carnival over the years acquired ancillary exhibitions of music, song, dance, mime, and the spoken word that have made it a grand theatrical spectacle and a repository of the nation's performing arts.

Carnival was brought to Spanish-held Trinidad by French colonial planters in the 1780s. Under British rule it continued to be observed by the white elite as a European-type festival, the free coloureds and black slaves having no part in it. When slavery ended in 1834, the black and coloured masses took over the festival and transformed it into an expression of their new-found freedom. Among the principal 19th-century masquerades were *canboulay* ('cannes-brûlées' or burnt canes) revellers reenacting scenes from slavery, dread stick-fighters whose music, dance, and pungent argot survive on the contemporary stage, military bands that satirized the armed forces, indigenous creatures of myth and folk-tale, and the ubiquitous calypsonian who emerged as carnival songster and public commentator. During this period repeated attempts by government to suppress the masquerade as a rowdy and indecent exhibition were strenuously resisted, sometimes with rioting and loss of life.

In the 20th century conditions slowly improved as English replaced French patois in song lyrics and the street parade gained respectability. Hierarchically structured costumed bands like the Wild Indians and Burroquites held pre-carnival meetings in backyard venues. To a growing public audience they rehearsed speeches, dances, mimes and playlets, and on carnival eve they installed the bands' royal rulers. Calypsonians, now universally recognized professional singers, gave nightly concerts which often ended with a comic sketch

Adoration of Hiroshima by Hugh Bernard, Trinidad Carnival, 1985.

that recounted in song a topical event of recent date. On carnival streets traditional maskers like the Midnight Robber harangued spectators with hair-raising encounters and threats until paid off. The Dragon Band performed an elaborate street ballet, the Pierrot Grenade gave its version of a Spelling B contest, Military Bands exhibited precise drills or made furious assaults on an imaginary enemy.

Carnival music kept pace with developments. Skin drums and wooden clappers used to accompany *canboulay* trampers and stickfighters gave way to shack-shack (gourd rattle) and bottle-and-spoon ensembles when drum beating was restricted. Then came the bamboo bands and finally the steel orchestras, made from discarded petrol drums, which have extended their musical repertoire from calypsoes to classics and have spread to countries abroad. Maskers who could afford them hired string bands and later jazz ensembles to accompany their parade, but the bamboo bands and steel orchestras were the creative response of the indigent masquerader whose meagre funds were carefully garnered to pay for his costume.

In recent years traditional performing masquerades have dwindled as newly conceived bands enrol thousands of members. Detailed ornamentation in costuming and theatrical presentation has been replaced by massed colour effects, except for competing carnival kings and queens whose costumes were so extravagantly constructed as to encumber the free movement of the mask-wearer. This trend has been effectively countered by the carnival designs of Peter Minshall who employs traditional mask-making techniques to free the performer to dance his costume. In addition

Snake Child by Roland St George, Trinidad Carnival, 1979.

Minshall has presented his masquerade bands as dramatic spectacles that pantomime contemporary concerns such as environmental pollution and nuclear war. EGH

See: B. Brereton, 'The Trinidad Carnival 1870–1900' in *Savacou*, September 1975; *Caribbean Quarterly*, Trinidad Carnival Issue, vol. 4 nos. 3 & 4, March/June 1956; E. Hill, *The Trinidad Carnival: Mandate for a National Theatre*, Austin, Texas, 1972; G. Rohlehr, 'Sparrow and the Language of Calypso' in *Savacou*, September 1970; K. Q. Warner, *Kaiso! The Trinidad Calypso: A Study of the Calypso as Oral Literature*, Washington, DC, 1982.

Trinity Square Repertory Company Founded in 1964 in Providence, Rhode Island, by a group of local citizens this ensemble has become one of the more adventurous of the regional theatres in the USA (with over 25 world premieres). Since 1965 its artistic director has been Adrian Hall, who in 1983 also assumed artistic control for the **Dallas Theatre Centre** in Texas. Before moving in 1973 into their present complex (The Lederer Theatre, a converted vaudeville/cinema house) the company performed primarily in a converted church. A federal grant in 1966 (Project Discovery) covered many of the theatre's expenses for three years, allowing it to reach true professional stature. A major grant from the National Endowment for the Arts allowed financial security for its theatre artists beginning with the 1985–6 season. A varied bill of approximately 12 productions is staged annually in two theatres. In 1978 a training programme for actors, directors, and playwrights was initiated, and in 1986 'Square' was removed from the theatre's name. DBW

Trissino, Gian Giorgio (1478–1550) Italian dramatist, academician and literary theorist. His two plays, the tragedy *Sofonisba* (1514–15) and the comedy *I Simillimi* (1548), written under strong classical influence, were highly regarded in their day, especially the former which was widely imitated. **Riccoboni** tried unsuccessfully to revive Italian interest in tragedy by staging the play in Venice in 1713. He was an active patron of the architect **Palladio**. LR

Tristan l'Hermite, François (c. 1601–55) French poet and dramatist. His first, and perhaps best, play, a tragedy entitled *La Mariane* on the subject of Herod's jealous love for his doomed wife, was performed with great success at the **Marais** only months before *Le Cid* and many contemporaries considered him to be **Corneille**'s equal at least; it remained in the repertoire until the end of the century. His later work, which included several tragedies, notably *La Mort de Sénèque* (*The Death of Seneca*, 1644), one of the plays staged by **Molière**'s ill-fated Illustre-Théâtre, a tragicomedy, a pastoral and an entertaining comedy, *Le Parasite* (1654), was also well received and he was elected to the Académie-Française in 1649. Of late a renewal of interest in his plays has led to several revivals. DR

Trotter, Catharine (1679–1749) English playwright. Highly educated and precocious, her first poems and novels were published in 1693 when she was 14. Her first play, *Agnes de Castro*, a romantic tragedy with an unusually classical style and centred on a pathetic heroine, was performed two years later. She

was mocked with **Mrs Pix** and Mrs Manley in *The Female Wits* in 1696. By this time she was admired by **Dryden** and **Congreve**. Her plays, mostly 'she-tragedies' with a distressed heroine, were often revised with help from Congreve. In 1700 she became a friend of Bishop Burnet and John Locke, publishing a pamphlet defending Locke's *Essay on Human Understanding* in 1703. Her marriage to a clergyman in 1708 ended her career as a playwright. PH

Tsegaye Gebre-Medhin (1936–) Ethiopian playwright. Graduated in law in the United States but worked in theatre in Britain and France. In 1960 he was appointed director of the Haile Selassie I Theatre in Addis Ababa, where many of his plays were staged. Their realism and oblique criticism of the feudal regime led to frequent imprisonment and ultimate dismissal. After the revolution he established himself as Ethiopia's foremost playwright, with many translations and original plays in Amharic, including *The Future Man* (first performed before the revolution in 1964), *ABC in Six ·Months* (an inspiring revolutionary drama performed in the year of the revolution), *Otello* (1982) and *Tewodros* (an epic about the emperor defeated by the British at the battle of Mekdela, performed in 1983). Two of his plays in English have been published – *Oda Oak Oracle* and *Collision of Altars*. His work is characterized by strong nationalism and the inventive power and at times difficulty of his Amharic dialogue. RK

Tsodzo, Thompson (1947–) Zimbabwean playwright, novelist and educational writer. Formerly a teacher, he joined the government at independence. Many of his plays in Shona have been televised. He also produced *The Storm* in 1982 with S. Chikwendere, commemorating Zimbabwe's struggle for independence. His published plays include *The Talking Calabash* (1976), *Tsano* (*The Brother-in-law*, 1982) and *Shanduko* (*Changes*, 1983). His focus is generally moralistic though *The Storm* and *Shanduko* show an interest in modern political developments in Zimbabwe. RK

Tucker, Sophie (Sophia Kalish) (1884–1966) American vaudeville singer, born in Russia; known as 'The Last of the Red-Hot Mammas'. She made her professional debut at the 116th St Music Hall, New York, in 1906 in blackface and won a reputation as a 'Coon Shouter', singing ragtime melodies. A brief moment in the 1909 *Ziegfeld Follies* (from which she was ejected when Nora Bayes found the competition too daunting) was followed by stardom in vaudeville, where she capitalized on her girth and her innuendo in such songs as 'He Hasn't Up to Yesterday, but I Guess He Will To-night'. In 1911 she introduced 'Some of These Days', which became her theme song. She moved easily from ragtime to jazz, made a huge success in England beginning in 1922, appeared in the musicals *Leave It to Me* (1938) and *High Kickers* (1941), and helped in organizing vaudevillians into the short-lived American Federation of Actors, which she served as President in 1938. LS

Tukak Theatre Founded in 1975 under the guidance of Norwegian actor–director Reidar Nilsson, this experimental theatre company is based in the remote village of Fjaltring on the north-west coast of Jutland,

Tukak Theatre, Denmark, in *Man and the Mask*.

Denmark. Its early identity grew primarily from its training of Greenlandic actors and its attempt to rediscover and adapt to the modern theatre (without falling into a nostalgic folklorism) the lost para-theatrical forms (including drum-dances, masks and story-telling) of Inuit Greenland before its colonization by Denmark. By the early 1980s, partly as a result of its successful international tours, it had broadened into an international theatre of and for native peoples in general, including North-American Indians and Inuit. By the mid-1980s, ex-company-members were involved in establishing the first permanent theatre-company in the Greenlandic capital Nuuk. Among Tukak's major productions have been *Inuit*, *Tupilak*, *Man and the Mask* and *Sinnattoq*. In 1980 the company participated in the founding of the Indigenous People's Theatre Association.   HL   AEG

Tunisia see **French-speaking North Africa**; **Middle East**

Turgenev, Ivan Sergeevich (1818–83) Russian writer and dramatist, whose subtle, lyrical character studies shifted narrative focus to internal action and helped pave the way for **Chekhov**'s psychological realism. A liberal and a Westernizer, Turgenev absorbed the romantic idealism of the 1840s without embracing its radicalism. Personal reticence and melancholia, conditioned by a sadistic mother, made him vulnerable to the exaltation produced by art and love and simultaneously prepared him for disillusionment. His narrative, *The Diary of a Superfluous Man* (1850), defined this as the characteristic literary type of his generation and one whose forebears he described in

an essay 'Hamlet and Don Quixote' (1860). While his gentility, his 'female genius', made him suspect among his politically committed contemporaries – Belinsky, Bakunin and Stankevich were early friends – his anti-serfdom stance and harsh criticism of the nobility and other classes made him unpopular with the Russian censor. With the publication of his great novel *Fathers and Sons* (1862), which alienated Slavophiles and Westernizers alike, Turgenev went into more or less permanent exile in France. He became the first Russian writer to find a large Western following for his work. Although he considered himself to be primarily a novelist, Turgenev came to drama first, writing a total of ten plays. His early efforts are Gogolian satires, genre parodies and vaudevilles of no real distinction. A number of them, including *The Charity Case* (1845), *Where It's Thin, There It Breaks* (1847), *The Bachelor* (1849) and *The Provincial Lady* (1850), were written with his friend and **Gogol**'s favourite comic actor **Shchepkin** in mind. They feature the 'insulted and injured' little man in whom are mingled the humour and pathos that were the actor's strong suit. His best play, the classic *A Month in the Country* (1850), is perhaps unfairly undervalued in relation to Chekhov's work which it clearly foreshadows in the following ways: conversational misdirection, leisurely pacing, verbal and visual counterpoint half-revealing an inner action; this inner focus creating a sense of *ennui* and uneventfulness centred around a single or series of nonevents; an oppressive rural environment in which an ineffectual ensemble enacts a tangled roundelay, energy is contrasted with enervation and change waits on the periphery.   SG

Turkey see **Middle East**

Turlupin (Henri Le Grand) see **Turlupinades**

Turlupinades Farces played at the **Hôtel de Bourgogne**, Paris, from 1618 to about 1630 by a famous trio of comedians. **Gros-Guillaume** (Robert Guérin, c. 1554–1635), allegedly a former baker's boy, was round and fat, in white garments and a red cap, his belly cinctured with two belts to suggest a barrel, his face powdered with flour. He played a foul-mouthed, good-natured drunkard, and occasionally a corpulent harridan. **Gaultier-Garguille** (Hugues Guéru, d. 1633) was said to be the son-in-law of **Tabarin**; his character was a modified Pantalone in black and red: tall, scrawny, with a pointed beard, lens-less spectacles and slippers. Although he published a collection of licentious songs (1632), he was praised as the first actor to lead a relatively thrifty and ordered private life. **Turlupin** (Henri Le Grand, c. 1587–1637) may have begun in fairbooths; a witty and malicious improviser, he wore a brick-red beard and a striped costume like Brighella's. All three played high comedy as well, Gros-Guillaume as Lafleur, Gaultier-Garguille as Fléchelles and Turlupin as Belleville. Legend has them renting a small tennis court at the Porte St-Jacques to give performances for school-boys; when the actors of the Hôtel de Bourgogne protested to **Cardinal Richelieu**, he was so delighted by the scene of an unfaithful wife pleading not to be killed that he enrolled the comedians in the official acting troupe. Dates do not support this: Gaultier-Garguille joined the Hôtel de

Bourgogne in 1606 and teamed with Gros-Guillaume only from 1612, Turlupin from 1618.   LS

Tussaud, Madame (Marie Grosholtz) see **Wax-works**

Tutin, Dorothy (1931–) British actress, who began her stage career in 1950. She joined the Shakespeare Memorial Theatre at Stratford in 1958 and on their subsequent tour of Russia, played Ophelia, Viola and Juliet. Her first major appearance in a contemporary play came in 1961, when she played the tormented Sister Jeanne in **John Whiting**'s *The Devils* at the Aldwych Theatre; and she stayed with the **Royal Shakespeare Company** to play Desdemona, Varya in *The Cherry Orchard*, Polly Peachum in *The Beggar's Opera* and in **John Barton**'s Shakespearian anthology on kingship, *The Hollow Crown*. This grounding in classical theatre helped her in her first major West End success, as Queen Victoria in *Portrait of a Queen* (1965), which went to New York in 1968; and her cool, controlled timing was a memorable feature of **Harold Pinter**'s *Old Times* at the Aldwych in 1971. As Lady Plyant in *The Double Dealer* (1978), she won the Society of West End Theatres Award, one of several roles played at the National Theatre in the late 1970s, including Madam Ranevsky in *The Cherry Orchard*. She played Hester in a revival of **Terence Rattigan**'s *The Deep Blue Sea* (1981) and appeared in the West End production of Pinter's *A Kind of Alaska* (1985). Among her film parts, she won the Variety Club of Great Britain's Film Actress Award as Sophie Breska in *Savage Messiah* and appeared in *The Shooting Party*. In 1967, she was awarded the CBE.   JE

Tyler, George Crouse (1867–1946) American manager and producer. Born in Ohio, Tyler managed his first theatre in Chillicothe at the age of 20. Afterwards, he moved to New York and worked as a dramatic reporter, advance agent, and producer. In 1897, he joined forces with Theodore A. Liebler to found Liebler and Company, which for the next 17 years produced some 300 plays; brought to America **Mrs Patrick Campbell**, **Eleonora Duse**, Madam **Réjane**, and the **Abbey Theatre**; and managed stars such as **Arnold Daly**, **James O'Neill** and **Gertrude Elliott**. After the firm failed in 1915, Tyler was associated with Klaw and Erlanger until he became an independent producer in 1918. His best known presentations include: **Booth Tarkington**'s *Clarence* (1919), **Eugene O'Neill**'s *Anna Christie* (1921), **Kaufman** and **Connelly**'s *Dulcy* (1921), and **O'Casey**'s *The Plough*

and the Stars (1927). His revival of *Macbeth* in 1928 was designed by **Gordon Craig**. Tyler is noted for bringing European talent to the United States, and for preferring new works to revivals.   TLM

Tyler, Royall (1758–1826) American playwright, author of *The Contrast* (1787), the first script by an American to receive a successful professional production. Born in Boston and educated at Harvard, Tyler showed some early literary talent and wrote *The Contrast* in three weeks after seeing his first stage production, a New York production of *The School for Scandal*. The script contrasts the effete world of fashion and the more manly types of Americans. The character Jonathan, a low comedy role played by **Wignell**, introduced the Yankee character to the American stage. Most of the script, which is seldom done today, consists of two-character scenes, and the plot is less than noteworthy, but the humour and dialogue are lively and original.   SMA

Tynan, Kenneth (Peacock) (1927–80) British theatre critic and literary adviser to the **National Theatre** (1963–9). After a flamboyant university career at Oxford, he briefly became the director of the Lichfield Repertory Company and an actor who appeared as First Player in *Hamlet* (1951) in which **Alec Guinness** played the Prince. He turned to journalism where his wit and unorthodox left-wing views made a powerful impression in the *Evening Standard* and, from 1954 to 1958, the *Observer*, where his theatre columns were outstanding. His liveliest journalism dates from this period, although he also wrote eloquently for the *New Yorker* (1958–60), the *Observer* again (1960–3) and as a freelance commentator until his death. **Laurence Olivier** invited him to join the National Theatre in 1963, when it was formed, and Tynan's influence was felt in the radical tone of the early seasons. He was an advocate of **Brecht** and **Beckett**, although he underrated the talents of **Harold Pinter**. He championed **Hochhuth**'s *Soldiers*, to the annoyance of Lord Chandos, then Chairman of the National Theatre's Board of Governors, for the play attacked Churchill, a friend and wartime colleague of Chandos. From then on, his place at the National Theatre was insecure and, after co-producing *Soldiers* in the West End in 1968, he brought together an evening of 'elegant erotica', *Oh, Calcutta!*, the first and most successful sex revue which came in the wake of the abolition of censorship in 1968. He published several essay and review collections, including *He That Plays the King* (1950), *Curtains* (1961) and *The Sound of Two Hands Clapping* (1975).   JE

U

Überbrettl see **Cabaret**

Udall, Nicholas (1505–56) English playwright, the
most famous of whose plays is *Ralph Roister Doister*, a
comedy about the amorous manoeuvrings of its
broadly drawn characters, with the robustness of the
comedies of **Terence** and **Plautus** which it imitated
and adapted to a truly English context. Udall wrote
other plays, but only *Ralph Roister Doister* can be
attributed to him with any certainty, and its date of
performance is not fully established. He taught at both
Eton and Westminster schools, and the play seems to
have been written for and performed by the boys at one
of these. MB

Uganda Despite the fact that Uganda is a multilingual
society there are common features in the traditions
from which recognizably Ugandan theatre is developing. Whether the culture is Bantu or Nilotic (the major
language divisions) all communities celebrate their
major occasions with dance and music in close conjunction. Both on religious and social occasions these
appear to be the natural emotional outlets. All the
community participates with lead (often solo) performers and a considerable emphasis on spontaneity.
Extempore composition within a pattern is valued.
Basic dance steps might be taught and practised (as in
Masaba circumcision dances), there is a set form for
some traditional stories, there were professional musicians and dancers at the royal courts (even a court jester
in Bunyoro) and there were travelling performers who
might be invited to weddings and other celebrations,
but here too individual improvisation was seen as a
mark of excellence. Story-telling was a family rather
than a marketplace entertainment and, while providing
a store of traditional material, remained a pre-theatre
form.

After 1877 Christian missionaries established
schools, and it was schools and colleges that saw the
first rehearsed performances in which spoken communication was an important feature, and for which there
was a specific audience. Side by side with 'set' plays in
English, improvised vernacular farces were popular
with students and parents, and in Community Centres
the development of musical dialogue between soloist
and chorus with vivid dance-type gesture marks the
beginnings of a form which combines dance drama and
musical play. While expatriate teachers were encouraging knowledge of Western drama, Mukono Theological College used a method which has proved more
creative. Taking the well-known Bible stories plays
were drawn from the imaginations of the students

working in their mother tongue: the most notable was
Were You There? (1949).

All forms of theatre have been encouraged since 1946
by organized competitions within and between youth
groups, schools, colleges, and at national level. At first,
drama was separated from other forms of theatre but
increasingly they have come together. Almost all the
known writers first reached the public in festivals. The
majority are graduates of Makerere University which
served all East Africa until the breakup of the East
African Community. Its Department of Literature not
only produced plays and encouraged writing, but
began a diploma in drama course which has become a
full Department of Music, Dance and Drama, offering
degree and postgraduate courses. Fifty per cent of the
one-year Creative Writing Fellows have been playwrights, and include **Serumaga**, Ruganda, Zirimu and
Kawadwa. Nonetheless theatre arts have remained
largely amateur activities despite attempts to establish a
national choir and theatre company. There has been a
national dance troupe and the most successful inter-
cultural training has been in dance and music.

The National Theatre building in Kampala was built
in 1959, before independence, and in its first five years
was used largely by expatriate groups. Stimulated by
radio serials and, after 1962, TV, a local audience began
to grow and by 1966 more local than expatriate groups
were performing, two landmarks on the way being the
premieres of *The Black Hermit* by **Ngugi wa Thiong'o**
(1962), the first full-length play by an East African in
English, and *Gwosussa Emwani* by Wycliffe Kiyingi-
Kagwe (1963), the first full-length Luganda play produced and acted entirely by Ugandans. The number of
original plays presented now became impressive,
although the increasing domination of one language
has led to the accusation that it is a regional rather than a
national theatre. There is now a taste for theatre
entertainment country-wide. Most major secondary
schools have an appropriate venue and until the fighting of the recent troubled years community centres
were increasingly catering for the performing arts.
Lack of maintenance and looting present problems but
Uganda is blessed with an equable climate and all that is
needed is an open space. In many parts a natural hill
amphitheatre is easily provided and travelling shows,
despite the prohibitive transport costs, perform to full
houses everywhere. The first travelling theatre came
from Makerere in 1965 and now all reputable groups
aim to tour annually. The standard of performance
varies and there is insufficient two-way traffic, more
Kampala groups going out than outside groups visiting
Kampala. There is a danger of inbreeding which the
strong satirical element in most theatre forms may

counter. Dance drama is increasingly popular since it solves the language problem. There is a large audience for farce, a safe form in periods of political oppression and encouraged by TV serials about office immorality, nagging wives, drunken husbands and trickery. Many presentations are scrappily scripted and ephemeral. Rivalry and fear of plagiarism, as well as the cost and difficulty of publication, bedevil literary developments, but there is no closet drama, all playwrights writing for performance, sometimes working through to a final script via group improvisation, including Elvania Zirimu, Nuwa Sentongo and Robert Serumaga. Byron Kawadwa and Wycliffe Kiyingi-Kagwe, by far the most popular dramatists, write in Luganda. Robert Serumaga attracted limited and 'intellectual' audiences in Uganda although he is probably the best-known theatre man overseas, but he saw the way forward to a theatre form dependent on movement, sound, music and dance rather than words, which is still taking shape. John Ruganda's influence in Uganda has been limited since he left the country although *The Burdens* is an examination text and therefore performed when not censored. Elvania Zirimu, herself a gifted actress and producer as well as lecturer in Theatre Arts, formed and led the Ngoma Players, and was a wider influence than her limited number of published plays suggests. Popular since 1980 are the comedies of Cliff Lubwa p'Chong, a lecturer at the National Teachers' College. The raising of standards of composition and performance in general is delayed by the proliferation of amateur groups exploiting the amazing but largely unselective taste for theatre entertainment in Kampala; but original and vigorous work is appearing, especially in Dance Drama and Musical Satire.   MMAC

See: M. Banham and C. Wake, *African Theatre Today*, London, 1976; D. Cook, *In Black and White*, EALB, Nairobi, 1976; D. Duerden and C. Pieterse, *African Writers Talking*, Heinemann, 1972; E. Jones, *African Literature Today, No. 8*, Heinemann, 1976; A. Roscoe, *Uhuru's Fire*, Cambridge, 1977.

Ulric, Lenore (1892–1970) American actress. Like **Blanche Bates**, **David Warfield**, and **Mrs Leslie Carter**, Lenore Ulric was a **David Belasco** creation. From her debut in 1916 as an Indian maiden in *The Heart of Wetona*, Belasco cast her as a temptress in a series of exotic pot-boilers. In *The Son-Daughter* (1919) she was a Chinese siren, in *Kiki* (1921) a Parisian chorus girl, in *Lulu Belle* (1925) a Harlem whore and in *Mima* (1928) a slinky mannikin. Raven-haired, with large dark eyes in an oval face, Ulric made a beguiling twenties vamp, sultry and sharp-tongued, voluptuous and swivel-hipped. She received good notices even when the primitive, scenically spectacular Belasco vehicles she starred in were critical howlers.   FH

Ulster Literary Theatre (1902–34, from 1915 the Ulster Theatre) Founded with no encouragement from **Yeats**, by Bulmer Hobson and David Parkhill (Lewis Purcell), both of whom contributed some plays. It proposed to enunciate a regional identity, a variant of the **Abbey**'s work, often in good-humoured satire. The company toured England and Ireland and gave the premieres of some 50 Northern Irish plays. Apart from

Rutherford Mayne, it cultivated no important dramatist and remained amateur to the end, though working to professional standards. Its demise was finally due to the lack of either private or government financing.   DM

Uncle Tom's Cabin No American play has had such a remarkable stage history. Mrs Stowe's novel was published in March 1852 (after its serialization), the first dramatization was performed in Baltimore in January 1852, the second in New York in August, and the third, by **George L. Aiken** (now the accepted version), with the **Howard family** in Troy, New York, in September. The Howards made a life's work of 'Tomming', as did a host of American actors.

'Tom' shows under canvas were on the road in 1854, in 1879 the *Dramatic Mirror* listed the routes of 49 companies, in 1893 a national exchange for 'Tom' actors opened in Chicago, in the 90s some 400 troupes were barnstorming across the country, and every season companies in the major cities called in the hounds to pursue Eliza across the Ohio River, a spectacle not included in the novel. Theatrical novelty became the 'Tommer's' stock-in-trade. In 1853 Captain Purdy labelled his theatre a 'Temple of Moral Drama', to accommodate strait-laced Puritans. Bloodhounds, 'Jubilee Singers', and dioramas became featured attractions; some troupes carried as few as three actors. In 1901 **William Brady**'s production dwarfed its predecessors with 200 buck-and-wing dancers and singers plus a transformation sequence of 21 scenes. A dozen companies were still on the road in 1927, and in 1933 a Players Club revival featured **Otis Skinner** and Fay Bainter.

In 1852 there were seven productions in London. The Howards appeared at the Marylebone in 1857, and in 1878 **Jarrett** and **Palmer**'s spectacle employed 'a hundred real American freed slaves'. Berlin saw the play in 1852 and Paris in 1853.   RN

Unibadan Masques (formerly the University of Ibadan's School of Drama Acting Company) Nigerian professional theatre company, subsidized by the University of Ibadan. It has encouraged the development of Nigerian theatre by giving professional performances of new Nigerian plays, and by linking these to detailed research of traditional performance, epitomised in Wale Ogunyemi's total theatre plays. Founded in 1967 as part of the School of Drama in the University, the first director, Geoffrey Axworthy, was succeeded by **Wole Soyinka** who could not take up his appointment because he had been detained without trial in the Civil War. On his instructions, Dexter Lyndersay, with the help of tutors in the School of Drama, set up 'the Six-Month Crash Programme of Training' which brought a company of 12 actors into being, six of whom had had training already in Soyinka's own Orisun Theatre. Even whilst training was in progress the Company performed weekly on television in the Orisun Television Series, directed by Dapo Adelugba, in order to meet some of its financial commitments. When Soyinka was released in 1969 he took over directing and, together with Adelugba, took the troupe to Waterford, Connecticut, where they premiered Soyinka's new play *Madmen and Specialists* (August 1970). The Company was disbanded in 1971. The

Company was formally reconstituted in October 1974 as Unibadan Masques, with Lyndersay as its Director. In its first season it presented a musical review by Wale Ogunyemi, *Day of Deities*, and **Osofisan**'s *Kolera Kolej*. Adelugba succeeded as Director, directing Ogunyemi's *Langbobo* for FESTAC in 1977, and taking it on tour in Europe in 1985. The Company has staged plays by 'Zulu Sofola, Wale Ogunyemi, Tunde Aiyegbusi and has introduced new writers like Femi Osofisan, Bode Sowande and Bode Osanyin. They were able to develop as playwrights through the combined *mise-en-scène* talents of Demas Nwoko (stage and scenic design). Nwoko subsequently set up his own fully professional private New Culture Studios which designed theatres and furniture and offered in-house training in the plastic and performance arts. These three theatre practitioners have severally made a considerable contribution to the present direction and status of theatre within Nigeria. ME

Union Square Theatre Union Square South, between Broadway and Fourth Ave, New York City. Sheridan Shook, the owner of the Union Place (later the Morton House) Hotel, installed a theatre within the hotel and opened it in 1871 as the Union Square Theatre. A year later, he entrusted it to **A. M. Palmer**. With no experience in theatrical management but with a passion for the theatre, Palmer succeeded in finding the right actors and in producing a succession of successful romantic melodramas to become a competitor of the nearby **Wallack's**. After he left the theatre in 1883, it passed to the management of J. M. Hill prior to its destruction by fire in 1888. When it was rebuilt, it was taken over by the Keith–Albee chain for continuous vaudeville in 1893. From 1908 to 1936, it served mainly as a movie house. When it was finally closed, the section of the theatre fronting 14th Street was rebuilt into shops, but the rear section was walled up and still stands. MCH

Unions, theatrical, USA Although performers had organized themselves for social and beneficial purposes since the middle of the 19th century, the stagehands were the first to achieve collective bargaining. The National Alliance of Theatrical and Stage Employees was formed in 1893 and became the International Alliance through affiliation with its Canadian counterpart (1898).

Though some performers resisted organization because work was abundant and salaries reasonable, working conditions at the end of the 19th century were intolerable. Actors were required to rehearse without pay for as long as necessary. There was no limit to the number of performances they were required to give during a week, but any cancellation meant a salary reduction. Moreover, actors furnished their own costumes in modern and standard period plays, they paid their own way to where a tour started, and they paid their own way home. Yet they played at the pleasure of the management. Disputes over wages and working conditions were settled by the management, and dismissal required neither notice nor reason.

The first performers to achieve collective bargaining were those in the Yiddish theatre. The Hebrew Actors' Union was founded in 1899 and recognized in 1902.

English-language players had formed the Actors' Society in 1896, but it failed to achieve a standard contract. Its last act was to authorize a study group, which then organized itself as Actors' Equity Association (1913). Their affiliation with the American Federation of Labour was delayed because the AFL had issued a charter for all performers to The White Rats vaudeville union in 1910. Formed in 1900, it had been crushed in a lock-out (1916–17). It surrendered its charter in 1919 and with AFL support Equity struck in the fall. They closed 13 productions that were running and another 30 in rehearsal, their membership swelled from 2,700 to 14,000, and the producers capitulated in a month. Subsequently, Equity won a closed shop (1924), and producer contributions to pension and welfare funds (1960).

New unions were created in response to new media. The Screen Actors Guild was formed in 1933. The American Federation of Radio Artists was born in 1937, and was expanded to include television (AFTRA) in 1952. The American Guild of Musical Artists was founded in 1936, and the American Guild of Variety Artists in 1939.

Organization of non-performers also emerged in the 20th century. The Dramatists' Guild of America became a separate branch of the Authors' League of America (founded in 1912) in 1920. In the same year the Screen Writers Guild was formed. Designers affiliated in the United Scenic Artists (1918), the Association of Theatrical Press Agents and Managers was formed in 1928, and the Society of Stage Directors and Choreographers in 1959. DMCD

United States of America

1. To the Civil War The early history of the American theatre is largely one of the transference of European traditions, primarily those of provincial England, and a gradual development toward self-identity which did not reach its full potential until after the First World War. Early settlers in the colonies, many representing the same anti-theatre element that existed in England, through the exigencies of the times diverted their energies into other and more complex channels than entertainment. As actors in the real-life drama of survival in hostile surroundings, colonists, with some notable exceptions, reflected Benjamin Franklin's attitude: 'After the first cares for the necessities of life are over, we shall come to think of the embellishments.'

The earliest records of theatre in the New World were not English in origin at all. Indeed, the initial dramatic performances were the rituals of North and South American Indians. More complex theatre, however, is tenuously documented as having occurred in Spanish as early as 1538 in the south-west and Mexico and by 1606 in French, in what is now Canada. With the establishment of the first settlement (Jamestown, Virginia, 1607) in what would become the USA, two traditions were quickly established among the English-speaking residents. The Southern colonies, especially the Royalist colony of Virginia, were more congenial to the theatre; Puritan New England and Quaker-dominated Pennsylvania were vehemently against this frivolous pastime, although William Penn's efforts were inevitably overturned by regal veto, the King and his court being strong supporters of the theatre in England.

Nonetheless, between 1700 and 1716 laws were passed against the theatre in various colonies with some effect. In Massachusetts, Increase Mather expressed the typical Puritan attitude when he wrote in 1687 that 'there is much discourse of beginning Stage-Plays in New England. The last year Promiscuous Dancing was openly practised.' Despite such outcries, there were local amateur theatricals from an early date. A non-extant piece called *Ye Bare and Ye Cubb*, the first recorded play in English presented in the colonies, was written by one William Darby of Accomac County, Virginia, and performed in 1665 by Darby, Cornelius Wilkinson and Philip Howard in Cowles Tavern, though this is the last recorded performance in Virginia until 1702. In 1687 a Boston innkeeper named John Wing attempted to outfit a room in his establishment for theatrical use but to no avail; attitudes like Mather's and the protests of Judge Samuel Sewall ended the brief experiment. There is evidence, however, that three years later a Harvard College student, Benjamin Colman, wrote the first play (*Gustavus Vasa*) by an American to be acted in the colonies. In Virginia students at William and Mary College offered in 1702 the recitation of a 'pastoral colloquy' before the governor. Other colloquies of this sort were offered at other institutions of higher learning. Between 1699 and 1702 a Richard Hunter petitioned for permission to produce plays in New York, then a town of 4,436 people; it was granted but no more is known. On 6 May 1709, however, the Governor's Council in New York forbade 'play acting and prize fighting', with no rationale provided.

Early evidence of professional efforts is scattered and imprecise. The British vagabond player **Anthony (Tony) Aston** is generally credited as the first professional actor in America; in 1703, in his early 20s, he acted in 'Charles Town', South Carolina, writing that he 'turn'd *Player* and *Poet*, and wrote one Play on the Subject of the Country'. He then claims to have gone to New York. His play is unknown and in 1704 he returned to London. In 1715, the first known play written and published in America appeared. Written by Governor Robert Hunter of New York, *Androboros* is a satire on the citizens of that city and the New York Senate. There is no record of performance.

For the next 35 years theatrical activity was sporadic. In 1716, in Williamsburg, Virginia, the most advanced town in the colonies to promote theatre, William Levingston, who ran a dancing school, built a theatre which was operated by his indentured servants William and Mary Stagg until Levingston's death in 1729. In 1724 a makeshift playhouse (The New Booth) was built in the Society Hill section of Philadelphia for 'roap dancing' and the traditional clown pieces called Pickleherring. The 1730s marks the advancement of Charleston as a theatrical centre and the erection of a theatre in Dock Street in 1735. During the same period there was limited activity in New York: in 1730 an amateur production of *Romeo and Juliet* was presented, the first **Shakespeare** in America; in 1732 a space above a commercial establishment was turned into a playing space; and in 1735 at 'The New Theatre' (a converted warehouse in Pearl Street) a season of recent English plays, including *The Beaux' Stratagem*, was presented.

A sustained record of professional theatre in Philadelphia, which quickly became America's theatrical

Plumstead's Warehouse, Philadelphia, the first building used for professional theatre in America.

centre until about 1825, dates from 1749 and is associated with the activities of the first professional company known in the colonies under Walter Murray and Thomas Kean, about whom we know virtually nothing. In August they performed in Plumstead's Warehouse, converted for use as a playhouse; by February they were performing in New York in a converted building in Nassau Street. In October 1751 they opened a new, crudely-built wooden playhouse in Williamsburg, played in Maryland the following year as The Virginia Company of Comedians, and then drifted into obscurity. They had, however, as historian Hugh F. Rankin indicates, acted 'as an advance agent for those to follow, whetting the appetite of the colonials for the drama and upon occasion wearing down religious and moralistic opposition'.

The next chapter in the history of theatre in America is the story of one company, The London Company of Comedians (renamed in 1763 The American Company of Comedians) and their total dominance of the theatrical scene for 50 years, beginning in 1752 under the leadership of **Lewis Hallam, Sr**, and continuing from 1758 under **David Douglass**, who married Hallam's widow. The Hallam Company, sent to America on speculation by Lewis's eldest brother William, who remained in London, arrived in Williamsburg with a completely professional company of 12 adults and three children, a complete repertoire of plays, and basic scenery and costumes. Operating on a sharing system, the company began their first season at Kean's old playhouse on 16 September with *The Merchant of Venice*; in July 1754 they moved to New York, carrying with them a letter of endorsement from Governor Dinwiddie to the governor of New York. Until October 1754 they played in New York, Philadelphia, Annapolis, and Charleston, spending the next three years in Jamaica, where Lewis Hallam died in 1755. Douglass, an erstwhile actor and printer, brought the company back to New York in 1758 and within six years had added 'American' to their name. Despite continued opposition from all quarters (Puritan, Quaker, Lutheran, Presbyterian, Baptist), Douglass, with **Lewis Hallam, Jr** as leading man, took his company up and down the East Coast, building new theatres or revamping old buildings, and introducing significant new British plays to the public. In the early

1760s Douglass even attempted an invasion of New England, first in Newport, Rhode Island, in 1761, and the next year in Providence, Rhode Island, both stops a challenge to his ingenuity. In order to avoid criticism, he advertised his plays as 'moral dialogues' and in Providence called his makeshift playhouse a 'schoolhouse'. Literally drummed out of town, Douglass returned to New York where he opened the temporary Chapel of Beekman Street Theatre in 1761, followed in 1766 and 1767 by the construction of two more important and permanent theatres.

The first permanent theatre on the American continent, the **Southwark Theatre** (1766), which stood until 1912, also was the scene for the first professionally produced play by a native author, Thomas Godfrey, whose *The Prince of Parthia*, a heroic tragedy in blank verse set in Parthia near the beginning of the Christian era and thus in no way American in subject matter, premiered on 24 April 1767. It was sheer chance that this play earned its historic position, for a play called *The Disappointment* by Thomas Forrest was to receive that honour but was abruptly withdrawn because it contained 'personal reflections unfit for the stage'. On 7 December 1767, Douglass's second major venture, the **John Street Theatre**, opened in New York City and remained that city's major playhouse for 30 years.

On 20 October 1774 the Continental Congress forbade all extravagance and dissipation, including stage entertainments; Douglass and his company returned to the West Indies the following year. Other than military theatricals, theatre ceased during the hostilities, though plays, many little more than political satire in dialogue form and the majority unperformed, were written during the period, including those by **Mercy Otis Warren**, **Hugh Henry Brackenridge**, **Robert Munford**, and anonymous pieces such as *The Blockheads*, inspired by the performance in Boston of General John Burgoyne's farce *The Blockade of Boston*, as well as John Leacock's *The Fall of British Tyranny* (both 1776). The real activity, however, took place among the military on both sides. In 1775 the John Street was renamed the Theatre Royal and presented a long series of dramatic productions performed by the British military, until their evacuations in 1783. The same was true in other major cities, such as Boston, where a theatre was organized in Faneuil Hall from 1775–7, and in Philadelphia a Captain Delancey and Captain John André, later involved with Benedict Arnold, were leaders of a theatrical group under General William Howe. Despite edicts to the contrary, the Continental Army performed too. At Valley Forge, for example, Washington's troops presented **Addison**'s *Cato* in 1778.

After the Revolution, in 1782, professionals began to return. Lewis Hallam, Jr brought back the Old American Company from Jamaica in 1784, picking up where they had been in 1774. Along with **John Henry**, they were the major actors of the day, joined soon by **Thomas Wignell**. On 16 April 1787 the reinstated company offered the first professional production of a native American comedy on an American subject, **Royall Tyler**'s *The Contrast*, which, among other firsts, introduced the stage Yankee, Jonathan, the prototype of many subsequent Yankees and the first native type to be developed. With the elimination of all repression, Philadelphia was stimulated as a theatre centre due to the efforts of Wignell and Alexander Reinagle, a musician who in 1794 opened the superior **Chestnut Street Theatre** with a new group of actors. After this period of reestablishment, the 1790s became a decade of rapid expansion. Wignell erected theatres in Baltimore (1794) and Washington (1800); in 1792 **John Hodgkinson** joined the Old American Company; with the repealing of restrictive laws in New England, Boston and Providence became important centres, especially with the opening of Boston's **Federal Street Theatre** in 1794, followed two years later by the Haymarket; other scattered activity spread theatre throughout the young country, including French-speaking theatres in Charleston (1794) and in New Orleans (1791; though not a part of the USA until 1803). In 1798 New York kept pace with Philadelphia with the opening of the **Park** (New) **Theatre** where **William Dunlap**, whose drama *The Father* had been performed at the John Street in 1789, initially became a partner of Lewis Hallam, Jr and John Hodgkinson but ultimately assumed the management, recording a career of ups and downs, ending in bankruptcy in 1805. After a brief period of management by the actor **Thomas Abthorpe Cooper**, **Stephen Price**, America's first professional manager, took control in 1809 and by encouraging star appearances, beginning with **George Frederick Cooke** in 1810, helped to undermine the stock system. Actors such as Cooper and **John Howard Payne** (remembered primarily as a playwright) exploited the starring possibilities, and, after the uncertainties of the War of 1812, a steady flow of actors from England appeared, including in the 1820s **Edmund Kean**, **Junius Brutus Booth**, **William B. Wood**, **William Warren, Sr**, **Tyrone Power**, **Laura Keene**, **Charles Kean**, and **John Brougham**, to mention only a few.

More significant than foreign imports of stars and plays, was the slow Americanization of the theatre which accelerated during the first half of the 19th century. Native-born stars began to emerge in the 1820s, beginning with **Edwin Forrest**, America's first great actor and the first native-born performer to create excitement abroad. In his footsteps came Augustus A. Addams, McKean Buchanan, John R. Scott, J. Hudson Kirby, and most significantly John E. McCullough, **E. L. Davenport**, **James Murdoch**, and, toward the end of this period, great actors like **Edwin Booth** and **Joseph Jefferson III**. Among the actresses of the period, none received more acclaim than Forrest's contemporary, **Charlotte Cushman**, who by the mid-century was the dominating tragic actress on the American stage and an international star. Other actresses of note during the first half of the century include **Mary Ann Duff**, Josephine Clifton, Clara Fisher, Maggie Mitchell, **Lotta Crabtree**, **Adah Isaacs Menken**, and **Anna Cora Mowatt**, remembered today for her play *Fashion* (1845), the most significant native comedy of manners of its time. The central character in *Fashion* is Trueman, another Yankee in the tradition of Jonathan. Numerous significant American comic actors specialized in playing such roles, including **James H. Hackett**, **George Handel Hill**, **Danforth Marble**, Joshua Silsbee, and later **John E. Owens** and **Denman Thompson**.

Parallel with the emergence of American-born actors is the growth of native plays and native characters. As a result of a playwriting contest sponsored first in 1828 by Forrest for 'the best tragedy, in five acts, of which the hero, or principal character shall be an original of the country', 200 plays were submitted overall and nine prizes were awarded, four retained in his repertoire. The first winner, **John Augustus Stone**'s *Metamora*, which echoes back to Major Robert Roger's 1766 play *Ponteach* and other early dramatic efforts to write plays about the noble red man, became the most durable of the dozens of Indian plays written and performed for the next half century. Stone was one of a number of notable playwrights of the period from Philadelphia. Others included **James Nelson Barker**, **Robert Montgomery Bird**, **Richard Penn Smith**, **Mordecai Manuel Noah**, **Robert T. Conrad**, and **Samuel Woodworth**. In addition to the Indian and the Yankee, a minor native character was the stage Negro, the first appearing in John Murdock's *The Triumphs of Love* (1795) and culminating in the many versions of **Uncle Tom's Cabin** beginning in 1852. Related to the dramatic development of black characters is the phenomenal popularity of Negro minstrelsy stimulated by **Thomas D. Rice** in the late 1820s. Two additional types emerged before the Civil War: the tough city lad, Mose the fire 'b'hoy as depicted in **Benjamin Baker**'s *A Glance at New York* (1848), and the stout-hearted frontiersman beginning with Col. Nimrod Wildfire in **James K. Paulding**'s *The Lion of the West* (1831). In addition to the development of native types, American drama up to the mid-century was dominated by the burlesques and dramas of immigrant playwright-actors like John Brougham and **Dion Boucicault** and advancements in writing techniques were made by **George Henry Boker**. Boker was arguably the best writer of romantic drama in the English-speaking world of the period, especially his *Francesca da Rimini* (1855), though Bird's romantic plays as performed by Forrest were more popular.

As the USA expanded its territory enterprising theatre entrepreneurs took small companies into the Ohio and Mississippi Valley, beginning in 1815 when **Samuel Drake** went from Albany, New York, into frontier settlements in Kentucky, Ohio and Tennessee. **James H. Caldwell** established a first-rate English-speaking theatre in New Orleans by 1819. The names **Noah Ludlow** and **Sol Smith** were familiar ones along the rivers and in the wild. Combining forces they established the first real theatre in St Louis in 1835. Chicago's first theatre dates from 1847. During the same period William Chapman was operating his Mississippi Floating Theatre. By the mid-century, thanks to the gold rush, theatre came to California. The first theatrical performance by professional actors was given in San Francisco in 1850 and by 1862 the Salt Lake Theatre (Utah) was established. The star system was unequivocally aided by this westward expansion, for Western managers paid higher salaries than in the East to attract the best talent available.

By 1800 a definite shift of influence from Philadelphia to New York had begun. Philadelphia's population in 1820 was 63,802, New York's 123,706; by 1840 it was 93,655 to 312,710 and by the mid-century New York boasted almost half a million people. The Chestnut Street Theatre, managed by William Warren and William B. Wood, began to lose dominance in Philadelphia in 1811, followed in 1828 by the **Arch Street**

The riot at the Astor Place Opera House, New York, 10 May 1849.

Theatre. Philadelphia could not support three major theatres and in 1828–9 all three went bankrupt. The country was rapidly changing with a growing urban lower-class audience on the rise, significant emigrations on the horizon, an active revolt against English domination of the stage in motion, and a major civil war around the corner. Gradually playwrights were able to gain a living writing plays, encouraged by the copyright law of 1856. The number and quality of playhouses increased, gas-lighting was introduced beginning in 1816, native scenic designers were gaining recognition, and greater realism, given impetus by the 1846 presentation of Charles Kean's *King John*, was sought. The Lafayette Theatre, built in New York in 1826, boasted of border lights and equipment for equestrian and aquatic drama. The second Park opened in 1821 with a 2,500 capacity, topped by the first **Bowery Theatre** in 1826 and its 3,500 capacity. The **Chatham Garden Theatre** opened in 1825; what became **Barnum's Museum** began operation in 1841; as did the famous **Boston Museum** which operated a most successful stock company for almost 50 years beginning in 1843; the **Astor Place Opera House** opened in 1847; Brougham's Lyceum in 1850. Some of the more successful managements up to the mid-century fought the growing trends of stars and long runs. For example, **William Mitchell** did so at the **Olympic Theatre** in New York from 1839 to 1850 and **William E. Burton**, who leased Palmo's Opera House in 1848 and opened it as Burton's, followed suit, dominating as the fashionable New York theatre until the emergence of the **Wallack's** stock company beginning in 1853.

By the Civil War the American theatre had undeniably established a strong, individualistic mainstream tradition, relatively free of foreign influence, despite strong impulses from New European migrations to America. After a brief curtailment of growth, the American theatre would experience a great period of prosperity following the War Between the States, lasting until about 1915.   DBW

2. The Civil War to the First World War The Civil War only disrupted theatrical activities in the East, and by early 1862 the theatres in New York, Boston, and Philadelphia were open and thriving. Such patriotic pieces as Charles Gayler's *Bull Run, or the Sacking of Fairfax Courthouse* (1861) appeared in New York at the **New Bowery Theatre** three weeks after the actual battle. Into the 1880s Wallack's continued as the leading New York playhouse offering a steady diet of old and new British comedies with a superb acting company which included Mme Elizabeth Ponisi, **Rose Coghlan**, Henry J. Montague, and **Charles Coghlan**. William Warren remained a fixture at the Boston Museum until his retirement in 1883, offering a wide range of comic roles, classic as well as contemporary. **Mrs John Drew** managed a talented company at the Arch Street Theatre in Philadelphia from 1861–92, establishing the careers of her son, **John Drew**, and her daughter, **Georgina Drew Barrymore**.

At the beginning of the decade, Edwin Forrest and Charlotte Cushman reigned as the leading tragedians in America although Forrest's position was being challenged by Edwin Booth, the son of the English-born tragedian, **J. B. Booth**. Young Booth had served his apprenticeship in California (1852–6) and returned east in 1856 to establish himself as a star. Success the following year in Boston and New York made him an actor to watch. In the fall of 1862 he played in New York at the same time as Forrest, inviting comparison with the older actor. Cultivated theatre patrons had long abandoned Forrest and found Booth's quiet, unassuming, intellectual and refined style more suitable for their ideal of a 'temple of the arts'. Booth's slight but handsome physique (dark hair and eyes) made him the ideal late Victorian tragedian as Forrest's muscular physique had attracted patrons 30 years earlier. Critic Nym Crinkle (**Andrew C. Wheeler**) thought Booth's Hamlet resembled a 19th-century gentleman more than a 16th-century courtier. While his most famous role was Hamlet – which he played for 100 performances at the **Winter Garden Theatre** during the 1864–5 season – he excelled in other roles requiring intellectual rather than emotional or physical force: Iago, Richard II, Shylock, Cardinal Richelieu (in **Bulwer-Lytton**'s play), and Bertuccio in **Tom Taylor**'s *The Fool's Revenge*. Booth departed from tradition in building his own theatre (1869) without a raked and grooved stage, and without an apron or proscenium doors. A better actor than manager, he succumbed to the financial panic of 1873 and lost the theatre through bankruptcy. Considered by historians as America's finest actor, Booth spent the last two decades of his life successfully touring as a star.

Booth was not the only actor challenging theatrical traditions. **Matilda Heron** became an overnight success in 1857 with her portrayal of Marguerite Gautier in **Dumas**'s *The Lady of the Camellias* (called *Camille* in New York), exhibiting a style of acting marked by excessive emotional display and a seeming lack of technique and control. For the next half-century, the style attracted such actresses as **Lucille Western**, **Clara Morris**, and **Mrs Leslie Carter**. Joseph Jefferson also broke with the traditional school in the 1860s with his portrayal of Rip Van Winkle in Boucicault's dramatization. After presenting it in London (1865) for 170 performances, Jefferson brought it to New York in 1866 and in the title role established himself as the leading comedian of his age as Booth was the leading tragedian. He endowed Rip with charm, humour, and pathos. His quiet, even casual style seemed free of all staginess with nothing forced or unnatural. And in 1874 **Frank Mayo** idealized the frontiersman in **Frank H. Murdoch**'s drama *Davy Crockett*. Like Jefferson, Mayo underplayed the emotional points and offered a style of acting which seemed natural to his audiences.

Dramatic tastes changed significantly in the 1860s. The historical costume dramas of Stone, Bird, **Knowles**, and Bulwer-Lytton began to go out of fashion. More popular were sensational melodramas which offered adventure, romance, and obligatory sensational events. In **Augustin Daly**'s most successful melodramas, suspense and novel disasters abound: a man tied to railroad tracks facing an approaching train (*Under the Gaslight*, 1867); the heroine stranded on a steamship about to explode (*A Flash of Lightning*, 1868); or the rescue of a man bound to a log entering a sawmill (*The Red Scarf*, 1868). These dramas had broad emotional appeal and played to a large popular audience.

The excitement over *Camille* and the new French drama resulted in numerous adaptations. There was a good reason why the new French drama achieved instant popularity: it dealt with contemporary events and discussed subjects formerly considered taboo (adultery for example). Dion Boucicault made a profession out of Anglicizing French plays. Augustin Daly was responsible in part or whole for 44 adaptations of French drama in addition to borrowing others from the German and English theatres. While the Dramatic Copyright Law of 1856 improved the playwright's legal rights, it was not until the International Copyright Agreement was accepted by the United States in 1891 that managers found it as profitable to produce native as foreign plays.

American social comedies and dramas in the 1870s reflected the important topics of the day: stock speculation, social climbing, the winning of the West, divorce and the family, and in a romantic way, the Civil War. Daly's big hit of 1875, *The Big Bonanza*, poked fun at those who naively attempted to make a 'killing' on Wall Street. **Bronson Howard** offered a more serious treatment of the subject in *The Banker's Daughter* (1878); and in *Young Mrs Winthrop* (1883) he touched upon the subjects of money, social status, and divorce. In *The Henrietta* (1887) he suggested that the country's obsession with making money was leading to moral decline, a theme which **David Belasco** and Henry De Mille explored in *Men and Women* (1890), and **Clyde Fitch** exploited in *The Climbers* (1901). A better play of the genre, **Langdon Mitchell**'s *The New York Idea* (1906), satirizes divorce and social customs among the wealthy. Historians have regarded Bronson Howard as the first professional playwright in America because he successfully made a living from his plays. His biggest hit, *Shenandoah* (1889), used the Civil War as a background for an essentially romantic plot as did **William Gillette**'s spy stories, *Held by the Enemy* (1886), and *Secret Service* (1896); Belasco's *The Heart of Maryland* (1895); and Clyde Fitch's *Barbara Frietchie* (1899).

The frontier and the winning of the West provided countless plots and characters including Davy Crockett and the American cowboy. Daly set his *Horizon* (1871) in the West as did **Bret Harte** for *Two Men of Sandy Bar* (1876); **Joaquin Miller** for *The Danites in the Sierras* (1887); **Bartley Campbell** for *My Partner* (1879); **Augustus Thomas** for *Arizona* (1899); and David Belasco for *The Girl of the Golden West* (1905). **William Vaughn Moody**'s *The Great Divide* (1906) contrasts the East and the West in what some historians regard as the first modern American play.

In the final years of the 19th century a more realistic treatment of subject began to replace melodrama. Playwrights rejected long-held conventions dearly loved by audiences including romantic plots, spine-chilling rescues, and happy endings in favour of a truthful depiction of life. The farce-comedies of **Edward Harrigan** in the 1870s and 1880s offered a theatrical but authentic portrait of life among the recent immigrants in New York. **William Dean Howells** called Harrigan the American **Goldoni**, and championed his plays. In the 1890s, the increased interest in **Ibsen** offended traditionalists like **William Winter** and **John Ranken Towse**, but the new drama was defended by critics Howells, Hamlin Garland, and **James Huneker**. **James A. Herne**'s *Margaret Fleming* (1890) presented a realistic portrait of the consequences of a husband's infidelity, and avoided a happy ending. Herne's more conventional *Shore Acres* (1892) maintained the externals of realism but returned in character and plot to sentimental melodrama, and was similar in style to Denman Thompson's *The Old Homestead* (1886). Augustus Thomas also combined the trappings of realism and local colour in *Alabama* (1891), *Arizona* (1899), *The Witching Hour* (1907), and *The Copperhead* (1918). More important are **Edward Sheldon**'s *Salvation Nell* (1908), *The Nigger* (1909), and *The Boss* (1911) which deal with social problems in a realistic framework.

The public's demand for popular entertainment was insatiable. Adah Isaacs Menken's *Mazeppa* (1861) thrilled the masculine element of the audience as she gave the illusion of riding nude on the back of a wild horse. *The Black Crook* (1866) created a vogue for elaborate musical spectacle, owing much of its success to a Parisian ballet troupe of one hundred 'beautiful girls' in flesh-coloured tights. **Lydia Thompson**'s 'British Blondes' Burlesque Company from London drew crowded houses in New York for seven months (1868-9). French companies presented the new *opéra bouffe* of Jacques Offenbach to New York audiences in the late 1860s, and Maurice Grau formed a company in the 1870s to present French operettas and French stars. *Evangeline* (1874) offered an American version of *opéra bouffe*. Written by Edward E. Rice and J. C. Godwin, it featured a scantily clad female chorus, elaborate scenery, and the comedian, **Nat Goodwin**. The success of the **Kiralfy** brothers' *Around the World in Eighty Days* (1875) set the standard for large scale spectacular theatre for the next two decades. The comic operettas of **Gilbert** and Sullivan found an audience in this country after the huge success of *Pinafore* in 1878-9. **Charles Hoyt**'s 'musical trifle', *A Trip to Chinatown* (1890), offered songs, dances, and risqué comedy in addition to a thin plot and ran for 650 performances. A decade later, an English import, *Florodora* (1900), survived for 505 performances and made famous its sextette of chorus girls. **Florenz Ziegfeld** inaugurated his Follies Revue in 1907 which featured beautiful girls, elaborate costumes and sets, and leading comedians. He discovered such talent as **Fannie Brice**, **W. C. Fields**, **Eddie Cantor**, and **Bert Williams**.

Operetta continued its hold on the American musical stage into the 1920s. **Victor Herbert** gained success with European styled pieces such as *Babes in Toyland* (1903) and *Mlle Modeste* (1905), and is regarded as America's first important composer of operetta. The proper setting for operetta remained in Central Europe with Franz Lehar's memorable *The Merry Widow* (1907); Rudolf Friml's *The Firefly* (1912), and *Rose Marie* (1924); and Sigmund Romberg's *Blossom Time* (1921), and *The Student Prince* (1924).

Specialists such as Lotta Crabtree charmed New York audiences from 1867-91 with her singing, dancing, and banjo playing. A master of the quick costume change, she played both Little Nell and the Marchioness in John Brougham's dramatic version of *The Old Curiosity Shop*, and six roles in *The Little Detective*. **George L. Fox** drew packed houses to the Olympic Theatre (1868) in the pantomime *Humpty Dumpty*, which he was to perform for 1,268 times in New York alone. **Eddie Foy** gained fame in the 1890s by clowning in such musical pieces as *Sinbad the Sailor* (1891) and *Ali Baba* (1892). **Tony Pastor** presented the top speciality acts at his vaudeville theatres in the 1870s and 1880s, including the Four Cohans, **Lillian Russell**, and the **Weber** and **Fields** comedy duo. **George M. Cohan** would move from vaudeville to the musical stage, establishing himself as a star in 1904-5 in his own *Little Johnny Jones*. Lillian Russell became a leading star on the American musical stage. Weber and Fields opened their own Music Hall in 1896, which for seven years was regarded as one of Broadway's brightest attractions. The future of the speciality acts in the 20th century, however, lay with B. F. Keith and Edward Albee, businessmen who introduced continuous vaudeville and organized the industry into a giant national circuit, gaining a near monopoly over it.

Economics and public taste after the Civil War dictated a change in the theatrical order. While Wallack and Burton were strong managers, the actor as star had been the most powerful force in the theatre. Realism and the demand for artistic unity made the rise of the modern director inevitable. During the 1869-70 season, Augustin Daly leased the **Fifth Avenue Theatre** and began developing his own company. He hired actors by type rather than by lines of business; cast plays without regard to tradition, lines of business, or possession of parts; rehearsed each play with careful attention to interpretation, blocking, costuming, and scenery; and while he opposed the star system, developed a succession of stars including Agnes Ethel, **Fanny Davenport**, Clara Morris, and **Ada Rehan**. At his own **Daly's Theatre** in the 1880s, he featured a quartet of actors including John Drew, Ada Rehan, **Mrs G. H. Gilbert**, and James Lewis. Known as the home of light comedy in New York, Daly's displaced Wallack's as the most fashionable playhouse in the city. In 1884 he toured his company to London – the first American to do so – and later to Paris and Germany. Four years later he produced *The Taming of the Shrew* at Stratford-upon-Avon in the Shakespeare Memorial Theatre. Historians consider him the first American *régisseur* in the style of the Duke of Saxe-**Meiningen**.

From 1872-83, **A. M. Palmer** tightly controlled

every aspect of his productions at the **Union Square Theatre**; the **Madison Square Theatre** from 1884–91; and Wallack's old theatre renamed Palmer's from 1888–96. Whereas Daly's Theatre was known as the home of comedy, Palmer's featured 'polite melodrama' which he mounted with taste and care. With the assistance of A. R. Cazauran, Palmer built a strong company by hiring established actors such as Agnes Ethel, Clara Morris, **Kate Claxton**, **Rose Eytinge**, Charles R. Throne, Jr, and **James O'Neill**. His most popular successes included Kate Claxton in *The Two Orphans* (1874); **Richard Mansfield** in *A Parisian Romance* (1883); and premieres of Clyde Fitch's *Beau Brummell* (1890), and Augustus Thomas's *Alabama* (1891).

Steele MacKaye also saw himself as an all-powerful manager who shaped every aspect of his productions. He designed the elevator stage at the Madison Square Theatre (1880), which allowed for an entire setting to be shifted in 40 seconds. He also built the **Lyceum Theatre** (1884–5) and taught the Delsarte system of expression. In 1887 he directed his own *Paul Kauvar* which demonstrated his skill in handling crowd scenes in the Meiningen manner. But MacKaye remains a controversial figure in the American theatre because he failed to finish most of his projects.

Through staging, lighting, and scenery, David Belasco attempted to create the illusion of real life. He served as stage manager of the Madison Square Theatre and Lyceum Theatre in the 1880s, after which he turned to producing in 1895. Also a successful playwright, Belasco excelled in writing sentimental melodramas which he tailored for specific stars, and interpolated with enough contemporary thought to make them seem modern. He starred Mrs Leslie Carter in *Zaza* (1899); **Blanche Bates** in *Madame Butterfly* (1900); Blanche Bates and **George Arliss** in *Sweet Kitty Bellairs* (1903); **David Warfield** in *The Return of Peter Grimm* (1911); and a replica of a Child's restaurant in *The Governor's Lady* (1912). Belasco used publicity to make stars out of his actors and is credited by some historians with being the most successful of American régisseurs. But while he involved himself directly in producing theatre, his business methods were little different from other commercial producers.

By the mid-1870s the resident stock company and repertory system had become unprofitable to maintain and were rapidly being replaced by 'combination companies'. A play would open in New York, run until attendance lagged, then be transported in its entirety – actors, sets, properties – from city to city. The number of such 'combination' companies steadily increased until the *New York Dramatic Mirror* reported nearly 100 companies on the road during the 1876–7 season. MacKaye's *Hazel Kirk* (1880) was sent out in three road companies while still running in New York. Interest in local plays, companies, and actors was replaced by interest in touring attractions. Theatrical trade papers in New York such as *Dramatic News* (1875) and *Dramatic Mirror* (1879) were established to cater for this interest.

Touring in America promised financial rewards for foreign and native actors alike. **Adelaide Ristori** made the first of several American tours in 1866, acting in Italian except for her last visit in 1884–5. The English actress **Adelaide Neilson** made her first of two

American appearances in 1872. **Tommaso Salvini** made his American debut in 1873, and returned four more times, playing with American actors in bilingual performances. Henry E. Abbey brought **Sarah Bernhardt** to the United States in 1880 for her first tour of seven months which covered 50 cities and 156 performances. In 1883 Abbey also brought **Henry Irving**, **Ellen Terry** and the Lyceum Company for the first of several visits. Irving's carefully mounted productions set a new standard for the American stage. **Eleonora Duse** imported her natural style of acting to New York for the first of four visits in 1893 and on her last international tour in 1924, died in Pittsburgh.

All major American stars toured. After the loss of his theatre in 1873, Edwin Booth spent the last two decades of his life touring in Shakespearian and pseudo-romantic plays including two seasons (1887–9) with **Lawrence Barrett**. **John McCullough**, an actor in the Forrest tradition, gave up management of the California Theatre (1875) to tour for the next nine seasons. Of the new generation of actors, Richard Mansfield toured in such eccentric parts as Baron Chevrial in *A Parisian Romance* (1883); and the title roles in *Prince Karl* (1886), *Dr Jekyll and Mr Hyde* (1887), *Richard III* (1889), *Beau Brummel* (1890), and *Cyrano de Bergerac* (1898). Mansfield introduced **Shaw** to an American audience as Bluntschli in *Arms and the Man* (1894); and later as Dick Dudgeon in *The Devil's Discipline* (1897). **Otis Skinner** had learned his trade in Booth's and Daly's companies and scrambled to play roles such as Hajj in *Kismet* (1911) which would best showcase his talents. **E. H. Sothern** made a hit with Edward Rose's romantic drama, *The Prisoner of Zenda* (1895), and later became a Shakespearian actor together with his second wife, **Julia Marlowe**. The public's loss of interest in the traditional repertory and demand for new plays left Mansfield and his generation scrambling to find suitable vehicles in which to star.

Establishing herself in the 1880s as a star in light comedy and melodrama, **Mrs Minnie Maddern Fiske** adjusted better to the demands of the new drama. She encouraged the production of **Ibsen** in America by acting Nora in *A Doll's House* (1894), the title role in *Hedda Gabler* (1903), Rebecca West in *Rosmersholm* (1907), and Mrs Alving in *Ghosts* (1927). She also created the title character in Edward Sheldon's *Salvation Nell* (1908). Probably more effective in comedy, Mrs Fiske was praised for her psychological truthfulness and simplicity of effects. Critics associated her in style with Duse. She and her husband, **Harrison Grey Fiske**, leased the Manhattan Theatre in 1903 and established an acting company which allowed them to remain independent of the **Theatrical Syndicate**.

Arnold Daly, like Mansfield, brought Shaw's plays before an American public. In 1903 he directed and starred in the American premiere of *Candida* which ran for 133 performances. In 1904–5 he organized a company which produced *You Never Can Tell*, *The Man of Destiny*, *How He Lied to Her Husband*, a revival of *Candida*, and *Mrs Warren's Profession*. The latter was considered an immoral play and led to Daly's arrest. While acquitted, he soon lost the zeal for dramatic reform and turned back to performing in standard works.

The growing power of the businessman in the American theatre can be evidenced in the 1890s with the demise of Palmer's and Daly's companies, and the rise of the **Frohman** brothers (**Daniel** and **Charles**) as New York's leading producers. Daniel had assumed control of the Lyceum Theatre from Steel MacKaye in 1885 and established a stock company and acting school which lasted from 1887 until 1902. His company included such stellar performers as E. H. Sothern, Virginia Harned, Mary Mannering, **William Faversham**, **Henrietta Crosman**, **Henry Miller**, Georgia Cayvan, Herbert Kelcey, and **James H. Hackett**. He minimized risks and maximized profits by producing bright new plays by established writers including Belasco and De Mille's *The Charity Ball* (1889); **Henry Arthur Jones**'s *The Dancing Girl* (1891); **Pinero**'s *Trelawny of the Wells* (1898); and Clyde Fitch's *The Moth and the Flame* (1898). Charles Frohman established two companies at Proctor's in 1890 to produce and tour new plays. He built the Empire Theatre in 1893 which quickly gained the reputation of being a 'star factory'. He hired John Drew from Daly's company in 1892 and added William Gillette to his stable of stars in 1894. And when required, he created stars such as **Maude Adams**, **Ethel Barrymore**, and Henry E. Dixey. His numerous hits include Belasci and Franklin Fyles's *The Girl I Left Behind Me* (1893); **James M. Barrie**'s *The Little Minister* (1897) and *Peter Pan* (1905) – both starring Maude Adams; and William Gillette's *Sherlock Holmes* (1899).

Charles Frohman is best known for organizing a theatrical trust in 1896 which consisted of three partnerships: Frohman and Al Hayman; the booking firm of Marc Klaw and Abraham L. Erlanger; and Philadelphia theatre owners, S. F. Nixon and J. Fred Zimmerman. Called the **Syndicate**, this trust gained a monopoly over the American theatre by controlling bookings, theatre buildings, and talent. In 1896 they either operated or directly controlled 33 first-class houses from coast to coast, and by 1903, had extended their holdings to 70. At the height of their power, they had exclusive rights to book over 700 theatres. The cancelling of engagements, double bookings, broken contracts, and general disorganization which characterized the theatre in the 1880s were eliminated. For 15 years Frohman and the Syndicate tightly controlled the American Theatre and ran it on 'big business' principles. They judged a play's worth solely on its ability to generate a profit. The **Shubert**s' (Lee, Sam and Jacob J.) 'Independent Movement' in 1900 challenged the position of the Syndicate. They also gained control over theatres from coast to coast; offered attractive bookings to independent managers; and began producing their own shows. Fierce competition between the two groups resulted in an oversupply of attractions and theatres. Cities built separate theatres for Syndicate and Independent productions. Economic disaster was averted by an agreement between the two parties in 1914. Frohman went down in the *Lusitania* in 1915, and afterwards the Syndicate declined in power. The **Shubert Organization** has remained a vital force in the 20th-century American theatre.

Critics Walter Prichard Eaton, Norman Hapgood, **Brander Matthews**, John Ranken Towse, and William Winter denounced the Syndicate's purely commercial policy in the early 1900s and envisaged a national theatre supported by either public or private funds. Interest grew in the idea with the *Arena* publishing a Symposium 'A National Art Theatre for America' in 1904. Four years later Heinrich Conried announced plans for such a company in New York, and despite his death the following year, money was raised and the **New Theatre** under **Winthrop Ames**'s direction opened 6 November 1909 with Julia Marlowe and E. H. Sothern in *Antony and Cleopatra*. The lack of a well-trained company and the New Theatre's poor acoustics contributed to its demise in 1911, although the project may have been doomed from the start: 20th-century theatre problems could not be solved with 19th-century solutions. This attempt to create an art theatre did express dissatisfaction with the triteness of the American stage. This attitude was reinforced through visits by foreign companies in the 1910s: the Irish Players of the **Abbey Theatre** (1911); **Max Reinhardt**'s company in *Sumurun* at the **Casino Theatre** (1912); **Granville Barker**'s productions at Wallack's Theatre for the New Stage Society of New York (1915); and **Jacques Copeau**'s **Vieux-Colombier** Company at the Old Garrick Theatre (1917). These companies demonstrated that theatre could be more than manufactured entertainment for mass tastes but could touch the human mind and spirit in an important way. **William Brady**, a commercial producer, presented Edward Sheldon's *The Boss* (1911), and Shaw's *Major Barbara* (1915). Amateur theatre groups were organized throughout the country, inspired by artists such as Maurice Browne of the Chicago Little Theatre (1912). In New York, the **Washington Square Players** (1914) led by **Lawrence Langner** and Edward Goodman produced the plays of Ibsen, **Chekhov**, and Shaw, and also important new works by American writers. In 1916 the **Provincetown Players** presented *Bound East for Cardiff*, the first **O'Neill** play to be staged. The same year, in Detroit, Sheldon Cheney founded *Theatre Arts*, a magazine dedicated to the art of the theatre. And in 1919, members of the now defunct Washington Square Players founded the **Theatre Guild**, the first professional art theatre in the United States. Led by Lawrence Langner, **Philip Moeller**, **Theresa Helburn** and others the Guild became an important theatre offering professional productions of plays not normally seen in the commercial theatre. TLM

3. The First World War to the present day After the First World War, Actors' Equity demanded improved working conditions in the theatre and pushed for unionization of the acting profession. This resulted in an actors' strike in 1919. Stage hands had first organized themselves into a union in 1886, and later had affiliated with the American Federation of Labour (1894). After several unsuccessful attempts, performers formed Actors' Equity in 1913. Producers, including George M. Cohan and the Shuberts, fought the union and were joined by many actors who considered themselves artists not labourers. But on 6 August 1919, Equity went out on strike, demanding official recognition and a closed shop for legitimate performers. They were supported by the stage hands and musicians, and by the AFL. The Theatre Guild met Equity's terms immediately, but all other producers resisted, and their plays closed. On 6 September, the producers capitulated and signed contracts which stipulated minimum contracts, improved rehearsal conditions, higher pay, and better working conditions.

In 1920 the Provincetown Players brought Eugene O'Neill's first full-length play, *Beyond the Horizon*, to Broadway, where it ran for 111 performances and won a Pulitzer Prize. Critics **George Jean Nathan** and Ludwig Lewisohn touted play and author as important new forces in the American theatre. O'Neill followed with *The Emperor Jones* (1920), an expressionistic drama which featured **Charles Gilpin** and the scenery of **Cleon Throckmorton**, and *Anna Christie* (1921), starring Pauline Lord. Working quickly, within three years he had added *The Straw* (1921), *The First Man* (1922), dominating the American theatre in the 1920s as no playwright had previously.

Popular successes in the 1920s include **Avery Hopwood** and Mary Roberts Rinehart's *The Bat* (1920) which ran over two years (867 performances), and **Anne Nichols**'s *Abie's Irish Rose* (1922) which received scathing reviews but survived for 2,327 performances. Hopwood made a fortune writing such risqué fluff as *The Gold Diggers* (1919) and *The Demi-Virgin* (1921). The *Ziegfeld Follies* began to look dated in the 1920s, but gaining in popularity were all-Negro revues such as **Noble Sissle** and **Eubie Blake**'s *Shuffle Along* (1921), and *Blackbirds* (1928), a compendium of songs and dances which made a star of hoofer **Bill 'Bojangles' Robinson**. Musical comedy survived because of pretty chorus girls and memorable songs by Vincent Youmans, **George Gershwin**, **Cole Porter** and **Richard Rodgers**, and superb showmen such as W. C. Fields, **Al Jolson**, **Ed Wynn**, Fanny Brice, Bert Williams, **Will Rogers**, **Bert Lahr**, and Jimmy Durante. **George** and **Ira Gershwin** created a new jazz style with hits such as *Lady, Be Good!* (1924), *Tip-Toes* (1925), and *Funny Face* (1927). The **Marx Brothers** clowned in such vehicles as *The Cocoanuts* (1925) by **George S. Kaufman** and **Irving Berlin**, and *Animal Crackers* (1928) by Kaufman, Morrie Ryskind, and others after which they took their buffoonery to Hollywood.

Operetta remained popular with long runs for Rudolf Friml's *Rose Marie* (1924), and Sigmund Romberg's *The Student Prince* (1924) and *The Desert Song* (1926). *Show Boat* (1928) by **Jerome Kern** and **Oscar Hammerstein II**, broke new ground by drawing on American musical traditions, and by better integrating the book, music, songs, and dances. Kern contributed such standards as 'Ol' Man River' and 'Can't Help Lovin' That Man' to a growing American art form. **Joseph Urban** designed the show, adding to his reputation for creating opulent sets for opera, theatre, and the *Ziegfeld Follies*.

In the early 1910s, the New Theatre had failed to create a more artistic American stage but efforts continued into the 1920s. **Arthur Hopkins**, **Robert Edmond Jones** and **John Barrymore** combined forces in 1920 to present Shakespeare's *Richard III*, and two years later to revive *Hamlet* in a somewhat untraditional interpretation by Barrymore. The production ran 101 performances and Barrymore repeated his success in London (1925). In 1923, the **Moscow Art Theatre**'s acting company visited New York. Critics pretended not to notice that they performed in Russian as they praised the company's ensemble training. Although the **Stanislavsky** system of acting was not unknown in the United States, demonstration of the MAT work to New York audiences had lasting impact. Two members of the company, Richard Boleslavsky and Maria Ouspenskaya, remained in America to teach in the **American Laboratory Theatre**. In 1924 **Walter Hampden** organized his own company at the Colonial (later the Hampden) Theatre and for five years offered Shakespeare, Ibsen, **Rostand**, and other less commercial playwrights. **Eva Le Gallienne** leased the 50-year-old **Fourteenth Street Theatre** in 1926, gathered together a company of veterans and newcomers, and opened with Chekhov's *The Three Sisters*. Few critics showed interest but Le Gallienne kept her Civic Repertory Theatre intact for six years, presenting 34 plays, most of which would have been fiscally impossible on Broadway.

Under the guidance of Lawrence Langner, the Theatre Guild emerged in the 1920s as America's most artistic producing organization. The company which at one time included **Alfred Lunt**, **Lynn Fontanne**, **Dudley Digges**, Helen Westley, **Lee Simonson** and Philip Moeller, presented a number of important world premieres including Shaw's *Heartbreak House* in 1920, and **Elmer Rice**'s expressionistic play *The Adding Machine* in 1923. In 1925 they opened their own Guild Theatre with a production of Shaw's *Caesar and Cleopatra*. Between 1920–30 the Guild offered 67 different productions, 15 the work of American playwrights.

American comedy became more worldly in the 1920 with George S. Kaufman, replacing its penchant for folksy, romantic, and sentimental nonsense with witty and irrelevant stabs at native society and culture. Kaufman and **Marc Connelly**'s *Dulcy* (1921) elevated Lynn Fontanne to stardom and was the first of their collaborations which included *To the Ladies* (1922), *Merton of the Movies* (1922), and *Beggar on Horseback* (1924), the latter an expressionistic satire on American business. Kaufman collaborated successfully with other writers, including Edna Ferber and **Moss Hart**, while Connelly enjoyed his greatest triumph with *The Green Pastures* (1930), which played for 640 performances. **George Kelly** attracted attention in 1922 with *The Torchbearers*, a satire on the **Little Theatre movement**, before writing his highly popular comedy *The Show-Off* two years later, and Pulitzer Prize-winning *Craig's Wife* in 1925. Philip Barry and **S. N. Behrman** wrote fashionable comedies with wit and style albeit a streak of sentimentality. Behrman's *The Second Man* (1927) featured Alfred Lunt and Lynn Fontanne in a comedy about an artist's choice between two women. Barry's *Paris Bound* (1927) and *Holiday* (1928) presented a charming portrait of the wealthy just before the stock market crash of 1929. His best play, *The Philadelphia Story* (1939), allowed **Katharine Hepburn** to look dazzling in a light-hearted treatment of life among the wealthy. The best American farce of the 1920s was Ben Hecht and Charles MacArthur's *The Front Page* (1928), a cynical and satirical look at big-city life in Chicago.

Serious drama probed the romantic assumptions underlying American life. War received a realistic and truthful depiction in **Maxwell Anderson** and Laurence Stalling's *What Price Glory?* (1924). George Jean Nathan thought it superior to every other play inspired by the First World War. In the same year,

O'Neill's *Desire Under the Elms* offered a Freudian interpretation of New England puritanism which relied for much of its power on Robert Edmond Jones's highly symbolic setting. The prolific O'Neill with mixed success examined other aspects of American life in *The Fountain* (1925), *The Great God Brown* (1926), and *Strange Interlude* (1928), the latter a nine act, five hour dramatic novel, which ran for 432 performances and won a Pulitzer. The same year, Maxwell Anderson and Harold Hickerson's *Gods of the Lightning* brought the Sacco and Vanzetti murder case before a New York audience. **Sidney Howard** dissected the American way of life in *They Knew What They Wanted* (1924), *Lucky Sam McCarver* (1925), *Ned McCobb's Daughter* (1926), and *Silver Cord* (1927), the latter a play about excessive maternal devotion. **Robert Sherwood** attracted attention in 1927 with *The Road to Rome*, a bittersweet reenactment of Hannibal''s march, starring **Jane Cowl**.

At the end of the decade, radio and motion pictures emerged as rivals for the American theatre audience. Radio had grown from its first regular broadcasts in 1920 to a full scale entertainment industry by 1930. Motion pictures added sound with *The Jazz Singer* in 1927, which made it possible to film stage plays and show them for a fraction of the cost of a theatre ticket. Between 1920 and 1930 theatres outside New York decreased in number from 1,500 to 500, many converting to film, as the professional theatre in America became almost exclusively located in Manhattan. The depression was radically to reduce what was left. During the 1927–8 season on Broadway, the number of stage productions reached a record of 280; by 1939–40 this had been reduced to 80.

The American theatre in the 1930s directly reflected the nation's political and economic crises. Leftist theatre groups proliferated including the New Playwrights' Theatre (1926), Workers' Drama League (1929), Workers' Laboratory Theatre (1930), League of Workers' Theatres (1932), and Theatre Union (1922) among the most active. They were founded by writers such as Michael Gold and **John Howard Lawson** who returned from Russia eager to form a theatre of the left. **Clifford Odets**'s inflammatory *Waiting for Lefty* (1935) drew its early sponsorship from the League of Workers' Theatres. The Theatre Union gained an early success with *Peace on Earth* (1933), an anti-war piece, and *Stevedore* (1934), a play dealing with the relationship between black and white workers. Left-wing theatre remained a short-lived phenomenon of the 1930s, as its writers and artists were absorbed into the main stream of American theatre and films. Many were blacklisted during the McCarthy Hearings in the 1950s.

The Harlem Renaissance of the 1920s generated a new interest in black literature which continued in the 1930s. Plays about blacks by whites – **Paul Green**'s *In Abraham's Bosom*, Marc Connelly's *Green Pastures*, and O'Neill's *The Emperor Jones* – had been more successful than plays by blacks until W. E. B. Dubois, **Langston Hughes**, and others organized black companies. Hughes's *Mulatto* (1935) was the most successful play by a black playwright in the 1930s. Negro units of the **Federal Theatre** offered new plays by black authors but are remembered mainly by the voodoo *Macbeth* and *Swing Mikado*, directed by **Orson Welles** in 1938.

Politically sensitive but more concerned with artistic ideals, the **Group Theatre** began in 1931 as a palace revolt inside the Guild Theatre by younger members, led by **Harold Clurman**, **Cheryl Crawford** and **Lee Strasberg**: 28 actors, who included Franchot Tone, **Morris Carnovsky**, Clifford Odets, Sanford Meisner, and **Stella Adler**, joined the three to set up a summer colony in Connecticut. Under the tutelage of Strasberg, the Group sought an acting technique for realistic plays which came to be known as the Method. After a summer of work and analysis, the Group Theatre produced Paul Green's *The House of Connelly* (1931) followed by John Howard Lawson's *Success Story* (1932) and **Sidney Kingsley**'s *Men in White* (1933). They discovered playwright Clifford Odets and produced his *Awake and Sing!* and *Waiting for Lefty*, both in 1935. They gave **William Saroyan** a hearing in 1939 with *My Heart's in the Highlands*, before running into financial problems in 1941 and disbanding.

In 1935 the Federal Theatre was organized by the Works Progress Administration to create jobs for out-of-work theatre people. Mrs Hallie Flanagan of the Vassar Experimental Theatre was appointed first director and charged with locating the unemployed and putting them to work. This, the first subsidized producing agency in United States history, was disbanded by the government in 1939 on grounds of leftist infiltration. The Federal Theatre made several distinctive contributions to the American Theatre, including the **Living Newspaper** productions.

The censorship and closing of the Federal Theatre's production of Marc Blitzstein's *The Cradle Will Rock* (1937) led to the resignations of Orson Welles and **John Houseman**, and to their creation of the **Mercury Theatre**. Welles had demonstrated a remarkable originality as a director with his voodoo *Macbeth* (1936) and **Marlowe**'s *Doctor Faustus* (1937). In 1937, he directed an impressive modern-dress *Julius Caesar* with fascist costumes and Abe Feder's lighting.

The depressed economy sharply reduced the number of Broadway productions, prompting five playwrights – Robert Sherwood, Maxwell Anderson, Sidney Howard, S. N. Behrman, and Elmer Rice – to join together in 1938 to form their own producing organization, the Playwrights' Company. Opening with Sherwood's *Abe Lincoln in Illinois* (1938), they presented Anderson's *Knickerbocker Holiday* (1938), Rice's *American Landscape* (1938), and Behrman's *No Time for Comedy* (1939), launching an ambitious programme which would survive until 1960. Together with the Theatre Guild, they set the standard for Broadway production in the late 1930s.

The successful musicals of the 1930s tended to be both stylish and topical. George S. Kaufman and Howard Dietz's *The Band Wagon* (1931) offered brilliant artistry – directing by Hassard Short, dancing by **Fred** and **Adele Astaire**, and memorable songs such as 'Dancing in the Dark' and 'The Beggar Waltz'. *Of Thee I Sing* (1931) by the Gershwins, George S. Kaufman, and Morrie Ryskind satirized the supreme court, president, vice-president, diplomatic corps, and the general humbug of American elections. In 1935, *Porgy and Bess* arrived on Broadway for 124 performances, making famous such songs as 'Summertime', 'A Woman is a Sometime Thing', 'I Got Plenty o' Nuttin'', and 'It Ain't Necessarily So'. In the 1940–1 season, *Pal Joey* by Richard Rodgers and **Lorenz Hart**,

A scene from George Gershwin's *Porgy and Bess*.

and *Lady in the Dark* by Moss Hart, Ira Gershwin, and Kurt Weill offered more mature subjects and a worldly tone. *Pal Joey* showcased Gene Kelly in the title role and offered a bitter and cynical look at urban life. Songs such as 'Bewitched, Bothered, and Bewildered' and 'I Could Write a Book' have become American standards. *Lady in the Dark* dealt with psychoanalysis in surrealistic dream sequences with superb performances by **Gertrude Lawrence** and Danny Kaye.

The depression gripped the nation spiritually as well as economically, and set the tone for serious drama. O'Neill wrote *Mourning Becomes Electra* (1931), a six-hour play based on the *Oresteia*. Philip Moeller directed, Robert Edmond Jones designed, and **Alla Nazimova**, **Alice Brady**, and Earle Larimore starred. The play ran for 150 performances. Two years later *Tobacco Road* opened for a seven-year run, based on Erskine Caldwell's steamy novel of Georgia backwoods' poor white trash, starring Henry Hull as Jeeter Lester. In 1935, Clifford Odets's *Awake and Sing*, Sidney Kingsley's *Dead End*, and Maxwell Anderson's *Winterset* offered a sombre picture of the American dream. **Lillian Hellman**'s *The Children's Hour* (1934) and *The Little Foxes* (1939), **John Steinbeck**'s *Of Mice and Men* (1937), and **Thornton Wilder**'s epic *Our Town* (1938) suggested the anxiety underlying American life.

Bad economic times produced some of America's best comic writing. O'Neill penned a domestic comedy in 1933, *Ah, Wilderness!*, which critics thought sentimental and moralistic but reassuring. Sam and Bella Spewack's *Boy Meets Girl* (1935) provided a light-hearted spoof of Hollywood. Clare Booth's *The Women* (1936) was a bitchy satire on idle and wealthy urban women. The George Kaufman and Moss Hart collaborations, *You Can't Take it With You* (1936) and *The Man Who Came to Dinner* (1939), were the funniest American comedies since *The Front Page*, and have remained classics. **Rachel Crothers** returned from Hollywood in 1937 to write *Susan and God*, a satire on the efforts of a wife to reform her alcoholic husband. *My Heart's in the Highlands* and *The Time of Your Life* (both 1939) established William Saroyan as an important playwright. **Howard Lindsay** and **Russel Crouse**'s *Life with Father* (1939), starring Lindsay and Dorothy Stickney, became a smash hit which ran for 3,216 performances, then a record. James Thurber and Elliott Nugent's *The Male Animal* appeared the same season and satirized intellectual as well as romantic notions of the nation.

America's favourite acting couple, Alfred Lunt and Lynn Fontanne, remained popular throughout the 1930s, playing comedy with elegance, grace, and perfect teamwork. **Katharine Cornell** and **Helen Hayes** were considered the First Ladies of the American stage for their beauty and ability to play classical as well as modern roles. Other important actresses included **Tallulah Bankhead**, Eva Le Gallienne, **Ruth Gordon**, and Katharine Hepburn. Except for Alfred Lunt and John Barrymore (before he went to Hollywood), the American stage lacked distinguished actors. The better younger players were opting for a career in films.

Broadway prospered during the Second World War. Irving Berlin's *This is the Army* (1942), Rodgers and Hammerstein's *Oklahoma!* (1943) and *Carousel* (1945), and **Leonard Bernstein**'s *On the Town* (1944) set the pace for musical entertainment. Much of America's serious drama depicted the war as simple melodrama, including Moss Hart's *Winged Victory* (1943), Maxwell Anderson's *Storm Operation* (1944), and James Gow and Arnaud D'Usseau's *Tomorrow the World* (1943), which were anti-fascist. In the spring of 1945, **Tennessee Williams**'s *A Glass Menagerie* opened on Broadway to excellent notices with fine performances by **Laurette Taylor**, **Eddie Dowling** and Julie Haydon. Comedies offered little more than escape except Thornton Wilder's *Skin of Our Teeth* (1942) which preached survival in a strange theatrical style. More typical were Joseph Kesselring's off-beat farce, *Arsenic and Old Lace* (1941), John van Druten's sentimental *I Remember Mama* (1944) and Mary Chase's fantastic *Harvey* (1944).

The immediate post-war period saw renewed activity by established writers including Eugene O'Neill's *The Iceman Cometh* (1946); Lillian Hellman's *Another Part of the Forest* (1946); Maxwell Anderson's *Anne of the Thousand Days* (1948); Clifford Odets's *The Country Girl* (1950); and Sidney Kingsley's *Darkness at Noon* (1951), adapted from Arthur Koestler's novel. At the time of O'Neill's death in 1953, his reputation was in a decline. A reevaluation of his work began with **José Quintero**'s revival of *The Iceman Cometh* at **Circle in the Square** in 1956. **Jason Robards**'s portrayal of Hickey drew widespread praise and launched his career. Later that year, O'Neill's *Long Day's Journey into Night* premiered at Circle in the Square under Quintero's direction and was hailed as the playwright's greatest work. *A Moon for the Misbegotten* followed in 1957 and *A Touch of the Poet* in 1958. In 1959, the Coronet Theatre in New York was renamed in O'Neill's honour.

Popular successes at the time reflected the public's continued interest in the war and its own idealism. Garson Kanin's comedy *Born Yesterday* (1946) ran for 1,642 performances and made a star of Judy Holliday. Other hits include William Wister Haines's melodrama, *Command Decision* (1947); Norman Krasna's farce, *John Loves Mary* (1947); Thomas Heggen and **Joshua Logan**'s comedy, *Mr Roberts* (1947), starring **Henry Fonda**; Donald Bevan and Edmund Trzcinski's thriller, *Stalag 17* (1951); and Herman Wouk's courtroom drama, *The Caine Mutiny Court Martial* (1954).

After the war, Tennessee Williams, **Arthur Miller**, and **William Inge** emerged as the major new playwrights. *A Streetcar Named Desire* (1947) with stellar performances by **Marlon Brando, Jessica Tandy**, Karl Malden and **Kim Hunter**, solidified Williams's reputation established with *The Glass Menagerie*, and won both the Pulitzer Prize and the Critics Circle Award. In 1947, Arthur Miller's *All My Sons* drew respectable notices and won the Drama Critics Award. Two years later his *Death of a Salesman* under **Elia Kazan**'s direction and with a brilliant performance by

Lee J. Cobb duplicated Williams's success. Williams and Miller depicted a society which had grown decadent, obsessed with materialism and power. Williams wrote with compassion and poetic insight about the people unable to cope, who seek escape through booze, drugs, daydreams, and sex. His plays in the 1950s include *The Rose Tattoo* (1951), *Cat on a Hot Tin Roof* (1955), *Orpheus Descending* (1957), *Sweet Bird of Youth* (1959), and *The Night of the Iguana* (1961). Later his reputation suffered from such lesser pieces as *The Milk Train Doesn't Stop Here Anymore* (1963), *Vieux Carré* (1977), and *Clothes for a Summer Hotel* (1980). Arthur Miller focused more on the larger social and political issues in *The Crucible* (1953), *A View from the Bridge* (1956), and *Incident at Vichy* (1964). His last plays – i.e., *The Creation of the World and Other Business* (1972) and *The American Clock* (1980) – were not well received. Inge's reputation has not worn as well as his two colleagues. In 1950 *Come Back, Little Sheba* established him as an important playwright and promoted the career of actress **Shirley Booth**. Inge would enjoy meteoric success with hits *Picnic* (1953), *Bus Stop* (1955), and *The Dark at the Top of the Stairs* (1957) before his star faded in the 1960s. His plays now seem sentimental and contrived.

After the war, Rodgers and Hammerstein continued their mastery of operetta with *South Pacific* (1949), which ran for 1,925 performances. *The King and I* (1951) made Yul Brynner a star and ran for 1,246 performances. Their last major collaboration, *The Sound of Music* (1959), ran for 1,443 performances. This was a golden age of the American musical. Hits by other composers include: Irving Berlin's *Annie Get Your Gun* (1946); **Lerner** and **Loewe**'s *Brigadoon* (1947); Harburg and Saidy's *Finian's Rainbow* (1947); Cole Porter's *Kiss Me Kate* (1948); **Frank Loesser**'s *Guys and Dolls* (1950); Irving Berlin's *Call Me Madam* (1950); Leonard Bernstein's *Wonderful Town* (1953); Lerner and Loewe's *My Fair Lady* (1956), starring **Rex Harrison** and Julie Andrews; Bernstein's *West Side Story* (1957) with choreography by **Jerome Robbins**; and Jule Styne's *Gypsy* (1959), starring **Ethel Merman**. The American musical possessed energy and style and was recognized as the nation's most original contribution to world theatre.

Comedy grew tame and unadventuresome in the 1950s relying on stock plots and comic devices. In 1952, Ronald Alexander's domestic comedy *Time Out for Ginger* was a minor hit (248 performances) the same year George Axelrod's sex farce, *Seven Year Itch*, ran for 1,141 presentations and made a star of Tom Ewell. Another smash hit, **John Patrick**'s *The Teahouse of the August Moon* (1953), endured for 1,027 performances and won both the Critics Circle and Pulitzer Prize. Samuel Taylor's two hits, *Sabrina Fair* (1953) and *Pleasure of his Company* (1958), reminded audiences of Philip Barry and S. N. Behrman. George S. Kaufman with Howard Teichmann wrote a mild satire about American business methods, *The Solid Gold Cadillac* (1953). Sidney Kingsley's farcical *Lunatics and Lovers* (1954) offered audiences a screwball comedy and Buddy Hackett. Thornton Wilder's *The Matchmaker* (1955) endured for 486 performances and later served as the book for *Hello, Dolly!* **Jerome Lawrence** and **Robert E. Lee**'s *Auntie Mame* (1956) ran for 639 performances before it was transformed into the musical *Mame*. In 1959, **Paddy Chayevsky**'s *The Tenth Man* provided mysticism and love in a plot which threatened to turn serious.

In the work of the **Actors Studio**, the post-war American theatre found an acting style in which to interpret the realistic plays of Williams, Miller, and Inge. Elia Kazan, **Robert Lewis** and Cheryl Crawford founded the Studio in 1947, joined by Lee Strasberg a year later. Strasberg's system of acting based on Stanislavsky's writings became known as the Method and attracted a generation of actors including Marlon Brando and **Geraldine Page**. Kazan became the prominent director of his age, mounting important premieres for Williams, Miller, and Inge. As if to underscore the passing of an era, in 1958 Alfred Lunt and Lynn Fontanne gave their farewell performance in *The Visit*.

In the 1920s, Robert Edmond Jones had set the standard for American stage scenery by evolving a style of simplified sets which suggested rather than reproduced reality. His successor, **Jo Mielziner**, dominated American stage design from 1930 until his death in 1976. Mielziner used transparent scenery in a cinematic way to complement the poetic quality of plays by Williams and Miller. Ming Cho Lee has followed Mielziner as the major influence upon contemporary stage design in a style which features collage, textured surfaces, and scaffolding. Other important scenic artists of the post-war era include **Boris Aronson**, **Oliver Smith**, **Jean Rosenthal**, **Santo Loquasto**, and **Eugene Lee**.

After the Second World War, high production costs on Broadway and efforts to establish professional theatre outside of New York resulted in the Off-Broadway and regional theatre movements. Off-Broadway recorded its first major success in 1952 with José Quintero's revival of Williams's *Summer and Smoke* at the Circle in the Square. The production reclaimed the play (which had earlier failed on Broadway) and made a star of Geraldine Page. Judith Malina and Julian Beck opened **The Living Theatre** in 1951; Norris Houghton and Edward Hambleton founded the Phoenix in 1953; and **Joseph Papp** created the most important Off-Broadway theatre in 1954, the **New York Shakespeare Festival**. Outside New York, in 1947 **Margo Jones** founded Theatre 47 in Dallas, and Nina Vance the **Alley Theatre** in Houston. In 1950 Zelda Fichandler and Edward Mangum created the **Arena Stage** in Washington, DC. Two years later Herbert Blau and Jules Irving established the Actors' Workshop in San Francisco. In 1955, the **American Shakespeare Festival** opened in Stratford, Connecticut, joining the Oregon Shakespeare Festival (1935–) as a major summer company dedicated to the production of Shakespeare's plays.

In the 1960s, the American stage faced a revolt which was aesthetic and social. A new artistic school rejected much of the American theatre for being too rational and psychological. They wanted a theatre experience which would tap into the unconscious, and make its appeal through the senses rather than the mind. Influenced by the writings of **Antonin Artaud**, these neo-romantics experimented with form, language, and space to understand the relationship between life and art. In composing music, John Cage used chance procedures and recordings of everyday noises to force his audience

to listen without pre-determining meaning. Allan Kaprow's Happenings were efforts to redefine the boundaries between art and life by blurring the distinction. The theatrical collectives of the Becks, Richard Schechner, and **Joseph Chaikin** were attempts to understand and shape audience–performer dynamics. Social revolt in the theatre reflected the larger society where affluent youth 'dropped out' of a materialistic world and 'turned-on' to drugs, sex, and rock music. Relaxed obscenity laws, improved birth control methods, the civil rights movement, and the Vietnam War helped define a generation who demanded that all forms of art be relevant to contemporary life, and who echoed Artaud's cry of 'No more masterpieces!' There was no longer one theatre audience but many as American culture fragmented in the face of rapid and explosive change.

The most successful playwright on Broadway was **Neil Simon**, with comic hits *Come Blow Your Horn* (1961), *Barefoot in the Park* (1963), *The Odd Couple* (1965), *Plaza Suite* (1968), *The Last of the Red Hot Lovers* (1969) plus books for musicals *Little Me* (1962), *Sweet Charity* (1966), and *Promises, Promises* (1968). **Edward Albee** emerged as the decade's major dramatist with *Who's Afraid of Virginia Woolf?* (1962) after early successes in one-acts *The Zoo Story* (1959) and *The American Dream* (1961). *Tiny Alice* (1964) and *Quotations from Chairman Mao Tse-Tung* (1968) were thought obscure but *Delicate Balance* (1966) won Albee the Pulitzer Prize. Both Simon and Albee wrote about deteriorating family and personal relationships and the inability of individuals to maintain community.

Rock music brought some change to musical theatre in the 1960s. *Hair* (1967) was a cultural as well as artistic event and spawned a wave of imitations. But traditional forms continued to set new attendance figures: *Fiddler on the Roof* (1964) ran for 3,242 performances; *Hello, Dolly!* (1964) for 2,844; and *Man of La Mancha* (1965) for 2,328 performances. Other hits included *Camelot* (1960), *She Loves Me* (1963), *Funny Girl* (1964), *Mame* (1966) and *Cabaret* (1966).

As production costs mounted in the late 1950s, artists turned lofts, churches, cafés, and garages into theatres in what was to be called the Off-Off Broadway movement. In 1958 Joe Cino's Caffé began presenting plays by new writers such as **Lanford Wilson** and **Sam Shepard**. Ellen Stewart's Café **La Mama** (1961–) proved more durable and has continued to produce new playwrights in addition to providing a platform for young directors such as Tom O'Horgan and **Andrei Serban**. The production of new plays gave purpose to Al Carmines's Judson Poets' Theatre (1961), Wynn Handman's **American Place Theatre** (1964), Ralph Cook's Theatre Genesis (1964), and Joseph Papp's New York Shakespeare Festival and its Public Theatre. Joseph Chaikin's **Open Theatre** (1963), and Richard Schechner's **Performance Group** (1968) were more concerned with the aesthetics of performance. The growth of the Off-Off Broadway movement led to an Alliance (OOBA) in 1972 for purposes of shared services. During the 1974–5 season, the *New York Times* reported 548 plays in 150 theatres Off-Off Broadway.

Resident non-profit professional theatre continued to grow at a rapid pace in the 1960s and early 1970s, receiving strong financial support from private foundations. Important regional companies include: **Guthrie Theatre** in Minneapolis (1963); **Actors Theatre of Louisville** (1964); **Trinity Square Repertory Company** of Providence, Rhode Island (1964); **Long Wharf** in New Haven, Connecticut (1965); the **Yale Repertory Theatre** (1966); and the American Conservatory Theatre** in San Francisco (1966). Cultural centres – i.e., the Lincoln Center in New York, **John F. Kennedy Centre** in Washington, DC, and Music Centre in Los Angeles – were built with theatres as part of their complexes. In New York the Shakespeare Festival's Public Theatre (1967), **Circle Repertory Company** (1969), **Manhattan Theatre Club** (1970), and **Acting Company** (1972) provided places for artists to experiment in non-commercial environments.

Theatre companies dedicated to radical politics proliferated in the 1960s embracing racial, homosexual, feminist, and anti-war causes. Black theatre benefited from the civil rights movement of the late 1950s which made desegregation and equal rights major issues in both politics and art. An important play for symbolic as well as aesthetic and political reasons, **Lorraine Hansberry**'s *Raisin in the Sun* (1959) ran for 530 performances on Broadway. Two years later, **Ossie Davis**'s *Purlie Victorious* also found a mainstream audience for a moderate run. The mood of black theatre then turned violent. **James Baldwin**'s *Blues for Mister Charlie* (1964) dealt with the death of a civil rights worker, anticipating the fierce plays of LeRoi Jones (**Imamu Amiri Baraka**): *Dutchman* (1964), *The Toilet* (1965), *The Slave* (1965), and *Slave Ship* (1969); and **Ed Bullins**: *How Do You Do* (1965), *Clara's Ole Man* (1965), and *The Electronic Nigger* (1968). Black women playwrights **Adrienne Kennedy** and **Ntozake Shange** wrote unsparingly about their experiences. White dramatists Martin Duberman (*In White America*, 1963) and Howard Sackler (*The Great White Hope*, 1968) raised social awareness about the effects of discrimination on black Americans. The availability of public and private monies in the 1960s supported the growth of black theatre companies including the Free Southern Theatre (1963), New Lafayette (1967), and **Negro Ensemble Company** (1967). The NEC has presented premieres of **Douglas Turner Ward**'s *Day of Absence* (1967), **Lonne Elder III**'s *Ceremonies in Dark Old Men* (1969); Joseph A. Walker's *The River Niger* (1972), and **Charles Fuller**'s *A Soldier's Play* (1981), which was awarded the Pulitzer Prize.

Other racial minorities have found theatre an effective tool in which to deal with discrimination. In 1965 **Luis Valdéz** established **El Teatro Campesino** in California to support the migrant farm workers' strike. In 1978 his play *Zoot Suit* about discrimination against the Chicano opened at the **Mark Taper Forum** in Los Angeles, and later played in New York. While its original purpose was economic, El Teatro Campesino has forged a new social identity for the Chicano caught between Mexican and American cultures. Hanay Geiogamah's Native American Theatre Ensemble in the 1970s evolved out of the American Indian Movement of the late 1960s.

Gay theatre groups were formed in the 1960s following the efforts of gay activists to gain recognition and respect for the homosexual lifestyle. While much of gay theatre has existed for its own sub-culture, Mark Crowley's *The Boys in the Band* (1968) ran for 1,000 performances Off-Broadway, suggesting a widespread interest in the gay community. The acceptance of homosexual subjects by mainstream audiences gained credibility in the 1980s when **Harvey Fierstein**'s *Torch Song Trilogy* (1982) won the Drama Critics Award and Tony for best play, and *La Cage aux Folles* (1983) received a Tony for best musical. Lesbian and gay Theatre Companies formed an Alliance in 1978 with 28 groups identified across the country in 1981.

Like black and gay theatre, feminist theatre has followed efforts by activists to gain equality for a minority. Organizations which have taken an active feminist position include Anselma Dell'Ollio's New Feminist Theatre, the Rhode Island Feminist Theatre, Omaha Magic Theatre, and the Women's Project of the American Place Theatre. Playwrights with a strong feminist vision include **Alice Childress**, **Megan Terry**, Corinne Jacker, **Maria Irene Fornes**, Ntozake Shange, **Rosalyn Drexler**, and **Marsha Norman**. Norman's *'night, Mother* won the Pulitzer Prize in 1983.

Anti-American plays proliferated at the end of the 1960s as the nation turned against the Vietnam War. In 1966–7 the San Francisco Mime Troupe, Yale Repertory Theatre and the Living Theatre responded to the conflict by performing agit-prop, anti-war material. They were joined by the **Bread and Puppet Theatre**, the Performance Group, La Mama ETC, the Open Theatre and others. Plays with an anti-war point of view include Megan Terry's *Viet Rock* (1966), Joseph Heller's *We Bombed in New Haven* (1968), and **David Rabe**'s *The Basic Training of Pavlo Hummel* (1968), *Sticks and Bones* (1971), and *Streamers* (1976). In vogue for a time were documentary plays which held up to question acts of the American government: Donald Freed's *Inquest* (1970), about the Rosenberg trial; Daniel Berrigan's *The Trial of the Catonsville Nine* (1971); Stanley R. Greenberg's *Pueblo* (1971); and **Eric Bentley**'s *Are You Now Or Have You Ever Been* (1972), about the McCarthy hearings of the 1950s. Plays which responded to the youth, sex, and drug culture of the time include: Jack Gelber's *The Connection* (1959), Dale Wasserman's *One Flew Over the Cuckoo's Nest* (1963); the rock musical, *Hair* (1967); the Performance Group's *Dionysus in '69* (1968); Robert Patrick's *Kennedy's Children* (1970); and **Michael Weller**'s *Moonchildren* (1972).

Since the early 1970s, theatre in America has become less a public than a private art. The leading figures of the avant-garde, **Richard Foreman**, **Robert Wilson**, and **Lee Breuer**, have shunned plot, character, and language to present highly personal images which resist conventional interpretation. Foreman's Ontological Hysteric Theatre (1968–) requires an audience to experience each moment without reducing everything to meaning. Wilson's best-known opera, *Einstein on the Beach* (1976), depends more on form and sound than character, plot, and language as he attempts to free audiences from a tendency to over-rationalize experience. Breuer's **Mabou Mines** Company uses pop art and media images to explore how the self invents its own definition. The use of mixed media to create a theatre of personal images also characterizes the work of **Spalding Gray**, **Meredith Monk**, Ping Chong, **JoAnne Akalaitis**, Martha Clarke, **Elizabeth LeCompte**, and the Wooster Group. Unlike O'Neill and Williams who used the conventions of the theatre to turn personal experience into drama, these artists shun conventions and present highly personal images from their experiences which must be turned into drama by their audiences.

Since the 1960s, Broadway has become an outlet where proven theatrical wares are merchandised to an affluent minority. Audiences have viewed an increasing number of revivals (especially musicals) and productions transferred from Off-Broadway, the regional theatres and from London. Neil Simon has continued his domination of American comedy with *The Prisoner of Second Avenue* (1971), *The Sunshine Boys* (1972), *California Suite* (1976), *Chapter Two* (1977), *Brighton Beach Memoirs* (1983), and *Biloxi Blues* (1984). Less successful have been his more serious *The Gingerbread Lady* (1970), *God's Favourite* (1974), *The Good Doctor* (1973), and *Fools* (1981). While Edward Albee won a Pulitzer Prize for *Seascape* (1975), the best drama has come from Off-Broadway and from the trio of Sam Shepard, Lanford Wilson, and **David Mamet**. Shepard's plays appear realistic on the surface, belying their vivid theatricality and close relationship with the absurd. He depicts a world where family, community, and love have lost their meanings while the words remain as part of the media culture. Alienated from their environment, Shepard's characters struggle towards some kind of transcendental experience. His plays do not depend on well-made plots but on highly personal images to which the audience must find connections. His best work to date includes: *Curse of the Starving Class* (1976), *Buried Child* (1978), *True West* (1980), *Fool for Love* (1983), and *A Lie of the Mind* (1985). Lanford Wilson's lyrical prose suggests the influence of Tennessee Williams. His *Balm in Gilead* (1965) at La Mama brought him recognition while *Hot l Baltimore* (1973) set a record Off-Broadway with 1,166 performances. His best play, *Fifth of July* (1978), became a metaphor for an entire generation coming to terms with its own failed idealism. Other works include *The Mound Builders* (1975), *Talley's Folly* (1979) which won a Pulitzer, and *Angel's Fall* (1983). Mamet uses language brilliantly to depict the spiritual emptiness which lies at the core of contemporary American life. He established his career in Chicago before winning the Drama Critics Award for *American Buffalo* (1977), and the Pulitzer Prize in 1984 for *Glengarry Glen Ross*, plays which suggest that there is little difference between commercial and criminal ethics in American society.

Dominating musical theatre since the mid-1970s, and widely regarded as the most original and innovative composer-lyricist now writing in the American theatre, is **Stephen Sondheim**. He avoids sentimentality and offers a bittersweet and satirical view of art and life. His major works include *Company* (1970); *Follies* (1971); *A Little Night Music* (1973) which contains his best known song, 'Send in the Clowns'; *Pacific Overtures* (1976); *Sweeney Todd* (1979); and *Sunday in the Park with George* (1984), which won a Pulitzer. He has worked closely with director **Harold Prince** in all but the latter. By the mid-1980s, the American musical has become less dependent upon a book than upon a concept or theme. This has elevated the choreographer-director to a new position of power. The best known of the new breed, **Bob Fosse**, created hits with *Pippin*

(1972), *Chicago* (1975), and *Dancin'* (1978). **Michael Bennett** developed the longest run show on Broadway in *Chorus Line* (1973), and assembled another hit in *Dreamgirls* (1981).

London successes have been seen frequently in New York since the early 1970s, including **Peter Shaffer**'s *Equus* and *Amadeus*; **David Storey**'s *The Changing Room* and *Home*; **Tom Stoppard**'s *Travesties* and *The Real Thing*; **Andrew Lloyd Webber** and **Tim Rice**'s *Jesus Christ Superstar* and *Evita*, as well as Webber's *Cats*; **Harold Pinter**'s *The Homecoming* and *Betrayal*; and plays by **David Hare**, **Simon Gray**, **Caryl Churchill** and C. P. Snow. The **Royal Shakespeare Company** has visited several times but is remembered especially for *The Life and Adventures of Nicholas Nickleby* in 1980.

The American theatre in the mid-1980s depends less on Broadway than at any time this century, and more on the non-profit resident theatres both inside and out of New York. New plays of distinction now originate regularly at such theatres as the New York Shakespeare Festival, **Playwrights Horizon**, Chicago's Steppenwolf Theatre Company and **Goodman Theatre**, the Yale Repertory Theatre, **American Repertory Theatre** at Harvard, Mark Taper Forum in Los Angeles, Actors Theatre of Louisville, and Long Wharf Theatre in New Haven, Conn. The *Burns Mantle Best Plays of 1984–5* reported that six of their ten best plays did not originate on Broadway. High costs make producing in Manhattan a risky business. During the 1984–5 season, a new musical, *Grind*, lost its entire investment of $4,750,000. The *New York Times* reported that a revival of *Arsenic and Old Lace* in 1986 cost $700,000 compared to the original amount in 1941 of $37,000. Even Off-Broadway plays are costing up to $400,000 to produce. Ticket prices of $40.00 to $50.00 for Broadway have become the norm.

Production values in the American theatre of the 1980s remain high. The Broadway musical has no equal, with a wide array of talented young performers including Bernadette Peters, Mandy Patinkin, Ben Vereen, and Tommy Tune. A more serious problem lies in the dearth of composers and writers who can attract a large enough audience to reward investors. A new generation of talented actors including Judith Ivey, John Lithgow, **Meryl Streep**, William Hurt, Pamela Reed, Lindsay Crouse, **Kevin Kline**, Mary Beth Hurt, **Glenn Close**, and Swoosie Kurtz promises distinguished performances in the future if they continue to appear on stage as well as in films. But the theatre is not attracting the younger playgoer. One estimate has placed the average age of the Broadway audience at 44. High ticket prices and the appeal of films are undoubtedly major reasons for this condition. With electronic media radically changing how we receive information, the future of the American stage may lie in directions in which innovators Richard Foreman, Robert Wilson, Lee Breuer, and others are pointing.   TLM

Various items referred to above are discussed in greater detail in separate entries, including: **Afro-American theatre**; **American musical theatre**; **Chicano theatre**; **Ethnic theatre**; **Feminist theatre**; **Frontier theatre**; **Little Theatre movement**; **Living Newspaper**; **Off-Broadway**; **Off-Off Broadway**; **Resident non-profit professional theatre**; **Theatrical Syndicate**; **United**

States: theatres in New York City; **Western theatre**; **Yankee theatre**.

Section 1

See: T. Bogard, R. Moody, W. J. Meserve, *The Revels History of Drama in English: Vol. VIII: American Drama*, London, 1977; J. S. Bost, *Monarchs of the Mimic World*, Orono, Maine, 1977; O. S. Coad and E. Mims, Jr, *The American Stage*, New Haven, CT, 1927; W. Dunlap, *A History of the American Theatre*, New York, 1832; B. Hewitt, *Theatre U. S. A., 1668 to 1957*, New York, 1959; G. Hughes, *A History of the American Theatre*, New York, 1951; B. McNamara, *The American Playhouse in the Eighteenth Century*, Cambridge, MA, 1969; W. J. Meserve, *An Outline History of American Drama*, Totowa, NJ, 1965; *idem, An Emerging Entertainment: The Drama of the American People to 1828*, Bloomington, IN, 1977; *idem, Heralds of Promise, The Drama of the American People in the Age of Jackson, 1829–1849*, Westport, CT, 1986; J. Y. Miller, *American Dramatic Literature*, New York, 1961; R. Moody, *America Takes the Stage*, Bloomington, IN, 1955; R. Moody (ed.), *Dramas From the American Theatre 1762–1909*, Cleveland, Ohio, 1969; G. C. D. Odell, *Annals of the New York Stage*, New York, 1927–49; A. H. Quinn, *A History of the American Drama from the Beginning to the Civil War*, New York, 1943; H. F. Rankin, *The Theatre in Colonial America*, Chapel Hill, Nth. Carolina, 1965; H. B. Williams (ed.), *The American Theatre: A Sum of Its Parts*, New York, 1971; G. B. Wilson, *Three Hundred Years of American Drama and Theatre*, Englewood Cliffs, NJ, 1982.

Section 2

See: B. Atkinson, *Broadway*, rev. ed., New York, 1974; D. Belasco, *Theatre Through Its Stage Door*, New York, 1919; A. L. Bernheim, *The Business of the Theatre*, New York, 1932; G. Bordman, *The American Musical Theatre*, Oxford, 1978; O. S. Coad and E. Mims, Jr, *The American Stage*, New Haven, CT, 1920; M. Felheim, *The Theatre of Augustin Daly*, Cambridge, MA, 1956; P. Hartnoll (ed.), *The Oxford Companion to the Theatre*, fourth ed., Oxford, 1983; M. C. Henderson, *The City and the Theatre*, Clifton, NJ, 1973; B. Hewitt, *Theatre U. S. A., 1668 to 1957*, New York, 1959; G. Hughes, *A History of the American Theatre*, New York, 1951; W. J. Meserve, *An Outline History of American Drama*, Totowa, NJ, 1965; R. Moody, *America Takes the Stage*, Bloomington, IN, 1955; E. Mordden, *The American Theatre*, New York, 1981; L. Morris, *Curtain Time*, New York, 1953; J. Moses and J. M. Brown, *The American Theatre as Seen by Its Critics, 1752–1934*, New York, 1934; G. C. D. Odell, *Annals of the New York Stage*, New York, 1927–49; A. H. Quinn, *A History of the American Drama from the Civil War to the Present Day*, 2nd ed., New York, 1949; C. H. Shattuck, *Shakespeare on the American Stage*, Washington, DC, 1976; C. Smith, *Musical Comedy in America*, New York, 1950; J. Stagg, *The Brothers Shubert*, New York, 1968; H. B. Williams (ed.), *The American Theatre: A Sum of Its Parts*, New York, 1971; G. B. Wilson, *A History of American Acting*, Bloomington, IN, 1966; *idem, Three Hundred Years of American Drama and Theatre*, Englewood Cliffs, NJ, 1982; W. Winter, *Life and Art of Edwin Booth*, New York, 1893.

Section 3

See: B. Atkinson, *Broadway*, rev. ed., New York, 1974; J. Beck, *The Life of the Theatre*, New York, 1972; G. M. Berkowitz, *New Broadways: Theatre Across America 1950–1980*, Totowa, NJ; C. W. E. Bigsby, *A Critical Introduction to Twentieth-Century American Drama*, 3 vols., Cambridge, 1982, 1984, 1985; H. Blau, *Take Up the Bodies: Theatre at the Vanishing Point*, Urbana, 1982; G. Bordman, *The American Musical Theatre*, Oxford, 1978; *idem, The Oxford Companion to American Theatre*, Oxford, 1984; S. Brecht, *The Theatre of Visions: Robert Wilson*, Frankfurt-am-Main, 1978; R. Cohn, *New American Dramatists*, London, 1982; R. G. Davis, 'The Radical Right in the American Theatre', *Theatre Quarterly*, v, xix (September–November 1975), 67–72; K. Davy, ed., *Richard Foreman: Plays and Manifestos*, New York, 1976; Spalding Gray, 'About Three Places in Rhode Island', *The Drama Review*, xxiii, i (March 1979), 31–42; P. Hartnoll (ed.), *The Oxford Companion to the Theatre*, fourth ed., Oxford, 1983; B. Hewitt, *Theatre U. S. A., 1668 to 1957*, New York, 1959; E. Hill, *The Theatre of Black Americans*, 2 vols., Englewood Cliffs, NJ, 1980; B. Marranca, *Animations: A Trilogy for Mabou Mines*, New York, 1979; J. Miles (ed.), *The Women's Project: Seven Plays by Women*, New York, 1980; E. Mordden, *The American Theatre*, New York, 1981; R. Schechner, *The End of Humanism*, New York, 1982; T. Shank, *American Alternative Theatre*, London, 1982; Luis Valdéz, *The Drama Review*, xi, iv (September 1967); G. B. Wilson, *Three Hundred Years of American Drama and Theatre*, second ed., Englewood Cliffs, NJ, 1982.

Supplementary bibliography

See: S. M. Archer (compiler), *American Actors and Actresses: A Guide to Information Sources*, Detroit, Michigan, 1983; W. Browne, F. A. Austin (eds.), *Who's Who on the Stage: The Dramatic Reference Book and Bibliographical Dictionary of the Theatre Containing Records of the Careers of Actors, Actresses, Managers, and Playwrights*, 1908; G. B. Bryan (compiler), *Stage Lives: A Bibliography and Index to Theatrical Biographies in English*, Westport, CT and London, 1985; B. N. Cohen-Sratyner, *Biographical Dictionary of Dance*, New York, 1982; C. Ghodes, *Literature and Theater of the States and Regions of the U.S.A.: An Historical Bibliography*, Durham, Nth. Carolina, 1967; I. Herbert (ed.), *Who's Who in the Theatre, Vol. 1, Biographies*, 17th edn, 1981; D. La Beau (ed.), *Theatre, Film and Television Biographies Master Index*, Detroit, 1979; C. F. W. Larson, *American Regional Theatre History to 1900: a Bibliography*, Metuchen, NJ and London, 1979; E. Mapp, *Directory of Blacks in the Performing Arts*, Metuchen, NJ and London, 1978; B. McNeil, M. C. Herbert (eds.), *Performing Arts Biography Master Index*, 2nd edn, Detroit, 1979; R. L. Moyer (compiler), *American Actors, 1861–1910: An Annotated Bibliography of Books published in the United States in English from 1861 through 1976*, Troy, New York, 1979; D. Mullin (ed.), *Victorian Actors and Actresses in View: A Dictionary of Contemporary Views of Representative British and American Actors and Actresses, 1837–1901*, Westport, CT and London, 1983; *New York Times Directory of the Theater*, New York, 1973; W. Rigdon (ed.), *The Biographical Encyclopedia and Who's Who of the American Theatre*, New York, 1966; H. T. Sampson, *Blacks in Blackface: A Source Book on Early Black Musical Shows*, Metuchen, NJ and London, 1980; L. Senelick, D. F. Cheshire, U. Schneider, *British Music Hall 1840–1923: A Bibliography and Guide to Sources, with a Supplement on European Music Hall*, Hamden, CT, 1981; C. H. Shattuck, *The Shakespeare Prompt Books: A Descriptive Catalogue*, Urbana and London, 1965; A. Slide, *The Vaudevillians: A Dictionary of Vaudeville Performers*, Westport, CT, 1981; R. Stoddard, *Stage Scenery, Machinery, and Lighting: A Guide to Information Sources*, Detroit, 1977; *idem, Theatre and Cinema Architecture: A Guide to Information Sources*, Detroit, 1978; C. J. Stratman (compiler), *A Bibliography of American Theatre, Excluding New York City*, Chicago, 1965; *idem, American Theatrical Periodicals, 1798–*

1967: A Bibliographical Guide, Durham, Nth. Carolina, 1970; J. Trapido (ed.), *An International Dictionary of Theatre Language*, Westport, CT and London, 1985; J. P. Wearing (compiler), *American and British Theatrical Biography: A Dictionary*, Metuchen, NJ, 1979; *Who Was Who in the Theatre: 1912–1976*, 4 vols., Detroit, 1978; D. B. Wilmeth, *The American Stage to World War I: A Guide to Information Sources*, Detroit, 1978; *idem*, *American and English Popular Entertainment: A Guide to Information Sources*, Detroit, 1980; *idem*, *Variety Entertainment and Outdoor Amusements: A Reference Guide*, Westport, CT and London, 1982.

United States of America: theatres in New York City

(General) From its inception, New York, or more properly, the island of Manhattan, was blessed with an air of cosmopolitanism. Settled by the Dutch at the toe of the island early in the 17th century, its population grew to include English, French, Irish, German and Jewish inhabitants plus Negro slaves. If, when the English took over the settlement later in the century, the Anglican church dominated its religious life, the tone had been set by the fundamentalism of the Dutch Reformed church. The arrival of the Presbyterians and Methodists served to strengthen the conservatism of the early population, which found its entertainment within the family and home and in simple outdoor pursuits and sports.

The creation of a miniature English court at the beginning of the 18th century plus the growing prosperity of the colonials brought people out of their homes and into society. Early records suggest amateur theatrical entertainment in and around the colonial court and, perhaps, itinerant performers in the early taverns. Then, in 1732, a newspaper advertisement refers to a theatre owned by 'the honourable Rip Van Dam' and later a map (1735) shows a playhouse close to the English fort, the site of the governor's residence. Both theatres were probably rudimentary and makeshift, but they point to a greater interest in theatrical activity among the colonial population.

By the mid-18th century, two theatrical companies visited New York, the second of which was composed of professional actors from London. They settled in a theatre on Nassau Street, which may well have been the Rip Van Dam warehouse theatre used by the amateurs some 20 years before. Although it still encountered religious opposition, a company assembled by **David Douglass** in Jamaica from the remnants of the old **Hallam** company returned to New York in 1758 and was emboldened by a palpable interest in theatrical entertainment to build three theatres in the next nine years. One of them, the Theatre in **John Street** built in 1767, was to serve Douglass until his withdrawal from the mainland before the Revolution and later used by the occupying English troops during the war. When **Lewis Hallam** the younger returned to New York in 1785, he reopened the theatre and used it until 1798.

The first substantial playhouse to be built in New York was subscribed by the city's important and wealthy citizens and located in a site destined to become an early municipal centre at a place where Broadway was to merge with The Bowery, the main road to Boston from the city. Here, in 1798, a new theatre was built, which came to be known as the **Park**. Here, theatre was established as a necessary concomitant of urban living. Designed by a French architect, Joseph Mangin, the playhouse had an ugly exterior but provided reasonable comfort for its patrons in the auditorium and represented a distinct improvement over the old unattractive and uncomfortable wooden John Street house.

While the Park dominated theatrical activity through the early years of the 18th century, it provided the spur for the building of other theatres in the burgeoning city. To the east and north of it, a more elegant theatre was built on **The Bowery**, but quickly fell out of favour with the fashionable class and survived into the 20th century as a 'neighbourhood house' catering for the tastes of its shifting and immigrant population. For the sixth and last time, it was destroyed by fire in 1929.

By 1825, New York had emerged as the premier theatre city of America. Theatres dotted the urban landscape but they never strayed too far from Broadway, the principal thoroughfare of the city. Stars from England and Europe generally made New York the first stop on their lucrative tours. When the fortunes of the Park waned, other theatres arose to take its place. The comedian **Billy Mitchell** made his Olympic Theatre the most popular theatre on Broadway in the late 1830s and early 1840s. Another comedian, **William E. Burton**, took over a little opera house on Chambers Street, dispensing his merry entertainment to enthusiastic audiences. Theatres tended to get bigger and more comfortable, culminating in the 4,500-seat **Broadway Theatre**, modelled on London's **Haymarket**.

As the city pushed northward, so did the theatres. By the mid-century, Broadway was no longer residential but mixed factories, office buildings, shops and department stores together with theatres along its way. Playhouses purveyed everything from minstrel shows to opera to urbane English comedy and became more attractive architecturally as they reflected the trends from Europe. **Niblo's Garden** had a grand foyer for its patrons and most theatres included refreshment stands. Seats were upholstered in the National Theatre and the pit was rendered into the orchestra and made respectable as the gallery became the family circle to combat the rowdyism of its early denizens. The familiar tiers of boxes atrophied into ceremonial sidewall appendages as the stage was pulled closer to the curtain line.

In the last decades of the 19th century, following the process of urbanization, a theatre district began to form around Union Square at the junction of Broadway and Fourth Avenue at 14th Street. The Academy of Music, **Wallack's Theatre**, and **Union Square** and **Tony Pastor**'s all offering different entertainment, formed a core around which a small support industry of agents, costumers, photographers, managers, restaurants, theatrical boarding houses and hotels sprang up. More theatres were built above Union Square, reaching to Herald Square and beyond, to satisfy an entertainment-hungry population. In 1869, **Edwin Booth** built his elegant theatre at the corner of Sixth Avenue and 23rd Street and provided a new look in theatres. (See **Booth's Theatre**.) Gone was the raked stage and with it, the wing-and-drop setting. In its place, illusory walls of canvas and lath were fastened to the stage floor to create rooms and scenes of extraordinary realistic detail.

In 1893, **Charles Frohman** built his **Empire Theatre** on Broadway at 40th Street and Oscar Hammerstein crossed 42nd Street to build his **Olympia** at 44th Street just two years later. Both structures signalled the development of a new theatre district around Longacre (later Times) Square. From 1900 to 1928, an unprecedented boom in theatre building ensued, providing New York's population with more playhouses than it could support. The new theatres reflected the change in theatrical production. The 19th-century stock company resident in its own theatre was supplanted by the 'combination system', or the assembling of a cast for the presentation of a single play to be produced at a rented theatre. Consisting of a stage, dressing rooms, a box office, an auditorium and a small lobby, the 20th-century playhouse served the new system. With fewer than 2,000 seats, they were well-suited for the plays and musicals presented on their stages.

Some 80 theatres were built during this era and filled Broadway from 39th Street to 54th Street and its side streets. Some were erected on odd-shaped parcels of land, others had proper facades designed in a variety of styles from Egyptian to Georgian and all are proscenium theatres. They were largely the architectural work of J. B. McElfatrick and Company and Herbert J. Krapp. Beginning with the depression and extending into the years beyond the Second World War, more than half of them fell victim to the competitive effects of movies and television and the rise of New York's alternative theatre, Off-Broadway and Off-Off Broadway. Some were torn down, others were converted to movie houses (those lining 42nd Street) and a few were rebuilt to serve other purposes.

With the recognition that New York's theatres were rapidly becoming an endangered species, a succession of the city's mayors began to take steps to protect the standing playhouses while stimulating the erection of others. Zoning laws were changed to permit the incorporation of theatres within tall office buildings, which resulted in the **Gershwin** and **Minskoff** Theatres and two smaller playhouses in the early 1970s. Only a few have been protected by the Landmark law and the fate of the others depends heavily on the availability of plays and musicals suitable for production and the willingness of investors to wager ever greater sums of money to mount them. In 1982, an advisory panel was appointed by Mayor Edward I. Koch to study the situation and to make recommendations for the preservation of the remaining theatres. MCH

United States theatre clubs By and large a gregarious group, actors in 19th-century America sought to organize themselves into social groups. The first of such clubs was the Actors' Order of Friendship, founded in Philadelphia in 1849. In 1888 a lodge was founded in New York City and almost immediately dominated the organization. Primarily designed to supply relief to indigent members, the organization eventually was replaced by the Actors' Fund of America.

The Benevolent and Protective Order of Elks began as a similar charitable organization in New York in 1868. By the turn of this century, however, the organization lost its theatrical nature.

The Lambs Club, primarily social in nature, was founded in 1874 and incorporated in 1877. The Lambs became famous for their Gambols, productions in their private theatre, the receipts from which were donated to charity. This convivial club experienced financial trouble in 1974, but still operates on a modest scale.

The Friars began in 1904 as the National Association of Press Agents, but in 1907 changed its name, widened its membership, and became a club for all theatrical workers. Like the Lambs, the Friars staged productions for charity on a regular basis. Now housed on East 55th Street in New York, the club has recently opened a Los Angeles branch.

Of the theatrical clubs in the USA, perhaps the most distinguished is the Players Club at 16 Gramercy Park, New York. Founded in 1888 by **Edwin Booth**, the club brought together actors and non-theatrical persons; among the charter members were Mark Twain and William Tecumseh Sherman. The clubhouse houses a magnificent collection of theatrical portraits and memorabilia. Booth, who lived in the club for the last five years of his life, donated his personal library to the Players, from which has grown an outstanding American theatre collection. The club for a time gave annual revivals of classic plays, but the practice has been curtailed in recent years.

The first actresses' club was the Twelfth Night Club, founded in 1891 in New York to supply aid and social opportunities for actresses. Another organization, the Professional Woman's League, began in 1892 to meet actresses' professional needs.

In 1907 the Charlotte Cushman Club offered lodging for actresses in Philadelphia, as it continues to do to this day. A large collection of **Cushman** papers and memorabilia are housed in the club. SMA

Uniti, Compagnia degli A commedia dell'arte troupe said to have been founded by Adriano Valerini (Aurelio) in the late 16th century. It circulated throughout northern Italy, under the protection of Vincenzo Gonzaga, Duke of Ferrara, and never toured abroad; it combined with the **Confidenti** in 1583. At various periods, its leading players included, in 1584, **Isabella Andreini**; in 1593, **Drusiano Martinelli** as Arlecchino; and, in 1614, **Silvio Fiorillo** as Captain Matamoros. The last notice of it occurs in 1640, after a long hiatus. LS

Unity Theatre (London) Developed from the Workers' Theatre Movement, it opened its first stage in a converted church hall in 1936 with the English premiere of **Odets**'s *Waiting for Lefty*, which became a model for left-wing theatre of the time with its agit-prop form, audience participation and theme of strikers' solidarity. Moving to a small 200-seat auditorium in 1937, Unity's political line was firmly established with the first of **Brecht**'s plays to be performed in London (*Senora Carrer's Rifles*), a satiric 'political pantomime' (*Babes in the Woods*), and the first English example of **Living Newspaper**, as well as the **Group Theatre**'s production of Spender's *Trial of a Judge* in 1938. It continued to introduce new radical works, including **O'Casey**'s *The Star Turns Red* (1940), **Sartre**'s *Nekrassov* (1956), **Adamov**'s *Spring '71* (1962) and Shatrov's *The Bolsheviks* (1970), until it was burnt down in 1975 while being rebuilt as a cultural centre for the Labour movement. CI

University and school drama (16th–18th centuries)

Drama in the schools and universities of the Middle Ages was usually satirical or celebratory in subject matter, often rowdy in performance, but with the dwindling of the religious theatre of church and town during the 16th century a new amateur drama of instruction developed side by side with the professional theatre of entertainment, and over the next two and a half centuries hundreds of plays were written and performed in universities, colleges and schools all over Europe, many of them in Latin or Greek, some of them polemical, most of them didactic.

The Latin comedies of **Plautus** and **Terence** were the models for the writers of the Christian Terence movement, such as Macropedius, Crocus and Gnaphaeus. Encouraged also by the 1501 edition by Conrad Celtis of the 9th-century Latin plays by the German oblate Hrotsvitha, they composed for their pupils plays on the stories of, for example, Joseph, Susanna and especially the Prodigal Son which was dramatized several times in both Latin and vernacular: the *Acolastus* by the Dutchman, Gnaphaeus, went through 31 editions between 1529 and 1577.

Writers such as the Scottish Catholic George Buchanan modelled their Latin dramas on **Seneca**'s tragedies. Two of Buchanan's plays, *Jepthes* and *Baptistes*, were composed between 1539 and 1542 for the Collège de Guienne in Bordeaux whose actors included the essayist Montaigne. *Baptistes*, in which a parallel is drawn between Herod's execution of John the Baptist and Henry VIII's treatment of Sir Thomas More, was also played in Cambridge in 1562 and, like many of the other Latin school plays, was frequently reprinted as well as being translated into English, French and German.

Catholics and Protestants alike used drama as an aid for teaching and preaching: Luther and the Pope both appear as Antichrist on the 16th-century stage. Medieval biblical and saints' plays were given a new look, either purged of tendentious elements or deliberately slanted for propaganda purposes. Between 1538 and 1621, the pupils of the Protestant college in Strasbourg regularly performed specially written plays in Latin and Greek, designed as pedagogical exercises for the boys but attracting enormous audiences from the surrounding districts. In 1546, Calvin and the Council in Geneva allowed the performance there of the *Acts of the Apostles*, while the *Abraham Sacrifiant* by Calvin's successor, Theodore of Beza, was published in Geneva in 1550 and reprinted in 1560. Towards the end of the 16th century Capuchin friars used specially written plays as part of a *Forty Hour Devotion of the Blessed Sacrament* in an attempt to win back the people of the region round Geneva to the Catholic faith. The Old Testament, the Acts and allegorical material are common sources for this drama, but the rarest subject in 16th-century didactic theatre is the life of Christ. A notable exception to this rule is the *Christus Redivivus* by the Cambridge graduate, Nicholas Grimald, who wrote his Resurrection play in Oxford in 1543. (It was subsequently published in Cologne and used by the **Oberammergau** reviser in the preparation for the text of the performance in 1664.)

Encouraged by Queen Elizabeth, the universities in England also played an important role in the development of the vernacular drama and the tradition continued in the post-Tudor period. Scores of plays were written and performed in the universities and schools of Europe during this period, but the most important single contribution to the school drama is undoubtedly that of the Jesuits who, from their foundation in 1540 to their suspension by the Pope in 1773, were a major force in education throughout Catholic Europe. Plays formed a regular part of the curriculum in all their colleges of which, by the end of the 17th century, there were more than 200. The plays were designed to improve the pupils' knowledge of Latin as well as their ability to speak and move well. The original instruction in the *Ratio studiorum* (1599) was that plays should be in Latin, pious in subject matter and 'very rare'. But the Jesuit drama rapidly became frequent in performance and more wide-ranging in subject matter, including stories from classical and medieval history; in parts of Spain, vernacular replaced Latin and the themes were often humorous and contemporary. A major innovation of the Jesuit drama throughout Europe was the introduction of Ballets as interludes in the Latin texts, thus providing spectacle and music for the benefit of the uneducated members of the public who flocked to see their children act.

Different traditions developed in different countries. In Germany, Austria and Poland where each college might give five to ten performances a year, Jesuit drama formed a part of the spectacular, sometimes fantastic or romantic baroque drama, with Bidemaker, Avancini and Masel being among the most important authors. In Italy and France, on the other hand, the school drama was closely associated with the more sober conventions of the classical theatre (**Jodelle**'s *Cléopâtre Captive*, the first 'classical' play, was performed in the Parisian Collège de Reims in 1552). Many of the Latin Jesuit plays in France were on classical themes and they also influenced the court ballets in their use of symbolism based on classical myth. The first play published was in Rome in 1587 but only a small proportion of the vast number of plays was ever printed, though the subject of many of them is known from the *periochae* or programme notes which gave a synopsis of the action for the benefit of the audience and also described the symbolism of the ballets and musical interludes. (Music plays an important part in other school drama: Purcell's *Dido and Aeneas* was composed for a girls' school in Chelsea and **Racine**'s two plays *Esther* (1689) and *Athalie* (1691), commissioned by Madame de Maintenon for the girls of St Cyr, both contain important choral sections.)

Nor was Jesuit drama entirely limited to Europe: German plays used material from the missions in Japan and the Congo, while from Spain (where the drama developed side by side with the professional theatre of the Golden Age) Jesuit missionaries carried the tradition of teaching by drama with them to the Far East and South America: the first Jesuit plays recorded from Manila in the Philippines date from 1610. LRM

See: L. B. Campbell, *Divine Poetry and Drama in Sixteenth Century England*, Cambridge, 1959; N. Griffin, *Jesuit School Drama, a checklist of critical literature*, Research bibliographies and checklists, 12. London, 1976; L.-V. Gofflot, *Le Théâtre au collège du moyen âge à nos jours*, Paris, 1907; J.-M. Valentin, *Le Théâtre des Jésuites dans les pays de langue allemande: Répertoire chronologique des pièces représentées et des documents conservés (1555–1773)*, Stuttgart, 2 vols., 1983–4.

University theatre (Britain)

1 Student drama During the first half of the century the opportunities for amateur theatre work in the universities were most notably provided by Cambridge University's Amateur Dramatic Company (ADC), formed in 1855, and the Oxford University Dramatic Society (OUDS) formed in 1885. Both societies have a long and impressive record of producing classics and experimental plays and of nurturing many famous actors and directors.

After the Second World War, student drama began to flourish at other institutions too, and in 1956 the *Sunday Times*-sponsored National Student Drama Festival was established to provide a platform for productions, a forum for the exchange of ideas and a means of national recognition for talented young directors, actors, writers and designers. The Festival, held annually at different campuses around the country, has steadily expanded and developed: polytechnics, colleges, acting schools and high schools now also enter productions.

2 Departments of drama The first such department was inaugurated in 1946–7 in the University of Bristol, financed partly by the Rockefeller Foundation. A small theatre studio was built, courses were organized in theatre history, dramatic literature and practical production approaches, and contacts were established with the **Bristol Old Vic** Theatre School. A chair was established in 1960 – occupied until 1984 by Glynne Wickham. It was not until 1961 that a second department was founded at the University of Manchester, with a grant from Granada Television and with **Hugh Hunt** as professor. The establishment of other drama departments then followed quickly: Hull in 1963, Birmingham in 1964, Bangor in 1965, Glasgow in 1966 and Exeter in 1968. Expansion continued through the 1970s with departments being set up at more universities and at polytechnics and colleges of higher education too. In 1985 there were almost 40 undergraduate and postgraduate degree courses in the higher education sector in which drama was a major if not the sole subject of study. There were many more in which drama formed a smaller element of a combined degree course.

3 Campus theatres During the era of university expansion (in the 1960s and early 70s), many universities built their own theatres to professional standards. They were designed to provide facilities for student drama and departmental productions and to be the venue for touring and sometimes semi-resident professional companies – a cultural centre for the area, university and town alike. In 1985 there were 18 such theatres, ranging from Exeter's Northcott Theatre and Manchester University Theatre, homes for professional repertory companies, to Stirling's Macrobert Centre and Warwick's Arts Centre housing both student productions and touring companies. AJ

University Wits
The name popularly given to a group of playwrights, among whom **Marlowe**, **Greene**, **Nash**, and **Peele** are the most prominent, who received their education at Oxford or Cambridge, lived rashly in London and contributed significantly to the rapid development of a national repertoire of plays.

Most of the University Wits were hostile to the rising generation of playwrights, which included **Jonson** and **Shakespeare**, who had lacked their educational advantages. PT

Urban, Joseph
(1871–1933) Austrian-American set designer. Many of the approaches and techniques adopted by **Robert Edmond Jones**, **Lee Simonson**, and others were first introduced in America by Urban. In the 1890s in Vienna he designed palaces, exposition pavilions and a bridge. In 1904 he began to work with the Vienna **Burgtheater** and spent the next years designing operas throughout Europe. He came to the USA in 1912 to design for the Boston Opera. He was discovered by showman **Florenz Ziegfeld** who persuaded him to design for the *Follies*. Urban's designs were simple in terms of line, but vibrant colour created a sense of lushness and complexity. He achieved this by applying pointillist techniques to scene painting – the juxtaposition of dots of colour. Not only did this add new dimensions to painted scenery but it allowed parts of the image to appear or disappear under different coloured lights. He was also one of the first to use platforms and portals – arched scenic units at the side of the stage, connected at the top. This framed and focused the stage while providing continuous elements for unit sets. AA

Uruguay
The theatre history of Uruguay is closely related to that of Argentina and is often combined in theatre histories under the designation 'River Plate Theatre'. Uruguay was created as a nation in 1828 as a buffer between Brazil and Argentina, both of whom disputed this rich agricultural territory which, in spite of its relatively flat terrain, is called 'Little Switzerland'. During the colonial period the scant population was insufficient to sustain theatrical activity, although there is record of a theatre that opened in Montevideo as early as 1793. Throughout most of the 19th century, years of tumult and confusion in politics and economics when the country lagged behind its more powerful neighbours, the theatre followed the romantic trends in vogue in other parts of the hemisphere. Many plays reflected the costumbristic tendencies of the times and recorded the history and society of this land dominated by the gaucho and wild outlaws. The fierce rivalry between two political parties, the *blancos* (whites) and the *colorados* (reds), struggling for power, tested the cohesion of this incipient democratic nation through difficult times, and did little to foment the theatre. The Teatro Solís opened in 1856 and several theatre groups or companies were registered in the latter half of the century.

The single event of greatest importance in the development of the River Plate Theatre occurred in 1884 when the Carlo Brothers' North American Circus, on tour in Argentina, incorporated the little Uruguayan clown José J. Podestá (1858–1937) into their initial rendition of *Juan Moreira*, a romanticized version of a gaucho whose adventures had been published serially by Eduardo Gutiérrez. The instantaneous success of the original pantomime version led subsequently to a more developed version with dialogue, recognized by the Uruguayans for its dramatic value. The national spirit spawned a host of imitations about upstanding and virtuous gauchos persecuted unjustly by the civil authorities.

The authors who best represent Uruguayan theatre in the second half of the 19th century are Samuel Blixen (1868–1911), who wrote romantic comedies and a seasonal tetralogy, Orosmán Moratorio (1852–98), author of **sainetes**, especially those with gaucho themes, and Elías Regules (1860–1929), who adapted the epic *Martín Fierro* and wrote other gaucho plays.

20th century Uruguay experienced waves of immigration similar to those of Argentina as thousands of Europeans, primarily Italians and Germans, arrived in the southern hemisphere. The influence of realism and naturalism in the European theatre was superimposed on local customs and life styles and the resulting dramatic form, known as the *sainete criollo*, marked a new direction in the theatre of the entire River Plate region. The best known playwright of all of South America, even at this point, is Florencio Sánchez (1875–1910), who spent his first 25 years in Uruguay, although the development of his theatre is normally associated with Argentina because of the greater opportunities for production that existed there. Sánchez wrote quickly and easily. His plays have been criticized for shallow characterization and flawed structures, but he was able to capture the heart and mind of his public with a vision of an emerging new culture that combined the immigrant urban population with the traditional rural society. *M'hijo el dotor* (*My Son the Lawyer*, 1903), *La gringa* (*The Foreign Girl*, 1904), and *Barranca abajo* (*Down the Gully*, 1905) are only three of the 20 plays he wrote during the brief career that catapulted him to fame, and changed the course of Uruguayan and Argentine theatre. Others followed and tried to imitate or surpass his work. Ernesto Herrera (1886–1917), another autodidactic playwright, wrote in a vein similar to Sánchez but with better developed characters, as in *El león ciego* (*The Blind Lion*, 1911), a powerful play about the misery and folly of war as an exercise in virility. Herrera's career paralleled that of Sánchez, including his early death by tuberculosis. Other major playwrights of the period included Víctor Pérez Petit (1871–1947) and José Pedro Bellán (1888–1930). The relationship with Argentina facilitated the development of their careers also during this period of costumbristic theatre in which the language patterns and the social mores of the incipient middle class were becoming more firmly established.

In the period after 1920, while the previous costumbristic tendencies continued, a theatre more attuned to universal concerns with a sound psychological basis began to emerge. Two of the major playwrights were contemporaries of the previous group: Francisco Imhof (1880–1937) revealed a Freudian influence in such plays as *Eutanasia* (*Euthanasia*, 1927), which integrated the subconscious and a mercy killing within a lovers' triangle. Vicente Martínez Cuitiño (1887–1964) was a prolific author whose early plays were naturalistic, the later ones more in the vanguard. His *Servidumbre* (*Servitude*, 1937) derives from the Italian tradition with its exploration of the cruelty of the society that mistreats young lovers for sadistic reasons. Yamandú Rodríguez (1889–1957) wrote historical plays in verse and Justino Zavala Muñiz (b. 1898) also picked up

creole issues, as in *En un rincón del Tacuari* (*In a Corner of the Tacuari*, 1938) with its theme of incest.

In the period following the Second World War, Uruguay's relationship with Argentina was ruptured by the strong-arm tactics of the latter's Juan Domingo Perón, who envisioned annexation of the territory. When rebuffed, he imposed economic sanctions on the little country which became a haven for Argentine political refugees, just as it had a century earlier during the period of Juan Manuel de Rosas. In the theatre, Uruguay responded to this new period by expanding its available performance space and by creating new theatre companies. The Comedia Nacional (National Comedy) was established by the municipal government of Montevideo in 1947 with the first resident theatre company in the country's history and a training programme designed by the famous Spanish actress Margarita Xirgú.

In 1949 the Teatro Galpón was created, a theatre group that has survived political harassment under the spiritual leadership of the indomitable Atahualpa del Cioppo and the direction of César Campodónico. The Galpón (so-named for the barn in which it started) spent eight years in exile, mostly in Mexico, but was able to return to Montevideo in 1984 by invitation of the newly-elected president Julio María Sanguinette. El Galpón's collective creation, *La reja* (*The Grille*, 1972), based on narrations by released prisoners, was important in the government's decision to close them down. In exile their production of *Artigas*, based on Uruguay's national hero, played in many countries.

The Teatro Circular (Arena Theatre), established in 1954, is also known for its quality productions, its actor training programme, and its promotion of both foreign and national plays. In recent years the group has published a theatre journal, *Escenario* (Stage). Another group of importance is the Teatro Alianza (Alliance Theatre), which since its creation in 1975 has occupied a flexible space in the Uruguay–USA Cultural Alliance building, where it has brought new staging techniques to a wide variety of plays.

In Walter Rela's documentation of all Uruguayan plays staged in the country between 1808 and 1968, the number of plays performed in the 1950s increased markedly as did the number of theatres in use. By the late 1960s, however, the proliferation of independent theatre groups had not succeeded in elevating the artistic quality of performances, and the military coup of 1973 stifled free expression by counterculture groups.

The post-war period spawned a new generation of playwrights, directors, actors and critics. Of the writers, **Carlos Maggi** (b. 1922), a lawyer and critic, commanded the greatest attention for a series of fine plays in which with humour and irony he was able to penetrate the foibles of Uruguayan society and politics within a larger universal context. *La biblioteca* (*The Library*, 1959) was an excellent prelude to *El patio de la Torcaza* (*The Patio of the Torcaza*, 1967) in which the black humour and acerbic style revealed his particular vision of the decadence and turmoil of contemporary Uruguay. Others have been even more overt in their criticism. Antonio Larreta (b. 1922) wrote existentialist as well as committed theatre. His *Juan Palmieri* (1972) is a semi-documentary account of an encounter between the bourgeoisie and a young *tupamaro* Revolutionary.

Mario Benedetti (b. 1920) manipulated a metatheatrical technique in *Ida y vuelta (Return Trip*, 1958) and then wrote a virulent play about torture, premiered by El Galpón in Mexico. Later made as a film in Mexico (1983), it analyses the emotions and responsibility of a torturer confronted with a resistant victim. *Primavera con una esquina rota (Springtime with a Broken Corner*, 1984) was adapted by the Chilean group ICTUS from one of his novels dealing with exile during a period of political repression. Other playwrights of particular note during this same period are Jacobo Langsner (b. 1927), Híber Conteris (b. 1933) and **Mauricio Rosencof** (b. 1933); the latter is worthy of note for his *Las ranas (The Frogs*, 1961) and *Los caballos (The Horses*, 1967).

The return of political stability permitted the celebration of an International Theatre Showcase in 1984 in which 20 plays by groups from South America and Europe were performed. Among the younger authors are Alberto Paredes with *Tres tristes tangos (Three Sad Tangos*) and *Devaluación (Devaluation*) and Alfredo de la Peña with *El novio de la nena (The Girl's Boyfriend*). Jorge Scheck and Pedro Corradi each wrote excellent monologues, *El santo y el muñeco (The Saint and the Puppet*) and *Retrato de dama con espejo (Portrait of a Lady with Mirror*), respectively. *Costumbres (Customs*, 1981) by Ernesto Castillo and *Doña Ramona* (1982) by Víctor Manuel Leites both provide microcosmic visions of family love and sexuality under conditions of rigid morality and religious fervour. Alberto Rowinsky (b. 1946) is an actor, director and author (for several years in Venezuela) whose play, *Reunión de muertos en familia (Reunion of the Family Dead*) was ironically in rehearsal with Héctor Duvauchelle at the time the latter was murdered.

A dependency on foreign tendencies at the expense of a national theatre movement has left Uruguay in an underdeveloped situation. **Molière**, **Brecht**, **García Lorca**, **Pirandello**, **Shaffer**, and **Williams** are more likely fare than local authors like Juan Graña and Jacobo Langsner. Political and economic conditions have not favoured the Uruguayan theatre in recent years, but an irrepressible talent and a long theatre tradition bode well for the future. GW

See: J. Cruz, *Genio y figura de Florencio Sánchez*, Buenos Aires, 1966; W. Rela, *Historia del teatro uruguayo, 1808–1968*, Montevideo, 1969; idem, *Repertorio bibliográfico del teatro uruguayo, 1816–1964*, Montevideo, 1965; C. Scosería, *Un panorama del teatro uruguayo*, Montevideo, 1963; C. Solórzano, *El teatro latinoamericano en el siglo XX*, Mexico, 1964.

Usigli, Rodolfo (1905–79) Mexican playwright, poet and diplomat, who during the 1930s and 1940s launched Mexican dramaturgy with plays of lasting significance. Unaffiliated, for the most part, with the independence theatre movement in Mexico, Usigli emulated the best of world theatre and earned accolades from **George Bernard Shaw**. His first major success was *El gesticulador (The Impostor*) (written 1937, performed 1947), a study of hypocrisy that transcends its Mexican ambiance. *Corona de sombre (Crown of Shadow*) (written 1943, performed 1947) is a revisionist historical play on the period of Maximilian and Carlota in Mexico. It forms a trilogy with *Corona de luz (Crown of Light*, 1960) and *Corona de fuego (Crown of Fire*, 1961) which deal with the Virgin of Guadalupe and Cuauhtémoc, respectively. Other major works include *El niño y la niebla (The Boy and the Mist*, 1936–51), *Jano es una muchacha (Jano is a Girl*, 1952), and *Buenos días, Señor presidente (Good Morning, Mr President*, 1972), the latter rooted in **Calderón**'s *La vida es sueño (Life Is a Dream*) and growing out of the 1968 Tlatelolco massacre in Mexico. Known also for his explanatory prologues and epilogues, Usigli wrote more than 40 plays in addition to several substantial books on the theatre itself. GW

V

Vagantes A term applied in medieval documents to disaffected and homeless clerics, students and Latin teachers, to distinguish them from ordinary rovers. They travelled throughout England, France and Germany in the 12th and 13th centuries, reciting disputatious poems and rollicking songs composed in vulgar Latin. In France these clerics were known as *Goliards*, and the Goliardic ballads are often forceful and obscene, sometimes anti-clerical in tone, praising wine and women in song. One set, the *Carmina burana*, was put to music by Carl Orff (1936). The *vagantes* were important in disseminating a classical influence throughout the folk culture of their time. LS

Vakhtangov, Evgeny Bagrationovich (1883–1923) Russian director-actor-teacher, disciple and reconciler of Stanislavskian psychological realism and Meyerholdian grotesque via his sytem of humane and joyous creation, 'fantastic realism'. Armenian born, Vakhtangov studied law at Moscow University before enrolling at A. I. Adashev's drama school, where he was taught by, among others, Leopold Sulerzhitsky. He was accepted into the **Moscow Art Theatre** (MAT) as an actor in 1911 where his former teacher Sulerzhitsky, for whom he assistant directed **Maeterlinck**'s *The Blue Bird*, and **Nemirovich-Danchenko**, whose work he observed, taught him much about the **Stanislavsky** system and theatricality, respectively. In time he became one of the system's leading teachers. His acting at MAT and its First Studio (founded in 1912) featured expressive, often grotesque outer form developed from psychological bases in such roles at Tackleton in **Dickens**'s *Cricket on the Hearth* (1914), Frazer in Berger's *The Flood* (1915) and Feste in *Twelfth Night* (1919). These same qualities, derived from the following principles, informed his work as a director-teacher: the actor's primacy in the theatre, his personality and imagination being his most significant tools in creating a performance that is expressive rather than a mere impersonation (Stanislavsky) on the one hand, or stylization (**Meyerhold**) on the other; this 'expressiveness' consists of the combination of the actor's subjective psychological belief in the character and the actor's objective consideration as a representative of his culture, of the character; the actor expresses the 'soul of the people' and 'the life of the nation' (reveals **Wagner**'s influence and points toward **Brecht**); the 'actor-eccentric' must first be an expert improviser, his performance – which includes the skills of singing, dancing, vaudeville and musical comedy – embodies controlled spontancity and quickly communicates to an audience via selected details an instantaneous, complex and vibrant impression of the character's essence;

'creative distortion' and child-like play in which emotion arises from action (achieved via rehearsal *études*) must replace MAT moodiness, sentimentalism, pseudo-psychological significance and naturalistic scenic effects as well as Meyerhold's and **Tairov**'s visual experimentation at the expense of the actor's inner life. A man of prodigious talent, energy and enthusiasm, Vakhtangov at the height of his brief career, in the face of serious personal illness and national famine, taught and directed at 14 theatres and studios, in addition to his work at MAT and its First and Second Studios. His best work was done at MAT's Third Studio (after 1926, the Vakhtangov Theatre) – **Chekhov**'s *The Wedding* (1920), his second version of Maeterlinck's *The Miracle of St Anthony* (1921), **Gozzi**'s *Princess Turandot* (1922) – and with the Jewish **Habimah** Theatre on **S. Anski**'s *The Dybbuk* (1922). He staged *The Wedding* as a tragicomic grotesque à la **Gogol**'s *The Inspector General*, reflecting his belief that Chekhov is crueller than is generally thought. *The Miracle of St Anthony* was presented as a black and white Daumier caricature filtered through the lighting and imagery of Goya and aimed at 'branding the bourgeoisie'. *The Dybbuk*, rehearsed in Russian but performed in Hebrew, also used a black and white pallette and was his most highly choreographed piece. *Turandot*, his final and most famous production, spoofed the play's romanticism via frank theatricality – Oriental conventions of scene, prop and costume changing, hand towels as beards and selected costume pieces over evening dress, a cubist set by Ignaty Nivinsky, accompanying music – designed to present the actor as being an ordinary man leading an extraordinary life. This production influenced Stanislavsky's ideas on tempo-rhythm. Among Vakhtangov's disciples are four members of the Students Drama Studio who achieved notable success and high state honours: **Yury Zavadsky**, from 1940 artistic director of the Mossoviet Theatre; N. M. Gorchakov, senior director at MAT; Boris Zakhava, from 1925 head of the Vakhtangov Theatre's Shchukin Theatre School; Ruben Simonov, the Vakhtangov Theatre's artistic director (1924–39). The last three have left valuable memoirs of their work with Vakhtangov. SG

Valdéz, Luis (1940–) Chicano director and playwright, he is responsible for the **Chicano theatre** revolution. University-trained and a student activist at San José State, he visited Cuba before joining the San Francisco Mime Troupe in 1964. Knowledgeable about **commedia dell'arte**, **Brecht** and pantomime, he used bilingual theatre to help César Chávez organize the migrant workers around Delano, California, in 1965. His efforts led to the *actos*, one-act revolutionary pieces, and the creation of the **Teatro Campesino** (Farmworkers' Theatre), which in turn inspired the formation of other Chicano theatre groups. His early titles include *Las dos caras del patroncito* (*The Boss's Two Faces*), *Quinta temporada* (*Fifth Season*), *No saco nada de la escuela* (*I Don't Get Anything out of School*), *Vietnam campesino* (*Vietnam Farmer*), *Soldado razo* (*Buck Private*) and *Huelguistas* (*Strikers*). *Zoot Suit* (1978), based on the Sleepy Lagoon murder trial during the Second World War, dramatized the stereotypical *pachuco* in a successful run in Los Angeles, but failed on Broadway. Teatro Campesino became professional and later moved into new facilities in San Juan Bautista. Valdéz's folk musical *Corridos*, based on popular Mexican folk ballad traditions, opened in 1983. GW

Valentin, Karl (Valentin Ludwig Fey) (1892–1948)

German comedian, the son of a Munich upholsterer, he made a start as a club comic and musical clown in 1899, and by 1907 was the leading Munich comedian in his own monologues and sketches. In 1911 he met Liesl Karlstadt (Elizabeth Welleno) (1892–1961) who, for 35 years, was his partner, playing both male and female roles. They worked together until 1941, in Munich and on tour in Zürich, Vienna and Berlin, parting temporarily in 1934 when their Panoptikum failed, leaving them bankrupt. Lanky, cranky Valentin created more than 500 skits and farces that raised Bavarian folk comedy to a sphere of universal significance. His comic world comprised the recalcitrance of inanimate objects, cross-purposes of language, the malignity of human nature. Often, by a scene's end, the stage – a record shop, a radio studio or a variety stage – would be totally demolished, in the wake of monstrous physical and logical complications. Most of his acts were filmed in detail after 1912; from 1941 to the end of the Second World War, Valentin was withdrawn, making only a few radio broadcasts thereafter. His admirers included **Brecht**, who compared him to Chaplin. LS

Valle-Inclán, Ramón del (1866–1936)

Spanish novelist and playwright from Galicia who moved to Madrid and joined a Bohemian circle of artists. His first play, *Cenizas* (*Ashes*, 1899), was a poetic melodrama revised as *El yermo de las almas* (*The Desert of Souls*) in 1908. This was followed by a rural Galician trilogy of *Comedias bárbaras*, depicting the fossilized nobility of the region, *Águila de blasón* (*The Emblazoned Eagle*, 1907), *Romance de lobos* (*Ballad of Wolves*, 1908) and *Cara de plata* (*Silver Countenance*, 1922). His growing interest in farces and the grotesque was evident from *La marquesa Rosalinda* (1912). Later farces included *La enamorada del rey* (*The Girl Who Loved the King*, 1920) and *Farsa y licencia de la reina castiza* (*Farce of the True Spanish Queen*, 1922), which satirizes the decadent and licentious court of Isabel II.

In 1920 *Luces de Bohemia* (*Lights of Bohemia*) was the first play to which Valle-Inclán gave the title *esperpento*, which he described as the systematic distortion of the norms of theatre and novel through the mathematics of the concave mirror. This he felt was necessary to portray corrupt society with enhanced truth, and foreshadows many elements of absurd drama. The play is a sombre evocation of the last days of the Bohemian poet Alejandro Sawa. Other *esperpento* plays are *Divinas palabras* (*Divine Words*, 1920) and *Los cuernos de don Friolero* (*Don Friolero the Cuckold*, 1921), a sour farce on the decadence of the military, using puppets and actors. These plays were certainly not the fare of the commercial theatre of the time, though they have since been seen as his most original and important contribution to the theatre. They were published together as *Martes de carnaval* (1930). CL

Valleran le Conte (fl. 1590–1614)

French actor-manager, one of the earliest for whom documentation is extant. He was a strolling player in the provinces in 1592–3 with a repertoire of biblical plays and works by **Jodelle** and in 1599 he brought a company to Paris, signing a three-month lease for the **Hôtel de Bourgogne**. Between then and 1612 his career alternated between provincial touring and repeated attempts to establish himself in the capital, but prosperity eluded him and on several occasions he was obliged to reform his troupe or to amalgamate it with another. The bulk of his repertoire probably consisted of tragedies and tragicomedies by **Alexandre Hardy**, whom he had engaged as company dramatist, and contracts signed with tradesmen provide evidence of the multiple stage decor that he used for their performance, though he is also reported to have appeared in farce. In 1612, perhaps tiring of the struggle to conquer Paris, he formed yet another company and returned to the provinces. DR

Vampilov, Aleksandr Valentinovich (1937–72)

Soviet dramatist who, on the basis of a short canon of plays which have been compared to those of **Gogol** and **Chekhov**, has been called the greatest playwright of his generation and has become a major influence on those who have followed him. A native Siberian and graduate of Irkutsk University (1960), Vampilov published his first collection of short stories and comic sketches on provincial life, *A Chain of Being* (1961), while pursuing a five-year career in journalism. His playwriting career, which included some early provincially published efforts – *Katya Kozlova's Happiness* (one-act, 1959) and *Tichaia Factory* (1960) – began in earnest when as a student at Moscow's Gorky Literary Institute his one-act comedy *The House Overlooking a Field* (1964) was published in the influential Moscow journal *Theatre*. The following year saw *Theatre's* publication of Vampilov's *Farewell in June* and Rostov's and **Arbuzov's** sponsorship of the young dramatist's membership in the Writer's Union. In these and his other plays Vampilov examined the problems of young and old in accepting societal values and institutions and responsibility for their own failed dreams and relationships, and the fall from grace precipitated by man's physical and spiritual separation from nature. Whereas the young protagonists of *Farewell in June* and *The Elder Son* (1967) are still capable of making a moral choice, the confirmed middle-aged egoists of Vampilov's best two plays, *Duck Hunting* (1967) and *Last Summer in Chulimsk* (1971), either no longer care or are no longer able to do so. In *Duck Hunting*, the last of his plays to be staged in the USSR (at the Theatre of Russian Drama in Riga, 1976) and the most bitter, Vampilov is credited with having created a model of the 'urban grotesque' which has been adapted by other Soviet dramatists such as Lyudmila Petrushevskaya, Semyon Zlotnikov, Mark Rozovsky, Viktor Slavkin, Arbuzov and **Volodin**. (See **Russia and the Soviet Union**.) *Duck Hunting*'s protagonist – an egocentric misfit and anti-hero – its flashback structure and telephone motif, tied to a cruel-joke premiss and a threatened suicide (reminiscent of **Erdman**'s *The Suicide*), is typical of the breed. The 'crippled personality', whom the Soviets regard as an aberration like the old duck who can no longer migrate, has failed on some profound level. This theme is echoed in Vampilov's *The Seagull* variant, *Last Summer in Chulimsk*, in which self-pitying and spiritless people living at the edge of breathtaking Siberian wilderness abuse it and one another. Vampilov's indebtedness to the traditional farce-vaudeville of Gogol, Chekhov and others, is demonstrated in his unfinished vaudeville *The Incomparable Nakonechnikov* (1971) and in the two plays published under the title *Provincial Anecdotes* (1971) – *Twenty Minutes with an Angel* (1962) and *An Incident with a Typesetter* (1970) – whose mistaken identity premiss and escalating frenzy of paranoia suggest *The Inspector General*. In 1974, two years after his death from a heart seizure precipitated by a boating accident, fully one-third of all 380 Soviet dramatic theatres were performing one or more of Vampilov's plays. SG

Van Itallie, Jean–Claude (1936–) American playwright, director, producer, and teacher. Born in Brussels, Belgium, Van Itallie became a naturalized American citizen in 1952. After studying at Harvard and the **Neighborhood Playhouse**, Van Itallie made his debut as a writer in 1963 with *War*. His *Motel* and *Pavanne* were produced at the Café **La Mama** in 1965, attracting considerable attention to him as a new talent. *American Hurrah* appeared at the Pocket Theatre, New York, in 1966; *The Serpent* premiered in Rome in 1968 and was produced by the **Open Theatre**, New York, in 1969. Other scripts include *King of the US* (1972), *Mystery Play* (1973), and his own version of *The Seagull* in 1973. Van Itallie has adapted two other **Chekhov** scripts, *The Cherry Orchard* (1977) and *The Three Sisters* (1979).

Van Itallie's affiliation with the Open Theatre and **Joseph Chaikin** placed him at the forefront of experimental dramaturgy in the 1960s and 1970s. Especially with the Open Theatre, Van Itallie merged European traditions with a poetic vision of American experience. SMA

Vanbrugh, Sir John (1664–1726) English dramatist and architect. Educated in England and France, he became an Ensign in the army in 1689 and was imprisoned in France for spying from 1689 to 1692, including a period in the Bastille. Appointed a Captain in 1696, he began his career as a playwright in the same year with *The Relapse*, ostensibly a sequel to **Cibber**'s *Love's Last Shift*, a comedy in which Cibber's characters' repentance and reformation are found to be temporary and the marriage problems left unresolved. In 1697 both parts of his satire on contemporary society, *Aesop*, were performed, as well as *The Provoked Wife*, his best play. Here Vanbrugh analyses the loveless marriage of convenience and the hopelessness of the spouses when divorce is effectively impossible.

Attacked by **Jeremy Collier** for the immorality and profanity of his plays, Vanbrugh defended himself in *A Short Vindication of The Relapse and The Provoked Wife* (1698), by turns wittily and disingenuously. He began his career as an architect in 1699 when he began the plans for Castle Howard in Yorkshire, the foundation-stone of which was laid in 1701 and which was subsequently completed in 1714. He adapted a play by **Dancourt** as a brilliant farce, *The Country House* (1698), **Fletcher**'s *The Pilgrim* (1700), another Dancourt play as *The Confederacy* (1705) and a **Molière** comedy as *Squire Trelooby* (1704) in collaboration with **Congreve** and William Walsh. His last play, an original comedy called *A Journey to London*, was left unfinished and completed by Cibber as *The Provoked Husband* in 1728. He adapted a play by **Dancourt** as a brilliant farce, *The Country House* (1698), **Fletcher**'s *The Pilgrim* (1700), another Dancourt play as *The Confederacy* (1705) and a **Molière** comedy as *Squire Trelooby* (1704) in collaboration with **Congreve** and William Walsh. His last play, an original comedy called *A Journey to London*, was left unfinished and completed by Cibber as *The Provoked Husband* in 1728. Vanbrugh designed the Queen's Theatre in the Haymarket, which opened in 1705, and Blenheim Palace, for which he was Surveyor from 1705 to 1716. Vanbrugh was licensed, with Congreve, to manage the Haymarket but its poor acoustics and distance from the centre of London made it financially disastrous. Vanbrugh continued to be involved in the confused world of theatre management at this time until he sold out his interests in 1708. He was knighted in 1714. PH

Vandenhoff, George (1813–85) British-born American actor and lawyer, son of the actor John Vandenhoff. After a debut at **Covent Garden** in 1839, George began his American career at the **Park Theatre** in 1842 as Hamlet. As an actor he was noted for his correctness but lacked power and apparently never liked the stage. After returning to England in 1853, where he and his new wife acted in the provinces, he retired from the stage in the mid-1850s. Although admitted to the New York Bar in 1858, he spent much of his time teaching elocution and giving public readings. In 1860 he published his reminiscences, *Leaves from an Actor's Notebook*. DBW

Variety The most widespread and widely attended form of urban entertainment in the 19th and early 20th century. The element of variety is common to popular theatre, which seeks to engage limited attention spans with a diversity of skills. Egypt in the 5th century BC had its sequences of musicians, dancers, acrobats, and female jugglers performing for rich men's guests; and the wandering minstrel of the Middle Ages was capable of a broad range of diversions. As a distinct genre, *variety* was organized in the 19th century in the music-halls and public houses of Europe and America, took on elements of circus, and ramified into cabaret and revue. A major contributory factor to its prominence was a new proletarian public, who had lost their communal village traditions and were receptive to less demanding, cheaper and more colourful amusement than the 'legitimate' theatre offered. Innovative forms of publicity and presentation developed to exploit the form's commercial potential.

Variety can be identified by its series of attractions, 'turns' or 'numbers', unconnected by any theme. In contrast to the modern dramatic theatre, the audience is encouraged to eat, drink and smoke during the performance. In Great Britain, the common form was the music-hall, which took to calling itself 'variety' as it gained respectability; in America, in contrast, 'variety' preferred to be known as vaudeville. Nomenclature is confused: the chief European terms are, in France, the *café concert* and *café chantant* and, later, the revue-like music-hall; in Germany, the low Singspielhalle and Tingeltangel and the more circus-like and spectacular Variété; in Russia, the disreputable *myuzik-kholl* and the all-encompassing *estrada*. In Spain variety remained closely linked to folkloric dance and song, in Italy to circus. Variety's apogee came before the First World War; afterwards it had to compete with and was absorbed by cinema, radio and television. Its influence on the literary drama has been enormous (e.g., **Brecht**), but more especially it has been a constant inspiration for experimental theatrical innovators, from the Italian futurists of the 1910s to radical feminist groups of the 1970s.   LS

See: J. Feschotte, *Histoire du music-hall*, Paris, 1965; E. Günther, *Geschichte des Variétés*, Berlin, 1978; Jacques-Charles, *Cent ans de music-hall*, Paris, 1956.

Vasari, Giorgio (1511–74) Italian architect, painter, stage designer and writer on art. One of the key figures in the development of perspective stage setting, after a period in the mid and late 1530s working as assistant to **Sangallo** in Florence, he worked elsewhere, particularly in Venice on a production of **Aretino**'s *La Talanta* (1541). Later, in Florence, he built the wooden theatre of the Palazzo Vecchio, devised the spectacular entertainments to celebrate the marriage of Francesco de'Medici and Giovanna d'Austria in 1566, and introduced an important innovation in stage decoration in 1569 with a system of rotating *periaktoi*. His *Vite de'piu Eccellenti Pittori, Scultori ed Architetti* (*Lives of the Most Excellent Painters, Sculptors and Architects*, 1530–68) is an invaluable source of information about the work of Renaissance painters, designers and architects.   KR

Vaudeville, American This essentially American form of variety has nothing to do with the French *vaudeville*, a farce studded with songs set to popular tunes; rather, the term attempted to lend a veneer of elegance to what was originally rough and ready entertainment. A so-called 'vaudeville' house had been opened by William Valentine in 1840, and H. J. Sargent's Great Vaudeville Co. was playing in Louisville in 1871, but the term did not catch on till later.

The usual venue for variety performances in the late 1860s was the concert saloon, its waiters and dancing-girls closely allied to the prostitutes that preyed on the all-male audience. Out-of-work minstrels and chorines unemployed after the decline of the leg-show drifted into these 'olio entertainments', as did newly formed doubles acts. Unlike European variety, where song was the standard unit, broad comedy and exuberant dance predominated here. This 'honky tonk' style permutated into burlesque, while respectable variety gained greater professionalism and urbanity between 1876 and 1893 to become *vaudeville*.

Tony Pastor, hoping to lure a family audience with giveaways and promises of clean amusement, was instrumental in this development, and the traditional, if debatable, date given for the birth of vaudeville is the opening of his 14th St Theatre, New York, on 24 October 1881. But the innovation was enlarged and expanded by Benjamin Franklin Keith (1846–1914) and his associate Edward F. Albee (1857–1930). Keith began with a 'store-show', the Gaiety Museum, Boston, and had Albee transform it in 1885 into a Japanese tea-garden offering a tabloid opera. So great was their success that they soon owned several theatres and in 1894 opened the first exclusively vaudeville house, the Boston Colonial, typical of the opulent palaces designed to lure the middle class spectator into a fairy-tale world of luxury. Keith and Albee eliminated offensive material, fining offenders, and introduced the continuous show, so that one could enter the theatre at any time between 9.30 am and 10.30 pm and see a performance. The invention of 'continuous vaudeville', well ensconced by 1896, is also attributed to F. F. Proctor, a sometime partner, who claimed 'to give the masses what they want', but forbade smoking and drinking in the auditorium.

Competing with these robber barons were Martin Beck, credited with establishing the touring vaudeville company, who backed 'class acts' to educate the public; Oscar Hammerstein I who aimed his Roof at an elitist and his Olympic at a more popular public; William Morris, J. J. Murdoch and Sylvester Poli. The Keith–Albee circuit dominated the eastern United States through its many theatres (over 400 by 1920) and booking offices; Beck's Orpheum circuit played the West, though he also built the New York **Palace**, which soon was regarded as vaudeville's Valhalla. In addition, there were thousands of small houses scattered throughout the nation, enabling performers to play one-night stands throughout the season. Vaudevillians became a nomadic race, living much of the year on railway carriages and platforms and in dreary boarding-houses.

By 1900 the typical 'polite vaudeville' bill had grown formulaic, and was divided into two parts by an intermission. The first part would open with a 'dumb act', animals or acrobats, whose effect would not be damaged by a noisy entering audience. The number three slot was intended to wake up the house, the number four to deliver the first solid punch, and the last before the interval a knockout that would bring them back wanting more. The prime position was 'next to closing', where the 'headliner' or star of stars appeared. The concluding act was meant as a 'chaser', often a cinematic offering, like a newsreel. Turns or 'numbers' seldom lasted more than 10 to 20 minutes, although some popular egoists like **Harry Lauder** and **Al Jolson** might usurp a whole hour. According to **George Burns**, a performer needed only 17 good minutes, which he could play year in, year out across the country, before the act became too pirated or shopworn for use. The diversity of performance was considerable: in addition to the song-and-dance and comedy acts, there were mimes, ventriloquists, eccentrics, musical virtuosi, acrobats and jugglers, male and female impersonators, miniature musicals, monologuists, trained animals, conjurers, demonstrations of new inventions, and even famous criminals discoursing on their lurid past.

Much of the comedy in vaudeville dealt in racial stereotypes, with the Dutch, Irish, Jewish, blackface, Swedish and Italian comics the most familiar, reflecting the melting-pot nature of urban American society; by 1910 many of the older types, including the hick and Bowery tough, were *passé*. Low comedy was categorized as 'jazz', a fast routine to speed up an act; 'hokum', crude fun verging on vulgarity. Despite the efforts of the managers, innuendo was often resorted to, particularly in the 1920s, when more sophisticated audiences expected it.

Dance tended to be acrobatic until the First World War, when adagio and exhibition ballroom dancing and even imitations of the Ballets Russes arrived. Singers were either sentimental or strenuous, but American audiences, unless exhorted by such devices as 'following the bouncing ball' on a projected song-sheet, seldom joined in the chorus, another token of the heterogeneity of the public. Among the leading performers spawned by vaudeville or trained in its excellent school were Eva Tanguay the 'I Don't Care' Girl, Elsie Janis, Nora Bayes, **W. C. Fields** who moved from juggling to comic skits, **Eddie Cantor** and Al Jolson who retained the corked face of minstrelsy, as did the black comedian **Bert Williams, George M. Cohan** whose family had been variety pioneers, **Will Rogers** with his lowkeyed commentary, and George Burns and Gracie Allen, whose doubles act refined the Dumb Dora creation of Ryan and Lee. As vaudeville increased in respectability and popularity, stars of the 'legit', like **Lillie Langtry, Ethel Barrymore** and **Alla Nazimova**, played 'tab' versions of their dramatic hits on the circuits.

The American language was enriched by vaudeville slang: a success was a wow, a panic or a riot, a failure a flop, all wet or all washed-up. Duffey and Sweeney originated the phrase, 'We died in . . .' to indicate an utter fiasco. The minstrel Billy Emerson's 'hoofer' for dancer became popular, along with the injunction 'Strut your stuff' and the exit 'Shuffle off to Buffalo'. Some terms were too technical to become widespread, such as 'grouch bag' for a purse pinned to the underwear for safety's sake, 'feeder' for 'straight man', 'split time' for three days' work in any theatre, or 'death trail' for a circuit of small towns. But 'coffin nails' for cigarettes, which came from Junie McCree's act, and 'belly laughs', coined by Jack Conway, entered the language.

Vaudeville was the dominant form of American entertainment by 1890, and grew exponentially: in 1896 New York had seven vaudeville theatres, by 1910, 22. It came to be clearly differentiated into the Big Time, with its two-a-day offerings of an eight or nine act bill, and the Small Time with fewer acts and a film played continuously. The empire-building of the leading managements created booking agencies which could blacklist performers who did not conform to the rules or who failed to kick back percentages of their salaries (often levies were imposed by the house manager before the salary was paid). Keith–Albee created the United Booking Office (UBO) in 1906, whose impositions were so outrageous that the performers banded into a protective society, the White Rats, which failed to sustain its strike in 1900. Astutely, Albee backed a new organization, the National Vaudeville Artists (NVA), in 1916, which ameliorated some of the abuses without seriously harming the managers' interests.

The decline of vaudeville is attributable to a number of factors. Between 1905 and 1912, the Big Time had grown in sophistication, putting its emphasis on glamour, novelty, and lavish wardrobes; the influence of

the musical comedy and revue could be felt. Before 1925, it reached its period of greatest growth, but the cinema proved a powerful rival for the lower class audiences made uncomfortable by vaudeville's aspirations to gentility and its increased admission prices (the Palace went as high as two dollars). The automobile, put within everyone's financial reach by Henry Ford, enabled city-dwellers to escape to the country. During Prohibition, the proliferation of night-clubs offered a sophisticated and alcoholic alternative to those bored by vaudeville's stale material. By the mid-1920s many vaudeville houses were converted to cinemas and the succumbing of the Palace in 1932, its *coup de grâce* delivered by the depression, is considered the symbolic terminus of the form. Some managers like Marcus Loew persisted in alternating films with live performance at their houses, but gradually vaudeville came to be regarded as the seedbed for mass media: many of the most popular comedians, singers and dancers in the movies, on the radio and, later, television had honed their skills in vaudeville. LS

See: C. Caffin, *Vaudeville*, NY, 1914; D. Gilbert, *American Vaudeville*, NY, 1940, 1963; J. Laurie, Jr, *Vaudeville: From the Honky-tonks to the Palace*, NY, 1953; A. Slide, *The Vaudevillians*, Westport, Conn., 1981; S. Staples, *Male-Female Comedy Teams in American Vaudeville 1865–1932*, Ann Arbor, 1984; C. W. Stein (ed.), *American Vaudeville As Seen by Its Contemporaries*, NY, 1984.

Vaughan, Kate (Catherine Candelin) (c. 1852–1903) English dancer and burlesque actress, who formed, with **Nellie Farren, Edward Terry** and **Edward Royce**, the famous **Gaiety** Quartette from 1876–83. She had been trained as a dancer, playing the music-halls as part of the Vaughan Troupe when **John Hollingshead** discovered her. After 1883, she devoted herself increasingly to straight acting in classical roles. PT

Vauthier, Jean (1910–) Belgian dramatist. First revealed to the Parisian public by André Reybaz in 1951, he is remembered for the creation of Capitaine Bada, a cross between the common man and the writer who struggles for control of his life and his language but becomes lost in a welter of baroque poetic prose. **Barrault** scored a personal triumph in *Le Personnage Combattant* (*The Fighting Character*, 1956) and *Capitaine Bada* was revived by **Maréchal** in 1966, who also commissioned *Le Sang* (*Blood*, 1970). Vauthier has made several dramatic adaptations, notably of **Shakespeare** and **Euripides**. DB

Vedrenne, John Eugene (1867–1930) British theatre manager who worked with **Frank Benson** and **Johnston Forbes-Robertson**, before becoming manager of the **Royal Court Theatre** where he brought in **Granville Barker** for the 1904 season. There and, in 1907, at the Savoy they mounted a series of productions that influenced the whole development of British theatre – not only establishing **Shaw** on the public stage, but introducing **Galsworthy** and **Hauptmann**. Their example encouraged the formation of the new repertory theatre movement in Britain, while Vedrenne's insistence on maximum expenses of £200 per production enforced simplified settings that focused attention on ensemble acting. After the partnership was dissolved in 1911 he became manager of the Royalty Theatre, and in 1920 of the Little Theatre.   CI

Veedhi Natakam (India) The term *veedhi* or *vithi*, as it is sometimes spelled, means 'street'. *Natakam* means 'drama'. At one time, *Veedhi Natakam* was considered the most popular form of traditional theatre in Andhra Pradesh, a state in south India. Not being a court-supported art, the artists moved freely among the people of the countryside where they found patronage. Because it was a rural form of theatre, its roots are uncertain. Even the date of its origin is in doubt. Scholars are fairly sure that it was in vogue at the height of the Vijayanagar Empire during the 16th century. It may have been the dramatic counterpart of **Yakshagana**, also of Andhra Pradesh, which emphasized music and dance in its early phase. **Kuchipudi** may have adapted the dramatic form of *Veedhi Natakam* to its own unique brand of sophisticated theatre tradition.

The stories performed in *Veedhi Natakam* are drawn from the epics and the *Puranas*. Troupes of players perform throughout the state from November to May, playing in the open air, usually in squares or before village temples. Today, the generally depressed condition of the form has led exponents to adapt popular film music in place of traditional folk melodies to the dramatic action. The actors sing all the songs and a chorus of musicians repeats various lines and phrases for emphasis. A harmonium provides the basic melodic line and the *tabla* drums keep the basic tempo. Performances are played in the open air and any space in the village large enough to accommodate a crowd. Rugs or mats demarcate the playing area which is shaped like an arena. The musicians sit on stage in full view of the spectators.

Spectators gather about and sit on mats on the ground. The women sit separately from the men. Children struggle to get a good seat close to the acting area. Older youths may climb a nearby tree to see the proceedings. Vendors hawk sweets, tobacco, tea and coffee throughout the long hours of the night.   FAR

Vega Carpio, Lope Félix de (Lope de Vega) (1562–1635) Spanish dramatist, poet and novelist,

Veedhi Natakam actors and musicians.

rivalling **Calderón** as the greatest of the Golden Age. Born in Madrid, the son of a craftsman, he was a child prodigy, composing verses even before he could write, who sustained an astonishing literary production throughout his life. He studied with the Jesuits and probably at the University of Alcalá, though in later life he liked to contrast his unschooled genius to the learning of others. By his twenties he was famous as a poet, and his earliest plays date from this time, but though lively they are often poor in construction and somewhat immoral. His great plays were written mainly from his late thirties onwards. He was married twice and had many scandalous affairs with actresses, even after becoming a priest in 1614 on the death of his second wife. He sailed with the Armada, and was secretary to the Duke of Alba (1590–5) and then to the Duke of Sessa till his death. His last years, marred by the ill-fortune of his children, produced some fine tragedies, and even the occasional successful comedy, though he wrote little after 1625.

Lope's claim to have written 1,500 plays is certainly an exaggeration, but modern criticism accepts as genuine at least 314 of the 500 plays ascribed to him which have survived. Many poor plays and some fine ones by other playwrights were given his name since it was a watchword for excellence during his lifetime. Lope published more than 20 volumes of his works between 1604 and 1635, but many are undated and only the analysis of the versification yields approximate dates.

By the force of his genius and success Lope developed and established the three-act verse **comedia** as the standard Spanish play of the period. The range of subjects treated was enormous, including comedy, tragedy, farce, lives of saints, pastoral and historical, though Lope tended to blur the often artificial distinctions between the genres. He had a gift for inventing or discerning good plots, some inspired merely by fragments of popular poetry, others taken from the Bible, history, ballads or Italian *novelle*. He established the practice of varying the metre according to the type of scene (for example the use of the sonnet for soliloquies) the main metre being the eight-syllable ballad metre which enabled him to introduce fragments of real ballads for dramatic effect.

Some of his views on drama are given in the laconic and ironical *Arte nuevo de hacer comedias en este tiempo* (*New Art of Play-writing for Today*) published in 1609. In this poem he defends his art against the attacks of the classicists, including his mixing of comic and tragic scenes, following **Guarini**. He recommends the unity of action, though not those of place and time, except that each act should not exceed one day if possible. He comments on types of theme and on plot construction, and gives a few recommendations on types of metre. Throughout he defends what practice has shown to be successful rather than the demands of theorists.

The largest group of Lope's plays are *capa y espada* comedies such as *La dama boba* (*The Idiot Lady*, 1613) whose protagonist is made wise by the effects of love, or *El acero de Madrid* (*Madrid Spa*, 1602–12) in which the gallant disguises himself as a doctor and prescribes daily visits to the spa for his lady so that they can meet. These plays are full of local and topical references which the Madrid audience could enjoy. He also wrote many court comedies, including the brilliant *El perro del hortelano* (*The Dog in the Manger*, 1613–15) in which a

Countess falls in love with her secretary, a commoner, but cannot bear either to marry below her station or to let him marry another. The problem is solved when a servant's stratagem convinces everyone that the secretary is of noble birth.

Some of the finest and most famous of Lope's plays are those in which a peasant is forced to defend his honour and his wife against a tyrannical overlord. In *Fuenteovejuna* (1612–14) the people of the town of that name rise in revolt against their Lord and murder him and his servants. Under torture they will only say 'Fuenteovejuna did it' and are eventually pardoned by the king since no culprit can be identified. The protagonist of *Peribáñez* (1605–8) is a wealthy peasant who kills the Lord who tries to seduce or rape his wife, and again is pardoned by the king. In *El mejor alcalde el rey* (*The King is the Best Justice*, 1620–3), the king himself goes in disguise to punish a rapacious noble. These plays certainly emphasize the need for a strong bond between monarch and peasant, but they are not as radical as has been claimed.

Lope wrote many plays on the theme of adultery and honour, ranging from the witty *El castigo del discreto* (*The Wise Man's Punishment*, 1598–1601), in which the husband dissuades his wife from adultery by disguising himself as her lover and giving her a thrashing, to the bloody ballad-inspired *Los comendadores de Córdoba* (*The Knights-Commander of Córdoba*, 1596), in which the wronged husband massacres not only the guilty but also the whole household even to the pets. It is unwise to derive Lope's view of the problem from such a play, however. One of his finest plays treats the theme as a true tragedy. In *El castigo sin venganza* (*Punishment Without Revenge*, 1631) an elderly libidinous Duke is obliged to procure the deaths of his young wife and his illegitimate son when he discovers their affair, which is a direct result of his neglect. In doing so he also loses any chance of an heir. Other fine tragedies include *El duque de Viseo* (*The Duke of Viseo*, 1608–9?) and the lyrical *El caballero de Olmedo* (*The Knight of Olmedo*, 1620–5?).

In the 19th century, Lope's works were rediscovered by the German romantics, and **Grillparzer** based his *Jüden von Toledo* on a Lope play. Lope's vivid characterization and apparent realism have made him frequently more popular than the supposedly more cerebral Calderón, though he is equally neglected outside Spanish-speaking areas. CL

Velten, Johannes (1640–?93) German actor. After receiving a university education, from 1685 Velten led a troupe of players under the patronage of the Elector of Saxony. He did much to raise standards of acting and of repertoire. He introduced, in German adaptation, some plays of **Corneille**, **Racine**, and **Molière**. His troupe combined both improvisational and scripted acting. Some years after his death, it was taken over by **Caroline Neuber**. SW

Venezuela Since 1914 Venezuela and oil have become inseparable concepts. The immense reserves of Lake Maracaibo have been both the boon and the curse of this century, permitting enormous growth and public projects while contributing to greed, bribery and venal public officials. Previously, coffee was the dominant product of this country crossed by the Andes, with huge plains to the east and a population concentrated in a few cities with vast areas mostly unsettled. In the 19th century, after independence led by the liberator, Simón Bolívar, the country was governed by inept and often corrupt leaders with dictatorial tendencies. In the 20th century, the dictatorships of Juan Vicente Gómez (1908–35) and Marcos Pérez Jiménez (1952–8) were separated by various military regimes. In spite of the favourable constitution with which Venezuela ('Little Venice') was established by Bolívar, democracy has been infrequent but notable under Isaías Obedina Bugarita (1941–5) and the 1945–8 Triennial resulting from Democratic Action's 'October Revolution'. Cultural development has lagged due to Venezuela's dependence on foreign economic and artistic systems.

Ethnologists have documented Indian theatre events in the region by Muku, Jirajara and the Arawaks, but activity was isolated and no influence is evident in later theatre development. In the colonial years local groups performed European religious and secular plays, and there is evidence of an anonymous **auto sacramental**, *Auto a Nuestra Señora del Rosario* in the 1760s. The first theatre building, constructed in 1784 and known as the Coliseo (Coliseum), or the Teatro del Conde (Theatre of the Count), was destroyed by an earthquake in 1812. In that theatre, Andrés Bello, the neoclassic grammarian, poet, humanitarian, and first playwright of importance in Venezuela, presented his *Venezuela consolada* (*Venezuela Consoled*, 1804); his later *España restaurada* (*Spain Restored*, 1808) was an allegorical defence of the Spanish monarchy of Fernando VII on the eve of independence. Although noteworthy because of Bello's reputation, his theatre in general was of limited quality.

The sparse population in Caracas did little to stimulate the production of a local theatre industry throughout the 19th century. Various theatres, such as the Caracas Theatre (1854, restored 1885) and the Guzmán Blanco Theatre (1881, now the Municipal Theatre), were constructed. Music and Italian opera flourished. Foreign plays were presented frequently, not only by Spanish playwrights such as **Zorrilla** and **Tamayo y Baus**, but also by French and English writers. Teresa Carreño, a talented pianist, gave brilliant performances as did her opera company, in collaboration with her husband, the baritone Tagliapietra. Martín de la Guardia (1836–1907) caught the public attention with a play called *Cosme II de Medicis*, written for the Caracas Dramatic Company and performed in 1848, which he followed with a long series of exotic works. For the most part the *sainete* was the most popular form of theatre in Venezuela during the 19th century. While history records the names of many writers during this period, no plays of great value are to be found.

20th century Romantic and sentimental tendencies continued into the early 20th century. In 1915 Rómulo Gallegos, celebrated novelist and short-term president of the country (1947–8), presented *El milagro del año* (*Miracle of the Year*). The year 1916 marked the end of a brilliant career for Miguel I. Leicibabaza, an impresario and promoter responsible for many theatrical events in Venezuela. In 1917 the company of María Guerrero and her husband Fernando Díaz de Mendoza arrived in

Caracas with a splendid retinue, offering plays by Spanish playwrights **Echegaray**, Marquina and the brothers **Álvarez Quintero**, but these productions did little to stimulate national dramaturgy.

The first half of the century failed to produce a strong theatre movement, although a sense of national identity began to coalesce within some particular groups. La Sociedad de Amigos de Teatro (Society of Friends of Theatre) in its short five years (1942–7) promoted more works by national authors than any previous group. Other groups, some formed earlier, such as the Teatro Obrero (Worker's Theatre) (1938), the Compañía Venezolana de Dramas y Comedias (Venezuelan Company of Plays and Comedies) (1939), and the Teatro Universitario (University Theatre) (1946) contributed to the renovation during a period dominated by *costumbrismo*, a familiar form that had captured popular character types and customs in Spanish traditions since the 19th century. Technically and psychologically superficial, the plays normally used humour to satirize the stereotypical figures within the society. Rafael Guinand (1881–1929) and Leopoldo Ayala Michelena relied on these popular costumbristic forms. Throughout the first half of the 20th century, Venezuela welcomed travelling companies from Spain, France and the Americas that brought conservative, often out-dated productions. **Ibsen** and **O'Neill** inspired a naturalistic orientation.

The so-called creole theatre left an important mark, but a new generation of authors and directors during the 50s sought to bring Venezuelan theatre abreast of contemporary developments on a world scale. Productions of **Cocteau**'s *The Indifferent Lover* in 1950 and **Miller**'s *Death of a Salesman* in 1951 provided new standards for Venezuelans to emulate in theme and style. Of transcendental importance was the arrival of three foreign directors who provided an original stamp and began to train another entire group. Alberto de Paz y Mateos arrived from his native Spain in 1945 and in the Liceo Fermín Toro joined the writer **Román Chalbaud** and director Nicolás Curiel. Jesús Gómez Obregón arrived two years later from Mexico to teach theatre courses in the Ministry of Education, where in short order (for political reasons he had to leave in 1950) he created disciples who have left their own mark: Humberto Orsini, Eduardo Moreno, Gilberto Pinto and Pedro Martán, among others. Juana Sujo arrived from Argentina in 1949 to make a film, staying until her death in 1961. In 1950 she established the Dramatic Studio Juana Sujo; in 1952 the Studio became the National Theatre School and in 1954 the Venezuelan Theatre Society, and the Latin branch of the Caracas Theatre Club. In 1959 she inaugurated the Los Caobos Theatre, the first stable professional theatre in Venezuela. Her students include, among others, Esteban Herrera, Margot Antillano, América Alonso, José Antonio Gutiérrez, and Porfirio Rodríguez. Later the Chilean Horacio Peterson added impetus by assuming the direction of the theatre section of the Ateneo de Caracas (Caracas Atheneum) in 1957.

César Rengifo, a talented artist, writer and director, is considered the father of the modern Venezuelan theatre. He evaluated the Venezuelan national past, creating analogies with contemporary situations through a series of historical trilogies focusing on different time periods.

The Venezuelan theatre began to acquire a sense of national identity. In the 1960s, playwrights experimented freely with absurdist, Artaudian and Brechtian techniques to uncover the realities of Venezuelan social, political and psychological problems. The Grupo Compás (Compás Group), directed by Romeo Costea, was instrumental in introducing these vanguard tendencies into Venezuela. The Venezuelan Theatre Union (1954) promoted the active development of both experimental and professional theatre groups, and the national theatre festivals, initiated in 1959 and repeated at irregular intervals thereafter, encouraged new playwrights and productions. **Isaac Chocrón**, Román Chalbaud and **José Ignacio Cabrujas** earned the epithet of the 'Holy Trinity' for their innovative work with the Nuevo Grupo (New Group, created in 1967) as they worked to elevate the national consciousness of theatre as an artistic form. Caracas's other major group, the **Rajatabla**, was created in 1971 as a subsidiary of the Caracas Atheneum and directed for many years by the Argentine Carlos Giménez. The National Theatre Company was created by presidential decree in 1984 with Isaac Chocrón as its first director.

In a flourishing economy, Venezuela sponsored an ambitious and exciting International Theatre Festival on a two-year cycle from 1973 to 1983, when fiscal considerations required its suspension. In 1977 CELCIT (Centro Latinoamericano de Creación e Investigación Teatral) (The Latin American Centre of Theatre Creativity and Research) was established as an adjunct of the Ateneo. Under the capable direction of Luis Molina and with the patronage of María Teresa Castillo, the organization began to coordinate theatre events, exchanges and publications throughout the Americas.

El Nuevo Grupo in Isaac Chocrón's *La Revolución*, Caracas, Venezuela, 1971.

Theatrical activity in the provinces was widespread, although two centres were most active. In Maracaibo the Sociedad Dramática de Aficionados (Amateur Dramatic Society) directed by Enrique León alternated classical plays (**Büchner**'s *Woyzeck,* **Jarry**'s *Ubu,* and **Sophocles**' *Oedipus Rex*) and regionalist plays, including folkloric works by César Chirinos whose *Traje de etiqueta (Tuxedo),* for example, captured coastal influences. In Valencia, the Teatro de Cámara de la Universidad de Carabobo (Chamber Theatre of the University of Carabobo), established in 1971 by Armando Gota, functioned under the direction of Héctor Vargas after 1973. Of similar importance was the Carabobo Theatre Association directed by Eduardo Moreno after 1966.

In Caracas, several groups in addition to those named continued to function in spite of difficult economic stresses. Armando Gota, Eduardo Gil, Nicolás Curiel, Antonio Costante, Enrique Porte and Ugo Ulive are important directors. José Simón Escalona is an author and director, founder of Grupo Theja, and Humberto Orsini established the Tabla Redonda, Teatro Estudio (Round Table, Studio Theatre) in 1981. **José Gabriel Núñez** and **Rodolfo Santana** are both prolific and committed playwrights. Three women playwrights have made exceptional contributions: Elizabeth Schön, Elisa Lerner, and **Mariela Romero**. Writers of the most recent promotion include Paúl Williams, Edilio Peña, Néstor Caballero and Ibsen Martínez.

The recent level of activity indicates that the Venezuelan theatre has come of age, perhaps somewhat later than in other developing Latin American countries. The quality and quantity associated with the current movement places the theatre of Venezuela into a category with solid values.   GW

See: L. Azparren Giménez, *El teatro venezolano y otros teatros,* Caracas, 1979; *Cabrujas en tres actos,* Caracas, 1983; S. Castillo, *El desarraigo en el teatro venezolano,* Caracas, 1980; I. Chocrón (ed.), *Nueva crítica de teatro venezolano,* Caracas, 1981; G. Hernández, *Tres dramaturgos venezolanos de hoy (Chalbaud, Cabrujas, Chocrón),* Caracas, 1979; R. Monasterios, *Un estudio crítico y longitudinal del teatro venezolano,* Caracas, 1974; idem, *Un enfoque crítico del teatro venezolano,* Caracas, 1975; *La miel y el veneno,* Valencia, 1971; L. F. Ramón y Rivera, *Teatro popular venezolano,* Quito, 1981; C. Salas, *Historia del teatro en Caracas,* Caracas, 1974.

Verdon, Gwen (1926–) American dancer, singer

and actress. Considered to be the finest musical comedy dancer of the 1950s, Verdon studied with choreographer **Jack Cole** and assisted him with the choreography for *Magdalena* (1948) and *Alive and Kicking* (1950), making her Broadway debut as a dancer in the latter. Given a supporting role in *Can-Can* (1953), Verdon stole the show with her exuberant dancing and her impish clowning. Following her success as the seductive Lola in *Damn Yankees* (1955), Verdon surprised critics and audiences with her poignant acting in *New Girl in Town* (1957), a musical version of **Eugene O'Neill**'s *Anna Christie.* She next appeared in *Redhead,* a vehicle written especially for her. In 1966 she created the role of Charity Hope Valentine in *Sweet Charity,* which was choreographed and directed by her husband, **Bob Fosse**. Despite reservations about the show's libretto, critics praised Verdon's performance for its innocence and vulnerability. Verdon's only

musical of the 1970s was the tawdry, flamboyant *Chicago* (1975), in which she was again directed by Fosse. In all of her musicals, Verdon's sinuous, energetic style of dance ideally suited the jazz choreography created for her by Jack Cole and Bob Fosse.   MK

Verga, Giovanni (1840–1922) Italian novelist and

dramatist. The foremost representative of late 19th-century Italian literary naturalism (*verismo*), much of his work depicted the lives of the peasants and fisher folk of his native Sicily, in a poetic, evocative and highly original prose. His best-known work is non-dramatic, *Vita dei Campi* (1880), *I Malavoglia* (1881), *Novelle Rusticane* (1883) and *Mastro Don Gesualdo* (1888), but he was an important figure in the late 19th-century Italian naturalistic theatre. His first stage success was the *Cavalleria Rusticana (Rustic Chivalry)* in 1884, which **Duse** was instrumental in getting performed and in which she enjoyed one of her greatest triumphs. Derived from one of his own short stories this one-act play was justly praised for the originality of its setting (a Sicilian village square) and formal qualities. Another of his major plays, *La Lupa* (1896), likewise taken from a short story, enjoyed stage success as a vehicle for strong female leads. A more ambitious three-act play, *Dal Tuo al Mio* (1903), attempted to treat of class conflict on a broader social canvas and provoked some controversy, but won only limited success.   LR

Verismo An Italian artistic and literary movement of

the late 19th and early 20th centuries, indebted to French naturalism, and of which the most significant figures in the Italian theatre were the dramatists **Giacosa** and **Verga**. Important too were the ideas of the Sicilian writer **Capuana**. In drama *verismo* had two broad manifestations: one was a region-based drama rooted in the observation of local life, sometimes in dialect, occasionally marred by folkloristic simplification but at its best a powerful representation of elemental passions and social conflict (as in Verga's *Cavalleria Rusticana (Rustic Chivalry)* and *La Lupa,* **Bracco**'s *Don Pietro Caruso,* and Bertolazzi's *El Nost Milan,* Capuana's *Malia,* and De Roberto's *Il Rosario*); the other was a bourgeois naturalistic drama, either with strong echoes of **Becque**, but less cynical and daring (**Praga**'s *La Moglie Ideale (The Ideal Wife),* Rovetta's *I Disonesti*), or near-Chekhovian in its dispassionate style and mood of melancholy (Giacosa's *Tristi Amori (Sad Loves)* and *Come le Foglie (Like the Leaves)*). *Verismo* produced the first distinctively national drama in Italy after decades of rather passive imitation of French *drame.* It called for, and helped to breed, a new school of actors who drew upon the example of the 'star' players' romantic realism, but accommodated that to more familiar locales and subject matter.   LR

Vestris, Madame (Lucy Elizabeth Barto-

lozzi) (1797–1856) English actress, singer and theatre manager who owed her stage name to her short-lived marriage to the French ballet-dancer, Armand Vestris, (1787–1825), who supervised his young wife's debut as a singer at the King's Theatre in 1815. It was in the 1820 revival of **Moncrieff**'s *Giovanni in London* (1817) at **Drury Lane** that she became a star, and it was her legs as well as her voice that attracted audiences. Played in travesty, the title-role became a **breeches part**. 'Handsome just above the knee', as a street-ballad insisted, the legs of Vestris were on display again that summer, when she played Macheath in *The Beggar's Opera* at the **Haymarket**, and she continued to combine a high-brow singing career at the King's with low-brow acting roles in breeches for several seasons. Her singing of 'Cherry Ripe' in **Poole**'s *Paul Pry* (1825) was the talk of the town, but however great her popularity, it was an act of extraordinary boldness to set herself up as the lessee of the **Olympic** in 1830. It was there (1831-9) that her innovations in the field of costume and stage decoration were first seen. She owed much to the advice of **J. R. Planché**, whose exquisite burlesque extravaganzas were the outstanding features of the Olympic repertoire and whose knowledge of historical costume was unscarred by pedantry, but her own visual sense was highly developed. The Olympic company included **Liston**, the **Keeleys**, Mrs Glover and, after 1835, **Charles James Mathews**, whom Vestris married in 1838 and with whom she shared the rest of her career. They toured New York and Philadelphia together (1838), jointly managed **Covent Garden** (1839-42), where their outstanding success was with **Boucicault**'s *London Assurance* (1841), after which they were jointly imprisoned for debt and returned to management together at the **Lyceum** (1847-55), during which time Vestris's uncertain health finally failed. There is some dispute about whether or not she was the first manager to employ a box set (was it in 1832 at the Olympic, 1841 for *London Assurance* at Covent Garden or never?), but none about the new impetus she gave to pictorial staging, which became the high achievement of the 19th-century stage. PT

Vianna Filho, Oduvaldo (1936-74) Brazilian playwright and actor, son of playwright Oduvaldo Vianna. In 1956 he joined São Paulo's Arena Theatre which produced his early plays. In 1964 he co-founded Rio's Opinion Theatre which with Arena and Workshop led the *engagé* theatre movement of the 60s. *Se correr o bicho pega, se ficar o bicho come* (*If You Run the Beast Will Catch You, If You Stay the Beast Will Eat You*, 1965) was a veiled reference to the military dictatorship (1964). Before his death, censorship prevented productions of his later plays, but *Rasga coração* (*Heart Stopping*, 1974), staged in 1979 by Arena founder José Renato, was a posthumous success. Along with **Boal** and **Guarnieri**, he established a legacy of well-crafted plays that communicated social consciousness through a Brazilian fusion of Brechtian technique and intense emotion. GW

Viau, Théophile de (1590-1626) French poet and dramatist. As a well-educated young man of Bohemian ways he was supposedly attached for a while to a company of itinerant actors and may have written more for the stage than the one play which has survived, a tragedy entitled *Pyrame et Thisbé* (*Pyramus and Thisbe*). Published in 1623, it was probably performed several years earlier and some measure of its popularity is suggested by the fact that it was still in the repertoire of the **Hôtel de Bourgogne** company in the early 1630s. It is a fine example of baroque tragedy, written in powerful, if contrived verse, and its text, taken in conjunction with the decor provided for it by **Mahe-**

lot, gives a clear insight into the way in which the multiple stage setting inherited from medieval drama was adapted and exploited in the early 17th-century professional theatre. DR

Vicente, Gil (c. 1460-c. 1539) Portuguese playwright, actor and director, who also wrote a number of plays wholly or partly in Spanish. He is generally allowed to have been the founder of the Portuguese theatre and continues to be thought of as Portugal's major dramatist. It could also be said of him that, owing to his greater range, inventiveness and feel for theatre, he is more truly the father of the Hispanic theatre as a whole than his immediate Spanish predecessors and contemporaries, who often furnished him with models for emulation.

Vicente was early on connected with the court, probably before the death of King John II in 1495. His rise in standing at court is arguably linked to his proven skill as a goldsmith and jeweller (although the identity of goldsmith and dramatist has been questioned – irrelevantly to our purposes). He contributed verses and wit to the court's *serões* (musical and poetic soirées). His talents as a man to organize show and spectacle around royal occasions such as anniversaries and entries into cities were often called upon, and it was probably owing to a fine stroke of perceptiveness on the part of the Dowager Queen Leonor that he was invited to bring his literary and theatrical skills together for his first essay into theatre.

The *Monólogo do Vaqueiro* (*Monologue of the Cowherd*) was recited or acted, possibly by Vicente himself, on the occasion of the birth of the future king John III in 1502. As in a similar play by **Encina**, a cowherd stumbles into the royal bedchamber, proclaims how dazzled he is by the magnificence of the palace, and with rustic humour and simplicity makes an offer of produce to the baby prince on behalf of the nation. The shepherd-play humour is to be found in a few more plays, with more or less of Renaissance pastoral in their confection. They are not, with the exception of the *Auto da Sibila Cassandra* (*Sibyl Cassandra's Play*, 1513), Vicente's most memorable work. The *Monólogo* is the first of over 40 works of varying lengths that Vicente wrote and produced for the court in a variety of palaces and settings. Two or three plays were aired more publicly, a further one had its first performance at a convent near Lisbon.

Vicente's religious theatre is a splendid synthesis of the themes and staging of the Middle Ages. The *Auto da Alma* (*Play of the Soul*, 1518) is almost pure morality, with Soul making her way to the safety of Mother Church, first pulled onward by Angel and then waylaid by a subtle tempter of a Devil who lures her into stiletto heels, heavy brocade and a plight from which she escapes narrowly. The trilogy known as the *Barcas* (1516, 1518, 1519) (*The Ship of Hell*, –*of Purgatory*, –*of Heaven*) puts the whole of humanity into the dock of individual judgement at the point of death. The three estates of society, or more strictly the emergent three social classes, are examined very fiercely before assignment to one of two boats bound one for Heaven the other to Hell. The *Breve Sumário da História de Deus* (*A Brief Summary of the Story of God*) is a consideration of the matière of the mystery cycles of Northern Europe. Time and World preside over the passage of humanity from Adam to Christ over the stage of this life, in a play calling for split-level simultaneous staging.

The many *farsas* (farces, some of them very close to comedy proper) deal with human, social and institutional foibles and abuses. *Quem Tem Farelos?*, 1508, (*Who Has Chaff? – for nags, no pun in Portuguese*) is a satire on the down-at-heel minor nobility and their designs upon richer but also earthy and shrewder women of lower class. The eponymous heroine of *Inês Pereira* (1523) buries her first such husband and then marries a dolt of a yeoman she literally rides off at the end of the play to his cuckolding. The *Auto da Índia* (*The Play of India*, 1509) is as slick and humorous as 20th-century bedroom farce. The protagonist of the *Juiz da Beira* (*The J. P. from Beira*, 1526) is a figure very much in the mould of **Brecht**'s Azdak in his ambivalent sentencings.

In these religious plays and comedies, as well as in chivalresque tragicomedies and court masques, Vicente deployed theatrical skills that were not equalled anywhere in Europe for another 60 or 70 years.   LK

Victoria Theatre, Stoke-on-Trent

Britain's first permanent theatre-in-the-round. Beginning life as **Stephen Joseph**'s touring Studio Theatre Company, in 1962 it became based in a converted cinema on the border between Stoke and Newcastle under Lyme. Peter Cheeseman, originally appointed manager, became artistic director in 1966 and has remained as such to this day. The company is best known for its documentary plays – entertaining blends of music, song and dramatized research into actual events in the area, past and present. Topics have included the building of the local railways (*The Knotty*) and the threatened closure of the nearby steelworks (*The Fight for Shelton Bar*). They have proved extraordinarily popular and helped to create strong bonds with the surrounding communities. The repertoire also includes the classics and new plays (sometimes by resident dramatists such as **Peter Terson**) and each season is organized on a true repertory basis. 1986 saw the opening of a new, purpose-built theatre-in-the-round, seating 600 instead of the old theatre's 389.   AJ

Viertel, Berthold

(1885–1955) Austrian director, instrumental in promoting the plays of **Hasenclever**, **Bronnen** and **Kaiser**. He produced **Brecht**'s *Fear and Suffering in the Third Reich* under the title of *The Private Life of the Master Race* in New York in 1945 and worked at the **Berliner Ensemble** before becoming director of the Vienna **Burgtheater** in 1951.   CI

Vietnam

This South-East Asian nation has a population of 61 million and borders on Kampuchea (formerly, Cambodia), Laos, and China. From the 1st to the 10th century the country was ruled by China: Mahayana Buddhism, Confucian values, and Taoist thought entered, while Chinese models affected performance of the court. The Hindu kingdom of Champa was incorporated into the country in the 14th century and musical features of Indian origin including the use of drum syllables, musical modes and improvisation technique seem to have been borrowed for theatre music from that time. From 1862–1945 the country was a French colony: early experiments in staging translations of French playwrights, like **Molière** and **Cor-**

neille, led to a lively spoken drama movement which continues to the present. Marxist socialist use of theatre as a tool of education and mass communication has helped raise the traditionally low status of performance in recent years.

Four major kinds of theatre exist in Vietnam: (1) folk performance (2) classical performance (3) popular theatre, and (4) spoken drama. All these forms exist at present, but the first two have a venerable history while the last two forms are the product of this century.

Folk performance Folk performance includes prototheatrical forms (including possession trance seances, courting songs, and story-telling) and folk theatricals. Spirit mediums in Buddhist temples might take up in ecstatic dances the attribute (knives, clubs, etc.) of the spirit they incarnated. Mediums' songs, *châu van* in the north, *hâu van* in the central region and *rôi bong* in the south, are now dying out, but flourished in times past. Courting songs were sung alternately by boys and girls in various areas. These dialogue songs, called *trông quân*, *quan ho*, and other names according to the area, were popular folk performances that laid the groundwork for more dramatic dialogues to develop. Storytelling, too, abounded: blind musicians (*xâm xoan*) travelled from village to village singing epic, historical, humorous and erotic songs. While the courtesan singer (*a dao*), accompanied by a musician on a lute (*dan day*), was another significant entertainer of times past.

Within the village environment a folk theatre, *hat cheo*, and water puppetry also emerged. The *hat cheo*, which is believed to have developed around the first century AD, remains significant in the northern part of the country. It was performed outside temples or *dinh*, places of worship for the tutelary god which simultaneously served as men's community houses. Maurice Durand and Nguyen Tran Huan see the performance developing out of both religious rites and the songs exchanged by young men and women at harvest festivals. By the 10th century the form included poetry, mime, singing and dancing. The rules of this form were laid down by the theorist Luong The Vinh in 1501. Prior to the 20th century performances were paid for by the communal fund or rich benefactors and were presented during the day in the forecourt of the community house. The stage area was separated from the audience by a rope, and costumes hung in full view of the audience. Performers were largely amateurs who showed skill at singing during work songs, but some performers risked the social opprobrium that was an actor's lot to join professional troupes which eked out an existence. The texts and songs were passed orally from one generation of performers to the next. The clown (*he*) improvised wittily, and this, with the graceful dance and song of the actors, made this a light entertainment form. Skits customarily showed the common man triumphing over greedy mandarin and emperor. These qualities endeared the form to the masses and eventually gave it favour with the socialist government of the Democratic Republic of Vietnam which took over the northern part of the country after the Second World War. Despite government favour, currently the popularity of the *hat cheo* is in decline.

Water puppetry (*muá rôi nuóe*) is another significant folk theatre passed through the oral tradition. According to Dinh Gia Khanh a stone inscription on a pillar in

Nan Ninh province proves the form was well developed by AD 1121. A pond forms the stage and music accompanies the presentation. Puppets of about 1½ ft are mounted on frames or attached to long poles that are submerged in the water, and manipulators work behind a stage house constructed for the occasion. Animals' battles, acrobatic feats, village activities, and popular tales, such as that of the Trung sisters who opposed Chinese tyranny, are depicted, and the puppet clown, Chu Teu, enlivens the performance with humour. Puppetry societies are village based with admission to the group by consensus of the members.

Classical performance The *hat bôi* (alternatively *hat tuông, tuồng*) is the classical theatre tradition that was fostered by the Vietnamese courts. Like the court dances, comprising the *van vu* (civil dance) and *vo vu* (military dance), the *hat bôi* derives from Chinese models. Tradition holds that the form dates from 1285 when a Chinese actor was captured by the Vietnamese general and taught his art to the Vietnamese.

The form served primarily as a court entertainment from the 13th to the 17th centuries for rulers in Hanoi. The actor Dao Duy Tu (1572–1634) is credited with popularizing the form by introducing musical styles of Champa, the Indian-influenced kingdom to the south. These tunes came to be called southern songs (*hat nam*) and their sad poignancy is felt to contrast with the more stirring tunes of *hat khach* (foreigners' songs). *Noi lôi* (stylized speaking) are patter songs which form the final category of singing in this operatic mode. Dao Duy Tu's transformation is said to have helped spread *hat bôi* to the southern area and popularized it among the people. He is also credited with composing the most loved play, *The Fort of Son Hou*, which recounts how political intrigue is resolved when the rightful heir is returned to the Vietnamese throne.

During the 18th and 19th centuries the form had the support of the Nguyen dynasty. Gia Long (1802–20) had the first theatre built in the imperial palace at Hue, the capital. Chinese influences were reinforced during the reign of Emperor Minh Mang (1820–41) who imported Chinese actors from Canton to the court to revise the genre. The current similarities between *hat bôi* and Cantonese opera in gestures, costumes, and makeup probably result from this reform. The colour symbolism used in painted-face characters corresponds closely, but not exactly, to Chinese practice. The use of falsetto voice; a bare stage with only a table and chairs to create the locale; stylized mimes for riding a horse or expressing emotion; costume practices; and character types are related to Chinese models. Likewise, the division of plays into ones based on the history of China and Vietnam and those dealing with commoners is related to Chinese categories of military and civil. The orchestral instrumentation and the Vietnamese of the plays, replete with sinicized words and Chinese literary references, shows borrowing too. But distinctive Vietnamese features are also apparent: women have always played female roles; many plays deal with Vietnamese history and events and utilize Vietnamese dress; 'water sleeves' and the associated movement techniques characteristic of Chinese opera are lacking; and, of course, songs retain the distinctive Vietnamese musical flavour.

The court troupe, *phuong nha tro*, operated until the demise of the courts in 1946. Plays tend to exalt the emperor, and uphold Confucian ethics and feudal values. This content has alienated more recent audiences from *hat bôi* as have Chinese features of the technique. Doan Quan Tan attempted a revision in the 1940s which involved the elimination of the falsetto voice and Chinese words. Up to the 1970s the form was still performed in Saigon, but lacked an enthusiastic audience.

Popular theatre Vietnamese *cai luong* (reformed theatre) is the popular musical theatre that prevailed from the 1920s to the advent of television in the late 1960s in the southern part of the country. Songs are the most significant feature of the performance, and these are memorized while the dialogue is improvised from a scenario. *Tu dai*, ballads in which one singer would perform a few lines and another sing a reply, form the base of *cai luong*. Around 1916 performers of one particular ballad 'The song of Nguyet Nga' are said to have begun presenting the song in a more dramatic style. Travelling circuses began including this dramatic playlet in their programmes. The greater part of the performance was given to the singing of the songs. The clown who developed his own business and monologues soon became an important element in the performance. The falsetto voice of *hat bôi* was abandoned but, since many of the early performers were trained in the classical theatre, southern songs were still used for sad scenes and some of the stirring, military songs were also incorporated. By the 1920s performers had incorporated a popular song 'Remembrances' ('Vong Cô') which figures prominently in the music of every performance to the present. Different parts of this song will occur in different sections of the play, and performers are judged by their singing of this tune.

Plays could be on social themes depicting current Vietnamese life, Chinese themes, or Western – especially Roman – themes. During the 1930s troupes introduced innovations to lure audiences: Western plays such as **Schiller**'s *Maria Stuart* and *Hamlet* were adapted. Miss Nam Phi introduced her version of **Folies-Bergère** dancing; and Hong Kong flying and sword fighting techniques were introduced by an actor named Mui Buu, giving rise to a new genre called 'flying plays'. Records of performances were released, and Tango and swing rhythms had their impact on music and dance. The use of scenery and proscenium stage was introduced from the West, and Western instruments might be incorporated into the orchestra.

The continuing political unrest after the partition of the country in 1954 was reflected in plays which criticized the French regime. The theatre declined in the 1960s and early 1970s, years during which the American military presence and escalating war debilitated the south. The stage was dominated by escapist sword fighting plays and melodramatic domestic dramas. During this period the Kim Chung troupe under the direction of Nguyen Viet Long was the most prominent group in the country with four touring troupes and one additional company stationed in Saigon. Popular plays included modern domestic dramas and traditional stories, such as the *The Story of Thuy Kieu*, the story of a virtuous woman who becomes a courtesan against her will and finally is reunited with her first love.

Spoken drama　Molière's *The Miser* was translated and staged in 1907, an event greeted by Vietnamese intellectuals. Thereafter, spoken drama plays called *kich nôi* were regularly presented. The first Vietnamese spoken drama was the 1921 play, *A Cup of Poison*, by Vu Dinh Long (1901–60). Since then the tradition has developed strongly in the country and there are now 23 professional spoken drama companies. Training is given in many schools including the Hanoi Institute of Theatre and Cinema opened in 1980. Mackerras viewing theatre in 1984 noted that the struggle with China, morality, self-sacrifice, and love between the sexes were currently favoured themes within this form which tends towards realistic portrayal of social problems.

In 1980 there were 62 state troupes in Vietnam. Spoken drama predominated, but 16 were devoted to *cheo*, 13 to *cai luong*, three to *hat bôi*, three to puppet theatre, and miscellaneous performance making up the remainder. The troupes in which performers are paid a wage comparable to professionals in teaching or medicine show the respect the current government accords to the arts which are seen as important channels of raising political and social consciousness.　KF

> *See*: J. Brandon, *The Theatre in Southeast Asia*, Cambridge, Mass., 1967; M. Durand and Nguyen Tran Huan, *An Introduction to Vietnamese Literature*, trans. by D. M. Hawke, New York, 1985; D. Hauch, 'The Cai Luong Theatre of Vietnam, 1915–1970', Ph.D. diss. Southern Illinois University, 1972 (University Microfilms); Huynh Khac Dung, *Hat Bôi, Théâtre traditionnel du Viêt-nam*, Saigon, 1970; C. Mackerras, 'Theatre in Vietnam', unpublished manuscript; Song-Ban, *The Vietnamese Theatre*, Hanoi, 1960; Trân Van Khê, 'Vietnam', *New Grove Dictionary of Music and Musicians*, ed. by S. Sadie, New York, 1980; 'Vietnamese Water Puppets', *Performing Arts Journal* 9, 1 (1985), and 'Le théâtre vietnamien', in *Les théâtres d'Asie*, ed. by J. Jacquot, Paris, 1968, 203–19.

Vieux-Colombier Theatre　A 19th-century theatre building in the street of that name on the Paris left bank, formerly known as the Athénée St Germain. It was renovated by **Copeau** in 1913 as the launching pad for his renewal of French theatre. It was again remodelled by **Jouvet** under Copeau's direction after the First World War so as to approximate an Elizabethan stage and here Copeau's company performed after their return from America 1920–4. After four years as a cinema the theatre was occupied by the **Compagnie des Quinze** in 1931 and then continued under commercial management until it closed in 1972. It always retained some of the prestige of Copeau's name and many important events have taken place there such as **Artaud**'s reading of his own work in 1947. It saw the first Paris performances of such influential plays as **Sartre**'s *In Camera* (1944), **T. S. Eliot**'s *Murder in the Cathedral* (1945), a production later revived at the **TNP**, and **Adamov**'s *Paolo Paoli* (see **Planchon**).　DB

Viganò, Salvatore (1769–1821) Italian choreographer and dancer. Born to the world of theatrical dance he made his debut as a choreographer at the age of 17 with an *intermezzo*. After several years of study, including particularly the theory of Noverre and the practice of Danberval, he joined his father in Venice in

1790, and at the San Samuele Theatre scored signal success as dancer and choreographer. After a period of working in Vienna, he toured Europe in the late 1790s, returning to Vienna in 1799 to create some of his most significant works, including *Die Gasehöpfe der Prometheus* (1801) to Beethoven's music, brilliantly fantastic and allegorical ballets. His Shakespearian subjects included an *Othello* in 1818.　KR

Vigarani, Gaspare (1586–1663) Italian theatre architect and stage designer. Although he had a well-established reputation in Italy, particularly for his theatre at Modena (1654), his most famous work was done in Paris where he had been summoned by Cardinal Mazarin in 1659 to supervise the performances in conjunction with the marriage of Louis XIV. This involved the creation of a new theatre to replace the **Petit-Bourbon** which was being torn down to make way for the Colonnade of the Louvre. The result was the **Salle des Machines**, based on the Modena theatre, and constructed in the Tuileries Palace. When it opened in 1662 with *Ercole Amante* (*Hercules in Love*) it was the largest theatre in Europe. It accommodated 7,000 spectators and had a stage 140 feet deep. The elaborate settings and machinery included a device that raised the entire royal family above the stage. Vigarani was very jealous of his rival **Giacomo Torelli** and had the latter's machinery removed from the Petit-Bourbon before it was demolished, ostensibly to use it in the new theatre. Instead he had it burned. After his death Vigarani was succeeded at court by his son Carlo (1623–1713) who held the post until 1680 and designed primarily at the Palace of Versailles. Carlo Vigarani's best-known work was **Molière** and **Lully**'s *Les Plaisirs de l'Ile Enchantée* (*Pleasures of the Enchanted Isle*, 1664), a spectacular three-day celebration.　AA

Vigny, Alfred de (1797–1863) French poet, dramatist and novelist. A leading figure in the French Romantic movement, Vigny's reputation as a dramatist rests on two plays: *Le More de Venise, Othello* (1829) and *Chatterton* (1835), both performed at the Théâtre-Français. The hostile reception of English actors playing **Shakespeare** ('an emissary of Wellington') in 1822 had encouraged a re-evaluation of Shakespeare in France (*vide* Stendhal's essay *Racine et Shakespeare*) and this was confirmed by a more successful visit in 1827. Vigny, in his *Othello*, did not attempt to assimilate Shakespeare's play into the forms of a neoclassical tragedy, as **Ducis** had done. Instead he offered a free, but generally faithful, translation (Gratiano and Bianca being the only significant characters to disappear). The same year his three-act version of *The Merchant of Venice* was accepted by the Ambigu-Comique, but not performed. In 1831, his historical drama, *La Maréchale d'Ancre*, with **Mlle George** in the title role, was performed at the **Odéon**. *Chatterton*, with its theme of a poet driven to suicide by a philistine society, was one of the great successes of the romantic theatre and offered a superb role to **Marie Dorval** (Vigny's mistress) as a sensitive soul who dies of a love she cannot express. In 1834 Vigny also wrote a dramatic proverb, *Quitte Pour La Peur* (*Getting off with a Fright*), for Dorval.　JMCC

Vilar, Jean (1912–71) French actor, and director. Vilar trained with **Dullin** and began to direct during the Occupation, when his time was divided between tours with La Roulotte and avant-garde productions in Paris which included two plays by **Strindberg**. In the late 1940s he continued to direct for the avant-garde (e.g. **Adamov**'s *L'Invasion* in 1950) but also founded the **Avignon theatre festival** in 1947, where he developed the virtues of **Copeau**'s bare stage, performing on a vast open-air stage in the courtyard of the papal palace. His uncluttered production style suited a revival of heroic tragedy (*Le Cid* 1949, *Danton's Death* 1948) but also enabled him to present **Molière**, **Marivaux** and **Musset** in a new light. His considerable gifts as an actor of mature roles complemented the passionate brilliance of the young **Gérard Philipe**: he played the old statesman to Philipe's young hero on many occasions. In 1951 he was put in control of the **Théâtre National Populaire** at **Chaillot**, where he extended the methods that had proved successful at Avignon. He made the theatre into as near as possible a classless space, transcending social divisions, in which all could join in a process of reflection, learning, and a celebration of common humanity. He insisted that theatre should be available to all: 'a public service in exactly the same way as gas, water or electricity'. His repertoire consisted of classics and modern classics and he regretted not being able to introduce more modern works: his few attempts, which included **Gatti**'s first performed play, *Le Crapaud-Buffle* 1959, were box-office failures. In 1963 he left the TNP to devote himself to a revitalization and extension of the Avignon festival but in 1968 he was fiercely attacked by young revolutionaries who mistook his lifelong left-wing commitment for compromise. Through his example he had a strong influence on many young actors and directors who have sought to reconcile social and political commitment with theatre art of the highest standards, notably **Mnouchkine**, **Planchon** and **Vitez**.   DB

Vildrac, Charles (1882–1971) French author and playwright whose first and best play *Le Paquebot Tenacity* (*The Steamboat Tenacity*, 1920) was one of the few new works to be produced by **Copeau**. His subsequent plays were produced by **Jouvet**, **Pitoëff** and the **Comédie-Française**. Together with Jean-Jacques Bernard and **Lenormand**, he helped to generate a vogue for the theatre of the unexpressed: plays telling the stories of simple people incapable of grand speeches, but whose silences gave eloquent expression to their feelings.   DB

Villaurrutia, Xavier (1903–50) Mexican playwright and poet involved in the renovation of Mexican drama. Co-founder with **Salvador Novo** of the **Teatro de Ulises** in 1928, he experimented with the most recent European techniques, and after the early demise of the Ulysses theatre, he continued with **Teatro de Orientación** in the same mould. His plays often show the influence of **Giraudoux** and **Lenormand**. The *Autos profanos*, five short pieces (1933–7), are humorous and playable with strong philosophical underpinings. Major plays are *La hiedra* (*The Ivy*, 1942) based on **Racine**'s *Phèdre* and *Invitación a la muerte* (*Invitation to Death*, 1940), with overtones of *Hamlet*.   GW

Villegas, Oscar (1943–) Mexican playwright and ceramicist, studied the plastic arts, completed the

directing programme at the National Institute of Fine Arts and dramatic theory and composition at the National University. His plays are highly experimental in form and language, greatly influenced by rock music in theme and structure, including *El renacimiento* (*The Renaissance*, 1967), *Santa Catarina* (*St Catherine*, 1969). His major work is *Atlántida* (*Atlantis*, 1976), a full-length play which examines values among youth outside mainstream society. The techniques used are daring and innovative, major themes are aspects of individual freedom and expression. *Mucho gusto en conocerlo* (*Pleased to Meet You*, 1985) is his most recent play.   GW

Vilna Troupe, The Celebrated co-operative company which opened in Russia in 1916 with two immediately successful productions of **Sholom Asch**'s *The Landsman* and **Peretz Hirshbein**'s *The Forsaken Nook*. With **David Herman** as director and **Jacob Ben-Ami** as leading actor, the company's achievements soon brought a much needed dignity to European Yiddish theatre and various 'Wings', or detachments, set out on world tours. Its most famous production, **Solomon Anski**'s *The Dybbuk*, toured continuously for many years. The Warsaw 'Wing' achieved its greatest success with Sholom Asch's *Kiddush Hashem*, whilst the Berlin 'Wing' toured a particularly striking production of Peretz Hirshbein's *The Haunted Inn*. There was also a Rumanian 'Wing' and an American 'Wing'.   AB

Vinaver, Michel (1927–) French novelist and playwright. His first plays were written in the 1950s, when *Les Coréens* (*The Koreans*, 1956) had some success, with four different productions by **Planchon**, **Serreau**, Joris and Monnet. But in between *Iphigénie Hotel* (written 1959) and *Par-dessus Bord* (*Overboard*) (written 1969, directed by Planchon 1973) he wrote no plays, devoting himself entirely to his job as a business executive. The world of business provides the material for most of his later plays e.g., *La Demande d'Emploi* (*Situation Vacant*, 1973); *Les Travaux et les Jours* (*Works and Days*, 1979); *A la Renverse* (*Bending over Backwards*, 1980). In these plot is reduced to a minimum, the plays consisting of ambiguous, fragmentary dialogues in which questions and answers do not necessarily correspond, and different streams of consciousness interweave to create a rich dramatic texture. Vinaver has been associated with the **théâtre du quotidien** because of the everyday concerns and realistic nature of his characters and also because of the use he makes of different linguistic codes. But in his more ambitious plays such as *Par-dessus Bord* mythical archetypes underlie modern stories and the drama's method of dealing with its subject matter is multiple, varying from naturalist representation to sequences in which the very possibility of representation is questioned. In the course of the 1970s he became associated particularly with Jacques Lassalle who directed a number of his plays but his most recent work has been directed by Alain Françon.   DB

Vincent, Jean-Pierre (1942–) French theatre director who founded the Théâtre de l'Espérance at the Montmartre Palace theatre in 1972 in collaboration with Jean Jourdheuil. Here he produced **Brecht**,

Büchner, **Vishnevsky**, as well as modern French works by Rezvani and **Grumberg**. In 1975 he became director of the Théâtre National de Strasbourg, which he modelled on German civic theatres, drawing the theatre school into close collaboration and appointing Bernard Chartreux and Michel Deutsch as dramaturges. His repertoire included translations of new German writing and French plays of the **quotidien** as well as adaptations from novels e.g., **Zola**'s *Germinal* (1975). In 1983 he was appointed director of the **Comédie-Française**, but he resigned three years later. DB

Virginia Theatre 245 West 52nd St, New York City [Architect: C. Howard Crane]. In 1925, with a good deal of ceremony, the **Theatre Guild** opened its new house, the Guild, which was intended for its own productions. For a number of reasons relating to the design of the theatre and the paucity of seats (under 1,000), it proved to be unpopular with actors and audiences and the Theatre Guild turned to other theatres for its most significant productions while leasing the Guild to other producers. From 1943 to 1950, it was rented as a radio playhouse, then sold to the American National Theatre and Academy to be operated by the ANTA board as a not-for-profit 'home for the living arts'. After extensive renovation, the newly named ANTA Playhouse was only intermittently used for ANTA-sponsored productions and more often leased to commercial producers. In 1981, the Jujamcyn Organization, founded in 1956, bought it from the ANTA board, renovated it and increased the seating, and renamed it the Virginia after the wife of the owner. MCH

Visconti, Luchino (1906–76) Italian film and theatre director: best known for his films, *La Terra Trema* (*The Earth Trembles*, 1948), *Rocco e si Suoi Fratelli* (*Rocco and his Brothers*, 1960), *Il Gattopardo* (*The Leopard*, 1963) and *Morte in Venezia* (*Death in Venice*, 1971), he was also a distinguished director in the 'straight' and musical theatre. Of aristocratic background but socialist political sympathies, both of which tended to be reflected in much of his work, he came to prominence only after the Second World War directing the kinds of drama which dominated the serious European stages of the late 1940s and 50s (**Miller**, **Williams**, **Sartre**, **Anouilh**), and discovering in classic plays dimensions of social realism hitherto ignored, as in his stage revaluation of **Goldoni**'s *La Locandiera* (1952). His early productions of **Shakespeare** included *Troilus and Cressida* (1949) and *Macbeth* (1958). At once lyrical and realistic, flamboyant and analytical, his work often aroused vigorous enthusiasm or hostility. His strong sense of the theatrical and emotionally powerful found further expression in his work for the musical stage, particularly with the operas of Verdi. Among his notable stage productions of the sixties and seventies were **Chekhov**'s *The Cherry Orchard* (1965) and **Pinter**'s *Old Times* (1973), in which directorial emphases explored the passage of time and its effects with an underlying melancholy that became increasingly prominent too in his film work. KR

Vishnevsky, Vsevolod Vitalievich (1900–51) Soviet prose writer and dramatist who drew upon his experiences fighting in the First World War, October Revolution and Russian Civil War as a member of the Red Army in composing dramas of epic sweep, monumental scale, passionate emotion and romantic-heroic perspective. His play *The First Horse Army* (1929), commemorating and mythologizing Red Cavalry leader Marshal Semyon Budyony's Rostov campaign of the Civil War, was meant to 'correct' **Babel**'s description of its brutality in his story collection *Red Cavalry*. Vishnevsky employs a sprawling, episodic structure with framing prologue and epilogue, a narrator and correspondence to bridge the 10-year gap between the date of the events being described and that of the play, as well as crowd scenes, a variety of sounds and musical selections, simultaneous staging and suggested screen projections. His most famous play, *An Optimistic Tragedy* (1934), about a heroic female commisar's sacrifice of her own life to instill discipline in a motley group of seamen and to insure the Baltic Fleet's victory during the Civil War, gave its name to a new type of play. Vishnevsky maintained that although Soviet Russia would undoubtedly continue to engage in a tragic conflict with anti-Bolshevik elements, the strength of the new socialist order inspires optimism in the outcome. This points towards the 'conflictless dramas' of socialist realism. The play's episodic structure is held together by two sailors who serve as choral figures. **Tairov**'s famous 1934 production at the Kamerny Theatre with his wife Alisa Koonen as the leather-jacketed lady commissar and a monumental, spirally ramped set by Vadim Ryndin, established the model for succeeding productions for years to come. Vishnevsky's earnestness and will to survive eclipsed his artistic integrity, resulting in blatant falsification of history as in his last play *Unforgotten 1919* (1949) which fabricates a heroic role for Stalin in the Revolution. SG

Vitez, Antoine (1930–90) French actor and director of Russian origins and strong Communist sympathies, he worked on the journal of **Vilar**'s **TNP**, *Bref*, acted and directed in the decentralized theatres and in the theatres of the Parisian red belt at Nanterre and Ivry, where he ran the Théâtre des Quartiers d'Ivry from 1971 to 1980. Unlike directors with a tendency to scenic extravagance (e.g., **Planchon**), Vitez achieved his effects by unusual direction of actors, encouraging them to seek for unexpected body movements, to play against the text, to break accepted conventions. This gave rise to productions of scintillating intelligence but also of considerable preciosity. He became a teacher at the Conservatoire in 1968 and influenced a large number of young French actors. His choice of repertoire was broad, from **Sophocles** to **Brecht**, from **Hugo** to **Claudel**, and also included many new plays and adaptations of novels. In 1981 he became director of the **Chaillot** theatre where he continued to direct experimental productions of both modern and classical plays. From 1988 he was director of the **Comèdie-Française**. DB

Vitrac, Roger (1899–1952) French poet and playwright, active in the dada movement, who founded the Théâtre Alfred Jarry with **Artaud** in 1926. Here two of his plays were performed, *Les Mystères de l'Amour* (*The Mysteries of Love*, 1927) and *Victor ou les Enfants au Pouvoir* (*Victor or Power to Children*, 1928). The latter can stand as a masterpiece of surrealist theatre, though it was not until the revival of the play in a production by **Anouilh** (1962) that its quality was generally recognized. Set in 1909, *Victor* satirizes middle-class manners, patriotism, and the conventions of boulevard comedy by means of a grotesque child, Victor, who is nine years old but already six feet tall and can see through all the social pretence that surrounds him. Later plays failed to achieve the brilliance of Vitrac's early work and he was not again involved in a practical theatre venture. DB

Vivian Beaumont and **Mitzi E. Newhouse Theatres** Lincoln Center, New York City [Architects: Eero Saarinen with **Jo Mielziner**]. Part of the Lincoln Center for the Performing Arts, the repertory theatre with its experimental appendage began under the aegis of **Elia Kazan** and **Robert Whitehead**, who spent two years planning it. Named after Mrs Vivian Beaumont Allen, its benefactress, the larger theatre opened in 1965. The playhouse was designed with 11,000 square feet of stage space (compared to 3,000 square of the **Martin Beck** on Broadway) and was intended to shift from being a proscenium to a thrust stage and to be able to store scenery for the repertory. All of the mechanical and electrical elements are concealed and the auditorium is gently amphitheatrical. The smaller stage, originally the Forum, with its 299 seats as compared to the flexible 1,090 to 1,140 seats of the larger Beaumont was designed with all of the structural, mechanical and electrical equipment exposed and was intended for experimental productions. Kazan and Whitehead resigned and were replaced by Herbt Blau and **Jules Irving** in the first year, then by Irving alone in 1967. He was succeeded by **Joseph Papp** (1973–7), who obtained operating funds from Mrs Mitzi E. Newhouse, after whom he renamed the Forum. Since Papp's departure, the theatres have been reopened only intermittently as the Lincoln Center management has struggled to find creative leaders and a purpose for the two theatres. In 1985, Gregory Mosher of the Chicago **Goodman Theatre** and Bernard Gersten, a Broadway and Off-Broadway producer, were named to guide its destiny. MCH

Viviani, Raffaele (1888–1950) Italian actor, director and dramatist who began his career as a singer and comic entertainer in the Neapolitan popular variety theatre. Naples is the setting for many realistic plays of powerful social criticism, written in the Neapolitan dialect, among the most outstanding of which are *'O Vico* (*The Alley*, 1917), *Tuledu'e Notte* (*Tuledu by Night*, 1918), *Festa di 'Piedigrotta* (*The Festival of Piedigrotta*, 1919). They present sharp and realistic portraits of working-class life and are crafted with great skill. One of the major figures of the Italian stage between the two World Wars, he was an extremely versatile *homme du théâtre*, combining the talents of playwright, director, composer and actor–manager. LR

Voaden, Herman (1903–84) A pioneering Canadian playwright, educator and cultural agitator. He combined a teaching career with important work in the community and little theatre movement. By the late 1920s he was using newspaper articles to conduct a crusade for a true Canadian drama and a new Canadian

theatrical art. During the 1930s he began writing and producing his own innovative and experimental multimedia works in a style he called 'symphonic expressionism' which tried to develop the ideas of **Appia** and **Craig** with a distinctively Canadian production of **Eliot**'s *Murder in the Cathedral*.

His career as a lobbyist for the arts began after the war as a founder and first president of the Canadian Arts Council (now the Canadian Conference of the Arts) which pressured the government to establish the Massey Commission which was to lead to the expansion of government support of the arts and, ultimately, the Canada Council. JA

Vodanović, Sergio (1926–) Chilean playwright, born to Yugoslavian immigrant parents and trained as a lawyer. Although he began with light, vaudevillian plays, his first major works are *El senador no es honorable* (*The Senator is not Honourable*, 1952) and *Deja que los perros ladren* (*Let the Dogs Bark*, 1959), both of which provide a penetrating criticism of political intrigue, corruption and venality through well-drawn characters. *Los fugitivos* (*The Fugitives*, 1965) resonates of *Tea and Sympathy* with the young lover/older woman syndrome. In his later plays, Vodanović becomes more virulent in his socio-political commentaries: *Perdón . . . ¡Estamos en guerra! (Sorry . . . We're at War!*, 1966) and *Nos tomamos la Universidad* (*We Took the University*, 1970). *¿Cuántos años tiene un día?* (*How many Years in a Day?*, 1978) written in conjunction with the ICTUS, contrasts the liberty of expression of former years with both the overt and covert oppression of a group of news reporters working for television in the Pinochet regime. GW

Volkov, Fyodor Grigorievich (1729–63) The first eminent Russian actor and named by the critic Belinsky as 'the father of the Russian theatre'. With the inheritance left him by his father, a factory owner, he established a public theatre in his native Yaroslavl (1750). In 1752 his troupe, which included his brother Grigory and **Ivan Dmitrevsky**, was brought to St Petersburg to perform the morality play *A Sinner's Repentance* by the high cleric **Dmitry Rostovsky** and some tragedies by **A. P. Sumarokov**. What was to have been a court theatre instead became in 1756 the Russian Patent Theatre, Russia's first permanent professional public theatre, under the direction of Sumarokov. Volkov became the company's leading tragic actor, impersonating the heroes in Sumarokov's plays, most notably Khorev and Hamlet. Recognizing Volkov's singular talent, his passionate temperament and naturalness of expression, Sumarokov adjusted his neoclassical verse form to accommodate him. Volkov had from the outset helped Sumarokov in the direction of the theatre, a role which became solely his upon the latter's dismissal in 1761. Volkov and his brother took part in the plot to overthrow Peter III for which they were rewarded with court offices. While organizing the festivities for the coronation of Catherine the Great (1763) which included the masquerade *Minerva Triumphant*, Volkov caught cold and died. SG

Volksbühne (People's Theatre) The generic label for a wide cultural movement as well as the name of those theatres affiliated with it. Founded in 1890 in Berlin as a subscription organization, its first title of the Freie (Free) Volksbühne reveals its origins as well as its unique contribution in bringing theatre to a mass audience. Growing out of **Otto Brahm**'s **Freie Bühne**, which followed the Théâtre Libre in experimental productions of **Ibsen** or **Hauptmann**, it was dedicated to providing art for the working classes and brought out the social content in the new naturalism. In politicizing drama its history raised – and partially resolved – many issues still plaguing alternate/political theatre today. The tension between ideological and artistic aims split the organization in 1892, and it took over two decades to create a working compromise. Disagreement over servicing cultural demands or acting as a catalyst for radicalizing the masses, which reached a head with the productions of **Erwin Piscator**, produced two parallel organizations in 1927, while its expansion demonstrates how size inhibits experimentation.

Beginning by booking special performances in commercial theatres, the organization not only came at times to control three of the regular Berlin stages, but built two major theatres specifically for its needs. The first, financed largely by personal subscription, opened as the Volksbühne on Bülowplatz in 1914. It provided 2,000 seats and a 40 metre-wide stage with a huge revolve, in which a permanent company could produce socially committed work. By 1930 there were over 300 local organizations with a nation-wide membership of half a million. As one of the dominant forces in the Weimar Republic, it helped to shape the whole direction of modern drama by employing such directors as **Reinhardt**, Jürgen Fehling or Piscator at the beginning of their careers, and by supporting new plays from a wide range of dramatists, including **Barlach** and **Toller**, or more recently **Hochhuth** and **Kipphardt**. It introduced **Shaw** to the German stage, and promoted early modern dance. The educational lectures that accompanied its first productions developed into influential periodicals, *Die Volksbühne* and *Die Schaubühne*, through which critics like Julius Bab and Herbert Jhering established high theatrical standards and encouraged as yet unknown playwrights like **Brecht**.

Socialist principles and responsiveness to members' aspirations meant that dictatorial regimes were unable to assimilate the Volksbühne. After taking it over in 1933, the Nazis were forced to dissolve it in 1937. Reestablished in 1947, it ceased to exist as a subscription organization in East Germany in 1957, although the rebuilt theatre on Bülowplatz continued to function under the Volksbühne title and became a showcase for the work of **Benno Besson**. The contemporary Freie Volksbühne was founded in opposition in 1949 in West Berlin, and moved into a newly designed theatre under Piscator in 1963, returning to the original ideals of the organization with the creation of post-war documentary drama. There are currently some 65 towns with resident Volksbühne companies in West Germany, as well as an international dimension through IATO (International Association of Theatre-Public Organizations). CI

Volksstück (Germany) A play written for popular audiences in their local dialect. Although several German cities have a *Volksstück* tradition, the genre is associated most consistently with Vienna, where, throughout the 18th and much of the 19th century, it flourished in the city's commercial theatres. Originating in the improvisational work of **Joseph Anton Stranitzky** and **Gottfried Prehauser** (1699–1769), the *Volksstück* gradually came to be scripted, partly in an attempt to introduce greater decorum into performance, partly in response to the demands of the censor. The most notable comic writer of the mid-18th century was Philipp Hafner (1735–64), whose *Megära, the Terrible Witch* (1755) was a great success. Johann Kurz (1717–83), in addition to writing over 300 plays and creating the popular role of Bernadon, continued the tradition of improvisation after it had officially been banned in 1768. The end of the 18th century saw the production of the single most famous example of the genre, Mozart and **Schikaneder**'s opera *The Magic Flute* (1791). Over the turn of the century, the theatres most associated with the performance of the *Volksstück* were established; of these the Theater in der Josefstadt, founded in 1788, and the Theater an der Wien, founded by Schikaneder in 1801, are still in use. The Theater in der Leopoldstadt, founded in 1781 by the actor Karl von Marinelli (1744–1803), was replaced in 1845 by the Carltheater, built by the actor–manager Karl Carl (1789–1854). In the 19th century, two distinct sub-genres of the *Volksstück* can be distinguished. First there is the *Zauberstück*, a 'magic play' with music and spectacle, generally chronicling the adventures of the ordinary Viennese citizen in a fairy-world, of which the plays of **Ferdinand Raimund** are the best example. Then there is the *Lokalstück*, a more realistic play that treats, sometimes moralistically, sometimes farcically, the local customs and habits of the Viennese. The vigorous, witty, and caustic comedies of **Johann Nestroy** are the finest examples of such comedy. Writers of the *Volksstück* were unusually prolific, due to the seemingly insatiable appetite of the Viennese for their work. Among the most successful of these dramatists were Karl Meisl (1775–1853), who probably wrote over 200 plays, Adolf Bäuerle (1786–1859), who also edited the famous *Theaterzeitung* from 1806 to 1859, and Friedrich Kaiser (1814–75), another very prolific dramatist. Towards the end of the 19th century, the *Volksstück* tradition began to lose its identity, being transformed on the one hand into operetta, on the other into commercial comedy. Nevertheless, its characteristic charm was remembered with painful poignancy by **Arthur Schnitzler** in *Liebelei* (1895) and with a sense of brutal reality by **Ödön von Horváth** in *Tales from the Vienna Woods* (1931). SW

Volodin (pseudonym of Lifshits), Aleksandr Moiseevich (1919–) Soviet dramatist whose lyrical dramas on the personal lives of ordinary people, related with a combination of gently ironic humour and pathos over lost innocence and failed romance, are characteristic of the post-Thaw period. Trained as a scenarist at the State Institute of Cinematography (1949), Volodin writes highly cinematic plays, replete with montage-like editing and dissolving of episodes, understatement of incident, evocative lighting, contrapuntal split-staging and parallel plotting, voice-over narration and musical accompaniment which together bring a formal sense of fable to otherwise quotidian content. His restless, individualistic characters must discover personal happiness and spiritual values for themselves, a task made difficult by an ideologically based society, the pressure of work, the fallibility of the human heart and the failure of such institutions as marriage. This basic situation is manifested in *The Factory Girl* (1956), *Five Evenings* (1957), *The Elder Sister* (1961), *The Idealist* (1962), *The Appointment* (1963) and *Never Part from Your Loved Ones* (1972). The last play, based upon Volodin's short-story account of his experience as a citizen judge at Leningrad divorce court proceedings, offers a strongly emotional central story, which culminates in the heroine's nervous breakdown, ironically counterpointed by an innocent, optimistic social games leitmotif added by Minsk director Nikolai Scheiko in the play's original production. Volodin has written three highly successful parable-plays, *Two Arrows*, *Little Lizard* and *Dulcinea of El Toboso* (1973), the last concerning Aldonsa and Sancho Panza's lives following Don Quixote's death and the basis for a highly popular stage musical at Leningrad's Lensoviet Theatre. Volodin has also written several film scenarios, including *Autumn Marathon* and *The Blonde*. SG

Voltaire (François-Marie Arouet) (1694–1778) French poet, dramatist, historian and philosopher, the most tireless man of letters of his century. His manifold interests and inquiring mind, to which he added an irritable outspokenness, occasioned numerous brushes with authority and led to periods of imprisonment or of self-imposed exile, in England, Prussia and Switzerland as well as the remote French provinces. The same circumstances help to explain the discontinuity of his career as a playwright, which began in 1718 with a tragedy, *Oedipe*, and, after only three further plays in the next decade, resumed with vigour in the early 1730s and again in the 1740s, continuing with intervals until his last performed tragedy, *Irène*, in 1778. He wrote librettos for a few operas and *divertissements* and some comedies and domestic dramas, but he was most respected in his day for his many tragedies, which probably constituted the most persuasive grounds for his election to the Académie-Française in 1746. That none of them holds the stage today is attributable to several factors, not least the extreme orthodoxy of his dramaturgic method, which was tenaciously neoclassical and impelled him to emulate **Corneille** and **Racine** without any of their creative originality. Even his few innovations, such as the choice of subject matter from indigenous French history (e.g., *Adélaïde du Guesclin*, 1734) or from exotic climes (e.g., *Alzire, ou les Américains*, 1736, set in Peru; *L'Orphelin de la Chine*, (*The Chinese Orphan*, 1755)), introduce only a superficial local colour, while his occasional borrowings from **Shakespeare**, whose work he learned to read in the original while in England and helped to popularize in France before disavowing it, now have an air of rather gauche melodrama (as in *Zaïre*, 1732, considered to be his masterpiece, and *La Mort de César* (*The Death of Caesar*, 1735)). His use of plays as vehicles for propaganda in his long, energetic onslaught upon religious bigotry and tyranny of all kinds (e.g., *Mahomet, ou le Fanatisme*, 1741), while estimable in itself, has proved inimical to their dramatic appeal. He produced a large

body of critical writing on the drama, notably the prefaces to his plays and the *Commentaires sur Corneille* (1764), and his genuine love of the stage was expressed in other ways, as in his building of several private theatres and his patronage of individual players, such as **Adrienne Lecouvreur** and **Lekain** whom he supported in a successful campaign against the fashionable practice of seating spectators on the stage.   DR

Vondel, Joost van den (1587–1679) Dutch playwright and poet, who has given the Golden Age in The Netherlands European standing. He had some influence on German baroque. In his turn, van den Vondel underwent the influence of the 'Rederijkers', **Seneca**, **Sophocles**, and **Euripides**.

In 1637, van den Vondel wrote *Gijsbrecht van Aemstel* to mark the opening of Amsterdam's new municipal theatre in 1638. It was performed there annually on New Year's Day, from 1638 until 1968.

In 1641, he was converted to the Roman Catholic Church. Consequently, many of the plays that followed bear witness to a deep religious feeling, for which he found a constant source of inspiration in the Bible. Some of these plays, such as *Lucifer* (1654) and *Adam in Exile* (1664), are still performed today.   MG WH

Vormingstoneel (politiek) ((political) educational drama) Since 1970 (see **Aktie Tomaat**) Dutch theatre companies, like Proloog (1964–83), De Nieuwe Komedie (1969–85), Sater (1971–85), and in Belgium, Kollektief **Internationale Nieuwe Scene**, Mannen van de Dam (Men of the Dam), Het Trojaanse Paard (The Trojan Horse), have been producing work with a strong political tendency. The aim is to stimulate an audience's social awareness and emancipation through the theatre. Inspired by **Brecht** and Marx, they see a theatre performance as a device in class-warfare, and as a contribution to a change in society.

The plays are often written by collective effort and frequently deal with the problems of a specific social group. If necessary, research is undertaken into the group which the production hopes to reach, and try-outs are given for a few of its representatives. After the performance, the company invites discussion; theatrical experience is analysed in view of the structure of society. To reach a potential audience, acting-space is created in all kinds of locations: schools, factories, local meeting-centres, and at demonstrations. In the eighties, the Dutch companies involved lost their subsidies. The reason given was that the performances did not have enough artistic quality. The Vormingstoneel was found to present gross simplifications and clichés, thereby failing to meet a satisfactory traditional theatrical standard. The question remains whether this judgement has done justice to the educational aspects of the Vormingstoneel. At all events, the decision has caused the disappearance of a very outspoken segment in the Dutch theatrical landscape.   MG HS

Voskovec, Jiří (Wachsmann) (1905–81) and **Jan Werich** (1905–80) Czech actors, dramatists and cabaret performers, who met while attending the law faculty of Prague's Karl University in 1927. With the composer Jaroslav Ježek, they founded the Independent Theatre, where they staged satires and political revues

Jiří Voskovec and Jan Werich in characteristic makeup, early 1930s.

until 1938, mixing parodies of film and theatrical clichés with social commentary. Werich usually played the robust, instinctual clown to Voskovec's more rational straightman, and their verbal comedy attacked middle-class values and fascist ideology. In 1938 they emigrated to the USA, broadcasting for the ČSR and touring, but returned to Prague in 1946 to perform in their own theatre. After 1948, Voskovec settled in the USA, working in theatre and film; Werich continued at the Prague Theatre of Satire until his retirement in 1968. LS

Vychodil, Ladislav (1920–) Czechoslovakian designer and teacher of scenography, and, since 1945, primary designer and technical chief of the Slovak National Theatre in Bratislava. Vychodil describes his work as 'poetism' – a lyrical yet restrained form with an emphasis on props and details over traditional decor. His style was strongly influenced by designer Frantisek Tröster. Except for a period of imposed socialist realism in the early 1950s, Vychodil's work is typified by a complex treatment of the floor and cyclorama – frequently covered with designs or projections – with an emphasis on light and colour, and the use of flown scenic pieces creating a layered look. In the late 1970s he began working with director Alfred Radok and the result has been a more spare look and an almost total de-emphasis of obvious design. AA

Vysotsky, Vladimir Semyonovich (1938–80) Hoarse, wiry Russian actor and chansonnier, who became a national idol shortly after joining the Taganka Theatre in Moscow. Closely associated with its director **Yury Lyubimov**, he played the aviator in *The Good Person of Setzuan* (1964), Kerensky in *Ten Days That Shook the World* (1965), Pugachev in a curtailed and cancelled play of that name by Esenin (1967); Hamlet (1971); and Svidrigailov in *Crime and Punishment*, his last role (1979), as well as Lopakhin in **Anatoly Efros**'s staging of *The Cherry Orchard* at the Taganka (1975). He married the French actress Marina Vlady on a tour to Paris in 1977. His more than 900 songs and poems were, according to Lyubimov, 'an irreplaceable chronicle of daily life in the Soviet Union for 20 years'; cassettes of his guitar-accompanied recitals were copied and recopied, but the authorities never allowed him to record officially. When his 'Wolf Hunt' was acclaimed in Voznesensky's *Cover Your Faces* (1970), the play was banned after four performances, and the homage production Lyubimov staged after his death received only private performances. LS

W

Wagner, (Wilhelm) Richard (1813–83) Wagner wrote to a friend, 'I am an artist and nothing but an artist – that is my blessing and my curse.' **Nietzsche** referred to him as 'the most outstanding theatrical genius that the Germans have ever had'. His major theatrical works, operas of which he wrote both librettos and scores, have a wide range of composition and first-performance dates: *Rienzi* (written 1838–40; performed 1842), *The Flying Dutchman* (1841; 1843), *Tannhäuser* (1843–5; 1845), *Lohengrin* (1846–8; 1850), '*The Rhinegold*' (1853–4; 1869), '*The Valkyrie*' (1854–6; 1870), '*Siegfried*' (1856–71; 1876), *Tristan and Isolde* (1857–9; 1865), *The Mastersingers of Nuremberg* (1862–7; 1868), '*The Twilight of the Gods*' (1869–74; 1876), *Parsifal* (1877–82; 1882). The four titles in quotes are those of the components of the great cycle *The Ring of the Nibelungs* which did not receive its first integral performance until 1876 although its ultimate origins can be traced back to 1848.

Wagner aimed to write music-dramas, the very term emphasizing his view that the effect of opera should be above all a dramatic effect. He abhorred the gratuitous in opera, however attractive this may be to audiences, and in this he included display singing and arias that were almost free-standing items, stage effects striking by their spectacle alone – in fact everything theatrical that was not justified by its contribution to the drama or that interrupted its flow or that flawed its organic unity. Instead of disposing his works in recitatives that supplied information and arias that expressed high points of feeling, he strove for a continuous flow of music in which voices express greater or less feeling, the mundane or the transcendent, as the progress of the drama demands. His concern for unity led him to exploit brief melodic components as binding features. Such a component might be the symbol of Siegfried's horn, Alberich's curse or the gold stolen from the Rhinemaidens. Its sounding in the orchestra makes a clear reference and brings forth a host of associations, even though what is referred to is neither present on the stage nor the immediate concern of the characters. The components are not merely reiterated in identical form. They act as germs that metamorphose into various strains and they appear in the score as integrated features in an overall design. The established term (not invented by Wagner) for one of these components is *leitmotif* or leading motive. Given the kind of opera that was familiar to audiences of the third quarter of the 19th century it is no surprise that many found the Wagner operas either incomprehensibly formless, because of their continuous flow in which climaxes come as a result of dramatic development and not because of a familiar formula, or just incomprehensible because of the allusions of the leading motives. Further, because Wagner's orchestra was not a mere accompanist nor, as some have claimed, a protagonist, but the definer of the ambience of the characters, the prop and stay of their world, there were those who found his operas 'too symphonic'. Wagner was single-mindedly, some would say ruthlessly, dedicated to art which for him found its highest expression in music-drama. In spite of his aspirations towards the total work of art (*Gesamtkunstwerk*) in which all the arts were to find expression, his own works are authentic operas in which the essential elements are the music and the characters.

Wagner was a man of enormous industry. His prose works run to some ten volumes and his correspondence was voluminous. Three of his celebrated essays are *Art and Revolution* (1849), *The Artwork of the Future* (1849) and *Opera and Drama* (1851). His writings as a whole do not express a single, unchanging and uncontradictory view, and they are often tortuous in expression. Nevertheless they are the vigorous and challenging product of a fine mind in its struggle to make sense of what has been intuitively grasped as valuable. The sweep of the foregoing titles tends to obscure the fact of Wagner's outstanding practical interests and skills. His essays *On the Performing of Tannhäuser* and *Remarks on Performing the Opera 'The Flying Dutchman'* (both 1852–3) are as careful guides to rehearsals, playing, singing, acting and staging as one could hope for. The composer-conductor Hans Pfitzner (1869–1949) maintained that whatever reservations might be held against Wagner the composer or librettist, he was infallible in his ideas of theatrical effectiveness.

Wagner the man has been accused of violent anti-semitism and vigorous proto-Nazism. How violent and how vigorous seems to be a matter of endless debate. It is noteworthy that many eminent Jews and anti-Nazis extol the genius of his operas, whose place in the repertoire is secure. Wagner remains one of the most outstanding phenomena of European musical theatre. It is necessary to refer to him as a phenomenon since from his own day until the present he has been acclaimed by some and loathed by others. It is hardly conceivable that anyone who pays attention to his works should remain indifferent to them.   GH

Wagner, Robin (1933–) American set designer. Wagner has been associated with some of the most successful musicals of the post-1960 period including *Hair*, *A Chorus Line*, and *Dreamgirls*. He began his career in San Francisco and worked with the Actors' Workshop where he was greatly influenced by director Herbert Blau and Brechtian aesthetics. His work at the **Arena Stage** in the mid-1960s led to explorations of stage space and moving scenery. Wagner is generally associated with spectacular sets, moving scenery, and stylish decor, but by and large his sets are minimal. It is the way in which the sets move and are integrated into the production that gives the illusion of a great deal of scenery. His best set (and best known) was for *A Chorus Line*. For most of the show it consisted of only a white line on the floor; in the final scene the upstage wall revealed mylar mirrors. This seemingly simple set was the result of over a year of stripping away excess and unnecessary scenic elements to arrive at a design that simply and boldly expressed the essence of the play. Wagner has never followed tradition or conventions – he has always explored new ideas, new materials, and new configurations of space. In addition to Broadway he has also designed for opera, dance, and rock concerts.   AA

Wagner, Wieland (1917–66) German director and designer, who staged all the major productions of his grandfather's operas at Bayreuth since its reopening in 1951, and established the contemporary style of Wagnerian interpretation with his *Ring* cycle in the same year. Freeing the operas from naturalism, he introduced symbolic lighting, sets and rhythms corresponding to the theories of **Adolphe Appia**.   CI

Walcott, Derek (1930–   ) The major West Indian playwright and a poet of world rank, Walcott has produced some 36 plays, half of which have appeared in print. He has also published 12 volumes of poetry and has received numerous prizes for his work. Born in St Lucia, Walcott began writing and directing plays while at high school. With his twin brother Roderick Walcott (also a playwright) he founded the St Lucia Arts Guild which performed his first published play *Henri Christophe* (1950) about the Haitian revolutionary leader. He attended the University of the West Indies in Jamaica (1950–4) and there wrote and staged a number of early plays several of which he later revised and retitled.

After graduating from college, Walcott taught for two years then became a feature writer and art and theatre critic for newspapers in Jamaica and later in Trinidad. In 1957 he was commissioned to write an epic drama *Drums and Colours* (1958) for the arts festival that heralded the birth of the West Indies federation. In 1958–9 he studied theatre in the United States under a Rockefeller Foundation fellowship and returned to Trinidad where he founded and became director of the Trinidad Theatre Workshop. For 17 years he wrote and directed plays with this company, taking productions on tour to other West Indian territories and to the United States and Canada. Among the most noteworthy of his plays are *The Sea at Dauphin* (1954), *Ti Jean and His Brothers* (1958), the highly acclaimed *Dream on Monkey Mountain* (1967) which received an Obie Award in its 1971 production by the **Negro Ensemble Company**, New York, *The Joker of Seville* (1974), *O, Babylon!* (1976) and *Remembrance* (1977).

In essence Walcott's dramas encompass a tension between instinct and intellect – the racial instinct stemming from an African heritage in conflict with an undiminished admiration for European intellectual and artistic achievement. His plays have been produced by theatre organizations in the United States and England including the Public Theatre in New York, the **Arena Stage** in Washington, DC, the **Mark Taper Forum** in Los Angeles, and elsewhere. In London the **Royal Court Theatre** has presented his works.

In 1981 Walcott accepted an appointment as a professor in creative writing at Boston University and moved to the United States. However, he returns regularly to the West Indies to work in theatre and in the summer of 1984 he directed an open-air production of his recent play, *Haitian Earth*, in his native St Lucia.   EGH

Waldoff, Claire (Clara Wortmann) (1884–1957) German music-hall performer. Born in Gelsenkirchen, she toured the provinces as an ingenue (1903–6) before moving to Berlin, where she had a phenomenally successful cabaret debut in 1907. In 1910 she became the star of the Linden-Cabaret, personifying the lower class types drawn by Heinrich Zille. Her throaty voice, red pageboy haircut and mannish suits contributed to the effect of such hits as 'Hermann heest er' ("Is Name's 'Erman'). A virtual symbol of Berlin wit and *joie de vivre*, she appeared in London in 1913 and 1933. After the latter tour, the Nazis banned her from the theatre, and she retired to lower Bavaria to live out her life in obscurity.   LS

Wales Welsh-language theatre has its root in the culture's strong bardic (poetic) tradition. The narration of epic tales, battle reportage, eulogies and elegies were given at court by the paid entertainer – the bard. He was a performer (*diddanwr*). Doubtless the oral tradition and its influence extends further back to the 4th century AD which gives us one such written version of the battle of Caterick (*Y Gododdin* – attributed to Aneurin). It is the primitive version of verse drama but unlike Homer's *Odyssey* designed to be enacted aloud by the court poet, sometimes accompanying himself by way of character illustration. It is argued forcibly that this is the tradition which held sway – crossbred with the litany and rites of Celtic catholicism – until the thirteenth century, its major literary manifestations being the work of the bards Teliesin and Llywarch Hen.

After these classical origins – though not explicitly manifest in 'dramatic form', Welsh-language theatre's history becomes undisciplined and irksome. The form subsides, its practitioners disperse and the heavy hand of literary verbal tyranny dominates. There are naturally enough exceptions, principal among these being *Tri Brenin o Gwlen*, a miracle play, and the interludes (*Anterliwtiau*) of Twm o'r Nant (who seems to have been elected as the father of Welsh-language theatre), whose period of productivity was abruptly ended by the Methodist revival of the early 19th century. Twm o'r Nant and his *anterliwtŵyr* were (like the bards) professional performers who moved from pub to market-place performing contemporary satirical plays. It is curious this tradition was prevalent in the North whilst the folk rites of the Mari Lwyd, a folk tradition with strong connections with the English mummers' performances, were confined to the South.

The prevalence of Methodism and a kind of puritanical morality stunted the development of the professional theatrical tradition. The next outcrop is amateur kitchen-sink drama of the late 19th and early 20th centuries whose emphasis was a pseudo-domestic realism. These were performed with enthusiasm but very little real theatrical sophistication, by village groups and societies. These plays are largely unexceptional apart from the fact that this remained the dominant mode of dramatic perception until the sixties and is still perceived as a kind of norm or standard in eisteddfodic circles. Its shadow still blights the professional theatre's development.

However, notable in the early years of this century and active after the post-war period, were a number of distinctive personalities who have left a significant mark on Welsh-language drama. Saunders Lewis (1893–1985), perhaps the only contender for the title of Wales's leading playwright, is chief among these. Born in Wallasey and educated at Liverpool University, where he gained a first in English, he lectured in Welsh at Swansea University from 1926 to 1939 and became president of the newly formed Nationalist Party (Plaid Cymru). During this period he was jailed for his political activity (allegedly burning the bomber school at Penybeth), lost his university post and from 1939–52 was a freelance writer and lecturer becoming the most distinguished literary critic of the period. He returned to lecturing at the University of Wales, in Cardiff, in 1952 and remained there until his retirement. His first essay in playwriting was the English play *The Eve of St John* (1921), but his greatest plays are undoubtedly *Blodeuwedd* (1923–5 and completed 1948) and *Siwan* (1956) both of which show Lewis exploring the older Celtic mythological tradition within the constraints of strict metre verse form and being strongly influenced by **Racine**.

During the fifties, Saunders Lewis was foremost among those who argued for the creation of a Welsh National Theatre. He was clearly aware that his plays were not adequately performed by the amateur companies (see the preface to *Problemau'r Prifysgol*, Llandybie 1968). In effect television with its six hours a week of Welsh-language broadcasting and BBC radio had become the main outlets of professional drama in Wales. Wilbert Lloyd Roberts said 'We are the only nation in the world to which television came before professional theatre' (*Daily Post*, 1974).

The national theatre movement in the English language had many complicated stops and starts. One of its manifestations was the Welsh Theatre Company in 1963 under Warren Jenkins. Wilbert Lloyd Roberts, a BBC producer, was responsible under this regime for the Welsh-language work which gained its independence in 1968 basing itself in Bangor, North Wales, under the title Theatre Cymru. A nationally touring company, it formed the first professional theatre ensemble and contributed enormously to the training of professional talent of both actors and writers. Notable amongst the latter was Gwenlyn Parry whose surrealist plays are probably the most significant development in Welsh-language drama. His drama required more sophisticated stage techniques incorporating film as in plays like *Y Twr* (1978). However, in general the work of Lloyd Roberts and his excessively touring company became inadequate, mainly artistically as touring constraints forced amateurish productions of an elementary dramatic nature which aped the prevalent styles of the English repertories. In 1972 one of the company's more adventurous directors and actors,

David Lyn, formed a fringe company, Theatr yr Ymylon, which although short-lived was notable for some of its productions such as *Siwan* directed by Hugh Thomas.

During the seventies a number of TIE and community groups emerged such as Bara Caws in North Wales (1977) and Theatr Crwban in Aberystwyth (1978), with an emphasis on revue style accessible work with a quasi-socialist edge. As with the previous companies, most of the works were indigenous, written by the new generation of writers or jointly written by the group members themselves.

It is not however until the eighties that European theatre emerged as a real influence on Welsh-language drama. Certainly there is strong evidence of a tradition of classics in translation ostensibly performed at the beginning of the century e.g. *Faust* and *Dychweledigion* (*Ghosts*) (translated by T. Gwyn Jones) and later the Saunders Lewis *Waiting for Godot*. But it is with the emergence of the **Grotowski**-influenced company Brith Gôf in 1981 that the influences become felt. The company's strong physical and emotional skills married to 'poor-style' stagings have contributed excitingly to Welsh-language drama with pieces like *Branwen* (1981), *Gwned neu Fara* (1982), *Ymfudwyr* (1985). It is perhaps the first Welsh-language company to join international status with its frequent European tours.

Concurrently, Theatre Cymru's new Artistic Director in 1982, Emily Davies, whose **Brook**-influenced work led her to form an ensemble of new generation young actors for Theatre Cymru, opened up the spectrum of drama to non-indigenous texts with presentations of **Friel**, **Obey** and, for the first time in Welsh, **Chekhov**'s *Three Sisters* professionally played and directed by her Associate Director, Ceri Sherlock. The company's vibrant beginnings were unfortunately stunted by financial problems which eventually resulted in closure in 1983 leaving a gap in mainstream product.

The ensemble regrouped under the banner of Theatrig to present 'classical' works such as *Miss Julie*, *A Doll's House*, *The Bear*, *Peer Gynt*, and most influentially Saunders Lewis's *Blodeuwedd* in 1985, directed by Ceri Sherlock, who had by then worked alongside some of the major European directors, most influential among whom was **Peter Stein** of the Schaubühne in Berlin.

New writing companies such as Hwyl a Fflag and Whare Teg also emerged to provide a different range of more conventional fare whilst Brith Gôf influenced groups such as Jeremy Turner's Cwmni Cyfri Tri and Gyrdd-der provide theatre pieces of a more stimulating non-literary, non-narrative nature.

Theatre writing as such continues to be largely television-influenced continuing in the tradition set by John Gwilym Jones, although there is an emergent style, some, like the work of Siôn Eirian, with direct connection to the contemporary style of Anglo-Welsh theatre writings of Alan Osborne and Ed Thomas, and others like John Glyn Owen from a more historico-literary background.

Of note too is the fact that the distinctive colour of Welsh-language drama is now being appreciated on its own terms albeit in the cinema, with actors like Dafydd Hywel, Richard Lynch and Iola Gregory gaining the kind of international recognition previously restricted to Welsh artists working through the medium of English. This will undoubtedly follow in Welsh-language theatre which will either emerge out of its current period as a significant contribution to European theatre or disappear once again into amateurishness.

See: D. Jones, *Black Book on Welsh Theatre*, Lausanne, 1985; G. Jones, *Three Welsh Religious Plays*, Bala, 1939; S. Lewis, *Blodeuwedd*, Llandybie, 1948, *Problemau'r Prifysgol*, Llandybie, 1968 and *The Plays of Saunders Lewis*, vols. 1–3, trans. J. P. Clancy, Llandybie, 1985; O. Llew Owain, *Hanes y Ddrama yng Nghymru 1943–1985*, Liverpool, 1948; G. Parry, *Y Twr*, Llandysul, 1978; T. Parry, ed., *The Oxford Book of Welsh Verse in translation*, Oxford, 1963; M. Stephens, ed., *Y Celfyddyday yng Nghymru 1950–1975*, Welsh Arts Council, 1979; T. Stephens, *The Literature of the Kymru*, London, 1876; S. Williams, 'Theatr Farddonol y Cymry', 1 (1985), Gomer.

Walker, George (1947–   ) One of Canada's most distinctive and prolific young playwrights. His first play, *The Prince of Naples* (1971), was produced by the newly-formed Factory Theatre Lab, as were his next six works, including *Beyond Mozambique* (1974). He was playwright in residence at the Factory until 1976. *Gossip* (1977), and his gothic comedy, *Zaztrozzi* (1977) were first seen at the Toronto Free Theatre and have enjoyed several other productions in the USA, Britain and Australia. His first directorial attempt was with his own *Ramona and the White Slaves* (1976), and he subsequently became an associate director of The Factory Lab. His plays are profoundly influenced by television and movies, and in his own words, 'try to walk that fine line between the serious and the comic', their characters finding their obsessions 'a way of coping with life and surviving'.   JA

Wall, Max (Maxwell George Lorimer) (1908–90) British actor and eccentric comedian. With a voice as mobile and disjointed as his limbs, with trousers too high and jackets too tight, and a face that expressed a fathomless range of experience, Wall turned the simplest act and the most innocent comment into anarchic and often disturbing comedy. His early reputation was established in the music hall and on radio from the 1920s to the 1950s. Thereafter he turned increasingly to 'straight' plays, appearing in such roles as Père Ubu (**Royal Court Theatre**, 1966), Archie Rice (Greenwich Theatre, 1974) and as Bludgeon in **John Arden**'s *Sergeant Musgrave's Dance* (**Old Vic**, 1984). He had a special affinity for **Beckett**, memorably instanced by his portrayal of Vladimir in the **Manchester Royal Exchange Theatre** production of *Waiting for Godot* (1981). He had previously played Krapp at Greenwich (1976) and went on to play Malone in John Elsom's version of Beckett's novel at the **Edinburgh Festival** in 1984. Wall often appeared as a solo artist, inventing Professor Wallofski, and presenting his one-man show *Aspects of Max Wall* (1974 and after).   MB

Wallace, Edgar (Horatio) (1875–1932) British novelist and dramatist, whose experience as a crime reporter gave a realistic basis to the ingenious plots of his popular detective thrillers, the most successful of which were *The Ringer* (1926), *On the Spot* (1930) and *The Case of the Frightened Lady* (1931).   CI

Wallace, Nellie (Eleanor Jane) (1870–1948) Scottish comedienne, billed as 'The Essence of Eccentricity'; she began her music-hall career clog-dancing at the age of 12 and was a star shortly after her first London appearance in 1903. Portraying a moth-eaten spinster with buckteeth and a ratty fur-piece ('my little bit of vermin'), she was one of the few actresses grotesque enough to play a pantomime dame successfully. Her best songs included 'The Blasted Oak', 'Tally Ho', 'A Boy's Best Friend is His Mother' and 'Let's Have a Tiddley at the Milk Bar'. She last performed publicly at the Royal Command Performance of 1948.   LS

Wallach, Eli (1915–   ) American actor, born in Brooklyn. Wallach made his New York debut as the crew chief in *Skydrift* (1945). He won stardom as Alvaro Mangiacavallo, a sexually driven truck driver in **Tennessee Williams**'s *The Rose Tattoo* (1951). Both Wallach and his wife, Anne Jackson (b. 1926), had substantial successes before their marriage in 1948, but were acclaimed as an acting duo in *The Typists* and *The Tiger* in 1963. Jackson made her professional debut in a touring production of *The Cherry Orchard*, later appearing with **Eva Le Gallienne**'s **American Repertory Theatre** in 1946. Jackson and Wallach appeared together in *Luv* (1964), a revival of *The Waltz of the Toreadors* (1973), and *Twice Around the Park* (1982). Both Jackson and Wallach have appeared in numerous films and television programmes.

Both members of the team use an internal intensity (both studied at the **Actors Studio**) suitable for drama or comedy. Of them in *Luv*, critics said 'Miss Jackson can play comedy as straight-faced and doggedly as if she were mining coal, but she turns up diamonds', and 'Mr Wallach has a flair for enduring indignities, whether of poverty or affluence, marriage or divorce'.   SMA

Wallack family A dynasty of actor-managers, of English origin, in the American theatre, inseparably linked with the history of the New York stage for over 50 years. **Henry John Wallack** (1790–1870), the eldest son of William H. Wallack and Elizabeth Field (Granger), popular performers at London's **Astley**'s Amphitheatre and later at the Surrey, came to the USA in 1819 with his first wife, dancer Fanny Jones. After lengthy stays in Baltimore, Philadelphia, and Washington, DC, Wallack made his debut in New York City at the Anthony Street Theatre in 1821; in 1824 he became leading man at the **Chatham Theatre**. From 1828–32, 34–6, and during the summer of 1840 and for some time afterwards he was back in England, acting sporadically. In 1837 he was stage manager, under his brother, at the National Theatre. He gained considerable acclaim for his Sir Peter Teazle in 1847 at New York's Broadway Theatre. One of his last roles was Falstaff in 1858. Though a versatile and accomplished actor, he did not win the fame of other family members in the USA. Two of his sisters were actors (Mary [Mrs Stanley] and Elizabeth [Mrs Pincott], mother of the actress Leonora, later known as Mrs Alfred Wigan) and his brother **James William Wallack** (?1795–1864), known as the

elder to distinguish him from his nephew. This Wallack, also born in England, appeared first in the USA at
the **Park Theatre** as Macbeth in 1818. For the next 35
years he shuttled between the USA and England,
though he was best known on the American stage. He
was admired for roles in tragedy and comedy, especially the latter. Although most historians categorize
him as a member of the **Kemble** school, **James E.
Murdoch** called him 'the first romantic actor of
America'. An exceedingly handsome actor, his Shylock and Jaques in *As You Like It* were considered
innovative. From 1837–9 he managed the National
Theatre and after its destruction by fire, **Niblo's
Garden** for a time. In 1851 he settled permanently in
New York City, assuming control the following year
of Brougham's Lyceum, as **Wallack's**. For nine years
this theatre prospered. For almost 35 years his company
was the leading American ensemble, first under his
leadership and later under his son Lester. In 1861 he
built the second Wallack's on Broadway at 13th Street.
James the elder was the most distinguished member of
this notable family. His nephew, **James William
Wallack, Jr** (1818–73), son of Henry and born in
London, became a credible actor in tragedy. More than
any other member of the family, he spent most of his
career away from New York, spreading the Wallack
name to all the major American theatrical centres,
retiring in 1872. Next to James the elder, **Lester
Wallack** (John Johnstone) (1820–88), his nephew,
made the greatest contribution to the American stage.
The only major member of the family born in the USA,
he nonetheless served his apprenticeship in England
and Ireland, making his USA debut in 1847 at the
Broadway Theatre as Sir Charles Coldstream in *Used
Up*. During his career with the Wallack company he
played nearly 300 roles, excelling as Benedick, Charles
Surface, Sir Andrew Aguecheek, and Sir Elliott Grey in
his own adaptation of *Rosedale* (1863). Lester stage
managed for his father at Wallack's Lyceum and
became the manager of the second Wallack's until 1882
when he opened a new Wallack's, remaining there until
1887. Although Lester did little to encourage native
American works, depending heavily on an English
repertoire, he was a highly honoured member of the
profession until his death. His important memoirs were
published posthumously in 1889.   DBW

Wallack's Theatre Broadway and 13th St, New
York City [Architect: John M. Trimble]. Although the
playhouse on 13th Street was the most famous of the
theatres bearing the name of Wallack, there were
actually three theatres associated with the Wallack
family. The first was built by **John Brougham** in 1850
at 485 Broadway, but passed to **James W. Wallack**
two years later and was operated by him as Wallack's
Lyceum for nine years. In 1861, a new Wallack's went
up in the theatre district forming around Union Square
and was managed by **Lester Wallack**. For nearly 20
years, it dispensed impeccably cast English plays with a
company of mainly English actors to an elitist audience. Lester Wallack was the principal star for many
years. Following a trend, Wallack relocated his company into a third theatre at the north-east corner of
Broadway and 30th Street, but fortune did not follow
him. In ill health and faced with an indifferent theatrical
public, he retired in 1887. A year later, Wallack died

James W. Wallack as Falconbridge in Shakespeare's *King John*,
1818.

and the house was leased to **A. M. Palmer**, who
changed the name to Palmer's but it reverted to its
original name in 1896. All three theatres were torn
down: the first in 1869; the second, which was renamed
the Star and continued to be leased to producers, in
1901; and the third house in 1915.   MCH

Waller, Emma (1820–99) British-born actress, she
married American actor Daniel Wilmarth Waller in
1849 and came with him to the USA in 1851. Her
earliest known performance was in 1855 on tour in
Australia, followed by a London debut in 1856. For her
American debut in 1857 at the **Walnut Street Theatre**
in Philadelphia she appeared on successive nights as
Ophelia to Mr Waller's Hamlet, Pauline in *The Lady of
Lyons*, and Lady Macbeth, the latter performed with an
'almost painful' intensity of passion. Fullness of characterization and a stately presence were her strengths in
roles like Queen Margaret and Queen Katharine and
Meg Merrilies in *Guy Mannering*. She also achieved
succès d'estime as Iago in the 1860s and 1870s. She and her
husband often performed together from her 1858 New
York debut as Marina in *The Duchess of Malfi* until her
retirement in 1878.   FHL DJW

Waller, Lewis (1860–1915) English actor-manager,
who became the supreme matinee idol at the turn of the
century and whose repertoire was constrained by the
need to gratify the KOW (Keen on Waller) Brigade. He
made his debut under **J. L. Toole** in 1883 and made his
first venture into management when he produced *An
Ideal Husband* at the **Haymarket** (1895). 'You make it
suit you', was **Wilde**'s ambiguous comment. As
D'Artagnan (1898) and as the eponymous hero of
Booth Tarkington's *Monsieur Beaucaire* (1902), he
was rapturously received and they became the basis of

his repertoire. But the modest Waller would have preferred to play more often in **Shakespeare** than his audiences allowed. He was an excellent Brutus and Faulconbridge and among the finest exponents of Henry V and Hotspur in the English theatre. To these parts, he added during his management of the Imperial (1903–6) and the **Lyric** (1907–11) that of Othello. PT

Walnut Street Theatre 9th and Walnut, Philadelphia. Miraculously eluding the American penchant for tearing down the old and building up the new, the Walnut Street survives today as the oldest functioning playhouse in America. It was opened in 1809 as a domed arena for the Pepin and Breschard circus, but in 1811 came the first of a string of renovations to transform it into a workable theatre. It was enlarged, fitted with a stage and orchestra pit and renamed the Olympic. In 1820, the dome was removed and the name changed to the Walnut Street and it briefly housed a company that rivalled the **Chestnut Street**. In 1828, John Haviland designed a new Greek-revival facade for it. Eventually, it passed to the ownership of **John Sleeper Clarke**, **Edwin Booth**'s brother-in-law, and remained in his estate until 1919. Intending to raze it and replace it with a new theatre, the new owner discovered that the building code restricted him to a smaller theatre and decided to rebuild the old house. In 1968, it was declared a National Landmark and money was raised to restore it to its 1828 version by Haviland, although the interior was thoroughly modernized. MCH

Walser, Martin (1927–) German dramatist and novelist. Influenced by Kafka as well as **Brecht**, his characteristic work presents an absurdist perspective on contemporary society and its roots in the Nazi era. After his first play *The Detour* (1961), in which marital infidelity represents the absence of values – a theme he returned to in *Home Front* (*Die Zimmerschlacht*, 1967, produced by **Kortner**, who helped Walser expand the play from the original television script) – he turned to parable drama with *Rabbit Race* (*Eiche und Angora*, 1962) and *The Black Swan* (1964). These form the initial parts of a projected 'German Chronicle', the first undermining popular images in a parodistic vision of the final days of the war, the second attacking the complacent attitudes of the present through a symbolic fable of the younger generation's traumatic guilt for the actions of their parents. Rejecting documentary drama as well as the overt theatricality of **Handke**, Walser's plays analyse social consciousness, continuing the alternation between grotesque naturalism and psychological parable in *Child's Play* (1970) or *In Goethe's Hand* (1982). CI

Walter, Eugene (1874–1941) American playwright and film writer. Associated as a business manager with numerous theatrical enterprises – minstrel shows, circuses, symphony orchestras – Walter contributed most importantly to American theatre with a score of successful, social realistic melodramas. Essentially, he portrayed the victims of overwhelming social and personal forces: the political machine in New York City (*The Undertow*, 1906); the power of business as a weak husband appeals to a strong wife (*Paid in Full*, 1908); money as corruption bringing ruin and death

(*Fine Feathers*, 1913). Walter's best play, *The Easiest Way* (1908), remembered for a realistic production by **David Belasco**, features a weak woman who understands her frailty. Walter's dramatic techniques were easily adapted to the writing of numerous film scenarios. In 1925 he published a series of lectures entitled *How to Write a Play*. WJM

Wälterlin, Oskar (1895–1961) Swiss director, actor and author. Educated at the University of Basle, he gained his PhD in 1918 with a thesis on '**Schiller** and the Public'. In January 1919 he played his first (small) professional part in *Wilhelm Tell* and in October he directed his first opera: Pergolesi's *La Serva Padrona*. His association with the Basel Stadttheater continued until his death: 1919–25, as actor; 1925–32 and 1942–4 as artistic director (a post which he was to take up for a third time in 1961), and as guest-director at other times. In Basle he is particularly remembered for **Wagner**'s *Ring* which he had prepared with **Adolphe Appia** for 1924–5, but only *Rhinegold* and *The Valkyrie* were presented following the hostile outcry of the conservative 'Wagner friends'. 1933–8 he directed mainly opera in Frankfurt-am-Main but returned to Switzerland in 1938 to take up the artistic and administrative direction of the Schauspielhaus, Zurich, where he remained until 1961. In Zurich he attracted the best German and Austrian actors and directors who were escaping from Nazi oppression. He created an impressive ensemble and evolved a style which established the Schauspielhaus as the main centre of German theatre from the late 30s to the early 60s. Under Wälterlin, Zurich saw the world premieres of **Brecht**'s *Mother Courage* (19 April 1942), *The Good Person of Setzuan* (4 February 1947), *Galileo* (9 September 1947) and *Puntila* (5 June 1949); **Zuckmayer**'s *Barbara Blomberg* (1948); the first German performance of **Wilder**'s *Our Town* and the first plays of two emerging Swiss playwrights, **Frisch**'s *Don Juan or The Love of Geometry* (1952), *The Fire Raisers* (1957) and **Dürrenmatt**'s *The Visit* (1955). CLS

War of the theatres The first salvo in the Poetomachia or war of the theatres may have been fired when the **Lord Chamberlain's Men** presented **Jonson**'s *Every Man out of His Humour* (1599), with its satirical portraits of **Marston** and **Dekker**, but the war was not declared until 1601, when Jonson was preparing a play for the **Children of the Chapel Royal** at the **Blackfriars**, Dekker for the Lord Chamberlain's Men at the **Globe** and Marston for the **Boys of St Paul's** at their indoor theatre. There is every likelihood that Jonson heard a rumour that he was to be pilloried in Dekker's *Satiromastix* and decided to get his blow in first with *Poetaster*. Marston countered, rather tamely, with *What You Will*, and tongues continued to wag throughout the year. It is possible that the Chamberlain's Men and the Paul's Boys were leagued in rivalry to the suddenly fashionable Chapel Children, and that Hamlet's abuse of the 'little eyases' is a reverberation from the Poetomachia. But *Hamlet* is an infinitely finer play than any of those directly provoked by the war. It has been plausibly suggested that the squabble was not much more than a publicity stunt. PT

Ward, Douglas Turner (1930–) Afro-American actor, director and playwright. Born in Louisiana but educated in the North, Ward trained at the Paul Mann Theatre Workshop in New York. He acted in Off-Broadway plays before accepting a minor role on Broadway in *A Raisin in the Sun* (1959). Working with Robert Hooks in 1965, Ward produced his two one-act satiric comedies, *Happy Ending* and *Day of Absence*, for a 14-month Off-Broadway run. In 1968 Ward, Hooks and Gerald Krone founded the **Negro Ensemble Company** where Ward continues as artistic director. He has directed and played leading roles in many of the company's productions, notably *Ceremonies in Dark Old Men* (1969) and *The River Niger* (1972), and has also written *The Reckoning* (1969) and *Brotherhood* (1970). EGH

Ward, Geneviève (Teresa) (1838–1922) American-born actress whose career belongs to the English theatre. As Ginevra Guerrabella, she made her professional debut in opera, but her voice failed and she turned to acting, though retaining much of the grandiose aura of a *prima donna*. She opened at Manchester in 1873 as Lady Macbeth (a part she played in French in Paris in 1877) and Constance in *King John*, at once announcing her Wagnerian scales, but it was in a forgotten play by Herman Merivale and F. C. Grove, *Forget-Me-Not* (1879), that she made her international reputation. In the part of Stephanie, a high-society Frenchwoman, she toured the English-speaking world, returning to the London stage as a celebrity. At **Tennyson**'s request, she played Eleanor of Aquitaine in **Irving**'s production of *Becket* (1893) and was Morgan le Fay to Irving's King in the **Lyceum**'s lavish *King Arthur* (1895). Her appearances were infrequent after that, and she was received as a monumental figure from the past when she played Queen Margaret for **John Martin-Harvey** in his 1916 *Richard III*, the part in which she made her farewell appearance with the **F. R. Benson** company in 1920, at the age of 82. She was, by a mysterious early marriage, the Countess de Guerbel, which may have encouraged the conservative English to create her DBE in 1921, the first actress to be so honoured. PT

Warde, Frederick (1851–1935) American actor. A successful English provincial actor, he made his American debut (1874) as a supporting player, and found success as a regional star after 1880. Like Thomas Keene, Louis James, Charles Hanford, Joseph Grismer, Phoebe Davis, Kathryn Kidder, and Marie Wainwright, his contemporaries who had similar careers, he played an older repertory in an elevated, declamatory style that was innocent of realism. He specialized in serious, older men. He continued on the stage and the lecture platform until 1915, and made films of *Richard III* and *King Lear* (1916). DMCD

Wardle, (John) Irving (1929–) British theatre critic, who studied at Oxford, and at the Royal College of Music in London. He entered journalism as a sub-editor on the *Times Educational Supplement* in 1956, and became the deputy drama critic on *The Observer* in 1960. In 1963, he joined *The Times*, where his thoughtful, persuasive columns set the standards for daily reviewing for more than 20 years. As a critic, Wardle uses superlatives only reluctantly, preferring to weigh each side to an argument before arriving at usually qualified conclusions; with the result that he is not the most-quoted critic in Britain. But his knowledge and integrity are rarely questioned, and best revealed in his biography of **George Devine**, *The Theatres of George Devine* (1978). Wardle's early play, *The Houseboy* (1974), received a successful production at the Open Space, and was later seen on television. From 1973–5, he was the editor of the theatre magazine, *Gambit*. JE

Warfield, David (1866–1951) American actor. **Belasco**'s one great male star was a native of San Francisco, who began acting with a travelling stock company in Napa, California (1888). He played a variety of parts in New York City and on tour until he became a member of the company at the **Casino Theatre** in 1893. He quickly became a specialist in musical parody, which led to an engagement as an eccentric ethnic comic with **Joe Weber** and **Lew Fields** (1899–1901). Belasco coached him in a series of pathetic older parts in which he was always the gentle, slightly humorous, forgiving victim. His first vehicle was *The Auctioneer* (1901), followed by *The Music Master* (1904), *The Return of Peter Grimm* (1911), and culminating in an unsuccessful production of *The Merchant of Venice* (1924), after which he retired. DMCD

Warren, Mercy Otis (1728–1814) American patriot and political satirist, the best representative of 'The War of Belles Lettres' during the Revolutionary War. Her propaganda plays, really dialogues without plot, character development or women, satirized British officials and American Loyalists and were published anonymously in Massachusetts periodicals and as political pamphlets. Several plays have been falsely attributed to Warren; she acknowledged authorship of only *The Group* (1775). Other plays which are identified as her work include: *The Adulateur: A Tragedy: As it is Now Acted in Upper Servia* (1772), which refers to the Boston Massacre and attacks Governor Thomas Hutchison; *The Defeat* (1773); and two blank verse historical tragedies, *The Ladies of Castille* and *The Sack of Rome*, both published in *Poems, Dramatic and Miscellaneous* (1790). FB

Warren, William the elder (1767–1832) British-born American actor and manager, whose 1784 debut was as Young Norval in *Douglas*. When engaged by **Tate Wilkinson** for his provincial company in 1788, Warren acted in support of **Sarah Siddons**. In 1796 he joined **Thomas Wignell**'s company. At the **Chestnut Street Theatre** he first appeared as Friar Lawrence in *Romeo and Juliet* and Bundle in *The Waterman*. Other than infrequent appearance in New York, the remainder of Warren's career, both as actor and manager, was associated with the theatres in Baltimore and Philadelphia. In 1806 he married the second of his three wives, the actress **Mrs Merry**. In partnership with **William B. Wood**, Warren's management in Philadelphia and Baltimore prospered until late in his career; in 1829 he retired from management. As an actor, Warren was especially adept at old men in comedy, but he was also capable in tragedy. He was noted especially for his performances as Old Dornton, Sir Robert Bramble,

Falstaff, and Sir Toby Belch. He had six children with his third wife, Esther Fortune, all of whom were associated with the stage.   DBW

Warren, William the younger (1812–88) American actor, son of the above, whose career is almost totally associated with the **Boston Museum**, the stock company he joined in 1847. During his 50-year career, until his retirement in 1883, he is reported to have given 13,345 performances and to have portrayed 577 characters. No actor of his period was identified so thoroughly with a single theatre and none received more respect and affection from the public. His versatility in comic roles was practically limitless, although his special talent was with eccentric types. His most famous roles included Dogberry, Polonius, Bob Acres, Sir Peter Teazle, Micawber, Touchstone, and Launcelot Gobbo, although he also appeared in leading roles in numerous forgettable contemporary plays.   DBW

Washington Square Players A pre-First World War American producing agency, founded in 1915 by amateurs (Edward Goodman, **Lawrence Langner**, etc.) to improve the level of drama in New York City. Their first three one-acts were produced at a cost of 35 dollars in a theatre seating 40 persons.

They received favourable reviews and continued, producing one-acts by **Chekhov**, **Musset**, Aikins, **Moeller**, and other then little-known playwrights. After a disastrous production of *The Seagull*, they moved to the Comedy Theatre, just off Broadway, seating 600. There they presented the first Broadway production of **Eugene O'Neill**'s *In the Zone*. Several important American actors began or worked with the Washington Square Players: Roland Young, Rollo Peters, Frank Conroy, Helen Westley, and **Katharine Cornell**. In 1918 the group disbanded, but reorganized in 1919 as the **Theatre Guild**, New York's most influential producing agency.   SMA

Wasserstein, Wendy (1950–) American playwright who portrays with wit and understanding the plight of the modern woman caught between feminism and traditionalism. *Uncommon Women and Others* (1977) depicts the reunion of five women graduates of Mt Holyoke and their hilarious reflections on their past college days. *Isn't It Romantic* (1983) follows two such uncommon, contemporary women as they confront their own unclear desires, their parents, and their lovers to make a choice about marriage and/or career.   FB

Watene, Kenneth (*fl.* 1970s) Kenyan playwright. His published plays include *My Son For My Freedom*, *The Haunting Past* and *The Broken Pot* (1973).   RK

Waterhouse, Keith see **Hall, Willis**

Waters, Ethel (1896–1977) Afro-American singer and actress. Born into poverty, Waters started at age 17 as a vaudeville singer in Baltimore for nine dollars a week. In 1933, she featured in **Irving Berlin**'s revue *As Thousands Cheer*. Moving from honky-tonks to cellar cafés to New York socialite clubs, Waters attained a glowing reputation as comedienne and singer of such songs as 'St Louis Blues', 'Dinah', and 'Stormy Weather'. Waters emerged as a superb dramatic actress of warmth and sensitivity in stage or film productions of *Mamba's Daughters* (1939), *Cabin in the Sky* (1940), *Pinky* (1949), and *The Member of the Wedding* (1950). Earl Dancer termed her 'the greatest artist of her generation'.   EGH

Waterston, Samuel A. (1940–) American actor. Born in Cambridge, Mass., and educated at Yale University, Waterston studied acting in Paris and New York before his New York debut in 1962 as Jonathan in *Oh Dad, Poor Dad*. He began a long association with the **New York Shakespeare Festival** in 1963 at the Delacorte as Silvius in *As You Like It*. After numerous stage appearances both in and out of New York, Waterston returned to the Delacorte in 1968 as Prince Hal in *Henry IV*, *Parts 1 and 2*, and again in 1971 as Cloten in *Cymbeline*. In 1972 his Benedick in *Much Ado* drew critical acclaim as a superb comic performance. Mel Gussow (*New York Times*) found him 'boyish – but not immature . . . sharptongued and headstrong, never losing sight of the character's . . . romantic nature'. Waterston added an interesting Prospero in 1974, but a lightweight Hamlet the following year as he sought to widen his range and versatility. Julius Novick (*New York Times*) characterized him as 'a warm, unassuming performer, easy to like and to sympathize with onstage', but not up to the intellectual demands of Hamlet. Appearances in *Chez Nous* (1977), *Waiting for Godot* (1978) and *The Three Sisters* (1982) received respectful notices. Waterston's film and television appearances include: *The Great Gatsby*, *The Glass Menagerie*, *Much Ado*, *Oppenheimer* (7-part BBC series), and *The Killing Fields*, which won him an Academy Award nomination in 1985.   TLM

Watts, Richard, Jr (1898–1981) American drama critic. Born in West Virginia and educated at Columbia University, Watts began his career as a reporter for the old Brooklyn *Times* in 1922. He became film critic for the *New York Herald* in 1924, a position he held until 1936 when he succeeded **Percy Hammond** as drama critic (1936–42). He spent the war years in the Far East (1942–6) to return as drama critic for the *New York Post* (1946–74). Succeeded by Martin Gottfried in 1974, Watts wrote a weekly column until his retirement in 1976. An early champion of **Tom Stoppard**, **Harold Pinter**, and **Edward Albee**, Watts has been characterized as a gentle, judicious, and civilized critic of taste who loved the theatre.   TLM

Waxworks The public exhibit of waxen effigies, first found in 16th-century Amsterdam, has two sources: anatomical cabinets for the display of medical anomalies, and state portraits that permit subjects a symbolic audience with their monarch. It was the portrait from life of Louis XIV by the Parisian Antoine Benoist (1632–1717) that popularized wax as a medium for such shows. Jacques de Vaucanson with his wax automata and Wolfgang von Kempelen with his wax chessplayer (1769) both achieved some popularity; but it was Johann Christian Curtius (Creutz) who added real showmanship. His Cabinet Palais-Royal (1783) exhibited figures of the nobility, while his Caverne des grands voleurs in the Boulevard du Temple was a resort of the people. During the Revolution, Curtius had licence to take death masks of heads fresh from the guillotine, a task carried out by his niece Marie Grosholtz (1760–1850). With this legacy of gruesome mementos, and as Madame Tussaud, she opened a gallery in London in 1833 which soon became world-famous. Its Chamber of Horrors, displaying the latest in murderers, is a forerunner of the news photo. Her success was soon emulated by the Musée Grévin, Paris (where the Raft of the Medusa boasted a wave effect produced by clever lighting); the Hamburg Panoptikum (still extant); Emil E. Harmer's Munich Panoptikum; Präuscher's Enkel Museum, Vienna; and the Eden Musée, New York. These housed historical tableaux along with the grotesque and unnerving models of foetuses and venereal afflictions usually found in so-called 'medical museums'. The Munich comedian **Karl Valentin** parodied this attraction in his Isar Tower panopticon of the 1930s which displayed nose-picking machines and Adam's original apple with a bite out of it. Tigerpark, founded in Singapore in 1946 by the Tiger Balsam millionaire Boon Haw, enhanced the traditional terrors of Hell and scenes from Chinese myth with up-to-date technology. Disneyland and Disneyworld have added synthetic flesh and computer-controlled movement and speech without appreciably surpassing the artistic results of their precursors. LS

Wayang see **Shadow puppets**

Wayburn, Ned (1874–1942) American director and choreographer. After starting out as a singer and dancer in vaudeville, Wayburn made his theatrical debut in *The Swell Miss Fitwell* (1897). He served as assistant director of *The Governor's Son* (1901), and was soon in demand as a producer, director and choreographer of musical comedies and revues. Among the shows he staged in New York were two editions of *The Passing Show* (1912, 1913), and six of *The Ziegfeld Follies* (1916–19, 1922, 1923). In addition to producing and staging hundreds of musicals, Wayburn operated dance studios which trained many of the musical theatre's finest dancers. MK

Weaver, Fritz (1926–) American actor who made his professional debut with the Barter Theatre and made his New York debut as Fainall in *The Way of the World*. After 1955, Weaver appeared frequently with **American Shakespeare Festival**. Weaver has also appeared in several films and numerous television network films and series. Among his awards are the Clarence Derwent Award for Flamineo in *The White Devil* (1955) and a *Theatre World* Award for Maitland in *The Chalk Garden* (1956). For *Child's Play* (1970), Weaver received the *Variety* Critics Poll, the Outer Critics Circle, the Drama Desk, and a Tony Award. SMA

Webb, John (1611–72) English architect and scene-designer who, as **Inigo Jones**'s pupil, assisted him in the preparation of masques for the Court of Charles I. Webb designed the scenery for **Davenant**'s *The Siege of Rhodes* (1656), contriving, on the small stage at Rutland House, five scene changes, including two scenes in relief. It was, as far as can be ascertained, the first use of perspective scenery on a public stage. Neither there nor in his designs for **Boyle**'s heroic tragedy *Mustapha*

(1665) at Court did Webb emulate the magnificence of the masques, but the surviving drawings strongly suggest that he took the first tentative steps towards scenic realism. PT

Weber, Joseph (1867–1942) and **Lew Fields** (1867–1941) American comedians. After learning their craft as child performers in museums, circuses, and variety houses, Weber and Fields evolved a knockabout 'Dutch comic' act in which the short, rotund, innocent Weber was the foil for the tall, skinny, bullying Fields. They toured for many years in vaudeville before playing their first legitimate theatre engagements at the Harlem Opera House and Hammerstein's **Olympia Theatre** in 1894. Two years later they opened the Weber and Fields Music Hall, where they offered hilarious burlesques of current Broadway successes. The Weber and Fields company, which at various times included such stars as **Lillian Russell**, Peter F. Dailey, Sam Bernard, **De Wolf Hopper**, **David Warfield**, **Fay Templeton** and Bessie McCoy, was also noted for the beauty and animation of its female chorus. Weber and Fields chose many talented writers, designers, and directors to assist them in mounting their shows.

In 1904 the partners separated, with Weber continuing at the Music Hall and Fields producing and starring in musical comedies. In 1912 they reunited for a 'jubilee' production at a new Music Hall, after which they toured with the show. Following some vaudeville appearances the partners again split up and concentrated on their producing careers.

The rough, acrobatic comic style of Weber and Fields, coupled with the fractured English they spoke in their 'Dutch' personas, made them favourites of audiences in New York and across the country in both legitimate theatres and vaudeville houses. MK

Webster, Benjamin (Nottingham) (1798–1882) English actor and theatre manager, one of the most intelligent, stubborn and admirable leaders of the mid-century theatre. He began as a provincial dancer and **Harlequin**, and had struggled his way into the **Drury Lane** company by 1823, but it was with **Madame Vestris** at the **Olympic** in 1832 that he got his first chance to display his skill in comedy, and it was as manager of the **Haymarket** (1837–53) that he demonstrated his exemplary concern to find good plays and to stage them conscientiously. He produced **Sheridan Knowles**'s lively comedy, *The Love Chase* (1837), to set the pattern, and subsequent Haymarket premieres included several plays by **Jerrold**, **Boucicault**'s *Old Heads and Young Hearts* (1844) and *Used Up* (1844), **Bulwer**'s *Money* (1840) and **Tom Taylor** and **Charles Reade**'s *Masks and Faces* (1852), which provided him with his favourite part as Triplet. No other theatre could match the repertoire of the Haymarket during Webster's management. More remarkable still was his production of *The Taming of the Shrew* (1844), in which he defied the taste for pictorial **Shakespeare** by setting the play on a decent approximation to current views of the original Elizabethan stage; and this was 40 years before **William Poel**'s first experiments. His management of the **Adelphi**, which he had shared with **Madame Céleste** since 1844, but took into his own hands from 1853 until his retirement in 1874, was less remarkable – the Adelphi audience was insistently low-brow. Webster would have liked to be a Shakespearian actor, but though he was an admired Dogberry, he found the better-born Petruchio beyond his range. PT

Webster, John (c. 1580–1634) Little is known of Webster's life. He received payments from **Henslowe** in 1602, for contributions to a lost play, but his earliest surviving work is probably the Induction to **Marston's** *The Malcontent*, written on the occasion of the play's revival by the King's Men in 1604. At much the same time, Webster was collaborating with **Dekker** on a play for the **Boys of St Paul's**. The success of this piece, *Westward Ho* (1604), was exploited by **Jonson**, **Chapman** and Marston with *Eastward Ho* (1605), written for the **Children of the Chapel Royal** at the Blackfriars. Both plays graft city comedy onto the older tradition of the 'journey play'. Webster and Dekker were less successful with their *Northward Ho* (1605). A further collaboration, on *The Famous History of Sir Thomas Wyatt* (published 1607), produced an untidy history play. But Webster was learning his craft, and his poetic gift and dramatic ingenuity were supremely exhibited in the two tragedies which he wrote alone, *The White Devil* (c. 1612) and *The Duchess of Malfi* (c. 1613). Violent and sensational according to the prevailing taste, both plays are also eloquent and compassionate. Webster chose their plots from catchpenny translations of Italian novellas, purporting to give 'true' accounts of recent crimes, but he perceived an almost Aeschylean pattern in these squalid stories of bloodthirsty family vengeance. It is clear from the detail and extent of his borrowings that he kept a careful commonplace book of striking lines from the work of other writers, improving almost everything that he stole.

There is nothing as impressive as these two tragedies in the rest of his work. *The Devil's Law Case* (published 1623) is a scrappy tragicomedy, with one astonishing scene. *Monuments of Honour* (1624) is no more impressive than other surviving Lord Mayor's Pageants. The rest of Webster's extant dramatic work is the outcome of collaborations, with **Thomas Heywood** on *Appius and Virginia* (c. 1608), with **Middleton** on *Any Thing for a Quiet Life* (c. 1621) and with **William Rowley** on *A Cure for a Cuckold* (c. 1624). He is, in addition, the putative author of some of the Overburian *Characters* (1614), including that of 'An Excellent Actor'. PT

Webster, Margaret (1905–72) Actress and director. The daughter of Benjamin Webster III and Dame May Whitty, she was the last member of a 150-year-old English theatrical dynasty. Her professional career began in *The Trojan Women* with **Sybil Thorndike** (1924), followed the next year with a small role in **John Barrymore**'s *Hamlet*. After several years of stock experience she joined the **Old Vic** in 1929, returning to play Lady Macbeth in 1932–3. In 1934 she began to direct and this became her chief endeavour, mostly in America. Notable United States productions under her direction included *Richard II* with **Maurice Evans** (1937), *Hamlet* (1938), *Twelfth Night* (1940), *Othello* with **Paul Robeson** (1943), *The Cherry Orchard* (1944), and *The Tempest* with **Canada Lee** as Caliban (1945). She founded with **Eva Le Gallienne** and **Cheryl**

Crawford the **American Repertory Theatre** (1946–8). In 1950 she began directing operas, becoming the first woman to direct at the New York Metropolitan Opera. She was the author of important books on theatre, including *The Same Only Different* (1969) and *Don't Put Your Daughter on the Stage* (1972). DBW

Wedekind, Frank (1864–1918) German playwright. Wedekind started his career working in business and in a circus. He then became an actor and singer, appearing with acclaim in the satirical cabaret *Die elf Scharfrichter* (*The Eleven Executioners*) in Munich. As a playwright, he was influenced initially by the naturalists, whose views on the imperativeness of the biological instinct in man he tended to retain throughout his life. But his plays were not rigorously realistic. Instead, adopting an episodic approach to plot and presenting character frequently through the means of grotesque caricature, Wedekind foreshadowed the expressionists. His first major play, *Spring's Awakening* (1891), was not produced until 1906, due to the bold and shocking manner in which he unfolded his theme, which was the need for a repressive society to recognize the stirrings of puberty in its children. The 'Lulu' plays, *Earth Spirit* (1895) and *Pandora's Box* (1904), while no less striking in their depiction of a society riven by the demands of lust and greed, are somewhat more ambiguous over the issue of sexuality. Of his several other plays, the one-act *The Court Singer* (1899) and *The Marquis of Keith* (1901) have been widely performed. In the past 20 years there has been a significant revival of Wedekind in the German and English theatres. However, his plays are likely to remain of limited appeal due to Wedekind's concern, especially later in life, to justify in them his outspoken position in German society. SW

Wei Liangfu Chinese musician and innovator. His dates are controversial and biographical data scanty. It is known that he was at work in the Kunshan area near Suzhou in Jiangsu province during the years 1522–73. There he carried out innovative research over a decade on the several musical modes which flourished in the southern area at that time. Their principal differences lay in a dialectal usage which affected the rhythm and tempo of song and speech forms. By synthesizing modal elements while refining articulation and vocalization to match speech tones with tempo and pitch he created the mellifluous, somewhat plaintive, singing to flute accompaniment which characterizes the musical content of **kunqu** drama. Wei was assisted in his researches by Zhang Yetang who was an authority on the northern modal repertoire which differed from that central to Wei's researches. An accomplished singer himself Wei created a new musical vogue which had a significant impact on the development of style and practice in the theatre. ACS

Weigel, Helene (1900–71) Austrian-born actress and theatre manager, who worked under **Jessner** and was **Brecht**'s leading actress, becoming his second wife in 1928. Her performances in *The Mother* (1932) and *Mother Courage and her Children* (1949) gave the definitive interpretation of his female proletarian characters. The nominal director of the **Berliner**

Helene Weigel in the title role of Brecht's *Mother Courage*, Berlin, 1949.

Ensemble, she took control of the company after Brecht's death and the tours she mounted established Brecht's international reputation.   CI

Weimar style A style of tragic acting cultivated by **Goethe** while he was director of the Weimar Court Theatre between 1791 and 1817. It was described in the 'Rules for Actors', which Goethe wrote down as guidelines, primarily for the actor **Wolff**. Goethe expected his actors to be models of decorum on stage, acting always with scrupulous attention to articulation, especially in the delivery of verse, and with constant grace and formality in stature and gesture. Goethe's rules were read by actors throughout the 19th century, and the style of acting they suggested was widely copied.   SW

Weise, Christian (1642–1708) German schoolmaster and playwright. His plays, which were written for his students at the Zittau gymnasium, demonstrate a striking realism in contrast to the formal, often turgid drama of the baroque era. Among his best-known works are the tragedy *Masaniello* (1683) and the comedy *Peasant Machiavel* (1679).   SW

Weisenborn, Günter (1902–63) German dramatist and novelist, who made his name with *Submarine S4* (1928), the earliest example of '**Living Newspaper**' dealing with the sinking of an American naval vessel. He continued this trend with plays such as *Outside the Law* (1945), which was the first play about the Nazi period to be performed in Berlin after the war.   CI

Weiss, Peter (1916–82) German dramatist, novelist and graphic artist, whose play the *Marat/Sade* (1964) brought him wide international recognition. Marking a bridge between early surrealist work influenced by Kafka, like *The Tower* (1949) or *Night with Guests* (1962), and documentary drama, the complexity of its structure is represented in the full title *The Persecution and Assassination of Marat as Performed by the Inmates of the Asylum of Charenton under the Direction of the Marquis de Sade*. The multi-layered action combines the two contrasting poles of 20th-century theatre, **Artaud** and **Brecht**, to present conflicting theses of revolution and repression, psychological freedom and social equality in the image of a mad-house world. Weiss's developing political commitment is represented by the differences in interpretation between the West Berlin premiere, **Peter Brook**'s London production of 1965, and the East German premiere later the same year – which emphasized respectively, the need for compromise and the danger of dictatorship; the extreme individualism of Sade's position; and the accuracy of Marat's arguments as the martyred spokesman of Communist liberation. His new commitment to Marxism underlies *The Investigation* (produced by **Piscator** and simultaneously on 16 other German stages in 1965). Using transcripts from the 1964 Frankfurt War Crimes trials, it focuses on the system responsible for Auschwitz to demonstrate that its values were still the norm in post-war society and that genocide was the logical extension of capitalism. The absence of conventional plot or individualistic characterization, and the apparently objective tone combined with clear political bias in the selection of purely factual material, established new criteria for documentary theatre. Subsequent plays extended the genre to its limits and created a new form of psychological documentary. Dealing with the history of colonialism in the examples of Portuguese Angola, *The Song of the Lusitanian Bogey* (1967), and the 2,500-year Vietnamese struggle for liberation, *Vietnam Discourse* (1968), tended toward abstraction and over-simplification in attempting to reveal the long-term patterns of developing revolutionary consciousness. These reintroduced theatricality in the use of masks, songs and revue elements; and perhaps as a response to the criticism that he was substituting art for political activism, Weiss turned to analysing the role of the revolutionary writer in *Trotsky in Exile* (1970), a piece with strong autobiographical overtones reflecting his own exile in Sweden, where he resided since 1939. The thesis that external political change cannot be effective without the internal liberation inspired by artistic vision is extended in *Hölderlin* (1971), where the artist is presented as the conscience of the revolution. An attempt to create a synthesis out of the opposition previously epitomized in the historical figures of Marat and Sade, this reuses the image of madness to expose the moral grotesqueness of 19th-century society, and Weiss returned again to earlier themes in his final play *The New Investigation* (1981).   CI

Weisse, Christian Felix (1726–1804) German dramatist. His highly successful *Richard III* (1759) was written, he claimed, without any knowledge of **Shakespeare**'s play. He also adapted, very severely, *Romeo and Juliet* (1767), which was the version most frequently performed in the 18th century. Weisse's *Singspielen*, especially *Hell Is Let Loose* (1752) and *The Hunt* (1770), were also very popular.   SW

Wekwerth, Manfred (1929–) East German director. Manager of the **Berliner Ensemble** (1977–) and director for that company from 1951. His *Coriolanus* for the **National Theatre** in London in 1971 complemented his production of **Brecht**'s version, which he directed in Berlin and brought to London in 1965. MB

Welfare State International British theatre company. Formed in Leeds in 1968, and now based in Ulverston, Cumbria, this loosely knit group of actors, sculptors, musicians, painters and pyrotechnologists, under the direction of John Fox and Boris Howarth, have been one of the most successful companies in fulfilling the 1960s dream of taking theatre to a mass audience – their spectacular processions regularly draw audiences in four figures. A principle of their work is that of the carnival, both aesthetically and socially. Socially, their performances are not merely commodities which people buy off the peg; as far as possible they are constructed around some local concern (in Northwich, Cheshire, they provided 'A Grand Salt Celebration') or festive date ('Scarecrow Zoo' in Bracknell, Hallowe'en to Bonfire Night 1982), and members of the local community are involved in their planning and realization. Aesthetically, a Welfare State performance is not a 'play', but an event incorporating processions, dramatic pieces, firework displays, social dancing, and communal eating and drinking, with a strong emphasis on powerful visual images, both sinister and ludicrous. In their pursuit of celebratory theatre, WSI have begun to undertake weddings and naming ceremonies as well as their more familiar civic entertainments. AEG

Well-made play A translation of the French *pièce bien faite*, the well-made play was first codified by **Eugène Scribe** (1791–1861). Since he (with assorted collaborators) wrote some 400 plays, he had little time for such frivolities as theory. By the mid-19th century, when the term came into common use, it was already derogatory, and yet its formulae have moulded some 150 years of Western drama.

The well-made play is skilfully crafted to arouse suspense. An outgrowth of the comedy of intrigue, its action is propelled through a concatenation of causally related events. Beginning with a detailed, faintly disguised exposition, it gathers momentum through complications and crises, with each act closing on a climactic curtain. A series of perils for the protagonist lead to the revelation of a secret in an obligatory scene – named and analysed by the French critic **Francisque Sarcey** some half-century after Scribe codified the practice. The well-made play then closes swiftly in a logical and plausible resolution, which implicitly accepts the ethic of the audience, even when the author's spokesman, the *raisonneur*, does not baldly voice it. Technically, the well-made play thrives on fortuitous entrances and exits, mistaken identity, and *quid pro quo*.

Scribe's structural influence is everywhere evident in 19th-century France – **Sardou**, **Augier**, **Dumas** *fils*, **Labiche**, **Feydeau** – and in those copyright-free days, the formula swiftly crossed the English Channel and is seen in plays by **Bulwer-Lytton**, **Taylor**, **Robertson**, not to mention Henry James and **Henrik Ibsen**. Even **Shaw**, who fulminated against 'Sardoodledom', manipulated the formula in both his Pleasant and Unpleasant Plays, and its carpentry has been learned by craftsmen as various as **Lillian Hellman**, **Terence Rattigan**, **Jean Anouilh**, and **Harvey Fierstein**. Shaw's dismissal of the obligatory scene has been

widely quoted: 'Once this scene was invented, nothing remained for the author to do except to prepare for it in a first act, and to use up its backwash in a third.' Yet that 'nothing' took considerable doing on the part of playwrights. RC

Weller, Michael (1942–   ) American playwright. Born in New York, Weller was educated at Brandeis and Manchester Universities. After productions at the **Edinburgh Festival** Fringe and at **Charles Marowitz**'s Open Space (London) in 1969, he premiered *Cancer* at the **Royal Court** in 1970. Renamed *Moonchildren*, it opened at the **Arena Stage** (Washington) in 1971, followed by productions both off and on Broadway in 1972. A popular critical success, *Moonchildren* depicts the hangups and idealism of the 'children of the sixties', a subject Weller returned to with *Loose Ends* in 1979. Premiering at the Arena Stage prior to its Broadway debut, *Loose Ends* expresses the disillusionment of the 1970s as young people attempt to reconcile their ideals with the demands of careers, marriages, and families. Weller's other plays include *23 Years Later*, *Fishing*, and *At Home*. He wrote the screenplay for *Hair* (1979) and *Ragtime* (1980). TLM

Welles, (George) Orson (1915–85) American actor and director whose place in history is assured as a result of youthful accomplishments. By 1941 the protean Welles had established himself as a major actor and brilliant theatre director, had directed, co-written and starred in *Citizen Kane* (1940), one of the most influential films in cinema history, and had inadvertently created a national panic with his radio version of H. G. Wells's *The War of the Worlds* (1938). Welles's career began with an appearance at Dublin's **Gate Theatre** in 1931 as the Duke of Wurtemburg in *Jew Süss*. After touring with **Katharine Cornell** in 1933–4, he made his New York debut in 1934 in *Romeo and Juliet* (Chorus and Tybalt). In 1936, as director of the Negro People's Theatre, New York, he staged a controversial 'Voodoo' version of *Macbeth* with an all black cast; in 1937, when appointed a director of the **Federal Theatre Project**, NY, he directed notable productions of *Dr Faustus* (and acted the title role) and *The Cradle Will Rock*. With **John Houseman** he co-founded the same year **The Mercury Theatre**, remembered primarily for its modern-dress production of *Julius Caesar*. Welles's theatre impact lessened after the Second World War, although he is remembered for his direction of *Native Son* (1941), his 1946 version of *Around the World in Eighty Days*, his first appearance in London in 1951 as Othello, his adaptation and direction of *Moby Dick* in London (1955) and New York (1962), his direction and acting in *King Lear* (1956) at New York's City Centre, and his direction at London's **Royal Court Theatre** of *Rhinoceros* (1960). Welles is the subject of two contradictory 1985 biographies by Barbara Leaming and Charles Higham. DBW

Wemyss, Francis Courtney (1797–1859) English-born American actor and manager. A year after his first London appearance in 1821, Wemyss made his American debut at the **Chestnut Street Theatre**. His forte was comedy and farce, and he excelled in roles such as Vapid in *The Dramatists*, Marplot in *The Busy Body*, and

Rover in *Wild Oats*. He later acted in New York with **Charlotte Cushman**, **William Macready**, **Joseph Jefferson**, and **Laura Keene**. In 1827 he turned to management, and was widely respected for his taste and integrity. He founded the Theatrical Fund to aid needy actors; edited 16 volumes of plays, published as the *Acting American Theatre*; and wrote an informative autobiography, *Twenty-six Years of the Life of an Actor and Manager* (1847).   TLM

Werfel, Franz (1890–1945) Austrian dramatist, novelist and poet, whose early work is among the most interesting examples of expressionism with its contemporary perspective on classical themes. His strongly pacifist adaptation of **Euripides'** *Trojan Women* (1915) was followed by a 'magic trilogy' updating **Goethe**'s *Faust* – *The Mirror Man* (1921), *The Goat Song* (1922), *The Silent One* (1923) – in which the revolt against authority typified by the plays of **Bronnen** or **Hasenclever** is given a psychological and highly critical perspective in grotesque images of the duality of man, with idealistic political aspiration liberating the demonic and bestial *alter ego*. After the tragic history of the Habsburg Emperor in Mexico *Juarez and Maximilian* (1925) won him an international reputation, *The Goat Song* was produced by the New York **Theatre Guild** in 1926, as was his war-time comedy of the rescue of an anti-semitic Polish officer by a Jewish refugee *Jacobowsky and the Colonel*. This reached Broadway in 1944 (the only play by an Austrian exile to establish itself on the foreign stage during the Nazi period), while his verse tragedy on the history of Jewish suffering culminating in their persecution under Hitler, *The Eternal Road*, was staged by **Reinhardt** at the Manhattan Opera House in 1937. But he is primarily remembered for his 1941 novel *The Song of Bernadette*.   CI

Werich, Jan see **Voskovec, Jiří**

Werkteater In Amsterdam in 1970, the 'cooperative society the Werkteater' was founded. The Werkteater (work-theatre) receives subsidy to investigate new possibilities in the theatre (see **Aktie Tomaat**; **Vormingstoneel**). The aims are to renew acting methods, from within, to find alternatives for acting methods taught at drama schools or used in repertory theatre which are seen as acting tricks, and to investigate the relationship between actors and audience. The working method is democratic and collective; many of the performances develop from improvisations built on the basis of the actor's personal experiences.

The Werkteater has a lot in common with the **Living Theatre** (the actor as a person merges with his part into a unity), and with **Jerzy Grotowski** (the actor is trained to develop his physical abilities, because the language of the body is considered to be *the* language of the theatre). Frequently, a high level of acting is reached. Their strong social involvement, which is apparent through plays like *Toestanden* (*Situations*, 1972), about situations in mental hospitals, *Bosch en Lucht* (*Forest and Air*, 1979), a play about 'ordinary' and mentally deficient people, and *Avondrood* (*Sunset Sky*, 1973), dealing with the issue of senior citizenship, is nowhere marked by the sharp line of approach seen in Vormingstoneel. The play *Je moet ermee leven*, about the treatment of a cancer patient in a hospital, has been

filmed as *Opname* by Erik van Zuylen (*In for Treatment*, 1979). In the early eighties, some members left and set up solo projects, of which Joop Admiraal's *U bent mijn moeder* (*You are my mother*) received great acclaim both in The Netherlands and abroad. It too has been adapted for film. Around Shireen Strooker, a new generation has come into existence: Werkteater II, who also focus their attention on existing plays.   MG HS

Werner, Zacharias (1763–1823) German playwright. Werner was the only romantic dramatist to achieve popular recognition. His most widely performed play *The Consecration of Power* (1807) is a five-act verse tragedy on the life of Martin Luther. His most famous, or notorious, play was the one-act *Schiksaltragödie*, *The 24th of February* (1810), which dramatizes with mordant and unrelieved grimness the working-out of a family curse.   SW

Wesker, Arnold (1932–) British dramatist, who served in the Royal Air Force and took various unskilled jobs before becoming a professional writer. His first three plays, *Chicken Soup with Barley* (1958), *Roots* (1959) and *I'm Talking about Jerusalem* (1960), were a partly autobiographical trilogy, which started with a Jewish family, the Kahns, in pre-war Hackney. All three expressed the unforced socialism of his childhood, where the enemy was fascism and the key to social progress lay in mass education. The trilogy was first staged in Coventry but transferred to the **Royal Court Theatre** in London, where **Joan Plowright** scored a personal triumph in *Roots* as Beatie, the Norfolk girl inspired by learning. In *The Kitchen* (1959) and *Chips with Everything* (1962), Wesker drew on his experiences as a chef and in the air force to provide vivid dramatic pictures of working lives, a kind of *théâtre trouvé* which was then rare but became popular. He became the Founder-Director of Centre 42, an arts centre established at the Round House at Chalk Farm, North London, deriving its name from Clause 42 in the Trade Union Charter. His frustrations in satisfactorily raising money for Centre 42 are reflected in *Their Very Own and Golden City* (1965) and *The Friends* (1970), both of which mourn the decline of utopian socialism in Britain; and Wesker's writing changes direction away from the social optimism of his early plays towards a more lyrical, disillusioned and sometimes introverted theatre. *The Four Seasons* (1965) is concerned with the waxing and waning of love, while *Love Letters on Blue Paper* (1976), *Caritas* (1981) and the one-woman trilogy of short plays, *Annie Wobbler* (1984), all concentrate on a particular person or state of mind. In contrast, however, *The Wedding Feast* (1974), *The Journalists* (1975) and *The Merchant* (1976) tackle major themes but, with their large casts, have yet to be seen in London. *The Old Ones* (1972) is Wesker's most successful recent play, describing the enforced seclusion of old people from the brutalities of daily life. Wesker also directs and has written extensively about the craft of writing.   JE

West, Mae (1893–1980) American actress and playwright, whose pose of unabashed but self-mocking sensuality made her a cult figure. A vaudeville headliner by 1911, she achieved notoriety in her first play *Sex* (1926), in which she took the lead. Attacked by the censors, she continued to defy them with *The Drag* (1927), the first American drama to depict a homosexual party; *Diamond Lil* (1928), a melodramatic comedy about white slavery; and *The Constant Sinner* (1931). Her Hollywood career in the 1930s increased her fame, but the limitations forced on her by production codes brought her back to Broadway in *Catherine Was Great* (1944). West always located her insatiable, man-eating temptresses safely in past eras, and her own attitude was one of worldly bemusement.   LS

West End theatres (London) The centre of English commercial theatre, gaining its name from its geographical relationship to the City of London. It contains over 25 theatres within a relatively small area, ranging in size from the **Coliseum** or the London Palladium with over 2,300 seats to the Windmill with 326 (though at one period the smallest was the Little Theatre, originally with only 250 seats), and in age from Drury Lane where the first theatre was erected in 1663 to the Westminster, converted from a cinema in 1931. Names have been reused or changed – there have been three theatres called the Globe and two Shaftesbury Theatres, while the Duke of York's was once the Trafalgar Square Theatre and **Sadler's Wells** has been at various times Miles's Musick House and the Aquatic Theatre. The older buildings have all been destroyed, demolished, reconstructed, and restored several times; but over half the theatres in the district were built between 1889 and 1909. Two, the Coliseum and **Covent Garden**, are now opera houses, while others have seldom held anything but musicals and revues, like the Shaftesbury, or the Windmill which was specifically constructed for non-stop variety and (until it became a theatre-restaurant in 1981) renowned mainly for the nude tableaux of 'the Windmill Girls'. Another, the **Lyceum** which under **Irving** became the leading London theatre, was turned into a dance hall in 1945.

Their reputations and the types of drama performed on their stages have changed with successive managements, and some have never had identifiable policy. These include the Criterion, which sank from producing **Henry Arthur Jones**'s plays in the 1890s to light comedy and became a BBC studio from 1939 to 1945, Wyndham's, mainly associated with **Edgar Wallace**'s thrillers (between 1926 and 1932), or the Ambassadors, which was almost entirely occupied by revues until the record-breaking run of **Agatha Christie**'s *The Mousetrap* in the 21 years up to 1973. Since the mid-1970s they have been used as transfer houses – like the Piccadilly, which was always a 'second run' stage apart from a period after 1941 when **Noël Coward**, Peter Ustinov and **Albee** were successfully produced there – and instead of originating productions they have been occupied by successful work from the **Royal Court**, the **Young Vic**, the Mermaid, the **Royal Shakespeare Company**, provincial companies or more recently various fringe theatre groups. So has the Duke of York's, which played a significant part in the development of English drama during the early part of the century, with the first productions of **Barrie**'s plays, seasons from 1910 to 1914 under **Frohman** with new works by **Galsworthy**, **Shaw**, **Granville Barker** and **Maugham**, and a short period when **Ashley Dukes**'s adaptations of contemporary German drama or John Van Druten's plays appeared there (1928–31). Similarly the **Haymarket**, once the province of the actor–manager from **Beerbohm Tree** to **John Gielgud**'s repertory season in 1944–5, has housed revivals or transfers from the **Chichester Festival** and the **Lyric, Hammersmith**, since 1960.

A second group represents theatres that have followed a consistent policy and stage a clearly identifiable type of work, like the Adelphi or the Shaftesbury, which have been almost continually occupied by pantomime, musical comedy or revues. The Savoy, the home of the D'Oyly Carte company from 1881 to 1907, when it was taken over by Granville Barker and **John Vedrenne**, has since then alternated between **Gilbert** and Sullivan and comedy by Coward, **Kaufman** and **Hart**, or **William Douglas Home**. St Martin's, where **Basil Dean** presented significant new drama in the 1920s, has been occupied by detective thrillers since 1970; while the Westminster, which under Anmer Hall introduced a wide range of English and foreign plays by Granville Barker, **T. S. Eliot**, **Denis Johnston** and **O'Neill**, was taken over by the 'Moral Rearmament' movement in 1946. In this group too is London's most famous theatre, **Drury Lane**. After opening the century with spectacular melodrama, it has housed an almost continuous series of musicals from *Rose Marie* and *The Desert Song* in the 1920s, through Ivor Novello and **Rodgers** and **Hammerstein** to *A Chorus Line* and *Sweeney Todd*.

Other theatres have offered varying but always interesting programmes. The Phoenix has staged a series of significant plays by **Thornton Wilder**, **Rattigan** and more recently **Stoppard**, as well as the musical version of Chaucer's *Canterbury Tales*. **St James's** which established an early reputation for stagecraft under **John Hare** and **George Alexander**, contributing to the success of **Pinero** and **Wilde**, continued with outstanding performances by **Sybil Thorndike**, **Edith Evans** or Noël Coward in the 1920s, plays by **Emlyn Williams** and Odets in the 1930s, and in 1950–2 productions by **Laurence Olivier** and **Vivien Leigh**, until it closed in 1957. The Apollo made its mark with **Harold Brighouse**, **Clemence Dane**, **Sherwood**, Emlyn Williams, Rattigan, influential productions of **Giraudoux** in the 1950s, and more recently performances of **Alan Bennett**, **David Storey** or **Alan Ayckbourn** with Gielgud or **Ralph Richardson**. The **Globe**, which presented plays by **A. A. Milne**, Maugham and Coward as well as visiting performers like **Moisiu** or the **Pitoëffs**, was taken over by H. M. Tennent in 1937 and by **Prince Littler** in 1960, under whom Rattigan, **Christopher Fry**, **Bolt**, **Peter Shaffer** and **Sartre** were staged, and has recently specialized in contemporary dramatists like **Michael Frayn** and Ayckbourn. The Lyric, which at the turn of the century had provided a stage for **Duse**, **Sarah Bernhardt** and **Forbes-Robertson**, as well as **Tallulah Bankhead** in the 1920s, offered productions of **Priestley**, Sherwood, **Housman**, Giraudoux and Charles Morgan in the 1930s, Rattigan and T. S. Eliot in the 1940s and 1950s, and became identified with comedy in the 1970s, notably by Ayckbourn, Bennett and **Ben Travers**. Her/His Majesty's, opened by Tree, has presented a wide range of significant new work from Shaw, Coward and Priestley to Rattigan and Shaffer, interspersed with long running musicals (**Oscar Ashe**'s *Chu Chin Chow*, or more recently *West Side Story*, *Fiddler on the Roof*).

Perhaps the most interesting theatre in this group is the Aldwych, which gave its name to the farces written by Travers between 1925 and 1933. It was also there that the **Stage Society** put on the first major English production of **Chekhov** in 1911, and from 1943 to 1954 it presented a series of significant productions – **Lillian Hellman**, Sherwood, **Tennessee Williams**, Christopher Fry and **Maxwell Anderson**. In 1960 it ceased to be a purely commercial theatre, becoming the London home of the Royal Shakespeare Company until their recent move to the new Barbican Centre; and during that time it not only presented transfers from the classical repertoire but significant new drama by **John Whiting**, **Harold Pinter**, Tom Stoppard, **Peter Nichols**, and (from abroad) **Anouilh**, **Brecht**, **Dürrenmatt**, **Hochhuth**, **Weiss** and Albee, in addition to housing the annual World Theatre Season between 1964 and 1973. But in general it has been theatres outside the West End, with non-commercial policies or (more recently) subsidized companies, that have established standards, recovered the heritage of traditional drama or been the leading edge of modern English developments – the **Old Vic** up to 1981, the Lyric in Hammersmith during the 1920s, the Greenwich Theatre since 1969, or in particular the Royal Court. This has been a vital catalyst from the Barker–Vedrenne seasons of 1904–7, through the productions of **Fagan** and **Barry Jackson** in the 1920s, to the English Stage Company under **George Devine** and **William Gaskill**, introducing the early plays of Shaw, **Galsworthy** and Maugham, **Osborne**, **Wesker**, Storey, **Bond**, **Barker**, and **Hare**.   CI

West Indian theatre The anglophone West Indies have had formal dramatic theatre for centuries. Jamaica, conquered by Britain in 1655, had a public theatre by 1682. Barbados had organized dramatics in 1728 and in 1751 gave a performance of **George Lillo**'s *The London Merchant* before George Washington who would become the first President of the United States. Antigua opened its first theatre in 1788 with *Venice Preserv'd*; coloured amateurs in Grenada staged a Shakespearian tragedy in 1828 and in 1832 St Lucia started a theatre for English- and French-speaking players. Trinidad, taken from Spain in 1797, boasted three theatres in the 1820s while Guyana built its first theatre by subscription of Dutch inhabitants in 1828.

Up to the abolition of slavery in 1834 and beyond, the West Indian theatre was merely a reflection of English and European stages. British, occasionally French and American players travelled to the then colonies with a repertoire of established plays including **Shakespeare**, **Molière**, and a quantity of farces and melodramas. Less frequently Spanish and Italian troupers brought musical plays and opera. The **Hallam** Company, for instance, which came to America from London in 1752, spent two extended tours in Jamaica between 1754–8 and 1775–85, returning to the mainland only at the end of the War of Independence.

Between the visits by professionals, local players known as 'gentlemen amateurs' occupied the theatres and performed similar works. British forces stationed in the territories also gave plays, at times combining their talents with amateurs to present spectacular dramas and pantomimes. Theatre audiences for these shows consisted primarily of the so-called 'upper-crust' of society: the planters, well-to-do merchants, military and naval officers, government officials and civic leaders.

From time to time plays romanticizing West Indian life and written by foreign authors would be produced such as **Cumberland**'s *The West Indian* (1771) set in London, **Bickerstaff**'s comic operetta *The Padlock* (1768), and the romantic musical *Inkle and Yarico* (1787) by **Colman the Younger**, set on a plantation in Barbados. Although some members of Hallam's Company wrote comic sketches of Jamaica which were played as afterpieces on their bills, the first attempts to produce an indigenous West Indian drama came later. In the 1820s Jamaican newspapers carried in serialized form some anonymous plays on the slavery issue meant to be read rather than performed, but in Trinidad E. L. Joseph, a Scottish resident, wrote and produced a group of plays including the musical farce *Martial Law* (1832). This play, which survives, pokes fun at the annual muster of troops which occurred during the Christmas holidays to safeguard against a slave rebellion. It drew characters from the different racial strains on the island and used native dialects. In Jamaica the newspaper reporter Charles Shanahan wrote a historical tragedy *The Spanish Warrior* (1853) that traced the late career and death of the new world Spanish explorer Balboa. The play was produced at Kingston's Theatre Royal along with an afterpiece, also written by Shanahan, titled *The Mysteries of Vegetarianism* that ridiculed a dietary fad then current in the city.

Throughout the 19th century attempts were made to establish permanent playhouses in West Indian towns. Theatre buildings that were erected or converted from existing halls after much debate and fund-raising were often destroyed by fire, storm, or creeping decay and painfully rebuilt. Native plays continued to appear sporadically for local consumption. In the 1860s and 70s Jamaica produced two monologuists in Henry Murray and his son Andrew who between them delighted town and country audiences for over 20 years with recitals of 'The Customs and Characters of Jamaican Society a Generation Ago'. Topics such as the annual troop muster, the Set Girls, John Canoe, and the Festival of the New Yam, written in sparkling dialect and skilfully presented with appropriate songs, were enormously popular.

Trinidad observed the centenary of British rule in 1897 with a drama festival that included two original sentimental plays. One, *Carmelita, the Belle of San Jose* by L. O. Inniss, was a love story set against the conquest of the island by British forces with the aid of native Indians. The other, *The Violet of Icacos*, was a play of domestic intrigue on a rural plantation, its author unknown. The next year Inniss returned to his theme of the noble savage despoiled by Spanish invaders with *Mura, the Cacique's Daughter*. Remarkably, his two dramas honouring 100 years of British control ignored the presence of blacks who, in the time-period of his plays, constituted some 80 per cent of the population.

The turn of the century saw a resurgence of touring professionals such as the **Frank Benson** Shakespeare Company and, some years later, the Florence Glossop-

Harris Dramatic Company. In 1911 **George Bernard Shaw** visited Jamaica and advised the country, if it wished to create a truly indigenous theatre, to 'do your own acting and write your own plays . . . with all the ordinary travelling companies from England and America kept out'. In fact serious interest in the native culture was already developing. J. A. Van Sertima of Guyana had printed his *Scenes and Sketches of Demerara Life* (1899), the anthropologist Walter Jekyll had published *Jamaican Song and Story* (1907) and the Jamaican Astley Clark in two years would print his lectures on *The Music and Musical Instruments of Jamaica* (1913). In Trinidad the carnival and calypso had begun their long march towards respectability and national acceptance. (See **Trinidad Carnival**.)

The focus on indigenous culture brought to the fore native comedians, notably Ernest Cupidon of Jamaica and Sam Chase of Guyana, both of whom wrote and performed comic sketches to popular and admiring audiences. Cupidon would later be the first to dramatize a favourite West Indian novel, H. G. DeLisser's *Susan Proudleigh* (1930), which played at Kingston's Ward Theatre and enjoyed numerous revivals with Cupidon himself performing the female lead. Other stage versions of prose works followed. At another level Tom Redcam (pen-name for T. H. McDermot, a respected Jamaican journalist and poet) hoped to create a literary drama with his historical play *San Gloria* (c. 1920s), written in prose and verse, and treating episodes in the third voyage of Columbus when the admiral's ships were driven aground on Jamaica's north coast. Many years would pass before other West Indian poets like Roger Mais and **Derek Walcott** would write for the stage.

At this time forces in the West Indies were beginning to challenge colonial overlordship. Strong leaders of grassroots political parties and labour unions emerged. Left-wing literary magazines began to appear. In the theatre a new self-awareness asserted itself as participation became more widespread. The Jamaican Marcus Garvey, leader of a global African uplift movement, opened a theatre for the masses in 1929 and presented a series of farce comedies written by the comedian Ranny Williams as well as three epic pageants on black nationhood by Garvey himself. Una Marson's play *Pocomania* (1938) dealt with the pervasiveness of a banned religious cult and Frank Hill's *Upheaval* (1939) spoke boldly of labour unrest leading to social revolution. The Guyanese writer Esme Cendrecourt produced her first play, *Romance of Kaiteur*, and her compatriot Norman Cameron began his series of quasi-religious-historical dramas with *Balthazar*, both in 1931.

In Trinidad, Cecil Cobham formed the Paragon Players in Port-of-Spain in the 1920s and presented a number of original pathetic dramas under such titles as *False Honeymoon*, *Retribution* and *Sold But Not Lost*. F. E. M. Hosein, Mayor of Arima, wrote and staged *Hyarima and the Saints* (1931), a martyr play on the killing of Spanish priests by Amerindians at their mission near the town. The schoolmaster Arthur Roberts produced a decade of delightful yet circumspect plays on topical issues such as divorce, slander, personal hygiene, and child-rearing which were performed by his boy pupils to tumultuous audiences. Another schoolteacher, DeWilton Rogers, dealt more

astutely with questions of colour prejudice and political chicanery in *Blue Blood and Black* (1936) and *Trikidad* (1937). New ground was broken when the historian and political activist C. L. R. James had his drama on the Haitian revolution, *Toussaint L'Ouverture* (1936), produced in London for a special showing by the **Stage Society**. In the cast were the American actor **Paul Robeson** as Toussaint, the Guyanese Robert Adams as Dessalines, John Ahuma as Christophe, and the Nigerian Orlando Martins as Boukman. Also in 1934 Trinidad calypsonians began annual visits to New York to cut recordings and appear on metropolitan boards.

In many respects the decade of the 30s represented a breakthrough for West Indian theatre. The need to show more local life and history on the dramatic stage was recognized. The theatre's ability not merely to entertain but to address issues of common concern was accepted. That plays of this nature could gain attention abroad had been demonstrated. Local drama groups in schools and communities were encouraged in their efforts. Colour and class barriers still existed in the theatre, but were steadily being dismantled. In particular, working class characters in plays frequently lacked dignity and dialect speech was allowed mainly for comic relief. However, as the outbreak of the Second World War brought an influx of American and British servicemen to the region, native entertainers catering to this new clientele with exhibitions of folk culture began to enjoy considerable kudos.

The next two decades witnessed steady progress towards the establishment of a West Indian theatre. Several important theatre groups came into being most of which are still extant. In Jamaica the Little Theatre Movement (LTM) was inaugurated in 1941 and the Caribbean Thespians in 1946. The LTM by 1961 had built its own theatre, laid the foundations for a national drama school, and had given the country its most unique theatre form, the Jamaican pantomime that performs annually to tens of thousands of playgoers. The Whitehall Players (later renamed the Company of Players) started in Trinidad in 1946, the St Lucia Arts Guild in 1950, and the Theatre Guild of Guyana in 1957.

In Barbados, Joyce Stuart began in 1950 her annual productions of West Indian 'customs, culture and folklore' under the title *Revuedeville* but this popular variety show lasted only four years. West Indian drama was gaining a foothold abroad. In New York William Archibald's *Carib Song* (1945) starring the dancer Katherine Dunham had a fair reception on Broadway and **Moss Hart**'s *Climate of Eden* (1952) dramatizing a novel by the Guyanese writer Edgar Mittelholzer was a gallant if unsuccessful attempt. In London, Derek Walcott's verse play *Henri Christophe* showed well in production at the Hans Crescent International House and Errol John, formerly of the Whitehall Players, won the *Observer* prize for the best Commonwealth play with *Moon on a Rainbow Shawl* (1957).

The new movement was distinguished by as serious a commitment to the craft of theatre as to the development of a West Indian dramatic form. Local companies sponsored training classes which were conducted by resident professionals, efforts that were reinforced by the timely appointment at the West Indies University of extramural drama tutors who travelled around the

Caribbean organizing workshops, summer schools and drama festivals. They collected, published and distributed locally written plays. The result of this activity was a cadre of skilled theatre artists and young dramatists who gave high promise for the future. Among playwrights to emerge at this period were Barry Reckord, Cicely Waite-Smith and Samuel Hillary of Jamaica, Jack Archibald, Errol Hill and Errol John of Trinidad, Derek Walcott and his twin brother Roderick of St Lucia, Frank Pilgrim and Sheik Sadeek of Guyana and others. At a 1957 drama festival held at the Ward Theatre in Kingston, the adjudicator could boast that 'side by side with plays from England, America and France, have been plays from Trinidad, Grenada, St Lucia and Jamaica – and we have not suffered by the comparison'. The work of this period peaked in 1958 with the staging in Trinidad of a commissioned epic drama *Drums and Colours* written by Derek Walcott and performed by the finest acting talent assembled from the region, at the inaugural ceremonies of the short-lived West Indies Federation.

Succeeding decades have witnessed the spread of West Indian theatre to metropolitan countries. The Trinidad Theatre Workshop, established in 1959, regularly toured its productions to neighbouring islands and to North America. Playwrights resident abroad such as Mustapha Matura and Michael Abbensetts in England, Lennox Brown and Lorris Elliott in Canada, Edgar White and Derek Walcott in the United States, as well as those who remain at home like Trevor Rhone of Jamaica now have their plays produced on metropolitan boards. Meanwhile the search for a narrative theatrical form that captures the expressive qualities of West Indian life continues. Elements of indigenous culture culled especially from the carnival, from folk religions and speech patterns are incorporated in plays. The Jamaica National Drama School focused part of its programme on developing an idiomatic West Indian theatre. In the tradition of the Anansi story-teller, solo dialect performers like the veteran Louise Bennett of Jamaica, Shake Keane of St Vincent and Paul Keens-Douglas of Trinidad continue to enjoy wide popularity. Paralleling the work of dramatists and actors is the contribution made by the choreographers in establishing theatrical dance forms based on West Indian material. Chief among these are Beryl McBurnie of the Little Carib Theatre in Trinidad, Ivy Baxter of Jamaica and Rex Nettleford of the Jamaican National Dance Theatre.   EGH

See: I. Baxter, *The Arts of An Island*, New Jersey, 1970; Wycliffe Bennett, 'The Jamaican Theatre: A Preliminary Overview' in *Jamaica Journal*, vol. 8 nos. 2 & 3, Summer 1974; E. K. Brathwaite, *Folk Culture of the Slaves in Jamaica*, London, 1971; K. Corsbie, *Theatre in the Caribbean*, London, 1984; E. Hill, 'The Emergence of a National Drama in the West Indies' in *Caribbean Quarterly*, vol. 18 no. 4, December, 1972; K. Omotoso, *The Theatrical Into Theatre: A Study of Drama and Theatre in the English-speaking Caribbean*, London, 1982; R. Wright, *Revels in Jamaica*, London, 1937.

Western, (Pauline) Lucille (1843–77) American actress. Born in New Orleans to comedian George Western and an actress later known as Mrs Jane English, Lucille Western spent her childhood performing with her younger sister, Helen, in a piece designed to show off their dancing and farcical impersonations. As an adult, she excelled in emotional roles such as Lady Isabel in *East Lynne*, Marguerite Gautier in *Camille*, the title roles in *Lucretia Borgia* and *Leah the Forsaken*, and her most popular role, Nancy, in *Oliver Twist*. A dark-eyed beauty, she relied on inspiration more than art and gave the impression of being impulsive and untamed.   TLM

Western theatre, USA Development of the trans-Mississippi west was similar to that of the east, but more extreme – distance was greater, population shift more volatile, and wealth more instantaneous and abundant. The following pattern was repeated several times: a principal city developed as the transportation, supply, and finance centre for a series of outlying communities in which the region's raw materials were exploited. If these outlying communities were sufficiently remote, intermediate supply towns developed as well. Theatre responded to this pattern. Permanent companies resided in large city theatres, and a dominant manager sent them on tour to the outlying communities. Intermediate towns were served in the same way, but on a more frequent basis. While playing conditions were conventional in the cities and towns, they were primitive in the small settlements. Actors travelled to them by wagon and pack animal, often slept in the open, and performed in stores, houses, tents. However crude the conditions, though, western audiences were noted for the prodigality of their response.

California was the first region to develop in this way. Its pioneer period began in 1849 and had passed its peak by 1857. The principal city was San Francisco, and the outlying communities were the gold mining camps in the Sierra Nevada. Lying between were the towns of Marysville, Sacramento, and Stockton. From 1850 to 1884 the Napoleon of California managers was Tom Maguire, an illiterate cab driver and saloon keeper. With only brief exceptions, he managed one or more theatres in the city, and at least one in each intermediate town, thereby assuring a smooth flow of attractions to the gold mines during the summer and early fall. Between 1859 and 1867 the silver mines of Nevada's Washoe Valley became an extension of the California region, and Maguire used Virginia City as an intermediate town for them.

The west's second mining frontier began in 1857 along the eastern slopes of the Rocky Mountains near the South Platte River, and spread north and east with the gold strikes in Montana during the 1860s and in the Dakotas in the 1870s. Denver was the region's city, and it was there that its most important manager, John Langrishe, first struck it rich. An actor seasoned by 15 years of barnstorming in the Mississippi Valley, Langrishe moved with his company in pursuit of bonanza: Denver (1859–67), Helena and Cheyenne (1867–71), and Deadwood (1876–9). The coming of the railroads divided this frontier into separate regions. Denver became the centre of the Silver Circuit, which included the mining and resort towns of Colorado and the Mormon communities of Utah. It peaked under the management of Peter McCoart (1885–95). Montana and Wyoming were controlled by John Maguire (no relation to Tom), with its centre in Helena (1884–1900), while the Dakotas developed their own identity under the management of C. P. 'Con' Walker in Fargo after 1892.

Both the north-west and the south-west waited for eastern rail links in the 1880s. Theatre followed population along the route of the Santa Fe Railroad in the south-west. Los Angeles, where Henry T. Wyatt was the principal manager, became a theatrical centre servicing adjacent regions: southern California, the central coast, the central valley, and Arizona–New Mexico. In the north-west development followed the line of the northern Pacific, which terminated in Seattle. A second centre was Portland, which was on the way to San Francisco. Calvin Heilig and John Cort were the leading managers in Seattle, while John Howe was the principal manager in Portland until the coming of the **Theatrical Syndicate**.

Western theatricals had two extensions beyond the continental United States. Players had passed through San Francisco to and from the British colonies since 1855, but the management of an American, **James Cassius Williamson**, in Sydney after 1879 developed the route from Honolulu to Cape Town. The west's final frontier was the Klondike region of Alaska, where there was a gold stampede from 1896 to 1910. Vancouver was the city for this region, and Dawson, Fairbanks, and Nome each had its turn as a principal town. DMCD

Wheatley, William (1816–76) American theatre manager and actor. Born into a theatrical family, Wheatley made his stage debut at the age of ten in 1826 at the **Park Theatre**, New York, as young Albert in **William Macready**'s production of *William Tell*. Following a tour with Macready, Wheatley returned to the Park and played the title role in *Tom Thumb* establishing himself as a leading juvenile actor. After acting in small roles at the **Bowery Theatre** (1833), he returned to the Park (1834) as a 'walking gentleman' to excel as Nicholas Nickleby, and Charles in *London Assurance*. For the 1842–3 season, Wheatley acted with the **Walnut Street Theatre** company in Philadelphia. After a brief retirement from the stage, he returned to Philadelphia in 1853, to co-manage the **Arch Street Theatre** with **John Drew**. He was sole manager in 1856 but two years later joined forces with **John Sleeper Clarke** who ran it with him until the outbreak of the Civil War. In 1862 he returned to New York and leased **Niblo's Garden** where he excelled in producing elaborate romantic dramas including *The Duke's Motto* and *Arrah-na-pogue*. His biggest hit came in 1866, however, when *The Black Crook* began its 475 performance run, creating a vogue for elaborate musical spectacle and making Wheatley a rich man. He retired from the stage in 1868. TLM

Wheeler, Andrew Carpenter (1832–1903) American drama critic also known as Trinculo and Nym Crinkle. Born in New York, Wheeler began his career as a reporter on the *New York Times* in 1857. After travelling in the midwest, he wrote for the *Milwaukee Daily Sentinel*, reported on the Civil War, and returned to New York to pursue a career in journalism. From 1869 to 1876 he reviewed plays for the *Sunday World*; beginning in 1870 he replaced **Henry Clapp**, Jr, as drama critic of *The Leader*; for 1876–7, he

followed Joseph Howard, Jr, on the *Sun*; his 'Nym Crinkle's Feuilleton' graced the *Dramatic Mirror* from 1886–9; and in 1889, he added a regular column to Deshler Welch's *The Theatre*. Wheeler returned to the *World* in 1883 when Joseph Pulitzer purchased the paper. He was known also as a playwright, novelist, and essayist on nature (under the pen-name of J. P. Mowbray). Called by **James Huneker** 'more brilliant than reliable', Wheeler popularized an aggressive style marked by devastating sarcasm. He opposed the Genteel Tradition, the aesthete views of **William Winter**, and the cultural shift of the country away from rugged individualism. TLM

White, George (1890–1968) American dancer and producer. As a producer of successful musical revues in the 1920s, White provided stiff competition for **Florenz Ziegfeld**. He started out as a dancer in Bowery saloons, gradually working his way up to vaudeville with a dancing act. Between 1910 and 1918 he appeared as a dancer in a number of musicals, including the *Ziegfeld Follies of 1915*. In 1919 he produced the *Scandals of 1919*, the first in a series of thirteen revues bearing the title of *Scandals*. Because of his own background as a dancer, White emphasized dance in his revues, introducing black dance steps such as the Charleston and the Black Bottom to white audiences. His fast-paced revues were also noted for the jazz music of **George Gershwin** and DeSylva, Brown and Henderson. White appeared as a dancer in several of the *Scandals*, and also contributed comedy sketches to several editions. MK

White, Jane (1922–) Afro-American actress. A Smith College graduate, White came early to Broadway as the female lead in *Strange Fruit* (1945). Thereafter she played mostly in Off-Broadway and regional theatres, taking lead roles in *Blithe Spirit*, *The Taming of the Shrew*, and *Dark of the Moon* for the Hayloft Theatre in Allentown, Pennsylvania, in 1948–9. In 1964 she appeared in three productions for the **New York Shakespeare Festival**: *Love's Labour's Lost*, *Troilus and Cressida* and *Coriolanus* for which she won an Obie Award as Volumnia. After engagements in Italy and France, she replaced Irene Pappas as Clytemnestra in the Off-Broadway *Iphigenia in Aulis* (1967). Her Goneril to **Morris Carnovsky**'s King Lear (1975) was hailed for its commanding intelligence, style and rich contralto voice. EGH

White, Patrick Victor Martindale (1912–90) Australian playwright. He was already an internationally known novelist when his four plays *The Ham Funeral* (1961), written in 1947, *The Season at Sarsaparilla* (1962), *A Cheery Soul* (1963) and *Night on Bald Mountain* (1964) were staged by university theatres in Adelaide and Melbourne. All make use of heightened language, expressionistic devices and larger-than-life characterization. His later plays were *Bit Toys* (1977), a comedy of Sydney high society; *Signal Driver* (1982) and *Netherwood* (1983). White was awarded the Nobel Prize for Literature in 1973. MW

Whitefriars Theatre, London Very little is known of this theatre, which was sometimes confused by Caroline commentators with its near neighbour in **Salisbury Court**. The poet Michael Drayton leased a portion of the Old Whitefriars monastery in c. 1605 and may have ordered conversion work to the refectory (85 ft x 35 ft), but it was a sign of hard times when the **Children of the Chapel Royal** took refuge there in 1608. They had lost control of their attractive playhouse in the **Blackfriars** precinct, and the move to the notoriously rough Whitefriars area was a downward step. As the Children of the King's Revels, the reconstituted company played in the Whitefriars from 1608–9, when they were succeeded by, or renamed, the Children of the Queen's Revels. It is likely that two of **Jonson**'s finest plays, *Epicoene* and *Bartholomew Fair*, were first performed at this obscure theatre, which was at best intermittently used after 1614 and not at all after 1621. PT

Whitehead, Robert (1916–) American producer. Born in Montreal and educated at Trinity College School in Canada, Whitehead began his theatrical career as an actor, making his Broadway debut in 1936. He turned to producing in 1947 when he co-presented *Medea* with **Judith Anderson**. In 1951 he served as managing director for ANTA. In 1953 he joined **Roger Stevens** and others in forming the Producers Theatre; and from 1960–4 he was a co-director of the Repertory Theatre of Lincoln Center with **Elia Kazan**. His more than 50 New York productions include: *Member of the Wedding* (1950), *Bus Stop* (1955), *The Visit* (1958), *A Touch of the Poet* (1958), *A Man for All Seasons* (1961), *The Price* (1968), *Old Times* (1972), *A Texas Trilogy* (1976), *Bedroom Farce* (1976), and *Medea* (1982) starring his wife, **Zoë Caldwell**. TLM

Whitehead, Ted (Edward Anthony) (1933–) British dramatist, whose plays for television and the theatre have concentrated on changing sexual manners, within and outside marriage, in contemporary Britain. *The Foursome* (1971) concerns two boys and two girls courting and eventually making love at the seaside; and Whitehead's clear and unsentimental study of male aggressive displays and female flirtatiousness carries a barbed authenticity. In *Alpha Beta* (1972), he describes the slow disintegration of a marriage over nine years, where step by step the two characters, Mr and Mrs Elliott, are drawn towards actions, such as threatening to kill the children, which express a melodramatic desperation. The horror of sexual frustration and despair extends on occasions to black farce, as in *Old Flames* (1975), where girl friends congregate to eat their common boyfriend in a celebratory feast; but Whitehead is seen at his best in his bleakly naturalistic studies which sometimes acquire, as in *The Sea-Anchor* (1974), a haunting atmosphere of loves lost and won. JE

Whitelaw, Billie (1932–) British actress. She has worked extensively with both the **National Theatre** and the **Royal Shakespeare Company** but it is her various appearances in the plays of **Samuel Beckett** that have been of especial importance. These have included *Play* (NT at the **Old Vic**, 1964), *Not I* (**Royal Court**, 1973 and 1975), *Footfalls* (Royal Court, 1976), *Happy Days* (Royal Court, 1979), *Rockaby* and *Enough*

(National Theatre, 1982). No other English actor has established such an authoritative command of the special qualities of Beckett's work. This emphasis should not, however, detract from the range of character and classical work which she has also undertaken, from Desdemona to Maggie Hobson (*Hobson's Choice*). MB

Whiting, John (Robert) (1917–63) British dramatist, who began his theatrical career as an actor, having studied at the Royal Academy of Dramatic Art. While serving in the Royal Artillery during the war, he started to write plays, poems and extracts of autobiography, and his first radio play, *Paul Southman*, was broadcast in 1946. Although his output as a stage dramatist was small, consisting of four major plays, he also wrote screenplays for films and television, and adapted some French plays (by **Obey** and **Anouilh**) for the British stage. He was highly conscious of his craft as a writer and at a time when, in the mid 1950s, proletarian roughness came into vogue, Whiting aspired towards elegant language, subtlety of thought, intricacy of dramatic techniques. His early plays were elegantly written in a style not dissimilar to that of **Christopher Fry**, erring towards flippancy in *A Penny for a Song* (1952) and religiosity in *Saint's Day* (1951), which won the Festival of Britain Award, but little praise from the critics or the public when it was first produced at the Arts Theatre Club. *Marching Song* (1954), however, handled the subject of post-war military guilt with originality and insight; while his best-known play, *The Devils*, based on Aldous Huxley's book, *The Devils of Loudun*, was an early success at the Aldwych Theatre, after it had been taken over as a London branch of the Shakespeare Memorial Company in 1961. *The Devils* proved that Whiting was ahead of his time in handling a complex historical narrative on an open stage; and that he was broadly liberal in his views, against all kinds of bigotry and intolerance. A revival by the **Royal Shakespeare Company** in their studio theatre in the Barbican in 1984 indicated that Whiting's language had dated, but that the general firmness of his technical control remained sound. JE

Wiehe, Michael (1820–64) Leading Danish actor at the **Kongelige Teater** and much admired by **Ibsen**. Amongst his varied repertoire (including **Shakespeare**, **Schiller** and **Holberg**), he excelled as melancholy romantic lovers, especially opposite **Johanne Luise Heiberg**, whose ironic style contrasted well with his apparent vulnerability. He was not an articulate theorist, but temporarily rebelled against what he felt was the Kongelige's frivolous repertoire by joining Frederik Høedt in his rival season at Christiansborg Court Theatre in 1855–6. His brother Wilhelm was also a successful actor. HL

Wieth, Mogens (1919–62) Danish actor of great virtuosity and sensitivity, whose career was hampered by ill-health; he died in London while rehearsing at the **Old Vic**. With his unusually expressive voice, Wieth established himself early at the **Kongelige Teater** as a specialist in such lyrical roles as Peer Gynt and Orpheus in **Anouilh**'s *Eurydice*. In the late 1940s he emerged as a major dramatic actor, especially in the brilliant seasons he shared with Bodil Kjer at the New Theatre, highlighted by *The Waltz of the Toreadors* and *The Misanthrope*. He was active in radio, TV and film, both in Scandinavia and in England, where his stage roles included a much admired Torvald in *A Doll's House*. HL

Wignell, Thomas (1753–1803) American actor, manager. Born in England, he joined his cousin **Lewis Hallam**'s American Company in 1774 and soon became its leading man. Known primarily as a comedian, he played the role of Jonathan in the original production of **Royall Tyler**'s *The Contrast* and created the prototype of the Yankee character. In 1791 he left the company and teamed up with Philadelphia musician Alexander Reinagle to form the **Chestnut Street Theatre**. When their building was finally constructed three years later it was recognized as one of the finest playhouses in the nation. Wignell recruited many of his players from England, including **James Fennell**, Mrs Oldmixon, **William Warren**, and **Thomas A. Cooper**. For many years the company made Philadelphia the theatrical capital of America and developed a touring circuit encompassing Maryland, northern Virginia, and occasional visits to New York City. When Wignell died, his share in the company passed to his widow. Although she and Reinagle were co-owners, management of the company was assumed by actors William Warren the elder and **William B. Wood**. Warren eventually married Mrs Wignell in 1806, and Wood joined him as owner of the company upon Reinagle's death in 1809. They finally disbanded in 1828. RAS

Wild West exhibition A recreation of American frontier life and skills popular in the late 19th century. Occasional exhibits of bronco-busting and Indian folkways were staged previously as museum attractions, but **P. T. Barnum** billed his Wild West extravaganza *Indian Life or A Chance for a Wife* in 1874 as a 'thrilling arenic contest'. The genre took its definitive shape under the guidance of Col. William Frederick 'Buffalo Bill' Cody (1846–1917), a former Indian fighter and buffalo-hunter, who, with the hack Ned Buntline, wrote a play *Scouts of the Prairie*, and starred in it at the **Bowery Theatre**, New York (1874). The interest shown in a frontier fair he put on in North Platte, Nebraska, in 1882 led him and crack shot dentist Dr W. F. Carver to organize a travelling show, The Wild West, which featured a programme of shooting, roping riding, and an attack on the Deadwood stage-coach. In his patent application Cody called it an 'equestrian drama', for he disliked the term 'show'. In 1884 it went on the road under the ownership of Cody, the shrewd theatrical producer Nate Salsbury (1846–1902) and the sharpshooter A. H. Bogardus, who gave it a coherent dramatic structure, culminating in its absorption into **Steele MacKaye**'s *Drama of Civilization* (Madison Square Garden, New York, 1885). From the first, it presented the white frontiersman as a civilizing factor in overcoming the savage elements of Nature and Amerinds. A European tour in 1887 (and again in 1903–6) made a deep impact, influencing the adventure novels of Karl May and, through him, the young **Bertolt Brecht**.

James A. Bailey took over Cody's Wild West in 1894 and used circus equipment and methods to enable it to make one-night stands; Cody added a 'Congress of Rough Riders of the World', with Cossacks, gauchos and Arabs bridging the gap between Sioux savagery and Plainsman nobility. The Buffalo Bill enterprise combined with Pawnee Bill's in 1909, but went into bankruptcy in 1913. A rival, the Miller Brothers and Edward Arlington's 101 Ranch Wild West Show, primarily a display of horsemanship minus the frontier-life romanticism, carried on in 1908–16, tried a revival in 1926 to no public interest, and folded in 1931. The cinema had taken over and expanded the depiction of cowboys and Indians, while authentic skills were relegated to the rodeo and circus 'after-shows'. One of Cody's stars, the sharp-shooter Annie Oakley (Phoebe Ann Moses, 1866–1926), was to inspire the **Irving Berlin** musical comedy *Annie Get Your Gun* (1946). **Arthur Kopit**'s play *Indians* (1969) paints a sardonic picture of the relationship between Cody's exhibitions and the plight of the native American. LS

See: D. Russell, *The Lives and Legends of Buffalo Bill*, Norman, O., 1960; *The Wild West*, Fort Worth, Tex., 1970.

Wildbrandt, Adolf (1837–1911) German playwright and director. During the 1870s and 1880s, Wildbrandt was closely associated with the **Burgtheater**, first as a writer of historical plays and of comedies, then, between 1881 and 1887, as director of the theatre. His finest play, *The Master of Palmyra* (1889), was written after he had retired from the Burgtheater. SW

Wilde, Oscar (Fingal O'Flahertie Wills) (1854–1900) Anglo-Irish playwright, poet, novelist, essayist and wit. Wilde's first play, *Vera: or, The Nihilists* (1883), has an adolescent clumsiness profoundly at odds with its social and literary reputation. It is a melodrama about a group of Russian revolutionary terrorists (or idealists – Wilde poses the alternatives). His second, *The Duchess of Padua* (1891), is a costume tragedy in ungainly blank verse, first staged, like *Vera*, in New York. Wilde's social performances were already familiar enough in the London of 1881 to tempt **W. S. Gilbert**'s satire in *Patience*, but it was not until 1892, the year after the publication of his controversial novel, *The Picture of Dorian Gray*, that he began to find his own voice in drama. *Lady Windermere's Fan* (1892), produced by **George Alexander** at the **St James's**, is formally a text-book example of the well-made play, in which the heroine's reputation rests on the discreet recovery of a fan. *A Woman of No Importance* (1893) and *An Ideal Husband* (1895) are, in terms of plot and subject matter, equally derivative. The contemporary drama of **Pinero** and **Henry Arthur Jones** offered a more overt challenge to Victorian morality. But the lively work of Wilde's plays is done in the dialogue. His upper-class dandies and dowagers have made so merry with the values that the plays purport to uphold that the saving of a marriage has, by the time it is achieved, little more significance than the saving of a cigarette card. Even so, the stagey contrivances are a constraint, and Wilde gives no indication of relishing the mechanical plotting of his drawing-room melodramas. It is quite otherwise with his brilliant masterpiece, *The Importance of Being Earnest* (1895). The contrariness of the title – if the play proves anything clearly, it is the importance of *not* being earnest – is sustained throughout the play. Nothing is what it seems, and the conventions of dramatic fiction become the subject rather than the disguise of the plot. Shortly after the brilliant opening of *The Importance of Being Earnest* at the St James's, Wilde sued the Marquess of Queensberry for slander and the first of two sensational trials began. As the evidence of Wilde's homosexual practices was revealed in court, George Alexander weakened, first removing Wilde's name from posters and programmes and then withdrawing the play altogether. It was during Wilde's spell of imprisonment in Reading Gaol that he begged **Sarah Bernhardt** to produce *Salomé* in Paris (1896). **Lugné-Poe** staged it instead. Wilde had written the play some years earlier, in overblown French prose-poetry. It is decadent purple, a symbolist extravaganza about the killing of John the Baptist. Bernhardt had planned a London production in 1892, but the Chamberlain's office banned the play because it used characters from the scriptures. The ban held until 1931, when the English version translated by Wilde's lover, Lord Alfred Douglas, was first publicly shown. Wilde is known to have planned several plays in prison, and Frank Harris's *Mr and Mrs Daventry* (1900) was probably based on a Wilde scenario, but, in the sad aftermath, he wrote only part of a one-act piece, *A Florentine Tragedy*, which was subsequently completed by T. Sturge Moore and produced in London in 1906. PT

Wildenbruch, Ernst von (1845–1909) German playwright. In the course of an active career in the military and diplomacy, Wildenbruch wrote several popular, nationalistic plays with historical settings, which were done by the Meininger. *The Quitzows* (1888), a play about the Hohenzollerns, was the most acclaimed, though his trilogy about the Emperor Henry IV (1896) was also a tremendous success. SW

Wilder, Clinton (1920–86) American producer. Born in Irvine, Pa., and educated at Princeton University, Wilder began his professional career as a stage-manager for *A Streetcar Named Desire* in 1947. He turned to producing with *Regina* (1949), *The Tender Trap* (1954), *Six Characters* (1955), and *A Visit to a Small Planet* (1957). He joined with Richard Barr to form a production company, Theatre 1960 (later 1961, 1962, etc.), to present non-commercial, avant-garde plays. Their achievements include: *The American Dream*, *The Death of Bessie Smith*, and *Happy Days* (1961); *Who's Afraid of Virginia Woolf?*, *Endgame*, *The Sandbox*, *Deathwatch*, and *Zoo Story* (1962). Joined by **Edward Albee** in 1963, they offered *The Dutchman* and *Tiny Alice* (1964); *Malcolm* and *The Long Christmas Dinner* (1966); *A Delicate Balance* (which won a Pulitzer Prize), *Rimers of Eldritch* and *Everything in the Garden* (1967); and *Seascape* (1975). TLM

Wilder, Thornton Niven (1897–1975) American novelist and playwright. While Wilder may be considered one of America's top ten playwrights, his reputation rests upon three full-length plays and a half-dozen one-acts, beginning in 1931 with the publication of *The Long Christmas Dinner & Other Plays in One Act*. In 1938 his Pulitzer Prize-winning *Our Town* opened on Broadway, employing many of the experimental techniques Wilder had used in his one-acts: minimal scenery, narrative descriptions, and the like. *Our Town*, which has been called America's most read and most produced play, examines in the first act small-town life in Grover's Corners, New Hampshire, for a single day in 1901. Succeeding acts complete the cycle of marriage, birth, and death, ending with Emily's conversation with the dead whom she has just joined.

Wilder's next play, *The Merchant of Yonkers* (revised as *The Matchmaker*, 1954), closed after only 39 performances, but was a smash hit in 1964 as the musical *Hello, Dolly!* Of more impact was *The Skin of Our Teeth* in 1942, a parable of the world's history centred around the Antrobus family. Act One is set in Excelsior, New Jersey, during the Ice Age; purposeful anachronisms mix with dinosaurs and refugees. Act Two on the broadwalk at Atlantic City closes with Mr Antrobus loading pairs of animals into his boat to avoid the Great Flood. Act Three finds the Antrobus family coping with the after-effects of a seven year war, but finding hope in their very existence. SMA

Wilkie, Allan (?1889–1970) Actor and manager. Born in Scotland; his first Australian **Shakespeare** season was in 1916, and from 1920–30 he toured Australia and New Zealand in Shakespeare and occasionally other classics. Wilkie's company, with his wife Frediswyde Hunter-Watts as leading lady, was known for its fine acting, with economical settings and elegant costumes. Unable to survive the depresion after 1930, the Wilkies moved to Canada and travelled through North America in Shakespeare recitals, eventually returning to Scotland. Wilkie was awarded a CBE in 1925. MW

Wilkinson, Tate (1739–1803) English actor and manager. He began acting at Harrow and was taken on by **John Rich**. He soon discovered that while his acting was poor his imitations of other actors were brilliant and he based his career on that talent, earning his dismissal by Rich because of **Mrs Woffington**'s irritation at his mimicry of her. Famed for his imitations he travelled to Dublin with **Foote** in 1757. His imitation of **Garrick** at **Covent Garden** infuriated Garrick and lost Wilkinson his friendship. In 1763 he was in York and joined Joseph Baker, the manager of the York theatre, investing heavily in the management. On Baker's death in 1770 he took on sole management of the York circuit of six theatres in the North of England, two of which, in York and Hull, had been made Theatres Royal in 1769. He reformed abuses in the theatres and employed most rising stars, including **Kemble** and his sister **Mrs Siddons**. His engaging *Memoirs* were published in 1790 and his account of the Yorkshire circuit, *The Wandering Patentee*, in 1795. PH

Williams, Barney (1823–76) Irish-born American actor whose first appearance on the New York stage was in 1836. In 1850 he married Maria Pray Mestayer (1828–1911), the widow of actor Charles Mestayer. For 20 years, the Williamses achieved considerable success, both in America and Great Britain, as a popular starring team in romantic Irish comedies such as *Born to Good Luck* and Samuel Lover's *Rory O'More*. Williams was regarded as unrivalled as the broadly comic, joking, hard-drinking, but appealing stage Irishman. For two seasons (1867–9) he managed the old **Wallack's Theatre** (the Broadway). His last appearance in *The Connie Soogah* and *The Fairy Circle* was at **Booth's Theatre** in New York on Christmas night, 1875. DJW

Williams, Bert (Egbert Austin Williams)

(1874–1922) Black American comedian, born in Nassau, British West Indies. He began in minstrel shows, where he had to affect blackface to conceal his light complexion and to learn the standard stage-darky dialect. From 1893 to 1908, he teamed with George Walker (1873–1911), who played the flashy free-spending urban sport to Williams's melancholy, shuffling fall-guy, both in vaudeville and a series of successful all-black musicals, including *Sons of Ham* (1900), *In Dahomey* (1902) and *Bandana Land* (1908). When Walker retired in 1909, the victim of advanced paresis, Williams went solo; already the first black comic to record for Victor (from 1901), he was known nation-wide for such lugubrious songs as 'I'm a Jonah Man' and 'Nobody', and founded the first all-black actors' friendly society in 1906. Over protests from some of the white cast, Williams became the first black performer in *The Ziegfeld Follies*, in which he played annually from 1910 to 1919 (missing only 1913 and 1918). 'The funniest man I ever saw and the saddest man I ever knew', as **W. C. Fields** called him, played in tandem with Leon Errol and **Eddie Cantor**, and never failed with his one-man poker game. LS

Williams, Emlyn

(1905–87) Welsh dramatist and actor, who established the psychological thriller with *A Murder Has Been Arranged* (1930) and *Night Must Fall* (1935), a line he continued with plays like *Someone Waiting* (1953). His best work is the semi-autobiographical study of the relationship between a young Welsh miner and his school-teacher, *The Corn is Green*, which ran for two years with himself in the lead role when it was first performed in 1935. He has also written adaptations, including his first farcical success *The Late Christopher Bean* (1933) and *The Master Builder* (for **Olivier** at the **National Theatre**, 1964), and his numerous other plays range from behind-the-scenes drama in **Shakespeare**'s theatre (*Spring 1600*, 1934 – rewritten in 1945) to the supernatural and religious (*The Wind of Heaven*, 1945; *Trespass*, 1947). Apart from acting in many of his own plays, some of which he also directed, he established a reputation as a performer in a wide variety of drama – starting with **Fagan**'s *And So To Bed* (1927), in Shakespearian roles with the **Old Vic** (1927) and at Stratford-upon-Avon (1956), in **Bolt**'s *A Man For All Seasons* (1962) and **Hochhuth**'s *The Deputy* (1964) in New York – winning international success with one-man shows, as **Dickens** (first performed, 1951), and after 1955 in *Growing Up*, based on readings from **Dylan Thomas**. CI

Williams, Jesse Lynch

(1871–1929) Journalist, writer and dramatist, is remembered as the winner of the first Pulitzer Prize for the best American play: *Why Marry?* (1917). Originally published as *And So They Were Married* (1914), *Why Marry?* first questioned and then carefully defended the institution of marriage as the best that society can offer. *Why Not?* (1922) scrutinized divorce through two mismated couples and arrived at the same conclusion. As other plays reveal – *The Lovely Lady* (1925), concerned with parents and children – Williams's comedic solution to society's problems remained conventional and distinct from the social realism of a later decade. WJM

Williams, Tennessee

(1911–83) American playwright. From 1945, with his first success *The Glass Menagerie*, Tennessee Williams has had a deep impact on the American theatre, bringing to it an original lyric voice and a new level of sexual frankness. The pleasure and the pain of sex was the great, inescapable subject of both his work and his life. In different moods and styles and with varying effectiveness, Williams returned repeatedly to the same neurotic conflicts embedded within the same character types: the spirits of Blanche Du Bois and Stanley Kowalski, the fierce antagonists of his masterpiece, *A Streetcar Named Desire* (1947), haunt practically all of his fables. Blanche is the lady of illusion and artifice, the fluttering Southern belle whose veneer of refinement masks emotional starvation and sexual rapacity. Desired and feared by Blanche as well as Williams, Stanley is the muscled male whose potency contains the promise of both salvation and destruction.

As in *Streetcar*, the battle between repression and release, between the puritan and the cavalier, is at the heart of Williams's most vibrant work (*Summer and Smoke*, 1948; *The Rose Tattoo*, 1951; and *Battle of Angels*,

Marlon Brando and Jessica Tandy in Tennessee Williams's *A Streetcar Named Desire*, New York, 1947.

1940, rewritten as *Orpheus Descending*, 1957). In some plays (*Battle of Angels*; *You Touched Me*, 1945; *Sweet Bird of Youth*, 1959) lusty men reanimate languishing women; in others (*Cat on a Hot Tin Roof*, 1955; *The Milk Train Doesn't Stop Here Anymore*, 1963) the refusal of desirable males to satisfy deprived women provides the central conflict. Sometimes, as in *Cat on a Hot Tin Roof* and *Suddenly Last Summer* (1958), men withhold sex from women because they are homosexual; sometimes, as in *Milk Train*, because they want to transcend sexual desire. The source of Williams's profound sexual conflicts was the war between his fatally mismatched parents, his mother a rector's prudish daughter, his father a blustery womanizer who called his sensitive son 'Miss Nancy'. Unable in the American theatre of the fifties and sixties to write openly about his own homosexual passion, Williams created nominally heterosexual dramas, transmuting tormented autobiography into artistic metaphor.

After *The Night of the Iguana* (1961), an uncharacteristic play of resolution and completion, Williams descended into a critical and commercial decline for the remaining 22 years of his life. Some of his later work, notably *The Gnädiges Fraulein* (1966), *In the Bar of a Tokyo Hotel* (1969), and *Outcry* (1973), chronicles the despair of creators who have lost control of their art. Other plays such as *Small-Craft Warnings* (1972) and especially *Vieux Carré* (1978) are attempts at self-restoration in which Williams returns to the delicacy of *The Glass Menagerie*. His Rabelaisian middle period is framed, as it were, by the directly autobiographical *Glass Menagerie* and *Vieux Carré*, in both of which Williams displays a healing compassion not only for others but also for himself as a young man. But neither the plays about disintegration nor the ones of partial affirmation have had the impact of his earlier work – audiences and critics have generally found the dramas too private.

In his later years Williams's personal life seriously deteriorated. He became increasingly dependent on drugs and alcohol and required periods of institutional confinement. Yet he continued to write daily, rigorously devoting himself to his craft. Despite the blurred focus, the occasional self-parody, the lack of control, there remains much of value in these later offerings, passages that testify to Williams's powerful sense of theatre and to his melodic gifts. Even the least of his plays is a vehicle for bravura acting, for in good plays and bad Williams created wonderfully actable neurotics. Twisted by desire, plagued by anxiety, Williams's victims and outsiders speak a poetry of the dispossessed flavoured with wit, irony, and gallantry.

Williams struggled through a long critical eclipse but his reputation is now secure. Among American playwrights his achievement is equalled only by that of **Eugene O'Neill**. FH

Williamson, David Keith (1942–) Australian playwright. His early plays *The Coming of Stork* (1970) and *The Removalists* (1971) were written while he was a thermodynamics lecturer; the latter won Sydney's Nimrod Theatre the 1971 British George Devine award for new playwriting. His astute observation of contemporary Australian society and ear for the vernacular's ironies and self-betrayals make him Australia's most successful playwright. His plays include *Don's Party*

(1971), *What if You Died Tomorrow* (1973), *The Club* (1977), *Travelling North* (1979), *The Perfectionist* (1982) and *Sons of Cain* (1985); and the television mini-series *The Last Bastion* (1984). He was made an Officer of the Order of Australia in 1983. MW

Williamson, James Cassius (1845–1913) Australian entrepreneur. Born in Pennsylvania, he was an actor-dancer in New York and San Francisco before touring Australia in 1874 with his wife Maggie Moore in *Struck Oil*. Returning to settle in 1879, he soon became Australia's leading manager, largely through importing overseas successes; his enforcing of his rights to *HMS Pinafore* and other pieces confirmed British copyright laws in Australia. Through various partnerships with George Musgrove, George Tallis, Gustave Ramaciotti, Hugh J. Ward and others, he established a firm which dominated Australian theatre until 1976. When he died, all Australian theatres remained dark for a night in his memory. MW

Williamson, Nicol (1938–) British actor, born in Scotland, who started his career with the Dundee Rep in 1960–1. After appearing at the **Royal Court** in London in *That's Us*, **Arden of Feversham** (1961) and two Shakespearian productions in 1962, he joined the **Royal Shakespeare Company**, playing in **Henry Livings**'s *Nil Carborundum* and **Gorky**'s *The Lower Depths*. His first major success came in 1964 as Maitland the tormented solicitor in **John Osborne**'s *Inadmissible Evidence*, which transferred from the Royal Court to the West End and Broadway. Williamson won the Evening Standard Best Actor Award and the New York Drama Critics Award for this performance, which revealed his talents to express a powerful if introverted personality, the inwardness which later, in 1969, allowed Williamson to become one of the most celebrated Hamlets of his generation. While that nervous tension was appropriate in *The Diary of a Madman* (1967), it did not prevent him from also being an excellent comic actor as in the New York production of *Plaza Suite* (1969) or from appearing in a wide variety of films. He rejoined the Royal Shakespeare Company in 1973, where he took the title roles in *Coriolanus* and *Macbeth*; while in 1974, he directed and played Vanya in a studio performance of *Uncle Vanya* with the RSC at Stratford-upon-Avon. In 1981, he appeared in London and New York in revivals of two Osborne plays, *Inadmissible Evidence* and *The Entertainer*. He also developed a solo performance, involving poetry readings, extracts from plays and singing in a quiet, intense style, which made him a highly effective cabaret performer. JE

Williamstown (Massachusetts) Theatre Festival Founded in 1955 by Yale Drama School professor Nikos Psacharopoulos, this festival has presented over 250 productions since its inception. Known for its appeal to established actors, many now primarily in films, as a place where they can return frequently to the stage, Williamstown also utilizes some of the best directors and designers in the United States and presents not only classics but avant-garde risks and unknown new plays. A rotating company of over 250 are associated with the Festival, including the likes of Christopher Reeve, **Colleen Dewhurst**, Frank Langella, Richard Thomas, **Geraldine Fitzgerald**, and Richard Chamberlain. A complex operation with at least six discrete production components, WTF has gained an international reputation and is considered by many the outstanding summer theatre establishment in the USA.   DBW

Willis, Nathaniel Parker (1806–67) American essayist and playwright. Willis began an intense but brief association with the theatre with *Bianca Visconti* (1837), the winner of Josephine Clifton's 1,000 dollar competition. *The Kentucky Heiress* (1837), also written for Clifton, failed. In 1839 Willis wrote *Tortesa the Usurer* for **James Wallack**, the story of a rich man who bargains for an aristocratic wife, one with a mind of her own, but accepts a glover's daughter. Audiences, however, did not appreciate Willis's literary comedy, and starring actors did not want plays with several starring roles. Enjoying a reputation as the foremost essayist in America, Willis stopped writing plays.   WJM

Wills, William Gorman (1828–91) Anglo-Irish playwright and painter, who provided **Henry Irving** with many of his **Lyceum** successes. These included *Charles I* (1872), *Eugene Aram* (1873), *Vanderdecken* (1878) and *Faust* (1885). Wills believed poetry to be a higher form than drama, and his attempts to combine the two impressed contemporaries more than they have posterity. A noted clubman and an endearingly generous, if somewhat anachronistic, Bohemian, he made more money by painting fashionable portraits than by writing plays. His only enduring success was *Olivia* (1878), an adaptation of **Goldsmith**'s novel, *The Vicar of Wakefield*, and even that endured only as long as **Ellen Terry** continued to perform in it.   PT

Wilson, August (1945–   ) American playwright whose position in the theatre rose meteorically in less than a five-year period. Winner of the 1987 Pulitzer Prize for Drama for *Fences*, he has written a series of plays each set in a different decade, evolving into a cycle of dramas which he terms his 'view of the black experience of the 20th century'. Wilson has focused on what he perceives as the largest idea that confronted blacks in each decade, drawing heavily on his own experience growing up in the Hill district of Pittsburgh, Pennsylvania, a black slum community. Wilson also is typical of an American playwright whose work has been fostered in the regions, with developmental work at the **Eugene O'Neill Theatre** Centre's National Playwrights Conference and premieres at the **Yale Repertory Theatre** under Lloyd Richards's direction, beginning with *Ma Rainey's Black Bottom* (1984) and including *Fences*, *Joe Turner's Come and Gone* (1986), and *The Piano Lesson* (1988).   DBW

Wilson, Francis (1854–1935) American comedian and singer. After an apprenticeship as a utility actor and low comedian with a stock company, Wilson made his musical theatre debut in *Our Goblins* (1880). From 1885–9 he appeared in comic operas with the McCaull

Opera Company, then established his own company. His greatest role was that of Cadeaux in *Erminie* (1886), a part he played nearly 1,300 times over 35 years. His other successes included *The Merry Monarch* (1890), *The Lion Tamer* (1891), *Half a King* (1896), and *The Toreador* (1902). From 1904 on, Wilson confined his efforts to comedy and drama. Because of his training in stock, Wilson brought to his musical roles the skills of a character actor, carefully preparing each move and gesture rather than trusting to improvisation. From 1913–21 he served as the first president of America's Actors' Equity. His autobiography was published in 1924.   MK

Wilson, Lanford (1937–   ) American playwright born in Lebanon, Missouri. After Wilson began writing plays at the University of Chicago, he became part of a group of playwrights at the Caffè Cino in New York. There his first script was produced, *So Long at the Fair*, in 1963. Since then his plays have been produced at the Café **La Mama** in New York, the **Mercury Theatre** in London, most of the regional United States theatres, and on Broadway.

Among his more successful scripts are *The Madness of Lady Bright* (1964), *Balm in Gilead* and *This is the Rill Speaking* (1965), *Rimers of Eldritch* (1966), *Lemon Sky* (1970), *The Great Nebula in Orion* (1971), *The Hot l Baltimore* (1973), *5th of July* (1978), and *Talley's Folly* (1979), the last winning Wilson the Pulitzer Prize for Drama and the New York Drama Critics Circle Award. His 1983 *Angel's Fall* was a critical, but not popular success.

Wilson was one of the founders of the **Circle Repertory Company**, which staged several of his scripts. *The Hot l Baltimore*, involving various social outcasts in a condemned hotel (the letter e is missing from its electric sign), ran 1,166 performances, the Off-Broadway record for a non-musical American play.

Besides the Pulitzer Prize, Wilson has won the Drama Desk Vernon Rice Award for *The Rimers of Eldritch*, the New York Drama Critics Circle Award, the Outer Circle Award, and an Obie for *The Hot l Baltimore*, and another Obie for *The Mound Builders*. In recent years Wilson has learned the Russian language in order to translate **Chekhov**.   SMA

Wilson, Robert (d. 1600) Actor and playwright, famous as an extemporizer. Wilson is known to have been with **Leicester's Men** after 1572 and with **Queen Elizabeth's Men** after 1583. Of several plays which he wrote or helped to write, the surviving three, *The Three Ladies of London* (c. 1581), *The Three Lords and Three Ladies of London* (c. 1589) and *The Cobbler's Prophecy* (c. 1594), are scholarly examples of a professional ability to adapt mid-century drama to the changing taste of the early public theatres.   PT

Wilson, Robert (1941–   ) American director whose training as a painter and architect is evident in his painterly theatre compositions. Wilson's work with brain-damaged children, using physical activity to influence mental activity, also influenced his dreamy pieces, especially their slow pace and repetition of simple movements. Christopher Knowles, an autistic adolescent, became a collaborator with Wilson on pieces like *A Letter to Queen Victoria* (1974) and *Einstein on the Beach* (1976). (In this piece, Wilson also worked with choreographers Andrew de Groat and Lucinda Childs, and composer Philip Glass.) Wilson was interested in Knowles's non-discursive use of language and sought to create on stage Knowles's unusual way of structuring perceptions. Operatic in scale, Wilson's streams of visual and aural images lack plots and characters in any conventional sense and often employ massive scenery, animals, and complex lighting effects. Nō-like in tone, they take place in slow motion, altering the audience's sense of time; a simple action like crossing the stage can take an hour. *Deafman Glance* (1970) lasted eight hours, and *Overture to Ka Mountain*, created for the 1972 Shiraz Festival in Iran, lasted a week. In the 1980s Wilson began centring his work in Europe where it was easier to find funding. There he created *The Man in the Raincoat* (1981, Cologne), *Great Day in the Morning* (1982, Paris), *The Golden Windows* (1982, Munich), and *the CIVIL warS* (*sic*) (1983, five countries).   AS

Wilton, Marie Effie (1839–1921) English actress and pioneering theatre manager, born into a theatrical family. As a child, she performed in provincial theatres, notably in Bristol, where she made an impression as Ophelia. In London, somewhat to her chagrin, she became a sex symbol, particularly during her years (1858–64) as the 'Queen of Burlesque' at the Strand Theatre, and it was primarily a determination to refashion for herself a career in legitimate drama that dictated her bold decision to enter into theatre management at the age of 25. With a borrowed £1,000, she bought the lease of the disreputable Queen's Theatre in Tottenham Street, sharing the management with the leading Strand dramatist, **H. J. Byron**, but sparing him the financial risk. An extraordinary intuition enabled her to recreate, in the small auditorium of the renamed **Prince of Wales's**, the atmosphere of decorous Victorian domesticity – ornamental flowers on each side of the proscenium, four rows of stalls complete with anti-macassars, carpeted aisles, rosebud chintz lining the circle – and audiences responded with enthusiasm. The crowning achievement was the staging in annual succession from 1865–70 of six comedies by **T. W. Robertson**. It was in the third of these, *Caste* (1867), that Marie Wilton created one of her finest roles, that of Polly Eccles. Her Captain Hawtree was **Squire Bancroft**, whom she married at the end of the run, and to whom she subsequently surrendered her managerial leadership. But hers is the primary credit for her theatre's contribution to the growth of ensemble acting, the raising of the status of actors and the increasing appropriateness of stage decor. The Bancrofts remained at the Prince of Wales's until 1879, after which they managed the **Haymarket** from 1880 until their wealthy retirement in 1885.   PT

Windust, Bretaigne (1906–60) American director and actor. Born in Paris, Windust grew up in New York and attended Princeton University. In 1928 he co-founded the University Players at Falmouth, Massachusetts. He began his professional career in 1929 as assistant stage manager with the **Theatre Guild**. In

1932 he staged the London production of *Strange Interlude*. He made his New York acting debut in 1933 and received good notices although the play failed. The **Lunts** noticed his work and hired him to play Tranio in *The Taming of the Shrew* (1935). His association with the Lunts continued in 1936 as he directed them in *Idiot's Delight* and a year later in *Amphitryon 38*. After staging a successful revival of *The Circle* with **Tallulah Bankhead** in 1938, Windust was to enjoy a decade of remarkable successes: *Life with Father* (1939), *Arsenic and Old Lace* (1941), *The Hasty Heart* (1945), *The State of the Union* (1945), and *Finian's Rainbow* (1947). Although he turned to films and television after 1947, Windust still enjoyed some success with *The Great Sebastians* (1956) and *The Girls in 509* (1958). His forte was comedy and his trademark was dramatic curtain-calls and post-curtain tableaux.   TLM

Winter, William (1836–1917) American drama critic, theatre historian, and biographer. Born in Gloucester, Massachusetts, and educated at Harvard University, Winter abandoned a law career for a literary one. Influenced by Henry Wadsworth Longfellow, Winter turned to writing poetry and reviewing books. In 1859 he moved to New York and worked as assistant editor and book reviewer for the *Saturday Press*. In 1860–1 he wrote briefly for *The Leader* before taking charge of the *Albion*'s dramatic department (1861–5), writing under the name of Mercutio. In 1865 he replaced Edward H. House as chief critic for the *New York Tribune*, a position he held until 1909, establishing himself as the foremost drama critic of his generation. The foundation of Winter's critical beliefs was essentially Aristotelian, tempered with 19th-century romantic idealism (later called 'the Genteel Tradition'). He considered acting the primary art of theatre, and the standard drama preferable to modern plays. He regarded the theatre as a temple of art to elevate and inspire mankind, and rejected the notion that art should depict real life. To Winter, beauty and morality were inseparable in art, and realism had banished both from the stage. Thus he saw Ibsenism as a 'rank, deadly pessimism . . . a disease, injurious alike to the stage and to the public . . . '. Winter prepared acting versions of **Shakespeare**'s plays for **Edwin Booth** and **Augustin Daly**. He wrote lengthy biographies on Edwin Booth (1893), **Ada Rehan** (1898), **Richard Mansfield** (1910), **Joseph Jefferson** (1913), and **Tyrone Power** (1913). His more than 50 books provide a comprehensive record of the late 19th-century American stage.   TLM

Winter Garden Theatre New York City theatre at 1634 Broadway, between 50th and 51st Streets. The Winter Garden, an important musical house, was designed for the **Shubert** brothers by architect William Swasey. It opened on 20 March 1911 with a double bill that included a curtain-raiser called *Bow Sing* and *La Belle Paree*, a revue. The Winter Garden was less a totally new theatre than an extensive remodelling of an existing building, the American Horse Exchange. The remodelled structure contained a cabaret, as well as a large theatre which was decorated in a garden motif and contained an unusual feature for the time, a runway extending from the stage into the auditorium. In 1912 the Winter Garden became the home of *The Passing Show* (an annual Shubert revue designed to compete with **Florenz Ziegfeld**'s *Follies*) which continued to be presented regularly through 1924. During the teens and early twenties, the theatre was also the home of a number of light musicals conceived as vehicles for Shubert star **Al Jolson**. The Winter Garden was extensively remodelled during the 1920s by theatre architect Herbert Krapp. During the 1930s it housed such important musical attractions as the Shubert-produced editions of the *Ziegfeld Follies* and the long running *Hellzapoppin'* starring Ole Olsen and Chic Johnson. From 1928 to 1933, and again from 1945 to 1948, the Winter Garden was used for motion picture showings. Following its second reconversion to live performance, the theatre has been the home of such major musicals as *West Side Story* (1957), *Gypsy* (1959), and *Cats* (1982). The Winter Garden, which seats some 1,500 spectators, is owned by the **Shubert Organization**. BMCN

Witkiewicz, Stanisław Ignacy (pseudonym, Witkacy) (1885–1939) Polish playwright, painter, novelist and philosopher who, unrecognized by his contemporaries, has emerged since 1956 as a seminal figure. He travelled to Australia in 1914 with the anthropologist Malinowski and then served in the Russian army, witnessing the Revolution of 1917. He wrote over 30 plays between 1918 and 1926, many

unpublished and unperformed. His theory of *Pure Form in the Theatre* (1920) seeks to liberate drama from story-telling and traditional psychology, and give it the formal possibilities of modern art and music. His works present an apocalyptic vision of the loss of metaphysical feelings in the coming anthill civilization, viewed with mocking irreverence and self-irony. Major plays are *They* (1920), *Gyubal Wahazar*, *The Water Hen* (1921), *The Madman and the Nun*, *The Crazy Locomotive* (1923), *The Mother* (1924), *The Beelzebub Sonata* (1925), *The Shoemakers* (1934). DG

Wodehouse, P[elham] G[renville] (1881–1975) British novelist and dramatist, who worked with John Bolton on many of the most successful English musical comedies between 1917 and 1935, as well as collaborating with **George Grossmith** and Ian Hay on a series of humorous farces. CI

Woffington, Margaret (Peg) (?1714–60) Irish actress. Her father died a pauper in 1720 and tradition says that she worked with Madame Violante's tightrope-walking act. She certainly acted with her children's company and played three roles, including Macheath, in *The Beggar's Opera* for her in London in 1732. In 1737 she was starring at the Smock Alley Theatre, particularly as Polly Peachum. In 1740 she was triumphant in the **breeches part** of Sir Harry Wildair in **Farquhar**'s *The Constant Couple*, a role she played in

Witkiewicz's *Gyubal Wahazar*, National Theatre, Warsaw, 1968. This production was censored and stopped after the dress rehearsal.

London for **Rich**. In 1742 she was Lady Anne to **Garrick**'s Richard III. She became his mistress and lived with him but he drew back on the verge of marriage. Facing fierce competition from **Mrs Clive** she eventually quarrelled with Garrick and left **Drury Lane** in 1748, beginning to play more roles in tragedies. Here rivalry with **Mrs Bellamy** reached a climax with a fight when they were playing *The Rival Queens* in 1756. She collapsed on stage as Rosalind when delivering the epilogue to *As You Like It* in 1757 and was ill until her death. PH

Wolf, Friedrich (1888–1953) German dramatist, later publisher of the journal *Volk und Kunst* and DDR ambassador to Poland, whose topical plays – *Cyanide* (1929), dealing with abortion from his experience as a medical practitioner, or *Tai Yang Awakes* on the Shanghai workers' uprising of 1927, staged by **Piscator** in 1931 – made him the rival of **Brecht** as the most significant political dramatist in the Weimar Republic. CI

Wolff, Egon (1926–) Chilean playwright, born of German parents, he has successfully maintained a career as a chemical engineer and owner of a small factory in Santiago while devoting himself to literature. His early plays focus on psychological problems, generational conflicts and social issues. Among many titles, two stand out. *Los invasores* (*The Invaders*, 1962), with a surrealistic technique and a touch of **J. B. Priestley**'s *An Inspector Calls*, portrays violently the threat of class revolution if the bourgeoisie continues to ignore social concerns. *Flores de papel* (*Paper Flowers*, 1970) deals with gratuitous violence and psychological violation in an obtuse class struggle. Later titles include *Kindergarten* (1977), *Espejismos* (*Mirages*, 1978), *José* (1980), and *La balsa de la Medusa* (*Medusa's Raft*, 1984). GW

Wolff, Pius Alexander (1782–1828) German actor. According to **Goethe**, Wolff was the only actor who fully mastered the **Weimar style**. He left the Weimar Court Theatre in 1816 for the **Berlin Royal Theatre**. Here his interpretations of Hamlet became legendary. Wolff was the author of the highly popular comedy, *Preziosa* (1821). SW

Wolfit, Donald (1902–68) British actor–manager. After an early career touring with Fred Terry, in London and with the Sheffield Repertory Company, mainly in melodrama, he established a reputation as a Shakespearian actor with the **Old Vic** in 1929–30, at Stratford-upon-Avon in 1936, and with his own company from 1937. He toured widely, giving memorable performances not only as Shylock in *The Merchant of Venice*, Macbeth and Lear, but also in the title role of **Jonson**'s *Volpone* and in **Massinger**'s *A New Way to Pay Old Debts*, and mounted a popular lunch-time series of scenes from **Shakespeare** in 1940. He also offered striking interpretations of modern plays, including **Hochwälder**'s *The Strong Are Lonely* (1955), **Ibsen**'s *Ghosts* (1959) and *John Gabriel Borkman* (1963), as well as classical drama such as *Oedipus Rex* and *Oedipus at Colonus* (1953). He was knighted in 1957. CI

Wood, Charles (Gerald) (1933–) British dramatist whose three short plays about the army, produced as *Cockade* in 1963, revealed his gift for terse, vivid dialogue and bitter satire. Wood, who served as a trooper in the Lancers from 1950–5, has written attacks on militarism, British imperialism and the class system embodied in the army ranks; and *Dingo* (1967), set in North Africa during the Second World War, and *H: Being Monologues at Front of Burning Cities* (1969), about the 'Christian' General Havelock who commanded the British forces in India at the time of the Indian mutiny, are epic tirades on the folly and hypocrisies of war. In a lighter vein, Wood has written amusing comedies about a run-down repertory theatre, *Fill the Stage with Happy Hours* (1966), the welfare state and the making of films, including *Veterans* (1972), based on his experiences in co-writing (with **John Osborne**) the screenplay for *The Charge of the Light Brigade*. *Has 'Washington' Legs?* was a farce about making a Hollywood flop, produced by the **National Theatre** in 1978. JE

Wood, John British actor, who studied at Oxford, becoming president of OUDS, before joining the **Old Vic** Company in 1954. A tall lean actor, with a characteristic acerbic delivery, Wood was not the easiest person to cast; and his appearances in *Camino Real* (1957), *The Making of Moo* (1957), *Brouhaha* (1958) and *The Fantasticks* (1961) were effective without giving a true indication of his talents. When he joined the **Royal Shakespeare Company** in 1971, however, he was offered parts in both Shakespearian and modern plays which revealed his exceptional intelligence and expressivity. In 1974, as Carr in **Tom Stoppard**'s *Travesties*, he won the Evening Standard Best Actor Award and, on Broadway, the Tony Award (1976), providing a brilliantly comic study of a bemused minor Foreign Office official in Zürich in 1917, matched by such dubious contemporaries as Lenin, Tristan Tzara and James Joyce. In 1979, he appeared at the **National Theatre** in Stoppard's version of a **Schnitzler** play, *Undiscovered Country*, as well as Richard III and in *The Provoked Wife* (1980). His film appearances include those in *Nicholas and Alexandra* (1971) and as a Thirties actor in Woody Allen's *The Purple Rose of Cairo*. JE

Wood, Mrs John (Matilda Charlotte Vining) (1831–1915) English actress and manager. Born in Liverpool, the future Mrs Wood acted on provincial English stages for 12 years before marrying the actor John Wood and coming to Boston in 1854. After their American debut at the Boston Theatre (September 1854), they appeared in New York at the Academy of Music (1856) before becoming regulars with the Boston Company. Mrs Wood played a guest engagement at **Wallack's Theatre** in late 1856, creating the role of Minnehaha in Charles Walcot's *Hi-A-Wa-tha*. At the end of the 1856–7 season, Mrs Wood and her husband left for San Francisco where she quickly became a star. After the couple separated, Mrs Wood returned East to play starring engagements for the next four years. In 1863 she began a three-year stint as manager of the Olympic Theatre. She returned to England in 1866 and acted only once more (1872–3) in America. Saucy, impudent, and fun-loving, Mrs Wood was called by

Lawrence Hutton 'one of the best burlesque actresses our stage has ever known'. TLM

Wood, William Burke (1779–1861) American actor and manager, born of English parents in Montreal, Canada. As a young man he joined **Thomas Wignell**'s Philadelphia company, despite ill-health and lack of theatrical experience. Unsuccessful in tragic roles, Wood proved better suited to genteel comedy and ultimately found his niche in management. After the death of Wignell in 1803, he became assistant to the acting manager of the **Chestnut Street Theatre**, **William Warren**. In 1804 he married Juliana Westray, a good actress who appeared under his management for many years. Warren and Wood shared a prosperous quarter-century together, bringing their Philadelphia, Baltimore and Washington theatres to international eminence. Wood sold his shares back to Warren before the 1826 season, but remained as a company member. He left in 1828 to manage the new **Arch Street Theatre**, Philadelphia; and from 1829 to 1846 he was at the **Walnut Street Theatre**, Philadelphia. His reminiscences are recorded in *Personal Recollections*, published in 1855. DBW

Woodworth, Samuel (1785–1842) American playwright. He is best known for his song 'The Old Oaken Bucket' and for *The Forest Rose* (1825, with music by John Davies), often called 'the first American musical hit', a light-hearted glorification of American farmers which became a vehicle for a host of 'Yankee' actors for forty years. He wrote seven other plays (e.g., *The Deed of Gift*, 1822; *LaFayette*, 1824; and *The Cannibals*, 1833), a patriotic novel, dedicatory addresses, sentimental ballads, and edited numerous periodicals and newspapers, notably the New York *Mirror* (1823–42). He received small profit from his literary endeavours and died in poverty. RM

Woollcott, Alexander (1887–1943) American dramatic critic. Woollcott made his debut as a critic for the *New York Times* in 1914, replacing Adolph Klauber. His battles with the **Shuberts** in 1915 made him a celebrity. After military service in Paris (1917–19), he returned to the *Times*, and helped establish that witty 'vicious circle' that met for lunch at the 'Algonquin Round Table'. In 1922 he was hired away by the *Herald*, and later reviewed for the *Sun* (1924–5) and the *World* (1925–8). In 1929 he established his 'Shouts and Murmurs' column in *The New Yorker*; began his radio show (later commanding up to $3,500 per programme for 'The Town Crier'); and collaborated on a play with **George S. Kaufman**. He also appeared frequently as an actor, playing, according to **Brooks Atkinson**, 'a sort of virtuoso fat man'. Woollcott remains best known as the model for Sheridan Whiteside in Kaufman and **Hart**'s *The Man Who Came to Dinner*. Vitality and urbanity were his trademarks. TLM

Worth, Irene (1916–) American-born actress, known equally on both sides of the Atlantic. She has accumulated most major awards for her acting and has been especially praised for the musicality of her voice and her commanding stage presence; her talent is held in high esteem by both critics and colleagues. After teaching school for several years, she turned to the stage, making her professional debut with a touring company in 1942, then appeared a year later on Broadway with **Elizabeth Bergner** in *The Two Mrs Carrolls*. Seeking classical training, she went to London in 1944 to study with Elsie Fogerty. Her first noteworthy appearance in London was as Ilona in **Molnár**'s *The Play's the Thing* (1947). She appeared as Celia in the premiere of *The Cocktail Party* at the **Edinburgh Festival** (1949). After working with the **Old Vic** Company (1951–3), she helped found with **Tyrone Guthrie** and **Alec Guinness** the **Stratford Ontario Shakespeare Festival** in 1953. Following a succession of critically acclaimed portrayals in London, New York, and Stratford Ontario, she joined the **Royal Shakespeare Company**, appearing as Goneril in **Peter Brook**'s production of *King Lear* (1962). Other notable appearances in the past quarter of a century have included *Tiny Alice* (New York, 1964; Royal Shakespeare Company, 1970), **Coward**'s *Suite in Three Keys* (London, 1966), *Heartbreak House* (Chichester, 1967), Brook's controversial *Oedipus* (**National Theatre**, 1968), *Hedda Gabler* (Stratford Ontario, 1970), *The Seagull* (Chichester, 1973), *The Cherry Orchard* (New York City, 1977), *John Gabriel Borkman* (New York City, 1980), and as a 'majestically unruffled' Volumnia in *Coriolanus* at London's National Theatre (1984). DBW

Wycherley, William (1641–1715) English playwright. Sent to France as part of his education, he was later trained for the law. His first play, *Love in a Wood* (1671), gained him both a high literary reputation and the Duchess of Cleveland as his mistress. After *The Gentleman Dancing-Master* for the Duke's Company (1672), Wycherley wrote the two masterpieces that confirmed his reputation as the most brilliant satiric dramatist of his day, *The Country Wife* (1675) and *The Plain Dealer* (1676). From this point his career went downhill and he did not write another play. Seriously ill in 1677 he lost favour at court after marrying the Countess of Drogheda against the King's wishes; she proved not to be the rich heiress he had supposed. Imprisoned for debt in 1685 after her death, Wycherley was released and given a pension by James II after a court performance of *The Plain Dealer*. He published a massive volume of poor poetry in 1704 and began a friendship with Pope who helped revise his later poems. His death-bed marriage, tricked by a distant relation, was almost a bizarre scene from one of his own plays. The genial satire of his first plays reached a climax in the verve of *The Country Wife* where, borrowing the device from **Terence**, the hero, Horner, pretends castration as a cover for his affairs, exposing the follies of society. It continued to be performed in the 18th century in **Garrick**'s anaemic adaptation, *The Country Girl* (1766). *The Plain Dealer* is a very dark rewriting of **Molière**'s *The Misanthrope*, an unwieldy play of enormous power tracing the deceptions of love and friendship with a central figure, Manley, an obsessive and savage satirist; it was prefaced when published with a dedicatory epistle to a famous London bawd. PH

Wyndham, Charles (1837–1919) English actor and theatre manager, who was already a qualified doctor when he made his debut on the professional stage in

1862. This first venture was short-lived, and Wyndham (born Charles Culverwell, he eventually legalized the name Wyndham in 1886) went to the USA, where he enlisted as a surgeon in the Federal army during the Civil War. From 1870–2, he took his own Comedy Company on a pioneering tour of mid-West theatres, presenting **T. W. Robertson**'s *Ours* and *Caste* and **James Albery**'s *Two Roses* to predominantly novice audiences. Wyndham's acting style in these early days was modelled on that of the quick-fire, gentlemanly **Charles James Mathews**. When Chicago audiences complained about his staid, English repertoire, he added the recent American hit, **Bronson Howard**'s *Saratoga*, and it was as bustling Bob Sackett in that play, revamped for London audiences by Frank Marshall as *Brighton*, that he began to establish his reputation after returning to England in 1872. The significant step into management came in 1875, at the Criterion, in which he retained an interest for the remaining 44 years of his life, bequeathing it to his son and step-son, Howard Wyndham and Bronson Albery. The Criterion was a small basement theatre and Wyndham had the good sense to exploit its intimacy in a series of society farces, the first being Albery's *The Pink Dominos* (1877), mostly taken from French originals whose impropriety was expurgated but still discernible. A handsome man, Wyndham retained a female fan-club for longer than seems likely. His favourite part was the virtuoso title-role of T. W. Robertson's *David Garrick*, but the Criterion is (and was) associated rather with the society comedies of **Henry Arthur Jones**, particularly *The Case of Rebellious Susan* (1894) and *The Liars* (1897), in both of which Wyndham excelled as a wise *raisonneur*. In 1899, the Prime Minister, the Marquis of Salisbury, agreed to the building of a theatre on land he owned only on condition that Wyndham would assume the management. Wyndham's Theatre opened the same year with a revival of *David Garrick*. It would later house Jones's *Mrs Dane's Defence* (1900), in which Wyndham as Sir Daniel Carteret coolly destroyed Mrs Dane in the famous cross-examination scene, and the first English performance of **Rostand**'s *Cyrano de Bergerac* (1903), in which the title-role was beyond his range (he was 66). Wyndham was knighted in 1902, and the following year a third theatre, the New, opened under his management. Three years before his death, he married his leading lady, Mary Moore (1869–1931), widow of the playwright James Albery. The marriage established a surviving theatrical dynasty.   PT

Wynn, Ed (Isaiah Edwin Leopold) (1886–1966) American comedian. Wynn began in vaudeville in 1901, later teaming up with Jack Lewis as two collegians in the act 'Rah, Rah, Boys'. Starting with *The Ziegfeld Follies of 1914* and *1915*, he found a comfortable solo niche in musical comedy, including *The Perfect Fool* (1921), which became his nickname, *Simple Simon* (1930), *The Laugh Parade* (1931) and *Hurray for What?* (1937). Wynn's stage persona wore horn-rimmed glasses and tiny pork-pie hats, spoke with a lisp, giggled and walked with a mincing gait. Many of Wynn's gags were predicated on an inability to complete an anecdote or a piece of music; his insane inventions included a typewriter carriage for eating corn-on-the-cob and a cigarette lighter that pointed out the nearest matches. From 1932 to 1937 Wynn was 'The Fire Chief' on radio; in the 1950s and 60s he played dramatic roles in films and television.   LS

Wyspiański, Stanisław (1869–1907) Polish painter, poet, playwright and man of the theatre who studied at the Cracow Academy of Fine Arts, and in Paris. Drawing upon Polish romantic drama, particularly **Mickiewicz**'s ideas, he revolutionized stage design and production in his work for the Cracow theatre. His *Study of Hamlet* (1905) calls for a synthesis of the arts, with stress on setting and costume. His plays, symbolist in orientation, interweave the real and fantastic, and join Polish history to Greek and biblical myth. Plays on national issues include *Song of Warsaw* (1898), *The Wedding*, *Deliverance* (1901), *November Night* (1903), *Acropolis* (1904) and *Legend* (1905); those on mythological themes are *Protesilas and Laodamia*, *Achilleis* (1903) and *The Return of Odysseus* (1907).   DG

Y

Yacine, Kateb (1929–) Algerian francophone playwright whose work is both densely poetic in texture and firmly committed to political struggle. Criticism of French colonial policies led to the banning of his early plays in the fifties but **Serreau** succeeded in producing *Le Cadavre Encerclé* (*The Surrounded Corpse*) in 1964 and *Les Ancêtres Redoublent de Férocité* (*Ancestors become more Ferocious*) in 1967 at the **TNP**. His play celebrating Ho Chi Minh *L'Homme aux Sandales de Caoutchouc* (*The Man with Rubber Sandals*) was deemed subversive enough for the Mayor of Lyon to cut **Maréchal**'s subsidy when he produced it in 1971. After his involvement with Théâtre de la Mer from 1970, he developed an idiosyncratic form of popular theatre in spoken Arabic and Berber, of which the outstanding example is *Mohamed, Prends ta Valise*, a constantly reworked play based on the experiences of immigrant Algerian workers. DB PT

Yakovlev, Aleksei Semyonovich (1773–1817) Russian actor. Along with **E. S. Semyonova**, one of the great St Petersburg actors of the day and a forerunner of the later romantic performance style. A pupil of **Dmitrevsky**, rival of and successor to Shusherin, Yakovlev was not one for careful preparation of a role or the continued development of craft over the course of a career. Instead he brought inspired emotionalism, manly good looks, a sonorous voice and wildly uneven play to his impersonation of **Kotzebue**'s sentimental characters and **Ozerov**'s noble heroes (Oedipus, Fingal and Dmitry Donskoi). He was the first Russian actor to appear in a series of roles adapted from **Shakespeare** and **Schiller**, including Othello in a translated French version (1806), Edgar in Gnedich's *King Lear* (1807), and Karl Moor (1814). Unrequited love for a married actress led to melancholia, drink, the destruction of his talent, attempted suicide and finally death. SG

Yakshagana (India) *Yakshagana* is a generic term referring to a variety of different theatre forms of south India, the best-known of which is found in the south Kanara region of Mysore state. The term *yaksha* means the demi-gods associated with Kubera, god of wealth, and *gana* is a song. Thus, *Yakshagana* means 'songs of the demi-gods'. Historical evidence suggests that *Yakshagana* of south Kanara may have originated in the early to mid-16th century, although some scholars argue that there is reason to suppose that it may have existed several centuries earlier.

Yakshagana is popular with rural audiences. All the companies are itinerant organizations under the management of temple authorities. The manager of the troupe contacts the players (a minimum of 15 people are required to produce a performance) and the musicians (a minimum of five are needed). Touring begins from the home temple and engagements are organized during the festival season which lasts approximately six months between November and May. The manager makes all the formal arrangements with a patron, including place of performance, cooking arrangements and living accommodations which are either in a local temple or the home of a Brahmin. During the initial contact, a ritual exchange takes place between patron and manager, usually on the morning of performance, and the full payment for the show is provided the morning after, just prior to the departure of the actors for their next engagement. The manager usually hires a staff of at least ten helpers to assist in the cooking, to prepare the accommodations and to transport the costume and prop boxes from place to place.

Yakshagana is a lively, fast-paced form in which songs, dances and improvised dialogue mix according to a prescribed structure. At the heart of the *Yakshagana* are the poetic songs (*prasanga*) sung by the chief musician (*bhagavata*), who controls the pace of the show. Popular *prasangas* have been transcribed and published, even those from hundreds of years ago; and, with their particular melody (*raga*) and metre intact, they constitute a major part of the historical record of the dramatic literature. Today, paperback editions of the *prasangas* are to be found on book stalls along the roadside in rural areas of Mysore state.

Expanding on the content of the songs is the improvised dialogue (*matu*) of the actor–dancers. Until recently, this portion was not recorded because it changed from night to night and from actor to actor depending on his skill and sensitivity to the demands of the audience. Most of the *prasangas* are based on stories from the great Hindu epics *Mahabharata* and *Ramayana* and from the *Puranas* and concern serious events from the lives of well-known epic figures. Humour is

The demon king in a *Yakshagana* production.

inserted in the performance by the clowns (*hasyagar*) through their comic antics and witty remarks.

The acting area (*rangasthala*) may be any space near the house of a patron, in a paddy field, cleared of stubble, or on open ground in front of a temple compound. The space is normally marked off as a rectangle 15 x 20 ft. Tall bamboo posts demarcate the four corners. Mango leaves, flowers, coconuts, plantains and coloured paper provide a festive, simple decoration. At the centre of one of the narrow ends of the acting area, a wooden table is placed on which the chief singer and the *maddale* drummer perform. Behind them is the *ratha*, a collapsible cart with four wheels which serves as the only functional piece of furniture and scenery used during performance. Standing between the musicians is a man who plays the *shruti*, which, like the harmonium, keeps the underlying pitch necessary to guide the singer's melodies. On the right side of the playing area, sitting on a chair facing the acting area, and the other musicians, is the *chende* drummer. The area between the pillar and the table upleft is used for entrances. Some distance away on the left side of the acting area, the actors gather in an improvised dressing room made of thatch walls. A space between the *chende* player and the table is reserved for exits.

The audience sits on three sides of the rectangle; the women and children sit separately from the men. Conventional shovel-shaped lamps are placed stage right and stage left facing the acting area but electric lights and petromax lanterns have become popular today to help the spectators to s : the action better. A simple curtain with the troupe's name embroidered on it is used for dance entrances of major characters or groups of dancing characters.

Admission is usually free to the public. Petty merchants display their wares, such as sweets, tea and snacks, outside the audience area and conduct a brisk business among the spectators through the long hours of the night. Shows generally begin with various ritual events about 9.30 or 10.00 pm and continue uninterrupted until sunrise when they are concluded by ritual prayers.

Some troupes give performances in a tent so that they may control attendance. Tickets are sold and folding chairs are provided for a fee. A raised proscenium stage is used for these performances and the style of dance and acting has assumed unique features which distinguish it from that of the open-air troupes. These performances are known as tent drama (*tent atta*).

During the monsoons which hit the area from June to September, *Yakshagana* is presented in the homes of patrons or in enclosed halls. The actors sit down on the ground and with musical accompaniment they sing the *prasangas* and perform truncated improvised dialogue. These events are known as *tala maddale*.

Costumes and makeup for the *Yakshagana* of this region are unique. Big heart-shaped headdresses are worn by the warriors, crowns of wood covered with tinsel paper are worn by kings and large impressive headdresses are worn by demons whose spiky makeup distorts the actor's facial features beyond recognition.

In the same region another style of *Yakshagana* is practised, called *Yakshagana Tekutittu* (the southern style of *Yakshagana*). The vigorous dances and music are reminiscent of the **Kathakali** dance-drama of neighbouring Kerala.

In Andhra Pradesh and Tamil Nadu states the origin and meaning of the term *Yakshagana* is just as obscure as it is in Mysore state. Some say that the term *isai* used in *Silappadikaram*, a famous Tamil epic poem of the 8th to 10th centuries AD, refers to a prototype of *Yakshagana* and that it comes from Kerala and imitates *Kathakali*. Others say that it originated in the 14th century and began as a dance interpretation of one character who took many roles. Later, it added a second character, the female counterpart. In this phase, the male was called *Yaksha* and the female was known as *Yakshi*. Then in the course of time, a clown was introduced to provide humour and finally a fortune teller came into the picture. At this stage, it is said that *Yakshagana* served as a model for **Kuchipudi** which 'upgraded' the form by bringing in classical Karnataka music and elaborate acted dances, according to the dictates of the *Natyasastra*.

The earliest written specimens of the form date from the first half of the 16th century when Kandukuru Rudrakavi wrote the play *Sugrivavijaya*, the story of the monkey king who overthrew his powerful brother, based on incidents adapted from the *Ramayana*. From what little is known or written on the subject and what little has been seen, the form found in Andhra is different from that found in Mysore and less sophisticated visually. FaR

Yale Repertory Theatre An adjunct to the Yale School of Drama (established as a graduate school in 1955) in New Haven, Connecticut, which in turn grew out of the Drama Department founded in 1925 by **George Pierce Baker**, this important non-profit professional theatre was founded in 1966 by **Robert Brustein**. In 1968 it moved into a church converted into a theatre with a thrust stage seating 487. Under Lloyd Richards, who was appointed Artistic Director in 1979, central to each season have been **Shakespeare**, **Athol Fugard**, **August Wilson**, and the Winterfest of New Plays. Among important new works premiered at Yale have been **Eric Bentley**'s *Are You Now Or Have You Ever Been. . . ?* (1972), **Robert Lowell**'s version of *Prometheus Bound* (1967), **Kopit**'s *Wings* (1978), three plays by **Edward Bond** (including *Bingo* in 1976), several plays of Fugard in the 1980s (*A Lesson from Aloes, Master Harold, The Road of Mecca*), and Wilson's *Ma Rainey's Black Bottom* (1984). DBW

Yankee theatre (USA) Yankee actors achieved their greatest popularity between 1825 and 1855, though Yankee characters appeared earlier and later. The first notable 'Jonathan' – the most common name (or nickname) – was in **Royall Tyler**'s *The Contract* (1787); the last, Joshua Whitcomb in **Denman Thompson**'s *The Old Homestead* (1886). The stage-Yankee possessed varying mixtures of the character attributes ascribed to rustic New Englanders ('downeasters'): simple, blundering, sentimental, parsimonious, patriotic, shrewd, critical of city folks, and devoted to tell-tales and picturesque speech. A storehouse of riches for eccentric comedians, many of whom began their careers as Yankee story-tellers before appearing in plays.

The English comedian **Charles Mathews** was the first to discover the gold-mine of good fun to be found in the Yankee in his *Trip to America* (1824) and *Jonathan in England* (1824).

Four American actors quickly followed his lead: **James H. Hackett** in his own *Sylvester Daggerwood* (1826), as Solomon Swap in *Jonathan in England* (1828), as Major Joe Bunker in *The Militia Muster* (1830), and as Lot Sap Sago in **Cornelius A. Logan**'s *Yankee Land* (1834).

George Handel 'Yankee' Hill, often called 'the most authentic', as John Bull disguised as Jonathan Doolittle in **William Dunlap**'s *Trip to Niagara* (1828), as Jonathan in **Samuel Woodworth**'s *The Forest Rose* (1832), in *Jonathan in England* (1832), as Jedediah Homebred in **J. S. Jones**'s *The Green Mountain Boy* (1833), as Sy Saco in **John Augustus Stone**'s *The Knight of the Golden Fleece, or The Yankee in Spain* (1834), as Hiram Dodge in *The Yankee Pedlar* (Anon., 1835), as Abner Tanner in J. S. Jones's *The Adventurer, or The Yankee in Tripoli* (1835), and as Solon Shingle in Jones's *The People's Lawyer* (1839).

Danforth Marble in E. H. Thompson and Marble's *Sam Patch* (1836), as Deuteronomy Dutiful in Cornelius A. Logan's *The Vermont Wool Dealer* (1838), as Jacob Jewsharp in J. P. Addams's *The Maiden's Vow, or The Yankee in Time* (1838), as Solon Shingle in Jones's *The People's Lawyer* (1839), and as Lot Sap Sago in Logan's *The Wag of Maine* (1842).

Joshua Silsbee in *The Forest Rose* (1840), in *The Yankee Pedlar* (1841), in *The Green Mountain Boy* (1853), and in *The Vermont Wool Dealer* (1853).

The Yankee actors were extremely popular in London in the 1830s and 40s; the critics found them not unlike 'our own canny Yorkshire lads'.   RM

Yeats, William Butler (1865–1939) Irish playwright. Yeats's ambition for Irish theatre was that it should stimulate, through his own plays, a poetic celebration of Irish legend and history, heroic and mythic in scale, yet with the ironic tone he admired in **Synge**. So in Yeats's *On Baile's Strand* (1904), the Blind Man and the Fool parody Conchubar and Cuchulain.

Formally, Yeats rejected the dominant theatrical realism, contemporary subjects, and painstakingly authentic sets. A bare stage with merely suggestive properties – a blue cloth for a well – would enable verse to make drama a sacred rite, expressed also through dance, music, masks. For this drama 'close to pure music' Yeats found precedents in the French symbolists, and from 1916, instructed by Ezra Pound, in Japanese **nō** plays. Throughout his career, however, his attachment remained to 'the sovereignty of words'.

These formal concerns did not imply a drama insulated from life. Yeats's early plays are in part political parables. *The Countess Cathleen* (1899) belongs to his myth of the Anglo-Irish aristocracy. *Cathleen ni Houlihan* (1903), is a patriotic allegory. *The King's Threshold* (1903) asserts the poet Seanchan's place among the lawmakers.

The burden of **Abbey Theatre** management impeded Yeats's own work. Between 1904 and 1910 his only major plays were *Deirdre* (1906), *The Golden Helmet* (1908) and its verse adaptation *The Green Helmet* (1910). Apart from *The Words Upon The Window Pane* (1930), conjuring Swift's ghost to a seance, in prose and a realistic setting, his later work experiments with verse, symbolist theatre. It has effective dramatic

moments. In *At the Hawk's Well* (1916) words unite with songs, Edmund Dulac's masks, and the hawk-dance performed by Michio Ito, to enact Cuchulain's heroic resolution. In *The Dreaming of the Bones* (1931) the dance and parting of Diarmuid and Grania, traitors 700 years dead, are memorably succinct. *Purgatory* (1938 – Yeats's last appearance at the Abbey) embodies in its fable of murderous family decadence Yeats's bitter judgement on modern Ireland. The problem remains, however, of a verse lyrical, expository, meditative, not dramatic.

Yeats's plays, infrequently performed, never won the popular audience for which he hoped. Nor did they revive verse drama in the 20th century. They are astonishing sketches, by an indisputably great poet, for a verse drama never fully realized. Yeats was awarded the Nobel Prize in 1923.   DM

Yiddish Art Theatre, The Maurice Schwartz's Company, which opened at the Irving Place Theatre in New York in 1918, subsequently moving to the Garden Theatre, and which rejected the improvisations of **Shund theatre** in favour of carefully rehearsed plays of quality, ensemble acting and a high standard of presentation. The first successes came with **Peretz Hirshbein**'s earthy pastoral play *The Forgotten Nook*, followed by the same writer's *The Blacksmith's Daughter*, another delicate, idyllic play of village life. During the second year 15 plays were added to the repertoire, including **Sholom Aleichem**'s *Tevye the Milkman* and four of **Jacob Gordin**'s plays including *God, Man and Devil*, based on the Faust legend. Inevitably 'stars' were created, like **Bertha Gerstein**, **Ludwig Satz**, Muni Weisenfreund (**Paul Muni**) and Anna Apfel. Several productions in English translation transferred to Broadway including Schwartz's greatest personal triumph, Israel Joshua Singer's *Yoshe Kalb*. The company continued until the late thirties.   AB

Yiddish theatre The appearance of an indigenous Jewish theatre was forbidden for centuries on religious grounds. Deuteronomy 22:5, which stated that 'a man shall not put on a woman's garments', was construed to prohibit dressing up in any clothes other than one's own, thus presenting an insuperable obstacle to theatrical performance. A connection was also invoked between drama and idol worship. A single exception was permitted during the Festival of Purim when Bible stories, particularly that of the deliverance of the Jewish people by Esther, could be told dramatically in the form of a *Purimspiel*. It was not until the last quarter of the 19th century that a general movement away from religious restriction had spread sufficiently to allow the belated beginnings of an endemic Jewish theatre. (See also **Hebrew theatre**.)

There had been plays written and published sporadically from as early as *The Exodus*, by Ezekiel, in the 2nd century BC, and particularly in Holland and Italy in the 16th and 17th centuries, but these were intended for reading, not performing. Aaron Halle Wolfsohn's *Frivolity and Hypocrisy*, for example, was published in 1798, intended as an alternative to the simple and often bawdy **Purim Plays**. The two published plays of greatest historical importance however were *Reb Henoch* by Isaac Eichel which appeared in Germany in 1793 and Solomon Ettinger's *Serkele*, written in Russia in 1825 but not published until 36 years later. The latter play, skilfully constructed and with closely observed characterization, received a school performance in 1861 in which the name part was played by a young student called **Abraham Goldfaden**, later to earn the title of 'Father of the Yiddish Theatre' by bravely presenting – in Rumania – the first public performance of a Yiddish play in October 1876. The play presented was almost certainly *The Recruits*, a Schweik type of broad comedy, although the subject was anything but funny at the time. Goldfaden had included many of his own songs, thus setting a pattern of musical theatre which was to last. The venture was a great success and the theatrical floodgates suddenly burst open. New companies sprang up everywhere, split up and multiplied, all following Goldfaden's pattern of musical plays written at a simple, folksy, emotional level, each company employing a resident 'writer' to supply story-lines and songs. The rest was improvised.

Stylistic traditions peculiar to Yiddish theatre were developed by Goldfaden for his unsophisticated audiences and adopted by all the companies. Thus a doctor always wore rimless spectacles, a simpleton had his shirt-tail hanging out, marriage-brokers carried an umbrella, students held a book and rich men a cane. Colour had special significance; a white robe with a blonde wig indicated an angel, a red outfit and a black wig signified a devil. Beggars always wore black, but a black robe indicated the Angel of Death. Villains wore red wigs and heroes black ones. The atmosphere at performances was close to that of a family gathering or a communal celebration, with a quite unique emotional rapport between actors and audience.

With the banning of all Yiddish theatre in Russia following the Assassination of Tsar Alexander II in 1883, and the escalation of Jewish persecution in Europe, a general exodus began. The theatre companies went with the people, establishing themselves in England, France, the Argentine etc., but particularly in America, where performances quickly became a vital social, educational and cultural influence amongst rapidly growing Yiddish-speaking communities. Theatres appeared in most of the large cities, particularly Chicago, Boston, Philadelphia and San Francisco. Within a short period of time no fewer than 11 Yiddish theatres were functioning in New York alone. Prolific writers like **Moishe Hurwitz** and **Jacob Lateiner** began churning out potboilers each of which combined pathos and comedy in the Goldfaden style, a form not dissimilar from the later work of Chaplin. Extrovert actor-managers like **Boris Thomashevski** and **Maurice Schwartz** became matinee idols.

The more cultured members of the community looked down upon this popular 'greenhorn' and 'peasant' theatre as unworthy, and movements towards a Jewish Art Theatre materialized in Europe and later in America, nurtured by the serious-minded Yiddish Drama and Literary Clubs and semi-professional groups such as **Folksbühne** and **Artef**, before spreading to the professional theatre. Jewish Art Theatre first manifested itself in Odessa in 1908, on the lifting of the 25-year ban on performances, when **Peretz Hirshbein** formed the Hirshbein Troupe, with **Jacob Ben-Ami** as leading actor. Rejecting improvisation, he directed plays by **Jacob Gordin**, **Sholom Asch**, **Isaac Loeb**

Peretz, **David Pinski**, **Sholom Aleichem**, in addition to his own plays. Hirshbein disbanded the company after two seminal years in order to devote more time to writing, but the main fruits of his labours were to come later in Vilna, Moscow and New York.

In 1916 the celebrated **Vilna Troupe** appeared, quickly achieving a style and character of its own. Under the direction of **David Herman**, Hirshbein's protégé, it developed a repertoire of over 100 plays, embarked on a brilliantly successful series of World Tours and built up an enviable reputation for distinctive stylization and ensemble playing. At about the same time **Esther Rachel Kaminska** and her Warsaw company were also producing some remarkable work which was continued by her daughter **Ida Kaminska** until the 1939 Nazi invasion. The company was re-formed after the war as the Polish State Yiddish Theatre and is one of the two remaining State-funded full-time Yiddish theatres, the other being the Rumanian State Yiddish Theatre. The **Moscow State Jewish Theatre** resulted from the wave of creative enthusiasm which·followed the Russian Revolution in 1917, and under the inspired leadership of Alexander Granowski, designers like Marc Chagall and Nathan Altman, composers like Alexander Krein and M. Milner, and actors like **Solomon Mikhoels** and Benjamin Zuskin it achieved world fame with productions of plays by Sholom Aleichem, Mendele Mocher Sforim, Goldfaden and particularly **Shakespeare**.

In America a quality Yiddish theatre flourished for two decades following the First World War, led by Maurice Schwartz and his **Yiddish Art Theatre**, which combined ensemble playing with high production values and brought forth actors of the calibre of **Celia Adler**, **Bertha Gerstein**, **Ludwig Satz**, Jacob Ben-Ami and Anna Apfel, designers like **Boris Aronson** and **Mordecai Gorelik** who went on to international fame, and plays by writers of quality such as Hirshbein, Gordin, Fishel Bimko and **Ossip Dimov** in addition to introducing many of the great European dramatists, in translation, to America. Jacob Ben-Ami's short-lived **Jewish Art Theatre** reached probably the highest point of theatrical achievement. **Emanuel Reicher**, who had been an associate of **Reinhardt** and later became Director of the **Theatre Guild**, was engaged as Director and the objectives of the company were closely modelled on those of the **Moscow Art Theatre**.

Yiddish theatre went into a world-wide decline in the 1930s, by which time the Yiddish language had virtually fallen into disuse. A large body of plays remain and although most of them, written for unsophisticated audiences, served their purpose and are better forgotten, there are many such as the plays of **Anski**, Hirshbein, Sholom Aleichem, Sholom Asch which will hold their own in any company.   AB

See: B. H. Clark & G. Freedley, *A History of Modern Drama*, New York, 1947; D. S. Lifson, *The Yiddish Theatre in America*, Cranberry, NJ, 1965; H. Madison, *Yiddish Literature, Its Scope and Major Writers*, New York, 1968; N. Sandrow, *Vagabond Stars*, New York, 1977; *The Drama Review, Jewish Theatre Issue*, vol. 24, no. 3, 1980.

Yorkshire Tragedy, A A tragedy, probably first performed in 1606, when it was part of the repertoire of the King's Men at the **Globe Theatre**. The title page of a 1608 edition claims **Shakespeare** as the author, but the most that can be supposed is that he had some hand in cutting the play down into the truncated form in which it has survived.

The play is based on the story of Walter Calverley, executed for murder in 1605. It describes with grim haste the passage from gambling debts to the attempted murder of all his family (wife and one son survive) to arrest and final repentance.   PT

Yoruba travelling theatres Nigerian professional theatre companies which travel around Nigeria performing to Yoruba-speaking audiences. These wholly commercial itinerant theatre groups started with the establishment of the Ogunde Theatre in 1945 and reached a peak in 1981 with as many as 120 separate companies. Companies tend to coalesce, break up, and then re-group with others. There are about 40 established companies (Jeyifo), including Ogunde Theatre and **Moses Olaiya Adejumo**'s Alawada Theatre; and as many groups still trying to find their audiences, including two led by actress-owners. Jeyifo estimates that about 3,600 professional actors, performers and organizers are employed full-time. Most companies are members of the Association of Theatre Practitioners of Nigeria (ATPN), founded by **Hubert Ogunde**, which acts as a theatre Chamber of Commerce.

The proliferation of companies followed in the wake of the rapid expansion of the Nigerian economy after independence which saw a threefold increase in the number of wage-earners in 12 years. Many of these were Yorubas who travelled to other cities in Nigeria to live and work. The Yoruba travelling theatres reflect and cater for the need for a Yoruba urban identity within the Nigerian polity: a sense of a Yoruba past with a contemporary urban style and morality. The audiences, therefore, determine the new theatre aesthetic through the thousands of performances of new plays, which they pay for. Jeyifo states that the travelling theatres are eclectic, and observes a process in which 'no dominant or "normative" style or structure of performance has emerged'.

A programme cover for Amos Tutuola's *The Palm-Wine Drinkard*, in a stage version by the Ogunmola Travelling Theatre, Ibadan, Nigeria.

Every company undertakes regular arduous itineraries but is not restricted to stage performances. Most perform regularly on television, sometimes on radio. Many make LPs for their performances, or publish them in the magazine format called 'photo-play'. Some make films for the cinema. All these successful commercial innovations indicate the dynamism of this immensely popular theatre.   ME

Young, Stark (1881–1963) American drama critic, translator, playwright, and director. Born in Mississippi, Young earned degrees in English at the University of Mississippi (1901) and at Columbia University (1902). After teaching in several universities, he became a contributing editor to *New Republic* in 1921, and an associate editor of **Theatre Arts** magazine from 1921 to 1940. Young took over as chief drama critic of the *New Republic* in early 1922 from Francis Hackett, and held the position (except for the 1924–5 season when he reviewed for the *New York Times*) until his retirement in 1947. He was an advocate of the New Stagecraft movement, and worked closely with **Eugene O'Neill**, Kenneth Macgowan, and **Robert Edmond Jones** at the Provincetown Playhouse. He staged the premiere of O'Neill's *Welded* in 1924. Young wrote several plays, none successful. He is better remembered for his translations of **Chekhov**'s plays, especially of *The Seagull* for the **Lunts** in 1938. His books include: *The Flower in Drama* (1923), *Glamour* (1925), *Theatre Practice* (1926), and *The Theatre* (1927).   TLM

Young People's Theatre (Britain) An umbrella term to cover all forms of theatre work for and with young people. The two major kinds of young people's theatre (YPT) are Children's Theatre and Theatre-in-Education (TIE), but among the variety of activities also undertaken are:

(a) 'Play Days' and 'Theatre Appreciation' programmes – work done by repertory and YPT companies designed *either* to provide a service to schools for the study of examination playtexts, *or* to stimulate an interest in and increase understanding of the theatre. Lectures, demonstrations, workshops, and performances of short plays or play extracts, on tour or in a theatre, are just some of the events that may be offered.

(b) 'Youth Theatre' – workshops and productions prepared and performed *by* young people, sometimes organized through the local repertory or YPT company, sometimes by the drama adviser of the local education authority and sometimes, on a larger scale, through an independent self-governing body such as, most notably, the **National Youth Theatre**.

Children's Theatre Professional theatre mainly for the younger age range (up to 14), consisting of self-contained performances given by touring or building-based companies before large numbers of children. Performances designed specifically for the older (15 plus) age range are now more usually described simply as 'young people's theatre', but for the sake of convenience will be included here under 'Children's Theatre'.

The early ventures into children's theatre in Britain, before the First World War, were almost exclusively devoted to encouraging an appreciation of **Shakespeare**. Foremost was **Ben Greet**'s company which performed Shakespeare in different parts of London at special low rates for schoolchildren, and simultaneously organized extremely popular competitions for the performance of scenes from Shakespeare by the pupils themselves. Immediately after the war the London County Council agreed to bear the cost of a season of Shakespeare matinees for schools at the **Old Vic** so that children could see the plays free of charge. An important precedent was thereby established: the Old Vic school matinees became a regular feature, and in 1924 the Board of Education officially agreed that school visits to see Shakespeare productions could be considered a legitimate part of children's education and subsidized accordingly.

Also in 1924, Bertha Waddell founded the Scottish Children's Theatre to present drama that could genuinely be enjoyed by children, especially young children, at their own level – not Shakespeare but short plays, dance, mime and song, drawing on folk tales, nursery rhymes and ballads with much emphasis on music, movement and colour. Such was the success of her work that in 1937 Glasgow education authority agreed to allow junior schoolchildren to attend performances free of charge within school hours.

Although other companies were formed during the thirties (notably Peter Slade's Parable Players in 1935), they mostly tended to be short-lived and cautious in their programming. During the final years of, and immediately following, the Second World War, however, the pace of development and innovation accelerated. Slade started a new company in 1945 (the Pear Tree Players) whose aim was not only to present scripted plays but to employ improvisation and teaching skills within its performances. Earlier, in 1943, the Children's Theatre Players were formed in Birmingham and the Motley Players in Aberdeen. Again in 1943 Brian Way, an actor with the Old Vic, began taking small presentations into schools while on tour, and the following year founded the West Country Children's Theatre whose productions deliberately avoided the use of the conventional stage and technical effects, encouraging instead a high degree of audience participation. Way's experience led him to found the influential Theatre Centre in 1954, based in London but touring with several companies up and down the country. Participation was a key element in their performances, and Way wrote many plays and adaptations to this end. Other schemes initiated at this time included Tom Clarke's Theatre for Youth at the Argyle Theatre in Birkenhead (1944); the Compass Players (1944–52) – touring; Glyndebourne Children's Theatre (1945–51) – touring; **The Young Vic** (1946–51) – touring; and Caryl Jenner's English Children's Theatre (1948). The latter was founded originally as a mobile theatre unit based in Amersham, and moved in 1967 to London, where it became the Unicorn Children's Theatre, based at the **Arts Theatre**, performing mainly during afternoons.

The post-war acceleration was however short-lived. Despite provision in the 1944 Education Act for the subsidy of theatre company visits to schools and of school visits to theatres, little money was forthcoming and many companies stopped in the early 1950s for want of funds. The companies that did survive did so on a shoestring: overworked, underpaid, short-stay actors and hastily rehearsed productions combined to produce much shoddy work. Standards were maintained primarily by the Theatre Centre and the Unicorn.

North West Spanner Theatre Company performing in *Safety First or Last?*, Manchester dry docks, mid 1970s.

In 1965 the **Arts Council** was persuaded by this unsatisfactory state of affairs to set up a committee of inquiry into the provision of theatre for young people. It noted that there were some 12 professional YPT companies in existence: some were touring companies while some (such as the Everyman in Liverpool) were based in a theatre building. Five companies were selected for immediate 'life-saving' grant aid and from 1967–8 a special allocation was made to help promote YPT schemes, including children's theatre, primarily through the repertory theatres. An upsurge of activity followed. A major new young people's theatre company was founded (the Young Vic, though with a bias mainly towards the older age range), and the range of work offered thenceforward into and throughout the seventies was considerable, if not always consistent in quality or quantity. Even in the 1980s, when government money for the performing arts was severely reduced in real terms, the attention given to young people by theatre companies remained substantial. In 1984–5, for example, there were approximately 25 companies offering children's theatre as their main or sole activity, in addition to which there were puppet and dance theatre companies and those TIE and community companies whose repertoire also included children's theatre work of some kind.

Accompanying and closely bound up with this increase in the number and type of such companies, has been a quite marked change in the content of the plays presented. Fantasy is still common, but more adventurous, contemporary and thought-provoking material is now often to be found, especially in the work of the specialist companies. Not only is there *Peter Pan* and the plays of the prolific David Wood, but there are, for example, the highly successful 'Peace Plays' by David Holman, toured by Theatre Centre in 1982, and the much acclaimed *Raj* (about the last days of British rule in India) by the Leeds Playhouse TIE Company, toured in 1983.

Theatre-in-Education Professional theatre work with specific educational aims, offering a unique educational resource to schools and colleges. Although it has roots in the work of such pioneers as **Joan Littlewood**, Peter Slade and Brian Way, the beginnings of TIE may be traced to the setting up of a pilot educational project at the Belgrade Theatre, Coventry, in 1965. The aim was to forge new links between the theatre and local schools, and to this end a small unit of 'actor-teachers' was formed to take programmes of work into classrooms and school halls, utilizing both drama teaching methods and performance skills. The objectives were educational and the means theatrical. The success of the scheme together with the availability of new money from the Arts Council for YPT led over the next five years to the formation of similar teams at repertory theatres in Bolton, Leeds, Nottingham, Edinburgh and Glasgow. The scale and adventurousness of the work grew and soon a number of Education Authorities decided to set up TIE units of their own, the Cockpit team within the Inner London Educational Authority being the most notable example. In due course some repertory-based teams found their relationship with their parent theatre inhibiting and became independent YPT or community/YPT companies. There are now about 28 fully-fledged TIE companies or YPT companies with a strong commitment to TIE. Many other community and touring companies include TIE within their schedules on a more occasional basis.

Kinds of TIE work range from straight performance of a play – devised specially for children of a particular age and followed by a workshop on its themes, discussion with the 'characters' of issues raised or a follow-up programme of work organized by the teacher in consultation with the company – to full participation programmes. It is the latter for which TIE has won its reputation as a pioneering force in education. Such programmes may last anything from one hour to a full day or even to a series of visits made to each class over a four-week period. The pupils will be involved in an experience *with* the characters – as witnesses or in role – and confronted with a series of problems to be solved, dilemmas faced, decisions reached. Learning through experience is a crucial tenet of the work. Subject-matter will range from conventional curriculum areas, such as local history or study of themes from an examination set text, to more general, sometimes sensitive matters of social concern such as racial prejudice, drugs, or the environment. Always the aim is to inform, to stimulate interest and to challenge preconceptions. Examples of particularly successful programmes are *Pow Wow* (Coventry Belgrade TIE), devised for 6- to 7-year-olds who participate in a Cowboy and Indian story that deals with racial prejudice and initiates classroom study of the American West and Indian culture; *Poverty Knocks* (Bolton Octagon TIE), devised for 10- to 12-year-olds – a two-visit programme about the Lancashire textile industry and the Chartist movement of the 1830s; *The Max Factor* (Lancaster Dukes Playhouse TIE) – a straight performance piece for 12- to 14-year-olds about a spastic child, seen from the child's point of view; and *Example – the case of Craig and Bentley* (Belgrade TIE) – a play followed by workshop for 16- to 19-year-olds about the operation of criminal justice.

Pit Prop Theatre in *Brand of Freedom*, a participation theatre-in-education programme in Wigan schools in 1984.

The material presented is always the product of much careful research and discussion with teachers and education advisers, and schools are fully involved in 'follow-up' work. But at the same time, the efficacy and power to stimulate of good TIE ultimately lie in its use of the theatrical medium and in its considerable measure of independence from the education system.

TIE has, until only recently, been a uniquely British phenomenon; there are now, however, companies established in Eire, Australia, Canada and the USA, and interest in TIE continues to grow. AJ

Young Vic, The There have been two Young Vic schemes. The first was initiated by **George Devine** as a touring children's theatre attached to the **Old Vic Company**. Its first production was in December 1946, and for five years under Devine's direction the company, aided by a small **Arts Council** grant, built up a high reputation for the standard of its productions. Audiences, mainly from 9 to 15 years of age and above, grew, but the problems of attracting new suitable plays, insufficient finance and disagreements over direction of the Old Vic as a whole brought the scheme to an end in 1951.

The second scheme began, as part of the **National Theatre**'s programme for young people, with the opening of the Young Vic Theatre – the first purpose-built young people's theatre in Britain – in 1970. The auditorium seats 450–500 people around a thrust stage and there is now additionally (since 1984) a small studio theatre seating 110. The purpose has been to make theatre of the highest standard – classics, specially written plays and experimental work – available to students and young people in an unpatronizing, exciting manner and at affordable prices. Frank Dunlop, the theatre's first director, established it as a completely independent organization in 1974. AJ

Yu Ch'i-jin (1905–74) Korean playwright, director, and producer. Born on the south-eastern sea-coast and educated at Rikyo University in Japan. In 1931 he became one of the founding members of the Kŭgyesul Yŏnguhoe Group. His first successful play was *T'omak*. He wrote more than 30 plays ranging from tragedy to comedy, becoming the most influential playwright until the 1950s. The most important subjects of his plays are the struggle against Japanese colonial policy, the struggle against occupying foreign military forces, satire against political feuds, and the national insistence upon ethnic identity. In 1950 he was appointed the first director of the newly established National Theatre. In 1962 he opened the Drama Centre which failed within a year. Some of his representative plays are *Maŭi t'aeja* (*Prince Maŭi*), *So* (*The Cow*), *Choguk* (*The Fatherland*), *Wŏnsulrang*, and *Pyŏl* (*The Star*). OKC

Yu Zhenfei (1902–) Chinese *xiaosheng* actor and **kunqu** specialist. He was born at Suzhou, the son of Yu Zonghai – an erudite *kunqu* authority – under whom he had his first lessons at the age of six. After serving his apprenticeship under both *kunqu* and **jingxi** master actors, he turned professional on the *jingxi* stage where he quickly became acclaimed for the perfection of his interpretations of the young scholar-hero roles of the

classical Beijing repertoire. He regularly partnered **Mei Lanfang** in this capacity. Through his long professional career Yu has worked indefatigably for the preservation and performance of *kunqu* to which he has made so distinguished a contribution. During the 1950s he was responsible for training a new generation of performers at the Shanghai Municipal Academy of Dramatic Art. Work there was disrupted by the Cultural Revolution but today Yu is active once again. He is an accomplished flute player as well as singer and actor. He has also written a treatise on *kunqu* techniques as a preface to a compilation he has made of his father's dramatic scores. ACS

Yueju (Guangdong Opera) The regional form of music-drama of Guangdong Province, popular also in southern Guangxi, Hong Kong and Macao and among those Overseas Chinese communities of North America, Australia and elsewhere whose ancestors came from Guangdong. The name *yueju* should not be confused with the **yueju** of Shaoxing Opera, a completely different style of Chinese music-drama. Although the two names sound identical, the first of the two characters is different.

Guangdong Opera belongs basically to the *pihuang* system of music-drama, although the two styles *erhuang* and *xipi* have been much changed under the influence of local music. Cantonese folksongs, **kunqu** and other tunes have also been absorbed into Guangdong Opera. Accompanying instruments include the end-blown flute and double-reeded *suona* as well as strings and percussion. In addition, such Western instruments as the violin and saxophone were added in about the 1920s and remain in use today. There is a certain mellifluousness in the texture of many of the singers' voices, as well as in the accompanying orchestra.

There are basically ten role-categories in the Guangdong Opera. Male characters are termed *mo* or *sheng* but, in contrast to most contemporary styles of Chinese music-drama, the latter is not normally the main one. The painted-face (*jing*) and female (*dan*) are as in other styles, but the *chou* lacks the white area on and around the nose found in the music-dramas of other regions.

The first famous actor of the Guangdong Opera was Zhang Wu of the 18th century, who came from Hubei Province. Possibly it was he who first introduced *pihuang* music to Guangdong, since that system was already familiar in Hubei during his lifetime. Zhang Wu settled in Foshan where he took on students and established a troupe; he was also the founder of a guildhall for actors called Qionghua. In due course further influxes of actors of *pihuang* music, from Anhui and Hunan Provinces, strengthened that system's impact on the music-drama of Guangdong.

In 1854 the well-known actor Li Wenmao (d. 1861), collected three armies and rebelled against the government in support of the Taiping uprising (1851–64). He even set up his own short-lived kingdom based on the town of Liuzhou in Guangxi. As a result of his activities, the Guangdong Opera was proscribed completely as subversive until the late 1860s. The Qionghua Guildhall was destroyed during the Taiping uprising and the centre of the revived Guangdong Opera was Guangzhou.

Because of Guangdong's proximity to the British colony of Hong Kong, Guangdong Opera has been more subject to foreign influences, especially the film, than any other form of Chinese music-drama. Early in this century urban actors began to experiment with more naturalistic movements and gestures, and to discard the traditional embroidery in favour of the more realistic costumes being used in the spoken drama and film. For the first time they used scenery on the stage. Some new items were directly political in their content; such as one in praise of the female anti-Manchu revolutionary Qiu Jin, who was beheaded in mid-1907.

Except for the Cultural Revolution decade (1966–76), Guangdong Opera has done well under the People's Republic. The state-run Guangdong Provincial Opera Company was established in 1958. There has been a tendency to return to traditional usage in some aspects of stagecraft such as costuming, movements and gestures. CPM

Yueju (Shaoxing Opera) A style of Chinese regional music-drama, usually termed Shaoxing Opera in English. It is not to be confused with the identically sounding **yueju**, Cantonese or Guangdong Opera, the first character of which is quite different.

Shaoxing Opera, also termed Sheng County Theatre, is so-called after its place or origin, Sheng County in Shaozing, east Zhejiang Province. It arose quite recently and does not belong to any of the major 'systems' of local Chinese drama (see **China**). It developed from peasant balladeers singing local folksongs early in the 20th century. Some formed themselves into drama troupes but the scale was small. Musical accompaniment was through percussion or chorus.

In 1916 the actor Wang Jinshui brought the Shaoxing Opera to Shanghai. He and others greatly expanded the scope of this form of music-drama by absorbing melodies from other local styles of eastern Zhejiang, adding string and other instruments to the accompanying orchestra and expanding the available rhythmic structures. In 1923 a training-school for girls was set up in Sheng County and from 1928 all-female companies began their period of prosperity in Shanghai. They competed with the male companies. By the mid-1930s the best-known feature of the Shaoxing Opera was that virtually all performers were female.

As a result romantic love stories are the strong point of the Shaoxing Opera. Military scenes and acrobatics are totally absent. The most famous of the early stories, which retains its popularity today, is that of the love between Liang Shanbo and Zhu Yingtai, who elope, later die under tragic circumstances and are transformed into butterflies, hence the name by which the piece is often known in English, 'the butterfly lovers'.

The 1940s was another era of reform, under the leadership of actresses like Yuan Xuefen. Lighting and scenery came to be extensively used in traditional or 'newly arranged historical' *yueju* music-dramas. A new method of costuming was introduced which combined influences from the **jingxi** and historical **huaju**. Specifically, in the designs of costumes for *dan* characters it copied old pictures of beautiful women rather extensively. Soft colours were emphasized in contrast to the bright colouring of the traditional costumes. Instead of satins, materials such as silks, crepe and georgette were

favoured. The new style of costuming was designed to accord more closely to the lyric beauty of the *yueju*'s romantic style.

The government of the People's Republic greatly encouraged the Shaoxing Opera at first. While it retained the emphasis on romantic stories it also encouraged male and female performers in the same troupe. During the Cultural Revolution the Shaoxing Opera companies were closed down. But with the fall of the 'gang of four' in 1976, Shaoxing Opera has revived like all other Chinese regional styles. In major professional performances of large-scale items, the accompanying orchestra now includes some Western instruments, especially the violoncello, aimed to provide a strong bass to the music. Actors now perform some male roles, especially evil ones, but actresses dominate strongly in most items, and in particular the scholar-lover (*xiaosheng*) roles are usually played by women. CPM

Yugoslavia The modern state of Yugoslavia was established in 1918 from the independent states of Serbia and Montenegro and from parts that belonged to the Austro-Hungarian monarchy. The country, whose name means 'the land of the South Slavs', contains several ethnic groups of common origin but of distinct traditions, languages and religions. The dividing line between the Eastern and Western Roman Empire and, later, between the Eastern and Western branches of Christianity, ran through the present state. After the period of Roman dominance on the Balkan Peninsula, from which some remains of Graeco-Roman theatres are still preserved, the cultural development of the population was strongly influenced by several neighbouring foreign powers whose rule or dominance lasted for centuries: Byzantium, Turkey, Italy (especially Venice), then Austria-Hungary. Thus it is virtually impossible to speak of one unifying theatrical tradition, as circumstances, conditions and influences varied to a great extent from one part to another. Continuous professional theatre activity started only in the mid-19th century, but since then theatre has played a significant role in the development of national identity, and has served as an influential forum for the dissemination of social ideas.

The popular rituals, dances and choral songs preserved in the villages contain noticeable paratheatrical elements, in both the Catholic and Orthodox traditions. Although even the most elaborate of these rituals rarely use masks, they do rely on very ornate costumes. Among ritual presentations, best known are the 'vertep', a nativity scene with three kings, and various forms of prayers for rain in the dry summer months. Elements of Christian belief are commonly intertwined with older strata – usually from the ancient religion of the Slavs or from the cults of the original non-Slavic inhabitants of the Balkans. Other forms sprang out of specific historical experiences, such as the 'moresca', a dance still performed on the Adriatic island of Korcula, which has a clear narrative line: the liberation of island maidens kidnapped by Moorish pirates.

In all probability, entertainers and jugglers from Byzantium appeared in the courts of medieval rulers and nobles in the 12th century. After the arrival of the Turks (14th–15th centuries), theatrical activity of any sort must have been quite scarce: clowns, called 'pelivans', dervish dances, puppet theatre of the **Karagöz** type. The Christian population under Turkish rule kept its cultural identity in marginal theatrical forms: public relations of epic folk poetry about medieval nobles and later heroes of the anti-Turkish resistance, accompanied by the 'gusle', a one-stringed instrument.

In the western mainly Catholic parts, religious plays were performed during the 14th century, utilizing Old Testament material and various apocrypha, with local vernaculars sometimes used instead of Latin. The earliest surviving dramatic text of a secular nature is *The Slave Woman* (1520) by Hannibal Lucić, an aristocrat from the island of Hvar, where a theatre building – still well preserved today – was erected in 1612.

The impact of the Italian Renaissance was felt all along the coastal area as well as the islands, but it was strongest in Dubrovnik; as a semi-independent city-state, Dubrovnik possessed an urban concentration and an active social life that favoured the appearances of guest players and entertainers, and encouraged the emergence of local amateur groups. The players, usually engaged and paid by the city government for celebrations such as the pre-Lenten carnival, were sometimes hired by local patrons for family festivities as well. The repertory of comedies and pastorals, influenced by Italian models, was set early in the mid-16th century, first of all by **Marin Držić**, then expanded in the 17th century by other local authors. In the 18th century, free adaptations of **Molière**'s comedies, altered to local circumstances and translated into the local dialect, were popular in Dubrovnik. Some of these have been revived successfully in recent times.

In the 18th century, theatre began to play a more political role in the struggles both for national emancipation of the South Slavs, and against the policies of cultural assimilation imposed by the Austrian Empire. Local Slavic languages were occasionally used in performances in schools, Jesuit seminaries and cultural societies. Still, while Hungarian and German troupes started to appear regularly in the northern parts of today's Yugoslavia, and Italian and sometimes French companies toured the coastal areas, the amateur performances of the local Slavs remained sporadic until the 1840s. After two uprisings, in 1804 and 1815, the Serbs won semi-independence from the Turks, and Joakim Vujić, a dilettante actor and one of the champions of itinerant amateur theatricals among the Serbs in Austria, crossed the Danube to found the Serbian Principal Theatre in Kragujevac in 1834. Although his effort was short-lived, and although Vujic himself was more an adapter than an original dramatist, his enthusiasm stimulated the formation of itinerant companies that within a few decades evolved into professional troupes, and further led to the establishment of the Serbian National Theatre in Novi Sad and of the Croatian National Theatre in Zagreb, both in 1861. These two theatres became important instruments in the struggle of Serbs and Croats in the Dual Monarchy for their cultural autonomy and ultimately their political independence. Belgrade became the site of the National Theatre in 1868, the year of the Turkish withdrawal from their garrisons in the young principality, and a similar Slovenian theatre society was soon formed in Ljubljana.

The first national playwright of importance, Jovan Sterija Popović, wrote a few tragedies inspired by national history and legend, combining neoclassicist and romantic elements, but his lasting popularity is based on his comedies of provincial life in the multi-ethnic towns of the Panonian valley. The National repertory of Slovenes, Croats and Serbs followed two major lines: historic or pseudohistoric plays of old glory, calling for the rebirth of long-lost independence; and comedies of bourgeois manners, often with mild satires of government corruption and incompetence, of yearning for class elevation and ennoblement. The heroic plays effectively protracted the romantic spirit all the way to the end of the century, agitating and glorifying, imitating the versification of popular epic poetry and leading to a performance style that was often loaded with displays of knightly bravado and with ranting rhetoric on patriotism, manliness and self-sacrifice. The comedies, more urbane and contemporary in their concerns, inaugurated a realistic style, even when they contained folkloric elements, and were enriched with songs, dances and shooting of rifles, as the old playbills proudly announced. This entertaining amalgam, similar to the German **Singspiel** or Spanish **zarzuela**, carried a new set of values to a society that was – while proclaiming its allegiance to the old heroic myths – eager to break through its agrarian matrix.

The establishment of national repertory companies with permanent ensembles permitted the steady introduction of foreign dramas, translated into Slovenian and Serbo-Croatian, often indirectly (i.e., English drama through German) and not always very competently. Beside standard classical works, theatre audiences were familiarized in the last three decades of the 19th century with the comedies, farces, vaudevilles and melodramas imported from the boulevard stages of Paris, Munich and Vienna. **Kotzebue**, **Scribe**, and their lesser followers helped establish among new theatregoers the bourgeois stage and its problems and concerns, clearing the way for the works of **Ibsen** and, later, **Hauptmann**. The transition to naturalism and later symbolism came at the turn of the century, mainly in Croatia and Slovenia, through German influences. The plays of Ivan Cankar are representative of this process. They contain strong attacks on the philistinism of petit-bourgeois Slovenia, its political conservatism, clericalism and social conformity (*Scandal in the St Florin Valley*, *The Servants*, *The Beautiful Vida*, 1907–11); but they also often possess a poetic detachment, a yearning for the kind of utopian beauty found only in national myths or in resigned daydreaming.

In organization and technology, the existing theatres mainly followed the practices of the Vienna **Burgtheater**; the standardized sets were initially ordered from Hungarian and Austrian workshops, while the acting and directing styles were inspired by the stages of Vienna and Munich.

In the new Yugoslav state, after 1918, the older theatres and the newly formed ones in other cities were entitled to a steady government subsidy that came with direct ministerial control. Theatre professionals were in fact treated as civil servants with yearly contracts. Traditional performing styles were modified by influences of German expressionism and Russian realism associated with **Stanislavsky**. Two visits by the **Moscow Art Theatre** in the 1920s, and the absorption of several Russian émigré designers, directors, choreographers, musicians and acting coaches, made this influence lasting.

The period between the two world wars was marked by the consolidation of theatre life, and by the emergence of directing as a clearly distinct task separate from acting, as embodied in the erudite and truly cosmopolitan figure of Branko Gavella, active in several Central European theatres. Painters and architects elevated the importance of the visual aspects of production. Famous international actors and companies made guest appearances. Opera and ballet became a regular part of the repertory, at least in the major theatres with resident ensembles. Theatre criticism in newspapers and magazines reached a new sophistication and competence.

Among playwrights of merit, only **Branislav Nŭsić** and **Miroslav Krleža** exercised a durable impact on the repertory. The 1941 occupation of the country by German and Italian forces and their Hungarian and Bulgarian allies, did not stop all theatre activity. However, many prominent artists chose to stay away from the stage in those times of mass humiliation and suffering; others joined Tito's partisan forces, as did most of the cast of a *Faust* production in 1942, running away from the Zagreb theatre to the liberated territory. They formed the core of the Theatre of National Liberation that was active in Tito's army throughout the war.

The contemporary situation The first post-war period brought many changes to the theatre life, as the liberation movement, lead by the Communist Party, was in fact a socialist revolution. New companies were formed in many places. All theatres were entitled to receive municipal and state subsidies and the combination of very low-priced tickets and the Party's educational policies brought in large masses of new theatregoers. There was a genuine and widespread enthusiasm for theatre art, despite the fact that strict ideological standards were in force. Initially, the repertory was dominated by domestic classics and works by Russian and Soviet authors, and Stanislavski's system – in its 'socialist-realism' version – was imposed on theatre as a binding model.

After Yugoslavia's break with Stalin in 1948 and her strategic orientation to own original and independent type of socialism (developed in defiance of the Soviet model), socialist realism was quickly abandoned and new venues for artistic expression were gradually opened and enlarged. This policy of aesthetic pluralism, tolerance and freedom of artistic creation – albeit unable to prevent occasional attempts of politicians, especially on the local level, to interfere in repertory matters – served to place the ultimate responsibility on theatre professionals within the permanent ensembles. Their 'self-management' authority had to accommodate the views and political opinions of delegates of various cultural institutions and organizations who sat on the theatre boards as watchdogs of supposed social interests, but in practice, interests of the Party. In 1990 the self-management was markedly reduced and more authority given to the artistic and managing directors. At the same time, in matters of subsidies and appointments, theatres became more dependent on the ministries of culture in each of the six federal republics.

When the Yugoslav Drama Theatre was formed in Belgrade in 1948, it was conceived as the central representative ensemble, the embodiment of the best features of the Yugoslav theatre. Under the energetic leadership of its director and designer, Bojan Stupica, it earned the first international credits with its successful appearance at the Paris **Théâtre des Nations** in 1954. Its reputation was further enhanced by several subsequent international tours. But since later 1950s, no one theatre can claim to represent the essence of Yugoslav stage as the federal structure of the country, together with a very high degree of decentralization, results in a checkered theatrical map, with distinct features evident in each individual federal republic. In Macedonia, for instance, the Macedonian language has been spoken regularly and legally on the stage only since 1945 – and sporadic efforts to use it instead of Turkish, Bulgarian or Serbian date from the turn of the century. Codification of Macedonian literary language, its grammar and orthography, almost paralleled the development of Macedonian drama (K. Čašule, G. Stefanovski, J. Plevneš). The long-lasting policy of full cultural and educational development of ethnic minorities has resulted in permanent professional ensembles that perform across the country in Hungarian, Albanian, Italian and Turkish, while amateur groups utilize almost a dozen languages, including Romany (Gypsy). The centres of the six federal republics have several repertory theatres each and at least one such theatre exists in another 30 cities. There is a total of over 80 repertory theatres, including ten operas with ballet and 20 theatres for children. Institutions for the training of theatre professionals were established in all major centres and integrated in the university system. There are several theatre museums and research centres, and among specialized periodicals *Scena* (Novi Sad), *Prolog* (Zagreb), *Teater* (Skopje) and *Maske* (Ljubljana) are the most important.

Although the contemporary theatre has never lacked great actors, and adventurous directors have been active throughout the whole post-war period (Milošević, Spaić, Belović, Korun, Paro, Mijač), the development of playwriting was noticeably delayed. Foreign works from the West had been shown frequently since early in the 1950s and had been received with enthusiasm. Coming as they did after a period of collective passions and experiences, these imported plays helped reintroduce to the Yugoslav stage individual concerns and intimate issues. Belgrade's Atelje 212, founded in 1956, conquered the last ideological suspicions toward the works of the European avant-garde, from **Jarry** to **Beckett** and **Genet**, yet lacked for a while similar works of domestic authors for its repertory.

Native Yugoslav playwrights made their post-war start only in 1950s (Matković, Marinoković); established themselves in the next decade (Smole, Hristić, Lukić); gained popularity in the 70s (Brešan, Popović, Jovanović); and finally conquered the repertories in the 80s (Šeligo, Šnajder, Kovačević), reducing the part of the classics and even of contemporary foreign works. This popularity of new domestic works was based on several factors: their candid and searching consideration of all significant issues of the society, including the most sensitive ones; their frequent reexamination of recent national history; and on the fact that these plays brought to the stage the debate about the destiny of the Yugoslav multi-ethnic community and its particular brand of socialism. Very few of these plays have been published or produced abroad, but some were seen by foreign audiences during the not-infrequent tours of Yugoslav theatres in Eastern and Western Europe, and, in a few instances, in North and South America and Australia.

Yet, despite the popularity of national drama, the still-prevailing model of repertory theatres, with its permanent ensemble and large administrative and technical staff, displayed in time some problems: routine, inertia, wastefulness, dependence on subsidies for 85–95% of the budget. The challenge to this system has come from an increasing number of independent groups, composed of freelance professionals and dissatisfied members of institutionalized troupes. They rely mainly on the box office for their survival (since public subsidies are as a matter of routine premarked for the established institutions) and yet often manage to present innovative, high-quality work. Even without a solid technical base and often with only a short lifespan, these groups managed to work with more efficiency and to tour extensively crossing both the linguistic and bureaucratic boundaries of regions and federal republics.

Until the outbreak of interethnic hostilities and a full-fledged civil war in 1991, several festivals used to connect the various realms of the Yugoslav theatre. The National Drama Festival, inaugurated in Novi Sad in 1956 with the explicit aim of stimulating Yugoslav playwriting and of enhancing its standing, had grown in an important theatre institution – Sterijino pozorje – which is active in publishing, documentation, international relations, and the organization of exhibits and conferences. The Dubrovnik Summer Festival must be

Miroslav Krleža's *Arethaeus*, performed at the Bokar fortress, Dubrovnik Summer Festival, 1972.

credited for the development of environmental theatre in the country – turning Dubrovnik's ancient courtyards, fortresses, squares and parks into performing sites for the plays of her own native sons, Držić and Ivo Vojnović, as well as for productions of **Shakespeare**, **Goldoni** and Krleža, and for operas, concerts, folklore, and classic and modern dance. Over 30 different sites in Dubrovnik have been used for performances so far. Summer festivals of international, national or regional importance are regularly held in other cities. Probably no festival has had more impact than Belgrade's BITEF, which has since 1967 featured the most important avant-garde works from all over the world. BITEF has served not only its Yugoslav audiences, but has also influenced such innovative directors as D. Jovanović, Lj. Ristić and S. Unkovski.

Ironically, the great diversity and vitality of the performing arts, sustained throughout the 1980s despite serious economic problems, suffered with the arrival of political pluralism and multi-partyism. Theatre lost its privileged position of a rare forum for the political debate, as political rallies, newly elected parliaments and increasingly pluralist media took over that role. Theatre professionals could derive their social prestige from the perception of the stage as a cornerstone of national culture but the escalation of national sentiment to chauvinist proportions forced theatre to serve the exclusivist ideologies and secessionist projects or to turn to a primarily entertainment role. Even before the outbreak of armed hostilities that damaged some theatre infrastructure, the Yugoslav performing arts community was broken, each part under the pressures of its own nationalist elites, with mutual communication and collaboration of artists and even touring made virtually impossible. As in other realms of public life, the essentially vivid and cosmopolitan atmosphere of Yugoslav theatre, visible in directorial and acting styles, in repertories and design, became threatened by self-imposed ghettoization, parochialism and conservative backlash in the name of separate ethnic identities – Serb, Croat, Slovene, Macedonian, Montenegrin, Albanian, Muslim, Hungarian. DK

See: BITEF catalogues, Belgrade, annually since 1967; *Bulletin, Choice of Yugoslav Plays, 1968–78*, Novi Sad and Belgrade, 1979; B. Mikasinovic, ed., *Five Modern Yugoslav Plays*, New York, 1977; *Scena*, Novi Sad, yearly issues in English since 1978.

Yurka, Blanche (1893–1974) American actress, born in Czechoslovakia and brought to the United States as an infant. She began acting in 1907 after training for opera. She applied to **David Belasco** successfully for work on the legitimate stage, her first leading role being in *Is Matrimony a Failure?* Over the next decade she shifted to tragic roles, appearing in 1925 as Gina in *The Wild Duck*, followed by a series of strong-willed female roles, winning praise for her emotional depth and vocal timbre. She played Gertrude to **John Barrymore**'s Hamlet. She was also an active member and organizer of Actors' Equity, being elected to a variety of positions in that organization. In 1955 she retired from the theatre, decrying the poverty of the theatre at that time, but soon returned to both films and Broadway. She often wrote and lectured about the theatre. SMA

Z

Zacconi, Ermete (1857–1948) Italian actor and company manager. Born to the profession, he was a child actor and acquired wide stage experience, notably with the actor–manager **Giovanni Emanuel**, by whose naturalistic style he was much influenced. In 1897 he formed his own company and his repertoire included much modern drama in the naturalistic vein (including **Ibsen**, **Tolstoi** and **Giacosa**), as well as Shakespearian tragedy, in which he was notable as Macbeth, Othello, Lear and Hamlet. For a time he worked with **Duse** in her attempts to launch the new poetic drama of **D'Annunzio**, and later appeared with her at the end of her career in Ibsen's *The Lady from the Sea* (1921). He continued to be a lead actor in the Italian theatre until the Second World War. His career in the cinema was lengthy and included silent film versions of his stage successes, such as Ibsen's *Ghosts* (1917). LR

Zadek, Peter (1926–) German theatre and film director, whose fast-paced highly theatrical and politically unconventional stagings of **Shakespeare**, **Brendan Behan** and **O'Casey** gave him a reputation as a radical iconoclast while artistic director in Bremen (1964–7) and Bochum (1972–5). His most successful productions have been his own adaptations of novels by Hans Fallada into satiric revues of the Nazi period, *Little Man – What Now?* (1972, together with **Tankred Dorst**) and *Each Dies for Himself Alone* (1981). CI

Zaire Zaire, the largest French-speaking country in Africa south of the Sahara, gained its independence from Belgium in 1960. The traumatic events that followed led to the murder of the country's first prime minister Patrice Lumumba, who as a result passed into legend as one of the heroes of Africa and became the subject of many plays and poems throughout the continent. The Belgian colonial authorities developed European education much later than their counterparts in the French and British colonies with the result that creative writing in French got off to a very slow start. Encouragement was, however, provided with the creation immediately after the Second World War of the official journal *La Voix du Congolais*, which became an important forum for Zairean writers of the colonial period, including some early playwrights.

The most successful of these was Albert Mongita who had the added advantage of being on the staff of the Belgian Congo Radio. His plays dealt with historical themes (*Soko Stanley*, 1954) as well as traditional and social (*La Quinzaine* (*The Fortnight*, 1957), *Mangengenge* 1956, and *Ngombe* 1957).

Pre-independence theatre was essentially amateur, and conventional in form. Since independence the range of activity has greatly widened and there is little doubt that live theatre, be it on the stage or on the radio or television, is a vital feature of contemporary Zairean cultural life. Amateur theatre continues to flourish, but alongside it there now exists amateur university theatre (particularly as represented by the Catharsis troupe at Lubumbashi University) and theatrical activity generously funded, for propaganda purposes, by General Mobutu's Party. On the professional side, there is the training provided by the drama sections of the state-financed Institut National des Arts and the Théâtre National. All these groups are as much, if not more interested in developing an essentially Zairean theatre drawing on indigenous theatrical traditions as in reflecting the European tradition. Catharsis has made a significant contribution to the former by going out into the rural areas recording traditional theatrical performances and studying traditional techniques, in addition to performing.

The majority of plays performed in Zaire are never published, but since independence there has nevertheless been a striking increase in the number of plays going into print, mostly in Zaire itself. The themes are fairly typical of contemporary African drama, ranging from the depiction of traditional and contemporary society, with the anxieties about social disintegration being reflected in an unusually large number of plays dealing with the role of women, to historical dramas and disguised or overt political comment. In the first category, M. Mikanza is among the best-known writers, with *Procès à Makala* (*Trial at Makala*, 1976) and *Monnaie d'Echange* (*Exchange Money*, 1979), along with Lisembe Elebe, with *Simon Kimbangu ou le Messie Noir* (*Simon Kimbangu or the Black Messiah*, 1972) and *Chant de la Terre, Chant de l'Eau* (*Song of the Earth/Song of Water*, 1973); less polished but very popular is Cheik Fita, the author of plays like *Psychanolove* (1979) and *Apocalypse 2000* (1979). Catharsis created its own historical play *Fulani* in 1977, and there are many others in this genre. The most difficult sphere to work in is the political theatre, because of the threat of censorship and even imprisonment – a fate suffered by Tandundu Bisikisi for his play *Quand les Afriques s'affrontent* (*When the Africas confront one another*, 1973; revised and expanded 1983). In order to overcome this problem, some writers use subjects from other parts of Africa to make indirect comment on events in Zaire; the life and death of the South African Steve Biko has proved very fruitful in this respect, as for example in N. Musangi's play *On crie à Soweto* (*They are crying in Soweto*, 1978). CW

See: R. Cornevin, *Le Théâtre en Afrique Noire et à Madagascar*, Paris, 1970; P. Ngandu, 'Le Théâtre: vers une dramaturgie fonctionnelle', *Notre Librairie*, no. 63, janvier–mars 1982, pp. 63–74.

Zaju Variety play. Chinese generic term for a style of entertainment in which dance, song, monologue, balladry and farcical skits were given an integrated presentation. The basis for archetypal roles was developed within this form along the broad division of comic and straight performance. The form has a complex history related to some of the earliest moves towards a style of dramatic representation. The genre attained significant advances in north China during the Jin dynasty (1115–1234) and the southern Song dynasty (1127–1279). The northern form also became designated *yuanpen*, meaning playscripts from the actors guild. *Zaju* reached its most creative metamorphosis during the Yuan dynasty (1234–1368). Yuan *zaju* (the description refers to the dynasty in this case) resulted in the emergence of a structured four-act style of play. It evoked the first definitive synthesis of song, music, versification and acting towards which the course of public entertainment had been moving by diverse routes for some time.

Due to the rise of a vigorous school of playwrights during the 13th century the foundations were laid for a formal dramatic structure which was to prevail. The Beijing theatre of modern times may be regarded as a legitimate descendant. The Yuan *zaju* was comparatively simple in form and followed the rules of prosody, rhyme and metre fundamental to all Chinese lyrical composition. In general a play had four acts plus what was known as a wedge. Each act was given a long suite of single stanza lyrics conforming to an identical musical mode but with a different mode for each act.

A wallpainting of a stage showing *zaju* actors, c. 1324.

Brick carvings showing costumed actors of Yuan dynasty *zaju*, c. 1279.

The wedge, a self-contained unity, allowed the dramatist a certain flexibility within the more rigid arrangement of the whole. It had a single song sequence with one or two stanzas only and could be situated at the beginning of the play or between any of the four acts although never after the last one. Only the leading performer, whether male or female, sang. The ancillary performers carried on the dialogue and action between the singing as well as enforcing the comic pace. The music of the Yuan plays has been lost to posterity and such knowledge of stage practices as we have must be deduced from existing playscripts. These in their rich diversity indicate that Yuan drama was a thriving popular entertainment catering for all levels of society. ACS

Zambia Zambia was formerly a British colony called Northern Rhodesia until independence on 24 October 1964. The population of 5.6 million can be grouped in six major language groups – Bemba, Nyanja, Lozi, Tonga, Lunda and Kaonde.

Before the advent of colonialism, traditional dances, dance-dramas and ritual plays were performed in seasonal and religious festivals and rites of passage, such as the *Makishi* masquerade of North Western Province and the *Nyau Kasinja* funeral dance of the Eastern Province. Other performances worth mentioning are the *nachisungu* ceremony – a puberty rite of the Northern Provinces, the *mutomboko* ceremony which celebrates the accession to the throne of Mwata Kazembe, king of the Lundas, *Kuomboka*, which marks the movement of the Lozi king from his winter to his summer capital, and the *Ncwala* ceremony, which is performed to commemorate the victories of the Ngoni during their migration from South Africa. In addition to these forms, there is a rich tradition of narrative, the most famous of which being the stories of Kalulu, the Hare.

With the advent of colonization and subsequent urbanization some of these forms were modified and in some cases new ones developed from the old. As with much cult drama in early societies – the rites of Dionysus in Greece and the Yoruba masquerades of Nigeria, for instance – the Nyau masquerades developed in line with social changes from a clan cult performance into a secret society, family guilds and ultimately professional performing groups. In the process new masks were added, comic and satiric plots elaborated and the original cult taboos set aside in favour of entertaining and inventive performances for money to multi-ethnic audiences with content devoid of the original meanings and functions.

Other syncretic modern performance forms based on the traditional culture were *kayowe* (a courtship dance based on a rooster and hen choreography), *kalela* (satirical of white dress and manners), *jwembu* (an acrobatic dance developed by soldiers returning from the Second World War) and *Kachala* (based on spirit possession (*Mashawe*) and puberty rites (*nachisungu*) and incorporating mimed satire of contemporary mores). During the period of agitation for independence the nationalist youth groups made effective use of these performing forms for political mobilization. They were then later incorporated into the repertoire of the National Dance Troupe, established in 1965, which under the directorship of Edwin Manda adopted a dynamic approach to the traditional forms, producing full-length dance-dramas such as *Nsombo Malimba* (the names of musical instruments). These in turn influenced other modern dramatists, including **Masautso Phiri** and **Stephen Chifunyise**.

The European settlers introduced Western theatre into Zambia, forming in 1952 the all-white Northern Rhodesia Drama Association, which with independence became the Theatre Association of Zambia (TAZ). Between 1954 and 1958 a number of theatres were built for the exclusive use of expatriate and settler communities. In 1958 a multi-racial group founded the Waddington Theatre Club and challenged the colonial colour bar by gaining membership of the white Association after heated debate.

Though the white settlers claimed that 'very little interest was shown by Africans in theatre', from 1958 to 1962 the Northern Rhodesian Youth Council held an annual drama and choir festival, which came to an end when the clubs became involved in the political campaigns of the nationalist organizations. In 1958, too, a 15-minute radio programme was introduced, broadcasting plays in a number of Zambian languages by among others Edward Kateka, Asaf Mvula, Y. L. Zulu, Wilfred Banda and Patterson Mukanda. Andreya Misiye was the first Zambian to write a full-length play, *The Many Lands of Kazembe*. A weekly series in Tonga, *Malikopo*, and another in Nyanja, *Tambwali*, became extremely popular.

Formed in the year before independence, the Zambia Arts Trust, a national association of indigenous theatre enthusiasts, toured the country on a grant from the new Zambian government with plays in English and Zambian languages including Gideon Lumpa's *Iyi eyali imikalile* (*The Way We Lived*), John Simbotwe's *Ifyabukaya* (*Our Customs*), **Kabwe Kasoma**'s *The Long Arm of the Law* and others by **Shaw**, **Soyinka**, **Rotimi** and Obutunde Ijimere. They organized theatre festivals and were virtually the only organization at the time performing plays in Zambian languages.

In 1969 a local publisher, Titus Mukopo, recruited **Yulisa Amadu Maddy** to found the Zambia Dance Company but the venture to establish a professional theatre company was not a success.

Possibly the most significant new development after independence was the development of drama at the new University of Zambia. A student dramatic society (UNZADRAMS) became active on the campus. Its policy was to emphasize the production of locally written plays. Their earliest productions included Kasoma's *The Long Arm of the Law*, Michael Etherton's adaptation of **Oyônô-Mbia**'s novel *Houseboy*, *Che Guevara* and *Kazembe and the Portuguese*.

In 1969 drama courses were established by Michael Etherton and Andrew Horn and with the construction of an open-air theatre the **Chikwakwa Theatre** was born. Chikwakwa took theatre in English and Zambian languages to the people by touring plays, developing plays with local schoolchildren and holding workshops and festivals. It also produced a journal, *The Chikwakwa Review*. The Chikwakwa tradition inspired many new developments and the concept of travelling theatre has been continued by the Centre for the Arts which was founded at the University in 1983.

Bazamai Theatre (1970–2) was a Chikwakwa outside university walls. Founded by Masautso Phiri and Stephen Moyo, it produced the dance-drama *Kuta*, Moyo's *The Last Prerogative* and an adaptation of Achebe's *Things Fall Apart*. Another development of Chikwakwa was Tikwiza founded in 1975. It became a de facto national company, dominating Zambian theatre for nine years and representing Zambian theatre at the 1972 FESTAC and in Cuba, Botswana and Kenya. Its actors include some of the best Zambia has produced e.g. Matildah Malamamfumu, Mumba Kapumpa and Haggai Chisulo. Its work was characterized by the political emphasis of plays such as Masautso's *Soweto* and Dickson Mwansa's *The Cell*.

The extent to which the Chikwakwa tradition had become the basis of an alternative indigenous Zambian theatre movement gained its organizational expression in the formation of the Zambian National Theatre Arts Association (ZANTAA). With a large membership in schools, colleges and community theatre groups, ZANTAA organized annual festivals following the Chikwakwa tradition. Over 87 plays were produced, mostly unpublished. In 1983 a national debate culminated in the dissolution of the two existing theatre organizations, TAZ and ZANTAA, in order to form a new one.

David Wallace's Theatre Circle deserves mention. Starting as an opponent of Chikwakwa, he developed into a leading advocate and practitioner of theatre based on traditional orature, especially the Kalulu (Hare) tales. Bakanda Theatre's production in 1980 of Dickson Mwansa's *The Cell*, Tithandize Theatre's performances of plays by Craig Lungu and ZANASE Theatre, a full-time company attached to the Zambian National Service, have all been influential.

Recently there has been spectacular growth in the area of community-based theatre in working-class residential areas. One of these groups, Kanyama Theatre, became Zambia's first full-time professional theatre group, touring Zambia and even Zimbabwe widely.

Finally a word on television drama. In the wake of government directives to scrap foreign material in favour of local work, Zambian television introduced the 'Play for Today' series, which, after initial problems, produced many effective Zambian works such as

Chifunyise's *I Resign* and *A Thorn in Our Flesh*, Mulenga N'gandu's *Jobless Existence*, Kwalela Ikafa's *Dambwa*, as well as a number of dance-dramas. The National Dance Troupe had an extremely influential weekly one-hour slot in which it performed dance, dance-drama and sketches, in Zambian languages, which constituted a breakthrough as previously only English had been used on television.

The future development of Zambian Theatre would seem to depend largely on the results of the TAZ/ZANTAA merger and the direction the new body pursues. DM SC RK

> See: M. Etherton, *The Development of African Drama*, London, 1982; 'The Dilemma of the Popular Playwright: The work of Kabwe Kasoma and V. E. Musinga', in *African Literature Today*, 8, London, 1976; *Chikwakwa Review*, Department of Literature and Languages, University of Zambia, Lusaka, various issues.

Zamyatin, Evgeny Ivanovich (1884–1937) Soviet-Russian novelist, short story writer, literary critic, dramatist and editor, best known in the West for his Wellsian anti-utopian novel *We* (1920), which antedated Huxley's *Brave New World* and inspired Orwell's *1984*. An engineer by training, an ironist by temperament, he wrote eloquently, satirically and passionately on artistic freedom, social ills and literary craft. An early Bolshevik, his anti-philistine polemical writing of the 1920s led to mounting official criticism of his work, culminating in the banning of his books from dissemination and further publication in 1929 and his emigration to Paris in 1931. Zamyatin wrote eight plays of which three were original works and five adaptations. His earliest play *The Society of Honorary Bell Ringers* (1925), derived from his novel *Islanders*, was produced at Leningrad's Mikhailovsky Theatre in 1925. That same year the **Moscow Art Theatre**'s Second Studio invited him to dramatize Nikolai Leskov's short story 'The Tale of the Cross-eyed Lefty from Tula and the Steel Flea'. The result was *The Flea*, directed by Aleksei Diky, a **commedia**-style depiction of Tsarist Russia and Victorian England meant to revitalize Russian folk comedy, which ran for six seasons. The tragedy *Attila* (1928), his last play, presents the Hun leader in a positive light and poetic style. It was banned while in rehearsal at the Leningrad Bolshoi Dramatic Theatre (1928), at which point Zamyatin returned to narrative writing. Zamyatin's essay 'The Modern Russian Theatre' (1932), originally a lecture delivered in Prague one month after his emigration (1931), offers critical assessments of Russian theatre's ensemble tradition, ideological playwriting, proletarian theatres and mass spectacles and the comparative strength of **Stanislavsky**'s and **Meyerhold**'s methods and influence. SG

Zanni (both singular and plural) The Italian term for the two servants in the **commedia dell'arte**. It is unlikely that the word derives from the *sanniones* of the ancient Atellan farces, but may come from the dialect forms of Giovanni (John): Gian, Zuan, or Zan. Originally they were servants from Bergamo speaking the local *patois*, and soon differentiated into two distinct types. The first became the clever, domineering intriguer, who motivated the plot through intrigues

and brainstorms; often characterized as an urban lackey he wore first a bright jerkin, later a stylized livery. His names were Brighella, Buffetto, Flautino, Coviello. The second was a knave from the village or the garden, a dolt not devoid of mother-wit, whose function was to be the fall-guy and provide the pratfalls. His clothes were patched or mended, and turned in time into a costume of polychrome rhomboids. His names were Arlecchino, Truffaldino, Pasquino, Tabarino, Tortellino, Mezzetino, Trappolino, Trivellino, Bagolino, Fritellino, and gradually he became the more important of the two. LS

Zapolska, Gabriela (1860–1921) Polish actress, director, manager, playwright and novelist, credited with introducing **Ibsen** in Russia, playing Nora in *A Doll's House* during a guest appearance of the Warsaw Theatre in 1883. She studied acting in Paris and appeared in minor roles at the Théâtre Libre (1892–4), returning to Poland as a proponent of naturalism. Her most popular play is *The Morality of Mrs Dulska* (1906), a mordant satire on bourgeois hypocrisy. *Małka Szwarcenkopf* (1897) portrays lower-class Jewish life; *Miss Maliczewska* (1910) deals with a young actress victimized by predatory males. DG

Zarzuela A musical comedy in one to three acts, probably invented by **Calderón**, *El mayor encanto amor* (*Love the Great Enchanter*, 1635) being one of the earliest. Usually performed in the open air, it took its name from the Palacio de la Zarzuela outside Madrid. Developing from the **sainete**, the musical element became the most important with aria and recitative alternating, in a stylized and often allegorical form. In the late 19th century the term was revived for a three-act self-contained form which was a light operetta, very popular until recent years, and still performed in the Teatro de la Zarzuela in Madrid. CL

Zavadsky, Yury Aleksandrovich (1894–1977) Soviet director who began his career as an actor in the Vakhtangov Studio (1915), performing the roles of Anthony in **Maeterlinck**'s *The Miracle of St Anthony* (1916) and Calaf in **Gozzi**'s *Princess Turandot* (1922). His training there as a designer later manifested itself in his attention to the outer form of his stage productions, many of which employed music generously, and especially in his early productions which he designed as well as directed. While acting at the **Moscow Art Theatre** (1924–31), Zavadsky formed his own studio (1924), reorganized in 1927 as the Zavadsky Studio which brought a **Stanislavsky–Vakhtangov**-based acting approach to plays by **G. B. Shaw**, Ostrovsky, Lavrenyov, **Sheridan**, Pervomaisky and **de Musset**. The Studio moved to Rostov in 1936, where it formed the core of the Gorky Theatre, and Zavadsky, who had already served as artistic director of the Moscow Central Theatre of the Red Army (1932–5), became its head (1936–40). From 1940 until the late 1970s Zavadsky was artistic director of Moscow's Mossoviet Theatre, which was founded in 1930 as the Theatre of the Moscow District of Soviet Trade Unions or MGSPS and renamed in 1938. A theatrical eminence more than an innovative director, Zavadsky attempted to recreate Vakhtangov's lyrical merger of psychological realism and vibrant theatricalism. His many productions at the Mossoviet include: **Shakespeare**'s *The Merry Wives of Windsor* (1957, 1967) and **Lermontov**'s *Masquerade* (1952, 1963, 1967), both of which won Zavadsky Lenin Prizes (1951, 1967); *Petersburg Dreams*, adapted from Dostoevsky's *Crime and Punishment* (1969), a popular success with its romanticized Raskolnikov (played by Gennady Bortnikov and a handsome multi-level set by A. Vasilyev); classics by **Chekhov**, **Goldoni**, Ostrovsky, Jack London, Shaw and Shakespeare; and Soviet dramas by **Afinogenov**, **Simonov**, **Korneichuk**, **Leonov**, Shtein, **Zorin**, and Virta. He wrote numerous articles and books between the 1940s and the 1970s, including *The Birth of a Production* and *Teachers and Students* (1975) and was named a 'People's Artist of the USSR' in 1948. From 1940 he taught at the Moscow State Institute of Theatrical Art (GITIS). Among his students was Polish director **Jerzy Grotowski**. SG

Zeffirelli, Franco (1923–) Italian stage and film designer and director. After a classical education in Florence, Zeffirelli began his career in 1945 as an actor, but after two years he became a designer. Working primarily on plays and films for **Luchino Visconti**, he designed also for the films of Michelangelo Antonioni and Vittorio de Sica. In 1951, Zeffirelli became a stage director and subsequently worked on such operas as *La Cenerentola* (La Scala, 1953), and *Don Giovanni* (**Covent Garden**, 1962), and such **Shakespeare** plays as *Romeo and Juliet* (1960), and *Much Ado About Nothing* (1965). As film director, Zeffirelli's abundantly romantic, yet realistically detailed style is evident in his widely acclaimed *Romeo and Juliet* (1968), as well as *The Taming of the Shrew* (1967), and *La Traviata* (1982) and *Otello* (1986). TM

Zemach, Nahum (1887–1939) Founder of the **Habimah** Theatre. Born in Bialystok, Russia. An ardent Zionist and lover of the Hebrew language, he conceived the idea of a professional Hebrew theatre which would disseminate the Zionist idea and ultimately settle in Palestine. Under his guidance, the collective of actors achieved world fame. But in 1927, during its tour of the USA, the troupe split in two, the majority of senior members going to Palestine and the minority, headed by Zemach, remaining in New York. Zemach, whose dream of establishing a Hebrew theatre in the Land of Israel had come true, ended his life staging performances in Yiddish and English in New York. HAS

Ziegfeld, Florenz (1869–1932) American producer. Ziegfeld's first venture into show business was as manager of **Sandow**, a vaudeville strongman. After meeting singer Anna Held in Europe, Ziegfeld brought her to New York and presented her in several musicals. At her suggestion, he created a Parisian-style revue called *Follies of 1907*, the first in a series that he continued to produce for the next quarter of a century. Initially presented on a modest scale, the *Follies* grew increasingly elaborate, eventually moving to the **New Amsterdam Theatre**, where designers such as **Joseph Urban** were given free reign to create ornate scenery and lavish costumes. In 1913 the show's title was changed to *The Ziegfeld Follies*. The motto 'Glorifying

the American Girl' underlines the *Follies*' emphasis on choruses of beautiful women in glittering production numbers. Many of the shows also feature first-rate comedians such as **Bert Williams**, **Fanny Brice**, **W. C. Fields**, **Will Rogers**, and **Eddie Cantor**, and popular singers and dancers such as Nora Bayes, **Marilyn Miller**, and **Ina Claire**.

Besides producing annual editions of the *Follies*, Ziegfeld presented some of the most successful musical comedies and operettas of the 1920s, including *Sally* (1920), *Kid Boots* (1923), *Sunny* (1925), *Rio Rita* (1927), *Show Boat* (1927), *Rosalie* (1928), *The Three Musketeers* (1928), and *Whoopee* (1928). Rarely innovative in his choice of material or his production methods, Ziegfeld built his reputation as a producer on his ability to discover and nurture talented performers, and the care and expense with which he mounted his shows. MK

Zimbabwe After years of bitter armed struggle against the white settler regime of Ian Smith, the new state of Zimbabwe (formerly Rhodesia) came into existence on 18 April 1980. The majority of its 7.5 million inhabitants speak Shona while Ndebele is a significant minority language and Tonga, Kalanga, Venda and English are also spoken.

When a soldier by the name of William King put up a variety concert soon after the Pioneer Column first occupied the country in 1890, he was said to have staged the 'first major theatrical entertainment in the country'. However indigenous theatre forms existed many years before the coming of the settlers, as illustrated by the wide practice of *mahumbwe* (Shona), a young people's harvest performance and the comic 'funeral drama' in which the deceased's major achievements are dramatized. In addition many other ritual ceremonies, dances, games and narratives contained significant dramatic elements.

By the 1950s the white settlers had established segregated theatre clubs in most major towns and in 1958 these formed the Association of Rhodesian Theatrical Societies, later to become the National Theatre Organization, holding an annual theatre festival adjudicated by 'experts' from Britain or South Africa. With few exceptions this organization confined itself to segregated colonial drama, a situation which has not changed a great deal with independence.

The organization of theatre amongst the black majority was left to the colonial government, which organized festivals of prescribed plays, the Salisbury City Council, which employed Basil Chidyamathamba to foster traditional dancing and establish the Neshamwari Festival of Music, Dance and Drama in 1965, various church organizations from whose activities emerged active personalities such as **Ben Sibenke**, Walter Muparutsa and Dominic Kanaventi, and a number of amateur clubs often associated with the mining companies, namely the Torwood African Theatre Society, the Wankie Dramatic and Choral Society and the Kamativi African Players.

Meanwhile in the 1970s the escalating war of liberation was restoring to the people a theatre practice based in the indigenous traditions of Zimbabwe. Political cadres of the nationalist movements organized dramas in the guerilla camps and all-night *pungwes* in the liberated zones, where songs, folk-tales, dance and drama articulated the motivations for the struggle. The theatre of the *pungwe* featured prominently the heroes of the first anti-colonial resistance of the 1980s, colonial repression and the new Zimbabwe that would emerge from the struggle.

Theatre in the post-independence period is characterized by a mixture of trends established in the colonial regime and new ones generated by the changed circumstances of independence. Artists who had been active in the colonial period found more room to expand. Whereas before independence N. Chipunza's *Svikiro* (1978), mangled by the white director into *My Spirit Sings*, was the only play written and performed by black Zimbabweans to be performed in a white theatre, now both the People's Company with locally written plays by Ben Sibenke and Karl Dorn and the Sundown Players, specializing in the plays of **Athol Fugard**, began competing in the previously all-white National Theatre Festival. In 1982 Basil Chidyamathamba's traditional musical, *Sounds of Zimbabwe*, was produced. In 1985 Kanaventi, Muparutsa and Sibenke came together to form the Zimbabwe Arts Productions with impressive performances of *Sizwe Banzi is Dead* and *The Island*.

It was the new government however which introduced trends which were new to the development of theatre in Zimbabwe, namely the National Dance Company, the community-based theatre movement organized by the Zimbabwe Foundation For Education With Production (ZIMFEP) and the work of the new Ministry of Youth, Sport and Culture.

The National Dance Company was formed in 1981 and its first production, *Mbuya Nehanda – the Spirit of Liberation*, choreographed by Peggy Harper, Karium Welsh-Asante and Emmanuel Ribeiro, continued the spirit of the revolutionary *pungwe*. Subsequently however the company has confined itself to the performance of indigenous dance.

In 1982 the then Ministry of Education and Culture employed the Kenyans, Ngugi wa Mirii and Kimani Gecau to develop a community-based theatre movement under the auspices of ZIMFEP. They produced *The Trials of Dedan Kimathi* (**Ngugi wa Thiong'o/ Micere Mugo**) in Shona and English with the Chindinduma School community and toured nationally, demonstrating widely the concept of community-based theatre. The Ministry followed this up with a UNESCO-sponsored African Workshop on Theatre for Development (see **Third World popular theatre**) in Murewa in 1983 involving local participants and theatre artists from 22 African countries.

Ngugi wa Mirii, with ZIMFEP, and **Stephen Chifunyise**, as Director of Arts and Crafts in the new Ministry of Youth, Sport and Culture, have continued the tradition by holding various theatre for development and drama skills workshops and forming community-based theatre groups. The Vashandi (Workers) Theatre Group, the Avondale Domestic Workers Theatre Group, Chindinduma School Drama Group and Habbakuk Musengezi's Centenary-based community theatre group are examples of this movement's growing importance. Other groups of course exist in various centres – Amakhosi Productions of Bulawayo, which is directed by Cont Mhlanga and produces work in Ndebele, is a representative example. Recently the majority of such theatre groups have come together to form the Zimbabwe Association of Community Theatre (ZACT).

An extremely influential new development has been the growth of indigenous television drama, including the regular Shona comedy series *Mhuri ya Mukadota* (the Mukadota Family) featuring Safirio Madzikatire and Susan Chenjerai, both veterans of Shona radio drama since the early 1960s, plays by Stephen Chifunyise and **Thompson Tsodzo** and MAWA Theatre Group's *Tshaka Zulu* (Ndebele). Madzikatire also has a very popular stage show which includes sketches and is the embryo of a Kente (see **South Africa**) or **Ogunde**-type popular theatre format.

Lastly, in 1984 the University of Zimbabwe created undergraduate courses in drama. Since then the university has produced *Mavambo* (*First Steps*), based on Wilson Katiyo's novel, *A Son of the Soil*, *The Adamant Eve* (a play on Zimbabwean women) and *Seri kwesasa/ Okusemsamo* (*Behind the Door*), a play about modern Zimbabwean life in both Shona and Ndebele. All these productions have been performed both at the university and in the community. The Faculty also works closely with the Ministry and ZIMFEP in the development of the community-based movement.

Since independence Zimbabwean publishers have devoted more attention to publishing plays, including those of Chifunyise, Bertha Msora and Habbakuk Musengezi. The University Faculty of Arts publishes a University Playscripts Series of cheap acting editions of Zimbabwean and African plays.

For many years indigenous theatre in Zimbabwe has been extremely depressed but there are signs of a considerable upsurge in interest and activity which may in a few years' time transform the situation.   SC   RK

See: G. P. Kahari, *The Imaginative Writings of Paul Chidyausiku*, Gweru, 1975; R. M. Zinyemba, *Zimbabwean Drama*, Gweru, 1986.

Zindel, Paul (1936–) American playwright. This former high school chemistry teacher is chiefly known for two plays that continue to provide actresses with exceptionally challenging roles. The first, *The Effect of Gamma Rays on Man-in-the-Moon Marigolds* (1970), was produced in Houston before moving to New York where it won the Pulitzer Prize and the Drama Critics' Circle Award. The less successful second, *And Miss Reardon Drinks a Little* (1971), continued his examina-

Paul Zindel's *The Effect of Gamma Rays on Man-in-the-Moon Marigolds*, Prague National Theatre, 1972. The designer was Josef Svoboda.

tion of fragile people who become a part of the madness surrounding them. Recently Zindel has turned to writing television plays and screenplays as well as highly-praised novels for young adults. LDC

Zipprodt, Patricia (1925–) American costume designer. Zipprodt has been designing since the mid-1950s and became well known in the 1960s with such productions as *Fiddler on the Roof, Cabaret,* and *Pippin,* and the film *The Graduate.* She adapts her style to the demands of the script and the director but if she has a trademark, it is textured clothes. Beginning with *Fiddler* she developed a technique of creating layers of paint and dye that gave a vibrant or shimmering sense of colour to costumes that would otherwise be drab. This approach continued through *Sunday in the Park with George* (1964) in which costumes were heavily textured with dye, paint, brocade, lace and fabric. AA

Zola, Emile (1840–1902) French novelist and critic. Zola's major literary importance is for his monumental series of novels, the *Rougon-Macquart* (1871–93), a chronicle of life under the Second Empire, one of which, *L'Assommoir* (1877), established him at the head of the naturalist movement. He also maintained a considerable interest in the theatre and was the major influence on **Antoine**'s Théâtre Libre. William Busnach's melodramatic adaptations of *L'Assommoir* (1879), *Nana* (1881) or *Pot Bouillé* (1883) drew large audiences to the Ambigu, but did little for Zola's reputation as a serious writer. Of his own original plays, *Thérèse Raquin* (1873), an adaptation of his novel, though not very successful on the stage, became a model for the naturalist play both in France and abroad. *Les Héritiers Rabourdin* (*The Rabourdin Heirs,* 1874) and *Bouton de Rose* (*Rosebud,* 1879) both showed his unsuitedness to the comic stage. His short story, *Jacques Damour,* adapted by Léon Hennique, opened the first season of the Théâtre Libre. His play *Madeleine* (1865), which became the novel *Madeleine Férat* (1868), was also performed by the Théâtre Libre. In the preface to *Thérèse Raquin,* Zola expressed the hope that the naturalist movement would establish itself in the theatre. In 1873 he was drama critic for four months for *L'Avenir National* and from 1876–80 for *Le Bien Public* and then *Le Voltaire.* His reviews from 1876–80 were published in two volumes, *Le Naturalisme au Théâtre* (*Naturalism in the Theatre*) and *Nos Auteurs Dramatiques* (*Our Dramatists,* 1881). Unlike critics who merely recorded performances, Zola used his weekly column to promote the new drama and to develop a critical methodology. For the well-made play he wished to substitute a drama of observation and scientific fact, using an analytic approach akin to that of such novelists as Balzac, Flaubert and himself. Anti-romantic, he saw a link with the logical approach of the classical theatre, but felt that modern theatre should deal with the particular rather than the general and that 'the modern naturalist drama should individualize, enter into experimental analysis and an anatomical study of each human being'. He saw scenery in the theatre as taking on the role of description in the novel, with a real function in the analysis of facts and characters. He objected to the conventional paraphernalia of wings and backdrops and even foresaw the abandonment of footlights. He also believed in the social and educa-

Zola's *Nana* was converted into popular melodrama in Busnach's adaptation at the Ambigu-Comique. The spirit may have been wrong, but the attention to detail of setting at the Ambigu contributed to the naturalist staging.

tional value of theatre and saw all great plays as containing a social thesis. The critic was recommended to look not merely at the work, but at the audience's reaction to it. In his last years Zola converted to socialism and devoted his attention to socialist and humanitarian propaganda, notably becoming involved in the Dreyfus affair, with his famous article *J'Accuse.* JMCC

Zorin, Leonid Genrikhovich (1924–) Soviet dramatist of the post-Thaw generation which brought a new lyricism and focus on personal relationships and ethical concerns to the theatre. Born in Baku and receiving early encouragement in his writing from **Gorky**, Zorin worked in the literary department of the Baku Russian theatre, where his first play *Falcons* was produced in 1941. In 1949 he graduated from the Gorky Literary Institute in Moscow and had his play *Youth* staged at the Maly Theatre. His play *The Guests* (1954) identifies a neo-bourgeois class of ruthless, privileged bureaucrats to which the son of a revolutionary father belongs, thus reversing the idea frequently espoused in earlier Soviet plays that the younger generation is more enlightened than the elder. The play, which alerted people to the inequities within the classless society and corruption in high places of revolutionary ideals, was attacked by the Ministry of Culture and by literary conservatives as part of a counter-offensive to the Thaw. *A Roman Comedy* (*Dion,* 1964) is a satirical comedy partially based on historical fact about a plainspoken ancient Roman poet-pundit and his on/off relationship with the emperor. *A Warsaw Melody* (1967) is a story of unfulfilled love between two young students, a Russian boy and a Polish girl, at first frustrated by a new law forbidding Soviet citizens to marry foreigners, then by their own conflicting personal responsibilities and finally by lost years which cannot be reclaimed. A typical 1960s drama, it played over 4,000 times during the 1968–9 season. *The Decembrists* is part of a trilogy commemorating the 50th anniversary of the October Revolution (1967) – the second and third parts are A. Svobodin's *The Populists* and Mikhail Shatrov's *The Bolsheviks*, respectively – which considers the use of terror in revolution. It brought to the stage of Moscow's Sovremennik Theatre, where it premiered, the human face of Russian history. Zorin has also written film scenarios, one of which, *Peace to the Newcomer*, won a gold medal at the 1961 Venice International Festival.   SG

Zorrilla y Moral, José (1817–93) Spanish poet and dramatist of the romantic period. Apart from two unsuccessful classical tragedies, his 33 plays are on Spanish history and legend. His most famous play is the mediocre *Don Juan Tenorio* (1844), a sentimental treatment of the legend ending in his repentance and salvation, and still performed every year in Spain around All Souls' Day. Much better is the two part *El zapatero y el rey* (*The Shoemaker and the King*, 1840–2) on Pedro the Cruel and the shoemaker Diego Pérez, while the one-act melodrama *El puñal del godo* (*The Dagger of the Goth*, 1843) is also interesting.   CL

Zuckmayer, Carl (1896–1977) German dramatist and novelist, who became a Swiss citizen in 1966. Although awarded the Kleist Prize for a dialect comedy *The Merry Vineyard* in 1925, his reputation is based on *The Captain from Köpenick* (1931) which has become a standard work of modern drama. Based on a true incident, its satire of Prussian militarism is a classic formulation of the common man's struggle against state bureaucracy. Recognized by **Hauptmann** as his successor, Zuckmayer completed Hauptmann's unfinished play, *Herbert Engelmann*. But his naturalistic treatments of the conflict between patriotic duty and resistance to the Nazi regime (*The Devil's General*, 1946) or nuclear physics and moral responsibility (*The Cold Light*, 1956, based on the Klaus Fuchs espionage case), successful as they were at the time, seem dated by comparison with less conventional treatments of the same subjects by **Weiss** or **Kipphardt**; while his experiment with a poetic 'requiem' *The Song in the Fiery Furnace* (1950) was only partially successful in coming to terms with the modern dramaturgy developed by **Thornton Wilder** or **Frisch**.   CI

Picture Acknowledgements

The publishers gratefully acknowledge the help of the many individuals and organizations who cannot be named in collecting the illustrations for this volume. We would like to thank especially those contributors who assisted beyond the call of duty, and the many people who lent us original photographs from their own collections.

Every effort has been made to obtain permission to use copyright materials; the publishers apologise for any errors and omissions and would welcome these being brought to their attention.

1 Michael Johnston; **4, 29, 30, 75, 135, 164, 270, 289, 339, 340, 418, 579, 613, 617, 657, 682, 697, 751, 758, 767, 826, 867, 993, 995, 1001** Collection Laurence Senelick; **14, 853, 854, 505** Courtesy of Prof. Herbert Marshall, Carbondale; **21, 433, 658, 833, 1022** The Billy Rose Theatre Collection, The New York Public Library at Lincoln Center; **24** Photo: Richard Feldman; **33** Courtesy of the Swiss Theatre Collection; **36** Ernesto Asheri, Fotografias; **50** Mansell Collection; **52** Australian Institute of Aboriginal Studies, Canberra (ref. AIAS N 2079.28); **56** Courtesy of the Melbourne Theatre Company; **67** Courtesy of the Royal Academy of Dancing; **68t** Photo: John R. Freeman/Courtesy of Ivor Guest; **68b** Crown Copyright, Victoria & Albert Museum (Theatre Museum); **71** Dominic Photography; **83, 84, 529, 825, 948, 992, 1074, 1057** Museum of the City of New York, Theatre Collection; **88** Photo: Jorge O. Vasquez; **92, 269, 495, 626** Theatre Museum, Victoria & Albert Museum, London; **94, 104, 108, 116, 202b, 257, 530t, 734, 762, 863, 986** Harvard Theatre Collection; **95, 96, 98, 478, 479, 480, 481, 569, 990, 1039, 1082** Courtesy of Farley Richmond; **100, 234, 244, 379, 411** Reproduced by courtesy of the Trustees of the British Museum; **105, 114t, 206, 219, 343, 364, 385, 584, 788, 1100** Bibliothèque Historique de la Ville de Paris/Courtesy of John McCormick; **111** Courtesy of Andrew Horn; **114b** Collection of Mary Henderson; **121t** Photo: Ana Amundaray; **121b** © Alix Jeffry/Harvard Theatre Collection; **131** Photo: Gerry Goodstein/Courtesy of Yale Repertory Theatre; **136, 763** Photo: D. Linder, Asia Society, New York; **147** Provincial Archives of British Colombia (HP8720, HP10081); **158, 1099** Courtesy of Jaromir Svoboda; **159, 338** The Shakespeare Centre Library; **173, 1041** Photo: Samuel Dembo; **188, 189, 190, 192, 195, 196, 198, 199, 1095** Courtesy of Charles Mackerras; **200, 218, 233, 583, 794** Courtesy of George Woodyard; **202t, 627** ET Archive Ltd; **217** Fotografia Jorge Hurtado L.; **223** Photo: Jean-Loup Charmet/Musée Carnavalet, Paris; **235t** Museo Nazionale, Naples; **235b** M. Chuzeville/Musée du Louvre; **236** MM Verlag/Salzburger Museum (Volkskundemuseum); **237, 239t, 277, 535, 809, 873** Deutsches Theatermuseum, Munich; **238** © BBC Hulton Picture Library; **239b** The Maugham Collection of Theatrical Paintings at the National Theatre, London; **240t** National Museums and Galleries on Merseyside (Walker Art Gallery); **240b** The Tate Gallery, London; **241** Courtesy of Robert Gordon Craig; **242** Joe Cocks Studio, Stratford-upon-Avon; **255** Photo: Cristóbal López; **256** Photo: Vidal Hernandez; **259, 985, 1052** Courtesy of Jarka Burian; **264, 436** University of Bristol Theatre Collection; **274** Courtesy of Gladsaxe Teater; **290** Courtesy of J. Kotsibilis-Davis; **291, 358, 426, 460, 606, 852, 866, 900** Becker Theater Library, Brown University, Providence, Rhode Island; **292** Photo: Beata Bergstrom/Drottningholms Teatermuseum; **296** Photo: Michael Mayhew/National Theatre Press Office; **328** Olga Lindgren-Nilsen Collection/Courtesy of Anne-Charlotte Harvey; **336** Photo: Barry Hicks/British Tourist Authority; **337** Johann Zoffany c.1734/5–1810 German. Elizabeth Farren as 'Hermione' in *A Winter's Tale* c.1780, oil on canvas, 245 × 167 cm. Everard Studley Miller Bequest 1966–7. Reproduced by permission of the National Gallery of Victoria, Melbourne; **346** Photo: Raimo Aro/Courtesy of the Finnish Centre of the International Theatre Institute; **382** Yale Center for British Art, Paul Mellon Collection; **390** Bildarchiv Preussischer Kulturbesitz; **396** Photo: Byron/The Byron Collection, Museum of the City of New York; **398, 417, 629, 857** Reproduced from Rudnitsky, *Meyerhold the Director*, trans. G. Petrov, ed. S. Schultze, 1981, by permission of Ardis, Publishers, USA; **409, 410** National Archaeological Museum, Athens; **413** Athens Theatrical Museum; **420, 539, 778** Courtesy of Daniel Gerould; **424** D. E. Bower Collection, Chiddingstone Castle, Kent; **454** K.B. Chan, Manager, Hong Kong Repertory Theatre, Hong Kong; **462** Courtesy of Barry Humphries; **483, 485, 486, 487, 610, 727** Photo: K. Foley; **492** Mauclair & Chelton/Agence de Presse Bernand; **517** Courtesy of Kubo Masa; **520** © Mikoshiba Shigeru; **530b** The Iveagh Bequest, Kenwood (English Heritage); **544, 551** National Portrait Gallery, London; **547** Guildhall Art Gallery, City of London; **553** Courtesy of Oh-Kon Cho; **556** Photo: Chris Davies; **575, 843, 905, 1086** Courtesy of Martin Banham; **575** Jersey Museums Service; **609** Courtesy of Robert McLaren;

611 Photo: Roger Long; 621 Don B. Wilmeth Collection; 628 Courtesy of Dev Virahsawmy; 685 The National Commission of the People's Socialist Republic of Albania for UNESCO; 701 Photo: J. Burian; 710 Photo: George E. Joseph; 728 Photo: Amy Pukunaga/East-West Center, Hawaii; 730 Photo: Peter Bysted/Courtesy of Odin Teatret; 750 Courtesy of Mike Patterson; 753 Courtesy of the New York Historical Society, NY; 759 Photo: Leon Myszkowski/Zaiks/Courtesy of Alec Baron; 761 Photo: H. Schwarz; 773 Photo: Lesly Hamilton/Gamma; 777 Enthoven Collection, Theatre Museum, Victoria & Albert Museum, London; 786 Courtesy of Lawrence Keates; 789 Photo: David Edwards/© BBC 1986; 792 Photo: John Vere Brown; 836 Courtesy of the Turkish National Tourist Office, London; 837 © Scala/Firenze; 844 Courtesy of Columbia University Press; 846 Photo: Kevin Cummins; 856b Society for Cultural Relations with the USSR, London; 856t Austrian National Library; 858, 859 Courtesy of Spencer Golub; 868 Photo: Miguel Gracia; 879 Courtesy of the Theatre National Daniel Sorano, Dakar; 890, 1015 The Library of Congress, NY; 901, 902 Reproduced from Collison, *Stage Sound*, by permission of Cassells Ltd.; 911 Courtesy of the Spanish National Tourist Office, London; 917 Suffolk Record Office, Eyre Collection; 919 Courtesy of Prof. Stanislaw Mossakowski, Director, Institute of Art, Polish Academy of Sciences; 920 Mary Evans Picture Library; 922 Photo: David I. Taylor; 924 Reproduced by permission of the Huntington Library, San Marino, California (ref. K-D 588); 929 Photo: Peter Smith/Courtesy of Stratford Festival Archives, Ontario, Canada; 925 Photo: Ruth Walz/Courtesy of Mike Patterson; 934t Photo: Ruth Walz/Courtesy of J. Burian; 934b Library of the University of Utrecht; 936 Photo: Erik Appelgren; 938 Photo: Marcel Imsand, Editions Payot Lausanne; 942 Wu Chin-Chi, Artistic Director, Lan Ling Ensemble, Taipei, Taiwan; 953 © BBC Enterprises; 954 Courtesy of Nippon Hoso Kyokai, Tokyo; 955t Courtesy of TV Globo Ltda., Rio de Janeiro; 955b Courtesy of Granada Television Ltd., Manchester; 958 Courtesy of the Royal Photographic Society, Bath; 963 Photo: S. Virulrak; 965, 966, 967, 970, 971 Reproduced from Leacroft, *Theatre and Playhouse*, by permission of Methuen, London; 975 Lauros-Giraudon/Condé Museum, Chantilly; 976 By permission of the Folger Shakespeare Library; 978 Bibliothèque et Musée de l'Opéra, Paris; 1006 Photos reproduced from TRINIDAD CARNIVAL, published by Key Caribbean Publications; 1008 Photo: Ole Jorgensen/ Courtesy of Tukak Teatret; 1013 Harry Ransom Humanities Research Center, University of Texas at Austin; 1063 Photo: Hainer Hill, Berlin; 1078 Photo: Z. Lubak; 1087 © Northwest Spanner; 1088 Photo: Arthur Thompson/Courtesy of Pit Prop Theatre; 1093 Courtesy of Prof. Enes Midzic.